KAPLAN & SADOCK'S

Synopsis of Psychiatry

Behavioral Sciences/Clinical Psychiatry

Eighth Edition

Drugs Used In Psychiatry

This guide contains color reproductions of some commonly prescribed major psychotherapeutic drugs. This guide mainly illustrates tablets and capsules. A † symbol preceding the name of the drug indicates that other doses are available. Check directly with the manufacturer. *(Although the photos are intended as accurate reproductions of the drug, this guide should be used only as a quick identification aid.)*

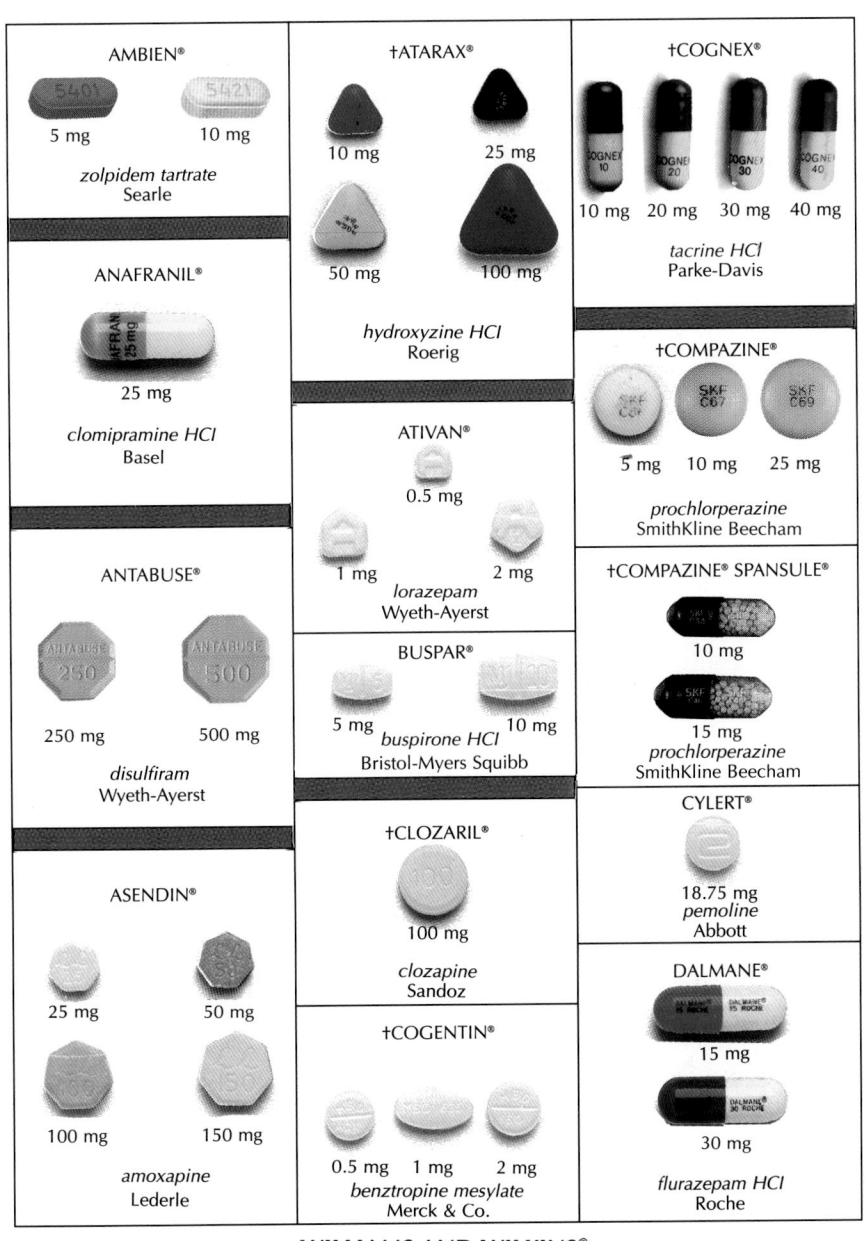

AMBIEN®

5 mg 10 mg

zolpidem tartrate
Searle

ANAFRANIL®

25 mg

clomipramine HCl
Basel

ANTABUSE®

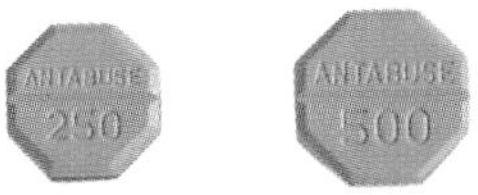
ANTABUSE 250
ANTABUSE 500

250 mg 500 mg

disulfiram
Wyeth-Ayerst

ASENDIN®

25 mg 50 mg

100 mg 150 mg

amoxapine
Lederle

†ATARAX®

10 mg 25 mg

50 mg 100 mg

hydroxyzine HCl
Roerig

ATIVAN®

0.5 mg

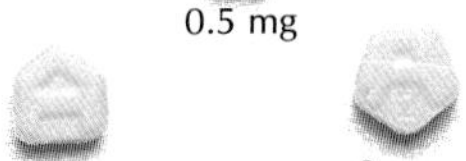

1 mg 2 mg

lorazepam
Wyeth-Ayerst

BUSPAR®

5 mg 10 mg

buspirone HCl
Bristol-Myers Squibb

†CLOZARIL®

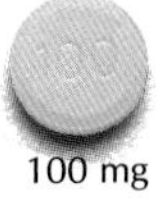

100 mg

clozapine
Sandoz

†COGENTIN®

0.5 mg 1 mg 2 mg

benztropine mesylate
Merck & Co.

†COGNEX®

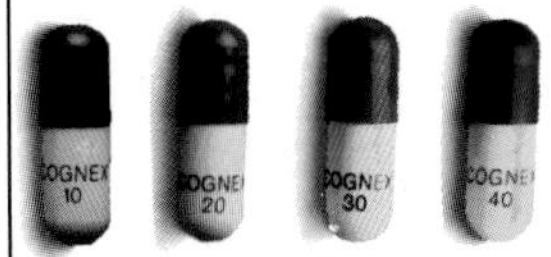

10 mg 20 mg 30 mg 40 mg

tacrine HCl
Parke-Davis

†COMPAZINE®

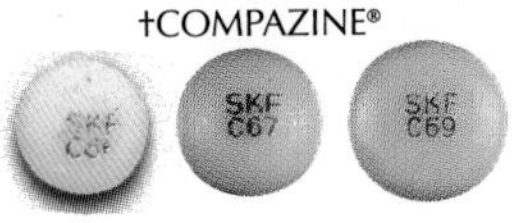
SKF C67
SKF C69

5 mg 10 mg 25 mg

prochlorperazine
SmithKline Beecham

†COMPAZINE® SPANSULE®

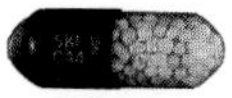

10 mg

15 mg

prochlorperazine
SmithKline Beecham

CYLERT®

18.75 mg

pemoline
Abbott

DALMANE®

15 mg

30 mg

flurazepam HCl
Roche

WILLIAMS AND WILKINS©

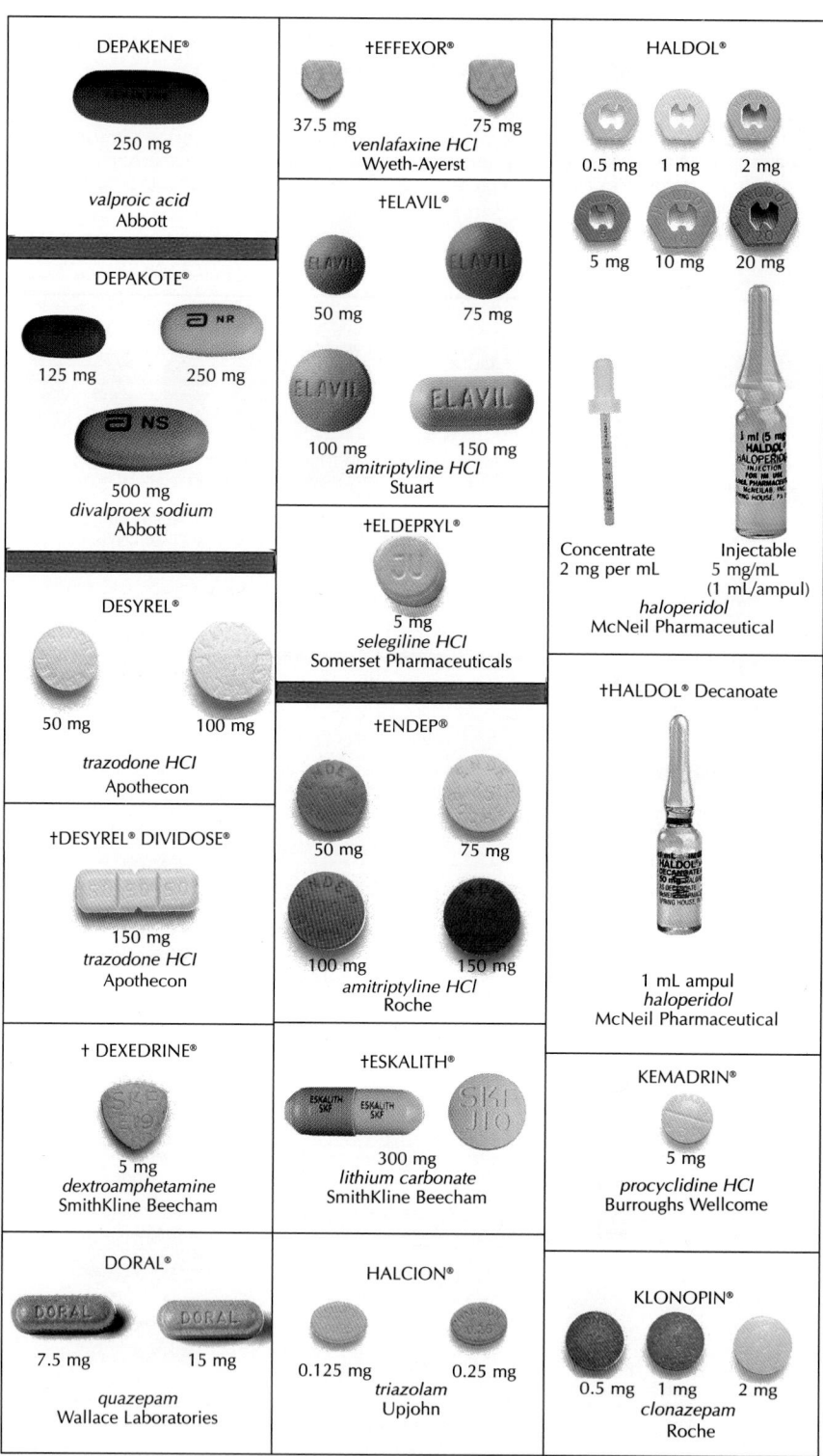

DEPAKENE®

250 mg

valproic acid
Abbott

DEPAKOTE®

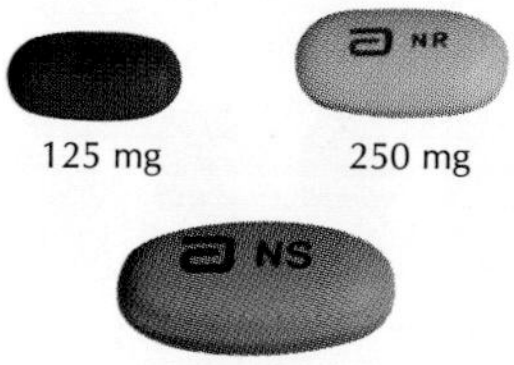
NR
NS

125 mg 250 mg

500 mg
divalproex sodium
Abbott

DESYREL®

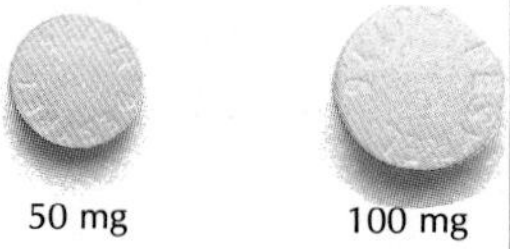

50 mg 100 mg

trazodone HCl
Apothecon

†DESYREL® DIVIDOSE®

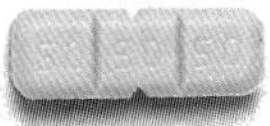

150 mg
trazodone HCl
Apothecon

† DEXEDRINE®

SKF
E19

5 mg
dextroamphetamine
SmithKline Beecham

DORAL®

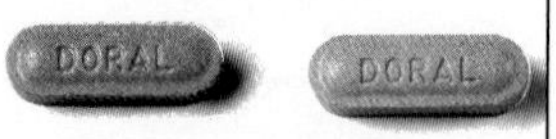
DORAL
DORAL

7.5 mg 15 mg

quazepam
Wallace Laboratories

†EFFEXOR®

37.5 mg 75 mg
venlafaxine HCl
Wyeth-Ayerst

†ELAVIL®

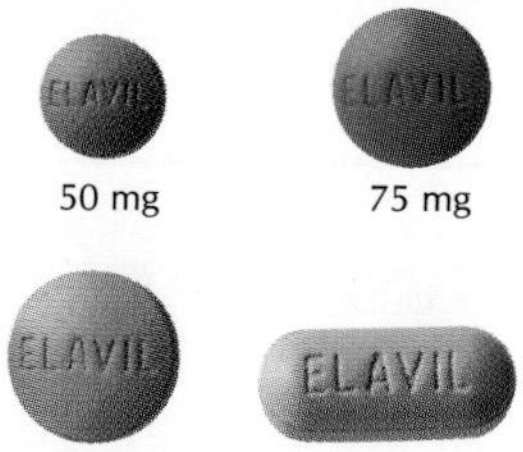
ELAVIL
ELAVIL
ELAVIL
ELAVIL

50 mg 75 mg

100 mg 150 mg
amitriptyline HCl
Stuart

†ELDEPRYL®

5 mg
selegiline HCl
Somerset Pharmaceuticals

†ENDEP®

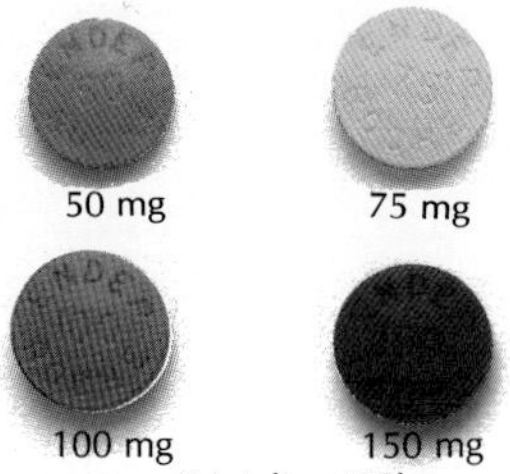

50 mg 75 mg

100 mg 150 mg
amitriptyline HCl
Roche

†ESKALITH®

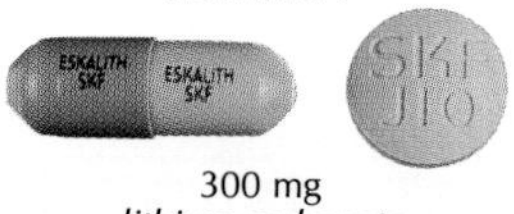
ESKALITH SKF
ESKALITH SKF
SKF
J10

300 mg
lithium carbonate
SmithKline Beecham

HALCION®

0.125 mg 0.25 mg
triazolam
Upjohn

HALDOL®

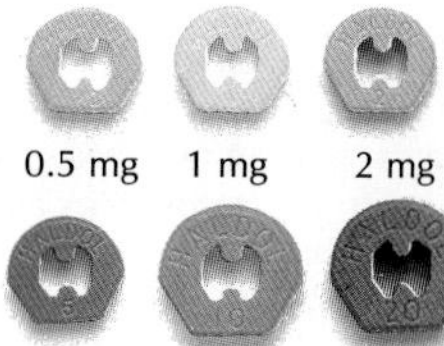

0.5 mg 1 mg 2 mg

5 mg 10 mg 20 mg

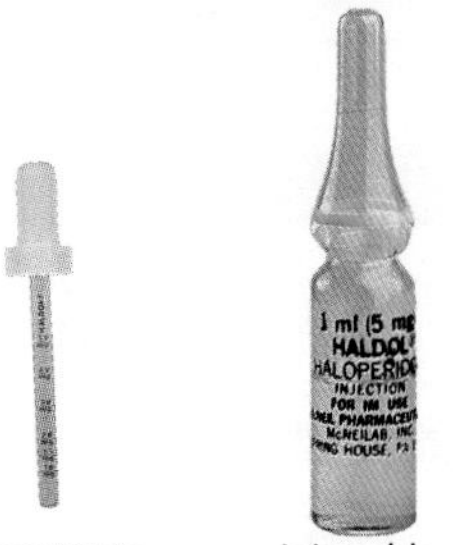

Concentrate
2 mg per mL

Injectable
5 mg/mL
(1 mL/ampul)

haloperidol
McNeil Pharmaceutical

†HALDOL® Decanoate

1 mL ampul
haloperidol
McNeil Pharmaceutical

KEMADRIN®

5 mg
procyclidine HCl
Burroughs Wellcome

KLONOPIN®

0.5 mg 1 mg 2 mg
clonazepam
Roche

WILLIAMS AND WILKINS©

LARODOPA®

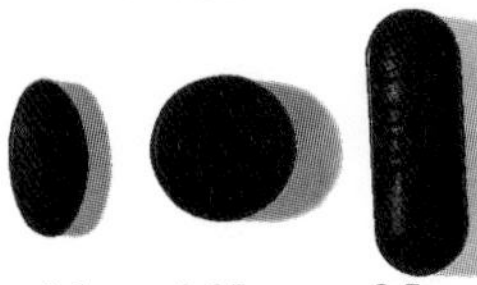

0.1 g 0.25 g 0.5 g

levodopa

Roche

†LIBRIUM®

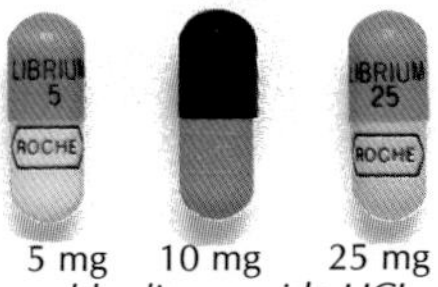
LIBRIUM 5
ROCHE
LIBRIUM 25
ROCHE

5 mg 10 mg 25 mg

chlordiazepoxide HCl

Roche

†LOXITANE®

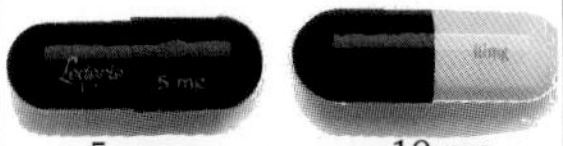

5 mg 10 mg

25 mg 50 mg

loxapine succinate

Lederle

LUDIOMIL®

25 mg 50 mg 75 mg

maprotiline HCl

Novartis

LUVOX®

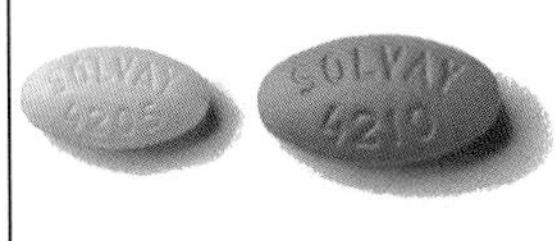
SOLVAY 4205
SOLVAY 4210

50 mg 100 mg

fluvoxamine maleate

Solvay

MARPLAN®

10 mg

isocarboxazid

Roche

(no longer manufactured)

†MELLARIL®

10 mg 15 mg 25 mg

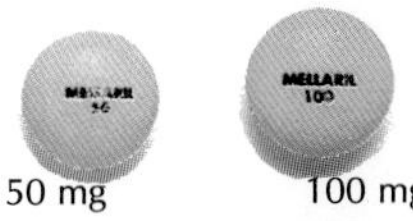

50 mg 100 mg

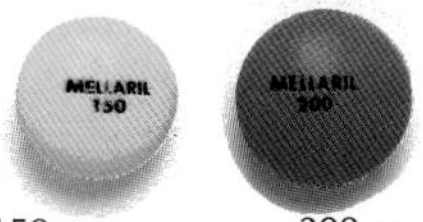
MELLARIL 150
MELLARIL 200

150 mg 200 mg

thioridazine

Sandoz

METHADONE HCl DISKET®

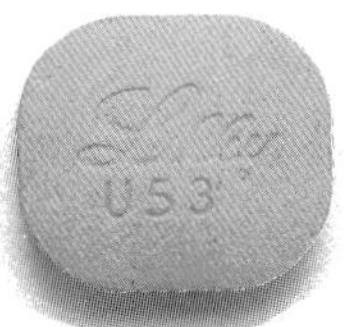
U53

Eli Lilly

†MOBAN®

50 mg

molindone HCl

Du Pont Multi-Source Products

NARDIL®

15 mg

phenelzine sulfate

Parke-Davis

†NAVANE®

ROERIG 571
ROERIG 573

1 mg 5 mg

10 mg

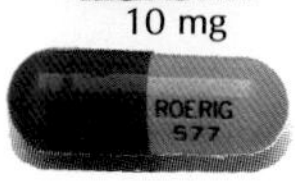
ROERIG 577

20 mg

thiothixene

Roerig

†NEMBUTAL®

CH

100 mg

pentobarbital sodium

Abbott

†NORPRAMIN®

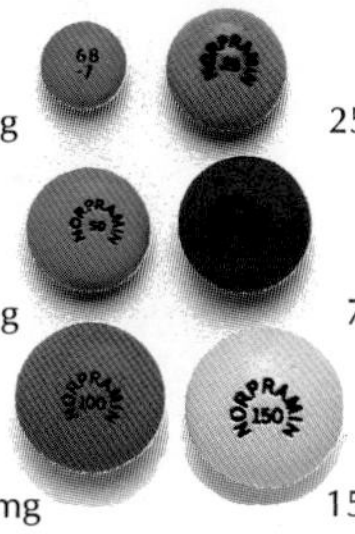

10 mg 25 mg

50 mg 75 mg

100 mg 150 mg

desipramine HCl

Marion Merrell Dow

†ORAP®

2 mg

pimozide

Gate

†PAMELOR®

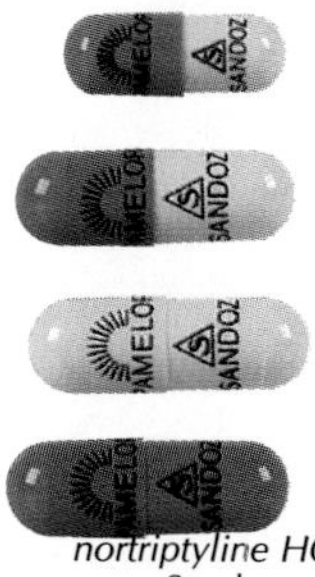
PAMELOR SANDOZ

10 mg

25 mg

50 mg

75 mg

nortriptyline HCl

Sandoz

†PARLODEL®

0.5 mg 2.5 mg

bromocriptine mesylate

Sandoz

PARNATE®

10 mg

tranylcypromine sulfate

SmithKline Beecham

WILLIAMS AND WILKINS©

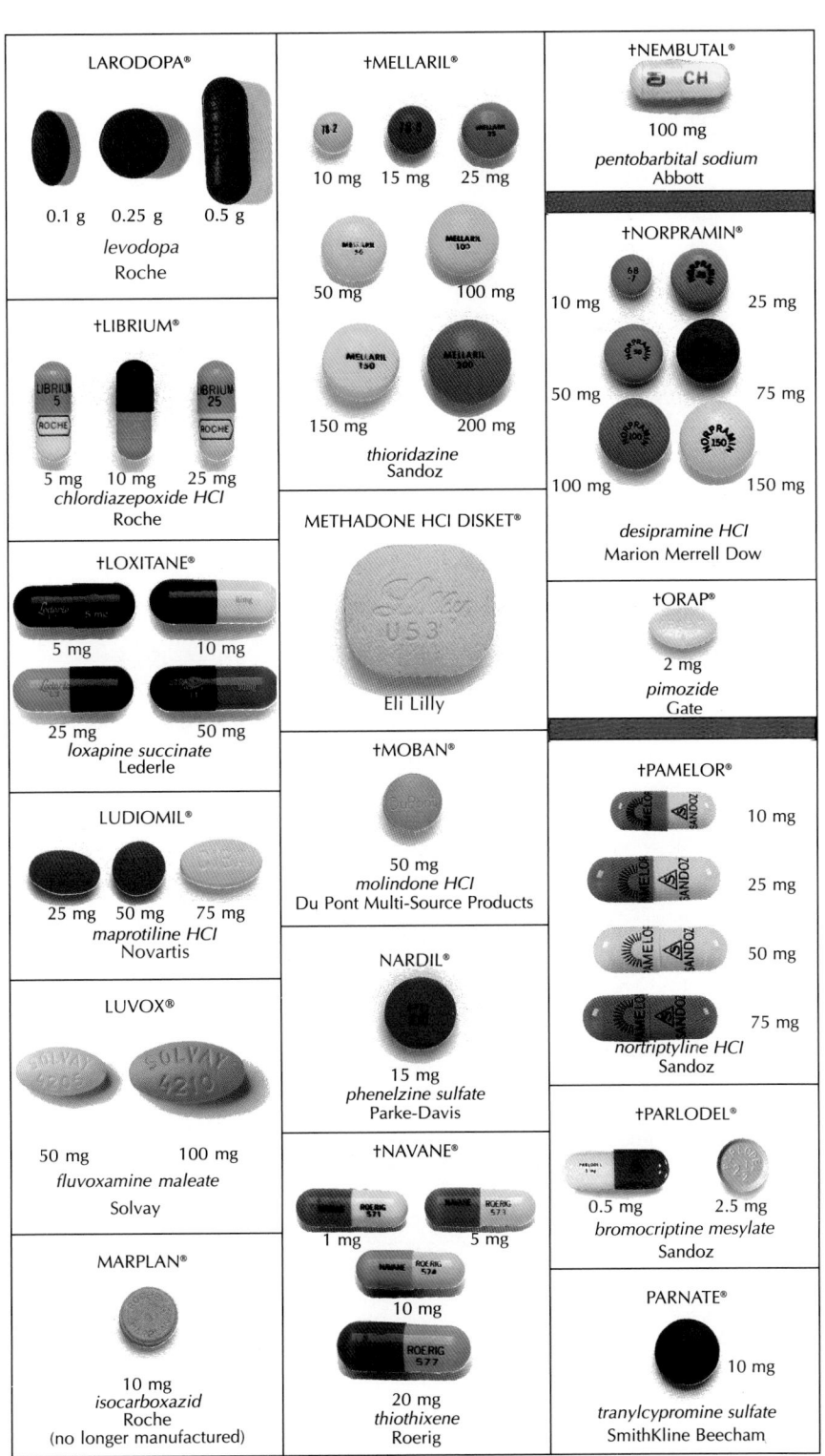

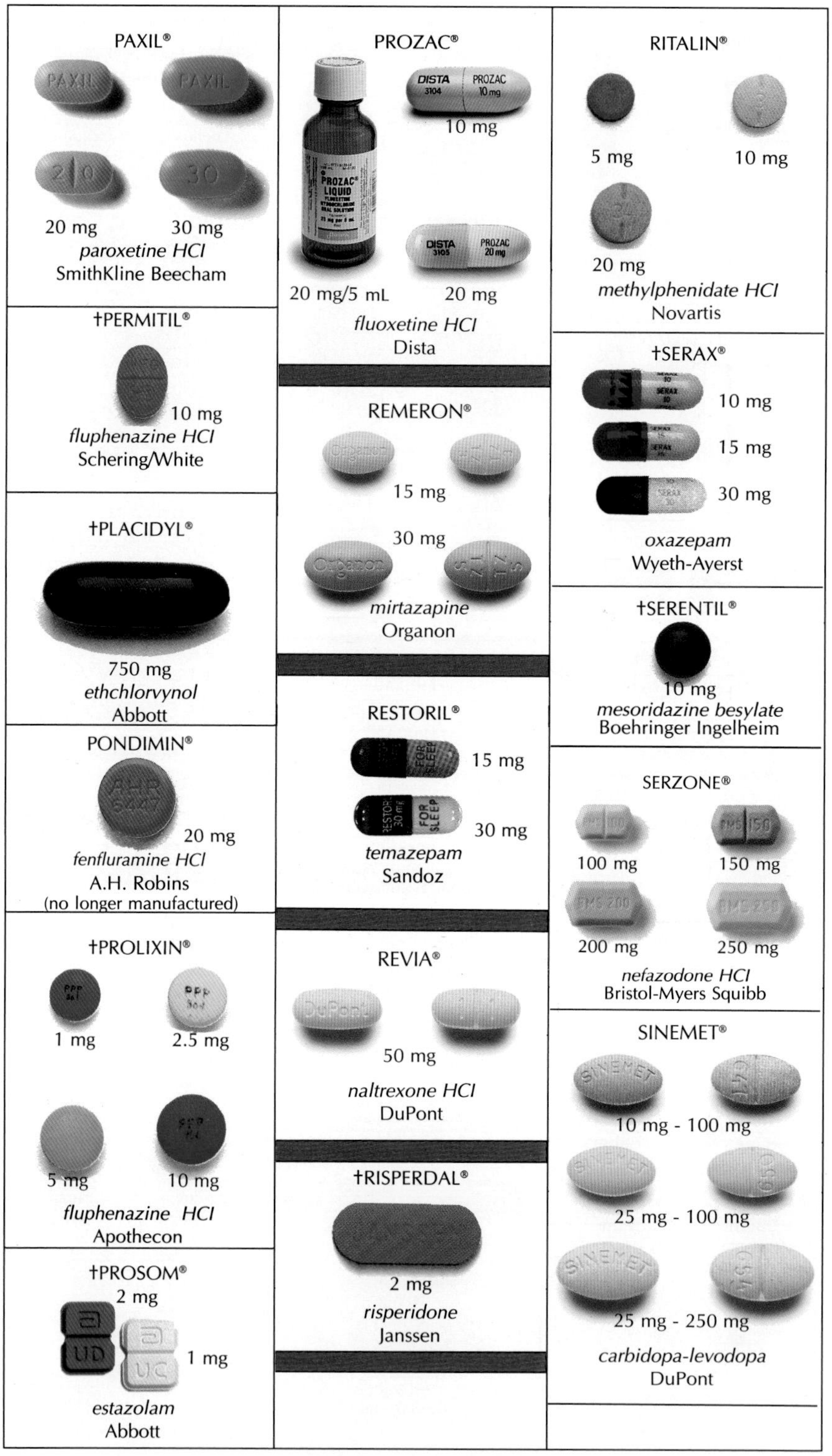
PAXIL®
20 mg
30 mg
paroxetine HCl
SmithKline Beecham
†PERMITIL®
10 mg
fluphenazine HCl
Schering/White
†PLACIDYL®
750 mg
ethchlorvynol
Abbott
PONDIMIN®
20 mg
fenfluramine HCl
A.H. Robins
(no longer manufactured)
†PROLIXIN®
1 mg
2.5 mg
5 mg
10 mg
fluphenazine HCl
Apothecon
†PROSOM®
2 mg
1 mg
estazolam
Abbott
PROZAC®
DISTA 3104 PROZAC 10 mg
10 mg
PROZAC® LIQUID
DISTA 3105 PROZAC 20 mg
20 mg/5 mL
20 mg
fluoxetine HCl
Dista
REMERON®
15 mg
30 mg
mirtazapine
Organon
RESTORIL®
15 mg
30 mg
temazepam
Sandoz
REVIA®
50 mg
naltrexone HCl
DuPont
†RISPERDAL®
2 mg
risperidone
Janssen
RITALIN®
5 mg
10 mg
20 mg
methylphenidate HCl
Novartis
†SERAX®
10 mg
15 mg
30 mg
oxazepam
Wyeth-Ayerst
†SERENTIL®
10 mg
mesoridazine besylate
Boehringer Ingelheim
SERZONE®
100 mg
150 mg
200 mg
250 mg
nefazodone HCl
Bristol-Myers Squibb
SINEMET®
10 mg - 100 mg
25 mg - 100 mg
25 mg - 250 mg
carbidopa-levodopa
DuPont

WILLIAMS AND WILKINS©

SINEMET® CR

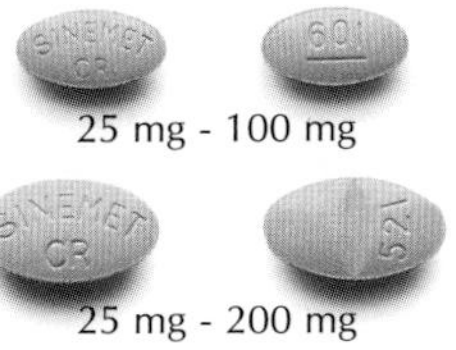

25 mg - 100 mg

25 mg - 200 mg

carbidopa-levodopa sustained release
DuPont

†SINEQUAN®

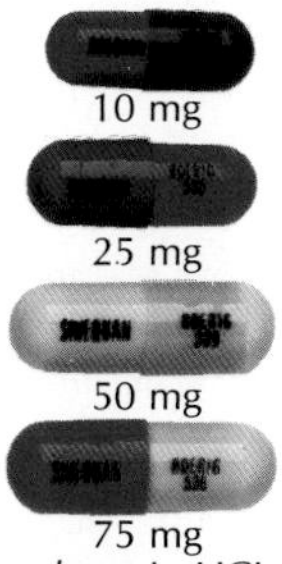

10 mg

25 mg

50 mg

75 mg

doxepin HCl
Roerig

†SPARINE®

25 mg

50 mg

100 mg

promazine HCl
Wyeth-Ayerst

†STELAZINE®

2 mg

trifluoperazine HCl
SmithKline Beecham

†SYMMETREL®

100 mg

amantadine HCl
Du Pont Multi-Source

†TARACTAN®

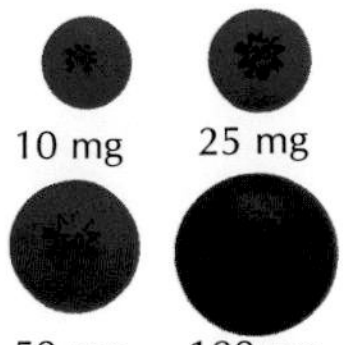

10 mg 25 mg

50 mg 100 mg

chlorprothixene
Roche

TEGRETOL®

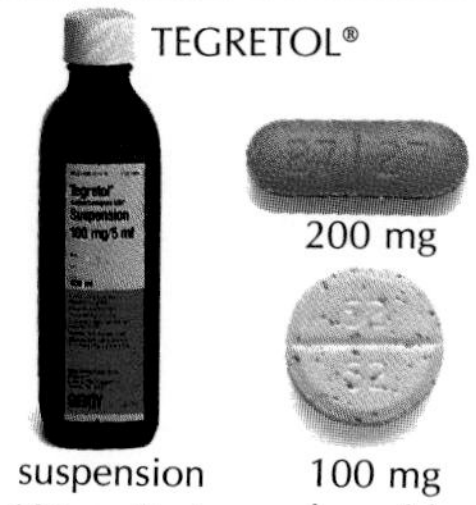

200 mg

suspension 100 mg/5mL

100 mg chewable

carbamazepine
Basel

†THORAZINE®

25 mg

chlorpromazine HCl
SmithKline Beecham

†TOFRANIL®

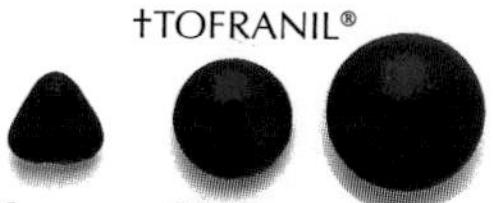

10 mg 25 mg 50 mg

imipramine HCl
Novartis

TOFRANIL-PM®

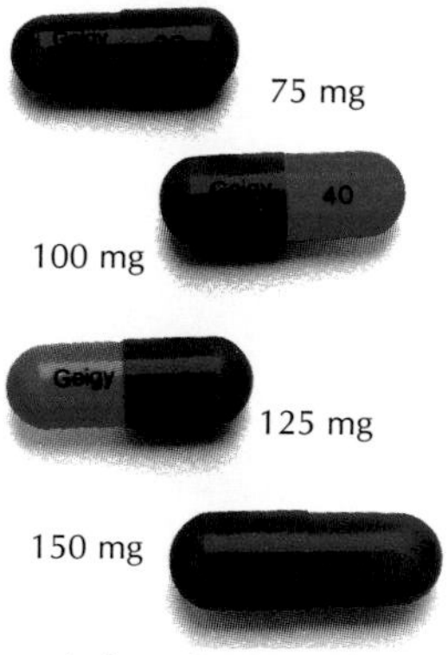

75 mg

100 mg

125 mg

150 mg

imipramine pamoate
Novartis

†TRANXENE® T-TAB®
Tablets

7.5 mg

clorazepate dipotassium
Abbott

TRIAVIL®

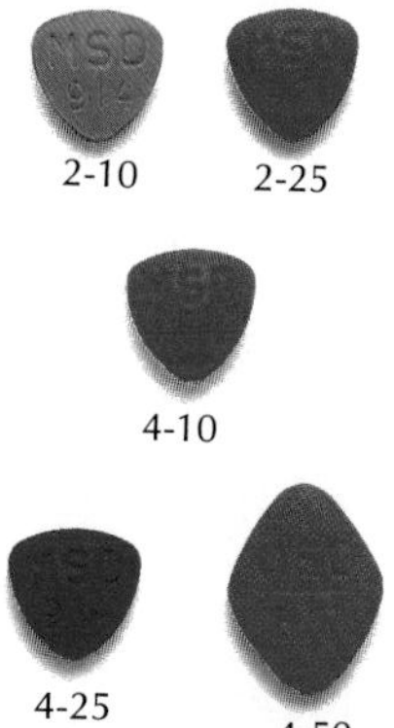

2-10 2-25

4-10

4-25 4-50

perphenazine-amitriptyline HCl
Merck & Co.

†TRILAFON®

4 mg

perphenazine
Schering

†VALIUM®

2 mg 5 mg 10 mg

diazepam
Roche

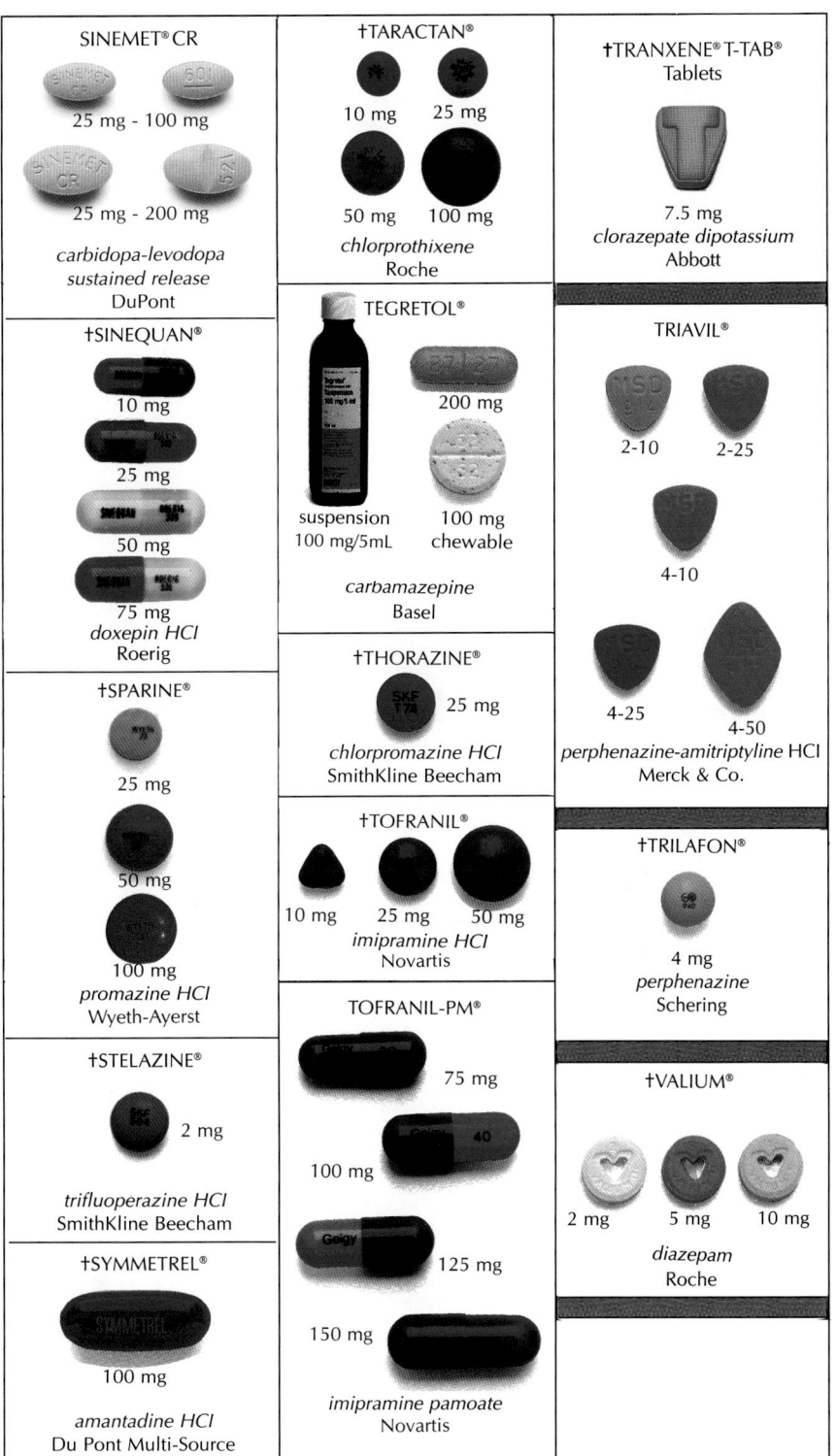

WILLIAMS AND WILKINS©

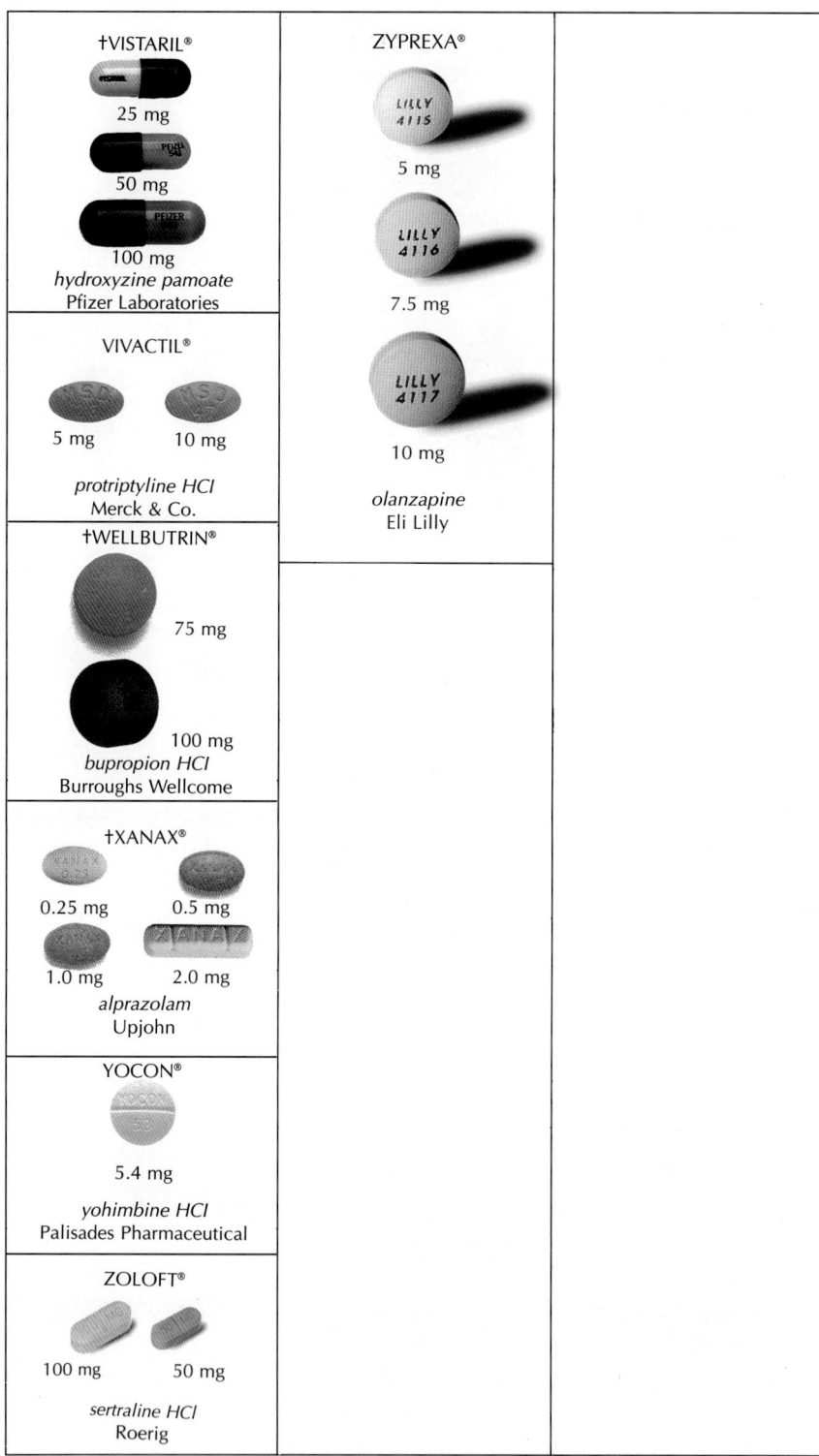

†VISTARIL®

25 mg

50 mg

100 mg

hydroxyzine pamoate

Pfizer Laboratories

VIVACTIL®

5 mg 10 mg

protriptyline HCl

Merck & Co.

†WELLBUTRIN®

75 mg

100 mg

bupropion HCl

Burroughs Wellcome

†XANAX®

0.25 mg 0.5 mg

1.0 mg 2.0 mg

alprazolam

Upjohn

YOCON®

5.4 mg

yohimbine HCl

Palisades Pharmaceutical

ZOLOFT®

100 mg 50 mg

sertraline HCl

Roerig

ZYPREXA®

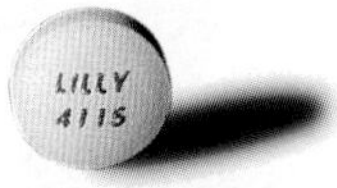
LILLY
4115

5 mg

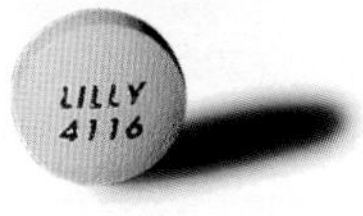
LILLY
4116

7.5 mg

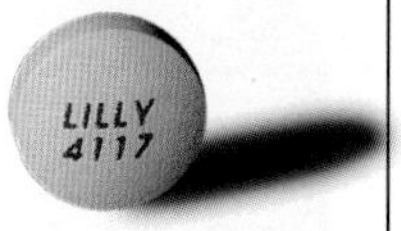
LILLY
4117

10 mg

olanzapine

Eli Lilly

KAPLAN & SADOCK'S

Synopsis of Psychiatry

Behavioral Sciences/Clinical Psychiatry

Eighth Edition

Senior Contributing Editor

Robert Cancro, M.D., Med.D.Sc.
Professor and Chairman, Department of Psychiatry, New York University School of Medicine; Director, Department of Psychiatry, Tisch Hospital, the University Hospital of the New York University Medical Center, New York, New York; Director, Nathan S. Kline Institute for Psychiatric Research, Orangeburg, New York

Contributing Editors

James Edmondson, M.D., Ph.D.
Clinical Assistant Professor of Neurology, Department of Neurology, College of Medicine, State University of New York Health Science Center at Brooklyn; Assistant Attending, Department of Neurology, Brooklyn Hospital Center; Assistant Attending, Department of Neurology, Long Island College Hospital, Brooklyn, New York

Glen O. Gabbard, M.D.
Distinguished Professor, Menninger Clinic; Distinguished Professor, Karl Menninger School of Psychiatry and Mental Health Sciences; Training and Supervising Analyst, Topeka Institute for Psychoanalysis, Topeka, Kansas; Clinical Professor of Psychiatry, Kansas University School of Medicine, Wichita, Kansas

Myrl Manley, M.D.
Associate Professor of Clinical Psychiatry and Director of Medical Student Education, New York University School of Medicine, New York, New York

Caroly S. Pataki, M.D.
Assistant Clinical Professor of Psychiatry and Associate Director of Training and Education for Child and Adolescent Psychiatry, University of California at Los Angeles School of Medicine; Attending Psychiatrist, UCLA Neuropsychiatric Institute, Los Angeles, California

Virginia A. Sadock, M.D.
Clinical Professor of Psychiatry and Director, Program in Human Sexuality and Sex Therapy, Department of Psychiatry, New York University School of Medicine; Attending Psychiatrist, Tisch Hospital, the University Hospital of the New York University Medical Center; Attending Psychiatrist, Bellevue Hospital Center, New York, New York

KAPLAN & SADOCK'S

Synopsis of Psychiatry

Behavioral Sciences/Clinical Psychiatry

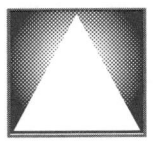

EIGHTH EDITION

Harold I. Kaplan, M.D.

Professor of Psychiatry,
New York University School of Medicine
Attending Psychiatrist, Tisch Hospital, the University Hospital
of the New York University Medical Center
Attending Psychiatrist, Bellevue Hospital Center
Consultant Psychiatrist, Lenox Hill Hospital
New York, New York

Benjamin J. Sadock, M.D.

Professor and Vice Chairman,
Department of Psychiatry, New York University School of Medicine
Attending Psychiatrist, Tisch Hospital, the University Hospital
of the New York University Medical Center
Attending Psychiatrist, Bellevue Hospital Center
Consultant Psychiatrist, Lenox Hill Hospital
New York, New York

LIPPINCOTT WILLIAMS & WILKINS
A **Wolters Kluwer** Company
Philadelphia • Baltimore • New York • London
Buenos Aires • Hong Kong • Sydney • Tokyo

Editor: Charles W. Mitchell
Managing Editor: Joyce A. Murphy
Marketing Manager: Daniell T. Griffin
Production Coordinator: Carol Lindley Eckhart
Project Editor: Bill Cady
Illustration Planner: Lorraine Wrzosek
Cover and Inside Designer: Paul Fry
Typesetter: Maryland Composition Co., Inc.
Printer and Binder: Quebecor World Taunton

351 West Camden Street
Baltimore, Maryland 21201-2436 USA

Rose Tree Corporate Center
1400 North Providence Road
Building II, Suite 5025
Media, Pennsylvania 19063-2043 USA

Notice. The indications and dosages of all drugs in this book have been recommended in the medical literature and conform to the practices of the general medical community. The medications described do not necessarily have specific approval by the Food and Drug Administration for use in the diseases and dosages for which they are recommended. The package insert for each drug should be consulted for use and dosage as approved by the FDA. Because standards for usage change, it is advisable to keep abreast of revised recommendations, particularly those concerning new drugs.

Printed in the United States of America

Previous Editions
First Edition 1972
Second Edition 1976
Third Edition 1981
Fourth Edition 1985
Fifth Edition 1988
Sixth Edition 1991
Seventh Edition 1994

Library of Congress Cataloging-in-Publication Data

Kaplan, Harold I.,
Kaplan and Sadock's synopsis of psychiatry ;n: behavioral sciences, clinical psychiatry / Harold I. Kaplan, Benjamin J. Sadock, —8th ed.
p. cm.
Includes bibliographical references and index.
ISBN 0-683-30330-9
1. Mental illness. 2. Psychiatry. I. Sadock, Benjamin J., . II. Title.
[DNLM: 1. Mental Disorders. WM 140 K17k 1997]
RC454.K35 1997
616.89—dc21
DNLM/DLC
for Library of Congress 97-9138
CIP

The publishers have made every effort to trace the copyright holders for borrowed material. If they have inadvertently overlooked any, they will be pleased to make the necessary arrangements at the first opportunity.

5 6 7 8 9 10

Dedicated to our wives,
Nancy Barrett Kaplan
and Virginia Alcott Sadock,
without whose help and sacrifice
this textbook would not have been possible

Preface

The first edition of *Kaplan and Sadock's Synopsis of Psychiatry* was published over 25 years ago; this edition is the eighth to appear. Since the first edition, psychiatry has undergone major transformations: New advances in neural sciences emerged and continue to do so at an ever-increasing rate, particularly in the areas of neuroanatomy, neurochemistry, neurophysiology, psychoneuroimmunology, and psychoendocrinology. Psychopharmacology established itself as an applied science. New information about the diagnosis and treatment of mental illness developed, and the range of psychotherapeutic approaches available to clinicians increased. Nosology changed significantly since the publication of the first edition of the American Psychiatric Association's *Diagnostic and Statistical Manual* (DSM-I) in 1952; and although many psychiatrists have been critical of the later revisions of DSM, it remains the "law of the land." Accordingly, the nomenclature and diagnostic criteria used in this textbook are based on the latest edition of DSM published in 1994 (DSM-IV). *Kaplan and Sadock's Synopsis of Psychiatry* has had the reputation of being a consistent, accurate, objective, and reliable chronicler of these and other new events in the field of psychiatry for over a quarter of a century. It is written to meet the needs of medical students, psychiatrists, neurologists, primary care and other nonpsychiatric physicians and mental health professionals from all fields—psychology, social work, and nursing, among others.

ICD-10

This is the first U.S. textbook to include the definitions and diagnostic criteria of mental disorders used in the tenth revision of *International Statistical Classification of Diseases and Related Health Problems* (ICD-10) published by the World Health Organization. DSM-IV is currently similar to the ninth revision of that manual (ICD-9), also known as ICD-9-CM (CM stands for clinical modifications). According to treaties between the United States and the World Health Organization, however, by the year 2000, DSM-IV diagnoses and codes must be identical with those used in ICD-10 (and ICD-10-CM) to ensure uniform reporting of national and international psychiatric statistics. Currently, both DSM-IV and ICD-9-CM diagnoses and numerical codes are accepted by Medicare, Medicaid, and private insurance companies for reimbursement purposes in the United States. Readers can find the DSM-IV classification list with the equivalent ICD-9-CM code numbers and the ICD-10 classification list in Chapter 9.

Philosophy

Throughout the years, an eclectic, multidisciplinary approach has been the hallmark of *Kaplan and Sadock's Synopsis of Psychiatry.* This edition maintains the same position; thus biological, psychological, and sociological factors in psychiatry are equitably presented as they affect the person in health and disease. The authors are committed to the philosophy of humanitarianism that stresses the inherent dignity, worth, and capacity for self-realization in each individual.

This edition continues the tradition of speaking out forcefully on sociopolitical issues that affect the delivery of health care. We expect this book to provide a forum about the many forces that affect medical practice. Readers can find discussions of physician-assisted suicide and euthanasia; the use, classification, and definition of controlled substances; the use of triplicate prescriptions; people who are homeless and mentally ill; deinstitutionalization; working conditions and the number of hours medical house staff are on duty; reductions in residency training positions; the role of managed care in medicine and psychiatry; and the increased regulation of medicine as represented by state offices of professional medical conduct. Both psychiatrists and nonpsychiatric practitioners have a special obligation to be informed about the sociopolitical issues affecting the physical and psychological well-being of their patients.

KAPLAN AND SADOCK TEACHING SYSTEM

This textbook forms one part of a comprehensive system developed by the authors to facilitate the teaching of psychiatry and the behavioral sciences. At the head of the system is *Comprehensive Textbook of Psychiatry,* which is global in depth and scope; it is designed for and used by psychiatrists, behavioral scientists, and all workers in the mental health field. *Kaplan and Sadock's Synopsis* is a relatively brief, highly modified, original, and current version useful for medical students, psychiatric residents, practicing psychiatrists, and mental health professionals. Another part of the system is *Study Guide and Self-Examination Review for Kaplan and Sadock's Synopsis of Psychiatry,* which consists of multiple-choice questions and answers; it is designed for students of psychiatry and for clinical psychiatrists who require a review of the behavioral sciences and general psychiatry in preparation for a variety of examinations. The questions are modeled after and consistent with the format used by the National Board of Medical Examiners and the United States Medical Licensing Examination. Other parts of the system are the pocket handbooks: *Pocket Handbook of Clinical Psychiatry, Pocket Handbook of Psychiatric Drug Treatment, Pocket Handbook of Emergency Psychiatric Medicine,* and *Pocket Handbook of Primary Care Psychiatry.* Those books cover the diagnosis and the treatment of psychiatric disorders, psychopharmacology, psychiatric emergencies, and primary care psychiatry, respectively, and are compactly designed and concisely written to be carried in the pocket by clinical clerks and practicing physicians, whatever their specialty, to provide a quick reference. Finally, *Comprehensive Glossary of Psychiatry and Psychology* provides simply written definitions for psychiatrists and other physicians, psychologists, students, other mental health professionals, and the general public.

Taken together, these books create a multiple approach to the teaching, study, and learning of psychiatry.

CHANGES IN THIS EDITION

Format. This edition is heavily illustrated to enrich the educational experience and to avoid having readers flounder in a sea of type. Some photographs of Sigmund Freud are published here for the first time. Color illustrations of all major psychiatric drugs and their various dosage forms, including those that were recently released, are included as they are in all Kaplan and Sadock books. To keep the text from being too unwieldy, we limited the reference lists and used small type in some sections to conserve space. Readers will find color cues to differentiate DSM-IV and ICD-10 diagnostic criteria.

New and Updated Sections. Chapter 3, ''The Brain and Behavior,'' is completely rewritten to provide the most up-to-date exposition of neurochemistry, neurophysiology, brain imaging, and behavioral genetics. New chapters that are relevant to current psychiatric theory and practice have been added: These include Chapter 18, ''Neurasthenia and Chronic Fatigue Syndrome,'' and Chapter 29, ''Alternative Medicine and Psychiatry.'' Two new sections, ''Psychosocial Treatment and Rehabilitation'' and ''Combined Psychotherapy and Pharmacotherapy,'' are included in the chapter on psychotherapies (Chapter 34). A discussion of the Persian Gulf War syndrome has been added to the section titled ''Posttraumatic Stress Disorder'' (Chapter 16.5). A review of the newly classified prion diseases appears in the section ''Mental Disorders Due to a General Medical Condition'' (Chapter 10.5). Extensive revisions were made in the sections on ''Public Psychiatry'' and ''Health Care Delivery,'' and a new section on ''Anabolic Steroid Abuse'' was added to Chapter 12 entitled ''Substance-Related Disorders.'' A new section on Obesity was added. All the sections on clinical psychiatry have been updated to include the latest information about diagnosing and treating mental disorders. The references are also completely up to date.

Biological Psychiatry. Drugs used to treat mental disorders are classified and discussed pharmacologically, rather than as antidepressants, antipsychotics, and the like. We employ this unique format to provide students with an understanding of the use of each drug according to its pharmacological activity as a discrete drug. Information about pharmacological agents used in psychiatry, including pharmacodynamics, pharmacokinetics, dosages, adverse effects, and drug–drug interactions, were thoroughly updated and include all newly approved drugs.

Childhood Disorders. Two new chapters, ''Adolescent Substance Abuse'' (Chapter 50) and ''Forensic Issues in Child Psychiatry'' (Chapter 55), were newly written for this edition. Pharmacological treatment for children was updated as have all sections on child and adolescent disorders.

Case Histories. Case histories were added to make clinical disorders more vivid in readers' minds. For the first time in a U.S. text, clinical cases from the *ICD-10 Casebook* are included in addition to cases from DSM-IV. We wish to thank the American Psychiatric Press and the World Health Organization for their permission to use these cases.

Acknowledgments. Jack Grebb, M.D., who joined us as coauthor in the last edition of *Synopsis,* was unable to again do so because of other commitments. He made himself available, however, as an active consultant to this edition, especially in the area of biological psychiatry.

We thank our contributing editors: Glen Gabbard, M.D., contributed to the chapters on psychoanalysis and the psychodynamics of clinical disorders and drug therapy. James Edmondson, M.D., contributed to the chapter on the brain and behavior and updated the psychopharmacological sections. Caroly Pataki, M.D., revised the sections on childhood and adolescent disorders. Myrl Manley, M.D., updated and condensed the behavioral science section. We extend our very special thanks to Virginia Sadock, M.D., who revised the sections on human sexuality and who served as assistant to the authors and participated in every editorial decision.

We also thank Norman Sussman, M.D., and Jay E. Kantor, Ph.D., for their help in the psychopharmacology and ethics sections, respectively. We thank Eugene Rubin, M.D., for his assistance in updating the sections on legal and ethical issues in psychiatry.

Justin Hollingsworth played a key role as editorial assistant. He was assisted by Jennifer Peters. We thank Linda Kenevich, who processed the manuscript. We also want to thank Ann Farkas for editing this textbook. We thank Waguih IsHak, M.D., Tal Burt, M.D., Philip Kaplan, M.D., Peter Kaplan, M.D., Victoria Sadock, M.D., Jennifer Kaplan, and James Sadock for their help. We also wish to thank Carol Bernstein, M.D., Director of Residency Training in Psychiatry and the following persons at NYU Medical Center for their help: Gary Collins, M.D., Preston Dess, M.D., Peter Farol, M.D., Sylvia Hafliger, M.D., Helen Rosengarten, M.D., Marjorie Waldbaum, M.D., and Gene Yen, M.D.

We also take this opportunity to acknowledge those who have translated this and other works of the authors into foreign languages. Current translations include French, German, Greek, Indonesian, Italian, Japanese, Polish, Portuguese, Russian, Spanish, and Turkish, in addition to a special Asian and international student edition.

We thank Robert Cancro, M.D., Professor and Chairman of the Department of Psychiatry at New York University School of Medicine, who participated as Senior Contributing Editor of this edition. Dr. Cancro's commitment to psychiatric education and psychiatric research is recognized throughout the world. He has been a source of great inspiration and friendship to us and has contributed immeasurably to this and previous books.

Finally, we wish to thank Susan Gay, Vice President and Publisher of Clinical Medicine in the Book Division at Williams & Wilkins and her staff for their cooperation in every aspect of the textbook.

October 20, 1997
New York University Medical Center
New York, New York

H.I.K.
B.J.S.

Contents

1

The Doctor–Patient Relationship and Interviewing Techniques

Diagnosis may be defined as the study of signs and symptoms of disorders and their classification into disease entities. Because the etiology of many medical disorders has been clarified and specific therapies are available, a medical diagnosis also often permits inferences about the etiology of a disorder, as well as the choice of a specific treatment procedure.

In the main, psychiatry has followed the medical tradition according to which diagnosis and assessment govern the initial phases of the doctor–patient encounter. On the other hand, the role of diagnosis in psychiatry is not quite analogous to its place in other fields of medicine; in contrast to the etiology of medical disorders, the etiology of many psychiatric syndromes is not yet fully understood, and treatment is often empirical. Thus, formal diagnosis in psychiatry does not always implicate specific etiology factors and facilitate treatment decisions.

Despite these limitations, accurate assessment does play an important role in psychiatry. Clinical experience has shown that, on the basis of such assessment, it is possible, with respect to certain diagnostic entities, to predict patients' responses to therapy with a fair degree of accuracy. For example, the acute symptoms of many patients with schizophrenia improve with appropriate antipsychotic medication, and certain hyperactivity disorders in children are likely to respond to treatment with amphetamines. Clearly, clinicians must accurately assess such cases to choose appropriate pharmacological therapy, as well as to differentiate between those patients who require drugs and those who may be treated exclusively with psychological forms of therapy.

Another difference between the role of diagnosis in general medicine and its role in psychiatry derives from the greater complexities of psychiatric assessment. Assessment of medical patients involves the diagnostic classification of their disorder and the choice of appropriate treatment methods. Psychiatric assessment extends beyond these considerations; psychiatric treatment often involves exploration of subtle aspects of patients' personalities, which, in turn, requires psychiatrists to understand patients in depth. Thus, apart from the criteria that usually serve as the basis for formal diagnosis (for example, the presence of specific symptoms such as hallucinations or delusions), psychiatrists in the course of assessment must also identify more subtle deviations in cognitive and affective functions: They must assess the quality of patients' relationships with others; and they must evaluate the degree to which patients are able to satisfy their sexual, creative, and material needs. Patients' typical modes of adaptation and the strength of their psychological defenses also constitute important data.

For diagnosing, managing, and treating patients' disorders, all physicians can summon many tools, which range from complicated laboratory investigations to highly sophisticated radiographic procedures. Although medical schools and residencies train students and newly graduated doctors in the complex and essential skills of their profession, they often treat one such skill superficially: the capacity for an effective doctor–patient relationship. This capacity requires a deep appreciation for the intricacies of human behavior and a rigorous education in the techniques of talking and listening to people.

To diagnose, manage, and treat a person's disorder, physicians must have learned to listen. Many physicians, whose training has taught them to be, first and foremost, active, aggressive, and in control, are not always comfortable with the act of listening. One of the supreme tasks of any medical training center is to help physicians acquire the skills of active listening, both to what doctor and patient say and to the undercurrents, the unspoken feelings, between the two. Physicians who continually monitor not only the *content* of the interaction (what patient and doctor say to each other) but also the *process* (what patient and doctor may not say but clearly convey in many other ways) realize that communication between two people simultaneously takes place on several levels. Physicians who are sensitive to the effects of history, culture, environment, and psychology on the doctor–patient relationship work with patients who are multifaceted people, not mere disease syndromes. When educators have failed to emphasize, respect, and convey the art and technique of active listening, they have failed to train physicians in the rudiments of establishing relationships with their patients, and patient care is the inevitable loser.

MODELS OF DISEASE

The most prominent proponent of the biopsychosocial model of disease has been George Engel, who has stressed an integrated systems approach to human behavior and to disease. The biopsychosocial model is derived from general systems theory: The biological system deals with the anatomical, structural, and molecular substrates of disease and the effects on patients' biological functioning; the psychological system treats the effects of psychodynamic factors, motivation, and personality on the experience of, and reaction to, illness; and the social system examines cultural, environmental, and familial influences on the expression and experience of illness.

Engel postulates that each system affects and is affected by all the others. Engel's model does not treat medical illness as a direct result of people's psychological and sociocultural makeup but, rather, promotes a comprehensive understanding of disease and treatment.

A dramatic example of Engel's concept of the biopsychosocial model was a 1971 study of the relation between sudden death and psychological factors. After investigating 170 sudden deaths over about 6 years, Engel observed that serious illness or even death may be associated with psychological stress or trauma. Among the potential triggering events he listed are the death of a close friend, grief, anniversary reactions, loss of self-esteem, personal danger or threat, the letdown after the threat has passed, and reunions or triumphs.

The doctor–patient relationship is a critical component of the biopsychosocial model. All physicians must not only have a working knowledge of patients' medical status but must also be familiar with how patients' individual psychology and sociocultural milieu affect the medical condition, the emotional responses to the condition, and the involvement with the doctor.

MEANING OF BEING SICK

The term *illness behavior* describes patients' reactions to the experience of being sick. Aspects of illness behavior have sometimes been termed the *sick role,* the role that society ascribes to sick people because they are ill. The sick role can include being excused from responsibilities and being expected to want to obtain help to get well. Edward Suchman described five stages of illness behavior: *the symptom experience stage,* in which a decision is made that something is wrong; *the assumption of the sick role stage,* in which a decision is made that a person is sick and needs professional care; *the medical care contact stage,* in which a decision is made to seek professional care; *the dependent-patient role stage,* in which a decision is made to transfer control to the doctor and to follow prescribed treatment; and *the recovery or rehabilitation stage,* in which a decision is made to give up the patient role.

Illness behavior and the sick role are affected by people's previous experiences with illness and by their cultural beliefs about disease. The influence of culture on reporting and presenting symptoms must be evaluated. For some disorders reporting and manifestation vary little from culture, whereas for others the way a person deals with the disorder may strongly shape the way the condition manifests itself. The relation of illness to family processes, class status, and ethnic identity is also important. The attitudes of peoples and cultures about dependency and helplessness greatly influence how and if a person asks for help, as do such psychological factors as personality type and the personal meaning attributed to the experience of being ill. People react to illness in different ways, which depend on their habitual modes of thinking, feeling, and behaving. Some people experience illness as overwhelming loss; others see in the same illness a challenge they must overcome or a punishment they deserve. Table 1–1 lists essential areas to be addressed in assessing illness behavior and helpful questions for making the assessment.

Table 1–1
Assessment of Individual Illness Behavior

Prior illness episodes, especially illnesses of standard severity (childbirth, renal stones, surgery)
Cultural degree of stoicism
Cultural beliefs concerning the specific problem
Personal meaning or beliefs about the particular problem
Specific questions to ask to elicit the patient's explanatory model:

1. What do you call your problem? What name does it have?
2. What do you think caused your problem?
3. Why do you think it started when it did?
4. What does your sickness do to you? How does it work?
5. How severe is it? Will it have a short or long course?
6. What do you fear most about your sickness?
7. What are the chief problems that your sickness has caused for you?
8. What kind of treatment do you think you should receive? What are the most important results you hope to receive from treatment?
9. What have you done so far to treat your sickness?

Courtesy of Mack Lipkin, Jr., M.D.

DOCTOR–PATIENT MODELS

The doctor–patient relationship has several potential models, which most often derive from the personalities, expectations, and needs of both doctor and patient. Often, neither doctor nor patient is fully conscious of choosing one or another model. That the personalities, the expectations, and the needs are largely unspoken and may be different for doctor and patient may lead to miscommunication and disappointment for both participants. Doctors must be aware of which model operates with which patient and must be able to shift models as the particular needs of specific patients and as the treatment requirements of specific clinical situations dictate.

Types

Models of the doctor–patient relationship include the active-passive model, the teacher–student (or parent–child, guidance–cooperation) model, the mutual participation model, and the friendship (or socially intimate) model.

The *active-passive model* implies a patient's complete passivity and a physician's taking control. In this model patients assume virtually no responsibility for their own care and take no part in treatment. The model is appropriate when patients are unconscious, immobilized, or delirious.

In the *teacher–student model* the physician's dominance is assumed and emphasized. The role of the physician is paternalistic and controlling; the role of the patient is essentially one of dependence and acceptance. This model is often observed during a patient's recovery from surgery.

The *mutual participation model* implies equality between doctor and patient; both participants require and depend on each other's input. The need for a doctor–patient relationship based on a model of mutual, active participation is most obvious in the treatment of such chronic illnesses as renal failure and diabetes, in which a patient's knowledge and acceptance of treatment ramifications are critical to the success of the treatment. The model may also be effective when patients have conditions such as pneumonia.

The *friendship model* of the doctor–patient relationship is generally considered dysfunctional if not unethical. It most often reflects a primary, underlying psychological problem in the physician, who may have an emotional need to turn the patient's care into a relationship of mutual sharing of personal information and love. The model often involves indeterminate perpetuation of the relationship rather than an appropriate ending and a blurring of boundaries between professionalism and intimacy.

General Considerations

Gaining conscious insight into the relationship between physicians and patients requires constant evaluation. The more that doctors understand themselves, the more secure they feel, and the better able they are to modify destructive attitudes. Doctors must empathize with patients, but not to the point of assuming their patients' burdens or unrealistically fantasizing that only they can be the patients' saviors. They should be able to leave behind their patients' problems when away from the office or the hospital and should not use their patients as substitutes for an intimacy or relationship that may be missing in their personal lives. Otherwise they are handicapped in their efforts to help sick people, who need sympathy and understanding, not sentimentality and overinvolvement.

Physicians are prone to some defensiveness, partly with good reason; many innocent doctors have been sued, attacked, and even killed because they did not give some patients the satisfaction they desired. Consequently, physicians may assume a defensive attitude toward all patients. Although such rigidity may create the image of thoroughness and efficiency, it is frequently inappropriate. Increased flexibility leads to a responsiveness to the subtle interplay between doctor and patient and also assumes a certain tolerance for the uncertainty present in any clinical situation with any patient. Physicians must learn to accept that, as much as they may wish to control everything in a patient's care, this wish can never be fully realized. In some situations a disease cannot be controlled, and death cannot be prevented, no matter how conscientious, competent, or caring a physician is. Physicians must also avoid sidestepping issues that they find difficult to deal with because of their own sensitivities, prejudices, or peculiarities, especially when these issues are important to a patient.

A medical student insisted on questioning a patient about her relationship with her 23-year-old son. The playback of a tape-recorded interview revealed that the patient wanted to talk about her problems with her husband. When the supervising doctor later interviewed the patient, she said: "The medical student was a nice fellow, but I could see that he was having trouble with his mother. It made me understand my own son more."

In such a complex interaction as the doctor–patient relationship, mistakes are usually not disastrous when they are relatively infrequent. When patients sense interest, enthusiasm, and goodwill on the part of an interviewer, they are apt to tolerate considerable inexperience.

INTERVIEWING EFFECTIVELY

One of a physician's most critical tools is the ability to interview effectively. Through a skillful interview, physicians can gather the data necessary to understand and treat patients and, in the process, to increase patients' understanding of and compliance with physicians' advice. Every interview has three main components, all of which require special techniques and skills: the beginning, the interview itself, and the closing of the interview.

Ekkehard Othmer and Sieglinde Othmer described psychiatric interviews as taking place in four dimensions—establishing rapport, assessing patients' mental status, using specific techniques, and diagnosing—with the interviewing process progressing through five stages. Table 1–2 summarizes their concept of an ideal interview. Othmer and Othmer stressed that the order of completion of the interview tasks is determined by following patients' needs; the order need not necessarily be that outlined in Table 1–2. In general, interviewers must convey an attitude that is nonjudgmental, interested, concerned, and kind; otherwise, potentially crucial information may not be obtained.

Many factors influence both the content and the process of interviews: Patients' personalities and character styles significantly influence reactions as well as the emotional context in which interviews unfold. Various clinical situations—including whether patients are seen on a general hospital ward, on a psychiatric ward, in an emergency room, or as outpatients—shape the questions asked and the recommendations offered. Technical factors—such as telephone interruptions, the use of an interpreter, note taking, and a patients' illness, be it in the most acute stage or during a remission—influence interviews' content and process. Interviewers' styles, orientations, and experiences have a significant influence on interviews. Even the timing of interjections such as "Uh-huh" can influence when patients speak and what they do or do not say, as they unconsciously try to follow the subtle leads and cues provided by a doctor.

Psychiatric Interviewing

Psychiatric interviews have two major technical goals: recognition of the psychological determinants of behavior and symptom classification. Othmer and Othmer described goals as encompassing two styles of interviewing: the insight-oriented or psychodynamic style and the symptom-oriented or descriptive style. *Insight-oriented interviewing* tends to emphasize eliciting and interpreting unconscious conflicts, anxieties, and defenses; the *symptom-oriented approach* emphasizes the classification of patients' complaints and dysfunctions as defined by specific diagnostic categories. The approaches are not mutually exclusive and, in fact, can be compatible.

Table 1–2
Five Phases of the Interview and the Four Components

Phase	Rapport	Technique	Mental Status	Diagnosis
1. Warm-up and screening of problem	Put patient at ease, set limits, empathize with suffering, become a compassionate listener	Select productive and broad screening questions	Observe appearance, psychomotor functions, speech, thinking, affect, orientation, memory, and explore mood, insight, memory, judgment	Note clues, classify the chief complaint; assess symptoms, severity, course, stressors; list differential diagnoses
2. Follow-up of preliminary impressions	Become an ally, make shifts in topics clear	Shift topics, progress from open- to closed-ended questions	Assess thinking, thought content, suicidality	Verify or exclude diagnoses
3. History and database	Show expertise, interest, thoroughness, leadership and motivate for testing	Shift topics, handle defenses, fill in gaps, follow up clues, reconcile inconsistencies	Evaluate judgment, memory, test specific mental status functions and IQ	Assess course of disorders, impact on social life, family and medical history
4. Diagnoses and feedback	Secure acceptance of diagnosis	Explain disorders and treatment options	Discuss mental status findings, explore compliance	Establish diagnoses on five axes
5. Prognosis and treatment contract	Assume the leadership role and assure compliance	Discuss treatment contract	Make inferences about insight, judgment, and compliance	Give prognosis; predict treatment effects

Reprinted with permission from Othmer E, Othmer SC: *The Clinical Interview Using DSM-IV,* p 273. American Psychiatric Press, Washington, 1994.

Patients' diagnoses can be described as precisely as possible by eliciting such details as symptoms, course of illness, and family history and by understanding patients' personalities, developmental histories, and unconscious conflicts.

Psychiatric versus Medical-Surgical Interviews

Similarities. **PSYCHOLOGICAL VERSUS MEDICAL SYMPTOMS.** Mack Lipkin, Jr., described three functions of medical interviews: to assess the nature of the problem, to develop and maintain a therapeutic relationship, and to communicate information and implement a treatment plan (Table 1–3). These functions are exactly the same as those of psychiatric and surgical interviews. Also universal are the predominant coping mechanisms, both adaptive and maladaptive. These mechanisms include such reactions as anxiety, depression, regression, denial, anger, and dependency (Table 1–4). Physicians must anticipate, recognize, and address such reactions if any treatment or intervention is to be effective. Many psychiatric problems appear as medical illnesses, and conversely, many medical and surgical problems are accompanied by psychiatric symptoms. For this reason alone, all physicians must recognize the importance of obtaining a comprehensive biopsychosocial history for each of their patients.

MEDICAL SYNDROMES WITH PSYCHIATRIC PRESENTATIONS. Lipkin defined psychogenic syndromes as "illnesses presenting as medical problems but characterized by strong evidence to suggest that the dominant role in the timing, etiology, and nature of the syndrome is that of psychological or social events, rather than biological ones." Examples include somatization disorder, factitious disorder with predominantly physical signs and symptoms, pain disorder, and hypochondriasis. Medical problems that can have psychiatric symptoms include acquired immune deficiency syndrome (AIDS) (depression, anxiety, cognitive deficits), multiple sclerosis (personality changes, mood swings, depression), and hypothyroidism (irritability, depression, paranoia, delusions, hallucinations).

Differences. Psychiatric patients must often contend with stresses and pressures different from those suffered by patients who do not have a psychiatric disorder. These stresses include the stigma attached to being a psychiatric patient (it is more acceptable to have a medical or surgical problem than to have a mental problem); difficulties in communicating because of disorders in thinking, which can include delusions, hallucinations, and disorganized thought processes; and oddities of behavior and impairments of insight and judgment, which make compliance with treatment particularly difficult. Because psychiatric patients often find it difficult to describe fully what is going on, physicians must be prepared to obtain information from other sources. Family members, friends, and spouses can provide critical data, such as past psychiatric history, responses to medication, and precipitating stresses that patients may not be able to provide themselves.

Psychiatric patients may not be able to tolerate a traditional interview format, especially in acute stages of a disorder. For instance, a patient suffering from increased agitation or depression may not be able to sit for 30 to 45 minutes of discussion or questioning. In such cases, physicians must be prepared to conduct multiple brief interactions over time—sitting or standing for as long as the patient is able, then stopping and returning when the patient appears able to tolerate more.

Physicians must be particularly prepared to use their powers of observation with psychiatric patients who are not able to communicate well verbally. Their specific observations should include patients' general appearance, behavior, and body language and the ways all these factors provide diagnostic clues.

According to the American Psychiatric Association's

Table 1–3
Three Functions of the Medical Interview

Functions	Objectives	Skills
I. Determining the nature of the problem	1. To enable the clinician to establish a diagnosis or recommend further diagnostic procedures, suggest a course of treatment, and predict the nature of the illness	1. Knowledge base of diseases, disorders, problems, and clinical hypotheses from multiple conceptual domains; biomedical, sociocultural, psychodynamic, and behavioral 2. Ability to elicit data for the above conceptual domains (encouraging the patient to tell his or her story; organizing the flow of the interview, the form of questions, the characterization of symptoms, the mental status examination) 3. Ability to perceive data from multiple sources (history, mental status examination, physician's subjective response to patient, nonverbal cues, listening at multiple levels) 4. Hypothesis generation and testing 5. Developing a therapeutic relationship (function II)
II. Developing and maintaining a therapeutic relationship	1. The patient's willingness to provide diagnostic information 2. Relief of physical and psychological distress 3. Willingness to accept treatment plan or a process of negotiation 4. Patient satisfaction 5. Physician satisfaction	1. Defining the nature of the relationship 2. Allowing the patient to tell his or her story 3. Hearing, bearing, and tolerating the patient's expression of painful feelings 4. Appropriate and genuine interest, empathy, support, and cognitive understanding 5. Attending to common patient concerns over embarrassment, shame, and humiliation 6. Elicitation of the patient's perspective 7. Determining the nature of the problem (function I) 8. Communicating information and recommending treatment (function III)
III. Communicating information and implementing a treatment plan	1. The patient's understanding of the nature of the illness 2. The patient's understanding of suggested diagnostic procedures 3. The patient's understanding of the treatment possibilities 4. Achievements of consensus between physician and patient over the above items 1 to 3 5. Achievement of informed consent 6. Improve coping mechanisms 7. Life-style change	1. Determining the nature of the problem (function I) 2. Developing a therapeutic relationship (function II) 3. Establishing the differences in perspective between physician and patient 4. Educational strategies 5. Clinical negotiations for conflict resolutions

Reprinted with permission from Lazare A, Bird J, Lipkin M Jr, Putnam S: Three functions of the medical interview: An integrative conceptual framework. In *The Medical Interview,* M Lipkin Jr, S Putnam, A Lazare, editors, p 103. Springer, New York, 1989.

''Practice Guideline for Psychiatric Evaluation of Adults,'' psychiatrists' assessment tool ''is the face-to-face interview of the patient: evaluations based solely on review of records and interviews of persons close to the patient are inherently limited.''

It is essential that all physicians who treat psychiatric patients be familiar with these guidelines (Table 1–5), because many nonpsychiatric physicians see psychiatric patients. Studies show that about 60 percent of all patients with mental disorders visit a nonpsychiatric physician during any 6-month period and that patients with mental disorders are twice as likely to visit a primary care physician as are other patients. Nonpsychiatric physicians should be knowledgeable about the special problems of psychiatric patients and the specific techniques used to treat them.

Rapport

Establishing rapport is the first step of a psychiatric interview, and interviewers often use their own empathic responses to facilitate the development of rapport. Othmer and Othmer defined the development of rapport as encompassing six strat-

Table 1–4
Predictable Reactions to Illness

Intrapsychic	Clinical
Lowered self-image → loss → grief	Anxiety
Threat to homeostasis → fear	Denial
Failure of (self) care → helplessness, hopelessness	Depression Bargaining and blaming
Sense of loss of control → shame (guilt)	Regression Isolation Dependency Anger Acceptance

Courtesy of Mack Lipkin, Jr., M.D.

egies: putting patients and interviewers at ease; finding patients' pain and expressing compassion; evaluating patients' insight and becoming an ally; showing expertise; establishing authority as physicians and therapists; and balancing the roles of empathic listener, expert, and authority. As part of a strategy for increasing rapport, Othmer and Othmer developed a checklist (Table 1–6) that enables interviewers to recognize problems and refine their skills in establishing rapport.

In one survey of 700 patients, patients substantially agreed that physicians do not have the time or inclination to listen and consider patients' feelings, that physicians do not have enough knowledge of the emotional problems and socioeconomic background of patients' families, and that physicians increase patients' fear by giving explanations in technical language.

Physician failures to establish good rapport with patients account for much of the ineffectiveness in care. Rapport implies that understanding and trust between doctor and patient are present. Psychosocial and economic factors exert a profound influence on human relations, and physicians should have as much understanding as possible of patients' subcultures. Differences in social, intellectual, and educational status can interfere seriously with rapport. Understanding—or not understanding—patients' beliefs, use of language, and attitudes toward illness influences the character of physicians' examinations.

Evaluating the social pressures in patients' early lives helps psychiatrists better understand patients. Emotional reactions, healthy or unhealthy, are the result of a constant interplay of biological, sociological, and psychological forces. Each stress leaves behind a trace of its influence and continues to manifest itself throughout life in proportion to the intensity of its effect and the susceptibility of the human being involved. Stresses and strains should be determined to the fullest extent possible. The significant point may not be a stress itself but, rather, a person's reactions to it. The establishment of genuine rapport also depends on a basic understanding of such complex interpersonal factors as transference and countertransference.

Transference. *Transference* is generally defined as the set of expectations, beliefs, and emotional responses that a patient brings to the doctor–patient relationship. Transference reflects not necessarily who a doctor is or how a doctor acts in reality but, rather, what persistent experiences a patient has had with other important authority figures throughout life.

TRANSFERENTIAL ATTITUDES. A patient's attitude toward a physician is apt to be a repetition of the attitude he or she has had toward authority figures. The attitude may range from one of realistic basic trust, with an expectation that the doctor has the patient's best interests at heart, through one of overidealization and even eroticized fantasy, to one of basic mistrust, with an expectation that the doctor will be contemptuous and potentially abusive. A patient may expect a doctor to do something—for example, to prescribe medication or to perform surgery—and can accept a doctor's care as sufficient and competent only if these actions occur. Inherent in this attitude is a patient's role as a passive recipient in relation to a doctor's role as an active bestower of help. A doctor has different expectations. Another patient may be active and expect to participate fully in treatment and, correspondingly, feels at odds with a doctor who does not want patient participation.

PSYCHIATRIST VERSUS NONPSYCHIATRIST. In many respects the role of psychiatrists is different from that of nonpsychiatric physicians, and

Table 1–5
Outline of the APA Practice Guideline for Psychiatric Evaluation

STATEMENT OF INTENT
SUMMARY
INTRODUCTION
I. PURPOSE OF EVALUATION
  A. General psychiatric evaluation
  B. Emergency evaluation
  C. Clinical consultation
  D. Other consultations
II. SITE OF THE CLINICAL EVALUATION
  A. Inpatient settings
  B. Outpatient settings
  C. General medical settings
  D. Other settings
III. DOMAINS OF THE CLINICAL EVALUATION
  A. Reason for the evaluation
  B. History of the present illness
  C. Past psychiatric history
  D. General medical history
  E. History of substance use
  F. Psychosocial developmental history (personal history)
  G. Social history
  H. Occupational history
  I. Family history
  J. Review of systems
  K. Physical examination
  L. Mental status examination
  M. Functional assessment
  N. Diagnostic tests
  O. Information derived from the interview process
IV. EVALUATION PROCESS
  A. Methods of obtaining information
  B. The process of assessment
V. SPECIAL CONSIDERATIONS
  A. Interactions with third-party payers and their agents
  B. Privacy and confidentiality
  C. Legal and administrative issues in institutions
  D. Evaluation of elderly persons
VI. DEVELOPMENT PROCESS

Reprinted with permission from American Psychiatric Association: Practice guidelines for psychiatric evaluation of adults. Am J Psychiatry *152* (11, Suppl): 66, 1995.

Table 1–6
Checklist

The following checklist allows clinicians to rate their skills in establishing and maintaining rapport. It helps them detect and eliminate weaknesses in interviews that failed in some significant way.

	Yes	No	N/A
1. I put the patient at ease.			
2. I recognized the patient's state of mind.			
3. I addressed the patient's distress.			
4. I helped the patient warm up.			
5. I helped the patient overcome suspiciousness.			
6. I curbed the patient's intrusiveness.			
7. I stimulated the patient's verbal production.			
8. I curbed the patient's rambling.			
9. I understood the patient's suffering.			
10. I expressed empathy for the patient's suffering.			
11. I tuned in on the patient's affect.			
12. I addressed the patient's affect.			
13. I became aware of the patient's level of insight.			
14. I assumed the patient's view of the disorder.			
15. I had a clear perception of the overt and the therapeutic goals of treatment.			
16. I stated the overt goal of treatment to the patient.			
17. I communicated to the patient that I am familiar with the illness.			
18. My questions convinced the patient that I am familiar with the symptoms of the disorder.			
19. I let the patient know that he or she is not alone with the illness.			
20. I expressed my intent to help the patient.			
21. The patient recognized my expertise.			
22. The patient respected my authority.			
23. The patient appeared fully cooperative.			
24. I recognized the patient's attitude toward the illness.			
25. The patient viewed the illness with distance.			
26. The patient presented as a sympathy-craving sufferer.			
27. The patient presented as a very important patient.			
28. The patient competed with me for authority.			
29. The patient was submissive.			
30. I adjusted my role to the patient's role.			
31. The patient thanked me and made another appointment.			

Reprinted with permission from Othmer E, Othmer SC: *The Clinical Interview Using DSM-IV*, p 41. American Psychiatric Press, Washington, 1994.

yet many patients expect the same from a psychiatrist as they do from other physicians. When they expect a doctor to take action, give advice, and prescribe medication to cure an illness, they may well expect the same interaction with a psychiatrist and may be disappointed or angry when their expectations are not fulfilled. For many reasons, transference reactions may be strongest with psychiatrists. For example, in intensive insight-oriented psychotherapy, the encouragement of transference feelings is an integral part of treatment. In some types of therapy, a psychiatrist is more or less neutral. The more neutral or less known a psychiatrist is, the more a patient's transferential fantasies and concerns are mobilized and projected onto the doctor. Once fantasies are stimulated and projected, psychiatrists can help patients gain insight into how these fantasies and concerns affect all the important relationships in their lives.

Although a nonpsychiatrist does not use or even need to understand transference attitudes in this intensive way, a solid understanding of the power and manifestations of transference is necessary for optimal treatment results in any doctor–patient relationship. Physicians' words and deeds have a power far beyond the commonplace because of their unique authority and patients' dependence on them. How a particular physician behaves and interacts has a direct bearing on a patient's emotional and even physical reactions. One patient repeatedly had high blood pressure readings when examined by a physician the patient considered cold, aloof, and stern but had normal blood pressure readings when seen by a doctor the patient regarded as warm, understanding, and sympathetic.

Countertransference. Just as patients bring transferential attitudes to doctor–patient relationships, doctors themselves often have countertransferential reactions to their patients. Countertransference may take the form of negative feelings that are disruptive to the doctor–patient relationship but may also encompass disproportionately positive, idealizing, or even eroticized reactions. Just as patients have expectations—such as competence, lack of exploitation, objectivity, comfort, and relief—physicians often have unconscious or unspoken expectations of patients. Most commonly, physicians think of patients as good when their expressed severity of symptoms correlates with an overtly diagnosable biological disorder, when they are compliant and generally do not challenge the treatment, when they are emotionally controlled, and when they are grateful. If these expectations are not met, physicians may blame patients and experience them as unlikable, untreatable, or bad.

DISLIKE. A psychiatrist who actively dislikes a patient is apt to be ineffective in dealing with him or her. Emotion breeds counteremotion. For example, if a physician is hostile, the patient becomes hostile; the physician then becomes even angrier than before, and the relationship deteriorates rapidly. If a physician can rise above such emotions and handle a resentful patient with equanimity, the interpersonal relationship may shift from one of mutual overt antagonism to one of at least increased acceptance and grudging respect. Rising above such emotions involves being able to step back from the intense countertransferential reactions and to dispassionately explore why a patient reacts to the doctor in such an apparently self-defeating way. After all, patients need doctors, and hostility ensures that the needed help does not occur. If the doctor can understand that a patient's antagonism is in some ways defensive or self-protective and most likely reflects transferential fears of disrespect, abuse, and disappointment, the doctor may be less angry and more empathic than otherwise.

Psychiatrists with strong unconscious needs to be all knowing and all powerful may have particular problems with certain types of patients: those who appear to repeatedly defeat attempts to help them (for example, patients with severe heart disease who continue to smoke or drink); those who are perceived as uncooperative (for example, patients who question or refuse treatment); those who request a second opinion; those who fail to recover in response to treatment; those who use physical or somatic complaints to mask emotional problems (for example, patients with somatization disorder, pain disorder, hypochondriasis, or factitious disorders); those with chronic cognitive disorders (for example, patients with dementia of the Alzheimer's type); and those who are dying or in chronic pain (for example, patients who represent a professional failure and are, thus, a threat to a physician's identity and self-esteem). These patients may be difficult for most physicians to deal with, but if a physician is as aware as possible of his or her own needs, capabilities, and limitations, the patients will not be threatening.

SEXUALITY. Psychiatrists are bound to like some patients more than others, but if a physician feels a strong attraction to a patient and is tempted to act on the attraction, stepping back and dispassionately assessing the situation is essential. In some medical specialties in which the doctor–patient relationship is not particularly intimate or intense, the prohibition against romantic involvement with patients may not be strong. In other specialties, however, especially psychiatry, the ethical and even legal prohibitions are important. Physicians are powerful figures in this country's culture and may trigger many unconscious fantasies of being rescued, taken care of, and loved. Doctors themselves may have their own unconscious fantasies of being, and needing to be, all powerful, rescuing, and lovable. These fantasies are not only inherently unrealistic and dehumanizing but are inevitably disappointed. The disappointments, if realized in a romantic relationship between a doctor and a patient, can be destructive, especially for the patient. (Sexual relationships between patients and therapists are discussed further in Chapter 56.)

Another aspect of sexuality as it pertains to countertransference issues relates to asking patients about sexual issues and to obtaining a sexual history. A reluctance to do so may reflect a physician's own anxiety about sexuality or even an unconscious attraction toward a patient. Moreover, the omission of these questions generally tells patients that a doctor is uncomfortable with the subject and thus leads to an inhibition about discussing any number of other sensitive subjects.

NEED TO SELF-MONITOR. Countertransference feelings need not always be perceived in negative terms. They also have the potential, if recognized and analyzed, to help psychiatrists better understand patients who have stimulated the feelings. For instance, if a doctor feels bored and restless when with a particular patient and has ascertained that the boredom is not secondary to his or her own preoccupations, the doctor may surmise that the patient is speaking about trivial or insignificant concerns to avoid real and potentially disturbing concerns.

PHYSICIAN PATIENTS. A special example of countertransference issues, which applies to psychiatrists and nonpsychiatrists alike, occurs when the patient being treated is a physician. Problems that can arise for the treating physician in this situation include the expectation that a physician-patient can take care of his or her own medications and treatment and the fear that the patient will criticize the treating doctor's skills or competence. Ill physicians are notoriously poor patients, most likely because they are trained to be in control of medical situations and to be the masters in the doctor–patient relationship. For a physician, being a patient may mean giving up control, becoming dependent, and appearing vulnerable and frightened—tendencies that most physicians are professionally trained to suppress. Physician-patients may be reluctant to become what they perceive as burdens to overworked colleagues, or they may be embarrassed to ask pertinent questions for fear of appearing ignorant or incompetent. Physician-patients may stimulate fear in the treating physicians who see themselves in the patient, an attitude that can lead to denial and avoidance on the part of the treating physician.

Beginning the Interview

How a physician begins an interview provides a powerful first impression to patients, and the manner in which a doctor opens communication with a patient has potentially powerful effects on the way the remainder of the interview proceeds. Patients are often anxious on first encounters with physicians and feel both vulnerable and intimidated. A physician who can establish rapport quickly, put the patient at ease, and show respect is well on the way to conducting a productive exchange of information. This exchange is critical to formulate a correct diagnosis and to establish treatment goals.

All physicians should initially make sure that they know the patients' names and that patients know physicians' names. Physicians should introduce themselves to any other people who have come with the patient. If relatives or friends accompany a patient, the physician should ascertain whether the patient would like another person to be present during the initial interview. If the patient states an emphatic desire for the presence of another person, this request should be respected; the other person's presence may alleviate the patient's anxiety about the interview. It may also help gain the trust of significant people in the patient's life, people who may be essential to the patient's continued compliance with and acceptance of the doctor. The physician, however, should also attempt to speak to the patient individually to make sure that the patient has a chance to say anything he or she may not want to say in front of others. One way to do this is to first see the patient along with a family member or friend and then say: "I very much appreciate speaking with you both and getting all your thoughts and input about what is going on with Mr. X. At this point, let me give Mr. X. a chance to speak with me alone, since he and I are going to work together closely in the coming weeks. If you would like to meet together with me again in the future, I would be happy to arrange such a meeting."

Patients have the right to know the position and professional status of the people involved with their care. For example, medical students should introduce themselves as such, not as doctors, and physicians should make it clear whether they are consultants (called in by another physician to see the patient), are covering for another physician, or are involved in the interview to teach students, rather than to treat the patient.

How to Begin

Once the introductions and other initial assessments have been made, a useful and appropriate opening remark is, "Can you tell me about the troubles that bring you in today?" or "Tell me about the problems you have been having." Following up this remark with a second one, such as, "What other problems have you been experiencing?," often elicits further information that patients were reluctant to give initially. It also indicates to patients that doctors are interested in hearing as much as patients want to say.

A less directive approach is to ask a patient, "Where shall we start?" or "Where would you prefer to begin?" If a patient has been referred by another doctor for consultation, the initial remarks can indicate that the consulting doctor already knows something about the patient. For instance, the consulting doctor may say, "Your doctor has told me something about what has been troubling you (such as cardiovascular symptoms or depression), but I'd like to hear from you in your own words about what is troubling you."

Most patients do not speak freely unless they have privacy and are sure that their conversations cannot be overheard. Physicians who make sure at the beginning of an interview that such factors as privacy, quiet, and a lack of interruptions are attended to convey to patients that what patients say is important and worthy of serious consideration.

A patient may appear frightened or resistant at the beginning of an interview and may not want to answer questions. If this seems to be the case, the physician may comment on this impression directly in a gentle and supportive way and encourage the patient to talk about his or her feelings about the interview itself. Acknowledging a patient's anxiety may be the first step in delineating what the anxiety is about and can enable a physician to offer appropriate reassurance. An example of what could be said is, "I can't help but notice that you seem to be feeling anxious about talking with me, and I wonder if there is anything I can do or any question I can answer that will make it easier for you." Or "I know that it can be difficult or frightening to talk to a doctor, especially one you have never met before, but I would like to make it as comfortable for you as possible. Is there anything that you can put your finger on that is making it tough for you to talk to me?"

Another important initial question is, "Why now?" A physician should be clear about why a patient has chosen that particular time to ask for help. The reason may be as simple as this was the first available appointment time. Very often, however, people seek out doctors as the result of particular events that have led to an increase in stress. These stressful events may be thought of as precipitants and are often significant contributors to patients' current problems. Examples of stressful precipitants include real or symbolic losses (such as death and separations), milestone events (such as significant birthdays), and physical changes (such as the initiation of a new diet or a new drug). Physicians who are unaware of such stresses in people's lives may miss unspoken fears and questions that can compromise the patient's care and well-being.

Interview Proper

In the interview proper, physicians discover in detail what is troubling patients. They must do so in a systematic way that facilitates the identification of relevant problems in the context of an ongoing empathic working alliance with patients.

Content versus Process. The *content* of an interview is literally what is said between doctor and patient: the topics discussed, the subjects mentioned. The *process* of the interview is what occurs nonverbally between doctor and patient: what is happening in the interview beneath the surface. Process involves feelings and reactions that are unacknowledged or unconscious. For example, a patient may use body language to express feelings he or she cannot express verbally—a clenched fist or nervous tearing at a tissue in the face of a patient with an apparently calm outward demeanor. A patient may shift the interview away from an anxiety-provoking subject onto a neutral topic without realizing that he or she is doing so. A patient may return again and again to a particular topic, regardless of what direction the interview appears to be taking. Trivial remarks and apparently casual asides may reveal serious underlying concerns, as, for example, "Oh, by the way, a neighbor of mine tells me that he knows someone with the same symptoms as my son, and that person has cancer."

Specific Techniques. **OPEN-ENDED VERSUS CLOSED-ENDED QUESTIONS.** Interviewing any patient involves a fine balance between allowing the patient's story to unfold at will and obtaining the necessary data for diagnosis and treatment. Most experts on interviewing agree that the ideal interview is one in which a interviewer begins with broad, open-ended questioning, continues by becoming specific, and closes with detailed direct questioning.

The early part of the interview is generally the most open ended, in that physicians allow patients to speak as much as possible in their own words. A closed-ended question or directive question is one that asks for specific information and that allows a patient few options in answering. Too many closed-ended questions, especially in the early part of an interview, can lead to a restriction of patients' responses. Sometimes, directive questions are necessary to obtain important data, but when they are used too often, a patient may think that information is to be given only in response to direct questioning by the doctor. An example of an open-ended question is, "Can you tell me more about that?" A closed-ended question, if a patient has stated that he or she has been feeling depressed, might be, "Your mother died recently, didn't she?" This question can be answered only by a yes or no, and the mother's death may or may not be the reason the patient is depressed. More information is likely to be obtained if the doctor responds with, "Tell me more about what you're feeling and what you think may be causing it."

Closed-ended questions, however, can be effective in generating specific and quick responses about a clearly delineated topic. Closed-ended questions have been shown to be effective in eliciting information about the absence of certain symptoms (for example, auditory hallucinations and suicidal ideation). Closed-ended questions have also been found to be effective in assessing such factors as the frequency, the severity, and the duration of symptoms. Table 1–7 summarizes some of the pros and cons of open-ended and closed-ended questions.

REFLECTION. In the technique of reflection, a doctor repeats to a patient in a supportive manner something that the patient has said. The purpose of

Table 1–7
Pros and Cons of Open-Ended and Closed-Ended Questions

Aspect	Broad, Open-Ended Questions	Narrow, Closed-Ended Questions
Genuineness	High They produce spontaneous formulations	Low They lead the patient
Reliability	Low They may lead to nonreproducible answers	High Narrow focus, but they may suggest answers
Precision	Low Intent of question is vague	High Intent of question is clear
Time efficiency	Low Circumstantial elaborations	High May invite yes or no answers
Completeness of diagnostic coverage	Low Patient selects the topic	High Interviewer selects the topic
Acceptance by patient	Varies Most patients prefer expressing themselves freely; others become guarded and feel insecure	Varies Some patients enjoy clear-cut checks; others hate to be pressed into a yes or no format

Reprinted with permission from Othmer E, Othmer SC: *The Clinical Interview Using DSM-IV,* p. 48. American Psychiatric Press, Washington, 1994.

reflection is twofold: to assure the doctor that he or she has correctly understood what the patient is trying to say and to let the patient know that the doctor is perceiving what is being said. It is an empathic response meant to allow the patient to know that the doctor is both listening to the patient's concerns and understanding them. For example, if a patient is speaking about fears of dying and the effects of talking about these fears with his or her family, the doctor may say, "It seems that you are concerned with becoming a burden to your family." This reflection is not an exact repetition of what the patient has said but, rather, a paraphrase that indicates that the doctor has perceived what the patient is trying to say.

FACILITATION. Doctors help patients continue in the interview by providing both verbal and nonverbal cues that encourage patients to keep talking. Nodding the head, leaning forward in the chair, and saying, "Yes, and then . . . ?" or "Uh-huh, go on," are all examples of facilitation.

SILENCE. Silence can be used in many ways in normal conversations, even to indicate disapproval or disinterest. In the doctor–patient relationship, however, silence may be constructive and in certain situations may allow patients to contemplate, to cry, or just to sit in an accepting, supportive environment where the doctor makes it clear that not every moment must be filled with talk.

CONFRONTATION. The technique of confrontation is meant to point out to a patient something that the doctor thinks the patient is not paying attention to, is missing, or is in some way denying. Confrontation must be done skillfully, so that patients are not forced to become hostile and defensive. The confrontation is meant to help patients face whatever needs to be faced in a direct but respectful way. For example, a patient who has just made a suicidal gesture but is telling the doctor that it was not serious may be confronted with the statement, "What you have done may not have killed you, but it's telling me that you are in serious trouble right now and that you need help so that you don't try suicide again."

CLARIFICATION. In clarification, doctors attempt to get details from patients about what they have already said. For example, a doctor may say: "You are feeling depressed. When is it that you feel most depressed?"

INTERPRETATION. The technique of interpretation is most often used when a doctor states something about a patient's behavior or thinking that a patient may not be aware of. The technique follows on the doctor's careful listening to the underlying themes and patterns in the patient's story. Interpretations usually help clarify interrelationships that the patient may not see. The technique is a sophisticated one and should generally be used only after the doctor has established some rapport with the patient and has a reasonably good idea of what some interrelationships are. For example, a doctor may say: "When you talk about how angry you are that your family has not been supportive, I think you're also telling me how worried you are that I won't be there for you either. What do you think?"

SUMMATION. Periodically during the interview, a doctor can take a moment and briefly summarize what a patient has said thus far. Doing so assures both patient and doctor that the doctor has heard the same information as the patient has actually conveyed. For example, the doctor may say, "OK, I just want to make sure that I've got everything right up to this point."

EXPLANATION. Doctors explain treatment plans to patients in easily understandable language and allow patients to respond and ask questions. For example, a doctor may say: "It is essential that you come into the hospital now because of the seriousness of your condition. You will be admitted tonight through the emergency room, and I will be there to make all the arrangements. You will be given a small dose of medication that will make you sleepy. The medication is called triazolam (Halcion), and the dose you will be getting is 0.125 mg. I will see you again first thing in the morning, and we'll go over all the procedures that will be required before anything else happens. Now, what are your questions? I know you must have some."

TRANSITION. The technique of transition allows doctors to convey the idea that enough information has been obtained on one subject; the doctor's words encourage patients to continue on to another subject. For example, a doctor may say: "You've given me a good sense of that particular time in your life. It would be good now if you told me a bit more about an even earlier time in your life."

SELF-REVELATION. Limited, discreet self-disclosure by physicians may be useful in certain situations, and physicians should feel at ease and should communicate a sense of self-comfort. Conveying this sense may involve answering a patient's questions about whether a physician is married and where he or she comes from. A doctor who practices self-revelation excessively, however, is using a patient to fulfill unfilled needs in his or her own life and is abusing the role of physician. If a doctor thinks that a piece of information will help a patient be more comfortable, the doctor can decide in each case whether to be self-revealing. It depends on whether the information will further a patient's care or whether it will provide nothing useful. Even if the doctor decides that self-revelation is not warranted, he or she should be careful not to make the patient feel embarrassed for asking. For example, the doctor may say: "I'm not sure whether you are really asking if I'm married. Let's talk about it a little more, so that I can understand why that information is important to you. Maybe it has more to do with some concerns you have about my commitment to your care.'' Or ''I am married, but let's talk a little about why it was important for you to know that. If we talk about it, I'll have a bit more information about who you are and what your concerns are regarding me and my involvement in your care.'' Perhaps the important point here is not to take patients' questions at face value alone. Many questions, especially personal ones, convey not just natural curiosity but also hidden concerns about the doctor, which should not be ignored.

POSITIVE REINFORCEMENT. The technique of positive reinforcement allows patients to feel comfortable in telling a doctor anything, even about such things as noncompliance with treatment. By encouraging a patient to feel that the doctor is not upset by whatever the patient has to say, the doctor facilitates an open exchange. For example, a doctor may say: ''I appreciate your telling me that you have stopped taking your medication. Can you tell me what the problem was with the medication? The more I know about what's going on with you, the better I'll be able to treat you in a way that you will feel comfortable with.''

REASSURANCE. Truthful reassurance of a patient can lead to increased trust and compliance and can be experienced as an empathic response of a concerned physician. False reassurance, however, is essentially lying to a patient and can badly impair the patient's trust and compliance. False reassurance is often given from a desire to make a patient feel better, but once a patient knows that a doctor has not told the truth, the patient is unlikely to accept or believe truthful reassurance. In an example of false reassurance, a patient with a terminal illness asks, ''Am I going to be all right, Doctor?'' and the doctor responds, ''Of course you'll be all right; everything is fine.'' In an example of truthful reassurance, the doctor responds: ''I am going to do everything to make you as comfortable as possible, and part of being comfortable is for you to know as much as I know about what is going on with you. We both know that what you have is serious. I'd like to know exactly what you think is happening to you and to clarify any questions or confusion you have.''

ADVICE. In many situations it is not only acceptable but desirable for physicians to give patients advice. To be effective and to be perceived as empathic rather than as inappropriate or intrusive, the advice should be given only after patients are allowed to talk freely about their problems, so that physicians have an adequate information base from which to make suggestions. At times, after a doctor has listened carefully to a patient, it becomes clear that the patient does not, in fact, want advice as much as an objective, caring, nonjudgmental ear. Giving advice too quickly can lead a patient to feel that the doctor is not really listening but, rather, is responding either out of anxiety or from the belief that the doctor inherently knows better than the patient what should be done in a particular situation. In an example of advice given too quickly, a patient says, ''I cannot take this medication; it's bothering me,'' and the physician responds: ''Fine. I think you should stop taking it, and I'll start you on something new.'' A more appropriate response is the following: ''I'm sorry to hear that. Tell me what about the medication is bothering you, so that I have a better idea of what we may do to make you feel more comfortable.'' In another example the patient says, ''I've really been feeling down lately,'' and the doctor responds, ''Well, I think in that case it would be a good idea for you to go out and really do some things that are fun, like going to the movies or walking in the park.'' In this case a more appropriate and helpful response is the following: ''Tell me what you mean by 'feeling down.' The more I know about what you're feeling, the more likely it will be that I can help.''

Psychotic Patients. Patients who are psychotic often have limited insight, are more concrete than abstract in their thinking, and are not always psychologically minded or introspective. Many psychotic patients experience insight and introspection as frightening and threatening, because their perceptions are distorted and they are unable to integrate certain feelings, fantasies, and ideas about themselves without decompensating (becoming more psychotic than before). Their internal psychological makeup is fragile or vulnerable, and certain psychological insights can impose too much stress for them to bear. If people who are psychotic can tolerate certain degrees of insight and introspection, they should be encouraged, although for the most part a physician's role with a psychotic person is supportive rather than insight oriented. The support, in part, involves increasing a patient's ability to test reality (to differentiate between fantasy and reality). Insight-oriented interventions, by contrast, often trigger disturbing fantasies. Psychotic patients often experience what has been termed the *need–fear dilemma,* both an overwhelming loneliness and a need for contact with others and a profound fear that contact with others is dangerous, overwhelming, and destructive.

There are specific therapy techniques to be used with patients who are psychotic. Do not attempt to talk patients out of delusional beliefs. Do not laugh at bizarre psychotic material; it may sound funny but is clearly not meant to be funny. Maintain a certain formality with patients, so that they do not feel threatened by what they perceive as frightening closeness. Focus on patients' achieving concrete, day-to-day survival and social skills. Decrease pressure on patients to achieve more than they may feel capable of achieving (including answering interview questions). Structure the interview sessions so that patients know what to expect and are not left, for instance, with long periods of silence if these periods seem to increase anxiety. Be sensitive to how easily humiliated or shamed patients may feel about relatively minor inadequacies (such as the inability to remember a past medication).

Ending the Interview

Physicians want patients to leave an interview feeling understood and respected and believing that all the pertinent and important information has been conveyed to an informed, empathic listener. To this end, doctors should give patients a chance to ask questions and should let patients know as much as possible about future plans. Doctors should thank patients for sharing the necessary information and let patients know that the information conveyed has been helpful in clarifying the next steps. Any prescription of medication should be clearly and simply spelled out, and doctors should ascertain whether patients understand the prescription and how to take it. Doctors should make another appointment or give a referral and some indication about how patients can reach help quickly if it is necessary before the next appointment.

COMPLIANCE

Compliance, also known as adherence, is the degree to which a patient carries out the clinical recommendations of a treating physician. Examples of compliance include keeping appointments, entering into and completing a treatment program, taking medications correctly, and following recommended changes in behavior or diet. Compliance behavior depends on the specific clinical situation, the nature of the illness, and the treatment program. In general, about one third of all patients comply with treatment, one third sometimes comply with certain aspects of treatment, and one third never comply with treatment. An overall figure assessed from a number of studies indicates that 54 percent of patients comply with treatment at any given time. One study found that up to 50 percent of patients with hypertension do not comply at all with treatment and that 50 percent of those who do follow up leave treatment within 1 year.

In an attempt to understand why such a high percentage of patients fails to comply regularly, researchers have investigated several variables. For example, an increased complexity of regimen, along with an increased number of required behavioral changes, appears to be associated with noncompliance. Psychiatric patients exhibit a higher degree of noncompliant behavior than do medical patients. There is no clear association, however, between compliance and a patient's sex, marital status, race, religion, socioeconomic status, intelligence, or educational level. Compliance is increased when physicians have such characteristics as enthusiasm and a permissive attitude. Age and experience are also important, as are time spent talking to patients and short waiting room time.

The doctor–patient relationship, or doctor–patient match, is the most important factor in compliance issues. When doctor and patient have different priorities and beliefs, different styles of communication (including a different understanding of medical advice), and different medical expectations, patients' compliance diminishes. Compliance can be increased when physicians explain to a patient the value of a particular treatment outcome and also emphasize that following the recommendation will produce this outcome. Compliance can also increase if patients know the names and effects of each drug they are taking.

A highly significant factor in compliance seems to be patients' subjective feelings of distress or illness, as opposed to doctors' often objective medical estimates of the disease and required therapy. Patients must believe that they are ill. Thus, asymptomatic patients, such as those with hypertension, are at greater risk for noncompliance than are patients with symptoms.

Simply stated, when there are problems in communication, compliance decreases; when there is effective communication, coupled with close patient supervision and a patient's subjective sense of satisfaction that a doctor has met expectations, compliance increases. Studies have shown that noncompliance is associated with physicians who are perceived as rejecting and unfriendly. Noncompliance is also associated with asking a patient for information without giving feedback and with failing to explain a diagnosis or the cause of a patient's symptoms. Doctors who are aware of patients' belief systems, feelings, and habits and who enlist the patient in establishing a treatment regimen increase compliant behavior.

Strategies suggested to improve compliance include asking patients directly to describe what they themselves believe is wrong with them, what they believe should be done, what they understand about what the doctor believes should be done, and what they believe to be the risks and the benefits of following the prescribed treatment. Common errors are patients' not taking medications as often or as long as they are supposed to and not taking the right number of pills or treatments. Patients are generally noncompliant if they have to take more than three types of medications a day or if their medications must be taken more than four times a day. Purely verbal instructions by doctors or the presentation of treatment prescriptions to patients in the few hours immediately before being discharged from a hospital is associated with increased error and noncompliance. Older people who may have trouble hearing or reading small type may become noncompliant if they cannot hear the verbal instructions or read the prescription labels. In these instances, it is helpful to print the instructions on a piece of paper, ask the patient to read them back, ask whether the patient has any questions, and ask the patient to explain when specifically and in what amounts the medication is to be taken.

Sometimes, instead of making errors, patients deliberately change the treatment regimen, for example, by not showing up for appointments or by taking medications in a manner different from that recommended. In these instances, in which there may be competing pressures from the family or from work or a lack of understanding about the details of the doctor's advice, the doctor needs to negotiate a compromise, a contract, with the patient. In this case, doctor and patient together specify what they can expect from each other. Implicit in this approach are the ideas that the contract can be renegotiated and the patient can be assured that suggestions can be made by either the doctor or the patient to improve compliance.

SPECIFIC ISSUES

Fees

Before physicians can establish an ongoing relationship with patients, they must address certain issues. For instance, they must openly discuss the matter of payment or fees at the beginning: the doctor's charges, whether the doctor is willing to directly accept insurance company payments (known as assignment), the doctor's policy about payment for missed appointments, and whether the doctor is a member of a managed care plan. Discussing these questions and any other questions about fees from the beginning of the relationship between the doctor and patient can minimize misunderstanding later.

Confidentiality

Physicians should discuss the extent and limitations of confidentiality with patients, so that patients are clear about what can and cannot remain confidential. As much as physicians must legally and ethically respect patients' confidentiality, confidentiality in some situations may be either partially or wholly broken. Doctors must make patients aware of these situations to avoid mistrust. For instance, if a patient makes clear that he or she intends to harm another person violently, the doctor has a legal responsibility to warn the intended victim. Other examples of issues related to confidentiality involve the patient's medical record and who has access to it; the extent of the information required by particular insurance companies (which may be highly detailed); and the degree, if any, to which a patient's case will be used in teaching medical students, residents, or others. In all such situations patients must give previous permission for using the medical records. (These issues are further discussed in Chapter 55.)

Supervision

It is both commonplace and necessary for doctors in training to receive supervision from experienced physicians. This practice is the norm in large teaching hospitals, and most patients are aware of it. When young doctors are receiving supervision from senior physicians, patients should know from the beginning. Informing patients is particularly important in psychiatry, in which the supervision of individual psychotherapy cases is a routine and established practice and in which the psychiatric resident is required to present verbatim accounts of an entire therapy session (process notes) to a senior supervisor. If a patient is curious about the level of the treating doctor's experience, the doctor or medical student should respond honestly and not mislead the patient. If the doctor is less than truthful and the patient later discovers this, the relationship between doctor and patient may become untenable.

Missed Appointments and Length of Sessions

Patients need to be informed about doctors' policies for the issue of missed appointments and the length of sessions. Psychiatrists, for example, generally see patients in regularly scheduled blocks of 20 to 45 minutes; at the end of this time, psychiatrists expect patients to accept the fact that the session is over. Nonpsychiatric physicians may schedule somewhat differently, by putting aside 30 minutes to an hour for an initial visit and then perhaps scheduling patient visits every 15 to 20 minutes for follow-up appointments. Psychiatrists who are treating psychotic inpatients may determine that a patient cannot tolerate a lengthy session and may decide to see the patient in a series of 10-minute sessions throughout the day. Whatever the policies, patients must be made aware of them to prevent misunderstandings.

The same can be said for doctors' policies on missed appointments, about which patients must be informed. Some doctors deal with the issue of missed appointments by asking patients to give 24 hours' notice to avoid being billed for a missed session. Other doctors bill for missed sessions regardless of notice. Still others decide on a case-by-case basis and perhaps state a 24-hour rule but make exceptions when warranted. Some doctors state that, if they receive notice and can fill the vacated time with another patient, they will not charge for the missed appointment; other doctors do not charge for missed appointments at all. The decision is up to the individual physician, but patients must know the doctor's policy in advance, to make an informed decision about whether to accept the policy or to choose another doctor.

Availability of the Doctor

What are doctors' obligations to be available to patients between scheduled appointments? Is it incumbent on physicians to be available 24 hours a day? Once a patient enters into a contract to receive care from a particular physician, it is the physician's responsibility to have a mechanism in place by which the patient can receive help if an emergency occurs outside the time of scheduled appointments. Patients should be explicitly informed what the mechanism is, whether it is an emergency phone number or a covering physician. If a physician is going to be away for a long time, coverage by another physician must be obtained, and patients must be informed about contacting the covering doctor. Patients should know that the doctor will be available between appointments to answer pressing questions and that, if necessary, extra appointments can be scheduled.

Within these general parameters, however, physicians must make their own individual decisions about their availability to specific patients. In some cases, doctors may have to place firm limits on availability between sessions. For instance, patients who repeatedly call at all hours with concerns that are best addressed in the context of a regularly scheduled appointment should be gently but definitely encouraged to bring up their problems only during scheduled sessions. In such cases, doctors may reassure patients that all concerns will be addressed and that, if there is not enough time during the regularly scheduled appointment, another appointment can be made but that nonemergency concerns will be postponed until the appointment.

Follow-up

Many events can disrupt the continuity of the doctor–patient relationship. Some of these events are routine (such as when residents end their training and move on to another hospital); others are out of the ordinary and thus unpredictable (such as when physicians become ill and can no longer take care of their patients). Patients must be assured that, regardless of what occurs in the course of a particular doctor–patient relationship, patients' care will be ongoing. If a doctor is a resident who will be serving as a patient's doctor for a finite time, the doctor should be explicit about this limit at the beginning of treatment. At the same time, the resident can make clear to the patient that, when he or she moves on, the patient's care will continue, albeit with a new doctor. It may help the patient's sense of continuity if the departing resident introduces the incoming resident to the patient.

A complex situation arises when physicians become ill and are unable to continue caring for patients. When physicians know in advance that they are going to have to interrupt therapy, clear arrangements for referral to other physicians can be made. Although there are arguments for both revealing and not revealing physicians' illnesses to patients, it seems best to inform patients truthfully why a doctor is discontinuing therapy. This information should be conveyed in as calm and nonthreatening a way as possible. The risk in not telling patients the truth is that many patients may fantasize about why a doctor has stopped seeing them and may then fear that something about them made the doctor want to leave. Nontruthfulness in the situation also encourages the view that being ill is something shameful or frightening and that doctors who cannot discuss or handle their own illnesses should not expect patients to be able to. It is not the role of patients, however, to take care of their doctors; informing patients should not carry with it any sense that a doctor's illness is a patient's burden.

Difficult Patients

Some patients, who can create undue stress if they are not managed effectively, require particular skill on the part of any physician. Inherent in the management of all these patients is the doctor's understanding of the covert emotions, fears, and conflicts that the patient's overt behavior represents. An appropriate understanding of what is hidden behind a particular patient's difficult behavior can guide doctors away from angry, contemptuous, or anxious responses and toward helpful interventions.

Depressed Patients. The most important factor in interviewing depressed patients is assessing the risk of suicide. Clinicians should pose questions geared to determining feelings of worthlessness, despair, and pessimism. A profound feeling of hopelessness is an ominous sign that many psychiatrists consider pathognomonic of suicidal risk. A history of past suicide attempts, the presence of chronic illness, especially if associated with pain, a recent life stressor, such as the loss of a loved one, and a family history of suicide are signs of increased risk. The myth that asking about suicidal ideation plants the seed for a suicide attempt should not stop physicians from asking patients whether they have thoughts that life is no longer worth living, that they want to harm themselves, or that they wish to die.

Depressed patients often demand reassurance from an interviewer but often do not respond to a physician's attempts to meet this need. Physicians should offer patients a realistic appraisal. When depression is present, doctors should tell patients so and should explain that therapeutic intervention, such as psychotherapy, drug therapy, or hospitalization (especially if a patient is suicidal), is necessary. Depression is a curable condition in 95 percent of cases, and patients and their families often respond positively to this fact.

Histrionic Patients. Histrionic patients are often seductive with doctors from an unconscious need for reassurance that they are still attractive, even if ill, and from fear that they will not be taken seriously unless they are found to be sexually desirable. They often appear overly emotional and intimate in their interactions with doctors. Physicians need to be calm, reassuring, firm, and nonflirtatious. Patients do not really want to seduce physicians, but they may not know any other way to get what they feel they need.

Dependent Patients. Dependent patients need a great amount of reassurance and yet are often resistant to any and all such offers. They are the patients most likely to make repeated, urgent calls between scheduled appointments and to demand that doctors provide special attention. They often become angry or frightened when they perceive that doctors are not taking their concerns seriously. Doctors must be prepared to set necessary limits within the context of an expressed willingness to listen and to care for patients.

Impulsive Patients. Impulsive patients have a difficult time delaying gratification and may demand that their discomfort be eliminated immediately. They are easily frustrated and may become petulant or even angry and aggressive when they do not get what they want as soon as they want it. They may impulsively do something self-destructive if they feel thwarted by the doctor, and they may appear manipulative and attention seeking. Underneath the surface manifestations, they may fear that they will never get what they need from others and thus must act in this inappropriately aggressive way. These patients can be particularly difficult for any doctor to treat; doctors must set firm, nonangry limits from the outset and define clearly acceptable and unacceptable behavior. They must treat patients with respect and care but must hold them responsible for their actions.

Narcissistic Patients. Narcissistic patients act as though they are superior to everyone around them, including the doctor. With their pressing need to appear perfect and their contemptuous attitude toward anyone whom they perceive to be imperfect, they may be rude, abrupt, arrogant, or demeaning. They may initially overidealize physicians in their need to have their doctors be as perfect as they are themselves, but the overidealization may quickly turn to disdain when they discover that doctors are human. Underneath their surface arrogance, these patients often feel inadequate, helpless, and empty, and they fear that others see through them.

Obsessive Patients. Obsessive and controlling patients are orderly, punctual, and overconcerned with detail. They often appear unemotional, even aloof, especially with regard to anything potentially disturbing or frightening. They may be resistant to any perceived control on the doctor's part because of their strong needs to be in control of everything in their environment. Underneath, these patients are often frightened of losing control and of being dependent and helpless. Physicians must be prepared to strengthen the patients' sense of control by including them as much as possible in their own care and treatment. Doctors should explain in detail what is going on and what is being planned.

Paranoid Patients. Paranoid and hypervigilant patients fear that people want to hurt them and intend to do them harm. Patients may misperceive cues in their environment to the degree that they see conspiracies in neutral events. They are critical, evasive, and suspicious. They are often called grievance seekers because they tend to blame others for everything bad that happens in their lives. They are extremely mistrustful and may question everything that doctors advise doing. Physicians must remain somewhat formal, albeit always respectful and courteous, with these patients, as they often view expressions of warmth and empathy with suspicion ("What does he want from me?"). As with obsessive patients, doctors should be prepared to explain in detail every decision and planned procedure and should react nondefensively to patients' suspicions.

Isolated Patients. Termed schizoid personalities, isolated and solitary patients appear detached and reclusive and do not appear to need or want much contact with other human beings. Intimate contact with a doctor is viewed with distaste by these patients, who would prefer to take care of themselves entirely on their own if they could. Doctors should treat the patients with as much respect for privacy as possible and should not expect them to respond to doctors' concerns in kind.

Demanding and Passive-Aggressive Patients. Demanding, martyrlike, and passive-aggressive patients appear to communicate solely through a litany of complaints and disappointments. They often covertly blame others for all their problems, and they make others feel guilty about not doing or caring enough. They are often not able to express angry feelings directly and, thus, express them indirectly or passively by being late for appointments or not making their payments on time. They often perceive themselves as being extremely self-sacrificing and as being taken advantage of by others, who are seen as selfish. They may unconsciously believe that the only way to be taken seriously or to be cared for or loved is to be sick. Doctors must be patient and tolerant with these patients, as difficult as they can sometimes be; they should take such patients' concerns seriously but without encouraging the sick role and should set firm limits on their availability (as with overly dependent patients). At the same time, doctors should reassure patients that they will listen to them during frequent, regularly scheduled appointments. Doctors must often be involved with patients' families; family members deal with patients' difficult styles every day and are likely to be angry, frustrated, and guilty themselves.

Malingering Patients. Malingering patients feign illness. They are often described in psychiatric terminology as antisocial personalities; they do not appear to experience appropriate guilt and, in fact, may not even be consciously aware of what it means to be guilty. On the surface they may appear charming, socially adept, and intelligent; but over many years they have perfected the behaviors they know to be appropriate, and they perform almost like an actor. They often have histories of criminal acts and get by in the world through lying and manipulation. They can be self-destructive and harm not only others but themselves in a perhaps unacknowledged expression of self-punishment. Antisocial patients often malinger, the term for consciously feigning illness for a clear secondary gain (for example, to obtain drugs, to get a bed for the night, or to hide from people pursuing them). They obviously do get sick, just as nonantisocial people do, and when they are sick, they need to be cared for in the same ways as others. Doctors must treat them with respect but also with a heightened sense of vigilance. These patients can inspire fear in others, often legitimately so, as many have violent histories. Doctors who feel threatened by patients should unashamedly seek assistance and not feel compelled to see the patients alone. Firm limits must be set on behavior (for example, no drugs in the hospital and no sexual activity with other patients), and the consequences of transgressing must be firmly stated and adhered to (for example, discharge from the hospital if the patient is medically stable, isolation if not). If inappropriate behavior is discovered, patients must be confronted directly and nonangrily, and they must be held responsible for their actions.

BURNOUT

Trained physicians not only have learned the knowledge base and techniques of the profession but also must confront, resolve, and incorporate many significant attitudinal issues involved in becoming skilled and effective in their fields. These issues encompass the ideals of balancing compassionate concern with dispassionate objectivity; the wish to relieve pain and distress with the ability to make difficult, often painful decisions; and the desire to cure or control with the acceptance of the limits on what they can realistically accomplish. Learning to balance these interrelated aspects of the physician's role is essential in allowing doctors to withstand, in a graceful and life-affirming way, the daily work of continually confronting illness, pain, sadness, fear, suffering, vulnerability, and death. A lack of balance can lead physicians to feel overwhelmed, depressed, and burned out. A sense of futility and failure can begin to permeate their attitudes and can set the stage for anger and frustration about their profession, their patients, and themselves. Many physicians are at risk for this lack of balance because of particular personality and coping styles prevalent among those drawn to the practice of medicine. For instance, many medical students are perfectionistic, controlling, and obsessive. These traits can be adaptive for physicians when balanced with healthy doses of self-knowledge, humility, humor, and kindness. When the balance is absent, many physicians travel the path of dispassion at the expense of compassion, and of willingness to be in charge at the expense of being supportive; they have a diminished capacity to tolerate the limits of what they can realistically and honestly accomplish.

References

American Psychiatric Association. Practice guideline for psychiatric evaluation of adults. Am J Psychiatry *152* (11, Suppl): 66, 1995.

Bishop J: Guidelines for a nonsexist (gender-sensitive) doctor–patient relationship. Can J Psychiatry *37:* 62, 1992.

Engel GL: The clinical application of the biopsychosocial model. Am J Psychiatry *137:* 535, 1980.

Freud S: Recommendations to physicians practicing psychoanalysis. In *Standard Edition of the Complete Psychological Works of Sigmund Freud,* vol 12, p 109. Hogarth, London, 1958.

Greengold NL, Ault M: Crossing the cultural doctor–patient barrier. Acad Med *71:* 112, 1995.

O'Brien R: The doctor–patient relationship. Ann NY Acad Sci *729:* 22, 1994.

Omer H: Enhancing the impact of therapeutic interventions. Am J Psychother *44:* 218, 1990.

Ong LM, de Haes JC, Hoos AM, Lammas FB: Doctor–patient communication: A review of the literature. Soc Sci Med *40:* 903, 1995.

Othmer E, Othmer SC: *The Clinical Interview Using DSM-IV.* American Psychiatric Press, Washington, 1994.

Silver A, Weiss D: Paternalistic attitudes and moral reasoning among physicians at a large teaching hospital. Acad Med *67:* 62, 1992.

Stoffelmayr B, Hoppe RB, Weber N: Facilitating patient participation: The doctor–patient encounter. Prim Care *16:* 265, 1989.

Strauss GD: The psychiatric interview, history, and mental status examination. In *Comprehensive Textbook of Psychiatry,* ed 6, HI Kaplan, BJ Sadock, editors, p 521. Williams & Wilkins, Baltimore, 1995.

Verhulst J, Tucker G: Medical and narrative approaches in psychiatry. Psychiatr Serv *46:* 513, 1995.

Walsh JM, McPhee SJ: A systems model of clinical preventive care: An analysis of factors influencing patient and physician. Health Educ Q *19:* 157, 1992.

West C: Reconceptualizing gender in physician–patient relationships. Soc Sci Med *36:* 57, 1993.

2 Human Development Throughout the Life Cycle

▲ 2.1 Life Cycle and Normality

Studying the human life cycle helps to clarify people's behavior, to understand the normal stages of development, and to predict complications and problems that can arise. In the early 20th century, psychiatrists began to investigate the human life cycle in connection with interest in personality development, particularly the role of internal psychological events and the effects of childhood experiences on shaping adults. Somewhat later, an added focus was the impact of social events on personality, along with the varieties of changes occurring throughout life. Today, discoveries in the biological sciences have emphasized the biological substrate of behavior, and investigations in this area have become the primary contributions to understanding the human life cycle.

LIFE-CYCLE THEORIES

Sigmund Freud

A handful of highly influential workers have shaped the study of the human life cycle. A seminal work on the subject is the developmental scheme introduced in 1905 by Sigmund Freud, in his *Three Essays on the Theory of Sexuality.* Freud's theory, which focused on the childhood period, was organized around his idea of libido. According to Freud, childhood phases of development correspond to successive shifts in the investment of sexual energy in areas of the body usually associated with eroticism: the mouth, the anus, and the genitalia. Freud's developmental stages were accordingly classified as the oral phase, birth to 1 year; the anal phase, ages 1 to 3 years; and the phallic phase, ages 3 to 5 years.

Freud also described a fourth period, latency, which extends from ages 5 and 6 years until puberty. Latency is marked by a diminution of sexual interest, which is reactivated at puberty. Freud believed that the successful resolution of these childhood phases was essential to normal adult functioning and that, by comparison, adult experiences are of relatively little consequence. (Freud's theories are discussed thoroughly in Chapter 6, Section 6.1.)

Carl Gustav Jung

Carl Gustav Jung viewed external factors as playing an important role in people's growth and adaptation. He described the process of individuation as the growth and expansion of personality which occurs through a person's realizing and learning what he or she intrinsically is. According to Jung, libido is every possible manifestation of psychic energy; it is not limited to sexuality or to aggression but includes religious and spiritual urges and the drive to seek a clear, deep understanding of the meaning of life.

Harry Stack Sullivan

Harry Stack Sullivan conceived of human development as largely shaped by external events, specifically by social interaction. According to his influential model of the life cycle, each phase of development is marked by a need for interactions with certain people, and the quality of these interactions influences human personality.

Erik Erikson

Although Erik Erikson accepted Freud's theory of infantile sexuality, he also thought that developmental potentials occurred at all stages of life. Erikson constructed a life-cycle model consisting of eight stages that extend into adulthood and old age:

Stage 1. Trust versus mistrust
Stage 2. Autonomy versus shame and doubt
Stage 3. Initiative versus guilt
Stage 4. Industry versus inferiority
Stage 5. Ego identity versus role confusion
Stage 6. Intimacy versus isolation
Stage 7. Generativity versus stagnation
Stage 8. Ego integrity versus despair

Erikson ascribed five of these psychological stages to childhood: trust, autonomy, initiative, industry, and identity, which correlate with Freud's psychosexual stages. In addition, Erikson added three stages that extend beyond young adulthood into old age: intimacy, generativity, and integrity. These eight stages have both positive and negative aspects; each stage has its specific emotional crises, and each is affected by the interaction of the person's biology, culture, and society. Every stage has two possible outcomes, one positive or healthy and the other negative or unhealthy. Under ideal circumstances, the crisis at each stage is resolved when people achieve a new and higher level of functioning at the positive end of the stage. According to Erikson, most people are unlikely to achieve perfect positive polarity, but they achieve more positive than negative results. Erikson described his theoretical developmental sequence as *epigenetic*. Each crisis must be negotiated before a person can move on to the next phase. (Erikson's theories are discussed in depth in Chapter 6, Section 6.3.)

Jean Piaget

Another major model is Jean Piaget's theory of cognitive (intellectual) development. By conducting intensive studies of the way children think and behave, Piaget formulated a theory of cognition, which he divided into the four stages of sensorimotor, preoperational thought, concrete operations, and formal operations. In the epigenetic view of development by workers like Piaget and Erikson, infants grow by predetermined steps through various stages. Each stage has its own characteristics and needs and must be negotiated successfully before going to the next phase. The sequence of stages is not automatic but depends on both central nervous system growth and life experiences. Ample evidence indicates that an unfavorable environment can delay some of the developmental stages, but particularly favorable environmental stimulators can accelerate progress through the stages. (Piaget's theories are discussed in depth in Chapter 4, Section 4.1.)

Daniel Levinson

Daniel Levinson and his coworkers at Yale University focused on personality development throughout the course of life. In a major study they set out to clarify the issues and characteristics of male personality development in early and middle adulthood. A total of 40 men were studied; their ages at the start of the investigation ranged from 35 to 45 years. The resulting observations caused Levinson to postulate a new scheme of the adult phases of the life cycle. He suggested that the human life cycle is composed of four major eras, each lasting about 25 years, with some overlap, so that a new era is starting as the previous one is ending. Levinson was able to identify a typical age of onset, that is, the age at which an era usually begins. The evolving sequence of eras and their age spans described by Levinson are childhood and adolescence, birth to 22 years; early adulthood, 17 to 45 years; middle adulthood, 40 to 65 years; and late adulthood, 65 years and beyond. Levinson also identified 4- to 5-year transitional periods between eras, which function as boundary zones during which a person terminates the outgoing era and initiates the incoming one.

These and other developmental theories are more heuristic than empirical; they are working models whose value is descriptive rather than prescriptive. Although they offer a way to conceptualize certain issues of development and provide a vocabulary for describing what otherwise would remain vague, the theories are not intended to describe objective realities as, for example, developmental neurobiology describes maturation of the central nervous system. Many theorists who once occupied a central position in psychology and psychiatry are now of greater historical interest than of clinical importance.

Longitudinal Studies of Human Development

Freud, Jung, and Erikson derived theories of development as much from philosophical speculation as from the direct observation of human subjects, and critics have argued that their observations were biased by preconceptions. None of these workers can be said to have engaged in controlled, empirical research in behavior and development.

For these reasons, traditional models of development are being supplemented by prospective longitudinal studies. A cohort of people is followed throughout life. Observations that include standardized ratings are made as people mature and pass from one phase of life to another, and correlations are made between life events and psychological and emotional outcomes.

George Vaillant and his group studied a cohort of men for more than 35 years. The study began when the men were freshmen at Harvard University. A happy childhood was found to correlate significantly with positive traits in middle life, manifested by little psychopathology, the capacity to play, and good interpersonal relationships.

Vaillant noted that a hierarchy of ego mechanisms was constructed as the men advanced in age. Defenses were organized along a continuum that reflected two aspects of the personality: immaturity versus maturity and psychopathology versus mental health. He found that the maturity of the defenses was related to both psychopathology and objective adaptation to the external environment. Moreover, defensive styles shifted as people matured.

Vaillant concluded that adaptive styles mature over the years and that the maturation depends more on development from within than on changes in the interpersonal environment. He has continued to study the impact of life events on health and development and has found, for example, that negative life events affect men's psychological health more than their physical health and that the extreme stress of military combat is associated with posttraumatic stress disorder but not with other forms of psychopathology.

Although prospective longitudinal studies do not yet confirm a coherent model for all aspects of development, they do provide important evidence of the complex, bidirectorial influence of genetic predisposition and environment. They already offer convincing evidence that change is possible throughout a lifetime and that early childhood experiences, although a powerful influence, do not uniquely determine adult personality.

Neurobiology of Development

Physical maturation profoundly affects psychological and emotional growth. The capacity for independent movement around the age of 1 year and the emergence of speech around the age of 2 shape social interactions in ways not possible before these milestones of neurological development. While developing infants learn to alter their environment through purposeful manipulation, environments also shape the children's developing brains.

Human infants are born with all the brain cells they will ever have: The number of neurons does not increase as children grow. Rather, the impressive increase in brain size (an infant's brain weighs about one third as much as an adult's) is due to the growth of existing neurons, which branch out and establish contact with one another. This process is referred to as arborization because of the analogy with the branching of tree limbs.

There is ample evidence that both the rate and pattern of interneuronal connections are influenced by environmental forces. *Plasticity* is the intrinsic capacity of brain cells to grow and branch in response to environmental stimuli. Plasticity allows the developing brain to achieve maximal fit with the environment in which it matures. For example, although infants are born with the capacity to discriminate all human vocal sounds (universal phonemic perception), by the age of 2 they have lost the ability to recognize sounds not heard in the spoken language of their environment. Normal environmental stimulation is necessary for normal brain development.

CONCEPT OF NORMALITY

Psychiatrists have long made a concerted effort to define mental health and normality. In years past, they implicitly assumed that mental health was the opposite of mental illness. With such an assumption, the absence of gross psychopathology was often equated with normal behavior. There is doubt about the usefulness of this assumption that has made it increasingly important for psychiatrists to provide precise concepts and definitions of mental health and normality.

The many theoretical and clinical concepts of normality seem to fall into four functional perspectives. Although each perspective is unique and has its own definition and description, the perspectives complement each other, and together they represent the totality of the behavioral science and social science approaches to normality. The four perspectives of normality, as formulated by Daniel Offer and Melvin Sabshin, are normality as health, normality as utopia, normality as average, and normality as process.

Normality as Health

The first perspective is the traditional medical-psychiatric approach to health and illness. Most physicians equate normality with health and view health as an almost universal phenomenon. Behavior is assumed to be within normal limits when no manifest psychopathology is present. If all behavior were to be put on a scale, normality would encompass most of the continuum, and abnormality would be the small remainder.

This definition of normality correlates with the traditional model of the doctor who attempts to free patients from grossly observable signs and symptoms of disease. To this physician the lack of signs or symptoms indicates health. In this context, health is a reasonable, rather than an optimal, state of functioning.

Normality as Utopia

The second perspective conceives of normality as the harmonious and optimal blending of the diverse elements of the mental apparatus which culminates in optimal functioning. Such a definition clearly emerges when psychiatrists or psychoanalysts talk about the ideal person or when they discuss their criteria for successful treatment. This approach can be traced directly back to Freud, who, when discussing normality, stated, "A normal ego is like normality in general, an ideal fiction."

Normality as Average

The third perspective is commonly used in normative studies of behavior and is based on the mathematical principle of the bell-shaped curve. In this approach the middle range of the curve is conceived of as normal, and both extremes are conceived of as deviant. The normative approach based on this statistical principle describes each person in terms of general assessment and total score. Variability is described only in the context of total groups, not within the context of a single person.

Normality as Process

The fourth perspective stresses that normal behavior is the end result of interacting systems. On the basis of this definition, temporal changes are essential to a complete definition of normality. In other words, the normality-as-process perspective stresses changes or processes, rather than a cross-sectional definition of normality.

Investigators who subscribe to this approach work in all the behavioral and social sciences. Typical of the concepts in this perspective are Erikson's theory of epigenesis of personality development and the eight developmental stages essential to attain mature adult functioning.

Longitudinal Studies

The understanding of normality has been advanced by several longitudinal studies. For example, Offer and Sabshin studied a group of adolescents throughout their high school years and identified three normal types of development: continuous growth, surgent growth, and tumultuous growth. Although people of each type are different, they can be placed along a continuum of normality. Offer and Sabshin formulated an operational definition of normality which is not absolute but, rather, is descriptive of one type of middle-class adolescent population. The criteria best describing the teenagers are

1. Almost complete absence of gross psychopathology, severe physical defects, and severe physical illness
2. Mastery of previous developmental tasks without serious setbacks
3. Ability to experience emotional states flexibly and to resolve conflicts actively with reasonable success
4. Relatively good relationships with parents, siblings, and peers
5. Feeling part of a larger cultural environment and being aware of its norms and values

Vaillant and others also use the developmental approach for adults. Studies of adaptation to marriage, parenthood, work, and leisure activities are increasingly prominent. Precise empirical studies are being conducted to explore developmental problems of old age.

The development of geriatric psychiatry has moved to a significant extent in a normative direction away from the deficit-focused orientation of early studies in gerontology. In a normative framework, researchers ask, in effect, "How do older people cope with the adaptational tasks of their 60s, 70s, and beyond?"

The developmental stages are customarily organized in chronological order: infancy; toddler period; preschool period; school or middle year period; early, middle, and late adolescence; and early, middle, and late adulthood (old age). Each developmental stage is discussed in detail in the sections that follow.

References

Colorusso CA, Nemiroff RA: *Adult Development: A New Dimension in Psychodynamic Theory and Practice.* Plenum, New York, 1981.

Craig GJ: *Human Development,* ed 7. Prentice-Hall, Upper Saddle River, NJ, 1996.

Cui X-J, Vaillant GE: Antecedents and consequences of negative life events in adulthood: A longitudinal study. Am J Psychiatry *153:* 21, 1996.

Dacey JS, Travers JF: *Human Development across the Lifespan,* ed 3. Brown & Benchmark, Madison, WI, 1996.

Erikson E: *Childhood and Society.* Norton, New York, 1950.

Freud A: *The Ego and the Mechanisms of Defense.* International Universities Press, New York, 1966.

Kelly SJ: Parenting stress and child maltreatment in drug-exposed children. Child Abuse Negl *16*: 317, 1992.

Lidz T: *The Person: His and Her Development Throughout the Life Cycle.* Basic Books, New York, 1976.

Maccoby EE: The role of gender identity and gender constancy in sex-differentiated development. New Dir Child Dev *47:* 5, 1990.

Notman MT: Menopause and adult development. Ann NY Acad Sci *592:* 149, 1990.

Offer D, Sabshin M: *Normality and the Life Cycle.* Basic Books, New York, 1984.

Robins LN, Rutter M, editors: *Straight and Devious Pathways from Childhood to Adulthood.* Cambridge University Press, Cambridge, 1989.

Vaillant GE, editor: *Empirical Studies of Ego Mechanism and Defense.* American Psychiatric Association Press, Washington, 1986.

Werner EE: The children of Kauai: Resiliency and recovery in adolescence and adulthood. J Adolesc Health *13:* 262, 1992.

Wolff S: Attachment and morality. Developing themes with different values. Br J Psychiatry *156:* 266, 1990.

▲ 2.2 Pregnancy, Childbirth, and Related Issues

PREGNANCY

Despite cultural, social, economic, and other factors that affect people's lives and that have made bearing and raising children problematic and costly in recent years, pregnancy is a major event in many people's lives. Although feminism has often promoted the tenet that women should free themselves from their traditional roles, women often experience childbirth as affirming their identity. New attitudes about men's roles as fathers have involved them more intimately in parenting experiences than earlier generations could have conceived.

Changes in Pregnancy

Pregnant women undergo marked biological, physiological, and psychological changes, and their attitudes toward pregnancy reflect deeply felt beliefs about reproduction and pregnancy (whether it has been planned and whether a baby is wanted). The relationship with the infant's father, her age, and her sense of identity also affect a woman's reaction to prospective motherhood. Prospective fathers face psychological challenges also.

Psychologically healthy women often find pregnancy a means of self-realization. Many women report that being pregnant is a creative act gratifying a fundamental need. Other women use pregnancy to diminish self-doubts about femininity or to reassure themselves that they can function as women in the most basic sense. Still others view pregnancy negatively; they may fear childbirth or feel inadequate about mothering. During early stages of their own development, women must undergo the experience of separating from their mothers and of establishing an independent identity; this experience later affects their own success at mothering. Women's unconscious fears and fantasies during early pregnancy often center on the idea of fusion with their own mothers. If a woman's mother was a poor role model, a woman's sense of maternal competence may be impaired, and she may lack confidence before and after her baby's birth.

Psychological attachment to the fetus begins in utero, and by the beginning of the second trimester most women have a mental picture of the infant. Even before being born, the fetus is viewed as a separate being, endowed with a prenatal personality. Many mothers talk to their unborn children. Recent evidence suggests that emotional talk with the fetus is related not only to early mother–infant bonding but also to the mother's efforts to have a healthy pregnancy, for example, by giving up cigarettes and caffeine. According to psychoanalytic theorists, the child-to-be is a blank screen on which a mother projects her hopes and fears. In rare instances these projections account for postpartum pathological states, such as a mother's wanting to harm her infant, whom she views as a hated part of herself. Normally, however, giving birth to a child fulfills a woman's need to create and nurture life.

Fathers are also profoundly affected by pregnancy. Impending parenthood demands a synthesis of such developmental issues as gender role and identity, separation-individuation from a man's own father, sexuality, and, as Erik Erikson proposed, generativity. Pregnancy fantasies in men and wishes to give birth in boys reflect early identifications with their mothers as well as the wish to be as powerful and creative as they perceive mothers to be. For some men, getting a woman pregnant is proof of their potency, a dynamic that plays a large part in adolescent fatherhood.

Marriage and Pregnancy

The prospective wife-mother and husband-father must redefine their roles as a couple and as individuals. They face readjustments in their relationships with friends and relatives and must deal with new responsibilities as caretakers to the newborn and to each other. Both parents may experience anxiety about their adequacy as parents; one or both partners may be consciously or unconsciously ambivalent about the addition of the child to the family and about the effects on the dyadic (two-person) relationship. A husband may feel guilty about his wife's discomfort during pregnancy and parturition, and some men experience jealousy or envy of the experience of pregnancy. Accustomed to gratifying each other's dependency needs, the couple must attend to the unremitting needs of a new infant and a developing child. Although most couples respond positively to these demands, some do not. Under ideal conditions the decision to become a parent and to have a child should be agreed on by both partners, but sometimes parenthood is rationalized as a way to achieve intimacy in a conflicted marriage or to avoid having to deal with other life circumstance problems.

The Pregnant Woman. In general, others' attitudes toward a pregnant woman reflect a variety of factors: intelligence, temperament, cultural practices, and myths of the society and the subculture into which both parents were born. Married men's responses to pregnancy are generally positive. For some men, however, reactions vary from a misplaced sense of pride that they are able to impregnate the woman to fear of increased responsibility and subsequent termination of the relationship. The risk that a woman will be abused by her husband or boyfriend increases during pregnancy. Domestic abuse adds significantly to the cost of health care during pregnancy: Abused women are more likely than nonabused controls to have histories of miscarriage, abortion, and neonatal death.

Alternative Lifestyle Pregnancy

Some lesbian couples may decide that one partner should become pregnant through artificial insemination. Societal attitudes may create stresses, but if the two women have a secure relationship, they tend to bond strongly together as a family unit. Long-term follow-up studies have shown that children of lesbian mothers do not differ from children of heterosexual mothers in emotional health or interpersonal relationships and the children are not more likely to be gay or lesbian themselves.

Similarly, some single, never-married women who do not wish to marry but do want to become pregnant may do so through artificial or natural insemination. Although few in number, such women constitute a group who believe that motherhood is the fulfillment of female identity, without which they view their lives to be incomplete and, in some cases, meaningless.

Sexual Behavior

The effects of pregnancy on sexual behavior vary. Some women experience an increased sex drive as pelvic vasocongestion produces an increased sexually responsive state. Others are more responsive than before the pregnancy because they no longer fear becoming pregnant. Some have diminished desire or lose interest in sexual activity altogether, either because of physical discomfort or because they associate motherhood with asexuality. Men with a Madonna complex view pregnant women as sacred and not to be defiled by the sexual act. Some men find a pregnant woman unattractive. Either a man or a woman may erroneously regard intercourse as potentially harmful to the developing fetus and, therefore, as something to be avoided. Men who have extramarital affairs during their wives' pregnancies usually do so during the last trimester.

Coitus. Most obstetricians place no prohibitions on coitus during pregnancy. Some suggest that sexual intercourse cease 4 to 5 weeks antepartum. If bleeding occurs early in pregnancy, it is usually, though not invariably, followed by a spontaneous abortion. In these cases an obstetrician prohibits coitus on a temporary basis as a therapeutic measure. The resulting abstinence can strain the marriage. Maternal deaths resulting from forcibly blowing air into the vagina during cunnilingus have been reported; the deaths presumably result from air emboli in the placental-maternal circulation, and such activity should be interdicted.

Medications and Breast Feeding. Lactation is influenced by many factors. Some women may feel obliged to nurse; others may nurse to please their husbands, friends, relatives, or physicians. In some cases women may feel guilty if they choose not to nurse or are physically unable to do so. There is no evidence of improved psychological or physical adjustment in breast-fed infants compared to those who are bottle fed. Currently, more than 50 percent of babies are breast fed; of this number about 30 percent are breast fed for 3 months or longer.

Many drugs can be transferred to infants through breast milk. Although most drugs are compatible with breast feeding, some can produce signs and symptoms in newborn infants (for example, antibiotics can produce rashes, and narcotics can produce sedation).

Biology of Pregnancy

The first presumptive sign of pregnancy is the absence of menses for one cycle. Other presumptive signs are breast engorgement and tenderness, changes in breast size and shape, nausea with or without vomiting (morning sickness), frequent urination, and fatigue. A diagnosis can be made 10 to 15 days after fertilization by testing for human chorionic gonadotropin (HCG), which is produced by the placenta. The definitive diagnosis requires a doubling of HCG levels, fetal heart sounds, and fetal movements. Ultrasound scanning can reveal a pregnant uterus as early as 4 weeks after fertilization.

Psychiatric Disorders and Pregnancy

Despite the tremendous physiological and psychological changes during pregnancy, most adult women tolerate the process remarkably well. Teenage mothers do not fare as well as adults and are also at increased risk for suicide. Before the widespread availability of contraception and legal abortions, pregnant women of all ages had a high risk of suicide, especially when they were unwed and without social supports.

Pica. Pica is the repeated ingestion of nonnutritive substances, such as dirt, clay, starch, sand, and feces. This eating disorder is most often seen in young children but is common in pregnant women in some subcultures, most notably among African-American women in the rural South, where the eating of clay or starch (for example, Argo) is common.

False Pregnancy. Pseudocyesis (false pregnancy) is a rare condition in which a person has the signs and symptoms of pregnancy, such as abdominal distention, breast enlargement, pigmentation, cessation of menses, and morning sickness. Pseudocyesis was first reported by Hippocrates; Mary Tudor, queen of England (1516–1558), allegedly had two episodes of pseudocyesis; and Sigmund Freud's patient Anna O. also suffered from pseudocyesis.

Pseudocyesis can occur at any age, in men as well as in women. Male pseudocyesis differs from couvade, a phenomenon that occurs in some primitive cultures; in couvade, a father takes to his bed during or shortly after the birth of his child, as though he himself had given birth.

The treatment of pseudocyesis should be undertaken in concert with a gynecologist or a primary care physician. Negative results on pregnancy tests (plasma or urine HCG and abdominal ultrasound) often result in a reduction of symptoms when the results are communicated to the patient in a compassionate manner. Reality-based supportive psychotherapy is the treatment of choice. Some patients respond to antipsychotic medications if their beliefs persist despite negative test results.

Antepartum (Prenatal) Care

Good prenatal care strongly correlates with healthy babies and satisfied mothers. Prenatal care should begin before conception so that prospective mothers' health can be assessed. Pregnant women can be examined to ensure fetal health and survival; they should receive information about the use of drugs (including the interdiction of alcohol, tobacco, and coffee) and about exercise and diet.

After pregnancy is diagnosed, clinicians may assess mothers' attitudes toward pregnancy: Was it planned? What are their attitudes toward having a child? Are children viewed as a burden or a joy? What are the husbands' feelings? If the women work, when do they plan to stop work? Do they plan to return to work? If so, when? How will a new baby affect the family finances? These and other questions can provide clues to the possible course of the pregnancy. Mothers who are under stress have a greater than usual risk of miscarriage, premature birth, and other complications. The risk of postpartum depression increases when there is a history of depression in the mother or her family or when the mother had a previous postpartum psychiatric illness.

There are significant differences in the proportion of women receiving prenatal care among racial and ethnic groups in the United States. In 1993, Native American, Mexican American, African-American, Hispanic, and Hawaiian mothers were less likely to receive prenatal care (63 to 71 percent) than were Chinese, White, Japanese, and Cuban mothers (85 to 89 percent). Nevertheless, there has been an overall increase in the proportion of women beginning prenatal care in the first trimester (from 76 to 79 percent between 1990 and 1993), with the greatest increase for those with the lowest levels of early care.

Infertility

Infertility is the inability of a couple to conceive after 1 year of coitus without the use of a contraceptive. In the United States, about 15 percent of married couples are unable to have children. The causes of infertility are attributed to disorders in women in 60 percent of cases and to disorders in men in 40 percent of cases. Tests in an infertility workup usually reveal the specific cause.

The inability to have a child can produce severe psychological stress on one or both partners in a marriage. They may feel defective and undesirable, have low self-esteem, and become depressed. Some may grieve for the lost infant they cannot have. Self-blame increases the likelihood of psychological problems. Men—but not women—are at increased risk for psychological distress if they are older and do not already have biological children. No statistics are available on infertility as a precipitating factor in divorce, but it does play a role. In couples in which one person (usually the woman) chooses adoption as an alternative choice but the other person (usually the man) is unwilling to do so, divorce may occur. Similarly, if one or both partners are unwilling to take advantage of assisted reproductive techniques, the marriage may falter. Various clinics report that 20 to 50 percent of couples presently facing infertility can be helped.

The most common medical causes of infertility are irregular ovulation, endometriosis, and damaged fallopian tubes. Until recently, women were blamed when couples did not have children, and feelings of guilt, depression, and inadequacy frequently accompanied the perception of being barren. Current practice encourages simultaneous investigations of factors preventing conception in both men and women, but frequently women still initiate an infertility workup.

A thorough sexual history of the couple—including such factors as frequency of contact, erectile or ejaculatory dysfunction, and coital position—must be obtained. Frequently, conception is less likely simply because the woman rises to void, wash, or even douche immediately after coitus. Coitus with the woman in the superior position is also not conducive to conception because of the lessened retention of semen.

A psychiatric evaluation of the couple may be advisable. Marital disharmony or emotional conflicts about intimacy, sexual relations, or parenting roles can directly affect endocrine function and such physiological processes as erection, ejaculation, and ovulation. There is no evidence, however, for any simple, causal relation between stress and infertility.

The stress of infertility itself in a couple who want children can lead to emotional disturbances. When a preexisting conflict gives rise to problems of identity, self-esteem, and guilt, the disturbance may be severe and may manifest itself through regression; extreme dependence on a physician, mate, or parent; diffuse anger; impulsive behavior; or depression. The problem is further complicated when hormone therapy is used to treat the infertility, because the therapy may temporarily increase depression in some patients.

People who have difficulty conceiving may experience shock, disbelief, and a general sense of helplessness, and they develop an understandable preoccupation with the problem. Involvement in the infertility workup and the development of expertise about infertility can be a constructive defense against feelings of inadequacy and the humiliating, sometimes painful aspects of the workup itself. Worries about attractiveness and sexual desirability are common. Partners may feel ugly or impotent, and episodes of sexual dysfunction and loss of desire are reported. These problems are aggravated when a couple is scheduling sexual relations according to temperature charts.

In addition, the couple must deal with a narcissistic blow to the sense of femininity or masculinity. An infertile partner may fear abandonment or feel that the spouse resents remaining in the relationship. Single people who are aware of their own infertility may shy away from relationships for fear of being rejected once their ''defect'' is known. People who are infertile may have particular difficulty in their adult relationships with their own parents. The identification and equality that come from sharing the experience of parenthood must be replaced by internal reserves and other generative aspects of their lives.

Professional intervention may be necessary to help infertile couples ventilate their feelings and go through the process of mourning for their lost biological functions and the children they cannot have. Couples who remain infertile must cope with an actual loss. Couples who decide not to pursue parenthood may develop a renewed sense of love, dedication, and identity as a pair. Others may need help in exploring the options of husband or donor insemination, laboratory implantation, and adoption.

Perinatal Death

Perinatal death is defined as death sometime between the 20th week of gestation and the first month of life and includes spontaneous abortion (miscarriage), fetal demise, stillbirth, and neonatal death. In previous years, the intense bond between the expectant or new parent and the fetus or neonate was underestimated, but perinatal loss is now recognized as a significant trauma for both parents. Parents who experience such a loss go through a period of mourning much like that experienced when any loved one is lost.

Intrauterine fetal death, which can occur at any time during the pregnancy, is an emotionally traumatic experience. In the early months of pregnancy, a woman is usually unaware of fetal death and learns of it only from her doctor. Later in pregnancy, after fetal movements and heart tones have been experienced, a woman may be able to detect fetal demise. When given the diagnosis of fetal death, most women want the dead fetus removed; depending on the trimester, labor may be induced, or the woman may have to wait for the spontaneous expulsion of the uterine contents. Many couples view sexual relations during the period of waiting as not only undesirable but psychologically unacceptable.

A sense of loss also accompanies the birth of a stillborn child as well as an induced abortion of an abnormal fetus detected by antenatal diagnosis. As mentioned earlier, attachment to an unborn child begins before birth, and grief and mourning occur after a loss at any time. The grief experienced after a third-trimester loss, however, is generally greater than that experienced after a first-trimester loss. Some parents do not wish to view a stillborn child, and their wishes should be respected. Others wish to hold the stillborn, and this act can assist the mourning process. A subsequent pregnancy may diminish overt feelings of grief but does not eliminate the need to mourn. So-called replacement children are at risk for overprotection and future emotional problems.

FAMILY PLANNING AND CONTRACEPTION

In present day society, more and more women work from economic necessity or from a desire for self-actualization. This fact and today's relative freedom of sexual expression have led to many women's postponing or avoiding pregnancy. Family planning is the process of choosing when and if to bear children; one form of family planning is contraception, the prevention of fecundation or fertilization of the ovum.

The choice of a contraceptive method is a complex decision involving both women and their partners. Factors influencing the decision include a woman's age and medical condition, her access to medical care, the couple's religious beliefs, and the need for spontaneity. The woman and her partner can weigh the risks and benefits of the various forms of contraception and make their decision on the basis of their current lifestyle and other factors. The success of contraceptive technology has enabled career-minded couples to delay childbearing into their 30s and 40s. Such a delay, however, may increase infertility problems. Consequently, many women with careers feel their biological clocks ticking and plan to have children in their early 30s to avoid the risk of not being able to have them at all. Table 2.2–1 provides information on current methods of contraception, and Figures 2.2–1 and 2.2–2 show some contraceptive modalities.

Induced Abortion

Induced abortion is the planned termination of a pregnancy. About 1.5 million abortions are performed in the United States

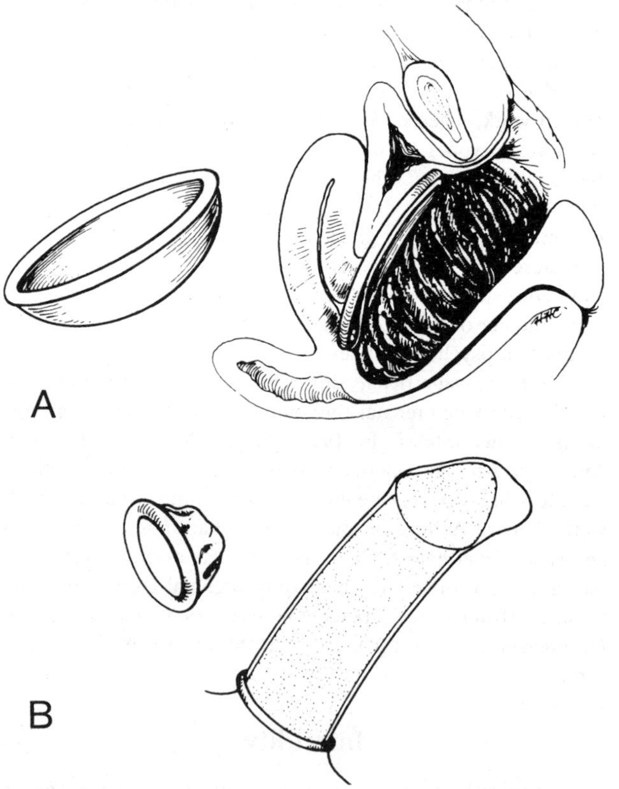
A
B

FIGURE 2.2–1

Pictorial representation of certain contraceptive modalities. **A.** The intravaginal diaphragm and its correct position as viewed during coition. **B.** The condom before and after being unrolled onto the erect penis.

Table 2.2–1
Current Methods of Contraception

Type	Method of Action	Effectiveness	Advantages	Disadvantages	Potential Complications
Fertility awareness method (FAM); rhythm	Timed abstinence; couple abstains 7 days before and after ovulation	Low	No cost or health risks; always available; no professional help required	Imposed coital timing (lack of spontaneity); continuous recording of menstrual cycle necessary; must learn to take basal body temperature and check cervical mucus	Essentially none
Withdrawal; coitus interruptus	Prevention of insemination	Low (but theoretically high)	No cost; always available; no professional help required	Regular coital use required; requires considerable attention and control by man, which may interfere with pleasure for both partners	Essentially none
Diaphragm	Rubber dome inserted into vagina; works as sperm barrier; used with spermicidal jelly; must be left in place for 6 hours after coitus (Fig. 2.2–1)	Medium to high	Inexpensive	Regular coital use required; possible interference with enjoyment; requires professional fitting; not anatomically adaptable to everyone; repeated intercourse requires new application of spermicide	Essentially none, but diaphragm can dislodge during coitus; urinary tract infections; used by 3.4 percent of women
Cervical cap	Rubber cap covers only cervical os; works as sperm barrier; works best with spermicidal jelly	Medium to high	Inexpensive: does not cover anterior vaginal wall, so may be more pleasurable for both partners; allows for repeated coitus without new application of spermicide	More difficult to fit and to insert than diaphragm; cannot be used if cervical lesions present	Essentially none, but may dislodge during coitus
Contraceptive sponge	Polyurethane sponge with spermicide inserted into vagina before intercourse; must be left in place for 6 hours after coitus	Medium	Easy to insert into vagina; vaginal walls not covered; must be left in place for 6 hours after intercourse; can be used for 24 hours with repeated coitus	Must be removed after 24 hours, or infection can develop	Chemical sensitivity to spermicide; sponge may break
Intravaginal foams, creams, jellies, and suppositories	Spermicidal	Low	Inexpensive; generally available; most effective when used with condom	Regular coital use required; possible messiness; possible interference with enjoyment	Essentially none; possible allergies

(continued)

Table 2.2–1 (*continued*)

Type	Method of Action	Effectiveness	Advantages	Disadvantages	Potential Complications
Condom	Sperm barrier (a female condom made of polyurethane is placed in the vaginal space before coitus and acts as a sperm barrier) (Fig. 2.2–2)	Medium	Inexpensive; latex condom protects against AIDS; generally available; no professional help required; decreased acquisition of coitally transmitted diseases	Regular coital use required; possible interference with enjoyment	Essentially none; may tear; 3 to 1,000 defective manufacture rate; allergy to latex is rare; used by 12.6 percent of couples
Intrauterine device (IUD)	Unknown (possibly prevents zygote implantation)	Medium	Inexpensive; only single decision required; not coitally connected; does not interfere with pleasure	Possible increase in bleeding and cramping; requires professional insertion; annual checkup required	Uterine perforation, pelvic infection, spontaneous expulsion; used by 10.2 percent of women
Oral (hormonal)	Prevention of ovulation (possible interference with sperm mobility); two types: (1) combined progesterone-estrogen, (2) progesterone only (minipill)	High (most commonly used method)	Inexpensive; potential absolute efficiency; not coitally connected	Possible side effects; daily ingestion; requires professional visit and prescription	Thromboembolism, hypertension, depression; used by 36.6 percent of women
Progestin implants (Norplant)	Suppresses ovulation; high change in cervical mucus	High	Effective for 5 years; no interference with spontaneity or pleasure	Requires minor surgery (local anesthesia) to implant and to remove	Menstrual irregularities, weight gain, headache
Postcoital hormonal method (RU-486)	Prevention of implantation of fertilized ovum	High	Cited as ideal contraceptive; can be used after coitus without contraception, after rape and incest	Not in widespread use in the United States (developed and used in France)	Excessive bleeding
Male sterilization (vasectomy)	Surgical interruption of vas deferens so that sperm cannot travel from testes to penis	High	Failure very rare; 20-minute office procedure	Morbidity in 1% to 2% of patients includes infections, clots	Can be reversed in only 80% of cases; rare neurotic impotence reaction; used by 10.4% of men
Female sterilization	Tubal ligation prevents transport of oocyte	High	Almost 100% protection; no impairment of sexual function or pleasure	More complex procedure than vasectomy; reversal is complicated and difficult	Surgical morbidity; used by 13.6 percent of women

Adapted and modified after data by Eugene C. Sandberg, M.D. Effectiveness is rated roughly as follows: low, more than 20 pregnancies for 100 women-years of use; medium, 1 to 20 pregnancies for 100 women-years of use; high, less than 1 pregnancy for 100 women-years of use.

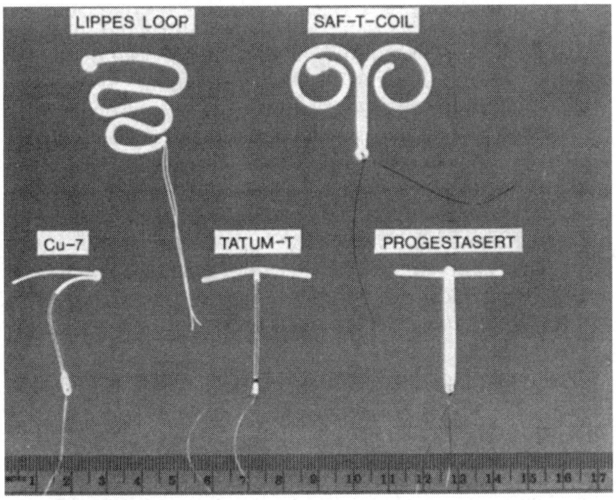
LIPPES LOOP
SAF-T-COIL
Cu-7
TATUM-T
PROGESTASERT

FIGURE 2.2–2
Intrauterine devices available in the United States. (Courtesy of Livia S. Wan, M.D., Judith E. Belsky, M.D., and Gordon W. Douglas, M.D.)

each year—380 abortions for every 1,000 live births. Since 1988, the number of abortions has declined by about 5 percent. In Western countries, most women who obtain abortions are young, unmarried, and primiparous; in emerging countries, abortion is most common among married women with two or more children.

Fifty percent of abortions are performed before 8 weeks of gestation, 25 percent between 9 and 10 weeks, and 10 percent between 11 and 12 weeks. The remainder occur after 13 weeks, with 1 percent occurring after 21 weeks. Table 2.2–2 summarizes the most common abortion techniques.

Abortion has become a political and philosophical issue in the United States; the country is sharply divided between pro-choice (pro-abortion) and pro-life (antiabortion) factions. In recent years, antiabortion demonstrators have picketed abortion clinics and have provoked angry confrontations with patients. The atmosphere of moral condemnation and intimidation may make the decision to terminate a pregnancy difficult. Nonetheless, recent studies have shown that most women who undergo a termination of pregnancy—particularly if they do so before the 12th week of gestation—do not suffer significant psychological sequelae. In fact, most women experience a sense of relief and have less of an emotional reaction than do those who maintain the pregnancy and give the baby up for adoption.

Second-trimester abortions are more psychologically traumatic than are first-trimester abortions. The most common reason for late abortions is the discovery (through amniocentesis or ultrasound) of a severe abnormality in the fetus. Thus, late abortions usually involve the loss of a wanted child with whom the mother has already formed a bond.

Before the legalization of abortion in the United States in 1973, many women sought illegal abortions, often performed by untrained practitioners under unsterile conditions. Considerable morbidity and mortality were associated with these abortions, and women who were denied abortion sometimes chose suicide over continuation of an unwanted pregnancy. When a woman is forced to carry a fetus to term, the risk of infanticide, abandonment, and neglect of the unwanted newborn increases.

Abortion can also be a significant experience for men. If a

Table 2.2–2
Abortion Techniques

Type	Benefits	Risks
Cervical dilation and evacuation of uterine contents by curettage or vacuum aspiration	Most commonly performed procedure for termination of pregnancy; can be done before 16 weeks gestation	Uterine perforation Cervical incompetence Adhesions Hemorrhage Infection Incomplete removal of fetus and placenta
Menstrual aspiration (miniabortion)	Can be done within 1 to 3 weeks of missed period	Implanted zygote not removed Uterine perforation (rare) Failure to recognize ectopic pregnancy
Medical induction (cervical dilation with laminaria followed by high dose of IV oxytocin)	Can be used for second-trimester abortions	Water intoxication Rupture of uterus, cervix, or isthmus
Intra-amniotic hyperosmotic solutions (salting out)	Can be used for second-trimester abortions	Hyperosmolar crisis Heart failure Peritonitis Hemorrhage Water intoxication Myometrial necrosis Accounts for only 2% of abortions
Prostaglandins (applied intravaginally, cervically, or intra-amniotically)	Noninvasive procedure	Expulsion of live fetus

man has a close relationship with the woman, he may wish to play an active role in the abortion, by accompanying her to the hospital or abortion clinic and providing emotional support. Fathers may experience considerable grief over the termination of a wanted pregnancy.

Sterilization

Sterilization is a procedure that prevents a man or a woman from producing offspring. In a woman the procedure is usually salpingectomy, ligation of the fallopian tubes, a procedure with low morbidity and low mortality. A man is usually sterilized by vasectomy, excision of part of the vas deferens. It is a simpler procedure than is salpingectomy and may be performed in a physician's office. Voluntary sterilization, especially vasectomy, has become the most popular form of birth control in couples married for more than 10 years.

A small proportion of patients who elect sterilization may suffer a neurotic poststerilization syndrome, which may manifest itself through hypochondriasis, pain, loss of libido, sexual unresponsiveness, depression, and concerns about masculinity or femininity. One study of a group of women who regretted sterilization reported they had chosen the procedure while in poor relationships, frequently with abusing husbands. Regret is most prevalent when a woman forms a new relationship and wishes to have a child with a new partner.

Psychiatric consultation may be necessary to separate people seeking sterilization for irrational or psychotic reasons from those who have made the decision after some time and thought.

In the United States, involuntary sterilization procedures have been performed to prevent the reproduction of traits considered genetically undesirable, and various statutes allowed the sterilization of hereditary criminals, sex offenders, syphilitic patients, mentally retarded people, and people with epilepsy. Some of these statutes have been declared unconstitutional, and in recent years human rights and civil liberties groups have challenged the legality and ethical standing of such sterilization procedures with increasing vigor.

The operative procedures for sterilization have assumed less importance than in the past because of the advent of contraceptives and the relative ease of obtaining abortions. Nonetheless, sterilization procedures are still chosen by men and women who, for a variety of reasons, want to permanently end their ability to produce children.

Vasectomy. In a vasectomy a man's vas deferens is ligated bilaterally, and a segment is removed. The procedure is done under local anesthesia and takes about 20 minutes. The procedure can be reversed in 80 to 90 percent of cases. A few men experience a postvasectomy syndrome consisting of decreased libido, impotence, identity confusion, and signs of depression. Most of these men had been depressed prior to the vasectomy, however. In most cases of male sterilization, no negative psychological sequelae are experienced.

Tubal Ligation. In tubal ligation the woman's fallopian tubes are cauterized by laparotomy. Reversal of the procedure is far less effective than is reversal of vasectomy in men. For a small proportion of women, a poststerilization syndrome consisting of hypochondria, pain, loss of libido, and doubt about female identity may develop, although this occurs generally in women with a preexisting psychopathological state.

Psychiatric consultation before sterilization is useful for evaluating motivations for the procedure (for example, coercion by a partner) and for ruling out preexisting psychopathology, such as depression, that may lead to postoperative syndrome.

CHILDBIRTH

According to the U.S. Department of Health and Human Services, 3,954,000 babies were born in the United States in the 12-month period ending March 1995. The birthrate was 15.1 per 1,000 people, a decline of 3 percent over the previous year. The number and rate of live births in the United States have been steadily declining since 1990. Advances in prenatal and perinatal care reduced the infant death rate to 7.9 per 1,000 live births in 1994 (down from 9.1 infant deaths per 1,000 live births in 1990 and 9.8 infant deaths per 1,000 live births in 1989). In 1993 the infant mortality rate for black infants (16.5) was more than twice that for white infants (6.8). Despite the declining infant mortality rate, in 1992 the rate was 88 percent higher in the United States than in Japan and 40 percent higher in the United States than in Canada. The fertility rate of 67.6 live births per 1,000 women ages 15 to 44 years in 1993 marked a decline over the previous 3 years. The decline in fertility among black women was nearly twice the decline for white women. Between 1991 and 1993 the birthrate for teenagers declined slightly and reversed a trend seen between 1986 and 1991.

The overwhelming majority of babies are born in hospitals with physicians in attendance (Fig. 2.2–3), but freestanding birthing centers with access to a hospital are an alternative for some couples. High-risk babies are best delivered in a hospital with a perinatal center, as these infants face the risk of neonatal morbidity and mortality.

The number of babies born by cesarean section increased steadily from about 5 percent in the 1960s to about 20 percent in the 1980s. Some of the increase reflected physicians' fear of malpractice suits. Prolonged labor, which is sometimes hazardous to the fetus, is also avoided with a cesarean section. Analgesic drugs given to the mother during labor enter the fetal bloodstream and sedate the newborn infant. A drug that depresses the mother's nervous system affects the infant's sucking reflex, sometimes for a few days. Since 1990, however, both the number and rate of cesarean sections have declined.

Lamaze Method

Also known as natural childbirth, the Lamaze method originated with the French obstetrician Fernand Lamaze. In this method, women are fully conscious during labor and delivery, and no analgesic or anesthetic is used. The expectant mother and father attend special classes, during which they are taught relaxation and breathing exercises designed to facilitate the

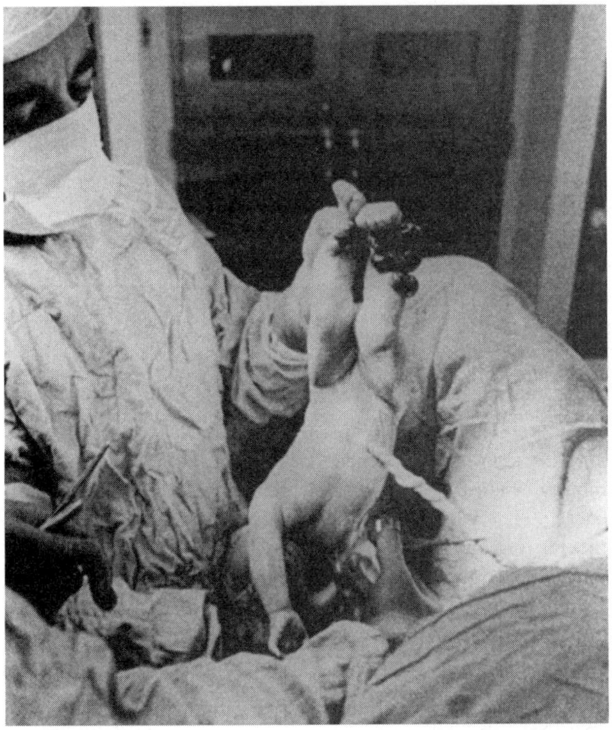

FIGURE 2.2–3

The moment of birth. (Reprinted with permission from Stone LJ, Church J: *Childhood and Adolescence,* ed 4, p 4. Random House, New York, 1979.)

birth process. Women who undergo such training often report minimal pain during labor and delivery.

Premature Births

Childbirth is a potentially hazardous time for both mother and child. Although most premature infants develop normally, a premature birth increases the risk of dysfunction. About 30 percent of premature infants suffer from one or more of the following: mental retardation, behavior problems, emotional disorders, blindness, hearing deficits, movement disorders, and sensorimotor problems, such as dyslexia. Also, premature babies are at a greater than usual risk for child abuse. Prematurity is defined as a birth weight under 2,500 grams or a gestation period less than 34 weeks. Prematurity is correlated with low socioeconomic status, poor maternal nutrition, and teenage pregnancy; it accounts for 7 percent of all births. High socioeconomic status correlates negatively with infant mortality. Low-birth-weight babies are most common in blacks (13.2 percent of all deliveries) and least common in whites (5.7 percent).

Attachment and Bonding. Because premature infants have a weakened sensorimotor system, less mother–infant interaction occurs with a premature infant than with a full-term baby. This difference may affect *attachment* (an infant's feelings toward the mother) and *bonding* (a mother's feelings toward the infant), both of which are partially dependent on the interaction between mother and infant. In addition, premature babies require more care than do full-term babies, and the strain on the new mother and father can be exceptionally burdensome.

Neonatal Intensive Care Units (NICUs). Infants who are kept in neonatal units receive intensive care with complex technological life-support systems. Most mothers are encouraged to have physical contact with their infants within a few hours of birth, but in some neonatal intensive care units, mothers may not be able to hold their babies for several days. Generally, fathers participate less than do mothers, and both have little to do because the neonatal intensive care unit staff attends to the infant. When possible, parents should be involved in nursing tasks and should be allowed to touch, clean, and stroke the neonates.

HIV Infection

About 7,000 human immunodeficiency virus (HIV)-infected women give birth every year. Mothers infected with HIV can transmit the virus to their children, who can be infected in utero or through breast feeding. About 85 percent of acquired immune deficiency syndrome (AIDS) cases in children under 13 are contracted from infected mothers. In the United States, most infected mothers are black or Hispanic women who became infected through intravenous (IV) drug use. AIDS is among the top 10 causes of death in children under 5 years of age, but when newborn infants have their mothers' antibodies, they can be protected from developing AIDS if they are not breast fed.

An amendment to the 1996 Ryan White Care Act, which would have required HIV testing of newborns in the United States, was defeated in committee. States are now merely "encouraged" to provide testing.

Depression and Psychosis in the Postpartum Period

About 20 to 40 percent of women report some emotional disturbance or cognitive dysfunction in the postpartum period. Many experience postpartum blues, a normal state of sadness, dysphoria, frequent tearfulness, and clinging dependence. These feelings, which may last several days, have been ascribed to rapid changes in women's hormonal levels, the stress of childbirth, and the awareness of the increased responsibility that motherhood brings.

A similar syndrome has been described in fathers who have mood changes during their wives' pregnancies or after the babies are born. Such a father is affected by several factors: added responsibility, diminished sexual outlet, decreased attention from his wife, and the belief that the child is a binding force in an unsatisfactory marriage. In rare cases (1 to 2 in 1,000 deliveries), a woman's postpartum depression is characterized by depressed feelings and suicidal ideation. In severe cases the depression may reach psychotic proportions, with hallucinations, delusions, and thoughts of infanticide. Although previous psychiatric problems put women at risk for postpartum disturbances, there is evidence to suggest that postpartum mood disorder is a specific concept, distinct from other psychiatric diagnoses. Most women with severe postpartum depressions do not suffer future nonpuerperal episodes if their previous psychiatric history was benign.

GENETIC COUNSELING

Genetic counseling provides people who plan to have children with information about genetically based disorders. For example, a person whose father has Huntington's disease may be concerned about having the disease. Huntington's disease follows mendelian rules of inheritance; a person whose parent has the disorder has a 50 percent chance of having the disease. Because the age of onset varies, the longer a person lives without becoming ill, the lower the risk. A chemical test for determining the gene carriers of Huntington's disease was recently developed, and people can now use this knowledge when deciding whether to have children.

Genetic counseling requires that clinicians be aware of patients' levels of maturity, individual conflicts, defense mechanisms, and ego strengths and weaknesses. Counselors must be ready to deal with depression, anger, anxiety, and other complex emotions related to the issues at hand.

References

Annas GJ: Protecting the liberty of pregnant patients. N Engl J Med *316:* 1213, 1987.

Berga SL, Parry PL: Psychiatry and reproductive medicine. In *Comprehensive Textbook of Psychiatry,* ed 6, HI Kaplan, BJ Sadock, editors, p 1693. Williams & Wilkins, Baltimore, 1995.

Cath SH, Gurwitt AR, Ross JM, editors: *Father and Child: Developmental and Clinical Perspective.* Little, Brown, Boston, 1982.

Connolly KJ, Edelman RJ, Cooke ID, Robson J: The impact of infertility on psychological functioning. J Psychosom Res *36:* 459, 1992.

Cook RJ: Abortion laws and policies: Challenges and opportunities. Int J Gynaecol Obstet *3* (Suppl): 61, 1989.

Friedman R, Gradstein B: *Surviving Pregnancy Loss.* Little, Brown, Boston, 1982.

Groome LJ, Swiber MJ, Bentz LS, Holland SB, et al: Maternal anxiety during pregnancy: Effect on fetal behavior at 38 to 40 weeks of gestation. Dev Behav Pediatr *16:* 391, 1995.

Hechtman L: Teenage mothers and their children: Risks and problems: A review. Can J Psychiatry *34:* 569, 1989.

Hoffman NS: Stress factors related to antenatal testing during high-risk pregnancy. J Perinatol *10:* 195, 1990.

Hutchison KE, Stevens VM, Collins FL: Cigarette smoking and the intention to quit among pregnant smokers. Behav Med *19:* 307, 1996.

Matthews KA, Rodin J: Pregnancy alters blood pressure responses to psychological and physical challenge. Psychophysiology *29:* 232, 1992.

McCormick MC, Brooks-Gunn J, Shorter T, Holmes JH, Wallace CY, Heagarty MC: Factors associated with smoking in low-income pregnant women: Relationship to birth weight, stressful life events, social support, health behaviors and mental distress. J Clin Epidemiol *43:* 441, 1990.

McDuffie RS Jr, Beck A, Bischoff K, Cross J, Orleans M: Effects of frequency of prenatal care visits on perinatal outcome among low-risk women: A randomized controlled trial. JAMA *275:* 847, 1996.

Molfese VJ, Holcomb LC: Predicting learning and other developmental disabilities: Assessment of reproductive and caretaking variables. Birth Defects *25:* 1, 1989.

Morrow KA, Thoreson RW, Penney LL: Predictors of psychological distress among infertility clinic patients. J Consult Clin Psychol *63:* 163, 1995.

Public Health Service: *United States Chartbook: Health 1995.* US Department of Health and Human Services, Washington, 1995.

Rofe Y, Blittner M, Lewin I: Emotional experiences during the three trimesters of pregnancy. J Clin Psychol *49:* 3, 1993.

Tasker F, Golumbok S: Adults raised as children in lesbian families. Am J Orthopsychiatry *65:* 203, 1995.

Victor SB, Fish MC: Lesbian mothers and the children: A review for school psychologists. School Psychol Rev *24:* 456, 1995.

Webster J, Chandler J, Battistutta D: Pregnancy outcomes and health care use: Effects of abuse. Am J Obstet Gynecol *142:* 760, 1996.

Whiteford LM, Gonzoles L: Stigma: The hidden burden of infertility. Soc Sci Med *40:* 27, 1995.

Young DD, Ehrhardt AA: *Psychosomatic Obstetrics and Gynecology.* Appleton-Century-Crofts, New York, 1980.

Zhang J, Cai W: Risk factors associated with antepartum fetal death. Early Hum Dev *28:* 193, 1992.

▲ 2.3 Prenatal Period, Infancy, and Childhood

Although various strands of science have contributed to modern theories of children's prenatal and postnatal experiences, most workers think of these experiences in developmental terms. The conventional stages of early development include the prenatal period, infancy (from birth to about 15 months), the toddler period (15 months to 2½ years), the preschool period (2½ to 6 years), and the middle years (6 to 12 years). These stages form a continuum along which development proceeds, and after birth there is rarely a clear-cut division between them.

Arnold Gesell described developmental schedules that are widely used in both pediatrics and child psychiatry. These schedules outline the qualitative sequence of children's motor, adaptive, and personal-social behavior from birth to 6 years (Table 2.3–1).

PRENATAL PERIOD

After implantation, the egg begins to divide and at this time is known as an *embryo.* Growth and development occur at a rapid pace; by the end of 8 weeks, the shape is recognizably human, and the embryo has become a *fetus.* Figure 2.3–1 illustrates the moment of conception.

Any view of mental disorders must consider the fetus's uteroplacental environment and neurobiological substrate. The fetus maintains an internal equilibrium that, with variable effects, interacts continuously with the intrauterine environment. In general, most disorders that occur are multifactorial—the result of a combination of effects, some of which may be additive. Damage at the fetal stage is usually more global in its impact than is damage after birth because rapidly growing organs are the most vulnerable. Boys are more vulnerable to developmental damage than are girls; geneticists recognize that, in humans and animals, girls show a propensity for greater biological vigor than do boys, possibly because of the girl's second X chromosome.

Fetal Life

A great deal of biological activity occurs in utero. A fetus is involved in a variety of behaviors that are necessary for adaptation outside the womb. For example, the fetus sucks on thumb and fingers; it folds and unfolds its body and eventually assumes a position in which its occiput is in an anterior vertex

Table 2.3–1
Landmarks of Normal Behavioral Development

Age	Motor and Sensory Behavior	Adaptive Behavior	Personal and Social Behavior
Birth to 4 weeks	Hand-to-mouth reflex, grasping reflex Rooting reflex (puckering lips in response to perioral stimulation), Moro reflex (digital extension when startled); sucking reflex, Babinski reflex (toes spread when sole of foot is touched) Differentiates sounds (orients to human voice) and sweet and sour tastes Visual tracking Fixed focal distance of 8 inches Makes alternating crawling movements Moves head laterally when placed in prone position	Anticipatory feeding-approach behavior at 4 days Responds to sound of rattle and bell Regards moving objects momentarily	Responsiveness to mother's face, eyes, and voice within first few hours of life Endogenous smile Independent play (until 2 years) Quiets when picked up Impassive face
4 weeks	Tonic neck reflex positions predominate Hands fisted Head sags but can hold head erect for a few seconds Visual fixation, stereoscopic vision (12 weeks)	Follows moving objects to the midline Shows no interest and drops objects immediately	Regards face and diminishes activity Responds to speech Smiles preferentially to mother
16 weeks	Symmetrical postures predominate Holds head balanced Head lifted 90 when prone on forearm Visual accommodation	Follows a slowly moving object well Arms activate on sight of dangling object	Spontaneous social smile (exogenous) Aware of strange situations
28 weeks	Sits steadily, leaning forward on hands Bounces actively when placed in standing position	One-hand approach and grasp of toy Bangs and shakes rattle Transfers toys	Takes feet to mouth Pats mirror image Starts to imitate mother's sounds and actions
40 weeks	Sits alone with good coordination Creeps Pulls self to standing position Points with index finger	Matches two objects at midline Attempts to imitate scribble	Separation anxiety manifest when taken away from mother Responds to social play, such as pat-a-cake and peekaboo Feeds self cracker and holds own bottle
52 weeks	Walks with one hand held Stands alone briefly	Seeks novelty	Cooperates in dressing
15 months	Toddles Creeps up stairs		Points or vocalizes wants Throws objects in play or refusal
18 months	Coordinated walking, seldom falls Hurls ball Walks up stairs with one hand held	Builds a tower of three or four cubes Scribbles spontaneously and imitates a writing stroke	Feeds self in part, spills Pulls toy on string Carries or hugs a special toy, such as a doll Imitates some behavioral patterns with slight delay
2 years	Runs well, no falling Kicks large ball Goes up and down stairs alone Fine motor skills increase	Builds a tower of six or seven cubes Aligns cubes, imitating train Imitates vertical and circular strokes Develops original behaviors	Pulls on simple garment Domestic mimicry Refers to self by name Says "no" to mother Separation anxiety begins to diminish Organized demonstrations of love and protest Parallel play (plays side by side but does not interact with other children)
3 years	Rides tricycle Jumps from bottom steps Alternates feet going up stairs	Builds tower of 9 or 10 cubes Imitates a three-cube bridge Copies a circle and a cross	Puts on shoes Unbuttons buttons Feeds self well Understands taking turns
4 years	Walks down stairs one step to a tread Stands on one foot for 5 to 8 seconds	Copies a cross Repeats four digits Counts three objects with correct pointing	Washes and dries own face Brushes teeth Associative or joint play (plays cooperatively with other children)
5 years	Skips, using feet alternately Usually has complete sphincter control Fine coordination improves	Copies a square Draws a recognizable person with a head, a body, limbs Counts 10 objects accurately	Dresses and undresses self Prints a few letters Plays competitive exercise games
6 years	Rides two-wheel bicycle	Prints name Copies triangle	Ties shoelaces

Adapted from Arnold Gesell, M.D., and Stella Chess, M.D.

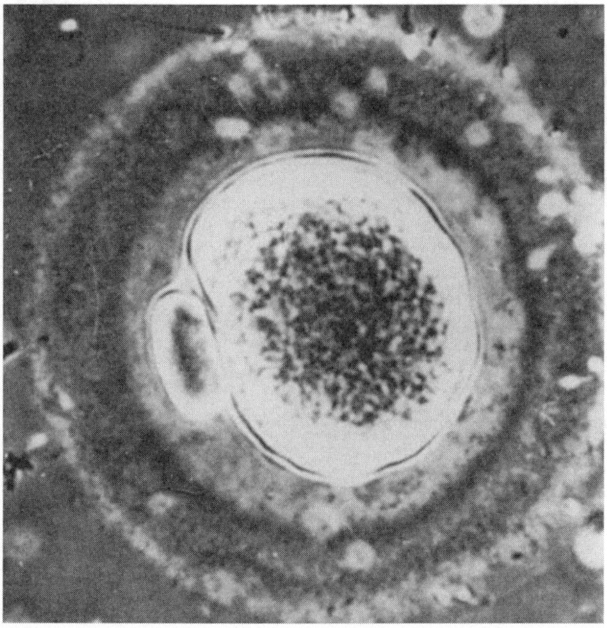

FIGURE 2.3–1

A human egg at the instant of fertilization. (Reprinted with permission from Stone LJ, Church J: *Childhood and Adolescence,* ed 4, p 106. Random House, New York, 1979.)

position, which is the position in which it usually exits the uterus.

Behavior. Pregnant women are extraordinarily sensitive to prenatal movements. They describe their unborn babies as active or passive, as kicking vigorously or rolling around, as quiet when the mothers are active but as kicking as soon as the mothers try to rest.

Women usually detect fetal movements at 16 to 20 weeks into the pregnancy; the fetus can be artificially set into total body motion by in utero stimulation of its ventral skin surfaces by the 14th week. The fetus may be able to hear by the 18th week, and it responds to loud noises with muscle contractions, movements, and an increased heart rate. Smell and taste are also developed at this time, and the fetus responds to substances that may be injected into the amniotic sac, such as contrast medium. Some reflexes present at birth exist in utero: the grasp reflex, which appears at 17 weeks; the Moro (startle) reflex, which appears at 25 weeks; and the sucking reflex, which appears at about 28 weeks.

Nervous System. The nervous system arises from the neural plate, which is a dorsal ectodermal thickening that appears at about the 16th day of gestation. By the sixth week, part of the neural tube becomes the cerebral vesicle, which later becomes the cerebral hemispheres.

The cerebral cortex begins to develop by the 10th week, but layers do not appear until the sixth month of pregnancy; the sensory cortex and the motor cortex are formed before the association cortex. In utero, some brain function has been detected by fetal encephalographic responses to sound. The weight of the human brain is about 350 grams at birth and 1,450 grams at full adult development, a fourfold increase, mainly in the neocortex. During fetal life and early infancy, the number and branching of dendrites and the number of synaptic junctions grow enormously. Uterine contractions may contribute to fetal neural development by causing the developing neural network to receive and transmit sensory impulses.

Maternal Stress

The fetus is vulnerable and reacts to stimuli such as drugs and maternal stress. Animal studies have shown that maternal stress during pregnancy affects behavior in offspring; the same effects are seen in humans. Maternal hormones cross the placenta and produce secondary effects in the fetus; if a mother is stressed, corticosteroids and other stress-related hormones may affect the cardiovascular system of the fetus, whose blood pressure is sensitive to external stimuli. Some correlation has been found between a woman's autonomic responses and the neonate's responses. Women with high anxiety levels are likely to produce babies who are hyperactive and irritable, have sleep disorders and low birth weight, and feed poorly.

Prenatal Disorders

In many cases, genetic counseling depends on prenatal diagnosis. The diagnostic techniques used include amniocentesis (transabdominal aspiration of fluid from the amniotic sac), ultrasound examinations, X-rays, fetoscopy (direct visualization of the fetus), fetal blood and skin sampling, chorionic villus sampling, and α-fetoprotein screening. In about 2 percent of the total number of women tested, the results are positive for some abnormality, including X-linked disorders, neural tube defects (detected by high levels of α-fetoprotein), chromosomal disorders (for example, trisomy 21), and various inborn errors of metabolism (for example, Tay-Sachs disease and lipoidoses).

Some diagnostic tests carry a risk; for instance, about 5 percent of women who undergo fetoscopy have miscarriages. Amniocentesis, which is usually performed between the 14th and 16th weeks of pregnancy, causes fetal damage or miscarriage in fewer than 1 percent of women tested. Fully 98 percent of all prenatal tests in pregnant women reveal no abnormality in the fetus. Prenatal testing is recommended for women over 35 and for those with a family history of a congenital defect.

Other Defects

Fetal alcohol syndrome affects about one third of all infants born to alcoholic women. The syndrome is characterized by growth retardation of prenatal origin (height, weight); minor anomalies, including microphthalmia (small eyeballs), short palpebral fissures, midface hypoplasia (underdevelopment), a smooth or short philtrum, and a thin upper lip; and central nervous system (CNS) manifestations, including microcephaly (head circumference below the third percentile), a history of delayed development, hyperactivity, attention deficits, learning disabilities, intellectual deficits, and seizures. The incidence of infants born with fetal alcohol syndrome was 0.4 per 1,000 live births in 1990, according to the U.S. Public Health Service.

Table 2.3–2
Causes of Human Malformations Observed During the First Year of Life

Suspected Cause	% of Total
Genetic	
Autosomal genetic disease	15–20
Cytogenetic (chromosomal abnormalities)	5
Unknown	65
Polygenic	
Multifactorial (genetic-environmental interactions)	
Spontaneous error of development	
Synergistic interactions of teratogens	
Environmental	
Maternal conditions: diabetes; endocrinopathies; nutritional deficiencies, starvation; drug and substance addictions	4
Maternal infections: rubella, toxoplasmosis, syphilis, herpes, cytomegalic inclusion disease, varicella, Venezuelan equine encephalitis, *Parvovirus* B19	3
Mechanical problems (deformations): abnormal cord constrictions, disparity in uterine size and uterine contents	1–2
Chemicals, drugs, radiation, hyperthermia	1
Preconception exposures (excluding mutagens and infectious agents)	1

Reprinted with permission from Brent RL, Beckman DA: Environmental teratogens. Bull NY Acad Med *66:* 125, 1990.

Smoking during pregnancy is associated with lower-than-average infant birth weight. Infants born to mothers dependent on narcotics go through a withdrawal syndrome at birth. When a woman is exposed to severe radiation during the first 20 weeks of her pregnancy, the baby will be born with gross deformities. Estimates are that 3 to 6 percent of all newborns have some sort of birth defect that is fatal at birth or that causes permanent disability. Table 2.3–2 lists malformations that occur during the first year of life.

Prenatal exposure to various medications can also result in abnormalities. Common drugs that have teratogenic effects include antibiotics (tetracycline), phenytoin, progesterone-estrogens, lithium, and warfarin.

INFANCY

The delivery of the fetus marks the start of infancy. The average newborn weighs about 3,400 grams (7½ pounds).

Small fetuses, defined as those with a birth weight below the 10th percentile for their gestational age, occur in about 7 percent of all pregnancies. At the 26th to the 28th week of gestation, the prematurely born fetus has a good chance of survival.

Premature infants are usually defined as those weighing between 1,000 and 2,500 grams. With each 100-gram increment of weight, beginning at about 1,000 grams, infants have a progressively better chance of survival. A 36-week-old fetus has less of a chance of survival than does a 3,000-gram fetus born close to term. The differences between normal and preterm infants are shown in Figure 2.3–2.

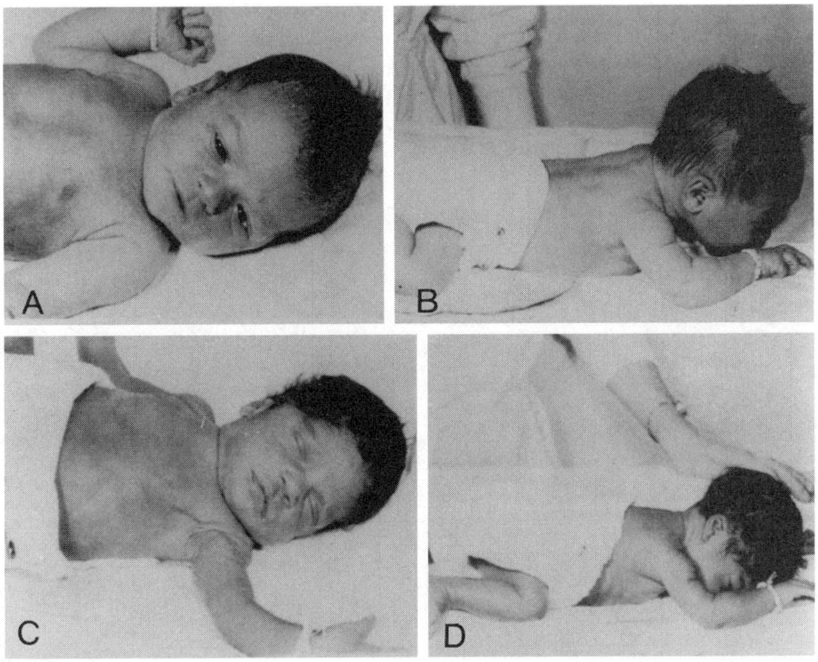
A
B
C
D

FIGURE 2.3–2
Contrast between full-term (**A** and **B**) and premature (**C** and **D**) infants. Note the limp sprawl of the baby in **C** and the difficulty in raising the head to clear nose and mouth in **D.** (Reprinted with permission from Stone LJ, Church J: *Childhood and Adolescence,* ed 4, p 7. Random House, New York, 1979.)

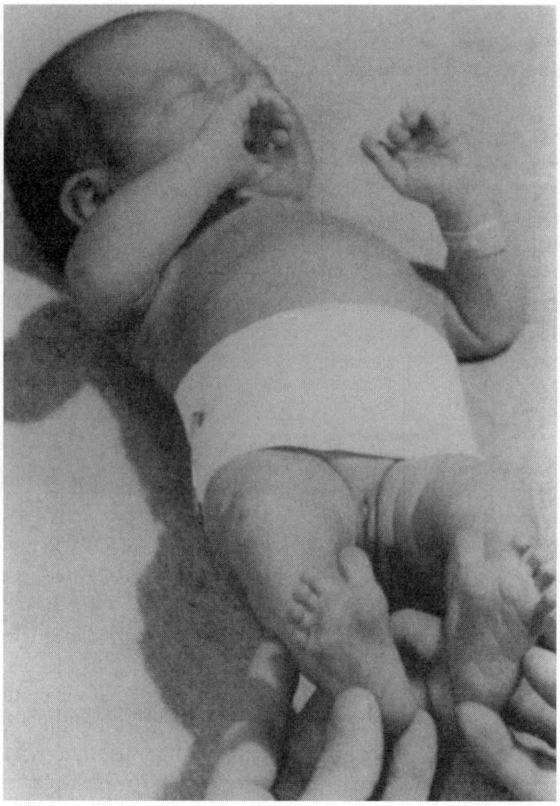

FIGURE 2.3–3
Babinski response. (Reprinted with permission from Stone LJ, Church J: *Childhood and Adolescence,* ed 4, p 7. Random House, New York, 1979.)

Postmature infants are defined as infants born 2 weeks or more beyond the expected date of birth. Because pregnancy at term is calculated as extending 40 weeks from the last menstrual period and as the exact time of fertilization varies, the incidence of postmaturity is high when based on menstrual history alone. The postmature baby typically has long nails, scanty lanugo hair, more than the usual amount of scalp hair, and increased alertness.

Developmental Landmarks

Reflexes and Survival Systems at Birth. Reflexes are present at birth. They include the rooting reflex (puckering of the lips in response to perioral stimulation), the grasp reflex, the plantar (Babinski) reflex (Fig. 2.3–3), the knee reflex, the abdominal reflexes, the startle (Moro) reflex (Fig. 2.3–4), and the tonic neck reflex. In normal children, the grasp reflex, the startle reflex, and the tonic neck reflex disappear by the fourth month.

Survival systems—breathing, sucking, swallowing, and circulatory and temperature homeostasis—are relatively functional at birth, but the sensory organs are incompletely developed. Further differentiation of neurophysiological functions depends on an active process of stimulatory reinforcement from the external environment, such as people touching and stroking the infant.

Language and Cognitive Development. At birth, infants are able to make noises, such as crying, but they do not vocalize until about 8 weeks (Fig. 2.3–5). At that time, guttural or babbling sounds occur spontaneously, especially in response to the mother. The persistence and further evolution of children's vocalizations depend on parental reinforcement. Language development occurs in well-delineated stages, as outlined in Table 2.3–3.

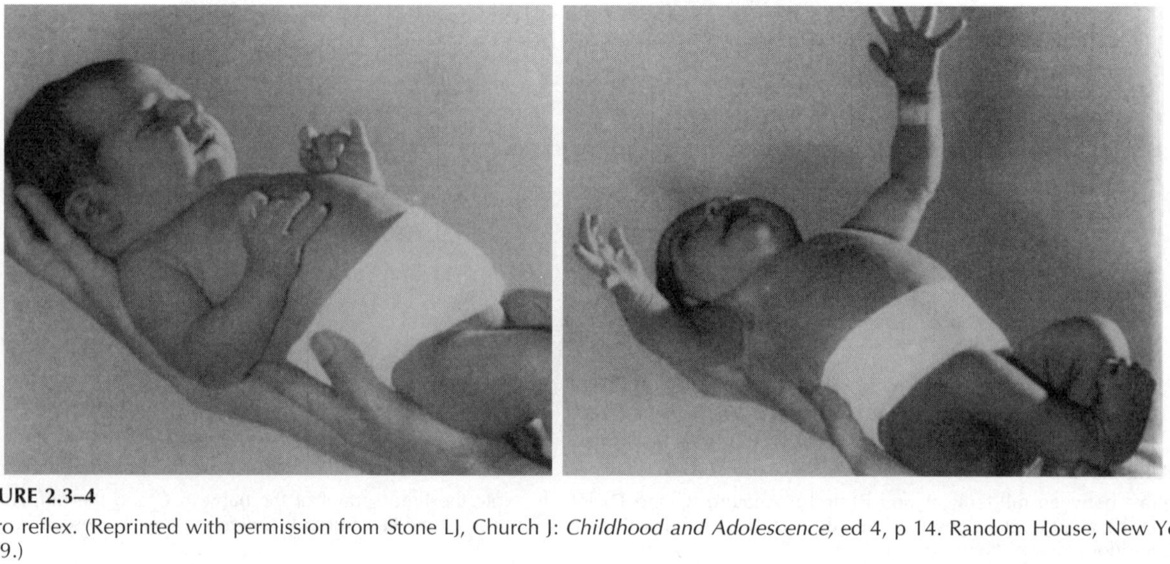

FIGURE 2.3–4
Moro reflex. (Reprinted with permission from Stone LJ, Church J: *Childhood and Adolescence,* ed 4, p 14. Random House, New York, 1979.)

Table 2.3–3
Language Development

Age and Stage of Development	Mastery of Comprehension	Mastery of Expression
0–6 months	Shows startle response to loud or sudden sounds Attempts to localize sounds, turning eyes or head Appears to listen to speakers, may respond with smile Recognizes warning, angry, and friendly voices Responds to hearing own name	Has vocalizations other than crying Has differential cries for hunger, pain Makes vocalizations to show pleasure Plays at making sounds Babbles (repeats a series of sounds)
7–11 months Attending-to-language stage	Shows listening selectivity (voluntary control over responses to sounds) Listens to music or singing with interest Recognizes "no," "hot," own name Looks at pictures being named for up to 1 minute Listens to speech without being distracted by other sounds	Responds to own name with vocalizations Imitates the melody of utterances Uses jargon (own language) Has gestures (shakes head for no) Has exclamation ("oh-oh") Plays language games (pat-a-cake, peekaboo)
12–18 months Single-word stage	Shows gross discriminations between dissimilar sounds (bell *vs.* dog *vs.* horn *vs.* mother's or father's voice) Understands basic body parts, names of common objects Acquires understanding of some new words each week Can identify simple objects (baby, ball, etc.) from a group of objects or pictures Understands up to 150 words by age 18 months	Uses single words (mean age of first word is 11 months; by age 18 months, child is using up to 20 words) "Talks" to toys, self, or others, using long patterns of jargon and occasional words Approximately 25% of utterances are intelligible All vowels articulated correctly Initial and final consonants often omitted
12–24 months Two-word messages stage	Responds to simple directions ("Give me the ball") Responds to action commands ("Come here," "Sit down") Understands pronouns (me, him, her, you) Begins to understand complex sentences ("When we go to the store, I'll buy you some candy")	Uses two-word utterances ("Mommy sock," "all gone," "ball here") Imitates environmental sounds in play ("moo," "mmm, mmm," etc.) Refers to self by name, begins to use pronouns Echoes two or more last words of sentences Begins to use three-word telegraphic utterances ("all gone ball," "me go now") Utterances 26% to 50% intelligible Uses language to ask for needs
24–36 months Grammar formation stage	Understands small body parts (elbow, chin, eyebrow) Understands family name categories (grandma, baby) Understands size (little one, big one) Understands most adjectives Understands functions (why do we eat, why do we sleep)	Uses real sentences with grammatical function words (can, will, the, a) Usually announces intentions before acting "Conversations" with other children, usually just monologues Jargon and echolalia gradually drop from speech Increased vocabulary (up to 270 words at 2 years, 895 words at 3 years) includes slang Speech 50% to 80% intelligible P, b, m articulated correctly Speech may show rhythmic disturbances
36–54 months Grammar development stage	Understands prepositions (under, behind, between) Understands many words (up to 3,500 at 3 years, 5,500 at 4 years) Understands cause and effect (What do you do when you're hungry?, cold?) Understands analogies (Food is to eat, milk is to ______)	Correct articulation of *n, w, ng, h, t, d, k, g* Uses language to relate incidents from the past Uses wide range of grammatical forms: plurals, past tense, negatives, questions Plays with language: rhymes, exaggerates Speech 90% intelligible, occasional errors in the ordering of sounds within words Able to define words Egocentric use of language rare Can repeat a 12-syllable sentence correctly Some grammatical errors still occur
55 months on True communication stage	Understands concepts of number, speed, time, space Understands left and right Understands abstract terms Is able to categorize items into semantic classes	Uses language to tell stories, share ideas, and discuss alternatives Increasing use of varied grammar; spontaneous self-correction of grammatical errors Stabilizing of articulation of *f, v, s, z, l, r, th,* and consonant clusters Speech 100% intelligible

Reprinted with permission from Rutter M, Hersov L, editors: *Child and Adolescent Psychiatry.* Blackwell, London, 1985.

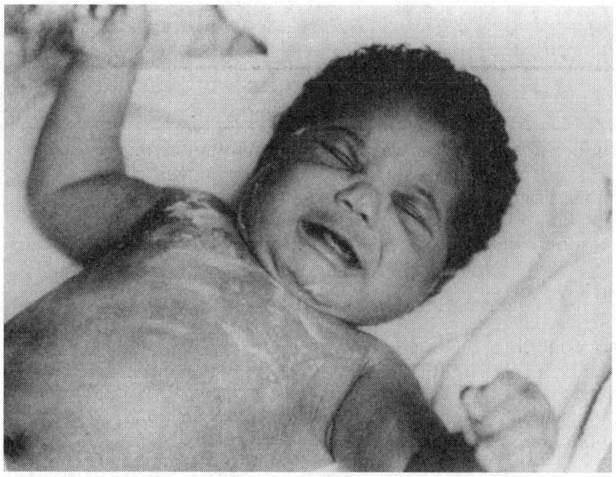

FIGURE 2.3–5
A neonate communicated distress by tearless crying. (Reprinted with permission from Stone LJ, Church J: *Childhood and Adolescence,* ed 4, p 5. Random House, New York, 1979.)

By the end of infancy (around 2 years), infants have transformed reflexes into voluntary actions that are the building blocks of cognition. They begin to interact with the environment, to experience feedback from their own bodies, and to become intentional in their actions. By the end of the second year of life, children begin to use symbolic play and language.

Jean Piaget (1896–1980), a Swiss psychologist, observed the growing capacity of young children (including his own) to think and to reason. An outline of the main stages of his theory of cognitive development is presented in Table 2.3–4.

Emotional and Social Development. By the age of 3 weeks, infants imitate the facial movements of adult caretakers. They open their mouths and thrust out their tongues in response to adults who do the same. By the third and fourth months of life, these behaviors are easily elicited. These imitative behaviors are believed to be the precursors of infants' emotional life. The smiling response occurs in two phases: The first phase is endogenous smiling, which occurs spontaneously within the first 2 months and is unrelated to external stimulation; the second phase is exogenous smiling, which is stimulated from the outside, usually by the mother, and occurs by the 16th week.

The stages of emotional development parallel those of cognitive development. Indeed, the caretaking person provides the major stimulus for both aspects of mental growth. Human infants are totally dependent on adults for survival. Through regular and predictable interaction, infants' behavioral repertoire expands as a consequence of caretakers' social responses (Table 2.3–5).

In the first year, infants' moods are highly variable and intimately related to internal states such as hunger. Toward the second two thirds of the first year, infants' moods grow increasingly related to external social cues; a parent can get even a hungry infant to smile. When the infant is internally comfortable, a sense of interest and pleasure in the world and in its primary caretakers should prevail. The development of infants' personal and social behavior is outlined in Table 2.3–1. Prolonged separation from the mother (or other primary caretaker) during the second 6 months of life can lead to depression that may persist into adulthood as part of an individual's character.

Temperamental Differences

There are strong suggestions of inborn differences and wide variability in autonomic reactivity and temperament among individual infants. Stella Chess and Alexander Thomas (husband and wife psychiatric collaborators) identified the following nine behavioral dimensions, from which reliable differences among infants can be observed:

Table 2.3–4
Stages of Cognitive Development Proposed by Piaget

1. Sensorimotor (birth to 2 years)
   From the outset, biology and experience blend to produce learned behavior. A stimulus is received, a response elicited, accompanied by awareness. As children become more mobile, these experiences build on one another.
   Critical achievements by the end of this period:
   a. Object permanence (objects have an existence independent of children's involvement with them)
   b. Symbolization, expressed in mental symbols and words
2. Preoperational thought (2 to 7 years)
   Children use symbols and language more extensively, but thinking and reasoning are intuitive. Children are unable to think logically or deductively.
   Characteristics:
   a. Sense of "immanent justice"—punishment for bad deeds is unavoidable
   b. Egocentrism—children see themselves as the center of the universe, are unable to understand another's point of view
   c. "Phenomenalistic causality"—events that occur together are thought to cause one another
   d. "Animistic thinking"—physical events and objects are endowed with feelings and intentions
3. Concrete operations (7 to 11 years)
   Egocentric thought is replaced by "operational" thought, which involves attending to information outside; children are able to understand another's point of view. Children in this stage can serialize, order, and group things according to common characteristics.
   Critical achievements:
   a. Conservation—recognizing that a ball of clay rolled out into a tube contains the same amount of clay
   b. Reversibility—ice can change to water and back to ice again
4. Formal operations (11 years through the end of adolescence)
   Children can think abstractly, reason deductively, and define abstract concepts. Not all children enter this stage at the same time or to the same degree.

1. Activity level—the motor component present in a given child's functioning
2. Rhythmicity—the predictability of such functions as hunger, feeding pattern, elimination, and the sleep–wake cycle
3. Approach or withdrawal—the nature of the response to a new stimulus, such as a food, toy, or person
4. Adaptability—the speed and ease with which a current behavior is able to be modified in response to altered environmental structuring
5. Intensity of reaction—the amount of energy used in mood expression
6. Threshold of responsiveness—the intensity level of stimulation required to evoke a discernible response to sensory stimuli, environmental objects, and social contacts
7. Quality of mood—pleasant, joyful, friendly behavior as contrasted with unpleasant, crying, unfriendly behavior
8. Distractibility—the effectiveness of extraneous environmental stimuli interfering with or altering the direction of ongoing behavior
9. Attention span and persistence—the length of time a particular activity is pursued by a child (attention span) and the continuation of an activity in the face of obstacles (persistence)

The ratings of individual children showed considerable stability over a 25-year follow-up period, but some temperamental traits did not persist over time. This finding was attributed to genetic effects on personality: Some gene actions were discontinuous. There is a complex interplay among the initial characteristics of infants, the mode of parental management, children's subsequent behavior, and even the appearance of symptoms. These connections support the concept of the importance of genetic endowment (nature) and environmental experience (nurture) in behavior.

Attachment

Infants in the first months after birth become attuned to social and interpersonal interaction. They show a rapidly increasing responsivity to the external environment and an ability to form a special relationship with significant primary caretakers—that is, to form an attachment.

Harry Harlow. Harry Harlow studied social learning and the effects of social isolation in monkeys. Harlow placed newborn rhesus monkeys with two types of surrogate mothers—one a wire-mesh surrogate with a feeding bottle and the other a wire-mesh surrogate covered with terry cloth. The monkeys preferred the terry-cloth surrogates, which provided contact and comfort, to the feeding surrogate. (When hungry, the infant monkeys would go to the feeding bottle but then would quickly return to the terry-cloth surrogate.) When frightened, terry-cloth–raised monkeys showed intense clinging behavior and appeared to be comforted, whereas wire-mesh–raised monkeys gained no comfort and appeared to be disorganized. Both types of surrogate-reared monkeys were subsequently unable to adjust to life in a monkey colony and had extraordinary difficulty in learning to mate. When impregnated, the females failed to mother their young. These behavioral peculiarities were attributed to the isolates' lack of mothering in infancy.

Table 2.3–5
Emotional Development from Infancy Through Childhood

Age	Emotional Capacity and Expression
Birth	Pleasure, surprise, disgust, distress
6–8 weeks	Joy
3–4 months	Anger
8–9 months	Sadness, fear
12–18 months	Tender affection, shame (begins at 18 months)
24 months	Pride
3–4 years	Guilt, envy
5–6 years	Insecurity, humility, confidence

Data adapted from Joseph Campas at the University of Denver and from other researchers.

John Bowlby. John Bowlby studied the attachment of infants to mothers and concluded that early separation of infants from their mothers had severe negative effects on children's emotional and intellectual development. He described *attachment behavior,* which develops during the first year of life, as the maintenance of physical contact between the mother and child when the child is hungry, frightened, or in distress.

Mary Ainsworth. Mary Ainsworth expanded on Bowlby's observations and found that the interaction between the mother and her baby during the attachment period significantly influences the baby's current and future behavior. Many observers believe that patterns of infant attachment affect future adult emotional relationships. Patterns of attachment vary among babies; for example, some babies signal or cry less than others. Sensitive responsiveness to infant signals, such as cuddling the baby when it cries, causes infants to cry less in later months. Close bodily contact with the mother when the baby signals for her is also associated with the growth of self-reliance, rather than with a clinging dependence, as the baby grows older. Unresponsive mothers produce anxious babies.

Ainsworth also confirmed that attachment serves the purpose of reducing anxiety. What she called the secure base effect enables a child to move away from the attachment figure and to explore the environment. Inanimate objects, such as a teddy bear or a blanket (called the transitional object by Donald Winnicott), also serve as a secure base, one that often accompanies children as they investigate the world. A growing body of literature derived from direct observation of mother–infant interactions and longitudinal studies has expanded on and refined Ainsworth's original descriptions. Maternal sensitivity and responsiveness are the main determinants of secure attachment. But when the attachment is insecure, the type of insecurity (avoidant, anxious, ambivalent) is determined by infant temperament. Overall, male infants are less likely to have secure attachments than are female infants and are also more vulnerable to changes in maternal sensitivity than are girls.

The attachment of the firstborn child is decreased by the birth of a second; but it is decreased much more so when the firstborn is 2 to 5 years of age, when the younger sibling is born, than when the firstborn is under 24 months. Not surprisingly, the degree of decrease is also modified by the mother's own sense of security, confidence, and mental health.

Social Deprivation Syndromes and Maternal Neglect. Investigators, especially René Spitz, have long documented the severe developmental retardation that accompanies maternal rejection and neglect. Infants in institutions characterized by low staff-to-infant ratios and frequent turnover of personnel tend to display marked developmental retardation, even with adequate physical care and freedom from infection. The same infants, placed in adequate foster or adoptive care, undergo a marked acceleration in development.

Fathers and Attachment. Babies become attached to fathers as well as to mothers, but the attachment is different. Generally, mothers hold babies for caretaking, and fathers hold babies for purposes of play. Given a choice of either parent after separation, infants usually go to the mother, but if the mother is unavailable, they turn to the father for comfort.

Stranger Anxiety. A fear of strangers is first noted in infants at about 26 weeks of age but does not develop fully until about 32 weeks (8 months). At the approach of a stranger, infants cry and cling to their mothers. Babies exposed to only one caretaker are more likely to have stranger anxiety than are those exposed to a variety of caretakers. Stranger anxiety is believed to result from a baby's growing ability to distinguish caretakers from all other people.

Separation anxiety, which occurs between 10 and 18 months of age, is related to stranger anxiety but is not identical to it. Separation from the person to whom the infant is attached precipitates separation anxiety. Stranger anxiety, however, occurs even when the infant is in the mother's arms. The infant learns to separate as it starts to crawl and move away from the mother, but the infant constantly looks back and frequently returns to the mother for reassurance.

Margaret Mahler (1897–1985) proposed a theory to describe how young children acquire a sense of identity separate from their mothers. The theory of separation-individuation was based on her observations of the interactions of children and their mothers. The theory is outlined in Table 2.3–6.

Table 2.3–6
Stages of Separation-Individuation Proposed by Mahler

1. Normal autism (birth to 2 months)
   Periods of sleep outweigh periods of arousal in a state reminiscent of intrauterine life.
2. Symbiosis (2 to 5 months)
   Developing perceptual abilities gradually enable infants to distinguish the inner from the outer world; mother-infant is perceived as a single fused entity.
3. Differentiation (5 to 10 months)
   Progressive neurological development and increased alertness draw infants' attention away from self to the outer world. Physical and psychological distinctiveness from the mother is gradually appreciated.
4. Practicing (10 to 18 months)
   The ability to move autonomously increases children's exploration of the outer world.
5. Rapprochement (18 to 24 months)
   As children slowly realize their helplessness and dependence, the need for independence alternates with the need for closeness. Children move away from their mothers and come back for reassurance.
6. Object constancy (2 to 5 years)
   Children gradually comprehend and are reassured by the permanence of mother and other important people, even when not in their presence.

Infant Care

Clinicians are now beginning to view infants as important actors in the family drama, ones who partly determine its course. Infants' behavior controls mothers' behavior, just as mothers' behavior modulates infants' behavior. A calm, smiling, predictable, good infant is a powerful reward for tender maternal care. A jittery, irregular, irritable infant tries a mother's patience. When a mother's capacities for giving are marginal, such infant traits may cause her to turn away from her child and thus complicate the child's already-troubled beginnings.

Parental Fit. Parental fit describes how well the mother or father relates to the newborn or developing infant; the idea takes into account temperamental characteristics of both parent and child. Each newborn has innate psychophysiological characteristics, which are known collectively as temperament. Chess and Thomas identified a range of normal temperamental patterns, from the difficult child at one end of the spectrum to the easy child at the other end.

Difficult children, who make up 10 percent of all children, have a hyperalert physiological makeup. They react intensely to stimuli (cry easily at loud noises), sleep poorly, eat at unpredictable times, and are difficult to comfort.

Easy children, who make up 40 percent of all children, are regular in eating, eliminating, and sleeping; are flexible; are able to adapt to change and to new stimuli with a minimum of distress; and are easily comforted when they cry. The other 50 percent of children are mixtures of these two types. The difficult child is harder to raise and places greater demands on the parent than does the easy child. Chess and Thomas used the term *goodness of fit* to characterize the harmonious and consonant interaction between a mother and a child in their motivations, capacities, and styles of behavior. Poorness of fit is likely to lead to distorted development and maladaptive functioning. A difficult child must be recognized because parents of such infants often have feelings of inadequacy and believe that something they are doing wrong accounts for the difficulty in sleeping and eating and the problems in comforting the child. In addition, a majority of difficult children have emotional disturbances later in life.

Good-Enough Mothering. Winnicott believed that infants begin life in a state of nonintegration, with unconnected and diffuse experiences, and that mothers provide the relationship that enables infants' incipient selves to emerge. Mothers supply a holding environment in which infants are contained and experienced. During the last trimester of pregnancy and for the first few months of a baby's life, the mother is in a state of primary maternal preoccupation, absorbed in fantasies about and experiences with her baby. The mother need not be perfect, but she must provide good-enough mothering. She plays a vital role in bringing the world to the child and in offering empathic anticipations of the infant's needs. If the mother is able to resonate with the infant's needs, the baby can become attuned to its own bodily functions and drives that afford the basis for the gradually evolving sense of self.

TODDLER PERIOD

The second year of life is marked by an acceleration of motor and intellectual development. The ability to walk confers on toddlers a degree of control over their own actions; this mobility enables children to determine when to approach and when to withdraw. The acquisition of speech profoundly extends their horizons. Typically, children learn to say "no" before they learn to say "yes." Toddlers' negativism plays a vital part in the development of independence. If persistent, however, oppositional behavior connotes a problem.

Developmental Landmarks

Language and Cognitive Development. Learning language is a crucial task in the toddler period. Vocalizations become distinct, and toddlers have the ability to name a few objects and to make needs known in one or two words. Near the end of the second year and into the third year, toddlers sometimes use short sentences. They begin to reason and to listen to explanations that can help them tolerate delay. Toddlers create new behaviors from old ones (originality) and engage in symbolic activities (for example, using words and playing with dolls when the dolls represent something, such as a feeding sequence). Toddlers have variable capacities for concentration and self-regulation.

Emotional and Social Development. In the second year, pleasure and displeasure become further differentiated. Toddlers show exploratory excitement, assertive pleasure, and pleasure in discovery and in developing new behavior (for example, new games), including teasing and surprising or fooling the parent (for example, hiding). The toddler has capacities for an organized demonstration of love (for example, running up and hugging, smiling, and kissing the parent at the same time) and protest (for example, turning away, crying, banging, biting, hitting, yelling, and kicking). Comfort with family and apprehension with strangers may increase. Anxiety appears to be related to disapproval and the loss of a loved caretaker and can be disorganizing. Additional information appears in Table 2.3–1.

Sexual Development. Sexual differentiation is evident from birth, when parents start dressing and treating infants differently because of the expectations evoked by sex typing. Through imitation, reward, and coercion, children assume the behaviors that their cultures define as appropriate for their sexual roles. Children exhibit curiosity about anatomical sex. When their curiosity is recognized as healthy and is met with honest and age-appropriate replies, children acquire a sense of the wonder of life and are comfortable with their own roles. If the subject of sex is taboo and children's questions are rebuffed, shame and discomfort may result. By the age of 2½ years, gender identity (the conviction of being a boy or a girl) becomes fixed. In general, play is determined by gender: Boys play with guns, and girls play with dolls and dollhouses, but cultural mores and social trends significantly influence children's choices of games and toys. There is also considerable individual variation, and boys playing with dolls or girls with guns are not abnormal.

Sphincter Control and Sleep. The second year of life is a period of increasing social demands on children. Toilet training serves as a paradigm of the family's general training practices; that is, the parent who is overly severe in the area of toilet training is likely to be punitive and restrictive in other areas also. Control of daytime urination is usually complete by the age of 2½, and control of nighttime urination is usually complete by the age of 4 years, when bowel control is usually accomplished. Since 1900, there have been pendulum swings between extremes of permissiveness and control in toilet training. The trend in the United States has been toward delayed training, but in the last few years this trend appears to be shifting back to early training.

Toddlers may have sleep difficulties related to fear of the dark, which can often be managed by the use of a nightlight. Most toddlers generally sleep about 12 hours a day, including a 2-hour nap. Parents must be aware that children of this age may need reassurance before going to bed and that the average 2 year old takes about 30 minutes to fall asleep.

Parenting

Parallel to the changing tasks for children are changing tasks for parents. In infancy, the major responsibility for parents is to meet the infant's needs in a sensitive and consistent fashion, without anticipating and fulfilling all the needs so that the child never experiences some amount of desirable tension. The parental task in the toddler stage requires firmness about the boundaries of acceptable behavior and encouragement of the child's progressive emancipation. Parents must be careful not to be too authoritarian at this stage; children must be allowed to operate for themselves and to learn from their mistakes and must be protected and assisted when challenges are beyond their abilities.

During the toddler period, children are likely to struggle for the exclusive affection and attention of their parents. This struggle includes rivalry both with siblings and with one or another parent for the star role in the family. Although children are beginning to be able to share, they do so with reluctance. When the demands for exclusive possession are not effectively resolved, the result is likely to be jealous competitiveness in relationships with peers and lovers. The fantasies aroused by the struggle lead to fear of retaliation and to displacement of fear onto external objects. In an equitable, loving family, a child elaborates a moral system of ethical rights. Parents need to set realistic limits on a toddler's behavior and to balance between punishment and permissiveness.

PRESCHOOL PERIOD

The preschool period is characterized by marked physical and emotional growth. Generally, between 2 and 3 years of age, children reach half their adult height. The 20 baby teeth are in place at the beginning of the stage, and by the end they begin to fall out. Children are ready to enter school by the time the stage ends at age 5 or 6. They have mastered the tasks of primary socialization—to control their bowels and urine, to dress and feed themselves, and to control their tears and temper outbursts, at least most of the time.

The term *preschool* for the age group of 2½ to 6 years may be a misnomer; many children are already in school-like settings, such as preschool nurseries and day care centers, where working mothers must often place their children. Preschool education can be of value, but too great a stress on academic advancement beyond a child's capabilities can be counterproductive.

Developmental Landmarks

Language and Cognitive Development. In the preschool period, children's use of language expands, and they use sentences. Individual words have regular and consistent meanings at the beginning of the period, and children begin to think symbolically. In general, however, their thinking is egocentric: They cannot place themselves in the position of another child and are incapable of empathy. Children think intuitively and prelogically and do not understand cause-and-effect relations.

Emotional and Social Behavior. At the start of the preschool period, children can express such complex emotions as love, unhappiness, jealousy, and envy, both preverbally and verbally. Their emotions are still easily influenced by somatic events, such as tiredness and hunger. Although they still think mostly egocentrically, children's capacity for cooperation and sharing is emerging. Anxiety is related to loss of a person who was loved and depended on and to loss of approval and acceptance. Although still potentially disorganizing, anxiety can be better tolerated than in the past. Four year olds are learning to share and to have concern for others. Feelings of tenderness are sometimes expressed. Anxiety over bodily injury and the loss of a loved person's approval is sometimes disruptive.

By the end of the preschool period, children have many relatively stable emotions. Expansiveness, curiosity, pride, and a gleeful excitement related to the self and the family are balanced with coyness, shyness, fearfulness, jealousy, and envy. Shame and humiliation are evident. Capacities for empathy and love are developed but fragile and easily lost if competitive or jealous strivings intervene. Anxiety and fears are related to bodily injury and loss of respect, love, and emerging self-esteem. Guilt feelings are possible. Additional information appears in Table 2.3–1.

Children between the ages of 3 and 6 years are aware of their bodies, of the genitalia, and of differences between the sexes. In their play, doctor–nurse games allow children to act out their sexual fantasies. Their awareness of their bodies extends beyond the genitalia; they show a preoccupation with illness or injury, so much so that the period has been called the Band-Aid phase: Every injury must be examined and taken care of by a parent.

Children develop a division between what they want and what they are told to do. The division increases until a gap grows between their set of expanded desires, their exuberance at unlimited growth, and their parents' restrictions; they gradually turn parental values into self-obedience, self-guidance, and self-punishment.

At the end of the preschool stage, children's conscience is established. The development of a conscience sets the tone for the moral sense of right and wrong. Until about 7 years of age, children experience rules as absolute and as existing for their own sake. They do not understand that there may be more than one point of view to a moral issue; a violation of the rules calls for absolute retribution—that is, children have the notion of imminent justice.

SIBLING RIVALRY. In the preschool period children relate to others in new ways. The birth of a sibling (a common occurrence during this time) tests a preschool child's capacity for further cooperation and sharing but may also evoke sibling rivalry, which is most likely to occur at this time. Sibling rivalry depends on child-rearing practices. Favoritism for any reason is a common outcome of such rivalry. Children who get special treatment because they are gifted, defective in some way, or of a preferred gender are likely to be the recipient of angry feelings from their siblings. Experiences with siblings may influence growing children's relationships with peers and authority. If, for example, the needs of a new baby prevent the mother from attending to a firstborn child's needs, a problem may result. If not handled properly, the displacement of the firstborn can be a traumatic event.

PLAY. In the preschool years, children begin to distinguish reality from fantasy, and play reflects this growing awareness. Pretend games are popular and help test real-life situations in a playful manner. Dramatic play in which children act out a role, such as that of a housewife or a truck driver, is common (Fig. 2.3–6). One-to-one play relationships advance to complicated patterns with rivalries, secrets, and two-against-one intrigues. Children's play behavior reflects their level of social development.

Between 3 and 6 years of age, growth can be traced through drawings. A child's first drawing of a human being is a circular line with marks for the mouth, nose, and eyes; later, ears and hair are added; next, arms and sticklike fingers appear; then legs appear. Last to appear is a torso in proportion to the rest of the body. Intelligent children can deal with details in their art. Drawings express

FIGURE 2.3–6
Children at play. (Courtesy of Caroly Pataki, M.D.)

creativity throughout children's development: They are representational and formal in early childhood, make use of perspective in middle childhood, and become abstract and affect laden in adolescence. Drawings also reflect children's body image concepts and sexual and aggressive impulses.

IMAGINARY COMPANIONS. Imaginary companions most often appear during preschool years, usually in children with above-average intelligence and usually in the form of people. Imaginary companions may also be things, such as toys that are anthropomorphized. Some studies indicate that up to 50 percent of children between the ages of 3 and 10 years have imaginary companions at one time or another. Their significance is not clear, but these figures are usually friendly, relieve loneliness, and reduce anxiety. In most instances, imaginary companions disappear by age 12, but they may occasionally persist into adulthood.

MIDDLE YEARS

During the middle years, children enter elementary school. The formal demands for academic learning and accomplishment become major determinants of further personality development.

Developmental Landmarks

Language and Cognitive Development. In the middle years, language expresses complex ideas with relations among several elements. Logical exploration tends to dominate fantasy, and children show an increased interest in rules and orderliness and an increased capacity for self-regulation.

During this period, children's conceptual skills develop, and thinking becomes organized and logical. The ability to concentrate is well established by age 9 or 10, and by the end of the period, children begin to think in abstract terms.

Improved gross motor coordination and muscle strength enable children to write with fluency and to draw artistically. They are also capable of complex motor tasks and activities, such as tennis, gymnastics, golf, baseball, and skateboarding.

Recent evidence has shown that changes in thinking and reasoning during the middle years result from maturational changes in the brain. Children are now capable of increased independence, learning, and socialization. Theorists consider moral development a gradual, stepwise process spanning childhood, adolescence, and young adulthood.

In the middle years, both girls and boys make new identifications with other adults, such as teachers and counselors. These identifications may so influence girls that their goals of wanting to marry and have babies, as their mothers did, may be combined with a desire for a career or may be postponed or abandoned entirely.

Girls who are unable to identify with their mothers or whose fathers are overly attached may become fixated at about a 6-year-old level; as a result, they may fear men or women or both or become seductively close to them. In either case, such girls may not be seen as normal during the school-age years. A similar situation may occur in boys who have been unable to identify successfully with fathers who were aloof, brutal, or absent. Perhaps his mother prevented a boy from identifying with his father by being overprotective or by binding the son too closely to herself. As a result, boys may enter this period with a variety of problems. They may be fearful of men, unsure of their sense of masculinity, or unwilling to leave their mothers (sometimes manifested by a school phobia); they may lack initiative, be unable to master school tasks, and thus incur academic problems.

The school-age period is a time in which peer interaction assumes major importance. Interest in relationships outside the family takes precedence over those within the family. Nevertheless, a special relationship exists with the same-sex parent, with whom children identify and who is now an ideal and a role model.

Empathy and concern for others begin to emerge early in the middle years; by the time children are 9 or 10, they have well-developed capacities for love, compassion, and sharing. They have a capacity for long-term, stable relationships with family, peers, and friends, including best friends. Emotions about sexual differences begin to emerge as either excitement or shyness with the opposite sex. School-age children prefer to interact with children of the same sex. This period has been referred to as a psychosexual and psychosocial moratorium—a lull before adolescents' pubescent sexual impulses. The moratorium is characterized by an absence of overt sexual behavior, which, according to Freud, is sublimated and expressed in other abilities, such as sports, studies, and nonsexual peer activities.

CHUM PERIOD. Harry Stack Sullivan postulated that a chum or buddy is an important phenomenon during the school years. By about 10 years of age, children develop a close same-sex relationship, which Sullivan believed is necessary for further healthy psychological growth. Moreover, Sullivan believed that an early harbinger of schizophrenia is the absence of a chum during the middle years of childhood.

SCHOOL REFUSAL. Some children refuse to go to school at this time, generally because of separation anxiety. A fearful mother may transmit her own fear of separation to a child, or a child who has not resolved dependence needs panics at the idea of separation. School refusal is usually not an isolated problem; children with the problem typically avoid many other social situations.

OTHER ISSUES IN CHILDHOOD

Sex Role Development

People's sex roles are similar to their gender identity: People see themselves as male or female. The sex role also involves identification with culturally acceptable masculine or feminine ways of behaving; but changing expectations in society (particularly in the United States) of what constitutes masculine and feminine behavior can create ambiguity.

Parents react differently to their male and female children. Independence, physical play, and aggressiveness are encouraged in boys; dependence, verbalization, and physical intimacy are encouraged in girls. Nowadays, however, boys are encouraged to be verbal about their feelings and to pursue interests traditionally associated with girls, while girls are encouraged to pursue careers traditionally dominated by men and to participate in competitive sports. As society grows more tolerant in its expectations of the sexes, roles become less rigid, and opportunities for boys and girls enlarge and broaden.

Biologically, boys are more physically aggressive than are girls; and parental expectations, particularly the expectations of fathers, reinforce this trait.

Sex differences also exist in play activities: Boys commonly play with guns and trucks, whereas girls commonly play with dolls and are interested in clothes. These differences appear as early as 2 or 3 years of age and remain fairly constant.

Boys are less tolerant of opposite-sex behavior by other boys (sissy behavior) than are girls who see other girls engage in opposite-sex behavior (tomboy behavior).

Dreams and Sleep

Children's dreams can have a profound effect on behavior. During the first year of life, when the differentiation between reality and fantasy is not yet fully achieved, dreams may be experienced as if they were or could be true. At age 3, many children believe dreams are directly shared by more than one person, but most 4 year olds understand that dreams are unique to each individual. Children view dreams either with pleasure or, as is most often reported, with fear. The dream content should be seen in connection with children's life experience, developmental stage, mechanisms used during dreaming, and sex.

Disturbing dreams peak when children are 3, 6, and 10 years old. Two-year-old children may dream about being bitten or chased; at the age of 4, they may have many animal dreams and also dream of people who either protect or destroy. At age 5 or 6, dreams of being killed or injured, of flying and being in cars, and of ghosts become prominent; the role of conscience, moral values, and increasing conflicts are concerned with these themes. In early childhood, aggressive dreams rarely seem to occur; instead, dreamers are in danger, a state that perhaps reflects children's dependent position. By about the age of 5, children realize that their dreams are not real; before then they believe them to be real events. By age 7, children know that they themselves create their dreams.

Between the ages of 3 and 6 years, children normally want to keep their bedroom door open or to have a nightlight, so that they can either maintain contact with their parents or view the room in a realistic, nonfearful way. At times, children resist going to sleep to avoid dreaming. Disorders associated with falling asleep, therefore, are often connected with dreaming. Children often create rituals as protective devices designed to make safe the withdrawal from the world of reality into the world of sleep. When somnambulism (sleepwalking) occurs, a dream's content seems to release motor discharge, and children go to those persons and places that can offer them protection.

Periods of rapid eye movement (REM) take place about 60 percent of the time during the first few weeks of life, a period when infants sleep two thirds of the time. Premature babies sleep even longer than do full-term babies, and a greater proportion of their sleep is REM sleep. The sleep–wake cycle of newborns is about 3 hours long. Among adults the dream-to-sleep ratio is stable: 20 percent of sleeping time is spent dreaming. Even newborns have brain activity similar to that of the dreaming state.

Spacing of Children

For women in the United States, 10 percent of conceptions that lead to live births are considered to be unwanted, and 20 percent are wanted but considered to be ill timed. The implications of these figures are that some couples may be poorly prepared or may feel guilty about not wanting to be parents. It is desirable to plan pregnancies and to have mutual agreement on the spacing of children. The typical number of children in a present-day family is two, half the typical number at the beginning of the century. Repeated childbearing prevents adequate recuperation from the birth process and places mothers at risk for complications and injury. New mothers require time to adapt; the period of adaptation may range from a few weeks to several months. The demands of other children at home can be taxing, and if these children are also young, the family may be stressed beyond its capacity.

Studies of children from large families (of four or five children) show that they are more likely to have conduct disorder and to have a slightly lower level of verbal intelligence than do children from small families. Decreased parental interaction and discipline may account for these findings.

Birth Order

The effects of birth order are variable. Firstborn children are often more highly valued than are subsequent children, particularly if the firstborn is male, especially in non-Western cultures, but also sometimes in the United States. Firstborns have been found to have higher intelligence quotients (IQs) than their younger siblings, a finding that may reflect parents' having more time to interact with a firstborn child. Firstborn children appear to be more achievement oriented than are subsequent children born to the same parents. As more children enter the family, parental time for each child diminishes; prenatal stress may also increase as more children have to be cared for.

Second and third children have the advantage of their parents' previous experience. Younger children also learn from their older siblings. For example, they may show more sophisticated use of pronouns at an earlier age than do firstborns. When children are spaced too closely together, however, there may not be enough lap time for each child. The arrival of new children in the family affects not only the parents but also the siblings. Firstborn children may resent the birth of a new sibling, who threatens their sole claim on parental attention. In some cases, regressive behavior, such as enuresis or thumb sucking, occurs.

In general, the oldest children achieve the most and are the most authoritarian; middle children usually receive the least attention in the home and may develop strong peer relationships to compensate; and the youngest children may receive too much attention and be spoiled. According to Frank Sulloway, firstborn children tend to be conservative and conformists; by contrast, youngest children tend to be independent and rebellious in regard to family and cultural norms. Sulloway found a high proportion of prominent people to have been lastborn children. He ascribes these differences to birth order and suggests that each child develops personality traits to fit an unfilled slot in the family tree. His findings need to be replicated.

Children and Divorce

Many children live in homes in which divorce has occurred. Approximately 30 percent of all children in the United States live in homes in which one parent (usually the mother) is the sole head of the household. Sixty-one percent of all children born in any given year can expect to live with only one parent before they reach the age of 18 years. A child's age at the time of the parents' divorce affects the child's reaction to the divorce. Immediately after a divorce, an increase in behavioral and emotional disorders appears in all age groups. Three- to six-year-old children do not understand what is happening, and those who do understand often assume that they are somehow responsible for the divorce. If divorce occurs when a child is between 7 and 12 years, school performance generally declines. Older children, especially adolescents, comprehend the situation and believe that they could have prevented the divorce had they intervened in some way—had they, in effect, served as surrogate marriage therapists—but they are still hurt, angry, and critical of their parents' behavior.

Some children harbor the fantasy that their parents will be reunited in the future. Such children show animosity toward a parent's real or potential new mate because they are forced to recognize that a reconciliation is not taking place. Recovery from and adaptation to the effects of divorce usually take 3 to 5 years, but about one third of all children from divorced homes have lasting psychological trauma. Among boys, physical aggression is a common sign of distress. Adolescents tend to spend more time away from the parental home after the divorce. Suicide attempts may occur as a direct result of the divorce; one of the predictors of suicide in adolescence is the recent divorce or separation of the parents. Children who adapt well to divorce do so if each parent makes an effort to continue to relate to the child in spite of the child's anger. To facilitate recovery, the divorced couple must avoid arguing with one another and must show consistent behavior toward the child. Despite childhood behavioral problems at the time of divorce, the prevalence of serious psychiatric problems such as depression or anxiety disorders is not increased among children from divorced homes when they reach adulthood.

Stepparents. When remarriage occurs, children must learn to adapt to the stepparent and to the so-called reconstituted family. Such adaptation is usually difficult, especially when the stepparent is nonsupportive or resentful of the stepchild or favors his or her own natural children. A natural child born to the new couple—a stepsibling—sometimes receives more attention than a stepchild and, as a result, is the object of sibling rivalry.

Adoption

Adoption is defined as the process by which a child is taken into a family by one or more adults who are not the biological parents but are recognized by law as the child's parents. About 2.5 million persons under 18 years of age are adopted each year. Fifty-two percent of children are adopted by persons not related to them by birth or marriage, and the remainder are adopted by relatives or stepparents. The majority of adopted children are born out of wedlock, and 40 percent of all such children are born to mothers between 15 and 19 years of age.

Adoptive parents most often tell their children of their status between the ages of 2 and 4 years. Informing children about their adoption reduces the possibility that the children learn of it from extrafamilial sources and then feel betrayed by their adoptive parents and abandoned by their biological parents.

Emotional and behavior disorders such as aggressive behavior, stealing, and learning disturbances have been reported to be higher among adopted rather than nonadopted children. The later the age of adoption, the higher the incidence and the more severe the degree of behavior problems.

Throughout childhood and adolescence, children may be preoccupied with fantasies of two sets of parents. An adopted child may split the two sets of parents into good and bad parents. Adopted children usually have a strong desire to know their biological parents; some children pattern themselves after their fantasies of their absent biological parents and create a conflict with their adoptive parents. In most cases in which adopted children have sought out and met their biological parents (and vice versa), the experience has been generally positive, especially if the child is in late adolescence or early adulthood.

Family Factors in Child Development

Family Stability. Parents and children living under the same roof in harmonious interaction is the expected cultural norm in Western society. Within this framework, childhood development presumably proceeds most expeditiously. Deviations from the norm (for example, divorced- and single-parent families) are associated with a broad range of problems in children, including low self-esteem, increased risk of child abuse, increased incidence of divorce when they eventually marry, and increased incidence of mental disorders, particularly depressive disorders and antisocial personality disorder as adults. Why some children from unstable homes are less affected than others (or even immune to these deleterious effects) is of great interest. Michael Rutter has postulated that vulnerability is influenced by sex (boys are more affected than are girls), age (older children are less vulnerable than younger ones), and inborn personality characteristics. For example, children who have a placid temperament are less likely to be victims of abuse within a family than are hyperactive children; by virtue of their placidity, they may be less affected by the emotional turmoil surrounding them.

Other Family Factors. In childhood and adolescence the death of a parent is associated with adverse effects, such as an increase in later emotional problems, particularly a susceptibility to depression and divorce. This finding is in sharp contrast to the results of separations that result from less traumatic events. For example, no evidence indicates that working mothers raise children who are less healthy than those brought up by mothers who stay at home. Home caretakers can act as surrogate mothers, and in such cases the children do not become more attached to the caretaker than to the parent.

The role of day care centers for children is under continuous investigation. Some studies show that children placed in day care centers before the age of 5 years are less assertive and less effectively toilet trained than are home-reared children. Other studies have shown that young children in day care are more advanced in social and cognitive development than are young children not in day care. Such studies must take into account the quality of both the day care center and the homes from which children come. For example, a child from a disadvantaged home may be better off in a day care center than is the child from an advantaged home. Similarly, a woman who wishes to leave the home to work for financial or other reasons and is unable to do so may resent being forced to remain in the home in a child-rearing role and, thus, may adversely affect the child.

TYPING OF PARENTING. Michael Rutter described four types of parenting styles: authoritarian, characterized by rigidity and strict rules, which can lead to depression in children; permissive, characterized by indulgence and no limit setting, which can lead to poor impulse control; indifferent, characterized by neglect and lack of involvement, leading to aggressive behavior; and reciprocal, characterized by shared decision making with behavior directed in a rational manner, which results in a sense of self-reliance.

In general, experimental studies indicate that the most effective parenting involves consistency and reward for good behavior and punishment for undesirable behavior, both of which should occur within the context of a warm, loving environment.

References

Ainsworth M, Bell SM, Stayton D: Infant–mother attachment and social development: Socialization as a product of reciprocal responsiveness to signals. In *The Integration of the Child into a Social World,* M Richards, editor, p 7. Cambridge University Press, Cambridge, UK, 1974.

Bowlby J: *Attachment and Loss:* vol 1. *Attachment.* Basic Books, New York, 1969.

Brandt P, Magyary D, Hammond M, Barnard K: Learning and behavioral-emotional problems of children born preterm at second grade. J Pediatr Psychol *17:* 291, 1992.

Brodzinsky DM, Schechter D, editors: *The Psychology of Adoption.* Oxford University Press, New York, 1988.

Buka SL, Tsuang MT, Lipsitt LP: Pregnancy–delivery complications and psychiatric diagnosis: A prospective study. Arch Gen Psychiatry *50:* 151, 1993.

Butler JA: Child health and the family. Bull NY Acad Med *65:* 285, 1989.

Chehrazi S, editor: *Psychosocial Issues in Day Care.* American Psychiatric Press, Washington, 1990.

Diener ML, Goldstein LH, Mangelsdorf SC: The role of prenatal expectations in parents' reports of infant temperament. Merrill-Palmer Q *41:* 172, 1995.

Dworkin PH: Behavior during middle childhood: Developmental themes and clinical issues. Pediatr Ann *1:* 347, 1989.

Erikson EH: *Childhood and Society,* ed 2. Norton, New York, 1963.

Feldman H: The development of thinking skills in school age children. Pediatr Ann *18:* 356, 1989.

Fish M, Stifter CA: Patterns of mother–infant interaction and attachment: A cluster-analytic approach. Infant Behav Dev *18:* 435, 1995.

Kasen S, Cohen P, Brook JS, Hartmark C: A multiple-risk interaction model: Effects of temperament and divorce on psychiatric disorders in children. Abnorm Child Psychol *24:* 121, 1996.

Kohnstamm GA, Bates JE, Rothbart MK, editors: *Temperament in Childhood.* Wiley, New York, 1989.

Lewis M: Emotional development in the preschool child. Pediatr Ann *18:* 316, 1989.

Lidz T: *The Person: His and Her Development Throughout the Life Cycle.* Basic Books, New York, 1976.

Newcomb AF, Bukowski WM, Pattee L: Children's peer relations: A meta-analytic review of popular, rejected, neglected, controversial, and average sociometric status. Psychol Bull *113:* 99, 1993.

O'Brien M: Child-rearing difficulties reported by parents of infants and toddlers. J Pediatr Psychol *21:* 433, 1996.

Smotherman WP, Robinson SR: The development of behavior before birth. Dev Psychol *32:* 425, 1996.

Susman-Stillman A, Kalkose M, Egeland B, Waldman I: Infant temperament and maternal sensitivity as predictors of attachment security. Infant Behav Dev *19:* 33, 1996.

Volkmar FR: Normal child development. In *Comprehensive Textbook of Psychiatry,* ed 6, HI Kaplan, BJ Sadock, editors, p 2154. Williams & Wilkins, Baltimore, 1995.

Zeanah CH: Beyond insecurity: A reconceptualization of attachment disorders in infancy. J Consult Clin Psychol *64:* 42, 1996.

▲ 2.4 Adolescence

Many societies have marked the beginning of adolescence with puberty rites, so-called rites of passage celebrating adolescents' attainment of adult status, with its corresponding duties and responsibilities. Although the complexities of modern life have postponed attaining adult status to the end of adolescence, the onset of the teens is sometimes celebrated with religious rites, and adolescence is an acknowledged stage of human development today. As a stage, however, adolescence is variable—in age of onset, in length, in rate of growth, in sexual development, in mental maturation. Jean Piaget, for example, had proposed that formal operational thinking—which involves deductive logic—inevitably begins in adolescence, but later researchers have shown that the ability to solve complex problems depends on education and knowledge, as well as on an innate facility.

Adolescence is characterized by profound biological, psychological, and social developmental changes. The biological onset of adolescence is signaled by the rapid acceleration of skeletal growth and the beginnings of physical sexual development. The psychological onset is characterized by an acceleration of cognitive development and consolidation of personality formation. Socially, adolescence is a period of intensified preparation for the coming role of young adulthood.

Adolescence is commonly divided into three periods: early (ages 11 to 14), middle (ages 14 to 17), and late (ages 17 to 20). These divisions are arbitrary; growth and development occur along a continuum that varies from person to person. Puberty, a physical process of change characterized by the development of secondary sex characteristics, differs from adolescence, largely a psychological process of change. Under ideal circumstances the processes are synchronous; when they do not occur simultaneously, as they often do not, adolescents must cope with the imbalance as an added stress. Adolescence terminates in adulthood.

PUBERTY

The onset of puberty, triggered by the maturation of the hypothalamic-pituitary-adrenal-gonadal axes, is marked by the secretion of sex steroids. This hormonal activity produces the manifestations of puberty, traditionally categorized as primary and secondary sex characteristics. The primary sex characteristics are those directly involved in coitus and reproduction: the reproductive organs and the external genitalia. The secondary sex characteristics include enlarged breasts and hips in girls and facial hair and lowered voices in boys. The increase in height and weight occurs earlier in girls than in boys; by age 12, girls are generally both taller and heavier than boys. Table 2.4–1 gives a summary of puberty changes.

Precocious or delayed growth, acne, obesity, and enlarged mammary glands in boys and small or overabundant breasts in girls are some deviations from the expected patterns of maturation. Although these conditions may not be medically significant, they often lead to psychological sequelae. Adolescents are sensitive to the opinions of their peers and constantly com-

Table 2.4–1
Pubertal Stages

Stage	Characteristics: Genital Development[a]	Pubic Hair Development	Breast Development[b]
1	Testes, scrotum, and penis are about the same size and shape as in early childhood.	The vellus over the pubis is not further developed than over the abdominal wall (ie, no pubic hair).	There is elevation of the papillae only.
2	Scrotum and testes are slightly enlarged. The skin of the scrotum is reddened and changed in texture. There is little or no enlargement of the penis at this stage.	There is sparse growth of long, slightly pigmented, tawny hair, straight or slightly curled, chiefly at the base of the penis or along the labia.	Breast bud stage. There is elevation of the breasts and papillae as small mounds. Areolar diameter is enlarged over that of stage 1.
3	Penis is slightly enlarged, at first mainly in length. Testes and scrotum are larger than in stage 2.	The hair is considerably darker, coarser, and more curled. It spreads sparsely over the pubis.	Breasts and areolae are both enlarged and elevate more than in stage 2 but with no separation of their contours.
4	Penis is further enlarged, with growth in breadth and development of glans. Testes and scrotum are larger than in stage 3; scrotum skin is darker than in earlier stages.	Hair is now adult in type, but the area covered is still considerably smaller than in the adult. There is no spread to the medial surface of the thighs.	The areolae and papillae form secondary mounds projecting above the contours of the breasts.
5	Genitalia are adult in size and shape.	The hair is adult in quantity and type, with distribution of the horizontal (or classically feminine) pattern. Spread is to the medial surface of the thighs but not up the linea alba or elsewhere above the base of the inverse triangle.	Mature stage. The papillae only project, with the areolae recessed to the general contours of the breasts.

Reprinted with permission from Brunstetter RW, Silver LB: Normal adolescent development. In *Comprehensive Textbook of Psychiatry*, ed 4, HI Kaplan, BJ Sadock, editors, p 1609. Williams & Wilkins, Baltimore, 1985.
[a] For boys.
[b] For girls.

pare themselves with others. Any deviation, real or imagined, can lead to feelings of inferiority, low self-esteem, and loss of confidence. Girls are more sensitive to early physical manifestations of puberty than are boys. For example, tall girls feel more self-conscious about their height than do tall boys when they compare themselves with their peers.

Onset of Puberty

The age of onset of puberty varies, with girls entering puberty 12 to 18 months earlier than do boys. The average age is 11 for girls (with a range of 8 to 13) and 13 for boys (with a range of 10 to 14). Twins of either sex tend to have later onset of puberty than do nontwins.

Changes in Hormones

Sex hormones increase slowly throughout adolescence and correspond to bodily changes. Follicle-stimulating hormone (FSH) and luteinizing hormone (LH) also increase throughout adolescence, but between ages 17 and 18, LH is frequently elevated above adult values. LH levels characteristic of adult functioning begin in late adolescence.

From ages 16 and 17, a large increase seems to occur in average testosterone levels, which then decrease to stabilize at the adult level. Testosterone is the hormone responsible for the masculinization of boys, and estradiol is the hormone responsible for the feminization of girls. Both hormones also influence central nervous system functioning, including mood and behavior. Decreased levels of estrogen may be associated with depressed mood (as happens in some women's premenstrual periods). High testosterone levels have been correlated with aggression and impulsivity in some men.

In adolescent boys, testosterone levels correlate with libido and are manifested by sex drive and masturbation. Adolescent girls are also influenced by androgens (produced by the adrenal gland) but to a lesser extent than are boys. Sexual intercourse in girls is determined almost entirely by psychosocial factors; hormones have much less influence on girls than on boys.

PSYCHOSEXUAL DEVELOPMENT

The sex drive is triggered by certain androgens, such as testosterone, which are at higher levels during adolescence than at any other time of life. According to William Masters and Virginia Johnson, the male sex drive peaks between 17 and 18 years of age. Early adolescents vent libidinal urges most often through masturbation, a safe way to satisfy sexual impulses.

Because girls enter puberty 2 years earlier than do boys, they may begin dating and having sexual intercourse at an earlier age; but adolescent girls are less sexually active than are boys of the same age. Boys are easily aroused by stimuli, and erections are frequent. For girls, the sexual impulse is associated with other feelings. Girls tend to view sex and love as related; boys find desire or lust and love to be separable.

Anna Freud described intellectualism and asceticism as two defense mechanisms commonly used by adolescents to deal with sexual drives. Intellectualization is manifested by involvement in ideas and books; asceticism is manifested by a retreat into grand ideas and a renunciation of bodily pleasures. Most adolescents struggle with the control of their libidinal drives. Early adolescents are still attached to their families and sometimes have a resurgence of oedipal feelings and even sexual fantasies about the same-sex or opposite-sex parent. These thoughts and feelings are generally repressed, and sexuality is directed outward; crushes, hero worship, and the idealization of movie and music stars are characteristic of this stage.

In middle adolescence, sexual behavior and experimentation with a variety of sexual roles are common. Masturbation occurs as a normal activity about equally in both sexes at this time, but a strict religious upbringing may engender strong feelings of guilt. Heterosexual crushes, often with an unattainable person of the same age or older, are common.

Homosexual experiences, usually transient, may also occur in middle adolescence. Many adolescents need reassurance about the normality of an isolated homosexual experience and confirmation that it is not an indication of a permanent homosexual orientation. For others, a homosexual orientation has already been predetermined by this time. These adolescents (estimated at between 1 and 4 percent of all adolescent boys and 0.5 to 2 percent of all adolescent girls) may require counseling about dealing with their sexual orientation.

Although many adolescents experiment with sex at an early age, recent surveys indicate that the average age for the first sexual intercourse in both sexes is 16 years. The trend in U.S. society is toward greater and more frequent sexual activity at earlier ages than in the past. A decade ago, for example, the average age for first sexual intercourse was 18, and only 55 percent of women had had sexual intercourse by that time. Currently, 80 percent of men and 70 percent of women have engaged in coitus by age 19.

Menarche

The onset of menarche is one of the pubertal changes in girls. The current trend is toward an earlier age of menarche than in the past. In the 1920s in the United States, the average age of menarche was 14.5 years; by the 1980s it had dropped to 13 years. The onset of menarche is determined by a complex interaction of biological and psychosocial factors. Good nutrition and overall good physical health promote earlier menarche. The mother's age of onset of menarche correlates loosely with that of her daughter's. Psychological or social distress has not been found to either delay or advance menarche. Cultural attitudes toward menarche vary from viewing it as a curse at one extreme to seeing it as a joyful affirmation of womanhood at the other. Most adolescent girls still do not receive information on the menses from their parents but rely on information from peers, schools, and the media.

COGNITIVE AND PERSONALITY DEVELOPMENT

At the beginning of adolescence, thinking usually becomes abstract, conceptual, and future oriented. Many adolescents show remarkable creativity, which they express in writing, music, art, and poetry. Creativity is also expressed in sports and in adolescents' interests in the world of ideas—humanitarian issues, morals, ethics, and religion. Keeping a personal diary is a common creative outlet during this period.

A major task of adolescence is to achieve a secure sense of self. *Identity diffusion* is a failure to develop a cohesive self or self-awareness. Adolescent identity crisis is partly resolved by the move from dependency to independence. The initial struggles often revolve around the established concepts of sex roles and gender identification. Old techniques that a child earlier used to master separation may return.

Negativism

"No, I can do it myself. Don't tell me how long my hair can be. Don't tell me how short my skirt can be." This negativism is a renewed attempt to tell parents and the world that young people have minds of their own. Negativism becomes an active, verbal way of expressing anger; adolescents may seize almost any issue to express their independence. Parents and adolescents may argue about the adolescents' choice of friends, peer groups, school plans and courses, and points of philosophy and etiquette. Members of each generation recall the clothes, hairstyles, and other external badges—the more shocking the better—used to define adolescents' differences from their parents.

Adolescents slowly blend values from many sources into their own belief systems, which must have the flexibility to change and grow to accommodate new life situations. As adolescents begin to feel independent of their families and as families support and encourage their emerging maturity, the questions of "Who am I?" and "Where am I going?" begin to be answered.

PEER GROUP

The school experience accelerates and intensifies the degree of separation from the family. More and more, adolescents live in a world unfamiliar to parents. Home is a base; the real world is school, and the most important relationships, besides an adolescent's family, are with people of similar ages and interests. Adolescents attempt to establish a personal identity separate from their parents but close enough to the family structure to be included. Although adolescents tend to rely on peers for day-to-day support, the social support provided by parents has a stress-buffering effect in emergency situations. Adolescents often view themselves through the eyes of their peers, and any deviation in appearance, dress code, or behavior can result in diminished self-esteem. Parents must be aware of the sudden, frequent changes in friendships, personal appearance, and interests but must abrogate their authority.

PARENTING

The concept of the generation gap between parents and children has emerged from people's experience of being parents of adolescents. The gap represents the differences in experiences and perceptions of life events. In addition to having to deal with the turmoil that accompanies adolescent development, parents of adolescents are usually middle aged and must also make adjustments to work, to marriage, and to their own parents. Many difficulties surround adolescents' needs to assume increased independence from home, a move that can be threatening to parents who cannot let go and who want to maintain control of their children. Some parents may be unable to set limits on behavior; others act out their hidden or unconscious fantasies through the lives of their children. Superego lacunae (gaps or holes in the conscience) in parents may engender similar lacunae in children, and these gaps are then acted out. Moreover, the strong emerging sexuality of adolescents may trigger anxiety in parents. A few parents may be attracted to their opposite-sex or same-sex offspring and deal with the subsequent anxiety in maladaptive ways, such as getting angry (reaction formation).

In spite of these possibilities, parents of adolescents report few major altercations and get along with their children. For the most part, adolescents are receptive to parental approval and disapproval, and the majority of adolescents and their parents can bridge the generation gap successfully. When they do not, the failure may arise from mental disorders in children, parents, or both. About 20 percent of adolescents have a diagnosable mental disorder. Among the most common diagnoses are adjustment disorders; anxiety disorders and depressive disorders are also common. These disorders are often associated with delinquent behavior, rebelliousness, and academic failure—all of which may contribute to family disharmony.

DEVELOPMENT OF MORALS

For most people, developing a well-defined sense of morality is a major accomplishment of late adolescence and adulthood. *Morality* is defined as conformity to shared standards, rights, and duties. When two socially accepted standards conflict, a person learns to make judgments based on an individualized sense of conscience. People are morally obliged to abide by established norms but only to the degree that they serve human ends. The adolescent stage of development internalizes ethical principles and the control of conduct.

Piaget described morality as developing gradually, in conjunction with the stages of cognitive development. Preschool children simply follow rules set forth by the parents; in the middle years, children accept rules but show an inability to allow for exceptions; during adolescence, young people recognize rules in terms of what is good for the society at large.

Lawrence Kohlberg integrated Piaget's concepts and described three major levels of morality. The first level is *preconventional morality,* in which punishment and obedience to the parent are the determining factors; the second level is *morality of conventional role-conformity,* in which children try to conform to gain approval and to maintain good relationships with others; and the third and highest level is *morality of self-accepted moral principles,* in which children voluntarily comply with rules on the basis of a concept of ethical principles and make exceptions to rules in certain circumstances.

CHOICE OF OCCUPATION

Occupational choice stems from the question, "Where am I going?" Both men and women need to feel independent, autonomous, and content with their vocational choices. Adolescents are beleaguered by peers, parents, teachers, and counselors, as well as by unconscious forces, in attempting to decide on a vocation. Whether there are opportunities for further schooling plays a role in their decisions. Among college graduates, 30 percent go on to some type of postcollege graduate education. Those adolescents who are unable to continue schooling are severely hampered in establishing a satisfactory vocational identity. Many are fated for lives of economic and emotional depression.

The psychological basis for a sense of individual worth as an adult rests on the acquisition of competence during adolescence. A sense of competence is acquired by experiencing success in a task that today's society views as important. The sustained motivation necessary for mastering a difficult work role is possible only when adolescents have a likelihood of fulfilling this role in adult life and of gaining the respect of others.

RISK-TAKING BEHAVIOR

Risk-taking behavior in adolescence can involve alcohol, tobacco, and other substance use; promiscuous sexual activity, which is especially dangerous in view of the risk of acquired immune deficiency syndrome (AIDS), and accident-prone behavior, such as fast driving, skydiving, and hang gliding. Most mortality statistics for teenagers cite accidents as the leading cause of death, with vehicular accidents accounting for about 40 percent of all teenage deaths. The reasons for risk-taking behavior are varied and relate to counterphobic dynamics, the fear of inadequacy, the need to affirm a sexual identity, and group dynamics, such as peer pressure. The behavior may also reflect some adolescents' omnipotent fantasies, in which they view themselves as invulnerable to harm and injury. Information alone does not decrease risk: High levels of knowledge about the human immunodeficiency virus (HIV) and AIDS do not correlate with decreased high-risk behaviors. Recently, a genetic predisposition to risk-taking behavior has been identified; as adolescence proceeds, risk-taking behavior abates, and responsible decision-making activity occurs.

USE OF DRUGS

Although the use of cocaine is declining among U.S. teenagers, the use of other drugs of abuse has increased. This increase reverses a trend of declining drug use since the peak years in the 1970s. In a 1994 survey of high school students, marijuana was the most popular illegal drug; 38.2 percent of high school seniors reported having used it. Alcohol use was reported by over 85 percent of seniors; 25 percent had five or more drinks in a row in the 2 weeks before the survey.

PREGNANCY

Each year about 1 million teenage girls become pregnant. Of this number, 600,000 give birth; the remainder—400,000 (40 percent)—obtain abortions. The number of teenagers who engage in sexual intercourse is increasing. Boys generally have more sexual partners than do girls, and boys are less likely than are girls to seek emotional attachments with their sexual partners.

Contrary to earlier beliefs, sexual abuse during childhood does not increase teenage pregnancy rates. (Sexually abused girls are, however, more likely to exhibit socially deviant behaviors and to have older boyfriends.) Among pregnant teenagers, minimal prenatal care is a major contributing factor in maternal morbidity and mortality. Only one third of sexually active teenagers use contraceptives; most are uneducated about contraceptive use or are unwilling or unable to obtain contraceptives. Table 2.4–2 lists reasons for contraceptive misuse or rejection.

In some subcultures, teenagers view pregnancy as a rite of passage into adulthood. An adolescent girl who is depressed, insecure about her attractiveness, or the child of a conflicted or divorced couple is more likely to become pregnant than is an adolescent from a stable background.

The average adolescent mother is unable to care for her child, who is either placed in foster care or raised by the teenager's already-overburdened parents or other relatives. Few girls marry the fathers of their children; the fathers, usually teenagers, are unable to care for themselves, much less the mothers of their children. If the two do marry, they usually divorce.

Abortion

Teenage girls often use abortion services. Almost all the girls are unwed mothers from low socioeconomic groups; their pregnancies result from sex with boys to whom they felt emotionally attached. Most teenagers elect to have abortions with their parents' consent, but laws of mandatory parental consent put two rights into competition: a girl's claim to privacy and a parent's need to know. Most adults believe that teenagers should have parental permission for an abortion; but when parents refuse to give their consent, most states prohibit the parents' vetoing of the teenagers' decisions.

Table 2.4–2
Factors in the Misuse or Rejection of Contraceptives

Factors	Comments
Denial	Belief that pregnancy will not or cannot occur
Opportunism	Taking advantage of the opportunity (possibly unexpected) for coitus without regard for the consequences
Love	Coitus is driven by passionate enthusiasm with the expectation of marriage if pregnancy occurs
Guilt	Contraceptive use represents planned coitus, which engenders feelings of guilt
Embarrassment	Self-consciousness about using condom or inserting diaphragm in front of the partner
Entrapment	Desire to impregnate or to become pregnant to force the partner to become attached emotionally
Eroticism	Belief that contraceptive use decreases or interferes with erotic pleasure
Nihilism	Belief that contraceptives are ineffective or useless
Fear and anxiety	Coitus is associated with high levels of anxiety; fear of performance ability interferes with contraceptive use
Abortion	Belief that, if one gets pregnant, abortion can be obtained; therefore, a contraceptive is not needed
Education	Lack of education about effective contraceptive use from parents and school
Availability	Access to or cost of contraceptive prohibits its use

PROSTITUTION

Teenagers constitute a large portion of all prostitutes, with estimates ranging up to 1 million teenagers involved in prostitution. Most adolescent prostitutes are girls, but boys are also involved as homosexual prostitutes. Most teenagers who enter into a life of prostitution come from broken homes or were abused as children. Many were victims of rape. Most teenagers ran away from home and were taken in by pimps and substance abusers; the adolescents themselves then became substance abusers. They are at high risk for AIDS, and many, up to 70 percent in some studies, are infected with HIV.

VIOLENCE

Although rates of violent crime have decreased throughout the United States in the past 5 years (dramatically so in some large cities: the homicide rate in New York City fell by almost 50 percent in 2 years), violent crimes by young offenders are on the increase. Homicides are the second cause of death among people of ages 15 to 25. (Accidents are first; suicides, third.) Black male teenagers are far more likely to be murder victims than are boys from any other racial or ethnic group or girls of any race. The factor most strongly associated with violence among adolescent boys is growing up in a household without a father or father surrogate. Aside from this factor, race, socioeconomic status, and education show no effect on the propensity toward violence.

EVOLUTION OF ADULTHOOD

The end of adolescence occurs when people begin to assume the tasks of young adulthood, which involve choosing an occupation and developing a sense of intimacy that leads, in most cases, to marriage and parenthood. Daniel Levinson described an early-adult transition between adolescence and adulthood in which a young person begins to leave home and live independently. This period sees a peaking of biological development, the assumption of new social roles, the socialization into these roles, which involves learning skills and attitudes required to perform the roles well, and the eventual assumption of an adult self and life structure.

References

Brent DA, Johnson B, Bartle S, Bridge J: Personality disorders, tendency to impulsive violence, and survival behavior in adolescents. J Am Acad Child Adolesc Psychiatry *32:* 69, 1993.

Campbell BC, Udry JR: Stress and age at menarche of mothers and daughters. J Biosoc Sci *27:* 127, 1995.

Flanagan CA, Eccles JS: Changes in parents' work status and adolescents' adjustment at school. Child Dev *64:* 246, 1993.

Freud A: Adolescence. Psychoanal Study Child *13:* 255, 1958.

Frey CU, Rothlisberger C: Social support in healthy adolescents. J Youth Adolesc *25:* 17, 1996.

Garber J, Weiss B, Shanley N: Cognitions, depressive symptoms, and development in adolescents. J Abnorm Psychol *102:* 47, 1993.

Graber JA, Brooks-Gunn J, Warren MP: The antecedents of menarcheal age: Heredity, family environment, and stressful life events. Child Dev *66:* 346, 1995.

Jarvinen DW, Nicholls JG: Adolescents' social goals, belief about the causes of social success, and satisfaction in peer relationships. Dev Psychol *32:* 432, 1996.

Murry VM: Incidence of first pregnancy among black adolescent females over three decades. Youth Soc *23:* 478, 1992.

Mussen PH, Conger JJ, Kagan J: Adolescence. In *Essentials of Child Development and Personality.* Harper & Row, New York, 1984.

Newcomb MD: Life change events among adolescents. J Nerv Ment Dis *175:* 280, 1986.

Rainey DY, Stevens-Simon C, Kaplan DW: Are adolescents who report prior sexual abuse at a higher risk for pregnancy? Child Abuse Negl *19:* 1283, 1995.

Shields G, Adams J: HIV/AIDS among youth: A community needs assessment study. Child Adolesc Soc Work J *12:* 361, 1995.

Takanishi R: The opportunities of adolescence: Research, interventions, and policy. Am Psychol *48:* 85, 1993.

Waughan VC, Litt IF: *Child and Adolescent Development.* Saunders, Philadelphia, 1990.

▲ 2.5 Adulthood

In modern Western societies, *adulthood* is the longest phase of human life. It is defined as the stage when people are presumably fully developed and mature, the period of peak potential for personal fulfillment. Although the exact age of onset varies from person to person, adulthood can be divided into three main parts: young or early adulthood (ages 20 to 40), middle adulthood (ages 40 to 65), and late adulthood or old age. This section deals with early and middle adulthood, when the processes of marriage, child rearing, and work are most significant—a time of changes dramatic and subtle, but always continuous.

EARLY ADULTHOOD

Usually considered to begin at the end of adolescence (about age 20) and to end at age 40, early adulthood is characterized by the peaking of biological development, the assumption of major social roles, and the evolution of an adult self and life structure. The successful passage into adulthood depends on the satisfactory resolution of childhood and adolescent crises.

During late adolescence, young people generally leave home and begin to function independently. Sexual relationships become serious, and the quest for intimacy begins. The transitional period to early adulthood involves many important events: graduating from high school, starting a job or entering college, and living independently. The 20s are spent, for the most part, exploring options for occupation, marriage, or alternative relationships and making commitments in various areas. But the choices made in the late teens and early 20s are tentative at best; young adults may make several false starts.

Developmental Tasks

During early adulthood, options for occupation and marriage (or other intimate relationships) are explored. For most young adults, selecting a mate and starting a family are of paramount importance.

Those in their 30s become increasingly concerned with achieving authority, independence, and self-sufficiency. The primary goal of early adulthood is to become more autonomous and less dependent on people and institutions.

At about age 30, young adults are likely to question their choices and may ask themselves whether the life they have is the one they really want. Daniel J. Levinson called this period of reappraisal the age 30 transition. Some young people who think that their lives are going well reaffirm their commitments and experience a smooth transition. Others, however, may experience a major crisis, manifested by marital problems, job changes, and psychiatric symptoms such as anxiety and depression. Levinson described developmental periods through all phases of adulthood (Fig. 2.5–1).

Roger Gould reported a similar process among persons in their late 20s and early 30s who discover new talents, wishes, tendencies, and interests not previously appreciated or acknowledged. This awareness may produce either disillusionment and depression or a new sense of self with a realistic appraisal of the person's strengths and weaknesses.

Vulnerability

It has long been observed that some individuals, despite serious adverse circumstances in childhood, grow up to be satisfied, socially integrated, productive adults. They have sometimes been called *the invulnerable ones,* and recent longitudinal studies have focused on factors that may protect against negative outcomes. Good adult adjustment despite a high-risk childhood correlates with high intelligence, absence of child-

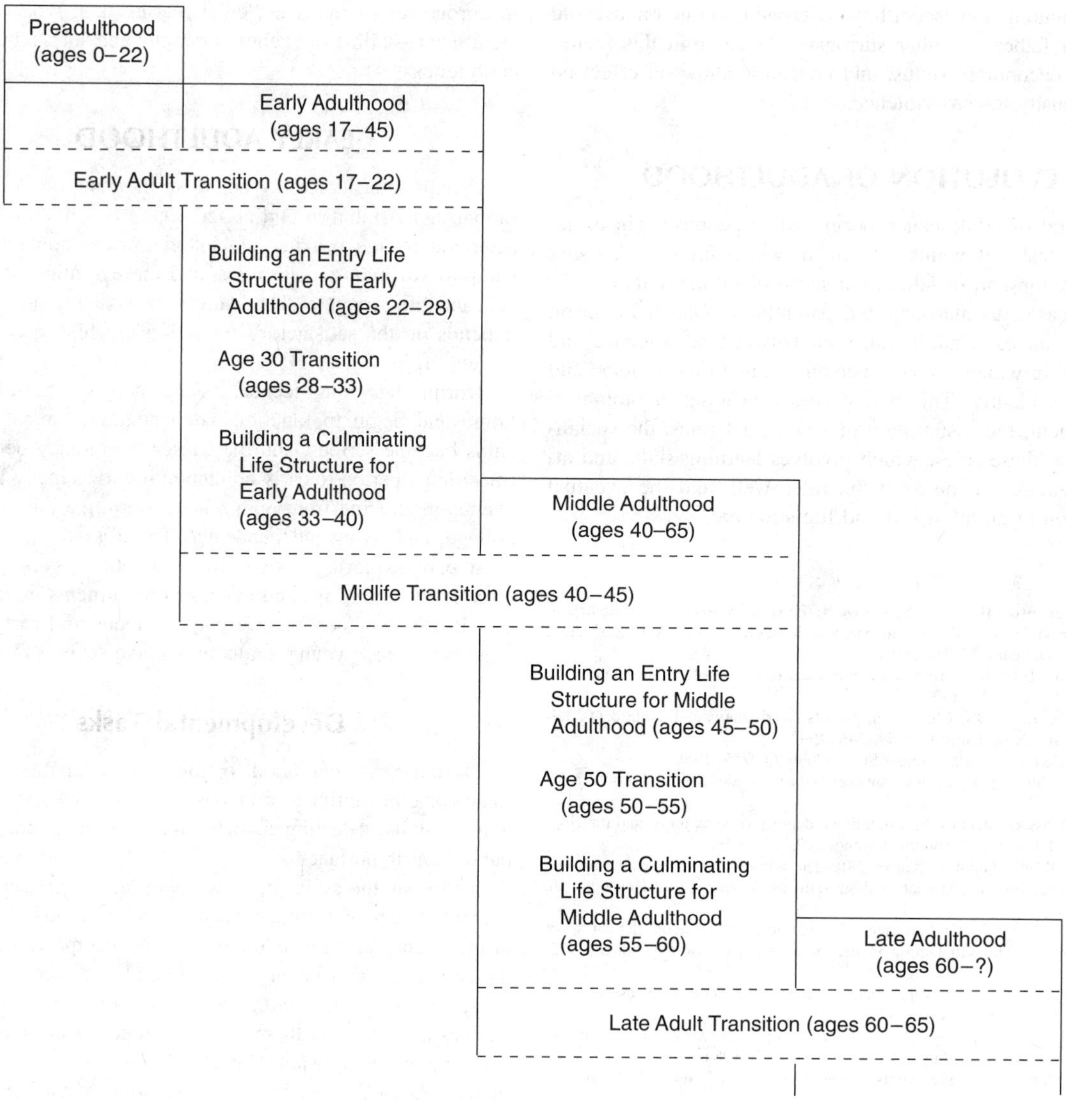
Preadulthood
(ages 0–22)
Early Adulthood
(ages 17–45)
Early Adult Transition (ages 17–22)
Building an Entry Life Structure for Early Adulthood (ages 22–28)
Age 30 Transition
(ages 28–33)
Building a Culminating Life Structure for Early Adulthood (ages 33–40)
Middle Adulthood
(ages 40–65)
Midlife Transition (ages 40–45)
Building an Entry Life Structure for Middle Adulthood (ages 45–50)
Age 50 Transition
(ages 50–55)
Building a Culminating Life Structure for Middle Adulthood (ages 55–60)
Late Adulthood
(ages 60–?)
Late Adult Transition (ages 60–65)

FIGURE 2.5–1
Developmental periods in the eras of early and middle adulthood. (Adapted from Levinson DJ, Darrow NC, Klein EB, Levinson MH, McKee B: *The Seasons of a Man's Life.* Knopf, New York, 1978.)

hood behavioral problems, the presence of rules and structure in the household of rearing, and good external social supports. In adulthood, the ability to bounce back from adversity is positively influenced by both personality factors, such as the ability to master stress, and by strong social supports.

Occupation. Socioeconomic group, gender, and race affect the pursuit and development of particular occupational choices. Blue-collar workers generally enter the work force directly after high school; white-collar workers and professionals usually enter the work force after college or professional school.

A healthy adaptation to work provides an outlet for creativity, satisfactory relationships with colleagues, pride in accomplishment, and increased self-esteem. Job satisfaction is not wholly dependent on money. In contrast, maladaptation can lead to a person's dissatisfaction with himself or herself and with the job, to insecurity, decreased self-esteem, anger, and resentment at having to work. Symptoms of job dissatisfaction are a high rate of job changes, absenteeism, mistakes at work, accident proneness, and even sabotage.

Members of minorities are frequently burdened with low socioeconomic status, which limits their opportunities for rewarding and satisfying work. They frequently begin their 20s with hopes of becoming successful but are often disappointed in this endeavor later in life.

ECONOMIC STATUS OF WOMEN. In the past 3 decades, women have become a significant economic force in the United States. Women's wages, compared to men's, have steadily increased, although in 1995 the typical hourly wage for women was still only 77 percent of that for men. More women have been entering the workplace. The proportion of working-age women with jobs has increased from 35 percent in 1960 to 55 percent in 1995. Even more impressive is the fact that the number of businesses owned by women increased 40 percent between 1987 and 1992 and accounted for one third of all businesses. Undoubtedly some but not all married women work only because of financial necessity. The greatest increase in working wives has been toward the top of the income scale.

Women's increasing economic power has been accompanied by increasing political power (if not yet widespread representation on the national level). The political gender gap (men and women voting for different parties) has widened; women disproportionately favor Democrats. Political observers noted numerous instances in which the 1996 presidential campaigns appealed specifically to women. The term *soccer moms* was coined to describe well-to-do, ethnically diverse suburbanite women balancing the demands of work and family. Soccer moms were supposedly hard headed and pragmatic; their votes were up for grabs. One pundit wrote, "As the soccer mom votes, so goes the election."

UNEMPLOYMENT. The effects of unemployment transcend those of loss of income; the psychological and physical tolls are enormous. The incidence of alcohol dependence, homicide, violence, suicide, and mental illness rises with unemployment. People's core identity, which is often tied to occupation and work, is seriously damaged when a job is lost, whether through firing, attrition, or early or regular retirement.

Marriage. Most people in the United States marry in their mid-20s; but the marriage rate is decreasing, and an increasing number of marriages in the United States end in divorce. Most divorced persons marry again—in most cases more successfully than the first time—an indication that the marital unit still provides the means for sustained intimacy, perpetuates the culture, and gratifies interpersonal needs. In the 1990s, nearly two thirds of all people in their 20s are married, nearly three quarters of all people in their 30s are married, and almost twice as many whites as blacks in the age range of 25 to 34 are married.

The change in mores from the 1950s' restrictive moral climate to the 1990s' permissive moral climate is seen in the number of unmarried adults who live together (cohabitation). In the 1960s, only 8 percent of couples lived together before marrying; currently, more than 50 percent of first marriages are preceded by cohabitation.

INTERRACIAL MARRIAGE. Mixed-race marriages were banned in 19 states until a Supreme Court decision in 1967. In 1970, they accounted for only 2 percent of all marriages involving at least one black partner. The trend has been steadily upward. In 1993, over 12 percent of all new black marriages involved a white partner. In more than two thirds of these mixed weddings, the groom was black and the bride was white.

Despite the trend toward more interracial marriages, they still remain a small proportion of all marriages. Most people are more likely to marry someone from the same racial and ethnic background. Marriages between Latinos and whites and between Asians and whites are more common than those between blacks and whites.

MARITAL ADJUSTMENT. In the United States a high value is placed on marital stability, love, and happiness. Although most people marry for love, it is not possible to predict who will marry whom and which marriages will be successful. Most people marry within their own socioeconomic group to persons from their own neighborhoods. The decision to marry also hinges on group and family pressures. Most persons are expected to marry in their 20s.

David Reed, who studied emotional adjustment in marriage and the factors that account for marital happiness, wrote:

> Most studies concur that happiness in a marriage implies happiness in the general relationship. However, those who report very happy marriages tend to dwell on their relationship in surveys, and those who are unhappy tend to indicate external sources to stress. None of this research includes objective observation of actual behavior. In relations in which need satisfaction is measured, researchers are inconclusive as to how emotional adjustment is achieved. It has become popular to advocate communication and verbal confrontation as important ingredients in emotional adjustment in marriage. Advocates of this view proselytize that openness, more talking, increased sensitivity to feelings, personalizing of language symbols, and keeping the communication channels open all contribute to happiness. Some studies agree with this view. . . . However, other studies report that communication can disturb a relationship, particularly when there is an emphasis on verbal overkill. Complete openness can be destructive. There may be a secret intolerance of weakness or an inability to perceive accurately the emotional strength of one's spouse. In such a relationship the verbally active partner becomes the better fighter who always wins. Thus, conflict is never well handled, and fights become a chronic source of despair. . . .
>
> [I]t is likely that there is a general correlation between happiness and stability. It is likely that in most relationships some form of success precedes general emotional fulfillment. By and large, this means that the husband needs to succeed in his role performance before there is an overwhelming concern with companionship. This is particularly true in disadvantaged families in which survival is an issue of far greater importance than pleasure. Moreover, satisfaction should not be confused with bliss, for satisfaction may include overt hostility more than peaceful companionship.

MARITAL PROBLEMS. Although marriage tends to be regarded as a permanent tie, unsuccessful unions may be terminated, as indeed they are in most societies. Nevertheless, many marriages that do not end in separation or divorce are disturbed.

In considering marital problems, clinicians are concerned not only with the people involved but also with the marital unit itself. How any marriage works out relates to the partners selected, the personality organization or disorganization of each, the interaction between them, and the original reasons for the union. People marry for a variety of reasons—emotional, social, economic, and political, among others. One person may look to the spouse to meet unfulfilled childhood needs for good parenting. Another may see the spouse as someone to be saved from an otherwise unhappy life. Irrational expectations between spouses increase the risk of marital problems.

MARRIAGE AND COUPLES THERAPY. When families consist of grandparents, parents, children, and other relatives living under the same roof, assistance for marital problems can sometimes be obtained from a member of the extended family with whom one or both partners have rapport. With the contraction of the extended family in recent times, however, this source of informal help is no longer as accessible as it once was. Similarly, religion once played a more important role than now in the maintenance of family stability. Wise religious leaders are available to provide counseling, but they are not sought out to the extent that they once were, a reflection of the decline in religious influence among large segments of the population. Formerly, both the extended family and religion not only provided guidance for couples in distress but also prevented dissolution of marriages by virtue of the social pressures that the extended family and religion exerted on couples to stay together. As family, religious, and societal pressures have relaxed, legal procedures for relatively easy separation and divorce have expanded. Concurrently, the need for formalized marriage counseling services has developed.

Marital therapy is a form of psychotherapy for married people in conflict with each other. A trained person establishes a professional contract with the patient-couple and, through definite types of communication, attempts to alleviate the disturbance, reverse or change maladaptive patterns of behavior, and encourage personality growth and development.

In *marriage counseling,* only a particular conflict related to the immediate concerns of the family is discussed; marriage counseling is conducted in a much more superficial manner and by people with less psychotherapeutic training than is marital therapy. In *marriage therapy,* there is greater emphasis on restructuring the interaction between the couple—including, at times, an exploration of the psychodynamics of each partner. Both therapy and counseling emphasize helping marital partners cope effectively with their problems.

Parenthood. By age 30, most people have established families and must deal with parent–child problems. In addition to the economic burden of raising a child (estimated to be more than $150,000 for a middle-class family whose child goes to college), there are emotional costs. Children may reawaken conflicts that parents themselves had as children, or children may have chronic illnesses that challenge families' emotional resources. In general, men have been more concerned with their work and advancement in their occupations than with child rearing, and women have been more concerned about their role as mothers than with advancement in their occupations; but this emphasis is changing dramatically for both sexes. A small but growing number of couples are choosing to split a job (or work at two part-time jobs) and share child-rearing duties.

For people in their 20s and 30s, parenting has been described as a continuing process of letting go. Children must be allowed to separate from parents and in some cases must be encouraged to do so. When parents are in their 20s, letting go involves the separation of children who are starting school. School phobias and school refusal syndromes that are accompanied by extreme separation anxiety may have to be dealt with. Often, a parent who is unable to let go of a child accounts for this situation: Some parents want their children to remain tightly bound to them emotionally. Family therapy in which these dynamics are explored may be necessary to resolve such problems.

As children get older and enter adolescence, the process of establishing identity assumes great importance. Peer relationships become crucial to children's development, and overprotective parents who keep the child from developing friendships or having the freedom to experiment with friends that the parents disapprove of can interfere with the children's passage through adolescence. Parents need not try to refrain from exerting influence over their children: Guidance and involvement are crucial. But they must recognize that adolescents especially need parental approval; although rebellious on the surface, adolescents are much more tractable than they appear, provided parents are not overbearing or generally punitive.

SINGLE-PARENT FAMILIES. There are more than 30 million families with one or more children under the age of 18; of these families, 20 percent are single-parent homes in which a woman is the sole head of the household. Although the majority of these children were left in the custody of their mothers by the courts in divorce proceedings, other children have been abandoned by their fathers. Among black families with one or more children under 18, almost 48 percent are headed by women with no spouse present.

ADOPTION. In the United States, adoption laws were enacted around 1850, and since the turn of the century, adoption or foster placement has replaced institutional care as the preferred way to raise children who are neglected, unwanted, or abandoned. Many couples who are unable to conceive (and some couples who already have children) turn to adoption.

In addition to the full range of normal parent–child developmental issues, adoptive parents face special problems. They must decide how and when to tell the child about the adoption. They must deal with the child's possible desire for information about biological parents. Recent high-profile cases in which children were removed from adoptive and psychological parents to be placed with biological parents may cast a shadow of uncertainty over the first few years of adoption. Whether these events have any impact on parent–child bonding or the child's subsequent emotional development has not been studied. Adopted children are more likely to develop conduct disorders, problems with drug abuse, and antisocial personality traits. It is unclear whether these problems result from the process of adoption or whether parents who give up children for adoption are more likely to pass along a genetic predisposition for these behaviors.

With widespread use of birth control and access to abortions, the number of infants available for adoption has steeply declined. Wealthy parents may prefer to arrange for private adoptions rather than wait many uncertain years for an institutional adoption. (In private adoptions a biological mother is paid for her legal and medical expenses but not for the baby. Baby selling is a felony in all states.) International adoptions (especially from Bosnia, Latin America, Eastern Europe, China) have also become more common. Questionable regulation in these countries has raised concern that some infants put up for adoption in poor countries may not be orphans but are being sold by destitute mothers.

Additional controversy has surrounded the adoption of black babies by white families. In 1972 the National Association of Black Social Workers issued a position paper condemning such adoptions in all circumstances. Several prospective studies have found that white parents can raise black children who have solid self-esteem and unambivalent racial identity.

MIDDLE ADULTHOOD

The ages that define middle adulthood vary among theorists, but the period typically spans the years from 40 to 65. Jung referred to age 40 as the noon of life. The task of terminating early adulthood involves a process of reviewing the past, considering how life has gone, and deciding what the future will be like. With regard to occupation, many people begin to experience the gap between early aspirations and current achievements. They may wonder whether the lifestyle and the commitments they chose in early adulthood are worth continuing; they may feel that they would like to live their remaining years in a different, more satisfying way, without knowing exactly how. As children grow up and leave home, parental roles change, and people redefine their roles as husbands and wives.

Important gender changes occur in middle adulthood. Many women, no longer needing to nurture young children, are able to release their energy into independent pursuits that require assertiveness and a competitive spirit, traits that were traditionally considered to be masculine. Alternatively, men in middle adulthood may develop qualities that enable them to express their emotions and recognize their dependence needs, traits that were traditionally considered to be feminine. The new balance of the masculine and the feminine may enable a person to relate more effectively than in the past to someone of the opposite sex.

Developmental Tasks

Robert Butler described several underlying themes in middle adulthood that appear to be present regardless of marital and family status, gender, or economic level (Table 2.5–1). These themes include aging, as changes in bodily functions are noticed in middle adulthood; taking stock of accomplishments and setting goals for the future; reassessing commitments to family, work, and marriage; dealing with the new generation and relationships with children; using accumulated power responsibly and ethically; dealing with parental illness and death; and attending to all the developmental tasks without losing capacity to experience pleasure or to engage in playful activity.

Erik Erikson. Eric Erikson described middle adulthood as characterized either by generativity or by stagnation. Erik-

Table 2.5–1
Features Salient to Middle Life

Issues	Positive Features	Negative Features
Prime of life	Responsible use of power; maturity; productivity	Winner–loser view; competitiveness
Stocktaking: what to do with the rest of one's life	Possibility; alternatives; organization of commitments; redirection	Closure; fatalism
Fidelity and commitments	Commitment to self, others, career, society; filial maturity	Hypocrisy, self-deception
Growth-death (to grow is to die); juvenescence and rejuvenation fantasies	Naturality regarding body, time	Obscene or frenetic efforts (eg, to be youthful); hostility and envy of youth and progeny; longing
Communication and socialization	Matters understood; continuity; picking up where left off; large social network; rootedness of relationships, places, and ideas	Repetitiveness; boredom; impatience; isolation; conservatism; confusion; rigidity

Adapted from Robert N. Butler, M.D.

son defined *generativity* as the process by which people guide the oncoming generation or improve society. This stage includes having and raising children, but wanting or having children does not ensure generativity. A childless person can be generative by helping others, by being creative, and by contributing to society. Parents must be secure in their own identity to raise children successfully: They cannot be preoccupied with themselves and act as if they were or wished to be the child in the family.

To be *stagnant* means that a person stops developing. For Erikson, stagnation was anathema, and he referred to adults without any impulses to guide the new generation or to those who produce children without caring for them as being "within a cocoon of self-concern and isolation." Such persons are in great danger. Because they are unable to negotiate the developmental tasks of middle adulthood, they are unprepared for the next stage of the life cycle, old age, which places more demands on the psychological and physical capacities than do all the preceding stages.

George Vaillant. In his longitudinal study of 173 men who were interviewed at 5-year intervals after they graduated from Harvard, George Vaillant found a strong correlation between physical and emotional health in middle age. In addition, those with the poorest psychological adjustment during college years had a high incidence of physical illness in middle age. No single factor in childhood accounted for adult mental health, but an overall sense of stability in the parental home predicted a well-adjusted adulthood. A close sibling relationship during college years was correlated with emotional and physical well-being in middle age. In another study Vaillant found that childhood and adult work habits were correlated and that adult mental health and good interpersonal relationships were associated with the capacity to work in childhood.

Sexuality

Sexuality is a major issue in midlife. Although William Masters and Virginia Johnson reported, as did Alfred Kinsey and others, that enjoyable sexual activity (including coitus) may continue well into old age, sexual functioning may decline. For some persons, however, the erroneous belief that vigorous sexual activity is the prerogative of youth is sufficient to interfere with their normal physiological sexual responses.

Fears and the reality of impotence are common problems in middle-aged men. The most common cause of impotence in the middle years is not aging but excessive alcohol intake, drugs (such as tranquilizers and antidepressants), and stress with fatigue and anxiety; 90 percent of the cases of chronic impotence in middle adulthood are due to psychological rather than organic causes.

Middle-aged women may also experience a decline in sexual functioning that is related to psychological more than to physical causes. Women do not reach their sexual prime until their mid-30s; consequently, they have a greater capacity for orgasm in middle than in young adulthood. Women, however, are more vulnerable than men to narcissistic blows to their self-esteem as they lose their youthful appearance, which is overvalued in today's society. During middle adulthood they may feel less sexually desirable than in early adulthood and, therefore, feel less entitled to an adequate sex life.

An inability to deal with changes in body image prompts many women and men to undergo cosmetic surgery in an effort to maintain their youthful appearance.

Climacterium

Middle adulthood is the time of the male and female *climacterium,* the period in life characterized by a decrease in biological and physiological functioning.

For women, the menopausal period is considered to be the climacterium and may start anywhere from the 40s to the early 50s. Bernice Neugarten studied this period and found that more than 50 percent of women described the menopause as an unpleasant experience, but a significant portion believed that their lives had not changed in any significant way, and many women experienced no adverse effects. Because they no longer had to worry about becoming pregnant, several women reported feeling more free after the menopause than before its onset. Generally, the female climacterium has been stereotyped as a sudden or radical psychophysiological experience; but it is more often a gradual experience as estrogen secretion decreases with changes in the flow, timing, and eventual cessation of the menses. Vasomotor instability (hot flashes) may occur, and the menopause may extend over a period of several years. Some women experience anxiety and depression, but usually a premenopausal personality structure predisposes people to the menopausal syndrome.

For men, the climacterium has no clear demarcation; male hormones stay fairly constant through the 40s and 50s. Nevertheless, men must adapt to a decline in biological functioning and overall physical vigor. The crisis can be mild or severe, characterized by a sudden drastic change in work or marital relationships, severe depression, increased use of alcohol or drugs, or a shift to an alternate lifestyle.

Normal turning points during middle age are usually mastered without distress. Only when life events are severe or unexpected—such as the death of a spouse, the loss of a job, or a serious illness—does a person experience an emotional disorder severe enough to warrant the term *midlife crisis.* Men and women who are most prone to midlife crises tend to come from families characterized by one or more of the following during their adolescence: parental discord, withdrawal by the same-sex parent, anxious parents, and impulsive parents with a low sense of responsibility.

Empty-Nest Syndrome. Another phenomenon described in middle adulthood has been called the empty-nest syndrome, a depression that occurs in men and women when their youngest child is about to leave home. Most parents, however, perceive the departure of the youngest child as a relief rather than a stress. If no compensating activities have been developed, particularly by the mother, some parents become depressed.

Other Tasks of Middle Adulthood

As persons approach the age of 50, they clearly define what they want from work, family, and leisure. Men who have reached their highest level of advancement in work may experience disillusionment or frustration when they realize that they can no longer anticipate new work challenges. For women who have invested themselves completely in mothering, this period leaves them with no suitable identity after the children leave home. Sometimes, social rules become rigidly established; lack of freedom in lifestyle and a sense of entrapment may lead to depression and a loss of confidence. There may also be unique financial burdens in middle age, produced by pressures to care for aged parents at one end of the spectrum and for children at the other end.

Levinson described a transitional period between the ages of 50 and 55 during which a developmental crisis may occur when people feel incapable of changing an intolerable life structure. Although no single event characterizes the transition, the physiological changes that begin to appear may have a dramatic effect on people's sense of self. For example, a person may experience a decrease in cardiovascular efficiency that accompanies aging. Chronological age and physical infirmity are not linear, however; those who exercise regularly, who do not smoke, and who eat and drink in moderation are able to maintain their physical health and emotional well-being.

Middle adulthood is the period when people frequently feel overwhelmed by too many obligations and duties, but it is also a time of great satisfaction for most persons. People have developed a wide array of acquaintances, friendships, and relationships. The satisfaction people express about their network of friends predicts positive mental health. Some social ties, however, may be a source of stress when demands either cannot be met or assault a person's self-esteem. Power, leadership, wisdom, and understanding are most generally possessed by people who are middle aged, and if their health and vitality remain intact, it is truly the prime of life.

DIVORCE

Divorce is a major crisis of adult life. Spouses often grow, develop, and change at different rates; one spouse may discover that the other is not the same as when they first married. In truth, both partners have changed and evolved, not necessarily in complementary directions. Frequently, one spouse blames a third person for alienation of affections and refuses to examine his or her own role in the marital problems. Certain aspects of marital deterioration and divorce seem to be related to specific qualities of middle life—need for change, weariness with acting responsibly, fear of facing up to oneself. The following cases by Butler are informative.

A 43-year-old woman was divorced after 21 years of marriage. She had brought up four children and felt she had contributed to the material success of her husband, who received all the credit. She was bitter and hurt over his failure to appreciate her but saw this failure as his problem alone. She was dismayed when he pressed for a divorce. Neither wanted marital counseling, and the end came quickly. They no longer even talked to each other. Neither of them could quite believe they were divorced.

Some men and women begin to seek a last fling or a last chance to experience something they feel they have missed. This phenomenon is not confined to heterosexual relationships.

Mary and Joan had lived together for 23 years. Their homosexuality was only part of their rich relationship together. They had lived through many painful public experiences, and they had developed good relationships with their neighbors. Mary had always struggled with the possibility of trying a heterosexual relationship and at 44 felt that she had little time left. When an opportunity arose, she seized the chance for a heterosexual affair. Joan was deeply hurt. Despite the long-standing success of their life together, they were not certain their relationship would survive this development. They jointly sought therapeutic help.

Types of Separation

Paul Bohannan, an anthropologist with expertise in marriage and divorce, described the types of separation that take place at the time of divorce.

Psychic Divorce. In psychic divorce the love object is given up, and a grief reaction about the death of the relationship occurs. Sometimes a period of anticipatory mourning sets in before the divorce. Separating from a spouse forces a person to become autonomous, to change from a position of dependence. The separation may be difficult to achieve, especially if both are used to being dependent on each other (as normally happens in marriage) or if one was so dependent as to be afraid or incapable of becoming independent. Most people report such feelings as depression, ambivalence, and mood swings at the time of divorce. Studies indicate that the process of recovery from divorce takes about 2 years; by then the ex-spouse may be viewed neutrally, and each spouse accepts his or her new identity as a single person.

Legal Divorce. Legal divorce involves going through the courts so that each of the parties is remarriageable. Seventy-five percent of divorced women and eighty percent of divorced men remarry within 3 years of divorce. No-fault divorce, in which neither person is judged to be the guilty party, has become the most widely used legal mechanism for divorce.

Economic Divorce. Major concerns are the division of the couple's property between them and economic support for the wife. Many men who are ordered by the courts to pay alimony or child support flout the law and create a major social problem.

Community Divorce. The social network of the divorced couple changes markedly. A few relatives and friends are retained from the community, and new ones are added. The task of meeting new friends is often difficult for divorced people, who may realize how dependent they were on their spouses for social exchanges.

Coparental Divorce. Coparental divorce is the separation of a parent from the child's other parent. Being a single parent is different from being a married parent.

Custody

The parental right doctrine is a legal concept that awards custody to the more fit natural parent and attempts to ensure that the best interest of the child is served. In the past, mothers were almost always awarded custody, but custody is now given to fathers in about 15 percent of cases. Custodial fathers are more likely to be white, married, older, and better educated than custodial mothers. Women who are granted custody have a better chance of being awarded child support and of actually receiving payments than do men who are granted custody. Nevertheless, women who receive payments still have lower incomes than men who receive payment.

The types of custody include joint custody, in which a child spends equal time with each parent, an increasingly common practice; split custody, in which siblings are separated and each parent has custody of one or more of the children; and single custody, in which the children live solely with one parent and the other parent has rights of visitation that may be limited in some ways by the court. Child support payments are more likely to be made when parents have joint custody or when the noncustodial parent is given visitation rights.

Problems may surface in the parent–child relationship with the custodial or the noncustodial parent. The presence of the custodial parent in the home represents the reality of the divorce, and this parent may become the target of the child's anger. The parent under such stress may not be able to deal with the child's increased needs and emotional demands.

The noncustodial parent must cope with limits placed on time spent with the child. This parent loses the day-to-day gratification and the responsibilities involved with parenting. Emotional distress is common in parent and child. Joint custody offers a solution with some advantages but requires a high degree of maturity on the part of the parents and can present some problems. Parents must separate their child-rearing practices from their postdivorce resentments, and they must develop a spirit of cooperation about rearing the child. They must also have the ability to tolerate frequent communication with the ex-spouse.

Reasons for Divorce

Divorce tends to run in families and is highest in couples who marry as teenagers or come from different socioeconomic backgrounds. Every marriage is psychologically unique, and so is each divorce. If a person's parents were divorced, he or she may choose to resolve a marital problem in the same way, through divorce. Expectations of the spouse may be unrealistic: One partner may expect the other to act as an all-giving mother or as a magically protective father. The parenting experience places the greatest strain on a marriage. In surveys of couples with and without children, those without children reported getting more pleasure from the spouse than did those couples with children. Illness in the child creates the greatest strain of all, and in marriages in which a child has died through illness or accident, more than 50 percent end in divorce.

Other causes of marital distress are problems about sex and money. Both areas may be used as a means of control, and withholding sex or money is a means of expressing aggression. There is also less social pressure now than in the past to remain married. As previously discussed, the easing of divorce laws and the declining influence of religion and the extended family make divorce an acceptable course of action today.

Intercourse Outside of Marriage. Adultery is defined as voluntary sexual intercourse between a married person and someone other than his or her spouse. A 1994 survey by the University of Chicago reported that 85 percent of married women and 75 percent of married men remain faithful to their spouses. These numbers are much higher than earlier researchers found. For men, the first extramarital affair is often associated with the wife's pregnancy, when coitus may be interdicted. Most of these incidents are kept secret from the spouse and, if known, rarely account for divorce. Nevertheless the infidelity may serve as the catalyst for basic dissatisfactions in the marriage to surface, and these problems may then lead to its dissolution. Adultery may decline, as potentially fatal sexually transmitted diseases such as acquired immune deficiency syndrome (AIDS) serve as sobering deterrents.

References

Bureau of the Census: *Who Receives Child Support?* US Department of Commerce, Washington, 1995.

Campbell M: Divorce at mid-life: Intergenerational issues. J Divorce *23:* 185, 1995.

Charny IM, Parnass S: The impact of extramarital relationships on the continuation of marriage. Sex Marital Ther *21:* 100, 1995.

Christensen A, Pasch L: The sequence of marital conflict: An analysis of seven phases of marital conflict in distressed and nondistressed couples. Clin Psychol Rev *13:* 3, 1993.

Fergusson DM, Lynskey M, Horwood LJ: The adolescent outcomes of adoption: A 16-year longitudinal study. J Child Psych Psychiatry *36:* 597, 1995.

Hornstein GA: The structuring of identity among midlife women as a function of their degree of involvement in employment. J Pers *54:* 551, 1986.

Kermani EJ, Weiss BA: Biological parents regaining their rights: A psycholegal analysis of a new era in custody disputes. Bull Am Acad Psychiatry Law *23:* 261, 1995.

Levinson DJ, Damow CN, Klein EB, Levinson MH, McKeeb B: *The Seasons of a Man's Life.* Knopf, New York, 1978.

Matthews KA, Wing RR, Kuller LH, Meilahn EN, Kelsey SF, Costello EJ, Caggiula AW: Influences of natural menopause on psychological characteristics and symptoms of middle-aged healthy women. J Consult Clin Psychol *58:* 345, 1990.

Nemiroff RA, Colarusso CA: Frontiers of adult development in theory and practice. J Geriatr Psychiatry *21:* 7, 1988.

Neugarten BL: *Personality in Middle and Late Life.* Atherton, New York, 1964.

Reed DM: Traditional marriage. In *The Sexual Experience,* BJ Sadock, HI Kaplan, AM Freedman, editors, p 217. Williams & Wilkins, Baltimore, 1976.

Repetti RL: Short-term effects of occupational stressors on daily mood and health complaints. Health Psychol *12:* 125, 1993.

Sullivan PF, Wells JE, Bushnell JA: Adoption as a risk factor for mental disorders. Acta Psychiatr Scand *92:* 119, 1995.

Vaillant GE, Vaillant CO: Natural history of male psychological health: 12. A 45-year study of predictors of successful aging at age 65. Am J Psychiatry *147:* 31, 1990.

Westman M, Eden D: Excessive role demand and subsequent performance. J Org Behav *13:* 519, 1992.

Wickrama K, Conger RD, Lorenz FO: Work, marriage, lifestyle, and changes in men's physical health. Behav Med *18:* 97, 1995.

Wilkinson SH: Psycholegal process and issues in international adoption. Am J Fam Ther *23:* 173, 1995.

Woodruff SI, Conway TL: A longitudinal assessment of the impact of health–fitness status and health behavior on perceived quality of life. Percept Mot Skills *75:* 3, 1992.

▲ 2.6 Late Adulthood (Old Age)

Older people are becoming the fastest growing age group in the United States. Robert N. Butler has described the phenomenon of people living longer now than ever before as a triumph of survivorship rather than a cause for despair.

Gerontology—the study of aging—has become a new specialization to accommodate to the changing demographic patterns. Late adulthood, or old age, usually refers to the stage of the life cycle that begins at age 65. Gerontologists divide older adults into two groups: young-old, ages 65 to 74; and old-old, ages 75 and beyond. Older adults can also be described as well-old, people who are healthy, and as sick-old, people who have an infirmity that interferes with functioning and requires medical or psychiatric attention. The health needs of older adults have grown enormously as the population ages, and geriatric physicians and psychiatrists play major roles in treating this population.

DEMOGRAPHICS

In 1994 an estimated 32 million people in the United States were more than 65 years old. Although the total population of the United States increased by 45 percent between 1960 and 1994, people of age 65 years or older increased by 100 percent. According to the U.S. Bureau of the Census, this figure will rise to more than 50 million persons over the age of 65 by the year 2030 and is a result of the aging of the baby-boom generation—those born between 1946 and 1964. By 2050 it is projected that there will be more people over than under age 65 and more people over 65 than under 14 living in the United States. Figures 2.6–1 and 2.6–2 show the U.S. population by age and sex in 1975 and 2050.

BIOLOGY OF AGING

The aging process, or senescence (from the Latin *senescere,* ''to grow old''), is characterized by a gradual decline in the functioning of all the body's systems—cardiovascular, respiratory, genitourinary, endocrine, and immune, among others. But the belief that old age is invariably associated with profound intellectual and physical infirmity is a myth. Most older people retain their cognitive abilities and physical capacities to a remarkable degree.

An overview of the biological changes that accompany old age is given in Table 2.6–1. The various decrements listed do not occur in a linear fashion in all systems. Not all organ systems deteriorate at the same rate, nor do they follow a similar pattern of decline for all people. Each person is genetically endowed with one or more vulnerable systems, or a system may become vulnerable because of environmental stressors or intentional misuse (for example, excessive ultraviolet exposure, smoking, alcohol). Moreover, not all organ systems deteriorate at the same time; a person does not disintegrate like the one-horse shay in Oliver Wendell Holmes's poem, *The Deacon's Masterpiece,* which ''went to pieces all at once.'' Rather, any one of a number of organ systems begins to deteriorate, and this deterioration then leads to illness or death.

Aging generally means the aging of cells. In the most commonly held theory, each cell has a genetically determined life span during which it can replicate itself a limited number of times before it dies. Structural changes in cells occur with age. In the central nervous system, for example, age-related cell changes occur in neurons, which show signs of degeneration. In senility (characterized by severe memory loss and a loss of intellectual functioning), signs of degeneration are much more severe and are known as neurofibrillary degeneration, seen most commonly in dementia of the Alzheimer's type.

Changes in the structure of deoxyribonucleic acid (DNA) and ribonucleic acid (RNA) are also found in aging cells; the cause has been attributed to genotypic programming, X-rays,

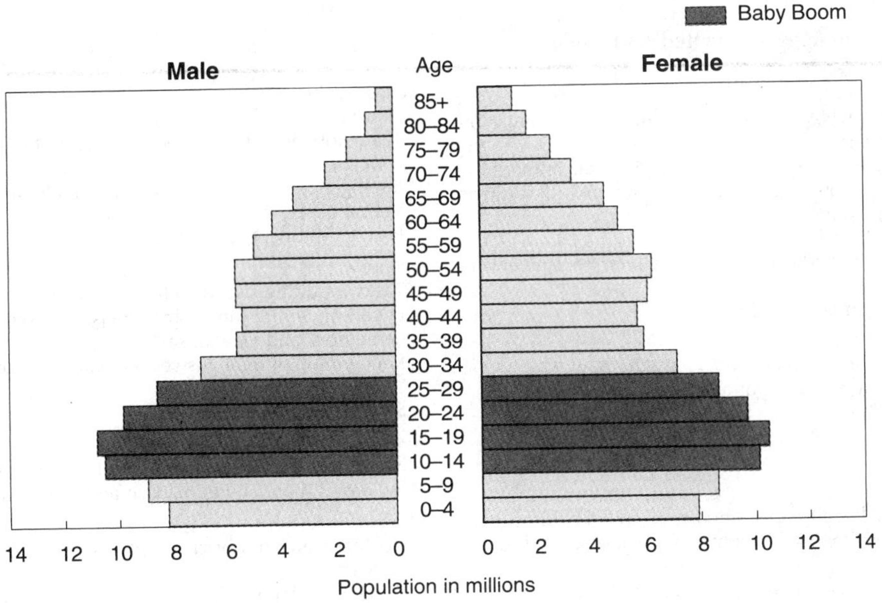
Baby Boom
Male
Age
Female
85+
80–84
75–79
70–74
65–69
60–64
55–59
50–54
45–49
40–44
35–39
30–34
25–29
20–24
15–19
10–14
5–9
0–4
14 12 10 8 6 4 2 0
0 2 4 6 8 10 12 14
Population in millions

FIGURE 2.6–1
U.S. population by age and sex: 1975. (Reprinted from US Bureau of the Census: *65+ in the United States,* p 2–6. Current Population Reports Series. US Government Printing Office, Washington, 1996.)

chemicals, and food products, among others. There is probably no single cause of aging, and all areas of the body are affected to some degree.

Genetic factors have been implicated in disorders that commonly occur in older people, such as hypertension, coronary artery disease, arteriosclerosis, and neoplastic disease. Family studies indicate inheritance factors for breast and stomach cancer, colon polyps, and certain mental disorders of old age. Huntington's disease shows an autosomal dominant mode of inheritance with complete penetrance. The average age of onset is between 35 and 40, but cases have occurred as late as 70 years of age.

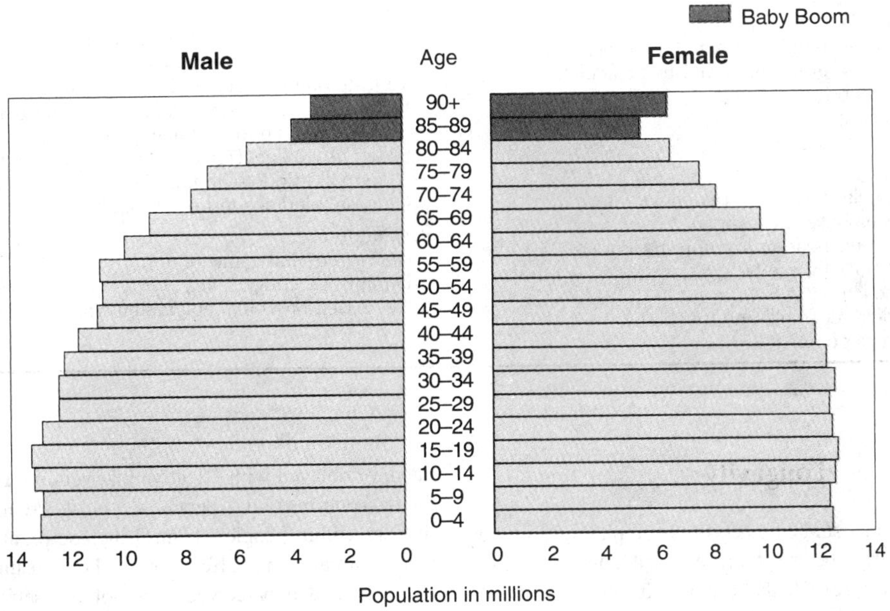
Baby Boom
Male
Age
Female
90+
85–89
80–84
75–79
70–74
65–69
60–64
55–59
50–54
45–49
40–44
35–39
30–34
25–29
20–24
15–19
10–14
5–9
0–4
14 12 10 8 6 4 2 0
0 2 4 6 8 10 12 14
Population in millions

FIGURE 2.6–2
U.S. population (projected) by age and sex: 2050. (Reprinted from US Bureau of the Census: *65+ in the United States,* p 2–7. Current Population Reports Series. US Government Printing Office, Washington, 1996.)

Table 2.6–1
Biological Changes Associated with Aging

Cellular level
- Change in cellular DNA and RNA structures: intracellular organelle degeneration
- Neuronal degeneration in central nervous system, primarily in superior temporal precentral and inferior temporal gyri; no loss in brainstem nuclei
- Receptor sites and sensitivity altered
- Decreased anabolism and catabolism of cellular transmitter substances
- Intercellular collagen and elastin increase

Immune system
- Impaired T-cell response to antigen
- Increase in function of autoimmune bodies
- Increased susceptibility to infection and neoplasia
- Leukocytes unchanged, T lymphocytes reduced
- Increased erythrocyte sedimentation (nonspecific)

Musculoskeletal
- Decrease in height because of shortening of spinal column (two-inch loss in both men and women from the second to the seventh decade)
- Reduction in lean muscle mass and muscle strength; deepening of thoracic cage
- Increase in body fat
- Elongation of nose and ears
- Loss of bone matrix, leading to osteoporosis
- Degeneration of joint surfaces may produce osteoarthritis
- Risk of hip fracture is 10–25% by age 90
- Continual closing of cranial sutures (parietomastoid suture does not attain complete closure until age 80)
- Men gain weight until about age 60, then lose; women gain weight until age 70, then lose

Integument
- Graying of hair results from decreased melanin production in hair follicles (by age 50, 50% of all persons male and female are at least 50% gray; pubic hair is last to turn gray)
- General wrinkling of skin
- Less active sweat glands
- Decrease in melanin
- Loss of subcutaneous fat
- Nail growth slowed

Genitourinary and reproductive
- Decreased glomerular filtration rate and renal blood flow
- Decreased hardness of erection, diminished ejaculatory spurt
- Decreased vaginal lubrication
- Enlargement of prostate
- Incontinence

Special senses
- Thickening of optic lens, reduced peripheral vision
- Inability to accommodate (presbyopia)
- High-frequency sound hearing loss (presbyacusis)—25% show loss by age 60, 65% by age 80
- Yellowing of optic lens
- Reduced acuity of taste, smell, and touch
- Decreased light-dark adaption

Neuropsychiatric
- Learning
  - Takes longer to learn new material, but complete learning still occurs
  - Intelligence quotient (IQ) remains stable until age 80
  - Verbal ability maintained with age
  - Psychomotor speed declines

Memory
- Tasks requiring shifting attentions performed with difficulty
- Encoding ability diminishes (transfer of short-term to long-term memory and vice versa)
- Recognition of right answer on multiple-choice tests remains intact
- Simple recall declines

Neurotransmitters
- Norepinephrine decreases in central nervous system
- Increased monoamine oxidase and serotonin in brain

Brain
- Decrease in gross brain weight, about 17% by age 80 in both sexes
- Widened sulci, smaller convolutions, gyral atrophy
- Ventricles enlarge
- Increased transport across blood-brain barrier
- Decreased cerebral blood flow and oxygenation

Cardiovascular
- Increase in size and weight of heart (contains lipofuscin pigment derived from lipids)
- Decreased elasticity of heart valves
- Increased collagen in blood vessels
- Increased susceptibility to arrhythmias
- Altered homeostasis of blood pressure
- Cardiac output maintained in absence of coronary heart disease

Gastrointestinal (GI) system
- At risk for atrophic gastritis, hiatal hernia, diverticulosis
- Decreased blood flow to gut, liver
- Diminished saliva flow
- Altered absorption from GI tract (at risk for malabsorption syndrome and avitaminosis)
- Constipation

Endocrine
- Estrogen levels decrease in women
- Adrenal androgen decreases
- Testosterone production declines in men
- Increase in follicle-stimulating hormone (FSH) and luteinizing hormone (LH) in postmenopausal women
- Serum thyroxine (T_4) and thyroid-stimulating hormone (TSH) normal, triiodothyronine (T_3) reduced
- Glucose tolerance test result decreases

Respiratory
- Decreased vital capacity
- Diminished cough reflex
- Decreased bronchial epithelium ciliary action

Longevity

Longevity has been studied since the beginning of recorded history and has always been a topic of great interest. The research about longevity reveals that a family history of longevity is the best indicator of a long life: Almost half the fathers of persons who live past 80 also lived past 80. Nevertheless, many conditions leading to a shortened life can be prevented, ameliorated, or delayed with effective intervention. Heredity is but one factor—one beyond a person's control. Predictors of longevity that are within people's control include regular medical checkups, minimal or no caffeine or alcohol consumption, work gratification, and a perceived sense of the self as being socially useful in an altruistic role, such as spouse, teacher, mentor, parent, or grandparent. Healthy eating and adequate exercise are also associated with health and longevity.

Life Expectancy

In the United States, the average life expectancy has increased in every decade—from 48 years in 1900 to 75.8 years in 1995. The projected life expectancy at birth and at age 65 is indicated in Table 2.6–2.

Changes in morbidity and mortality have also occurred. Over the past 30 years, for example, there has been a 60 percent decline in mortality from cerebrovascular disease and a 30 percent decline in mortality from coronary artery disease. In contrast, mortality from cancer, which rises steeply with age, has increased, especially cancer of the lung, colon, stomach, skin, and prostate.

The prediction of mortality is important to actuaries and insurance companies, among others. All mortality formulas have flaws, but the one that has been most accepted is the law of human mortality. Proposed in 1825 by Benjamin Gompertz, the formula holds that mortality in a given population rises exponentially with the passage of time, and after age 30 the mortality rate doubles about every 8.5 years. The death rate in the United States for all ages is 879.3 deaths a year per 100,000 population from all causes. In the age group 65 to 74, it is 2,590.9 per 100,000; in the age group 74 to 85, it is 5,909.7 per 100,000; and in the age group 85 and over, it is 15,312.6 per 100,000.

The oldest old, people over 85 years of age, are the most rapidly growing segment of the older population. Between 1960 and 1994 the population of all older people increased by 100 percent compared with 45 percent for the entire U.S. population, but the increase for the 85 and older group was 274 percent. It is expected that by 2050 the oldest old will make up 24 percent of the elderly population and 5 percent of the total population in the United States. Figure 2.6–3 gives projected numbers for the average annual growth rate of the elderly population to the year 2050.

The leading causes of death among older people are heart disease, cancer, and stroke. Accidents were the seventh leading cause of death of people over 65 in 1993. Most fatal accidents are caused by falls, pedestrian incidents, and burns. Falls are most commonly the result of cardiac arrhythmias and hypotensive episodes.

Some gerontologists consider death in very old people (over 85) to be the result of an aging syndrome characterized by diminished elastic-mechanical properties of the heart, arteries, lungs, and other organs. Death results from trivial tissue injuries that would not be fatal to a younger person; accordingly, senescence is viewed as the cause of death.

Ethnicity and Race

The proportion of older people in the black, Hispanic, and Asian population is smaller than in the white population but is increasing at a fast rate. In 1994, 10 percent of older people were other than white. This proportion should rise to 20 percent by 2050, and the proportion of older people who are Hispanic will increase from 4 to approximately 14 percent over the same period (Fig. 2.6–4).

Sex Ratios

On the average, women live longer than men and are more likely than men to live alone. The number of men per 100 women decreases sharply from age 65 to 85 (Fig. 2.6–5).

Geographic Distribution

The most populous states have the largest number of older people. California has the most (3.3 million), followed by New York, Pennsylvania, Texas, Michigan, Illinois, Florida, and Ohio, each with more than 1 million (Fig. 2.6–6). States with high proportions of older people include Pennsylvania, Florida, Nebraska, and North Dakota. The high proportion in Florida is due to those who move into the state for retirement; in the others it is due to young people moving out.

Exercise, Diet, and Health

Diet and exercise play a role in preventing or ameliorating chronic diseases of older people, such as arteriosclerosis and hypertension.

Hyperlipemia correlates with coronary artery disease and can be controlled by reducing body weight, decreasing the in-

Table 2.6–2
Projected Life Expectancy at Birth and Age 65, by Sex: 1990–2050 (In years)

	At Birth			At Age 65		
Year	Men	Women	Difference	Men	Women	Difference
1990	72.1	79.0	6.9	15.0	19.4	4.4
2000	73.5	80.4	6.9	15.7	20.3	4.6
2010	74.4	81.3	6.9	16.2	21.0	4.8
2020	74.9	81.8	6.9	16.6	21.4	4.8
2030	75.4	82.3	6.9	17.0	21.8	4.8
2040	75.9	82.8	6.9	17.3	22.3	5.0
2050	76.4	83.3	6.9	17.7	22.7	5.0

Reprinted from Spencer G: Projections of the population of the United States, by age, sex and race: 1988 to 2080. In *Current Population Reports,* p 43. US Bureau of the Census, Washington, 1989.

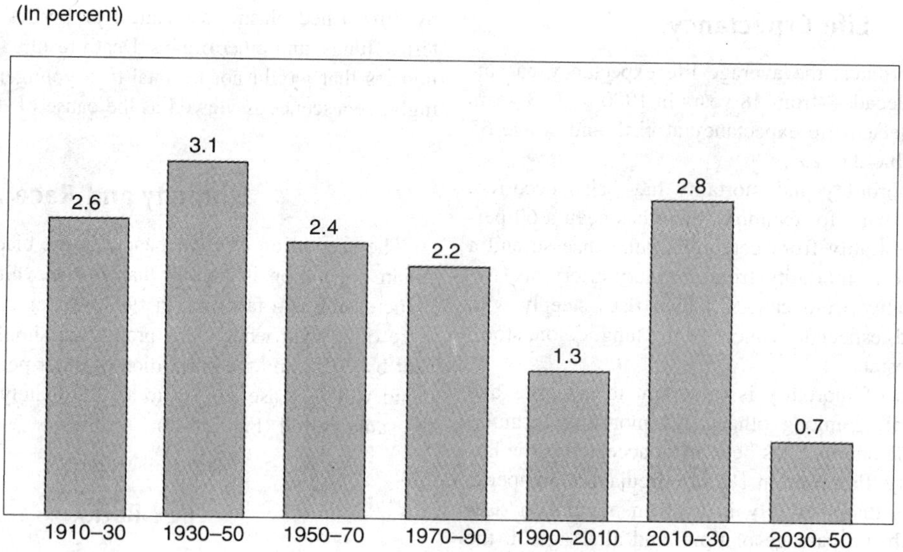
(In percent)
2.6
3.1
2.4
2.2
1.3
2.8
0.7
1910–30
1930–50
1950–70
1970–90
1990–2010
2010–30
2030–50

FIGURE 2.6–3

Average annual growth rate of the elderly population: 1910–30 to 1930–50 (in percent). (Reprinted from US Bureau of the Census: *65+ in the United States,* p 2–2. Current Population Reports Series. US Government Printing Office, Washington, 1996.)

take of saturated fat, and limiting the intake of cholesterol. Increasing the daily intake of dietary fiber can also help decrease serum lipoprotein levels. A daily intake of 1 ounce (about 30 mL) of alcohol has been correlated with longevity and elevated high-density lipoproteins (HDL).

Reduced salt intake (less than 3 grams a day) is associated with a lowered risk of hypertension. Hypertensive geriatric patients can often correct their condition by moderate exercise and decreased salt intake without the addition of drugs.

A regimen of daily moderate exercise (walking for 30 minutes a day) has been associated with a reduction in cardiovascular disease, a decreased incidence of osteoporosis, improved respiratory function, the maintenance of ideal weight, and a general sense of well-being. Even among the very old, exercise has been shown to improve strength and function. In many cases a disease process has been reversed and even cured by diet and exercise, without additional medical or surgical intervention.

Table 2.6–3 lists the biological changes associated with diet and exercise. A comparison with Table 2.6–1 reveals that almost every biological change associated with aging is positively affected by diet and exercise.

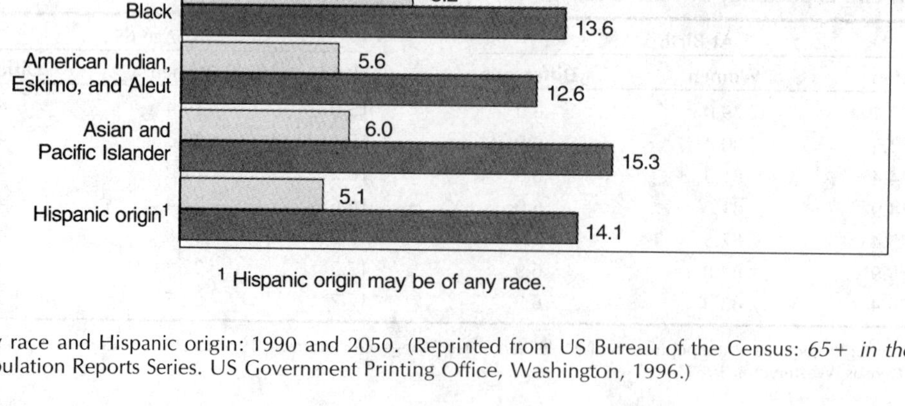
1990
2050
All races
12.5
20.4
White
13.4
22.8
Black
8.2
13.6
American Indian, Eskimo, and Aleut
5.6
12.6
Asian and Pacific Islander
6.0
15.3
Hispanic origin¹
5.1
14.1
¹ Hispanic origin may be of any race.

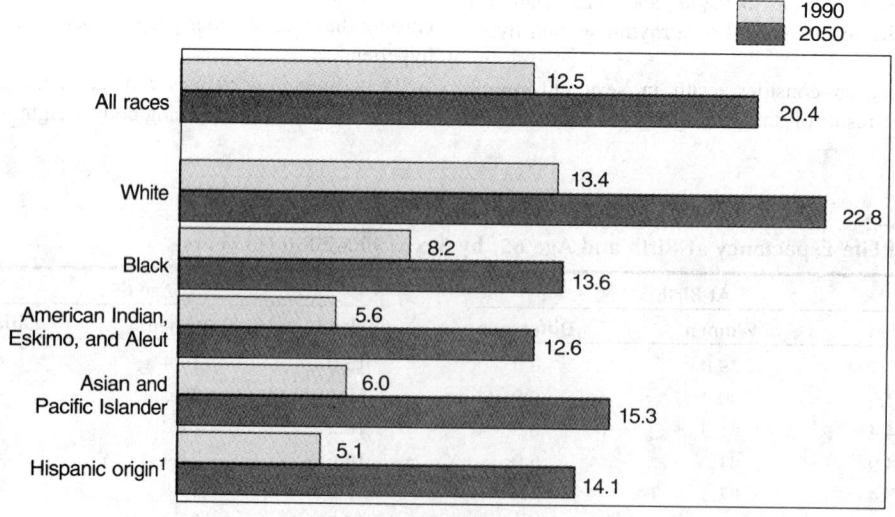

FIGURE 2.6–4

Percent elderly by race and Hispanic origin: 1990 and 2050. (Reprinted from US Bureau of the Census: *65+ in the United States,* p 2–18. Current Population Reports Series. US Government Printing Office, Washington, 1996.)

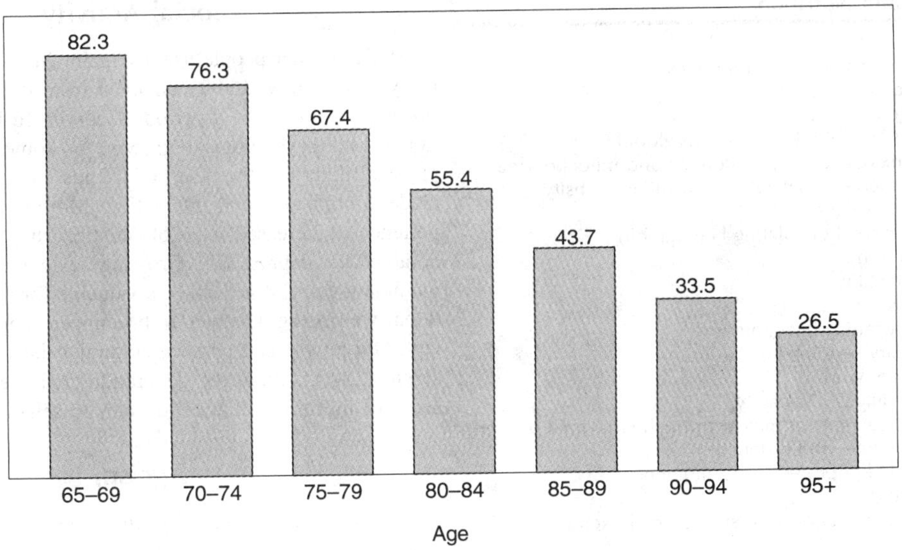
82.3
76.3
67.4
55.4
43.7
33.5
26.5
65–69
70–74
75–79
80–84
85–89
90–94
95+
Age

FIGURE 2.6–5

Number of men per 100 women by age: 1994. (Reprinted from US Bureau of the Census: *65+ in the United States,* p 2–10. Current Population Reports Series. US Government Printing Office, Washington, 1996.)

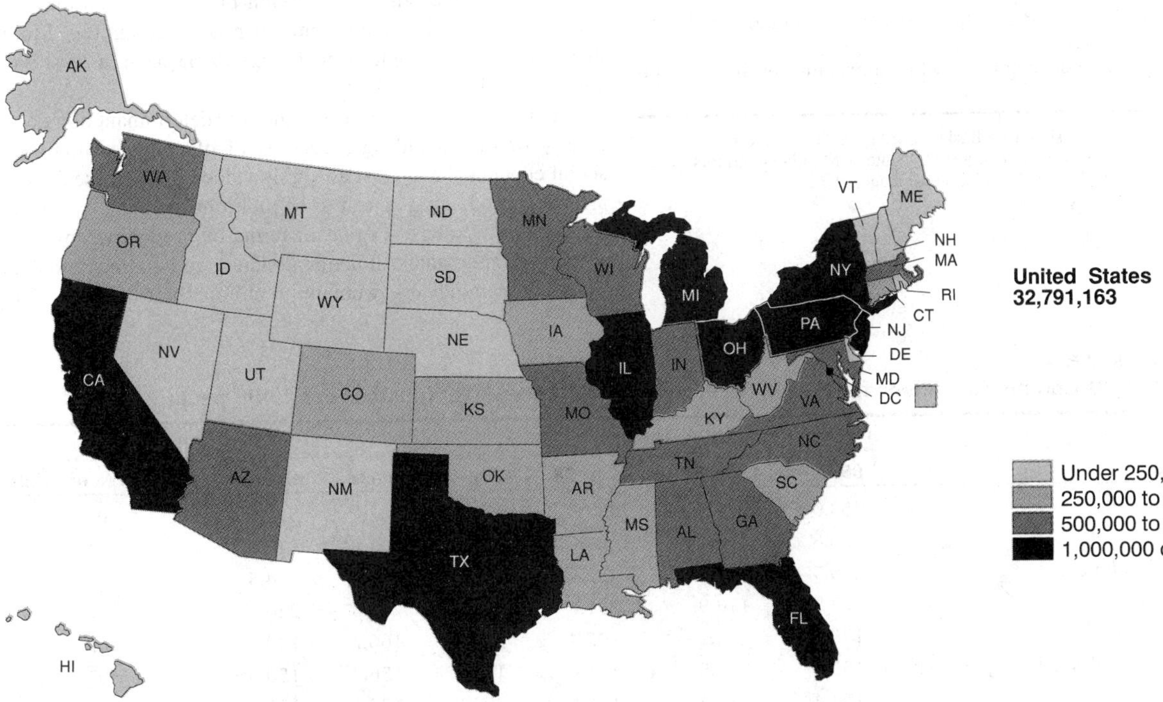
AK
WA
OR
CA
NV
ID
MT
WY
UT
CO
AZ
NM
ND
SD
NE
KS
OK
TX
MN
IA
MO
AR
LA
WI
IL
MS
MI
IN
OH
KY
TN
AL
GA
FL
SC
NC
VA
WV
PA
NY
VT
ME
NH
MA
RI
CT
NJ
DE
MD
DC
HI
United States
32,791,163
Under 250,000
250,000 to 499,999
500,000 to 999,999
1,000,000 or more

FIGURE 2.6–6

Total population aged 65 years and over: 1993. (Reprinted from US Bureau of the Census: *65+ in the United States,* p 5–6. Current Population Reports Series. US Government Printing Office, Washington, 1996.)

Table 2.6–3
Positive and Healthy Physiological Effects of Exercise and Nutrition

Increases
- Strength of bones, ligaments, and muscles
- Muscle mass and body density
- Articular cartilage thickness
- Skeletal muscle ATP, CRP, K+, and myoglobin
- Skeletal muscle oxidative enzyme content and mitochondria
- Skeletal muscle arterial collaterals and capillary density
- Heart volume and weight
- Blood volume and total circulating hemoglobin
- Cardiac stroke volume
- Myocardial contractility
- Maximal CO_2(A-V)
- Maximal blood lactate concentration
- Maximal pulmonary ventilation
- Maximal respiratory work
- Maximal oxygen diffusing capacity
- Maximal exercise capacity as measured by the maximal oxygen intake, exercise time, and distance
- Serum high-density lipoprotein concentration
- Anaerobic threshold
- Plasma insulin concentration with submaximal exercise

Decreases
- Heart rate at rest and during submaximal exercise
- Blood lactate concentration during submaximal exercise
- Pulmonary ventilation during submaximal work
- Respiratory quotient during submaximal work
- Serum triglyceride concentration
- Body fatness
- Serum low-density lipoprotein concentration
- Systolic blood pressure
- Core temperature threshold for initiation of sweating
- Sweat sodium and chloride content
- Plasma epinephrine and norepinephrine with submaximal exercise
- Plasma glucagon and growth hormone concentrations with submaximal exercise
- Relative hemoconcentration with submaximal exercise in the heat

Reprinted with permission from Buskirk ER: In *Diet and Exercise: Synergism in Health Maintenance*, PL White, T Monderka, editors, p 133. American Medical Association, Chicago, 1982.

PSYCHOSOCIAL ASPECTS OF AGING

Social Activity

Healthy older people usually maintain a level of social activity that is only slightly changed from that of earlier years. For many, old age is a period of continued intellectual, emotional, and psychological growth. In some cases, however, physical illness or the death of friends and relatives may preclude continued social interaction. Moreover, as persons experience an increased sense of isolation, they may become vulnerable to depression. Growing evidence indicates that maintaining social activities is valuable for physical and emotional well-being. Contact with younger people is also important. Old people can pass on cultural values and provide care services to the younger generation and thereby maintain a sense of usefulness that contributes to self-esteem.

Ageism

Ageism, a term coined by Butler, refers to the discrimination toward old persons and to the negative stereotypes about old age that are held by younger adults. Old people may themselves resent and fear other old people and discriminate against them. In Butler's scheme, people often associate old age with loneliness, poor health, senility, and general weakness or infirmity. The experience of older people, however, does not consistently support this attitude. For example, although 50 percent of young adults expect poor health to be a problem for those over 65 years old, 75 percent of people 65 to 74 years of age describe their health as good. Two thirds of people 75 and older feel the same way. Health problems, when they do exist, more often involve chronic than acute conditions. More than four of five people over the age of 65 have at least one chronic condition (Table 2.6–4).

Good health, however, is not the sole determinant of a good quality of life in old age. Surveys of old people show that social contacts are at least as highly valued. In fact, the factors affecting good aging appear to be multidimensional. A. J. Garfein defined "robust" aging in terms of productive involvement, affective status, functional status, and cognitive status. These four indicators were only minimally correlated. The

Table 2.6–4
Top 10 Chronic Conditions for People 65+, by Age and Race: 1989 (number per 1,000 people)

	Age				Race (65+)		
Condition	65+	45 to 64	65 to 74	75+	White	Black	Black as % of White
Arthritis	483.0	253.8	437.3	554.5	483.2	522.6	108
Hypertension	380.6	229.1	383.8	375.6	367.4	517.7	141
Hearing impairment	286.5	127.7	239.4	360.3	297.4	174.5	59
Heart disease	278.9	118.9	231.6	353.0	286.5	220.5	77
Cataracts	156.8	16.1	107.4	234.3	160.7	139.8	87
Deformity or orthopedic impairment	155.2	155.5	141.4	177.0	156.2	150.8	97
Chronic sinusitis	153.4	173.5	151.8	155.8	157.1	125.2	80
Diabetes	88.2	58.2	89.7	85.7	80.2	165.9	207
Visual impairment	81.9	45.1	69.3	101.7	81.1	77.0	95
Varicose veins	78.1	57.8	72.6	86.6	80.3	64.0	80

Reprinted from National Center for Health Statistics: Current estimates from the National Health Interview Survey, 1989. In *Vital and Health Statistics*, p 31. National Center for Health Statistics, Washington, 1990.

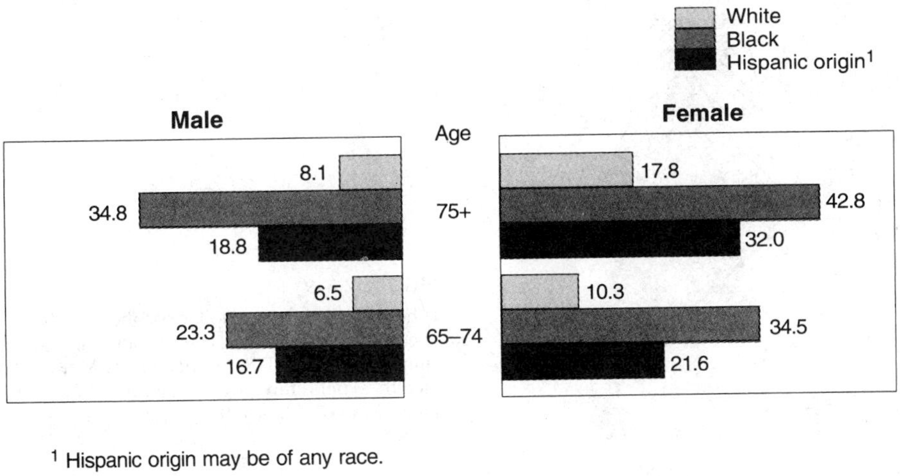
White
Black
Hispanic origin[1]
Male
Age
Female
8.1
34.8
18.8
75+
17.8
42.8
32.0
6.5
23.3
16.7
65–74
10.3
34.5
21.6
[1] Hispanic origin may be of any race.

FIGURE 2.6–7
Percent of poor elderly by age, sex, race, and Hispanic origin: 1992. (Reprinted from US Bureau of the Census: *65+ in the United States,* p 4–19. Current Population Reports Series. Government Printing Office, Washington, 1996.)

most robustly aging individuals reported greater social contact, better health and vision, and fewer significant life events in the past 3 years than did less robustly aging counterparts. There is a linear, age-related decrease in robustness, but it can still be found among the oldest old.

George Vaillant followed up a group of Harvard freshmen into old age and found the following about emotional health at age 65: Having been close to brothers and sisters during college correlated with emotional well-being; undergoing early traumatic life experiences, such as the death of a parent or parental divorce, did not correlate with poor adaptation in old age; being depressed at some point between ages 21 and 50 predicted emotional problems at age 65; and possessing the personality traits of pragmatism and dependability as a young adult was associated with a sense of well-being at age 65.

Countertransference

Physicians' feelings and attitudes toward older people stem from a variety of sources: countertransference, societal attitudes, and patients' attitudes about being old. Countertransference feelings about aging are determined by a physician's needs and past experiences, and they function on both a conscious and an unconscious level. Physicians may have fears about their own old age or may have had conflicts about the aging or death of parents or grandparents. Physicians must be aware of these feelings, especially negative ones: Some older people may act out the poor expectations held by their physicians; they may lose confidence in their abilities and appear to be what, in fact, they are not.

Socioeconomics

The economics of old age is of paramount importance to older people themselves and to society at large. Over the past 30 years there has been a dramatic decline in the proportion of the U.S. elderly population who are poor, primarily as a result of Medicare, Social Security, and private pensions. In 1959, 35.2 percent of people over 65 lived below the poverty line, but by 1995 this figure had declined to 10.5 percent, the first time that the poverty rate for older people dipped below that for people of working age. People over age 65 make up 12 percent of the population, but they include only 9 percent of those living at low socioeconomic levels. Women are more likely than men to be poor (Fig. 2.6–7). Figure 2.6–8 provides income sources for persons of age 65 and older. Despite overall economic gains, many older people are so preoccupied by money worries that their enjoyment of life is lessened. Obtaining proper medical care may be especially difficult when personal funds are not available or sufficient.

Medicare (Title 18) provides both hospital and medical insurance for those over age 65 (Fig. 2.6–9). About 150 million medical bills are reimbursed under the Medicare program each year; but only about 40 percent of all medical expenses incurred by older people is covered under Medicare. The rest is paid by private insurance, state insurance, or personal funds.

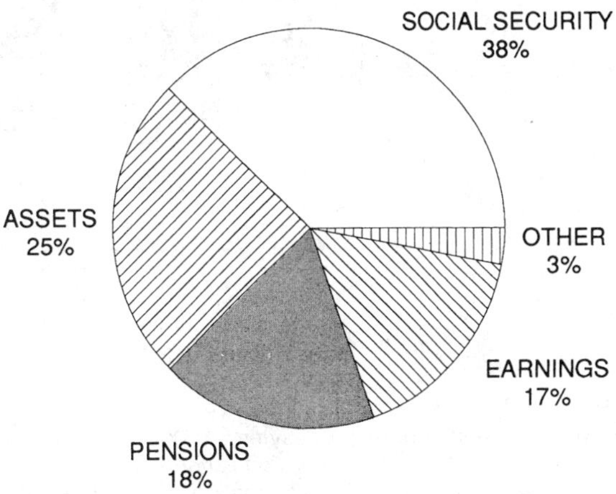
SOCIAL SECURITY
38%
ASSETS
25%
OTHER
3%
EARNINGS
17%
PENSIONS
18%

FIGURE 2.6–8
Income sources of persons age 65+: 1988. (Reprinted from Grad S: *Income of the Population 65 or Over, 1988,* p 26. US Government Printing Office, Washington, 1990.)

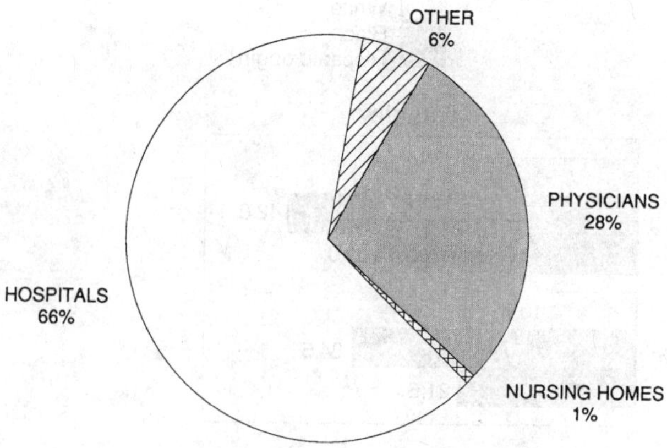
OTHER
6%
PHYSICIANS
28%
HOSPITALS
66%
NURSING HOMES
1%

FIGURE 2.6–9

Where the Medicare dollar for the elderly goes: 1987 (total exceeds 100 percent because of rounding). (Reprinted with permission from Waldo DR, Sonnefeld ST, McKusick DR, Arnett RH III: Health expenditures by age group, 1977 and 1987. Health Care Finan Rev *10:* 98, 1989.)

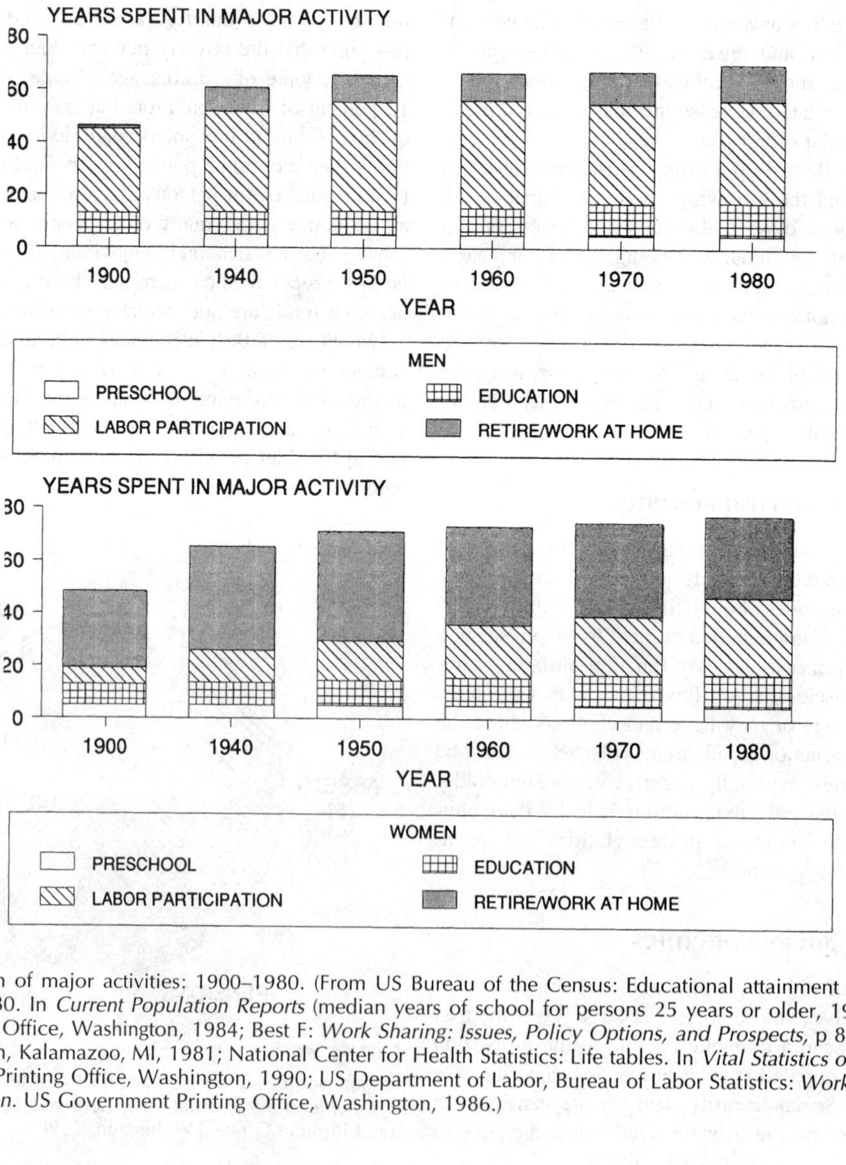
YEARS SPENT IN MAJOR ACTIVITY
80
60
40
20
0
1900
1940
1950
1960
1970
1980
YEAR
MEN
PRESCHOOL
EDUCATION
LABOR PARTICIPATION
RETIRE/WORK AT HOME
YEARS SPENT IN MAJOR ACTIVITY
80
60
40
20
0
1900
1940
1950
1960
1970
1980
YEAR
WOMEN
PRESCHOOL
EDUCATION
LABOR PARTICIPATION
RETIRE/WORK AT HOME

FIGURE 2.6–10

Life cycle distribution of major activities: 1900–1980. (From US Bureau of the Census: Educational attainment in the United States: March 1981 and 1980. In *Current Population Reports* (median years of school for persons 25 years or older, 1940–1980), p 32. US Government Printing Office, Washington, 1984; Best F: *Work Sharing: Issues, Policy Options, and Prospects,* p 8. Upjohn Institute for Employment Research, Kalamazoo, MI, 1981; National Center for Health Statistics: Life tables. In *Vital Statistics of the United States,* p 48. US Government Printing Office, Washington, 1990; US Department of Labor, Bureau of Labor Statistics: *Worklife Estimates: Effects of Race and Education.* US Government Printing Office, Washington, 1986.)

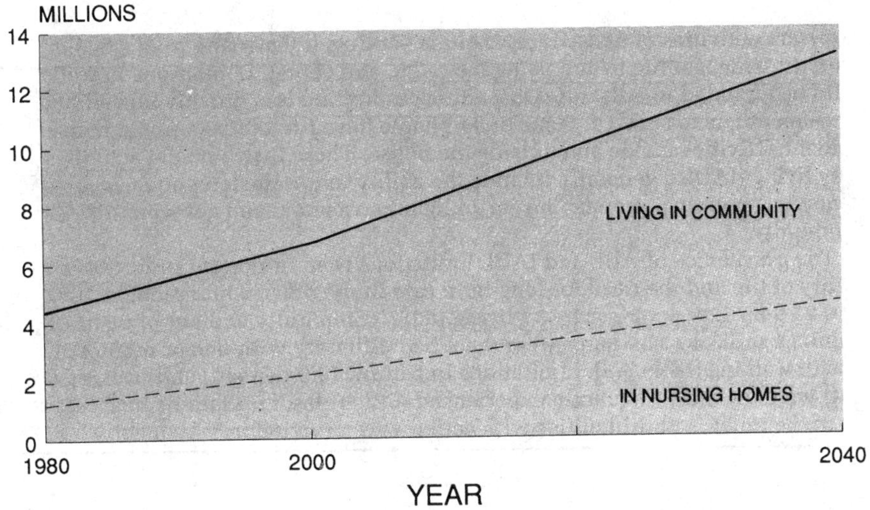
MILLIONS
14
12
10
8
6
4
2
0
1980
2000
2040
YEAR
LIVING IN COMMUNITY
IN NURSING HOMES

FIGURE 2.6–11
People age 65+ in need of long-term care: 1980–2040. (Reproduced with permission from Manton B, Soldo J: Dynamics of health changes in the oldest old: New perspectives and evidence. Milbank Q *63:* 12, 1985.)

Some services—such as outpatient psychiatric treatment, skilled nursing care, physical rehabilitation, and preventive physical examinations—are covered minimally or not at all.

In addition to Medicare, the Social Security program pays benefits to persons over age 65 (over age 66 in the year 2009 and age 67 in 2027) and pays benefits at reduced rates from age 62 on. Benefits payable to retired workers average about $500 a month. To qualify for benefits, a person must have worked long enough to become insured: A worker must have worked for 10 years to be eligible for benefits. Benefits are also paid to widows, widowers, and dependent children if those receiving benefits or contributing to Social Security die (survivor benefits). Social Security is not a pension scheme but a pay-as-you-go income supplement to prevent mass destitution among older people. Benefits are paid by those currently working to those retired. Serious difficulties for Social Security are forecast for the next 3 decades, when the number of baby boomers reaching old age will greatly exceed the number of younger workers paying into the plan.

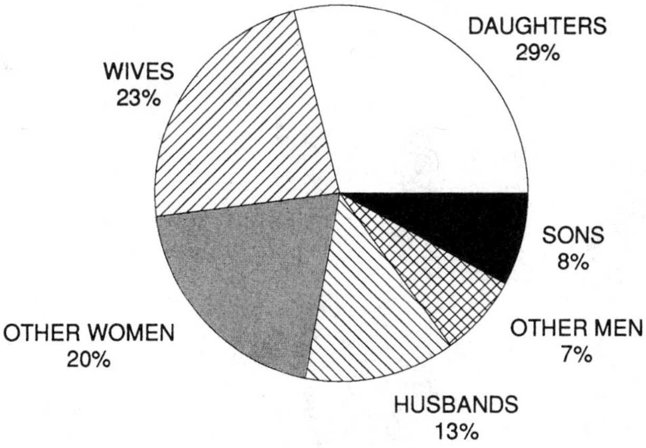
DAUGHTERS
29%
WIVES
23%
SONS
8%
OTHER WOMEN
20%
OTHER MEN
7%
HUSBANDS
13%

FIGURE 2.6–12
Caretakers and their relationship to the elderly care recipient: 1982 (caretaker population includes primary and secondary caretakers). (From Select Committee on Aging, US House of Representatives: *Exploding the Myths: Caregiving in America,* p 60. US Government Printing Office, Washington, 1987.)

Retirement

For many older people, retirement is a time for the pursuit of leisure and for freedom from the responsibility of previous working commitments. For others, it is a time of stress, especially when retirement results in economic problems or a loss of self-esteem. Ideally, employment after age 65 should be a matter of choice. With the passage of the Age Discrimination in Employment Act of 1967 and its amendments, forced retirement at age 70 has been virtually eliminated in the private sector, and it is not legal in federal employment.

Of those who voluntarily retire, a majority reenter the work force within 2 years, for a variety of reasons—negative reactions to being retired, feelings of being unproductive, economic hardship, and loneliness.

The amount of time spent in retirement has increased as the life span has nearly doubled since 1900. Figure 2.6–10 shows the time spent in retirement compared with other activities as part of the life cycle.

Sexual Activity

An estimated 70 percent of men and 20 percent of women over age 60 are sexually active; sexual activity is usually limited by the absence of an available partner. Longitudinal studies have found that the sex drive does not decrease as men and women age; in fact, some report an increase in sex drive. William Masters and Virginia Johnson reported sexual functioning among those in their 80s. Expected physiological changes in men include a longer time for erection to occur, decreased

Table 2.6–5
Old Age Developmental Theorists

Sigmund Freud	Increasing control of the ego and id with aging results in increased autonomy. Regression may permit primitive modes of functioning to reappear.
Erik Erikson	The central conflict in old age is between *integrity,* the sense of satisfaction people feel reflecting on a life productively lived, and *despair,* the sense that life has little purpose or meaning. Contentment in old age comes only with getting beyond narcissism and into intimacy and generativity.
Heinz Kohut	Old people must continually cope with narcissistic injury as they attempt to adapt to the biological, psychological, and social losses associated with the aging process. The maintenance of self-esteem is a major task of old age.
Bernice Neugarten	The major conflict of old age relates to giving up the position of authority and evaluating achievements and former competence. It is a time of reconciliation with others and resolution of grief over the death of others and the approaching death of self.
Daniel Levinson	Ages 60–65 is a transition period ("the late adult transition"). People who are narcissistic and too heavily invested in body appearance are liable to become preoccupied with death. Creative mental activity is a normal and healthy substitute for reduced physical activity.

penile turgidity, and ejaculatory seepage; in women, decreased vaginal lubrication and vaginal atrophy are associated with lowered estrogen levels. Medications can also adversely affect sexual behavior. A significant finding was that the more active a person's sex life was in early adulthood, the more likely it is to be active in old age.

Long-Term Care

Many older people who are infirm require institutional care. Although only 5 percent are institutionalized in nursing homes at any one time, about 35 percent of older people require care in a long-term facility at some time during their lives (Fig. 2.6–11). Older nursing home residents are mainly widowed women, and about 50 percent are over age 85.

Nursing home care costs are not covered by Medicare; they range from $20,000 to $50,000 a year. About 20,000 long-term nursing care institutions are available in the United States—not enough to meet the need. Those older persons who do not require skilled nursing care can be managed in other types of health-related facilities, such as centers they attend during the daytime hours, but the need for care far exceeds the availability of such centers.

Outside institutions, care for older people is provided by their children (primarily their daughters and daughters-in-law), their wives, and other women (Fig. 2.6–12). Over 50 percent of these women caregivers also work in jobs outside the home, and about 40 percent also care for their own children. In general, women end up as caretakers more often than do men because of cultural and societal expectations. According to the American Association of Retired Persons, daughters with jobs spend an average of 12 hours a week providing care and currently spend about $120 a month for travel, telephone calls, special foods, and medication for older people.

PSYCHIATRIC PROBLEMS OF OLDER PEOPLE

Loss is the predominant theme that characterizes the emotional experiences of older people (Table 2.6–5). They must deal with the grief of multiple losses (death of a spouse,

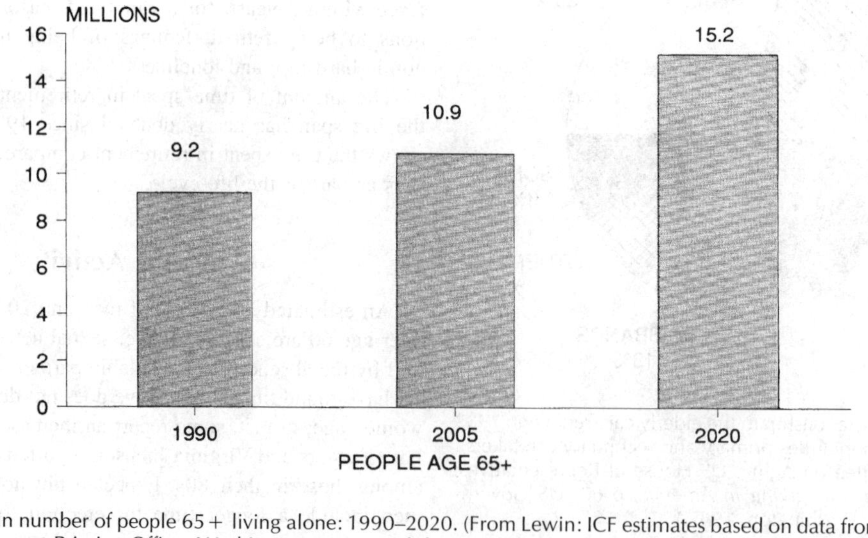
MILLIONS
16
14
12
10
8
6
4
2
0
9.2
10.9
15.2
1990
2005
2020
PEOPLE AGE 65+

FIGURE 2.6–13
Projected increase in number of people 65+ living alone: 1990–2020. (From Lewin: ICF estimates based on data from *Current Population Survey.* US Government Printing Office, Washington, 1990; and the Brookings/ICF Long-Term Care Financing Model, 1990.)

friends, family, and colleagues), change of work status and prestige, and decline of physical abilities and health. They expend enormous amounts of emotional and physical energy in grieving, resolving grief, and adapting to the changes that result from loss. Living alone is a major stress that affects about 10 percent of older people (Fig. 2.6–13). For both sexes the likelihood of living alone increases with age. Thirty two percent of women 65 to 74 years of age live alone, compared with 57 percent of women over 85.

Despite the ubiquity of loss in old age, the prevalence of major depressive disorder and dysthymia is actually less than for younger age groups. Several explanations for this phenomenon have been proposed: rarity of late-onset depression, higher mortality among people with depression, and a general decrease in disorders caused by emotional upheavals or substance abuse in older people. Depression in old people is often accompanied by physical symptoms or cognitive changes that may mimic dementia.

The incidence of suicide among older people is high (40 per 100,000 population) and is highest for older white men. The suicide of older people is perceived differently by surviving friends and family members on the basis of gender: Men are thought to have been physically ill, and women are thought to have been mentally ill.

The relation between good mental and good physical health is clear in older people. Adverse effects on the course of chronic medical illness are correlated with emotional problems. (An extensive discussion of psychiatric problems in older people appears in Chapter 54.)

References

Aging America: Trends and Projections. US Government Printing Office, Washington, 1991.

Andrews GR: Cross-cultural studies: An important development in aging research. J Am Geriatr Soc *37:* 483, 1989.

Blair KA: Aging. Physiological aspects and clinical implications. Nurse Pract *15:* 14, 1990.

Bromley DB: The idea of ageing: An historical and psychological analysis. Compr Gerontol *2:* 30, 1988.

Buagher E, Lamison-White L: *Poverty in the United States: 1995,* p 60–194. Current Population Reports Series, 1995 and 1996. US Bureau of the Census, Washington, 1996.

Busse EW, Pfeiffer, editors: *Behavior and Adaptation in Late Life.* Little, Brown, Boston, 1969.

Butler RN, Lewis MI: *Aging and Mental Health; Positive Psychosocial and Biomedical Approaches,* ed 3. Mosby, St. Louis, 1982.

Casper RC: Nutrition and its relationship to aging. Exp Gerontol *30:* 299, 1995.

Economics and Statistics Administration: *Statistical Brief: Sixty-five plus in the United States.* US Department of Commerce, Washington, 1995.

Erikson EH, Erikson JM, Kivnick HG: *Vital Involvement in Old Age.* Norton, New York, 1986.

Ernst C, Angst J: Depression in old age. Is there a real decrease in prevalence? A review. Eur Arch Psychiatry Clin Neurosci *245:* 272, 1995.

Farquhar M: Elderly people's definitions of quality of life. Soc Sci Med *41:* 1439, 1995.

Garfein AJ, Herzog AR: Robust aging among the young-old, old-old, and oldest-old. J Gerontol B Psychol Sci Soc Sci *50:* S77, 1995.

Nemiroff RA, Colarusso CA: *The Race Against Time: Psychotherapy and Psychoanalysis in the Second Half of Life.* Plenum, New York, 1985.

Pollock GM: Aging or aged: Development or pathology? In *The Course of Life: Psychoanalytic Contributions Toward Understanding Personality Development,* SI Greenspan, GM Pollock, editors, vol 3, p 549. US Department of Health and Human Services, Mental Health Study Center, Adelphi, MD, 1981.

Pruchno R, Kleban MH: Caring for an institutionalized parent: The role of coping strategies. Psychol Aging *8:* 18, 1993.

Rinn WE: Mental decline in normal aging: A review. J Geriatr Psychiatry Neurol *1:* 144, 1988.

Schiavi RC, Schreiner-Engel P, Mandeli J, Schanzer H, Cohen E: Healthy aging and male sexual function. Am J Psychiatry *147:* 766, 1990.

Stoller EP, Forster E, Portugal S: Self-care responses to symptoms by older people: A healthy diary study of illness behavior. Med Care *31:* 24, 1993.

Uchino BN, Keicolt-Glaser JK, Cacioppo JT: Age-related changes in cardiovascular response as a function of a chronic stressor and social support. J Pers Soc Psychol *63:* 839, 1992.

West RL, Crook TH, Barron KL: Everyday memory performance across the life span: Effects of age and noncognitive individual differences. Psychol Aging *7:* 72, 1992.

▲ 2.7 Thanatology: Death and Bereavement

Thanatology, the study of the experiences of dying and bereavement, has evolved in the last several decades. Although people in every culture have always speculated about death, religion and philosophy have been considered the proper areas for dealing with the subject. Systematic study of death has been avoided until the late 20th century, and even now people in Western cultures often resist exploring their own mortality. Nonetheless, researchers have begun to develop a psychology of death as well as therapies and other treatments for both those who are dying and those who will be bereaved.

Most practicing physicians regularly confront death, dying, and grief; these phenomena are ongoing realities in their lives. Nevertheless, medical training programs often address this reality inadequately so that doctors must learn to contend with the problems of death on their own. As a result, the treatment of dying patients can be needlessly painful for patients, family and friends, physicians, and medical personnel. Thus, in addition to thanatology per se, physicians must study the reactions of caretakers to death and grief in their work with patients and must explore the ways that caretakers can learn to accept their own fears and sense of loss.

REACTIONS TO DEATH

People react to death partly according to its context. For instance, people may experience death as timely or untimely: *timely* when a person's expected survival and actual lifespan are approximately equal; and *untimely* when a person's death is unexpected or premature. Those left to grieve a timely death are usually not surprised or shocked by it, unlike those who grieve an untimely death, such as that of a young person, a person who dies suddenly, or a person whose catastrophic death is associated with violence, an accident, or utter meaninglessness.

Death can also be thought of as intentional (suicide), unintentional (trauma or disease), and subintentional (substance abuse, alcohol dependence, cigarette smoking). Death may have multiple psychological meanings, both for the person who is dying and for society in general. In Susan Sontag's formulation, death may even take on the power of metaphor. For example, some view death as deserved punishment for what are perceived as immoral or sinful lifestyles.

PSYCHOGENIC DEATH

Emotional factors alone may be sufficient to trigger sudden death in certain people not otherwise at risk. For instance, ventricular fibrillation and myocardial infarction may follow sudden psychic stress. Voodoo death or death secondary to a hex occurs when a person who is thought to have the psychic power to cause death puts a curse on another who believes in the person's power. In such cases, the hypothalamic-pituitary-adrenal axis and the autonomic nervous system probably become dysfunctional because of emotional stress, which causes the cessation of vital functions. Unless a healer removes the curse, a person under such a spell or hex may die.

Out-of-Body Experiences

Many people believe in an afterlife, and afterlife phenomena have been reported throughout history. In recent years large numbers of people have claimed near-death experiences: As many as 40 percent of people in the United States have described such events. The manner of the brush with death (illness, accident, or attempted suicide), the demographics (age, education, race, sex), and religious beliefs did not predispose one group over another to report the events.

Descriptions of near-death experience are often strikingly similar; they can involve an out-of-body experience of a person's viewing his or her own body and overhearing conversations; feelings of peace and quiet; hearing a distant noise; entering a dark tunnel; leaving the body behind; meeting dead loved ones; witnessing beings of light; returning to life to complete unfinished business; and a deep sadness on leaving the new dimension. The experience is almost always described as peaceful and loving; it feels real to the participants, who distinguish it from dreams and hallucinations. Such experiences may provoke sweeping lifestyle changes. Because they have been widely reported in the popular press, patients may want to discuss such events with their physicians.

LEGAL ASPECTS OF DEATH

According to law, physicians must sign the death certificate, which attests to the cause of death (for example, congestive heart failure or pneumonia). They must also classify death as occurring from natural, accidental, suicidal, homicidal, or unknown causes. Anyone who dies unattended by a physician must be examined by the appointed medical examiner, coroner, or pathologist; an autopsy must be performed to determine the cause of death. In some cases, a *psychological autopsy* is performed: A person's sociocultural and psychological background is examined retrospectively by interviewing friends, relatives, and doctors to determine whether a mental illness, such as a depressive disorder, was present. A determination can be made that a person died because he or she was pushed (murder) or because he or she jumped (suicide) from a high building. Each situation has clear medical and legal implications.

IMPENDING DEATH

Many researchers have studied dying people's reactions to death; an early and useful organization of reactions to impending death was made by the psychiatrist and thanatologist Elisabeth Kübler-Ross. Seldom does a dying patient follow a regular series of responses that can be clearly identified; no established sequence is applicable to all patients. Nevertheless, the following five stages proposed by Kübler-Ross are widely encountered.

Stage 1—Shock and Denial

On being told that they are dying, people initially react with shock. They may appear dazed at first and then may refuse to believe the diagnosis; they may deny that anything is wrong. Some people never pass beyond this stage and may go from doctor to doctor until they find one who supports their position. The degree to which denial is adaptive or maladaptive appears to depend on whether a patient continues to obtain treatment even while denying the prognosis. In such cases, physicians must communicate to patients and their families, respectfully and directly, basic information about the illness, its prognosis, and the options for treatment. Inherent in effective communication is physicians' allowing for patients' emotional responses and reassuring them that they will not be abandoned.

Stage 2—Anger

People become frustrated, irritable, and angry that they are ill. They commonly ask, "Why me?" They may become angry at God, their fate, a friend, or a family member; they may even blame themselves. They may displace their anger onto the hospital staff members and the doctor, whom they blame for the illness. Patients in the stage of anger are difficult to treat. Doctors who have difficulty in understanding that anger is a predictable reaction and is really a displacement may withdraw from patients or transfer them to other doctors' care.

Physicians treating angry patients must realize that the anger being expressed cannot be taken personally. An empathic, nondefensive response can help defuse patients' anger and can help them refocus on their own deep feelings (such as grief, fear, loneliness) that underlie the anger. Physicians should also recognize that anger may represent patients' desires for control in a situation in which they feel completely out of control.

Stage 3—Bargaining

Patients may attempt to negotiate with physicians, friends, or even God: In return for a cure, they promise to fulfill one or many pledges, such as giving to charity and attending church regularly. Another aspect of bargaining is that patients believe that, if they are good (compliant, nonquestioning, cheerful), the doctor will make them better. The treatment of such patients involves making it clear that they will be taken care of to the best of the doctor's abilities and that everything that can be done will be done, regardless of any action or behavior on the patients' part. Patients must also be encouraged to participate as partners in their treatment and to understand that being a good patient means being as honest and straightforward as possible.

Stage 4—Depression

In the fourth stage, patients show clinical signs of depression—withdrawal, psychomotor retardation, sleep disturbances, hopelessness, and, possibly, suicidal ideation. The depression may be a reaction to the effects of the illness on their lives (for example, the loss of jobs, economic hardship, helplessness, hopelessness, and isolation from friends and family), or it may be in anticipation of the loss of life that will eventually occur. When a major depressive disorder with vegetative signs and suicidal ideation develops, treatment with antidepressant medication or electroconvulsive therapy (ECT) may be indicated. All people feel some degree of sadness at the prospect of their own deaths, and normal sadness does not require biological intervention. But major depressive disorder and active suicidal ideation can be alleviated and should not be accepted as mere normal reactions to impending death. A person who suffers from major depressive disorder may be unable to sustain hope, which can alter longevity and can enhance the dignity and quality of life.

Stage 5—Acceptance

In this stage, patients realize that death is inevitable, and they accept the universality of the experience. Their feelings may range from a neutral to a euphoric mood. Under ideal circumstances, patients resolve their feelings about the inevitability of death and are able to talk about facing the unknown. Those with strong religious beliefs and a conviction of life after death can find comfort in the ecclesiastical maxim: Fear not death; remember those who have gone before you and those who will come after.

COMPASSIONATE CARE

Physicians' abilities to care compassionately and effectively for patients who are dying depend, in large part, on their awareness of their own attitudes toward death and dying. Some physicians have dysfunctional attitudes about death and the dying patient that may be reinforced by their medical training. When training focuses almost entirely on the control and eradication of disease at the expense of the care and comfort of the person with the disease, death, and dying, the patients become the enemy. They may be equated with failure and may thus reflect the doctor's inadequacy and limitations. When this reaction occurs, it is no surprise that the dying patient is avoided or is experienced as a source of irritation, impatience, and fear.

Because of their extensive knowledge of the human body and their technical expertise in controlling many disease states, physicians may unconsciously begin to feel omnipotent and all powerful about preventing death. When these physicians confront death, they may feel threatened and defensive because their self-image has been badly injured. These physicians view dying patients as painful reminders of their own fallibility.

Some physicians enter the practice of medicine because of their own unconscious fears of death. These doctors unconsciously hope that, through the study and mastery of medicine, they may achieve some control over their own mortality. Although these doctors must deal with dying patients, they may feel an inordinate amount of anxiety, coupled with a strong need to avoid them. These physicians may attempt to deal with their underlying fear of death through extensive intellectualization; for instance, they may provide dying patients with minute and often unnecessary details about the day-to-day vicissitudes of the illness while sidestepping any discussion of the patients' fears, worries, and feelings.

The major task of physicians caring for dying patients is to provide compassionate concern and continuing support. The hallmarks of appropriate care are visiting the patients regularly, maintaining eye contact, touching appropriately, listening to what the patients have to say, and being willing to answer all questions in as respectful a way as possible. Tactful honesty is doctors' most important aid. Most patients want their doctors to be truthful with them; they prefer to know, for example, that they have cancer. Honesty, however, does not preclude hope. If 85 percent of patients with a particular disease die in 5 years, 15 percent are still alive after that time. Doctors may ask patients how much they want to know about the illness and should respond to patients' wishes; some people do not want to know the facts of their illness.

Physicians must consider other factors in caring for patients who are dying. Pain management should be vigorous for those who are terminally ill. People who are dying need to function as effectively as possible and can do so more easily when they are relatively free of pain. Physicians should use narcotics as liberally as they are needed and tolerated, so that patients can attend to any business with a minimum of discomfort. In addition, physicians should not take personally the complaints of a patient who may be in the anger phase of dying and should help the members of the dying patient's family deal with their feelings about the patient's illness. Family members are the main source of emotional support for many patients and are far more available to and knowledgeable about the patient than is the doctor on the case.

Family Interventions

The first step in working with the family members of a patient who is dying is to develop an alliance with them by allowing the family members to talk about their own lives and stresses and by offering them understanding. Physicians should try to assess to what degree the family members want direction or help and to what degree they prefer a sense of autonomy.

At times of great external stress, such as the impending death of a family member, family conflicts may intensify. A physician can help the family refocus attention on confronting the external stress rather than on mutual blame and argument. Opening communication channels among family members can be helpful.

Family members may be reluctant to talk to patients who are dying about their impending death for fear of being too upset themselves or of upsetting the patients. Conversely, people who are dying may be reluctant to talk about their own impending death for fear of burdening the family. In this situation a physician can let each party know what the others are feeling and can encourage discussion or even raise the topic when all parties are present.

DEATH CRITERIA AND LIVING WILLS

The Uniform Determination of Death Act states that "an individual who has sustained either (a) irreversible cessation of circulatory and respiratory functions, or (b) cessation of function of the entire brain, including the brain stem, is dead.

Table 2.7–1
Advance Directive Living Will and Health Care Proxy

Death is a part of life. It is a reality like birth, growth and aging. I am using this advance directive to convey my wishes about medical care to my doctors and other people looking after me at the end of my life. It is called an advance directive because it gives instructions in advance about what I want to happen to me in the future. It expresses my wishes about medical treatment that might keep me alive. I want this to be legally binding.

If I cannot make or communicate decisions about my medical care, those around me should rely on this document for instructions about measures that could keep me alive.

I do not want medical treatment (including feeding and water by tube) that will keep me alive if:

- I am unconscious and there is no reasonable prospect that I will ever be conscious again (even if I am not going to die soon in my medical condition), or
- I am near death from an illness or injury with no reasonable prospect of recovery.

I do want medicine and other care to make me more comfortable and to take care of pain and suffering. I want this even if the pain medicine makes me die sooner.

I want to give some extra instructions: *[Here list any special instructions, eg, some people fear being kept alive after a debilitating stroke. If you have wishes about this, or any other condition, please write them here.]*

The legal language in the box that follows is a health care proxy. It gives another person the power to make medical decisions for me.

I name ______________________________,
who lives at ______________________________,
phone number ________________, to make medical decisions for me if I cannot make them myself. This person is called a health care "surrogate," "agent," "proxy," or "attorney in fact." This power of attorney shall become effective when I become incapable of making or communicating decisions about my medical care. This means that this document stays legal when and if I lose the power to speak for myself, for instance, if I am in a coma or have Alzheimer's disease.

My health care proxy has power to tell others what my advance directive means. This person also has power to make decisions for me based either on what I would have wanted, or, if this is not known, on what he or she thinks is best for me.

If my first choice health care proxy cannot or decides not to act for me, I name ______________________________,
address ______________________________,
phone number ________________, as my second choice

I have discussed my wishes with my health care proxy, and with my second choice if I have chosen to appoint a second person. My proxy(ies) has(have) agreed to act for me.

I have thought about this advance directive carefully. I know what it means and want to sign it. I have chosen two witnesses, neither of whom is a member of my family, nor will inherit from me when I die. My witnesses are not the same people as those I named as my health care proxies. I understand that this form should be notarized if I use the box to name (a) health care proxy(ies).

Signature ______________________________
Date ______________________________
Address ______________________________
Witness' signature ______________________________
Witness' printed name ______________________________
Address ______________________________
Witness' signature ______________________________
Witness' printed name ______________________________
Address ______________________________
Notary [to be used if proxy is appointed] ______________________________

 (Choice in Dying is a national not-for-profit organization that works for the rights of patients at the end of life. In addition to this generic advance directive, Choice in Dying distributes advance directives that conform to each state's specific legal requirements and maintains a national Living Will Registry for completed documents.)

A determination of death must be made in accordance with acceptable medical standards."

Physicians must anticipate the wishes of patients and their families about the use of life-sustaining procedures. Moreover, physicians should discuss the patients' wishes with the patients and family members while the patients are still competent. Patients may ask that their lives not be prolonged by artificial means (for example, "Do not resuscitate [DNR] if in extremis").

Living wills are legal documents in which patients give instructions to their physicians about withholding life-support measures. But physicians must use their best judgment, even in the absence of a living will. If major questions arise about any decisions, physicians should consult the hospital administrators or lawyers. A sample living will and health care proxy is given in Table 2.7–1.

The American Medical Association states that doctors can withhold all means of life-prolonging medical treatment, including food and water, from patients in irreversible comas, provided adequate safeguards are taken to confirm the accuracy of the diagnosis. This decision is made in conjunction with the patient's family or legal guardians. In such cases, a physician lets a terminally ill patient die; the physician does not intentionally cause death. Persons are brain dead when they suffer irreversible cessation of the functions of the entire brain, including the brain stem, even if the heart and the lungs continue to function.

ATTITUDES TOWARD DEATH ACROSS THE LIFE CYCLE

The stages of children's emotional and cognitive development play a significant role in their perception, interpretation, and understanding of death. Children's ability to understand death reflects their ability to understand any abstract concept. Preschool children under the age of 5 years (Jean Piaget's preoperational phase) are animistic: They believe that everything, even an inanimate object, is alive, and they are aware of death only in the sense that it is a separation similar to sleep. Between the ages of 5 and 10 years (concrete operations), children have a developing sense of inevitable human mortality; they fear that their parents will die and that they will be abandoned. Around the age of 9 or 10, children conceptualize death as something that can happen to a child as well as to a parent. Usually by puberty, children are able to conceptualize death as universal, irreversible, and inevitable, as do adults.

In contrast to parents in other parts of the world, middle-class parents in the United States tend to shield children from a knowledge of death. Rather than protecting children, the air of mystery surrounding death in such instances may create irrational fears in them.

Adolescents may be preoccupied with issues related to body image and control of the environment; thus, they may appear to focus on what adults perceive to be concerns more trivial than death itself. Treating dying adolescents may be difficult because of their intense need at times for independence and control.

Young adults, in Erikson's stage of intimacy versus isolation, are in the process of developing new, deep relationships. They may focus on such issues as missing the chance to marry or to have children and therefore may feel threatened by the potential isolation. Young adult parents fear that their untimely deaths will result in their children's growing up alone. They also fear that they will not experience the role of grandparent.

Middle-aged adults, in Erikson's stage of generativity versus stagnation, may feel frustrated in their hopes to become involved with the next generation and in their plans to enjoy hard-earned pleasure. Older people, facing Erikson's stage of conflict between integrity and despair, must confront the increasing reality of their own mortality through the deaths of family members and friends.

Children with fatal illnesses create major emotional stresses on their caretakers, be they parents, relatives, hospital staff members, or physicians. A consistently present, trusted person is essential in providing optimal care for a dying child. The separation of a child from its mother is as traumatic an event for the hospitalized child as the illness itself, perhaps even more so. As John Bowlby pointed out, having the mother or an equally valued and familiar caretaker room with a hospitalized child can help alleviate the child's anxiety and can facilitate necessary medical care.

GRIEF, MOURNING, AND BEREAVEMENT

Grief, mourning, and bereavement are terms that apply to the psychological reactions of those who survive a significant loss. *Grief* is the subjective feeling precipitated by the death of a loved one. The term is used synonymously with mourning, although, in the strictest sense, *mourning* is the process by which grief is resolved; it is the societal expression of post-bereavement behavior and practices. *Bereavement* literally means the state of being deprived of someone by death and refers to being in the state of mourning. Regardless of the fine points that differentiate these terms, there are sufficient similarities in the experiences of grief and bereavement to warrant a syndrome that has signs, symptoms, a demonstrable course, and an expected resolution.

The expression of grief encompasses a wide range of emotions, depending on cultural norms and expectations (for example, some cultures encourage or demand an intense display of emotions, whereas others expect just the opposite) and on the circumstances of the loss (for example, a sudden unexpected death versus one that is clearly anticipated). Grief work is a complex psychological process of withdrawing attachment and working through the pain of bereavement. (Grief and bereavement are discussed further in Chapter 30.) Figure 2.7–1 summarizes one concept of some recognizable and predictable manifestations of the phases of uncomplicated grief.

Normal Grief

Uncomplicated grief is a normal response in view of the predictability of its symptoms and its course. Initial grief is often manifested as a state of shock that may be expressed as a feeling of numbness and a sense of bewilderment. This apparent inability to comprehend what has happened may be short lived and is followed by such expressions of suffering and distress as sighing and crying; in Western cultures this feature of grief is less common among men than among women. Feelings of weakness, decreased appetite, weight loss, and difficulty in concentrating, breathing, and talking also appear. Sleep disturbances may include difficulty in falling asleep, waking up during the night, and awakening early. Dreams of the deceased person often occur, after which the dreamer awakens with a sense of disappointment in finding that the experience was only a dream.

Self-reproach is common, although it is less intense in normal than in pathological grief. Self-reproachful thoughts usually center on some relatively minor act of omission or commission toward the deceased. A phenomenon known as *survivor guilt* occurs in those who are relieved that someone other than they themselves has died. Survivors sometimes believe that they should have been the person who died and may (if the guilt persists) have difficulty in establishing new intimate relationships from fear of betraying the deceased person. Forms of denial occur throughout the period of bereavement; often, the bereaved person inadvertently denies the death or

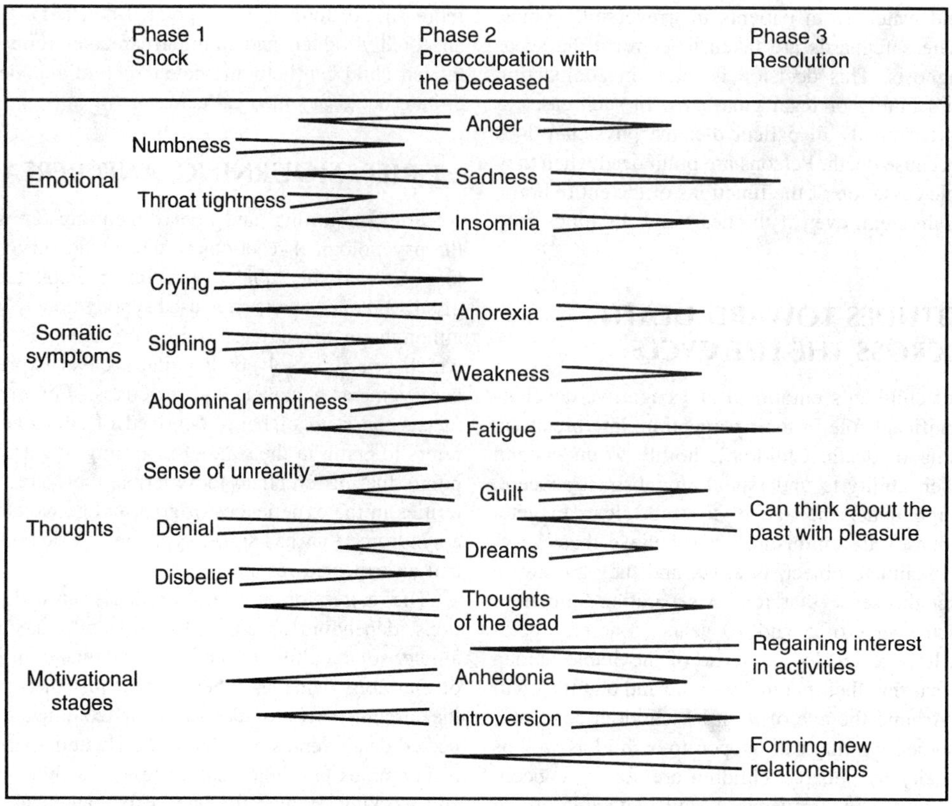
Phase 1
Shock
Phase 2
Preoccupation with the Deceased
Phase 3
Resolution
Emotional
Numbness
Throat tightness
Anger
Sadness
Insomnia
Somatic symptoms
Crying
Sighing
Abdominal emptiness
Anorexia
Weakness
Fatigue
Thoughts
Sense of unreality
Denial
Disbelief
Guilt
Dreams
Thoughts of the dead
Can think about the past with pleasure
Motivational stages
Anhedonia
Introversion
Regaining interest in activities
Forming new relationships

FIGURE 2.7–1
Phases of uncomplicated grief. (Reprinted with permission from Brown JT, Stoudemire A: Normal and pathological grief. JAMA *250:* 378, 1983.)

acts as if the loss had not occurred. Efforts to perpetuate the lost relationship are evidenced by an investment in objects that were treasured by the deceased person or that remind the grief-stricken person of the one who has died (linkage objects).

A sense of the deceased person's presence may be so intense that it constitutes an illusion or a hallucination (for example, hearing the deceased person's voice or feeling the person's presence). In normal grief, however, the survivor realizes that the perception is not real. As part of what has been labeled *identification phenomena,* a survivor may take on the qualities, mannerisms, or characteristics of the deceased person to perpetuate the person in some concrete way. This maneuver can reach potentially pathological expression with the development of physical symptoms similar to those that were experienced by the person who died or to ones suggestive of the illness from which the deceased person died.

Bowlby hypothesized four stages of bereavement: *Stage 1* is an early phase of acute despair characterized by numbness and protest. Denial may be immediate, and outbursts of anger and distress are common. The stage may last moments to days and may be periodically revisited by the grieving person throughout the mourning process. *Stage 2* is a phase of intense yearning and searching for the person who has died. It is characterized by a physical restlessness and an all-consuming preoccupation with the deceased. The phase may last several months or even years in an attenuated form. In *Stage 3,* which has been described as a phase of disorganization and despair, the reality of the loss begins to sink in. A sense of going through the motions of living is dominant, and the grieving person appears to be withdrawn, apathetic, and listless. Insomnia and weight loss often occur, as does a feeling that life has lost its meaning. The grieving person constantly relives memories of the deceased; an associated inevitable feeling of disappointment occurs when the bereaved person recognizes that the memories are just memories. *Stage 4* is a phase of reorganization during which the acutely painful aspects of grief begin to recede and the grieving person begins to feel like returning to life. The deceased person is now remembered with a sense of joy as well as sadness, and the image of the lost person becomes internalized.

Grief Period

Because people vary greatly in their expressions of grief, the signs, symptoms, and phases of mourning and bereavement are not as discrete as their characterizations may imply. Nevertheless, the manifestations of grief usually tend to subside over time. The length and intensity of grief, especially the acute phases, can be shaped by the suddenness of the death. If death occurs without warning, shock and disbelief may last for a long time; when death has been long anticipated, much of the mourning process may have already occurred by the time death intervenes. Traditionally, grief lasts about 6 months to 1 year, as the grieving person experiences the calendar year at least once without the lost person. Some signs and symptoms of grief may persist much longer than 1 or 2 years, and a survivor may have various grief-related feelings, symptoms, and behavior throughout life. Eventually, however, normal grief resolves, and people return to a state of productivity and relative well-being. In general, the acute grief symptoms gradually lessen, and within 1 or 2 months the grieving person is able to eat, sleep, and return to functioning.

Anticipatory Grief

Anticipatory grief is expressed in advance of a loss perceived as inevitable, as distinguished from grief that occurs at or after the loss. By definition, anticipatory grief ends with the occurrence of the anticipated loss, regardless of what reactions follow. Unlike conventional grief, which diminishes in intensity with the passage of time, anticipatory grief may either increase or decrease in intensity as the expected loss becomes imminent. In some instances, particularly when the occurrence of the loss is delayed, anticipatory grief may be expended, and the bereaved person shows few manifestations of acute grief when the loss occurs. Once anticipatory grief has been expended, the bereaved person may find it difficult to reestablish a previous relationship; this phenomenon is experienced with the return of persons long gone (for example, to war or confined to concentration camps) and of persons thought to have been dead.

Pathological (Abnormal) Grief

For some people the course of grief and mourning is abnormal. Pathological grief can take several forms, ranging from absent or delayed grief to excessively intense and prolonged grief to grief associated with suicidal ideation or frank psychotic symptoms. Those at greatest risk for an abnormal grief reaction are those who suffer a loss suddenly or through horrific circumstances, those who are socially isolated, those who believe they are responsible (whether the responsibility is real or imagined) for the death, those with a history of traumatic losses, and those with an intensely ambivalent or dependent relationship to the person who died.

Some relationships, regardless of their public appearances, are sufficiently negative to render reduced or absent grief a normal and appropriate response. In these cases, the consequences of the death of a spouse or a parent may be decidedly positive for the survivor.

Other forms of abnormal grief occur when some of the aspects of normal grieving are distorted or intensified to psychotic proportions. Identifying with the deceased person, such as taking on certain admired traits or treasuring certain possessions, is normal; a person's believing that he or she is the deceased or is dying of exactly what the deceased person died of (if, in fact, this is untrue) is not normal. Hearing a fleeting, transient voice of a deceased person may be normal; persistent, intrusive, complex auditory hallucinations are not normal. Denial of certain aspects of the death is normal; denial that includes the belief that the dead person is still alive is not normal.

Grief versus Depression

Grief and depression share many features: sadness, tearfulness, loss of appetite, poor sleep, diminished interest in the world. There are, however, sufficient differences that psychiatrists regard them as separate syndromes. The mood disturbance in depression is typically pervasive and unremitting. If there are mood fluctuations, they are relatively minor. Fluctuations in grief are common. People often describe grief coming in waves, washing over them, and then subsiding. Even in intense grief, moments of lightheartedness and happy reminiscence are possible.

Shame and guilt are common in depression. When they occur in grief, it is usually because of not having done enough for the deceased before his or her death, rather than because of a person's fundamental belief that he or she is wicked or worthless, so common in depression. Of great importance is the realization that grief is time limited. Many people suffering from major depression are hopeless: They cannot imagine ever feeling better. People who have experienced previous depressions are at risk for becoming depressed at times of major loss, and a bereaved person's clinical history may be helpful in judging a current reaction. Depressed persons threaten suicide more often than do grieving persons, who, except in unusual instances—for example, physically dependent and older persons—do not seriously wish to die, even if they claim that life is unbearable.

Physicians must determine when grief has become pathological and has evolved into major depressive disorder. Grief is a normal, albeit intensely painful, state that is responsive to support, empathy, and the passage of time. Major depressive disorder is potentially a medical emergency that requires immediate intervention to forestall a complication like suicide.

Childhood Grief

Bowlby also studied the bereavement process in children, a process similar to that in adults, especially once a child can understand the irrevocability of death. The mourning process resembles that of separation in that there are three phases: protest, despair, and detachment. In the *protest phase,* a child has a strong desire for the mother or other caretaker who died and cries for her return; in the *despair phase,* a child begins to feel hopeless about the mother's return, crying is intermittent, and withdrawal and apathy set in. In the *detachment phase,* a child begins to relinquish some emotional attachment to the dead parent and to show a reawakening of interest in the surroundings.

In dealing with bereaved children, physicians should recognize the children's need to find a person to substitute for the lost parent. Children may transfer their need for a parent to several adults rather than to one. If there is no consistently available person, severe psychological damage to the children may result, so that they no longer look for or expect intimacy in any relationship. The importance of managing grief reactions in children is highlighted by the increased evidence that depressive disorders and suicide attempts occur more frequently in adults who in early childhood experienced the death of a parent.

The question of whether children should attend funerals is

a common one, and no hard and fast rule is available. Most child experts agree that, if a child expresses a desire to go, the wish should be respected; if a child is reluctant or refuses to go, this wish should also be respected. In most circumstances it is probably best to encourage a child to attend so that the ritual is not enveloped in a frightening and distorted fantasy or mystery.

Parental Grief

Parents react to a child's death or to the birth of a malformed infant in stages similar to those that Kübler-Ross described in terminal illness: shock, denial, anger, bargaining, depression, and acceptance. The death of a child is often a more intense emotional experience than the death of an adult. Parental feelings of guilt and helplessness may be overwhelming; parents may believe that somehow they did not protect their children and have unnaturally outlived them. Lost hopes, wishes, and fulfillments associated with a new generation cause additional pain. Manifestations of the grief may well last a lifetime.

A sudden death is often more traumatic than a prolonged death, because anticipatory grief can occur when death is expected. A parent may become overprotective toward a dying child or shower the child with gifts that were previously denied. The stress of dealing with a child's death may cause a marriage that has had conflicts to disintegrate. One parent may blame the other for the child's fatal illness, especially if the child's disease had a hereditary basis. Physicians should be alert to these patterns of dissension. Some studies indicate that up to 50 percent of marriages in which a child dies or is born malformed end in divorce.

Psychodynamics

In 1917, Freud wrote in *Mourning and Melancholia* that normal grief (mourning) results from the withdrawal of the libido from its attachment to the lost object. In normal mourning, the loss is clearly and unambivalently perceived, and the person who died is eventually, through the grief work, internalized as a loving and loved object. In abnormal grief (melancholia), the lost object is not given up but is incorporated in the survivor's psyche as an object infused with negative feelings. These negative feelings toward the deceased person are experienced as part of the self, and the survivor becomes depressed, has low self-esteem, feels worthless, and becomes self-accusatory, with possible delusional expectations of punishment. Freud's distinction between mourning and melancholia is still considered valid—that is, an exaggerated loss of self-esteem is not part of normal grieving.

Other psychoanalytic theorists have stressed the role of unconscious dynamics in grief reactions. The greater the role of unconscious and ambivalent factors (for example, anger toward a person who died), the greater is the likelihood of an abnormal grief reaction. Karl Abraham described the introjection of an ambivalently loved lost object and the subsequent direction of anger toward the introjected object.

Biology of Grief

Grief is a physiological as well as an emotional response. During acute grief (as with other stressful events), people may suffer disruption of biological rhythms. Grief is also accompanied by impaired immune functioning: decreased lymphocyte proliferation and impaired functioning of natural killer cells. Whether the immune changes are clinically significant has not been established, but the mortality rate for widows and widowers following the death of a spouse is increased compared to the general population. Widowers appear to be at risk longer than are widows.

How to Deal with Grief

Physicians play an important role in dealing with bereaved spouses, relatives, and friends. First, they may have to prepare the family for the probability that a loved one will die. In the event of a patient's death, a physician should encourage the family's ventilation of feelings. If this emotional expression is inhibited, in all likelihood the feelings will later be intensely expressed. Outcomes of bereavement are most favorable if a grief-stricken person can interact with others who share or empathize with their feelings of loss.

Persons in normal grief seldom seek psychiatric help because they accept their reactions and behavior as appropriate. Accordingly, an attending physician should not routinely recommend that a bereaved person see a psychiatrist unless a markedly divergent reaction to the loss is noted. For example, under usual circumstances a bereaved person does not make a suicide attempt. Should a suicide be attempted, psychiatric intervention is indicated.

When professional assistance is sought, it usually involves a request for sleeping medication from a family physician. A mild sedative to induce sleep may be useful in some situations, but antidepressant medication or antianxiety agents are rarely indicated in normal grief. Bereaved people may have to go through the mourning process, however painful it is, for a successful resolution to occur. To narcotize patients with drugs interferes with the normal process that ultimately can lead to a favorable outcome.

Physicians' Responses. The reactions of physicians to patients who are dying often reflect underlying attitudes toward death. When a physician experiences death as a personal failure or a threat to a feeling of personal immortality, he or she is likely to avoid the dying patient. Sadness on the part of a physician in response to a patient's death is normal and expectable; but if sadness or a sense of helplessness interferes with the ability to provide optimal care, the physician needs to seek support, advice, or consultation from colleagues. Both excessive, inappropriate intervention and a complete withdrawal of hope can reflect the underlying imbalance in a physician's attitude toward accepting the inevitability of death.

Grief Therapy

Because grief reactions may develop into a depressive disorder or pathological mourning, specific counseling sessions for those who are bereaved are often valuable. Grief therapy is an increasingly important skill. In regularly scheduled sessions, grieving people are encouraged to talk about feelings of loss and about the person who has died. Many bereaved people have difficulty in recognizing and expressing angry or ambivalent feelings toward a deceased person, and they must be reassured that these feelings are normal.

During grief therapy, an attachment to the therapist usually occurs; this attachment provides a person who is bereaved with temporary support until a sense of confidence about the future develops. The therapist gradually encourages the patient to take on new responsibilities and to develop a sense of autonomy. To do grief therapy, therapists must be comfortable in dealing with the issues of death and dying and must be able to handle patients' intense emotional reactions of sadness, anger, guilt, and self-denigration. In addition, grief therapy requires that therapists be active and participate in the decision-making process with patients, especially in decisions that guide patients toward independence.

Grief therapy need not be conducted only on a one-to-one basis; group counseling is also effective. Self-help groups have value in certain cases. About 30 percent of widows and widowers report that they become isolated from friends, withdraw from social life, and, thus, experience feelings of isolation and loneliness. Self-help groups offer companionship, social contacts, and emotional support; they eventually enable their members to reenter society in a meaningful way. Bereavement care and grief therapy have been most effective with widows and widowers. The necessity for this therapy stems, in part, from the contraction of the family unit; extended family members were once able to provide the needed emotional support and guidance during the mourning period.

Hospice Movement

A *hospice* is a domicile in which dying patients are given care; hospices primarily emphasize the physical and psychological comfort of people who are terminally ill. Hospice care may be provided in an institution or at home. The central concept of the hospice is the humanization of terminal care by helping dying patients and their families carry out final choices with dignity and control.

The hospice movement began in the early 1960s, when Dame Cicely Saunders established a small residential unit in England to care for people who were terminally ill. At present, about 1,800 such units are active in the United States. Most hospices are sponsored by hospitals or are affiliated with home health care agencies; some are approved by Medicare, which, with certain restrictions, reimburses patients for hospice care. A multidisciplinary team of physicians, psychiatrists, social workers, and trained volunteers provides round-the-clock coverage.

A hospice program has many positive features. A supervised, organized routine provides intensive care for both patient and family. The control of pain is a primary goal, and narcotics are given without the fear of addiction. Group support is provided for patients, who are not as isolated as they are in general hospitals.

Because the bereavement process is a major focus, hospice care also helps prevent pathological grief from occurring in surviving family members. Several studies have indicated that hospice care has a more favorable effect than does standard hospital care on family members' abilities to cope and adapt. The *burned-out syndrome,* in which health care providers become uninterested and irritable with terminally ill patients who require almost constant attention, rarely occurs in hospice care. When a patient is in home hospice care, visiting nurses provide relief for overburdened family members.

Medicare pays for hospice care when a patient's doctor states that the patient has a life expectancy of 6 months or less. In one study by C. M. Parks, however, predictions about the length of survival for patients referred to a hospice did not correlate with the actual length of survival. Doctors could not be more precise than to state that patients with incurable cancer would die within a relatively short time. Unfortunately, current federal regulations do not provide for financing hospital care once federally sponsored hospice care has begun; thus, a patient who uses a hospice's care is not insured on reentry to a hospital if the need arises.

The hospice movement is in its ascendancy, especially because it costs more to keep a terminally ill patient in a general hospital than it does to provide hospice benefits. It is also a more compassionate and humane method for treating preterminal and terminal patients than is general hospital care.

Human Immunodeficiency Virus (HIV) Infections

People in social communities representing the high-risk groups for HIV infection are subject to repeated bereavement. Indeed, some surveys find that almost one of three gay men has suffered the loss of two or more members of his social network during the preceding 12 months, as compared with none of a heterosexual lower-risk comparison group. Furthermore, it has been noted that approximately 20 percent of these bereaved persons can be characterized as carrying *unresolved grief* (that is, a persisting experience of grief for the deceased, difficulty with adjustment to the loss, and an inability to discuss the loss without distress). Persons with unresolved grief are more likely to have more depressive and anxious symptoms than are those with resolved grief. Clinicians should routinely inquire into their patients' history of bereavement and loss, especially because some may be experiencing multiple bereavements. The ultimate impact of these bereavements on adaptation to illness, compliance with medical treatment, and adherence to safe sexual practices and health outcome is unknown. People with acquired immune deficiency syndrome (AIDS) provide a special example of the need for many more hospice care centers for terminally ill patients. The AIDS epidemic poses profound challenges to the medical care system, to the mental health care system, and to social service agencies, as well as to patients and their families. AIDS has a devastating effect on most areas of human functioning, and many patients are debilitated for long periods before death. Many patients' needs overwhelm the capabilities of their own social networks, just as the needs of AIDS patients are overwhelming the capacities of the existing traditional health care facilities. Furthermore, the incidence of the burned-out or chronic professional stress syndrome in caretakers of people with AIDS is high and presents a major challenge to the development and maintenance of an adequate care system for these patients. Recent improvements in AIDS treatment, however, may alleviate the disease's demands on the health care system and on those concerned with caring for people with AIDS.

EUTHANASIA AND PHYSICIAN-ASSISTED SUICIDE

In the Hippocratic oath, physicians swear not to prescribe a deadly drug or to give advice to a patient that may cause death. As a result, physicians must walk a fine line between their responsibilities to relieve pain and suffering and their obligation to preserve life.

With developments in technology and life-support systems and the increase in longevity, various groups are trying to develop a comprehensive policy about euthanasia that is acceptable to patients, physicians, lawyers, and theologians, among others. Euthanasia and physician-assisted suicide have become sources of continuing controversy and are likely to be so for the foreseeable future.

Euthanasia

Euthanasia is defined as a physician's deliberate act to cause a patient's death by directly administering a lethal dose of medication or other agent. Because such patients are thought of as hopelessly ill or injured, euthanasia has been called mercy killing.

On the basis of the doctor's action and the patient's condition, four types of euthanasia have been described: *active euthanasia,* in which a physician deliberately intends to kill a patient to alleviate or prevent uncontrollable suffering; *passive euthanasia,* in which a physician withholds artificial life-sustaining measures so that a patient dies a natural death; *voluntary euthanasia,* in which the person who is to die is competent to give consent and does so; and *involuntary euthanasia,* in which the person who is to die is incompetent or incapable of giving consent.

Suicide

Suicide is a person's deliberately taking his or her own life. Assisted suicide is the imparting of information or means that enable a person to deliberately take his or her own life. When such assistance is provided by a physician, the suicide is physician assisted. Assisted suicide and euthanasia should not be confused with palliative care designed to alleviate the suffering of patients who are dying. Palliative care includes giving a patient pain relief and emotional, social, and spiritual support, as well as psychiatric care if indicated. The intent of palliative care is to relieve pain and suffering, not to end a patient's life, even though death may result from palliative care.

The issue of physician-assisted suicide came to national attention in 1990, when Jack Kevorkian, a physician in Michigan, connected Janet Adkins, a victim of dementia of the Alzheimer's type, to a so-called suicide machine that enabled her to give herself an infusion of potassium chloride (KCl) that ended her life. Since then, Kevorkian has helped over 40 people take their own lives. In Michigan, where Kevorkian practiced, his medical license was revoked; he was indicted for assisted suicide in that state but was acquitted.

Ethical Issues

In the United States, physician-assisted suicide and euthanasia have been consistently opposed by the American Psychiatric Association, the American Medical Association, the American Nurses Association, the National Legal Center for the Disabled, and the Roman Catholic Church. The World Medical Association issued the following declaration on euthanasia in October 1987:

> Euthanasia, that is the act of deliberately ending the life of a patient, even at his own request or at the request of his close relatives, is unethical. This does not prevent the physician from respecting the will of a patient to allow the natural process of death to follow its course in the terminal phase of sickness.

The New York State Committee of Bioethical Issues is also opposed to euthanasia but has stated that physicians have an obligation to provide effective treatment to relieve pain and suffering, even though the treatment may on occasion hasten death. The committee stated the following:

> The principle of patient autonomy requires that physicians respect the decision of a patient who possesses decision-making capacity to forgo life-sustaining treatment. Life-sustaining treatment is defined as any medical treatment that serves to prolong life without reversing the underlying medical condition. Life-sustaining treatment includes, but is not limited to, mechanical ventilation, renal dialysis, blood transfusions, chemotherapy, antibiotics, and artificial nutrition and hydration.

Physicians are obligated to relieve pain and suffering and to promote the dignity and autonomy of dying patients in their care. This obligation includes providing effective palliative treatment, even though it may occasionally hasten death. But physicians should not perform euthanasia or participate in assisted suicide. Support, comfort, respect for patient autonomy, good communication, and adequate pain control may dramatically decrease the demand for euthanasia and assisted suicide. In certain carefully defined circumstances, it is humane to recognize that death is certain and suffering is great. Nevertheless, the societal risks of involving physicians in medical interventions to cause patients' deaths is too great to condone active euthanasia or physician-assisted suicide.

In the Netherlands, physicians are allowed to participate in active euthanasia, provided certain conditions are met: Patients must make repeated requests that are well informed and enduring. Patients' mental or physical condition must be considered incurable. All other options for care must have been exhausted. The assisting physician must have the agreement of another physician. About 3 percent of all deaths in Holland result from euthanasia.

In the United States, a group called the Hemlock Society actively promotes the practice of euthanasia. Its founder, Derek Humphry, in his book *Final Exit,* gave explicit directions on suicide techniques. The book has been a bestseller in this country and abroad and attests to the interest and controversy surrounding the issue. Similar right-to-die societies include Choice in Dying and Americans for Death with Dignity, among others.

The American Association of Suicidology in its 1996 *Report of the Committee on Physician-Assisted Suicide and Euthanasia* concluded that involuntary euthanasia can never be condoned; the report also stated, however, that "intolerable, prolonged suffering of persons in extremis should never be insisted upon, against their wishes, in single-minded efforts to preserve life at all cost." This position acknowledges that patients may die as a result of treatment given to them for the explicit purpose of relieving suffering; but death associated with palliative care differs greatly from physician-assisted suicide, in that death is not the goal of treatment and is not intentional.

Legal Issues

At one time, suicide was considered a type of murder, although no one was or is prosecuted for the crime. Assisted suicide, however, is a crime, and in some states, such as California, can be prosecuted as murder. Over 40 states in the United States, however, currently consider aiding and abetting suicide a crime without clarifying it as murder. In 1996 in both New York and California, a state court held that a person had the right to bring about his or her death through assisted suicide. And in 1994 the people of Oregon approved a referendum permitting physicians to prescribe lethal medication for terminally ill patients (the Oregon Death with Dignity Act). All these decisions have been overturned in federal court, and the U.S. Supreme Court ruled in June 1997 that there is no constitutional right to assisted suicide.

Psychiatric Issues

Some surveys among U.S. physicians have found 25 to 30 percent in favor of euthanasia; but most U.S. physicians oppose the practice. In Oregon, two thirds of physicians (including psychiatrists) surveyed in 1996 believed that physician-assisted suicide for competent terminally ill persons should be permitted in some circumstances, but this number represents only a tiny fraction of U.S. doctors.

Most psychiatrists view suicide as an irrational act that is the product of mental illness, usually of depression. In almost every case in which a patient asks to be put to death, there is depression associated with an incurable medical condition that causes the patient intolerable pain. In these instances, every effort should be made to alleviate both conditions: antidepressants or psychostimulants for depression and opioids for pain. Psychotherapy, spiritual counseling, or both may be needed. In addition, family therapy to deal with the stress of a dying patient may be necessary. Some patients may ask to be put to death because they do not wish to be a burden to their families; others may be coerced by their families into believing that they are or will be a burden and may choose death as a result. Currently, no professional codes countenance euthanasia or assisted suicide in the United States. Therefore, psychiatrists must stand on the side of responsible rescue and treatment while recognizing that is it is lawful and ethical to provide palliative care designed to relieve emotional and physical pain or suffering, even if death is a possible side effect of these efforts.

References

Aarli J: The immune system and the nervous system. J Neurol *229:* 137, 1983.

Baker JE, Sedney MA, Gross E: Psychological tasks for bereaved children. Am J Orthopsychiatry *62:* 105, 1992.

Conwell Y, Caine ED: Rational suicide and the right to die: Reality and myth. N Engl J Med *325:* 1100, 1991.

Council on Ethical and Judicial Affairs: *Current Opinions.* American Medical Association, Chicago, 1992.

deWachter MM: Active euthanasia in the Netherlands. JAMA *262:* 3316, 1989.

Duberstein PR, Conwell Y, Cox C, Podgorski CA, Glazer RS, Caine ED: Attitudes toward self-determined death; a survey of primary care physicians. J Am Geriatr Soc *43:* 395, 1995.

Ganzini L, Fenn DS, Lee MA, Heintz RT, Bloom JD: Attitudes of Oregon psychiatrists toward physician-assisted suicide. Am J Psychiatry *153:* 11, 1996.

Hendin H, Klerman G: Physician-assisted suicide: The dangers of legalization. Am J Psychiatry *150:* 143, 1993.

Hinohara S: Sir William Osler's philosophy on death. Ann Intern Med *118:* 639, 1993.

Horowitz MJ: Depression after the death of a spouse. Am J Psychiatry *149:* 579, 1992.

Humphry D: *Final Exit: The Practicalities of Self-Deliverance and Assisted Suicide for the Dying.* Hemlock Society, Eugene, OR, 1991.

Jeret JS: Discussing dying: Changing attitudes among patients, physicians, and medical students. Pharos *52:* 15, 1989.

Kaplan KJ, Dewitt J: Kevorkian's list: Gender bias or what? News Link Am Link Assoc Suicidol *22:* 1, 1996.

Kübler-Ross E: *On Death and Dying.* Macmillan, New York, 1969.

Lazar TS: Physician-assisted suicide and the state of the law in California. Action Rep Med Board Calif *59:* 5, 1996.

Lee MA, Nelson HD, Tilden VP, Ganzini L, Schmidt TA, Tolle SW: Legalizing assisted suicide—Views of physicians in Oregon. N Engl J Med *334:* 310, 1994.

Leming MR, Dickinson GE: *Understanding Dying, Death and Bereavement.* Holt, Rinehart & Winston, New York, 1985.

Ness DE, Pfeffer CR: Sequelae of bereavement resulting from suicide. Am J Psychiatry *147:* 279, 1990.

Nuss WS, Zubenko GS: Correlates of persistent depressive symptoms in widows. Am J Psychiatry *149:* 346, 1992.

Parkes CM, Weiss RS: *Recovery from Bereavement.* Basic Books, New York, 1983.

Quill TE, Cassel CK, Meier DE: Care of the hopelessly ill: Proposed clinical criteria for physician-assisted suicide. N Engl J Med *327:* 1380, 1992.

Roberts G, Owen J: The near-death experience. Br J Psychiatry *153:* 607, 1988.

Rosner F, Rogatz P: Physician-assisted suicide: Committee on Bioethical Issues of the Medical Society of the State of New York. NY State J Med *92:* 388, 1992.

Schleifer SJ, Keller SE, Camerino M, et al: Suppression of lymphocyte stimulation following bereavement. JAMA *250:* 374, 1983.

Speece MW, Brent SB: The acquisition of a mature understanding of three components of the concept of death. Death Stud *16:* 211, 1992.

Tedeschi RG, Calhoun LG: Using the support group to respond to the isolation of bereavement. J Ment Health Counsel *15:* 47, 1993.

Weiss L, Frischer L, Richman J: Parental adjustment to intrapartum and delivery room loss: The role of hospital-based support program. Clin Perinatol *16:* 1009, 1989.

3 The Brain and Behavior

▲ 3.1 Neuroanatomy

THREE LEVELS OF NEUROANATOMICAL STUDY

Histology

The cell types of the brain are broadly classified as neurons and glial cells.

Neurons. *Neurons* are polarized, elongated cells that are uniquely capable of instantaneous, intercellular communication (Fig. 3.1–1). Each neuron is polarized with respect to transmission of information. The reception of information, in the form of extracellular signals, occurs through cellular receptors located on the *dendrites.* The receptors activate or inactivate ion channels within the membrane and thus regulate the voltage potential across the membrane. The passage of ions, especially calcium ions, alters the intracellular ion concentrations and activates intracellular second messenger cascades. Simultaneously, activation of other cell surface receptors influences the phosphorylation and activation of other intracellular signaling pathways. This information is integrated in the *cell body,* where it is translated into variations in levels of gene expression, which can alter the composition of proteins and other cellular components within the cell. If the membrane potential at the axon hillock immediately adjacent to the cell body rises above a threshold because of the actions of the dendritic ion channels, an action potential is generated. Action potentials are instantaneous pulses of membrane depolarization that are rapidly transmitted along axons to the synaptic terminals, in some cases more than several centimeters away from the cell body. The rate of action potential propagation along the axon is increased by the presence of the myelin sheath, which serves as an electrical insulation. At the synaptic terminal, the action potential triggers the release of chemical neurotransmitters, which enter the synaptic cleft and bind to receptors on the dendrites of neighboring neurons. (Neurotransmission is discussed in depth in Section 3.2.)

There are two broad classes of neurons: *interneurons,* which form local circuits within a brain region, and *projection neurons,* which extend beyond the confines of a particular brain region to communicate with other areas. Consistent with the computational and associative functions of the brain, most neurons are interneurons. Each of the 10^{11} neurons in the adult human brain receives, on average, 10^3 to 10^4 synapses from 10^3 other neurons. In addition to this immense interconnectivity, each presynaptic neuron is capable of exerting an infinitesimal shading of stimulatory and inhibitory influence on each postsynaptic neuron. The combined result of these nuances in intercellular communication is the most complex computational structure known.

The collections of neuronal cell bodies within the nervous system constitute the *gray matter,* and the myelinated axonal tracts constitute the *white matter.* In the spinal cord, the gray matter is encircled by white matter fibers. In the brainstem, numerous discrete nuclei of gray matter are interdigitated among white matter tracts. Located immediately beneath the cortex, the basal ganglia and thalamus make up a set of gray matter nuclei that have extensive reciprocal connections with specific regions of the cortex. The highest computational region is the *cerebral cortex,* in which the gray matter is located on the surface. The cortex is folded into gyri and sulci to fit its entire surface into the skull (Fig. 3.1–2).

Glial Cells. *Glia,* or ''glue'' cells, are the nonneuronal elements of the nervous system; they function to regulate the extracellular neural environment. Three types of glial cells are recognized: astrocytes, oligodendrocytes, and microglial cells. *Astrocytes* serve a structural role in forming and stabilizing the gray-white pattern during development. They envelop individual synapses to ensure uncontaminated synaptic communication and regulate the extracellular ion concentrations to maintain the fidelity of neurotransmission. In cases of brain injury, astrocytes may proliferate and absorb neuronal debris. *Oligodendrocytes* ensheathe axons with myelin, a hydrophobic membrane that serves to insulate individual fibers in bundled fiber tracts. Together, the glia create a homeostatic environment in which neuronal communication may proceed with maximum accuracy. *Microglia* are actually immune system cells that perform surveillance in cases of infection.

Cytoarchitectonics and Cortical Columns

Most of the cerebral cortex consists of a six-layered arrangement of neurons (Fig. 3.1–3). The term *cytoarchitectonics* refers to the local organization of neurons and glial cells in discrete domains of the cortex. Korbinian Brodmann divided the cerebral cortex into 47 cytoarchitectonic areas, based on subtle differences in the number and size of the cells in each of the six layers of the cortex throughout the cerebrum (Fig. 3.1–4). The cortex is assembled on a columnar scaffolding established by the radial arms of radial astrocytic cells during

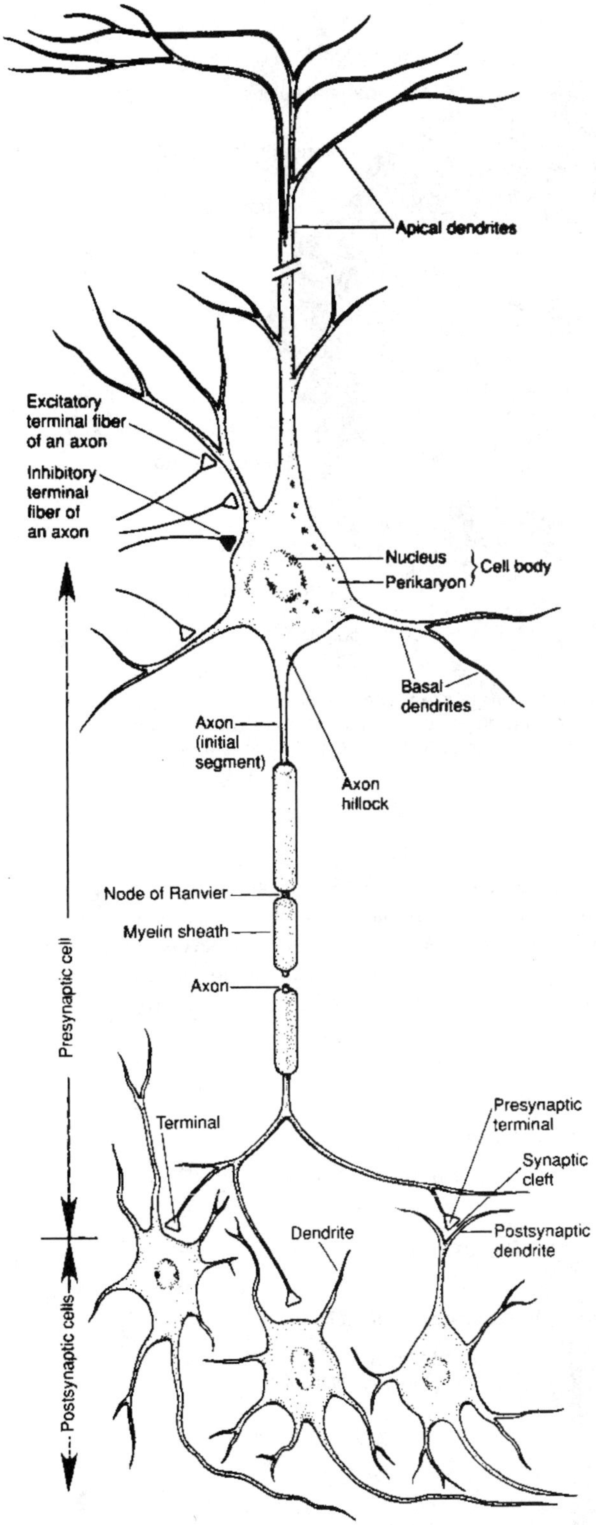

Apical dendrites
Excitatory terminal fiber of an axon
Inhibitory terminal fiber of an axon
Nucleus
Perikaryon
Cell body
Basal dendrites
Axon (initial segment)
Axon hillock
Node of Ranvier
Myelin sheath
Axon
Presynaptic cell
Terminal
Presynaptic terminal
Synaptic cleft
Dendrite
Postsynaptic dendrite
Postsynaptic cells

FIGURE 3.1–1

Features of a typical neuron. The *apical dendrites* receive synaptic input of either *excitatory* or *inhibitory* nature; the input acts on membrane ion channels and determines the intracellular voltage potential. The *cell body* houses the *nucleus* and the protein synthetic machinery. The *axon hillock* consists of the origin of the *axon* from the cell body and is the site of origin of the action potential. The axon transmits the action potential; the insulating function of the *myelin sheath* facilitates this transmission. Some axons extend over 1 meter in length. The *axon terminal* houses the synaptic vesicles, from which neurotransmitters are released into the *synaptic cleft.* (Reprinted with permission from Kandel ER: Nerve cells and behavior. In *Principles of Neural Science,* ed 3, ER Kandel, JH Schwartz, TM Jessell, editors, p 19. Elsevier, New York, 1991. Copyright ©1996 by Appleton and Lange.)

development. This columnar arrangement retains a functional importance in the mature cortex: Cells along a radial axis tend to respond and act in concert during information processing. The columnar organization of the cortex is most obvious in the visual system, where stripes and arrays of cortical columns in the occipital, parietal, and temporal cortices compartmentalize the extraction of features from the images registered by the eyes. In the inferior temporal cortex, for example, parallel cortical columns responding to distinct facial movements and to the angle at which another's face is turned enable the brain to recognize facial expressions (Fig. 3.1–5). This cortical specialization appears to operate immediately upon birth and is therefore largely established in the absence of experience. In contrast, the ocular dominance columns of the primary visual cortex, in which the input from each eye is neatly segregated from the input of the other eye, arise postnatally and require coherent input from each eye (Fig. 3.1–6). In an animal that is deprived of this binocular experience in the critical postnatal period, the functional organization of the cortical columns is dramatically altered. The cortical columns of the brain thus acquire specific functions through a combination of nature and nurture.

Behavioral Neuroanatomy

Two thousand years ago, Aristotle remarked that "there is nothing in our minds that does not go through the senses." The *nervous system* may be considered as a set of functional units classified as sensory, motor, and association. By processing external stimuli into neuronal impulses, *sensory systems* create an internal representation of the external world. A separate map is formed for each sensory modality. *Motor systems* enable people to manipulate their environment and to influence others' behavior through communication. In the brain, sensory input, representing the external world, is integrated with internal drives and emotional stimuli in *association units,* which in turn drive the actions of motor units. Although psychiatry is primarily concerned with the brain's association function, an appreciation of the sensory and motor systems' information processing is essential for sorting logical thought from the distortions introduced by psychopathology.

SENSORY SYSTEMS

The external world offers an infinite amount of potentially relevant information. In this overwhelming volume of sensory information in the environment, the sensory systems must both detect and discriminate stimuli; they winnow relevant information from the mass of confounding input by applying filtration at all levels. Sensory systems first transform external stimuli into neural impulses and then filter out irrelevant information to create an internal image of the environment,

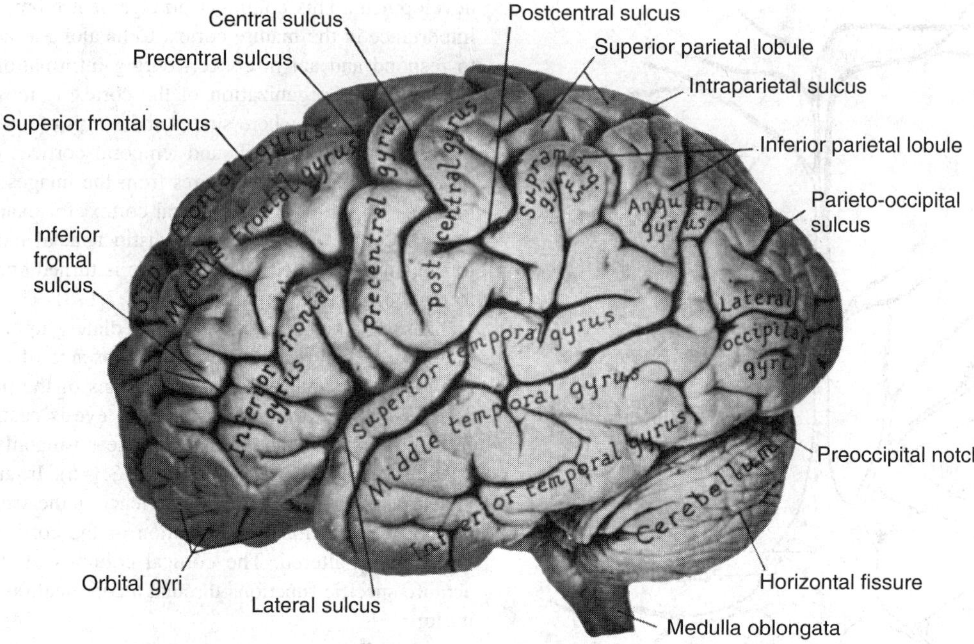
Central sulcus
Postcentral sulcus
Superior parietal lobule
Precentral sulcus
Intraparietal sulcus
Superior frontal sulcus
Inferior parietal lobule
Parieto-occipital sulcus
Inferior frontal sulcus
Preoccipital notch
Orbital gyri
Lateral sulcus
Horizontal fissure
Medulla oblongata
Sup. frontal gyrus
Middle frontal gyrus
Precentral gyrus
Postcentral gyrus
Supramarg. gyrus
Angular gyrus
Lateral occipital gyri
Inferior frontal gyrus
Superior temporal gyrus
Middle temporal gyrus
Inferior temporal gyrus
Cerebellum

FIGURE 3.1–2
Lateral surface of the brain. The principal sulci and gyri of the cerebral cortex are labeled. The *lateral sulcus* divides the *temporal lobe* from the *frontal* and *parietal* lobes. The central sulcus forms the posterior border of the frontal lobe and the anterior border of the parietal lobe. The occipital lobe is bounded by the *parieto-occipital sulcus.* (Reprinted with permission from Carpenter MB: *Core Text of Neuroanatomy,* ed 4, p 25. Williams & Wilkins, Baltimore, 1991.)

which serves as a basis for reasoned thought. Feature extraction is the quintessential role of sensory systems. They achieve this task with their hierarchical organizations, which first transform physical stimuli into neural activity in the primary sense organs and then refine and narrow the neural activity in a series of higher cortical processing areas. This neural processing eliminates irrelevant data from higher representations and reinforces crucial features. At the highest levels of sensory processing, neural images are transmitted to the association areas to be acted on in the light of emotions and drives.

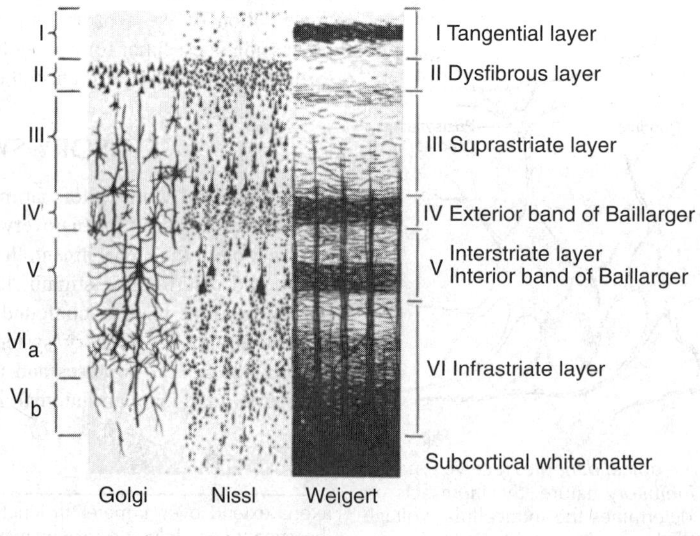
I
II
III
IV
V
VIa
VIb
I Tangential layer
II Dysfibrous layer
III Suprastriate layer
IV Exterior band of Baillarger
V Interstriate layer
Interior band of Baillarger
VI Infrastriate layer
Subcortical white matter
Golgi
Nissl
Weigert

FIGURE 3.1–3
The six layers of the cerebral cortex. *Golgi* staining reveals the entire boundary of the cell and shows the relative size of the cells of each layer. *Nissl* staining shows the perinuclear substance of the cell bodies. *Weigert* staining shows axon tracts. The relative abundance of cells of each layer varies over the cortex and gives rise to the various cytoarchitectonic regions (for example, Brodmann areas). (Reprinted with permission from Carpenter MB: *Core Text of Neuroanatomy,* ed 4, p 391. Williams & Wilkins, Baltimore, 1991.)

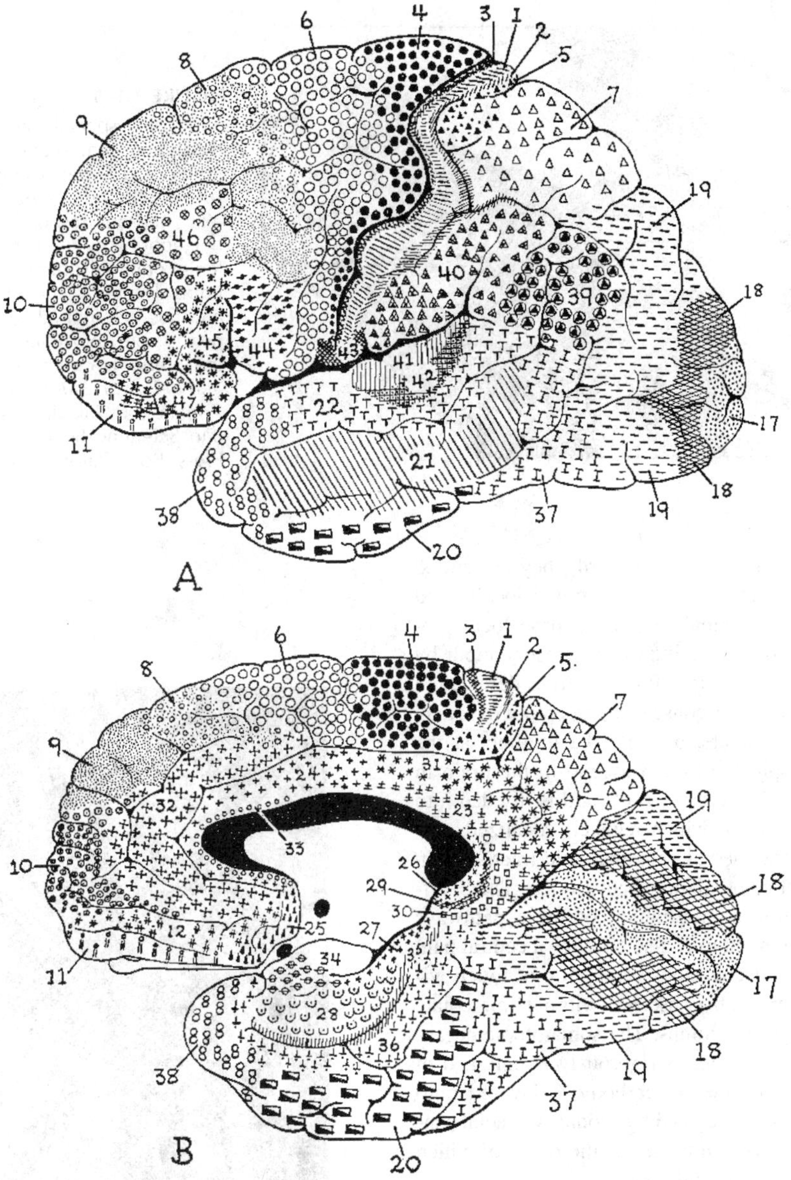
6
4
3
1
2
5
7
8
9
46
10
45
44
43
40
39
41
42
22
21
11
47
38
20
37
19
18
17
A
6
4
3
1
2
5
7
8
9
24
31
32
23
33
10
26
29
30
25
27
12
11
34
28
36
35
38
20
37
19
18
17
B

FIGURE 3.1–4

Cytoarchitectonic regions of the brain according to Brodmann. **A.** Lateral surface. **B.** Medial surface. (Reprinted with permission from Carpenter MB: *Core Text of Neuroanatomy,* ed 4, p 399. Williams & Wilkins, Baltimore, 1991.)

The Five Primary Senses

Somatosensory System. Beginning in the 1950s, the *somatosensory system,* an intricate array of parallel point-to-point connections from the body surface to the brain, was the first sensory system to be understood in anatomical detail. There are six somatosensory modalities: light touch, pressure, pain, temperature, vibration, and proprioception (position sense). The organization of nerve bundles and synaptic connections in the somatosensory system encodes spatial relationships at all levels, so that the organization is strictly *somatotopic* (Fig. 3.1–7). Within a given patch of skin, various receptor nerve terminals act in concert to mediate distinct modalities. The mechanical properties of the skin's mechanoreceptors and thermoreceptors generate neural impulses in response to dynamic variations in the environment while they suppress static input. Nerve endings are either fast or slow response; their depth in the skin also determines their sensitivity to sharp or blunt stimuli. Thus, the representation of the external world is significantly refined at the level of the primary sensory organs.

The receptor organs generate coded neural impulses that travel proximally along the sensory nerve axons to the spinal cord. These far-flung routes are susceptible to varying systemic medical conditions and to pressure palsies. Pain, tingling, and numbness are the typical presenting symptoms of peripheral neuropathies.

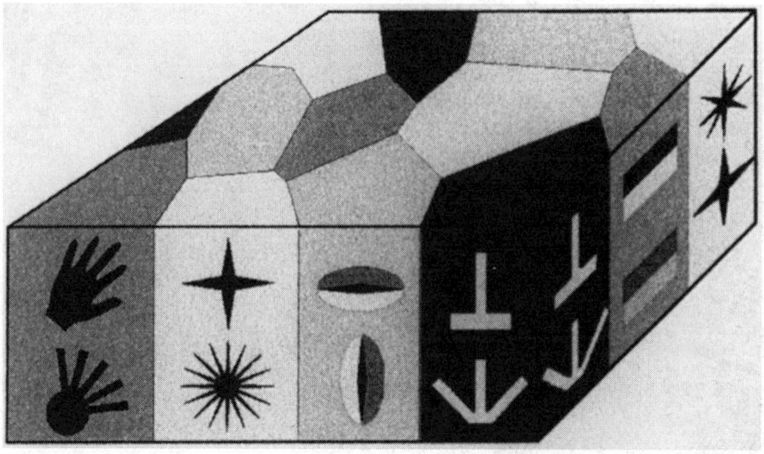

FIGURE 3.1–5
Functional specialization of cortical columns in the inferior temporal cortex. Within a gyrus, columns of 0.4-mm average width selectively respond to different visual stimuli. Along the radial axis, neurons respond to similar shapes, while neighboring columns may have significantly different optimal stimuli. These feature-specific columns develop in the absence of visual input and are thus determined genetically. (Reprinted with permission from Fujita I: The warp and weft in the inferior temporal cortex. In *Emotion, Memory and Behavior: Studies on Human and Nonhuman Primates,* T Nakajima, T Ono, editors, p 82. Japan Scientific Societies Press, Tokyo, and CRC Press, Boca Raton, 1995.)

After sensory fibers enter the spinal cord, they are sorted into one of three fiber tracts. Some fibers travel locally and synapse within one or two spinal segments; these local projections participate in further filtering of the sensory input by suppressing unwanted "noise" to allow a sharper delineation of the signal. Second, fibers for conscious perception of touch, pain, and temperature decussate, or cross the midline, at the level of entry into the spinal cord and ascend to the brain in the spinothalamic tract. The perception of pain is divided into the lateral spinothalamic tract, which registers localized, discrete, acute pains, and the medial spinothalamic tract, which, along with the spinoreticulothalamic pathway, registers diffuse, chronic pains. Surgical interruption of these pathways may ablate pain perception but may also produce a central pain syndrome. Third, fibers for conscious perception of touch, vibration sense, and proprioception ascend, without immediate decussation, in the posterior columns. The somatotopic organization of the sensory projections is rigorously maintained in the spinal cord; input from the upper body is layered onto fibers from the legs and is segregated by modality. Facial sensation is mediated by the trigeminal nerve, the fibers of which are laid atop those of the arms and legs.

All somatosensory fibers project to and synapse in the thalamus. The thalamic neurons preserve the somatotopic representation by projecting fibers to the somatosensory cortex, located immediately posterior to the sylvian fissure in the parietal lobe (Fig. 3.1–4, Brodmann areas 1, 2, and 3). Despite considerable overlap, several bands of cortex roughly parallel to the sylvian fissure are segregated by somatosensory modality. Within each band is the sensory "homunculus," the culmination of the careful somatotopic segregation of the sensory fibers at the lower levels. The clinical syndrome of *tactile agnosia (astereognosis)* is defined by the inability to recognize objects based on touch, although the primary somatosensory modalities—light touch, pressure, pain, temperature, vibration, and proprioception—are intact. This syndrome, localized at the border of the somatosensory and association areas in the posterior parietal lobe, appears to represent an isolated failure of only the highest order of feature extraction, with preservation of the more basic levels of the somatosensory pathway.

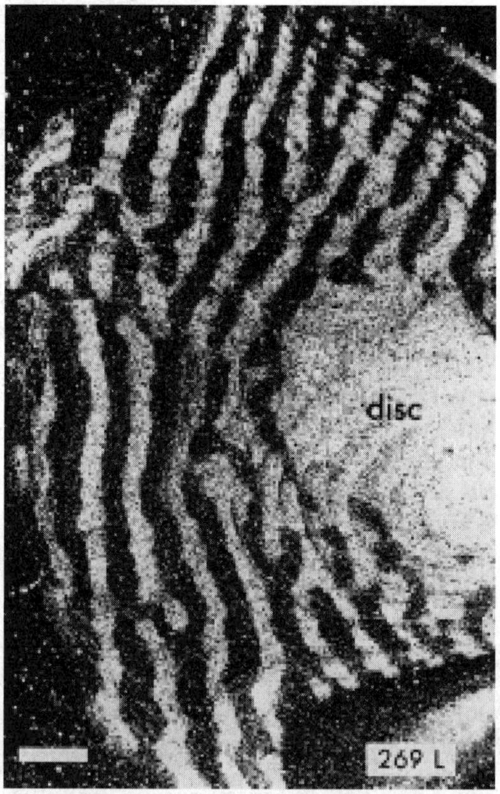
disc
269 L

FIGURE 3.1–6
Ocular dominance columns. Projection of the retina onto the visual cortex in the occipital lobe. Axons from the left eye are labeled black; axons from the right eye are unlabeled. In the cortex, the retinal projections form a neatly ordered alternating pattern called the ocular dominance columns. These columns form as a result of postnatal visual activity and are thus determined through a combination of genetics and experience. (Reprinted with permission from Carpenter MB: *Core Text of Neuroanatomy,* ed 4, p 412. Williams & Wilkins, Baltimore, 1991.)

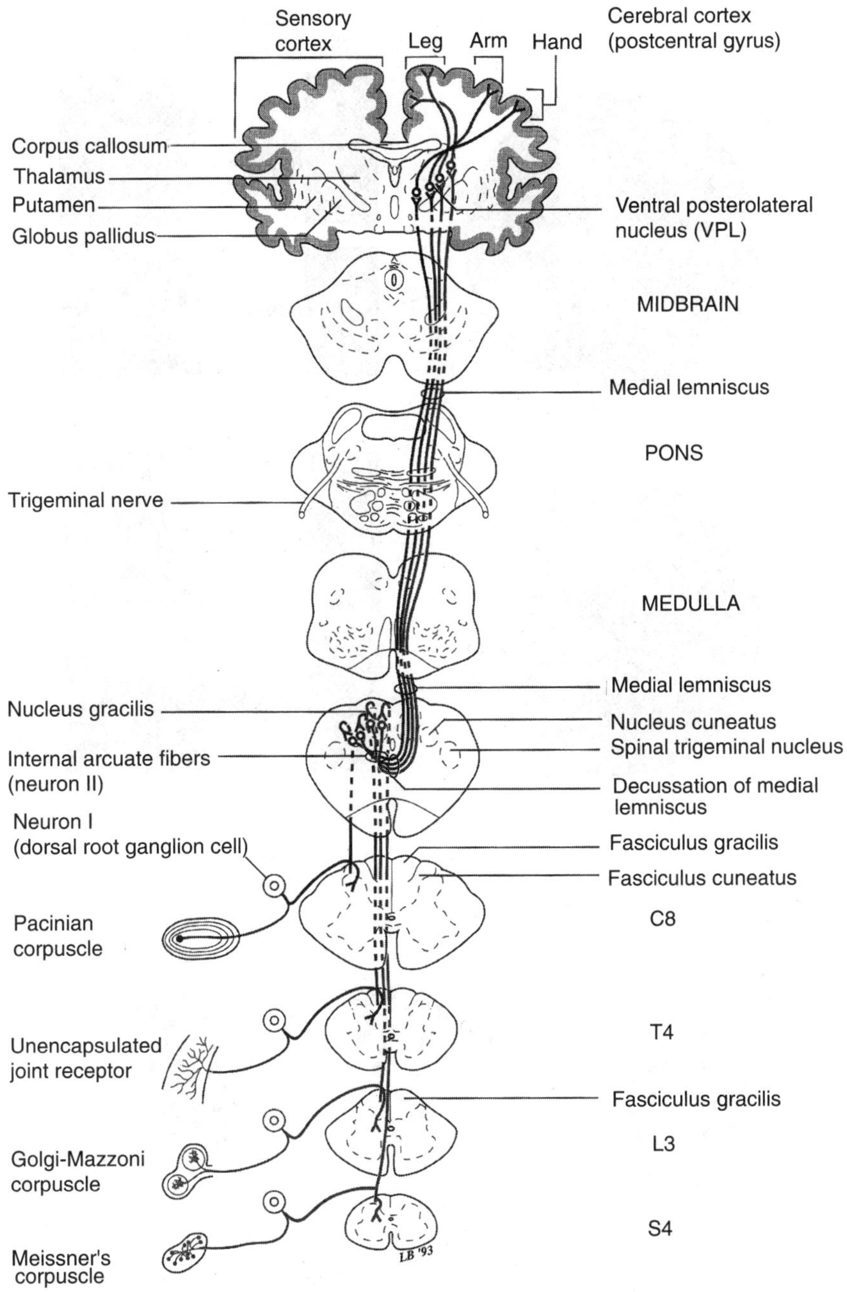
Sensory cortex
Leg
Arm
Hand
Cerebral cortex (postcentral gyrus)
Corpus callosum
Thalamus
Putamen
Globus pallidus
Ventral posterolateral nucleus (VPL)
MIDBRAIN
Medial lemniscus
PONS
Trigeminal nerve
MEDULLA
Medial lemniscus
Nucleus gracilis
Nucleus cuneatus
Spinal trigeminal nucleus
Internal arcuate fibers (neuron II)
Decussation of medial lemniscus
Neuron I (dorsal root ganglion cell)
Fasciculus gracilis
Fasciculus cuneatus
C8
Pacinian corpuscle
T4
Unencapsulated joint receptor
Fasciculus gracilis
L3
Golgi-Mazzoni corpuscle
S4
Meissner's corpuscle
LB '93

FIGURE 3.1–7
Somatotopic organization of the somatosensory system. Each somatosensory modality is carefully segregated from the other modalities, and the fibers of different spinal levels are segregated as they ascend to the somatosensory cortex. (Reprinted with permission from Parent A: *Carpenter's Human Neuroanatomy*, ed 9, p 369. Williams & Wilkins, Baltimore, 1996.)

Reciprocal connections are a key anatomical feature of crucial importance to conscious perception: As many fibers project down from the cortex to the thalamus as fibers that project up from the thalamus to the cortex. These reciprocal fibers play a critical role in the filtering of sensory input. In normal states, they facilitate the sharpening of internal representations, but in pathological states, they may generate false signals or inappropriately suppress sensation. Such cortical interference with sensory perception is thought to underlie many psychosomatic syndromes, such as the hemisensory loss that characterizes conversion disorder.

The prenatal development of the strict point-to-point pattern that characterizes the somatosensory system remains an area of active study. Patterns of sensory innervation result from a combination of axonal guidance by particular molecular cues and pruning of exuberant synaptogenesis based on an organ-

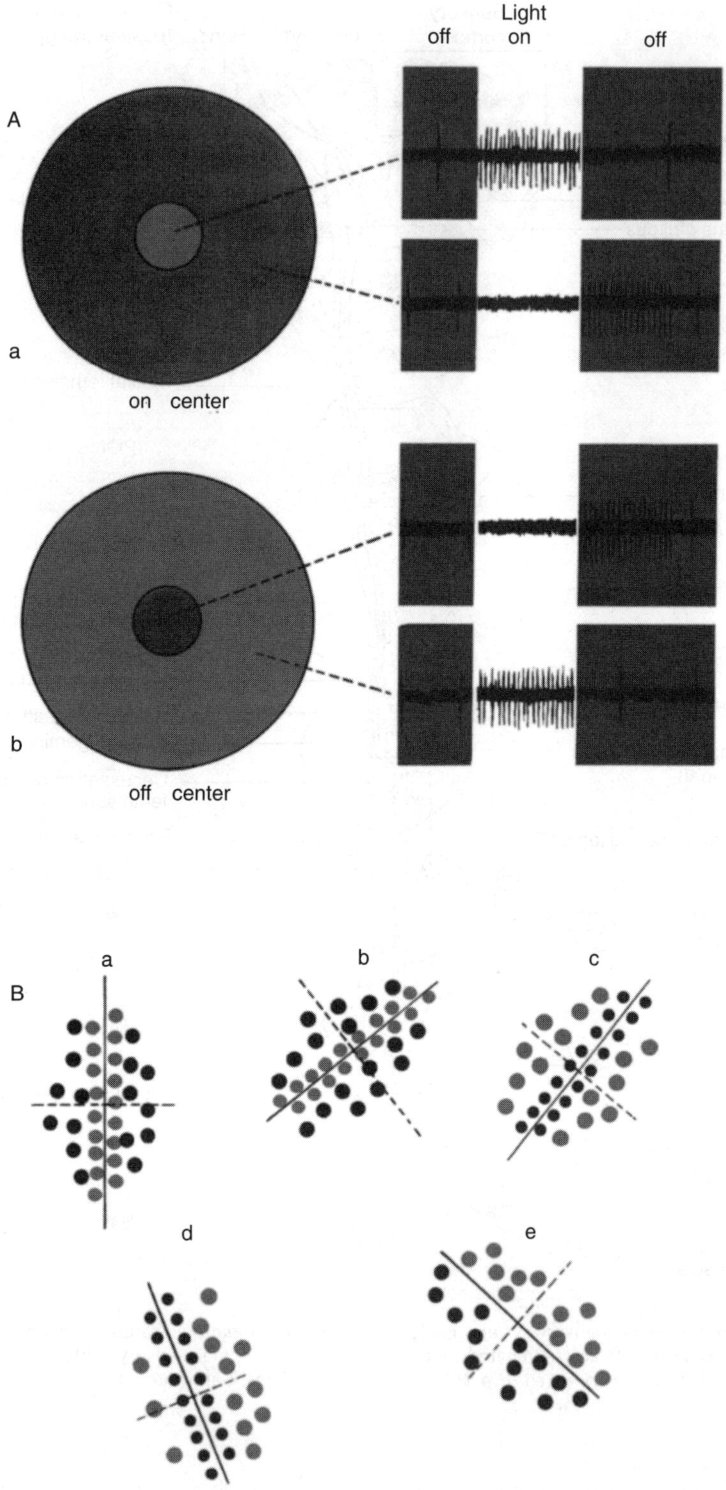
Light
off
on
off
A
a
on center
b
off center
B
a
b
c
d
e

FIGURE 3.1–8

Center–surround response of retinal cells. **A-a.** One retinal ganglion cell fires rapidly when light hits directly *(top tracing at right),* and when light hits the surrounding retina, the cell is inactive. **A-b.** The opposite pattern is seen for a second retinal ganglion cell. Lateral dendritic connections in the retina suppress neighboring cells to sharpen the contrast of edges in the visual field. This is the first stage of visual feature extraction. **B.** Five orientation columns in the primary visual cortex. Each cortical column extracts lines of a different axis from the visual image. This is the second stage of visual feature extraction. (Reprinted with permission from Carpenter MB: *Core Text of Neuroanatomy,* ed 4, 408. Williams & Wilkins, Baltimore, 1991.)

ism's experience. Leading hypotheses weigh contributions from a genetically determined molecular map, in which the arrangement of fiber projections is organized by fixed and diffusible chemical cues, against contributions from the modeling and remodeling of projections based on coordinated neural activity. Thumbnail calculations suggest that the 80,000 genes in each human chromosome are far too few to encode completely the position of all the trillions of synapses in the brain. In fact, genetically determined positional cues probably steer growing fibers toward the general target, and fine tuning of the pattern of projections is accomplished by activity-dependent mechanisms. Recent data suggest that well-established adult thalamocortical sensory projections can be gradually remodeled as a result of a reorientation of coordinated sensory input or in response to loss of part of the somatosensory cortex, for instance, in stroke.

Visual System. Visual images are transduced into neural activity within the retina and are processed through a series of brain cells, which respond to increasingly complex features, from the eye to the higher visual cortex. The neurobiological basis of feature extraction is best understood in finest detail in the visual system. Beginning with classical work in the 1960s, research in the visual pathway has produced two main paradigms for all sensory systems. The first paradigm, previously mentioned with respect to the somatosensory system, weighs the contributions of genetics and experience, or nature and nurture, to the formation of the final synaptic arrangement. Transplantation experiments, resulting in an accurate point-to-point pattern of connectivity even when the eye was surgically inverted, suggested an innate, genetically determined mechanism of synaptic pattern formation. The crucial role of early visual experience in the establishment of the adult pattern of visual connections, on the other hand, crystallized the hypothesis of activity-dependent formation of synaptic connectivity. The final adult pattern is the result of both factors.

The second main paradigm, most clearly revealed in the visual system, is that of highly specialized brain cells that respond exclusively to extremely specific stimuli. Recent work, for example, has defined cells in the inferior temporal cortex that respond only to faces viewed at a specific angle (Fig. 3.1–5). Extrapolating this specialization to an extreme, researchers have postulated a "grandmother cell," a cell that would fire only when a subject was regarding his or her own grandmother. Such a cell, representing a fixed site for important memories, has not yet been identified, perhaps simply because scientists have not yet found it or, more significantly, perhaps because evoking the memory of a person's responding to the presence of his or her grandmother may require the activity of large neural networks and may not be limited to a single neuron. Nevertheless, the cellular localization of specific feature extraction is of critical importance in defining the boundary between sensory and association systems, but only in the visual system has this significant question been posed experimentally.

In the visual pathway, light passes through the eye and stimulates the photoreceptor cells. In response to light, the receptor molecules change conformation and trigger an intracellular cascade that generates neural impulses. Feature extraction begins in the retina, where stimulating a point immediately suppresses the response of the circle of neighboring cells, termed a *center–surround response* (Fig. 3.1–8). This response sharpens edges in the image. The retina consists of rods, which respond only to the intensity of light, and three types of cones, each of which is tuned to respond most strongly to one of the three primary colors. Perception of color ultimately emerges in the cortex, from comparisons of the ratio of intensities of signals from each of the three classes of cones. An exact point-to-point visuotopic projection, from the halves of each retina that respond to the same half of the visual field, travels to the lateral geniculate nucleus (LGN), where additional center–surround sharpening occurs. The optic tracts project from the LGN to the primary visual cortex at the posterior pole of the occipital lobe. In the visual cortex of each hemisphere, the input from each eye is segregated into ocular dominance columns: Radial columns of cortex that are activated by input from only one eye are adjacent to columns that respond only to the other eye (Fig. 3.1–6). This segregation may underlie the stereoscopic localization of objects in space.

In the primary visual cortex, columns of cells respond specifically to lines of a specific orientation. The cells of the primary visual cortex project to the secondary visual cortex, where cells respond specifically to particular movements of lines and to angles. In turn, these cells project to two association areas, where additional features are extracted and conscious awareness of images forms (Fig. 3.1–9). The inferior temporal lobe detects the shape, form, and color of the object—the *what* questions; the posterior parietal lobe tracks the location, motion, and distance—the *where* questions. The posterior parietal lobe contains distinct sets of neurons that signal the intention either to look into a certain part of visual space or to reach for a particular object. In the inferior temporal cortices (ITCs), adjacent cortical columns respond to complex forms: Responses to facial features tend to occur in the left ITC, and responses to complex shapes tend to occur in the right ITC. The brain devotes specific cells to the recognition

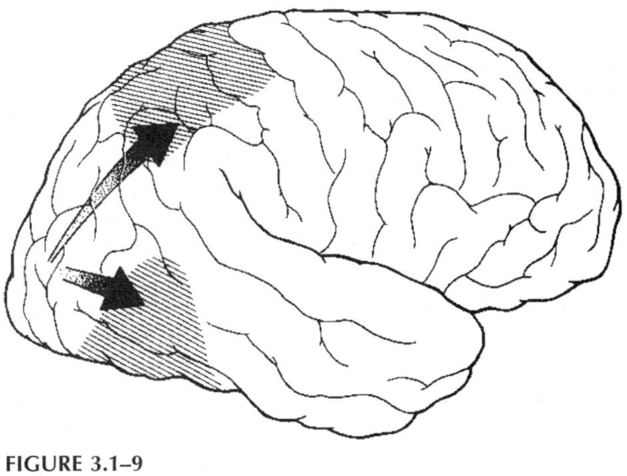

FIGURE 3.1–9

Visual association areas. At the far left pole of the cortex, impulses from the primary visual cortex spread both to the parietal lobe *(upper shaded area),* which tracks *where* the image is in space, and to the temporal lobe *(lower shaded area),* which determines *what* the image is. (Reprinted with permission from Filley CM: *Neurobehavioral Anatomy,* p 107. University Press of Colorado, Niwot, CO, 1995.)

of facial expressions and to the aspect and position of faces of others with respect to the individual (Fig. 3.1–5). Other body parts have a less complete representation among feature-specific cells, and inanimate objects occupy another set of cellular addresses.

At this time, the crucial connections between the feature-specific cells and the association areas involved in memory and conscious thought remain to be delineated. Much elucidation of feature recognition is based on invasive animal studies. In humans, the clinical syndrome of *prosopagnosia* describes the inability to recognize faces, in the presence of preserved recognition of other environmental objects. On the basis of pathological and radiological examination of individual cases, prosopagnosia is thought to result from a disconnection of the left ITC from the visual association area in the left parietal lobe. Such lesional studies are useful in identifying necessary components of a mental pathway, but they may be inadequate to identify the entire pathway. One newer, noninvasive technique, which is currently being perfected and which may begin to reveal the full anatomic relation of the human visual system to conscious thought and memory, is functional neuroimaging (Chapter 3, Section 3.3).

As is true for language, there appears to be a hemispheric asymmetry for certain components of visuospatial orientation. Although both hemispheres cooperate in the perceiving and drawing of complex images, the right hemisphere, especially the parietal lobe, contributes the overall contour, perspective, and right-left orientation; and the left hemisphere adds internal detail, embellishment, and complexity.

Neurological conditions such as strokes and other focal lesions have permitted the definition of several disorders of visual perception. *Apperceptive visual agnosia* is the inability to identify and draw items using visual cues, with preservation of other sensory modalities. It represents a failure of transmission of information from the higher visual sensory pathway to the association areas and is due to bilateral lesions in the visual association areas. *Associative visual agnosia* is the inability to name or use objects despite the ability to draw them. It is caused by bilateral medial occipitotemporal lesions and may occur along with other visual impairments. Color perception may be ablated in lesions of the dominant occipital lobe that include the splenium of the corpus callosum. *Color agnosia* is the inability to recognize a color despite being able to match it. *Color anomia* is the inability to name a color despite being able to point to it. *Central achromatopsia* is a complete inability to perceive color. *Anton's syndrome* is a failure to acknowledge blindness, possibly owing to interruption of fibers involved in self-assessment. It is seen with bilateral occipital lobe lesions. The most common causes are hypoxic injury, stroke, metabolic encephalopathy, migraine, herniation resulting from mass lesions, trauma, and leukodystrophy. *Balint's syndrome* consists of a triad of optic ataxia (the inability to direct optically guided movements), oculomotor apraxia (inability to direct gaze rapidly), and simultanagnosia (inability to integrate a visual scene to perceive it as a whole). Balint's syndrome is seen in bilateral parieto-occipital lesions. *Gerstmann syndrome* includes agraphia, calculation difficulties (acalculia), right-left disorientation, and finger agnosia. It has been attributed to lesions of the dominant parietal lobe.

Auditory System. Sounds are instantaneous, incremental changes in ambient air pressure. The pressure changes cause the ear's tympanic membrane to vibrate; the vibration is then transmitted to the ossicles (malleus, incus, and stapes) and thereby to the endolymph or fluid of the cochlear spiral. Vibrations of the endolymph move cilia on hair cells, which generate neural impulses. The hair cells respond to sounds of different frequency in a tonotopic manner within the cochlea, like a long spiral piano keyboard. Neural impulses from the hair cells travel in a tonotopic arrangement to the brain in the fibers of the cochlear nerve. They enter the brainstem cochlear nuclei, are relayed through the lateral lemniscus to the inferior colliculi, and then to the medial geniculate nucleus (MGN) of the thalamus. MGN neurons project to the primary auditory cortex in the posterior temporal lobe. Dichotic listening tests, in which different stimuli are presented to each ear simultaneously, demonstrate that most of the input from one ear activates the contralateral auditory cortex and that the left hemisphere tends to be dominant for auditory processing.

In the auditory system, the temporal and tonotopic pattern of cortical projections to the primary auditory cortex encodes pitch and begins to localize sounds in space. Sound localization relative to the ears is achieved by subtle comparisons of sound intensity and phase between the two ears. This function occurs in a brain region that is spatially distinct from the primary auditory cortex and that has cells that respond specifically to movements of the sound source relative to the listener. There is evidence that this task is mediated by the right hemisphere. The helices of the pinna facilitate localization by producing characteristic echoes, depending on the angle at which the sound hits the ear.

Extraction of sonic features is achieved through a combination of mechanical and neural filters. The representation of sound is roughly tonotopic in the primary auditory cortex, whereas *lexical processing,* the extraction of vowels, consonants, and words from the auditory input occurs in higher language association areas, especially in the left temporal lobe (Fig. 3.1–10). The syndrome of *word deafness,* characterized by intact hearing for voices but an inability to recognize speech, may reflect damage to the left parietal cortex. This syndrome is thought to result from a disconnection of the auditory cortex from Wernicke's area. A rare, complementary syndrome, *auditory sound agnosia,* is defined as the inability to recognize nonverbal sounds, such as a horn or a cat's meow, in the presence of intact hearing and speech recognition. Researchers consider this syndrome to be the right hemisphere correlate of pure word deafness.

Olfaction. Odorants, or volatile chemical cues, enter the nose, are solubilized in the nasal mucus, and bind to odorant receptors displayed on the surface of the sensory neurons of the olfactory epithelium. Each neuron in the epithelium displays a unique odorant receptor, and cells displaying a given receptor are randomly arranged within the olfactory epithelium. Humans possess several hundred distinct receptor molecules that bind the huge variety of environmental odorants; workers estimate that humans can discriminate 10,000 different odors. Odorant binding generates neural impulses, which travel

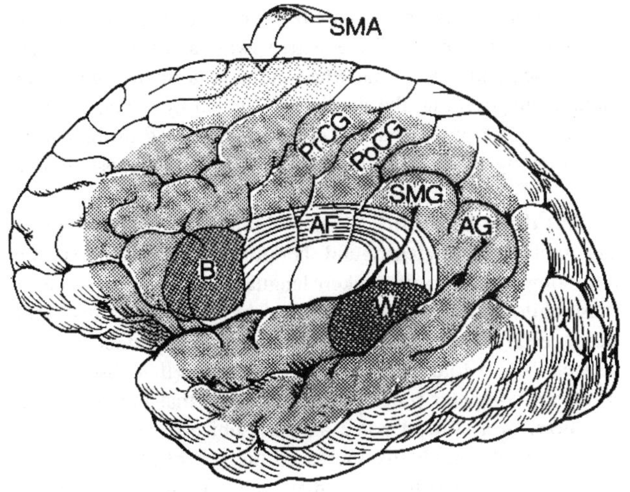
SMA
PrCG
PoCG
SMG
AF
AG
B
W

FIGURE 3.1–10
Language areas of the left hemisphere: *B,* Broca's area; *W,* Wernicke's area; *AF,* arcuate fasciculus; *SMA,* supplementary motor area; *PrCG,* precentral gyrus; *PoCG,* postcentral gyrus; *SMG,* supramarginal gyrus; and *AG,* angular gyrus. Language comprehension occurs in Wernicke's area, which is connected to Broca's area by the arcuate fasciculus. Generation of speech occurs in Broca's area. (Reprinted with permission from Filley CM: *Neurobehavioral Anatomy,* p 76. University Press of Colorado, Niwot, CO, 1995.)

along the axons of the sensory nerves through the cribriform plate to the olfactory bulb. Within the bulb, all axons corresponding to a given receptor converge onto only 1or 2 of 3,000 processing units called *glomeruli.* Because each odorant activates several receptors that activate a characteristic pattern of glomeruli, the identity of external chemical molecules is represented internally by a spatial pattern of neural activity in the olfactory bulb.

The central projections of fibers from the olfactory bulb are less well understood. Unlike the signals of the somatosensory system, vision, and hearing, olfactory signals do not pass through the thalamus but project directly to the frontal lobe and the limbic system, especially the pyriform cortex. The connections to the limbic system (amygdala, hippocampus, pyriform cortex) are significant: Olfactory cues stimulate strong emotional responses and may evoke powerful memories.

Olfaction is the most ancient sense in evolutionary terms and is tightly associated with sexual and reproductive responses. A related chemosensory structure, the vomeronasal organ, is thought to detect *pheromones,* chemical cues that trigger unconscious, stereotyped responses. In some animals, ablation of the vomeronasal organ in early life may prevent the onset of puberty. Recent studies have suggested that humans also respond to pheromones in a manner that varies according to the menstrual cycle. The structures of higher olfactory processing in phylogenetically more primitive animals have evolved in humans into the limbic system, the center of the emotional brain and the gate through which experience is admitted into memory according to emotional significance. The elusive basic animal drives with which clinical psychiatry constantly grapples may therefore, in fact, originate from the ancient centers of higher olfactory processing.

Taste. Soluble chemical cues in the mouth bind to receptors in the tongue and stimulate the gustatory nerves, which project to the nucleus solitarius in the brainstem. Only very broad classes of stimuli are thought to be discriminated by the sense of taste: sweet, sour, bitter, and salty. Each modality is mediated through a unique set of cellular receptors and channels. The detection and discrimination of foods, for example, involves a combination of the senses of taste, olfaction, touch, vision, and hearing. Taste fibers activate the medial temporal lobe, but the higher cortical localization of taste is only poorly understood.

Autonomic Sensory System

The autonomic nervous system monitors the basic functions necessary for life. The activity of visceral organs, blood pressure, cardiac output, blood glucose levels, and body temperature are all transmitted to the brain by autonomic fibers. Most autonomic sensory information remains unconscious; if such information rises to conscious levels, it is only as a vague sensation, in contrast to the capacity of the primary senses to transmit sensations rapidly and exactly.

Activity-Dependent Modulation of Sensory Networks in Development and in Adulthood

Somatosensory System. There is a strict somatotopic representation at each level of the somatosensory system. During development, neurons extend axons to connect to distant brain regions; after arriving at the destination, a set of axons must therefore sort itself to preserve the somatotopic organization. A classical experimental paradigm for this developmental process is the representation of a mouse's whiskers in the somatosensory cortex. The murine somatosensory cortex contains a barrel field of cortical columns, each of which corresponds to one whisker. When mice are inbred to produce fewer whiskers, fewer somatosensory cortex barrels also appear. Each barrel is expanded in area, and the entire barrel field covers the same area of the somatosensory cortex as in normal animals. This experiment demonstrates that certain higher cortical structures may form in response to peripheral input and that different complexities of input determine different patterns of synaptic connectivity. Although the mechanisms by which peripheral input molds cortical architecture are largely unknown, animal model paradigms are beginning to yield clues. For example, in a mutant mouse that lacks monoamine oxidase A and that therefore has extremely high cortical levels of serotonin, barrels fail to form in the somatosensory cortex. This result indirectly implicates serotonin in the mechanism of barrel field development.

In adults, the classic mapping studies of Wilder Penfield suggested the existence of a homunculus, an immutable cortical representation of the body surface. More recent experimental evidence from primate studies and from stroke patients, however, has promoted a more plastic conception than was

Penfield's. There are minor variations in the cortical pattern of normal individuals, yet dramatic shifts in the map can occur in response to loss of cortex from stroke or injury. When a stroke ablates a significant fraction of the somatosensory homunculus, the homuncular representation begins to contract and shift proportionately to fill the remaining intact cortex.

Moreover, the cortical map can be rearranged solely in response to a change in the pattern of tactile stimulation of the fingers. The somatotopic representation of the proximal and distal segments of each finger normally forms a contiguous map, presumably because both segments contact surfaces simultaneously. But under experimental conditions in which the distal segments of all fingers are simultaneously stimulated while contact of the distal and proximal parts of each finger is separated, the cortical map gradually shifts 90 degrees to reflect the new sensory experience. In the revised map, the cortical representation of the proximal segment of each finger is no longer contiguous with that of the distal segment. These data support the notion that the internal representation of the external world, while static in gross structure, may be continuously modified at the level of synaptic connectivity to reflect relevant sensory experiences. The cortical representation also tends to shift to fit entirely into the available amount of cortex.

These results support the notion that cortical representations of sensory input or of memories may be holographic rather than spatially fixed: The pattern of activity, rather than the physical structure, may encode information. In sensory systems, this plasticity of cortical representation allows for recovery from brain lesions; the phenomenon may also underlie learning.

Visual System. In humans, the initial projections from both eyes intermingle in the cortex. During the development of visual connections in the early postnatal period, there is a window of time during which binocular visual input is required for development of ocular dominance columns in the primary visual cortex. Occlusion of one eye during this critical period completely eliminates the persistence of its fibers in the cortex and allows the fibers of the active eye to innervate the entire visual cortex. In contrast, when normal binocular vision is allowed during the critical development window, the usual dominance columns form; occluding one eye after the completion of innervation of the cortex produces no subsequent alteration of the ocular dominance columns. This paradigm crystallizes the importance of early childhood experience on the formation of adult brain circuitry.

Ocular dominance columns are stripes of cortex that receive input from only one eye, separated by stripes innervated only by fibers from the other eye (Fig. 3.1–6). The mechanism of the formation of dominance columns is the strengthening of synapses that fire simultaneously and the pruning of synapses that fire asynchronously. Images entering one eye stimulate coordinated activity of adjacent neural fibers; this activity solidifies their cortical connections. Information from the other eye does not benefit from simultaneous firing of adjacent fibers, and its input is eliminated from the area.

An interesting experimental twist occurs in frogs, where each visual cortex is normally innervated by only one eye. If a third eye is grafted onto the brain before development of the visual connections and if its fibers arrive at the cortex coincidentally with those of the native eyes, a pattern of ocular dominance columns forms where none is normally seen. This finding suggests that the neural mechanism by which competing inputs are organized and compartmentalized in the cortex is a property with a high degree of evolutionary conservation.

Auditory System. Certain children are unable to process auditory input clearly and therefore have impaired speech and comprehension of spoken language. Studies on some of these children have determined that they can in fact discriminate speech if the consonants and vowels—the phonemes—are slowed 2- to 5-fold by a computer. Based on this observation, a tutorial computer program was designed that initially asked questions in a slowed voice and, as subjects answered questions correctly, gradually increased the rate of phoneme presentation to approximate normal rates of speech. Subjects gained some abilities to discriminate routine speech over a period of 2 to 6 weeks and appeared to retain these skills after the period of tutoring was completed. This finding probably has therapeutic applicability to 5 to 8 percent of children with speech delay, but ongoing studies may expand the eligible group of students. This finding, moreover, suggests that neuronal circuits required for auditory processing can be recruited and be made more efficient long after language is normally learned, provided that the circuits are allowed to finish their task properly, even if this requires slowing the rate of input. Circuits thus functioning with high fidelity can then be trained to speed their processing.

A recent report has extended the age at which language acquisition may be acquired for the first time. A boy who suffered from intractable epilepsy of one hemisphere was mute because the uncontrolled seizure activity precluded the development of organized language functions. At the age of 9 years he had the abnormal hemisphere removed to cure the epilepsy. Although he had not spoken to that point of his life, he initiated an accelerated acquisition of language milestones beginning at that age and ultimately gained language abilities only a few years delayed relative to his chronological age. Researchers cannot place an absolute upper limit on the age at which language abilities may be learned, although acquisition at ages beyond the usual childhood period is usually incomplete. Anecdotal reports document acquisition of reading skills after the age of 80 years.

Olfaction. During normal development, axons from the nasal olfactory epithelium project to the olfactory bulb and segregate into about 3,000 equivalent glomeruli. If in the early postnatal period an animal is exposed to a single dominant scent, then one glomerulus expands massively within the bulb at the expense of the surrounding glomeruli. Thus, as was discussed above with reference to the barrel fields of the somatosensory cortex, the size of brain structures may reflect the environmental input.

Alteration of Conscious Sensory Perception Through Hypnosis

Hypnosis is a state of heightened suggestibility attainable by a certain proportion of the population. Under a state of hypnosis, gross distortions of perception in any sensory modality can be achieved on an instantaneous timescale. The anatomy of the sensory system does not change, yet the same specific stimuli may be perceived with diametrically opposed emotional value before and after induction of the hypnotic state. For example, under hypnosis a person may savor an onion as if it were a luscious chocolate truffle, only to reject the onion as abhorrently pungent seconds later, when the hypnotic suggestion is reversed. The localization of the hypnotic switch has not been determined, but it presumably involves sensory as well as association areas of the brain. Experiments in human volunteers, in which neural pathways are traced through functional neuroimaging, have demonstrated that shifts in attention in an environmental setting determine changes in the regions of the brain that are activated, on an instantaneous timescale. Thus the organizing centers of the brain may route conscious and unconscious thoughts through different sequences of neural processing centers, depending on a person's ultimate goals and emotional state. These attention-mediated variations in synaptic utilization can occur on an instantaneous timescale. A similar alteration in the routing of associational processing may occur in hypnotic states.

MOTOR SYSTEMS

Layers of Evolutionary Sophistication

The movements of the body muscles are controlled by the lower motor neurons, which extend axons, some as long as 1 meter in length, to the muscle fibers. The firing of the lower motor neurons is regulated by the summation of upper motor neuron activity. In the brainstem, primitive systems produce gross coordinated movements of the entire body. Activation of the rubrospinal tract stimulates flexion of all limbs, whereas activation of the vestibulospinal tract causes all limbs to extend. In newborn infants, for example, all limbs are held tightly flexed, presumably through the dominance of the rubrospinal system. In fact, the movements of an anencephalic infant, who completely lacks a cerebral cortex, may be indistinguishable from the movements of a normal newborn. In the first few months of life, the flexor spasticity is gradually mitigated by the opposite actions of the vestibulospinal fibers, and more limb mobility occurs.

At the top of the motor hierarchy is the corticospinal tract, which controls fine movements and which eventually dominates the brainstem system during the first years of life. The upper motor neurons of the corticospinal tract reside in the posterior frontal lobe, in a section of cortex known as the *motor strip* (Fig. 3.1–4, Brodmann area 4). Planned movements are conceived in the association areas of the brain, and, in consultation with the basal ganglia and cerebellum, the motor cortex directs their smooth execution. The importance of the corticospinal system becomes immediately evident in strokes, where spasticity returns as the cortical influence is ablated and the actions of the brainstem motor systems are released from cortical modulation.

Basal Ganglia

The *basal ganglia,* a subcortical group of gray matter nuclei, appear to mediate postural tone. There are four functionally distinct ganglia: the striatum, the pallidum, the substantia nigra, and the subthalamic nucleus. Collectively known as the corpus striatum, the caudate and putamen harbor components of both motor and association systems. The caudate nucleus plays an important role in the modulation of motor acts. Anatomic and functional neuroimaging studies have correlated decreased activation of the caudate with obsessive-compulsive behavior. When functioning properly, the caudate nucleus acts as a gatekeeper to allow the motor system to perform only those acts that are goal directed. When it fails to perform its gatekeeper function, extraneous acts are performed as in obsessive-compulsive disorder or in the tic disorders, such as Tourette's disorder. Overactivity of the striatum owing to lack of dopaminergic inhibition, for example in parkinsonian conditions, results in *bradykinesia,* an inability to initiate movements. The caudate, in particular, shrinks dramatically in Huntington's disease. This disorder is characterized by rigidity, on which is gradually superimposed choreiform or "dancing" movements. Psychosis may be a prominent feature of Huntington's disease, and suicide is not uncommon. The caudate is also thought to influence associative, or cognitive, processes.

The globus pallidus contains two parts linked in series. In a cross section of the brain, the internal and external parts of the globus pallidus are nested within the concavity of the putamen. The globus pallidus receives input from the corpus striatum and projects fibers to the thalamus. This structure may be severely damaged in Wilson's disease and in carbon monoxide poisoning, which are characterized by dystonic posturing and flapping movements of the arms and legs.

The substantia nigra is named the black substance because the presence of melanin pigment causes it to appear black to the naked eye. It has two parts, one of which is functionally equivalent to the globus pallidus interna. The other part degenerates in Parkinson's disease. Parkinsonism is characterized by rigidity and tremor and is associated with depression in over 30 percent of cases.

Finally, lesions in the subthalamic nucleus yield ballistic movements, sudden limb jerks of such velocity that they are compared to projectile movement.

Together, the nuclei of the basal ganglia appear capable of initiating and maintaining the full range of useful movements. Workers have speculated that the nuclei serve to configure the activity of the overlying motor cortex to fit the purpose of the association areas. In addition, they appear to integrate proprioceptive feedback to maintain an intended movement.

Cerebellum

The cerebellum consists of a simple six-cell pattern of circuitry that is replicated roughly 10 million times. Simultaneous recordings of the cerebral cortex and the cerebellum have shown that the cerebellum is activated several milliseconds before a planned movement. Moreover, ablation of the cerebellum renders intentional movements coarse and tremulous. These data suggest that the cerebellum carefully modulates the tone of agonistic and antagonistic muscles by predicting the relative degrees of contraction needed for smooth motion. This prepared motor plan is used to ensure that exactly the right amount of flexor and extensor stimuli is sent to the muscles.

Recent functional imaging data have shown that the cerebellum is active even during the mere imagination of motor acts, when no movements ultimately result from its calculations. The cerebellum harbors two, and possibly more, distinct "homunculi" or cortical representations of the body plan.

Motor Cortex

Penfield's groundbreaking work defined a motor homunculus in the precentral gyrus, Brodmann area 4 (Fig. 3.1–4), where a somatotopic map of the motor neurons is found. Individual cells within the motor strip cause contraction of single muscles. The brain region immediately anterior to the motor strip is called the *supplementary motor area,* Brodmann area 6. This region contains cells that when individually stimulated can trigger more complex movements, by influencing a firing sequence of motor strip cells.

The skillful use of the hands is called *praxis,* and deficits in skilled movements are termed *apraxias.* The three levels of apraxia are limb kinetic, ideomotor, and ideational. *Limb-kinetic apraxia* is the inability to use the contralateral hand in the presence of preserved strength; it results from isolated lesions in the supplementary motor area, which contains neurons that stimulate functional sequences of neurons in the motor strip.

Ideomotor apraxia is the inability to perform an isolated motor act upon command, despite preserved comprehension, strength, and spontaneous performance of the same act. Ideomotor apraxia simultaneously affects both limbs and involves functions so specialized that they are localized to only one hemisphere. Conditions in two separate areas can produce this apraxia: Disconnection of the language comprehension area, Wernicke's area, from the motor regions causes an inability to follow spoken commands; and lesions to the left premotor area may impair the actual motor program as it is generated by the higher order motor neurons. This program is transmitted across the corpus callosum to the right premotor area, which directs the movements of the left hand. A lesion in this callosal projection may also cause an isolated ideomotor apraxia in the left hand. This syndrome implies the representation of specific motor acts within discrete sections of the left premotor cortex. Thus, just as some cells respond selectively to specific environmental features in the higher sensory cortices, some cells in the premotor cortex direct specific complex motor tasks.

Ideational apraxia obtains when the individual components of a sequence of skilled acts can be performed in isolation, but the entire series cannot be organized and executed as a whole. For example, the sequence of opening an envelope, removing the letter, unfolding it, and placing it on the table cannot be performed in order, even though the individual acts can be performed in isolation. The representation of the concept of a motor sequence may involve several areas, specifically the left parietal cortex, but it likely also relies on the sequencing and executive functions of the prefrontal cortex. This apraxia is a typical finding of diffuse cortical degeneration, such as Alzheimer's disease.

Autonomic Motor System

The *autonomic system* is divided into two branches, the sympathetic and the parasympathetic. As a rule, organs are innervated by both types of fibers, which often serve antagonistic roles. The *parasympathetic system* slows the heart rate and begins the process of digestion. In contrast, the *sympathetic system* mediates the fight or flight response, with increased heart rate, shunting of blood away from the viscera, and increased respiration. The sympathetic system is highly activated by sympathomimetic drugs, such as amphetamine and cocaine, and may also be activated by withdrawal from sedating drugs, such as alcohol, benzodiazepines, and opioids. Investigators who have found an increased risk of heart attacks in people with high levels of hostility have suggested that chronic activation of the sympathetic fight or flight response, with elevated secretion of adrenaline, may underlie this association.

The brain center that drives the autonomic motor system is the *hypothalamus,* which houses a set of paired nuclei that appear to control appetite, rage, temperature, blood pressure, perspiration, and sexual drive. For example, lesions to the ventromedial nucleus, the satiety center, produce a voracious appetite and rage. In contrast, lesions to the upper region of the lateral nucleus, the hunger center, produce a profound loss of appetite. Numerous research groups are making intense efforts to define the biochemical regulation of appetite and obesity and frequently target the role of the hypothalamus.

In the regulation of sexual attraction, the role of the hypothalamus has also become an area of active research. At the beginning of this decade, three groups independently reported neuroanatomical differences between certain of the hypothalamic nuclei of heterosexual and homosexual men. Researchers interpreted this finding to suggest that human sexual orientation has a neuroanatomical basis, and this result has stimulated several follow-up studies of the biological basis of sexual orientation. At present, however, these controversial findings are not accepted without question, and no clear consensus has emerged about whether the structure of the hypothalamus consistently correlates with male sexual orientation. In animal studies, early nurturing and sexual experiences have been shown to consistently alter the size of specific hypothalamic nuclei. Because of the central role of sexual behavior in clinical psychiatry, this area of neuroscience research promises to yield interesting and controversial findings in coming years.

ASSOCIATION SYSTEMS

Primitive Reflex Circuit

Sensory pathways function as extractors of specific features from the overwhelming multitude of environmental stimuli, whereas motor pathways carry out the wishes of the organism. These pathways may be linked directly, as, for example, in the spinal cord, where a primitive reflex arc may mediate the brisk withdrawal of a limb from a painful stimulus, without immediate conscious awareness. In this loop, the peripheral stimulus activates the sensory nerve, the sensory neuron synapses on and directly activates the motor neuron, and the motor neuron drives the muscle to contract. This response is strictly local and all-or-none. Such primitive reflex arcs, however, rarely generate an organism's behaviors. In most behaviors, sensory systems project to association areas, where sensory information is interpreted in terms of internally determined memories, motivations, and drives. The exhibited behavior results from a plan of action determined by the association components and carried out by the motor systems.

Basic Organization of the Brain

Many theorists have subdivided the brain into functional systems. Brodmann defined 47 areas based on cytoarchitectonic distinctions, a cataloguing that has been remarkably durable as the functional anatomy of the brain has emerged (Fig. 3.1–4). A separate function, based on data from lesion studies and from functional neuroimaging, has been assigned to nearly all Brodmann areas. At the other extreme, certain experts have distinguished only three processing blocks: The brainstem and the thalamic reticular activating system provide arousal and set up attention; the posterior cortex integrates perceptions and generates language; and at the highest level, the frontal cortex generates programs and executes plans like an orchestra conductor.

Hemispheric lateralization of function is a key feature of higher cortical processing: The primary sensory cortices for touch, vision, hearing, smell, and taste are represented bilaterally, and the first level of abstraction for these modalities is also usually represented bilaterally. The highest levels of feature extraction, however, are generally unified in one brain hemisphere only. For example, recognition of familiar and unfamiliar faces appears localized to the left inferior temporal cortex, and cortical processing of olfaction occurs in the right frontal lobe. The clearest known example of hemispheric lateralization is the localization of language functions to the left hemisphere. Starting with the work of Broca and Wernicke in the 19th century, researchers have drawn a detailed map of language comprehension and expression (Fig. 3.1–10). At least eight types of aphasias in which one or more components of the language pathway are injured have been defined (Table 3.1–1). *Prosody,* the emotional and affective components of language, or "body language," appears to be localized in a mirror set of brain units in the right hemisphere.

The *limbic system,* a circuit of phylogenetically ancient structures, is responsible for generating and modifying memories and for assigning emotional weight to sensory and recalled experience (Fig. 3.1–11). One nucleus in the limbic system, the *amygdala,* receives fibers from all sensory areas and appears to serve as a gate for the assignment of emotional significance to memories. The limbic structures in lower animals are devoted in large measure to processing olfactory input, a role superseded in humans by memory functions.

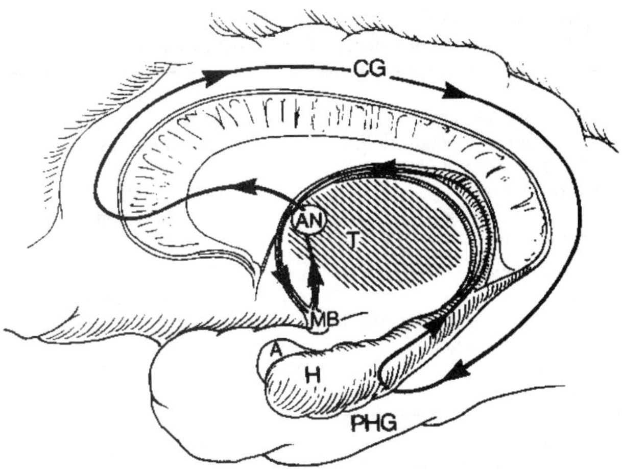
CG
AN
T
MB
A
H
PHG

FIGURE 3.1–11

Papez circuit. *H,* hippocampus; *A,* amygdala; *PHG,* parahippocampal gyrus; *CG,* cingulate gyrus; *AN,* anterior nucleus of the thalamus; *MB,* mamillary body; and *T,* thalamus. (Reprinted with permission from Filley CM: *Neurobehavioral Anatomy,* p 132. University Press of Colorado, Niwot, CO, 1995.)

Hypotheses about the flow of thought in the brain are based on few experimental data, although this scarcity of findings has not impeded numerous theoreticians from speculating about functional neuroanatomy. Several roles have been tentatively assigned to specific lobes of the brain, on the basis of the functional deficits resulting from localized injury. These data indicate that certain regions of cortex may be necessary for a specific function, but they do not define the complete set of structures sufficient for a complex task. Anecdotal evidence from surface electrocorticography for the study of epilepsy, for example, suggests that a right parietal seizure impulse may shoot immediately to the left frontal lobe and then to the right temporal lobe before spreading locally to the remainder of the parietal lobe. This evidence illustrates the limitations of na-

Table 3.1–1
Localization of Aphasia Syndromes

Aphasia Type	Spontaneous Speech	Auditory Comprehension	Repetition	Naming	Localization (Left Hemisphere)
Broca's	Nonfluent	Good	Poor	Poor	Broca's area
Wernicke's	Fluent	Poor	Poor	Poor	Wernicke's area
Conduction	Fluent	Good	Poor	Poor	Arcuate fasciculus
Global	Nonfluent	Poor	Poor	Poor	Perisylvian region
Transcortical motor	Nonfluent	Good	Good	Poor	Anterior border zone
Transcortical sensory	Fluent	Poor	Good	Poor	Posterior border zone
Anomic	Fluent	Good	Good	Poor	Angular gyrus
Mixed transcortical	Nonfluent	Poor	Good	Poor	Anterior and posterior border zone

Reprinted with permission from Filley CM: *Neurobehavioral Anatomy,* p 80. University Press of Colorado, Niwot, CO, 1995.

Table 3.1–2
Regional Functions of the Human Brain

Frontal lobes	Parietal lobes
Voluntary movement	Tactile sensation
Language production (left)	Visuospatial function (right)
Motor prosody (right)	Reading (left)
Comportment	Calculation (left)
Executive function	Occipital lobes
Motivation	Vision
Temporal lobes	Visual perception
Audition	
Language comprehension (left)	
Sensory prosody (right)	
Memory	
Emotion	

Reprinted with permission from Filley CM: *Neurobehavioral Anatomy,* p 6. University Press of Colorado, Niwot, CO, 1995.

ively assigning a mental function to a single brain region. Functional neuroimaging studies frequently reveal simultaneous activation of disparate brain regions during the performance of even a simple cognitive task. Nevertheless, particularly in the processing of vision and language, fairly well defined lobar syndromes have been confirmed (Table 3.1–2).

Localization of Specific Brain Functions

Arousal and Attention. *Arousal,* or the establishment and maintenance of an awake state, appears to require at least three brain regions. Within the brainstem, the ascending reticular activating system (ARAS), a diffuse set of neurons, appears to set the level of consciousness. The ARAS projects to the intralaminar nuclei of the thalamus, and these nuclei in turn project widely throughout the cortex. Electrophysiological studies show that both the thalamus and the cortex fire rhythmical bursts of neuronal activity at the rates of 20 to 40 cycles per second. During sleep, these bursts are not synchronized. During wakefulness, the ARAS stimulates the thalamic intralaminar nuclei, which in turn coordinate the oscillations of different cortical regions. The greater the synchronization, the higher the level of wakefulness. The absence of arousal produces stupor and coma. In general, small discrete lesions of the ARAS may produce a stuporous state, whereas at the hemispheric level, large bilateral lesions are required to cause the same depression in alertness. One particularly unfortunate but instructive condition involving extensive, permanent bilateral cortical dysfunction is the persistent vegetative state. Sleep–wake cycles may be preserved, and the eyes may appear to gaze; but there is no registering of the external world and no evidence of conscious thought. This condition would represent the expression of the isolated actions of the ARAS and the thalamus.

The maintenance of attention appears to require an intact right frontal lobe. For example, a widely used test of persistence requires scanning and identifying only the letter *A* from a long list of random letters. Normal people can usually maintain performance of such a task for several minutes, but in patients with right frontal lobe dysfunction, this capacity is severally curtailed. Lesions of similar size in other regions of the cortex usually do not affect persistence tasks. In contrast, the more generally adaptive skill of maintaining a coherent line of thought is diffusely distributed throughout the cortex. Many medical conditions may affect this skill and may produce acute confusion or delirium (Table 3.1–3).

One widely diagnosed disorder of attention is attention-deficit/hyperactivity disorder (ADHD). No pathological findings have been consistently associated with this disorder. Functional neuroimaging studies, however, have variously documented either frontal lobe or right hemisphere hypometabolism in ADHD patients, when compared to normal controls. These findings strengthen the notion that the frontal lobes, especially the right frontal lobe, are essential to the maintenance of attention.

Memory. The clinical assessment of memory should test three periods, which have distinct anatomical correlates. *Immediate memory* functions over a period of seconds; *recent memory* applies on the scale of minutes to days; and *remote memory* encompasses months to years. Immediate memory is implicit in the concept of attention and the ability to follow a train of thought. This ability has been divided into phonological and visuospatial, and functional imaging has localized these components of immediate memory to the left and right hemispheres, respectively. A related concept, incorporating immediate and recent memory, is working memory. Working memory is defined as the ability to store information for several seconds, while other, related cognitive operations take place on this information. Recent studies have shown that single neurons in the dorsolateral prefrontal cortex not only record features necessary for working memory, but also record the certainty with which the information is known and the degree of expectation assigned to the permanence of a particular en-

Table 3.1–3
Major Causes of Acute Confusion

Toxic	Vascular
Prescription drugs	Stroke
Nonprescription drugs	Subarachnoid hemorrhage
Drug withdrawal	Traumatic
Metabolic	Concussion
Hypoxia	Severe traumatic brain injury
Hypoglycemia	Neoplastic
Uremia	Deep midline tumors
Hepatic disease	Increased intracranial pressure
Thiamine deficiency	Postsurgical
Electrolyte disturbances	Preoperative atropine
Endocrinopathies	Hypoxia
Infectious and inflammatory	Analgesics
Meningitis	Electrolyte imbalance
Encephalitis	Fever
Vasculitis	
Abscess	
Epileptic	
Postictal state	
Complex partial status epilepticus	
Absence status epilepticus	

Reprinted with permission from Filley CM: *Neurobehavioral Anatomy,* p 52. University Press of Colorado, Niwot, CO, 1995.

vironmental feature. Some neurons fire rapidly for an item that is eagerly awaited, but may cease firing if hopes are dashed unexpectedly. The encoding of the emotional value of an item contained in the working memory may be of great usefulness in determining goal-directed behavior. Some researchers localize working memory predominantly to the left frontal cortex. Clinically, however, bilateral prefrontal cortex lesions are required for severe impairment of working memory.

Three brain structures are critical to the formation of memories; the medial temporal lobe, certain diencephalic nuclei, and the basal forebrain. The *medial temporal lobe* houses the *hippocampus,* an elongated, highly repetitive network. The amygdala is adjacent to the anterior end of the hippocampus. The *amygdala* has been suggested to rate the emotional importance of an experience and to activate the level of hippocampal activity accordingly. Thus, an emotionally intense experience is indelibly etched in memory, but indifferent stimuli are quickly disregarded.

Animal studies have defined a hippocampal place code, a pattern of cellular activation in the hippocampus that corresponds to the animal's location in space. When the animal is introduced to a novel environment, the hippocampus is broadly activated. As the animal explores and roams, the firing of certain hippocampal regions begins to correspond to specific locations in the environment. In about 1 hour, a highly detailed internal representation of the external space (a "cognitive map") appears in the form of specific firing patterns of the hippocampal cells. These patterns of neuronal firing may bear little spatial resemblance to the environment they represent; rather, they may appear randomly arranged in the hippocampus. If the animal is manually placed in a certain part of a familiar space, only the corresponding hippocampal regions show intense neural activity. When recoding continues into sleep periods, firing sequences of hippocampal cells outlining a coherent path of navigation through the environment are registered, even though the animal is motionless. If the animal is removed from the environment for several days and then returned, the previously registered hippocampal place code is immediately reactivated. A series of animal experiments has dissociated the formation of the hippocampal place code from either visual, auditory, or olfactory cues, although each of these modalities may contribute partially to place code generation. Other factors may include internal calculations of distances based on counting footsteps or other proprioceptive information. Data from targeted genetic mutations in mice have implicated both the *N*-methyl-D-aspartate (NMDA) glutamate receptors and the calcium-calmodulin kinase II (CaMKII) in the proper formation of hippocampal place fields. These data suggest that the hippocampus is a significant site for formation and storage of immediate and recent memories. It is conceivable that, although no data yet support the notion, the hippocampal cognitive map is inappropriately reactivated during a déjà-vu experience.

The most famous human subject in the study of memory is H. M., a man with intractable epilepsy, to alleviate which both his hippocampi and amygdalae were surgically removed. The epilepsy was controlled, but he was left with a complete inability to form and recall memories of facts. The finding that H. M.'s learning and memory skills were relatively preserved has lead to the suggestion that declarative or factual memory may be separate within the brain from procedural or skill-related memory. A complementary deficit in procedural memory with preservation of declarative memory may be seen in people with Parkinson's disease, in whom dopaminergic neurons of the nigrostriatal tract degenerate. Because this deficit in procedural memory can be ameliorated with treatment with levodopa, which is thought to potentiate dopaminergic neurotransmission in the nigrostriatal pathway, a role has been postulated for dopamine in procedural memory. Additional case reports have further implicated the amygdala and the afferent and efferent fiber tracts of the hippocampus as being essential to the formation of memories. Lesional studies have also suggested a mild lateralization of hippocampal function in which the left hippocampus is more efficient at forming verbal memories and the right hippocampus tends to form nonverbal memories. After unilateral lesions in humans, however, the remaining hippocampus may compensate to a large extent. Medical causes of amnesia include alcoholism, seizures, migraine, drugs, vitamin deficiencies, trauma, strokes, tumors, infections, and degenerative diseases.

The motor system within the cortex receives directives from the association areas. The performance of a novel act requires constant feedback from the sensory and association areas for completion, and functional neuroimaging studies have demonstrated widespread activation of the cortex during unskilled acts. Memorized motor acts initially require activation of the medial temporal lobe. With practice, however, the performance of ever larger segments of an act necessary to achieve a goal become encoded within discrete areas of the premotor and parietal cortices, particularly the left parietal cortex, with the result that a much more limited activation of the cortex is seen during highly skilled acts and the medial temporal lobe is bypassed. This process is called the corticalization of motor commands. In lay terms, the process suggests a neuroanatomical basis for the adage "practice makes perfect."

Within the diencephalon, the dorsal medial nucleus of the thalamus and the mamillary bodies appear necessary for memory formation. These two structures are damaged in thiamine deficiency states usually seen in chronic alcoholics, and their inactivation is associated with Korsakoff's syndrome. This syndrome is characterized by severe inability to form new memories and a variable inability to recall remote memories. A colorful tendency to confabulate to resolve contradictions introduced by gaps in memory has been described. A case report supporting the role of the thalamic dorsal medial nucleus in memory is that of the patient N. A., who suffered a penetrating injury to his left dorsal medial nucleus in a fencing mishap and was left with a selective deficit in verbal memory.

The most common clinical disorder of memory is Alzheimer's disease. Alzheimer's disease is characterized pathologically by the degeneration of neurons and their replacement by senile plaques and neurofibrillary tangles. Clinicopathological studies have suggested that the cognitive decline is best correlated with the loss of synapses. Initially, the parietal and temporal lobes are affected, with relative sparing of the frontal lobes. This pattern of degeneration correlates with the early loss of memory, which is largely a temporal lobe function. Also, syntactical language comprehension and visuospatial organization, functions that rely heavily on the parietal lobe, are impaired early in the course of Alzheimer's disease. In contrast, personality changes, which reflect frontal lobe function, are relatively late consequences of Alzheimer's disease. Alzheimer's disease is discussed in Chapter 3, Section 3.4, and in Chapter 10. A rarer, complementary cortical degeneration syndrome, Pick's disease, first affects the frontal lobes while sparing the temporal and parietal lobes. In Pick's disease, there are early disinhibition and impaired language expression, which are signs of frontal dysfunction, with relatively preserved language comprehension and memory.

Memory loss can also result from disorders of the subcortical gray matter structures, specifically the basal ganglia and the brainstem nuclei, from disease of the white matter, or from disorders that affect both gray and white matter.

Language. Because of the major role of verbal and written language in human communication, the neuroanatomical basis of language is the most completely understood association function. Language disorders, also called aphasias, are readily diagnosed in routine conversation, whereas perceptual disorders may escape notice except during detailed neuropsychological testing, although these disorders may be due to injury of an equal volume of cortex. Among the earliest models of cortical localization of function were Broca's 1865 description of a loss of fluent speech caused by a lesion in the left inferior frontal lobe and Wernicke's 1874 localization of language comprehension to the left superior temporal lobe. Subsequent analyses of patients rendered aphasic by strokes, trauma, or tumors have led to the definition of the entire language association pathway from sensory input through the motor output (Fig. 3.1–10).

Language most clearly demonstrates hemispheric localization of function. In most people, the hemisphere dominant for language also directs the dominant hand. Ninety percent of the population is right-handed, and ninety-nine percent of right-handers have left hemispheric dominance for language. Of the 10 percent who are left-handers, 67 percent also have left hemispheric language dominance; the other 33 percent have either mixed or right hemispheric language dominance. This innate tendency to lateralization of language in the left hemisphere is highly associated with an asymmetry of the planum temporale, a triangular cortical patch on the superior surface of the temporal lobe that appears to harbor Wernicke's area. In patients with mixed hemispheric dominance for language, there is an absence of the expected asymmetry of the planum temporale. The fact that asymmetry has been observed in prenatal brains suggests a genetic determinant. Indeed, the absence of asymmetry runs in families, although both genetic and intrauterine influences probably contribute to the final pattern.

Language comprehension is processed at three levels. First, in *phonological processing,* individual sounds, such as vowels or consonants, are recognized in the inferior gyrus of the frontal lobes. Phonological processing improves if lip reading is allowed, if speech is slowed, or if contextual clues are provided. Second, *lexical processing* matches the phonological input with recognized words or sounds in the individual's memory. Lexical processing determines whether a sound is a word or not. Recent evidence has localized lexical processing to the left temporal lobe, where the representations of lexical data are organized according to semantic category. Third, *semantic processing* connects the words to their meaning. People with an isolated defect in semantic processing may retain the ability to repeat words in the absence of an ability to understand or spontaneously generate speech. Semantic processing activates the middle and superior gyri of the left temporal lobe, whereas the representation of the conceptual content of words is widely distributed in the cortex. Language production proceeds in the opposite direction, from the cortical semantic representations through the left temporal lexical nodes to either the oromotor phonological processing area, for speech, or the graphomotor system, for writing. Each of these areas may be independently or simultaneously damaged by stroke, trauma, infection, or tumor, resulting in a specific type of aphasia.

The garbled word salad or illogical utterances of an aphasic patient leave little uncertainty about the diagnosis of left-sided cortical injury, but the right hemisphere contributes a somewhat more subtle, but equally important, affective quality to language. For example, the phrase "I feel good" may be spoken with an infinite variety of shadings, each of which is differently understood. The perception of prosody and the appreciation of the associated gestures or "body language" appear to require an intact right hemisphere. Behavioral neurologists have mapped an entire pathway for prosody association in the right hemisphere that mirrors the language pathway of the left hemisphere. Patients with right hemisphere lesions, who have impaired comprehension or expression of prosody, may find it difficult to function in society despite their intact language skills.

Developmental dyslexia is defined as an unexpected difficulty with learning in the context of adequate intelligence, motivation, and education. Whereas speech consists of the logical combination of 44 basic phonemes of sounds, reading requires a broader set of brain functions and is thus more prone to disruption. The awareness of specific phonemes develops around the age of 4 to 6 years and appears to be a prerequisite to the acquisition of reading skills. Inability to recognize distinct phonemes has been shown to be the best predictor of a reading disability. Functional neuroimaging studies have localized the identification of letters to the occipital lobe adjacent to the primary visual cortex. Phonological processing occurs in the inferior frontal lobe, and semantic processing requires the superior and middle gyri of the left temporal lobe. A recent finding of uncertain significance is that phonological processing in men activates only the left inferior frontal gyrus, whereas phonological processing in women activates the inferior frontal gyrus bilaterally. Careful analysis of an individual's particular reading deficits can guide remedial tutoring efforts that can focus on weaknesses and thus attempt to bring the reading skills up to the general level of intelligence and verbal skills.

In children, developmental nonverbal learning disorder is postulated to result from right hemisphere dysfunction. Nonverbal learning disorder is characterized by poor fine motor control in the left hand, deficits in visuoperceptual organization, problems with mathematics, and incomplete or disturbed socialization.

Patients with nonfluent aphasia, who cannot complete a simple sentence, may be able to sing an entire song, apparently because many aspects of music production are localized to the right hemisphere. Music is represented predominantly in the right hemisphere, but the full complexity of musical ability seems to involve both hemispheres. Trained musicians appear to transfer many musical skills from the right hemisphere to the left as they gain proficiency in musical analysis and performance.

Emotion. People's emotional experiences occupy the attention of all mental health professionals. Emotion derives from basic drives, such as feeding, sex, reproduction, pleasure, pain, fear, and aggression, which all animals share. The neuroanatomical basis for these drives appears to be centered in the limbic system. Distinctly human emotions, such as affection, pride, guilt, pity, envy, and resentment, are largely learned and most likely are represented in the cortex. The regulation of drives appears to require an intact frontal cortex. The complex interplay of the emotions, however, is far beyond the understanding of functional neuroanatomists. Where, for example, are the representations of the id, the ego, and the superego? Through what pathway are ethical and moral judgments shepherded? What processes allow beauty to be in the eye of the beholder? These philosophical questions represent a true frontier of human discovery.

Within the cortex, several studies have suggested a hemispheric dichotomy of emotional representation. The left hemisphere houses the analytical mind but may have a limited emotional repertoire. For example, lesions to the right hemisphere, which cause profound functional deficits, may be noted with indifference by the intact left hemisphere. The denial of illness and of the inability to move the left hand in cases of right hemisphere injury is call *anosognosia.* In contrast, left hemisphere lesions, which cause profound aphasia, may trigger a catastrophic depression, as the intact right hemisphere struggles with the realization of the loss. The right hemisphere also appears dominant for affect, socialization, and body image.

Damage to the left hemisphere produces intellectual disorder and a loss of the narrative aspect of dreams. Damage to the right hemisphere produces affective disorders, loss of the visual aspects of dreams, and a failure to respond to humor, shadings of metaphor, and connotations. In dichotic vision experiments, two scenes of varied emotional content were displayed simultaneously to each half of the visual field and were perceived separately by each hemisphere. A more intense emotional response attended the scenes displayed to the left visual field that were processed by the right hemisphere. Moreover, hemisensory changes representing conversion disorders have been repeatedly noted to involve the left half of the body more often than the right, an observation that suggests an origin in the right hemisphere.

Within the hemispheres, the temporal and frontal lobes play a prominent role in emotion. The temporal lobe exhibits a high frequency of epileptic foci, and temporal lobe epilepsy (TLE) has presented an interesting model for the role of the temporal lobe in behavior. In studies of epilepsy, abnormal brain activation is analyzed, rather than the deficits in activity analyzed in classical lesional studies. TLE is of particular interest in psychiatry because temporal lobe seizures may often manifest bizarre behavior without the classic grand mal shaking movements caused by seizures in the motor cortex. A proposed TLE personality is characterized by hyposexuality, emotional intensity, and a perseverative approach to interactions, termed *viscosity.* Patients with left TLE may generate references to personal destiny and philosophical themes and may display a humorless approach to life. In contrast, patients with right TLE may display excessive emotionality, ranging from elation to sadness. Although TLE patients may display excessive aggression between seizures, the seizure itself may evoke fear.

The inverse of a TLE personality appears in people with bilateral injury to the temporal lobes after head trauma, cardiac arrest, herpes simplex encephalitis, or in Pick's disease. This lesion resembles the one described in the Klüver-Bucy syndrome, an experimental model of temporal lobe ablation in monkeys. Behavior in this syndrome is characterized by hypersexuality, placidity, a tendency to explore the environment with the mouth, inability to recognize the emotional significance of visual stimuli, and constantly shifting attention, called *hypermetamorphosis.* In contrast to the aggression-fear spectrum sometimes seen in patients with TLE, complete experimental ablation of the temporal lobes appears to produce a uniform, bland reaction to the environment, possibly due to inability to access memories.

The prefrontal cortices influence mood in a complementary way. Whereas activation of the left prefrontal cortex appears to lift the mood, activation of the right prefrontal cortex causes depression. A lesion to the left prefrontal area, at either the cortical or the subcortical level, abolishes the normal mood-elevating influences and produces depression and uncontrollable crying. In contrast, a comparable lesion to the right prefrontal area may produce laughter, euphoria, and *witzelsucht,* a tendency to joke and make puns. Effects opposite to those caused by lesions appear during seizures, in which there is an abnormal excessive activation of either prefrontal cortex. A seizure focus within the left prefrontal cortex may cause gelastic seizures, for example, in which the ictal event is laughter. Functional neuroimaging has documented left prefrontal hypoperfusion during depressive states, which normalized once the depression was successfully treated.

The limbic system was delineated by Papez in 1937. The Papez circuit consists of the hippocampus, the fornix, the mamillary bodies, the anterior nucleus of the thalamus, and the cingulate gyrus (Fig. 3.1–11). The boundaries of the limbic system were subsequently expanded to include the amygdala, septum, basal forebrain, nucleus accumbens, and orbitofrontal cortex. Although this schema creates an anatomical loop for emotional processing, the specific contributions of the individual components other than the hippocampus or even whether a given train of neural impulses actually travels along the entire pathway is unknown.

The amygdala appears to be a critically important gate through which internal and external stimuli are integrated. Information from the primary senses is interwoven with internal drives, such as hunger and thirst, to assign an emotional significance to sensory experiences. The amygdala may mediate learned fear responses, such as anxiety and panic, and may direct the expression of certain emotions by producing a particular affect. Neuroanatomical data suggest that the amygdala exerts a more powerful influence on the cortex, to stimulate or suppress cortical activity, than the cortex exerts on the amygdala. Pathways from the sensory thalamic relay stations separately send sensory data to the amygdala and the cortex, but the subsequent effects of the amygdala on the cortex is the more potent of the two reciprocal connections. In contrast, damage to the amygdala has been reported to ablate the ability to distinguish fear and anger in other people's voices and facial expressions. People with such injuries may have a preserved ability to recognize happiness, sadness or disgust. The limbic system appears to house the emotional association areas, which direct the hypothalamus to express the motor and endocrine components of the emotional state.

The limbic system has been particularly implicated in neuropathological studies of schizophrenia. Bleuler's well-known four *As* of schizophrenia—affect, associations, ambivalence, and autism—refer to brain functions served in part by limbic structures. Several clinicopathological studies have found a reduction in the brain weight of the gray matter but not of the white matter in people with schizophrenia. In pathological as well as in magnetic resonance imaging (MRI) reports, people with schizophrenia may have reduced volume of the hippocampus, amygdala, and parahippocampal gyrus. Schizophrenia may be a late sequela of a temporal epileptic focus, with some studies reporting an association in 7 percent of patients with TLE. Finally, functional neuroimaging studies have suggested a selective reduction of frontal lobe activity in patients with schizophrenia.

The dense set of connections between the limbic system and the frontal lobe has also received intense scrutiny by workers studying schizophrenia. Functional neuroimaging studies have demonstrated decreased activation of the frontal lobes in a large number of patients with schizophrenia, particularly during tasks requiring willed action. A reciprocal increase in activation of the temporal lobe may occur during willed actions, such as finger movements or speaking, in people with schizophrenia. Neuropathological studies have shown a decreased density of neuropil, the intertwined axons and dendrites on the neurons, in the frontal lobes of these patients. During development, the density of neuropil is highest around age 1 and then is reduced somewhat through synaptic pruning; the density plateaus throughout childhood and is further reduced to adult levels in adolescence. One hypothesis of the appearance of schizophrenia in the late teenage years is that the adolescent synaptic pruning proceeds in excess and results in too low a level of frontolimbic activity. Some experts have suggested that hypometabolism and paucity of interneuronal connections in the prefrontal cortex may reflect inefficiencies in working memory, which thus permits the disjointed discourse and loosening of associations that characterize schizophrenia. At present, the molecular basis for the regulation of the density of synapses within the neuropil is unknown. Other lines of investigation aimed at understanding the biological basis of schizophrenia have documented inefficiencies of the formation of cortical synaptic connections in the middle of the second trimester of gestation, which may be due to a viral infection or malnutrition. Neurodevelopmental surveys administered during childhood have found an increased incidence of subtle neurological abnormalities prior to the appearance of the thought disorder in people who subsequently presented signs of schizophrenia.

In one intriguing study, positron emission tomography (PET) scanning was used to identify the brain regions that are activated when a person hears spoken language. A consistent set of cortical and subcortical structures demonstrated increased metabolism when speech was processed. The researchers then studied a group of patients with schizophrenia who were experiencing active auditory hallucinations. During the hallucinations, the same cortical and subcortical structures were activated as were activated by the actual sounds, including the primary auditory cortex. At the same time, there was decreased activation of areas thought to monitor speech, including the left middle temporal gyrus and the supplementary motor area. This study raises the questions of what brain structure is activating the hallucinations and by what mechanism do neuroleptic drugs suppress the hallucinations. Clearly, functional imaging has much to tell about the neuroanatomic basis of schizophrenia.

Frontal Lobe Function

The *frontal lobes,* the region that determines how the brain acts on its knowledge, constitute a category unto themselves. In comparative neuroanatomical studies, the massive size of the frontal lobes is the main feature that distinguishes the human brain from that of other primates and that lends it uniquely human qualities. There are four subdivisions of the frontal lobes. The first three, the motor strip, the supplemental motor area, and Broca's area, have already been mentioned in the discussion of the motor system and language. The fourth, most anterior, division is the prefrontal cortex. Within the prefrontal cortex, there are three regions, lesions of which produce distinct syndromes: the *orbitofrontal,* the *dorsolateral,* and the *medial.* Dye-tracing studies have defined dense reciprocal connections between the prefrontal cortex and all other brain regions. Therefore, to the extent that anatomy can predict function, the prefrontal cortex is ideally connected to allow the sequential utilization of the entire palette of brain functions in the execution of goal-directed activity. Indeed, frontal lobe injury usually impairs the executive functions: motivation, attention, and sequencing of actions.

Bilateral lesions of the frontal lobes are characterized by changes in personality—how people interact with the world. The *frontal lobe syndrome,* which is most commonly produced by trauma, infarcts, tumors, lobotomy, multiple sclerosis, or Pick's disease, consists of slowed thinking, poor judgment, decreased curiosity, social withdrawal, and irritability. Patients typically manifest an apathetic indifference to experience that can suddenly explode into impulsive disinhibition. Unilateral frontal lobe lesions may be largely unnoticed because the intact lobe can compensate with high efficiency.

Frontal lobe dysfunction may be difficult to detect by means of highly structured, formal neuropsychological tests. Intelligence, as reflected in the intelligence quotient (IQ), may be normal, and functional neuroimaging studies have shown that the IQ seems to require mostly parietal lobe activation. For example, during administration of the Wechsler Adult Intelligence Scale-Revised (WAIS-R), the highest levels of increased metabolic activity during verbal tasks occurred in the left parietal lobe, whereas the highest levels of increased metabolic activity during performance skills occurred in the right parietal lobe. In contrast, frontal lobe pathology may become apparent only under unstructured, stressful, real-life situations.

Researchers have recently created neuropsychological tests

that are inherently ambiguous rather than clearly defined, yet generate a numerical score. In such a test, the subject must first decide by what criteria two figures must be compared and then must make the comparison. The first step of this task simulates a real-life dilemma and draws on prefrontal functions not normally tested on structured tests. Specifically, a subject could choose to define the task in terms of the immediately preceding context, a definition that would draw heavily on the working memory. Alternatively, the subject could interpret the task in terms of context-independent cues, an interpretation driven by the subject's own internal, associative memory. In normal people, the interpretation of the task balances both strategies.

In one study of right-handed males, lesions of the right prefrontal cortex eliminated the tendency to use internal, associative memory cues and led to an extreme tendency to interpret the task at hand in terms of its immediate context. In contrast, right-handed males who had lesions of the left prefrontal cortex produced no context-dependent interpretations and interpreted the tasks entirely in terms of the subject's internal drives. A mirror image of the functional lateralization appeared in left-handed subjects. This test thus revealed the clearest known association of higher cortical functional lateralization with the subjects' dominant hand. Future experiments in this vein will attempt to reproduce these findings with functional neuroimaging. If corroborated, these studies suggest a remarkable complexity of functional localization within the prefrontal cortex and may also give implications for the understanding of psychiatric diseases in which prefrontal pathology has been postulated, such as schizophrenia and mood disorders.

The heavy innervation of the frontal lobes by dopamine-containing nerve fibers is of interest because of the action of antipsychotic medications. At the clinical level, antipsychotic medications may help to organize the rambling associations of a patient with schizophrenia. At the neurochemical level, most typical antipsychotic medications block the actions of dopamine at the dopamine type 2 (D_2) receptors. Therefore, the frontal lobes may be a major therapeutic site of action for antipsychotic medications.

Specific Prefrontal Lobe Syndromes

Orbitofrontal Region. Dysfunction of the orbitofrontal area causes disinhibition, irritability, lability, euphoria, and a lack of remorse. Insight and judgment are impaired; patients are distractible. These features are reminiscent of the diagnoses of antisocial personality disorder, intermittent explosive disorder, and episodic dyscontrol syndrome. The orbitofrontal syndrome also may produce a state of "pseudopsychopathy."

Dorsolateral Region. The dorsolateral area appears to be the executive headquarters of the brain. Lesions in this region lead to deficiencies of planning, monitoring, flexibility, and motivation. Patients may be unable to use foresight and feedback and to maintain goal directedness, focus, and sustained effort. They appear inattentive and undermotivated, cannot plan novel cognitive activity, and exhibit a tendency to linger on a trivial thought. They may merely echo the examiner's question and react primarily to details of environmental stimuli. They miss the forest for the trees. Dorsolateral frontal lobe injury may also produce mood disorders. On formal neuropsychological testing, however, patients may exhibit intact memory, language, and visuospatial skills, which are functions of the occipital, temporal and parietal lobes.

Medial Region. The medial area appears to initiate a wide range of activities. Ablation of this region may produce a profound apathy characterized by limited spontaneous movement, gesture, and speech. In the extreme, there may be a state of akinetic mutism, without any initiation of activity at all.

DEVELOPMENT

The nervous system is divided into the central and peripheral nervous systems (CNS and PNS). The CNS consists of the brain and spinal cord; the PNS refers to all the sensory, motor, and autonomic fibers and ganglia outside the CNS. During development, both divisions arise from a common precursor, the neural tube, which in turn is formed through folding of the neural plate, a specialization of the ectoderm, the outermost of the three layers of the primitive embryo. During embryonic development, the neural tube itself becomes the CNS, while the ectoderm immediately superficial to the neural tube becomes the neural crest, which gives rise to the PNS. The formation of these structures requires chemical communication between the neighboring tissues in the form of cell surface molecules and diffusible chemical signals. In many cases, an earlier-formed structure, such as the notocord, is said to *induce* the surrounding ectoderm to form a later structure, in this case the neural plate. Identification of the chemical mediators of tissue induction is an active area of research. Investigators have begun to examine whether failures of the interactions of these mediators and their receptors could underlie errors in brain development that cause psychopathology.

Central Nervous System

The life cycle of a neuron consists of cell birth, migration to the adult position, extension of an axon, elaboration of dendrites, synaptogenesis, and, finally, the onset of chemical neurotransmission. Individual neurons are born in proliferative zones generally located along the inner surface of the neural tube. At the peak of neuronal proliferation in the middle of the second trimester, 250,000 neurons are born each minute. Postmitotic neurons migrate outward to their adult locations in the cortex, guided by radially oriented astrocytic glial fibers. Glial-guided neuronal migration in the cerebral cortex occupies much of the first 6 months of gestation. For some neurons in the prefrontal cortex, migration occurs over a distance 5,000 times the diameter of the neuronal cell body. Neuronal migration requires a complex set of cell–cell interactions and is susceptible to errors in which neurons fail to reach the cortex and instead reside in ectopic positions. A group of such incorrectly placed neurons is called a *heterotopia.* Neuronal heterotopias have been shown to cause epilepsy and are highly associated with mental retardation. In a neuropathological study of the planum temporale of four consecutive patients with dyslexia, heterotopias were a common finding. Recently, heterotopic neurons within the frontal lobe have been postulated to play a causal role in some cases of schizophrenia.

Many neurons lay an axon down as they migrate, while others do not initiate axon outgrowth until they have reached their cortical targets. Thalamic axons that project to the cortex initially synapse on a transient layer of neurons called the subplate neurons. In normal development, the axons subsequently detach from the subplate neurons and proceed superficially to synapse on the true cortical cells. The subplate neurons then degenerate. Some brains from people with schizophrenia reveal an abnormal persistence of subplate neurons, suggesting a failure to complete axonal pathfinding in the brains of people with schizophrenia. This finding did not correlate with the presence of schizophrenia in every case, however. Elaboration of a characteristic branched dendritic tree occurs once the neuron has completed migration. Synaptogenesis occurs at a furious rate from the second trimester through the first 10 years or so of life. The peak of synaptogenesis occurs within the first 2 postnatal years, when as many as 30 million synapses form each second. Ensheathment of axons by myelin begins prenatally; it is largely complete in early childhood but does not reach its full extent until late in the third decade of life.

Neuroscientists are tremendously interested in the effect of experience on the formation of brain circuitry in the first years of life. As already noted, there are many examples of the impact of early sensory experience on the wiring of cortical sensory processing areas. Similarly, early movement patterns are known to reinforce neural connections in the supplemental motor area that drive specific motor acts. Neurons rapidly form a fivefold excess of synaptic connections; then, through a darwinian process of elimination, only those synapses that serve a relevant function persist. This synaptic pruning appears to preserve input in which the presynaptic cell fires in synchrony with the postsynaptic cell, a process that reinforces repeatedly activated neural circuits. One molecular component that is thought to mediate synaptic reinforcement is the postsynaptic *N*-methyl-D-aspartate (NMDA) glutamate receptor. This receptor allows the influx of calcium ions only when activated by glutamate at the same time as the membrane in which it sits is depolarized. Thus, binding of glutamate without membrane depolarization, or membrane depolarization without binding of glutamate, fails to trigger calcium influx. NMDA receptors open in dendrites that are exposed to repeated activation, and their activation stimulates stabilization of the synapse. Calcium is a crucial intracellular messenger that initiates a cascade of events, including gene regulation and the release of trophic factors that strengthen particular synaptic connections. Although there is less experimental evidence for the role of experience in modulating synaptic connectivity of association areas than has been demonstrated in sensory and motor areas, neuroscientists assume that similar activity-dependent mechanisms apply in all areas of the brain.

An emerging concept of great significance in both child and adult psychiatry is the existence of early windows of time during which the brain establishes the basic circuitry for language, emotion, logic, mathematics, movements, and music. These windows open within the first few months of life and may close in some cases by 1 year of age. For example, a "perceptual map" of *phonemes,* the building blocks of language, is formed in the higher auditory processing regions of Wernicke's area during the first 12 months of life.

Certain sounds used by non–English-speaking people do not occur in English. Studies in the United States have shown that babies less than 6 months of age can be taught to discriminate these non-English sounds, but babies older than 6 months are no longer capable of hearing them. Moreover, the map for English differs, for instance, from that for Japanese in the location of neurons that respond to the sounds *ra* and *la.* In English, these neurons are located far apart within the somatosensory cortex, whereas in Japanese people, who have difficulty distinguishing these sounds, the neurons are so closely intertwined as to be virtually overlapping. Thus, to a Japanese person, *la* and *ra* elicit nearly the same pattern of neural activity, a fact that may underlie the difficulties of Japanese speakers in discriminating these sounds. Within the English language, studies have shown that babies of mothers who spoke loquaciously to them acquired a larger vocabulary than did babies of taciturn mothers. These findings suggest that very early experiences may establish the density and fidelity of neural circuits for specific brain functions, the consequences of which may affect people for the rest of their lives.

Workers have recently studied a particular learning disorder, the auditory processing defect, with electroencephalography. Patients with this defect may have difficulty discriminating the phonemes *da* and *ga.* When the string *da-da-da-ga* is played to normal subjects while an electroencephalogram is recorded, a change in the brain wave pattern accompanies the transition from *da* to *ga.* In contrast, the same stimulus fails to alter the brain waves of subjects with the auditory processing defect. Nevertheless, with proper training over the course of several weeks, many people with the auditory processing defect acquired the ability to discriminate the two sounds. This finding illustrates the notion that in some cases, with intensive modification of experience, neural circuits may be at least partially altered after the window of development has closed.

In the realm of emotion, early childhood experiences have been suspected to be at the root of psychopathology since the earliest theories of Sigmund Freud. Freud's psychoanalytic method aimed to trace the threads of a patient's earliest childhood memories to allow him or her to relive them in a less pathological environment, a process known as a "corrective emotional experience." Although neuroscientists have no data that demonstrate this method's operating at the level of neurons and circuits, emerging results demonstrate a profound effect of early caregivers on an adult individual's emotional repertoire. For example, the concept of attunement is defined as the process by which caregivers "play back a child's inner feelings." If a baby's emotional expressions are reciprocated in a consistent and sensitive manner, certain emotional circuits are reinforced. These circuits likely include the limbic system, in particular, the amygdala, which serves as a gate to the hippocampal memory circuits for emotional stimuli. In one anecdote, for example, a baby whose mother repeatedly failed to mirror her level of excitement emerged from childhood an extremely passive girl, who was unable to experience a thrill or a feeling of joy.

The relative contributions of nature and nurture are perhaps nowhere more indistinct than in the maturation of emotional responses, partly because the localization of emotion within the adult brain is only poorly understood. It is reasonable to assume, however, that the reactions of caregivers during a child's first 2 years of life are eventually internalized as distinct neural circuits, which may be only incompletely subject to modification through subsequent experience. For example, axonal connections between the prefrontal cortex and the limbic system, which probably play a role in modulating basic drives, are established between the ages of 10 and 18 months. Recent work suggests that a pattern of terrifying experiences in infancy may flood the amygdala and drive memory circuits to be specifically alert to threatening stimuli, at the expense of circuits for language and other academic skills. Thus, infants raised in a chaotic and frightening home may be neurologically disadvantaged for the acquisition of complex cognitive skills in school.

An adult correlate to this cascade of detrimental overactivity of the fear response is found in the posttraumatic stress disorder, in which people exposed to an intense trauma involving death or injury may have feelings of fear and helplessness for years after the event. A PET scanning study of posttraumatic stress disorder patients revealed abnormally high activity in the right amygdala while the patients were reliving their traumatic memories. The researchers hypothesized that the stressful hormonal milieu present during the registration of the memories may have served to burn the memories into the brain and to prevent their erasure by the usual memory modulation circuits. As a result, the traumatic memories exerted a pervasive influence and led to a state of constant vigilance, even in safe, familiar settings.

Workers in the related realms of mathematics have produced results documenting the organizing effects of early experiences on internal representations of the external world. Since the time of Pythagoras, music has been considered a branch of mathematics. A series of recent studies has shown that groups of children who were given 8 months of intensive classical music lessons during preschool years later showed significantly improved spatial and mathematical reasoning in school compared to a control group. Nonmusical tasks such as navigating mazes, drawing geometric figures, and copying patterns of two-color blocks were performed significantly more skillfully by the musical children. Early exposure to music may thus be an ideal preparation for later acquisition of complex mathematical and engineering skills.

These tantalizing observations suggest a neurological basis for the developmental theories of Jean Piaget, Erik Erikson, Margaret Mahler, John Bowlby, Sigmund Freud, and others. Erikson's epigenetic theory states that normal adult behavior results from the successful, sequential completion of each of several infantile and childhood stages (see Chapter 6, Section 6.3). According to the epigenetic model, the failure to complete an early stage is reflected in subsequent physical, cognitive, social, or emotional maladjustment. By analogy, the experimental data just discussed suggest that early experience, particularly during the critical window of opportunity for establishing neural connections, primes the basic circuitry for language, emotions, and other advanced behaviors. Clearly, miswiring of an infant's brain may later lead to severe handicaps when the person attempts to relate to the world as an adult. These findings support the vital need for adequate public financing of Early Intervention and Head Start programs, programs that may be the most cost-effective means to improving people's mental health.

References

Aggleton JP: *The Amygdala: Neurobiological Aspects of Emotion, Memory, and Mental Dysfunction.* Wiley-Liss, New York, 1992.

Aggleton JP: The contribution of the amygdala to normal and abnormal emotional states. Trends Neurosci *16:* 328, 1993.

Baxter LR, Mazziotta JC, Grafton ST, St George-Hyslop P, Haines JL, Gusella JF, Szuba MP, Selin CE, Guze BH, Phelps ME: Psychiatric, genetic, and positron emission tomographic evaluation of persons at risk for Huntington's disease. Arch Gen Psychiatry *49:* 148, 1992.

Biller J, Kathol RG, editors: The interface of psychiatry and neurology. Psychiatr Clin North Am *15:* 1, 1992.

Calne DB: Treatment of Parkinson's disease. N Engl J Med *329:* 1021, 1993.

Convit A, Czobor P, Volaka J: Lateralized abnormality in the EEG of persistently violent psychiatric inpatients. Biol Psychiatry *30:* 363, 1991.

Cummings JL: *Clinical Neuropsychiatry.* Grune & Stratton, Orlando, 1985.

Cummings JL: Depression and Parkinson's disease: A review. Am J Psychiatry *149:* 443, 1992.

Davis M: The role of the amygdala in fear-potentiated startle: Implications for animal models of anxiety. Trends Pharmacol Sci *13:* 35, 1992.

Delwaide PJ, Pepin JL, Maertens de Noordhout A: From basal ganglia to motoneurons: Probable involvement of pathways relaying in the medulla. Adv Neurol *69:* 111, 1996.

Feinberg TE, Farah MJ: *Behavioral Neurology and Neuropsychology.* McGraw-Hill, New York, 1997.

Filley CM: *Neurobehavioral Anatomy.* University Press of Colorado, Niwot, CO, 1995.

Fornazzari L, Farcnik K, Smith I, Heasman GA, Ishise M: Violent visual hallucinations and aggression in frontal lobe dysfunction: Clinical manifestations of deep orbitofrontal foci. J Neuropsychiatry Clin Neurosci *4:* 42, 1992.

Gazzaniga M: *The Cognitive Neurosciences.* MIT Press, Cambridge, MA, 1995.

He X, Rosenfeld MG: Mechanisms of complex transcriptional regulation: Implications for brain development. Neuron *7:* 183, 1991.

Heimer L, de Olmos J, Alheid GF, Zaborszky L: "Perestroika" in the basal forebrain: Opening the border between neurology and psychiatry. Prog Brain Res *87:* 109, 1991.

Hoover JE, Strick PL: Multiple output channels in the basal ganglia. Science *159:* 819, 1993.

Kandel ER, Schwartz JH, Jessell TM: *Principles of Neural Science,* ed 3. Elsevier, New York, 1991.

Komuro H, Rakic P: Modulation of neuronal migration by NMDA receptors. Science *260:* 95, 1993.

Lauder JM: Neurotransmitters as growth regulatory signals: Role of receptors and second messengers. Trends Neurosci *16:* 233, 1993.

Markham CH, editor: Parkinson's disease. Clin Neurosci *1:* 2, 1993.

McKay RDG: The origins of cellular diversity in the mammalian central nervous system. Cell *58:* 815, 1989.

Mesulam MM: *Principles of Behavioral Neurology.* Davis, Philadelphia, 1985.

Pramstaller PP, Mardsen CD: The basal ganglia and apraxia. Brain *119:* 319, 1996.

Redburn DA, Rowe-Rendleman C: Developmental neurotransmitters: Signals for shaping neuronal circuitry. Invest Ophthalmol Vis Sci *37:* 1479, 1996.

Roberts JKA: *Differential Diagnosis in Neuropsychiatry.* Wiley, New York, 1984.

Strub RL, Black FW: *Neurobehavioral Disorders: A Clinical Approach.* Davis, Philadelphia, 1988.

Tonkonogy JM, Geller JL: Hypothalamic lesions and intermittent explosive disorder. J Neuropsychiatry Clin Neurosci *4:* 45, 1992.

Walsh C, Cepko CL: Widespread dispersion of neuronal clones across functional regions of the cerebral cortex. Science *255:* 434, 1992.

▲ 3.2 Neurophysiology and Neurochemistry

The brain maintains and modifies an internal representation of the external world through a bewildering number of infinitesimal chemical changes during each moment of life. In the previous section, the gross structure of the brain is defined, and the various functional units of the brain are presented as being generally stable for the life of the organism. Indeed, the anatomical relationships between neurons undoubtably play a major role in determining personality traits and thought processes. At a finer level of analysis, however, an equally important determinant of the quality of thought is the efficiency of information processing by individual neurons. Single neurons communicate by interpreting their chemical environment, by instantly changing the chemical cues to electrical activity for transport down axons, and finally by efficiently translating the electrical data into finely modulated secreteable chemical emissions with which to influence other neuronal or nonneuronal cells. Therefore, electrical impulses facilitate instantaneous responses, and the chemical milieu is of paramount importance to maintenance of the fidelity of the brain's image of the world.

History

The study of chemical interneuronal communication is called *neurochemistry.* With the acceptance in the late 19th century of the neuronal theory of Santiago Ramon y Cajal, which stated that the brain consists of individual cells rather than a syncytium of cytoplasm, a search was initiated for the mediators of intercellular communication. At the turn of the century, Lewandowsky and Lashley independently described the effects of extracts of the adrenal gland on sympathetic nerve tissue, and they and others soon discovered chemicals in the brain—neurotransmitters—with similar stimulatory actions. With the postulation that cells also contained inhibitory and excitatory "receptive substances," Lashley envisioned the entire basic apparatus of chemical neurotransmission: neurotransmitters and specific receptor molecules. In the first half of this century, the major biogenic amine neurotransmitters were first characterized, whereas the more abundant amino acid neurotransmitters were not recognized as transmitters until much more recently. In recent years, a massive proliferation in known peptide neurotransmitters and receptors has been reported, and novel classes of neurotransmitters have been defined, including nucleotides, prostaglandins, and gases. Through advanced molecular cloning techniques, dozens of orphan receptor genes have been sequenced, for which no known ligand exists. Moreover, in addition to their role in modulation of cellular electrical excitability, molecules defined initially as neurotransmitters, for example, serotonin, have been shown to influence gene expression and synapse formation. The field of neurochemistry has therefore exploded into a massive complexity of molecules and has breached the bounds of the mere study of the chemical mediation of nerve impulses into a broad discipline that overlaps with neuroanatomy, developmental neurobiology, and behavioral genetics.

In psychopharmacology, the major available therapeutic interventions center around modification of biogenic amine neurotransmission and, to a lesser extent, amino acid neurotransmission. While these systems are discussed in detail later, it is important for students of psychiatry to be aware of the entire range of neurochemistry, because it is quite probable that many new classes of psychopharmacological agents, which act on more recently defined neurotransmitter systems, will emerge in the near future. Moreover, neuronal electrical activity is continuously modulated by excitatory and inhibitory neurotransmitters, by circulating hormones, by immune surveillance, by general medical homeostasis, and by chronobiological rhythms, each of which may be influenced with existing therapeutic methods. Neuronal electrical activity, along with the chemical factors, simultaneously modifies the abundance and phosphorylation status of cellular proteins, the level of expression of certain genes, and the connectivity of a neuron to thousands of neighboring neurons. It remains possible that each of these avenues of therapeutic influence will open in the future.

BASIC ELECTROPHYSIOLOGY

Membranes and Charge

In the resting state the intracellular compartment of a neuron is negatively charged in comparison with the extracellular compartment. The charge gradient is maintained across the hydrophobic plasma membrane, which consists of a lipid bilayer, in which are embedded cholesterol molecules that modify membrane rigidity, and numerous proteins including ion pumps, ion channels, and neurotransmitter receptors. Ion pumps and ion channels maintain a gradient of cations: potassium ions are 15 to 20 times more concentrated inside neurons, while sodium ions are 8 to 15 times less concentrated inside neurons with respect to the extracellular space. The principal ion pump is the energy-requiring sodium-potassium ATPase exchange pump; the principal ion channels are the sodium, potassium, calcium, and chloride ion channels. The membrane is said to be semipermeable because it is selective regarding which ions can pass through it. The semipermeable property of the membrane is the basis for its functional role, which is similar to the role of a capacitor. A capacitor stores an electrical charge by isolating positive and negative ions with an insulator. The hydrophobic neuronal membrane serves this insulator role. The charge can be released by bypassing the insulator, which occurs in neurons by the opening of channels that allow passage of ions through the membrane. The electrical potential of the membrane follows the equations of *Ohm's law,* $E = IR$. In this equation, E is the transmembrane potential, I is the current, and R is the resistance.

Ion Channels

The rapid transmission of information along neuronal axons, which may exceed a velocity of 60 meters per second, is mediated by instantaneous changes in membrane potential called action potentials. These changes in membrane potential occur when the charge gradients maintained by the insulator function of the membrane are allowed to flow unimpeded through protein pores called *ion channels.* Ion channels are selective for specific ions, such as sodium channels that may not allow passage of potassium ions. In the resting state, ion channels are closed. Ion channels open in response to binding of ligands to receptors—*ligand-gated ion channels*—or in response to changes in membrane potential—*voltage-gated ion channels.* Among ligand-gated ion channels, certain ligands, called *excitatory neurotransmitters,* open cation channels that depolarize the membrane and increase the likelihood of the generation of an action potential. These ligands are said to elicit excitatory postsynaptic potentials (EPSPs). Other ligands, called *inhibitory neurotransmitters,* open chloride channels that hyperpolarize the membrane and decrease the likelihood of the generation of an action potential. These ligands are said to elicit inhibitory postsynaptic potentials (IPSPs). In the central nervous system (CNS), the binding of a single ligand to a ligand-gated ion channel may change the neuronal membrane potential by 1 mV. Therefore, the combined activation of several ligand-gated channels is needed to trigger an action potential. In clinical medicine, sodium channel blockers are used as local anesthetics and antiarrhythmics, and blockers of potassium channels are used as antiarrhythmics. In psychiatry, blockers of CNS calcium channels are used to treat bipolar disorder. A blocker of calcium channels in skeletal muscle, dantrolene, is used to treat neuroleptic malignant syndrome.

The ion channels themselves are glycoproteins (proteins with sugar moieties) that span the neuronal membrane and contain a pore that can be opened and closed and through which specific ions can flow. The ligand-gated channels are particularly relevant in the study of psychiatry, since many psychotherapeutic and psychoactive drugs affect these channels directly (Table 3.2–1). There are three general types of ligand-gated channels: direct-coupled, G protein-coupled, and second-messenger–coupled (Fig. 3.2–1). The neurotransmitter acts directly on direct-coupled, ligand-gated ion channels. With G protein-coupled ion channels the neurotransmitter acts on its receptor protein, which then activates a G protein, which activates the ion channel. The second-messenger–coupled ion channel is activated by a second-messenger product of some physically removed neurotransmitter receptor.

Action Potentials

In the resting state the intracellular compartment of the neuron is negatively charged at a potential of −70 to −80 mV, but during an action potential this membrane potential reverses in a thin zone immediately adjacent to the membrane. For an action potential to be generated by a neuron, ligand-gated ion channels open, and sodium ions begin to enter the cell and gradually make the inner surface of the membrane less negatively charged relative to the outside. The point at which the interior of the membrane is sufficiently less negatively charged to cause the opening of adjacent voltage-gated sodium channels is called the *spike threshold* and is characteristically approximately −55 mV. The inward flow of sodium ions then rapidly depolarizes the membrane and initiates an action potential, which propagates itself along the membrane by sequentially triggering adjacent voltage-gated sodium channels. The action potential itself is a brief (0.1 to 2 ms) wave of reversal of membrane potential that moves along an axon (Fig. 3.2–2). During an action potential the interior of the membrane is positively charged in comparison with the outside of the membrane. The initial ion channel involved in the action potential is the Na^+ channel, which, when opened, allows positively charged sodium ions to enter the neuron. The Ca^{2+} channels are next to open, thus allowing the positively charged calcium ions to enter the neuron and further contribute to the spike of the action potential. Not only does the entry of calcium ions affect the membrane potential, but the calcium ion is also an important second-messenger molecule that is involved in initiating protein–protein interactions and gene regulation. Entry of the calcium ion into the synaptic terminal is also critical for the release of neurotransmitter molecules. And calcium ion entry activates ion channels that carry an outgoing flow of potassium ions that are involved in arresting the action potential. The activation of those K^+ channels results in the afterhyperpolarization of the membrane after an action potential. During the afterhyperpolarization the inside of the membrane is even more negatively charged than it was at baseline. The afterhyperpolarization contributes to the refractory period of a neuron after an action potential; during this period, another action potential cannot be generated.

The rate of local spread of an action potential determines the rate of conduction of the impulse along the nerve. A bare

Table 3.2–1
Some Ligand-Gated Ion Channels

Neurotransmitter	Receptor Subtype	G Protein or Direct[a]	Ion Channel Activated	Physiological Response[b]
Acetylcholine	Nicotinic	D	Na^+/K^+	E
	Muscarinic	G	K^+	E
Dopamine	D_2	G	K^+	I
Norepinephrine	α_1	G	K^+	E
	α_2	G	K^+	I
	β	G	K^+	E
Serotonin	5-HT_{1A}	G	K^+	I
	$5\text{-HT}_{1C/2}$	G	K^+	E
	5-HT_3	D	Na^+/K^+	E
GABA	$GABA_A$	D	Cl^-	I
Glutamate	AMPA	D	Na^+/K^+	E
	Kainate	D	Na^+/K^+	E
	NMDA	D	Ca^{2+}	E
Opioid	μ, δ	G	K^+	I
Substance P	NK	G	K^+	E

[a] D, direct-coupled; G, G protein-coupled.
[b] E, excitatory; I, inhibitory.

axon may conduct an action potential at a velocity of 1 meter per second. At this rate, for example, only about three new visual images could reach the visual cortex per second, and polysynaptic image processing would be considerably slower. However, the brain can distinguish up to 50 new images per second. The increase in nerve conduction velocity that accounts for the rapid processing capabilities of the brain is due to the presence of myelin sheaths, which encircle larger axons. *Myelin* is a highly hydrophobic substance that completely prevents the passage of ions. It is laid down in segments along the axon, which are separated by gaps of bare axonal membrane called *nodes of Ranvier.* The local changes in membrane charge that constitute the action potential occur at the nodes of Ranvier, and they then jump over the myelin segment to the next node of Ranvier. For a given distance of axon, for example, the presence of myelin segments reduces the number of times the action potential must trigger neighboring voltage-gated ion channels in order to conduct an impulse along that distance of axon. The nerve conduction velocity may therefore increase to as high as 65 meters per second in large, myelinated fibers.

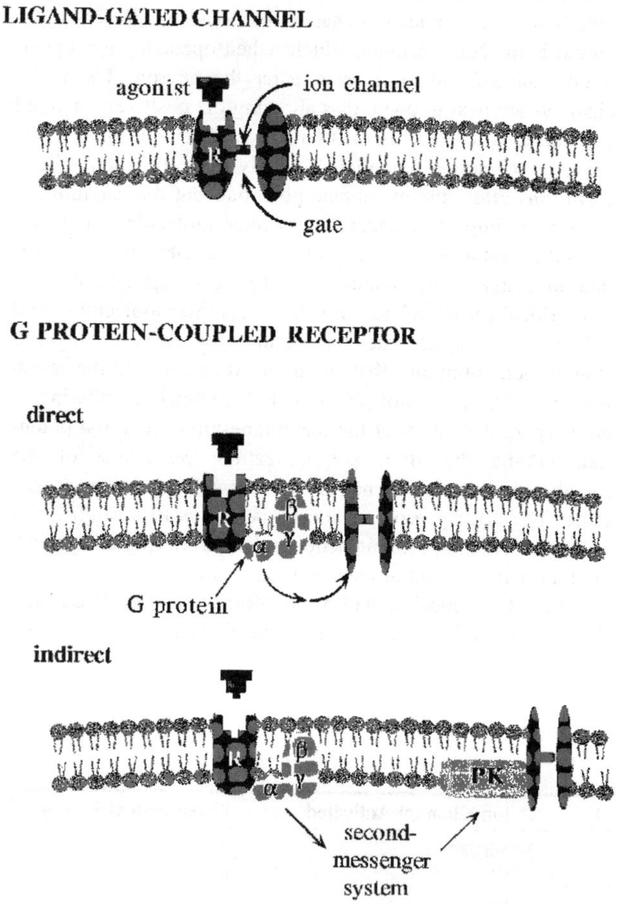
LIGAND-GATED CHANNEL
agonist
ion channel
R
gate
G PROTEIN-COUPLED RECEPTOR
direct
R
β
γ
α
G protein
indirect
R
β
γ
α
PK
second-
messenger
system

FIGURE 3.2–1

Modes of coupling of receptors and ion channels. At the *top,* an agonist (a neurotransmitter) binds directly to the protein complex of the channel itself, causing the gate to open and allowing specific ions to flow down a concentration gradient. The nicotinic acetylcholine receptor is an example of this class. The *lower panels* show separate receptors *(R),* which open channels through binding to G proteins, which may open channels directly, as in the *middle panel,* or indirectly, through a second-messenger system, such as cAMP, cGMP, or IP_3, as in the *bottom panel.* G protein-coupled receptors typically have seven transmembrane domains, and their genes form the largest superfamily yet discovered within the human genome, with several hundred distinct receptors. Nearly all receptors for the biogenic amines are of this latter class. (Reprinted with permission from Aghajanian GK, Alreja M: Basic electrophysiology. In *Comprehensive Textbook of Psychiatry,* ed 6, HI Kaplan, BJ Sadock, editors, p 68. Williams & Wilkins, Baltimore, 1995.)

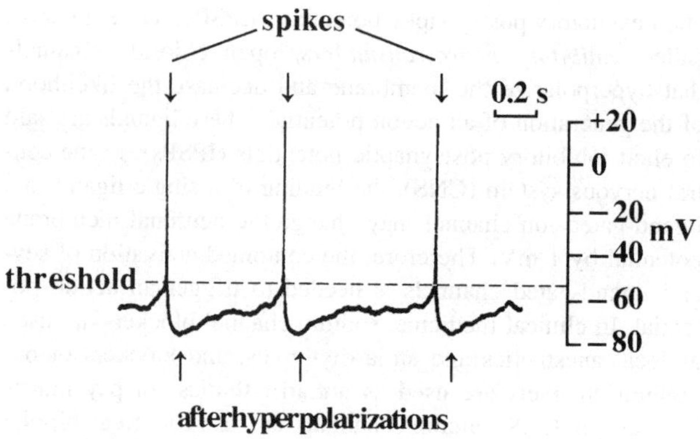
spikes
0.2 s
+20
0
−20
−40
−60
−80
mV
threshold
afterhyperpolarizations

FIGURE 3.2–2

Action potentials. An oscilloscope trace shows a repetitively firing neuron recorded intracellularly *in vivo.* This example was taken from a serotonergic neuron in the dorsal raphe nucleus of the rat midbrain. As can be seen from the trace, when the membrane potential, in millivolts, reaches the spike threshold (−55 mV), an all-or-none spike occurs. After each spike, an afterhyperpolarization moves the cell away from the threshold into a more negative potential (near −80 mV). As the afterhyperpolarization decays, the cell again approaches the spike threshold. (Reprinted with permission from Aghajanian GK, Alreja M: Basic electrophysiology. In *Comprehensive Textbook of Psychiatry,* ed 6, HI Kaplan, BJ Sadock, editors, p 65. Williams & Wilkins, Baltimore, 1995.)

Translation of the Action Potential into Chemical Neurotransmission

At the synaptic terminus of the axon, action potentials trigger the release of neurotransmitters (Fig. 3.2–3) into the synaptic cleft, where they may act on other neurons or muscles. The presynaptic nerve terminals contain voltage-gated calcium channels that locally raise the intracellular calcium concentration. This initiates a cascade of protein–protein and protein–lipid interactions in which neurotransmitter-containing synaptic vesicles fuse with the presynaptic membrane and release their contents into the synaptic cleft. In muscles, voltage-gated calcium channels, which are opened by the arriving action potentials, trigger the movement of myosin on actin fibers, a process called *excitation–contraction coupling.* In each of these instances, the electrical impulse causes changes in local calcium concentrations, which in turn rapidly trigger physical changes in the ultrastructure of the cell.

SYNAPSES

The propagation of an action potential along an axon is described as an *all-or-none phenomenon;* that is, once an action potential has been triggered, it is propagated at full strength for the entire length of the axon. Subtleties of neuronal processing are therefore generally not represented by modulation of the intensity of the action potential. An exception to this rule may occur at axoaxonal synapses. In most neurons, however, the essence of neuronal processing occurs in the regulation of whether an action potential is generated. This determination is the summation of excitatory and inhibitory chemical influences that act on the *axon hillock,* which originates the action potential. The *synapse* is the site at which stimuli are given and received and where the finest shadings of neuronal activity are negotiated.

The components of the synapse are the axon terminal of the presynaptic neuron, the synaptic cleft, and the dendrite of the postsynaptic neuron. When an action potential develops in the presynaptic neuron, the action potential moves down the axon to the axon terminal or to other functionally similar regions of the axons called *axonal varicosities.* The action potential causes the release of neurotransmitter molecules into the *synaptic cleft,* the small space between the presynaptic neuron and the postsynaptic neuron. The neurotransmitter molecules diffuse across the synaptic cleft and then bind to their specific receptors on the external membrane of the dendrite of the postsynaptic neuron. The most common type of synapse involves the termination of the presynaptic neuronal axon on the postsynaptic neuronal cell body, an axon, or a dendrite. These synapses are called *axosomatic, axoaxonic,* and *axodendritic,* respectively. In addition to the chemical synapses, electrical synapses, also called *gap junctions,* allow the direct transfer of ions between two neurons as a form of intraneuronal neurochemical communication. Conjoint synapses are synapses that have both electrical and chemical characteristics.

During development, a severalfold excess of synapses forms, and only those synapses of functional relevance survive into adulthood. In the adult, synaptic relationships are constantly remodeled through increases or decreases in the size and strength of individual synapses, as well as the formation

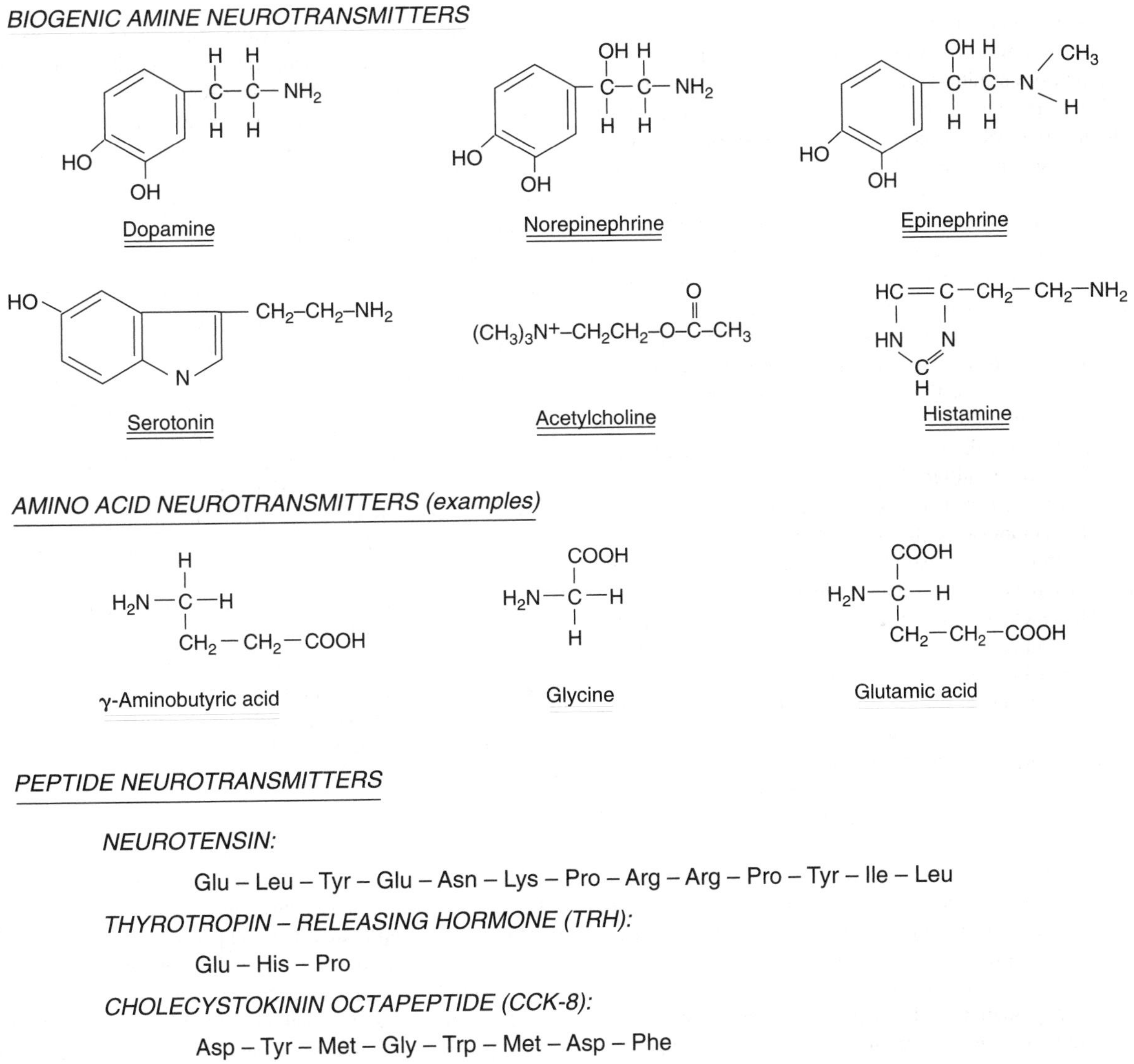
BIOGENIC AMINE NEUROTRANSMITTERS
Dopamine
Norepinephrine
Epinephrine
Serotonin
Acetylcholine
Histamine
AMINO ACID NEUROTRANSMITTERS (examples)
γ-Aminobutyric acid
Glycine
Glutamic acid
PEPTIDE NEUROTRANSMITTERS
NEUROTENSIN:
Glu – Leu – Tyr – Glu – Asn – Lys – Pro – Arg – Arg – Pro – Tyr – Ile – Leu
THYROTROPIN – RELEASING HORMONE (TRH):
Glu – His – Pro
CHOLECYSTOKININ OCTAPEPTIDE (CCK-8):
Asp – Tyr – Met – Gly – Trp – Met – Asp – Phe

FIGURE 3.2–3
Three classes of neurotransmitters.

of new synapses and the elimination of unnecessary synapses. The mechanical adhesive properties of synapses are mediated by various combinations of the calcium-dependent cadherin family of adhesion molecules. Changes in the structure of synapses are mediated by trophic substances known as *growth factors,* which act on specific receptors to regulate local protein–protein interactions and to modify levels of gene expression. Therefore, not only do neurotransmitters subtly modulate intercellular communication, but also trophic substances constantly remodel the synaptic channels through which chemical neurotransmission occurs. *N*-Methyl-D-aspartate (NMDA) glutamate receptors are of particular importance to the process of synaptic remodeling. NMDA receptors are essential to certain forms of long-term potentiation (LTP) in which coordinated neuronal activity strengthens certain synapses. Based on a large amount of electrophysiological data, LTP has been proposed to be the cellular correlate of long-term memory, although molecular biological experiments suggest that other systems must also contribute.

Presynaptic Components

The presynaptic terminals contain the synthetic machinery responsible for the synthesis of all neurotransmitters except peptide neurotransmitters, which are synthesized in the cell body. Neurotransmitter synthesis may be stimulated by influx of calcium ions, variations in levels of the second-messenger cyclic adenosine monophosphate (cAMP), or changes in levels of circulating hormones. Once synthesized, neurotransmitters are packaged into synaptic vesicles, which may store a mixture of amine and peptide neurotransmitters. Available data have generally confirmed the long-held belief of Dale and Eccles that all termini of a single neuron secrete the same combination of neurotransmitters. In practice, however, probably a minority of neurons have more than one axonal terminus and newer techniques suggest that there may be heterogeneity of neurotransmitter composition among different vesicles in a single neuron. Energy for the synthesis, storage, release, and degradation of neurotransmitters is provided by mitochondria. The life cycle of specific neurotransmitters is discussed below. The presynaptic membrane contains ion channels, neurotransmitter receptors, and neurotransmitter transporters. Voltage-gated calcium channels trigger vesicle release. Presynaptic neurotransmitter receptors mediate feedback inhibition of neurotransmitter synthesis and release. For example, many norepinephrine-releasing neurons have presynaptic, α_2 receptors, which, when occupied by the released norepinephrine, cause the releasing neuron to decrease or stop the release of norepinephrine. Transporters take neurotransmitters up from the synaptic cleft for recycling or degradation. Additional transporters in the membranes of storage vesicles load the vesicles with neurotransmitters.

Neurotransmitter storage vesicles in the presynaptic terminal fuse with the presynaptic membrane and release their components into the synaptic cleft in a process called *exocytosis.* Many details of synaptic vesicle fusion have become known recently. The synapsins and Rab3 control the localization of vesicles. Synaptotagmin and synaptobrevin, components of the vesicle membrane, and neurexins and syntaxins, components of the plasma membrane, mediate the fusion of the vesicle to the inner surface of the presynaptic membrane. Synaptophysin aids in the creation of a pore in the presynaptic membrane.

Once a monoamine neurotransmitter such as norepinephrine, dopamine, or serotonin has been released into the synaptic cleft, it acts until it diffuses away or, more commonly, is removed by reuptake mechanisms. Specific presynaptic transmembrane transporter molecules return free monoamine neurotransmitters to the nerve terminal, where they are either repackaged into vesicles for release in response to subsequent action potentials or degraded by monoamine oxidases (MAOs). Transporters have gained increasing appreciation in psychopharmacology as the sites of the major mechanism of action of both therapeutic and illicit drugs. They form a family of integral membrane proteins with 12 transmembrane domains and several intracellular sites of potential phosphorylation. The tricyclic antidepressants, discovered almost 40 years ago, are thought to inhibit the norepinephrine and serotonin reuptake mechanisms. Based on this fact, several newer antidepressant medications have been identified in assays specifically designed to detect the inhibition of monoamine reuptake through transporters. The most widely used of these are the serotonin-specific reuptake inhibitors, also called selective serotonin reuptake inhibitors (SSRIs), while others have more recently been developed with varying ratios of inhibitory activity on the dopamine, norepinephrine, and serotonin transporters. Cocaine appears to block all three monoamine transporters. A recent study has found a correlation between a genetic variant serotonin transporter, which is present in lower amounts on the presynaptic membrane, and increased levels of anxiety and neuroticism. Decreased numbers of transporter molecules would be expected to reduce the rate of reuptake of serotonin. Based on a relatively small patient sample, the genetic variant was calculated to account for 3 to 4 percent of the behavioral variation for anxiety in the population of normal subjects. This result appears to conflict with the fact that pharmacological blockers of serotonin transporters, such as fluoxetine (Prozac), which would be expected to have the same net effect as the mutation, specifically the lowering of reuptake and therefore the increasing of synaptic serotonin activity, nevertheless reduce rather than increase anxiety. Clearly, more research is needed to understand the role of serotonin in anxiety and mood disorders.

Degradation of recycled biogenic amine neurotransmitters is mediated principally by MAOs, which are attached to the outer mitochondrial membrane. MAO type A (MAO_A) metabolizes norepinephrine and serotonin, and its inhibition by MAO inhibitors is associated with an elevation in mood. MAO type B (MAO_B) metabolizes dopamine.

Synapse

Although it comprises less than 1 percent of the total volume of the brain, the *synaptic compartment*—the space between the presynaptic and postsynaptic membranes—contains the mixture of neurotransmitters with the greatest influence on thought and behavior. These molecules are available to act on specific receptors and to initiate or inhibit the generation of action potentials in the postsynaptic cell. The list of neurotransmitters runs into the hundreds of distinct molecules, including amino acids (glutamate, γ-aminobutyric acid [GABA], glycine, aspartate, homocysteate), biogenic amines (norepinephrine, serotonin, dopamine, epinephrine, acetylcholine, histamine), neuropeptides (vasopressin, oxytocin, enkephalins, endorphins, substance P, neurotensin, and several hundred others), nucleotides (adenosine, cAMP), gases (nitric oxide [NO], carbon monoxide [CO], ammonia [NH_3]), and prostaglandins.The synaptic cleft of cholinergic synapses harbors acetylcholinesterase, which inactivates acetylcholine by cleaving it into acetate and choline. The concentrations of various neurotransmitters in the synaptic cleft are carefully regulated by feedback inhibition of transmitter release and by reuptake into the presynaptic terminal by transporter molecules. This regulation is critically important because the concentration of each neurotransmitter determines the degree to which it activates its specific receptors.

Postsynaptic Components

Receptors. Neurotransmitter receptors are the sites of action for many of the psychotherapeutic and psychoactive drugs used today. The techniques of molecular biology have led to the identification and sequencing of many new subtypes of receptors. The importance of those advances lies in the long-standing hypothesis that the ability to subtype receptors would refine both the hunt for pathology in disease states and the design of specifically acting drugs.

The principal function of postsynaptic neurotransmitter receptors is to alter the electrical transmembrane potential: either to increase or to decrease the likelihood of triggering an action potential. Excitatory neurotransmitters cause depolarization of the postsynaptic membrane. Because the binding of a single neurotransmitter results in a change of only 1 mV, there is much room for subtle modulation of the postsynaptic response by the combined actions of several neurotransmitters before the membrane potential is raised from the resting potential of −70 to −80 mV to the threshold potential of −55 mV. The fine modulation of receptor activation results from changes in the synaptic concentration of neurotransmitters, in combination with variations in the efficiency of the translation of receptor binding to the opening of ion channels, which are due to chemical modulations of the intracellular segments of the receptor, the association of the receptor with other cellular proteins, the number of receptors, or levels of second messengers. Once the threshold potential is reached at the axon hillock, however, the all-or-none action potential is initiated by the opening of voltage-gated sodium channels, and there is virtually no further chance for modification of the impulse.

Two terms often used in conjunction with receptors are "supersensitivity" and "subsensitivity." These terms refer, respectively, to a greater than usual response and a less than usual response of the receptor to a constant amount of neurotransmitter. The sensitivity of a receptor may be due to the number of receptors present, the affinity of the receptor for the neurotransmitter, and the efficiency with which the binding of the neurotransmitter to the receptor is translated into an intraneuronal message. All these steps in receptor function are variable and subject to regulation.

Fundamentally, there are two types of neurotransmitter receptors: seven-transmembrane-domain receptors, which require G proteins to open channels, and ligand-gated ion channels, in which the channel is an integral part of the complex that binds the ligand. Many of the receptors located directly on ion channels are listed in Table 3.2–1. Many of the biogenic amine receptors, regardless of whether they are associated with G proteins or directly with ion channels, are listed in Table 3.2–2. The seven-transmembrane-domain receptors all have a characteristic structure in which the NH_2-terminal end of the protein is located extracellularly and the COOH-terminal end of the protein is located intracellularly. Moreover, the third intracytoplasmic loop of the receptor tends to be the largest loop. Occasionally, the second intracytoplasmic loop is also fairly large. The first intracytoplasmic loop seems invariably to be the smallest. The length of the COOH-terminal intracytoplasmic tail is variable. The large intracytoplasmic loops and the COOH-tail contain identified or potential sites of phosphorylation, a feature that is involved in the regulation of receptor function. For example, when a β-adrenergic receptor is activated, it is rapidly inactivated by phosphorylation of the third intracytoplasmic loop by β-adrenergic receptor kinase, which then allows the binding of an inhibitor protein called β-arrestin.

Another type of postsynaptic membrane receptor, which does not cause changes in membrane potential, is the family of tyrosine kinase receptors, which have an extracellular ligand-binding component, a single transmembrane domain, and an intracellular tyrosine kinase, which phosphorylates both itself and other cytoplasmic proteins and so triggers a cascade of intracellular phosphorylations that ultimately lead to changes in gene expression. Tyrosine kinase receptors often associate as dimers, either homodimers or heterodimers. There is a vast diversity of tyrosine kinase receptors; much of this diversity is due to various combinations of modular segments of the receptor genes that have arisen during evolution. Tyrosine kinase receptors bind growth factors and mediate the plasticity of synaptic associations. Two such factors are nerve growth factor (NGF) and brain-derived neurotropic factor (BDNF), which have been shown to have opposite effects on the size of developing cortical somatosensory receptive fields and thus may collaborate in the remodeling of neuronal circuits that underlies synaptic plasticity during development and in adults.

Postsynaptic cells also are regulated by circulating hormones, such as thyroid hormone or steroids. These hormones diffuse through the membrane and bind to cytoplasmic receptors, which then are translocated into the nucleus, where they regulate gene expression.

G Proteins. G proteins are a family of guanosine triphosphate (GTP)-binding proteins with similar structures, which interact with members of the very large family of seven-transmembrane-domain receptors, of which the adrenergic receptor is a prototype. GTP is interconvertible with guanosine diphosphate (GDP). The G proteins themselves consist of three smaller proteins, called the α, β, and γ subunits. When an intact G protein (all three subunits, with GDP bound to the α subunit) binds to a receptor, the receptor is converted into a state with a high affinity for the neurotransmitter molecule. When the neurotransmitter binds to this complex, it triggers

Table 3.2–2
Receptor Subtypes for Biogenic Amine Neurotransmitters

Neurotransmitter	Receptor Subtype	G/I[a]	Effector Mechanism[b]
Acetylcholine	M_1	G	IP_3/DG, increase cGMP
	M_2	G	Decrease cAMP, increase K^+ conductance
	M_3	G	IP_3/DG, increase cGMP
	M_4	G	Decrease cAMP
	M_5	G	IP_3/DG
	Nicotinic	I	Na^+/K^+
Dopamine	D_1	G	Increase cAMP
	D_2	G	Decrease cAMP, increase K^+ conductance
	D_3	G	?Decrease cAMP
	D_4	G	?Decrease cAMP
	D_5	G	Increase cAMP
Epinephrine and Norepinephrine	$\alpha_{1a, b, c, and d}$	G	IP_3/DG
	$\alpha_{2a, b, and c}$	G	Decrease cAMP, increase K^+ conductance
	$\beta_{1, 2, and 3}$	G	Increase cAMP
Histamine	H_1	G	IP_3/DG
	H_2	G	Increase cAMP
	H_3	?	?
Serotonin	5-HT_{1A}	G	Decrease cAMP, increase K^+ conductance
	5-HT_{1B}	G	Decrease cAMP
	5-HT_{1C}	G	IP_3 DG
	5-HT_{1D}	G	Increase cAMP
	5-HT_{1E}	G	Decrease cAMP
	5-HT_{1F}	G	Decrease cAMP
	5-HT_{2A}	G	IP_3/DG
	5-HT_{2B}	G	IP_3/DG
	5-HT_{2C}	G	IP_3/DG
	5-HT_3	I	Na^+/K^+
	5-HT_4	G	Increase cAMP
	5-HT_{5A}	G	?
	5-HT_{5B}	G	?
	5-HT_6	G	Increase cAMP
	5-HT_7	G	Increase cAMP

[a] G, G protein-linked; I, direct linkage to an ion channel.
[b] IP_3, stimulation of phosphoinositide turnover, resulting in an increase in the concentrations of inositol triphosphate and diacylglycerol.

the replacement of GDP with GTP on the α subunit, thereby destabilizing the associations among the neurotransmitter, the receptor, and the G protein. The G protein further dissociates into the GTP-binding α subunit and the $\beta\gamma$ subunit, which contains both the β and γ subunits. The GTP-associated α subunit is the active fragment involved in activating or inhibiting a particular effector molecule (for example, adenylyl cyclase or an ion channel). Because that α subunit itself has the ability to convert GTP to GDP, the activity of the GTP-associated α subunit is stopped when the GTP is converted to GDP. The conversion of GTP to GDP permits the reassociation of the α subunit with a $\beta\gamma$ subunit.

The family of G proteins is created by the diversity of subunit types that have been identified. The greatest diversity has been found for the α subunit, although an increasing number of reports describe diversity of the β and γ subunits. The classically described α subunits have been α_s, α_i, and α_o. The α_s subunit has been associated with the stimulation of adenylyl cyclase activity; the α_i subunit has been associated with the inhibition of adenylyl cyclase activity; and the α_o subunit has been associated with the stimulation of the phosphoinositol second-messenger system. At least 10 other α subunit genes have been sequenced.

Second Messengers. The neurotransmitters themselves are conceptualized as the first messengers that bring a signal to a neuron. For the neuron to act on the signal, the first-messenger signal must be translated into an intraneuronal signal through the formation of second-messenger molecules. The most classic second messengers are the cyclic nucleotides (cyclic adenosine monophosphate [cAMP] and cyclic guanosine monophosphate [cGMP]), the calcium ion (Ca^{2+}), and the phosphoinositol metabolites (inositol triphosphate [IP_3] and diacylglycerol [DAG]). Another increasingly appreciated class of second messengers is the eicosanoid metabolites. Gases, such as NO and CO, not only mediate interneuronal communication but also serve as intraneuronal second-messenger molecules.

CYCLIC NUCLEOTIDES. Cyclic AMP is produced from ATP by the enzyme adenylyl cyclase. Adenylyl cyclase is linked to receptors by G proteins. The G_s protein stimulates the activity of adenylyl cyclase, and the G_i protein inhibits the activity of adenylyl cyclase. Once formed, cAMP has its biological effects; then the cAMP activity is terminated by its conversion into 5′-AMP by phosphodiesterase. An exactly analogous pathway is involved in the formation of cGMP, where the involved enzyme is guanylyl cyclase. Cyclic AMP binds to a cAMP-responsive element binding protein (CREBP), which is a transcription factor that stimulates transcription from several genes, including the synthetic machinery for certain neurotransmitters. Based on studies from mutant ''knockout'' mice that lack CREBP, CREBP appears to mediate learning and memory, as well as opiate addiction, which may be viewed as an extreme form of associative learning.

CALCIUM. In the resting cell, the intracellular calcium concentration is maintained at a very low level (10^{-7} M) relative to the extracellular concentration (10^{-3} M). Calcium, as a second messenger, can come from two sources. First, calcium can enter the cell from the extracellular space through either voltage-gated or ligand-gated ion channels. Second, calcium can be released from intraneuronal storage vesicles by the action of a phosphoinositol metabolite, IP_3. Calcium can act either alone as a second messenger or in tandem with a variety of calcium-binding proteins (for example, calmodulin). Calcium stimulates the formation of nitric oxide (NO) and may trigger excitotoxic cellular damage under some circumstances. Very small increases in the intraneuronal calcium concentration can have profound biological effects. Recent data have demonstrated that significant changes in intracellular calcium concentrations may be very localized, for example to a single dendrite, without involving the entirety of the cellular domain. This ability to sequester calcium may underlie local changes in synaptic efficiency and may provide a subcellular basis for learning and memory.

PHOSPHOINOSITOL METABOLITES. In a manner analogous to adenylyl cyclase, another receptor-activated enzyme, phospholipase C, converts a membrane lipid, phosphatidylinositol 4,5-bisphosphate, into two active metabolites, IP_3 and DAG. As mentioned above, the major effect of IP_3 is to cause the release of calcium from intraneuronal stores of calcium in the endoplasmic reticulum. The major activity of DAG is to activate a specific protein kinase.

EICOSANOIDS. In a manner analogous to phospholipase C, another receptor-activated enzyme, phospholipase A_2, converts membrane phospholipids into free arachidonic acid. Arachidonic acid can then be cleaved by cyclo-oxygenase and other enzymes to produce a wide array of second-messenger molecules, including several types of prostaglandins, cyclic endoperoxides (for example, prostacyclins and thromboxanes), and leukotrienes. These three classes of molecules have a variety of second-messenger activities that are the subject of many ongoing basic science investigations.

GASES. Nitric oxide (NO) is formed from L-arginine and molecular oxygen by the enzyme nitric oxide synthase, of which there are at least four recognized forms. NO was originally discovered because of its ability to relax vascular muscle, and it may mediate local increases in cerebral blood flow associated with neuronal activity. NO diffuses readily within cells and between cells, and among its activities is the potent activation of guanylyl cyclase. NO synthase is stimulated by nitroprusside and inhibited by nitroarginine and methyl arginine. Carbon monoxide (CO) also activates guanylyl cyclase and is formed in neurons by heme oxygenase.

JAK-STAT. The Janus kinase (Jak) is a receptor for cytokines. Upon activation by its ligand, Jak phosphorylates members of the signal transducers and activators of transcription (STAT) family of transcription factors, which then translocate directly into the nucleus, where they regulate gene expression. This system is unusual in that it does not utilize one of the common second messengers but, rather, allows for very specific communication between the cytokine ligand and the resulting regulation of gene transcription. This distinction raises one perplexing issue regarding the regulation of gene expression by the common transcription factors: how a general increase in a small molecule could elicit a specific change in gene expression. One answer given to this problem has been that the response of a particular cell to a rise in second-messenger levels is determined by the state of differentiation of the cell, such that only a small number of genes may be regulated by a common second messenger at any one time. The Jak-STAT mechanism may represent an alternative pathway in which a variety of second messengers may be independently utilized, depending on the extracellular stimulus. In the brain, the Jak-STAT system has so far only been shown to mediate trophic signals that support neuronal survival. Researchers are actively investigating other possible roles for this novel second-messenger system.

Protein Phosphorylation. One of the primary activities of the second-messenger molecules is to activate a class of molecules known as the protein kinases. *Protein kinases* catalyze the transfer of the terminal phosphate group of ATP onto protein molecules (Fig. 3.2–4). Each of the second-messenger molecules is associated with the activation of a specific protein kinase. Four protein kinases (cAMP-dependent protein kinase [PKA], cGMP-dependent protein kinase [PKG], calcium/calmodulin-dependent protein kinase [CaMK], and calcium/phosphatidylserine-dependent protein kinase, also known as protein kinase C [PKC]) phosphorylate proteins on serine or threonine residues. In contrast, the receptor tyrosine kinases phosphorylate proteins on tyrosine residues without involving a second messenger. Tyrosine kinases are activated by the binding of growth factors to specific transmembrane receptors.

Protein phosphorylation is the best-studied example of how a reversible, posttranslational modification of a protein can change the function of the protein. Protein phosphorylation is reversible by the activities of another class of enzymes, the protein phosphatases, that remove the phosphate group from the protein (Fig. 3.2–4). The addition or the deletion of the negatively charged phosphate group changes the charge and can change the shape of the protein molecule. This change in charge and shape can affect the function of the protein and essentially serves as a molecular on-off switch for the function of the protein. Moreover, proteins are usually phosphorylated on multiple sites by different protein kinases; therefore, fine adjustment of the function of the protein is possible, in addition to simply turning the protein on or off. An example of regulation by phosphorylation is the β-adrenergic receptor. The sensitivity of this receptor to its ligand is regulated by the state of the receptor's phosphorylation.

Protein phosphorylation has been traced through many metabolic pathways in which a cascade of phosphorylations regulates a chain of enzymatic reactions. The regulation of glucose metabolism and the citric acid cycle are two examples. Kinases also play an important role in the regulation of cellular proliferation—many oncogenes are kinases—and in the regulation of numerous other genes. In psychiatry, lithium therapy has been shown to reduce the activity of protein kinase C in

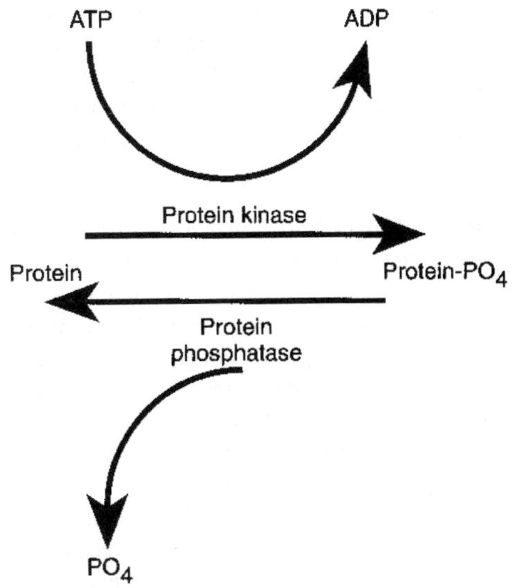
ATP
ADP
Protein kinase
Protein
Protein-PO4
Protein
phosphatase
PO4

FIGURE 3.2–4
Regulation of protein function by phosphorylation. Numerous cellular proteins are activated or inactivated by the addition of a phosphate group (PO_4) from adenosine triphosphate (ATP). Addition of the phosphate is catalyzed by specific protein kinases, while removal of the phosphate is catalyzed by protein phosphatases. (Courtesy of Jack A. Grebb, M.D.)

Table 3.2–3
Criteria for a Neurotransmitter

1. The molecule is synthesized in the neuron.
2. The molecule is present in the presynaptic neuron and is released on depolarization in physiologically significant amounts.
3. When administered exogenously as a drug, the exogenous molecule mimics the effects of the endogenous neurotransmitter.
4. A mechanism in the neurons or the synaptic cleft acts to remove or deactivate the neurotransmitter.

concert with its salutary effects on bipolar disorder. It is very likely that ongoing investigations will implicate kinases in the etiology of other psychiatric disorders.

NEUROTRANSMITTERS

For a molecule to be classified as a neurotransmitter, it must meet a number of criteria (Table 3.2–3). These criteria must usually be met through a variety of basic science and clinical research studies. Some substances, which have been shown to meet a few of the criteria, are referred to as *putative neurotransmitters,* meaning that all the criteria have not been demonstrated as yet.

Chemical Neurotransmission

Chemical neurotransmission is the process involving the release of a neurotransmitter by one neuron and the binding of the neurotransmitter molecule to a receptor on another neuron. The process of chemical neurotransmission is affected by most drugs used in psychiatry. All antipsychotics, with the exception of the serotonin-dopamine antagonists, are believed to have their effects mainly by blocking dopamine type 2 (D_2) receptors; virtually all antidepressants are believed to have their effects by increasing the amount of serotonin or norepinephrine or both in the synaptic cleft; and almost all benzodiazepine anxiolytics are believed to have their effects on the $GABA_A$ receptors that are linked to chloride ion channels.

Neuromodulators and Neurohormones. The most common word used to denote the chemical signals that flow between neurons is "neurotransmitter," although the words "neuromodulators" and "neurohormones" are also used in some cases to emphasize specific characteristics. In contrast to the characteristically immediate and short-lived effects of a neurotransmitter, a neuromodulator substance, as the name implies, modulates the response of a neuron to a neurotransmitter. The modulatory effect may be present for a longer time than is usual for a neurotransmitter molecule to be present. Thus, a neuromodulating substance may have an effect on a neuron over a long period of time, and that effect may be more involved with fine tuning than with activating or directly inhibiting the generation of an action potential. A neurohormone is distinguished by the fact that it is released into the bloodstream rather than into the extraneuronal space in the brain. Once in the bloodstream, the neurohormone can then diffuse into the extraneuronal space and have its effects on neurons.

Classification. The three major types of neurotransmitters in the brain are the biogenic amines, the amino acids, and the peptides (Fig. 3.2–3). The biogenic amines are the best known and most understood neurotransmitters because they were the first to be discovered. However, they constitute the neurotransmitter substance in only a small percentage of neurons. The amino acid neurotransmitters were late in being discovered, principally because of the difficulty in differentiating amino acids present in most proteins from the same amino acids acting separately as neurotransmitters. The amino acid neurotransmitters are present in upward of 70 percent of neurons. The peptide neurotransmitters are intermediate in terms of the percentage of neurons that contain a peptide neurotransmitter but far surpass the other two categories in the sheer number (about 200 to 300) of peptide neurotransmitters that have been putatively identified. The full neurotransmitter criteria have been met for only a few of those peptides at this time (Table 3.2–3). Nevertheless, the evidence indicating that the putative peptide neurotransmitters are, in fact, neurotransmitters is generally robust. Recent data have led to the identification of at least four other classes of neurotransmitters—nucleotides, gases, eicosanoids, and anandamides—and have hinted at receptors for others, including so-called sigma (Σ) receptors.

It can be seen, therefore, that the current psychopharmacological agents influence only a small fraction of the neurons in the brain. This may represent a fortunate coincidence, as drugs which influence amino acid neurotransmitters generally have toxic side effects at low doses, and relatively few drugs have been found to act on peptide receptors, most notably the opiates. The small number of biogenic amine-containing neurons belies their significant functional importance, because they project widely throughout the brain and modulate activity in practically every brain region.

BIOGENIC AMINE NEUROTRANSMITTERS. The six biogenic amine neurotransmitters are dopamine, norepinephrine, epinephrine, serotonin, acetylcholine, and histamine. Dopamine, epinephrine, and norepinephrine are all synthesized from the same amino acid precursor, tyrosine, and are classified as a group as the catecholamines (Fig. 3.2–5). Serotonin is synthesized from the amino acid precursor tryptophan and is an indolamine (Fig. 3.2–6). Serotonin is also known as 5-hydroxytryptamine (5-HT). Therefore, the abbreviation for serotonin is often written as 5-HT. A common feature of all the biogenic amine neurotransmitters is that they are synthesized in the axon terminal. The enzymes necessary for their synthesis are synthesized in the cell body but are transported down the axon, so that the actual production of the neurotransmitter occurs at the site of its release. Upon release, a significant amount of norepinephrine, serotonin, and dopamine within the synaptic cleft is taken up again by a presynaptic transporter protein. Many antidepressant medications prevent this reuptake by blocking the transporters. Different classes of antidepressant drugs selectively or predominantly block either serotonin or norepinephrine transporters or both. This has the immediate effect of raising synaptic levels of the neurotransmitter, especially serotonin and norepinephrine, and increasing the activation of postsynaptic receptors. Because the therapeutic benefit requires 2 to 4 weeks, however, other biochemical changes must follow the reuptake inhibition. For biological reasons that probably relate to reciprocal patterns of innervation, potentiation of only the serotonin or only the norepinephrine system results in efficient activation of the other system. Cocaine also blocks the reuptake of serotonin, norepinephrine, and dopamine by binding to their respective transporters.

AMINO ACID NEUROTRANSMITTERS. Amino acids constitute the building blocks of proteins. Because of their abundance, it was long assumed that they could not also serve as neurotransmitters. However, glutamate and

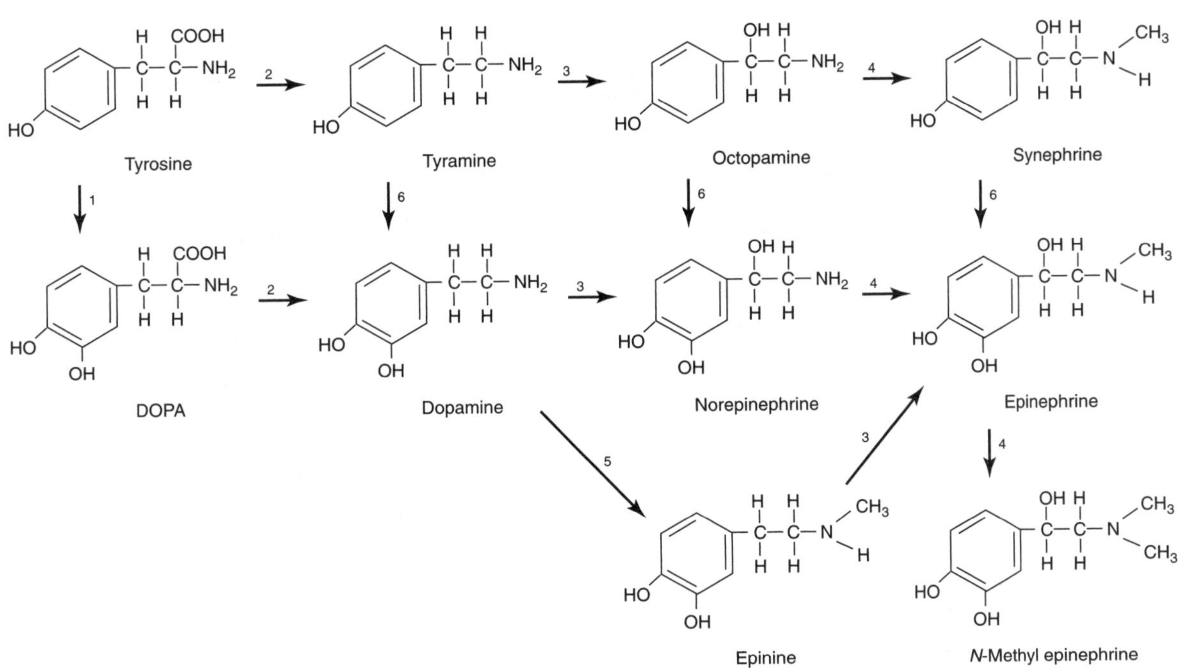
Tyrosine
Tyramine
Octopamine
Synephrine
DOPA
Dopamine
Norepinephrine
Epinephrine
Epinine
N-Methyl epinephrine

FIGURE 3.2–5
Primary and alternative pathways for the formation of catecholamines: (1) tyrosine hydroxylase; (2) aromatic amino acid decarboxylase; (3) dopamine-β-hydroxylase; (4) phenylethanolamine-*N*-methyltransferase; (5) nonspecific *N*-methyltransferase in lung and folate-dependent *N*-methyltransferase in brain; (6) catechol-forming enzyme. (Reprinted with permission from Cooper JR, Bloom FE, Roth RH: *The Biochemical Basis of Neuropharmacology,* ed 7, p 232. Oxford University Press, New York, 1996.)

aspartate are present in disproportionately high concentrations in the brain, and in the past 10 years, their roles as neurotransmitters have been broadly accepted. The two major amino acid neurotransmitters are γ-aminobutyric acid (GABA) and glutamate. GABA is an inhibitory amino acid, and glutamate is an excitatory amino acid. It is occasionally suggested that a simplified way to look at the brain is as a balance between just those two neurotransmitters, with all the biogenic amine and peptide neurotransmitters simply involved in modulating that balance. Recent discoveries have further increased the importance of the study of amino acid neurotransmitters. These discoveries include the observations that the benzodiazepines, barbiturates, and several anticonvulsants act primarily through GABAergic mechanisms and that an important substance of abuse, phencyclidine (PCP), acts at glutamate receptors. One of the most active areas of recent neuroscience research is the role of NMDA glutamate receptors in learning and memory. These observations have led to an intensive study of these receptors with regard to major psychiatric disorders, such as anxiety disorders and schizophrenia.

PEPTIDE NEUROTRANSMITTERS. Peptide refers to the chemical bond between the carboxylic acid group and the amino group of adjacent amino acids in a protein. Short chains of amino acids are generally referred to as *peptides,* although they actually are short proteins. Peptides differ from the other two major types of neurotransmitters in that peptides must be made in the cell body, where the genetic information for making them resides. Peptide neurotransmitters are usually first synthesized as longer forms called preprohormones and are further processed during their transport to the axon terminals. First, the preprohormones are cleaved to make prohormones; then the prohormones are cleaved to make the final hormones. Unlike replenishing the biogenic amine neurotransmitters, replenishing released neuroactive peptides takes a comparably long time because they are synthesized in the cell body and must be transported to the synapse, but cannot be recycled. Peptide neurotransmitters may have a longer duration of action than either biogenic amine neurotransmitters or amino acid neurotransmitters. In this sense, peptide neurotransmitters may serve a neuromodulatory role at some synapses. In addition to cleavage of the long forms to make the final forms of the peptides, other posttranslational modifications can modify the structure and the function of the peptides. These posttranslational modifications include such biochemical reactions as phosphorylation, glycosylation, sulfation, disulfide bond formation, and COOH-terminal amidation.

NUCLEOTIDES. Of the four nucleotides in deoxyribonucleic acid (DNA) the purine adenosine and its high-energy phosphorylated form, adenosine triphosphate (ATP), have also been shown to be neurotransmitters. Receptors for purines have been found in the brain. P_1 receptors have a high affinity for adenosine, and P_2 receptors have a high affinity for ATP. Two subtypes of the P_1 receptor are the adenosine A_1 and A_2 receptors, both of which are G protein-linked receptors. Binding of adenosine to A_1 receptors results in opposite cellular responses to binding of adenosine to A_2 receptors in some systems. The P_1 receptors are blocked by xanthines, such as caffeine and theophylline. Adenosine is concentrated in specific cellular layers of discrete regions of the brain and appears to have the general effect of inhibiting the release of most other neurotransmitters. During a seizure, it is released from cells and appears to act to terminate the seizure. The actions of adenosine, which are opposite to those of caffeine, have led to various research efforts to study adenosine analogues for use as anticonvulsants or sedatives. In clinical use as a cardiac antiarrhythmic agent, intravenous adenosine has a half-life on the order of less than 5 minutes. ATP itself may also serve as a neurotransmitter. It is stored in synaptic vesicles along with catecholamines and is released when the catecholamines are released. It preferentially acts on P_2 receptors, and data show that at least one function of ATP is the opening of Na^+, K^+, and Ca^{2+} ion channels.

GASES. The recent discovery that the gas nitric oxide (NO) apparently serves both as an intraneuronal second messenger and as a neurotransmitter has been one of the most interesting discoveries in neuroscience. NO is formed from the amino acid L-arginine by the actions of NO synthase (NOS). One of the first observations regarding the effects of NO was its role as an endothelial-derived factor that relaxed vascular tone. When acetylcholine acts on receptors on the

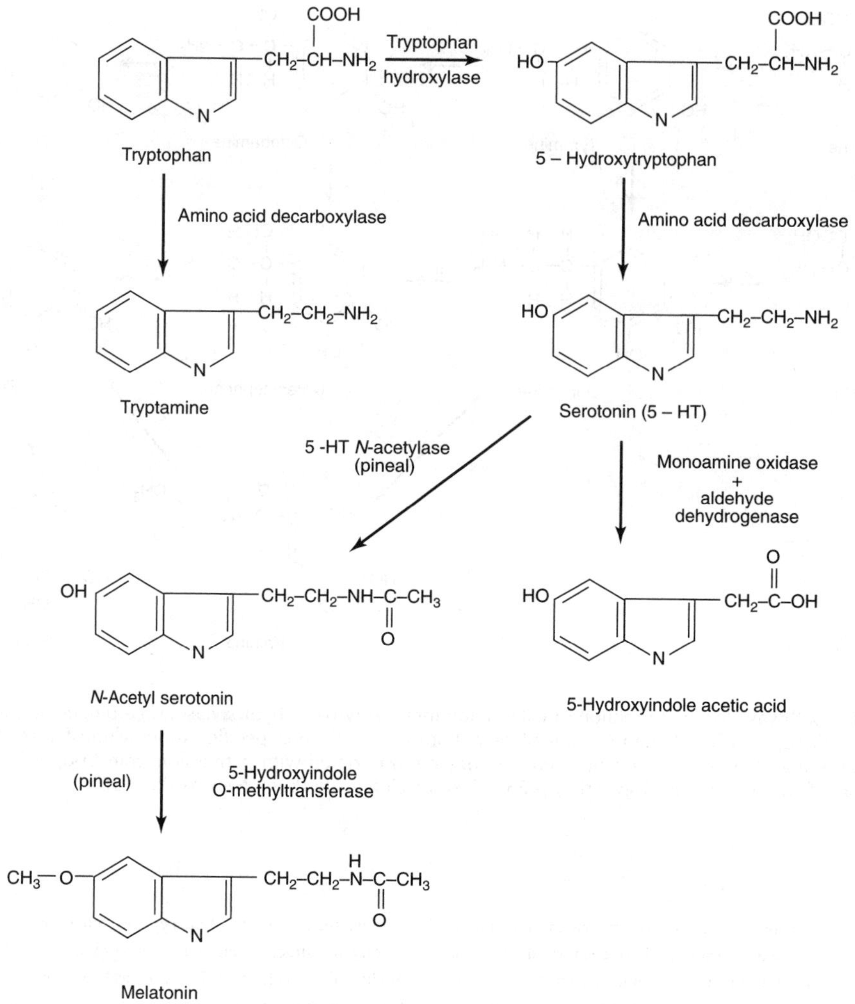

COOH
CH2–CH–NH2
Tryptophan
hydroxylase
HO
COOH
CH2–CH–NH2
N
Tryptophan
5 – Hydroxytryptophan
Amino acid decarboxylase
Amino acid decarboxylase
CH2–CH2–NH2
HO
CH2–CH2–NH2
Tryptamine
Serotonin (5 – HT)
5 -HT N-acetylase
(pineal)
Monoamine oxidase
+
aldehyde
dehydrogenase
OH
CH2–CH2–NH–C–CH3
O
HO
CH2–C–OH
N-Acetyl serotonin
5-Hydroxyindole acetic acid
(pineal)
5-Hydroxyindole
O-methyltransferase
CH3–O
H
CH2–CH2–N–C–CH3
Melatonin

FIGURE 3.2–6

Synthetic and metabolic pathways of serotonin. (Reprinted with permission from Cooper JR, Bloom FE, Roth RH: *The Biochemical Basis of Neuropharmacology,* ed 7, p 355. Oxford University Press, New York, 1996.)

endothelium, NO is formed in the endothelial cells and then diffuses to the adjacent smooth muscle, in which it causes an increase in the concentration of cyclic guanosine monophosphate (cGMP) and the relaxation of the muscle.

NO and NOS have been described in the brain. Two types of NOS can be found in specific, discrete regions of the brain, particularly in the striatum, the hypothalamus, the basal forebrain, and the cerebellum. The best understood pathway resulting in the generation of NO starts at the NMDA receptor subtype of glutamate. Activation of this receptor allows calcium to enter the neuron, thereby activating a variety of calcium-mediated events. One of the calcium-mediated events is the activation of NOS and the generation of NO. NO then acts on the iron molecule contained in guanylyl cyclase and results in the formation of cGMP, a potent second-messenger molecule. Data suggest that NO can diffuse to adjacent neurons, in which it can then result in cGMP formation in neighboring neurons. Excessive exposure to glutamate may overstimulate certain neurons and result in the release of large amounts of calcium and the production of large amounts of NO. NO may be metabolized into toxic free radicals, which act, along with intracellular calcium, to injure or kill neurons in a phenomenon called *excitotoxicity.* The role of NO in excitotoxicity is illustrated in the striatum, which contains an apparently random mixture of NOS and non–NOS-containing neurons. Interestingly, under conditions of glutamate excess, those neurons that produce large amounts of NO are somehow spared excitotoxic cell death, while neighboring neurons into which NO diffuses are killed.

NO is an unusual putative neurotransmitter. It is not stored in synaptic vesicles but is generated as needed and diffuses away rapidly. It is not necessarily released only on depolarization. Its receptors are the iron molecule and perhaps other reactive metals. Inhibitors of NOS may be useful in reducing ischemic damage after a stroke. Other experimental data suggest that NO is involved in learning and memory. Another gaseous neurotransmitter about which relatively little is known is carbon monoxide (CO). CO is present in a discrete set of neurons and glial cells. CO is formed by the actions of heme oxygenase on hemoglobin, and, like NO, CO stimulates guanylyl cyclase.

EICOSANOIDS. The metabolites of arachidonic acid, prostaglandins, prostacyclins, thromboxane, and leukotrienes, also called eicosanoids or prostanoids, are all present in the brain. To date, eight prostanoid receptors have been identified in various neural and nonneural tissues: the thromboxane A_2 receptor, prostacyclin receptor, prostaglandin F receptor, prostaglandin D receptor, and four subtypes of prostaglandin E receptors (EP_1R to EP_4R). They are coupled to different signal transduction systems. In addition, leukotriene-binding sites have been found in brain. Although these substances have not yet fulfilled all the criteria for neurotransmitters, efforts are being made to explore this possible role.

ANANDAMIDES. A novel compound formed from arachidonic acid and ethanolamine, *N*-arachidonoylethanolamine (anandamide), is now recognized as an endogenous ligand for the cannabinoid receptor family. Cannabinoids are the active ingredients in marijuana, and a lengthy search for an endogenous ligand for the cannabinoid receptor has recently ended. There are two types of cannabinoid receptors, central (CB_1) and peripheral (CB_2), each of which has several subtypes. These receptors are members of the seven-transmembrane-domain, G protein-linked family of receptors, and they bind tetrahydrocannabinol (THC), the active ingredient of marijuana. Anandamides generally exhibit less potent, but similar, pharmacological effects compared with THC, including lowering of intraocular pressure, decreases in activity level, and relief of pain. The co-localization of anandamides and cannabinoid receptors in the thalamus suggests that anandamides may act as neurotransmitters. Researchers are continuing to seek more potent endogenous ligands.

SIGMA RECEPTORS. The Σ receptor site has been defined pharmacologically but has not yet been purified or cloned, and the endogenous ligand for the receptors has not been identified. Only recently has the site now known as the Σ receptor been distinguished from the PCP receptor. It is now clear that the principal site of action for PCP is the *N*-methyl-D-aspartate (NMDA) glutamate receptor, where PCP binding results in an indirect inhibition of calcium ion influx. The Σ site binds pentazocine (Talwin) and haloperidol (Haldol), which belong to distinct drug classes. Although the study of the Σ-binding characteristic remains an area of active research, consistent results from efforts to purify the receptor have been elusive.

Amino Acid Neurotransmitters

Amino acid neurotransmitters are the most abundant neurotransmitters in the brain. The major excitatory amino acid (EAA) is glutamate, although aspartate, *N*-acetylaspartylglutamate (NAAG), cysteate, and homocysteate are also EAAs. The major inhibitory amino acid (IAA) is GABA, although glycine, taurine, and β-alanine are also inhibitory amino acids of increasing interest to researchers. All EAAs are dicarboxylic amino acids, and all IAAs are monocarboxylic amino acids. That structural difference is thought to be a major contributor to the differential activities of the two classes of amino acids.

Glutamate. SYNTHESIS, METABOLISM, AND PATHWAYS.

Glutamate is synthesized from glucose and glutamine in presynaptic neuron terminals and is stored in synaptic vesicles. Once released into the synaptic cleft, it acts on receptors, and its action is terminated by highly efficient uptake into the presynaptic neuron or into adjacent glia. Glutamate is the primary neurotransmitter in cerebellar granule cells, the striatum, the cells of the hippocampal molecular layer and entorhinal cortex, the pyramidal cells of the cortex, and the thalamocortical and corticostriatal projections. Glutamate release is stimulated by nicotine.

GLUTAMATE RECEPTORS AND DRUGS. There are five major types of glutamate receptors. The *N*-methyl-D-aspartate (NMDA) receptor is the best understood and most complex of the receptors, because it may play an essential role in learning and memory, as well as psychopathology. The other four receptor types are therefore referred to as the non-NMDA glutamate receptors. The NMDA receptor allows the passage of sodium, potassium, and calcium. It opens only under conditions where it is bound by two molecules of glutamate and a molecule of glycine at the same time as the potential of the membrane in which it sits rises above −65 mV, which allows the magnesium ion that normally blocks the ion pore to fall off (Fig. 3.2–7). Since most cells that respond to glutamate display both NMDA and non-NMDA receptors, the initial depolarization response is mediated by the non-NMDA receptors until the membrane potential rises above −65 mV, at which time the NMDA receptors open. The NMDA receptor is also blocked by physiological concentrations of magnesium, PCP, and PCP-related substances (for example, MK-801). The requirement of simultaneous membrane depolarization and glutamate receptor occupancy for activation of NMDA-mediated calcium flux has piqued the interest in the receptor as the essential feature of the cellular mechanism of memory. In this model, a prolonged set of temporally coordinated stimuli is required for NMDA receptor opening, which uniquely triggers a cascade of intracellular events leading to the expression of a certain set of genes, and this in turn reinforces and stabilizes the synapses responsible for the initial receptor activation. Thus, a physical change in the synaptic relationships results from a specific pattern of receptor stimulation. Although the details of this pathway remain to be completely elucidated, NMDA receptor antagonists have been shown to prevent the formation of memory.

Two of the other receptors are the α-amino-3-hydroxy-5-methyl-4-isoxazole propionic acid (AMPA) and the kainate receptors, which share depolarization as their principal effect with the NMDA receptor. The two remaining types of glutamate receptors are the AP4 (1-2-amino-4-phosphorobutyrate) and ACPD (*trans*-1-aminocyclopentane-1-3-dicarboxylic acid) receptors. The AP4 receptor is thought to be an inhibitory autoreceptor. The ACPD receptor (also called the metabotropic receptor) is a seven-transmembrane-domain, G protein-linked receptor that has its effects through the phosphoinositol second-messenger system.

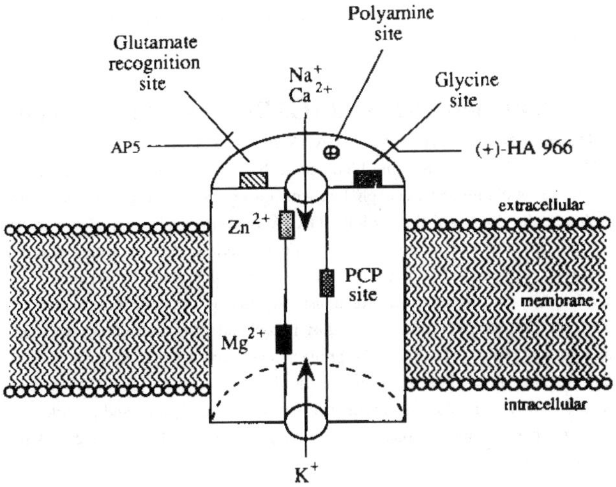
Polyamine site
Glutamate recognition site
Na^+
Ca^{2+}
Glycine site
AP5
(+)-HA 966
extracellular
Zn^{2+}
PCP site
membrane
Mg^{2+}
intracellular
K^+

FIGURE 3.2–7
N-Methyl-D-aspartate (NMDA) receptor. The flow of sodium (Na^+) and calcium (Ca^{2+}) ions is gated by Mg^{2+} in a voltage-dependent fashion. K^+ is the counterion. The NMDA receptor channel is blocked by PCP and MK-801, and the complex is regulated at two modulatory sites by glycine and Zn^{2+}. AP5 and CPP are competitive antagonists at the NMDA site. (+)-HA 966 is a selective antagonist at the glycine site. (Reprinted with permission from Cooper JR, Bloom FE, Roth RH: *The Biochemical Basis of Neuropharmacology,* ed 7, p 182. Oxford University Press, New York, 1996.)

GLUTAMATE AND PSYCHOPATHOLOGY. The major pathophysiological conditions currently associated with the glutamate systems are excitotoxicity and schizophrenia. *Excitotoxicity* is the hypothesis that excessive stimulation of glutamate receptors leads to prolonged and excessive intraneuronal concentrations of calcium and NO. Such conditions activate many enzymes, especially proteases, that are destructive to neuronal integrity. The association with schizophrenia is partly due to the psychotomimetic effects observed with PCP. In this model, a reduction in NMDA receptor activity is thought to cause psychotic symptoms. Attempts to reduce excitotoxicity during strokes with the NMDA receptor blocker MK-801 were terminated because of the precipitation of psychosis. It seems, therefore, that the glutamate neurotransmitter–receptor system is poorly suited to be a target for psychotherapeutic drugs: Too much NMDA receptor activity kills neurons, and too little NMDA receptor activity induces psychosis. A few NMDA receptor inhibitors with a reassuring safety profile are under development, including remacemide. Some basic science studies show that dopamine and glutamate have opposing effects. Because of that association or because of the sensitivity of nigral dopamine-containing neurons to excitotoxicity, glutamate may be involved in the pathophysiology of Parkinson's disease.

γ-Aminobutyric Acid (GABA).

SYNTHESIS, METABOLISM, AND PATHWAYS. GABA is found almost exclusively in the CNS, and it does not cross the blood–brain barrier. The highest concentrations are in the midbrain and diencephalon, with lower amounts in the cerebral hemispheres, the pons, and the medulla. GABA is synthesized from glutamate by the rate-limiting enzyme glutamic acid decarboxylase (GAD), which requires pyridoxine (vitamin B_6) as a cofactor. Once released into the synaptic cleft, GABA is taken up by a specific transporter into the presynaptic neuron and adjacent glia, where it is metabolized by mitochondrial-associated GABA transaminase (GABA-T). GABA is the primary neurotransmitter in intrinsic neurons that function as local mediators for the inhibitory feedback loops. GABA commonly coexists with biogenic amine neurotransmitters, glycine, and peptide neurotransmitters, including somatostatin, neuropeptide Y (NPY), cholecystokinin (CCK), substance P, and vasoactive intestinal peptide (VIP).

RECEPTORS AND DRUGS. There are three types of GABA receptors, $GABA_A$, $GABA_B$, and $GABA_C$, each with a discrete pattern of expression in the brain. The $GABA_B$ receptor is a G protein-associated receptor; $GABA_A$ and $GABA_C$ are directly acting, ligand-gated chloride ion channels that act to increase membrane polarization (Fig. 3.2–8). $GABA_A$ is the predominant species, consisting of five subunits in variable combinations. The $GABA_B$ receptor agonist baclofen is used to treat spasticity. The $GABA_A$ receptor antagonists bicuculline and picrotoxin strongly induce seizures. Because GABA is thought to suppress seizure activity, anxiety, and mania, considerable effort has been devoted to the synthesis of drugs that potentiate GABA activity. One such drug, progabide, is a hydrophobic GABA receptor agonist with good brain penetration, which has anticonvulsant activity. Tiagabine, which inhibits the GABA transporter, and vigabatrin (Sabril), which inhibits GABA-T, raise the effective synaptic levels of GABA and exhibit anticonvulsant activity. The anticonvulsant topiramate (Topamax) potentiates $GABA_A$ receptor activity by unclear mechanisms. Gabapentin (Neurontin), a GABA derivative, is an effective anticonvulsant with good brain penetration; yet, curiously, it has no activity at GABA receptors or the GABA transporter. The $GABA_A$ receptor has binding sites for GABA, the benzodiazepines, and the barbiturates. The benzodiazepines increase the affinity of the $GABA_A$ receptor for GABA. The benzodiazepine receptors are sometimes referred to as the omega (ω) receptors. The β-carbolines are a class of drugs that are inverse agonists of the benzodiazepine receptors; thus, their activity results in anxiety and convulsions. Flumazenil (Romazicon) is a benzodiazepine antagonist that is currently being used in hospital emergency rooms as a treatment for benzodiazepine overdoses.

PSYCHOPATHOLOGY. Clinical research on the GABAergic system, because it is associated with benzodiazepines, has focused on its potential role in the pathophysiology of anxiety disorders. Many of the standard anticonvulsants also have their effects on the GABA system; therefore, researchers in epilepsy also are actively studying the GABA system. The success of the anticonvulsants carbamazepine (Tegretol) and valproic acid (Depakote) for the treatment of rapid cycling bipolar I disorder has stimulated trials of the GABAergic anticonvulsants listed above for this indication.

Glycine.

Glycine is synthesized primarily from serine by the actions of serine *trans*-hydroxymethylase and β-glycerate dehydrogenase, both of which are rate-limiting. Glycine does double duty as a mandatory adjunctive neurotransmitter for glutamate activity and as an independent inhibitory neurotransmitter at its own receptors. The excitatory amino acid-binding site for glycine on the NMDA glutamate receptor is referred to as the nonstrychnine-sensitive glycine receptor, and it contrasts with the strychnine-sensitive glycine receptor, which is an inhibitory receptor. Improvement of NMDA receptor activity by occupancy of the glycine-binding site has been hypothesized to present an adjunctive mode for the treatment of schizophrenia. Some, but not all, clinical trials of this hypothesis have shown a reduction of the negative symptoms of schizophrenia by glycine or glycine analogues. The glycine receptor proper is a chloride ion channel similar in general structure and function to the nicotinic or GABA receptors. It

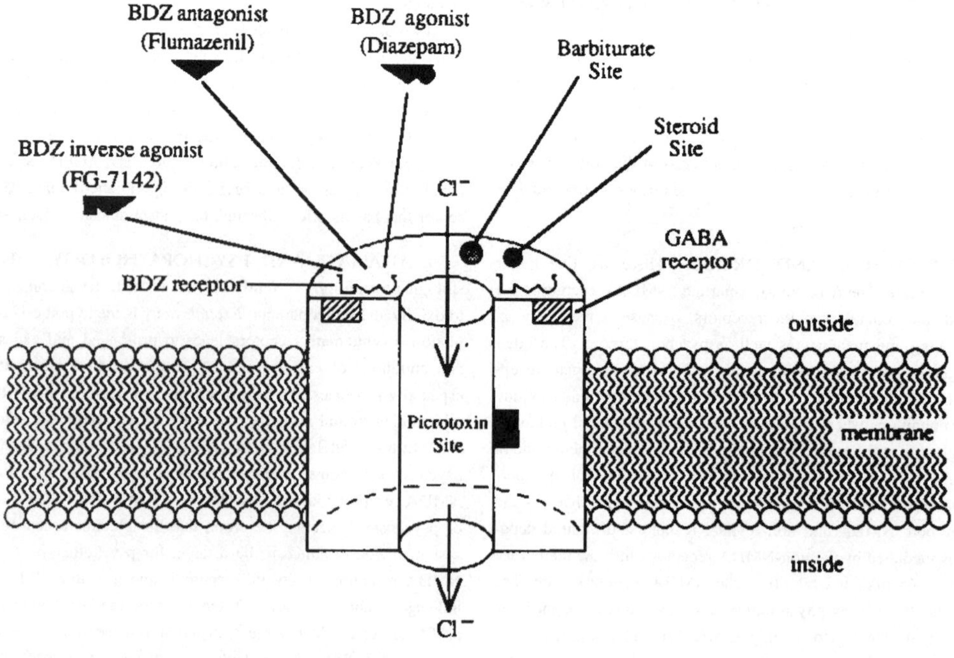
BDZ antagonist
(Flumazenil)
BDZ agonist
(Diazepam)
Barbiturate
Site
Steroid
Site
BDZ inverse agonist
(FG-7142)
Cl⁻
GABA
receptor
BDZ receptor
outside
Picrotoxin
Site
membrane
inside
Cl⁻

FIGURE 3.2–8
GABA-A receptor complex. *BDZ* (benzodiazepine). (Reprinted with permission from Cooper JR, Bloom FE, Roth RH: *The Biochemical Basis of Neuropharmacology,* ed 71, p 141. Oxford University Press, New York, 1996.)

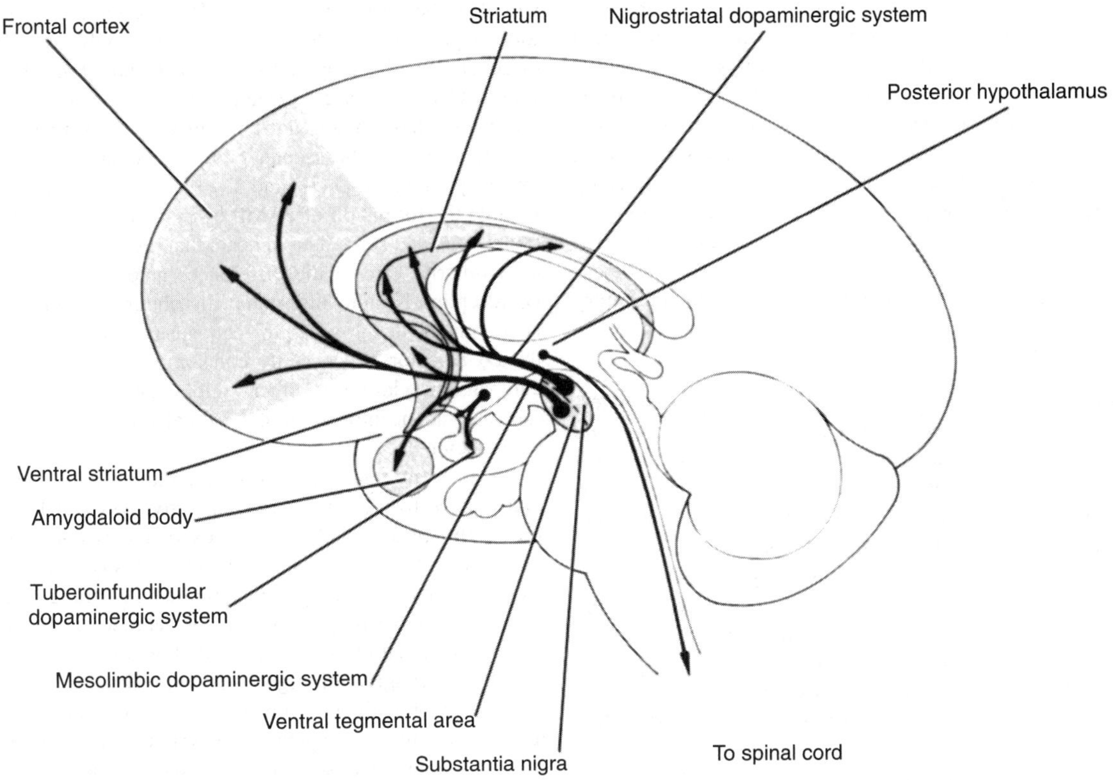
Frontal cortex
Striatum
Nigrostriatal dopaminergic system
Posterior hypothalamus
Ventral striatum
Amygdaloid body
Tuberoinfundibular dopaminergic system
Mesolimbic dopaminergic system
Ventral tegmental area
Substantia nigra
To spinal cord

FIGURE 3.2–9

Dopaminergic (DA) pathways. The nigrostriatal DA system originates in the substantia nigra and terminates in the main dorsal part of the striatum. The ventral tegmental area gives rise to the mesolimbic DA system, which terminates in the ventral striatum, the amygdaloid body, the frontal lobe, and some other basal forebrain areas. The tuberoinfundibular system innervates the median eminence and the posterior and intermediate lobes of the pituitary, and dopamine neurons in the posterior hypothalamus project to the spinal cord. (Reprinted with permission from Heimer L: *The Human Brain and Spinal Cord.* Springer, New York, 1983.)

is present in highest quantities in the spinal cord. Mutations in the glycine receptor cause a rare neurological condition called *hyperekplexia,* which is characterized by an exaggerated, i.e., poorly inhibited, startle response.

BIOGENIC AMINES

Each of these neurotransmitters is synthesized in a discrete nucleus of neurons from which axons project widely throughout the brain and spinal cord. They therefore exert a disproportionate influence on the activity of the brain, and they are of central importance to the pharmacological therapy of thought disorders, mood disorders, and anxiety disorders. Dopamine, norepinephrine, and epinephrine are products of the catecholamine synthetic pathway (Fig. 3.2–5), whereas serotonin (Fig. 3.2–6), acetylcholine, and histamine are derived from distinct precursors. A full understanding of the role of these neurotransmitters in psychiatry includes knowledge of their anatomy, life cycle (synthesis, secretion, reuptake, and degradation), receptors, and the drugs that modify their activity.

Dopamine

CNS Dopaminergic Tracts. The three most important dopaminergic tracts for psychiatry are the nigrostriatal tract, the mesolimbic-mesocortical tract, and the tuberoinfundibular tract (Fig. 3.2–9). The nigrostriatal tract projects from its cell bodies in the substantia nigra to the corpus striatum. When the D_2 receptors at the end of this tract are blocked by classic antipsychotic drugs, parkinsonian side effects emerge. In Parkinson's disease the nigrostriatal tract degenerates, resulting in the motor symptoms of the disease. Because of the significant association between Parkinson's disease and depression, the nigrostriatal tract may somehow be involved with the control of mood, in addition to its classic role in motor control.

D_2 receptors in the caudate nucleus suppress the activity of the caudate nucleus. The caudate neurons regulate motor acts by gating which intended acts are actually carried out. The absence of D_2 receptor activity allows the caudate to dampen motor activity excessively, resulting in the bradykinesia that typifies parkinsonism. At the other extreme, excess dopamine activity in the caudate removes the gating control and may result in extraneous motor acts, such as tics. A recent study of Tourette's syndrome patients, for example, correlated increased caudate dopamine analogue binding, which reflects increased numbers of the D_2 receptors, with more prominent clinical tics.

The mesolimbic-mesocortical tract projects from its cell bodies in the ventral tegmental area (VTA), which lies adjacent to the substantia nigra, to most areas of the cerebral cortex and the limbic system. Because the tract projects to the limbic system and the neocortex, the tract may be involved in mediating the antipsychotic effects of antipsychotic drugs.

The cell bodies of the tuberoinfundibular tract are in the arcuate nucleus and the periventricular area of the hypothalamus and project to the infundibulum and the anterior pituitary. Dopamine acts as a release-inhibiting factor in the tract by inhibiting the release of prolactin from the anterior pituitary. Patients who take typical antipsychotic drugs often have roughly threefold elevated prolactin levels because the blockade of dopamine receptors in the tract eliminates the inhibitory effect of dopamine.

Dopamine Life Cycle. The dopaminergic axon terminal is the site of synthesis for dopamine. Dopamine is one of the three catecholamine neurotransmitters that is synthesized starting with the amino acid tyrosine. The other two catecholamine neurotransmitters are norepinephrine and epinephrine (Fig. 3.2–5). The rate-limiting enzymatic step in the synthesis of any of the catecholamines is tyrosine hydroxylase. Therefore, dietary changes in tyrosine levels do not influence the synthesis of catecholamines. Tyrosine hydroxylase is a phosphoprotein that is subject to regulation by a range of protein kinases and protein phosphatases. Tyrosine hydroxylase transforms tyrosine into 3,4-dihydroxyphenylalanine (DOPA). Because it is beyond the rate-limiting synthetic step, DOPA may be administered orally to increase the rate of synthesis of its product, dopamine. DOPA is used for this purpose to treat Parkinson's disease. Once dopamine is produced, it is taken into synaptic vesicles by specific transporters and then released into the synaptic cleft on depolarization of the axon terminal.

The actions of dopamine are terminated by two general routes. First, dopamine can be taken back up into the presynaptic neuron and recycled as a neurotransmitter; this pathway is generally referred to as the reuptake mechanism. Reuptake occurs by the passage of the dopamine molecule from the synaptic space, through the presynaptic dopamine transporter, into the intracellular space, where it is packaged into vesicles. Second, dopamine can be metabolized. The two major enzymes involved in the metabolism of dopamine are monoamine oxidase (MAO) and, less importantly, catechol-*O*-methyltransferase (COMT). MAO is localized on the outer mitochondrial membrane principally in the presynaptic terminal, where it acts on dopamine that has been taken up into the presynaptic terminal but not yet repackaged into vesicles. COMT is a soluble enzyme localized in the cytoplasm of the postsynaptic cell and of glial cells and, possibly also, extracellularly. When dopamine is metabolized extraneuronally by COMT, the resulting metabolites are then taken back into the neuron and further metabolized by MAO. The two types of MAO are MAO_A and MAO_B, of which MAO_B selectively metabolizes dopamine. The primary metabolite of dopamine is homovanillic acid (HVA), and many research studies of cerebrospinal fluid, urine, and serum attempt to assess CNS dopamine activity by measuring concentrations of HVA.

Dopamine Receptors. The five subtypes of dopamine receptors are listed in Table 3.2–2. The five subtypes can be put into two groups. In the first group the D_1 and D_5 receptors stimulate the formulation of cAMP by activating the stimulatory G protein, G_s. The D_5 receptor has only recently been discovered, and less is known about it than about the D_1 receptor. One difference between these two receptors is that the D_5 receptor has a much higher affinity for dopamine than does the D_1 receptor. The second group of dopamine receptors is made up of the D_2, D_3, and D_4 receptors. The D_2 receptor inhibits the formation of cAMP by activating the inhibitory G protein, G_i, and some data indicate that the D_3 and D_4 receptors act similarly. One of the differences among the D_2, D_3, and D_4 receptors is their differential distribution. The D_2 receptor is prominent in the striatum (caudate nucleus and putamen), the D_3 receptor is especially concentrated in the nucleus accumbens, in addition to other regions, and the D_4 receptor is especially concentrated in the frontal cortex, in addition to other regions.

In a recent study, a scale of emotional detachment, with high values for aloofness and vindictiveness and low values for overly nurturing behavior and excessive exploitability, was used to rate 24 individuals, and then the density of D_2 receptors was determined in each person's putamen. A strong correlation was found between high levels of detachment and a low density of putaminal D_2 receptors, while low levels of detachment correlated strongly with high D_2 receptor density. This finding is in keeping with the clinical observation that D_2 receptor antagonists (that is, typical antipsychotic drugs) reduce the positive symptoms of schizophrenia, such as hallucinations and delusions, but may worsen the negative symptoms, such as social ambivalence and catatonia. In another study, experts postulate that dopamine activity may act in the medial left prefrontal cortex to suppress signals of emotional distress. A recent report supporting this hypothesis correlated a genetic polymorphism in the D_4 receptor with differences in subjective reports of mood.

Dopamine and Drugs. In the past the potency of antipsychotic compounds has been correlated with their affinity for the D_2 receptor. Since blockade of dopamine receptors, particularly the D_2 receptor, has been associated with the efficacy of antipsychotic drugs, long-term administration of dopamine receptor antagonists results in an upregulation in the number of dopamine receptors present. This upregulation may be involved in the development of tardive dyskinesia. The development of a new class of highly effective antipsychotic agents, called the serotonin-dopamine antagonists because they block predominantly the serotonin type 2 ($5\text{-}HT_2$) and, to a lesser extent, the D_2 receptors, has led to a reassessment of the D_2 receptor affinity hypothesis of antipsychotic potency. Serotonin-dopamine antagonists are associated with a greatly reduced risk of development of parkinsonian side effects and tardive dyskinesia, and not only do they treat the positive symptoms of schizophrenia effectively treated by pure D_2 receptor antagonists (psychosis, hallucinations, agitation), but they also improve the negative symptoms of schizophrenia (blunted affect, ambivalence, catatonia).

Other substances that affect the dopamine system are amphetamine and cocaine. Amphetamines cause the release of dopamine, and cocaine blocks the uptake of dopamine. Thus, the substances increase the amount of dopamine present in the synapse. Cocaine and methamphetamine (Desoxyn) are among the most addicting substances. Their use may permanently deplete the brain's stores of dopamine. The dopaminergic systems may be particularly involved in the brain's so-called reward system, and this involvement may explain the high addiction potential of cocaine. Mutant "knockout mice," in which the dopamine transporter gene has been experimentally deleted, do not respond biochemically or behaviorally to cocaine. This suggests that the dopamine transporter is necessary for the pharmacological effects of cocaine. Studies in rats showed that D_2 receptor agonists increased cocaine self-administration, while D_1 receptor agonists lowered the desire for cocaine. Nicotine, the most psychoactive ingredient in cigarette smoke, stimulates the release of dopamine and glutamate. Epidemiological studies have found that smokers have a reduced risk of developing Parkinson's disease, Alzheimer's disease, and ulcerative colitis. A nicotine analogue that stimulates dopamine release is under study for treatment of Parkinson's disease, and the nicotine transdermal patch is being studied to counteract the cognitive impairment caused by treatment with haloperidol.

The dopamine transporter may be blocked by benztropine (Cogentin) and bupropion (Wellbutrin), though it is unlikely that sufficient CNS concentrations of these drugs are routinely obtained to see an appreciable effect on dopamine transport. The transporter is the portal of entry of the neurotoxin methylphenyltetrahydropyridine (MPTP), which may cause parkinsonism by killing the nigral dopaminergic neurons. Dopamine-containing storage vesicles are depleted irreversibly by reserpine (Serpasil) and reversibly by tetrabenazine.

Dopamine and Psychopathology. The *dopamine hypothesis of schizophrenia* grew from the observations that drugs that block dopamine receptors (for example, haloperidol) have antipsychotic activity and that drugs that stimulate dopamine activity (for example, amphetamine) can, when given in high enough doses, induce psychotic symptoms in nonschizophrenic persons. The dopamine hypothesis remains the leading neurochemical hypothesis for schizophrenia, but room is being made for a role for serotonin, based on the therapeutic success of the serotonin-dopamine antagonists. A recent series of studies showed that plasma concentrations of HVA are, in fact, reduced in many schizophrenic patients who respond to antipsychotic drugs. A major problem with the hypothesis is that blockade of dopamine receptors reduces psychotic symptoms in virtually any disorder, such as psychosis associated with a brain tumor and psychosis associated with mania. Thus, some as yet unrecognized neurochemical abnormality in schizophrenia may be unique to the condition. Dopamine may also be involved in the pathophysiology of mood disorders. Dopamine activity may be low in depression and high in mania. Amphetamines, which potentiate dopamine activity, are highly effective antidepressants. The observation that levodopa (Larodopa) can cause mania and psychosis in some parkinsonian patients also supports the hypothesis. Some studies have found low levels of dopamine metabolites in depressed patients.

Norepinephrine and Epinephrine

Although norepinephrine and epinephrine are discussed together, norepinephrine is the more important and more abundant of the two related neurotransmitters in the brain, although adrenally derived epinephrine is more abundant than norepinephrine in the serum. The norepinephrine system and the epinephrine system are also referred to as, respectively, the noradrenergic system and the adrenergic system. The receptors are referred to simply as adrenergic receptors, however, because they are receptors for both epinephrine and norepinephrine.

CNS Noradrenergic Tracts. The major concentration of noradrenergic (and adrenergic) cell bodies that project upward in the brain is in the compact locus ceruleus in the pons (Fig. 3.2–10). The axons of these neurons project through the medial forebrain bundle to the cerebral cortex, the limbic system, the thalamus, and the hypothalamus.

Norepinephrine and Epinephrine Life Cycle. Norepinephrine and epinephrine, along with dopamine, constitute the catecholamines. The catecholamines are synthesized from tyrosine, and the rate-limiting enzyme is tyrosine hydroxylase (Fig. 3.2–5). In neurons that release norepinephrine, the enzyme dopamine β-hydroxylase converts dopamine to norepinephrine; neurons that release dopamine lack this enzyme. In neurons that release epinephrine, the enzyme phenylethanolamine-*N*-methyltransferase (PNMT) converts norepinephrine into epinephrine. Neurons that release either dopamine or norepinephrine do not have PNMT.

Once norepinephrine or epinephrine is formed, it is taken through specific transporter proteins into synaptic vesicles, from which it is released on depolarization of the axonal terminal. As with dopamine, the two major routes of deactivation are uptake back into the presynaptic neuron and metabolism by MAO and COMT. The MAO_A subtype preferentially metabolizes norepinephrine and epinephrine, as well as serotonin.

Noradrenergic and Adrenergic Receptors. The two broad groups of adrenergic and noradrenergic receptors, often just referred to as adrenergic receptors, are the α-adrenergic receptors and the β-adrenergic receptors (Table 3.2–2). The advances of molecular biology have now subtyped these receptors into four types of α_1 receptors (α_{1a}, α_{1b}, α_{1c}, and α_{1d}), three types of α_2 receptors (α_{2a}, α_{2b}, and α_{2c}), one type of α_3 receptor, and three types of β receptors (β_1, β_2, and β_3). Although the field is changing rapidly, all α_1 receptors seem to be linked to the phosphoinositol turnover system, α_2 receptors seem to inhibit the formation of cAMP, and β receptors seem to stimulate the formation of cAMP. The surface availability and the efficiency of signal transduction of the adrenergic receptors are constantly regulated by phosphorylations and changes in protein–protein interactions. Significant data have long been available on the β_1 and β_2 receptors, which regulate the function of nearly every organ in the body, often in antagonism to the effects of the α-adrenergic receptors. The β_3 receptors have recently been found to regulate energy metabolism. They are expressed in adipocytes, and their activation by agonists reduces the amount of body fat. They are therefore a target for the development of antiobesity drugs.

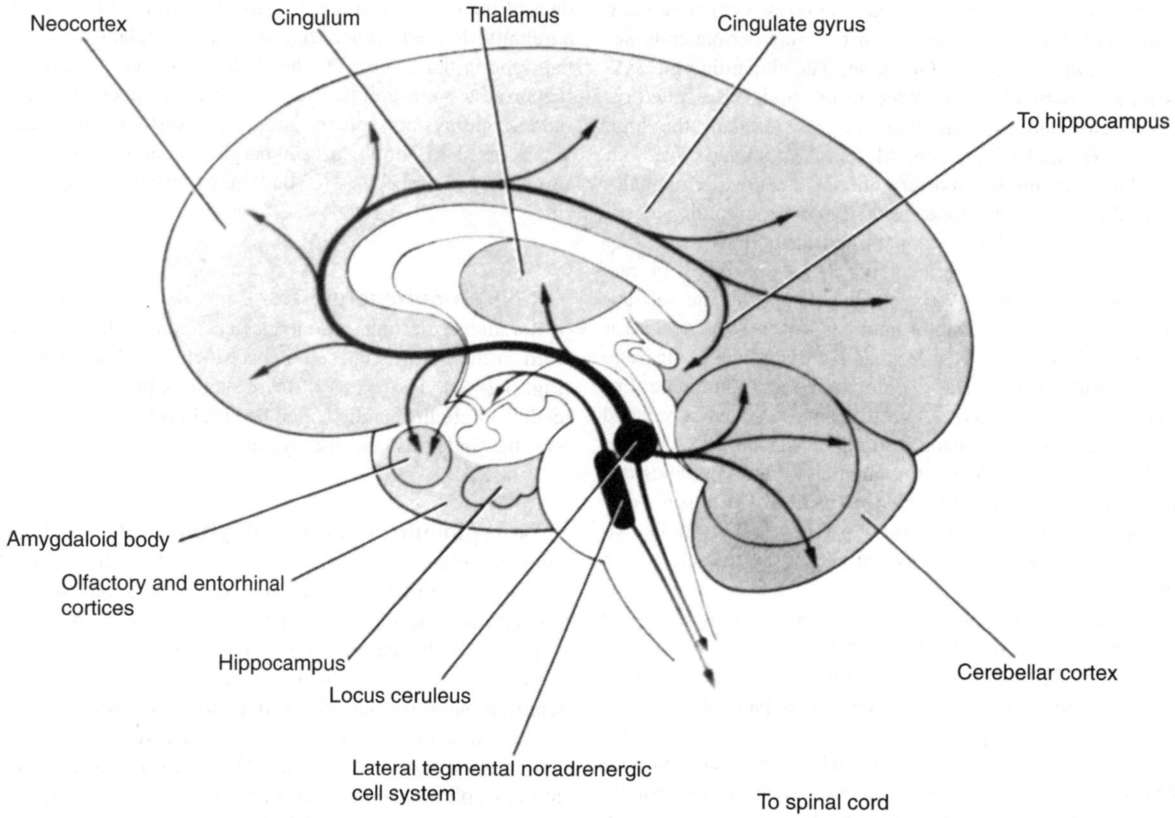
Neocortex
Cingulum
Thalamus
Cingulate gyrus
To hippocampus
Amygdaloid body
Olfactory and entorhinal cortices
Hippocampus
Locus ceruleus
Lateral tegmental noradrenergic cell system
To spinal cord
Cerebellar cortex

FIGURE 3.2–10
Noradrenergic pathways. The locus ceruleus, which is located immediately underneath the floor of the fourth ventricle in the rostrolateral part of the pons, is the most important noradrenergic nucleus in the brain. Its projections reach many areas in the forebrain, the cerebellum, and the spinal cord. Noradrenergic neurons in the lateral brainstem tegmentum innervate several structures in the basal forebrain, including the hypothalamus and the amygdaloid body. (Reprinted with permission from Heimer L: *The Human Brain and Spinal Cord.* Springer, New York, 1983.)

Norepinephrine and Drugs. The psychiatric drugs that are most associated with norepinephrine are the classic antidepressant drugs, the tricyclic drugs and the MAO inhibitors (MAOIs), and, more recently, venlafaxine (Effexor), mirtazapine (Remeron), bupropion, and nefazodone (Serzone). The tricyclic drugs, venlafaxine, bupropion, and nefazodone, block the reuptake of norepinephrine (and serotonin) into the presynaptic neuron, and the MAOIs block the catabolism of norepinephrine (and serotonin). Thus, the immediate effect of tricyclic drugs and MAOIs is to increase the concentrations of norepinephrine (and serotonin) in the synaptic cleft. Since antidepressants take 2 to 4 weeks to exert their therapeutic effects, it is obviously not the immediate effect alone that results in their beneficial effects. However, the immediate effects may eventually lead to a downregulation of the number of postsynaptic β-adrenergic receptors, and this downregulation of postsynaptic β-adrenergic receptors has been correlated with clinical improvement. Mirtazapine acts by blocking the presynaptic α_2 receptors and thus removing the feedback inhibition normally exerted on the release of norepinephrine. The net effect of mirtazapine is to increase norepinephrine secretion.

The α-adrenergic system is also involved in the production of some of the adverse events that can be seen with many psychotherapeutic drugs. Blockade of the α_1-adrenergic receptors is commonly associated with sedation and postural hypotension. Another drug that affects the α-adrenergic system is clonidine (Catapres), which is an α_2 receptor agonist. The α_2-adrenergic receptors are generally located on the presynaptic neuron in the CNS, and activation of these receptors downregulates the production and the release of norepinephrine. The sympatholytic actions of clonidine have been used for a variety of psychiatric disorders, including opioid withdrawal. The antihypertensive agent methyldopa (Aldomet) is a competitive inhibitor of L-aromatic amino acid decarboxylase, which transforms methyldopa to methyldopamine and eventually to methylnorepinephrine, which displaces norepinephrine from storage vesicles. Methylnorepinephrine acts as an α_2 receptor agonist to lower blood pressure. The α_2 receptor antagonist yohimbine (Yocon) is used to reverse the antisexual effects of antidepressants, especially those of the serotonergic class.

The β-adrenergic antagonists, such as propranolol (Inderal), have also been used in psychiatry. In general, β-adrenergic receptors are located postsynaptically, and inhibition of their

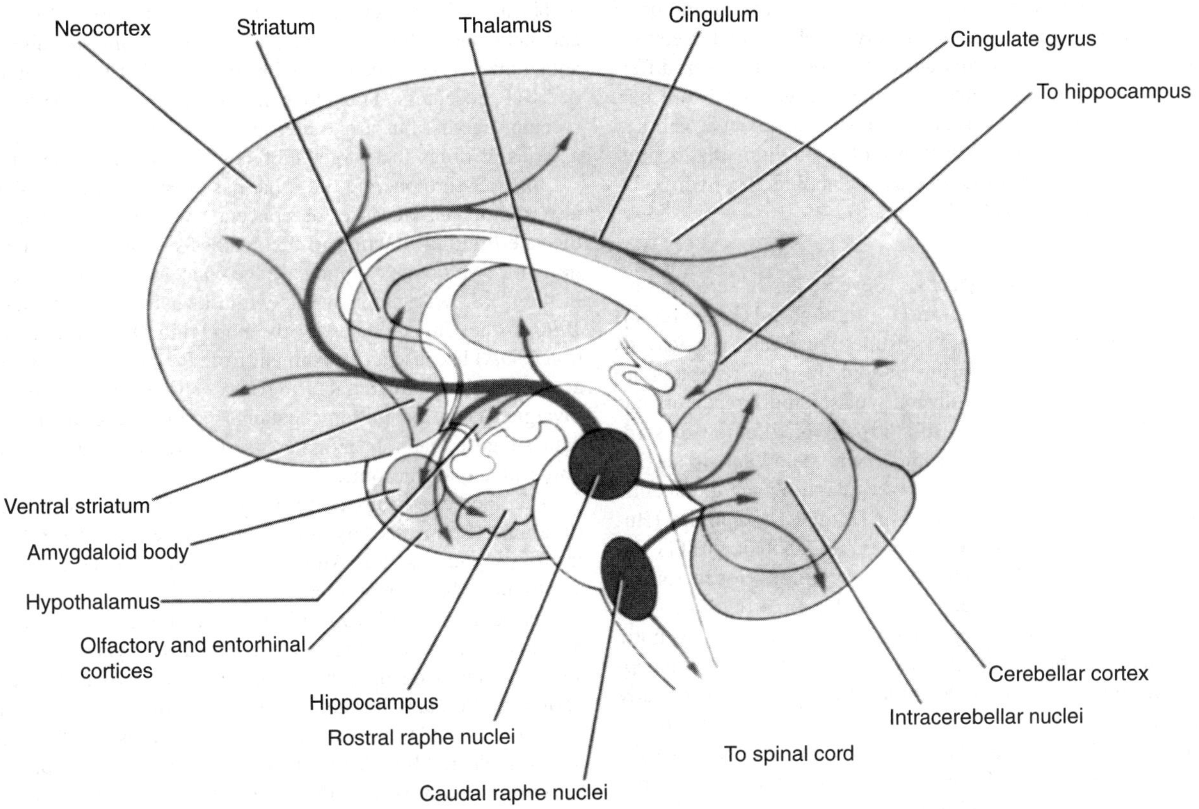

Neocortex
Striatum
Thalamus
Cingulum
Cingulate gyrus
To hippocampus
Ventral striatum
Amygdaloid body
Hypothalamus
Olfactory and entorhinal cortices
Hippocampus
Rostral raphe nuclei
Caudal raphe nuclei
To spinal cord
Intracerebellar nuclei
Cerebellar cortex

FIGURE 3.2–11
Serotonergic (5-HT) pathways. The raphe nuclei form a more-or-less continuous collection of cell groups close to the midline throughout the brainstem, but for the sake of simplicity, they have been subdivided into a rostral group and a caudal group in the drawing. The rostral raphe nuclei project to a large number of forebrain structures. The fibers that project laterally through the internal and external capsules to widespread areas of the neocortex are not indicated in this highly schematic drawing. (Reprinted with permission from Heimer L: *The Human Brain and Spinal Cord.* Springer, New York, 1983.)

activity results in a decrease in cAMP formation in the postsynaptic neuron. The β-adrenergic antagonists have been used to treat social phobia (for example, performance anxiety), akathisia (a movement disorder associated with antipsychotic compounds), and lithium-induced tremor.

Norepinephrine and Psychopathology. The *biogenic amine hypothesis of mood disorders* was based on the observation that the tricyclic drugs and the MAOIs are effective in alleviating the symptoms of depression. What the relative roles of serotonin and norepinephrine are in the pathophysiology of depression is still unclear. Drugs that affect both neurotransmitters are effective, and drugs that affect primarily norepinephrine—for example, desipramine (Norpramin)—and drugs that affect primarily serotonin—for example, fluoxetine—are also effective. When noradrenergic neurons are destroyed in experimental animal models, however, drugs that affect serotonin do not have their usual effects; and when serotonergic neurons are destroyed, drugs that affect norepinephrine do not have their usual effects. These experimental results indicate that the interrelationships between serotonergic and noradrenergic neurons are incompletely understood.

Serotonin

CNS Serotonergic Tracts. The major site of serotonergic cell bodies is in the upper pons and the midbrain—specifically, the median and dorsal raphe nuclei, and, to a lesser extent, the caudal locus ceruleus, the area postrema, and the interpeduncular area (Fig. 3.2–11). These neurons project to the basal ganglia, the limbic system, and the cerebral cortex.

Serotonin Life Cycle. As with the catecholamines, serotonin is synthesized in the axonal terminal (Fig. 3.2–6). The precursor amino acid is tryptophan. In contrast to the catecholamines, the availability of tryptophan is the rate-limiting function, and the enzyme tryptophan hydroxylase is not rate-limiting. Therefore, dietary variations in tryptophan can measurably affect serotonin levels in the brain. For example, tryptophan depletion causes irritability and hunger, whereas tryptophan supplementation may induce sleep, relieve anxiety, and increase a sense of well-being. Once synthesized, serotonin is packaged into vesicles for release upon the arrival of an action potential. The synaptic action of serotonin is terminated by reuptake into the presynaptic terminal by the plasma membrane transporter. As discussed earlier, the promotor of the transporter gene contains a polymorphism that creates a twofold variation in the amount of transporter between different individuals that in some way may account for 3 to 4 percent of the biological variation in levels of anxiety. The key enzyme involved in the metabolism of serotonin is MAO, preferentially MAO_A, and the primary metabolite is 5-hydroxyindoleacetic acid (5-HIAA) (Fig. 3.2–6).

Serotonergic Receptors. Seven types of serotonin receptors are now recognized—5-HT_1 through 5-HT_7—with numerous subtypes, totalling 14 distinct receptors. The various functional effector mechanisms of some of these receptors are listed in Table 3.2–2. The diversity of serotonin receptors has initiated a significant effort to study the distribution of serotonin receptor subtypes in pathological states and to design subtype-specific drugs that may be of particular therapeutic benefit in specific conditions. For example, buspirone (BuSpar), a clinically effective anxiolytic, is a potent 5-HT_{1A} agonist, and other 5-HT_{1A} agonists are being developed for the treatment of anxiety and depression. Clozapine (Clozaril), the prototypical serotonin-dopamine antagonist antipsychotic agent, has significant activity as an antagonist of 5-HT_2 receptors, and this observation has initiated a major effort to study the role of this serotonin receptor subtype and to develop drugs that are 5-HT_2 antagonists for the treatment of schizophrenia. Antagonists of the 5-HT_3 receptor are also under study as potential antianxiety and antipsychotic compounds. The distributed serotonin receptors are sometimes responsible for the side effects of serotonergic drugs, many of which nonspecifically raise serotonin levels and thus indiscriminately increase receptor activation. Serotonin receptors in the basal ganglia may be responsible for akathisia and agitation; 5-HT_3 receptors in the brainstem vomiting center (area postrema) and/or the hypothalamus may cause nausea and vomiting; receptors in the limbic system may cause an initial increase in anxiety; receptors in various of the brainstem sleep centers may produce either insomnia or somnolence; spinal cord pathways may produce sexual dysfunction; receptors in the intestines (where 90 percent of the body's serotonin is found) may cause gastrointestinal upset and diarrhea; and receptors in the cranial blood vessel may cause headache. It has not been possible to predict which adverse effects, if any, will occur in a particular patient.

Serotonin and Drugs. Some of the new relations between serotonin and drugs under development are discussed above; however, the historical association of serotonin and psychotropic drugs was first made with the tricyclic drugs and the MAOIs, as described for norepinephrine and epinephrine. The tricyclic drugs and the MAOIs, respectively, block the uptake and the metabolism of serotonin and norepinephrine, thus increasing the concentration of both neurotransmitters in the synaptic cleft. Fluoxetine is one of the serotonin-specific reuptake inhibitors (SSRIs) that are used in the treatment of depression. Other drugs in that class include paroxetine (Paxil), sertraline (Zoloft), fluvoxamine (Luvox), and citalopram, all of which are usually associated with minimal adverse effects, especially in comparison with the tricyclic drugs and the MAOIs. Venlafaxine blocks the reuptake of both serotonin and norepinephrine. With respect to serotonin, both trazodone (Desyrel) and nefazodone block the reuptake of serotonin and directly antagonize 5-HT_2 receptors, with the net effect of stimulation of 5-HT_1 receptors. Trazodone and nefazodone and the 5-HT_1 receptor agonist buspirone are the first of what will likely be a series of drugs that target subtypes of serotonin receptors.

Another serotonergic drug that has been used in psychiatry is L-tryptophan. Because the concentration of L-tryptophan is the rate-limiting function in the synthesis of serotonin, ingestion of L-tryptophan can increase the concentration of serotonin in the CNS. L-Tryptophan was withdrawn from the market in 1990 in the United States by the Food and Drug Administration (FDA) because a contaminant from the production process at one particular manufacturing site caused an eosinophilia-myalgia syndrome in some patients taking the drug. Recent data suggest that L-tryptophan itself may cause the eosinophilia-myalgia syndrome.

The anorectic drugs fenfluramine (Pondimin) and dexfenfluramine (Redux) act by stimulating the release of serotonin from synaptic vesicles. Another serotonin reuptake inhibitor, sibutramine, has potent anorexigenic qualities.

Serotonin is also involved in the mechanism of at least two major substances of abuse, lysergic acid diethylamide (LSD) and 3,4-methylenedioxymethamphetamine (MDMA), also known as "ecstacy." The serotonin system is the major site of action for LSD, but exactly how LSD exerts its effects remains unclear. MDMA has dual effects as an uptake blocker to serotonin and as an inducer of the massive release of the serotonin contents of serotonergic neurons.

Serotonin and Psychopathology. The principal association for serotonin with a psychopathological condition is with depression, as suggested in the biogenic amine hypothesis of mood disorders. This hypothesis is simply that depression is associated with too little serotonin and that mania is associated with too much serotonin. As explained above for norepinephrine, that simplified view is undoubtedly not entirely accurate. The *permissive hypothesis* postulates that low levels of serotonin permit abnormal levels of norepinephrine to cause depression or mania. With the introduction of a variety of new drugs, serotonin is one of the most exciting areas for research in the anxiety disorders and schizophrenia, in addition to its role in depression. For example, early theories about the causes of anxiety focused on the GABA system because the first effective anxiolytics were the benzodiazepines, which potentiate GABAergic neurotransmission. With the recent success of SSRIs and buspirone, which are effective antianxiety agents, room has had to be made in the theory of anxiety for a role for serotonin. Similarly, schizophrenia was previously thought to result from an imbalance of dopamine, but since the therapeutic success of the serotonin-dopamine antagonists, schizophrenia is now thought to result from misregulation of both dopamine and serotonin function. It is likely that the theories will need to be reconceived several times in the near future as agents become available for modification of particular receptor subtypes.

Acetylcholine

CNS Cholinergic Tracts. A group of cholinergic neurons in the nucleus basalis of Meynert projects to the cerebral cortex and the limbic system. Additional cholinergic neurons in the reticular system project to the cerebral cortex, the limbic system, the hypothalamus, and the thalamus. Some patients with dementia of the Alzheimer's type or Down's syndrome appear to have a specific degeneration of the neurons in the nucleus basalis of Meynert.

Acetylcholine Life Cycle. Acetylcholine is synthesized in the cholinergic axon terminal from acetylcoenzyme A (acetyl-CoA) and choline by the enzyme choline acetyltransferase. Once made, acetylcholine is packaged into storage vesicles for release when triggered by an action potential. Acetylcholine is metabolized in the synaptic cleft by acetylcholinesterase, and the resulting choline is taken back up into the presynaptic neuron and is recycled to make new acetylcholine molecules. Acetylcholinesterase is affected by the drugs currently in use for the treatment of Alzheimer's disease.

Cholinergic Receptors. The two major subtypes of cholinergic receptors are muscarinic and nicotinic (Table 3.2–2). There are five recognized types of muscarinic receptors with various effects on phosphoinositol turnover, cAMP and cGMP production, and potassium ion channel activity. Muscarinic receptors are antagonized by atropine and by the anticholinergic drugs. The nicotinic receptors are ligand-gated ion channels that have the receptor site directly on the ion channel itself. The nicotinic receptor is actually made up of four subunits (α, β, γ, and δ). Nicotinic receptors can vary in the number of each of those subunits; thus, there is a multitude of subtypes of nicotinic receptors, based on the specific configuration of the subunits.

Acetylcholine and Drugs. The most common use of anticholinergic drugs in psychiatry is as a treatment of the motor abnormalities caused by the use of classic antipsychotic drugs (for example, haloperidol). The efficacy of the drugs for that indication is determined by the balance between acetylcholine activity and dopamine activity in the basal ganglia. In normal people, the activity of the nigrostriatal dopamine pathway is partially balanced by the activity of cholinergic pathways in the basal ganglia. Blockade of D_2 receptors in the striatum upsets this balance, but the balance may be partially restored, albeit at a lower set point, by antagonism of muscarinic receptors. Blockade of muscarinic cholinergic receptors is a common pharmacodynamic effect of many psychotropic drugs. Blockade of these receptors leads to the commonly seen side effects of blurred vision, dry mouth, constipation, and difficulty in initiating urination. Excessive blockade of CNS cholinergic receptors causes confusion and delirium. Drugs that increase cholinergic activity by blocking breakdown by acetylcholinesterase (for example, donepezil [Aricept]) have been shown to be effective in the treatment of dementia of the Alzheimer's type.

When bound by nicotine, CNS presynaptic nicotinic receptors mediate a large influx of calcium and therefore cause neurotransmitter release in many types of neurons. Recent evidence has shown that nicotine increases the strength of synaptic connections in the hippocampus, the brain region that supports short-term memory. Several nicotine-like compounds that stimulate acetylcholine release are under study as cognitive enhancers for treatment of Alzheimer's disease.

Acetylcholine and Psychopathology. The most common association with acetylcholine is dementia of the Alzheimer's type and other dementias. Anticholinergic agents can impair learning and memory in normal people. With the recent identification of the protein structures of the various muscarinic and nicotinic receptors, many researchers are working on specific muscarinic and nicotinic agonists that may prove to be of some benefit in the treatment of dementia of the Alzheimer's type. Acetylcholine may also be involved in mood and sleep disorders.

Histamine

Neurons that release histamine as their neurotransmitter are located in the hypothalamus and project to the cerebral cortex, the limbic system, and the thalamus. There are three types of histamine receptors: H_1 receptor stimulation increases the production of IP_3 and DAG; H_2 stimulation increases the production of cAMP; and the H_3 receptor may regulate vascular tone. Blockade of H_1 receptors is the mechanism of action for allergy medications and is partly the mechanism for commonly observed side effects—such as sedation, weight gain, and hypotension—seen with some psychotropic drugs.

PEPTIDE NEUROTRANSMITTERS

As many as 300 peptide neurotransmitters may be in the human brain. A peptide is a short protein consisting of fewer than 100 amino acids. Peptides are made in the neuronal cell body by the transcription and translation of a genetic message. Peptides are stored in synaptic vesicles and are released from the axon terminals. The activity of peptides is terminated by the action of enzymes, peptidases, that cleave the peptides between specific amino acid residues. In addition to the regulatory mechanisms shared with other neurotransmitters, neuroactive peptides are subject to additional refinements in regulation. Differential ribonucleic acid (RNA) processing of the RNA first transcribed from the deoxyribonucleic acid (DNA) (heterogeneous nuclear RNA [hnRNA]) can result in different messenger RNAs (mRNAs). Most of these initial mRNAs for peptide neurotransmitters actually code for much longer peptides, called preprohormones, which are cleaved in the cell body before they are packaged as prohormones into vesicles for transport to the axon terminals. During the transport phase, the prohormone is usually further cleaved to form the final form of the peptide, which can then be subject to additional posttranslational modifications. Peptide receptors are members of the seven-transmembrane-domain, G protein-linked receptor family. In addition, most if not all peptide neurotransmitters coexist in storage vesicles with other neurotransmitters.

Selected Peptide Neurotransmitters

Endogenous Opioids. The remarkable analgesic and psychological effects of opium have been recognized since biblical times. The isolation of the alkaloid morphine in 1806 led in this century to the development of extensive pharmacological assays for opiate agents and raised the question of whether there were endogenous opiate-like compounds. In the mid-1970s, peptides isolated from brain extracts were shown to interact with opioid receptors and were called *opioids*. The endogenous opioids act on three major receptors, μ, κ, and δ and are believed to be involved in the regulation of stress, pain, and mood. Until this year, three classes of endogenous opioids were recognized, the enkephalins, endorphins, and dynorphins. Recently, the endomorphins, which at last rival morphine itself in potency, were discovered. These range in size from the 31-amino acid β-endorphin down to the tetrapeptide endomorphins. These peptides bind to members of the opioid receptor family. Enkephalins bind strongly to δ opioid receptors and with less affinity to μ receptors. The β-endorphin binds with modest affinity to μ and δ receptors. Dynorphins bind strongly to κ and μ receptors. None of these binds as strongly as morphine nor elicits as strong an analgesic response as the plant alkaloid, however, which led for many years to questions as to whether they in fact represented the true endogenous opioids. Endomorphins 1 and 2, in contrast, equal the affinity of morphine for the μ receptors and also the analgesic activity of morphine in animals. It is therefore postulated that endogenous ligands of high affinity for the δ and κ receptors remain to be discovered. The enkephalins, endorphins, and dynorphins are derived by processing of their respective precursor polypeptides, proopiomelanocortin (POMC), proenkephalin, and prodynorphin. Processing of POMC results in adrenocorticotrophic hormone (ACTH), melanocyte-stimulating hormones, and β-endorphin. Processing of proenkephalin produces met-enkephalin and leuenkephalin, and processing of prodynorphin produces β-neoendorphin and dynorphin. The precursor molecule or molecules for endomorphins have not been discovered but are assumed also to be larger polypeptides. Although evidence of opioids as true neurotransmitters has been difficult to distinguish from their potentiating effects on glutamatergic or adrenergic neurotransmission, a true role for endogenous opioid neurotransmission has been established in the hippocampus, where associative learning may contribute to addiction. Endogenous opioid-containing neurons are found in several brain regions, including the medial hypothalamus, diencephalon, pons, hippocampus, and midbrain, and their axons project both locally and widely. Examination of enkephalins, endorphins, and dynorphins in models of addiction have failed to yield insight in the form of variations in levels of ligands. This may be because they are not the endogenous ligands of highest affinity and specificity. Emerging data on endomorphins and other, so far undiscovered, ligands may yet unlock the mystery of addiction.

Substance P. Substance P is the primary neurotransmitter in most primary afferent sensory neurons and in the striatonigral pathway. They are most prominently associated with mediation of the perception of pain. Abnormalities affecting substance P have been hypothesized for Huntington's disease, dementia of the Alzheimer's type, and mood disorders.

Neurotensin. Neurotensin has been hypothesized to be involved in the pathophysiology of schizophrenia, mostly because of its coexistence with dopamine in some axon terminals. Some preliminary reports suggest that neurotensin-related peptides or drugs have beneficial effects for some psychotic symptoms.

Cholecystokinin. Like neurotensin and for the same reasons, cholecystokinin (CCK) has been hypothesized to be involved in the pathophysiology of schizophrenia. CCK has also been implicated in the pathophysiologies of eating disorders and movement disorders. CCK causes anxiety and triggers panic attacks in people with panic disorder. CCK antagonists are under study as possible anxiolytic agents.

Somatostatin. Somatostatin is also known as growth hormone-inhibiting factor. Somatostatin has been implicated by postmortem studies in Huntington's disease and dementia of the Alzheimer's type.

Vasopressin and Oxytocin. Vasopressin and oxytocin, two related peptides, have been postulated to be involved in the regulation of mood. They are both synthesized in the hypothalamus and are released in the posterior pituitary.

Neuropeptide Y. This peptide has been shown to stimulate the appetite, and development of neuropeptide Y receptor antagonists is an active area of interest for obesity researchers.

PSYCHONEUROENDOCRINOLOGY

Three related areas involving peptides and psychiatry need to be differentiated. First, neuroactive peptide neurotransmitters are a class of peptides that function like classic neurotransmitters. Second, the hormones of the classic neuroendocrine axes (for example, the limbic-hypothalamic-pituitary-adrenal axis) can feed back to the brain through the bloodstream to affect neuronal function. Third, specific psychiatric syndromes are associated with hyperactivity and hypoactivity of those same classic neuroendocrine axes. The first and second areas are discussed here. The third area is covered in Chapter 10.

Hormone Receptors

There are a variety of hormone receptors. It is instructive, however, to describe the steroid receptor. Steroid hormones are produced by the ovaries (estrogen and progestins), the testes (androgens), and the adrenal cortex (glucocorticoids). After secretion, steroid hormones are tightly bound to steroid-binding proteins in the blood, from which the steroid hormones can diffuse into the cytoplasm of cells, including neurons. Once inside the cell, the steroid hormones can bind to receptor proteins that are specific to each type of cell. Therefore, although the steroid hormones can diffuse into any cell, only those cells with the appropriate receptors will respond. Once bound to its appropriate receptor, the steroid receptor complex can diffuse through the nuclear membrane. Once inside the nucleus, the steroid can interact with DNA and regulate RNA synthesis. Steroids are an example of hormones with nuclear receptors; other hormones have conventional surface receptors; and still other hormones have both types of receptors.

Selected Hormonal Axes

Adrenal Axis. The components of the adrenal axis are corticotropin-releasing hormone (CRH), also called corticotropin-releasing factor (CRF), from the hypothalamus, ACTH from the anterior pituitary, and cortisol from the adrenal gland. The plasma concentrations of cortisol are at their highest in the early morning (around 6 AM) and at their lowest values in the late afternoon and evening. The adrenal axis reacts to stress by increasing the secretion of cortisol. The released cortisol performs many peripheral functions, as well as feeding back to the brain itself to induce new protein synthesis, presumably adaptive to handling stressful situations. CRH secretion may increase in major depression, anorexia nervosa, and anxiety-related disorders. Excessive CRH may produce Cushing's syndrome, whereas CRH deficiency may cause Addison's syndrome.

Thyroid Axis. The components of the thyroid axis are thyrotropin-releasing hormone (TRH) from the hypothalamus, thyroid-stimulating hormone (TSH) from the anterior pituitary, and thyroid hormone from the thyroid gland. The active forms of thyroid hormone, thyroxine (T_4) and Triiodothyronine (T_3), are deactivated when they are converted into reverse T_3 (rT_3). There are both surface and nuclear receptors for thyroid hormones. The absence of thyroid hormone in early infancy results in a severe form of mental retardation called *cretinism.* The administration of TRH has brief mood-elevating effects in depressed patients, and some antidepressant-nonresponsive patients are converted into antidepressant-responsive patients with the addition of T_3 to their antidepressant regimen. Experimental data indicate that the additional T_3 acts by modulating the function of the β-adrenergic receptor.

Growth Hormone. The components of the growth hormone axis are growth hormone-releasing hormone (GHRH) and growth hormone–release-inhibiting factor (GHRIF), also known as somatostatin, from the hypothalamus, and growth hormone itself from the anterior pituitary. Growth hormone is released in pulses throughout the day, but the pulses are closer together during the first hours of sleep than at other times. Growth hormone regulation has been studied particularly in schizophrenia and mood disorders, in which some data suggest a disordered regulation of the growth hormone axis.

Prolactin. The release of prolactin from the anterior pituitary is regulated by prolactin-releasing factors (PRFs) and prolactin-inhibiting factor (PIF), which is the neurotransmitter dopamine. Especially with the novel antipsychotic drugs under development, interest is increasing in correlating the effects of antipsychotic drugs on the release of prolactin with therapeutic effects.

Melatonin. Melatonin is released by the pineal body, which also contains many other peptides and hormones. Melatonin is secreted when the eyes perceive darkness, and its release is inhibited when the eyes perceive light. Melatonin is synthesized from serotonin by the action of two enzymes: serotonin-*N*-acetylase and 5-hydroxyindole-*O*-methyltransferase. Melatonin is involved in the regulation of circadian rhythms and has been implicated in the pathophysiology of depression.

Estrogens. A few small studies have demonstrated that estrogen replacement in postmenopausal women reduces the development of Alzheimer's disease. Estrogen receptors, which are members of the steroid receptor family, are present in high levels in the basal forebrain and may interact with receptors for nerve growth factor to support the survival of cholinergic neurons. Further, larger studies are needed to determine whether the effect is due to estrogen or to some other factor. Because of the reluctance of some women to be assigned to the placebo arm of such a study for several years, however, concern is mounting that the necessary data will not be collected, and estrogen will be given based in part on its emotional significance.

Endocrine Dysregulation in Psychiatric Disorders

Some patients with psychiatric disorders, particularly depressive disorders and schizophrenia, have abnormal regulation of some of their neuroendocrine axes. The unresolved question is whether the abnormal regulation is involved in the pathophysiology and the cause of the disorder or is merely reflective of abnormal brain function. The latter case is likely for two reasons: First, the biogenic amine neurotransmitters, which are affected by most psychotherapeutic drugs, are also key regulators of the neuroendocrine axes. Second, most neuroendocrine abnormalities return to normal baseline values once the psychotic or depressive episode has passed, suggesting that the abnormality is a state marker (reflective of the condition) rather than a trait marker (reflective of an underlying predisposition to the illness).

Endocrine Assessment

Neuroendocrine function can be studied by assessing baseline measures and by measuring the response of the axis to some neurochemical or hormonal challenge. The first method has two approaches: One approach is to measure a single time point, for example, morning levels of growth hormone; this approach is subject to significant error because of the pulsatile nature of the release of most hormones. The second approach is to collect blood samples at multiple points or to collect 24-hour urine samples; these measurements are less prone to major errors. The best approach, however, is to do a neuroendocrine challenge test, in which the person is given a drug or a hormone that perturbs the endocrine axis in some standard way. Nondiseased persons show much less variation in their responses to such challenge studies than in their baseline measurements.

PSYCHONEUROIMMUNOLOGY AND MIND–BODY MEDICINE

The nervous system and the immune system represent two networks within the body. Each contains a massive diversity of cell types and utilizes a large pharmacopoeia of chemical signals. Until about 20 years ago, these two systems were considered to act as parallel, but independent entities. In the past 2 decades, however, a small but growing number of elegant studies has revealed a set of direct interactions between the two systems and has spawned the field of psychoneuroimmunology (PNI). The effects of mood and thought on disease processes has had a long history throughout the centuries. Until this century, physicians strove to "comfort always, cure seldom." The reassuring laying on of hands was the therapeutic principal established by Hippocrates and followed to this day by sensitive clinicians. Successful physicians would draw inner strength from their patients to help them fight disease and relieve their suffering.

The power of suggestion that is incorporated into all physician–patient interactions is called the *placebo effect.* It is considered such a forceful influence on the outcome of medical therapies that all new treatments must be compared in randomized, double-blind clinical trials against a placebo, which is a chemically neutral treatment. It is not uncommon for the placebo arm of the study to show a significant positive clinical response, sometimes in as much as 50 percent of the placebo group, which must be attributed to the influence of the mental state, the mood and the attitude of the patient, towards recovery. This poorly understood factor represents a potent therapeutic modality, and harnessing it for specific purposes is the aim of mind–body medicine. The increasing economic pressure to hasten patient contacts imposed by health maintenance organizations threatens to limit the role of the placebo effect in clinical practice, which represents the tragic loss of a highly effective treatment.

In recent decades, the revolutionary success of biological and pharmacological treatment modalities has reduced the emphasis on emotional appeals to the patient's inner resources in clinical practice. As recently as the 1980's, the majority of editorial commentary in prestigious journals dismissed the influence of emotional factors on the common medical maladies, such as cancer, heart disease, and infectious diseases, as anecdotal and lacking in rigorous scientific proof.

The roots of PNI can be traced from the beginning of this century. The fight or flight response to stress, which is now known to be mediated by a surge of catecholamines, was first described during World War I. One hormonal change resulting from increased systemic catecholamines is a rise in the levels of adrenal corticosteroids, which suppress T-cell number and activity level. A person under repeated or chronic stress may become sufficiently clinically immunosuppressed to be at risk for infectious diseases. In the 1960s, for example, the U.S. Navy completed a study correlating a recent history of serious life changes, such as divorce, moving, or loss of job, with an increased likelihood of serious illness in the months following the stressful event. Subsequent studies have found a higher risk of illness and early death in people without a social network. A 1991 study, for example, tested the likelihood that volunteers would contract viral illnesses after being inoculated with measured doses of one of five viruses or placebo. The likelihood of clinical disease was directly proportional to the amount of life stresses reported in the previous year. Recent animal data show that chronic exposure to glucocorticoids causes permanent loss of hippocampal neurons and thus may impair learning and memory. Similarly, a 1996 neuroimaging study found a positive correlation between hippocampal atrophy in people and duration of either depression, Cushing's syndrome, or combat stress, three states characterized by increased levels of glucocorticoids.

The clinical study that signaled the beginnings of the acceptance of quantifiable benefits of psychotherapy to the treatment of cancer was published in 1989 and consisted of long-term follow-up of a study begun in the mid-1970s. In the initial study, a series of women with breast cancer was randomized to receive the standard surgery and chemotherapy either alone or in combination with supportive group therapy. At the time, the patients in the group therapy setting scored higher on indices of the quality of life than those who received only medical treatment. About a decade later, in an effort to discredit theories of the effect of psychotherapy on mortality, the author surveyed the long-term outcome of the two groups of women, expecting to find no difference in mean survival time. To his surprise, however, the women in the group therapy lived an average of 18 months longer than the control group, a beneficial effect that exceeded that of any of the chemotherapeutic agents. This remarkable result remains to be rigorously duplicated, but it represents a watershed event in the field of mind–body medicine.

Long-term clinical trials such as the breast cancer study provide the most clinically useful information, but they are difficult and time-consuming to perform. In an effort to detect beneficial effects of a positive mental state on the immune system, a number of laboratory indices of immune function have been used. The ratio of the number of T-helper cells, which stimulate the immune response, to T-suppressor cells, which reduce the immune response, is a readily quantified index of activation of the immune system. The activation of individual T lymphocytes can be assayed by measuring the release of chemical mediators called cytokines in response to certain exogenous compounds. A subset of T cells will divide when exposed to mitogens, and this proliferative response depends on the level of T-cell activation. Natural killer (NK) cell numbers are maintained by interferon gamma levels, and each of these values reflects the level of immune surveillance of infections and tumors. The humoral arm of the immune system, represented by antibody titers and regulated by interferons and cytokines, presents another quantifiable measure of immune system activity. Each of these laboratory assays has been demonstrated to be influenced by the emotional state of the patient, though not always in the same direction in separate studies. The main shortcoming of the laboratory approach is the lack of a clearly demonstrable clinical correlate to the variations in immune activity documented in the test tube. Ultimately, all hypotheses must be subjected to full-scale clinical trials.

The animal study that began the field of PNI was performed in 1974. In an effort to condition rats to avoid saccharine-flavored water, the flavored water was presented simultaneously with an injection of cyclophosphamide, to induce nausea. While the method succeeded in engendering an aversion to saccharine, the immunosuppressive effect of cyclophosphamide also became a conditioned response. Thus, conditioned rats, when given saccharine-flavored water, suppressed their T cells, contracted infectious diseases, and died unexpectedly. Several elegant follow-up studies showed that several aspects of immune system function can be conditioned to unrelated stimuli. This conditioning may have a correlate in suggestible individuals, such as those with allergies, who may begin to sneeze when presented with plastic flowers.

The broad notion of a "disease-prone personality" has received scientific support, but only one specific condition has been correlated convincingly to a particular personality trait. Coronary artery disease appears more common in individuals who score higher on scales detecting hostility, a reaction that may have a basis in the surges of adrenalin that accompany angry outbursts. The general disease-prone personality requires other environmental or genetic factors to determine diseases such as asthma, ulcerative colitis, and rheumatoid arthritis. Studies have correlated emotional stresses to flare-ups of herpes virus infections and to the likelihood of contracting infectious mononucleosis. Recent evidence has suggested that depression may be as powerful a risk factor for heart attack as are preexisting heart disease, cardiac arrhythmias, or congestive heart failure. Yet, depression is often unrecognized and untreated by primary care physicians and cardiologists. Additional controlled studies are needed to confirm these initial findings.

A series of experimental findings that provide evidence for PNI have been recently summarized. At the anatomical level, autonomic nerve endings are found within the bone marrow, thymus, spleen, and lymph nodes. The autonomic motor centers in the hypothalamus may regulate the immune response. Autonomic sensory centers are activated during the generation of an immune response and reach a peak of activity coincident with the highest levels of antibodies. The rapid febrile response to the presence of immune mediators in the peritoneal cavity can be ablated by sectioning of the vagus nerve. At the neurochemical level, corticosteroids and growth hormone affect immune responsivity. The hormones that change during emotional stresses, steroids and endorphins, have been shown to bind to specific receptors on the surface of immune system cells. Conversely, lymphocytes may produce tiny amounts of hormones normally seen in the pituitary gland. The interleukins and interferons, with which immune cells communicate, also bind to certain brain cells. Beside the above-mentioned studies relating psychosocial support and stresses to susceptibility or recovery from disease, hypnosis has been shown to be capable of regulating allergic skin reactions. Antibody titers induced by vaccines are likely to be higher in patients who are relatively free of stress.

In 1997, the results of a 15-year study of 1,600 people that tracked use of specific drugs and correlated this with the risk of development of Alzheimer's disease were reported. The data showed that people who used nonsteroidal anti-inflammatory drugs (NSAIDs), such as ibuprofen (Motrin), developed Alzheimer's disease half as frequently as people who did not use NSAIDs. Because this was not a controlled trial, the possibility of other causes for the apparent protective effects of NSAIDs could not be excluded, and the investigators indicated that controlled trials would be necessary prior to recommendations of widespread use of these drugs to prevent Alzheimer's disease. Because NSAIDs reduce inflammation, the fact that they may prevent Alzheimer's disease supports an immune mechanism as one step in the development of amyloid plaques and neurofibrillary tangles.

Human immunodeficiency virus (HIV) infection and acquired immune deficiency syndrome (AIDS), as well as other immune deficiency states, may allow the spread of viral, bacterial, fungal or parasitic infections in the central and peripheral nervous systems. This failure of the immune surveillance of brain regions necessary for cognition and emotion represents another facet of the influence of the immune system on the mind. The appearance of opportunistic infections in the brain creates an additional stress in patients who are struggling to come to grips with the apparent inevitability of their disease.

PNI studies may be difficult to interpret not only because of the placebo effect but also because a patient's frame of mind may powerfully influence his or her seeking of and compliance with medical treatments. To the extent that a healthy lifestyle can reduce the risk of potentially life-threatening illnesses, a person's motivation to eat well and avoid smoking or alcohol can be a significant variable in their clinical outcome. Relatively few PNI studies have successfully controlled for all these variables, but well-controlled studies are certainly needed for widespread acceptance within the medical community. A far greater number of reports are anecdotal or ambiguous, yet are promoted with great zeal.

There is a risk that well-meaning proponents of a causal link between emotion and the incidence of cancer or other serious illnesses may overstate their case to the degree that victims of serious illness may question whether they may have caused their illness through a "lack of self-love" or a "need to be ill." The judicious application of common sense and sensitivity to misfortune remains an invaluable clinical skill. In this context, the positive use of the insights of PNI may be even more influential than any medication for cancer, AIDS, and other immune-related maladies.

BIOLOGICAL RHYTHMS AND CHRONOBIOLOGY

Biological systems constantly oscillate between different states at different rates. The obvious physical cycles to which people's biological rhythms conform include the day–night cycle, the lunar month, the solar year, and biophysical constraints, such as the rate of pulmonary gas diffusion that determines the respiratory rate and the cardiac contractile parameters that dictate the heart rate. Patterned mealtimes and the 9-to-5 workday are examples of other exogenous influences. The brain is filled with oscillations, some of which provide a constant drone over which others weave an elaborate melody. Theorists of higher perception and thought are increasingly interested in how the brain may use rhythmical patterns of neuronal firing to encode information, in addition to using different spatial combinations of synaptic connections. Thus, biological rhythms range from the monthly menstrual cycle to brain oscillations occurring at the rate of 30 to 60 times per second. In psychiatry, much work has been aimed at understanding circadian rhythms and the relation between sleep and psychopathology.

Sleep is one of several biological rhythms within the body. Circadian biological rhythms are set by both internal and external forces, generally called *zeitgebers* (time givers, time clues, synchronizers), which constitute a widely distributed set of nuclei. The principal circadian influences emanate from the pontine reticular formation, as well as the suprachiasmatic nuclei of the hypothalamus. Recent evidence has shown that the suprachiasmatic nucleus can entrain circadian rhythms even in the absence of physical synaptic connections with the remainder of the hypothalamus, suggesting that this zeitgeber may act through elaboration of diffusible substances. In the absence of exogenous clues, the period of human circadian rhythms is a bit longer than a day (24.5 hours).

The sleep–wake cycle, hormonal levels, the body temperature, and the menstrual cycle are all examples of biological rhythms in the human body that can be measured. When a person is in a healthy state, all the rhythms have a natural relation, and they are said to be in phase. When the system is perturbed (by staying up all night, for example), certain biological rhythms are thrown off (for example, those for growth hormone and cortisol), and the rhythms are then considered to be out of phase. The state of having one's biological rhythms out of phase contributes to the ill effects experienced by the person. Some disorders have phase perturbations as part of their symptoms. When rhythms are disordered, a particular rhythm may have an *abnormal phase advance,* in which it begins earlier than usual, or a *phase delay,* in which it begins later than usual. Under experimental conditions a phase responsive curve for a biological rhythm may show that a particular stimulation (for example, light) causes either a phase advance or a phase delay when it is delivered at different times in a cycle (for example, the sleep–wake cycle). Lithium and many of the tricyclic drugs and MAOIs delay rhythms in experimental animal models, supporting the hypothesis that at least some forms of depression represent phase-advance disorders.

Sleep is an essential phase of human daily existence in which a great amount of mental activity occurs. While most of the period of sleep remains unconscious, dream states may engrave vivid and bizarre memories. Freud, in "The Interpretation of Dreams," called dreams the "royal road to the unconscious." The sleep–wake cycle is synchronized with cyclic changes in the levels of several circulating hormones. Serum cortisol levels are lowest at the onset of sleep and highest in morning. Thyroid-stimulating hormone secretion is suppressed by the onset of sleep, while melatonin is secreted at night and terminates upon retinal stimulation by sunlight. Growth hormone levels surge during deep sleep, and this stimulus for growth gradually ceases by late adult life as deep sleep disappears. Prolactin and luteinizing hormone also are found at their highest levels during sleep.

The necessity for sleep is demonstrated by experiments in which animals deprived of sleep die within a few weeks. Humans deprived of sleep for 60 to 200 hours begin to demonstrate a breakdown in concentration, motor skills, self-care, attention, judgment, and eventually communication. Hallucinations and illusions may appear. There is, however, a wide variation in the requirements for sleep, which is determined by genetic factors, habits formed early in life, and particular physical and emotional states. The circadian (24-hour) rhythm appears in the first few months of life and remains intact until old age, when it may begin to fragment.

Depression is the psychiatric symptom that has been most associated with disruptions in biological rhythms. Early morning awakening, decreased latency of rapid eye movement (REM) sleep, and neuroendocrine perturbations that are seen in depression can all be conceptualized as reflecting a disorder of coordination in biological rhythms. One hypothesis is that depression occurs in some persons when the sleep-sensitive phase of the circadian system advances from the first hours of awakening to the last hours of sleep. Research indicates that alterations in the light-dark cycle (by exposing the patient to artificial light or by changing the patient's sleep–wake cycle) can relieve the symptoms.

Reproduction is tightly linked to olfaction, and the menstrual cycle appears to modulate the sexual response of women and men to olfactory cues. Studies indicate that women usually dislike the scent of androstenone, a major component of male perspiration, except when the women are ovulating. In this way, women may be more likely to accept sexual overtures at the time they are fertile. Conversely, inhalation of aerosolized vaginal secretions by men tends to generate positive perceptions of pictures of women, and vaginal secretions collected from women during ovulation are most potent in this regard. Thus, to the male nose, female ovulation is not concealed, as ovulatory scents raised male salivary testosterone levels.

REFERENCES

Bloom FE, Kupfer DJ: *Psychopharmacology, Fourth Generation of Progress.* Raven Press, New York, 1995.

Brown BL, Dobson PRM: *Advances in Second Messenger and Phosphoprotein Research.* Raven Press, New York, 1993.

Cooper JR, Bloom FE, Roth RH: *The Biochemical Basis of Neuropharmacology,* ed 7. Oxford University Press, New York, 1996.

Elsworth JD, Roth RH: *The Dopamine Receptors.* Human Press, Totowa, NJ, 1995.

Goleman D, Gurin J: *Mind/Body Medicine: How to Use Your Mind for Better Health.* Consumers Union, Yonkers, NY, 1993.

Hardman JG, Limbird LE, et al: *Goodman & Gilman's The Pharmacological Basis of Therapeutics,* ed 9. McGraw-Hill, New York, 1996.

▲ 3.3 Neuroimaging

Mental processes reflect the activity of the brain, which as a bodily organ is subject to the effects of medical conditions. Psychiatric symptoms may result from primary mental disorders but may also represent variations in the brain function in response to metabolic, infectious, or structural abnormalities (see Chapter 10). The initial presentation of psychiatric symptoms requires a thorough medical and neurological evaluation. Often, such an evaluation includes neuroimaging, the study of the brain structure.

Technical advances in neuroimaging increasingly permit localization and analysis of specific chemical and electrical activities within the brain during normal mental processing as well as during psychiatric dysfunction. This field of study is called functional neuroimaging. For instance, routine computed tomography (CT) and magnetic resonance imaging (MRI) scans give information about the gross structure of the brain. Under specific circumstances, however, functional MRI (fMRI) can reveal which brain regions are particularly activated during the performance of defined mental tasks. In addition, two methods requiring radioactive tracer compounds, positron emission tomography (PET) and single photon emission computed tomography (SPECT), have been used extensively in psychiatry, both to localize mental activity within the brain and to identify binding sites of neurotransmitters and psychopharmacological agents. The electrical activity of the brain can be mapped at high temporal, but low-spatial, resolution with electroencephalography and magnetoencephalography (MEG). The correlation of changes in brain electrical activity with specific environmental or mental stimuli yields event-related potentials (ERPs), which may be further correlated with fMRI, PET, or SPECT scans to trace the path of a defined thought through the brain.

USES OF NEUROIMAGING

Indications for Ordering Neuroimaging in Clinical Practice

Neurological Deficits. In a neurological examination, any change that can be localized to the brain or spinal cord requires neuroimaging. Neurological examination includes mental status, cranial nerves, motor system, coordination, sensory system, and reflex components. The mental status examination assesses arousal, attention, and motivation; memory; language; visuospatial function; complex cognition; and mood and affect. Consultant psychiatrists should consider a workup including neuroimaging for patients with new-onset psychosis and acute changes in mental status. The clinical examination always assumes priority, and neuroimaging is ordered based on a clinical suspicion of a central nervous system (CNS) disorder.

Dementia. Loss of memory and of cognitive abilities affect more than 10 million people in the United States and will affect an increasing number as the population ages. Reduced mortality from cancer and heart disease has increased life expectancy and has allowed people to survive to the age of onset of degenerative brain disorders, which have proven more difficult to treat. Depression, anxiety, and psychosis are common in cases of dementia. The most common cause of dementia is Alzheimer's disease, which does not have a characteristic appearance on routine neuroimaging but, rather, is associated with diffuse loss of brain volume.

One treatable cause of dementia that requires neuroimaging for diagnosis is *normal pressure hydrocephalus.* This condition is a disorder of the drainage of cerebrospinal fluid; the condition does not progress to the point of acute increased intracranial pressure but stabilizes at a pressure at the upper end of the normal range. The dilated ventricles, which may be readily seen with CT or MRI, exert pressure on the frontal lobes. A gait disorder is almost uniformly present; dementia, which may be indistinguishable from that of Alzheimer's disease, appears less consistently. Relief of the increased cerebrospinal fluid pressure may completely restore gait and mental function.

Infarction of the cortical or subcortical areas, or stroke, may produce focal neurological deficits, including cognitive and emotional changes. Strokes are easily seen on MRI scans. Depression is very common among stroke patients, either because of direct damage to the emotional centers of the brain or because of a patient's reaction to his or her disability. Depression, in turn, may cause a pseudodementia. In addition to large strokes, extensive atherosclerosis in brain capillaries may cause countless tiny infarctions of brain tissue; patients with this phenomenon may develop dementia as fewer and fewer neural pathways participate in cognition. This state is called vascular dementia and is characterized on MRI scans as patches of increased signal in the white matter. Recent clinicopathological studies of brain tissue with typical Alzheimer's disease changes (senile plaques and neurofibrillary tangles) have suggested that dementia results from these changes plus microscopic infarctions. Patients with Alzheimer's neuropathology but without strokes may not have dementia.

Certain degenerative disorders of basal ganglia structures, associated with dementia, may have a characteristic appearance on MRI scans. Huntington's disease typically produces atrophy of the caudate nucleus; thalamic degeneration may interrupt the neural links to the cortex.

Space-occupying lesions can cause dementia. Chronic subdural hematomas and cerebral contusions, caused by head trauma, may produce focal neurological deficits or may only produce dementia. Brain tumors can affect cognition in several ways. Skull-based meningiomas can compress the underlying cortex and impair its processing. Infiltrative glial cell tumors, such as astrocytoma or glioblastoma multiforme, may cut off communication between brain centers by interrupting white matter tracts. Tumors located near the ventricular system can obstruct the flow of cerebrospinal fluid and gradually increase the intracranial pressure.

Chronic infections, including neurosyphilis, cryptococcosis, tuberculosis, and Lyme disease, may cause symptoms of dementia and may produce a characteristic enhancement of the meninges, especially at the base of the brain. Serological studies are needed to complete the diagnosis. Human immunodeficiency virus (HIV) infection can cause dementia directly, in which case there is a diffuse loss of brain volume, or can allow the proliferation of the JC virus to yield progressive multifocal leukoencephalopathy, which affects white matter tracts and appears as increased white matter signal on MRI scans.

Chronic demyelinating diseases, such as multiple sclerosis, may affect cognition because of white matter disruption. Multiple sclerosis plaques are easily seen on MRI scans as periventricular patches of increased signal intensity.

Any evaluation of dementia should consider medication effects, metabolic derangements, infections, and nutritional causes that may not produce abnormalities on neuroimaging.

Indications for Neuroimaging in Clinical Research

Systematic Analysis of Clinically Defined Groups of Patients. Psychiatric research aims to categorize patients with psychiatric disorders to facilitate the discovery of neuroanatomical and neurochemical bases of mental illness. Researchers have used functional neuroimaging to study groups of patients with such psychiatric conditions as schizophrenia, affective disorders, and anxiety disorders, among others. In schizophrenia, for example, neuropathological volumetric analyses have suggested a loss of brain weight, specifically of gray matter. There appears to be a paucity of axons and dendrites in the cortex, and CT and MRI may show compensatory enlargement of the lateral and third ventricles. Specifically, the temporal lobes of people with schizophrenia appear to suffer the most loss of volume relative to normal people. Recent studies have found that the left temporal lobe is generally more affected than the right. The frontal lobe may also have abnormalities, but these are not in the volume of the lobe but, rather, in the level of activity detected by functional neuroimaging. People with schizophrenia consistently exhibit decreased metabolic activity in the frontal lobes, especially during tasks that require the prefrontal cortex.

Disorders of mood and affect may also be associated with loss of brain volume and decreased metabolic activity in the frontal lobes. Inactivation of the left prefrontal cortex appears to depress mood; inactivation of the right prefrontal cortex elevates it. Among anxiety disorders, studies of obsessive-compulsive disorder with conventional CT and MRI have shown either no specific abnormalities or reduced size of the caudate nucleus. Functional PET and SPECT studies suggest abnormalities in the corticolimbic, basal ganglia, and thalamic structures in the disorder. When patients are experiencing obsessive-compulsive disorder symptoms, the orbital prefrontal cortex shows abnormal activity. A partial normalization of caudate glucose metabolism appears in patients taking medications such as fluoxetine (Prozac) and clomipramine (Anafranil) or undergoing behavior modification.

Functional neuroimaging studies of people with attention-deficit/hyperactivity disorder (ADHD) have either been normal or have shown decreased volume of the right prefrontal cortex and the right globus pallidus. In addition, whereas normally the right caudate nucleus is larger than the left caudate nucleus, people with ADHD may have caudate nuclei of equal size. These findings suggest dysfunction of the right prefrontal-striatal pathway for control of attention.

Analysis of Brain Activity During Performance of Specific Tasks. Many original conceptions of different brain region functions emerged from observing deficits caused by local injuries, tumors, or strokes. Functional neuroimaging has permitted researchers to review and reassess classical teachings in the intact brain. Most work, to date, has been aimed at language and vision. Although many technical peculiarities and limitations of SPECT, PET, and fMRI have been overcome, none of these techniques has demonstrated a clear superiority. Studies require carefully controlled conditions, which subjects may find arduous. Nonetheless, functional neuroimaging has contributed major conceptual advances, and the methods are now limited mainly by the creativity of the investigative protocols.

Studies have been designed to understand the functional neuroanatomy of all sensory modalities, gross and fine motor skills, language, memory, calculations, learning, and disorders of thought, mood, and anxiety. Unconscious sensations transmitted by the autonomic nervous system have been localized to specific brain regions. These analyses provide a basis for comparison with studies of clinically defined patient groups and may lead to improved therapies for mental illnesses.

SPECIFIC TECHNIQUES

Computed Tomography (CT) Scans

The appearance of CT scanning in 1972 revolutionized diagnostic neuroradiology by permitting imaging of the brain tissue in live patients. CT scanners are currently the most widely available and convenient imaging tools available in clinical practice; practically every hospital emergency room has immediate access to a CT scanner at all times. CT scanners effectively take a series of head X-ray pictures from all vantage points, 360 degrees around a patient's head. The amount of radiation that passes through, or is not absorbed, from each angle is digitized and entered into a computer. The computer uses matrix algebra calculations to assign a specific density to each point within the head and displays these data as a set of two-dimensional images. When viewed in sequence, the images allow a mental reconstruction of the shape of the brain.

The CT image is determined only by the degree to which tissues absorb X-irradiation. The bony structures absorb high amounts of irradiation and tend to obscure details of neighboring structures, an especially troublesome problem in the brainstem, which is surrounded by a thick skull base. Within the brain itself, there is relatively little difference in the attenuation of X-rays between gray matter and white matter. Although the gray-white border is usually distinguishable, details of the gyral pattern may be difficult to appreciate in CT scans. Certain tumors may be invisible on CT because they absorb as much irradiation as the surrounding normal brain.

Appreciation of tumors and areas of inflammation, which may cause changes in behavior, can be increased with the intravenous infusion of iodine-containing contrast agents. Iodinated compounds, which absorb much more irradiation than does the brain, appear white. The intact brain is separated from the bloodstream by the blood–brain barrier, which normally prevents the passage of the highly charged contrast agents. The blood–brain barrier, however, breaks down in the presence of inflammation or fails to form within tumors and thus allows accumulation of contrast agents. These sites appear whiter than the surrounding brain. Iodinated contrast agents must be used with caution in patients who are allergic to the agents or to shellfish.

With the introduction of MRI scanning, CT scans have been supplanted as the nonemergency neuroimaging study of choice. The increased resolution and delineation of detail afforded by MRI scanning is often required for diagnosis in psychiatry. In addition, the most detailed study available should be performed to inspire the most confidence in the analysis. The only component of the brain better seen on CT scanning is calcification, which may be invisible on MRI (Fig. 3.3–1).

Magnetic Resonance Imaging (MRI) Scans

MRI scanning entered clinical practice in 1982 and soon became the test of choice for clinical psychiatrists and neurologists. The technique does not rely on the absorption of X-rays but is based on nuclear magnetic resonance (NMR). The principle of NMR is that the nuclei of all atoms are thought to spin about an axis, which is randomly oriented in space. When atoms are placed in a magnetic field, the axes of all odd-numbered nuclei align with the magnetic field. The axis of a nucleus deviates away from the magnetic field when exposed to a pulse of radiofrequency electromagnetic radiation oriented at 90 or 180 degrees to the magnetic field. When the pulse terminates, the axis of the spinning nucleus realigns itself with the magnetic field, and during this realignment, it emits its own radiofrequency signal. MRI scanners collect the emis-

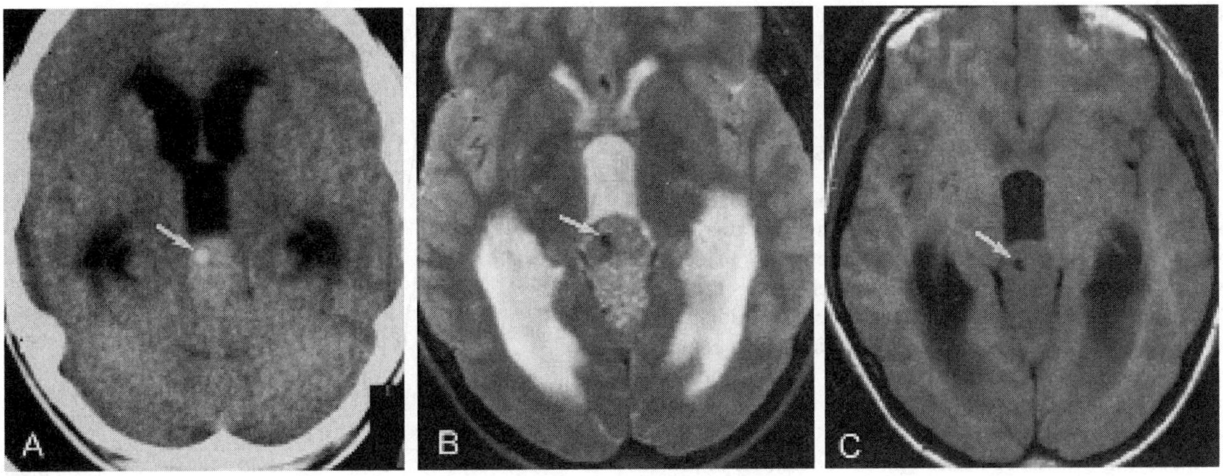
A
B
C

FIGURE 3.3–1

Comparison of CT and MRI. **A.** Computed tomography (CT) scan in the axial plane at the level of the third ventricle. The cerebrospinal fluid (CSF) within the ventricles appears black, the brain tissue appears gray, and the skull appears white. There is very poor discrimination between the gray and white matter of the brain. The *arrow* indicates a small calcified lesion in a tumor of the pineal gland. Detection of calcification is one role in which CT is superior to MRI. **B.** T_2-weighted image of the same patient at roughly the same level. With T_2, the CSF appears white, the gray matter appears gray, the white matter is clearly distinguished from the gray matter, and the skull and indicated calcification appear black. Much more detail of the brain is visible than with CT. **C.** T_1-weighted image of the same patient at roughly the same level. With T_1, the CSF appears dark, the brain appears more uniformly gray, and the skull and indicated calcification appear black. T_1 MRI images are the most similar to CT images. (Reprinted with permission from Grossman CB: *Magnetic Resonance Imaging and Computed Tomography of the Head and Spine,* ed 2, p 101. Williams & Wilkins, Baltimore, 1996.)

sion of individual, realigning nuclei and use computer analysis to generate a series of two-dimensional images that represent the brain. The images may be in the axial, coronal, or sagittal planes.

By far the most abundant odd-numbered nucleus in the brain is that of hydrogen. The rate of realignment of the axis of hydrogen is determined by its immediate environment, a combination of both the nature of the molecule of which it is a part and the degree to which it is surrounded by water. Thus, hydrogen nuclei within fat realign rapidly, and hydrogen nuclei within water realign slowly. Hydrogen nuclei in proteins and carbohydrates realign at intermediate rates.

Routine MRI studies use three different radiofrequency pulse sequences. The two parameters that are varied are the duration of the radiofrequency excitation pulse and the duration of the time collection of data from the realigning nuclei. Because T1 pulses are brief and data collection is brief, hydrogen nuclei in hydrophobic environments are emphasized. Thus, fat is bright on T1, and cerebrospinal fluid is dark. The T1 image most closely resembles that of CT scans and is most useful for the assessment of overall brain structure. T1 is also the only sequence that allows contrast enhancement with the contrast agent, gadolinium-diethylenetriamine pentaacetic acid (gadolinium-DTPA). Like the iodinated contrast agents used in CT scanning, gadolinium remains excluded from the brain by the blood–brain barrier, except in areas where this barrier breaks down, such as inflammation or tumor. On T1 images, gadolinium-enhanced structures appear white.

T2 pulses last four times longer than do T1 pulses, and the collection times are also extended, to emphasize the signal from hydrogen nuclei surrounded by water. Thus, brain tissue is dark, and cerebrospinal fluid is white on T2 images. Areas within the brain tissue that have abnormally elevated water content, such as tumors, inflammation, or strokes, appear brighter on T2 images. T2 images reveal brain pathology most clearly. The third routine pulse sequence is the proton density, or balanced, sequence. In this sequence, a short radio pulse is followed by a prolonged period of data collection, which equalizes the density of the cerebrospinal fluid and the brain and allows distinction of tissue changes immediately adjacent to the ventricles.

An additional technique, sometimes used in clinical practice for specific indications, is inversion recovery. In this method, the T1 image is inverted and added to the T2 image, to double the image contrast between gray matter and white matter. Inversion recovery imaging is useful for detecting sclerosis of the hippocampus caused by temporal lobe epilepsy, as well as for the localization of areas of abnormal metabolism in degenerative neurological disorders.

MRI magnets are rated in teslas, units of magnetic field strength. MRI scanners in clinical use range from 0.3 tesla to 2.0 teslas. Higher field-strength scanners produce images of markedly higher resolution. In research settings for humans, magnets as powerful as 4.7 teslas are used; for animals, magnets up to 12 teslas are used. Unlike the well-known hazards of X-irradiation, exposure to electromagnetic fields of the strength used in MRI machines has not been shown to cause damage to biological tissues.

MRI scans may not be used for patients with pacemakers or implants of ferromagnetic metals. MRI involves enclosing a patient in a narrow tube, where the patient must remain motionless for up to 20 minutes. The radiofrequency pulses create a loud banging noise, which may be obscured by music played in headphones. A significant number of patients cannot tolerate the claustrophobic conditions of routine MRI scanners and may need an open MRI scanner, which is of lower power and therefore produces images of lower resolution. The resolution of brain tissue of even the lowest-power MRI scan, however, is superior to that of CT scanning.

Magnetic Resonance Spectroscopy (MRS)

Although routine MRI detects hydrogen nuclei to determine brain structure, MRS is capable of detecting several odd-numbered nuclei (Table 3.3–1). The ability of MRS to detect a wide range of biologically important nuclei permits the use of the technique to study many metabolic processes. Although the resolution and sensitivity of MRS machines are poor compared with currently available PET and SPECT devices, the use of stronger magnetic fields will improve this feature to some extent in the future.

MRS is able to image nuclei with an odd number of protons and neutrons (Table 3.3–1). The unpaired protons and neutrons (nucleons) appear naturally and are nonradioactive. As in MRI, in the strong magnetic field produced by an MRS device, the nuclei align themselves with the magnetic field. A radiofrequency pulse causes the nuclei of interest to absorb and then emit energy. The readout of an MRS device is usually in the form of a spectrum, such as those for phosphorus-31 (Fig. 3.3–2) and hydrogen-1 nuclei, although the spectrum can also be converted into a pictorial image of the brain. The multiple peaks for each nucleus reflect the fact that the same nucleus is exposed to different electron environments (electron clouds) in different molecules. The hydrogen-1 nuclei in a molecule of creatine, therefore, have a different chemical shift (position

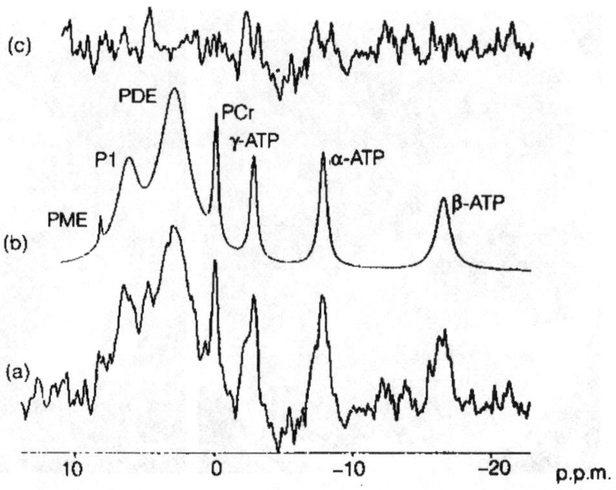
(c)
PDE
PCr
γ-ATP
P1
α-ATP
PME
β-ATP
(b)
(a)
10
0
−10
−20
p.p.m.

FIGURE 3.3–2

An in vivo ^{31}P spectrum of brain tissue: **(a)** original processed spectrum, **(b)** the spectrum after a computerized curve-fitting routine, and **(c)** original spectrum with the fitted spectrum subtracted. The spectrum represents in vivo phosphorus metabolism in cortical gray and white matter. The broad hump underlying the PME, Pi, PDE, and PCr resonances is derived from tissue phospholipids and mineral phosphates in bone. The phosphorus metabolites are not in solution and are, therefore, unable to resonate freely. *ATP,* adenosine triphosphate (γ, α, and β positions of ^{31}P nucleus); *PCr,* phosphocreatine; *PDE,* phosphodiester; *Pi,* inorganic phosphate; *PME,* phosphomonoester. (Reprinted with permission from Lock T, Abou-Saleh MT, Edwards RHT: Psychiatry and the new magnetic resonance era. Br J Psychiatry *157*(9, Suppl): 41, 1990.)

Table 3.3–1
Nuclei Available for in Vivo Magnetic Resonance Spectroscopy (MRS)[a]

Nucleus	Natural Abundance	Relative Sensitivity	Potential Clinical Uses
^{1}H	99.99	1.00	MRI Analysis of metabolism Identification of unusual metabolites Characterization of hypoxia
^{19}F	100.00	0.83	Measurement of pO_2 Analysis of glucose metabolism Measurement of pH Noninvasive pharmacokinetics
^{7}Li	92.58	0.27	Pharmacokinetics
^{23}Na	100.00	0.09	MRI
^{31}P	100.00	0.07	Analysis of bioenergetics Identification of unusual metabolites Characterization of hypoxia Measurement of pH
^{14}N	93.08	0.001	Measurement of glutamate, urea, ammonia
^{39}K	93.08	0.0005	?
^{13}C	1.11	0.0002	Analysis of metabolite turnover rate Pharmacokinetics of labeled drugs
^{17}O	0.04	0.00001	Measurement of metabolic rate
^{2}H	0.02	0.000002	Measurement of perfusion

Reprinted with permission from Dager SR, Steen RG: Applications of magnetic resonance spectroscopy to the investigation of neuropsychiatric disorders. Neuropsychopharmacology *6:* 249, 1992.

[a] Natural abundance is given as percent abundance of the isotope of interest. Nuclei are tabulated in order of decreasing relative sensitivity; relative sensitivity is calculated by multiplying the relative sensitivity for equal numbers of nuclei (at a given field strength) by the natural abundance of that nucleus. A considerable gain in relative sensitivity can be obtained by isotopic enrichment of the nucleus of choice or by the use of novel pulse sequences.

in the spectrum) than do the hydrogen-1 nuclei in a choline molecule, for example. Thus, the position in the spectrum (the chemical shift) indicates the identity of the molecule in which the nuclei are present. The height of the peak, when compared with the height of a reference standard of the molecule, indicates the amount of the molecule present.

MRS of the hydrogen-1 nuclei is best at measuring *N*-acetylaspartate (NAA), creatine, and choline-containing molecules; but MRS can also detect glutamate, glutamine, lactate, and *myo*-inositol. Although glutamate and γ-aminobutyric acid (GABA), the major amino acid neurotransmitters, can be detected by MRS, the biogenic amine neurotransmitters (for example, dopamine) are present in concentrations too low to be detected with the technique. MRS of phosphorus-31 can be used to determine the pH of brain regions and the concentrations of phosphorus-containing compounds (such as adenosine triphosphate [ATP] and guanosine triphosphate [GTP]), which are important in the energy metabolism of the brain.

MRS has revealed decreased concentrations of NAA in the temporal lobes and increased concentrations of inositol in the occipital lobes of people with dementia of the Alzheimer's type. In a series of subjects with schizophrenia, decreased concentrations of NAA were found in the temporal and frontal lobes. MRS has been used to trace the levels of ethanol in various brain regions. In panic disorder, MRS has been used to record the levels of lactate, intravenous infusion of which can precipitate panic episodes in about three-fourths of patients with either panic disorder or major depression. Brain lactate concentrations have been shown to be elevated during panic attacks, even in the absence of provocative infusion.

Additional indications include the use of MRS to measure concentrations of psychotherapeutic drugs in the brain. One study used MRS to measure lithium concentrations in the brains of patients with bipolar disorder and found that the brain lithium concentrations were half those in the plasma during depressed and euthymic periods but rose to greater than those in the plasma during manic episodes. Some compounds, such as fluoxetine and trifluoperazine (Stelazine), contain fluorine-19, and this can also be detected in the brain and measured by using the MRS technique. For example, MRS has demonstrated that fluoxetine requires 6 months of steady use to reach maximum brain concentrations, which equilibrate at about 20 times the serum concentrations.

Functional Magnetic Resonance Imaging (fMRI)

Recent advances in data collection and computer data processing have reduced the acquisition time for an MRI image to less than 1 second. A new sequence of particular interest to psychiatrists is the T2* sequence, which detects levels of oxygenated hemoglobin in the blood. It has long been known that neuronal activity within the brain causes a local increase in blood flow, which in turn brings higher local levels of hemoglobin. Although neuronal metabolism extracts more oxygen in active areas of the brain, the net effect of neuronal activity is to raise the local amount of oxygenated hemoglobin. This change can be detected essentially in real time with the T2* sequence, which thus detects the functionally active brain regions. This process is the basis for the technique of fMRI.

What fMRI detects is not brain activity per se, but blood flow. The volume of brain in which blood flow increases exceeds the volume of activated neurons by about 1 to 2 cm and limits the resolution of the technique. Thus, two tasks that activate clusters of neurons 5 mm apart, such as recognizing two different faces, yield overlapping signals on fMRI and therefore are usually indistinguishable by this technique. Functional MRI is useful to localize neuronal activity to a particular lobe or subcortical nucleus and has even been able to localize activity to a single gyrus. The method detects tissue perfusion, not neuronal metabolism. In contrast, PET scanning may give information specifically about neuronal metabolism.

No radioactive isotopes are administered in fMRI, a great advantage over PET and SPECT. A subject can perform a variety of tasks, both experimental and control, in the same imaging session. First, a routine T1 MRI image is obtained; then the T2* images are superimposed to allow the most precise localization. Acquisition of enough images for study may require 20 minutes to 3 hours, during which time the subject's head must remain in exactly the same position. Several methods, including a frame around the head and a special mouthpiece, have been used. Although realignments of images can correct for some amount of head movement, small changes in head position may lead to erroneous interpretations of brain activation.

Functional MRI has recently revealed unexpected details about the organization of language within the brain. Using a series of language tasks requiring semantic, phonemic, and rhyming discrimination, one study found that rhyming, but not other types of language processing, produced a different pattern of activation in men and women. Rhyming activated the inferior frontal gyrus bilaterally in women, but only on the left in men. In another study, fMRI revealed a previously suspected, but unproven, neural circuit for lexical categories, interpolated between the representations for concepts and those for phonemes. This novel circuit was located in the left anterior temporal lobe. Still other data for patients with dyslexia studied during simple rhyming tasks have demonstrated a failure to activate Wernicke's area and the insula, which were active in normal subjects during the same task (Fig. 3.3–3).

Sensory functions have also been mapped in detail with fMRI. The activation of the visual and auditory cortices has been visualized in real time. In a recent intriguing study, the areas that were activated while a subject with schizophrenia listened to speech were also activated during auditory hallucinations. These areas included the primary auditory cortex as well as higher-order auditory processing regions.

Single Photon Emission Computed Tomography (SPECT) Scanning

Single photon emission computed tomography (SPECT) uses manufactured radioactive compounds to study regional differences in cerebral blood flow within the brain. This high-resolution imaging technique records the pattern of photon emission from the bloodstream according to the level of perfusion in different regions of the brain. Like fMRI, it provides information on the cerebral blood flow, which is highly correlated with the rate of glucose metabolism, but does not measure neuronal metabolism directly.

SPECT uses compounds that have been labeled with single photon-emitting isotopes: iodine-123, technetium-99m, and xenon-133. Xenon-133 is a noble gas that is inhaled directly. The xenon quickly enters the blood and is distributed to areas of the brain as a function of regional blood flow. Xenon-SPECT may therefore be referred to as the regional cerebral blood flow (rCBF) technique. Because of technical factors, xenon-SPECT can measure blood flow only on the surface of the brain. This is an important limitation: Many mental tasks require communication between the cortex and subcortical structures, and this activity is poorly measured by xenon-SPECT.

Assessment of blood flow over the whole brain with SPECT requires the injectable tracers, technetium-99m–*d,l*-hexamethylpropyleneamine oxime (HMPAO [Ceretec]) or iodoamphetamine (Spectamine). These isotopes are attached to molecules that are highly lipophilic and that rapidly cross the blood–brain barrier and enter cells. Once inside the cell, the ligands are enzymatically converted to charged ions, which remain trapped in the cell. Thus, over time, the tracers are concentrated in areas of relatively higher blood flow. Although blood flow is usually assumed to be the major variable tested in HMPAO SPECT, local variations in the permeability of the blood–brain barrier and in the enzymatic conversion of the ligands within cells also contribute to regional differences in signal levels.

In addition to these compounds used for measuring blood flow, iodine-123 (^{123}I)-labeled ligands for the muscarinic, dopaminergic, and serotonergic receptors, for example, can be used to study these receptors by using SPECT technology.

Once photon-emitting compounds reach the brain, their light-emitting property can be detected by detectors surrounding the patient's head. This information is relayed to a computer, which constructs a two-dimensional image of the isotope's distribution within a slice of the brain. A key point of differentiation between SPECT and PET is that in SPECT a single particle is emitted, whereas in PET two particles are emitted; the latter reaction gives a more precise location of the event and better resolution of the image. For both SPECT and PET studies, investigators are increasingly performing prestudy MRI or CT studies, then superimposing the SPECT or PET image on the MRI or CT image to obtain a more accurate anatomical location of the functional information (Fig. 3.3–4).

Positron Emission Tomography (PET) Scanning

The isotopes used in PET decay by emitting positrons, antimatter particles that bind with and annihilate electrons, and in so doing give off photons that travel in 180-degree opposite directions. Because detectors have twice as much signal from which to generate an image as SPECT scanners have, the resolution of the PET image is higher. A wide range of compounds can be used in PET studies, and the resolution of PET continues to be refined closer to its theoretical minimum of 3 mm, which is the distance positrons move before colliding

FIGURE 3.3–3

Functional MRI during rhyming tasks in normal people and people with dyslexia. The left hemisphere is depicted in green. Normal *(top)* and dyslexic *(bottom)* subjects were shown two letters and asked to determine whether the letters rhymed (B-T) or not (B-K). To perform the task, the subjects had to translate the letters into sounds, or phonemes, (/bee/,/tee/), then compare only the rhyming part of the phonemes (/ee/). In normals, three contiguous areas were activated, including Broca's area, Wernicke's area, and the intervening insula. In those with dyslexia, only Broca's area was activated. Dyslexic patients required much more time to complete the task and were more prone to make errors. (Reprinted with permission from Frith C, Frith U: A biological marker for dyslexia. Nature *382:* 19,1996.)

FIGURE 3.3–4

Stages of the superimposition of a SPECT cerebral blood-flow image **(A),** which has been redefined **(B),** and an MRI T_1-weighted image **(C),** to produce a combination **(D).** (Reprinted with permission from Besson JAO: Magnetic resonance imaging and its application in neuropsychiatry. Br J Psychiatry *157* (9, Suppl): 25, 1990.)

FIGURE 3.3–5

PET scans with [^{18}F]fluorodeoxyglucose in a control *(top)* and six patients with neurological disorders. The three images from the control show transverse sections of the brain at a high level through the parietal lobes *(left),* an intermediate level through the basal ganglia and the thalamus *(center),* and a low level through the base of the frontal lobes, the temporal lobes, and the cerebellum *(right).* The level of each image corresponds approximately to the level of the scans below. The *bar* indicates the level of glucose metabolic activity in the images, with colors on the left indicating low levels of metabolism and colors on the right indicating high levels. The middle and bottom scans are from patients with multi-infarct dementia *(MID)* (also known as vascular dementia), Alzheimer's disease *(AD),* temporal lobe epilepsy, brain tumor (primitive neuroectodermal tumor), Huntington's disease *(HD),* and olivopontocerebellar atrophy *(OPCA).* A small region of absent glucose metabolism is seen in the patient with multi-infarct dementia *(arrow);* PET scans at other levels in the patient revealed a number of similar areas, which represent small focal infarctions. The scan in the patient with Alzheimer's disease shows hypometabolism in both parietal lobes *(arrows).* The image in the patient with epilepsy shows hypometabolism in the right temporal lobe *(arrow),* which is the site of origin of the seizure disorder. The scan in the patient with a tumor shows a region of hypermetabolism in the thalamus, which is the location of the tumor *(arrow).* The image in the patient with Huntington's disease shows hypometabolism in the caudate nuclei bilaterally *(arrows).* The scan in the patient with olivopontocerebellar atrophy shows hypometabolism in the cerebellum *(arrows)* and the brainstem. (Reprinted with permission from Gilman S: Advances in neurology. N Engl J Med *326:* 1610, 1992.)

FIGURE 3.3–6

PET images showing radioactivity in a horizontal brain section through the striatal level after an intravenous injection of [^{11}C]raclopride, a dopamine receptor agonist, into a healthy volunteer. **A.** PET image before medication. Corresponding PET images at different time points after the administration of 4 mg haloperidol are shown after 3 hours **(B),** after 6 hours **(C),** and after 27 hours **(D).** (Reprinted with permission from Nordström A-L, Farde L, Halldin D: Time course of D_2-dopamine receptor occupancy examined by PET after single oral doses of haloperidol. Psychopharmacology *106:* 436, 1992.)

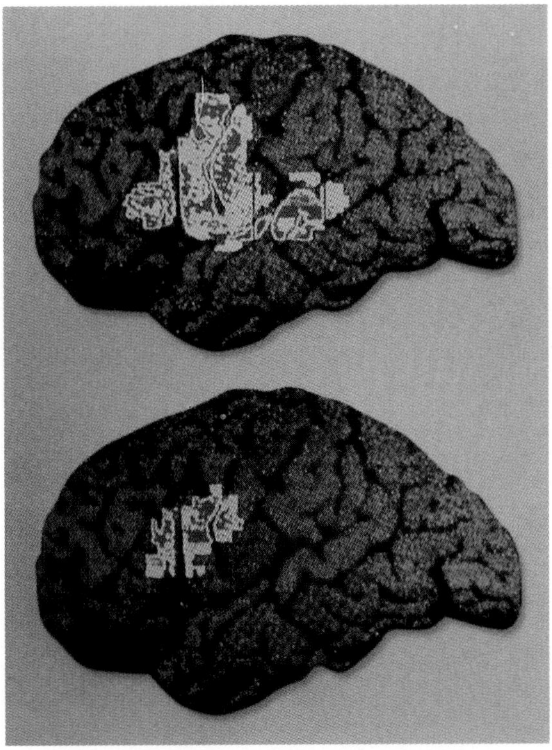

FIGURE 3.3–3

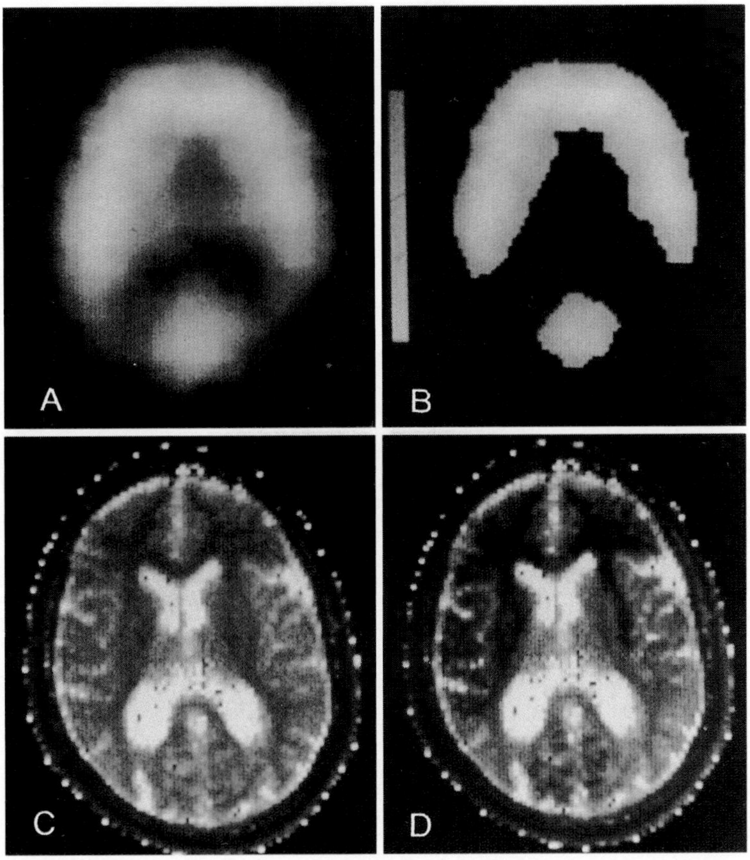
A
B
C
D

FIGURE 3.3–4

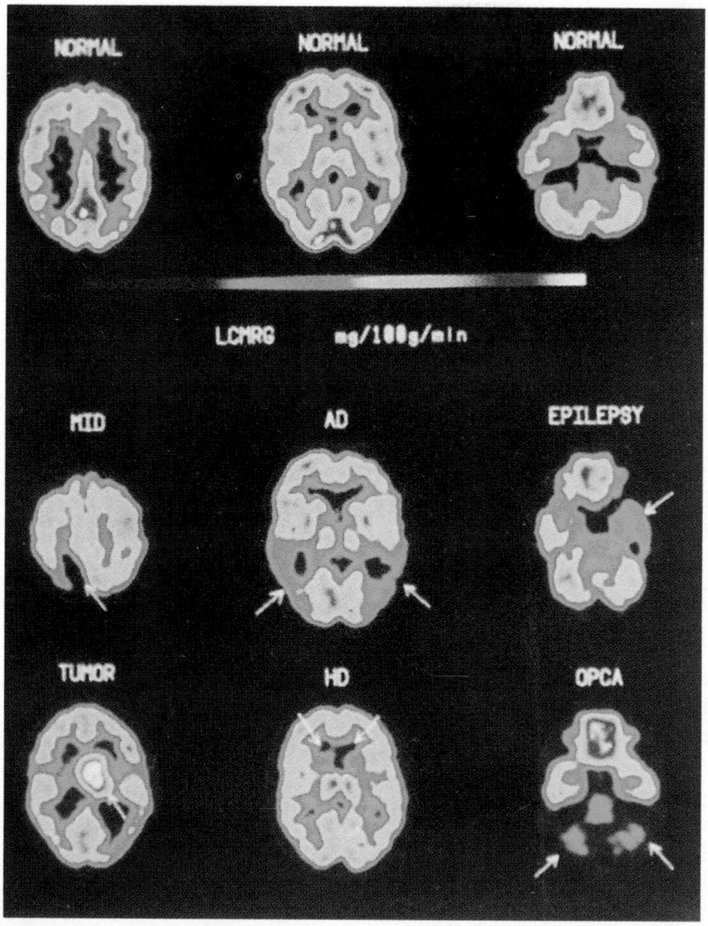
NORMAL
NORMAL
NORMAL
LCMRG mg/100g/min
MID
AD
EPILEPSY
TUMOR
HD
OPCA

FIGURE 3.3–5

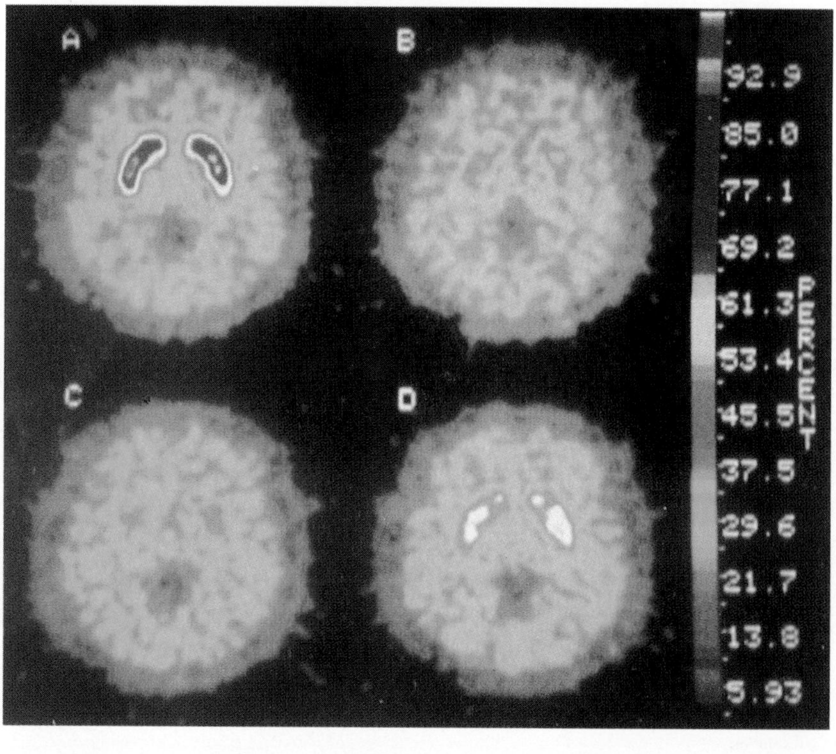
A
B
C
D
92.9
85.0
77.1
69.2
61.3
53.4
45.5
37.5
29.6
21.7
13.8
5.93
PERCENT

FIGURE 3.3–6

with an electron. PET scanners remain relatively few in number because they require an on-site cyclotron with which to make the isotopes.

The most commonly used isotopes in PET are fluorine-18, nitrogen-13, and oxygen-15. These isotopes are usually linked to another molecule, except in the case of oxygen-15 (^{15}O). The most commonly reported ligand has been [^{18}F]fluorodeoxyglucose (FDG), an analogue of glucose that the brain cannot metabolize. Thus, the brain regions with the highest metabolic rate and the highest blood flow take up the most FDG but are unable to metabolize and excrete the usual metabolic products. The concentration of ^{18}F builds up in these neurons and is detected by the PET camera. Water-15 ($H_2{}^{15}O$) and nitrogen-13 (^{13}N) are used to measure blood flow, and oxygen-15 (^{15}O) can be used to determine metabolic rate. Glucose is by far the predominant energy source available to brain cells, and its utilization is therefore a highly sensitive indicator of the rate of brain metabolism. [^{18}F]-labeled DOPA, the fluorinated precursor to dopamine, has been used to localize dopaminergic neurons.

PET has been increasingly used to study normal brain development and function as well as to study neuropsychiatric disorders. With regard to brain development, PET studies have found that glucose use is greatest in the sensorimotor cortex, thalamus, brainstem, and cerebellar vermis when an infant is 5 weeks of age or younger. By 3 months of age, most areas of the cortex show increased use except for the frontal and association cortices, which do not begin to increase until the infant is 8 months old. An adult pattern of glucose metabolism is achieved by the age of 1 year, but the cortex continues to rise above adult levels until the child is about 9 years old, when the cortex begins to decrease, and reaches its final adult level in the late teen years. In another study, subjects listened to a rapidly presented list of thematically related words. When asked to recall words in the thematic category that may or may not have been on the list, some subjects falsely recalled that they had heard words that were actually not on the list. By PET scanning, the hippocampus was active during both true and false recollections, whereas the auditory cortex was only active during recollection of words that were actually heard. When pressed to determine whether memories were true or false, subjects activated the frontal lobes. FDG studies have also been used to study pathology in neurological disorders and psychiatric disorders (Fig. 3.3–5). Two other types of studies use precursor molecules and receptor ligands. With the dopamine precursor DOPA, pathology has been visualized in patients with Parkinson's disease. Radiolabeled ligands for receptors have been useful in determining the occupancy of receptors by specific psychotherapeutic drugs (Fig. 3.3–6).

Issues Common to PET and SPECT

Image Resolution. Four major factors affect the resolution level of both PET and SPECT techniques: Compton scattering, signal attenuation, anatomical resolution, and partial volume effects.

COMPTON SCATTERING. The emitted photons in both PET and SPECT are deviated from a straight path by tissue through which they pass, a fact that limits the anatomical resolution of both PET and SPECT.

SIGNAL ATTENUATION. Not only are the photons deviated from their straight path by the tissue, but also the energy of the photons is dissipated by bone, air, fluid, and brain tissue. In fact, the most carefully done PET and SPECT studies use prestudy CT examinations to correct for variable attenuations or for the signal caused by differences in patients' head sizes.

ANATOMICAL RESOLUTION. A common term used in describing the resolution for both PET and SPECT is *full width at half maximum* (FWHM), which refers to the width of the curve of distribution for the signal at 50 percent of the maximal signal. For PET studies, FWHM is about 5 to 6 mm; for SPECT studies, FWHM is about 8 to 9 mm and thus reflects the better resolution of the PET technique compared with the SPECT technique.

PARTIAL VOLUME EFFECTS. For both PET and SPECT, areas of interest within the slice are selected, but the signal from each area of interest also affects the neighboring areas of interest. In some studies of SPECT and PET, investigators use various computer modeling programs to subtract the energy contribution of neighboring areas from the areas of interest.

Pharmacological and Neuropsychological Probes

With both PET and SPECT and eventually with MRS, more studies and possibly more diagnostic procedures will use pharmacological and neuropsychological probes. The purpose of such probes is to stimulate particular regions of brain activity, so that, when compared with a baseline, workers can reach conclusions about the functional correspondence to particular brain regions. One example of the approach is the use of PET to detect regions of the brain involved in the processing of shape, color, and velocity in the visual system. Another example is the use of cognitive activation tasks (for example, the Wisconsin Card Sorting Test) to study frontal blood flow in patients with schizophrenia. A key consideration in the evaluation of reports that measure blood flow is the establishment of a true baseline value in the study design. Typically, the reports use an awake, resting state, but there is a variability in whether the patients have their eyes closed or their ears blocked; both conditions can affect brain function. There is also variability in such baseline brain function factors as gender, age, anxiety about the test, nonpsychiatric drug treatment, vasoactive medications, and time of day.

Electroencephalography

Neural electrical activity consists of patterned changes in electrical potential across cell membranes. Individual cells generate membrane potentials that can be detected only within a few micrometers of the cell, but assemblies of brain cells that fire synchronously may generate potentials on the order of microvolts, which can be detected through the skull and skin with an array of scalp electrodes. The regional variation in electrical potential across the scalp forms the basis of *electroencephalography,* which is the recording of the electrical activity of the brain. Electroencephalography is used in clinical psychiatry principally to evaluate the presence of seizures, particularly temporal lobe or frontal lobe seizures, which may produce complex behaviors.

The summation of the electrical potential changes in the cortex is thought to occur at the radially oriented large pyramidal cells of the cortex. When two scalp electrodes are placed sufficiently widely apart, at least several millimeters, they subsume a sufficient number of pyramidal cell generators to detect changes in the electrical potential on the order of 2 to 200 microvolts. Although a random pattern of voltage changes might be expected, the normal human electroencephalogram (EEG), in fact, contains rhythmical activity at frequencies of 1 Hz (1 cycle per second) to 50 Hz. The most obvious rhythm in adults is the alpha rhythm of 9 to 10 Hz, present over the occipital lobe. On the basis of animal experiments in which stimulation or ablation of the thalamus was noted to stimulate or abolish rhythmical cortical activity, respectively, researchers have concluded that rhythmical cortical activity detected by the EEG originates in thalamocortical circuits driven by thalamic pacemaker cells. The nuclei of the thalamus may project widely or to discrete regions of the cortex and may also project branches that stimulate thalamic inhibitory interneurons. Certain of these interneurons inhibit the thalamic projection for a period of one tenth of a second, which according to one theory may be the basis of the 10-Hz alpha rhythm. In an alternative view, cortical-cortical interactions alone have cortical rhythmicity; this view is based on observations that cortical activity may be better synchronized to activity in other parts of the cortex than to the thalamus. Besides the thalamus and cortex, lesional studies have demonstrated that an intact brainstem ascending reticular activating system (ARAS) is necessary for cortical rhythms. Finally, cortical rhythms in humans may be abolished by arousal, heightened attention, drowsiness, or sleep.

The principal source of EEG activity is the electrical potential of the brain. Activity immediately below the scalp electrodes contributes most to the recording, but distant brain activity may modulate the tracing. The EEG must be recorded with the patient as motionless as possible, to eliminate the introduction of muscle artifact. Muscle contraction, of course, also involves electrical activity, and muscle twitching, especially of the face and scalp muscles, may generate electrical potentials of such magnitude that brain electrical activity is completely obscured. Other sources of muscle artifact include eye movements; eye movements are a normal component of the rapid eye movement (REM) stage of sleep and may clue an electroencephalographer to the presence of REM sleep. As artifacts may also be introduced from a strong source of alternating current, the EEG is usually recorded in a shielded room.

The electrodes normally used for recording the EEG are attached to the scalp with a conductive paste. Under special circumstances, needle electrodes may be placed into the nasopharynx or the masseter muscle to approximate the temporal lobes. With the realization that surgical removal of an epileptic focus within the brain may cure epilepsy in a patient otherwise refractory to medical management, several epilepsy centers have refined the use of strips or arrays of electrodes applied directly to the surface of the brain at craniotomy, from which discharges are recorded for several days. To localize deeper epileptogenic foci, depth electrodes may be inserted into the brain. These invasive recording methods offer greatly improved spatial resolution of epileptiform activity. They may also be used to stimulate the brain to map out the sites of critical functions, to guide the hand of the neurosurgeon during the resection of diseased brain.

In routine electroencephalography, the international 10–20 system of electrode placement provides a uniform assessment of the entire scalp. With lines drawn between bony landmarks, each of which is divided into segments of either 10 or 20 percent of its length, a grid is plotted to cover the scalp. The standard array consists of 21 electrodes, but extra electrodes may be interpolated on the grid for finer spatial resolution. Three montages are used to represent cortical activity. In the longitudinal bipolar montage, each channel registers positive or negative signals by comparing the potential of adjacent electrodes, which are oriented in anterior-posterior chains. In the transverse bipolar montage, the chains are connected from left to right across the head. The deflection of adjacent electrodes in opposite directions, called a *phase reversal,* localizes the site of a spike in electrical potential in the bipolar montage. *Bipolar montages* allow the best localization of cerebral activity. In contrast to the bipolar montage, the *referential montage* compares the electrical potential of each electrode to a common ground electrode, usually located at one ear. The advantage of the referential montage is that it may reveal potentials with a wider distribution across the brain.

The normal EEG consists of a mixture of frequencies, which are divided into four bandwidths. Delta waves oscillate below 4 Hz, and theta waves oscillate from 4 to 8 Hz; activity below 8 Hz is also called slow wave activity. Alpha waves, the frequency of the posterior dominant rhythm, are from 8 to 13 Hz. Beta waves (fast activity) are over 13 Hz. Normal activity contains a posterior alpha rhythm with the eyes closed; more anterior regions have random admixtures of theta, alpha, or beta activity. The appearance of delta activity is abnormal, except in sleep, and may reflect an underlying structural lesion. Upon alerting and eye opening, the posterior alpha is replaced by random activity.

Abnormal discharges suggestive of a seizure focus consist of rapid changes in potential, or spikes, which may be organized in rhythmical patterns. The spikes may be followed by a broad slow wave, yielding a spike–wave pattern. If spike or spike–wave activity is localized to one area of the montage, the underlying brain is referred to as a potentially epileptogenic focus. Such a focus may originate a focal seizure, which is a series of spikes or spike–wave complexes that persists to the point of affecting a patient's movements or behavior. If the seizure focus recruits neighboring brain tissue and spreads throughout the cortex, it is said to generalize; generalized seizures are accompanied by loss of consciousness. Generalized seizures may not be preceded by focal cortical seizure activity but may appear throughout the EEG simultaneously. Such generalized-onset seizures are thought to originate in deep structures, such as the thalamus.

Routine surface electroencephalography is useful in the evaluation of epilepsy. In patients with epileptic seizures, a single EEG will be abnormal 70 percent of the time. After three routine EEGs, the sensitivity increases to 95 percent. Therefore, an abnormal EEG may be highly suggestive of epilepsy, but a normal EEG does not rule out the disorder. In patients with episodes of bizarre behavior who do not exhibit the classical tonic-clinic seizure movements, it may be very difficult to diagnose seizure activity based on history alone. When routine EEGs do not show epileptiform activity, it may be necessary to record the EEG for a prolonged period, as much as several days, with closed-circuit television (CCTV) observation, to capture an actual seizure event. This method is called *24-hour CCTV electroencephalographic monitoring.* It is performed in specified epilepsy monitoring units at major referral centers or on an ambulatory basis in the home.

In clinical psychiatry, electroencephalography is useful to distinguish temporal lobe seizures from pseudoseizures. Another indication for electroencephalography is in the differentiation of dementia from pseudodementia caused by depression. In dementia, the EEG reveals excessive slow wave activity, whereas in depression the recording is normal. For most psychiatric patients, however, electroencephalography is of little value. Electroencephalography is used during electroconvulsive therapy (ECT) to monitor the success of the stimulus in the production of seizure activity. The EEG is an essential part of the polysomnogram, or sleep study, used in the evaluation of sleep disorders. The definition of sleep stages is based on the EEG patterns.

The EEG has been used in research settings to evaluate the registration of sensations by the cortex. If the responses to a sufficient series of stimuli are summed, the subconscious registration of environmental events may be detected with an EEG. As a tool for establishment of the function of different brain regions, the EEG provides excellent temporal resolution, but it yields only poor spatial resolution. Because of the constant random brain activity seen over most parts of the brain, it has not been possible to localize the activation of specific brain regions during complex cognitive tasks with the EEG, in the manner afforded by fMRI, SPECT, or PET scanning.

In theory, a sufficiently detailed recording of the electrical activity of the brain should reveal a specific pattern of activity when a person thinks of a specific word or idea. In practice, however, this level of interpretive sophistication is many years away. Preliminary efforts have succeeded in interpreting EEG activity in terms of simple conscious thought. In an effort to harness the complexity of brain waves to direct computers and machines, for instance as a tool of communication for patients unable to speak because of severe spasticity, researchers have categorized the frequency and wave forms of the EEG during thoughts. Alpha waves (8 to 13 Hz) appear when the eyes close, and they attenuate when the eyes open or the person concentrates on vivid imagination. Beta waves (fast waves, usually 14 to 30 Hz) increase with heightened mental activity and may reach 50 Hz during intense thought. Theta waves (4 to 7 Hz) appear during emotional stress, especially frustration or disappointment. Delta waves (less than 4 Hz) occur during deep sleep.

A particular type of alpha-range waves, called mu waves, are recorded over the motor cortex, and they attenuate in amplitude with actual or imagined movements. In the past decade, researchers have trained individuals to regulate the amplitude of their mu waves by visualizing various motions, such as chewing, swallowing, or smiling. EEG electrodes placed over the motor strip and attached to an amplitude analyzer can determine the size of the mu waves with sufficient precision to guide a computer cursor and operate a program solely by means of their thoughts. Other EEG-computer machines use the presence or absence of alpha waves, determined by unfocusing or focusing attention, to operate an electronic switch. With time and the application of increased computer-processing power, researchers may begin to decipher the electrical signature of complex cognition.

Magnetoencephalography (MEG) and Transcranial Magnetic Stimulation (TMS)

Physics teaches that every electrical field has a corresponding magnetic field oriented at right angles to it. This fact applies to the electrical activity of the brain and forms the basis for magnetoencephalography (MEG). Much of the previous discussion of electroencephalography can be translated for MEG. The changes in membrane potential of neurons during normal activity generate tiny magnetic fields. When the activities of the billions of neurons in the cortex are summed, the changes in magnetic field can be detected with special magnets placed on the scalp. But although electroencephalography uses simple wires and can be performed almost anywhere, MEG requires supercooled magnets, called single superconducting quantum interference devices (SQUIDs), which operate near absolute zero temperature. The technique is therefore limited to a handful of facilities.

MEG offers the best temporal and the lowest spatial resolution of any technique currently available. It also detects only tangentially flowing fields, complementary to electroencephalography, which detects radially oriented fields. MEG is the superior technique for detection of activity deep within the brain because the fields are less attenuated by the skull and scalp tissues. In addition, as it is a true monopolar technique, it does not require a reference electrode and therefore can avoid certain artifacts. The fields registered by MEG are tiny; recordings need careful shielding and extensive computerized computational algorithms for maximum localization within the brain. MEG thus remains almost exclusively a research tool.

The major area in which the existence of magnetic fields in the brain provides a unique opportunity for study is the ability to alter the magnetic fields by transcranial magnetic stimulation (TMS). In theory, applying electrical fields to the brain is also possible, and this is the central therapeutic intervention in ECT. In practice, however, attenuation of the scalp and nonneural tissues, which generates heat and pain and may produce burns, limits the usefulness of electrical stimulation. TMS involves a strong electromagnet, in which the field is oscillated at 0.1 Hz to 60 Hz. The frequency, pulse duration, and intensity of the magnetic field all contribute to the amount of neuronal stimulation caused by TMS. Low frequency (0.1 Hz to 5 Hz) pulses may in some cases reduce metabolism in the underlying cortex, whereas higher frequency pulses (15 Hz to 25 Hz) may increase local cerebral metabolism. Pulse rates above 25 Hz are associated with the induction of seizures and are avoided in human subjects. When accurately applied in a single pulse, TMS can inactivate neural activity. When given as a train of pulses, it can transiently inhibit discrete regions of the brain, which then rebound and exhibit prolonged increased activity, sometimes for as long as days to months. For example, a pulse aimed at a specific part of the basal ganglia can eliminate the tremor of Parkinson's disease.

In psychiatric research, the prevailing view that the left hemisphere generates positive emotions and the right hemisphere mediates negative emotions has been addressed with TMS. Pulses that inactivate brain regions, when directed toward the left frontal lobe, suppress positive thoughts and elicit sadness. When the right frontal lobe is suppressed by TMS, subjects feel happier and more energetic. In tests, these mood changes lasted a few hours. In another experimental paradigm, severely depressed patients, who might otherwise have been candidates for ECT, instead received TMS over the left frontal lobe for 20 minutes a day over 2 weeks. A significant number of patients reported an improvement in mood for a few days, whereas patients subjected to sham treatments showed no improvement. As a practical therapy for depression, TMS would have to be readministered frequently. Researchers are attempting to prolong the effects.

An interesting application of TMS and electroencephalography or MEG is for timing the flow of neural impulses through the brain. When one part of the brain is stimulated with TMS, the transmission of this information to distant brain regions can be registered to millisecond accuracy with either electroencephalography, MEG, or both. This process may allow a systematic functional mapping of intracortical circuits, to build on the scaffolding of cortical connections defined by classical neuroanatomical methods.

Evoked Potentials (EPs) and Event-Related Potentials (ERPs)

Sensory EPs, reflecting the brain's electrical response to reproducible sensory stimuli, are extracted from the EEG by computer-assisted signal averaging. The recording of EPs uses similar electrode and recording arrangements to those used in electroencephalography. Sensory EPs provide a measure of how the cortex responds to particular sensory stimuli. In the evaluation of demyelinating disorders, such as multiple sclerosis, well-established protocols exist for somatosensory evoked potentials (SEPs), brainstem auditory evoked potentials (BAEPs), and visual evoked potentials (VEPs). In EP testing, a stimulus from one sensory modality (for example, a mild electric shock, a click, or a light flash) is presented multiple times while the resulting neural evoked potentials are recorded at various levels over the sensory pathway, always including electrodes over the corresponding sensory cortex. Because of the inherent random and rhythmical brain activity recorded by scalp electrodes, it is necessary to average the cortical responses to 100 to 2000 identical repetitions of a particular sensory stimulus. The random activity tends to cancel itself out, whereas the sensory response adds up to a recognizable waveform. The result is a smooth curve (the EP) that includes peaks and valleys.

Positive waves are the downward deflections, and negative waves are the upward deflections. Particular waves are further identified by the number of milliseconds that occur after the stimulus. The P300 wave, therefore, is a downward (positive) deflection that occurs approximately 300 ms after the stimulus. The magnitude and the timing of EP waves constitute the basis of the clinical and research evaluation of an EP recording.

The EP waves have been classified into early (50 ms after the stimulus), middle (50 to 250 ms), and late (250 ms) components. The relay of sensory information as it passes from a sensory organ (for example, the eyes) to the primary sensory cortex and to the association cortex is reflected in the early EP components. Increasingly complex cognitive and psychological processing of sensory information is reflected in the late EP components. EP recordings are especially subject to contamination by various artifacts in addition to those affecting EEG recordings. Attention, compliance, fatigue, coffee and cigarette consumption, the age of the person, and diurnal variations have all been reported to affect the data from EP recordings.

In research settings, a dense (64-channel) EEG electrode array, recording brain activity in a time-locked fashion during cognitive tasks such as reading, is used to correlate late EP components with higher cognitive processing. In one study, when subjects read a passage and recording began at the arrival at a certain trigger word, the ERP began at about 70 ms with bilateral positive current sources over the occipitoparietal visual processing areas. A negative potential then followed at about 180 ms over the left temporal lobe, accompanied by an anterior positivity. A separate posterior positive pattern then emerged that seemed to repeat the topography of the initial positive current. Next, at about 350 ms, the ERP for the trigger word developed a diffuse positivity over the superior surface of the head and several negativities over inferior regions. This superior source–inferior sink pattern, called the P300 or the late positive component (LPC), was greater over the left hemisphere. Under similar recording conditions, when the trigger word was replaced with a semantically unexpected word, the brain electrical activity showed no potential at 350 ms, but then developed an LPC at 400 ms, which remained relatively symmetrical over the two hemispheres.

In a further refinement of this approach, ERPs, which have relatively poor spatial resolution, nevertheless provide enough spatial discrimination to permit the temporal ordering of the activation of several brain regions that are identified as essential to the performance of a task by functional MRI or PET. In one example of this approach, functional brain imaging studies with PET identified blood flow changes in widely separated areas of the brain during the performance of word-related tasks. ERPs were then used to investigate the temporal relationships among cortical areas previously identified by PET to be differentially activated when performing a language task. ERPs showed strong task-related differences over left and middle inferior frontal and left parietotemporal regions. Frontal and left parietotemporal channels revealed these differences around 200 and 700 ms, respectively, after word presentation. These results provided the time course for parts of the anatomical circuit involved in generating the meaning of a word.

Although labor intensive, studies combining functional neuroimaging and ERP hold great promise for understanding the neuroanatomical basis for normal and abnormal human cognition.

References

Abou-Saleh MT, editor: Brain imaging in psychiatry. Br J Psychiatry *157* (9, Suppl): 1, 1990.

Aine CJ: A conceptual overview and critique of functional neuroimaging techniques in humans: I. MRI/FMRI and PET. Crit Rev Neurobiol *9:* 229, 1995.

Andreasen NC, Cohen G, Harris G, Cizadlo T, Parkkinen J, Rezai K, Swayze VW: Image processing for the study of brain structure and function: Problems and programs. J Neuropsychiatry Clin Neurosci *4:* 125, 1992.
Corbetta M, Miezin FM, Dobmeyer S, Shulman GL, Petersen SE: Attentional modulation of neural processing of shape, color, and velocity in humans. Science *248:* 1556, 1990.
Dager SR, Steen RG: Applications of magnetic resonance spectroscopy to the investigation of neuropsychiatric disorders. Neuropsychopharmacology *6:* 249, 1992.
Devous MD: SPECT functional brain imaging: Technical considerations. J Neuroimaging *5* (1, Suppl): S2, 1995.
Garber HJ, Weilburg JB, Duffy FH, Manschreck TL: Clinical use of topographic brain electrical activity mapping in psychiatry. J Clin Psychiatry *50:* 205, 1989.
Gevins A, Leong H, Smith ME, Le J, Du R: Mapping cognitive brain function with modern high-resolution electroencephalography. Trends Neurosci *18:* 429, 1995.
Gilman S: Advances in neurology. N Engl J Med *326:* 1608, 1992.
Gur RC, Edwin RJ, Gur RE: Neurobehavioral probes for physiologic neuroimaging studies. Arch Gen Psychiatry *49:* 409, 1992.
Holman LB, Tumeh SS: Single-photon emission computed tomography (SPECT): Applications and potential. JAMA *263:* 561, 1990.
Horwitz B, McIntosh AR, Haxby JV, Grady CL: Network analysis of brain cognitive function using metabolic and blood flow data. Behav Brain Res *66:* 187, 1995.
Kato T, Takahashi S, Inubushi T: Brain lithium concentration by ^{7}Li- and ^{1}H-magnetic resonance spectroscopy in bipolar disorder. Psychiatry Res Neuroimaging *45:* 53, 1992.
Keshavan MS, Kapur S, Pettegrew JW: Magnetic resonance spectroscopy in psychiatry: Potential, pitfalls, and promise. Am J Psychiatry *148:* 967, 1991.
Kotrla KJ, Weinberger DR: Brain imaging in schizophrenia. Annu Rev Med *46:* 113, 1995.
Kuikka JT, Belliveau JW, Hari R: Future of functional brain imaging. Eur J Nucl Med *23:* 737, 1996.
Levin JM, Ross MH, Renshaw PF: Clinical applications of functional MRI in neuropsychiatry. J Neuropsychiatry Clin Neurosci *7:* 511, 1995.
Lock T, Abou-Saleh MT, Edwards RHT: Psychiatry and the new magnetic resonance area. Br J Psychiatry *157:* 38, 1990.
Moonen CTW, Van Zijl PCM, Frank JA, Le Bihan D, Becker ED: Functional magnetic resonance imaging in medicine and physiology. Science *250:* 53, 1990.
Reeve A, Rose DF, Weinberger DR: Magnetoencephalography: Applications in psychiatry. Arch Gen Psychiatry *46:* 573, 1989.
Therapeutics and Technology Assessment Subcommittee of the American Academy of Neurology: Assessment: Magnetoencephalography (MEG). Neurology *42:* 1, 1992.
Villringer A, Dirnagl U: Coupling of brain activity and cerebral blood flow: Basis of functional neuroimaging. Cerebrovasc Brain Metab Rev *7:* 240, 1995.
Warner MD, Boutros NN, Peabody CA: Usefulness of screening EEGs in psychiatric inpatient population. J Clin Psychiatry *51:* 363, 1990.

▲ 3.4 Molecular Biology and Behavioral Genetics

Many philosophers and psychiatrists have viewed behavior and emotion as products of the mind, a whole that is somehow greater than its parts. This perspective has seemingly assumed that behavior will never be fully understood in terms of specific biochemical interactions. Although such a reductionist notion, that thoughts may be defined in terms of specific protein–protein binding, seems mechanical in the extreme, application of the increasingly powerful tools of molecular genetics to human behavior may yet yield profound insights into psychiatric disorders. The psychiatric disorders with perhaps the broadest, unambiguous molecular basis are Alzheimer's disease, in which four genetic loci may account for a large percentage of the risk of occurrence, and Huntington's disease, in which the risk is fully accounted for by an abnormality in a single dominant gene. Only a small amount of the genetic variation for major thought and mood disorders, in contrast, has been associated with a single genetic locus in isolated pedigrees, the significance of which for the general population is unclear.

BASIC MOLECULAR BIOLOGY

The central dogma of molecular biology is ''DNA makes RNA makes protein.'' Deoxyribonucleic acid (DNA) is a genetic code consisting of a series of bases, adenine (A), cytosine (C), guanine (G), and thymine (T), which are covalently linked in series to form extremely long molecules. *Genes* consist of strings of DNA code that specify a series of base triplets, called *codons,* that determine a specific sequence of *amino acids,* the building blocks of proteins. DNA resides in the nucleus, where it serves as a template for the formation of messenger ribonucleic acid (mRNA) molecules. Messenger RNA is assembled according to the DNA code by the stepwise addition of bases according to a complementation algorithm. Ribonucleic adenine (rA) is complementary to deoxyribonucleic thymine (T), rG to C, rC to G, and ribonucleic uracil (rU) to adenine (A). Thus, the DNA string ATGTCTTAG would encode the mRNA string UACAGAAUC. Messenger RNA has stretches of protein-coding sequences, called *exons,* which are interrupted by noncoding sequences, called *introns.* Soon after the mRNA is transcribed from the DNA, the exons are spliced together to form a continuous stretch of coding sequence. The mRNA moves into the cytoplasm and binds to ribosomes, which read the triplet codons and assemble a string of amino acids to form a specific protein. There are 20 common amino acids, each with a different atomic configuration. Depending on the primary amino acid sequence, the protein folds into a three-dimensional molecule that interacts specifically with other proteins, carbohydrates, nucleic acids, or lipids to carry out the functions of the cell.

The regulation of the relative abundance of various proteins in the cell may occur at the level of the rate of mRNA transcription, at the level of mRNA translation into protein, or at the level of the degradation of the protein molecules. Messenger RNA transcriptional control is the most common type of specific gene regulation. The initiation of mRNA transcription involves general factors, called *transcription factors,* common to all genes, but it is regulated by specific transcription factors that bind only to certain genes and are themselves regulated by intracellular and extracellular signals. Thus, thyroid hormones diffuse into the cell and bind to the thyroid receptors, and the hormone–receptor complex, which acts as a transcription factor, enters the nucleus and activates certain genes by binding to specific DNA sequences immediately adjacent to these genes. There is much interest in psychiatry in gene regulation by neurotransmitters and in the regulation of the synaptic neurochemical milieu by variations in the levels of gene transcription.

The human genetic material consists of 3 billion bases of DNA, which are divided into units of roughly 60 million bases, called *chromosomes.* The normal cell nucleus contains 23 pairs of chromosomes. A typical gene spans about 10,000 bases, and the longest known gene covers 2 million bases. Humans are estimated to have about 80,000 distinct genes. The site on the chromosomes where a gene is located is called a *locus.* Thus, about one third of the total DNA encodes genes that may be translated into proteins, and the remaining two thirds is noncoding "junk" DNA. The function of only a few thousand of the genes is known at this time. Some genes encode proteins that play housekeeping roles within the cell; that is, they are present in all cells and are essential to the survival of the cell. Other genes play specific regulatory roles and are cell-type specific. Among these latter genes are those of particular interest to psychiatrists. Intense research is under way to identify those genes that, when altered, may cause psychiatric illness, as well as to identify those that may determine normal emotional behaviors and responses. At this time, these goals tax and in most cases exceed the data processing capabilities of even the most sophisticated investigators. Yet, the methods currently in use were almost inconceivable only 15 years ago, and major technical advances are appearing at a rapid rate. Most gene experts now anticipate significant advances in the identification of the genetic basis of complex human behaviors early in the 21st century.

PREMISES OF BEHAVIORAL GENETICS

Many major psychiatric disorders have been shown to have a strong hereditary predisposition. In the case of schizophrenia, for example, a first-degree relative of an affected patient has about a 10 percent chance of having the illness, far in excess of the 1 percent risk to the general population. Monozygotic twins display nearly 50 percent concordance rate for schizophrenia. Bipolar I disorder and major depressive disorder exhibit similar familial clustering, in that first-degree relatives are 8 to 18 times more likely to have a mood disorder than is the general population, and monozygotic twins show a 33 to 90 percent concordance rate. Tourette's disorder shows an even more convincing genetic association. Several family pedigrees have been constructed in which transmission of the disorder is consistent with an autosomal dominant mode with penetrance of 99 percent in males and 70 percent in females. Only 10 percent of patients with Tourette's disorder do not have an affected family member. These facts stimulate the expectation that a specific genetic basis will emerge for certain psychiatric diseases.

Medicine has provided many models of genetically determined pathology. There are thousands of examples of inherited human traits and disorders, many of which have been traced to a single aberrant gene. One classic model is sickle cell anemia. A mutation at a single point in the β-globin gene causes this disorder by producing a single amino acid substitution in the β-globin protein, which forms half of hemoglobin. The mutation promotes crystallization of hemoglobin red blood cells and causes them to assume the shape of a sickle. Clinically, this effect leads to sludging in capillaries and bone pain, as well as ischemic events such as strokes. The sickle cell anemia model is unusual among genetic diseases for the detail in which the molecular abnormality is known and for the simplicity with which the clinical syndrome can be traced to the biochemical mutation. Nevertheless, sickle cell anemia displays a wide clinical variability, ranging from patients who are asymptomatic to patients with severe impairments who die prematurely. This fact demonstrates the clinical variability introduced by *modifier genes,* which encode proteins that the aberrant protein interacts with. Two variants of sickle cell anemia, sickle-thalassemia and hemoglobin SC disease, have been traced to specific modifier genes, but most clinical variability is due to unknown factors. Thus, sickle cell anemia demonstrates the incompleteness of even the most clearly understood genetic determination for human disease. This model tempers the optimism of researchers pursuing the genetic basis of behavior and emotion, which are considerably less well defined at a clinical level than is sickle cell anemia.

Traits are clinically defined features, such as sickle crises or blue eyes. Some traits are determined by a single gene, whereas others emerge from the interactions of the products of, in some cases, hundreds of genes. Behavior very likely is the expression of the products of thousands of genes, although specific single gene mutations may influence certain behaviors in consistent ways. Studies of animal behavior, especially of the fruit fly and the laboratory mouse, have documented many behaviors inherited as single gene traits. These heritable behaviors have often been traced to a specific gene, whereas others are only known to be heritable. Fortunately, the former category is rapidly expanding at the expense of the latter. Identifying a gene that determines a specific behavioral trait requires a rigorous clinical definition of the trait and the largest possible pedigree or family tree in which the pattern of the trait's inheritance is unambiguously defined. Mapping genes essentially involves correlating the inheritance of the trait with the inheritance of molecular markers scattered throughout an animal's genetic material. This method is called *linkage analysis* or *positional cloning.*

For traits determined by single genes, three common inheritance patterns are recognized: autosomal dominant, autosomal recessive, and X-linked recessive transmission. In *autosomal dominant transmission,* only one of the two copies of the gene in the cell nucleus needs to mutate to produce the clinical trait. A parent with one copy of a dominant mutation has a 50 percent chance of passing the trait to a child. In *autosomal recessive transmission,* the trait can be passed on only when both copies are mutated. Thus a parent with an autosomal recessive trait can transmit it to a child only when the other parent also passes on the mutant gene. In *X-linked recessive transmission,* the gene is found on an unpaired X chromosome and is thus the only copy of the gene in the nucleus. An X-linked recessive trait therefore occurs in males, who have only one X chromosome; females are carriers, but they do not display the clinical traits because they have a second, normal X chromosome.

In psychiatry, the largest hurdle in the process of assigning behavioral traits to specific genes is the rigorous clinical definition of psychiatric traits. The fourth edition of *Diagnostic and Statistical Manual of Mental Disorders* (DSM-IV), which provides a very exact categorization for most psychiatric disorders, nonetheless probably includes a genetically heterogeneous population of patients under each diagnostic category. The situation is further muddled by the lack of objective, quantifiable tests for psychiatric disorders. Moreover, because familial clustering of certain behavioral traits can be due to either genetics (nature) or upbringing (nurture), the construction of accurate pedigrees strictly according to genetic criteria may be impossible. Finally, the multigenetic determination of behavioral traits serves to increase exponentially the complexity of analysis. If all hurdles can be overcome, the process of screening chromosomes for linkage between a trait and a specific chromosome location is virtually automated.

At this time, pedigrees have been assembled for each of the main psychiatric disorders, and chromosomal linkage has been sought with the tools of molecular genetics. Even in the apparently straightforward case of Tourette's disorder, screening of almost all chromosomes has failed to identify a specific genetic location always inherited with the clinical behavior. This finding suggests that Tourette's syndrome is a *multigenic trait,* that is, a disorder that may be due to the combined influences of several genes. Ongoing studies are screening for mutations in genes for components of the dopamine pathway in patients with Tourette's syndrome, as well as other disorders in the spectrum of anxiety disorders, focusing on the dopamine D_2 receptor, the synthetic enzyme dopamine β-hydroxylase, and the dopamine transporter.

Genetic causes are being sought for other psychiatric disorders. Based on an analysis of 22 pedigrees, a locus that confers an increased risk of bipolar disorder has been identified on chromosome 18. The correlation is not robust, which indicates a need for further investigation. For the personality trait of anxiety, a genetic variant of the serotonin transporter gene has been described that alters the number of transporter molecules in the presynaptic membrane of serotonergic neurons. This alternative version of the transporter has been calculated to account for less than 5 percent of the genetic variance for anxiety in the general population. A genetic basis for the development of cortical processing for spatial representation in the parietal lobe has been described from an analysis of people with Williams syndrome, some of whom have defective spatial abilities. Poor spatial abilities in Williams syndrome are thought to be due to a mutation in the LIM kinase-1 gene. The way in which the gene defect perturbs development of the parietal lobe remains to be elucidated.

People with schizophrenia may have difficulties with filtering auditory input to screen out extraneous sounds. A carefully performed positional cloning project has identified a locus on chromosome 15 that encodes the α_7 nicotinic acetylcholine receptor that appears to account for the abnormality in auditory processing in several pedigrees of patients with schizophrenia. Another study, examining the previously described negative association between schizophrenia and rheumatoid arthritis, found that the human lymphocyte antigen (HLA) DRB1*04 allele was significantly associated with a reduced risk of schizophrenia in 94 unrelated patients with schizophrenia. Another study of 265 Irish families with a high incidence of schizophrenia found two loci, one on chromosome 8 and the other on chromosome 6, each of which accounted for the vulnerability to schizophrenia in a separate 10 to 30 percent of the families. Each of these findings should be viewed as preliminary, and each will require further work.

Alzheimer's disease can be definitively diagnosed only by pathological examination of brain tissue, either at autopsy or from brain biopsy. Whereas shrinkage of neuronal volume without loss of neurons is a feature of normal aging, loss of neurons is typical of Alzheimer's disease. The two characteristic neuropathological features are senile plaques and neurofibrillary tangles. A recent clinicopathological study found that elderly nuns with senile plaques and neurofibrillary tangles do not always have dementia, but the risk is greatly increased, from 57 percent to 93 percent, if they also have suffered strokes. A separate nun study showed that the complexity of writing style at age 20 years predicted the onset of dementia (presumably Alzheimer's) over the age of 70 years. Nuns with a simple writing style in their youth were more likely subsequently to develop dementia than nuns with a complex command of written language. These two studies illustrate that dementia of the Alzheimer's type likely results from a combination of genetically determined and acquired damage to neurons.

Four genetic loci have been associated with the risk of Alzheimer's disease. Ten percent of cases of Alzheimer's disease are hereditary, and the remaining 90 percent are sporadic. Of the hereditary cases, 70 to 80 percent are attributable to mutations in the presenilin 1 gene, located on chromosome 14, which causes onset of symptoms at age 40 to 50 years. Another 20 to 30 percent are attributable to mutations in a related gene, presenilin 2, located on chromosome 1, which causes onset of symptoms at age 50 years. A final 2 to 3 percent of the familial cases are attributable to mutations in the β-amyloid precursor protein (βAPP) gene, located on chromosome 21, which causes onset of symptoms at age 50 years. βAPP and a cytoskeletal protein called *tau* are prominent components of senile plaques and neurofibrillary tangles in both familial and sporadic cases of Alzheimer's disease. Tau protein appears to polymerize into the paired helical filaments that are the main components of neurofibrillary tangles if it is not protected from phosphorylation. This protection is afforded by apolipoprotein E (apo ϵ), the gene for which, on chromosome 19, has three alleles. The $\epsilon 2$ allele is protective of tau, whereas the $\epsilon 3$ and, especially, the $\epsilon 4$ alleles do not associate as strongly with tau and leave it susceptible to phosphorylation and eventual polymerization. Presence of the $\epsilon 3/\epsilon 4$ or of the $\epsilon 4/\epsilon 4$ alleles has been claimed to account for 10 to 50 percent of the risk of sporadic Alzheimer's disease, with onset of symptoms around age 60 years. Such individuals seem to have a particular loss of acetylcholine-containing neurons and therefore may be less likely to respond to acetylcholinesterase inhibitors, such an donepezil (Aricept). In summary, the known genetic risk factors for Alzheimer's disease so far account for less than 50 percent of the cases.

The process of correlating a specific gene to a clinical trait by linkage analysis is called *positional cloning.* Positional cloning may involve identifying a change in 1 base of the 3 billion bases of DNA in the human nucleus, potentially a highly tedious task. Presently, researchers have identified well in excess of 6,000 unique DNA markers, which are scattered evenly across the chromosomes at an average interval of 500,000 bases. To establish linkage of a trait with one of these markers, each member of a pedigree is tested for the presence of the markers, and patterns of inheritance of the markers are correlated with presence or absence of the trait of interest. This task is now almost fully automated but still requires several months of work for even a small pedigree. Although positional cloning projects for human behavioral traits have been begun several times, no psychiatric disorder has been completely analyzed.

To carry out the experimental method of positional cloning, once a researcher identifies a marker that is inherited exactly as is the trait, the genetic mutation can be assumed to lie within 1 million bases of the marker. In this interval, several dozen genes may need to be individually isolated and sequenced, a process that can consume several years of intense work. This step is expected to be simplified by the complete sequencing of the human genome, which is expected in the year 2005. In each gene, each variant in the primary sequence could represent the critical mutation; therefore, each must be systematically tested in all members of the pedigree. If a mutation is determined to be likely to cause the trait, the mutation can be artificially produced in mice to assay whether the clinical trait is reproduced, within the limitations of the behavioral repertoire of laboratory mice. The entire process resembles searching for a needle in a haystack, with clues obtainable only at great effort and expense.

ANIMAL MODELS OF HUMAN BEHAVIOR

Researchers have customarily used small mammals and birds in screening and testing pharmacological agents. Animals share many neurotransmitter systems acted on by psychiatric drugs and are thus good models for pharmacokinetic studies. Numerous behavioral assays have been devised to test activity levels, aggression and passivity, exploration and withdrawal, and other basic behavioral tendencies. Nevertheless, animals are poor models for many complex human behavioral traits. This fact is explained partly by neuroanatomy; small mammals and birds lack a prefrontal cortex, a part of the human brain that is increasingly thought necessary for complex behaviors as well as for psychiatric abnormalities.

Animals can be bred for specific traits and may rapidly provide extensive pedigrees for positional cloning projects. Among the genes recently discovered in this manner are those that control obesity in mice. Breeding of the *ob* mouse strain with a normal strain led to the discovery of *leptin,* a hormone made by fat cells, which acts on the brain to suppress eating behavior. Leptin is also found in humans, although its role in human obesity is still unclear, and it remains to be seen whether exogenous administration of leptin can reduce overeating in humans. Hundreds of mutant mouse strains have been isolated on the basis of unusual behavior, and positional cloning projects are slowly identifying specific mutant genes that determine the behavioral variation. The techniques of positional cloning are becoming ever more powerful and efficient, and a proliferation of reports on genes that influence animal behavior can be expected in the next few years.

On the basis of pharmacological evidence, some genes have been assumed to encode proteins needed for behavior, such as neurotransmitter receptors. Methods of gene targeting, called *knockout technology,* can assess the contribution of specific candidate genes to mouse behavior. Gene targeting allows the creation of mice with deletions or modifications of a specific candidate gene. The resulting mutant mice have one of three phenotypes. Some have no detectable abnormalities, either because the gene is redundant or because the abnormality is too subtle to be detected. Some gene knockouts are lethal in the embryonic period and cannot be assayed in adulthood. Neither of these outcomes is particularly informative about behavior. Sometimes, however, the mutant animals display specific behavioral abnormalities against a background of otherwise normal behavior. In some cases, the abnormalities are predictable, whereas in other cases they are unexpected.

Calcium-calmodulin kinase II (CaMKII) was thought to be a critical component of the intracellular signaling pathway during learning and memory, on the basis of biochemical data. CaMKII knockout mice, in which this protein is completely absent, are unable to learn a maze easily mastered by normal mice. They also show an abnormal impersistence of the hippocampal place code, which is an internal map representing the external environment that normally can be recalled for most of an animal's life span. This example of a predicted outcome is unfortunately a relatively rare result. In another example, based on the fact that cocaine blocks the serotonin transporter and raises synaptic levels of serotonin, a deletion was made in the serotonin 1B (5-hydroxytryptamine 1B [5-HT_{1B}]) receptor, and cocaine was administered. Normal mice become very active and aggressive when given a dose of cocaine, but the 5-HT_{1B}–receptor knockout mice failed to respond to injections of the same dose. This result confirms the role of the 5-HT_{1B} receptors in the response to cocaine. Mice that lack the dopamine transporter show excessive locomotor activity reminiscent of the behavior of mice given amphetamine, which stimulates dopamine release into the synapse.

Targeted deletion of another serotonin receptor, the 5-HT_{2C} receptor, yielded mice that were obese and aggressive. This result was interesting because it was not fully expected based on the pharmacological data. The deletion of monoamine oxidase type B (MAO_B), the enzyme that metabolizes serotonin and catecholamines, caused failure of formation of the barrel fields in the somatosensory cortex. This finding was associated with significantly elevated amounts of serotonin in the cortex, and the results suggest that careful modulation of serotonin levels may be necessary for the proper formation of certain cortical circuits during development. This result was quite unexpected. Another unexpected finding was that mice lacking the transcription factor *fosB* grew and developed apparently normally but failed to nurture their young. A defect in olfactory imprinting in mothers was thought to be responsible for this behavior.

There are presently hundreds of ongoing knockout projects targeted to known candidate genes; as more such genes are isolated, hundreds more knockout projects will undoubtably commence. Because most mouse genes have a human counterpart, inferences can be made about the role of particular candidate genes in human behavior, on the basis of the mouse data. This approach is limited, however, by the fact that human genes cannot be manipulated; the assumptions must remain untested, unless a human mutation appears coincidentally.

NEW METHODS FOR ISOLATION OF HUMAN GENES RESPONSIBLE FOR BEHAVIORAL TRAITS

The most significant project currently underway in behavioral genetics is the Human Genome Project. The ultimate goal of this project is to determine the sequence of all 3 billion bases in human DNA. At present, researchers are creating an ordered library of fragments of chromosomes that are of a convenient size for sequencing. Sequencing can presently be achieved only on short pieces of DNA, less than 1,000 bases at a time. With sufficient automation and data processing and storage, all chromosomes are expected to be sequenced by the year 2005. This procedure will facilitate the identification of new candidate genes. The technology will simplify the task of testing candidate genes within a pedigree and may yield novel options for determining genetic linkage in psychiatric disorders.

The major need in behavioral genetics is clinical research to better define the genetic subtypes of major disease categories. Only with a more complete understanding of clinical phenotypes can breakthroughs in behavioral genetics arise. Once clinical research can tease out inherited components from environmental influences and can construct reliable pedigrees, the mechanical task of finding a specific genetic mutation that is inherited with the behavioral trait is almost an afterthought.

To speculate on the uses of a specific genetic linkage, beyond the intellectual satisfaction of the discovery, researchers must consider drugs and gene therapy. Although pharmacologists have probably tested millions of known biochemical compounds to assess their clinical effectiveness, it is conceivable that a specific genetic linkage may suggest a novel class of drugs that has not yet been tried. With respect to gene therapy, this hypothetical method would use a gene delivery system, most likely a modified virus, to insert a functional copy of a mutant gene into those brain cells that require the gene for normal function. This prospect is unlikely to be realized for a long while.

References

Brown JR, Ye H, Bronson RT, Dikkes P, Greenberg ME: A defect in nurturing in mice lacking the immediate early gene *fosB*. Cell *86:* 297, 1996.

Collins FS: Positional cloning moves from perditional to traditional. Nature Genet *9:* 347, 1995.

Frangiskakis JM, Ewart AK, Morris CA, Mervis CB, Bertrand J, Robinson BF, Klein BP, Ensing GJ, Everett LA, Green ED, Proschel C, Gutowski NJ, Noble M, Atkinson DL, Odelberg SJ, Keating MT: LIM-kinase 1 hemizygosity implicated in impaired visuospatial constructive cognition. Cell *86:* 59, 1996.

Gilger JW: Behavioral genetics: Concepts for research and practice in language development disorders. J Speech Hear Res *38:* 1126, 1995.

Giros B, Jaber M, Jones SR, Wightman PM, Caron MG: Hyperlocomotion and indifference to cocaine and amphetamine in mice lacking the dopamine transporter. Nature *396:* 606, 1996.

Greenspan RJ: Understanding the genetic construction of behavior. Sci Am *272:* 72, 1995.

Kendler KS, MacLean CJ, O'Neill A, Burke J, Murphy B, Duke F, Shinkwin R, Easter SM, Webb BT, Zhang J, Walsh D, Straubb RE: Evidence for a schizophrenia vulnerability locus on chromosome 8p in the Irish study of high-density schizophrenia families. Am J Psychiatry *153:* 1534, 1996.

Lendon CL, Ashall F, Goate AM: Exploring the etiology of Alzheimer disease using molecular genetics. JAMA *277:* 825, 1997.

Lesch K-P, Bengel D, Heils A, Sabol SZ, Greenberg BD, Petri S, Benjamin J, Müller CR, Hamer DH, Murphy DL: Association of anxiety-related traits with a polymorphism in the serotinin transporter gene regulatory region. Science *274:* 1527, 1996.

Selkoe DJ: Alzheimer's disease: Geneotypes, phenotype, and treatment. Science *275:* 630, 1997.

Snowdon DA, Greiner LH, Mortimer JA, Riley KP, Greiner PA, Markesbery WR: Brain infarction and the clinical expression of Alzheimer disease: The nun study. JAMA *277:* 813, 1997.

Snowdon DA, Kemper SJ, Mortimer JA, Griener LH, Wekstein DR, Markesbery WR: Linguistic ability in early life and cognitive function and Alzheimer's disease in late life: Findings from the nun study. JAMA *275:* 528, 1996.

Wright P, Donaldson PT, Underhill JA, Choudhuri K, Doherty DG, Murray RM: Genetic association of the HLA DRB1 gene locus on chromosome 6p21.3 with schizophrenia. Am J Psychiatry *153:* 1530, 1996.

4 Contributions of the Psychosocial Sciences to Human Behavior

▲ 4.1 Jean Piaget

Jean Piaget (1896–1980) was born in Neuchâtel, Switzerland, where he studied at the university and received a doctorate in biology at the age of 22 (Fig. 4.1–1). Becoming interested in psychology, he studied and carried out research at several centers, including the Sorbonne in Paris, and worked with Eugen Bleuler at the Burghöltzli Psychiatric Hospital. Piaget created a broad theoretical system for the development of cognitive abilities; in this sense, his work was similar to that of Sigmund Freud, but Piaget emphasized the ways that children think and acquire knowledge.

Piaget referred to his theory as *genetic epistemology,* which he defined as the study of the acquisition, modification, and growth of abstract ideas and abilities on the basis of an inherited or biological substrate, an intelligent functioning that makes the growth of abstract thought possible. Piaget derived his theories from directly observing children (including his own) and by questioning them about their thinking (Fig. 4.1–2). He was less interested in whether children answered correctly than in how they arrived at their answers. Piaget viewed intelligence as an extension of biological adaptation that has a logical structure. Central to his theory is the concept of *epigenesis:* Growth and development occur in a series of stages, each of which is built on the successful mastery of the preceding stage. Every stage occurs at a certain age, and children show a higher level of thought organization during each successive stage of development.

ORGANIZATION OF COGNITION

Cognitive organization is the process of learning and knowing that occurs in a predictable manner. The major process involved in cognitive organization is *adaptation,* people's ability to adjust to and interact with the environment. Adaptation occurs as a result of the two complementary processes, assimilation and accommodation. In *assimilation* people take in new experiences through their own system of knowledge, a process comparable to eating and digesting food, which then becomes part of the organism's substance. In *accommodation,* people adjust their system of knowledge to the reality demands of the environment. Together, the two processes, which are in dynamic equilibrium, create *schemata* or specific cognitive structures, each with a behavioral pattern. Piaget spoke of a schema of sucking, grasping, and seeing.

Early schemata become more complex as infants grow. Later schemata, which Piaget referred to as *operations,* include imitation, abstraction, and higher intelligence. As infants and children grow, they continue to adapt to the outside world and to react with increasingly complex patterns of cognitive organization.

Organization is both biological and psychological; all species inherit the ability to organize, but what is organized differs for different species. Birds organize flying, and human babies organize crawling. Organization varies among individual members of a species, but its function is constant. For instance, every baby crawls in its own way, but crawling is constant.

Organization occurs in stages, each of which represents a stage of cognitive development, described with the approximate ages at which they first occur.

COGNITIVE DEVELOPMENT STAGES

Piaget described four major stages leading to the capacity for adult thought. Each stage is a prerequisite for the following one, but the rate at which different children move through different stages varies with their native endowment and environmental circumstances. Piaget's four stages are the sensorimotor stage, the stage of preoperational thought, the stage of concrete operations, and the stage of formal operations.

Sensorimotor Stage (Birth to 2 Years)

Piaget used the term *sensorimotor* to describe the first stage: Infants begin to learn through sensory observation, and they gain control of their motor functions through activity, exploration, and manipulation of the environment. Piaget divided this stage into six substages, listed in Table 4.1–1.

From the outset, biology and experience blend to produce learned behavior. For example, infants are born with a sucking reflex, but a type of learning occurs when infants alter the shape of their mouths and discover the location of the nipple. A stimulus is received, and a response results, accompanied by a sense of awareness that is the first schema or elementary concept. As infants become more mobile, one schema is built on another, and new and more complex schemata are developed. Infants' spatial, visual, and tactile worlds expand during this period; children actively interact with the environment and

FIGURE 4.1–1
Jean Piaget. (Reprinted with permission from the Jean Piaget Society, Temple University, Philadelphia, PA.)

FIGURE 4.1–2.
Piaget *(far left)* observes children on a playground.

use previously learned behavior patterns. For example, having learned to use a rattle, infants shake a new toy like the rattle they have already learned to use. Infants also use the rattle in new ways.

The critical achievement of this period is the development of *object permanence* or the *schema of the permanent object.* This phrase relates to a child's ability to understand that objects have an existence independent of the child's involvement with them. Infants learn to differentiate themselves from the world and are able to maintain a mental image of an object, even when it is not present and visible.

When an object is dropped in front of infants, they look down to the ground to search for the object; that is, they behave for the first time as though the object has a reality outside themselves.

At about 18 months, infants begin to develop mental symbols and to use words, a process known as *symbolization.* Infants are able to create a visual image of a ball or a mental symbol of the word *ball* to stand for or signify the real object. Such mental representations allow children to operate on new conceptual levels. The attainment of object permanence marks the transition from the sensorimotor stage to the preoperational stage of development.

Stage of Preoperational Thought (2 to 7 Years)

During the stage of preoperational thought, children use symbols and language more extensively than in the sensorimotor stage. Thinking and reasoning are intuitive; children learn without the use of reasoning. They are unable to think logically or deductively, and their concepts are primitive; they can name objects but not classes of objects. Preoperational thought is midway between socialized adult thought and the completely autistic freudian unconscious. Events are not linked by logic. Early in this stage, if children drop a glass that then breaks, they have no sense of cause and effect. They believe that the glass was ready to break, not that they broke the glass. Children in this stage are also unable to grasp the sameness of an object in different circumstances: The same doll in a carriage, a crib, or a chair is perceived to be three different ob-

Table 4.1–1
Piaget's Sensorimotor Period of Cognitive Development

Age	Characteristics
Birth–2 months	Uses inborn motor and sensory reflexes (sucking, grasping, looking) to interact and accommodate to the external world
2–5 months	Primary circular reaction—coordinates activities of own body and five senses (eg, sucking thumb); reality remains subjective—does not seek stimuli outside of its visual field; displays curiosity
5–9 months	Secondary circular reaction—seeks out new stimuli in the environment; starts both to anticipate consequences of own behavior and to act purposefully to change the environment; beginning of intentional behavior
9 months–1 year	Shows preliminary signs of object permanence; has a vague concept that objects exist apart from itself; plays peekaboo; imitates novel behaviors
1 year–18 months	Tertiary circular reaction—seeks out new experiences; produces novel behaviors
18 months–2 years	Symbolic thought—uses symbolic representations of events and objects; shows signs of reasoning (e.g., uses one toy to reach for and get another); attains object permanence

Adapted from Ginsburg HP: Jean Piaget. In *Comprehensive Textbook of Psychiatry,* ed 4, HI Kaplan, BJ Sadock, editors, p 179. Williams & Wilkins, Baltimore, 1985.

jects. During this time, things are represented in terms of their function. For example, a child defines a bike as "to ride" and a hole as "to dig."

In this stage, children begin to use language and drawings in more elaborate ways. From one-word utterances, two-word phrases, made up of either a noun and a verb or a noun and an objective, develop. A child may say, "Bobby eat," or "Bobby up."

Children in the preoperational stage are unable to deal with moral dilemmas, although they have a sense of what is good and bad. For example, when asked, "Who is more guilty: The person who breaks one dish on purpose or the person who breaks 10 dishes by accident?," a young child usually answers that the person who breaks 10 dishes by accident is more guilty because more dishes are broken. Children in this stage have a sense of *immanent justice,* the belief that punishment for bad deeds is inevitable.

Children in this developmental stage are *egocentric:* They see themselves as the center of the universe; they have a limited point of view; and they are unable to take the role of another person. Children are unable to modify their behavior for someone else; for example, children are not being negativistic when they do not listen to commands to be quiet because their brother has to study. Instead, egocentric thinking prevents an understanding of their brother's point of view.

During this stage, children also use a type of magical thinking, called *phenomenalistic causality,* in which events that occur together are thought to cause one another (for example, thunder causes lightning, and bad thoughts cause accidents). In addition, children use *animistic thinking,* which is the tendency to endow physical events and objects with lifelike psychological attributes, such as feelings and intentions.

Semiotic Function. The semiotic function emerges during the preoperational period. With this new ability, children can represent something—such as an object, an event, or a conceptual scheme—with a signifier, which serves a representative function (for example, language, mental image, symbolic gesture). That is, children use a symbol or sign to stand for something else. Drawing is a semiotic function initially done as a playful exercise but eventually signifying something else in the real world.

Stage of Concrete Operations (7 to 11 Years)

The stage of concrete operations is so named because in this period children operate and act on the concrete, real, and perceivable world of objects and events. Egocentric thought is replaced by *operational thought,* which involves dealing with a wide array of information outside the child. Therefore, children can now see things from someone else's perspective.

Children in this stage begin to use limited logical thought processes and are able to serialize, order, and group things in classes on the basis of common characteristics. *Syllogistic reasoning,* in which a logical conclusion is formed from two premises, appears during this stage; for example, all horses are mammals (premise); all mammals are warm blooded (premise); therefore, all horses are warm blooded (conclusion). Children are able to reason and to follow rules and regulations. They are able to regulate themselves, and they begin to develop a moral sense and a code of values.

Children who become overly invested in rules may show obsessive-compulsive behavior; children who resist a code of values often seem willful and inactive. The most desirable development outcome in this stage is that a child attain a healthy respect for rules and understand that there are legitimate exceptions to rules.

Conservation is the ability to recognize that, although the shape of objects may change, the objects still maintain or conserve other characteristics that enable them to be recognized as the same. For example, if a ball of clay is rolled into a long and thin sausage shape, children recognize that each form contains the same amount of clay. An inability to conserve (which is characteristic of the preoperational stage) is observed when a child declares that there is more clay in the sausage-shaped piece because it is longer. *Reversibility* is the capacity to understand the relation between things, to realize that one thing can turn into another and back again—for example, ice and water.

The most important sign that children are still in the preoperational stage is that they have not achieved conservation or reversibility. The ability of children to understand concepts of quantity is one of Piaget's most important cognitive developmental theories. Measures of quantity include measures of substance, length, number, liquids, and area (Fig. 4.1–3).

The 7- to 11-year-old child must organize and order occurrences in the real world. Dealing with the future and its possibilities occurs in the formal operational stage.

Stage of Formal Operations (11 Years Through the End of Adolescence)

The stage of formal operations is so named because young people's thinking operates in a formal, highly logical, systematic, and symbolic manner. This stage is characterized by the ability to think abstractly, to reason deductively, and to define concepts and also by the emergence of skills in dealing with permutations and combinations: Young people can grasp the concept of probabilities. Adolescents attempt to deal with all possible relations and hypotheses to explain data and events. During this stage, language use is complex, follows formal rules of logic, and is grammatically correct. Abstract thinking is shown by adolescents' interest in a variety of issues: philosophy, religion, ethics, and politics.

Hypotheticodeductive Thinking. This thinking is the highest organization of cognition and enables people to make a hypothesis or proposition and to test it against reality. *Deductive reasoning* moves from the general to the particular and is a more complicated process than *inductive reasoning,* which moves from the particular to the general.

Because young people can reflect on their own and other people's thinking, they are prone to self-conscious behavior. As adolescents attempt to master new cognitive tasks, they may return to egocentric thought, but on a higher level than

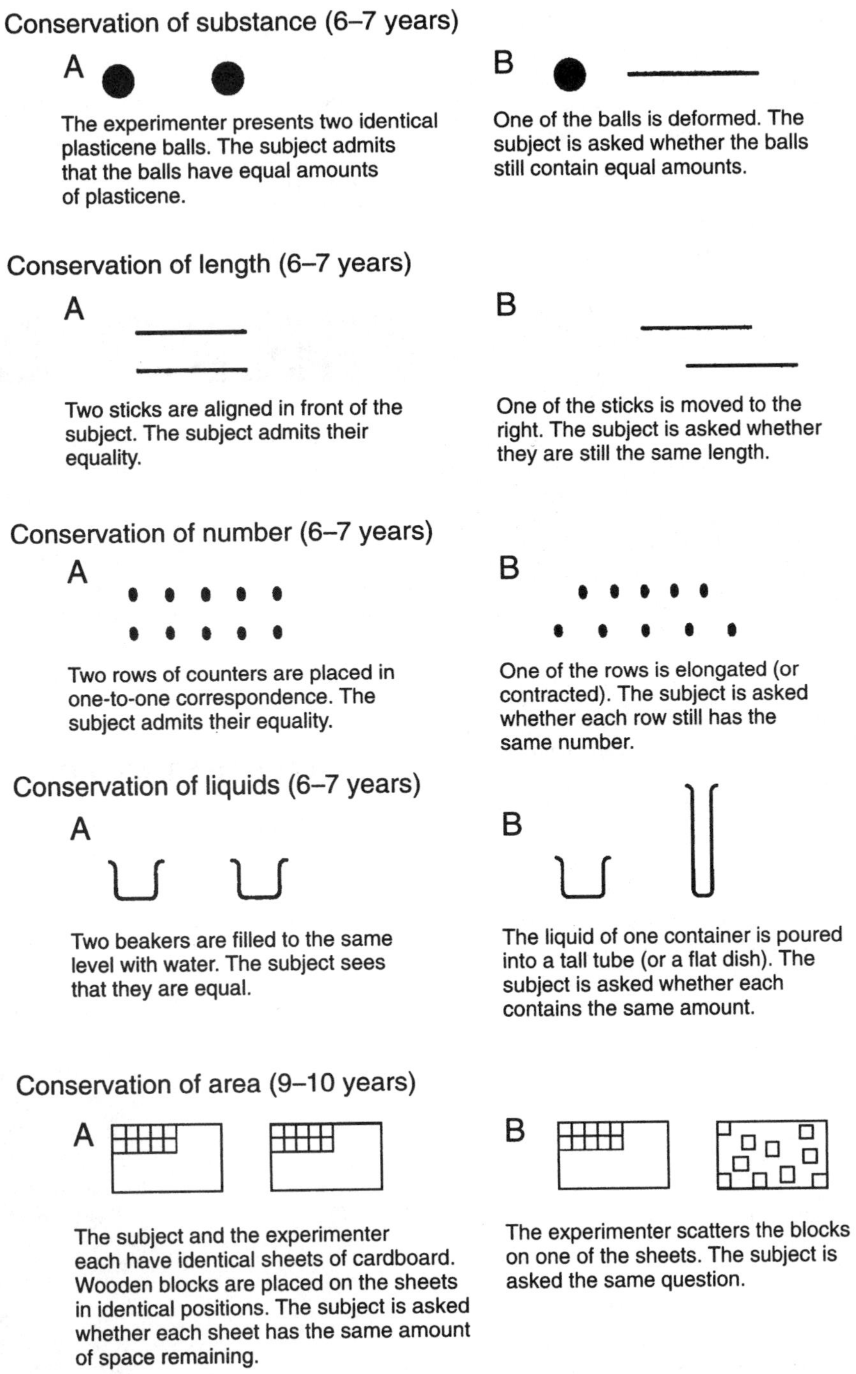
Conservation of substance (6–7 years)
A
The experimenter presents two identical plasticene balls. The subject admits that the balls have equal amounts of plasticene.
B
One of the balls is deformed. The subject is asked whether the balls still contain equal amounts.
Conservation of length (6–7 years)
A
Two sticks are aligned in front of the subject. The subject admits their equality.
B
One of the sticks is moved to the right. The subject is asked whether they are still the same length.
Conservation of number (6–7 years)
A
Two rows of counters are placed in one-to-one correspondence. The subject admits their equality.
B
One of the rows is elongated (or contracted). The subject is asked whether each row still has the same number.
Conservation of liquids (6–7 years)
A
Two beakers are filled to the same level with water. The subject sees that they are equal.
B
The liquid of one container is poured into a tall tube (or a flat dish). The subject is asked whether each contains the same amount.
Conservation of area (9–10 years)
A
The subject and the experimenter each have identical sheets of cardboard. Wooden blocks are placed on the sheets in identical positions. The subject is asked whether each sheet has the same amount of space remaining.
B
The experimenter scatters the blocks on one of the sheets. The subject is asked the same question.

FIGURE 4.1–3
Some simple tests for conservation, with approximate ages of attainment. When the sense of conservation is achieved, the child answers that **B** contains the same quantity as that in **A.** (Reprinted with permission from Lefrancois GR: *Of Children: An Introduction to Child Development,* p 305. Wadsworth, Belmont, CA, 1973.)

in the past. For example, adolescents may think that they can accomplish everything or can change events by thought alone. Not all adolescents enter the stage of formal operations at the same time or to the same degree. Depending on individual capacity and intervening experience, some may not reach the stage of formal operational thought at all and may remain in the concrete operational mode throughout life.

PSYCHIATRIC APPLICATIONS

Piaget's theories have many psychiatric implications. Hospitalized children who are in the sensorimotor stage have not achieved object permanence and, therefore, suffer from separation anxiety. They are best off if their mothers are allowed to stay with them overnight. Children at the preoperational stage, who are unable to deal with concepts and abstractions, benefit more from role-playing proposed medical procedures and situations than by having them verbally described in detail. For example, a child who is to receive intravenous therapy is helped by acting out the procedure with a toy intravenous set and dolls.

Because children at the preoperational stage do not understand cause and effect, they may interpret physical illness as punishment for bad thoughts or deeds; and because they have not yet mastered the capacity to conserve and do not understand the concept of reversibility (which normally occurs during the concrete operational stage), they cannot understand that a broken bone mends or that blood lost in an accident is replaced.

Adolescents' thinking, during the stage of formal operations, may appear overly abstract when it is, in fact, a normal developmental stage. Adolescent turmoil may not herald a psychotic process but may well be the result of a normal adolescent's coming to grips with newly acquired abilities to deal with the unlimited possibilities of the surrounding world.

Adults under stress may regress cognitively as well as emotionally: Their thinking can become preoperational, egocentric, and sometimes animistic.

Despite their psychiatric applications, Piaget's theories have been applied more widely in the area of education. Piaget's concepts have been used to resolve educational problems, such as assessing intellectual development, scholastic aptitude, grade placement, and reading readiness. Innovative early school programs such as Head Start, which provide an enriched environment for children from families at low socioeconomic levels, can be traced to Piaget's belief that experience plays a major role in the maturation of cognitive functioning. Throughout his writings, Piaget emphasized that the greater the richness, complexity, and diversity of the environment, the greater the likelihood that high levels of mental functioning are achieved.

REFERENCES

Chapman M: *Constructive Evolution: Origins and Development of Piaget's Thought.* Cambridge University Press, Cambridge, UK, 1988.

Elkind D: Piagetian psychology and the practice of child psychiatry. J Am Acad Child Psychiatry *21:* 435, 1982.

Feinstein SC, Berndt DJ: Assimilating Piaget. Cognitive structures and depressive reaction to loss. Adolesc Psychiatry *20:* 23, 1995.

Flavell J: *The Developmental Psychology of Jean Piaget.* Van Nostrand, New York, 1963.

Ginsburg H, Brant SO: *Piaget's Theory of Intellectual Development,* ed 3. Prentice-Hall, Englewood Cliffs, NJ, 1988.

Greenspan ST, Curry JF: Piaget's approach to intellectual functioning. In *Comprehensive Textbook of Psychiatry,* ed 5, HI Kaplan, BJ Sadock, editors, p 256. Williams & Wilkins, Baltimore, 1989.

Kitchener RF: *Piaget's Theory of Knowledge: Genetic Epistemology and Scientific Reason.* Yale University Press, New Haven, 1986.

Matteson MA, Linton AD, Barnes SJ, Cleary BL, Lichtenstein MJ: The relationship between Piaget and cognitive levels in persons with Alzheimer's disease and related disorders. Aging *8:* 61, 1996.

Moses N, Klein HB, Altman E: An approach to assessing and facilitating causal language in adults with learning disabilities based on piagetian theory. J Learn Disabil *23:* 220, 1990.

Piaget J: *Genetic Epistemology.* Columbia University Press, New York, 1973.

Piaget J: *The Grasp of Consciousness.* Harvard University Press, Cambridge, MA, 1976.

Piaget J: *Judgement and Reasoning in the Child.* Harcourt, New York, 1926.

Piaget J: *The Language and Thought of the Child.* Routledge & Kegan Paul, London, 1926.

Piaget J: *Logic and Psychology.* Basic Books, New York, 1957.

Piaget J: *The Moral Judgement of the Child.* Harcourt, New York, 1932.

Piaget J: *The Origins of Intelligence in Children.* International Universities Press, New York, 1952.

Piaget J: *Play, Dreams, and Imitation in Childhood.* Norton, New York, 1951.

Piaget J, Inhelder B: *Memory and Intelligence.* Basic Books, New York, 1973.

Piaget J, Inhelder B: *The Origin of the Idea of Chance in Children.* Norton, New York, 1975.

Piaget J, Inhelder B: *The Psychology of the Child.* Basic Books, New York, 1969.

Richards R: Beyond Piaget: Accepting divergent, chaotic, and creative thought. New Dir Child Dev *72:* 67, 1996.

Soffer J: Jean Piaget and George Kelly: Toward a stronger constructivism. Int J Construct Psychol *6:* 59, 1993.

▲ 4.2 Attachment Theory

A secure attachment between mother and child in infancy affects people's ability to form healthy relationships in life. Human social groups, primates, and many other animals develop attachments in infancy.

Attachment can be defined as the emotional tone between children and their caregivers and is evidenced by an infant's seeking and clinging to the caregiving person, usually the mother. By their first month, infants usually have begun to show such behavior, which is designed to promote proximity to the desired person.

ATTACHMENT AND DEVELOPMENT

John Bowlby, a British psychoanalyst (1907–1990), formulated the theory that normal attachment in infancy is crucial to people's healthy development (Fig. 4.2–1). According to

FIGURE 4.2–1
John Bowlby.

Bowlby, attachment occurs when there is a "warm, intimate and continuous relationship with the mother in which both find satisfaction and enjoyment." Being monotropic, infants tend to attach to one person; but they may form attachments to several people, such as the father or a surrogate. Attachment develops gradually; it results in an infant's wanting to be with a preferred person, who is perceived as stronger, wiser, and able to reduce anxiety or distress. Attachment thus gives infants feelings of security. The process is facilitated by interaction between mother and infant; the amount of time together is less important than the amount of activity between the two.

The term *bonding* is sometimes used synonymously with attachment, but the two are different phenomena. *Bonding* concerns the mother's feelings for her infant and differs from attachment: Mothers do not normally rely on their infants as a source of security, as is the case in attachment behavior. Much research reveals that the bonding of mother to infant occurs when there is skin-to-skin contact between the two or when other types of contact, such as voice and eye contact, are made. Some workers have concluded that a mother who has skin-to-skin contact with her baby immediately after birth shows a stronger bonding pattern and may provide more attentive care than does a mother who does not have this experience. Some researchers have even proposed a critical period immediately after birth, during which such skin-to-skin contact must occur if bonding is to take place. This concept is much disputed: Many mothers are clearly bonded to their infants and display excellent maternal care even though they did not have skin-to-skin contact immediately postpartum. Because human beings can develop representational models of their babies in utero and even before conception, this representational thinking may be as important to the bonding process as is skin, voice, or eye contact.

Signal Indicators

Signal indicators are infants' signs of distress that prompt or elicit a behavioral response in the mother. The primary signal is crying; there are three types: hunger (the most common), anger, and pain. Some mothers are able to distinguish between them, but most mothers generalize the hunger cry to represent distress from pain, frustration, or anger. Other signal indicators that reinforce attachment are smiling, cooing, and looking. The sound of an adult human voice can prompt these indicators.

Ethological Studies

Bowlby suggested a darwinian evolutionary basis for attachment behavior: Such behavior ensures that adults protect their young. Ethological studies show that nonhuman primates and other animals show attachment behavior patterns that are presumably instinctual and are governed by inborn tendencies. An example of an instinctual attachment system is *imprinting,* in which certain stimuli are capable of eliciting innate behavior patterns during the first few hours of an animal's behavioral development; thus, the animal offspring becomes attached to its mother at a critical period early in its development. A similar sensitive or critical period during which attachment occurs has been postulated for human infants. The presence of imprinting behavior in humans is highly controversial, but bonding and attachment behavior during the first year of life closely approximate the critical period; in humans, however, this period occurs over a span of years rather than hours.

Harry Harlow. Harry Harlow's work with monkeys is relevant to attachment theory. Harlow demonstrated the emotional and behavioral effects of isolating monkeys from birth and keeping them from forming attachments. The isolates were withdrawn, unable to relate to peers, unable to mate, and incapable of caring for their offspring. (Harlow's work is discussed further in Section 4.5.)

PHASES OF ATTACHMENT

In the first attachment phase, sometimes called the *preattachment stage* (birth to 8 or 12 weeks), babies orient to their mothers, follow them with their eyes over a 180-degree range, and turn toward and move rhythmically with their mother's voices. In the second phase, sometimes called *attachment in the making* (8 or 12 weeks to 6 months), infants become attached to one or more people in the environment. In the third phase, sometimes called *clear-cut attachment* (6 through 24 months), infants cry and show other signs of distress when separated from the caretaker or mother; this phase may occur as early as 3 months in some infants. On being returned to the mother, the infant stops crying and clings, as if to gain further assurance of the mother's return. Sometimes, seeing the mother after a separation is sufficient for crying to stop. In the fourth phase (25 months and beyond), the mother figure is seen as independent, and a more complex relationship between the mother and the child develops.

Table 4.2–1 summarizes the development of normal attachment from birth through 3 years.

Separation

Separation from the attachment figure may or may not produce intense anxiety, depending on children's developmental levels and their current phases of attachment.

Expressed as tearfulness or irritability, *separation anxiety* is the response of a child who is isolated or separated from its mother or caretaker. It is most common at 10 to 18 months of age and disappears generally by the end of the third year. Somewhat earlier (at about 8 months) *stranger anxiety,* an anxiety response to someone other than the caregiver, appears.

ANXIETY

Bowlby's theory of anxiety holds that children's sense of distress during separation is perceived and experienced as anxiety and is the prototype of anxiety. Any stimuli that alarm children and cause fear (such as loud noises, falling, and cold blasts of air) mobilize signal indicators (for example, crying) that cause the mother to respond in a caring way by cuddling and reassuring the child. The mother's ability to relieve the infant's anxiety or fear is fundamental to the growth of attachment in the infant. When the mother is close to the child and the child experiences no fear, the child gains a sense of *security,* the opposite of anxiety. When the mother is unavailable to the infant because of physical absence (for example, if the

Table 4.2–1
Normal Attachment

Birth to 30 Days
- Reflexes at birth
  - Rooting
  - Head turning
  - Sucking
  - Swallowing
  - Hand-mouth
  - Grasp
  - Digital extension
  - Crying—signal for particular kind of distress
  - Responsiveness and orientation to mother's face, eyes, and voice
- 4 days—anticipatory approach behavior at feeding
- 3 to 4 weeks—infant smiles preferentially to mother's voice

Age 30 Days Through 3 Months
- Vocalization and gaze reciprocity further elaborated from 1 to 3 months; babbling at 2 months, more with the mother than with a stranger
- Social smile
- In strange situation, increased clinging response to mother

Age 4 Through 6 Months
- Briefly soothed and comforted by sound of mother's voice
- Spontaneous, voluntary reaching for mother
- Anticipatory posturing to be picked up
- Differential preference for mother intensifies
- Subtle integration of responses to mother

Age 7 Through 9 Months
- Attachment behaviors further differentiated and focused specifically on mother
- Separation distress, stranger distress, strange-place distress

Age 10 Through 15 Months
- Crawls or walks toward mother
- Subtle facial expressions (coyness, attentiveness)
- Responsive dialogue with mother clearly established
- Early imitation of mother (vocal inflections, facial expression)
- More fully developed separation distress and mother preference
- Pointing gesture
- Walking to and from mother
- Affectively positive reunion responses to mother after separation or, paradoxically, short-lived, active avoidance or delayed protest

Age 16 Months Through 2 Years
- Involvement in imitative jargon with mother (12 to 14 months)
- Head-shaking "no" (15 to 16 months)
- Transitional object used during the absence of mother
- Separation anxiety diminishes
- Mastery of strange situations and persons when mother is near
- Evidence of delayed imitation
- Object permanence
- Microcosmic symbolic play

Age 25 Months Through 3 Years
- Able to tolerate separations from mother without distress when familiar with surroundings and given reassurances about mother's return
- Two- and three-word speech
- Stranger anxiety much reduced
- Object consistency achieved—maintains composure and psychosocial functioning without regression in absence of mother
- Microcosmic play and social play; cooperation with others begins

Based on material by Justin Call, M.D.

mother is in prison) or because of psychological impairment (such as severe depression), anxiety develops in the infant.

Mary Ainsworth

Mary Ainsworth expanded on Bowlby's observations and found that the interaction between the mother and her baby during the attachment period significantly influences the baby's current and future behavior. Patterns of attachments vary among babies; for example, some babies signal or cry less than others. Sensitive responsiveness to infant signals, such as cuddling a crying baby, causes infants to cry less in later months, rather than reinforcing crying behavior. Close bodily contact with the mother when the baby signals for her is also associated with the growth of self-reliance, rather than a clinging dependence, as the baby grows older. Unresponsive mothers produce anxious babies; these mothers often have lower intelligence quotients (IQs) and are emotionally more immature and younger than responsive mothers.

Ainsworth also confirmed that attachment serves the purpose of reducing anxiety. What she called the secure base effect enables children to move away from attachment figures and to explore the environment. Inanimate objects, such as a teddy bear and a blanket (called the *transitional object* by Donald Winnicott), also serve as a secure base, one that often accompanies them as they investigate the world.

Strange Situation. Ainsworth developed *strange situation,* the research protocol for assessing the quality and security of an infant's attachment. In this procedure, the infant is exposed to escalating amounts of stress: For example, the infant and the parent enter an unfamiliar room; an unfamiliar adult then enters the room, and the parent leaves the room. The protocol has seven steps (Table 4.2–2). According to Ainsworth's studies, about 65 percent of infants are securely attached by the age of 24 months.

ATTACHMENT THROUGHOUT THE LIFE CYCLE

As Bowlby hypothesized, attachment behavior persists throughout life, from the cradle to the grave. Clinical studies

Table 4.2–2
The Strange Situation

Episode[a]	Persons Present	Change
1	Parent, infant	Enter room
2	Parent, infant, stranger	Unfamiliar adult joins the dyad
3	Infant, stranger	Parent leaves
4	Parent, infant	Parent returns, stranger leaves
5	Infant	Parent leaves
6	Infant, stranger	Stranger returns
7	Parent, infant	Parent returns, stranger leaves

Reprinted with permission from Lamb ME, Nash A, Teti DM, Bornstein MH: Infancy. In *Child and Adolescent Psychiatry: A Comprehensive Textbook,* M Lewis, editor, ed 2, p 256. Williams & Wilkins, Baltimore, 1996.

[a] All episodes are usually three minutes long, but episodes 3, 5, and 6 can be curtailed if the infant becomes too distressed, and episodes 4 and 7 are sometimes extended.

have shown attachment behavior in middle childhood, adolescence, and adulthood. College students away from home for the first time make good social adjustments if their early attachments to caretakers were secure. Low self-esteem, poor social relatedness, and emotional vulnerability to stress are associated with insecure attachments during the first year of life.

Human beings continue to be attached to their parents, regardless of whether their early attachments were optimal. At various stages in life, attachments are made to others—such as teachers, relatives, coaches, and older siblings—especially when parental attachments are poor or inadequate. These attachment figures are cast in the parental role and may be mentors or even therapists. By inspiring trust, they provide a secure base from which people gain confidence in themselves and in their ability to deal with the outside world. Thus, new attachment figures promote corrective emotional experiences. In addition, George Vaillant's finding that early, close sibling relationships are related to adult mental health points to the importance of developing and maintaining attachments.

Affectional bonds that later develop between children and people other than parents have attachment components in them. Sharing experiences is important in many attachment bonds, such as those between siblings, friends, relatives, and marital pairs. The adult attachment bond, however, is unique in that it provides a sense of being able to give. Nevertheless, the absence of the attachment figure makes a person feel lonely or anxious. Love relationships are a major factor in maintaining emotional stability throughout life.

Day Care

The effect of day care experiences on infants' attachment processes is controversial. Some studies have shown that day care of more than 20 hours a week during the first year results in insecure attachments, but no consistent findings have emerged. In view of the fact that most infants in day care are securely attached to their mothers, such programs seem to have no adverse effects, provided they are of high quality and have competent, nurturing caregivers. (See Chapter 30 for a further discussion of day care.)

Losing Attachments

People's reactions to the death of a parent or a spouse can be traced to the nature of their past and present attachment to the lost figure. An absence of demonstrable grief may be due to real experiences of rejection and to the lack of closeness in the relationship. The person may even consciously offer an idealized picture of the deceased. People who show no grief usually try to present themselves as independent and as disinterested in closeness and attachment.

Sometimes, however, the severing of attachments is traumatic. The death of a parent or a spouse can precipitate a depressive disorder, and even suicide, in some people. The death of a spouse increases the chance that the surviving spouse will experience a physical or mental disorder during the next year. The onset of depression and other dysphoric states often involves having been rejected by a significant figure in a person's life.

DISORDERS OF ATTACHMENT

Attachment disorders are characterized by biopsychosocial pathology that results from maternal deprivation, a lack of care by and interaction with the mother or caregiver. Failure-to-thrive syndromes, psychosocial dwarfism, separation anxiety disorder, avoidant personality disorder, depressive disorders, delinquency, academic problems, and borderline intelligence have been traced to negative attachment experiences. When maternal care is deficient because a mother is mentally ill, because a child is institutionalized for a long time, or because the primary object of attachment dies, children suffer emotional damage. Bowlby originally thought that the damage was permanent and invariable, but he revised his theories to take into account the time at which the separation occurred, the type and degree of separation, and the level of security that the child experienced before the separation.

Bowlby described a predictable set and sequence of behavior patterns in children who are separated from their mothers for long periods (more than 3 months): *protest,* in which the child protests against the separation by crying, calling out, and searching for the lost person; *despair,* in which the child appears to lose hope that the mother will return; and *detachment,* in which the child emotionally separates himself or herself from the mother. Bowlby believed that this sequence involves ambivalent feelings toward the mother; the child both wants her and is angry at her for her desertion.

Children in the detachment stage respond in an indifferent manner when the mother returns; the mother has not been forgotten, but the child is angry at her for having gone away in the first place and fears that she will go away again. Some children have affectionless personalities characterized by emotional withdrawal, little or no feeling, and a limited ability to form affectionate relationships.

Anaclitic Depression

Anaclitic depression, also known as hospitalism, was first described by René Spitz in infants who had made normal attachments but were then suddenly separated from their mothers for varying times and placed in institutions or hospitals. The children became depressed, withdrawn, nonresponsive, and vulnerable to physical illness but recovered when their mothers returned or when surrogate mothering was available.

CHILD MALTREATMENT

Abused children often maintain their attachments to abusive parents. Studies of dogs have shown that severe punishment and maltreatment increase attachment behavior. When children are hungry, sick, or in pain, they too show clinging attachment behavior. Similarly, when children are rejected by their parents or are afraid of them, their attachment may increase; some children want to remain with an abusive parent. Nevertheless, when a choice must be made between a punishing and a nonpunishing figure, the nonpunishing person is the preferable choice, especially if the person is sensitive to the child's needs. (Child abuse is discussed at length in Chapter 31.)

PSYCHIATRIC APPLICATIONS

The applications of attachment theory in psychotherapy are numerous. When a patient is able to attach to a therapist, a secure base effect is seen. The patient may then be able to take risks, mask anxiety, and practice new patterns of behavior that otherwise might not have been attempted. Patients whose impairments can be traced to never having made an attachment in early life may do so for the first time in therapy, with salutary effects.

Patients whose pathology stems from exaggerated early attachments may attempt to replicate them in therapy. Therapists must enable such patients to recognize the ways their early experiences have interfered with the patients' ability to achieve independence.

For patients who are children and whose attachment difficulties may be more apparent than those in adults, therapists represent consistent and trusted figures who can engender a sense of warmth and self-esteem in children, often for the first time.

References

Ainsworth MS: Attachments across the life span. Bull NY Acad Med *61:* 792, 1985.

Bowlby J: *Attachment and Loss,* vols 1, 2, 3. Basic Books, New York, 1969, 1973, 1980.

Bowlby J: *Maternal Care and Mental Health.* World Health Organization, Geneva, 1951.

Bowlby J: The nature of the child's tie to his mother. Int J Psychoanal *39:* 350, 1958.

Crittenden PM: Children's strategies for coping with adverse home environments: An interpretation using attachment theory. Child Abuse Negl *16:* 329, 1992.

DeFrain JD, Jakub DK, Mendoza BL: The psychological effects of sudden infant death on grandmothers and grandfathers. Omega J Death Dying *24:* 165, 1992.

George C: A representational perspective of child abuse and prevention: Internal working models of attachment and caregiving. Child Abuse Negl *20:* 411, 1996.

High H: Impediments to the development of attachment. Psychoanal Psychother *6:* 107, 1992.

Klaus MH, Kennell JH: *Bonding: The Beginnings of Parent–Infant Attachment.* Mosby, St. Louis, 1983.

Klaus MH, Kennell JH: *Parent–Infant Bonding,* ed 2. Mosby, St. Louis, 1982.

Papovsek KH, Papovsek M: The evolution of parent–infant attachment: New psychobiological perspectives. In *Frontiers of Infant Psychiatry,* JD Can, editor, vol 2, p 276. Saunders, Philadelphia, 1984.

Routh CP, Hill JW, Steele H, Elliott CE, Dewey ME: Maternal attachment status, psychosocial stressors and problem behaviour: Follow-up after parent training courses for conduct disorder. J Child Psychol Psychiatry *36:* 1179, 1995.

Ward MJ, Carlson EA: Associations among adult attachment representations, maternal sensitivity, and infant-mother attachment in a sample of adolescent mothers. Child Dev *66:* 69, 1995.

▲ 4.3 Learning Theory

Strictly defined, *learning* is a behavioral change in a specific situation, produced by repeated experiences of the situation, as long as the changed behavior is not dependent on native response tendencies, maturation, or temporary state. Cognition, environment, and behavior interact to produce the learned change.

Measuring an aspect of performance, such as the accuracy of a motor skill or the ability to recognize and repeat words, is a means of assessing learning. Learning and performance are related but should not be confused: When performance is adversely affected by insufficient motivation or by anxiety, learning that has occurred may not be demonstrable. Performance may also be impaired in *state-dependent learning*—the facilitated recall of information by a person in the same internal state or external environment in which the information was first acquired. When a behavior is acquired under the influence of a pharmacological agent and tests for learning are carried out in the absence of the drug, there may be little or no evidence of acquisition. When the learning test is carried out under the influence of the drug, however, performance may change, and learning may then be demonstrated.

Among the building blocks of learning theory are classical and operant conditioning. In *classical conditioning,* learning is thought to take place as a result of the contiguity of environmental events: When events occur closely together in time, people will probably come to associate the two. In the case of *operant conditioning,* learning is thought to occur as a result of the consequences of a person's actions and the resultant effect on the environment. As B. F. Skinner (1904–1990) stated, "A person does not act upon the world, the world acts upon him." Skinner, in his definition of the sphere of interest of psychology, specifically eschewed the role of intervening variables such as thoughts. *Social learning theory* incorporates both classical and operant models of learning but also considers a reciprocal interaction between the person and the environment. Cognitive processes are viewed as important factors in modulating people's responses to environmental events.

Psychoanalytic theory and practice developed concurrently with learning theory, and attempts have been made over the past half century to integrate the two theoretical approaches. For example, in 1950 John Dollard and Neal Miller reformulated many psychoanalytic concepts in terms of learning theory. Such attempts, however, have had little lasting influence on psychoanalytic thought or therapy.

Workers recently have shown much interest in the neurophysiological and biochemical components of learning. Eric Kandel's research with simple organisms, such as the *Aplysia,* a sea snail, has revealed that the learning of avoidance behavior alters the chemical structure of cells in the nervous system. When the avoidance is unlearned, these chemical changes are reversed. Such research provides a foundation for understanding the neurochemistry of learning and for exploring reciprocal interactions between ongoing biological processes in the central nervous system and behavior changes resulting from environmental influences.

CONDITIONING

Researchers have described two types of conditioning: classical and operant.

Classical or Respondent Conditioning

Classical or respondent conditioning results from the repeated pairing of a neutral (conditioned) stimulus with one that evokes a response (unconditioned stimulus), such that the neutral stimulus eventually comes to evoke the response. The time relation between the presentation of the conditioned and unconditioned stimuli is important and varies for optimal learning from a fraction of a second to several seconds.

The Russian physiologist and Nobel prize winner, Ivan Petrovich Pavlov (1849–1936) (Fig. 4.3–1), observed in his work on gastric secretion that a dog salivated not only when food

FIGURE 4.3–1.
Ivan Pavlov.

was placed in its mouth but also at the sound of the footsteps of the person coming to feed the dog, even though the dog could not see or smell the food. Pavlov analyzed these events and called the saliva flow that occurred with the sound of footsteps a *conditioned response* (CR)—a response elicited under certain conditions by a particular stimulus.

In a typical pavlovian experiment, a *stimulus* (S) that had no capacity to evoke a particular response before training did so after consistent association with another stimulus. For example, under normal circumstances, a dog does not salivate at the sound of a bell, but when the bell sound is always followed by the presentation of food, the dog ultimately pairs the bell and the food. Eventually, the bell sound alone elicits salivation (CR).

Because the food naturally produces salivation, it is referred to as an *unconditioned stimulus* (UCS). Salivation, a response that is reliably elicited by food (UCS), is referred to as an *unconditioned response* (UCR). The bell, which was originally unable to evoke salivation but came to do so when paired with food, is referred to as a *conditioned stimulus* (CS). Classical conditioning is most often applied to responses mediated by the autonomic nervous system.

Classical conditioning is diagramed as follows:

Before Conditioning

Food (UCS) → Salivation (UCR)

Bell (CS) paired with food (UCS) → Salivation (UCR)

After Conditioning

Bell (CS) → Salivation (CR)

Extinction. Extinction occurs when the conditioned stimulus is constantly repeated without the unconditioned stimulus until the response evoked by the conditioned stimulus gradually weakens and eventually disappears. In the previous example, extinction would occur if the bell (CS) is repeatedly rung without the food (UCS) being given. Eventually, salivation (CR) does not occur when the bell sounds, and extinction occurs. Extinction, however, does not completely destroy a conditioned response. If an animal is rested after extinction, the conditioned response returns, although less strong than originally, a phenomenon known as *partial recovery*.

The American psychologist John B. Watson (1878–1958) used Pavlov's theory of classical conditioning to explain certain aspects of human behavior. In 1920, Watson described producing a phobia in an 11-month-old boy called Little Albert. At the same time that the boy was shown a white rat that he initially did not fear, he was exposed to a loud, frightening noise. After several such pairings, Albert became fearful of the white rat even when he heard no loud noise. Watson and his colleagues obtained the same results using a white rabbit and eventually managed to generalize the response to any furry object. Many theorists believe that this process accounts for the development of childhood phobias, which are considered learned responses based on classical conditioning.

Stimulus Generalization. *Stimulus generalization* describes a process whereby a conditioned response is transferred from one stimulus to another. Animals respond to stimuli similar to the original conditioned stimulus: A dog conditioned to respond to a bell also responds to the sound of a tuning fork. The theory of stimulus generalization is sometimes used to explain higher learning by showing how people learn similarities. For example, a street sign is recognized whether it is on a pole, a building, or a curb because there is sufficient stimulus similarity for generalization to occur.

Discrimination. *Discrimination* is the process of recognizing and responding to differences between similar stimuli. If the two stimuli are sufficiently different, an animal can learn to respond to one and not to the other; for example, an animal can learn to respond differentially to similar bells. A child learns to discriminate four-legged animals (the common stimulus) into dogs, cats, cows, and other quadrupeds.

When learning is viewed as a balance of generalization and discrimination, some disorders of thinking can be considered to stem from difficulties with these two processes. A person who had a traumatic childhood experience with a person who wore a moustache may transfer these negative feelings to all men with moustaches; this example shows both faulty discrimination and stimulus generalization.

Operant Conditioning

Skinner's theory of learning and behavior is known as operant or instrumental conditioning. Whereas in classical conditioning an animal is passive or restrained and behavior is reinforced by the experimenter, in operant conditioning the animal is active and behaves in a way that produces a reward; thus learning occurs as a consequence of action. For example, a rat receives a reinforcing stimulus (food) only when it correctly responds by pressing a lever. Food, approval, praise, good grades, or any other response that satisfies a need in an animal or a person can serve as a reward.

Operant conditioning is related to trial-and-error learning, as described by the American psychologist Edward L. Thorndike (1874–1949). In trial-and-error learning, a person or an animal attempts to solve a problem by trying different actions until one proves successful: A freely moving organism behaves in a way that is instrumental in producing a reward. For example, a cat in a Thorndike puzzle box must learn to lift a latch to escape from the box. For this reason, operant conditioning is sometimes called *instrumental conditioning.* Thorndike's law of effect states that certain responses are reinforced by reward and the organism learns from these experiences.

Four kinds of instrumental or operant conditioning are described in Table 4.3–1: primary reward conditioning, escape conditioning, avoidance conditioning, and secondary reward conditioning.

Respondent and Operant Behavior. Skinner described two types of behavior: *respondent behavior,* which results from known stimuli (for example, the knee jerk reflex to patellar stimulation or the pupillary constriction to light), and *operant behavior,* which is independent of a stimulus (for example, the random movements of an infant or the aimless movements of a laboratory rat in a cage). Skinner took advantage of operant behavior by placing a rat in a Skinner box (named after him, its developer). The rat was deprived of food; in the course of moving around the box, it randomly pressed a bar. At some point in the experiment, food was released by the experimenter when the bar was pressed. The food reinforced the bar pressing, which increased or decreased in rate depending on the level of reinforcement given by the experimenter. A *reinforcer* is anything that maintains a response or increases its strength; the term is used synonymously with *reward.* Some workers, however, distinguish between the two and point out that responses are reinforced, whereas subjects are rewarded.

Table 4.3–1
Four Kinds of Operant or Instrumental Conditioning

Primary reward conditioning	The simplest kind of conditioning. The learned response is instrumental in obtaining a biologically significant reward, such as a pellet of food or a drink of water.
Escape conditioning	The organism learns a response that is instrumental in getting out of some place it prefers not to be.
Avoidance conditioning	The kind of learning in which a response to a cue is instrumental in avoiding a painful experience. A rat on a grid, for example, may avoid a shock if it quickly pushes a lever when a light signal goes on.
Secondary reward conditioning	The kind of learning in which instrumental behavior to get at a stimulus has no biological usefulness itself but has in the past been associated with a biologically significant stimulus. For example, chimpanzees learn to press a lever to obtain poker chips, which they insert into a slot to secure grapes. Later, they work to accumulate poker chips even when they are not interested in grapes.

Reinforcement Schedule (Programming). Reinforcers are described as *primary* when independent of previous learning (for example, the need for food or water) or *secondary* when based on previously rewarded learning (for example, giving money to a child with good grades). In operant conditioning, it is possible to vary the schedule of reward or reinforcement for a behavioral pattern in a process known as programming. The intervals between reinforcements may be *fixed* (for example, every third response is rewarded) or *variable* (for example, sometimes, the third response is rewarded; at other times, the sixth response is rewarded).

A *continuous reinforcement* (also called contingency reinforcement or management) schedule, in which every response is reinforced, leads to the most rapid acquisition of a behavior. Reinforcing a response only a fraction of the times the behavior occurs is called *partial reinforcement.* Partial or intermittent reinforcement is effective in maintaining behavior that is resistant to extinction. For example, a person uses a gambling slot machine most frequently when the reward is partially reinforced—that is, when money is won at variable times. This procedure keeps the gambler guessing or trying to anticipate when a payoff will occur. The strength of operant learning is reflected in the frequency of responses: A high response frequency indicates strong operant learning, and a decrease in frequency indicates that extinction is occurring. Table 4.3–2 lists the effects of various reinforcement schedules on behavior.

In operant conditioning, *positive reinforcement* is the process by which certain consequences of a response increase the probability that the response will recur. Food, water, praise, and money are positive reinforcers. On the other hand, events aversive to some may be reinforcing for others. For example, the behavior of some children is reinforced by scolding, which, after all, is a form of attention. Many substances also appear to be positive reinforcers, including opium, cocaine, nicotine, and barbiturates.

Negative reinforcement is a process by which a response that leads to the removal of an aversive event is increased. For example, a teenager mows the lawn to avoid parental complaints, or an animal jumps off a grid to escape a painful shock. Any behavior that enables a person or another animal to avoid or escape a punishing consequence is strengthened.

Negative reinforcement is not punishment. *Punishment* is an aversive stimulus (for example, a slap) that is presented specifically to weaken or suppress an undesired response; punishment reduces the probability that a response will recur. The usual use of the term *punishment* must be distinguished from the technical use of the term. In learning theory, the punishing event delivered is always contingent on performance and demonstrably reduces the frequency of the behavior being punished. This meaning differs from the use of the term to denote

Table 4.3–2
Reinforcement Schedules in Operant Conditioning

Reinforcement Schedule	Example	Behavioral Effect
Fixed-ratio (FR) schedule	Reinforcement occurs after every 10 responses (10:1 ratio); 10 bar presses release a food pellet; workers are paid for every 10 items they make.	Rapid rate of response to obtain the greatest number of rewards. Animal knows that the next reinforcement depends on a certain number of responses being made.
Variable-ratio (VR) schedule	Variable reinforcement occurs (eg, after the third, sixth, then second response, and so on).	Generates a fairly constant rate of response because the probability of reinforcement at any given time remains relatively stable.
Fixed-interval (FI) schedule	Reinforcement occurs at regular intervals (eg, every 10 minutes or every third hour).	Animal keeps track of time. Rate of responding drops to near 0 after reinforcement and then increases at about the expected time of reward.
Variable-interval (VI) schedule	Reinforcement occurs after variable intervals (eg, every 3, 6, and then 2 hours), similar to VR schedule.	Response rate does not change between reinforcements. Animal responds at a steady rate to get the reward when it is available; common in trout fishermen, use of slot machines, checking mailbox.

imprisonment, for example, because the prison sentence follows long after the crime has been committed and may not affect future criminal behavior.

Aversive Control. In aversive control or conditioning, an organism changes its behavior to avoid a painful, noxious, or aversive stimulus. Electric shocks are common aversive stimuli used in laboratory experiments. Any behavior that avoids an aversive stimulus is reinforced as a result.

Escape Learning and Avoidance Learning. Negative reinforcement is related to two types of learning, escape learning and avoidance learning. In *escape learning,* an animal learns a response to get out of a place where it does not want to be (for example, an animal jumps off an electric grid whenever the grid is charged). *Avoidance learning* requires an additional response. The rat on the grid learns to avoid a shock if it quickly pushes a lever when a light signal goes on. To move from escape learning to avoidance learning, an animal must make an *anticipatory response* to prevent the punishment. Escape learning and avoidance learning are two forms of aversive control: Behavior that terminates the source of aversive stimuli is strengthened and maintained.

Shaping Behavior. Shaping involves changing behavior in a deliberate and predetermined way. By reinforcing those responses that are in the desired direction, an experimenter shapes an animal's behavior. When an experimenter wants to train a seal to ring a bell with its nose, the experimenter can give a food reinforcement as the animal's random behavior brings its nose near the bell. To teach a mute schizophrenic patient to talk, a therapist may first reward the patient for simply looking at the therapist; later the therapist reinforces any vocalizations and then simple speech. The closer the time of the reinforcement to the operant behavior, the better the learning. Shaping is also called successive approximation.

Adventitious Reinforcement. Responses accidentally reinforced by coincidental pairing of response and reinforcement are adventitious. Such events may have clinical implications in the development of phobias and other behavior.

Premack's Principle. A concept developed by David Premack states that a behavior engaged in at a high frequency can be used to reinforce a low-frequency behavior. In one experiment, Premack observed that children spent more time playing with a pinball machine than eating candy when both were freely available. When he made playing with the pinball machine contingent on eating a certain amount of candy, the children increased the amount of candy they ate. In a therapeutic application of this principle, patients with schizophrenia were observed to spend more time in a rehabilitation center sitting down doing nothing than they did working at a simple task. When 5 minutes of sitting down was made contingent on a certain amount of work, the work output was considerably increased, as was skill acquisition. This principle is also known as Grandma's rule (''If you eat your spinach, you can have dessert'').

Psychiatric Applications

In 1950, Joseph Wolpe defined anxious behavior as persistent habits of learned or conditioned responses acquired in anxiety-generating situations. If a response inhibitory to anxiety can occur in the presence of anxiety-evoking stimuli, it weakens the connection between the stimuli and the anxiety response. Wolpe referred to this process as *reciprocal inhibition.* Relaxation, for instance, is considered incompatible with anxiety and, therefore, inhibits it.

Anxiety Hierarchy. In Wolpe's method of therapy, known as systematic desensitization, the goal is to eliminate maladaptive anxiety and behavior. To accomplish this goal, Wolpe asked his patients to imagine the least disturbing item on a list of potentially anxiety-evoking stimuli and then to proceed step by step up the list to the most disturbing stimulus. For example, a patient with a fear of heights ranked the sight of a tall building lower in the anxiety hierarchy than standing on a high ledge; being on the 10th floor of a building fell somewhere in between. In a relaxed state (usually induced by hypnosis but sometimes induced by drugs), the patient was instructed to visualize the least anxiety-producing situation; if this visualization did not produce anxiety, the person moved up the hierarchy. Eventually, the patient was desensitized to the source of anxiety.

Tension Reduction Theory. John Dollard and Neal Miller attempted to reconcile behavioral theory and freudian psychodynamics by stressing the commonalities between the two. Subscribing to the tension reduction theory of behavior, they considered behavior as motivated by an organism's attempt to reduce tension produced by unsatisfied or unconscious drives. Sigmund Freud's pleasure principle is a tension-reducing force and, consequently, is a strong motivator. When repressed, fear is learned and transformed into anxiety. In either case, it acts as an acquired drive; thus, a person's behavior may be motivated by an attempt to reduce fear. Early childhood events may be traumatic and may cause anxiety. When such events are repressed, adults may avoid situations that are likely to stimulate anxiety, but they may be completely unaware of their avoidance patterns. Therapy, in part, is an unlearning process. The patient learns that certain behaviors can reduce anxiety, and avoidance patterns are replaced by approach patterns.

Table 4.3–3 gives a comparison of the behavioral and psychoanalytic models.

Learned Helplessness Model of Depression. A laboratory animal may be classically conditioned to accept a painful stimulus when restrained. Such restraint eventually teaches the animal that it has no way to avoid the aversive stimulus. A condition known as learned helplessness develops when an organism learns that no behavioral pattern can influence the environment. The learned helplessness paradigm has been used to explain depression in humans who feel helpless, without options, and unable to control events.

Brain Stimulation and Reinforcement. When certain areas of the hypothalamus are electrically stimulated, intense pleasure is experienced by both humans and other animals. When nonhuman primates were provided with a method by which they could stimulate pleasure centers in their brains, they preferred stimulating themselves to eating or drinking. In human beings, similar phenomena occur; in one case, a patient stimulated his brain 1,000 times in a 6-hour period until he was forced to stop.

COGNITIVE LEARNING

Cognition is the process of obtaining, organizing, and using intellectual knowledge. People perform mental operations and store bits of information in memory to be retrieved later. Cognitive learning theories focus on the role of understanding: Cognition implies an understanding of the connection between cause and effect, between action and the consequences of the action. *Cognitive strategies* are mental plans people use to understand themselves and the environment.

Table 4.3–3
Behavioral and Psychoanalytic Models

Behavioral Model	Psychoanalytic Model
Behavior is determined by current contingencies, reinforcement history, and genetic endowment.	Behavior is determined by intrapsychic processes.
Problem behavior is the focus of study and treatment.	Behavior is but a symbol of intrapsychic processes and a symptom of unconscious conflict. The underlying conflict is the focus of treatment.
Contemporary variables, such as contingencies of reinforcement, are the focus of the analysis.	Historical variables, such as childhood experiences, are the focus of the analysis.
Treatment entails the application of the principles of operant or classical conditioning.	Treatment consists of bringing unconscious conflicts into consciousness.
Objective observation, measurement, and experimentation are the methods used. The focus is on observable behavior and environmental events (antecedents and consequences).	Subjective methods of interpretation of behavior and inference regarding unobservable events (eg, intrapsychic processes) are used.
Theory is based on experimentation.	Theory is predominantly based on case histories.
Tenets can be formulated into testable hypotheses and evaluated through experimentation.	Many tenets cannot be formulated into testable hypotheses to be evaluated through experimentation.

Reprinted with permission from Dorsett PG: Behavioral and social learning psychology. In *Human Behavior: An Introduction for Medical Students,* A Stoudemire, editor, p 105. Lippincott, Philadelphia, 1990.

The cognitive strategy of patients with depression focuses on what is wrong rather than what is right. A form of cognitive therapy developed by Aaron Beck for the treatment of depression teaches patients to recognize and value their assets and alerts them to the cognitive pattern that causes their depression. Beck described the cognitive triad that exists in depression as consisting of a person's negative view of self, negative interpretation of experience, and negative expectation of the future.

Many theorists, such as Jean Piaget, have defined a series of stages in cognitive growth. Another approach toward cognition is *information processing,* a sequence of mental operations involving input, storage, and output of information. Cognition involves calling up and processing relevant information from stored memory.

Behavior can change through techniques in which people learn by listening to or reading instructions. Therapeutic instructions modify both people's outcome and efficacy expectations. For example, patients told that their blood pressure readings would drop if they followed certain relaxation procedures showed a decline in blood pressure. To learn new patterns of behavior, people can monitor their behavior by charting events, such as when they eat or smoke. Self-monitoring also reduces the rate of relapse. If a therapist helps patients define and set realistic and well-specified goals, they have a greater likelihood of achieving them than if goals are poorly defined or unrealistic. Goal attainment enhances self-efficacy, which in turn positively affects future performance.

ATTRIBUTION THEORY

Attribution theory is a cognitive approach concerned with how people perceive the causes of behavior. According to attribution theory, people are likely to attribute their own behavior to situational causes but are likely to attribute others' behavior to stable internal dispositions (personality traits); the particular cause that a person attributes to a given event influences subsequent feelings and behavior. In psychiatry, attribution theory may help explain why some persons attribute a change in behavior to an external event (situation) or to a change in internal state (disposition or ability). Similarly, behavioral change may be attributed to the results of taking a drug or to interpersonal events. Research on drug effects by attribution theorists have shown that it may be unwise to describe a drug as very strong or as very effective because, if it does have the desired effect, patients may believe that is the only reason they got better.

SOCIAL LEARNING THEORY

Social learning theory relies on role modeling, identification, and human interactions. A person can learn by imitating the behavior of another person, but personal factors are involved. When a person dislikes a role model, imitative behavior is not likely to occur. Social learning theorists combine operant and classical conditioning theories. For example, although the observation of models may be a major factor in the learning process, imitation of the model must be reinforced or rewarded if the behaviors are to become part of the person's repertoire.

Albert Bandura is a major proponent of the social learning school. According to Bandura, behavior occurs as a result of the interplay between cognitive and environmental factors, a concept known as *reciprocal determinism.* People learn by observing others, intentionally or accidentally; this process is described as *modeling* or learning through imitation. People's choices of model are influenced by a variety of factors, such as age, sex, status, and similarity. If a chosen model reflects healthy norms and values, the person develops *self-efficacy,* the capacity to adapt to normal, everyday life as well as to threatening situations. It is possible to eliminate negative behavior patterns by having a person learn alternative techniques from other role models. For example, fearful children become less fearful when they watch other children acting fearlessly in the same situation. Similarly, demonstrating a fearless approach to a phobic situation may be useful to motivate a patient's approach to the feared object or situation.

Modeling has also been used in weight reduction and smoking cessation programs and is an important component of group treatment plans in which members of the group learn from one another.

NEUROPHYSIOLOGY

One of the first theorists to explore the neurophysiological aspects of learning was Clark L. Hull (1884–1952), who developed a drive reduction theory of learning. Hull postulated that neurophysiological connections established in the central nervous system reduce the level of a drive (for example, obtaining food reduces hunger). An external stimulus stimulates an efferent system and elicits a motor impulse. The critical connection is between the stimulus and the motor response, which is a neurophysiological reaction that leads to what Hull called a habit. Habits are strengthened when a response leads to a further reduction in the drive associated with the aroused need.

By exploring the human brain, researchers such as Pierre Broca and Karl Wernicke identified specific areas of the brain involved in the development and retention of speech and language. Electrical stimulation of certain brain sites evoked vivid mental imagery in patients, and lesions of the amygdaloid nucleus in animals interfered with learning. Learning produces changes in the structure and function of nerve cells. In one study, monkeys that were trained to use a particular finger to obtain food showed hypertrophy of the area of the brain responsible for finger control.

Habituation and Sensitization

In the study of the snail *Aplysia,* Eric Kandel showed how simple forms of learning, such as habituation and sensitization, can occur. Kandel studied a defensive reflex involving the withdrawal of the snail's siphon when the animal is tactually stimulated. If the snail is touched repeatedly, it is subject to habituation and learns not to withdraw its siphon and gill. Habituation causes the organism to stop responding reflexively as a result of the repeated stimulus.

Aplysia can also be sensitized; that is, a reflex response can be made more sensitive, so that a subthreshold stimulus elicits a response. If the snail receives a strong stimulus (for example, an electric shock), it becomes sensitized; then, even a previously subthreshold stimulation causes the animal to withdraw its gill and siphon. Experimental work with *Aplysia* has also shown that habituation develops before sensitization.

Memory Formation and Storage

The neurobiological basis of learning is located in the structures of the brain involved in forming and storing information, which include the hippocampus, the cortex, and the cerebellum. One hundred billion neurons in the brain are involved in forming memories, including a layer of 4.6 million cells in the hippocampus.

Learning begins with the senses taking in an environmental stimulus that is eventually transformed into a memory trace or memory link. An electrical or chemical impulse, passing through a neuron when the brain receives information, triggers the formation of connections between synapses. Animal experiments have shown an increase in synaptic connections when learning occurs.

Long-term memories have increased time to link with many locations in the cortex and thus are retained longer than short-term memories. The more connections, the better the chance of contacting a neural pathway leading to the memory. Repeated reliving of a memory enhances its permanence.

Storage is the key to a good memory. Relating material to something that is already known creates more pathways and increases the storage power. Processing information at a semantic level involves more of the mind than does rote memorization. The semantic information decays at a slower rate than does information superficially memorized, without meaning and comprehension.

Memory is divided into short term and long term; long-term memory is also known as recent memory, recent past memory, remote memory, and secondary memory. Short-term memory—also called immediate memory, working memory, primary memory, and buffer memory—is adversely affected by chronic emotional stress, psychological exhaustion, or too much input. Short-term and long-term memory differ in the amount of information that can be stored. The capacity of short-term memory is limited (five to nine bits of information).

Smell and emotion may underlie long-term memories. Scent conveys information through the olfactory nerve to the hippocampus, which plays a role in the control of emotions. Learning and memory are affected by stress. The increase in adrenaline resulting from stress can enhance learning, but if stress is too great, learning is inhibited. A person's mood affects the learning and recall of material; a person learning material in a happy mood enhances his or her memory and has better recall. Those childhood memories that survive are memories associated with the time the child learned to speak, between the ages of 3 and 5 years. Before then, only memories associated with traumatic events or with smell are likely to be remembered.

MOTIVATION

Motivation is a state of being that produces a tendency toward action. The state may be one of deprivation (for example, hunger), a value system, or a strongly held belief (for example, religion). In the mediation of learning and perception, biological mechanisms play an important role in motivating behavior. An organism tries to maintain homeostasis or internal balance against any disturbance of equilibrium (for example, a thirsty animal is motivated to find water and drink). Social motives, such as the need for recognition and achievement, also account for behavioral patterns (for example, studying hard in order to get good grades). But the intensity of motivation to achieve any task in a particular situation is determined by at least two factors: the achievement motive (desire to achieve) and the likelihood of success.

People show marked individual differences in the values placed on objects and goals. Some students strive for *A*s; others depreciate the importance of grades and place higher value on intellectual satisfactions or on extracurricular activities. The expectancy factor refers to the subjective probability that, with the expenditure of sufficient effort, the object may be acquired or the goal reached.

Cognitive Dissonance

Cognitive dissonance means incongruity or disharmony among a person's beliefs, knowledge, and behavior. When dissonance becomes too great, people change their ways of thinking or behaving to lessen the disharmony. An example of cognitive dissonance is people's unwillingness to believe that a car for which they paid a great deal of money or that is considered a status symbol could have anything wrong with it or could be defective in any way. Another example is believing strongly in a decision after it has been made. Dissonance generally occurs when there is a palpable disparity between two experimental or behavioral elements. Cognitive dissonance apparently produces an uncomfortable tension state (like hunger) that people are motivated to change.

References

Agras WS: Learning theory. In *Comprehensive Textbook of Psychiatry,* ed 5, HI Kaplan, BJ Sadock, editors, p 262. Williams & Wilkins, Baltimore, 1989.

Byrnes JP: Categorizing and combining theories of cognitive development and learning. Educ Psychol Rev *4:* 309, 1992.

Cattell RB: *Psychotherapy by Structured Learning Theory.* Springer, New York, 1987.

Daum I, Schugens M: On the cerebellum and classical conditioning. Curr Dir Psychol Sci *5:* 58, 1996.

Dunn AJ: Neurochemistry of learning and memory. An evaluation of recent data. Annu Rev Psychol *33:* 343, 1982.

Ettenberg A: Dopamine, neuroleptics, and reinforced behavior. Neurosci Biobehav Rev *13:* 105, 1989.

Hall G: Learning about associatively activated stimulus representations: Implications for acquired equivalence and perceptual learning. Anim Learn Behav *24:* 233, 1996.

Lovibond PF: Animal learning theory and the future of human pavlovian conditioning. Biol Psychol *27:* 199, 1988.

Mowrer OH: *Learning Theory and Behavior.* Wiley, New York, 1960.

Pavlov IP: *Conditioned Reflexes.* Oxford University Press, London, 1927.

Raine A, Venables PH, Williams M: Better autonomic conditioning and faster electrodermal half-recovery time at age 15 years as possible protective factors against crime at age 29 years. Dev Psychol *32:* 624, 1996.

Rescorla RA, Holland PC: Behavioral studies of associative learning in animals. Annu Rev Psychol *33:* 265, 1982.

Skinner BF: *Science and Human Behavior.* Macmillan, New York, 1953.

Slangen JL, Early B, Jaffard R, Richelle M, Olton DS: Behavioral models of memory and amnesia. Pharmacopsychiatry *23:* 81, 1990.

Walker S: *Learning Theory and Behavior Modification.* Methuen, London, 1984.

Watson JB, Rayner R: Conditioned emotional reactions. J Exp Psychol *3:* 1, 1920.

Windholz G: Pavlov's conceptualization of learning. Am J Psychol *105:* 459, 1992.

▲ 4.4 Aggression and Accidents

AGGRESSION

Aggressive behavior in humans assumes the form of violent actions against others, who may avoid such treatment or may fight back. Aggression implies the intent to harm or otherwise injure another person, an implication inferred from events preceding or following the act of aggression. As compared to aggression in animals, which is instinctive and can be understood to serve the purpose of species survival, human aggression is thought by some workers to be learned and is difficult to rationalize in terms of benefit to the species.

Aggression and violence occur in many clinical situations, ranging from alcohol and other substance intoxication to cognitive disorders to child abuse to chronic antisocial acts. When the balance collapses between impulses and internal control, violence breaks out (Fig. 4.4–1).

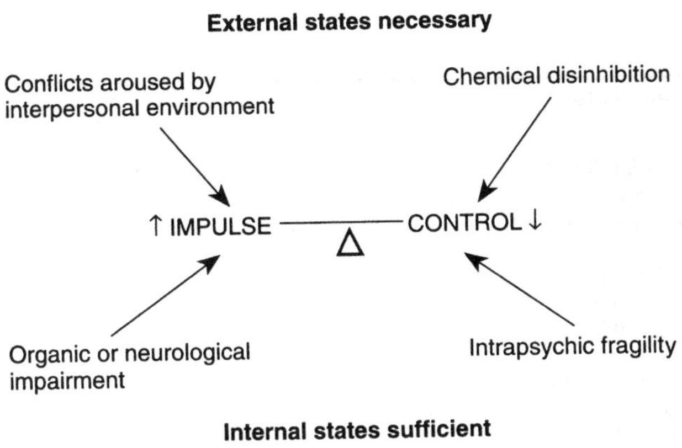
External states necessary
Conflicts aroused by interpersonal environment
Chemical disinhibition
↑ IMPULSE
Δ
CONTROL ↓
Organic or neurological impairment
Intrapsychic fragility
Internal states sufficient

FIGURE 4.4–1
Mechanisms of violence.

People may have violent thoughts or fantasies, but unless they lose control, thoughts do not become acts. Any set of conditions that produce increased aggressive impulses in the context of diminished control may produce violent acts. Situations with combinations of factors include toxic and organic states, developmental disabilities, florid psychosis, conduct disorder, and overwhelming psychological and environmental stress. Table 4.4–1 outlines some of the disorders listed in the fourth edition of *Diagnostic and Statistical Manual of Mental Disorders* (DSM-IV) that have been associated with violent and aggressive behavior.

Several investigators have attempted to apply their understanding of the forces shaping violent acts to predict who will become violent. Tables 4.4–2 and 4.4–3 summarize some of the best-known concepts of violence predictors. Many investigators summarize all the findings into the simple conceptualization that the best predictor of violent acts is a previous violent act. Any predictor, however, is merely a guideline for the possibility of an increased risk for violence, and many potentially violent people do not fit any predictors.

Table 4.4–1
Some DSM-IV Disorders Associated with Aggression

Mental retardation
Attention-deficit/hyperactivity disorder
Conduct disorder
Cognitive disorders
Delirium
Dementia
Psychotic disorders
Schizophrenia
Psychotic disorder not otherwise specified
Mood disorders
Mood disorder due to a general medical condition
Substance-induced mood disorder
Intermittent explosive disorder
Adjustment disorder with disturbance of conduct
Personality disorders
Paranoid personality disorder
Antisocial personality disorder
Borderline personality disorder
Narcissistic personality disorder
Axis V conditions
Childhood, adolescent, or adult antisocial behavior

Table 4.4–2
Commonly Cited Predictors of Dangerousness to Others

High degree of intent to harm
Presence of a victim
Frequent and open threats
Concrete plan
Access to instruments of violence
History of loss of control
Chronic anger, hostility, or resentment
Enjoyment in watching or inflicting harm
Lack of compassion
Self-view as victim
Resentful of authority
Childhood brutality or deprivation
Decreased warmth and affection in home
Early loss of parent
Fire setting, bed-wetting, and cruelty to animals
Prior violent acts
Reckless driving

Incidence

According to the 1995 Federal Bureau of Investigation (FBI) *Uniform Crime Reports,* 1.8 million violent crimes (murder, rape, forcible robbery, and aggravated assault) were committed in the United States. Of this number, 97,464 crimes were rape, and 21,597 crimes were homicide. These statistics have decreased by 13 percent since 1991. Violent crime rates are highest in large metropolitan areas and lowest in rural areas.

Violent acts are most often committed by persons who know or knew each other. Homicides are most prevalent among strangers (55 percent); more than 70 percent of homicides are committed with handguns. In the United States, homicide is the second leading cause of death among people 15 to 24 years of age. Furthermore, a young black man is 8 times more likely to be murdered than is a white man of the same age. Much lower rates of homicide have been reported in such countries as England, Sweden, Japan, and Canada, which all have strict handgun-control laws. Homicide is most prevalent in low socioeconomic groups and is more commonly committed by men than by women.

One national survey of high school students reported that 28 percent of the boys and 7 percent of the girls had been in a physical fight in the previous month. Nearly 35 percent of those surveyed reported having been in at least one physical fight that resulted in an injury requiring medical attention.

Table 4.4–3
Assessing the Risk of Committing a Homicide[a]

Clinical Characteristics	Low Risk	Medium Risk	High Risk
Hostility indicators (history)			
Family life	Wanted child, good loving family	Some family disruption, loss of a parent or one-parent family	Early violence, battered child, poor parent model
Significant others	Several reliable family members or friends available	Few or one available	None available
Daily functioning	Good in most activities	Moderately good in some activities	Not good in any activities
Lifestyle	Stable	Moderately stable	Unstable
Socioeconomic	Upper	Middle	Lower
Employment	Employed	Employment history fairly stable	Unemployed
Education	High school graduate or more (university or technical training)	High school dropout, can read and write	School dropout, semiliterate to illiterate
Housing	Lives in adequate housing, clean environment and space	Fair housing, some overcrowding	Poor housing, crowded, slums
Isolation or withdrawal	Able to relate well to others, outgoing	Mild, some withdrawal and feelings of hopelessness	Long history of being a loner, antisocial, withdrawn, hopeless and helpless feelings
Alcohol or other substance use	Nondrinker, occasional social use	Social drinker or user to occasional abuse	Chronic abuse
Psychological help	No history of need for or use of psychiatric hospitalization	Some outpatient psychiatric help, moderately satisfied with self	History of psychiatric hospitalization, negative view of help
Personal history	No history of violence or impulsive behavior	Occasional history of violence or impulsive behavior	Frequent history of violence or impulsive behavior
Perturbation (negative emotional states)			
Anxiety	Low, good emotional control	Occasional feelings of anxiety	Easily aroused to anxiety, high or panic state
Depression	Low	Occasional depression	Severe, chronically moody
Self-esteem	Good, has reinforcements from others	Usually good	Chronically poor self-image
Hostility	Low	Some	Marked, aggressive
Impulse control	Controlled	Some impulsive acting out not physically violent	Feels need for violence
Constriction (narrowing of vision)			
Coping strategies and devices being used	Able to cope with stress and outside irritating influences; well-developed defense mechanisms	Usually can cope under most pressures; sometimes becomes constrictive in thinking and acts out	Becomes constrictive under most stress; acts out in destructive, socially unacceptable ways
Disorientation and disorganization	None, is in good contact with what is happening	Little to moderate	Marked, losing contact with reality
Resources	Able to make good use of resources available	Some use of resources, aware of most resources	Unable either to use resources available or to recognize that help is available
Cessation (stop the person causing the problem)			
Previous arrests	*None*	*Has been arrested, has not served time*	*Multiple arrest history, served time in prison, would murder to avoid going back to prison*
Previous homicide	*None*	*Has exhibited aggressive behavior; been in fights but no attempt to kill another*	*Yes, looks at the killing of another as a feasible act*
Homicide plan	*None*	*Has held fleeting thoughts of killing another, no definite plan*	*Frequent or constant thoughts with a specific plan*
Weapon available	*None that person thinks of*	*Yes, person aware of weapons in immediate environment but not seriously considering use*	*Yes, and planning on use (a loaded gun should be considered highly lethal)*

Adapted from Allen N: *Homicide: Perspectives on Prevention.* Human Sciences, New York, 1979.
[a] No one clinical characteristic predicts homicide. However, the greater the number of clinical characteristics in the medium-risk and high-risk categories, the greater is the risk.

Predictors of Aggression

Most adults with and without mental disorders who commit aggressive acts are likely to do so against people they know, usually family members. This fact indicates that aggression is not indiscriminately directed. A possible exception to the familiar-person generalization is reported among male adolescents, who often behave aggressively against casual acquaintances or strangers.

Generally, the probability of aggressive behavior increases when people become psychologically decompensated and perhaps also when the onset of a mental disorder is rapid. Otherwise, little is known about the relation between the course of illness and aggression. Episodic decompensation may occur in those who ingest large quantities of alcohol; more than 50 percent of people who commit criminal homicides and who engage in assaultive behavior are reported to have imbibed significant amounts of alcohol immediately beforehand.

Researchers have recently turned their attention to sex differences in the predisposition to and frequency of aggression. For aggression classified as homicide, battery, assault with a weapon, or rape, the frequency among males clearly exceeds that among females. For domestic violence, in which one marital partner acts to hurt another, the frequency among men and women is about equal. Studies of people who are hospitalized in psychiatric facilities for long periods indicate that the prevalence of male and female aggression is about equal.

Theory of Aggressive Behavior

Instinctive Behavior.

FREUD'S VIEW. In his early writings, Sigmund Freud held that all human behavior stems either directly or indirectly from Eros—the life instinct—whose energy, or libido, is directed toward the enhancement or reproduction of life. In this framework, aggression was viewed simply as a reaction to the blocking or thwarting of libidinal impulses and was neither an automatic nor an inevitable part of life.

After the tragic events of World War I, Freud gradually came to adopt a gloomier position about the nature of human aggression. He proposed the existence of a second major instinct—Thanatos, the death force—the energy of which is directed toward the destruction or termination of life. According to Freud, all human behavior stems from the complex interplay of Thanatos and Eros and the constant tension between them.

Because the death instinct, if unrestrained, soon results in self-destruction, Freud hypothesized that through mechanisms such as displacement, the energy of Thanatos is redirected outward and serves as the basis for aggression against others. Thus in Freud's latest view, aggression stems primarily from the redirection of the self-destructive death instinct away from the self and toward others.

LORENZ'S VIEW. According to Konrad Lorenz, aggression that causes physical harm to others springs from a fighting instinct that humans share with other organisms. The energy associated with this instinct is spontaneously produced in organisms at a more or less constant rate. The probability of aggression increases as a function of the amount of stored energy and the presence and strength of aggression-releasing stimuli. Aggression is inevitable, and, at times, spontaneous eruptions occur.

Learned Behavior.

From another perspective, aggression is primarily a learned form of social behavior—one that is acquired and maintained in much the same manner as other forms of activity. According to Albert Bandura, neither innate urges toward violence nor aggressive drives aroused by frustration are the roots of human aggression. Rather, people engage in assaults against others because they acquired aggressive responses through past experience; they receive or anticipate various forms of reward for performing such actions; or they are directly instigated to aggression by specific social or environmental conditions. In contrast to instinct and drive theories (the psychological representation of a need that impels an organism to seek a goal), the social learning perspective does not attribute aggression to one or a few potential causes but suggests that the roots of such behavior are varied and involve an aggressor's past experience, learning, and a wide range of external situational factors. For example, soldiers receive medals for killing enemy troops during times of war, and professional athletes attain widespread admiration and large financial rewards by competing aggressively (Table 4.4–4).

Neuroanatomical Damage.

Increasingly, several investigators are hypothesizing that, for certain chronically aggressive people, the root of their aggressive behavior is organic brain damage. This perspective is an elaboration of the theory that aggression is a learned social behavior, in that people who have been the victims of severe physical abuse themselves may suffer neurological sequelae secondary to the abuse, and the sequelae biologically predispose them to violent behavior. In 1986, Dorothy Lewis reported that every death-row inmate studied by her team of researchers had a history of head injury, often inflicted by abusive parents. This study concluded that death-row inmates constitute an especially neuropsychiatrically impaired prison population. Researchers investigating the association between head injury and violent behavior have been careful to point out that the linkage of physical abuse, head injury, and violence is uncertain, although most studies do

Table 4.4–4
Theoretical Perspectives on Aggression

Theory	Assumed Source of Aggression	Possibility of Preventing or Controlling Aggression
Instinct theory	Innate tendencies or instincts	Low: aggressive impulses are constantly generated and impossible to avoid
Drive theory	Externally elicited aggressive drive	Low: external sources of aggressive drive are common (eg, frustration) and impossible to eliminate
Social learning theory	Present social or environmental conditions plus past social learning	Moderate to high: appropriate changes in current social and environmental conditions or in reinforcement contingencies can reduce or prevent overt aggressive actions

Courtesy of Robert A. Baron, Ph.D.

show an association between early physical abuse and later aggressive behavior. Some researchers speculate that the combination of brain injury and a history of undergoing and observing chronic severe abuse is particularly lethal.

Causes

Social. FRUSTRATION. The single most potent means of inciting human beings to aggression is frustration. Widespread acceptance of this view stems mainly from John Dollard's frustration–aggression hypothesis. In its original form, the hypothesis indicated that frustration always leads to a form of aggression and that aggression always stems from frustration.

Frustrated people, however, do not always respond with aggressive thoughts, words, or deeds. They may show a wide variety of reactions, ranging from resignation, depression, and despair to attempts to overcome the sources of their frustration. And not all aggression results from frustration. People (for example, boxers and football players) act aggressively for many reasons and in response to many stimuli.

An examination of the evidence indicates that whether frustration increases or fails to enhance overt aggression depends largely on two factors: First, frustration appears to increase aggression only when the frustration is intense. When it is mild or moderate, aggression may not be enhanced. Second, frustration is likely to facilitate aggression when it is perceived as arbitrary or illegitimate, rather than when it is viewed as deserved or legitimate.

DIRECT PROVOCATION. Evidence indicates that physical abuse and verbal taunts from others often elicit aggressive actions. Once aggression begins, it often shows an unsettling pattern of escalation; as a result, even mild verbal slurs or glancing blows may initiate a process in which stronger and stronger provocations are exchanged.

AGGRESSION. A link between aggression and exposure to televised violence has been noted. The more televised violence children watch, the greater is their level of aggression against others. The strength of the relation appears to increase over time; this finding points to the cumulative effects of media violence. The processes that account for the effects of filmed and televised violence on the behavior of viewers are outlined in Table 4.4–5.

Environmental. AIR POLLUTION. Exposure to noxious odors, such as those produced by chemical plants and other industries, may increase personal irritability and, therefore, aggression, although this effect appears to be true only up to a point. If the odors in question are truly foul, aggression appears to decrease—perhaps because escaping from the unpleasant environment becomes a dominant goal for those involved.

Table 4.4–5
Mechanisms Underlying the Effects of Televised and Filmed Violence on the Behavior of Viewers

Mechanism	Effects
Observational learning	Viewers acquire new means of harming others not previously present in their behavior repertoires.
Disinhibition	Viewers' restraints or inhibitions against performing aggressive actions are weakened as a result of observing others engaging in such behavior.
Desensitization	Viewers' emotional responsivity to aggressive actions and their consequences—signs of suffering on the part of victims—is reduced. As a result, they show little, if any, emotional arousal in response to such stimuli.

Courtesy of Robert A. Baron, Ph.D.

NOISE. Several studies have reported that people exposed to loud and irritating noise direct stronger assaults against others than do those not exposed to such environmental conditions.

CROWDING. Some studies indicate that overcrowding may produce elevated levels of aggression, but other investigations have failed to obtain evidence of such a link. Crowding may enhance the likelihood of aggressive outbursts when typical reactions are negative (for example, annoyance, irritation, and frustration).

Situational. HEIGHTENED PHYSIOLOGICAL AROUSAL. Some research indicates that heightened arousal stemming from such diverse sources as participation in competitive activities, vigorous exercise, and exposure to provocative films enhances overt aggression.

SEXUAL AROUSAL. Recent investigations indicate that the effects of sexual arousal on aggression strongly depend on the erotic materials used to induce such reactions and on the precise nature of the reactions themselves. When the erotica viewed are mild, such as photos of attractive nudes, aggression is reduced. When they are explicit, such as films of couples engaged in various acts of lovemaking, aggression is enhanced.

PAIN. Physical pain may arouse an aggressive drive—the motive to harm or injure others. This drive, in turn, may find expression against any available target, including those not in any way responsible for the aggressor's discomfort. This hypothesis may partly explain why people exposed to aggression act aggressively toward others.

Hormones, Drugs, and Other Substances. Aggression has been linked in animals with testosterone, progesterone, luteinizing hormone, renin, β-endorphin, prolactin, melatonin, norepinephrine, dopamine, epinephrine, acetylcholine, serotonin, 5-hydroxyindoleacetic acid (5-HIAA), and phenylacetic acid, among others.

Some studies have related the level of aggression to androgen levels. These studies point to the androgen insensitivity syndrome (in which there is defective binding of androgens to proteins, resulting in male offspring with a feminine appearance and a decreased propensity for rough-and-tumble play) and to the adrenogenital syndrome (in which the mother's adrenal cortex exposes the fetus to elevated adrenal androgens, resulting in masculinization, partly evidenced by increased rough-and-tumble play in masculinized girls).

In regard to drugs and substances of abuse, the following generalizations appear to hold: Small doses of alcohol inhibit aggression, and large doses facilitate it; barbiturate effects are similar to the effects of alcohol; aerosol and commercial solvent effects also resemble alcohol's effects; anxiolytics generally inhibit aggression, although paradoxical aggression is sometimes observed; opioid dependence (but not opioid intoxication) is associated with increased aggression, as is the use of stimulants, cocaine, hallucinogens, and, in some cases, variable doses of marijuana.

Neurotransmitters. Generally, cholinergic and catecholaminergic mechanisms seem to be involved in the induction and enhancement of predatory aggression, whereas serotonergic systems and γ-aminobutyric acid (GABA) seem to inhibit such behavior. The catecholaminergic and serotonergic systems evidently modulate affective aggression. Dopamine seems to facilitate aggression, whereas norepinephrine and serotonin appear to inhibit it. Recently, serotonin has again gained attention as a potentially important mediating factor in aggression. Rapid declines in serotonin levels or function are associated with increased irritability and, in nonhuman primates, with increased aggression. Some human studies have indicated that 5-HIAA levels in cerebrospinal fluid inversely correlate with the frequency of aggression, particularly among people who commit suicide.

Genetics. TWIN STUDIES. Research involving monozygotic twins indicates a hereditary component to aggressive behavior. Thus far, most studies have focused on nonpsychiatric populations, in which the concordance rates for monozygotic twins exceed the rates for dizygotic twins.

PEDIGREE STUDIES. Several studies show that people with family histories of mental disorders are more prone to mental disorders and engage in more aggressive behavior than do those without such histories. Those with low intelligence quotient (IQ) scores appear to have a higher frequency of delinquency and aggression than do those with normal IQ scores. Observed correlations between aggressive behavior and other atypical behaviors indicate that genetic predispositions to atypical behavior, including behaviors associated with mental disorders, are associated with atypical physiological functions, one consequence of which is an increase in the probability of aggression.

CHROMOSOME INFLUENCES. Behavior research involving the influence of chromosomes has concentrated primarily on abnormalities in X and Y chromosomes, particularly the 47-chromosome XYY syndrome. Early studies indicated that people with the syndrome could be characterized as tall, of below-average intelligence, and likely to be apprehended and in prison for engaging in criminal behavior. Subsequent studies indicated, however, that, at most, the XYY syndrome contributes to aggressive behavior in only a small percentage of cases. Studies of the androgen and gonadotropin characteristics of people with XYY syndrome have been inconclusive and have not established that such people are biochemically atypical.

Certain inborn metabolic disorders, genetic in origin, that diffusely involve the nervous system have been reported to be associated with aggressive personalities. Examples include Sanfilippo's syndrome (increased mucopolysaccharide storage), Vogt syndrome (a diffuse neuronal storage disorder with increased ganglioside storage), and phenylketonuria.

Prevention and Control

For physicians, the prevention of death and disability resulting from aggressive, violent, or homicidal behavior begins at the individual level. For instance, violence within a family (such as sexual and physical abuse of children, wife beating, and self-destructive behavior) is often revealed through sensitive questioning and a high index of suspicion on the clinician's part. Preventive interventions include psychiatric referral, notification of the proper legal or other authorities (mandatory in such cases as child abuse and specific threats of harm to people), and skilled counseling by appropriately trained therapists.

Punishment. Punishment is sometimes effective as a deterrent to overt aggression. Research findings indicate that the frequency or intensity of such behavior can be reduced by even mild forms of punishment, such as social disapproval; but punishment may not always or even usually produce such effects.

The recipients of punishment often interpret it as an attack against them. To the extent that it is so, aggressors may respond even more aggressively. Strong punishment is more likely to provoke desires for revenge or retribution than to instill lasting restraints against violence. People who administer punishment may serve as aggressive models for those on the receiving end of such discipline, and as noted earlier, exposure to such models may potentiate violent acts. Because of the conditions under which it is usually administered (a long time after the aggression is committed), punishment may only temporarily reduce the strength or frequency of aggressive behavior. Once the punishment is discontinued, the aggressive acts quickly reappear. For these reasons, certain punishments may backfire and actually enhance, rather than inhibit, the dangerous actions they are designed to prevent.

Catharsis. For many years workers have widely believed that providing angry people with an opportunity to engage in expressive but noninjurious behaviors reduces their tension or arousal and weakens their tendency to engage in overt and potentially dangerous acts of aggression—the so-called catharsis hypothesis. Although Sigmund Freud accepted the existence of such catharsis, he was relatively pessimistic about its usefulness in preventing overt aggression. At present, catharsis is thought to help some people discharge aggression; other people may become more aggressive as a result of the expressive behaviors.

Training in Social Skills. A major reason why many people become involved in repeated aggressive encounters is their lack of basic social skills. These people do not know how to communicate effectively; therefore, they adopt an abrasive style of self-expression. Their ineptness in performing such basic tasks as making requests, engaging in negotiations, and lodging complaints often irritates friends, acquaintances, and strangers. Their severe social deficits seem to ensure that they experience repeated frustration and that they frequently anger those with whom they have direct contact. A technique for reducing the frequency of such behavior involves providing such people with the social skills that they sorely lack. Social skills training has been applied to diverse groups, including highly aggressive teenagers, police, and even child-abusing parents. In many cases, dramatic changes in the targeted behaviors have been produced (for example, enhanced interpersonal communication and improved ability to handle rejection and stress), and reductions in aggressive behavior related to these shifts have frequently been observed. The results are encouraging and indicate that training in appropriate social skills can offer a promising approach to the reduction of human violence.

Induction of Incompatible Responses. EMPATHY. When aggressors attack other people in face-to-face confrontations, the aggressors may block out, ignore, or deny signs of pain and suffering on the part of their victims. If aggressors are exposed to such feedback, they may feel empathy and subsequently reduce further aggression. In several experiments, exposure to signs of pain or discomfort on the victim's part has inhibited further aggression.

HUMOR. Informal observation indicates that anger can often be reduced through exposure to humorous material, and some laboratory studies support this hypothesis. Several types of humor, presented in various formats, may induce reactions or emotions incompatible with aggression among the people who observe the humor.

Table 4.4–6
Schematic Differential Diagnosis and the Pharmacological Treatment of Violence

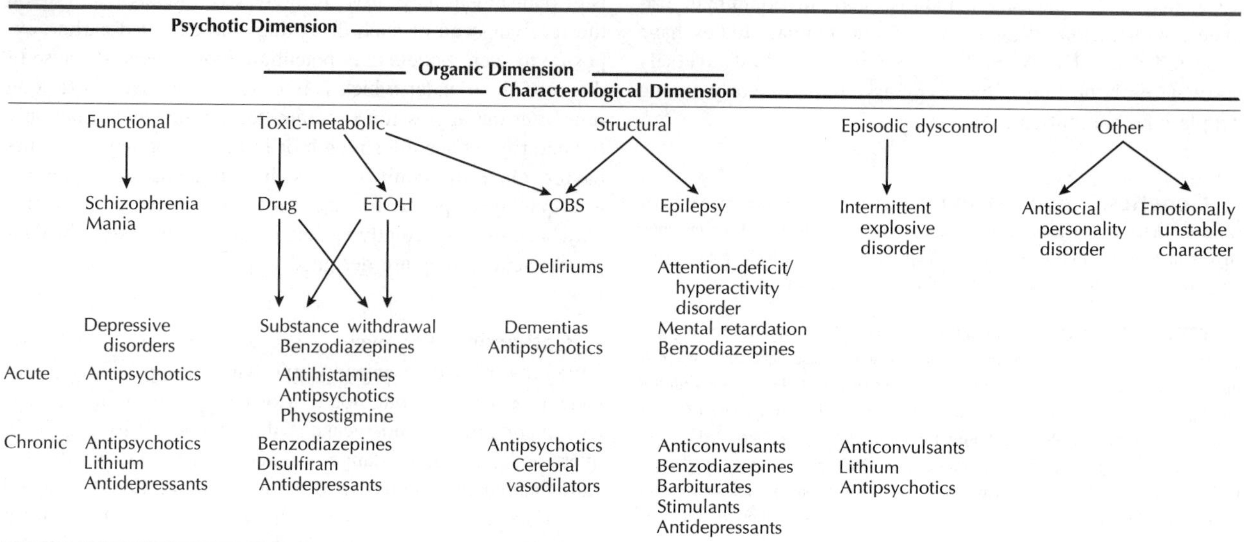
Psychotic Dimension
Organic Dimension
Characterological Dimension
Functional
Toxic-metabolic
Structural
Episodic dyscontrol
Other
Schizophrenia
Mania
Drug
ETOH
OBS
Epilepsy
Intermittent explosive disorder
Antisocial personality disorder
Emotionally unstable character
Deliriums
Attention-deficit/ hyperactivity disorder
Depressive disorders
Substance withdrawal
Dementias
Mental retardation
Benzodiazepines
Antipsychotics
Benzodiazepines
Acute
Antipsychotics
Antihistamines
Antipsychotics
Physostigmine
Chronic
Antipsychotics
Lithium
Antidepressants
Benzodiazepines
Disulfiram
Antidepressants
Antipsychotics
Cerebral vasodilators
Anticonvulsants
Benzodiazepines
Barbiturates
Stimulants
Antidepressants
Anticonvulsants
Lithium
Antipsychotics

Adapted from Skodol A: Emergency management of potentially violent patients. In *Emergency Psychiatry: Concepts, Methods and Practice,* E Bassuk, A Birk, editors. Plenum, New York, 1984.
ETOH, ethanol; OBS, organic brain syndrome.

OTHER FACTORS. Many other reactions may also be incompatible with anger or overt aggression. As already noted, mild sexual arousal sometimes operates in this fashion. Similarly, feelings of guilt about the performance of aggressive actions often reduce such behavior. Participation in absorbing cognitive tasks, such as solving mathematics problems, may induce reactions incompatible with anger and aggressive actions.

Drug Treatment. Several types of drugs and clinical monitoring—for example, blood pressure and electroencephalogram (EEG)—are essential for the optimal treatment of specific aggressive people. Lithium (Eskalith) appears to be a drug of major promise for some violent patients, especially delinquent adolescent boys. Anticonvulsants occasionally reduce seizure-induced forms of aggression, and they may have the same effect on people who do not have epilepsy. Antipsychotic medications seem to reduce aggression in both psychotic and nonpsychotic violent patients. Antidepressants may be effective in reducing violence in some depressed patients. Antianxiety agents appear to have a limited role in reducing aggression. Antiandrogen agents may be effective in the treatment of aggressive sex offenders. β-Blockers and stimulants may be effective in aggressive children. And electroconvulsive therapy may be effective in a small group of selected patients.

Table 4.4–6 outlines some possible psychopharmacological interventions for aggression.

Table 4.4–7
Aftermath of Crime: Main Emotional Effects

Sense of helplessness: The world seems unsafe; victims lack confidence in their judgment and competence to deal with the world.

Rage at being a victim: Intense anger is usually expressed toward family members and those who try to help; conversely, sometimes the victim is unable to express any anger at anything.

Sense of being permanently damaged: Rape victims, for example, may feel that they will never be attractive again.

Inability to trust or to be intimate with others: The effect can include a loss of faith in institutions like the police and the courts.

Persistent preoccupation with the crime: Excessive concern with the crime and its details may reach the point of obsession.

Loss of belief that the world is just: The effect may include self-blame and a sense of having done something to deserve being a victim.

Courtesy of Stuart Kleinman, M.D.

Victims

An estimated 18 million people in the United States at some time have suffered psychiatric disturbance as a result of crime. At any given moment, up to 5 million people in the United States may suffer from crime-related symptoms. The National Institute of Justice estimates that a 12-year-old American has an 80 percent chance of being the victim of a serious crime at some point in his or her life. Recent research indicates that many victims of violent crimes are at increased risk for major psychiatric problems. Long-term depressive disorders and phobias are two mental disorders reported to occur more frequently in victims of crime than in the general population. Many researchers believe that distinct and characteristic emotional effects are associated with being the victim of a crime and that these effects are related to the fact that victims are the targets of another person's intentional aggression. Table 4.4–7 lists the main emotional aftereffects of crime.

ACCIDENTS

An accident is an event that occurs by chance or unexpectedly, without conscious planning. Studies of accidents show that causes can sometimes be determined and possibly corrected, but they are often multiple and require a many-faceted approach to the problem. For instance, both behavioral and psychological characteristics can be related to the occurrence of accidents. These characteristics include anxiety, boredom, fatigue, and the ingestion of substances that alter concentration and motor coordination. In 1992, according to the National Safety Council, a total of 83,000 deaths and 17.1 million disabling injuries resulted from accidents.

For people 15 to 24 years of age, accidents are the most common cause of death in the United States. Accidents are the fifth most common cause of death overall in the United States. The most recent national data on the cost of injuries reported that for the noninstitutionalized population intentional and unintentional accidents were the second leading cause of direct medical costs (second only to heart disease and exceeding cancer) and also accounted for major indirect costs, such as work loss and disability.

Vehicular accidents, industrial accidents, and home accidents were the most frequent types of injury. One third of all injury deaths are secondary to automobile accidents, and one third are secondary to other accidents; the remaining one third are evenly divided between suicide and homicide. After motor vehicle accidents, the most common causes of accidental death are falls, followed by fire, drowning, and poisoning.

Psychophysiological Considerations

Victims' psychophysiological states must be considered in all injuries and accidents. A physical condition such as fatigue may lead either to distraction or to an inability to respond quickly enough to avoid an accident. Such toxic factors as barbiturates, antihistamines, marijuana, and particularly alcohol are important. About one half of reported automobile accidents occur in conjunction with alcohol intake. People with diabetes, epilepsy, cardiovascular disease, and mental disorders are involved in more than twice the number of accidents per 1,000 miles of driving than are those who do not have these illnesses.

Age-related impairments, both motor and cerebral function deficits, may lead to potentially impaired judgment, which contributes to fatal accidents among people 65 and older.

Motivations

From a motivational point of view, the first writings on the subject of an accident-prone personality date to Freud's *The Psychopathology of Everyday Life* (1904):

> Many apparently accidental injuries that happen to such patients are really instances of self-injuries. What happens is an impulse to self-punishment, which is constantly on the watch and which normally finds expression in self-reproach or contributes to the formation of a symptom, takes ingenious advantage of an external situation that chance happens to offer, or lends *assistance* [italics added] to that situation until the desired injurious effect is brought about.

Many retrospective studies have explored the personality characteristics of people who have had severe or frequent accidents. In these studies, workers have speculated that people repeatedly involved in accidents may have an underlying self-destructive tendency suggestive of the existence of depression, poor control of hostility, a tendency to be more action oriented and less reflective than the general population, and a propensity for intrapsychic or interpersonal difficulties at least partially resolved by the occurrence of the accident. The concept of an unconscious sense of guilt and a need to atone or to be punished for such guilt feelings may provide the motivation of many unintended accidents. Motivations other than an unconscious sense of guilt may be found by examining the life situations of people involved in accidents. An unconscious wish to escape or to avoid something is often apparent. The desire to escape may be related to external situations in which an accident provides a convenient way of avoiding a possibly humiliating experience. One such example is the man who has an accident on his way to a job interview and thereby avoids the possible humiliation of not obtaining the position he was seeking. Accidents help a person to avoid new responsibilities by providing a convenient and acceptable rationale for not entering into the new situation without losing self-esteem or the esteem of others.

REFERENCES

Berkowitz L: On the formation and regulation of anger and aggression: A cognitive-neoassociationistic analysis. Am Psychol *45:* 494, 1990.

Callahan CM, Rivara FP: Urban high school youth and handguns: A school-based survey. JAMA *267:* 3038, 1992.

Council on Scientific Affairs: Assault weapons as a public health hazard in the United States. JAMA *267:* 3067, 1992.

Crusio WE: The neurobehavioral genetics of aggression. Behav Genet *26:* 459, 1996.

Cueva JE, Overall JE, Small AM, Armenteros JL, Perry R, Campbell M: Carbamazepine in aggressive children with conduct disorder: A double-blind and placebo-controlled study. Child Adolesc Psychiatry *35:* 480, 1996.

Eichelman BS: Neurochemical and psychopharmacologic aspects of aggressive behavior. Annu Rev Med *41:* 149, 1990.

Elliott FA: Violence: The neurologic contribution: An overview. Arch Neurol *49:* 595, 1992.

Else L, Wonderlich SA, Beatty WW, Christie DW, et al: Personality characteristics of men who physically abuse women. Hosp Community Psychiatry *44:* 54, 1993.

Federal Bureau of Investigation: *Uniform Crime Reports.* US Government Printing Office, Washington, 1995.

Gentry J, Eron LD: American Psychological Association Commission on Violence and Youth. Am Psychol *48:* 89, 1993.

Ghaziuddin M, Ghaziuddin N: Violence against staff by mentally retarded inpatients. Hosp Community Psychiatry *43:* 503, 1992.

Kinzie JD, Boehnlein JK: Psychotherapy of the victims of massive violence: Countertransference and ethical issues. Am Psychother *47:* 90, 1993.

Liebert RM: *The Early Window: Effects of Television on Children and Youth,* ed 3. Allyn & Bacon, Needham Heights, MA, 1992.

Lion JR: Aggression. In *Comprehensive Textbook of Psychiatry,* ed 6, HI Kaplan, BJ Sadock, editors, p 310. Williams & Wilkins, Baltimore, 1995.

National Center for Environmental Health and Injury Control: Physical fighting among high school students: United States, 1990. MMWR Morb Mortal Wkly Rep *41:* 91, 1992.

Parkes CM: Psychiatric problems following bereavement by murder or manslaughter. Br J Psychiatry *162:* 49, 1993.

Serbin LA, Peters PL, Schwartzman AE: Longitudinal study of early childhood injuries and acute illnesses in the offspring of adolescent mothers who were aggressive, withdrawn, or aggressive-withdrawn in childhood. Abnorm Psychol *105:* 500, 1996.

Tardiff K, Marzuk PM, Leon AC, Portera L, Weiner C: Violence by patients admitted to a private psychiatric hospital. Am J Psychiatry *154:* 88, 1997.

Weil DS, Hemenway D: Loaded guns in the home: Analysis of a national random survey of gun owners. JAMA *267:* 3033, 1992.

▲ 4.5 Ethology, Experimental Disorders, and Sociobiology

Knowledge of human psychological behavior has been enriched by studies of ethology, experimental disorders, and sociobiology. A review of these areas' contributions to human physiological function is of interest to the field of psychiatry.

Ethologists, who study animal behavior and its origins, have found several schemes that shape animal behavior through genetic programming: releasers, motor programs, drive, and programmed learning. Ethologists have generally observed animals in their natural environments to measure behavior but have also used other techniques, such as introducing experimental factors into a natural environment and conducting laboratory investigations.

The work of three ethologists who were also 1973 Nobel laureates in medicine is described in this section.

KONRAD LORENZ

Born in Austria, Konrad Lorenz (1903–1988) is best known for his studies of imprinting. *Imprinting* implies that, during a certain short period of development, a young animal is highly sensitive to a certain stimulus that then, but not at other times, provokes a specific behavior pattern. Lorenz described newly hatched goslings that are programmed to follow a moving object and thereby become rapidly imprinted to follow it and possibly similar objects. Typically, the mother is the first moving object the gosling sees, but should it see something else first, the gosling follows it. For instance, a gosling imprinted by Lorenz followed him and refused to follow a goose (Fig. 4.5–1). Imprinting is an important concept for psychiatrists to understand in their effort to link early developmental experiences with later behaviors.

FIGURE 4.5–1
In a famous experiment, Konrad Lorenz demonstrated that goslings responded to him as if he were the natural mother. (Reprinted with permission from Hess EH: Imprinting: An effect of an early experience. Science *130:* 133, 1959.)

Lorenz also studied the behaviors that function as sign stimuli—that is, social releasers—in communications between individual animals of the same species. Many signals have the character of fixed motor patterns that appear automatically; the reaction of other members of the species to the signals is equally automatic.

Lorenz is also well known for his study of aggression. He wrote about the practical function of aggression, such as territorial defense by fish and birds. Aggression among members of the same species is common, but Lorenz pointed out that, in normal conditions, it seldom leads to killing or even to serious injury. Although animals attack one another, a certain balance appears between tendencies to fight and flight, with the tendency to fight being strongest in the center of the territory and the tendency to flight strongest at a distance from the center.

In many works, Lorenz tried to draw conclusions from his ethological studies of animals that can also be applied to human problems. The postulation of a primary need for aggression in humans, cultivated by the pressure of selection, is a primary example. Such a need may have served a practical purpose at an early time, when human beings lived in small groups that had to defend themselves from other groups. Competition with neighboring groups could become an important factor of selection. Lorenz pointed out, however, that this need has survived the advent of weapons that can be used not merely to kill individuals but to wipe out all human beings.

NIKOLAAS TINBERGEN

Born in the Netherlands, Nikolaas Tinbergen (1907–1988), a British zoologist, conducted a series of experiments to analyze various aspects of animals' behavior. He was also successful in quantifying behavior and in obtaining measures of the power or strength of various stimuli in eliciting specific behavior. Tinbergen described displacement activities, which have been studied mainly in birds. For example, in a conflict situation, when the needs for fight and for flight are of roughly equal strength, birds sometimes do neither. Rather, they display behavior that appears to be irrelevant to the situation (for example, a herring gull defending its territory can start to pick grass). Displacement activities of this kind vary according to the situation and the species concerned. Human beings can engage in displacement activities when under stress.

Lorenz and Tinbergen described *innate releasing mechanisms,* animals' responses triggered by releasers, which are specific environmental stimuli. Releasers (including shapes, colors, and sounds) evoke sexual, aggressive, or other responses. For example, big eyes in human infants evoke more caretaking behavior than do small eyes.

In his later work, Tinbergen, along with his wife, studied early childhood autistic disorder. They began by observing the behavior of autistic and normal children when they meet strangers, analogous to the techniques used in observing animal behavior. In particular, they observed in animals the conflict that arises between fear and the need for contact and noted that the conflict can lead to behavior similar to that of autistic children. They hypothesized that, in certain predisposed children, fear can greatly predominate and can also be provoked by stimuli that normally have a positive social value for most children. This innovative approach to studying infantile autistic disorder opened up new avenues of inquiry. Although their conclusions about preventive measures and treatment must be considered tentative, their method shows another way in which ethology and clinical psychiatry can relate to each other.

KARL VON FRISCH

Born in Austria, Karl von Frisch (1886–1982) conducted studies on changes of color in fish and demonstrated that fish could learn to distinguish among several colors and that their sense of color was fairly congruent with that of human beings. He later went on to study the color vision and behavior of bees and is most widely known for his analysis of how bees communicate with one another—that is, their language, or what is known as their dances. His description of the exceedingly complex behavior of bees prompted an investigation of information systems in other animal species.

EXPERIMENTAL MODELS

Pharmacological Syndromes

With the emergence of biological psychiatry, many researchers have used pharmacological means to produce syndrome analogues in animal subjects. Two classic examples are the reserpine (Serpasil) model of depression and the amphetamine psychosis model of paranoid schizophrenia. In the depression studies, animals given the norepinephrine-depleting drug reserpine exhibited behavioral abnormalities analogous to those of major depressive disorder in humans. The behavioral abnormalities produced were generally reversed by antidepressant drugs. These studies tended to corroborate the theory that depression in humans is, in part, the result of diminished levels of norepinephrine. Similarly, animals given amphetamines acted in a stereotyped, inappropriately aggressive, and apparently frightened manner that was similar to paranoid psychotic symptoms in humans. Both these models are thought to be too simplistic in their concepts of cause, but they remain as early paradigms for this type of research.

Studies have also been made on the effects of catecholamine-depleting drugs on monkeys during separation and reunion periods. These studies showed that catecholamine depletion and social separation can interact in a highly synergistic fashion and can yield depressive symptoms in subjects for whom mere separation or low-dosage treatment by itself is not sufficient to produce depression.

Stress Syndromes

Several researchers, including Ivan Petrovich Pavlov in Russia and W. Horsley Gantt and Howard Scott Liddell in the United States, studied the effects of stressful environments on animals, such as dogs and sheep. Pavlov produced a phenomenon in dogs, which he labeled *experimental neurosis,* by the use of a conditioning technique that led to symptoms of extreme and persistent agitation. The technique involved teaching dogs to discriminate between a circle and an ellipse and then progressively diminishing the difference between the two. Gantt used the term *behavior disorders* to describe the reactions he elicited from dogs forced into similar conflictual learning situations. Liddell described the stress response he obtained in sheep, goats, and dogs as *experimental neurasthenia,* which was produced in some cases by merely doubling the number of daily test trials in an unscheduled manner.

Learned Helplessness. The learned helplessness model of depression, developed by Martin Seligman, is a good example of an experimental disorder. Dogs were exposed to electric shocks from which they could not escape. The dogs eventually gave up and made no attempt to escape new shocks. The apparent giving up generalized to other situations, and eventually the dogs always appeared to be helpless and apathetic. Because the cognitive, motivational, and affective deficits displayed by the dogs resembled symptoms common to human depressive disorders, learned helplessness, although controversial, was proposed as an animal model of human depression. In connection with learned helplessness and the expectation of inescapable punishment, research on subjects has revealed brain release of endogenous opiates, destructive effects on the immune system, and elevation of the pain threshold.

A social application of this concept involves school children who have learned that they fail in school no matter what they do; they view themselves as helpless losers, and this self-concept causes them to stop trying. Teaching them to persist may reverse the process, with excellent results in self-respect and school performance.

Unpredictable Stress. Rats subjected to chronic unpredictable stress (crowding, shocks, irregular feeding, and interrupted sleep time) show decreases in movement and exploratory behavior; this finding illustrates the roles of unpredictability and lack of environmental control in producing stress. These behavioral changes can be reversed by antidepressant medication. Animals under experimental stress (Fig. 4.5–2) become tense, restless, hyperirritable, or inhibited in certain conflict situations.

Dominance. Animals in a dominant position in a hierarchy have certain advantages (such as in mating and feeding). Being more dominant than peers is associated with ela-

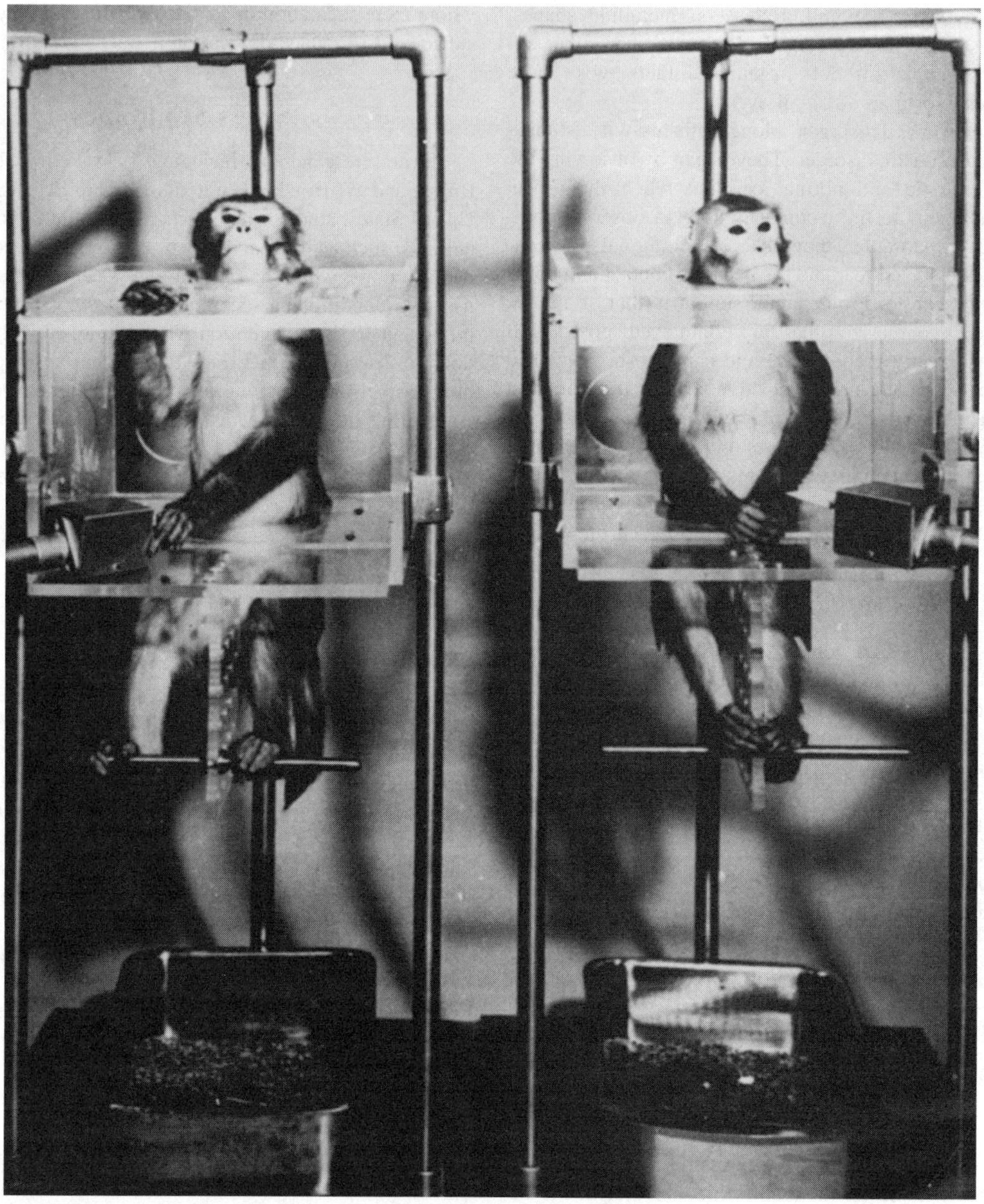

FIGURE 4.5–2
The monkey on the *left,* known as the executive monkey, controls whether or not both will receive an electric shock. The decision-making task produces a state of chronic tension. Note the more relaxed attitude of the monkey on the *right.* (From U.S. Army photographs.)

tion, and a fall in position in the hierarchy is associated with depression. When people lose jobs, are replaced in organizations, or otherwise have their dominance or hierarchical status changed, they can experience depression.

Temperament. Temperament mediated by genetics plays a role in behavior. For example, one group of pointer dogs was bred for fearfulness and a lack of friendliness toward people, and another group was bred for the opposite characteristics. The phobic dogs were extremely timid and fearful and showed decreased exploratory capacity, increased startle response, and cardiac arrhythmias. Benzodiazepines diminished these fearful, anxious responses. Amphetamines and cocaine aggravated the responses of genetically nervous dogs to a greater extent than they did the responses of the stable dogs.

Brain Stimulation. Pleasurable sensations have been produced in both humans and animals through self-stimulation of certain brain areas, such as the medial forebrain bundle, the septal area, and the lateral hypothalamus. Rats have engaged in repeated self-stimulation (2,000 stimulations per hour) to gain rewards. Catecholamine production increases with self-

FIGURE 4.5–3
Social isolate after removal of isolation screen.

stimulation of the brain areas, and drugs that decrease catecholamines decrease the process. The centers for sexual pleasure and opioid reception are closely related anatomically.

DEVELOPMENTAL PROCESSES IN MONKEYS

An area of animal research that has relevance to human behavior and psychopathology is the longitudinal study of nonhuman primates. Monkeys have been observed from birth to maturity, not only in their natural habitats and laboratory facsimiles but also in laboratory settings that involve various degrees of social deprivation early in life. Social deprivation has been produced through two predominant conditions: social isolation and separation. Socially isolated monkeys are raised in varying degrees of isolation and are not permitted to develop normal attachment bonds. Monkeys separated from their primary caretakers thereby experience a disruption in an already-developed bond. Social isolation techniques illustrate the effects of an infant's early social environment on subsequent development (Figs. 4.5–3 and 4.5–4), and separation techniques illustrate the effects of loss of a significant attachment figure. The name most associated with isolation and separation studies is Harry Harlow. A summary of Harlow's work is presented in Table 4.5–1.

In a series of experiments, Harlow separated rhesus monkeys from their mothers during their first weeks of life. During this time, the monkey infant depends on its mother for nourishment and protection, as well as for physical warmth and emotional security—contact comfort, as Harlow first termed it in 1958. Harlow substituted a surrogate mother made from wire or cloth for the real mother. The infants preferred the cloth-covered surrogate mother, which provided contact comfort, to the wire-covered surrogate, which provided food but no contact comfort (Fig. 4.5–5).

Treatment of Abnormal Behavior

In 1972, Stephen Suomi demonstrated that monkey isolates can be rehabilitated if they are exposed to monkeys that promote physical contact without threatening the isolates with aggression or overly complex play interactions. These monkeys

FIGURE 4.5–4
Choo-choo phenomenon in peer-only–reared infant rhesus monkeys.

Table 4.5–1
Social Deprivation in Nonhuman Primates

Type of Social Deprivation	Effect
Total isolation (not allowed to develop caretaker or peer bond)	Self-orality, self-clasping, very fearful when placed with peers, unable to copulate (Fig. 4.5–3). If impregnated, female is unable to nurture young (motherless mothers). If isolation goes beyond 6 months, no recovery is possible.
Mother-only–reared	Fails to leave mother and explore. Terrified when finally exposed to peers. Unable to play or to copulate.
Peer-only–reared	Engages in self-orality, grasps others in clinging manner, easily frightened, reluctant to explore, timid as adult, play is minimal (Fig. 4.5–4).
Partial isolation (can see, hear, and smell other monkeys)	Stares vacantly into space, engages in self-mutilation, stereotyped behavior patterns.
Separation (taken from caretaker after bond has developed)	Initial protest stage changing to despair 48 hours after separation; refuses to play. Rapid reattachment when returned to mother.

Adapted from work of Harry Harlow, M.D.

were called therapist monkeys. To fill such a therapeutic role, Suomi chose young normal monkeys that would play gently with the isolates and approach and cling to them. Within 2 weeks, the isolates were reciprocating the social contact, and their incidence of abnormal self-directed behaviors began to decline significantly. By the end of the 6-month therapy period, the isolates were actively initiating play bouts with both the therapists and each other, and most of their self-directed behaviors had disappeared. The isolates were observed closely for the next 2 years, and their improved behavioral repertoires did not regress over time. The results of this and subsequent monkey–therapist studies underscored the potential reversibility of early cognitive and social deficits at the human level. The studies also served as a model for developing therapeutic treatments for socially retarded and withdrawn children.

Several investigators have argued that social separation manipulations with nonhuman primates provide a compelling basis for animal models of depression and anxiety. Some monkeys react to separations with behavioral and physiological symptoms similar to those seen in depressed human patients; both electroconvulsive therapy (ECT) and tricyclic drugs are effective in reversing the symptoms in monkeys. Not all separations produce depressive reactions in monkeys, just as separation does not always precipitate depression in humans, young and old.

Individual Differences

Recent research has revealed that some rhesus monkey infants consistently display fearfulness and anxiety in situations in which similarly reared peers show normal exploratory behavior and play. These situations generally involve exposure to a novel object or situation. Once the object or situation has become familiar, any behavioral differences between the anxiety-prone or timid infants and their outgoing peers disappear, but the individual differences appear to be stable during development. Infant monkeys at 3 to 6 months of age that are at high risk for fearful or anxious reactions tend to remain at high risk for such reactions, at least until adolescence.

Long-term follow-up study of these monkeys has revealed

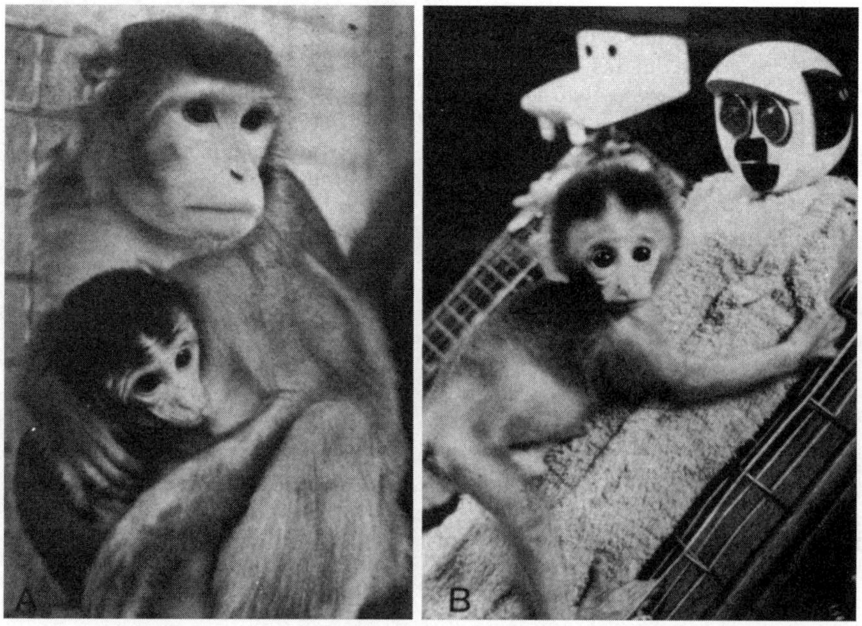
A
B

FIGURE 4.5–5
Monkey infant with mother *(left)* and with cloth-covered surrogate *(right)*.

some behavioral differences between fearful and nonfearful female monkeys when they become adults and have their first infants. Fearful female monkeys who grow up in socially benign and stable environments typically become fine mothers, but fearful female monkeys who have reacted with depression to frequent social separations during childhood are at high risk for maternal dysfunction; more than 80 percent of these mothers either neglect or abuse their first offspring. Yet nonfearful female monkeys that encounter the same number of social separations but do not react to any of these separations with depression subsequently turn out to be good mothers.

SENSORY DEPRIVATION

The history of sensory deprivation and its potentially deleterious effects evolved from instances of aberrant mental behavior in explorers, shipwrecked sailors, and prisoners in solitary confinement. Toward the end of World War II, startling confessions, induced by brainwashing prisoners of war, caused a rise of interest in this psychological phenomenon brought about by the deliberate diminution of sensory input.

To test the hypothesis that an important element in brainwashing is prolonged exposure to sensory isolation, D. O. Hebb and his coworkers brought solitary confinement into the laboratory and demonstrated that volunteer subjects—under conditions of visual, auditory, and tactile deprivation for periods of up to 7 days—reacted with increased suggestibility. Some subjects also showed characteristic symptoms of the sensory deprivation state: anxiety, tension, inability to concentrate or organize thoughts, increased suggestibility, body illusions, somatic complaints, intense subjective emotional distress, and vivid sensory imagery—usually visual and sometimes reaching the proportions of hallucinations with a delusionary quality.

Psychological Theories

Anticipating psychological explanations, Sigmund Freud wrote: "It is interesting to speculate what could happen to ego function if the excitations or stimuli from the external world were either drastically diminished or repetitive. Would there be an alteration in the unconscious mental processes and an effect upon the conceptualization of time?"

Indeed, under conditions of sensory deprivation, the abrogation of such ego functions as perceptual contact with reality and logical thinking brings about confusion, irrationality, fantasy formation, hallucinatory activity, and wish-dominated mental reactions. In the sensory deprivation situation the subject becomes dependent on the experimenter and must trust the experimenter for the satisfaction of such basic needs as feeding, toileting, and physical safety. A patient undergoing psychoanalysis may be in a kind of sensory deprivation room (for example, a soundproof room with dim lights and a couch) in which primary process mental activity is encouraged through free association.

Physiological Theories

The maintenance of optimal conscious awareness and accurate reality testing depends on a necessary state of alertness. This alert state, in turn, depends on a constant stream of changing stimuli from the external world, mediated through the ascending reticular activating system in the brainstem. In the absence or impairment of such a stream, as occurs in sensory deprivation, alertness drops away, direct contact with the outside world diminishes, and impulses from the inner body and the central nervous system may gain prominence. For example, idioretinal phenomena, inner ear noise, and somatic illusions may take on a hallucinatory character.

Other Theories

Personality. Personality theories attempt to explain not the phenomena of sensory deprivation but, rather, the variation in these phenomena from subject to subject. For example, why do some volunteers in experiments quit sooner than others? Various approaches are offered by various investigators—introversion-extroversion, body-field orientation, and optimal stimulation level.

Expectation. The expectation hypotheses involve social influences, including the important role played by the experimenter. Modern researchers place great emphasis on anticipation, instructional set, and the demand characteristics of the experimental situation (tacit and overt suggestion).

Cognitive. Cognitive theories stress the fact that the organism is an information-processing machine, the purpose of which is optimal adaptation to the perceived environment. Lacking sufficient information, the machine is unable to form a cognitive map against which current experience is matched. Disorganization and maladaptation then result. To monitor their own behavior and to attain optimal responsiveness, people must receive continuous feedback; otherwise they are forced to project outward idiosyncratic themes that have little relation to reality. This situation is similar to that of many psychotic patients.

SOCIOBIOLOGY

Sociobiology, a relatively new discipline that integrates principles of evolution, genetics, ecology, and ethology, is the study of the biological basis of social behavior. Sociobiologists find many similarities in animal and human behavior, such as competition, territoriality, aggression, reproduction, mate selection, male-female differences, parenting, and altruism. Sociobiologists postulate that human behavior has evolved to achieve maximum fitness and adaptation: *Fitness* is defined as the highest measure of evolutionary success, in that the best genes are passed from one generation to the next. *Inclusive fitness* is the sum of a person's personal fitness and that of the person's relatives compared with the rest of the population.

Evolution

Evolution is described as any change in the genetic makeup of a population. Evolution occurs through natural (darwinian) selection, which is the reproduction of those genes produced by mutation that account for the most successful offspring. Lamarckian evolution, which occurs through the inheritance of acquired characteristics, describes the evolution of culture.

Competition

Animals vie with one another for resources and territory, the area that is defended for the exclusive use of the animal and that ensures access to food and reproduction. The ability of one animal to defend a disputed territory or resource is called *resource holding potential;* and the greater this potential, the more successful is the animal.

Aggression

Aggression serves both to increase territory and to eliminate competitors. Defeated animals can emigrate, disperse, or remain in the social group as subordinate animals. A dominance hierarchy in which animals are associated with one another in subtle but well-defined ways is part of every social pattern.

Reproduction

Because behavior is influenced by heredity, those behaviors that promote reproduction and survival of the species are among the most important. Males usually compete for the females with other males, a process that produces fit offspring. Male-male competition can take various forms; for example, sperm can be thought of as competing for access to the ovum. Females compete with females but in more subtle ways, primarily in terms of dominance, nest-building ability, and breeding potential. *Sexual dimorphism,* or different behavioral patterns between males and females, evolves to ensure the maintenance of resources and reproduction.

Altruism

Behavior that is altruistic benefits others and appears to enhance others' success, with no benefit for the altruist. Sociobiologists explain altruism as a way of maintaining the gene pool at its highest level. In a sense, altruism is selfishness at the level of the gene rather than at the level of the individual animal. A classic case of altruism is the female worker classes of certain wasps, bees, and ants. These workers are sterile and do not reproduce but labor altruistically for the reproductive success of the queen.

Another possible mechanism for the evolution of altruism is group selection. If groups containing altruists are more successful than those composed entirely of selfish members, the altruistic groups succeed at the expense of the selfish ones, and altruism evolves. But within each group, altruists are at a severe disadvantage relative to selfish members, however well the group as a whole is able to do.

References

Ainsworth MS, Bowlby J: An ethological approach to personality development. Am Psychol *46:* 333, 1991.

Braff DL, Geyer MA: Sensorimotor gaiting and schizophrenia. Human and animal studies. Arch Gen Psychiatry *47:* 181, 1990.

Fine TH, Turner JW Jr: The effect of brief restricted environmental stimulation therapy in the treatment of essential hypertension. Behav Res Ther *20:* 567, 1982.

Gardner R: Sociobiology and its applications to psychiatry. In *Comprehensive Textbook of Psychiatry,* HI Kaplan, BJ Sadock, editors, ed 6, p 365. Williams & Wilkins, Baltimore, 1995.

Harlow HF: The nature of love. Am Psychol *13:* 673, 1958.

Kraemer GW, Ebert MH, Schmidt DE, McKinney WT: Strangers in a strange land: A psychobiological study of infant monkeys before and after separation from real or inanimate mothers. Child Dev *62:* 548, 1991.

Lerner RM, von Eye A: Sociobiology and human development: Arguments and evidence. Hum Dev *35:* 12, 1992.

Lieberman L, Reynolds LT, Friedrich D: The fitness of human sociobiology: The future utility of four concepts in four subdisciplines. Soc Biol *39:* 158, 1992.

Lister RG: Ethologically based animal models of anxiety disorders. Pharmacol Ther *46:* 321, 1990.

Lorenz KZ: *The Foundations of Ethology.* Springer, New York, 1981.

McGuire MT, Marks I, Nesse RM, Troisi A: Evolutionary biology: A basic science for psychiatry? Acta Psychiatrica Scand *86:* 89, 1992.

McKinney WT: Animal research and its relevance to psychiatry. In *Comprehensive Textbook of Psychiatry,* ed 6, HI Kaplan, BJ Sadock, editors, p 3970. Williams & Wilkins, Baltimore, 1995.

Pavlov IP: *Conditioned Reflexes.* Oxford University Press, London, 1927.

Price JS, Sloman L, Gardner R Jr, Gilbert P, Rohde P: The social competition hypothesis of depression. Br J Psychiatry *164:* 309, 1994.

Slavin MO, Kriegman D: *The Adaptive Design of the Human Psyche: Psychoanalysis, Evolutionary Biology, and the Therapeutic Process.* Guilford, New York, 1992.

Smith CUM: Evolutionary biology and psychiatry. Br J Psychiatry *162:* 149, 1993.

Spear NE, Miller JS, Jagielo JA: Animal memory and learning. Annu Rev Psychol *41:* 169, 1990.

Swerdlow NR, Braff DL, Taaid N, Geyer MA: Assessing the validity of an animal model of deficient sensorimotor gating in schizophrenic patients. Arch Gen Psychiatry *51:* 139, 1994.

Tinbergen N: *The Study of Instinct.* Clarendon, Oxford, UK, 1989.

Yehuda R, Antelman SM: Criteria for rationally evaluating animal models of posttraumatic stress disorder. Biol Psychiatry *33:* 479, 1993.

▲ 4.6 Anthropology and Psychiatry

Anthropology (the study of human beings) and psychiatry both deal with human behavior. Anthropologists study, among other things, the origin and distribution of human beings and explore their physical remains, their environmental and social relations, and their culture, which may be defined as the external expression of people's mental life in the form of language, beliefs, customs, technology, human relationships, and many other factors. Cultures show great variety in all their aspects, from their definitions of health and sickness to their relations with nature to their beliefs about child rearing, women's and men's roles, exchange of goods, and almost every other aspect of life (Fig. 4.6–1).

Researchers in human behavior often turn to anthropology for examples of normal and maladaptive behavior in various cultures. Because psychiatric theorists have long predicted that cultural variables influence behavior, these variables may help further the understanding of the nature–nurture controversy: Which aspects of human beings are innate and biological, which aspects are shaped by the environment, and how the constant feedback between these two aspects create human beings.

In the past decades, the fields of anthropology and psychiatry have both undergone many changes. In psychiatry, the increasingly acknowledged evidence of biological factors has altered the view of people as largely determined by the outcome of relationships shaping children's earliest years. And although anthropological cross-cultural studies have focused on differences as well as similarities in human beings, some anthropologists have emphasized that people cannot be independent of their cultures and that even the attempt to study cross-cultural behavior is a culturally bound viewpoint.

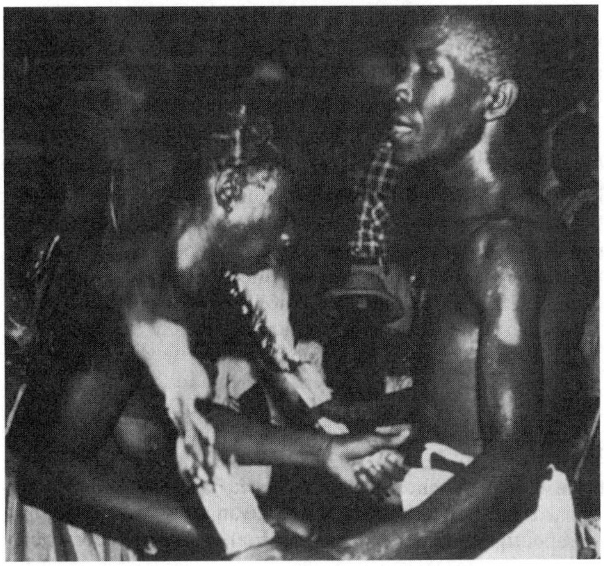

FIGURE 4.6–1
A voodoo shaman and shamaness, Houngan and Mambo, in Haiti, undergo an ordeal by fire while possessed by spirits in an altered state of consciousness. (Courtesy of Wolfgang Jilek, M.D., Vancouver, British Columbia.)

PSYCHOANALYTICAL THEORY

Beginning with Sigmund Freud, psychoanalysts have applied their insights to cultural data. In Freud's 1913 work *Totem and Taboo,* he described the earliest humans as a group of brothers who killed and devoured their violent primal father. This criminal act and the so-called totem meal made the brothers feel guilty. Consequently, they formulated rules to prevent similar acts from recurring, and these rules were the beginning of social organization. Carl Gustav Jung's writings include many anthropological references, especially to archaeology and mythology. In *Symbols and Transformations,* written in 1912, Jung traced patients' fantasies back to earliest human artifacts. Neither Freud nor Jung had field experience, but Erik Erikson, for one example, did. Erikson is best known for his psychocultural biographies of Mohandas Gandhi and Martin Luther and for his 1950 book *Childhood and Society,* in which he attempted to integrate individual psychosexual development with cultural influences. Many of his conclusions were based on his experiences with the Pine Ridge Indians in the Dakotas and the Yurok Indians in Oregon.

George Devereux studied American Plains Indians and provided insights into the problems that arise in dealing with patients from diverse ethnic backgrounds. In the 1930s and the 1940s, Abraham Kardiner worked with the concept of national character and suggested that each culture is associated with a common (or at least widely shared) personality structure. Kardiner believed that the adult Russian personality, for example, is characterized by depressive and manic traits. Other such generalities about national character were set forth by various workers, but these descriptions were often used to foster political, ideological, or discriminatory attitudes and so have fallen out of favor. The current consensus is that a clinically meaningful prediction about personality cannot be made on the basis of nationality alone. But as Ruth Benedict wrote in *Patterns of Culture,* personality types may reflect a culture's configuration because people are malleable and they assume a society's expected behavior pattern.

Bronislaw Malinowski and Margaret Mead were among the anthropologists who examined the psychoanalytic concept that adult personality and mental functioning are largely determined during childhood. Malinowski examined childhood and adult sexuality in the Trobriand Islanders and claimed that he found no evidence of the Oedipus complex, which at the time was believed to be universal. Margaret Mead examined gender and sex-role behavior. She observed three tribes in New Guinea and found different patterns of sex-role behavior for men and women in each tribe. According to Mead, behavior is relative, and a society can create deviance by either condoning or condemning certain behavior patterns. Mead believed the Oedipus complex to be a useful concept in its widest meaning, which is that in all societies adults are involved in the growing child's sexual attitudes, especially toward the parent of the opposite sex.

Margaret Mead

In Margaret Mead's *Coming of Age in Samoa* published in 1928, Mead described a society in the South Pacific in which adolescent turmoil—widely believed at the time to be universal—appeared not to exist. This was the result, she argued, of the unusual Samoan culture that nurtured open, nonpossessive sexual relationships among adolescents, encouraged communal child rearing, and denigrated aggressiveness and competitiveness. Growing up was ''so easy,'' she stated, because of ''the general casualness of the whole society.''

Widely publicized and discussed, Mead's observations helped to entrench a belief in cultural determinism that persisted for decades. Research has shown, however, that Mead's methodology was seriously flawed and her conclusions were questionable. When Mead went to Samoa at the age of 23, she spoke no Samoan language, and her data were based, not on direct observation, but on the hearsay reports of adolescent and preadolescent girls from nearby villages.

Rather than an idyllic paradise of free love among gentle people, most observers, including Samoans themselves, describe a competitive society marked by interfamily and intervillage networks in which female virginity is highly prized at the time of marriage. Ample evidence (such as teenage delinquency and suicide rates) shows that during the 1920s ''adolescent turmoil'' was not only present, but pronounced. One critic has described Mead's Samoan study as an example of how ''as evidence is sought to substantiate a cherished doctrine, the deeply held beliefs of those involved may lead them unwillingly into error.''

The absolute cultural determinism advocated by Mead arose in response to the absolute biological determinism of an earlier generation. Neither extreme is believed credible by behavioral researchers today.

UNIVERSALS AND VARIATIONS IN PSYCHOSOCIAL GROWTH

The effects of early life experiences on adult mental health and the explanations for deviance or maladaptive behavior are still controversial issues. Psychodynamic psychiatrists and theorists rely on historical data about adverse experiences to explain later behavior; but new work shows that few experiences are irreversible. Some affection-deprived children described by John Bowlby were able to grow up capable of forming attachments if other experiences later in life were favorable. Similarly, many successful adults come from deprived or otherwise toxic homes and appear to be or are invulnerable to these stressors.

Freud postulated a universal sequence of emotional development. Beyond some very general elements (the existence of infantile sexuality, the formation of an attachment to a primary caretaker who is usually the mother, the ubiquity of conflicts and jealousies within the family) this allegedly universal sequence has never found empirical support in cross-cultural studies of human behavioral psychological development. Such studies have, however, produced extensive evidence supporting empirically grounded putative universals of psychosocial growth.

Among the well-established cross-cultural universals of psychosocial development, the best supported and most plausibly related to underlying neural or neuroendocrine maturational events are the emergence of sociality, as heralded by social smiling, during the first 4 months of life, in parallel with the maturation of basal ganglia and cortical motor circuits; the emergence of strong attachments, as well as of feats of separation and of recognition of strangers, in the second half of the first year of life, in parallel with the maturation of the major fiber tracts of the limbic system; the emergence of language during the second year and after, in parallel with the maturation of the thalamic projection to the auditory cortex among other circuits; the emergence of a sex difference in physical aggressiveness in early and middle childhood, with male children on the average exceeding female children, a consequence in part of prenatal androgenization of the hypothalamus; the emergence of adult sexual motivation and functioning in adolescence, in parallel with and following the maturation of the hypothalamic-pituitary-gonadal axis at puberty, against the background of the previously mentioned prenatal androgenization of the hypothalamus.

As for the effect of early life experiences on psychological development, recent work has established an extraordinary fact. In rigorous twin, adoption, and family studies, variance in personality as well as in mental ability can be statistically apportioned among various sources. The results routinely accord a large proportion of the variance to environmental influence (roughly half in numerous studies). The effect of family relationships on personality and mental ability, however, appears to be minimal.

The portion of the variance in outcome measure (such as behavior and questionnaire results) attributable to environment is composed almost entirely of within-family variance, such as sibling differences. Identical twins reared together are routinely found to be no more similar in personality than identical twins reared in separate families; sometimes, the separately reared twins are found to be more similar. To the extent that children in different families differ in personality, the difference can be explained almost entirely by their genetic differences. Differences between nonidentical twin siblings, however, cannot be explained by their genetic differences alone but require environmental explanations as well, such as birth order.

This conclusion seems to indicate that parents' attempts to treat their children similarly (rules, religion, schooling, toys, television) do not make their offspring more similar in personality, or more different from their counterparts in other families, than they would be on the basis of genes alone. No one understands the reason for this phenomenon. Whatever the explanation, the challenge posed by the extremely small magnitude of measurable between-family variance poses a major challenge to the explanatory paradigms of child psychiatry, psychodynamic theory, and developmental psychology.

CROSS-CULTURAL UNIVERSALS OF HUMAN BEHAVIOR, MIND, AND CULTURE

Although cultural anthropologists have described and analyzed cross-cultural variation, they have also studied the features of human behavior that do not vary. The concept of universals has at least five different meanings. Behaviors such as coordinated bipedal walking or smiling in social greeting are exhibited by all normal members of every known society. Behaviors are universal within an age or sex class, such as the Moro reflex in all normal neonates or the ejaculatory motor action pattern in all postpubertal males. Population characteristics apply to all populations but not to all individual members of the populations, such as the sex difference in physical aggressiveness. Universal features of culture rather than of behavior exist, such as the taboos against incest and homicide, or the highly variable but always present institution of marriage, or the social construction of illness and attempts at healing (Fig. 4.6–2). Characteristics, although unusual or even rare, are found at some low level in every population, such as homicidal violence, thought disorder, depression, suicide, and incest.

The search for societies without violence, or without gender differences that go beyond reproduction, or without mental ill-

FIGURE 4.6–2
Psychotic woman in Laos. She was kept in stocks for several months to prevent her from running off into the forest, a well-known fatal outcome of psychosis in the area. (Courtesy of Joseph Westermeyer, M.D.)

ness has been a vain one. Although there is convincing documentation of variation in the incidence or context of expression of most human behaviors, the existence of a large core of always-present, if variable, features constitutes a demonstration of the reality of human nature and its validity as a scientific construct.

References

Al-Issa I, editor: *Handbook of Culture and Mental Illness: An International Perspective.* International Universities Press, Madison, CT, 1995.

Andrews GR: Cross cultural studies: An important development in aging research. J Am Geriatr Soc *37:* 483, 1989.

Armelagos GJ, Leatherman T, Ryan M, Sibley L: Biocultural synthesis in medical anthropology. Med Anthropol *14:* 35, 1992.

Bracken PJ: Post-empiricism and psychiatry: Meaning and methodology in cross-cultural research. Soc Sci Med *36:* 265, 1993.

Erikson E: *Childhood and Society.* Norton, New York, 1950.

Fabrega H Jr: Culture and the psychosomatic tradition. Psychosom Med *54:* 561, 1992.

Fabrega H Jr: An ethnomedical perspective of Anglo-American psychiatry. Am J Psychiatry *146:* 588, 1989.

Freud S: Totem and taboo. In *Standard Edition of the Complete Psychological Works of Sigmund Freud,* vol 13, p 1. Hogarth, London, 1955.

Fullilove MT: Psychiatric implications of displacement: Contributions from the psychology of place [Review]. Am J Psychiatry *153:* 1516, 1996.

Jung C: *Symbols and Transformations,* ed 2. Princeton University Press, Princeton, NJ, 1967.

Kirmayer LJ: Cultural variations in the response to psychiatric disorders and emotional distress. Soc Sci Med *29:* 327, 1989.

Koegel P: Through a different lens: An anthropological perspective on the homeless mentally ill. Cult Med Psychiatry *16:* 1, 1992.

Konner M: Anthropology and psychiatry. In *Comprehensive Textbook of Psychiatry,* ed 6, HI Kaplan, BJ Sadock, editors, p 337. Williams & Wilkins, Baltimore, 1995.

Landrine H, Klonoff EA: Culture and health-related schemas: A review and proposal for interdisciplinary integration. Health Psychol *11:* 267, 1992.

Mooij A: Towards an anthropological psychiatry. Theoret Med *16:* 73, 1995.

Parron DL: DSM-IV: Making it culturally relevant. In *Anxiety Disorders in African Americans,* S Friedman, editor, p 15. Springer, New York, 1994.

▲ 4.7 Epidemiology, Biostatistics, and Social Psychiatry

The *scientific method* is the process by which events in epidemiology, biostatistics, and social psychiatry are observed, described, and recorded. Several philosophic schools have contributed to the scientific method of psychology and psychiatry: empiricism, rationalism, and determinism, among others. *Empiricism* is the doctrine that although all knowledge is derived from experience, people's minds and inner experiences affect their perceptions of the world. *Rationalism,* by contrast, holds that people can grasp basic truths about the world by reason alone, unaided by experience. In *determinism,* people are thought to be products of their histories and experiences.

Workers in psychology and psychiatry use scientific methods to ensure that their work adheres strictly to principles of honesty, accuracy, and controlled experimentation. *Experiments* are defined as tests of the validity or probability of a hypothesis or theory that is demonstrated by inductive and deductive reasoning. *Inductive reasoning* works from the particular to the general, so that a new hypothesis is formed after observations. *Deductive reasoning* works from the general to the particular, so that a new conclusion about a specific case is formed from accepted premises. Although in deductive logic the truth of the conclusion is in a sense contained in the premise, in inductive logic the link between the conclusion and the premises is only probable. The theory of parsimony, or Ockham's razor, is also applied in the behavioral sciences to prune the logical tree. The theory of *parsimony* in medicine, for instance, states that two diagnoses need not be made when one alone can account for all the signs and symptoms. Human behavior and experience, however, are often so complex that a single explanation cannot capture them.

EPIDEMIOLOGY

Epidemiology is the study of the distribution, incidence, prevalence, and duration of disease. In psychiatry, epidemiological methods contribute to an understanding of the causes, treatment, and prevention of mental disorders. Such methods also help define and evaluate strategies to prevent and control disease and disability.

Epidemiological surveys reveal that about one third of all people in the United States have had or will have a mental disorder at some time in their lives. Most common are anxiety disorders, followed by depressive disorders and alcohol or other substance abuse. Surveys have also found that about 15 percent of all patients whom nonpsychiatric physicians see for a medical or surgical problem have an associated emotional disorder, most often depression or alcohol abuse or both.

Epidemiology advances psychiatric research by correlating clinical findings with such sociodemographic variables as age, gender, and socioeconomic status. For example, higher rates of almost every mental disorder are found in persons under age 45 than in those over 45. In general, women have significantly higher rates than do men for all depression and generalized anxiety disorders. Men, however, have higher rates of substance-related disorders and antisocial personality disorder. Schizophrenia, which affects about 1 percent of the population, shows similar rates for men and women.

Epidemiological studies are also used to compare the incidence and prevalence of diseases internationally and cross-culturally. Prevalence refers to the number of existing cases of a disorder; incidence refers to the number of new cases (discussed later). In general, the prevalence of mental disorders appears to be fairly constant, regardless of nationality or cultural background; but schizophrenia has a better prognosis and outcome in less-developed third-world countries than it does in societies such as the United States and the United Kingdom.

Types of Studies

Clinical and epidemiological studies in psychiatry attempt to answer questions about the etiology, treatment, course, prognosis, and prevention of various disorders. Two main types of studies are *observational,* in which the natural course of an illness is followed without any intervention, and *experimental,* in which some or all factors under study are controlled by the investigator. Most studies are experimental in design; but because of the many variables involved in mental disorders, it is difficult to design well-controlled experimental studies. The most common types of experimental designs used in psychiatry are described next.

Cohort Study. A *cohort* is a group chosen from a well-defined population that is studied over a long time. Cohort studies are also known as longitudinal studies. An example is the study by Stella Chess and Alexander Thomas of temperamental characteristics of the same group of infants at ages 3 months, 2 years, 5 years, and 20 years. In this study the cohort was the group born and studied in the year the study began. The researchers were able to discern a relation between infants' initial characteristics and a subgroup of children who eventually had clinical psychiatric problems.

Cohort studies provide direct estimates of risk associated with a suspected causal factor. They are more time consuming and expensive to perform than are case-history studies, which are usually quick and inexpensive. Cohort studies are usually conducted when ample evidence from case-history studies indicates a relation between a risk factor and a disorder. For example, in the relation between lung cancer and smoking, many case-history studies had been published before the first cohort study was published.

Retrospective and Prospective Studies. Prospective studies, also called longitudinal studies, are based on observing events as they occur. A major problem in psychiatric longitudinal studies is that some people are lost to follow-up over time. Retrospective studies are based on past data or past events.

Cross-sectional Study. Cross-sectional studies provide information about the prevalence of disease in a representative study population at a particular point in time. For this reason, they are also known as prevalence studies.

Case-History Study. A case-history study is a retrospective study that examines persons with a particular disease.

Case-Control Study. A case-control study is a retrospective study that examines persons without a particular disease.

Clinical Trial. In a clinical trial, specially selected patients receive a course of treatment, and another group does not. Eligible patients are assigned to the treatment and control groups on a random basis, and the goal of the study is to determine the effects of a given treatment.

Double-Blind Study. A double-blind study helps eliminate bias; neither the patients nor the other persons involved in the study know which, if any, treatment is being given to the patients. In drug studies, a control group of patients may receive a *placebo,* an inert substance prepared to resemble the active drug being tested in the experiment. A response to the placebo may represent the psychological effect of taking a pill, a response not caused by any psychopharmacological property (so-called *placebo effect*). Even the investigators do not know the treatment given, in that the drugs are identified by special codes unknown to them. The assessment of the outcome may be made by people other than those administering the treatment—so-called blind evaluators. Control subjects may receive an alternative comparison treatment rather than just a placebo.

Crossover Study. A crossover study is a variation of the double-blind study. The treatment group and the control or placebo group change at some point, so that the placebo group gets the treatment and the first treatment group gets the placebo. This procedure eliminates bias because if the treatment group improves in each instance and the placebo group does not, then the makeup of both groups was truly random. Each group serves as its own control.

Diagnostic Reliability and Validity

Medical and psychiatric diagnoses are clinically useful only when they are reliable and valid. *Diagnostic reliability* refers to consistency. It describes the extent to which different examiners give the same diagnosis for a given patient and the extent to which this patient continues to receive the same diagnosis over time. *Validity* refers to the accuracy of a diagnosis. Reliability must be established before validity can be determined. If 100 psychiatrists all conclude that a patient is suffering from schizophrenia, this diagnosis is reliable. If the patient actually suffers from a cocaine-induced psychosis, the diagnosis is not valid.

The reliability and validity of psychiatric diagnoses have suffered from the absence of external validating criteria—biological markers or laboratory tests that confirm or refute a diagnosis independent of a clinician's judgment. When a diagnosis rests wholly on the judgment of individual examiners, reliability may suffer. The year 1980 marked a watershed in U.S. psychiatry: The third edition of the *Diagnostic and Statistical Manual of Mental Disorders* (DSM-III), published by the American Psychiatric Association, deliberately turned from a diagnostic system strongly influenced by psychoanalytic theory to a phenomenological and descriptive system based only on signs, symptoms, and clinical course. DSM-III (and later editions) attempted to enhance diagnostic reliability by formulating precise, descriptive diagnostic criteria and minimizing the degree of inference needed to make a diagnosis.

Several types of diagnostic validity can be described. *Face validity* refers to a general consensus among experienced researchers and clinicians that a particular disorder exists. (The editors of DSM-III for the most part selected categories on the basis of face validity.) *Descriptive validity* implies that a disorder can be described by features characteristic enough to distinguish it from other disorders. For a medical or psychiatric diagnosis to be of clinical use, it must have *predictive validity:* The diagnosis allows clinicians to accurately predict treatment response and clinical course. *Construct validity* bases the diagnosis on an understanding of the underlying pathophysiology and can be confirmed with biological markers. The diagnosis of pneumonia, for instance, has construct validity: It relates the fever, shortness of breath, and chest pain to known pathological processes of the invading organism and can be confirmed through chest X-rays and sputum cultures. On the other hand, the diagnosis of bipolar I disorder has both descriptive and predictive validity but lacks construct validity. The mechanisms of symptom production remain unknown, and biological markers have not yet been identified.

Biological markers and other external validating criteria must be *sensitive;* that is, they must be able to detect the thing being evaluated (for example, to diagnose a disorder when it is present). When a marker detects a disorder in a person who does not have the disorder, the result is called a false positive rather than a true positive. Tests must also be *specific;* that is, they must not detect things not being evaluated. For example, tests must be able to detect the absence of a disorder in a person who does not have the disorder, a result called true negative. A disorder reported to be absent in a person when it is actually present is called a false-negative result. Markers and other assessment instruments should also have good *predictive value,* which is the proportion of true-positive or true-negative results. Predictive values indicate what percentage of test outcomes are expected to coincide with assigned diagnoses. Table 4.7–1 summarizes the interpretation of the concepts of sensitivity, specificity, and predictive value.

BIOSTATISTICS

Biostatistics is the mathematical science of describing, organizing, and interpreting data related to medicine. Epidemiology relies on statistics to enable investigators to examine possible causes of disease and to evaluate treatment strategies.

The principles of statistics are beyond the scope of this book; but a glossary of statistical terms used in most elementary textbooks of statistics is presented here. A knowledge of such terms is necessary not only for understanding epidemiological concepts but also for accurately assessing statistical methods that appear in scientific publications.

Statistical Overview

The two major types of statistics are descriptive and inferential. *Descriptive statistics* are numerical values for summarizing, organizing, and describing observations (for example, the average number of symptoms associated with an anxiety disorder). Examples include mean, standard deviation, and variance. *Inferential statistics* are numerical values used to draw general conclusions about probabilities on the basis of a sample (for example, the influences of drug A versus drug B in the treatment of a group of depressed patients). Examples include the analysis of variance, probability, and probability (*P*) value.

Data are factual information derived from a population or a sample. A *population* is the entire collection of a set of objects, people, or events in a particular context (for example, all patients with schizophrenia in a particular hospital). A *sample* is a subset selected from this population (for example, one half of the patients with schizophrenia in a particular hospital). Data can be *nominal* (organized into categories), *ordinal* (ranked in order), or *organized into interval ratios* (measured on a scale, graph, or table).

Glossary of Statistical Terms

Analysis of Variance (ANOVA). A set of statistical procedures designed to compare two or more groups of observations. It determines whether the differences between groups are due to experimental influence or to chance alone.

Control Group. A group that does not receive treatment and is used as a standard of comparison.

Correlation Coefficient. A measurement of the direction and strength of the relationship between two variables. Two of the most commonly used are the Spearman rank order coefficient for ordinal data and the Pearson correlation coefficient for nominal data. The Pearson correlation coefficient (*r*) takes any value between −1 and +1. A positive correlation means that as one variable increases (or decreases) the other

Table 4.7–1
Definitions and Calculations for Interpreting Performance of Diagnostic Tests

Term	Definition	Calculation
True positive (TP)	Diseased person with abnormal test results	
True negative (TN)	Nondiseased person with normal test results	
False positive (FP)	Nondiseased person with abnormal test results	
False negative (FN)	Diseased person with normal test results	
Referent value	A value to which laboratory results can be referred and from which the probability of disease or predictive value can be calculated	
Sensitivity	True positive rate	$\frac{TP}{TP + FN} \times 100$
Specificity	True negative rate	$\frac{TN}{TP + FP} \times 100$
Predictive value of abnormal test results (PV +)	Proportion of abnormal test results that are true positive	$\frac{TP}{TP + FP} \times 100$
Predictive value of normal test results (PV −)	Proportion of normal test results that are true negative	$\frac{TN}{TN + FN} \times 100$
Efficiency	Percentage of all results that are true results, whether positive or negative	$\frac{TP + TN}{\text{Grand Total}} \times 100$

Courtesy of John F. Greden, M.D.

moves in the same direction. A negative r indicates that the variables move in opposite directions. A correlation approaching -1 or $+1$ indicates a strong relationship; a correlation approaching 0 indicates a weak relationship. Correlation coefficients indicate only the degree of relationship; they say nothing about cause and effect.

Distribution. A series or range of values that can be organized according to their frequency of occurrence (*frequency distribution*). A symmetrical, bell-shaped frequency distribution of scores is called a *normal distribution* (the bell curve).

Incidence. The number of new cases occurring over a specified time. The most common period used is 1 year, which produces an annual incidence calculated as follows:

$$\text{Incidence} = \frac{\text{Number of new cases of a disease (over a 1-year period)}}{\text{Total number of people at risk (over a 1-year period)}}$$

A study of incidence is more difficult to do than a study of prevalence cases because those who already have the disease must be excluded from the incidence numerator; they cannot be considered new cases. As those who have had the disease are no longer at risk for it, they also must be excluded from the denominator. A broader concept of total incidence includes those with a new episode of illness, regardless of whether they have had previous episodes.

Lifetime expectancy is the total probability of a person's having a disorder during a lifetime. Prevalence and incidence vary for sex and age; thus, sex-specific and age-specific rates are used to express the relative frequency of cases in each category.

Measure of Central Tendency. A central value in a distribution around which other values are distributed. Three measures of central tendency are the mean, the median, and the mode.

MEAN. A statistical measurement derived from adding a set of scores and then dividing by the number of scores. The mean is the average score.

MEDIAN. The value in the middle of a set of measurements. For example, in the series 2, 3, 5, 11, 21, the number 5 is the median value.

MODE. The value that appears most frequently in a set of measurements.

Null Hypothesis. The assumption that there is no significant difference between two random samples of a population. When the null hypothesis is rejected, observed differences between groups are deemed to be improbable by chance alone.

Percentile Rank. The percentage of scores in a distribution exceeded by any particular score. For example, a percentile rank of 80 for a given score means that this score exceeds 80 percent of all scores in the distribution.

Power. The probability of rejecting the null hypothesis when, in the real world, it should have been rejected. Power is the probability of identifying a true difference.

Prevalence. The number of existing cases of a disorder. There are several types of prevalence.

POINT PREVALENCE. The number of people who have a disorder at a specified point in time. The point can be a certain calendar day (for example, April 1, 1993) or any day during a particular study (for example, the fourth day of the study), regardless of the calendar day. It is calculated as follows:

$$\text{Point prevalence} = \frac{\text{Number of people with a disorder at a specified point in time}}{\text{Total population at specified point in time}}$$

PERIOD PREVALENCE. The number of people who have a disorder at any time during a specified period (longer than a calendar day or a point in time). It is calculated as follows:

$$\text{Period prevalence} = \frac{\text{Number of people with a disorder during a time period}}{\text{Total population during time period}}$$

The numerator includes any existing cases at the start of the period and any new cases that develop during the period. Period prevalence may be used to determine the number of people with a disorder, the number of those in treatment, and the duration of an illness.

LIFETIME PREVALENCE. A measure at a point in time of the number of people who had a disorder at some time during their lives. A potential problem with determining lifetime prevalence is that it is almost always based on subject recall, which can be inaccurate.

TREATED PREVALENCE. The number of people being treated for a disorder, arrived at by counting all those in a defined geographic area who are receiving treatment. Treated point prevalence (for example, the number of patients being treated for a disorder in a clinic on a certain day) or treated period prevalence (for example, the number of patients being treated for a disorder at a clinic over the past year) can be measured.

Probability. A quantitative statement of the likelihood that an event will occur. A probability of 0 means that the event is certain not to occur; a probability of 1 means that the event will occur with certainty.

***P* Value.** The probability of obtaining a result by chance alone. A P value of .01 means that the probability of obtaining a result by chance alone is 1 in 100; a value of .05 means that the result will occur 5 times out of every 100 times by chance alone.

Randomization. The process allowing each patient in a clinical trial to have an equal chance to be assigned to a control or experimental treatment group. It protects against selection bias and guarantees the validity of statistical tests of significance.

Regression Analysis. A method for obtaining a prediction from observed data to predict the value of one variable (x) in relation to the value of another variable (y).

Risk Factor. A disorder-associated factor that may support a causal connection. A risk may be factor specific (for example, it occurs in only one sex) or factor related (for example, it is likely to occur in a certain environment). A causal connection between a risk factor and a disorder is shown by temporality, in which a factor precedes the disorder being studied; the repeated appearance of the same risk factor in multiple studies; specificity, in which a risk factor is associated with one disorder only; and a determination that the experimental intervention eliminating the risk factor also eliminates the disorder. Determining what factor or factors account for the increased risk of a disorder is one of the challenges of psychiatric epidemiology.

RELATIVE RISK. The ratio of the incidence of the disease among people exposed to the risk factor to the incidence among those not exposed. For example, the relative risk of lung cancer is much greater for heavy smokers than for nonsmokers.

ATTRIBUTABLE RISK. The absolute incidence of the disease in exposed people that can be attributed to the exposure. The measure is derived by subtracting the incidence of the disease in question among unexposed people from its total incidence among those exposed. For example, the lung cancer death rate for nonsmokers may be subtracted from the total community lung cancer death rate. The results are the attributable community risk for lung cancer. Attributable risk is a useful concept that shows what may be expected if the risk is removed. For example, on the basis of available data, the attributable risk for deaths from lung cancer could be avoided if smoking were eliminated.

Sensitivity. The number of true positives divided by the sum of the number of true positives and false negatives. It is the proportion of patients with the condition in question which the test can detect.

Specificity. The number of true negatives divided by the sum of the number of true negatives and false positives. It is the proportion of patients without the condition, which the test finds negative.

Standard Deviation (SD). A measure of variation derived by squaring each deviation in a set of scores, taking the average of these squares, and then taking the square root of the result. The standard deviation is represented by the Greek letter sigma (σ). In a normal distribution, $\pm$ 1 SD includes 68 percent of the population; $\pm$ 2 SD includes 95 percent of the population; and $\pm$ 3 SD includes 99 percent of the population.

Type I Error. The error that occurs when the null hypothesis is rejected when it should have been retained; the false claim of a true difference because the observed difference is due entirely to chance.

Type II Error. The error that occurs when the null hypothesis is retained when it should have been rejected; the false acceptance of the null hypothesis when, in fact, there is a true difference, but the difference is so small that it falls within the acceptance region of the null hypothesis.

Variable. A characteristic that can assume different values in different experimental situations. In research, *independent variables* are those qualities that the experimenter systematically varies (for example, time, age, sex, type of drug) in the experiment. *Dependent variables* are those qualities that measure the influence of the independent variable or the outcome of the experiment (for example, the measurement of a person's specific physiological reactions to a drug).

References

Bird HR: Epidemiology of childhood disorders in a cross-cultural context. Child Psychol Psychiatry *37:* 35, 1996.

Cooper B: Epidemiology and prevention in the mental health field. Soc Psychiatry Psychiatr Epidemiol *25:* 9, 1990.

Doll B: Prevalence of psychiatric disorders in children and youth: An agenda for advocacy by school psychology. School Psychol Q *11:* 20, 1996.

Fenton WS, Robinowitz CB, Leaf PJ: Male and female psychiatrists and their patients. Am J Psychiatry *144:* 358, 1987.

Grant I, Kaplan RM: Statistics and experimental design. In *Comprehensive Textbook of Psychiatry,* ed 6, HI Kaplan, BJ Sadock, editors, p 412. Williams & Wilkins, Baltimore, 1995.

Gurland B: Epidemiology of psychiatric disorders. In *Comprehensive Review of Geriatric Psychiatry—II,* ed 2, J Sadavoy, LW Lazarus, LF Jarvik, GT Grossberg, editors, p 3, American Psychiatric Press, Washington, 1996.

Henderson AS: The present state of psychiatric epidemiology. Aust NZ J Psychiatry *30:* 9, 1996.

Kessler RC: Sociology and psychiatry. In *Comprehensive Textbook of Psychiatry,* ed 6, HI Kaplan, BJ Sadock, editors, p 356. Williams & Wilkins, Baltimore, 1995.

Klerman GL: Paradigm shifts in USA psychiatric epidemiology since World War II. Soc Psychiatry Psychiatr Epidemiol *25:* 27, 1990.

Regier DA, Burke JD: Epidemiology. In *Comprehensive Textbook of Psychiatry,* ed 6, HI Kaplan, BJ Sadock, editors, p 377. Williams & Wilkins, Baltimore, 1995.

Roger JL, Howard KI, Vesey JT: Using significance test to evaluate equivalence between two experimental groups. Psychol Bull *113:* 553, 1993.

Samuels JF, Nestadt G: Epidemiology: The distribution of mental disorders in the community. In *Integrated Mental Health Services: Modern Community Psychiatry,* WR Breakey, editor, p 71. Oxford University Press, New York, 1996.

Visotsky HM: Courage, creativity, and cost-effectiveness: The challenge for a psychiatric program administration. New Dir Ment Health Serv *49:* 51, 1991.

▲ 4.8 Public Psychiatry

The present idea of public psychiatry was largely shaped by federal regulations passed in the 1960s to offer people who were mentally ill financial support in their communities and to establish community mental health centers. Rather than isolating people with mental disorders for long periods in state hospitals (Fig. 4.8–1), legislators thought it preferable to treat these people in the community and to hospitalize them only briefly and under certain restrictions. Thus *public psychiatry* refers to treating mentally ill people in the community, where all aspects of care, from hospitalization, case management, and crisis intervention to day treatment and supportive living arrangements, fall under the public umbrella and are sponsored by the government.

One unfortunate result of this approach is the numerous homeless, mentally ill people who would once have lived in state institutions but are now left to the understaffed, financially limited, often grossly inadequate public health services. Public psychiatry must grapple with the almost unsolvable problem of providing these people with continuous, comprehensive integrated care at a time when federal, state, and local budgets are sharply curtailed.

BACKGROUND

In 1963, under the leadership of President John F. Kennedy, Congress passed the Community Mental Health Centers Act, which provided funds for the construction of community mental health centers with specified catchment areas (geographic regions with a population of 75,000 to 200,000). Each com-

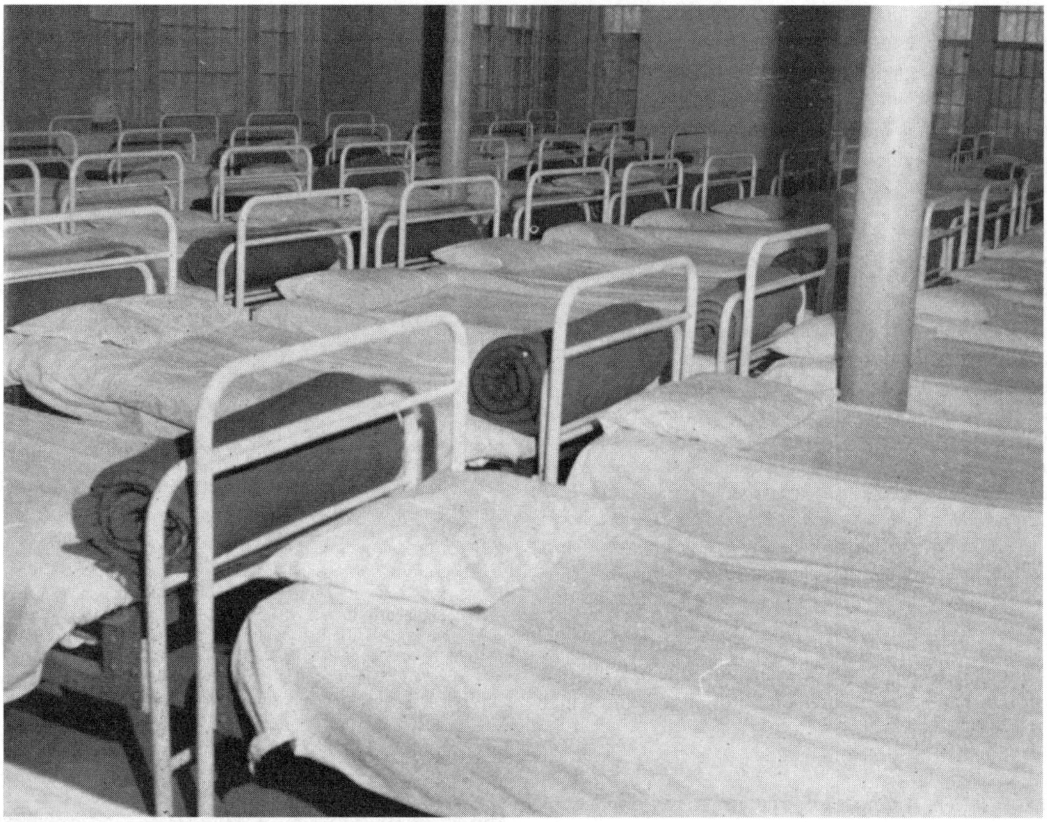

FIGURE 4.8–1
The crowded sleeping area in this illustration of a state hospital ward in the 1960s was antitherapeutic and exerted an unfavorable influence on both patients and staff. (National Association of Mental Health, New York, NY.)

munity mental health center must provide five basic psychiatric services: inpatient care, emergency services (on a 24-hour basis), community consultation, day care (including partial hospitalization programs, halfway houses, aftercare services, and a broad range of outpatient services), and research and education. In 1975, Congress added the requirements of services for children and older people, prehospitalization, screening, follow-up services for those who have been hospitalized, transitional housing, and alcoholism and drug-abuse services to the community centers' responsibilities. By the early 1980s, the community mental health center movement had strongly influenced mental health services, the practice of psychiatry, and the other mental health professions. At that time, about 800 centers were in operation, more than half in urban areas. Currently, because of severe financial constraints, the community mental health centers are severely limited and are considered by many to be ineffective.

In 1981, a block grant program was created to provide federal funds to states for drug abuse, alcohol abuse, and other mental health programs. Several states established community support systems to help furnish needed mental health services; these programs are currently available nationwide. In spite of such efforts, state mental hospitals still receive most state-allocated mental health dollars, and financial limitations have interfered with the block grant and state programs.

COMMUNITY MENTAL HEALTH CENTER FACTORS

Commitment

Commitment to a population's health care implies a responsibility for planning. Commitment suggests that the plan should identify all the mental health needs of the population, inventory the resources available to meet these needs, and organize a system of care; that citizens and political figures should be involved in the planning process; that prevention is at least as important as direct treatment; and that all the population, including children, older people, minorities, people who are chronically and acutely ill, and those who live in geographically remote areas, should receive care.

The federal requirement that mental health services be located close to people's residences or workplaces is meant to make it easy for people to get treatment and to identify illness early so that hospitalization, when required, is likely brief.

Services

Public mental health is a total system, not a single service. To be effective, services must be integrated and balanced, so that appropriate treatment modalities are available to fit patients' needs. A lack of services in one area (such as community placements) can delay other services (such as hospital discharges) and can lead to lack of services for some patients (for example, those who cannot gain admission to overcrowded hospitals). A central authority must provide the needed integration.

The public mental health team includes psychiatrists (including child psychiatrists), clinical psychologists, psychiatric social workers, psychiatric nurses, administrative and clerical staff members, and occupational and recreational therapists for inpatient and partial hospitalization programs. Links to welfare workers, the clergy, family agencies, schools, and other human services groups are also maintained.

Long-Term Care

Because of concerns about the fragmentation of care and the tendency to keep patients hospitalized or unnecessarily restricted to one type of service, public mental health programs must encourage continuity of care. Continuity of care enables a single clinician to follow a patient through emergency services, hospitalization, partial hospitalization as a transition to the community, and outpatient treatment as follow-up. Continuity also provides an exchange of information and team responsibility for the patient when various therapists, for reasons of convenience or economy, treat the patient in several settings. A free exchange of clinical information between centers and a liaison between agencies are also part of the total system of care.

Case Management

Intensive case managers are clinicians who can provide continuity of care by following patients through all the phases of treatment while helping them negotiate a complex and fragmented system. Intensive case managers provide support, advocacy, and systems management. They engage patients in treatment through outreach in single-room-occupancy residences and shelters; they ensure continuing treatment by initiating contact during hospitalization and continuing support through aftercare; and they serve as liaisons between patients and other mental health providers and between the providers themselves. Ideally, intensive care managers should have small caseloads that allow for intensive contact with their patients.

Community Participation

Communities should participate in decisions about their mental health care needs and programs instead of having them defined solely by professionals. Mental health services are sensitive to the needs of those served when the public is actively involved. The National Mental Health Association (NMHA) and the National Alliance for the Mentally Ill (NAMI) are two lay advocacy groups working at local, state, and national levels to improve care for people who are mentally ill. Liaisons with these groups can provide links to the general public and facilitate outreach and educational efforts.

Consultation

Consultations range from attention to or treatment of a person's emotional problems to using knowledge about human behavior to help organizations achieve their professional goals with their programs and patients. Consultants offer assistance to mental health professionals who work in outpatient centers or agencies and also provide direct educational activities, liaison with consumer and advocacy groups, and administrative services.

Evaluation and Research

Evaluation is the process of obtaining information about a total community mental health program and its effects on people, institutions, and communities. Program evaluation should also provide feedback to planners and decision makers, so that operating programs can be modified and new ones planned. Evaluation is an activity required for federally funded centers, which must spend at least 2 percent of their budgets on it.

Research may focus specifically on key issues rather than on a total program and may address a particular disorder or a treatment method.

PREVENTION

The disabilities associated with chronic mental illness are major social, economic, and public health problems. In the United States, these disabilities afflict more than 3 million people; they are costly and create suffering for those affected, their families, and society. Although the term *chronic mental illness* has traditionally been associated with older patients who have a long history of mental hospitalization, it has recently been broadened to include young adults with a variety of mental disorders who have grown up in the era of deinstitutionalization. Many of these people have never been hospitalized, but their ability to lead productive lives in the community is severely impaired. Psychiatric rehabilitation addresses the medical, psychiatric, and social needs of people who are persistently mentally ill.

Preventive psychiatry is part of public psychiatry. The goal of prevention is to decrease the onset (incidence), duration (prevalence), and residual disability of mental disorders. The prevention of mental disorders is based on public health principles and is divided into primary, secondary, and tertiary prevention.

Primary Prevention

The goal of *primary prevention* is to prevent the onset of a disease or disorder and thereby reduce its incidence (the ratio of new cases to the population in a specific period). This goal is reached by eliminating causative agents, reducing risk factors, enhancing host resistance, and interfering with disease transmission. For some physical disorders, the identification and modification of one or more of these factors revolutionized health care, exemplified by the virtual elimination of many infectious diseases and vitamin deficiency states and by the reduction of some forms of cancer, heart disease, and lung disease.

Examples of primary prevention to help people cope with life include mental health education programs (such as parent training in child development and alcohol and drug education programs); efforts at competence building (such as Outward

Bound, Head Start, and other enriched day-care programs for disadvantaged children); the development and use of social support systems to reduce the effects of stress on those at high risk (for example, widow-to-widow programs); anticipatory guidance programs to assist people to prepare for expected stressful situations (such as counseling Peace Corps volunteers); and crisis intervention after stressful life events, such as bereavement, marital separation, divorce, traumas, and group disasters. The hostage-release program, in which U.S. hostages released from captivity are prepared for reentry into society, is another example of primary prevention.

Primary prevention programs also aim at eradicating stressful agents and reducing stress. Such programs include prenatal and perinatal care to decrease the incidence of mental retardation and cognitive disorders in children (for example, advice about improved nutrition and abstinence from alcohol and other substances during pregnancy, improved obstetrical services, specific dietary modification for neonates vulnerable to phenylketonuria); strict lead-elimination laws to reduce the incidence of lead encephalopathy; modification of divorce, adoption, and child abuse laws to provide a healthy environment for child development; enrichment or replacement of institutional settings for infants, children, and older people; modification of certain risk factors for mental disorders that appear to be associated with low socioeconomic status; genetic counseling for parents at high risk for chromosomal abnormalities to prevent the unwitting conception of compromised infants; and efforts to reduce the spread of certain sexually transmitted diseases (for example, acquired immune deficiency syndrome [AIDS] and syphilis) that can lead to mental disorders.

Secondary Prevention

Secondary prevention is defined as the early identification and prompt treatment of an illness or disorder, with the goal of reducing the prevalence (the proportion of existing cases in the population at risk at a specified time) of the condition by shortening its duration. Crisis intervention and public education are components of secondary prevention. In psychiatry, secondary prevention targets children who are emotionally ill for early intervention. The National Institute of Mental Health's (NIMH) Child and Adolescent Services System identifies and treats these children to support their family structures and prevent or reduce later disability.

Tertiary Prevention

The goal of *tertiary prevention* is to reduce the prevalence of residual defects and disabilities caused by an illness or a disorder. In the case of mental disorders, tertiary prevention enables those with chronic mental illnesses to reach the highest feasible level of functioning.

DEINSTITUTIONALIZATION

Deinstitutionalization is the process by which large numbers of patients are discharged from public psychiatric hospitals back into the community to receive outpatient care. This policy, which began in the late 1950s, resulted in a decrease in the state psychiatric hospital population from more than 560,000 beds at that time to roughly 100,000 beds today. Many patients were released into various aftercare clinics, where they continued to receive psychiatric treatment and rehabilitative services. Others were placed in new types of institutions, such as halfway houses, board and care facilities, and public housing units. Many had to be rehospitalized, and a revolving-door policy developed, with up to 80 percent of patients being readmitted within 2 years of discharge.

Transinstitutionalization is the transfer of state hospital patients to other facilities. Many workers believe that one set of problems has been exchanged for another without solving the problem of people who are chronically mentally ill. As the number of state hospital beds has been reduced, the number of general hospital psychiatric beds has increased to 48,000, the number of private psychiatric beds has increased to 67,000, and the number of Veterans Administration beds has increased to 25,000.

A significant percentage of people who are mentally ill receive psychiatric services as prison inmates, and incarceration remains a significant component of transinstitutionalization. One study estimated that 31 percent of mentally ill people in an urban jail were homeless before arrest. Severe mental illness is 2 to 3 times more prevalent in prison populations than among the general public. Many of the incarcerated homeless mentally ill people are arrested for minor crimes that are survival strategies (for example, trespassing in buildings or cars as a means of obtaining shelter) or for behavior directly produced by psychosis.

Several studies have found that, without an active, multifaceted treatment system that assumes ongoing responsibility for all facets of patients' care, mentally ill patients regress in the community as they did in state hospitals. A major problem faced by chronically ill patients is that their illnesses interfere with their coping skills and render them particularly likely to drift downward into even more stressful, impoverished environments. The end result is an increase in homeless people in urban areas.

Deinstitutionalized patients need extensive social support, such as vocational and recreational counseling, comprehensive psychiatric treatment, paying jobs, and affordable housing. This support has not been given to the extent that planners and supporters of deinstitutionalization think necessary, primarily because of the lack of adequate funding on federal, state, and local levels. It is scandalous that funding for aftercare community services for those who are mentally ill continues to decline; unless this trend is reversed, deinstitutionalization will remain a failed public policy. Some have suggested that the limited funds available be channeled into improving existing state hospitals, so that chronically mentally ill patients and homeless mentally ill people can be referred to the system and receive appropriate care.

HOMELESS MENTALLY ILL PEOPLE

The homeless mentally ill population continues to grow; one major survey found a 7 percent rise in urban homeless people who are mentally ill over a 19-month period, with a concurrent decline in the number of shelter beds.

An average of 33 percent of homeless people are mentally ill. The percentage ranges from 15 percent of homeless people in Kansas City, Missouri, to 70 percent of homeless single adults in Boston. On average, 45 percent of homeless mentally ill people are also dependent on alcohol or other substances. The estimated percentage of these people with dual diagnoses ranges from 23 percent in Philadelphia to more than 60 percent in several major cities. There was a 9 percent rise in the number of dually diagnosed homeless people during a recent 19-month period, with a concurrent increase in the average length of time of homelessness for those who are homeless and mentally ill.

Qualities

Like those who are chronically mentally ill, homeless mentally ill people are a heterogeneous population, with no uniformity in diagnosis, demographics, functional performance, or residential history. One categorization divides them into street people, episodically homeless people, and situationally homeless people. Street people usually have schizophrenia or substance dependence or both, a history of psychiatric hospitalization, and a variety of health problems. Episodically homeless people are usually younger than street people and are likely to be regarded as difficult patients with personality disorders, substance abuse, and mood disorders; they sporadically use a wide variety of mental health services. Situationally homeless people have problems of situational stress more than of psychopathology.

Homeless mentally ill people are not simply undomiciled: They are often totally disaffiliated, with few, if any, links to the community. They are unemployed, socially isolated, and out of contact with their families. Homeless women may be more likely than are men to have intact social skills and social networks. In general, homeless mentally ill people are difficult to treat because of their high levels of withdrawal and suspicion, psychopathology, homeless lifestyle, or negative past experiences with the mental health system.

In one group of homeless mentally ill patients studied, the majority suffered from schizophrenia and schizoaffective disorder. Many patients had histories of alcohol and other substance abuse. Close to one third had concomitant physical illnesses that were secondary to alcohol dependence. The patients also suffered from significant medical problems, including anemia, lice infestation, nutritional deficiencies (B_{12}, folate, and iron deficiencies), cellulitis, and evidence of exposure to and an increased incidence of tuberculosis.

A 35-year-old man with a 10-year history of paranoid schizophrenia complicated by alcohol abuse resided in a city-run shelter, where he was identified as psychotic on the basis of his bizarre behavior related to hallucinations. He was enrolled in an intensive case management program. Through repeated outreach efforts, his intensive case manager helped the patient obtain benefits and begin treatment with fluphenazine (Prolixin), as prescribed by a visiting psychiatrist.

After the patient stabilized, his intensive case manager placed him in a supportive residence with on-site social workers and psychiatric staff members. The residence acted as the representative payee of the patient's entitlement check. At the same time, the patient attended an intensive program for mentally ill substance abusers at a nearby city hospital. He remained in the program and continued taking his medication for 2 years before leaving the program because of his desire for more control over his finances.

One year later, an outreach team found him bizarrely posturing and talking to himself in a city train terminal. He accepted a sandwich and voluntary transport to a specialized ward for the treatment of homeless mentally ill people. After stabilization, he was transferred to a state hospital for intermediate care. As his insight into the interplay of his psychiatric illness and his alcohol abuse improved, community placement was sought.

Treatment

Some people who are homeless and mentally ill remain within geographic limits; others travel from one part of the country to another. Because demography, epidemiology, history, and treatment needs vary, no single treatment method is recommended. In addition to the full range of traditional services—evaluation, crisis intervention, medication review, psychosocial skills training, and housing—homeless mentally ill patients may require less traditional services, such as a mailbox where welfare checks can be delivered, bathing facilities, and delousing services.

Traditional mental health service systems may present barriers to access for homeless mentally ill people. Sometimes the barriers are simply the result of a lack of services to meet patients' special needs or of geographic or functional limitations. Housing programs for chronically mentally ill people are often limited to high-functioning patients and thereby screen out poorly functioning street people. Effective service programs include provisions for shelter and food, drop-in centers, outreach contact, and a cooperative endeavor between mental health agencies and other agencies in the community (for example, the Salvation Army and church-affiliated organizations).

Homeless mentally ill people can be treated through outreach programs and treatment geared to their specific needs. Effective treatment can be achieved with appropriate community placements and mentally ill substance abuser programs. Many patients cannot function in the community, even with significant support; for them, long-term state hospitalization may be the only way to safeguard their well-being. Governments must accept this reality if the patients' needs are to be met.

Outreach Programs

Street outreach programs are crucial components in addressing the problems of homeless mentally ill people, as many people do not use shelters. Those who do use shelters require shelter-based outreach programs, because they rarely seek treatment by traditional routes.

Street outreach programs have succeeded by using a multidisciplinary team of psychiatrists, social workers, and nurses. They approach homeless mentally ill people by making repeated brief contacts while offering food and concrete services as a means of engagement. Street people do not tolerate a standard psychiatric interview; therefore, assessment must be made by observation, with particular attention to self-care, bizarre behavior, possible physical problems, and changing trends in appearance or behavior over time. Collateral histories from the police and workers in the community are often valuable.

Hospitalization

Those who are suicidal, homicidal, or unable to care for themselves to the point of constituting a danger to themselves require hospitalization. Involuntary hospitalization under these circumstances is controversial because of the infringement of patients' rights; but for many of these patients, involuntary hospitalization is lifesaving. Outreach teams must have strong links with local law enforcement officials, and some outreach physicians may be legally empowered to involuntarily transport patients to designated hospitals. Once the patients are hospitalized, they need comprehensive assessment, with particular attention to concomitant medical problems, substance abuse, and cognitive disorders. Psychotropic medication and a therapeutic milieu that emphasizes nursing observation, activity therapy, and psychoeducation are all helpful.

Many homeless mentally ill patients are nonverbal and profoundly regressed. As a result, they may require more than short-term hospitalization and may need transfers to state facilities. Other patients improve so much that they can function in the community. The most appropriate placements for such people are community residences with on-site social workers and psychiatric services combined with some degree of structure. Discharging patients to a shelter or an unsupervised apartment is inadequate. Such a practice is reprehensible and unfair to sick patients who require help, and it is disastrous to urban communities where homeless people are found on every corner. Assigning patients to intensive case managers before discharge can ease the transition and provide needed support and continuity of care. Attention to the patients' individual needs is essential if a long-term plan is to be effective. It is tragic that funding such long-term planning is an unresolved political issue.

PSYCHOGERIATRIC LONG-TERM CARE

The elderly population will increase an estimated 125 percent by the year 2030 and will need 3 times the nursing home care now available. The cost of such care will grow from $44 billion in 1990 to an estimated $187 billion in 2030. The growing need for professional care results from the increasing proportion of older people who will lack family supports. As a result, future long-term care financing is a major problem.

Some have suggested private-sector solutions, which include making long-term care insurance affordable through tax incentives, insurance regulations, and an increased emphasis on the provision of home care as a substitute for nursing home care, to decrease insurance payments and premiums. Others have called for a national long-term care program as part of a national health plan. At present, much of the burden of elderly long-term care falls on families: More than 70 percent of the people receiving long-term care rely on unpaid caretakers. It is clear that sweeping changes in the financing and delivery of long-term care will be needed to meet the increasing needs of this growing portion of the population.

OUTPATIENT COMMITMENT PROGRAM (OCP)

Mental patients discharged from public hospitals are often noncompliant about attending outpatient clinics for continued psychosocial or psychopharmacological treatment. In 1993, a program was begun at Bellevue Hospital Center to provide for involuntary outpatient treatment of mentally ill persons, the goals of which are to help patients live and function in the community and to avoid relapse resulting in rehospitalization. Involuntary outpatient treatment is mandated by a judge, and patients report to the clinic for medication, individual or group therapy, psychosocial therapy, and vocational training. In addition, living arrangements are made for the patient and a case manager is assigned. The court may order medication if the patient lacks the capacity to make a treatment decision. All court mandated outpatient commitment procedures are made after the patient is evaluated by the psychiatrist. Noncompliance is minimal because of close supervision and the patient's preference for OCP over involuntary hospitalization.

REFERENCES

Bachrach LL: What we know about homelessness among mentally ill persons: An analytical review and commentary. Hosp Community Psychiatry *43:* 453, 1992.

Breakey WR, editor: *Integrated Mental Health Services: Modern Community Psychiatry.* Oxford University Press, New York, 1996.

Burns BJ, Taube JE, Permutt T, Rudin SC, Mulcare ME, Harbin HT, Goldman HH: Evaluation of a Maryland fiscal incentive plan for placing state hospital patients in nursing homes. Hosp Community Psychiatry *42:* 1228, 1991.

Dencker K, Gottfries C-G: The closure of a major psychiatric hospital: Can psychiatric patients in long-term care be integrated into existing nursing homes? J Geriatr Psychiatry Neurol *4:* 149, 1991.

Elpers JR: Community psychiatry. In *Comprehensive Textbook of Psychiatry,* ed 6, HI Kaplan, BJ Sadock, editors, p 2663. Williams & Wilkins, Baltimore, 1995.

Goering P, Wasylenski D, St Onge M, Paduchak D, Lancee W: Gender differences among clients of a case management program for the homeless. Hosp Community Psychiatry *43:* 160, 1992.

Hess R, Morgan J, editors: *Prevention in Community Mental Health Centers.* Haworth, New York, 1990.

Katz SE, Nardacci D, Sabatini A, editors: *Intensive Treatment of the Homeless Mentally Ill.* American Psychiatric Press, Washington, 1993.

Marshall EJ, Reed JL: Psychiatric morbidity in homeless women. Br J Psychiatry *160:* 761, 1992.

Menninger WW: Role of the psychiatric hospital in the treatment of mental illness. In *Comprehensive Textbook of Psychiatry,* ed 6, HI Kaplan, BJ Sadock, editors, p 2690. Williams & Wilkins, Baltimore, 1995.

Moak GS, Fisher WH: Geriatric patients and services in state hospitals: Data from a national survey. Hosp Community Psychiatry *42:* 273, 1992.

Moffic HS: Cultural issues in community psychiatry. In *Practicing Psychiatry in the Community: A Manual,* JV Vaccaro, GH Clark Jr, editors, p 407. American Psychiatric Press, Washington, 1996.

Okin RL, Borus JF: Primary, secondary, and tertiary prevention of mental disorders. In *Comprehensive Textbook of Psychiatry,* ed 5, HI Kaplan, BJ Sadock, editors, p 2067. Williams & Wilkins, Baltimore, 1989.

Saathoff GB, Cortina JA, Jacobson R, Aldrich CK: Mortality among elderly patients discharged from a state hospital. Hosp Community Psychiatry *43:* 280, 1992.

Solomon PL, Drain JN, Marcenko MO, Meyerson AT: Homelessness in a mentally ill urban jail population. Hosp Community Psychiatry *43:* 169, 1992.

Zedlewski SR, McBride TD: The changing profile of the elderly: Effects on future long-term care needs and financing. Milbank Q *70:* 247, 1992.

▲ 4.9 Health Care Delivery in Psychiatry and Medicine

In theory, an ideal health care delivery system in the United States would provide high-quality medical care for all citizens while promoting medical research and new technology. Social and economic factors, however, significantly affect a nation's health status and delivery of health services. Health, according to the World Health Organization (WHO), is not merely the absence of disease but a state of complete physical, mental, and social well-being. To affect the factors that shape a population's health, illness, and death rate, the population must be studied to ascertain health care needs, future facilities and programs, and optimal financial allocations for carrying out these intentions.

Currently, workers in health care emphasize prevention and promoting good health as well as diagnosing and treating medical disorders. Escalating health care costs, however, have become one of the most significant obstacles to fulfilling the requirements of an ideal health care system: The need to focus on cost control affects distribution of funds, delivery of services, and mechanisms for reimbursing medical personnel for these services.

SOCIAL FACTORS

Personal Habits

Personal habits and lifestyle are major factors in the causes of illness and death in the United States; they account for about 70 percent of all illness, both mental and physical. Obesity, for example, is related to heart disease and diabetes, and a person's weight bears a direct relation to habit patterns of eating and exercise.

Many cancer deaths have been related to both poor dietary habits and chewing and smoking of tobacco. According to the 1994 National Health Interview Survey, an estimated 48 million U.S. adults (25.3 million men and 22.7 million women) currently smoke. The prevalence rate remained statistically the same in 1994 (25.5 percent) as in 1993 (25.0 percent), the first time in over a decade that there has not been an annual decrease. Forty-six million adults were former smokers, and nearly 70 percent of current smokers reported that they wanted to quit smoking completely. Of current daily adult smokers in 1994, 18.1 million (46.4 percent) had stopped smoking for at least 1 day during the past year.

Regular physical activity has a positive effect on stress reduction. It is also useful in treating and preventing such mental problems as anxiety disorders and depressive disorders and such physical problems as obesity, heart disease, diabetes, and high blood pressure. A trend in this country over the past 2 decades indicates that, although the number of adults involved in a daily exercise regimen is rising, less than half of all school-age children are exercising on a daily basis.

Accident prevention would also prevent many premature deaths. Education about safe driving habits, especially the need to abstain from alcohol when driving, would save more than 100,000 lives each year, especially among young adults.

Age

The incidence of illness is affected by age. Eighty-six percent of people more than 65 years of age have one or more chronic conditions. The three leading chronic conditions of old age are arthritis, hypertension, and heart disease. Hearing impairments, diabetes, cataracts, and varicose veins are also common chronic problems. Mental health problems increase with age also. Although chronicity is a factor among older people, young people are more predisposed than older people to acute illnesses. The three most common acute medical problems, across age groups, are upper respiratory conditions, influenza, and injuries.

Age influences the use of all health care services. Both young people (ages 20 to 30) and people over 65 tend to have more illnesses and health care needs than do people in middle adulthood. Young children's health care habits are often modeled after those of their parents. Previous experiences with health care influence future attitudes and behavior.

Education about accidents in the home would save about 28,000 lives each year, especially among older people, who account for two thirds of all accidents that occur at home.

Socioeconomic Status

People's socioeconomic status (SES) is not based solely on income but includes such factors as education, occupation, and lifestyle. The incidence of physical illness is affected by SES. Those in low SES groups are likely to be afflicted with hypertension, arthritis, upper respiratory illness, speech difficulties, and eye diseases. They also have a reduced life expectancy, as longevity is positively correlated to SES level.

A positive correlation exists between SES and mental health; consequently, people with high SES have better mental health than do persons of low SES. With regard to the incidence of psychopathology, some studies have found a slightly higher than usual percentage of bipolar I disorder among high SES people and a greater number than usual of people with schizophrenia in low SES groups.

Poverty

Poverty is associated with many long-term problems, such as poor health and increased mortality, mental disorders, school failure, crime, and substance abuse. The Bureau of the Census defines poverty status by a set of income thresholds that vary by family size and composition. Families or individuals with incomes below their appropriate poverty thresholds are classified as poor. In 1995, there were 36.4 million poor people (13.8 percent), a significant decrease from 38.1 million (14.5 percent) in 1994. Almost half of poor people (49 percent) were either under 18 years of age or 65 and over. The poverty rate was 11.2 percent for all whites, 8.5 percent for non-Hispanic whites, 29.3 percent for blacks, and 14.6 percent for Asians and Pacific Islanders.

Sex

Regardless of age, women seek health care and are hospitalized more often than are men. Women are most frequently hospitalized for heart disease, cancer, and childbirth, whereas men are hospitalized for heart disease, cancer, and pneumonia. The three leading chronic conditions that can limit activity for men are heart conditions, arthritis, and impairment of the back or the spine; for women, the leading chronic conditions are arthritis, heart conditions, and hypertension.

Race

Race affects the use of health care facilities, and minorities are less likely to obtain medical treatment. In 1994, the average number of physician contacts per person was 6.0, the same number reported for 1993. The rate of physician contacts was higher for white people than for black people (6.1 as compared to 5.7).

In 1993, a survey of women 40 years of age or older showed that 59.7 percent had obtained a mammogram in the past 2 years. By race, the percentages were 60.6 percent for whites, 59.2 percent for blacks, and 50.9 percent for Hispanics.

Environment

The environment is estimated to contribute to about one quarter of today's health problems. The exposure to such environmental risks as toxic waste, natural disasters, lead, asbestos, and dioxins is a major source of disease and death in humans. Waterborne diseases, especially those occurring in shellfish from polluted waters, are a major cause of morbidity and mortality.

About 75 percent of all carcinogens come from the environment. One of the highest incidences of bladder cancer occurs in certain industrial sites in New Jersey, where 25 percent of all workers are employed in the chemical industry. Nearly 67 percent of the men who die from coal workers' pneumoconiosis live in Pennsylvania.

Between 1985 and 1996, lead emissions declined by almost 60 percent, from 21,000 to 9,000 metric tons a year, in large part because of Environmental Protection Agency (EPA) rules requiring petroleum refineries to lower the lead content of gasoline.

With regard to mental health, mental disorders generally rise among people as their environments change from the suburban community to the inner city.

GENERAL HEALTH TRENDS

The health status and the health needs of a population can be assessed by examining general health trends, including death rates, causes of death, and longevity. The existence of certain medical disorders influences the need for particular health care delivery systems, programs, and personnel. A population's general health status determines the overall need for services and dollars.

The National Center for Health Statistics reports that in 1995, the age-adjusted death rate was 503.7 per 100,000 U.S. standard million population, a record low for the United States. In 1994, the rate was 507.4 per 100,000 U.S. standard million population. The decline from 1994 to 1995 reflects reduced mortality for white males, black males and females, as well as Hispanic males. The mortality of white and Hispanic females did not change significantly.

The three leading causes of death in 1995 were heart disease, cancer, and stroke, in decreasing order. Reductions between 1994 and 1995 occurred in the mortality from heart disease and cancer. For both causes of death, which combined accounted for a total of over 1.3 million deaths, the declines in age-adjusted death rates were over 1 percent. Age-adjusted death rates increased for four leading causes of death: Alzheimer's disease, septicemia, kidney disease, and diabetes.

The number of deaths caused by human immunodeficiency virus (HIV) infection increased from 42,114 in 1994 to approximately 42,506 in 1995, the largest number reported in a single year; but the age-adjusted death rate from this cause did not change from the 1994 rate. This is the first time the age-adjusted death rate for HIV infections has held steady between 2 years since 1987, when this cause of death was first uniquely classified in the morbidity and mortality statistics of the United States.

Mortality rates differ considerably by race and sex. Females have lower mortality rates than do males in all age groups, but the difference has been decreasing in recent years. Racial minorities within a given population have higher death rates than does the majority population. The primary cause of death for each of the sex and race groups is heart disease. The mortality rate of heart disease, cancer, and stroke is greatest among black men and is higher for men than for women.

The most common cause of death among adolescents and young adults (ages 15 to 24) is accidents; for children under the age of 14, the leading causes of death are accidents, cancer, and homicide.

Infant Mortality

Infant mortality in the United States is high compared with other countries, although the preliminary rate of 7.5 infant deaths per 1,000 live births in 1995 represents a 6 percent reduction from the 1994 rate. Between 1994 and 1995 the mortality rate for white infants fell from 6.6 to 6.3 per 1,000 live births, while the rate for black infants fell from 15.8 to 14.9 per 1,000 live births.

Good prenatal care contributes to a low infant mortality rate. In 1995, the percentage of mothers beginning prenatal care in the first trimester was 81.2 percent, a gain from the 1994 level of 80.2 percent. The proportions of black (70.3 percent) and Hispanic (70.4 percent) women receiving early prenatal care rose 1 to 3 percent compared with the percentages in 1994.

The three leading causes of infant death are congenital anomalies, sudden infant death syndrome, and disorders relating to short gestation and unspecified low birth weight.

Life Expectancy

According to the National Center for Health Statistics, life expectancy in the United States for all age, sex, and race groups has been steadily increasing since the turn of the century. In 1995, the average life expectancy from birth was 75.8 years. Black men have the shortest life expectancy from birth (64.9 years). White men (72.9 years), black women (74.1 years), and white women (79.6 years) all live longer than black men. Although the life expectancy of women is greater than that of men (79 years versus 72.3 years), this difference has been diminishing in recent years.

HEALTH CARE PROVIDERS

Health care providers include a broad array of people from a variety of professions who care for the sick. In addition to physicians, health care personnel include nurses, dentists, psychologists, social workers, podiatrists, speech therapists, and vocational therapists. More than 3 million people are employed in health-related occupations.

Physician Supply

In 1994, there were about 684,000 physicians, 151,000 dentists, and 1.9 million nurses practicing in the United States. The proportion of female physicians to total physicians nearly tripled between 1970 and 1994—from 7.6 percent to 19.5 percent. About 22 percent of M.D.s were educated outside the United States or Canada, a figure that has remained fairly constant since 1980. Psychiatrists number about 37,000. There is an excess number of physicians, and there is a problem in their distribution. High physician–patient ratios exist in the Northeast and in California; low concentrations are the norm in the South and in the mountain states. Psychiatrists tend to be concentrated in urban areas.

Primary care physicians are usually defined as general practitioners, family practitioners, internists, and pediatricians. Primary care is defined as a type of medical care delivery that emphasizes first-contact care and assumes ongoing responsibility for patients in both health maintenance and therapy. Many believe that psychiatry should also be classified as a primary care specialty, but this is not currently the case.

U.S. Physician Needs

Projections through the year 2000 show surpluses in physician needs around the country in almost every specialty. About 35 percent of U.S. physicians are primary care generalists; but the Council on Graduate Medical Education estimates eventual shortages. Most U.S. physicians are specialists, and some estimates suggest that by the year 2000 there will be a surplus of 165,000 specialists in the United States. In 1997, 50 percent of U.S. medical school graduates applied for primary care residency positions. The distribution of physicians shows that rural areas and inner cities have a shortage of all types of physicians, both generalists and specialists. Like most people in the United States, doctors prefer metropolitan areas; there is no incentive for them to practice in rural areas where they are generally in solo practice without other professionals with whom they can interact. An oversupply of physicians enables managed care companies to obtain lower prices from doctors and hospitals in exchange for referring patients.

Physician Earnings

The median physician net income in 1995 was $160,000 a year, a 6.7 percent increase over 1994. Neurosurgery, orthopedic surgery, and cardiothoracic surgery are the highest-paid specialties; pediatrics, general practice, and psychiatry are the lowest paid specialties (Table 4.9–1).

Physician Earnings in Context. The American Medical Association made the following observations about physician income:

> In assessing the level of physician income relative to that of the typical worker, it is important to bear in mind several factors.
>
> Physicians work long hours, often under stress, and must continually keep up with new medical developments. The average number of hours worked per week was 58.3 in 1994, about 46 percent in excess of the typical 40-hour week.
>
> Physicians do not begin their careers until later in life. In 1994, the average age of a medical school graduate was 28. Counting postgraduate education, many physicians are in their early 30s before beginning to practice. In addition, most physicians incur high educational debt before they begin to practice. In 1994, 79 percent of graduates reported some level of debt, with the average for those with indebtedness amounting to $63,885.

Liability Insurance

One of the most expensive components of physician practices is liability insurance. From 1990 to 1994, average premiums increased from $14,500 to $15,100. The high premiums result from the increased incidence of malpractice claims and high jury awards. According to latest statistics, over 95 percent of self-employed physicians paid malpractice premiums in 1994. More then one third of all physicians have been sued at least once during their medical careers. Physicians who have the highest risk of liability are obstetricians and surgeons; at low risk are pathologists and psychiatrists. Physicians who have a positive relationship with their patients have fewer liability suits than those who do not establish good rapport with their patients.

Table 4.9–1
Average Physician Net Income by Speciality (1995)[a]

Specialty	Yearly Income (in thousands of $)
General/family practice	131.2
Pediatrics	140.5
Psychiatry	137.2
Internal medicine	185.7
Pathology	209.4
Obstetrics/gynecology	244.3
Anesthesiology	215.1
Radiology	244.4
Surgery	269.4

Data are from the American Medical Association.
[a] *After expenses and before taxes.*

Patient Visits

Physician services tend to be underused. Twenty-two percent of the population do not see a physician at all in a given year. Of the 78 percent who do, most are very young or old or are women. Men average 5.2 physician contacts a year; women average 6.7 contacts. Whites visit doctors more often than do blacks. Most visits are made to general practitioners and internists. Approximately 60 percent of Americans visit a dentist at least twice a year. Physician visits may take place in doctors' offices; hospital outpatient departments, including emergency rooms; over the telephone; and at home. As family income rises, the rates of office and phone consultations increase, and the rate of hospital outpatient visits decreases. The five leading reasons for office visits are a general examination, a prenatal examination, throat problems, hypertension, and postoperative visits, in descending order of frequency.

People in the United States do not use physician services as much as those in other countries do. Germans visit doctors an average number of 14 times a year; the French, 7 times; and Americans, 6 times. Americans give as their reason for not seeking care the cost of an office visit. Both Germany and France have national health systems that cover the bulk of medical care.

Working Hours of Interns and Residents

Teaching hospitals often rely on interns and residents to perform services such as phlebotomies and intravenous therapy and to serve as messengers and transporters, tasks that are more appropriately performed by ancillary personnel. In addition, house staff are often required to work long hours, and sleep-deprivation can impair their judgment and clinical skills. Because of this, in 1988, a limit on the number of hours interns and residents may work was set forth by the U.S. Health Care Financing Administration (HCFA). Their work rules are: (1) Residents are limited to no more than 12 consecutive hours per assignment in emergency services. (2) Residents may not work more than 80 hours per week over a 4-week period and cannot be scheduled to work more than 24 consecutive hours. (3) Scheduled rotations must be separated by not less than 8 nonworking hours and with at least one 24-hour period of nonworking time provided for each week. Nonworking time is time away from training and patient care activities.

The HCFA also defined medical student responsibilities as follows: (1) Students can take histories and perform physical examinations with the approval of the patient's attending physician. (2) They may write in the patient's chart, but all entries must be countersigned by the attending physicians. (3) Medical or surgical procedures may be performed if they are under direct in-person supervision.

Many medical educators believe that the current HCFA rules do not go far enough and that interns and residents are not properly used by many teaching hospitals. It is not uncommon for a resident in cardiac surgery to be assisting at an operation for 14 hours and then to stay on duty an additional 10 hours. Similarly, a pediatric resident may be in the emergency room for 24 hours without sleep. Even though their hours fall within the HCFA guidelines, they are not conducive to a high level of functioning in either situation; nor do they contribute to the resident's education in view of the inevitable fatigue that will occur when a person is without sleep for 24 hours. For those residents with families, especially those who are mothers, work schedules as they currently exist are disruptive to both marital harmony and child rearing. This added stress interferes with optimal functioning. There are no easy answers to these problems, but the current situation clearly presents a problem.

Decrease in Residency Training Programs

In 1997, the HCFA approved a proposal to cut New York State residency programs, reducing the number of medical residents by 20 to 25 percent over a period of 6 years. To offset the loss of Medicare revenues, which are intended to be used for teaching purposes, each hospital would receive about $100,000 to compensate for each resident not trained. Each hospital will determine which residency specialty program to cut. The cuts are most likely to affect international medical graduates (IMGs) trained abroad who make up over 50 percent of residents in all specialties in New York.

The demonstration project was proposed in an attempt to reduce the number of physicians in the United States. New York's teaching hospitals train 15 percent of all U.S. physicians, more than any other state. The full effects of the plan to reduce the number of physicians will not be felt for many years.

HEALTH CARE COSTS

The provision of adequate, cost-effective services to the U.S. public is a critical concern. Spending for all types of health care, including the care of people who are mentally ill, continues to escalate. The growth rate of health care expenditures continues to outdistance the pace of growth of the economy. Health care has become increasingly expensive as a result of inflation, population growth, and advanced technology.

In 1995, statistics showed a growth in health spending. National health expenditures were approximately $988 billion, a 5.4 percent increase from the previous year. Spending per person amounted to $3,510, 5.4 percent higher than the 1993 level. Government paid $421 billion (44 percent) of the expense, while private expenditure totaled $529 billion (55 percent). The federal government's monetary contribution to health care has grown steadily over the years. Medicare now accounts for 17.8 percent of the public national health expenditure, and Medicaid represents 13.6 percent. Current estimates are that the Medicare trust fund will be exhausted by 2001 and requires, therefore, major reorganization.

Mental disorders account for a large proportion of health care expenditures: about $2.5 billion a year. Hospitals use the largest proportion of health care dollars. In general, hospital costs and general medical care services have risen at a far greater rate than have physicians' fees.

As many as 85 percent of people in the United States have some form of health insurance. In 1994, private health insurance premiums totaled $313.3 billion, up 5.7 percent from 1993 (the fourth year of single-digit growth). The slow growth was a result, in part, of a shift by employees to lower-cost managed care plans offered through the workplace. In general,

Table 4.9–2
Aspects of Hospital Organization

Criteria	Voluntary Hospital	Investor-Owned Hospital	State Mental Hospital System	Municipal Hospital System	Federal Hospital System	Special Hospital
Patient population	All illnesses	All illnesses, although hospital may specialize	Mental illness	All illnesses	All illnesses	70% of facility must be for single diagnosis
Profit orientation	Nonprofit	For profit	Nonprofit	Nonprofit	Nonprofit	For profit or nonprofit
Ownership	Private management board	Private corporation; may be owned by medical doctors	State	City government	Federal government	Private or public
Affiliation	Church-affiliated; privately owned or university sponsored	May be owned by large chains such as Humana Corporation, Columbia/HCA	Free-standing or affiliated with various medical schools	Voluntary teaching hosiptals and medical schools	Department of Defense, Public Health Service, Coast Guard, Prison, Merchant Marine, Indian Health Service, Veterans Administration (VA)	Optional affiliation with medical schools
Other	Provide bulk of care in U.S.	Increasing in importance nationally	Deinstitutionalization—number of patients has been reduced	Most physicians at municipal hospitals are employed by their affiliated medical school	VA hospitals usually have affiliations with medical schools	Less regulated than other types of hospitals

Notes: (1) To be designated a teaching hospital, a hospital must offer at least four types of approved residencies, clinical experiences for medical students, and an affiliation with a medical school. (2) Short-term hospitals have an average patient stay of less than 30 days; long-term hospitals, an average of longer duration. (3) Special hospitals include obstetrics and gynecology; eye, ear, nose, and throat. They do not include psychiatric hospitals or substance abuse hospitals.

the scope of insurance coverage has widened as more people enroll in managed care plans that more fully cover preventive services. About 60 percent of Americans working for medium-sized and large companies are enrolled in managed care plans.

HEALTH CARE ORGANIZATIONS

Hospitals

Hospitals are the institutional providers of general medical and surgical services in the U.S. health care system. There are currently more than 6,000 hospitals of all types in the United States, with about 1 million beds. About 66 percent of all beds are occupied at any one time. According to the World Health Organization (WHO), hospitals must have physician staff, offer continuous medical and nursing care to patients, and maintain inpatient facilities. Because hospitals consume the biggest percentage of health dollars, their use is the focus of current cost-containment strategies.

The number of yearly hospital admissions had been falling steadily since 1981. A slight future increase may be expected as the number of people of age 65 and older, with their greater needs for health services, continues to grow. Technological advances and the growth of managed care, however, have prompted the shift of care to less costly outpatient settings.

In 1994, the average length of stay for inpatients in community hospitals fell to a new low of 6.7 days. Possible explanations for this drop include the expansion of managed care among the Medicare and Medicaid populations, as well as improved integration of services through networking, which may allow hospitals to discharge patients to more appropriate settings for their continued recovery.

The classification of hospitals may be based on ownership, length of stay, or the nature of the service offered. Table 4.9–2 presents an overview of important aspects of hospital organization.

Nursing Homes

There are about 25,000 nursing homes with about 1,500,000 beds in the United States. Nursing homes are classified by the intensity of the care they offer: nursing care homes, which employ one or more full-time registered or licensed practical nurses and provide nursing care to at least half the residents; personal care homes with nursing, which employ one or more registered or licensed practical nurses and provide medications and treatments in accordance with physicians' orders; personal care homes without nursing; domiciliary care homes, which primarily provide supervisory care but also provide one or two personal services; skilled nursing facilities, which provide the most intensive nursing care available outside a hospital, such as the application of dressings or bandages, bowel and bladder care, catheterization, enemas, intramuscular and intravenous injections, irrigation, nasal feeding, and oxygen therapy; and intermediate care facilities, which are certified by the Medicaid and Medicare programs to provide health-related services on a regular basis to Medicaid-eligible persons who do not require hospital or skilled nursing facility care but who do require institutional care above the level of room and board.

REGULATION OF HEALTH CARE

Hospital Standards and Performance

A group of agencies, such as the Joint Commission on Accreditation of Healthcare Organizations (JCAHO) and the Liaison Committee on Medical Education (LCME), influence the standards of hospital care and performance. In addition, hospitals must comply with government regulations (city and state health rules). The JCAHO inspects hospitals every 2 years and is also responsible for determining the requirements for hospital accreditation. Hospital reimbursements from Medicare and Medicaid are contingent on meeting these standards, but the accreditation is done on a voluntary basis. The LCME and the Liaison Committee on Graduate Education are charged with accrediting medical schools and residency training programs, respectively. The two accrediting committees review education and training programs every 4 years; the procedure is voluntary.

Currently, all the hospitals in a community tend to be monitored as a single health entity and community resource. Thus no one unit has the prerogative to develop new facilities without concern for the services offered by the other hospitals in the area.

Hospital Utilization Review. This in-house evaluation process was created to make sure that institutions provide efficient, quality health care that meets patients' needs. The members of the utilization review committee consist of hospital administrators, physicians, and nurses. The committee reviews each patient's chart within a specified number of days of admission. The appropriateness of the admission, treatment strategies, and the length of the hospital stay are reviewed to facilitate the patient's discharge. Through this process the utilization review committee determines whether a particular admission was really indicated and whether the hospital stay was longer than necessary. A hospital must conduct utilization reviews to be eligible for JCAHO accreditation.

Professional Standards Review Organization. The Professional Standards Review Organization (PSRO) was set up by the federal government to review and monitor care received by patients whose care is paid for with government funds. PSROs made up of physicians elected by local medical societies have been established by local medical associations and serve several functions: They attempt to ensure high-quality care, control costs, determine maximum lengths of stay by patients in hospitals, conduct utilization reviews, and censure physicians who do not adhere to established guidelines. A PSRO may conduct a medical audit to evaluate the quality of care retrospectively by carefully examining charts.

Peer Review Organization. In the early 1980s, the Peer Review Organization (PRO) replaced PSROs as the federal review organization for hospitals receiving Medicare funds. To promote compliance with federal guidelines for health and hospital care, PROs conduct independent utilization reviews and quality-of-care studies, validate diagnosis-related group (DRG) assignments, and review hospital admissions and readmissions.

Federally mandated and funded, the PROs have greater authority than the PSROs. PROs can impose sanctions on hospitals for inadequate care; they can even recommend the termination of federal funding to hospitals that consistently violate federal standards. In addition, PROs can adjust or refuse payment for health services that they consider unnecessary.

PROs operate on a statewide level and can be either nonprofit or for profit. To reduce costs, a PRO is chosen through a competitive bidding process from among qualified physician-sponsored organizations.

Health Systems Agency. Health systems agencies (HSAs) are nonprofit organizations mandated by the federal government and set up on a statewide basis. HSAs promote or limit the development of health services and facilities, depending on the needs of a particular locality or state. They are made up of consumers and have considerable power in medicine. For example, before a new hospital can be built or an existing hospital can be extensively renovated, the HSA must approve a certificate of need (CON). Before a CON is issued, the necessity for a new facility in a specified locale must be established. HSAs control capital expenditures and, therefore, the availability of health resources. In each state, HSAs develop both long-term and short-term goals and plans, approve health care proposals requesting federal funding, review existing facilities and services, and suggest future construction and renovation projects on the basis of their findings.

Reimbursement Programs

Medicare (Title 18). Set up by the Federal Social Security Act of 1965, Medicare is a federally funded health insurance program. It provides both hospital and medical insurance for people 65 years of age and older and for people with certain disabilities (for example, blindness and renal disease). Medicare consists of two parts: Part A covers inpatient hospital care, home health services, dialysis, and nursing home care after hospitalization. Funding is derived from a federal trust fund, which, in turn, receives its funds from Social Security contributions. Part B is optional medical insurance that can be purchased to cover such services as physicians' fees, medical supplies, home health care, outpatient hospital care, and therapy services. Benefits and eligibility standards of Medicare are uniform throughout the United States, and more than 34 million people are covered by Medicare. The benefits available to Medicare members are listed in Table 4.9–3.

Medicaid (Title 19). Mandated by the federal government in 1965, Medicaid is an assistance program for certain needy and low-income people. It is financed by both federal and state governments, but each state defines its requirements

Table 4.9–3
Medicare Benefits

Below is a chart of the major Medicare benefits provided under Part A (hospital insurance benefits) and Part B (medical insurance benefits) as of January 1995.

There are gaps in Medicare coverage. The following charges are not covered by either Medicare Part A or Part B:

- ▲ Physician charges above the Medicare-approved amount;
- ▲ Long-term custodial care, either at home or in a skilled nursing facility; and
- ▲ Many preventive health care services, such as routine physicals; vision exams and eyeglasses; routine dental care and dentures; hearing aids; and routine foot care.

A special claims note: Effective September 1, 1990, all Part B providers *must* file claims to the Medicare carrier.

Benefits—Part A	**Current Provisions**
Hospital	Currently, the beneficiary is responsible for a Part A deductible ($716 in 1995). Medicare covers almost all hospital expenses for the first 60 days. Medicare then pays all covered costs except $179 per day for days 61–90 and $358 per day for days 91–150. Medicare pays nothing after 150 days.
Skilled nursing facility (SNF) care	Medicare pays all SNF care for the first 20 days if a beneficiary has been hospitalized for at least 3 days before the SNF care. From days 21–100 Medicare pays all but $89.50 per day. After 100 days, Medicare pays nothing.
Home health care	Medicare covers home health care on a part-time or intermittent basis if beneficiaries meet restrictive eligibility requirements. The beneficiary must be homebound, in need of skilled nursing care, or physical or speech therapy. Services must be ordered and regularly reviewed by a physician.
Hospice care	Medicare covers up to 210 days of hospice care for a terminally ill Medicare beneficiary. Additional coverage is available if necessary.
Benefits—Part B	**Current Provisions**
Doctor bills	After a beneficiary meets an annual $100 deductible, Medicare Part B pays 80% of an amount based on a government fee schedule for doctor services. The beneficiary is responsible for the remaining 20% and any amount of the bill which exceeds Medicare's approved fee schedule up to new caps established in 1991 (120% in 1992 and 115% thereafter).
Prescription drugs	Medicare pays only for prescription drugs administered in the hospital and in limited outpatient situations.
Special Protections for Low-Income Elderly and Spouses of Nursing Home Residents	
Low-income protection (qualified Medicare beneficiaries [QMB] and specified low-income Medicare beneficiary [SLMB])	A number of low-income elderly persons do not receive benefits because they cannot afford to pay the premiums, deductibles, and coinsurance. In 1995, state Medicaid programs are required to pay the Medicare premiums, deductibles, and coinsurance for QMB beneficiaries with incomes at or below 100% of the federal poverty level ($613 per month for an individual in 1994). Assets must also fall below $4,000 for individuals and $6,000 for couples. Beginning January 1, 1995, states must pay the Medicare premiums for those SLMB persons with incomes up to 120% of the poverty level. New poverty levels are set in February of each year.
Spousal impoverishment	In most states, when one spouse is in a nursing home and the other is not, the institutionalized spouse has to deplete his/her income and assets before Medicaid will cover the cost of nursing home care. If the spouse remaining at home is financially dependent upon the institutionalized spouse, he/she is left impoverished. In 1995, the spouse of a Medicaid-eligible nursing home resident is allowed to keep at least $1,230 of monthly income and at least $14,964 of the couple's assets, in addition to their home. States are given the option of allowing the spouse at home to keep one half of the assets up to $74,820 (in 1995). These amounts will increase each year.

for eligibility and is responsible for its administration. Although benefits vary from state to state, federal provisions require that Medicaid cover inpatient and outpatient hospital care (including psychiatric care), physicians' services, laboratory tests, diagnostic imaging, home health care services, and nursing home care. Additional services may be provided at a state's option. Increasingly tight eligibility requirements have left many low-income people without coverage and unable to pay. Currently, about 25 million people are covered by Medicaid.

Blue Cross Association. The Blue Cross Association (BCA) of more than 80 independent insurance plans around the country pays primarily for inpatient hospital service. Blue Shield pays for physician services during the patient's hospital stay. In contrast to commercial insurance carriers, BCA is a nonprofit organization regulated by state insurance departments. BCA premiums cover administrative expenses and benefits and provide a reserve to cover financial losses. Benefits for psychiatric services are severely limited, compared with those for other medical illnesses, although inpatient psychiatric care is less limited than is outpatient care. BCAs are attempting to become for-profit organizations, a change that requires legislative approval and is likely to occur by 2000. Half of all Blue Cross enrollees are now part of a managed care system that requires that mandatory second opinions be obtained for surgical procedures and that precertification of need be obtained before a patient is admitted to a hospital.

Self-Pay. People contract with commercial insurance companies to cover both inpatient and outpatient costs, including physicians' fees, diagnostic procedures, and laboratory tests. For this type of insurance, self-pay patients pay a premium that may be based on an experience rating determined by the risk or previous record for reimbursement on insurance claims or a community rating system in which each participant pays the same premium because the plan's cost is divided equally among group members.

HEALTH CARE ORGANIZATIONS

Health Maintenance Organizations

A *health maintenance organization* (HMO) is an organized system providing comprehensive (both inpatient and outpatient) health care in all specialties, including psychiatry. Members voluntarily enroll in the plan and pay a prepayment or capitation fee to cover all health care services for a fixed period (a month or a year). There are more than 500 HMOs in the United States with an enrollment of about 45 million people (Fig. 4.9–1).

There are three types of HMOs: the *staff model,* in which physicians receive a salary to provide services in the HMO's own facility; the *group model,* in which health care is furnished by one or more groups of doctors, and payment is received on a contractual basis at a predetermined rate; the *individual practice association* (IPA) *network model,* in which the HMO negotiates with individual physicians to receive a capitation fee for providing services to each IPA member seen in their private offices. Physicians retain their office-based private practices when they join an IPA. Physicians in staff and group models often own stock in their HMOs.

Preferred Provider Organizations. Like HMOs, a preferred provider organization (PPO) uses a prospective payment system. In PPO, however, a corporation or an insurance company makes an agreement with a particular group of community hospitals and doctors to supply health services to PPO members at a previously determined rate lower than their usual rates. Patients who enroll in a PPO select their physicians from among the list of participating doctors that includes both specialists and primary care physicians. Inpatient care is provided

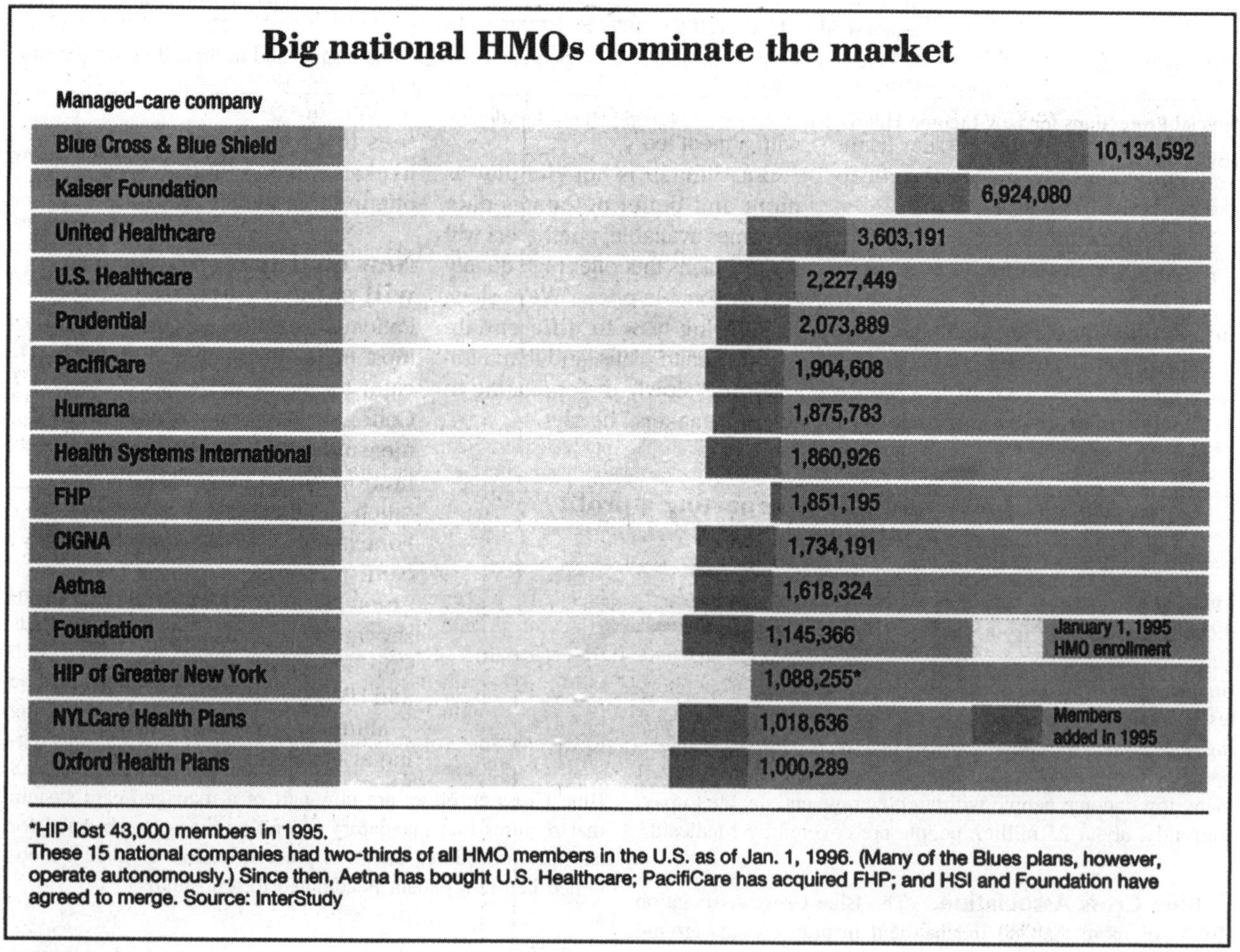
Big national HMOs dominate the market
Managed-care company
Blue Cross & Blue Shield
10,134,592
Kaiser Foundation
6,924,080
United Healthcare
3,603,191
U.S. Healthcare
2,227,449
Prudential
2,073,889
PacifiCare
1,904,608
Humana
1,875,783
Health Systems International
1,860,926
FHP
1,851,195
CIGNA
1,734,191
Aetna
1,618,324
Foundation
1,145,366
January 1, 1995 HMO enrollment
HIP of Greater New York
1,088,255*
NYLCare Health Plans
1,018,636
Members added in 1995
Oxford Health Plans
1,000,289
*HIP lost 43,000 members in 1995.
These 15 national companies had two-thirds of all HMO members in the U.S. as of Jan. 1, 1996. (Many of the Blues plans, however, operate autonomously.) Since then, Aetna has bought U.S. Healthcare; PacifiCare has acquired FHP; and HSI and Foundation have agreed to merge. Source: InterStudy

FIGURE 4.9–1
Big national HMOs dominate the market. (Reprinted with permission from Terry K: You can thrive under managed care. Med Economics *74:* 21, 1997.)

at the designated hospital that a patient chooses. There are about 1,000 PPOs in the United States at this time.

Managed Care

Managed care is a system by which a health care insurer and providers work together to ensure cost containment. The goal of managed care is to eliminate unnecessary medical procedures and to obtain discounted services from physicians and hospitals. Business and insurance companies have advocated managed care in an effort to cut their medical costs for employees and insurance beneficiaries. The number of doctors participating in managed care has increased rapidly. Over 80 percent of doctors have a managed care contract.

The cost-cutting procedures used by HMOs involve payment arrangements for hospitals, physicians, and pharmaceutical services. Oversight procedures are put in place to evaluate doctors' decisions, to restrict coverage of certain kinds of care deemed experimental or cosmetic, and to limit the range of medications available to patients for various illnesses. By these procedures, HMOs can control costs. HMOs also decrease health care costs by limiting the number of new hospitalizations and by discharging patients from hospitals earlier than usual. The emphasis on prevention and health promotion and on performing as much diagnosis and therapy as possible on an outpatient basis further helps control expenses.

Most HMOs are for-profit corporations, shares of which are traded on the New York Stock Exchange and other exchanges, and their motivation to cut costs and increase earnings is strong. Because they are businesses, they have a large number of nonmedical employees, many of whom receive large salaries—far in excess of what physicians earn.

According to a report in *Consumers Union,* the CEO of Health Net, an HMO based in California, received more than $3 million in annual and long-term compensation in 1994. Columbia/HCA Healthcare Corporation, the largest for-profit health care organization in the United States, reported revenues of $4.88 billion in 1996 (*The New York Times,* November 7, 1996), an increase of 12 percent over 1995. In 1997, federal agents began investigating the company for fraud. The increased number of patients enrolled in HMOs, coupled with decreased medical costs in the form of lower fees to doctors and hospitals, contributed to HMOs' revenue growth. In addition to executive compensation, HMOs spend over $40 million annually on advertising and marketing their product. They have introduced a level of bureaucracy consisting of care managers and utilization review personnel, who not only must be paid but who also serve as intermediaries between doctor and patient.

Obviously, health care has become a lucrative business in the United States; but the profits often come from denying medical, surgical, and drug reimbursement services; reducing payments to doctors and hospitals; and introducing complex procedures that serve to discourage patients and providers from pursuing denied claims.

An egregious example of cost cutting by HMOs was the provision that allowed only 24 hours of hospitalization for newborn deliveries. In 1996, the U.S. Congress agreed to legislation that prohibits the insurance company practice known as drive-through deliveries. Under the law, the decision about how long a mother and her newborn child remain in the hospital is now made by the mother and her physician. This new law represents a strong first step by the federal government toward ensuring that cost containment will not be allowed to be the primary or sole consideration in determining how and which health care services will be paid for in the new era of managed care. Similarly, some HMOs insisted that women not be allowed an overnight stay in a hospital for a mastectomy but that it be performed as an outpatient procedure. This policy was also changed by legislation to allow for 2 days of hospitalization. The problem remains, however, that medical procedures are being legislated by Congress and physicians are losing their authority in making clinical decisions. For example, some women require prolonged hospitalization after a mastectomy, but the law makes no provision for such differences.

Relation of Medicare and Medicaid to HMOs. It is now possible for those eligible to receive fee-for-service Medicare and Medicaid benefits to become members of HMOs. Nationwide, Medicare HMO enrollment is about 3 million or about 10 percent of the elderly population. A problem encountered by people over 65 who switch to HMOs is that they no longer can visit the doctors of their choice; access to specialists is also restricted. Furthermore, most HMOs do not cover members who live outside the HMO area. Disputes arise about unapproved emergency room visits, specialist referrals, and nursing home stays. The advantages claimed for HMO membership are that people with Medicare HMO coverage do not have to pay a deductible of 20 percent of doctor bills but only a small copayment of $5 to $15. For some people with chronic illness, the yearly cost of medication may be less for those in HMOs. HMOs are anxious to enroll medical beneficiaries because they receive over $4,000 annually for each enrollee.

Primary Care Physicians. Every patient enrolled in an HMO must choose a primary care physician, who has usually received training in internal medicine, family medicine, or pediatrics. Primary care physicians are fast becoming the foundation on which the current system of health delivery in the United States is based. These physicians deal not only with the physical complaints of their patients but also with their mental, emotional, and social concerns—a field called primary care psychiatry. Unfortunately, most primary care physicians have limited knowledge of the full range of psychiatric disorders and therapeutic options. A challenge faced by psychiatric educators is to attempt to upgrade the skills of primary care physicians in managing mental illness, particularly in prescribing psychotropic medications, more of which are dispensed by primary care physicians in the United States than by psychiatrists. Psychiatrists use potent pharmacologic agents with a wide range of side effects, some of which may be fatal. Nonpsychiatric physicians must have an in-depth knowledge of these agents to practice psychopharmacologic therapy effectively and safely.

Gatekeeper. The term *gatekeeper* has been applied to primary care physicians who, as part of providing total care for patients, must decide when to refer a patient to a specialist.

To make a specialist referral most HMOs require that ''preapproval'' be obtained: Primary care physicians must request permission from the HMO to refer the patient. Some plans have utilization committees (which may or may not include physicians) whose goal is to review physician referrals to see whether they are indicated; these committees developed as protection against soaring health care expenditures. Most physicians acknowledge the need for accountability but view the procedures as cumbersome and inequitable. Doctors may have to deal with 10 to 20 review organizations, each of which has its own criteria as to what constitutes a necessary medical procedure or specialist referral for which it is willing to allow payment.

One troubling aspect of review organizations is the denial of payment that occurs for some treatments labeled experimental but actually considered advisable treatment by medical experts. Payment denials of this sort are increasing and threaten to interfere with both innovative medical treatment and traditional medical care. Another particularly troubling issue resulting from these oversight activities has been the breaching of confidentiality in doctor–patient relationships. Moreover, denials of payment, demands to justify clinical decisions, and requirements for previous approval of procedures undermine professional decision making and contribute to a growing sense of frustration among physicians in all specialties. Most complaints by patients about HMOs involve decisions by utilization review committees not to approve certain treatments; thereby HMOs force patients to forgo the therapy or pay for it out of pocket, neither of which is a satisfactory option.

Quality of Care

Quality of care has several definitions ranging from patient satisfaction with health care to rate of death associated with a particular procedure, such as coronary bypass grafting. A database currently exists to record individual physicians' performance, but physicians are concerned that the data are flawed because severity of illness, other concurrent illness, or case mix may not be taken into account. It is unfair to attempt to rate the competence of a psychiatrist based on the number of suicide attempts in his or her practice if one psychiatrist's caseload is composed mainly of patients with severe mood disorders and another's is composed mainly of anxiety disorders. Similarly, rating cardiovascular surgeons based on the mortality rate of their patients without considering severity of illnesses and coexisting illness is illusory. One result of the release of these data to the public is that some cardiovascular surgeons have refused to operate on patients who are considered high risk because of the chance of adversely affecting their standing. At present, there are no valid reliable or useful techniques to assess quality of care.

Attempts to outline guidelines for the treatment of psychiatric disorders have been made by the American Psychiatric Association (APA), but the APA is careful to point out that their guidelines are not ''official'' and are not meant to be slavishly followed. Thus psychiatrists have the latitude to develop treatment plans individualized to particular patients. When a physician deviates from published guidelines, however, it is important to document the reasons for the alternative method of care. By doing so, the physician can justify and maintain his or her autonomy.

Patients' Reactions to HMOs. In a 1993 nationwide study of 17,000 patients enrolled in HMOs, the patients voiced widespread dissatisfaction with the care they received. Independent doctors, the patients said, were easier to reach by telephone, were more apt to schedule office appointments on short notice, and spent more time with patients than did doctors who worked in large medical groups and HMOs. Managed-care organizations typically restrict payments to specialists unless care is approved in advance by a designated primary care doctor. This practice also contributed to patient dissatisfaction, because people are prevented from seeking a specialist of their own choosing.

In an attempt to deal with patients' desires to have a free choice of physician, most HMOs (up from about 20 percent in 1992 to 75 percent in 1996) offer a point-of-service (POS) plan. Under such plans, patients may see any doctor they choose without a referral. POS plans are more expensive for patients and do not reimburse doctors at the same rate as those doctors who belong to the HMO system. The U.S. government, in an effort to cut Medicare and Medicaid costs, is encouraging beneficiaries to enroll in managed care plans; however, those over 75 and those who are sick are unlikely to do so. Also, there are plans to reduce Medicare HMO-reimbursement dollars, which will decrease the managed care for-profit motive to continue to enroll the sick elderly.

PSYCHIATRIC CARE DELIVERY

Psychiatric care is provided by a variety of mental health organizations in addition to private practitioners. The organizations include psychiatric hospitals, including Veterans Administration psychiatric hospitals, state and county mental hospitals, and private mental hospitals; psychiatric units of general hospitals; residential treatment centers for emotionally disturbed children; federally funded community mental health centers; and independent psychiatric outpatient clinics, where a psychiatrist has medical responsibility for all patients in the program. Most psychiatric patients are seen in one of these organizations; fewer than 5 percent of all psychiatric patients are seen by psychiatrists in private practice.

Based on recent studies, over 30 million people in the United States have anxiety disorders, and 17.5 million have depression. There are 2 million patients with schizophrenia and 5 million with severe cognitive impairment, such as Alzheimer's disease. HMOs clearly cannot handle such a large and serious caseload.

Mental health care is usually provided as part of the health benefit package offered by employers to their employees. It is also offered as a Medicare and Medicaid service. In almost all instances, however, mental health benefits are reviewed by so-called managed behavioral health care companies in an effort to reduce the costs of care and to provide some type of quality control over service. In doing their job, however, managed care programs seriously interfere with the practice of psychiatry as it is known today.

Many programs limit the number of psychotherapy visits

to 5 to 20 sessions a year, and although some types of psychotherapy can be conducted within this framework, other types, such as insight or psychodynamic therapies, require frequent visits over an extended period. In addition, patients must be referred to a psychiatrist by their primary care physician, who is encouraged to try to deal with the patients' problems before making a referral. During this time pharmacotherapy rather than psychotherapy is most likely to be prescribed; most primary care physicians have neither the training nor the time to provide therapy. When a referral to a psychiatrist is made, the psychiatrist must provide an initial report to the managed care company about the patient's condition and must submit periodic reports thereafter, a process that violates a basic tenet of successful psychotherapy, that of confidentiality. Finally, managed care companies encourage primary care physicians to refer patients to nonpsychiatrists, such as psychologists and social workers, for psychotherapy because they accept lower fees than do psychiatrists. Psychiatrists are used primarily to prescribe medication or to treat patients who require hospitalization. Managed behavioral health care companies receive a predetermined annual fee or, more often, a percentage of the amount of money saved as payment for their services, practices that have led to charges of conflict of interest.

Claims Review

When psychiatric (or other medical) benefits are denied or curtailed, a claims review may be initiated by a patient or doctor. The first level of claims review generally consists of a clerical examination to determine whether the bill shows the necessary administrative information and whether the claimant is covered for the prescribed treatment. There is no determination of the appropriateness of the care given. The second level of claims review is generally done by trained personnel, often nurses. Here the claims reviewer compares the treatment rendered with previously established criteria for treatment that have been established as appropriate for the condition.

The second-level reviewer may approve payment for the claim. If the second-level reviewer has questions or if the treatment is considered inappropriate according to the criteria, the claim is reviewed by a third-level group or a true peer review committee. Here a professional determination is made as to the appropriateness of the care rendered. The peer review committee—one or more psychiatrists, for example, review each claim—may approve or disapprove. There are levels of appeal for the practitioner who is dissatisfied with the committee determination. The appeals process often goes to a special committee of the county or state medical society.

Parity of Mental Health Services

Most employer health benefits set an annual and lifetime payment cap for mental illness that is less than for physical illness. In 1996, Congress passed a bill (sponsored by Senators Peter Domenici and Paul Wellstone) that sought to achieve total equality or parity between benefits for mental and physical illness. Some disparity remains; not all mental disorders are included, and substance abuse and alcoholism are excluded from the mental illness parity requirement. The bill also prohibits health plans from imposing lifetime financial limits on mental health benefits that are less than for physical health.

Gag Rule

Managed care plans prohibit doctors enrolled in their plans from advising patients about treatments not covered by the HMO, such as specialized or experimental procedures; doctors are also forbidden to refer patients to physicians who are experts in certain rare diseases but who are not members of an HMO. These and other prohibitions (including criticizing HMOs) are collectively known as the gag rule. Many states have passed laws prohibiting gag rules in contracts between HMOs and physicians, and the issue is currently under legislative review by the U.S. Congress. Several major HMOs have eliminated gag clauses as a result of public and professional pressure. The American Medical Association (AMA) has launched a major effort to achieve bipartisan elimination of health plan gag clauses. According to the AMA, there is intense lobbying by the insurance industry against implementation of gag clause legislation.

In an effort to regain control of the medical decision process, some states prohibit nonphysicians from making clinical decisions. The Texas State Board of Medical Examiners (Board) adopted a position statement (Oct. 5, 1996) on what constitutes the practice of medicine in that state. According to the statement, "the determination of medical necessity appropriateness of proposed care so as to effect the diagnosis or treatment of a patient is the practice of medicine."

The Board warns that individuals or entities who make determinations of medical necessity or appropriateness who do not have a Texas medical license may be subject to investigation, criminal prosecution, injunctive action, and possibly monetary penalties. In concluding its statement, the Board warned, "To avoid a violation of the law regarding unlicensed practice, reviewers, insurers, medical directors, and managed care gatekeepers should be particularly conscientious in allowing physician providers to exercise independent medical judgment to the greatest extent possible."

Some experts believe that the future of managed care is bleak over the long term. Managed care firms lack a social conscience, in that they do not contribute to teaching, research, or care of the poor. As governmental regulation of managed care policies and practices increases to ensure the social good, the profit-making goals of managed care companies and big business become more difficult to achieve. If they are to have a stronger presence in the future, as Jerome P. Kassner pointed out in the *New England Journal of Medicine* (April 8, 1997), "managed care plans will have to show that they have become better citizens: that they care about more than profits, that they do not skimp on care, that they support their just share of teaching, research, and the care of the poor, that they no longer muzzle physicians, and that they offer something special (including control of costs) by managing care."

THE FUTURE OF HEALTH CARE

In 1993, President Bill Clinton proposed the American Health Security Bill to guarantee comprehensive coverage for all people in the United States. Under the bill, which was defeated by the Congress and did not become law, health coverage would have continued without interruption if a person lost or changed a job, moved from one area to another, became ill, or confronted a family crisis. Networks of doctors, hospitals, and insurers would then negotiate with regional or corporate health alliances to obtain health care service. The bill was opposed by both private industry and organized medicine; but in the wake of its defeat, private industry led by insurance companies saw an opportunity to enter the health care field. Insurance companies already had the infrastructure to develop a computerized database enabling them, with the help of the HMOs, to direct the flow of patients to more efficient (and thus more profitable) providers of service.

A new concept of medical services as *market driven* has emerged. This concept now dominates the health care industry and will do so for the foreseeable future. Paradoxically, the role of government must increase as legislation is required to regulate this new industry, whose preoccupation is the cost of health. There is a growing conflict between medicine, whose expertise is in the quality of health, and industry; ultimately the U.S. Congress will become the arbiters between the consumers of health care (patients), the providers (physicians and other health professionals), and the payers (insurance companies and HMOs). In this sense, society and the body politic will determine the future of the nature and quality of health care in the United States.

References

Enthoven A, Kronick R: A consumer-choice health plan for the 1990s: Universal health insurance in a system designed to promote quality and economy. N Engl J Med *320:* 29, 1989.

Flaskerud JH, Hu L: Racial-ethnic identity and amount and type of psychiatric treatment. Am J Psychiatry *149:* 379, 1992.

Ginsberg E, Ostow M: Managed care—A look back and a look ahead. N Engl J Med *336:* 1019, 1997.

Gonzales ML, editor: *Socioeconomic Characteristics of Medical Practice, 1995.* American Medical Association, Chicago, 1995.

Health Insurance Institute: *Source Book of Health Insurance Data.* Health Insurance Institute, New York, 1989.

Himmelstein DU, Woolhandler S: A national health program for the United States: A physicians' proposal. N Engl J Med *320:* 102, 1989.

Kassirer JD: Is managed care here to stay? N Engl J Med *336:* 1013, 1997.

National Center for Health Statistics: *Health, United States, 1995.* Public Health Service, Hyattsville, MD, 1995.

Riggs RT: HMOs and the seriously mentally ill: A view from the trenches. Community Ment Health J *32* (3): 213, 1996.

Rosenberg S: Health maintenance organization penetration and general hospital psychiatric services: Expenditure and utilization trends. Prof Psychol Res Pract *27:* 345, 1996.

5

Psychology and Psychiatry: Psychometric and Neuropsychological Testing

▲ 5.1 Psychological Testing of Intelligence and Personality

Psychometric and neurological tests are designed to measure specific aspects of people's intelligence, thinking, or personality. Psychologists specifically trained in the tests' use and interpretation generally administer them. These tests play a relatively minor role in establishing a psychiatric diagnosis, which is based primarily on observable signs and symptoms and clinical interviews. Because of expense, the tests are usually reserved for special situations: Intelligence testing is necessary to establish the degree of mental retardation; neuropsychological tests help to quantify and localize brain damage. Some tests may highlight areas of conflict or concern in a person's life that should be a focus of therapeutic attention; certain tests may reveal severely disordered thinking not otherwise evident.

Most commonly used assessment instruments are standardized against normal control subjects, who are required to respond to the same stimuli or set of questions. Their responses are tabulated into a normal distribution pattern against which new subjects are compared. With standardization, test administration and scoring are invariant across time and examiners. Related to the standardization of any test are the available data that presumably show whether the test is valid and reliable. Reliability assesses the reproducibility of results; validity assesses whether the test measures what it purports to measure (see Chapter 4, Section 4.7).

TYPES OF TESTS

Objective Tests

Objective tests are typically pencil-and-paper tests based on specific items and questions. They yield numerical scores and profiles easily subjected to mathematical or statistical analysis. An example is the Minnesota Multiphasic Personality Inventory (MMPI).

Projective Tests

Projective tests present stimuli whose meanings are not immediately obvious; some degree of ambiguity forces people to project their own needs into the test situation. Projective tests presumably have no right or wrong answers. Those being tested impute meanings to the stimulus, apparently based on psychological and emotional factors. Examples include the Thematic Apperception Test (TAT), the Draw-a-Person test, the Rorschach test, and the Sentence Completion Test.

INTELLIGENCE TESTING

Intelligence can be defined as the ability to assimilate factual knowledge; to recall either recent or remote events; to reason logically; to manipulate concepts (either numbers or words); to translate the abstract to the literal and the literal to the abstract; to analyze and synthesize forms; and to deal meaningfully and accurately with problems and priorities deemed important in a particular setting. Intelligence varies tremendously from person to person.

In 1905, Alfred Binet introduced the concept of the mental age (MA), which is the average intellectual level of a particular age. The intelligence quotient (IQ) is the ratio of MA over CA (chronological age), multiplied by 100 to eliminate the decimal point; it is represented by the following equation:

$$IQ = \frac{MA}{CA} \times 100$$

An IQ of 100, or average, results when chronological and mental ages are equal. Because it is impossible to measure age-associated changes in intellectual power after the age of 15 with available intelligence tests, the highest divisor in the IQ formula is 15. One way of expressing a person's relative standing within a group is by using percentile. The higher the percentile, the higher the rank within a group. An IQ of 100 corresponds to the 50th percentile in intellectual ability for the general population.

As measured by most intelligence tests, IQ is an interpretation or classification of a total test score in relation to norms established by a group. IQ is a measure of present functioning ability, not necessarily of future potential. Although under ordinary circumstances the IQ is stable throughout life, there is no absolute certainty about its predictive properties. A person's IQ must be examined in the light of past experiences and future opportunities.

The IQ itself is no indicator of the origins of its reflected capacities, genetic (innate) or environmental. The most useful intelligence test must measure a variety of skills and abilities, including verbal and performance, early learned and recently learned, timed and untimed, culture free, and culture bound. No intelligence test is totally culture free, although tests do differ significantly in degree.

Wechsler Adult Intelligence Scale (WAIS)

The Wechsler Adult Intelligence Scale (WAIS) is the best standardized and most widely used intelligence test in clinical practice today. It was constructed by David Wechsler at New York University Medical Center and Bellevue Psychiatric Hospital. Designed in 1939, the original WAIS has gone through several revisions. A scale for children ages 5 through 15 years has been devised (WISC—Wechsler Intelligence Scale for Children) and a scale for children ages 4 to 6½ years (WPPSI—Wechsler Preschool and Primary Scale of Intelligence).

The WAIS comprises 11 subtests made up of six verbal subtests and five performance subtests, which yield a verbal IQ, a performance IQ, and a combined or full-scale IQ. Intelligence levels are based on the assumption that intellectual abilities are normally distributed (in a bell-shaped curve) throughout the population (Fig. 5.1–1). Verbal and performance IQs and the full-scale IQ are determined by the use of separate tables for each of the seven age groups (from 16 to 64 years) on which the test was standardized. Variability in functioning is revealed through discrepancies between verbal and performance IQs and by the scatter pattern between subtests.

Construction of the Test. The following subtests are described in the order in which they are presented to the subject.

VERBAL SKILLS. *Information.* This subtest covers general information and knowledge and is subject to cultural variables. Persons from low socioeconomic groups with little schooling do not perform as well as those from high socioeconomic groups with more schooling.

Comprehension. This sububtest measures subjects' ability to adhere to social conventions and to understand social judgment by answering questions about proverbs and how people ought to behave under certain circumstances.

Arithmetic. The ability to do arithmetic and other simple calculations is reflected on this subtest, which is adversely influenced by anxiety and poor attention and concentration.

Similarities. This subtest is a sensitive indicator of intelligence. It covers the ability to abstract by asking subjects to explain the similarity between two things.

Digit Span. Immediate retention is measured in this subtest. Subjects are asked to learn a series of two to nine digits, which are immediately recalled both forward and backward. Anxiety, poor attention span, and brain dysfunction interfere with recall.

Vocabulary. Subjects are asked to define 35 vocabulary words of increasing difficulty. Intelligence has a high correlation with vocabulary, which is related to level of education. Idiosyncratic definitions of words may give clues to personality structure.

PERFORMANCE. *Picture Completion.* This subtest initiates the performance part of the WAIS and consists of completing a picture in which a part is missing. Visuoperceptive defects become evident when mistakes are made on this test.

Block Design. This subtest requires subjects to match colored blocks and visual designs. Brain dysfunction involving impairment of left-right dominance interferes with performance.

Picture Arrangement. Subjects are required to arrange a series of pictures in a sequence that tells a story (for example, a person committing a crime). In addition to testing performance, this subtest provides data about subjects' cognitive styles.

Object Assembly. Subjects must assemble objects, such as the figure of a woman or an animal, in the proper order and organization. Visuoperception, somatoperception, and manual dexterity are tested.

Digit Symbol. In this final subtest of the WAIS, subjects receive a code

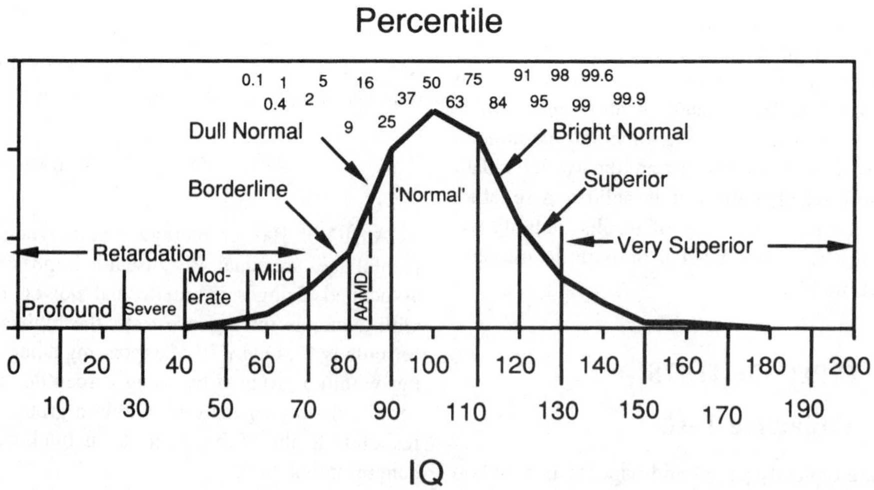
Percentile
0.1 1 5 16 50 75 91 98 99.6
0.4 2 37 63 84 95 99 99.9
9 25
Dull Normal
Bright Normal
Borderline
'Normal'
Superior
Retardation
Very Superior
Mod-erate
Mild
AAMD
Profound
Severe
0 20 40 60 80 100 120 140 160 180 200
10 30 50 70 90 110 130 150 170 190
IQ

FIGURE 5.1–1
The distribution of Wechsler Adult Intelligence Scale IQ categories. (Adapted from Matarazzo JD: *Wechsler's Measurement and Appraisal of Adult Intelligence,* ed 5, p 124. Oxford University Press, New York, 1972.)

that pairs symbols with digits. The test consists of matching a series of digits to their corresponding symbols in as little time as possible.

Distribution of IQ Scores. The average or normal range of IQ is 90 to 110; IQ scores of at least 120 are considered superior (Table 5.1–1). According to the American Association of Mental Deficiency (AAMD) and the fourth edition of *Diagnostic and Statistical Manual of Mental Disorders* (DSM-IV), mental retardation is defined as an IQ of less than 70, which corresponds to the lowest 2.2 percent of the population. Consequently, 2 out of every 100 people have IQ scores consistent with mental deficiency, which can range from mild to profound.

Reliability and Validity. The reliability of the WAIS is very high. Retesting of people 18 years and older rarely reveals changes in IQ scores.

The verbal scale of the IQ measures the retention of previously acquired factual information, and the performance scale measures visuospatial capacity and visuomotor speed in problem-solving tasks. The performance scale is more sensitive to normal aging than is the verbal scale, which is more sensitive to education. Arithmetic and memory for digits are adversely affected by anxiety. The validity of the WAIS is high in identifying mental retardation and in predicting future school performance. A disparity between the verbal test and the performance test (usually greater than 15 points) may indicate psychopathology, such as attention-deficit/hyperactivity disorder, which requires further testing.

Lewis Terman at Stanford University devised the Stanford-Binet Test in 1916. It is a comprehensive intelligence test that is used in psychiatry and education, although less widely used than is the WAIS.

ADULT PERSONALITY ASSESSMENT

Objective Personality Assessment

The objective approach to personality assessment is characterized by the reliance on structured, standardized measurement devices, which typically are of a self-report nature. *Structured* reflects the tendency to use straightforward test stimuli, such as direct questions about people's opinions of themselves and unambiguous instructions about completing the test.

Response sets are attitudes or styles in responding to personality questionnaires. Some people answer incorrectly to present themselves in a more favorable light or to please the examiner. Other people attempt to look worse than is truly the case. Well-designed tests, such as the Minnesota Multiphasic Personality Inventory (MMPI), have built-in scales designed to detect such response sets and to adjust scores accordingly.

Minnesota Multiphasic Personality Inventory (MMPI). This self-report inventory is the most widely used and most thoroughly researched objective personality assessment instrument. The MMPI was developed in 1937 by Starke Hathaway, a psychologist, and J. Charnley McKinley, a psychiatrist. The test was recently updated and is now called the MMPI-2. The test consists of more than 500 statements—such as, "I worry about sex matters"; "I sometimes tease animals"; "I believe I am being plotted against"—to which subjects must respond with "true," "false," or "cannot say." The test may be used in card or booklet form, and several computer programs exist to process responses.

The MMPI gives scores on 10 standard clinical scales, each of which was derived empirically (that is, homogeneous criterion groups of psychiatric patients were used in developing the scales). The items for each scale were selected for their ability to separate medical and psychiatric patients from normal control subjects.

CLINICAL SCALES. The clinical scales are numbered and are often referred to by number rather than by name, particularly in coding deviantly high scores. A high score on a particular scale does not mean that a subject has the illness. For example, an elevated 8 (schizophrenia) score does not indicate that a patient necessarily has schizophrenia. The scales are listed in Table 5.1–2.

INTERPRETATION. An accurate interpretation requires great experience in administering the test and some understanding of the social, educational, and socioeconomic backgrounds of patients. Recent evidence indicates that religion and race are both potential variables in MMPI responses.

Although the MMPI was initially viewed as a diagnostic aid (that is, a patient with major depressive disorder would show an elevation on the depression scale), the advantages of a configural approach to interpretation quickly became apparent. The configural approach, which involves interpretation based on the patterning of the entire profile, has become the preferred method and has increased the effectiveness of the MMPI as a personality measurement device. Various researchers have identified numerous personality correlates of various MMPI scale configurations, frequently by using the two highest scales as the basis for interpretive statements.

Actuarial research of such nature has also served as the basis for computerized interpretative services. These services, although not a substitute for a comprehensive personality evaluation, can assist clinicians in hypothesis formulation. Computerized services are especially useful when the MMPI is to be interpreted by a person knowledgeable in all aspects of the MMPI and in the nature of the development of the computerized program. Blind use of these services by professionals not trained in the use of the MMPI, however, is clearly inappropriate and perhaps even unethical.

The fact that the MMPI is the most widely used and researched psychological personality measurement device is undoubtedly one of its major strengths. Several hundred research papers on the MMPI appear in the literature each year, and it has been used extensively in cross-cultural clinical and research applica-

Table 5.1–1
Classification of Intelligence by IQ Range

Classification	IQ Range
Profound mental retardation (MR)[a]	Below 20 or 25
Severe MR[a]	20–25 to 35–40
Moderate MR[a]	35–40 to 50–55
Mild MR[a]	50–55 to about 70
Borderline	70–79
Dull normal	80 to 90
Normal	90 to 110
Bright normal	110 to 120
Superior	120 to 130
Very superior	130 and above

[a] According to the fourth edition of *Diagnostic and Statistical Manual of Mental Disorders* (DSM-IV).

Table 5.1–2
MMPI Validity and Clinical Scales

Validity

- **L: Lie Scale** A nonempirically derived social desirability scale. Items tend to reflect behaviors that are considered socially desirable but rarely practiced. The score can suggest defensiveness, illiteracy, psychosis, or personality processes, depending on various factors.
- **F: Infrequency Scale** Measures a tendency to endorse selected items that are statistically rare responses (less than 10 percent of the original normal sample). Useful in identifying illiteracy, malingering, panic, confusion, psychosis, and personality processes.
- **K: Suppressor Scale** Used to adjust mathematically certain clinical scales to decrease false positives and false negatives. The scale is also useful in determining overall test-taking attitude and is an indication of personality variables.

Clinical

- **1: Hypochondriasis** Reflects somatic concerns and preoccupation with bodily functioning. Interpretation needs to take into account such factors as age and actual health status. As with all MMPI scales, interpretation is furthered by looking at its relation to other scales.
- **2: Depression** Tends to reflect depression as a mood disorder. The fact that the scale is sensitive to situational variables suggests that it may be a good index of state personality status.
- **3: Hysteria** Involves the identification of classic histrionic symptoms, including the presence of physical symptoms coupled with indifference, denial, repression, and inhibition. The scale does not necessarily measure other popularly conceived traits, such as liability and melodramatic attitude.
- **4: Psychopathic Deviance** Developed to assess the amorality and asociality aspects of psychopathy, rather than the criminal or antisocial. Its meaning depends on other scale configurations. The scale provides good information on the quality of interpersonal relationships.
- **5: Masculinity-Femininity** Originally developed to identify homosexuality but rarely used for that purpose, although it does provide information on gender identity. The scale reflects a variety of personality and interest areas, such as dependence, sensitivity, intellectuality, and tendencies toward introspection.
- **6: Paranoia** Developed by the empirical identification of classic paranoiacs, assesses vigilance, sensitivity, delusional thought, distrust, and suspicion. Except for the paranoid areas, the members of the original criterion group were considered functional in their lives.
- **7: Psychasthenia** A diverse scale designed to measure anxiety and obsessive-compulsive traits. Endorsed items can reflect fear, obsessive-compulsive symptoms, interpersonal hostility, tension, specific phobias, and impaired concentration.
- **8: Schizophrenia** Reflects the acute positive symptoms of psychotic breaks with reality, rather than the chronic negative symptoms. The scale also assesses alienation, impaired self-identity, and isolation.
- **9: Hypomania** Measures the classic symptoms of mania, including elated and unstable mood, psychomotor excitement, and flight of ideas. It also appears to reflect narcissistic personality traits. In general, the scale provides information on the degree of drivenness of the person's personality characteristics. It has a strong age component.
- **10: Social Introversion** Provides information on social withdrawal, shyness, leadership, talkativeness, levels of gregariousness, and, to a small degree, self-concept and neurotic tendencies. It is more two-dimensional and bipolar (introversion versus extroversion) than the other scales.

Special

- **A: Anxiety** The first general factor extracted from factor analytic studies on the MMPI. It is thought to reflect generalized endorsement of psychopathology.
- **R: Repression** The second factor that is found on factor analytic studies of the MMPI. It can be conceptualized as measuring the tendency to engage in denial.
- **ES: Ego Strength** Provides an index of how functional the patient may be in terms of work and other social areas, regardless of level of psychopathology.
- **MAS**: *McAndrews Alcoholism Scale* Estimates the person's degree of addiction proneness, especially with alcohol, opiates, and opioids. It is especially sensitive to daily substance abuse, rather than episodic abuse.

Courtesy of Robert W. Butler, Ph.D., and Paul Salz, Ph.D., with the assistance of Alex Caldwell, Ph.D.

tions. The huge body of literature generated has resulted in a catalog of MMPI correlates on a wide variety of clinical cases, which provides descriptive, predictive, diagnostic, and prognostic information. Another strength of the MMPI is its atheoretical nature, a characteristic that probably increases its usefulness over a broad spectrum. The presence of validity scales designed to assess test-taking attitude, in addition to clinical and personality information, is a distinct advantage that the MMPI maintains over many personality assessment tools.

The MMPI has been restandardized on the basis of a contemporary sample of normal people, and questions and language have been updated to reflect current cultural views.

Structured Clinical Diagnostic Assessments. Several structured and semistructured interviews based on DSM-IV criteria have been designed to provide numerical scores on diagnostic scales. The scales are useful in establishing the severity of illness and in monitoring recovery. Although used clinically, their greatest use is as research instruments: They help to standardize a subject cohort and provide objective outcome measures for assessing treatment response. Among the instruments are the Hamilton Rating Scale for Depression, the Hamilton Anxiety Rating Scale, the Yale-Brown Obsessive-Compulsive Scale (YBOCS), and the Structural Clinical Interview for DSM-IV Dissociative Disorders (SCID-D).

Projective Personality Assessment

The projective approach to personality assessment is defined by the use of unstructured, often ambiguous test stimuli. A basic assumption is that, when confronted with a vague stimulus and required to respond to it in some manner, people cannot help but reveal information about themselves—not only in the process by which the ambiguity is confronted but also in the content of their responses.

The projective approach is essentially idiographic, and the tests most commonly are not interpreted by comparing a person's responses with a set of criterion-referenced normative data. Typically, interpretation is based on a theory of human behavior and personality; it is assumed that people bring certain needs, characteristics, defenses, and other qualities that become apparent through the testing process.

Several semistructured situations and projective-type stimuli have been developed, including perceiving inkblots, drawing pictures, and telling stories on the basis of presented pictures.

Rorschach Test. The Rorschach test was devised by Hermann Rorschach, a Swiss psychiatrist, who around 1910 (Fig. 5.1–2) began to experiment with ambiguous inkblots. A standard set of 10 inkblots serves as stimuli for associations; one inkblot is shown in Figure 5.1–3. In the standard series, the blots are reproduced on cards 7 by 9½ inches and are numbered from I to X. Five of the blots are in black and white; the other five include colors. The cards are shown to a patient in a particular order, and the psychologist keeps a record of the patient's verbatim responses, along with initial reaction times and total time spent on each card. After completion of what is called the free-association phase, the examiner conducts an inquiry phase to determine important aspects of each response that are crucial to its scoring. Table 5.1–3 contains examples of responses to Rorschach stimuli.

SCORING. The scoring of responses converts the important aspects of each response into a symbol system related to location areas, determinants, content areas, and popularity.

Location. Location is scored in terms of which portion of the blot was used as the basis for a response (for example, the whole blot, a common detail of the blot, an unusual detail of the blot, or an area of white space). Attention to the whole blot with accurate form perception reflects good organizational ability and high intelligence. Overattention to detail is common in obsessive and paranoid subjects.

Determinants. The determinants of each response reflect the features of the blot that make it look the way the patient thought it looked (for example, form, shading, color, movement of either humans or animals, inanimate movements, or combinations of these determinants with varying emphasis). Overemphasis on form suggests rigidity and constriction of the personality. Color responses relate to the emotional reactions of the person to the environment and to the control of emotion.

Content. Responses are scored in terms of the content they reflect—human, animal, anatomy, sex, food, nature, and so on. In general, content areas reflect the subject's breadth and range of interests.

Popularity. Certain responses to the cards are more popular than others.

INTERPRETATION. The Rorschach test brings subjects' thinking and association patterns clearly into focus because the ambiguity of the stimulus provides relatively few cues about conventional, standard, or normal responses. Proper interpretation, however, requires a great deal of experience. There is a high reliability among experienced clinicians who administer the test. In proper hands, the test is extremely useful, especially in eliciting psychodynamic formulations, defense mechanisms, and subtle disorders of thinking.

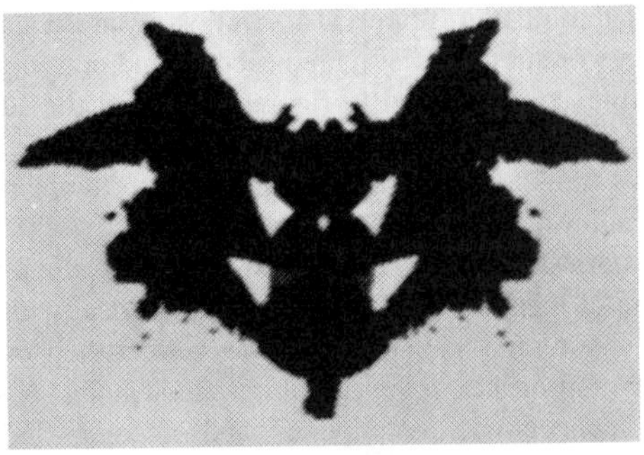

FIGURE 5.1–3
Plate 1 of the Rorschach test. (Reprinted with permission from Huber Medical Publisher, Bern.)

FIGURE 5.1–2
Herman Rorschach. (Courtesy of New York Academy of Medicine, New York, NY.)

Thematic Apperception Test (TAT). This test was designed by Henry Murray and Christiana Morgan as part of a normal personality study conducted at the Harvard Psychological Clinic in 1943. The TAT consists of a series of 30 pictures and one blank card, but not all the pictures are used. The choice depends on what conflict area the examiner wishes to clarify with a patient. Examples of TAT pictures are a young woman seated on a couch looking up at an older man, a man standing beside a nude woman in a bed, a gray-haired man looking at a younger man, and an older woman standing behind a younger woman (Fig. 5.1–4).

Although most of the pictures depict people and all are representational (making the test stimuli more structured than are the inkblots of the Rorschach test), there is ambiguity in each picture. Unlike the Rorschach blots to which patients are asked to associate, the TAT requires that patients construct or create a story.

As the test was originally conceived, an important aspect of each story was the figure (the hero) with whom subjects seemed to identify and to whom they presumably attributed their own wishes, strivings, and conflicts. The characteristics of people other than the hero were considered to represent subjects' views of other people in their environment. It is now assumed that all the figures in a TAT story are equally representative of subjects; the more accepted and conscious traits and motives are attributed to figures closest to the subject in age, sex, and appearance, and the more unacceptable and unconscious traits and motives are attributed to figures most unlike the subject.

The stories must be considered from the standpoint of unusualness of theme or plot. Whether subjects deal with a common or uncommon theme, their stories reflect their own idiosyncratic approaches to organization, sequence, vocabulary, style, preconceptions, assumptions, and outcome. TAT cards have varying stimulus values and can be assumed to elicit data pertaining to various areas of functioning. Generally, the TAT is more useful as a technique for inferring motivational aspects of behavior than as a basis for making a diagnosis.

FIGURE 5.1–4
Care 12F of the Thematic Apperception Test. (Courtesy of Harvard University Press, Cambridge, MA.)

Sentence Completion Test (SCT). This test is designed to tap patients' conscious associations to areas of functioning in which clinicians may be interested. The SCT is composed of a series of sentence stems (usually 75 to 100)—such as, ''I like . . .''; ''Sometimes I wish . . .''—that patients are asked to complete in their own words.

Table 5.1–3
Responses to Rorschach Card I by Five Male Patients

Free Association		Inquiry
Patient A:	A bug with two witches attached to it.	This whole thing in the middle, just the way it looks. [Points] Just the wings here. Looks like a witch.
	Also a halloween mask. About all I can see.	That the whole thing. The eyes, the mouth [White space] [?] Nothing else about it.
Patient B:	A bat, a bug.	Bat. [Whole] The blackness and the wings. Bug—that was just a pure reference to the color. I just see it as unpleasant.
	One of the furies. A headless woman with black wings, grasping hands, claws, whatever. Bottom part of her torso is compressed, held in, like she's reaching forward.	Furies. [Whole] The central portion could represent legs pressed together. She represents a figure of death launching forward, and the head gets lost. Sort of snakelike, and the outer parts are reaching forth at the shadow of the earth.
Patient C:	It looks like a monster bat. It has pincers. And an ass over here.	The whole thing. It has wings, It's kind of ragged, that's all. [Top center] Arches. Just shaped that way. Feel uptight, knowing I'm taking a test[?] Shape, two mounds.
	And a butterfly.	Whole object. The wings, the shape. I just feel I want to get out of here.
Patient D:	Two dancers and two children in between them like they're dancing around them.	[Whole] Head, cape, clothing, legs. Matching heads. A pair of children or a pair of dancers, since it's symmetrical, one on one side and one on the other.
Patient E:	Looks like a bat? That's all I can make of it.	Whole blot. The middle makes it look like a body. And it looks like he has a tail and two short feet.

This table gives the Rorschach responses, both free associations and inquiries, given to Card I by five male patients. The extracted test responses are reported primarily to illustrate the range given by various patients to the same stimulus. As such, the responses may not themselves always delineate the varying DSM-IV diagnoses represented.

Patient A: 26 years old, multiple psychiatric hospitalizations within past 4 years. Unable to care for himself, believing himself controlled by a force that makes him act inappropriately. Suffers from chronic delusions, obsessional thinking, and social withdrawal. Schizophrenia.

Patient B: 23 years old, long history of social isolation, repetitive self-destructive behavior, depression, and inability to function academically. Has shown depersonalization and derealization phenomena but no admitted delusions or hallucinations. Schizotypal personality disorder.

Patient C: 28 years old, complaints of chronic and overwhelming anxiety, feelings of loneliness, and ambivalence about homosexual identification. History of excessive use of psychotropic medication. Borderline personality disorder.

Patient D: 20 years old, presently hospitalized for manic episode, with history of two clear-cut manic and depressive episodes, followed by remissions. Bipolar I disorder.

Patient E: 33 years old, hospitalized on neurology service for cognitive disorder assumed to be related to occupational hazard: mercury poisoning. Prior history of behavior difficulties.

Table by Arthur C. Carr, Ph.D.

Time pressure is usually applied; patients are instructed to write down the first thing that comes to mind. In other instances, the test is administered orally by the examiner, as in the word-association technique. Sentence stems vary in their ambiguity; hence, some items serve as projective test stimuli (''Sometimes I . . .''). Others closely resemble direct-response questionnaires (''My greatest fear is . . .'').

With the individual protocol, most clinicians use an inspection technique and note particularly those responses that are expressive of strong affects, that tend to be given repetitively, or that are unusual or particularly informative in any way. Areas in which denial operates are often revealed through omissions, bland expressions, or factual reports (''My mother is a woman''). Humor may also reflect an attempt to deny anxiety about a particular issue, person, or event. Important historical material is sometimes revealed directly (''I feel guilty about the way my sister was drowned'').

Word-Association Technique. Carl Gustav Jung devised the word-association technique. Jung presented stimulus words to patients and had them respond with the first word that came to mind. After the initial administration of the list, some clinicians today repeat the list and ask the patient to respond with the same words that he or she used previously; discrepancies between the two administrations may reveal associational difficulties. Complex indicators include long reaction times, blocking difficulties in making responses, unusual responses, repetition of the stimulus word, apparent misunderstanding of the word, slang associations, perseveration of earlier responses, and ideas or unusual mannerisms or movements accompanying a response. Because it is easily quantified, the test continues to be used as a research instrument, although its popularity has diminished greatly over the years.

Draw-a-Person Test. This test was first used as a measure of intelligence in children. Detail was correlated with intelligence and developmental level. It has since become useful as an adult test. The Draw-a-Person test is easily administered, usually with the instructions, ''I'd like you to draw a picture of a person; draw the best person you can.'' After the completion of the first drawing, the patient is asked to draw a picture of a person of the sex opposite to that of the figure in the drawing. Some clinicians use an interrogation procedure in which the patient is questioned about his or her drawings. (''What is he doing?'' ''What are her best qualities?'') Modifications include asking for a drawing of a house and a tree (House-Tree-Person test), of the patient's family, and of an animal.

A general assumption is that the drawing of a person represents the expression of the self or of the body in the environment. Interpretive principles rest largely on the assumed functional significance of each body part. Most clinicians use drawings primarily as a screening technique, particularly for the detection of brain damage.

INTEGRATION OF TEST FINDINGS

The integration of test findings into a comprehensive, meaningful report is probably the most difficult aspect of psychological evaluation. Inferences from various tests must be related to one another in terms of clinicians' confidence in them and of a patient's presumed level of awareness that consciousness is being tapped.

Most clinicians follow some general outline in preparing a psychological report, such as test behavior, intellectual functioning, personality functioning (reality-testing ability, impulse control, manifest depression and guilt, manifestations of major dysfunction, major defenses, overt symptoms, interpersonal conflicts, self-concept, affects), inferred diagnosis, degree of present overt disturbance, prognosis for social recovery, motivation for personality change, primary assets and weaknesses, recommendations, and summary.

References

Archer RP, Krishnamurthy R: A review of MMPI and Rorschach inter-relationships in adult samples. J Pers Assess *61:* 277, 1993.

Bremner J, Steinberg M, Southwick SM, Johnson DR, Charney DS: Use of the Structured Clinical Interview for DSM-IV Dissociative Disorders for systematic assessment of dissociative symptoms in posttraumatic stress disorder. Am J Psychiatry *150:* 1011, 1993.

Butler RW, Satz P: Personality assessment of adults and children. In *Comprehensive Textbook of Psychiatry,* ed 6, HI Kaplan, BJ Sadock, editors, p 544. Williams & Wilkins, Baltimore, 1995.

Chick D, Sheaffer CI, Goggin WC, Sison GF: The relationship between MCMI personality scales and clinician-generated DSM-III-R personality disorder diagnoses. J Pers Assess *61:* 264, 1993.

Edwards DW, Morrison TL, Weissman HN: The MMPI and MMPI-2 in an outpatient sample: Comparisons of code types, validity scales and clinical scales. J Pers Assess *61:* 1, 1993.

Fischer J, Corcoran K: *Measures for Clinical Practice: A Sourcebook,* ed 2, vol 1: *Couples, Families and Children.* Free Press, New York, 1994.

Fischer J, Corcoran K: *Measures for Clinical Practice: A Sourcebook,* ed 2, vol 2: *Adults.* Free Press, New York, 1994.

Goldstein G, Hersen M, editors: *Handbook of Psychological Assessment.* Pergamon, New York, 1990.

Graham JR: *Assessing Personality and Psychopathology.* Oxford University Press, New York, 1990.

Kardum I, Hudek-Knezevic J: The relationship between Eysenck's personality traits, coping styles and moods. Pers Indiv Diff *20:* 341, 1996.

Katon W, Sullivan MD, Clark MR: Cardiovascular disorders. In *Comprehensive Textbook of Psychiatry,* ed 6, HI Kaplan, BJ Sadock, editors, p 1491. Williams & Wilkins, Baltimore, 1995.

Lezak MD: *Neuropsychological Assessment,* ed 2. Oxford University Press, New York, 1983.

McCann JR: Convergent and discriminant validity of the MCMI-II and MMPI personality disorder scales. Psych Asess 3: *9,* 1991.

Rorschach H: *Psychodiagnostik.* Bircher, Bern, 1921.

Schnurr PP, Friedman MJ, Rosenberg SD: Preliminary MMPI scores as predictors of combat-related PTSD symptoms. Am J Psychiatry *150:* 479, 1993.

Steinberg M: *The Structured Clinical Interview for DSM-IV Dissociative Disorders.* American Psychiatric Press, Washington, 1993.

▲ 5.2 Neuropsychological Assessment of Adults

The aim of neuropsychological tests is to achieve quantifiable and reproducible results that can be compared to the test scores of normal people whose age and demographic background are similar to those of the person tested. Standardized techniques for assessing adult functioning include psychological tests, scales that rate behavior, and controlled interviews.

Neuropsychological assessment is indicated to identify cognitive defects, to differentiate incipient depression from dementia, to determine the course of an illness, to assess neurotoxic effects (such a memory impairment by substance abuse), to evaluate the effects of treatment (for example, surgery for epilepsy, pharmacotherapy), and to evaluate learning disorders.

REASONING, CONCEPT FORMATION, AND PROBLEM SOLVING

Patients with cerebral disease are likely to show a loss of the capacity to reason abstractly and a lack of flexibility in problem solving or in adapting to changed situations. Frontal lobe disease is often associated with impaired abstract reasoning, although other areas of the brain may also be involved. Workers can use many tests to assess the capacity for concept formation.

Wisconsin Card Sorting Test (WCST)

The Wisconsin Card Sorting Test assesses abstract reasoning and flexibility in problem solving. Stimulus cards of different color, form, and number are presented to patients for sorting into groups according to a principle established by the examiner but unknown to the patient (for example, to sort by color, ignoring form and number). As the patient sorts the cards, he or she is told whether the responses are correct or incorrect, and the number of trials required to achieve 10 consecutive correct responses is recorded. When (or if) the patient has mastered the task, the examiner changes the principle of sorting, and the number of trials required to achieve correct sorting is recorded. The procedure is repeated several times, and measures of the capacity for abstract thinking (that is, the number of trials required to achieve a solution) and of flexibility (perseverative errors on successive sorting trials) are derived. Abnormal responses appear in people with damage to the frontal lobes or to the caudate and in some people with schizophrenia.

MEMORY

Impairment of various types of memory, most notably short-term and recent memory, is a prominent behavioral deficit in patients with brain damage. In addition, it is often the first sign of cerebral disease and of aging. Memory is a comprehensive term that covers the retention of all types of material over various times and involves diverse forms of response. Consequently, a neuropsychological examiner is more inclined to give specific memory tests and evaluate them separately than to use an omnibus battery that provides a brief assessment of a large variety of performances and yields a single score.

Types of Memory

Immediate (or *short-term*) *memory* may be defined as the reproduction, recognition, or recall of perceived material within a period of up to 30 seconds after presentation. It is most often assessed by digit repetition and reversal (auditory) and memory-for-designs (visual) tests. Both an auditory-verbal task, such as digit span or memory for words or sentences, and a nonverbal visual task, such as memory for designs or for objects or faces, should be given to assess a patient's immediate memory. Patients can also be asked to listen to a standardized story and then to repeat it as accurately as possible. Patients with lesions of the right hemisphere are likely to show more severe defects on visual nonverbal tasks than on auditory verbal tasks. Conversely, patients with left hemisphere disease, including those who are not aphasic, are likely to show severe deficits on the auditory verbal tests, with variable performance on the visual nonverbal tasks.

Recent memory concerns events over the past few hours or days and can be tested by asking patients what they had for breakfast and who visited with them in the hospital.

Recent past memory concerns the retention of information over the past few months. Patients can be asked questions about current events.

Remote memory is the ability to remember events in the distant past. It is commonly believed that remote memory is well preserved in patients who show pronounced defects in recent memory, but the remote memory of senile and amnestic patients is usually significantly inferior to that of normal people of comparable age and education. Even patients who appear to be able to recount their past fairly accurately show, on close examination, gaps and inconsistencies in their recitals.

Memory theorists have described three other types of memory: episodic, for specific events (for example, a telephone message); semantic, for knowledge and facts (for example, the first President of the United States); and implicit, for automatic skills (for example, speaking grammatically or driving a car). Semantic and implicit memory do not decline with age, and people continue to accumulate information over a lifetime. A minimal decline in episodic memory with aging may relate to impaired frontal lobe functioning.

Testing Memory

Wechsler Memory Scale. The Wechsler Memory Scale-Revised (WMS-R) is the most widely used memory test battery for adults. It is a composite of verbal paired associate and paragraph retention, visual memory for designs, orientation, digit span, rote recall of the alphabet, and counting backward. The scale yields a memory quotient (MQ), which is corrected for age and generally approximates the Wechsler Adult Intelligence Scale intelligence quotient (WAIS IQ); amnestic conditions, such as Korsakoff's syndrome, are characterized by a disproportionately low MQ but a relatively preserved IQ.

Benton Visual Retention Test. The Benton Visual Retention Test is sensitive to short-term memory loss (Fig. 5.2–1).

ORIENTATION

Orientation for person or place is rarely disturbed in brain-damaged patients who are not psychotic or severely demented, although defects in temporal orientation, which can reflect the integrity of recent memory, are common. Clinical examiners often miss these defects because of the tendency to regard as

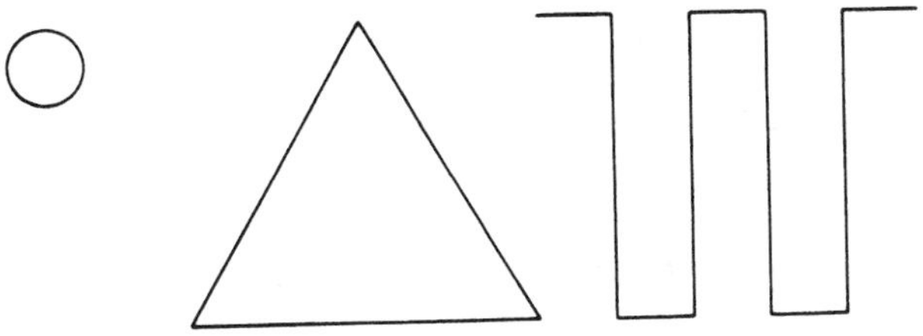

FIGURE 5.2–1

Test item from the Benton Visual Retention Test. The most frequently used testing condition involves the presentation of each geometric figure for 10 seconds, after which the patient attempts to draw the figure from memory. (Reprinted with permission from Benton AL: *The Revised Visual Retention Test: Clinical and Experimental Applications,* 4th ed, p 32. Psychological Corporation, New York, 1974.)

inconsequential slight inaccuracies in giving the day of the week or the date of the month. About 25 percent of nonpsychotic patients with hemispheric cerebral disease, however, are likely to show significantly decreased performance with respect to the precision of temporal orientation. A simple test for orientation is outlined in Table 5.2–1.

Table 5.2–1
Temporal Orientation Schedule

Administration

What is today's date? (The patient is required to give month, day, and year.)

What day of the week is it?

What time is it now? (Examiner makes sure that the patient cannot look at a watch or clock.)

Scoring

Day of week: 1 error point for each day removed from the correct day to a maximum of 3 points

Day of month: 1 error point for each day removed from the correct day to a maximum of 15 points

Month: 5 error points for each month removed from the correct month with the qualification that, if the stated date is within 15 days of the correct date, no points are scored for the incorrect month (for example, May 29 for June 2 = 4 points off)

Year: 10 error points for each year removed from the correct year to a maximum of 60 points with the qualification that, if the stated date is within 15 days of the correct date, no points are scored for the incorrect year (for example, December 26, 1982, for January 2, 1983 = 7 points off)

Time of day: 1 error point for each 30 minutes removed from the correct time to a maximum of 5 points

Courtesy of Arthur L. Benton, Ph.D.

PERCEPTUAL AND PERCEPTUOMOTOR PERFORMANCE

Many patients with brain disease show an impaired ability to analyze complex stimulus constellations or an inability to translate their perception into appropriate motor action. Unless the impairment is of a gross nature, as in visual object agnosia or dressing apraxia, or unless it interferes with a specific occupation skill, these deficits are not likely to be the subject of spontaneous complaint. Appropriate testing, however, discloses a remarkably high incidence of impaired performance on visuoanalytic, visuospatial, and visuoconstructive tasks in brain-damaged patients, particularly in people with disease involving the right hemisphere. This type of impairment also extends to tactile and auditory perceptual task performances.

Visuoperceptive and visuoconstructive capacity and somatoperceptual defects can be assessed by tests. Double simultaneous stimulation is tested by lightly touching one of the patient's cheeks with one hand and simultaneously touching the back of one of the patient's hands with the other. A patient with brain dysfunction is unable to recognize one or both of the stimuli. The double simultaneous stimulation is a general test of defective capacity for perceptual integration.

Perceptuomotor tests often help localize cerebral lesions. A significant portion of patients with lesions of the right hemisphere who do not show obvious impairment in language functions perform poorly on perceptual tests (Fig. 5.2–2).

Bender Visual Motor Gestalt Test

This test of visuomotor coordination is useful for both children and adults. It was designed in 1938 by Lauretta Bender of New York University Medical Center and Bellevue Psychiatric Hospital, who used it to evaluate maturational levels in children. Developmentally, a child younger than 3 years of age is generally unable to reproduce any of the test's designs meaningfully. Around 4 years of age, a child may be able to copy several designs but does so poorly. At about age 6, a child should produce some recognizable, although still uneven, representations of all the designs. By age 10 and certainly by age 12, a child's copies should be reasonably accurate and well organized. Bender also presented studies of adults with cognitive disorders, mental retardation, aphasias, psychoses, neuroses, and malingering.

The test material consists of nine separate designs, adapted from those used by Max Wertheimer in his studies in Gestalt psychology. Each design is printed against a white background on a separate card (Fig. 5.2–3). Presented with unlined paper, patients are asked to copy each design with the card in front of them. There is no time limit. This phase of the test is highly structured and does not investigate memory function, because the cards remain in front of patients while they copy them. Many clinicians include a subsequent recall phase, in which (after an interval of 45 to 60 seconds) patients are asked to reproduce as many of the designs as they can from memory. This phase not only investigates visual memory, but also presents a less structured situation, in which patients must rely essentially on their own resources. It is often particularly helpful to compare the patient's functioning under the two conditions.

The Bender gestalt test is probably used most frequently with adults as a screening device for signs of organic dysfunction. Evaluation of the protocol depends on the form of the reproduced figures and on their relation to one another and to the whole spatial background (Figs. 5.2–4 and 5.2–5).

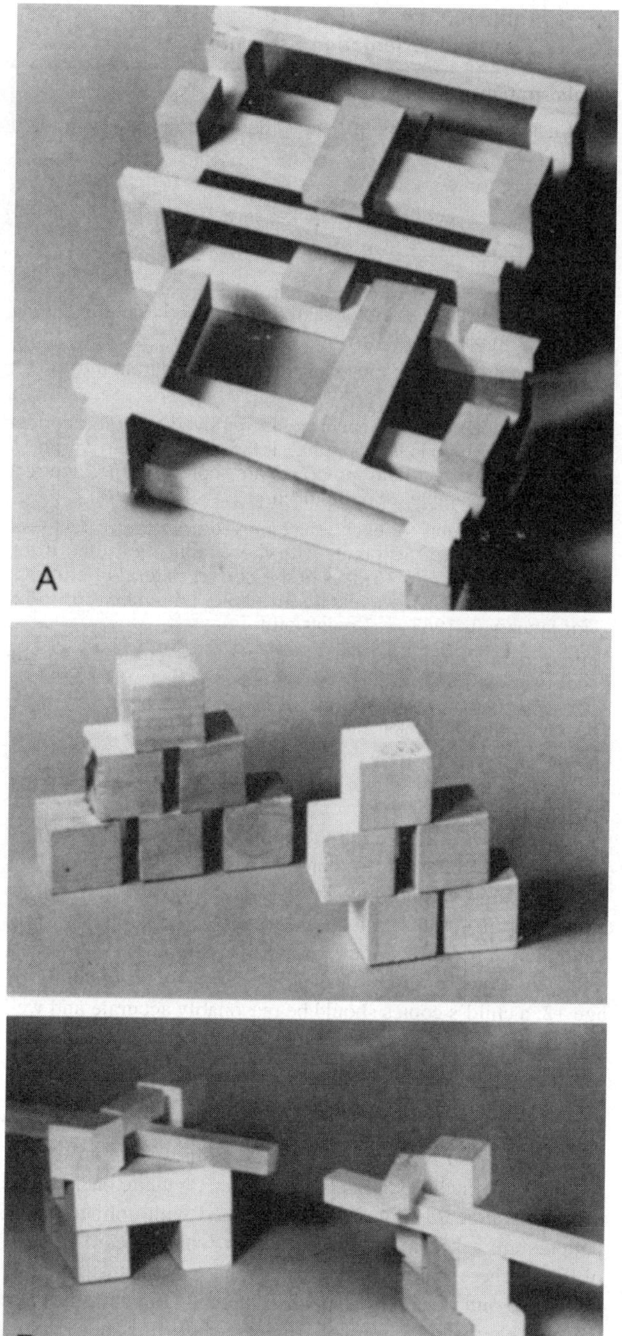
A
B

FIGURE 5.2–2

Examples of "closing-in" error **(A)** and neglect of left side **(B)** on the three-dimensional constructional praxis test. (Reprinted with permission from Benton AL, Sivan AB, Hamsher KdeS, Varney NR, Spreen O: *Contributions to Neuropsychological Assessment,* 2nd ed, p 121. Oxford University Press, New York, 1983.)

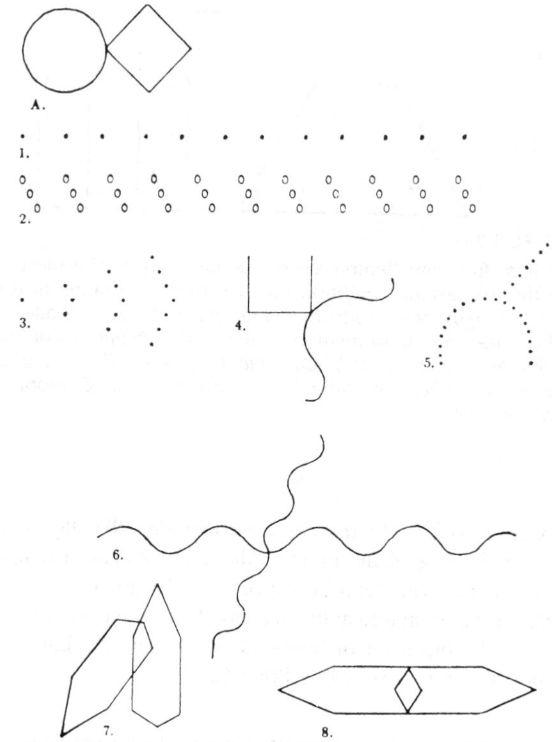
A.
1.
2.
3.
4.
5.
6.
7.
8.

FIGURE 5.2–3

Text figures from the Bender Visual Motor Gestalt test, adapted from Max Wertheimer. (From Bender L: *A Visual Motor Gestalt Test and Its Clinical Use,* p 33. American Orthopsychiatric Association, New York, 1938.)

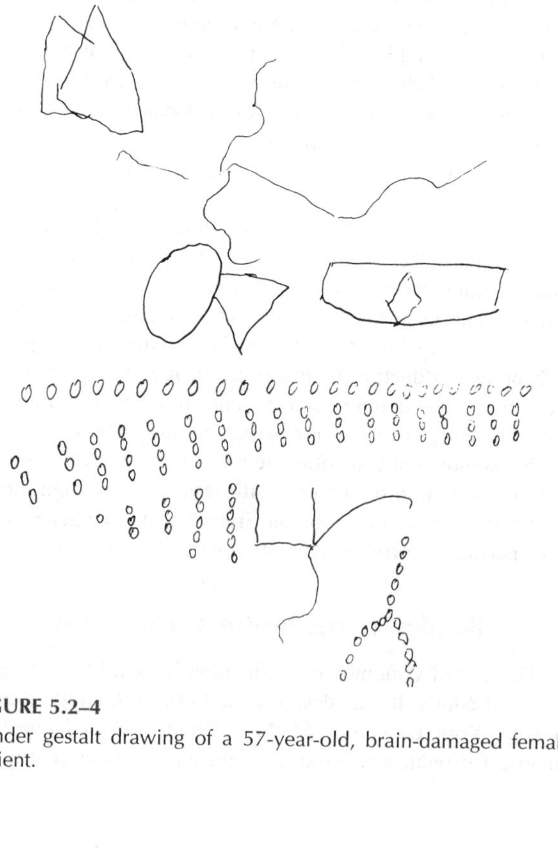

FIGURE 5.2–4

Bender gestalt drawing of a 57-year-old, brain-damaged female patient.

FIGURE 5.2–5
Bender gestalt recall of the 57-year-old, brain-damaged female patient in Figure 5.2–4.

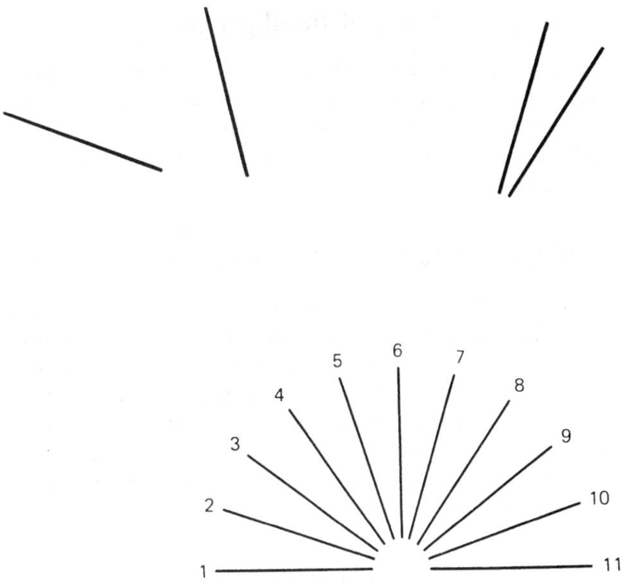
1
2
3
4
5
6
7
8
9
10
11

FIGURE 5.2–6
Double-line stimuli that are matched to the multiple choice card below on the Judgment of Line Orientation Test. (Reprinted with permission from Benton AL, Sivan AB, Hamsher KdeS, Varney NR, Spreen O: *Contributions to Neuropsychological Assessment. A Clinical Manual,* 2nd ed. Oxford University Press, New York, 1994.)

Complex Visual Discrimination

Although the inability to recognize familiar faces (prosopagnosia) is an uncommon disorder, defective discrimination of unfamiliar faces is a common finding in patients with right-hemisphere or bilateral lesions. The Facial Recognition Test, in which a patient is required to identify a photograph of a face originally presented in a front view when it is included in various displays (for example, side view and a front view with shadows), produces a high frequency of failure in patients with posterior right-hemisphere lesions. Performance is generally intact in patients with left-hemisphere lesions (provided that receptive language is not seriously limited) and in patients with schizophrenia.

The Judgment of Line Orientation Test has been found to demonstrate failing performance in an impressive proportion of patients with right-hemisphere disease. The test requires matching the slope of visually presented lines or pairs of lines. As depicted in Figure 5.2–6, the patient points to or verbally identifies the lines of the display that correspond to the angular orientation of each pair of lines. As with facial recognition, patients with right-hemisphere lesions are frequently defective in visuospatial tests, whereas patients with left-hemisphere disease perform within normal range.

LANGUAGE

Relatively minor defects in the use of language may be valid indicators of the presence of brain disease. The dominant hemisphere controls language function. The affective part of speech that conveys mood is called prosody and is controlled by the nondominant hemisphere. Fluency is tested by asking patients to give all the words they can think of beginning with a given letter of the alphabet. Aphasic patients with left-hemisphere disease fail this task. Variables influencing language tests are educational background, sex, and age. Reading and writing are also associated with the dominant hemisphere and are tested by asking patients to read aloud from prepared material and to write their names or a brief passage. Dyslexia and dysgraphia are suspected if patients have difficulties in performing these tasks.

The Boston Diagnostic Aphasia Examination includes a speech rating scale that is useful for comparing with test scores and a brief schedule of items for assessing ideomotor praxis—that is, symbolic buccofacial and limb movements to exhibit gestures and to demonstrate the use of imagined or real objects.

ATTENTION AND CONCENTRATION

The capacity to sustain a maximal level of attention over a period is sometimes impaired in brain-damaged patients, and this impairment is reflected in an oscillation in performance level for a continuous or repeated activity. Some evidence indicates that the instability in performance is related to an electroencephalographic abnormality and that an inexplicable decline in performance is related temporally to the occurrence of certain types of abnormal electrical activity. Simple reaction time provides a convenient measure of the variability and speed of simple responses.

The reaction time needed to respond to a stimulus is impaired in 40 to 45 percent of brain-damaged patients and is a sensitive indicator of overall cerebral integrity. Comparison of the reaction times of the right and left hands often provides an indication of the site of the lesion in a patient and of unilateral cerebral disease.

BEHAVIORAL INDEXES OF BRAIN DAMAGE IN CHILDREN

If present, the behavioral consequences of early brain damage may take many forms, of which attention-deficit/hyperactivity disorder is only one. Early brain damage may result in little or no behavioral deficit; when such a deficit does appear, it usually is less severe than that caused by a comparable lesion in adults. Thus, many brain-damaged children may not be identified by current methods of behavioral assessment.

General Intelligence

The most frequently used batteries are the WISC, the Stanford-Binet Test, and the Wechsler Preschool and Primary Scale of Intelligence (WPPSI). A relatively low level of general intelligence is probably the most constant behavioral result of brain damage in children.

Perceptual and Perceptuomotor Performances

Many brain-damaged children with adequate verbal skills show strikingly defective visuoperceptive and visuomotor performance. The test most frequently used is the copying of designs, either from a model or from memory. About 25 percent of brain-damaged school children of adequate verbal intelligence perform defectively. The task helps discriminate between brain-damaged children and those suffering from presumably psychogenic emotional disturbances.

Language

Considerable evidence indicates that children who show gross maldevelopment of oral language abilities, as compared with their general mental levels, suffer from brain damage. Perinatal brain injury may be a causative factor in at least some cases of developmental dyslexia or generalized learning disability. The finding of a relatively high incidence of electroencephalographic abnormalities in children with learning disorders points to the same conclusion.

Motor Performances

Motor awkwardness and inability to carry out movement sequences on command or by imitation are commonly seen in brain-damaged children. A variety of tests are available for the assessment of manual dexterity (for example, manipulations with tweezers, paper cutting, and peg placing).

Motor impersistence—the inability to sustain an action initiated on command, such as keeping the eyes closed—is seen in a relatively small proportion of adult patients with cerebral disease. It is seen with high frequency, however, in nondefective brain-damaged children. Many children with mental defects also show excessive motor impersistence, particularly those children with brain damage.

COMPREHENSIVE TESTING

Several test batteries have been developed to help in neuropsychological and neuropsychiatric evaluation. Among them are the Luria-Nebraska and the Halstead-Reitan neuropsychological test batteries.

Luria-Nebraska Neuropsychological Battery

Based on the work of the Russian neuropsychologist Alexander Luria, the Luria-Nebraska Neuropsychological Battery was developed at the University of Nebraska. The test assesses a wide range of cognitive functions: memory; motor functions; rhythm; tactile, auditory, and visual functions; receptive and expressive speech; writing; spelling; reading; and arithmetic. The test is designed for people who are at least 15 years of age, and a children's version can be used with 8 to 12 year olds. The test is extremely sensitive for identifying specific types of problems (for example, dyslexia and dyscalculia), rather than being limited to global impressions of brain dysfunction. It also helps localize the various cortical zones that are involved in a particular function and is useful in establishing left or right cerebral dominance.

Halstead-Reitan Battery of Neuropsychological Tests

In the early 1940s, Ward Halstead and his student Ralph Reitan developed a battery of tests that were used to determine the location and the effects of specific brain lesions. The battery is composed of 10 tests.

1. Category test: Patients must discover the common element in a set of pictures; the test measures concept function, abstraction, and visual acuity.
2. Tactual performance test: Patients place shapes in a form board while blindfolded and then must recall the arrangement of the board; the performance tests dexterity, spatial memory, and tactual discrimination.
3. Rhythm test: Patients identify 30 pairs of rhythmic beats as either the same or different to test auditory perception, attention, and concentration.
4. Finger-oscillation test: Patients tap the index finger of each hand in a measured 10-second period; the test measures dexterity and motor speed.
5. Speech-sounds perception test: Patients match 60 nonsense syllables that they hear with several printed alternatives; the test measures auditory discrimination and phonetic skills.
6. Trail-making test: Patients first connect 25 numbered circles in order and then connect 25 lettered and numbered circles in order, alternating between numbered and alphabetical circles; the procedure tests visuomotor perception and motor speed.
7. Critical flicker frequency: Patients note when a flickering light becomes steady for a test of visual perception.
8. Time sense test: Patients judge, without looking, the time it takes for the second hand of a watch to make several revolutions as a test of memory and spatial perception.
9. Aphasia screening test: Patients must name objects, read, write, calculate, draw shapes, identify body parts, perform acts, and differentiate between left and right as a means of testing a wide range of verbal and nonverbal brain functions.
10. Sensory-perceptual tests: Patients perform several tasks with eyes closed—such as identifying where they are touched simultaneously on the hand and the face (simultaneous sensory stimulation test), which finger is touched (finger localization), what coins are placed in the hand (stereognosis), and what numbers are written on the skin (tactile perception).

The Halstead-Reitan battery has the advantage of providing a uniform profile of scores that must be weighed against the considerable time required for administration. The test is able to differentiate those who are brain damaged from neurologically intact people. People with schizophrenia tend to perform above the level of subacutely brain-damaged patients but not differently from those with chronic brain damage. Moreover, the pattern of deficits on the Halstead-Reitan battery is similar in patients with brain damage and with schizophrenia.

RELIABILITY AND VALIDITY

The reliability and validity of neuropsychological tests may be affected by many factors. Mood states, especially anxiety and depression, may change scores from one test administration to the next. Reliability is also affected by motivation, effort, and cooperation, and changes in clinical status can alter test–retest performance.

Results may be confounded by medication effects. Anticonvulsants typically decrease performance in all areas. Antipsychotics, however, have either negligible or mildly positive effects in patients with schizophrenia.

REFERENCES

Axelrod BN, Goldman RS, Henry RR: Sensitivity of the Mini-Mental State Examination to frontal lobe dysfunction in normal aging. J Clin Psychol *48:* 68, 1992.

Bryson GJ, Silverstein ML, Nathan A, Stephen L: Differential rate of neuropsychological dysfunction in psychiatric disorders: Comparison between the Halstead-Reitan and Luria-Nebraska batteries. Percept Mot Skills *76:* 305, 1993.

Chouinard MJ, Braun CM-J: A meta analysis of the relative sensitivity of neuropsychological screening tests. J Clin Exp Neuropsychol *15:* 591, 1993.

Crossen JR, Wiens AN: Comparison of the Auditory-Verbal Learning Test (AVLT) and California Verbal Learning Test (CVLT) in a sample of normal subjects. J Clin Exp Neuropsychol *16:* 190, 1995.

Goldberg TE, Hyde TM, Kleinman JE, Weinberger DR: Course of schizophrenia: Neuropsychological evidence for a static encephalopathy. Schizophr Bull *19:* 797, 1993.

Grant I, Adams KM: *Neuropsychological Assessment of Neuropsychiatric Disorders,* ed 2. Oxford University Press, New York, 1996.

Hanson SL, Tucker DM: *Neuropsychological Assessment.* Hanley & Belfus, Philadelphia, 1992.

Heilman KM, Valenstein E, editors: *Clinical Neuropsychology,* ed 3. Oxford University Press, New York, 1993.

Kempen JM, Kritchevsky M, Feldman ST: Effect of visual impairment on neuropsychological test performance. J Clin Exp Neuropsychol *16:* 223, 1994.

Levin HS, Soukup VM, Benton AL, Fletcher JM, Satz P: Neuropsychological and intellectual assessment of adults. In *Comprehensive Textbook of Psychiatry,* ed 6, HI Kaplan, BJ Sadock, editors, p 562. Williams & Wilkins, Baltimore, 1995.

Lezak MD: *Neuropsychological Assessment,* ed 3. Oxford University Press, New York, 1995.

Mittenberg W, Azrin R, Millsaps C, Heilbronner R: Identification of malingered head injury on the Weschsler Memory Scale–Revised. Psychol Assess *5:* 34, 1993.

Reitan RM, Wolfson D: Conventional intelligence measurements and neuropsychological concepts of adaptive abilities. J Clin Psychol *48:* 521, 1992.

6 Theories of Personality and Psychopathology

▲ 6.1 Sigmund Freud: Founder of Classic Psychoanalysis

Psychoanalysis is a theory of the personality, a method of investigation, and a scientific discipline. As it is practiced today, it is a pluralistic endeavor drawing from diverse theoretical perspectives that revolve around several fundamental controversies in the field. Is the origin of a patient's difficulties based in conflict or deficit? Is psychoanalysis fundamentally a one-person or a two-person psychology? Is the database of psychoanalysis limited to a patient's subjective experience, or should it be expanded to include the analyst's experience as well? Does psychopathology originate primarily from traumatic reality events, or does it stem largely from the role of fantasy in distorting real events? Do symptomatic expressions derive from the oedipal phase of development or from much earlier experiences?

The current debates in the field and the plethora of theories associated with these debates would undoubtedly baffle Sigmund Freud, were the founder of psychoanalysis alive today. Yet all the theories and modifications of technique are clearly traceable to Freud's monumental work in the latter part of the 19th century and the first 40 years of the 20th century. Nevertheless, he always preserved certain fundamental tenets.

Freud stipulated that for a technique to be psychoanalytic, it has to involve the principles of transference and resistance. Transference is the patient's displacement onto the analyst of early wishes and feelings toward other people. Although patients may begin their analyses with the understanding that their analysts are helpful professionals, they soon begin to experience the analyst as a significant figure from the past, such as a parent. Contemporary analysts also recognize that transference is affected in part by the analyst's real characteristics so that the transference perception is an admixture of the real relationship with the analyst and of relationships with figures from the past whom patients unconsciously bring into the present.

Freud originally identified resistance when he asked his patients to use the technique of free association, which involved saying whatever comes to mind without censoring the thoughts. Freud noted that many patients could not carry out these instructions and in some cases would ''go blank.'' Ultimately, he came to realize that these patients were unconsciously opposing the treatment every step of the way. Many patients are ambivalent about getting better and about cooperating with the clinician who intends to be helpful. Modern psychiatrists see resistance in the acts of patients who forget to fill prescriptions, refuse to take medication, miss appointments, and otherwise engage in noncompliant behaviors.

These principles of technique, transference, and resistance derive from basic theoretical notions inherent in psychoanalysis. First and foremost, much of people's intrapsychic world is *unconscious.* People like to think they are in control of their lives, but factors outside conscious awareness often influence behavior. A simple example is the New Year's resolution that people have every conscious intention to keep, yet consistently undermine as they try to carry out their pledge. The unconscious is also revealed through slips of the tongue, termed *parapraxes,* which unwittingly exhibit to everyone what is going on in a speaker's unconscious. A politician blurted out, ''I have this information from an impeachable source''; instead, he meant to say that his source was unimpeachable.

Dreams and many nonverbal behaviors also reveal unconscious conflicts and wishes. Just as the unconscious is implicated in the principles of transference and resistance, so are other notions central to psychoanalytic theory. The fact that childhood experiences are repeated throughout life reflects the developmental underpinnings of psychoanalytic theory. As Wordsworth noted, ''The Child is father of the Man.'' Behavior has meaning and is determined in part by unconscious conflicts, although of course it is also influenced by biological factors and cultural considerations. The domain of psychoanalysis, however, involves *meanings,* and psychoanalysts are always interested in patients' uniquely individual interpretation of thoughts, feelings, and external events. Psychoanalytic theory and technique take their place alongside neurosciences, social theories, behaviorism, and other diverse elements of contemporary psychiatry; yet the principles originally outlined by Freud continue to be of great value in understanding and treating psychiatric disorders and in addressing people who are ill.

LIFE OF FREUD

Sigmund Freud was born on May 6, 1856, in Freiburg, a small town in Moravia, which is now a part of the Czech

Republic. When Freud was 4 years old, his father, a Jewish wool merchant, moved the family to Vienna, where Freud spent most of his life. Following medical school, he specialized in neurology and studied for a year in Paris with Jean-Martin Charcot. He was also influenced by Ambroise-August Liebault and Hippolyte-Marie Bernheim, both of whom taught him hypnosis while he was in France. After his education in France, he returned to Vienna and began clinical work with hysterical patients. Between 1887 and 1897, his work with these patients led him to develop psychoanalysis. Figures 6.1–1 through 6.1–9 trace the highlights of Freud's life.

BEGINNINGS OF PSYCHOANALYSIS

Freud's early career as a neurologist inevitably led him to wonder about the interface between mind and body. In conjunction with his colleague Joseph Breuer, he treated a series of female patients suffering from hysterical symptoms that defied neurological explanation. One particular patient, Bertha Pappenheim, who was treated by Breuer as Anna O., intrigued Freud and led him to investigate the use of hypnosis as a routine part of his clinical practice. In 1889, Freud turned to the cathartic method, which he used in conjunction with hypnosis. Using this approach, Freud attempted to remove symptoms through a process of recovering and verbalizing suppressed feelings with which the symptoms were associated. This method came to be known as *abreaction.*

Through his experiments with abreaction and catharsis, Freud learned that his patients were often unable or unwilling

FIGURE 6.1–2
Sigmund Freud and his bride, Martha Bernays, in 1886. (Courtesy of Menninger Foundation Archives, Topeka, KS.)

FIGURE 6.1–1
Sigmund Freud as a boy in 1870. (Courtesy of Menninger Foundation Archives, Topeka, KS.)

FIGURE 6.1–3
Sigmund Freud in 1903. (Courtesy of Menninger Foundation Archives, Topeka, KS.)

FIGURE 6.1–4
Sigmund Freud in 1911. (Courtesy of Menninger Foundation Archives, Topeka, KS.)

FIGURE 6.1–5
Sigmund Freud with his grandson in 1922. (Courtesy of Menninger Foundation Archives, Topeka, KS.)

FIGURE 6.1–6
Sigmund Freud in 1935. (Courtesy of Menninger Foundation Archives, Topeka, KS.)

FIGURE 6.1–7
Sigmund Freud at work in his office in 1936. (Courtesy of Menninger Foundation Archives, Topeka, KS.)

to recount memories that subsequently proved to be very significant. Freud referred to this reluctance as *resistance,* and later determined that resistance was caused by largely unconscious, active forces in patients' minds. Freud described this active process of excluding distressing material from conscious awareness as *repression,* which he came to regard as essential to symptom formation. Because of the forces of repression and resistance, Freud abandoned his cathartic method and switched to *free association*—inviting his patients to say whatever came into their minds without censoring their thoughts.

Freud's treatment of patients with hysteria during the early 1890s convinced him that childhood sexual seduction played a major role in causing the neuroses. Many of his patients reported such seductions by nursemaids, fathers, and caretakers, and Freud believed that repressed memories of actual sexual traumata created neurotic symptoms.

In the later 1890s, however, he began to reconsider these views; ultimately, he shifted his thinking. The idea that sexual seduction by parental figures was a fantasy began to displace his theory that actual seduction was a pivotal pathogenic factor in neuroses. This shift seemed to be influenced by Freud's own self-analysis, in which he became convinced of childhood sexual fantasies in himself as well as in his patients. Moreover, some patients' reports of abuse sounded so fantastic that it became difficult for Freud to distinguish truth from fiction in such accounts. Contrary to recent reports by Freud's critics, however, he never actually abandoned his belief that real incest was a factor contributing to psychopathology in adults, and throughout his career he reasserted that he was convinced of actual sexual seductions of children by parents. Nevertheless,

FIGURE 6.1–8
Sigmund Freud with two pet chows in 1938. (Courtesy of Menninger Foundation Archives, Topeka, KS.)

FIGURE 6.1–9
Sigmund Freud's couch in Freud Museum. (Courtesy of Menninger Foundation Archives, Topeka, KS.)

he placed much greater emphasis on childhood sexual fantasies as the core of neuroses. Freud's self-analysis also was instrumental in his deciphering of dreams and led to the appearance in 1900 of perhaps his most monumental work, *The Interpretation of Dreams.*

THE INTERPRETATION OF DREAMS

Freud became aware of the significance of dreams when he noted that patients frequently reported their dreams in the process of free association. Through their further associations to the dream content, he learned that dreams were definitely meaningful, even though meanings were often hidden or disguised. Most of all, Freud was struck by the intimate connection between dream content and unconscious memories or fantasies that were long repressed. This observation led Freud to declare that the interpretation of dreams was the royal road to understanding the unconscious.

In *The Interpretation of Dreams,* Freud asserted that a dream is the disguised fulfillment of an unconscious childhood wish that is not readily accessible to conscious awareness in waking life. In attempting to characterize the psychology of dreaming, Freud laid the foundations for ego psychology. He suggested that unconscious childhood wishes can be transformed into disguised conscious manifestations only if a censor exists in the mind. The censor, acting in the service of the ego, functions to preserve sleep. By disguising disturbing thoughts and feelings, the censor makes sure that the dreamer's sleep is not disturbed. Moreover, early forms of defense mechanisms in the ego were delineated by Freud's investigation of the different methods of disguise used by the ego—for example, displacement, condensation, and symbolic representation. Freud drew beginning parallels between dream mechanisms and pathological thoughts of psychotic patients in the waking state.

The analysis of dreams elicits material that has been repressed. These unconscious thoughts and wishes include nocturnal sensory stimuli (sensory impressions such as pain, hunger, thirst, urinary urgency), the day residue (thoughts and ideas that are connected with the activities and preoccupations of the dreamer's current waking life), and repressed unacceptable impulses. For these nocturnal mental activities to give rise to a dream, they must be associated with one or more repressed wishes so that a dreamer continues sleeping instead of waking. Because motility is blocked by the sleep state, the dream enables partial but limited gratification of the repressed impulse that gives rise to the dream.

Freud distinguished between two layers of dream content. The *manifest* content refers to what is recalled by the dreamer; the *latent* content involves the unconscious thoughts and wishes that threaten to awaken the dreamer. Freud described the unconscious mental operations by which latent dream content is transformed into manifest dream as the *dream work.* Repressed wishes and impulses must attach themselves to innocent or neutral images to pass the scrutiny of the dream censor. This process involves the selection of apparently meaningless or trivial images from the dreamer's current experience, images that are dynamically associated with the latent images that they resemble in some respect.

Condensation

In condensation, several unconscious impulses, wishes, or feelings can be combined and attached to one manifest dream image. For example, a composite character may appear in the dream with a name like one person in the dreamer's life, a beard like another person, and a musical instrument that reflects a third person.

Displacement

In displacement, the energy or intensity associated with one object is diverted to a substitute object that is associatively related but more acceptable to the dreamer's ego. Murderous wishes toward the dreamer's mother, for example, may be redirected toward a neutral or insignificant person in life. Thus, the dream censor displaces affective energy in such a way that the dreamer's sleep can continue undisturbed. Projection, a special instance of displacement, involves the attribution of the dreamer's own unacceptable impulses or wishes to another character in the dream.

Symbolic Representation

Freud noted that the dreamer would often represent highly charged ideas or objects by using innocent images that were in some way connected with the idea or object being represented. In this manner, an abstract concept or a complex set of feelings toward a person could be symbolized by a simple, concrete, or sensory image. Freud noted that symbols have unconscious meanings that can be discerned through the patient's associations to the symbol, but he also believed that certain symbols have universal meanings.

Secondary Revision

The mechanisms of condensation, displacement, and symbolic representation are characteristic of a type of thinking that Freud referred to as *primary process.* This primitive mode of cognitive activity is characterized by illogical, bizarre, and absurd images that seem incoherent. Freud believed that a more mature and reasonable aspect of the ego works during dreams to organize primitive aspects of dreams into a more coherent form. *Secondary revision* is Freud's name for this process, in which dreams become somewhat more rational. The process is related to mature activity characteristic of waking life, which Freud termed *secondary process.*

Affects in Dreams

Secondary emotions may not appear in the dream at all, or they may be experienced in somewhat altered form. For example, repressed rage toward a person's father may take the form of mild annoyance. Feelings may also appear as their opposites.

Anxiety Dreams

Freud's dream theory preceded his development of a comprehensive theory of the ego. Hence, his understanding of dreams stresses the importance of discharging drives or wishes through the hallucinatory contents of the dream. He viewed such mechanisms as condensation, displacement, symbolic representation, projection, and secondary revision primarily as facilitating the discharge of latent impulses, rather than as protecting dreamers from anxiety and pain. Freud understood anxiety dreams as reflecting a failure in the protective function of the dream-work mechanisms. In other words, the repressed impulses succeed in working their way into the manifest content in a more or less recognizable manner.

Punishment Dreams

Dreams in which dreamers experience punishment represented a special challenge for Freud because they appear to represent an exception to his wish fulfillment theory of dreams. He came to understand such dreams as reflective of a compromise between the repressed wish and the repressing agency or conscience. In a punishment dream, the ego anticipates condemnation on the part of the dreamer's conscience if the latent unacceptable impulses are allowed direct expression in the manifest dream content. Hence, it is the wish for punishment on the part of the patient's conscience that is satisfied by giving expression to punishment fantasies.

TOPOGRAPHIC MODEL OF THE MIND

The publication of *The Interpretation of Dreams* in 1900 heralded the arrival of Freud's topographic model of the mind, in which he divided the mind into three regions: the conscious system, the preconscious system, and the unconscious system. Each system has its own unique characteristics.

The Conscious

The conscious system in Freud's topographic model is the part of the mind in which perceptions coming from the outside world or from within the body or mind are brought into awareness. Consciousness is a subjective phenomenon whose content can be communicated only by means of language or behavior. Freud assumed that consciousness employed a form of neutralized psychic energy that he referred to as *attention cathexis.* In other words, people were aware of a particular idea or feeling as a result of investing a discrete amount of psychic energy in the idea or feeling.

The Preconscious

The preconscious system is composed of those mental events, processes, and contents capable of being brought into conscious awareness by the act of focusing attention. Although most people are not consciously aware of the appearance of their first-grade teacher, they ordinarily can bring this image to mind by deliberately focusing attention on the memory. Conceptually, the preconscious interfaces with both unconscious and conscious regions of the mind. To reach conscious awareness, contents of the unconscious must become linked with words and thus become preconscious. The preconscious also serves to maintain the repressive barrier and to censor unacceptable wishes and desires.

The Unconscious

The unconscious system is dynamic: Its mental contents and processes are kept from conscious awareness through the force of censorship or repression. The unconscious is closely related to instinctual drives. At this point in Freud's theory of development, instincts were thought to consist of sexual and self-preservative drives, and the unconscious was thought to contain primarily the mental representations and derivatives of the sexual instinct.

The content of the unconscious is limited to wishes seeking fulfillment. These wishes provide the motivation for dream and neurotic symptom formation. This view is now considered reductionist.

The unconscious system is characterized by *primary process thinking,* which has as its principal aim the facilitation of wish fulfillment and instinctual discharge. It is governed by the pleasure principle and therefore disregards logical connections, has no concept of time, represents wishes as fulfillments, permits contradictions to exist simultaneously, and denies the existence of negatives. The primary process is also characterized by extreme mobility of drive cathexis: The investment of psychic energy can shift from object to object without opposition. Memories in the unconscious have been divorced from their connection with verbal symbols. Hence, when words are reapplied to forgotten memory traits, as in psychoanalytic treatment, the verbal recathexis allows the memories to reach consciousness again.

The contents of the unconscious can become conscious only by passing through the preconscious; when censors are overpowered, the elements can enter consciousness.

Limitations of the Topographic Theory

Freud soon realized that two main deficiencies in the topographic theory limited its usefulness. First, many patients' defense mechanisms that guard against distressing wishes, feelings, or thoughts were themselves not initially accessible to consciousness. Repression, then, cannot be identical with the preconscious, because by definition this region of the mind is accessible to consciousness. Second, Freud's patients frequently demonstrated an unconscious need for punishment. This clinical observation made it unlikely that the moral agency making the demand for punishment could be allied with anti-instinctual forces that were available to conscious awareness in the preconscious. These difficulties led Freud to discard the topographic theory, but certain concepts derived from the theory continue to be useful, particularly those of primary and secondary thought processes, the fundamental importance of wish fulfillment, the existence of a dynamic unconscious, and a tendency toward regression under frustrating conditions.

INSTINCT OR DRIVE THEORY

After the development of the topographic model, Freud turned his attention to the complexities of instinct theory. Freud was determined to anchor his psychological theory in biology. His choice led to terminological and conceptual difficulties when he used terms derived from biology to denote psychological constructs. Instinct, for example, refers to a pattern of species-specific behavior that was genetically derived and therefore is more or less independent of learning. Modern research demonstrating that instinctual patterns are modified through experiential learning, however, has made Freud's instinctual theory problematic. Further confusion has stemmed from the ambiguity inherent in a concept on the borderland between the biological and the psychological: Should the mental representation aspect of the term and the physiological component be integrated or separated? Although *drive* may have been closer than *instinct* to Freud's meaning, in contemporary usage, the two terms are often used interchangeably.

In Freud's view, an instinct has four principal characteristics: source, impetus, aim, and object. The *source* refers to the part of the body from which the instinct arises. The *impetus* is the amount of force or intensity associated with the instinct. The *aim* refers to any action directed toward tension discharge or satisfaction, and the *object* is the target (often a person) for this action.

Instincts

Libido. Freud defined *libido* as "that force by which the sexual instinct is represented in the mind." The association of libido with sexuality is somewhat misleading: Freud's intent was to encompass the general notion of pleasure as well as sexuality and to include both the physiological underpinnings and the mental representations. The linkage of genital sexuality with libido was viewed as the end result of a course of development in which libidinal expression took a variety of forms.

Ego Instincts. From 1905 on, Freud maintained a dual instinct theory, subsuming sexual instincts and ego instincts connected with self-preservation. Until 1914, with the publication of *On Narcissism,* Freud had paid little attention to ego instincts; in this communication, however, Freud invested ego instinct with libido for the first time by postulating an ego libido and an object libido. Freud thus viewed narcissistic investment as an essentially libidinal instinct and called the remaining nonsexual components the ego instincts.

Aggression. When psychoanalysts today discuss the dual instinct theory, they are generally referring to libido and aggression. Freud, however, originally conceptualized aggression as a component of the sexual instincts in the form of sadism. As he became aware that sadism had nonsexual aspects to it, he made finer gradations, which enabled him to categorize aggression and hate as part of the ego instincts and the libidinal aspects of sadism as components of the sexual instincts. Finally, in 1923, to account for the clinical data he was observing, he was compelled to conceive of aggression as a separate instinct in its own right. The source of this instinct, according to Freud, was largely in skeletal muscles, and the aim of the aggressive instincts was destruction.

Life and Death Instincts. Before designating aggression as a separate instinct, Freud, in 1920, subsumed the ego instincts under a broader category of life instincts. These were juxtaposed with death instincts and were referred to as Eros and Thanatos in *Beyond the Pleasure Principle*. The life and death instincts were regarded as forces underlying the sexual and aggressive instincts. Although Freud could not provide clinical data that directly verified the death instinct, he thought the instinct could be inferred by observing *repetition compulsion,* people's tendency to repeat past traumatic behavior. Freud thought that the dominant force in biological organisms had to be the death instinct. In contrast to the death instinct, Eros (the life instinct) refers to the tendency of particles to reunite or bind to one another, as in sexual reproduction. The prevalent view today is that the dual instincts of sexuality and aggression are sufficient to explain most clinical phenomena without recourse to a death instinct.

Pleasure and Reality Principles

In 1911, Freud described two basic tenets of mental functioning, the pleasure principle and the reality principle. He essentially recast the primary process and secondary process dichotomy into the pleasure and reality principles and thus took an important step toward solidifying the notion of the ego. Both principles, in Freud's view, are aspects of ego functioning. The *pleasure principle* is defined as an inborn tendency of the organism to avoid pain and to seek pleasure through the discharge of tension. The *reality principle,* on the other hand, is considered to be a learned function closely related to the maturation of the ego; this principle modifies the pleasure principle and requires the delay or postponement of immediate gratification.

Infantile Sexuality

Freud set forth the three major tenets of psychoanalytic theory when he published *Three Essays on the Theory of Sexuality.* First, he broadened the definition of sexuality to include forms of pleasure that transcend genital sexuality. Second, he established a developmental theory of childhood sexuality that delineated the vicissitudes of erotic activity from birth through puberty. Third, he forged a conceptual linkage between neuroses and perversions.

Throughout its 100-year history, Freud's notion that children are influenced by sexual drives has made some people reluctant to accept psychoanalysis. Freud noted that infants are capable of erotic activity from birth, but the earliest manifestations of infantile sexuality are basically nonsexual and are associated with such bodily functions as feeding and bowel-bladder control. As libidinal energy shifts from the oral zone to the anal zone to the phallic zone, each stage of development is thought to build on and to subsume the accomplishments of the preceding stage. The *oral stage* occupies the first 12 to 18 months of life, centers on the mouth and lips, and is manifested in chewing, biting, and sucking. The dominant erotic activity of the *anal stage,* from 18 to 36 months of age, involves bowel function and control. The *phallic stage,* from 3 to 5 years of life, initially focuses on urination as the source of erotic activity. Freud suggested that phallic erotic activity in boys is a preliminary stage leading to adult genital activity. Whereas the penis remains the principal sexual organ throughout male psychosexual development, Freud postulated that females have two principal erotogenic zones, the vagina and the clitoris. He thought that the clitoris was the chief erotogenic focus during the infantile genital period but that erotic primacy shifted to the vagina after puberty. Studies of human sexuality have subsequently questioned the validity of this distinction.

Freud discovered that in the psychoneuroses, only a limited number of the sexual impulses that had undergone repression and were responsible for creating and maintaining the neurotic symptoms were normal. For the most part, these were the same impulses that were given overt expression in the perversions. The neuroses, then, were the negative of perversions.

Object Relationships in Instinct Theory

Freud suggested that the choice of a love object in adult life, the love relationship itself, and the nature of all other object relationships depend primarily on the nature and quality of children's relationships during the early years of life. In describing the libidinal phases of psychosexual development, Freud repeatedly referred to the significance of a child's relationships with parents and other significant people in the environment.

The awareness of the external world of objects develops gradually in infants. Soon after birth, they are primarily aware of physical sensations, such as hunger, cold, and pain, that give rise to tension, and caregivers are regarded primarily as persons who relieve their tension or remove painful stimuli. Recent infant research, however, suggests that awareness of others begins much sooner than Freud originally thought. Table 6.1–1 provides a summary of the stages of psychosexual development and the object relationships associated with each stage. Although the table goes only as far as young adulthood, development is now recognized as continuing throughout adult life.

Concept of Narcissism

According to Greek myth, Narcissus, a beautiful youth, fell in love with his own reflection in the water of a pool and drowned in his attempt to embrace his beloved image. Freud used the term *narcissism* to describe situations in which an individual's libido was invested in the ego itself rather than in other people. This concept of narcissism presented him with vexing problems for his instinct theory and essentially violated his distinction between libidinal instincts and ego or self-preservative instincts. Freud's understanding of narcissism led him to use the term to describe a wide array of psychiatric disorders, very much in contrast to the term's contemporary use to describe a specific personality disorder. Freud lumped several disorders together as the narcissistic neuroses, in which a person's libido is withdrawn from objects and turned inward. He believed that this withdrawal of libidinal attachment to objects accounted for the loss of reality testing in psychotic patients; grandiosity and omnipotence in such patients reflected excessive libidinal investment in the ego.

Freud did not limit his use of narcissism to psychoses. In states of physical illness and hypochondriasis, he observed that libidinal investment was frequently withdrawn from external objects and from outside activities and interests. Similarly, he suggested that in normal sleep, libido was also withdrawn and

Table 6.1–1
Stages of Psychosexual Development

Oral Stage			
Definition	The earliest stage of development in which the infant's needs, perceptions, and modes of expression are primarily centered in the mouth, lips, tongue, and other organs related to the oral zone.	Objectives	To establish a trusting dependence on nursing and sustaining objects, to establish comfortable expression and gratification of oral libidinal needs without excessive conflict or ambivalence from oral sadistic wishes.
Description	The oral zone maintains its dominant role in the organization of the psyche through approximately the first 18 months of life. Oral sensations include thirst, hunger, pleasurable tactile stimulations evoked by the nipple or its substitute, sensations related to swallowing, and satiation. Oral drives consist of two separate components: libidinal and aggressive. States of oral tension lead to a seeking for oral gratification, typified by quiescence at the end of nursing. The oral triad consists of the wish to eat, to sleep, and to reach that relaxation that occurs at the end of sucking just before the onset of sleep. Libidinal needs (oral erotism) are thought to predominate in the early parts of the oral phase, whereas they are mixed with more aggressive components later (oral sadism). Oral aggression may express itself in biting, chewing, spitting, or crying. Oral aggression is connected with primitive wishes and fantasies of biting, devouring, and destroying.	Pathological traits	Excessive oral gratifications or deprivation can result in libidinal fixations that contribute to pathological traits. Such traits can include excessive optimism, narcissism, pessimism (often seen in depressive states), and demandingness. Oral characters are often excessively dependent and require others to give to them and to look after them. Such persons want to be fed but may be exceptionally giving to elicit a return of being given to. Oral characters are often extremely dependent on objects for the maintenance of their self-esteem. Envy and jealousy are often associated with oral traits.
		Character traits	Successful resolution of the oral phase provides a basis in character structure for capacities to give to and receive from others without excessive dependence or envy and a capacity to rely on others with a sense of trust, as well as with a sense of self-reliance and self-trust.
Anal Stage			
Definition	The stage of psychosexual development that is prompted by maturation of neuromuscular control over sphincters, particularly the anal sphincters, thus permitting more voluntary control over retention or expulsion of feces.	Objectives	The anal period is essentially a period of striving for independence and separation from the dependence on and control by the parent. The objectives of sphincter control without overcontrol (fecal retention) or loss of control (messing) are matched by the child's attempts to achieve autonomy and independence without excessive shame or self-doubt from loss of control.
Description	This period, which extends roughly from 1 to 3 years of age, is marked by a recognizable intensification of aggressive drives mixed with libidinal components and in sadistic impulses. Acquisition of voluntary sphincter control is associated with an increasing shift from passivity to activity. The conflicts over anal control and the struggle with the parent over retaining or expelling feces in toilet training give rise to increased ambivalence, together with a struggle over separation, individuation, and independence. Anal erotism refers to the sexual pleasure in anal functioning, both in retaining the precious feces and in presenting them as a precious gift to the parent. Anal sadism refers to the expression of aggressive wishes connected with discharging feces as powerful and destructive weapons. These wishes are often displayed in such children's fantasies as bombing and explosions.	Pathological traits	Maladaptive character traits, often apparently inconsistent, are derived from anal erotism and the defenses against it. Orderliness, obstinancy, stubbornness, willfulness, frugality, and parsimony are features of the anal character derived from a fixation on anal functions. When defenses against anal traits are less effective, the anal character reveals traits of heightened ambivalence, lack of tidiness, messiness, defiance, rage, and sadomasochistic tendencies. Anal characteristics and defenses are most typically seen in obsessive-compulsive neuroses.
		Character traits	Successful resolution of the anal phase provides the basis for the development of personal autonomy, a capacity for independence and personal initiative without guilt, a capacity for self-determining behavior without a sense of shame or self-doubt, a lack of ambivalence and a capacity for willing cooperation without either excessive willfulness or sense of self-diminution or defeat.

(continued)

Table 6.1–1 *(continued)*

Urethral Stage	
Definition	This stage was not explicitly treated by Freud but is envisioned as a transitional stage between the anal and the phallic stages of development. It shares some of the characteristics of the preceding anal stage and some from the subsequent phallic stage.
Description	The characteristics of the urethral stage are often subsumed under those of the phallic stage. Urethral erotism, however, is used to refer to the pleasure in urination, as well as the pleasure in urethral retention analogous to anal retention. Similar issues of performance and control are related to urethral functioning. Urethral functioning may also be invested with a sadistic quality, often reflecting the persistence of anal sadistic urges. Loss of urethral control, as in enuresis, may frequently have regressive significance that reactivates anal conflicts.
Objectives	Issues of control and urethral performance and loss of control. It is not clear whether or to what extent the objectives of urethral functioning differ from those of the anal period.
Pathological traits	The predominant urethral trait is that of competitiveness and ambition, probably related to the compensation for shame due to loss of urethral control. In control this may be the start for the development of penis envy, related to the feminine sense of shame and inadequacy in being unable to match the male urethral performance. This is also related to issues of control and shaming.
Character traits	Besides the healthy effects analogous to those from the anal period, urethral competence provides a sense of pride and self-competence derived from performance. Urethral performance is an area in which the small boy can imitate and match his father's more adult performance. The resolution of urethral conflicts sets the stage for budding gender identity and subsequent identifications.
Phallic Stage	
Definition	The phallic stage of sexual development begins sometime during the third year of life and continues until approximately the end of the fifth year.
Description	The phallic phase is characterized by a primary focus of sexual interests, stimulation, and excitement in the genital area. The penis becomes the organ of principal interest to children of both sexes, with the lack of a penis in the female being considered as evidence of castration. The phallic phase is associated with an increase in genital masturbation accompanied by predominantly unconscious fantasies of sexual involvement with the opposite-sex parent. The threat of castration and its related castration anxiety arise in connection with guilt over masturbation and oedipal wishes. During this phase the oedipal involvement and conflict are established and consolidated.
Objectives	The objective of this phase is to focus erotic interest in the genital area and genital functions. This focusing lays the foundation for gender identity and serves to integrate the residues of previous stages of psychosexual development into a predominantly genital-sexual orientation. The establishing of the oedipal situation is essential for the furtherance of subsequent identifications that will serve as the basis for important and enduring dimensions of character organization.
Pathological traits	The derivation of pathological traits from the phallic-oedipal involvement are sufficiently complex and subject to such a variety of modifications that it encompasses nearly the whole of neurotic development. The issues, however, focus on castration in males and on penis envy in females. The other important focus of developmental distortions in this period derives from the patterns of identification that are developed out of the resolution of the oedipal complex. The influence of castration anxiety and penis envy, the defenses against both, and the patterns of identification that emerge from the phallic phase are the primary determinants of the development of human character. They also subsume and integrate the residues of previous psychosexual stages, so that fixations or conflicts that derive from any of the preceding stages can contaminate and modify the oedipal resolution.
Character traits	The phallic stage provides the foundations for an emerging sense of sexual identity, a sense of curiosity without embarrassment, initiative without guilt, as well as a sense of mastery not only over objects and persons in the environment but also over internal processes and impulses. The resolution of the oedipal conflict at the end of the phallic period gives rise to powerful internal resources for regulation of drive impulses and their direction to constructive ends. This internal source of regulation is the superego, and it is based on identifications derived primarily from parental figures.

(continued)

Table 6.1–1 *(continued)*

	Latency Stage		
Definition	The stage of relative quiescence or inactivity of the sexual drive during the period from the resolution of the Oedipus complex until pubescence (from about 5–6 years until about 11–13 years).	Pathological traits	The danger in the latency period can arise either from a lack of development of inner controls or an excess of them. The lack of control can lead to a failure of the child to sufficiently sublimate energies in the interests of learning and development of skills; an excess of inner control, however, can lead to premature closure of personality development and the precocious elaboration of obsessive character traits.
Description	The institution of the superego at the close of the oedipal period and the further maturation of ego functions allow for a considerably greater degree of control of instinctual impulses. Sexual interests during this period are generally thought to be quiescent. This is a period of primarily homosexual affiliations for both boys and girls, as well as a sublimation of libidinal and aggressive energies into energetic learning and play activities, exploring the environment, and becoming more proficient in dealing with the world of things and persons around them. It is a period for the development of important skills. The relative strength of regulatory elements often gives rise to patterns of behavior that are somewhat obsessive and hypercontrolling.	Character traits	The latency period has frequently been regarded as a period of relatively unimportant inactivity in the developmental scheme. Recently, great respect has been gained for the developmental processes that take place in this period. Important consolidations and additions are made to the basic postoedipal identifications. It is a period of integrating and consolidating previous attainments in psychosexual development and establishing decisive patterns of adaptive functioning. The child can develop a sense of industry and a capacity for mastery of objects and concepts that allows autonomous function and with a sense of initiative without running the risk of failure or defeat or a sense of inferiority. These important attainments need to be further integrated, ultimately as the essential basis for a mature adult life of satisfaction in work and love.
Objectives	The primary objective in this period is the further integration of oedipal identifications and a consolidation of sex-role identity and sex roles. The relative quiescence and control of instinctual impulses allow for the development of ego apparatuses and mastery skills. Further identificatory components may be added to the oedipal ones on the basis of broadening contacts with other significant figures outside the family, such as teachers, coaches, and other adults.		
	Genital Stage		
Definition	The genital or adolescent phase of psychosexual development extends from the onset of puberty from ages 11–13 until the person reaches young adulthood. In current thinking, there is a tendency to subdivide this stage into preadolescent, early adolescent, middle adolescent, late adolescent, and even postadolescent periods.	Pathological traits	The pathological deviations due to a failure to achieve successful resolution of this stage of development are multiple and complex. Defects can arise from the whole spectrum of psychosexual residues, since the developmental task of the adolescent period is in a sense a partial reopening and reworking and reintegrating of all those aspects of development. Previous unsuccessful resolutions and fixations in various phases or aspects of psychosexual development will produce pathological defects in the emerging adult personality. A more specific defect from a failure to resolve adolescent issues has been described by Erikson as identity diffusion.
Description	The physiological maturation of systems of genital (sexual) functioning and attendant hormonal systems leads to an intensification of drives, particularly libidinal drives. This produces a regression in personality organization, which reopens conflicts of previous stages of psychosexual development and provides the opportunity for a reresolution of these conflicts in the context of achieving a mature sexual and adult identity.	Character traits	The successful resolution and reintegration of previous psychosexual stages in the adolescent, fully genital phase sets the stage normally for a fully mature personality with a capacity for full and satisfying genital potency and a self-integrated and consistent sense of identity. Such a person has reached a satisfying capacity for self-realization and meaningful participation in the areas of work and love and in the creative and productive application to satisfying and meaningful goals and values. Only in the last few years has the presumed relationship between psychosexual genitality and maturity of personality functioning been put in question.
Objectives	The primary objectives of this period are the ultimate separation from dependence on and attachment to the parents and the establishment of mature, nonincestuous object relations. Related to this are the achievement of a mature sense of personal identity and acceptance and the integration of a set of adult roles and functions that permit new adaptive integrations with social expectations and cultural values.		

Adapted by Glen O. Gabbard, M.D., from Meissner WW: Theories of personality and psychopathology. In *Comprehensive Textbook of Psychiatry*, ed 4, HI Kaplan, BJ Sadock, editors, vol 1, p 360. Williams & Wilkins, Baltimore, 1985.

reinvested in a sleeper's own body. Freud regarded homosexuality as an instance of a narcissistic form of object choice, in which people fall in love with an idealized version of themselves projected onto another person. He also found narcissistic manifestations in the beliefs and myths of primitive people, especially those involving the ability to influence external events through the magical omnipotence of thought processes. In the course of normal development, children also exhibit this belief in their own omnipotence.

Freud postulated a state of primary narcissism at birth in which the libido is stored in the ego. He viewed the neonate as completely narcissistic, with the entire libidinal investment in physiological needs and their satisfaction. He referred to this self-investment as *ego libido.* The infantile state of self-absorption changes only gradually, according to Freud, with the dawning awareness that a separate person—the mothering figure—is responsible for gratifying an infant's needs. This realization leads to the gradual withdrawal of the libido from the self and its redirection toward the external object. Hence, the development of object relations in infants parallels the shift from primary narcissism to object attachment. The libidinal investment in the object is referred to as *object libido.* If a developing child suffers rebuffs or trauma from the caretaking figure, object libido may be withdrawn and reinvested in the ego. Freud called this regressive posture *secondary narcissism.*

Freud used the term *narcissism* to describe many different dimensions of human experience. At times, he used it to describe a perversion in which persons used their own bodies or body parts as objects of sexual arousal. At other times, he used the term to describe a developmental phase, as in the state of primary narcissism. In still other instances, the term referred to a particular object choice. Freud distinguished love objects who are chosen ''according to the narcissistic type,'' in which case the object resembles the subject's idealized or fantasied self-image, from objects chosen according to the ''anaclitic,'' in which the love object resembles a caretaker from early in life. Finally, Freud also used the word *narcissism* interchangeably and synonymously with *self-esteem.*

EGO PSYCHOLOGY

Although Freud had used the construct of the ego throughout the evolution of psychoanalytic theory, ego psychology as it is known today really began with the publication in 1923 of *The Ego and the Id.* This landmark publication also represented a transition in Freud's thinking from the topographic model of the mind to the tripartite structural model of ego, id, and superego. He had observed repeatedly that not all unconscious processes can be relegated to a person's instinctual life. Elements of the conscience, as well as functions of the ego, are clearly unconscious as well.

Structural Theory of the Mind

The structural model of the psychic apparatus is the cornerstone of ego psychology. The three provinces—id, ego, and superego—are distinguished by their different functions (Fig. 6.1–10).

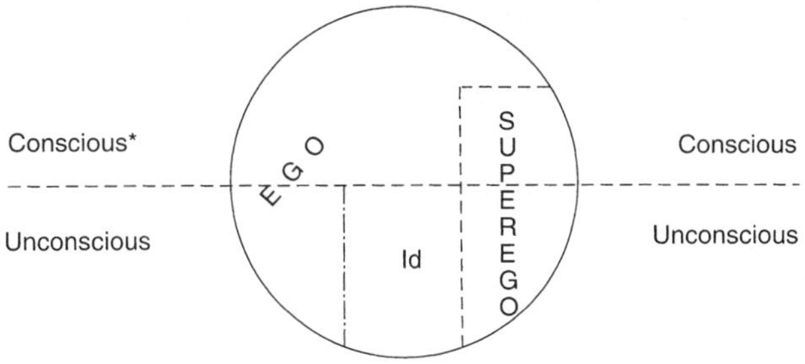
Conscious*
Unconscious
EGO
Id
SUPEREGO
Conscious
Unconscious

*The preconscious has been deleted for the sake of simplicity.

FIGURE 6.1–10

Freud's structural model. (Reprinted with permission from Gabbard GO: *Psychodynamic Psychiatry in Clinical Practice: The DSM-IV Edition,* p 31. American Psychiatric Press, Washington, 1994.)

Id. Freud used this term to refer to a reservoir of unorganized instinctual drives. Operating under the domination of the primary process, the id lacks the capacity to delay or modify the instinctual drives with which an infant is born. The id should not, however, be viewed as synonymous with the unconscious because both the ego and the superego have unconscious components.

Ego. The ego spans all three topographic dimensions of conscious, preconscious, and unconscious. Logical and abstract thinking and verbal expression are associated with conscious and preconscious functions of the ego. Defense mechanisms reside in the unconscious domain of the ego. The ego is the executive organ of the psyche and controls motility, perception, contact with reality, and, through the mechanisms of defense available to it, the delay and modulation of drive expression.

Freud believed that the modification of the id occurs as a result of the impact of the external world on the drives. The pressures of external reality enable the ego to appropriate the energies of the id to do its work. As the ego brings influences from the external world to bear on the id, it simultaneously substitutes the reality principle for the pleasure principle. Freud emphasized the role of conflict within the structural model and observed that conflict occurs initially between the id and the outside world, only to be transformed later to conflict between the id and the ego.

The third component of the tripartite structural model is the superego. The superego establishes and maintains an individual's moral conscience based on a complex system of ideals and values internalized from parents. Freud viewed the superego as the heir to the Oedipus complex: Children internalize parental values and standards around the age of 5 or 6 years. The superego then serves as an agency that provides ongoing scrutiny of a person's behavior, thoughts, and feelings; makes comparisons with expected standards of behavior; and offers approval or disapproval. These activities occur largely unconsciously.

The ego ideal is often regarded as a component of the superego: It is an agency that prescribes what a person should do according to internalized standards and values. The superego, by contrast, is an agency of moral conscience that *proscribes*—that is, dictates what a person should *not* do. Throughout the latency period and thereafter, people continue to build on early identifications through their contact with admired figures who contribute to the formation of moral standards, aspirations, and ideals.

Functions of the Ego

Modern ego psychologists have identified a set of basic ego functions that characterize the operations of the ego. These descriptions reflect the ego activities that are generally regarded as fundamental.

Control and Regulation of Instinctual Drives. The development of the capacity to delay or postpone drive discharge, like the capacity to test reality, is closely related to the early childhood progression from the pleasure principle to the reality principle. This capacity is also an essential aspect of the ego's role as mediator between the id and the outside world. Part of infants' socialization to the external world is the acquisition of language and secondary process or logical thinking.

Judgment. A closely related ego function is judgment, which involves the ability to anticipate the consequences of actions. As with control and regulation of instinctual drives, judgment develops in parallel with the growth of *secondary process thinking.* The ability to think logically allows for an assessment of how contemplated behavior may impact others.

Relation to Reality. The mediation between the internal world and external reality is a crucial function of the ego. Relations with the outside world can be divided into three aspects: the sense of reality, reality testing, and adaptation to reality. The *sense of reality* develops in concert with an infant's dawning awareness of bodily sensations. The ability to distinguish what is outside the body from what is inside is an essential aspect of the sense of reality, and disturbances of body boundaries, such as depersonalization, reflect impairment in this ego function. *Reality testing* is an ego function of paramount importance that refers to the capacity to distinguish internal fantasy from external reality. This function differentiates psychotic from nonpsychotic people. *Adaptation to reality* involves people's ability to use their resources to develop effective responses to changing circumstances on the basis of previous experiences with reality.

Object Relationships. The capacity to form mutually satisfying relationships is related in part to patterns of internalization stemming from early interactions with parents and other significant figures. This ability is also a fundamental function of the ego, in that satisfying relatedness depends on the ability to integrate positive and negative aspects of others and self and to maintain an internal sense of others even in their absence. Similarly, mastery of drive derivatives is also crucial to the achievement of satisfying relationships. Although Freud did not develop an extensive object relations theory, British psychoanalysts, such as Ronald Fairbairn (1889–1964) and Michael Balint (1886–1970), elaborated greatly on the early stages in infants' relationships with need-satisfying objects and on the gradual development of a sense of separateness from the mother. Another of their British colleagues, Donald W. Winnicott (1897–1971), described the *transitional object* (such as a blanket, a teddy bear, a pacifier) as the link between developing children and their mothers. A child is able to separate from the mother because a transitional object provides feelings of security in her absence.

The stages of human development and object relations theory are summarized in Figure 6.1–11.

Synthetic Function of the Ego. First described by Herman Nunberg in 1931, the synthetic function refers to the ego's capacity to integrate diverse elements into an overall unity. Different aspects of self and others, for example, are synthesized into a consistent representation that endures over time. The function also involves organizing, coordinating, and generalizing or simplifying large amounts of data.

Primary Autonomous Ego Functions. A direct outgrowth of the work of Heinz Hartmann, the primary autonomous functions refer to rudimentary apparatuses that are present at birth and that develop independently of intrapsychic conflict between drives and defenses, provided that what Hartmann referred to as an *average expectable environment* is available to an infant. These functions include perception, learning, intelligence, intuition, language, thinking, comprehension, and motility. In the course of development, some of these conflict-free aspects of the ego may eventually become involved in conflict if they encounter opposing forces.

Secondary Autonomous Ego Functions. Hartmann originally used the concept of the conflict-free sphere of ego functioning to identify areas of primary autonomy, but these areas may be enlarged by functions that originally arise in the service of defense against drives but subsequently become independent of them. These functions are referred to as *secondary autonomous ego functions.* For example, a child may develop caretaking functions as a reaction formation against murderous wishes during the first few years of life. Later, the defensive functions of this style may be neutralized or deinstinctualized when the child grows up to be a social worker and cares for homeless people.

Defense Mechanisms

Freud acknowledged the existence of several defense mechanisms, but his writings focused predominantly on repression, which he regarded as the queen of the defenses. His daughter Anna wrote the first comprehensive study of defense mechanisms. In her landmark contribution, *The Ego and the Mechanisms of Defense,* she maintained that everyone, normal or neurotic, uses a characteristic repertoire of defense mechanisms. She also insisted that the ego should be the focus of psychoanalytic treatment, in addition to the uncovering of repressed drive derivatives. Her famous observation that "there is depth in the surface" reflected her appreciation of the complexity of the ego's defensive aspects.

At each phase of libidinal development, specific drive components evoke characteristic ego defenses. The anal phase, for example, is associated with reaction formation, as manifested

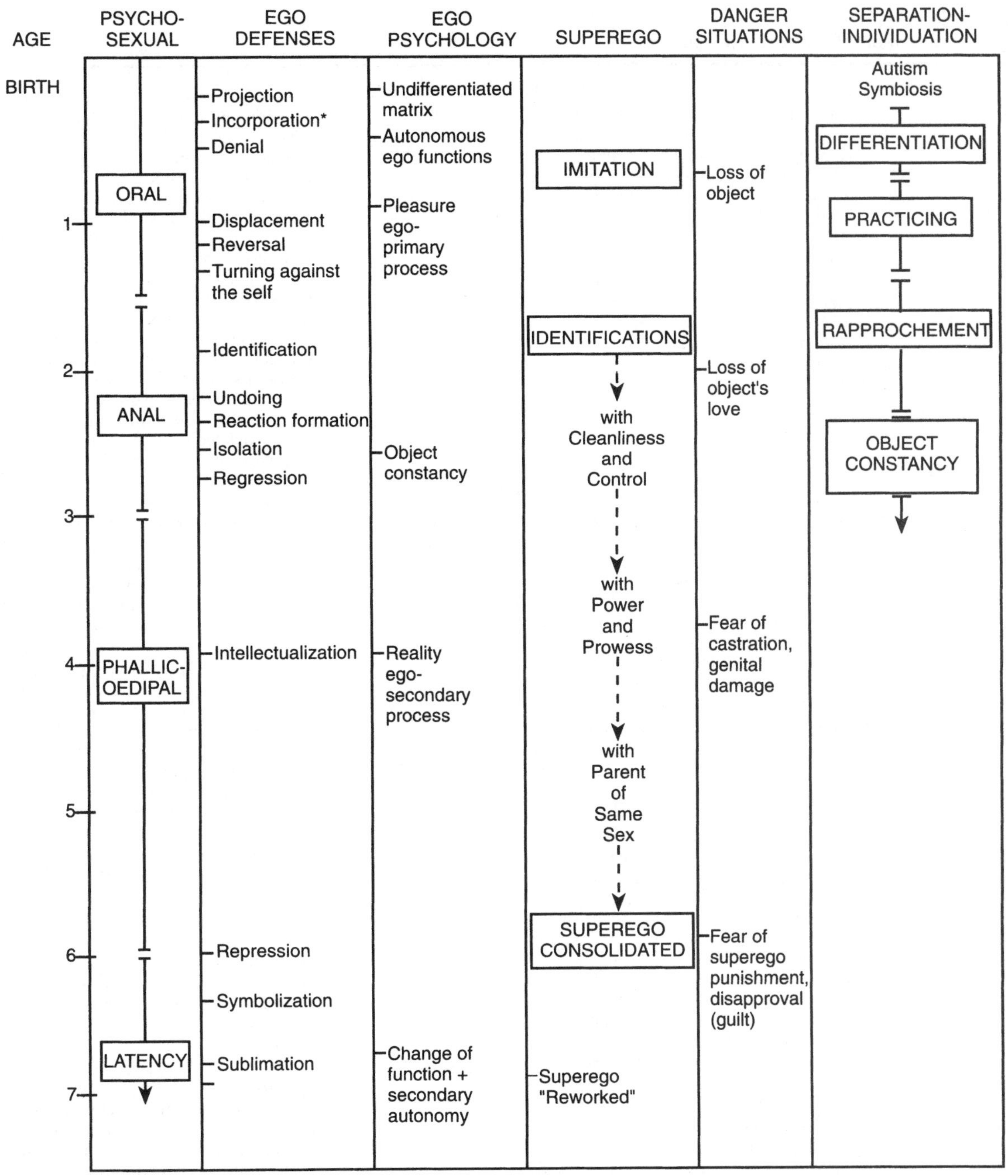
AGE
PSYCHO-SEXUAL
EGO DEFENSES
EGO PSYCHOLOGY
SUPEREGO
DANGER SITUATIONS
SEPARATION-INDIVIDUATION
BIRTH
1
2
3
4
5
6
7
ORAL
ANAL
PHALLIC-OEDIPAL
LATENCY
Projection
Incorporation*
Denial
Displacement
Reversal
Turning against the self
Identification
Undoing
Reaction formation
Isolation
Regression
Intellectualization
Repression
Symbolization
Sublimation
Undifferentiated matrix
Autonomous ego functions
Pleasure ego-primary process
Object constancy
Reality ego-secondary process
Change of function + secondary autonomy
IMITATION
IDENTIFICATIONS
with Cleanliness and Control
with Power and Prowess
with Parent of Same Sex
SUPEREGO CONSOLIDATED
Superego "Reworked"
Loss of object
Loss of object's love
Fear of castration, genital damage
Fear of superego punishment, disapproval (guilt)
Autism
Symbiosis
DIFFERENTIATION
PRACTICING
RAPPROCHEMENT
OBJECT CONSTANCY

FIGURE 6.1–11

Parallel lines of human development. *Asterisk* indicates also introjection. (Reprinted with permission from Inderbitzin LB, Luke CM, James ME: Psychoanalytic psychotherapy. In *Human Behavior: An Introduction for Medical Students,* A Stoudemire, ed, p 74. Lippincott, Philadelphia, 1990.)

by the development of shame and disgust in relation to anal impulses and pleasures.

Defenses can be grouped hierarchically according to the relative degree of maturity associated with them. Narcissistic defenses are the most primitive and appear in children and people who are psychotically disturbed. Immature defenses are seen in adolescents and some nonpsychotic patients. Neurotic defenses are encountered in obsessive-compulsive and hysterical patients as well as in adults under stress. Table 6.1–2 lists the defense mechanisms according to Vaillant's classification of the four types.

Theory of Anxiety

Freud initially conceptualized anxiety as "dammed up libido." In other words, a physiological increase in sexual ten-

Table 6.1–2
Classification of Defense Mechanisms

Narcissistic Defenses[a]	
Denial	Avoiding the awareness of some painful aspect of reality by negating sensory data. Although repression defends against affects and drive derivatives, denial abolishes external reality. Denial may be used in both normal and pathological states.
Distortion	Grossly reshaping external reality to suit inner needs (including unrealistic megalomanic beliefs, hallucinations, wish-fulfilling delusions) and using sustained feelings of delusional superiority or entitlement.
Projection	Perceiving and reacting to unacceptable inner impulses and their derivatives as though they were outside the self. On a psychotic level, this defense mechanism takes the form of frank delusions about external reality (usually persecutory) and includes both perception of one's own feelings in another and subsequent acting on the perception (psychotic paranoid delusions). The impulses may derive from the id or the superego (hallucinated recriminations) but may undergo transformation in the process. Thus, according to Freud's analysis of paranoid projections, homosexual libidinal impulses are transformed into hatred and then projected onto the object of the unacceptable homosexual impulse.
Immature Defenses	
Acting out	Expressing an unconscious wish or impulse through action to avoid being conscious of an accompanying affect. The unconscious fantasy is lived out impulsively in behavior, thereby gratifying the impulse, rather than the prohibition against it. Acting out involves chronically giving in to an impulse to avoid the tension that would result from the postponement of expression.
Blocking	Temporarily or transiently inhibiting thinking. Affects and impulses may also be involved. Blocking closely resembles repression but differs in that tension arises when the impulse, affect, or thought is inhibited.
Hypochondriasis	Exaggerating or overemphasizing an illness for the purpose of evasion and regression. Reproach arising from bereavement, loneliness, or unacceptable aggressive impulses toward others is transformed into self-reproach and complaints of pain, somatic illness, and neurasthenia. In hypochondriasis, responsibility can be avoided, guilt may be circumvented, and instinctual impulses are warded off. Because hypochondriacal introjects are ego-alien, the afflicted person experiences dysphoria and a sense of affliction.
Introjection	Internalizing the qualities of an object. Although vital to development, introjection also serves specific defensive functions. When used as a defense, it can obliterate the distinction between the subject and the object. Through the introjection of a loved object, the painful awareness of separateness or the threat of loss may be avoided. Introjection of a feared object serves to avoid anxiety when the aggressive characteristics of the object are internalized, thus placing the aggression under one's own control. A classic example is identification with the aggressor. An identification with the victim may also take place, whereby the self-punitive qualities of the objects are taken over and established within one's self as a symptom or character trait.
Passive-aggressive behavior	Expressing aggression toward others indirectly through passivity, masochism, and turning against the self. Manifestations of passive-aggressive behavior include failure, procrastination, and illnesses that affect others more than oneself.
Regression	Attempting to return to an earlier libidinal phase of functioning to avoid the tension and conflict evoked at the present level of development. It reflects the basic tendency to gain instinctual gratification at a less-developed period. Regression is a normal phenomenon as well, as a certain amount of regression is essential for relaxation, sleep, and orgasm in sexual intercourse. Regression is also considered an essential concomitant of the creative process.
Schizoid fantasy	Indulging in autistic retreat in order to resolve conflict and to obtain gratification. Interpersonal intimacy is avoided, and eccentricity serves to repel others. The person does not fully believe in the fantasies and does not insist on acting them out.
Somatization	Converting psychic derivatives into bodily symptoms and tending to react with somatic manifestations, rather than psychic manifestations. In desomatization, infantile somatic responses are replaced by thought and affect; in resomatization, the person regresses to earlier somatic forms in the face of unresolved conflicts.

(continued)

Table 6.1–2 (*continued*)

Neurotic Defenses			
Controlling	Attempting to manage or regulate events or objects in the environment to minimize anxiety and to resolve inner conflicts.	Dissociation	Temporarily but drastically modifying a person's character or one's sense of personal identity to avoid emotional distress. Fugue states and hysterical conversion reactions are common manifestations of dissociation. Dissociation may also be found in counterphobic behavior, dissociative identity disorder, and the use of pharmacological highs or religious joy.
Displacement	Shifting an emotion or drive cathexis from one idea or object to another that resembles the original in some aspect or quality. Displacement permits the symbolic representation of the original idea or object by one that is less highly cathected or evokes less distress.	Reaction formation	Transforming an unacceptable impulse into its opposite. Reaction formation is characteristic of obsessional neurosis, but it may occur in other forms of neuroses as well. If this mechanism is frequently used at any early stage of ego development, it can become a permanent character trait, as in an obsessional character.
Externalization	Tending to perceive in the external world and in external objects elements of one's own personality, including instinctual impulses, conflicts, moods, attitudes, and styles of thinking. Externalization is a more general term than projection.		
Inhibition	Consciously limiting or renouncing some ego functions, alone or in combination, to evade anxiety arising out of conflict with instinctual impulses, the superego, or environmental forces or figures.	Repression	Expelling or withholding from consciousness an idea or feeling. Primary repression refers to the curbing of ideas and feelings before they have attained consciousness: secondary repression excludes from awareness what was once experienced at a conscious level. The repressed is not really forgotten in that symbolic behavior may be present. This defense differs from suppression by effecting conscious inhibition of impulses to the point of losing and not just postponing cherished goals. Conscious perception of instincts and feelings is blocked in repression.
Intellectualization	Excessively using intellectual processes to avoid affective expression or experience. Undue emphasis is focused on the inanimate in order to avoid intimacy with people, attention is paid to external reality to avoid the expression of inner feelings, and stress is excessively placed on irrelevant details to avoid perceiving the whole. Intellectualization is closely allied to rationalization.	Sexualization	Endowing an object or function with sexual significance that it did not previously have or possessed to a smaller degree in order to ward off anxieties associated with prohibited impulses or their derivatives.
Isolation	Splitting or separating an idea from the affect that accompanies it but is repressed. Social isolation refers to the absence of object relationships.		
Rationalization	Offering rational explanations in an attempt to justify attitudes, beliefs, or behavior that may otherwise be unacceptable. Such underlying motives are usually instinctually determined.		
Mature Defenses			
Altruism	Using constructive and instinctually gratifying service to others to undergo a vicarious experience. It includes benign and constructive reaction formation. Altruism is distinguished from altruistic surrender, in which a surrender of direct gratification or of instinctual needs takes place in favor of fulfilling the needs of others to the detriment of the self, and the satisfaction can only be enjoyed vicariously through introjection.	Humor	Using comedy to overtly express feelings and thoughts without personal discomfort or immobilization and without producing an unpleasant effect on others. It allows the person to tolerate and yet focus on what is too terrible to be borne; it is different from wit, a form of displacement that involves distraction from the affective issue.
Anticipation	Realistically anticipating or planning for future inner discomfort. The mechanism is goal-directed and implies careful planning or worrying and premature but realistic affective anticipation of dire and potentially dreadful outcomes.	Sublimation	Achieving impulse gratification and the retention of goals but altering a socially objectionable aim or object to a socially acceptable one. Sublimation allows instincts to be channeled, rather than blocked or diverted. Feelings are acknowledged, modified, and directed toward a significant object or goal, and modest instinctual satisfaction occurs.
Asceticism	Eliminating the pleasurable effects of experiences. There is a moral element in assigning values to specific pleasures. Gratification is derived from renunciation, and asceticism is directed against all base pleasures perceived consciously.	Suppression	Consciously or semiconsciously postponing attention to a conscious impulse or conflict. Issues may be deliberately cut off, but they are not avoided. Discomfort is acknowledged but minimized.

Adapted by Glen O. Gabbard, M.D., from Vaillant GE: *Adaptation to Life*, Little Brown, Boston, 1977; Semrad E: The operation of ego defenses in object loss. In *The Loss of Loved Ones*, DM Moriarity, editor. Charles C Thomas, Springfield, IL, 1967; and Bibring GL, Dwyer TF, Huntington DS, Valenstein AA: A study of the psychological process in pregnancy and of the earliest mother–child relationship: Methodological considerations. *Psychoanal Stud Child 16:* 25, 1961.

[a] The categorization of these defenses as narcissistic is controversial. Many psychoanalysts would subsume them under "Immature Defenses."

sion leads to a corresponding increase in libido, the mental representation of the physiological event. (See Chapter 18 for a discussion of neurasthenia.) The *actual neuroses* are caused by this buildup. Later, with the development of the structural model, Freud developed a new theory of a second type of anxiety that he referred to as *signal anxiety.* In this model, anxiety operates at an unconscious level and serves to mobilize the ego's resources to avert danger. Either external or internal sources of danger may produce such a signal that leads the ego to marshal specific defense mechanisms to guard against or reduce the degree of instinctual excitation.

Freud's later theory of anxiety explains neurotic symptoms as the ego's partial failure to cope with distressing stimuli. The drive derivatives associated with danger may not have been adequately contained by the defense mechanisms used by the ego. In phobias, for example, Freud explained that fear of an external threat (such as dogs or snakes) is an externalization of an internal danger.

Danger situations can also be linked to developmental stages and thus can create a developmental hierarchy of anxiety. The earliest danger situation is a fear of disintegration or annihilation, often associated with concerns about fusion with an external object. As infants mature and recognize the mothering figure as a separate person, separation anxiety or fear of the loss of the object becomes more prominent. During the oedipal psychosexual stage, girls are most concerned about losing the love of the most important figure in their lives, their mother. Boys are primarily anxious about bodily injury or castration. After the resolution of the oedipal conflict, a more mature form of anxiety occurs, often termed *superego anxiety.* This latency-age concern involves the fear that internalized parental representations, contained in the superego, will cease to love or will angrily punish the child.

Character

In 1913, Freud distinguished between neurotic symptoms and personality or character traits. *Neurotic symptoms* develop as a result of the failure of repression; *character traits* owe their existence to the success of repression, that is, to the defense system that achieves its aim through a persistent pattern of reaction formation and sublimation. In 1923, Freud also observed that the ego can only give up important objects by identifying with them or introjecting them. This accumulated pattern of identifications and introjections also contributes to character formation. Freud specifically emphasized the importance of superego formation in the construction of character.

Contemporary psychoanalysts regard character as a person's habitual or typical pattern of adaptation to internal drive forces and to external environmental forces. *Character* and *personality* are used interchangeably and are distinguished from the ego in that they largely refer to styles of defense and of directly observable behavior rather than to feeling and thinking.

Character is also influenced by constitutional temperament, the interaction of drive forces with early ego defenses and with environmental influences, and various identifications with and internalizations of other people throughout life. The extent to which the ego has developed a capacity to tolerate the delay of impulse discharge and to neutralize instinctual energy determines the degree to which such character traits emerge in later life. The exaggerated development of certain character traits at the expense of others may lead to personality disorders or produce a vulnerability or predisposition to psychosis.

CLASSIC PSYCHOANALYTIC THEORY OF NEUROSES

The classic view of neurosogenesis regards conflict as essential. The conflict may arise between instinctual drives and external reality or between internal agencies, such as the id and the superego or the id and the ego. Moreover, because the conflict has not been worked through to a realistic solution, the drives or wishes that seek discharge have been expelled from consciousness through repression or another defense mechanism. Their expulsion from conscious awareness, however, does not make the drives any less powerful or influential. As a result, the unconscious tendencies (such as the disguised neurotic symptoms) fight their way back into consciousness. This theory of the development of neurosis assumes that a rudimentary neurosis based on the same type of conflict existed in early childhood.

Deprivation during the first few months of life because of absent or impaired caretaking figures may adversely affect ego development. This impairment, in turn, may result in the failure to make appropriate identifications. The resulting ego difficulties create problems mediating between the drives and the environment. Lack of capacity for constructive expression of drives, especially aggression, may lead some children to turn their aggression on themselves and become overtly self-destructive. Parents who are inconsistent, excessively harsh, or overly indulgent may influence children to develop disordered superego functioning. Severe conflict that cannot be managed through symptom formation may lead to extreme restrictions in ego functioning and to a fundamental impairment of the capacity to learn and develop new skills.

Traumatic events that seem to threaten survival may break through defenses when the ego has been weakened. Greater amounts of libidinal energy are then required to master the excitation that results. The libido thus mobilized, however, is withdrawn from the supply that is normally applied to external objects. This withdrawal further diminishes the strength of the ego and produces a sense of inadequacy. Frustrations or disappointments in adults may revive infantile longings that are then dealt with through symptom formation or further regression.

TREATMENT AND TECHNIQUE

The cornerstone of psychoanalytic technique is *free association,* in which patients say whatever comes to mind. Free association does more than provide content for the analysis: It also induces the necessary regression and dependency connected with establishing and working through the transference neurosis. When this development occurs, all the original wishes, drives, and defenses associated with the infantile neurosis are transferred to the person of the analyst.

As patients attempt to free associate, they soon learn that they have difficulty saying whatever comes to mind without censoring certain thoughts. They develop conflicts about their wishes and feelings toward the analyst that reflect childhood conflicts. The *transference* that develops toward the analyst may also serve as a resistance to the process of free association. Freud discovered that *resistance* was not simply a stoppage of a patient's associations, but also an important revelation of the patient's internal object relations as they were externalized and manifested in the transference relationship with the analyst. The systematic analysis of transference and resistance is the essence of psychoanalysis. Freud was also aware that the analyst might have transferences to the patient, which he called *countertransference.* Countertransference, in Freud's view, was an obstacle that the analyst needed to understand so that it did not interfere with treatment. In this spirit, he recognized the need for all analysts to have been analyzed themselves.

Analysts after Freud began to recognize that countertransference was not only an obstacle, but also a source of useful information about the patient. In other words, the analyst's feelings in response to the patient reflect how other people respond to the patient as well as provide some indication of the patient's own internal object relations. By understanding the intense feelings that occur in the analytic relationship, the analyst can help the patient broaden understanding of past and current relationships outside the analysis. The development of insight into neurotic conflicts also expands the ego and provides an increased sense of mastery. (Psychoanalysis and other techniques derived from it are discussed in greater detail in Chapter 33, Section 34.1.)

References

Brenner C: *The Mind in Conflict.* International Universities Press, New York, 1982.
Fenichel O: *The Psychoanalytic Theory of Neurosis.* Norton, New York, 1945.
Freud A: *The Ego and the Mechanisms of Defense* (1936). In *The Writings of Anna Freud,* vol 2, rev ed. International Universities Press, New York, 1966.
Freud S: *Beyond the Pleasure Principle.* Norton, New York, 1961.
Freud S: *The Ego and the Id.* Norton, New York, 1960.
Freud S: *An Outline of Psycho-Analysis.* Norton, New York, 1969.
Freud S: *The Standard Edition of the Complete Psychological Works of Sigmund Freud,* vols 1–24. Hogarth, London, 1953–1966.
Gabbard GO: Psychoanalysis. In *Comprehensive Textbook of Psychiatry,* ed 6, HI Kaplan, BJ Sadock, editors, p 431. Williams & Wilkins, Baltimore, 1995.
Gabbard GO: *Psychodynamic Psychiatry in Clinical Practice: The DSM-IV Edition.* American Psychiatric Press, Washington, 1994.
Holt RR: *Freud Reappraised: A Fresh Look at Psychoanalytic Theory.* Guilford, New York, 1989.
Winnicott DW: *Playing and Reality.* Basic Books, New York, 1971.

▲ 6.2 Schools Derived from Psychoanalysis and Psychology

KARL ABRAHAM (1877–1925)

Karl Abraham, one of Sigmund Freud's earliest disciples, was the first psychoanalyst in Germany. He is best known for his explication of depression from a psychoanalytic perspective and for his elaboration of Freud's stages of psychosexual development. Abraham divided the oral stage into a biting phase and a sucking phase; the anal stage into a destructive-expulsive (anal-sadistic) phase and a mastering-retentive (anal-erotic) phase; and the phallic stage into an early phase of partial genital love (true phallic phase) and a later mature genital phase. Abraham also linked the psychosexual stages to specific syndromes. For example, he postulated that obsessional neurosis was the result of fixation at the anal-sadistic phase and depression the result of fixation at the oral stage.

ALFRED ADLER (1870–1937)

Alfred Adler (Fig. 6.2–1) was one of Freud's prized pupils, but theoretical differences led to their eventual estrangement. Adler thought that Freud had overemphasized the sexual theory of neurosis and that aggression was of far more importance, specifically in its manifestation as a striving for power, which he believed to be a masculine trait. He introduced the term *masculine protest* to describe the tendency to move from a passive and feminine role to a masculine and active role. Adler's theories are collectively known as *individual psychology.*

Adler coined the term *inferiority complex* to refer to a sense of inadequacy and weakness that is universal and inborn. A developing child's self-esteem is compromised by a physical defect, and Adler referred to this phenomenon as *organ inferiority.* He also thought that a basic inferiority tied to children's oedipal longings could never be gratified.

Adler was one of the first developmental theorists to recognize the importance of children's birth order in their families of origin. The firstborn child reacts with anger to the birth of siblings and struggles against giving up the powerful position of only child. The second-born child must constantly strive to compete with the firstborn. Adler thought that a child's sibling position results in lifelong influences on character and lifestyle.

The primary therapeutic approach in adlerian therapy is

FIGURE 6.2–1
Alfred Adler.

encouragement, through which Adler believed his patients could overcome feelings of inferiority. Consistent human relatedness, in his view, leads to greater hope, less isolation, and greater affiliation with society. He believed that patients needed to develop a greater sense of their own dignity and worth and a renewed appreciation for their abilities and strengths.

FRANZ ALEXANDER (1891–1964)

Franz Alexander (Fig. 6.2–2) emigrated from his native Germany to the United States, where he settled in Chicago and founded the Chicago Institute for Psychoanalysis. He wrote extensively about the association between specific personality traits and certain psychosomatic ailments, a point of view that came to be known as the *specificity hypothesis.* Alexander fell out of favor with classical analysts for advocating the *corrective emotional experience* as part of analytic technique. In this approach, Alexander suggested that an analyst must deliberately adopt a particular mode of relatedness with a patient to counteract noxious childhood influences from the patient's parents. He believed that the trusting, supportive relationship between patient and analyst enabled the patient to master childhood traumas and to grow from the experience.

GORDON ALLPORT (1896–1967)

Gordon Allport, a psychologist in the United States, is known as the founder of the *humanistic school* of psychology, which holds that each person has an inherent potential for autonomous function and growth. At Harvard University, he taught the first course in the psychology of personality offered at a college in the United States.

FIGURE 6.2–2
Franz Alexander. (Courtesy of Franz Alexander.)

Allport believed that a person's only real guarantee of personal existence is a sense of self. Selfhood develops through a series of stages, from awareness of the body to self-identity. Allport used the term *propriem* to describe strivings related to the maintenance of self-identity and self-esteem. He used the term *traits* to refer to the chief units of personality structure. *Personal dispositions* are individual traits that represent the essence of an individual's unique personality. *Maturity* is characterized by a capacity to relate to others with warmth and intimacy and an expanded sense of self. In Allport's view, mature people have security, humor, insight, enthusiasm, and zest. Psychotherapy is geared to helping patients realize these characteristics.

MICHAEL BALINT (1896–1970)

Michael Balint was considered a member of the independent or middle group of object relations theorists in the United Kingdom. Balint believed that the urge for the primary love object underlies virtually all psychological phenomena. Infants wish to be loved totally and unconditionally, and when a mother is not forthcoming with appropriate nurturance, a child devotes his or her life to a search for the love missed in childhood. According to Balint, the *basic fault* is the feeling of many patients that something is missing. Like Ronald Fairbairn and Donald W. Winnicott, Balint understood this deficit in internal structure to be the result of maternal failures. He viewed all psychological motivations as stemming from the failure to receive adequate maternal love.

Unlike Fairbairn, however, Balint did not entirely abandon drive theory. He suggested that libido, for example, is both pleasure seeking and object seeking. He also worked with seriously disturbed patients, and like Winnicott, he thought that certain aspects of psychoanalytic treatment occur at a more profound level than that of the ordinary verbal explanatory interpretations. Although some material involving genital psychosexual stages of development can be interpreted from the perspective of intrapsychic conflict, Balint believed that certain preverbal phenomena are reexperienced in analysis and that the relationship itself is decisive in dealing with this realm of early experience.

ERIC BERNE (1910–1970)

Eric Berne (Fig. 6.2–3) began his professional life as a training and supervising analyst in classic psychoanalytic theory and technique, but ultimately developed his own school, known as transactional analysis. A *transaction* is a stimulus presented by one person that evokes a corresponding response in another. Berne defined psychological *games* as stereotyped and predictable transactions that people learn in childhood and continue to play throughout their lives. *Strokes,* the basic motivating factors of human behavior, consist of specific rewards, such as approval and love. All people have three ego states that exist within them: the *Child,* which represents primitive elements that become fixed in early childhood; the *Adult,* which is the part of the personality capable of objective appraisals of reality; and the *Parent,* which is an introject of a person's actual parents' values. The therapeutic process is geared to help patients understand whether they are functioning

FIGURE 6.2–3
Eric Berne. (Courtesy of Grove Press.)

in the child, adult, or parent mode in their interactions with others. As patients learn to recognize characteristic games played again and again throughout life, they can ultimately function in the adult mode as much as possible in interpersonal relationships.

WILFRED BION (1897–1979)

Wilfred Bion expanded Klein's concept of *projective identification* to include an interpersonal process in which a therapist feels coerced by a patient into playing a particular role in the patient's internal world. He also developed the notion that the therapist must contain what has been projected by the patient so that it is processed and returned to the patient in modified form. Bion believed that a similar process occurs between mother and infant. He also observed that ''psychotic'' and ''nonpsychotic'' aspects of the mind function simultaneously as suborganizations. Bion is probably best known for his application of psychoanalytic ideas to groups. Whenever a group gets derailed from its task, it deteriorates into one of three *basic states:* dependency, pairing, or fight-flight.

RAYMOND CATTELL (b. 1905)

Raymond Cattell obtained his Ph.D. in England before moving to the United States. He introduced the use of *multivariate analysis* and *factor analysis*—statistical procedures that simultaneously examine the relations among multiple variables and factors—to the study of personality. By objectively examining the person's life record, using personal interviewing and questionnaire data, Cattell described a variety of traits that represent the building blocks of personality.

Traits are both biologically based and environmentally determined or learned. Biological traits include sex, gregariousness, aggression, and parental protectiveness. Environmentally learned traits include cultural ideas, such as work, religion, intimacy, romance, and identity. An important concept is the *law of coercion to the biosocial mean,* which holds that society exerts pressure on genetically different persons to conform to social norms. For example, a person with a strong genetic tendency toward dominance is likely to receive social encouragement for restraint, whereas the naturally submissive person will be encouraged toward self-assertion.

RONALD FAIRBAIRN (1889–1964)

Ronald Fairbairn, a Scottish analyst who worked most of his life in relative isolation, was one of the major psychoanalytic theorists in the British school of object relations. He suggested that infants are not primarily motivated by the drives of libido and aggression but by an object-seeking instinct. Fairbairn replaced the freudian ideas of energy, ego, and id with the notion of *dynamic structures.* When an infant encounters frustration, a portion of the ego is defensively split off in the course of development and functions as an entity in relation to internal objects and to other subdivisions of the ego. He also stressed that not only an object but also an object *relationship* is internalized during development, so that a self is always in relationship to an object, and the two are connected with an affect.

SÁNDOR FERENCZI (1873–1933)

Although Sándor Ferenczi, a Hungarian analyst, had been analyzed by Freud and was influenced by him, he later discarded Freud's techniques and introduced his own method of analysis. He understood the symptoms of his patients as related to sexual and physical abuse in childhood and proposed that analysts need to love their patients in a way that compensates them for the love they did not receive as children. He developed a procedure known as *active therapy,* in which he encouraged patients to develop an awareness of reality through active confrontation by the therapist. He also experimented with *mutual analysis,* in which he would analyze his patient for a session and then allow the patient to analyze him for a session.

ERICH FROMM (1900–1980)

Erich Fromm (Fig. 6.2–4) came to the United States in 1933 from Germany, where he had received his Ph.D. He was instrumental in the founding of the William Alanson White Institute for Psychiatry in New York. Fromm identified five character types that are common to and determined by Western culture; each person may possess qualities from one or more types. The types are (1) the *receptive personality,* who is passive; (2) the *exploitative personality,* who is manipulative; (3) the *marketing personality,* who is opportunistic and changeable; (4) the *hoarding personality,* who saves and stores; and (5) the *productive personality,* who is mature and enjoys love and work. The therapeutic process involves strengthening the person's sense of ethical behavior toward others and devel-

FIGURE 6.2–4
Erich Fromm. (Courtesy of Erich Fromm.)

oping productive love, which is characterized by care, responsibility, and respect for other persons.

MERTON M. GILL (1914–1994)

Merton M. Gill began his career at the Menninger Clinic in the 1940s, working with David Rappaport on the elaboration of ego psychology. As his career evolved, he became a leader in what is now termed the *social constructivist* view. Gill suggested that the facts within the psychoanalytic process are not objectively or authoritatively observed by the analyst but, rather, are a matter of agreement between analyst and analysand. Gill advocated two major elements of the social constructivist perspective: A patient's transference perception of the analyst is to some degree based on the analyst's *real* behavior, and the analyst's ongoing personal participation in the analytic process has a continuous effect on the patient and on how the analyst understands the patient.

In this regard, Gill moved psychoanalysis away from an objectivist or logical positivist philosophical framework. In other words, he regarded reality as a subjectively constructed entity rather than as something objective and "out there." Hence, the analyst's "objectivity" was also a myth. Gill was instrumental in bringing the psychoanalytic profession to the point of recognizing that psychoanalysis is both a one-person (intrapsychic) and a two-person (interpersonal) psychology.

KURT GOLDSTEIN (1878–1965)

Kurt Goldstein was born in Germany and received his M.D. from the University of Breslau. He was influenced by existentialism and Gestalt psychology: Every organism has dynamic properties, which are energy supplies that are relatively constant and evenly distributed. When states of tension-disequilibrium occur, an organism automatically attempts to return to its normal state. What happens in one part of the organism affects every other part, a phenomenon known as *holocoenosis.*

Self-actualization was a concept Goldstein used to describe people's creative powers to fulfill their potentialities. Because each person has a different set of innate potentialities, people strive for self-actualization along different paths.

Sickness severely disrupts self-actualization. Responses to the disruption of an organism's integrity may be rigid and compulsive; regression to more primitive modes of behavior is characteristic. One of Goldstein's major contributions was his identification of the *catastrophic reaction* to brain damage, in which a person becomes fearful and agitated and refuses to perform simple tasks because of the fear of possible failure.

KAREN HORNEY (1885–1952)

Born and educated in Germany, Karen Horney (Fig. 6.2–5) taught at the Institute of Psychoanalysis in Berlin before immigrating to the United States. Horney believed that a person's current personality attributes are the result of the interaction between the person and the environment and are not solely based on infantile libidinal strivings carried over from childhood. Her theory, known as *holistic psychology,* maintains that a person needs to be seen as a unitary whole who influences and is influenced by the environment. She thought that the Oedipus complex was overvalued in terms of its contribution to adult psychopathology, but she also believed that

FIGURE 6.2–5
Karen Horney. (Courtesy of the Association for the Advancement of Psychoanalysis, New York.)

rigid parental attitudes about sexuality led to excessive concern with the genitals.

She proposed three separate concepts of the self: the *actual self,* the sum total of a person's experience; the *real self,* the harmonious, healthy person; and the *idealized self,* the neurotic expectation or glorified image that a person feels he or she should be. A person's *pride system* alienates him or her from the real self by overemphasizing prestige, intellect, power, strength, appearance, sexual prowess, and other qualities that can lead to self-effacement and self-hatred. Horney also established the concepts of *basic anxiety* and *basic trust.* The therapeutic process, in her view, aims for *self-realization* by exploring distorting influences that prevent the personality from growing.

EDITH JACOBSON (1897–1978)

Edith Jacobson, a psychiatrist in the United States, believed that the structural model and an emphasis on object relations are not fundamentally incompatible. She thought that the ego, self-images, and object images exert reciprocal influences on each other's development. She also stressed that the infant's disappointment with the maternal object is not necessarily related to the mother's actual failure. In Jacobson's view, disappointment is related to a specific, drive-determined demand, rather than to a global striving for contact or engagement. She viewed an infant's experience of pleasure or unpleasure as the core of the early mother–infant relationship. Satisfactory experiences lead to the formation of good or gratifying images, whereas unsatisfactory experiences create bad or frustrating images. Normal and pathological development is based on the evolution of these self-images and object images. Jacobson believed that the concept of *fixation* refers to modes of object relatedness, rather than to modes of gratification.

CARL GUSTAV JUNG (1875–1961)

Carl Gustav Jung (Fig. 6.2–6), a Swiss psychiatrist, formed a psychoanalytic school known as analytic psychology, which includes basic ideas related to but going beyond Freud's theories. After initially being Freud's disciple, Jung broke with Freud over the latter's emphasis on infantile sexuality. He expanded on Freud's concept of the unconscious by describing the *collective unconscious* as consisting of all humankind's common, shared mythological and symbolic past. The collective unconscious includes *archetypes*—representational images and configurations with universal symbolic meanings. Archetypal figures exist for the mother, father, child, and hero, among others. Archetypes contribute to *complexes,* feeling-toned ideas that develop as a result of personal experience interacting with archetypal imagery. Thus, a mother complex is determined not only by the mother–child interaction but also by the conflict between archetypal expectation and actual experience with the real woman who functions in a motherly role.

Jung noted that there are two types of personality organizations: introversion and extroversion. *Introverts* focus on their inner world of thoughts, intuitions, emotions, and sensations; *extroverts* are more oriented toward the outer world, other people, and material goods. Each person has a mixture of both components. The *persona,* the mask covering the personality, is the face a person presents to the outside world. The persona may become fixed and the real person hidden from himself or herself. *Anima* and *Animus* are unconscious traits possessed by men and women, respectively, and are contrasted with the persona. *Anima* refers to a man's undeveloped femininity, whereas *animus* refers to a woman's undeveloped masculinity.

FIGURE 6.2–6

Carl Jung (print includes signature). (From the National Library of Medicine, Bethesda, MD.)

The aim of jungian treatment is to bring about an adequate adaptation to reality, which involves a person's fulfilling his or her creative potentialities. The ultimate goal is to achieve *individuation,* a process continuing throughout life whereby people develop a unique sense of their own identity. This developmental process may lead them down new paths away from their previous directions in life.

OTTO KERNBERG (b. 1928)

Otto Kernberg is perhaps the most influential object relations theorist in the United States. Influenced by both Melanie Klein and Edith Jacobson, much of his theory is derived from his clinical work with patients who have borderline personality disorder. Kernberg has placed great emphasis on the splitting of the ego and the elaboration of good and bad self-configurations and object configurations. Although he has continued to use the structural model, he views the id as composed of self-images, object images, and their associated affects. Drives appear to manifest themselves only in the context of internalized interpersonal experience. Good and bad self-representations and object relations become associated, respectively, with libido and aggression. Not only do object relations constitute the building blocks of structure, but they are also the building blocks of drives. Goodness and badness in relational experiences precede drive cathexis. In other words, the dual instincts of libido and aggression arise from object-directed affective states of love and hate.

Kernberg proposed the term *borderline personality organization* for a broad spectrum of patients characterized by a lack of an integrated sense of identity, ego weakness, absence of superego integration, reliance on primitive defense mechanisms such as splitting and projective identification, and a tendency to shift into primary process thinking. He suggested a specific type of psychoanalytic psychotherapy for such patients in which transference issues are interpreted early in the process.

MELANIE KLEIN (1882–1960)

Melanie Klein (Fig. 6.2–7) was born in Vienna, worked with Abraham and Ferenczi, and later moved to London. Klein evolved a theory of internal object relations which was intimately linked to drives. Her unique perspective grew largely from her psychoanalytic work with children, in which she became impressed with the role of unconscious intrapsychic fantasy. She postulated that the ego undergoes a splitting process to deal with the terror of annihilation. She also thought that Freud's concept of the death instinct was central to understanding aggression, hatred, sadism, and other forms of "badness," all of which she viewed as derivatives of the death instinct.

Klein viewed projection and introjection as the primary defensive operations in the first months of life. Infants project derivatives of the death instinct into the mother and then fear attack from the "bad mother," a phenomenon that Klein referred to as *persecutory anxiety.* This anxiety is intimately associated with the *paranoid-schizoid position,* infants' mode of organizing experience in which all aspects of infant and mother are split into good and bad elements. As the disparate views are integrated, infants become concerned that they may have harmed or destroyed the mother through the hostile and sadistic fantasies directed toward her. At this developmental point, children have arrived at the *depressive position,* in which the mother is viewed ambivalently as having both positive and negative aspects and as being the target of a mixture of loving and hateful feelings.

Klein was also instrumental in the development of child analysis, which evolved from an analytic play technique in which children would use toys and play in a symbolic fashion that allowed analysts to make interpretations of the play.

FIGURE 6.2–7
Melanie Klein. (Courtesy of Melanie Klein and Douglas Glass.)

HEINZ KOHUT (1913–1981)

Heinz Kohut is best known for his writings on narcissism and the development of self psychology. He viewed the development and maintenance of self-esteem and self-cohesion as more important than sexuality or aggression. Kohut described Freud's concept of narcissism as judgmental in that development was supposed to proceed toward object relatedness and away from narcissism. He conceived of two separate lines of development, one moving in the direction of object relatedness and the other in the direction of greater enhancement of the self.

In infancy, children fear losing the protection of the early mother–infant bliss and resort to one of three pathways to save the lost perfection: the grandiose self, the alter ego or twinship, and the idealized parental image. These three poles of the self manifest themselves in psychoanalytic treatment in terms of characteristic transferences, known as *self-object transferences.* The *grandiose self* leads to a *mirror transference,* in which patients attempt to capture the gleam in the analyst's eye through exhibitionistic self-display. The *alter ego* leads to the *twinship transference,* in which patients perceive the analyst as a twin. The *idealized parental imago* leads to an *idealizing transference,* in which patients feel enhanced self-esteem by being in the presence of the exalted figure of the analyst.

Kohut suggested that empathic failures in the mother lead to a developmental arrest at a particular stage when children need to use others to perform self-object functions. Although Kohut originally applied this formulation to narcissistic personality disorder, he later expanded it to apply to all psychopathology.

JACQUES LACAN (1901–1981)

Born in Paris and trained as a psychiatrist, Jacques Lacan founded his own institute, the Freudian School of Paris. He attempted to integrate the intrapsychic concepts of Freud with concepts related to linguistics and semiotics, the latter being the study of language and symbols. Whereas Freud saw the unconscious as a seething cauldron of needs, wishes, and instincts, Lacan saw it as a sort of language that helps to structure the world. Two of his principal concepts are that the unconscious is structured like a language and that the unconscious is a discourse. Primary process thoughts are actually uncontrolled free-flowing sequences of meaning. Symptoms are signs or symbols of underlying processes. The role of the therapist is to interpret the semiotic text of the personality structure. Lacan's most basic phase is the mirror stage; it is here that infants learn to recognize themselves by taking the perspective of others. In that sense, the ego is not part of the self but, rather, is something outside of and viewed by the self. The ego comes to represent parents and society, more than it represents the actual self of the person.

Lacan's therapeutic approach involves the need to become less alienated from the self and more involved with others. Relationships are often fantasized, which distorts reality and which must be corrected. Among his most controversial beliefs was that the resistance to understanding the real relationship can be reduced by shortening the length of the therapy session and that psychoanalytic sessions need to be standardized not to time but, rather, to content and process.

KURT LEWIN (1890–1947)

Kurt Lewin received his Ph.D. in Berlin, came to the United States in the 1930s, and taught at Cornell, Harvard, and the Massachusetts Institute of Technology. He adapted the field approach of physics to a concept called *field theory.* A *field* is the totality of coexisting, mutually interdependent parts. Behavior becomes a function of people and their environment, which together make up the *life space.* The life space represents a field in constant flux, with *valences* or needs that require satisfaction. A hungry person is more aware of restaurants than is someone who has just eaten, and a person who wants to mail a letter is aware of mailboxes.

Lewin applied field theory to groups. *Group dynamics* refers to the interaction among members of a group, each of whom is dependent on the others. The group is capable of exerting pressure on a person to change behavior, but the person also influences the group when change occurs.

ABRAHAM MASLOW (1908–1970)

Abraham Maslow was born in Brooklyn, New York, and completed both his undergraduate and graduate work at the University of Wisconsin. Along with Kurt Goldstein, Maslow believed in *self-actualization theory*—the need to understand the totality of a person. A leader in humanistic psychology, Maslow described a hierarchical organization of needs present in everyone. As the more primitive needs, such as hunger and thirst, are satisfied, more advanced psychological needs, such as affection and self-esteem, become the primary motivators. Self-actualization is the highest need.

A *peak experience,* frequently occurring in self-actualizers, is an episodic, brief occurrence in which a person suddenly experiences a powerful transcendental state of consciousness: a sense of heightened understanding, an intense euphoria, an integrated nature, unity with the universe, and an altered perception of time and space. This powerful experience tends to occur most often in the psychologically healthy and may produce long-lasting beneficial effects.

KARL A. MENNINGER (1893–1990)

Karl A. Menninger was one of the first physicians in the United States to receive psychiatric training. With his brother, Will, he pioneered the concept of a psychiatric hospital based on psychoanalytic principles and founded the Menninger Clinic in Topeka, Kansas. He also was a prolific writer: *The Human Mind,* one of his most popular books, brought psychoanalytic understanding to the lay public. He made a compelling case for the validity of Freud's death instinct in *Man Against Himself. The Vital Balance* was his magnum opus, in which he formulated a unique theory of psychopathology. Menninger maintained a life-long interest in the criminal justice system and argued in *The Crime of Punishment* that many convicted criminals needed treatment rather than punishment. Finally, his volume entitled *Theory of Psychoanalytic Technique* was one of the few books to examine the theoretical underpinnings of psychoanalysts' interventions.

ADOLPH MEYER (1866–1950)

Adolph Meyer (Fig. 6.2–8) came to the United States from Switzerland in 1892 and eventually became director of the psychiatric Henry Phipps Clinic of Johns Hopkins Medical School. Although he did not entirely reject Freud's theoretical emphasis of mental functioning, Meyer preferred to examine the verifiable and objective aspects of a person's life. His theory of psychobiology explained disordered behavior as reactions to genetic, physical, psychological, environmental, and social stresses. Meyer introduced the concept of *common sense psychiatry,* and focused on ways in which a patient's current life situation can be realistically improved. He coined the concept of *ergasia,* the action of the total organism. His goal in therapy was to aid patients' adjustment by helping them modify unhealthy adaptations. One of Meyer's tools was an autobiographical life chart constructed by the patient during therapy.

FIGURE 6.2–8
Adolf Meyer, 1866–1950. (From the National Library of Medicine, Bethesda, MD.)

GARDNER MURPHY (1895–1979)

Gardner Murphy was born in Ohio and received his Ph.D. at Columbia University. He was among the first to publish a comprehensive history of psychology and made major contributions to social, general, and educational psychology.

According to Murphy, three essential stages of personality development are the stage of undifferentiated wholeness, the stage of differentiation, and the stage of integration. This development is frequently uneven, with both regression and progression occurring along the way.

There are four inborn human needs: visceral, motor, sensory, and emergency-related. These needs become increasingly specific in time as they are molded by a person's experiences in various social and environmental contexts. *Canalization* brings about these changes by establishing a connection between a need and a specific way of satisfying the need.

Murphy was interested in parapsychology. States such as sleep, drowsiness, certain drug and toxic conditions, hypnosis, and delirium tend to be favorable to paranormal experiences. Impediments to paranormal awareness include various intrapsychic barriers, conditions in the general social environment, and a heavy investment in ordinary sensory experiences.

FIGURE 6.2–9
Sandor Rado. (Courtesy of New York Academy of Medicine, New York, NY.)

HENRY MURRAY (1893–1988)

Henry Murray was born in New York City, attended medical school there, and was a founder of the Boston Psychoanalytic Institute. He proposed the term *personology* to describe the study of human behavior. He focused on *motivation,* a need that is aroused by internal or external stimulation; once aroused, motivation produces continued activity until the need is reduced or satisfied. He developed the *Thematic Apperception Test* (TAT), a projective technique used to reveal both unconscious and conscious mental processes and problem areas.

FREDERICK S. PERLS (1893–1970)

Gestalt theory developed in Germany under the influence of several men: Max Wertheimer (1880–1943), Wolfgang Köhler (1887–1967), and Kurt Lewin (1890–1947).

Frederick "Fritz" Perls applied Gestalt theory to a therapy that emphasizes the current experiences of the patient in the here and now, as contrasted to the there and then of psychoanalytic schools. In terms of motivation, patients learn to recognize their needs at any given time and the ways that the drive to satisfy these needs may influence their current behavior. According to the Gestalt point of view, behavior represents more than the sum of its parts. A *gestalt,* or a whole, both includes and goes beyond the sum of smaller, independent events; it deals with essential characteristics of actual experience, such as value, meaning, and form.

SANDOR RADO (1890–1972)

Sandor Rado (Fig. 6.2–9) came to the United States from Hungary in 1945 and founded the Columbia Psychoanalytic Institute in New York. His theories of *adaptational dynamics* hold that the organism is a biological system operating under hedonic control, which is somewhat similar to Freud's pleasure principle. Cultural factors often cause excessive hedonic control and disordered behavior by interfering with the organism's ability for *self-regulation.* In therapy, the patient needs to relearn how to experience pleasurable feelings.

OTTO RANK (1884–1939)

An Austrian psychologist and a protégé of Sigmund Freud, Otto Rank (Fig. 6.2–10) broke with Freud in his 1924 publication, *The Trauma of the Birth,* and developed a new theory, which he called birth trauma. Anxiety is correlated with separation from the mother—specifically, with separation from the womb, the source of effortless gratification. This painful experience results in primal anxiety. Sleep and dreams symbolize the return to the womb.

The personality is divided into impulses, emotions, and will. Children's impulses seek immediate discharge and gratification. As impulses are mastered, as in toilet training, children begin the process of will development. If will is carried too far, pathological traits—such as stubbornness, disobedience, and inhibitions—may develop.

WILHELM REICH (1897–1957)

Wilhelm Reich (Fig. 6.2–11), an Austrian psychoanalyst, made major contributions to psychoanalysis in the area of character formation and character types. The term *character armor* refers to the personality's defenses that serve as a resistance to self-understanding and change. There are four major character types: The *hysterical character* is sexually seductive, anxious, and fixated at the phallic phase of libido development; the *compulsive character* is controlled, distrustful, indecisive, and fixated at the anal phase; the *narcissistic character* is fix-

FIGURE 6.2–10
Otto Rank. (Courtesy of New York Academy of Medicine, New York, NY.)

ated at the phallic state of development, and if the person is male, there is a contempt for women; and the *masochistic character* is long-suffering, complaining, and self-deprecatory, with an excessive demand for love.

The therapeutic process—called *will therapy*—emphasizes the relationship between patient and therapist; the goal of treatment is to help patients accept their separateness. A definite termination date for therapy is used to protect against excessive dependence on the therapist.

CARL ROGERS (1902–1987)

Carl Rogers received his Ph.D. in psychology at Columbia University. After attending Union Theological Seminary in New York, Rogers studied for the ministry. His name is most clearly associated with the *person-centered theory* of personality and psychotherapy, in which the major concepts are self-actualization and self-direction. Specifically, people are born with a capacity to direct themselves in the healthiest way, toward a level of completeness called self-actualization. From his person-centered approach, Rogers viewed personality not as a static entity composed of traits and patterns but as a dynamic phenomenon involving ever-changing communications, relationships, and self-concepts.

Rogers developed a treatment program called *client-centered psychotherapy.* Therapists attempt to produce an atmosphere in which clients can reconstruct their strivings for self-actualization. Therapists hold clients in *unconditional positive regard,* which is the total nonjudgmental acceptance of clients as they are. Other therapeutic practices include attention to the present, focus on clients' feelings, emphasis on process, trust in the potential and self-responsibility of clients, and a philosophy grounded in a positive attitude toward them, rather than a preconceived structure of treatment.

JEAN-PAUL SARTRE (1905–1980)

Born in Paris, Jean-Paul Sartre wrote plays and novels before turning to psychology. He was a German prisoner of war from 1940 to 1941 during World War II. Influenced by the

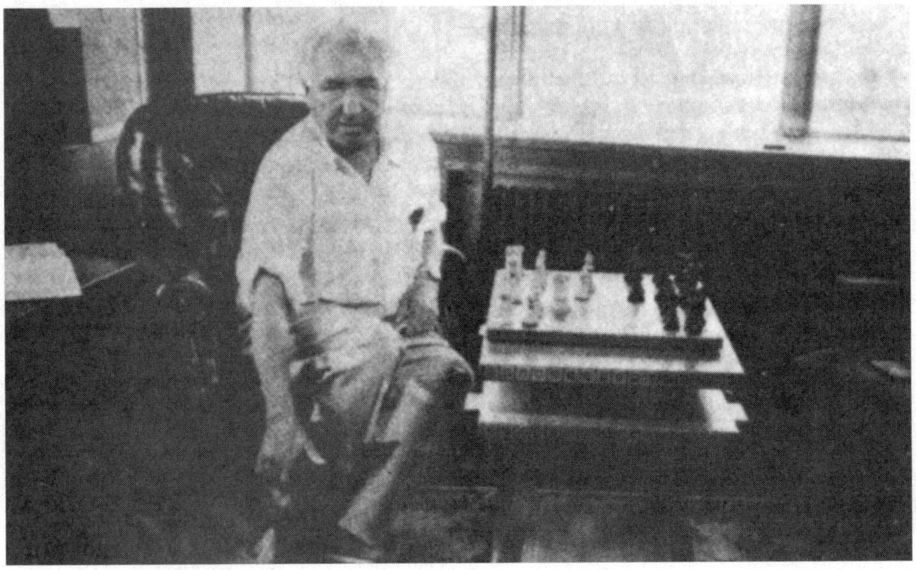

FIGURE 6.2–11
Wilhelm Reich at home. (Courtesy of Farrar, Straus & Giroux, Inc.)

ideas of Martin Heidegger, he developed what he called existential psychoanalysis. The *reflective self* was a key concept in Sartre's psychology. He recognized that humans alone could reflect on themselves as objects, so that the experience of Being in humans is unique in the natural world. This capacity to reflect leads humans to impose a meaning on existence. For Sartre, this meaning allows a human being to create his or her own essence.

Sartre denied the realm of the unconscious; he thought that human beings were condemned to be free and to face the fundamental existential dilemma—their aloneness without a god to provide meaning. As a result, each individual creates values and meanings. Neurosis is an escape from freedom, which is the key to maintaining psychological health.

Sartre made no distinction between philosophy and psychology. Psychologists, like philosophers, search for the truth about the world. Part of this truth, in Sartre's view, was the dialectic between consciousness and Being: Consciousness introduces nothingness and is a negation of being-in-itself. Ideals are revealed in actions, not in professed beliefs.

B. F. SKINNER (1904–1990)

Burrhus Frederic Skinner (Fig. 6.2–12), commonly known as B. F. Skinner, received his Ph.D. in psychology from Harvard University, where he taught for many years. It was Skinner's seminal work in operant learning that laid much of the groundwork for many current methods of behavior modification, programmed instruction, and general education. His global beliefs about the nature of behavior have been applied more widely, it can be argued, than those of any other theorist except, perhaps, Freud. His impact has been impressive in scope and magnitude.

Skinner's approach to personality was derived more from his basic beliefs about behavior than from a specific theory of personality per se. To Skinner, personality was not different from other behaviors or sets of behaviors; it is acquired, maintained, and strengthened or weakened according to the same rules of reward and punishment that alter any other form of behavior. *Behaviorism,* as Skinner's basic theory is most commonly known, is concerned only with observable, measurable, and operationalizable behavior. Many abstract and mentalistic hallmarks of other dominant personality theories have little place in Skinner's framework. Concepts such as self, ideas, and ego are considered unnecessary for understanding behavior and are shunned. Through the process of operant conditioning and the application of basic principles of learning, people are believed to develop sets of behavior that characterize their responses to the world of stimuli that they face in their lives. Such a set of responses is called *personality.*

FIGURE 6.2–12
B. F. Skinner.

HARRY STACK SULLIVAN (1892–1949)

Harry Stack Sullivan (Fig. 6.2–13) received his training in psychiatry in the United States in the 1920s and 1930s, during the early years of Freud's profound influence on American psychiatry. Like Adolf Meyer, under whom he studied, however, Sullivan insisted on formulating his concepts on observable data.

Sullivan described three modes of experiencing and thinking about the world. The *prototaxic mode* is undifferentiated thought that is unable to separate the whole into parts or to use symbols. It occurs normally in infancy and also appears in

FIGURE 6.2–13
Harry Stack Sullivan. (Courtesy of New York Academy of Medicine, New York, NY.)

patients with schizophrenia. In the *parataxic mode,* events are causally related because of temporal or serial connections. Logical relationships, however, are not perceived. The *syntaxic mode* is the logical, rational, and most mature type of cognitive functioning of which a person is capable. These three types of thinking and experiencing occur side by side in all people; it is the rare person who functions exclusively in the syntaxic mode.

The total configuration of personality traits is known as the *self-system,* which develops in various stages and is the outgrowth of interpersonal experiences, rather than an unfolding of intrapsychic forces. During infancy, anxiety occurs for the first time when infants' primary needs are not satisfied. During childhood, from 2 to 5 years, a child's main tasks are to become educated as to the requirements of the culture and to learn how to deal with powerful adults. As a juvenile, from 5 to 8 years, a child has a need for peers and must learn how to deal with them. In preadolescence, from 8 to 12 years, the development of the capacity for love and for collaboration with another person of the same sex develops. This so-called chum period is the prototype for a sense of intimacy. In the history of patients with schizophrenia, this experience of chums is often missing. During adolescence, major tasks include the separation from the family, the development of standards and values, and the transition to heterosexuality.

The therapy process requires the active participation of the therapist, who is known as a *participant observer.* Modes of experience, particularly the parataxic, need to be clarified, and new patterns of behavior need to be implemented. Ultimately, people need to see themselves as they really are, instead of what they think they are or what they want others to think they are.

Sullivan is best known for his creative psychotherapeutic work with severely disturbed patients. He believed that even the most psychotic patients with schizophrenia could be reached through the human relationship of psychotherapy.

DONALD W. WINNICOTT (1897–1971)

Donald W. Winnicott was one of the central figures in the British school of object relations theory. His theory of *multiple self-organizations* included a *true self,* which develops in the context of a responsive *holding environment* provided by a *good-enough mother.* When infants experience a traumatic disruption of their developing sense of self, however, a false self emerges and monitors and adapts to the conscious and unconscious needs of the mother; it thus provides a protected exterior behind which the true self is afforded a privacy that it requires to maintain its integrity.

Winnicott also developed the notion of the *transitional object.* Ordinarily, a pacifier, blanket, or teddy bear, this object serves as a substitute for the mother during infants' efforts to separate and become independent. It provides a soothing sense of security in the absence of the mother. Winnicott viewed the transitional space in which the transitional object functions as the source of art, creativity, and religion.

REFERENCES

Adler A: *The Individual Psychology of Alfred Adler: A Systematic Presentation in Selections from His Writings,* HL Ansbacher, RR Ansbacher, editors. Basic Books, New York, 1956.

Baker HS, Baker MN: Heinz Kohut's self psychology: An overview. Am J Psychiatry *144:*1, 1987.

Chessick R: *What Constitutes the Patient in Psychotherapy: Alternative Approaches to Understanding.* Jason Aronson, Northvale, NJ, 1992.

Gabbard GO: Psychoanalysis. In *Comprehensive Textbook of Psychiatry,* ed 6, HI Kaplan, BJ Sadock, editors, p 431. Williams & Wilkins, Baltimore, 1995.

Gabbard GO: *Psychodynamic Psychiatry in Clinical Practice: The DSM-IV Edition.* American Psychiatric Press, Washington, 1994.

Gill MM: *Psychoanalysis in Transition: A Personal View.* Analytic Press, Hillsdale, NJ, 1994.

Groskurth P: *Melanie Klein: Her World and Her Work.* Knopf, New York, 1986.

Horney K: *The Neurotic Personality of Our Time.* Norton, New York, 1937.

Jung CG: *Memories, Dreams, Reflections.* Random House, New York, 1961.

Menninger KA: *The Vital Balance: The Life Process in Mental Health and Illness.* Viking, New York, 1963.

Millon T: *Theories of Psychopathology,* pt 2. Saunders, Philadelphia, 1967.

Ogden TH: The concept of internal object relations. Int J Psychoanal *64:* 227, 1983.

Perry HS: *Psychiatrist of America: The Life of Harry Stack Sullivan.* Belknap Press, Harvard University Press, Cambridge, MA, 1982.

Rayner E: *The Independent Mind in British Psychoanalysis.* Jason Aronson, Northvale, NJ, 1991.

Segal H: *Melanie Klein.* Viking, New York, 1980.

Smith S: *Ideas of the Great Psychologists.* Harper & Row, Philadelphia, 1983.

▲ 6.3 Erik Erikson

Erik Homburger Erikson (Fig. 6.3–1) was born in 1902 in Frankfurt, Germany. His father, a Danish Protestant, and his mother, a Danish Jew, separated before he was born, and he grew up in the home of his mother and German-Jewish step-

FIGURE 6.3–1
Erik Erikson.

father, Theodore Homburger, a pediatrician. Erikson trained as a lay psychoanalyst in Europe and was schooled in the Montessori method of education.

Erikson immigrated to the United States in 1933. He worked at the Austen Riggs Center in Stockbridge, Massachusetts, and conducted research at Harvard, Yale, and the University of California at Berkeley. He became interested in the influence of culture on child development, and as a result of his studies in the 1930s and the 1940s, including anthropological work with the Sioux in South Dakota and the Yurok in northern California, his book *Childhood and Society* was published in 1950. In this publication, he presented a psychosocial theory of development that describes crucial steps in people's relationships with the social world, based on the interplay between biology and society.

Erikson drew on much of freudian psychology, but he added to Sigmund Freud's theory of infantile sexuality by concentrating on children's development beyond puberty. Erikson concluded that human personality is determined not only by childhood experiences, but also by those of adulthood. Erikson stated: "If everything goes back into childhood, then everything is somebody else's fault and taking responsibility for oneself is undermined." Most important, Erikson formulated a theory of human development that covers the entire span of the life cycle, from infancy and childhood through old age and senescence.

EPIGENETIC PRINCIPLE

Erikson's formulations were based on the concept of epigenesis, a term borrowed from embryology. His *epigenetic principle* holds that development occurs in sequential, clearly defined stages, and that each stage must be satisfactorily resolved for development to proceed smoothly. According to the epigenetic model, if successful resolution of a particular stage does not occur, all subsequent stages reflect the failure in the form of physical, cognitive, social, or emotional maladjustment.

Relation to Freudian Theory

Erikson accepted Freud's concepts of instinctual development and infantile sexuality. For each of Freud's psychosexual stages (for example, oral, anal, phallic), Erikson described a corresponding zone with a specific pattern or mode of behavior. Thus, the oral zone is associated with sucking or taking-in behavior; the anal zone is associated with holding on and letting go. Erikson emphasized that the development of the ego is more than the result of intrapsychic wants or inner psychic energies. It is also a matter of mutual regulation between growing children and a society's culture and traditions.

Stages of the Life Cycle

Erikson described eight stages of the life cycle (Table 6.3–1). Each stage is marked by one or more internal crises, defined as turning points—periods when people are in a state of increased vulnerability. Ideally, when a crisis is mastered successfully, people gain strength and move on to the next stage.

Erikson's stages are not fixed in time. Development is continuous; a particular stage may dominate at a certain time, but a person may have residual problems carried from one stage to the next or may be under severe stress and regress wholly or in part to an earlier stage. The time boundaries of each stage represent approximations agreed on by most workers in the field.

Stage 1: Basic Trust Versus Basic Mistrust (Birth to About 1 Year). Trust versus mistrust is the first crisis infants must face. Erikson wrote in *Growth and Crisis of the Healthy Personality:*

> For the first component of a healthy personality I nominate a sense of basic trust which I think is an attitude toward oneself and the world derived from the experience of the first year of life. Trust is the expectation that one's needs will be taken care of and that the world or outer providers can be relied upon.

This period coincides with Freud's oral stage of development, in which the mouth is the most sensitive zone of the body. Finding the nipple, sucking, and taking in nutrients fill the infant's primary needs. The trust-inducing mother attends to these needs assiduously and thus lays the groundwork for the infant's future positive expectations of the world. Erikson added the term *sensory* to Freud's oral stage (calling it oral-sensory) because the parent also attends to the infant's senses—sight, taste, smell, touch, and hearing. Through this interaction, infants develop the feeling of trust that their wants will be satisfied, or, if the mother is not attentive, they develop the mistrustful sense that they are not going to get what they want.

ORAL CRISIS. Toward the second half of the first year, the oral crisis occurs: Infants' teeth develop, and a drive to bite emerges. Infants progress from simply being passive to becoming active. If an infant bites too aggressively, however, the nipple is taken away. The mother's responses are influenced in part by the child's behavior, and the infant learns that it must control the urge to bite. As a result, infants learn that they can influence the environment, and they begin to develop a sense of themselves as individuals separate from the environment. In today's culture, weaning from the breast or the bottle begins toward the end of this phase. Erikson believed that the separation is the basis of a sense of sorrow, nostalgia, or homesickness. If basic trust is strong, however, the child develops a sense of hope, optimism, and confidence.

DEVELOPMENT OF TRUST. An affectionate, loving mother or surrogate mother who gives consistent, high-quality care provides the basis for the development of trust. According to Erikson, infants' first social achievement is the willingness to let the mother out of sight without undue anxiety or rage. This process occurs because the mother becomes an inner certainty in the infant's mental representation. Erikson's idea is parallel to Jean Piaget's concept of object permanence, which is children's ability to maintain mental images of people or objects when they are not present and not visible, and to Margaret Mahler's concept of object constancy, in which children have mental representations of the mother as reliable and stable. (This developmental phase occurs at 24 to 36 months, according to Mahler.)

Stage 2: Autonomy Versus Shame and Doubt (About 1 to 3 Years). Autonomy concerns children's sense of mastery over themselves and over their drives and impulses. Toddlers gain a sense of their separateness from others. "I," "you," "me," and "mine" are common words used by children during this period. Children have a choice of holding on or letting go, of being cooperative or stubborn. This period coincides with Freud's anal stage of development. For

Table 6.3–1
Erik Erikson's Stages of the Life Cycle

Stage 1. Basic Trust versus Basic Mistrust
(birth to about 1 year)
- Corresponds to the oral psychosexual stage
- Trust shown by ease of feeding, depth of sleep, bowel relaxation
- Depends on consistency and sameness of experiences provided by caretaker or outerprovider
- Second 6 months: teething and biting move infant from getting to taking
- Weaning leads to nostalgia for lost paradise
- If basic trust is strong, child maintains hopeful attitude, develops self-confidence
- Oral zone associated with mode of being satisfied

Stage 2. Autonomy versus Shame and Doubt
(about 1 to 3 years)
- Corresponds to the muscular-anal stage
- Biologically includes learning to walk, feed self, talk
- Need for outer control, firmness of caretaker before development of autonomy
- Shame occurs when child is overly self-conscious through negative exposure and punishment
- Self-doubt can evolve if parents overly shame child, eg, about elimination
- Anal zone associated with mode of holding on and letting go

Stage 3. Initiative versus Guilt
(3 to 5 years)
- Corresponds to the phallic psychosexual stage
- Initiative arises in relation to tasks for the sake of activity, both motor and intellectual
- Guilt may arise over goals contemplated (especially aggressive goals)
- Desire to mimic adult world; involvement in oedipal struggle leads to resolution through social role identification
- Sibling rivalry frequent
- Phallic zone associated with mode of competition and aggression

Stage 4. Industry versus Inferiority
(6 to 11 years)
- Corresponds to the latency psychosexual stage
- Child is busy building, creating, accomplishing
- Receives systematic instruction and fundamentals of technology
- Danger of sense of inadequacy and inferiority if child despairs of tools, skills, and status among peers
- Socially decisive age
- No dominant zone or mode

Stage 5. Identity versus Role Diffusion
(11 years through end of adolescence)
- Struggle to develop ego identity (sense of inner sameness and continuity)
- Preoccupation with appearance, hero worship, ideology
- Group identity (with peers) develops
- Danger of role confusion, doubts about sexual and vocational identity
- Psychosexual moratorium, stage between morality learned by the child and the ethics developed by the adult
- No dominant zone or mode

Stage 6. Intimacy versus Isolation
(21 to 40 years)
- Tasks are to love and to work
- Intimacy is characterized by self-abandonment, mutuality of sexual orgasm, intense friendship, attachments that are lifelong
- Isolation is marked by separation from others and view that others are dangerous
- General sense of productivity in this stage
- No dominant zone or mode

Stage 7. Generativity versus Stagnation
(40 to 65 years)
- Generativity includes raising children, guiding new generation, creativity, altruism
- Stagnation not prevented by having a child; parent must provide nurturance and love
- Self-concern, isolation, and absence of intimacy are characteristic of stagnation
- No dominant zone or mode

Stage 8. Integrity versus Despair
(over 65 years)
- Integrity is a sense of satisfaction that life has been productive and worthwhile
- Despair is a loss of hope that produces misanthropy and disgust
- Persons in the state of despair are fearful of death
- An acceptance of one's place in the life cycle is characteristic of integrity

Erikson, it is the time for children either to retain feces (holding in) or to eliminate feces (letting go); both behaviors have an effect on the mother.

Children in the second and third years of life learn to walk alone, to feed themselves, to control the anal sphincter, and to talk. Muscular maturation sets the tone for this stage of development. When parents permit children to function with some autonomy and are supportive without being overprotective, toddlers gain self-confidence and feel that they can control themselves and their world. But if toddlers are punished for being autonomous or are overcontrolled, they feel angry and ashamed. If parents show approval when children show self-control, children's self-esteem is enhanced, and a sense of pride develops. Parental overcontrol or children's loss of self-control, also called muscular and anal impotence by Erikson, produces a sense of doubt and shame. Shame implies that a child is looked down on by the outside world. It exploits children's sense of being small as they stand upright for the first time. Feeling small, children are easily shamed by poor parenting experiences.

Stage 3: Initiative Versus Guilt (3 to 5 Years). This stage corresponds to Freud's phallic-oedipal phase. Children's growing sense of sexual curiosity is manifested by engaging in group sex play or touching their own genitalia or those of a peer. If parents do not make an issue of these childhood impulses (Erikson gives this example: "If you touch it, the doctor will cut it off"), the impulses are eventually repressed and reappear during adolescence as part of puberty. If parents make too much of the impulses, children may become sexually inhibited.

As children approach the end of the third year, they are able to initiate both motor and intellectual activities. Whether initiative is reinforced depends on how much physical freedom children are given and on how well their intellectual curiosity is satisfied. If toddlers are made to feel inadequate about their behavior or interests, they may emerge from this period with a sense of guilt about self-initiative activity. Conflicts over initiative can prevent developing children from experiencing their full potential and can interfere with their sense of ambition, which develops during this stage.

Children are able to move independently and vigorously by the end of this stage. By playing with peers, they learn how to interact with others. If aggressive fantasies have been managed properly (neither punished nor encouraged), children develop a sense of initiative and ambition.

At the end of the stage of initiative versus guilt, a child's conscience (Freud's superego) is established. Children learn not only that there are limits to their behavioral repertoire (for example, that a boy cannot sleep with his mother or murder his father) but also that aggressive impulses can be expressed in constructive ways, such as healthy competition, playing games, and using toys. The development of a conscience sets the tone for the moral sense of right and wrong. Excessive punishment, however, can restrict children's imagination and initiative. Children who develop too strong a superego, one with an all-or-nothing quality, may insist as adults that others adhere to their moral code, and, therefore, may become dangers to themselves and others. If the crisis of initiative is successfully resolved, a sense of responsibility, dependability, and self-discipline develops.

Stage 4: Industry Versus Inferiority (6 to 11 Years). This stage is the school-age period, during which children begin to participate in an organized program of learning. It is equivalent to Freud's latency period, when biological drives are dormant and peer interaction prevails. In all cultures, children receive formal instruction at about the age of 6; in Western culture, children learn to be literate and technical. In other societies, learning may involve becoming familiar with tools and weapons or learning to prepare food.

Industry, the ability to work and acquire adult skills, is the keynote of the stage. Children learn that they are able to make things and, most important, able to master and complete a task. When too great an emphasis is placed on rules, regulations, shoulds, or oughts, children develop a sense of duty at the expense of a natural desire to work. Productive children learn the pleasure of work completion and the pride of doing something well.

A sense of inadequacy and inferiority, the potential negative outcome of this stage, results from several sources: Children may be discriminated against at school; children may be told that they are inferior; children may be overprotected at home or excessively dependent on the emotional support of their families; children may compare themselves unfavorably with the same-sex parent. Good teachers and good parents who encourage children to value diligence and productivity and to persevere in difficult enterprises are bulwarks against a sense of inferiority. Whereas Freud placed most of the blame or credit for a child's development squarely on the shoulders of the parents, Erikson emphasized that sensitive social situations may counteract nonsupportive parents. Conversely, a school environment that denigrates or discourages children can diminish their self-esteem, even if their parents reward their industriousness at home.

Stage 5: Identity Versus Role Diffusion (11 Years Through End of Adolescence). Developing a sense of identity is the main task of this period, which coincides with puberty and adolescence. Identity is described as the characteristics that establish who people are and where they are going. Healthy identity is built on success in passing through earlier stages. Children's success in attaining trust, autonomy, initiative, and industry has much to do with their developing a sense of identity. Identifying with either healthy parents or parent surrogates facilitates the process.

ESTABLISHING IDENTITY. Identity implies a sense of inner solidarity with the ideas and values of a social group. Adolescents live in a psychosocial moratorium between childhood and adulthood, a time during which they test various roles. They may make several false starts before deciding on an occupation; they may drop out of school, to return at a later date to complete a course of study. Moral values may change, but eventually, an ethical system is consolidated into a coherent organizational framework.

IDENTITY CRISIS. An identity crisis occurs at the end of adolescence. Erikson calls the crisis normative because it is a normal event. Failure to negotiate this stage leaves adolescents without a solid identity; they suffer from identify diffusion or role confusion, characterized by not having a sense of self and by confusion about their place in the world. Role confusion may manifest itself in such behavioral abnormalities as running away, criminality, and overt psychosis. Problems in gender identity and sexual role may manifest at this time. Adolescents may defend against role diffusion by joining cliques or cults or by identifying with folk heroes.

Stage 6: Intimacy Versus Self-Absorption or Isolation (21 to 40 Years). This period extends from late adolescence through early middle age. Erikson pointed out that a major psychosocial conflict can arise during this stage and that, as in previous stages, success or failure depends on how well the groundwork has been laid in earlier periods and on how young adults interact with the environment. The intimacy of sexual relations, friendships, and other deep associations are not frightening to people with resolved identity crises. In contrast, people who reach the adult years in a state of continued role confusion cannot become involved in intense and long-term relationships. Without a friend, significant-other, or a partner in marriage, a person may become self-absorbed and self-indulgent; as a result, a sense of isolation may grow to dangerous proportions.

In true intimacy, there is mutuality, a quality reminiscent of the first stage of life. When a child achieves initiative in genitality, the sensual pleasure of childhood merges with the idea of genital orgasm, and the young adult is able to make and share love with another person. Through the crisis of intimacy versus isolation, people transcend the exclusivity of earlier dependencies and establish a mutuality with an extended and diverse social group.

Erikson quoted Freud's view that normal people must be able to love and work (*lieben und arbeiten*). Erikson believed that meaningful work, procreation, and recreation within a loving relationship represent utopia.

Stage 7: Generativity Versus Stagnation (40 to 65 Years). During the decades of the middle years of life, adults choose between generativity and stagnation. Generativity not only concerns a person's having or raising children, but also includes a vital interest outside the home in establishing and guiding the oncoming generation or in improving society. Childless people can be generative when they develop a sense of altruism and creativity. Most people, if able, want to continue their personalities and energies in the production and care of offspring. Wanting or having children, however, does not ensure generativity. Parents need to have achieved successful identities themselves to be truly generative.

Adults who have no interest in guiding or establishing the oncoming generation are likely to look obsessively for intimacy that is not truly intimate. Such people may marry and even produce children but only within a cocoon of self-concern and isolation. They become preoccupied with and pamper themselves as if they themselves were the children. Indeed, parents who do not truly believe that life in a given society is worthwhile may find that their children absorb this message only too well, the result being a lack of grandchildren.

Stagnation is a barren state. The inability to transcend the lack of creativity is dangerous because people are unable to accept the eventuality of not being and the idea that death is inescapably a part of life.

Stage 8: Integrity Versus Despair and Isolation (Over 65 Years). Old age is Erik Erikson's eighth stage of the life cycle. The stage is described as the conflict between integrity (the sense of satisfaction that a person feels in reflecting on a life productively lived) and despair (the sense that life has had little purpose or meaning). Late adulthood can be a period of contentment—a time to enjoy grandchildren, to contemplate life's major efforts, and perhaps to see personal accomplishments being put to good use by the next generation. Integrity allows people to accept their place in the life cycle and to realize that life is each person's responsibility. People accept who their parents are or were and understand how they lived their lives. Those who are misanthropic or otherwise contemptuous of people, those who lack the conviction that life has been meaningful and that they have made a contribution, either by producing happy children or by giving to the next generation, fear death and have a sense of despair or disgust.

Erikson recently wrote about the problem of those over age 85 who must balance autonomy with the real need for help (for example, physical and economic assistance). People must recognize that growing old requires active preparation, which must begin at an earlier stage of life. Because society is not yet prepared to meet the needs of very old people, a great responsibility remains with the individual. In a concluding remark about this stage in *Childhood and Society,* Erikson wrote the following: ''Healthy children will not fear life if their parents have integrity enough not to fear death.''

PSYCHOPATHOLOGY

Each stage of the life cycle has its own psychopathological outcome if it is not mastered successfully.

Basic Trust

An impairment of basic trust leads to basic mistrust. In infants, social trust is characterized by ease of feeding, depth of sleep, smiling, and general physiological homeostasis. Prolonged separation during infancy can lead to hospitalism or anaclitic depression (see Chapter 4, Section 4.2). In later life, this lack of trust may be manifested by dysthymic disorder, a depressive disorder, or a sense of hopelessness. People who develop and rely on the defense of projection—in which, according to Erikson, ''we endow significant people with the evil which actually is in us''—experienced a sense of social mistrust in the first years of life and are likely to develop paranoid or delusional disorders. Basic mistrust is a major contribution to the development of schizoid personality disorder and, in most severe cases, to the development of schizophrenia. Substance-related disorders can also be traced to social mistrust; substance-dependent personalities have strong oral-dependency needs and use chemical substances to satisfy themselves because of their belief that human beings are unreliable and, at worst, dangerous. If not nurtured properly, infants may feel empty, starved not just for food but also for sensual and visual stimulation. They may become, as adults, seekers after stimulating thrills that do not involve intimacy and that help ward off feelings of depression.

Autonomy

The stage in which children attempt to develop into autonomous beings is often called the *terrible 2s,* referring to toddlers' willfulness at this period of development. If shame and doubt dominate over autonomy, compulsive doubting may occur. The inflexibility of the obsessive personality also results from an overabundance of doubt. Too rigorous toilet training, commonplace in today's society, which requires a clean, punctual, and deodorized body, can produce an overly compulsive personality that is stingy, meticulous, and selfish. Known as anal personalities, such people are parsimonious, punctual, and perfectionistic (the three Ps).

Too much shaming causes children to feel evil or dirty and may pave the way for delinquent behavior. In effect, children say, ''If that's what they think of me, that's the way I'll behave.'' Paranoid personalities feel that others are trying to control them, a feeling that may have its origin during the stage of autonomy versus shame and doubt. When coupled with mistrust, the seeds are planted for persecutory delusions. Impulsive disorder may be explained as a person's refusing to be inhibited or controlled.

Initiative

Erikson stated: ''In pathology, the conflict over initiative is expressed either in hysterical denial, which causes the repression of the wish or the abrogation of its executive organ by paralysis or impotence; or in overcompensatory showing off, in which the scared individual, so eager to 'duck,' instead 'sticks his neck out.' '' In the past, hysteria was the usual form of pathological regression in this area, but a plunge into psychosomatic disease is now common.

Excessive guilt may lead to a variety of conditions, such as generalized anxiety disorder and phobias. Patients feel guilty because of normal impulses, and they repress these impulses, with resulting symptom formation. Punishments or severe prohibitions occurring during the stage of initiative versus guilt can produce sexual inhibitions. Conversion disorder or specific phobia may result when the oedipal conflict is not resolved. As sexual fantasies are accepted as unrealizable, children may punish themselves for these fantasies by fearing harm to their genitals. Under the brutal assault of the developing superego, they may repress their wishes and begin to deny them. If this pattern is carried forward, paralysis, inhibition, or impotence can result. Sometimes, in fear of not being able to live up to what others expect, children may turn to psychosomatic disease.

Industry

Erikson described industry as a "sense of being able to make things and make them well and even perfectly." When children's efforts are thwarted, they are made to feel that personal goals cannot be accomplished or are not worthwhile, and a sense of inferiority develops. In adults, this sense of inferiority can result in severe work inhibitions and a character structure marked by feelings of inadequacy. For some people, the feelings may result in a compensatory drive for money, power, and prestige. Work can become the main focus of life, at the expense of intimacy.

Identity

Many disorders of adolescence can be traced to identity confusion. The danger is role diffusion. Erikson stated:

> Where this is based on a strong previous doubt as to one's sexual identity, delinquent and outright psychotic incidents are not uncommon. If diagnosed and treated correctly, those incidents do not have the same fatal significance that they have at other ages. It is primarily the inability to settle on an occupational identity that disturbs young people. Keeping themselves together, they temporarily overidentify, to the point of apparent complete loss of identity, with the heroes of cliques and crowds.

Other disorders during the stage of identity versus role diffusion include conduct disorder, disruptive behavior disorder, gender identity disorder, schizophreniform disorder, and other psychotic disorders. The ability to leave home and live independently is an important task during this period. An inability to separate from the parent and prolonged dependence may occur.

Intimacy

The successful formation of a stable marriage and family depends on the capacity to become intimate. The years of early adulthood are crucial for deciding whether to get married and to whom. Gender identity determines object choice, either heterosexual or homosexual, but making an intimate connection with another person is a major task. People with schizoid personality disorder remain isolated from others because of fear, suspicion, the inability to take risks, or the lack of a capacity to love.

Generativity

From about 40 to 65 years, the period of middle adulthood, specific disorders are less clearly defined than in the other stages described by Erikson. People who are middle aged show a higher incidence of depression than do younger adults, a finding that may be related to middle-aged people's disappointments and failed expectations as they review the past, consider their lives, and contemplate the future. The increased use of alcohol and other psychoactive substances also occurs during this time.

Integrity

Anxiety disorders often develop in older people. In Erikson's formulation, this development may be related to people's looking back on their lives with a sense of panic. Time has run out, and chances are used up. The decline in physical functions can contribute to psychosomatic illness, hypochondriasis, and depression. The suicide rate is highest over the age of 65. People facing dying and death may find it intolerable not to have been generative or able to make significant attachments in life. Integrity, for Erikson, is characterized by an acceptance of life. Without acceptance, people feel despair and hopelessness that can result in severe depressive disorders.

TREATMENT

Although no independent eriksonian psychoanalytic school exists in the same way as do freudian and jungian schools, Erikson made many important contributions to the therapeutic process. Among his most important contributions is his belief that establishing a state of trust between doctor and patient is the basic requirement for successful therapy. When psychopathology stems from basic mistrust (for example, depression), a patient must re-establish trust with the therapist, whose task, like that of the good mother, is to be sensitive to the patient's needs. The therapist must have a sense of personal trustworthiness that can be transmitted to the patient.

Techniques

For Erikson, a psychoanalyst is not a blank slate in the therapeutic process, as he or she commonly is in freudian psychoanalysis. To the contrary, effective therapy requires that therapists actively convey to patients the belief that they are understood. This is done not only through empathetic listening but also by verbal assurances, which enable a positive transference, built on mutual trust to develop.

Beginning as an analyst for children, Erikson tried to provide this mutuality and trust while he observed children recreating their own worlds by structuring dolls, blocks, vehicles, and miniature furniture into the dramatic situations that were bothering them. Then Erikson correlated his observations with statements by the children and their family members. He began the treatment of a child only after eating an evening meal with the entire family, and his therapy was usually conducted with much cooperation from the family. After each regressive episode in the treatment of a schizophrenic child, for instance, Erikson discussed with every member of the family what had been going on with them before the episode. Only when he was thoroughly satisfied that he had identified the problem did treatment begin. Erikson sometimes provided corrective information to the child—for instance, telling a boy who could not release his feces and had made himself ill from constipation that food is not an unborn infant.

Erikson often turned to play, which, along with specific recommendations to parents, proved fruitful as a treatment modality. Play, for Erikson, is diagnostically revealing and thus helpful for a therapist who seeks to promote a cure, but it is also curative in its own right. Play is a function of the ego and gives children a chance to synchronize social and bodily processes with the self. Children playing with blocks or adults playing out an imagined dramatic situation can manipulate the environment and develop the sense of control that the ego needs. Play therapy is not the same for children and adults, however. Children create models in an effort to gain control of reality; they look ahead to new areas of mastery. Adults use play to correct the past and to redeem their failures.

Mutuality, which is important in Erikson's system of health, is also vital to a cure. Erikson applauded Freud for the moral choice of abandoning hypnosis, as hypnosis heightens the demarcation between the healer and the sick and heightens the inequality that Erikson compares to the inequality of child and adult. Erikson urged that the relationship of the healer to the sick person be one of equals "in which the observer who has learned to observe himself teaches the observed to become self-observant."

Goals

Erikson discussed four dimensions of the psychoanalyst's job. The patient's desire to be cured and the analyst's desire to cure is the first dimension. There is mutuality in that patient and therapist are motivated by cure, and there is a division of labor. The goal is always to help the patient's ego get stronger and cure itself. The second dimension Erikson called objectivity-participation. Therapists must keep their minds open. "Neuroses change," wrote Erikson. New generalizations must be made and arranged in new configurations. The third dimension runs along the axis of knowledge-participation. The therapist "applies selected insights to more strictly experimental approaches." The fourth dimension is tolerance-indignation. Erikson stated: "Identities based on Talmudic argument, on messianic zeal, on punitive orthodoxy, on faddist sensationalism, on professional and social ambition" are harmful and tend to control patients. Control widens the gap of inequality between the doctor and the patient and makes the realization of the recurrent idea in Erikson's thought—mutuality—difficult.

According to Erikson, therapists have the opportunity to work through past unresolved conflicts in the therapeutic relationship. Erikson encouraged therapists not to shy away from guiding patients; he believes that therapists must offer patients both prohibitions and permissions. Nor should therapists be so engrossed in patients' past life experiences that current conflicts are overlooked.

The goal of therapy is to recognize how patients have passed through the various stages of the life cycle and how the various crises in each stage have or have not been mastered. Equally important, future stages and crises must be anticipated, so that they can be negotiated and mastered appropriately. Unlike Freud, Erikson does not believe that the personality is so inflexible that change cannot occur in middle and late adulthood. For Erikson, psychological growth and development occur throughout the entire span of the life cycle.

References

Coles R: *Erik Erikson: The Growth of His Work.* Little, Brown, Boston, 1970.

Erikson E: *Childhood and Society.* Norton, New York, 1950.

Erikson E: The dream specimen of psychoanalysis. J Am Psychoanal Assoc *2:* 5, 1954.

Erikson E: The first psychoanalyst. Yale Rev *46:* 40, 1956.

Erikson E: Freud's "The Origin of Psychoanalysis." Int J Psychoanal *36:* 1, 1995.

Erikson E: *Gandhi's Truth.* Norton, New York, 1969.

Erikson E: Hitler's imagery and German youth. Psychiatry *5:* 475, 1942.

Erikson E: *Identity and the Life Cycle.* Norton, New York, 1980.

Erikson E: *Identity: Youth and Crisis.* Norton, New York, 1968.

Erikson E: *Insight and Responsibility.* Norton, New York, 1964.

Erikson E: *Life History and the Historical Moment.* Norton, New York, 1975.

Erikson E: Observations on Sioux education. J Psychol *7:* 101, 1939.

Erikson E: The problem of ego identity. Psychol Issues *1:* 22, 1959.

Erikson E: *Young Man Luther.* Norton, New York, 1962.

Erikson E, Erikson J, Kivnik H: *Vital Involvement in Old Age.* Norton, New York, 1986.

Evans R: *Dialogue with Erik Erikson.* Harper & Row, New York, 1967.

Ginsburg HJ: Childhood injuries and Erikson's psychosocial stages. Soc Behav Pers *20:* 95, 1992.

Schein S, editor: *Erik Erikson: A Way of Looking at Things.* Norton, New York, 1987.

7 Clinical Examination of the Psychiatric Patient

▲ 7.1 Psychiatric Interview, History, and Mental Status Examination

INTERVIEW OF PSYCHIATRIC PATIENT

To formulate diagnoses, psychiatrists conduct interviews in which they explore the factors—genetic, temperamental, biological, developmental, social, and psychological—that have influenced their patients. In a successful interview, a psychiatrist communicates empathy, respect, competence, and interest to the patient and thus creates the atmosphere of trust that encourages the patient to talk honestly about his or her innermost feelings and thoughts. Psychiatrists who have developed their interviewing skills and techniques give patients the chance to reveal the signs and symptoms that make up the potentially definable and treatable syndromes.

Some techniques can be used in any interview; other techniques are tailored for specific patients. Psychiatrists must be prepared to treat a range of patients—from those who speak clearly and articulately and are easy to engage to those whose thoughts are disordered to those who are paranoid, respond to internal stimuli, or are severely disorganized. Clinicians whose interviewing techniques match the challenges of each patient and who thereby elicit the necessary histories will make accurate, reliable diagnoses. These psychiatrists will be able to treat their patients effectively—whether with medications, environmental manipulations, or psychodynamic psychotherapy.

Nancy Andreasen and Donald Black have listed 11 techniques common to most psychiatric interview situations (Table 7.1–1).

Time Management

The initial consultation lasts for 30 minutes to 1 hour, depending on the circumstances. Interviews with patients who are psychotic or medically ill are brief because patients may find the interview stressful; when a long interview is necessary, it may be carried out in the emergency room. Second visits and ongoing therapeutic interviews also vary in length. The American Board of Psychiatry and Neurology, in its clinical oral examination in psychiatry, allows 30 minutes for a psychiatric examination.

Patients' management of appointment times reveals important aspects of personality and coping. Most often, patients arrive a few minutes before their appointments. An anxious patient may arrive as much as 30 minutes early. When a patient arrives very early, the clinician may want to explore the reasons. The patient who arrives significantly late for an appointment poses potential questions. The first time a patient is late, the clinician may listen to the explanation offered and respond sympathetically if the lateness is due to circumstances beyond the patient's control. A patient who states, ''I forgot all about the appointment,'' however, is offering a clue that something about going to the doctor makes the patient anxious or uncomfortable. This reaction needs to be explored further. The psychiatrist may ask, ''Did you feel reluctant to come in today?'' If the answer is, ''Yes,'' the psychiatrist can begin to explore the possible reasons for the patient's reluctance. If the answer is, ''No,'' it is probably best to drop the direct questioning about the lateness and just listen to the patient. By listening carefully, the psychiatrist can usually detect themes that the patient may not recognize. These themes can then be explored by both the patient and the psychiatrist in an attempt to understand better what the patient is experiencing.

A psychiatrist's handling of time is also an important factor in the interview. Carelessness about time indicates a lack of concern for the patient. If a psychiatrist is unavoidably detained for an interview, it is appropriate to express regret at having kept the patient waiting.

Arrangement of Seating

The arrangement of chairs in the psychiatrist's office affects the interview. Both chairs should be of approximately equal height, so that neither person looks down on the other. Most psychiatrists think that it is desirable to place the chairs without any furniture between the clinician and the patient. If the room contains several chairs, the psychiatrist indicates his or her own chair and then allows the patient to choose the chair in which he or she will feel most comfortable.

If the patient being interviewed is potentially dangerous, the door to the interview room should be left open. The psychiatrist should sit closest to the open door, with nothing obstructing the space from the clinician to the door; if necessary,

Table 7.1–1
Common Interview Techniques

1. Establish rapport as early in the interview as possible.
2. Determine the patient's chief complaint.
3. Use the chief complaint to develop a provisional differential diagnosis.
4. Rule the various diagnostic possibilities out or in by using focused and detailed questions.
5. Follow up on vague or obscure replies with enough persistence to accurately determine the answer to the question.
6. Let the patient talk freely enough to observe how tightly the thoughts are connected.
7. Use a mixture of open-ended and closed-ended questions.
8. Don't be afraid to ask about topics that you or the patient may find difficult or embarrassing.
9. Ask about suicidal thoughts.
10. Give the patient a chance to ask questions at the end of the interview.
11. Conclude the initial interview by conveying a sense of confidence and, if possible, of hope.

Reprinted with permission from Andreasen NC, Black DW: *Introductory Textbook of Psychiatry*. American Psychiatric Association Press, Washington, 1991.

a third person should be asked to stand outside or even inside the room, to be available if there is trouble.

Arrangement of Office

A psychiatrist can never remain entirely unknown to patients, and his or her office can tell patients a good deal about the doctor's personality. The colors in the office, paintings ands diplomas on the wall, the furniture, plants, books, and personal photographs—all describe the psychiatrist in ways that are not directly verbalized. Patients often have reactions to their doctors' offices that may or may not be distortions, and carefully listening to any comments can help a psychiatrist understand the patient. Studies have shown that patients respond more positively to male physicians who wear jackets and ties than to those who do not. No studies have been done on the dress of female physicians, but, by extrapolation, a positive response would probably be elicited by professional attire.

Taking of Notes

For legal and medical reasons, an adequate written record of each patient's treatment must be maintained. The patient's record also aids the psychiatrist's memory. Each clinician must establish a system of record keeping and decide which information to record. Many psychiatrists make complete notes during the first few sessions while eliciting historical data. Afterward, most psychiatrists record only new historical information, important events in the patient's life, medications prescribed, dreams, and general comments about the patient's progress. Some psychiatrists maintain detailed process notes (verbatim record of a session) for specific patients by writing out immediately after a session as much of the session as they can remember. Process notes make it much easier to determine trends in the treatment (with regard to transference and countertransference issues) and to go back over the session to pick up ideas that may have been missed. Process notes are also helpful if a psychiatrist is working with a supervisor or a consultant who needs an accurate presentation of a particular session.

Most psychiatrists do not recommend taking extensive notes during a session; writing can cut down on the ability to listen. Some patients, however, may express resentment if a psychiatrist does not write notes during an interview; they may fear that their comments were not important enough to record or that the psychiatrist was not interested in them. As not taking notes during a session presumably has no relation to the psychiatrist's listening, this feeling on a patient's part can be further explored to understand the fear of not being taken seriously.

Follow-up Interviews

Interviews after the initial one allow patients to correct any misinformation provided in the first meeting. It is often helpful to start the second interview by asking a patient whether he or she has thought about the first interview and what were the reactions to the experience. Another variation is to say: "Frequently, people think of additional things they wanted to discuss after they leave. What thoughts have you had?"

Psychiatrists often learn something of value when they ask patients whether they have discussed the interview with anyone else. If the patient has done so, the details of the conversation and the person with whom the patient spoke are enlightening. There are no set rules about which topics are best deferred until the second interview. In general, as patients' comfort and familiarity with the psychiatrist increase, they become increasingly able to reveal the intimate details of their lives.

Interviewing Variations

The manner in which an interview is conducted—the specific techniques and structure—varies depending on the setting in which the interview takes place, the purpose of the interview, and the strengths, weaknesses, and diagnosis of the particular patient. Psychiatrists are trained to be flexible in modifying their interview style to fit the existing situation. Patients with varying psychiatric diagnoses differ in their capacities to participate in an interview and differ in the challenges they present to the interviewing psychiatrist. Certain consistent themes are often observed in interviews with patients who have the same diagnosis, although, even with the same diagnosis, patients may require subtly different interview strategies.

Depressed and Potentially Suicidal Patients. Depressed patients are often unable to provide an adequate account of their illness spontaneously because of such factors as psychomotor retardation and hopelessness. A psychiatrist must be prepared to ask a depressed person specifically about history and symptoms related to depression, including questions about suicidal ideation, which the patient may not initially volunteer. Another reason for being specific when questioning a depressed patient is that the patient may not realize that such symptoms as waking during the night or increased somatic complaints are related to depressive disorders.

FEELINGS OF HOPELESSNESS. One of the most difficult aspects of dealing with people who are depressed is experiencing their hopelessness. Many severely depressed patients believe that their current feelings will continue indefinitely and that there is no hope. Psychiatrists must be careful not to reassure such patients prematurely that everything is going to be fine; patients most likely experience this reassurance as an indication that the psychiatrist does not understand the degree of their pain. A reasonable approach is for the psychiatrist to indicate that he or she is aware how bad their patients are feeling, that help is certainly possible, and that it is understandable that patients do not always believe that they can be helped. Furthermore, the psychiatrist must make it clear that he or she is committed to helping patients feel better, that all specific and effective pharmacological and psychological tools will be used, and that patients will not be abandoned during what may be a lengthy period of recovery.

Up to this point, everything patients have done to relieve their distress has not worked, and, by the time the psychiatrist interviews them, they may be desperate. Depressed patients may be relieved when the psychiatrist truthfully tells them that their depression can be treated, but that it may take a little work and time for the psychiatrist to find the most effective method of treating their specific depressive disorder. This message conveys not a false sense of reassurance, which could make depressed patients feel even more depressed than before, but a sense that the psychiatrist is committed to understanding who the patient is and what treatment works most quickly and most effectively. Every depressed person hopes, consciously or unconsciously, that the psychiatrist will magically and immediately produce a cure, but most people are willing to proceed along a therapeutic path, even when one part of them believes there is no hope. The interviewing psychiatrist must be careful not to promise that a specific treatment is the answer. If the recommended treatment does not work, the disappointment may eliminate the patient's last hope.

SUICIDE. Of special concern when interviewing depressed patients is the potential for suicide. Being mindful of the possibility of suicide is imperative when interviewing any depressed patient, even if there is no apparent suicidal risk. The psychiatrist must inquire in some detail about the presence of suicidal thoughts. The psychiatrist should ask specifically, "Are you suicidal now, or do you have plans to take your own life?" A suicide note, a family history of suicide, or previous suicidal behavior on the part of the patient increases the risk for suicide. Evidence of impulsivity or of pervasive pessimism about the future also places patients at risk.

When a psychiatrist decides that a patient is in imminent risk for suicidal behavior, the patient must be hospitalized or otherwise protected. A difficult situation arises when there does not seem to be an immediate risk but the potential for suicide is present as long as the patient remains depressed. If the patient is not hospitalized immediately, the psychiatrist should insist that the patient promise to call at any time suicidal pressure mounts. In such situations, the patient commonly has a crisis after midnight and calls the psychiatrist, who should assure the patient that he or she is reachable at all times. Having determined that the psychiatrist is, in fact, available, the patient is often reassured and can control the impulses and use regularly scheduled sessions for exploration of the suicidal feelings.

Aggressive Patients. Potentially aggressive or violent patients should be approached with some of the same attitudes and techniques used with suicidal patients. For example, a psychiatrist's indicating that he or she is capable of dealing with the patient's capacity for violence is important. This message conveys that the physician is accustomed to the unpleasant, as well as the pleasant, in life, and that part of his or her job is to help patients stay in control and to make sure that neither the patient nor anyone else gets hurt.

A psychiatrist frequently encounters a violent patient in a hospital setting. For example, when police bring a patient into an emergency room, the patient is often in some type of physical restraint (such as handcuffs). The psychiatrist must establish whether effective verbal contact can be made with the patient or whether the patient's sense of reality is so impaired that effective interviewing is impossible. If impaired reality testing is an issue, the psychiatrist may have to medicate the patient before any attempt at interviewing can begin. If reality testing is not severely impaired, however, one of the first questions to address is whether it is safe to remove the physical restraints from the patient. This question can be addressed in a straightforward manner, expressing concern for the safety of the patient and other persons in the surrounding area. Many psychiatrists opt to leave restraints on the patient until some history has been obtained and some rapport established. Should a decision be made to undo the restraints, the psychiatrist must carefully monitor what is happening to the patient as the restraints are loosened. If the patient remains calm and seems to be relieved, the process of removing the restraints can continue. If the patient does or says anything that indicates that the removal of the restraints is leading to increased agitation, the decision to remove them should be reassessed immediately.

With or without restraints, a violent patient should not be interviewed alone; at least one other person should always be present, and in some situations the other person should be a security guard or a police officer. Other precautions include leaving the interview room's door open and sitting between the patient and the door, so that the interviewer has unrestricted access to an exit should it become necessary. The psychiatrist must make it clear, in a firm but nonangry manner, that the patient may say or feel anything but is not free to act in a violent way. This statement must be backed up by a unified, calm, consistent staff presence that the patient understands is there to lend support in efforts to maintain control, by physical means if necessary.

A 35-year-old man who had been jailed repeatedly for assaultive behavior appeared in an emergency room. He was intoxicated, edgy, and threatening, trying to provoke staff members into a fight, and asserting that he had previously injured several policemen and security guards in similar situations. His wife confirmed the history. Ushered into a seclusion room and sedated, he pounded on the walls, bruising his hands, until he fell asleep. The next morning, he was sheepish and apologetic and said that he could hardly remember the events of the previous night.

A 35-year-old schizoid man, who had been battered as a child, avoided intimacy with people, because he feared that he would be unable to relate well. He bought two dogs and hoped to teach himself to be socialized. To his horror he found that he became jealous when one dog paid attention to the other dog rather than to him; he sadistically beat the dog, while realizing that he was repeating the pattern of his father's abuse toward him. When beating the dog, he would imagine feeling the same sadistic rage that his father must have felt.

Confrontation with a violent patient is to be assiduously avoided, as is any behavior that could be construed as demeaning or disrespectful of the patient. Within the limits of safety, the interviewer should respect as much as possible the patient's need for space.

Specific questions that psychiatrists need to ask violent patients include those pertaining to their previous acts of violence and to violence experienced as a child. The psychiatrist should determine under what specific conditions the patient resorts to violence and should obtain corroboration about critical aspects of the patient's history from friends and family members. Table 7.1–2 summarizes the dos and don'ts of treating violent patients.

Interview of Delusional Patients. A patient's delusion should never be directly challenged. Delusions may be thought of as a patient's defensive and self-protective, albeit maladaptive, strategy against overwhelming anxiety, lowered self-esteem, and confusion. Challenging a delusion by insisting that it is untrue or impossible only increases a patient's anxiety and often leads the threatened patient to defend the belief ever more desperately. It is also inadvisable, however, to pretend to believe the patient's delusion. A psychiatrist can often help by indicating that he or she understands that the patient believes the delusion to be true but that the psychiatrist does not hold the same belief. It is probably most productive to focus on the feelings, fears, and hopes that underlie the delusional belief to understand the delusion's particular function. The more that patients feel that the psychiatrist respects, understands, and listens to them, the more likely they are to talk about themselves, not about the delusion.

Delusions may be excessively fixed, immutable, and chronic, or they may be subject to question and doubt by a patient and may last only a relatively brief time. A patient may or may not be influenced by the delusional beliefs and may be able to recognize their effects.

A man with chronic schizophrenia revealed the simple delusion that his ultimate mission in life was to raise the dead to herald the coming of a new age. He denied ever seeing signs in his environment that referred to his mission, nor did he have auditory hallucinations telling him about

Table 7.1–2
Dos and Don'ts of Treating Violent Patients

Do	Don't
Anticipate possible violence from hostile, threatening, agitated, restless, abusive patients or from those who lack control for any reason.	Don't ignore your gut feeling that a patient may be dangerous.
Heed your gut feeling. If you feel frightened or uneasy, discontinue the interview and get help.	Don't see angry, threatening, restless persons right away.
Summon as many security guards or orderlies as possible at the first sign of violence. Patients who see that you take them seriously often will not act out further. If they do, you will be prepared.	Don't compromise your ability to escape a dangerous situation. Don't sit behind a desk.
Ask if the patient is carrying a weapon. Weapons must be surrendered to security personnel. Never see an armed patient.	Don't antagonize the patient by responding angrily or being patronizing.
Offer help, food, medication. Bolster the patient by commenting on his or her strength and self-control.	Don't touch or startle the patient or approach quickly without warning.
If restraint becomes necessary, assign one team member each to the patient's head and to each extremity. Be humane but firm, and do not bargain. Search the patient for psychoactive substances and weapons.	Don't try to restrain a patient without sufficient backup.
If the patient refuses oral medication, offer an injection after a few moments. Be prepared to administer it if the patient continues to refuse.	Don't neglect looking for organic causes of violence.
Keep a close eye on patients who are sedated or restrained. Restrained patients should never be left alone.	Don't bargain with a violent person about the need for restraints, medication, or psychiatric admission.
Hospitalize patients who state their intention to harm anyone, refuse to answer questions about their intent to harm, are abusing alcohol or other substances, are psychotic, have a cognitive disorder, or refuse to cooperate with treatment.	Don't forget medicolegal concerns, such as full documentation of all interventions and the duty to warn and protect. If the patient is transferred, tell the admitting physician about any specific threats and victims.
Warn potential victims of threatened violence, and notify the appropriate protection agencies.	Don't overlook family and friends as important sources of information.
Follow up on any violent person, and document it in the chart.	

Reprinted with permission from Dwyer B, Weissberg M: Treating violent patients. Psychiatric Times p 11, December 1988.

it. The delusion persisted as an isolated psychotic symptom during long, quiescent phases of his disorder. The delusion also appeared during his schizophrenic exacerbations, at which times the patient had many other complicated and bizarre psychotic ideas. During the chronic phases of his disorder, the patient worked at low-level jobs and had a few ongoing but superficial relationships. The patient's behavior in no way revealed the presence of his delusion.

Delusions, as with most psychiatric symptoms, occur on a spectrum from severe to mild and must be evaluated for the degree of severity, fixedness, elaborateness, power to influence the patient's actions, and deviation from normal beliefs. Andreasen and Black have suggested some helpful methods for eliciting delusional beliefs from patients (Table 7.1–3).

Interview of Relatives. Interviews with family members of a patient can be both valuable and fraught with difficulties. For example, a spouse may be so closely identified with the patient that anxiety overwhelms the spouse's ability to provide coherent information. Family members may not realize that certain information is best provided by an observer and that other kinds of information may be obtained only from the patient; for example, family members may be able to describe the patient's social activity, but only the patient can describe what he or she is thinking and feeling. The psychiatrist must be highly sensitive to discussions with family members; if these discussions are not handled properly by the psychiatrist, the relationship between the patient and the clinician may break down.

Interviews with family members can be viewed from several perspectives. If a clinician's goal is to diagnose a disorder, then the more facts at his or her disposal, the easier it will be to formulate a diagnosis, prognosis, and treatment. From the dynamic or analytical viewpoint, however, a physician who sees patients' problems as largely influenced by interactions with important figures in their lives considers external reality as less important than the patients' own perceptions. In general, the more serious a patient's presenting situation (for example, major depressive disorder, suicidal ideation, or psychotic disorder), the more likely and perhaps the more appropriate it is for the psychiatrist to deal with family members.

One of the most important aspects related to talking with family members has to do with confidentiality. Ultimately, a physician must learn to elicit information and to offer hope to family members without revealing information about the patient that the patient does not want revealed. Betraying a confidence can make treating a patient impossible. If the issues concern suicidal or homicidal ideation, however, the patient must understand that such information cannot remain

Table 7.1–3
Methods for Eliciting Delusional Beliefs

Delusions	Questions
Persecutory delusions (eg, one is being followed, one's mail is being opened, one's home is bugged, one is being monitored by the government)	Have you had trouble getting along with people? Have you felt that people were against you? Has anyone been trying to harm you or plot against you?
Delusions of jealousy (eg, one's mate is having an affair)	Have you worried that your partner may be unfaithful? What evidence do you have?
Delusions of sin or guilt (eg, one has committed a terrible sin, one is responsible for an unpardonable act, one deserves to be punished)	Have you felt that you have done some terrible thing? Is anything bothering your conscience? What is it? Do you feel you deserve to be punished for it?
Grandiose delusions (eg, one is possessed of special powers, abilities, identities)	Do you have any special powers, talents, or abilities? Do you feel that you are going to achieve great things?
Somatic delusions (eg, one believes one's body is diseased, abnormal, or changed)	Is anything wrong with the way your body is working? Have you noticed any change in your appearance? What has caused it?
Ideas and delusions of reference (eg, one believes that insignificant remarks, statements, or events refer back to one or have some special meaning)	Have you walked into a room and thought people were talking about you or laughing at you? Have you seen things in magazines or on TV that refer to you or contain special meaning for you? Have you received special messages in other ways?
Thought broadcasting, thought insertion, and thought withdrawal	Have you heard your thoughts out loud, as if there were a voice outside your head? Have you felt that your thoughts were being broadcast so that others could hear them? Have you felt that thoughts were being put into your head by some outside source or person? Have you felt that your thoughts were being taken away by some outside source or person?

Reprinted with permission from Andreasen NC, Black D: *Introductory Textbook of Psychiatry,* American Psychiatric Association Press, Washington, 1991.

entirely confidential, for the protection of the patient and others.

THE PSYCHIATRIC HISTORY

The psychiatric history is the record of the patient's life; it allows a psychiatrist to understand who the patient is, where the patient has come from, and where the patient is likely to go in the future. The history is the patient's life story told to the psychiatrist in the patient's own words from his or her own point of view. Many times, the history also includes information about the patient obtained from other sources, such as a parent or a spouse. Obtaining a comprehensive history from a patient and, if necessary, from informed sources is essential to making a correct diagnosis and formulating a specific and effective treatment plan. A psychiatric history differs slightly from histories taken in medicine or surgery. In addition to gathering the concrete and factual data related to the chronology of symptom formation and to psychiatric and medical history, a psychiatrist strives to derive from the history the elusive picture of patients' individual personality characteristics, including both their strengths and their weaknesses. The psychiatric history provides insight into the nature of relationships with those closest to the patients and includes all the important people in their lives. A reasonably comprehensive picture of the patients' development, from the earliest formative years until the present, can usually be elicited.

The most important technique for obtaining a psychiatric history is to allow patients to tell their own stories in their own words in the order that they feel is most important. Skillful interviewers recognize the points, as patients relate their stories, at which they can introduce relevant questions about the areas described in the outline of the history and mental status examination.

The structure presented in this section is not intended as a rigid plan for interviewing a patient; it is intended as a guide for organizing the patient's history when it is written up. Several acceptable and standard formats for a psychiatric history are available; one such format is presented in Table 7.1–4.

Table 7.1–4
Outline of Psychiatric History

I. Identifying data
II. Chief complaint and problem
III. Present illness
    1. Onset
    2. Precipitating factors
IV. Past illnesses
    A. Psychiatric
    B. Medical
    C. Alcohol and other substance history
V. Personal history (anamnesis)
    A. Prenatal and perinatal
    B. Early childhood (through age 3)
    C. Middle childhood (ages 3–11)
    D. Late childhood (puberty through adolescence)
    E. Adulthood
        1. Occupational history
        2. Marital and relationship history
        3. Military history
        4. Educational history
        5. Religion
        6. Social activity
        7. Current living situation
        8. Legal history
    F. Sexual history
    G. Family history
    H. Fantasies and dreams

Identifying Data

The identifying data provide a succinct demographic summary of the patient by name, age, marital status, sex, occupation, language if other than English, ethnic background and religion insofar as they are pertinent, and current circumstances of living. The information can also include in what place or situation the current interview took place, the sources of the information, the reliability of the source, and whether the current disorder is the first episode for the patient. The psychiatrist should indicate whether the patient came in on his or her own, was referred by someone else, or was brought in by someone else. The identifying data are meant to provide a thumbnail sketch of potentially important patient characteristics that may affect diagnosis, prognosis, treatment, and compliance.

An example of the written report of the identifying data is as follows:

> Mr. J. Jones is a 25-year-old white, single Catholic man, currently unemployed and homeless, living in public shelters and on the street. The current interview occurred in the emergency room (ER) with the patient in four-point restraints in the presence of two clinical staff members and one police officer. It was the 10th such visit to the ER for Mr. Jones in the past year. The sources of information on Mr. Jones included the patient himself and the police officer who brought Mr. Jones to the ER. The police officer had witnessed the patient on the street and knew him from previous episodes.

Chief Complaint

The chief complaint, in the patient's own words, states why he or she has come or been brought in for help. It should be recorded even if the patient is unable to speak, and a description of the person who provided the information should be included. The patient's explanation, regardless of how bizarre or irrelevant it is, should be recorded verbatim in the section on the chief complaint. The other individuals present as sources of information can then give their versions of the presenting events in the section on the history of the present illness.

Examples of chief complaints follow:

"I was feeling very depressed and thinking about killing myself." "Every car outside my house has a license plate number that is sending me hidden messages concerning a plot to kill the President." "There's nothing wrong with me; it's her that's crazy." The patient was mute.

History of Present Illness

This part of the psychiatric history provides a comprehensive and chronological picture of the events leading up to the current moment in the patient's life. This part of the history is probably the most helpful in making a diagnosis: When was the onset of the current episode, and what were the immediate precipitating events or triggers? An understanding of the history of the present illness helps answer the question, "Why now?" Why did the patient come to the doctor at this time? What were the patient's life circumstances at the onset of the symptoms or behavioral changes, and how did they affect the patient so that the presenting disorder became manifest? Knowing the previously well patient's personality also helps give perspective on the currently ill patient.

The evolution of the patient's symptoms should be determined and summarized in an organized and systematic way. Symptoms not present should also be delineated. The more detailed the history of the present illness, the more likely the clinician is to make an accurate diagnosis. What past precipitating events were part of the chain leading up to the immediate events? In what ways has the patient's illness affected his or her life activities (for example, work, important relationships)? What is the nature of the dysfunction (for example, details about changes in such factors as personality, memory, speech)? Are there psychophysiological symptoms? If so, they should be described in terms of location, intensity, and fluctuation. Any relation between physical and psychological symptoms should be noted. Evidence of secondary gain—the extent to which illness serves some additional purpose—should also be noted. A description of the patient's current anxieties, whether they are generalized and nonspecific (free floating) or are specifically related to particular situations, is helpful. How does the patient handle these anxieties? Frequently, a relatively open-ended question—such as, "How did this all begin?"—leads to an adequate unfolding of the history of the present illness. A well-organized patient is generally able to present a chronological account of the history, but a disorganized patient is difficult to interview, as the chronology of events is confused. In this case, contacting other informants, such as family members and friends, can be a valuable aid in clarifying the patient's story.

Past Illness

This section of the psychiatric history is a transition between the story of the present illness and the patient's personal history (anamnesis). Past episodes of both psychiatric and medical illnesses are described. Ideally, a detailed account of the patient's preexisting and underlying psychological and biological substrates is given at this point, and important clues and evidence of vulnerable areas in the patient's functioning are provided. The patient's symptoms, extent of incapacity, type of treatment received, names of hospitals, length of each illness, effects of previous treatments, and degree of compliance should all be explored and recorded chronologically. Particular attention should be paid to the first episode that signaled the onset of illness, because first episodes can often provide crucial data about precipitating events, diagnostic possibilities, and coping capabilities.

With regard to medical history, the psychiatrist should obtain a medical review of symptoms and note any major medical or surgical illnesses and major traumas, particularly those requiring hospitalization. Episodes of craniocerebral trauma, neurological illness, tumors, and seizure disorders are especially relevant to psychiatric histories, and so is a history of having tested positive for the human immunodeficiency virus (HIV) or of having acquired immune deficiency syndrome (AIDS). Specific questions need to be asked about the presence of a seizure disorder, episodes of loss of consciousness, changes in usual headache patterns, changes in vision, and episodes of confusion and disorientation. A history of infection with syphilis is critical and relevant.

Causes, complications, and treatment of any illness and the effects of the illness on the patient should be noted. Specific questions about psychosomatic disorders should be asked and noted. Included in this category are hay fever, rheumatoid arthritis, ulcerative colitis, asthma, hyperthyroidism, gastrointestinal upsets, recurrent colds, and skin conditions. All patients must be asked about alcohol and other substance use, including details about the quantity and frequency of use. It is often advisable to frame questions in the form of an assumption of use, such as, "How much alcohol would you say you drink in a day?" rather than "Do you drink?" The latter question may put the patient on the defensive, concerned about what the physician will think if the answer is yes. If the physician assumes that drinking is a fact, the patient is likely to feel comfortable admitting use.

Personal History (Anamnesis)

In addition to studying the patient's present illness and current life situation, the psychiatrist needs a thorough understanding of the patient's past and its relations to the present emotional problem. The anamnesis or personal history is usually divided into the major developmental period, late childhood, and adulthood. The predominant emotions associated with the different life periods (for example, painful, stressful, conflictual) should be noted. Depending on time and situation, the psychiatrist may go into detail with regard to each of those areas.

Prenatal and Perinatal History. The psychiatrist considers the nature of the home situation into which the patient was born and whether the patient was planned and wanted. Were there any problems with the mother's pregnancy and delivery? Was there any evidence of defect or injury at birth? What was the mother's emotional and physical state at the time of the patient's birth? Were there any maternal health problems during pregnancy? Was the mother abusing alcohol or other substances during her pregnancy?

Early Childhood (Birth Through Age 3 Years). The early childhood period consists of the first 3 years of the patient's life. The quality of the mother–child interaction during feeding and toilet training is important. It is frequently possible to learn whether the child presented problems in these areas. Early disturbances in sleep patterns and signs of unmet needs, such as head banging and body rocking, provide clues about possible maternal deprivation or developmental disability. In addition, the psychiatrist should obtain a history of human constancy during the first 3 years. Was there psychiatric or medical illness present in the parents that may have interfered with parent–child interactions? Did persons other than the mother care for the patient? Did the patient exhibit excessive problems at an early period with stranger anxiety or separation anxiety? The patient's siblings and the details of his or her relationship to them should be explored. The emerging personality of the child is also a topic of crucial importance. Was the child shy, restless, overactive, withdrawn, studious, outgoing, timid, athletic, friendly? The clinician should seek data about the child's ability to concentrate, to tolerate frustration, and to postpone gratification. The child's preference for active or passive roles in physical play should also be noted. What were the child's favorite games or toys? Did the child prefer to play alone, with others, or not at all? What is the patient's earliest memory? Were there any recurrent dreams or fantasies during this period? A summary of the important areas to be covered follows:

FEEDING HABITS. Breast fed or bottle fed, eating problems.

EARLY DEVELOPMENT. Walking, talking, teething, language development, motor development, signs of unmet needs, sleep pattern, object constancy, stranger anxiety, maternal deprivation, separation anxiety, other caretakers in the home.

TOILET TRAINING. Age, attitude of parents, feelings about it.

SYMPTOMS OF BEHAVIOR PROBLEMS. Thumb sucking, temper tantrums, tics, head bumping, rocking, night terrors, fears, bed wetting or bed soiling, nail biting, excessive masturbation.

PERSONALITY AS A CHILD. Shy, restless, overactive, withdrawn, persistent, outgoing, timid, athletic, friendly, patterns of play.

EARLY OR RECURRENT DREAMS OR FANTASIES.

Middle Childhood (Ages 3 to 11 Years).

In this section, the psychiatrist can address such important subjects as gender identification, punishments used in the home, and the people who provided the discipline and influenced early conscience formation. The psychiatrist must inquire about the patient's early school experiences, especially how the patient first tolerated being separated from his or her mother. Data about the patient's earliest friendships and personal relationships are valuable. The psychiatrist should identify and define the number and the closeness of the patient's friends, describe whether the patient took the role of a leader or a follower, and describe the patient's social popularity and participation in group or gang activities. Was the child able to cooperate with peers, to be fair, to understand and comply with rules, and to develop an early conscience? Early patterns of assertion, impulsiveness, aggression, passivity, anxiety, or antisocial behavior emerge in the context of school relationships. A history of the patient's learning to read and of the development of other intellectual and motor skills is important. A history of learning disabilities, their management, and their effects on the child are of particular significance. The presence of nightmares, phobias, bed wetting, fire setting, cruelty to animals, and excessive masturbation should also be explored.

Late Childhood (Puberty Through Adolescence).

During late childhood, people begin to develop independence from their parents through relationships with peers and in group activities. The psychiatrist should attempt to define the values of the patient's social groups and to determine who were the patient's idealized figures. This information provides useful clues about the patient's emerging idealized self-image.

It is helpful to explore the patient's school history, relationships with teachers, and favorite studies and interests, both in school and in extracurricular areas. The psychiatrist should ask about the patient's participation in sports and hobbies and inquire about any emotional or physical problems that may have first appeared during this phase. Examples of the types of questions that are commonly asked include the following: What was the patient's sense of personal identity? How extensive was the use of alcohol and other substances? Was the patient sexually active, and what was the quality of the sexual relationships? Was the patient interactive and involved with school and peers, or was he or she isolated, withdrawn, perceived as odd by others? Did the patient have a generally intact self-esteem, or was there evidence of excessive self-loathing? What was the patient's body image? Were there suicidal episodes? Were there problems in school, including excessive truancy? How did the patient use private time? What was the relationship with the parents? What were the feelings about the development of secondary sex characteristics? What was the response to menarche? What were the attitudes about dating, petting, crushes, parties, and sex games? One way to organize the diverse and large amount of information is to break late childhood into subsets of behavior (for example, social relationships, school history, cognitive and motor development, emotional and physical problems, and sexuality), as described next.

SOCIAL RELATIONSHIPS. Attitudes toward sibling(s) and playmates, number and closeness of friends, leader or follower, social popularity, participation in group or gang activities, idealized figures, patterns of aggression, passivity, anxiety, antisocial behavior.

SCHOOL HISTORY. How far the patient progressed, adjustment to school, relationships with teachers—teacher's pet versus rebel—favorite studies or interests, particular abilities or assets, extracurricular activities, sports, hobbies, relations of problems or symptoms to any social period.

COGNITIVE AND MOTOR DEVELOPMENT. Learning to read and other intellectual and motor skills, minimal cerebral dysfunctions, learning disabilities—their management and effects on the child.

EMOTIONAL AND PHYSICAL PROBLEMS. Nightmares, phobias, masturbation, bed wetting, running away, delinquency, smoking, alcohol or other substance use, anorexia, bulimia, weight problems, feelings of inferiority, depression, suicidal ideas and acts.

SEXUALITY. Early curiosity, infantile masturbation, sex play; acquisition of sexual knowledge, attitude of parents toward sex, sexual abuse; onset of puberty, feelings about it, kind of preparation, feelings about menstruation, development of secondary sex characteristics; adolescent sexual activity: crushes, parties, dating, petting, masturbation, nocturnal emissions, and attitudes toward them; attitudes toward opposite sex: timid, shy, aggressive, needed to impress, seductive, sexual conquests, anxiety; sexual practices: sexual problems, paraphilias, promiscuity; sexual orientation: homosexual experiences in both heterosexual and homosexual adolescents, gender identity issues, self-esteem.

Adulthood. **OCCUPATIONAL HISTORY.** The psychiatrist should describe the patient's choice of occupation, the requisite training and preparation, any work-related conflicts, and the long-term ambitions and goals. The interviewer should also explore the patient's feelings about his or her current job and relationships at work (with authorities, peers, and, if applicable, subordinates) and describe the job history (for example, number and duration of jobs, reasons for job changes, and changes in job status). What would the patient do for work if he or she could freely choose?

A 40-year-old physician in a successful general practice also had many business ventures in which he invested a great deal of the money he had earned from property development. The ventures frequently entangled him in legal disputes. He spent 12 to 14 hours in his medical office each day seeing patients, completed his charting and paperwork on weekends, and snatched odd moments to conduct complicated business transactions with his attorney. He was snappy and irritable with his family; he expected them to be at his beck and call and to notice his "self-sacrificing" on their behalf. Reducing his practice, taking on an associate, and limiting his business activities were all unacceptable to him.

MARITAL AND RELATIONSHIP HISTORY. In this section, the psychiatrist describes the history of each marriage, legal or common law. Significant relationships with persons with whom the patient has lived for a protracted period are also included. The story of the marriage or long-term relationship should give a description of the evolution of the relationship, including the age of the patient at the beginning of the marriage or the long-term relationship. The areas of agreement and disagreement—including the management of money, housing difficulties, the roles of the in-laws, and attitudes toward raising children—should be described. Other questions include: Is the patient currently in a long-term relationship? How long is the longest relationship that the patient has had? What is the quality of the patient's sexual relationship (for example, is the patient's sexual life experienced as satisfactory or inadequate)? What does the patient look for in a partner? Is the patient able to initiate a relationship or to approach someone he or she feels attracted to or compatible with? How does the patient describe the current relationship in terms of its positive and negative qualities? How does the patient perceive failures of past relationships in terms of understanding what went wrong and who was or was not to blame?

A 32-year-old woman had a series of relationships in which she was ultimately abused, always emotionally and often physically and sexually. Despite her conscious intent to find a caring man with whom she could have a less abusive relationship, the pattern repeated itself. Her mother had been chronically beaten by her abusive father. She recalled that her mother warned her repeatedly, "A woman's role is to give in to her husband and put up with the crap as best we can."

MILITARY HISTORY. The psychiatrist should inquire about the patient's general adjustment to the military, whether he or she saw combat or sustained an injury, and the nature of the discharge. Was the patient ever referred for psychiatric consultation, and did he or she suffer any disciplinary action during the period of service?

A 22-year-old soldier returning from Vietnam claimed to have no memory of his last month in combat. He had been assigned to a squad conducting a long-range patrol; only three of eight soldiers returned alive. Through repeated amobarbital interviews conducted in a supportive setting, gradually and with much emotion he recalled that his squad had been ambushed, that early in the firefight he had killed two or three 12- or 13-year-old Vietnamese boys who were in the attacking group, and that at a certain point he turned and ran away, leaving one or two of his wounded buddies behind, pleading with him to help.

EDUCATION HISTORY. The psychiatrist needs to have a clear picture of the patient's educational background. This information can provide clues about the patient's social and cultural background, intelligence, motivation, and any obstacles to achievement. For instance, a patient from an economically deprived background who never had the opportunity to attend the best schools and whose parents never graduated from high school shows strength of character, intelligence, and tremendous motivation by graduating from college. A patient who dropped out of high school because of violence and substance use displays creativity and determination by going to school at night to obtain a high school diploma while working during the day as a drug counselor. How far did the patient go in school? What was the highest grade or graduate level attained? What did the patient like to study, and what was the level of academic performance? How far did the other members of the patient's family go in school, and how do they compare with the patient's progress? What is the patient's attitude toward academic achievement?

RELIGION. The psychiatrist should describe the religious background of both parents and the details of the patient's religious instruction. Was the family's attitude toward religion strict or permissive, and were there any conflicts between the parents over the child's religious education? The psychiatrist should trace the evolution of the patient's adolescent religious practices to present beliefs and activities. Does the patient have a strong religious affiliation, and, if so, how does this affiliation affect the patient's life? What does the patient's religion say about the treatment of psychiatric or medical illness? What is the religious attitude toward suicide?

SOCIAL ACTIVITY. The psychiatrist should describe the patient's social life and the nature of friendships, with an emphasis on the depth, duration, and quality of human relationships. What social, intellectual, and physical interests does the patient share with friends? What relationships does the patient have with people of the same sex and the opposite sex? Is the patient essentially isolated and asocial? Does the patient prefer isolation, or is the patient isolated because of anxieties and fears about other people? Who visits the patient in the hospital and how frequently?

An attractive, successful 32-year-old woman reported having a long string of admiring suitors and a series of intimate sexual relationships since the age of 17. Although several of the suitors to whom she was strongly attracted had proposed marriage, she felt unable to commit herself; she was never sufficiently in love with any of them and hoped that she would someday meet Mr. Perfect.

CURRENT LIVING SITUATION. The psychiatrist should ask the patient to describe where he or she lives in terms of the neighborhood and the residence. He or she should include the number of rooms, the number of family members living in the home, and the sleeping arrangements. The psychiatrist should inquire as to how issues of privacy are handled, with particular emphasis on parental and sibling nudity and bathroom arrangements. He or she should ask about the sources of family income and any financial hardships. If applicable, the psychiatrist may inquire about public assistance and the patient's feelings about it. If the patient has been hospitalized, have provisions been made so that he or she will not lose a job or an apartment? The psychiatrist should ask who is caring for the children at home, who visits the patient in the hospital, and how frequently.

LEGAL HISTORY. Has the patient ever been arrested and, if so, for what? How many times? Was the patient ever in jail? For how long? Is the patient on probation, or are charges pending? Is the patient mandated to be in treatment as part of a stipulation of probation? Does the patient have a history of assault or violence? Against whom? Using what? What is the patient's attitude toward the arrests or prison terms? An extensive legal history, as well as the patient's attitude toward it, may indicate an antisocial personality disorder. An extensive history of violence may alert the psychiatrist to the potential for violence in the future.

Sexual History. Much of the history of infantile sexuality is not recoverable, although many patients are able to recall curiosities and sexual games played from the ages of 3 to 6 years. The psychiatrist should ask how the patient learned about sex and what he or she felt were parents' attitudes about sexual development. The interviewer can also inquire whether the patient was sexually abused in childhood. Some material discussed in this section may also be covered in the section on adolescent sexuality. It is not important where in the history it is covered, as long as it is included.

The onset of puberty and the patient's feelings about this milestone are important. Adolescent masturbatory history, including the nature of the patient's fantasies and feelings about them, is of significance. Attitudes toward sex should be described in detail. Is the patient shy, timid, aggressive? Or does the patient need to impress others and boast of sexual conquests? Did the patient experience anxiety in the sexual setting? Was there promiscuity? What is the patient's sexual orientation?

The sexual history should include any sexual symptoms, such as anorgasmia, vaginismus, impotence, premature or retarded ejaculation, lack of sexual desire, and paraphilias (for example, sexual sadism, fetishism, voyeurism). Attitudes toward fellatio, cunnilingus, and coital techniques may be discussed. The topic of sexual adjustment should include a description of how sexual activity is usually initiated, the frequency of sexual relations, and sexual preferences, variations, and techniques. It is usually appropriate to inquire whether the patient has engaged in extramarital relationships and, if so, under what circumstances and whether the spouse knew of the affair. If the spouse did learn of the affair, the psychiatrist should ask the patient to describe what happened. The reasons underlying an extramarital affair are just as important as an understanding of its effect on the marriage.

Attitudes toward contraception and family planning are important. What form of contraception does the patient use? The psychiatrist, however, should not assume that the patient uses birth control. If an interviewer asks a lesbian patient to describe what type of birth control she uses (on the assumption that she is heterosexual), the patient may surmise that the interviewer will not be understanding or accepting of her sexual orientation. A more helpful question is "Do you need to use birth control?" or "Is contraception something that is part of your sexuality?"

The psychiatrist should ask whether the patient wants to mention other areas of sexual functioning and sexuality. Is the patient aware of the issues involved in safe sex? Does the patient have a sexually transmitted disease, such as herpes or AIDS? Does the patient worry about being HIV positive?

Family History. A brief statement about any psychiatric illnesses, hospitalizations, and treatments of the patient's immediate family members should be placed in this part of the report. Is there a family history of alcohol and other substance abuse or of antisocial behavior? In addition, the family history should provide a description of the personalities and intelligence of the various people living in the patient's home from childhood to the present as well as descriptions of the various households in which the patient lived. The psychiatrist should also define the role each person has played in the patient's upbringing and this person's current relationship with the patient. What were and are the family ethnic, national, and religious traditions? Informants other than the patient may be available to contribute to the family history, and the source should be cited in the written record. Various members of the family often give different descriptions of the same people and events. The psychiatrist should determine the family's attitude toward and insight into the patient's illness. Does the patient feel that the family members are supportive, indifferent, or destructive? What is the role of illness in the family?

Other questions that provide useful information in this section include the following: What are the patient's attitudes toward his or her parents and siblings? The psychiatrist should ask the patient to describe each family member. Whom does the patient mention first? Whom does the patient leave out? What does each of the parents do for a living? What do the siblings do? How do siblings' occupations compare with the patient's work, and how does the patient feel about it? Whom does the patient feel he or she is most like in the family and why?

Fantasies and Dreams. Sigmund Freud stated that dreams are the royal road to the unconscious. Repetitive dreams are of particular value. If the patient has nightmares, what are their repetitive themes? Some of the most common dream themes are food, examinations, sex, helplessness, and impotence. Can the patient describe a recent dream and discuss its possible meanings? Fantasies and daydreams are another valuable source of unconscious material. As with dreams, the psychiatrist can explore and record all manifest details and attendant feelings.

What are the patient's fantasies about the future? If the patient could make any change in his or her life, what would it be? What are the patient's most common or favorite current fantasies? Does the patient experience daydreams? Are the patient's fantasies grounded in reality, or is the patient unable to tell the difference between fantasy and reality?

The psychiatrist may inquire about the patient's system of values—both social and moral—including values about work, money, play, children, parents, friends, sex, community concerns, and cultural issues. For instance, are children a burden or a joy? Is work a necessary evil, an avoidable chore, or an opportunity? What is the patient's concept of right and wrong?

MENTAL STATUS EXAMINATION

The mental status examination is the part of the clinical assessment that describes the sum total of the examiner's observations and impressions of the psychiatric patient at the time of the interview. Whereas the patient's history remains stable, the patient's mental status can change from day to day or hour to hour. The mental status examination is the description of the patient's appearance, speech, actions, and thoughts during the interview. Even when a patient is mute, incoherent, or refusing to answer questions, the clinician can obtain a wealth of information through careful observation. Although practitioners' organizational formats for writing up the mental status examination vary slightly, the format must contain certain categories of information. One such format is outlined in Table 7.1–5.

General Description

Appearance. In this category, the psychiatrist describes the patient's appearance and overall physical impression, as reflected by posture, poise, clothing, and grooming. If the patient appears particularly bizarre, the clinician may ask, "Has anyone ever commented on how you look?" "How would you describe how you look?" "Can you help me understand some of the choices you make in how you look?"

Examples of items in the appearance category include body type, posture, poise, clothes, grooming, hair, and nails. Common terms used to describe appearance are healthy, sickly, ill at ease, poised, old looking, young looking, disheveled, childlike, and bizarre. Signs of anxiety are noted: moist hands, perspiring forehead, tense posture, wide eyes.

Table 7.1–5
Outline of the Mental Status Examination

I. General description
    A. Appearance
    B. Overt behavior and psychomotor activity
    C. Attitude
II. Mood and affectivity
    A. Mood
    B. Affect
    C. Appropriateness of affect
III. Speech characteristics
IV. Perception
V. Thought content and mental trends
    A. Thought process
    B. Thought content
VI. Sensorium and cognition
    A. Consciousness
    B. Orientation and memory
    C. Concentration and attention
    D. Reading and writing
    E. Visuospatial ability
    F. Abstract thought
    G. Information and intelligence
VII. Impulsivity
VIII. Judgment and insight
IX. Reliability

Overt Behavior and Psychomotor Activity. This category refers to both the quantitative and qualitative aspects of the patient's motor behavior. Included are mannerisms, tics, gestures, twitches, stereotyped behavior, echopraxia, hyperactivity, agitation, combativeness, flexibility, rigidity, gait, and agility. Restlessness, wringing of hands, pacing, and other physical manifestations are described. Psychomotor retardation or generalized slowing down of body movements should be noted. Any aimless, purposeless activity should be described.

Attitude Toward Examiner. The patient's attitude toward the examiner can be described as cooperative, friendly, attentive, interested, frank, seductive, defensive, contemptuous, perplexed, apathetic, hostile, playful, ingratiating, evasive, or guarded; any number of other adjectives can be used. The level of rapport established should be recorded.

Mood and Affect

Mood. *Mood* is defined as a pervasive and sustained emotion that colors the person's perception of the world. The psychiatrist is interested in whether the patient remarks voluntarily about feelings or whether it is necessary to ask the patient how he or she feels. Statements about the patient's mood should include depth, intensity, duration, and fluctuations. Common adjectives used to describe mood include depressed, despairing, irritable, anxious, angry, expansive, euphoric, empty, guilty, awed, futile, self-contemptuous, frightened, and perplexed. Mood may be labile, fluctuating or alternating rapidly between extremes (for example, laughing loudly and expansively one moment, tearful and despairing the next).

Affect. *Affect* may be defined as the patient's present emotional responsiveness, inferred from the patient's facial expression, including the amount and the range of expressive behavior. Affect may or may not be congruent with mood. Affect can be described as within normal range, constricted, blunted, or flat. In the normal range of affect, there is variation in facial expression, tone of voice, use of hands, and body movements. When affect is constricted, the range and intensity of expression are reduced. Similarly, in blunted affect, emotional expression is further reduced. To diagnose flat affect, there should be virtually no signs of affective expression; the patient's voice should be monotonous, and the face should be immobile. *Blunted, flat,* and *constricted* are terms used to refer to the apparent depth of emotion; *depressed, proud, angry,* *fearful, anxious, guilty, euphoric,* and *expansive* are terms used to refer to particular moods. The psychiatrist should note the patient's difficulty in initiating, sustaining, or terminating an emotional response.

Appropriateness of Affect. The psychiatrist can consider the appropriateness of the patient's emotional responses in the context of the subject the patient is discussing. Delusional patients who are describing a delusion of persecution should be angry or frightened about the experiences they believe are happening to them. Anger or fear in this context is an appropriate expression. Some psychiatrists have reserved the term *inappropriateness of affect* for a quality of response found in some schizophrenic patients, in which the patient's affect is incongruent with what the patient is saying (for example, flattened affect when speaking about murderous impulses).

Speech Characteristics

This part of the report describes the physical characteristics of speech. Speech can be described in terms of its quantity, rate of production, and quality. The patient may be described as talkative, garrulous, voluble, and taciturn, unspontaneous, or normally responsive to cues from the interviewer. Speech may be rapid or slow, pressured, hesitant, emotional, dramatic, monotonous, loud, whispered, slurred, staccato, or mumbled. Impairments of speech, such as stuttering, are included in this section. Unusual rhythms (termed *dysprosody*) and any accent that may be present should be noted. Is the patient's speech spontaneous or not?

Perception

Perceptual disturbances, such as hallucinations and illusions, may be experienced in reference to the self or the environment. The sensory system involved (for example, auditory, visual, olfactory, or tactile) and the content of the illusion or the hallucinatory experience should be described. The circumstances of the occurrence of any hallucinatory experience are important; hypnagogic hallucinations (occurring as a person falls asleep) and hypnopompic hallucinations (occurring as a person awakens) are of much less serious significance than are other types of hallucinations. Hallucinations may also occur in particular times of stress for individual patients. Feelings of depersonalization and derealization (extreme feelings of detachment from the self or the environment) are other examples of perceptual disturbance. Formication, the feeling of bugs crawling on or under the skin, is seen in cocainism.

Examples of questions used to elicit the experience of hallucinations include the following: Have you ever heard voices or other sounds that no one else could hear or when no one else was around? Have you experienced any strange sensations in your body that others do not seem to experience? Have you ever had visions or seen things that other people do not seem to see?

A young man with schizophrenia heard an insistent voice repeatedly telling him to stop his antipsychotic medication. After resisting the command for many weeks, the patient felt that he could no longer fight the voice, and he discontinued treatment. Two months later, he was hospitalized involuntarily and near cardiovascular collapse. He later said that, once he stopped the medication, the voice further insisted that he should stop eating and drinking in order to be pure.

A terrified 37-year-old man in acute delirium tremens glanced agitatedly about the room. He pointed out the window and said: "My God, the Spanish armada is on the lawn. They're about to attack." He experienced the hallucination as real, and it persisted intermittently for 3 days before abating. Subsequently, the patient had no memory of the experience.

Thought Content and Mental Trends

Thought can be divided into process (or form) and content. Process refers to the way in which a person puts together ideas and associations, the form in which a person thinks. Process or form of thought may be logical and coherent or completely illogical and even incomprehensible. Content refers to what a person is actually thinking about: ideas, beliefs, preoccupations, obsessions. Table 7.1–6 lists common disorders of thought, divided into process and content.

Thought Process (Form of Thinking). The patient may have either an overabundance or a poverty of ideas. There may be rapid thinking, which, if carried to the extreme, is called a *flight of ideas.* A patient may exhibit slow or hesitant

Table 7.1–6
Examples of Disorders of Thought

Process (or Form) of Thought
Loosening of associations or derailment
Flight of ideas
Racing thoughts
Tangentiality
Circumstantiality
Word salad or incoherence
Neologisms
Clang associations
Punning
Thought blocking
Vague thought
Content of Thought
Delusions
Paranoia
Preoccupations
Obsessions and compulsions
Phobias
Suicidal or homicidal ideas
Ideas of reference and influence
Poverty of content

thinking. Thought may be vague or empty. Do the patient's replies really answer the questions asked, and does the patient have the capacity for goal-directed thinking? Are the responses relevant or irrelevant? Is there a clear cause-and-effect relation in the patient's explanations? Does the patient have *loose associations* (for example, do the ideas expressed appear to be unrelated and idiosyncratically connected)? Disturbances of the continuity of thought include statements that are tangential, circumstantial, rambling, evasive, and perseverative.

Blocking is an interruption of the train of thought before an idea has been completed; the patient may indicate an inability to recall what was being said or intended to be said. *Circumstantiality* indicates the loss of capacity for goal-directed thinking; in the process of explaining an idea, the patient brings in many irrelevant details and parenthetical comments but eventually does get back to the original point. *Tangentiality* is a disturbance in which the patient loses the thread of the conversation and pursues tangential thoughts stimulated by various external or internal irrelevant stimuli and never returns to the original point. Thought process impairments may be reflected by incoherent or incomprehensible connections of thoughts (*word salad*), *clang associations* (association by rhyming), *punning* (association by double meaning), and *neologisms* (new words created by the patient through the combination or condensation of other words).

Thought Content. Disturbances in content of thought include delusions, preoccupations (which may involve the patient's illness), obsessions (''Do you have ideas that are intrusive and repetitive?''), compulsions (''Are there things you do over and over, in a repetitive manner?'' ''Are there things you must do in a particular way or order?'' ''If you do not do them that way, must you repeat them?'' ''Do you know why you do things that way?''), phobias, plans, intentions, recurrent ideas about suicide or homicide, hypochondriacal symptoms, and specific antisocial urges.

> A 32-year-old woman with a mild viral syndrome picked up a carton of milk in the supermarket and then returned it to its shelf, after deciding not to buy it. Over the next few days, she spent increasing amounts of time thinking about the act. She could not stop herself from thinking that the mother of a young child picked up the same container, contracted the patient's virus, and gave it to her child, who may then have become ill and died as a result of a fulminant infection. Despite knowing that this sequence of events was extremely unlikely, the woman could not stop replaying the scenario in her mind.

Does the patient have thoughts of doing harm to himself or herself? Is there a plan? A major category of disturbances of thought content involves delusions. *Delusions*—fixed, false beliefs out of keeping with the patient's cultural background—may be *mood congruent* (in keeping with a depressed or elated mood) or mood incongruent. The content of any delusional system should be described, and the psychiatrist should attempt to evaluate its organization and the patient's conviction as to its validity. The manner in which it affects the patient's life is appropriately described in the history of the present illness. Delusions may be bizarre and may involve beliefs about external control. Delusions may have themes that are persecutory or paranoid, grandiose, jealous, somatic, guilty, nihilistic, or erotic. Ideas of reference and of influence should also be described. Examples of *ideas of reference* include a person's belief that the television or radio is speaking to or about him or her. Examples of *ideas of influence* are beliefs about another person or force controlling some aspect of a person's behavior.

> A young man with schizophrenia, a college dropout who could work only part-time at low-level jobs and who lived with his high-achieving family, believed he was the Messiah. He was fully convinced that his struggles and lack of occupational success were merely God's tests until the patient's true identity would be revealed. As he improved, he would, if asked, say that he was God's chosen but, when questioned further, would admit the slight possibility that he was wrong. On reaching his best clinical state, he would muse on the possibility that he was the Messiah but state that he was not sure.

Sensorium and Cognition

This portion of the mental status examination seeks to assess organic brain function and the patient's intelligence, capacity for abstract thought, and level of insight and judgment.

The Mini-Mental State Examination (MMSE) is a brief instrument designed to grossly assess cognitive functioning. It assesses orientation, memory, calculations, reading and writing capacity, visuospatial ability, and language. The patient is measured quantitatively on these functions; a perfect score is 30 points. The MMSE is widely used as a simple, quick assessment of possible cognitive deficits. (See Table 10.1–2 for an example of the MMSE.)

Consciousness. Disturbances of consciousness usually indicate organic brain impairment. *Clouding of consciousness* is an overall reduced awareness of the environment. A patient may be unable to sustain attention to environmental stimuli or to maintain goal-directed thinking or behavior. Clouding or obtunding of consciousness is frequently not a fixed mental state. A patient typically manifests fluctuations in the level of awareness of the surrounding environment. The patient who has an altered state of consciousness often shows some impairment of orientation as well, although the reverse is not necessarily true. Some terms used to describe the patient's level of consciousness are clouding, somnolence, stupor, coma, lethargy, alertness, and fugue state.

Orientation and Memory. Disorders of orientation are traditionally separated according to time, place, and person. Any impairment usually appears in this order (that is, sense of time is impaired before sense of place); similarly, as the patient improves, the impairment clears in the reverse order. The psychiatrist must determine whether patients can give the approximate date and time of day. In addition, if patients are in a hospital, do they know how long they have been there? Do the patients behave as though they are oriented to the present? In questions about patients' orientation to place, it is not sufficient that they be able to *state* the name and the location of the hospital correctly; they should also *behave* as though they know where they are. In assessing orientation for person, the psychiatrist asks patients whether they know the names of the people around them and whether they understand their roles in relationship to them. Do they know who the examiner is? It is only in the most severe instances that patients do not know who they themselves are.

A 42-year-old alcoholic man in delirium tremens, examined in a California hospital in 1995, was asked the date and where he was. He replied: "I'm standing on a street corner in Kansas City in 1966 minding my own business. Why don't you mind yours?"

Memory functions have traditionally been divided into four areas: remote memory, recent past memory, recent memory, and immediate retention and recall. Recent memory may be checked by asking patients about their appetite and then about what they had for breakfast or for dinner the previous evening. Patients may be asked at this point if they recall the interviewer's name. Asking patients to repeat six digits forward and then backward is a test for immediate retention. Remote memory can be tested by asking patients for information about their childhoods that can be later verified. Asking patients to recall important news events from the past few months checks recent past memory. Often in cognitive disorders, recent or short-term memory is impaired first, and remote or long-term memory is impaired later. If there is impairment, what are the efforts made to cope with it or to conceal it? Is denial, confabulation, catastrophic reaction, or circumstantiality used to conceal a deficit? Reactions to the loss of memory can give important clues to underlying disorders and coping mechanisms. For instance, a patient who appears to have memory impairment but, in fact, is depressed is more likely to be concerned about memory loss than is someone with memory loss secondary to dementia.

A 40-year-old, chronically alcoholic man, whose memory on the mental status examination was markedly impaired, frantically demanded to be released from the hospital, saying that his wife had just been in an automobile accident and that he had to rush to another hospital to see her. He said it with sincere conviction and appropriate fearful concern; for the patient, at least, the story was real. In fact, his wife had been dead for 15 years. The patient told the same story over and over again, always with evident conviction, in spite of the fact that staff members confronted him with the reality that his wife had been dead for years. The patient was never influenced by their assertions, because he could not register new memories. Although his past memory was patchy at best, he could repeatedly recall the story of his wife's emergency.

Confabulation (unconsciously making up false answers when memory is impaired) is most closely associated with cognitive disorders. Table 7.1–7 gives a summary of memory tests.

Concentration and Attention. A patient's concentration may be impaired for many reasons. A cognitive disorder, anxiety, depression, and internal stimuli, such as auditory hallucinations—all may contribute to impaired concentration. Subtracting serial 7s from 100 is a simple task that requires intact concentration and cognitive capacities. Was the patient able to subtract 7 from 100 and keep subtracting 7s? If the patient could not subtract 7s, could 3s be subtracted? Were easier tasks accomplished—4 × 9, 5 × 4? The examiner must always assess whether anxiety, some disturbance of mood or consciousness, or a learning deficit is responsible for the difficulty.

Attention is assessed by calculations or by asking the patient to spell the word *world* (or others) backward. The patient can also be asked to name five things that start with a particular letter.

During his most recent manic episode, a 48-year-old man with bipolar disorder had intense grandiose, psychotic ideas. He was convinced that he could control the traffic in Los Angeles by driving on certain freeways at specified times and willing others to leave the road. After the manic episode ended and during the depressive episode that immediately followed, he could recall virtually no details of his previous thought content while he was manic. Later, when euthymic, he remembered only a few hazy images. A year later, the beginning of a new hypomanic period was heralded by the patient's spontaneously remembering and describing in great detail the psychotic plans of the previous episode.

Table 7.1–7
Summary of Memory Tests

Try to assess whether the process of registration, retention, or recollection of material is involved.

Remote memory: childhood data, important events known to have occurred when the patient was younger or free of illness, personal matters, neutral material

Recent past memory: the past few months

Recent memory: the past few days, what the patient did yesterday, the day before; what the patient had for breakfast, lunch, dinner

Immediate retention and recall: digit-span measures; ability to repeat six figures after examiner dictates them—first forward, then backward (patients with unimpaired memory can usually repeat six digits backward); ability to repeat three words immediately and 3 to 5 minutes later

Reading and Writing. The patient should be asked to read a sentence (for example, "Close your eyes") and then to do what the sentence says. The patient should also be asked to write a simple but complete sentence.

Visuospatial Ability. The patient should be asked to copy a figure, such as a clock face or interlocking pentagons.

Abstract Thought. Abstract thinking is the ability to deal with concepts. Patients may have disturbances in the manner in which they conceptualize or handle ideas. Can patients explain similarities, such as those between an apple and a pear or those between truth and beauty? Are the meanings of simple proverbs, such as "A rolling stone gathers no moss," understood? Answers may be concrete (giving specific examples to illustrate the meaning) or overly abstract (giving too generalized an explanation). Appropriateness of answers and the manner in which answers are given should be noted. In a catastrophic reaction, brain-damaged patients become extremely emotional and cannot think abstractly.

Information and Intelligence. If a possible cognitive impairment is suspected, does the patient have trouble with mental tasks, such as counting the change from $10 after a purchase of $6.37? If this task is too difficult, are easy problems (such as how many nickels are in $1.35) solved? The patient's intelligence is related to vocabulary and general fund of knowledge (for example, the distance from New York to Paris, Presidents of the United States). The patient's education level (both formal and self-education) and socioeconomic status must be taken into account. Handling of difficult or sophisticated concepts can reflect intelligence, even in the absence of formal education or an extensive fund of information. Ultimately, the psychiatrist estimates the patient's intellectual capability and capacity to function at the level of basic endowment.

Impulsivity

Is the patient capable of controlling sexual, aggressive, and other impulses? An assessment of impulse control is critical in ascertaining the patient's awareness of socially appropriate behavior and is a measure of the patient's potential danger to self and others. Patients may be unable to control impulses secondary to cognitive and psychotic disorders or resulting from chronic characterological defects, as observed in the personality disorders. Impulse control can be estimated from information in the patient's recent history and from behavior observed during the interview.

Judgment and Insight

Judgment. During the course of history-taking, the psychiatrist should be able to assess many aspects of the patient's capability for social judgment. Does the patient understand the likely outcome of his or her behavior, and is he or she influenced by this understanding? Can the patient predict what he or she would do in imaginary situations? For instance, what would the patient do if he or she smelled smoke in a crowded movie theater?

Insight. Insight is a patient's degree of awareness and understanding about being ill. Patients may exhibit a complete denial of their illness or may show some awareness that they are ill but place the blame on others, on external factors, or even on organic factors. They may acknowledge that they have an illness but ascribe it to something unknown or mysterious in themselves.

> An 18-year-old man went to an emergency room with the belief that he was controlled by a computer on an Enterprise-like starship, an elaboration from the television series *Star Trek.* He was convinced that all his thoughts, actions, and feelings were being programmed on board the starship, which was located light years away and, therefore, could never be detected by anyone else.

Intellectual insight is present when patients can admit that they are ill and acknowledge that their failures to adapt are, in part, due to their own irrational feelings. Patients' inability to apply their knowledge to alter future experiences, however, is the major limitation to intellectual insight. True emotional insight is present when patients' awareness of their own motives and deep feelings leads to a change in their personality or behavior patterns.

A summary of levels of insight follows:

- Complete denial of illness.
- Slight awareness of being sick and needing help but denying it at the same time.
- Awareness of being sick but blaming it on others, on external factors, or on organic factors.
- Awareness that illness is due to something unknown in the patient.
- *Intellectual insight:* admission that the patient is ill and that symptoms or failures in social adjustment are due to the patient's own particular irrational feelings or disturbances without applying this knowledge to future experiences.
- *True emotional insight:* emotional awareness of the motives and feelings within the patient and the important people in his or her life, which can lead to basic changes in behavior.

Reliability

The mental status part of the report concludes with the psychiatrist's impressions of the patient's reliability and capacity to report his or her situation accurately. It includes an estimate of the psychiatrist's impression of the patient's truthfulness or veracity. For instance, if the patient is open about significant active substance abuse or about circumstances that the patient knows may reflect badly (for example, trouble with the law), the psychiatrist may estimate the patient's reliability to be good.

CASE REPORT

When the psychiatrist has completed a comprehensive psychiatric history and mental status examination, the information obtained is written up and organized into the psychiatric report. The report follows the outline of the standard psychiatric history and mental status examination. In the psychiatric report, the examiner addresses the critical questions of further diagnostic studies that must be performed; adds a summary of both positive and negative findings; makes a tentative multiaxial diagnosis; gives a prognosis; gives a psychodynamic formulation; and gives a set of management recommendations.

Further Diagnostic Studies

Other useful studies include:

- Physical examination.
- Neurological examination.
- Additional psychiatric diagnostic interviews.
- Interviews with family members, friends, or neighbors by a social worker.
- Psychological, neurological, or laboratory tests as indicated: electroencephalogram, computed tomography scan, magnetic resonance imaging, tests of other medical conditions, reading comprehension and writing tests, tests for aphasia, projective psychological tests, dexamethasone-suppression test, 24-hour urine test for heavy-metal intoxication.

Summary of Findings

Mental symptoms, historical data (for example, family history), medical and laboratory findings, and psychological and neurological test results, if available, are summarized.

Diagnosis

Diagnostic classification is made according to the fourth edition of the *Diagnostic and Statistical Manual of Mental Disorders* (DSM-IV). DSM-IV uses a multiaxial classification scheme consisting of five axes, each of which should be covered in the diagnosis.

Axis I consists of all clinical syndromes (for example, mood disorders, schizophrenia, generalized anxiety disorder) and other conditions that may be a focus of clinical attention.

Axis II consists of personality disorders, mental retardation, and defense mechanisms.

Axis III consists of any general medical conditions (for example, epilepsy, cardiovascular disease, endocrine disorders).

Axis IV refers to psychosocial and environmental problems (for example, divorce, injury, death of a loved one) relevant to the illness.

Axis V relates to the global assessment of functioning exhibited by the patient during the interview (for example, social, occupational, and psychological functioning); a rating scale with a continuum from 100 (superior functioning) to 1 (grossly impaired functioning) is used.

(The DSM-IV multiaxial classification scheme is discussed in detail in Chapter 9.)

Prognosis

The prognosis is an opinion about the probable immediate and future course, extent, and outcome of the disorder. The good and bad prognostic factors, as known, are listed.

Psychodynamic Formulation and Defense Mechanisms

The psychodynamic formulation is a summary of proposed psychological influences on or causes of the patient's disturbance; influences in the patient's life that contributed to the present disorder; environmental and personality factors relevant to determining the patient's symptoms and how these influences have interacted with the patient's genetic, temperamental, and biological makeup; primary and secondary gains. An outline of the major defense mechanisms used by the patient should be listed.

Treatment Plan

A treatment plan is very important and is required by many health management organizations (HMOs) before they approve payment. In formulating the treatment plan, the clinician should note whether the patient requires psychiatric treatment at the time and, if so, at which problems and target symptoms the treatment is aimed; what kind of treatment or combination of treatments the patient should receive; and what treatment setting seems most appropriate. For instance, the examiner evaluates the role of medication, inpatient or outpatient treatment, frequency of sessions, probable duration of therapy, and type of psychotherapy (individual, group, or family therapy). Specific goals of therapy are noted. If hospitalization is recommended, the clinician should specify the reasons for hospitalization, the type of hospitalization indicated, the urgency with which the patient must be hospitalized, and the anticipated duration of inpatient care. The clinician should also estimate the length of treatment.

If either the patient or family members are unwilling to accept the recommendations for treatment and the clinician thinks that the refusal of the recommendations may have serious consequences, the patient (or the parent or guardian) should sign a statement that the recommended treatment was refused.

References

Alarcon RD: Culture and psychiatric diagnosis. Impact on DSM-IV and ICD-10. Psychiatr Clin North Am *18:* 449, 1995.

American Psychiatric Association: *Diagnostic and Statistical Manual of Mental Disorders,* ed 4. American Psychiatric Association, Washington, 1994.

Corty E, Lehman AF, Myers CP: Influence of psychoactive substance use on the reliability of psychiatric diagnosis. J Consult Clin Psychol *61:* 165, 1993.

Janca A, Hiller W: ICD-10 checklists—a tool for clinician's use of the ICD-10 classification of mental and behavioral disorders. Compr Psychiatry *37:* 180, 1996.

Kosten TA, Rounsaville BJ: Sensitivity of psychiatric diagnosis based on the best estimate procedure. Am J Psychiatry *149:* 1225, 1992.

Lewis NDC: *Outlines for Psychiatric Examinations,* ed 3. New York State Department of Mental Hygiene, Albany, 1943.

MacKinnon RA, Yudofsky SC: *The Psychiatric Interview in Clinical* Practice. Lippincott, Philadelphia, 1986.

Shaffer D, Gould MS, Fisher P, Trautman P, Moreau D, Kleinman M, Flory M: Psychiatric diagnosis in child and adolescent suicide. Arch Gen Psychiatry *53:* 339, 1996.

Strauss GD: The psychiatric interview, history, and mental status examination. In *Comprehensive Textbook of Psychiatry,* ed 6, HI Kaplan, BJ Sadock, editors, p 521. Williams & Wilkins, Baltimore, 1995.
Tangalos EG, Smith GE, Ivnik RJ, Petersen RC, Kokmen E, Kurland LT, Offord KP, Parisi JE: The Mini-Mental State Examination in general medical practice: clinical utility and acceptance. Mayo Clin Proc *71:* 829, 1996.
Zarin DA, Earls F: Diagnostic decision making in psychiatry. Am J Psychiatry *150:* 197, 1993.

▲ 7.2 Laboratory Tests in Psychiatry

The crucial skill of clinical assessment in psychiatry can be supported by laboratory data gained through tests. Tests may eliminate potential organic causes for psychiatric symptoms, such as impaired copper metabolism in Wilson's disease and a positive result on an antinuclear antibody (ANA) test in systemic lupus erythematosus (SLE). Laboratory tests are also useful in monitoring treatment; they can measure blood levels of antidepressant medications and assess the effects of lithium (Eskalith) on electrolytes, thyroid metabolism, and renal function.

Compared to other medical specialists, psychiatrists depend more on clinical examinations and patients' signs and symptoms than on laboratory tests. No test can establish or rule out a diagnosis of schizophrenia, bipolar I disorder, or major depressive disorder. Nevertheless, advances in neuropsychiatry and biological psychiatry have made laboratory tests more and more useful to psychiatrists as well as to biological researchers.

BASIC SCREENING TESTS

Before initiating psychiatric treatment, a clinician should undertake a routine medical evaluation for the purposes of screening for concurrent disease, ruling out organicity, and establishing baseline values of functions to be monitored. Such an evaluation includes a medical history and routine medical laboratory tests, such as a complete blood count (CBC); hematocrit and hemoglobin; renal, liver, and thyroid function; electrolytes; and blood sugar.

Thyroid disease and other endocrinopathies may appear as a mood disorder or a psychotic disorder; cancer or infectious disease, as depression; infection and connective tissue diseases, as short-term changes in mental status. In addition, a psychiatrist may see patients with a range of organic mental and neurological conditions. These conditions include multiple sclerosis, Parkinson's disease, dementia of the Alzheimer's type, Huntington's disease, dementia due to human immunodeficiency virus (HIV) disease, and temporal lobe epilepsy. Any suspected medical or neurological condition should be thoroughly evaluated with appropriate laboratory tests and consultation.

NEUROENDOCRINE TESTS

Thyroid Function Tests

Several thyroid function tests are available, including tests for thyroxine (T_4) by competitive protein binding (T_4D) and by radioimmunoassay (T_4RIA) involving a specific antigen–antibody reaction. Table 7.2–1 lists some common thyroid function tests. More than 90 percent of T_4 is bound to serum protein and is responsible for thyroid-stimulating hormone (TSH) secretion and for cellular metabolism. Other thyroid measures include the free T_4 index (FT_4I), triiodothyronine uptake, and total serum triiodothyronine measured by radioimmunoassay (T_3RIA). These tests are used to rule out hypothyroidism, which can appear with symptoms of depression. In some studies, up to 10 percent of patients complaining of depression and associated fatigue had incipient hypothyroid disease. Other associated signs and symptoms common to both depression and hypothyroidism include weakness, stiffness, poor appetite, constipation, menstrual irregularities, slowed speech, apathy, impaired memory, and even hallucinations and delusions. Lithium can cause hypothyroidism and, more rarely, hyperthyroidism. Table 7.2–2 outlines the suggested monitoring of thyroid function for patients taking lithium. Neonatal hypothyroidism results in mental retardation and is preventable if the diagnosis is made at birth. Table 7.2–3 lists the thyroid function test changes associated with hypothyroidism.

The thyrotropin-releasing hormone (TRH) stimulation test is indicated in patients whose marginally abnormal thyroid test results suggest subclinical hypothyroidism, which may account for clinical depression. The test is also used for patients with possible lithium-induced hypothyroidism. The procedure entails an intravenous (IV) injection of 500 μg of TRH, which produces a sharp rise in serum TSH when measured at 15, 30, 60, and 90 minutes. Table 7.2–4 summarizes one suggested TRH test protocol. An increase in serum TSH of from 5 to 25 μIU/mL above the baseline is normal. An increase of less than 7 μIU/mL is considered a blunted response, which may correlate with a diagnosis of a depressive disorder. Eight percent of all patients with depressive disorders have some thyroid illness.

Dexamethasone-Suppression Test

Dexamethasone is a long-acting synthetic glucocorticoid with a long half-life. About 1 mg of dexamethasone is equivalent to 25 mg of cortisol. The dexamethasone-suppression test (DST) is used to help confirm a diagnostic impression of major depressive disorder.

Procedure. The patient is given 1 mg of dexamethasone by mouth at 11 PM, and plasma cortisol is measured at 8 AM, 4 PM, and 11 PM. Plasma cortisol above 5 μg/dL (known as nonsuppression) is considered abnormal (that is, positive). Suppression of cortisol indicates that the hypothalamic-adrenal-pituitary axis is functioning properly. Since the 1930s, dysfunction of this axis has been known to be associated with stress.

The DST can be used to follow a depressed person's response to treatment. Normalization of the DST, however, is not an indication to stop antidepressant treatment, because the DST may normalize before the depression resolves.

Reliability. The problems associated with the DST include varying reports of sensitivity and specificity. False-pos-

Table 7.2–1
Common Thyroid Function Tests[a]

Type of Test	Normal Values	Cost ($)	Interference
In vitro (serum tests)			
T_4	4.5–13 μg/100 mL 58–167 nmol/L	7–22	Changes in TBG, drugs, etc.
Resin T_3 uptake	25–35%	3–10	Changes in TBG, drugs, etc.
T_7 and ETR	Combinations of values for T_4 and resin T_3 uptake		
TSH	0–10 μIU/mL 2–7 μIU/mL	39	Pituitary disease
T_3RIA	80–200 ng/100 mL 1.2–3.1 nmol/L	41	Changes in TBG, drugs, etc.
Autoantibodies	Absent	30–60	
In vivo tests			
Radioiodine uptake (^{131}I, ^{123}I)	10–25%/24 hours	60–95	Never use in pregnancy: iodides T_3 and T_4 therapy, antithyroid drugs, thyroiditis
Thyroid scan radioiodine	Both lobes homogeneous	80	Iodides T_3, T_4: never use in pregnancy
TRH injection	TSH increase to 2x control	115	
TSH stimulation	No effect or increased uptake	115	
T_4 suppression	Uptake reduced to half of original value	115	Heart disease or other contraindication of T_4 therapy
Histology (biopsy)			
Fine needle aspiration biopsy	Normal cytology	28	Inadequate sample
Cutting needle biopsy	Normal cytology	*b*	Significant danger of hemorrhage

Reprinted with permission from MacKinnon RA, Yudofsky SC: *Principles of the Psychiatric Evaluation*, p 96. Lippincott, Philadelphia, 1991.
[a] Tests are listed in order of decreasing frequency of practical application. Adapted from Halsted JA, Halsted CH, editors: *The Laboratory in Clinical Medicine: Interpretation and Application*, ed 2. Saunders, Philadelphia, 1981.
[b] Cost data vary from laboratory to laboratory.

itive and false-negative results are common and are listed in Table 7.2–5. The sensitivity of the DST is considered to be 45 percent in major depressive disorders and 70 percent in major depressive episodes with psychotic features. The specificity is 90 percent compared with controls and 77 percent compared with other psychiatric diagnoses. Figure 7.2–1 illustrates the suppression of plasma cortisol in a patient with major depressive disorder before and 6 weeks after the initiation of treatment with a tricyclic drug. Some evidence indicates that patients with a positive DST result (especially 10 μg/dL) will have a good response to somatic treatment, such as electroconvulsive therapy (ECT) or cyclic antidepressant therapy.

Table 7.2–2
Thyroid Monitoring for Patients Taking Lithium

Evaluation	Before Treatment	Repeat at 6 months	Repeat Yearly
Medical			
1. Careful medical and family history to detect family history of thyroid disease	x		
2. Review of symptoms of hyperthyroidism and hypothyroidism	x	x	x
3. Physical examination, including palpation of thyroid	x		x
Laboratory			
T_3RU	x		x
T_4RIA	x		x
T_2I (free thyroxine index)	x		x
TSH	x	x	x
Antithyroid antibodies	x		x

Reprinted with permission from MacKinnon RA, Yudofsky SC: *Principles of the Psychiatric Evaluation*, p 104. Lippincott, Philadelphia, 1991.

Other Endocrine Tests

Many other hormones affect behavior. Exogenous hormonal administration has been shown to affect behavior, and known endocrine diseases have associated mental disorders.

Table 7.2–3
Thyroid Function Test Changes in Patients with Hypothyroidism

1. Serum T_4 concentration is decreased.
2. Serum-free thyroxine is decreased.
3. Serum T_3 concentration is decreased.
4. Serum T_3 uptake is decreased.
5. Serum PBI is decreased.
6. Serum thyroxine-binding globulin is normal.
7. Serum T_3-T_4 ratio is increased.
8. Serum thyroid-stimulating hormone is increased.

Reprinted with permission from MacKinnon RA, Yudofsky SC: *Principles of the Psychiatric Evaluation*, p 97. Lippincott, Philadelphia, 1991.

Table 7.2–4
TRH Test Protocol

1. Patient takes nothing by mouth after midnight and is at rest in bed at 8:30 AM.
2. Indwelling venous catheter is placed, and a normal saline drip is started to keep the line open.
3. At 8:59 AM, blood is taken through a three-way stopcock for determination of T_3RU, T_3RIA, T_4, and TSH levels (reverse T_3 is optional).
4. At 9 AM, intravenous TRH (protirelin) 500 μg is given slowly over 30 seconds. Side effects from the infusions may include a transient sensation of warmth, desire to urinate, nausea, metallic taste, headache, dry mouth, chest tightness, or a pleasant genital sensation. Those effects are generally short-lived and mild.
5. Blood samples are taken through the stopcock before the TRH is administered and at 15, 30, 60, and 90 minutes after infusion to measure changes in TSH.

Reprinted with permission from MacKinnon RA, Yudofsky SC: *Principles of the Psychiatric Evaluation,* p 94. Lippincott, Philadelphia, 1991.

In addition to thyroid hormones, these hormones include the anterior pituitary hormone prolactin, growth hormone, somatostatin, gonadotrophin-releasing hormone (GnRH), the sex steroids—luteinizing hormone (LH), follicle-stimulating hormone (FSH), testosterone, and estrogen. Melatonin from the pineal gland has been implicated in seasonal affective disorder (called mood disorder with seasonal pattern in DSM-IV).

Symptoms of anxiety or depression may be explained in some patients on the basis of unspecified changes in endocrine function or homeostasis.

Catecholamines

The level of serotonin metabolite 5-hydroxyindoleacetic acid (5-HIAA) is elevated in the urine of patients with carcinoid tumors. Elevated levels are noted at times in patients who take phenothiazine medication and in those who eat foods high in serotonin (for example, walnuts, bananas, avocados). The amount of 5-HIAA in cerebrospinal fluid is low in some people who are in a suicidal depression and in postmortem studies of those who have committed suicide in particularly violent ways. Low cerebrospinal fluid 5-HIAA levels are associated with violence in general. Norepinephrine and its metabolic products—metanephrine, normetanephrine, and vanillylmandelic acid (VMA)—can be measured in the urine, the blood, and the plasma. Plasma catecholamine levels are markedly elevated in pheochromocytoma, which is associated with anxiety, agitation, and hypertension. Some cases of chronic anxiety may share elevated blood norepinephrine and epinephrine levels. Some depressed patients have a low urinary norepinephrine to epinephrine ratio (NE:E).

High levels of urinary norepinephrine and epinephrine have been found in some patients with posttraumatic stress disorder. The norepinephrine metabolite 3-methoxy-4-hydroxyphenylglycol (MHPG) level is decreased in patients with severe depressive disorders, especially in those patients who attempt suicide.

Renal Function Tests

Creatinine clearance detects early kidney damage and can be serially monitored to follow the course of renal disease. Blood urea nitrogen (BUN) is also elevated in renal disease and is excreted by way of the kidneys; the serum BUN and creatinine are monitored in patients taking lithium. If the serum BUN or creatinine is abnormal, the patient's 2-hour creatinine clearance and ultimately the 24-hour creatinine clearance are tested. Table 7.2–6 outlines a suggested protocol for monitoring renal function in patients taking lithium. Table 7.2–7 summarizes other laboratory testing for patients taking lithium.

Liver Function Tests

Total bilirubin and direct bilirubin values are elevated in hepatocellular injury and intrahepatic bile stasis, which can occur with phenothiazine or tricyclic medication and with alcohol and other substance abuse. Certain drugs—for example, phenobarbital (Luminal)—may decrease serum bilirubin concentration. Liver damage or disease, which is reflected by abnormal findings in liver function tests (LFTs), may manifest

Table 7.2–5
Medical Conditions and Pharmacological Agents That May Interfere with Results of the Dexamethasone-Suppression Test

False-positive results are associated with
- Phenytoin
- Barbiturates
- Meprobamate
- Glutethimide
- Carbamazepine
- Cardiac failure
- Hypertension
- Renal failure
- Disseminated cancer and serious infections
- Recent major trauma or surgery
- Fever
- Nausea
- Dehydration
- Temporal lobe disease
- High-dosage estrogen treatment
- Pregnancy
- Cushing's disease
- Unstable diabetes mellitus
- Extreme weight loss (malnutrition, anorexia nervosa)
- Alcohol abuse
- Benzodiazepine withdrawal
- Tricyclic drug withdrawal
- Dementia
- Bulimia nervosa
- Acute psychotic disorder
- Advanced age

False-negative results are associated with
- Hypopituitarism
- Addison's disease
- Long-term synthetic steroid therapy
- Indomethacin
- High-dosage cyproheptadine treatment
- High-dosage benzodiazepine treatment

Reprinted with permission from Young M, Stanford J: The dexamethasone suppression test for the detection, diagnosis, and management of depression. Arch Intern Med *100:* 309, 1984.

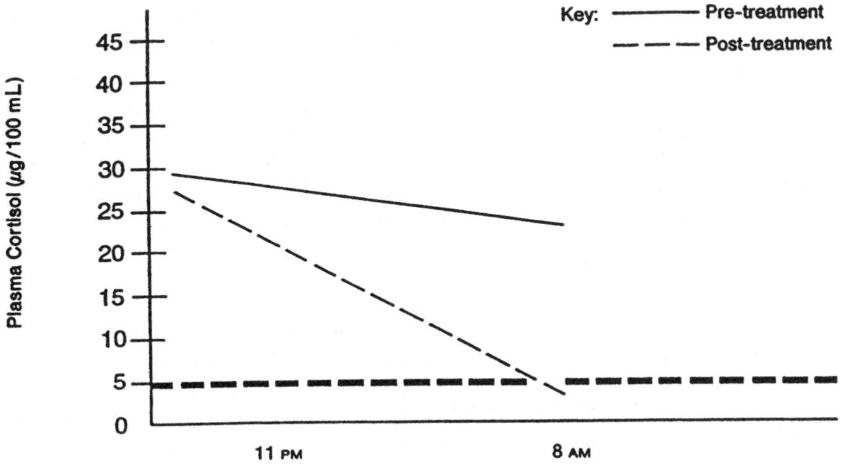
Key: Pre-treatment
Post-treatment
Plasma Cortisol (μg/100 mL)
45
40
35
30
25
20
15
10
5
0
11 PM
8 AM

FIGURE 7.2–1

Dexamethasone-suppression test results for a patient with major depressive disorder. (Reprinted with permission from MacKinnon RA, Yudofsky SC: *Principles of the Psychiatric Evaluation.* Lippincott, Philadelphia, 1991.)

with signs and symptoms of a cognitive disorder, including disorientation and delirium. Impaired hepatic function may increase the elimination half-lives of certain drugs, including some benzodiazepines, so that the drug may stay in a patient's system longer than it would under normal circumstances. LFTs must be monitored routinely when using certain drugs, such as carbamazepine (Tegretol) and valproate (Depakene).

Table 7.2–6
Renal Monitoring for Patients Taking Lithium

Evaluation	Before Treatment	Repeat at 6 months	Repeat Yearly
Medical			
1. Careful medical and family history to detect presence of familial kidney disease or predisposition to kidney disease (diabetes, hypertension)	x		
2. Specific comprehensive review of genitourinary system symptoms	x	x	x
3. Physical examination	x		x
Laboratory			
BUN	x		x
Creatinine	x	x	x
Creatinine clearance (24-hour urine) urinalysis	x		x
24-hour urine volume	x		x
12-hour fluid deprivation test	x		

Reprinted with permission from MacKinnon RA, Yudofsky SC: *Principles of the Psychiatric Evaluation*, p 103. Lippincott, Philadelphia, 1991.

BLOOD TEST FOR SEXUALLY TRANSMITTED DISEASES

The Venereal Disease Research Laboratory (VDRL) test is used as a screening test for syphilis. If positive, the result is confirmed by using the specific fluorescent treponemal antibody-absorption test (FTA-ABS test), in which the spirochete *Treponema pallidum* is used as the antigen. Central nervous system VDRL is measured in patients with suspected neurosyphilis. A positive HIV test result indicates that a person has been exposed to infection with the virus that causes acquired immune deficiency syndrome (AIDS).

TESTS RELATED TO PSYCHOTROPIC DRUGS

In caring for patients receiving psychotropic medication, there is a trend to take regular measurements of their plasma levels of the prescribed drug. For some drugs, such as lithium, the monitoring is essential; for other drugs, such as antipsychotics, it is mainly of academic or research interest. A clinician need not practice defensive medicine by insisting that all

Table 7.2–7
Other Laboratory Testing for Patients Taking Lithium

Test	Frequency
1. Complete blood count	Before treatment and yearly
2. Serum electrolytes	Before treatment and yearly
3. Fasting blood glucose	Before treatment and yearly
4. Electrocardiogram	Before treatment and yearly
5. Pregnancy testing for women of childbearing age[a]	Before treatment

Reprinted with permission from MacKinnon RA, Yudofsky SC: *Principles of the Psychiatric Evaluation*, p 106. Lippincott, Philadelphia, 1991.

[a] Take more frequently when compliance with treatment plan is uncertain.

patients receiving psychotropic drugs have blood levels taken for medicolegal purposes. The current status of psychopharmacological treatment is such that a psychiatrist's clinical judgment and experience, except in rare instances, is a better indication of a drug's therapeutic efficacy than is a plasma-level determination. Moreover, the reliance on plasma levels cannot replace clinical skills and the need to maintain the humanitarian aspects of patient care. The major classes of drugs and the suggested guidelines are outlined in the following discussion.

Benzodiazepines

No special tests are needed for patients taking benzodiazepines. Among the benzodiazepines metabolized in the liver by oxidation, impaired hepatic function increases the half-life. Baseline LFTs are indicated in patients with suspected liver damage. Urine testing for benzodiazepines is used routinely in cases of substance abuse.

Antipsychotics

Antipsychotics can cause leukocytosis, leukopenia, mild anemia, and, in rare cases, agranulocytosis. A baseline may be desirable; but, because bone marrow side effects can occur abruptly, even when the dosage of a drug has remained constant, a baseline normal CBC is not conclusive. Antipsychotics are metabolized in the liver, so LFTs may be useful. Antipsychotic plasma levels do not correlate with clinical response, although there is a possible correlation between high plasma levels and toxic side effects, especially with chlorpromazine (Thorazine) and haloperidol (Haldol). A known relation exists between antipsychotic levels and tardive dyskinesia. Plasma levels are currently of clinical use only to detect noncompliance and nonabsorption and, thus, may be useful in identifying a nonresponder.

Clozapine. Because of the risk of agranulocytosis (1 to 2 percent), patients who are being treated with clozapine (Clozaril) must have a baseline white blood cell (WBC) and differential count before the initiation of treatment, a WBC count every week throughout treatment, and a WBC count for 4 weeks after the discontinuation of clozapine. Physicians and pharmacists who provide clozapine are required to be registered through the Clozaril National Registry (1-800-448-5938). Table 7.2–8 summarizes the clinical management of reduced WBC, leukopenia, and agranulocytosis for patients treated with clozapine.

Tricyclic and Tetracyclic Drugs

An electrocardiogram (ECG) should be given before starting a regimen of cyclic drugs to assess for conduction delays, which may lead to heart block at therapeutic levels. Some clinicians believe that all patients receiving prolonged cyclic drug therapy should have an annual ECG. At therapeutic levels, the drugs suppress arrhythmias through a quinidine-like effect.

Blood levels should be tested routinely when using imipramine (Tofranil), desipramine (Norpramin), or nortriptyline (Pamelor) in the treatment of depressive disorders. Taking blood levels may also be of use in patients with a poor response at normal dosage ranges and in high-risk patients for whom there is an urgent need to know whether a therapeutic or toxic plasma level of the drug has been reached. Blood level tests should also include the measurement of active metabolites (for example, imipramine is converted to desipramine, amitriptyline [Elavil] to nortriptyline). Some characteristics of tricyclic drug plasma levels are described as follows.

Imipramine. The percentage of favorable responses correlates with plasma levels in a linear manner between 200 and 250 ng/mL, but some patients may respond at a lower level. At levels that exceed 250 ng/mL, there is no improved favorable response, and side effects increase.

Nortriptyline. The therapeutic window (the range within which a drug is most effective) is between 50 and 150 ng/mL. There is a decreased response rate at levels greater than 150 ng/mL.

Desipramine. Levels greater than 125 ng/mL correlate with a higher percentage of favorable responses.

Amitriptyline. Different studies have produced conflicting results with regard to blood levels, but they range from 75 to 175 ng/mL.

Procedure for Taking Blood Levels. The blood specimen should be drawn 10 to 14 hours after the last dose, usually in the morning after a bedtime dose. Patients must be receiving stable daily dosage for at least 5 days for the test to be valid. Some patients are unusually poor metabolizers of cyclic drugs and may have levels as high as 2,000 ng/mL, while taking normal dosages and before showing a favorable clinical response. Such patients must be monitored closely for cardiac side effects. Patients with levels greater than 1,000 ng/mL are generally at risk for cardiotoxicity.

Monoamine Oxidase Inhibitors

Patients taking monoamine oxidase inhibitors (MAOIs) are instructed to avoid tyramine-containing foods because of the danger of a potential hypertensive crisis. A baseline normal blood pressure (BP) must be recorded, and the BP must be monitored during treatment. MAOIs may also cause orthostatic hypotension as a direct drug side effect unrelated to diet. Other than their potential for causing elevated BP when taken with certain foods, MAOIs are relatively free of other side effects. A test used both in a research setting and in current clinical practice involves correlating the therapeutic response with the degree of platelet monoamine oxidase inhibition.

Lithium

Patients receiving lithium should have baseline thyroid function tests, electrolyte monitoring, a WBC, renal function

Table 7.2–8
Clinical Management of Reduced White Blood Cell Count, Leukopenia, and Agranulocytosis

Problem Phase	WBC Findings	Clinical Findings	Treatment Plan
Reduced WBC	WBC count reveals a significant drop (even if WBC count is still in normal range). "Significant drop" = (1) drop of more than 3,000 cells from prior test or (2) three or more consecutive drops in WBC counts	No symptoms of infection	1. Monitor patient closely 2. Institute twice-weekly CBC tests with differentials if deemed appropriate by attending physician 3. Clozapine therapy may continue
Mild leukopenia	WBC = 3,000–3,500	Patient may or may not show clinical symptoms, such as lethargy, fever, sore throat, weakness	1. Monitor patient closely 2. Institute a minimum of twice-weekly CBC tests with differentials 3. Clozapine therapy may continue
Leukopenia or granulocytopenia	WBC = 2,000–3,000 or granulocytes = 1,000–1,500	Patient may or may not show clinical symptoms, such as fever, sore throat, lethargy, weakness	1. Interrupt clozapine at once 2. Institute daily CBC tests with differentials 3. Increase surveillance, consider hospitalization 4. Clozapine therapy may be reinstituted after normalization of WBC
Agranulocytosis (uncomplicated)	WBC count less than 2,000 or granulocytes less than 1,000	The patient may or may not show clinical symptoms, such as fever, sore throat, lethargy, weakness	1. Discontinue clozapine at once 2. Place patient in protective isolation in a medical unit with modern facilities 3. Consider a bone marrow specimen to determine if progenitor cells are being suppressed 4. Monitor patient every 2 days until WBC and differential counts return to normal (about 2 weeks) 5. Avoid use of concomitant medications with bone marrow-suppressing potential
Agranulocytosis (with complications)	WBC count less than 2,000 or granulocytes less than 1,000	Definite evidence of infection, such as fever, sore throat, lethargy, weakness, malaise, skin ulcerations, etc.	6. Consult with hematologist or other specialist to determine appropriate antibiotic regimen 7. Start appropriate therapy; monitor closely
Recovery	WBC count more than 4,000 and granulocytes more than 2,000	No symptoms of infection	1. Once-weekly CBC with differential counts for 4 consecutive normal values 2. Clozapine must not be restarted

Reprinted with permission of Sandoz Pharmaceuticals Corporation and MacKinnon RA, Yudofsky SC: *Principles of the Psychiatric Evaluation,* p 118. Lippincott, Philadelphia, 1991.

tests (specific gravity, BUN, and creatinine), and a baseline ECG. The rationale for these tests is that lithium can cause renal concentrating defects, hypothyroidism, and leukocytosis; sodium depletion can cause toxic lithium levels; and about 95 percent of lithium is excreted in the urine. Lithium has also been shown to cause ECG changes, including various conduction defects.

Lithium is most clearly indicated in the prophylactic treatment of manic episodes (its direct antimanic effect may take up to 2 weeks) and is commonly coupled with antipsychotics for the treatment of acute manic episodes. Lithium itself may also have antipsychotic activity. The maintenance level is 0.6 to 1.2 mEq/L, although acutely manic patients can tolerate up to 1.5 to 1.8 mEq/L. Some patients may respond at lower levels, whereas others may require higher levels. A response below 0.4 mEq/L is probably a placebo. Toxic reactions may occur with levels over 2.0 mEq/L. Regular lithium monitoring is essential; there is a narrow therapeutic range beyond which cardiac problems and central nervous system (CNS) effects can occur.

Lithium levels are drawn 8 to 12 hours after the last dose, usually in the morning after the bedtime dose. The level should be measured at least twice a week while stabilizing the patient and may be drawn monthly thereafter.

Carbamazepine

A pretreatment CBC including platelet count should be done. Reticulocyte count and serum iron tests are also desirable. These tests should be repeated weekly during the first 3 months of treatment and monthly thereafter. Carbamazepine can cause aplastic anemia, agranulocytosis, thrombocytopenia, and leukopenia. Because of the minor risk of hepatotoxicity, LFTs should be done every 3 to 6 months. The medication should be discontinued if the patient shows any signs of bone marrow suppression as measured with periodic CBCs. The therapeutic level of carbamazepine is 8 to 12 ng/mL, with toxicity most often reached at levels of 15 ng/mL. Most clinicians report that levels as high as 12 ng/mL are hard to achieve. Table 7.2–9 summarizes one suggested protocol for the laboratory monitoring of patients taking carbamazepine.

Valproate

Serum levels of valproic acid (Depakene) and divalproex (Depakote) are therapeutic in the range of 45 to 50 ng/mL. Above 125 ng/mL, side effects occur, including thrombocytopenia. Serum levels should be obtained periodically, and LFTs should be obtained every 6 to 12 months.

Tacrine

Tacrine (Cognex) may cause liver damage. A baseline of liver function should be established, and follow-up serum transaminase levels should be obtained every other week for about 5 months. Patients who develop jaundice or who have bilirubin levels higher than 3 mg/dL must be withdrawn from the drug.

PROVOCATION OF PANIC ATTACKS WITH SODIUM LACTATE

Up to 72 percent of patients with panic disorder have a panic attack when administered an intravenous (IV) injection of sodium lactate. Therefore, lactate provocation is used to confirm a diagnosis of panic disorder. Lactate provocation has also been used to trigger flashbacks in patients with posttraumatic stress disorder. Hyperventilation, another known trigger of panic attacks in predisposed persons, is not as sensitive as lactate provocation in inducing panic attacks. Carbon dioxide (CO_2) inhalation also precipitates panic attacks in those so predisposed. Panic attacks triggered by sodium lactate are not inhibited by peripherally acting β-blockers but are inhibited by alprazolam (Xanax) and tricyclic drugs.

DRUG-ASSISTED INTERVIEW

Interviews with amobarbital (Amytal) have both diagnostic and therapeutic indications. Diagnostically, the interviews are helpful in differentiating nonorganic and organic conditions, particularly in patients with symptoms of catatonia, stupor, and muteness. Organic conditions tend to worsen with infusions of amobarbital, but nonorganic or psychogenic conditions tend to get better because of disinhibition, decreased anxiety, or increased relaxation. Therapeutically, amobarbital interviews are useful in disorders of repression and dissociation—for example, in the recovery of memory in psychogenic amnestic disorders and fugue, in the recovery of function in conversion disorder, and in the facilitation of emotional expression in posttraumatic stress disorder. Benzodiazepines can be substituted for amobarbital in the infusion.

LUMBAR PUNCTURE

Lumbar puncture is of use in patients who have a sudden manifestation of new psychiatric symptoms, especially changes in cognition. The clinician should be especially vigilant if there is fever or neurological symptoms such as seizures. Lumbar puncture is of use in diagnosing CNS infection (for example, meningitis).

Table 7.2–9
Laboratory Monitoring of Patients Taking Carbamazepine

Test	Frequency
1. Complete blood count	Before treatment and every 2 weeks for the first 2 months of treatment; thereafter, once every 3 months
2. Platelet count and reticulocyte count	Before treatment and yearly
3. Serum electrolytes	Before treatment and yearly
4. Electrocardiogram	Before treatment and yearly
5. SGOT, SGPT, LDH alkaline phosphatase	Before treatment and every month for the first 2 months of treatment; thereafter, every 3 months
6. Pregnancy test for women of childbearing age	Before treatment and as frequently as monthly in noncompliant patients

Reprinted with permission from MacKinnon RA, Yudofsky SC: *Principles of the Psychiatric Evaluation*, p 108. Lippincott, Philadelphia, 1991.

Table 7.2–10
Substances of Abuse That Can Be Tested in Urine

Substance	Length of Time Detected in Urine
Alcohol	7–12 hours
Amphetamine	48 hours
Barbiturate	24 hours (short-acting) 3 weeks (long-acting)
Benzodiazepine	3 days
Cannabis	3 days to 4 weeks (depending on use)
Cocaine	6–8 hours (metabolites 2–4 days)
Codeine	48 hours
Heroin	36–72 hours
Methadone	3 days
Methaqualone	7 days
Morphine	48–72 hours
Phencyclidine (PCP)	8 days
Propoxyphene	6–48 hours

Table 7.2–11
Blood Level Data for Clinical Assessment

Substance	Therapeutic or Normal (%)	Blood Levels Toxic (%)	Blood Levels Lethal (%)
Acetaminophen (Tylenol)	1.0–2.0 mg	15.0 mg	150.0 mg
Acetylsalicylic acid (salicylate)	10–30.0 mg	39.0 mg	50.0 mg
Aminophylline (theophylline)	1.0–2.0 mg	3.0–4.0 mg	21.0–25.0 mg
Amitriptyline (Elavil)	5.0–20.0 μg	50.0 μg	1.0–2.0 mg
Amphetamines	2.0–3.0 μg	50.0 μg	200.0 μg
Arsenic	0.0–2.0 μg	0.10 mg	1.5 mg
Barbiturates			
Short acting	0.1 mg	0.7 mg	1.0 mg
Intermediate-acting	0.1–0.5 mg	1.0–3.0 mg	3.0 mg
Phenobarbital	1.5–3.9 mg	4.0–6.0 mg	8.0– 15 mg
Barbital	1.0 mg	6.0–8.0 mg	10.0 mg
Bromide	5.0–30 mg	50–150 mg	200 mg
Carbamazepine (Tegretol)	0.8–1.2 mg	1.5 mg	
Chloral hydrate (Noctec)	0.2–1.0 mg	10.0 mg	25.0 mg
Chlordiazepoxide (Librium)	0.1–0.3 mg	0.55 mg	2.0 mg
Chlorpromazine (Thorazine)	0.05 mg	0.1–0.2 mg	0.3–1.2 mg
Cocaine	5.0–15.0 μg	90.0 μg	0.1–2.0 mg
Codeine	2.5–12.0 μg		20.0–60.0 μg
Desipramine (Norpramin)	15.0–30.0 μg	50.0 μg	1.0–2.0 mg
Diazepam (Valium)	0.05–0.25 mg	0.5–2.0 mg	2.0 mg
Digoxin	0.06–0.20 μg	0.21–0.90 μg	1.5 μg
Diphenhydramine (Benadryl)	1.0–10.0 μg	0.5 mg	1.0 mg
Doxepin (Sinequan)	10.0–25.0 μg	50.0–200.0 μg	1.0 mg
Ethanol		100.0 mg (legal intoxication)	350.0 mg
Glutethimide (Doriden)	0.02–0.08 mg	1.0–8.0 mg	3.0–10.0 mg
Haloperidol (Haldol)	0.05–0.9 μg	1.0–4.0 mg	
Imipramine (Tofranil)	15.0–25.0 μg	50.0–150.0 μg	0.2 mg
Lead	0.0–30.0 μg	130 μg	110.0–350.0 μg
Lithium	0.42–0.83 mg (0.6–1.2 mEq/L)	1.39 mg (2.0 mEq/L)	3.47 mg (4.0 mEq/L)
LSD		0.1–0.4 μg	
Meperidine (Demerol)	0.03–0.10 mg	0.5 mg	3.0 mg
Meprobamate	0.8–2.4 mg	6.0–10.0 mg	14.0–35.0 mg
Mercury	0.0–8 μg	100 μg	600.0 μg
Methadone (Dolophine)	30.0–110.0 μg	0.2 mg	0.4 mg
Methamphetamine	0.02–0.06 mg	0.06–0.5 mg	1.0–4.0 mg
Methanol		20.0 mg	89.0 mg
Methaqualone (Quaalude)	0.3–0.6 mg	1.0–3.0 mg	3.0 mg
Methylphenidate (Ritalin)	1.0–6.0 μg	80.0 μg	230.0 μg
Morphine	10.0 μg		5.0–400 μg (free morphine from heroin)
Nortriptyline (Pamelor)	12.0–16.0 μg	0.05 mg	1.3 mg
Oxycodone (Percodan)	1.7–3.6 μg	20.0–500.0 μg	
Paraldehyde	2.0–11.0 mg	20.0–40.0 mg	50.0 mg
Pentazocine (Talwin)	0.01–0.06 mg	0.2–0.5 mg	1.0–2.0 mg
Perphenazine (Trilafon)	0.5 μg	100.0 μg	
Phencyclidine (PCP)		0.7–24.0 μg	100.0–500.0 μg
Phenytoin (Dilantin)	1.0–2.0 mg	2.0–5.0 mg	10 mg
Primidone (Mysoline)	0.5–1.2 mg	5.0–8.0 mg	10.0 mg
Propoxyphene (Darvon)	5.0–20.0 μg	30.0–60.0 μg	80.0–200.0 μg
Propranolol (Inderal)	2.5–20.0 μg		0.8–1.2 mg
Quinidine	0.03–0.6 mg	1.0 mg	3.0–5.0 mg
Quinine	0.18 mg		1.2 mg
Thioridazine (Mellaril)	0.10–0.15 mg	1.0 mg	2.0–8.0 mg
Trifluoperazine (Stelazine)	0.08 mg	0.12–0.3 mg	0.3–0.8 mg

Reprinted with permission from Winek L: *Drug and Chemical Blood-Level Data*. Fisher Scientific, Pittsburgh, 1985.

Table 7.2–12
Other Laboratory Tests

Test	Major Psychiatric Indications	Comments
Acid phosphatase	Organic workup for cognitive disorders	Increased in prostate cancer, benign prostatic hypertrophy, excessive platelet destruction, bone disease
Adrenocorticotropic hormone (ACTH)	Organic workup	Increased in steroid abuse; may be increased in seizures, psychotic disorders, Cushing's disease, and in response to stress Decreased in Addison's disease
Alanine aminotransferase (ALT) (formerly called serum glutamic-pyruvic transaminase [SGPT])	Organic workup	Increased in hepatitis, cirrhosis, liver metastases Decreased in pyridoxine (vitamin B_6) deficiency
Albumin	Organic workup	Increased in dehydration Decreased in malnutrition, hepatic failure, burns, multiple myeloma, carcinomas
Aldolase	Eating disorders Schizophrenia	Increased in patients who abuse ipecac (e.g., bulimic patients), schizophrenia (60–80%)
Alkaline phosphatase	Organic workup Use of psychotropic medications	Increased in Paget's disease, hyperparathyroidism, hepatic disease, hepatic metastases, heart failure, phenothiazine use Decreased in pernicious anemia (vitamin B_{12} deficiency)
Ammonia, serum	Organic workup	Increased in hepatic encephalopathy
Amylase, serum	Eating disorders	May be increased in bulimia nervosa
Antinuclear antibodies	Organic workup	Found in systemic lupus erythematosus (SLE) and drug-induced lupus (e.g., secondary to phenothiazines, anticonvulsants); SLE can be associated with delirium, psychotic disorders, mood disorders
Aspartate aminotransferase (AST) (formerly SGOT)	Organic workup	Increased in heart failure, hepatic disease, pancreatitis, eclampsia, cerebral damage, alcohol dependence Decreased in pyridoxine (vitamin B_6) deficiency, terminal stages of liver disease
Bicarbonate, serum	Panic disorder Eating disorders	Decreased in hyperventilation syndrome, panic disorder, anabolic steroid abuse May be elevated in patients with bulimia nervosa, in laxative abuse, in psychogenic vomiting
Bilirubin	Organic workup	Increased in hepatic disease
Blood urea nitrogen (BUN)	Delirium Use of psychotropic medications	Elevated in renal disease, dehydration Elevations associated with lethargy, delirium If elevated, can increase toxic potential of psychiatric medications, especially lithium and amantadine (Symmetrel)
Bromide, serum	Dementia Psychosis	Bromide intoxication can cause psychosis, hallucinations, delirium Part of dementia workup, especially when serum chloride is elevated
Caffeine level, serum	Anxiety	Evaluation of patients with suspected caffeinism
Calcium (Ca), serum	Organic workup Mood disorders Psychosis Eating disorders	Increased in hyperparathyroidism, bone metastases Increase associated with delirium, depression, psychosis Decreased in hypoparathyroidism, renal failure Decrease associated with depression, irritability, delirium, long-term laxative abuse
Carotid ultrasound	Dementia	Occasionally included in dementia workup, especially to rule out multi-infarct dementia Primary value is in search for possible infarct causes
Catecholamines, urinary and plasma	Panic attacks Anxiety disorders	Elevated in pheochromocytoma
Cerebrospinal fluid (CSF)	Organic workup	Increased protein and cells in infection, positive VDRL in neurosyphilis, bloody CSF in hemorrhagic conditions
Ceruloplasmin, serum; copper, serum	Organic workup	Low in Wilson's disease (hepatolenticular disease)
Chloride (Cl), serum	Eating disorders Panic disorder	Decreased in patients with bulimia nervosa and psychogenic vomiting Mild elevation in hyperventilation syndrome, panic disorder

(continued)

Table 7.2–12 *(continued)*

Test	Major Psychiatric Indications	Comments
Cholecystokinin (CCK)	Eating disorders	Compared with controls, blunted in bulimic patients after eating meal (may normalize after treatment with antidepressants)
CO_2 inhalation; sodium bicarbonate infusion	Anxiety	Panic attacks produced in subgroup of patients
Coombs test, direct and indirect	Hemolytic anemias secondary to psychotropic medications	Evaluation of drug-induced hemolytic anemias, such as those secondary to chlorpromazine, phenytoin, levodopa, and methyldopa
Copper, urine	Organic workup	Elevated in Wilson's disease
Cortisol (hydrocortisone)	Organic workup Mood disorders	Excessive level may indicate Cushing's disease associated with anxiety, depression, and a variety of other conditions
Creatine phosphokinase (CPK)	Use of antipsychotics Use of restraints Substance abuse	Increased in neuroleptic malignant syndrome, intramuscular injection, rhabdomyolysis (secondary to substance abuse), patients in restraints, patients experiencing dystonic reactions; asymptomatic elevations seen with use of antipsychotics
Creatinine, serum	Organic workup	Elevated in renal disease
Dopamine (DA) (L-dopa stimulation of dopamine)	Depression	Inhibits prolactin Test used to assess functional integrity of dopaminergic system, which is impaired in Parkinson's disease, depression
Doppler ultrasound	Impotence Organic workup	Carotid occlusion, transient ischemic attack (TIA), reduced penile blood flow in impotence
Echocardiogram	Panic disorder	10–40% of patients with panic disorder show mitral valve prolapse
Electroencephalogram (EEG)	Organic workup	Seizures, brain death, lesions; shortened REM latency in depression High-voltage activity in stupor; low-voltage fast activity in excitement; in functional nonorganic cases (eg, dissociative disorders), alpha activity is present in the background, which responds to auditory and visual stimuli Biphasic or triphasic slow bursts seen in dementia of Creutzfeldt-Jakob disease
Epstein-Barr virus (EBV); cytomegalovirus (CMV)	Organic workup Chronic fatigue Mood disorders	Part of herpes virus group EBV is causative agent for infectious mononucleosis, which can present with depression and personality change CMV can produce anxiety, confusion, mood disorders EBV associated with chronic mononucleosis-like syndrome associated with chronic depression and fatigue; may be association between EBV and major depressive disorder
Erythrocyte sedimentation rate (ESR)	Organic workup	An increase in ESR represents a nonspecific test of infectious, inflammatory, autoimmune, or malignant disease; sometimes recommended in the evaluation of anorexia nervosa
Estrogen	Mood disorder	Decreased in menopausal depression and premenstrual syndrome; variable changes in anxiety
Ferritin, serum	Organic workup	Most sensitive test for iron deficiency
Folate (folic acid), serum	Alcohol abuse Use of specific medications	Usually measured with vitamin B_{12} deficiencies associated with psychotic disorders, paranoia, fatigue, agitation, dementia, delirium Associated with alcohol dependence, use of phenytoin, oral contraceptives, estrogen
Follicle-stimulating hormone (FSH)	Depression	High normal in anorexia nervosa, higher values in postmenopausal women; low levels in patients with panhypopituitarism
Glucose, fasting blood (FBS)	Panic attacks Anxiety Delirium Depression	Very high FBS associated with delirium Very low FBS associated with delirium, agitation, panic attacks, anxiety, depression
Glutamyl transaminase, serum	Alcohol abuse Organic workup	Increased in alcohol abuse, cirrhosis, liver disease
Gonadotropin-releasing hormone (GnRH)	Depression Anxiety Schizophrenia	Decreased in schizophrenia; increased in anorexia nervosa; variable in depression, anxiety

(continued)

Table 7.2–12 *(continued)*

Test	Major Psychiatric Indications	Comments
Growth hormone (GH)	Depression Schizophrenia	Blunted GH responses to insulin-induced hypoglycemia in depressed patients; increased GH responses to dopamine agonist challenge in schizophrenic patients; increased in some cases of anorexia nervosa
Hematocrit (Hct); hemoglobin (Hb)	Organic workup	Assessment of anemia (anemia may be associated with depressive and psychotic disorders)
Hepatitis A viral antigen (HAAg)	Mood disorders Organic workup	Less severe, better prognosis than hepatitis B; may present with anorexia nervosa, depression
Hepatitis B surface antigen (HBsAg); hepatitis Bc antigen (HBcAg)	Mood disorders Organic workup	Active hepatitis B infection indicates greater degree of infectivity and of progression to chronic liver disease May present with depression
Holter monitor	Panic disorder	Evaluation of panic-disordered patients with palpitations and other cardiac symptoms
Human immunodeficiency virus (HIV)	Organic workup	CNS involvement: AIDS dementia, personality change due to a general medical condition, mood disorder due to a general medical condition, acute psychotic disorders
17-Hydroxycorticosteroid	Depression	Deviations detect hyperadrenocorticalism, which can be associated with major depressive disorder Increased in steroid abuse
5-Hydroxyindoleacetic acid (5-HIAA)	Depression Suicide Violence	Decrease in CSF in aggressive or violent patients with suicidal or homicidal impulses May be indicator of decreased impulse control and predictor of suicide
Iron, serum	Organic workup	Iron-deficiency anemia
Lactate dehydrogenase (LDH)	Organic workup	Increased in myocardial infarction, pulmonary infarction, hepatic disease, renal infarction, seizures, cerebral damage, megaloblastic (pernicious) anemia, factitious elevations secondary to rough handling of blood specimen tube
Lupus anticoagulant (LA)	Use of phenothiazines	An antiphospholipid antibody, which has been described in some patients using phenothiazines, especially chlorpromazine
Lupus erythematosus (LE) test	Depression Psychosis Delirium Dementia	Positive test associated with systemic LE, which may present with various psychiatric disturbances, such as psychotic disorders, depressive disorders, delirium, dementia; also tested for with antinuclear antibody (ANA) and anti-DNA antibody tests
Luteinizing hormone (LH)	Depression	Low in patients with panhypopituitarism; decrease associated with depression
Magnesium, serum	Alcohol abuse Organic workup	Decreased in alcohol dependence; low levels associated with agitation, delirium, seizures
MAO, platelet	Depression	Low in depression
MCV (mean corpuscular volume) (average volume of a red blood cell)	Alcohol abuse	Elevated in alcohol dependence, vitamin B_{12}, folate deficiency
Melatonin	Mood disorder with seasonal pattern	Produced by light and pineal gland and decreased in mood disorder with seasonal pattern
Metal (heavy) intoxication (serum or urinary)	Organic workup	Lead—apathy, irritability, anorexia nervosa, confusion Mercury—psychosis, fatigue, apathy, decreased memory, emotional lability, "mad hatter" Manganese—manganese madness, Parkinson-like syndrome Aluminum—dementia Arsenic—fatigue, blackouts, hair loss
3-Methoxy-4-hydroxyphenylglycol (MHPG)	Depression Anxiety	Most useful in research; decreases in urine may indicate decreases centrally
Myoglobin, urine	Phenothiazine use Substance abuse Use of restraints	Increased in neuroleptic malignant syndrome; in PCP, cocaine, or lysergic acid diethylamide (LSD) intoxication; in patients in restraints
Nicotine	Anxiety Nicotine addiction	Anxiety, smoking

(continued)

Table 7.2–12 *(continued)*

Test	Major Psychiatric Indications	Comments
Nocturnal penile tumescence	Impotence	Quantification of penile circumference changes, penile rigidity, frequency of penile tumescence Evaluation of erectile function during sleep Erections associated with rapid eye movement (REM) sleep Helpful in differentiation between organic and functional causes of impotence
Parathyroid (parathormone) hormone	Anxiety Organic workup	Low level causes hypocalcemia and anxiety Dysregulation associated with wide variety of cognitive disorders
Phosphorus, serum	Organic workup Panic disorder	Increased in renal failure, diabetic acidosis, hypoparathyroidism, hypervitamin D Decreased in cirrhosis, hypokalemia, hyperparathyroidism, panic attack, hyperventilation syndrome
Platelet count	Use of psychotropic medications	Decreased by certain psychotropic medications (carbamazepine, clozapine, phenothiazines)
Porphobilinogen (PBG)	Organic workup	Increased in acute porphyria
Porphyria synthesizing enzyme	Psychosis Organic workup	Acute panic attack or a cognitive disorder can occur in acute porphyria attack, which may be precipitated by barbiturates, imipramine
Potassium (K), serum	Organic workup Eating disorders	Increased in hyperkalemic acidosis; increase is associated with anxiety in cardiac arrhythymia Decreased in cirrhosis, metabolic alkalosis, laxative abuse, diuretic abuse; decrease is common in bulimic patients and in psychogenic vomiting, anabolic steroid abuse
Prolactin, serum	Use of antipsychotic medications Cocaine use Pseudoseizures	Antipsychotics, by decreasing dopamine, increase prolactin synthesis and release, especially in women Elevated prolactin levels may be seen secondary to cocaine withdrawal Lack of prolactin rise after seizure suggests pseudoseizure
Protein, total serum	Organic workup Use of psychotropic medications	Increased in multiple myeloma, myxedema, lupus Decreased in cirrhosis, malnutrition, overhydration Low serum protein can result in greater sensitivity to conventional doses of protein-bound medications (lithium is not protein-bound)
Prothrombin time (PT)	Organic workup	Elevated in significant liver damage (cirrhosis), patients with lupus anticoagulant, which can be found in certain patients receiving antipsychotic medications, especially chlorpromazine
Reticulocyte count (estimate of red blood cell production in bone marrow)	Organic workup Use of carbamazepine	Low in megaloblastic or iron deficiency anemia and anemia of chronic disease Must be monitored in patient taking carbamazepine
Salicylate, serum	Psychotic disorder due to a general medical condition with hallucinations Suicide attempts	Toxic levels may be seen in suicide attempts and may cause psychotic disorder due to a general medical condition with hallucinations
Sodium (NA), serum	Organic workup	Decreased with water intoxication; SIADH Increased with excessive salt intake; diabetes Decreased in hypoadrenalism, myxedema, congestive heart failure, diarrhea, polydipsia, use of carbamazepine, anabolic steroids Low levels associated with greater sensitivity to conventional dose of lithium
Testosterone, serum	Impotence Hypoactive sexual desire disorder	Increase in anabolic steroid abuse Follow-up of sex offenders treated with medroxyprogesterone May be decreased in organic workup of impotence Decrease may be seen in hypoactive sexual desire disorder Decreased with medroxyprogesterone treatment
Thyroid function tests	Organic workup Depression	Detection of hypothyroidism or hyperthyroidism Abnormalities can be associated with depression, anxiety, psychosis, dementia, delirium
Urinalysis	Organic workup Pretreatment workup of lithium Drug screening	Provides clues to cause of various cognitive disorders (assessing general appearance, pH, specific gravity, bilirubin, glucose, blood, ketones, protein, etc.); specific gravity may be affected by lithium

(continued)

Table 7.2–12 *(continued)*

Test	Major Psychiatric Indications	Comments
Urinary creatinine	Organic workup Substance abuse Lithium use	Increased in renal failure, dehydration Part of pretreatment workup for lithium
Venereal Disease Research Laboratory (VDRL)	Syphilis	Positive (high titers) in secondary syphilis (may be positive or negative in primary syphilis) Low titers (or negative) in tertiary syphilis
Vitamin A, serum	Depression Delirium	Hypervitaminosis A is associated with a variety of mental status changes
Vitamin B_{12}, serum	Organic workup Dementia	Part of workup of megaloblastic anemia and dementia B_{12} deficiency associated with psychosis, paranoia, fatigue, agitation, dementia, delirium Often associated with chronic alcohol abuse
White blood cell (WBC)	Use of psychotropic medications	Leukopenia and agranulocytosis associated with certain psychotropic medications, such as phenothiazines, carbamazepine, clozapine Leukocytosis associated with lithium and neuroleptic malignant syndrome

URINE TESTING FOR SUBSTANCE ABUSE

A number of substances may be detected in a patient's urine if the urine is tested within a specific (and variable) period after ingestion. Knowledge of urine substance testing is becoming crucial for practicing physicians in view of the controversial issue of mandatory or random substance testing. Table 7.2–10 provides a summary of substances of abuse that can be tested in urine.

Laboratory tests are also used in the detection of substances that may be contributing to cognitive disorders. Table 7.2–11 is an outline of therapeutic, toxic, and lethal levels of substances most commonly implicated in cognitive disorders.

OTHER LABORATORY TESTS

Laboratory tests not already discussed are covered in Table 7.2–12 in terms of their indications and significance in medical conditions that affect behavior. See Chapter 11 for information about human immunodeficiency virus (HIV) testing.

References

Anfinson TJ, Kathol RG: Screening laboratory evaluation in psychiatric patients: A review. Gen Hosp Psychiatry *14* (4, Suppl): 248, 1992.

Appleby L, Luchins DJ, Dyson V: Effects of mandatory drug screens on substance use diagnoses in a mental hospital population. J Nerv Ment Dis *183:* 183, 1995.

Belkin B, Miller NS: Agreement among laboratory tests, self-reports, and collateral reports of alcohol and drug use. Ann Clin Psychiatry *4:* 33, 1992.

Bowden CL, Janicak PG, Orsulak P, et al: Relation of serum valproate concentration to response in mania. Am J Psychiatry *153:* 765, 1996.

Brower KJ, Catlin DH, Blow FC, Eliopulos GA, Beresford TP: Clinical assessment and urine testing for anabolic-androgenic steroid abuse and dependence. Am J Drug Alcohol Abuse *17:* 161, 1991.

Davidson M, Kahn RS, Knott P, Kaminsky R, Cooper M, DuMont K, Apter S, Davis KL: Effects of neuroleptic treatment on symptoms of schizophrenia and plasma homovanillic acid concentrations. Arch Gen Psychiatry *48:* 910, 1991.

Heuser I, Yassouridis A, Holsboer F: The combined dexamethasone/CRH test: A refined laboratory test for psychiatric disorders. J Psychiatr Res *28:* 341, 1994.

Hughes JR: A review of the usefulness of the standard EEG in psychiatry. Clin Electroencephalogr *27:* 35, 1996.

Mookhoek EJ, Sterrenburg CM: Annual laboratory screening for chronic hospitalized elderly psychiatric patients: Habit or necessity? Int J Geriatr Psychiatry *11:* 477, 1996.

Rosse RB, Deutsch LH, Deutsch SI: Medical assessment and laboratory testing in psychiatry. In *Comprehensive Textbook of Psychiatry,* ed 6, HI Kaplan, BJ Sadock, editors, p 601. Williams & Wilkins, Baltimore, 1995.

▲ 7.3 Physical Examination in Psychiatry

Although psychiatrists do not perform routine physical examinations on their patients, they should be able to distinguish physical diseases that mimic psychiatric disorders and vice versa. They also should be able to recognize the symptoms of some physical illnesses that have psychiatric signs or symptoms. A chief complaint of anxiety, for instance, may be associated with mitral valve prolapse, which is discovered by cardiac auscultation.

Some psychiatrists insist that every patient have a complete medical workup; others may not. Whatever their policy, psychiatrists should consider patients' medical status at the outset of a psychiatric evaluation. Psychiatrists must often decide whether a patient needs a medical examination and, if so, what it should include—most commonly, a thorough medical history, a review of systems, general observations, physical examination, and diagnostic laboratory studies.

HISTORY OF MEDICAL ILLNESS

In the course of conducting a psychiatric evaluation, information should be gathered about known bodily diseases or dysfunctions; hospitalizations and operative procedures; medications taken recently or at present; personal habits and occupational history; family history of illnesses; and specific physical complaints. Information about medical illnesses should be gathered from both the patient and the referring physician.

Information about previous episodes of illness may provide valuable clues about the nature of the present disorder. For example, if the present disorder is distinctly delusional, the patient has a history of several similar episodes, and each responded promptly to diverse forms of treatment, the possibility of substance-induced psychotic disorder is strongly suggested. To pursue this lead, the psychiatrist should order a drug screen. The history of a surgical procedure may also be useful; for instance, a thyroidectomy suggests hypothyroidism as the cause of depression.

Depression is a side effect of several medications prescribed for hypertension. Medication taken in a therapeutic dosage occasionally reaches high blood levels. Digitalis intoxication, for example, may occur under such circumstances and result in impaired mental functioning. Proprietary drugs may cause or contribute to an anticholinergic delirium. Therefore, the psychiatrist must inquire about over-the-counter remedies, as well as prescribed medications.

An occupational history may provide essential information. Exposure to mercury may result in complaints suggesting a psychosis, and exposure to lead, as in smelting, may produce a cognitive disorder. The latter clinical picture can also result from imbibing moonshine with a high lead content.

In eliciting information about specific symptoms, the psychiatrist brings medical and psychological knowledge into full play. For example, the psychiatrist should elicit sufficient information from the patient complaining of headache to predict, with considerable certainty, whether the pain is the result of intracranial disease. Also, the psychiatrist should be able to recognize that the pain in the right shoulder of a hypochondriacal patient with abdominal discomfort may be the classic referred pain of gallbladder disease.

REVIEW OF SYSTEMS

An inventory by systems should follow the open-ended inquiry. The review may be organized according to organ systems (for example, liver, pancreas), functional systems (for example, gastrointestinal), or a combination of the two, as in the following outline. In all cases, the review should be comprehensive and thorough.

Head

Many patients give a history of headache; its duration, frequency, character, location, and severity should be ascertained. Headaches often result from substance abuse, including alcohol, nicotine, and caffeine. Vascular (migraine) headaches are precipitated by stress. Temporal arteritis causes unilateral throbbing headaches and may lead to blindness. Brain tumors are associated with headaches as a result of increases in intracranial pressure. A history of head injury may result in subdural hematoma and in boxers can cause progressive dementia with extrapyramidal symptoms. The headache of subarachnoid hemorrhage is sudden, severe, and associated with changes in the sensorium. Normal pressure hydrocephalus may follow a head injury or encephalitis and may be associated with dementia and a shuffling gait.

Eye, Ear, Nose, and Throat

Visual acuity, diplopia, hearing problems, tinnitus, glossitis, and bad taste are covered in this area. A patient taking antipsychotics who gives a history of twitching about the mouth or disturbing movements of the tongue may be in the early and potentially reversible stage of tardive dyskinesia. Impaired vision may occur with thioridazine (Mellaril) in high dosages. A history of glaucoma contraindicates drugs with anticholinergic side effects. Aphonia may be hysterical in nature. The late stage of cocaine abuse can result in perforations of the nasal septum and difficulty in breathing. A transitory episode of diplopia may herald multiple sclerosis. Delusional disorder is more common in hearing-impaired people than in those with normal hearing.

Respiratory System

Cough, asthma, pleurisy, hemoptysis, dyspnea, and orthopnea are considered in this section. Hyperventilation is suggested if the patient's symptoms include all or a few of the following: onset at rest, sighing respirations, apprehension, anxiety, depersonalization, palpitations, inability to swallow, numbness of the feet and hands, and carpopedal spasm. Dyspnea and breathlessness may occur in depression. In pulmonary or obstructive airway disease, the onset of symptoms is usually insidious, whereas in depression, it is sudden. In depression, breathlessness is experienced at rest, shows little change with exertion, and may fluctuate within a matter of minutes; the onset of breathlessness coincides with the onset of a mood disorder and is often accompanied by attacks of dizziness, sweating, palpitations, and paresthesias.

In obstructive airway disease, only the patients with the most advanced respiratory incapacity experience breathlessness at rest. Most striking and of greatest assistance in making a differential diagnosis is the emphasis placed on the difficulty in inspiration experienced by patients with depression and on the difficulty in expiration experienced by patients with pulmonary disease. Bronchial asthma has sometimes been associated with childhood histories of extreme dependence on the mother. Patients with bronchospasm should not receive propranolol (Inderal) because it may block catecholamine-induced bronchodilation; propranolol is specifically contraindicated for patients with bronchial asthma because epinephrine given to such patients in an emergency will not be effective.

Cardiovascular System

Tachycardia, palpitations, and cardiac arrhythmia are among the most common signs of anxiety about which the patient may complain. Pheochromocytoma usually produces symptoms that mimic anxiety disorders, such as rapid heart beat, tremors, and pallor. Increased urinary catecholamines are diagnostic of pheochromocytoma. Patients taking guanethidine (Micronase) for hypertension should not receive tricyclic drugs, which reduce or eliminate the antihypertensive effect of guanethidine. A history of hypertension may preclude the use of monoamine oxidase inhibitors (MAOIs) because of the risk of a hypertensive crisis if such hypertensive patients inadvertently ingest foods high in tyramine. Patients with a suspected cardiac disease should have an electrocardiogram before tricyclics or lithium (Eskalith) is prescribed. A history of substernal pain should be evaluated, and the clinician should keep in mind that psychological stress can precipitate angina-type chest pain in the presence of normal coronary arteries. Patients taking opioids should never receive MAOIs, a combination that can cause cardiovascular collapse.

Gastrointestinal System

This area covers such topics as appetite, distress before or after meals, food preferences, diarrhea, vomiting, constipation, laxative use, and abdominal pain. A history of weight loss is common in depressive disorders; but depression may accompany the weight loss caused by ulcerative colitis, regional enteritis, and cancer. Anorexia nervosa is accompanied by severe weight loss in the presence of normal appetite. Avoidance of certain foods may be a phobic phenomenon or part of an obsessive ritual. Laxative abuse and induced vomiting are common in bulimia nervosa. Constipation can be caused by opioid dependence and by psychotropic drugs with anticholinergic side effects. Cocaine or amphetamine abuse causes a loss of appetite and weight loss. Weight gain occurs under stress. Polyphagia, polyuria, and polydipsia are the triad of diabetes mellitus. Polyuria, polydipsia, and diarrhea are signs of lithium toxicity.

Genitourinary System

Urinary frequency, nocturia, pain or burning on urination, and changes in the size and the force of the stream are some of the signs and symptoms in this area. Anticholinergic side effects associated with antipsychotics and tricyclic drugs may cause urinary retention in men with prostate hypertrophy. Erectile difficulty and retarded ejaculation are also common side effects of these drugs, and retrograde ejaculation occurs with thioridazine. A baseline level of sexual responsiveness before using pharmacological agents should be obtained. A history of venereal diseases—for example, gonorrheal discharge, chancre, herpes, and pubic lice—may indicate sexual promiscuity. In some cases, the first symptom of acquired immune deficiency syndrome (AIDS) is the gradual onset of mental confusion leading to dementia. If a psychotic patient remains incontinent after treatment for several days with a psychotropic medication, some cause other than a mental disorder should be suspected.

Menstrual History

A menstrual history should include the age of the onset of menarche and menopause; the interval, regularity, duration, and amount of flow of periods; irregular bleeding; dysmenorrhea; and abortions. Amenorrhea is characteristic of anorexia nervosa and also occurs in women who are psychologically stressed. Women who are afraid of becoming pregnant or who have a wish to be pregnant may have delayed periods. Pseudocyesis is false pregnancy with complete cessation of the menses. Perimenstrual mood changes (for example, irritability, depression, and dysphoria) should be noted. Painful menstruation can result from uterine disease (for example, myomata), from psychological conflicts about the menses, or from a combination of the two. Many women report a premenstrual increase in sexual desire. The emotional distress that some women experience after an abortion is usually mild and self-limited.

GENERAL OBSERVATION

An important part of the medical examination is subsumed under the broad head of general observation—visual, auditory, and olfactory. Such nonverbal clues as posture, facial expression, and mannerisms should also be noted.

Vision

Scrutiny of the patient begins at the first encounter. When the patient goes from the waiting room to the interview room, the psychiatrist should observe the patient's gait. Is the patient unsteady? Ataxia suggests diffuse brain disease, alcohol or other substance intoxication, chorea, spinocerebellar degeneration, weakness based on a debilitating process, and an underlying disorder, such as myotonic dystrophy. Does the patient walk without the usual associated arm movements and turn in a rigid fashion, like a toy soldier, as is seen in early Parkinson's disease? Does the patient have an asymmetry of gait, such as turning one foot outward, dragging a leg, or not swinging one arm, suggesting a focal brain lesion?

As soon as the patient is seated, the psychiatrist should direct attention to grooming. Is the patient's hair combed, are the nails clean, and are the teeth brushed? Has clothing been chosen with care, and is it appropriate? Although inattention to dress and hygiene is common in mental disorders—in particular, depressive disorders—it is also a hallmark of cognitive disorders. Lapses—such as mismatching socks, stockings, or shoes—may suggest a cognitive disorder.

The patient's posture and automatic movements or the lack of them should be noted. A stooped, flexed posture with a paucity of automatic movements may be due to Parkinson's disease, diffuse cerebral hemispheric disease, or the side effects of antipsychotics. An unusual tilt of the head may be adopted to avoid eye contact, but it can also result from diplopia, a visual field defect, or focal cerebellar dysfunction. Frequent quick, purposeless movements are characteristic of anxiety disorders, but they are equally characteristic of chorea and hyperthyroidism. Tremors, although commonly seen in anxiety disorders, may point to Parkinson's disease, essential tremor, or side effects of psychotropic medication. Patients with essential tremor sometimes seek psychiatric treatment because they believe the tremor must be due to unrecognized fear or anxiety, as others often suggest. Unilateral paucity or excess of movement suggests focal brain disease.

The patient's appearance is then scrutinized to assess general health. Does the patient appear to be robust, or is there a sense of ill health? Does looseness of clothing indicate recent weight loss? Is the patient short of breath or coughing? Does the patient's general physiognomy suggest a specific disease? Men with Klinefelter's syndrome have a feminine fat distribution and lack the development of secondary male sex characteristics. Acromegaly is usually immediately recognizable.

What is the patient's nutritional status? Recent weight loss, although often seen in depressive disorders and schizophrenia, may be due to gastrointestinal disease, diffuse carcinomatosis, Addison's disease, hyperthyroidism, and many other somatic disorders. Obesity may result from either emotional distress or organic disease. Moon facies, truncal obesity, and buffalo hump are striking findings in Cushing's syndrome. The puffy, bloated appearance seen in hypothyroidism and the massive obesity and periodic respiration seen in Pickwickian syndrome are easily recognized in patients referred for psychiatric help.

The skin frequently provides valuable information. The yellow discoloration of hepatic dysfunction and the pallor of anemia are reasonably distinctive. Intense reddening may be due to carbon monoxide poisoning or to photosensitivity resulting from porphyria or phenothiazines. Eruptions may be manifestations of such disorders as systemic lupus erythematosus, tuberous sclerosis with adenoma sebaceum, and sensitivity to drugs. A dusky purplish cast to the face, plus telangiectasia, is almost pathognomonic of alcohol abuse.

A young woman, complaining of depression and listlessness, mentioned in an off-hand manner that she had a skin rash. An on-the-spot examination of her skin revealed petechial hemorrhages on both arms and both legs. Further inquiry disclosed information about bleeding from several sites. Her blood platelet count was $4,000/mm^3$. The diagnosis was thrombocytopenia.

Careful observation may reveal clues that lead to the correct diagnosis in patients who create their own skin lesions. For example, the location and shape of the lesions and the time of their appearance may be characteristic of dermatitis factitia.

The patient's face and head should be scanned for evidence of disease. Premature whitening of the hair occurs in pernicious anemia, and thinning and coarseness of the hair occur in myxedema. Pupillary changes are produced by various drugs—constriction by opioids and dilation by anticholinergic agents and hallucinogens. The combination of dilated and fixed pupils and dry skin and mucous membranes should immediately suggest the likelihood of atropine use or atropine-like toxicity. Diffusion of the conjunctiva suggests alcohol abuse, cannabis abuse, or obstruction of the superior vena cava. Flattening of the nasolabial fold on one side or weakness of one side of the face—as manifested in speaking, smiling, and grimacing—may be the result of focal dysfunction of the contralateral cerebral hemisphere.

The patient's state of alertness and responsiveness should be carefully evaluated. Drowsiness and inattentiveness may be due to a psychological problem, but they are more likely to result from an organic brain dysfunction, whether secondary to an intrinsic brain disease or to an exogenous factor, such as substance intoxication.

Hearing

Listening intently is just as important as looking intently for evidence of somatic disorders. Slowed speech is characteristic not only of depression but also of diffuse brain dysfunction and subcortical dysfunction; unusually rapid speech is characteristic not only of manic episodes and anxiety disorders but also of hyperthyroidism. A weak voice with monotony of tone may be a clue to Parkinson's disease in patients who complain mainly of depression. A slow, low-pitched, hoarse voice should suggest the possibility of hypothyroidism; this voice quality has been described as sounding like a bad record of a drowsy, slightly intoxicated person with a bad cold and a plum in the mouth.

Difficulty in initiating speech may be due to anxiety or stuttering or may indicate Parkinson's disease or aphasia. Easy fatigability of speech may sometimes be a manifestation of an emotional problem, but it is also characteristic of myasthenia gravis. Patients with these complaints are likely to be seen by a psychiatrist before the correct diagnosis is made.

Word production, as well as the quality of speech, is important. When words are mispronounced or incorrect words are used, the possibility of aphasia caused by a lesion of the dominant hemisphere should be entertained. The same possibility exists when the patient perseverates, has trouble finding a name or a word, or describes an object or an event in an indirect fashion (paraphasia). When not consonant with the patient's socioeconomic and educational levels, coarseness, profanity, or inappropriate disclosures may indicate loss of inhibition caused by dementia.

Smell

Much less is learned through the sense of smell than through the senses of sight and hearing, but smell occasionally provides useful information. The unpleasant odor of a patient who fails to bathe suggests a cognitive disorder or a depressive disorder. The odor of alcohol or of substances used to hide it is revealing in a patient who attempts to conceal a drinking problem. Occasionally, a uriniferous odor calls attention to bladder dysfunction secondary to a nervous system disease. Characteristic odors are also noted in patients with diabetic acidosis, uremia, and hepatic coma.

PHYSICAL EXAMINATION

Patient Selection

The nature of the patient's complaints is critical to determine whether a complete physical examination is required. Complaints fall into the three categories of body, mind, and social interactions.

Bodily symptoms—such as headaches, erectile disorder, and palpitations—call for a thorough medical examination to determine what part, if any, somatic processes play in causing the distress. The same can be said for mental symptoms—such as depression, anxiety, hallucinations, and persecutory delusions—which can be expressions of somatic processes. If the problem is clearly limited to the social sphere—as in long-standing difficulties in interactions with teachers, employers, parents, or a spouse—there may be no special indication for a physical examination.

Psychological Factors

Even a routine physical examination may evoke adverse reactions; instruments, procedures, and the examining room may be frightening. A simple running account of what is being done can prevent much needless anxiety. Moreover, if the patient is consistently forewarned of what will be done, the dread of being suddenly and painfully surprised recedes. Comments such as, ''There's nothing to this'' and ''You don't have to be afraid because this won't hurt'' leave the patient in the dark and are much less reassuring than a few words about what actually will be done.

Although the physical examination is likely to engender or intensify a reaction of anxiety, it can also stir up sexual feelings. Some women with fantasies of being seduced may misinterpret an ordinary movement in the physical examination as a sexual advance. Similarly, a delusional man with homosexual fears may perceive a rectal examination as a sexual attack.

Lingering over the examination of a particular organ because an unusual but normal variation has aroused the physician's scientific curiosity is likely to raise concern in the patient that a serious pathological process has been discovered. Such a reaction in an anxious or hypochondriacal patient may be profound.

The physical examination occasionally serves a psychotherapeutic function. An anxious patient may be relieved to learn that, in spite of troublesome symptoms, there is no evidence of the serious illness that is feared. The young person who complains of chest pain and is certain that the pain heralds a heart attack can usually be reassured by the report of normal findings after a physical examination and electrocardiogram. The reassurance relieves only the worry occasioned by the immediate episode, however. Unless psychiatric treatment succeeds in dealing with the determinants of the reaction, recurrent episodes are likely.

Sending a patient who has a deeply rooted fear of malignancy for still another test that is intended to be reassuring is usually unrewarding. Some patients may have a false fixed belief that a disorder is present.

> In spite of repeated examinations, a patient who was a physician was convinced that he had carcinoma of the pharynx. A colleague, in an effort to produce positive proof, biopsied the area of complaint. When the patient was shown a microscopic section of normal tissue, he immediately declared that the normal section had been substituted for one showing malignant cells.

During the performance of the physical examination, an observant physician may note indications of emotional distress. For instance, during genital examinations, a patient's behavior may reveal information about sexual attitudes and problems, and these reactions may be used later to open this area for exploration.

Timing of the Physical Examination

Circumstances occasionally make it desirable or necessary to defer a complete medical assessment. For example, a delusional or manic patient may be combative or resistive or both. In this instance, a medical history should be elicited from a family member if possible, but, unless there is a pressing reason to proceed with the examination, it should be deferred until the patient is tractable.

For psychological reasons, it may be ill-advised to recommend a medical assessment at the time of an initial office visit. In view of today's increased sensitivity and openness about sexual matters and a proneness to turn quickly to psychiatric help, young men may complain about their failure to consummate a sexual relationship in an initial attempt. After taking a detailed history, the psychiatrist may conclude that the failure has been prematurely defined as a problem requiring attention. If so, neither a physical examination nor psychotherapy should be recommended; they would have the undesirable effect of reinforcing the notion of pathology.

Neurological Examination

If the psychiatrist suspects that the patient has an underlying somatic disorder, such as diabetes mellitus or Cushing's syndrome, referral is usually made to a medical physician for diagnosis and treatment. The situation is different when a cognitive disorder is suspected. The psychiatrist often chooses to assume responsibility in these cases, even though neurological evaluation may be especially difficult when a brain disease is in an early stage.

During the history-taking process in such cases, the patient's level of awareness, attentiveness to the details of the examination, understanding, facial expression, speech, posture, and gait are noted. It is also assumed that a thorough mental status examination will be performed. The neurological examination should then be carried out with two objectives in mind: to elicit signs pointing to focal, circumscribed cerebral dysfunction and to elicit signs suggesting diffuse, bilateral cerebral disease. The first objective is met by the routine neurological examination, which is designed primarily to reveal asymmetries in the motor, perceptual, and reflex functions of the two sides of the body caused by focal hemispheric disease. The second objective is met by seeking to elicit signs that have been attributed to diffuse brain dysfunction and to frontal lobe disease. These signs include the suckling, snout, palmomental, and grasp reflexes and the persistence of the glabella tap response. Regrettably, with the exception of the grasp reflex, such signs do not correlate strongly with the presence of underlying brain pathology.

Other Findings

Psychiatrists should be able to evaluate the significance of findings uncovered by consultants. With a patient who complains of a lump in the throat (globus hystericus) and who is found on examination to have hypertrophied lymphoid tissue, it is tempting to wonder about a cause-and-effect relation. How can a clinician be sure that the finding is not incidental? Has the patient been known to have hypertrophied lymphoid tissue at a time when no complaint was made? Do many people with hypertrophied lymphoid tissue never experience the sensation of a lump in the throat?

With a patient with multiple sclerosis who complains of an inability to walk but, on neurological examination, has only mild spasticity and a unilateral Babinski's sign, it is tempting to ascribe the symptom to the neurological disorder, but the evidence of a neurological abnormality is out of keeping with manifest dysfunction. The same holds true for a patient with profound dementia in whom a small frontal meningioma is seen on a computed tomography (CT) scan. The knowledgeable psychiatrist should recognize that profound dementia may not result from such a small lesion so situated.

A lesion is often found that can account for a symptom, but the psychiatrist should make every effort to separate an incidental finding from a causative one, to separate a lesion merely found in the area of the symptom from a lesion producing the symptom.

PATIENTS UNDERGOING PSYCHIATRIC TREATMENT

While patients are being treated for psychiatric disorders, psychiatrists should be alert to the possibility of intercurrent illnesses that call for diagnostic studies. Patients in psychotherapy, particularly those in psychoanalysis, may be all too willing to ascribe their new symptoms to emotional causes. Attention should be given to the possible use of denial, especially if the symptoms seem to be unrelated to the conflicts currently in focus.

At a time of increased psychological stress, a patient had urinary frequency, which she ascribed to her current situation. Only after much urging did she agree to see a urologist, who diagnosed and treated her cystitis.

Not only may patients in psychotherapy be prone to attribute new symptoms to emotional causes, but sometimes their therapists do so as well. The danger of providing psychodynamic explanations for physical symptoms is ever present.

A disturbed young woman in a psychiatric unit, who would curl up in a clothes basket and remain there for long periods, was described as regressing and assuming the fetal position. Later, when the diagnosis of meningoencephalitis was confirmed, it seemed that a better explanation for her behavior was the need to relieve pressure on nerve roots.

Symptoms such as drowsiness and dizziness and signs such as a skin eruption and a gait disturbance, common side effects of psychotropic medication, call for a medical reevaluation if the patient fails to respond in a reasonable time to changes in the dosage or the kind of medication prescribed. If patients who are receiving tricyclic or antipsychotic drugs complain of blurred vision, usually an anticholinergic side effect, and if the condition does not recede with a reduction in dosage or a change in medication, they should be evaluated to rule out other causes. In one case, the diagnosis proved to be *Toxoplasma* chorioretinitis. The absence of other anticholinergic side effects, such as a dry mouth and constipation, is an additional clue alerting the psychiatrist to the possibility of a concomitant medical illness.

Early in an illness, there may be few if any positive physical or laboratory results. In such instances, especially if the evidence of psychic trauma or emotional conflicts is glaring, all symptoms are likely to be regarded as psychosocial in origin and new symptoms also seen in this light. Indications for repeating portions of the medical workup may be missed unless the psychiatrist is alert to clues suggesting that some symptoms do not fit the original diagnosis and point, instead, to a medical illness. Occasionally, a patient with an acute illness, such as encephalitis, is hospitalized with the diagnosis of schizophrenia; or a patient with a subacute illness, such as carcinoma of the pancreas, is treated in a private office or clinic with the diagnosis of a depressive disorder. Although it may not be possible to make the correct diagnosis at the time of the initial psychiatric evaluation, continued surveillance and attention to clinical details usually provide clues leading to the recognition of the cause.

The likelihood of intercurrent illness is greater with some psychiatric disorders than with others. Substance abusers, for example, because of their life patterns, are susceptible to infection and are likely to suffer from the adverse effects of trauma, dietary deficiencies, and poor hygiene.

When somatic and psychological dysfunctions are known to coexist, the psychiatrist should be thoroughly conversant with the patient's medical status. In cases of cardiac decompensation, peripheral neuropathy, and other disabling disorders, the nature and the degree of the impairment that can be attributed to the physical disorder should be assessed. It is important to answer the question: Does the patient exploit a disability, or is it ignored or denied with resultant overexertion? To answer this question, the psychiatrist must assess the patient's capabilities and limitations, rather than make sweeping judgments based on a diagnostic label.

Special vigilance about medical status is required for some patients in treatment for somatoform and eating disorders. Such is the case for patients with ulcerative colitis who are bleeding profusely and for patients with anorexia nervosa who are losing appreciable weight. These disorders can become life threatening.

Importance of Medical Illness

Numerous articles have called attention to the need for thorough medical screening of patients seen in psychiatric inpatient services and clinics. (A similar need has been shown to exist for the psychiatric evaluation of patients seen in medical inpatient services and clinics.)

Among identified psychiatric patients, anywhere from 24 to 60 percent have been shown to suffer from associated physical disorders. In a survey of 2,090 psychiatric clinic patients, 43 percent were found to have associated physical disorders; of these, almost half the physical disorders had not been diagnosed by the referring sources. (In this study, 69 patients were found to have diabetes mellitus, but only 12 of the cases of diabetes had been diagnosed before referral.)

Expecting all psychiatrists to be experts in internal medicine is unrealistic, but expecting them to recognize physical disorders when present is realistic. Moreover, they should make appropriate referrals and collaborate in treating patients who have both physical and mental disorders.

Psychiatric symptoms are nonspecific; they can herald medical as well as psychiatric illness. Moreover, psychiatric symptoms often precede the appearance of definitive medical symptoms. Some psychiatric symptoms—such as visual hallucinations, distortions, and illusions—should call forth a high level of suspicion.

The medical literature abounds with case reports of patients whose disorders were initially considered emotional but ultimately proved to be organic. The data in most of the reports revealed features pointing toward organicity. Diagnostic errors arose because such features were accorded too little weight.

References

D'Ercole A, Skodol AE, Struening E, Curtis J, Millman J: Diagnosis of physical illness in psychiatric patients using Axis III and a standardized medical history. Hosp Community Psychiatry *42:* 395, 1991.

Ellenhorn MJ, Barceloux DG: *Medical Toxicology: Diagnosis and Treatment of Human Poisoning.* Elsevier, New York, 1988.

Kaaya S, Goldberg D, Gask L: Management of somatic presentations of psychiatric illness in general medical settings: Evaluation of a new training course for general practitioners. Med Educ *26:* 138, 1992.

Kirch DG: Medical assessment and laboratory testing in psychiatry. In *Comprehensive Textbook of Psychiatry,* ed 5, HI Kaplan, BJ Sadock, editors, p 525. Williams & Wilkins, Baltimore, 1989.

Osterloh JD, Becker CE: Chemical dependency and drug testing in the workplace. West J Med *152:* 506, 1990.

Waddington D: GP monitoring of lithium levels. Br J Psychiatry *168:* 383, 1996.

Weinberger DR: Brain disease and psychiatric illness: When should a psychiatrist order a CT scan? Am J Psychiatry *141:* 1521, 1984.

8

Typical Signs and Symptoms of Psychiatric Illness Defined

Psychiatrists develop their ability to detect people's mental conditions for several reasons: to make accurate diagnoses; to carry out effective treatments of patients; to offer reliable prognoses; to analyze psychiatric issues as fully as possible; and to communicate fruitfully with other clinicians. To accomplish these aims, they must become experts in the language of psychiatry; they must learn to recognize and define behavioral and emotional signs and symptoms and must then become masters at rigorously observing and articulately describing the mental phenomena of psychiatry.

Signs are clinicians' observations and objective findings, such as a patient's constricted affect or psychomotor retardation. *Symptoms* are the subjective experiences described by patients, such as depressed mood or lack of energy. A *syndrome* is a group of signs and symptoms that together make up a recognizable condition, which can be more equivocal than a specific disorder or disease.

The following outline is a comprehensive list of signs and symptoms, each of which has a precise definition or description. Most psychiatric signs and symptoms are rooted in normal behavior and can be understood as various points on a spectrum of behavior ranging from normal to pathological. Table 8–1 presents an alphabetical list of the mental phenomena and the signs and symptoms of psychiatric illness outlined in this chapter. The right-hand column contains numbers and letters that refer to the location in this chapter of each term's definition.

I. **Consciousness:** state of awareness.
   A. **Disturbances of consciousness:** apperception is perception modified by a person's own emotions and thoughts; sensorium is the state of cognitive functioning of the special senses (sometimes used as a synonym for consciousness); disturbances of consciousness are most often associated with brain pathology.
      1. Disorientation: disturbance of orientation in time, place, or person.
      2. Clouding of consciousness: incomplete clear-mindedness with disturbances in perception and attitudes.
      3. Stupor: lack of reaction to and unawareness of surroundings.
      4. Delirium: bewildered, restless, confused, disoriented reaction associated with fear and hallucinations.
      5. Coma: profound degree of unconsciousness.
      6. Coma vigil: coma in which a patient appears to be asleep but ready to be aroused (also known as akinetic mutism).
      7. Twilight state: disturbed consciousness with hallucinations.
      8. Dreamlike state: often used as a synonym for complex partial seizure or psychomotor epilepsy.
      9. Somnolence: abnormal drowsiness.
      10. Confusion: disturbance of consciousness in which reactions to environmental stimuli are inappropriate; manifested by a disordered orientation in relation to time, place, or person.
      11. Drowsiness: a state of impaired awareness associated with a desire or inclination to sleep.
      12. Sundowning: syndrome in older people that usually occurs at night and is characterized by drowsiness, confusion, ataxia, and falling as the result of being overly sedated with medications; also called sundowner's syndrome.
   B. **Disturbances of attention:** attention is the amount of effort exerted in focusing on certain portions of an experience; ability to sustain a focus on one activity; ability to concentrate.
      1. Distractibility: inability to concentrate attention; state in which attention is drawn to unimportant or irrelevant external stimuli.
      2. Selective inattention: blocking out only those things that generate anxiety.
      3. Hypervigilance: excessive attention and focus on all internal and external stimuli, usually secondary to delusional or paranoid states.
      4. Trance: focused attention and altered consciousness, usually seen in hypnosis, dissociative disorders, and ecstatic religious experiences.
   C. **Disturbances in suggestibility:** compliant and uncritical response to an idea or influence.
      1. Folie à deux (or *folie à trois*): communicated emotional illness between two (or three) persons.
      2. Hypnosis: artificially induced modification of consciousness characterized by a heightened suggestibility.

Table 8–1
Index to Signs and Symptoms of Psychiatric Illness (This table lists in alphabetical order the mental phenomena and the signs and symptoms of psychiatric illness discussed in this chapter. The numbers and letters in the right-hand column refer to the place in the chapter where each item is defined.)

Abreaction	II, C, 9	Bradykinesia	III, 22
Abulia	III, 15	Broca's aphasia	V, B, 1
Acalculia	VIII, B, 1	Bulimia	II, D, 11
Acrophobia	IV, C, 11c	Catalepsy	III, 2a
Acting out	III, 14	Cataplexy	III, 4
Adiadochokinesia	VI, B, 8	Catatonia	III, 2
Affect	II, A	Catatonic excitement	III, 2b
Aggression	III, 13	Catatonic posturing	III, 2e
Agitation	II, C, 4	Catatonic rigidity	III, 2d
Agnosia	VI, B	Catatonic stupor	III, 2c
Agoraphobia	IV, C, 11d	Cenesthesic hallucination	VI, A, 1, h
Agraphia	VIII, B, 2	*Cerea flexibilitas* (waxy flexibility)	III, 21
Ailurophobia	IV, C, 11f	Chorea	III, 23
Akathisia	III, 10e	Circumstantiality	IV, B, 3
Akinesia	III, 2g	Clang association	IV, B, 14
Akinetic mutism	I, A, 6	Claustrophobia	IV, C, 11i
Alexia	VIII, B, 3	Clérambault–Kandinsky complex	IV, C, 31
Alexithymia	II, B, 12	Clonic convulsion	III, 24, a
Algophobia	IV, C, 11e	Clouding of consciousness	I, A, 2
Alogia	V, B, 7	Cluttering	V, A, 10
Ambivalence	II, C, 8	Coma	I, A, 5
Amnesia	VII, A, 1	Coma vigil	I, A, 6
Amnestic aphasia	V, B, 3	Command automatism	III, 8
Anergia	III, 16	Command hallucination	VI, A, 1o
Anhedonia	II, B, 10	Complex partial seizure	III, 25, c
Anomia	V, B, 3	Compulsion	IV, C, 9; III, 10f
Anorexia	II, D, 1	Conation	III
Anosognosia	VI, B, 1	Concrete thinking	VIII, D
Anterograde amnesia	VII, A, 1a	Condensation	IV, B, 9
Anxiety	II, C, 1	Confabulation	VII, A, 2c
Apathy	II, C, 7	Confusion	I, A, 10
Aphasic disturbances	V, B	Consciousness	I
Apperception	I	Constipation	II, D, 7
Appropriate affect	II, A, 1	Constricted affect	II, A, 4
Apraxia	VI, B, 6	Conversion phenomena	VI, C
Astasia abasia	III, 17	Convulsion	III, 24
Astereognosis	VI, B, 4	Coprolalia	IV, C, 10
Ataxia	III, 10g	Copropregia	V, B, 8
Attention	I, B	Coprophagia	III, 18
Auditory hallucination	VI, A, 1c	*Déjà entendu*	VII, A, 2e
Aura	VI, B, 9	*Déjà pensé*	VII, A, 2f
Autistic thinking	IV, A, 7	Déjà vu	VII, A, 2d
Automatic judgment	X, B	Delirium	I, A, 4
Automatic obedience	III, 8	Delirium tremens	VI, A, 1l
Automatism	III, 7	Delusion	IV, C, 3
Autotopagnosia	VI, B, 2	Delusion of control	IV, C, 3j
Bizarre delusion	IV, C, 3a	Delusion of grandeur	IV, C, 3h, ii
Blackout	VII, A, 8	Delusion of infidelity	IV, C, 3k
Blocking	IV, B, 15	Delusion of persecution	IV, C, 3h, i
Blunted affect	II, A, 3	Delusion of poverty	IV, C, 3f

(*continued*)

Table 8–1 (*continued*)

Delusion of reference	IV, C, 3h, iii
Delusion of self-accusation	IV, C, 3i
Delusional jealousy	IV, C, 3k
Dementia	VIII, B
Dementia syndrome of depression	VIII, C
Depersonalization	VI, C, 4
Depression	II, B, 9
Derailment	IV, B, 12
Derealization	VI, C, 5
Dereism	IV, A, 6
Diminished libido	II, D, 6
Dipsomania	III, 10f, i
Disorientation	I, A, 1
Dissociation	VI, C, 8
Dissociative identity disorder	V1, C, 7
Distractibility	I, B, 1
Disturbances associated with cognitive disorder	VI, B
Disturbances associated with conversion and dissociative phenomena	VI, C
Disturbances in content of thought	IV, C
Disturbances in form of thinking	IV, A
Disturbances in speech	V, A
Disturbances in suggestibility	I, C
Disturbances of attention	I, B
Disturbances of consciousness	I, A
Disturbances of memory	VII, A
Diurnal variation	II, D, 5
Dreamlike state	I, A, 8
Drowsiness	I, A, 10
Dysarthria	V, A, 7
Dyscalculia	VIII, B, 1
Dysgraphia	VIII, B, 2
Dyskinesia	III, 19
Dysphoric mood	II, B, 1
Dysprosody	V, A, 6
Dystonia	III, 26
Echolalia	IV, B, 8
Echopraxia	III, 1
Ecstasy	II, B, 8
Egomania	IV, C, 5
Eidetic image	VII, A, 4
Elation	II, B, 14
Elevated mood	II, B, 6
Emotion	II
Emotional insight	IV, A, 10
Erotomania	IV, C, 3l
Erythrophobia	IV, C, 11g
Euphoria	II, B, 7
Euthymic mood	II, B, 2
Excessively loud or soft speech	V, A, 8
Expansive mood	II, B, 3
Expressive aphasia	V, B, 1
False memory	VII, A, 2h
Fatigue	II, D, 8
Fausse reconnaissance	VII, A, 2a
Fear	II, C, 3
Flat affect	II, A, 5
Flight of ideas	IV, B, 13
Fluent aphasia	V, B, 2
Folie à deux (folie à trois)	I, C, 1
Formal thought disorder	IV, A, 4
Formication	VI, A, 1g
Free-floating anxiety	II, C, 2
Freudian slip	IV
Fugue	VI, C, 6
Generalized tonic-clonic seizure	III, 25, a
Global aphasia	V, B, 6
Glossolalia	IV, B, 16
Grief	II, B, 11
Guilt	II, C, 11
Gustatory hallucination	VI, A, 1f
Hallucination	VI, A, 1
Hallucinosis	VI, A, 1l
Haptic hallucination	VI, A, 1g
Hyperactivity (hyperkinesis)	III, 10b
Hypermnesia	VII, A, 3
Hyperphagia	II, D, 2
Hypersomnia	II, D, 4
Hypervigilance	I, B, 3
Hypnagogic hallucination	VI, A, 1a
Hypnopompic hallucination	VI, A, 1b
Hypnosis	I, C, 2
Hypoactivity (hypokinesis)	III, 11
Hypochondria	IV, C, 7
Hysterical anesthesia	VI, C, 1
Idea of reference	IV, C, 3h, iii
Illogical thinking	IV, A, 5
Illusion	VI, A, 2
Immediate memory	VII, B, 1
Impaired insight	IX, C
Impaired judgment	X, C
Impulse control	II, C, 12
Inappropriate affect	II, A, 2
Incoherence	IV, B, 5
Increased libido	II, D, 6
Initial insomnia	II, D, 3a
Insight	IX
Insomnia	II, D, 3
Intellectual insight	IX, A
Intelligence	VIII
Irrelevant answer	IV, B, 10
Irritable mood	II, B, 4
Jamais vu	VII, A, 2g

(*continued*)

Table 8–1 (*continued*)

Jargon aphasia	V, B, 5	Persecutory delusion	IV, C, 3h, i
Kleptomania	III, 10f, ii	Perseveration	IV, B, 6
Labile affect	II, A, 6	Phantom limb	VI, A, 1g
Labile mood	II, B, 5	Phobia	IV, C, 11
Lethologica	VII, A, 7	Physiological disturbances associated with mood	II, D
Lilliputian hallucination	VI, A, 1i	Pica	II, D, 9
Logorrhea	V, A, 2	Polyphagia	III, 10h
Loosening of associations	IV, B, 11	Posturing	III, 2e
Macropsia	VI, C, 2	Poverty of content of speech	V, A, 5
Magical thinking	IV, A, 8	Poverty of speech	V, A, 3
Mannerism	III, 6	Preoccupation of thought	IV, C, 4
Melancholia	II, C, 13	Pressure of speech	V, A, 1
Memory	VII	Primary process thinking	IV, A, 9
Mental disorder	IV, A, 1	Prosopagnosia	VI, B, 5
Mental retardation	VIII, A	Pseudocyesis	II, D, 10
Micropsia	VI, C, 3	Pseudodementia	VIII, C
Middle insomnia	II, D, 3b	Pseudologia phantastica	IV, C, 3m
Mimicry	III, 12	Psychomotor agitation	III, 10a
Monomania	IV, C, 6	Psychosis	IV, A, 2
Mood	II, B	Reality testing	IV, A, 3
Mood-congruent delusion	IV, C, 3c	Recent memory	VII, B, 2
Mood-congruent hallucination	VI, A, 1j	Recent past memory	VII, B, 3
Mood-incongruent delusion	IV, C, 3d	Receptive aphasia	V, B, 2
Mood-incongruent hallucination	VI, A, 1k	Remote memory	VII, B, 4
Mood swings	II, B, 5	Repression	VII, A, 6
Motor aphasia	V, B, 1	Restricted affect	II, A, 4
Motor behavior (conation)	III	Retrograde amnesia	VII, A, 1b
Mourning	II, B, 11	Retrospective falsification	VII, A, 2b
Multiple personality	VI, C, 7	Rigidity	III, 2d
Munchausen syndrome	IV, C, 3m	Ritual	III, 10f, vi
Muscle rigidity	III, 20	Rumination	IV, C, 8
Mutism	III, 9	Satyriasis	III, 10f, iv
Needle phobia	IV, C, 111	Screen memory	VII, A, 5
Negativism	III, 3	Seizure	III, 25
Neologism	IV, B, 1	Selective inattention	I, B, 2
Nihilistic delusion	IV, C, 3e	Sensorium	I
Noesis	IV, C, 12	Sensory aphasia	V, B, 2
Nominal aphasia	V, B, 3	Shame	II, C, 10
Nonfluent aphasia	V, B, 1	Simple partial seizure	III, 25, b
Nymphomania	III, 10f, iii	Simultagnosia	VI, B, 7
Obsession	IV, C, 8	Sleepwalking	III, 10d
Olfactory hallucination	VI, A, 1e	Social phobia	IV, C, 11b
Overactivity	III, 10	Somatic delusion	IV, C, 3g
Overvalued idea	IV, C, 2	Somatic hallucination	VI, A, 1h
Panic	II, C, 6	Somatopagnosia	VI, B, 2
Panphobia	IV, C, 11h	Somnambulism	III, 10d
Paramnesia	VII, A, 2	Somnolence	I, A, 9
Paranoid delusions	IV, C, 3h	Speaking in tongues	IV, B, 16
Paranoid ideation	IV, C, 3h	Specific disturbances in form of thought	IV, B
Parapraxis	IV	Specific phobia	IV, C, 11a
Pathological jealousy	IV, C, 3k	Stereotypy	III, 5
Perception	VI		

(*continued*)

Table 8–1 (*continued*)

Stupor	I, A, 3; III, 2c	Trailing phenomenon	VI, A, 1n
Stuttering	V, A, 9	Trance	I, B, 4
Suicidal ideation	II, B, 13	Tremor	III, 10i
Sundowning	I, A, 12	Trend of thought	IV, C, 4
Synesthesia	VI, A, 1m	Trichotillomania	III, 10f, v
Syntactical aphasia	V, B, 4	True insight	IX, B
Systematized delusion	IV, C, 3b	Twilight state	I, A, 7
Tactile (haptic) hallucination	VI, A, 1g	Twirling	III, 21
Tangentiality	IV, B, 4	*Unio mystica*	IV, C, 13
Tension	II, C, 5	Vegetative signs	II, D
Terminal insomnia	II, D, 3c	Verbigeration	IV, B, 7
Thinking	IV	Visual agnosia	VI, B, 3
Thought broadcasting	IV, C, 3j, iii	Visual hallucination	VI, A, 1d
Thought control	IV, C, 3j, iv	Volubility	V, A, 2
Thought deprivation	IV, B, 15	Waxy flexibility	III, 2f
Thought insertion	IV, C, 3j, ii	Wernicke's aphasia	V, B, 2
Thought withdrawal	IV, C, 3j, i	Word salad	IV, B, 2
Tic	III, 10c	Xenophobia	IV, C, 11j
Tonic convulsion	III, 24, b	Zoophobia	IV, C, 11k

II. Emotion: complex feeling state with psychic, somatic, and behavioral components that is related to affect and mood.

A. Affect: observed expression of emotion, possibly inconsistent with patient's description of emotion.

1. Appropriate affect: condition in which the emotional tone is in harmony with the accompanying idea, thought, or speech; also further described as broad or full affect in which a full range of emotions is appropriately expressed.
2. Inappropriate affect: disharmony between the emotional feeling tone and the idea, thought, or speech accompanying it.
3. Blunted affect: disturbance in affect manifested by a severe reduction in the intensity of externalized feeling tone.
4. Restricted or constricted affect: reduction in intensity of feeling tone less severe than blunted affect but clearly reduced.
5. Flat affect: absence or near absence of any signs of affective expression; voice monotonous, face immobile.
6. Labile affect: rapid and abrupt changes in emotional feeling tone, unrelated to external stimuli.

B. Mood: a pervasive and sustained emotion, subjectively experienced and reported by a patient and observed by others; examples include depression, elation, anger.

1. Dysphoric mood: an unpleasant mood.
2. Euthymic mood: normal range of mood, implying absence of depressed or elevated mood.
3. Expansive mood: a person's expression of feelings without restraint, frequently with an overestimation of their significance or importance.
4. Irritable mood: a state in which a person is easily annoyed and provoked to anger.
5. Mood swings (labile mood): oscillations between euphoria and depression or anxiety.
6. Elevated mood: air of confidence and enjoyment; a mood more cheerful than usual.
7. Euphoria: intense elation with feelings of grandeur.
8. Ecstasy: feeling of intense rapture.
9. Depression: psychopathological feeling of sadness.
10. Anhedonia: loss of interest in and withdrawal from all regular and pleasurable activities, often associated with depression.
11. Grief or mourning: sadness appropriate to a real loss.
12. Alexithymia: a person's inability to or difficulty in describing or being aware of emotions or mood.
13. Suicidal ideation: thoughts or act of taking one's own life.
14. Elation: feelings of joy, euphoria, triumph, intense self-satisfaction, or optimism.

C. Other emotions.

1. Anxiety: feeling of apprehension caused by anticipation of danger, which may be internal or external.
2. Free-floating anxiety: pervasive, unfocused fear not attached to any idea.
3. Fear: anxiety caused by consciously recognized and realistic danger.

4. Agitation: severe anxiety associated with motor restlessness.
5. Tension: increased and unpleasant motor and psychological activity.
6. Panic: acute, episodic, intense attack of anxiety associated with overwhelming feelings of dread and autonomic discharge.
7. Apathy: dulled emotional tone associated with detachment or indifference.
8. Ambivalence: coexistence of two opposing impulses toward the same thing in the same person at the same time.
9. Abreaction: emotional release or discharge after recalling a painful experience.
10. Shame: failure to live up to self-expectations.
11. Guilt: emotion secondary to doing what is perceived as wrong.
12. Impulse control: ability to resist an impulse, drive, or temptation to perform an action.
13. Melancholia: severe depressive state; used in the term *involutional melancholia* both descriptively and also in reference to a distinct diagnostic entity.

D. Physiological disturbances associated with mood: signs of somatic (usually autonomic) dysfunction, most often associated with depression (also called vegetative signs).

1. Anorexia: loss of or decrease in appetite.
2. Hyperphagia: increase in appetite and intake of food.
3. Insomnia: lack of or diminished ability to sleep.
   a. Initial: difficulty in falling asleep.
   b. Middle: difficulty in sleeping through the night without waking up and difficulty in going back to sleep.
   c. Terminal: early morning awakening.
4. Hypersomnia: excessive sleeping.
5. Diurnal variation: mood is regularly worst in the morning, immediately after awakening, and improves as the day progresses.
6. Diminished libido: decreased sexual interest, drive, and performance (increased libido is often associated with manic states).
7. Constipation: inability to defecate or difficulty in defecating.
8. Fatigue: a feeling of weariness, sleepiness, or irritability following a period of mental or bodily activity.
9. Pica: craving and eating of nonfood substances, such as paint and clay.
10. Pseudocyesis: rare condition in which a patient has the signs and symptoms of pregnancy, such as abdominal distention, breast enlargement, pigmentation, cessation of menses, and morning sickness.
11. Bulimia: insatiable hunger and voracious eating; seen in bulimia nervosa and atypical depression.

III. Motor behavior (conation): aspect of the psyche that includes impulses, motivations, wishes, drives, instincts, and cravings, as expressed by a person's behavior or motor activity.

1. Echopraxia: pathological imitation of movements of one person by another.
2. Catatonia and postural abnormalities: seen in catatonic schizophrenia and some cases of brain diseases, such as encephalitis.
   a. Catalepsy: general term for an immobile position that is constantly maintained.
   b. Catatonic excitement: agitated, purposeless motor activity, uninfluenced by external stimuli.
   c. Catatonic stupor: markedly slowed motor activity, often to a point of immobility and seeming unawareness of surroundings.
   d. Catatonic rigidity: voluntary assumption of a rigid posture, held against all efforts to be moved.
   e. Catatonic posturing: voluntary assumption of an inappropriate or bizarre posture, generally maintained for long periods.
   f. *Cerea flexibilitas* (waxy flexibility): condition of a person who can be molded into a position that is then maintained; when an examiner moves the person's limb, the limb feels as if it were made of wax.
   g. Akinesia: lack of physical movement, as in the extreme immobility of catatonic schizophrenia; may also occur as an extrapyramidal side effect of antipsychotic medication.
3. Negativism: motiveless resistance to all attempts to be moved or to all instructions.
4. Cataplexy: temporary loss of muscle tone and weakness precipitated by a variety of emotional states.
5. Stereotypy: repetitive fixed pattern of physical action or speech.
6. Mannerism: ingrained, habitual involuntary movement.
7. Automatism: automatic performance of an act or acts generally representative of unconscious symbolic activity.
8. Command automatism: automatic following of suggestions (also automatic obedience).
9. Mutism: voicelessness without structural abnormalities.
10. Overactivity.
    a. Psychomotor agitation: excessive motor and cognitive overactivity, usually nonproductive and in response to inner tension.
    b. Hyperactivity (hyperkinesis): restless, aggressive, destructive activity, often associated with some underlying brain pathology.
    c. Tic: involuntary, spasmodic motor movement.
    d. Sleepwalking (somnambulism): motor activity during sleep.

e. Akathisia: subjective feeling of muscular tension secondary to antipsychotic or other medication, which can cause restlessness, pacing, repeated sitting and standing; can be mistaken for psychotic agitation.
f. Compulsion: uncontrollable impulse to perform an act repetitively.
   i. Dipsomania: compulsion to drink alcohol.
   ii. Kleptomania: compulsion to steal.
   iii. Nymphomania: excessive and compulsive need for coitus in a woman.
   iv. Satyriasis: excessive and compulsive need for coitus in a man.
   v. Trichotillomania: compulsion to pull out hair.
   vi. Ritual: automatic activity, compulsive in nature, anxiety reducing in origin.
g. Ataxia: failure of muscle coordination; irregularity of muscle action.
h. Polyphagia: pathological overeating.
i. Tremor: rhythmical alteration in movement, which is usually faster than one beat a second; typically, tremors decrease during periods of relaxation and sleep and increase during periods of anger and increased tension.

11. Hypoactivity (hypokinesis): decreased motor and cognitive activity, as in psychomotor retardation; visible slowing of thought, speech, and movements.
12. Mimicry: simple, imitative motor activity of childhood.
13. Aggression: forceful, goal-directed action that may be verbal or physical; the motor counterpart of the affect of rage, anger, or hostility.
14. Acting out: direct expression of an unconscious wish or impulse in action; living out unconscious fantasy impulsively in behavior.
15. Abulia: reduced impulse to act and think, associated with indifference about consequences of action; a result of neurological deficit.
16. Anergia: lack of energy (anergy).
17. Astasia abasia: the inability to stand or walk in a normal manner, even though normal leg movements can be performed in a sitting or lying down position. The gait is bizarre and is not suggestive of a specific organic lesion; seen in conversion disorder.
18. Coprophagia: eating of filth or feces.
19. Dyskinesia: difficulty in performing voluntary movements, as in extrapyramidal disorders.
20. Muscle rigidity: state in which the muscles remain immovable; seen in schizophrenia.
21. Twirling: a sign present in autistic children who continually rotate in the direction in which their head is turned.
22. Bradykinesia: slowness of motor activity with a decrease in normal spontaneous movement.
23. Chorea: random and involuntary quick, jerky, purposeless movements.
24. Convulsion: An involuntary, violent muscular contraction or spasm.
    a. Clonic convulsion: convulsion in which the muscles alternately contract and relax.
    b. Tonic convulsion: convulsion in which the muscle contraction is sustained.
25. Seizure: an attack or sudden onset of certain symptoms, such as convulsions, loss of consciousness, and psychic or sensory disturbances; seen in epilepsy and can be substance-induced.
    a. Generalized tonic-clonic seizure: generalized onset of tonic-clonic movements of the limbs, tongue biting, and incontinence followed by slow, gradual recovery of consciousness and cognition; also called grand mal seizure and psychomotor seizure.
    b. Simple partial seizure: localized ictal onset of seizure without alterations in consciousness.
    c. Complex partial seizure: localized ictal onset of seizure with alterations in consciousness.
26. Dystonia: slow, sustained contractions of the trunk or limbs; seen in medication-induced dystonia.

IV. Thinking: goal-directed flow of ideas, symbols, and associations initiated by a problem or task and leading toward a reality-oriented conclusion; when a logical sequence occurs, thinking is normal; parapraxis (unconsciously motivated lapse from logic is also called a freudian slip) considered part of normal thinking.

A. General disturbances in form or process of thinking.

1. Mental disorder: clinically significant behavior or psychological syndrome associated with distress or disability, not just an expected response to a particular event or limited to relations between a person and society.
2. Psychosis: inability to distinguish reality from fantasy; impaired reality testing, with the creation of a new reality (as opposed to neurosis: mental disorder in which reality testing is intact; behavior may not violate gross social norms, but is relatively enduring or recurrent without treatment).
3. Reality testing: objective evaluation and judgment of the world outside the self.
4. Formal thought disorder: disturbance in the form of thought rather than the content of thought; thinking characterized by loosened associations, neologisms, and illogical constructs; thought process is disordered, and the person is defined as psychotic.
5. Illogical thinking: thinking containing erroneous conclusions or internal contradictions; psychopathological only when it is marked and

when not caused by cultural values or intellectual deficit.
6. Dereism: mental activity not concordant with logic or experience.
7. Autistic thinking: preoccupation with inner, private world; term used somewhat synonymously with dereism.
8. Magical thinking: a form of dereistic thought; thinking similar to that of the preoperational phase in children (Jean Piaget), in which thoughts, words, or actions assume power (for example, to cause or prevent events).
9. Primary process thinking: general term for thinking that is dereistic, illogical, magical; normally found in dreams, abnormally in psychosis.
10. Emotional insight: deep level of understanding or awareness that is likely to lead to positive changes in personality and behavior.

B. Specific disturbances in form of thought.

1. Neologism: new word created by a patient, often by combining syllables of other words, for idiosyncratic psychological reasons.
2. Word salad: incoherent mixture of words and phrases.
3. Circumstantiality: indirect speech that is delayed in reaching the point but eventually gets from original point to desired goal; characterized by an overinclusion of details and parenthetical remarks.
4. Tangentiality: inability to have goal-directed associations of thought; speaker never gets from desired point to desired goal.
5. Incoherence: thought that generally is not understandable; running together of thoughts or words with no logical or grammatical connection, resulting in disorganization.
6. Perseveration: persisting response to a previous stimulus after a new stimulus has been presented; often associated with cognitive disorders.
7. Verbigeration: meaningless repetition of specific words or phrases.
8. Echolalia: psychopathological repeating of words or phrases of one person by another; tends to be repetitive and persistent; may be spoken with mocking or staccato intonation.
9. Condensation: fusion of various concepts into one.
10. Irrelevant answer: answer that is not in harmony with question asked (person appears to ignore or not attend to question).
11. Loosening of associations: flow of thought in which ideas shift from one subject to another in a completely unrelated way; when severe, speech may be incoherent.
12. Derailment: gradual or sudden deviation in train of thought without blocking; sometimes used synonymously with loosening of associations.
13. Flight of ideas: rapid, continuous verbalizations or plays on words produce constant shifting from one idea to another; ideas tend to be connected, and in the less severe form a listener may be able to follow them.
14. Clang association: association of words similar in sound but not in meaning; words have no logical connection; may include rhyming and punning.
15. Blocking: abrupt interruption in train of thinking before a thought or idea is finished; after a brief pause, person indicates no recall of what was being said or was going to be said (also known as thought deprivation).
16. Glossolalia: expression of a revelatory message through unintelligible words (also known as speaking in tongues); not considered a disturbance in thought if associated with practices of specific Pentecostal religions.

C. Specific disturbances in content of thought.

1. Poverty of content: thought that gives little information because of vagueness, empty repetitions, or obscure phrases.
2. Overvalued idea: unreasonable, sustained false belief maintained less firmly than a delusion.
3. Delusion: false belief, based on incorrect inference about external reality, not consistent with patient's intelligence and cultural background; cannot be corrected by reasoning.
   a. Bizarre delusion: an absurd, totally implausible, strange false belief (for example, invaders from space have implanted electrodes in a person's brain).
   b. Systematized delusion: false belief or beliefs united by a single event or theme (for example, a person is being persecuted by the CIA, the FBI, or the Mafia).
   c. Mood-congruent delusion: delusion with mood-appropriate content (for example, a depressed patient believes that he or she is responsible for the destruction of the world).
   d. Mood-incongruent delusion: delusion with content that has no association to mood or is mood neutral (for example, a depressed patient has delusions of thought control or thought broadcasting).
   e. Nihilistic delusion: false feeling that self, others, or the world is nonexistent or coming to an end.
   f. Delusion of poverty: a person's false belief that he or she is bereft or will be deprived of all material possessions.
   g. Somatic delusion: false belief involving functioning of the body (for example, belief that the brain is rotting or melting).
   h. Paranoid delusions: includes persecutory delusions and delusions of reference, control, and grandeur (distinguished from para-

noid ideation, which is suspiciousness of less than delusional proportions).

i. Delusion of persecution: a person's false belief that he or she is being harassed, cheated, or persecuted; often found in litigious patients who have a pathological tendency to take legal action because of imagined mistreatment

ii. Delusion of grandeur: a person's exaggerated conception of his or her importance, power, or identity.

iii. Delusion of reference: a person's false belief that the behavior of others refers to himself or herself; that events, objects, or other people have a particular and unusual significance, usually of a negative nature; derived from idea of reference, in which a person falsely feels that others are talking about him or her (for example, belief that people on television or radio are talking to or about the person).

i. Delusion of self-accusation: false feeling of remorse and guilt.

j. Delusion of control: false feeling that a person's will, thoughts, or feelings are being controlled by external forces.

i. Thought withdrawal: delusion that thoughts are being removed from a person's mind by other people or forces.

ii. Thought insertion: delusion that thoughts are being implanted in a person's mind by other people or forces.

iii. Thought broadcasting: delusion that a person's thoughts can be heard by others, as though they were being broadcast over the air.

iv. Thought control: delusion that a person's thoughts are being controlled by other people or forces.

k. Delusion of infidelity (delusional jealousy): false belief derived from pathological jealousy about a person's lover being unfaithful.

l. Erotomania: delusional belief, more common in women than in men, that someone is deeply in love with them (also known as Clérambault-Kandinsky complex).

m. Pseudologia phantastica: a type of lying in which a person appears to believe in the reality of his or her fantasies and acts on them; associated with Munchausen syndrome, repeated feigning of illness.

4. Trend or preoccupation of thought: centering of thought content on a particular idea, associated with a strong affective tone, such as a paranoid trend or a suicidal or homicidal preoccupation.
5. Egomania: pathological self-preoccupation.
6. Monomania: preoccupation with a single object.
7. Hypochondria: exaggerated concern about health that is based not on real organic pathology but, rather, on unrealistic interpretations of physical signs or sensations as abnormal.
8. Obsession: pathological persistence of an irresistible thought or feeling that cannot be eliminated from consciousness by logical effort; associated with anxiety.
9. Compulsion: pathological need to act on an impulse that, if resisted, produces anxiety; repetitive behavior in response to an obsession or performed according to certain rules, with no true end in itself other than to prevent something from occurring in the future.
10. Coprolalia: compulsive utterance of obscene words.
11. Phobia: persistent, irrational, exaggerated, and invariably pathological dread of a specific stimulus or situation; results in a compelling desire to avoid the feared stimulus.
    a. Specific phobia: circumscribed dread of a discrete object or situation (for example, dread of spiders or snakes).
    b. Social phobia: dread of public humiliation, as in fear of public speaking, performing, or eating in public.
    c. Acrophobia: dread of high places.
    d. Agoraphobia: dread of open places.
    e. Algophobia: dread of pain.
    f. Ailurophobia: dread of cats.
    g. Erythrophobia: dread of red (refers to a fear of blushing).
    h. Panphobia: dread of everything.
    i. Claustrophobia: dread of closed places.
    j. Xenophobia: dread of strangers.
    k. Zoophobia: dread of animals.
    l. Needle phobia: the persistent, intense, pathological fear of receiving an injection.
12. Noesis: a revelation in which immense illumination occurs in association with a sense that a person has been chosen to lead and command.
13. *Unio mystica:* an oceanic feeling of mystic unity with an infinite power; not considered a disturbance in thought content if congruent with person's religious or cultural milieu.

V. Speech: ideas, thoughts, feelings as expressed through language; communication through the use of words and language.

A. Disturbances in speech.

1. Pressure of speech: rapid speech that is increased in amount and difficult to interrupt.
2. Volubility (logorrhea): copious, coherent, logical speech.
3. Poverty of speech: restriction in the amount of speech used; replies may be monosyllabic.
4. Nonspontaneous speech: verbal responses given only when asked or spoken to directly; no self-initiation of speech.

5. Poverty of content of speech: speech that is adequate in amount but conveys little information because of vagueness, emptiness, or stereotyped phrases.
6. Dysprosody: loss of normal speech melody (called prosody).
7. Dysarthria: difficulty in articulation, not in word finding or in grammar.
8. Excessively loud or soft speech: loss of modulation of normal speech volume; may reflect a variety of pathological conditions ranging from psychosis to depression to deafness.
9. Stuttering: frequent repetition or prolongation of a sound or syllable, leading to markedly impaired speech fluency.
10. Cluttering: erratic and dysrhythmic speech, consisting of rapid and jerky spurts.

B. Aphasic disturbances: disturbances in language output.

1. Motor aphasia: disturbance of speech caused by a cognitive disorder in which understanding remains but ability to speak is grossly impaired; halting, laborious, and inaccurate speech (also known as Broca's, nonfluent, and expressive aphasia).
2. Sensory aphasia: organic loss of ability to comprehend the meaning of words; fluid and spontaneous but incoherent and nonsensical speech (also known as Wernicke's, fluent, and receptive aphasia).
3. Nominal aphasia: difficulty in finding correct name for an object (also termed anomia and amnestic aphasia).
4. Syntactical aphasia: inability to arrange words in proper sequence.
5. Jargon aphasia: words produced are totally neologistic; nonsense words repeated with various intonations and inflections.
6. Global aphasia: combination of a grossly nonfluent aphasia and a severe fluent aphasia.
7. Alogia: inability to speak because of a mental deficiency or an episode of dementia.
8. Copropregia: involuntary use of vulgar or obscene language; seen in Tourette's disorder and some cases of schizophrenia.

VI. Perception: process of transferring physical stimulation into psychological information; mental process by which sensory stimuli are brought to awareness.

A. Disturbances of perception.

1. Hallucination: false sensory perception not associated with real external stimuli; there may or may not be a delusional interpretation of the hallucinatory experience.
   a. Hypnagogic hallucination: false sensory perception occurring while falling asleep; generally considered nonpathological phenomenon.
   b. Hypnopompic hallucination: false perception occurring while awakening from sleep; generally considered nonpathological.
   c. Auditory hallucination: false perception of sound, usually voices but also other noises, such as music; most common hallucination in psychiatric disorders.
   d. Visual hallucination: false perception involving sight consisting of both formed images (for example, people) and unformed images (for example, flashes of light); most common in medically determined disorders.
   e. Olfactory hallucination: false perception of smell; most common in medical disorders.
   f. Gustatory hallucination: false perception of taste, such as unpleasant taste, caused by an uncinate seizure; most common in medical disorders.
   g. Tactile (haptic) hallucination: false perception of touch or surface sensation, as from an amputated limb (phantom limb); crawling sensation on or under the skin (formication).
   h. Somatic hallucination: false sensation of things occurring in or to the body, most often visceral in origin (also known as cenesthesic hallucination).
   i. Lilliputian hallucination: false perception in which objects are seen as reduced in size (also termed micropsia).
   j. Mood-congruent hallucination: hallucination in which the content is consistent with either a depressed or a manic mood (for example, a depressed patient hears voices saying that the patient is a bad person; a manic patient hears voices saying that the patient is of inflated worth, power, and knowledge).
   k. Mood-incongruent hallucination: hallucination in which the content is not consistent with either depressed or manic mood (for example, in depression, hallucinations not involving such themes as guilt, deserved punishment, or inadequacy; in mania, hallucinations not involving such themes as inflated worth or power).
   l. Hallucinosis: hallucinations, most often auditory, that are associated with chronic alcohol abuse and that occur within a clear sensorium, as opposed to delirium tremens (DTs), hallucinations that occur in the context of a clouded sensorium.
   m. Synesthesia: sensation or hallucination caused by another sensation (for example, an auditory sensation accompanied by or triggering a visual sensation; a sound experienced as being seen or a visual experience experienced as heard).
   n. Trailing phenomenon: perceptual abnormality associated with hallucinogenic drugs in which moving objects are seen as a series of discrete and discontinuous images.
   o. Command hallucination: false perception of

orders that a person may feel obliged to obey or unable to resist.

2. Illusion; misperception or misinterpretation of real external sensory stimuli.

B. Disturbances associated with cognitive disorder and medical conditions: agnosia—an inability to recognize and interpret the significance of sensory impressions.

1. Anosognosia (ignorance of illness): a person's inability to recognize a neurological deficit as occurring to himself or herself.
2. Somatopagnosia (ignorance of the body): a person's inability to recognize a body part as his or her own (also called autotopagnosia).
3. Visual agnosia: inability to recognize objects or persons.
4. Astereognosis: inability to recognize objects by touch.
5. Prosopagnosia: inability to recognize faces.
6. Apraxia: inability to carry out specific tasks.
7. Simultagnosia: inability to comprehend more than one element of a visual scene at a time or to integrate the parts into a whole.
8. Adiadochokinesia: inability to perform rapid alternating movements.
9. Aura: warning sensations such as automatisms, fullness in the stomach, blushing, and changes in respiration, cognitive sensations, and affective states usually experienced before a seizure; a sensory prodrome that precedes a classic migraine headache.

C. Disturbances associated with conversion and dissociative phenomena: somatization of repressed material or the development of physical symptoms and distortions involving the voluntary muscles or special sense organs; not under voluntary control and not explained by any physical disorder.

1. Hysterical anesthesia: loss of sensory modalities resulting from emotional conflicts.
2. Macropsia: state in which objects seem larger than they are.
3. Micropsia: state in which objects seem smaller than they are (both macropsia and micropsia can also be associated with clear organic conditions, such as complex partial seizures).
4. Depersonalization: a person's subjective sense of being unreal, strange, or unfamiliar.
5. Derealization: a subjective sense that the environment is strange or unreal; a feeling of changed reality.
6. Fugue: taking on a new identity with amnesia for the old identity; often involves travel or wandering to new environments.
7. Multiple personality: one person who appears at different times to be two or more entirely different personalities and characters (called dissociative identity disorder in the fourth edition of *Diagnostic and Statistical Manual of Mental Disorders* [DSM-IV]).
8. Dissociation: unconscious defense mechanism involving the segregation of any group of mental or behavioral processes from the rest of the person's psychic activity; may entail the separation of an idea from its accompanying emotional tone, as seen in dissociative and conversion disorders.

VII. Memory: function by which information stored in the brain is later recalled to consciousness.

A. Disturbances of memory.

1. Amnesia: partial or total inability to recall past experiences; may be organic or emotional in origin.
   a. Anterograde: amnesia for events occurring after a point in time.
   b. Retrograde: amnesia for events occurring before a point in time.
2. Paramnesia: falsification of memory by distortion of recall.
   a. *Fausse reconnaissance:* false recognition.
   b. Retrospective falsification: memory becomes unintentionally (unconsciously) distorted by being filtered through a person's present emotional, cognitive, and experiential state.
   c. Confabulation: unconscious filling of gaps in memory by imagined or untrue experiences that a person believes but that have no basis in fact; most often associated with organic pathology.
   d. Déjà vu: illusion of visual recognition in which a new situation is incorrectly regarded as a repetition of a previous memory.
   e. *Déjà entendu:* illusion of auditory recognition.
   f. *Déjà pensé:* illusion that a new thought is recognized as a thought previously felt or expressed.
   g. *Jamais vu:* false feeling of unfamiliarity with a real situation that a person has experienced.
   h. False memory: a person's recollection and belief by the patient of an event that did not actually occur.
3. Hypermnesia: exaggerated degree of retention and recall.
4. Eidetic image: visual memory of almost hallucinatory vividness.
5. Screen memory: a consciously tolerable memory covering for a painful memory.
6. Repression: a defense mechanism characterized by unconscious forgetting of unacceptable ideas or impulses.
7. Lethologica: temporary inability to remember a name or a proper noun.
8. Blackout: amnesia experienced by alcoholics about behavior during drinking bouts; usually indicates that reversible brain damage has occurred.

B. Levels of memory.

1. Immediate: reproduction or recall of perceived material within seconds to minutes.
2. Recent: recall of events over past few days.
3. Recent past: recall of events over past few months.
4. Remote: recall of events in distant past.

VIII. Intelligence: ability to understand, recall, mobilize, and constructively integrate previous learning in meeting new situations.

A. Mental retardation: lack of intelligence to a degree in which there is interference with social and vocational performance: mild (IQ of 50 or 55 to approximately 70), moderate (IQ of 35 or 40 to 50 or 55), severe (IQ of 20 or 25 to 35 or 40), or profound (IQ below 20 or 25); obsolete terms are idiot (mental age less than 3 years), imbecile (mental age of 3 to 7 years), and moron (mental age of about 8).

B. Dementia: organic and global deterioration of intellectual functioning without clouding of consciousness.

1. Dyscalculia (acalculia): loss of ability to do calculations; not caused by anxiety or impairment in concentration.
2. Dysgraphia (agraphia): loss of ability to write in cursive style; loss of word structure.
3. Alexia: loss of a previously possessed reading facility; not explained by defective visual acuity.

C. Pseudodementia: clinical features resembling a dementia not caused by an organic condition; most often caused by depression (dementia syndrome of depression).

D. Concrete thinking: literal thinking; limited use of metaphor without understanding of nuances of meaning; one-dimensional thought.

E. Abstract thinking: ability to appreciate nuances of meaning; multidimensional thinking with ability to use metaphors and hypotheses appropriately.

IX. Insight: a person's ability to understand the true cause and meaning of a situation (such as a set of symptoms).

A. Intellectual insight: understanding of the objective reality of a set of circumstances without the ability to apply the understanding in any useful way to master the situation.

B. True insight: understanding of the objective reality of a situation, coupled with the motivation and the emotional impetus to master the situation.

C. Impaired insight: diminished ability to understand the objective reality of a situation.

X. Judgment: ability to assess a situation correctly and to act appropriately in the situation.

A. Critical judgment: ability to assess, discern, and choose among various options in a situation.

B. Automatic judgment: reflex performance of an action.

C. Impaired judgment: diminished ability to understand a situation correctly and to act appropriately.

References

Andreasen NC: The clinical assessment of thought, language, and communication disorders: I. The definition of terms and evaluation of their reliability. Arch Gen Psychiatry *36:* 1315, 1979.

Campbell RJ: *Psychiatric Dictionary,* ed 6. Oxford University Press, New York, 1989.

Cassano GB, Perugi G, Musetti L, Akiskal HS: The nature of depression presenting concomitantly with panic disorder. Compr Psychiatry *30:* 473, 1989.

Coleman M, Gillberg C: *The Schizophrenias; A Biological Approach to the Schizophrenia Spectrum Disorders.* Springer, New York, 1996.

Geschwind N: Aphasia. N Engl J Med *284:* 654, 1971.

Kaplan HI, Sadock BJ: Typical signs and symptoms of psychiatric illness. In *Comprehensive Textbook of Psychiatry,* ed 6, HI Kaplan, BJ Sadock, editors, p 535. Williams & Wilkins, Baltimore, 1995.

Sadler JZ, Hulgus UF: Clinical problem solving and the biopsychosocial model. Am J Psychiatry *149:* 1315, 1992.

Spitzer RL, Gibbon M, Skodol AE, Williams JBW, First MB: *DSM-IV Casebook: A Learning Companion to the Diagnostic and Statistical Manual of Mental Disorders, Fourth Edition.* American Psychiatric Press, Washington, 1994.

9

Classification in Psychiatry and Psychiatric Rating Scales

Systems of classification for psychiatric diagnoses have several purposes: to distinguish one psychiatric diagnosis from another, so that clinicians can offer the most effective treatment; to provide a common language among health care professionals; and to explore the causes of the many mental disorders that are still unknown. The two most important psychiatric classifications are the *Diagnostic and Statistical Manual of Mental Disorders* (DSM) (Table 9–1) and the International Classification of Diseases (ICD) (Table 9–2).

ICD-10

The 10th revision of *International Statistical Classification of Diseases and Related Health Problems* (ICD-10), published by the World Health Organization (WHO) in 1992, is a comprehensive classification system of medical conditions and mental disorders. The International Classification of Diseases (ICD) is the official medical and psychiatric nosology used throughout most of the world. However, some countries (for example, Japan, United States) use compatible or modified classifications.

DSM-IV

The fourth edition of *Diagnostic and Statistical Manual of Mental Disorders* (DSM-IV), published in 1994 by the American Psychiatric Association (APA), is the official psychiatric coding system used in the United States. Although many psychiatrists have been critical of the many versions of DSM that have appeared since the first edition (DSM-I) appeared in 1952, DSM-IV is the official U.S. nomenclature. All terminology used in this textbook conforms to DSM-IV nomenclature. DSM-IV is compatible with the ninth revision of International Classification of Diseases (ICD-9), published by the World Health Organization (WHO), and with ICD-9-CM (CM stands for Clinical Modification), published by the U.S. Department of Health and Human Services.

According to treaties between the United States and WHO, ICD-10 will be used in the United States (probably in the year 2000). To facilitate the reader's understanding of this transition, this textbook also includes tables and diagnostic criteria from ICD-10. Currently, DSM-IV diagnostic codes are compatible with ICD-9-CM and are used in the United States by Medicare, Medicaid, and insurance companies for reimbursement purposes.

History

The various classification systems used in psychiatry date back to Hippocrates, who introduced the terms *mania* and *hysteria* as forms of mental illness in the fifth century B.C. Since then, each era has introduced its own psychiatric classification. The first U.S. classification was introduced in 1869 at the annual meeting of the American Medico-Psychological Association, which was then the name of the American Psychiatric Association.

In 1952, the American Psychiatric Association's Committee on Nomenclature and Statistics published the first edition of DSM (DSM-I). Four editions have been published since then: DSM-II (1968); DSM-III (1980); a revised DSM-III, DSM-III-R (1987); and DSM-IV (1994).

Basic Features

Descriptive Approach. The approach to DSM-IV is atheoretical with regard to causes. Thus, DSM-IV attempts to describe the manifestations of the mental disorders and only rarely attempts to account for how the disturbances come about. The definitions of the disorders usually consist of descriptions of clinical features.

Diagnostic Criteria. Specified diagnostic criteria are provided for each specific mental disorder. These criteria include a list of features that must be present for the diagnosis to be made. Such criteria increase the reliability of clinicians' process of diagnosis.

Systematic Description. DSM-IV also systematically describes each disorder in terms of its associated features: specific age, cultural, and gender-related features; prevalence, incidence, and risk; course; complications; predisposing factors; familial pattern; and differential diagnosis. In some instances, when many specific disorders share common features, this information is included in the introduction to the entire section. Laboratory findings and associated physical examination signs and symptoms are described when relevant. DSM-IV does not purport to be a textbook: No mention is made of theories of causes, management, or treatment, and the controversial issues surrounding a particular diagnostic category are not discussed.

Table 9–1
DSM-IV Classification of Mental Disorders, Updated to Include ICD-9-CM Numerical Codes

Code	Disorder
DISORDERS USUALLY FIRST DIAGNOSED IN INFANCY, CHILDHOOD, OR ADOLESCENCE	
Mental Retardation	
Note: *These are coded on Axis II.*	
317	Mild mental retardation
318.0	Moderate mental retardation
318.1	Severe mental retardation
318.2	Profound mental retardation
319	Mental retardation, severity unspecified
Learning Disorders	
315.00	Reading disorder
315.1	Mathematics disorder
315.2	Disorder of written expression
315.9	Learning disorder NOS
Motor Skills Disorder	
315.4	Developmental coordination disorder
Communication Disorders	
315.31	Expressive language disorder
315.32	Mixed receptive-expressive language disorder
315.39	Phonological disorder
307.0	Stuttering
307.9	Communication disorder NOS
Pervasive Developmental Disorders	
299.00	Autistic disorder
299.80	Rett's disorder
299.10	Childhood disintegrative disorder
299.80	Asperger's disorder
299.80	Pervasive developmental disorder NOS
Attention-Deficit and Disruptive Behavior Disorders	
314.xx	Attention-deficit/hyperactivity disorder
.01	combined type
.00	predominantly inattentive type
.01	predominantly hyperactive-impulsive type
314.9	Attention-deficit/hyperactivity disorder NOS
312.xx	Conduct disorder
.81	childhood-onset type
.82	adolescent-onset type
.89	unspecified type
313.81	Oppositional defiant disorder
312.9	Disruptive behavior disorder NOS
Feeding and Eating Disorders of Infancy or Early Childhood	
307.52	Pica
307.53	Rumination disorder
307.59	Feeding disorder of infancy or early childhood
Tic Disorders	
307.23	Tourette's disorder
307.22	Chronic motor or vocal tic disorder
307.21	Transient tic disorder
307.20	Tic disorder NOS
Elimination Disorders	
—	Encopresis
787.6	with constipation and overflow incontinence
307.7	without constipation and overflow incontinence
307.6	Enuresis (not due to a general medical condition)
Other Disorders of Infancy, Childhood, or Adolescence	
309.21	Separation anxiety disorder
313.23	Selective mutism
313.89	Reactive attachment disorder of infancy or early childhood
307.3	Stereotypic movement disorder
313.9	Disorder of infancy, childhood, or adolescence NOS
DELIRIUM, DEMENTIA, AND AMNESTIC AND OTHER COGNITIVE DISORDERS	
Delirium	
293.0	Delirium due to a general medical condition
—.—	Substance intoxication delirium (*refer to substance-related disorders for substance-specific codes*)
—.—	Substance withdrawal delirium (*refer to substance-related disorders for substance-specific codes*)
—.—	Delirium due to multiple etiologies (*code each of the specific etiologies*)
780.09	Delirium NOS
Dementia	
290.xx	Dementia of the Alzheimer's type, with early onset (*also code 331.0 Alzheimer's disease on Axis III*)
.10	uncomplicated
.11	with delirium
.12	with delusions
.13	with depressed mood
290.xx	Dementia of the Alzheimer's type, with late onset (*also code 331.0 Alzheimer's disease on Axis III*)
.0	uncomplicated
.3	with delirium
.20	with delusions
.21	with depressed mood
290.xx	Vascular dementia
.40	uncomplicated
.41	with delirium
.42	with delusions
.43	with depressed mood
Dementia Due to Other General Medical Conditions	
294.1	Dementia due to HIV disease (*also code 042 HIV infection on Axis III*)
294.1	Dementia due to head trauma (*also code 854.00 head injury on Axis III*)
294.1	Dementia due to Parkinson's disease (*also code 332.0 Parkinson's disease Axis III*)
294.1	Dementia due to Huntington's disease (*also code 333.4 Huntington's disease on Axis III*)
290.10	Dementia due to Pick's disease (*also code 331.1 Pick's disease on Axis III*)
290.10	Dementia due to Creutzfeldt-Jakob disease (*also code 046.1 Creutzfeldt-Jakob disease on Axis III*)
294.1	Dementia due to other general medical condition (*also code the general medical condition on Axis III*)
—.—	Substance-induced persisting dementia (*refer to substance-related disorders for substance-specific codes*)
—.—	Dementia due to multiple etiologies (*code each of the specific etiologies*)
294.8	Dementia NOS
Amnestic Disorders	
294.0	Amnestic disorder due to a general medical condition
—.—	Substance-induced persisting amnestic disorder (*refer to substance-related disorders for substance-specific codes*)
294.8	Amnestic disorder NOS
Other Cognitive Disorders	
294.9	Cognitive disorder NOS

(*continued*)

Table 9–1 (*continued*)

MENTAL DISORDERS DUE TO A GENERAL MEDICAL CONDITION NOT ELSEWHERE CLASSIFIED	
293.89	Catatonic disorder due to a general medical condition
310.1	Personality change due to a general medical condition
293.9	Mental disorder NOS due to a general medical condition
SUBSTANCE-RELATED DISORDERS	
Alcohol-Related Disorders	
Alcohol Use Disorders	
303.90	Alcohol dependence
305.00	Alcohol abuse
Alcohol-Induced Disorders	
303.00	Alcohol intoxication
291.81	Alcohol withdrawal
291.0	Alcohol intoxication delirium
291.0	Alcohol withdrawal delirium
291.2	Alcohol-induced persisting dementia
291.1	Alcohol-induced persisting amnestic disorder
291.x	Alcohol-induced psychotic disorder
.5	with delusions
.3	with hallucinations
291.81	Alcohol-induced mood disorder
291.81	Alcohol-induced anxiety disorder
291.81	Alcohol-induced sexual dysfunction
291.81	Alcohol-induced sleep disorder
291.9	Alcohol-related disorder NOS
Amphetamine (or Amphetamine-like)-Related Disorders	
Amphetamine Use Disorders	
304.40	Amphetamine dependence
305.70	Amphetamine abuse
Amphetamine-Induced Disorders	
292.89	Amphetamine intoxication
292.0	Amphetamine withdrawal
292.81	Amphetamine intoxication delirium
292.xx	Amphetamine-induced psychotic disorder
.11	with delusions
.12	with hallucinations
292.84	Amphetamine-induced mood disorder
292.89	Amphetamine-induced anxiety disorder
292.89	Amphetamine-induced sexual dysfunction
292.89	Amphetamine-induced sleep disorder
292.9	Amphetamine-related disorder NOS
Caffeine-Related Disorders	
Caffeine-Induced Disorders	
305.90	Caffeine intoxication
292.89	Caffeine-induced anxiety disorder
292.89	Caffeine-induced sleep disorder
292.9	Caffeine-related disorder NOS
Cannabis-Related Disorders	
Cannabis Use Disorders	
304.30	Cannabis dependence
305.20	Cannabis abuse
Cannabis-Induced Disorders	
292.89	Cannabis intoxication
292.81	Cannabis intoxication delirium
292.xx	Cannabis-induced psychotic disorder
.11	with delusions
.12	with hallucinations
292.89	Cannabis-induced anxiety disorder
292.9	Cannabis-related disorder NOS
Cocaine-Related Disorders	
Cocaine Use Disorders	
304.20	Cocaine dependence
305.60	Cocaine abuse
Cocaine-Induced Disorders	
292.89	Cocaine intoxication
292.0	Cocaine withdrawal
292.81	Cocaine intoxication delirium
292.xx	Cocaine-induced psychotic disorder
.11	with delusions
.12	with hallucinations
292.84	Cocaine-induced mood disorder
292.89	Cocaine-induced anxiety disorder
292.89	Cocaine-induced sexual dysfunction
292.89	Cocaine-induced sleep disorder
292.9	Cocaine-related disorder NOS
Hallucinogen-Related Disorders	
Hallucinogen Use Disorders	
304.50	Hallucinogen dependence
305.30	Hallucinogen abuse
Hallucinogen-Induced Disorders	
292.89	Hallucinogen intoxication
292.89	Hallucinogen persisting perception disorder (flashbacks)
292.81	Hallucinogen intoxication delirium
292.xx	Hallucinogen-induced psychotic disorder
.11	with delusions
.12	with hallucinations
292.84	Hallucinogen-induced mood disorder
292.89	Hallucinogen-induced anxiety disorder
292.9	Hallucinogen-related disorder NOS
Inhalant-Related Disorders	
Inhalant Use Disorders	
304.60	Inhalant dependence
305.90	Inhalant abuse
Inhalant-Induced Disorders	
292.89	Inhalant intoxication
292.81	Inhalant intoxication delirium
292.82	Inhalant-induced persisting dementia
292.xx	Inhalant-induced psychotic disorder
.11	with delusions
.12	with hallucinations
292.84	Inhalant-induced mood disorder
292.89	Inhalant-induced anxiety disorder
292.9	Inhalant-related disorder NOS
Nicotine-Related Disorder	
Nicotine Use Disorder	
305.10	Nicotine dependence
Nicotine-Induced Disorder	
292.0	Nicotine withdrawal
292.9	Nicotine-related disorder NOS
Opioid-Related Disorders	
Opioid Use Disorders	
304.00	Opioid dependence
305.50	Opioid abuse
Opioid-Induced Disorders	
292.89	Opioid intoxication
292.0	Opioid withdrawal
292.81	Opioid-intoxication delirium
292.xx	Opioid-induced psychotic disorder
.11	with delusions
.12	with hallucinations
292.84	Opioid-induced mood disorder
292.89	Opioid-induced sexual dysfunction
292.89	Opioid-induced sleep disorder
292.9	Opioid-related disorder NOS

(*continued*)

Table 9–1 (*continued*)

Phencyclidine (or Phencyclidine-like) Related Disorders	
Phencyclidine Use Disorders	
304.60	Phencyclidine dependence
305.90	Phencyclidine abuse
Phencyclidine-induced Disorders	
292.89	Phencyclidine intoxication
292.81	Phencyclidine intoxication delirium
292.xx	Phencyclidine-induced psychotic disorder
.11	with delusions
.12	with hallucinations
292.84	Phencyclidine-induced mood disorder
292.89	Phencyclidine-induced anxiety disorder
292.9	Phencyclidine-related disorder NOS
Sedative-, Hypnotic-, or Anxiolytic-Related Disorders	
Sedative, Hypnotic, or Anxiolytic Use Disorders	
304.10	Sedative, hypnotic, or anxiolytic dependence
305.40	Sedative, hypnotic, or anxiolytic abuse
Sedative-, Hypnotic-, or Anxiolytic-Induced Disorders	
292.89	Sedative, hypnotic, or anxiolytic intoxication
292.0	Sedative, hypnotic, or anxiolytic withdrawal
292.81	Sedative, hypnotic, or anxiolytic intoxication delirium
292.81	Sedative, hypnotic, or anxiolytic withdrawal delirium
292.82	Sedative-, hypnotic-, or anxiolytic-induced persisting dementia
292.83	Sedative-, hypnotic-, or anxiolytic-induced persisting amnestic disorder
292.xx	Sedative-, hypnotic-, or anxiolytic-induced psychotic disorder
.11	with delusions
.12	with hallucinations
292.84	Sedative-, hypnotic-, or anxiolytic-induced mood disorder
292.89	Sedative-, hypnotic-, or anxiolytic-induced anxiety disorder
292.89	Sedative-, hypnotic-, or anxiolytic-induced sexual dysfunction
292.89	Sedative-, hypnotic-, or anxiolytic-induced sleep disorder
292.9	Sedative-, hypnotic-, or anxiolytic-related disorder NOS
Polysubstance-Related Disorder	
304.80	Polysubstance dependence
Other (or Unknown) Substance-Related Disorders	
Other (or Unknown) Substance Use Disorders	
304.90	Other (or unknown) substance dependence
305.90	Other (or unknown) substance abuse
Other (or Unknown) Substance-Induced Disorders	
292.89	Other (or unknown) substance intoxication
292.0	Other (or unknown) substance withdrawal
292.81	Other (or unknown) substance-induced delirium
292.82	Other (or unknown) substance-induced persisting dementia
292.83	Other (or unknown) substance-induced persisting amnestic disorder
292.xx	Other (or unknown) substance-induced psychotic disorder
.11	with delusions
.12	with hallucinations
292.84	Other (or unknown) substance-induced mood disorder
292.89	Other (or unknown) substance-induced anxiety disorder
292.89	Other (or unknown) substance-induced sexual dysfunction
292.89	Other (or unknown) substance-induced sleep disorder
292.9	Other (or unknown) substance-related disorder NOS
SCHIZOPHRENIA AND OTHER PSYCHOTIC DISORDERS	
295.xx	Schizophrenia
.30	paranoid type
.10	disorganized type
.20	catatonic type
.90	undifferentiated type
.60	residual type
295.40	Schizophreniform disorder
295.70	Schizoaffective disorder
297.1	Delusional disorder
298.8	Brief psychotic disorder
297.3	Shared psychotic disorder
293.xx	Psychotic disorder due to a general medical condition
.81	with delusions
.82	with hallucinations
—.—	Substance-induced psychotic disorder (*refer to substance-related disorders for substance-specific codes*)
298.9	Psychotic disorder NOS
MOOD DISORDERS	
Code current state of major depressive disorder or bipolar I disorder in fifth digit:	
1 mild	
2 moderate	
3 severe, without psychotic features	
4 severe with psychotic features	
5 in partial remission	
6 in full remission	
0 unspecified	
Depressive Disorders	
296.xx	Major depressive disorder
.2x	single episode
.3x	recurrent
300.4	Dysthymic disorder
311	Depressive disorder NOS
Bipolar Disorders	
296.xx	Bipolar I disorder
.0x	single manic episode
.40	most recent episode hypomanic
.4x	most recent episode manic
.6x	most recent episode mixed
.5x	most recent episode depressed
.7	most recent episode unspecified
296.89	Bipolar II disorder
301.13	Cyclothymic disorder
296.80	Bipolar disorder NOS
293.83	Mood disorder due to a general medical condition
—.—	Substance-induced mood disorder (*refer to substance-related disorders for substance-specific codes*)
296.90	Mood disorder NOS
ANXIETY DISORDERS	
300.01	Panic disorder without agoraphobia
300.21	Panic disorder with agoraphobia
300.22	Agoraphobia without history of panic disorder
300.29	Specific phobia
300.23	Social phobia
308.3	Obsessive-compulsive disorder
309.81	Posttraumatic stress disorder
300.3	Acute stress disorder
300.02	Generalized anxiety disorder
293.84	Anxiety disorder due to a general medical condition
—.—	Substance-induced anxiety disorder (*refer to substance-related disorders for substance-specific codes*)
300.00	Anxiety disorder NOS

(*continued*)

Table 9–1 (*continued*)

SOMATOFORM DISORDERS	
300.81	Somatization disorder
300.82	Undifferentiated somatoform disorder
300.11	Conversion disorder
307.xx	Pain disorder
.80	associated with psychological factors
.89	associated with both psychological factors and a general medical condition
300.7	Hypochondriasis
300.7	Body dysmorphic disorder
300.82	Somatoform disorder NOS
FACTITIOUS DISORDERS	
300.xx	Factitious disorder
.16	with predominantly psychological signs and symptoms
.19	with predominantly physical signs and symptoms
.19	with combined psychological and physical signs and symptoms
300.19	Factitious disorder NOS
DISSOCIATIVE DISORDERS	
300.12	Dissociative amnesia
300.13	Dissociative fugue
300.14	Dissociative identity disorder
300.6	Depersonalization disorder
300.15	Dissociative disorder NOS
SEXUAL AND GENDER IDENTITY DISORDERS	
Sexual Dysfunctions	
Sexual Desire Disorders	
302.71	Hypoactive sexual desire disorder
302.79	Sexual aversion disorder
Sexual Arousal Disorders	
302.72	Female sexual arousal disorder
302.72	Male erectile disorder
Orgasmic Disorders	
302.73	Female orgasmic disorder
302.74	Male orgasmic disorder
302.75	Premature ejaculation
Sexual Pain Disorders	
302.76	Dyspareunia (not due to a general medical condition)
306.51	Vaginismus (not due to a general medical condition)
Sexual Dysfunction Due to a General Medical Condition	
625.8	Female hypoactive sexual desire disorder due to a general medical condition
608.89	Male hypoactive sexual desire disorder due to a general medical condition
607.84	Male erectile disorder due to a general medical condition
625.0	Female dyspareunia due to a general medical condition
608.89	Male dyspareunia due to a general medical condition
625.8	Other female sexual dysfunction due to a general medical condition
608.89	Other male sexual dysfunction due to a general medical condition
—.—	Substance-induced sexual dysfunction (*refer to substance-related disorders for substance-specific codes*)
302.70	Sexual dysfunction NOS
Paraphilias	
302.4	Exhibitionism
302.81	Fetishism
302.89	Frotteurism
302.2	Pedophilia
302.83	Sexual masochism
302.84	Sexual sadism
302.3	Transvestic fetishism
302.82	Voyeurism
302.9	Paraphilia NOS
Gender Identity Disorders	
302.xx	Gender identity disorder
.6	in children
.85	in adolescents or adults
302.6	Gender identity disorder NOS
302.9	Sexual disorder NOS
EATING DISORDERS	
307.1	Anorexia nervosa
307.51	Bulimia nervosa
307.50	Eating disorder NOS
SLEEP DISORDERS	
Primary Sleep Disorders	
Dyssomnias	
307.42	Primary insomnia
307.44	Primary hypersomnia
347	Narcolepsy
780.59	Breathing-related sleep disorder
307.45	Circadian rhythm sleep disorder
307.47	Dyssomnia NOS
Parasomnias	
307.47	Nightmare disorder
307.46	Sleep terror disorder
307.46	Sleepwalking disorder
307.47	Parasomnia NOS
Sleep Disorders Related to Another Mental Disorder	
307.42	Insomnia related to another mental disorder
307.44	Hypersomnia related to another mental disorder
Other Sleep Disorders	
780.xx	Sleep disorder due to a general medical condition
.52	insomnia type
.54	hypersomnia type
.59	parasomnia type
.59	mixed type
—.—	Substance-induced sleep disorder (*refer to substance-related disorders for substance-specific codes*)
IMPULSE-CONTROL DISORDERS NOT ELSEWHERE CLASSIFIED	
312.34	Intermittent explosive disorder
312.32	Kleptomania
312.33	Pyromania
312.31	Pathological gambling
312.39	Trichotillomania
312.30	Impulse-control disorder NOS
ADJUSTMENT DISORDERS	
309.xx	Adjustment disorder
.0	with depressed mood
.24	with anxiety
.28	with mixed anxiety and depressed mood
.3	with disturbance of conduct
.4	with mixed disturbance of emotions and conduct
.9	Unspecified

(*continued*)

Table 9–1 (*continued*)

PERSONALITY DISORDERS	
Note: *These are coded on Axis II.*	
301.0	Paranoid personality disorder
301.20	Schizoid personality disorder
301.22	Schizotypal personality disorder
301.7	Antisocial personality disorder
301.83	Borderline personality disorder
301.50	Histrionic personality disorder
301.81	Narcissistic personality disorder
301.82	Avoidant personality disorder
301.6	Dependent personality disorder
301.4	Obsessive-compulsive personality disorder
301.9	Personality disorder NOS
OTHER CONDITIONS THAT MAY BE A FOCUS OF CLINICAL ATTENTION	
316	Psychological factors affecting medical condition
	Choose name based on nature of factors:
	Mental disorder affecting medical condition
	Psychological symptoms affecting medical condition
	Personality traits or coping style affecting medical condition
	Maladaptive health behaviors affecting medical condition
	Stress-related physiological response affecting medical condition
	Other or unspecified psychological factors affecting medical condition
Medication-Induced Movement Disorders	
332.1	Neuroleptic-induced parkinsonism
333.92	Neuroleptic malignant syndrome
333.7	Neuroleptic-induced acute dystonia
333.99	Neuroleptic-induced acute akathisia
333.82	Neuroleptic-induced tardive dyskinesia
333.1	Medication-induced postural tremor
333.90	Medication-induced movement disorder NOS
Other Medication-Induced Disorder	
995.2	Adverse effects of medication NOS
Relational Problems	
V61.9	Relational problem related to a mental disorder or general medical condition
V61.20	Parent-child relational problem
V61.10	Partner relational problem
V61.8	Sibling relational problem
V62.81	Relational problem NOS
Problems Related to Abuse or Neglect	
V61.21	Physical abuse of child (*code 995.54 if focus of attention is on victim*)
V61.21	Sexual abuse of child (*code 995.53 if focus of attention is on victim*)
V61.21	Neglect of child (*code 995.52 if focus of attention is on victim*)
V61.1	Physical abuse of adult
V61.12	(if by partner)
V62.83	(if by person other than partner)
V61.1	Sexual abuse of adult
V61.12	(if by partner)
V62.83	(if by person other than partner)
Additional Conditions That May Be a Focus of Clinical Attention	
V15.81	Noncompliance with treatment
V65.2	Malingering
V71.01	Adult antisocial behavior
V71.02	Childhood or adolescent antisocial behavior
V62.89	Borderline intellectual functioning
780.9	Age-related cognitive decline
V62.82	Bereavement
V62.3	Academic problem
V62.2	Occupational problem
313.82	Identity problem
V62.89	Religious or spiritual problem
V62.4	Acculturation problem
V62.89	Phase of life problem
ADDITIONAL CODES	
300.9	Unspecified mental disorder (nonpsychotic)
V71.09	No diagnosis or condition on Axis I
799.9	Diagnosis or condition deferred on Axis I
V71.09	No diagnosis on Axis II
799.9	Diagnosis deferred on Axis II

Reprinted with permission from American Psychiatric Association: *Diagnostic and Statistical Manual of Mental Disorders,* ed 4. Copyright, American Psychiatric Association, Washington, 1994.

Diagnostic Uncertainties. DSM-IV provides explicit rules to be used when the information is insufficient (diagnosis to be deferred or provisional) or the patient's clinical presentation and history do not meet the full criteria of a prototypical category (an atypical, residual, or not otherwise specified type within the general category).

Multiaxial Evaluation

DSM-IV is a multiaxial system that evaluates patients along several variables and contains five axes. Axis I and Axis II make up the entire classification of mental disorder: 17 major classifications and more than 300 specific disorders (Table 9–3). In many instances, patients have a disorder on both axes. For example, a patient may have major depressive disorder noted on Axis I and obsessive-compulsive personality disorder on Axis II.

Axis I. Axis I consists of clinical disorders and other conditions that may be a focus of clinical attention (Table 9–4).

Axis II. Axis II consists of personality disorders and mental retardation (Table 9–5). The habitual use of a particular defense mechanism can be indicated on Axis II.

Axis III. Axis III lists any physical disorder or general medical condition that is present in addition to the mental disorder. The physical condition may be causative (for example, kidney failure causing delirium), the result of a mental disorder (for example, alcohol gastritis secondary to alcohol dependence), or unrelated to the mental disorder. When a medical condition is causative or causally related to a mental disorder, a mental disorder due to a general condition is listed on Axis I and the general medical condition is listed on both Axis I

Table 9–2
ICD-10 Classification of Mental Disorders

F00–F09
Organic, including symptomatic, mental disorders

F00 Dementia in Alzheimer's disease
F00.0 Dementia in Alzheimer's disease with early onset
F00.1 Dementia in Alzheimer's disease with late onset
F00.2 Dementia in Alzheimer's disease, atypical or mixed type
F00.9 Dementia in Alzheimer's disease, unspecified

F01 Vascular dementia
F01.0 Vascular dementia of acute onset
F01.1 Multi-infarct dementia
F01.2 Subcortical vascular dementia
F01.3 Mixed cortical and subcortical vascular dementia
F01.8 Other vascular dementia
F01.9 Vascular dementia, unspecified

F02 Dementia in other diseases classified elsewhere
F02.0 Dementia in Pick's disease
F02.1 Dementia in Creutzfeldt-Jakob disease
F02.2 Dementia in Huntington's disease
F02.3 Dementia in Parkinson's disease
F02.4 Dementia in human immunodeficiency virus [HIV] disease
F02.8 Dementia in other specified diseases classified elsewhere

F03 Unspecified dementia
A fifth character may be added to specify dementia in F00–F03, as follows:
.x 0 Without additional symptoms
.x 1 Other symptoms, predominantly delusional
.x 2 Other symptoms, predominantly hallucinatory
.x 3 Other symptoms, predominantly depressive
.x 4 Other mixed symptoms

F04 Organic amnestic syndrome, not induced by alcohol and other psychoactive substances

F05 Delirium, not induced by alcohol and other psychoactive substances
F05.0 Delirium, not superimposed on dementia, so described
F05.1 Delirium, superimposed on dementia
F05.8 Other delirium
F05.9 Delirium, unspecified

F06 Other mental disorders due to brain damage and dysfunction and to physical disease
F06.0 Organic hallucinosis
F06.1 Organic catatonic disorder
F06.2 Organic delusional [schizophrenia-like] disorder
F06.3 Organic mood [affective] disorders
.30 Organic manic disorder
.31 Organic bipolar disorder
.32 Organic depressive disorder
.33 Organic mixed affective disorder
F06.4 Organic anxiety disorder
F06.5 Organic dissociative disorder
F06.6 Organic emotionally labile [asthenic] disorder
F06.7 Mild cognitive disorder
F06.8 Other specified mental disorders due to brain damage and dysfunction and to physical disease
F06.9 Unspecified mental disorder due to brain damage and dysfunction and to physical disease

F07 Personality and behavioral disorders due to brain disease, damage and dysfunction
F07.0 Organic personality disorder
F07.1 Postencephalitic syndrome
F07.2 Postconcussional syndrome
F07.8 Other organic personality and behavioral disorders due to brain disease, damage and dysfunction
F07.9 Unspecified organic personality and behavioral disorder due to brain disease, damage and dysfunction

F09 Unspecified organic or symptomatic mental disorder

F10–F19
Mental and behavioral disorders due to psychoactive substance use

F10.—Mental and behavioral disorders due to use of alcohol

F11.—Mental and behavioral disorders due to use of opioids

F12.—Mental and behavioral disorders due to use of cannabinoids

F13.—Mental and behavioral disorders due to use of sedatives or hypnotics

F14.—Mental and behavioral disorders due to use of cocaine

F15.—Mental and behavioral disorders due to use of other stimulants, including caffeine

F16.—Mental and behavioral disorders due to use of hallucinogens

F17.—Mental and behavioral disorders due to use of tobacco

F18.—Mental and behavioral disorders due to use of volatile solvents

F19.—Mental and behavioral disorders due to multiple drug use and use of other psychoactive substances

Four- and five-character categories may be used to specify the clinical conditions, as follows:
F1x.0 Acute intoxication
.00 Uncomplicated
.01 With trauma or other bodily injury
.02 With other medical complications
.03 With delirium
.04 With perceptual distortions
.05 With coma
.06 With convulsions
.07 Pathological intoxication
F1x.1 Harmful use
F1x.2 Dependence syndrome
.20 Currently abstinent
.21 Currently abstinent, but in a protected environment
.22 Currently on a clinically supervised maintenance or replacement regime [controlled dependence]
.23 Currently abstinent, but receiving treatment with aversive or blocking drugs
.24 Currently using the substance [active dependence]
.25 Continuous use
.26 Episodic use [dipsomania]
F1x.3 Withdrawal state
.30 Uncomplicated
.31 Convulsions
F1x.4 Withdrawal state with delirium
.40 Without convulsions
.41 With convulsions
F1x.5 Psychotic disorder
.50 Schizophrenia-like
.51 Predominantly delusional
.52 Predominantly hallucinatory
.53 Predominantly polymorphic
.54 Predominantly depressive symptoms
.55 Predominantly manic symptoms
.56 Mixed
F1x.6 Amnestic syndrome
F1x.7 Residual and late-onset psychotic disorder
.70 Flashbacks
.71 Personality or behavior disorder
.72 Residual affective disorder
.73 Dementia
.74 Other persisting cognitive impairment
.75 Late-onset psychotic disorder
F1x.8 Other mental and behavioral disorders
F1x.9 Unspecified mental and behavioral disorder

(*continued*)

Table 9–2 (*continued*)

F20–F29
Schizophrenia, schizotypal and delusional disorders

F20 Schizophrenia
F20.0 Paranoid schizophrenia
F20.1 Hebephrenic schizophrenia
F20.2 Catatonic schizophrenia
F20.3 Undifferentiated schizophrenia
F20.4 Postschizophrenic depression
F20.5 Residual schizophrenia
F20.6 Simple schizophrenia
F20.8 Other schizophrenia
F20.9 Schizophrenia, unspecified

A fifth character may be used to classify course:
.x 0 Continuous
.x 1 Episodic with progressive deficit
.x 2 Episodic with stable deficit
.x 3 Episodic remittent
.x 4 Incomplete remission
.x 5 Complete remission
.x 8 Other
.x 9 Period of observation less than one year

F21 Schizotypal disorders

F22 Persistent delusional disorders
F22.0 Delusional disorder
F22.8 Other persistent delusional disorders
F22.9 Persistent delusional disorder, unspecified

F23 Acute and transient psychotic disorders
F23.0 Acute polymorphic psychotic disorder without symptoms of schizophrenia
F23.1 Acute polymorphic psychotic disorder with symptoms of schizophrenia
F23.2 Acute schizophrenia-like psychotic disorder
F23.3 Other acute predominantly delusional psychotic disorders
F23.8 Other acute transient psychotic disorders
F23.9 Acute and transient psychotic disorders unspecified

A fifth character may be used to identify the presence or absence of associated acute stress:
.x 0 Without associated acute stress
.x 1 With associated acute stress

F24 Induced delusional disorder

F25 Schizoaffective disorders
F25.0 Schizoaffective disorder, manic type
F25.1 Schizoaffective disorder, depressive type
F25.2 Schizoaffective disorder, mixed type
F25.8 Other schizoaffective disorders
F25.9 Schizoaffective disorder, unspecified

F28 Other nonorganic psychotic disorders

F29 Unspecified nonorganic psychosis

F30–F39
Mood [affective] disorders

F30 Manic episode
F30.0 Hypomania
F30.1 Mania without psychotic symptoms
F30.2 Mania with psychotic symptoms
F30.8 Other manic episodes
F30.9 Manic episode, unspecified

F31 Bipolar affective disorder
F31.0 Bipolar affective disorder, current episode hypomanic
F31.1 Bipolar affective disorder, current episode manic without psychotic symptoms
F31.2 Bipolar affective disorder, current episode manic with psychotic symptoms
F31.3 Bipolar affective disorder, current episode mild or moderate depression
.30 Without somatic symptoms
.31 With somatic symptoms
F31.4 Bipolar affective disorder, current episode severe depression without psychotic symptoms
F31.5 Bipolar affective disorder, current episode severe depression with psychotic symptoms
F31.6 Bipolar affective disorder, current episode mixed
F31.7 Bipolar affective disorder, currently in remission
F31.8 Other bipolar affective disorders
F31.9 Bipolar affective disorder, unspecified

F32 Depressive episode
F32.0 Mild depressive episode
.00 Without somatic symptoms
.01 With somatic symptoms
F32.1 Moderate depressive episode
.10 Without somatic symptoms
.11 With somatic symptoms
F32.2 Severe depressive episode without psychotic symptoms
F32.3 Severe depressive episode with psychotic symptoms
F32.8 Other depressive episodes
F32.9 Depressive episode, unspecified

F33 Recurrent depressive disorder
F33.0 Recurrent depressive disorder, current episode mild
.00 Without somatic symptoms
.00 With somatic symptoms
F33.1 Recurrent depressive disorder, current episode moderate
.10 Without somatic symptoms
.11 With somatic symptoms
F33.2 Recurrent depressive disorder, current episode severe without psychotic symptoms
F33.3 Recurrent depressive disorder, current episode severe with psychotic symptoms
F33.4 Recurrent depressive disorder, currently in remission
F33.8 Other recurrent depressive disorders
F33.9 Recurrent depressive disorder, unspecified

F34 Persistent mood [affective] disorders
F34.0 Cyclothymia
F34.1 Dysthymia
F34.8 Other persistent mood [affective] disorders
F34.9 Persistent mood [affective] disorder, unspecified

F38 Other mood [affective] disorders
F38.0 Other single mood [affective] disorders
.00 Mixed affective episode
F38.1 Other recurrent mood [affective] disorders
.10 Recurrent brief depressive disorder
F38.8 Other specified mood [affective] disorders

F39 Unspecified mood [affective] disorder

F40–F48
Neurotic stress-related and somatoform disorders

F40 Phobic anxiety disorders
F40.0 Agoraphobia
.00 Without panic disorder
.01 With panic disorder
F40.1 Social phobias
F40.2 Specific (isolated) phobias
F40.8 Other phobic anxiety disorders
F40.9 Phobic anxiety disorder, unspecified

F41 Other anxiety disorders
F41.0 Panic disorder [episodic paroxysmal anxiety]
F41.1 Generalized anxiety disorder
F41.2 Mixed anxiety and depressive disorder
F41.3 Other mixed anxiety disorders
F41.8 Other specified anxiety disorders
F41.9 Anxiety disorder, unspecified

(*continued*)

Table 9–2 (*continued*)

F242 Obsessive-compulsive disorder
F42.0 Predominantly obsessional thoughts or ruminations
F42.1 Predominantly compulsive acts [obsessional rituals]
F42.2 Mixed obsessional thoughts and acts
F42.8 Other obsessive-compulsive disorders
F42.9 Obsessive-compulsive disorder, unspecified

F43 Reaction to severe stress, and adjustment disorders
F43.0 Acute stress reaction
F43.1 Posttraumatic stress disorder
F43.2 Adjustment disorders
.20 Brief depressive reaction
.21 Prolonged depressive reaction
.22 Mixed anxiety and depressive reaction
.23 With predominant disturbance of other emotions
.24 With predominant disturbance of conduct
.25 With mixed disturbance of emotions and conduct
.28 With other specified predominant symptoms
F43.8 Other reactions to severe stress
F43.9 Reaction to severe stress, unspecified

F44 Dissociative [conversion] disorders
F44.0 Dissociative amnesia
F44.1 Dissociative fugue
F44.2 Dissociative stupor
F44.3 Trance and possession disorders
F44.4 Dissociative motor disorders
F44.5 Dissociative convulsions
F44.6 Dissociative anesthesia and sensory loss
F44.7 Mixed dissociative [conversion] disorders
F44.8 Other dissociative [conversion] disorders
.80 Ganser's syndrome
.81 Multiple personality disorder
.82 Transient dissociative [conversion] disorders occurring in childhood and adolescence
.88 Other specified dissociative [conversion] disorders
F44.9 Dissociative [conversion] disorder, unspecified

F45 Somatoform disorders
F45.0 Somatization disorder
F45.1 Undifferentiated somatoform disorder
F45.2 Hypochondriacal disorder
F45.3 Somatoform autonomic dysfunction
.30 Heart and cardiovascular system
.31 Upper gastrointestinal tract
.32 Lower gastrointestinal tract
.33 Respiratory system
.34 Genitourinary system
.38 Other organ or system
F45.4 Persistent somatoform pain disorder
F45.8 Other somatoform disorders
F45.9 Somatoform disorder, unspecified

F48 Other neurotic disorders
F48.0 Neurasthenia
F48.1 Depersonalization-derealization syndrome
F48.8 Other specified neurotic disorders
F48.9 Neurotic disorder, unspecified

F50–F59
Behavioral syndromes associated with physiological disturbances and physical factors

F50 Eating disorders
F50.0 Anorexia nervosa
F50.1 Atypical anorexia nervosa
F50.2 Bulimia nervosa
F50.3 Atypical bulimia nervosa
F50.4 Overeating associated with other psychological disturbances
F50.5 Vomiting associated with other psychological disturbances
F50.8 Other eating disorders
F50.9 Eating disorder, unspecified

F51 Nonorganic sleep disorders
F51.0 Nonorganic insomnia
F51.1 Nonorganic hypersomnia
F51.2 Nonorganic disorder of the sleep-wake schedule
F51.3 Sleepwalking [somnambulism]
F51.4 Sleep terrors [night terrors]
F51.5 Nightmares
F51.8 Other nonorganic sleep disorders
F51.9 Nonorganic sleep disorder, unspecified

F52 Sexual dysfunction, not caused by organic disorder or disease
F52.0 Lack or loss of sexual desire
F52.1 Sexual aversion and lack of sexual enjoyment
.10 Sexual aversion
.11 Lack of sexual enjoyment
F52.2 Failure of genital response
F52.3 Orgasmic dysfunction
F52.4 Premature ejaculation
F52.5 Nonorganic vaginismus
F52.6 Nonorganic dyspareunia
F52.7 Excessive sexual drive
F52.8 Other sexual dysfunction, not caused by organic disorders or disease
F52.9 Unspecified sexual dysfunction, not caused by organic disorder or disease

F53 Mental and behavioral disorders associated with the puerperium, not elsewhere classified
F53.0 Mild mental and behavioral disorders associated with the puerperium, not elsewhere classified
F53.1 Severe mental and behavioral disorders associated with the puerperium, not elsewhere classified
F53.8 Other mental and behavioral disorders associated with the puerperium, not elsewhere classified
F53.9 Puerperal mental disorder, unspecified

F54 Psychological and behavioral factors associated with disorders or diseases classified elsewhere

F55 Abuse of non-dependence-producing substances
F55.0 Antidepressants
F55.1 Laxatives
F55.2 Analgesics
F55.3 Antacids
F55.4 Vitamins
F55.5 Steroids or hormones
F55.6 Specific herbal or folk remedies
F55.8 Other substances that do not produce dependence
F55.9 Unspecified

F59 Unspecified behavioral syndromes associated with physiological disturbances and physical factors

F60–69
Disorders of adult personality and behavior

F60 Specific personality disorders
F60.0 Paranoid personality disorder
F60.1 Schizoid personality disorder
F60.2 Dissocial personality disorder
F60.3 Emotionally unstable personality disorder
.30 Impulsive type
.31 Borderline type
F60.4 Histrionic personality disorder
F60.5 Anankastic personality disorder
F60.6 Anxious [avoidant] personality disorder
F60.7 Dependent personality disorder
F60.8 Other specific personality disorders
F60.9 Personality disorder, unspecified

F61 Mixed and other personality disorders
F61.0 Mixed personality disorders
F61.1 Troublesome personality changes

(*continued*)

Table 9–2 (*continued*)

F62 Enduring personality changes, not attributable to brain damage and disease
- F62.0 Enduring personality change after catastrophic experience
- F62.1 Enduring personality change after psychiatric illness
- F62.8 Other enduring personality changes
- F62.9 Enduring personality change, unspecified

F63 Habit and impulse disorders
- F63.0 Pathological gambling
- F63.1 Pathological fire-setting [pyromania]
- F63.2 Pathological stealing [kleptomania]
- F63.3 Trichotillomania
- F63.8 Other habit and impulse disorders
- F63.9 Habit and impulse disorder, unspecified

F64 Gender identity disorders
- F64.0 Transsexualism
- F64.1 Dual-role transvestism
- F64.2 Gender identity disorder of childhood
- F64.8 Other gender identity disorders
- F64.9 Gender identity disorder, unspecified

F65 Disorders of sexual preference
- F65.0 Fetishism
- F65.1 Fetishistic transvestism
- F65.2 Exhibitionism
- F65.3 Voyeurism
- F65.4 Pedophilia
- F65.5 Sadomasochism
- F65.6 Multiple disorders of sexual preference
- F65.8 Other disorders of sexual preference
- F65.9 Disorder of sexual preference, unspecified

F66 Psychological and behavioral disorders associated with sexual development and orientation
- F66.0 Sexual maturation disorder
- F66.1 Egodystonic sexual orientation
- F66.2 Sexual relationship disorder
- F66.8 Other psychosexual development disorders
- F66.9 Psychosexual development disorder, unspecified

A fifth character may be used to indicate association with:
- .x 0 Heterosexuality
- .x 1 Homosexuality
- .x 2 Bisexuality
- .x 8 Other, including prepubertal

F68 Other disorders of adult personality and behavior
- F68.0 Elaboration of physical symptoms for psychological reasons
- F68.1 Intentional production or feigning of symptoms or disabilities, either physical or psychological [factitious disorder]
- F68.8 Other specified disorders of adult personality and behavior

F69 Unspecified disorder of adult personality and behavior

F70–F79
Mental retardation

F70 Mild mental retardation

F71 Moderate mental retardation

F72 Severe mental retardation

F73 Profound mental retardation

F78 Other mental retardation

F79 Unspecified mental retardation

A fourth character may be used to specify the extent of associated behavioral impairment:
- F7x.0 No, or minimal, impairment of behavior
- F7x.1 Significant impairment of behavior requiring attention or treatment
- F7x.8 Other impairments of behavior
- F7x.9 Without mention of impairment of behavior

F80–F89
Disorders of psychological development

F80 Specific developmental disorders of speech and language
- F80.0 Specific speech articulation disorder
- F80.1 Expressive language disorder
- F80.2 Receptive language disorder
- F80.3 Acquired aphasia with epilepsy [Landau-Kleffner syndrome]
- F80.8 Other developmental disorders of speech and language
- F80.9 Developmental disorder of speech and language, unspecified

F81 Specific developmental disorders of scholastic skills
- F81.0 Specific reading disorder
- F81.1 Specific spelling disorder
- F81.2 Specific disorder of arithmetical skills
- F81.3 Mixed disorder of scholastic skills
- F81.8 Other developmental disorders of scholastic skills
- F81.9 Developmental disorder of scholastic skills, unspecified

F82 Specific developmental disorder of motor function

F83 Mixed specific developmental disorders

F84 Pervasive developmental disorders
- F84.0 Childhood autism
- F84.1 Atypical autism
- F84.2 Rett's syndrome
- F84.3 Other childhood disintegrative disorder
- F84.4 Overactive disorder associated with mental retardation and stereotyped movements
- F84.5 Asperger's syndrome
- F84.8 Other pervasive developmental disorders
- F84.9 Pervasive developmental disorder, unspecified

F88 Other disorders of psychological development

F89 Unspecified disorder of psychological development

F90–F98
Behavioral and emotional disorders with onset usually occurring in childhood and adolescence

F90 Hyperkinetic disorders
- F90.0 Disturbance of activity and attention
- F90.1 Hyperkinetic conduct disorder
- F90.8 Other hyperkinetic disorders
- F90.9 Hyperkinetic disorder, unspecified

F91 Conduct disorders
- F91.0 Conduct disorder confined to the family context
- F91.1 Unsocialized conduct disorder
- F91.2 Socialized conduct disorder
- F91.3 Oppositional defiant disorder
- F91.8 Other conduct disorders
- F91.9 Conduct disorder, unspecified

F92 Mixed disorders of conduct and emotions
- F92.0 Depressive conduct disorder
- F92.8 Other mixed disorders of conduct and emotions
- F92.9 Mixed disorder of conduct and emotions, unspecified

F93 Emotional disorders with onset specific to childhood
- F93.0 Separation anxiety disorder of childhood
- F93.1 Phobic anxiety disorder of childhood
- F93.2 Social anxiety disorder of childhood
- F93.3 Sibling rivalry disorder
- F93.8 Other childhood emotional disorders
- F93.9 Childhood emotional disorder, unspecified

F94 Disorders of social functioning with onset specific to childhood and adolescence
- F94.0 Elective mutism
- F94.1 Reactive attachment disorder of childhood
- F94.2 Disinhibited attachment disorder of childhood
- F94.8 Other childhood disorders of social functioning
- F94.9 Childhood disorders of social functioning, unspecified

(*continued*)

Table 9–2 (*continued*)

F95 Tic disorders
- F95.0 Transient tic disorder
- F95.1 Chronic motor or vocal tic disorder
- F95.2 Combined vocal and multiple motor tic disorder [de la Tourette's syndrome]
- F95.8 Other tic disorders
- F95.9 Tic disorder, unspecified

F98 Other behavioral and emotional disorders with onset usually occurring in childhood and adolescence
- F98.0 Nonorganic enuresis
- F98.1 Nonorganic encopresis
- F98.2 Feeding disorder of infancy and childhood
- F98.3 Pica of infancy and childhood
- F98.4 Stereotyped movement disorders
- F98.5 Stuttering [stammering]
- F98.6 Cluttering
- F98.8 Other specified behavioral and emotional disorders with onset usually occurring in childhood and adolescence
- F98.9 Unspecified behavioral and emotional disorders with onset usually occurring in childhood and adolescence

F99
Unspecified mental disorder

F99 Mental disorder, not otherwise specified

Reprinted with permission from World Health Organization: *The ICD-10 Classification of Mental and Behavioral Disorders: Clinical Descriptions and Diagnostic Guidelines.* World Health Organization, Geneva, 1992.

and Axis III. In DSM-IV's example—a case in which hypothyroidism is a direct cause of major depressive disorder—the designation on Axis I is mood disorder due to hypothyroidism with depressive features, and hypothyroidism is listed again on Axis III (Table 9–6).

Axis IV. Axis IV is used to code the psychosocial and environmental problems that significantly contribute to the development or exacerbation of the current disorder (Table 9–7).

The evaluation of stressors is based on a clinicians' assessment of the stress that an average person with similar sociocultural values and circumstances would experience from the psychosocial stressors. This judgment is based on the amount of change that the stressor causes in the person's life, the degree to which the event is desired and under the person's control, and the number of stressors. Stressors may be positive (such as a job promotion) or negative (such as the loss of a loved one). Information about stressors may be important in formulating a treatment plan that includes attempts to remove the psychosocial stressors or to help the patient cope with them.

Table 9–3
Classes or Groups of Conditions in DSM-IV

Disorders usually first diagnosed in infancy, childhood, or adolescence
Delirium, dementia, and amnestic and other cognitive disorders
Mental disorders due to a general medical condition not elsewhere classified
Substance-related disorders
Schizophrenia and other psychotic disorders
Mood disorders
Anxiety disorders
Somatoform disorders
Factitious disorders
Dissociative disorders
Sexual and gender identity disorders
Eating disorders
Sleep disorders
Impulse-control disorders not elsewhere classified
Adjustment disorders
Personality disorders
Other conditions that may be a focus of clinical attention

Table 9–4
DSM-IV Axis I: Clinical Disorders and Other Conditions That May Be a Focus of Clinical Attention

Disorders usually first diagnosed in infancy, childhood, or adolescence (excluding mental retardation, which is diagnosed on Axis II)
Delirium, dementia, and amnestic, and other cognitive disorders
Mental disorders due to a general medical condition
Substance-related disorders
Schizophrenia and other psychotic disorders
Mood disorders
Anxiety disorders
Somatoform disorders
Factitious disorders
Dissociative disorders
Sexual and gender identity disorders
Eating disorders
Sleep disorders
Impulse-control disorders not elsewhere classified
Adjustment disorders
Other conditions that may be a focus of clinical attention

Reprinted with permission from American Psychiatric Association: *Diagnostic and Statistical Manual of Mental Disorders,* ed 4. Copyright, American Psychiatric Association, Washington, 1994.

Table 9–5
DSM-IV Axis II: Personality Disorders and Mental Retardation

Paranoid personality disorder
Schizoid personality disorder
Schizotypal personality disorder
Antisocial personality disorder
Borderline personality disorder
Histrionic personality disorder
Narcissistic personality disorder
Avoidant personality disorder
Dependent personality disorder
Obsessive-compulsive personality disorder
Personality disorder not otherwise specified
Mental retardation

Reprinted with permission from American Psychiatric Association: *Diagnostic and Statistical Manual of Mental Disorders,* ed 4. Copyright, American Psychiatric Association, Washington, 1994.

Axis V. Axis V is a global assessment of functioning (GAF) scale in which clinicians judge patients' overall levels of functioning during a particular time (for example, the patient's level of functioning at the time of the evaluation or the patient's highest level of functioning for at least a few months during the past year). Functioning is considered a composite of three major areas: social functioning, occupational functioning, and psychological functioning. The GAF scale, based on a continuum of mental health and mental illness, is a 100-point scale, 100 representing the highest level of functioning in all areas (Table 9–8).

People who had a high level of functioning before an episode of illness generally have a better prognosis than do those who had a low level of functioning.

Table 9–6
DSM-IV Axis III: ICD-9-CM General Medical Conditions

Infectious and parasitic diseases (001–139)
Neoplasms (140–239)
Endocrine, nutritional, and metabolic diseases and immunity disorders (240–279)
Diseases of the blood and blood-forming organs (280–289)
Diseases of the nervous system and sense organs (320–389)
Diseases of the circulatory system (390–459)
Diseases of the respiratory system (460–519)
Diseases of the digestive system (520–579)
Diseases of the genitourinary system (580–629)
Complications of pregnancy, childbirth, and the puerperium (630–676)
Diseases of the skin and subcutaneous tissue (680–709)
Diseases of the musculoskeletal system and connective tissue (710–739)
Congenital anomalies (740–759)
Certain conditions originating in the perinatal period (760–779)
Symptoms, signs, and ill-defined conditions (780–799)
Injury and poisoning (800–999)

Reprinted with permission from American Psychiatric Association: *Diagnostic and Statistical Manual of Mental Disorders,* ed 4. Copyright, American Psychiatric Association, Washington, 1994.

Table 9–7
DSM-IV Axis IV: Psychosocial and Environmental Problems

Problems with primary support group
Problems related to the social environment
Educational problems
Occupational problems
Housing problems
Economic problems
Problems with access to health care services
Problems related to interaction with the legal system/crime
Other psychosocial and environmental problems

Reprinted with permission from American Psychiatric Association; *Diagnostic and Statistical Manual of Mental Disorders,* ed 4. Copyright, American Psychiatric Association, Washington, 1994.

Multiaxial Evaluation Report Form. Table 9–9 shows the DSM-IV Multiaxial Evaluation Report form. Examples of how to record the results of a DSM-IV multiaxial evaluation are given in Table 9–10.

Nonaxial Format

DSM-IV also allows clinicians who do not wish to use the multiaxial format to list the diagnoses serially, with the principal diagnosis listed first (Table 9–11).

Severity of Disorder

Depending on the clinical picture, the presence or absence of signs and symptoms, and their intensity, the severity of a disorder may be mild, moderate, or severe, and the disorder may be in partial or full remission. The following guidelines are used by DSM-IV.

Mild. Few, if any, symptoms in excess of those required to make the diagnosis are present, and symptoms result in no more than minor impairment in social or occupational functioning.

Moderate. Symptoms or functional impairment between *mild* and *severe* are present.

Severe. Many symptoms in excess of those required to make the diagnosis or several particularly severe symptoms are present, or the symptoms result in marked impairment in social or occupational functioning.

In Partial Remission. The full criteria for the disorder were previously met, but currently only some of the symptoms or signs of the disorder remain.

In Full Remission. There are no longer any symptoms or signs of the disorder but it is still clinically relevant to note the disorder. . . . The differentiation of *in full remission* from *recovered* requires consideration of many factors, including the characteristic course of the disorder, the length of time since the last period of disturbance, the total duration of the disturbance, and the need for continued evaluation or prophylactic treatment.

Table 9–8
DSM-IV Global Assessment of Functioning (GAF) Scale

Consider psychological, social, and occupational functioning on a hypothetical continuum of mental health-illness. Do not include impairment in functioning due to physical (or environmental) limitations.

Code	(**Note:** Use intermediate codes when appropriate, eg, 45, 68, 72.)
100–91	Superior functioning in a wide range of activities, life's problems never seem to get out of hand, is sought out by others because of his or her many positive qualities. No symptoms.
90–81	Absent or minimal symptoms (eg, mild anxiety before an exam), good functioning in all areas, interested and involved in a wide range of activities, socially effective, generally satisfied with life, no more than everyday problems or concerns (eg, an occasional argument with family members).
80–71	If symptoms are present, they are transient and expectable reactions to psychosocial stressors (eg, difficulty concentrating after family argument): no more than slight impairment in social, occupational, or school functioning (eg, temporarily falling behind in schoolwork).
70–61	Some mild symptoms (eg, depressed mood and mild insomnia) OR some difficulty in social, occupational, or school functioning (eg, occasional truancy, or theft within the household), but generally functioning pretty well, has some meaningful interpersonal relationships.
60–51	Moderate symptoms (eg, flat affect and circumstantial speech, occasional panic attacks) OR moderate difficulty in social, occupational, or school functioning (eg, few friends, conflicts with peers or coworkers).
50–41	Serious symptoms (eg, suicidal ideation, severe obsessional rituals, frequent shoplifting) OR any serious impairment in social, occupational, or school functioning (eg, no friends, unable to keep a job).
40–31	Some impairment in reality testing or communication (eg, speech is at times illogical, obscure, or irrelevant) OR major impairment in several areas, such as work or school, family relations, judgment, thinking, or mood (eg, depressed man avoids friends, neglects family, and is unable to work; child frequently beats up younger children, is defiant at home, and is failing at school).
30–21	Behavior is considerably influenced by delusions or hallucinations OR serious impairment in communication or judgment (eg, sometimes incoherent, acts grossly inappropriately, suicidal preoccupation) OR inability to function in almost all areas (eg, stays in bed all day; no job, home, or friends).
20–11	Some danger of hurting self or others (eg, suicide attempts without clear expectation of death, frequently violent, manic excitement) OR occasionally fails to maintain minimal personal hygiene (eg, smears feces) OR gross impairment in communication (eg, largely incoherent or mute).
10–1	Persistent danger of severely hurting self or others (eg, recurrent violence) OR persistent inability to maintain minimal personal hygiene OR serious suicidal act with clear expectation of death.
0	Inadequate information.

Reprinted with permission from American Psychiatric Association: *Diagnostic and Statistical Manual of Mental Disorders,* ed 4. Copyright, American Psychiatric Association, Washington, 1994.
The GAF Scale is a revision of the GAS (Endicott J, Spitzer RL, Fleiss JL, Cohen J: The Global Assessment Scale: A procedure for measuring overall severity of psychiatric disturbance. Arch Gen Psychiatry *33:* 766, 1976) and CGAS (Shaffer D, Gould MS, Brasio J, Ambrosini P, Fisher P, Bird H, Aluwahlia S: Children's Global Assessment Scale (CGAS). Arch Gen Psychiatry *40:* 1228, 1983). They are revisions of the Global Scale of the Health-Sickness Rating Scale (Luborsky L: Clinicians' judgments of mental health. Arch Gen Psychiatry *7:* 407, 1962).

Multiple Diagnoses

When a person has more than one Axis I disorder, the principal diagnosis is indicated by listing it first. According to DSM-IV:

> The remaining disorders are listed in order of focus of attention and treatment. When a person has both an Axis I and an Axis II diagnosis, the principal diagnosis or the reason for visit will be assumed to be on Axis I unless the Axis II diagnosis is followed by the qualifying phrase "(Principal diagnosis)" or "(Reason for visit)."

DSM-IV also states:

> When more than one diagnosis for an individual is given in an inpatient setting, the *principal diagnosis* is the condition established after study to be chiefly responsible for occasioning the admission of the individual. When more than one diagnosis is given for an individual in an outpatient setting, the *reason for visit* is the condition that is chiefly responsible for the ambulatory care medical services received during the visit. In most cases, the principal diagnosis or the reason for visit is also the main focus of attention or treatment. It is often difficult (and somewhat arbitrary) to determine which diagnosis is the principal diagnosis or the reason for visit, especially in situations of "dual diagnosis" (a substance-related diagnosis like Amphetamine Dependence accompanied by a non-substance-related diagnosis like Schizophrenia). For example, it may be unclear which diagnosis should be considered "principal" for an individual hospitalized with both Schizophrenia and Amphetamine Intoxication, because each condition may have contributed equally to the need for admission and treatment.

Provisional Diagnosis

According to DSM-IV:

> The modifier *provisional* can be used when there is a strong presumption that the full criteria will ultimately be met for a disorder, but not enough infor-

Table 9–9
DSM-IV Multiaxial Evaluation Report Form

The following form is offered as one possibility for reporting multiaxial evaluations. In some settings, this form may be used exactly as is; in other settings, the form may be adapted to satisfy special needs.

AXIS I: Clinical Disorders
Other Conditions that May Be a Focus of Clinical Attention

Diagnostic code ___ ___ ___ . ___ ___ DSM-IV name ______________
___ ___ ___ . ___ ___ ______________
___ ___ ___ . ___ ___ ______________

AXIS II: Personality Disorders
Mental Retardation

Diagnostic code ___ ___ ___ . ___ ___ DSM-IV name ______________
___ ___ ___ . ___ ___ ______________

AXIS III: General Medical Conditions

ICD-9-CM code ___ ___ ___ . ___ ___ ICD-9-CM name ______________
___ ___ ___ . ___ ___ ______________
___ ___ ___ . ___ ___ ______________

AXIS IV: Psychosocial and Environmental Problems

Check:
- ☐ Problems with primary support group *Specify*: ______________
- ☐ Problems related to the social environment *Specify*: ______________
- ☐ Educational problems *Specify*: ______________
- ☐ Occupational problems *Specify*: ______________
- ☐ Housing problems *Specify*: ______________
- ☐ Economic problems *Specify*: ______________
- ☐ Problems with access to health care services *Specify*: ______________
- ☐ Problems related to interaction with the legal system/crime *Specify*: ______________
- ☐ Other psychosocial and environmental problems *Specify*: ______________

AXIS V: Global Assessment of Functioning Scale
Score: ______
Time frame: ______

Reprinted with permission from American Psychiatric Association: *Diagnostic and Statistical Manual of Mental Disorders*, ed 4. Copyright, American Psychiatric Association, Washington, 1994.

mation is available to make a firm diagnosis. The clinician can indicate the diagnostic uncertainty by writing "(Provisional)" following the diagnosis. For example, the individual appears to have a Major Depressive Disorder, but is unable to give an adequate history to establish that the full criteria are met. Another use of the term *provisional* is for those situations in which differential diagnosis depends exclusively on the duration of illness. For example, a diagnosis of Schizophreniform Disorder requires a duration of less than 6 months and can only be given provisionally if assigned before remission has occurred.

Prior History

According to DSM-IV:

For some purposes, it may be useful to note a history of the criteria having been met for a disorder even when the individual is considered to be recovered from it. Such past diagnosis of mental disorder would be indicated by using the specifier Prior History (e.g., Separation Anxiety Disorder, Prior History, for an individual with a history of Separation Anxiety Disorder who has no current disorder or who currently meets criteria for Panic Disorder).

Not Otherwise Specified Categories

According to DSM-IV, "not otherwise specified" categories are used as follows:

Because of the diversity of clinical presentations, it is impossible for the diagnostic nomenclature to cover every possible situation. For this reason, each diagnostic class has at least one Not Otherwise Specified (NOS) category and some classes have several NOS categories. There are four situations in which an NOS diagnosis may be appropriate:

- The presentation conforms to the general guidelines for a mental disorder in the diagnostic class, but the symptomatic picture does not meet the criteria for any of the specific disorders. This would occur either when the symptoms are below the diagnostic threshold for one of the specific disorders or when there is an atypical or mixed presentation.

Table 9–10
DSM-IV Examples of How to Record the Results of a DSM-IV Multiaxial Evaluation

Example 1:		
Axis I	296.23	Major depressive disorder, single episode, severe without psychotic features
	305.00	Alcohol abuse
Axis II	301.6	Dependent personality disorder
		Frequent use of denial
Axis III		None
Axis IV		Threat of job loss
Axis V	GAF = 35	(current)
Example 2:		
Axis I	300.4	Dysthymic disorder
	315.00	Reading disorder
Axis II	V71.09	No diagnosis
Axis III	382.9	Otitis media, recurrent
Axis IV		Victim of child neglect
Axis V	GAF = 53	(current)
Example 3:		
Axis I	293.83	Mood disorder due to hypothyroidism, with depressive features
Axis II	V71.09	No diagnosis, histrionic personality features
Axis III	244.9	Hypothyroidism
	365.23	Chronic angle-closure glaucoma
Axis IV		None
Axis V	GAF = 45	(on admission)
	GAF = 65	(at discharge)
Example 4:		
Axis I	V61.1	Partner relational problem
Axis II	V71.09	No diagnosis
Axis III		None
Axis IV		Unemployment
Axis V	GAF = 83	(highest level past year)

Reprinted with permission from American Psychiatric Association: *Diagnostic and Statistical Manual of Mental Disorders*, ed 4. Copyright, American Psychiatric Association, Washington, 1994.

Table 9–11
DSM-IV Nonaxial Format

Clinicians who do not wish to use the multiaxial format may simply list the appropriate diagnoses. Those choosing this option should follow the general rule of recording as many coexisting mental disorders, general medical conditions, and other factors that are relevant to the care and treatment of the individual. The principal diagnosis or the reason for visit should be listed first.

The examples below illustrate the reporting of diagnoses in a format that does not use the multiaxial system.

Example 1:	
296.23	Major depressive disorder, single episode, severe without psychotic features
305.00	Alcohol abuse
301.6	Dependent personality disorder
	Frequent use of denial
Example 2:	
300.4	Dysthymic disorder
315.00	Reading disorder
382.9	Otitis media, recurrent
Example 3:	
293.83	Mood disorder due to hypothyroidism, with depressive features
244.9	Hypothyroidism
365.23	Chronic angle-closure glaucoma
	Histrionic personality features
Example 4:	
V61.1	Partner relational problem

Reprinted with permission from American Psychiatric Association: *Diagnostic and Statisical Manual of Mental Disorders*, ed. 4. Copyright American Psychiatric Association, Washington, 1994.

- The presentation to a symptom pattern that has not been included in the DSM-IV classification but that causes clinically significant distress or impairment. Research criteria for some of these symptom patterns have been included in Appendix B (''Criteria Sets and Axes Provided for Further Study''), in which case a page reference to the suggested research criteria set in Appendix B is provided.
- There is uncertainty about etiology (i.e., whether the disorder is due to a general medical condition, is substance induced, or is primary).

Frequently Used Criteria

Criteria Used to Exclude Other Diagnoses and to Suggest Differential Diagnoses. Most criteria sets used in DSM-IV include exclusion criteria to establish boundaries between disorders and to clarify differential diagnoses. The wordings of the exclusion criteria reflect the various types of relations between disorders:

- ''Criteria have never been met for . . .'' This exclusion criterion is used to define a lifetime hierarchy between disorders. For example, a diagnosis of Major Depressive Disorder can no longer be given once a Manic Episode has occurred and must be changed to a diagnosis of Bipolar I Disorder.
- ''Criteria are not met for . . .'' This exclusion criterion is used to establish a hierarchy between disorders (or subtypes) defined cross-sectionally. For example, the specifier With Melancholic Features takes precedence over With Atypical Features for describing the current Major Depressive Episode.
- ''does not occur exclusively during the course of . . .'' This exclusion criterion prevents a disorder from being diagnosed when its symptom presentation occurs only during the course of another disorder. For example, dementia is not diagnosed separately if it occurs only during delirium; Conversion Disorder is not diagnosed separately if it occurs only during Somatization Disorder; Bulimia Nervosa is not diagnosed separately if it occurs only during Anorexia Nervosa. This exclusion criterion is typically used in situations in which the symptoms of one disorder are associated features or a subset of the symptoms of the preempting disorder. The clinician should consider periods of partial remission as part of the ''course of another disorder.'' It should be noted that the excluded diagnosis can be given at times when it occurs independently (e.g., when the excluding disorder is in full remission).
- ''not due to the direct physiological effects of a substance (e.g., a drug of abuse, a medication) or a general medical condition.'' This exclusion criterion is used to indicate that a substance-induced and general medical etiology must be considered and ruled out before the disorder can be diagnosed (e.g., Major Depressive Disorder can be diagnosed only after etiologies based on substance use and a general medical condition have been ruled out).
- ''not better accounted for by . . .'' This exclusion criterion is used to indicate that the disorders mentioned in the criterion must be considered in the differential diagnosis of the presenting psychopathology and that, in boundary cases, clinical judgment will be necessary to determine which disorder provides the most appropriate diagnosis. In such cases, the ''Differential Diagnosis'' section of the text for the disorders should be consulted for guidance.

The general convention in DSM-IV is to allow multiple diagnoses to be assigned for those presentations that meet criteria for more than one DSM-IV disorder. In three situations, the previous exclusion criteria help to establish a diagnostic hierarchy (and thus prevent multiple diagnoses) or to highlight differential diagnostic considerations (and thus discourage multiple diagnoses):

- When a Mental Disorder Due to a General Medical Condition or a Substance-Induced Disorder is responsible for the symptoms, it preempts the diagnosis for the corresponding primary disorder with the same symptoms (e.g., Cocaine-Induced Mood Disorder preempts Major Depressive Disorder). In such cases, an exclusion criterion containing the phrase ''not due to the direct effects of . . .'' is included in the criteria set for the primary disorder.
- When a more pervasive disorder (e.g., Schizophrenia) has among its defining symptoms (or associated symptoms) what are the defining symptoms of a less pervasive disorder (e.g., Dysthymic Disorder), one of the following three exclusion criteria appears in the criteria set of the less pervasive disorder, indicating that only the more pervasive disorder is diagnosed: ''Criteria have never been met for . . .'', ''Criteria are not met for . . .'', ''does not occur exclusively during the course of . . .''
- When there are particularly difficult differential diagnostic boundaries, the phrase ''not better accounted for by . . .'' is included to indicate that clinical judgment is necessary to determine which diagnosis is most appropriate. For example, Panic Disorder With Agoraphobia includes the criterion ''not better accounted for by Social Phobia'' and Social Phobia includes the criterion ''not better accounted for by Panic Disorder With Agoraphobia'' in recognition of the fact that this is a particularly difficult boundary to draw. In some cases, both diagnoses might be appropriate.

Criteria for Substance-Induced Disorders. It is often difficult to determine whether presenting symptomatology is substance induced, that is, the direct physiological consequence of Substance Intoxication or Withdrawal, medication use, or toxin exposure. In an effort to provide some assistance in making this determination, two criteria have been added to each of the Substance-Induced Disorders. These criteria are intended to provide general guidelines, but at the same time allow for clinical judgment in determining whether or not the presenting symptoms are best accounted for by the direct physiological effects of the substance:

- There is evidence from the history, physical examination, or laboratory findings of either or:
  1. The symptoms developed during, or within a month of, Substance Intoxication or Withdrawal.
  2. Medication use is etiologically related to the disturbance.
- The disturbance is not better accounted for by a disorder that is not substance induced. Evidence that the symptoms are better accounted for by a disorder that is not substance induced might include the following: symptoms precede the onset of the substance use (or medication use); symptoms persist for a substantial period of time (about 1 month) after the cessation of acute withdrawal or severe intoxication or are substantially in excess of what would be expected given the type, duration, or amount of the substance used; or other evidence suggests the existence of an independent non–substance-induced disorder (a history of recurrent non–substance-related episodes).

Criteria for a Mental Disorder Due to a General Medical Condition. The following criterion is necessary to establish the etiological requirements for each of the Mental Disorders Due to a General Medical Condition (such as Mood Disorder Due to Hypothyroidism) . . .

There is evidence from the history, physical examination, or laboratory findings that the disturbance is the direct physiological consequence of a general medical condition.

DSM-IV Classification of Mental Disorders

Table 9–1 presents the DSM-IV classification of mental disorders (Axis I and Axis II).

Definition of Mental Disorder. According to DSM-IV:

[E]ach of the mental disorders is conceptualized as a clinically significant behavioral or psychological syndrome or pattern that occurs in an individual and that is associated with present distress (e.g., a painful symptom) or disability (i.e., impairment in one or more important areas of functioning) or with a significantly increased risk of suffering death, pain, disability, or an important loss of freedom. In addition, this syndrome or pattern must not be merely an expectable and culturally sanctioned response to a particular event, for example, the death of a loved one. Whatever its original cause, it must currently be considered a manifestation of a behavioral, psychological, or biological dysfunction in the individual. Neither deviant behavior (e.g., political, religious, or sexual) nor conflicts that are primarily between the individual and society are mental disorders unless the deviance or conflict is a symptom of a dysfunction in the individual, as described above . . .

Distinction Between Mental Disorder *and* General Medical Condition. The terms *mental disorder* and *general medical condition* are used throughout this manual. The term *mental disorder* is explained above. The term *general medical condition* is used merely as a convenient shorthand to refer to conditions and disorders that are listed outside the ''Mental and Behavioral Disorders'' chapter of ICD. It should be recognized that these are merely terms of convenience and should not be taken to imply that there is any fundamental distinction between mental disorders and general medical conditions, that mental disorders are unrelated to physical or biological factors or processes, or that general medical conditions are unrelated to behavioral or psychosocial factors or processes.

Organization. The DSM-IV organizational plan is described as follows:

The first section is devoted to ''Disorders Usually First Diagnosed in Infancy, Childhood, or Adolescence.'' This division of the Classification according to age at presentation is for convenience only and is not absolute. Although disorders in this section are usually first evident in childhood and adolescence, some individuals diagnosed with disorders located in this section (e.g., Attention-Deficit/Hyperactivity Disorder) may not present for clinical attention until adulthood. In addition, it is not uncommon for the age at onset for many disorders placed in other sections to be during childhood or adolescence (e.g., Major Depressive Disorder, Schizophrenia, Generalized Anxiety Disorder). Clinicians who work primarily with children and adolescents should therefore be familiar with the entire manual, and those who work primarily with adults should also be familiar with this section.

The next three sections—''Delirium, Dementia, and Amnestic and Other Cognitive Disorders''; ''Mental Disorders Due to a General Medical Condition''; and ''Substance-Related Disorders''—were grouped together in DSM-III-R under the single heading of ''Organic Mental Syndromes and Disorders.'' . . . As in DSM-III-R, these sections are placed before the remaining disorders in the manual because of their priority in differential diagnosis (e.g., substance-related causes of depressed mood must be ruled out before making a diagnosis of Major Depressive Disorder). To facilitate differential diagnosis, complete lists of Mental Disorders Due to a General Medical Condition and Substance-Related Disorders appear in these sections, whereas the text and criteria for these disorders are placed in the diagnostic sections with disorders with which they share phenomenology. For example, the text and criteria for Substance-Induced Mood Disorder and Mood Disorder Due to a General Medical Condition are included in the Mood Disorders section.

The organizing principle for all the remaining sections (except for Adjustment Disorders) is to group disorders based on their shared phenomenological features in order to facilitate differential diagnosis. The ''Adjustment Disorders'' section is organized differently in that these disorders are grouped based on their common etiology (e.g., maladaptive reaction to a stressor). Therefore, the Adjustment Disorders include a variety of heterogeneous clinical presentations (e.g., Adjustment Disorder With Depressed Mood, Adjustment Disorder With Anxiety, Adjustment Disorder With Disturbance of Conduct).

Finally, DSM-IV includes a section for Other Conditions That May Be a Focus of Clinical Attention.

Psychosis and Neurosis

Psychosis. Although the traditional meaning of the term *psychotic* emphasized loss of reality testing and impairment of mental functioning—manifested by delusions, hallucinations, confusion, and impaired memory—two other meanings have evolved during the past 50 years. In the most common psychiatric use of the term, *psychotic* became synonymous with severe impairment of social and personal functioning characterized by social withdrawal and inability to perform the usual household and occupational roles. The other use of the term specifies the degree of ego regression as the criterion for psychotic illness. As a consequence of these multiple meanings, the term has lost its precision in current clinical and research practice.

According to the glossary of the American Psychiatric Association, the term *psychotic* means grossly impaired in reality testing. The term may be used to describe the behavior of a person at a given time or a mental disorder in which at some time during its course all people with the disorder have grossly impaired reality testing. With gross impairment in reality testing, people incorrectly evaluate the accuracy of their perceptions and thoughts and make incorrect inferences about external reality, even in the face of contrary evidence. The term *psychotic* does not apply to minor distortions of reality that involve matters of relative judgment. For example, depressed people who underestimate their achievements are not described as psychotic, whereas those who believe that they have caused natural catastrophes are so described.

Direct evidence of psychotic behavior is the presence of either delusions or hallucinations without insight into their pathological nature. The term *psychotic* is sometimes appropriate when behavior is so grossly disorganized that it is reasonable to infer that reality testing is disturbed. Examples include markedly incoherent speech without apparent awareness by the person that the speech is not understandable and the agitated, inattentive, and disoriented behavior seen in alcohol intoxication delirium. A person with a nonpsychotic mental disorder may exhibit psychotic behavior, although rarely. For example, a person with obsessive-compulsive disorder may at times come to believe in the reality of the danger of being contaminated by shaking hands with strangers.

In DSM-IV, the psychotic disorders include pervasive developmental disorders, schizophrenia, schizophreniform disorder, schizoaffective disorder, delusional disorder, brief psychotic disorder, shared psychotic disorder, psychotic disorder due to a general medical condition, substance-induced psychotic disorder, and psychotic disorder not otherwise specified. In addition, some severe mood disorders have psychotic features.

Neurosis. A neurosis is a chronic or recurrent nonpsychotic disorder characterized mainly by anxiety. The disorder is experienced or expressed directly or is altered through defense mechanisms; it appears as a symptom, such as an obsession, a compulsion, a phobia, or a sexual dysfunction. Although not used in DSM-IV, the term *neurosis* is still found in the literature and in ICD-10. In the third edition of DSM (DSM-III), a neurotic disorder was defined as follows:

> A mental disorder in which the predominant disturbance is a symptom or group of symptoms distressing to the individual and recognized by him or her as unacceptable and alien (ego dystonic); reality testing is grossly intact. Behavior does not actively violate gross social norms (although it may be quite disabling). The disturbance is relatively enduring or recurrent without treatment, and is not limited to a transitory reaction to stressors. There is no demonstrable organic etiology or factor.

In DSM-IV, no overall diagnostic class is called *neuroses,* but many clinicians consider the following diagnostic categories to be neuroses: anxiety disorders, somatoform disorders, dissociative disorders, sexual disorders, and dysthymic disorder. The term *neuroses* encompasses a broad range of disorders with various signs and symptoms. As such, it has lost any degree of precision except to signify that a person's gross reality testing and personality organization are intact. A neurosis, however, can be and usually is sufficient to impair the person's functioning in several areas. The authors believe that the term is useful in contemporary psychiatry and should be retained.

ICD-10. In ICD-10, a class called neurotic, stress-related, and somatoform disorders encompasses the following: phobic anxiety disorders, other anxiety disorders (including panic disorder, generalized anxiety disorder, and mixed anxiety and depressive disorder), obsessive-compulsive disorder, adjustment disorders, dissociative (conversion) disorders, and somatoform disorders. In addition, ICD-10 includes neurasthenia as a neurotic disorder, characterized by mental and physical fatigability, a sense of general instability, irritability, anhedonia, and sleep disturbances. Many of the cases so diagnosed outside the United States fit the descriptions of anxiety disorders and depressive disorders and are diagnosed as such by U.S. psychiatrists.

An appendix was added to DSM-IV to reflect the influence of culture and ethnicity on psychiatric assessment and diagnosis. This appendix describes culturally specific symptom patterns, preferred idioms for describing distress, and prevalence when such information is available. It also provides clinicians with guidance on how clinical presentations may be influenced by patients' cultural settings.

Appendix H lists the corresponding ICD-10 codes for DSM-IV disorders.

New and Controversial Categories

Proposed new categories that were considered controversial or for which there was insufficient information to warrant inclusion in DSM-IV were placed in Appendix B, "Criteria Sets and Axes Provided for Further Study." Not all psychiatrists agree that these categories are discrete psychological disorders, and they do not agree on the essential diagnostic features. Each category requires systematic research to determine whether it will eventually be included in the official nomenclature. Nevertheless, clinicians should be familiar with the conditions, some of which are already included in ICD-10.

In addition to the following categories, DSM-IV includes a list of defense mechanisms that can be added to the principal diagnosis when a clinician chooses.

Postconcussional Disorder. This disorder is discussed in Chapter 10, Section 10.5. In ICD-10, it is referred to as postconcussional syndrome, which occurs after head trauma that usually is sufficiently severe to result in loss of consciousness. Symptoms include headache, dizziness (usually lacking the features of true vertigo), fatigue, irritability, difficulty in concentrating and performing mental tasks, memory impairment, insomnia, and reduced tolerance for stress, emotional excitement, and alcohol abuse.

Mild Neurocognitive Disorder. This condition is discussed in Chapter 10, Section 10.1.

Caffeine Withdrawal. This disorder is covered in Chapter 12, Section 12.4.

Postpsychotic Depressive Disorder of Schizophrenia. This disorder is discussed in Chapter 14, Section 14.1. In ICD-10, postschizophrenic depression is described as follows:

> A depressive episode, which may be prolonged, arising in the aftermath of a schizophrenic illness. Some schizophrenic symptoms must still be present but no longer dominate the clinical picture. These persisting schizophrenic symptoms may be "positive" or "negative," though the latter are more common. It is uncertain, and immaterial to the diagnosis, to what extent the depressive symptoms have merely been uncovered by the resolution of earlier psychotic symptoms (rather than being a new development) or are an intrinsic part of schizophrenia rather than a psychological reaction to it. They are rarely sufficiently severe or extensive to meet criteria for a severe depressive episode, and it is often difficult to decide which of the patient's symptoms are due to depression and which to neuroleptic medication or to the impaired volition and affective flattening of schizophrenia itself. This depressive disorder is associated with an increased risk of suicide.

Simple Deteriorative Disorder. This disorder is covered in Chapter 14, Section 14.1. In ICD-10, it is described as an uncommon disorder characterized by oddities of conduct, an inability to meet the demands of society, blunting of affect, loss of volition, and social impoverishment. Delusions and hallucinations are not evident.

Minor Depressive Disorder, Recurrent Brief Depressive Disorder, and Premenstrual Dysphoric Disorder. These disorders are covered in Chapter 15, Section 15.1. Minor depressive disorder is associated with comparatively mild symptoms, such as worry and overconcern with minor autonomic symptoms (for example, tremor and palpitations). Most cases never come to medical or psychiatric attention. In ICD-10, recurrent brief depressive disorder is characterized by recurrent episodes of depression, each of which lasts less than 2 weeks (typically 2 to 3 days) and each of which ends with complete recovery.

Mixed Anxiety-Depressive Disorder. This disorder is covered in Chapter 16, Section 16.1. Mixed anxiety and depressive disorder is listed in ICD-10, where it is described as encompassing symptoms of both anxiety and depression, neither of which predominates.

Factitious Disorder by Proxy. This disorder, also known as Munchausen syndrome by proxy, is discussed in Chapter 19. In the disorder, parents feign illness in their children.

Dissociative Trance Disorder. The dissociative disorders are discussed in Chapter 20. ICD-10 lists trance and possession disorders, in which a patient experiences a temporary loss of both the sense of personal identity and full awareness of the surroundings. The disorders are involuntary or unwanted. In some cases, patients act as if taken over by another personality, spirit, or force.

Binge-Eating Disorder. This disorder is a variant of bulimia nervosa, which is discussed in Chapter 23, Section 23.2. It consists of recurrent episodes of binge eating without compensatory behavior, such as self-induced vomiting and laxative abuse.

Depressive Personality Disorder and Passive-Aggressive Personality Disorder. These personality disorders are classified in the not otherwise specified category of personality disorders. Each disorder is described in Chapter 27.

Medication-Induced Movement Disorders. These disorders are caused by the adverse effects of medication. They include parkinsonism, neuroleptic malignant syndrome, acute dystonia, acute akathisia, tardive dyskinesia, postural tremor, and not otherwise specified movement disorder. These disorders are discussed in Chapter 35, Section 35.2.

Culture-Bound Syndromes

An appendix of culturally related syndromes includes the name for each condition, the culture in which it was first described, a brief description of its psychopathology, and a list of possibly related DSM-IV categories. Chapter 14, Section 14.1 includes a discussion of culture-bound syndromes.

The implication of culture and its relation to diagnosis is set forth in DSM-IV as follows:

> Diagnostic assessment can be especially challenging when a clinician from one ethnic or cultural group uses the DSM-IV Classification to evaluate an individual from a different ethnic or cultural group. A clinician who is unfamiliar with the nuances of an individual's cultural frame of reference may incorrectly judge as psychopathology those normal variations in behavior, belief, or experience that are particular to the individual's culture. For example, certain religious practices or beliefs (e.g., hearing or seeing a deceased relative during bereavement) may be misdiagnosed as manifestations of a Psychotic Disorder. Applying Personality Disorder criteria across cultural settings may be especially difficult because of the wide cultural variation in concepts of self, styles of communication, and coping mechanisms.

Guidelines

Cautionary Statement. The American Psychiatric Association has issued a cautionary statement about the proper use and interpretation of the diagnostic categories in DSM-IV. It reads as follows:

> The specified diagnostic criteria for each mental disorder are offered as guidelines for making diagnoses, because it has been demonstrated that the use of such criteria enhances agreement among clinicians and investigators. The proper use of these criteria requires specialized clinical training that provides both a body of knowledge and clinical skills.
>
> These diagnostic criteria and the DSM-IV Classification of mental disorders reflect a consensus of current formulations of evolving knowledge in our field.

They do not encompass, however, all the conditions for which people may be treated or appropriate topics for research efforts.

The purpose of DSM-IV is to provide clear descriptions of diagnostic categories in order to enable clinicians and investigators to diagnose, communicate about, study, and treat people with various mental disorders. It is to be understood that inclusion here, for clinical and research purposes, of a diagnostic category such as Pathological Gambling or Pedophilia does not imply that the condition meets legal or other nonmedical criteria for what constitutes mental disease, mental disorder, or mental disability. The clinical and scientific considerations involved in categorization of these conditions as mental disorders may not be wholly relevant to legal judgments, for example, that take into account such issues as individual responsibility, disability determination, and competency.

Caveats. DSM-IV describes specific caveats regarding its use:

LIMITATIONS OF THE CATEGORICAL APPROACH. DSM-IV is a categorical classification that divides mental disorders into types based on criteria sets with defining features. This naming of categories is the traditional method of organizing and transmitting information in everyday life and has been the fundamental approach used in all systems of medical diagnosis. A categorical approach to classification works best when all members of a diagnostic class are homogeneous, when there are clear boundaries between classes, and when the different classes are mutually exclusive. Nonetheless, the limitations of the categorical classification system must be recognized.

In DSM-IV, there is no assumption that each category of mental disorder is a completely discrete entity with absolute boundaries dividing it from other mental disorders or from no mental disorder. There is also no assumption that all individuals described as having the same mental disorder are alike in all important ways. The clinician using the DSM-IV should therefore consider that individuals sharing a diagnosis are likely to be heterogeneous even in regard to the defining features of the diagnosis and that boundary cases will be difficult to diagnose in any but a probabilistic fashion. This outlook allows greater flexibility in the use of the system, encourages more specific attention to boundary cases, and emphasizes the need to capture additional clinical information that goes beyond diagnosis. In recognition of the heterogeneity of clinical presentations, DSM-IV often includes polythetic criteria sets, in which the individual need only present with a subset of items from a longer list (e.g., the diagnosis of Borderline Personality Disorder requires only five out of nine items).

USE OF CLINICAL JUDGMENT. DSM-IV is a classification of mental disorders that was developed for use in clinical, educational, and research settings. The diagnostic categories, criteria, and textual descriptions are meant to be employed by individuals with appropriate clinical training and experience in diagnosis. It is important that DSM-IV not be applied mechanically by untrained individuals. The specific diagnostic criteria included in DSM-IV are meant to serve as guidelines to be informed by clinical judgment and are not meant to be used in a cookbook fashion. For example, the exercise of clinical judgment may justify giving a certain diagnosis to an individual even though the clinical presentation falls just short of meeting the full criteria for the diagnosis as long as the symptoms that are present are persistent and severe. On the other hand, lack of familiarity with DSM-IV or excessively flexible and idiosyncratic application of DSM-IV criteria or conventions substantially reduces its utility as a common language for communication.

USE OF DSM-IV IN FORENSIC SETTINGS. When the DSM-IV categories, criteria, and textual descriptions are employed for forensic purposes, there are significant risks that diagnostic information will be misused or misunderstood. These dangers arise because of the imperfect fit between the questions of ultimate concern to the law and the information contained in a clinical diagnosis. In most situations, the clinical diagnosis of a DSM-IV mental disorder is not sufficient to establish the existence for legal purposes of a "mental disorder," "mental disability," "mental disease," or "mental defect." In determining whether an individual meets a specified legal standard (e.g., for competence, criminal responsibility, or disability), additional information is usually required beyond that contained in the DSM-IV diagnosis. This might include information about the individual's functional impairments and how these impairments affect the particular abilities in question. It is precisely because impairments, abilities, and disabilities vary widely within each diagnostic category that assignment of a particular diagnosis does not imply a specific level of impairment or disability.

Nonclinical decision-makers should also be cautioned that a diagnosis does not carry any necessary implications regarding the causes of the individual's mental disorder or its associated impairments. Inclusion of a disorder in the Classification (as in medicine generally) does not require that there be knowledge about its etiology. Moreover, the fact that an individual's presentation meets the criteria for a DSM-IV diagnosis does not carry any necessary implication regarding the individual's degree of control over the behaviors that may be associated with the disorder. Even when diminished control over one's behavior is a feature of the disorder, having the diagnosis in itself does not demonstrate that a particular individual is (or was) unable to control his or her behavior at a particular time.

It must be noted that DSM-IV reflects a consensus about the classification and diagnosis of mental disorders derived at the time of its initial publication. New knowledge generated by research or clinical experience will undoubtedly lead to an increased understanding of the disorders included in DSM-IV, to the identification of new disorders, and to the removal of some disorders in future classifications. The text and criteria sets included in DSM-IV will require reconsideration in light of evolving new information.

The use of DSM-IV in forensic settings should be informed by an awareness of the risks discussed above. When used appropriately, diagnoses and diagnostic information can assist decision-makers in their determinations. For example, when the presence of a mental disorder is the predicate for a subsequent legal determination (e.g., involuntary civil commitment), the use of an established system of diagnosis enhances the value and reliability of the determination. By providing a compendium based upon a review of the pertinent clinical and research literature, DSM-IV may facilitate the legal decision-makers' understanding of the relevant characteristics of mental disorders. The literature related to diagnoses also serves as a check on ungrounded speculation about mental disorders and about the functioning of a particular individual. Finally, diagnostic information regarding longitudinal course may improve decision-making when the legal issue concerns an individual's mental functioning at a past or future point in time.

Decision Trees

Decision trees, also known as algorithms, are diagrammatic tracks that organize a clinician's thinking so that all differential diagnoses are considered and ruled in or out, and thus result in a presumptive diagnosis. Beginning with specific signs or symptoms, the psychiatrist follows the positive or negative track down the tree (by answering yes or no) until a point in the tree with no outgoing branches (known as a leaf) is found. This point is the final diagnosis. Figure 9–1 is an example of a decision tree for psychotic disorders. DSM-IV includes an appendix of diagnostic decision trees.

PSYCHIATRIC RATING SCALES

Psychiatric rating scales, also called rating instruments, provide a way to quantify aspects of a patient's psyche, behavior, and relationships with individuals and society. The measurement of pathology in these areas of a person's life may initially seem to be less straightforward than is the measurement

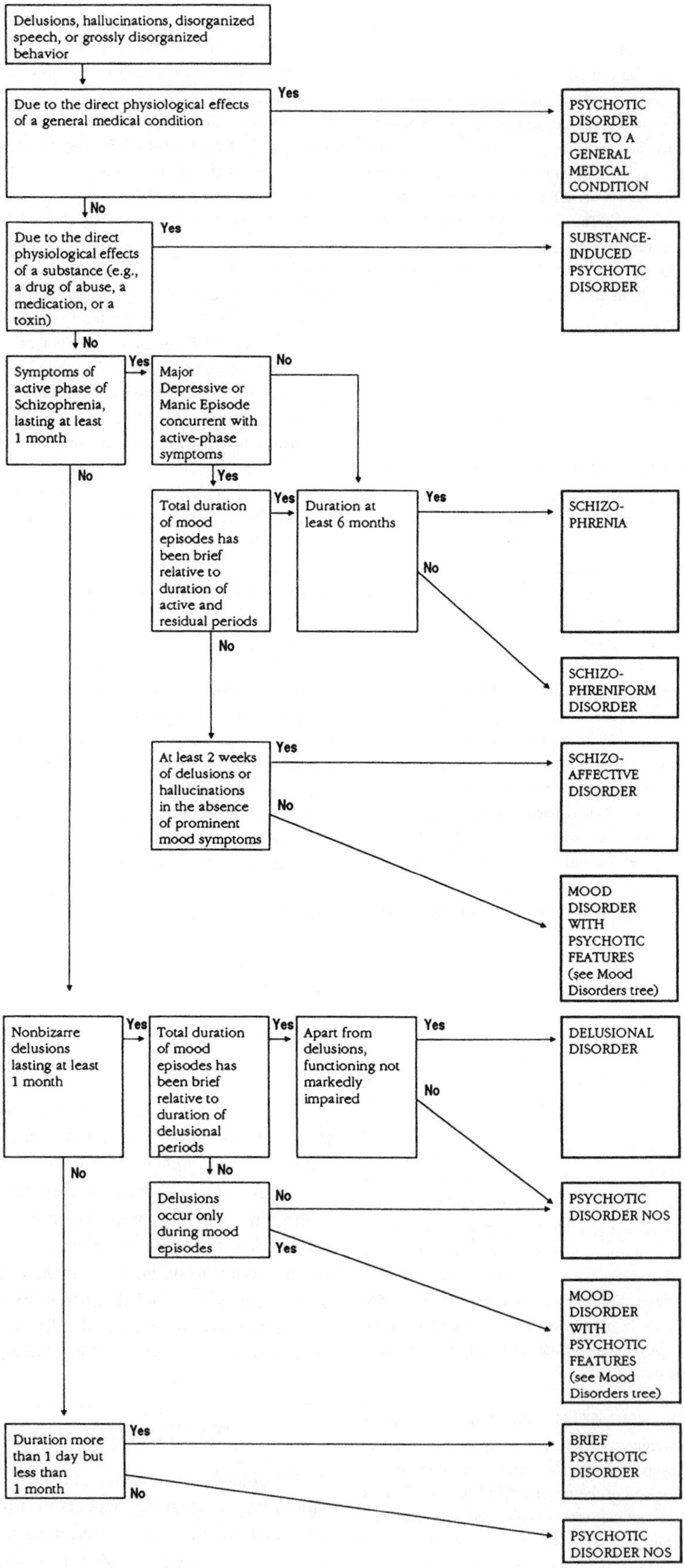
Delusions, hallucinations, disorganized speech, or grossly disorganized behavior
Due to the direct physiological effects of a general medical condition
Yes
PSYCHOTIC DISORDER DUE TO A GENERAL MEDICAL CONDITION
No
Due to the direct physiological effects of a substance (e.g., a drug of abuse, a medication, or a toxin)
Yes
SUBSTANCE-INDUCED PSYCHOTIC DISORDER
No
Symptoms of active phase of Schizophrenia, lasting at least 1 month
Yes
Major Depressive or Manic Episode concurrent with active-phase symptoms
No
Yes
Total duration of mood episodes has been brief relative to duration of active and residual periods
Yes
Duration at least 6 months
Yes
SCHIZO-PHRENIA
No
SCHIZO-PHRENIFORM DISORDER
No
At least 2 weeks of delusions or hallucinations in the absence of prominent mood symptoms
Yes
SCHIZO-AFFECTIVE DISORDER
No
MOOD DISORDER WITH PSYCHOTIC FEATURES (see Mood Disorders tree)
No
Nonbizarre delusions lasting at least 1 month
Yes
Total duration of mood episodes has been brief relative to duration of delusional periods
Yes
Apart from delusions, functioning not markedly impaired
Yes
DELUSIONAL DISORDER
No
PSYCHOTIC DISORDER NOS
No
Delusions occur only during mood episodes
No
Yes
MOOD DISORDER WITH PSYCHOTIC FEATURES (see Mood Disorders tree)
No
Duration more than 1 day but less than 1 month
Yes
BRIEF PSYCHOTIC DISORDER
No
PSYCHOTIC DISORDER NOS

FIGURE 9–1

Differential diagnosis of psychotic disorders. (Reprinted with permission from American Psychiatric Association: *Diagnostic and Statistical Manual of Mental Disorders,* ed 4. American Psychiatric Association, Washington, 1994.)

Table 9–12
Psychiatric Rating Scales

Scale	Source
Rating Scales Used for Schizophrenia and Psychosis	
Brief Psychiatric Rating Scale	Psychological Reports *10:* 799, 1962
Schedule for Affective Disorders and Schizophrenia (SADS)	Archives of General Psychiatry *35:* 837, 1978
Scale for the Assessment of Negative Symptoms (SANS)	University of Iowa Press, 1983
Scale for the Assessment of Thought, Language, and Communication (TLC)	University of Iowa Press, 1978
Thought Disorder Index (TDI)	Archives of General Psychiatry *40:* 1281, 1983
Quality of Life Scale (QLS)	Schizophrenia Bulletin *10:* 383, 1984
Chestnut Lodge Prognostic Scale for Chronic Schizophrenia	Schizophrenia Bulletin *13:* 277, 1987
Rating Scales Used for Mood Disorders	
Beck Depression Inventory	Archives of General Psychiatry *4:* 561, 1961
Standard Assessment of Depressive Disorders (SADD)	Psychological Medicine *10:* 743, 1979
Zung Self-Rating Scale for Depression	Archives of General Psychiatry *12:* 63, 1965
Carroll Rating Scale for Depression	British Journal of Psychiatry *138:* 194, 1981
Montgomery-Asberg Scale	British Journal of Psychiatry *134:* 382, 1979
Raskin Depression Rating Scale	Journal of Nervous and Mental Disease *148:* 87, 1969
Inventory to Diagnose Depression	Archives of General Psychiatry *43:* 1976, 1986
Mania Rating Scale	Journal of Clinical Psychiatry *44:* 98, 1983
Manic State Rating Scale	Archives of General Psychiatry *25:* 256, 1971
Rating Scales Used for Anxiety Disorders	
Brief Outpatient Psychopathology Scale	Journal of Clinical Pharmacology *9:* 187, 1969
Physicians Questionnaire	Psychopharmacologia *17:* 338, 1970
Covi Anxiety Scale	Psychopharmacology Bulletin *18:* 69, 1982
Anxiety States Inventory	Psychosomatics *12:* 371, 1971
Fear Questionnaire	Behavioral Research and Therapeutics *17:* 263, 1979
Mobility Inventory for Agoraphobia	Behavioral Research and Therapeutics *23:* 35, 1985
Social Avoidance and Distress Scale	Journal of Consulting and Clinical Psychology *33:* 448, 1969
Acute Panic Inventory	Archives of General Psychiatry *41:* 764, 1984
Leyton Obsessional Inventory	Psychological Medicine *1:* 48, 1970
Maudsley Obsessional-Compulsive Inventory	Behavioral Research and Therapeutics *15:* 389, 1977
Fear Thermometer	Journal of Consulting and Clinical Psychiatry *15:* 488, 1983
Impact of Events Scale	Psychosomatic Medicine *41:* 209, 1979
Other Rating Scales	
Child and adolescent patients	
General reference for adult scales that have been modified for children	Psychopharmacology Bulletin *21:* 737, 1985
Adverse effects of drugs	
Systematic Assessment for Treatment of Emergent Events (SAFTEE):	Psychopharmacology Bulletin *22:* 343, 1986
General Inquiry (GI)	
Systematic Inquiry (SI)	
Quality of Life	
Patterns of Individual Change Scale (PICS)	Archives of General Psychiatry *42:* 703, 1985
Dissociative disorders	
Structured Clinical Interview for DSM-IV Dissociative Disorders (SCID-IV)	American Journal of Psychiatry *150:* 1011, 1993

of pathology—hypertension, for example—by other medical specialists. Nevertheless, many psychiatric rating scales are able to measure carefully chosen features of well-formulated concepts. Moreover, psychiatrists who do not use these rating scales are left with only their clinical impressions, which are difficult to record in a manner that allows for reliable future comparison and communication. Without psychiatric rating scales, quantitative data in psychiatry are crude (for example, length of hospitalization or other treatment, discharge and readmission to hospital, length to relationships or employment, and presence of legal troubles).

Table 9–12 lists a variety of rating scales and the initial reference source for each. Some commonly used instruments are found in Tables 9–13 through 9–18.

Characteristics of Rating Scales

Rating scales can be specific or comprehensive, and they can measure both internally experienced variables (for example, mood) and externally observable variables (for example, behavior). Specific scales measure discrete thoughts, moods, or behaviors, such as obsessive thoughts and temper tantrums; comprehensive scales measure broad abstractions, such as depression and anxiety.

Table 9–13
Brief Psychiatric Rating Scale

DIRECTIONS: Place an X in the appropriate box to represent level of severity of each symptom.

PATIENT ______________________________

RATER ______________________________

NO. ______________________________

DATE ______________________________

	0 Not Present = 0	1 Very Mild = 1	2 Mild = 2	3 Moderate = 3	4 Mod. Severe = 4	5 Severe = 5	6 Extremely Severe = 6
1. Somatic concern—preoccupation with physical health, fear of physical illness, hypochondriases	☐	☐	☐	☐	☐	☐	☐
2. Anxiety—worry, fear, overconcern for present or future	☐	☐	☐	☐	☐	☐	☐
3. Emotional withdrawal—lack of spontaneous interaction, isolation, deficiency in relating to others	☐	☐	☐	☐	☐	☐	☐
4. Conceptual disorganization—thought processes confused, disconnected, disorganized, disrupted	☐	☐	☐	☐	☐	☐	☐
5. Guilt feelings—self-blame, shame, remorse for past behavior	☐	☐	☐	☐	☐	☐	☐
6. Tension—physical and motor manifestations or nervousness, overactivation, tension	☐	☐	☐	☐	☐	☐	☐
7. Mannerisms and posturing—peculiar, bizarre, unnatural motor behavior (not including tic)	☐	☐	☐	☐	☐	☐	☐
8. Grandiosity—exaggerated self-opinion, arrogance, conviction of unusual power or abilities	☐	☐	☐	☐	☐	☐	☐
9. Depressive mood—sorrow, sadness, despondency, pessimism	☐	☐	☐	☐	☐	☐	☐
10. Hostility—animosity, contempt, belligerence, disdain for others	☐	☐	☐	☐	☐	☐	☐
11. Suspiciousness—mistrust, belief that others harbor malicious or discriminatory intent	☐	☐	☐	☐	☐	☐	☐
12. Hallucinatory behavior—perceptions without normal external stimulus correspondence	☐	☐	☐	☐	☐	☐	☐
13. Motor retardation—slowed, weakened movements or speech, reduced body tone	☐	☐	☐	☐	☐	☐	☐
14. Uncooperativeness—resistance, guardedness, rejection of authority	☐	☐	☐	☐	☐	☐	☐
15. Unusual thought content—unusual, odd, strange, bizarre thought content	☐	☐	☐	☐	☐	☐	☐
16. Blunted affect—reduced emotional tone, reduction in normal intensity of feelings, flatness	☐	☐	☐	☐	☐	☐	☐
17. Excitement—heightened emotional tone, agitation, increased reactivity	☐	☐	☐	☐	☐	☐	☐
18. Disorientation—confusion or lack of proper association for person, place, or time	☐	☐	☐	☐	☐	☐	☐

Courtesy of John E. Overall, Ph.D.

Table 9–14
Hamilton Anxiety Rating Scale

Instructions: This checklist is to assist the physician or psychiatrist in evaluating each patient as to his degree of anxiety and pathological condition. Please fill in the appropriate rating:

NONE = 0 MILD = 1 MODERATE = 2 SEVERE = 3 SEVERE, GROSSLY DISABLING = 4

Item		Rating	Item		Rating
Anxious	Worries, anticipation of the worst, fearful anticipation, irritability	______	Somatic (sensory)	Tinnitus, blurring of vision, hot and cold flushes, feelings of weakness, picking sensation	______
Tension	Feelings of tension, fatigability, startle response, moved to tears easily, trembling, feelings of restlessness, inability to relax	______	Cardiovascular symptoms	Tachycardia, palpitations, pain in chest, throbbing of vessels, fainting feelings, missing beat	______
Fears	Of dark, of strangers, of being left alone, of animals, of traffic, of crowds	______	Respiratory symptoms	Pressure or constriction in chest, choking feelings, sighing, dyspnea	______
Insomnia	Difficulty in falling asleep, broken sleep, unsatisfying sleep and fatigue on waking, dreams, nightmares, night-terrors	______	Gastrointestinal symptoms	Difficulty in swallowing, wind, abdominal pain, burning sensations, abdominal fullness, nausea, vomiting, borborygmi, looseness of bowels, loss of weight, constipation	______
Intellectual (cognitive)	Difficulty in concentration, poor memory	______	Genitourinary symptoms	Frequency of micturition, urgency of micturition, amenorrhea, menorrhagia, development of frigidity, premature ejaculation, loss of libido, impotence	______
Depressed mood	Loss of interest, lack of pleasure in hobbies, depression, early waking, diurnal swing	______	Autonomic symptoms	Dry mouth, flushing, pallor, tendency to sweat, giddiness, tension headache, raising of hair	______
Somatic (muscular)	Pains and aches, twitching, stiffness, myoclonic jerks, grinding of teeth, unsteady voice, increased muscular tone	______	Behavior at interview	Fidgeting, restlessness or pacing, tremor of hands, furrowed brow, strained face, sighing or rapid respiration, facial pallor, swallowing, belching, brisk tendon jerks, dilated pupils, exophthalmos	______

ADDITIONAL COMMENTS

Investigator's signature:

Reprinted with permission from Hamilton M: The assessment of anxiety states by rating. Br J Psychiatry *32:* 50, 1959.

Table 9–15
Hamilton Rating Scale for Depression

For each item select the "cue" which best characterizes the patient.

1: Depressed Mood (Sadness, hopeless, helpless, worthless)
- 0 Absent
- 1 These feeling states indicated only on questioning
- 2 These feeling states spontaneously reported verbally
- 3 Communicates feeling states nonverbally—ie, through facial expression, posture, voice, and tendency to weep
- 4 Patient reports VIRTUALLY ONLY these feeling states in his spontaneous verbal and nonverbal communication

2: Feelings of Guilt
- 0 Absent
- 1 Self-reproach, feels he has let people down
- 2 Ideas of guilt or rumination over past errors or sinful deeds
- 3 Present illness is a punishment. Delusions of guilt
- 4 Hears accusatory or denunciatory voices and/or experiences threatening visual hallucinations

3: Suicide
- 0 Absent
- 1 Feels life is not worth living
- 2 Wishes he were dead or any thoughts of possible death to self
- 3 Suicide ideas or gesture
- 4 Attempts at suicide (any serious attempt rates 4)

4: Insomnia early
- 0 No difficulty falling asleep
- 1 Complains of occasional difficulty falling asleep—ie, more than 1/4 hour
- 2 Complains of nightly difficulty falling asleep

5: Insomnia middle
- 0 No difficulty
- 1 Patient complains of being restless and disturbed during the night
- 2 Waking during the night—any getting out of bed rates 2 (except for purpose of voiding)

(*continued*)

Table 9–15 (*continued*)

6: Insomnia late
- 0 No difficulty
- 1 Waking in early hours of the morning but goes back to sleep
- 2 Unable to fall asleep again if gets out of bed

7: Work and activities
- 0 No difficulty
- 1 Thoughts and feelings of incapacity, fatigue or weakness related to activities, work, or hobbies
- 2 Loss of interest in activity, hobbies, or work—either directly reported by patient, or indirect in listlessness, indecision and vacillation (feels he has to push self to work or activities)
- 3 Decrease in actual time spent in activities or decrease in productivity. In hospital, rate 3 if patient does not spend at least three hours a day in activities (hospital job or hobbies) exclusive of ward chores
- 4 Stopped working because of present illness. In hospital, rate 4 if patient engages in no activities except ward chores, or if patient fails to perform ward chores unassisted

8: Retardation (Slowness of thought and speech; impaired ability to concentrate; decreased motor activity)
- 0 Normal speech and thought
- 1 Slight retardation at interview
- 2 Obvious retardation at interview
- 3 Interview difficult
- 4 Complete stupor

9: Agitation
- 0 None
- 1 "Playing with" hands, hair, etc.
- 2 Hand-wringing, nail biting, hair pulling, biting of lips

10: Anxiety psychic
- 0 No difficulty
- 1 Subjective tension and irritability
- 2 Worrying about minor matters
- 3 Apprehensive attitude apparent in face or speech
- 4 Fears expressed without questioning

11: Anxiety somatic

0 Absent	Physiological concomitants of anxiety, such as:
1 Mild	Gastrointestinal—dry mouth, wind, indigestion, diarrhea, cramps, belching
2 Moderate	Cardiovascular—palpitations, headaches
3 Severe	Respiratory—hyperventilation, sighing
4 Incapacitating	Urinary frequency
	Sweating

12: Somatic symptoms gastrointestinal
- 0 None
- 1 Loss of appetite but eating without staff encouragement. Heavy feelings in abdomen
- 2 Difficulty eating without staff urging. Requests or requires laxatives or medication for bowels or medication for G.I. symptoms

13: Somatic symptoms general
- 0 None
- 1 Heaviness in limbs, back or head. Backaches, headache, muscle aches. Loss of energy and fatigability
- 2 Any clear cut symptom rates 2

14: Genital symptoms

0 Absent	Symptoms such as:
1 Mild	Loss of libido
2 Severe	Menstrual disturbances

15: Hypochondriasis
- 0 Not present
- 1 Self-absorption (bodily)
- 2 Preoccupation with health
- 3 Frequent complaints, requests for help, etc
- 4 Hypochondriacal delusions

16: Loss of weight
- A: When rating by history
- 0 No weight loss
- 1 Probable weight loss associated with present illness
- 2 Definite (according to patient) weight loss
- B: On weekly ratings by ward psychiatrist, when actual weight changes are measured
- 0 Less than 1 lb weight loss in week
- 1 Greater than 1 lb weight loss in week
- 2 Greater than 2 lb weight loss in week

17: Insight
- 0 Acknowledges being depressed and ill
- 1 Acknowledges illness but attributes cause to bad food, climate, overwork, virus, need for rest, etc
- 2 Denies being ill at all

18: Diurnal variation

AM	PM		
0	0	Absent	If symptoms are worse in the morning or evening, note which it is and rate severity of variation
1	1	Mild	
2	2	Severe	

19: Depersonalization and derealization

0 Absent	
1 Mild	Such as:
2 Moderate	Feeling of unreality
3 Severe	Nihilistic ideas
4 Incapacitating	

20: Paranoid symptoms
- 0 None
- 1, 2 Suspiciousness
- 3 Ideas of reference
- 4 Delusions of reference and persecution

21: Obsessional and compulsive symptoms
- 0 Absent
- 1 Mild
- 2 Severe

22: Helplessness
- 0 Not present
- 1 Subjective feelings which are elicited only by inquiry
- 2 Patient volunteers his helpless feelings
- 3 Requires urging, guidance, and reassurance to accomplish ward chores or personal hygiene
- 4 Requires physical assistance for dress, grooming, eating, bedside tasks, or personal hygiene

23: Hopelessness
- 0 Not present
- 1 Intermittently doubts that "things will improve" but can be reassured
- 2 Consistently feels "hopeless" but accepts reassurances
- 3 Expresses feelings of discouragement, despair, pessimism about future, which cannot be dispelled
- 4 Spontaneously and inappropriately perseverates "I'll never get well" or its equivalent

24: Worthlessness (Ranges from mild loss of esteem, feelings of inferiority, self-depreciation to delusional notions of worthlessness)
- 0 Not present
- 1 Indicates feelings of worthlessness (loss of self-esteem) only on questioning
- 2 Spontaneously indicates feelings of worthlessness (loss of self-esteem)
- 3 Different from 2 by degree. Patient volunteers that he is "no good," "inferior," etc.
- 4 Delusional notions of worthlessness—ie, "I am a heap of garbage" or its equivalent

Reprinted with permission from Hamilton M: A rating scale for depression. J Neurol Neurosurg Psychiatry *23:* 56, 1960.

Table 9–16
Yale-Brown Obsessive-Compulsive Scale

For each item circle the number identifying the response which best characterizes the patient.

1. Time occupied by obsessive thoughts
   How much of your time is occupied by obsessive thoughts? How frequently do the obsessive thoughts occur?
   0 None
   1 Mild (less than 1 hr day) or occasional (intrusion occurring no more than 8 times a day)
   2 Moderate (1 to 3 hr day) or frequent (intrusion occurring more than 8 times a day, but most of the hours of the day are free of obsessions)
   3 Severe (greater than 3 and up to 8 hr day) or very frequent (intrusion occurring more than 8 times a day and occurring during most of the hours of the day)
   4 Extreme (greater than 8 hr day) or near consistent intrusion (too numerous to count and an hour rarely passes without several obsessions occurring)
2. Interference due to obsessive thoughts
   How much do your obsessive thoughts interfere with your social or work (or role) functioning? Is there anything that you don't do because of them?
   0 None
   1 Mild, slight interference with social or occupational activities, but overall performance not impaired
   2 Moderate, definite interference with social or occupational performance but still manageable
   3 Severe, causes substantial impairment in social or occupational performance
   4 Extreme, incapacitating
3. Distress associated with obsessive thoughts
   How much distress do your obsessive thoughts cause you?
   0 None
   1 Mild, infrequent and not too disturbing
   2 Moderate, frequent and disturbing but still manageable
   3 Severe, very frequent and very disturbing
   4 Extreme, near constant and disabling distress
4. Resistance against obsessions
   How much of an effort do you make to resist the obsessive thoughts?
   How often do you try to disregard or turn your attention away from these thoughts as they enter your mind?
   0 Makes an effort to always resist, or symptoms so minimal doesn't need to actively resist
   1 Tries to resist most of the time
   2 Makes some effort to resist
   3 Yields to all obsessions without attempting to control them, but does so with some reluctance
   4 Completely and willingly yields to all obsessions
5. Degree of control over obsessive thoughts
   How much control do you have over your obsessive thoughts? How successful are you in stopping or diverting your obsessive thinking?
   0 Complete control
   1 Much control, usually able to stop or divert obsessions with some effort and concentration
   2 Moderate control, sometimes able to stop or divert obsessions
   3 Little control, rarely successful in stopping obsessions
   4 No control, experienced as completely involuntary, rarely able to even momentarily divert thinking
6. Time spent performing compulsive behaviors
   How much time do you spend performing compulsive behaviors? How frequently do you perform compulsions?
   0 None
   1 Mild (less than 1 hr day performing compulsions) or occasional (performance of compulsions occurring no more than 8 times a day)
   2 Moderate (1 to 3 hr day performing compulsions) or frequent (performance of compulsions occurring more than 8 times a day, but most of the hours of the day are free of compulsive behaviors)
   3 Severe (greater than 3 and up to 8 hr day performing compulsions) or very frequent (performance of compulsions occurring more than 8 times a day and occurring during most of the hours of the day)
   4 Extreme (greater than 8 hr day performing compulsions) or near consistent performance of compulsions (too numerous to count and an hour rarely passes without several compulsions being performed)
7. Interference due to compulsive behaviors
   How much do your compulsive behaviors interfere with your social or work (or role) functioning? Is there anything that you don't do because of the compulsions?
   0 None
   1 Mild, slight interference with social or occupational activities, but overall performance not impaired
   2 Moderate, definite interference with social or occupational performance but still manageable
   3 Severe, causes substantial impairment in social or occupational performance
   4 Extreme, incapacitating
8. Distress associated with compulsive behavior
   How would you feel if prevented from performing your compulsions?
   How anxious would you become? How anxious do you get while performing compulsions until you are satisfied they are completed?
   0 None
   1 Mild, only slightly anxious if compulsions prevented or only slightly anxious during performance of compulsions
   2 Moderate, reports that anxiety would mount but remain manageable if compulsions prevented or that anxiety increases but remains manageable during performance of compulsions
   3 Severe, prominent and very disturbing increase in anxiety if compulsions interrupted or prominent and very disturbing increases in anxiety during performance of compulsions
   4 Extreme, incapacitating anxiety from any intervention aimed at modifying activity or incapacitating anxiety develops during performance of compulsions
9. Resistance against compulsions
   How much of an effort do you make to resist the compulsions?
   0 Makes an effort to always resist, or symptoms so minimal doesn't need to actively resist
   1 Tries to resist most of the time
   2 Makes some effort to resist
   3 Yields to all compulsions without attempting to control them but does so with some reluctance
   4 Completely and willingly yields to all compulsions
10. Degree of control over compulsive behavior
   0 Complete control
   1 Much control, experiences pressure to perform the behavior but usually able to exercise voluntary control over it
   2 Moderate control, strong pressure to perform behavior, can control it only with difficulty
   3 Little control, very strong drive to perform behavior, must be carried to completion, can only delay with difficulty
   4 No control, drive to perform behavior experienced as completely involuntary

Reprinted with permission from Goodman WK, Price LH, Rasmussen SA, et al. The Yale-Brown Obsessive-Compulsive Scale, I: Development, use, and reliability. Arch Gen Psychiatry *46:* 1006, 1989.

Table 9–17
Scale for the Assessment of Negative Symptoms (SANS)

0 = None 1 = Questionable 2 = Mild 3 = Moderate 4 = Marked 5 = Severe

Affective flattening or blunting	
1 *Unchanging facial expression* The patient's face appears wooden, changes less than expected as emotional content of discourse changes.	0 1 2 3 4 5
2 *Decreased spontaneous movements* The patient shows few or no spontaneous movements, does not shift position, move extremities, etc.	0 1 2 3 4 5
3 *Paucity of expressive gestures* The patient does not use hand gestures, body position, etc., as an aid to expressing his ideas.	0 1 2 3 4 5
4 *Poor eye contact* The patient avoids eye contact or "stares through" interviewer even when speaking.	0 1 2 3 4 5
5 *Affective nonresponsivity* The patient fails to smile or laugh when prompted.	0 1 2 3 4 5
6 *Lack of vocal inflections* The patient fails to show normal vocal emphasis patterns, is often monotonic.	0 1 2 3 4 5
7 *Global rating of affective flattening* This rating should focus on overall severity of symptoms, especially unresponsiveness, eye contact, facial expression, and vocal inflections.	0 1 2 3 4 5
Alogia	
8 *Poverty of speech* The patient's replies to questions are restricted in *amount*, tend to be brief, concrete, and unelaborated.	0 1 2 3 4 5
9 *Poverty of content of speech* The patient's replies are adequate in amount but tend to be vague, overconcrete, or overgeneralized, and convey little information.	0 1 2 3 4 5
10 *Blocking* The patient indicates, either spontaneously or with prompting, that his [her] train of thought was interrupted.	0 1 2 3 4 5
11 *Increased latency of response* The patient takes a long time to reply to questions; prompting indicates the patient is aware of the question.	0 1 2 3 4 5
12 *Global rating of alogia* The core features of alogia are poverty of speech and poverty of content.	0 1 2 3 4 5
Avolition-apathy	
13 *Grooming and hygiene* The patient's clothes may be sloppy or soiled, and he [she] may have greasy hair, body odor, etc.	0 1 2 3 4 5
14 *Impersistence at work or school* The patient has difficulty seeking or maintaining employment, completing school work, keeping house, etc. If an inpatient, cannot persist at ward activities, such as occupational therapy, playing cards, etc.	0 1 2 3 4 5
15 *Physical anergia* The patient tends to be physically inert. He [she] may sit for hours and does not initiate spontaneous activity.	0 1 2 3 4 5
16 *Global rating of avolition-apathy* Strong weight may be given to one or two prominent symptoms if particularly striking.	0 1 2 3 4 5
Anhedonia-asociality	
17 *Recreational interests and activities* The patient may have few or no interests. Both the quality and quantity of interests should be taken into account.	0 1 2 3 4 5
18 *Sexual activity* The patient may show a decrease in sexual interest and activity, or enjoyment when active.	0 1 2 3 4 5
19 *Ability to feel intimacy and closeness* The patient may display an inability to form close or intimate relationships, especially with the opposite sex and family.	0 1 2 3 4 5
20 *Relationships with friends and peers* The patient may have few or no friends and may prefer to spend all of his time isolated.	0 1 2 3 4 5
21 *Global rating of anhedonia-asociality* This rating should reflect overall severity, taking into account the patient's age, family status, etc.	0 1 2 3 4 5
Attention	
22 *Social inattentiveness* The patient appears uninvolved or unengaged. He [she] may seem spacey.	0 1 2 3 4 5
23 *Inattentiveness during mental status testing* Tests of "serial 7s" (at least five subtractions) and spelling *world* backwards: Score: 2 = 1 error; 3 = 2 errors; 4 = 3 errors.	0 1 2 3 4 5
24 *Global rating of attention* This rating should assess the patient's overall concentration, clinically and on tests.	0 1 2 3 4 5

Bracketed words are our addition.

Table 9–18
Scale for the Assessment of Positive Symptoms (SAPS)

0 = None 1 = Questionable 2 = Mild 3 = Moderate 4 = Marked 5 = Severe

Hallucinations	
1 *Auditory hallucinations* The patient reports voices, noises, or other sounds that no one else hears.	0 1 2 3 4 5
2 *Voices commenting* The patient reports a voice which makes a running commentary on his [her] behavior or thoughts.	0 1 2 3 4 5
3 *Voices conversing* The patient reports hearing two or more voices conversing.	0 1 2 3 4 5
4 *Somatic or tactile hallucinations* The patient reports experiencing peculiar physical sensations in the body.	0 1 2 3 4 5
5 *Olfactory hallucinations* The patient reports experiencing unusual smells which no one else notices.	0 1 2 3 4 5
6 *Visual hallucinations* The patient sees shapes or people that are not actually present.	0 1 2 3 4 5
7 *Global rating of hallucinations* This rating should be based on the duration and severity of the hallucinations and their effects on the patient's life.	0 1 2 3 4 5
Delusions	
8 *Persecutory delusions* The patient believes he [she] is being conspired against or persecuted in some way.	0 1 2 3 4 5
9 *Delusions of jealousy* The patient believes his [her] spouse is having an affair with someone.	0 1 2 3 4 5
10 *Delusions of guilt or sin* The patient believes that he [she] has committed some terrible sin or done something unforgivable.	0 1 2 3 4 5
11 *Grandiose delusions* The patient believes he [she] has special powers or abilities.	0 1 2 3 4 5
12 *Religious delusions* The patient is preoccupied with false beliefs of a religious nature.	0 1 2 3 4 5
13 *Somatic delusions* The patient believes that somehow his [her] body is diseased, abnormal, or changed.	0 1 2 3 4 5
14 *Delusions of reference* The patient believes that insignificant remarks or events refer to him [her] or have some special meaning.	0 1 2 3 4 5
15 *Delusions of being controlled* The patient feels that his [her] feelings or actions are controlled by some outside force.	0 1 2 3 4 5
16 *Delusions of mind reading* The patient feels that people can read his [her] mind or know his [her] thoughts.	0 1 2 3 4 5
17 *Thought broadcasting* The patient believes that his [her] thoughts are broadcast so that he himself [she herself] or others can hear them.	0 1 2 3 4 5
18 *Thought insertion* The patient believes that thoughts that are not his [her] own have been inserted into his [her] mind.	0 1 2 3 4 5
19 *Thought withdrawal* The patient believes that thoughts have been taken away from his [her] mind.	0 1 2 3 4 5
20 *Global rating of delusions* This rating should be based on the duration and persistence of the delusions and their effect on the patient's life.	0 1 2 3 4 5
Bizarre behavior	
21 *Clothing and appearance* The patient dresses in an unusual manner or does other strange things to alter his [her] appearance.	0 1 2 3 4 5
22 *Social and sexual behavior* The patient may do things considered inappropriate according to usual social norms (eg, masturbating in public).	0 1 2 3 4 5
23 *Aggressive and agitated behavior* The patient may behave in an aggressive, agitated manner, often unpredictably.	0 1 2 3 4 5
24 *Repetitive or stereotyped behavior* The patient develops a set of repetitive actions or rituals that he [she] must perform over and over.	0 1 2 3 4 5
25 *Global rating of bizarre behavior* This rating should reflect the type of behavior and the extent to which it deviates from social norms.	0 1 2 3 4 5
Positive formal thought disorder	
26 *Derailment* A pattern of speech in which ideas slip off track onto ideas obliquely related or unrelated.	0 1 2 3 4 5
27 *Tangentiality* Replying to a question in an oblique or irrelevant manner.	0 1 2 3 4 5
28 *Incoherence* A pattern of speech which is essentially incomprehensible at times.	0 1 2 3 4 5
29 *Illogicality* A pattern of speech in which conclusions are reached which do not follow logically.	0 1 2 3 4 5
30 *Circumstantiality* A pattern of speech which is very indirect and delayed in reaching its goal idea.	0 1 2 3 4 5
31 *Pressure of speech* The patient's speech is rapid and difficult to interrupt; the amount of speech produced is greater than that considered normal.	0 1 2 3 4 5
32 *Distractible speech* The patient is distracted by nearby stimuli which interrupt his [her] flow of speech.	0 1 2 3 4 5
33 *Clanging* A pattern of speech in which sounds rather than meaningful relationships govern word choice.	0 1 2 3 4 5
34 *Global rating of positive formal thought disorder* This rating should reflect the frequency of abnormality and degree to which it affects the patient's ability to communicate.	0 1 2 3 4 5
Inappropriate affect	
35 *Inappropriate Affect* The patient's affect is inappropriate or incongruous, not simply flat or blunted.	0 1 2 3 4 5

Bracketed words are our addition.

Table 9–19
Social and Occupational Functioning Assessment Scale (SOFAS)

Consider social and occupational functioning on a continuum from excellent functioning to grossly impaired functioning. Include impairments in functioning due to physical limitations, as well as those due to mental impairments. To be counted, impairment must be a direct consequence of mental and physical health problems; the effects of lack of opportunity and other environmental limitations are not to be considered.

Code	(**Note:** Use intermediate codes when appropriate, eg, 45, 68, 72.)
100–91	Superior functioning in a wide range of activities.
90–81	Good functioning in all areas, occupationally and socially effective.
80–71	No more than a slight impairment in social, occupational, or school functioning (eg, infrequent interpersonal conflict, temporarily falling behind in schoolwork).
70–61	Some difficulty in social, occupational, or school functioning, but generally functioning well, has some meaningful interpersonal relationships.
60–51	Moderate difficulty in social, occupational, or school functioning (eg, few friends, conflicts with peers or co-workers).
50–41	Serious impairment in social, occupational, or school functioning (eg, no friends, unable to keep a job).
40–31	Major impairment in several areas, such as work or school, family relations (eg, depressed man avoids friends, neglects family, and is unable to work; child frequently beats up younger children, is defiant at home, and is failing at school).
30–21	Inability to function in almost all areas (eg, stays in bed all day; no job, home, or friends).
20–11	Occasionally fails to maintain minimal personal hygiene; unable to function independently.
10–1	Persistent inability to maintain minimal personal hygiene. Unable to function without harming self or others or without considerable external support (e.g., nursing care and supervision).
0	Inadequate information.

Note: The rating of overall psychological functioning on a scale of 0–100 was operationalized by Luborsky in the Health-Sickness Rating Scale. (Luborsky L: Clinicians' judgments of mental health. Arch Gen Psychiatry *7*:407, 1962). Spitzer and colleagues developed a revision of the Health-Sickness Rating Scale called the Global Assessment Scale (GAS) (Endicott J, Spitzer RL, Fleiss JL, et al.: The Global Assessment Scale: A procedure for measuring overall severity of psychiatric disturbance. Arch Gen Psychiatry *33*:766, 1976). The SOFAS is derived from the GAS and its development is described in Goldman HH, Skodol AE, Lave TR: Revising Axis V for DSM-IV: A review of measures of social functioning. Am J Psychiatry *149*:1148–1156, 1992.

Table 9–20
DSM-IV Global Assessment of Relational Functioning (GARF)

INSTRUCTIONS: The GARF Scale can be used to indicate an overall judgment of the functioning of a family or other ongoing relationship on a hypothetical continuum ranging from competent, optimal relational functioning to a disrupted, dysfunctional relationship. It is analogous to Axis V (Global Assessment of Functioning Scale) provided for individuals in DSM-IV. The GARF Scale permits the clinician to rate the degree in which a family or other ongoing relational unit meets the affective and/or instrumental needs of its members in the following areas:

A. *Problem solving*—skills in negotiating goals, rules, and routines; adaptability to stress; communication skills; ability to resolve conflict.

B. *Organization*—maintenance of interpersonal roles and subsystem boundaries; hierarchical functioning, coalitions and distribution of power, control and responsibility.

C. *Emotional climate*—tone and range of feelings; quality of caring, empathy, involvement and attachment/commitment; sharing of values; mutual affective responsiveness, respect, and regard; quality of sexual functioning.

In most instances, the GARF Scale should be used to rate functioning during the current period (ie, the level of relational functioning at the time of the evaluation). In some settings, the GARF Scale may also be used to rate functioning for other time periods (ie, the highest level of relational functioning for at least a few months during the past year). **Note**: Use specific, intermediate codes when possible, for example, 45, 68, 72. If detailed information is not adequate to make specific ratings, use midpoints of the five ranges, that is, 90, 70, 50, 30, or 10.

(81–100) Overall: Relational unit is functioning satisfactorily from self-report of participants and from perspectives of observers.

Agreed-on patterns or routines exist that help meet the usual needs of each family/couple member; there is flexibility for change in response to unusual demands or events; occasional conflicts and stressful transitions are resolved through problem-solving communication and negotiation.

There is a shared understanding and agreement about roles and appropriate tasks; decision making is established for each functional area, and there is recognition of the unique characteristics and merit of each subsystem (eg, parents/spouses, siblings, and individuals).

There is a situationally appropriate, optimistic atmosphere in the family; a wide range of feelings is freely expressed and managed within the family; there is a general atmosphere of warmth, caring, and sharing of values among all family members. Sexual relations of adult members are satisfactory.

(61–80) Overall: Functioning of relational unit is somewhat unsatisfactory. Over a period of time, many but not all difficulties are resolved without complaints.

Daily routines are present but there is some pain and difficulty in responding to the unusual. Some conflicts remain unresolved, but do not disrupt family functioning.

Decision making is usually competent, but efforts at control of one another quite often are greater than necessary or are ineffective. Individuals and relationships are clearly demarcated but sometimes a specific subsystem is depreciated or scapegoated.

A range of feeling is expressed, but instances of emotional blocking or tension are evident. Warmth and caring are present but are marred by a family member's irritability and frustrations. Sexual activity of adult members may be reduced or problematic.

(41–60) Overall: Relational unit has occasional times of satisfying and competent functioning together, but clearly dysfunctional, unsatisfying relationships tend to predominate.

Communication is frequently inhibited by unresolved conflicts that often interfere with daily routines; there is significant difficulty in adapting to family stress and transitional change.

Decision making is only intermittently competent and effective; either excessive rigidity or significant lack of structure is evident at these times. Individual needs are quite often submerged by a partner or coalition.

Pain or ineffective anger or emotional deadness interfere with family enjoyment. Although there is some warmth and support for members, it is usually unequally distributed. Troublesome sexual difficulties between adults are often present.

(21–40) Overall: Relational unit is obviously and seriously dysfunctional; forms and time periods of satisfactory relating are rare.

Family/couple routines do not meet the needs of members; they are grimly adhered to or blithely ignored. Life cycle changes, such as departures or entries into the relational unit, generate painful conflict and obviously frustrating failures of problem solving.

Decision making is tyrannical or quite ineffective. The unique characteristics of individuals are unappreciated or ignored by either rigid or confusingly fluid coalitions.

There are infrequent periods of enjoyment of life together; frequent distancing or open hostility reflect significant conflicts that remain unresolved and quite painful. Sexual dysfunction among adult members is commonplace.

(1–20) Overall: Relational unit has become too dysfunctional to retain continuity of contact and attachment.

Family/couple routines are negligible (eg, no mealtime, sleeping, or waking schedule); family members often do not know where others are or when they will be in or out; there is little effective communication among family members.

Family/couple members are not organized in such a way that personal or generational responsibilities are recognized. Boundaries of relational unit as a whole and subsystems cannot be identified or agreed upon. Family members are physically endangered or injured or sexually attacked.

Despair and cynicism are pervasive; there is little attention to the emotional needs of others; there is almost no sense of attachment, commitment, or concern about one another's welfare.

0 Inadequate information.

Table 9–21
DSM-IV Defensive Functioning Scale

High adaptive level. This level of defensive functioning results in optimal adaptation in the handling of stressors. These defenses usually maximize gratification and allow the conscious awareness of feelings, ideas, and their consequences. They also promote an optimum balance among conflicting motives. Examples of defenses characteristically at this level are
- anticipation
- affiliation
- altruism
- humor
- self-assertion
- self-observation
- sublimation
- suppression

Mental inhibitions (compromise formation) level. Defensive functioning all this level keeps potentially threatening ideas, feelings, memories, wishes, or fears out of awareness. Examples are
- displacement
- dissociation
- intellectualization
- isolation of affect
- reaction formation
- repression
- undoing

Minor image-distorting level. This level is characterized by distortions in the image of the self, body, or others that may be employed to regulate self-esteem. Examples are
- devaluation
- idealization
- omnipotence

Disavowal level. This level is characterized by keeping unpleasant or unacceptable stressors, impulses, ideas, affect, or responsibility out of awareness with or without a misattribution of these to external causes. Examples are
- denial
- projection
- rationalization

Major image-distorting level. This level is characterized by gross distortion or misattribution of the image of self or others. Examples are
- autistic fantasy
- projective identification
- splitting of self-image or image of others

Action level. This level is characterized by defensive functioning that deals with internal or external stressors by action or withdrawal. Examples are
- acting out
- apathetic withdrawal
- help-rejecting complaining
- passive aggression

Level of defensive dysregulation. This level is characterized by failure of defensive regulation to contain the individual's reaction to stressors, leading to a pronounced break with objective reality. Examples are
- delusional projection
- psychotic denial
- psychotic distortion

Signs and Symptoms. Classic items from the mental status examination are the most frequently assessed items on rating scales. These items include thought disorders, mood disturbances, and gross behaviors. Another type of information covered by rating scales is the assessment of adverse effects from psychotherapeutic drugs. Social adjustments (for example, occupational success and quality of relationships) and psychoanalytic concepts (for example, ego strength and defense mechanisms) are also measured by some rating scales, although the reliability and the validity of such scales are lowered by the absence of agreed-on norms, the high level of inference required on some items, and the lack of independence between measures.

Other Characteristics. Other characteristics of rating scales include the time covered, the level of judgment required, and the method of recording answers. The time covered by a rating scale must be specified, and the rate must adhere to this period. For example, a particular rating scale may rate a 5-minute observation period, a week-long period, or a patient's entire life.

The most reliable rating scales require a limited amount of judgment or inference on the part of the rater. Whatever the level of judgment required, clear definitions of the answer scale, preferably with clinical examples, should be provided by the developer of the scale and should be read by the rater.

The actual answer given may be recorded as either a dichotomous variable (for example, true or false, present or absent) or a continuous variable. Continuous items may ask the rater to choose a term to describe severity (absent, slight, mild, moderate, severe, or extreme) or frequency (never, rarely, occasionally, often, very often, or always). Although many psychiatric symptoms are thought of as existing in dichotomous states—for example, the presence or absence of delusions—most experienced clinicians know that the world is not so simple.

Rating Scales Used in DSM-IV

Rating scales form an integral part of DSM-IV. The rating scales used are broad and measure the overall severity of a patient's illness.

GAF Scale. Axis V in DSM-IV uses the Global Assessment of Functioning (GAF) Scale (see Table 9–7). This axis is used for reporting a clinician's judgment of a patient's overall level of functioning. The information is used to decide on a treatment plan and later to measure the plan's effect.

Social and Occupational Functioning Assessment Scale. This scale can be used to track a patient's progress in social and occupational areas (Table 9–19). It is independent of the psychiatric diagnosis and of the severity of the patient's psychological symptoms.

Other Scales. Two other scales that may be useful are the Global Assessment of Relational Functioning (GARF) Scale and the Defensive Functioning Scale (Tables 9–20 and 9–21).

References

American Psychiatric Association: *Diagnostic and Statistical Manual of Mental Disorders,* ed 4. American Psychiatric Association, Washington, 1994.

Berrios GE, Hauser R: The early development of Kraepelin's ideas on classification: A conceptual history. Psychol Med *18:* 813, 1988.

Bryan KJ, Rounsaville B, Spitzer RL, Williams JB: Reliability of dual diagnosis: Substance dependence and psychiatric disorders. J Nerv Ment Dis *180:* 251, 1992.

Burros OK, editor: *Personality Tests and Reviews.* Gryphon, Highland Park, NJ, 1970.

Frances A: An introduction of DSM-IV. Hosp Community Psychiatry *41:* 49, 1990.

Janca A, Hiller W: ICD-10 checklists—A tool for clinician's use of the ICD-10 classification of mental and behavioral disorders. Compr Psychiatry *37:* 180, 1996.

Kaplan HI, Sadock BJ: The classification of mental disorders. In *Comprehensive Textbook of Psychiatry,* ed 6, HI Kaplan, BJ Sadock, editors, p 671. Williams & Wilkins, Baltimore, 1995.

Lyerly SB: *Handbook of Psychiatric Rating Scales,* ed 2. National Institute of Mental Health, Bethesda, MD, 1973.

Wilson M: DSM-III and the transformation of American psychiatry. A history. Am J Psychiatry *150:* 399, 1993.

World Health Organization: *The ICD-10 Classification of Mental and Behavioral Disorders: Clinical Descriptions and Diagnostic Guidelines.* World Health Organization, Geneva, 1992.

World Health Organization: *The ICD-10 Classification of Mental and Behavioural Disorders: Diagnostic Criteria for Research.* World Health Organization, Geneva, 1992.

Zarin DA, Earls F: Diagnostic decision making in psychiatry. Am J Psychiatry *150:* 197, 1993.

Zimmerman M: Is DSM-IV needed at all? Am J Psychiatry *147:* 974, 1990.

Zimmerman M, Coryell W, Black D: Variability in the application of contemporary diagnostic criteria: Endogenous depression as an example. Am J Psychiatry *147:* 1173, 1990.

10

Delirium, Dementia, and Amnestic and Other Cognitive Disorders and Mental Disorders Due to a General Medical Condition

▲ 10.1 Overview

In its section on delirium, dementia, and amnestic and other cognitive disorders, the fourth edition of *Diagnostic and Statistical Manual of Mental Disorders* (DSM-IV) defines the predominant disturbance as a ''clinically significant deficit in cognition or memory that represents a significant change from a previous level of functioning.'' The origin of the disorders is a medical condition, although the precise condition may not always be identifiable.

DSM-IV describes delirium as a disturbance of consciousness and a cognitive change that develop during a short time. Dementia is characterized by several cognitive deficits including impaired memory. In amnestic disorders, there is only an impairment of memory, without other cognitive impairments. DSM-IV also offers the diagnosis of cognitive disorder not otherwise specified.

Traditionally, organic brain disorders have been defined as disorders for which there is an identifiable pathologic condition such as brain tumor, cerebrovascular disease, or drug intoxication. Those brain disorders with no generally accepted organic basis (such as schizophrenia or depression) have been called functional disorders. Historically, the field of neurology has been associated with the treatment of organic disorders and psychiatry has been associated with the treatment of functional disorders.

The authors of DSM-IV believe that the century-old distinction between organic and functional disorders is outdated and should be deleted from the nomenclature. The medical, neurological, and psychiatric journals, as well as this and other textbooks, contain a preponderance of data about the organic basis of the major psychiatric disorders. The only unbiased conclusion to be made from evaluation of the available data is that every psychiatric disorder has an organic (that is, biological) component. Because of this reassessment of the data, the concept of functional disorders has been determined to be misleading, and both the term *functional* and its historical opposite, *organic,* are no longer used in that context in the DSM-IV.

The term *functional* is also used in basic science, wherein functional abnormalities are contrasted with structural abnormalities. This distinction is antiquated as well because neuroscientists can identify the structural correlates of functional abnormalities at the level of genes and other molecules. The structural-functional division rests solely on the biological level arbitrarily chosen as the cutoff point. This ''dichotomy'' is best resolved by acknowledging that each biological disorder, including mental illness, has a structural abnormality at some level or assortment of levels and that the structural abnormality is reflected as a disorder of function or regulation.

COGNITIVE DISORDERS

In DSM-IV, three groups of disorders—delirium, dementia, and the amnestic disorders—form a broad category characterized by the primary symptoms common to all the disorders, that is, an impairment in cognition (as in memory, language, or attention). Although DSM-IV acknowledges that other psychiatric disorders can exhibit a degree of cognitive impairment as a symptom, cognitive impairment is the cardinal symptom in delirium, dementia, and the amnestic disorders. Within each of these diagnostic categories, DSM-IV delimits specific types (Table 10.1–1).

For each of the three major groups (delirium, dementia, and amnestic disorders), there are subcategories for disorders caused by general medical conditions, substance use, and causes not otherwise specified. For delirium and dementia, DSM-IV also includes a diagnostic category for multiple causes, which is a commonly encountered clinical situation. For dementia, DSM-IV includes seven general medical conditions as diagnostic possibilities.

Evaluation

Although formal evaluation of cognitive impairment requires time-consuming consultation with an expert in psychological testing, one practical and clinically useful test for practitioners is the Mini-Mental State Examination (MMSE) (Table 10.1–2). The MMSE is a screening test that can be

Table 10.1–1
DSM-IV Cognitive Disorders

- Delirium
  - Delirium due to a general medical condition
  - Substance-induced delirium
  - Delirium due to multiple etiologies
  - Delirium not otherwise specified
- Dementia
  - Dementia of the Alzheimer's type
  - Vascular dementia
  - Dementia due to other general medical conditions
    - Dementia due to HIV disease
    - Dementia due to head trauma
    - Dementia due to Parkinson's disease
    - Dementia due to Huntington's disease
    - Dementia due to Pick's disease
    - Dementia due to Creutzfeldt-Jakob disease
    - Dementia due to other general medical conditions
  - Substance-induced persisting dementia
  - Dementia due to multiple etiologies
  - Dementia not otherwise specified
- Amnestic disorders
  - Amnestic disorder due to a general medical condition
  - Substance-induced persisting amnestic disorder
  - Amnestic disorder not otherwise specified
  - Cognitive disorder not otherwise specified

used during a patient's clinical examination. It is also a practical test to track the changes in a patient's cognitive state. Out of a possible 30 points, a score of less than 25 suggests impairment, and a score of less than 20 indicates definite impairment.

Cognitive Disorder Not Otherwise Specified

DSM-IV allows for the diagnosis of cognitive disorders that do not fit any other category. These disorders fit into the not otherwise specified category (Table 10.1–3). Patients with syndromes of cognitive impairment that do not meet the criteria for delirium, dementia, or amnestic disorders are classified in the not otherwise specified category. The causes of these syndromes are presumed to involve either a specific general medical condition or a pharmacologically active agent, or possibly both.

MENTAL DISORDERS DUE TO A GENERAL MEDICAL CONDITION

DSM-IV introduces two major changes to the nomenclature. First, the term *organic* is substituted with the phrase *due to a general medical condition.* Second, the psychiatric disorders due to a general medical condition are included within the DSM-IV diagnostic categories that contain other disorders with the same primary symptom. For example, anxiety disorder due to a general medical condition is included within the anxiety disorders section of DSM-IV. The inclusion of the secondary psychiatric disorder within the general anxiety disorders section is meant to facilitate the clinician's formulation of the differential diagnoses of patients who exhibit a particular set of symptoms. Delirium, dementia, or amnesia due to a general medical condition is contained in the diagnostic section on delirium, dementia, and amnestic and other cognitive disorders.

Use of the phrase *due to a general medical condition* is meant to convey a clinician's opinion that a particular psychiatric symptom (such as depression) is probably primarily related to a specific nonpsychiatric disorder (for example, pancreatic cancer) and the DSM-IV–defined disorder (such as mood disorder due to pancreatic cancer, with depressive features) is a distinct diagnosis that requires its own treatment plan. The phrase *due to a general medical condition* does not imply a specific temporal relation to the associated nonpsychiatric condition. In the previous example, depression associated with pancreatic cancer may be the presenting complaint and thus may be identified before the pancreatic cancer is diagnosed. The use of the phrase can perhaps be criticized as being overly simplistic: It disregards the other variables that may affect the appearance of a psychiatric symptom in association with a general medical condition. Such other variables

Table 10.1–2
Mini-Mental State Examination (MMSE) Questionnaire

Orientation (score 1 if correct)	
Name this hospital or building.	______
What city are you in now?	______
What year is it?	______
What month is it?	______
What is the date today?	______
What state are you in?	______
What county is this?	______
What floor of the building are you on?	______
What day of the week is it?	______
What season of the year is it?	______
Registration (Score 1 for each object correctly repeated)	
Name three objects and have the patient repeat them. Score number repeated by the patient. Name the three objects several more times if needed for the patient to repeat correctly (record trials ______).	______
Attention and calculation	
Subtract 7 from 100 in serial fashion to 65. Maximum score = 5	______
Recall (score 1 for each object recalled)	
Do you recall the three objects named before?	______
Language tests	
Confrontation naming: watch, pen = 2	______
Repetition: "No ifs, ands, or buts" = 1	______
Comprehension: Pick up the paper in your right hand, fold it in half, and set it on the floor = 3	______
Read and perform the command "close your eyes" = 1	______
Write any sentence (subject, verb, object) = 1	______
Construction	
Copy the design below = 1	______

Total MMSE questionnaire score (maximum = 30)	______

Adapted from Folstein MF, Folstein S, McHugh PR: Mini-mental state: A practical method for grading the cognitive state of patients for the clinician. J Psychiatr Res *12:* 189, 1975.

Table 10.1–3
DSM-IV Diagnostic Criteria for Cognitive Disorder Not Otherwise Specified

This category is for disorders that are characterized by cognitive dysfunction presumed to be due to the direct physiological effects of a general medical condition that do not meet criteria for any of the specific deliriums, dementias, or amnestic disorders listed in this section and that are not better classified as delirium not otherwise specified, dementia not otherwise specified, or amnestic disorder not otherwise specified. For cognitive dysfunction due to a specific or unknown substance, the specific substance-related disorder not otherwise specified category should be used.

Examples include

1. Mild neurocognitive disorder: impairment in cognitive functioning as evidenced by neuropsychological testing or quantified clinical assessment, accompanied by objective evidence of a systemic general medical condition or central nervous system dysfunction.
2. Postconcussional disorder: following a head trauma, impairment in memory or attention with associated symptoms.

may include other biological factors (such as a genetic diathesis to depression), psychosocial problems, prescribed or illicit drug use, and psychological stressors. Any diagnostic nosological system must reduce the available information somewhat, and the intent of the updated DSM-IV is to highlight the principal causative factor involved.

In the DSM-IV, most mental disorders due to a general medical condition are listed with other diagnoses for the major symptom, including psychotic disorder due to a general medical condition, mood disorder due to a general medical condition, anxiety disorder due to a general medical condition, sexual dysfunction due to a general medical condition, and sleep disorder due to a general medical condition. The three disorders listed in the DSM-IV section called mental disorders due to a general medical condition not elsewhere classified are catatonic disorder due to a general medical condition, personality change due to a general medical condition, and mental disorder not otherwise specified due to a general medical condition.

ICD-10

Unlike in the DSM-IV, organic (including symptomatic) mental disorders are organized in the 10th revision of the *International Statistical Classification of Diseases and Related Health Problems* (ICD-10) based on "their common, demonstrable etiology in cerebral disease, brain injury, or other insult leading to cerebral dysfunction." In the ICD-10, rather than being deleted, the term *organic* "does not imply that . . . 'nonorganic'" disorders have "no cerebral substrate." *Organic* in ICD-10 implies only that "the syndrome . . . can be attributed to an independently diagnosable cerebral or systemic disease or disorder." Primary dysfunctions affect the brain directly; secondary dysfunctions occur as a result of diseases or disorders attacking several organs or body systems *including* the brain. According to ICD-10, all the disorders can be divided into two groups: one in which the invariable and most prominent features are disturbances of cognitive functions or of the sensorium and one in which the most conspicuous manifestations are in the areas of perception, thought contents, or mood and emotion or in the overall pattern of personality and behavior.

Consequently, categories included as organic mental disorders, including symptomatic ones, in ICD-10 are dementia in Alzheimer's disease; vascular dementia; dementia in other diseases classified elsewhere (such as dementia in Pick's disease); unspecified dementia; organic amnesia syndrome, not induced by alcohol and other psychoactive substances; delirium, not induced by alcohol and other psychoactive substances; other mental disorders due to brain damage and dysfunction and due to physical disease (such as organic mood disorder, mild cognitive disorder); personality and behavioral disorders due to brain disease, damage, and dysfunction; and unspecified organic or symptomatic mental disorder. Alcohol- and drug-caused brain disorders are discussed in a separate section.

References

Cane ED: Delirium, dementia, and amnestic and other cognitive disorders and mental disorders due to a general medical condition. In *Comprehensive Textbook of Psychiatry,* ed 6, HI Kaplan, BJ Sadock, editors, p 705. Williams & Wilkins, Baltimore, 1995.

Caine ED: Should age-associated cognitive decline be included in DSM-IV? J Neuropsychiatry Clin Neurosci *5:* 1, 1993.

Frances A, Pincus HA, Widiger TA, Davis WW, First MB: DSM-IV: Work in progress. Am J Psychiatry *147:* 1439, 1990.

Lopowski ZJ: Is "organic" obsolete? Psychosomatics *31:* 342, 1990.

Reynolds EH: Structure and function in neurology and psychiatry. Br J Psychiatry *157:* 481, 1990.

Spitzer RL, First MB, Williams JBW, Kendler K, Pincus HA, Tucker G: Now is the time to retire the term "organic mental disorders." Am J Psychiatry *149:* 240, 1992.

Spitzer RL, Williams JBW, First MB, Kendler KS: A proposal for DSM-IV: Solving the "organic/nonorganic problems." J Neuropsychiatry *147:* 947, 1990.

Sullivan MD: Organic or functional? Why psychiatry needs a philosophy and mind. Psychiatr Ann *20:* 271, 1990.

▲ 10.2 Delirium

In the fourth edition of the *Diagnostic and Statistical Manual of Mental Disorders* (DSM-IV), delirium is "characterized by a disturbance of consciousness and a change in cognition that develop over a short . . . time." The hallmark symptom of delirium is an impairment of consciousness, usually occurring in association with global impairments of cognitive functions. Abnormalities of mood, perception, and behavior are common psychiatric symptoms; tremor, asterixis, nystagmus, incoordination, and urinary incontinence are common neurological symptoms. Classically, delirium has a sudden onset (hours or days), a brief and fluctuating course, and a rapid improvement when the causative factor is identified and eliminated, but each of these characteristic features can vary in individual patients.

Delirium is a syndrome, not a disease, and it has many

causes, all of which result in a similar pattern of symptoms relating to the patient's level of consciousness and cognitive impairment. Most of the causes of delirium arise outside the central nervous system, for example, in renal or hepatic failure. Delirium remains an underrecognized and underdiagnosed clinical disorder. Part of the problem is that the syndrome has a variety of other names, for example, acute confusional state, acute brain syndrome, metabolic encephalopathy, toxic psychosis, and acute brain failure. The intent of DSM-IV has been to help consolidate the myriad of terms into a single diagnostic label.

Physicians must recognize delirium to identify and treat the underlying cause and to avert the development of delirium-related complications. Such complications include accidental injury because of the patient's clouded consciousness or impaired coordination or because of the unnecessary use of restraints. The disruption of ward routine is an especially troubling problem on nonpsychiatric units, such as intensive care units and general medical and surgical wards.

EPIDEMIOLOGY

Delirium is a common disorder. Approximately 10 to 15 percent of patients on general surgical wards and 15 to 25 percent of patients on general medical wards experience delirium during their hospital stays. Approximately 30 percent of patients in surgical intensive care units and cardiac intensive care units and 40 to 50 percent of patients who are recovering from surgery for hip fractures have an episode of delirium. The highest rate of delirium is found in postcardiotomy patients, more than 90 percent in some studies. An estimated 20 percent of patients with severe burns and 30 percent of patients with acquired immune deficiency syndrome have episodes of delirium while they are hospitalized. The causes of postoperative delirium include the stress of surgery, postoperative pain, insomnia, pain medication, electrolyte imbalances, infection, fever, and blood loss.

Advanced age is a major risk factor for the development of delirium. Approximately 30 to 40 percent of hospitalized patients older than age 65 have an episode of delirium. Other predisposing factors for the development of delirium are young age (that is, children), preexisting brain damage (such as dementia, cerebrovascular disease, tumor), a history of delirium, alcohol dependence, diabetes, cancer, sensory impairment (such as blindness), and malnutrition.

The presence of delirium is a poor prognostic sign. The 3-month mortality rate of patients who have an episode of delirium is estimated to be 23 to 33 percent. The 1-year mortality rate for patients who have an episode of delirium may be as high as 50 percent.

ETIOLOGY

The major causes of delirium are central nervous system disease (such as epilepsy), systemic disease (such as cardiac failure), and either intoxication or withdrawal from pharmacological or toxic agents (Table 10.2–1). When evaluating patients with delirium, clinicians should assume that any drug that a patient has taken may be causatively relevant to the delirium.

Table 10.2–1
Causes of Delirium

- Intracranial causes
  - Epilepsy and postictal states
  - Brain trauma (especially concussion)
  - Infections
    - Meningitis
    - Encephalitis
  - Neoplasms
  - Vascular disorders
- Extracranial causes
  - Drugs (ingestion or withdrawal) and poisons
    - Anticholinergic agents
    - Anticonvulsants
    - Antihypertensive agents
    - Antiparkinsonian agents
    - Antipsychotic drugs
    - Cardiac glycosides
    - Cimetidine
    - Clonidine
    - Disulfiram
    - Insulin
    - Opiates
    - Phencyclidine
    - Phenytoin
    - Ranitidine
    - Salicylates
    - Sedatives (including alcohol) and hypnotics
    - Steroids
  - Poisons
    - Carbon monoxide
    - Heavy metals and other industrial poisons
  - Endocrine dysfunction (hypofunction or hyperfunction)
    - Pituitary
    - Pancreas
    - Adrenal
    - Parathyroid
    - Thyroid
  - Diseases of nonendocrine organs
    - Liver
      - Hepatic encephalopathy
    - Kidney and urinary tract
      - Uremic encephalopathy
    - Lung
      - Carbon dioxide narcosis
      - Hypoxia
    - Cardiovascular system
      - Cardiac failure
      - Arrhythmias
      - Hypotension
  - Deficiency diseases
    - Thiamine, nicotinic acid, B_{12}, or folic acid deficiencies
  - Systemic infections with fever and sepsis
  - Electrolyte imbalance of any cause
  - Postoperative states
  - Trauma (head or general body)

Adapted from Charles E. Wells, M.D.

The major neurotransmitter hypothesized to be involved in delirium is acetylcholine, and the major neuroanatomical area is the reticular formation. Several studies have reported that a variety of delirium-inducing factors result in decreased acetylcholine activity in the brain. One of the most common causes of delirium is toxicity from too many prescribed medications with anticholinergic activity. In addition to the anticholinergic drugs themselves, amitriptyline (Elavil), doxepin (Sinequan),

Table 10.2–2
DSM-IV Diagnostic Criteria for Delirium Due to a General Medical Condition

A. Disturbance of consciousness (ie, reduced clarity of awareness of the environment) with reduced ability to focus, sustain, or shift attention.

B. A change in cognition (such as memory deficit, disorientation, language disturbance) or the development of a perceptual disturbance that is not better accounted for by a preexisting, established, or evolving dementia.

C. The disturbance develops over a short period of time (usually hours to days) and tends to fluctuate during the course of the day.

D. There is evidence from the history, physical examination, or laboratory findings that the disturbance is caused by the direct physiological consequences of a general medical condition.

Coding note: Include the name of the general medical condition on Axis I, eg, delirium due to hepatic encephalopathy; also code the general medical condition on Axis III.

nortriptyline (Aventyl), imipramine (Tofranil), thioridazine (Mellaril), and chlorpromazine (Thorazine) are among the anticholinergic drugs most used in psychiatry. The reticular formation of the brain stem is the principal area regulating attention and arousal; the major pathway implicated in delirium is the dorsal tegmental pathway, which projects from the mesencephalic reticular formation to the tectum and thalamus.

Researchers have suggested other pathophysiological mechanisms for delirium. In particular, the delirium associated with alcohol withdrawal has been associated with hyperactivity of the locus ceruleus and its noradrenergic neurons. Other neurotransmitters that have been implicated are serotonin and glutamate.

Lithium-Induced Delirium

Patients with lithium serum concentrations greater than 1.5 mEq/L are at risk for delirium. The onset of delirium in these patients may be heralded by general lethargy, stammering, stuttering, and muscle fasciculations that develop over the course of several days to a week. Lithium-induced delirium may take up to 2 weeks to resolve even after lithium administration has been stopped. The appearance of seizures and episodes of stupor during recovery is common. In addition to stopping lithium administration, the primary treatments are maintenance of the patient's electrolyte balance, facilitation of lithium excretion, and supportive therapy. The use of proximal segment-acting drugs (such as aminophylline, acetazolamide [Diamox]) is more effective than the use of distal tubule–acting drugs. The most effective way to eliminate lithium from the patient's body is by hemodialysis, especially if done early in the course of the disorder.

DIAGNOSIS

DSM-IV strives to group all the causes of delirium under one section. Thus, delirium due to a general medical condition

Table 10.2–3
DSM-IV Diagnostic Criteria for Substance Intoxication Delirium

A. Disturbance of consciousness (ie, reduced clarity of awareness of the environment) with reduced ability to focus, sustain, or shift attention.

B. A change in cognition (such as memory deficit, disorientation, language disturbance) or the development of a perceptual disturbance that is not better accounted for by a preexisting, established, or evolving dementia.

C. The disturbance develops over a short period of time (usually hours to days) and tends to fluctuate during the course of the day.

D. There is evidence from the history, physical examination, or laboratory findings of either (1) or (2):
(1) the symptoms in criteria A and B developed during substance intoxication
(2) medication use is etiologically related to the disturbance

Note: This diagnosis should be made instead of a diagnosis of substance intoxication only when the cognitive symptoms are in excess of those usually associated with the intoxication syndrome and when the symptoms are sufficiently severe to warrant independent clinical attention.
Note: The diagnosis should be recorded as substance-induced delirium if related to medication use.

Code: [Specific substance] intoxication delirium (Alcohol; amphetamine [or amphetamine-like substance]; cannabis; cocaine; hallucinogen; inhalant; opioid; phencyclidine [or phencyclidine-like substance]; sedative, hypnotic, or anxiolytic; other [or unknown] substance [eg, cimetidine, digitalis, benztropine])

Table 10.2–4
DSM-IV Diagnostic Criteria for Substance Withdrawal Delirium

A. Disturbance of consciousness (ie, reduced clarity of awareness of the environment) with reduced ability to focus, sustain, or shift attention.

B. A change in cognition (such as memory deficit, disorientation, language disturbance) or the development of a perceptual disturbance that is not better accounted for by a preexisting, established, or evolving dementia.

C. The disturbance develops over a short period of time (usually hours to days) and tends to fluctuate during the course of the day.

D. There is evidence from the history, physical examination, or laboratory findings that the symptoms in criteria A and B developed during, or shortly after, a withdrawal syndrome.

Note: This diagnosis should be made instead of a diagnosis of substance withdrawal only when the cognitive symptoms are in excess of those usually associated with the withdrawal syndrome and when the symptoms are sufficiently severe to warrant independent clinical attention.

Code: [Specific substance] withdrawal delirium: (Alcohol; sedative, hypnotic, or anxiolytic; other [or unknown] substance)

Table 10.2–5
DSM-IV Diagnostic Criteria for Delirium Due to Multiple Etiologies

A. Disturbance of consciousness (ie, reduced clarity of awareness of the environment) with reduced ability to focus, sustain, or shift attention.

B. A change in cognition (such as memory deficit, disorientation, language disturbance) or the development of a perceptual disturbance that is not better accounted for by a preexisting, established, or evolving dementia.

C. The disturbance develops over a short period of time (usually hours to days) and tends to fluctuate during the course of the day.

D. There is evidence from the history, physical examination, or laboratory findings that the delirium has more than one etiology (eg, more than one etiological general medical condition, a general medical condition plus substance intoxication or medication side effect).

Coding note: Use multiple codes reflecting specific delirium and specific etiologies, eg, delirium due to viral encephalitis, alcohol withdrawal delirium.

(Table 10.2–2), substance intoxication delirium (Table 10.2–3), substance withdrawal delirium (Table 10.2–4), and delirium due to multiple etiologies (Table 10.2–5) are included in the section on delirium. A diagnostic category of delirium not otherwise specified (Table 10.2–6) is included for states of delirium due to causes not included in the other categories. DSM-IV gives delirium related to sensory deprivation as an example of such a situation. DSM-IV has moved closer to the 10th revision of *International Statistical Classification of Diseases and Related Health Problems* (ICD-10) by making impairment of consciousness the cardinal feature of delirium. As to which impairments of cognition are present, DSM-IV merely requires a change in cognition that is ''not better accounted for by a preexisting, established, or evolving dementia.''

Substance intoxication delirium and substance withdrawal delirium are included in the section on delirium in DSM-IV (Tables 10.2–3 and 10.2–4, although clinicians are referred to the specific substance causing delirium within the substance-related disorders section in DSM-IV regarding the specific drug causing delirium). When the diagnosis of substance-related delirium is made, the specific substance should be noted.

Table 10.2–6
DSM-IV Diagnostic Criteria for Delirium Not Otherwise Specified

This category should be used to diagnose a delirium that does not meet criteria for any of the specific types of delirium described in this section.

Examples include

1. A clinical presentation of delirium that is suspected to be due to a general medical condition or substance use but for which there is insufficient evidence to establish a specific etiology.
2. Delirium due to causes not listed in this section (eg, sensory deprivation).

ICD-10

The ICD-10 criteria for delirium, not induced by alcohol and other psychoactive substances, are presented in Table 10.2–7. In ICD-10, deliriums associated with the use of a sub-

Table 10.2–7
ICD-10 Diagnostic Criteria for Delirium, Not Induced by Alcohol and Other Psychoactive Substances

A. There is clouding of consciousness, ie, reduced clarity of awareness of the environment, with reduced ability to focus, sustain, or shift attention.

B. Disturbance of cognition is manifest by both:
   (1) impairment of immediate recall and recent memory, with relatively intact remote memory;
   (2) disorientation in time, place, or person.

C. At least one of the following psychomotor disturbances is present:
   (1) rapid, unpredictable shifts from hypoactivity to hyperactivity;
   (2) increased reaction time;
   (3) increased or decreased flow of speech;
   (4) enhanced startle reaction.

D. There is disturbance of sleep or of the sleep–wake cycle, manifest by at least one of the following:
   (1) insomnia, which in severe cases may involve total sleep loss, with or without daytime drowsiness, or reversal of the sleep–wake cycle;
   (2) nocturnal worsening of symptoms;
   (3) disturbing dreams and nightmares, which may continue as hallucinations or illusions after awakening.

E. Symptoms have rapid onset and show fluctuations over the course of the day.

F. There is objective evidence from history, physical and neurological examination, or laboratory tests of an underlying cerebral or systemic disease (other than psychoactive substance-related) that can be presumed to be responsible for the clinical manifestations in criteria A–D.

Comments

Emotional disturbances such as depression, anxiety or fear, irritability, euphoria, apathy, or wondering perplexity, disturbances of perception (illusions or hallucinations, often visual), and transient delusions are typical but are not specific indications for the diagnosis. A fourth character may be used to indicate whether or not the delirium is superimposed on dementia:

Delirium, not superimposed on dementia

Delirium, superimposed on dementia

Other delirium

Delirium, unspecified

stance are classified under mental and behavioral disorders due to psychoactive substance use as a withdrawal state with delirium, as a subtype of acute intoxication (such as acute intoxication due to the use of alcohol with delirium), and as an additional specifier to alcohol withdrawal state and sedative or hypnotic withdrawal state (see Table 12.1–5).

Physical and Laboratory Examinations

Delirium is usually diagnosed at the bedside and is characterized by the sudden onset of symptoms. A bedside mental status examination—such as the Mini-Mental State Examination (see Table 10.1–2), the Mental Status Examination, or the Face-Hand Test—can be used to document the cognitive impairment and to provide a baseline from which to measure the patient's clinical course. The physical examination often reveals clues to the cause of the delirium (Table 10.2–8). The presence of a known physical illness or a history of head trauma or alcohol or other substance dependence increases the likelihood of the diagnosis.

The laboratory workup of a patient with delirium should include standard tests and additional studies indicated by the clinical situation (Table 10.2–9). In delirium, the electroencephalogram (EEG) characteristically shows a generalized slowing of activity and may be useful in differentiating delirium from depression or psychosis. The EEG of a delirious patient sometimes shows focal areas of hyperactivity. In rare cases, it may be difficult to differentiate delirium related to epilepsy from delirium related to other causes.

CLINICAL FEATURES

As discussed, a key feature of delirium is an impairment of consciousness, which DSM-IV describes as a ''reduced clarity of awareness of the environment,'' with reduced ability to focus, sustain, or shift attention. Some investigators have suggested that the inability of delirious patients to maintain attention is the central feature of delirium. Most commonly, the impairment of consciousness and the inability to attend fluctuate over the course of a day, so that relatively lucid periods alternate with symptomatic periods. The development of anxiety, drowsiness, insomnia, transient hallucinations, nightmares, and restlessness may precede the delirious state by a few days. The appearance of these symptoms in patients at risk for delirium should prompt clinicians to monitor a patient carefully. Moreover, patients who have had a previous episode of delirium are likely to have a recurrent episode under the same conditions.

Abnormal Arousal

Two patterns of abnormal arousal have been noted in patients with delirium. One pattern is characterized by hyperactivity associated with increased alertness, the other by hypoactivity associated with decreased alertness. Patients with delirium related to substance withdrawal often have the hyperactive delirium, which can also be associated with autonomic signs, such as flushing, pallor, sweating, tachycardia, dilated pupils, nausea, vomiting, and hyperthermia. Patients with hypoactive symptoms are occasionally classified as being depressed, catatonic, or demented. Clinicians may also encounter patients with a mixed symptom pattern of hypoactivity and hyperactivity.

Impaired Orientation

Orientation to time, place, and person should be tested in a patient with delirium. Orientation to time is commonly lost, even in mild cases of delirium. In severe cases, patients may lose orientation to place and the ability to recognize others (such as the physician, family members). A delirious patient rarely loses orientation to self.

Language Abnormalities

Patients with delirium often have language abnormalities that include rambling, irrelevant or incoherent speech, and an impaired ability to comprehend speech. DSM-IV no longer requires the presence of an abnormality of language for diagnosis; however, such an abnormality may be impossible to diagnosis in a mute patient.

Other cognitive functions that may be impaired in patients with delirium include memory and generalized cognitive functions. The ability to register, retain, and recall memories may be impaired, although the recall of remote memories may be preserved. In addition to decreased attention, patients may have a dramatically decreased cognitive output as a characteristic of the hypoactive symptoms of delirium. Delirious patients have impaired problem-solving abilities and may also have unsystematized, often paranoid, delusions.

Perception

Patients with delirium often have a generalized inability to discriminate sensory stimuli and to integrate present perceptions with their past experiences. Therefore, they are often distracted by irrelevant stimuli or become agitated when presented with new information. Hallucinations are also relatively common in delirious patients. The hallucinations are most often visual or auditory, although they can also be tactile or olfactory. The visual hallucinations can range from simple geometric figures or colored patterns to fully formed people and scenes. Visual and auditory illusions are common in delirium.

Mood

Patients with delirium often have abnormalities in the regulation of mood. The most common symptoms are anger, rage, and unwarranted fear; other abnormalities are apathy, depression, and euphoria. In some patients, these emotions rapidly alternate within the course of a day.

Associated Symptoms

Sleep–Wake Disturbances. The sleep of patients with delirium is characteristically disturbed. Patients are often drowsy and nap during the day. The sleep of delirious patients, however, is almost always short and fragmented. Sometimes the sleep–wake cycle of patients with delirium is reversed. Patients may have an exacerbation of delirious symptoms at bedtime, a clinical situation known as sundowning. The night-

Table 10.2–8
Physical Examination of the Delirious Patient

Parameter	Finding	Clinical Implication
1. Pulse	Bradycardia	Hypothyroidism Stokes-Adams syndrome Increased intracranial pressure
	Tachycardia	Hyperthyroidism Infection Heart failure
2. Temperature	Fever	Sepsis Thyroid storm Vasculitis
3. Blood pressure	Hypotension	Shock Hypothyroidism Addison's disease
	Hypertension	Encephalopathy Intracranial mass
4. Respiration	Tachypnea	Diabetes Pneumonia Cardiac failure Fever Acidosis (metabolic)
	Shallow	Alcohol or other substance intoxication
5. Carotid vessels	Bruits or decreased pulse	Transient cerebral ischemia
6. Scalp and face	Evidence of trauma	
7. Neck	Evidence of nuchal rigidity	Meningitis Subarachnoid hemorrhage
8. Eyes	Papilledema	Tumor Hypertensive encephalopathy
	Pupillary dilatation	Anxiety Autonomic overactivity (eg, delirium tremens)
9. Mouth	Tongue or cheek lacerations	Evidence of generalized tonic-clonic seizures
10. Thyroid	Enlarged	Hyperthyroidism
11. Heart	Arrhythmia	Inadequate cardiac output, possibility of emboli
	Cardiomegaly	Heart failure Hypertensive disease
12. Lungs	Congestion	Primary pulmonary failure Pulmonary edema Pneumonia
13. Breath	Alcohol	
	Ketones	Diabetes
14. Liver	Enlargement	Cirrhosis Liver failure
15. Nervous system		
a. Reflexes—muscle stretch	Asymmetry with Babinski's signs	Mass lesion Cerebrovascular disease Preexisting dementia
	Snout	Frontal mass Bilateral posterior cerebral artery occlusion
b. Abducent nerve (sixth cranial nerve)	Weakness in lateral gaze	Increased intracranial pressure
c. Limb strength	Asymmetrical	Mass lesion Cerebrovascular disease
d. Autonomic	Hyperactivity	Anxiety Delirium

Reprinted with permission from Strub RL, Black FW: *Neurobehavioral Disorders: A Clinical Approach*, p 120. Davis, Philadelphia, 1981.

mares and disturbing dreams of delirious patients occasionally continue into wakefulness as hallucinatory experiences.

Neurological Symptoms. Patients with delirium commonly have associated neurological symptoms, including dysphasia, tremor, asterixis, incoordination, and urinary incontinence. Focal neurological signs can also be seen as part of the symptom pattern of patients with delirium.

A 74-year-old African American woman, Ms. Richardson, was brought to a city hospital emergency room by the police. She is unkempt, dirty, and foul smelling. She does

Table 10.2–9
Laboratory Workup of Patient with Delirium

Standard studies
- Blood chemistries (including electrolytes, renal and hepatic indexes, and glucose)
- Complete blood count with white cell differential
- Thyroid function tests
- Serologic tests for syphilis
- Human immunodeficiency virus (HIV) antibody test
- Urinalysis
- Electrocardiogram
- Electroencephalogram
- Chest radiograph
- Blood and urine drug screens

Additional tests when indicated
- Blood, urine, and cerebrospinal fluid (CSF) cultures
- B_{12}, folic acid concentrations
- Computed tomography or magnetic resonance imaging brain scan
- Lumbar puncture and CSF examination

not look at the interviewer and is apparently confused and unresponsive to most of his questions. She knows her name and address, but not the day or the month. She is unable to describe the events that led to her admission.

The police reported that they were called by neighbors because Ms. Richardson had been wandering around the neighborhood, not taking care of herself. The medical center mobile crisis unit went to her house twice but could not get in, and presumed she was not at home. Finally the police came and broke into the apartment, where they were met by a snarling German shepherd. They shot the dog with a tranquilizing gun, and then found Ms. Richardson hiding in the corner, wearing nothing but a bra. The apartment was filthy, the floor littered with dog feces. The police found a gun, which they took into custody.

The following day, while Ms. Richardson was awaiting transfer to a medical unit for treatment of her out-of-control diabetes, the supervising psychiatrist attempted to interview her. Her facial expression was still mostly unresponsive, and she still didn't know the month and couldn't say what hospital she was in. She reported that the neighbors had called the police because she was ''sick,'' and indeed she had felt sick and weak, with pains in her shoulder; in addition, she had not eaten for 3 days. She remembered that the police had shot her dog with a tranquilizer, and said the dog was now in ''the shop'' and would be returned to her when she got home. She refused to give the name of a neighbor who was a friend, saying, ''he's got enough troubles of his own.'' She denied ever being in a psychiatric hospital or hearing voices but acknowledged that she had at one point seen a psychiatrist ''near Lincoln Center'' because she couldn't sleep. He had prescribed medication that was too strong so she didn't take it. She didn't remember the name, so the interviewer asked if it was Thorazine. She said no, it was ''allal.'' ''Haldol?'' asked the interviewer. She nodded. The interviewer was convinced that was the drug, but other observers thought she might have said yes to anything that sounded remotely like it, such as ''Elavil.'' When asked about the gun, she denied, with some annoyance, that it was real and said it was a toy gun that had been brought to the house by her brother, who had died 8 years ago. She was still feeling weak and sick, complained of chest pains in her shoulder, and apparently had trouble swallowing. She did manage to smile as the team left her bedside.

DISCUSSION

When this patient was seen initially in the emergency room, her most prominent symptoms were disorientation, inability to focus attention, and a history of disorganized behavior that probably developed over a relatively short period of time. These are the characteristic features of delirium; that diagnosis is further supported by the information gained on the second day, that her diabetes had been out of control, and her improved mental status with treatment of the diabetes.

A valiant attempt was made to obtain follow-up information to determine whether the delirium was superimposed on a more chronic disorder, such as schizophrenia or dementia. Although the staff on the medical unit recalled having seen the patient previously, they could offer no additional information, and both the patient and her chart were nowhere to be found. (From *DSM-IV Casebook.*)

DIFFERENTIAL DIAGNOSIS

Delirium versus Dementia

A number of clinical features help distinguish delirium from dementia (Table 10.2–10). In contrast to the sudden onset

Table 10.2–10
Frequency of Clinical Features of Delirium Contrasted with Dementia

Feature	Delirium	Dementia
Impaired memory	+ + +	+ + +
Impaired thinking	+ + +	+ + +
Impaired judgment	+ + +	+ + +
Clouding of consciousness	+ + +	−
Major attention deficits	+ + +	+[a]
Fluctuation over course of a day	+ + +	+
Disorientation	+ + +	+ +[a]
Vivid perceptual disturbances	+ +	+
Incoherent speech	+ +	+[a]
Disrupted sleep–wake cycle	+ +	+[a]
Nocturnal exacerbation	+ +	+[a]
Insight	+ +[b]	+[b]
Acute or subacute onset	+ +	−[c]

Reprinted with permission from Liston EH: Diagnosis and management of delirium in the elderly patient. Psychiatr Ann *14:* 117, 1984.

+ + +, always present; + +, usually present; +, occasionally present; −, usually absent

[a] More frequent in advanced stages of dementia.

[b] Present during lucid intervals or on recovery from delirium; present during early stages of dementia.

[c] Onset may be acute or subacute in some dementias, eg, multi-infarction, hypoxemia, certain reversible dementias.

of delirium, the onset of dementia is usually insidious. Although both conditions include cognitive impairment, the changes in dementia are more stable over time and, for example, do not fluctuate over the course of a day. A patient with dementia is usually alert; a patient with delirium has episodes of decreased consciousness. Occasionally, delirium occurs in a patient with dementia, a condition known as beclouded dementia. A diagnosis of delirium can be made when there is a definite history of preexisting dementia.

Delirium versus Schizophrenia or Depression

Delirium must also be differentiated from schizophrenia and depressive disorder. Patients with factitious disorders may attempt to simulate the symptoms of delirium but usually reveal the factitious nature of their symptoms by inconsistencies on their mental status examinations, and an EEG can easily separate the two diagnoses. Some patients with psychotic disorders, usually schizophrenia or manic episodes, may have periods of extremely disorganized behavior difficult to distinguish from delirium. In general, however, the hallucinations and delusions of patients with schizophrenia are more constant and better organized than are those of patients with delirium. Patients with schizophrenia usually experience no change in their level of consciousness or in their orientation. Patients with hypoactive symptoms of delirium may appear somewhat similar to severely depressed patients but can be distinguished on the basis of an EEG. Other psychiatric diagnoses to consider in the differential diagnosis of delirium are brief psychotic disorder, schizophreniform disorder, and dissociative disorders.

COURSE AND PROGNOSIS

Although the onset of delirium is usually sudden, prodromal symptoms (such as restlessness and fearfulness) may occur in the days preceding the onset of florid symptoms. The symptoms of delirium usually persist as long as the causally relevant factors are present, although delirium generally lasts less than a week. After identification and removal of the causative factors, the symptoms of delirium usually recede over a 3- to 7-day period, although some symptoms may take up to 2 weeks to resolve completely. The older a patient and the longer the patient has been delirious, the longer the delirium takes to resolve. Recall of what transpired during a delirium, once it is over, is characteristically spotty; a patient may refer to the episode as a bad dream or a nightmare only vaguely remembered. As stated in the discussion on epidemiology, the occurrence of delirium is associated with a high mortality rate in the ensuing year, primarily because of the serious nature of the associated medical conditions that lead to delirium.

Whether delirium progresses to dementia has not been demonstrated in carefully controlled studies, although many clinicians believe that they have seen such a progression. A clinical observation that has been validated by some studies, however, is that periods of delirium are sometimes followed by depression or posttraumatic stress disorder.

TREATMENT

In treating delirium, the primary goal is to treat the underlying cause. When the underlying condition is anticholinergic toxicity, the use of physostigmine salicylate (Antilirium), 1 to 2 mg intravenously or intramuscularly, with repeated doses in 15 to 30 minutes may be indicated. The other important goal of treatment is to provide physical, sensory, and environmental support. Physical support is necessary so that delirious patients do not get into situations in which they may have accidents. Patients with delirium should be neither sensory deprived nor overly stimulated by the environment. They are usually helped by having a friend or relative in the room or by the presence of a regular sitter. Familiar pictures and decorations, the presence of a clock or a calendar, and regular orientations to person, place, and time help make patients with delirium be comfortable. Delirium can sometimes occur in older patients wearing eye patches after cataract surgery (black-patch delirium). Such patients can be helped by placing pinholes in the patches to let in some stimuli or by occasionally removing one patch at a time during recovery.

Pharmacotherapy

The two major symptoms of delirium which may require pharmacological treatment are psychosis and insomnia. The drug of choice for psychosis is haloperidol (Haldol), a butyrophenone antipsychotic drug. Depending on a patient's age, weight, and physical condition, the initial dose may range from 2 to 10 mg intramuscularly, repeated in an hour if the patient remains agitated. As soon as the patient is calm, oral medication in liquid concentrate or tablet form should begin. Two daily oral doses should suffice, with two thirds of the dose being given at bedtime. To achieve the same therapeutic effect, the oral dose should be approximately 1.5 times higher than the parenteral dose. The effective total daily dosage of haloperidol may range from 5 to 50 mg for most patients with delirium.

Droperidol (Inapsine) is a butyrophenone available as an alternative intravenous formulation, although careful monitoring of the electrocardiogram may be prudent with this treatment. Phenothiazines should be avoided in delirious patients: These drugs are associated with significant anticholinergic activity.

Insomnia is best treated with either benzodiazepines with short half-lives or with hydroxyzine (Vistaril), 25 to 100 mg. Benzodiazepines with long half-lives and barbiturates should be avoided unless they are being used as part of the treatment for the underlying disorder (such as alcohol withdrawal).

References

Caine ED: Delirium, dementia, and amnestic and other cognitive disorders and mental disorders due to a general medical condition. In *Comprehensive Textbook of Psychiatry,* ed 6, HI Kaplan, BJ Sadock, editors, p 705. Williams & Wilkins, Baltimore, 1995.

Francis J, Kapoor WN: Delirium in hospitalized elderly. J Gen Intern Med *5:* 65, 1990.

Francis J, Martin D, Kapoor WN: A prospective study of delirium in hospitalized elderly. JAMA *263:* 1097, 1990.

Lipowski ZJ: Update on delirium. Psychiatr Clin North Am *15:* 335, 1992.

Liptzin B, Levkoff SE, Cleary PD, Pilgrim DM, Reilly CH, Albert M, Wetle TT: An empirical study of diagnostic criteria for delirium. Am J Psychiatry *148:* 454, 1991.

Metzger E, Friedman R: Prolongation of the corrected QT and torsades de pointes cardiac arrhythmia associated with intravenous haloperidol in the mentally ill. J Clin Psychopharmacol *13:* 128, 1993.

Parikh SS, Chung F: Postoperative delirium in the elderly. Anesth Analg *80:* 1223, 1995.

Pompei P: Delirium in hospitalized elderly patients. Hosp Pract (Off Ed) *28:* 69, 1993.

Rummans TA, Evans JM, Krahn LE, Fleming KC: Delirium in elderly patients: Evaluation and management. Mayo Clin Proc *70:* 989, 1995.
Shapira J, Roper J, Schulzinger J: Managing delirious patients. Nursing *23:* 78, 1993.
Smith LW, Dimsdale JE: Postcardiotomy delirium: Conclusions after 25 years? Am J Psychiatry *146:* 452, 1989.
Taylor D, Lewis S: Delirium. J Neurol Neurosurg Psychiatry *56:* 742, 1993.

▲ 10.3 Dementia

In the fourth edition of *Diagnostic and Statistical Manual of Mental Disorders* (DSM-IV), dementia is "characterized by multiple cognitive defects that include impairment in memory," without impairment in consciousness. The cognitive functions that can be affected in dementia include general intelligence, learning and memory, language, problem solving, orientation, perception, attention and concentration, judgment, and social abilities. A person's personality is also affected. A person with an impairment of consciousness probably fits the diagnostic criteria for delirium. In addition, a diagnosis of dementia, according to DSM-IV, requires that the symptoms result in a significant impairment in social or occupational functioning and that they represent a significant decline from a previous level of functioning.

The critical clinical points of dementia are the identification of the syndrome and the clinical workup of its cause. The disorder may be progressive or static, permanent or reversible. An underlying cause is always assumed, although in rare cases it is impossible to determine a specific cause. The potential reversibility of dementia is related to the underlying pathological condition and to the availability and application of effective treatment. Approximately 15 percent of people with dementia have reversible illnesses if treatment is initiated before irreversible damage takes place.

EPIDEMIOLOGY

Dementia is essentially a disease of older people. In the United States, approximately 5 percent of people older than age 65 have severe dementia and 15 percent have mild dementia. Of those older than age 80, approximately 20 percent have severe dementia. Of all patients with dementia, 50 to 60 percent have the most common type of dementia, dementia of the Alzheimer's type. About 5 percent of everyone who reaches age 65 has dementia of the Alzheimer's type, compared with 15 to 25 percent of everyone age 85 or older. Patients with dementia of the Alzheimer's type occupy more than 50 percent of nursing home beds. Over 2 million persons with dementia are cared for in these homes. The risk factors for the development of dementia of the Alzheimer's type include being female, having a first-degree relative with the disorder, and having a history of head injury. Down's syndrome is also characteristically associated with the development of dementia of the Alzheimer's type. According to the 1997 American Psychiatric Association (APA) *Practice Guideline for the Treatment of Patients with Alzheimer's Disease and the Dementia of Late Life,* the onset of the disease generally occurs in late life, most commonly in the 60s, 70s, and 80s and beyond, but in rare instances the disorder appears in the 40s and 50s (known as early-onset dementia). The incidence of Alzheimer's disease also increases with age, and it is estimated at 0.5 percent per year from age 65 to 69, 1 percent per year from age 70 to 74, 2 percent per year from age 75 to 79, 3 percent per year from 80 to 84, and 8 percent per year from age 85 onward. Progression is gradual but steadily downward, with an average duration from onset of symptoms to death of 8 to 10 years. Plateaus may occur, but progression generally resumes after 1 to several years.

The second most common type of dementia is vascular dementia, which is causally related to cerebrovascular diseases. Hypertension predisposes a person to the disease. Vascular dementias account for 15 to 30 percent of all dementia cases. Vascular dementia is most common in people between the ages of 60 and 70 and is more common in men than in women. Approximately 10 to 15 percent of patients have coexisting vascular dementia and dementia of the Alzheimer's type.

Other common causes of dementia, each representing 1 to 5 percent of all cases, include head trauma, alcohol-related dementias, and various movement disorder-related dementias such as Huntington's disease and Parkinson's disease (Table 10.3–1). Because dementia is a fairly general syndrome, it has many causes, and clinicians must embark on a careful clinical workup of a patient with dementia to establish its cause.

The current annual cost of caring for patients with dementia is $15 billion, which is likely to increase. By the year 2030, an estimated 20 percent of the population will be older than age 65.

ETIOLOGY

Dementia has many causes (see Table 10.3–1), but dementia of the Alzheimer's type and vascular dementia together represent as many as 75 percent of all cases. Other causes of dementia specified in DSM-IV are Pick's disease, Creutzfeldt-Jakob disease, Huntington's disease, Parkinson's disease, human immunodeficiency virus (HIV), and head trauma.

Dementia of the Alzheimer's Type

In 1907, Alois Alzheimer first described the condition that later assumed his name. He described a 51-year-old woman with a 4½-year course of progressive dementia. The final diagnosis of Alzheimer's disease is based on a neuropathological examination of the brain; nevertheless, dementia of the Alzheimer's type is commonly diagnosed in the clinical setting after other causes of dementia have been excluded from diagnostic consideration.

Genetic Factors. Although the cause of dementia of the Alzheimer's type remains unknown, progress has been made in understanding the molecular basis of the amyloid deposits that are a hallmark of the disorder's neuropathology. Some studies have indicated that as many as 40 percent of patients have a family history of dementia of the Alzheimer's type; thus, genetic factors are presumed to play a part in the development of the disorder, at least in some cases. Additional support for a genetic influence is the concordance rate for mon-

Table 10.3–1
Disorders That May Produce Dementia

Alzheimer's disease[a]
Vascular dementia[b]
  Varieties: Multiple infarcts (called multi-infarct dementia)
    Lacunae
    Binswanger's disease
    Cortical microinfarction
Drugs and toxins (including chronic alcoholic dementia)[c]
Intracranial masses: tumors, subdural masses, brain abscesses[c]
Anoxia
Trauma
  Head injury[c]
  Dementia pugilistica (punch-drunk syndrome)
Normal-pressure hydrocephalus[c]
Neurodegenerative disorders
  Parkinson's disease[d]
  Huntington's disease[d]
  Progressive supranuclear palsy[d]
  Pick's disease[d]
  Amyotrophic lateral sclerosis
  Spinocerebellar degenerations
  Olivopontocerebellar degeneration
  Ophthalmoplegia plus
  Metachromatic leukodystrophy (adult form)
  Hallervorden-Spatz disease
  Wilson's disease
Infections
  Creutzfeldt-Jakob disease
  AIDS[d]
  Viral encephalitis
  Progressive multifocal leukoencephalopathy
  Behçet's syndrome
  Neurosyphilis
  Chronic bacterial meningitis
  Cryptococcal meningitis
  Other fungal meningitides
Nutritional disorders
  Wernicke-Korsakoff syndrome (thiamine deficiency)[c]
  Vitamin B_{12} deficiency
  Folate deficiency
  Pellagra
  Marchiafava-Bignami disease
  ?Zinc deficiency
Metabolic disorders
  Metachromatic leukodystrophy
  Adrenal leukodystrophy
  Dialysis dementia
  Hypothyroidism and hyperthyroidism
  Renal insufficiency, severe
  Cushing's syndrome
  Hepatic insufficiency
  Parathyroid disease
Chronic inflammatory disorders[d]
  Lupus and other collagen-vascular[d] disorders with intracerebral vasculitis
  Multiple sclerosis
  Whipple's disease

Reprinted with permission from Bosser M: Dementia. In *Diseases of the Nervous System: Clinical Neurobiology*, ed 2, AK Asbury, GM McKhann, WI McDonald, editors, p 789. Saunders, Philadelphia, 1992.
[a] Accounts for 50 to 60 percent of cases.
[b] Accounts for 10 to 20 percent of cases.
[c] Accounts for 1 to 5 percent of cases.
[d] Accounts for about 1 percent of cases.
No symbol: less than 1 percent of cases.

ozygotic twins, which is higher than the rate for dizygotic twins (43 percent versus 8 percent, respectively). In several well-documented cases, the disorder has been transmitted in families through an autosomal dominant gene, although such transmission is rare.

AMYLOID PRECURSOR PROTEIN. The gene for amyloid precursor protein is on the long arm of chromosome 21. Through the process of differential splicing, there are four forms of amyloid precursor protein. The β/A4 protein, the major constituent of senile plaques, is a 42-amino acid peptide that is a breakdown product of amyloid precursor protein. In Down's syndrome (trisomy 21), there are three copies of the amyloid precursor protein gene, and in a disease in which there is a mutation at codon 717 in the amyloid precursor protein gene, a pathological process results in the excessive deposition of β/A4 protein. Whether the processing of abnormal amyloid precursor protein is of primary causative significance in Alzheimer's disease is unknown, but many research groups are studying both the normal metabolic processing of amyloid precursor protein and its processing in patients with dementia of the Alzheimer's type in an attempt to answer this question.

MULTIPLE E4 GENES. In one study, gene E4 was implicated in the etiological origin of Alzheimer's disease. People with one copy of the gene have Alzheimer's disease 3 times more frequently than do those with no E4 gene, and people with two E4 genes have the disease 8 times more frequently than do those with no E4 gene. Diagnostic testing for this gene is not currently recommended because it is found in persons without dementia and not found in all cases of dementia.

Neuropathology. The classic gross neuroanatomical observation of a brain from a patient with Alzheimer's disease is diffuse atrophy (Fig. 10.3–1) with flattened cortical sulci and enlarged cerebral ventricles. The classic and pathognomonic microscopic findings are senile plaques, neurofibrillary tangles, neuronal loss (particularly in the cortex and the hippocampus), synaptic loss (perhaps as much as 50 percent in the cortex), and granulovascular degeneration of the neurons. Neurofibrillary tangles are composed of cytoskeletal elements, primarily phosphorylated tau protein, although other cytoskeletal proteins are also present. Neurofibrillary tangles are not unique to Alzheimer's disease, but also occur in Down's syndrome, dementia pugilistica (punch-drunk syndrome), Parkinson–dementia complex of Guam, Hallervorden-Spatz disease, and the brains of normal people as they age. Neurofibrillary tangles are commonly found in the cortex, the hippocampus, the substantia nigra, and the locus ceruleus.

Senile plaques, also referred to as amyloid plaques, are much more indicative of Alzheimer's disease, although they are also seen in Down's syndrome and, to some extent, in normal aging. Senile plaques are composed of a particular protein, β/A4, and astrocytes, dystrophic neuronal processes, and microglia. The number and the density of senile plaques present in postmortem brains have been correlated with the severity of the disease that affected the person.

Neurotransmitters. The neurotransmitters that are most often implicated in the pathophysiological condition of Alzheimer's disease are acetylcholine and norepinephrine, both of which are hypothesized to be hypoactive in Alzheimer's disease. Several studies have reported data consistent with the hypothesis that a specific degeneration of cholinergic neurons is present in the nucleus basalis of Meynert in people with

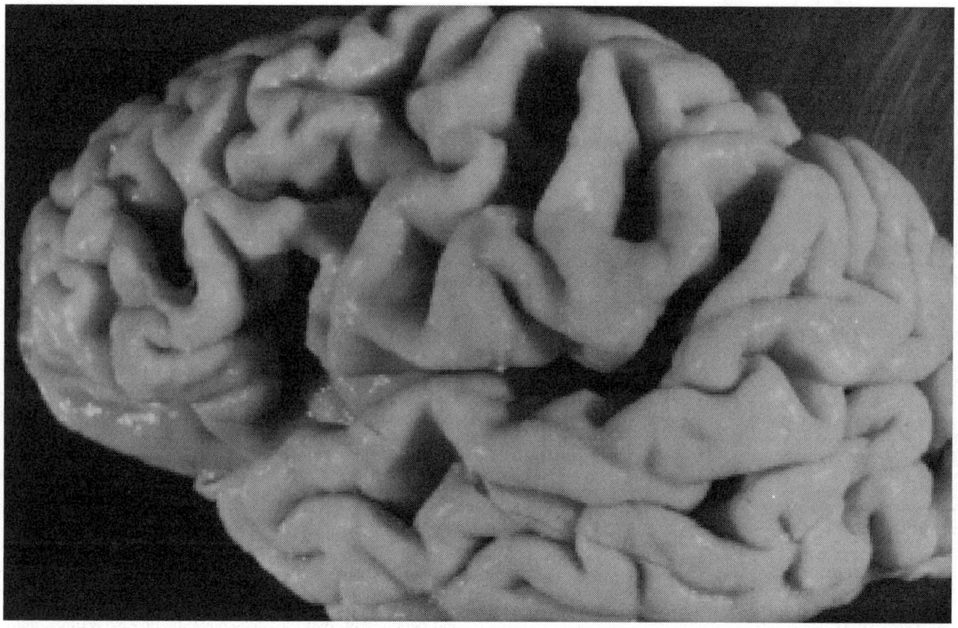

FIGURE 10.3–1
Gross external appearance of the brain of a patient who had dementia of the Alzheimer's type, with late onset. The leptomeninges have been removed so that the generalized atrophy may be fully appreciated. (Courtesy of Daniel P. Perl, M.D.)

Alzheimer's disease. Other data in support of a cholinergic deficit in Alzheimer's disease are those that demonstrate decreases in acetylcholine and choline acetyltransferase concentrations in the brain. Choline acetyltransferase is the key enzyme for the synthesis of acetylcholine, and a reduction in choline acetyltransferase concentrations suggests a decrease in the number of cholinergic neurons present. Additional support for the cholinergic deficit hypothesis comes from the observation that cholinergic antagonists, such as scopolamine and atropine, impair cognitive abilities, whereas cholinergic agonists, such as physostigmine and arecoline, enhance cognitive abilities. The decrease in norepinephrine activity in Alzheimer's disease is suggested by the decrease in norepinephrine-containing neurons in the locus ceruleus found in some pathological examinations of brains from people with Alzheimer's disease. Two other neurotransmitters implicated in the pathophysiological condition of Alzheimer's disease are the neuroactive peptides somatostatin and corticotropin, both of which have been reported to be decreased in Alzheimer's disease.

Other Causes. Other causative theories have been proposed to explain the development of Alzheimer's disease. One theory is that an abnormality in the regulation of membrane phospholipid metabolism results in membranes that are less fluid—that is, more rigid—than normal. Several investigators are using molecular resonance spectroscopic imaging to assess this hypothesis directly in patients with dementia of the Alzheimer's type. Aluminum toxicity has also been hypothesized to be a causative factor, because high levels of aluminum have been found in the brains of some patients with Alzheimer's disease; but this is not considered a significant etiological factor.

Familial Multiple System Taupathy with Presenile Dementia. A recently discovered type of dementia, familial multiple system taupathy, shares some brain abnormalities found in people with Alzheimer's disease. The gene that causes the disorder is thought to be carried on chromosome 17. The symptoms of the disorder include short-term memory problems and difficulty maintaining balance and walking. The onset of disease occurs in people's 40s and 50s, and people with the disease live an average 11 years after the onset of symptoms.

As in Alzheimer's disease patients, tau protein builds up in neurons and glial cells of people with familial multiple system taupathy. Eventually, the protein buildup kills brain cells. The disorder is not associated with the senile plaques associated with Alzheimer's disease.

Vascular Dementia

The primary cause of vascular dementia, formerly referred to as multi-infarct dementia, is presumed to be multiple cerebral vascular disease, resulting in a symptom pattern of dementia. Vascular dementia is most common in men, especially those with preexisting hypertension or other cardiovascular risk factors. The disorder affects primarily small- and medium-sized cerebral vessels, which undergo infarction and produce multiple parenchymal lesions spread over wide areas of the brain (Fig. 10.3–2). The causes of the infarctions may include occlusion of the vessels by arteriosclerotic plaque or thromboemboli from distant origins (such as heart valves). An examination of a patient may reveal carotid bruits, funduscopic abnormalities, or enlarged cardiac chambers.

Binswanger's Disease. Binswanger's disease, also known as subcortical arteriosclerotic encephalopathy, is char-

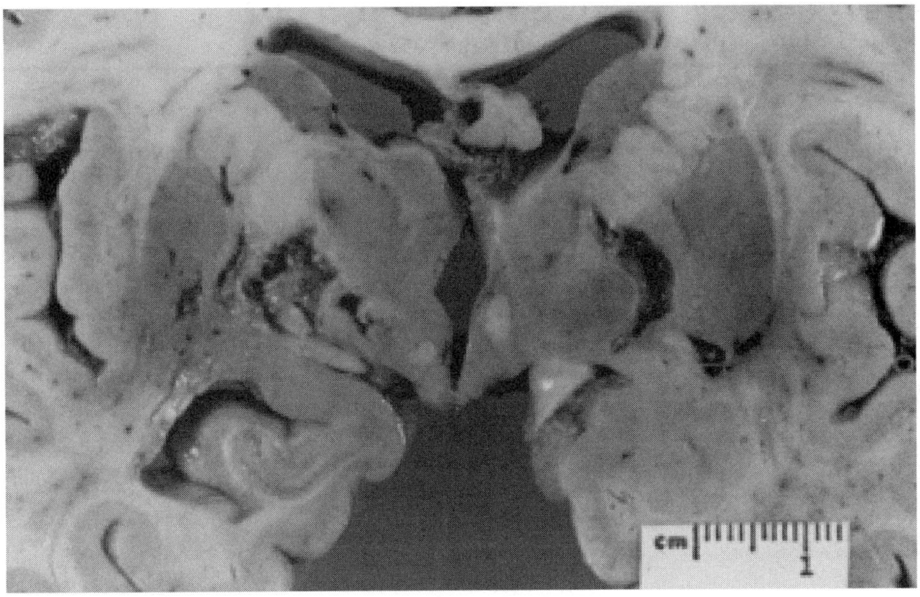
cm
1

FIGURE 10.3–2
Gross appearance of the cerebral cortex on coronal section from a case of vascular dementia. The multiple bilateral lacunar infarcts involve the thalamus, the internal capsule, and the globus pallidus. (Courtesy of Daniel P. Perl, M.D.)

acterized by the presence of many small infarctions of the white matter that spare the cortical regions. Although Binswanger's disease was previously considered a rare condition, the advent of sophisticated and powerful imaging techniques, such as magnetic resonance imaging (MRI), has revealed that the condition is more common than was previously thought.

Pick's Disease

In contrast to the parietal-temporal distribution of pathological findings in Alzheimer's disease, Pick's disease is characterized by a preponderance of atrophy in the frontotemporal regions. These regions also have neuronal loss, gliosis, and the presence of neuronal Pick's bodies, which are masses of cytoskeletal elements. Pick's bodies are seen in some postmortem specimens but are not necessary for the diagnosis. The cause of Pick's disease is unknown, but the disease constitutes approximately 5 percent of all irreversible dementias. It is most common in men, especially those who have a first-degree relative with the condition. Pick's disease is difficult to distinguish from dementia of the Alzheimer's type, although the early stages of Pick's disease are more often characterized by personality and behavioral changes, with a relative preservation of other cognitive functions. Features of Klüver-Bucy syndrome (such as hypersexuality, placidity, and hyperorality) are much more common in Pick's disease than in Alzheimer's disease.

Lewy Body Disease

Lewy body disease is a dementia clinically similar to Alzheimer's disease and often characterized by hallucinations, parkinsonian features, and extrapyramidal signs. Lewy inclusion bodies are found in the cerebral cortex. The exact incidence is unknown. These patients show marked adverse effects when given antipsychotic medications.

Huntington's Disease

Huntington's disease is classically associated with the development of dementia. The dementia seen in this disease is the subcortical type of dementia, characterized by more motor abnormalities and fewer language abnormalities than in the cortical type of dementia (Table 10.3–2). The dementia of Huntington's disease exhibits psychomotor slowing and difficulty with complex tasks, but memory, language, and insight remain relatively intact in the early and middle stages of the illness. As the disease progresses, however, the dementia becomes complete; the features distinguishing it from dementia of the Alzheimer's type are the high incidence of depression and psychosis, in addition to the classic choreoathetoid movement disorder.

Parkinson's Disease

Like Huntington's disease, parkinsonism is a disease of the basal ganglia commonly associated with dementia and depression. An estimated 20 to 30 percent of patients with Parkinson's disease have dementia, and an additional 30 to 40 percent have a measurable impairment in cognitive abilities. The slow movements of people with Parkinson's disease are paralleled in the slow thinking of some affected patients, a feature that clinicians may refer to as bradyphrenia.

Table 10.3–2
Distinguishing Features of Subcortical and Cortical Dementias

Characteristic	Subcortical Dementia	Cortical Dementia	Recommended Tests
Language	No aphasia (anomia, if severe)	Aphasia early	FAS test Boston Naming test WAIS-R vocabulary test
Memory	Impaired recall (retrieval) recognition (encoding)	Recall and recognition impaired	Wechsler memory scale; Symbol Digit Paired Associate Learning (Brandt)
Attention and immediate recall			WAIS-R digit span
Visuospatial skills	Impaired	Impaired	Picture arrangement, object assembly and block design; WAIS subtests
Calculation	Preserved until late	Involved early	Mini-Mental State
Frontal systems abilities (executive function)	Disproportionately affected	Degree of impairment consistent with other involvement	Wisconsin Card Sorting Test; Odd Man Out test: Picture Absurdities
Speed of cognitive processing	Slowed early	Normal until late in disease	Trail making A and B: Paced Auditory Serial Addition Test (PASAT)
Personality	Apathetic, inert	Unconcerned	MMPI
Mood	Depressed	Euthymic	Beck and Hamilton depression scales
Speech	Dysarthric	Articulate until late	Verbal fluency (Rosen, 1980)
Posture	Bowed or extended	Upright	
Coordination	Impaired	Normal until late	
Motor speed and control	Slowed	Normal	Finger-tap; grooved pegboard
Adventitious movements	Chorea, tremor tics, dystonia	Absent (Alzheimer's dementia—some myoclonus)	
Abstraction			Category test (Halstead Battery)

Reprinted with permission from Pajeau AK, Román GC: HIV encephalopathy and dementia. In *The Psychiatric Clinics of North America: The Interface of Psychiatry and Neurology*, vol 15, J Biller, RG Kathol, editors, p 457. Saunders, Philadelphia, 1992.

HIV-Related Dementia

Infection with human immunodeficiency virus (HIV) commonly leads to dementia and other psychiatric symptoms. Patients infected with HIV experience dementia at an annual rate of approximately 14 percent. An estimated 75 percent of patients with acquired immune deficiency syndrome have involvement of the central nervous system at the time of autopsy. The development of dementia in people infected with HIV is often paralleled by the appearance of parenchymal abnormalities in MRI scans. Other infectious dementias are caused by *Cryptococcus.*

Head Trauma-Related Dementia

Dementia can be a sequela of head trauma, as can a wide range of neuropsychiatric syndromes including neurosyphilis.

DIAGNOSIS

DSM-IV

The dementia diagnoses in DSM-IV are dementia of the Alzheimer's type (Table 10.3–3), vascular dementia (Table 10.3–4), dementia due to other general medical conditions (Table 10.3–5), substance-induced persisting dementia (Table 10.3–6), dementia due to multiple etiologies (Table 10.3–7), and dementia not otherwise specified (Table 10.3–8).

Dementia of the Alzheimer's Type. The DSM-IV diagnostic criteria for dementia of the Alzheimer's type emphasize the presence of memory impairment and the associated presence of at least one other symptom of cognitive decline (aphasia, apraxia, agnosia, or abnormal executive functioning). The diagnostic criteria also require a continuing and gradual decline in functioning, impairment in social or occupational functioning, and the exclusion of other causes of dementia. The authors of DSM-IV suggest that the age of onset be characterized as early (at age 65 or younger) or late (after age 65) and that a predominant behavioral symptom be coded with the diagnosis, if appropriate.

Vascular Dementia. The general symptoms of vascular dementia are the same as those for dementia of the Alzheimer's type, but the diagnosis of vascular dementia requires

Table 10.3–3
DSM-IV Diagnostic Criteria for Dementia of the Alzheimer's Type

A. The development of multiple cognitive deficits manifested by both
  (1) memory impairment (impaired ability to learn new information and to recall previously learned information)
  (2) one (or more) of the following cognitive disturbances:
    (a) aphasia (language disturbance)
    (b) apraxia (impaired ability to carry out motor activities despite intact motor function)
    (c) agnosia (failure to recognize or identify objects despite intact sensory function)
    (d) disturbance in executive functioning (ie, planning, organizing, sequencing, abstracting)

B. The cognitive deficits in criteria A1 and A2 each cause significant impairment in social or occupational functioning and represent a significant decline from a previous level of functioning.

C. The course is characterized by gradual onset and continuing cognitive decline.

D. The cognitive deficits in criteria A1 and A2 are not due to any of the following:
  (1) other central nervous system conditions that cause progressive deficits in memory and cognition (eg, cerebrovascular disease, Parkinson's disease, Huntington's disease, subdural hematoma, normal-pressure hydrocephalus, brain tumor)
  (2) systemic conditions that are known to cause dementia (eg, hypothyroidism, vitamin B_{12}, or folic acid deficiency, niacin deficiency, hypercalcemia, neurosyphilis, HIV infection)
  (3) substance-induced conditions

E. The deficits do not occur exclusively during the course of a delirium.

F. The disturbance is not better accounted for by another Axis I disorder (eg, major depressive disorder, schizophrenia).

Code based on type of onset and predominant features:
With early onset: if onset is at age 65 years or below
With delirium: if delirium is superimposed on the dementia
With delusions: if delusions are the predominant feature
With depressed mood: if depressed mood (including presentations that meet full symptom criteria for a major depressive episode) is the predominant feature. A separate diagnosis of mood disorder due to a general medical condition is not given.
Uncomplicated: if none of the above predominates in the current clinical presentation
With late onset: if onset is after age 65 years
With delirium: if delirium is superimposed on the dementia
With delusions: if delusions are the predominant feature
With depressed mood: if depressed mood (including presentations that meet full symptom criteria for a major depressive episode) is the predominant feature. A separate diagnosis of mood disorder due to a general medical condition is not given.
Uncomplicated: if none of the above predominates in the current clinical presentation

Specify if:
With behavioral disturbance
Coding note: Also code Alzheimer's disease on Axis III.

the presence of either clinical or laboratory evidence supportive of a vascular cause of the dementia.

Dementia Due to Other General Medical Conditions. DSM-IV lists six specific causes of dementia that can be coded directly: HIV disease, head trauma, Parkinson's disease, Huntington's disease, Pick's disease, and Creutzfeldt-Jakob disease. A seventh category allows clinicians to specify other nonpsychiatric medical conditions associated with dementia.

Substance-Induced Persisting Dementia. To facilitate the clinician's thinking about differential diagnosis, substance-induced persisting dementia is listed in two places in the DSM-IV, with the dementias and with the substance-re-

Table 10.3–4
DSM-IV Diagnostic Criteria for Vascular Dementia

A. The development of multiple cognitive deficits manifested by both
  (1) memory impairment (impaired ability to learn new information or to recall previously learned information)
  (2) one (or more) of the following cognitive disturbances:
    (a) aphasia (language disturbance)
    (b) apraxia (impaired ability to carry out motor activities despite intact motor function)
    (c) agnosia (failure to recognize or identify objects despite intact sensory function)
    (d) disturbance in executive functioning (ie, planning, organizing, sequencing, abstracting)

B. The cognitive deficits in criteria A1 and A2 each cause significant impairment in social or occupational functioning and represent a significant decline from a previous level of functioning.

C. Focal neurological signs and symptoms (eg, exaggeration of deep tendon reflexes, extensor plantar response, pseudobulbar palsy, gait abnormalities, weakness of an extremity) or laboratory evidence indicative of cerebrovascular disease (eg, multiple infarctions involving cortex and underlying white matter) that are judged to be etiologically related to the disturbance.

D. The deficits do not occur exclusively during the course of a delirium.

Code based on predominant features:
With delirium: if delirium is superimposed on the dementia
With delusions: if delusions are the predominant feature
With depressed mood: if depressed mood (including presentations that meet full symptom criteria for a major depressive episode) is the predominant feature. A separate diagnosis of mood disorder due to a general medical condition is not given.
Uncomplicated: if none of the above predominates in the current clinical presentation

Specify if:
With behavioral disturbance
Coding note: Also code cerebrovascular condition on Axis III.

Table 10.3–5
DSM-IV Diagnostic Criteria for Dementia Due to Other General Medical Conditions

A. The development of multiple cognitive deficits manifested by both
   (1) memory impairment (impaired ability to learn new information and to recall previously learned information)
   (2) one (or more) of the following cognitive disturbances:
      (a) aphasia (language disturbance)
      (b) apraxia (impaired ability to carry out motor activities despite intact motor function)
      (c) agnosia (failure to recognize or identify objects despite intact sensory function)
      (d) disturbance in executive functioning (ie, planning, organizing, sequencing, abstracting)

B. The cognitive deficits in criteria A1 and A2 each cause significant impairment in social or occupational functioning and represent a significant decline from a previous level of functioning.

C. There is evidence from the history, physical examination, or laboratory findings that the disturbance is the direct physiological consequence of one of the general medical conditions listed below.

D. The deficits do not occur exclusively during the course of a delirium.

Dementia due to HIV disease

Coding note: Also code HIV infection on Axis III.

Dementia due to head trauma

Coding note: Also code head injury on Axis III.

Dementia due to Parkinson's disease

Coding note: Also code Parkinson's disease on Axis III.

Dementia due to Huntington's disease

Coding note: Also code Huntington's disease on Axis III.

Dementia due to Pick's disease

Coding note: Also code Pick's disease on Axis III.

Dementia due to Creutzfeldt-Jakob disease

Coding note: Also code Creutzfeldt-Jakob disease on Axis III.

Dementia due to . . . [indicate the general medical condition not listed above]
For example, normal pressure hydrocephalus, hypothyroidism, brain tumor, vitamin B_{12} deficiency, intracranial radiation

Coding note: Also code the general medical condition on Axis III.

Table 10.3–6
DSM-IV Diagnostic Criteria for Substance-Induced Persisting Dementia

A. The development of multiple cognitive deficits manifested by both
   (1) memory impairment (inability to learn new information and to recall previously learned information)
   (2) one (or more) of the following cognitive disturbances:
      (a) aphasia (language disturbance)
      (b) apraxia (impaired ability to carry out motor activities despite intact motor function)
      (c) agnosia (failure to recognize or identify objects despite intact sensory function)
      (d) disturbance in executive functioning (ie, planning, organizing, sequencing, abstracting)

B. The cognitive deficits in criteria A1 and A2 each cause significant impairment in social or occupational functioning and represent a significant decline from a previous level of functioning.

C. The deficits do not occur exclusively during the course of a delirium and persist beyond the usual duration of substance intoxication or withdrawal.

D. There is evidence from the history, physical examination, or laboratory findings that the deficits are etiologically related to the persisting effects of substance use (eg, a drug of abuse, a medication).

Code: (Specific substance)-induced persisting dementia: (Alcohol; inhalant; sedative, hypnotic, or anxiolytic; other [or unknown] substance)

lated disorders. The specific substances that DSM-IV cross-references are alcohol; inhalant; sedative, hypnotic, or anxiolytic; and other or unknown substances.

ICD-10

Except for dementia due to head trauma, all the dementias included in DSM-IV are also in the 10th revision of *International Statistical Classification of Diseases and Related Health Problems* (ICD-10). ICD-10 also includes general criteria for dementia (Table 10.3–9). Dementia in Alzheimer's disease is divided into four types (Table 10.3–10). ICD-10 divides vascular dementia into nine types based on the nature of the vascular disease (Table 10.3–11). ICD-10 includes two residual categories—dementia in other diseases classified elsewhere (such as dementia in Pick's disease) (Table 10.3–12) and unspecified dementia (dementia with an unknown cause).

Clinical Diagnosis

The diagnosis of dementia is based on a patient's clinical examination, including a mental status examination, and on information from the patient's family, friends, and employers. Complaints of a personality change in a patient older than age 40 suggest that a diagnosis of dementia should be carefully considered.

Clinicians should note patients' complaints about intellectual impairment and forgetfulness as well as evidence of patients' evasion, denial, or rationalization aimed at concealing cognitive deficits. Excessive orderliness, social withdrawal, or a tendency to relate events in minute detail can be characteristic, and sudden outbursts of anger or sarcasm may occur. Patients' appearance and behavior should be observed. Lability of emotions, sloppy grooming, uninhibited remarks, silly jokes, or a dull, apathetic, or vacuous facial expression and manner suggest the presence of dementia, especially when coupled with memory impairment.

Table 10.3–7
DSM-IV Diagnostic Criteria for Dementia Due to Multiple Etiologies

A. The development of multiple cognitive deficits manifested by both
  (1) memory impairment (inability to learn new information and to recall previously learned information)
  (2) one (or more) of the following cognitive disturbances:
    (a) aphasia (language disturbance)
    (b) apraxia (impaired ability to carry out motor activities despite intact motor function)
    (c) agnosia (failure to recognize or identify objects despite intact sensory function)
    (d) disturbance in executive functioning (ie, planning, organizing, sequencing, abstracting)

B. The cognitive deficits in criteria A1 and A2 each cause significant impairment in social or occupational functioning and represent a significant decline from a previous level of functioning.

C. There is evidence from the history, physical examination, or laboratory findings that the disturbance has more than one etiology (eg, head trauma plus chronic alcohol use, dementia of the Alzheimer's type with the subsequent development of vascular dementia).

D. The deficits do not occur exclusively during the course of delirium.

Coding note: Use multiple codes based on specific dementias and specific etiologies, eg, dementia of the Alzheimer's type, with late onset uncomplicated; vascular dementia, uncomplicated.

Table 10.3–8
DSM-IV Diagnostic Criteria for Dementia Not Otherwise Specified

This category should be used to diagnose a dementia that does not meet criteria for any of the specific types described in this section.

An example is a clinical presentation of dementia for which there is insufficient evidence to establish a specific etiology.

CLINICAL FEATURES

At the initial stages of dementia, patients show fatigue, difficulty in sustaining mental performance, and a tendency to fail when a task is novel or complex or requires a shift in problem-solving strategy. The inability to perform tasks becomes increasingly severe and spreads to everyday tasks, such as grocery shopping, as the dementia progresses. Eventually, patients with dementia may require constant supervision and help to perform even the most basic tasks of daily living. The major defects in dementia involve orientation, memory, perception, intellectual functioning, and reasoning, and all these functions become progressively affected as the disease process advances. Affective and behavioral changes, such as defective control of impulses and lability of mood, are frequent, as are accentuations and alterations of premorbid personality traits.

Memory

Memory impairment is typically an early and prominent feature in dementia, especially in dementias involving the cortex, such as dementia of the Alzheimer's type. Early in the course of dementia, memory impairment is mild and is usually most marked for recent events; people forget telephone numbers, conversations, and events of the day. As the course of dementia progresses, memory impairment becomes severe, and only the earliest learned information (such as a person's place of birth) is retained.

Orientation

Inasmuch as memory is important for orientation to person, place, and time, orientation can be progressively affected during the course of a dementing illness. For example, patients with dementia may forget how to get back to their rooms after going to the bathroom. No matter how severe the disorientation seems, however, patients show no impairment in their level of consciousness.

Language Changes

Dementing processes that affect the cortex, primarily dementia of the Alzheimer's type and vascular dementia, can affect patients' language abilities. DSM-IV includes aphasia as one of the diagnostic criteria. The language difficulty may be characterized by a vague, stereotyped, imprecise, or circumstantial locution, and patients may also have difficulty in naming objects.

Personality Changes

Changes in the personality of a person with dementia are especially disturbing for the families of affected patients. Preexisting personality traits may be accentuated during the development of a dementia. Patients with dementia may also become introverted and may seem to be less concerned than they previously were about the effects of their behavior on others. People with dementia who have paranoid delusions are generally hostile to family members and caretakers. Patients with frontal and temporal involvement are likely to have marked personality changes and may be irritable and explosive.

Hallucinations and Delusions

An estimated 20 to 30 percent of patients with dementia, primarily patients with dementia of the Alzheimer's type, have hallucinations, and 30 to 40 percent have delusions, primarily of a paranoid or persecutory and unsystematized nature, although complex, sustained, and well-systematized delusions are also reported by these patients. Physical aggression and

Table 10.3–9
ICD-10 Diagnostic Criteria for for Dementia

G1. There is evidence of each of the following:

(1) A decline in memory, which is most evident in the learning of new information, although, in more severe cases, the recall of previously learned information may also be affected. The impairment applies to both verbal and nonverbal material. The decline should be objectively verified by obtaining a reliable history from an informant, supplemented, if possible, by neuropsychological tests or quantified cognitive assessments. The severity of the decline, with mild impairment as the threshold for diagnosis, should be assessed as follows:

Mild. The degree of memory loss is sufficient to interfere with everyday activities, though not so severe as to be incompatible with independent living. The main function affected is the learning of new material. For example, the individual has difficulty in registering, storing, and recalling elements involved in daily living, such as where belongings have been put, social arrangements, or information recently imparted by family members.

Moderate. The degree of memory loss represents a serious handicap to independent living. Only highly learned or very familiar material is retained. New information is retained only occasionally and very briefly. Individuals are unable to recall basic information about their own local geography, what they have recently been doing, or the names of familiar people.

Severe. The degree of memory loss is characterized by the complete inability to retain new information. Only fragments of previously learned information remain. The individual fails to recognize even close relatives.

(2) A decline in other cognitive abilities characterized by deterioration in judgment and thinking, such as planning and organizing, and in the general processing of information. Evidence for this should ideally be obtained from an informant and supplemented, if possible, by neuropsychological tests or quantified objective assessments. Deterioration from a previously higher level of performance should be established. The severity of the decline, with mild impairment as the threshold for diagnosis, should be assessed as follows:

Mild. The decline in cognitive abilities causes impaired performance in daily living, but not to a degree that makes the individual dependent on others. Complicated daily tasks or recreational activities cannot be undertaken.

Moderate. The decline in cognitive abilities makes the individual unable to function without the assistance of another in daily living, including shopping and handling money. Within the home, only simple chores can be performed. Activities are increasingly restricted and poorly sustained.

Severe. The decline is characterized by an absence, or virtual absence, of intelligible ideation.

The overall severity of the dementia is best expressed as the level of decline in memory *or* other cognitive abilities, whichever is the more severe (eg, mild decline in memory *and* moderate decline in cognitive abilities indicate a dementia of moderate severity).

G2. Awareness of the environment (ie, absence of clouding of consciousness [as defined in delirium, not induced by alcohol and other psychoactive substances, criterion A]) is preserved during a period sufficiently long to allow the unequivocal demonstration of the symptoms in criterion G1. When there are superimposed episodes of delirium, the diagnosis of dementia should be deferred.

G3. There is a decline in emotional control or motivation, or a change in social behavior manifest as at least one of the following:

(1) emotional lability
(2) irritability
(3) apathy
(4) coarsening of social behavior

G4. For a confident clinical diagnosis, the symptoms in criterion G1 should have been present for at least 6 months; if the period since the manifest onset is shorter, the diagnosis can be only tentative.

Comments

The diagnosis is further supported by evidence of damage to other higher cortical functions, such as aphasia, agnosia, apraxia.

Judgment about independent living or the development of dependence (upon others) should take account of the cultural expectation and context.

Dementia is specified here as having a minimum duration of 6 months to avoid confusion with reversible states with identical behavioral syndromes, such as traumatic subdural hemorrhage, normal pressure hydrocephalus, and diffuse or focal brain injury.

A fifth character may be used to indicate the presence of additional symptoms: Dementia in Alzheimer's disease, vascular dementia, dementia in diseases classified elsewhere, unspecified dementia, as follows:

Without additional symptoms
With other symptoms, predominantly delusional
With other symptoms, predominantly hallucinatory
With other symptoms, predominantly depressive
With other mixed symptoms

A sixth character may be used to indicate the severity of the dementia:

Mild
Moderate
Severe

As mentioned above, the overall severity of the dementia depends on the level of memory *or* intellectual impairment, whichever is the more severe.

Table 10.3–10
ICD-10 Diagnostic Criteria for Dementia in Alzheimer's Disease

A. The general criteria for dementia G1–G4 must be met.

B. There is no evidence from the history, physical examination, or special investigations for any other possible cause of dementia (eg, cerebrovascular disease, HIV disease, Parkinson's disease, Huntington's disease, normal pressure hydrocephalus), a systemic disorder (eg, hypothyroidism, vitamin B_{12} or folic acid deficiency, hypercalcemia), or alcohol or drug abuse.

Comments

The diagnosis is confirmed by postmortem evidence of neurofibrillary tangles and neuritic plaques in excess of those found in normal aging of the brain.

The following features support the diagnosis, but are not necessary elements: involvement of cortical functions as evidenced by aphasia, agnosia or apraxia; decrease of motivation and drive, leading to apathy and lack of spontaneity; irritability and disinhibition of social behavior; evidence from special investigations that there is cerebral atrophy, particularly if this can be shown to be increasing over time. In severe cases there may be Parkinson-like extrapyramidal changes, logoclonia, and epileptic fits.

Specification of features for possible subtypes

Because of the possibility that subtypes exist, it is recommended that the following characteristics be ascertained as a basis for a further classification: age at onset; rate of progression; configuration of the clinical features, particularly the relative prominence (or lack) of temporal, parietal, or frontal lobe signs; any neuropathological or neurochemical abnormalities, and their pattern.

The division of Alzheimer's disease into subtypes can at present be accomplished in two ways: first by taking only the age of onset and labeling the disease as either early or late, with an approximate cut-off point at 65 years; or second, by assessing how well the individual conforms to one of the two putative syndromes, early- or late-onset type.

It should be noted that a sharp distinction between early- and late-onset types is unlikely. Early-onset type may occur in late life, just as late-onset type may occasionally have an onset before the age of 65. The following criteria may be used to differentiate dementia in Alzheimer's disease with early and late onset, but it should be remembered that the status of this subdivision is still controversial.

Dementia in Alzheimer's diseases with early onset

1. The criteria for dementia in Alzheimer's disease must be met, and the age at onset must be below 65 years.
2. In addition, at least one of the following requirements must be met:
   (a) evidence of a relatively rapid onset and progression;
   (b) in addition to memory impairment, there must be aphasia (amnesic or sensory), agraphia, alexia, acalculia, or apraxia (indicating the presence of temporal, parietal, and/or frontal lobe involvement).

Dementia in Alzheimer's disease with late onset

1. The criteria for dementia in Alzheimer's disease must be met and the age at onset must be 65 years or more.
2. In addition, at least one of the following requirements must be met:
   (a) evidence of a very slow, gradual onset and progression (the rate of the latter may be known only retrospectively after a course of 3 years or more);
   (b) predominance of memory impairment G1(1), over intellectual impairment G1(2) (see general criteria for dementia).

Dementia in Alzheimer's disease, atypical or mixed type

This term and code should be used for dementias that have important atypical features or that fulfill criteria for both early- and late-onset types of Alzheimer's disease. Mixed Alzheimer's and vascular dementia are also included here.

Dementia in Alzheimer's disease, unspecified

other forms of violence are common in demented patients who also have psychotic symptoms.

Other Signs and Symptoms

Psychiatric. In addition to psychosis and personality changes, depression and anxiety are major symptoms in an estimated 40 to 50 percent of patients with dementia, although the full syndrome of depressive disorder may be present in only 10 to 20 percent. Patients with dementia may also exhibit pathological laughter or crying—that is, extremes of emotions—with no apparent provocation.

Neurological. In addition to the aphasias in patients with dementia, apraxias and agnosias are common, and they are included as potential diagnostic criteria in DSM-IV. Other neurological signs that can be associated with dementia are seizures, seen in approximately 10 percent of patients with dementia of the Alzheimer's type and in 20 percent of patients with vascular dementia, and atypical neurological presentations, such as nondominant parietal lobe syndromes. Primitive reflexes—such as the grasp, snout, suck, tonic-foot, and palmomental reflexes—may be present on neurological examination, and myoclonic jerks are present in 5 to 10 percent of patients.

Patients with vascular dementia may have additional neurological symptoms, such as headaches, dizziness, faintness, weakness, focal neurological signs, and sleep disturbances, possibly attributable to the location of the cerebrovascular disease. Pseudobulbar palsy, dysarthria, and dysphagia are also more common in vascular dementia than in other dementing conditions.

Catastrophic Reaction. Patients with dementia also exhibit a reduced ability to apply what Kurt Goldstein called the abstract attitude. Patients have difficulty in generalizing from a single instance, in forming concepts, and in grasping similarities and differences among concepts. Furthermore, the ability to solve problems, to reason logically, and to make sound judgments is compromised. Goldstein also described a catastrophic reaction, marked by agitation secondary to the subjective awareness of intellectual deficits under stressful cir-

Table 10.3–11
ICD-10 Diagnostic Criteria for Vascular Dementia

G1. The general criteria for dementia (G1–G4) must be met.

G2. Deficits in higher cognitive functions are unevenly distributed, with some functions affected and others relatively spared. Thus, memory may be markedly affected while thinking, reasoning, and information processing may show only mild decline.

G3. There is clinical evidence of focal brain damage, manifest as at least one of the following:
(1) unilateral spastic weakness of the limbs;
(2) unilaterally increased tendon reflexes;
(3) extensor plantar response;
(4) pseudobulbar palsy.

G4. There is evidence from the history, examination, or tests of a significant cerebrovascular disease, which may reasonably be judged to be etiologically related to the dementia (eg, a history of stroke, evidence of cerebral infarction).

The following criteria may be used to differentiate subtypes of vascular dementia, but it should be remembered that the usefulness of this subdivision may not be generally accepted.

Vascular dementia of acute onset

A. The general criteria for vascular dementia must be met.

B. The dementia develops rapidly (ie, usually within 1 month, but within no longer than 3 months) after a succession of strokes or (rarely) after a single large infarction.

Multi-infarct dementia

A. The general criteria for vascular dementia must be met.

B. The onset of the dementia is gradual (ie, within 3–6 months), following a number of minor ischemic episodes.

Comments

It is presumed that there is an accumulation of infarcts in the cerebral parenchyma. Between the ischemic episodes there may be periods of actual clinical improvement.

Subcortical vascular dementia

A. The general criteria for vascular dementia must be met.

B. There is a history of hypertension.

C. There is evidence from clinical examination and special investigations of vascular disease located in the deep white matter of the cerebral hemispheres, with preservation of the cerebral cortex.

Mixed cortical and subcortical vascular dementia

Mixed cortical and subcortical components of the vascular dementia may be suspected from the clinical features, the results of investigations (including autopsy), or both.

Other vascular dementia

Vascular dementia, unspecified

Reprinted with permission from World Health Organization: *The ICD-10 Classification of Mental and Behavioural Disorders: Diagnostic Criteria for Research.* Copyright, World Health Organization, Geneva, 1993.

cumstances. People usually attempt to compensate for defects by using strategies to avoid demonstrating failures in intellectual performance; they may change the subject, make jokes, or otherwise divert the interviewer. Lack of judgment and poor impulse control commonly appear, particularly in dementias that primarily affect the frontal lobes. Examples of these impairments include coarse language, inappropriate jokes, the neglect of personal appearance and hygiene, and a general disregard for the conventional rules of social conduct.

A 61-year-old, high-school science department head who was an experienced and enthusiastic camper and hiker became extremely fearful while on a trek in the mountains. Gradually, over the next few months, he lost interest in his usual hobbies. Formerly a voracious reader, he stopped reading. He had difficulty doing computations and made gross errors in home financial management. On several occasions he became lost while driving in areas that were formerly familiar to him. He began to write notes to himself so that he would not forget to do errands. Very abruptly, and in uncharacteristic fashion, he decided to retire from work, without discussing his plans with his wife. Intellectual deterioration gradually progressed. He spent most of the day piling miscellaneous objects in one place and then transporting them to another spot in the house. He became stubborn and querulous. Eventually he required assistance in shaving and dressing.

When examined 6 years after the first symptoms had developed, the patient was alert and cooperative. He was disoriented with respect to place and time. He could not recall the names of four or five objects after a 5-minute interval of distraction. He could not remember the names of his college and graduate school or the subject in which he had majored. He could describe his job by title only. In 1978 he thought that Kennedy was president of the United States. He did not know Stalin's nationality. His speech was fluent and well articulated, but he had considerable difficulty finding words and used many long, essentially meaningless phrases. He called a cup a vase, and identified the rims of glasses as "the holders." He did simple calculations poorly. He could not copy a cube or draw a house. His interpretation of proverbs was concrete, and he had no insight into the nature of his disturbance.

An elementary neurological examination revealed nothing abnormal, and routine laboratory tests were also negative. A computed tomography scan, however, showed marked cortical atrophy.

DISCUSSION

This patient has memory impairment, impairment in abstract thinking (concrete interpretation of proverbs), and other disturbances in higher cortical functioning (aphasia). These signs of global cognitive impairment, severe enough to interfere significantly with work and social activities and not occurring exclusively during the course of delirium, indicate a dementia. There is an insidious onset, beginning before age 65, with a generally progressive, deteriorating course and no specific cause. Thus the diagnosis is dementia of the Alzheimer type, with early onset. The following subtypes are provided to allow the clinician to indicate a specific feature that sometimes predominates in cases of dementia: delirium, delusions, and depressed mood. Because none of these predominate in this case, the subtype uncomplicated is used.

Because some degree of supervision is necessary, the

Table 10.3–12
ICD-10 Diagnostic Criteria for Dementia in Other Diseases Classified Elsewhere

Dementia in Pick's disease

A. The general criteria for dementia (G1–G4) must be met.

B. Onset is slow with steady deterioration.

C. Predominance of frontal lobe involvement is evidenced by two or more of the following:
(1) emotional blunting;
(2) coarsening of social behavior;
(3) disinhibition;
(4) apathy or restlessness;
(5) aphasia.

D. In the early stages, memory and parietal lobe functions are relatively preserved.

Dementia in Creutzfeldt–Jakob disease

A. The general criteria for dementia (G1–G4) must be met.

B. There is very rapid progression of the dementia, with disintegration of virtually all higher cerebral functions.

C. One or more of the following types of neurological symptoms and signs emerge, usually after or simultaneously with the dementia:
(1) pyramidal symptoms;
(2) extrapyramidal symptoms;
(3) cerebellar symptoms;
(4) aphasia;
(5) visual impairment.

Comments

An akinetic and mute state is the typical terminal stage. An amyotrophic variant may be seen, where the neurological signs precede the onset of the dementia. A characteristic electroencephalogram (periodic spikes against a slow and low-voltage background), if present in association with the above clinical signs, increases the probability of the diagnosis. However, the diagnosis can be confirmed only by neuropathological examination (neuronal loss, astrocytosis, and spongiform changes). Because of the risk of infection, this should be carried out only under special protective conditions.

Dementia in Huntington's disease

A. The general criteria for dementia (G1–G4) must be met.

B. Subcortical functions are affected first and dominate the picture of dementia throughout; subcortical involvement is manifested by slowness of thinking or movement and personality alteration with apathy or depression.

C. There are involuntary choreiform movements, typically of the face, hands, or shoulders, or in the gait. The patient may attempt to conceal them by converting them into a voluntary action.

D. There is a history of Huntington's disease in one parent or a sibling, or a family history that suggests the disorder.

E. There are no clinical features that otherwise account for the abnormal movements.

Comments

In addition to involuntary choreiform movements, there may be development of extrapyramidal rigidity or of spasticity with pyramidal signs.

Dementia in Parkinson's disease

A. The general criteria for dementia (G1–G4) must be met.

B. A diagnosis of Parkinson's disease has been established.

C. None of the cognitive impairment is attributable to anti-parkinsonian medication.

D. There is no evidence from the history, physical examination, or special investigations for any other possible cause of dementia, including other forms of brain disease, damage, or dysfunction (eg, cerebrovascular disease, HIV disease, Huntington's disease, normal pressure hydrocephalus), a systemic disorder (eg, hypothyroidism, vitamin B_{12} or folic acid deficiency, hypercalcemia), or alcohol or drug abuse.

If criteria are also fulfilled for dementia in Alzheimer's disease with late onset, that category should be used in combination with Parkinson's disease.

Dementia in human immunodeficiency virus (HIV) disease

A. The general criteria for dementia (G1–G4) must be met.

B. A diagnosis of HIV infection has been established.

C. There is no evidence from the history, physical examination, or special investigations for any other possible cause of dementia, including other forms of brain disease, damage, or dysfunction (eg, Alzheimer's disease, cerebrovascular disease, Parkinson's disease, Huntington's disease, normal pressure hydrocephalus), a systemic disorder (e.g. hypothyroidism, vitamin B_{12} or folic acid deficiency, hypercalcemia), or alcohol or drug abuse.

Dementia in other specified diseases classified elsewhere

Dementia can occur as a manifestation or consequence of a variety of cerebral and somatic conditions. To specify the etiology, the ICD-10 code for the underlying condition should be added.

severity of the dementia is noted as moderate. We note the presence of the neurological disease, Alzheimer's disease, on Axis III.

FOLLOW-UP

This man's condition progressed, and he required admission to the hospital within a year of his initial assessment. Over the next year, he became essentially mute, and mental status testing was virtually impossible. He had a tendency to pace back and forth constantly in the ward; on one occasion he managed to get out of the locked ward and was found some miles from the hospital.

His retained physical appearance was in striking contrast to his devastated intellectual capacities for a long time, but eventually he began to lose weight, took to bed, and developed contractures (permanent muscular contractions).

He died at age 72 of pneumonia. Autopsy revealed cerebral atrophy and, microscopically, the plaques and tangles diagnostic of Alzheimer's disease. (From *DSM-IV Casebook.*)

Sundowner Syndrome. Sundowner syndrome is characterized by drowsiness, confusion, ataxia, and accidental falls. It occurs in older people who are overly sedated and in patients with dementia who react adversely to even a small dose of a psychoactive drug. The syndrome also occurs in demented patients when external stimuli, such as light and interpersonal orienting cues, are diminished. It most commonly occurs as a result of benzodiazepines.

DIFFERENTIAL DIAGNOSIS

A comprehensive laboratory workup must be performed when evaluating a patient with dementia (Table 10.3–13). The purposes of the workup are to detect reversible causes of dementia and to provide the patient and family with a definitive diagnosis. The continued improvements in brain imaging techniques, particularly MRI, have, in some cases, made the differentiation between dementia of the Alzheimer's type and vascular dementia somewhat more straightforward than in the past. An active area of research is the use of single photon emission computed tomography (SPECT) to detect patterns of brain metabolism in various types of dementia; the use of SPECT images may soon help in the clinical differential diagnosis of dementing illnesses.

Table 10.3–13
Comprehensive Workup of Dementia

- Physical examination including thorough neurological examination
- Vital signs
- Mental status examination
- Mini-Mental State Examination (MMSE)
- Review of medications and drug levels
- Blood and urine screens for alcohol, drugs, and heavy metals[a]
- Physiological workup
  - Serum electrolytes/glucose/Ca^{2+}, Mg^{2+}
  - Liver, renal function tests
  - SMA-12 or equivalent serum chemistry profile
  - Urinalysis
  - Complete blood cell count with differential cell type count
  - Thyroid function tests (including TSH level)
  - RPR (serum screen)
  - FTA-ABS (if CNS disease is suspected)
  - Serum B_{12}
  - Folate levels
  - Urine corticosteroids[a]
  - Erythrocyte sedimentation rate (Westergren)
  - Antinuclear antibody[a] (ANA), C_3C_4, Anti-DS DNA[a]
  - Arterial blood gases[a]
  - HIV screen[a,b]
  - Urine porphobilinogens[a]
- Chest radiograph
- Electrocardiogram
- Neurological workup
  - CT or MRI scan of head[a]
  - SPECT[b]
  - Lumbar puncture[a]
  - EEG[a]
- Neuropsychological testing[d]

Adapted with permission from Stoudemire A, Thompson TL: Recognizing and treating dementia. Geriatrics *36*: 112, 1981.
[a] All indicated by history and physical examination.
[b] Requires special consent and counseling.
[c] May detect cerebral blood flow perfusion deficits.
[d] May be useful in differentiating dementia from other neuropsychiatric syndromes if it cannot be done clinically.

Dementia of the Alzheimer's Type versus Vascular Dementia

Classically, vascular dementia has been distinguished from dementia of the Alzheimer's type by the decremental deterioration that may accompany cerebrovascular disease over time. Although the discrete, stepwise deterioration may not be apparent in all cases, focal neurological symptoms are more common in vascular dementia than in dementia of the Alzheimer's type, as are the standard risk factors for cerebrovascular disease.

Vascular Dementia versus Transient Ischemic Attacks (TIAs)

TIAs are brief episodes of focal neurological dysfunction lasting less than 24 hours (usually 5 to 15 minutes). Although a variety of mechanisms may be responsible, the episodes are frequently the result of microembolization from a proximal intracranial arterial lesion that produces transient brain ischemia, and the episodes usually resolve without significant pathological alteration of the parenchymal tissue. Approximately one third of people whose TIAs were untreated experience a brain infarction later; therefore, recognition of TIAs is an important clinical strategy to prevent brain infarction.

Clinicians should distinguish episodes involving the vertebrobasilar system from those involving the carotid arterial system. In general, symptoms of vertebrobasilar disease reflect a transient functional disturbance in either the brain stem or the occipital lobe; carotid distribution symptoms reflect unilateral retinal or hemispheric abnormality. Anticoagulant therapy, antiplatelet agglutinating drugs such as acetylsalicylic acid (aspirin), and extracranial and intracranial reconstructive vascular surgery have been reported to be effective in reducing the risk of infarction in patients with transient ischemic attacks.

Delirium

Differentiating between delirium and dementia can be more difficult than the DSM-IV classification indicates. In general, delirium is distinguished by rapid onset, brief duration, fluctuation of cognitive impairment during the course of the day, nocturnal exacerbation of symptoms, marked disturbance of the sleep–wake cycle, and prominent disturbances in attention and perception.

Depression

Some patients with depression have symptoms of cognitive impairment difficult to distinguish from symptoms of dementia. The clinical picture is sometimes referred to as pseudodementia, although the term *depression-related cognitive dysfunction* is preferable and more descriptive (Table 10.3–14). Patients with depression-related cognitive dysfunction generally have prominent depressive symptoms, have more insight into their symptoms than do demented patients, and often have a past history of depressive episodes.

Table 10.3–14
Major Clinical Features Differentiating Pseudodementia from Dementia

Pseudodementia	Dementia
Clinical course and history	
Family always aware of dysfunction and its severity	Family often unaware of dysfunction and its severity
Onset can be dated with some precision	Onset can be dated only within broad limits
Symptoms of short duration before medical help is sought	Symptoms usually of long duration before medical help is sought
Rapid progression of symptoms after onset	Slow progression of symptoms throughout course
History of previous psychiatric dysfunction common	History of previous psychiatric dysfunction unusual
Complaints and clinical behavior	
Patients usually complain much of cognitive loss	Patients usually complain little of cognitive loss
Patients' complaints of cognitive dysfunction usually detailed	Patients' complaints of cognitive dysfunction usually vague
Patients emphasize disability	Patients conceal disability
Patients highlight failures	Patients delight in accomplishments, however trivial
Patients make little effort to perform even simple tasks	Patients struggle to perform tasks
	Patients rely on notes, calendars, etc., to keep up
Patients usually communicate strong sense of distress	Patients often appear unconcerned
Affective change often pervasive	Affect labile and shallow
Loss of social skills often early and prominent	Social skills often retained
Behavior often incongruent with severity of cognitive dysfunction	Behavior usually compatible with severity of cognitive dysfunction
Nocturnal accentuation of dysfunction uncommon	Nocturnal accentuation of dysfunction common
Clinical features related to memory, cognitive, and intellectual dysfunctions	
Attention and concentration often well preserved	Attention and concentration usually faulty
"Don't know" answers typical	Near-miss answers frequent
On tests of orientation, patients often give "don't know" answers	On tests of orientation, patients often mistake unusual for usual
Memory loss for recent and remote events usually severe	Memory loss for recent events usually more severe than for remote events
Memory gaps for specific periods or events common	Memory gaps for specific periods unusual[a]
Marked variability in performance on tasks of similar difficulty	Consistently poor performance on tasks of similar difficulty

Reprinted with permission from Wells CE: Pseudodementia. Am J Psychiatry *36*: 898, 1979.
[a] Except when caused by delirium, trauma, seizures, etc.

Factitious Disorder

Persons who attempt to simulate memory loss, as in factitious disorder, do so in an erratic and inconsistent manner. In true dementia, memory for time and place is lost before memory for person, and recent memory is lost before remote memory.

Schizophrenia

Although schizophrenia may be associated with some degree of acquired intellectual impairment, its symptoms are much less severe than are the related symptoms of psychosis and thought disorder seen in dementia.

Normal Aging

Aging is not necessarily associated with any significant cognitive decline, but a minor degree of memory problems can occur as a normal part of aging. These normal occurrences are sometimes referred to as benign senescent forgetfulness or age-associated memory impairment. They are distinguished from dementia by their minor severity and by the fact that they do not significantly interfere with a person's social or occupational behavior.

Other Disorders

Mental retardation does not include memory impairment and occurs in childhood. Amnestic disorder is characterized by circumscribed loss of memory and no deterioration. Major depression in which there is impaired memory responds to medication. Malingering and pituitary disorder must be ruled out but are unlikely.

COURSE AND PROGNOSIS

The classic course of dementia is an onset in a patient's 50s or 60s, with gradual deterioration over 5 to 10 years, leading eventually to death. The age of onset and the rapidity of deterioration vary among different types of dementia and within individual diagnostic categories. The mean survival expectation for patients with dementia of the Alzheimer's type is approximately 8 years, with a range of 1 to 20 years. Data suggest that people with an early onset of dementia or with a family history of dementia are likely to have a rapid course. Once dementia is diagnosed, patients must undergo a complete medical and neurological workup, because 10 to 15 percent of all patients with dementia have a potentially reversible condition if treatment is initiated before permanent brain damage occurs.

The most common course of dementia begins with a number of subtle signs that may, at first, be ignored by both the patient and the people closest to the patient. A gradual onset of symptoms is most commonly associated with dementia of the Alzheimer's type, vascular dementia, endocrinopathies, brain tumors, and metabolic disorders. Conversely, the onset of dementia resulting from head trauma, cardiac arrest with cerebral hypoxia, or encephalitis may be sudden. Although the symptoms of the early phase of dementia are subtle, the symptoms become conspicuous as the dementia progresses, and family members may then bring a patient to a physician's attention. People with dementia may be sensitive to the use of benzodiazepines or alcohol, which can precipitate agitated, aggressive, or psychotic behavior. In the terminal stages of dementia, patients become empty shells of their former selves—profoundly disoriented, incoherent, amnestic, and incontinent of urine and feces.

With psychosocial and pharmacological treatments and possibly because of self-healing properties of the brain, the symptoms of dementia may progress slowly for a time or may even recede somewhat. The regression of symptoms is certainly a possibility in reversible dementias (dementias caused by hypothyroidism, normal pressure hydrocephalus, and brain tumors) once treatment is initiated. The course of the dementia varies from a steady progression (commonly seen with dementia of the Alzheimer's type) to an incrementally worsening dementia (commonly seen with vascular dementia) to a stable dementia (as may be seen in dementia related to head trauma).

Psychosocial Determinants

The severity and course of dementia can be affected by psychosocial factors. The greater a person's premorbid intelligence and education, the better the ability to compensate for intellectual deficits. People who have a rapid onset of dementia use fewer defenses than do those who experience an insidious onset. Anxiety and depression may intensify and aggravate the symptoms. Pseudodementia occurs in depressed people who complain of impaired memory but are, in fact, suffering from a depressive disorder. When the depression is treated, the cognitive defects disappear.

Dementia of the Alzheimer's Type

Dementia of the Alzheimer's type may begin at any age. In DSM-IV, the age of onset is specified and classified as early onset (at age 65 or younger) or as late (after age 65). Approximately half of all patients with dementia of the Alzheimer's type experience their first symptoms between the ages of 65 and 70. The course of the disorder is characteristically one of gradual decline over 8 to 10 years, although the course may be much more rapid or much more gradual. Once the symptoms of dementia have become severe, death often follows in a short time.

Vascular Dementia

In contrast to the onset of dementia of the Alzheimer's type, the onset of vascular dementia is likely to be sudden. Also in contrast to dementia of the Alzheimer's type, there is a greater preservation of personality in patients with vascular dementia. The course of vascular dementia has previously been described as stepwise and patchy, but refinements in brain imaging techniques have revealed that patients with vascular dementia can have clinical courses that are as gradual and smooth as the clinical course characteristically associated with dementia of the Alzheimer's type. About 8 percent of persons who have a stroke after age 60 develop dementia within 1 year.

TREATMENT

Some cases of dementia are regarded as treatable because the dysfunctional brain tissue may retain the capacity for recovery if treatment is timely. A complete medical history, physical examination, and laboratory tests, including appropriate brain imaging, should be undertaken as soon as the diagnosis is suspected (see Table 10.3–13). If a patient is suffering from a treatable cause of dementia, therapy is directed toward treating the underlying disorder.

The general treatment approach to patients with dementia is to provide supportive medical care, emotional support for the patients and their families, and pharmacological treatment for specific symptoms, including disruptive behavior. The maintenance of a patient's physical health, a supportive environment, and symptomatic psychopharmacological treatment are indicated in the treatment of most types of dementia. Symptomatic treatment also includes the maintenance of a nutritious diet, proper exercise, recreational and activity therapies, attention to visual and auditory problems, and treatment of associated medical problems, such as urinary tract infections, decubitus ulcers, and cardiopulmonary dysfunction. Particular attention must be provided to caretakers and family members who deal with frustration, grief, and psychological burnout as they care for a patient over a long period.

When the diagnosis of vascular dementia is made, risk factors contributing to cerebrovascular disease should be identified and therapeutically addressed. These factors include hypertension, hyperlipidemia, obesity, cardiac disease, diabetes, and alcohol dependence. Patients who smoke should be encouraged to stop; smoking cessation is associated with improved cerebral perfusion and cognitive functioning. A summary of treatment approaches is given in Table 10.3–15.

Pharmacotherapy

Currently Available Treatments. Clinicians may prescribe benzodiazepines for insomnia and anxiety, antidepressants for depression, and antipsychotic drugs for delusions and hallucinations, but they should be aware of possible idiosyncratic drug effects in older people (such as paradoxical excitement, confusion, and increased sedation). In general, drugs with high anticholinergic activity should be avoided, although some data indicate that thioridazine (Mellaril), which does have high anticholinergic activity, may be an especially effective drug in controlling behavior in demented patients when given in low dosages. Short-acting benzodiazepines in small dosages are the preferred anxiolytic and sedative medication for demented patients. In addition, zolpidem (Ambien) may also be used for sedative purposes.

Tacrine has been approved by the Food and Drug Administration as a treatment for Alzheimer's disease. The drug is a

Table 10.3–15
Practice Guideline for Treatment of Dementia of Alzheimer's Type

A. General principles
   1. Identify and treat general medical conditions (eg, thyroid, B_{12}, tertiary syphilis, HIV).
   2. See patient on regular basis: once a week when starting therapy, once a month thereafter.
   3. Evaluate for suicidal potential or self-harm (eg, falling or wandering).
   4. Restrict driving.
   5. Educate family about disease, financial decisions, living wills, support groups, community organizations.

B. Psychosocial treatment
   1. Stimulation-oriented treatment: recreational activity, art therapy, dance therapy, pet therapy.
   2. Reminiscence therapy: talking about past can improve mood.
   3. Cognitive or reality therapy: correct cognitive errors (may cause frustration).

C. Drug therapy for cognitive defects
   1. Cholinesterase inhibitors
      a) Tacrine: dosages over 120 mg/day effective in decreasing cognitive defects in 60 percent of patients; risk of liver damage high; side effects prevent compliance in 20 percent of patients.
      b) Donepezil (Aricept): dosages of 5–10 mg/day effective in increasing cognitive performance; less severe side effects than tacrine.
   2. Vitamin E: dosages of 200–2000 IU/day decrease rate of functional decline.
   3. Selegiline
      a) MAO_B inhibitor that delays cognitive deterioration; 5–10 mg/day.
      b) Major side effect is orthostatic hypotension; no food limitations as in other MAOIs.
   4. Ergot mesylates (Hydergine): improves behavior, not cognition, but of questionable efficacy; routine use not recommended.

D. Drug therapy for psychosis and agitation
   1. Antipsychotic medication (no evidence that one is superior to another)
      a) Risperidone: less extrapyramidal effects; use low doses 0.5–2.0 mg/day.
      b) Clozapine: risk of agranulocytosis requires regular WBC counts; efficacy similar to other antipsychotics; sertindole and quetiapine to be released in future may also be of use.
   2. Benzodiazepines: lorazepam (0.5–1.0 mg every 4–6 hr) and oxazepam (7.5–15.0 mg 4 times per day) preferred to diazepam because they are less likely to produce sedation and falls (sundowner syndrome).
   3. Anticonvulsant agents: carbamazepine (100 mg 2–4 times per day); valproate (150–250 mg 2–3 times per day) reported to decrease agitation.
   4. Hormones: antiandrogens (medroxyprogesterone) may be useful to treat disinhibited sexual behavior in men.

E. Drugs used to treat depression
   1. SSRIs: first-line treatment because of few adverse side effects; avoid amitriptyline and imipramine because of anticholinergic effects that the elderly cannot tolerate.
   2. Trazodone: used at bedtime (25–100 mg at bedtime) for agitated depression and insomnia.
   3. Bupropion and venlafaxine: used in apathetic patients because of stimulating effects.
   4. MAOIs: use only if other drugs fail; observe caution with tryptamine-containing foods to prevent hypertensive crisis.
   5. Psychostimulants: amphetamines (2.5–5 mg every 4–6 hours) useful in patients with medical illness and depression.
   6. Bromocriptine and amantadine: may improve apathy.
   7. Buspirone: used for agitation and anxiety associated with depression (total dose 5–60 mg/day).

F. ECT
   1. May be useful in severe depression associated with dementia that does not respond to drugs.
   2. Rule out pseudodementia.
   3. Given 2 times per week; less memory loss with unilateral than with bilateral electrode placement.

G. Treatment of sleep disturbances
   1. Pay attention to sleep hygiene and habits.
   2. Use drugs sparingly
      a) Zolpidem: fast-acting, nonbenzodiazepine hypnotic (5 mg at bedtime).
      b) Benzodiazepines or sedative-hypnotics such as chloral hydrate or barbiturates not recommended because of risk of daytime sedation and sundowner syndrome.

H. Other drugs: Aspirin, NSAIDs, melatonin, ginkgo biloba (botanical herb), chelating agents of no demonstrated use; estrogen replacement therapy can delay onset of dementia in postmenopausal women.

I. Treatment plan
   1. Mild impairment: borderline functioning in several areas but definite impairment in none; able to do simple tasks.
      a) Provide orientation aids (calendars, TV).
      b) Restrict driving.
      c) Provide support groups for caregivers.
      d) Trial of tacrine or donepezil.
      e) Evaluate for depression and suicidality.
      f) Make arrangements for wills, advance directives, power of attorney, and general estate matters.
   2. Moderate impairment: unable to do simple tasks, eg, food preparation; require assistance with tasks of daily living.
      a) Risk of self-harm from accidents, falls, fires.
      b) Prevent driving at all costs, eg, take away keys, immobilize car.
      c) Continue use of tacrine or donepezil if response noted; vitamin E may delay progression.
      d) Treat agitation, depression, and psychotic symptoms if present.
   3. Severe and profound impairment: total incapacitation with complete reliance on caregivers for tasks of daily living.
      a) Patient needs help with dressing, bathing, feeding; ensure that hygiene is maintained.
      b) Medications for dementia (eg, tacrine) of no use in this stage.
      c) Treat medical conditions vigorously, especially decubitus ulcers.
      d) Long-term facility (including hospice) necessary if caregivers not available.
      e) 30 percent of family caregivers develop depressive disorders secondary to stress; use of home health aides and day care to relieve stress in caregivers is essential.

Adapted from American Psychiatric Association: Practice guideline for the treatment of patients with Alzheimer's disease and other dementias of late life. Am J Psychiatry *154* (Suppl, 5): 1, 1997.

MAO_B, monoamine oxidase type B; MAOIs, monoamine oxidase inhibitors; WBC, white blood cell; SSRIs, serotonin-specific reuptake inhibitors; ECT, electroconvulsive therapy; NSAIDs, nonsteroidal anti-inflammatory drugs.

moderately long-acting inhibitor of cholinesterase activity, and well-controlled trials have shown a clinically significant improvement in 20 to 25 percent of patients who take it. Because of the cholinomimetic activity of the drug, some patients are not able to tolerate the side effects. Others must discontinue the drug because of elevations in liver enzymes. A new drug, donepezil (Aricept), also improves cognition and has fewer adverse effects. Neither drug, however, prevents progressive neuronal degeneration. (Chapter 35, Section 35.3–1 presents a detailed discussion of drugs used to treat the cognitive deficits in dementia.)

Experimental Treatment Approaches. A wide variety of experimental pharmacological treatments for the cognitive decline of dementia are being developed by pharmaceutical companies. Many of the compounds are designed to enhance the functioning of the cholinergic neurotransmitter system. Some drugs that are being tested for cognitive-enhancing activity include general cerebral metabolic enhancers, calcium channel blockers, and serotonergic agents. Recent studies have demonstrated that vitamin E (1,000 mg a day) or selegiline (Eldepryl) (10 mg a day) may slow the advance of this disease.

Psychotherapy

The deterioration of mental faculties has significant psychological meaning for patients with dementia. The experience of a person's having continuity over time depends on memory. Recent memory is lost before remote memory in most cases of dementia, and many patients are highly distressed by clearly recalling how they used to function while observing their obvious deterioration. At the most fundamental level, the self is a product of brain functioning. Patients' identities begin to fade as the illness progresses, and they can recall less and less of their past. Emotional reactions ranging from depression to severe anxiety to catastrophic terror can stem from the realization that the sense of self is disappearing.

Patients often benefit from a supportive and educational psychotherapy in which the nature and course of their illness are clearly explained. They may also benefit from assistance in grieving and accepting the extent of their disability and from attention to self-esteem issues. Any areas of intact functioning should be maximized by helping patients identify activities in which successful functioning is possible. A psychodynamic assessment of defective ego functions and cognitive limitations can also be useful. Clinicians can assist patients to find ways to deal with the defective ego functions, such as keeping calendars for orientation problems, making schedules to help structure activities, and taking notes for memory problems.

Psychodynamic interventions with family members of patients with dementia may be of great assistance. Those who take care of a patient struggle with feelings of guilt, grief, anger, and exhaustion as they watch a family member gradually deteriorate. A common problem that develops among caregivers involves their self-sacrifice in caring for a patient. The gradually developing resentment from this self-sacrifice is often suppressed because of the guilt feelings it produces. Clinicians can help caregivers understand the complex mixture of feelings associated with seeing a loved one decline and can provide understanding as well as permission to express these feelings. Clinicians must also be aware of the caregivers' tendencies to blame themselves or others for patients' illnesses and must appreciate the role that patients with dementia play in the lives of family members.

References

Almkvist O, Bäckman L: Detection and staging of early clinical dementia. Acta Neurol Scand *88:* 10, 1993.

American Psychiatric Association: Practice guidelines for the treatment of patients with Alzheimer's disease and other dementia of late life. Am J Psychiatry *154* (5, Suppl): 1, 1997.

Bondareff W, Raval J, Woo B, Hauser DL, Colletti PM: Magnetic resonance imaging and the severity of dementia in older adults. Arch Gen Psychiatry *47:* 47, 1990.

Burns A, Jacoby R, Levy R: Psychiatric phenomena in Alzheimer's disease: I–IV. Br J Psychiatry *157:* 72, 1990.

Caine ED: Delirium, dementia, and amnestic and other cognitive disorders and mental disorders due to a general medical condition. In *Comprehensive Textbook of Psychiatry,* ed 6, HI Kaplan, BJ Sadock, editors, p 705. Williams & Wilkins, Baltimore, 1995.

Chatterjee A, Strauss ME, Smyth KA, Whitehouse PJ: Personality changes in Alzheimer's disease. Arch Neurol *49:* 486, 1992.

Corder EH, Saunders AM, Strittmatter WJ, Schmechel DE, Gaskell PC, Small GW, Roses AD, Haines JL, Pericak-Vance MA: Gene dose of apolipoprotein E type 4 allele and the risk of Alzheimer's disease in late onset families. Science *261:* 921, 1993.

Davidson M, editor: Alzheimer's disease. Psychiatr Clin North Am *14* (2, Suppl): 1, 1991.

Davis RE, Emmerling MR, Jaen JC, Moos WH, Spiegel K: Therapeutic intervention in dementia. Crit Rev Neurobiol *7:* 41, 1993.

Day JJ, Grant I, Atkinson JH, Bryst LT, McClutchan JA, Hesselink JR, Heaton RK, Weinrich JD, Spector SA, Richman DD: Incidence of AIDS dementia in a two-year follow-up of AIDS and ARC patients on an initial phase II AZT placebo-controlled study: San Diego cohort. J Neuropsychiatry Clin Neurosci *4:* 16, 1992.

Deutsch L, Bylsma FW, Royner BW, Steele C, Folstein MF: Psychosis and physical aggression in probable Alzheimer's disease. Am J Psychiatry *148:* 1159, 1991.

Flint AJ: Delusions in dementia: A review. J Neuropsychiatry Clin Neurosci *3:* 121, 1991.

Gabbard GO: *Psychodynamic Psychiatry in Clinical Practice: The DSM-IV Edition.* American Psychiatric Press, Washington, 1994.

Gandy S, Greengard P: Amyloidognesis in Alzheimer's disease: Some possible therapeutic opportunities. Trends Pharmacol Sci *13:* 108, 1992.

Ghetti B: Familial multiple system taupath with presenile dementia. Proc Natl Acad Sci USA *94:* 4113, 1997.

Greenmyre JT, Maragos WF: Neurotransmitter receptors in Alzheimer disease. Cerebrovasc Brain Metab Rev *5:* 61, 1993.

Harper RG, Chacko RC, Kotik-Harper D, Kirby HB: Comparison of two cognitive screening measures for efficacy in differentiating dementia from depression in a geriatric inpatient population. J Neuropsychiatry Clin Neurosci *4:* 179, 1992.

Hyman BT, Tanzi RE: Amyloid dementia and Alzheimer's disease. Curr Opin Neurol Neurosurg *5:* 88, 1992.

Luchins DJ, Cohen D, Hanrahan P, Eisdorfer C, Pavaza G, Ashford JW, Gorelich P, Hirschman R, Freels S, Levy P, Semla T, Shaw H: Are there clinical differences between familial and non familial Alzheimer's disease? Am J Psychiatry *149:* 1023, 1992.

O'Connor DW, Pollitt PA, Roth M, Brook PB, Reiss BB: Memory complaints and impairments in normal, depressed, and demented elderly persons identified in a community survey. Arch Gen Psychiatry *47:* 224, 1990.

Pajeau AK, Roman GC: HIV encephalopathy and dementia. Psychiatr Clin North Am *15:* 455, 1992.

Reed KR, Rogers RL, Meyer JS: Cerebral magnetic resonance imaging compared in Alzheimer's and multi-infarct dementia. J Neuropsychiatry Clin Neurosci *3:* 51, 1991.

Sano M, Ernesto C, Thomas RG, Klauber MR, Schafer K, Grundman M, Woodbury P, Growdon J, Cotman CW, Pfeiffer E, Schneider LS, Thal LJ, for Members of the Alzheimer's Disease Cooperative Study: A controlled trial of selegiline, alpha-tocopherol, or both as treatment for Alzheimer's disease. N Engl J Med *336:* 1216, 1997.

Simonian NA, Hyman BT: Functional alterations in neural circuits in Alzheimer's disease. Neurobiol Aging *16:* 305, 1995.

Stern GM: New drug interventions in Alzheimer's disease. Curr Opin Neurol Neurosurg *5:* 100, 1992.

Will RG, Ironside JW, Zeidler M, Cousens SN, Estibeiro K, Alpervitch A, Poser

S, Pocchiari M, Hofman A, Smith PG: A new variant of Creutzfeldt-Jakob disease in the UK. Lancet *347:* 921, 1996.
World Health Organization consultation on public health issues related to bovine spongiform encephalopathy and the emergence of a new variant of Creutzfeldt-Jakob disease. MMWR Morb Mortal Wkly Rep *45:* 295, 303, 1996.
Yesauage J: Differential diagnosis between depression and dementia. Am J Med *94* (Suppl 5): 235, 1993.

▲ 10.4 Amnestic Disorders

In the fourth edition of *Diagnostic and Statistical Manual of Mental Disorders* (DSM-IV), amnestic disorder is ''characterized by memory impairment in the absence of other significant cognitive impairments.'' The amnestic disorders are characterized primarily by the single symptom of a memory disturbance that causes significant impairment in social or occupational functioning. The diagnosis of amnestic disorder cannot be made when a patient has other signs of cognitive impairment, such as those seen in dementia, or when a patient has impaired attention or consciousness, such as that seen in delirium. The amnestic disorders are differentiated from the dissociative disorders (such as dissociative amnesia, dissociative fugue, and dissociative identity disorder) by the identified or presumed presence of a causally related general medical condition, such as a history of head trauma or carbon monoxide poisoning.

EPIDEMIOLOGY

No adequate studies have reported on the incidence or prevalence of amnestic disorders. Some studies, however, note the incidence or the prevalence of memory impairments in specific disorders (such as multiple sclerosis). Amnesia is most commonly found in alcohol use disorders and in head injury. In general practice and hospital settings, there has been a decrease in the frequency of amnesia related to chronic alcohol abuse and an increase in the frequency of amnesia related to head trauma.

ETIOLOGY

The major neuroanatomical structures involved in memory and in the development of an amnestic disorder are particular diencephalic structures such as the dorsomedial and midline nuclei of the thalamus and midtemporal lobe structures such as the hippocampus, the mamillary bodies, and the amygdala. Although amnesia is usually the result of bilateral damage to these structures, some cases of unilateral damage result in an amnestic disorder, and evidence indicates that the left hemisphere may be more critical than the right hemisphere in the development of memory disorders. Many studies of memory and amnesia in animals have suggested that other brain areas may also be involved in the symptoms accompanying amnesia. Frontal lobe involvement may result in such symptoms as confabulation and apathy, which can be seen in patients with amnestic disorders.

Amnestic disorders have many potential causes (Table 10.4–1). Thiamine deficiency, hypoglycemia, hypoxia (including carbon monoxide poisoning), and herpes simplex encephalitis all have a predilection to damage the temporal lobes, particularly the hippocampi, and thus can be associated with the development of amnestic disorders. Similarly, when tumors, cerebrovascular diseases, surgical procedures, or multiple sclerosis plaques involve the diencephalic or temporal regions of the brain, the symptoms of an amnestic disorder may develop. General insults to the brain such as seizures, electroconvulsive therapy (ECT), and head trauma may also result in memory impairments. Transient global amnesia is presumed to be a cerebrovascular disorder involving transient impairment in blood flow through the vertebrobasilar arteries.

Table 10.4–1
Major Causes of Amnestic Disorders

Systemic medical conditions
Thiamine deficiency (Korsakoff's syndrome)
Hypoglycemia
Primary brain conditions
Seizures
Head trauma (closed and penetrating)
Cerebral tumors (especially thalamic and temporal lobe)
Cerebrovascular diseases (especially thalamic and temporal lobe)
Surgical procedures on the brain
Encephalitis due to herpes simplex
Hypoxia (including nonfatal hanging attempts and carbon monoxide poisoning)
Transient global amnesia
Electroconvulsive therapy
Multiple sclerosis
Substance-related causes
Alcohol use disorders
Neurotoxins
Benzodiazepines (and other sedative-hypnotics)
Many over-the-counter preparations

Many drugs have been associated with the development of amnesia, and clinicians should review all drugs taken, including nonprescription drugs, in the diagnostic workup of a patient with amnesia. The benzodiazepines are the most commonly used prescription drugs associated with amnesia. One benzodiazepine in particular, the short-acting hypnotic triazolam (Halcion), has inaccurately been singled out as being associated with anterograde amnesia. A review of the scientific data has concluded that all benzodiazepines can be associated with amnesia and that the association is related to dosage. When triazolam is used in doses (generally less than or equal to 0.25 mg) equivalent to standard doses of other benzodiazepines, amnesia is no more often associated with triazolam than with other benzodiazepines.

DIAGNOSIS

For the diagnosis of amnestic disorder, DSM-IV requires the ''development of memory impairment as manifested by impairment in the ability to learn new information or the inability to recall previously learned information,'' and the ''memory disturbance [must cause] . . . significant impairment in social or occupational functioning.'' A diagnosis of amnestic disorder due to a general medical condition (Table 10.4–2)

Table 10.4–2
DSM-IV Diagnostic Criteria for Amnestic Disorder Due to a General Medical Condition

A. The development of memory impairment as manifested by impairment in the ability to learn new information or the inability to recall previously learned information.

B. The memory disturbance causes significant impairment in social or occuaptional functioning and represents a significant decline from a previous level of functioning.

C. The memory disturbance does not occur exclusively during the course of a delirium or a dementia.

D. There is evidence from the history, physical examination, or laboratory findings that the disturbance is the direct physiological consequence of a general medical condition (including physical trauma).

Specify if:

Transient: if memory impairment lasts for 1 month or less
Chronic: if memory impairment lasts for more than 1 month

Coding note: Include the name of the general medical condition on Axis I, eg, amnestic disorder due to head trauma; also code the general medical condition on Axis III.

Table 10.4–3
DSM-IV Diagnostic Criteria for Substance-Induced Persisting Amnestic Disorder

A. The development of memory impairment as manifested by impairment in the ability to learn new information or the inability to recall previously learned information.

B. The memory disturbance causes significant impairment in social or occupational functioning and represents a significant decline from a previous level of functioning.

C. The memory disturbance does not occur exclusively during the course of a delirium or a dementia and persists beyond the usual duration of substance intoxication or withdrawal.

D. There is evidence from the history, physical examination, or laboratory findings that the memory disturbance is etiologically related to the persisting effects of substance use (eg, a drug of abuse, a medication).

Code: (Specific substance)-induced persisting amnestic disorder: (Alcohol; sedative, hypnotic, or anxiolytic; other [or unknown] substance)

is made when there is evidence of a causatively relevant specific medical condition (including physical trauma). DSM-IV further categorizes the diagnosis as being transient or chronic. A diagnosis of substance-induced persisting amnestic disorder is made when there is evidence that the symptoms are causatively related to the use of a substance (Table 10.4–3). DSM-IV refers clinicians to specific diagnoses within substance-related disorders: alcohol-induced persisting amnestic disorder; sedative, hypnotic, or anxiolytic-induced persisting amnestic disorder; and other (or unknown) substance-induced persisting amnestic disorder. DSM-IV also provides for the diagnosis of amnestic disorder not otherwise specified (Table 10.4–4).

ICD-10

The criteria for organic amnesic syndrome, not induced by alcohol and other psychoactive substances, in the 10th revision of *International Statistical Classification of Diseases and Related Health Problems* (ICD-10) are presented in Table 10.4–5. In ICD-10, deliriums associated with the use of a substance are classified under the category of mental and behavioral disorders due to psychoactive substance use as a withdrawal state with delirium, as a subtype of acute intoxication (for example, acute intoxication due to the use of alcohol with delirium), and as an additional specifier to alcohol withdrawal state and sedative or hypnotic withdrawal state (see Chapter 12, Table 12.1–5).

CLINICAL FEATURES AND SUBTYPES

The central symptom of amnestic disorders is the development of a memory disorder characterized by impairment in the ability to learn new information (anterograde amnesia) and the inability to recall previously remembered knowledge (retrograde amnesia). The symptom must result in significant problems for patients in their social or occupational functioning. The time for which a patient is amnestic may begin directly at the point of trauma or may include a period before the trauma. Memory for the time during the physical insult (as during a cerebrovascular event) may also be lost.

Short-term and recent memory are usually impaired. Patients cannot remember what they had for breakfast or lunch, the name of the hospital, or their doctors. In some patients, the amnesia is so profound that they cannot orient themselves to city and time, although orientation to person is seldom lost in amnestic disorders. Memory for overlearned information or events from the remote past, such as childhood experiences, is good; but memory for events from the less remote past (over the past decade) is impaired. Immediate memory (tested, for example, by asking a patient to repeat six numbers) remains intact. With improvement, patients may experience a gradual

Table 10.4–4
DSM-IV Amnestic Disorder Not Otherwise Specified

This category should be used to diagnose an amnestic disorder that does not meet criteria for any of the specific types described in this section.

An example is a clinical presentation of amnesia for which there is insufficient evidence to establish a specific etiology (ie, dissociative, substance induced, or due to a general medical condition).

Table 10.4–5
ICD-10 Diagnostic Criteria for Organic Amnesic Syndrome, Not Induced by Alcohol and Other Psychoactive Substances

A. There is memory impairment, manifest in both
   1. A defect of recent memory (impaired learning of new material) to a degree sufficient to interfere with daily living
   2. A reduced ability to recall past experiences

B. There is no
   1. Defect in immediate recall (as tested, for example, by the digit span)
   2. Clouding of consciousness and disturbance of attention. Delirium, not induced by alcohol and other psychoactive substances
   3. Global intellectual decline (dementia)

C. There is objective evidence (from physical and neurological examination, laboratory tests) and/or history of an insult to, or a disease of, the brain (especially involving bilaterally the diencephalic and medial temporal structures but other than alcohol encephalopathy) that can reasonably be presumed to be responsible for the clinical manifestations

Comments: Associated features, including confabulations, emotional changes (apathy, lack of initiative), and lack of insight are useful additional pointers to the diagnosis but are not invariably present.

Adapted with permission from World Health Organization: *The ICD-10 Classification of Mental and Behavioural Disorders: Diagnostic Criteria for Research.* Copyright, World Health Organization, Geneva, 1993.

shrinking of the time for which memory has been lost, although some patients experience a gradual improvement in memory for the entire period.

The onset of symptoms may be sudden, as in trauma, cerebrovascular events, and neurotoxic chemical assaults, or gradual, as in nutritional deficiency and cerebral tumors. The amnesia can be of short duration (specified by DSM-IV as transient if lasting 1 month or less) or of long duration (specified by DSM-IV as persistent if lasting more than 1 month).

A variety of other symptoms can be associated with amnestic disorders. For patients with other cognitive impairments, a diagnosis of dementia or delirium is more appropriate than a diagnosis of an amnestic disorder. Both subtle and gross changes in personality can accompany the symptoms of memory impairment in amnestic disorders. Patients may be apathetic, lack initiative, have unprovoked episodes of agitation, or appear to be overly friendly or agreeable. Patients with amnestic disorders may also appear bewildered and confused and may attempt to cover their confusion with confabulatory answers to questions. Characteristically, patients with amnestic disorders do not have good insight into their neuropsychiatric conditions.

Cerebrovascular Diseases

Cerebrovascular diseases affecting the hippocampus involve the posterior cerebral and basilar arteries and their branches. Infarctions are rarely limited to the hippocampus; they often involve the occipital or parietal lobes. Thus, common accompanying symptoms of cerebrovascular diseases in this region are focal neurological signs involving vision or sensory modalities. Cerebrovascular diseases affecting the bilateral medial thalamus, particularly the anterior portions, are often associated with symptoms of amnestic disorders. A few case studies report amnestic disorders from ruptures of an aneurysm of the anterior communicating artery, resulting in an infarction of the basal forebrain region.

Multiple Sclerosis

The pathophysiological process of multiple sclerosis involves the seemingly random formation of plaques within the brain parenchyma. When the plaques occur in the temporal lobe and the diencephalic regions, symptoms of memory impairment can occur. In fact, the most common cognitive complaints in patients with multiple sclerosis involve impaired memory, which occurs in 40 to 60 percent of patients. Characteristically, digit span memory is normal, but immediate recall and delayed recall of information are impaired. The memory impairment can affect both verbal and nonverbal material.

Korsakoff's Syndrome

Korsakoff's syndrome is an amnestic syndrome caused by thiamine deficiency, most commonly associated with the poor nutritional habits of people with chronic alcohol abuse. Other causes of poor nutrition (such as starvation), gastric carcinoma, hemodialysis, hyperemesis gravidarum, prolonged intravenous hyperalimentation, and gastric plication may also result in thiamine deficiency. Korsakoff's syndrome is often associated with Wernicke's encephalopathy, which is the associated syndrome of confusion, ataxia, and ophthalmoplegia. In patients with these thiamine deficiency-related symptoms, the neuropathological findings include hyperplasia of the small blood vessels with occasional hemorrhages, hypertrophy of astrocytes, and subtle changes in neuronal axons. Although the delirium clears up within a month or so, the amnestic syndrome either accompanies or follows untreated Wernicke's encephalopathy in approximately 85 percent of all cases.

The onset of Korsakoff's syndrome may be gradual. Recent memory tends to be affected more than is remote memory, but this feature is variable. Confabulation, apathy, and passivity are often prominent symptoms in the syndrome. With treatment, patients may remain amnestic for up to 3 months and then gradually improve over the ensuing year. The administration of thiamine may prevent the development of additional amnestic symptoms, but rarely is the treatment able to reverse severe amnestic symptoms once they are present. Approximately one third to one fourth of all patients recover completely, and approximately one fourth of all patients have no improvement of their symptoms.

Alcoholic Blackouts

In some people with severe alcohol abuse, the syndrome commonly referred to as an alcoholic blackout may occur. Characteristically, the person awakens in the morning with a conscious awareness of being unable to remember a time the night before during which the person was intoxicated. Sometimes, specific behaviors (hiding money in a secret place and provoking fights) are associated with the blackouts.

Electroconvulsive Therapy

ECT treatments are usually associated with a retrograde amnesia for a period of several minutes before the treatment and an anterograde amnesia after the treatment. The anterograde amnesia usually resolves within 5 hours. Mild memory deficits may remain for 1 to 2 months after a course of ECT treatments, but the symptoms are completely resolved 6 to 9 months after treatment.

Head Injury

Head injuries (both closed and penetrating) can result in a wide range of neuropsychiatric symptoms, including dementia, depression, personality changes, and amnestic disorders. Amnestic disorders caused by head injuries are commonly associated with a period of retrograde amnesia leading up to the traumatic incident and amnesia for the traumatic incident itself. The severity of the brain injury is somewhat correlated with the duration and severity of the amnestic syndrome, but the best correlate of eventual improvement is the degree of clinical improvement of the amnesia during the first week after the patient regains consciousness.

Transient Global Amnesia

Transient global amnesia is characterized by the abrupt loss of the ability to recall recent events or to remember new information. The syndrome is often characterized by a lack of insight into the problem, a clear sensorium, a mild degree of confusion, and, occasionally, the ability to perform some well-learned complex tasks. Episodes last from 6 to 24 hours. Studies suggest that transient global amnesia occurs in 5 to 10 cases per 100,000 people per year, although, for patients older than age 50, the rate may be as high as 30 cases per 100,000 people per year. The pathophysiology is unknown, but it is likely to involve ischemia of the temporal lobe and the diencephalic brain regions. Several studies of patients with single photon emission computed tomography have shown decreased blood flow in the temporal and parietal-temporal regions, particularly in the left hemisphere (Fig. 10.4–1). Patients with transient global amnesia almost universally experience complete improvement, although one study found that approximately 20 percent of patients may have a recurrence of the episode, and another study found that approximately 7 percent of patients may have epilepsy. Patients with transient global amnesia have been differentiated from patients with transient ischemic attacks in that fewer patients have diabetes, hypercholesterole-

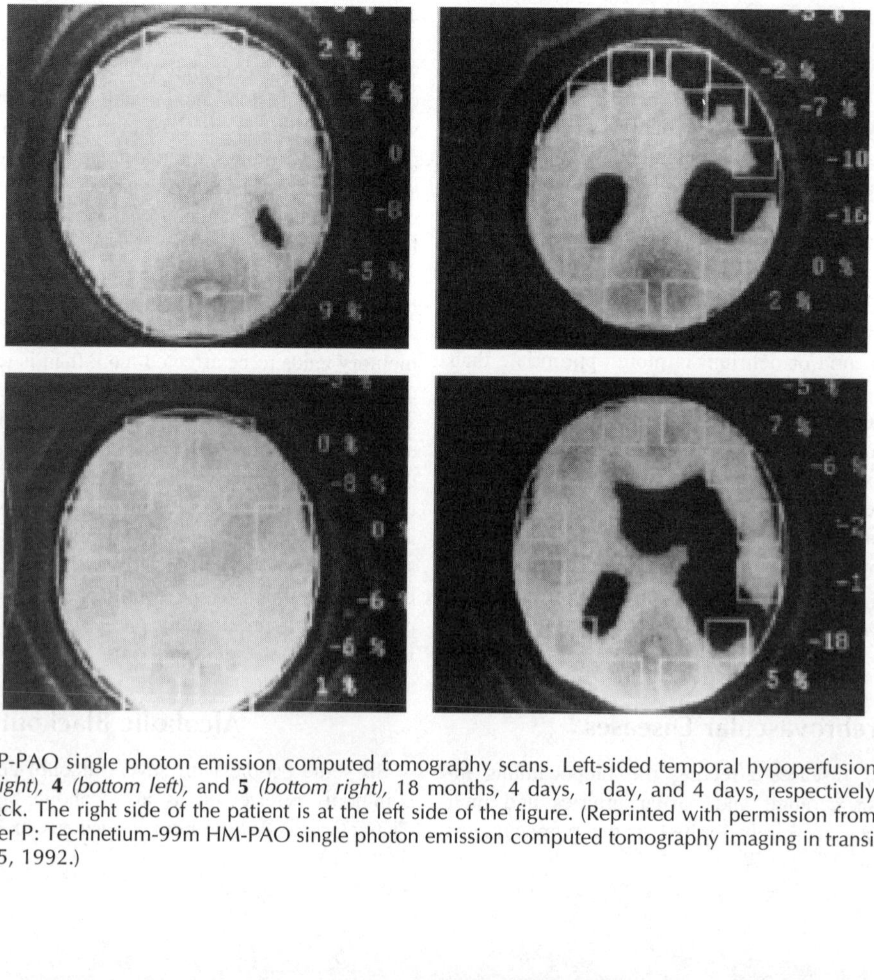

FIGURE 10.4–1

Technetium-99m HP-PAO single photon emission computed tomography scans. Left-sided temporal hypoperfusion is seen in **patients 2** *(top left),* **3** *(top right),* **4** *(bottom left),* and **5** *(bottom right),* 18 months, 4 days, 1 day, and 4 days, respectively, after the transient global amnestic attack. The right side of the patient is at the left side of the figure. (Reprinted with permission from Laloux P, Brichant C, Cauwe F, Decoster P: Technetium-99m HM-PAO single photon emission computed tomography imaging in transient global amnesia. Arch Neurol *49:* 545, 1992.)

mia, and hypertriglyceridemia but more have hypertension and migrainous episodes.

DIFFERENTIAL DIAGNOSIS

Table 10.4–1 lists the major causes of amnestic disorders. To make the diagnosis, clinicians must obtain a patient's history, conduct a complete physical examination, and order all appropriate laboratory tests. Other diagnoses, however, can be confused with the amnestic disorders.

Dementia and Delirium

Clinicians must differentiate amnestic disorders from dementia and delirium. Memory impairment is commonly present in dementia but is accompanied by other cognitive deficits. Memory impairment is also commonly present in delirium but occurs in the setting of an impairment in attention and consciousness.

Normal Aging

Some minor impairment in memory may accompany normal aging, but the DSM-IV requirement that the memory impairment cause significant impairment in social or occupational functioning should exclude normal aging in patients from the diagnosis.

Dissociative Disorders

The dissociative disorders can sometimes be difficult to differentiate from the amnestic disorders. Patients with dissociative disorders, however, are more likely to have lost their orientation to self and may have more selective memory deficits than do patients with amnestic disorders. For example, patients with dissociative disorders may not know their names or home addresses but may still be able to learn new information and remember selected past memories. Dissociative disorders are also often associated with emotionally stressful life events involving money, the legal system, or troubled relationships.

Factitious Disorders

Patients with factitious disorders who are mimicking an amnestic disorder often have inconsistent results on memory tests and have no evidence of an identifiable cause. These findings, coupled with evidence of primary or secondary gain for a patient, should suggest a factitious disorder.

COURSE AND PROGNOSIS

The specific cause of the amnestic disorder determines the course and the prognosis for a patient. The onset may be sudden or gradual, the symptoms may be transient or persistent, and the outcome can range from no improvement to complete recovery. Transient amnestic disorder with full recovery is common in temporal lobe epilepsy, ECT, the intake of such drugs as benzodiazepines and barbiturates, and resuscitation from cardiac arrest. Permanent amnestic syndromes may follow a head trauma, carbon monoxide poisoning, a cerebral infarction, a subarachnoid hemorrhage, and herpes simplex encephalitis.

TREATMENT

The primary approach to treating amnestic disorders is to treat the underlying cause. Although a patient is amnestic, supportive prompts about the date, the time, and the patient's location can be helpful and can reduce the patient's anxiety. After the resolution of the amnestic episode, psychotherapy of some type (cognitive, psychodynamic, or supportive) may help patients incorporate the amnestic experience into their lives.

Psychotherapy

Psychodynamic interventions may be of considerable value for patients suffering from amnestic disorders that result from insults to the brain. Understanding the course of recovery in such patients helps clinicians be sensitive to the narcissistic injury inherent in damage to the central nervous system.

The first phase of recovery, in which patients are incapable of processing what happened because the ego defenses are overwhelmed, requires clinicians to serve as a supportive auxiliary ego who explains to a patient what is happening and provides missing ego functions. In the second phase of recovery, as the realization of the injury sets in, patients may become angry and feel victimized by the malevolent hand of fate. They may view others, including the clinician, as bad or destructive, and clinicians must contain these projections without becoming punitive or retaliatory. Clinicians can build a therapeutic alliance with patients by explaining slowly and clearly what happened and by offering an explanation for a patient's internal experience. The third phase of recovery is integrative. As a patient accepts what happened, a clinician can help the patient form a new identity by connecting current experiences of the self with past experiences. Grieving over the lost faculties may be an important feature of the third phase.

Most patients who are amnestic because of brain injury engage in denial. Clinicians must respect and empathize with the patient's need to deny the reality of what has happened. Insensitive and blunt confrontations destroy any developing therapeutic alliance and may cause patients to feel attacked. In a sensitive approach, clinicians help patients accept their cognitive limitations by exposing them to these deficits bit by bit over time. When patients fully accept what has happened, they may need assistance in forgiving themselves and any others involved, so that they can get on with their lives. Clinicians must also be wary of being seduced into thinking that all of the patient's symptoms are directly related to the brain insult. An evaluation of preexisting personality disorders, such as borderline, antisocial, and narcissistic personality disorders, must be part of the overall assessment; many patients with personality disorders place themselves in situations that predispose them to injuries. These personality features may become a crucial part of the psychodynamic psychotherapy.

References

Caine ED: Amnesic disorders. J Neuropsychiatry Clin Neurosci *5:* 6, 1993.

Caine ED: Delirium, dementia, and amnestic and other cognitive disorders and mental disorders due to a general medical condition. In *Comprehensive Textbook of Psychiatry,* ed 6, HI Kaplan, BJ Sadock, editors, p 705. Williams & Wilkins, Baltimore, 1995.

Erickson KR: Amnestic disorders: Pathophysiology and patterns of memory dysfunction. West J Med *152:* 159, 1990.

Gabbard GO: *Psychodynamic Psychiatry in Clinical Practice: The DSM-IV Edition.* American Psychiatric Press, Washington, 1994.

Gandolofo C, Caponnetto C, Conti M, Dagino N, Del Sette M, Primivera A: Prognosis of transient global amnesia: A long-term follow-up study. Eur Neurol *32:* 52, 1992.
Gasquonine PG: Learning in post-traumatic amnesia following extremely severe closed head injury. Brain Inj *5:* 169, 1991.
Hodges JR, McCarthy RA: Loss of remote memory: A cognitive neuropsychological perspective. Curr Opin Neurobiol *5:* 178, 1995.
Hodges JR, Warlow CP: The aetiology of transient global amnesia: A case-control study of 114 cases with prospective follow-up. Brain *113:* 639, 1990.
Hodges JR, Warlow CP: Syndromes of transient amnesia: Towards a classification: A study of 153 cases. J Neurol Neurosurg Psychiatry *53:* 834, 1990.
Jonides J, Smith EE, Koeppe RA, Awh E, Minoshima S, Mintun MA: Spatial working memory in humans as revealed by PET. Nature *363:* 623, 1993.
Kin JJ, Fanselow MS: Modality-specific retrograde amnesia of fear. Science *256:* 675, 1992.
Kirk T, Roache JD, Griffiths RR: Dose-response evaluation of the amnestic effects of triazolam and pentobarbital in normal subjects. J Clin Psychopharmacol *10:* 161, 1990.
Krupa DJ, Thompson JK, Thompson RF: Localization of a memory trace in the mammalian brain. Science *260:* 989, 1993.
Laloux P, Brichant C, Cauwe F, Decoster P: Technetium-99m HM-PAO single photon emission computed tomography imaging in transient global amnesia. Arch Neurol *49:* 543, 1992.
Melo TP, Ferro JM, Ferro H: Transient global amnesia: A case control study. Brain *115:* 261, 1992.
Saneda DL, Corrigan JD: Predicting clearing of post-traumatic amnesia following closed-head injury. Brain Inj *6:* 167, 1992.
Squire LR, Amaral DG, Press GA: Magnetic resonance imaging of the hippocampal formation and mammillary nuclei distinguish medial temporal lobe and diencephalic amnesia. J Neurosci *10:* 3106, 1990.
Squire LR, Zola-Morgan S: The medical temporal lobe memory system. Science *253:* 1380, 1991.

▲ 10.5 Mental Disorders Due to a General Medical Condition

In the fourth edition of *Diagnostic and Statistical Manual of Mental Disorders* (DSM-IV), the authors introduced the phrase *due to a general medical condition* as part of a resolve to eliminate the long-standing but misleading distinction between organic and functional disorders. An assessment that a mental disorder is due to a general medical condition indicates that a clinician, on the weight of the available data, thinks that the psychiatric symptoms are part of a syndrome caused by a nonpsychiatric medical condition. An example is the depression associated with Cushing's disease. The diagnosis of a mental disorder due to a general medical condition also implies that the clinician thinks the psychiatric symptom severe enough to warrant treatment as an identified problem.

In DSM-IV, the approach to categorizing the mental disorders due to a general medical condition differs from earlier editions. In DSM-IV, each mental disorder due to a general medical condition is classified within the category that most resembles the symptoms (Table 10.5–1). For example, the diagnosis of psychotic disorder due to a general medical condition is found in the DSM-IV section on schizophrenia and other psychotic disorders. The symptom-based organization of DSM-IV is meant to facilitate clinical decision making about the differential diagnosis of symptoms. A clinician who is evaluating a patient with depression can refer to the DSM-IV section on mood disorders and find *mood disorder due to a general medical condition* as one of the diagnoses. This diagnosis should help clarify the importance of considering the possibility of a mental disorder due to a general medical condition for almost all psychiatric presentations.

DSM-IV has three additional diagnostic categories for clinical presentations of mental disorders due to a general medical condition which do not meet the diagnostic criteria for specific diagnoses. The first of the diagnoses is catatonic disorder due to a general medical condition (Table 10.5–2), the second is personality change due to a general medical condition (Table 10.5–3), and the third is mental disorder not otherwise specified due to a general medical condition (Table 10.5–4).

In addition to the mental disorders due to a general medical condition within the DSM-IV symptom categories, there are also diagnoses for substance-induced psychiatric disorders. Specifically, DSM-IV allows for the diagnosis of intoxication-related or withdrawal-related substance-induced disorders with features of psychotic, mood, anxiety, and sleep disorders.

As a general rule, the differential diagnosis for a mental syndrome in a patient should always include consideration of any general medical disease or disorder that a patient may have and consideration of any prescription, nonprescription, or il-

Table 10.5–1
Mental Disorders Due to a General Medical Condition

DSM-IV Category	Mental Disorders Due to a General Medical Condition	Section
Delirium, dementia, amnestic, and other cognitive disorders	Delirium due to a general medical condition Dementia due to other general medical conditions Amnestic disorder due to a general medical condition	10.2 10.3 10.4
Schizophrenia and other psychotic disorders	Psychotic disorder due to a general medical condition	14.1
Mood disorders	Mood disorder due to a general medical condition	15.1
Anxiety disorders	Anxiety disorder due to a general medical condition	16.1
Sexual disorders	Sexual dysfunction due to a general medical condition	21.2
Sleep disorders	Sleep disorder due to a general medical condition	24.2
Mental disorders due to a general medical condition not elsewhere classified	Catatonic disorder due to a general medical condition Personality change due to a general medical condition Mental disorder not otherwise specified due to a general medical condition	10.5 10.5 10.5

Table 10.5–2
DSM-IV Diagnostic Criteria for Catatonic Disorder Due to a General Medical Condition

A. The presence of catatonia as manifested by motoric immobility, excessive motor activity (that is apparently purposeless and not influenced by external stimuli), extreme negativism or mutism, peculiarities of voluntary movement, or echolalia or echopraxia.

B. There is evidence from the history, physical examination, or laboratory findings that the disturbance is the direct physiological consequence of a general medical condition.

C. The disturbance is not better accounted for by another mental disorder (eg, a manic episode).

D. The disturbance does not occur exclusively during the course of a delirium.

Coding note: Include the name of the general medical condition on Axis I, eg, catatonic disorder due to hepatic encephalopathy; also code the general medical condition on Axis III.

legal substances that a patient may be taking. Although some general medical conditions have classically been associated with mental syndromes, a much larger number of general medical conditions have been associated with mental syndromes in case reports and small studies.

ICD-10

In the 10th revision of *International Classification of Diseases and Related Health Problems* (ICD-10) mental disorders related to medical conditions are covered by two categories: personality and behavioral disorders due to brain disease, damage, and dysfunction (Table 10.5–5) and other mental disorders due to brain damage and dysfunction and to physical disease (Table 10.5–6).

DEGENERATIVE DISORDERS

Degenerative disorders affecting the basal ganglia are commonly associated not only with movement disorders but also with depression, dementia, and psychosis. The most widely known examples of the degenerative disorders are Parkinson's disease, Huntington's disease, Wilson's disease, and Fahr's disease. Parkinson's disease involves a degeneration of primarily the substantia nigra and usually has an unknown cause. Huntington's disease involves primarily degeneration of the caudate nucleus and is an autosomal dominant disease. Wilson's disease is an autosomal recessive disease that results in the destructive deposition of copper in the lenticular nuclei. Fahr's disease is a rare hereditary disorder involving the calcification and destruction of the basal ganglia.

EPILEPSY

Epilepsy is the most common chronic neurological disease in the general population and affects approximately 1 percent

Table 10.5–3
DSM-IV Diagnostic Criteria for Personality Change Due to a General Medical Condition

A. A persistent personality disturbance that represents a change from the individual's previous characteristic personality pattern. (In children, the disturbance involves a marked deviation from normal development or a significant change in the child's usual behavior patterns lasting at least 1 year.)

B. There is evidence from the history, physical examination, or laboratory findings that the disturbance is the direct physiological consequence of a general medical condition.

C. The disturbance is not better accounted for by another mental disorder (including other mental disorders due to a general medical condition).

D. The disturbance does not occur exclusively during the course of a delirium and does not meet criteria for a dementia.

E. The disturbance causes clinically significant distress or impairment in social, occupational, or other important areas of functioning.

Specify type:
- **Labile type:** if the predominant feature is affective lability
- **Disinhibited type:** if the predominant feature is poor impulse control as evidenced by sexual indiscretions, etc.
- **Aggressive type:** if the predominant feature is aggressive behavior
- **Apathetic type:** if the predominant feature is marked apathy and indifference
- **Paranoid type:** if the predominant feature is suspiciousness or paranoid ideation
- **Other type:** if the predominant feature is not one of the above, eg, personality change associated with a seizure disorder
- **Combined type:** if more than one feature predominates in the clinical picture
- **Unspecified type**

Coding note: include the name of the general medical condition on Axis I, eg, personality change due to temporal lobe epilepsy, also code the general medical condition on Axis III.

Table 10.5–4
DSM-IV Mental Disorder Not Otherwise Specified Due to a General Medical Condition

This residual category should be used for situations in which it has been established that the disturbance is caused by the direct physiological effects of a general medical condition, but the criteria are not met for a specific mental disorder due to a general medical condition (eg, dissociative symptoms due to a complex partial seizure).

Coding note: Include the name of the general medical condition on Axis I, eg, mental disorder not otherwise specified due to HIV disease; also code the general medical condition on Axis III.

Table 10.5–5
ICD-10 Diagnostic Criteria for Personality and Behavioral Disorders Due to Brain Disease, Damage and Dysfunction

G1. There must be objective evidence (from physical and neurological examination and laboratory tests) and/or history of cerebral disease, damage, or dysfunction.

G2. There is no clouding of consciousness or significant memory deficit.

G3. There is insufficient evidence for an alternative causation of the personality or behavior disorder that would justify its placement in disorders of adult personality and behavior category.

Organic personality disorder

A. The general criteria for personality and behavioral disorders due to brain disease, damage, and dysfunction must be met.

B. At least three of the following features must be present over a period of 6 months or more:
- (1) Consistently reduced ability to persevere with goal-directed activities, especially those involving relatively long periods and postponed gratification;
- (2) one or more of the following emotional changes:
  - (a) emotional lability (uncontrolled, unstable, and fluctuating expression of emotions);
  - (b) euphoria and shallow, inappropriate jocularity, unwarranted by the circumstances;
  - (c) irritability and/or outbursts of anger and aggression;
  - (d) apathy;
- (3) disinhibited expression of needs or impulses without consideration of consequences or of social conventions (the individual may engage in dissocial acts such as stealing, inappropriate sexual advances, or voracious eating, or exhibit extreme disregard for personal hygiene);
- (4) cognitive disturbances, typically in the form of:
  - (a) excessive suspiciousness and paranoid ideas;
  - (b) excessive preoccupation with a single theme such as religion, or rigid categorization of other people's behavior in terms of "right" and "wrong";
- (5) marked alteration of the rate and flow of language production, with features such as circumstantiality, overinclusiveness, viscosity, and hypergraphia;
- (6) altered sexual behavior (hyposexuality or change in sexual preference).

Specification of features for possible subtypes

Option 1. A marked predominance of the symptoms in criteria (1) and (2)(d) is thought to define a pseudoretarded or apathetic type; a predominance of (1), (2)(c), and (3) is considered a pseudopsychopathic type; and a combination of (4), (5) and (6) is regarded as characteristic of the limbic epilepsy personality syndrome. None of these entities has yet been sufficiently validated to warrant a separate description.

Option 2. If desired, the following types may be specified: labile type, disinhibited type, aggressive type, apathetic type, paranoid type, mixed type, and other.

Postencephalitic syndrome

A. The general criteria for personality and behavioral disorders due to brain disease, damage, and dysfunction must be met.

B. At least one of the following residual neurological dysfunctions must be present:
- (1) paralysis;
- (2) deafness;
- (3) aphasia;
- (4) constructional apraxia;
- (5) acalculia.

C. The syndrome is reversible, and its duration rarely exceeds 24 months.

Comments

Criterion C constitutes the main difference between this disorder and organic personality disorder.

Residual symptoms and behavioral change following either viral or bacterial encephalitis are nonspecific and do not provide a sufficient basis for a clinical diagnosis. They may include: general malaise, apathy, or irritability; some lowering of cognitive functioning (learning difficulties); disturbances in the sleep–wake pattern; or altered sexual behavior.

Postconcussional syndrome

Note. The nosological status of this syndrome is uncertain, and criterion G1 of the introduction to this rubric is not always ascertainable. However, for those undertaking research into this condition, the following criteria are recommended:

A. The general criteria of personality and behavioral disorders due to brain disease, damage, and dysfunction must be met.

B. There must be a history of head trauma with loss of consciousness, preceding the onset of symptoms by a period of up to 4 weeks. (Objective EEG, brain imaging, or oculonystagmographic evidence for brain damage may be lacking.)

C. At least three of the following features must be present:
- (1) complaints of unpleasant sensations and pains, such as headache, dizziness (usually lacking the features of true vertigo), general malaise, and excessive fatigue, or noise intolerance;
- (2) emotional changes, such as irritability, emotional lability (both easily provoked or exacerbated by emotional excitement or stress), or some degree of depression and/or anxiety;
- (3) subjective complaints of difficulty in concentration and in performing mental tasks, and of memory problems (without clear objective evidence, eg, psychological tests, of marked impairment);
- (4) insomnia;
- (5) reduced tolerance to alcohol;
- (6) Preoccupation with the above symptoms and fear of permanent brain damage, to the extent of hypochondriacal, overvalued ideas and adoption of a sick role.

Other organic personality and behavioral disorders due to brain disease, damage, and dysfunction

Brain disease, damage, or dysfunction may produce a variety of cognitive, emotional, personality, and behavioral disorders, some of which may not be classifiable under organic personality disorder, postencephalitic syndrome, postconcussional syndrome. However, since the nosological status of the tentative syndromes in this area is uncertain, they should be coded as "other." A fifth character may be added, if necessary, to identify presumptive individual entities.

Unspecified organic personality and behavioral disorder due to brain disease, damage, and dysfunction

Table 10.5–6
ICD-10 Diagnostic Criteria for Other Mental Disorders Due to Brain Damage and Dysfunction and Due to Physical Disease

G1. There is objective evidence (from physical and neurological examination and laboratory tests) and/or history of cerebral disease, damage, or dysfunction, or of systemic physical disorder known to cause cerebral dysfunction, including hormonal disturbances (other than alcohol- or other psychoactive substance-related) and nonpsychoactive drug effects.

G2. There is a presumed relationship between the development (or marked exacerbation) of the underlying disease, damage, or dysfunction, and the mental disorder, the symptoms of which may have immediate onset or may be delayed.

G3. There is recovery from or significant improvement in the mental disorder following removal or improvement of the underlying presumed cause.

G4. There is insufficient evidence for an alternative causation of the mental disorder, eg, a strong family history of a clinically similar or related disorder.

If criteria G1, G2, and G4 are met, a provisional diagnosis is justified; if, in addition, there is evidence of G3, the diagnosis can be regarded as certain.

Organic hallucinosis

A. The general criteria for other mental disorders due to brain damage and dysfunction and to physical disease must be met.

B. The clinical picture is dominated by persistent or recurrent hallucinations (usually visual or auditory).

C. Hallucinations occur in clear consciousness.

Comments

Delusional elaboration of the hallucinations, as well as full or partial insight, may or may not be present: these features are not essential for the diagnosis.

Organic catatonic disorder

A. The general criteria for other mental disorders due to brain damage and dysfunction and to physical disease must be met.

B. One of the following must be present:
   (1) Stupor, ie, profound diminution or absence of voluntary movements and speech, and of normal responsiveness to light, noise, and touch, but with normal muscle tone, static posture, and breathing maintained (and often limited coordinated eye movements);
   (2) negativism (positive resistance to passive movement of limbs or body or rigid posturing).

C. There is catatonic excitement (gross hypermotility of a chaotic quality, with or without a tendency to assaultiveness),

D. There is rapid and unpredictable alternation of stupor and excitement.

Comments

Confidence in the diagnosis is increased if additional catatonic phenomena are present, eg, stereotypies, waxy flexibility, and impulsive acts. Care should be taken to exclude delirium; however, it is not known whether an organic catatonic state always occurs in clear consciousness, or whether it represents an atypical manifestation of a delirium in which criteria A, B, and D are only marginally met, whereas criterion C is prominent.

Organic delusional (schizophrenia-like) disorder

A. The general criteria for other mental disorders due to brain damage and dysfunction and to physical disease must be met.

B. The clinical picture is dominated by delusions (of persecution, bodily change, disease, death, jealousy), which may exhibit a varying degree of systematization.

C. Consciousness is clear and memory is intact.

Comments

Further features that complete the clinical picture but that are not invariably present include: hallucinations (in any modality); schizophrenic-type thought disorder; isolated catatonic phenomena such as stereotypies, negativism, or impulsive acts.

The clinical picture may meet the symptomatic criteria for schizophrenia, persistent delusional disorder, or acute and transient psychotic disorders. However, if the state also meets the general criteria for a presumptive organic etiology laid down in the introduction to other mental disorders due to brain damage and dysfunction and to physical disease, it should be classified here. Marginal or nonspecific findings such as enlarged cerebral ventricles or "soft" neurological signs *do not qualify as evidence* for criterion G1 of other mental disorders due to brain damage and dysfunction and to physical disease.

Organic mood (affective) disorder

A. The general criteria for other medical disorders due to brain damage and dysfunction and to physical disease must be met.

B. The condition must meet the criteria for one of the affective disorders.

The diagnosis of the affective disorder may be specified by using a fifth character:

Organic manic disorder
Organic bipolar disorder
Organic depressive disorder
Organic mixed affective disorder

Organic anxiety disorder

A. The general criteria for other medical disorders due to brain damage and dysfunction and to physical disease must be met.

B. The condition must meet the criteria for either panic disorder or generalized anxiety disorder.

Organic dissociative disorder

A. The general criteria for other mental disorders due to brain damage and dysfunction and to physical disease must be met.

B. The condition must meet the criteria for one of the dissociative (conversion) disorders categories.

Organic emotionally labile (asthenic) disorder

A. The general criteria for other mental disorders due to brain damage and dysfunction and to physical disease must be met.

B. The clinical picture is dominated by emotional lability (uncontrolled, unstable, and fluctuating expression of emotions).

C. There is a variety of unpleasant physical sensations such as dizziness or pains and aches.

Comments

Fatigability and listlessness (asthenia) are often present but are not essential for the diagnosis.

(continued)

Table 10.5–6 *(continued)*

Mild cognitive disorder *Note:* The status of this construct is being examined. Specific research criteria must be viewed as tentative. One of the principal reasons for its inclusion is to obtain further evidence, allowing its differentiation from disorders such as dementia, organic amnesic syndrome, delirium, and several disorders in personality and behavioral disorders due to brain disease, damage, and dysfunction. A. The general criteria for other mental disorders due to brain damage and dysfunction and to physical disease must be met. B. There is a disorder in cognitive function for most of the time over a period of at least 2 weeks, as reported by the individual or a reliable informant. The disorder is exemplified by difficulties in any of the following areas: (1) memory (particularly recall) or new learning; (2) attention or concentration; (3) thinking (eg, slowing in problem solving or abstraction); (4) language (eg, comprehension, word finding); (5) visual-spatial functioning. C. There is an abnormality or decline in performance in quantified cognitive assessments (eg, neuropsychological tests or mental status examination). D. None of the difficulties listed in criterion B (1)–(5) is such that a diagnosis made of dementia, organic amnesic syndrome, delirium, postencephalitic syndrome, postconcussional syndrome, or other persisting cognitive impairment due to psychoactive substance use.	**Comments** If criterion G1 for other mental disorders due to brain damage and dysfunction and to physical disease is fulfilled by the presence of central nervous system dysfunction, it is usually presumed that this is the cause of the mild cognitive disorder. If criterion G1 is fulfilled by the presence of a systemic physical disorder, it is often unjustified to assume that there is a direct causative relationship. Nevertheless, it may be useful in such instances to record the presence of the systemic physical disorder as "associated," without implying a necessary causation. An additional fifth character may be used for this: **Not associated with a systemic physical disorder** **Associated with a systemic physical disorder** The systemic physical disorder should be recorded separately by its appropriate ICD-10 code. **Other specified mental disorders due to brain damage and dysfunction and to physical disease** Examples of this category are transient or mild abnormal mood states occurring during treatment with steroids or antidepressants which do not meet the criteria for organic mood disorder. **Unspecified mental disorder due to brain damage and dysfunction and to physical disease**

of the population in the United States. For psychiatrists, the major concerns about epilepsy are consideration of an epileptic diagnosis in psychiatric patients, the psychosocial ramifications of a diagnosis of epilepsy for a patient, and the psychological and cognitive effects of commonly used antiepileptic drugs. With regard to the first of these concerns, 30 to 50 percent of all people with epilepsy have psychiatric difficulties sometime during the course of their illness. The most common behavioral symptom of epilepsy is a change in personality; psychosis, violence, and depression occur much less commonly in epileptic disorders.

Definitions

A seizure is a transient paroxysmal pathophysiological disturbance of cerebral function caused by a spontaneous, excessive discharge of neurons. Patients are said to have epilepsy if they have a chronic condition characterized by recurrent seizure. The ictus or ictal event of a seizure is the seizure itself. The nonictal periods can be categorized as preictal, postictal, and interictal. The symptoms present during the ictal event are determined primarily by the site of origin in the brain for the seizure and by the pattern of the spread of seizure activity through the brain. Interictal symptoms are influenced by the ictal event and other neuropsychiatric and psychosocial factors, such as coexisting psychiatric or neurological disorders, the presence of psychosocial stressors, and premorbid personality traits.

Classification

The two major categories of seizures are partial and generalized. Partial seizures involve epileptiform activity in localized brain regions (Fig. 10.5–1). Generalized seizures involve the entire brain; a classification system for seizures is outlined in Table 10.5–7.

Generalized Seizures. Generalized tonic-clonic seizures exhibit the classic symptoms of loss of consciousness, generalized tonic-clonic movements of the limbs, tongue biting, and incontinence. Although the diagnosis of the ictal events of the seizure is relatively straightforward, the postictal state, characterized by a slow, gradual recovery of consciousness and cognition, occasionally presents a diagnostic dilemma for a psychiatrist in an emergency room. The period of recovery from a generalized tonic-clonic seizure ranges from a few minutes to many hours, and the clinical picture is that of a gradually clearing delirium. The most common psychiatric problems associated with generalized seizures involve helping patients adjust to a chronic neurological disorder and assessing the cognitive or behavioral effects of antiepileptic drugs.

ABSENCES (PETIT MAL). A difficult type of generalized seizure for a psychiatrist to diagnose is an absence or petit mal seizure. The epileptic nature of the episodes may go unrecognized, because the characteristic motor or sensory manifestations of epilepsy may be absent or so slight that they do not arouse suspicion. Petit mal epilepsy usually begins in childhood between the ages of 5 and 7 years and ceases by puberty. Brief disruptions of consciousness, during

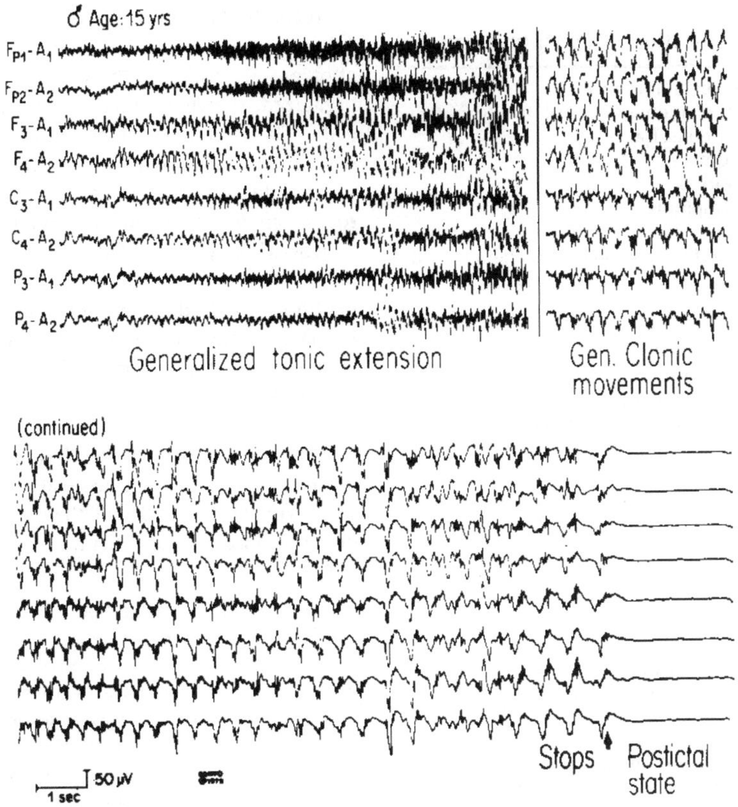
♂ Age: 15 yrs
Fp1-A1
Fp2-A2
F3-A1
F4-A2
C3-A1
C4-A2
P3-A1
P4-A2
Generalized tonic extension
Gen. Clonic movements
(continued)
Stops
Postictal state
50 µV
1 sec

FIGURE 10.5–1

Electroencephalographic recording during generalized tonic-clonic seizure, showing rhythmic sharp waves and muscles artifact during tonic phase, spike and wave discharges during clonic phase, and attenuation of activity during postictal state. (Courtesy of Barbara F. Westmoreland, M.D.)

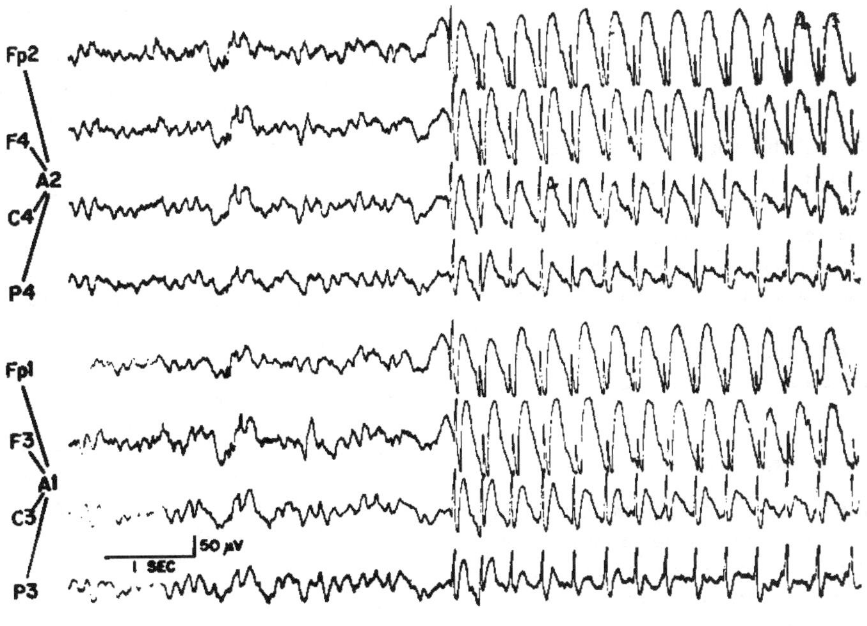
Fp2
F4
A2
C4
P4
Fpl
F3
Al
C3
P3
50 µV
1 SEC

FIGURE 10.5–2

Petit mal epilepsy characterized by bilaterally synchronous, 3-Hz spike and slow-wave activity.

Table 10.5–7
International Classification of Epileptic Seizures

- I. Partial seizures (seizures beginning locally)
  - A. Partial seizures with elementary symptoms (generally without impairment of consciousness)
    - 1. With motor symptoms
    - 2. With sensory symptoms
    - 3. With autonomic symptoms
    - 4. Compound forms
  - B. Partial seizures with complex symptoms (generally with impairment of consciousness; temporal lobe or psychomotor seizures)
    - 1. With impairment of consciousness only
    - 2. With cognitive symptoms
    - 3. With affective symptoms
    - 4. With psychosensory symptoms
    - 5. With psychosensory symptoms (automatisms)
    - 6. Compound forms
  - C. Partial seizures secondarily generalized
- II. Generalized seizures (bilaterally symmetrical and without local onset)
  - A. Absences (petit mal)
  - B. Myoclonus
  - C. Infantile spasms
  - D. Clonic seizures
  - E. Tonic seizures
  - F. Tonic-clonic seizures (grand mal)
  - G. Atonic seizures
  - H. Akinetic seizures
- III. Unilateral seizures
- IV. Unclassified seizures (because of incomplete data)

Adapted from Gastaut H: Clinical and electroencephalographical classification of epileptic seizures. Epilepsia *11*:102, 1970.

which the patient suddenly loses contact with the environment, are characteristic of petit mal epilepsy, but the patient has no true loss of consciousness and no convulsive movements during the episodes. The electroencephalogram (EEG) produces a characteristic pattern of three-per-second spike-and-wave activity (Fig. 10.5–2). In rare instances, petit mal epilepsy begins in adulthood. Adult-onset petit mal epilepsy can be characterized by sudden, recurrent psychotic episodes or deliriums that appear and disappear abruptly. The symptoms may be accompanied by a history of falling or fainting spells.

Partial Seizures. Partial seizures are classified as either simple (without alterations in consciousness) or complex (with an alteration in consciousness). Somewhat more than half of all patients with partial seizures have complex partial seizures. Other terms used for complex partial seizures are temporal lobe epilepsy, psychomotor seizures, and limbic epilepsy; these terms, however, are not accurate descriptions of the clinical situation. Complex partial epilepsy, the most common form of epilepsy in adults, affects approximately 3 in 1,000 persons.

Symptoms

Preictal Symptoms. Preictal events (auras) in complex partial epilepsy include autonomic sensations (such as fullness in the stomach, blushing, and changes in respiration), cognitive sensations (such as déjà vu, *jamais vu,* forced thinking, and dreamy states), affective states (such as fear, panic, depression, and elation), and, classically, automatisms (such as lip smacking, rubbing, and chewing).

Ictal Symptoms. Brief, disorganized, and uninhibited behavior characterizes the ictal event. Although some defense attorneys may claim otherwise, rarely does a person exhibit organized, directed violent behavior during an epileptic episode. The cognitive symptoms include amnesia for the time during the seizure and a period of resolving delirium after the seizure. In patients with complex partial epilepsy, a seizure focus can be found on an EEG in 25 to 50 percent of all patients (Fig. 10.5–3). The use of sphenoidal or anterior temporal electrodes and of sleep-deprived EEGs may increase the likelihood of finding an EEG abnormality. Multiple normal EEGs are often obtained for a patient with complex partial epilepsy; therefore, normal EEGs cannot be used to exclude a diagnosis of complex partial epilepsy. The use of long-term EEG recordings (usually 24 to 72 hours) can help clinicians detect a seizure focus in some patients. Most studies show that the use of nasopharyngeal leads does not add much to the sensitivity of an EEG, but they do add to the discomfort of the procedure for the patient.

Interictal Symptoms. PERSONALITY DISTURBANCES. The most frequent psychiatric abnormalities reported in epileptic patients are personality disorders, and they are especially likely to occur in patients with epilepsy of temporal lobe origin. The most common features are religiosity, a heightened experience of emotions—a quality usually called viscosity of personality—and changes in sexual behavior. The syndrome in its complete form is relatively rare, even in those with complex partial seizures of temporal lobe origin. Many patients are not affected by personality disturbances; others suffer from a variety of disturbances that differ strikingly from the classic syndrome.

A striking religiosity may be manifested not only by increased participation in overtly religious activities but also by unusual concern for moral and ethical issues, preoccupation with right and wrong, and heightened interest in global and philosophical concerns. The hyperreligious features can sometimes seem like the prodromal symptoms of schizophrenia and can result in a diagnostic problem in an adolescent or a young adult.

The symptom of viscosity of personality is usually most noticeable in a patient's conversation, which is likely to be slow, serious, ponderous, pedantic, overly replete with nonessential details, and often circumstantial. The listener may grow bored but be unable to find a courteous and successful way to disengage from the conversation. The speech tendencies, often mirrored in the patient's writing, result in a symptom known as hypergraphia, which some clinicians consider virtually pathognomonic for complex partial epilepsy.

Changes in sexual behavior may be manifested by hypersexuality; deviations in sexual interest, such as fetishism and transvestism; and, most commonly, hyposexuality. The hyposexuality is characterized both by a lack of interest in sexual matters and by reduced sexual arousal. Some patients with the onset of complex partial epilepsy before puberty may fail to reach a normal level of sexual interest after puberty, although this characteristic may not disturb the patient. For patients with the onset of complex partial epilepsy after puberty, the change in sexual interest may be bothersome and worrisome.

PSYCHOTIC SYMPTOMS. Interictal psychotic states are more common than are ictal psychoses. Schizophrenia-like interictal episodes can occur in patients with epilepsy, particularly those with temporal lobe origins. An estimated 10 to 30 percent of all patients with complex partial epilepsy have psychotic symptoms. Risk factors for the symptoms include female gender, left-handedness, the onset of seizures during puberty, and a left-sided lesion.

The onset of psychotic symptoms in epilepsy is variable. Classically, psychotic symptoms appear in patients who have had epilepsy for a long time, and the onset of psychotic symptoms is preceded by the development of personality changes related to the epileptic brain activity. The most characteristic symptoms of the psychoses are hallucinations and paranoid delusions. Patients usually remain warm and appropriate in affect, in contrast to the abnormalities of affect commonly seen in patients with schizophrenia. The thought disorder symptoms in patients with psychotic epilepsy are most commonly those involving concep-

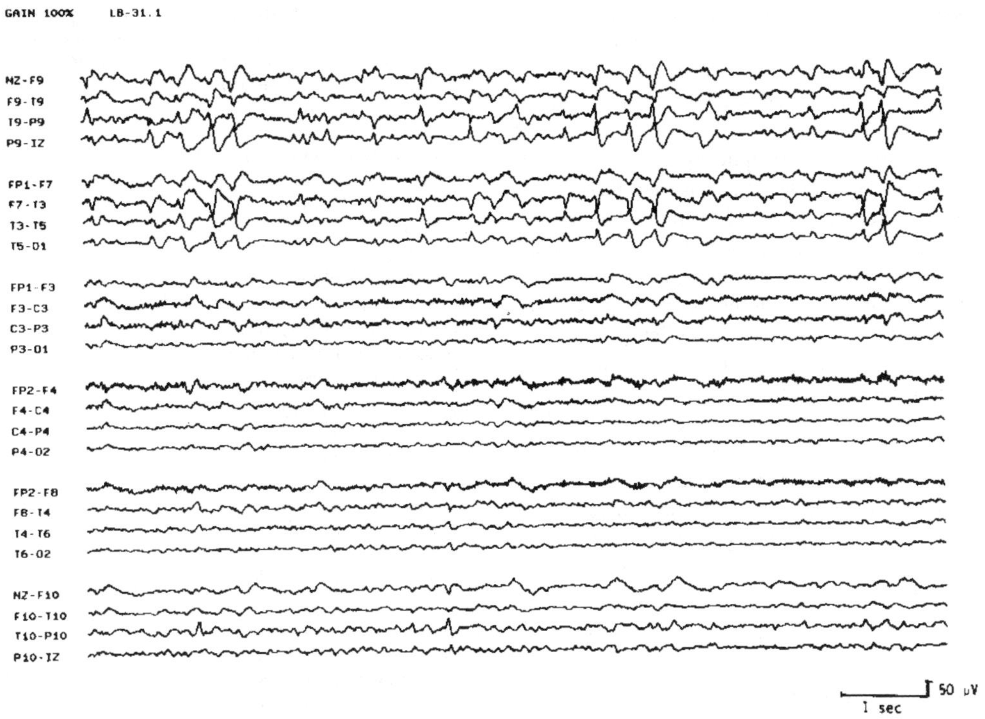
GAIN 100%
LB-31.1
NZ-F9
F9-T9
T9-P9
P9-IZ
FP1-F7
F7-T3
T3-T5
T5-O1
FP1-F3
F3-C3
C3-P3
P3-O1
FP2-F4
F4-C4
C4-P4
P4-O2
FP2-F8
F8-T4
T4-T6
T6-O2
NZ-F10
F10-T10
T10-P10
P10-IZ
50 μV
1 sec

FIGURE 10.5–3
An interictal encephalograph in a patient with complex partial seizures reveals frequent left-temporal spike discharges and rare, independent right-temporal sharp-wave activity. (Reprinted with permission from Cascino GD: Complex partial seizures: Clinical features and differential diagnosis. Psychiatr Clin North Am *15:* 377, 1992.)

tualization and circumstantiality, rather than the classic schizophrenic symptoms of blocking and looseness.

VIOLENCE. Episodic violence has been a problem in some patients with epilepsy, especially epilepsy of temporal and frontal lobe origin. Whether the violence is a manifestation of the seizure itself or is of interictal psychopathological origin is uncertain. Most evidence points to the extreme rarity of violence as an ictal phenomenon. Only in rare cases should an epileptic patient's violence be attributed to the seizure itself.

MOOD DISORDER SYMPTOMS. Mood disorder symptoms, such as depression and mania, are seen less often in epilepsy than are schizophrenia-like symptoms. The mood disorder symptoms that do occur tend to be episodic and appear most often when the epileptic foci affect the temporal lobe of the nondominant cerebral hemisphere. The importance of mood disorder symptoms may be attested to by the increased incidence of attempted suicide in people with epilepsy.

Diagnosis

A correct diagnosis of epilepsy can be particularly difficult when the ictal and interictal symptoms of epilepsy are severe manifestations of psychiatric symptoms in the absence of significant changes in consciousness and cognitive abilities. Therefore, psychiatrists must maintain a high level of suspicion during the evaluation of a new patient and must consider the possibility of an epileptic disorder, even in the absence of the classic signs and symptoms. Another differential diagnosis to consider is that of pseudoseizure, in which a patient has some conscious control over mimicking the symptoms of a seizure (Table 10.5–8).

Table 10.5–8
Differentiating Features of Pseudoseizures and Epileptic Seizures

Feature	Epileptic Seizures	Pseudoseizure
Clinical features		
Nocturnal seizure	Common	Uncommon
Stereotyped aura	Usually	None
Cyanotic skin changes during seizures	Common	None
Self-injury	Common	Rare
Incontinence	Common	Rare
Postictal confusion	Present	None
Body movements	Tonic or clonic or both	Nonstereotyped and asynchronous
Affected by suggestion	No	Yes
EEG features		
Spike and waveforms	Present	Absent
Postictal slowing	Present	Absent
Interictal abnormalities	Variable	Variable

Reprinted with permission from Stevenson JM, King JH: Neuropsychiatric aspects of epilepsy and epileptic seizures. In *American Psychiatric Press Textbook of Neuropsychiatry,* RE Hales, SC Yodofsky, editors, p 220. American Psychiatric Press, Washington, 1987.

For patients who have previously received a diagnosis of epilepsy, the appearance of new psychiatric symptoms should be considered as possibly representing an evolution in their epileptic symptoms. The appearance of psychotic symptoms, mood disorder symptoms, personality changes, or symptoms of anxiety (such as panic attacks) should cause a clinician to evaluate the control of the patient's epilepsy and to assess the patient for the presence of an independent mental disorder. In such circumstances, the clinician should evaluate the patient's compliance with the antiepileptic drug regimen and should consider whether the psychiatric symptoms could be toxic effects from the antiepileptic drugs themselves. When psychiatric symptoms appear in a patient who has had epilepsy diagnosed or considered as a diagnosis in the past, the clinician should obtain one or more EEG examinations.

In patients who have not previously received a diagnosis of epilepsy, four characteristics should cause a clinician to be suspicious of the possibility: the abrupt onset of psychosis in a person previously regarded as psychologically healthy, the abrupt onset of delirium without a recognized cause, a history of similar episodes with abrupt onset and spontaneous recovery, and a history of previous unexplained falling or fainting spells.

Treatment

The drugs of choice for various types of seizures are listed in Table 10.5–9. Carbamazepine (Tegretol) and valproic acid (Depakene) may be helpful in controlling the symptoms of irritability and outbursts of aggression, as are the typical antipsychotic drugs. Psychotherapy, family counseling, and group therapy may be useful in addressing the psychosocial issues associated with epilepsy. In addition, clinicians should be aware that many antiepileptic drugs cause a mild to moderate degree of cognitive impairment, and an adjustment of the dosage or a change in medications should be considered if symptoms of cognitive impairment are a problem in a patient.

Table 10.5–9
Drugs of Choice for Various Types of Seizures

Generalized tonic-clonic (grand mal) seizures
Carbamazepine (Tegretol)
Phenytoin (Dilantin)
Valproic acid (Depakote)
Phenobarbital (Luminal)
Vigabatrin (Sabril)
Topiramate (Topamax)
Gabapentin (Neurontin)
Lamotrigine (Lamictal)
Tiagabine (Gabitril)
Absence (petit mal) seizures
Ethosuximide (Zarontin)
Valproic acid (Depakote)
Lamotrigine (Lamictal)
Simple partial seizures
Phenytoin (Dilantin)
Carbamazepine (Tegretol)
Vigabatrin (Sabril)
Topiramate (Topamax)
Tiagabine (Gabitril)
Lamotrigine (Lamictal)
Gabapentin (Neurontin)
Phenobarbital (Luminal)
Complex partial seizures
Phenytoin (Dilantin)
Carbamazepine (Tegretol)
Valproic acid (Depakote)
Vigabatrin (Sabril)
Topiramate (Topamax)
Tiagabine (Gabitril)
Lamotrigine (Lamictal)
Gabapentin (Neurontin)
Phenobarbital (Luminal)
Myoclonic, atonic, akinetic, and atypical absence seizures
Valproic acid (Depakote)
Clonazepam (Klonopin)
Topiramate (Topamax)
Lamotrigine (Lamictal)
Infantile spasms
Adrenocorticotropic hormone
Valproic acid (Depakote)
Clonazepam (Klonopin)
Vigabatrin (Sabril)
Lamotrigine (Lamictal)
Status epilepticus
Phenytoin (Dilantin)
Phenobarbital (Luminal)
Diazepam (Valium)
Lorazepam (Ativan)
Fosphenytoin (Cerebyx)
Paraldehyde
General anesthesia

BRAIN TUMORS

Brain tumors and cerebrovascular diseases can cause virtually any psychiatric symptom or syndrome, but cerebrovascular diseases, by the nature of their onset and symptom pattern, are rarely misdiagnosed as mental disorders. In general, tumors are associated with much less psychopathological affectations than are cerebrovascular diseases affecting a similar volume of brain tissue. The two key approaches to the diagnosis of either condition are a comprehensive clinical history and a complete neurological examination. Performance of the appropriate brain imaging technique is usually the final diagnostic procedure; the imaging should confirm the clinical diagnosis, not discover an unsuspected cause.

Clinical Features, Course, and Prognosis

Mental symptoms are experienced at some time during the course of illness in approximately 50 percent of patients with brain tumors. In approximately 80 percent of these patients with mental symptoms, the tumors are located in frontal or limbic brain regions rather than in parietal or temporal regions. Meningiomas are likely to cause focal symptoms by compressing a limited region of the cortex, whereas gliomas are likely to cause diffuse symptoms. Delirium is most often a component of rapidly growing, large, or metastatic tumors. If a patient's history and a physical examination reveal bowel or bladder incontinence, a frontal lobe tumor should be suspected; if the history and examination reveal abnormalities in memory and speech, a temporal lobe tumor should be suspected.

Cognition. Impaired intellectual functioning often accompanies the presence of a brain tumor, regardless of its type or location.

Language Skills. Disorders of language function may be severe, particularly if tumor growth is rapid. In fact, defects of language function often obscure all other mental symptoms.

Memory. Loss of memory is a frequent symptom of brain tumors. Patients with brain tumors exhibit Korsakoff's syndrome and retain no memory of events that occurred since the illness began. Events of the immediate past, even painful ones, are lost. Patients, however, retain old memories and are unaware of their loss of recent memory.

Perception. Prominent perceptual defects are often associated with behavioral disorders, especially because patients must integrate tactile, auditory, and visual perceptions to function normally.

Awareness. Alterations of consciousness are common late symptoms of increased intracranial pressure caused by a brain tumor. Tumors arising in the upper part of the brain stem may produce a unique symptom called akinetic mutism or vigilant coma. The patient is immobile and mute, yet alert.

Colloid Cysts

Although they are not brain tumors, colloid cysts located in the third ventricle can exert physical pressure on structures within the diencephalon and produce such mental symptoms as depression, emotional lability, psychotic symptoms, and personality changes. The classic associated neurological symptoms are position-dependent intermittent headaches.

HEAD TRAUMA

Head trauma can result in an array of mental symptoms and can lead to a diagnosis of dementia due to head trauma or to mental disorder not otherwise specified due to a general medical condition (such as postconcussional disorder). The postconcussive syndrome remains controversial, because it focuses on the wide range of psychiatric symptoms, some serious, that can follow what seem to be minor head traumas. DSM-IV includes a set of research criteria for postconcussional disorder in an appendix (Table 10.5–10).

Table 10.5–10
DSM-IV Diagnostic Criteria for Postconcussional Disorder

A. A history of head trauma that has caused significant cerebral concussion.
Note: The manifestations of concussion include loss of consciousness, posttraumatic amnesia, and less commonly, posttraumatic onset of seizures. The specific method of defining this criterion needs to be established by further research.

B. Evidence from neuropsychological testing or quantified cognitive assessment of difficulty in attention (concentrating, shifting focus of attention, performing simultaneous cognitive tasks) or memory (learning or recalling information).

C. Three (or more) of the following occur shortly after the trauma and last at least 3 months.
(1) becoming fatigued easily
(2) disordered sleep
(3) headache
(4) vertigo or dizziness
(5) irritability or aggression on little or no provocation
(6) anxiety, depression, or affective lability
(7) changes in personality (eg, social or sexual inappropriateness)
(8) apathy or lack of spontaneity

D. The symptoms in criteria B and C have their onset following head trauma or else represent a substantial worsening of preexisting symptoms.

E. The disturbance causes significant impairment in social or occupational functioning and represents a significant decline from a previous level of functioning. In school-age children, the impairment may be manifested by a significant worsening in school or academic performance dating from the trauma.

F. The symptoms do not meet criteria for dementia due to head trauma and are not better accounted for by another mental disorder (eg, amnestic disorder due to head trauma, personality change due to head trauma).

Pathophysiology

Head trauma is a common clinical situation; an estimated 2 million incidents involve head trauma each year. Head trauma most commonly occurs in people 15 to 25 years of age and has a male-to-female predominance of approximately 3 to 1. Gross estimates based on the severity of the head trauma suggest that virtually all patients with serious head trauma, more than half of patients with moderate head trauma, and about 10 percent of patients with mild head trauma have ongoing neuropsychiatric sequelae resulting from the head trauma. Head trauma can be divided grossly into penetrating head trauma (such as trauma produced by a bullet) and blunt trauma, in which there is no physical penetration of the skull. Blunt trauma is far more common than penetrating head trauma. Motor vehicle accidents account for more than half of all the incidents of blunt central nervous system (CNS) trauma, and falls, violence, and sports-related head trauma account for most of the remaining cases.

Whereas brain injury from penetrating wounds is usually localized to the areas directly affected by the missile, brain injury from blunt trauma involves several mechanisms. During the actual head trauma, the head usually moves back and forth violently, so that the brain crashes repeatedly against the skull as it and the skull are mismatched in their rapid deceleration and acceleration. This crashing results in focal contusions, and the stretching of the brain parenchyma produces diffuse axonal injury. Later-developing processes, such as edema and hemorrhaging, may result in further damage to the brain.

Symptoms

The two major clusters of symptoms related to head trauma are those of cognitive impairment and of behavioral sequelae. After a period of posttraumatic amnesia, there is usually a 6- to 12-month period of recovery, after which the remaining symptoms are likely to be permanent. The most common cognitive problems are a decreased speed in information processing, decreased attention, increased distractibility, deficits in problem solving and in the ability to sustain effort, and problems with memory and learning new information. A variety of language disabilities may also be present.

Behaviorally, the major symptoms involve depression, increased impulsivity, increased aggression, and changes in personality. These symptoms may be further exacerbated by the use of alcohol, which is often involved in the head trauma event itself. A debate has ensued about how preexisting character and personality traits affect the development of behavioral symptoms after a head trauma. The critical studies needed to answer the question definitively have not yet been done, but the weight of opinion is leaning toward a biologically and neuroanatomically based association between the head trauma and the behavioral sequelae.

Treatment

The treatment of the cognitive and behavioral disorders in head trauma patients is basically similar to the treatment approaches used in other patients with these symptoms. One difference is that head trauma patients may be particularly susceptible to the side effects associated with psychotropic drugs; therefore, these agents should be initiated in lower dosages than usual and should be titrated upward more slowly than usual. Standard antidepressants can be used to treat depression, and either anticonvulsants or antipsychotics can be used to treat aggression and impulsivity. Other approaches to the symptoms include lithium (Eskalith), calcium channel blockers, and β-adrenergic antagonists.

Clinicians must support patients through individual or group psychotherapy and should support the major caretakers through couples and family therapy. Especially with minor and moderate head traumas, the patients rejoin their families and restart their jobs; therefore, all involved parties need help to adjust to any changes in the affected patient's personality and mental abilities.

DEMYELINATING DISORDERS

Multiple sclerosis (MS) is the major demyelinating disorder. Other demyelinating disorders include amyotrophic lateral sclerosis (ALS), metachromatic leukodystrophy, adrenoleukodystrophy, gangliosidoses, subacute sclerosing panencephalitis, and Kufs' disease. All these disorders can be associated with neurological, cognitive, and behavioral symptoms.

Multiple Sclerosis

MS is characterized by multiple episodes of symptoms, pathophysiologically related to multifocal lesions in the white matter of the CNS. The cause remains unknown, but studies have focused on slow viral infections and disturbances in the immune system. The estimated prevalence of multiple sclerosis in the Western Hemisphere is 50 per 100,000 people. The disease is much more frequent in cold and temperate climates than in the tropics and subtropics and more common in women than in men; it is predominantly a disease of young adults. In most patients, the onset occurs between the ages of 20 and 40 years.

The neuropsychiatric symptoms of MS can be divided into cognitive and behavioral types. Research reports have found that 30 to 50 percent of patients with MS have some cognitive impairment and that 20 to 30 percent of MS patients have serious cognitive impairments. Although evidence indicates that MS patients experience a decline in their general intelligence, memory is the most commonly affected cognitive function. The severity of the memory impairment does not seem to be correlated with the severity of the neurological symptoms or the duration of the illness. Other cognitive impairments can be seen in MS, as is expected for a disease in which any part of the brain can be affected by the white matter lesions.

The behavioral symptoms associated with MS are euphoria, depression, and personality changes. Psychosis is a rare complication. Approximately 25 percent of people with MS exhibit a euphoric mood that is not hypomanic in severity but, rather, somewhat more cheerful than their situation warrants and not necessarily in character with their disposition before the onset of MS. Only 10 percent of MS patients have a sustained and elevated mood, although it is still not truly hypomanic in severity. Depression, however, is common; it affects 25 to 50 percent of patients with MS and results in a higher rate of suicide than is seen in the general population. Risk factors for suicide in MS patients are male sex, onset of MS before age 30, and a relatively recent diagnosis of the disorder. Personality changes are also common in MS patients; they affect 20 to 40 percent of patients and are often characterized by increased irritability or apathy.

Amyotrophic Lateral Sclerosis

ALS is a progressive, noninherited disease of asymmetrical muscle atrophy. It begins in adult life and progresses over months or years to involve all the striated muscles except the cardiac and ocular muscles. In addition to muscle atrophy, patients have signs of pyramidal tract involvement. The illness is rare and occurs in approximately 1.6 persons per 100,000 a year. A few patients have concomitant dementia. The disease progresses rapidly, and death generally occurs within 4 years of onset.

INFECTIOUS DISEASES

Herpes Simplex Encephalitis

Herpes simplex encephalitis is the most common type of focal encephalitis and most commonly affects the frontal and temporal lobes. The symptoms often include anosmia, olfactory and gustatory hallucinations, and personality changes and can also involve bizarre or psychotic behaviors. Complex partial epilepsy may also develop in patients with herpes simplex encephalitis. Although the mortality rate for the infection has decreased, many patients exhibit personality changes, symptoms of memory loss, and psychotic symptoms.

Rabies Encephalitis

The incubation period for rabies ranges from 10 days to 1 year, after which symptoms of restlessness, overactivity, and agitation can develop. Hydrophobia, present in up to 50 percent of patients, is characterized by an intense fear of drinking water. The fear develops from the severe laryngeal and diaphragmatic spasms that the patients experience when they drink water. Once rabies encephalitis develops, the disease is fatal within days or weeks.

Neurosyphilis

Neurosyphilis (also known as general paresis) appears 10 to 15 years after the primary *Treponema* infection. Since the advent of penicillin, neurosyphilis has become a rare disorder, although acquired immune deficiency syndrome (AIDS) is associated with reintroducing neurosyphilis into medical practice in some urban settings. Neurosyphilis generally affects the frontal lobes and results in personality changes, the development of poor judgment, irritability, and decreased care for self. Delusions of grandeur develop in 10 to 20 percent of affected patients. The disease progresses with the development of dementia and tremor, until patients are paretic. The neurological symptoms include Argyll-Robertson pupils, which are small, irregular, and unequal and have light–near reflex dissociation; tremor; dysarthria; and hyperreflexia. A cerebrospinal fluid examination shows lymphocytosis, increased protein, and a positive result on a Venereal Disease Research Laboratory test.

Chronic Meningitis

Chronic meningitis is also seen more often than it has in the recent past because of the immunocompromised condition of people with AIDS. The most usual causative agents are *Mycobacterium tuberculosis, Cryptococcus,* and *Coccidioides.* The usual symptoms are headache, memory impairment, confusion, and fever.

Subacute Sclerosing Panencephalitis

Subacute sclerosing panencephalitis is a disease of childhood and early adolescence, with a 3 to 1 male-to-female ratio. The onset usually follows either an infection with measles or a vaccination for measles. The initial symptoms may be behavioral change, temper tantrums, sleepiness, and hallucinations, but the classic symptoms of myoclonus, ataxia, seizures, and intellectual deterioration eventually develop. The disease relentlessly progresses to coma and death in 1 to 2 years.

Prion Disease

Creutzfeldt-Jakob Disease Creutzfeldt-Jakob disease is a rare degenerative brain disease caused by a slow virus infection or a mutation in the prion protein gene. A progressive dementia occurs, accompanied by ataxia, extrapyramidal signs, choreoathetosis, and dysarthria. Men and women are equally affected. The disease is most common in adults in their 50s, and death occurs usually within 1 year after the diagnosis is made. No treatment is known. Computed tomography scans show cerebellar and cortical atrophy, and specific EEG changes occur in the late stages. Death usually occurs within 6 months after onset. Creutzfeldt-Jakob disease can be transmitted by use of contaminated dura matter and corneal grafts and treatment with infected cadaver-derived pituitary growth hormone and gonadotrophin.

In 1996, a new variant of Creutzfeldt-Jakob disease was identified in young people in the United Kingdom. It is characterized by psychiatric changes in behavior and personality, early ataxia, and eventual severe dementia and death. The disease was found to have been transmitted to humans by cattle with bovine spongiform encephalopathy. Bovine spongiform encephalopathy is an encephalopathy that is transmitted between cattle and to other animals by feed containing animal parts, particularly brain and spinal cord. Both kuru and Creutzfeldt-Jakob disease are known as *prion diseases* because they affect the prion protein gene, which can be altered through inherited mutations or viral transmission. Prion diseases are characterized by spongiform change, loss of neurons, and proliferation of astrocytes.

Kuru. Kuru is a progressive dementia accompanied by extrapyramidal signs. It is found among inhabitants of New Guinea who practice cannibalistic rites. By eating the brains of infected people, the natives take in the slow virus that produces the fatal disease. Kuru has a long incubation period (up to 40 years). Death occurs within 1 year of the onset of symptoms.

IMMUNE DISORDERS

The major immune disorder in contemporary society is AIDS, but other immune disorders can also present diagnostic and treatment challenges to mental health clinicians.

Systemic Lupus Erythematosus

Systemic lupus erythematosus (SLE) is an autoimmune disease that involves a sterile inflammation of multiple organ systems. The officially accepted diagnosis of SLE requires a patient to have 4 of 11 criteria that have been defined by the American Rheumatism Association. Between 5 and 50 percent of SLE patients have mental symptoms at the initial presentation, and approximately 50 percent of patients eventually show neuropsychiatric manifestations. The major symptoms are depression, insomnia, emotional lability, nervousness, and confusion. Treatment with steroids commonly induces further psychiatric complications, including mania and psychosis.

ENDOCRINE DISORDERS

Thyroid Disorders

Hyperthyroidism is characterized by confusion, anxiety, and an agitated depressive syndrome. Patients may also complain of being easily fatigued and of feeling generally weak. Insomnia, weight loss despite increased appetite, tremulousness, palpitations, and increased perspiration are also common symptoms. Serious psychiatric symptoms include impairments in memory, orientation, and judgment; manic excitement; delusions; and hallucinations.

In 1949, Irvin Asher named hypothyroidism *myxedema madness.* In its most severe form, hypothyroidism is characterized by paranoia, depression, hypomania, and hallucinations. Slowed thinking and delirium can also be symptoms. The physical symptoms include weight gain, a deep voice, thin and dry hair, loss of the lateral eyebrow, facial puffiness, cold intolerance, and impaired hearing. Approximately 10 percent of all patients have residual neuropsychiatric symptoms after hormone replacement therapy.

Parathyroid Disorders

Dysfunction of the parathyroid gland results in the abnormal regulation of calcium metabolism. Excessive secretion of the parathyroid hormone causes hypercalcemia, which can result in delirium, personality changes, and apathy in 50 to 60 percent of patients and in cognitive impairments in approximately 25 percent of patients. Neuromuscular excitability, which depends on proper calcium ion concentration, is reduced, and muscle weakness may appear.

Hypocalcemia can occur with hypoparathyroid disorders and can result in neuropsychiatric symptoms of delirium and personality changes. If the calcium level decreases gradually, clinicians may see the psychiatric symptoms without the characteristic tetany of hypocalcemia. Other symptoms of hypocalcemia are cataract formation, seizures, extrapyramidal symptoms, and increased intracranial pressure.

Adrenal Disorders

Adrenal disorders disturb the normal secretion of hormones from the adrenal cortex and produce significant neurological and psychological changes. Patients with chronic adrenocortical insufficiency (Addison's disease), which is most frequently the result of adrenocortical atrophy or granulomatous invasion caused by tuberculous or fungal infection, exhibit mild mental symptoms, such as apathy, easy fatigability, irritability, and depression. Occasionally, confusion or psychotic reactions develop. Cortisone or one of its synthetic derivatives is effective in correcting such abnormalities.

Excessive quantities of cortisol produced endogenously by an adrenocortical tumor or hyperplasia (Cushing's syndrome) lead to a secondary mood disorder, a syndrome of agitated depression, and, often, suicide. Decreased concentration and memory deficits may also be present. Psychotic reactions, with schizophrenia-like symptoms, are seen in a small number of patients. The administration of high doses of exogenous corticosteroids typically leads to a secondary mood disorder similar to mania. Severe depression may follow the termination of steroid therapy.

Pituitary Disorders

Patients with total pituitary failure can exhibit psychiatric symptoms, particularly postpartum women who have hemorrhaged into the pituitary, a condition known as Sheehan's syndrome. Patients have a combination of symptoms, especially of thyroid and adrenal disorders, and can show virtually any psychiatric symptom.

METABOLIC DISORDERS

A common cause of organic brain dysfunction, metabolic encephalopathy is capable of producing alterations in mental processes, behavior, and neurological functions. The diagnosis should be considered whenever recent and rapid changes in behavior, thinking, and consciousness have occurred. The earliest signals are likely to be impairment of memory, particularly recent memory, and impairment of orientation. Some patients become agitated, anxious, and hyperactive; others become quiet, withdrawn, and inactive. As metabolic encephalopathies progress, confusion or delirium gives way to decreased responsiveness, to stupor, and, eventually, to death.

Hepatic Encephalopathy

Severe hepatic failure can result in hepatic encephalopathy, characterized by, asterixis, hyperventilation, EEG abnormalities, and alterations in consciousness. The alterations in consciousness can range from apathy to drowsiness to coma. Associated psychiatric symptoms are changes in memory, general intellectual skills, and personality.

Uremic Encephalopathy

Renal failure is associated with alterations in memory, orientation, and consciousness. Restlessness, crawling sensations on the limbs, muscle twitching, and persistent hiccups are also associated symptoms. In young people with brief episodes of uremia, the neuropsychiatric symptoms tend to be reversible; in elderly people with long episodes of uremia, the neuropsychiatric symptoms can be irreversible.

Hypoglycemic Encephalopathy

Hypoglycemic encephalopathy can be caused either by the excessive endogenous production of insulin or by excessive exogenous insulin administration. The premonitory symptoms, which do not occur in every patient, include nausea, sweating, tachycardia, and feelings of hunger, apprehension, and restlessness. As the disorder progresses, disorientation, confusion, and hallucinations, as well as other neurological and medical symptoms, can develop. Stupor and coma may occur, and a residual and persistent dementia can sometimes be a serious neuropsychiatric sequela of the disorder.

Diabetic Ketoacidosis

Diabetic ketoacidosis begins with feelings of weakness, easy fatigability, and listlessness and with increasing polyuria and polydipsia. Headache and sometimes nausea and vomiting appear. Patients with diabetes mellitus have an increased likelihood of chronic dementia with general arteriosclerosis.

Acute Intermittent Porphyria

The porphyrias are disorders of heme biosynthesis which result in the excessive accumulation of porphyrins. The triad of symptoms is acute, colicky abdominal pain, motor polyneuropathy, and psychosis. Acute intermittent porphyria is an autosomal dominant disorder that affects more women than men and that has its onset between ages 20 and 50. The psychiatric symptoms include anxiety, insomnia, lability of mood, depression, and psychosis. Some studies have found that between 0.2 and 0.5 percent of chronic psychiatric patients may have undiagnosed porphyrias. Barbiturates precipitate or aggravate the attacks of acute porphyria, and the use of barbiturates for any reason is absolutely contraindicated in a person with acute intermittent porphyria and in anyone who has a relative with the disease.

NUTRITIONAL DISORDERS

Niacin Deficiency

Dietary insufficiency of niacin (nicotinic acid) and its precursor, tryptophan, is associated with pellagra, a globally occurring nutritional deficiency disease seen in association with alcohol abuse, vegetarian diets, and extreme poverty and starvation. The neuropsychiatric symptoms of pellagra include apathy, irritability, insomnia, depression, and delirium; the medical symptoms include dermatitis, peripheral neuropathies, and diarrhea. The course of pellagra has traditionally been described as five *D*s: dermatitis, diarrhea, delirium, dementia, and death. The response to treatment with nicotinic acid is rapid; but dementia from prolonged illness may improve only slowly and incompletely.

Thiamine Deficiency

Thiamine (vitamin B_1) deficiency leads to beriberi, characterized chiefly by cardiovascular and neurological changes, and to Wernicke-Korsakoff syndrome, which is most often associated with chronic alcohol abuse. Beriberi occurs primarily in Asia and in areas of famine and poverty. The psychiatric symptoms include apathy, depression, irritability, nervousness, and poor concentration; severe memory disorders can develop with prolonged deficiencies.

Cobalamin Deficiency

Deficiencies in cobalamin (vitamin B_{12}) arise because of the failure of the gastric mucosal cells to secrete a specific substance, intrinsic factor, required for the normal absorption of vitamin B_{12} in the ileum. The deficiency state is characterized by the development of a chronic macrocytic megaloblastic anemia (pernicious anemia) and by neurological manifestations resulting from degenerative changes in the peripheral nerves, the spinal cord, and the brain. Neurological changes are seen in approximately 80 percent of all patients. These changes are commonly associated with megaloblastic anemia, but they occasionally precede the onset of hematological abnormalities.

Mental changes such as apathy, depression, irritability, and moodiness are common. In a few patients, encephalopathy and its associated delirium, delusions, hallucinations, dementia, and sometimes paranoid features are prominent and are sometimes called megaloblastic madness. The neurological manifestations of vitamin B_{12} deficiency can be completely and rapidly arrested by the early and continued administration of parenteral vitamin therapy.

TOXINS

Environmental toxins are becoming an increasingly serious threat to physical and mental health in contemporary society. Although the delirium and dementia associated with arsenic is of historical interest, mercury poisoning is an increasingly important differential diagnosis.

Mercury

Mercury poisoning can be caused by either inorganic or organic mercury. Inorganic mercury poisoning results in the Mad Hatter syndrome (previously seen in workers in the lead industry who softened mercury by putting it in their mouths), with depression, irritability, and psychosis. Associated neurological symptoms are headache, tremor, and weakness. Organic mercury poisoning can be caused by contaminated fish or grain and can result in depression, irritability, and cognitive impairments. Associated symptoms are sensory neuropathies, cerebellar ataxia, dysarthria, paresthesias, and visual field defects. Mercury poisoning in pregnant women causes abnormal fetal development.

Lead

Lead poisoning occurs when the amount of lead ingested exceeds the ability to eliminate it. It takes several months for toxic symptoms to appear.

The signs and symptoms of lead poisoning depend on the level of lead in the blood. When lead reaches levels above 200 μg/mL, symptoms of severe lead encephalopathy occur, with dizziness, clumsiness, ataxia, irritability, restlessness, headache, and insomnia. Later, an excited delirium, with associated vomiting and visual disturbances, occurs, progressing to convulsions, lethargy, and coma.

Treatment of lead encephalopathy should be instituted as rapidly as possible, even without laboratory confirmation, because of the high mortality. The treatment of choice to facilitate lead excretion is the intravenous administration of calcium disodium edetate (calcium disodium versenate) daily for 5 days. One gram is given in each dose.

Manganese

Early manganese poisoning produces manganese madness, with symptoms of headache, irritability, joint pains, and somnolence. An eventual picture appears of emotional lability, pathological laughter, nightmares, hallucinations, and compulsive and impulsive acts associated with periods of confusion and aggressiveness. Lesions involving the basal ganglia and pyramidal system result in gait impairment, rigidity, monotonous or whispering speech, tremors of the extremities and tongue, masked facies (manganese mask), micrographia, dystonia, dysarthria, and loss of equilibrium. The psychological effects tend to clear 3 or 4 months after the patient's removal from the site of exposure, but neurological symptoms tend to remain stationary or to progress. There is no specific treatment for manganese poisoning, other than removal from the source of poisoning.

Thallium

Thallium poisoning initially causes severe pains in the legs, diarrhea, and vomiting. Within a week, delirium, convulsions, cranial nerve palsies, blindness, choreiform movements, and coma may occur. Behavioral changes include paranoid thinking and depression, with suicidal tendencies. Alopecia is a common and important diagnostic clue. Treatment is generally symptomatic.

References

Biller J, Kathol RH: The interface of psychiatry and neurology. Psychiatr Clin North Am *15* (2)*:* 283, 1992.

Caine ED: Delirium, dementia, and amnestic and other cognitive disorders and mental disorders due to a general medical condition. In *Comprehensive Textbook of Psychiatry,* ed 6, HI Kaplan, BJ Sadock, editors, p 705. Williams & Wilkins, Baltimore, 1995.

Chiu HF: Psychiatric aspects of progressive supranuclear palsy. Gen Hosp Psychiatry *17:* 135, 1995.

Currier MB, Murray GB, Elch CC: Electroconvulsive therapy for poststroke depressed geriatric patients. J Neuropsychiatry Clin Neurosci *4:* 140, 1992.

Dunlop TW, Udvarhelyi GB, Stedem AFA, O'Connor JMC, Isaacs ML, Puig JG, Mather JH: Comparison of patients with and without emotional/behavioral deterioration during first year after traumatic brain injury. J Neuropsychiatry Clin Neurosci *3:* 150, 1991.

Fedoroff JP, Startstein SE, Forrester AW, Giesler FH, Jorge RE, Arndt SV, Robinson RG: Depression in patients with acute traumatic brain injury. Am J Psychiatry *149:* 918, 1992.

Fornazzari L, Farcnik K, Smith I, Heasman GA, Ichise M: Violent visual hallucinations and aggression in frontal lobe dysfunction: Clinical manifestations of deep orbitofrontal foci. J Neuropsychiatry Clin Neurosci *4:* 42, 1992.

Fricchione GL, Carbone L, Bennett WI: Psychotic disorder caused by a general medical condition, with delusion: Secondary ''organic'' delusional syndromes. Psychiatr Clin North Am *18:* 363, 1995.

Herman BP, Seidenberg M, Haltiner A, Wyler AR: Mood state in unilateral temporal lobe epilepsy. Biol Psychiatry *30:* 1205, 1991.

Iverson GL: Psychopathology associated with systemic lupus erythematosus: A methodological review. Semin Arthritis Rheum *22:* 242, 1993.

Jorge RE, Robinson RG, Starkstein SE, Arndt SV: Depression and anxiety following traumatic brain injury. J Neuropsychiatry *5:* 369, 1993.

Lishman WA: *Organic Psychiatry: The Psychological Consequences of Cerebral Disorder,* ed 2. Blackwell Scientific, Oxford, UK, 1987.

Masand P, Murray GB, Pickett P: Psychostimulants in post-stroke depression. J Neuropsychiatry Clin Neurosci *3:* 23, 1991.

Stenager EN, Stenager E, Kock-Henriksen N, Bronnum-Hansen H, Hyllested K, Jensen K, Bille-Brahe U: Suicide and multiple sclerosis: An epidemiological investigation. J Neurol Neurosurg Psychiatry *55:* 542, 1992.

11

Neuropsychiatric Aspects of Human Immunodeficiency Virus (HIV) Infection and Acquired Immune Deficiency Syndrome (AIDS)

Acquired immune deficiency syndrome (AIDS)- and human immunodeficiency virus (HIV)-related disorders have profoundly altered the nature of health care throughout the world. Mental health clinicians have played an important part in efforts to cope with these disorders in three areas: First, workers have reported pathological involvement of the brain in 75 to 90 percent of autopsies performed on those who had had AIDS. At least 50 percent of patients have neuropsychiatric complications, such as HIV encephalopathy; in about 10 percent of patients such complications are the first sign of the disorder. Second, because classic psychiatric syndromes such as anxiety and depressive disorders and psychotic disorders are commonly associated with HIV-related disorders, mental health clinicians must assess and treat these syndromes both pharmacologically and psychotherapeutically. Third, everyone in the mental health field is involved in helping society deal with this modern plague. Mental health organizations and professionals have worked to educate people about the societal effects of the disorders and about the necessity to change private behaviors, such as sexual and substance-using actions.

AIDS results from HIV infection. Infection with HIV produces a variety of manifestations that range from no symptoms at one end of the spectrum to AIDS at the other end. HIV allows the body to be susceptible to a broad array of medical conditions, such as infections and tumors, and to neuropsychiatric syndromes. HIV was isolated and identified in 1983 as a ribonucleic acid (RNA)-containing retrovirus that infects cells of the immune and nervous systems. Infection of T4 (helper) lymphocytes eventually produces impaired cell-mediated immunity and dramatically limits the body's ability to protect itself from other infectious agents and to prevent the development of specific neoplastic disorders. Infection of cells (primarily astrocytes) within the central nervous system (CNS) causes neuropsychiatric syndromes to develop. These syndromes are further complicated in patients with AIDS by the neuropsychiatric effects of opportunistic CNS infections and neoplasms, antiviral treatment-related adverse effects, independent psychiatric syndromes, and myriad psychosocial stresses associated with having an HIV-related disorder.

HIV AND ITS TRANSMISSION

HIV is a retrovirus related to the human T-cell leukemia viruses (HTLV) and to retroviruses that infect animals, including nonhuman primates. At least two types of HIV have been identified, HIV type 1 (HIV-1) and HIV type 2 (HIV-2). HIV-1 is the causative agent for most HIV-related diseases; HIV-2, however, seems to be causing an increasing occurrence of infection in Africa. There may be other subtypes of HIV, which are now classified as HIV type O (HIV-O). HIV is present in blood, semen, cervical and vaginal secretions, and, to a lesser extent, in saliva, tears, breast milk, and the cerebrospinal fluid of those who are infected. Transmission of HIV most often occurs through sexual intercourse or through the transfer of contaminated blood from one person to another. Unprotected anal or vaginal sex are the sexual activities most likely to transmit the virus. Oral sex has also been implicated, but rarely. Health providers should be aware of the guidelines for safe sexual practices and should advise their patients to practice safe sex (Table 11–1).

The chance of becoming infected after a single exposure to an HIV-infected person is relatively low: 0.8 percent to 3.2 percent for unprotected receptive anal intercourse, 0.05 percent to 0.15 percent with unprotected vaginal sex, 0.32 percent after puncture with an HIV-contaminated needle, and 0.67% after using a contaminated needle to inject drugs. However, the probability of transmission could be higher depending on the viral load of the contact person, which tends to be higher at the beginning and end of the illness' course, or if there are also other factors, such as sexually transmitted diseases. The presence of sexually transmitted diseases, such as herpes, syphilis, or other lesions that compromise the integrity of skin or mucosa, further increases the risk of transmission. Transmission also occurs through exposure to contaminated needles, thus accounting for the high incidence of HIV infection among drug users. HIV is also transmitted by infusions of whole blood, plasma, and clotting factors but not from immune serum globulin or hepatitis B vaccine.

Although male-to-male transmission has been the most common route of sexual transmission in North America, male-

Table 11–1
AIDS Safe-Sex Guidelines

Remember: Any activity that allows for the exchange of body fluids of one person through the mouth, anus, vagina, bloodstream, cuts, or sores of another person is considered unsafe at this time.

Safe-Sex Practices
- Massage, hugging, body-to-body rubbing
- Dry social kissing
- Masturbation
- Acting out sexual fantasies (that do not include any unsafe-sex practices)
- Using vibrators or other instruments (provided they are not shared)

Low-Risk Sex Practices
These activities are not considered completely safe:
- French (wet) kissing (without mouth sores)
- Mutual masturbation
- Vaginal and anal intercourse while using a condom
- Oral sex, male (fellatio), while using a condom
- Oral sex, female (cunnilingus), while using a barrier
- External contact with semen or urine, provided there are no breaks in the skin

Unsafe-Sex Practices
- Vaginal or anal intercourse without a condom
- Semen, urine, or feces in the mouth or the vagina
- Unprotected oral sex (fellatio or cunnilingus)
- Blood contact of any kind
- Sharing sex instruments or needles

Reprinted with permission from Moffatt B, Spiegel J, Parrish S, Helquist M: *AIDS: A Self-Care Manual*, p 125. IBS Press, Santa Monica, CA, 1987.

to-female and female-to-male transmissions represent an increasingly large percentage of the transmission routes and represent the majority of transmission routes worldwide. Some studies have shown that about 50 percent of the regular sex partners of people with HIV infections become infected themselves, a statistic suggesting that some people have an as-yet-not-understood immunity or resistance to HIV infection.

Transmission by contaminated blood most often occurs when those abusing an intravenous (IV) substance share hypodermic needles without proper sterilization techniques. Transmission of HIV through blood transfusions, organ transplantation, and artificial insemination is no longer a problem now that donors are tested for HIV infection. Tragically, many hemophiliacs received transfusions of HIV-infected blood products before HIV was identified as the causative agent. The risk among health care workers infected after a needle-stick is very rare, less than 0.3 percent.

Children can be infected in utero or through breast feeding when their mothers are infected with HIV. Zidovudine and protease inhibitors prevent perinatal transmission when taken by the HIV-infected pregnant woman in over 95 percent of cases. Health workers are theoretically at risk because of potential contact with bodily fluids from HIV-infected patients. In practice, however, the incidence of such transmission is very low, and almost all reported cases have been traced to accidental needle punctures with contaminated hypodermic needles. No evidence has been found that HIV can be contracted through casual contact, such as by sharing a living space or a classroom with a person who is infected, although direct and indirect contact with an infected person's body fluids, such as blood and semen, should be avoided (Table 11–2).

After infection with HIV, AIDS is estimated to develop in 8 to 11 years, although this time is gradually increasing because of early implementation of treatment. Once a person is infected with HIV, the virus primarily targets T4 (helper) lymphocytes, also called CD4 + lymphocytes, to which the virus binds because a glycoprotein (gp-120) on the viral surface has a high and selective affinity for the CD4 receptor on T4 lymphocytes. After binding, the virus is able to inject its RNA into the infected lymphocyte; there, the RNA is transcribed into deoxyribonucleic acid (DNA) by the action of reverse transcriptase. The resultant DNA can then be incorporated into the host cell's genome and translated and eventually transcribed, once the lymphocyte is stimulated to divide. After viral proteins have been produced by lymphocytes, the various components of the virus assemble, and new mature viruses bud off from the host cell. Although the process of budding may cause lysis of the lymphocyte, other HIV pathophysiological mechanisms can gradually disable a patient's entire complement of T4 lymphocytes.

Table 11–2
Centers for Disease Control and Prevention (CDC) Guidelines for the Prevention of HIV Transmission from Infected to Uninfected Persons

Infected persons should be counseled to prevent the further transmission of HIV by:

1. Informing prospective sex partners of their infection with HIV, so they can take appropriate precautions. Abstention from sexual activity with another person is one option that would eliminate any risk of sexually transmitted HIV infection.
2. Protecting a partner during any sexual activity by taking appropriate precautions to prevent that person's coming into contact with the infected person's blood, semen, urine, feces, saliva, cervical secretions, or vaginal secretions. Although the efficacy of using condoms to prevent infections with HIV is still under study, the consistent use of condoms should reduce the transmission of HIV by preventing exposure to semen and infected lymphocytes.
3. Informing previous sex partners and any persons with whom needles were shared of their potential exposure to HIV and encouraging them to seek counseling and testing.
4. For IV drug abusers, enrolling or continuing in programs to eliminate the abuse of IV substances. Needles, other apparatus, and drugs must never be shared.
5. Never sharing toothbrushes, razors, or other items that could become contaminated with blood.
6. Refraining from donating blood, plasma, body organs, other tissue, or semen.
7. Avoiding pregnancy until more is known about the risks of transmitting HIV from the mother to the fetus or newborn.
8. Cleaning and disinfecting surfaces on which blood or other body fluids have spilled, in accordance with previous recommendations.
9. Informing physicians, dentists, and other appropriate health professionals of antibody status when seeking medical care, so that the patient can be appropriately evaluated.

Reprinted from MMWR Morb Mortal Wkly Rep *35:* 152, 1986.

AIDS

As researchers have learned more about the disease, the definition of AIDS has changed over time. The Centers for Disease Control and Prevention (CDC) describes AIDS as the presence of a disease associated with a defect in cell-mediated immunity, occurring in a person with no known cause for diminished resistance to that disease other than HIV. Such diseases include Kaposi's sarcoma (KS), *Pneumocystis carinii* pneumonia, and other serious opportunistic infections. Other conditions considered indicative of AIDS are HIV encephalopathy, HIV wasting syndrome, recurrent salmonella septicemia, lymphoid interstitial pneumonia, extrapulmonary tuberculosis, and multiple and recurrent pyogenic infections in children.

Epidemiology

The first case of AIDS was reported in 1981; analysis of specimens retained from people who had died before 1981, however, has shown that cases of HIV infection were present as early as 1959. This fact suggests that in the 1960s and 1970s, HIV-related disorders and AIDS were increasingly common but unrecognized, particularly in Africa and North America. At the end of 1995, more than 510,000 new cases of AIDS were reported (including more than 320,000 deaths), and an estimated total of 1 million people were infected with HIV in the United States. The ratio of men to women who are infected is estimated to be 6 to 1, but the number of infected women is growing 4 times faster than the number of infected men. At the end of 1996, the World Health Organization (WHO) estimated that, worldwide, 2.5 million adults and 1 million children had AIDS and about 22 million people were infected with HIV. Although estimates of future cases have varied widely, it appears likely that by the year 2000, 30 to 40 million people worldwide will be infected with HIV.

In the United States the major groups at risk have been gay and bisexual men and IV substance abusers; they accounted for about 60 percent and 20 percent, respectively, of the first 100,000 cases of AIDS. Because of changes in sexual behaviors by homosexual and bisexual men and because of the continued spread of the virus through heterosexual sex, the percentage of total cases for gay and bisexual men has gradually declined, but the percentage of total cases for other groups has increased—specifically, IV substance users, women, heterosexual men, children, and minority groups (particularly African Americans and Hispanics). More women are now being infected through heterosexual intercourse than through IV substance use. Some reports have shown a link between the use of crack cocaine and HIV infection in women. Although the geographic distribution is heavily skewed toward large urban centers—with the cities of New York, Los Angeles, San Francisco, and Miami accounting for more than 50 percent of all cases—cases of AIDS have been reported in every state of the United States.

Diagnosis

Serum Testing. Two assay techniques are now widely available to detect the presence of anti-HIV antibodies in human serum. Both health care workers and their patients must understand that the presence of HIV antibodies is indicative of infection, not of immunity to infection. Those with a positive finding on an HIV test have been exposed to the virus, have the virus within their bodies, have the potential to transmit the virus to another person, and will almost certainly eventually develop AIDS. Those with a negative HIV test result have either not been exposed to the HIV virus and are not infected or were exposed to the HIV virus but have not yet developed antibodies, a possibility if the exposure occurred less than a year before the testing.

The two assay techniques used are the enzyme-linked immunosorbent assay (ELISA) and the Western blot assay. The ELISA is used as an initial screening test because it is less expensive than the Western blot assay and more easily used to screen a large number of samples. The ELISA is sensitive and reasonably specific; although it is unlikely to report a false-negative result, it may indicate a false-positive one. For this reason, positive results from an ELISA are confirmed by using the more expensive and cumbersome Western blot assay, which is sensitive and specific.

Seroconversion is the change, after infection with HIV, from a negative HIV antibody test result to a positive HIV antibody test result. Seroconversion most commonly occurs between 6 and 12 weeks after infection, although in rare cases seroconversion can take 6 to 12 months.

Counseling. The major issues in counseling people about HIV serum testing are who, in general, should be tested; why a particular person should or should not be tested; what the test results signify; and what the implications are. Although specific groups of people are at high risk for contracting HIV and should be tested (Table 11–3), any one person who wants to be tested should probably be tested. The reasons for requesting a test should be ascertained to detect unspoken concerns and motivations that may merit psychotherapeutic intervention. Counseling both before and after testing should be

Table 11–3
Possible Indications for HIV Testing

1. Patients who belong to a high-risk group: (1) men who have had sex with another man since 1977; (2) intravenous drug abusers since 1977; (3) hemophiliacs and other patients who have received since 1977 blood or blood product transfusions not screened for HIV; (4) sexual partners of people from any of those groups; (5) sexual partners of people with known HIV exposure—people with cuts, wounds, sores, or needlesticks whose lesions have had direct contact with HIV-infected blood.
2. Patients who request testing. Not all patients admit to the presence of risk factors (eg, because of shame, fear).
3. Patients with symptoms of AIDS.
4. Women belonging to a high-risk group who are planning pregnancy or who are pregnant.
5. Blood, semen, or organ donors.

Adapted with permission from Rosse RB, Giese AA, Deutsch S, Morihisa JM. *Laboratory and Diagnostic Testing in Psychiatry*, p 54. American Psychiatric Press. Washington, 1989.

done in person, not over the telephone, and should cover both the significance of the test results and their implications for behavioral changes. It is good practice to repeat the meaning of the test results and their implications several times at both pretest and posttest interviews; many people are so anxious at these sessions that they may miss something told to them only once.

During pretest counseling, counselors should review past practices that may have put the testee at risk for HIV infection and should discuss safe sexual practices (Table 11–4). During posttest counseling (Table 11–5), counselors should advise that a negative test finding implies that safe sexual behavior and the avoidance of shared hypodermic needles are recommended for the person to remain free of HIV infection. A positive test result indicates that the person is infected with HIV and can spread the disease. Those with positive results must receive counseling about safe practices and potential treatment options. They may need additional psychotherapeutic interventions if anxiety or depressive disorders develop after they discover that they are infected. Common issues and concerns are fear of disclosure, relationships with friends and family, employment and financial security, medical condition, and such psychological issues as self-esteem and self-blame. A person may react to a positive HIV test finding with a syndrome similar to that of posttraumatic stress disorder. Concern about minor physical symptoms, insomnia, and dependence on health care workers commonly arise. Adjustment disorder with anxiety or depressed mood may develop in as many as 25 percent of those informed of a positive HIV test result. Clinical interactions with patients should emphasize the meaning of a positive test result and should encourage the reestablishment of emotional and functional stability.

Couples who are considering taking the HIV antibody test must decide who will be tested and whether to go alone or together. The therapist should ask why they are considering taking the test; partners often for the first time discuss issues of commitment, honesty, and trust, such as sexual contacts outside the relationship. They need to be prepared for the possibility that one or both are infected and must discuss what effect this will have on their relationship.

L. and M. met 6 months ago, started dating, and had a few safe-sex encounters (mutual masturbation). Both men had been tested for HIV more than a year ago; and both had tested HIV negative. They convinced each other to be tested again to allow more open and relaxed sexual interaction and to herald the possible start of a committed relationship. The testing results, however, did not follow their expectations: L. tested HIV negative, but M. tested HIV positive. The men sought couples counseling to deal with the crisis. The evaluation explored their fears, anger, and hurt, their sense of betrayal and deception, and their lack of trust. They decided, however, to remain together and to take care of each other, and they terminated therapy prematurely. (From Klinger and Cabaj.)

Table 11–5
Posttest HIV Counseling

1. Interpretation of test result:
   Clarify distortion (eg, "a negative test still means you could contract the virus at a future time; it does not mean you are immune from AIDS").
   Ask questions about the patient's understanding and emotional reaction to the test result.
2. Recommendations for prevention of transmission (careful discussion of high-risk behaviors and guidelines for prevention of transmission).
3. Recommendations on the follow-up of sexual partners and needle contacts.
4. If test result is positive, recommendations against donating blood, sperm, or organs and against sharing razors, toothbrushes, and anything else that may have blood on it.
5. Referral for appropriate psychological support: HIV-positive patients often need access to a mental health team (assess need for inpatient versus outpatient care; consider individual or group supportive therapy). Common themes include the shock of the diagnosis, the fear of death, and social consequences, grief over potential losses, and dashed hopes for good news. Also look for depression, hopelessness, anger, frustration, guilt, and obsessional themes. Activate supports available to patient (eg, family, friends, community services).

Reprinted with permission from Rosse RB, Giese AA, Deutsch SI, Morihisa JM: *Laboratory and Diagnostic Testing in Psychiatry,* p 58. American Psychiatric Press, Washington, 1989.

Table 11–4
Pretest HIV Counseling

1. Discuss meaning of a positive result and clarify distortions (eg, the test detects exposure to the AIDS virus; it is not a test for AIDS).
2. Discuss the meaning of a negative result (eg, seroconversion requires time, recent high-risk behavior may require follow-up testing).
3. Be available to discuss the patient's fears and concerns (unrealistic fears may require appropriate psychological intervention).
4. Discuss why the test is necessary. (Not all patients will admit to high-risk behaviors.)
5. Explore the patient's potential reactions to a positive result (eg, "I'll kill myself if I'm positive"). Take appropriate necessary steps to intervene in a potentially catastrophic reaction.
6. Explore past reactions to severe stresses.
7. Discuss the confidentiality issues relevant to the testing situation (eg, is it an anonymous or nonanonymous setting?). Inform the patient of other possible testing options where the counseling and testing can be done completely anonymously (eg, where the result is not made a permanent part of a hospital chart). Discuss who has access to the test results.
8. Discuss with the patient how being seropositive can potentially affect social status (eg, health and life insurance coverage, employment, housing).
9. Explore high-risk behaviors and recommend risk-reducing interventions.
10. Document discussions in chart.
11. Allow the patient time to ask questions.

Reprinted with permission from Rosse RB, Giese AA, Deutsch SI, Morihisa JM: *Laboratory and Diagnostic Testing in Psychiatry,* p 55. American Psychiatric Press, Washington, 1989.

Confidentiality. Confidentiality is a key issue in serum testing. No person should be given HIV tests without previous knowledge and consent, although various jurisdictions and organizations, such as the military, now require HIV testing for all inhabitants or members. The results of an HIV test can be shared with other members of a medical team, although the information should be provided to no one else except in the special circumstances to be discussed. The patient should be advised against too readily disclosing the results of HIV testing to employers, friends, and family members; the information could result in discrimination in employment, housing, and insurance.

The major exception to restriction of disclosure is the need to notify potential and past sexual or IV substance partners. Most HIV-positive patients act responsibly. If, however, a treating physician knows that an HIV-infected patient is putting another person at risk of becoming infected, the physician may try either to hospitalize the infected person involuntarily (to prevent danger to others) or to notify the potential victim. Clinicians should be aware of the laws about such issues, which vary among the states. These guidelines also apply to inpatient psychiatric wards when an HIV-infected patient is believed to be sexually active with other patients.

CLINICAL FEATURES

Nonneurological Factors

About 30 percent of people infected with HIV experience a flulike syndrome 3 to 6 weeks after becoming infected; most never notice any symptoms immediately or shortly after their infection. When symptoms do appear, the flulike syndrome includes fever, myalgia, headaches, fatigue, gastrointestinal symptoms, and sometimes a rash. The syndrome may be accompanied by splenomegaly and lymphadenopathy. Rarely, an acute aseptic meningitis develops shortly after infection, as does an encephalopathy or Guillain-Barré syndrome.

In the United States, the median duration of the asymptomatic stages is 10 years, although nonspecific symptoms—lymphadenopathy, chronic diarrhea, weight loss, malaise, fatigue, fevers, night sweats—may variably appear. During the asymptomatic period, however, the T4 cell count almost always declines from normal values (1,000/mm^3) to grossly abnormal values (200/mm^3).

The most common infection affecting those HIV-infected people who have AIDS is *Pneumocystis carinii* pneumonia, which is characterized by a chronic, nonproductive cough and dyspnea sometimes severe enough to result in hypoxemia and its resultant cognitive effects. Diagnosis is made with fiberoptic bronchoscopy and alveolar lavage. The pneumonia is usually treatable with trimethoprim and sulfamethoxazole (Bactrim, Septra) or pentamidine isethionate (Pentam), which can also be used for prophylaxis against the pneumonia. The other disease that was initially associated with the development of AIDS is Kaposi's sarcoma, a previously rare, blue-purple–tinted skin lesion. For unknown reasons, Kaposi's sarcoma is less commonly associated with cases of recently diagnosed AIDS.

Although *Pneumocystis carinii* pneumonia and Kaposi's sarcoma are the two classic AIDS-related infectious and neoplastic disorders, the severely disabled cellular immune system of HIV-infected patients permits the development of a staggering array of infections and neoplasms. The most common infections are from protozoa such as *Toxoplasma gondii,* fungi such as *Cryptococcus neoformans* and *Candida albicans,* bacteria such as *Mycobacterium avium-intracellulare,* and viruses such as cytomegalovirus and herpes simplex virus.

For psychiatrists, the importance of these nonneurological, nonpsychiatric complications lies in their biological effects on patients' brain functions (such as hypoxia with *Pneumocystis carinii* pneumonia) and their psychological effects on patients' moods and states of anxiety. Further, as each of the conditions is usually treated by an additional drug, psychiatrists need to be aware of the adverse CNS effects of the large armamentarium of medications.

Neurological Factors

An extensive array of disease processes can affect the brain of a patient infected with HIV (Table 11–6). The most important disease for mental health workers to be aware of is HIV encephalopathy, which is associated with the development of a subcortical type of dementia and which may affect 50 percent

Table 11–6
Conditions Associated with HIV Infection

Bacterial infections, multiple or recurrent[a]
Candidiasis of bronchi, trachea, or lungs
Candidiasis, esophageal
Cervical cancer, invasive[b]
Coccidioidomycosis, disseminated or extrapulmonary
Cryptococcosis, extrapulmonary
Cryptosporidiosis, chronic intestinal (1 month's duration)
Cytomegalovirus disease (other than liver, spleen, or nodes)
Cytomegalovirus retinitis (with loss of vision)
Encephalopathy, HIV-related
Herpes simplex, chronic ulcers (1 month's duration); or bronchitis, pulmonitis, or esophagitis
Histoplasmosis, disseminated or extrapulmonary
Isosporiasis, chronic intestinal (1 month's duration)
Kaposi's sarcoma
Lymphoid interstitial pneumonia and/or pulmonary lymphoid hyperplasia[a]
Lymphoma, Burkitt's (or equivalent term)
Lymphoma, immunoblastic (or equivalent term)
Lymphoma, primary, of brain
Mycobacterium avium complex or *M. kansasii,* disseminated or extrapulmonary
Mycobacterium tuberculosis, any site (pulmonary[b] or extrapulmonary)
Mycobacterium, other species or unidentified species, disseminated or extrapulmonary
Pneumocystis carinii pneumonia
Pneumonia, recurrent[b]
Progressive multifocal leukoencephalopathy
Salmonella septicemia, recurrent
Toxoplasmosis of brain
Wasting syndrome due to HIV

Adapted from 1993 revised classification system for HIV infection and expanded surveillance, case definition for AIDS among adolescents and adults. MMWR Morb Mortal Wkly Rep *41:* 1992.

[a] Children 13 years old.

[b] Added in the 1993 expansion of the AIDS surveillance case definition for adolescents and adults.

of HIV-infected patients to some degree. Other diseases and complications of treatment must also be considered in the differential diagnosis of an HIV-infected patient with neuropsychiatric symptoms. Symptoms such as photophobia, headache, stiff neck, motor weakness, sensory loss, and changes in level of consciousness should alert a mental health worker that the patient should be examined for the possible development of a CNS opportunistic infection or a CNS neoplasm. HIV infection can also result in a variety of peripheral neuropathies that should prompt mental health clinicians to reconsider the extent of CNS involvement.

HIV Encephalopathy. Although the means by which HIV enters the CNS remains controversial, it is known that when HIV does enter, it infects primarily glial cells, particularly astrocytes. The virus is also harbored within immune cells in the CNS. The neuropathological picture includes multinucleated giant cells, microglial nodules, diffuse astrocytosis, perivascular lymphocyte cuffing, cortical atrophy, and white matter vacuolation and demyelination (Fig. 11–1). HIV encephalopathy was previously referred to as AIDS dementia complex, but the fact that HIV-related encephalopathy and dementia can develop in a patient who does not meet the diagnostic criteria for AIDS makes *HIV encephalopathy* a preferable term.

CLINICAL SYMPTOMS. HIV encephalopathy is a subacute encephalitis that results in a progressive subcortical dementia without focal neurological signs. The differentiation between cortical dementia and subcortical dementia is presented in Table 10.3–2. The major differentiating feature between the two types of dementia is the absence of classic cortical symptoms such as aphasia until late in the illness. Patients with HIV encephalitis or their friends usually notice subtle mood and personality changes, problems with memory and concentration, and some psychomotor slowing. Additional symptoms include apathy, distractibility, confusion, malaise, anhedonia, and social withdrawal. Some of these symptoms are virtually indistinguishable from those of depressive disorders, although careful cognitive testing may help suggest the correct diagnosis. In addition to an overlap with the symptoms of depressive disorders, HIV encephalopathy can result in a delirium whose symptoms suggest manic episodes or schizophrenia. The presence of motor symptoms may also suggest a diagnosis of HIV encephalopathy. Motor symptoms associated with subcortical dementia include hyperreflexia, spastic or ataxic gait, paraparesis, and increased muscle tone.

Symptoms in Children. Children infected in utero with HIV have a variety of symptoms, including microcephaly, severe cognitive defects, weakness, failure to reach developmental milestones, pseudobulbar palsy, extrapyramidal rigidity, and seizures.

HIV LEVELS IN SALIVA OF INFECTED CHILDREN. Studies have shown that contact with saliva of HIV-infected children and adolescents does not pose a health threat. Only 1 of 13 saliva samples of children infected with the AIDS virus yielded positive results for traces of HIV genetic material. The lack of infectious risk from exposure to salivary secretions reinforces guidelines stating that HIV-1–infected children can safely attend day care centers and schools.

DIFFERENTIAL DIAGNOSIS. The differential diagnosis for HIV encephalopathy includes aseptic meningitis and all the other CNS-related conditions listed in Table 11–6. Aseptic meningitis occurs shortly after HIV infection and is characterized by a flulike illness in the presence of fluctuating levels of consciousness, meningeal signs, and facial palsies. Diagnostic testing should in-

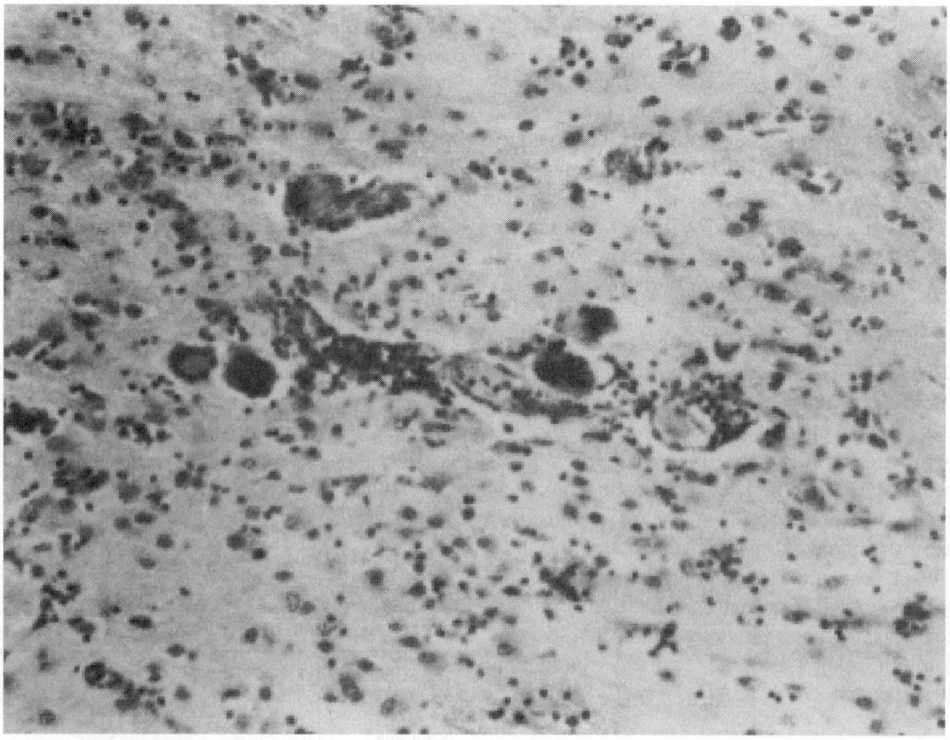

FIGURE 11–1

Typical multinucleated giant cells formed by macrophage-derived cells. (Reprinted with permission from Pajeau AK, Román GC: HIV encephalopathy and dementia. Psychiatr Clin North Am *15:* 461, 1992.)

clude detailed psychometric testing (Table 10.3–2), cerebrospinal fluid (CSF) examination, and brain-imaging studies. The CSF examination may show slight elevations in protein concentrations and, in about one quarter of all patients infected with HIV, a mononuclear pleocytosis. Magnetic resonance imaging (MRI) and computed tomography (CT) studies of patients often show cortical atrophy, ventricular enlargement, and areas of demyelination within the white matter (Fig. 11–2). Positron emission tomography (PET) and single photon emission computed tomography (SPECT) studies have reported hypermetabolism of the basal ganglia early in the course of HIV encephalopathy; this hypermetabolism progresses to subcortical and cortical hypometabolism later in the course of the illness. Electroencephalograms (EEGs) usually show generalized slowing, and evoked potential (EP) studies may show a delay in the P300 wave.

Psychiatric Syndromes

Dementia. The fourth edition of *Diagnostic and Statistical Manual of Mental Disorders* (DSM-IV) allows for the diagnosis of dementia due to HIV disease when there is ''the presence of a dementia that is judged to be the directed pathophysiological consequence of human immunodeficiency virus (HIV) disease.'' (See Table 10.3–12.)

Although HIV encephalopathy is found in a large proportion of patients infected with HIV, other causes of dementia in these patients must be considered. These causes include CNS infections, CNS neoplasms, CNS abnormalities caused by systemic disorders and endocrinopathies, and adverse CNS responses to drugs. The development of dementia is generally a poor prognostic sign, and 50 to 75 percent of patients with dementia die within 6 months.

ICD-10. In the 10th revision of *International Statistical Classification of Diseases and Related Health Problems* (ICD-10), dementia in HIV disease is briefly covered under organic, including symptomatic, mental disorders (see Chapter 10). Here the dementia is defined as ''a disorder characterized by cognitive deficits meeting the clinical diagnostic criteria for dementia, in the absence of concurrent illness or condition other than HIV infection that could explain the findings.'' AIDS–dementia complex and HIV encephalopathy or subacute encephalitis are also included in this dementia.

Delirium. Delirium can result from the same causes that lead to dementia in patients infected with HIV (Table 11–6). Clinicians have classified delirious states characterized by both increased and decreased activity. Delirium in HIV-infected patients is probably underdiagnosed but should always precipitate a medical workup of an HIV-infected patient to determine whether a new CNS-related process has begun.

Anxiety Disorders. Patients with HIV infection may have any of the anxiety disorders, but generalized anxiety disorder, posttraumatic stress disorder, and obsessive-compulsive disorder are particularly common.

Adjustment Disorder. Adjustment disorder with anxiety or depressed mood has been reported to occur in 5 to 20 percent of patients infected with HIV. The incidence of adjustment disorder in people infected with HIV is higher than usual in some special populations, such as military recruits and prison inmates.

Depressive Disorders. A range of 4 to 40 percent of HIV-infected patients have been reported to meet the diagnostic criteria for depressive disorders. The pre-HIV infection prevalence of depressive disorders may be higher than usual in some groups who are at risk for contracting HIV. Another

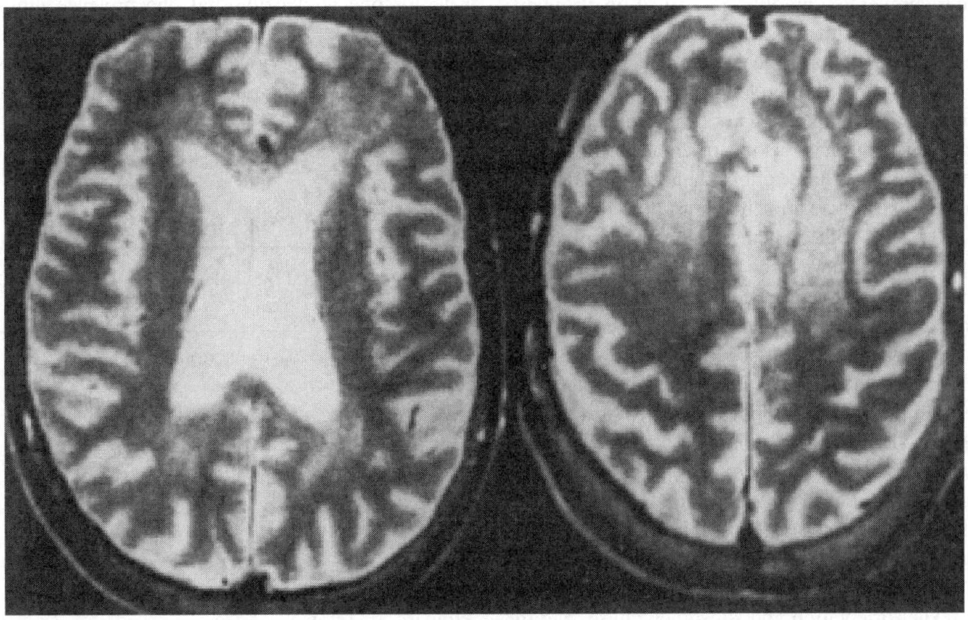

FIGURE 11–2

T2-weighted (3000/80) spin echo axial magnetic resonance images at the level of the lateral ventricles and centrum semiovale. Bilateral, relatively symmetrical, supratentorial white matter disease is visible. Those areas of increased signal intensity often show a frontal lobe predilection. The cortical sulci and ventricles are prominent for the patient's age (34-year-old HIV-positive man). (Reprinted with permission from Pajeau AK, Román GC: HIV encephalopathy and dementia. Psychiatr Clin North Am *15:* 458, 1992.)

reason for the reported variation in prevalence rates is the variable application of the diagnostic criteria; some of the criteria for depressive disorders (poor sleep and weight loss) can also be caused by the HIV infection itself.

Substance Abuse. Substance abuse is a problem not only for IV substance abusers who contract HIV-related diseases but also for all other patients with HIV, who may have used illegal substances only occasionally in the past but who may be tempted to use them regularly in an attempt to deal with depression or anxiety.

Suicide. Suicidal ideation and suicide attempts may increase in patients with HIV infection and AIDS. The risk factors for suicide among people infected with HIV are having friends who died from AIDS, recent notification of HIV seropositivity, relapses, difficult social issues relating to homosexuality, inadequate social and financial support, and the presence of dementia or delirium.

Worried Well. The *worried well* are those in high-risk groups who, although they are seronegative and disease free, are anxious or have an obsession about contracting the virus. Some people are reassured by repeated negative serum test results, but others obsess about the possible long incubation period and cannot be reassured. Their symptoms can include generalized anxiety, panic attacks, obsessive-compulsive disorder, and hypochondriasis.

TREATMENT

Prevention is the primary approach to HIV infection. Primary prevention involves protecting people from getting the disease; secondary prevention involves modification of the disease's course. All people with any risk of HIV infection should be informed about safe-sex practices and about the necessity to avoid sharing contaminated hypodermic needles. Preventive strategies, however, are complicated by the complex societal values surrounding sexual acts, sexual orientation, birth control, and substance abuse. Many public health officials have advocated condom distribution in schools and the distribution of clean needles to drug addicts. These issues remain controversial, although condoms have been shown to be a fairly (although not completely) safe and effective preventive strategy against HIV infection. Those who are conservative and religious argue that the educational message should be sexual abstinence. Many university laboratories and pharmaceutical companies are attempting to develop a vaccine to protect people from infection by HIV. The development of such a vaccine, however, is probably at least a decade away.

The assessment of patients infected with HIV should include a complete sexual and substance-abuse history, a psychiatric history, and an evaluation of the support systems available to them. Clinicians must understand a patient's history with regard to sexual orientation and substance abuse, and the patient must feel that the therapist is not judging past or present behaviors. A therapist can often encourage a sense of trust and empathy in the patient by asking specific, well-informed, and straightforward questions about the homosexual or substance-using culture. The therapist must also determine the patient's knowledge about HIV and AIDS.

The homosexual community has provided a significant support system for those infected with HIV, particularly for people who are gay and bisexual. Public education campaigns within this community have resulted in significant (more than 50 percent) reductions in the highest-risk sexual practices, although some gay men still practice high-risk sex. Homosexual men are likely to practice safe sex if they know the safe-sex guidelines, have access to a support group, are in a steady relationship, and have a close relationship with a person with AIDS. Partly because of the many biases against them, IV substance users with AIDS have received little support, and there has been little progress in educating these people who are a major reservoir from which the virus is spreading to women, heterosexual men, and children.

Pharmacotherapy

More than any other factor, plasma viral (HIV-1 RNA) load governs the rate of CD4 + cell count decline. Thus, the ultimate goal of medical treatment remains full viral suppression for the longest time with the least toxicity. The Food and Drug Administration (FDA) has recently approved several new drugs for the treatment of HIV infection, and single-drug therapy is no longer the treatment of choice. The reverse transcriptase inhibitors and the protease inhibitors are the two common classes of drugs used to treat HIV infection (Table 11–7). Some studies indicate that triple-drug therapy with two nucleosides and one protease inhibitor is the most potent antiretroviral treatment available. In one study of HIV-infected patients, treatment with saquinavir (Invirase), zalcitabine (Hivid), and zidovudine (Retrovir) reduced HIV-1 replication and increased CD4 + cell counts. Double-drug treatment with two nucleosides or one nucleoside and one protease inhibitor may also be effective.

Zidovudine, previously known as azidothymidine (AZT), an inhibitor of reverse transcriptase, was for many years a pri-

Table 11–7
Selected Drugs for HIV Infection

Class/Generic Name	Trade Name	Typical Daily Dosage (mg/day)
Nucleoside analogue transcriptase inhibitors		
Didanosine	Videx	400
Lamivudine	Epivir	300
Stavudine	Zerit	80
Zalcitabine	Hivid	2.25
Zidovudine	Retrovir	600
Nonnucleoside transcriptase inhibitors		
Delavirdine	Rescriptor	1,200
Viviratine	Viramune	400
Protease inhibitors		
Indinavir	Crixivan	2,400
Ritonavir	Norvir	1,200
Saquinavir	Invirase	1,800

mary medication for patients infected with HIV and was shown to often slow the course of the disease and to prolong survival. The use of zidovudine is frequently limited by its associated severe adverse effects. The prophylactic use of aerosolized pentamidine (NebuPent) and of trimethoprim-sulfamethoxazole (Bactrim) to prevent the development of *Pneumocystis carinii* pneumonia is also now common practice. Other drugs used to prevent opportunistic infections include dapsone, rifabutin (Mycobutin), fluconazole (Diflucan), and acyclovir (Zovirax). In addition, most physicians advise patients to get adequate nutrition, rest, and exercise and to minimize their use of alcohol and other psychoactive substances. Many other drugs not approved by the FDA are used by AIDS patients; therefore, a careful medication history is imperative.

Several studies have reported that treatment with antiretroviral agents such as zidovudine prevents or reverses the neuropsychiatric symptoms associated with HIV encephalopathy, and zidovudine has been found to be effective in preventing the onset of HIV encephalopathy in some studies. Because patients infected with HIV are susceptible to delirium, the use of psychoactive medications with significant anticholinergic activity should be avoided. Although dopamine antagonists such as haloperidol (Haldol) may be required for the control of agitation, they should be used in as low a dosage as possible because of patients' increased sensitivity for extrapyramidal effects and because patients may develop neuroleptic malignant syndrome.

Clinicians can attempt to treat some aspects of patients' anxiety disorders with an appropriate psychotherapeutic technique, but the use of anxiolytic drugs—benzodiazepine or nonbenzodiazepine (such as buspirone [BuSpar]) sedatives—or the use of antidepressant drugs may become necessary. When treatment with a benzodiazepine is necessary, most clinicians prefer to prescribe one with either a short or a medium half-life.

According to many physicians, depressive disorders in patients infected with HIV should be aggressively treated with antidepressant medications. The starting dose of antidepressants should be about one quarter of that normally used in adults, and the dosage should be raised in small increments every 2 to 3 days until a therapeutic effect is reached. Patients have effectively used both tricyclic drugs and serotonin-specific reuptake inhibitors. The use of sympathomimetic drugs such as amphetamine is also a reasonable treatment approach, especially for late-onset encephalopathy and depression. Electroconvulsive therapy (ECT) is a reasonable treatment if a neurological examination confirms the absence of increased intracranial pressure or space-occupying CNS lesions.

Manic and psychotic symptoms may require the use of typical antipsychotic drugs to control grossly disorganized behavior or to reduce delusions or hallucinations. HIV-infected patients are sensitive to the adverse effects of these drugs; therefore, both initial and maintenance dosages should be lower than usual. Patients who had previously been treated with lithium for the control of bipolar I disorder can continue to take lithium; the lithium concentrations, however, must be monitored closely, especially if the patient has significant gastrointestinal disturbances (such as vomiting and diarrhea) that may affect lithium absorption and excretion. Anticonvulsants such as carbamazepine (Tegretol) and valproic acid (Depakene) may also effectively treat mania and episodic behavioral dyscontrol.

Immunity. Detection of HIV-specific responses in people who are HIV negative but who have often been exposed to the virus suggests that in rare instances the natural immune responses to HIV may be protective. Understanding the correlates of protective immunity to HIV infection is critical to efforts to develop preventive HIV vaccines as well as to determine the feasibility of treating HIV infection by boosting immunity to the virus.

Psychotherapy

Major psychodynamic themes for patients infected with HIV involve self-blame, self-esteem, and issues about death. Some patients feel that they are being punished for a deviant lifestyle; psychiatrists can help patients deal with feelings of guilt for behaviors that contributed to the development of AIDS. Difficult health care decisions, such as whether to participate in an experimental drug trial and the nature of terminal care and life-support systems, should be explored. Practical concerns for patients include employment, medical benefits, life insurance, career plans, and relationships with families and friends. The entire range of psychotherapeutic approaches may be appropriate for patients with HIV-related disorders. Both individual and group therapy can be effective. Individual therapy may be short term or long term and may be supportive, cognitive, behavioral, or psychodynamic. Group therapy techniques can range from psychodynamic to completely supportive in nature.

Adjustment disorder in patients infected with HIV is usually treated with individual or group psychotherapy, sometimes supplemented with short-term (2 to 3 weeks) use of anxiolytic drugs. Direct counseling about substance abuse and its potential adverse effects on the patient's health is indicated. Specific treatments for particular substance abuse disorders should be initiated, if necessary, for the patient's well-being.

Some concern among healthy members of high-risk groups is appropriate, but when the concern evolves into psychological symptoms that impair functioning, psychiatric attention is warranted. Supportive or insight-oriented psychotherapy is indicated in these cases.

Therapists must evaluate countertransference issues and explore their own attitudes toward sexual identity, past behaviors, eventual death, and substance abuse so that these issues do not interfere with treating patients. Therapists who treat many patients infected with HIV must also explore the possibility of burnout, which can begin to lessen their effectiveness. Studies have shown that therapists who see many HIV-infected patients during a short period are more affected by stress than are those who see fewer such patients over a longer time.

Treatment of Children. Children with AIDS may require special schooling, and those from single-parent homes or those with parents who are unable to provide care may need foster care placement. HIV-infected children who are not severely neurologically impaired can attend regular schools without putting fellow classmates at risk for infection as long as reasonable guidelines are followed.

Involvement of Significant Others. Patients' families, lovers, and close friends are often important allies in treatment. A patient's spouse or lover may have guilt feelings about possibly having infected the patient or may experience anger toward the patient for possibly being infected by the partner. Members of a patient's support group can help a therapist assess the patient's cognitive function and can also aid in planning financial and living arrangements. Patients' significant others may themselves benefit from the attention of a therapist who helps them cope with the illness and the impending loss of a friend or family member.

Legal Issues. Mental health care workers are often enlisted to help patients deal with legal matters, such as making a will and taking care of hospital and other medical expenses. The resolution of these matters is of such practical importance that it is well worth mental health workers' time to make sure that patients address the issues satisfactorily.

References

Angrist B, d'Hollosy M, Sanfilipo M, Santriano J, Diamond G, Simberkoff M, Weinreb H: Central nervous system stimulants as symptomatic treatments for AIDS-related neuropsychiatric impairments. J Clin Psychopharmacol *12:* 268, 1992.

Batki SL: Buspirone in drug use with AIDS or AIDS-related complex. J Clin Psychopharmacol *10:* 111S, 1990.

Day JJ, Grant I, Atkinson JH, Brysk LT, McCutchan JA, Hesselink JR, Weinrich JD, Spector SA, Richman DD: Incidence of AIDS dementia in a two-year follow-up of AIDS and ARC patients on an initial phase II AZT-placebo–controlled study. San Diego cohort. J Neuropsychiatry Clin Neurosci *4:* 15, 1992.

Empfield M, Cournos F, Meyer I, McKinnon K, Horwarth E, Silver M, Schrage H, Herman R: HIV seroprevalence among homeless patients admitted to a psychiatric inpatient unit. Am J Psychiatry *150:* 47, 1993.

Goldfinger SM, Robinowitz CB, editors: AIDS and HIV infections. In *American Psychiatric Press Review of Psychiatry,* vol 9, A Tasman, SM Goldfinger, CA Kaufmann, editors, p 571. American Psychiatric Press, Washington, 1990.

Graham NMH, Zeger SL, Park LP, Vermund SH, Detels R, Rinalso CR, Phair JP: The effects on survival of early treatment of human immunodeficiency virus infection. N Engl J Med *326:* 1037, 1992.

Handelsman L, Aronson M, Maurer G, Weiner J, Jacobson J, Bernstein D, Ness R, Herman S, Losonczy M, Song IS, Holloway K, Horvath T, Donnelley N, Hirschowitz J, Rowan AJ: Neuropsychological and neurological manifestations of HIV-1 dementia in drug users. J Neuropsychiatry Clin Neurosci *4:* 21, 1992.

Harris MJ, Jests DV, Gleghorn A, Sewell DD: New-onset psychosis in HIV-infected patients. J Clin Psychiatry *52:* 369, 1991.

Hirsch MS, D'Aquilla RT: Therapy for human immunodeficiency virus infection. N Engl J Med *328:* 1686, 1993.

Jansen RS, St Louis ME, Satten GA, Critchley SE, Petersen LR, Stafford RS, Ward JW, Hanson DL, Olivo N, Schable CA, Dondero TJ, Hospital HIV Surveillance Group: HIV infection among patients in US acute care hospitals. N Engl J Med *327:* 445, 1992.

Katz MH, Gerberding JL: Postexposure treatment of people exposed to the human immunodeficiency virus through sexual contact or injection-drug use. N Engl J Med *336:* 1097, 1997.

Kieburtz K, Zettelmaier AE, Ketonen L, Tuite M, Caine ED: Manic syndrome in AIDS: Am J Psychiatry *148:* 1068, 1991.

Klinger RL, Cabaj RP: Characteristics of gay and lesbian relationships. In *American Psychiatric Press Review of Psychiatry,* vol 12, JM Oldham, MB Riba, A Tasman, editors, p 112. American Psychiatric Press, Washington, 1993.

Mapou RL, Law WA, Martin A, Kampen D, Salazar AM, Rundell JR: Neuropsychological performance, mood, and complaints of cognitive and motor difficulties in individuals infected with the human immunodeficiency virus. J Neuropsychiatry Clin Neurosci *5:* 86, 1993.

McKegny FP, O'Dowd MA: Suicidality and HIV status. Am J Psychiatry *149:* 396, 1992.

Pajeau AK, Román GC: HIV encephalopathy and dementia. Psychiatry Clin North Am *15:* 455, 1992.

Perry S, Fishman B, Jacobsberg L, Frances A: Relationships over 1 year between lymphocyte subsets and psychosocial variables among adults with infection by human immunodeficiency virus. Arch Gen Psychiatry *49:* 396, 1992.

Sacks M, Dermatis H, Looser-Ott S, Burton W, Perry S: Undetected HIV infection among acutely ill psychiatric inpatients. Am J Psychiatry *149:* 544, 1992.

Silverman DC: Psychosocial impact of HIV-related caregiving on health providers: A review and recommendations for the role of psychiatry. Am J Psychiatry *150:* 705, 1993.

Van Gorp EG, Mandlekern MA, Gee M, Hinkin CH, Stern CF, Paz DK, Dizon W, Evans G, Flynn F, Frederick CJ, Ropchan JR, Blahd WH: Cerebral metabolic dysfunction in AIDS: Findings in a sample with and without dementia. J Neuropsychiatry Clin Neurosci *4:* 280, 1992.

12 Substance-Related Disorders

▲ 12.1 Overview

In a recent National Institute on Drug Abuse (NIDA) survey, some 37 percent of the population reported using one or more illicit substances in their lifetimes; 13 percent had used illicit substances in the past year, and 6 percent had used them in the month before the survey. More than two thirds of people ages 18 to 25 have used an illegal substance and more than 15 percent of the U.S. population older than 18 years of age have serious substance use problems. About two thirds of this group abuses primarily alcohol, the other one third primarily other substances. In the late 1990s, the substance use problem's total annual cost to society is estimated at almost $200 billion.

It is almost impossible to calculate the effect of illegal substance use on society. The effects are various and widespread and may take decades to reveal themselves. For instance, people whose parents took illicit substances have a greater chance of developing both physical and psychological difficulties, which will have an impact on the fabric of society as measured by education, employment, and socioeconomic levels in the population.

Aside from the staggering cost to society, the phenomenon of substance abuse has many implications for brain research, and for clinical psychiatry. Simply stated, some substances can affect both internally perceived mental states, such as mood, and externally observable activities, such as behavior. The ramifications of this simple statement, however, are astonishing. The substances can cause neuropsychiatric symptoms indistinguishable from those of common psychiatric disorders with no known causes (for example, schizophrenia and mood disorders), and thus primary psychiatric disorders and disorders involving the use of substances are possibly related. If the depressive symptoms seen in some people who have not taken a brain-altering substance are indistinguishable from the depressive symptoms in a person who has taken a brain-altering substance, there may be a brain-based commonality between substance-taking behavior and depression. The very existence of brain-altering substances is a fundamental clue to the ways in which the brain works in both normal and abnormal states.

Although she stopped short of endorsing such a radical reversal of the nation's drug policy, the former U.S. surgeon general, Joycelyn Elders, M.D., recommended that the government study the possibility of legalizing drugs of abuse and suggested that doing so might reduce the incidence of violent crimes. According to *The New York Times* (December 7, 1993), Dr. Elders stated:

> I do feel that we would markedly reduce our crime rate if drugs were legalized . . . But I don't know all of the ramifications of this. I do feel that we need to do some studies. And in some of the countries that have legalized drugs and made it legal, they certainly have shown that there has been a reduction in their crime rate and there has been no increase in their drug use rate.

Dr. Elders' comments revived a perennial debate about the most effective way to handle drug problems. In the past few years, a small but growing number of government officials, commentators, and academics have argued that the present policy of aggressively prosecuting drug sellers and users should be reconsidered. They have compared the current state of drug policy to that of the prohibition of alcohol from 1920 to 1934, and have argued that abolishing drug laws would eliminate the profit motive, the gangs, and the drug dealers.

COMPARATIVE NOSOLOGY

Substance-Related Disorders

The complexity of the subject of illicit substance use is reflected in the associated terminology, which seems to change regularly as various professional and governmental committees convene to discuss the problem. One question is what to call the brain-altering substances. The fourth edition of *Diagnostic and Statistical Manual of Mental Disorders* (DSM-IV) refers to brain-altering substances as *substances* and to the related disorders as *substance-related disorders.* In the DSM-IV, the concept of psychoactive substance does not include chemicals with brain-altering properties such as organic solvents, which may be ingested either on purpose or by accident. Legal substances cannot be separated from illegal substances; many legal substances, such as morphine, are often obtained by illegal means and used for nonprescribed purposes. The word *substance* is generally preferable to the word *drug,* because *drug* implies a manufactured chemical, whereas many substances associated with abuse patterns occur naturally (for example, opium) or are not meant for human consumption (for example, airplane glue). Thus, in DSM-IV, the topic is described by the general heading of substance-related disorders.

In DSM-IV, the substance-related disorders are cross-referenced in the DSM-IV categories that cover these particular symptoms or syndromes (Table 12.1–1). For example, a patient with depression related to cocaine withdrawal receives a diagnosis of cocaine-induced mood disorder with depressive features, with onset during withdrawal; this diagnosis is also

Table 12.1–1
DSM-IV Substance-Induced Disorders Outside of Substance-Related Disorders Category

Diagnosis	DSM-IV Category	Synopsis Section
Substance intoxication delirium	Delirium, dementia, and amnestic and other cognitive disorders	10.2
Substance withdrawal delirium	Delirium, dementia, and amnestic and other cognitive disorders	10.2
Substance-induced persisting dementia	Delirium, dementia, and amnestic and other cognitive disorders	10.3
Substance-induced persisting amnestic disorder	Delirium, dementia, and amnestic and other cognitive disorders	10.4
Substance-induced psychotic disorder	Schizophrenia and other psychotic disorders	14
Substance-induced mood disorder	Mood disorders	15.1
Substance-induced anxiety disorder	Anxiety disorders	16.1
Substance-induced sexual dysfunction	Sexual and gender identity disorders	21.2
Substance-induced sleep disorder	Sleep disorders	24.2

cross-referenced within the DSM-IV section on mood disorders. The cross-referencing emphasizes the differential diagnosis of mood disorder symptoms while emphasizing that a single substance of abuse can result in many neuropsychiatric symptoms and syndromes.

Although all substances considered by DSM-IV in the substance-related disorders category are associated with a pathological intoxication state, the substances vary as to whether a pathological state is associated with withdrawal or persists after the elimination of the substance from the body (Table 12.1–2). Within the DSM-IV system, patients who are experiencing substance intoxication or withdrawal accompanied by psychiatric symptoms but who do not meet the criteria for a specific syndromal pattern of symptoms (for example, depression) receive the diagnosis of substance intoxication (Table 12.1–3) or substance withdrawal (Table 12.1–4), possibly along with dependence or abuse.

ICD-10

The 10th revision of *International Statistical Classification of Diseases and Related Health Problems* (ICD-10) uses an approach somewhat different from DSM-IV. In the section titled ''Mental and Behavioral Disorders Due to Psychoactive Substance Use,'' the term *psychoactive substance* refers to alcohol, opioids, cannabinoids, sedatives and hypnotics, cocaine, other stimulants such as caffeine, hallucinogens, tobacco, volatile solvents, multiple drugs, and other psychoactive substances (Table 12.1–5). Thus, solvents are considered psychoactive, although their accidental ingestion is not mentioned. ICD-10 does not distinguish between legal and illegal substances but stipulates that the substances may or may not have been medically prescribed.

The disorder related to psychoactive substance use are described as mental and behavioral, with diagnostic guidelines provided for identifying the substance and for determining the specific nature of the disorder. When appropriate, references to other categories are given. For instance, under *psychotic disorder* in the substance use section, ICD-10 mentions schizophrenia, mood disorder, and paranoid or schizoid personality disorder as possible diagnoses for mental disorders ''aggravated or precipitated by psychoactive substance use.'' In addition, ICD-10 includes a separate category for non–dependence-producing substances (Table 12.1–6), including antidepressants, laxatives, analgesics, and vitamins, among others. DSM-IV does not contain a similar category.

Substance Dependence

In 1964, the World Health Organization concluded that the term *addiction* is no longer a scientific term and recommended substituting the term *drug dependence.* The concept of substance dependence has had many officially recognized and commonly used meanings over the decades. Two concepts have been used to define aspects of dependence: behavioral and physical. In behavioral dependence, substance-seeking activities and related evidence of pathological use patterns are emphasized, whereas physical dependence refers to the physical (physiological) effects of multiple episodes of substance use. In definitions stressing physical dependence, ideas of tolerance or withdrawal appear in the classification criteria.

Somewhat related to *dependence* are the related words *addiction* and *addict.* The word *addict* has acquired a distinctive, unseemly, and pejorative connotation that ignores the concept of substance abuse as a medical disorder. *Addiction* has also been trivialized in popular usage, as in the phrases *TV addiction* and *money addiction.* Although these connotations have helped to avoid use of the word *addiction* in officially sanctioned nomenclature, there may be common neurochemical and neuroanatomical substrates among all the addictions, whether to substances or to gambling, sex, stealing, and eating. These various addictions may have similar effects on the activities of specific reward areas of the brain, such as the ventral tegmental area, the locus ceruleus, and the nucleus accumbens.

DSM-IV allows clinicians to specify whether symptoms of physiological dependence are present (Table 12.1–7). The presence or absence of physiological dependence need not be distinguished from, respectively, physical and psychological dependence. Such a distinction parallels the flawed organic-functional distinction; psychological or behavioral dependence undoubtedly reflects physiological changes in the behavioral centers of the brain. DSM-IV also allows clinicians to assess the current state of the substance dependence by providing a list of course modifiers (Table 12.1–8). *Psychological depend-*

Table 12.1–2
DSM-IV Substance-Induced Disorders Distributed in Other DSM-IV Sections with Phenomenologically Similar Disorders

	Dependence	Abuse	Intoxication	Withdrawal	Intoxication Delirium	Withdrawal Delirium	Dementia	Amnestic Disorder	Psychotic Disorders	Mood Disorders	Anxiety Disorders	Sexual Dysfunctions	Sleep Disorders
Alcohol	X	X	X	X	I	W	P	P	I/W	I/W	I/W	I	I/W
Amphetamines	X	X	X	X	I				I	I/W	I	I	I/W
Caffeine			X								I		I
Cannabis	X	X	X		I				I		I		
Cocaine	X	X	X	X	I				I	I/W	I/W	I	I/W
Hallucinogens	X	X	X		I				I[a]	I	I		
Inhalants	X	X	X		I		P		I	I	I		
Nicotine	X			X									
Opioids	X	X	X	X	I				I	I		I	I/W
Phencyclidine	X	X	X		I				I	I	I		
Sedatives, hypnotics, or anxiolytics	X	X	X	X	I	W	P	P	I/W	I/W	W	I	I/W
Polysubstance	X												
Other	X	X	X	X	I	W	P	P	I/W	I/W	I/W	I	I/W

Reprinted with permission from American Psychiatric Association: *Diagnostic and Statistical Manual of Mental Disorders,* ed 4. Copyright, American Psychiatric Association, Washington, 1994.

Note: X, I, W, I/W, and P indicate that the category is recognized in DSM-IV. In addition, *I* indicates the specifier "with onset during intoxication" may be noted for the category (except for intoxication delirium); *W* indicates that the specifier "with onset during withdrawal" may be noted for the category (except for withdrawal delirium); and *I/W* indicates that either "with onset during intoxication" or "with onset during withdrawal" may be noted for the category; *P* indicates that the disorder is "persisting."

[a] Also hallucinogen persisting perception disorder (flashbacks)

Table 12.1–3
DSM-IV Criteria for Substance Intoxication

A. The development of a reversible substance-specific syndrome due to recent ingestion of (or exposure to) a substance. **NOTE:** Different substances may produce similar or identical syndromes.

B. Clinically significant maladaptive behavioral or psychological changes that are due to the effect of the substance on the central nervous system (eg, belligerence, mood lability, cognitive impairment, impaired judgment, impaired social or occupational functioning) and develop during or shortly after use of the substance.

C. The symptoms are not due to a general medical condition and are not better accounted for by another mental disorder.

Reprinted with permission from American Psychiatric Association: *Diagnostic and Statistical Manual of Mental Disorders,* ed 4. Copyright, American Psychiatric Association, Washington, 1994.

Table 12.1–4
DSM-IV Criteria for Substance Withdrawal

A. The development of a substance-specific syndrome due to the cessation of (or reduction in) substance use that has been heavy and prolonged.

B. The substance-specific syndrome causes clinically significant distress or impairment in social, occupational, or other important areas of functioning.

C. The symptoms are not due to a general medical condition and are not better accounted for by another mental disorder.

Reprinted with permission from American Psychiatric Association: *Diagnostic and Statistical Manual of Mental Disorders,* ed 4. Copyright, American Psychiatric Association, Washington, 1994.

ence, also referred to as habituation, is characterized by a continuous or intermittent craving for the substance to avoid a dysphoric state.

Substance Abuse

DSM-IV defines substance abuse as characterized by the presence of at least one specific symptom indicating that substance use has interfered with the person's life (Table 12.1–9). People cannot meet the diagnosis of substance abuse for a particular substance if they have ever met the criteria for dependence on the same substance.

EPIDEMIOLOGY

A large recent survey showed that the lifetime prevalence of a diagnosis of substance abuse or dependence among the U.S. population older than age 18 was 16.7 percent. The lifetime prevalence for alcohol abuse or dependence was 13.8 percent; for nonalcohol substances, it was 6.2 percent. In 1995, 6.1 percent of the population age 12 years or older were current illicit drug users (used an illegal drug in the previous month). Alcohol and nicotine (cigarettes) are the most commonly used substances, but marijuana, hashish, and cocaine are also commonly used. In general, however, for all four of these substances—alcohol, marijuana, cigarettes, and cocaine—there has been a gradual but consistent decrease in use from a high around 1980 to 1992 (Fig. 12.1–1). Since 1993, however, substance abuse has been increasing among children and adolescents under age 18.

Abuse and dependence on substances are more common in men than in women, with the difference more marked for nonalcohol substances than for alcohol. Substance abuse is also higher among people who are unemployed and among some minority groups than among people who are employed and among majority groups. Substance use is not limited to adults. A recent survey of high school seniors showed that about 30 percent had tried a nonalcohol substance at least once and about 16 percent had tried a nonalcohol, nonmarijuana substance (such as amphetamines, inhalants, hallucinogens, sedatives, or cocaine) at least once.

Substance use is more common among medical professionals than among nonmedical professionals of equal levels of training (such as lawyers). A possible explanation for the difference is simply the relatively easy access that medical professionals have to some classes of substances (such as sedatives and stimulants).

The following data for 1995 comes from the Substance Abuse and Mental Health Services Administration.

Illicit Drug Use

In 1995, an estimated 12.8 million people in the United States were current illicit drug users, having used an illicit drug in the month preceding the interview. This figure represents no change from 1994, when the estimate was 12.6 million. The number of illicit drug users was at its highest level of 25 million in 1979.

Between 1994 and 1995, the rate of past month illicit drug use among adolescents increased, from 8.2 to 10.9 percent. This rate has doubled since 1992. Significant increases in past month marijuana use (from 6.0 to 8.2 percent), cocaine use (from 0.3 to 0.8 percent), and hallucinogen use (from 1.1 to 1.7 percent) occurred among adolescents between 1994 and 1995.

An estimated 2.3 million people started using marijuana in 1994. The annual number of marijuana initiates has risen since 1991. Marijuana is the most common illicit drug, used by 77 percent of current illicit drug users. Approximately 57 percent of current illicit drug users used marijuana only; 20 percent used marijuana and another illicit drug; and the remaining 23 percent used only an illicit drug other than marijuana in the past month. An estimated 5.6 million people (2.6 percent of the U.S. population) were current users of illicit drugs other than marijuana and hashish.

There were an estimated 582,000 (0.3 percent of the population) frequent cocaine users in 1995. Frequent use, defined as use on 51 or more days during the past year, was not significantly different from that in 1994 (734,000) or 1985 (781,000). The estimated number of occasional cocaine users (people who used in the past year but on fewer than 12 days), however, has sharply declined from 7.1 million in 1985 to 2.5 million in 1995.

Alcohol Use

In 1995, 111 million people in the United States age 12 and older had used alcohol in the past month (52 percent of the population). About 32 million engaged in binge drinking (5 or more drinks on at least one occasion in the past month), and about 11 million were heavy drinkers (drinking five or more drinks per occasion on 5 or more days in the past 30 days). About 10 million current drinkers were under age 21 in 1995. Of these, 4.4 million were binge drinkers, including 1.7 million heavy drinkers.

Table 12.1–5
ICD-10 Diagnostic Criteria for Mental and Behavioral Disorders Due to Psychoactive Substance Use

Mental and behavioral disorders due to use of alcohol

Mental and behavioral disorders due to use of opioids

Mental and behavioral disorders due to use of cannabinoids

Mental and behavioral disorders due to use of sedatives or hypnotics

Mental and behavioral disorders due to use of cocaine

Mental and behavioral disorders due to use of other stimulants, including caffeine

Mental and behavioral disorders due to use of hallucinogens

Mental and behavioral disorders due to use of tobacco

Mental and behavioral disorders due to use of volatile solvents

Mental and behavioral disorders due to multiple drug use and use of other psychoactive substances

Acute intoxication

G1. There must be clear evidence of recent use of a psychoactive substance (or substances) at sufficiently high dose levels to be consistent with intoxication.

G2. There must be symptoms or signs of intoxication compatible with the known actions of the particular substance (or substances), as specified below, and of sufficient severity to produce disturbances in the level of consciousness, cognition, perception, affect, or behavior that are of clinical importance.

G3. The symptoms or signs present cannot be accounted for by a medical disorder unrelated to substance use, and are not better accounted for by another mental or behavioral disorder.

Acute intoxication frequently occurs in persons who have more persistent alcohol- or drug-related problems in addition. Where there are such problems, eg, harmful use,, dependence syndrome, or psychotic disorder, they should also be recorded.

The following may be used to indicate whether the acute intoxication was associated with any complications:

Uncomplicated

Symptoms are of varying severity, usually dose dependent.

With trauma or other bodily injury

With other medical complications

Examples are hematemesis, inhalation of vomit.

With delirium

With perceptual distortions

With coma

With convulsions

Pathological intoxication
Applies only to alcohol

Acute intoxication due to use of alcohol

A. The general criteria for acute intoxication must be met.

B. There must be dysfunctional behavior, as evidenced by at least one of the following:
   (1) disinhibition
   (2) argumentativeness
   (3) aggression
   (4) lability of mood
   (5) impaired attention
   (6) impaired judgment
   (7) interference with personal functioning

C. At least one of the following signs must be present:
   (1) unsteady gait
   (2) difficulty in standing
   (3) slurred speech
   (4) nystagmus
   (5) decreased level of consciousness (eg, stupor, coma)
   (6) flushed face
   (7) conjunctival injection

Comment

When severe, acute alcohol intoxication may be accompanied by hypotension, hypothermia, and depression of the gag reflex. If desired, the blood alcohol level may be specified.

Pathological alcohol intoxication

Note. The status of this condition is being examined. These research criteria must be regarded as tentative.

A. The general criteria for acute intoxication must be met, with the exception that pathological intoxication occurs after drinking amounts of alcohol insufficient to cause intoxication in most people.

B. There is verbally aggressive or physically violent behavior that is not typical of the person when sober.

C. The intoxication occurs very soon (usually a few minutes) after consumption of alcohol.

D. There is no evidence of organic cerebral disorder or other mental disorders.

Comment

This is an uncommon condition. The blood alcohol levels found in this disorder are lower than those that would cause acute intoxication in most people, ie, below 40 mg/100 mL.

Acute intoxication due to use of opioids

A. The general criteria for acute intoxication must be met.

B. There must be dysfunctional behavior, as evidenced by at least one of the following:
   (1) apathy and sedation
   (2) disinhibition
   (3) psychomotor retardation
   (4) impaired attention
   (5) impaired judgment
   (6) interference with personal functioning

C. At least one of the following signs must be present:
   (1) drowsiness
   (2) slurred speech
   (3) pupillary constriction (except in anoxia from severe overdose, when pupillary dilatation occurs)
   (4) decreased level of consciousness (eg, stupor, coma)

Comment

When severe, acute opioid intoxication may be accompanied by respiratory depression (and hypoxia), hypotension, and hypothermia.

Acute intoxication due to use of cannabinoids

A. The general criteria for acute intoxication must be met.

B. There must be dysfunctional behavior or perceptual abnormalities, including at least one of the following:
   (1) euphoria and disinhibition
   (2) anxiety or agitation
   (3) suspiciousness or paranoid ideation
   (4) temporal slowing (a sense that time is passing very slowly, and/or the person is experiencing a rapid flow of ideas)
   (5) impaired judgment
   (6) impaired attention
   (7) impaired reaction time
   (8) auditory, visual, or tactile illusions
   (9) hallucinations with preserved orientation
   (10) depersonalization
   (11) derealization
   (12) interference with personal functioning

C. At least one of the following signs must be present:
   (1) increased appetite
   (2) dry mouth
   (3) conjunctival injection
   (4) tachycardia

(continued)

Table 12.1–5 (*continued*)

Acute intoxication due to use of sedatives or hypnotics

A. The general criteria for acute intoxication must be met.

B. There is dysfunctional behavior, as evidenced by at least one of the following:
  (1) euphoria and disinhibition
  (2) apathy and sedation
  (3) abusiveness or aggression
  (4) lability of mood
  (5) impaired attention
  (6) anterograde amnesia
  (7) impaired psychomotor performance
  (8) interference with personal functioning

C. At least one of the following signs must be present:
  (1) unsteady gait
  (2) difficulty in standing
  (3) slurred speech
  (4) nystagmus
  (5) decreased level of consciousness (eg, stupor, coma)
  (6) erythematous skin lesions or blisters

Comment

When severe, acute intoxication from sedative or hypnotic drugs may be accompanied by hypotension, hypothermia, and depression of the gag reflex.

Acute intoxication due to use of cocaine

A. The general criteria for acute intoxication must be met.

B. There must be dysfunctional behavior or perceptual abnormalities, as evidenced by at least one of the following:
  (1) euphoria and sensation of increased energy
  (2) hypervigilance
  (3) grandiose beliefs or actions
  (4) abusiveness or aggression
  (5) argumentativeness
  (6) lability of mood
  (7) repetitive stereotyped behaviors
  (8) auditory, visual, or tactile illusions
  (9) hallucinations, usually with intact orientation
  (10) paranoid ideation
  (11) interference with personal functioning

C. At least two of the following signs must be present:
  (1) tachycardia (sometimes bradycardia)
  (2) cardiac arrhythmias
  (3) hypertension (sometimes hypotension)
  (4) sweating and chills
  (5) nausea or vomiting
  (6) evidence of weight loss
  (7) pupillary dilatation
  (8) psychomotor agitation (sometimes retardation)
  (9) muscular weakness
  (10) chest pain
  (11) convulsions

Comment

Interference with personal functioning is most readily apparent from the social interactions of cocaine users, which range from extreme gregariousness to social withdrawal.

Acute intoxication due to use of other stimulants, including caffeine

A. The general criteria for acute intoxication must be met.

B. There must be dysfunctional behavior or perceptual abnormalities, as evidenced by at least one of the following:
  (1) euphoria and sensation of increased energy
  (2) hypervigilance
  (3) grandiose beliefs or actions
  (4) abusiveness or aggression
  (5) argumentativeness
  (6) lability of mood
  (7) repetitive stereotyped behaviors
  (8) auditory, visual, or tactile illusions
  (9) hallucinations, usually with intact orientation
  (10) paranoid ideation
  (11) interference with personal functioning.

C. At least two of the following signs must be present:
  (1) tachycardia (sometimes bradycardia)
  (2) cardiac arrhythmias
  (3) hypertension (sometimes hypotension)
  (4) sweating and chills
  (5) nausea or vomiting
  (6) evidence of weight loss
  (7) pupillary dilatation
  (8) psychomotor agitation (sometimes retardation)
  (9) muscular weakness
  (10) chest pain
  (11) convulsions

Comment

Interference with personal functioning is most readily apparent from the social interactions of the substance users, which range from extreme gregariousness to social withdrawal.

Acute intoxication due to use of hallucinogens

A. The general criteria for acute intoxication must be met.

B. There must be dysfunctional behavior or perceptual abnormalities, as evidenced by at least one of the following:
  (1) anxiety and fearfulness
  (2) auditory, visual, or tactile illusions or hallucinations occurring in a state of full wakefulness and alertness
  (3) depersonalization
  (4) derealization
  (5) paranoid ideation
  (6) ideas of reference
  (7) lability of mood
  (8) hyperactivity
  (9) impulsive acts
  (10) impaired attention
  (11) interference with personal functioning

C. At least two of the following signs must be present:
  (1) tachycardia
  (2) palpitations
  (3) sweating and chills
  (4) tremor
  (5) blurring of vision
  (6) pupillary dilatation
  (7) incoordination

Acute intoxication due to use of tobacco [acute nicotine intoxication]

A. The general criteria for acute intoxication must be met.

B. There must be dysfunctional behavior or perceptual abnormalities, as evidenced by at least one of the following:
  (1) insomnia
  (2) bizarre dreams
  (3) lability of mood
  (4) derealization
  (5) interference with personal functioning

C. At least one of the following signs must be present:
  (1) nausea or vomiting
  (2) sweating
  (3) tachycardia
  (4) cardiac arrhythmias

(continued)

Table 12.1–5 (*continued*)

Acute intoxication due to use of volatile solvents

A. The general criteria for acute intoxication must be met.

B. There must be dysfunctional behavior, evidenced by at least one of the following:
  (1) apathy and lethargy
  (2) argumentativeness
  (3) abusiveness or aggression
  (4) lability of mood
  (5) impaired judgment
  (6) impaired attention and memory
  (7) psychomotor retardation
  (8) interference with personal functioning

C. At least one of the following signs must be present:
  (1) unsteady gait
  (2) difficulty in standing
  (3) slurred speech
  (4) nystagmus
  (5) decreased level of consciousness (eg, stupor, coma)
  (6) muscle weakness
  (7) blurred vision or diplopia

Comment

Acute intoxication from inhalation of substances other than solvents should also be coded here.

When severe, acute intoxication from volatile solvents may be accompanied by hypotension, hypothermia, and depression of the gag reflex.

Acute intoxication due to multiple drug use and use of other psychoactive substances

This category should be used when there is evidence of intoxication caused by recent use of other psychoactive substances (eg, phencyclidine) or of multiple psychoactive substances where it is uncertain which substance has predominated.

Harmful use

A. There must be clear evidence that the substance use was responsible for (or substantially contributed to) physical or psychological harm, including impaired judgment or dysfunctional behavior, which may lead to disability or have adverse consequences for interpersonal relationships.

B. The nature of the harm should be clearly identifiable (and specified).

C. The pattern of use has persisted for at least 1 month or has occurred repeatedly within a 12-month period.

D. The disorder does not meet the criteria for any other mental or behavioral disorder related to the same drug in the same time period (except for acute intoxication).

Dependence syndrome

A. Three or more of the following manifestations should have occurred together for at least 1 month or, if persisting for periods of less than 1 month, should have occurred together repeatedly within a 12-month period:
  (1) a strong desire or sense of compulsion to take the substance
  (2) impaired capacity to control substance-taking behavior in terms of its onset, termination, or levels of use, as evidenced by: the substance being often taken in larger amounts or over a longer period than intended; or by a persistent desire or unsuccessful efforts to reduce or control substance use
  (3) a physiological withdrawal state when substance use is reduced or ceased, as evidenced by the characteristic withdrawal syndrome for the substance, or by use of the same (or closely related) substance with the intention of relieving or avoiding withdrawal symptoms
  (4) evidence of tolerance to the effects of the substance, such that there is a need for significantly increased amounts of the substance to achieve intoxication or the desired effect, or a marked diminished effect with continued use of the same amount of the substance;
  (5) preoccupation with substance use, as manifested by important alternative pleasures or interests being given up or reduced because of substance use; or a great deal of time being spent in activities necessary to obtain, take, or recover from the effects of the substance
  (6) persistent substance use despite clear evidence of harmful consequences, as evidenced by continued use when the individual is actually aware, or may be expected to be aware, of the nature and extent of harm

Diagnosis of the dependence syndrome may be further specified by the following:

Currently abstinent
  Early remission
  Partial remission
  Full remission

Currently abstinent but in a protected environment (eg, in hospital, in a therapeutic community, in prison, etc)

Currently on a clinically supervised maintenance or replacement regime (controlled dependence) (eg, with methadone; nicotine gum or nicotine patch)

Currently abstinent, but receiving treatment with aversive or blocking drugs (eg, naltrexone or disulfiram)

Currently using the substance (active dependence)
  Without physical features
  With physical features

The course of the dependence may be further specified, if desired, as follows:

Continuous use

Episodic use (dipsomania)

Withdrawal state

G1. There must be clear evidence of recent cessation or reduction of substance use after repeated, and usually prolonged and/or high-dose, use of that substance.

G2. Symptoms and signs are compatible with the known features of a withdrawal state from the particular substance or substances (see below).

G3. Symptoms and signs are not accounted for by a medical disorder unrelated to substance use, and not better accounted for by another mental or behavioral disorder.

The diagnosis of withdrawal state may be further specified by using the following:

Uncomplicated

With convulsions

Alcohol withdrawal state

A. The general criteria for withdrawal state must be met.

B. Any three of the following signs must be present:
  (1) tremor of the tongue, eyelids, or outstretched hands
  (2) sweating
  (3) nausea, retching, or vomiting
  (4) tachycardia or hypertension
  (5) psychomotor agitation
  (6) headache
  (7) insomnia
  (8) malaise or weakness
  (9) transient visual, tactile, or auditory hallucinations or illusions
  (10) grand mal convulsions

(continued)

Table 12.1–5 (*continued*)

Comment
If delirium is present, the diagnosis should be alcohol withdrawal state with delirium (delirium tremens).

Opioid withdrawal state
A. The general criteria for withdrawal state must be met. (Note that an opioid withdrawal state may also be induced by administration of an opioid antagonist after a brief period of opioid use.)
B. Any three of the following signs must be present:
(1) craving for an opioid drug
(2) rhinorrhea or sneezing
(3) lacrimation
(4) muscle aches or cramps
(5) abdominal cramps
(6) nausea or vomiting
(7) diarrhea
(8) pupillary dilatation
(9) piloerection, or recurrent chills
(10) tachycardia or hypertension
(11) yawning
(12) restless sleep

Cannabinoid withdrawal state
Note. This is an ill-defined syndrome for which definitive diagnostic criteria cannot be established at the present time. It occurs following cessation of prolonged high-dose use of cannabis. It has been reported variously as lasting from several hours to up to 7 days.

Symptoms and signs include anxiety, irritability, tremor of the outstretched hands, sweating, and muscle aches.

Sedative or hypnotic withdrawal state
A. The general criteria for withdrawal state must be met.
B. Any three of the following signs must be present:
(1) tremor of the tongue, eyelids, or outstretched hands
(2) nausea or vomiting
(3) tachycardia
(4) postural hypotension
(5) psychomotor agitation
(6) headache
(7) insomnia
(8) malaise or weakness
(9) transient visual, tactile, or auditory hallucinations or illustrations
(10) paranoid ideation
(11) grand mal convulsions

Comment
If delirium is present, the diagnosis should be sedative or hypnotic withdrawal state with delirium.

Cocaine withdrawal state
A. The general criteria for withdrawal state must be met.
B. There is dysphoric mood (for instance, sadness or anhedonia).
C. Any two of the following signs must be present:
(1) lethargy and fatigue
(2) psychomotor retardation or agitation
(3) craving for cocaine
(4) increased appetite
(5) insomnia or hypersomnia
(6) bizarre or unpleasant dreams

Withdrawal state from other stimulants, including caffeine
A. The general criteria for withdrawal state must be met.
B. There is dysphoric mood (for instance, sadness or anhedonia).
C. Any two of the following signs must be present:
(1) lethargy and fatigue
(2) psychomotor retardation or agitation
(3) craving for stimulant drugs
(4) increased appetite
(5) insomnia or hypersomnia
(6) bizarre or unpleasant dreams

Hallucinogen withdrawal state
Note: There is no recognized hallucinogen withdrawal state.

Tobacco withdrawal state
A. The general criteria for withdrawal state must be met.
B. Any two of the following signs must be present:
(1) craving for tobacco (or other nicotine-containing products
(2) malaise or weakness
(3) anxiety
(4) dysphoric mood
(5) irritability or restlessness
(6) insomnia
(7) increased appetite
(8) increased cough
(9) mouth ulceration
(10) difficulty in concentrating

Volatile solvents withdrawal state
Note: There is inadequate information on withdrawal states from volatile solvents for research to be formulated.

Multiple drugs withdrawal state

Withdrawal state with delirium
A. The general criteria for withdrawal state must be met.
B. The criteria for delirium must be met.

The diagnosis of withdrawal state with delirium may be further specified by using the following:
Without convulsions
With convulsions

Psychotic disorder
A. Onset of psychotic symptoms must occur during or within 2 weeks of substance use.
B. The psychotic symptoms must persist for more than 48 hours.
C. Duration of the disorder must not exceed 6 months.

The diagnosis of psychotic disorder may be further specified by using the following:

Schizophrenia-like
Predominantly delusional
Predominantly hallucinatory
Predominantly polymorphic
Predominantly depressive symptoms
Predominantly manic symptoms
Mixed

For research purposes it is recommended that change of the disorder from a nonpsychotic to a clearly psychotic state be further specified as either abrupt (onset within 48 hours) or acute (onset in more than 48 hours but less than 2 weeks).

(continued)

Table 12.1–5 (*continued*)

Amnesic syndrome A. Memory impairment is manifest in both: (1) a defect of recent memory (impaired learning of new material) to a degree sufficient to interfere with daily living (2) a reduced ability to recall past experiences B. All of the following are absent (or relatively absent): (1) defect in immediate recall (as tested, for example, by the digit span) (2) clouding of consciousness and disturbance of attention, as defined in delirium, not induced by alcohol and other psychoactive substances, criterion A (3) global intellectual decline (dementia). C. There is no objective evidence from physical and neurological examination, laboratory tests, or history of a disorder or disease of the brain (especially involving bilaterally the diencephalic and medial temporal structures), other than that related to substance use, that can reasonably be presumed to be responsible for the clinical manifestations described under criterion A. **Residual and late-onset psychotic disorder** A. Conditions and disorders meeting the criteria for the individual syndromes listed below should be clearly related to substance use. Where onset of the condition or disorder occurs subsequent to use of psychoactive substances, strong evidence should be provided to demonstrate a link.	***Comments*** In view of the considerable variation in this category, the characteristics of such residual states or conditions should be clearly documented in terms of their type, severity, and duration. For research purposes full descriptive details should be specified. If required, use as follows: Flashbacks Personality or behavior disorder B. The general criteria for personality and behavioral disorder due to brain disease, damage and dysfunction must be met. Residual affective disorder B. The criteria for organic mood (affective) disorder must be met. Dementia B. The general criteria for dementia must be met. Other persisting cognitive impairment B. The criteria for mild cognitive disorder must be met, except for the exclusion of psychoactive substance use in criterion D. Late-onset psychotic disorder B. The general criteria for psychotic disorder must be met, except with regard to the onset of the disorder, which is more than 2 weeks but not more than 6 weeks after substance use. **Other mental and behavioral disorders** **Unspecified mental and behavioral disorder**

Reprinted with permission from World Health Organization: *The ICD-10 Classification of Mental and Behavioural Disorders: Diagnostic Criteria for Research.* Copyright, World Health Organization, Geneva, 1993.

Cigarette Use

An estimated 61 million people in the United States were current smokers in 1995 (a smoking rate of 29 percent). The rate of current cigarette smoking did not change between 1994 and 1995. An estimated 20 percent of youths ages 12 through 17 (4.5 million adolescents) were current smokers in 1995.

Current smokers are more likely to be heavy drinkers and illicit drug users than are nonsmokers. Among smokers in 1995, 12.6 percent were heavy drinkers, and 13.6 percent were illicit drug users. Among nonsmokers, 2.7 percent were heavy drinkers, and 3.0 percent were illicit drug users.

Women of Childbearing Age

Overall, 7.3 percent (4.3 million) of women ages 15 to 44 in 1995 had used an illicit drug in the past month. The corresponding rate for men ages 15 to 44 was 11.6 percent. Of the 4.3 million women ages 15 to 44 who were current illicit drug users in 1995, more than 1.6 million had children living with them, including 390,000 with at least one child younger than 2 years of age.

Among women ages 15 to 44 who had no children and were not pregnant, 9.3 percent were current illicit drug users. Only 2.3 percent of pregnant women were current drug users; thus, most women may reduce their drug use when they become pregnant. But women who recently gave birth (had a child less than 2 years old and were not pregnant) had a rate of use of 5.5 percent. Many women thus resume their drug use after giving birth.

Age

Rates of drug use show substantial variation by age. Among adolescents ages 12 to 13, 4.5 percent were current illicit drug users. The highest rate was found among young people ages 16 to 17 (15.6 percent) and ages 18 to 20 (18.0 percent). Rates of use were lower in each successive age group, with only about 1 percent of those age 50 and older reporting current illicit use.

Race and Ethnicity

The rate of current illicit drug use for blacks (7.9 percent) remained somewhat higher than for whites (6.0 percent) and Hispanics (5.1 percent) in 1995. Among adolescents, however, the rates of use are about the same for the three groups. Most current illicit drug users were white. An estimated 9.6 million whites (75 percent of all users), 1.9 million blacks (15 percent), and 1.0 million Hispanics (8 percent) were current illicit drug users in 1995.

Gender

As in 1994, men continued to have a higher rate of current illicit drug use than did women (7.8 percent versus 4.5 percent) in 1995.

Region and Urbanicity

The current illicit drug use rate ranges from 7.8 in the West to 4.9 percent in the Northeast. There was little difference in rates of use in large metropolitan areas, small metropolitan areas, and nonmetropolitan areas.

Education

Illicit drug use rates remain highly correlated with educational status. Among young adults ages 18 to 34 years in 1995, those who had not completed high

Table 12.1–6
ICD-10 Diagnostic Criteria for Abuse of Non–Dependence-Producing Substances

A wide variety of medicaments and folk remedies may be involved, but the particularly important groups are: psychotropic drugs that do not produce dependence, such as antidepressants; laxatives, and analgesics that may be purchased without medical prescription, such as aspirin and paracetamol. Although the medication may have been medically prescribed or recommended in the first instance, prolonged, unnecessary, and often excessive dosage develops, which is facilitated by the availability of the substances without medical prescription.

Persistent and unjustified use of these substances is usually associated with unnecessary expense, often involves unnecessary contacts with medical professionals or supporting staff, and is sometimes marked by the harmful physical effects of the substances. Attempts to discourage or forbid the use of the substance are often met with resistance; for laxatives and analgesics this may be in spite of warnings about (or even the development of) physical harm such as renal dysfunction or electrolyte disturbances. Although it is usually clear that the patient has a strong motivation to take the substance, no dependence or withdrawal symptoms develop as in the case of the psychoactive substances specified in mental and behavioral disorders due to psychoactive substance use.

Identify the type of substance involved:

Antidepressants
(such as tricyclic and tetracyclic antidepressants and monoamine oxidase inhibitors)

Laxatives

Analgesics
(such as aspirin, paracetamol, phenacetin, not specified as psychoactive mental and behavioral disorders due to psychoactive substance use)

Antacids

Vitamins

Steroids or hormones

Specific herbal or folk remedies

Other substances that do not produce dependence
(such as diuretics)

Unspecified

Reprinted with permission from World Health Organization: *The ICD-10 Classification of Mental and Behavioural Disorders: Diagnostic Criteria for Research.* Copyright, World Health Organization, Geneva, 1993.

school had the highest rate of use (15.4 percent), and college graduates had the lowest rate of use (5.9 percent). Nevertheless, young adults at different educational levels are equally as likely to have tried illicit drugs in their lifetime (50 percent of those not completing high school and 52 percent of college graduates).

Employment

Current employment status is also highly correlated with rates of illicit drug use; 14.3 percent of unemployed adults (age 18 and older) were current illicit drug users in 1995, compared with 5.5 percent of full-time employed adults. The rate for full-time employed adults decreased significantly between 1994 (6.7 percent) and 1995 (5.5 percent).

COMORBIDITY

Comorbidity (also known as dual diagnosis) is the diagnosis of two or more psychiatric disorders in a single patient. A recent large community survey reported that 76 percent of men and 65 percent of women with a diagnosis of substance abuse or dependence had an additional psychiatric diagnosis. The most common comorbidity involves two substances of abuse, usually alcohol and another substance. Other psychiatric diagnoses commonly associated with substance abuse are antisocial personality disorder, phobias (and other anxiety disorders), major depressive disorder, and dysthymic disorder. In general, the most potent and dangerous substances have the highest comorbidity rates. For example, comorbidity of psychiatric disorders is more common for opioid and cocaine use than for marijuana use.

Table 12.1–7
DSM-IV Diagnostic Criteria for Substance Dependence

A maladaptive pattern of substance use, leading to clinically significant impairment or distress, as manifested by three (or more) of the following, occurring at any time in the same 12-month period:

(1) tolerance, as defined by either of the following:
  (a) a need for markedly increased amounts of the substance to achieve intoxication or desired effect
  (b) markedly diminished effect with continued use of the same amount of the substance

(2) withdrawal, as manifested by either of the following:
  (a) the characteristic withdrawal syndrome for the substance (refer to criteria A and B of the criteria sets for withdrawal from the specific substances)
  (b) the same (or closely related) substance is taken to relieve or avoid withdrawal symptoms

(3) the substance is often taken in larger amounts or over a longer period than was intended

(4) there is a persistent desire or unsuccessful efforts to cut down or control substance use

(5) a great deal of time is spent in activities necessary to obtain the substance (eg, visiting multiple doctors or driving long distances), use the substance (eg, chain-smoking), or recover from its effects

(6) important social, occupational, or recreational activities are given up or reduced because of substance use

(7) the substance use is continued despite knowledge of having a persistent or recurrent physical or psychological problem that is likely to have been caused or exacerbated by the substance (eg, current cocaine use despite recognition of cocaine-induced depression, or continued drinking despite recognition that an ulcer was made worse by alcohol consumption)

Specify if:
with physiological dependence: evidence of tolerance or withdrawal (ie, either item 1 or 2 is present)
without physiological dependence: no evidence of tolerance or withdrawal (ie, neither item 1 nor 2 is present)

Course specifiers:
Early full remission
Early partial emission
Sustained full remission
Sustained partial remission
On agonist therapy
In a controlled environment

Reprinted with permission from American Psychiatric Association: *Diagnostic and Statistical Manual of Mental Disorders,* ed 4. Copyright, American Psychiatric Association, Washington, 1994.

Table 12.1–8
DSM-IV Course Modifiers for Substance Dependence

Six course specifiers are available for substance dependence. The four remission specifiers can be applied only after none of the criteria for substance dependence of substance abuse have been present for at least 1 month. The definition of these four types of remission is based on the interval of time that has elapsed since the cessation of dependence (early versus sustained remission) and whether there is continued presence of one or more of the items included in the criteria sets for dependence or abuse (partial versus full remission). Because the first 12 months following dependence is a time of particularly high risk for relapse, this period is designated early remission. After 12 months of early remission have passed without relapse to dependence, the person enters into sustained remission. For both early remission and sustained remission, a further designation of full is given if no criteria for dependence or abuse have been met during the period of remission; a designation of partial is given if at least one of the criteria for dependence or abuse has been met, intermittently or continuously, during the period of remission. The differentiation of sustained full remission from recovered (no current substance use disorder) requires consideration of the length of time since the last period of disturbance, the total duration of the disturbance, and the need for continued evaluation. If, after a period of remission or recovery, the individual again becomes dependent, the application of the early remission specifier requires that there again be at least 1 month in which no criteria for dependence or abuse are met. Two additional specifiers have been provided: on agonist therapy and in a controlled environment. For an individual to qualify for early remission after cessation of agonist therapy or release from a controlled environment, there must be a 1-month period in which none of the criteria for dependence or abuse are met.

The following remission specifiers can be applied only after no criteria for dependence or abuse have been met for at least 1 month. Note that these specifiers do not apply if the individual is on agonist therapy or in a controlled environment (see below).

Early full remission. This specifier is used if, for at least 1 month, but for less than 12 months, no criteria for dependence or abuse have been met.

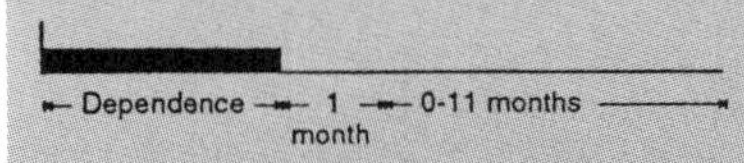
Dependence
1 month
0-11 months

Early partial remission. This specifier is used if, for at least 1 month, but less than 12 months, one or more criteria for dependence or abuse have been met (but the full criteria for dependence have not been met).

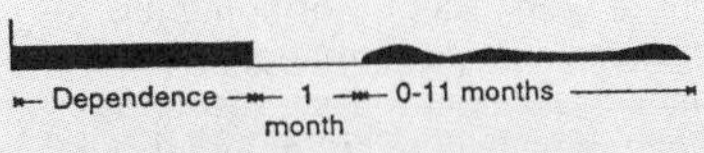
Dependence
1 month
0-11 months

Sustained full remission. This specifier is used if none of the criteria for dependence or abuse have been met at any time during a period of 12 months or longer.

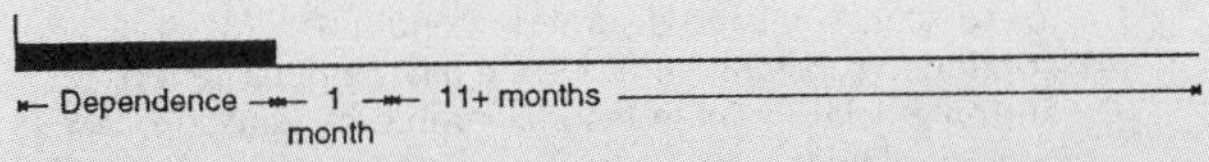
Dependence
1 month
11+ months

Sustained partial remission. This specifier is used if full criteria for dependence have not been met for a period of 12 months or longer; however, one or more criteria for dependence or abuse have been met.

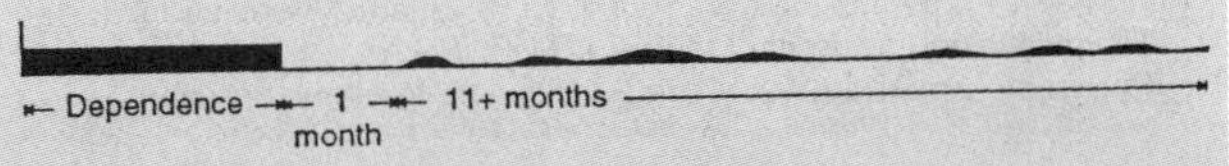
Dependence
1 month
11+ months

The following specifiers apply if the individual is on agonist therapy or in a controlled environment:

On agonist therapy. This specifier is used if the individual is on a prescribed agonist medication, and no criteria for dependence or abuse have been met for the class of medication for at least the past month (except tolerance to, or withdrawal from, the agonist). This category also applies to those being treated for dependence using a partial agonist or an agonist/antagonist.

In a controlled environment. This specifier is used if the individual is in an environment where access to alcohol and controlled substances is restricted, and no criteria for dependence or abuse have been met for at least the past month. Examples of these environments are closely supervised and substance-free jails, therapeutic communities, or locked hospital units.

Reprinted with permission from American Psychiatric Association: *Diagnostic and Statistical Manual of Mental Disorders,* ed 4. Copyright, American Psychiatric Association, Washington, 1994.

Antisocial Personality Disorder

In various studies, a range of 35 to 60 percent of patients with substance abuse or substance dependence also meet the diagnostic criteria for antisocial personality disorder. The range is even higher when investigators include people who meet all the antisocial personality disorder diagnostic criteria except the requirement that the symptoms started at an early age. That is, a high percentage of patients with substance abuse or substance dependence diagnoses have a pattern of antisocial behavior, whether it was present before the substance use started or developed during the course of the substance use. Patients with substance abuse or substance dependence diagnoses who have antisocial personality disorder are likely to use more illegal substances; to have more psychopathology; to be less satisfied with their lives; and to be more impulsive, isolated, and depressed than are other patients with antisocial personality disorders alone.

Depression and Suicide

Depressive symptoms are common among people diagnosed with substance abuse or substance dependence. About one third to one half of all those with opioid abuse or opioid dependence and about 40 percent of those with alcohol abuse or alcohol dependence meet the criteria for major depressive disorder sometime during their lives. Substance use is also a major precipitating factor for suicide. People who abuse sub-

Table 12.1–9
DSM-IV Criteria for Substance Abuse

A. A maladaptive pattern of substance use leading to clinically significant impairment or distress, as manifested by one (or more) of the following, occurring within a 12-month period:

(1) recurrent substance use resulting in a failure to fulfill major role obligations at work, school, or home (eg, repeated absences or poor work performance related to substance use; substance-related absences, suspensions, or expulsions from school; neglect of children or household)
(2) recurrent substance use in situations in which it is physically hazardous (eg, driving an automobile or operating a machine when impaired by substance use)
(3) recurrent substance-related legal problems (eg, arrests for substance-related disorderly conduct)
(4) continued substance use despite having persistent or recurrent social or interpersonal problems caused or exacerbated by the effects of the substance (eg, arguments with spouse about consequences of intoxication, physical fights)

B. The symptoms above never met the criteria for substance dependence for this class of substance.

stances are about 20 times more likely to die by suicide than are the general population. About 15 percent of people with alcohol abuse or alcohol dependence have been reported to commit suicide. This frequency of suicide is second only to the frequency in patients with major depressive disorder.

ETIOLOGY

At one level, substance abuse and substance dependence result from a person's taking a particular substance in an abusive pattern, but such simplification does not answer questions about why only some people and not others have substance abuse or substance dependence. As with all psychiatric disorders, the initial causative theories grew from psychodynamic models; subsequent models invoked behavioral, genetic, or neurochemical explanations. Most recent causative models for substance abuse invoke the entire range of theory (Fig. 12.1–2).

Psychodynamic Factors

The range of psychodynamic theories about substance abuse reflects the various popular theories during the past 100 years. According to classic theories, substance abuse is a masturbatory equivalent, a defense against homosexual impulses, or a manifestation of oral regression. Recent psychodynamic formulations relate substance use to depression or treat substance use as a reflection of disturbed ego functions.

Psychodynamic approaches to people with substance abuse are more widely valued and accepted than they are in the treatment of patients with alcohol abuse. In contrast to alcoholic patients, individuals with polysubstance abuse are more likely to have had unstable childhoods, more likely to self-medicate with substances, and more likely to benefit from psychotherapy. Considerable research links personality disorders with the development of substance dependence.

Other psychosocial theories invoke relationships with the family and with society in general, and there are many reasons to suspect a societal role in the development of patterns of

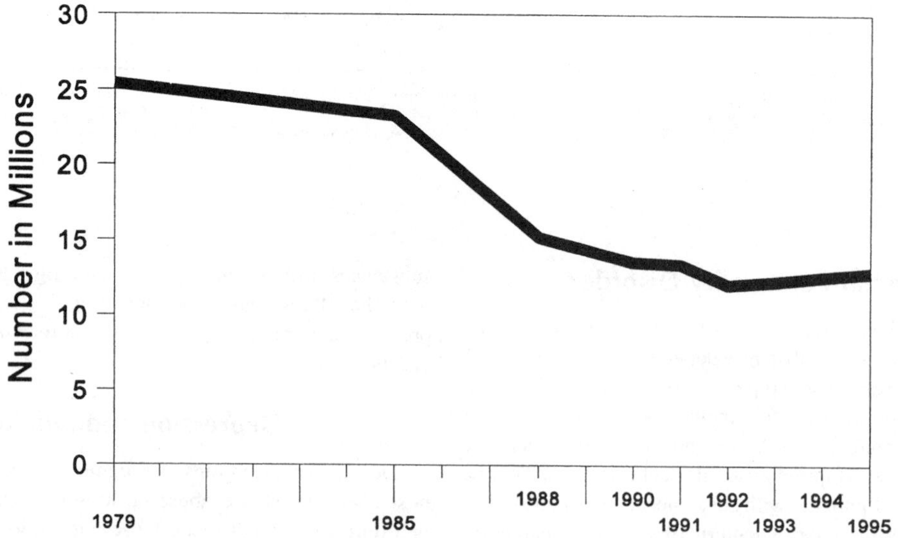
Number in Millions
30
25
20
15
10
5
0
1979
1985
1988
1990
1991
1992
1993
1994
1995

FIGURE 12.1–1
Number of people age 12 and older using illicit drugs in the past month, 1979–1995. The number of current illicit drug users did not change between 1994 and 1995 (12.6 and 12.8 million, respectively). The number of current illicit drug users was at its highest level in 1979 (25.4 million, 14.1 percent), declined until 1992 (12.0 million, 5.8 percent), and has since remained at approximately the same level. (From Substance Abuse and Mental Health Services Administration Office of Applied Studies: *Preliminary Estimates from the 1995 National Household Survey on Drug Abuse.* US Department of Health and Human Services, Washington, 1996.)

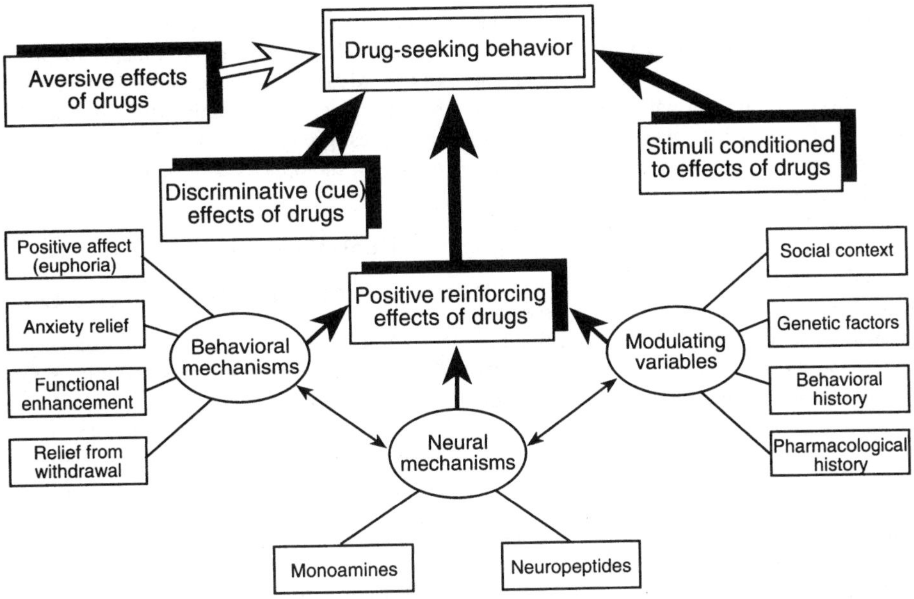
Drug-seeking behavior
Aversive effects of drugs
Discriminative (cue) effects of drugs
Stimuli conditioned to effects of drugs
Positive affect (euphoria)
Anxiety relief
Functional enhancement
Relief from withdrawal
Behavioral mechanisms
Positive reinforcing effects of drugs
Modulating variables
Social context
Genetic factors
Behavioral history
Pharmacological history
Neural mechanisms
Monoamines
Neuropeptides

FIGURE 12.1–2
A psychopharmacological model of dependence as substance-seeking behavior controlled by four main processes: positive reinforcing and discriminative effects of substances and of stimuli associated with them (which facilitate substance seeking) and aversive effects of substances (which weaken the behavior). The four processes are common to substances of many classes. A detailed framework for analyzing positive reinforcing effects is shown (similar analyses could be made for discriminative and aversive effects); at this level, the relative importance of the factors shown in the diagram varies considerably between classes of substances. (Reprinted with permission from Stolerman I: Drugs of abuse: Behavioral principles, methods, and terms. Trends Pharmacol Sci *13:* 171, 1992.).

substance abuse and substance dependence. Urban newspapers are filled with gripping stories about the drug culture permeating areas of urban poverty. Such articles often describe children brought into this culture at early ages. Yet even under these social pressures, not every child receives a diagnosis of substance abuse or substance dependence, a fact that suggests the involvement of other causal factors.

Coaddiction. The concept of coaddiction or codependence has become popularized in recent years, although some experts in the addiction field reject this concept as invalid. Coaddiction occurs when people, usually a couple, have a relationship that is primarily responsible for maintaining addictive behavior in at least one of the persons. Each person may exhibit enabling behaviors that help perpetuate the situation, and denial of the situation is a prerequisite for such a dyadic relationship to develop. The treatment of a coaddictive situation involves directly addressing the elements of the enabling behavior and the denial.

Behavioral Theories. Some behavioral models of substance abuse have focused on substance-seeking behavior rather than on the symptoms of physical dependence (see Fig. 12.1–2). For a behavioral model to have relevance to all substances, the model must not depend on the presence of withdrawal symptoms or of tolerance; many substances of abuse are not associated with the development of physiological dependence. Some researchers hypothesize that four major behavioral principles work to induce substance-seeking behavior. The first two principles are the positive reinforcing qualities and the adverse effects of some substances. Most substances of abuse produce a positive experience after their first use, and thus the substance acts as a positive reinforcer for substance-seeking behavior. Many substances also result in adverse effects, which act to reduce substance-seeking behavior. According to principles three and four, a person must be able to discriminate the substance of abuse from other substances, and almost all substance-seeking behavior is associated with cues that become connected with the substance-taking experience.

Genetic Factors

Strong evidence from studies of twins, adoptees, and siblings brought up separately indicates that the cause of alcohol abuse has a genetic component. Many less conclusive data show that other types of substance abuse or substance dependence have a genetic pattern in their development. Researchers recently have used the technology of restriction fragment length polymorphism (RFLP) in the study of substance abuse and substance dependence, and a few reports of RFLP associations have been published.

Neurochemical Factors

Receptors and Receptor Systems. For most substances of abuse, with the exception of alcohol, researchers have identified particular neurotransmitters through which, or neurotransmitter receptors on which, the substances have their effects. Some researchers base their studies on such hypotheses. The opiates, for example, act on opiate receptors. A person with too little endogenous opiate activity (such as low concentrations of endorphins) or with too much activity of an endogenous opiate antagonist may be at risk for the development of opioid dependence. Even in a person with completely normal endogenous receptor function and neurotransmitter concentration, the long-term use of a particular substance of abuse may eventually modulate receptor systems in the brain, which then requires the presence of the exogenous substance to maintain homeostasis. Such a receptor-level process may be the mechanism for developing tolerance within the central nervous system (CNS). Modulation of neurotransmitter release and neurotransmitter receptor function has proved to be difficult to demonstrate, however, and recent research focuses on the effects of substances on the second-messenger system and on gene regulation.

Pathways and Neurotransmitters. The major neurotransmitters possibly involved in developing substance abuse and substance dependence are the opioid, catecholamine (particularly dopamine), and γ-aminobutyric acid (GABA) systems (Fig. 12.1–3). Of particular importance are the dopaminergic neurons in the ventral tegmental area. These neurons project to the cortical and limbic regions, especially the nucleus accumbens. This pathway is probably involved in the sensation of reward and may be the major mediator of the effects of such substances as amphetamine and cocaine. The locus ceruleus, the largest group of adrenergic neurons, probably mediates the effects of the opiates and the opioids.

RESIDUAL DIAGNOSTIC CATEGORIES

Other Substance Use Disorders

DSM-IV includes a diagnostic category for substances not listed in the specific sections and allows for a complete range of substance-induced syndromes caused by other or unknown substances (Table 12.1–10). DMS-IV also permits the diagnosis of other (or unknown) substance-use disorders not otherwise specified to cover any syndrome that is assessed to be causally related to any substance.

Gamma Hydroxybutyrate (GHB). GHB is a naturally occurring transmitter in the brain that is related to sleep

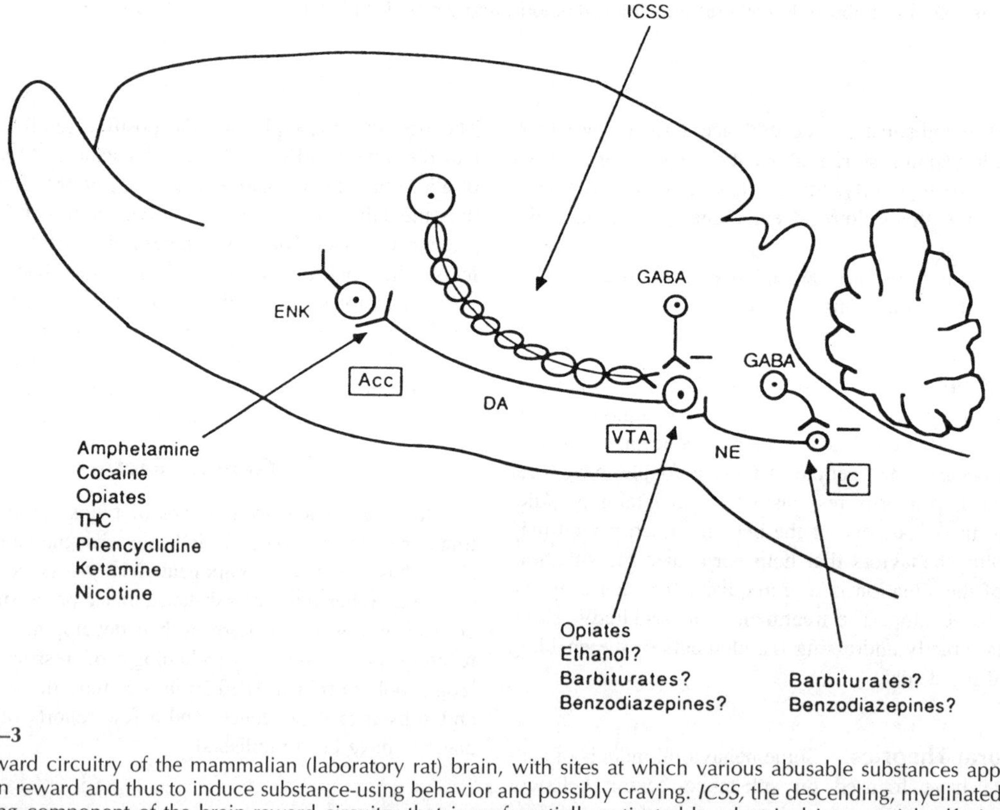
ICSS
ENK
GABA
GABA
Acc
DA
VTA
NE
LC
Amphetamine
Cocaine
Opiates
THC
Phencyclidine
Ketamine
Nicotine
Opiates
Ethanol?
Barbiturates?
Benzodiazepines?
Barbiturates?
Benzodiazepines?

FIGURE 12.1–3

The brain-reward circuitry of the mammalian (laboratory rat) brain, with sites at which various abusable substances appear to act to enhance brain reward and thus to induce substance-using behavior and possibly craving. *ICSS,* the descending, myelinated, moderately fast-conducting component of the brain-reward circuitry that is preferentially activated by electrical intracranial self-stimulation; *DA,* the subcomponent of the ascending mesolimbic dopaminergic system that appears to be preferentially activated by abusable substances; *LC,* locus ceruleus; *VTA,* ventral tegmental area; *Acc,* nucleus accumbens; *ENK,* enkephalins, *NE,* nonadrenergic fibers, which originate in the locus ceruleus and synapse into the general vicinity of the ventral mesencephalic DA cell fields; *GABA,* the GABAergic inhibitory fiber systems synapsing on both the locus ceruleus nonadrenergic fibers and the ventral mesencephalic DA cell fields. (Reprinted with permission from Gardner E: Brain reward mechanism. In *Substance Abuse: A Comprehensive Textbook,* ed 2, JH Lowinson, P Ruiz, RB Millman, editors, p 87. Williams & Wilkins, Baltimore, 1992.)

Table 12.1–10
DSM-IV Criteria for Other (or Unknown) Substance-Related Disorders

The other (or unknown) substance-related disorders category is for classifying substance-related disorders associated with substances not listed above. Examples of these substances, which are described in more detail below, include anabolic steroids, nitrite inhalants ("poppers"), nitrous oxide, over-the-counter and prescription medications not otherwise covered by the 11 categories (eg, cortisol, antihistamines, benztropine), and other substances that have psychoactive effects. In addition, this category may be used when the specific substance is unknown (eg, an intoxication after taking a bottle of unlabeled pills).

Anabolic steroids sometimes produce an initial sense of enhanced well-being (or even euphoria), which is replaced after repeated use by lack of energy, irritability, and other forms of dysphoria. Continued use of these substances may lead to more severe symptoms (eg, depressive symptomatology) and general medical conditions (liver disease).

Nitrite inhalants ("poppers"—forms of amyl, butyl, and isobutyl nitrite) produce an intoxication that is characterized by a feeling of fullness in the head, mild euphoria, a change in the perception of time, relaxation of smooth muscles, and a possible increase in sexual feelings. In addition to possible compulsive use, these substances carry dangers of potential impairment of immune functioning, irritation of the respiratory system, a decrease in the oxygen-carrying capacity of the blood, and a toxic reaction that can include vomiting, severe headache, hypotension, and dizziness.

Nitrous oxide ("laughing gas") causes rapid onset of an intoxication that is characterized by lightheadedness and a floating sensation that clears in a matter of minutes after administration is stopped. There are reports of temporary but clinically relevant confusion and reversible paranoid states when nitrous oxide is used regularly.

Other substances that are capable of producing mild intoxication include **catnip,** which can produce states similar to those observed with marijuana and which in high doses is reported to result in LSD-type perceptions; **betel nut,** which is chewed in many cultures to produce a mild euphoria and floating sensation; and **kava** (a substance derived from the South Pacific pepper plant), which produces sedation, incoordination, weight loss, mild forms of hepatitis, and lung abnormalities. In addition, individuals can develop dependence and impairment through repeated self-administration of **over-the-counter** and **prescription drugs,** including **cortisol, antiparkinsonian agents** that have anticholinergic properties, and **antihistamines.**

Texts and criteria sets have already been provided to define the generic aspects of substance dependence, substance abuse, substance intoxication, and substance withdrawal that are applicable across classes of substances. The other (or unknown) substance-induced disorders are described in the sections of the manual with disorders with which they share phenomenology (eg, other (or unknown) substance-induced mood disorder is included in the mood disorders section). Listed below are the other (or unknown) substance use disorders and the other (or unknown) substance-induced disorders.

Other (or unknown) substance use disorders

Other (or unknown) substance dependence

Other (or unknown) substance abuse

Other (or unknown) substance-induced disorders

Other (or unknown) substance intoxication
Specify if:
With perceptual disturbances

Other (or unknown) substance withdrawal
Specify if:
With perceptual disturbances

Other (or unknown) substance-induced delirium

Other (or unknown) substance-induced persisting dementia

Other (or unknown) substance-induced persisting amnestic disorder

Other (or unknown) substance psychotic disorder, with delusions
Specify if:
With onset during intoxication
With onset during withdrawal

Other (or unknown) substance-induced psychotic disorder, with hallucinations
Specify if:
With onset during intoxication
With onset during withdrawal

Other (or unknown) substance-induced mood disorder
Specify if:
With onset during intoxication
With onset during withdrawal

Other (or unknown) substance-induced anxiety disorder
Specify if:
With onset during intoxication
With onset during withdrawal

Other (or unknown) substance-induced sexual dysfunction
Specify if:
With onset during intoxication

Other (or unknown) substance-induced sleep disorder
Specify if:
With onset during intoxication

Other (or unknown) substance-related disorder not otherwise specified

regulation. GHB increases dopamine levels in the brain. In general, GHB is a central nervous system (CNS) depressant and has effects through the endogenous opioid system. It is used for induction of anesthesia and long-term sedation, but its unpredictable duration of action limits its use. It has recently been studied for the treatment of alcohol and opioid withdrawal and narcolepsy.

Until 1990, GHB was sold in U.S. health food stores, and body builders used it as a steroid alternative. Reports have indicated, however, that GHB has been abused for its intoxicating effects. It is variously referred to as GHB, GBH, and liquid ecstasy and is sold illicitly in various forms (such as powder and liquid). Adverse effects include nausea, vomiting, respiratory problems, seizures, comas, and death. In some reports, GHB abuse has been linked to Wernicke-Korsakoff–like syndrome.

Nitrite Inhalants. The nitrite inhalants include amyl, butyl, and isobutyl nitrites, all of which are called *poppers* in popular jargon. Like anesthetic gas use, nitrite inhalant use is specifically excluded from inhalant use disorders; the intoxication syndromes seen with nitrites can be markedly different from the syndromes seen with the standard inhalant substances, such as lighter fluid and airplane glue. Nitrite inhalants are used by people seeking the associated mild euphoria, altered sense of time, feeling of fullness in the head, and, possibly, increased sexual feelings. The nitrite compounds are used by some gay men to reduce sexual inhibitions, to delay orgasm, and to relax the anal sphincter for penile penetration. Under such circumstances, a person may inhale the substance from a small bottle for a few or a dozen times within several hours. Adverse reactions include a toxic syndrome characterized by nausea, vomiting, headache, hypotension, drowsiness, and irritation of the respiratory tract. Some evidence indicates that nitrite inhalants may adversely affect immune function.

Nitrous Oxide. Nitrous oxide, commonly known as laughing gas, is a widely available anesthetic agent that is subject to abuse because of its ability to produce feelings of lightheadedness and of floating, sometimes experienced as pleasurable. With long-term abuse patterns, nitrous oxide use has been associated with delirium and paranoia. Female dental assistants exposed to high levels of nitrous oxide have reportedly experienced reduced fertility.

Other Substances. The spice nutmeg can be ingested in a number of preparations. When nutmeg is taken in sufficiently high doses, it can induce depersonalization, derealization, and a feeling of heaviness in the limbs. In high-enough doses, morning glory seeds can produce a syndrome similar to that seen with lysergic acid diethylamide (LSD), characterized by altered sensory perceptions and mild visual hallucinations. Catnip can produce cannabis-like intoxication in low doses and LSD-like intoxication in high doses. Betel nuts, when chewed, can produce a mild euphoria and a feeling of floating in space. Kava, derived from a pepper plant native to the South Pacific, produces sedation and incoordination and is associated with hepatitis, lung abnormalities, and weight loss. DSM-IV notes that some people abuse over-the-counter and prescription medications such as cortisol, antiparkinsonian agents, and antihistamines. Ephedra, a natural substance found in herbal tea, acts like epinephrine and when abused produces cardiac arrhythmia and fatalities.

Polysubstance-Related Disorder

Substance users often abuse more than one substance. In DSM-IV, a diagnosis of polysubstance dependence is appropriate if, for a period of at least 12 months, a person has repeatedly used substances from at least three categories (not including nicotine and caffeine), even if the diagnostic criteria for a substance-related disorder are not met for any single substance, as long as, during this period, the criteria for substance dependence have been met for the substances considered as a group (Table 12.1–11).

Table 12.1–11
DSM-IV Criteria for Polysubstance Dependence

This diagnosis is reserved for behavior during the same 12-month period in which the person was repeatedly using at least three groups of substances (not including caffeine and nicotine), but no single substance has predominated. Further, during this period, the dependence criteria were met for substances as a group but not for any specific substance.

Reprinted with permission from American Psychiatric Association: *Diagnostic and Statistical Manual of Mental Disorders,* ed 4. Copyright, American Psychiatric Association, Washington, 1994.

TREATMENT AND REHABILITATION

Treatment Approaches and Goals

Treatment approaches for substance abuse vary according to substances, patterns of abuse, availability of psychosocial support systems, and patients' individual features. Two major treatment goals for substance abuse have been determined. The first goal is abstinence from the substance. Although some people have been able to change from an abusive pattern to a moderate pattern of use, they are exceptions to most abusers, for whom complete abstinence is the only way to control the problem. The second goal is the physical, psychiatric, and psychosocial well-being of the patient. Significant damage has often been done to a patient's support systems during prolonged periods of substance abuse. For a patient to stop a pattern of substance abuse successfully, adequate psychosocial supports must be in place to foster the difficult change in behavior.

Initial treatment approaches to substance abuse may be conducted in either an inpatient or outpatient setting. Although an outpatient setting is more naturalistic than is an inpatient setting, the temptations available to an outpatient may present too high a hurdle for the initiation of treatment. Inpatient treatment is also indicated in the case of severe medical or psychiatric symptoms, a history of failed outpatient treatments, a lack of psychosocial supports, or a particularly severe or long-term history of substance abuse. After an initial period of detoxification, patients need a sustained period of rehabilitation. Throughout treatment, individual, family, and group therapies can be effective. Education about substance abuse and support for patients' efforts are essential factors in treatment. In some cases, the use of a psychotherapeutic drug may be indicated to discourage patients from using the abused substance (such as disulfiram [Antabuse]), to reduce the effects of withdrawal (such as methadone), or to treat a presumptive underlying psychiatric disorder (such as antidepressants). The current trend is to shorten the number of inpatient treatment days and to effect outpatient treatment as much as possible.

Psychotherapy

The role of psychotherapy in alcohol dependence is highly controversial, but some patients who cannot or will not make use of Alcoholics Anonymous (AA) may require psychotherapeutic intervention. Alcohol dependence is a heterogeneous disorder, and the individual with the disorder must always be taken into account in treatment planning. Although no specific personality traits are connected with alcohol dependence, clinicians have observed that alcohol may replace missing psychological structures and therefore may restore a sense of self-esteem in patients. For some patients, psychotherapy and Alcoholics Anonymous work synergistically—AA helps them achieve abstinence, and psychotherapy deals with psychological and interpersonal factors that cause distress in their lives.

A view of most substance abuse as adaptive and defensive rather than as regressive has replaced the early psychoanalytic interpretation of substance abuse as a regression to the oral stage of psychosexual development. Regressive states may actually be reversed by using substances because the substance reinforces weakened defenses against intense affects such as shame and rage. Moreover, those with substance dependence tend to have significant deficits in self-care, which result from early developmental disturbances contributing to the impaired internalization of parental figures. As a consequence, people with substance dependence find it difficult to soothe themselves and to regulate impulse control and self-esteem.

Methodologically rigorous research has shown that the addition of psychotherapy to the overall treatment plan of people with opioid dependence has a greater benefit than do treatment plans without psychotherapy. Patients with significant psychiatric symptoms make little or no progress with counseling alone but are the best candidates for psychotherapy and benefit the most from it. Abstinence from the abused substance, however, is required for psychotherapy to be effective in dealing with the underlying psychiatric disturbances.

References

Bagatell CJ, Bremner WJ: Androgens in men—uses and abuses. N Engl J Med *334:* 707, 1996.

Brooner RK, Schmidt CW, Felch LJ, Bigelow FE: Antisocial behavior of intravenous drug abusers: Implications for diagnosis of antisocial personality disorder. Am J Psychiatry *149:* 482, 1992.

Ferras SD, Tedeschi L, Frison G, Rossi A: Fatality due to gamma-hydroxybutyric acid (GHB) and heroin intoxication. J Forensic Sci *40:* 501, 1995.

Friedman J, Westlake R, Furman M: "Grievous bodily harm:" gamma hydroxybutyrate abuse leading to a Wernicke-Korsakoff syndrome. Neurology *46:* 469, 1996.

Gabbard GO: *Psychodynamic Psychiatry in Clinical Practice: The DSM-IV Edition.* American Psychiatric Press, Washington, 1994.

Gamma hydroxy butyrate use—New York and Texas, 1995–1996. MMWR Morb Mortal Wkly Rep *46:* 281, 1997.

Gerstley LJ, Alterman AI, McLellan AT, Woody GE: Antisocial personality disorder in patients with substance abuse disorders: A problematic diagnosis? Am J Psychiatry *147:* 173, 1990.

Goldstein A, Kalant H: Drug policy: Striking the right balance. Science *249:* 1513, 1990.

Group for the Advancement of Psychiatry Committee on Alcoholism and the Addictions: Substance abuse disorders: A psychiatric priority. Am J Psychiatry *148:* 1291, 1991.

Grove WM, Eckert ED, Heston L, Bouchard TJ Jr, Segal N, Lykken DT: Heritability of substance abuse and antisocial behavior: A study of monozygotic twins reared apart. Biol Psychiatry *27:* 1293, 1990.

Hughes PH, Baldwin DC, Sheehan DV, Conrad S, Storr CL: Resident physician substance use, by specialty. Am J Psychiatry *149:* 1348, 1992.

Jaffe JH: Introduction and overview. In *Comprehensive Textbook of Psychiatry,* ed 6, HI Kaplan, BJ Sadock, editors, p 755. Williams & Wilkins, Baltimore, 1995.

Kaufman E: Diagnosis and treatment of drug and alcohol abuse in women. Am J Obstet Gynecol *174:* 21, 1996.

Kolb LC: The 100 years war. Psychiatr Ann *21:* 499, 1991.

Koob GF: Drugs of abuse: Anatomy, pharmacology and function of reward pathways. Trends Pharmacol Sci *13:* 177, 1992.

Meyer RE: The disease called addiction: Emerging evidence in a 200-year debate. Lancet *347:* 162, 1996.

Nace EP, Davis CW, Gaspari JP: Axis II comorbidity in substance abusers. Am J Psychiatry *148:* 118, 1991.

National Institute on Drug Abuse: *National Household Survey on Drug Abuse: Highlights, 1991.* US Government Printing Office, Washington, 1991.

Nestler EJ: Molecular mechanisms of drug addiction. J Neurosci *12:* 2439, 1992.

Rowland AS, Baird DD, Weinberg CR, Shore DL, Shy CM, Wilcox AJ: Reduced fertility among women employed as dental assistants exposed to high levels of nitrous oxide. N Engl J Med *327:* 993, 1992.

Satel SL, Kosten TR, Schuckit MA, Fischman MW: Should protracted withdrawal from drugs be introduced in DSM-IV? Am J Psychiatry *150:* 695, 1993.

Smith SS, O'Hara BF, Persico AM, Gorelick DA, Newlin DB, Vlahov D, Soloman L, Pickens R, Uhl GR: Genetic vulnerability to drug abuse. Arch Gen Psychiatry *49:* 723, 1992.

Stephens BG, Baselt RC: Driving under the influence of GHB? J Anal Toxicol *18:* 357, 1994.

Stolerman I: Drugs of abuse: Behavioral principles, methods and terms. Trends Pharmacol Sci *13:* 170, 1992.

Substance Abuse and Mental Health Services Administration Office of Applied Studies: *Preliminary Estimates from the 1995 National Household Survey on Drug Abuse.* US Government Printing Office, Washington, 1995.

Uhl G, Blum K, Noble E, Smith S: Substance abuse vulnerability and D_2 receptor genes. Trends Neurosci *16:* 83, 1993.

Warner LA, Kessler RC, Hughes M, Anthony JC, Nelson CB: Prevalence and correlates of drug use and dependency in the United States. Results from the National Comorbidity Survey. Arch Gen Psychiatry *52:* 219, 1995.

▲ 12.2 Alcohol-Related Disorders

The fourth edition of *Diagnostic and Statistical Manual of Mental Disorder* (DSM-IV) describes alcohol as "the most frequently used brain depressant" in most cultures and a "cause of considerable morbidity and mortality." The extent of alcohol-related disorders in the United States is generally well known, but the costs to society are probably not. The direct and indirect social costs of these disorders are estimated at more then $150 billion, about $600 per capita. They are by far the most common substance-related disorders in the United States.

Although alcohol abuse and dependence are commonly called alcoholism, DSM-IV does not use the term because it lacks a precise definition.

EPIDEMIOLOGY

Drinking alcohol-containing beverages is generally considered an acceptable and common habit in the United States. About 85 percent of all U.S. residents have had an alcohol-containing drink at least once in their lives, and about 51 percent of all U.S. adults are current users of alcohol. After heart disease and cancer, alcohol-related disorders constitute the third largest health problem in the United States today; beer accounts for about one half of all alcohol consumption, liquor for about one third, and wine for about one sixth. About 30 to 45 percent of all adults in the United States have had at least one transient episode of alcohol-related problems, usually an alcohol-induced amnestic episode like a blackout, driving a motor vehicle while intoxicated, or missing school or work because of excessive drinking. About 10 percent of women and 20 percent of men have met the diagnostic criteria for alcohol abuse during their lifetimes, and 3 to 5 percent of women and 10 percent of men have met the diagnostic criteria for the more serious diagnosis of alcohol dependence during their lifetimes. About 200,000 deaths each year are directly related to alcohol abuse. The common causes of death among people with the alcohol-related disorders are suicide, cancer, heart disease, and hepatic disease. Although people involved in automotive fatalities do not always meet the diagnostic criteria for an alcohol-related disorder, drunken drivers are connected with about 50 percent of all automotive fatalities and this percentage increases to about 75 percent when only accidents occurring in the late evening are considered. Alcohol use and alcohol-related disorders are also associated with about 50 percent of all homicides and 25 percent of all suicides. Alcohol abuse reduces life expectancy by about 10 years; alcohol leads all other substance in substance-related deaths.

Statistical Factors

The following data for 1995 came from the Substance Abuse and Mental Health Administration:

In 1995, approximately 111 million people age 12 and over were current (at least one drink in the past month [includes binge and heavy use]) alcohol users; this number was about 52 percent of the total population of age 12 and older. About 32 million people (15.8 percent) engaged in binge drinking (five or more drinks on the same occasion at least once in the past month [includes heavy use]), and about 11 million people (5.5 percent of the population) were heavy (five or more drinks on the same occasion on at least five different days in the past month) drinkers. About 10 million current drinkers were under age 21 in 1995. Of these, 4.4 million were binge drinkers, including 1.7 million heavy drinkers. Alcohol usage rates were not significantly different between 1994 and 1995.

The level of alcohol use was strongly associated with illicit drug use in 1995, as in previous years. Of the 11.3 million heavy drinkers, 25 percent (2.8 million people) were current illicit drug users. Among binge (but not heavy) drinkers, 18 percent (3.8 million) were illicit drug users. Other drinkers (past month but not binge) had a rate of 5.5 percent (3.9 million) for illicit drug use, while only 1.9 percent (1.9 million) of nondrinkers were illicit drug users.

Rates of current alcohol use were above 60 percent for age groups 21 through 25, 26 through 29, 30 through 34, 35 through 39, and 40 through 44 in 1995. For younger and older age groups, rates were lower. Young adults (18 to 25 years old) drinkers were the most likely to binge or drink heavy. About one half the drinkers in this age group were binge drinkers and about one in five were heavy drinkers.

Race and Ethnicity. In 1995, whites continued to have the highest rate of alcohol use at 56 percent. Rates for Hispanics and blacks were 45 percent and 41 percent, respectively. The rate of binge use was lower among blacks (11.2 percent) than among whites (16.6 percent) and Hispanics (17.2 percent). Heavy use showed no statistically significant differences by race or ethnicity (5.7 percent for whites, 6.3 percent for Hispanics, and 4.6 percent for blacks).

Gender. Sixty percent of men were past month alcohol users, compared with 45 percent of women. Men were much more likely than were women to be binge drinkers (23.8 percent and 8.5 percent, respectively) and heavy drinkers (9.4 and 2.0 percent, respectively).

Region and Urbanicity. The rate of current alcohol use was 59 percent in the North Central region, 54 percent in the Northeast region, 53 percent in the West, and 47 percent in the South in 1995. Rates of binge use were 20 percent in the North Central region, 16 percent in the West, and 14 percent in the South and Northeast. Heavy alcohol use rates were 7.0 percent in the North Central region, 5.6 percent in the West, 4.9 percent in the Northeast, and 4.8 percent in the South.

The rate of past month alcohol use was 56 percent in large metropolitan areas, 52 percent in small metropolitan areas, and 46 percent in nonmetropolitan areas. There was little variation in binge and heavy alcohol use rates by population density.

Education. In contrast to the pattern for illicit drugs, the higher the level of educational attainment, the more likely was the current use of alcohol. In 1995, 68 percent of adults with college degrees were current drinkers, compared with only 42 percent of those having less than a high school education. Binge alcohol use rates were similar across different levels of education. The rate of heavy alcohol use, however, was 3.7 percent among adults who had completed college and 7.1 percent among adults who had not completed high school.

Psychosocial Factors

Alcohol-related disorders appear among people of all socioeconomic classes. In fact, people who are stereotypical skid-row alcoholics constitute less than 5 percent of those with alcohol-related disorders in the United States. Moreover, these disorders are particularly frequent in people with advanced academic degrees and of upper socioeconomic standing.

Among high school students, alcohol-related problems are correlated with a history of school difficulties. High school dropouts and people with a record of frequent truancy and delinquency appear to be at particularly high risk for alcohol abuse. These epidemiological data are consistent with the high comorbidity between alcohol-related disorders and antisocial personality disorder.

Comorbidity

The psychiatric diagnoses most commonly associated with the alcohol-related disorders are other substance-related disorders, antisocial personality disorder, mood disorders, and anxiety disorders. Although the data are somewhat controversial, most suggest that people with alcohol-related disorders have a markedly higher suicide rate than do the general population.

Antisocial Personality Disorder. A relation between antisocial personality disorder and alcohol-related disorders has frequently been reported. Some studies have suggested that antisocial personality disorder is particularly common in men with an alcohol-related disorder and can precede the development of the alcohol-related disorder. Other studies, however, have suggested that antisocial personality disorder and alcohol-related disorders are completely distinct entities that are not causally related.

Mood Disorders. About 30 to 40 percent of people with an alcohol-related disorder meet the diagnostic criteria for major depressive disorder sometime during their lifetimes. Depression is more common in women than in men with these disorders. Several studies reported that depression is likely to occur in patients with alcohol-related disorders who have a high daily consumption of alcohol and who have a family history of alcohol abuse. People with alcohol-related disorders and major depressive disorder are at great risk for attempting suicide and are likely to have other substance-related disorder diagnoses. Some clinicians recommend that depressive symptoms that remain after 2 to 3 weeks of sobriety be treated with antidepressant drugs. Patients with bipolar I disorder are thought to be at risk for developing an alcohol-related disorder; they may use alcohol to self-medicate their manic episodes. Some studies have shown that people with both alcohol-related disorder and depressive disorder diagnoses have low cerebrospinal fluid (CSF) concentrations of dopamine metabolites (homovanillic acid) and γ-aminobutyric acid (GABA).

Anxiety Disorders. Many people use alcohol for its efficacy in alleviating anxiety. Although the comorbidity between alcohol-related disorders and mood disorders is fairly widely recognized, it is less well known that perhaps 25 to 50 percent of all people with alcohol-related disorders also meet the diagnostic criteria for an anxiety disorder (Table 12.2–1). Phobias and panic disorder are particularly frequent comorbid diagnoses in these patients. Some data indicate that alcohol may be used in an attempt to self-medicate symptoms of agoraphobia or social phobia, but an alcohol-related disorder is likely to precede the development of panic disorder or generalized anxiety disorder.

Suicide. Most estimates of the prevalence of suicide among people with alcohol-related disorders range from 10 to 15 percent, although alcohol use itself may be involved in a much higher percentage of suicides. Some investigators have questioned whether the suicide rate among people with alcohol-related disorders is as high as the numbers suggest. Factors that have been associated with suicide among people with alcohol-related disorders include the presence of a major depressive episode, weak psychosocial support systems, a serious coexisting medical condition, unemployment, and living alone.

ETIOLOGY

Alcohol-related disorders, like virtually all other psychiatric conditions, probably represent a heterogeneous group of disease processes. In any individual case, psychosocial, genetic, or behavioral factors may be more important than are other factors. Within any single set of factors, such as biological factors, one element, such as a neurotransmitter receptor gene, may be more critically involved than another element, such as a neurotransmitter uptake pump. Except for research purposes, it is not necessary to identify the single causative factor; treating alcohol-related disorders requires taking whatever approaches are effective, regardless of theory.

Childhood History

Researchers have identified several factors in the childhood histories of people with later alcohol-related disorders and in children at high risk for having an alcohol-related disorder because one or both of their parents are affected. In experimental studies, children at high risk for alcohol-related disorders have been found to possess, on average, a range of deficits on neurocognitive testing, a decreased amplitude of the P300 wave on evoked potential testing, and a variety of abnormalities on electroencephalogram (EEG) recordings. Studies of high-risk offspring in their 20s have also shown a generally blunted effect of alcohol compared with the effect seen in people whose parents have not been diagnosed with alcohol-related disorder. These findings suggest that a heritable biological brain function may predispose a person to an alcohol-related disorder.

A childhood history of attention-deficit/hyperactivity disorder or conduct disorder or both increases a child's risk for an alcohol-related disorder as an adult. Personality disorders, especially antisocial personality disorder, as earlier noted, also predispose a person to an alcohol-related disorder.

Psychodynamic Factors

Psychodynamic theories of alcohol-related disorders have centered on hypotheses about overly punitive superegos and fixation at the oral stage of psychosexual development. According to psychoanalytic theory, people with harsh superegos who are self-punitive turn to alcohol as a way of diminishing unconscious stress. Anxiety in people fixated at the oral stage may be reduced by taking substances, such as alcohol, by mouth. Some psychodynamic psychiatrists describe the general personality of a person with an alcohol-related disorder as shy, isolated, impatient, irritable, anxious, hypersensitive, and sexually repressed. According to a common psychoanalytic aphorism, the superego is soluble in alcohol. On a less theoretical level, alcohol may be abused by some people to reduce tension, anxiety, and psychic pain. Alcohol consumption can also lead to a sense of power and increased self-worth.

Social and Cultural Factors

Some social settings commonly lead to excessive drinking. College dormitories and military bases are two such examples; in these settings, excessive and frequent drinking is often completely normal and socially expected. Colleges and universities have recently tried to educate students about the health risks of drinking large quantities of alcohol. Some cultural and eth-

Table 12.2–1
Anxiety Disorders Found in Inpatient Alcoholic Samples

Study	N	Sex	Diagnostic Method, Criteria, and Time Frame	Anxiety Disorder	Patients with Disorder (%)
Mullaney and Trippett	102	M and F	Self-report; criteria and time frame not specified	Agoraphobia	42.2
				Social phobia	56.8
				Agoraphobia or social phobia	68.7
Powell et al.	565	M	Psychiatric diagnostic interview; criteria not specified; lifetime history	Phobic disorder	10.0
				Panic attacks	13.0
				Obsessive-compulsive disorder	12.0
Bowen et al.	48	M and F	SADS; RDC; lifetime history	Agoraphobia	12.5
				Social phobia	8.3
				Simple phobia	6.2
				Panic disorder	8.3
				Generalized anxiety disorder	22.9
				Any anxiety disorder	44.0
Hesselbrock et al.	321	M and F	DIS; DSM-III; lifetime history	Simple phobia	17.0
				Panic disorder	6.0
				Obsessive-compulsive disorder	5.0
				Agoraphobia	15.0
Smail et al.	60	M and F	Self-report; criteria and time frame not specified	Social phobia	39.0
				Agoraphobia	41.0
				Social phobia or agoraphobia	53.0
Weiss and Rosenberg	84	M and F	Structured clinical interview; DSM-III; lifetime history	Simple phobia	7.1
				Generalized anxiety disorder	8.3
				Panic disorder	2.4
				Agoraphobia	2.4
				Social phobia	2.4
				Any anxiety disorder	22.6
Stravynski et al.	173	—[a]	Structured clinical interview; DSM-III; lifetime history	Agoraphobia	8.5
				Social phobia	7.5
Chambless et al.	75	—[a]	SADS; RDC; lifetime history	Agoraphobia	8.0
				Simple phobia	9.3
				Panic disorder	9.3
				Obsessive-compulsive disorder	2.7
				Social phobia	18.7
				Any anxiety disorder	37.3
Ross et al.	370[b]	M and F	DIS; criteria not specified; lifetime history	Panic disorder	10.8
				Phobias[c]	36.5
				Generalized anxiety disorder	56.2
				Obsessive-compulsive disorder	10.8

[a] Data not given.
[b] Of the 501 patients described by Ross et al., this table represents only the findings for a subsample of 370 patients who reported an alcohol or alcohol and drug problem. Also, this study sample was an unspecified mix of inpatients and outpatients.
[c] Agoraphobia with and without panic attacks, simple phobia, and social phobia.

nic groups are more restrained than others about alcohol consumption. For example, Asians and people who are conservative Protestants use alcohol less frequently than do those who are liberal Protestants and Catholics.

Behavioral and Learning Factors

Just as cultural factors can affect drinking habits, so can the habits within a family, specifically parental drinking habits. Some evidence indicates, however, that familial drinking habits that affect children's drinking habits are less directly linked to the development of alcohol-related disorders than was previously thought. From a behavioral viewpoint, the positive reinforcing aspects of alcohol can induce feelings of well-being and euphoria and can reduce fear and anxiety, which may further encourage drinking.

Genetic and Other Biological Factors

The data strongly indicate a genetic component in at least some forms of alcohol-related disorders. The data for the heritability of alcohol-related disorders in men are stronger than are the data for the heritability of alcohol-related disorders in women. Both the design of the studies and the interpretation of their results are complicated, however, by the likely heterogeneity of the disorders and by the likely polygenic causes. Many studies have shown that persons with first-degree relatives affected with an alcohol-related disorder are three to four times more likely to have an alcohol-related disorder than are people without affected first-degree relatives. And patients with alcohol-related disorders with family histories of alcohol abuse are likely to have severe forms of the disorder and to have higher rates of alcohol intake and more alcohol-related problems than do patients without such family histories. This finding is supported by studies of monozygotic and dizygotic twins, which consistently show a much higher concordance rate among monozygotic than among dizygotic twins, who are no more likely to be concordant for alcohol-related disorder than are siblings who are not twins.

The effects of shared environmental factors have been explored through adoptee studies, which clearly demonstrate that the children of parents with alcohol-related disorders are at risk for an alcohol-related disorder event when brought up by families in which the parental figures do not have alcohol-related disorder. Moreover, children whose biological parents do not have an alcohol-related disorder are not at increased risk for the disorder if they are raised in households in which the paternal figures do have an alcohol-related disorder.

Genetic studies of families affected with alcohol-related disorder have used the technique of restriction fragment length polymorphism (RFLP). Some studies report an association between alcohol-related disorders and the dopamine type 2 (D_2) receptors, although these results have not been consistently replicated. This finding is attractive from a theoretical viewpoint because of its implication of pathology in the reward mechanisms of the ventral tegmental area and the nucleus accumbens in the pathophysiology of alcohol-related disorders. The association between alcohol-related disorders and D_2 receptors may occur in a subset of affected people, and subsequent studies may find additional associations between particular RFLP markers and alcohol-related disorders.

The biological consequences of genetic inheritance are unknown. As discussed previously, some evidence indicates that the brains of children with parents who have alcohol-related disorders exhibit unusual qualities in terms of electrophysiological measures—for example, evoked potentials and EEGs—and response to alcohol infusions. Neurotransmitter receptors such as the D_2 receptors may be factors in the inheritance of alcohol-related disorders. In some studies, abnormal concentrations of neurotransmitters and neurotransmitter metabolites were found in the cerebrospinal fluid (CSF) of patients with alcohol-related disorders. Results of many of these studies demonstrated decreased concentrations of serotonin, dopamine, and GABA or their metabolites.

EFFECTS OF ALCOHOL

The term *alcohol* refers to a large group of organic molecules that have a hydroxyl group (—OH) attached to a saturated carbon atom. Ethyl alcohol, also called ethanol, is the common form of alcohol; sometimes referred to as beverage alcohol, ethyl alcohol is used for drinking. The chemical formula for ethanol is CH_3—CH_2—OH.

The characteristic tastes and flavors of alcohol-containing beverages are the results of their methods of production, which result in various congeners in the final product. The congeners include methanol, butanol, aldehydes, phenols, tannins, and trace amounts of various metals. Although the congeners may confer some differential psychoactive effects on the various alcohol-containing beverages, these differences are minimal compared with the effects of ethanol itself. A single drink is usually considered to contain about 12 grams of ethanol, which is the content of 12 ounces of beer (7.2-proof, 3.6 percent ethanol in the United States), one 4-ounce glass of nonfortified wine, or 1 to 1.5 ounces of an 80-proof (40 percent ethanol) liquor (for example, whiskey or gin). In calculating patients' alcohol intake, however, clinicians should be aware that beers vary in their alcohol content, that beers are available in small and big cans and mugs, that glasses of wine range from 2 to 6 ounces, and that mixed drinks at some bars and in most homes contain 2 to 3 ounces of liquor. Nonetheless, using the moderate sizes of drinks, clinicians can estimate that a single drink increases the blood alcohol level of a 150-pound man 15 to 20 mg/dL, which is about the concentration of alcohol that an average person can metabolize in 1 hour.

Publicity has been given, especially by the makers and the distributors of alcohol, to the possible beneficial effects of alcohol intake. Most attention has been focused on some epidemiological data that suggest that one or two glasses of red wine each day lower the incidence of cardiovascular disease; these findings, however, are highly controversial.

Absorption

About 10 percent of consumed alcohol is absorbed from the stomach, the remainder from the small intestine. Peak blood concentration of alcohol is reached in 30 to 90 minutes and usually in 45 to 60 minutes, depending on whether the alcohol was taken on an empty stomach, which enhances absorption, or with food, which delays absorption. The time to peak blood concentration is also a factor of the time during which the alcohol was consumed; a short time reduces the time to peak concentration, and a long time increases the time to peak concentration. Absorption is most rapid with 15 to 30 percent (30- to 60-proof) alcohol-containing beverages. There is some dispute about whether carbonation (such as in champagne and in drinks mixed with seltzer) enhances the absorption of alcohol.

The body has protective devices against inundation by alcohol. For example, if the concentration of alcohol in the stomach becomes too high, mucus is secreted, and the pyloric valve closes. These actions slow the absorption and keep the alcohol from passing into the small intestine, where there are no significant restraints to absorption. Thus, a large amount of alcohol can remain unabsorbed in the stomach for hours. Furthermore, pylorospasm often results in nausea and vomiting.

Once alcohol is absorbed into the bloodstream, it is distributed to all body tissues. Because alcohol is uniformly dissolved in the body's water, tissues containing a high proportion of water receive a high concentration of alcohol. The intoxicating effects are greater when the blood alcohol concentration is rising than when it is falling (the Mellanby effects). For this reason, the rate of absorption bears directly on the intoxication response.

Metabolism

About 90 percent of absorbed alcohol is metabolized through oxidation in the liver; the remaining 10 percent is excreted unchanged by the kidneys and the lungs. The rate of oxidation by the liver is constant and independent of the body's energy requirements. The body is capable of metabolizing about 15 mg/dL per hour, with a range of 10 to 34 mg/dL per hour. Stated another way, the average person oxidizes three fourths of an ounce of 40 percent (80-proof) alcohol in an hour. In people with a history of excessive alcohol consumption, an upregulation of the necessary enzymes results in fast metabolism of alcohol.

Alcohol is metabolized by two enzymes: alcohol dehydrogenase (ADH) and aldehyde dehydrogenase. ADH catalyzes the conversion of alcohol into acetaldehyde, which is a toxic compound; aldehyde dehydrogenase catalyzes the conversion of acetaldehyde into acetic acid. Aldehyde dehydrogenase is inhibited by disulfiram (Antabuse), often used in the treatment of alcohol-related disorders. Some studies have shown that women have a lower ADH blood content than do men; this fact may account for women's tendency to become more intoxicated than do men after drinking the same amount of alcohol. The decreased function of alcohol-metabolizing enzymes in some Asian people can also lead to easy intoxication and toxic symptoms.

Effects on the Brain

Biochemistry. In contrast to most other substances of abuse with identified receptor targets—such as the *N*-methyl-D-aspartate (NMDA) receptor of phencyclidine (PCP)—no single molecular target has been identified as the mediator for the effects of alcohol. The long-standing theory about the biochemical effects of alcohol concerns its effects on the membranes of neurons. Data support the hypothesis that alcohol produces its effects by intercalating itself into membranes and thus increasing fluidity of the membranes with short-term use. With long-term use, however, the theory hypothesizes that the membranes become rigid or stiff. The fluidity of the membranes is critical to normal functioning of receptors, ion channels, and other membrane-bound functional proteins. In recent studies, researchers have attempted to identify specific molecular targets for the effects of alcohol. Most attention has been focused on the effects of alcohol at ion channels. Specifically, studies have found that alcohol ion channel activities associated with the nicotinic acetylcholine, serotonin (5-hydroxytryptamine) type 3 (5-HT_3), and GABA type A ($GABA_A$) receptors are enhanced by alcohol, whereas ion channel activities associated with glutamate receptors and voltage-gated calcium channels are inhibited.

Behavioral Effects. As the net result of the molecular activities, alcohol functions as a depressant much like the barbiturates and the benzodiazepines, with which alcohol has some degree of cross-tolerance and cross-dependence. At a level of 0.05 percent alcohol in the blood, thought, judgment, and restraint are loosened and sometimes disrupted. At a concentration of 0.1 percent, voluntary motor actions usually become perceptibly clumsy. In most states, legal intoxication ranges from 0.1 to 0.15 percent blood alcohol level. At 0.2 percent, the function of the entire motor area of the brain is measurably depressed; the parts of the brain that control emotional behavior are also affected. At 0.3 percent, a person is commonly confused or may become stuporous; at 0.4 to 0.5 percent the person falls into a coma. At higher levels, the primitive centers of the brain that control breathing and heart rate are affected, and death ensues secondary to direct respiratory depression or to the aspiration of vomitus. People with long-term histories of alcohol abuse, however, can tolerate much higher concentrations of alcohol than can alcohol-naive people; their alcohol tolerance may cause them to falsely appear less intoxicated than they really are.

Sleep Effects. Although alcohol consumed in the evening usually results in an increased ease of falling asleep (decreased sleep latency), alcohol also has adverse effects on sleep architecture. Specifically, alcohol use is associated with decreased rapid eye movement sleep (REM or dream sleep), decreased deep sleep (stage 4), and increased sleep fragmentation, with more and longer episodes of awakening. Therefore, that drinking alcohol helps people fall asleep is a myth.

Other Physiological Effects

Liver. The major adverse effects of alcohol use are related to liver damage. Alcohol use, even as short as week-long episodes of increased drinking, can result in an accumulation of fats and proteins, which produce the appearance of a fatty liver, sometimes found on physical examination as an enlarged liver. The association between fatty infiltration of the liver and serious liver damage remains unclear. Alcohol use, however, is associated with the development of alcoholic hepatitis and hepatic cirrhosis.

Gastrointestinal System. Long-term heavy drinking is associated with developing esophagitis, gastritis, achlorhydria, and gastric ulcers. The development of esophageal varices can accompany particularly heavy alcohol abuse; the rupture of the varices is a medical emergency often resulting in death by exsanguination. Disorders of the small intestine occasionally occur and pancreatitis, pancreatic insufficiency, and pancreatic cancer are also associated with heavy alcohol use. Heavy alcohol intake may interfere with the normal processes of food digestion and absorption; as a result, consumed food is inadequately digested. Alcohol abuse also appears to inhibit the intestine's capacity to absorb various nutrients, such as vitamins and amino acids. This effect, coupled with the often poor dietary habits of those with alcohol-related disorders, can cause serious vitamin deficiencies, particularly of the B vitamins.

Other Bodily Systems. Significant intake of alcohol

has been associated with increased blood pressure, dysregulation of lipoproteins and triglycerides, and increased risk for myocardial infarctions and cerebrovascular diseases. Alcohol has been shown to affect the hearts of nonalcoholic people who do not usually drink, increasing the resting cardiac output, the heart rate, and the myocardial oxygen consumption. Evidence indicates that alcohol intake can adversely affect the hematopoietic system and can increase the incidence of cancer, particularly head, neck, esophageal, stomach, hepatic, colonic, and lung cancer. Acute intoxication may also be associated with hypoglycemia, which, when unrecognized, may be responsible for some of the sudden deaths of people who are intoxicated. Muscle weakness is another side effect of alcoholism. Recent evidence shows that alcohol intake raises the blood concentration of estradiol in women. The increase in estradiol correlates with the blood alcohol level.

Laboratory Tests. The adverse effects of alcohol appear in common laboratory tests, which can be useful diagnostic aids in identifying people with alcohol-related disorders. The γ-glutamyl transpeptidase levels are elevated in about 80 percent of all those with alcohol-related disorders, and the mean corpuscular volume (MCV) is elevated in about 60 percent, more so in women than in men. Other laboratory test values that may be elevated in association with alcohol abuse are those of uric acid, triglycerides, serum glutamic-oxaloacetic transaminase (SGOT) (also called aspartate aminotransferase [AST]), and serum glutamic-pyruvic transaminase (SGPT) (also called alanine aminotransferase [ALT]).

Drug Interactions

The interaction between alcohol and other substances can be dangerous, even fatal. Certain substances such as alcohol and phenobarbital (Luminal) are metabolized by the liver, and their prolonged use may lead to an acceleration of their metabolism. When people with alcohol-related disorders are sober, this accelerated metabolism makes them unusually tolerant to many drugs such as sedatives and hypnotics; when they are intoxicated, however, these drugs compete with the alcohol for the same detoxification mechanisms, and potentially toxic blood levels of all involved substances can accumulate.

The effects of alcohol and other central nervous system (CNS) depressants are usually synergistic. Sedatives, hypnotics, and drugs that relieve pain, motion sickness, head colds, and allergy symptoms must be used with caution by people with alcohol-related disorders. Narcotics depress the sensory areas of the cerebral cortex, and can produce pain relief, sedation, apathy, drowsiness, and sleep; high doses can result in respiratory failure and death. Increasing the dosages of sedative-hypnotic drugs such as chloral hydrate (Noctec) and benzodiazepines, especially when they are combined with alcohol, produces a range of effects from sedation to motor and intellectual impairment to stupor, coma, and death. Because sedatives and other psychotropics can potentiate the effects of alcohol, patients should be instructed about the dangers of combining CNS depressants and alcohol, particularly when they are driving or operating machinery.

DISORDERS

DSM-IV lists the alcohol-related disorders (Table 12.2–2) and specifies the diagnostic criteria for alcohol intoxication (Table 12.2–3) and alcohol withdrawal (Table 12.2–4). The diagnostic criteria for the other alcohol-related disorders are listed in DSM-IV under the major symptom. For example, the diagnostic criteria for alcohol-induced anxiety disorder are found in the anxiety disorders category, under the heading ''substance-induced anxiety disorder.''

Alcohol Dependence and Alcohol Abuse

Diagnosis and Clinical Features. In DSM-IV, all substance-related disorders use the same criteria for dependence and abuse (see Tables 12.1–7, 12.1–8, and 12.1–9). In

Table 12.2–2
DSM-IV Alcohol-Related Disorders

Alcohol use disorders
Alcohol dependence
Alcohol abuse
Alcohol-induced disorders
Alcohol intoxication
Alcohol withdrawal
  Specify if:
    With perceptual disturbances
Alcohol intoxication delirium
Alcohol withdrawal delirium
Alcohol-induced persisting dementia
Alcohol-induced persisting amnestic disorder
Alcohol-induced psychotic disorder, with delusions
  Specify if:
    With onset during intoxication
    With onset during withdrawal
Alcohol-induced psychotic disorder, with hallucinations
  Specify if:
    With onset during intoxication
    With onset during withdrawal
Alcohol-induced mood disorder
  Specify if:
    With onset during intoxication
    With onset during withdrawal
Alcohol-induced anxiety disorder
  Specify if:
    With onset during intoxication
    With onset during withdrawal
Alcohol-induced sexual dysfunction
  Specify if:
    With onset during intoxication
Alcohol-induced sleep disorder
  Specify if:
    With onset during intoxication
    With onset during withdrawal
Alcohol-related disorder not otherwise specified

Reprinted with permission from American Psychiatric Association: *Diagnostic and Statistical Manual of Mental Disorders,* ed 4. Copyright, American Psychiatric Association, Washington, 1994.

Table 12.2–3
DSM-IV Diagnostic Criteria for Alcohol Intoxication

A. Recent ingestion of alcohol.

B. Clinically significant maladaptive behavior or psychological changes (eg, inappropriate sexual or aggressive behavior, mood lability, impaired judgment, impaired social or occupational functioning) that developed during, or shortly after, alcohol ingestion.

C. One (or more) of the following signs, developing during, or shortly after, alcohol use:
(1) slurred speech
(2) incoordination
(3) unsteady gait
(4) nystagmus
(5) impairment in attention or memory
(6) stupor or coma

D. The symptoms are not due to a general medical condition and are not better accounted for by another mental disorder.

Reprinted with permission from American Psychiatric Association: *Diagnostic and Statistical Manual of Mental Disorders,* ed 4. Copyright, American Psychiatric Association, Washington, 1994.

alcohol dependence and alcohol abuse, the need for the daily use of large amounts of alcohol for adequate functioning, a regular pattern of heavy drinking limited to weekends, and long periods of sobriety interspersed with binges of heavy alcohol intake lasting for weeks or months are strongly suggestive of those alcohol use disorders. The drinking patterns are often associated with certain behaviors: the inability to cut down or stop drinking; repeated efforts to control or reduce excessive drinking by going on the wagon (periods of temporary abstinence) or by restricting drinking to certain times of the day; binges (remaining intoxicated throughout the day for at least 2 days); the occasional consumption of a fifth of spirits (or its equivalent in wine or beer); amnestic periods for events occurring while intoxicated (blackouts); the continuation of drinking despite a serious physical disorder that the person knows is exacerbated by alcohol use; and the drinking of nonbeverage alcohol, such as fuel and commercial products containing alcohol. In addition, people with alcohol dependence and alcohol abuse show impaired social or occupational functioning because of alcohol use, such as violence while intoxicated, absence from work, job loss, legal difficulties such as arrest for intoxicated behavior and traffic accidents while intoxicated, and arguments or difficulties with family members or friends about excessive alcohol consumption.

Subtypes of Alcohol Dependence. Various researchers have attempted to divide alcohol dependence into subtypes, based primarily on phenomenological characteristics. One recent classification notes that *type A* alcohol dependence is characterized by late onset, few childhood risk factors, relatively mild dependence, few alcohol-related problems, and little psychopathology. *Type B* alcohol dependence is characterized by many childhood risk factors, severe dependence, an early onset of alcohol-related problems, much psychopathology, a strong family history of alcohol abuse, frequent polysubstance abuse, a long history of alcohol treatment, and a high number of severe life stresses. Some researchers have found that type *A* people who are alcohol dependent may respond to interactional psychotherapies, whereas type *B* people who are alcohol dependent may respond to the training of coping skills.

Other subtyping schemes of alcohol dependence have received fairly wide recognition in the literature. One group of investigators proposed three subtypes: *early-stage problem drinkers,* who do not yet have complete alcohol dependence syndromes; *affiliative drinkers,* who tend to drink daily in moderate amounts in social settings; and *schizoid-isolated drinkers,* who have severe dependence and tend to drink in binges and often alone.

Another investigator has described *gamma* alcohol dependence, which is thought to be common in the United States and is representative of the alcohol dependence seen in those who are active in Alcoholics Anonymous (AA). This variant concerns control problems in which people are unable to stop drinking once they start. When drinking is terminated as a result of ill health or lack of money, these people are capable of abstaining for varying periods. In *delta* alcohol dependence, perhaps more common in Europe than in the United States, people who are alcohol dependent must drink a certain amount each day but are unaware of a lack of control. The alcohol use disorder may not be discovered until a person who must stop drinking for some reason exhibits withdrawal symptoms.

Still another researcher has suggested a *type I, male-limited* variety of alcohol dependence, characterized by late onset, more evidence of psychological than of physical dependence, and the presence of guilt feelings. *Type II, male-limited* alcohol dependence is characterized by an onset at an early age, the spontaneous seeking of alcohol for consumption, and a socially disruptive set of behaviors when the person is intoxicated.

Table 12.2–4
DSM-IV Diagnostic Criteria for Alcohol Withdrawal

A. Cessation of (or reduction in) alcohol use that has been heavy and prolonged.

B. Two (or more) of the following, developing within several hours to a few days after criterion A:
(1) autonomic hyperactivity (eg, sweating or pulse rate greater than 100)
(2) increased hand tremor
(3) insomnia
(4) nausea or vomiting
(5) transient visual, tactile, or auditory hallucinations or illusions
(6) psychomotor agitation
(7) anxiety
(8) grand mal seizures

C. The symptoms in criterion B cause clinically significant distress or impairment in social, occupational, or other important areas of functioning.

D. The symptoms are not due to a general medical condition and not better accounted for by another mental disorder.

Specify if:
With perceptual disturbances

Reprinted with permission from American Psychiatric Association: *Diagnostic and Statistical Manual of Mental Disorders,* ed 4. Copyright, American Psychiatric Association, Washington, 1994.

Yet another investigator has postulated four subtypes of alcoholism. The first is *antisocial alcoholism,* typically with a predominance in men, a poor prognosis, an early onset of alcohol-related problems, and a close association with antisocial personality disorder. The second is *developmentally cumulative alcoholism,* with a primary tendency for alcohol abuse that is exacerbated with time as cultural expectations foster increased opportunities to drink. The third is *negative-affect alcoholism,* which is more common in women than in men; according to this hypothesis, women are likely to use alcohol for mood regulation and to help ease social relationships. The fourth is *developmentally limited alcoholism,* with frequent bouts of consuming large amounts of alcohol; the bouts become less frequent as people age and respond to the increased expectations of society about their jobs and families.

Alcohol Intoxication

Diagnosis and Clinical Features. DSM-IV establishes formal criteria for diagnosing alcohol intoxication (see Table 12.2–3): sufficient alcohol consumption, specific maladaptive behavioral changes, signs of neurological impairment, and the absence of other confounding diagnoses or conditions.

Alcohol intoxication is not a trivial condition and in extreme cases can lead to coma, respiratory depression, and death, from respiratory arrest or because of the aspiration of vomitus. Treatment for severe alcohol intoxication requires mechanical ventilatory support in an intensive care unit, with attention to the patient's acid-base balance, electrolytes, and temperature. Some studies of cerebral blood flow (CBF) during alcohol intoxication have found a modest increase in CBF after the ingestion of small amounts of alcohol, but CBF decreases with continued drinking.

The severity of alcohol intoxication symptoms correlates roughly with the blood concentration of alcohol, which reflects the alcohol concentration in the brain. With the onset of intoxication, some people become talkative and gregarious; others become withdrawn and sullen or belligerent. Some patients show lability of mood with intermittent episodes of laughing and crying. The person may show a short-term tolerance to alcohol and seem to be less intoxicated after many hours of drinking than after only a few hours.

The medical complications of intoxication include those that result from falls such as subdural hematomas and fractures. Telltale signs of frequent bouts of intoxication are facial hematomas, particularly about the eyes, the result of falls or fights while drunk. In cold climates, hypothermia and death may occur when a person is exposed to the elements. A person with alcohol intoxication may also be predisposed to infections secondary to a suppressed immune system.

Alcohol Withdrawal

Diagnosis and Clinical Features. Alcohol withdrawal, even without delirium, can be serious and can include seizures and autonomic hyperactivity. Conditions that may predispose to or aggravate withdrawal symptoms include fatigue, malnutrition, physical illness, and depression. The DSM-IV criteria for alcohol withdrawal (Table 12.2–4) require the cessation or reduction of alcohol use that was heavy and prolonged as well as the presence of specific physical or neuropsychiatric symptoms. The DSM-IV diagnosis also allows for the specification "with perceptual disturbances." One recent positron emission tomographic (PET) study of blood flow during alcohol withdrawal in otherwise healthy people with alcohol dependence reported a globally low rate of metabolic activity (Fig. 12.2–1), although, with further inspection of the data, the authors concluded that activity was especially decreased in the left parietal and right frontal areas.

The classic sign of alcohol withdrawal is tremulousness, although the spectrum of symptoms can expand to include psychotic and perceptual symptoms (such as delusions and hallucinations), seizures, and the symptoms of delirium tremens (DTs), called alcohol withdrawal delirium in DSM-IV. Tremulousness (commonly called the shakes or the jitters) develops 6 to 8 hours after the cessation of drinking, the psychotic and perceptual symptoms begin in 8 to 12 hours, seizures in 12 to 24 hours, and DTs during 72 hours, although physicians should watch for the development of DTs for the first week of withdrawal. The syndrome of withdrawal sometimes skips the usual progression and, for example, goes directly to DTs.

The tremor of alcohol withdrawal can be similar either to physiological tremor, with a continuous tremor of great amplitude and of more than 8 Hz, or to familial tremor, with bursts of tremor activity slower than 8 Hz. Other symptoms of withdrawal include general irritability, gastrointestinal symptoms (such as nausea and vomiting), and sympathetic autonomic hyperactivity, including anxiety, arousal, sweating, facial flushing, mydriasis, tachycardia, and mild hypertension. Patients experiencing alcohol withdrawal are generally alert but may startle easily.

Withdrawal Seizures. Seizures associated with alcohol withdrawal are stereotyped, generalized, and tonic-clonic in character. Patients often have more than one seizure 3 to 6 hours after the first seizure. Status epilepticus is relatively rare and occurs in less than 3 percent of all patients. Although anticonvulsant medications are not required in the management of alcohol withdrawal seizures, the cause of the seizures is difficult to establish when a patient is first assessed in the emergency room; thus, many patients with withdrawal seizures receive anticonvulsant medications, which are then discontinued once the cause of the seizures is recognized. Seizure activity in patients with known alcohol abuse histories should still prompt clinicians to consider other causative factors, like head injuries, CNS infections, CNS neoplasms, and other cerebrovascular diseases; long-term severe alcohol abuse can result in hypoglycemia, hyponatremia, and hypomagnesemia—all of which can also be associated with seizures.

Treatment. The primary medications for the control of alcohol withdrawal symptoms are the benzodiazepines (Table 12.2–5). Many studies have found that benzodiazepines help control seizure activity, delirium, anxiety, tachycardia, hypertension, diaphoresis, and tremor associated with alcohol withdrawal. Benzodiazepines can be given either orally or parenterally; neither diazepam (Valium) nor chlordiazepoxide (Librium), however, should be given intramuscularly (IM) because of their erratic absorption by this route. Clinicians must titrate the dosage of the benzodiazepine, starting with a high

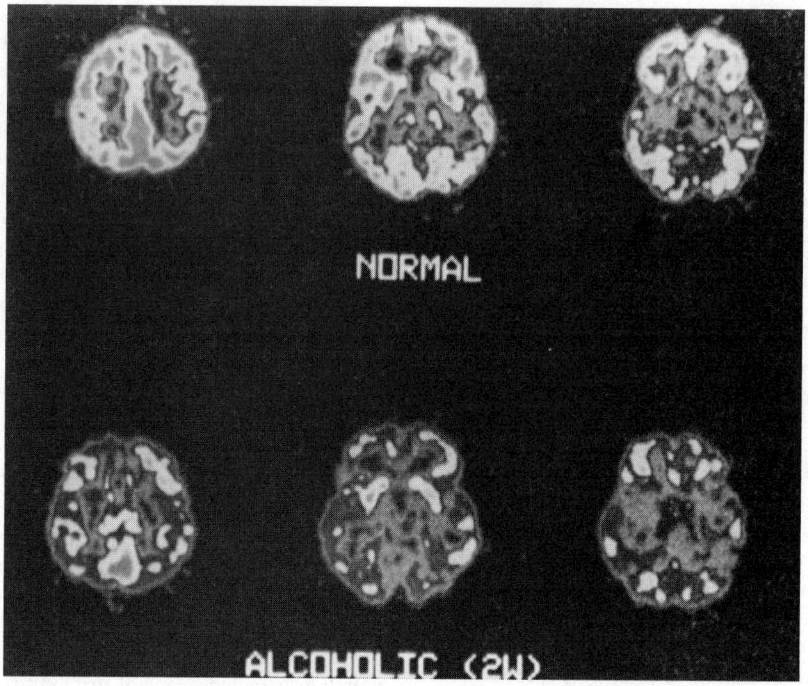
NORMAL
ALCOHOLIC (2W)

FIGURE 12.2–1
Brain PET metabolic images in a normal control subject and an alcoholic subject tested 2 weeks after the last use of alcohol. Notice the decreased cortical metabolic activity in the alcoholic person. (Reprinted with permission from Volkow ND, Hitzemann R, Wang G-J, Fowler JS, Burr G, Pascani K, Dewey SL, Wolf A: Decreased brain metabolism in neurologically intact healthy alcoholics. Am J Psychiatry *149:* 1019, 1992.)

dosage and lowering the dosage as the patient recovers. Sufficient benzodiazepines should be used to keep patients calm and sedated but not so sedated that they cannot be aroused for clinicians to perform appropriate procedures, including neurological examinations.

Although benzodiazepines are the standard treatment for alcohol withdrawal, studies have shown that carbamazepine (Tegretol) in dosages of 800 mg per day is as effective as benzodiazepines and has the added benefit of minimal abuse liability. The use of carbamazepine is gradually becoming common in the United States and Europe. The β-adrenergic receptor antagonists and clonidine (Catapres) have also been used to block the symptoms of sympathetic hyperactivity, but neither drug is an effective treatment for seizures or delirium.

Table 12.2–5
Drug Therapy for Alcohol Intoxication and Withdrawal

Clinical Problem	Drug	Route	Dosage	Comment
Tremulousness and mild to moderate agitation	Chlordiazepoxide	Oral	25–100 mg every 4–6 hrs	Initial dose can be repeated every 2 hours until patient is calm; subsequent doses must be individualized and titrated
	Diazepam	Oral	5–20 mg every 4–6 hrs	
Hallucinosis	Lorazepam	Oral	2–10 mg every 4–6 hrs	
Extreme agitation	Chlordiazepoxide	Intravenous	0.5 mg/kg at 12.5 mg/min	Give until patient is calm; subsequent doses must be individualized and titrated
Withdrawal seizures	Diazepam	Intravenous	0.15 mg/kg at 2.5 mg/min	
Delirium tremens	Lorazepam	Intravenous	0.1 mg/kg at 2.0 mg/min	

Adapted from Koch-Weser J, Sellers EM, Kalant J: Alcohol intoxication and withdrawal. N Engl J Med *294:* 757, 1976.

Delirium

Diagnosis and Clinical Features. DSM-IV contains the diagnostic criteria for alcohol intoxication delirium in the category of substance intoxication delirium and the diagnostic criteria for alcohol withdrawal delirium in the category of substance withdrawal delirium (see Chapter 10, Section 10.2). Patients with recognized alcohol withdrawal symptoms should be carefully monitored to prevent progression to alcohol withdrawal delirium, the most severe form of the withdrawal syndrome, also known as DTs. Alcohol withdrawal delirium is a medical emergency that can result in significant morbidity and mortality. Patients with delirium are a danger to themselves and to others. Because of the unpredictability of their behavior, patients with delirium may be assaultive or suicidal or may act on hallucinations or delusional thoughts as if they were genuine dangers. Untreated, DTs has a mortality rate of 20 percent, usually as a result of an intercurrent medical illness such as pneumonia, renal disease, hepatic insufficiency, or heart failure. Although withdrawal seizures commonly precede the development of alcohol withdrawal delirium, delirium can also appear unheralded. The essential feature of the syndrome is delirium occurring within 1 week after a person stops drinking or reduces the intake of alcohol. In addition to the symptoms of delirium, the features of alcohol intoxication delirium include autonomic hyperactivity such as tachycardia, diaphoresis, fever, anxiety, insomnia, and hypertension; perceptual distortions, most frequently visual or tactile hallucinations; and fluctuating levels of psychomotor activity, ranging from hyperexcitability to lethargy.

About 5 percent of people with alcohol-related disorders who are hospitalized have DTs. Because the syndrome usually develops on the third hospital day, a patient admitted for an unrelated condition may unexpectedly have an episode of delirium, as the first sign of a previously undiagnosed alcohol-related disorder. Episodes of DTs usually begin in a patient's 30s or 40s after 5 to 15 years of heavy drinking, typically of the binge type. Physical illness (for example, hepatitis or pancreatitis) predisposes to the syndrome; a person in good physical health rarely has DTs during alcohol withdrawal.

A 43-year-old divorced carpenter was examined in a hospital emergency observation ward. The patient's sister was available to provide some information. She reported that the patient had had a reasonably stable home life and job record until his wife had left him for another man 5 years before but had been consuming more than a fifth of cheap wine a day since his divorce. He often had blackouts from drinking and missed days from work; consequently, he had been fired from several jobs. Fortunately for him, carpenters are in great demand, and he had been able to provide marginally for himself during these years. Three days before hospitalization, however, he had run out of money and wine and had to beg on the street to buy a meal. The patient had been poorly nourished, eating perhaps one meal a day and evidently relying on wine for nourishment.

The morning after his last day of drinking (3 days earlier), he felt increasingly tremulous; his hands were shaking so grossly that he could hardly light a cigarette. He also had an increasing sense of inner panic and was virtually unable to sleep. A neighbor became concerned about the patient when he seemed not to be making sense and was clearly unable to take care of himself. The neighbor called the sister, who brought him to the hospital.

On examination, the patient alternated between apprehension and chatty, superficial warmth. He was keyed up and talked almost constantly in a rambling and unfocused manner. At times he recognized the doctor, but at other times he got confused and thought the doctor was his older brother. Twice during the examination he called the doctor by his older brother's name and asked when he had arrived; evidently he had entirely lost track of the interview up to that point. He had a gross hand tremor at rest and sometimes picked at "bugs" he saw on the bedsheets. He was disoriented and thought that he was in a supermarket parking lot rather than in a hospital. He indicated that he felt he was fighting against a terrifying sense of the world ending in a holocaust. Every few minutes, he was startled by sounds and scenes of fiery car crashes (evidently provoked by the sounds of carts rolling in the hall). Efforts to test his memory and his calculation ability failed because his attention shifted rapidly. An EEG indicated a pattern of diffuse encephalopathy.

DISCUSSION

This carpenter, with a long history of heavy alcohol use, develops severe withdrawal symptoms after he stops drinking. He has the characteristic symptoms of a delirium: difficulty sustaining attention and other cognitive deficits including disorganized thinking (rambling), perceptual disturbances (he sees scenes of car crashes provoked by the sound of rolling carts in the hall), and disorientation to place and person (mistakes the doctor for his brother and the hospital for a parking lot). The appearance of a delirium with marked autonomic hyperactivity (hand tremors) shortly after cessation or reduction of heavy alcohol ingestion indicates alcohol withdrawal delirium.

Although the treatment will initially be directed at the alcohol withdrawal delirium, the additional diagnosis of alcohol dependence can be assumed from the information that he has been a heavy daily user of alcohol for more than 5 years, has lost jobs because of his alcohol use, and has been poorly nourished. The alcohol dependence is noted as severe because he almost certainly has many of the symptoms of dependence and they interfere markedly with his occupational and social functioning. (From *DSM-IV Casebook.*)

Treatment. The best treatment for DTs is prevention. Patients withdrawing from alcohol who exhibit withdrawal phenomena should receive a benzodiazepine, such as 25 to 50 mg of chlordiazepoxide (Librium) every 2 to 4 hours until they seem to be out of danger. Once the delirium appears, however, 50 to 100 mg of chlordiazepoxide should be given every 4 hours orally, or intravenous lorazepam (Ativan) should be used if oral medication is not possible (Table 12.2–5). Antipsychotic medications that may reduce the seizure threshold in patients should be avoided. A high-calorie, high-carbohydrate diet supplemented by multivitamins is also important.

Physically restraining patients with the DTs is risky; they may fight against the restraints to a dangerous level of exhaustion. When patients are disorderly and uncontrollable, a seclusion room can be used. Dehydration, often contributed to by diaphoresis and fever, can be corrected with fluids given by mouth or intravenously. Anorexia, vomiting, and diarrhea often occur during withdrawal. Antipsychotic medications should be avoided because they may reduce the seizure threshold in the patient. The emergence of focal neurological symptoms, lateralizing seizures, increased intracranial pressure, or evidence of skull fractures or other indications of CNS pathology should prompt clinicians to examine a patient for additional neurological diseases. Nonbenzodiazepine anticonvulsant medication is not useful in preventing or treating alcohol withdrawal convulsions, although benzodiazepines are generally effective.

The need for warm, supportive psychotherapy in the treatment of DTs is essential. Patients are often bewildered, frightened, and anxious because of their tumultuous symptoms and skillful verbal support is imperative.

Alcohol-Induced Persisting Dementia

The legitimacy of the concept of alcohol-induced persisting dementia remains controversial; some clinicians and researchers believe that it is difficult to separate the toxic effects of alcohol abuse from the CNS damage done by poor nutrition and multiple trauma, and that following the malfunctioning of other bodily organs such as the liver, the pancreas, and the kidneys. Although several studies have found enlarged ventricles and cortical atrophy in people with dementia and a history of alcohol dependence, the studies do not help clarify the cause of the dementia. Nonetheless, DSM-IV includes the diagnosis of alcohol-induced persisting dementia (see Table 10.3–6). The controversy about the diagnosis should encourage clinicians to complete a diagnostic assessment of the dementia before concluding that the dementia was caused by alcohol.

Alcohol-Induced Persisting Amnestic Disorder

Diagnosis and Clinical Features. The diagnostic criteria of alcohol-induced persisting amnestic disorder are contained in the DSM-IV category of substance-induced persisting amnestic disorder (see Table 10.4–3). The essential feature of alcohol-induced persisting amnestic disorder is a disturbance in short-term memory caused by the prolonged heavy use of alcohol. Because the disorder usually occurs in persons who have been drinking heavily for many years, the disorder is rare in people younger than the age of 35.

Wernicke-Korsakoff Syndrome. The classic names for alcohol-induced persisting amnestic disorder are Wernicke's encephalopathy (a set of acute symptoms) and Korsakoff's syndrome (a chronic condition). Whereas Wernicke's encephalopathy is completely reversible with treatment, only about 20 percent of patients with Korsakoff's syndrome recover. The pathophysiological connection between the two syndromes is thiamine deficiency, caused either by poor nutritional habits or by malabsorption problems. Thiamine is a cofactor for several important enzymes and may also be involved in the conduction of the axon potential along the axon and in synaptic transmission. The neuropathological lesions are symmetrical and paraventricular, involving the mammillary bodies, the thalamus, the hypothalamus, the midbrain, the pons, the medulla, the fornix, and the cerebellum.

Wernicke's encephalopathy, also called alcoholic encephalopathy, is an acute neurological disorder characterized by ataxia (affecting primarily the gait), vestibular dysfunction, confusion, and a variety of ocular motility abnormalities, including horizontal nystagmus, lateral rectal palsy, and gaze palsy. Those eye signs are usually bilateral but not necessarily symmetrical. Other eye signs may include a sluggish reaction to light and anisocoria. Wernicke's encephalopathy may clear spontaneously in a few days or weeks or may progress into Korsakoff's syndrome.

Treatment. In the early stages, Wernicke's encephalopathy responds rapidly to large doses of parenteral thiamine, which is believed to be effective in preventing the progression into Korsakoff's syndrome. The dosage of thiamine is usually initiated at 100 mg by mouth two to three times daily and is continued for 1 to 2 weeks. In patients with alcohol-related disorders who are receiving intravenous (IV) administrations of glucose solution, it is good practice to include 100 mg of thiamine in each liter of the glucose solution.

Korsakoff's syndrome is the chronic amnestic syndrome that can follow Wernicke's encephalopathy, and the two syndromes are believed to be pathophysiologically related. The cardinal features of Korsakoff's syndrome are impaired mental syndrome (especially recent memory) and anterograde amnesia in an alert and responsive patient. The patient may or may not have the symptom of confabulation. Treatment of Korsakoff's syndrome is also thiamine given 100 mg by mouth two to three times daily; the treatment regimen should continue for 3 to 12 months. Few patients who progress to Korsakoff's syndrome ever fully recover, although a substantial proportion have some improvement in their cognitive abilities with thiamine and nutritional support.

Blackouts. Alcohol-related blackouts are not included in DSM-IV's diagnostic classification, although the symptom of alcohol intoxication is common. Blackouts are similar to episodes of transient global amnesia (see Chapter 10, Section 10.4) in that they are discrete episodes of anterograde amnesia, which occur in association with alcohol intoxication. The periods of amnesia can be particularly distressing when people fear that they have unknowingly harmed someone or behaved imprudently while intoxicated. During a blackout, people have relatively intact remote memory but experience a specific short-term memory deficit in which they are unable to recall events that happened in the previous 5 or 10 minutes. Because their other intellectual faculties are well preserved, they can perform complicated tasks and appear normal to casual observers. The neurobiological mechanisms for alcoholic blackouts are now known at the molecular level; alcohol blocks the consolidation of new memories into old memories, a process that is thought to involve the hippocampus and related temporal lobe structures.

Two couples in their later 20s were having drinks while playing bridge. The wives sipped wine but their husbands drank scotch to the point where they lost interest in the bridge game. The husbands began telling jokes. Husband A told the group a joke and they all laughed. Husband B told a joke and again they all laughed. The husband A repeated the same joke that he had told a few minutes previously. Husband B laughed but the two wives looked at each other in puzzlement. Then husband B told the same joke *he* had just told previously and husband A laughed, and the wives now felt that the situation was utterly ridiculous. The next day, neither husband had any recollection of telling the jokes.

DISCUSSION

Both husbands, in short, had had a blackout. The cause illustrates how alcohol can obliterate short-term memory while leaving other intellectual facilities intact. Both husbands could remember the jokes and tell them well, but soon after telling them, they forgot that they had done so. Neither of the men, incidentally, was alcoholic, nor was either of them ordinarily even a heavy drinker. This illustrates how blackouts can occur in more or less normal drinkers who drink excessively on some occasion. (Courtesy of Marc A. Schuckit, M.D.)

Alcohol-Induced Psychotic Disorder

Diagnosis and Clinical Features. The diagnostic criteria for alcohol-induced psychotic disorders, such as delusions and hallucinations, are found in the DSM-IV category of substance-induced psychotic disorder (see Table 14.1–2). DSM-IV further allows the specification of onset (during intoxication or withdrawal) and whether hallucinations or delusions are present (see Table 12.2–2). The most common hallucinations are auditory, usually voices, but they are often unstructured. The voices are characteristically maligning, reproachful, or threatening, although some patients report that the voices are pleasant and nondisruptive. The hallucinations usually last less than a week, although during that week impaired reality testing is common. After the episode, most patients realize the hallucinatory nature of the symptoms.

Hallucinations after alcohol withdrawal are considered rare, and the syndrome is distinct from that of alcohol withdrawal delirium. The hallucinations can occur at any age but usually appear in people abusing alcohol for a long time. Although the hallucinations usually resolve within a week, some may linger; in these cases, clinicians must consider other psychotic disorders in the differential diagnosis. Alcohol withdrawal-related hallucinations are differentiated from the hallucinations of schizophrenia by the temporal association with alcohol withdrawal, the absence of a classic history of schizophrenia, and their usually short-lived duration. Alcohol withdrawal-related hallucinations are differentiated from the DTs by the presence of a clear sensorium in patients.

A 39-year-old male letter carrier was brought to an emergency room by the police after he behaved in an unusual fashion at home and complained that his neighbors were trying to kill him. The history obtained from the patient and his wife revealed that his psychotic thinking developed slowly over the preceding 3 weeks; he began with feelings that people were looking at him at work, progressed to vague feelings that people were against him, and went on to frank auditory hallucinations that people at work and in the neighboring houses were talking about their plans to kill him. He has no insight into those paranoid delusions and auditory hallucinations.

DISCUSSION

The relatively abrupt onset of the syndrome in his late 30s pointed to a potential organic cause, and further probing documented his daily drinking of between 6 and 18 beers for at least 10 weeks. A diagnosis of alcohol-induced psychotic disorder with onset during intoxication was made, and both clinical conditions disappeared after 3 weeks of abstinence. After alcohol treatment, the man stayed sober for the next 8 months. Unfortunately, he later resumed heavy drinking and has a reoccurrence of both his hallucinations and his delusions. (Courtesy of Marc A. Schuckit, M.D.)

Treatment. The treatment of alcohol withdrawal-related hallucinations is much like the treatment of DTs—benzodiazepines, adequate nutrition, and fluids if necessary. If this regimen fails or in long-term cases, antipsychotics may be used.

Other Alcohol-Related Disorders

Alcohol-Induced Mood Disorder. DSM-IV allows for the diagnosis of alcohol-induced mood disorder with manic, depressive, or mixed features (see Table 15.1–11) and also for the specification of onset during either intoxication or withdrawal. As with all the secondary and substance-induced disorders, clinicians must consider whether the abused substance and the symptoms have a causal relation.

A 27-year-old male dockworker was brought to an emergency room after telling his family that he was going to kill himself. His history revealed more than 2 weeks of depressive symptoms, including crying spells, feelings of hopelessness, difficulties in concentrating, insomnia, and loss of appetite. The review of his life problems taken from both the patient and his wife and a series of blood tests all pointed to the regular intake of at least two six-packs of beer on most days for the preceding 3 months. Because he showed no evidence of daily severe depression interfering with his functioning except in the context of his heavy drinking, the hospital personnel assumed that the hospitalization for severe suicidal thoughts would be relatively short and that the depressive symptoms would begin to lift fairly rapidly without antidepressant medication or cognitive therapy.

DISCUSSION

At the end of several weeks, most alcoholic patients are no longer depressed all day every day. However, they are left with mood swings or intermittent symptoms of sadness that can resemble cyclothymic disorder or dysthymic disorder. Even those mild and intermittent depressive symptoms are likely to diminish and disappear with time. The presence of the dysthymic symptoms usually indicates the normal course of a withdrawal syndrome and not an independent mood disorder.

The man was diagnosed with alcohol-induced mood disorder and was discharged to an alcohol treatment program 4 days after his psychiatric admission to the hospital. (Courtesy of Marc A. Schuckit, M.D.)

Alcohol-Induced Anxiety Disorder. DSM-IV allows for the diagnosis of alcohol-induced anxiety disorder (see Table 16.1–5) and suggests that the diagnosis specify whether the symptoms are those of generalized anxiety, panic attacks, obsessive-compulsive symptoms, or phobic symptoms and whether the onset was during intoxication or during withdrawal. The association between alcohol use and anxiety symptoms has already been discussed (see Table 12.2–1); deciding whether the anxiety symptoms are primary or secondary can be difficult.

Alcohol-Induced Sexual Dysfunction. In DSM-IV, the formal diagnosis of symptoms of sexual dysfunction associated with alcohol intoxication is alcohol-induced sexual dysfunction (see Table 21.2–17).

Alcohol-Induced Sleep Disorder. In DSM-IV, the diagnostic criteria for alcohol-induced sleep disorders with an onset during either alcohol intoxication or alcohol withdrawal are found in the sleep disorders section (see Table 24.2–21).

Alcohol-Related Use Disorder Not Otherwise Specified. DSM-IV allows for the diagnosis of alcohol-related disorder not otherwise specified for alcohol-related disorders that do not meet the diagnostic criteria for any of the other diagnoses (Table 12.2–6).

Idiosyncratic Alcohol Intoxication. Whether there is such a diagnostic entity as idiosyncratic alcohol intoxication in under debate; DSM-IV does not recognize this category as an official diagnosis. Several well-controlled studies of people who supposedly have the disorder have raised questions about the validity of the designation. The condition has been variously called pathologic, complicated, atypical, and paranoid alcohol intoxication; all these terms indicate that a severe behavioral syndrome rapidly develops after a person consumes a small amount of alcohol that would have minimal behavioral effects on most people. The diagnosis is important in the forensic arena as alcohol intoxication is not generally accepted as a reason for judging people not responsible for their activities. Idiosyncratic alcohol intoxication, however, can be used in a person's defense if a defense lawyer can successfully argue that the defendant has an unexpected, idiosyncratic, and pathological reaction to a minimal amount of alcohol.

Table 12.2–6
DSM-IV Diagnostic Criteria for Alcohol-Related Disorder Not Otherwise Specified

The alcohol-related disorder not otherwise specified category is for disorders associated with the use of alcohol that are not classifiable as alcohol dependence, alcohol abuse, alcohol intoxication, alcohol withdrawal, alcohol intoxication delirium, alcohol withdrawal delirium, alcohol-induced persisting dementia, alcohol-induced persisting amnestic disorder, alcohol-induced psychotic disorder, alcohol-induced mood disorder, alcohol-induced anxiety disorder, alcohol-induced sexual dysfunction, or alcohol-induced sleep disorder.

Reprinted with permission from American Psychiatric Association: *Diagnostic and Statistical Manual of Mental Disorders,* ed 4. Copyright, American Psychiatric Association, Washington, 1994.

In anecdotal reports, people with idiosyncratic alcohol intoxication have been described as confused, disoriented, and as experiencing illusions, transitory delusions, and visual hallucinations. People may display greatly increased psychomotor activity and impulsive, aggressive behavior; they may be dangerous to others. They may also exhibit suicidal ideation and make suicide attempts. The disorder, usually described as lasting for a few hours, terminates in a prolonged sleep, and those affected are unable to recall the episodes on awakening. The cause of the condition is unknown but is reported to be most common in people with high levels of anxiety. According to one hypothesis, alcohol causes sufficient disorganization and loss of control to release aggressive impulses. Another suggestion is that brain damage, particularly encephalitic or traumatic damage, predisposes some people to an intolerance for alcohol and thus to abnormal behavior after they ingest only small amounts. Other predisposing factors may include advancing age, using sedative-hypnotic drugs, and feeling fatigued. A person's behavior while intoxicated tends to be atypical; after one weak drink, a quiet, shy person becomes belligerent and aggressive.

In treating idiosyncratic alcohol intoxication, clinicians must help to protect patients from harming themselves and others. Physical restraint may be necessary but is difficult because of the abrupt onset of the condition. Once a patient has been restrained, injection of an antipsychotic drug, such as haloperidol (Haldol), is useful for controlling assaultiveness. This condition must be differentiated from other causes of abrupt behavioral change, such as complex partial epilepsy. Some people with the disorder have been reported to show temporal lobe spiking on an EEG after ingesting small amounts of alcohol.

Other Alcohol-Related Neurological Disorders

Only the major neuropsychiatric syndromes associated with alcohol use have been discussed here. The complete list of neurological syndromes is lengthy (Table 12.2–7).

Alcoholic pellagra encephalopathy is one diagnosis of potential interest to psychiatrists presented with a patient who appears to be afflicted with Wernicke-Korsakoff syndrome but who has no response to thiamine treatment. The symptoms of alcoholic pellagra encephalopathy include confusion, clouding

Table 12.2–7
Neurological and Medical Complications of Alcohol Use

Alcohol intoxication
- Acute intoxication
- Pathological intoxication (atypical, complicated, unusual)
- Blackouts

Alcohol withdrawal syndromes
- Tremulousness (the shakes or the jitters)
- Alcoholic hallucinosis (horrors)
- Withdrawal seizures (rum fits)
- Delirium tremens (shakes)

Nutritional diseases of the nervous system secondary to alcohol abuse
- Wernicke-Korsakoff syndrome
- Cerebellar degeneration
- Peripheral neuropathy
- Optic neuropathy (tobacco-alcohol amblyopia)
- Pellagra

Alcoholic diseases of uncertain pathogenesis
- Central pontine myelinolysis
- Marchiafava-Bignami disease
- Fetal alcohol syndrome
- Myopathy
- Alcoholic dementia (?)
- Alcoholic cerebral atrophy

Systemic diseases due to alcohol with secondary neurological complications
- Liver disease
  - Hepatic encephalopathy
  - Acquired (non-Wilsonian) chronic hepatocerebral degeneration
- Gastrointestinal diseases
  - Malabsorption syndromes
  - Postgastrectomy syndromes
  - Possible pancreatic encephalopathy
- Cardiovascular diseases
  - Cardiomyopathy with potential cardiogenic emboli and cerebrovascular disease
  - Arrhythmias and abnormal blood pressure leading to cerebrovascular disease
- Hematological disorders
  - Anemia, leukopenia, thrombocytopenia (could possibly lead to hemorrhagic cerebrovascular disease)
- Infectious disease, especially meningitis (especially pneumococcal and meningococcal)
- Hypothermia and hyperthermia
- Hypotension and hypertension
- Respiratory depression and associated hypoxia
- Toxic encephalopathies, including alcohol and other substances
- Electrolyte imbalances leading to acute confusional states and rarely focal neurological signs and symptoms
  - Hypoglycemia
  - Hyperglycemia
  - Hyponatremia
  - Hypercalcemia
  - Hypomagnesemia
  - Hypophosphatemia

Increased incidence of trauma
- Epidural, subdural, and intracerebral hematoma
- Spinal cord injury
- Posttraumatic seizure disorders
- Compressive neuropathies and brachial plexus injuries (Saturday night palsies)
- Posttraumatic symptomatic hydrocephalus (normal pressure hydrocephalus)
- Muscle crush injuries and compartmental syndromes

Reprinted with permission from Rubino FA: Neurologic complications of alcoholism. Psychiatr Clin North Am *15:* 361, 1992.

of consciousness, myoclonus, oppositional hypertonias, fatigue, apathy, irritability, anorexia, insomnia, and sometimes delirium. Patients suffer from a deficiency of niacin (nicotinic acid), and the specific treatment is 50 mg of niacin by mouth four times daily or 25 mg parenterally two to three times daily.

Fetal Alcohol Syndrome

Data indicate that women who are pregnant or are breast-feeding should not drink alcohol. Fetal alcohol syndrome occurs when fetuses are exposed in utero to alcohol by their mothers' drinking alcohol. This syndrome is the leading cause of mental retardation in the United States. The presence of alcohol inhibits intrauterine growth and postnatal development. Microcephaly, craniofacial malformations, and limb and heart defects are common in affected infants. Short adult stature and the development of a range of adult maladaptive behaviors have also been associated with fetal alcohol syndrome.

Women with alcohol-related disorders have a 35 percent risk of having a child with defects. Although the precise mechanism of the damage to the fetus is unknown, the damage seems to be the result of exposure in utero to ethanol or to its metabolites; alcohol may also cause hormone imbalances that increase the risk of abnormalities.

TREATMENT AND REHABILITATION

Although some clinicians and some groups support the concept of controlled drinking, most clinicians and most well-controlled research studies indicate that complete abstinence from alcohol must be the centerpiece of a successful treatment strategy for alcohol abuse. People with alcohol-related disorders usually come to treatment because of pressure from a spouse or an employer or because of fear that continued drinking will have a fatal outcome. The patients who are persuaded, encouraged, or even coerced into treatment by those important to them are more apt to remain in treatment and to have a better prognosis than are those who are not so pressured. Affected people who voluntarily come to a mental health worker after realizing that they are alcoholics and that they need help have the best prognosis, however.

Psychotherapy

When therapists use psychotherapy to focus on the reasons that a person drinks, the therapy is more successful than when it focuses on vague psychodynamic issues. To explore the reasons for drinking, therapists must focus on the situations in which the patient drinks, on the motivating forces behind the drinking, on the results expected from drinking, and on alternate ways of dealing with these situations. Involving an interested and cooperative spouse, companion, friend, or family member in conjoint therapy for at least some of the sessions is highly effective.

The nature of the initial contact between therapists and people with alcohol-related disorders is crucial to successful treatment. In early encounters, therapists must be active and supportive; patients with alcohol problems often anticipate rejection and may misinterpret a passive therapeutic role as rejecting. Patients often have an ambivalent relation to therapy and may miss appointments or relapse into drinking. Many therapists attempt to view alcohol abuse less in terms of the individual patient and more in terms of the patient's interactions with family members, work or school colleagues, and society in general.

Therapists must also deal with the use of alcohol for a psychological defense; removing the emotional and intellectual barriers between patient and therapist should be an early goal. Therapists must be prepared to have the therapeutic bond tested again and again; they cannot hide behind a screen of a patient's lack of motivation when relapses become threatening to the therapist. The therapist's active, supportive role can counter depression, as can the addition of antidepressant drug medication.

Pharmacotherapy

Disulfiram. Disulfiram (Antabuse) competitively inhibits the enzyme aldehyde dehydrogenase; even a single drink usually causes a toxic reaction because of acetaldehyde accumulation in the blood. Administration of the drug should not begin until 24 hours have elapsed since the patient's last drink. The patient must be in good health, highly motivated, and cooperative, and the physician must warn the patient about the consequences of ingesting alcohol while taking the drug and for as long as 2 weeks thereafter. Those who drink while taking the 250 mg daily dose of disulfiram experience flushing and feelings of heat in the face, the sclera, the upper limbs, and the chest. They may become pale, hypotensive, and nauseated and experience serious malaise. They may also experience dizziness, blurred vision, palpitations, air hunger, and numbness of the extremities. The most serious potential consequence is severe hypotension. Patients may also have a response to alcohol ingested in such substances as sauces and vinegars and even to inhaled alcohol vapors from after-shave lotions. The syndrome, once elicited, typically lasts some 30 to 60 minutes but can persist longer. With dosages of more than 250 mg, toxic psychoses can occur, with memory impairment and confusion. The drug can also exacerbate psychotic symptoms in some patients with schizophrenia in the absence of alcohol intake. Naltrexone decreases alcohol craving, probably by blocking the release of endogenous opioids. A dosage of 50 mg once daily is recommended for most patients. It aids in achieving the goal of abstinence by preventing relapse and decreasing alcohol consumption.

Other Drug Treatment. Both antianxiety agents and antidepressants may be useful in the treatment of anxiety and depressive symptoms in patients with alcohol-related disorders. The possibility of using psychoactive drugs to control the sensation of craving for alcohol, however, is receiving increasing attention. Several trials of lithium (Eskalith) in patients who have both an alcohol-related disorder and a mood disorder of any type have shown a reduction in both the desire to drink and the mood cycles. Other studies with lithium have not consistently confirmed these results, but in difficult or complex cases a trial of lithium may be warranted.

There is also increasing interest in the use of serotonergic drugs to control drinking and alcohol craving. Some evidence indicates that the serotonin-specific reuptake inhibitors or trazodone (Desyrel) may be effective. Recent research focuses on specific serotonin receptor agonists and on serotonin type 3 ($5\text{-}HT_3$) receptor antagonists. Some data indicate that dopaminergic agonists, such as low dosages of apomorphine or bromocriptine (Parlodel), may also be effective in reducing a patient's craving. For the most part, however, treatment strategies directed at reducing the craving are still in early stages of research and require further validation.

Behavior Therapy

Behavior therapy teaches people with alcohol-related disorders other ways to reduce anxiety. Relaxation training, assertiveness training, self-control skills, and new strategies to master the environment are emphasized. Operant conditioning programs condition people with alcohol-related disorders to modify their drinking behavior or to stop drinking. The reinforcements have included monetary rewards, an opportunity to live in an enriched inpatient environment, and access to pleasurable social interactions.

Alcoholics Anonymous

Alcoholics Anonymous (AA) is a voluntary supportive fellowship of hundreds of thousands of persons with alcohol-related disorders; two alcohol-dependent men, a stockbroker and a surgeon, founded AA in 1935. Physicians should refer patients to AA as part of a multiple-treatment approach. Frequently, patients who initially object when AA is suggested later derive benefit from the organization and become enthusiastic participants. Its members make a public admission of their alcohol-related disorder, and abstinence is the rule.

Al-Anon

Al-Anon is an organization for the spouses of people with alcohol-related disorders and is structured along the same lines as AA. Al-Anon aims, through group support, to assist the efforts of the spouses to regain self-esteem, to refrain from feeling responsible for a spouse's drinking, and to develop a rewarding life for themselves and their families. Alateen, directed toward the children of people with alcohol dependence, helps them understand their parents' alcohol dependence.

Halfway Houses

Discharging patients with alcohol-related disorders from hospitals often poses serious placement problems. Home or other familiar environments may be counterproductive, unsupportive, or too unstructured. A halfway house is an important treatment resource that provides emotional support, counseling, and progressive entry back into society.

References

Alcoholism in the elderly. Council on Scientific Affairs, American Medical Association. JAMA *275:* 797, 1996.

Babor TF, Hofman M, DelBoca FK, Hesselbrock V, Meyer RE, Dolinsky ZS, Rounsaville B: Types of alcoholics: I. Evidence for an empirically derived typology based on indicators of vulnerability and severity. Arch Gen Psychiatry *49:* 599, 1992.

Chick J, Gough K, Falkowski W, Kershaw P, Hore B, Mehta B, Ritson B, Ropner R, Torley D: Disulfiram treatment of alcoholism. Br J Psychiatry *161:* 84: 1992.

Limson R, Goldman D, Roy A, Lamparski D, Ravitz B, Adinoff B, Linnoila M: Personality and cerebrospinal fluid monoamine metabolites in alcoholics and controls. Arch Gen Psychiatry *48:* 437, 1991.

Litt MD, Babor TF, DelBoca FK, Kadden RM, Cooney NL: Types of alcoholics: II. Application of an empirically derived typology to treatment matching. Arch Gen Psychiatry *49:* 609, 1992.

Litten RZ, Allen JP: Pharmacotherapies for alcoholism: Promising agents and clinical issues. Alcohol Clin Exp Res *15:* 620, 1991.

McGrath PJ, Nunes EV, Stewart JW, Goldman D, Agosti V, Ocepek-Welikson K, Quitkin PM: Imipramine treatment of alcoholics with primary depression: A placebo-controlled clinical trial. Arch Gen Psychiatry *53:* 232, 1996.

Murphy GE, Wetzel RD, Robins E, McEvoy L: Multiple risk factors predict suicide in alcoholism. Arch Gen Psychiatry *49:* 459, 1992.

Noble EP: The D_2 dopamine receptor gene: A review of association studies in alcoholism. Behav Genet *23:* 119, 1993.

Pickens RW, Svikis DC, McGue M, Lykken DT, Heston LL, Clayton PJ: Heterogeneity in the inheritance of alcoholism: A study of male and female twins. Arch Gen Psychiatry *48;* 19, 1991.

Roy A, DeJong J, Lamparski D, George T, Linnoila M: Depression among alcoholics: Relationship to clinical and cerebrospinal fluid variables. Arch Gen Psychiatry *48:* 428, 1991.

Rubino FA: Neurologic complications of alcoholism. Psychiatr Clin North Am *15:* 359, 1992.

Schuckit MA: Alcohol-related disorders. In *Comprehensive Textbook of Psychiatry,* ed 6, HI Kaplan, BH Sadock, editors, p 775. Williams & Wilkins, Baltimore, 1995.

Schuckit MA, Smith TL, Anthenelli R, Irwin M: Clinical course of alcoholism in 636 male inpatients. Am J Psychiatry *150;* 786, 1993.

Sellers EM, Higgins GA, Sobell M B: 5-HT and alcohol abuse. Trends Pharmacol Sci *13:* 69, 1992.

Substance Abuse and Mental Health Services Administration Office of Applied Studies: *Preliminary Estimates from the 1995 National Household Survey on Drug Abuse.* U.S. Government Printing Office, Washington, 1995.

Uhl GR, Persico AM, Smith SS: Current excitement with D_2 dopamine receptor gene alleles in substance abuse. Arch Gen Psychiatry *49:* 157, 1992.

Vaillant GE: A long-term follow-up of male alcohol abuse. Arch Gen Psychiatry *53:* 243, 1996.

Volkow ND, Hitzemann R, Wang G-J, Fowler J S, Burr G, Pascani K, Dewey SL, Wolf A: Decreased brain metabolism in neurologically intact healthy alcoholics. Am J Psychiatry *149:* 1016, 1992.

▲ 12.3 Amphetamine (or Amphetamine-like)-Related Disorders

Amphetamines were first synthesized for therapeutic use and are used legitimately to treat a variety of medical and psychiatric conditions (for example, narcolepsy, attention-deficit disorders and depression). The racemate amphetamine sulfate (Benzedrine) was first synthesized in 1887 and was introduced to clinical practice in 1932 as an over-the-counter inhaler for the treatment of nasal congestion and asthma. In 1937, amphetamine sulfate tablets were introduced for the treatment of narcolepsy, postencephalitic parkinsonism, depression, and lethargy. In the 1970s, a variety of social and regulatory factors began to curb widespread amphetamine distribution. The currently approved indications for amphetamine are limited to attention-deficit/hyperactivity disorder, narcolepsy, and depressive disorders. Amphetamines are also used in the treatment of obesity, although their efficacy and safety for this indication are controversial.

PREPARATIONS

The major amphetamines currently available and used in the United States are dextroamphetamine (Dexedrine), methamphetamine (Desoxyn), and methylphenidate (Ritalin). These drugs go by such street names as ice, crystal, crystal meth, and speed. As a general class, the amphetamines are also referred to as sympathomimetics, stimulants, and psychostimulants. The typical amphetamines are used to increase performance and to induce a euphoric feeling, for example, by students studying for examinations, by long-distance truck drivers on trips, by business people with important deadlines, and by athletes in competition. Although not as addictive as cocaine, amphetamines are nonetheless addictive drugs.

Other amphetamine-like substances are ephedrine and propranolamine, which are available over the counter in the United States as nasal decongestants. Phenylpropranolamine (PPA) is also available as an appetite suppressant. Although less potent than the classic amphetamines, ephedrine and propranolamine are subject to abuse, partly because of their easy availability and low price. Both drugs, propranolamine in particular, can dangerously exacerbate hypertension, precipitate a toxic psychosis, or result in death. The safety margin for propranolamine is particularly narrow, and three to four times the normal dose can result in life-threatening hypertension.

Amphetamine-Like Substances

The classic amphetamine drugs (dextroamphetamine, methamphetamine, and methylphenidate) exert their major effects through the dopaminergic system. Substituted, so-called designer amphetamines have neurochemical effects on both the serotonergic and the dopaminergic systems and have behavioral effects that reflect a combination of amphetamine-like and hallucinogen-like activities. Some psychopharmacologists classify the substituted amphetamines as hallucinogens; in this textbook, however, they are classified with the amphetamines to which they are closely related structurally. Examples of the substituted amphetamines include 3,4-methylenedioxyamphet amine (MDMA), also referred to as ecstasy, XTC, and Adam; *N*-ethyl-3,4-methylenedioxyamphetamine (MDEA), also referred to as Eve; 5-methoxy-3,4-methylenedioxyamphetamine (MMDA); and 2,5-dimethoxy-4-methylamphetamine (DOM), also referred to as STP. Of these drugs, MDMA has been studied most closely and is perhaps the most widely available.

Methamphetamine. Ice is a pure form of methamphetamine that abusers of the substance inhale, smoke, or inject intravenously. Methamphetamine has been used most heavily on the West Coast and in Hawaii. Its psychological effects last for hours and are described as particularly powerful. Unlike crack cocaine, which must be imported, ice is a synthetic drug that can be manufactured domestically in illicit laboratories. Some law enforcement agencies and urban emergency room physicians think that ice may become a widespread drug of abuse over the next several years.

Khat

The fresh leaves of the East African bush *Catha edulis* are chewed for their stimulant effects. Cathinone is the active ingredient in Khat and has most of the CNS and peripheral actions of amphetamine. Clandestine laboratories have begun synthesizing methcathinone, which has effects similar to cathinone. Methcathinone (also known as crank) is easily synthesized from ephedrine or pseudoephedrine.

EPIDEMIOLOGY

In 1991, about 7 percent of the U.S. population had used stimulants at least once, although fewer than 1 percent were current users. In 1995, about 2 percent of the U.S. population have tried methamphetamine. The 18- to 25-year-old age group reported the highest level of use, with 9 percent reporting use at least once and 1 percent describing themselves as current users. Use among the 12- to 17-year-old age group appears at an alarmingly high level, with 3 percent reporting use at least once and 1 percent reporting current use. Amphetamine use occurs in all socioeconomic groups, and the trend for amphetamine use among white professionals is at a high level. Because amphetamines are available by prescription for specific indications, prescribing physicians must be aware of the risk of amphetamine abuse by others, including friends and family members of the patient receiving the amphetamine. No reliable data are available on the epidemiology of designer amphetamine use.

According to the Centers for Disease Control (CDC), the number of amphetamine-related deaths nearly tripled between 1991 and 1994, and emergency room visits at reporting hospitals rose from 4,900 to 17,400 for treating amphetamine-related symptoms.

NEUROPHARMACOLOGY

All the amphetamines are rapidly absorbed orally and have a rapid onset of action, usually within 1 hour when taken orally. The classic amphetamines are also taken intravenously and have an almost immediate effect by this route. Nonprescribed amphetamines and designer amphetamines are also ingested by inhaling (snorting). Tolerance develops with both classic and designer amphetamines, although amphetamine users often overcome the tolerance by taking more of the drug. Amphetamine is less addictive than cocaine, as evidenced by experiments on rats in which not all animals spontaneously self-administered low doses of amphetamine. The further study of such animal models may help clinicians understand the susceptibility of some patients to amphetamine dependence.

The classic amphetamines (dextroamphetamine, methamphetamine, and methylphenidate) produce their primary effects by causing the release of catecholamines, particularly dopamine, from presynaptic terminals. The effects are particularly potent for the dopaminergic neurons projecting from the ventral tegmental area to the cerebral cortex and the limbic areas. This pathway has been termed the reward pathway, and its activation is probably the major addicting mechanism for the amphetamines.

The designer amphetamines (such as MDMA, MDEA, MMDA, and DOM) cause the release of catecholamines (dopamine and norepinephrine) and of serotonin, the neurotransmitter implicated as the major neurochemical pathway for hallucinogens. Therefore, the clinical effects of designer amphetamines blend the effects of classic amphetamines and those of hallucinogens. The pharmacology of MDMA is the best understood of this group. MDMA is taken up in serotonergic neurons by the serotonin transporter responsible for serotonin reuptake. Once in the neuron, MDMA causes a rapid release of a bolus of serotonin and inhibits the activity of serotonin-producing enzymes.

DIAGNOSIS

The fourth edition of *Diagnostic and Statistical Manual of Mental Disorders* (DSM-IV) lists many amphetamine (or amphetamine-like)-related disorders (Table 12.3–1) but specifies diagnostic criteria only for amphetamine intoxication (Table 12.3–2), amphetamine withdrawal (Table 12.3–3), and amphetamine-related disorder not otherwise specified (Table 12.3–4) in the section on amphetamine (or amphetamine-like)-related disorders. The diagnostic criteria for the other amphetamine (or amphetamine-like)-related disorders are contained in the DSM-IV sections dealing with the primary phenomenological symptom (for example, psychosis).

Amphetamine Dependence and Amphetamine Abuse

The DSM-IV criteria for dependence and abuse are applied to amphetamine and its related substances (see Tables 12.1–7,

Table 12.3–1
DSM-IV Amphetamine (or Amphetamine-like)-Related Disorders

Amphetamine use disorders
Amphetamine dependence
Amphetamine abuse
Amphetamine-induced disorders
Amphetamine intoxication
Specify if:
With perceptual disturbances
Amphetamine withdrawal
Amphetamine intoxication delirium
Amphetamine-induced psychotic disorder, with delusions
Specify if:
With onset during intoxication
Amphetamine-induced psychotic disorder, with hallucinations
Specify if:
With onset during intoxication
Amphetamine-induced mood disorder
Specify if:
With onset during intoxication
With onset during withdrawal
Amphetamine-induced anxiety disorder
Specify if:
With onset during intoxication
Amphetamine-induced sexual dysfunction
Specify if:
With onset during intoxication
Amphetamine-induced sleep disorder
Specify if:
With onset during intoxication
With onset during withdrawal
Amphetamine-related disorder not otherwise specified

Table 12.3–2
DSM-IV Diagnostic Criteria for Amphetamine Intoxication

A. Recent use of amphetamine or a related substance (eg, methylphenidate).

B. Clinically significant maladaptive behavioral or psychological changes (eg, euphoria or effective blunting; changes in sociability; hypervigilance; interpersonal sensitivity; anxiety, tension, or anger; stereotyped behaviors; impaired judgment; or impaired social or occupational functioning) that developed during, or shortly after, use of amphetamine or a related substance.

C. Two (or more) of the following, developing during, or shortly after, use of amphetamine or related substance:
(1) tachycardia or bradycardia
(2) pupillary dilation
(3) elevated or lowered blood pressure
(4) perspiration or chills
(5) nausea or vomiting
(6) evidence of weight loss
(7) psychomotor agitation or retardation
(8) muscular weakness, respiratory depression, chest pain, or cardiac arrhythmias
(9) confusion, seizures, dyskinesias, dystonias, or coma

D. The symptoms are not due to a general medical condition and not better accounted for by another mental disorder.

Specify if:
With perceptual disturbances

12.1–8, and 12.1–9). Amphetamine dependence can result in a rapid down-spiral of a person's abilities to cope with work- and family-related obligations and stresses. A person who abuses amphetamines requires increasingly high doses of amphetamine to obtain the usual high, and physical signs of amphetamine abuse (such as decreased weight and paranoid ideas) almost always develop with continued abuse.

Amphetamine Intoxication

The intoxication syndromes of cocaine (which blocks dopamine reuptake) and amphetamines (which cause the release of dopamine) are similar. Because more rigorous and in-depth research has been done on cocaine abuse and intoxication than on amphetamines, the clinical literature on amphetamines has been strongly influenced by the clinical findings of cocaine abuse. In DSM-IV, the diagnostic criteria for amphetamine intoxication (see Table 12.3–2) and cocaine intoxication (see Table 12.6–2) are separated but are virtually the same. DSM-IV specifies perceptual disturbances as a symptom of amphetamine intoxication. If intact reality testing is absent, a diagnosis of amphetamine-induced psychotic disorder with onset during intoxication is indicated. The symptoms of amphetamine intoxication are mostly resolved after 24 hours and are generally completely resolved after 48 hours.

Amphetamine Withdrawal

After amphetamine intoxication, a crash occurs with symptoms of anxiety, tremulousness, dysphoric mood, lethargy, fatigue, nightmares (accompanied by rebound rapid eye movement [REM] sleep), headache, profuse sweating, muscle cramps, stomach cramps, and insatiable hunger. The withdrawal symptoms generally peak in 2 to 4 days and are resolved in 1 week. The most serious withdrawal symptom is depression, which can be particularly severe after the sustained use of high doses of amphetamine and which can be associated with suicidal ideation or behavior. The DSM-IV diagnostic criteria for amphetamine withdrawal (see Table 12.3–3) specify that a dysphoric mood and physiological changes are necessary for the diagnosis.

Table 12.3–3
DSM-IV Diagnostic Criteria for Amphetamine Withdrawal

A. Cessation of (or reduction in) of amphetamine (or related substance) use which has been heavy and prolonged.

B. Dysphoric mood and two (or more) of the following physiological changes, developing within a few hours to several days after criterion A:
(1) fatigue
(2) vivid, unpleasant dreams
(3) insomnia or hypersomnia
(4) increased appetite
(5) psychomotor retardation or agitation

C. The symptoms in criterion B cause clinically significant distress or impairment in social, occupational, or other important areas of functioning.

D. The symptoms are not due to a general medical condition and not better accounted for by another mental disorder.

Amphetamine Intoxication Delirium

Under substance-related disorder, DSM-IV includes a diagnosis of amphetamine intoxication delirium (see Table 10.2–3). Delirium associated with amphetamine usually results from high doses of amphetamine or from its sustained use so that sleep deprivation affects the clinical presentation. The combination of amphetamines with other substances and the use of

Table 12.3–4
DSM-IV Diagnostic Criteria for Amphetamine-Related Disorder Not Otherwise Specified

The amphetamine-related disorder not otherwise specified category is for disorders associated with the use of amphetamine (or a related substance) that are not classifiable as amphetamine dependence, amphetamine abuse, amphetamine intoxication, amphetamine withdrawal, amphetamine intoxication delirium, amphetamine-induced psychotic disorder, amphetamine-induced mood disorder, amphetamine-induced anxiety disorder, amphetamine-induced sexual dysfunction, or amphetamine-induced sleep disorder.

amphetamines by a person with preexisting brain damage can also cause delirium to develop.

Amphetamine-Induced Psychotic Disorder

The clinical similarity of amphetamine-induced psychosis to paranoid schizophrenia has prompted researchers to extensively study the neurochemistry of amphetamine-induced psychosis to understand the pathophysiology of paranoid schizophrenia. The hallmark of amphetamine-induced psychotic disorder is the presence of paranoia. Amphetamine-induced psychotic disorder can be distinguished from paranoid schizophrenia by several differentiating characteristics associated with the former, including a predominance of visual hallucinations, generally appropriate affects, hyperactivity, hypersexuality, confusion and incoherence, and little evidence of disordered thinking (such as looseness of associations). In several studies, investigators also noted that, although the positive symptoms of amphetamine-induced psychotic disorder and schizophrenia are similar, amphetamine-induced psychotic disorder generally lacks the effective flattening and alogia of schizophrenia. Clinically, however, acute amphetamine-induced psychotic disorder can appear completely indistinguishable from schizophrenia, and only the resolution of the symptoms in a few days or a positive finding in a urine drug screen test eventually reveals the correct diagnosis.

The treatment of choice for amphetamine-induced psychotic disorder is the short-term use of dopamine receptor antagonists—for example, haloperidol (Haldol). DSM-IV lists the diagnostic criteria for amphetamine-induced psychotic disorder with the other psychotic disorders (see Table 14.1–7) and allows clinicians to specify whether delusions or hallucinations are the predominant symptoms.

Amphetamine-Induced Mood Disorder

According to DSM-IV, the onset of amphetamine-induced mood disorder can occur during intoxication or withdrawal (see Table 15.1–11). In general, intoxication is associated with manic or mixed mood features, whereas withdrawal is associated with depressive mood features.

Amphetamine-Induced Anxiety Disorder

In DSM-IV, the onset of amphetamine-induced anxiety disorder can also occur during intoxication or withdrawal (see Table 16.1–5). Amphetamine, like cocaine, can induce symptoms similar to those seen in obsessive-compulsive disorder, panic disorder, and phobic disorders, in particular.

Amphetamine-Induced Sexual Dysfunction

Although amphetamine is often used to enhance sexual experiences, high doses and long-term use are associated with impotence and other sexual dysfunctions. These dysfunctions are classified in DSM-IV as amphetamine-induced sexual dysfunction with onset during intoxication (see Table 21.2–17)

Amphetamine-Induced Sleep Disorder

The diagnostic criteria for amphetamine-induced sleep disorder with onset during intoxication or withdrawal are found in the DSM-IV section on sleep disorders (see Table 24.2–21). Amphetamine intoxication can produce insomnia and sleep deprivation, whereas people undergoing amphetamine withdrawal can experience hypersomnolence and nightmares.

Disorders Not Otherwise Specified

If an amphetamine (or amphetamine-like)-related disorder does not meet the criteria of one or more of the previous discussed categories, it can be diagnosed as an amphetamine-related disorder not otherwise specified (see Table 12.3–4). With the increasing illicit use of designer amphetamines, syndromes may arise that do not meet the criteria outlined in DSM-IV and that necessitate the frequent use of the not otherwise specified category.

CLINICAL FEATURES

Amphetamines

In people who have not previously used amphetamines, a single 5 mg dose increases the sense of well-being and induces elation, euphoria, and friendliness. Small doses generally improve attention and increase performance on written, oral, and performance tasks. There is also an associated decrease in fatigue, an induction of anorexia, and a heightening of the pain threshold. Undesirable effects accompany the use of high doses for long times.

Substituted Amphetamines

Because of their effects on the dopaminergic system, substituted amphetamines are activating and energizing. Their effects on the serotonergic system, however, color the experience of these drugs with a hallucinogenic character. Substituted amphetamines are associated with much less disorientation and perceptual distortion than are the classic hallucinogens such as lysergic acid diethylamide (LSD). A sense of closeness with other people and of personal comfort and an increased luminescence of objects are effects commonly reported by those who ingest MDMA (Table 12.3–5). Some psychotherapists have used and have advocated further research into the use of designer amphetamines as adjuvants to psychotherapy. This suggestion is controversial; other clinicians emphasize the potential dangers of using of such drugs.

Adverse Effects

Amphetamines. **PHYSICAL.** Amphetamine abuse can produce adverse effects, the most serious of which include cerebrovascular, cardiac, and gastrointestinal effects. Among the specific life-threatening conditions are myocardial infarction, severe hypertension, cerebrovascular disease, and ischemic colitis. A continuum of neurological symptoms, from twitching to tetany to seizures to coma and death, is associated with increasingly high amphetamine doses. The intravenous use of amphetamines can serve to transmit human immunodeficiency virus (HIV) and hepatitis and to further the development of lung abscesses, endocarditis, and necrotizing angiitis. Several studies have shown that abusers of amphetamines knew little about safe-sex practices and the use of condoms. The less-than-life-threatening adverse effects of amphetamine abuse include flushing, pallor, cyanosis, fever, headache, tachycardia, palpitations, nausea, vomiting, bruxism (teeth grinding), shortness of breath, tremor, and ataxia.

Table 12.3–5
Short-Term Effects of MDMA

Subjective Sensation	Subjects Affected[a]
Sense of "closeness" with other people	90
Trismus	75
Tachycardia	72
Bruxism	65
Dry mouth	61
Increased alertness	50
Luminescence of objects	42
Tremor	42
Palpitations	41
Diaphoresis	38
Difficulty in concentrating	38
Paresthesias	35
Insomnia	33
Hot or cold flashes	31
Increased sensitivity to cold	27
Dizziness or vertigo	24
Visual hallucinations	20
Blurred vision	20

Reprinted with permission from Peroutka SJ, Newman H, Harris H: Subjective effects of 3, 4-methylenedioxymethamphetamine in recreational users. Neuropsychopharmacology *1:* 275, 1988.
[a] Total number tested: 100.

Table 12.3–6
Moderate-Term Effects of MDMA

Subjective Sensation	Subjects Affected[a]
Drowsiness	36
Muscle aches or fatigability	32
Sense of "closeness" with other people	22
Depression	21
Tight jaw muscles	21
Difficulty in concentrating	21
Headache	17
Dry mouth	14
Anxiety, worry, or fear	12
Irritability	12

Reprinted with permission from Peroutka SJ, Newman H, Harris H: Subjective effects of 3, 4-methylenedioxymethamphetamine in recreational users. Neuropsychopharmacology *1:* 275, 1988.
[a] Total number tested: 100.

When pregnant women use amphetamines, the babies often have low birth weight, small head circumference, early gestational age, and growth retardation.

PSYCHOLOGICAL. The adverse psychological effects associated with amphetamine use include restlessness, dysphoria, insomnia, irritability, hostility, and confusion. Symptoms of anxiety disorders such as generalized anxiety disorder and panic disorder can be induced by amphetamine use as can ideas of reference, paranoid delusions, and hallucinations.

Substituted Amphetamines. Substituted amphetamines produce many of the same adverse effects as do classic amphetamines, but several other adverse effects have also been associated with designer drugs (Tables 12.3–5 and 12.3–6).

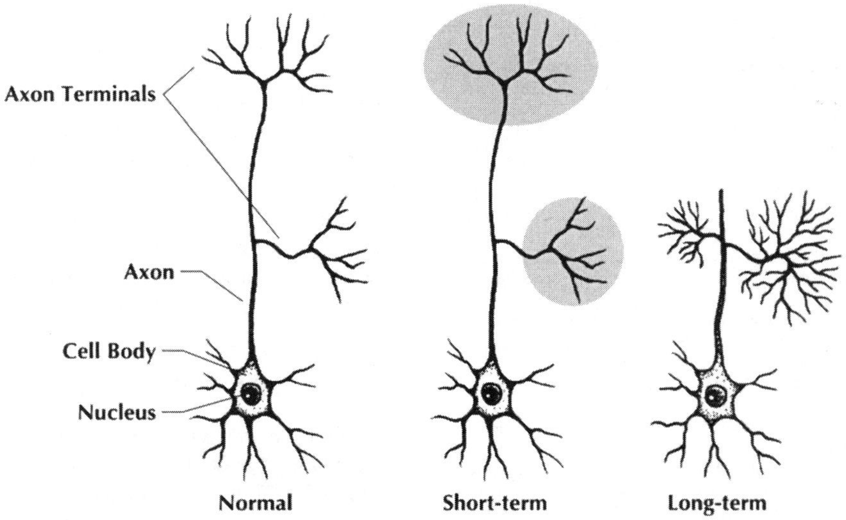
Axon Terminals
Axon
Cell Body
Nucleus
Normal
Short-term
Long-term

FIGURE 12.3–1

Neurotoxic effects of MDMA. Studies have found that MDMA damages serotonin-producing neurons in the brains of nonhuman primates. The *illustration* on the *left* shows a normal neuron. The *shaded area* in the *middle illustration* shows the axon terminals of the neuron that are damaged by MDMA. The *illustration* on the *right* shows how, 12 to 18 months after being damaged by MDMA, serotonin-producing nerve fibers have regrown excessively in some areas and not at all in others. (Reprinted from Mathias R: Like mathamphetamine, "ecstasy" may cause long-term brain damage. NIDA Notes *11* (5): 7, 1996.

MDMA causes hyperthermia, which is exacerbated by such excessive activity as wildly dancing in a crowded, hot room, an event known as a rave. Several deaths associated with MDMA use have been reported under such circumstances. MDMA is reported to cause damage to serotonergic neurons (Fig. 12.3–1), but researchers are divided in their opinions about whether MDMA causes neurotoxicity in the doses used by humans.

TREATMENT AND REHABILITATION

The treatment of amphetamine (or amphetamine-like)-related disorders shares with cocaine-related disorders the difficulty of helping patients remain abstinent from the drug, which is powerfully reinforcing and induces craving. An inpatient setting and the use of multiple therapeutic methods (individual, family, and group psychotherapy) are usually necessary to achieve lasting abstinence. The treatment of specific amphetamine-induced disorders (such as amphetamine-induced psychotic disorder and amphetamine-induced anxiety disorder) with specific drugs (such as antipsychotics and anxiolytics) may be necessary on a short-term basis. Antipsychotics, either a phenothiazine or haloperidol, may be prescribed for the first few days. In the absence of psychosis, diazepam (Valium) is useful to treat patients' agitation and hyperactivity.

Physicians should establish a therapeutic alliance with patients to deal with the underlying depression or personality disorder or both. Because many patients are heavily dependent on the drug, however, psychotherapy may be especially difficult.

REFERENCES

Beebe DK, Walley E: Smokable methamphetamine (''ice''): an old drug in a different form. Am Fam Physician *51:* 449, 1995.

Cox DE: ''Rave'' to the grave. Forensic Sci Int *60:* 5, 1993.

Dackis CA, Gold MS: Addictiveness of central stimulants. Adv Alcohol Subst Abuse *9:* 9, 1990.

Derlet RW, Heischober B: Methamphetamine: Stimulant of the 1990s? West J Med *153:* 625, 1990.

Gillogley KM, Evans AT, Hansen RL, Samuels SJ, Batra KK: The perinatal impact of cocaine, amphetamine, and opiate use detected by universal intrapartum screening. Am J Obstet Gynecol *163:* 1535, 1990.

Green AR, Cross AJ, Goodwin GM: Review of the pharmacology and clinical pharmacology of 3,4-methylenedioxymethamphetamine (MDMA or ''Ecstasy''). Psychopharmacology *119:* 247, 1995.

Grob CS, Bravo GL, Walsh RN, Liester MB: The MDMA-neurotoxicity controversy: Implications for clinical research with novel psychoactive drugs. J Nerv Ment Dis *180:* 355, 1992.

Hall W, Darke S, Ross M, Wodak A: Patterns of drug use and risk-taking among injecting amphetamine and opioid drug users in Sydney, Australia. Addiction *88:* 509, 1993.

Heishman SJ, Henningfield JE: Discriminative stimulus effects of *d*-amphetamine, methylphenidate, and diazepam in humans. Psychopharmacology *103:* 436, 1991.

Jaffe JH: Amphetamine (or amphetamine-like)-related disorder. In *Comprehensive Textbook of Psychiatry,* ed 6, HI Kaplan, BJ Sadock, editors, p 791. Williams & Wilkins, Baltimore, 1995.

Klee H: A new target for behavioral research: Amphetamine misuse. Br J Addict *87:* 439, 1992.

Koelega HS: Stimulant drugs and vigilance performance: A review. Psychopharmacology *111:* 1, 1993.

Liester MB, Grob CS, Bravo GL, Walsh RN: Phenomenology and sequelae of 3, 4-methylenedioxymethamphetamine use. J Nerv Ment Dis *180:* 345, 1992.

Lynch J, House MA: Cardiovascular effects of methamphetamine. J Cardiovasc Nurs *6:* 12, 1992.

Parran TV, Jasinski DR: Intravenous methylphenidate abuse: Prototype for prescription drug abuse. Arch Intern Med *151:* 171, 1991.

Ragland AS, Ismail Y, Arsura EL: Myocardial infarction after amphetamine use. Am Heart J *125:* 247, 1993.

Rudnick G, Wall SC: The molecular mechanism of ''ecstasy'' (3,4-methylenedioxymethamphetamine [MDMA]: Serotonin transporters are targets for MDMA-induced serotonin release. Proc Natl Acad Sci USA *89:* 1817, 1992.

Sato M: A lasting vulnerability to psychosis in patients with previous methamphetamine psychosis. Ann NY Acad Sci *654:* 160, 1992.

Sato M, Numachi Y, Hamamura T: Relapse of paranoid psychotic state in methamphetamine model of schizophrenia. Schizophr Bull *18:* 115, 1992.

Substance Abuse and Mental Health Services Administration Office of Applied Studies: *Preliminary Estimates from the 1995 National Household Survey on Drug Abuse.* U.S. Government Printing Office, Washington, 1995.

▲ 12.4 Caffeine-Related Disorders

Caffeine, usually in the form of coffee or tea, is the most widely used psychoactive substance in Western countries. About 80 percent of North American adults regularly drink caffeine-containing beverages. Although caffeine is a mild stimulant, it can cause agitation, heart palpitations, and insomnia. The fourth edition of *Diagnostic and Statistical Manual of Mental Disorders* (DSM-IV) includes diagnoses of caffeine intoxication, caffeine-induced anxiety disorder, and caffeine-induced sleep disorder. DSM-IV does not have diagnostic categories for caffeine dependence or caffeine withdrawal, in spite of the fact that studies have reported data consistent with the presence of caffeine-related physical dependence and withdrawal phenomena. DSM-IV does, however, include research criteria for caffeine withdrawal in an appendix.

EPIDEMIOLOGY

Caffeine is contained in drinks, foods, prescription medicines, and over-the-counter medicines (Table 12.4–1). An adult in the United States consumes about 200 mg of caffeine per day on average, although 20 to 30 percent of all adults consume more than 500 mg per day. The per capita use of coffee in the United States is 10.2 pounds per year. A cup of coffee generally contains 100 to 150 mg of caffeine; tea contains about one third as much. Many over-the-counter medications contain one third to one half as much caffeine as that in a cup of coffee, and some migraine medications and over-the-counter stimulants contain *more* caffeine than does a cup of coffee. Significant amounts of caffeine are contained in cocoa, chocolate, and soft drinks, enough to cause some symptoms of caffeine intoxication in small children when they ingest a candy bar and a 12-ounce cola drink.

NEUROPHARMACOLOGY

Caffeine, a methylxanthine, is more potent than another commonly used methylxanthine, theophylline (Primatene). The half-life of caffeine in the human body is 3 to 10 hours, and the time of peak concentration is 30 to 60 minutes. Caffeine readily crosses the blood–brain barrier. Caffeine's primary mechanism of action is as an antagonist of the adenosine receptors. Activation of adenosine receptors activates an inhibitory G protein (G_i), and thus inhibits the formation of the sec-

Table 12.4–1
Common Sources of Caffeine and Representative Decaffeinated Products

Source	Caffeine per Unit (mg)
Beverages and foods (5–6 oz)	
Fresh drip coffee, brewed coffee	90–140
Instant coffee	66–100
Tea (leaf or bagged)	30–100
Cocoa	5–50
Decaffeinated coffee	2–4
Chocolate bar or ounce of baking chocolate	25–35
Soft drinks (8–12 oz)	
Pepsi, Coke, Tab, Royal Crown, Dr. Pepper, Mountain Dew	25–50
Canada Dry Ginger Ale, Caffeine-Free Coke, Caffeine-Free Pepsi, 7-Up, Sprite, Squirt, Caffeine-Free Tab	0
Prescription medications (1 tablet or capsule)	
Cafergot, Migralam	100
Anoquan, Aspir-code, BAC, Darvon, Fiorinal	32–50
Over-the-counter analgesics and cold preparations (1 tablet or capsule)	
Excedrin	60
Aspirin compound, Anacin, B-C powder, Capron, Cope, Dolor, Midol, Nilain, Norgesic, PAC, Trigesic, Vanquish	~30
Advil, aspirin, Empirin, Midol 200, Nuprin, Pamprin	0
Over-the-counter stimulants and appetite suppressants (1 tablet or capsule)	
Caffin-TD, Caffedrine	250
Vivarin, Ver	200
Quick-Pep	140–150
Amostat, Anorexin, Appedrine, Nodoz, Wakoz	100

Adapted from table by Jerome H. Jaffe, M.D.

ond-messenger cyclic adenosine monophosphate (cAMP). Caffeine intake, therefore, results in an increase in intraneuronal cAMP concentrations in neurons with adenosine receptors. Three cups of coffee are estimated to deliver so much caffeine to the brain that about 50 percent of the adenosine receptors are occupied by caffeine. Several experiments indicate that caffeine, especially at high doses or concentrations, can affect dopamine and noradrenergic neurons. Specifically, dopamine activity may be enhanced by caffeine, a hypothesis that can explain clinical reports associating caffeine intake with an exacerbation of psychotic symptoms in patients with schizophrenia. Activation of noradrenergic neurons has been hypothesized to be involved in the mediation of some symptoms of caffeine withdrawal.

Caffeine as a Substance of Abuse

Caffeine evidences all the traits associated with commonly accepted substances of abuse. First, caffeine can act as a positive reinforcer, particularly at low doses. Caffeine doses of about 100 mg induce a mild euphoria in humans and repeated substance-seeking behavior effects in other animals. Caffeine doses of 300 mg, however, do not act as positive reinforcers and can produce increased anxiety and mild dysphoria. Second, studies in animals and humans have reported that caffeine can be discriminated from a placebo in blind experimental conditions. Third, both animal and human studies have shown that physical tolerance to some effects of caffeine does develop and that withdrawal symptoms do occur.

Effects on Cerebral Blood Flow

Most studies have found that caffeine results in global cerebral vasoconstriction, with a resultant decrease in cerebral blood flow (CBF), although this effect may not occur in people over 65 years of age. According to one recent study, tolerance does not develop to these vasoconstrictive effects, and the CBF shows a rebound increase after withdrawal from caffeine.

DIAGNOSIS

The diagnosis of caffeine intoxication or other caffeine-related disorders depends primarily on a clinician's taking a comprehensive history of a patient's intake of caffeine-containing products. The history should cover whether a patient has experienced any symptoms of caffeine withdrawal during periods when caffeine consumption was either stopped or severely reduced. The differential diagnosis for caffeine-related disorders should include the following psychiatric diagnoses: generalized anxiety disorder, panic disorder with or without agoraphobia, bipolar II disorder, attention-deficit/hyperactivity disorder, and sleep disorders. The differential diagnosis should include the abuse of caffeine-containing over-the-counter medications, anabolic steroids, and other stimulants, such as amphetamines and cocaine. A urine sample may be needed to screen for these substances. The differential diagnosis should also include hyperthyroidism and pheochromocytoma.

DSM-IV lists the caffeine-related disorders (Table 12.4–2) and provides diagnostic criteria for caffeine intoxication (Table 12.4–3) but does not formally recognize a diagnosis of caffeine withdrawal, which is classified as a caffeine-related disorder not otherwise specified. The diagnostic criteria for other caffeine-related disorders are contained in the sections specific for the principal symptom (for example, as a substance-induced anxiety disorder for caffeine-induced anxiety disorder).

Table 12.4–2
DSM-IV Caffeine-Related Disorders

Caffeine-Induced Disorders
- **Caffeine intoxication**
- **Caffeine-induced anxiety disorder**
  - *Specify if:*
    - With onset during intoxication
- **Caffeine-induced sleep disorder**
  - *Specify if:*
    - With onset during intoxication
- **Caffeine-related disorder not otherwise specified**

Table 12.4–3
DSM-IV Diagnostic Criteria for Caffeine Intoxication

A. Recent consumption of caffeine, usually in excess of 250 mg (eg, more than 2–3 cups of brewed coffee).

B. Five (or more) of the following signs, developing during, or shortly after, caffeine use:
(1) restlessness
(2) nervousness
(3) excitement
(4) insomnia
(5) flushed face
(6) diuresis
(7) gastrointestinal disturbance
(8) muscle twitching
(9) rambling flow of thought and speech
(10) tachycardia or cardiac arrhythmia
(11) periods of inexhaustibility
(12) psychomotor agitation

C. The symptoms in criterion B cause clinically significant distress or impairment in social, occupational, or other important areas of functioning.

D. The symptoms are not due to a general medical condition and are not better accounted for by another mental disorder (eg, an anxiety disorder).

Reprinted with permission from American Psychiatric Association: *Diagnostic and Statistical Manual of Mental Disorders,* ed 4.

Caffeine Intoxication

DSM-IV specifies the diagnostic criteria for caffeine intoxication (Table 12.4–3), including the recent consumption of caffeine, usually in excess of 250 mg. The annual incidence of caffeine intoxication is an estimated 10 percent, although some clinicians and investigators suspect that the actual incidence is much higher. The common symptoms associated with caffeine intoxication include anxiety, psychomotor agitation, restlessness, irritability, and psychophysiological complaints, such as muscle twitching, flushed face, nausea, diuresis, gastrointestinal distress, excessive perspiration, tingling in the fingers and toes, and insomnia. The consumption of more than 1 gram of caffeine can produce rambling speech, confused thinking, cardiac arrhythmias, inexhaustibleness, marked agitation, tinnitus, and mild visual hallucinations (light flashes). The consumption of more than 10 grams of caffeine can cause generalized tonic-clonic seizures, respiratory failure, and death.

Caffeine Withdrawal

In spite of the fact that DSM-IV does not include a diagnosis of caffeine withdrawal, several well-controlled studies indicate that caffeine withdrawal is a real phenomenon, and DSM-IV gives research criteria for caffeine withdrawal (Table 12.4–4). The appearance of withdrawal symptoms reflects the tolerance and physiological dependence that develop with continued caffeine use. Several epidemiological studies have reported symptoms of caffeine withdrawal in 50 to 75 percent of all caffeine users studied. The most common symptoms are headache and fatigue; other symptoms include anxiety, irritability, mild depressive symptoms, impaired psychomotor performance, nausea, vomiting, craving for caffeine, and muscle pain and stiffness. The number and severity of the withdrawal symptoms are correlated with the amount of caffeine ingested and the abruptness of the withdrawal. Caffeine withdrawal symptoms have their onset 12 to 24 hours after the last dose; the symptoms peak in 24 to 48 hours and resolve within 1 week.

The induction of caffeine withdrawal can sometimes be iatrogenic. Physicians often ask their patients to discontinue caffeine intake before certain medical procedures, such as endoscopy, colonoscopy, and cardiac catheterization. Physicians also often recommend that patients with anxiety symptoms, cardiac arrhythmias, esophagitis, hiatal hernias, fibrocystic disease of the breast, and insomnia stop caffeine intake. Some people simply decide that it would be good for them to stop using caffeine-containing products. In all these situations, caffeine users should taper the use of caffeine-containing products over a 7- to 14-day period rather than stop abruptly.

Other Caffeine-Related Disorders

Caffeine-Induced Anxiety Disorder. Caffeine-induced anxiety disorder, which can occur during caffeine intoxication, is a DSM-IV diagnosis (see Table 16.1–5). The anxiety related to caffeine use can appear similar to that of generalized anxiety disorder. Patients with the disorder may be perceived as wired, overly talkative, and irritable; they may complain of not sleeping well and of having energy to burn. Although caffeine induces and exacerbates panic attacks in people with a panic disorder, a causative association between caffeine and a panic disorder has not yet been demonstrated.

Caffeine-Induced Sleep Disorder. Caffeine-induced sleep disorder, which can occur during caffeine intoxication, is a DSM-IV diagnosis (see Table 24.2–21). Caffeine is associated with a delay in falling asleep, an inability to remain asleep, and early morning awakening.

Table 12.4–4
DSM-IV Research Criteria for Caffeine Withdrawal

A. Prolonged daily use of caffeine.

B. Abrupt cessation of caffeine use, or reduction in the amount of caffeine used, closely followed by headache and one (or more) of the following symptoms:
(1) marked fatigue or drowsiness
(2) marked anxiety or depression
(3) nausea or vomiting

C. The symptoms in criterion B cause clinically significant distress or impairment in social, occupational, or other important areas of functioning.

D. The symptoms are not due to the direct physiological effects of a general medical condition (eg, migraine, viral illness) and are not better accounted for by another mental disorder.

Reprinted with permission from American Psychiatric Association: *Diagnostic and Statistical Manual of Mental Disorders,* ed 4.

Caffeine-Related Disorder Not Otherwise Specified. DSM-IV contains a residual category for caffeine-related disorders: caffeine-related disorder not otherwise specified (Table 12.4–5). The category covers caffeine-related diagnoses that do not meet the criteria for caffeine intoxication, caffeine-induced anxiety disorder, or caffeine-induced sleep disorder.

Table 12.4–5 DSM-IV Diagnostic Criteria for Caffeine-Related Disorder Not Otherwise Specified

The caffeine-related disorder not otherwise specified category is for disorders associated with the use of caffeine that are not classifiable as caffeine intoxication, caffeine-induced anxiety disorder, or caffeine-induced sleep disorder. An example is caffeine withdrawal.

Other Substance-Related Disorders

People with caffeine-related disorders are more likely to have additional substance-related disorders than are those without diagnoses of caffeine-related disorders. About two thirds of the people who consume large amounts of caffeine every day also use sedative and hypnotic drugs.

CLINICAL FEATURES

Signs and Symptoms

After the ingestion of 50 to 100 mg of caffeine, common symptoms include increased alertness, a mild sense of well-being, and a sense of improved verbal and motor performance. Caffeine ingestion is also associated with diuresis, cardiac muscle stimulation, increased intestinal peristalsis, increased gastric acid secretion, and a usually mild increase in blood pressure.

Adverse Effects

Although caffeine is not associated with cardiac-related risks in healthy people, those with preexisting cardiac disease are often advised to limit their caffeine intake because of a possible association between cardiac arrhythmias and caffeine. Caffeine is clearly associated with increased gastric acid secretion, and clinicians usually advise patients with gastric ulcers not to ingest any caffeine-containing products. Limited data suggest that caffeine is associated with fibrocystic disease of the breasts in women. Although the question of whether caffeine is associated with birth defects remains controversial, women who are pregnant or breast-feeding should probably avoid caffeine-containing products. No solid data link caffeine intake with cancer.

TREATMENT

The primary treatment of caffeine-related disorders is either eliminating or severely reducing the use of caffeine-containing products. Education of patients regarding the wide range of products that contain caffeine is essential for therapeutic success. Clinicians can advise patients to substitute other beverages—water, decaffeinated soft drinks, decaffeinated coffee—for coffee frequently consumed during the day. Spouses or significant others can often help patients stop their caffeine use; the spouses or significant others usually agree to eliminate caffeine from their own diets.

Analgesics, such as aspirin, are almost always sufficient to control the headaches and muscle aches that may accompany caffeine withdrawal. Rarely do patients require benzodiazepines to relieve withdrawal symptoms. If benzodiazepines are used for this purpose, they should be used in small dosages for a brief time, about 7 to 10 days at the longest.

References

Ammon HP: Biochemical mechanism of caffeine tolerance. Arch Pharm (Weinheim) *324:* 261, 1991.

Battig K: Acute and chronic cardiovascular and behavioral effects of caffeine, aspirin and ephedrine. Int J Obes Related Metab Disord *17* (2, Suppl): 61, 1993.

Battig K: Coffee, cardiovascular and behavioral effects: Current research trends. Rev Environ Health *9:* 53, 1992.

Bradley JR, Petree A: Caffeine consumption, expectancies of caffeine-enhanced performance, and caffeinism symptoms among university students. J Drug Educ *20:* 319, 1990.

Greden JF, Pomerleau O: Caffeine-related disorders and nicotine-related disorders. In *Comprehensive Textbook of Psychiatry,* ed 6, HI Kaplan, BJ Sadock, editors, p 799. Williams & Wilkins, Baltimore, 1995.

Holtzman SG: Caffeine as a model drug of abuse. Trends Pharmacol Sci *11:* 355, 1990.

Hughes JR, Higgins ST, Bickel WK, Hunt WK, Fenwick JW, Gulliver SB, Mireault GC: Caffeine self-administration, withdrawal, and adverse effects among coffee drinkers. Arch Gen Psychiatry *48:* 611, 1991.

Hughes JR, Oliveto AH, Bickel WK, Higgins ST, Badger GJ: Caffeine self-administration and withdrawal: Incidence, individual differences and interrelationships. Drug Alcohol Depend *32:* 239, 1993.

Hughes JR, Oliveto AH, Helzer JE, Higgins ST, Bickel WK: Should caffeine abuse, dependence, or withdrawal be added to DSM-IV and ICD-10? Am J Psychiatry *149:* 33, 1992.

Jacobson BH, Thurman-Lacey SR: Effects of caffeine on motor performance by caffeine-naive and -familiar subjects. Mot Skills *74:* 151, 1992.

Kozlowski LT, Henningfield JE, Keenan RM, Lei H, Leight G, Jelinek LC, Pope MA, Haertzen CA: Patterns of alcohol, cigarette, and caffeine and other drug use in two drug abusing populations. J Subst Abuse Treat *10:* 171, 1993.

Lucas PB, Pickar D, Kelsoe J, Rapaport M, Pato C. Hommer D: Effects of the acute administration of caffeine in patients with schizophrenia. Biol Psychiatry *28:* 35, 1990.

Matthew RJ, Wilson WH: Behavioral and cerebrovascular effects of caffeine in patients with anxiety disorders. Acta Psychiatr Scand *82:* 17, 1990.

Rogers PJ, Richardson NJ, Dernoncourt C: Caffeine use: Is there a net benefit for mood and psychomotor performance? Neuropsychobiology *31:* 195, 1995.

Silverman K, Evans SM, Strain EC, Griffiths RR: Withdrawal syndrome after the double-blind cessation of caffeine consumption. N Engl J Med *327:* 1109, 1992.

Silverman K, Griffiths RR: Low-dose caffeine discrimination and self-reported mood effects in normal volunteers. J Exp Anal Behav *57:* 91, 1992.

Yu G, Maskray V, Jackson SH, Swift CG, Tiplady B: A comparison of the central nervous system effects of caffeine and theophylline in elderly subjects. Br J Clin Pharmacol *32:* 341, 1991.

▲ 12.5 Cannabis-Related Disorders

According to the fourth edition of *Diagnostic and Statistical Manual of Mental Disorders* (DSM-IV), cannabis is probably the world's most common illicit substance. Its euphoric effects have been known for thousands of years: The Greek historian Herodotus (fifth century B.C.) described a tribe of nomads who inhaled the smoke of hemp seeds roasted in a brazier set up inside a small tent and exited the tent shouting for joy. The potential medicinal effects of cannabis as an analgesic, anticonvulsant, and hypnotic were recognized in the 19th and early 20th centuries.

Cannabis is the abbreviated name for the hemp plant *Cannabis sativa.* All parts of the plant contain psychoactive cannabinoids, of which (-)-Δ^9-tetrahydrocannabinol (Δ^9-THC) is most abundant. The most potent forms of cannabis come from the flowering tops of the plants or from the dried, black-brown, resinous exudate from the leaves, which is referred to as hashish or hash. The cannabis plant is usually cut, dried, chopped, and rolled into cigarettes (commonly called joints), which are then smoked. The common names for cannabis are marijuana, grass, pot, weed, tea, and Mary Jane. Other names, which describe cannabis types of various strengths, are hemp, chasra, bhang, ganja, dagga, and sinsemilla.

Recently, cannabis and its primary active component, Δ^9-THC, have been used successfully to treat nausea secondary to cancer treatment drugs and to stimulate appetite in patients with acquired immune deficiency syndrome (AIDS). Some less convincing reports concern the use of Δ^9-THC in the treatment of glaucoma. In 1996, referenda conducted in California and Arizona gave physicians the right to prescribe cannabis in the form of marijuana cigarettes for the treatment of a variety of diseases. The referendum was opposed by the American Medical Association and is being reviewed by federal courts.

EPIDEMIOLOGY

The following data for 1995 came from the Substance Abuse and Mental Health Services Administration:

In 1995, an estimated 9.8 million people in the United States were current (past month) marijuana or hashish users. This figure represents 4.7 percent of the population age 12 years and older. Marijuana is by far the most common drug used by illicit drug users; approximately three quarters (77 percent) of current illicit drug users were marijuana or hashish users in 1995. Trends and demographic differences are generally similar for any illicit drug use and marijuana-hashish use.

Between 1994 and 1995, the rate of marijuana use among adolescents ages 12 to 17 increased from 6.0 to 8.2 percent and continued a trend that began during 1992–1993. Since 1992, the rate of use among adolescents has more than doubled. Similar trends are evident among both boys and girls; among whites, blacks, and Hispanics; in all four geographic regions; and in metropolitan and nonmetropolitan areas.

Frequent use of marijuana, defined as use on at least 51 days during the past year, remained unchanged from 1994 to 1995 at just over 5 million users (5.3 million, 2.5 percent of the population in 1995), but frequency of use was significantly lower than in 1985, when there were an estimated 8.4 million frequent users (4.4 percent of the population).

NEUROPHARMACOLOGY

As stated previously, the principal component of cannabis is Δ^9-THC; however, the cannabis plant contains more than 400 chemicals, of which about 60 are chemically related to Δ^9-THC. In humans, Δ^9-THC is rapidly converted into 11-hydroxy-Δ^9-THC, the metabolite that is active in the central nervous system (CNS).

A specific receptor for the cannabinols has been identified, cloned, and characterized. The cannabinoid receptor, a member of the G protein-linked family of receptors, is linked to the inhibitory G protein (G_i), which is linked to adenylyl cyclase in an inhibitory fashion. The cannabinoid receptor is found in highest concentrations in the basal ganglia, the hippocampus, and the cerebellum, with lower concentrations in the cerebral cortex (Fig. 12.5–1). It is not found in the brainstem, a fact consistent with cannabis's minimal effects on respiratory and cardiac functions. Studies in animals have shown that the cannabinoids affect the monoamine and γ-aminobutyric acid (GABA) neurons.

According to most studies, animals do not self-administer cannabinoids as they do most other substances of abuse. Moreover, there is some debate about whether the cannabinoids stimulate the so-called reward centers of the brain, such as the dopaminergic neurons of the ventral tegmental area. Tolerance to cannabis, however, does develop, and psychological dependence has been found, although the evidence for physiological dependence is not strong. Withdrawal symptoms in humans are limited to modest increases in irritability, restlessness, insomnia, anorexia, and mild nausea; all these symptoms appear only when a person abruptly stops taking high doses of cannabis.

When cannabis is smoked, the euphoric effects appear within minutes, peak in about 30 minutes, and last 2 to 4 hours. Some motor and cognitive effects last 5 to 12 hours. Cannabis can also be taken orally when it is prepared in food, such as brownies and cakes. About two to three times as much cannabis must be taken orally to be as potent as cannabis taken by inhaling its smoke. Many variables affect the psychoactive properties of cannabis, including the potency of the cannabis used, the route of administration, the smoking technique, the effects of pyrolysis on the cannabinoid content, the dose, the setting, the user's past experience, the user's expectations, and the user's unique biological vulnerability to the effects of cannabinoids.

DIAGNOSIS AND CLINICAL FEATURES

The most common physical effects of cannabis are dilation of the conjunctival blood vessels (red eye) and a mild tachycardia. At high doses, orthostatic hypotension may appear. Increased appetite—often referred to as the munchies—and dry mouth are other common effects of cannabis intoxication. A reflection of the substance's lack of effect on the respiratory rate is the fact that there has never been a clearly documented case of death caused by cannabis intoxication alone. The most serious potential adverse effects of cannabis use are those caused by inhaling the same carcinogenic hydrocarbons present in conventional tobacco, and some data indicate that heavy cannabis users are at risk for chronic respiratory disease and

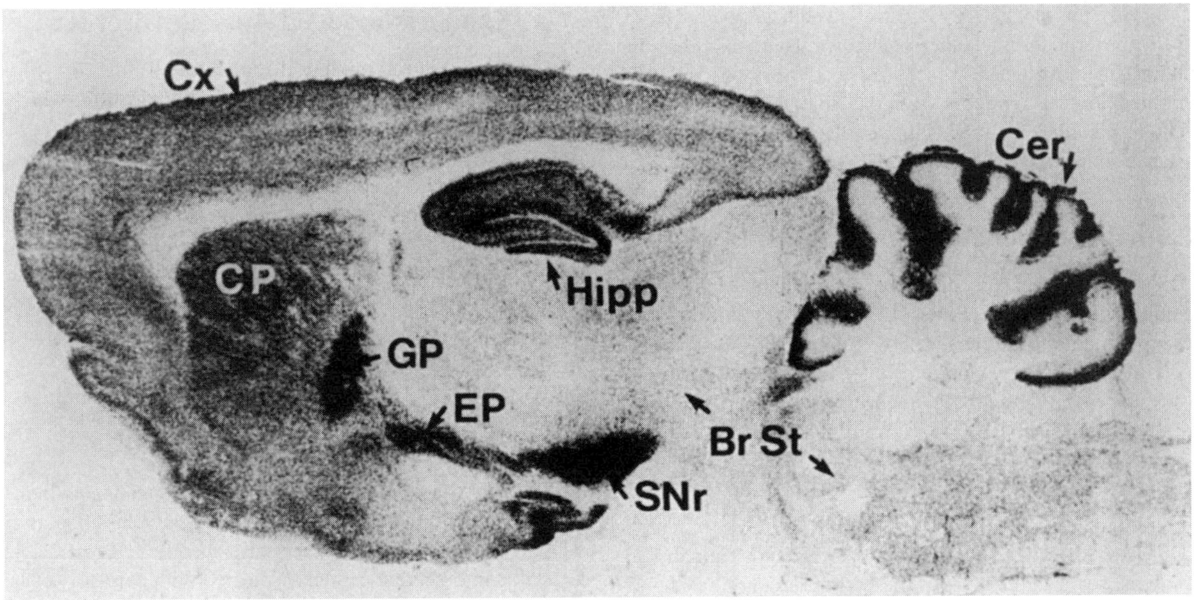
Cx
Cer
CP
Hipp
GP
EP
Br St
SNr

FIGURE 12.5–1
Autoradiography of cannabinoid receptor distribution in a sagittal section of rat brain. Binding of tritiated ligand is dense in the hippocampus *(Hipp)*, the globus pallidus *(GP)*, the entopeduncular nucleus *(EP)*, the substantia nigra pars reticulata *(SNr)*, and the cerebellum *(Cer)*. Binding is moderate in the cerebral cortex *(Cx)* and the caudate putamen *(CP)* and sparse in the brainstem *(Br St)* and spinal cord. (Reprinted with permission from Howlett AC, Bidaut-Russell M, DeVane WA, Melvin LS, Johnson MR, Herkenham M: The cannabinoid receptor: Biochemical anatomical, and behavioral characterization. Trends Neurosci *13:* 422, 1990.)

lung cancer. The practice of smoking cannabis-containing cigarettes to their very ends, so-called roaches, further increases the intake of tar (particulate matter). Many reports indicate that long-term cannabis use is associated with cerebral atrophy, seizure susceptibility, chromosomal damage, birth defects, impaired immune reactivity, alterations in testosterone concentrations, and dysregulation of menstrual cycles; these reports, however, have not been conclusively replicated, and the association between them and cannabis use is uncertain.

DSM-IV lists the cannabis-related disorders (Table 12.5–1) but has specific criteria within the cannabis-related disorders

Table 12.5–1
DSM-IV Cannabis-Related Disorders

Cannabis use disorders
Cannabis dependence
Cannabis abuse
Cannabis-induced disorders
Cannabis intoxication
Specify if:
With perceptual disturbances
Cannabis intoxication delirium
Cannabis-induced psychotic disorder, with delusions
Specify if:
With onset during intoxication
Cannabis-induced psychotic disorder, with hallucinations
Specify if:
With onset during intoxication
Cannabis-induced anxiety disorder
Specify if:
With onset during intoxication
Cannabis-related disorder not otherwise specified

Reprinted with permission from American Psychiatric Association: *Diagnostic and Statistical Manual of Mental Disorders,* ed 4. Copyright, American Psychiatric Association, Washington, 1994.

Table 12.5–2
DSM-IV Diagnostic Criteria for Cannabis Intoxication

A. Recent use of cannabis.
B. Clinically significant maladaptive behavioral or psychological changes (eg, impaired motor coordination, euphoria, anxiety, sensation of slowed time, impaired judgment, social withdrawal) that develop during, or shortly after, cannabis use.
C. Two (or more) of the following signs, developing within 2 hours of cannabis use:
(1) conjunctival injection
(2) increased appetite
(3) dry mouth
(4) tachycardia
D. The symptoms are not due to a general medical condition and are not better accounted for by another mental disorder.

Specify if:
With perceptual disturbances

Reprinted with permission from American Psychiatric Association: *Diagnostic and Statistical Manual of Mental Disorders,* ed 4. Copyright, American Psychiatric Association, Washington, 1994.

section only for cannabis intoxication (Table 12.5–2). The diagnostic criteria for the other cannabis-related disorders are contained in those DSM-IV sections that focus on the major phenomenological symptom—for example, cannabis-induced psychotic disorder, with delusions, in the DSM-IV section on substance-induced psychotic disorder (see Table 14.1–1).

Cannabis Dependence and Cannabis Abuse

DSM-IV includes the diagnoses of cannabis dependence and cannabis abuse (see Tables 12.1–7, 12.1–8, and 12.1–9). The experimental data clearly show tolerance to many of the effects of cannabis; the data, however, are less supportive of the presence of physical dependence. Psychological dependence on cannabis use does develop in long-term users.

Cannabis Intoxication

DSM-IV formalizes the diagnostic criteria for cannabis intoxication (see Table 12.5–2). These criteria state that the diagnosis can be augmented with the phrase "with perceptual disturbances." If intact reality testing is not present, the diagnosis is cannabis-induced psychotic disorder.

Cannabis intoxication commonly heightens users' sensitivities to external stimuli, reveals new details, makes colors seem brighter and richer than in the past, and subjectively slows the appreciation of time. In high doses, users may experience depersonalization and derealization. Motor skills are impaired by cannabis use, and the impairment in motor skills remains after the subjective, euphoriant effects have resolved. For 8 to 12 hours after using cannabis, users' impaired motor skills interfere with the operation of motor vehicles and other heavy machinery. Moreover, these effects are additive to those of alcohol, which is commonly used in combination with cannabis.

Cannabis Intoxication Delirium

Cannabis intoxication delirium is a DSM-IV diagnosis (see Table 10.2–3). The delirium associated with cannabis intoxication is characterized by marked impairment on cognition and performance tasks. Even modest doses of cannabis result in impairment in memory, reaction time, perception, motor coordination, and attention. High doses that also impair users' levels of consciousness have marked effects on cognitive measures.

Cannabis-Induced Psychotic Disorder

Cannabis-induced psychotic disorder (see Table 14.1–2) is diagnosed in the presence of a cannabis-induced psychosis. Cannabis-induced psychotic disorder is rare; transient paranoid ideation is more common. Florid psychosis is somewhat common in countries in which some people have long-term access to cannabis of a particularly high potency. The psychotic episodes are sometimes referred to as hemp insanity. Cannabis use rarely causes a bad-trip experience, which is often associated with hallucinogen intoxication. When cannabis-induced psychotic disorder does occur, it may be correlated with a preexisting personality disorder in the affected person.

Cannabis-Induced Anxiety Disorder

Cannabis-induced anxiety disorder (see Table 16.1–5) is a common diagnosis for acute cannabis intoxication, which in many people induces short-lived anxiety states often provoked by paranoid thoughts. In such circumstances, panic attacks may be induced, based on ill-defined and disorganized fears. The appearance of anxiety symptoms is correlated with the dose and is the most frequent adverse reaction to the moderate use of smoked cannabis. Inexperienced users are much more likely to experience anxiety symptoms than are experienced users.

Cannabis-Related Disorder Not Otherwise Specified

DSM-IV does not formally recognize cannabis-induced mood disorders; therefore, such disorders are classified as cannabis-related disorders not otherwise specified (Table 12.5–3). Cannabis intoxication can be associated with depressive symptoms, although such symptoms may suggest long-term cannabis use. Hypomania, however, is a common symptom in cannabis intoxication.

DSM-IV also does not formally recognize cannabis-induced sleep disorders or cannabis-induced sexual dysfunction; therefore, both are classified as cannabis-related disorders not otherwise specified. When either sleep disorder or sexual dysfunction symptoms are present and related to cannabis use, they almost always resolve within days or a week after cessation of cannabis use.

Flashbacks. Persisting perceptual abnormalities after cannabis use are not formally classified in DSM-IV, although there are case reports of people who have experienced—at times significantly—sensations related to cannabis intoxication after the short-term effects of the substance have disappeared. Continued debate concerns whether flashbacks are related to cannabis use alone or to the concomitant use of hallucinogens or of cannabis tainted with phencyclidine (PCP).

Amotivational Syndrome. Another controversial cannabis-related syndrome is amotivational syndrome. Whether the syndrome is related to cannabis use or reflects characterological traits in a subgroup of people regardless of cannabis

Table 12.5–3
DSM-IV Diagnostic Criteria for Cannabis-Related Disorder Not Otherwise Specified

The cannabis-related disorder not otherwise specified category is for disorders associated with the use of cannabis that are not classifiable as cannabis dependence, cannabis abuse, cannabis intoxication, cannabis intoxication delirium, cannabis-induced psychotic disorder, or cannabis-induced anxiety disorder.

use is under debate. Traditionally, the amotivational syndrome has been associated with long-term heavy use and has been characterized by people's unwillingness to persist in a task—be it at school, at work, or in any setting that requires prolonged attention or tenacity. People are described as becoming apathetic and anergic, usually gaining weight, and appearing slothful.

TREATMENT AND REHABILITATION

Treatment of cannabis use rests on the same principles as does treatment of other substances of abuse—abstinence and support. Abstinence can be achieved through direct interventions, such as hospitalization, or through careful monitoring on an outpatient basis by the use of urine drug screens, which can detect cannabis for up to 4 weeks after use. Support can be achieved through the use of individual, family, and group psychotherapies. Education should be a cornerstone for both abstinence and support programs. A patient who does not understand the intellectual reasons for addressing a substance-abuse problem has little motivation to stop. For some patients, an antianxiety drug may be useful for short-term relief of withdrawal symptoms. For other patients, cannabis use may be related to an underlying depressive disorder that may respond to specific antidepressant treatment.

THERAPEUTIC USE OF MARIJUANA

The use of marijuana to treat disease can be found in ancient Chinese medical texts dating to 2500 BC. In the 19th century, the drug was part of the U.S. pharmacopoeia and, until 1941, was prescribed legally as an analgesic, anticonvulsant, and muscle relaxant. George Beard thought it to be a useful treatment in certain cases of neuraesthenia. Recently, cannabis and its primary active component, Δ^9-THC, have been used successfully to treat nausea secondary to cancer treatment drugs, to stimulate appetite in patients with acquired immune deficiency syndrome (AIDS), and in the treatment of glaucoma.

Dronabinol contains the active ingredient in marijuana, is taken orally, and is available by prescription; however, it is not considered as effective as smoking marijuana, which produces a much more rapid blood level of the drug than the oral tablet.

In 1996, voters in Arizona and California approved referenda allowing physicians in those states to prescribe marijuana for the medical conditions mentioned above in addition to chronic pain. Shortly thereafter, President Clinton's Secretary of Health, Donna Shalala, and Attorney General Janet Reno announced that any doctor who prescribed the drug would be prosecuted for a Federal crime and could lose their license. The *New England Journal of Medicine* in a strongly worded 1997 editorial urged that "Federal authorities should rescind their prohibition of the medical use of marijuana for seriously ill patients and allow physicians to decide which patients to treat." They concluded the editorial commenting on the role of the physician:

> Some physicians will have the courage to challenge the continued proscription of marijuana for the sick. Eventually, their actions will force the courts to adjudicate between the rights of those at death's door and the absolute power of bureaucrats whose decisions are based more on reflexive ideology and political correctness than on compassion.

REFERENCES

Abood ME, Martin BR: Neurobiology of marijuana abuse. Trends Pharmacol Sci *13:* 201, 1992.

Bailey SL, Flewelling RL, Rachal JV: Predicting continued use of marijuana among adolescents: The relative influence of drug-specific and social context factors. J Health Soc Behav *33:* 51, 1992.

Chait LD, Zacny JP: Reinforcing and subjective effects of oral delta 9-THC and smoked marijuana in humans. Psychopharmacology *107:* 255, 1992.

Chaudry HR, Moss HB, Bashir A, Suliman T: Cannabis psychosis following bhang ingestion. Br J Addict *86:* 1075, 1991.

Friedman H, Klein TW, Newton C, Daaka Y: Marijuana, receptors and immunomodulation. Adv Exp Med Biol *373:* 103, 1995.

Gardner EL, Lowinson JH: Marijuana's interaction with brain reward systems: Update 1991. Pharmacol Biochem Behav *40:* 571, 1991.

Hammer T, Vaglum P: Users and nonusers within a high risk milieu of cannabis use: A general population study. Int J Addict *26:* 595, 1991.

Heishman SJ, Huestis MA, Henningfield JE, Cone EJ: Acute and residual effects of marijuana: Profiles of plasma THC levels: Physiological, subjective, and performance measures. Pharmacol Biochem Behav *37:* 561, 1990.

Howlett AC, Bidaut-Russell M, DeVane WA, Melvin LS, Johnson MR, Herkenham M: The cannabinoid receptor: Biochemical, anatomical, and behavioral characterization. Trends Neurosci *13:* 420, 1990.

Imade AG, Ebie JC: A retrospective study of symptom patterns of cannabis-induced psychosis. Acta Psychiatr Scand *83:* 134, 1991.

Kassirer JP: Editorial: Federal foolishness and marijuana. N Engl J Med *5:* 336, 1997.

Munro S, Thomas KL, Abu-Shaar M: Molecular characterization of a peripheral receptor for cannabinoids. Nature *365:* 61, 1993.

Nahas G, Latour C: The human toxicity of marijuana. Med J Aust *156:* 495, 1992.

National Institute on Drug Abuse: *National Household Survey on Drug Abuse: Highlights, 1991.* US Government Printing Office, Washington, 1991.

Perez-Reyes M, White WR, McDonald SA, Hicks RE, Jeffcoat AR, Cook CE: The pharmacologic effects of daily marijuana smoking in humans. Pharmacol Biochem Behav *40:* 691, 1991.

Schwartz RH, Lewis DC, Hoffman NG, Kyriazi N: Cocaine and marijuana use by medical students before and during medical school. Arch Intern Med *150:* 883, 1990.

Stacy AW, Newcomb MD, Bentler PM: Cognitive motivation and drug use: A 9-year longitudinal study. J Abnorm Psychol *100:* 502, 1991.

Stenbacka M, Allebeck P, Romelsjo A: Do cannabis drug abusers differ from intravenous drug abusers? The role of social and behavioral risk factors. Br J Addict *87:* 259, 1992.

Substance Abuse and Mental Health Services Administration Office of Applied Studies: *Preliminary Estimates from the 1995 National Household Survey on Drug Abuse.* US Government Printing Office, Washington, 1995.

Tashkin DP, Gliederer F, Rose J, Chang P, Hui KK, Yu JL, Wu TC: Tar, CO and delta 9 THC delivery from the 1st to 2nd halves of a marijuana cigarette. Pharmacol Biochem Behav *40:* 657, 1991.

Vulcano BA, Barnes GE, Langstaff P: Predicting marijuana use among adolescents. Int J Addict *25:* 531, 1990.

Woody GE, MacFadden W: Cannabis-related disorders. In *Comprehensive Textbook of Psychiatry,* ed 6, HI Kaplan, BJ Sadock, editors, p 810. Williams & Wilkins, Baltimore, 1995.

▲ 12.6 Cocaine-Related Disorders

Cocaine is one of the most addictive of commonly abused substances and one of the most dangerous. Cocaine—variously referred to as snow, coke, girl, and lady—is a white powder that is inhaled; in its most potent forms, freebase and crack (crack cocaine), it is smoked, and the substance can be injected as well. It is an alkaloid derived from the shrub *Erythroxylon coca,* which is indigenous to South America where the leaves of the shrub are chewed by local inhabitants to obtain the stimulating effects. The cocaine alkaloid was first isolated in 1860 and first used as a local anesthetic in 1880. It is still used as a local anesthetic, especially for eye, nose, and throat surgery, for which its vasoconstrictive effects are helpful. In 1884, Sigmund Freud made a study of cocaine's general pharmacological effects. In the 1880s and 1890s, cocaine was widely touted as a cure for many ills. In 1914, however, cocaine was classified as a narcotic, along with morphine and heroin, once its addictive and adverse effects had been recognized.

EPIDEMIOLOGY

About 1.9 million people in the United States, including 1.9 percent of high school seniors, have used cocaine within the past month. Current cocaine use, however, is on the decline. This decrease in cocaine use in the United States is primarily due to increased awareness of cocaine's risks, as well as a comprehensive public campaign about cocaine and its effects. The societal effects of the decrease in cocaine use, however, have been somewhat offset by the frequent use over the past years of crack, a highly potent form of cocaine. Crack use is most common in people ages 18 to 25, who are particularly attracted to the low street price of a single 50 to 100 mg dose, usually around $10. Cocaine generally sells for around $100 to $150 for each 1 gram vial.

In 1995, an estimated 1.5 million people in the United States were current cocaine users. This figure represents 0.7 percent of the population age 12 and older. The number of cocaine users did not change between 1994 and 1995 (1.4 million in 1994). The number had declined from 5.7 million in 1985 (3.0 percent of the population) to 1.4 million (0.7 percent of the population) in 1992.

An estimated 582,000 people (0.3 percent of the population) were frequent cocaine users in 1995. Frequent use, defined as use on 51 or more days during the past year, was not significantly different from 1994, when there were an estimated 634,000 frequent cocaine users. Since this measure of frequent cocaine use was first estimated in 1985, no significant increases or decreases have been detected. It should be noted that these estimates are subject to large sampling error and potentially large nonsampling error.

The estimated number of occasional cocaine users (people who used in the past year but on fewer than 12 days) was 2.5 million in 1995, similar to what it had been in 1994. The number of users was down significantly from 1985, when it was 7.1 million. The estimated number of current crack users was about 400,000 in 1995, and there have been no statistically significant changes since 1988.

As in the past, the rate of current cocaine use in 1995 was highest among people ages 18 to 25 years (1.3 percent) and ages 26 to 34 years (1.2 percent). Rates were 0.8 percent for ages 12 to 17 years and 0.4 percent for adults age 35 years and older. Except for adolescents, all these rates were similar to rates in 1994. The past month cocaine use prevalence rate for the 12- to 17-year age group increased from 0.3 percent in 1994 to 0.8 percent in 1995. Before 1994, the rate among adolescents had declined from 1.9 percent in 1982.

The annual number of new cocaine users remained stable from 1990 to 1994, but at a lower level than during the early 1980s. In 1994, an estimated 530,000 were new users, and during 1980 to 1984, there had been about 1.3 million cocaine initiates per year. The rate of initiation by different age groups, however, has been changing. With the age group 18 to 25 showing a decrease in the rate of first use from 1980 to 1994, the rate of first use for this group is now similar to that for the 12 to 17 age group (about 10 per 1,000 person years). For crack cocaine, the estimated annual number of new users has remained stable in recent years.

NEUROPHARMACOLOGY

Cocaine's primary pharmacodynamic action that is related to its behavioral effects is competitive blockade of dopamine reuptake by the dopamine transporter. This blockade increases the concentration of dopamine in the synaptic cleft and results in increased activation of both dopamine type 1 (D_1) and dopamine type 2 (D_2) receptors. The effects of cocaine on the activity mediated by D_3, D_4, and D_5 receptors is not yet well understood, but at least one preclinical study has implicated the D_3 receptor. Although the behavioral effects are thought to be mediated primarily by the blockade of dopamine reuptake, cocaine also blocks the reuptake of the other major catecholamine, norepinephrine, and the reuptake of serotonin. The behavioral effects related to these activities are receiving increased attention in the scientific literature. The effects of cocaine on cerebral blood flow and cerebral glucose use have also been studied. In most studies, results generally showed that cocaine is associated with decreased cerebral blood flow and possibly with the development of patchy areas of decreased glucose use.

The behavioral effects of cocaine are felt almost immediately and last for a relatively brief time (30 to 60 minutes); thus, users require repeated doses of the drug to maintain the feelings of intoxication. Despite the short-lived behavioral effects, metabolites of cocaine may be present in the blood and urine for up to 10 days.

Cocaine has powerful addictive qualities. Because of its potency as a positive reinforcer of behavior, a psychological dependence on cocaine can develop after a single use. With repeated administration, both tolerance and sensitivity to various effects of cocaine can arise, although the development of tolerance or sensitivity is apparently due to many factors and is not easily predicted. Physiological dependence on cocaine does occur, although cocaine withdrawal is mild compared with the effects of withdrawal from opiates and opioids.

Researchers recently reported that positron emission tomography (PET) scans of the brains of patients being treated for cocaine addiction show high activation in the mesolimbic dopamine system when addicts profoundly crave a drug. Researchers exposed patients to cues that had previously caused them to crave cocaine, and patients described feelings of intense cravings for the drug while PET scans showed activation in areas from the amygdala and the anterior cingulate to the tip of both temporal lobes. Some researchers claim that the mesolimbic dopamine system is also active in cases of nicotine addiction, and the same system has been linked to cravings for heroin, morphine, amphetamines, marijuana, and alcohol.

D_2 receptors in the mesolimbic dopamine system have been

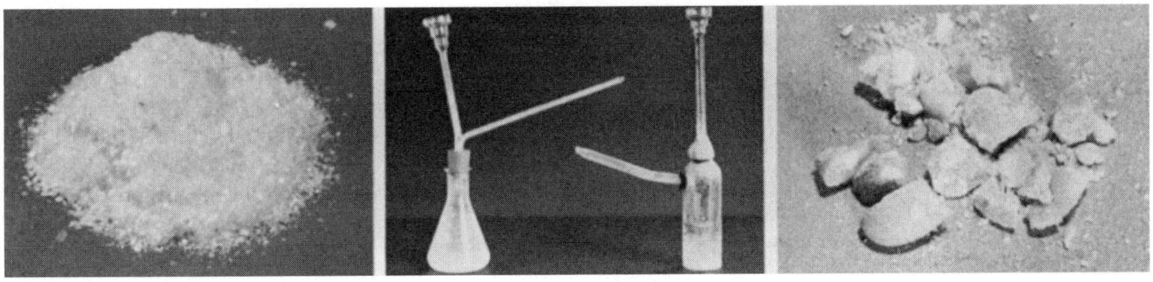

FIGURE 12.6–1
Pure cocaine *(left)* and typical freebasing pipes *(middle)* used to synthesize crack *(right)*. (Reprinted with permission from Woolverton WL, Johnson KM: Neurobiology of cocaine abuse. Trends Pharmacol Sci *13:* 194, 1992.)

held responsible for the heightened activity during periods of craving. PET scans of patients recovering from cocaine addiction are reported to show a drop in neuronal activity consistent with a lessened ability to receive dopamine, and the reduction in this ability, although it decreases over time, is apparent as long as a year and a half after withdrawal. The pattern of reduced brain activity reflects the course of the craving; between the third and fourth weeks of withdrawal, the activity is at its lowest level, and the risk of patient relapse is highest. After about 1 year, the brains of former addicts are almost back to normal, although whether the dopamine cells ever return to a completely normal state is debatable.

Table 12.6–1
DSM-IV Cocaine Use Disorders

Cocaine use disorders
Cocaine dependence
Cocaine abuse
Cocaine-induced disorders
Cocaine intoxication
Specify if:
With perceptual disturbances
Cocaine withdrawal
Cocaine intoxication delirium
Cocaine-induced psychotic disorder, with delusions
Specify if:
With onset during intoxication
Cocaine-induced psychotic disorder, with hallucinations
Specify if:
With onset during intoxication
Cocaine-induced mood disorder
Specify if:
With onset during intoxication
With onset during withdrawal
Cocaine-induced anxiety disorder
Specify if:
With onset during intoxication
With onset during withdrawal
Cocaine-induced sexual dysfunction
Specify if:
With onset during intoxication
Cocaine-induced sleep disorder
Specify if:
With onset during intoxication
With onset during withdrawal
Cocaine-related disorder not otherwise specified

Reprinted with permission from American Psychiatric Association: *Diagnostic and Statistical Manual of Mental Disorders,* ed 4. Copyright, American Psychiatric Association, Washington, 1994.

METHODS OF USE

Because drug dealers often dilute cocaine powder with sugar or procaine, street cocaine varies greatly in purity (Fig. 12.6–1). Cocaine is sometimes cut with amphetamine. The most common method of using cocaine is inhaling the finely chopped powder into the nose, a practice referred to as snorting or tooting. Other methods of ingesting cocaine are subcutaneous or intravenous (IV) injection and smoking (freebasing). Freebasing involves mixing street cocaine with chemically extracted pure cocaine alkaloid (the freebase) to get an increased effect. Smoking is also the method used for ingesting crack cocaine. Inhaling is the least dangerous method of cocaine use; IV injection and smoking are the most dangerous. The most direct methods of ingestion are often associated with cerebrovascular diseases, cardiac abnormalities, and death. Although cocaine can be taken orally, it is rarely ingested via this the least effective route.

Crack

Crack, a freebase form of cocaine, is extremely potent. It is sold in small, ready-to-smoke amounts, often called rocks (Fig. 12.6–1). Crack cocaine is highly addictive; even one or two experiences with the drug can cause intense craving for more. Users have been known to resort to extremes of behavior to obtain the money to buy more crack. Anecdotal reports from urban emergency rooms have also associated extremes of violence with crack abuse.

DIAGNOSIS AND CLINICAL FEATURES

The fourth edition of *Diagnostic and Statistical Manual of Mental Disorders* (DSM-IV) lists many cocaine use disorders (Table 12.6–1) but specifies the diagnostic criteria for only cocaine intoxication (Table 12.6–2) and cocaine withdrawal (Table 12.6–3) within the cocaine-related disorders section. The diagnostic criteria for the other cocaine-related disorders

Table 12.6–2
DSM-IV Diagnostic Criteria for Cocaine Intoxication

A. Recent use of cocaine.
B. Clinically significant maladaptive behavioral or psychological changes (eg, euphoria or affective blunting; changes in sociability; hypervigilance; interpersonal sensitivity; anxiety, tension, or anger; stereotyped behaviors; impaired judgment; or impaired social or occupational functioning) that developed during, or shortly after, use of cocaine.
C. Two (or more) of the following, developing during, or shortly after, cocaine use:
(1) tachycardia or bradycardia
(2) pupillary dilation
(3) elevated or lowered blood pressure
(4) perspiration or chills
(5) nausea or vomiting
(6) evidence of weight loss
(7) psychomotor agitation or retardation
(8) muscular weakness, respiratory depression, chest pain, or cardiac arrhythmias
(9) confusion, seizures, dyskinesias, dystonias, or coma
D. The symptoms are not due to a general medical condition and not better accounted for by another mental disorder.

Specify if:
With perceptual disturbances

Reprinted with permission from American Psychiatric Association: *Diagnostic and Statistical Manual of Mental Disorders,* ed 4. Copyright, American Psychiatric Association, Washington, 1994.

are in the DSM-IV sections that focus on the principal symptom—for example, cocaine-induced mood disorder in the mood disorders section (see Table 15.1–11).

DSM-IV uses the general guidelines for substance dependence and substance abuse to diagnose cocaine dependence and cocaine abuse (see Tables 12.1–7, 12.1–8, and 12.1–9). Clinically and practically, cocaine dependence or cocaine abuse can be suspected in patients who evidence unexplained changes in personality. Common changes associated with cocaine use are irritability, impaired ability to concentrate, compulsive behavior, severe insomnia, and weight loss. Colleagues at work and family members may notice a person's general and increasing inability to perform the expected tasks associated with work and family life. The patient may show new evidence of increased debt or inability to pay bills on time because of the large sums used to buy cocaine. Cocaine abusers often excuse themselves from work or social situations every 30 to 60 minutes to find a secluded place to inhale more cocaine. Because of the vasoconstricting effects of cocaine, users almost always develop nasal congestion, which they may attempt to self-medicate with decongestant sprays.

Comorbidity

As with other substance-related disorders, cocaine-related disorders are often accompanied by additional psychiatric disorders. The development of mood disorders and alcohol-related disorders usually follows the onset of cocaine-related disorders, whereas anxiety disorders, antisocial personality disorder, and attention-deficit/hyperactivity disorder are thought to precede the development of cocaine-related disorders. Most studies of comorbidity in patients with cocaine-related disorders have shown that major depressive disorder, bipolar II disorder, cyclothymic disorder, anxiety disorders, and antisocial personality disorder are the most commonly associated psychiatric diagnoses. The percentages of comorbidity in one study of 298 cocaine users who sought treatment are presented in Table 12.6–4.

Adverse Effects

A common adverse effect associated with cocaine use is nasal congestion, although serious inflammation, swelling, bleeding, and ulceration of the nasal mucosa can also occur. Long-term use of cocaine can also lead to perforation of the nasal septa. Freebasing and smoking crack can cause damage to the bronchial passages and the lungs. The IV use of cocaine can result in infection, embolisms, and the transmission of human immunodeficiency virus (HIV). Minor neurological complications with cocaine use include the development of acute dystonia, tics, and migrainelike headaches. The major complications of cocaine use, however, are its cerebrovascular, epileptic, and cardiac effects. About two thirds of these acute toxic effects occur within 1 hour of intoxication; about one fifth occur in 1 to 3 hours, and the remainder occur up to several days later.

Cerebrovascular Effects. The most common cerebrovascular diseases associated with cocaine use are nonhemorrhagic cerebral infarctions. When hemorrhagic infarctions do occur, they can include subarachnoid hemorrhages, intraparenchymal hemorrhages, and intraventricular hemorrhages. Transient ischemic attacks have also been associated with cocaine use. Although these vascular disorders usually affect the brain, spinal cord hemorrhages have also been reported. The

Table 12.6–3
DSM-IV Diagnostic Criteria for Cocaine Withdrawal

A. Cessation of (or reduction in) cocaine use that has been heavy and prolonged.
B. Dysphoric mood and two (or more) of the following physiological changes, developing within a few hours to several days after criterion A:
(1) fatigue
(2) vivid, unpleasant dreams
(3) insomnia or hypersomnia
(4) increased appetite
(5) psychomotor retardation or agitation
C. The symptoms in criterion B cause clinically significant distress or impairment in social, occupational, or other important areas of functioning.
D. The symptoms are not due to a general medical condition and are not better accounted for by another mental disorder.

Reprinted with permission from American Psychiatric Association: *Diagnostic and Statistical Manual of Mental Disorders,* ed 4. Copyright, American Psychiatric Association, Washington, 1994.

Table 12.6–4
Current and Lifetime Rates of Psychiatric Disorders (Research Diagnostic Criteria) in Treatment-Seeking Cocaine Abusers

	Number (%)	
Characteristic	**Current**	**Lifetime**
Total	298 (100.0)	298 (100.0)
Any psychiatric disorder (excluding drug disorders, alcoholism, or childhood disorders)	166 (55.7)	221 (73.5)
Affective disorders		
Major depression	14 (4.7)	91 (30.5)
Minor depression	2 (0.7)	35 (11.7)
Intermittent depressive personality	33 (11.1)	33 (11.1)
Chronic depressive personality	22 (7.4)	22 (7.4)
Intermittent hyperthymic personality	27 (9.1)	21 (9.1)
Chronic hyperthymic personality	21 (7.1)	21 (7.1)
Intermittent cyclothymic personality	8 (2.7)	8 (2.7)
Chronic cyclothymic personality	3 (1.0)	3 (1.0)
Mania	0 (0.0)	11 (3.7)
Hypomania	6 (2.0)	22 (7.4)
Any affective disorder	132 (44.3)	181 (60.7)
Anxiety disorders		
Panic	1 (0.3)	5 (1.7)
Generalized anxiety	11 (3.7)	21 (7.0)
Generalized anxiety with depression	3 (1.0)	4 (1.3)
Obsessive-compulsive disorder	1 (0.3)	1 (0.3)
Phobia	35 (11.7)	40 (13.4)
Any anxiety disorder	47 (15.8)	62 (20.8)
Schizophrenic disorders		
Schizophrenia	0 (0.0)	1 (0.3)
Schizoaffective, depressed	1 (0.3)	2 (0.7)
Schizoaffective, manic	0 (0.0)	1 (0.3)
Alcoholism (Research Diagnostic Criteria)	86 (28.9)	184 (61.7)
Personality disorders		
Antisocial personality	23 (7.7)	23 (7.7)
Briquet's syndrome	0 (0.0)	0 (0.0)
Childhood disorders		
Attention-deficit disorder	0 (0.0)	104 (34.9)
Gambling disorder	7 (2.3)	44 (14.8)
Suicide gestures or attempts	—	67 (22.5)

Reprinted with permission from Rounsaville BJ, Anton SF, Carroll K, Budde D, Prusoff BA, Gawin F: Psychiatric diagnoses of treatment-seeking cocaine abusers. Arch Gen Psychiatry *48:* 45, 1991.

obvious pathophysiological mechanism for these vascular disorders is vasoconstriction, but other pathophysiological mechanisms have also been proposed.

Seizures. Seizures have been reported to account for 3 to 8 percent of cocaine-related emergency room visits. Cocaine is the substance of abuse most commonly associated with seizures; the second most common substance is amphetamine. Cocaine-induced seizures are usually single events, although multiple seizures and status epilepticus are also possible. A rare and easily misdiagnosed complication of cocaine use is partial complex status epilepticus, which should be considered as a diagnosis in a patient who seems to have cocaine-induced psychotic disorder with an unusually fluctuating course. The risk of having cocaine-induced seizures is highest in patients with a history of epilepsy who use high doses of cocaine as well as crack.

Cardiac Effects. Myocardial infarctions and arrhythmias are perhaps the most common cocaine-induced cardiac abnormalities. Cardiomyopathies can develop with long-term use of cocaine, and cardioembolic cerebral infarctions can be a further complication of cocaine-induced myocardial dysfunction.

Death. High doses of cocaine are associated with seizures, respiratory depression, cerebrovascular diseases, and myocardial infarctions—all of which can lead to death in people who use cocaine. Users may experience warning signs of syncope or chest pain but may ignore these signs because of the irrepressible desire to take more cocaine. Deaths have also been reported with the ingestion of speedballs, which are combinations of opioids and cocaine.

Cocaine Intoxication

DSM-IV specifies the diagnostic criteria for cocaine intoxication (Table 12.6–2) and emphasizes the behavioral and physical signs and symptoms of cocaine use. The DSM-IV diagnostic criteria allow for the specification of the presence of perceptual disturbances. If hallucinations are present in the absence of intact reality testing, the appropriate diagnosis is cocaine-induced psychotic disorder, with hallucinations.

People use cocaine for its characteristic effects of elation, euphoria, heightened self-esteem, and perceived improvement on mental and physical tasks. Some studies have indicated that low doses of cocaine can actually be associated with improved performance on some cognitive tasks. With high doses, however, the symptoms of intoxication include agitation, irritability, impaired judgment, impulsive and potentially dangerous sexual behavior, aggression, a generalized increase in psychomotor activity, and, potentially, symptoms of mania. The major associated physical symptoms are tachycardia, hypertension, and mydriasis.

Cocaine Withdrawal

After cessation of cocaine use or after acute intoxication, postintoxication depression (crash) may be associated with symptoms of dysphoria, anhedonia, anxiety, irritability, fatigue, hypersomnolence, and sometimes agitation. With mild to moderate cocaine use, these withdrawal symptoms end within 18 hours. With heavy use, like that of cocaine dependence, withdrawal symptoms can last up to a week (Fig. 12.6–2) but usually peak in 2 to 4 days. Some patients as well as anecdotal reports have described cocaine withdrawal syn-

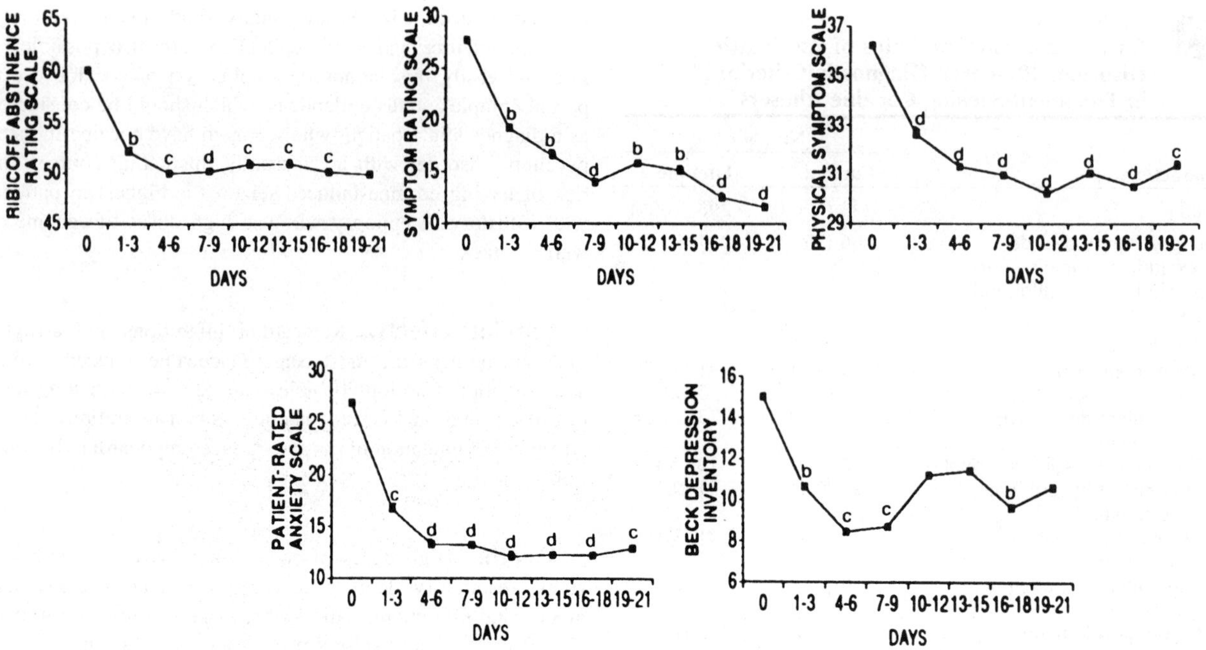
RIBICOFF ABSTINENCE RATING SCALE
SYMPTOM RATING SCALE
PHYSICAL SYMPTOM SCALE
PATIENT-RATED ANXIETY SCALE
BECK DEPRESSION INVENTORY
0 1-3 4-6 7-9 10-12 13-15 16-18 19-21
DAYS

FIGURE 12.6–2

Mean symptom scores of 22 cocaine-dependent patients during the initial 3 weeks of abstinence. The ranges of possible scores were as follows: Ribicoff Abstinence Rating Scale, 41–205; Symptom Rating Scale, 0–72; Physical Symptom Scale, 27–108; Patient-Rated Anxiety Scale, 0–144; Beck Depression Inventory, 0–63. The *p* values are based on paired *t* tests, time point versus baseline: *b–p* 0.05, *c–p* 0.005, *d–p* 0.001. (Reprinted with permission from Satel SL, Price LH, Palumbo JM, McDougle CJ, Krystal JH, Gawin F, Charney DS, Heninger GR, Kleber HD: Clinical phenomenology and neurobiology of cocaine abstinence: A prospective inpatient study. Am J Psychiatry *148:* 1714, 1991.)

dromes that have lasted for weeks or months. The withdrawal symptoms can also be associated with suicidal ideation in affected people. A person in the state of withdrawal can experience powerful and intense cravings for cocaine, especially because taking cocaine can eliminate the unpleasant withdrawal symptoms. People experiencing cocaine withdrawal often attempt to self-medicate with alcohol, sedatives, hypnotics, or antianxiety agents such as diazepam (Valium). DSM-IV has formalized the diagnostic criteria for cocaine withdrawal (Table 12.6–3).

Cocaine Intoxication Delirium

DSM-IV has specified a diagnosis for cocaine intoxication delirium (see Table 10.2–3). Cocaine intoxication delirium is most common when high doses of cocaine are used; when cocaine has been used over a short time, so that cocaine blood concentrations rapidly increase; or when cocaine is mixed with other psychoactive substances (such as amphetamine, opiates, opioids, and alcohol). People with preexisting brain damage (often resulting from previous episodes of cocaine intoxication) are also at increased risk for cocaine intoxication delirium.

Cocaine-Induced Psychotic Disorder

Paranoid delusions and hallucinations may occur in as many as 50 percent of all persons who use cocaine. The occurrence of these psychotic symptoms depends on the dose, the duration of use, and the individual user's sensitivity to the substance. Cocaine-induced psychotic disorders are most common with IV users and crack users. Men are much more likely to have psychotic symptoms than are women. Paranoid delusions are the most frequent psychotic symptoms. Auditory hallucinations are also common, but visual and tactile hallucinations may be less common than are paranoid delusions. The sensation of bugs crawling just beneath the skin (formication) has been reported to be associated with cocaine use. The development of psychotic disorders can occur with grossly inappropriate sexual and generally bizarre behavior and homicidal or other violent actions related to the content of the paranoid delusions or hallucinations. The DSM-IV diagnostic criteria of cocaine-induced psychotic disorders are listed in Table 14.1–2. Clinicians can further specify whether delusions or hallucinations are the predominant symptoms.

Cocaine-Induced Mood Disorder

DSM-IV allows for the diagnosis of cocaine-induced mood disorder (see Table 15.1–11), which can begin during either intoxication or withdrawal. Classically, the mood disorder symptoms associated with intoxication are hypomanic or manic; the mood disorder symptoms associated with withdrawal are characteristic of depression.

Cocaine-Induced Anxiety Disorder

DSM-IV also allows for the diagnosis of cocaine-induced anxiety disorder (see Table 16.1–5). Common anxiety disorder symptoms associated with cocaine intoxication or withdrawal are those of obsessive-compulsive disorder, panic disorders, and phobias.

Cocaine-Induced Sexual Dysfunction

DSM-IV allows for the diagnosis of cocaine-induced sexual dysfunction (see Table 21.2–17), which can begin when a person is intoxicated with cocaine. Although cocaine is used as an aphrodisiac and as a way to delay orgasm, its repeated use can result in impotence.

Cocaine-Induced Sleep Disorder

Cocaine-induced sleep disorder, which can begin during either intoxication or withdrawal, is described under the heading of substance-induced sleep disorder (see Table 24.2–21). Cocaine intoxication is associated with the inability to sleep; cocaine withdrawal is associated with disrupted sleep or hypersomnolence.

Cocaine-Related Disorder Not Otherwise Specified

DSM-IV provides a diagnosis of cocaine-related disorder not otherwise specified for cocaine-related disorders that cannot be classified into one of the previously discussed diagnoses (Table 12.6–5).

Table 12.6–5
DSM-IV Diagnostic Criteria for Cocaine-Related Disorder Not Otherwise Specified

The cocaine-related disorder not otherwise specified category is for disorders associated with the use of cocaine that are not classifiable as cocaine dependence, cocaine abuse, cocaine intoxication, cocaine withdrawal, cocaine intoxication delirium, cocaine-induced psychotic disorder, cocaine-induced mood disorder, cocaine-induced anxiety disorder, cocaine-induced sexual dysfunction, or cocaine-induced sleep disorder.

TREATMENT AND REHABILITATION

Many cocaine users do not come to treatment voluntarily. Their experience with the substance is too positive, and the negative effects are perceived as too minimal, to warrant seeking treatment. One study of cocaine users who sought treatment compared with those who did not seek treatment found that those who did not seek treatment more often had polysubstance-related disorder, fewer negative consequences associated with cocaine use, fewer work-related or family-related obligations, and increased contact with the legal system and with illegal activities.

The major hurdle to overcome in the treatment of cocaine-related disorders is the user's intense craving for the drug. Although animal studies have shown that cocaine is a powerful inducer of self-administration, these studies have also shown that animals limit their use of cocaine when negative reinforcers are experimentally linked to the cocaine intake. In humans, negative reinforcers may take the form of work and family-related problems brought on by cocaine use. Therefore, clinicians must take a broad treatment approach and include social, psychological, and perhaps biological strategies in the treatment program.

To attain abstinence from cocaine in their patients, clinicians may have to institute complete or partial hospitalization to remove patients from the usual social settings in which they had obtained or used cocaine. Frequent and unscheduled urine testing is almost always necessary to monitor patients' continued abstinence, especially in the first weeks and months of treatment. Relapse prevention therapy (RPT) is a therapy that relies on cognitive and behavioral techniques in addition to hospitalization and outpatient therapy to achieve the goal of abstinence.

Psychological intervention usually involves individual, group, and family modalities. In individual therapy, therapists should focus on the dynamics leading to cocaine use, the perceived positive effects of the cocaine, and other ways for achieving these effects. Group therapy and support groups, such as Narcotics Anonymous, often focus on discussions with other people who use cocaine and on sharing past experiences and effective coping methods. Family therapy is often an essential component of the treatment strategy. Common issues discussed in family therapy are the ways the patient's past behavior has harmed the family and the responses of family members to these behaviors. Therapy should also focus, however, on the future and on changes in the family's activities that may help the patient stay off the drug and direct energies in different directions. This approach can be used on an outpatient basis.

A variety of pharmacological strategies have been used to help people who use cocaine to resist the urge to take it. The two most successful classes of drugs are the dopaminergic agonists and some of the tricyclic drugs. Commonly used dopaminergic agonists are amantadine (Symmetrel), 100 mg twice daily, and bromocriptine (Parlodel), 2.5 mg twice daily. Both agents have been reported to reduce patients' craving, to increase energy, and to normalize sleep. Bupropion (Wellbutrin) has also been used with variable outcome. Carbamazepine (Tegretol) has also been used as a pharmacological approach to cocaine detoxification.

Further pharmacotherapy of cocaine-related disorders may involve the immune system. Researchers have developed a cocainelike compound that produces cocaine antibodies in rats. These antibodies block the stimulant and the adverse effects of cocaine. Whether immunotherapy reduces the dependence potential of cocaine, however, is unknown.

Sympathomimetics, such as methylphenidate (Ritalin), have been used to withdraw patients from cocaine. In patients with adult residual attention-deficit/hyperactivity disorder, psychostimulants may be useful.

References

Brady KT, Lydiard RB, Malcolm R, Ballenger JC: Cocaine-induced psychosis. J Clin Psychiatry *52:* 509, 1991.

Burke WM, Ravi NV, Dhopesh V, Vandegrift B, Maany I: Prolonged presence of metabolite in urine after compulsive cocaine use. J Clin Psychiatry *51:* 145, 1990.

Caine SB, Koob GF: Modulation of cocaine self-administration in the rat through D-3 dopamine receptors. Science *260:* 1814, 1993.

Carrera MRA, Ashley JA, Parsons LH, Wirsching P, Koob GF, Janda KD: Suppression of psychoactive effects of cocaine by active immunization. Nature *378:* 727, 1995.

Carroll KM, Rounsaville BJ: Contrast of treatment-seeking and untreated cocaine abusers. Arch Gen Psychiatry *49:* 464, 1992.

Crosby RD, Pearson VL, Eller C, Winegarden T, Graves NL: Phenytoin in the treatment of cocaine abuse: A double-blind study. Clin Pharmacol Ther *59:* 458, 1996.

Gallanter M, Egelko S, De Leon G, Rohrs C, Franco H: Crack-cocaine abusers in the general hospital: Assessment and initiation of care. Am J Psychiatry *149:* 810, 1992.

Gawin FH: Cocaine addiction: Psychology and neurophysiology. Science *251:* 1580, 1991.

Higgins ST, Budney AJ, Bickel WK, Hughes JR, Foerg F, Badger G: Achieving cocaine abstinence with a behavioral approach. Am J Psychiatry *150:* 763, 1993.

Jaffe JH: Cocaine-related disorders. In *Comprehensive Textbook of Psychiatry,* ed 6, HI Kaplan, BJ Sadock, editors, p 817. Williams & Wilkins, Baltimore, 1995.

Kang S-Y, Kleinman PH, Woody GE, Millman RB, Todd TC, Kemp J, Lipton DS: Outcomes for cocaine abusers after once-a-week psychosocial therapy. Am J Psychiatry *148:* 630, 1991.

McKelway R, Vieweg V, Westerman P: Sudden death from acute cocaine intoxication in Virginia in 1988. Am J Psychiatry *147:* 1667, 1990.

National Institute on Drug Abuse: *National Household Survey on Drug Abuse: Highlights, 1991.* US Government Printing Office, Washington, 1991.

Rounsaville BJ, Anton SF, Carroll K, Budde D, Prusoff BA, Gawin F: Psychiatric diagnoses of treatment-seeking cocaine abusers. Arch Gen Psychiatry *48:* 43, 1991.

Satel SL, Price LH, Palumbo JM, McDougle CJ, Krystal JH, Gawin F, Charney DS, Heninger GR, Kleber HD: Clinical phenomenology and neurobiology of cocaine abstinence: A prospective inpatient study. Am J Psychiatry *148:* 1712, 1991.

Satel SL, Southwick SM, Gawin FH: Clinical features of cocaine-induced paranoia. Am J Psychiatry *148:* 495, 1991.

Self DW: Cocaine abuse takes a shot. Nature *378:* 666, 1995.

Silverman K, Higgins ST, Brooder RK, Manda ID, Cone EJ, Schuster CR, Preston KL: Sustained cocaine abstinence in methadone maintenance patients through voucher-based reinforcement therapy. Arch Gen Psychiatry *53:* 409, 1996.

Strung J, Johns A, Can W: Cocaine in the UK—1991. Br J Psychiatry *162:* 1, 1993.

Substance Abuse and Mental Health Services Administration Office of Applied Studies: *Preliminary Estimates from the 1995 National Household Survey on Drug Abuse.* US Government Printing Office, Washington, 1995.

Volkow ND, Fowler JS, Wolf AP, Hitzeman R, Dewey S, Bendriem B, Alpert R, Hoff A: Changes in brain glucose metabolism in cocaine dependence and withdrawal. Am J Psychiatry *148:* 621, 1991.

Withers NW, Pulvirenti L, Koob GF, Gillin JC: Cocaine abuse and dependence. J Clin Psychopharmacol *15:* 63, 1995.

Woolverton WL, Johnson KM: Neurobiology of cocaine abuse. Trends Pharmacol Sci *13:* 193, 1992.

▲ 12.7 Hallucinogen-Related Disorders

People use any of more than 100 natural and synthetic hallucinogens that are variously called psychedelics or psychotomimetics because, besides inducing hallucinations, they produce a loss of contact with reality and an experience of expanded and heightened consciousness. The hallucinogens are classified as schedule I drugs; the Food and Drug Administration (FDA) has decreed that they have no medical use and a high abuse potential. The classic naturally occurring hallucinogens are psilocybin (from some mushrooms) and mescaline (from peyote cactus); others are harmine, harmaline, ibogaine, and dimethyltryptamine (DMT). The classic synthetic hallucinogen is lysergic acid diethylamide (LSD), synthesized in 1938 by Albert Hoffman, who later accidentally ingested some of the drug and experienced the first LSD-induced hallucinogenic episode. Some researchers classify the substituted or so-called designer amphetamines, such as 3,4-methylenedioxyamphetamine (MDMA), as hallucinogens. However, because these drugs are structurally related to amphetamines, this textbook classifies them as amphetamine-like substances (see section 12.3).

EPIDEMIOLOGY

In 1991, an estimated 8.1 percent of the people in the United States had used a hallucinogen at least once; 1.2 percent had used a hallucinogen in the preceding year, and 0.3 percent had used a hallucinogen in the preceding month. Hallucinogen use is most common among young (15 to 35 years of age) white men. The ratio of whites to blacks who have used a hallucinogen is 2 to 1, the white to Hispanic ratio is around 1.5 to 1. Men represent 62 percent of those persons who have used a hallucinogen at some time and 75 percent of those who have used a hallucinogen in the preceding month, a pattern of use more frequent than that of women. Persons 26 to 34 years of age show the highest use of hallucinogens, with 15.5 percent having used a hallucinogen at least once. Those persons 18 to 25 years of age have the highest recent use of a hallucinogen—1.2 percent of the age group. Cultural factors influence the use of hallucinogens; their use in the western United States is significantly higher than in the southern United States. Hallucinogen use is associated with less morbidity and less mortality than are some other substances. For example, one study found that only 1 percent of substance-related emergency room visits were related to hallucinogens, compared with 40 percent for cocaine-related problems. Of those people visiting the emergency room for hallucinogen-related reasons, however, more than 50 percent were younger than 20 years of age. A resurgence in the popularity of hallucinogens has been reported.

The following epidemiological data for 1991 to 1995 come from the National Institute on Drug Abuse (NIDA) and the Substance Abuse and Mental Health Service Administration:

In 1991, young adults (ages 18 to 25) were much more likely than were adolescents (ages 12 to 17) or older adults to report that they had used hallucinogens at sometime. In 1991, an estimated 13.1 percent of young adults, 7.8 percent of older adults, and 3.3 percent of adolescents (ages 12 to 17) reported that they had used hallucinogens. For past-month use, the prevalence rates among adolescents and young adults were significantly higher than those of the older age groups. The rates of use in the past month, however, were low in all age groups (less than 1 percent).

The lifetime rates of use were highest in 1979 for young adults and adolescents and decreased thereafter. The rates of lifetime use steadily increased among older adults from 1974 to 1991. This increase in lifetime rates among adults older than age 25 is expected, because the rates reflect the experience of this group in previous years, when rates of substance abuse were high.

Between 1990 and 1991, the percentages of each age group using hallucinogens in their lifetimes and in the past month were relatively stable. Although the percentage of past-month users rose slightly among young adults ages 18 to 25 (from 0.8 to 1.2 percent), there were no significant changes for any age group. There were an estimated 912,000 new hallucinogen users in 1994. The rate among adolescents ages 12 to 17 increased between 1991 and 1994, from 11.2 to 23.3 per 1,000 person years.

NEUROPHARMACOLOGY

Although most hallucinogenic substances vary in their pharmacological effects, LSD can serve as a hallucinogenic prototype. The pharmacodynamic effect of LSD remains controversial, although it is generally well accepted that the drug acts on the serotonergic system, whether as an antagonist or as an agonist. Data at this time suggest that LSD acts as a partial agonist at postsynaptic serotonin receptors.

Most hallucinogens are well absorbed after oral ingestion, although some are ingested by inhalation, smoking, or intravenous injection. Tolerance for LSD and other hallucinogens develops rapidly and is virtually complete after 3 or 4 days of continuous use. Tolerance also reverses quickly, usually in 4 to 7 days. Neither physical dependence nor withdrawal symptoms occur with hallucinogens, but a user can develop a psychological dependence on the insight-inducing experiences of episodes of hallucinogen use.

DIAGNOSIS

The fourth edition of *Diagnostic and Statistical Manual of Mental Disorders* (DSM-IV) lists a number of hallucinogen-related disorders (Table 12.7–1) but contains specific diagnostic criteria only for hallucinogen intoxication (Table 12.7–2) and for hallucinogen persisting perception disorder (flashbacks) (Table 12.7–3). The diagnostic criteria for the other hallucinogen use disorders are contained in the DSM-IV sections that are specific to each symptom—for example, hallucinogen-induced mood disorder (see Table 15.1–11).

Table 12.7–1
DSM-IV Hallucinogen-Related Disorders

Hallucinogen use disorders
Hallucinogen dependence
Hallucinogen abuse
Hallucinogen-induced disorders
Hallucinogen intoxication
Hallucinogen persisting perception disorder (flashbacks)
Hallucinogen intoxication delirium
Hallucinogen-induced psychotic disorder, with delusions
Specify if:
With onset during intoxication
Hallucinogen-induced psychotic disorder, with hallucinations
Specify if:
With onset during intoxication
Hallucinogen-induced mood disorder
Specify if:
With onset during intoxication
Hallucinogen-induced anxiety disorder
Specify if:
With onset during intoxication
Hallucinogen-related disorder not otherwise specified

Reprinted with permission from American Psychiatric Association: *Diagnostic and Statistical Manual of Mental Disorders,* ed 4. Copyright, American Psychiatric Association, Washington, 1994.

Table 12.7–2
DSM-IV Diagnostic Criteria for Hallucinogen Intoxication

A. Recent use of a hallucinogen.

B. Clinically significant maladaptive behavioral or psychological changes (eg, marked anxiety or depression, ideas of reference, fear of losing one's mind, paranoid ideation, impaired judgment, or impaired social or occupational functioning) that developed during, or shortly after, hallucinogen use.

C. Perceptual changes occurring in a state of full wakefulness and alertness (eg, subjective intensification of perceptions, depersonalization, derealization, illusions, hallucinations, synesthesias) that developed during, or shortly after, hallucinogen use.

D. Two (or more) of the following signs, developing during, or shortly after, hallucinogen use:
  (1) pupillary dilation
  (2) tachycardia
  (3) sweating
  (4) palpitations
  (5) blurring of vision
  (6) tremors
  (7) incoordination

E. The symptoms are not due to a general medical condition and are not better accounted for by another mental disorder.

Reprinted with permission from American Psychiatric Association: *Diagnostic and Statistical Manual of Mental Disorders,* ed 4. Copyright, American Psychiatric Association, Washington, 1994.

Hallucinogen Dependence and Hallucinogen Abuse

Long-term hallucinogen use is not common. As stated previously, there is no physical addiction. Although psychological

Table 12.7–3
DSM-IV Diagnostic Criteria for Hallucinogen Persisting Perception Disorder (Flashbacks)

A. The reexperiencing, following cessation of use of a hallucinogen, of one or more of the perceptual symptoms that were experienced wile intoxicated with the hallucinogen (eg, geometric hallucinations, false perceptions of movement in the peripheral visual fields, flashes of color, intensified colors, trails of images of moving objects, positive afterimages, halos around objects, macropsia, and micropsia).

B. The symptoms in criterion A cause clinically significant distress or impairment in social, occupational, or other important areas of functioning.

C. The symptoms are not due to a general medical condition (eg, anatomical lesions and infections of the brain, visual epilepsies) and are not better accounted for by another mental disorder (eg, delirium, dementia, schizophrenia) or hypnopompic hallucinations.

Reprinted with permission from American Psychiatric Association: *Diagnostic and Statistical Manual of Mental Disorders,* ed 4. Copyright, American Psychiatric Association, Washington, 1994.

dependence occurs, it is rare, in part because each LSD experience is different and in part because there is no reliable euphoria. Nonetheless, hallucinogen dependence and hallucinogen abuse are genuine syndromes, defined by DSM-IV criteria (see Tables 12.1–7, 12.1–8, and 12.1–9).

Hallucinogen Intoxication

Intoxication with hallucinogens is defined in DSM-IV as characterized by maladaptive behavioral and perceptual changes and by certain physiological signs (Table 12.7–2). The differential diagnosis for hallucinogen intoxication includes anticholinergic and amphetamine intoxication and alcohol withdrawal. The preferred treatment for hallucinogen intoxication is *talking down* the patient; during this process, guides can reassure patients that the symptoms are drug induced, that the patients are not going crazy, and that the symptoms will resolve shortly. In the most severe cases, dopaminergic antagonists—for example, haloperidol (Haldol)—or benzodiazepines—for example, diazepam (Valium)—can be used for a limited time. Hallucinogen intoxication usually lacks a withdrawal syndrome.

Hallucinogen Persisting Perception Disorder

Long after ingesting a hallucinogen, a person can experience a flashback of hallucinogenic symptoms. This syndrome is diagnosed as hallucinogen persisting perception disorder (Table 12.7–3) in DSM-IV. According to studies, from 15 to 80 percent of users of hallucinogens report having experienced flashbacks. The differential diagnosis for flashbacks includes migraine, seizures, visual system abnormalities, and posttraumatic stress disorder. The following can trigger a flashback: emotional stress; sensory deprivation, such as monotonous driving; or use of another psychoactive substance, such as alcohol or marijuana.

Flashbacks are spontaneous, transitory recurrences of the substance-induced experience. Most flashbacks are episodes of visual distortion, geometric hallucinations, hallucinations of sounds or voices, false perceptions of movement in peripheral fields, flashes of color, trails of images from moving objects, positive afterimages and halos, macropsia, micropsia, time expansion, physical symptoms, or relived intense emotion. The episodes usually last a few seconds to a few minutes but can sometimes last longer. Most often, even in the presence of distinct perceptual disturbances, the person has insight into the pathological nature of the disturbance. Suicidal behavior, major depressive disorder, and panic disorders are potential complications.

Hallucinogen Intoxication Delirium

DSM-IV allows for the diagnosis of hallucinogen intoxication delirium (see Table 10.2–3), a relatively rare disorder beginning during intoxication in those who have ingested pure hallucinogens. Hallucinogens are often mixed with other substances, however, and the other components or their interactions with the hallucinogens can produce a clinical delirium.

Hallucinogen-Induced Psychotic Disorders

If psychotic symptoms are present in the absence of retained reality testing, a diagnosis of hallucinogen-induced psychotic disorder may be warranted (see Table 14.1–2). DSM-IV also allows clinicians to specify whether hallucinations or delusions are the prominent symptoms. The most common adverse effect of LSD and related substances is a "bad trip," an experience resembling the acute panic reaction to cannabis but sometimes more severe; a bad trip can occasionally produce true psychotic symptoms. The bad trip generally ends when the immediate effects of the hallucinogen wear off, but its course is variable. Occasionally, a protracted psychotic episode is difficult to distinguish from a nonorganic psychotic disorder. Whether a chronic psychosis after a drug ingestion is the result of the drug ingestion, is unrelated to the drug ingestion, or is a combination of both the drug ingestion and predisposing factors is currently an unanswerable question.

Occasionally, the psychotic disorder is prolonged, a reaction thought to be most common in people with preexisting schizoid personality disorder and prepsychotic personalities, an unstable ego balance, or much anxiety. Such people cannot cope with the perceptual changes, body-image distortions, and symbolic unconscious material stimulated by the hallucinogen. The rate of previous mental instability in people hospitalized for LSD reactions is high. Adverse reactions occurred in the late 1960s when LSD was being promoted as a self-prescribed psychotherapy for emotional crises in the lives of seriously disturbed people. Now that this practice is less frequent, prolonged adverse reactions are less common.

Hallucinogen-Induced Mood Disorder

DSM-IV provides a diagnostic category for hallucinogen-induced mood disorder (see Table 15.1–11). Unlike cocaine-induced mood disorder and amphetamine-induced mood disorder, in which the symptoms are somewhat predictable, mood disorder symptoms accompanying hallucinogen abuse can be variable. Abusers may experience maniclike symptoms with grandiose delusions or depression-like feelings and ideas or mixed symptoms. As with the hallucinogen-induced psychotic disorder symptoms, the symptoms of hallucinogen-induced mood disorder usually resolve once the drug has been eliminated from the person's body.

Hallucinogen-Induced Anxiety Disorder

Hallucinogen-induced anxiety disorder (see Table 16.1–5) is also variable in its symptom pattern, but few data about symptom patterns are available. Anecdotally, emergency room physicians who treat patients with hallucinogen-related disorders frequently report panic disorder with agoraphobia.

Hallucinogen-Related Disorder Not Otherwise Specified

When a patient with a hallucinogen-related disorder does not meet the diagnostic criteria for any of the standard hallucinogen-related disorders, the patient may be classified as hav-

Table 12.7–4
DSM-IV Diagnostic Criteria for Hallucinogen-Related Disorder Not Otherwise Specified

The hallucinogen-related disorder not otherwise specified category is for disorders associated with the use of hallucinogens that are not classifiable as hallucinogen dependence, hallucinogen abuse, hallucinogen intoxication, hallucinogen persisting perception disorder, hallucinogen intoxication delirium, hallucinogen-induced psychotic disorder, hallucinogen-induced mood disorder, or hallucinogen-induced anxiety disorder.

ing hallucinogen-related disorder not otherwise specified (Table 12.7–4). DSM-IV does not have a diagnostic category of hallucinogen withdrawal, but some clinicians anecdotally report a syndrome with depression and anxiety after cessation of frequent hallucinogen use. Such a syndrome may best fit the diagnosis of hallucinogen-related disorder not otherwise specified.

CLINICAL FEATURES

The onset of action of LSD occurs within an hour, peaks in 2 to 4 hours, and lasts 8 to 12 hours. The sympathomimetic effects of LSD include tremors, tachycardia, hypertension, hyperthermia, sweating, blurring of vision, and mydriasis. Death caused by cardiac or cerebrovascular pathology related to hypertension or hyperthermia can occur with hallucinogenic use. A syndrome similar to neuroleptic malignant syndrome has reportedly been associated with LSD. Death can also be caused by a physical injury when LSD use impairs judgment about, for example, traffic or a person's ability to fly. The psychological effects are usually well tolerated, but when people cannot recall experiences or appreciate that the experiences are substance induced, they may fear the onset of insanity.

With hallucinogen use, perceptions become unusually brilliant and intense. Colors and textures seem to be richer than in the past, contours sharpened, music more emotionally profound, and smells and tastes heightened. Synesthesia is common; colors may be heard or sounds seen. Changes in body image and alterations of time and space perception also occur. Hallucinations are usually visual, often of geometric forms and figures, but auditory and tactile hallucinations are sometimes experienced. Emotions become unusually intense and may change abruptly and often; two seemingly incompatible feelings may be experienced at the same time. Suggestibility is greatly heightened, and sensitivity or detachment from other people may arise. Other common features are a seeming awareness of internal organs, the recovery of lost early memories, the release of unconscious material in symbolic form, and regression and the apparent reliving of past events, including birth. Introspective reflection and feelings of religious and philosophical insight are common. The sense of self is greatly changed, sometimes to the point of depersonalization, merging with the external world, separation of self from body, or total dissolution of the ego in mystical ecstasy.

There is no clear evidence of drastic personality change or chronic psychosis produced by long-term LSD use in moderate users not otherwise predisposed to these conditions. Some heavy users of hallucinogens, however, may experience chronic anxiety or depression and may benefit from a psychological or pharmacological approach that addresses the underlying problem.

Many people maintain that a single experience with LSD has given them increased creative capacity, new psychological insight, relief from neurotic or psychosomatic symptoms, or a desirable change in personality. In the 1950s and 1960s, psychiatrists showed great interest in LSD and related substances, both as potential models for functional psychosis and as possible pharmacotherapeutic agents. The availability of these compounds to researchers in the basic neurosciences has led to many scientific advances.

TREATMENT AND REHABILITATION

The treatment of choice for the acute psychiatric symptoms associated with hallucinogen intoxication is supportive counseling, so-called talking down. A person having a severely unpleasant experience under the influence of LSD requires protection, companionship, and reassurance. Occasionally, a short course of psychotherapeutic drugs may be necessary, usually with dopamine receptor antagonists for psychotic symptoms or with benzodiazepines for anxiety symptoms. When a hallucinogen-induced drug experience is temporally related to the onset of a persisting psychiatric condition (such as a depressive disorder, manic episodes, or schizophrenia), the treatment of the persisting psychiatric condition should generally follow the usual guidelines for that diagnosis.

References

Behan WM, Bakheit AM, Behan PO, More IA: The muscle findings in the neuroleptic malignant syndrome associated with lysergic acid diethylamide. J Neurol Neurosurg Psychiatry *54:* 741, 1991.

Cousineau D, Savard M, Allard D: Illicit drug use among adolescent students. A peer phenomenon? Can Fam Physician Med Fam Can *39:* 523, 1993.

Crowley TJ: Hallucinogen-related disorders. In *Comprehensive Textbook of Psychiatry,* ed 6, HI Kaplan, BJ Sadock, editors, p 831. Williams & Wilkins, Baltimore, 1995.

Dinges MM, Oetting ER: Similarity in drug use patterns between adolescents and their friends. Adolescence *28:* 253, 1993.

Glennon RA: Do classical hallucinogens act as 5-HT_2 agonists or antagonists? Neuropsychopharmacology *3:* 509, 1990.

Johnston LD, O'Malley PM, Bachman JG: Drug abuse among American high school seniors, college students, and young adults, 1975–1990. Department of Health and Human Services, Washington, 1991.

Kulig K: LSD. Emerg Med Clin North Am *8:* 551, 1990.

National Institute on Drug Abuse: *National Household Survey on Drug Abuse: Highlights, 1991.* US Government Printing Office, Washington, 1991.

Pierce PA, Peroutka SJ: Antagonist properties of *d*-LSD at 5-$hydroxytryptamine_2$ receptors. Neuropsychopharmacology *3:* 503, 1990.

Popik P, Layer RT, Skolnick P: 100 years of ibogaine: Neurochemical and pharmacological actions of a putative anti-addictive drug. Pharmacol Rev *47:* 235, 1995.

Schwartz RH: LSD: Its rise, fall, and renewed popularity among high school students. Pediatr Clin North Am *42:* 403, 1995.

Spoerke DG, Hall AH: Plants and mushrooms of abuse. Emerg Med Clin North Am *8:* 579, 1990.

Substance Abuse and Mental Health Services Administration Office of Applied Studies: *Preliminary Estimates from the 1995 National Household Survey on Drug Abuse.* US Government Printing Office, Washington, 1995.

Ulrich RF, Patten BM: The rise, decline, and fall of LSD. Perspect Biol Med *34:* 561, 1991.

▲ 12.8 Inhalant-Related Disorders

In the fourth edition of *Diagnostic and Statistical Manual of Mental Disorders* (DSM-IV), the category of inhalant-related disorders includes the psychiatric syndromes resulting from the use of solvents, glues, adhesives, aerosol propellants, paint thinners, and fuels. Among specific examples of these substances are gasoline, varnish remover, lighter fluid, airplane glue, rubber cement, cleaning fluid, spray paint, shoe conditioner, and typewriter correction fluid. A resurgence of inhalants' popularity among young people has been reported. The active compounds in these inhalants include toluene, acetone, benzene, trichloroethane, perchloroethylene, trichloroethylene, 1,2-dichloropropane, and halogenated hydrocarbons. DSM-IV specifically excludes anesthetic gases (such as nitrous oxide and ether) and short-acting vasodilators (such as amyl nitrite) from the inhalant-related disorders, which are classified as other (or unknown) substance-related disorders.

EPIDEMIOLOGY

Inhalant substances are easily available and are legal and inexpensive. These three factors contribute to the high use of inhalants among people who are poor and among young people. In 1991, about 5 percent of the people in the United States had used inhalants at least once, and about 1 percent were current users. Among young adults 18 to 25 years old, 11 percent had used inhalants at least once, and 2 percent were current users. Among adolescents 12 to 17 years old, 7 percent had used inhalants at least once, and 2 percent were current users. In one study of high school seniors, 18 percent reported having used inhalants at least once, and 2.7 percent reported having used inhalants within the preceding month. White users of inhalants are more common than are either black or Hispanic users. Some data suggest that inhalant use may be more common in suburban communities in the United States than in urban communities.

Inhalant use accounts for 1 percent of all substance-related deaths and fewer than 0.5 percent of all substance-related emergency room visits. About 20 percent of the emergency room visits for inhalant use involve people younger than 18 years of age. Inhalant use among adolescents may be most common in those whose parents or older siblings use illegal substances. Inhalant use among adolescents is also associated with an increased likelihood of conduct disorder or antisocial personality disorder.

The following epidemiological data for 1991 come from the Substance Abuse and Mental Health Services Administration:

For inhalants, the overall rate of past month use was 0.4 percent in both 1994 and 1995. There were an estimated 666,000 new inhalant users in 1994, up from 428,000 in 1991. The rate of first use among adolescents ages 12 to 17 rose significantly from 1991 to 1994, from 11.2 to 22.2 per 1,000 person years in 1994.

NEUROPHARMACOLOGY

People usually use inhalants with a tube, a can, a plastic bag, or an inhalant-soaked rag, through or from which a user can sniff the inhalant through the nose or huff it through the mouth. Inhalants generally act as a central nervous system (CNS) depressant. Tolerance for inhalants can develop, although withdrawal symptoms are usually fairly mild and are not classified in DSM-IV as a disorder.

Inhalants are rapidly absorbed through the lungs and rapidly delivered to the brain. The effects appear within 5 minutes and may last for 30 minutes to several hours, depending on the inhalant substance and the dose. For example, 15 to 20 breaths of a 1 percent solution of gasoline may result in a high of several hours. The blood concentrations of many inhalant substances are increased when used in combination with alcohol, perhaps because of competition for hepatic enzymes. Although about one fifth of an inhalant substance is excreted unchanged by the lungs, the remainder is metabolized by the liver. Inhalants are detectable in the blood for 4 to 10 hours after use, and blood samples should be taken in the emergency room when inhalant use is suspected.

Much like alcohol, inhalants have specific pharmacodynamic effects that are not well understood. Because their effects are generally similar and additive to the effects of other CNS depressants (such as ethanol, barbiturates, and benzodiazepines), some investigators have suggested that inhalants operate by enhancing the γ-aminobutyric acid (GABA) system. Other investigators have suggested that inhalants work through membrane fluidization, which has also been hypothesized to be a pharmacodynamic effect of ethanol.

DIAGNOSIS

DSM-IV lists a number of inhalant-related disorders (Table 12.8–1) but contains specific diagnostic criteria only for inhalant intoxication (Table 12.8–2) within the inhalant-related disorders section. The diagnostic criteria of other inhalant-related disorders are specified in the DSM-IV sections that specifically address the major symptoms—for example, inhalant-induced psychotic disorders (see Table 14.1–2).

Inhalant Dependence and Inhalant Abuse

Most people probably use inhalants for a short time without developing a pattern of long-term use resulting in dependence and abuse. Nonetheless, dependence and abuse of inhalants occur and are diagnosed according to the standard DSM-IV criteria for those syndromes (see Tables 12.1–7, 12.1–8, and 12.1–9).

Inhalant Intoxication

The DSM-IV diagnostic criteria for inhalant intoxication (Table 12.8–2) specify the presence of maladaptive behavioral changes and at least two physical symptoms. The intoxicated state is often characterized by apathy, diminished social and occupational functioning, impaired judgment, and impulsive or aggressive behavior, and it can be accompanied by nausea,

Table 12.8–1
DSM-IV Inhalant-Related Disorders

Inhalant use disorders
Inhalant dependence
Inhalant abuse
Inhalant-induced disorders
Inhalant intoxication
Inhalant intoxication delirium
Inhalant-induced persisting dementia
Inhalant-induced psychotic disorder, with delusions
Specify if:
With onset during intoxication
Inhalant-induced psychotic disorder, with hallucinations
Specify if:
With onset during intoxication
Inhalant-induced mood disorder
Specify if:
With onset during intoxication
Inhalant-induced anxiety disorder
Specify if:
With onset during intoxication
Inhalant-related disorder not otherwise specified

Reprinted with permission from American Psychiatric Association: *Diagnostic and Statistical Manual of Mental Disorders,* ed 4. Copyright, American Psychiatric Association, Washington, 1994.

anorexia, nystagmus, depressed reflexes, and diplopia. With high doses and long exposures, a user's neurological status can progress to stupor and unconsciousness, and a person may later be amnestic for the period of intoxication. Clinicians can sometimes identify a recent user of inhalants by rashes around the patient's nose and mouth; unusual breath odors; the residue of the inhalant substances on the patient's face, hands, or clothing; and irritation of the patient's eyes, throat, lungs, and nose.

Inhalant Intoxication Delirium

DSM-IV provides a diagnostic category for inhalant intoxication delirium (see Table 10.2–3). Delirium can be induced by the effects of the inhalants themselves, by pharmacodynamic interactions with other substances, and by the hypoxia that may be associated with either the inhalant or its method of inhalation. If the delirium results in severe behavioral disturbances, short-term treatment with a dopamine receptor antagonist, such as haloperidol (Haldol), may be necessary. Benzodiazepines should be avoided because of the possibility of increasing the patient's respiratory depression.

Inhalant-Induced Persisting Dementia

Inhalant-induced persisting dementia (see Table 10.3–6), like delirium, may be due to the neurotoxic effects of the inhalants themselves; the neurotoxic effects of the metals, such as lead, commonly used in inhalants; or the effects of frequent and prolonged periods of hypoxia. The dementia caused by inhalants is likely to be irreversible in all but the mildest cases.

Inhalant-Induced Psychotic Disorder

Inhalant-induced psychotic disorder is a DSM-IV diagnosis (see Table 14.1–2). Clinicians can specify hallucinations or delusions as the predominant symptoms. Paranoid states are probably the most common psychotic syndromes during inhalant intoxication.

Inhalant-Induced Mood Disorder and Inhalant-Induced Anxiety Disorder

Inhalant-induced mood disorder (see Table 15.1–11) and inhalant-induced anxiety disorder (see Table 16.1–5) are DSM-IV diagnoses that allow the classification of inhalant-related disorders characterized by prominent mood and anxiety symptoms. Depressive disorders are the most common mood disorders associated with inhalant use, and panic disorders and generalized anxiety disorder are the most common anxiety disorders.

Inhalant-Related Disorder Not Otherwise Specified

The diagnosis of inhalant-related disorder not otherwise specified is the recommended DSM-IV diagnosis for inhalant-related disorders that do not fit into one of the previously discussed diagnostic categories (Table 12.8–3).

Table 12.8–2
DSM-IV Diagnostic Criteria for Inhalant Intoxication

A. Recent intentional use or short-term, high-dose exposure to volatile inhalants (excluding anesthetic gases and short-acting vasodilators).
B. Clinically significant maladaptive behavioral or psychological changes (eg, belligerence, assaultiveness, apathy, impaired judgment, impaired social or occupational functioning) that developed during, or shortly after, use of or exposure to volatile inhalants.
C. Two (or more) of the following signs, developing during, or shortly after, inhalant use or exposure:
(1) dizziness
(2) nystagmus
(3) incoordination
(4) slurred speech
(5) unsteady gait
(6) lethargy
(7) depressed reflexes
(8) psychomotor retardation
(9) tremor
(10) generalized muscle weakness
(11) blurred vision or diplopia
(12) stupor or coma
(13) euphoria
D. The symptoms are not due to a general medical condition and are not better accounted for by another mental disorder.

Reprinted with permission from American Psychiatric Association: *Diagnostic and Statistical Manual of Mental Disorders,* ed 4. Copyright, American Psychiatric Association, Washington, 1994.

Table 12.8–3
DSM-IV Diagnostic Criteria for Inhalant-Related Disorder Not Otherwise Specified

The inhalant-related disorder not otherwise specified category is for disorders associated with the use of inhalants that are not classifiable as inhalant dependence, inhalant abuse, inhalant intoxication, inhalant intoxication delirium, inhalant-induced persisting dementia, inhalant-induced psychotic disorder, inhalant-induced mood disorder, or inhalant-induced anxiety disorder.

Reprinted with permission from American Psychiatric Association: *Diagnostic and Statistical Manual of Mental Disorders,* ed 4. Copyright, American Psychiatric Association, Washington, 1994.

CLINICAL FEATURES

In small initial doses, inhalants may be disinhibiting and may produce feelings of euphoria and excitement and pleasant floating sensations, the effects for which people presumably use the drugs. High doses of inhalants can cause other psychological symptoms of fearfulness, sensory illusions, auditory and visual hallucinations, and distortions of body size. The neurological symptoms can include slurred speech, decreased speed of talking, and ataxia. Use over a long period can be associated with irritability, emotional lability, and impaired memory.

Tolerance for the inhalants does develop; although not recognized by DSM-IV, a withdrawal syndrome can accompany the cessation of inhalant use. The withdrawal syndrome does not occur frequently; when it does, it can be characterized by sleep disturbances, irritability, jitteriness, sweating, nausea, vomiting, tachycardia, and, sometimes, delusions and hallucinations.

Adverse Effects

Inhalants are associated with many potentially serious adverse effects, the most serious of which is death. Death can result from respiratory depression, cardiac arrhythmias, asphyxiation, aspiration of vomitus, or accident or injury (for example, driving while intoxicated with inhalants). Other serious adverse effects of long-term inhalant use include irreversible hepatic or renal damage and permanent muscle damage associated with rhabdomyolysis. The combination of organic solvents and high concentrations of copper, zinc, and heavy metals has been associated with the development of brain atrophy, temporal lobe epilepsy, decreased intelligence quotient (IQ), and electroencephalogram (EEG) changes. Several studies of house painters and factory workers who have been exposed to solvents for long periods have shown evidence of brain atrophy on computed tomography (CT) scans and of decreases in cerebral blood flow. Additional adverse effects include cardiovascular and pulmonary symptoms (such as chest pain and bronchospasm), gastrointestinal symptoms (such as pain, nausea, vomiting, and hematemesis), and other neurological signs and symptoms (such as peripheral neuritis, headache, paresthesia, cerebellar signs, and lead encephalopathy). There are reports of brain atrophy, renal tubular acidosis, and long-term motor impairment in toluene users. Several reports concern serious adverse effects on fetal development when a pregnant woman uses or is exposed to inhalant substances.

TREATMENT AND REHABILITATION

Use of inhalants is usually relatively short lived. These people may cease substance-taking activity or move on to other substances of abuse. The identification of inhalant use in an adolescent is an indication that the teenager should receive counseling and education about the general topic of substance use. The presence of an associated diagnosis of conduct disorder or antisocial personality disorder should prompt clinicians to address the situation in depth because of the increased likelihood that the adolescent will become further involved in substance use. For the most part, however, those with inhalant abuse or inhalant dependence are older, debilitated people who need substantial social interventions as part of the treatment approach.

References

Anonymous: Inhalant abuse. American Academy of Pediatrics, Committee on Substance Abuse and Committee on Native American Child Health. Pediatrics *97:* 420, 1996.

Byrne A, Kirby B, Zibin T, Ensminger S: Psychiatric and neurological effects of chronic solvent abuse. Can J Psychiatry *36:* 735, 1991.

Crowley TJ: Inhalant-related disorders. In *Comprehensive Textbook of Psychiatry,* ed 6, HI Kaplan, BJ Sadock, editors, p 838. Williams & Wilkins, Baltimore, 1995.

Dinwiddie SH, Reich T, Cloninger CR: The relationship of solvent use to other substance use. Am J Drug Alcohol Abuse *17:* 173, 1991.

Dinwiddie SH, Reich T, Cloninger CR: Solvent use and psychiatric comorbidity. Br J Addict *85:* 1647, 1990.

Donnelly N, Oldenburg B, Quine S, Macaskill P, Flaherty B, Spooner C, Lyle D: Changes in reported drug prevalence among New South Wales secondary school students, 1983–1989. Aust J Public Health *16:* 50, 1992.

Espeland K: Identifying the manifestations of inhalant abuse. Nurs Pract *20:* 49, 1995.

Espeland K: Inhalant abuse: Assessment guidelines. J Psychosoc Nurs Ment Health Serv *31:* 11, 1993.

Evans EB, Balster RL: CNS depressant effects of volatile organic solvents. Neurosci Biobehav Rev *15:* 233, 1991.

Farrow JA, Schwartz RH: Adolescent drug and alcohol usage: A comparison of urban and suburban pediatric practices. J Natl Med Assoc *84:* 409, 1992.

Flanagan RJ, Ruprah M, Meredith TJ, Ramsey JD: An introduction to the clinical toxicology of volatile substances. Drug Saf *5:* 359, 1990.

Griesel RD, Jansen P, Richter LM: Electro-encephalographic disturbances due to chronic toxin abuse in young people, with special reference to glue-sniffing. S Afr Med J *78:* 544, 1990.

Johns A: Volatile substance abuse and 963 deaths. Br J Addict *86:* 1053, 1991.

Lindren CH: Volatile substances of abuse. Emerg Med Clin North Am *8:* 559, 1990.

Miller NS, Gold MS: Organic solvent and aerosol abuse. Am Fam Physician *44:* 183, 1991.

National Institute on Drug Abuse: *National Household Survey on Drug Abuse: Highlights, 1991.* US Government Printing Office, Washington, 1991.

Pollard TG: Relative addiction potential of major centrally-active drugs and drug classes: Inhalants and anesthetics. Adv Alcohol Subst Abuse *9:* 149, 1990.

Prasher VP, Corbett JA: Aerosol addiction. Br J Psychiatry *157:* 922, 1990.

Substance Abuse and Mental Health Services Administration Office of Applied Studies: *Preliminary Estimates from the 1995 National Household Survey on Drug Abuse.* US Government Printing Office, Washington, 1995.

Tenenbein M, Pillay N: Sensory evoked potentials in inhalant (volatile solvent) abuse. J Pediatr Child Health *29:* 206, 1993.

Wheeler MG, Rozycki AA , Smith RP: Recreational propane inhalation in an adolescent male. J Toxicol Clin Toxicol *30:* 135, 1992.

▲ 12.9 Nicotine-Related Disorders

Published in 1988, *The Surgeon General's Report on the Health Consequences of Smoking: Nicotine Addiction* stated that nicotine is an addicting drug, just as cocaine and heroin are addicting drugs. As a result of this report and of other public health information campaigns, the percentage of people in the United States who smoke has decreased from 44 percent in 1964 to approximately 29 percent in 1995. The fact that 29 percent of all people in the United States continue to smoke in spite of the mountain of data showing how dangerous the habit is to their health is testament to the powerfully addictive properties of nicotine. The ill effects of cigarette and cigar smoking are reflected in the estimate that 60 percent of the direct health care costs in the United States go to treat tobacco-related illnesses and amount to an estimated $1 billion a day.

In 1995 President Bill Clinton announced proposed rules that will allow the Food and Drug Administration (FDA) to govern the sale and distribution of nicotine-containing cigarettes and smokeless tobacco products to children and adolescents by reducing easy access and decreasing the appeal of these products. The proposed rule would not restrict the use of tobacco products by adults.

EPIDEMIOLOGY

The World Health Organization (WHO) estimates there are 1 billion smokers worldwide, and they smoke 6 trillion cigarettes a year. The WHO also estimates that tobacco kills more than 3 million people each year. Although the number of people in the United States who smoke is decreasing, the number of people smoking in developing countries is increasing, and it is estimated that 22 percent of the U.S. population will still be smoking in the year 2000. The rate of quitting smoking has been highest among well-educated white men and less high among women, blacks, teenagers, and those with low levels of education.

Tobacco is the most common form of nicotine. It is smoked in cigarettes, cigars, and pipes and used as snuff and chewing tobacco (also called smokeless tobacco), both of which are increasingly popular in the United States. About 3 percent of all people in the United States are current users of snuff or chewing tobacco, but about 6 percent of young adults ages 18 to 25 use those forms of tobacco.

The following data for 1995 come from the Substance Abuse and Mental Health Services Administration:

An estimated 61 million people in the United States were current smokers in 1995. This number represents a smoking rate of 29 percent for the population age 12 and older.

Current smokers were more likely to be heavy drinkers and illicit drug users. Among smokers, the rate of heavy alcohol use (5 or more drinks on 5 or more days in the past month) was 12.6 percent, and the rate of current illicit drug use was 13.6 percent. Among nonsmokers, only 2.7 percent were heavy drinkers, and 3.0 percent were illicit drug users.

An estimated 6.9 million people (3.3 percent of the U.S. population) were current users of smokeless tobacco in 1995.

Age

Approximately 4.5 million adolescents ages 12 to 17 were current smokers in 1995. The rate of smoking among adolescents ages 12 to 17 was 20 percent. The rate was 18.9 percent in 1994, but this increase does not represent a statistically significant change. Adolescents ages 12 to 17 who smoked were about 8 times as likely to use illicit drugs and 11 times as likely to drink heavily as were nonsmoking adolescents.

Race and Ethnicity

In 1995, no significant differences in smoking rates by race or ethnicity were found. Smokeless tobacco use was more prevalent among whites (3.9 percent) than among blacks (1.3 percent) or Hispanics (1.2 percent).

Gender

Among adults, men had somewhat higher rates of smoking than did women, but rates of smoking were similar for men and women ages 12 to 17. The rate of smokeless tobacco use was significantly higher for men than for women in 1995 (6.2 versus 0.6 percent). Greater than 90 percent of smokeless tobacco users were men.

Region and Urbanicity

The rate of current cigarette use was 32 percent in the North Central region, 29 percent in the South, 28 percent in the Northeast, and 26 percent in the West. The rate of smoking was 27 percent in large metropolitan areas.

Education

Level of education attainment was correlated with tobacco usage. Thirty-seven percent of adults who had not completed high school smoked cigarettes, whereas only 17 percent of college graduates smoked.

Psychiatric Patients

Psychiatrists must be particularly concerned and knowledgeable about nicotine dependence because of the high proportion of psychiatric patients who smoke. Approximately 50 percent of all psychiatric outpatients, 70 percent of outpatients with bipolar I disorder, and almost 90 percent of outpatients with schizophrenia smoke. Moreover, data indicate that patients with depressive disorders or anxiety disorders are less successful in their attempt to quit smoking than are other people; thus, a holistic health approach for such people probably includes helping patients address their smoking habits in addition to the primary mental disorder. The reason so many schizophrenic patients smoke has been attributed to the ability of nicotine to reduce extraordinary sensitivity to outside sensory stimuli and to increase concentration in such patients.

Death

Death is the primary adverse effect of cigarette smoking. Tobacco use is associated with approximately 400,000 premature deaths each year in the United States—25 percent of all deaths. The causes of death include chronic bronchitis and emphysema (51,000 deaths), bronchogenic cancer (106,000 deaths), 35 percent of fatal myocardial infarctions (115,000 deaths), cerebrovascular disease, cardiovascular disease, and almost all cases of chronic obstructive pulmonary disease and lung cancer. The increased use of chewing tobacco and snuff (smokeless tobacco) has been associated with the development of oropharyngeal cancer, and the resurgence of cigar smoking is likely to lead to an increase in the occurrence of this type of cancer.

Researchers have found that 30 percent of U.S. cancer deaths are caused by tobacco smoke, the single most lethal carcinogen in the United States. Smoking (mainly cigarette smoking) causes cancer of the lung, upper respiratory tract, esophagus, bladder, pancreas, and probably of the stomach, liver, and kidney. Smokers are 8 times more likely than are nonsmokers to develop lung cancer, and lung cancer has recently surpassed breast cancer as the leading cause of cancer-related deaths in women. Between 1973 and 1992, the mortality rate for lung cancer in women rose by more than 135 percent. Even second-hand smoke causes a few thousand cancer deaths each year in the United States, about the same number as the deaths caused by radon exposure. Despite these staggering statistics, people can dramatically lower their chances of developing smoke-related cancers simply by stopping smoking.

NEUROPHARMACOLOGY

The psychoactive component of tobacco is nicotine, which affects the central nervous system (CNS) by acting as an agonist at the nicotinic subtype of acetylcholine receptors. About 25 percent of the nicotine inhaled during smoking reaches the bloodstream, through which nicotine reaches the brain within 15 seconds. The half-life of nicotine is about 2 hours. Nicotine is believed to produce its positive reinforcing and addictive properties by activating the dopaminergic pathway projecting from the ventral tegmental area to the cerebral cortex and the limbic system. In addition to activating this dopamine reward system, nicotine causes an increase in the concentrations of circulating norepinephrine and epinephrine and an increase in the release of vasopressin, β-endorphin, adrenocorticotropic hormone (ACTH), and cortisol. These hormones are thought to contribute to the basic stimulatory effects of nicotine on the CNS.

DIAGNOSIS

The fourth edition of *Diagnostic and Statistical Manual of Mental Disorders* (DSM-IV) lists three nicotine-related disorders (Table 12.9–1) but contains specific diagnostic criteria for only nicotine withdrawal (Table 12.9–2) in the nicotine-related disorders section. The other nicotine-related disorders recognized by DSM-IV are nicotine dependence and nicotine-related disorder not otherwise specified.

Table 12.9–1
DSM-IV Nicotine-Related Disorders

Nicotine use disorder
Nicotine dependence
Nicotine-induced disorder
Nicotine withdrawal
Nicotine-related disorder not otherwise specified

Reprinted with permission from American Psychiatric Association: *Diagnostic and Statistical Manual of Mental Disorders,* ed 4. Copyright, American Psychiatric Association, Washington, 1994.

Table 12.9–2
DSM-IV Diagnostic Criteria for Nicotine Withdrawal

A. Daily use of nicotine for at least several weeks.
B. Abrupt cessation of nicotine use, or reduction in the amount of nicotine used, followed within 24 hours by at least four of the following signs:
 (1) dysphoric or depressed mood
 (2) insomnia
 (3) irritability, frustration, or anger
 (4) anxiety
 (5) difficulty concentrating
 (6) restlessness
 (7) decreased heart rate
 (8) increased appetite or weight gain
C. The symptoms in criterion B cause clinically significant distress or impairment in social, occupational, or other important areas of functioning.
D. The symptoms are not due to a general medical condition and are not better accounted for by another mental disorder.

Reprinted with permission from American Psychiatric Association: *Diagnostic and Statistical Manual of Mental Disorders,* ed 4. Copyright, American Psychiatric Association, Washington, 1994.

Nicotine Dependence

DSM-IV allows for the diagnosis of nicotine dependence (see Tables 12.1–7 and 12.1–8) but not nicotine abuse. Dependence on nicotine develops quickly, probably because of nicotine's activation of the ventral tegmental area dopaminergic system, the same system affected by cocaine and amphetamine. The development of dependence is enhanced by strong social factors that encourage smoking in some settings and by the powerful effects of tobacco company advertising. People are likely to smoke if their parents or siblings smoke and serve as role models. Several recent studies have also suggested a genetic diathesis toward nicotine dependence. Most people who smoke want to quit and have tried many times to quit but have been unsuccessful in their efforts.

Nicotine Withdrawal

DSM-IV does not have a diagnostic category for nicotine intoxication but does have a diagnostic category for nicotine withdrawal (Table 12.9–2). Withdrawal symptoms can develop within 2 hours of smoking the last cigarette, generally peak in the first 24 to 48 hours, and can last for weeks or months. The common symptoms include an intense craving for nicotine, tension, irritability, difficulty in concentrating, drowsiness and paradoxical trouble in sleeping, decreased heart rate and blood pressure, increased appetite and weight gain, decreased motor performance, and increased muscle tension. A mild syndrome of nicotine withdrawal can appear when a smoker switches from regular to low-nicotine cigarettes.

Table 12.9–3
DSM-IV Diagnostic Criteria for Nicotine-Related Disorder Not Otherwise Specified

The nicotine-related disorder not otherwise specified category is for disorders associated with the use of nicotine that are not classifiable as nicotine dependence or nicotine withdrawal.

Table 12.9–4
Treatments for Smoking

First line
- Nicotine patch
- Nicotine gum
- Nicotine patch and gum

Second line
- Nicotine nasal spray
- Nicotine inhaler
- Clonidine
- Buproprion

Adapted from American Psychiatric Association: Practice guidelines for the treatment of nicotine dependence. Am J Psychiatry *153* (10, Suppl): 1, 1996.

Nicotine-Related Disorder Not Otherwise Specified

Nicotine-related disorder not otherwise specified is a diagnostic category for nicotine-related disorders that do not fit into one of the categories previously discussed (Table 12.9–3). Such diagnoses may include nicotine intoxication, nicotine abuse, and mood disorders and anxiety disorders associated with nicotine use.

CLINICAL FEATURES

Behaviorally, the stimulatory effects of nicotine produce improved attention, learning, reaction time, and problem-solving ability. Tobacco users also report that cigarette smoking lifts their mood, decreases tension, and lessens depressive feelings. In studies of the effects of nicotine on cerebral blood flow (CBF), results suggest that short-term nicotine exposure increases the CBF without changing cerebral oxygen metabolism but that long-term nicotine exposure decreases the CBF. In contrast to its stimulatory CNS effects, nicotine acts as a skeletal muscle relaxant.

Adverse Effects

Nicotine is a highly toxic alkaloid. Doses of 60 mg in an adult are fatal secondary to respiratory paralysis; doses of 0.5 mg are delivered by smoking an average cigarette. In low doses the signs and symptoms of nicotine toxicity include nausea, vomiting, salivation, pallor (caused by peripheral vasoconstriction), weakness, abdominal pain (caused by increased peristalsis), diarrhea, dizziness, headache, increased blood pressure, tachycardia, tremor, and cold sweats. Toxicity is also associated with an inability to concentrate, confusion, and sensory disturbances. Nicotine is further associated with a decrease in the user's amount of rapid eye movement (REM) sleep. Tobacco use during pregnancy has been associated with an increased incidence of low-birth-weight babies and an increased incidence of newborns with persistent pulmonary hypertension.

Health Benefits of Smoking Cessation

In a 1990 Surgeon General's report on the health benefits of smoking cessation, the following conclusions were reached: Smoking cessation has major and immediate health benefits for people of all ages and provides benefits for people with and without smoking-related diseases. Former smokers live longer than do those who continue to smoke. Smoking cessation decreases the risk for lung cancer and other cancers, myocardial infarction, cerebrovascular diseases, and chronic lung diseases. Women who stop smoking before pregnancy or during the first 3 to 4 months of pregnancy reduce their risk for having low-birth-weight infants to that of women who never smoked. The health benefits of smoking cessation substantially exceed any risks from the average 5-pound (2.3-kg) weight gain or any adverse psychological effects after quitting.

TREATMENT

The combined use of systemic nicotine administration and behavioral counseling has resulted in sustained abstinence rates of 60 percent in well-controlled clinical trials. Nicotine is delivered to the body systemically via transdermal absorption (Nicoderm), intramucosally via nasal inhaler (Nicotrol), and orally via chewing gum or via an oral inhaler (Nicorette Inhaler). Dependence on these products has been reported in up to 20 percent of patients; therefore, careful supervision by the physician of amount and duration of use is necessary. Whether these products should be sold over the counter is open to serious question. This figure is significantly greater than the estimated 5 to 10 percent success rate for people who quit cigarette smoking without specific support treatment. The most effective behavioral support programs address such issues as how to perform common daily activities (such as eating, driving, and socializing) without smoking and how to cope with the dysphoric mood and the weight gain that can accompany smoking cessation. A further advantage of systemic nicotine use is that doses of the nicotine can be individually titrated to patients' needs and their experiences of nicotine withdrawal symptoms. A variety of other psychopharmacological agents have also been used with some success in maintaining abstinence and reducing withdrawal symptoms from nicotine (Table 12.9–4). These agents include clonidine (Catapres); antidepressants, particularly fluoxetine (Prozac), and buspirone (BuSpar). Bupropion (Zyban) was approved in 1996 by the Food and Drug Administration as a treatment for nicotine dependence. In addition, people who successfully discontinue smoking are likely to have been encouraged by someone close to them (such as a spouse or children), to have been fearful of the ill effects of smoking, and to have joined a support group of some type for ex-smokers. Encouragement from a nonsmoking physician is also highly correlated with abstinence.

References

Brautbar N: Direct effects of nicotine on the brain: Evidence for chemical addiction. Arch Environ Health *50:* 263, 1995.

Breslau N, Kilbey MM, Andreski P: Nicotine withdrawal symptoms and psychiatric disorders: Findings from an epidemiologic study of young adults. Am J Psychiatry *149:* 464, 1992.

Carmell D, Swan GE, Robinette D, Fabsitz R: Genetic influence on smoking: A study of male twins. N Engl J Med *327:* 829, 1992.

DeGrandpre RJ, Bickel WK Rizvi SA, Hughes JR: Effects of income on drug choice in humans. J Exp Anal Behav *59:* 483, 1993.

Fiore MC: Trends in cigarette smoking in the United States: The epidemiology of tobacco use. Med Clin North Am *76:* 289, 1992.

Ginsberg D, Hall SM, Rosinski M: Partner support, psychological treatment, and nicotine gum in smoking treatment: An incremental study. Int J Addict *27:* 503, 1992.

Greden JF, Pomerleau OF: Caffeine-related disorders and nicotine-related disorders. In *Comprehensive Textbook of Psychiatry,* ed 6, HI Kaplan, BJ Sadock, editors, p 799. Williams & Wilkins, Baltimore, 1995.

Hall SM, Tunstall CD, Vila KL, Duffy J: Weight gain prevention and smoking cessation: Cautionary findings. Am J Public Health *82:* 799, 1992.

Hatsukami DK, Skoog K, Huber M, Hughes J: Signs and symptoms from nicotine gum abstinence. Psychopharmacology *104:* 496, 1991.

Hughes JR, Gust SW, Skoog K, Keenan RM, Fenwick JW: Symptoms of tobacco withdrawal: A replication and extension. Arch Gen Psychiatry *48:* 52, 1991.

Kessler DA: Nicotine addition in young people. N Engl J Med *333:* 186, 1995.

Le Houezec J, Benowitz NL: Basic and clinical psychopharmacology of nicotine. Clin Chest Med *12:* 681, 1991.

Miller GH, Golish JA, Cox CE: A physician's guide to smoking cessation. J Fam Pract *34:* 759, 1992.

National Institute on Drug Abuse: *National Household Survey on Drug Abuse: Highlights, 1991.* US Government Printing Office, Washington, 1991.

Newhouse PA, Hughes JR: The role of nicotine and nicotinic mechanisms in neuropsychiatric disease. Br J Addict *86:* 521, 1991.

Perkins KA, Grobe JE, Epstein LH, Caggiula A, Stiller RL, Jacob RG: Chronic and acute tolerance to subjective effects of nicotine. Pharmacol Biochem Behav *45:* 375, 1993.

Pomerleau DF: Nicotine and the central nervous system: Biobehavioral effects of cigarette smoking. Am J Med *93* (1A): 2S, 1992.

Russell MA, Stapleton JA, Feyerabend C, Wiseman SM, Gustavsson G, Sawe U, Connor P: Targeting heavy smokers in general practice: Randomised controlled trial of transdermal nicotine patches. BMJ *306:* 1308, 1993.

Schelling TC: Addictive drugs: The cigarette experience. Science *255:* 430, 1992.

Schwartz JL: Methods of smoking cessation. Med Clin North Am *76:* 451, 1992.

Srivastava ED, Russell MA, Feyerabend C, Masterson JG, Rhodes J: Sensitivity and tolerance to nicotine in smokers and nonsmokers. Psychopharmacology *105:* 63, 1991.

Stolerman IP, Shoaib M: The neurobiology of tobacco addiction. Trends Pharmacol Sci *12:* 467, 1991.

Substance Abuse and Mental Health Services Administration Office of Applied Studies: *Preliminary Estimates from the 1995 National Household Survey on Drug Abuse.* US Government Printing Office, Washington, 1995.

Vaughan DA: Frontiers in pharmacologic treatment of alcohol, cocaine, and nicotine dependence. Psychiatr Ann *20:* 695, 1990.

Warburton DM: Nicotine as a cognitive enhancer. Prog Neuropsychopharmacol Biol Psychiatry *16:* 181, 1992.

▲ 12.10 Opioid-Related Disorders

In addition to the morbidity and mortality associated directly with the opioid-related disorders, the association between the transmission of the human immunodeficiency virus (HIV) and intravenous opioid and opiate use is now recognized as a leading national health concern. The words *opiate* and *opioid* come from the word *opium,* the juice of the opium poppy, *Papaver somniferum,* which contains approximately 20 opium alkaloids, including morphine. (The fourth edition of *Diagnostic and Statistical Manual of Mental Disorders* [DSM-IV] and this textbook use the word *opioid* to encompass *opiate,* any preparation or derivative of opium, as well as *opioid,* a synthetic narcotic that resembles an opiate in action but that is not derived from opium.) Naturally occurring opiates are smuggled into the United States from Colombia and Asia, where the opium poppy is a major revenue-producing crop in several regions. Other naturally occurring opiates or opiates that are synthesized from naturally occurring opiates are heroin (diacetylmorphine), codeine (3-methoxymorphine), and hydromorphone (Dilaudid). Heroin is about twice as potent as morphine and is the most commonly used opiate in persons with opioid-related disorders. In the 1970s, the purity of heroin sold in the United States averaged 7 percent (too low to be effective unless administered intravenously). Currently, the purity of heroin sold in the United states averages 80 percent, which gives users a more potent high without injecting.

Heroin, which is pharmacologically similar to morphine, induces analgesia, drowsiness, and changes in mood. Although the manufacture, sale, and possession of heroin are illegal in the United States, attempts have been made to make heroin available to pain-ridden terminal cancer patients because of its excellent analgesic and euphoric effects. Many people, including some legislators, favor a change in the law, but such legislation has been repeatedly voted down by the U.S. Congress.

Many synthetic opioids have been manufactured, including meperidine (Demerol), methadone (Dolophine), pentazocine (Talwin), and propoxyphene (Darvon). Methadone is the current gold standard in the treatment of opioid dependence. Opioid antagonists have been synthesized to treat opioid overdose and opioid dependence. This class of drugs includes naloxone (Narcan), naltrexone (ReVia), nalorphine, levallorphan, and apomorphine. Compounds with mixed agonist and antagonist activity at opioid receptors have been synthesized and include pentazocine, butorphanol (Stadol), and buprenorphine (Buprenex). Studies have found buprenorphine to be an effective treatment for opioid dependence.

EPIDEMIOLOGY

People with opioid dependence most widely use heroin. In 1991, an estimated 1.3 percent of the U.S. population had used heroin at least once. In the United States, there are about 500,000 people with opioid dependence, about half of them in New York City. The male-to-female ratio of people with opioid dependence is about 3 to 1. Users of opioids typically started to use substances in their teens and early 20s; currently, most people with opioid dependence are in their 30s and 40s. In the United States, people tend to experience their first opioid-induced experience in their early teens or even as young as 10 years old. Such early induction into the drug culture is likely to happen in communities in which substance abuse is rampant and in families in which the parents are substance abusers. A heroin habit can cost a person hundreds of dollars a day; thus, a person with opioid dependence needs to obtain money through criminal activities and prostitution. The involvement of people with opioid dependence in prostitution accounts for much of the spread of HIV.

The following epidemiological data come from the National Institute on Drug Abuse (NIDA) and the Substance Abuse and Mental Health Administration:

There were an estimated 122,000 new heroin users in 1994. Estimates of heroin incidence are subject to wide variability and do not show any clear trend, although the 1994 estimate of new users is larger than estimates for previous recent years. This finding is consistent with anecdotal reports of an increasing number of new heroin users.

In 1991, an estimated 1.3 percent of the population reported that they had ever used heroin at some time; and the reported use in the past month was so low that reliable estimates could not be developed. The rates of use of heroin in their lifetimes were significantly higher among adults ages 26 to 34 (1.8 percent) than among adults ages 18 to 25 (0.8 percent) or adolescents ages 12 to 17 (0.3 percent). Between 1990 and 1991, the prevalence of lifetime heroin use among adults ages 35 and older increased significantly, from 0.7 to 1.5 percent. No other changes for specific age groups were statistically significant.

NEUROPHARMACOLOGY

The primary effects of the opioids are mediated through the opioid receptors, which were discovered in the second half of the 1970s. The μ-opioid receptors are involved in the regulation and mediation of analgesia, respiratory depression, constipation, and dependence; the κ-opioid receptors, with analgesia, diuresis, and sedation; and the Δ-opioid receptors, possibly with analgesia.

In 1974, enkephalin, an endogenous pentapeptide with opioid-like actions, was identified. This discovery led to the identification of three classes of endogenous opioids within the brain, including the endorphins and the enkephalins. Endorphins are involved in neural transmission and pain suppression. They are released naturally in the body when a person is physically hurt and account in part for the absence of pain during acute injuries.

The opiates and opioids also have significant effects on the dopaminergic and noradrenergic neurotransmitter systems. Several types of data indicate that the addictive rewarding properties of opiates and opioids are mediated through the activation of the ventral tegmental area dopaminergic neurons that project to the cerebral cortex and the limbic system.

Heroin is the most commonly abused opioid and is more potent and lipid soluble than morphine. Because of those properties, heroin crosses the blood–brain barrier in less time and has a more rapid onset than does morphine. Heroin was first introduced as a treatment for morphine addiction, but heroin, in fact, is more dependence producing than is morphine. Codeine, which occurs naturally as about 0.5 percent of the opiate alkaloids in opium, is absorbed easily through the gastrointestinal tract and is subsequently transformed into morphine in the body. Results of at least one study using positron emission tomography (PET) has suggested that one effect of all opioids is a decrease in cerebral blood flow in selected brain regions in people with opioid dependence (Fig. 12.10–1).

Tolerance and Dependence

Tolerance to opioids develops rapidly and can be so profound, for example, that terminally ill cancer patients may need 200 to 300 mg a day of morphine, whereas a dose of 60 mg can easily be fatal to an opiate-naive person. The symptoms of opioid withdrawal, however, do not appear unless a person has been using opiates or opioids for a long time or when cessation is particularly abrupt, as functionally occurs when an opiate antagonist is given. The long-term use of opiates or opioids results in changes in the number and sensitivity of

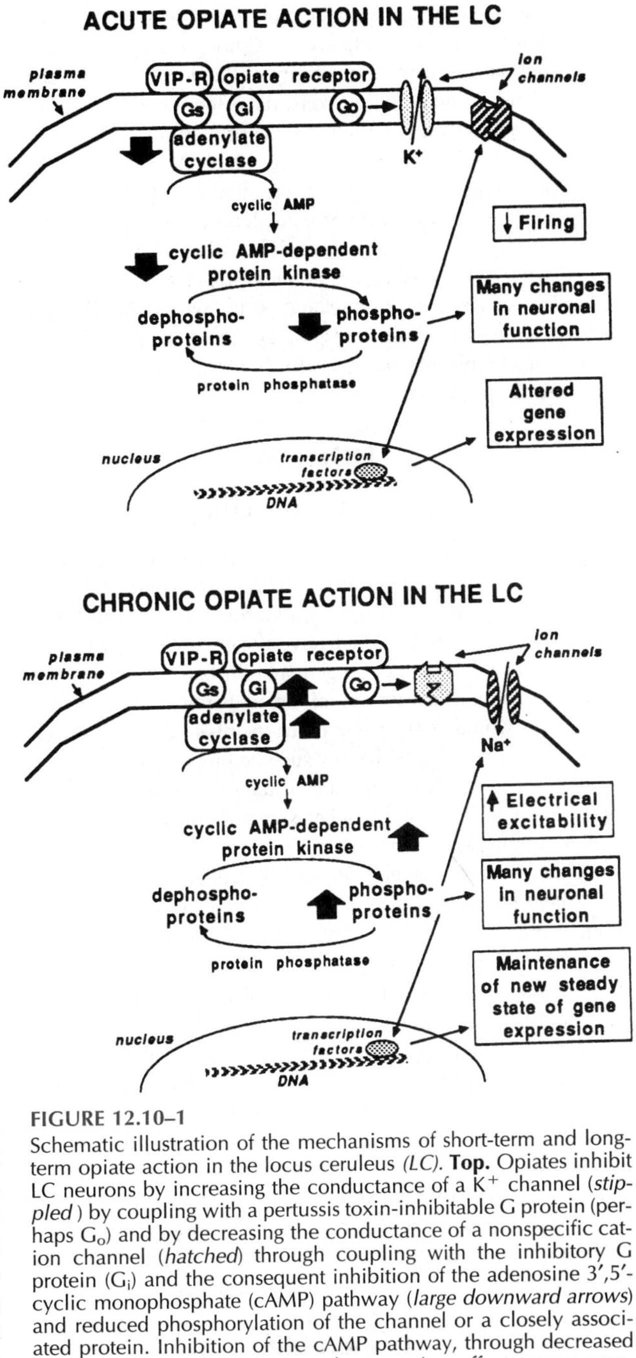
ACUTE OPIATE ACTION IN THE LC
plasma membrane
VIP-R
opiate receptor
Gs
Gi
Go
ion channels
adenylate cyclase
K+
cyclic AMP
↓ Firing
cyclic AMP-dependent protein kinase
Many changes in neuronal function
dephospho-proteins
phospho-proteins
protein phosphatase
Altered gene expression
nucleus
transcription factors
DNA
CHRONIC OPIATE ACTION IN THE LC
plasma membrane
VIP-R
opiate receptor
Gs
Gi
Go
ion channels
adenylate cyclase
Na+
cyclic AMP
↑ Electrical excitability
cyclic AMP-dependent protein kinase
Many changes in neuronal function
dephospho-proteins
phospho-proteins
protein phosphatase
Maintenance of new steady state of gene expression
nucleus
transcription factors
DNA

FIGURE 12.10–1

Schematic illustration of the mechanisms of short-term and long-term opiate action in the locus ceruleus *(LC)*. **Top.** Opiates inhibit LC neurons by increasing the conductance of a K^+ channel (*stippled*) by coupling with a pertussis toxin-inhibitable G protein (perhaps G_o) and by decreasing the conductance of a nonspecific cation channel (*hatched*) through coupling with the inhibitory G protein (G_i) and the consequent inhibition of the adenosine 3′,5′-cyclic monophosphate (cAMP) pathway (*large downward arrows*) and reduced phosphorylation of the channel or a closely associated protein. Inhibition of the cAMP pathway, through decreased phosphorylation of numerous other proteins, affects many processes in the neuron; in addition to reducing the firing rates, for example, it initiates alterations in gene expression through regulation of transcription factors. **Bottom.** Long-term administration of opiates leads to a compensatory upregulation of the cAMP pathway (*large upward arrows*), which contributes to opiate dependence in the neurons by increasing their intrinsic excitability through increased activation of the nonspecific cation channel. In addition, upregulation of the cAMP pathway is presumably associated with persistent changes in transcription factor that maintain the long-term morphine-treated state. Long-term opiate administration also leads to a relative decrease in the degree of activation of the K^+ channel because of tolerance, the mechanism of which is unknown. Also shown in the figure are VIP-R, a vasoactive intestinal polypeptide receptor (VIP is a major activator of the cAMP pathway in the LC), and G_s, the stimulatory G protein that activates adenylate cyclase. (Reprinted with permission from Nestler EJ: Molecular mechanisms of drug addiction. J Neurosci *12:* 2441, 1992.)

opioid receptors, which are mediators for at least some of the effect of tolerance and withdrawal. Although long-term use is associated with increased sensitivity of the dopaminergic, cholinergic, and serotonergic neurons, the effect of opioids on the noradrenergic neurons is probably the primary mediator of the symptoms of opioid withdrawal (Fig. 12.10–2). Short-term use of opioids apparently decreases the activity of the noradrenergic neurons in the locus ceruleus; long-term use activates a compensatory homeostatic mechanism within the neurons; and opioid withdrawal results in a rebound hyperactivity. This hypothesis also provides an explanation for why clonidine (Catapres), an α_2-adrenergic receptor agonist that decreases the release of norepinephrine, is useful in the treatment of opioid withdrawal symptoms.

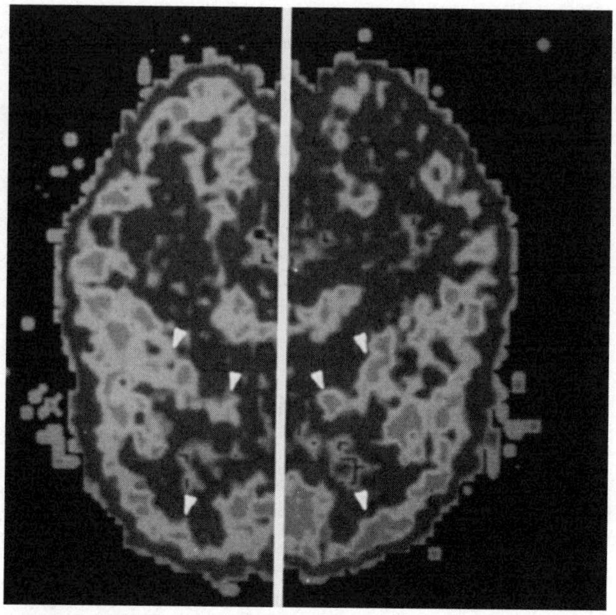

FIGURE 12.10–2
Glucose utilization, as revealed by PET, in the brain of a heroin addict. High rates are pictured as *light areas.* On the *left,* the addict was given a placebo. On the *right,* the addict was given 30 mg of morphine intramuscularly. (Courtesy of E. D. London, Ph.D.)

ETIOLOGY

Psychosocial Factors

Opioid dependence is not limited to low socioeconomic classes, although the incidence of opioid dependence is greater in these groups than in higher socioeconomic classes. Social factors associated with urban poverty probably contribute to opioid dependence. About 50 percent of urban heroin users are children of single parents or divorced parents and are from families in which at least one other member has a substance-related disorder. Children from such settings are at high risk for opioid dependence, especially if they also evidence behavioral problems in school or other signs of conduct disorder.

Some consistent behavior patterns seem to be especially pronounced in adolescents with opioid dependence. These patterns have been called the *heroin behavior syndrome:* underlying depression, often of an agitated type and frequently accompanied by anxiety symptoms; impulsiveness expressed by a passive-aggressive orientation; fear of failure; use of heroin as an antianxiety agent to mask feelings of low self-esteem, hopelessness, and aggression; limited coping strategies and low frustration tolerance, accompanied by the need for immediate gratification; sensitivity to drug contingencies, with a keen awareness of the relation between good feelings and the act of drug taking; feelings of behavioral impotence counteracted by momentary control over the life situation by means of substances; disturbances in social and interpersonal relationships with peers maintained by mutual substance experiences.

Comorbidity

About 90 percent of people with opioid dependence have an additional psychiatric disorder. The most common comorbid psychiatric diagnoses are major depressive disorder, alcohol use disorders, antisocial personality disorder, and anxiety disorders. About 15 percent of people with opioid dependence attempt to commit suicide at least once. The high prevalence of comorbidity with other psychiatric diagnoses highlights the need to develop a broad-based treatment program that also addresses patients' associated psychiatric disorders.

Biological and Genetic Factors

A person with an opioid-related disorder may have had a genetically determined hypoactivity of the opiate system. Researchers are investigating the possibility that such hypoactivity may be caused by opioid receptors that were too few or were less sensitive than possible; by too little release of endogenous opioid; or by having too high concentrations of a hypothesized endogenous opioid antagonist. A biological predisposition to an opioid-related disorder may also be associated with abnormal functioning in either the dopaminergic or the noradrenergic neurotransmitter system. Because of the difficulties inherent in the study of substance-related disorders, the data are still limited; some data, however, do support the idea that there are genetic determinants for developing of opioid-related disorders.

Psychodynamic Theory

In psychoanalytic literature, the behavior of people addicted to narcotics has been described in terms of libidinal fixation, with regression to pregenital, oral, or even more archaic levels of psychosexual development. The need to explain the relation of drug abuse, defense mechanisms, impulse control, affective disturbances, and adaptive mechanisms led to the shift from psychosexual formulations to formulations emphasizing ego psychology. Serious ego pathology is often thought to be associated with substance abuse and is considered to be indicative of profound developmental disturbances. Problems of the relation between the ego and affects emerge as a key area of difficulty.

DIAGNOSIS

DSM-IV lists several opioid-related disorders (Table 12.10–1) but contains specific diagnostic criteria only for

Table 12.10–1
DSM-IV Opioid-Related Disorders

Opioid use disorders
Opioid dependence
Opioid abuse
Opioid-induced disorders
Opioid intoxication
Specify if:
With perceptual disturbances
Opioid withdrawal
Opioid intoxication delirium
Opioid-induced psychotic disorder, with delusions
Specify if:
With onset during intoxication
Opioid-induced psychotic disorder, with hallucinations
Specify if:
With onset during intoxication
Opioid-induced mood disorder
Specify if:
With onset during intoxication
Opioid-induced sexual dysfunction
Specify if:
With onset during intoxication
Opioid-induced sleep disorder
Specify if:
With onset during intoxication
With onset during withdrawal
Opioid-related disorder not otherwise specified

Reprinted with permission from American Psychiatric Association: *Diagnostic and Statistical Manual of Mental Disorders,* ed 4. Copyright, American Psychiatric Association, Washington, 1994.

opioid intoxication (Table 12.10–2) and opioid withdrawal (Table 12.10–3) within the section on opioid-related disorders. The diagnostic criteria for the other opioid-related disorders are contained within the DSM-IV sections that deal specifically with the predominant symptom—for example, opioid-induced mood disorder (see Table 15.1–11).

Opioid Dependence and Opioid Abuse

Opioid dependence and opioid abuse are defined in DSM-IV according to the general criteria for these disorders (see Tables 12.1–7, 12.1–8, and 12.1–9).

A 42-year-old executive in a public relations firm was referred for psychiatric consultation by his surgeon, who discovered him sneaking large quantities of a codeine-containing cough medicine into the hospital. The patient had been a heavy cigarette smoker for 20 years and had a chronic hacking cough. He had come to the hospital for a hernia repair and found the pain from the incision unbearable when he coughed.

An operation on his back 5 years ago had led his doctor to prescribe codeine to help relieve the incisional pain. Over the intervening 5 years, however, the patient had continued to use codeine-containing tablets and had increased his intake to 60 to 90 tablets (5 mg) daily. He stated that he often "just took them by the handful—not to feel good, you understand, just to get by." He had spent considerable time and effort developing a circle of physicians and pharmacists to whom he would make the rounds at least 3 times a week to obtain new supplies of pills. He had tried several times to stop using codeine but had failed. He had lost two jobs because of lax work habits, and he had been divorced by his wife of 11 years.

Table 12.10–2
DSM-IV Diagnostic Criteria for Opioid Intoxication

A. Recent use of an opioid.
B. Clinically significant maladaptive behavioral or psychological changes (eg, initial euphoria followed by apathy, dysphoria, psychomotor agitation or retardation, impaired judgment, or impaired social or occupational functioning) that developed during, or shortly after, opioid use.
C. Pupillary constriction (or pupillary dilation due to anoxia from severe overdose) and one (or more) of the following signs, developing during, or shortly after, opioid use:
 (1) drowsiness or coma
 (2) slurred speech
 (3) impairment in attention or memory
D. The symptoms are not due to a general medical condition and are not better accounted for by another mental disorder.

Specify if:
With perceptual disturbances

Reprinted with permission from American Psychiatric Association: *Diagnostic and Statistical Manual of Mental Disorders,* ed 4. Copyright, American Psychiatric Association, Washington, 1994.

Table 12.10–3
DSM-IV Diagnostic Criteria for Opioid Withdrawal

A. Either of the following:
 (1) cessation of (or reduction in) opioid use that has been heavy and prolonged (several weeks or longer)
 (2) administration of an opioid antagonist after a period of opioid use
B. Three (or more) of the following, developing within minutes to several days after criterion A:
 (1) dysphoric mood
 (2) nausea or vomiting
 (3) muscle aches
 (4) lacrimation or rhinorrhea
 (5) pupillary dilation, piloerection, or sweating
 (6) diarrhea
 (7) yawning
 (8) fever
 (9) insomnia
C. The symptoms in criterion B cause clinically significant distress or impairment in social, occupational, or other important areas of functioning.
D. The symptoms are not due to a general medical condition and are not better accounted for by another mental disorder.

Reprinted with permission from American Psychiatric Association: *Diagnostic and Statistical Manual of Mental Disorders,* ed 4. Copyright, American Psychiatric Association, Washington, 1994.

Opioid Intoxication

DSM-IV defines opioid intoxication as including maladaptive behavioral changes and some specific physical symptoms of opioid use (Table 12.10–2). In general, an altered mood, psychomotor retardation, drowsiness, slurred speech, and impaired memory and attention in the presence of other indicators of recent opioid use strongly suggest a diagnosis of opioid intoxication. DSM-IV allows for the specification of "with perceptual disturbances."

Opioid Withdrawal

The general rule about the onset and duration of withdrawal symptoms is that substances with short durations of action tend to produce short, intense withdrawal syndromes and substances with long durations of action produce prolonged but mild withdrawal syndromes. As an exception to the rule, narcotic antagonist-precipitated withdrawal after long-acting opioid dependence can be severe.

An abstinence syndrome can be precipitated by the administration of an opioid antagonist. The symptoms may begin within seconds of such an intravenous injection and may peak in about 1 hour. Opioid craving rarely occurs in the context of analgesic administration for pain from physical disorders or surgery. The full withdrawal syndrome, including intense craving for opioids, usually occurs only secondary to an abrupt cessation of use in people with opioid dependence.

Morphine and Heroin. The morphine and heroin withdrawal syndrome begins in 6 to 8 hours after the last dose, usually after a 1- to 2-week period of continuous use or after the administration of a narcotic antagonist. The withdrawal syndrome reaches its peak intensity during the second or third day and subsides during the next 7 to 10 days, but some symptoms may persist for 6 months or longer.

Meperidine. The withdrawal syndrome from meperidine begins quickly, reaches a peak in 8 to 12 hours, and comes to an end in 4 to 5 days.

Methadone. Methadone withdrawal usually begins 1 to 3 days after the last dose and comes to an end in 10 to 14 days.

Symptoms. Opioid withdrawal is defined in DSM-IV (see Table 12.10–3). The disorder consists of severe muscle cramps and bone aches, profuse diarrhea, abdominal cramps, rhinorrhea, lacrimation, piloerection or gooseflesh (from which comes the term *cold turkey* for the abstinence syndrome), yawning, fever, pupillary dilation, hypertension, tachycardia, and temperature dysregulation, including hypothermia and hyperthermia. People with opioid dependence seldom die from opioid withdrawal, unless they have a severe preexisting physical illness such as cardiac disease. Residual symptoms—such as insomnia, bradycardia, temperature dysregulation, and a craving for opioids—may persist for months after withdrawal. Associated features of opioid withdrawal include restlessness, irritability, depression, tremor, weakness, nausea, and vomiting. At any time during the abstinence syndrome, a single injection of morphine or heroin eliminates all the symptoms.

Opioid Intoxication Delirium

Opioid intoxication delirium is a diagnostic category within DSM-IV (Table 10.2–3). Opioid intoxication delirium is most likely to happen when opioids are used in high doses, are mixed with other psychoactive compounds, or are used by a person with preexisting brain damage or a central nervous system (CNS) disorder (for example, epilepsy).

Opioid-Induced Psychotic Disorder

Opioid-induced psychotic disorder can begin during opioid intoxication. The DSM-IV diagnostic criteria are contained in the section on schizophrenia and other psychotic disorders (see Table 14.1–2). Clinicians can specify whether hallucinations or delusions are the predominant symptoms.

Opioid-Induced Mood Disorder

Opioid-induced mood disorder, which can begin during opioid intoxication, is a diagnostic category in DSM-IV (see Table 15.1–11). Opioid-induced mood disorder symptoms may be of a manic, depressed, or mixed nature, depending on a person's response to opiates or opioids. A person coming to psychiatric attention with opioid-induced mood disorder usually has mixed symptoms, combining irritability, expansiveness, and depression.

Opioid-Induced Sleep Disorder and Opioid-Induced Sexual Dysfunction

Opioid-induced sleep disorder (see Table 24.2–2) and opioid-induced sexual dysfunction (see Table 21.2–17) are diagnostic categories in DSM-IV. Hypersomnia is likely to be a more common sleep disorder with opioids than is insomnia. The most common sexual dysfunction is likely to be impotence.

Opioid-Related Disorder Not Otherwise Specified

DSM-IV includes diagnoses for opioid-related disorders with symptoms of delirium, abnormal mood, psychosis, abnormal sleep, and sexual dysfunction. Clinical situations that do not fit into these categories are examples of appropriate cases for the use of the DSM-IV diagnosis of opioid-related disorder not otherwise specified (Table 12.10–4).

CLINICAL FEATURES

Opioids can be taken orally, snorted intranasally, and injected intravenously (IV) (Fig. 12.10–3) or subcutaneously (Fig. 12.10–4). Opioids are subjectively addictive because of the euphoric high (the *rush*) that users experience, especially those who take the substances intravenously. The associated symptoms include a feeling of warmth, heaviness of the extremities, dry mouth, itchy face (especially the nose), and facial

Table 12.10–4
DSM-IV Diagnostic Criteria for Opioid-Related Disorder Not Otherwise Specified

The opioid-related disorder not otherwise specified category is for disorders associated with the use of opioids that are not classified as opioid dependence, opioid abuse, opioid intoxication, opioid withdrawal, opioid intoxication delirium, opioid-induced psychotic disorder, opioid-induced mood disorder, opioid-induced sexual dysfunction, or opioid-induced sleep disorder.

flushing. The initial euphoria is followed by a period of sedation, known in street parlance as *nodding off.* For opioid-naive people, the use of opioids can induce dysphoria, nausea, and vomiting.

The physical effects of opiates and opioids include respiratory depression, pupillary constriction, smooth muscle contraction (including the ureters and the bile ducts), constipation, and changes in blood pressure, heart rate, and body temperature. The respiratory depressant effects are mediated at the level of the brainstem.

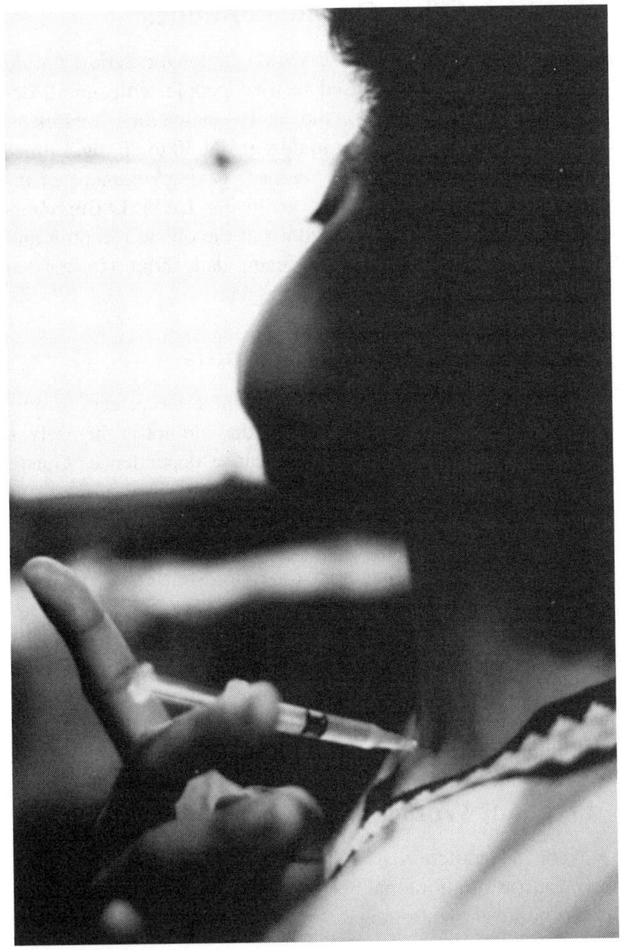

FIGURE 12.10–3
A heroin user puffs her cheeks to force blood into the jugular vein. (Courtesy of Steve Raymer, Copyright, National Geographic Society, 1985.)

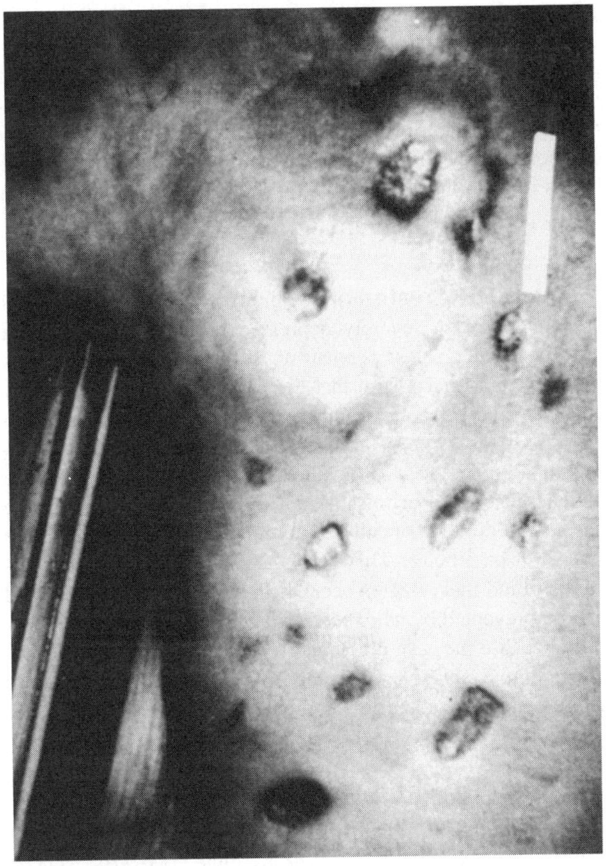

FIGURE 12.10–4
Skin-popper; circular depressed scars, often with underlying chronic abscesses, on the back of a subcutaneous user. Thighs are also commonly used skin-popping areas. (Courtesy of Michael Baden, M.D.)

Adverse Effects

The most common and most serious adverse effect associated with the opioid-related disorders is the potential transmission of hepatitis and HIV through the use of contaminated needles by more than one person. People can experience idiosyncratic allergic reactions to opioids, which result in anaphylactic shock, pulmonary edema, and death if they do not receive prompt and adequate treatment. Another serious adverse effect is an idiosyncratic drug interaction between meperidine and monoamine oxidase inhibitors (MAOIs), which can produce gross autonomic instability, severe behavioral agitation, coma, seizures, and death. Opioids and MAOIs should not be given together for this reason.

Opioid Overdose

Death from an overdose of an opiate or opioid is usually attributable to respiratory arrest from the respiratory depressant effect of the drug. The symptoms of overdose include marked unresponsiveness, coma, slow respiration, hypothermia, hypotension, and bradycardia. When presented with the clinical triad of coma, pinpoint pupils, and respiratory depression, clinicians should consider opiate or opioid overdose as a primary diagnosis. They can also inspect the patient's body for needle tracks in the arms, legs, ankles, groin, and even the dorsal vein of the penis.

Overdose Treatment. Opioid overdose is a medical emergency. With severely depressed respiration, the patient may be semicomatose, comatose, or in shock. A clinician's first task is to make sure that the patient has an open airway and that vital signs are maintained. An opioid antagonist, naloxone 0.4 mg IV, can be administered. This dose can be repeated 4 to 5 times within the first 30 to 45 minutes. The patient generally becomes responsive but, because naloxone has a short duration of action, may relapse into a semicomatose state in 4 or 5 hours. Therefore, careful observation is imperative. Grand mal seizures occur with meperidine overdose and can be prevented by naloxone. Antagonists must be used carefully because they can precipitate a severe withdrawal reaction. Other opioid antagonists useful in the treatment of overdose include nalorphine and levallorphan.

MPTP-Induced Parkinsonism

In 1976, after ingesting an opioid contaminated with *N*-methyl-4-phenyl-1,2,3,6-tetrahydropyridine (MPTP), several people developed a syndrome of irreversible parkinsonism. The mechanism for the neurotoxic effect is as follows: MPTP is converted into 1-methyl-4-phenylpyridinium (MPP^+) by the enzyme monoamine oxidase and is then taken up by dopaminergic neurons. Because MPP^+ binds to melanin in substantia nigra neurons, MPP^+ is concentrated in these neurons and eventually kills the cells. PET studies of people who ingested MPTP but remained asymptomatic have shown a decrease in the number of dopamine-binding sites in the substantia nigra. This decrease reflects a loss in the number of dopaminergic neurons in that region.

TREATMENT AND REHABILITATION

Education and Needle Exchange

Although the essential treatment of opioid use disorders is encouraging people to abstain from opiates and opioids, education about the transmission of HIV must receive equal attention. People with opioid dependence who use intravenous or subcutaneous routes of administration must be educated about available safe-sex practices. Free needle-exchange programs are often subject to intense political and societal pressures but, where allowed, should be made available to people with opioid dependence. Several studies have indicated that unsafe needle sharing is common when it is difficult to obtain a sufficient supply of clean needles and is also common in people with legal difficulties, severe substance problems, and psychiatric symptoms. These are just the people most likely to be involved in transmitting HIV.

Methadone

Methadone is a synthetic narcotic (an opioid) that substitutes for heroin and can be taken orally. When given to addicts to replace their usual substance of abuse, the drug suppresses withdrawal symptoms. A daily dosage of 20 to 80 mg is sufficient to stabilize a patient, although daily dosages of up to 120 mg have been used. Methadone has a duration of action exceeding 24 hours; thus, once-daily dosing is adequate. Methadone maintenance is continued until the patient can be withdrawn from methadone, which itself causes dependence. An abstinence syndrome occurs with methadone withdrawal, but patients are detoxified from methadone more easily than from heroin. Clonidine (Catapres) (0.1 to 0.3 mg 3 to 4 times a day) is usually given during the detoxification period.

Methadone maintenance has several advantages. First, it frees people with opioid dependence from using injectable heroin and thus reduces the chance of spreading HIV through contaminated needles. Second, methadone produces minimal euphoria and rarely causes drowsiness or depression when taken for a long time. Third, methadone allows patients to engage in gainful employment instead of criminal activity. The major disadvantage of methadone use is that patients remain dependent on a narcotic.

Other Opioid Substitutes

Levo-α-acetylmethadol (LAMM), a longer acting opioid than methadone, is also used to treat people with opioid dependence. In contrast to the daily methadone treatment, LAMM can be administered in dosages of 30 to 80 mg 3 times a week; because of this less frequent dosing regimen, an increasing number of programs are using LAMM. Buprenorphine is a mixed agonist-antagonist at the opiate receptor, and several studies have yielded promising data about its use as an opioid substitute in treatment strategies.

Opioid Antagonists

Opioid antagonists block or antagonize the effects of opiates and opioids. Unlike methadone, they do not in themselves exert narcotic effects and do not cause dependence. Opiate antagonists include naloxone, which is used in the treatment of opioid overdose because it reverses the effects of narcotics, and naltrexone, the longest acting (72 hours) antagonist. The theory for using an antagonist for opioid-related disorders is that the blocking of opiate agonist effects, particularly euphoria, discourages people with opioid dependence from substance-seeking behavior and thus deconditions this behavior. The major weakness of the antagonist treatment model is the lack of any mechanism that compels a person to continue to take the antagonist.

Pregnant Women with Opioid Dependence

Neonatal addiction is a significant problem in that about three fourths of all infants born to addicted mothers experience the withdrawal syndrome.

Neonatal Withdrawal. Although opioid withdrawal rarely is fatal for the otherwise healthy adult, it is hazardous to the fetus and can lead to miscarriage or fetal death. Maintaining a pregnant woman with opioid dependence on a low dosage of methadone (10 to 40 mg daily) may be the least hazardous course to follow. At this dosage, neonatal withdrawal is usually mild and can be managed with low doses of paregoric. If pregnancy begins while a woman is taking high doses of methadone, the dosage should be reduced slowly (for example, 1 mg every 3 days), and fetal movements should be monitored. If withdrawal is necessary or desired, it is accomplished with least hazard during the second trimester.

Fetal AIDS Transmission. AIDS is the other major risk to the fetus of a woman with opioid dependence. Pregnant women can pass HIV, the causative agent of AIDS, to the fetus through the placental circulation. An HIV-infected mother can also pass HIV to the infant through breast feeding.

Psychotherapy

The entire range of psychotherapeutic modalities is appropriate for treating opioid-related disorders. Individual psychotherapy, behavioral therapy, cognitive-behavioral therapy, family therapy, support groups (such as Narcotics Anonymous), and social skills training may all prove to be effective for specific patients. Social skills training should be particularly emphasized for patients with few social skills. Family therapy is usually indicated when the patient lives with family members.

Therapeutic Communities

Therapeutic communities are residences in which all members have a problem of substance abuse. Abstinence is the rule; in order to be admitted to such a community, a person must show a high level of motivation. The goals are to effect a complete change of lifestyle, including abstinence from substances; to develop personal honesty, responsibility, and useful social skills; and to eliminate antisocial attitudes and criminal behavior.

The staff members of most therapeutic communities are people with former substance dependence who often put a prospective candidate through a rigorous screening process to test the person's motivation. Self-help through the use of confrontational groups and isolation from the outside world and from friends associated with the drug life are emphasized. The prototypical community for people with substance dependence is Phoenix House, where the residents live for long periods (usually 12 to 18 months) while receiving treatment. They are allowed to return to their old environments only when they have demonstrated their ability to handle increased responsibility within the therapeutic community. Therapeutic communities can be effective but require large staffs and extensive facilities. Moreover, dropout rates are high; as many as 75 percent of those who enter therapeutic communities leave within the first month.

References

Darke S, Wodak A, Hall W, Heather N, Ward J: Prevalence and predictors of psychopathology among opioid users. Br J Addict *87:* 771, 1992.

Di Chiara G, North RA: Neurobiology of opiate abuse. Trends Pharmacol Sci *13:* 185, 1992.

Gintzler AR: Relevance of opioid bimodality to tolerance/dependence formation: From transmitter release to second messenger formation. Adv Exp Med Biol *373:* 73, 1995.

Goldstein A: Heroin addiction: Neurobiology, pharmacology, and policy. J Psychoactive Drugs *23:* 123, 1991.

Hurt PH, Ritchie EC: A case of ketamine dependence. Am J Psychiatry *151:* 779, 1994.

Jaffe JH: Opioid-related disorders. In *Comprehensive Textbook of Psychiatry,* ed 6, HI Kaplan, BJ Sadock, editors, p 842. Williams & Wilkins, Baltimore, 1995.

Kane S: HIV, heroin and heterosexual relations. Soc Sci Med *32:* 1037, 1991.

Koob GF, Maldonado R, Stinus L: Neural substrates of opiate withdrawal. Trends Neurosci *15:* 186, 1992.

Kosten TA, Bianchi MS, Kosten TR: The predictive validity of the dependence syndrome in opiate abusers. Am J Drug Alcohol Abuse *18:* 145, 1992.

Kosten TR, Rosen MI, Schottenfeld R, Ziedonis D: Buprenorphine for cocaine and opiate dependence. Psychopharmacol Bull *28:* 15, 1992.

Kreek MJ: Rationale for maintenance pharmacotherapy of opiate dependence. Res Publ Assoc Res Nerv Ment Dis *70:* 2, 1992.

Ling W, Wesson DR: Drugs of abuse: Opiates. West J Med *152:* 565, 1990.

London ED, Broussolle EPM, Links JM, Wong DF, Cascella NG, Dannals RF, Sano M, Herning R, Snyder FR, Rippetoe LR, Toung TJK, Jaffe JH: Morphine-induced metabolic changes in human brain: Studies with positron emission tomography and [fluorine 18] fluorodeoxyglucose. Arch Gen Psychiatry *47:* 73, 1990.

Luthar SS, Anton SF, Merikangas KR, Rounsaville BJ: Vulnerability to substance abuse and psychopathology among siblings of opioid abusers. J Nerv Ment Dis *180:* 153, 1992.

Metzger D, Woody G, De Philippis D, McLellan AT, O'Brien CP, Platt JJ: Risk factors for needle sharing among the methadone-treated patients. Am J Psychiatry *148:* 636, 1991.

National Institute on Drug Abuse: *National Household Survey on Drug Abuse: Highlights, 1991.* US Government Printing Office, Washington, 1991.

Neslter EJ: Molecular mechanisms of drug addiction. J Neurosci *12:* 2439, 1992.

Novick DM, Joseph H: Medical maintenance: The treatment of chronic opiate dependence in general medical practice. J Subst Abuse Treat *8:* 233, 1991.

Platt JJ, Husband SD, Taube D: Major psychotherapeutic modalities for heroin addiction: A brief overview. Int J Addict *25:* 1453, 1990.

Resnick RB, Galanter M, Pycha C, Cohen A, Grandison P, Flood N: Buprenorphine: An alternative to methadone for heroin dependence treatment. Psychopharmacol Bull *28:* 109, 1992.

Rounsaville BJ, Hosten TR, Weissman MM, Prusoff B, Pauls D, Anton SF, Merikangas K: Psychiatric disorders in relatives of probands with opiate addictions. Arch Gen Psychiatry *48:* 33, 1991.

Substance Abuse and Mental Health Services Administration Office of Applied Studies: *Preliminary Estimates from the 1995 National Household Survey on Drug Abuse.* US Government Printing Office, Washington, 1995.

Trujillo KA, Akil H: Opiate tolerance and dependence: Recent findings and synthesis. New Biol *3:* 915, 1991.

▲ 12.11 Phencyclidine (or Phencyclidine-like)-Related Disorders

Phencyclidine (PCP) [1-(1-phenylcyclohexy-1)piperidine] is the most commonly abused arylcyclohexylamine. PCP is also referred to as angel dust, crystal, peace, supergrass (when sprinkled on a cannabis cigarette), hog, rocket fuel, and horse tranqs. PCP was developed and is classified as a dissociative anesthetic. Its use as an anesthetic in humans, however, was associated with disorientation, agitation, delirium, and unpleasant hallucinations on awakening. Therefore, PCP is no longer used as an anesthetic in humans, although it is used in some countries as an anesthetic in veterinary medicine. A related compound, ketamine (Ketalar), also referred to as special K, is still used as a human anesthetic in the United States; it has not been associated with the same adverse effects, although ketamine is also subject to abuse by humans.

PCP was first used illicitly in San Francisco in the late 1960s. Since then, about 30 chemical analogues have been produced and are intermittently available on the streets of major U.S. cities. The effects of PCP are similar to those of such hallucinogens as lysergic acid diethylamide (LSD). Because of differing pharmacology and some difference in clinical effects, however, DSM-IV classifies the arylcyclohexylamines as a separate category. PCP has also been of interest to schizophrenia researchers, who have used PCP-induced chemical and behavioral changes in animals as a possible model of schizophrenia.

EPIDEMIOLOGY

PCP and some related substances are relatively easy to synthesize in illegal laboratories and relatively inexpensive to buy on the streets. The variable quality of the laboratories, however, results in a range of potency and purity. PCP use varies most markedly as a factor of geography. Some areas of some cities have a 10-fold higher usage rate of PCP than do other areas. The highest PCP use in the United States is in Washington, DC, where PCP accounts for 18 percent of all substance-related deaths. In Los Angeles, Chicago, and Baltimore, the comparable figure is 6 percent, and the national average is 3 percent. PCP is generally used by men ages 20 to 40, who are members of a minority group. Most users of PCP also use other substances, particularly alcohol, but also opiates, opioids, marijuana, amphetamines, and cocaine.

NEUROPHARMACOLOGY

PCP and its related compounds are variously sold as a crystalline powder, paste, liquid, or drug-soaked paper (blotter). PCP is most commonly used as an additive to a cannabis- or parsley-containing cigarette. Experienced users report that the effects of 2 to 3 mg of smoked PCP occur in about 5 minutes and plateau in 30 minutes. PCP has a bioavailability of about 75 percent when taken by intravenous administration and a bioavailability of about 30 percent when smoked. The half-life of PCP in humans is about 20 hours, and the half-life of ketamine in humans is about 2 hours.

The primary pharmacodynamic effect of PCP and ketamine is as an antagonist at the *N*-methyl-D-aspartate (NMDA) subtype of glutamate receptors. PCP binds to a site within the NMDA-associated calcium channel and prevents the influx of calcium ions. Another effect of PCP is the activation of the dopaminergic neurons of the ventral tegmental area, which project to the cerebral cortex and the limbic system. The activation of these neurons is usually involved in mediating the reinforcing qualities of PCP.

Tolerance for the effects of PCP occurs in humans, although physical dependence generally does not occur. In animals that are administered more PCP per pound for longer times than in virtually any humans, however, PCP does induce physical dependence, with marked withdrawal symptoms of lethargy, depression, and craving. Physical symptoms of withdrawal in humans are rare, probably as a function of dose and duration of use. Although physical dependence on PCP is rare in humans, psychological dependence on PCP, as well as ketamine, is common, and some users become psychologically dependent on the PCP-induced psychological state.

The fact that PCP is made in illicit laboratories contributes to the increased likelihood of impurities in the final product. One such contaminant is 1-piperidenocyclohexane carbonitrite, which releases hydrogen cyanide in small quantities when ingested. Another contaminant is piperidine, which can be recognized by its strong, fishy odor.

DIAGNOSIS

The fourth edition of *Diagnostic and Statistical Manual of Mental Disorders* (DSM-IV) lists a number of PCP (or PCP-like)-related disorders (Table 12.11–1) but outlines the specific diagnostic criteria for only PCP intoxication (Table 12.11–2) within the PCP (or PCP-like)-related disorders section. Their diagnostic criteria of other PCP (or PCP-like)-related disorders are listed in the sections that deal with specific symptoms—for example, PCP-induced anxiety disorder in the anxiety disorders section of DSM-IV (see Table 16.1–5).

PCP Dependence and PCP Abuse

DSM-IV uses the general criteria for PCP dependence and PCP abuse (see Tables 12.1–7, 12.1–8, and 12.1–9). Some long-term users of PCP are said to be crystallized, a syndrome characterized by dulled thinking, decreased reflexes, loss of memory, loss of impulse control, depression, lethargy, and impaired concentration.

Table 12.11–1
DSM-IV Phencyclidine-Related Disorders

Phencyclidine use disorders
Phencyclidine dependence
Phencyclidine abuse
Phencyclidine-induced disorders
Phencyclidine intoxication
Specify if:
With perceptual disturbances
Phencyclidine intoxication delirium
Phencyclidine-induced psychotic disorder, with delusions
Specify if:
With onset during intoxication
Phencyclidine-induced psychotic disorder, with hallucinations
Specify if:
With onset during intoxication
Phencyclidine-induced mood disorder
Specify if:
With onset during intoxication
Phencyclidine-induced anxiety disorder
Specify if:
With onset during intoxication
Phencyclidine-related disorder not otherwise specified

Table 12.11–2
DSM-IV Diagnostic Criteria for Phencyclidine Intoxication

A. Recent use of phencyclidine (or a related substance).

B. Clinically significant maladaptive behavioral changes (eg, belligerence, assaultiveness, impulsiveness, unpredictability, psychomotor agitation, impaired judgment, or impaired social or occupational functioning) that developed during, or shortly after, use of phencyclidine.

C. Within an hour (less when smoked, "snorted," or used intravenously), two (or more) of the following signs:
(1) vertical or horizontal nystagmus
(2) hypertension or tachycardia
(3) numbness or diminished responsiveness to pain
(4) ataxia
(5) dysarthria
(6) muscle rigidity
(7) seizures or coma
(8) hyperacusis

D. The symptoms are not due to a general medical condition and are not better accounted for by another mental disorder.

Specify if:
With perceptual disturbances

PCP Intoxication

Short-term PCP intoxication can have potentially severe complications and must often be considered a psychiatric emergency. DSM-IV gives specific criteria for PCP (Table 12.11–2). Clinicians can specify the presence of perceptual disturbances.

Some patients may be brought to psychiatric attention within hours of ingesting PCP, but often 2 to 3 days elapse before psychiatric help is sought. The long interval between drug ingestion and the appearance of the patient in a clinic usually reflects the attempts of friends to deal with the psychosis by talking down. People who lose consciousness are brought for help earlier than are those who remain conscious. Most patients recover completely within a day or two, but some remain psychotic for as long as 2 weeks. Patients who are first seen in a coma often manifest disorientation, hallucinations, confusion, and difficulty in communication on regaining consciousness. These symptoms may also be seen in noncomatose patients, but their symptoms appear to be less severe than are those of comatose patients. Behavioral disturbances sometimes are severe; they may include public masturbation, stripping off clothes, violence, urinary incontinence, crying, and inappropriate laughing. Patients frequently have amnesia for the entire period of the psychosis.

PCP Intoxication Delirium

PCP intoxication delirium is included as a diagnostic category in DSM-IV (see Table 10.2–3). An estimated 25 percent of all PCP-related emergency room patients may meet the criteria for the disorder, which can be characterized by agitated, violent, and bizarre behavior.

PCP-Induced Psychotic Disorder

PCP-induced psychotic disorder is included as a diagnostic category in DSM-IV (see Table 14.1–2). Clinicians can further specify whether the predominant symptoms are delusions or hallucinations. An estimated 6 percent of PCP-related emergency room patients may meet the criteria for the disorder. About 40 percent of these patients have physical signs of hypertension and nystagmus, and 10 percent have been injured accidentally during the psychosis. The psychosis can last from 1 to 30 days, with an average of 4 to 5 days.

PCP-Induced Mood Disorder

PCP-induced mood disorder is included as a diagnostic category in DSM-IV (see Table 15.1–11). An estimated 3 percent of PCP-related emergency room patients meet the criteria for the disorder, with most fitting the criteria for a maniclike episode. About 40 to 50 percent have been accidentally injured during the course of their manic symptoms.

PCP-Induced Anxiety Disorder

PCP-induced anxiety disorder is included as a diagnostic category in DSM-IV (see Table 16.1–5). Anxiety is probably the most common symptom causing a PCP-intoxicated person to seek help in an emergency room.

PCP-Related Disorder Not Otherwise Specified

The diagnosis of PCP-related disorder not otherwise specified is the appropriate diagnosis for a patient who does not fit into any of the previously described diagnoses (Table 12.11–3).

CLINICAL FEATURES

The amount of PCP varies greatly from PCP-laced cigarette to cigarette; 1 gram may be used to make as few as four or as

Table 12.11–3
DSM-IV Diagnostic Criteria for Phencyclidine-Related Disorder Not Otherwise Specified

The phencyclidine-related disorder not otherwise specified category is for disorders associated with the use of phencyclidine that are not classifiable as phencyclidine dependence, phencyclidine abuse, phencyclidine intoxication, phencyclidine intoxication delirium, phencyclidine-induced psychotic disorder, phencyclidine-induced mood disorder, or phencyclidine-induced anxiety disorder.

many as several dozen cigarettes. Less than 5 mg of PCP is considered a low dose, and doses above 10 mg are considered high. The variability of dose makes it difficult to predict the effect, although smoking PCP is the easiest and most reliable way users can titrate the dose.

Clinical Signs and Symptoms

People who have just taken PCP are frequently uncommunicative, appear to be oblivious, and report active fantasy production. They experience speedy feelings, euphoria, bodily warmth, tingling, peaceful floating sensations, and, occasionally, feelings of depersonalization, isolation, and estrangement. Sometimes, they have auditory and visual hallucinations. They often have striking alterations of body image, distortions of space and time perception, and delusions. They may experience an intensification of dependence feelings, confusion, and disorganization of thought. Users may be sympathetic, sociable, and talkative at one moment but hostile and negative at another. Anxiety is sometimes reported; it is often the most prominent presenting symptom during an adverse reaction. Nystagmus, hypertension, and hyperthermia are common effects of PCP. Head-rolling movements, stroking, grimacing, muscle rigidity on stimulation, repeated episodes of vomiting, and repetitive chanting speech are sometimes observed.

The short-term effects last 3 to 6 hours and sometimes give way to a mild depression in which the user becomes irritable, somewhat paranoid, and occasionally belligerent, irrationally assaultive, suicidal, or homicidal. The effects can last for several days. Users sometimes find that it takes 1 to 2 days to recover completely; laboratory tests show that PCP may remain in the patient's blood and urine for more than a week.

Adverse Effects

As with the other effects of PCP, neurological and physiological symptoms are dose related. Doses of more than 20 mg are likely to cause convulsions, coma, and death. Death can also be caused by hyperthermia and autonomic instability, for which benzodiazepine treatment may be useful. Another serious adverse effect of PCP use is rhabdomyolysis with associated renal failure, which may occur in 2 percent of all PCP users. A mild increase in muscle-derived creatinine phosphokinase occurs in about 70 percent of all PCP users. Among the common symptoms seen in emergency rooms are hypertension, increased pulse rate, and nystagmus (horizontal or vertical or both). At low doses, patients may experience dysarthria, gross ataxia, and muscle rigidity, particularly of the face and neck. Increased deep tendon reflexes and diminished response to pain are commonly observed. High doses may lead to massive heat production and fatal hyperthermia, agitated and repetitive movements, athetosis or clonic jerking of the extremities, and occasionally opisthotonic posturing. With even higher doses, patients may be drowsy, stuporous with their eyes open, comatose, and, in some instances, responsive only to noxious stimuli. Clonic movements and muscle rigidity sometimes precede generalized seizure activity, and status epilepticus has been reported. Cheyne-Stokes breathing has also been observed; respiratory arrest can occur, sometimes with death. Vomiting, probably of central origin, may occur. Hypersalivation and diaphoresis are occasional symptoms, and ptosis, usually bilateral, has been observed.

DIFFERENTIAL DIAGNOSIS

Depending on a patient's status at the time of admission, the differential diagnosis may include sedative or narcotic overdose, psychotic disorder as a consequence of the use of psychedelic drugs, and brief psychotic disorder. Laboratory analysis may be helpful in establishing the diagnosis, particularly in the many cases in which the substance history is unreliable or unattainable.

TREATMENT AND REHABILITATION

The treatment for each of the PCP (or PCP-like)-related disorders is symptomatic. Talking down, which may work after hallucinogen use, is generally not useful for PCP intoxication. Benzodiazepines and dopamine receptor antagonists are the drugs of choice for controlling behavior pharmacologically. Physicians must monitor the patient's level of consciousness, blood pressure, temperature, and muscle activity and must be ready to treat severe medical abnormalities as necessary.

Clinicians must carefully monitor unconscious patients, particularly those who have toxic reactions to PCP; excessive secretions may interfere with already compromised respiration. In an alert patient who has recently taken PCP, gastric lavage presents a risk of inducing laryngeal spasm and aspiration of emesis. Muscle spasms and seizures are best treated with diazepam (Valium). The environment should afford minimal sensory stimulation. Ideally, one person stays with the patient in a quiet, dark room. Four-point restraint is dangerous because it may lead to rhabdomyolysis; total body immobilization may occasionally be necessary. A benzodiazepine is often effective in reducing agitation, but a patient with severe behavioral disturbances may require short-term treatment with a dopamine receptor antagonist—for example, haloperidol (Haldol). For patients with severe hypertension, a hypotensive-inducing drug such as phentolamine (Regitine) may be needed. Ammonium chloride in the early stage and ascorbic acid or cranberry juice later on are used to acidify the patient's urine and to promote the elimination of the substance, although the efficacy of the procedure is controversial.

If the symptoms are not severe and if the clinician can be certain that enough time has elapsed so that all the PCP has been absorbed, the patient may be monitored in the outpatient department and, if the symptoms improve, released to family or friends. Even at low doses, however, symptoms may worsen, and the person should be hospitalized to prevent violence and suicide.

References

Baldridge EB, Bessen HA: Phencyclidine. Emerg Med Clin North Am *8:* 541, 1990.

Carroll ME: PCP and hallucinogens. Adv Alcohol Subst Abuse *9:* 167, 1990.

Crowley TJ: Phencyclidine (or phencylidinelike)-related disorders. In *Comprehensive Textbook of Psychiatry,* ed 6, HI Kaplan, BJ Sadock, editors, p 864. Williams & Wilkins, Baltimore, 1995.

Gorelick DA, Wilkins JN: Inpatient treatment of PCP abusers and users. Am J Drug Alcohol Abuse *15:* 1, 1989.

Gorelick DA, Wilkins JN, Wong C: Outpatient treatment of PCP abusers. Am J Drug Alcohol Abuse *15:* 367, 1989.
Jansen KL: Ketamine: Can chronic use impair memory? Int J Addict *25:* 133, 1990.
Javitt DC, Zukin SR: Recent advances in the phencyclidine model of schizophrenia. Am J Psychiatry *148:* 1301, 1991.
National Institute on Drug Abuse: *National Household Survey on Drug Abuse: Highlights, 1991.* US Government Printing Office, Washington, 1991.
Polkis A, Graham M, Maginn D, Branch CA, Gantner GE: Phencyclidine and violent deaths in St. Louis, Missouri: A survey of medical examiners' cases from 1977 through 1986. Am J Drug Alcohol Abuse *16:* 265, 1990.
Rahbar F, Fomufod A, White D, Westney LS: Impact of intrauterine exposure to phencyclidine (PCP) and cocaine on neonates. J Natl Med Assoc *85:* 349, 1993.
Tabor BL, Smith-Wallace T, Yonekura ML: Perinatal outcome associated with PCP versus cocaine use. Am J Drug Alcohol Abuse *16:* 337, 1990.

▲ 12.12 Sedative-, Hypnotic-, or Anxiolytic-Related Disorders

Sedatives are drugs that reduce subjective tension and induce mental calmness. The term *sedative* is virtually synonymous with the term *anxiolytic,* a drug that reduces anxiety. Hypnotics are drugs used to induce sleep. The differentiation between anxiolytics and sedatives as daytime drugs and hypnotics as nighttime drugs is not accurate. When sedatives and anxiolytics are given in high doses, they can induce sleep just as the hypnotics do. Conversely, when hypnotics are given in low doses, they can induce daytime sedation just as the sedatives and anxiolytics do. In some literature, especially older literature, the sedatives, anxiolytics, and hypnotics are grouped together as the minor tranquilizers. This term is poorly defined and subject to ambiguous meanings and, therefore, is best avoided.

The drugs associated with this class of substance-related disorders are the benzodiazepines (for example, diazepam [Valium], flunitrazepam [Rohypnol]), barbiturates (for example, secobarbital [Seconal]), and the barbiturate-like substances, which include methaqualone (Quaalude), meprobamate (Equanil), and glutethimide (Doriden). The major nonpsychiatric indications for these drugs are as antiepileptics, muscle relaxants, anesthetics, and anesthetic adjuvants. Alcohol and all drugs of this class are cross-tolerant, and their effects are additive. Physical and psychological dependence develop to all the drugs, and all are associated with withdrawal symptoms.

SUBSTANCES

Benzodiazepines

Many benzodiazepines, differing primarily in their half-lives, are available in the United States. Examples of benzodiazepines are diazepam, flurazepam (Dalmane), oxazepam (Serax), and chlordiazepoxide (Librium). Benzodiazepines are used primarily as anxiolytics, hypnotics, antiepileptics, and anesthetics, as well as for alcohol withdrawal. After their introduction in the United States in the 1960s, benzodiazepines rapidly became the most prescribed drugs; about 15 percent of all people in this country have had a benzodiazepine prescribed by a physician. Increasing awareness of the risks for dependence on benzodiazepines and increased regulatory requirements, however, have caused a decrease in the number of benzodiazepine prescriptions. All benzodiazepines are classified as schedule IV controlled substances by the Drug Enforcement Agency (DEA).

Flunitrazepam (also known as roofies), a benzodiazepine used in Mexico, South America, and Europe but not available in the United States, has become a drug of abuse. When taken with alcohol, it has been associated with promiscuous sexual behavior and rape. It is illegal to bring flunitrazepam into the United States. Although misused in the United States, it remains a standard anxiolytic in many countries.

Barbiturates

Before the introduction of benzodiazepines, barbiturates were frequently prescribed, but because of their high abuse potential, their use is much rarer today than in the past. Secobarbital (popularly known as reds, red devils, seggies, and downers), pentobarbital (Nembutal) (known as yellow jackets, yellows, and nembies), and a combination of secobarbital and amobarbital (Amytal) (known as reds and blues, rainbows, double-trouble, and tooies) are easily available on the street from drug dealers. Pentobarbital, secobarbital, and amobarbital are now under the same federal legal controls as morphine.

The first barbiturate, barbital (Veronal), was introduced in the United States in 1903. Barbital and phenobarbital (Luminal), which was introduced shortly thereafter, are long-acting drugs with half-lives of 12 to 24 hours. Amobarbital is an intermediate-acting barbiturate with a half-life of 6 to 12 hours. Pentobarbital and secobarbital are short-acting barbiturates with half-lives of 3 to 6 hours.

Barbiturate-like Substances

The most commonly abused barbiturate-like substance is methaqualone, which is no longer manufactured in the United States. Methaqualone is often used by young people who believe that the substance heightens the pleasure of sexual activity. Abusers of methaqualone commonly take one or two standard tablets (usually 300 mg per tablet) to obtain the desired effects. The street names for methaqualone include mandrakes (from the U.K. preparation Mandrax) and soapers (from the brand name Sopor). Luding out (from the brand name Quaalude) means getting high on methaqualone, which is often combined with excessive alcohol intake.

EPIDEMIOLOGY

About one quarter to one third of all substance-related emergency room visits involve substances of this class. The patients have a female-to-male ratio of 3 to 1 and a white-to-black ratio of 2 to 1. Some people use benzodiazepines alone, but people who use cocaine often use benzodiazepines to reduce withdrawal symptoms, and opiate and opioid abusers use

Table 12.12–1
DSM-IV Sedative-, Hypnotic-, or Anxiolytic-Related Disorders

Sedative, hypnotic, or anxiolytic use disorders
Sedative, hypnotic, or anxiolytic dependence
Sedative, hypnotic, or anxiolytic abuse
Sedative-, hypnotic-, or anxiolytic-induced disorders
Sedative, hypnotic, or anxiolytic intoxication
Sedative, hypnotic, or anxiolytic withdrawal
Specify if:
With perceptual disturbances
Sedative, hypnotic, or anxiolytic intoxication delirium
Sedative, hypnotic, or anxiolytic withdrawal delirium
Sedative-, hypnotic-, or anxiolytic-induced persisting dementia
Sedative-, hypnotic-, or anxiolytic-induced psychotic disorder, with delusions
Specify if:
With onset during intoxication
With onset during withdrawal
Sedative-, hypnotic-, or anxiolytic-induced psychotic disorder, with hallucinations
Specify if:
With onset during intoxication
With onset during withdrawal
Sedative-, hypnotic-, or anxiolytic-induced mood disorder
Specify if:
With onset during intoxication
With onset during withdrawal
Sedative-, hypnotic-, or anxiolytic-induced anxiety disorder
Specify if:
With onset during withdrawal
Sedative-, hypnotic-, or anxiolytic-induced sexual dysfunction
Specify if:
With onset during intoxication
Sedative-, hypnotic-, or anxiolytic-induced sleep disorder
Specify if:
With onset during intoxication
With onset during withdrawal
Sedative-, hypnotic-, or anxiolytic-related disorder not otherwise specified

them to enhance the euphoric effects of opiates and opioids. Because they are easily obtained, benzodiazepines are also used by abusers of stimulants, hallucinogens, and phencyclidine (PCP) to help reduce the anxiety effects that can be caused by those substances.

Whereas barbiturate abuse is common among mature adults who have long histories of abuse of these substances, benzodiazepines are abused by a younger age group, usually under 40 years of age. This group may have a slight male predominance and a white-to-black ratio of about 2 to 1. Benzodiazepines are probably not abused as frequently as are other substances for the purpose of getting high in the sense of inducing a euphoric feeling. Rather, they are used when a person wishes to experience a relaxed evening.

NEUROPHARMACOLOGY

The benzodiazepines, barbiturates, and barbiturate-like substances all have their primary effects on the γ-aminobutyric acid (GABA) type A ($GABA_A$) receptor complex, which contains a chloride ion channel, a binding site for GABA, and a well-defined binding site for benzodiazepines. The barbiturates and barbiturate-like substances are also believed to bind somewhere on the $GABA_A$ receptor complex. When a benzodiazepine, barbiturate, or barbiturate-like substance does bind to the complex, the effect is to increase the affinity of the receptor for its endogenous neurotransmitter, GABA, and to increase the flow of chloride ions through the channel into the neuron. The influx of negatively charged chloride ions into the neuron is inhibitory, and hyperpolarizes the neuron relative to the extracellular space.

Although all the substances in this class induce tolerance and physical dependence, the mechanisms behind these effects are best understood for the benzodiazepines. After long-term benzodiazepine use, there is an attenuation of the receptor effects caused by the agonist. Specifically, GABA stimulation of the $GABA_A$ receptors results in less influx of chloride than was caused by GABA stimulation before the benzodiazepine administration. This downregulation of receptor response is not due to a decrease in receptor number or to a decrease in the affinity of the receptor for GABA. The basis for the downregulation seems to be in the coupling between the GABA binding site and the activation of the chloride ion channel. This decreased efficiency in coupling may be regulated within the $GABA_A$ receptor complex itself or by other neuronal mechanisms.

DIAGNOSIS

The fourth edition of *Diagnostic and Statistical Manual of Mental Disorders* (DSM-IV) lists a number of sedative-, hyp-

Table 12.12–2
DSM-IV Diagnostic Criteria for Sedative, Hypnotic, or Anxiolytic Intoxication

A. Recent use of a sedative, hypnotic, or anxiolytic.
B. Clinically significant maladaptive behavioral or psychological changes (eg, inappropriate sexual or aggressive behavior, mood lability, impaired judgment, impaired social or occupational functioning) that developed during, or shortly after sedative, hypnotic, or anxiolytic use.
C. One (or more) of the following signs, developing during, or shortly after, sedative, hypnotic, or anxiolytic use:
   (1) slurred speech
   (2) incoordination
   (3) unsteady gait
   (4) nystagmus
   (5) impairment in attention or memory
   (6) stupor or coma
D. The symptoms are not due to a general medical condition and are not better accounted for by another mental disorder.

notic-, or anxiolytic-related disorders (Table 12.12–1), but includes specific diagnostic criteria only for sedative, hypnotic, or anxiolytic intoxication (Table 12.12–2) and sedative, hypnotic, or anxiolytic withdrawal (Table 12.12–3). Their diagnostic criteria for other sedative-, hypnotic-, or anxiolytic-related disorders are outlined in those DSM-IV sections that are specific for the major symptom—for example, sedative-, hypnotic-, or anxiolytic-induced psychotic disorder (see Table 14.1–7).

Dependence and Abuse

Sedative, hypnotic, or anxiolytic dependence and sedative, hypnotic, or anxiolytic abuse are diagnosed according to the general criteria in DSM-IV for substance dependence and substance abuse (see Tables 12.1–7, 12.1–8, and 12.1–9).

Intoxication

DSM-IV contains a single set of diagnostic criteria for intoxication by any sedative, hypnotic, or anxiolytic substance (Table 12.12–2). Although the intoxication syndromes induced by all these drugs are similar, subtle clinical differences are observable, especially with intoxications that involve low doses. The diagnosis of intoxication by one of this class of substances is best confirmed by obtaining a blood sample for substance screening.

Benzodiazepines. Benzodiazepine intoxication can be associated with behavioral disinhibition, potentially resulting in hostile or aggressive behavior in some people. The effect is perhaps most common when benzodiazepines are taken in combination with alcohol. Benzodiazepine intoxication is associated with less euphoria than is intoxication by other drugs in this class. This characteristic is the basis for the lower abuse and dependence potential of benzodiazepines when compared with the barbiturates.

Barbiturates and Barbiturate-like Substances. When barbiturates and barbiturate-like substances are taken in relatively low doses, the clinical syndrome of intoxication is indistinguishable from that associated with alcohol intoxication. The symptoms include sluggishness, incoordination, difficulty in thinking, poor memory, slowness of speech and comprehension, faulty judgment, disinhibition of sexual aggressive impulses, a narrowed range of attention, emotional lability, and an exaggeration of basic personality traits. The sluggishness usually resolves after a few hours, but depending primarily on the half-life of the abused substance, impaired judgment, distorted mood, and impaired motor skills may remain for 12 to 24 hours. Other potential symptoms are hostility, argumentativeness, moroseness, and, occasionally, paranoid and suicidal ideation. The neurological effects include nystagmus, diplopia, strabismus, ataxic gait, positive Romberg's sign, hypotonia, and decreased superficial reflexes.

Table 12.12–3
DSM-IV Diagnostic Criteria for Sedative, Hypnotic, or Anxiolytic Withdrawal

A. Cessation of (or reduction in) sedative, hypnotic, or anxiolytic use that has been heavy and prolonged.

B. Two (or more) of the following, developing within several hours to a few days after criterion A:
  (1) autonomic hyperactivity (eg, sweating or pulse rate greater than 100)
  (2) increased hand tremor
  (3) insomnia
  (4) nausea or vomiting
  (5) transient visual, tactile, or auditory hallucinations or illusions
  (6) psychomotor agitation
  (7) anxiety
  (8) grand mal seizures

C. The symptoms in criterion B cause clinically significant distress or impairment in social, occupational, or other important areas of functioning.

D. The symptoms are not due to a general medical condition and are not better accounted for by another mental disorder.

Specify if:
With perceptual disturbances

Withdrawal

DSM-IV contains a single set of diagnostic criteria for withdrawal from any sedative, hypnotic, or anxiolytic substance (Table 12.12–3). Clinicians can specify "with perceptual disturbances" if illusions, altered perceptions, or hallucinations are present but accompanied by intact reality testing. Two important issues to remember about withdrawal are that benzodiazepines are associated with a withdrawal syndrome and that withdrawal from barbiturates can be life threatening. Withdrawal from benzodiazepines can also result in serious medical complications, such as seizures.

Benzodiazepines. The severity of the withdrawal syndrome associated with the benzodiazepines varies significantly according to the average dose and the duration of use, but a mild withdrawal syndrome can follow even short-term use of relatively low doses of benzodiazepines. A significant withdrawal syndrome is likely to occur at the cessation of dosages in the 40-mg-a-day range for diazepam, for example, although 10 to 20 mg a day, taken for a month, can also result in a withdrawal syndrome when the drug is stopped. The onset of withdrawal symptoms usually occurs 2 to 3 days after the cessation of use, but with long-acting drugs, such as diazepam, the latency before onset may be 5 or 6 days. The symptoms include anxiety, dysphoria, intolerance for bright lights and loud noises, nausea, sweating, muscle twitching, and sometimes seizures (generally at dosages of 50 mg a day or more of diazepam).

Barbiturates and Barbiturate-like Substances. The withdrawal syndrome for barbiturate and barbiturate-like substances ranges from mild symptoms (such as anxiety, weakness, sweating, and insomnia) to severe symptoms (such as seizures, delirium, cardiovascular collapse, and death). People who have been abusing phenobarbital in the range of 400 mg a day may experience mild withdrawal symptoms; those who have been abusing the substance in the range of 800 mg a day experience orthostatic hypotension, weakness, tremor, and severe anxiety. About 75 percent of these people have withdrawal-related seizures. Users of dosages even higher than 800 mg a day may experience anorexia, delirium, hallucinations, and repeated seizures.

Most symptoms appear in the first 3 days of abstinence, and seizures generally occur on the second or third day, when the symptoms are worst. If seizures do occur, they always precede the development of delirium. The symptoms rarely occur more than a week after stopping the substance. A psychotic disorder, if it develops, starts on the third to eighth day. The various associated symptoms generally run their course within 2 to 3 days but may last as long as 2 weeks. The first episode of the syndrome usually occurs after 5 to 15 years of heavy substance use.

Delirium

DSM-IV allows for the diagnosis of sedative, hypnotic, or anxiolytic intoxication delirium and sedative, hypnotic, or anxiolytic withdrawal delirium (see Table 10.2–4). Delirium that is indistinguishable from delirium tremens associated with alcohol withdrawal is more commonly seen with barbiturate withdrawal than with benzodiazepine withdrawal. Delirium associated with intoxication can be seen with either barbiturates or benzodiazepines if the dosages are high enough.

Persisting Dementia

DSM-IV allows for the diagnosis of sedative-, hypnotic-, or anxiolytic-induced persisting dementia (see Table 10.3–6). The existence of the disorder is controversial, inasmuch as there is uncertainty whether a persisting dementia is due to the substance use itself or to associated features of the substance use. It is necessary to evaluate the diagnosis further by using DSM-IV criteria to ascertain validity.

Persisting Amnestic Disorder

DSM-IV allows for the diagnosis of sedative-, hypnotic-, or anxiolytic-induced persisting amnestic disorder (see Table 10.4–3). Amnestic disorders associated with sedatives, hypnotics, and anxiolytics may be underdiagnosed. One exception has been the increased number of reports of amnestic episodes associated with the short-term use of benzodiazepines with short half-lives (such as triazolam [Halcion]).

Psychotic Disorders

The psychotic symptoms of barbiturate withdrawal can be indistinguishable from those of alcohol-associated delirium tremens. Agitation, delusions, and hallucinations are usually visual, but sometimes tactile or auditory features develop after about 1 week of abstinence. Psychotic symptoms associated with intoxication or withdrawal are more common with barbiturates than with benzodiazepines and are diagnosed as sedative-, hypnotic-, or anxiolytic-induced psychotic disorders (see Table 14.1–2). Clinicians can further specify whether delusions or hallucinations are the predominant symptoms.

Other Disorders

Sedative, hypnotic, and anxiolytic use has also been associated with mood disorders (See Table 15.1–9), anxiety disorders (see Table 16.1–5), sleep disorders (see Table 24.2–21), and sexual dysfunctions (see Table 21.2–17). When none of the previously discussed diagnostic categories is appropriate for a person with a sedative, hypnotic, or anxiolytic use disorder, the appropriate diagnosis is sedative-, hypnotic-, or anxiolytic-related disorder not otherwise specified (Table 12.12–4).

CLINICAL FEATURES

Patterns of Abuse

Oral Use. Sedatives, hypnotics, and anxiolytics can all be taken orally, either occasionally to achieve a time-limited specific effect or regularly to obtain a constant, usually mild, intoxication state. The occasional use pattern is associated with young people who take the substance to achieve specific effects—relaxation for an evening, intensification of sexual activities, and a short-lived period of mild euphoria. The user's personality and expectations about the substance's effects and the setting in which the substance is taken also affect the substance-induced experience. The regular use pattern is associated with middle-aged, middle-class people who usually obtain the substance from a family physician as a prescription for

Table 12.12–4
DSM-IV Diagnostic Criteria for Sedative-, Hypnotic-, or Anxiolytic-Related Disorder Not Otherwise Specified

The sedative-, hypnotic-, or anxiolytic-related disorder not otherwise specified category is for disorders associated with the use of sedatives, hypnotics, or anxiolytics that are not classifiable as sedative, hypnotic, or anxiolytic dependence; sedative, hypnotic, or anxiolytic abuse; sedative, hypnotic, or anxiolytic intoxication; sedative, hypnotic, or anxiolytic withdrawal; sedative, hypnotic, or anxiolytic intoxication delirium; sedative, hypnotic, or anxiolytic withdrawal delirium; sedative-, hypnotic-, or anxiolytic-induced persisting dementia; sedative-, hypnotic-, or anxiolytic-induced persisting amnestic disorder; sedative-, hypnotic-, or anxiolytic-induced psychotic disorder; sedative-, hypnotic-, or anxiolytic-induced mood disorder; sedative-, hypnotic-, or anxiolytic-induced anxiety disorder; sedative-, hypnotic-, or anxiolytic-induced sexual dysfunction; or sedative-, hypnotic-, or anxiolytic-induced sleep disorder.

insomnia or anxiety. Abusers of this type may have prescriptions from several physicians, and the pattern of abuse may go undetected until obvious signs of abuse or dependence are noticed by the person's family, coworkers, or physicians.

Intravenous Use. A severe form of abuse involves the intravenous use of this class of substances. The users are mainly young adults intimately involved with illegal substances. Intravenous barbiturate use is associated with a pleasant, warm, drowsy feeling, and users may be inclined to use barbiturates more than opioids because barbiturates are less costly. The physical dangers of injection include the transmission of the human immunodeficiency virus (HIV), cellulitis, vascular complications from accidental injection into an artery, infections, and allergic reactions to contaminants. Intravenous use is associated with a rapid and profound degree of tolerance and dependence and with a severe withdrawal syndrome.

Overdose

Benzodiazepines. In contrast to the barbiturates and the barbiturate-like substances, the benzodiazepines have a large margin of safety when taken in overdoses, a feature that contributed significantly to their rapid acceptance. The ratio of lethal dose to effective dose is about 200 to 1 or higher because of the minimal degree of respiratory depression associated with the benzodiazepines. Even when grossly excessive amounts (more than 2 grams) are taken in suicide attempts, the symptoms include only drowsiness, lethargy, ataxia, some confusion, and mild depression of the user's vital signs. A much more serious condition prevails when benzodiazepines are taken in overdose in combination with other sedative-hypnotic substances, such as alcohol. In such cases, small doses of benzodiazepines can cause death. The availability of flumazenil (Romazicon), a specific benzodiazepine antagonist, has reduced the lethality of the benzodiazepines. Flumazenil can be used in emergency rooms to reverse the effects of the benzodiazepines.

Barbiturates. Barbiturates are lethal when taken in overdose because of their induction of respiratory depression. In addition to intentional suicide attempts, accidental or unintentional overdoses are common. Barbiturates in home medicine cabinets are a common cause of fatal drug overdoses in children. As with benzodiazepines, the lethal effects of the barbiturates are additive to those of other sedatives or hypnotics, including alcohol and benzodiazepines. Barbiturate overdose is characterized by the induction of coma, respiratory arrest, cardiovascular failure, and death.

The lethal dose varies with the route of administration and the degree of tolerance for the substance after a history of long-term abuse. For the most commonly abused barbiturates, the ratio of lethal dose to effective dose ranges between 3 to 1 and 30 to 1. Dependent users often take an average daily dose of 1.5 grams of a short-acting barbiturate, and some have been reported to take as much as 2.5 grams a day for months. The lethal dose is not much greater for the long-term abuser than for the neophyte. Tolerance develops quickly to the point at which withdrawal in a hospital becomes necessary to prevent accidental death from overdose.

Barbiturate-like Substances. The barbiturate substances vary in their lethality and are usually intermediate between the relative safety of the benzodiazepines and the high lethality of the barbiturates. An overdose of methaqualone, for example, may result in restlessness, delirium, hypertonia, muscle spasms, convulsions, and, in very high doses, death. Unlike barbiturates, methaqualone rarely causes severe cardiovascular or respiratory depression, and most fatalities result from combining methaqualone with alcohol.

TREATMENT AND REHABILITATION

Withdrawal

Benzodiazepines. Because some benzodiazepines are eliminated from the body slowly, the symptoms of withdrawal may continue to develop for several weeks. To prevent seizures and other withdrawal symptoms, clinicians should gradually reduce the dosage. Several reports indicate that carbamazepine (Tegretol) may be useful in the treatment of benzodiazepine withdrawal.

Barbiturates. To avoid sudden death during barbiturate withdrawal, clinicians must follow conservative clinical guidelines. Clinicians should not give barbiturates to a comatose or grossly intoxicated patient. A clinician should attempt to determine a patient's usual daily dose of barbiturates and then verify the dosage clinically. For example, a clinician can give a test dose of 200 mg of pentobarbital every hour until a mild intoxication is present but withdrawal symptoms are absent. The clinician can then taper the total daily dose at a rate of about 10 percent of the total daily dose. Once the correct dosage is determined, a long-acting barbiturate can be used for the detoxification period. During this process, the patient may

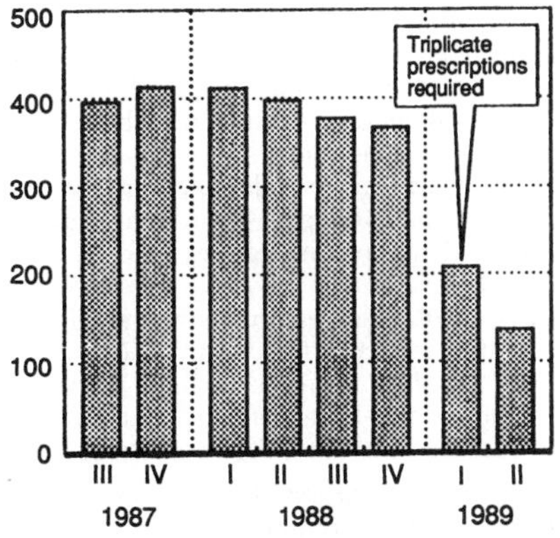

500
400
300
200
100
0
Triplicate prescriptions required
III
IV
I
II
III
IV
I
II
1987
1988
1989

FIGURE 12.12–1

Number (in thousands) of prescriptions paid for by New York State Medicaid for benzodiazepines, including diazepam (Valium) and alprazolam (Xanax). (From New York State Department of Health, Courtesy of *The Wall Street Journal*, Jan. 30, 1990.)

begin to experience withdrawal symptoms, in which case the clinician should halve the daily decrement.

In the withdrawal procedure, phenobarbital may be substituted for the more commonly abused short-acting barbiturates. The effects of phenobarbital last longer, and because there is less fluctuation of barbiturate blood levels, phenobarbital does not cause observable toxic signs or a serious overdose. An adequate dose is 30 mg of phenobarbital for every 100 mg of the short-acting substance. The user should be maintained for at least 2 days at that level before the dosage is reduced further. The regimen is analogous to the substitution of methadone for heroin.

After withdrawal is complete, the patient must overcome the desire to start taking the substance again. Although it has been suggested that nonbarbiturate sedatives or hypnotics be substituted for barbiturates as a preventive therapeutic measure, doing so often results in replacing one substance dependence with another. If a user is to remain substance-free, follow-

Table 12.12–5
Physicians' Reactions to Triplicate Prescriptions

New York State's triplicate prescription program has not only failed to reduce prescription drug abuse but it has also hampered prescribing of clinically indicated medications, according to data presented at a recent symposium sponsored by the Medical Society of the State of New York.

According to their proponents, triplicate prescription programs in New York and other states have caused a significant decline in the prescribing of regulated drugs. They attributed this reduction largely to decreases in inappropriate prescribing and in diversion of these drugs to street use. But the preponderance of evidence supports the opposite view, according to the data presented at the symposium. These data show that triplicate prescription programs do not reduce prescription drug abuse. In addition, these programs have several important unintended negative consequences.

Triplicate prescription programs inhibit physicians from prescribing drugs for patients whose medical conditions warrant them

- According to a Gallup poll, since 1989, when New York State extended its triplicate prescription program to cover benzodiazepines, 49% of responding physicians have reduced their prescribing of these agents—even though 56% of the physicians were concerned about patients being denied access to appropriate medication. Some physicians said that they felt pressured to prescribe alternative medications that were less safe (42%) or more expensive (31%).
- Prescription data show that in New York, use of outmoded or ineffective alternative medications to benzodiazepines, such as meprobamate, chloral hydrate, butabarbital, and fluoxetine, has increased markedly. In one study, 25% of nursing home residents taking benzodiazepines were switched to antipsychotic medications, which have more severe long-term adverse effects.
- Some physicians say that they are afraid to prescribe scheduled drugs because the criteria for government-agency review of their prescribing patterns are arbitrary and because of concerns about record-keeping and security requirements. Many physicians—particularly those in high-crime neighborhoods—do not even have triplicate prescription pads, because they fear their offices will be burglarized for the forms.
- Many cancer patients require multiple controlled drugs, often in high doses, to control severe pain. Fear of sanctions may prevent some physicians from treating cancer pain as aggressively as these patients deserve.
- In Texas, during 1982, the year following the adoption of a triplicate prescription program, there was a 60% decrease in the prescribing of Schedule II analgesics and a corresponding increase in the prescribing of less effective Schedule III analgesics and a potent nonsteroidal anti-inflammatory drug (NSAID).

Triplicate prescription programs threaten the confidentiality of the physician-patient relationship

- According to a Gallup survey, 63% of physicians felt that triplicate prescriptions violate patient confidentiality.
- Patients with epilepsy, anxiety disorders, depression, and other medical conditions requiring controlled medications express concern that triplicate prescriptions are an invasion of their privacy and may worsen the stigmatization they experience because of their illness.

Triplicate prescription programs are costly to operate and provide no useful information on prescribing that is not available elsewhere, at lower cost

- Triplicate prescription programs have financial costs that often go unrecognized by proponents—not only the programs' administrative costs, estimated at $1 per prescription, but also the "hidden" costs of alternative drugs, out-of-pocket expenses to patients for nonreimbursed drugs and additional visits, and untreated illnesses that may eventually require more intensive medical care.
- Several alternative prescription-monitoring programs already exist that can accomplish the same goals as triplicate prescription—at far lower cost. These include systems available from the American Medical Association, the Drug Enforcement Administration, and the U.S. Department of Health and Human Services.

Triplicate prescription programs do not reduce prescription drug diversion and abuse

- California has had a triplicate prescription program for more than 50 years. Recent analysis of data from the Epidemiologic Catchment Area study, sponsored by the National Institute of Mental Health, suggests that Los Angeles does not have a lower rate of illicit use of Schedule II prescription drugs than four other cities in states that do not have triplicate prescription. Furthermore, nearly 100% of abused prescription drugs in all cities surveyed were illicitly obtained, not prescribed by physicians.
- New York's triplicate prescription program has not affected the ability of drug abusers to obtain controlled agents from street dealers, who can easily find alternative sources for drugs, including overseas manufacturers, diversion from other states, and illicit laboratories.
- Adding benzodiazepines to the triplicate prescription program did not reduce the number of emergency room admissions for tranquilizer overdoses reported to the New York City Poison Control Center.

The Conclusion: Triplicate Prescription Jeopardizes Patient Care

Measures to adopt or discard triplicate prescription programs are before state and federal legislators this year. Lawmakers who hear only the testimony of regulatory and drug enforcement agencies may not be aware of the drawbacks of triplicate prescription. Legislators should also know of physicians' serious reservations about triplicate prescription, the harm these regulations do to patients, and the evidence that these programs are not the most effective way to control prescription drug abuse.

Reprinted with permission from Highlights of the Symposium, "Triplicate Prescription: Issues and Answers," sponsored by the Medical Society of the State of New York, February 28, 1991.

up treatment, usually with psychiatric help and community support, is vital. Otherwise, a patient will almost certainly return to barbiturates or to a substance with similar hazards.

Overdose

The treatment of overdose of this class of substances involves gastric lavage, activated charcoal, and careful monitoring of vital signs and central nervous system (CNS) activity. Overdose patients who come to medical attention while awake should be kept from slipping into unconsciousness. Vomiting should be induced, and activated charcoal should be administered to delay gastric absorption. If a patient is comatose, the clinician must establish an intravenous fluid line, monitor the patient's vital signs, insert an endotracheal tube to maintain a patent airway, and provide mechanical ventilation, if necessary. Hospitalization of a comatose patient in an intensive care unit is usually required during the early stages of recovery from such overdoses.

LEGAL ISSUES

State and federal agencies have attempted to restrict the distribution of benzodiazepines by requiring special reporting forms. For example, through the use of New York State triplicate prescription forms, the names of doctors and patients are kept on file in a data bank. Governments have taken such measures to stem the tide of abuse. But most abuse is the result of the illicit manufacture, sale, and diversion of substances, particularly to cocaine and opioid addicts, not from physicians' prescriptions or legitimate pharmaceutical companies. The attempt to curtail the use of substances with unquestionable and invaluable therapeutic benefits exemplifies increasing government interference in the practice of medicine and in the confidential relationship between doctor and patient. Such restrictions do little to curb cocaine, opioid, or benzodiazepine abuse.

The number of benzodiazepine prescriptions has decreased in New York State (Fig. 12.12–1), but whether this decrease is due to improved medical prescribing standards of practice or to the intimidation of physicians is open to question. New York is now among 10 states that regulate schedule II controlled substances with multiple-copy prescriptions (triplicates). California has the oldest triplicate program (established in 1939), but in 1989, New York, with its reported high prescription abuse rate, became the first state to extend triplicate regulation to benzodiazepines against the recommendation of most physicians in the state. In 1991, a symposium sponsored by the Medical Society of the State of New York concluded that triplicate prescriptions jeopardize patient care (Table 12.12–5). The advantages and disadvantages of New York's triplicate prescription program were summarized after conducting a survey of 1,513 physicians (Tables 12.12–6 and 12.12–7).

Table 12.12–6
Advantages of New York's Triplicate Prescription Program

	%[a]
Reduces inappropriate prescribing of benzodiazepines	77
Targets patients who abuse benzodiazepines	43
Represents a cost benefit to New York State	15
Other advantages	19
Reduces abuse of other controlled substances	
Allows more active control of medicine by the state	
Provides accurate record of prescriptions written	
Subjects MDs to peer review	
Provides reason for not prescribing benzodiazepines to patients	

Reprinted with permission from Highlights of the Symposium, "Triplicate Prescription: Issues and Answers," sponsored by the Medical Society of the State of New York, February 28, 1991.
[a] Percentages reflect proportion of those (N = 328) who thought that the triplicate prescription program had any advantages.

Table 12.12–7
Disadvantages of New York's Triplicate Prescription Program

	%[a]
Inappropriately allows legislators to dictate practice of medicine	75
Consumes too much physician time	74
Violates physician-patient confidentiality	64
Imposes unnecessary physician monitoring	56
Increases cost burden to patients	49
Poses benzodiazepine withdrawal concerns	29
Other disadvantages	20
Increases possibility of robbery and assault	
Requires physician to practice defensive or reactive medicine	
Increases expense to physician	
Has not been proven to eliminate drug abuse	
Increases possibility of malpractice liability	
Forces prescribing of less efficacious, more hazardous medications	
Sets precedent for further government controls	
Coerces patient to seek alternative sources of drugs	

Reprinted with permission from Highlights of the Symposium, "Triplicate Prescription: Issues and Answers," sponsored by the Medical Society of the State of New York, February 28, 1991.
[a] Percentages reflect proportion of those (N = 1,185) who thought that the triplicate prescription program had any advantages.

REFERENCES

American Psychiatric Association: *Benzodiazepine Dependence, Toxicity, and Abuse.* American Psychiatric Association, Washington, 1990.

Ciraulo DA, Greenblatt DJ: Sedatives-, hypnotic-, or anxiolytic-relates disorders. In *Comprehensive Textbook of Psychiatry,* ed 6, HI Kaplan, BJ Sadock, editors, p 872. Williams & Wilkins, Baltimore, 1995.

Cole JO, Chaiarello RJ: The benzodiazepines as drugs of abuse. J Psychiatr Res *24* (3, Suppl 2): 135, 1990.

Juergens SM: Benzodiazepines and addiction. Psychiatr Clin North Am *16:* 75, 1993.

Klein RL, Whiting PJ, Harris RA: Benzodiazepine treatment causes uncoupling of recombinant GABA-A receptors expressed in stably transfected cells. J Neurochem *63:* 2349, 1994.

Lader M, Farr I, Morton S: A comparison of alpidem and placebo in relieving benzodiazepine withdrawal symptoms. Int Clin Psychopharmacol *8:* 31, 1993.

Nutt DJ: Pharmacological mechanisms of benzodiazepine withdrawal. J Psychiatr Res *24* (3, Suppl 2): 105, 1990.

Patterson JF: Withdrawal from alprazolam dependency using clonazepam: Clinical observations. J Clin Psychiatry *51* (9, Suppl): 47, 1990.

Piper A Jr: Addiction to benzodiazepines—how common? Arch Fam Med *4:* 964, 1995.
Rickels K, Schweizer E, Case WG, Greenblatt DJ: Long-term therapeutic use of benzodiazepines: I. Effects of abrupt discontinuation. Arch Gen Psychiatry *47:* 899, 1990.
Rickels K, Warren GC, Schweizer E, Garcia-España F, Fridman R: Long-term benzodiazepine users 3 years after participation in a discontinuation program. Am J Psychiatry *148:* 757, 1991.
Romach M, Busto U, Somer G, Kaplan HL, Sellers E: Clinical aspects of chronic use of alprazolam and lorazepam. Am J Psychiatry *152:* 1161, 1995.
Schweizer E, Rickels K, Case WG, Greenblatt DJ: Carbamazepine treatment in patients discontinuing long-term benzodiazepine therapy: Effects on withdrawal severity and outcome. Arch Gen Psychiatry *48:* 448, 1991.
Schweizer E, Rickels K, Case WG, Greenblatt DJ: Long-term therapeutic use of benzodiazepines: II. Effects of gradual taper. Arch Gen Psychiatry *47:* 908, 1990.
Seiverwright N, Dougal W: Withdrawal symptoms from high dose benzodiazepines in poly drug users. Drug Alcohol Depend *32:* 15, 1993.
Staley KJ, Soldo BL, Proctor WR: Ionic mechanisms of neuronal excitation by inhibitory $GABA_A$ receptors. Science *269:* 977, 1995.

▲ 12.13 Anabolic Steroid Abuse

The naturally occurring anabolic-androgenic steroid in men is testosterone. Many synthetic anabolic steroids, such as Dianabol, Anavar, and Winstrol-V, are now available in oral, transdermal, and intramuscular formulations. Anabolic steroids are schedule III drugs and therefore are subject to the same regulatory dispensing requirements as are narcotics. Although anabolic steroids have legitimate medical uses, they are illegally used to enhance physical performance and appearance and to increase muscle bulk. Illegal sales of anabolic steroids in the United States are an estimated $400-million-a-year business. Many young athletes, some as young as 10 years of age, spend money on *blanks*—useless and sometimes harmful nonsteroid formulations. Although virtually every athletic regulatory agency has officially forbidden the use of anabolic steroids, sophisticated athletes and less-than-honest trainers have developed the use of steroids to a fine art and can adjust the amount and timing of doses to remain undetected by currently used screening tests.

EPIDEMIOLOGY

An estimated 1 million people in the United States have used illegal steroids at least once. Users are primarily middle class and white. Male users of anabolic steroids greatly outnumber female users by approximately 50 to 1; about half the users started before the age of 16. In a 1993 National Household Survey on Drug Abuse, 1.5 percent of people surveyed reported a lifetime nonmedical use of these drugs. The highest use was among 18 to 25 year olds, with 26 to 34 year olds having the next highest rate of use. Estimates for the rate of use in body builders have ranged up to 50 to 80 percent.

NEUROPHARMACOLOGY

After oral administration of testosterone, only small amounts of the drug reach systemic circulation unchanged. The low bioavailability of orally administered testosterone results from metabolism of the drug in the gastrointestinal mucosa during first pass through the liver. The synthetic androgens (such as fluoxymesterone and methyltestosterone) are also less extensively metabolized following oral administration. In plasma, testosterone is 98 percent bound to a specific testosterone-estradiol–binding globulin. The plasma half-life of testosterone reportedly ranges from 10 to 100 minutes. Testosterone is metabolized principally in the liver to various 17-ketosteroids.

ETIOLOGY

People drawn to use these drugs are usually involved in activities that require strength and endurance. These users include athletes involved in track and field, weight lifters, and others who desire extraordinary performance, usually in competitive sports settings. Reinforcement of use occurs if the drug-taking behavior results in a desired result, such as increased muscle mass or prolonged endurance. Psychodynamic vulnerability to anabolic steroid misuse includes low self-esteem and disturbances in the image and appearance of the body. Adolescent users—both heterosexual and homosexual—equate an Adonis-like body with the ability to attract sexual partners. These drugs may also be used to deny perceived narcissistic deficiencies.

DIAGNOSIS AND CLINICAL FEATURES

Because of their psychiatric effects, anabolic steroids have come to the attention of psychiatrists. Steroids may initially induce euphoria and hyperactivity. After relatively short periods, however, their use can become associated with increased anger, arousal, irritability, hostility, anxiety, somatization, and depression (especially during times when steroids are not used). Several studies have demonstrated that from 2 to 15 percent of anabolic steroid abusers experience hypomanic or manic episodes, and a smaller percentage may have clearly psychotic symptoms. Also disturbing is a correlation between steroid abuse and violence, so-called *roid rage* in the parlance of users. Steroid abusers with no record of antisocial behavior or violence have committed murders and other violent crimes.

Steroids are addictive substances. When abusers stop taking steroids, they can become depressed, anxious, and concerned about their bodies' physical state. Some similarities have been noted between athletes' views of their muscles and the views of patients with anorexia nervosa about their bodies; to an observer, both groups seem to distort realistic assessment of the body.

Iatrogenic addiction is a consideration in view of the increasing number of geriatric patients who are receiving testosterone from their physicians in an attempt to increase libido and reverse some aspects of aging.

Adverse Effects

Anabolic Steroids. Anabolic steroid use has obvious physical effects. Steroid use causes rapid development and enhancement of muscle bulk, definition, and power. Men who abuse steroids may have acne, premature balding, yellowing of the skin and the eyes, gynecomastia, and decreased size of the testicles and the prostate. Young boys abusing steroids can have painful enlargement of the genitalia. The use of steroids in young adolescents can also lead to stunted growth by causing premature closure of the bone plates. In women who abuse steroids, the voice may deepen, the breasts shrink, the clitoris enlarge, and the menstrual cycle become irregular.

Anabolic steroid use can also produce abnormal liver function tests, decreased high-density lipoprotein blood levels, and increased low-density lipoprotein blood levels. Decreased spermatogenesis has been reported, as has an association between anabolic steroid abuse and myocardial infarction and cerebrovascular diseases.

In women, adverse effects include clitoral enlargement, which may be irreversible, menstrual problems, alopecia or hirsutism, deepened voice (also irreversible) and acne.

Dehydroepiandrosterone (DHEA). DHEA is an adrenal androgen marketed as a food supplement and sold over the counter in health food stores. It is not approved or regulated by the Food and Drug Administration. DHEA is a steroid precursor of both androgens and estrogens; people taking the substance report an increase in physical and psychological well-being. The adverse effects of the drug are similar to those of anabolic steroids and include voice change, acne, hirsutism, and prostatic cancer. Because DHEA is available in U.S. health food stores and may have addictive potential, increased reports of misuse and adverse effects should be expected.

TREATMENT

There are no specific treatment guidelines for anabolic steroid abuse. Abstinence is the desired goal, and frequent urine testing is indicated for compliance. A successful outcome is more likely with psychotherapy than without, especially if, as is usually the case, there is underlying psychopathology.

A unique aspect of treatment is the need to deal with profound physical side effects in long-term users, such as nonreversible gynecomastia, which may require corrective surgery. Other medical problems, such as renal damage, may also necessitate treatment. Finally, patients may have to alter their lifestyles, either by giving up a favored activity, such as weight training, or by lowering their performance expectations, such as in running slower times. Correcting body image distortions are issues that may be improved through psychotherapy.

References

Abromowitz M: Dehydroepiandrosterone (DHEA). Med Lett Drug Ther *38:* 91, 1996

Brower KJ: Anabolic steroids: A mind-body problem. Psychiatry Ann *22:* 2, 1992.

Clancy GP, Yates WR: Anabolic steroid use among substance abusers in treatment. J Clin Psychiatry *53:* 97, 1992.

DuRant RH, Rickert VI, Ashworth CS, Newman C, Slavens G: Use of multiple drugs among adolescents who use anabolic steroids. N Engl J Med *328:* 922, 1993.

13 Schizophrenia

In the fourth edition of *Diagnostic and Statistical Manual of Mental Disorders* (DSM-IV), schizophrenia is described as "a disturbance that lasts for at least 6 months and includes at least a month of active-phase symptoms (that is, two [or more] of the following: delusions, hallucinations, disorganized speech, grossly disorganized or catatonic behavior, negative symptoms)." Over the years, major progress in the description of schizophrenia has occurred in three major areas: brain-imaging techniques, research into atypical antipsychotic drugs, and inquiry into the psychosocial factors affecting the disorder. In the first area, magnetic resonance imaging (MRI) and refinements in neuropathological techniques have emphasized the limbic system as central to the pathophysiology of schizophrenia. Study of the brain areas of interest—the amygdala, the hippocampus, and the parahippocampal gyrus—increasingly generates testable hypotheses about schizophrenia. In the second area, a significant amount of research on other atypical antipsychotic drugs, particularly risperidone, followed the introduction of clozapine (Clozaril), an atypical antipsychotic with minimal neurological side effects. These and other atypical drugs, such as sertindole (Serlect) and quetiapine (Seroquel, Zeneca), may be more effective than the commonly used medications for reducing the negative symptoms of schizophrenia and could be associated with a low incidence of adverse neurological effects. In the third area, with improved drug treatments and with the broad acceptance of schizophrenia as biologically based, the psychosocial factors in schizophrenia, such as those affecting onset, relapse, and treatment outcome, have received much attention.

HISTORY

The magnitude of the clinical problem of schizophrenia has consistently attracted the attention of major figures in psychiatry and neurology throughout the history of the disorder. Two of these people were Emil Kraepelin (1856–1926) and Eugen Bleuler (1857–1939). Earlier, Benedict Morel (1809–1873), a French psychiatrist, had used the term *démence précoce* for deteriorated patients whose illness began in adolescence; Karl Ludwig Kahlbaum (1828–1899) had described the symptoms of catatonia; Ewold Hacker (1843–1909) had written about the bizarre behavior of patients with hebephrenia.

Emil Kraepelin

Kraepelin (Fig. 13–1) translated Morel's *démence précoce* to *dementia precox,* a term that emphasized the distinct cognitive process (dementia) and early onset (precox) of the disorder. Patients with dementia precox were described as having a long-term deteriorating course and the common clinical symptoms of hallucinations and delusions. Kraepelin distinguished these patients from those classified as having manic-depressive psychosis who underwent distinct episodes of illness alternating with periods of normal functioning. The major symptoms of patients with paranoia were persistent persecutory delusions, and these patients were described as lacking the deteriorating course of dementia precox and the intermittent symptoms of manic-depressive psychosis. Although Kraepelin had acknowledged that about 4 percent of his patients recovered completely and 13 percent had significant remissions, later researchers sometimes mistakenly stated that he had considered dementia precox to have an inevitable deteriorating course.

Eugen Bleuler

Bleuler (Fig. 13–2) coined the term *schizophrenia,* which replaced *dementia precox* in the literature. He chose the term to express the presence of schisms between thought, emotion, and behavior in patients with the disorder. Bleuler stressed that, unlike Kraepelin's concept of dementia precox, schizophrenia need not have a deteriorating course. Before the publication of the third edition of DSM (DSM-III), the incidence of schizophrenia increased in the United States (where psychiatrists followed Bleuler's principles) to perhaps as much as twice the incidence in Europe (where psychiatrists followed Kraepelin's principles). After the publication of DSM-III, the diagnosis of schizophrenia in the United States moved toward Kraepelin's concept. Bleuler's term *schizophrenia,* however, has become the internationally accepted label for the disorder. This term is often misconstrued, especially by laypeople, to mean split personality. Split personality, now called *dissociative identity disorder,* is categorized in DSM-IV as a dissociative disorder and thus differs completely from schizophrenia.

The Four *As*. Bleuler identified specific *fundamental (or primary) symptoms* of schizophrenia to develop his theory about the internal mental schisms of patients. These symptoms included associational disturbances, especially looseness, affective disturbances, autism, and ambivalence, summarized as the four *A*s: *a*ssociations, *a*ffect, *a*utism, and *a*mbivalence. Bleuler also identified *accessory (secondary) symptoms,* which included those symptoms that Kraepelin saw as major indicators of dementia precox: hallucinations and delusions.

FIGURE 13–1
Emil Kraepelin. (Reprinted with permission from Davison GC, Neale JM: *Abnormal Psychology: An Experimental Clinical Approach.* Wiley, New York, 1974.)

FIGURE 13–2
Eugen Bleuler. (Reprinted with permission from Davison GC, Neale JM: *Abnormal Psychology: An Experimental Clinical Approach.* Wiley, New York, 1974.)

Other Theorists

Adolf Meyer, Harry Stack Sullivan, Ernst Kretschmer, Gabriel Langfeldt, Kurt Schneider, and Karl Jaspers added much to the understanding of schizophrenia. Meyer, the founder of psychobiology, saw schizophrenia and other mental disorders as reactions to life stresses and called the syndrome a schizophrenic reaction. Sullivan, who founded the interpersonal psychoanalytic school, emphasized social isolation as a cause and a symptom of schizophrenia.

Kretschmer compiled data to support the idea that schizophrenia occurred more often among people with asthenic, athletic, or dysplastic body types rather than among people with pyknic body types; the latter, he thought, were more likely to incur bipolar disorders. His observations may seem strange, but they are not inconsistent with a superficial impression of the body types in many homeless persons.

Langfeldt classified patients with major psychotic symptoms into two groups, those with true schizophrenia and those with a schizophrenia-like psychosis. In his description of *true schizophrenia,* Langfeldt stressed several factors: insidious onset, feelings of derealization and depersonalization, autism, and emotional blunting (see Table 13–7). Researchers after Langfeldt gave *true schizophrenia* other names: nuclear schizophrenia, process schizophrenia, and nonremitting schizophrenia.

Schneider contributed a description of first-rank symptoms, which, he stressed, were not specific for schizophrenia and were not to be rigidly applied but were useful for making diagnoses (see Table 13–7). He emphasized that in patients who showed no first-rank symptoms, the disorder could be diagnosed exclusively on the basis of second-rank symptoms and an otherwise typical clinical appearance. Clinicians frequently ignore his warnings and sometimes see the absence of first-rank symptoms during a single interview as evidence that a person does not have schizophrenia.

Jaspers, a psychiatrist and philosopher, played a major role in developing existential psychoanalysis. In his view, psychopathology had no fixed concepts or basic principles. Thus his theories of schizophrenia were free of traditional concepts like subject and object, cause and effect, and reality and fantasy, and his philosophic attitude led to an interest in the content of psychiatric patients' delusions.

EPIDEMIOLOGY

In the United States, the lifetime prevalence of schizophrenia has been variously reported as ranging from 1 to 1.5 percent; consistent with this range, the National Institute of Mental Health–sponsored Epidemiologic Catchment Area (ECA) study reported a lifetime prevalence in the range of 0.6 to 1.9 percent. About 0.025 to 0.05 percent of the total population is treated for schizophrenia in any single year. Although two thirds of treated patients require hospitalization, only about half of all patients with schizophrenia obtain treatment, in spite of the severity of the disorder.

Age and Sex

Schizophrenia is equally prevalent in men and women. The two sexes differ, however, in the onset and course of illness.

Onset is earlier in men than in women. More than half of all male schizophrenic patients but only a third of all female schizophrenic patients are first admitted to a psychiatric hospital before age 25. The peak ages of onset are 15 to 25 years for men and 25 to 35 years for women. Onset of schizophrenia before age 10 or after age 50 is extremely rare. About 90 percent of the patients in treatment for schizophrenia are between 15 and 55 years old. Some studies have indicated that men are more likely to be impaired by negative symptoms than are women and that women are more likely to have better social functioning than are men. In general, the outcome for female schizophrenic patients is better than the outcome for male schizophrenic patients.

Seasonality of Birth

A robust finding in schizophrenia research is that people who later have schizophrenia are more likely to have been born in the winter and early spring and less likely to have been born in late spring and summer. In the Northern Hemisphere, including the United States, people with schizophrenia are more often born in the months from January to April. In the Southern Hemisphere, people with schizophrenia are more often born in the months from July to September. Various hypotheses to explain these observations have been put forward. One hypothesis is that a season-specific risk factor, such as a virus or a seasonal change in diet, may be operative. Another hypothesis is that people with a genetic predisposition for schizophrenia have an increased biological advantage to survive season-specific insults.

Geographical Distribution

Schizophrenia is not evenly distributed throughout the United States or the world. Historically, the prevalence of schizophrenia in the northeastern and western United States was greater than in other areas, although this unequal distribution has eroded. Some geographical regions of the world have an unusually high prevalence of schizophrenia, and researchers have interpreted these geographical pockets of schizophrenia as possible support for an infective (for example, viral) cause of schizophrenia.

Reproduction Rates

The use of psychotherapeutic drugs, the open-door policies in hospitals, the deinstitutionalization in state hospitals, the emphasis on rehabilitation, and the community-based care for patients with schizophrenia have all led to an increase in the marriage and fertility rates among people with schizophrenia. Because of these factors, the number of children born to schizophrenic parents doubled from 1935 to 1955. The fertility rate for schizophrenic people is close to that for the general population.

Medical Illness

People with schizophrenia have a higher mortality rate from accidents and natural causes than does the general population. Institution-related or treatment-related variables do not explain the increased mortality rate, but the higher rate may be related to the fact that the diagnosis and treatment of medical and surgical conditions in schizophrenic patients can be clinical challenges. Several studies have shown that up to 80 percent of all schizophrenic patients have significant concurrent medical illnesses and that up to 50 percent of these conditions may be undiagnosed.

Suicide

Suicide is a common cause of death among patients with schizophrenia, partly because clinicians still tend to associate suicide more with mood disorders than with psychotic disorders. About 50 percent of all patients with schizophrenia attempt suicide at least once in their lifetimes, and 10 to 15 percent of schizophrenic patients die by suicide during a 20-year follow-up period. Male and female schizophrenic patients are equally likely to commit suicide. The major risk factors for suicide among people with schizophrenia include the presence of depressive symptoms, young age, and high levels of premorbid functioning (especially a college education). People in this risk group may realize the devastating significance of their illness more than do other groups of schizophrenic patients and may see suicide as a reasonable alternative. Treatment approaches to such patients may include pharmacological treatment of the depression, treatment of loss issues in psychotherapy, and the use of support groups to help direct patients' ambitions toward an obtainable goal.

Associated Substance Use and Abuse

Cigarette Smoking. Most surveys have reported that more than three fourths of all schizophrenic patients smoke cigarettes, compared with less than half of psychiatric patients as a whole. In addition to the well-known health risks associated with smoking, cigarette smoking affects other aspects of a schizophrenic patient's care. Several studies have reported that cigarette smoking is associated with the use of high dosages of antipsychotic drugs, possibly because cigarette smoking increases the metabolism rate of these drugs. On the other hand, cigarette smoking is associated with a decrease in antipsychotic drug-related parkinsonism, possibly because of nicotine-dependent activation of dopamine neurons. Recent studies have demonstrated that nicotine may decrease positive symptoms, such as hallucinations, in schizophrenic patients by its effect on nicotine receptors in the brain that reduce the perception of outside stimuli, especially noise.

Other Substance Abuse. Comorbidity of schizophrenia and other substance-related disorders is common, although the implications of substance abuse in schizophrenic patients are unclear. About 30 to 50 percent of patients with schizophrenia may meet the diagnostic criteria for alcohol abuse or alcohol dependence; the two most commonly used other substances are cannabis (about 15 to 25 percent) and cocaine (about 5 to 10 percent). Patients report that they use these substances to obtain pleasure and to reduce their depression and anxiety. Most studies have associated the comorbidity of substance-related disorders in patients who have schizophrenia with poor prognosis.

Population Density

The prevalence of schizophrenia has been correlated with local population density in cities with populations of more than 1 million people. The correlation is weaker in cities of 100,000 to 500,000 people and is absent in cities with fewer than 10,000 people. The effect of population density is consistent with the observation that the incidence of schizophrenia in children of either one or two schizophrenic parents is twice as high in cities as in rural communities. These observations suggest that social stressors in urban settings affect the development of schizophrenia in people at risk.

Cultural and Socioeconomic Considerations

Schizophrenia has been described in all cultures and socioeconomic status groups. In industrialized nations, a disproportionate number of schizophrenic patients are in the low socioeconomic groups, an observation explained by two alternative hypotheses. The *downward drift hypothesis* suggests that affected people move into, or fail to rise out of, a low socioeconomic group because of this illness. The *social causation hypothesis* proposes that stresses experienced by members of low socioeconomic groups contribute to the development of schizophrenia.

Some investigators have presented data indicating that, in addition to the stress of industrialization as a causes of schizophrenia, the stress of immigration can lead to a schizophrenia-like condition. Some studies report a high prevalence of schizophrenia among recent immigrants, a finding implicating abrupt cultural change as a stressor involved in the cause of schizophrenia. Perhaps consistent with both hypotheses is the observation that the prevalence of schizophrenia increases among Third-World populations as contact with technologically advanced cultures increases.

Theorists advocating a social cause for schizophrenia argue that cultures may be more or less schizophrenogenic, depending on the perceptions of mental illness in the culture, the nature of the patient's role, the system of social and family supports, and the complexity of social communication. Schizophrenia has been reported to be prognostically more benign in developing countries where patients are reintegrated into their communities and families more completely than they are in highly developed Western societies.

Homelessness. The problem of people who are homeless in large cities seems related to the deinstitutionalization of schizophrenic patients who were not adequately followed up. Although the exact percentage of homeless persons who are schizophrenic is difficult to obtain, an estimated one third to two thirds of homeless people are probably afflicted with schizophrenia.

Financial Cost to Society. The estimation of an illness's cost to society is a complex task; nevertheless, the financial cost of schizophrenia to the United States economy is widely acknowledged to be enormous. About 1 percent of the national income goes toward the treatment of mental illness (excluding substance-related disorders). Schizophrenia accounts for 2.5 percent of all health care expenditures. Costs of treatment and indirect costs to society (for example, lost production and mortality) amount to almost $50 billion annually. About 75 percent of people with severe schizophrenia are unable to work and are unemployed.

Mental-Hospital Beds. The development of effective antipsychotic drugs and changes in political and popular attitudes toward the treatment and the rights of people who are mentally ill have resulted in a dramatic change in the patterns of hospitalization for schizophrenic patients over the past 4 decades. The probability of readmission within 2 years after discharge from the first hospitalization is about 40 to 60 percent. Patients with schizophrenia occupy about 50 percent of all mental-hospital beds and account for about 16 percent of all psychiatric patients who receive any treatment.

ETIOLOGY

Schizophrenia is discussed as if it were a single disease, but the diagnostic category includes a group of disorders, probably with heterogeneous causes, but with somewhat similar behavioral symptoms. Patients with schizophrenia show differing clinical presentations, treatment responses, and courses of illness.

Stress–Diathesis Model

According to the stress–diathesis model for the integration of biological, psychosocial, and environmental factors, a person may have a specific vulnerability (diathesis) that, when acted on by a stressful influence, allows the symptoms of schizophrenia to develop. In the most general stress–diathesis model, the diathesis or the stress can be biological, environmental, or both. The environmental component can be either biological (for example, an infection) or psychological (for example, a stressful family situation or the death of a close relative). The biological basis of a diathesis can be further shaped by epigenetic influences, such as substance abuse, psychosocial stress, and trauma.

Biological Factors

The cause of schizophrenia is unknown. In the past decade, however, an increasing amount of research has indicated a pathophysiological role for certain areas of the brain, including the limbic system, the frontal cortex, and the basal ganglia. These three areas are interconnected, so that dysfunction in one area may involve a primary pathological process in another. Brain imaging of living people and neuropathological examination of postmortem brain tissue have implicated the limbic system as a potential site for the primary pathological process in at least some, perhaps even most, schizophrenic patients.

Two areas of active research are the time that a neuropathological lesion appears in the brain and the interaction of the lesion with environmental and social stressors. The basis for the appearance of the brain abnormality may lie in abnormal development (for example, abnormal migration of neurons along the radial glial cells during development) or in degeneration of neurons after development (for example, abnormally early preprogrammed cell death, as appears to occur in Huntington's disease). The fact that monozygotic twins have a 50 percent discordance rate, however, implies a little-understood interaction between the environment and the development of schizophrenia. On the other hand, the factors regulating gene expression are just beginning to be understood. Although monozygotic twins have the same genetic information, differential gene regulation during their lives perhaps allows one monozygotic twin to have schizophrenia, whereas the other does not.

General Research Principles. Researchers often design biological research in schizophrenia to measure a biological variable in a group of patients with schizophrenia and in a group of nonpsychiatrically ill people or in a group of nonschizophrenic psychiatric patients. They then compare the means of these measures to determine whether the schizophrenic group differs from the control group. This research approach has several drawbacks. First, because the schizophrenic group has been affected by drug treatments and psychosocial situations that most control populations have not experienced, a control group truly matched to the schizophrenic group is difficult to find. Second, the significance of a difference discovered by comparing the means of measure is difficult to assess. The demonstration of a between-group difference does not indicate that the measure is causally related to schizophrenia; the difference could be secondary to the disease process or to the treatment.

In clinical neurology, a single type of lesion that results in a range of psychological states is not a rare event. For example, many people have cerebrovascular diseases, but some have no psychological symptoms, some have depressive disorders, and others have mania or psychosis. In Huntington's disease, the disorder can be strictly neurological or associated with every diagnosis in DSM-IV. Conversely, a specific abnormality in the brain can have many different causes. Parkinson's disease, for example, has idiopathic, infectious, traumatic, and toxic causes.

Integration of Biological Theories. The major brain areas implicated in schizophrenia are the limbic structures, the frontal lobes, and the basal ganglia. Also implicated are the thalamus, because of its role as an integrating mechanism, and the brainstem, which, with the midbrain, is the primary location for the ascending aminergic neurons. The limbic system, however, is increasingly the focus of many theory-building exercises. For example, one study of sets of twins who were discordant for schizophrenia used both MRI and the measurement of regional cerebral blood flow. The investigators had previously determined that the hippocampal area of almost every affected twin was smaller than that of the unaffected twin and that the affected twin also had a smaller increase in blood flow to the dorsolateral prefrontal cortex while performing a psychological-activation procedure. The study found a correlation between these two abnormalities, which thus may be related or may be affected by a third factor.

Dopamine Hypothesis. The simplest formulation of the *dopamine hypothesis of schizophrenia* posits that schizophrenia results from too much dopaminergic activity. The theory evolved from two observations. First, the efficacy and the potency of most antipsychotic drugs, (that is, the dopamine receptor antagonists) are correlated with their abilities to act as antagonists of the dopamine type 2 (D_2) receptor. Second, drugs that increase dopaminergic activity, notably amphetamine, are psychotomimetic. The basic theory does not elaborate on whether the dopaminergic hyperactivity is due to too much release of dopamine, too many dopamine receptors, hypersensitivity of the dopamine receptors to dopamine, or a combination of these mechanisms. Which dopamine tracts in the brain are involved is also not specified in the theory, although the mesocortical and mesolimbic tracts are most often implicated. The dopaminergic neurons in these tracts project from their cell bodies in the midbrain to dopaminoceptive neurons in the limbic system and the cerebral cortex.

A significant role for dopamine in the pathophysiology of schizophrenia is consistent with studies that have measured plasma concentrations of the major dopamine metabolite, homovanillic acid. Several preliminary studies have indicated that under carefully controlled experimental conditions, plasma homovanillic acid concentrations can reflect central nervous system (CNS) concentrations of homovanillic acid. These studies have reported a positive correlation between high pretreatment concentrations of homovanillic acid and two factors: the severity of the psychotic symptoms and the treatment response to antipsychotic drugs. Studies of plasma homovanillic acid have also reported that after a transient increase, plasma homovanillic acid concentrations decline steadily. This decline is correlated with symptom improvement in at least some patients.

The dopamine hypothesis of schizophrenia continues to be refined and expanded. The dopamine type 1 (D_1) receptor may play a role in negative symptoms, and some researchers are interested in using D_1 agonists as a treatment approach for these symptoms. The recently discovered dopamine type 5 (D_5) receptor is related to the D_1 receptor and may merit research. Similarly the dopamine type 3 (D_3) and dopamine type 4 (D_4) receptors are related to the D_2 receptor and will be the subject of increasing research as specific agonists and antagonists are developed for these receptors. At least one study has reported an increase in D_4 receptors in postmortem brain samples from schizophrenic patients.

Although the dopamine hypothesis of schizophrenia has stimulated schizophrenia research for more than 2 decades and remains the leading neurochemical hypothesis, the hypothesis poses two major problems. First, dopamine antagonists are effective in treating virtually all psychotic and severely agitated patients, regardless of diagnosis. Dopaminergic hyperactivity is therefore not unique to schizophrenia. Second, some electrophysiological data suggest that dopaminergic neurons increase their firing rate in response to long-term exposure to antipsychotic drugs. These data imply that the initial abnormality in schizophrenia involves a hypodopaminergic state.

Other Neurotransmitters. Although the neurotransmitter dopamine has received the most attention in schizophrenia research, increasing attention is being paid to other neurotransmitters for at least two reasons. First, because schizophrenia is likely to be a heterogeneous disorder, it is possible that abnormalities in different neurotransmitters lead to the same behavioral syndrome. For instance, hallucinogenic substances that affect serotonin, such as lysergic acid diethylamide (LSD), and high doses of substances that affect dopamine, such as amphetamine, can cause psychotic symptoms that are difficult to distinguish from schizophrenia. Second, neuroscience research has shown that a single neuron may contain more than one neurotransmitter and may have neurotransmitter receptors for a half dozen more neurotransmitters. Thus, the various neurotransmitters in the brain are involved in complex interactional relations, and abnormal functioning may result from changes in any single neurotransmitter.

SEROTONIN. Serotonin has received much attention in schizophrenia research since the observation was made that the serotonin-dopamine antagonist drugs (for example, clozapine, risperidone, sertindole) have potent serotonin-related activities. Specifically, antagonism at the serotonin (5-hydroxytryptamine) type 2 (5-HT_2) receptor has been emphasized as important in reducing psychotic symptoms and in mitigating against the development of D_2-antagonism–related movement disorders. Examination of the receptor affinity profiles for each of the serotonin-dopamine antagonists reveals no uniform pattern or ratio of activities other than their relatively higher affinity for serotonin 5-HT_2 receptors than for D_2 receptors. Clozapine has its greatest affinity for histamine receptors, whereas quetiapine binds most tightly to α_1-adrenergic receptors, and ziprasidone is the only member of the group to interact strongly with 5-HT_1 receptors. The affinity for 5-HT_2 and D_2 receptors varies over more than a 100-fold range within this class of drugs. Yet each is a more effective antipsychotic agent than hundreds of related compounds that differ only slightly in their affinities. It appears, therefore, that multiple neurotransmitter systems interact in a particular balance of activity levels to regulate the signs and symptoms of schizophrenia and, moreover, that antipsychotic drugs can modulate these circuits by subtly perturbing any of several neurotransmitter systems. As suggested in the research on mood disorders, serotonin activity has been implicated in suicidal and impulsive behavior that can also be seen in schizophrenic patients.

NOREPINEPHRINE. Several investigators have reported that long-term antipsychotic drug administration decreases the activity of noradrenergic neurons in the locus ceruleus and that the therapeutic effects of some antipsychotic drugs may involve their activities at α_1-adrenergic and α_2-adrenergic receptors. Although the relation between dopaminergic and noradrenergic activity remains unclear, an increasing amount of data suggest that the noradrenergic system modulates the dopaminergic system in such a way that abnormalities of the noradrenergic system predispose a patient to relapse frequently.

AMINO ACIDS. The inhibitory amino acid neurotransmitter γ-aminobutyric acid (GABA) has also been implicated in the pathophysiology of schizophrenia. The available data are consistent with the hypothesis that some patients with schizophrenia have a loss of GABAergic neurons in the hippocampus. The loss of inhibitory GABAergic neurons could theoretically lead to the hyperactivity of dopaminergic and noradrenergic neurons.

The excitatory amino acid neurotransmitter glutamate has also been reported to be involved in the biological basis of schizophrenia. The hypotheses proposed about glutamate include those of hyperactivity, hypoactivity, and glutamate-induced neurotoxicity.

Neuropathology. In the 19th century, neuropathologists failed to find a neuropathological basis for schizophrenia, and thus they classified schizophrenia as a functional disorder. For more than 20 years, however, researchers have made significant strides in revealing a potential neuropathological basis for schizophrenia, primarily in the limbic system and the basal ganglia, although several controversial reports concern neuropathological or neurochemical abnormalities in the cerebral cortex, the thalamus, and the brainstem. The loss of brain volume widely reported in schizophrenic brains appears to result from a reduced density of neuropil—the axons, dendrites, and synapses that mediate associative functions of the brain. Synaptic density is highest at age 1, then is pared down to adult values in early adolescence. One theory, based in part on the observation that patients often develop schizophrenic symptoms during adolescence, holds that schizophrenia results from an excessive pruning of synapses during this phase of development.

LIMBIC SYSTEM. Because of its role in controlling emotions, the limbic system has been hypothesized to be involved in the pathophysiological basis of schizophrenia. In fact, this area of the brain has proved to be the most fertile for neuropathological studies of schizophrenia. Many well-controlled studies of postmortem schizophrenic brain samples have shown a decrease in the size of the region including the amygdala, the hippocampus, and the parahippocampal gyrus. This neuropathological finding agrees with the observations made by MRI study of patients with schizophrenia. A disorganization of the neurons within the hippocampus of schizophrenic patients has also been reported (Fig. 13–3).

BASAL GANGLIA. The basal ganglia have been of theoretical interest

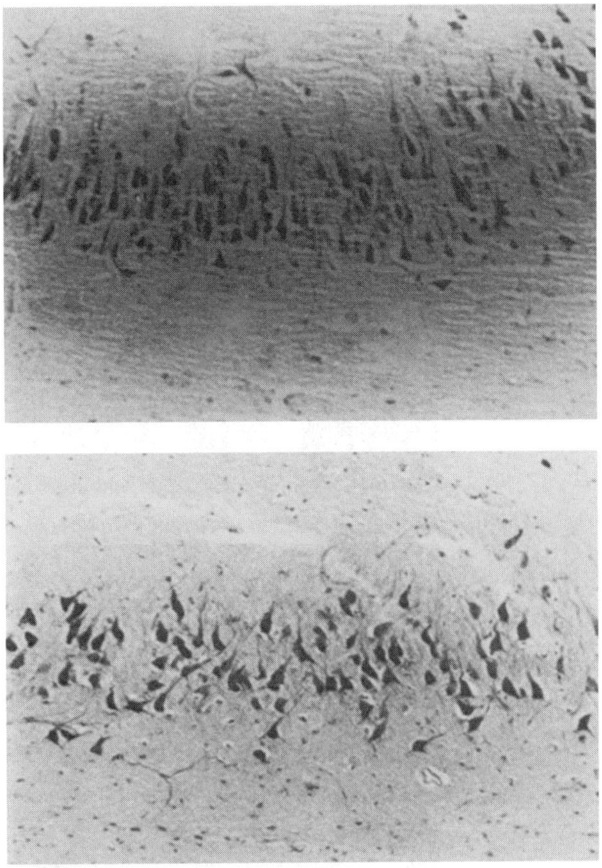

FIGURE 13–3

Comparison of cell orientation patterns of hippocampal pyramids at the CA1 to CA2 interface between nonschizophrenic control subjects **(top)** and schizophrenic subjects **(bottom)** (cresylecht violet stain, original magnification ×250). Positives were overexposed to enhance contrast. (Reprinted with permission from Conrad AJ, Abebe T, Austin R, Forsythe S, Scheibel AB: Hippocampal pyramidal cell disarray in schizophrenia as a bilateral phenomenon. Arch Gen Psychiatry *48:* 415, 1991.)

in schizophrenia for at least two reasons. First, many patients with schizophrenia show odd movements, even in the absence of medication-induced movement disorders (for example, tardive dyskinesia). The odd movements can include an awkward gait, facial grimacing, and stereotypies. Inasmuch as the basal ganglia are involved in the control of movement, disease in the basal ganglia is thereby implicated in the pathophysiology of schizophrenia. Second, of all the neurological disorders that can have psychosis as an associated symptom, the movement disorders involving the basal ganglia (for example, Huntington's disease) are the ones most commonly associated with psychosis in affected patients. Furthermore, the basal ganglia are reciprocally connected to the frontal lobes, and the abnormalities in frontal lobe function seen in some brain-imaging studies may be due to disease in the basal ganglia rather than in the frontal lobes themselves.

Neuropathological studies of the basal ganglia have produced variable and inconclusive reports about cell loss or the reduction of volume of the globus pallidus and the substantia nigra. In contrast, many studies have shown an increase in the number of D_2 receptors in the caudate, the putamen, and the nucleus accumbens. The question remains, however, whether the increase is secondary to the patients' having received antipsychotic medications. Some investigators have begun to study the serotonergic system in the basal ganglia; a role for serotonin in psychotic disorders is suggested by the clinical usefulness of antipsychotic drugs with serotonergic activity (for example, clozapine, risperidone).

Brain Imaging. Before the advent of brain-imaging technologies, the study of schizophrenia depended on the distant measurement of brain activity—for example, the measurement of neurotransmitters in cerebrospinal fluid, plasma, or urine—in living patients or the direct measurement of the brain in deceased persons. Brain-imaging techniques now allow researchers to make specific measurements of neurochemicals or brain function in living patients. Calculations of the data derived from the brain-imaging machines are constructed from many assumptions, however, and differences in these mathematical models between two research groups can potentially lead to different conclusions about the same data. To protect against this possibility, researchers constantly exchange their ideas about appropriate mathematical models.

COMPUTED TOMOGRAPHY. The initial studies using computed tomography (CT) in schizophrenic populations may have produced the earliest and most convincing data that schizophrenia is a bona fide brain disease. These studies have consistently shown that the brains of patients with schizophrenia have lateral and third ventricular enlargement and some degree of reduction in cortical volume. These findings can be interpreted as consistent with a decrease in the usual amount of brain tissue in affected patients; whether this decrease is due to abnormal development or to degeneration is unknown.

Other CT studies have reported abnormal cerebral asymmetry, reduced cerebellar volume, and brain density changes in patients with schizophrenia. Many CT studies have correlated the presence of CT scan abnormalities with the pres-

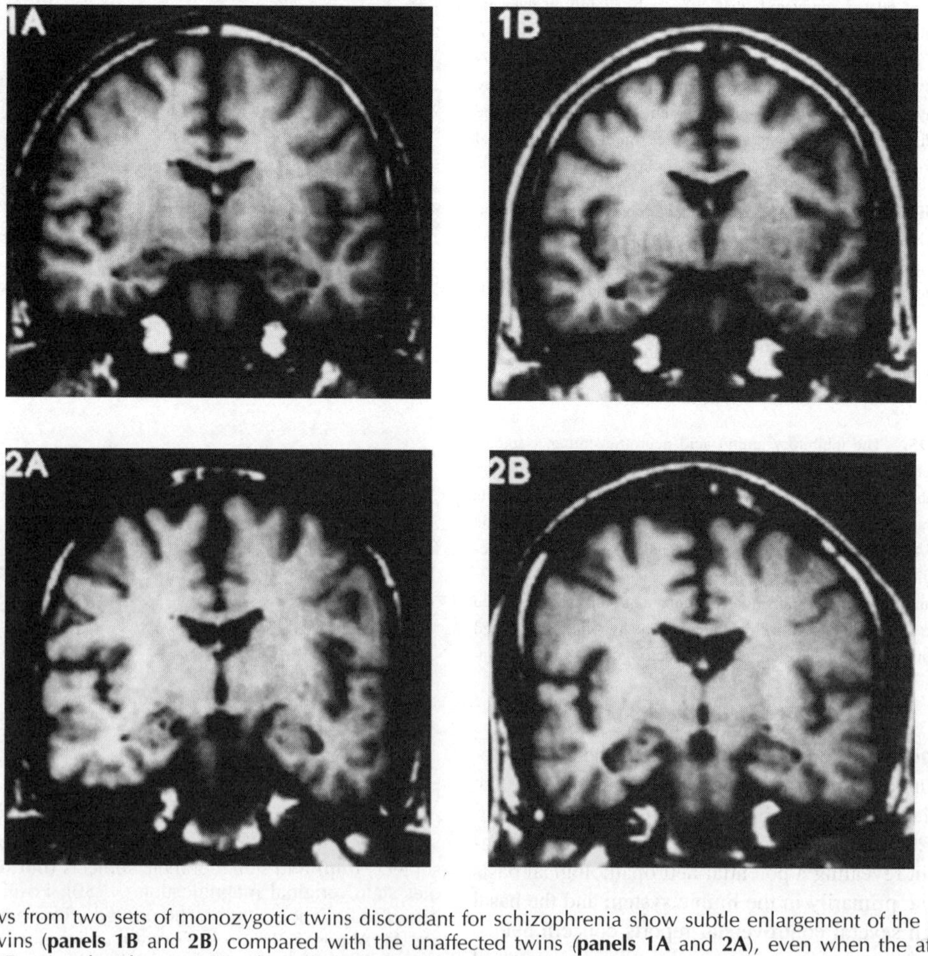
1A
1B
2A
2B

FIGURE 13–4

MRI coronal views from two sets of monozygotic twins discordant for schizophrenia show subtle enlargement of the lateral ventricles in the affected twins (**panels 1B** and **2B**) compared with the unaffected twins (**panels 1A** and **2A**), even when the affected twin had small ventricles. (Reprinted with permission from Suddath RL, Christison GW, Torrey EF, Casanova MF, Weinberger DR: Anatomical abnormalities in the brains of monozygotic twins discordant for schizophrenia. N Engl J Med *322:* 789, 1990.)

ence of negative or deficit symptoms, neuropsychiatric impairment, increased neurological signs, frequent extrapyramidal symptoms from antipsychotic drugs, and poor premorbid adjustment. Although not all CT studies have confirmed these associations, it makes sense to conclude that the greater the evidence of neuropathological disease, the more serious the symptoms. The abnormalities reported in CT studies of patients with schizophrenia, however, have also been reported in other neuropsychiatric conditions, including mood disorders, alcohol-related disorders, and dementias. Thus, these changes are unlikely to be specific for the pathophysiological processes underlying schizophrenia.

Several investigators have attempted to determine whether the abnormalities detected by CT are progressive or static. Some studies have concluded that the lesions observed on CT scan are present at the onset of the illness and do not progress. Other studies, however, have concluded that the pathological process visualized on CT scan continues to progress during the illness. Thus, whether an active pathological process is continuing to evolve in schizophrenic patients is still uncertain.

Although the enlarged ventricles in schizophrenic patients are apparent when groups of patients and controls are used, the difference between affected and unaffected people is variable and usually small. Therefore, the use of CT in the diagnosis of schizophrenia is limited. Some data indicate, however, that ventricles are more enlarged in patients with tardive dyskinesia than in patients without it, and some data show that the enlargement of ventricles is more frequent in male patients than in female patients.

MAGNETIC RESONANCE IMAGING (MRI). MRI was initially used to verify the findings of the CT studies but has subsequently served to expand the knowledge about the pathophysiology of schizophrenia. One of the most important MRI studies examined monozygotic twins who were discordant for schizophrenia (Fig. 13–4). The study found that virtually all the affected twins had larger cerebral ventricles than did the nonaffected twins, although the cerebral ventricles of most affected twins fell within a normal range.

Investigators have used MRI in schizophrenia research for its properties of superior resolution compared with CT and for the qualitative information obtainable by using various signal sequences to get T1- or T2-weighted images, for example. As a result of the superior resolution of MRI, several reports have shown that the volumes of the hippocampal–amygdala complex and the parahippocampal gyrus are reduced in patients with schizophrenia. One recent study found a reduction of these brain areas in the left hemisphere (Fig. 13–5) and not in the right, although other studies have found bilateral reductions in volume. Some studies have correlated the reduction in limbic system volume with the degree of psychopathology or other measures of severity of illness. There have also been reports of differential T1 and T2 relaxation times in schizophrenic patients, particularly as measured in the frontal and temporal regions.

MAGNETIC RESONANCE SPECTROSCOPY (MRS). Magnetic resonance spectroscopy (MRS) is a technique that allows the measurement of the concentrations of specific molecules—for example, adenosine triphosphate (ATP)—in the brain. Although the technique is still early in its development, several preliminary reports about using MRS to study schizophrenia have been published. One study that used MRS imaging of the dorsolateral prefrontal cortex found that, compared with a control group, patients with schizophrenia had lower levels of phosphomonoesters and inorganic phosphate and higher levels of phosphodiesters and adenosine triphosphate. These data about the metabolism of phosphate-containing compounds were consistent with hypoactivity of that brain region and supported the findings of other brain-imaging studies—for example, those of positron emission tomography (PET).

POSITRON EMISSION TOMOGRAPHY (PET). Although many studies using PET to study schizophrenia have been reported, few clear conclusions can be drawn at this time. Most PET studies have measured either glucose use or cerebral blood flow, and the positive findings have included hypoactivity of the frontal lobes, impaired activation of certain brain areas after psychological test stimulation, and hyperactivity of the basal ganglia relative to the cerebral cortex. Other studies, however, have failed to replicate these findings, although the abnormal-activation results seem to be robust. In these studies a person's blood flow is assayed by using PET, single photon emission computed tomography (SPECT), or regional cerebral blood flow (rCBF) brain-imaging systems.

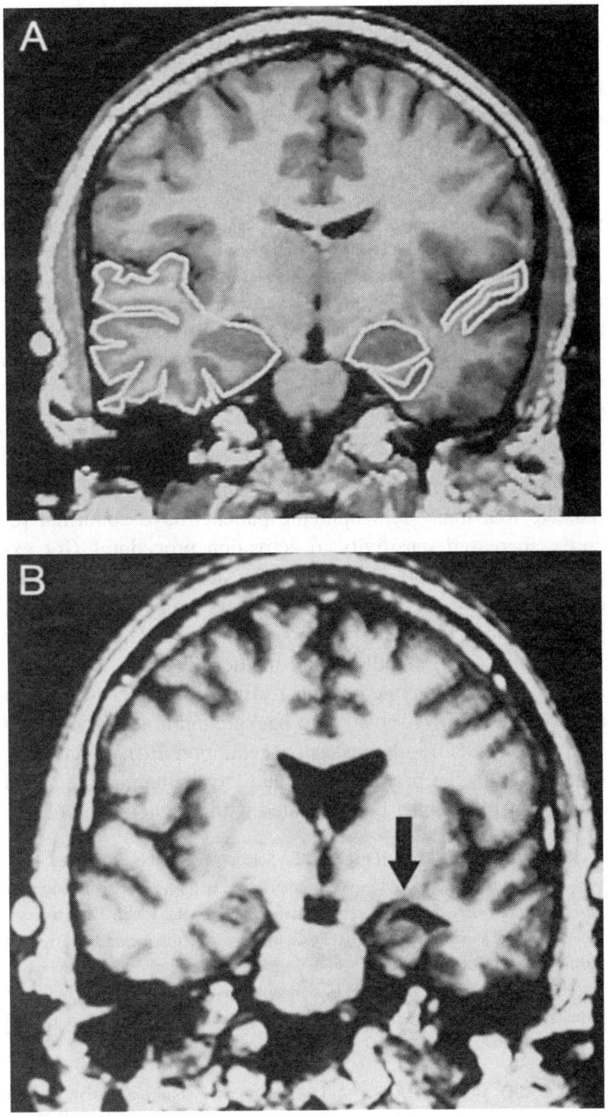
A
B

FIGURE 13–5

Coronal slice (1.5 mm) of the temporal lobe of a control **(A)** and a patient with schizophrenia **(B)**. In **A,** the regions of interest used to evaluate the temporal lobe have been outlined; the neocortical gray matter of the superior temporal gyrus is on the subject's left (the viewer's right); more medially, the amygdala–hippocampal complex is shown as an almondlike shape, with the parahippocampal gyrus underneath. The temporal lobe is outlined on the subject's right. In **B,** the amount of cerebrospinal fluid *(black area)* surrounding the left superior temporal gyrus (sylvian fissure) is increased compared with the amount in the control. Tissue is lost in the parahippocampal gyrus, and the size of the temporal horn surrounding the amygdala–hippocampal complex *(arrow)* is increased. (Reprinted with permission from Shenton ME, Kikinis R, Jolesz FA, Pollak SD, LeMay M, Wible CG, Hokama H, Martin J, Metcalf D, Coleman M, McCarley RW: Abnormalities of the left temporal lobe and thought disorder in schizophrenia. N Engl J Med *327:* 606, 1992.)

While the cerebral blood flow is being measured, the patient performs a psychological task that presumably activates a particular part of the cerebral cortex in normal control subjects. One of the best-controlled studies of this design found that patients with schizophrenia, in contrast to the control group, failed to increase blood flow to the dorsolateral prefrontal cortex while performing the Wisconsin Card Sorting Test.

A second type of PET study has used radioactive ligands to estimate the quantity of D_2 receptors present. The two most discussed studies disagree. One group reported an increased number of D_2 receptors in the basal ganglia, and the other group reported no change in the number of D_2 receptors in the basal ganglia. The difference between the two studies may involve the use of different ligands, different types of patients with schizophrenia, or other differences in method or data analysis. The controversy remains unresolved. The technique will, however, continue to be used in the study of schizophrenia, and subsequent research reports will use ligands for other neurotransmitter systems, such as the noradrenergic and glutamate systems.

Electrophysiology. Electroencephalographic studies indicate that many schizophrenic patients have abnormal records, increased sensitivity to activation procedures (for example, frequent spike activity after sleep deprivation), decreased alpha activity, increased theta and delta activity, possibly more than usual epileptiform activity, and possibly more than usual left-sided abnormalities. There is also an inability for schizophrenic patients to filter out irrelevant sounds and to be extremely sensitive to background noise. The flooding of sound that results makes concentration difficult and may be a factor in the production of auditory hallucinations. This sound sensitivity may be associated with a genetic defect.

COMPLEX PARTIAL EPILEPSY. Schizophrenia-like psychoses have been reported to occur more frequently than expected in patients with complex partial seizures, especially seizures involving the temporal lobes. Factors associated with the development of psychosis in these patients include a left-sided seizure focus, medial temporal location of the lesion, and early onset of seizures. The first-rank symptoms described by Schneider may be similar to symptoms of patients with complex partial epilepsy and may reflect the presence of a temporal lobe disorder when seen in patients with schizophrenia.

EVOKED POTENTIALS. A large number of abnormalities in evoked potential among patients with schizophrenia have been described. The P300 has been most studied and is defined as a large, positive evoked-potential wave that occurs about 300 ms after a sensory stimulus is detected. The major source of the P300 wave may be located in the limbic system structures of the medial temporal lobes. In patients with schizophrenia, the P300 has been reported to be statistically smaller and later than in comparison groups. Abnormalities in the P300 wave have also been reported to be more common in children who, because they have affected parents, are at high risk for schizophrenia. Whether the characteristics of the P300 represent a state or a trait phenomenon remains controversial. Other evoked potentials reported to be abnormal in patients with schizophrenia are the N100 and the contingent negative variation. The N100 is a negative wave that occurs about 100 ms after a stimulus, and the contingent negative variation is a slowly developing, negative-voltage shift following the presentation of a sensory stimulus that is a warning for an upcoming stimulus. The evoked-potential data have been interpreted as indicating that although patients with schizophrenia are unusually sensitive to a sensory stimulus (larger early-evoked potentials), they compensate for the increased sensitivity by blunting the processing of information at higher cortical levels (indicated by smaller late-evoked potentials).

Eye Movement Dysfunction. The inability to accurately follow a moving visual target is the defining basis for the disorders of smooth visual pursuit and disinhibition of saccadic eye movements seen in patients with schizophrenia. Eye movement dysfunction may be a trait marker for schizophrenia; it is independent of drug treatment and clinical state and is also seen in first-degree relatives of schizophrenic probands. Various studies have reported abnormal eye movements in 50 to 85 percent of patients with schizophrenia, compared with about 25 percent in nonschizophrenic psychiatric patients and less than 10 percent in nonpsychiatrically ill control subjects. Because eye movement is partly controlled by centers in the frontal lobes, a disorder in eye movement is consistent with theories that implicate a frontal lobe pathological process in schizophrenia.

Psychoneuroimmunology. Several immunological abnormalities have been associated with patients who have schizophrenia. The abnormalities include decreased T-cell interleukin-2 production, reduced number and responsiveness of peripheral lymphocytes, abnormal cellular and humoral reactivity to neurons, and the presence of brain-directed (antibrain) antibodies. The data can be interpreted variously as representing the effects of a neurotoxic virus or of an endogenous autoimmune disorder. Most carefully conducted investigations that have searched for evidence of neurotoxic viral infections in schizophrenia have had negative results, although epidemiological data show a high incidence of schizophrenia after prenatal exposure to influenza during several epidemics of the disease. Other data supporting a viral hypothesis are an increased number of physical anomalies at birth, an increased rate of pregnancy and birth complications, seasonality of birth consistent with viral infection, geographical clusters of adult cases, and seasonality of hospitalizations. Nonetheless, the inability to detect genetic evidence of viral infection reduces the significance of all circumstantial data. The possibility of autoimmune brain antibodies has some data to support it; the pathophysiological process, if it exists, however, probably explains only a subset of the population with schizophrenia.

Psychoneuroendocrinology. Many reports describe neuroendocrine differences between groups of patients with schizophrenia and groups of control subjects. For example, the dexamethasone-suppression test has been reported to be abnormal in various subgroups of patients with schizophrenia, although the practical or predictive value of the test in schizophrenia has been questioned. One carefully done report, however, has correlated persistent nonsuppression on the dexamethasone-suppression test in schizophrenia with a poor long-term outcome.

Some data suggest decreased concentrations of luteinizing hormone–follicle stimulating hormone (LH/FSH), perhaps correlated with age of onset and length of illness. Two additional reported abnormalities may be correlated with the presence of negative symptoms: a blunted release of prolactin and growth hormone to gonadotropin-releasing hormone (GnRH) or thyrotropin-releasing hormone (TRH) stimulation and a blunted release of growth hormone to apomorphine stimulation.

Genetic Factors

A wide range of genetic studies strongly suggests a genetic component to the inheritance of schizophrenia. In the 1930s, classic studies of the genetics of schizophrenia showed that a person is likely to have schizophrenia when other members of the family have the disorder and that the likelihood of the person's having schizophrenia is correlated with the closeness of the relationship (for example, first-degree or second-degree relative; Table 13–1). Monozygotic twins have the highest concordance rate. In studies of adopted monozygotic twins, twins reared by adoptive parents are seen to have schizophrenia at the same rate as their twin siblings brought up by their biological parents. This finding suggests that the genetic influence outweighs the environmental influence, a finding corroborated by the observation that the more severe the schizophrenia, the more likely the twins are to be concordant for the disorder. One study supports the stress–diathesis model and shows that adopted monozygotic twins who later had schizophrenia were likely to have been adopted by psychologically disordered families.

Chromosomal Markers. Current approaches in genetics are directed toward identifying long pedigrees of affected people and investigating the families for restriction fragment length polymorphisms that segregate with disease phenotype. Many associations between chromosomal sites and schizophrenia have been reported since the application of the techniques of molecular biology became widespread. More than half of all chromosomes have been associated with schizophrenia in various reports, but the long arms of chromosomes 5, 11, and 18, the short arm of chromosome 19, and the X chromosome have most commonly been implicated. The literature is best summarized as indicating a potentially heterogeneous genetic basis for schizophrenia.

Psychosocial Factors

The rapidly evolving understanding of the biology of schizophrenia and the introduction of effective and safe pharmacological treatments have further emphasized the need for exploring individual, family, and social issues that affect patients with schizophrenia. If schizophrenia is a disease of the brain, it is likely to parallel diseases of other organs (for example, myocardial infarctions and diabetes) whose courses are affected by psychosocial stress. Also like other chronic diseases (for example, chronic congestive pulmonary disease), drug therapy alone is rarely sufficient to obtain maximal clinical improvement. Thus, clinicians should consider the psychosocial factors affecting schizophrenia. Although, historically, theorists have attributed the development of schizophrenia to psychosocial factors, contemporary clinicians can benefit from using the relevant theories and guidelines of these past observations and hypotheses.

Theories about Individual Patients. Regardless of the controversies over the causes of schizophrenia, the disorder affects individual patients, each of whom has a unique psychological makeup. Although many psychodynamic theories about the pathogenesis of schizophrenia seem out of date, perceptive clinical observations can help contemporary clinicians understand how the disease may affect a patient's psyche.

PSYCHOANALYTIC THEORIES. Sigmund Freud postulated that schizophrenia resulted from developmental fixations that occurred earlier than those culminating in the development of neuroses. Freud also postulated that an ego defect contributed to the symptoms of schizophrenia. Ego disintegration in schizophrenia represents a return to the time when the ego was not yet, or had just begun to be, established. Thus, intrapsychic conflict arising from the early fixations and the ego defect, which may have resulted from poor early object relations, fuel the psychotic symptoms. Central to Freud's theories of schizophrenia were a decathexis of objects and a regression in response to frustration and conflict with others. Many of Freud's ideas about schizophrenia were colored by his lack of intensive involvement with schizophrenic patients. In contrast, Harry Stack Sullivan engaged schizophrenic patients in intensive psychoanalysis and concluded that the disorder was caused by early interpersonal difficulties, particularly those related to what he considered faulty, overanxious mothering.

In the general psychoanalytic view of schizophrenia, the ego defect affects the interpretation of reality and the control of inner drives, such as sex and aggression. The disturbances occur as a consequence of distortions in the reciprocal relationship between the infant and the mother. As described by Margaret Mahler, the child is unable to separate from and to progress beyond the closeness and complete dependence that characterize the mother–child relationship in the oral phase of development. A person with schizophrenia never achieves object constancy, which is characterized by a sense of secure identity and which results from a close attachment to the mother during infancy. Paul Federn concluded that the fundamental disturbance in schizophrenia is the patient's early inability to achieve self–object differentiation. Some psychoanalysts hypothesize that the defect in rudimentary ego functions permits intense hostility and aggression to distort the mother–infant relationship and leads to a personality organization vulnerable to stress. The onset of symptoms during adolescence occurs when teenagers need a strong ego to function independently, to separate from the parents, to identify tasks, to control increased internal drives, and to cope with intense external simulation.

Psychoanalytic theory also postulates that the various symptoms of schizophrenia have symbolic meaning for individual patients. For example, fantasies of the world coming to an end may indicate a perception that a person's internal world has broken down. Feelings of grandeur may reflect reactivated narcissism, in which people believe that they are omnipotent. Hallucinations may be substitutes for patients' inability to deal with objective reality and may represent their inner wishes or fears. Delusions, similar to hallucinations, are regressive, restitutive attempts to create a new reality or to express hidden fears or impulses.

PSYCHODYNAMIC THEORIES. Genetic studies clearly suggest that schizophrenia is an illness with a biological substrate. Nevertheless, studies of monozygotic twins repeatedly show that environmental and psychological factors have some importance in development of the disorder because many twins are discordant for the illness. Freud viewed schizophrenia as a regressive response to overwhelming frustration and conflict with people in the environment, a regression involving a withdrawal of emotional investment or *cathexis* from both internal object representations and actual people and leading to a return to an autoerotic stage of development. The patient's cathexis, reinvested in the self, thus gives the appearance of autistic withdrawal. Freud later added that although neurosis involves a conflict between the ego and the id, psychosis can be viewed as a conflict between the ego and the external world in which reality is disavowed and subsequently remodeled.

Table 13–1
Prevalence of Schizophrenia in Specific Populations

Population	Prevalence (%)
General population	1.0
Nontwin sibling of a schizophrenic patient	8.0
Child with one schizophrenic parent	12.0
Dizygotic twin of a schizophrenic patient	12.0
Child of two schizophrenic parents	40.0
Monozygotic twin of a schizophrenic patient	47.0

Unlike Freud's complex model, later psychodynamic views of schizophrenia tend to regard the constitutionally based hypersensitivity to perceptual stimuli as deficit. Indeed, much research suggests that patients with schizophrenia find it difficult to screen out various stimuli and to focus on one piece of information. This defective stimulus barrier causes difficulty throughout every phase of development during childhood and places particular stress on interpersonal relatedness. Psychodynamic views of schizophrenia are often mistakenly seen as emphasizing the parents' role in the disorder, but such views actually focus on the schizophrenic patient's psychological and neurophysiological difficulties that create problems for most people in close relationships with them.

Regardless of theoretical model, all psychodynamic approaches are founded on the premise that psychotic symptoms have meaning in schizophrenia. Patients, for example, may become grandiose after an injury to their self-esteem. Similarly, all theories recognize that human relatedness may be terrifying for people with schizophrenia. Although the research on the efficacy of psychotherapy with schizophrenia shows mixed results, concerned people who offer compassion and a sanctuary in a confusing world must be a cornerstone of any overall treatment plan. Long-term follow-up studies show that some patients who bury psychotic episodes probably do not benefit from exploratory psychotherapy, but those who are able to integrate the psychotic experience into their lives may benefit from some insight-oriented approaches.

LEARNING THEORIES. According to learning theorists, children who later have schizophrenia learn irrational reactions and ways of thinking by imitating parents who have their own significant emotional problems. In learning theory, the poor interpersonal relationships of people with schizophrenia develop because of poor models for learning during childhood.

Theories about the Family.

No well-controlled evidence indicates that a specific family pattern plays a causative role in the development of schizophrenia. Clinicians must understand this important point: Many parents of schizophrenic children harbor anger against the psychiatric community for formerly correlating dysfunctional families with the development of schizophrenia. Some patients with schizophrenia do come from dysfunctional families, just as many nonpsychiatrically ill people do. It is also clinically relevant, however, not to overlook pathological family behavior that can significantly increase the emotional stress with which a vulnerable patient with schizophrenia must cope.

DOUBLE BIND. The double bind concept was formulated by Gregory Bateson to describe a hypothetical family in which children receive conflicting parental messages about their behavior, attitudes, and feelings. In Bateson's hypothesis, children withdraw into a psychotic state to escape the unsolvable confusion of the double bind. Unfortunately, the family studies that were conducted to validate the theory were seriously flawed methodologically. The theory has value only as a descriptive pattern, not as an etiological explanation of schizophrenia.

SCHISMS AND SKEWED FAMILIES. Theodore Lidz described two abnormal patterns of family behavior. In one family type, with a prominent schism between the parents, one parent is overly close to a child of the opposite sex. In the other family type, a skewed relationship between a child and one parent involves a power struggle between the parents and the resulting dominance of one parent.

PSEUDOMUTUAL AND PSEUDOHOSTILE FAMILIES. As described by Lyman Wynne, some families suppress emotional expression by consistently using a pseudomutual or pseudohostile verbal communication. In such families, a unique verbal communication develops, and when a child leaves home and must relate to other people, problems may arise. The child's verbal communication may be incomprehensible to outsiders.

EXPRESSED EMOTION. Parents or other caretakers may behave with criticism, hostility, and overinvolvement toward a person with schizophrenia. Many studies have indicated that in families with high levels of expressed emotion (often abbreviated EE), the relapse rate for schizophrenia is high. The assessment of expressed emotion involves analyzing both what is said and the manner in which it is said.

Social Theories.

Some theories have suggested that industrialization and urbanization are involved in the causes of schizophrenia. Although some data support such theories, these stresses are now thought to have their major effects on the timing of the onset and severity of the illness.

DIAGNOSIS

DSM-IV contains the American Psychiatric Association's official diagnostic criteria for schizophrenia (Table 13–2). The criteria in other diagnostic systems appear in Table 13–7. Of particular note are the diagnostic criteria of Ming T. Tsuang and George Winokur, who in 1974 made a distinction between paranoid and nonparanoid schizophrenic patients.

The DSM-IV diagnostic criteria include course specifiers that offer clinicians several options and describe actual clinical situations (Table 13–2). The presence of hallucinations or delusions is not necessary for the diagnosis of schizophrenia; a patient's disorder is diagnosed as schizophrenia when the patient exhibits two of the symptoms listed as symptoms 3 through 5 in criterion A (Table 13–2). Criterion B requires that impaired functioning, although not deteriorations, be present during the active phase of the illness. DSM-IV stipulates that symptoms must persist for at least 6 months and that a diagnosis of schizoaffective disorder or mood disorder must be absent.

Subtypes

DSM-IV classifies the subtypes of schizophrenia as paranoid, disorganized, catatonic, undifferentiated, and residual (Table 13–3), based predominantly on clinical presentation. These subtypes are not closely correlated with different prognoses; for such differentiation, specific predictors of prognosis are best consulted (Table 13–4). ICD-10, by contrast, uses nine subtypes: paranoid schizophrenia, hebephrenia, catatonic schizophrenia, undifferentiated schizophrenia, postschizophrenic depression, residual schizophrenia, simple schizophrenia, other schizophrenia, and schizophrenia, unspecified, with eight possibilities for classifying the course of the disorder, ranging from continuous to complete remission.

Paranoid Type.

DSM-IV specifies that the paranoid type of schizophrenia is characterized by preoccupation with one or more delusions of frequent auditory hallucinations and that specific behaviors suggestive of the disorganized or catatonic type are absent. Classically, the paranoid type of schizophrenia is characterized mainly by the presence of delusions of persecution or grandeur. Patients with paranoid schizophrenia usually have their first episode of illness at an older age than do patients with catatonic or disorganized schizophrenia. Patients in whom schizophrenia occurs in the late 20s or 30s have usually established a social life that may help them through their illness, and the ego resources of paranoid patients tend to be greater than those of patients with catatonic and

Table 13–2
DSM-IV Diagnostic Criteria for Schizophrenia

A. *Characteristic symptoms:* Two (or more) of the following, each present for a significant portion of time during a 1-month period (or less if successfully treated):
(1) delusions
(2) hallucinations
(3) disorganized speech (eg, frequent derailment or incoherence)
(4) grossly disorganized or catatonic behavior
(5) negative symptoms, ie, affective flattening, alogia, or avolition
Note: Only one criterion A symptom is required if delusions are bizarre or hallucinations consist of a voice keeping up a running commentary on the person's behavior or thoughts, or two or more voices conversing with each other.

B. *Social/occupational dysfunction:* For a significant portion of the time since the onset of the disturbance, one or more major areas of functioning, such as work, interpersonal relations, or self-care, are markedly below the level achieved prior to the onset (or when the onset is in childhood or adolescence, failure to achieve expected level of interpersonal, academic, or occupational achievement).

C. *Duration:* Continuous signs of the disturbance persist for at least 6 months. This 6-month period must include at least 1 month of symptoms (or less if successfully treated) that meet criterion A (ie, active-phase symptoms) and may include periods of prodromal or residual symptoms. During these prodromal or residual periods, the signs of the disturbance may be manifested by only negative symptoms or two or more symptoms listed in criterion A present in an attenuated form (eg, odd beliefs, unusual perceptual experiences).

D. *Schizoaffective and mood disorder exclusion:* Schizoaffective disorder and mood disorder with psychotic features have been ruled out because either: (1) no major depressive, manic, or mixed episodes have occurred concurrently with the active-phase symptoms; or (2) if mood episodes have occurred during active-phase symptoms, their total duration has been brief relative to the duration of the active and residual periods.

E. *Substance/general medical condition exclusion:* The disturbance is not due to the direct physiological effects of a substance (eg, a drug of abuse, a medication) or a general medical condition.

F. *Relationship to a pervasive developmental disorder:* If there is a history of autistic disorder or another pervasive developmental disorder, the additional diagnosis of schizophrenia is made only if prominent delusions or hallucinations are also present for at least a month (or less if successfully treated).

Classification of longitudinal course (can be applied only after at least 1 year has elapsed since the initial onset of active-phase symtpoms):
Episodic with interepisode residual symtpoms (episodes are defined by the reemergence of prominent psychotic symptoms); *also* specify *if:* **with prominent negative symptoms**
Episodic with no interepisode residual symtpoms
Continuous (prominent psychotic symptoms are present thourhgout the period of observation); *also* specify *if:* **with prominent negative symptoms**
Single episode in partial remission; *also* specify *if:* **with prominent negative symtpoms**
Single episode in full remission
Other or unspecified pattern

disorganized schizophrenia. Patients with paranoid type of schizophrenia show less regression of their mental faculties, emotional responses, and behavior than do patients with other types of schizophrenia.

Patients with paranoid schizophrenia are typically tense, suspicious, guarded, reserved and sometimes hostile or aggressive, but they can occasionally conduct themselves adequately in social situations. Their intelligence in areas not invaded by their psychosis tends to remain intact.

Table 13–3
DSM-IV Diagnostic Criteria for Schizophrenia Subtypes

Paranoid Type
A type of schizophrenia in which the following criteria are met:

A. Preoccupation with one or more delusions or frequent auditory hallucinations
B. None of the following is prominent: disorganized speech, disorganized or catatonic behavior, or flat or inappropriate affect.

Disorganized Type
A type of schizophrenia in which the following criteria are met:

A. All of the following are prominent:
(1) disorganized speech
(2) disorganized behavior
(3) flat or inappropriate affect
B. The criteria are not met for catatonic type.

Catatonic Type
A type of schizophrenia in which the clinical picture is dominated by at least two of the following:
(1) motoric immobility as evidenced by catalepsy (including waxy flexibility) or stupor
(2) excessive motor activity (that is apparently purposeless and not influenced by external stimuli)
(3) extreme negativism (an apparently motiveless resistance to all instructions or maintenance of a rigid posture against attempts to be moved) or mutism
(4) peculiarities of voluntary movement as evidenced by posturing (voluntary assumption of inappropriate or bizarre postures), stereotyped movements, prominent mannerisms, or prominent grimacing
(5) echolalia or echopraxia

Undifferentiated Type
A type of schizophrenia in which symptoms that meet criterion A are present, but the criteria are not met for the paranoid, disorganized, or catatonic type.

Residual Type
A type of schizophrenia in which the following criteria are met:

A. Absence of prominent delusions, hallucinations, disorganized speech, and grossly disorganized or catatonic behavior.
B. There is continuing evidence of the disturbance, as indicated by the presence of negative symptoms or two or more symptoms listed in criterion A for schizophrenia, present in an attenuated form (eg, odd beliefs, unusual perceptual experiences).

Table 13–4
Features Weighting Toward Good to Poor Prognosis in Schizophrenia

Good Prognosis	Poor Prognosis
Late onset	Young onset
Obvious precipitating factors	No precipitating factors
Acute onset	Insidious onset
Good premorbid social, sexual, and work histories	Poor premorbid social, sexual, and work histories
Mood disorder symptoms (especially depressive disorders)	Withdrawn, autistic behavior
Married	Single, divorced, or widowed
Family history of mood disorders	Family history of schizophrenia
Good support systems	Poor support systems
Positive symptoms	Negative symptoms
	Neurological signs and symptoms
	History of perinatal trauma
	No remissions in three years
	Many relapses
	History of assaultiveness

Mrs. Nicolet is a 55-year-old Frenchwoman.

Problem. Mrs. Nicolet was brought to the emergency department by her family physician, who explained that he had tried for years to convince her to see a psychiatrist. This time he wanted to make sure that his patient would be hospitalized and that she would receive proper treatment at last. Mrs. Nicolet had called him in the middle of the night complaining that the situation had gotten out of hand, that "they" were really behaving quite badly now, and that something had to be done to put an end to their tricks. "They" were using some kind of invisible rays, laughing all the time and making obscene comments as they sent electricity into her genitalia and tried to get her sexually excited.

Mrs. Nicolet's family physician explained that for the previous 3 years his patient had been hearing voices almost continuously, but until the present she had obstinately refused to take any drugs or to see a specialist. She had always asserted that the voices did not really bother her and that, because she now lived all alone, she had come to enjoy their company.

History. Mrs. Nicolet was born and brought up in Paris. She had worked as a typist until her marriage. Her husband was a railway ticket collector. They had no children. There was no history of mental illness in Mrs. Nicolet's family, and she had never been treated for a psychiatric disorder.

The patient's problems began about a year after her husband died of lung cancer. She lived alone, she no longer had any relatives in Paris, and she had no real friends, as neither she nor her husband had ever cared much for company. She noticed one day that two voices in her head were commenting on what she was doing. She became rather upset by this at first and decided that it obviously had to do with the parabolic antenna that her neighbors had recently installed not far from her window. She took care to shut the blinds, but then she noticed that her radiators seemed to have become charged with electricity. She asked her physician to check whether she might have been contaminated by some strange rays. He could find nothing wrong with her, and the blood tests and other investigations, including a brain scan, were negative. He advised her to see a psychiatrist, and when she refused to do so, he gave her a prescription for haloperidol. The drug made her drowsy, so she stopped taking it after a few days. In the end, she decided to live with her voices, and because they were polite and friendly, she stopped worrying about them after a while and gradually grew accustomed to their company.

Mrs. Nicolet had always been in good physical health. She did not smoke or take drugs. She had shared an occasional bottle of wine with her husband but completely stopped drinking any alcoholic beverages after he died.

Mrs. Nicolet's family physician had known his patient for more than 20 years. She had consulted him occasionally for minor physical ailments, and of course he had seen more of her during her husband's illness. She had always been somewhat withdrawn and had not been inclined to talk more than was necessary, but the physician never noticed anything strange or abnormal in the way she spoke or behaved. Even after she started hearing voices, she was still able to function normally in her everyday life.

Findings. Mrs. Nicolet was oriented in time, place, and person. She got angry at her voices, telling them from time to time to "please stop it now," but she talked in a perfectly coherent way. She explained that she heard voices in her head and that they usually limited themselves to commenting on her thoughts and actions, or talked about her between themselves. At times they gave her advice or even instructions, or they put thoughts into her mind that she knew were not her own. However, because most of the time these instructions were quite sensible, she did not object to this. On a few occasions the voices had been unpleasant, and she had to call them to order. Mrs. Nicolet also reported that she frequently felt strange sensations in her body, something such as electricity, radio waves, or invisible rays, and then she knew that "they" were experimenting on her. Those sensations did not become particularly disagreeable until the preceding few weeks before she came to the hospital.

Mrs. Nicolet was neither depressed nor anxious. She gave a coherent account of her past and current life, and she asserted that she would be perfectly able to take care of herself as soon as her voices had started being reasonable once more.

The physical examination revealed no abnormality. Results of blood tests (including thyroid function) were within normal limits, as were all other special investigations, including an electroencephalogram and a new brain scan.

Course. Mrs. Nicolet was treated with 20 mg of haloperidol for the first 2 weeks. Her voices gradually diminished in frequency and prominence, and her somatic sensations disappeared completely. She began to accept that her voices were related to an illness but seemed somewhat disappointed when they stopped completely. She explained that, after all, the voices had been "good company" most of the time.

DISCUSSION

The significant features of Mrs. Nicolet's disorder were prominent auditory hallucinations of voices commenting on her thoughts and actions or discussing her between themselves. Other important features included somatic hallucinations and experiences of thought insertion. Mrs. Nicolet's affect was appropriate, and she was not depressed.

The psychiatrist who examined the patient made a diagnosis of chronic hallucinatory psychosis. This concept was introduced by the French psychiatrist Ballet and further developed by de Clérambault as a nonschizophrenic chronic delusional disorder with predominantly hallucinatory symptoms. Psychiatrists who continue to differentiate the concept from paranoid schizophrenia emphasize that chronic hallucinatory psychosis occurs at a later stage of life, is not accompanied by formal thought disorder, and has a better patient prognosis.

Mrs. Nicolet presented typical schizophrenic symptoms that had persisted for several years. The subtype is classified as paranoid because of the prominence of hallucinations and delusions and the absence of formal thought disorder and flat or inappropriate affect. (From *ICD-10 Casebook.*)

Disorganized Type. The disorganized (formerly called hebephrenic) type of schizophrenia is characterized by a marked regression to primitive, disinhibited, and unorganized behavior and by the absence of symptoms that meet the criteria for the catatonic type. The onset of this subtype is generally early, before age 25. Disorganized patients are usually active but in an aimless, nonconstructive manner. Their thought disorder is pronounced, and their contact with reality is poor. Their personal appearance and their social behavior are dilapidated, their emotional responses are inappropriate, and they often burst into laughter without any apparent reason. Incongruous grinning and grimacing are common in these patients, whose behavior is best described as silly or fatuous.

A 15-year-old girl attended a summer camp, where she had difficulties in getting along with the other children and developed animosity toward one of the counselors. On her return home, she refused to listen to her parents and said that she heard the voice of a man talking to her, although she could not see him. She rapidly began to show bizarre behavior characterized by grimacing, violent outbursts, and inability to take care of herself.

Her school record had always been good, and she was fluent in three languages. Her parents described her as having been a quiet, rather shut-in child, with no abnormal traits in childhood. Family relationships were reported as having been satisfactory.

When the patient was admitted to a psychiatric hospital, her speech was incoherent. She showed marked disturbances of formal thinking and blocking of thoughts. She was impulsive and seemed to be hallucinating. She stated that she heard voices in her right ear and that a popular singer was running after her with a knife. She also thought that her father was intent on killing her and that she was pregnant because she had hugged one of the residents.

Two months of neuroleptic treatment brought no apparent improvement. She was then given a course of intensive electroconvulsive therapy and continuous sleep treatment. Over a period of a year, she received close to 200 electroconvulsive treatments and 50 subcoma insulin treatments, with little improvement. She was then transferred to another mental hospital, where her behavior has, for almost 20 years, continued to be very disturbed.

At this hospital she has often been incontinent and has neglected her physical appearance most of the time. Occasionally, however, she has spent hours dressing herself, looking in the mirror, and putting on excessive makeup. At times, she has been discovered eating her feces. Occasionally, she has adopted the role of a singer or a dancer. She has made such statements as: "Will I live forever? Nurse, I didn't throw my love away. It is in my stomach, and it hurts." In the dining room she has attempted to grasp the genitals of male patients. High doses of neuroleptics are continuously required to control her behavior. The ultimate prognosis is very poor. (Courtesy of Heinz E. Lehmann, M.D., and Robert Cancro, M.D., Med.Sc.)

Catatonic Type. The catatonic type of schizophrenia, which was common several decades ago, has become rare in Europe and North America. The classic feature of the catatonic type is a marked disturbance in motor function; this disturbance may involve stupor, negativism, rigidity, excitement, or posturing (Fig. 13–6). Sometimes, the patient shows a rapid alteration between extremes of excitement and stupor. Associated features include stereotypies, mannerisms, and waxy flexibility. Mutism is particularly common. During catatonic stupor or excitement, patients need careful supervision to prevent them from hurting themselves or others. Medical care may be needed because of malnutrition, exhaustion, hyperpyrexia, or self-inflicted injury.

A young, unmarried woman, age 20, was admitted to a psychiatric hospital because she had become violent toward her parents, had been observed gazing into space with a rapt expression, and had been talking to invisible persons. She had been seen to strike odd postures. Her speech had become incoherent.

She had been a good student in high school, then went to business school, and, a year before admission to the hospital, started to work in an office as a stenographer. She had always been shy, and although she was quite attractive, she did not date much. She began to be influenced by another girl who worked in the same office and who told her about boys and petting. The second girl, she believed, was able to communicate with her from across the room. Even when they went home at night, the patient heard voice messages telling her to do certain things. Then she began to see pictures on the wall, most of them ugly and sneering.

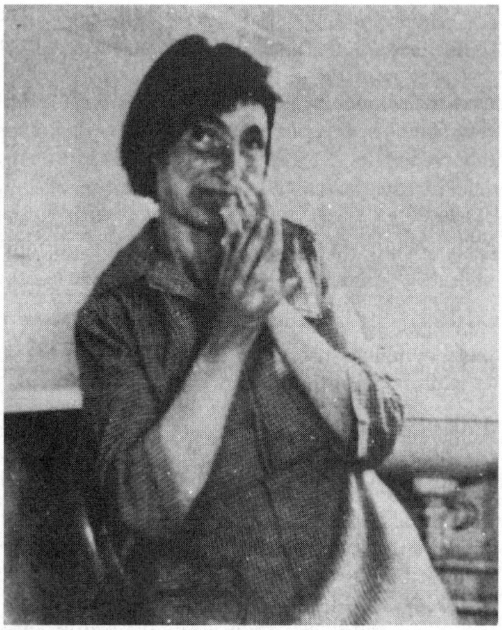

FIGURE 13–6
A 44-year-old chronic schizophrenic woman showing characteristic mannerism and facial grimacing. (Courtesy of New York Academy of Medicine, New York, NY.)

Those pictures had names—one was named shyness, another distress, another envy. The patient believed her office friend sent her messages to knock at the wall, so as to hit the pictures.

The patient was agitated, noisy, and uncooperative in the hospital for several weeks after she arrived and required sedation. She was given a course of insulin coma therapy, with no significant or sustained improvement. Later, she received several courses of electroconvulsive treatment, which also failed to influence the schizophrenic process to any significant degree. Ten years later, when neuroleptic drugs became available, she received pharmacotherapy.

Despite all those therapeutic efforts, her condition throughout her many years' stay in a mental hospital has remained one of chronic catatonic stupor. She is mute and practically devoid of any spontaneity, but she responds to simple requests. She stays in the same position for hours or sits in a chair in a curled-up position. Her facial expression is fixed and stony. (Courtesy of Heinz E. Lehmann, M.D., and Robert Cancro, M.D., Med.Sc.)

Undifferentiated Type. Frequently, patients who are clearly schizophrenic cannot be easily fitted into one or another type. DSM-IV classifies these patients as having schizophrenia of the undifferentiated type.

A 15-year-old girl was seen at the request of her school district authorities for advice on placement. She had recently moved into the area with her family and, after a brief period in a regular class, was placed in a class for students with emotional disturbances. She proved difficult, had a poor understanding of schoolwork, and functioned at about the fifth-grade level despite an apparently good vocabulary. She disturbed the class by making animal noises and telling fantastic stories, which caused other students to laugh at her.

At home, the patient was aggressive and bit or hit her parents or brother when frustrated. She was often bored, had no friends, and found it difficult to occupy herself. She spent a lot of time drawing pictures of robots, spaceships, and fantastic or futuristic inventions. Sometimes, she said she would like to die, but she never made any attempt at suicide and apparently had not thought of killing herself. Her mother said that from birth she had been different and that the onset of her current behavior had been so gradual that no definite date could be assigned to it.

The patient's prenatal and parental histories were unremarkable. Her developmental milestones were delayed, and she did not use single words until she was 4 or 5 years of age. When she first entered school, teachers and counselors had been concerned about her ability. Repeated evaluations had suggested an intelligence quotient (IQ) in the low 70s, but her achievement was somewhat behind what was expected at that level of ability. Because her father was in military service, the family had moved many times, and the results of her earlier evaluations were unavailable.

The parents reported that the patient had always been difficult and restless. Several physicians had said that she was not just mentally retarded but also had a serious mental disorder. An evaluation of the patient at the age of 12, made because of difficulties in school, showed evidence of bizarre thought processes and a fragmented ego structure. At that time, she was sleeping well at night and was not getting up with nightmares or bizarre requests, although she had apparently done so earlier, when she had reportedly slept poorly and disturbed the household nightly by getting up and wandering around. Her mother emphasized that the patient was unpredictable, told odd stories, and talked to herself in "funny voices." Her mother regarded her daughter's stories as childish make-believe and paid little attention to them. The mother reported that since the patient had seen the movie *Star Wars,* she had been obsessed with ideas about space, spaceships, and the future.

Her parents were in their early 40s. Her father, after retiring from military service, worked as an engineer. The patient's mother had many unusual beliefs about herself and was loquacious and circumstantial when giving her history. She dwelled on her strange childhood experiences: She claimed to have grown up in India and to have had a bizarre early childhood, full of dramatic and violent episodes. Many of these episodes seemed improbable. Her husband, in contrast, refused to let her talk about her past in his presence and tried to play down this material as well as the patient's problems. The parents appeared to have a restricted relationship. The father played the role of a taciturn, masterful head of household, and the mother bore the brunt of everyday family duties.

In the interview, the patient was seen to be a tall, overweight, pasty-looking teenager, dressed untidily and with a somewhat disheveled appearance. She complained vociferously of her insomnia, although it was difficult to elicit details of the sleep disturbance, and talked at length about her interests and occupations. She said that when she made a robot in the basement, it ran amok and almost caused damage before she could stop it by remote control. She claimed to have built the robot from spare computer parts, which she acquired from the local museum.

When asked for details about how the robot worked, the patient became increasingly vague. In a response to a request to draw a picture of one of her inventions, she drew a picture of an overhead railway and, to substantiate the structural details, went into what appeared to be complex mathematical calculations. These consisted of meaningless repetitions of symbols (plus, minus, division, multiplication). To the interviewer's expression of gentle incredulity, she blandly responded that many people did not believe that she was a supergenius. She also talked about her unusual ability to hear things that other people could not hear and about her communication with a creature who perhaps haunted her or who was a being from another planet. She could hear his voice talking to her and asking her questions, but he did not attempt to tell her what to do. The voice was outside her head and was inaudible to others. The questions asked her during the interview did not upset her or make her angry or frightened.

Her teacher commented that although the patient was apparently at the fifth-grade level, her comprehension was much lower. She read what was not there and sometimes changed the meanings of paragraphs. Her spelling was at about the third-grade level, her mathematics a little lower. She worked hard but slowly at school. When her teachers put pressure on her, she became upset, and her work deteriorated.

DISCUSSION

When the patient was seen at her school's request, she exhibited several psychotic symptoms. She was apparently delusional, believing she had made a complicated invention and was in communication with "some sort of creature." She had auditory hallucinations of voices talking to her and asking her questions. The presence of delusions and hallucinations, in the absence of a specific organic factor that initiated and maintained the disturbance or of a full mood disorder, raised the question of schizophrenia.

The DSM-IV diagnostic criteria for schizophrenia require that "for a significant portion of the time since the onset of the disturbance, one or more major areas of functioning such as work, interpersonal relations, or self-care are markedly below the level achieved before the onset (or, when the onset is in childhood or adolescence, failure to achieve expected level of interpersonal, academic, or occupational achievement)." The onset of the patient's illness was certainly in childhood, and she failed to achieve the expected level of social development for her age group. Therefore, the patient's condition was diagnosed as schizophrenia. Because her delusions had many different themes, they were not systematized, and a diagnosis of schizophrenia of the paranoid type was ruled out; the absence of prominent catatonic features ruled out a diagnosis of schizophrenia of the catatonic type; and the absence of flat or grossly inappropriate affect ruled out a diagnosis of schizophrenia of the disorganized type. Thus, a diagnosis of schizophrenia of the undifferentiated type was appropriate.

The patient's IQ level of more than 70 spared her from an additional diagnosis of mild mental retardation. A diagnosis of borderline intellectual functioning could be argued for, but the patient's bizarre behavior, not her intellectual abilities, was creating difficulties at school.

Residual Type. According to DSM-IV, the residual type of schizophrenia is characterized by the presence of continuing evidence of the schizophrenic disturbance in the absence of a complete set of active symptoms or of sufficient symptoms to meet the diagnosis of another type of schizophrenia (Table 13–3). Emotional blunting, social withdrawal, eccentric behavior, illogical thinking, and mild loosening of associations commonly appear in the residual type. When delusions or hallucinations occur, they are neither prominent nor accompanied by strong affect.

Positive and Negative Symptoms

In 1980, T. J. Crow proposed a classification of schizophrenic patients into types I and II, based on the presence or the absence of positive (or productive) and negative (or deficit) symptoms (Table 13–5). Although the system was not accepted as part of the DSM-IV classification, the clinical distinction of the two types has significantly influenced psychiatric research. The *positive symptoms* include delusions and hallucinations. The *negative symptoms* include affective flattening or blunting, poverty of speech (alogia) or speech content, blocking, poor grooming, lack of motivation, anhedonia, and social withdrawal. Type I patients tend to have mostly positive symptoms, normal brain structures on CT scans, and relatively good responses to treatment. Type II patients tend to have mostly negative symptoms, structural brain abnormalities on CT scans, and poor responses to treatments. A third category, disorganized, was added recently that includes disorganized speech (thought disorder), disorganized behavior, cognitive defects, and attention deficits.

Other Subtypes

The subtyping of schizophrenia has had a long history; other subtyping schemes appear in the literature, especially literature from countries other than the United States.

The names of some of these subtypes are self-explanatory. *Late-onset schizophrenia* is usually defined as schizophrenia with an onset after age 45. In DSM-IV, schizophrenia with a *childhood onset* is called simply schizophrenia, although even in the United States the literature tends to refer to *childhood* schizophrenia. *Process schizophrenia* describes schizophrenia with a particularly debilitating and deteriorating course.

Bouffée Délirante **(Acute Delusional Psychosis).** This French diagnostic concept differs from a diagnosis of schizophrenia primarily on the basis of a symptom duration

Table 13–5
Percentage of Patients with Negative and Positive Symptoms (111 Consecutively Admitted Schizophrenic Patients)

Symptoms	Mild or Moderate	Severe or Extreme
Negative symptoms		
Affective flattening		
Unchanging facial expression	54	33
Decreased spontaneous movements	37	14
Paucity of expressive gestures	34	24
Poor eye contact	39	16
Affective nonresponsivity	18	18
Inappropriate affect	29	22
Lack of vocal inflections	40	9
Alogia		
Poverty of speech	20	20
Poverty of content of speech	33	6
Blocking	12	3
Increased response latency	17	6
Avolition–apathy		
Grooming and hygiene	33	41
Impersistence at work or school	13	74
Physical anergia	36	31
Anhedonia–asociality		
Recreational interests, activities	38	41
Sexual interest, activity	11	23
Intimacy, closeness	24	35
Relationship with friends, peers	25	63
Attention		
Social inattentiveness	25	32
Inattentiveness during testing	33	19
Positive symptoms		
Hallucinations		
Auditory	19	51
Voices commenting	22	12
Voices conversing	27	12
Somatic-tactile	10	6
Olfactory	5	1
Visual	16	15
Delusions		
Persecutory	19	47
Jealousy	2	1
Guilt, sin	16	2
Grandiose	15	15
Religious	12	11
Somatic	11	11
Delusions of reference	13	21
Delusions of being controlled	25	12
Delusions of mind reading	19	14
Thought broadcasting	11	2
Thought insertion	15	4
Thought withdrawal	11	6
Bizarre behavior		
Clothing, appearance	8	4
Social, sexual behavior	17	7
Aggressive/agitated behavior	14	6
Repetitive/stereotyped behavior	7	4
Positive formal thought disorder		
Derailment	30	4
Tangentiality	28	4
Incoherence	9	1
Illogicality	10	1
Circumstantiality	14	0
Pressure of speech	14	0
Distractible speech	12	1
Clanging	1	0

Adapted from Andreasen NC: The diagnosis of schizophrenia. Schizophr Bull *13:* 9, 1987.

of less than 3 months. The diagnosis is similar to the DSM-IV diagnosis of schizophreniform disorder. French clinicians report that about 40 percent of patients with a diagnosis of *bouffée délirante* progress in their illness and are eventually classified as having schizophrenia.

Latent. The concept of latent schizophrenia was developed during a time when theorists conceived of the disorder in broad diagnostic terms. Currently, patients must be very mentally ill to warrant a diagnosis of schizophrenia, but with a broad diagnostic concept of schizophrenia, the condition of patients who would not currently be thought of as severely ill could have received a diagnosis of schizophrenia. Latent schizophrenia, for example, was often the diagnosis used for patients with what are now called schizoid and schizotypal personality disorders. These patients may occasionally show peculiar behaviors or thought disorders but do not consistently manifest psychotic symptoms. In the past, the syndrome was also termed *borderline schizophrenia.*

Oneiroid. The oneiroid state refers to a dreamlike state in which patients may be deeply perplexed and not fully oriented in time and place. The term *oneiroid schizophrenic* has been used for patients who are deeply engaged in their hallucinatory experiences to the exclusion of involvement in the real world. When an oneiroid state is present, clinicians should be particularly careful to examine patients for medical or neurological causes of the symptoms.

Paraphrenia. This term is sometimes used as a synonym for *paranoid schizophrenia* or for either a progressively deteriorating course of illness or the presence of a well-systemized delusional system. The multiple meanings of the term render it ineffective in communicating information.

Pseudoneurotic. Occasionally, patients who initially have such symptoms as anxiety, phobias, obsessions, and compulsions later reveal symptoms of thought disorder and psychosis. These patients are characterized by symptoms of pananxiety, panphobia, panambivalence, and sometimes a chaotic sexuality. Unlike people with anxiety disorders, pseudoneurotic patients have free-floating anxiety that rarely subsides. In clinical descriptions, the patients seldom become overtly and severely psychotic. Most of these patients are currently diagnosed as having borderline personality disorder.

Simple Schizophrenia. Like the term *latent schizophrenia,* the term *simple schizophrenia* was used when schizophrenia had a broad diagnostic conceptualization. Simple schizophrenia is characterized by a gradual, insidious loss of drive and ambition. Patients with the disorder are usually not overtly psychotic and do not experience persistent hallucinations or delusions. Their primary symptom is withdrawal from social and work-related situations. The syndrome may reflect depression, a phobia, a dementia, or an exacerbation of personality traits. Clinicians should be sure that patients truly meet the diagnostic criteria for schizophrenia before making the diagnosis. In spite of these reservations, simple deteriorative disorder (simple schizophrenia) appears as a diagnostic category in an appendix of DSM-IV (see Table 14.1–4).

A 27-year-old unmarried man was brought to a mental hospital because he had on several occasions become violent toward his father.

For a few weeks he had experienced hallucinations and heard voices. The voices eventually ceased, but he then adopted a strange way of life. He would sit up all night, sleep all day, and become very angry when his father tried to get him out of bed. He did not shave or wash for weeks, smoked continuously, ate very irregularly, and drank enormous quantities of tea.

In the hospital, he adjusted rapidly to the new environment and was found to be generally cooperative. He showed no marked abnormalities of mental state or behavior, except for his lack of concern for just about everything. He kept to himself as much as possible and conversed little with patients and staff. His personal hygiene had to be supervised by the nursing staff; otherwise, he would quickly become dirty and very untidy.

Twenty years after his admission to the hospital, he is described as shiftless and careless, sullen and unreasonable. He lies on a couch all day long. Neuroleptic treatment has failed to alter his mental state or behavior. Although many efforts have been made to get the patient to accept therapeutic work assignments, he refuses to consider any kind of regular occupation. In the summer, he wanders about the hospital grounds or lies under a tree. In the winter, he wanders through the tunnels connecting the various hospital buildings and is often seen stretched out for hours under the warm pipes that carry steam through the tunnels. (Courtesy of Heinz E. Lehmann, M.D., and Robert Cancro, M.D., Med.Sc.)

ICD-10

The 10th revision of *International Statistical Classification of Diseases and Related Health Problems* (ICD-10) distinguishes schizotypal disorder from schizophrenic disorders, although both types of disorder are probably genetically related, and ICD-10 describes delusional disorders as mostly unrelated to schizophrenia. According to ICD-10, nine groups of symptoms are important for diagnosing schizophrenia: (1) thought echo, insertion, withdrawal, and broadcasting; (2) delusions of control, influence, or passivity; (3) hallucinatory voices; (4) other persistent delusions that are culturally inappropriate and impossible; (5) persistent hallucinations; (6) breaks or interpolation in thinking; (7) catatonic behavior; (8) "negative" symptoms resulting in social withdrawal and poor social performance but not caused by depression or medication; (9) consistent, overall change in behavior. Unlike requirements in DSM-IV for a diagnosis of schizophrenia, ICD-10 requires one clear symptom or two less clear symptoms from any one of groups 1 through 4 or symptoms from at least two of groups 5 through 8 to be present for most of the time during 1 month or more. Similar conditions lasting less than a month should be diagnosed as schizophrenia-like disorders. DSM-IV defines schizophrenia as a disturbance of at least 6 months' duration, with two or more symptoms active for at least a month. A disorder diagnosed as schizophrenia under ICD-10 standards may be diagnosed as schizophreniform disorder under DSM-IV standards. The latter disorder is, according to DSM-IV, equivalent to schizophrenia except for its duration, which is 1 to 6 months, and for the absence of functional decline.

The ICD-10 general criteria for schizophrenia (Table 13–6) apply to all ICD-10 subtypes except simple schizophrenia. The ICD-10 diagnostic criteria for the schizophrenia subtypes are also presented in Table 13–6, and ICD-10 includes two residual categories: other schizophrenia (cenesthopathic schizophrenia [a disorder in which patients complain about or have delusions of a general sense of bodily existence]) and unspecified schizophrenia.

Other Diagnostic Criteria

A variety of research clinicians, some of whom have already been mentioned (for example, Langfeldt, Schneider, and Jaspers), constructed their own criteria to describe the essential features of schizophrenia. Table 13–7 lists some of these schema, many of which are still in active use. The Present State Examination is among those most extensively used by researchers.

Psychological Tests

In general, patients with schizophrenia perform similarly to patients with neurologically caused mental disorders. The data are consistent with the idea that schizophrenia is a brain disease that disrupts the normal functioning of many cognitive abilities. Patients with schizophrenia generally perform poorly on a wide range of neuropsychological tests. One recent study, however, compared the neuropsychological performances of schizophrenic monozygotic twins with those of their nonaffected counterparts. The study found that vigilance, memory, and concept formation were most affected and suggested that the pattern was most consistent with pathological involvement in the frontotemporal cortex. Moreover, the study found that these impairments were most related to the disease process itself and were not attributable to genetic trait markers or environmental factors.

Neuropsychological Testing. Formal neuropsychological assessment of cognitive functions in schizophrenic patients can often provide data for clinical use. Objective measures of neuropsychological performance, such as the Halstead-Reitan battery and the Luria-Nebraska battery, often give abnormal findings, but the results can suggest practical approaches that take into account patients' cognitive weaknesses. The test results are generally consistent with bilateral frontal and temporal lobe dysfunction, including impairments in attention, retention time, and problem-solving ability.

Intelligence Tests. When groups of patients with schizophrenia are compared with groups of nonschizophrenic

Table 13–6
ICD-10 Diagnostic Criteria for Schizophrenia

This overall category includes the common varieties of schizophrenia, together with some less common varieties and closely related disorders.

General criteria for paranoid, hebephrenic, catatonic, and undifferentiated schizophrenia

G1. Either *at least one* of the syndromes, symptoms, and signs listed under (1) below, *or* at least two of the symptoms and signs listed under (2) should be present for most of the time during an episode of psychotic illness lasting for at least 1 month (or at some time during most of the days).
- (1) At least one of the following must be present:
  - (a) thought echo, thought insertion or withdrawal, or thought broadcasting;
  - (b) delusions of control, influence, or passivity, clearly referred to body or limb movements or specific thoughts, actions, or sensations; delusional perception;
  - (c) hallucinatory voices giving a running commentary on the patient's behavior, or discussing the patient among themselves, or other types of hallucinatory voices coming from some part of the body;
  - (d) persistent delusions of other kinds that are culturally inappropriate and completely impossible (eg being able to control the weather, or being in communication with aliens from another world).
- (2) *Or* at least two of the following:
  - (a) persistent hallucinations in any modality, when occurring every day for at least 1 month, when accompanied by delusions (which may be fleeting or half-formed) without clear affective content, or when accompanied by persistent overvalued ideas;
  - (b) neologisms, breaks, or interpolations in the train of thought, resulting in incoherence or irrelevant speech;
  - (c) catatonic behavior, such as excitement, posturing or waxy flexibility, negativism, mutism, and stupor;
  - (d) "negative" symptoms, such as marked apathy, paucity of speech, and blunting or incongruity of emotional responses (it must be clear that these are not due to depression or to neuroleptic medication).

G2. *Most commonly used exclusion clauses*
- (1) If the patient also meets criteria for manic episode or depressive episode, the criteria listed under G1(1) and G1(2) above must have been met *before* the disturbance of mood developed.
- (2) The disorder is not attributable to organic brain disease or to alcohol- or drug-related intoxication, dependence, or withdrawal.

Comments

In evaluating the presence of these abnormal subjective experiences and behavior, special care should be taken to avoid false-positive assessments, especially where culturally or subculturally influenced modes of expression and behavior or a subnormal level of intelligence are involved.

Pattern of course

In view of the considerable variation of the course of schizophrenic disorders it may be desirable (especially for research) to specify the *pattern of course* by using a fifth character. Course should not usually be coded unless there has been a period of observation of at least 1 year.

Continuous

No remission of psychotic symptoms throughout the period of observation.

Episodic with progressive deficit

Progressive development of "negative" symptoms in the intervals between psychotic episodes.

Episodic with stable deficit

Persistent but nonprogressive "negative" symptoms in the intervals between psychotic episodes.

Episodic remittent

Complete or virtually complete remissions between psychotic episodes.

Incomplete remission

Complete remission

Other

Course uncertain, period of observation too short

Paranoid schizophrenia

- A. The general criteria for schizophrenia must be met.
- B. Delusions or hallucinations must be prominent (such as delusions of persecution, reference, exalted birth, special mission, bodily change, or jealousy; threatening or commanding voices, hallucinations of smell or taste, sexual or other bodily sensations.)
- C. Flattening or incongruity of affect, catatonic symptoms, or incoherent speech must not dominate the clinical picture, although they may be present to a mild degree.

Hebephrenic szhizophrenia

- A. The general criteria for schizophrenia must be met.
- B. Either of the following must be present:
  - (1) definite and sustained flattening or shallowness of affect;
  - (2) definite and sustained incongruity or inappropriateness of affect.
- C. Either of the following must be present:
  - (1) behavior that is aimless and disjointed rather than goal-directed;
  - (2) definite thought disorder, manifesting as speech that is disjointed, rambling, or incoherent.
- D. Hallucinations or delusions must not dominate the clinical picture, although they may be present to a mild degree.

Catatonic schizophrenia

The general criteria for schizophrenia must eventually be met, although this may not be possible initially if the patient is uncommunicative.

For a period of at least 2 weeks one or more of the following catatonic behaviors must be prominent:

- (1) stupor (marked decrease in reactivity to the environment and reduction of spontaneous movements and activity) or mutism;
- (2) excitement (apparently purposeless motor activity, not influenced by external stimuli);
- (3) posturing (voluntary assumption and maintenance of inappropriate or bizarre postures);
- (4) negativism (an apparently motiveless resistance to all instructions or attempts to be moved, or movement in the opposite direction);
- (5) rigidity (maintenance of a rigid posture against efforts to be moved);
- (6) waxy flexibility (maintenance of limbs and body in externally imposed positions);
- (7) command automatism (automatic compliance with instruction).

Undifferentiated schizophrenia

The general criteria for schizophrenia must be met.
Either of the following must apply:

- (1) insufficient symptoms to meet the criteria for any of the subtypes
- (2) so many symptoms that the criteria for more than one of the subtypes listed above are met.

(*continued*)

Table 13–6 *(continued)*

Postschizophrenic depression The general criteria for schizophrenia must have been met within the past 12 months but are not met at the present time. One of the conditions in criterion G1(2) a, b, c, or d for general schizophrenia must still be present. C. The depressive symptoms must be sufficiently prolonged, severe, and extensive to meet criteria for at least a mild depressive episode. **Residual schizophrenia** A. The general criteria for schizophrenia must have been met at some time in the past but are not met at the present time. B. At least four of the following "negative" symptoms have been present throughout the previous 12 months: (1) psychomotor slowing or underactivity; (2) definite blunting of affect; (3) passivity and lack of initiative; (4) poverty of either the quantity or the content of speech; (5) poor nonverbal communicatin by facial expression, eye contact, voice modulation, or posture; (6) poor social performance or self-care.	**Simple schizophrenia** A. There is slow but progressive development, over a period of at least 1 year, of all three of the following: (1) a significant and consistent change in the overall quality of some aspects of personal behavior, manifest as loss of drive and interests, aimlessness, idleness, a self-absorbed attitude, and social withdrawal; (2) gradual appearance and deepening of "negative" symptoms such as marked apathy, paucity of speech, underactivity, blunting of affect, passivity and lack of initiative, and poor nonverbal communication (by facial expression, eye contact, voice modulation, and posture); (3) marked decline in social, scholastic, or occupational performance. B. At no time are there any of the symptoms referred to in criterion G1 for general schizophrenia, nor are there hallucinations or well-formed delusions of any kind; ie, the individual must never have met the criteria for any other type of schizophrenia or for any other psychotic disorder. C. There is no evidence of dementia or any other organic mental disorder. **Other schizophrenia** **Schizophrenia, unspecified**

Reprinted with permission from World Health Organization: *The ICD-10 Classification of Mental and Behavioural Disorders: Diagnostic Criteria for Research.* Copyright, World Health Organization, Geneva, 1993.

psychiatric patients or with the general population, the schizophrenic patients tend to score lower on intelligence tests. Statistically, the evidence suggests that low intelligence is often present at the onset, and intelligence may continue to deteriorate with the progression of the disorder.

Projective and Personality Tests. Projective tests, such as the Rorschach test and the Thematic Apperception Test (TAT), may indicate bizarre ideation. Personality inventories, such as the Minnesota Multiphasic Personality Inventory (MMPI), often give abnormal results in schizophrenia, but the contribution to diagnosis and treatment planning is minimal.

CLINICAL FEATURES

A discussion of the clinical signs and symptoms of schizophrenia raises three key issues. First, no clinical sign or symptom is pathognomonic for schizophrenia; every sign or symptom seen in schizophrenia occurs in other psychiatric and neurological disorders. This observation is contrary to the often-heard clinical opinion that certain signs and symptoms are diagnostic of schizophrenia. Therefore, a patient's history is essential for the diagnosis of schizophrenia; clinicians cannot diagnose schizophrenia simply by a mental status examination. Second, a patient's symptoms change with time. For example, a patient may have intermittent hallucinations and a varying ability to perform adequately in social situations, or significant symptoms of a mood disorder may come and go during the course of schizophrenia. Third, clinicians must take into account the patient's educational level, intellectual ability, and cultural and subcultural membership. An impaired ability to understand abstract concepts, for example, may reflect either the patient's education or his or her intelligence. Religious organizations and cults may have customs that seem strange to outsiders but that are normal to those within the cultural setting.

Premorbid Signs and Symptoms

In theoretical formulations of the course of schizophrenia, premorbid signs and symptoms appear before the prodromal phase of the illness. The differentiation implies that premorbid signs and symptoms exist before the disease process evidences itself and that the prodromal signs and symptoms are parts of the evolving disorder. In the typical but not invariable premorbid history of schizophrenia, patients have had schizoid or schizotypal personalities characterized as quiet, passive, and introverted; as children they had few friends. Preschizophrenic adolescents may have no close friends and no dates and may avoid team sports. They may enjoy watching movies and television or listening to music to the exclusion of social activities. Some adolescent patients may show an acute onset of obsessive-compulsive behavior or a prodromal picture.

The validity of the prodromal signs and symptoms, almost invariably recognized after the diagnosis of schizophrenia has been made, is uncertain; once schizophrenia is diagnosed, the retrospective remembrance of early signs and symptoms is affected. Nevertheless, although the first hospitalization is often thought to mark the beginning of the disorder, signs and symptoms have often been present for months or even years. The

Table 13–7
Essential Features of Various Diagnostic Criteria for Schizophrenia

KURT SCHNEIDER CRITERIA

1. First-rank symptoms
   a. Audible thoughts
   b. Voices arguing or discussing or both
   c. Voices commenting
   d. Somatic passivity experiences
   e. Thought withdrawal and other experiences of influenced thought
   f. Thought broadcasting
   g. Delusional perceptions
   h. All other experiences involving volition, made affects, and made impulses
2. Second-rank symptoms
   a. Other disorders of perception
   b. Sudden delusional ideas
   c. Perplexity
   d. Depressive and euphoric mood changes
   e. Feelings of emotional impoverishment
   f. ". . . and several others as well"

GABRIEL LANGFELDT CRITERIA

1. Symptom criteria
   Significant clues to a diagnosis of schizophrenia are (if no sign of cognitive impairment, infection, or intoxication can be demonstrated):
   a. Changes in personality, which manifest themselves as a special type of emotional blunting followed by lack of initiative, and altered, frequently peculiar behavior. (In hebephrenia, especially, the changes are characteristic and are a principal clue to the diagnosis.)
   b. In catatonic types, the history and the typical signs in periods of restlessness and stupor (with negativism, oily facies, catalepsy, special vegetative symptoms, etc.)
   c. In paranoid psychoses, essential symptoms of split personality (or depersonalization symptoms) and a loss of reality feeling (derealization symptoms) or primary delusions
   d. Chronic hallucinations
2. Course criterion
   A final decision about diagnosis cannot be made before a follow-up period of at least 5 years has shown a long-term course of disease

NEW HAVEN SCHIZOPHRENIA INDEX

1. a. Delusions: not specified or other-than-depressive	2 points
b. Auditory hallucinations c. Visual hallucinations d. Other hallucinations	any one: 2 points
2. a. Bizarre thoughts b. Autism or grossly unrealistic private thoughts c. Looseness of associations, illogical thinking, overinclusion	any one: 2 points
d. Blocking e. Concreteness	either: 2 points
f. Derealization g. Depersonalization	each: 1 point
3. Inappropriate affect	1 point
4. Confusion	1 point
5. Paranoid ideation (self-referential thinking, suspiciousness)	1 point
6. Catatonic behavior a. Excitement b. Stupor c. Waxy flexibility d. Negativism e. Mutism f. Echolalia g. Stereotyped motor activity	Any one: 1 point

Scoring: To be considered part of the schizophrenic group, the patient must score on Item 1 or Item 2a, 2b, or 2c and must receive a total score of at least 4 points.

(continued)

Table 13–7 *(continued)*

FLEXIBLE SYSTEM

Minimum number of symptoms required can be four to eight, depending on investigator's choice:

1. Restricted affect
2. Poor insight
3. Thoughts aloud
4. Poor rapport
5. Widespread delusions
6. Incoherent speech
7. Unreliable information
8. Bizarre delusions
9. Nihilistic delusions
10. Absence of early awakening (1 to 3 hours)
11. Absence of depressed facies
12. Absence of elation

RESEARCH DIAGNOSTIC CRITERIA

Criteria 1 through 3 required for diagnosis:

1. At least two of the following for definite illness and one for probable (not counting those occurring during period of drug or alcohol abuse or withdrawal):
   a. Thought broadcasting, insertion, or withdrawal
   b. Delusions of being controlled or influenced, other bizarre delusions, or multiple delusions
   c. Delusions other than persecution or jealousy lasting at least one month
   d. Delusions of any type if accompanied by hallucinations of any type for at least one week
   e. Auditory hallucinations in which either a voice keeps up a running commentary on subject's behaviors or thoughts as they occur or two or more voices converse with each other
   f. Nonaffective verbal hallucinations spoken to subject
   g. Hallucinations of any type throughout day for several days or intermittently for at least one month
   h. Definite instances of marked formal thought disorders accompanied by blunted or inappropriate affect, delusions, or hallucinations of any type or grossly disorganized behavior
2. One of the following:
   a. Current period of illness lasted at least 2 weeks from onset of noticeable change in subject's usual condition
   b. Subject has had previous period of illness lasting at least two weeks, during which he or she met criteria, and residual signs of illness have remained (eg, extreme social withdrawal, blunted or inappropriate affect, formal thought disorder, or unusual thoughts or perceptual experiences)
3. At no time during active period of illness being considered did subject meet criteria for probable or definite manic or depressive syndrome to the degree that it was a prominent part of illness

ST. LOUIS CRITERIA

1. Both necessary:
   a. Chronic illness with at least 6 months of symptoms before index evaluation without return to premorbid level of psychosocial adjustment
   b. Absence of period of depressive or manic symptoms sufficient to qualify for mood disorder or probable mood disorder
2. At least one of the following:
   a. Delusions or hallucinations without significant perplexity or disorientation
   b. Verbal production that makes communication difficult owing to lack of logical or understandable organization (in presence of muteness, diagnostic decision must be deferred)
3. At least three for definite, two for probable, illness:
   a. Never married
   b. Poor premorbid social adjustment or work history
   c. Family history of schizophrenia
   d. Absence of alcohol or other substance abuse within one year of onset
   e. Onset before age 40

(continued)

Table 13–7 *(continued)*

TAYLOR AND ABRAMS CRITERIA

All criteria must be met for diagnosis:

1. Duration of episode greater than 6 months
2. Clear consciousness
3. Presence of delusions, hallucinations, or formal thought disorder (verbigeration, non sequiturs, word approximations, neologisms, blocking, and derailment)
4. Absence of broad affect
5. Absence of signs and symptoms sufficient to make diagnosis of mood disorder
6. No alcohol or other substance abuse within one year of index episode
7. Absence of focal signs and symptoms of coarse brain disease or major medical illness known to produce significant behavioral changes

PRESENT STATE EXAMINATION

The following 12 items from the Present State Examination correspond to a 12-point diagnostic system for schizophrenia, with varying levels of certainty of diagnosis based on the cut-off score determined by the examiner. Nine of the symptoms are scored 1 point each when present (+), and three are scored 1 point each when absent (−).

1. Restricted affect (+)
2. Poor insight (+)
3. Thoughts aloud (+)
4. Awaking early (−)
5. Poor rapport (+)
6. Depressed facies (−)
7. Elation (−)
8. Widespread delusions (+)
9. Incoherent speech (+)
10. Unreliable information (+)
11. Bizarre delusions (+)
12. Nihilistic delusions (+)

TSUANG AND WINOKUR CRITERIA

I. Hebephrenic (A through D must be present):
- A. Age of onset and sociofamilial data (one of the following):
  1. Age of onset before 25 years
  2. Unmarried or unemployed
  3. Family history or schizophrenia
- B. Disorganized thought
- C. Affect changes (either 1 or 2):
  1. Inappropriate affect
  2. Flat affect
- D. Behavioral symptoms (either 1 or 2):
  1. Bizarre behavior
  2. Motor symptoms (either a or b):
     - a. Hebephrenic traits
     - b. Catatonic traits (if present, subtype may be modified to hebephrenia with catatonic traits)

II. Paranoid (A through C must be present):
- A. Age of onset and sociofamilial data (one of the following):
  1. Age of onset after 25 years
  2. Married or employed
  3. Absence of family history of schizophrenia
- B. Exclusion criteria:
  1. Disorganized thoughts must be absent or of mild degree, such that speech is intelligible
  2. Affective and behavioral symptoms, as described in hebephrenia, must be absent or of mild degree
- C. Preoccupation with extensive, well-organized delusions or hallucinations

The criteria of Schneider and Langfeld are reprinted with permission from World Psychiatric Association: *Diagnostic Criteria for Schizophrenic and Affective Psychoses.* American Psychiatric Press, Washington, 1983. The criteria of St. Louis, Research Diagnostic Criteria, New Haven Schizophrenia Index, Flexible, and Taylor and Abrams are reprinted with permission from Endicott J Nee J, Fleiss L, Cohen J, Williams JBW, Simon R: Diagnostic criteria for schizophrenia. Arch Gen Psychiatry *39:* 884, 1982. The criteria for Tsuang and Winokur are reprinted with permission from Tsuang MT, Winokur G: Criteria for hebephrenic and paranoid schizophrenia. Arch Gen Psychiatry *31:* 43, 1974.

signs may have started with complaints about somatic symptoms, such as headache, back and muscle pain, weakness, and digestive problems. The initial diagnosis may be malingering or somatization disorder. Family and friends may eventually notice that the person has changed and is no longer functioning well in occupational, social, and personal activities. During this stage, a patient may begin to develop an interest in abstract ideas, philosophy, the occult, or religious questions. Additional prodromal signs and symptoms can include markedly peculiar behavior, abnormal affects, unusual speech, bizarre ideas, and strange perceptual experiences.

Mental Status Examination

General Description. The appearance of a patient with schizophrenia can range from that of a completely disheveled, screaming, agitated person to an obsessively groomed, completely silent, and immobile person. Between these two poles, patients may be talkative and may exhibit bizarre postures (Figs. 13–6 and 13–7). Their behavior may become agitated or violent, apparently in an unprovoked manner but usually in response to hallucinations. By contrast, in catatonic stupor, often referred to as *catatonia,* patients seem completely lifeless and may exhibit such signs as muteness, negativism, and automatic obedience. Waxy flexibility, once a common sign in catatonia, has become rare (Figs. 13–8 and 13–9). A person with a less extreme subtype of catatonia may show marked social withdrawal and egocentricity, lack of spontaneous speech or movement, and an absence of goal-directed behavior (Fig. 13–10). Patients with catatonia may sit immobile and speechless in their chairs, respond only with short answers to questions, and move only when directed to. Other obvious behavior may include an odd clumsiness or stiffness in body movements, signs now seen as possibly indicating a disease process in the basal ganglia. Patients with schizophrenia often are poorly groomed, fail to bathe, and dress much too warmly for the prevailing temperatures. Other odd behaviors include tics, stereotypies, mannerisms, and, occasionally, *echopraxia,* in which patients imitate the posture or the behaviors of the examiner.

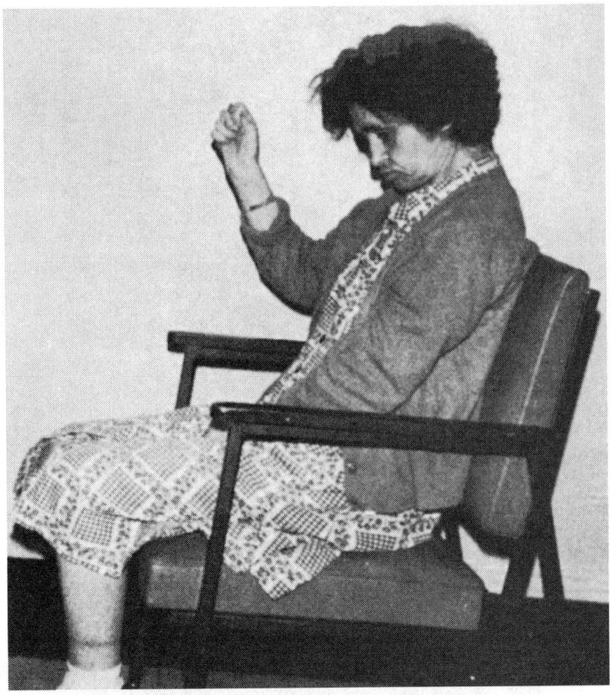

FIGURE 13–8
Long-term catatonic patient. This patient is immobile, demonstrating waxy flexibility. Her arm is in an uncomfortable position, elevated without support, and her stony facial expression has a *Schnauzkrampf* or frozen snout. (Courtesy of Heinz E. Lehmann, M.D.)

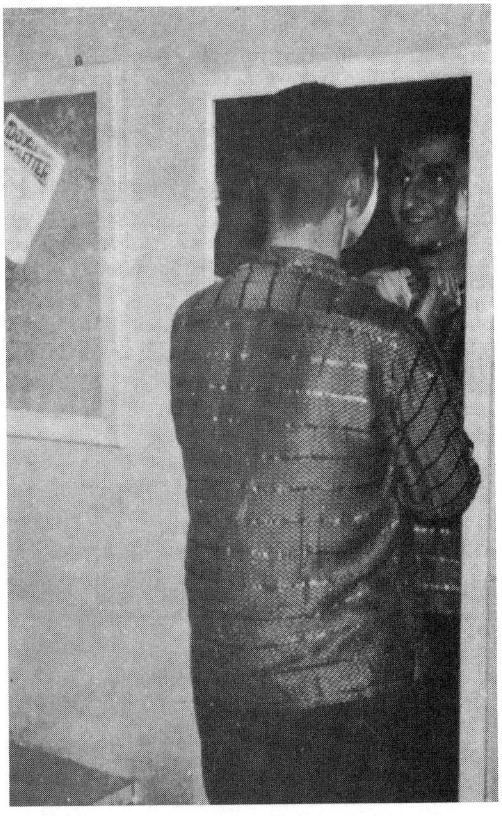

FIGURE 13–7
Hebephrenic patient. Posturing, grimacing, and mirror gazing are symptomatic of the disease. (Courtesy of Heinz E. Lehmann, M.D.)

PRECOX FEELING. Some clinicians report a precox feeling, an intuitive experience of their inability to establish an emotional rapport with a patient. Although the experience is common, no data indicate that it is a valid or reliable criterion in the diagnosis of schizophrenia.

Mood, Feelings, and Affect. Depression can be a feature of acute psychosis and an aftermath of a psychotic episode. The depressive symptoms are sometimes referred to as *secondary depression* in schizophrenia or as *postpsychotic depressive disorder of schizophrenia.* Some studies indicate that about 25 percent of all schizophrenic patients meet carefully defined criteria for postpsychotic depressive disorder of schizophrenia. Data show that depression correlates with the pres-

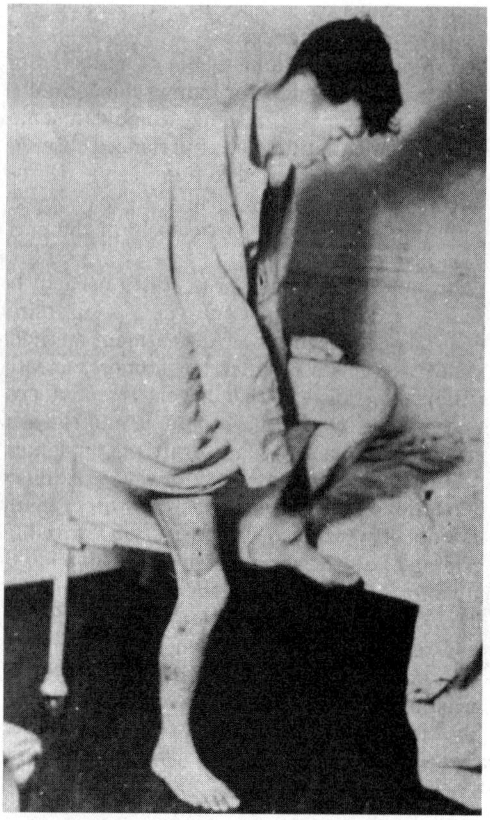

FIGURE 13–9
A chronic schizophrenic patient stands in a cataleptic position. He maintained this uncomfortable position for hours. (Courtesy of New York Academy of Medicine, New York, NY.)

ence of antipsychotic-induced extrapyramidal symptoms. These data may suggest that schizophrenic patients with depressive features are sensitive to the extrapyramidal side effects of antipsychotic drugs. Other feeling tones include perplexity, terror, a sense of isolation, and overwhelming ambivalence. (Postpsychotic depressive disorder of schizophrenia is further discussed in Chapter 14, Section 14.1.)

OTHER AFFECTIVE SYMPTOMS. Two other common affective symptoms in schizophrenia are reduced emotional responsiveness, sometimes severe enough to warrant the label of anhedonia, and overly active and inappropriate emotions such as extremes of rage, happiness, and anxiety. A flat or blunted affect can be a symptom of the illness itself, of the parkinsonian side effects of antipsychotic medications, or of depression, and differentiating these symptoms can be a clinical challenge. Overly emotional patients may describe exultant feelings of omnipotence, religious ecstasy, terror at the disintegration of their souls, or paralyzing anxiety about the destruction of the universe.

Perceptual Disturbances. Any of the five senses may be affected by hallucinatory experiences in patients with schizophrenia. The most common hallucinations, however, are auditory, with voices that are often threatening, obscene, accusatory, or insulting. Two or more voices may converse among themselves, or a voice may comment on the patient's life or behavior. Visual hallucinations are common, but tactile, olfactory, and gustatory hallucinations are unusual; their presence should prompt the clinician to consider the possibility of an underlying medical or neurological disorder that is causing the entire syndrome.

CENESTHETIC HALLUCINATIONS. Cenesthetic hallucinations are unfounded sensations of altered states in bodily organs. Examples of cenesthetic hallucinations include a burning sensation in the brain, a pushing sensation in the blood vessels, and a cutting sensation in the bone marrow.

ILLUSIONS. As differentiated from hallucinations, *illusions* are distortions of real images or sensations, whereas *hallucinations* are *not* based on real images or sensations. Illusions can occur in schizophrenic patients during active phases, but they can also occur during the prodromal phases and during periods of remission. Whenever illusions or hallucinations occur, clinicians should consider the possibility of a substance-related cause for the symptoms, even when patients have already received diagnoses of schizophrenia.

Thought. Disorders of thought are the most difficult symptoms for many clinicians and students to understand but may be the core symptoms of schizophrenia. Dividing the disorders of thought into disorders of thought content, form of thought, and thought process is one way to clarify them.

THOUGHT CONTENT. Disorders of thought content reflect the patient's ideas, beliefs, and interpretations of stimuli. Delusions, the most obvious example of a disorder of thought content, are varied in schizophrenia and may

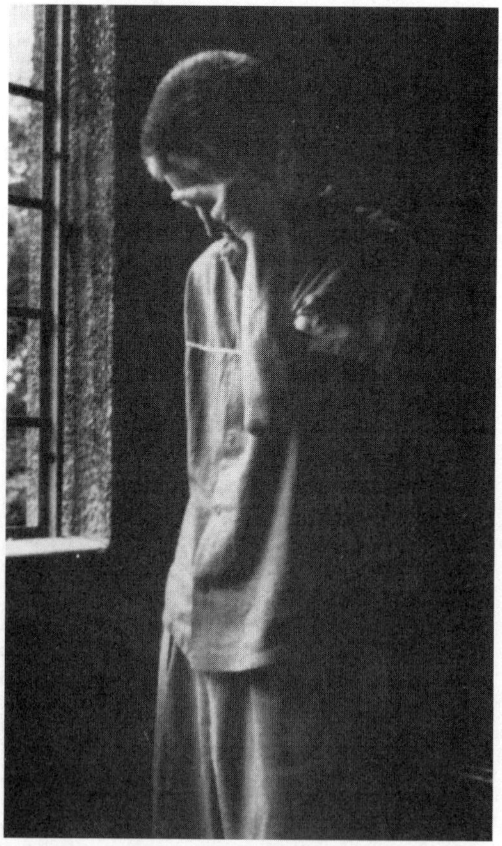

FIGURE 13–10
"Schizophrenic withdrawal." (Courtesy of Sid Bernstein, Research Facility, Orangeburg, NY.)

assume persecutory, grandiose, religious, or somatic forms. Patients may believe that an outside entity controls their thoughts or behavior or conversely, that they control outside events in an extraordinary fashion (for example, by causing the sun to rise and set or by preventing earthquakes). Patients may have an intense and consuming preoccupation with esoteric, abstract, symbolic, psychological, or philosophical ideas (Figs. 13–11 and 13–12). Patients may also worry about allegedly life-threatening but bizarre and implausible somatic conditions, such as the presence of aliens inside the patient's testicles, affecting his ability to father children.

The phrase *loss of ego boundaries* describes the lack of a clear sense of where the patient's own body, mind, and influence end and where those of other animate and inanimate objects begin. For example, patients may think that other people, the television, or the newspapers are making reference to them *(ideas of reference).* Other symptoms of the loss of ego boundaries include the sense that the patient has physically fused with an outside object (for example, a tree or another person) or that the patient has disintegrated and fused with the entire universe. With such a state of mind, some patients with schizophrenia doubt their sex or their sexual orientation. These symptoms should not be confused with transvestism, transsexuality, or homosexuality.

FORM OF THOUGHT. Disorders of the form of thought are objectively observable in patients' spoken and written language. The disorders include looseness of associations, derailment, incoherence, tangentiality, circumstantiality, neologisms, echolalia, verbigeration, word salad, and mutism. Although looseness of associations was once described as pathognomonic for schizophrenia, the symptom is frequently seen in mania. Distinguishing between looseness of associations and tangentiality can be difficult for even the most experienced clinicians.

THOUGHT PROCESS. Disorders in thought process concern the way ideas and language are formulated. The examiner infers a disorder from what and how the patient speaks, writes, or draws. The examiner may also assess the patient's thought process by observing his or her behavior, especially in carrying out discrete tasks, for example, in occupational therapy. Disorders of thought process include flight of ideas, thought blocking, impaired attention, poverty of thought content, poor abstraction abilities, perseveration, idiosyncratic associations (for example, identical predicates and clang associations), overinclusion, and circumstantiality.

Impulsiveness, Violence, Suicide, and Homicide.

Patients with schizophrenia may be agitated and have little impulse control when ill. They may also have decreased social sensitivity and appear to be impulsive when, for example, they grab another patient's cigarettes, change television channels abruptly, or throw food on the floor. Some apparently impulsive behavior, including suicide and homicide attempts, may be in response to hallucinations commanding the patient to act.

VIOLENCE. Violent behavior (excluding homicide) is common among untreated schizophrenic patients. Delusions of a persecutory nature, previous episodes of violence, and neurological deficits are risk factors for violent or impulsive behavior. Management includes appropriate antipsychotic medication. Emergency treatment consists of restraints and seclusion. Acute sedation with lorazepam, 1 to 2 mg intramuscularly, repeated every hour as needed, may be necessary to prevent the patient from doing harm to others. If a clinician finds himself being fearful in the presence of a schizophrenic patient, that should be taken as an internal clue that the patient may be on the verge of acting out violently. In such cases, the interview should be terminated or conducted with an attendant at the ready.

SUICIDE. About 50 percent of all schizophrenic patients attempt suicide, and 10 to 15 percent of patients with schizophrenia die by suicide. Perhaps the most underappreciated factor involved in the suicide of these patients is depression that has been misdiagnosed as flat affect or as a medication side effect. Other precipitants of suicide include feelings of absolute emptiness, a need to

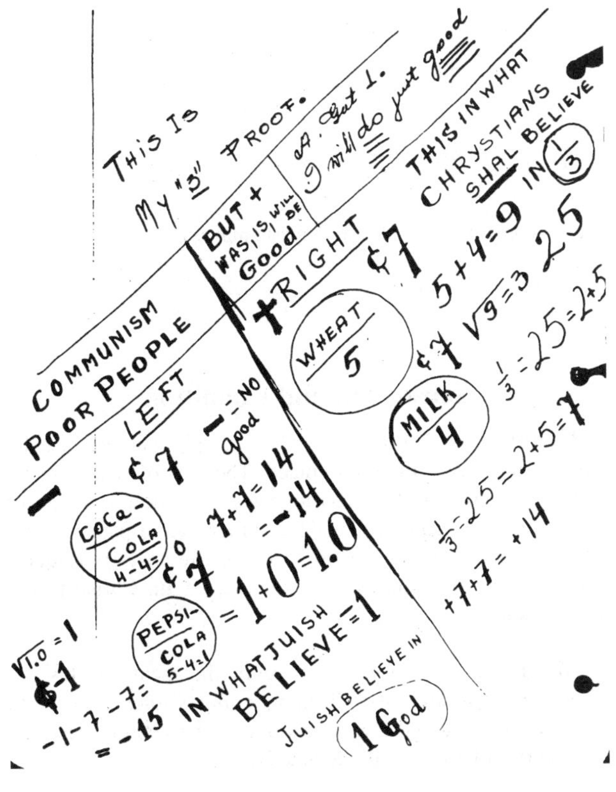
THIS IS
MY "3" PROOF.
BUT + WAS, IS, WILL BE Good
THIS IN WHAT CHRYSTIANS SHAL BELIEVE IN 1/3
COMMUNISM
POOR PEOPLE
LEFT
RIGHT
WHEAT 5
MILK 4
COCA-COLA 4-4=0
PEPSI-COLA 5-4=1
5+4=9
IN WHAT JUISH BELIEVE=1
JUISH BELIEVE IN 1 God

FIGURE 13–11

Schizophrenic patient's schema. It illustrates his fragmented, abstract, and overly inclusive thinking and preoccupation with religious ideologies and mathematical proofs. (Courtesy of Heinz E. Lehmann, M.D.)

What time is it?
JULY
AND THE TOURISTS INVADE OLD ORCHARD BEACH MAINE

FIGURE 13–12
A 25-year-old schizophrenic man produced this eerie-looking mixture of commercial poster and existential quandary about time. (Courtesy of Heinz E. Lehmann, M.D.)

escape from mental torture, or auditory hallucinations that command patients to kill themselves. The risk factors for suicide are the patient's awareness of the illness, male sex, college education, young age, a change in the course of the disease, an improvement after a relapse, dependence on the hospital, overly high ambitions, previous suicide attempts early in the course of the illness, and living alone. In the hospital, patients should be monitored closely if they are suicidal.

HOMICIDE. In spite of the sensational attention that the news media provide when a patient with schizophrenia murders someone, the available data indicate that these patients are no more likely to commit homicide than is a member of the general population. When a patient with schizophrenia does commit homicide, it may be for unpredictable or bizarre reasons based on hallucinations or delusions. Possible predictors of homicidal activity are a history of previous violence, dangerous behavior while hospitalized, and hallucinations or delusions involving such violence.

Sensorium and Cognition

Orientation. Patients with schizophrenia are usually oriented to person, time, and place. The lack of such orientation should prompt clinicians to investigate the possibility of a medical or neurological brain disorder. Some patients with schizophrenia may give incorrect or bizarre answers to questions about orientation, as, for example, "I am Christ; this is heaven; and it is A.D. 35."

Memory. Memory, as tested in the mental status examination, is usually intact. It may be impossible, however, to get a patient to attend closely enough to the memory tests for the ability to be assessed adequately.

Judgment and Insight. Classically, patients with schizophrenia are described as having poor insight into the nature and the severity of their disorder. The so-called lack of insight is associated with poor compliance with treatment. When examining schizophrenic patients, clinicians should carefully define various aspects of insight, such as awareness of symptoms, trouble in getting along with people, and the reasons for these problems. Such information can be clinically useful in tailoring a treatment strategy and theoretically useful in postulating what areas of the brain contribute to the observed lack of insight (for example, the parietal lobes).

Reliability. A patient with schizophrenia is no less reliable than is any other psychiatric patient. The nature of the disorder, however, requires the examiner to verify important information through additional sources.

Neurological Findings

Localizing and nonlocalizing neurological signs (also known as hard and soft signs, respectively) have been reported to be present more commonly in patients with schizophrenia than in other psychiatric patients. Nonlocalizing signs include dysdiadochokinesia, astereognosis, mirror sign, primitive reflexes, and diminished dexterity. The presence of neurological signs and symptoms correlates with increased severity of illness, affective blunting, and a poor prognosis. Other abnormal neurological signs include tics, stereotypies, grimacing, impaired fine motor skills, abnormal motor tone, and abnormal movements. One study has found that only about 25 percent of patients with schizophrenia are aware of their own abnormal involuntary movements and that the lack of awareness is correlated with lack of insight about the primary psychiatric disorder and the duration of illness.

Eye Examination. In addition to the disorder of smooth ocular pursuit, patients with schizophrenia have an elevated blink rate. The elevated blink rate is thought to reflect hyperdopaminergic activity. In primates, blinking can be increased by dopamine agonists and reduced by dopamine antagonists.

Speech. Although the disorders of speech in schizophrenia (for example, looseness of associations) are classically thought of as indicating a thought disorder, they may also indicate a forme fruste of an aphasia, perhaps implicating the dominant parietal lobe. The inability of schizophrenic patients to perceive the prosody of speech or to inflect their own speech can be seen as a neurological symptom of a disorder in the nondominant parietal lobe. Other parietal lobe-like symptoms in schizophrenia include the inability to carry out tasks (that is, *apraxia*), right-left disorientation, and lack of concern about the disorder.

Other Physical Findings

An increased incidence of minor physical anomalies is associated with the diagnosis of schizophrenia. Such anomalies, most likely associated with early stages of embryonic and fetal growth, usually during the first trimester, have been reported in 30 to 75 percent of patients with schizophrenia, compared with 0 to 13 percent of the general population. Some current studies suggest that the anomalies are more common in men than in women and are probably associated with genetic factors, although obstetric complications cannot be ruled out as causative factors. Compulsive water drinking may occur in some patients who can consume up to 10 L a day and develop hyponatremia.

DIFFERENTIAL DIAGNOSIS

Secondary Psychotic Disorders

A wide range of nonpsychiatric medical conditions and a variety of substances can induce symptoms of psychosis and catatonia (Table 13–8). The most appropriate diagnosis for

Table 13–8
Differential Diagnosis of Schizophrenia-Like Symptoms

Medical and Neurological
- Substance-induced—amphetamine, hallucinogens, belladonna alkaloids, alcohol hallucinosis, barbiturate withdrawal, cocaine, phencyclidine (PCP)
- Epilepsy—especially temporal lobe epilepsy
- Neoplasm, cerebrovascular disease, or trauma—especially frontal or limbic
- Other conditions
  - Acquired immune deficiency syndrome
  - Acute intermittent porphyria
  - B_{12} deficiency
  - Carbon monoxide poisoning
  - Cerebral lipoidosis
  - Creutzfeldt-Jakob disease
  - Fabry's disease
  - Fahr's disease
  - Hallervorden-Spatz disease
  - Heavy metal poisoning
  - Herpes encephalitis
  - Homocystinuria
  - Huntington's disease
  - Metachromatic leukodystrophy
  - Neurosyphilis
  - Normal pressure hydrocephalus
  - Pellagra
  - Systemic lupus erythematosus
  - Wernicke-Korsakoff syndrome
  - Wilson's disease

Psychiatric
- Atypical psychosis
- Autistic disorder
- Brief psychotic disorder
- Delusional disorder
- Factitious disorder with predominantly psychological signs and symptoms
- Malingering
- Mood disorders
- Normal adolescence
- Obsessive-compulsive disorder
- Personality disorders—schizotypal, schizoid, borderline, paranoid
- Schizoaffective disorder
- Schizophrenia
- Schizophreniform disorder

such psychosis or catatonia is *psychotic disorder due to a general medical condition, catatonic disorder due to a general medical condition, or substance-induced psychotic disorder.* The psychiatric manifestations of many nonpsychiatric medical conditions can come early in the course of the illness, often before the development of other symptoms. Therefore, clinicians must consider a wide range of nonpsychiatric medical conditions in the differential diagnosis of psychosis, even in the absence of obvious physical symptoms. Patients with neurological disorders generally have more insight into their illnesses and more distress from their psychiatric symptoms than do patients with schizophrenia. This fact can help clinicians distinguish the two groups of patients.

When evaluating a patient with psychotic symptoms, clinicians should follow the general guidelines for assessing nonpsychiatric conditions. First, clinicians should aggressively pursue an undiagnosed nonpsychiatric medical condition when a patient exhibits any unusual or rare symptoms or any variation in the level of consciousness. Second, clinicians should attempt to obtain a complete family history, including a history of medical, neurological, and psychiatric disorders. Third, clinicians should consider the possibility of a nonpsychiatric medical condition, even in patients with previous diagnoses of schizophrenia. A patient with schizophrenia is just as likely to have a brain tumor that produces psychotic symptoms as is a nonschizophrenic patient.

Malingering and Factitious Disorders

In a patient who imitates the symptoms of schizophrenia but does not actually have the disorder, either malingering or a factitious disorder may be an appropriate diagnosis. People have faked schizophrenic symptoms and have been admitted into and treated at psychiatric hospitals. The condition of patients who are completely in control of their symptom production may qualify for a diagnosis of malingering; such patients usually have some obvious financial or legal reason to be considered insane. The condition of patients who are less in control of their falsification of psychotic symptoms may qualify for a diagnosis of a factitious disorder. Some patients with schizophrenia, however, may falsely complain of an exacerbation of psychotic symptoms to obtain increased assistance benefits or to gain admission to a hospital. (Factitious disorders are the subject of Chapter 19.)

Other Psychotic Disorders

The psychotic symptoms of schizophrenia can be identical with those of schizophreniform disorder, brief psychotic disorder, schizoaffective disorder, and delusional disorders. *Schizophreniform disorder* differs from schizophrenia in that the symptoms have a duration of at least 1 month but less than 6 months. *Brief psychotic disorder* is the appropriate diagnosis when the symptoms have lasted at least 1 day but less than 1 month and when the patient has returned to the premorbid state of functioning within that time. When a manic or depressive syndrome develops concurrently with the major symptoms of schizophrenia, *schizoaffective disorder* is the appropriate diagnosis. Nonbizarre delusions present for at least 1 month without other symptoms of schizophrenia or a mood disorder warrant the diagnosis of *delusional disorder.*

Mood Disorders

The differential diagnosis of schizophrenia and mood disorders can be difficult but must be made because of the availability of specific and effective treatments for mania and depression. Compared with the duration of the primary symptoms, affective or mood symptoms in schizophrenia should be brief. Before making a premature diagnosis of schizophrenia, and without more information than that gleaned from a single mental status examination, clinicians should delay a final diagnosis or should assume the presence of mood disorder. After remission of a schizophrenic episode, some patients experience a postpsychotic or secondary depression. Treatment with a serotonin-specific reuptake inhibitor or a tricyclic antidepressant is indicated in that situation.

Personality Disorders

Various personality disorders may have some features of schizophrenia. Schizotypal, schizoid, and borderline personality disorders are the personality disorders with the most similar symptoms. Severe obsessive-compulsive personality disorder may mask an underlying schizophrenic process. Personality disorders, unlike schizophrenia, have mild symptoms and a history of occurring throughout a patient's life; they also lack an identifiable date of onset.

COURSE AND PROGNOSIS

Course

A premorbid pattern of symptoms may be the first evidence of illness, although the import of the symptoms is usually recognized only retrospectively. Characteristically, the symptoms begin in adolescence and are followed by the development of prodromal symptoms in days to a few months. Social or environmental changes, such as going away to college, using a substance, or a relative's death, may precipitate the disturbing symptoms and the prodromal syndrome may last a year or more before the onset of overt psychotic symptoms.

The classic course of schizophrenia is one of exacerbations and remissions. After the first psychotic episode, a patient gradually recovers and may then function relatively normally for a long time. Patients usually relapse, however, and the pattern of illness during the first 5 years after the diagnosis generally indicates the patient's course. A further deterioration in the patient's baseline functioning follows each relapse of the psychosis. This failure to return to baseline functioning after each relapse is the major distinction between schizophrenia and the mood disorders. Sometimes, a clinically observable postpsychotic depression follows a psychotic episode, and the schizophrenic patient's vulnerability to stress is usually lifelong. Positive symptoms tend to become less severe with time, but the socially debilitating negative or deficit symptoms may increase in severity. Although about one third of all schizophrenic patients have some marginal or integrated social existence, most have lives characterized by aimlessness, inactivity, frequent hospitalizations, and, in urban settings, homelessness and poverty.

Prognosis

Several studies have shown that over the 5- to 10-year period after the first psychiatric hospitalization for schizophrenia, only about 10 to 20 percent of patients can be described as having a good outcome. More than 50 percent of patients can be described as having a poor outcome, with repeated hospitalizations, exacerbations of symptoms, episodes of major mood disorders, and suicide attempts. In spite of these glum figures, schizophrenia does not always run a deteriorating course, and several factors have been associated with a good prognosis (Table 13–4).

Reported recovery rates range from 10 to 60 percent, and a reasonable estimate is that 20 to 30 percent of all schizophrenic patients are able to lead somewhat normal lives. About 20 to 30 percent of patients continue to experience moderate symptoms, and 40 to 60 percent of patients remain significantly impaired by their disorder for their entire lives. Patients with schizophrenia do much less well than do patients with mood disorders, although 20 to 25 percent of mood disorder patients are also severely disturbed at long-term follow-up.

TREATMENT

Three observations about schizophrenia warrant attention when clinicians consider the treatment of the disorder. First, regardless of cause, schizophrenia occurs in a person with a unique individual, familial, and social psychological profile. Two factors—how the patient has been affected by the disorder and how the patient will be helped by the treatment—must shape the treatment approach. Second, many investigators consider that a 50 percent concordance rate for schizophrenia among monozygotic twins suggests that unknown but probably specific environmental and psychological factors have contributed to the development of the disorder. Thus, just as pharmacological agents are used to treat presumed chemical imbalances, nonpharmacological strategies must treat nonbiological issues. Third, the complexity of schizophrenia usually renders any single therapeutic approach insufficient to deal with the multifaceted disorder.

Although antipsychotic medications are the mainstay of the treatment for schizophrenia, research has found that psychosocial interventions can augment the clinical improvement. Psychosocial modalities should be carefully integrated into the drug treatment regimen and should support it. Most patients with schizophrenia benefit from the combined use of antipsychotic drugs and psychosocial treatment.

Hospitalization

Hospitalization is indicated primarily for diagnostic purposes, for stabilization of medications, for patients' safety because of suicidal or homicidal ideation, and for grossly disorganized or inappropriate behavior, including the inability to take care of basic needs such as food, clothing, and shelter. Establishing an effective association between patients and community support systems is a primary goal of hospitalization. Other aspects of clinical management flow logically from medical models of the disorder. Because physicians are concerned with a patient's rehabilitation and adjustment, they must consider their specific disabilities when planning treatment strategies. Physicians must also educate patients and their families and caretakers about schizophrenia.

Hospitalization decreases patients' stress and helps them structure their daily activities. The severity of a patient's illness and the availability of outpatient treatment facilities determine the length of the hospital stay. Research has shown that short stays of 4 to 6 weeks are just as effective as long-term hospitalizations and that hospital settings with active behavioral approaches produce better results than do custodial institutions and insight-oriented therapeutic communities.

Hospital treatment plans should be oriented toward practical issues of self-care, quality of life, employment, and social relationships. During hospitalization, patients should be coordinated with aftercare facilities including their family homes, foster families, board-and-care homes, and halfway houses. Day care centers and home visits by counselors can sometimes help patients to remain out of the hospital for long periods and can improve the quality of their daily lives.

Biological Therapies

Pharmacotherapy. Antipsychotic medications, introduced in the early 1950s, have revolutionized the treatment of schizophrenia. About 2 to 4 times as many patients relapse when treated with a placebo as do those treated with antipsychotic drugs. These medications, however, treat the symptoms of the disorder and do not cure schizophrenia.

Antipsychotics. The antipsychotic drugs include two major classes: dopamine receptor antagonists (for example, chlorpromazine [Thorazine], haloperidol [Haldol], sulpiride) and serotonin-dopamine antagonists (for example, risperidone [Risperdal] and clozapine [Clozaril]). Antipsychotic drugs are sometimes called *neuroleptics,* an acceptable term. The term *major tranquilizers,* however, has been applied to various drugs; it inaccurately implies that the antipsychotic drugs have a sedative or tranquilizing effect as a major mode of action; the term *major tranquilizers* should therefore be avoided.

CHOICE OF DRUG. The classic (standard) antipsychotic drugs are the dopamine receptor antagonists, which are effective in the treatment of schizophrenia, particularly of the positive symptoms (for example, delusions). The drugs have two major shortcomings. First, only a small percentage of patients (perhaps 25 percent) are helped enough to recover a reasonable amount of normal mental functioning. As noted earlier, even with treatment, about 50 percent of patients with schizophrenia lead severely debilitated lives. Second, the dopamine receptor antagonists are associated with both annoying and serious adverse effects. The most common annoying effects are akathisia and parkinsonian-like symptoms of rigidity and tremor. The potential serious effects include tardive dyskinesia and neuroleptic malignant syndrome.

The serotonin-dopamine antagonists, also called atypical antipsychotic drugs, appear to be effective for a broader range of patients with schizophrenia than are the typical dopamine receptor antagonist antipsychotic agents. They are at least as effective as haloperidol for positive symptoms of schizophrenia, are uniquely effective for the negative symptoms, and cause few, if any, extrapyramidal symptoms. Three serotonin-dopamine antagonists, clozapine, risperidone, and olanzapine (Zyprexa), have been FDA-approved, and three others, sertindole, quetiapine, and ziprasidone (Pfizer), are in the approval process. These drugs are likely to replace the dopamine receptor antagonists as the drugs of first choice for treatment of schizophrenia.

Risperidone is an effective antipsychotic medication with a mild profile of adverse effects. It is the most widely used serotonin-dopamine antagonist. At doses commonly used, it is not associated with extrapyramidal symptoms. It causes less sedation and anticholinergic effects than do dopamine receptor antagonists. A growing body of evidence supports its role as a first-line agent for first-break, mildly to moderately ill patients and for severely ill, treatment-refractory patients.

Clozapine, a serotonin-dopamine antagonist, is probably the most effective for severely ill patients, but it is a second-line drug because of its significant adverse effects, which are not found in the serotonin-dopamine antagonists. Clozapine is associated with potentially life-threatening agranulocytosis in 1 to 2 percent of patients, which requires weekly monitoring of the neutrophil count. It also presents a high risk for seizures and has significant anticholinergic effects. Clozapine remains useful for patients refractory to any other antipsychotic drug and for patients with tardive dyskinesia. Clozapine has extremely little antagonist activity at the D_2 receptor and appears to reduce the symptoms of tardive dyskinesia without worsening the condition.

Olanzapine is an effective medication for treatment of schizophrenia, with a mild, but somewhat different, profile of adverse effects compared to risperidone. It is less likely to produce extrapyramidal effects but is more likely to produce sedation, weight gain, orthostatic hypotension, and constipation. Data comparing olanzapine directly with other serotonin-dopamine antagonists for a wide range of patient populations have not been reported. It is a useful first-line agent, in that patients who do not respond to one serotonin-dopamine antagonist may respond to another.

Sertindole is an effective agent, with a favorable profile of adverse effects, most of which are transient. It must be slowly titrated upward to avoid orthostatic hypotension. It may also cause sinus tachycardia, nasal congestion, and decreased ejaculatory volume. It causes little weight gain and does not cause anticholinergic symptoms. Its half-life of 3 days makes it ideal for poorly compliant patients. Data on long-term use have not been reported.

Quetiapine is an effective antipsychotic drug associated with no increased risk of extrapyramidal symptoms. The main adverse effects include sedation, tachycardia, weight gain, and agitation. The initial doses must be titrated upward over 4 days to avoid orthostatic hypotension and syncope.

Ziprasidone is an effective drug for treatment of schizophrenia. It has potential additional benefits for patients with affective symptoms, because it blocks reuptake of serotonin and norepinephrine, and for patients with anxiety, because it is an agonist for 5-HT_{1A} receptors. Adverse effects include sedation, nausea, dizziness, and light-headedness, but not weight gain. It is the only serotonin-dopamine antagonist suitable for a depot formulation.

THERAPEUTIC PRINCIPLES. The use of antipsychotic medications in schizophrenia should follow five major principles. (1) Clinicians should carefully define the target symptoms to be treated. (2) An antipsychotic that has worked well in the past for a patient should be used again. In the absence of such information, the choice of an antipsychotic is usually based on the side effect profile. Currently available data indicate that serotonin-dopamine antagonists may offer a superior side effect profile and the possibility of superior efficacy. Within the standard dopaminergic antagonists, all members of the class are equally efficacious. (3) The minimum length of an antipsychotic trial is 4 to 6 weeks at adequate dosages. If the trial is unsuccessful, a different antipsychotic drug, usually from a different class, can be tried. An unpleasant reaction by the patient to the first dose of an antipsychotic drug, however, correlates strongly with future poor response and noncompliance. Negative experiences can include a peculiar subjective negative feeling, oversedation, or an acute dystonic reaction. When a severe and negative initial reaction is observed, clinicians may consider switching to a different antipsychotic drug in less than 4 weeks. (4) In general, the use of more than one antipsychotic medication at a time is rarely, if ever, indicated, although some psychiatrists use thioridazine (Mellaril) for treating insomnia in a patient who is receiving another antipsychotic drug for the treatment of schizophrenic symptoms. In especially treatment-resistant patients, combinations of antipsychotics with other drugs—for example, carbamazepine (Tegretol)—may be indicated. (5) Patients should be maintained on the lowest possible effective dosage of medication. The maintenance dosage is often lower than that used to achieve symptom control during the psychotic episode.

A decision tree for the use of antipsychotic medication is given in Figure 13–13.

INITIAL WORKUP. In spite of the annoyance of the neurological effects and the looming possibility of tardive dyskinesia, antipsychotic drugs are remarkably safe, especially when given during a relatively short period. Thus, in emergency situations, clinicians can administer the drugs, with the exception of clozapine, without conducting a physical or laboratory examination of the patient. In the usual assessment, however, clinicians should obtain a complete blood count (CBC) with white blood cell indexes, liver function tests, and an electrocardiogram (ECG), especially in women older than 40 and men older than 30. The major contraindications to antipsychotic drugs are (1) a history of serious allergic response, (2) the possibility that a patient has ingested a substance that will interact with the antipsychotic to induce CNS depression (for example, alcohol, opioids, opiates, barbiturates, benzodiazepines) or anticholinergic delirium (for example, drugs containing atropine, scopolamine, and possibly phencyclidine [PCP]), (3) the presence of a severe cardiac abnormality, (4) a high risk for seizures from organic or idiopathic causes, and (5) the presence of narrow-angle glaucoma if an antipsychotic drug with significant anticholinergic activity is to be used.

TREATMENT OF REFRACTORY ILLNESS. In the acute state, virtually all patients eventually respond to repeated doses of an antipsychotic drug—every 1 to 2 hours by intramuscular (IM) administration or every 2 to 3 hours by mouth. A benzodiazepine is sometimes needed to sedate the patient further. The failure of a patient to respond in the acute state should cause clinicians to consider the possibility of an organic lesion.

Noncompliance with antipsychotic drugs is a major reason for relapse and for failure of a drug trial. Another major reason for a failed drug trial is insufficient time for the trial. It is generally a mistake to increase the dosage or to change antipsychotic medications in the first 2 weeks of treatment. If a patient is improving on the current regimen at the end of 2 weeks, continued treatment with the same regimen will probably result in steady clinical improvement. If, however, a patient has shown little or no improvement in 2 weeks, the possible reasons for a drug failure, including noncompliance, should be considered. In a noncompliant patient, the use of a liquid preparation or depot forms of fluphenazine (Prolixin) or haloperidol (Haldol) may be indicated. Because of the diversity in the metabolism of drugs, clinicians should obtain plasma levels when the laboratory capability is available. Plasma levels of antipsychotic drugs provide only a gross measure of compliance, absorption, and metabolism. There are no clearly defined therapeutic blood level ranges for antipsychotic drugs similar to those for some antidepressants. Because neurological side effects are a common reason for noncompliance in patients with schizophrenia and a major cause of relapse, the more favorable side effect profiles of atypical agents may lead to improved compliance and better outcome.

Having eliminated other possible reasons for the therapeutic failure of an antipsychotic drug, clinicians may try a second antipsychotic drug with a chemical structure different from that of the first one. Additional strategies include supplementing the antipsychotic drug with lithium (Eskalith), an anticonvulsant such as carbamazepine or valproate (Depakene), or a benzodiazepine. The use of so-called megadose antipsychotic therapy (for example, 100 to 200 mg of haloperidol) is rarely indicated because almost no data support the practice.

Other Drugs. If adequate trials with at least one dopaminergic receptor antagonist are unsuccessful, a serotonin-dopamine antagonist may be tried. Combination therapy with one of these drugs and an adjuvant medication may also be

If a patient has a specific contraindication to any medication, remove that medication from the possibilities for that patient.

At each point in the algorithm, medications are chosen on the basis of
- Past response
- Side effects
- Patient preference
- Planned route of administration

GROUP 1: Conventional antipsychotic medications
GROUP 2: Risperidone
GROUP 3: Clozapine
GROUP 4: New antipsychotic medications–olanzapine, sertindole, quetiapine

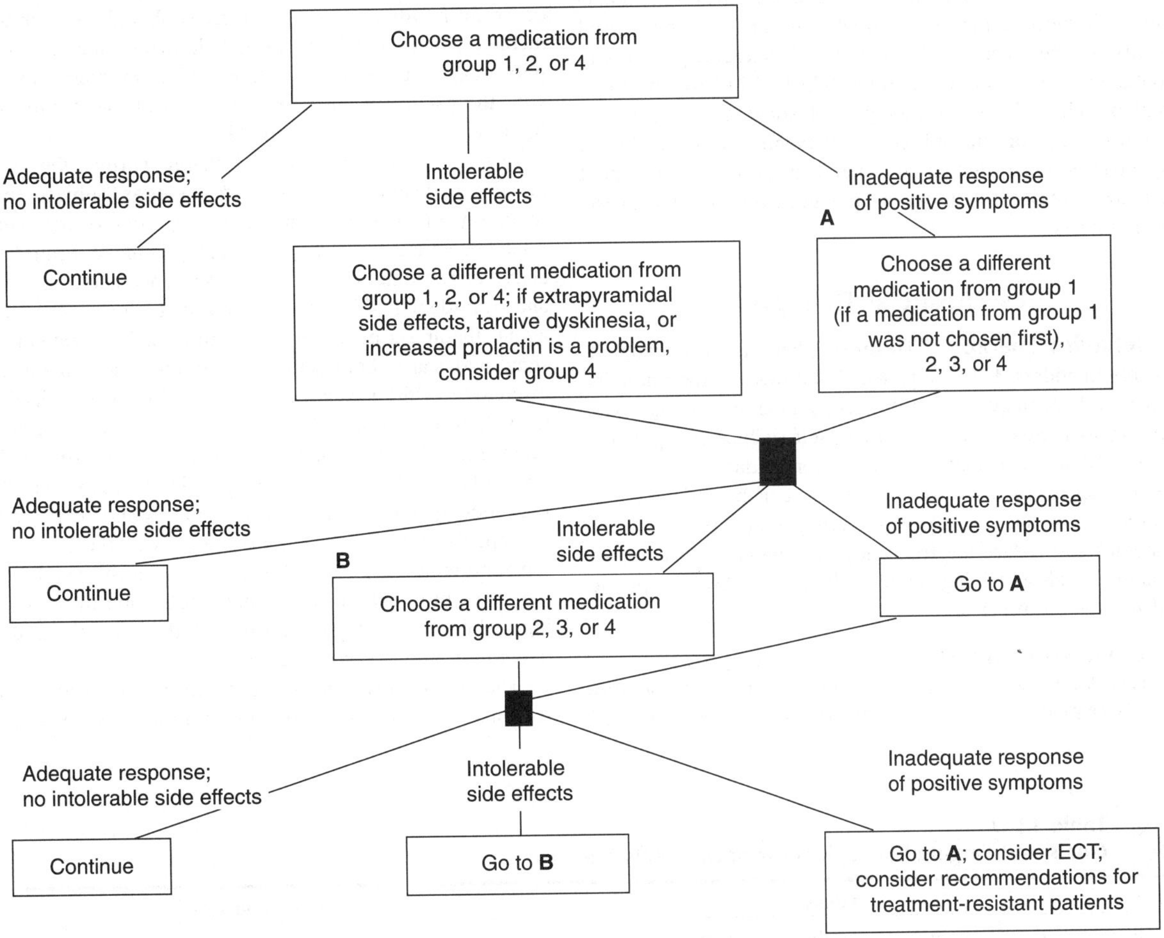
Choose a medication from group 1, 2, or 4
Adequate response; no intolerable side effects
Intolerable side effects
Inadequate response of positive symptoms
A
Continue
Choose a different medication from group 1, 2, or 4; if extrapyramidal side effects, tardive dyskinesia, or increased prolactin is a problem, consider group 4
Choose a different medication from group 1 (if a medication from group 1 was not chosen first), 2, 3, or 4
Adequate response; no intolerable side effects
Intolerable side effects
Inadequate response of positive symptoms
B
Continue
Choose a different medication from group 2, 3, or 4
Go to A
Adequate response; no intolerable side effects
Intolerable side effects
Inadequate response of positive symptoms
Continue
Go to B
Go to A; consider ECT; consider recommendations for treatment-resistant patients

FIGURE 13–13
Pharmacological treatment of schizophrenia. (Reprinted with permission from American Psychiatric Association: Practice guideline for the treatment of patients with schizophrenia. Am J Psychiatry *154* (4, Suppl): 1, 1997.)

tried. The adjuvant medications with the most supportive data are lithium, two anticonvulsants (carbamazepine and valproate), and the benzodiazepines.

LITHIUM. Lithium may be effective in further reducing psychotic symptoms in up to 50 percent of patients with schizophrenia. It is usually added with an antipsychotic drug that the patient is already taking. Lithium may also be a reasonable drug to try in patients who are unable to take any of the antipsychotic medications.

ANTICONVULSANTS. Carbamazepine or valproate is usually not used alone but is used in combination with lithium or an antipsychotic. Although neither of the anticonvulsants has been shown to be effective in reducing psychotic symptoms in schizophrenia when used alone, data suggest that the anticonvulsants reduce episodes of violence in some schizophrenic patients. Because of their effects on hepatic enzymes, anticonvulsants decrease antipsychotic blood levels.

BENZODIAZEPINES. Data support the practice of coadministering alprazolam (Xanax) with antipsychotic drugs to patients who have not responded to antipsychotic administration alone. There are also reports of schizophrenic patients' responding to high dosages of diazepam (Valium) alone. The severity of the psychosis may, however, be exacerbated after the withdrawal of a benzodiazepine. Lorazepam (Ativan) may be preferable to diazepam becasue it is shorter acting and has less abuse potential.

Other Biological Therapies. Although much less effective than antipsychotic drugs, electroconvulsive therapy may be indicated for catatonic patients and for patients who for some reason cannot take antipsychotic drugs. Patients who have been ill for less than 1 year are most likely to respond.

In the past, schizophrenia was treated with insulin- and barbiturate-induced coma. These treatments are no longer used because of the associated hazards. Psychosurgery, particularly frontal lobotomy, was used from 1935 to 1955 for the treatment of schizophrenia. Although sophisticated approaches to psychosurgery for schizophrenia may eventually be developed, psychosurgery is no longer considered an appropriate treatment of schizophrenia. It is, however, practiced on a limited experimental basis.

Psychosocial Therapies

Behavior Therapy. Treatment planning for schizophrenia should address both the patients' abilities and their deficits. Behavioral techniques use token economies and social skills training to increase social abilities, self-sufficiency, practical skills, and interpersonal communication. Adaptive behaviors are reinforced by praise or tokens that can be redeemed for desired items, such as hospital privileges and passes. These strategies can reduce the frequency of maladaptive or deviant behavior, such as talking loudly, talking to oneself in public, and bizarre posturing.

SOCIAL SKILLS TRAINING. Social skills training is sometimes referred to as behavioral skills therapy. The therapy can be directly supportive and useful to the patient along with pharmacological therapy (Table 13–9). In addition to the symptoms seen in patients with schizophrenia, some of the most noticeable symptoms involve the person's relationships with others, including poor eye contact, unusual delays in response, odd facial expressions, lack of spontaneity in social situations, and inaccurate perceptions or lack of perception of emotions in other people. Behavioral skills training addresses these behaviors through the use of videotapes of others and of the patient, role playing in therapy, and homework assignments for the specific skills being practiced.

Family-Oriented Therapies. Several family-oriented therapies are helpful in treating schizophrenia. Because patients with schizophrenia are often discharged in an only partially remitted state, a family to which a patient returns can often benefit from a brief but intensive (as often as daily) course of family therapy. The therapy should focus on the immediate situation and should include identifying and avoiding potentially troublesome situations. When problems do emerge with the patient in the family, the aim of the therapy should be to resolve the problem quickly.

After the immediate postdischarge period, the recovery process, its length, and its rate are important subjects to cover in family therapy. In wanting to help, family members too often encourage a relative with schizophrenia to resume regular activities too quickly, both from ignorance about the disorder and from denial of its severity. Without being overly discouraging, therapists must help the family and the patient understand and learn about schizophrenia and must encourage the discussion of the psychotic episode and the events leading up to it. Ignoring the psychotic episode, a common occurrence, often increases the shame associated with the event and does not exploit the freshness of the episode to understand it better. Psychotic symptoms often frighten family members, and talking openly with the psychiatrist and with the relative with schizophrenia often eases all parties. Therapists can direct later family therapy toward long-range application of stress-reducing and coping strategies and toward the patient's gradual reintegration into everyday life.

Therapists must control the emotional intensity of family sessions with patients with schizophrenia. The excessive ex-

Table 13–9
Goals and Targeted Behaviors for Social Skills Therapy

Phase	Goals	Targeted Behaviors
Stabilization and assessment	Establish therapeutic alliance Assess social performance and perception skills Assess behaviors that provoke expressed emotion	Empathy and rapport Verbal and nonverbal communication
Social performance within family	Express positive feelings within family Teach effective strategies for coping with conflict	Compliments, appreciation, interest in others Avoidance response to criticism, stating preferences and refusals
Social perception in the family	Correctly identify content, context, and meaning of messages	Reading a message Labeling an idea Summarizing other's intent
Extrafamilial relationships	Enhance socialization skills Enhance prevocational and vocational skills	Conversational skills Dating Recreational activities Job interviewing, work habits
Maintenance	Generalize skills to new situations	

Adapted with permission from Hogarty GE, Anderson CM, Reiss DJ, Kornblith SJ, Greenwald DP, Javna CD, Madonia MJ: Family psychoeducation, social skills training and maintenance chemotherapy: I. One-year effects of a controlled study on relapse and expressed emotion. Arch Gen Psychiatry *43:* 633, 1986.

pression of emotion during a session can damage a patient's recovery process and can undermine potentially successful future family therapy. Several studies have shown that family therapy is especially effective in reducing relapses. Each study, however, used a different type of family therapy. And the commonality among therapies remains unclear. In controlled studies, family therapy dramatically reduced the annual relapse rate, which is 25 to 50 percent for patients not undergoing family therapy, compared with 5 to 10 percent for those who undergo the therapy.

NATIONAL ALLIANCE FOR THE MENTALLY ILL (NAMI). NAMI and similar organizations are support groups for family members and friends of patients who are mentally ill and for patients themselves. Useful sources to which to refer family members, these organizations offer emotional and practical advice about obtaining care in the sometimes complex health care delivery system. NAMI has also waged a campaign to destigmatize mental illness and to increase government awareness of the needs and rights of people who are mentally ill and of their families.

Case Management. Because a variety of professionals with specialized skills, such as psychiatrists, social workers, and occupational therapists, among others, are involved in a treatment program, it is helpful to have one person aware of all the forces acting on the patient. The case manager ensures that their efforts are coordinated and that the patient keeps appointments and complies with treatment plans; the case manager may make home visits and even accompany the patient to work. The success of the program depends on the educational background, training, and competence of the case manager, which is variable. Case managers often have too many cases to manage effectively. The ultimate benefits of the program have yet to be demonstrated. (For a further discussion of other social and community interventions including dialectical therapy, see Section 34.9.)

Group Therapy. Group therapy for people with schizophrenia generally focuses on real-life plans, problems, and relationships. Groups may be behaviorally oriented, psychodynamically or insight oriented, or supportive. Some investigators doubt that dynamic interpretation and insight therapy are valuable for typical patients with schizophrenia. But group therapy is effective in reducing social isolation, increasing the sense of cohesiveness, and improving reality testing for patients with schizophrenia. Groups led in a supportive manner, rather than in an interpretative way, appear to be most helpful for schizophrenic patients.

Cognitive Therapy. Cognitive therapy has been used in schizophrenic patients to improve cognitive distortions, reduce distractibility, and correct errors in judgment. There are reports of ameliorating delusions and hallucinations in some patients using this method; however, its use in schizophrenia requires further study. See Section 34.8 for a more extensive discussion of cognitive therapy.

Individual Psychotherapy (Supportive and Insight-Oriented). The best-conducted studies of the effects of individual psychotherapy in the treatment of schizophrenia have provided data that the therapy is helpful and is additive to the effects of pharmacological treatment. The therapies most thoroughly studied include supportive psychotherapy and insight-oriented psychotherapy. In psychotherapy with a schizophrenic patient, developing a therapeutic relationship that the patient experiences as safe is critical. The therapist's reliability, the emotional distance between the therapist and the patient, and the genuineness of the therapist as interpreted by the patient all affect the therapeutic experience. Inexperienced psychotherapists often provide interpretations too quickly to patients with schizophrenia. The psychotherapy for a schizophrenic patient should be thought of in terms of decades, rather than sessions, months, or even years. This situation means that residency training programs allow only a few years, at most, for residents to spend with schizophrenic patients.

Some clinicians and researchers have emphasized that the ability of a patient with schizophrenia to form a therapeutic alliance with a therapist can predict the outcome. At least one study found that schizophrenic patients who were able to form a good therapeutic alliance were likely to remain in psychotherapy, to remain compliant with their medications, and to have good outcomes at a 2-year follow-up evaluation.

The relationship between clinicians and patients differs from that encountered in the treatment of nonpsychotic patients. Establishing a relationship is often difficult. People with schizophrenia are desperately lonely, yet defend against closeness and trust; they are likely to become suspicious, anxious, or hostile or to regress when someone attempts to draw close. Therapists should scrupulously observe a patient's distance and privacy and should demonstrate simple directness, patience, sincerity, and sensitivity to social conventions in preference to premature informality and the condescending use of first names. The patient is likely to perceive exaggerated warmth or professions of friendship as attempts at bribery, manipulation, or exploitation.

In the context of a professional relationship, however, flexibility is essential in establishing a working alliance with the patient. A therapist may have meals with the patient, sit on the floor, go for a walk, eat at a restaurant, accept and give gifts, play table tennis, remember the patient's birthday, or just sit silently with the patient. The major aim is to convey the idea that the therapist is trustworthy, wants to understand the patient and tries to do so, and has faith in the patient's potential as a human being, no matter how disturbed, hostile, or bizarre the patient may be at the moment. Mandred Bleuler stated that the correct therapeutic attitude toward patients with schizophrenia was to accept them rather than to observe them as people who are unintelligible to and different from the therapist.

REFERENCES

Abi-Dargham A, Laruelle M, Lipska B, Jaskiw GE, Wong DT, Roberston DW, Weinberger DR, Kleinman JE: Serotonin 5-HT_3 receptors in schizophrenia: A postmortem study in the amygdala. Brain Res *616:* 53, 1993.

Addington DE, Addington JM: Attempted suicide and depression in schizophrenia. Acta Psychiatr Scand *85:* 288, 1992.

Adler LE, Griffith JM: Concurrent medical illness in the schizophrenia patient: Epidemiology, diagnosis, and management. Schizophr Res *4:* 91, 1991.

Amador XF, Strauss DH, Yale SA, Gorman JA: Awareness of illness in schizophrenia. Schizophr Bull *17:* 113, 1991.

American Psychiatric Association: Practice guidelines for the treatment of patients with schizophrenia. Am J Psychiatry *154* (4, Suppl): 1, 1997.

American Psychiatric Association: Tardive Dyskinesia: A Task Force Report of the American Psychiatric Association. American Psychiatric Association, Washington, 1992.

Andreasen NC, Flaum M: Schizophrenia: The characteristic symptoms. Schizophr Bull *17:* 27, 1991.

Baldessarini RJ, Frankenburg FR: Clozapine: A novel antipsychotic agent. N Engl J Med *324:* 746, 1991.

Beasley CM, Sanger T, Satterlee WG, et al: Olanzapine versus placebo: Results of a double-blind fixed-dose trial. Psychopharmacology *124:* 59, 1996.

Beasley CM Jr, Tollefson G, Tran P, et al: Olanzapine versus placebo and haloperidol: Acute phase results of the North American double-blind olanzapine trial. Neuropsychopharmacology *14:* 11, 1996.

Bogerst B, Lieberman JA, Ashtari M, Bilder RM, Degreef G, Lerner G, Johns C, Masiar S: Hippocampus–amygdala volumes and psychopathology in chronic schizophrenia. Biol Psychiatry *33:* 236, 1993.

Breier A, Schreiber JL, Dyer J, Pickar D: National Institute of Mental Health longitudinal study of chronic schizophrenia: Prognosis and predictors of outcome. Arch Gen Psychiatry *48:* 239, 1991.

Buchsbaum MS: The frontal lobes, basal ganglia, and temporal lobes as sites for schizophrenia. Schizophr Bull *16:* 379, 1990.

Bymaster FP, Calligaro DO, Falcone JF, et al: Radio receptor binding profile of the atypical antipsychotic olanzapine. Neuropsychopharmacology *14:* 87, 1996.

Carone BJ, Harrow M, Westermeyer JF: Posthospital course and outcome in schizophrenia. Arch Gen Psychiatry *48:* 247, 1991.

Carpenter WT: The deficit syndrome. Am J Psychiatry *151:* 327, 1994.

Ceskova E, Svestka J: Double-blind comparison of risperidone and haloperidol in schizophrenic and schizoaffective psychoses. Pharmacopsychiatry *26:* 121, 1993.

Dixon L, Haas G, Weiden P, Sweeney J, Frances A: Acute effects of drug abuse in schizophrenic patients: Clinical observations and patient's self-reports. Schizophr Bull *16:* 69, 1990.

Fenton WS, McGlashan TH: Natural history of schizophrenia subtypes: I. Longitudinal study of paranoid, hebephrenic, and undifferentiated schizophrenia. Arch Gen Psychiatry *48:* 969, 1991.

Fenton WS, McGlashan TH: Natural history of schizophrenia subtypes: II. Positive and negative symptoms and long-term course. Arch Gen Psychiatry *48:* 978, 1991.

Fleischhacker WW, Roth SD, Kane JM: The pharmacologic treatment of neuroleptic-induced akathisia. J Clin Psychopharmacol *10:* 12, 1990.

Frank AF, Gunderson JG: The role of the therapeutic alliance in the treatment of schizophrenia. Arch Gen Psychiatry *47:* 228, 1990.

Gabbard GO: *Psychodynamic Psychiatry in Clinical Practice: The DSM-IV Edition.* American Psychiatric Press, Washington, 1994.

Goff DC, Henderson DC, Amico E: Cigarette smoking in schizophrenia: Relationships to psychopathology and medication side effects. Am J Psychiatry *149:* 1189, 1992.

Goldberg TE, Gold JM, Greenberg R, Griffin S, Schultz SC, Pickar D, Kleinman JE, Weinberger DR: Contrasts between patients with affective disorders and patients with schizophrenia on a neuropsychological test battery. Am J Psychiatry *150:* 1355, 1993.

Goldstein JM, Tsuang MT: Gender and schizophrenia: An introduction and synthesis of findings. Schizophr Bull *16:* 179, 1990.

Gur RE, Pearlson GD: Neuroimaging in schizophrenia research. Schizophr Bull *19:* 337, 1993.

Harrison PJ: On the neuropathology of schizophrenia and its dementia: Neurodevelopmental, neurodegenerative, or both? Neurodegeneration *4:* 1, 1995.

Heinrichs RW, Awad G: Neurocognitive subtypes of chronic schizophrenia. Schizophr Res *9:* 49, 1993.

Holland D, Watanabe MD, Sharma R: Atypical antipsychotics. Psychiatr Med *9:* 5, 1991.

Kane JM: Schizophrenia. N Engl J Med *334:* 34, 1996.

Kapur S, Remington G: Serotonin–dopamine interaction and its relevance to schizophrenia [review]. Am J Psychiatry *153:* 466, 1996.

Kavanagh DJ: Recent developments in expressed emotion and schizophrenia. Br J Psychiatry *160:* 601, 1992.

Keck PE, McElroy SL: The new antipsychotics and their therapeutic potential. Psychiatr Ann *27:* 320, 1997.

Keck PE Jr, McElroy SL: Olanzapine: A novel antipsychotic medication. Today's Ther Trends *14:* 63, 1996.

Kendler KS, Diehl SR: The genetics of schizophrenia: A current, genetic-epidemiologic perspective. Schizophr Bull *19:* 261, 1993.

Kinon BJ, Lieberman JA: Mechanisms of action of atypical antipsychotic drugs: A critical analysis. Psychopharmacology *124:* 2, 1996.

Lieberman JA, Koreen AR: Neurochemistry and neuroendocrinology of schizophrenia: A selective review. Schizophr Bull *19:* 371, 1993.

Lipton AA, Cancro R: Schizophrenia: Clinical features. In *Comprehensive Textbook of Psychiatry,* ed 6, HI Kaplan, BJ Sadock, editors, p 968. Williams & Wilkins, Baltimore, 1995.

Maas JW, Contreras SA, Miller AL, Berman N, Bowden CL, Javors MA, Seleshi E, Weintraub S: Studies of catecholamine metabolism in schizophrenia/psychosis: I. Neuropsychopharmacology *8:* 97, 1993.

Marden SR, Wirshing WC, Van Putten T: Drug treatment of schizophrenia: Overview of recent research. Schizophr Res *4:* 81, 1991.

McCarley RW, Faux SF, Shenton ME, Nestor PR, Adams J: Event-related potentials in schizophrenia: Their biological and clinical correlates and a new model of schizophrenia pathophysiology. Schizophr Res *4:* 209, 1991.

McClellan J, Werry J: Practice parameters for the assessment and treatment of children and adolescents with schizophrenia. J Am Acad Child Adolesc Psychiatry *33:* 616, 1994.

McGlashan TH, Fenton WS: Subtype progression and pathophysiologic deterioration in early schizophrenia. Schizophr Bull *19:* 17, 1993.

McGlashan TH, Fenton WS: The positive/negative distinction in schizophrenia: Review of natural history validators. Arch Gen Psychiatry *49:* 63, 1992.

McGlashan TH, Krystal JH: Schizophrenia-related disorders and dual diagnosis. In *Treatments of Psychiatric Disorders,* ed 2, GO Gabbard, editor, vol 1, p 1039. American Psychiatric Press, Washington, 1995.

Meltzer HY: The mechanism of action of clozapine in relation to its clinical advantages. In *Novel Antipsychotic Drugs,* HY Meltzer, editor, p 1. Raven Press, New York, 1992.

Meltzer HY, Nash JF: Effects of antipsychotic drugs on serotonin receptors. Pharmacol Rev *43:* 587, 1991.

Moller HJ: Neuroleptic treatment of negative symptoms in schizophrenia patients: Efficacy problems and methodological difficulties. Eur Neuropsychopharmacol *3:* 1, 1993.

Montgomery S, Beasley CM Jr, Tye NC: Olanzapine: An open-label study in schizophrenia. Presented at the Second International Conference on Schizophrenia, Vancouver, BC, 1992.

Moore NA, Calligaro DO, Wong DT, Bymaster F, Tye NC: The pharmacology of olanzapine and other new antipsychotic agents. Curr Opin Invest Drugs *2:* 281, 1993.

Nordstrom AL, Farde L, Wiesel FA, Forslund K, Pauline S, Halldin C, Uppfeldu G: Central D_2-dopamine receptor in relation to antipsychotic drug effects: A double-blind PET study of schizophrenic patients. Biol Psychiatry *33:* 227, 1993.

O'Callaghan E, Larkin C, Kinsella A, Waddington JL: Familial, obstetric, and other clinical correlates of minor physical anomalies in schizophrenia. Am J Psychiatry *148:* 479, 1991.

Pettegrew JW, Keshaven MS, Panchanlingam K, Strychor S, Kaplan DB, Tretta MG, Allen M: Alterations in brain high-energy phosphate and membrane phospholipid metabolism in first-episode, drug-naive schizophrenics. Arch Gen Psychiatry *48:* 563, 1991.

Peuskens J: Risperidone in the treatment of patients with chronic schizophrenia: A multi-national, multi-centre, double-blind, parallel-group study versus haloperidol. Br J Psychiatry *166:* 712, 1995.

Roberts GW, Done DJ, Brunton C, Crow TJ: A "mock up" of schizophrenia: Temporal lobe epilepsy and schizophrenia-like psychosis. Biol Psychiatry *28:* 127, 1990.

Schröder J, Niethammer R, Geider F-J, Reitz C, Binkert M, Jauss M, Sauer H: Neurological soft signs in schizophrenia. Schizophr Res *6:* 25, 1992.

Sedvall G: The current status of PET scanning with respect to schizophrenia. Neuropsychopharmacology *7:* 41, 1992.

Seeman P, Guan H-C, Van Tol HHM: Dopamine D_4 receptors elevated in schizophrenia. Science *365:* 441, 1993.

Seeman P, Van Tol HM: Dopamine receptor pharmacology. Curr Opin Neurol *6:* 602, 1993.

Shalev A, Hermesh H, Rothberg J, Munitz H: Poor neuroleptic response in acutely exacerbated schizophrenic patients. Acta Psychiatr Scand *87:* 86, 1993.

Sharma RP, Javaid JI, Pandey GN, Janicak PG, Davis JM: Behavioral and biochemical effects of methylphenidate in schizophrenic and non-schizophrenic patients. Biol Psychiatry *30:* 459, 1991.

Shenton ME, Kikinis R, Jolesz FA, Pollak SD, LeMay M, Wible CG, Hokama H, Martin J, Metcalf D, Coleman M, McCarley RW: Abnormalities of the left temporal lobe and thought disorder in schizophrenia: A quantitative magnetic resonance imaging study. N Engl J Med *327:* 604, 1992.

Siegel BV, Buchsbaum MS, Bunney WE, Gottschalk LA, Haier RJ, Lohr JB, Lottenberg S, Najafi A, Neuchterlein KH, Potkin SG, Wu JC: Cortical-striatal-thalamic circuits and brain glucose metabolic activity in 70 unmedicated male schizophrenic patients. Am J Psychiatry *150:* 1325, 1993.

Siris SG: Diagnosis of secondary depression in schizophrenia: Implications for DSM-IV. Schizophr Bull *17:* 65, 1991.

Stoll AL, Tohen M, Baldessarini RJ, Goodwin DC, Stein S, Katz S, Greenes D, Swinson RP, Goethe JW, McGlashan T: Shifts in diagnostic frequencies of schizophrenia and major affective disorders at six North American psychiatric hospitals, 1972–1988. Am J Psychiatry *150:* 1668, 1993.

Szymanski S, Kane JM, Lieberman JA: A selective review of biological markers in schizophrenia. Schizophr Bull *17:* 99, 1991.

Szymanski SR, Cannon TD, Gallacher F, Erwin RJ, Gur RE: Course of treatment response in first-episode and chronic schizophrenia. Am J Psychiatry *153:* 519, 1996.

Tandon R, Mazzara C, DeQuardo J, Craig KA, Meador-Woodruff JH, Goldman R, Greden JF: Dexamethasone suppression test in schizophrenia: Relationship to symptomatology, ventricular enlargement, and outcome. Biol Psychiatry *29:* 953, 1991.

Tsuang MT, Gilbertson MW, Faraone SV: The genetics of schizophrenia: Current knowledge and future directions. Schizophr Res *4:* 157, 1991.

Turner WM, Tsuang MT: Impact of substance abuse on the course and outcome of schizophrenia. Schizophr Bull 16: 87, 1990.

van Kammen DP, Kelly M: Dopamine and norepinephrine activity in schizophrenia: A integrative perspective. Schizophr Res *4:* 173, 1991.

van Kammen DP, Marder SR: Clozapine: A novel antipsychotic agent. In *Comprehensive Textbook of Psychiatry,* ed 6, HI Kaplan, BJ Sadock, editors, vol 2, p 1979. Williams & Wilkins, Baltimore, 1995.

Weinberger DR, Berman KF, Suddath R, Torrey EF: Evidence of dysfunction of a prefrontal-limbic network in schizophrenia: A magnetic resonance imaging and regional cerebral blood flow study of discordant monozygotic twins. Am J Psychiatry *140:* 890, 1992.

Woerner MG, Saltz BL, Kane JM, Lieberman JA, Alvir JM: Diabetes and development of tardive dyskinesia. Am J Psychiatry *150:* 66, 1993.

Zipursky RB, Lim KO, Sullivan EV, Brown BW, Pfefferbaum A: Widespread cerebral gray matter volume deficits in schizophrenia. Arch Gen Psychiatry *49:* 195, 1992.

14 Other Psychotic Disorders

▲ 14.1 Overview

In the fourth edition of *Diagnostic and Statistical Manual of Mental Disorders* (DSM-IV), the various meanings of the term *psychotic* are discussed, usually in connection with the disorder of schizophrenia. In the narrowest sense, psychotic refers to "delusions or prominent hallucinations," without "insight into their pathological nature." A somewhat broader definition would include hallucinations that a person recognizes as unreal. Both these definitions are based on symptoms. A still broader definition would include other positive symptoms of schizophrenia. A conceptual definition of psychotic focuses on the "loss of ego boundaries or a gross impairment in reality testing." The "other psychotic disorders" described in DSM-IV "emphasize different aspects of the various definitions of psychotic." In schizophrenia disorder, schizoaffective disorder, and brief psychotic disorder, the term *psychotic* refers to "delusions, any prominent hallucinations, disorganized speech, or disorganized or catatonic behavior." In psychotic disorder due to a general medical condition and in substance-induced psychotic disorder, "psychotic refers to delusions or only those hallucinations . . . not accompanied by insight." In delusional disorder and shared psychotic disorder, "psychotic is equivalent to delusional."

Schizophrenia is both the classic and the most common psychotic disorder. There are, however, many other psychotic syndromes that do not meet the diagnostic criteria for schizophrenia, the major ones being schizophreniform disorder, schizoaffective disorder, delusional disorder, and brief psychotic disorder. Briefly, the symptoms of schizophreniform disorder are identical to those of schizophrenia except that the symptoms have been present for at least 1 month but less than 6 months. Schizoaffective disorder is characterized by the presence of a complete syndrome of symptoms for both schizophrenia and a mood disorder. Delusional disorder, like schizophrenia, is a chronic disorder but is characterized by the presence of delusions as the predominant symptom. Brief psychotic disorder is characterized primarily by the brief duration (at least 1 day but less than 1 month) of schizophrenic symptoms.

In the evaluation of any psychotic patient, the possibility that the psychosis is caused by a general medical condition or is induced by a substance must be considered. These two situations are classified in DSM-IV as psychotic disorder due to a general medical condition and substance-induced psychotic disorder, respectively. DSM-IV also includes a diagnosis of catatonic disorder due to a general medical condition to emphasize the special considerations of the differential diagnosis of catatonic symptoms (see Table 10.5–2).

In an appendix, DSM-IV introduces two new psychotic disorder diagnoses: postpsychotic depressive disorder of schizophrenia and simple deteriorative disorder (simple schizophrenia). Postpsychotic depressive disorder of schizophrenia is characterized by the presence of all the symptoms of a major depressive episode during the residual phase of schizophrenia. Simple deteriorative disorder (simple schizophrenia), a still controversial diagnostic category, is described as the progressive development of symptoms of social withdrawal and other symptoms similar to the deficit symptoms of schizophrenia.

In addition to the common psychotic disorders and the newly introduced DSM-IV diagnoses, some rare or atypical psychotic disorders have been either officially or clinically recognized. DSM-IV includes diagnostic criteria for shared psychotic disorder, in which psychotic symptoms develop in one person because of that person's association with another psychotic person. Postpartum psychosis occurs in some women after the delivery of a child. In addition to these and other atypical psychoses, there are culture-bound psychotic syndromes, such as amok and koro.

The main thrust of treatment for this group of psychotic disorders is a comprehensive treatment plan that attends to the biological, psychological, and environmental factors of the disorders. Medication is a major part of treatment, but 25 to 50 percent of all patients do not comply with the medication as prescribed. Psychodynamic approaches may be helpful in uncovering the reasons for noncompliance. In some cases, states of ego-syntonic grandiosity are so pleasurable that patients prefer psychosis to stabilization on medication. When there has been only one psychotic episode, patients may refuse to comply with medication regimens; that is, they are dealing with a serious psychotic disorder by denying it. In their minds, taking a medication may translate into the stigma of mental illness.

Other psychodynamic factors that must be assessed in this group of psychotic disorders include the precipitating stressors and the interpersonal environment. In the course of taking a history and examining a patient, clinicians should pay attention to any changes or stresses in the patient's interpersonal environment. Patients who are susceptible to psychosis need to maintain a certain interpersonal distance; frequently, others' encroachment on the patient may create overwhelming stress that leads to decompensation. Similarly, any recent successes or losses may be important stressors in particular cases. Often a relatively minor event has profound psychological meaning, and dynamic exploration of the meaning of events is, therefore, crucial in assessing triggers of psychotic episodes.

PSYCHOTIC DISORDER DUE TO A GENERAL MEDICAL CONDITION AND SUBSTANCE-INDUCED PSYCHOTIC DISORDER

The evaluation of a psychotic patient requires consideration of the possibility that the psychotic symptoms result from a general medical condition such as a brain tumor or the ingestion of a substance such as phencyclidine (PCP).

Epidemiology

Relevant epidemiological data about psychotic disorder due to a general medical condition and substance-induced psychotic disorder are lacking. The disorders are most often encountered in patients who abuse alcohol or other substances on a long-term basis. The delusional syndrome that may accompany complex partial seizures is more common in women than in men.

Etiology

Physical conditions such as cerebral neoplasms, particularly of the occipital or temporal areas, can cause hallucinations. Sensory deprivation, as in people who are blind or deaf, can also result in hallucinatory or delusional experiences. Lesions involving the temporal lobe and other cerebral regions, especially the right hemisphere and the parietal lobe, are associated with delusions.

Psychoactive substances are common causes of psychotic syndromes. The most commonly involved substances are alcohol, indole hallucinogens such as lysergic acid diethylamide, amphetamine, cocaine, mescaline, PCP, and ketamine. Many other substances, including steroids and thyroxine, can produce hallucinations. (See Table 13–8 for a list of general medical conditions and substances that can be associated with psychotic symptoms.)

Diagnosis

Psychotic Disorder Due to a General Medical Condition. The DSM-IV diagnosis of psychotic disorder due to a general medical condition (Table 14.1–1) is defined in DSM-IV by specifying the predominant symptoms. When the diagnosis is used, the medical condition, along with the predominant symptoms pattern, should be included in the diagnosis, for example, psychotic disorder due to a brain tumor, with delusions. The DSM-IV criteria further specify that the disorder does not occur exclusively while a patient is delirious or demented and that the symptoms are not better accounted for by another mental disorder.

Catatonic Disorder Due to a General Medical Condition. DSM-IV has a separate diagnostic category for catatonic symptoms secondary to a general medical condition (see Table 10.5–2).

Table 14.1–1
DSM-IV Diagnostic Criteria for Psychotic Disorder Due to a General Medical Condition

A. Prominent hallucinations or delusions.

B. There is evidence from the history, physical examination, or laboratory findings that the disturbance is the direct physiological consequence of a general medical condition.

C. The disturbance is not better accounted for by another mental disorder.

D. The disturbance does not occur exclusively during the course of a delirium.

Code based on predominant symptom:
With delusions: if delusions are the predominant symptom
With hallucinations: if hallucinations are the predominant symptom

Coding note: Include the name of the general medical condition on Axis I, eg, psychotic disorder due to malignant lung neoplasm, with delusions; also code the general medical condition on Axis III.

Coding note: If delusions are part of a preexisting dementia, indicate the delusions by coding the appropriate subtype of the dementia if one is available, eg, dementia of the Alzheimer's type, with late onset, with delusions.

Substance-Induced Psychotic Disorder. The diagnostic category of substance-induced psychotic disorder in DSM-IV (Table 14.1–2) is reserved for those with substance-induced psychotic symptoms and impaired reality testing. People with substance-induced psychotic symptoms (for example, hallucinations) but with intact reality testing should be classified as having a substance-related disorder (for example, PCP intoxication with perceptual disturbances). The diagnosis of substance-induced psychotic disorder is included with the other psychotic disorder diagnoses in DSM-IV to prompt clinicians to consider the possibility that a substance is causally involved in the production of psychotic symptoms. The full diagnosis of substance-induced psychotic disorder should include the type of substance involved, the stage of substance use when the disorder began (for example, during intoxication or withdrawal), and the clinical phenomena (for example, hallucinations or delusions).

Clinical Features

Hallucinations. Hallucinations may occur in one or more sensory modalities. Tactile hallucinations (such as the sensation of bugs crawling on the skin) are characteristic of cocaine use. Auditory hallucinations are usually associated with psychoactive substance abuse; auditory hallucinations may also occur in people who are deaf. Olfactory hallucinations can result from temporal lobe epilepsy; visual hallucinations may occur in people who are blind because of cataracts. Hallucinations are either recurrent or persistent and are experienced in a state of full wakefulness and alertness; a hallucinating patient shows no significant changes in cognitive functions. Visual hallucinations often take the form of scenes

Table 14.1–2
DSM-IV Diagnostic Criteria for Substance-Induced Psychotic Disorder

A. Prominent hallucinations or delusions. **Note:** Do not include hallucinations if the person has insight that they are substance induced.

B. There is evidence from the history, physical examination, or laboratory findings of either (1) or (2):
(1) the symptoms in criteria A developed during, or within a month of, substance intoxication or withdrawal
(2) medication use is etiologically related to the disturbance

C. The disturbance is not better accounted for by a psychotic disorder that is not substance induced. Evidence that the symptoms are better accounted for by a psychotic disorder that is not substance induced might include the following: the symptoms precede the onset of the use (or medication use); the symptoms persist for a substantial period of time (eg, about a month) after the cessation of acute withdrawal or severe intoxication, or are substantially in excess of what would be expected given the type or amount of the substance used or the duration of use; or there is other evidence that suggests the existence of an independent non–substance-induced psychotic disorder (eg, a history of recurrent non–substance-related episodes).

D. The disturbance does not occur exclusively during the course of a delirium.

Note: This diagnosis should be made instead of a diagnosis of substance intoxication or substance withdrawal only when the symptoms are in excess of those usually associated with the intoxication or withdrawal syndrome and when the symptoms are sufficiently severe to warrant independent clinical attention.

Code: [Specific substance]-induced psychotic disorder (Alcohol, with delusions; alcohol, with hallucinations; amphetamine [or amphetamine-like substance], with delusions; amphetamine [or amphetamine-like substance] with hallucinations; cannabis, with delusions; cannabis, with hallucinations; cocaine, with delusions; cocaine, with hallucinations; hallucinogen, with delusions; hallucinogen, with hallucinations; inhalant, with delusions; inhalant, with hallucinations; opioid, with delusions; opioid, with hallucinations; phencyclidine [for phencyclidine-like substance], with delusions; phencyclidine [or phencyclidine-like substance], with hallucinations; sedative, hypnotic or anxiolytic, with delusions; sedative, hypnotic or anxiolytic, with hallucinations; other [or unknown] substance, with delusions; other [or unknown] substance, with hallucinations)

Specify if:
With onset during intoxication: if criteria are met for intoxication with the substance and the symptoms develop during the intoxication syndrome
With onset during withdrawal: if criteria are met for withdrawal from the substance and the symptoms develop during, or shortly after, a withdrawal syndrome

involving diminutive (lilliputian) human figures or small animals. Rare musical hallucinations typically feature religious songs. Patients with psychotic disorder due to a general medical condition and substance-induced psychotic disorder may act on their hallucinations. In alcohol-related hallucinations, threatening, critical, or insulting third person voices speak about the patients and may tell them to harm either themselves or others. Such patients are dangerous and are at significant risk for suicide or homicide. Patients may or may not believe that the hallucinations are real.

Delusions. Secondary and substance-induced delusions are usually present in a state of full wakefulness. Patients experience no change in the level of consciousness, although mild cognitive impairment may be observed. Patients may appear confused, disheveled, or eccentric, with tangential or even incoherent speech. Hyperactivity and apathy may be present and an associated dysphoric mood is thought to be common. The delusions may be systematized or fragmentary, with varying content, but persecutory delusions are the most common.

Differential Diagnosis

Psychotic disorder due to a general medical condition and substance-induced psychotic disorder must be distinguished from delirium, in which patients have a clouded sensorium, from dementia, in which patients have major intellectual deficits, and from schizophrenia, in which patients have other symptoms of thought disorder and impaired functioning. Psychotic disorder due to a general medical condition and substance-induced psychotic disorder must also be differentiated from psychotic mood disorders, in which other affective symptoms are pronounced.

Treatment

Treatment involves identifying the general medical condition or the particular substance involved. At this point, treatment is directed toward the underlying condition and the patient's immediate behavioral control. Hospitalization may be necessary to evaluate patients completely and to ensure their safety. Antipsychotic agents (for example, olanzapine [Zyprexa], haloperidol [Haldol]) may be necessary for immediate and short-term control of psychotic or aggressive behavior, although benzodiazepines may also be useful for controlling agitation and anxiety.

PSYCHOTIC DISORDERS IN DSM-IV APPENDIX

Postpsychotic Depressive Disorder of Schizophrenia

Postpsychotic depressive disorder in schizophrenic patients is categorized in an appendix in DSM-IV (Table 14.1–3).

Epidemiology. In the absence of specific diagnostic criteria, the reported incidence of postpsychotic depression of schizophrenia varies widely from less than 10 percent to more than 70 percent. A reasonable estimate based on large studies is about 25 percent, although a definitive incidence figure must wait for controlled studies using the DSM-IV criteria.

Table 14.1–3
DSM-IV Research Criteria for Postpsychotic Depressive Disorder of Schizophrenia

A. Criteria are met for a major depressive episode.
Note: The major depressive episode must include criterion A1: depressed mood. Do not include symptoms that are better accounted for as medication side effects or negative symptoms of schizophrenia.

B. The major depressive episode is superimposed on and occurs only during the residual phase of schizophrenia.

C. The major depressive episode is not due to the direct physiological effects of a substance or a general medical condition.

Prognostic Significance. The prognostic significance of the DSM-IV diagnosis is uncertain, because studies using the official diagnostic category have not yet been conducted. Nonetheless, data from other studies indicate that patients with postpsychotic depressive disorder of schizophrenia are likely to have had poor premorbid adjustment, marked schizoid personality disorder traits, and an insidious onset of their psychotic symptoms. They are also likely to have first-degree relatives with mood disorders. Although the findings have not been consistent, postpsychotic depressive disorder of schizophrenia has been associated with a less favorable prognosis, a higher likelihood of relapse, and an increased incidence of suicide than is seen in schizophrenic patients without postpsychotic depressive disorder. Some data indicate that schizophrenic patients with and without postpsychotic depressive disorder may differ in several biological variables, for example, in dexamethasone-suppression test and thyrotropin-releasing hormone test results and in monoamine oxidase activity, but the validity and usefulness of these tests in the diagnosis are still uncertain.

Diagnosis and Differential Diagnosis. The clinical boundaries of the diagnosis are hard to define operationally. The symptoms of postpsychotic depressive disorder of schizophrenia can closely resemble the symptoms of the residual phase of schizophrenia as well as the side effects of commonly used antipsychotic medications. Distinguishing the diagnosis from schizoaffective disorder, depressive type, is also difficult. The DSM-IV criteria specify that the criteria for a major depressive episode be met and that the symptoms occur only during the residual phase of schizophrenia. The symptoms cannot be substance induced or part of a mood disorder due to a general medical condition.

The disorder may be almost entirely caused by antipsychotic medications, but several types of data indicate that antipsychotic medications cannot explain the entire extent of the symptoms. First, depressive symptoms are often present during the psychotic episode itself and, generally, decrease in severity, along with the psychotic symptoms, with successful antipsychotic treatment. Second, the severity of depressive symptoms in postpsychotic schizophrenic patients has not been correlated with the dosage of antipsychotic medication. Third, depressive symptoms have been frequently reported in nonmedicated schizophrenic patients recovering from psychotic episodes. Nonetheless, clinicians should not confuse the antipsychotic-induced side effects of akathisia and akinesia as symptoms of postpsychotic depressive disorder of schizophrenia.

Treatment. The use of antidepressants (for example, fluoxetine [Prozac]) in the treatment of postpsychotic depressive disorder of schizophrenia has been reported in several studies. About half the studies have reported positive effects, and the other half have reported no effects in the relief of the depressive symptoms. Antidepressant medications probably relieve depressive symptoms in some patients, but the mixed results of the studies reflect the current inability to distinguish those patients who will respond from those who will not.

Simple Deteriorative Disorder (Simple Schizophrenia)

Simple deteriorative disorder (simple schizophrenia) (Table 14.1–4) is a controversial diagnostic category. The use of the DSM-IV research criteria in subsequent studies will help either refute or support the reliability and the validity of the diagnostic category. The research criteria outline the gradual and progressive onset of symptoms similar to the deficit symptoms and the cognitive decline in schizophrenia. Hallucinations and delusions are not part of the proposed symptom pattern.

Although few clinicians would say that they have not seen patients who meet the research criteria of simple schizophrenia, many researchers and clinicians have raised serious concerns about the diagnosis. The term *simple schizophrenia* may incorrectly imply a close relation to schizophrenia and may unfairly stigmatize patients given the diagnosis. The criteria

Table 14.1–4
DSM-IV Research Criteria for Simple Deteriorative Disorder (Simple Schizophrenia)

A. Progressive development over a period of at least of all of the following:
(1) marked decline in occupational or academic functioning
(2) gradual appearance and deepening of negative symptoms such as affective flattening, alogia, and avolition
(3) poor interpersonal rapport, social isolation, or social withdrawal

B. Criterion A for schizophrenia has never been met.

C. The symptoms are not better accounted for by schizotypal or schizoid personality disorder, a psychotic disorder, a mood disorder, an anxiety disorder, a dementia, or mental retardation and are not due to the direct physiological effects of a substance or a general medical condition.

may define an overinclusive group of patients, who may be better classified as having major depressive disorder, dysthymic disorder, substance abuse, or personality disorder. The obvious overlap with these other diagnostic categories necessitates the use of variable and unpredictable clinical judgment in deciding among the diagnostic alternatives. The lack of scientific literature on the criteria limits their usefulness for predicting prognosis or suggesting treatment.

Researchers may eventually show that the diagnostic category of simple deteriorative disorder has prognostic and treatment implications. While clinicians wait for the appropriate studies to be completed, they should use the diagnosis with caution and forethought.

ATYPICAL PSYCHOTIC DISORDERS

Shared Psychotic Disorder

Shared psychotic disorder, perhaps better known as *folie à deux,* is rare. A patient is classified as having shared psychotic disorder when the patient's psychotic symptoms developed during a long-term relationship with another person who had a similar psychotic syndrome before the onset of symptoms in the patient with shared psychotic disorder. The disorder most commonly involves two people—a dominant person (the inducer, the principal, or the primary patient) and a submissive person, who is the patient with shared psychotic disorder. Cases involving more than two people have occasionally been reported; these are called *folie à trois, folie à quatre, folie à cinq,* and so on. One case involved an entire family (*folie à famille*) of 12 people (*folie à douze*).

In 1860, Jules G. F. Baillarger first described the syndrome and called it *folie à communiquée,* although the first description is commonly attributed to Ernest Charles Lasègue and Jules Falret, who described the condition in 1877 and gave it the name folie à deux. The syndrome has also been called communicated insanity, contagious insanity, infectious insanity, psychosis of association, and double insanity. Marandon de Montyel divided folie à deux into three groups (*folie imposée, folie simultanée,* and *folie communiquée*—imposed, simultaneous, and transmitted *folie*), and Heinz Lehmann added a fourth group, *folie induite* (induced *folie*).

Folie imposée is the most common and classic form of the disorder. A delusional system develops in a dominant person who then progressively imposes the system onto a usually younger and more passive person. In folie simultanée, similar delusional systems develop independently in two closely associated people. In contrast to folie imposée, in which separation often produces an improvement of the symptoms in the submissive person, in folie simultanée, separation of the two people does not lead to improvement in either. In folie communiquée the dominant person is involved in inducting of a delusional system in the submissive person, but the submissive person develops his or her own delusional system, which does not remit after the separation of the two. In *folie induite,* the delusions of one person are extended by taking on another's delusions. The various folies are difficult to differentiate in practice and are of more historical than clinical interest.

Epidemiology. More than 95 percent of all cases of shared psychotic disorder involve two members of the same family. About one third of the cases involve two sisters; another one third involve a husband and a wife or a mother and her child. Two brothers, a brother and a sister, and a father and his child have been reported less frequently. The dominant person is usually affected by schizophrenia or a similar psychotic disorder. In about 25 percent of all cases, the submissive person is affected with physical disabilities, including deafness, cerebrovascular diseases, or other disability that increases the submissive person's dependence on the dominant person. Shared psychotic disorder may be more common in low than in high socioeconomic groups and is more common in women than in men.

Etiology. Although the primary theory about the disorder is psychosocial, because more than 95 percent of cases involve people in the same family, a significant genetic component to the disorder has been suggested. A modest amount of data indicate that affected people often have a family history of schizophrenia.

The dominant member of the dyad has a preexisting psychotic disorder, almost always schizophrenia or a related psychotic disorder, and rarely an affective or dementia-related psychosis. The dominant person is usually older, more intelligent, and better educated and has stronger personality traits than the submissive person, who is usually dependent on the dominant person. The two (or more) people inevitably live together or have an extremely close personal relationship, associated with shared life experiences, common needs and hopes, and, often, a deep emotional rapport with each other. The relationship between the people involved is usually somewhat or completely isolated from external societal and cultural inputs.

The submissive person may be predisposed to a mental disorder and may have a history of a personality disorder with dependent or suggestible qualities as well as a history of depression, suspiciousness, and social isolation. The relationship between the two, although one of dependence, may also be characterized by ambivalence, with deeply held feelings of both love and hate. The dominant person may be moved to induce the delusional system in the submissive person as a mechanism for maintaining contact with another, despite the dominant person's psychosis. The dominant person's psychotic symptoms may develop in the submissive person through the process of identification. By adopting the psychotic symptoms of the dominant person, the submissive person gains acceptance by the other. The submissive person's admiration for the dominant person, however, may evolve into hatred, which the submissive person considers unacceptable; when the hatred is directed inward, depression and sometimes suicide can result.

Diagnosis. The DSM-IV criteria for shared psychotic disorder (Table 14.1–5) include the development of delusions in a person who has a close relationship with a person who already has a similar delusional system. The person with shared psychotic disorder does not have a preexisting psychotic disorder.

Clinical Features. The key symptom of shared psychotic disorder is the unquestioning acceptance of another per-

Table 14.1–5
DSM-IV Diagnostic Criteria for Shared Psychotic Disorder

A. A delusion develops in an individual in the context of a close relationship with another person(s), who has an already-established delusion.

B. The delusion is similar in content to that of the person who already has the established delusion.

C. The disturbance is not better accounted for by another psychotic disorder (eg, schizophrenia) or a mood disorder with psychotic features and is not due to the direct physiological effects of a substance (eg, a drug of abuse, a medication) or a general medical condition.

son's delusions. The delusions themselves are often in the realm of possibility and usually not as bizarre as those seen in many patients with schizophrenia. The content of the delusions is often persecutory or hypochondriacal. Symptoms of a coexisting personality disorder may be present, but signs and symptoms that meet the diagnostic criteria for schizophrenia, mood disorders, and delusional disorder are absent. The patient may have ideation about suicide or pacts about homicide; clinicians must elicit this information during the interview.

A 52-year-old man was referred by the court for inpatient psychiatric examination, charged with disturbing the peace. He had been arrested for disrupting a trial, complaining of harassment by various judges. He had walked into a courtroom, marched to the bench, and begun to berate the probate judge. While in the hospital, he related a detailed account of conspiratorial goings-on in the local judiciary. A target of certain judges, he claimed he had been singled out for a variety of reasons for many years: He knew what was going on; he had kept records of wrongdoings; and he understood the significance of the whole matter. He refused to elaborate on the specific nature of the conspiracy. He had responded to it with frequent letters to newspapers, the local bar association, and even to a Congressional subcommittee. His mental state, apart from his story and a mildly depressed mood, was entirely normal.

A family interview revealed that his wife and several grown children shared the belief in a judicial conspiracy directed against the patient. There was no change in delusional thinking in the patient or the family after 10 days of observation. The patient refused follow-up.

DISCUSSION

In this case, the diagnosis is shared psychotic disorder because protection is provided by others who share the delusion and believe in the reasonableness of the response; such cases are uncommon, if not rare. (Courtesy of Theo C. Manschreck, M.D.)

Differential Diagnosis. Malingering, factitious disorder with predominantly psychological signs and symptoms, psychotic disorder due to a general medical condition, and substance-induced psychotic disorder must be considered in the differential diagnosis of the condition. The boundary between shared psychotic disorder and generic group madness, such as the Jonestown massacre in Guyana, is unclear.

Course and Prognosis. The nature of the disorder suggests that separation of the submissive person, the person with shared psychotic disorder, from the dominant person should result in the resolution and disappearance of the submissive person's psychotic symptoms. However, this course probably characterizes less than 40 percent of all cases and perhaps is true of only 10 percent. Often, the submissive person requires treatment with antipsychotic drugs, just as the dominant person needs antipsychotic drug treatment for his or her psychotic disorder. Because the people are almost always in the same family, they usually move back together after release from a hospital.

Treatment. The initial step in treatment is to separate the affected person from the source of the delusions, the dominant partner. Patients may need significant support to compensate for the loss and should be observed for the remission of the delusional symptoms. Antipsychotic drugs can be used if these symptoms have not abated in 1 or 2 weeks.

Psychotherapy with nondelusional members of the patient's family should be undertaken, and psychotherapy with both the patient with shared psychotic disorder and the dominant partner may be indicated later in the course of treatment. In addition, the mental disorder of the dominant partner should be treated. To prevent the recurrence of the syndrome, clinicians must use family therapy and social support to modify the family dynamics and to prevent redevelopment of the syndrome. It is often useful to make sure that the family unit is exposed to input from outside sources to decrease the family's isolation.

Other Atypical Psychotic Disorders

Autoscopic Psychosis. The characteristic symptom of autoscopic psychosis is a visual hallucination of all or part of the person's own body. The hallucinatory perception, which is called a phantom, is usually colorless and transparent, and because the phantom imitates the person's movements, it is perceived as though appearing in a mirror. The phantom tends to appear suddenly and without warning.

EPIDEMIOLOGY. Autoscopy is a rare phenomenon. Some people have an autoscopic experience only once or a few times; others have the experience more often. Although the data are limited, sex, age, heredity, and intelligence do not seem to be related to the occurrence of the syndrome.

ETIOLOGY. The cause of the autoscopic phenomenon is unknown. A biological hypothesis is that abnormal, episodic activity in areas of the temporoparietal lobes is involved with the sense of self, perhaps combined with abnormal activity in parts of the visual cortex. Psychological theories have associated the syndrome with personalities characterized by imagination, visual sensitivity, and, possibly, narcissistic personality disorder traits. Such people may be likely to experience autoscopic phenomena during periods of stress.

COURSE AND PROGNOSIS. The classic descriptions of the phenomenon indicate that in most cases the syndrome is neither progressive nor incapacitating. Affected people usually maintain some emotional distance from the phenomenon, an observation that suggests a specific neuroanatomical lesion. Rarely do the symptoms reflect the onset of schizophrenia or other psychotic disorders.

Capgras's Syndrome. The characteristic symptom of Capgras's syndrome is the delusion that other people, usually closely related to the affected person, have been replaced by exact doubles who are impostors. The syndrome was originally described in 1923 by the French psychiatrist Jean Marie Joseph Capgras, who called it *l'illusion des sosies,* the illusion of doubles.

EPIDEMIOLOGY. This rare syndrome occurs more frequently in women than in men. The condition is sometimes classified as a delusional disorder, although in some patients it may also be a symptom of schizophrenia.

ETIOLOGY. Capgras explained that the nature of the delusion resulted from feelings of strangeness combined with a paranoid tendency to distrust. A biological hypothesis might explain the syndrome as a neurobiological dysfunction in the brain areas that usually relate perceptions to the recognition of people. According to a psychoanalytic hypothesis, patients' feelings about the people confronting them (such as anger or fear) are displaced to the doubles, who are impostors and therefore may be safely and righteously rejected.

PROGNOSIS AND TREATMENT. The symptoms of Capgras's syndrome respond to antipsychotic treatment, but when Capgras's syndrome is the sole symptom of a psychotic disorder, clinicians should perform an extensive neuropsychological workup to identify any organic lesions that may be causing the syndrome.

Cotard's Syndrome. In the 19th century, the French psychiatrist Jules Cotard described several patients who suffered from a syndrome called *délire de négation,* sometimes referred to as nihilistic delusional disorder. Patients with the syndrome complain of having lost not only possessions, status, and strength but also their heart, blood, and intestines. The world beyond them is reduced to nothingness.

EPIDEMIOLOGY. This relatively rare syndrome is usually considered a precursor to a schizophrenic or depressive episode. With the common use today of antipsychotic drugs, the syndrome is seen even less frequently than in the past.

ETIOLOGY. In its pure form, the syndrome appears in patients with depression, schizophrenia, and psychotic disorder caused by a general medical condition, often associated with dementia.

PROGNOSIS AND TREATMENT. The syndrome usually lasts only a few days or weeks and responds to treatment directed at the underlying disorder. Long-term forms of the syndrome are usually associated with dementing syndromes such as dementia of the Alzheimer's type.

Atypical Schizophrenia. A particular form of schizophrenia described by R. Gjessing was called periodic catatonia. Patients affected with the disorder have periodic bouts of stuporous or excited catatonia, which Gjessing believed were related to metabolic shifts in nitrogen balance. The syndrome is rarely seen, responds well to standard antipsychotic agents, and is prevented by maintenance medication.

CULTURE-BOUND PSYCHOTIC SYNDROMES

Various culture-bound psychotic syndromes have been described (Table 14.1–6). In general, these syndromes fit into one or another ICD-10 or DSM-IV diagnosis, including psychotic disorder not otherwise specified, but at the same time they imply two possibilities. First, if the syndromes are unique and limited to specific cultures, specific cultural or biological factors may contribute to the psychosis. Second, if the syndromes are forms of standard diagnoses such as schizophrenia, the content of their delusions and hallucinations may be strongly influenced by society.

Amok

The Malayan word *amok* means a "murderous frenzy." The amok syndrome consists of a sudden, unprovoked outburst of wild rage in which those affected run about madly and indiscriminately attack and maim any people and animals in their way. The savage homicidal attack is generally preceded by a period of preoccupation, brooding, and mild depression. After the attack, the person feels exhausted, has no memory of the attack, and often commits suicide. The Malayan natives also refer to the attack as *mata elap,* "darkened eye." In the United States, the behavior of people with a syndrome similar to amok is commonly reported in the newspapers; they are often found to be suffering from schizophrenia, a bipolar disorder, or a depressive disorder. In other cases, the cause may be a general medical condition, such as epilepsy or another brain lesion. In cultural explanation of the syndrome, a culture that imposes strict restrictions on adolescents and adults but allows children free rein to express their aggression may be especially prone to psychopathological reactions of the amok type. A cultural belief in magical possession by demons and evil spirits may be another factor contributing to the development of the amok syndrome.

The only immediate treatment consists of overpowering amok people and gaining complete physical control over them. The attack is usually over within a few hours; afterward, the patient may require treatment for a chronic psychotic disorder, which may have been the underlying cause.

Koro

Koro is characterized by a patient's delusion that his penis is shrinking and may disappear into his abdomen and that he may die. The koro syndrome occurs among people in Southeast Asia and in some areas of China, where it is known as *suk-yeong.* A corresponding disorder in women involves complaints of the shrinkage of the vulva, the labia, and the breasts. Occasional cases of koro syndrome among people in a Western culture have been reported. Koro has usually been thought of as a psychogenic disorder resulting from interacting of cultural, social, and psychodynamic factors in especially predisposed people. Culturally elaborated fears about nocturnal emission, masturbation, and sexual overindulgence seem to give rise to the condition. Alternatively, the disorder may be seen as a delusional disorder or as a symptom of another psychotic disorder.

Patients have been given treatment with psychotherapy, antipsychotic drugs, and, in a few cases, electroconvulsive therapy. As with other psychiatric disorders, the prognosis is related to the patient's premorbid personality adjustment and to any associated pathological condition. Some cultures prescribe fellatio as a cure for Koro in men. It has been reported in the United States.

Table 14.1–6
Culture-Bound Syndromes

Diagnosis	Country or Culture	Characteristics
Amok	Southeast Asia, Malaysia	Sudden rampage, usually including homicide and suicide; occurs in males; ends in exhaustion and amnesia
Bouffée délirante	France	Transient psychosis with elements of trance or dream states
Brain fag	Sub-Saharan Africa	Headache, agnosia, chronic fatigue, visual difficulties, anxiety; seen in male students
Bulimia nervosa	North America	Food binges, self-induced vomiting; may occur with depression, anorexia nervosa, or substance abuse
Colera	Mayan Indians (Guatemala)	Temper tantrums, violent outbursts, gasping, stuporousness, hallucinations, delusions
Empacho	Mexican and Cuban American	Inability to digest and excrete recently ingested food
Grisi siknis	Miskito of Nicaragua	Headache, anxiety, anger, aimless running
Hi-Wa itck	Mohave American Indian	Anorexia nervosa, insomnia, depression, suicide associated with unwanted separation from loved one
Involutional paraphrenia	Spain, Germany	Paranoid disorder occurring in midlife; distinct from schizophrenia but may have elements of both schizophrenia and paranoia
Koro	Asia	Fear that the penis will withdraw into the abdomen, causing death
Latah	Southeast Asia, Malaysia, Bantu of Africa, Ainu of Japan	Automatic obedience reaction with echopraxia and echolalia precipitated by a sudden minimal stimulus; occurs in females; also called a startle reaction
Mal de ojo	Mediterranean	Vomiting, fever, restless sleep; caused by evil eye
Nervios	Costa Rica and Latin America	Headache, insomnia, anorexia, fears, anger, diarrhea, despair
Piblokto (Arctic hysteria, pibloktoq)	Eskimos of northern Greenland	MIxed anxiety and depression, confusion, depersonalization, derealization; occurs mainly in females; ends in stuporous sleep and amnesia
Reactive psychosis	Scandinavia	Psychosis precipitated by psychosocial stress; sudden onset with good prognosis, premorbid personality intact
Shinkeishitsu	Japan	Syndrome marked by obsessions, perfectionism, ambivalence, social withdrawal, neurasthenia, and hypochondriasis
Susto	Latin America	Severe anxiety, restlessness, fear of black magic and of evil eye
Tabanka	Trinidad	Depression in men abandoned by their wives; high risk of suicide
Taijin-kyofusho	Japan	Anxiety, fear of rejection, easy blushing, fear of eye contact, concern about body odor
Uqamairineq	Inuits	Paralysis associated with borderline sleep states, accompanied with agitation, anxiety, hallucinations
Wihtigo or windigo	Native American Indians (Algonkian)	Fear of being turned into a cannibal through possession by supernatural monster, the windigo

Piblokto

Occurring among the Inuit and sometimes referred to as Arctic hysteria, piblokto is characterized by attacks lasting from 1 to 2 hours, during which affected people (usually women) begin to scream and tear off and destroy their clothing. While imitating the cry of an animal or bird, affected people may throw themselves on the snow or run wildly about on the ice, although the temperature may be well below zero degrees. After the attack, the affected person appears to be normal and usually has no memory of the episode. The Inuit are reluctant to touch afflicted people during the attacks because of the evil spirits involved. Piblokto is almost certainly a hysterical state of a dissociative disorder and has become much less frequent among the Inuit.

Wihtigo

Wihtigo or windigo psychosis is a psychiatric disorder confined to the Cree, Ojibwa, and Salteaux of North America. Affected people believe that they have been transformed into a wihtigo, a giant monster that eats human flesh. During times of starvation, they may feel and express a craving for human flesh. Because of a person's belief in the possibility of such a transformation, symptoms connected with the alimentary tract, such as loss of appetite and nausea from trivial causes, may sometimes cause a person to become greatly excited for fear of being transformed into a wihtigo.

PSYCHOTIC DISORDER NOT OTHERWISE SPECIFIED

Psychotic disorder not otherwise specified is the DSM-IV category applied to patients with psychotic symptoms such as delusions, hallucinations, and disorganized speech and behavior who do not meet the diagnostic criteria for other specifically defined psychotic disorders. In some cases, the diagnosis of psychotic disorder not otherwise specified may be used when not enough information is available to make a specific

Table 14.1–7
DSM-IV Psychotic Disorder Not Otherwise Specified

This category includes psychotic symptomatology (ie, delusions, hallucinations, disorganized speech, grossly disorganized or catatonic behavior) about which there is inadequate information to make a specific diagnosis or about which there is contradictory information, or disorders with psychotic symptoms that do not meet the criteria for any specific psychotic disorder.

Examples include:

1. Postpartum psychosis that does not meet criteria for mood disorder with psychotic features, brief psychotic disorder, psychotic disorder due to a general medical condition, or substance-induced psychotic disorder
2. Psychotic symptoms that have lasted for less than 1 month but that have not yet remitted, so that the criteria for brief psychotic disorder are not met
3. Persistent auditory hallucinations in the absence of any other features
4. Persistent nonbizarre delusions with periods of overlapping mood episodes that have been present for a substantial portion of the delusional disturbance
5. Situations in which the clinician has concluded that a psychotic disorder is present, but is unable to determine whether it is primary, due to a general medical condition, or substance induced

diagnosis. DSM-IV lists some examples of the diagnosis to help guide clinicians (Table 14.1–7).

Postpartum Psychosis

Postpartum psychosis, an example of psychotic disorder not otherwise specified, occurs in women who have recently delivered a baby; the syndrome is most often characterized by the mother's depression, delusions, and thoughts of harming either her infant or herself. Such ideation of suicide or infanticide must be carefully monitored; some mothers have acted on these ideas. Most available data suggest a close relation between postpartum psychosis and the mood disorders, particularly bipolar disorders and major depressive disorder.

Epidemiology. The incidence of postpartum psychosis is about 1 per 1,000 childbirths, although some reports have indicated that the incidence may be as high as 2 per 1,000. About 50 to 60 percent of affected women have just had their first child, and about 50 percent of cases involve deliveries associated with nonpsychiatric perinatal complications. About 50 percent of the affected women have a family history of mood disorders. Although postpartum psychosis is fundamentally a disorder of women, some rare cases affect fathers. In these instances, a husband may feel displaced by the child and may compete for the mother's love and attention. Such men, however, probably have a coexisting major mental disorder that has been exacerbated by the stress of fatherhood.

Etiology. The most robust data indicate that an episode of postpartum psychosis is essentially an episode of a mood disorder, usually a bipolar disorder but possibly a depressive disorder. Relatives of those with postpartum psychosis have an incidence of mood disorders that is similar to the incidence in relatives of people with mood disorders. Schizoaffective disorder and delusional disorder are rarely appropriate diagnoses. The validity of diagnoses of mood disorders is usually verified in the year after the birth, when as many as two thirds of the patients have a second episode of the underlying disorder. The delivery process may best be seen as a nonspecific stress that causes the development of an episode of a major mood disorder, perhaps through a major hormonal mechanism.

A few instances of postpartum psychosis result from a general medical condition associated with perinatal events, such as infection, drug intoxication from, for example, scopolamine (Donnagel) and meperidine (Demerol), toxemia, and blood loss. The sudden decrease in estrogen and progesterone concentrations immediately after delivery may also contribute to the disorder, but treatment with these hormones has not been effective.

Some investigators have claimed that a purely psychosocial causal mechanism is suggested by the preponderance of primiparous mothers and by the association between postpartum psychosis and recent stressful events. Psychodynamic studies of postpartum mental illness have also suggested the presence of conflicted feelings in the mother about her mothering experience. Some women may not have wanted to become pregnant; others may feel trapped in unhappy marriages by motherhood. Marital discord during pregnancy has been associated with an increased incidence of illness, although the discord may be related to the slow development of mood disorder symptoms in the mother.

Diagnosis. Specific diagnostic criteria are not included in DSM-IV. The diagnosis can be made when psychosis occurs in close temporal association with childbirth, although a DSM-IV diagnosis of a mood disorder should be considered in the differential diagnosis. Characteristic symptoms include delusions, cognitive deficits, motility disturbances, mood abnormalities, and occasional hallucinations. The content of the psychotic material revolves around mothering and pregnancy. DSM-IV also allows for the diagnoses of brief psychotic disorder and mood disorders with postpartum onset (see Table 15.2–22).

Clinical Features. The symptoms of postpartum psychosis can often begin within days of the delivery, although the mean time to onset is 2 to 3 weeks and almost always within 8 weeks of delivery. Characteristically, patients begin to complain of fatigue, insomnia, and restlessness and may have episodes of tearfulness and emotional lability. Later, suspiciousness, confusion, incoherence, irrational statements, and obsessive concerns about the baby's health and welfare may be present. Delusions may be present in 50 percent of all patients and hallucinations in about 25 percent. Complaints regarding the inability to move, stand, or walk are also common.

Patients may have feelings of not wanting to care for the baby, of not loving the baby, and, in some cases, of wanting to do harm to the baby or to themselves or both. Delusional material may involve the idea that the baby is dead or defective. Patients may deny the birth and express thoughts of being unmarried, virginal, persecuted, influenced, or perverse. Hallucinations with similar content may involve voices telling the patient to kill the baby.

Differential Diagnosis. As with any psychotic disorder, clinicians should consider the possibility of either a psychotic disorder due to a general medical condition or a substance-induced psychotic disorder. Potential general medical conditions include hypothyroidism and Cushing's syndrome. Substance-induced psychotic disorder may be associated with the use of pain medications such as pentazocine (Talwin) or of antihypertensive drugs during pregnancy. Other potential medical causes include infections, toxemia, and neoplasms.

Women with a history of a mood disorder should be classified as having a recurrence of the disorder. Postpartum psychosis should not be confused with the so-called postpartum blues, a normal condition that occurs in up to 50 percent of women after childbirth. Postpartum blues is self-limited, lasts only a few days, and is characterized by tearfulness, fatigue, anxiety, and irritability that begin shortly after childbirth and lessen in severity over the course of a week.

Course and Prognosis. The onset of florid psychotic symptoms is usually preceded by prodromal signs such as insomnia, restlessness, agitation, lability of mood, and mild cognitive deficits. Once the psychosis occurs, the patient may be a danger to herself or to her newborn, depending on the content of her delusional system and her degree of agitation. In one study, 5 percent of the patients committed suicide and 4 percent committed infanticide. A favorable outcome is associated with a good premorbid adjustment and a supportive family network.

Because an episode of postpartum psychosis is most likely an episode of a mood disorder, the course of the syndrome is similar to that seen in patients with mood disorders. Specifically, mood disorders are usually episodic disorders, and patients with postpartum psychosis often experience another episode of symptoms within a year or 2 of the birth. Subsequent pregnancies are associated with an increased risk of another episode.

Treatment. Postpartum psychosis is a psychiatric emergency. Antidepressants and lithium (Eskalith), sometimes in combination with an antipsychotic, are the treatments of choice. No pharmacological agents should be prescribed to a woman who is breast-feeding. Suicidal patients may require transfer to a psychiatric unit to help prevent a suicide attempt.

The mother is usually helped by contact with her baby if she so desires, but the visits must be closely supervised, especially if the mother is preoccupied with harming the infant. Psychotherapy is indicated after the period of acute psychosis, and therapy is usually directed at the conflictual areas that have become evident during the evaluation. Therapy may involve helping the patient accept and be at ease with the mothering role. Changes in environmental factors may also be indicated. Increased support from the husband and others in the environment may help reduce the woman's stress. Most studies report high rates of recovery from the acute illness.

ICD-10

The 10th revision of *International Statistical Classification of Diseases and Related Health Problems* (ICD-10) includes the same disorders that appear in DSM-IV, although the organization reflects a different approach. Under schizophrenia, schizotypal, and delusional disorders in ICD-10, the schizophreniform disorder of DSM is included in the diagnosis of schizophrenia, which is defined as having a duration of at least 1 month. Schizotypal disorder—a disorder with eccentric behavior and anomalies of thought and affect similar to those seen in schizophrenia, but without any defining schizophrenic anomalies—can be diagnosed when symptoms have been pres-

Table 14.1–8
ICD-10 Diagnostic Criteria for Delusional Disorders

Delusional disorder

A. A delusion or a set of related delusions, other than those listed as typically schizophrenic in criterion G1(1)b or d for paranoid, hebephrenic, or catatonic schizophrenia (ie, other than completely impossible or culturally inappropriate), must be present. The commonest examples are persecutory, grandiose, hypochondriacal, jealous (zelotypic), or erotic delusions.

B. The delusion(s) in criterion A must be present for at least 3 months.

C. The general criteria for schizophrenia are not fulfilled.

D. There must be no persistent hallucinations in any modality (but there may be transitory or occasional auditory hallucinations that are not in the third person or giving a running commentary).

E. Depressive symptoms (or even a depressive episode) may be present intermittently, provided that the delusions persist at times when there is no disturbance of mood.

F. *Most commonly used exclusion clause.* There must be no evidence of primary or secondary organic mental disorder as listed under organic, including symptomatic, mental disorders, or of a psychotic disorder due to psychoactive substance use.

Specification for possible subtypes

The following types may be specified if desired: persecutory; litiginous; self-referential; grandiose; hypochondriacal (somatic); jealous; erotomanic.

Other persistent delusional disorders

This is a residual category for persistent delusional disorders that do not meet the criteria for delusional disorder. Disorders in which delusions are accompanied by persistent hallucinatory voices or by schizophrenic symptoms that are insufficient to meet criteria for schizophrenia should be coded here. Delusional disorders that have lasted for less than 3 months should, however, be coded, at least temporarily, under acute and transient psychotic disorders.

Persistent delusional disorder, unspecified

Reprinted with permission from World Health Organization: *The ICD-10 Classification of Mental and Behavioural Disorders: Diagnostic Criteria for Research.* Copyright, World Health Organization, Geneva, 1993.

Table 14.1–9
ICD-10 Diagnostic Criteria for Acute and Transient Psychotic Disorders

G1. There is acute onset of delusions, hallucinations, incomprehensible or incoherent speech, or any combination of these. The time interval between the first appearance of any psychotic symptoms and the presentation of the fully developed disorder should not exceed 2 weeks.

G2. If transient states of perplexity, misidentification, or impairment of attention and concentration are present, they do not fulfill the criteria for organically caused clouding of consciousness as specified for delirium, not induced by alcohol and other psychoactive substances, criterion A.

G3. The disorder does not meet the symptomatic criteria for manic episode, depressive episode, or recurrent depressive disorder.

G4. There is insufficient evidence of recent psychoactive substance use to fulfill the criteria for intoxication, harmful use, dependence, or withdrawal states. The continued moderate and largely unchanged use of alcohol or drugs in amounts or with the frequency to which the individual is accustomed does not necessarily rule out the use of acute and transient psychotic disorders; this must be decided by clinical judgment and the requirements of the research project in question.

G5. *Most commonly used exclusion clause.* There must be no organic mental disorder or serious metabolic disturbances affecting the central nervous system (this does not include childbirth).

A fifth character should be used to specify whether the acute onset of the disorder is associated with acute stress (occurring 2 weeks or less before evidence of first psychotic symptoms):

Without associated acute stress

With associated acute stress

For research purposes, it is recommended that change of the disorder from a nonpsychotic to a clearly psychotic state is further specified as either abrupt (onset within 48 hours) or acute (onset in more than 48 hours but less than 2 weeks).

Acute polymorphic psychotic disorder without symptoms of schizophrenia

A. The general criteria for acute and transient psychotic disorders must be met.

B. Symptoms change rapidly in both type and intensity from day to day or within the same day.

C. Any type of either hallucinations or delusions occurs, for at least several hours, at any time from the onset of the disorder.

D. Symptoms from at least two of the following categories occur at the same time:
   (1) emotional turmoil, characterized by intense feelings of happiness or ecstasy, or overwhelming anxiety or marked irritability;
   (2) perplexity, or misidentification of people or places;
   (3) increased or decreased motility, to a marked degree.

E. If any of the symptoms listed for schizophrenia, criterion G(1) and (2), are present, they are present only for a minority of the time from the onset; ie, criterion B of acute polymorphic psychotic disorder with symptoms of schizophrenia is not fulfilled.

F. The total duration of the disorder does not exceed 3 months.

Acute polymorphic psychotic disorder with symptoms of schizophrenia

A. Criteria A, B, C, and D of acute polymorphic psychotic disorder must be met.

B. Some of the symptoms for schizophrenia must have been present for the majority of the time since the onset of the disorder, although the full criteria need not be met, ie, at least one of the symptoms in criteria G1(1)a to G1(2)c.

C. The symptoms of schizophrenia in criterion B above do not persist for more than 1 month.

Acute schizophrenia-like psychotic disorder

A. The general criteria for acute and transient psychotic disorders must be met.

B. The criteria for schizophrenia are met, with the exception of the criterion for duration.

C. The disorder does not meet criteria B, C, and D for acute polymorphic psychotic disorder.

D. The total duration of the disorder does not exceed 1 month.

Other acute predominantly delusional psychotic disorders

A. The general criteria for acute and transient psychotic disorders must be met.

B. Relatively stable delusions and/or hallucinations are present but do not fulfill the symptomatic criteria for schizophrenia.

C. The disorder does not meet the criteria for acute polymorphic psychotic disorder.

D. The total duration of the disorder does not exceed 3 months.

Other acute and transient psychotic disorders

Any other acute psychotic disorders that are not classifiable under any other category in acute and transient psychotic disorders (such as acute psychotic states in which definite delusions or hallucinations occur but persist for only small proportions of the time) should be coded here. States of undifferentiated excitement should also be coded here if more detailed information about the patient's mental state is not available, provided that there is no evidence of an organic cause.

Acute and transient psychotic disorder, unspecified

Table 14.1–10
ICD-10 Diagnostic Criteria for Schizoaffective Disorders

Note. This diagnosis depends upon an approximate "balance" between the number, severity, and duration of the schizophrenic and affective symptoms.

G1. The disorder meets the criteria for one of the affective disorders of moderate or severe degree, as specified for each category.

G2. Symptoms from at least one of the groups listed below must be clearly present for most of the time during a period of at least 2 weeks (these groups are almost the same as for schizophrenia):

(1) thought echo, thought insertion or withdrawal, thought broadcasting (criterion G1(1)a for paranoid, hebephrenic, or catatonic schizophrenia);

(2) delusions of control, influence, or passivity, clearly referred to body or limb movements or specific thoughts, actions, or sensations (criterion G1(1)b for paranoid, hebephrenic, or catatonic schizophrenia);

(3) hallucinatory voices giving a running commentary on the patient's behavior or discussing the patient among themselves, or other types of hallucinatory voices coming from some part of the body (criterion G1(1)c for paranoid, hebephrenic, or catatonic schizophrenia);

(4) persistent delusions of other kinds that are culturally inappropriate and completely impossible, but not merely grandiose or persecutory (criterion G1(1)d for paranoid, hebephrenic, or catatonic schizophrenia), eg, has visited other worlds; can control the clouds by breathing in and out; can communicate with plants or animals without speaking;

(5) grossly irrelevant or incoherent speech, or frequent use of neologisms (a marked form of criterion G1(2)b for paranoid, hebephrenic, or catatonic schizophrenia);

(6) intermittent but frequent appearance of some forms of catatonic behavior, such as posturing, waxy flexibility, and negativism (criterion G1(2)c for paranoid, hebephrenic, or catatonic schizophrenia).

G3. Criteria G1 and G2 above must be met within the same episode of the disorder, and concurrently for at least part of the episode. Symptoms from both G1 and G2 must be prominent in the clinical picture.

G4. *Most commonly used exclusion clause.* The disorder is not attributable to organic mental disorder, or to psychoactive substance-related intoxication, dependence, or withdrawal.

Schizoaffective disorder, manic type

A. The general criteria for schizoaffective disorder must be met.

B. Criteria for a manic disorder must be met.

Other schizoaffective disorders

Schizoaffective disorder, unspecified

Comments

If desired, further subtypes of schizoaffective disorder may be specified, according to the longitudinal development of the disorder, as follows:

Concurrent affective and schizophrenic symptoms only
Symptoms as defined in criterion G2 for schizoaffective disorders.

Concurrent affective and schizophrenic symptoms beyond the duration of affective symptoms

Reprinted with permission from World Health Organization: *The ICD-10 Classification of Mental and Behavioural Disorders: Diagnostic Criteria for Research.* Copyright, World Health Organization, Geneva, 1993.

Table 14.1–11
ICD-10 Diagnostic Criteria for Induced Delusional Disorder

A. The individual(s) must develop a delusion or delusional system originally held by someone else with a disorder classified in schizophrenia, schizotypal disorder, persistent delusional disorder, or acute and transient psychotic disorders.

B. The people concerned must have an unusually close relationship with one another, and be relatively isolated from other people.

C. The individual(s) must not have held the belief in question before contact with the other person, and must not have suffered from any other disorder classified in schizophrenia, schizotypal disorder, persistent delusional disorder, or acute and transient psychotic disorders in the past.

Reprinted with permission from World Health Organization: *The ICD-10 Classification of Mental and Behavioural Disorders: Diagnostic Criteria for Research.* Copyright, World Health Organization, Geneva, 1993.

ent for at least 2 years. The disorder occasionally develops into schizophrenia and may be "part of the genetic 'spectrum' of schizophrenia." Because the hallucinations and other behavioral disturbances of schizophrenia are absent, the "disorder does not always come to medical attention." DSM-IV classifies this disorder under the section on personality disorders because of the absence of delusions and hallucinations rather than within the section on schizophrenia and other psychotic disorders. This diagnosis perhaps illustrates the tendency to overlook the exact nature of the disorder, as noted in ICD-10.

According to ICD-10, most delusional disorders are "probably unrelated to schizophrenia, although they may be difficult to distinguish clinically, particularly in their early stages." In ICD-10, these disorders are grouped on the basis of duration into persistent delusional disorders (Table 14.1–8) and acute and transient psychotic disorders (Table 14.1–9), equivalent to the delusional and brief psychotic disorders of DSM-IV. Schizoaffective disorders (Table 14.1–10), which ICD-10 considers controversial, are nevertheless included in the section on schizotypal and delusional disorders. Organic catatonic disorder and psychotic disorder due to a medical condition are classified

Table 14.1–12
ICD-10 Diagnostic Criteria for Other Nonorganic Psychotic Disorders

Psychotic disorders that do not meet the criteria for schizophrenia or for psychotic types of mood (affective) disorders, and psychotic disorders that do not meet the symptomatic criteria for persistent delusional disorder should be coded here (persistent hallucinatory disorder is an example). Combinations of symptoms not covered by the previous categories, such as delusions other than those listed as typically schizophrenic under criterion G1(1)b or d for schizophrenia (ie, other than completely impossible or culturally inappropriate) plus catatonia, should also be included here.

Reprinted with permission from World Health Organization: *The ICD-10 Classification of Mental and Behavioural Disorders: Diagnostic Criteria for Research.* Copyright, World Health Organization, Geneva, 1993.

under the organic mental disorders; psychotic disorder caused by substance use appears under disorders due to psychoactive substance use in ICD-10; and postschizophrenic depression and simple schizophrenia appear as categories of schizophrenia. Induced delusional disorder (Table 14.1–11), equivalent to shared psychotic disorder in DSM-IV, is a category of schizotypal and delusional disorders, but postpartum depression is treated separately, under behavioral syndromes. ICD-10 also includes two residual categories, other nonorganic psychotic disorders (Table 14.1–12) and unspecified nonorganic psychosis. According to ICD-10, the subdivisions of schizophrenia, schizotypal, and delusional disorders are provisional.

References

Anis-ur-Rehman, St Clair D, Platz C: Puerperal insanity in the 19th and 20th centuries. Br J Psychiatry *156:* 861, 1990.

Bandelow B, Müller P, Frick U, Gaebel W, Linden M, Müller-Spahn F, Pietzcker A, Tegeler J: Depressive syndromes in schizophrenic patients under neuroleptic therapy. Eur Arch Psychiatry Clin Neurosci *241:* 291, 1992.

Cox JL, Murray D, Chapman C: A controlled study of the onset, duration, and prevalence of postnatal depression. Br J Psychiatry *163:* 27, 1993.

Dippel B, Kemper J, Berger M: Folie à six: A case report on induced psychotic disorder. Acta Psychiatr Scand *83:* 137, 1991.

Enoch MD, Trethowan W: *Uncommon Psychiatric Syndromes,* ed 3. Butterworth-Heinemann, Oxford, 1991.

Glover V, Liddle P, Taylor A, Adams D, Sandler M: Mild hypomania (the highs) can be a feature of the first postpartum week—association with later depression. Br J Psychiatry *164:* 517, 1994.

McClellan JM, Werry JS, Ham M: A follow-up study of early onset psychosis: Comparison between outcome diagnoses of schizophrenia, mood disorders, and personality disorders. J Autism Dev Disord *23:* 243, 1993.

Popkin MK, Tucker GJ: ''Secondary'' and drug-induced mood, anxiety psychotic, catatonic, and personality disorders: A review of the literature. J Neuropsychiatry Clin Neurosci *4:* 369, 1992.

Siris SG: Diagnosis of secondary depression in schizophrenia: Implications for DSM-IV. Schizophr Bull *17:* 75, 1991.

Wisner KL, Peindl K, Hanusa BH: Symptomatology of affective and psychotic illnesses related to childbearing. J Affect Disord *30:* 77, 1994.

▲ 14.2 Schizophreniform Disorder

Schizophreniform disorder is identical to schizophrenia except that its symptoms last at least 1 month but less than 6 months. Patients with schizophreniform disorder return to their baseline level of functioning once the disorder has resolved. In contrast, for a patient to meet the diagnostic criteria for schizophrenia, the symptoms must have been present for at least 6 months.

HISTORY

The term *schizophreniform* was coined in 1939 by Gabriel Langfeldt, working at the University Psychiatric Clinic in Oslo. Langfeldt emphasized that schizophreniform psychosis defined a heterogeneous group of patients characterized only by the similarity of their symptoms to those of schizophrenia and a good clinical outcome. Before Langfeldt's arrival at the clinic, patients with schizophrenia had been classified as having either typical schizophrenia or schizophrenia (?? . . .), in which the number of question marks was a semiofficial method of denoting the questionableness of the diagnosis. Using sound scientific methods, Langfeldt studied a group of typical schizophrenic patients and a group of schizophrenic (?) patients and concluded that a group of patients with schizophrenic symptoms had a good outcome. He classified this group as having schizophreniform disorder. Langfeldt noted that these patients often had good premorbid adjustment, an abrupt onset of symptoms, the frequent presence of a psychosocial stressor, and a good prognosis.

EPIDEMIOLOGY

Little is known about the incidence, prevalence, and sex ratio of schizophreniform disorder. Some clinicians have the impression that the disorder is most common in adolescents and young adults, and most investigators believe that the disorder is less than half as common as schizophrenia. A lifetime prevalence rate of 0.2 percent and a 1-year prevalence rate of 0.1 percent have been reported.

Family History

Several studies have shown that the relatives of patients with schizophreniform disorder are at high risk of having psychiatric disorders but that the distribution of the disorders differs from the distribution seen in the relatives of patients with schizophrenia and bipolar disorders. Specifically, the relatives of patients with schizophreniform disorders are more likely to have mood disorders than are the relatives of patients with schizophrenia. In addition, the relatives of patients with schizophreniform disorder are more likely to have a diagnosis of a psychotic mood disorder than are the relatives of patients with bipolar disorders.

ETIOLOGY

As in all the classic psychotic disorders, the cause of schizophreniform disorder is not known. As Langfeldt noted in 1939, the group of patients with the diagnostic label are likely to be heterogeneous. In general, some patients have a disorder similar to schizophrenia, whereas others have a disorder similar to a mood disorder. Because of the generally good outcome, the disorder probably has similarities to the episodic nature of mood disorders. Some data, however, indicate a close relation to schizophrenia.

In support of the relation to mood disorders, several studies have shown that patients with schizophreniform disorder, as a group, have more affective symptoms (especially mania) and a better outcome than do patients with schizophrenia. Also, the increased presence of mood disorders in the relatives of patients with schizophreniform disorder indicates a relation to mood disorders. Thus, the biological and epidemiological data are most consistent with the hypothesis that the current diagnostic category defines a group of patients, some of whom have a disorder similar to schizophrenia and others of whom have a disorder similar to a mood disorder.

Brain Imaging

As has been reported for schizophrenia, a relative activation deficit in the inferior prefrontal region of the brain while the patient is performing a region-specific psychological task (the Wisconsin Card Sorting Test) has been reported in patients with schizophreniform disorder (Fig. 14.2–1). One study showed that the deficit was limited to the left hemisphere and also found impaired striatal activity suppression, also limited to the left hemisphere, during the activation procedure. The data can be interpreted to indicate a physiological similarity between the psychosis of schizophrenia and the psychosis of schizophreniform disorder. Additional central nervous system (CNS) factors, as yet unidentified, may lead to either the long-term course of schizophrenia or the foreshortened course of schizophreniform disorder.

Although some data indicate that patients with schizophreniform disorder may have enlarged cerebral ventricles, as determined by computed tomography and magnetic resonance imaging, other data indicate that, unlike the enlargement seen in schizophrenia, the ventricular enlargement in schizophreniform disorder is not correlated with outcome measures or other biological measures.

Other Biological Measures

Although brain imaging studies point to a similarity between schizophreniform disorder and schizophrenia, at least

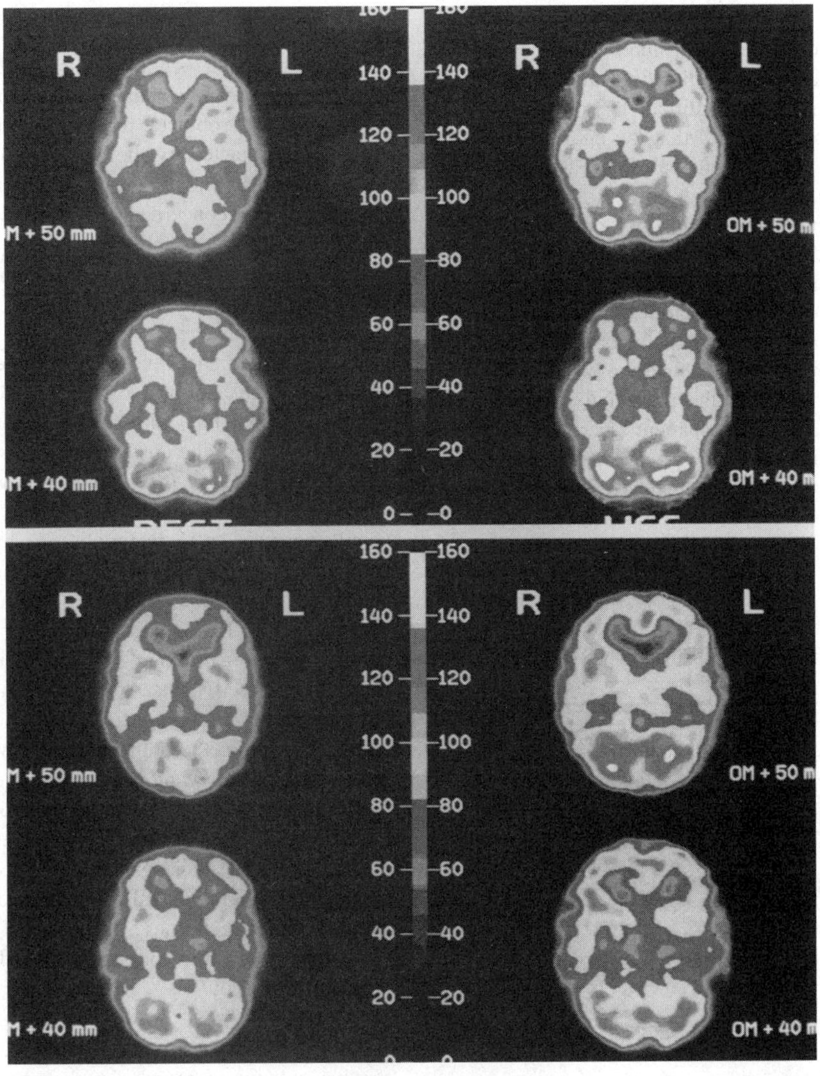
R
L
R
L
R
L
R
L
OM + 50 mm
OM + 40 mm

FIGURE 14.2–1

Regional cerebral blood flow distribution at rest *(left)* and during cerebral activation with the Wisconsin Card Sorting Test *(right)* in a patient with schizophreniform disorder **(top)** and a healthy volunteer **(bottom).** *OM* indicates orbitomeatal line. (Reprinted with permission from Rubin P, Holm S, Friberg L, Videbech P, Andersen HS, Bendsen BB, Strømsø N, Larsen JK, Lassen NA, Hemmingsen R: Altered modulation of prefrontal and subcortical brain activity in newly diagnosed schizophrenia and schizophreniform disorder. Arch Gen Psychiatry *48:* 992, 1991.)

one study of electrodermal activity has indicated a difference. Patients with schizophrenia born during the winter and spring months (a period of high risk for the birth of these patients) had hyporesponsive skin conductances, but this association was absent in patients with schizophreniform disorder. The significance and the meaning of this single study are difficult to interpret, but the results do suggest caution in assuming similarity between patients with schizophrenia and those with schizophreniform disorder. Data from at least one study of eye tracking in the two groups also indicate that they may differ in some biological measures.

DIAGNOSIS

The diagnostic criteria for schizophreniform disorder in the fourth edition of *Diagnostic and Statistical Manual of Mental Disorders* (DSM-IV) (Table 14.2–1) include three criteria identical to those for schizophrenia. The first criterion is the presence of active symptoms (such as delusions, hallucinations, and flat affects) for 1 month. The next two are exclusion criteria for schizoaffective disorder, mood disorder with psychotic features, substance-related disorders, and mental disorders due to a general medical condition. The other criteria for schizophreniform disorder specify that the entire episode, including the prodromal and residual phases, last at least 1 month but less than 6 months.

The diagnosis of provisional schizophreniform disorder is made while the clinician waits for the symptoms to resolve. When the clinician cannot obtain a reliable history from a patient about the duration of the symptoms, a diagnosis of schizophreniform disorder is more accurate than a diagnosis of schizophrenia. A patient's personal history of prodromal symptoms, however, may misdirect the physician from a correct diagnosis of schizophrenia, and a patient's personal history of affective symptoms may cause the physician to miss a diagnosis of a mood disorder or schizoaffective disorder.

Table 14.2–1
DSM-IV Diagnostic Criteria for Schizophreniform Disorder

A. Criteria A, D, and E of schizophrenia are met.

B. An episode of the disorder (including prodromal, active, and residual phases) lasts at least 1 month but less than 6 months. (When the diagnosis must be made without waiting for recovery, it should be qualified as "provisional.")

Specify if:

Without good prognostic features

With good prognostic features as evidenced by two (or more) of the following:

(1) onset of prominent psychotic symptoms within 4 weeks of the first noticeable change in usual behavior or functioning
(2) confusion or perplexity at the height of the psychotic episode
(3) good premorbid social and occupational functioning
(4) absence of blunted or flat affect

Reprinted with permission from American Psychiatric Association: *Diagnostic and Statistical Manual of Mental Disorders,* ed 4. Copyright, American Psychiatric Association, Washington, 1994.

Prognostic Subtypes

DSM-IV allows for specifying the presence or absence of good prognostic features (Table 14.2–1). These features include a rapid onset, a degree of cognitive impairment, good premorbid adjustment, and the absence of deficit affective symptoms. One study found that schizophreniform disorder patients with poor prognoses exhibit affective flattening, alogia (inability to speak), and poor eye contact with examiners.

CLINICAL FEATURES

The clinical signs and symptoms and the mental status examination for a patient with schizophreniform disorder are identical to those for a patient with schizophrenia, but the presence of affective symptoms may predict a favorable course. Alternatively, a flat or blunted affect may predict an unfavorable course.

A 35-year-old, single, unemployed, college-educated, African American woman, Ms. Fielding, was escorted to the emergency room by the mobile crisis team. The team had been contacted by the patient's sister after she failed to persuade Ms. Fielding to visit an outpatient psychiatrist. Her sister was concerned about the patient's increasingly erratic work patterns and, more recently, her bizarre behavior since the death of their father 2 years ago. The patient's only prior psychiatric contact had been brief psychotherapy in college.

The patient had not worked since losing her job 3 months ago. According to her boyfriend and roommate (both of whom live with her), she had become intensely preoccupied with the upstairs neighbors. A few days earlier she had banged on their front door with an iron for no apparent reason. She told the mobile crisis unit that the family upstairs was harassing her by "accessing" her thoughts and then repeating them to her. The crisis team brought her to the emergency room for evaluation of "thought broadcasting." Though she denied having any trouble with her thinking, she conceded that she had been feeling "stressed" since losing her job and might benefit from more psychotherapy.

After reading the admission note, which described the patient's bizarre symptoms, the emergency room psychiatrists were surprised to encounter a poised, relaxed, and attractive young woman, stylishly dressed and appearing perfectly normal. She greeted them with a courteous, if somewhat superficial, smile. She related to the doctors with nonchalant respectfulness. When asked why she was there, she ventured a timid shrug and replied, "I was hoping to find out from you!"

Ms. Fielding had been working as a secretary and attributed her job loss to the sluggish economy. She denied having any recent mood disturbance and answered no to questions about psychotic symptoms, punctuating each query with a polite but incredulous laugh. Wondering if perhaps the crisis team's assessment was of a different patient, the interviewer asked, somewhat apologetically, if the patient ever wondered whether people could read her mind. She replied, "Oh yes, it happens all the time," and described how, on one occasion, she was standing in her kitchen planning dinner in silence, only to hear, moments later, voices of people on the street below reciting the entire menu. She was convinced of the reality of the experience, having verified it by looking out the window and observing them speaking her thoughts aloud.

The patient was distressed not so much by people "accessing" her thoughts as by her inability to exercise control over the process. She believed that most people developed telepathic powers in childhood and that she was a "late bloomer" who had just become aware of her abilities and was currently overwhelmed by them. Although she had begun having telepathic experiences 2 years ago, they had become almost constant in the 3 months since losing her job. She was troubled most by her upstairs neighbors, who would not only repeat her thoughts but would bombard her with their own devaluing and critical comments, such as "You're no good!" and "You have to leave." They had begun to intrude upon her mercilessly, at all hours of the night and day.

She was convinced that the only solution was for the family to move away. When asked if she had contemplated other possibilities, she reluctantly admitted she had spoken to her boyfriend about hiring a hit man to "threaten" or, if need be, "eliminate" the couple. She hoped she would be able to spare their two children, whom she felt were not involved in this invasion of her "mental boundaries." This concern for the children was the only insight she demonstrated into the gravity of her symptoms. She did agree, however, to admit herself voluntarily to the hospital.

DISCUSSION

It is extremely unusual for patients with bizarre delusions, such as Ms. Fielding's delusion that her thoughts were "accessed" by others, to appear otherwise perfectly normal. Nevertheless, the presence of bizarre delusions, hallucinations, and social and occupational impairment for at least 1 month, but less than 6 months, in the absence of a mood disorder, substance, or general medical condition that could account for the disturbance, justifies a diagnosis of schizophreniform disorder. Her good premorbid functioning and the absence of blunted or flat affect indicate the further specification of "with good prognostic features." When the diagnosis is made without waiting for recovery, as in this case, it is further qualified as "provisional," because if continuous signs of the disturbance persist for at least 6 months, the diagnosis would change to that of schizophrenia.

FOLLOW-UP

Once admitted to the hospital, Ms. Fielding immediately began pressing for discharge and disavowed her previous symptoms. Her behavior, thinking, and affect seemed otherwise normal. After 2 weeks of observation, she was discharged to her treating physician's clinic. Within a month, however, she again admitted having frightening experiences of hearing voices and of reading other people's thoughts, as well as a general inability to plan for finding work. She agreed to try medication.

She was treated with an antipsychotic drug, and her frightening hallucinations, as well as the belief that she was clairvoyant, remitted. Within 3 months following discharge, she had obtained work with a temporary employment agency. Soon afterward, feeling completely well, she stopped attending the clinic and was lost to follow-up.

Although the total duration of the illness approaches 6 months, we would give her the benefit of the doubt and retain the diagnosis of schizophreniform disorder. (From *DSM-IV Casebook.*)

DIFFERENTIAL DIAGNOSIS

The differential diagnosis for schizophreniform disorder is identical to that for schizophrenia. Factitious disorder with predominantly psychological signs and symptoms, psychotic disorder caused by a general medical condition, and substance-induced psychotic disorder must be ruled out. One general medical condition to be considered is infection with human immunodeficiency virus. Temporal lobe epilepsy, CNS tumors, and cerebrovascular diseases can also be associated with relatively short-lived psychotic episodes. The increasing frequency of reports of psychosis associated with the use of anabolic steroids by young men who are attempting to build up their musculature to perform better in athletic endeavors should also be noted.

COURSE AND PROGNOSIS

The prognosis of schizophreniform disorder varies, a fact that is addressed in DSM-IV by distinguishing patients with and without good prognostic features. The good prognostic features noted in DSM-IV have been gathered from literature sources, but the validity of these features has been questioned. Confusion or perplexity at the height of the psychotic episode is the feature best correlated with a good outcome. The validity of the other features remains uncertain.

In addition to the predictors of a good prognosis in DSM-IV, the shorter the period of illness, the better the prognosis is likely to be. There is a significant risk of suicide in patients with schizophreniform disorder. They are likely to have a period of depression after the psychotic period, and psychotherapy addressed to helping the patient understand the psychotic episode is likely to improve the prognosis and speed the patient's recovery.

By definition, schizophreniform disorder resolves within 6 months with a return to baseline mental functioning. Studies have indicated that the requirement for at least 6 months of symptoms in schizophrenia weighs heavily toward a poor prognosis; therefore, patients with schizophreniform disorder have a better prognosis than do most patients with schizophrenia.

TREATMENT

Hospitalization is often necessary in treating patients with schizophreniform disorder and allows for an effective assessment, treatment, and supervision of a patient's behavior. The psychotic symptoms can usually be treated by a 3- to 6-month course of antipsychotic drugs (for example, risperidone [Risperdal]). Several studies have shown that patients with schizophreniform disorder respond much more rapidly to antipsychotic treatment than do patients with schizophrenia. One study found that about 75 percent of patients with schizophreniform disorder, compared with only 20 percent of the patients with schizophrenia, responded to antipsychotic medications within 8 days. Electroconvulsive therapy may be indicated for some patients, especially those with marked catatonic or depressed features. A trial of lithium (Eskalith), carbamazepine (Tegretol), or valproate (Depakene) may be warranted for treatment and prophylaxis if a patient has a recurrent episode. Psychotherapy is usually necessary to help patients integrate the psychotic experience into their understanding of their minds, brains, and lives.

References

Bergem ALM, Dahl AA, Guldberg C, Hansen H: Langfeldt's schizophreniform psychoses fifty years later. Br J Psychiatry *157:* 351, 1990.

Coryell WH, Tsuang MT: DSM-III schizophreniform disorder: Comparisons with schizophrenia and affective disorder. Arch Gen Psychiatry *39:* 66, 1982.

Cuesta MJ, Peralta V: Does formal thought disorder differ among patients with schizophrenic, schizophreniform and manic schizoaffective disorders? Schizophr Res *10:* 151, 1993.

Guldberg CA, Dahl AA, Hansen H, Bergem M: Predictive value of the four prognostic features in DSM-III-R schizophreniform disorder. Acta Psychiatr Scand *82:* 23, 1990.

Iacono WG, Moreau M, Beiser M, Fleming JA, Lin TY: Smooth-pursuit eye tracking in first-episode psychotic patients and their relatives. J Abnorm Psychol *101:* 104, 1992.

Katsanis J, Ficken J, Iacono WG, Beiser M: Season of birth and electrodermal activity in functional psychoses. Biol Psychiatry *31:* 841, 1992.

Katsanis J, Iacono WG, Beiser M: Relationship of lateral ventricular size to psychophysiological measures and short-term outcome. Psychiatry Res *37:* 115, 1991.

Marengo JT, Harrow M, Westermeyer JF: Early longitudinal course of acute-chronic and paranoid-undifferentiated schizophrenia subtypes and schizophreniform disorder. J Abnorm Psychol *100:* 600, 1991.

McDermott BE, Sautter FJ, Garver DL: Heterogeneity of schizophrenia: Relationship to latency of neuroleptic response. Psychiatry Res *37:* 97, 1991.

Pulver AE, Brown CH, Wolyniec PS, McGrath JA, Tam D: Psychiatric morbidity in the relatives of patients with DSM-III schizophreniform disorder: Comparisons with the relatives of schizophrenic and bipolar disorder patients. J Psychiatr Res *25:* 19, 1991.

Rao ML, Gross G, Halaris A, Huber G, Marler M, Strebel B, Braunig P: Hyperdopaminergia in schizophreniform psychosis: A chronobiological study. Psychiatry Res *47:* 187, 1993.

Rubin P, Holm S, Friberg L, Videbech P, Andersen HS, Bendsen BB, Strømsø N, Larsen JK, Lassen NA, Hemmingsen R: Altered modulation of prefrontal and subcortical brain activity in newly diagnosed schizophrenia and schizophreniform disorder: A regional cerebral blood flow study. Arch Gen Psychiatry *48:* 987, 1991.

Sautter F, McDermott B, Garver D: The course of DSM-III-R schizophreniform disorder. J Clin Psychol *49:* 339, 1993.

Siris SG, Lavin MR: Schizoaffective disorder, schizophreniform disorder, and brief psychotic disorder. In *Comprehensive Textbook of Psychiatry,* ed 6, HI Kaplan, BJ Sadock, editors, p 1019. Williams & Wilkins, Baltimore, 1995.

Troisi A, Pasini A, Bersani G, Mauro M, Ciani N: Negative symptoms and visual behavior in DSM-III-R prognostic subtypes of schizophreniform disorder. Acta Psychiatr Scand *83:* 391, 1991.

▲ 14.3 Schizoaffective Disorder

As the term implies, schizoaffective disorder has features of both schizophrenia and affective disorders (now called mood disorders). The diagnostic criteria for schizoaffective disorder have changed over time, mostly as a reflection of changes in the diagnostic criteria for schizophrenia and the mood disorders. Regardless of the mutable nature of the diagnosis, it remains the best diagnosis for patients whose clinical syndrome would be distorted if it were considered as only schizophrenia or only a mood disorder.

HISTORY

George H. Kirby, in 1913, and August Hoch, in 1921, both described patients with mixed features of schizophrenia and affective (mood) disorders. Because their patients did not have the deteriorating course of dementia precox, Kirby and Hoch classified them in Emil Kraepelin's manic-depressive psychosis group.

In 1933, Jacob Kasanin introduced the term *schizoaffective disorder* to refer to a disorder with symptoms of both schizophrenia and mood disorders. In patients with the disorder, the onset of symptoms was sudden and often occurred in adolescence. The patients tended to have a good premorbid level of functioning, and often a specific stressor preceded the onset of symptoms. The family histories of the patients often included a mood disorder. Because Eugen Bleuler's broad concept of schizophrenia had eclipsed Kraepelin's narrow concept, Kasanin believed that the patients had a type of schizophrenia. From 1933 to about 1970, patients whose symptoms were similar to those of Kasanin's patients were variously classified as having schizoaffective disorder, atypical schizophrenia, good prognosis schizophrenia, remitting schizophrenia, and cycloid psychosis—terms that emphasized a relation to schizophrenia.

Around 1970, two sets of data shifted the view of schizoaffective disorder from that of a schizophrenic illness to that of a mood disorder. First, lithium carbonate (Eskalith) was shown to be an effective and specific treatment for both bipolar disorders and some cases of schizoaffective disorder. Second, the United States–United Kingdom study published in 1968 by John Cooper and his colleagues showed that the variation in the number of patients classified as schizophrenic in the United States and in the United Kingdom was the result of an overemphasis in the United States on the presence of psychotic symptoms as a diagnostic criterion for schizophrenia.

EPIDEMIOLOGY

The lifetime prevalence of schizoaffective disorder is less than 1 percent, possibly in the range of 0.5 to 0.8 percent. These figures, however, are estimates; various studies of schizoaffective disorder have used varying diagnostic criteria. In clinical practice, a preliminary diagnosis of schizoaffective disorder is frequently used when a clinician is uncertain of the diagnosis.

Gender and Age Differences

The literature describing gender and age differences among patients with schizoaffective disorder is limited, but some preliminary observations may eventually be replicated in studies. The depressive type of schizoaffective disorder may be more common in older people than in younger people, and the bipolar type may be more common in young adults than in older adults. The prevalence of the disorder has been reported to be lower in men than in women, particularly married women; the age of onset for women is later than the age for men, as in schizophrenia. Men with schizoaffective disorder are likely to exhibit antisocial behavior and to have marked flatness or inappropriateness of affect.

ETIOLOGY

The cause of schizoaffective disorder is unknown, but four conceptual models have been advanced. Schizoaffective disorder may be either a type of schizophrenia or a type of mood disorder. Schizoaffective disorder may be the simultaneous expression of schizophrenia and a mood disorder. Schizoaffective disorder may be a distinct third type of psychosis, one that is not related to either schizophrenia or a mood disorder. The most likely possibility is that schizoaffective disorder is a heterogenous group of disorders encompassing all the first three possibilities.

Studies designed to explore these possibilities have examined family histories, biological markers, short-term treatment responses, and long-term outcomes. Most studies have considered patients with schizoaffective disorder as a homogeneous group, but recent studies have examined the bipolar and depressive types of schizoaffective disorder separately.

Although much of the family and genetic research in schizoaffective disorder is based on the premise that schizophrenia and the mood disorders are completely separate entities, some data indicate that they may be genetically related. Some confusion arising in the family studies of schizoaffective disorder patients may reflect the nonabsolute distinction between the two primary disorders. Not surprisingly, therefore, studies of the relatives of patients with schizoaffective disorder have reported inconsistent results. An increased prevalence of schizophrenia is not found among the relatives of probands with schizoaffective disorder, bipolar type; the relatives of patients with schizoaffective disorder, depressive type, however, may be at higher risk for schizophrenia than for a mood disorder.

Depending on the type of schizoaffective disorder studied, an increased prevalence of schizophrenia or mood disorders may be found in the relatives of schizoaffective disorder probands. The possibility that schizoaffective disorder is distinct from schizophrenia and mood disorders is not supported by the observation that only a small percentage of the relatives of schizoaffective disorder probands have schizoaffective disorder.

As a group, patients with schizoaffective disorder have a better prognosis than do patients with schizophrenia and a worse prognosis than do patients with mood disorders. As a group, patients with schizoaffective disorder respond to lithium and tend to have a nondeteriorating course.

Consolidation of Data

A reasonable conclusion from the available data is that patients with schizoaffective disorder are a heterogeneous group: some have schizophrenia with prominent affective symptoms, others have a mood disorder with prominent schizophrenic symptoms, and still others have a distinct clinical syndrome. The hypothesis that schizoaffective disorder patients have both schizophrenia and a mood disorder is untenable, because the calculated co-occurrence of the two disorders is much lower than is the incidence of schizoaffective disorder.

DIAGNOSIS

Because the concept of schizoaffective disorder involves the diagnostic concepts of both schizophrenia and the mood disorders, the evolution in the diagnostic criteria for schizoaffective disorder partly reflects the changes that have occurred in the diagnostic criteria for the other two conditions. According to the primary diagnostic criterion for schizoaffective disorder in the fourth edition of *Diagnostic and Statistical Manual of Mental Disorders* (DSM-IV) (Table 14.3–1), the patient must meet the diagnostic criteria for a major depressive episode or a manic episode concurrently with meeting the diagnostic criteria for the active phase of schizophrenia. In addition, the patient must have had delusions or hallucinations for at least 2 weeks in the absence of prominent mood disorder symptoms. The mood disorder symptoms must also be present for a substantial part of the active and residual psychotic periods. Essentially, the criteria are written to help clinicians avoid diagnosing a mood disorder with psychotic features as schizoaffective disorder. DSM-IV also allows clinicians to specify whether the patient had schizoaffective disorder, bipolar type, or schizoaffective disorder, depressive type. A patient is classified as having the bipolar type if the condition includes a manic mixed episode (with or without major depressive episodes). Otherwise, the patient is classified as having a depressive type.

CLINICAL FEATURES

The clinical signs and symptoms of schizoaffective disorder include all the signs and symptoms of schizophrenia, manic

Table 14.3–1
DSM-IV Diagnostic Criteria for Schizoaffective Disorder

A. An uninterrupted period of illness during which, at some time, there is either a major depressive episode, a manic episode, or a mixed episode concurrent with symptoms that meet criterion A for schizophrenia.

Note: The major depressive episode must include criterion A1: depressed mood.

B. During the same period of illness, there have been delusions or hallucinations for at least 2 weeks in the absence of prominent mood symptoms.

C. Symptoms that meet criteria for a mood episode are present for a substantial portion of the total duration of the active and residual periods of the illness.

D. The disturbance is not due to the direct physiological effects of a substance (eg, a drug of abuse, a medication) or a general medical condition.

Specify if:

Bipolar type: if the disturbance includes a manic or a mixed episode (or a manic or a mixed episode and major depressive episodes)

Depressive type: if the disturbance only includes major depressive episodes

episodes, and depressive disorders. The schizophrenic and mood disorder symptoms can appear together or in an alternating fashion. The course can vary from one of exacerbations and remissions to one of a long-term deteriorating course.

Many researchers and clinicians have speculated about the mood-incongruent psychotic features; the psychotic content (hallucinations or delusions) is not consistent with the prevailing mood. In general, the presence of mood-incongruent psychotic features in a mood disorder is likely to indicate a poor prognosis. This association is likely to be true for schizoaffective disorder as well, although the data are limited.

Ms. R. E., an unmarried woman with the bipolar type of schizoaffective disorder, was first hospitalized in 1972 when she was 26 years old. She was taken to the hospital emergency room by the local police, who found her in a city park wearing only the bottom part of a bikini bathing suit. She told the police that she was out looking for men and that thousands of men wished to date her. She was a university graduate student with no prior psychiatric history.

When examined, her mood alternated between euphoria and irritability, depending on the degree of frustration she experienced. She was unable to sit still. Although now fully clothed, she remained seductive and suggested that she possessed an unusual sexual capability. She exhibited flight of ideas and was vague, circumstantial, and delusional. A Protestant herself, she was preoccupied with the historical persecution of Jews and wished to convert to Judaism.

The diagnosis of schizophrenia, schizoaffective type, was made according to the diagnostic practice prevalent at that time. She was given a combination of trifluoperazine (Stelazine) and lithium and responded within a few weeks.

Her course over the ensuing 15 years has been marked by several recurrences, either primarily manic or depressive in nature. These have always been associated with some disorder of thinking and some mood-incongruent delusions.

Although she has generally done well and is free of either affective or schizophrenic symptoms between episodes, she has some persistent deficits. She has clearly not lived up to the potential of someone with an advanced degree (Ph.D.) from a major university. She has had difficulty breaking away from home and establishing an independent existence. She has almost always held a job, although never for more than a few years at a time, and her jobs have not tapped her considerable intellectual resources. Finally, she has never formed a very close heterosexual relationship.

She has no known family history of major mental illness. The patient's father was a merchant marine ship officer who was most likely alcoholic. (Courtesy of Samuel G. Siris, M.D., and Michael R. Lavin, M.D.)

Mr. H. L., a 36-year-old man with the depressive type of schizoaffective disorder, has a 15-year history of psychiatric illness. He has been married for 5 years and has two children. His current presentation to an outpatient clinic was the result of depressive ideation concerning his inadequacies as a husband and provider. Mr. H. L. is the only child of Eastern European immigrant parents who built an impressive financial empire, but he has not been able to keep a job on his own, despite having a college degree. He is employed in a largely ceremonial job, with a large salary, in the family business. He is distinctly aware of the superficial nature of his duties, which is a substantial blow to his self-esteem.

Mr. H. L. has been hospitalized 6 times during the past 15 years with a relatively consistent history of depressive ideation, motor retardation, insomnia, and appetite and weight loss. He also engages in considerable ruminative, and often circumstantial, thinking. Mood-incongruent delusions are also present. For example, he was convinced during his last admission that certain colors had special and unique meaning for him and that they indicated certain actions that should be taken by the family business. He was unable to be more specific.

Mr. H. L. has been given a wide variety of medications, including tricyclic antidepressants, antipsychotic drugs, and lithium. He usually receives tricyclic antidepressants during the acute episodes, which require hospitalization. Between episodes, he has done best when given low to moderate dosages of high-potency antipsychotic medication, usually haloperidol (Haldol) or fluphenazine (Prolixin). When his dosage was lowered, his depressive and mood-incongruent psychotic symptoms returned. Mr. H. L. has no known family history of major mental illness. The patient's father died at age 64 and had been given the diagnosis of Alzheimer's disease. (Courtesy of Samuel G. Siris, M.D., and Michael R. Lavin, M.D.)

DIFFERENTIAL DIAGNOSIS

All the conditions listed in the differential diagnoses of schizophrenia and mood disorders should be considered in the differential diagnosis of schizoaffective disorder. Patients undergoing treatment with steroids, abusers of amphetamine and phencyclidine (PCP), and some patients with temporal lobe epilepsy are particularly likely to have concurrent schizophrenic and mood disorder symptoms.

The psychiatric differential diagnosis also includes all the possibilities usually considered for schizophrenia and mood disorders. In clinical practice, psychosis at the time of presentation may hinder the detection of current or past mood disorder symptoms. Therefore, clinicians may delay making a final psychiatric diagnosis until the most acute symptoms of psychosis have been controlled.

COURSE AND PROGNOSIS

As a group, patients with schizoaffective disorder have prognoses that are between those of patients with schizophrenia and those of patients with mood disorders. As a group, patients with schizoaffective disorder have much worse prognoses than do patients with depressive disorders and patients with bipolar disorders, and they have better prognoses than do patients with schizophrenia. These generalities have been supported by several studies that followed up patients for 2 to 5

Table 14.3–2
Overall Outcome for Patients with Schizoaffective Disorder and Patients in Other Major Diagnostic Groups at Two Follow-up Times

	First Follow-up (2 years after hospitalization)				Second Follow-up (4–5 years after hospital discharge)			
	Overall Score on Strauss-Carpenter Scale[a]		Patients with Very Poor Outcome[b]		Overall Score on Strauss-Carpenter Scale[a]		Patients with Very Poor Outcome[b]	
Diagnostic Group	**Mean**	**SD**	**N**	**%**	**Mean**	**SD**	**N**	**%**
Schizoaffective disorder (N = 41)	9.68	4.0	17/40	43	9.73	3.3	17/40	43
Schizophrenia (N = 20)	9.40	4.7	11/20	55	8.60	3.9	11/20	55
Bipolar disorder (N = 20)	10.40	4.0	7/20	35	10.08	3.5	4/14	29
Major depressive disorder (N = 20)	10.60	3.4	2/20	10	10.20	3.5	2/15	13

Reprinted with permission from Grossman LS, Harrow M, Goldberg JF, Fichtner CG: Outcome of schizoaffective disorder at two long-term follow-ups: Comparisons with outcome of schizophrenia and affective disorders. Am J Psychiatry *148:* 1361, 1991.
[a] On this 16-point scale, higher scores reflect better functioning.
[b] LKP scale score of 7 or higher.

years after the index episode and that assessed social and occupational functioning as well as the course of the disorder itself. The results of one such study are shown in Tables 14.3–2 and 14.3–3.

Data indicate that patients with schizoaffective disorder, bipolar type, have prognoses similar to those for patients with bipolar I disorder and that patients with schizoaffective disorder, depressive type, have prognoses similar to those for patients with schizophrenia. Regardless of the type, the following variables weigh toward a poor prognosis: a poor premorbid history; an insidious onset; no precipitating factor; a predominance of psychotic symptoms, especially deficit or negative symptoms; an early onset; an unremitting course; and a family history of schizophrenia. The opposite of each of these characteristics weighs toward a good outcome. The presence or the absence of schneiderian first-rank symptoms does not seem to predict the course.

Although there do not appear to be gender-related differences in outcome for schizoaffective disorder, some data indicate that suicidal behavior may be more common in women with schizoaffective disorder than in men with the disorder. The incidence of suicide among patients with schizoaffective disorder is thought to be at least 10 percent.

TREATMENT

The major treatment modalities for schizoaffective disorder are hospitalization, medication, and psychosocial interventions. The basic principles underlying pharmacotherapy for schizoaffective disorder are that antidepressant and antimanic protocols be followed if at all indicated and that antipsychotic medications be used only as needed for short-term control. If thymoleptic protocols are not effective in controlling the symptoms on an ongoing basis, antipsychotic medications (for

Table 14.3–3
Rehospitalization of Patients with Schizoaffective Disorder and Patients in Other Major Diagnostic Groups at Two Follow-up Times

	First Follow-up (2 years after hospitalization)				Second Follow-up (4–5 years after hospital discharge)			
	Rehospitalization Score on Strauss-Carpenter Scale[a]		Patients Rehospitalized		Rehospitalization Score on Strauss-Carpenter Scale[a]		Patients Rehospitalized	
Diagnostic Group	**Mean**	**SD**	**N**	**%**	**Mean**	**SD**	**N**	**%**
Schizoaffective disorder (N = 41)	3.24	1.2	16	39	3.46	0.9	15	37
Schizophrenia (N = 20)	3.10	0.8	9	45	3.55	0.5	8	40
Bipolar disorder (N = 20)	3.45	0.8	9	45	3.60	0.6	7	35
Major depressive disorder (N = 20)	3.65	0.7	5	25	3.75	0.6	4	20

Reprinted with permission from Grossman LS, Harrow M, Goldberg JF, Fichtner CG: Outcome of schizoaffective disorder at two long-term follow-ups: Comparisons with outcome of schizophrenia and affective disorders. Am J Psychiatry *148:* 1363, 1991.
[a] On this 5-point subscale, higher scores reflect better functioning.

example, haloperidol [Haldol], risperidone [Risperdal]) may be indicated. Patients with schizoaffective disorder, bipolar type, should receive trials of lithium, carbamazepine (Tegretol), valproate (Depakene), or some combination of these drugs if one alone is not effective. Patients with schizoaffective disorder, depressive type, should be given trials of antidepressants and electroconvulsive therapy before they are determined to be unresponsive to antidepressant treatment.

References

Bardenstein KK, McGlashan TH: Gender differences in affective, schizoaffective, and schizophrenic disorders: A review. Schizophr Res *3:* 159, 1990.

Beatty WW, Jocic Z, Monson N, Staton RD: Memory and frontal lobe dysfunction in schizophrenia and schizoaffective disorder. J Nerv Ment Dis *181:* 448, 1993.

del Rio Vega JM, Ayuso-Gutierrez JL: Course of schizoaffective psychosis: Further data from a retrospective study. Acta Psychiatr Scand *85:* 328, 1992.

Grossman LS, Harrow M, Goldberg JF, Fichtner CG: Outcome of schizoaffective disorder at two long-term follow-ups: Comparisons with outcome of schizophrenia and affective disorders. Am J Psychiatry *148:* 1359, 1991.

Kendler KS: Mood-incongruent psychotic affective illness: A historical and empirical review. Arch Gen Psychiatry *48:* 362, 1991.

Lapensée MA: A review of schizoaffective disorder: I. Current concepts. Can J Psychiatry *37:* 335, 1992.

Lapensée MA: A review of schizoaffective disorder: II. Somatic treatment. Can J Psychiatry *37:* 347, 1992.

Maier W, Lichtermann D, Minges J, Heun R, Hallmayer J, Benkert O: Schizoaffective disorder and affective disorders with mood-incongruent psychotic features: Keep separate or combine? Evidence from a family study. Am J Psychiatry *149:* 1666, 1992.

Maj M, Perris C: Patterns of course in patients with a cross-sectional diagnosis of schizoaffective disorder. J Affect Disord *20:* 71, 1990.

Marneros A, Deister A, Rohde A: Stability of diagnoses in affective, schizoaffective and schizophrenic disorders: Cross-sectional versus longitudinal diagnosis. Eur Arch Psychiatry Clin Neurosci *241:* 187, 1991.

McGlashan TH, Williams PV: Predicting outcome in schizoaffective psychosis. J Nerv Ment Dis *178:* 518, 1990.

Retzer A, Simon FB, Weber G, Stierlin H, Schmidt G: A follow-up study of manic-depressive and schizoaffective psychoses after systematic family therapy. Fam Process *30:* 139, 1991.

Simhandl C, Meszaros K: The use of carbamazepine in the treatment of schizophrenic and schizoaffective psychoses: A review. J Psychiatry Neurosci *17:* 1, 1992.

Siris SG, Lavin MR: Schizoaffective disorder, schizophreniform disorder, and brief psychotic disorder. In *Comprehensive Textbook of Psychiatry,* ed 6, HI Kaplan, BJ Sadock, editors, p 1019. Williams & Wilkins, Baltimore, 1995.

Smith TE, Deutsch A, Schwartz F, Terkelsen KG: The role of personality in the treatment of schizophrenic and schizoaffective disorder inpatients: A pilot study. Bull Menninger Clin *57:* 88, 1993.

Strakowski SM: Diagnostic validity of schizophreniform disorder. Am J Psychiatry *151:* 815, 1994.

Taylor MA: Are schizophrenia and affective disorder related? A selective literature review. Am J Psychiatry *149:* 22, 1992.

Tsuang MT: Morbidity risks of schizophrenia and affective disorders among first-degree relatives of patients with schizoaffective disorders. Br J Psychiatry *158:* 165, 1991.

Zaudig M: Cycloid psychoses and schizoaffective psychoses: A comparison of different diagnostic classification systems and criteria. Psychopathology *23:* 233, 1990.

▲ 14.4 Delusional Disorder

Delusional disorder is defined as a psychiatric disorder in which the predominant symptoms are delusions. Delusional disorder was formerly called paranoia or paranoid disorder. These terms, however, incorrectly imply that the delusions are always persecutory in content, and this is not the case. The delusions in delusional disorder can also be grandiose, erotic, jealous, somatic, and mixed in primary content.

Delusional disorder must be differentiated from both mood disorders and schizophrenia. Although patients with delusional disorder may have a mood that is consistent with the content of their delusions, they do not evidence the pervasiveness of the effective symptoms seen in the mood disorders. Similarly, patients with delusional disorder differ from patients with schizophrenia in the nonbizarre nature of their delusions (for example, ''being followed by the FBI,'' which is unlikely but possible, versus ''being controlled by Martians,'' which is not possible). Patients with delusional disorder also lack other symptoms seen in schizophrenia, such as prominent hallucinations, affective flattening, and additional symptoms of thought disorder.

HISTORY

The former term for delusional disorder, *paranoia,* was derived from the Greek words meaning ''beside'' and ''mind.'' In this sense, paranoia was historically used to describe a variety of mental states, including dementia and delirium. In modern usage, paranoia is taken to mean extreme suspiciousness, usually not based on a realistic assessment of the situation. Often, however, the term *paranoia* is used in a casual way by both laypeople and mental health professionals to mean any type of suspiciousness. In mental health settings, it is preferable to limit the use of the word *paranoid* to those clinical situations in which the degree of paranoia is delusional.

In 1818, Johann Christian Heinroth introduced the basic concept of paranoia into psychiatry when he described disorders of the intellect under the term *Verrücktheit.* In 1838, the French psychiatrist Jean Etienne Dominique Esquirol coined the term *monomania* to characterize delusions with no associated defect in logical reasoning or general behavior.

Karl Ludwig Kahlbaum

In 1863, Karl Ludwig Kahlbaum used the term *paranoia,* which he characterized as uncommon but distinct. Kahlbaum referred to the condition as a partial insanity that affects the intellect but not other areas of mental functioning. Patients with paranoia, according to Kahlbaum, are characterized by a persistent delusional system that remains relatively static throughout the disorder.

Emil Kraepelin

Emil Kraepelin also recognized a condition that he called *paranoia,* characterized by a persistent delusional system in the absence of hallucinations and personality deterioration. Kraepelin, however, considered the disorder rare. Kraepelin also identified two other paranoid disorders: paraphrenia and dementia paranoides. Paraphrenia was differentiated from paranoia by the presence of hallucinations and a later onset but was similar to paranoia in the absence of a deteriorating course. Dementia paranoides was characterized by an early onset of symptoms that resembled those of paranoia but then progressed to a disorder with a deteriorating course, perhaps akin to paranoid schizophrenia.

Eugen Bleuler

Eugen Bleuler, who coined the term *schizophrenia,* was responsible for broadening the range of people who could be given the diagnosis of the disorder. Bleuler considered paranoia, as distinct from schizophrenia, to be such a rare condition that it did not warrant a separate diagnostic category.

Sigmund Freud

Sigmund Freud's formulation of the development of paranoid symptoms was an important milestone in the development of the concept. Freud used the autobiographical writings of a noted judge, Daniel Paul Schreber, as illustrations to prove his hypothesis that paranoid delusions develop from repressed homosexual impulses. Freud did not define any types of paranoia and suggested that the term *paraphrenia* be used solely to describe schizophrenia.

EPIDEMIOLOGY

An accurate assessment of the epidemiology of delusional disorder is hampered by the relative rareness of the disorder, as well as by its changing definitions in recent history. Moreover, delusional disorder may be underreported because delusional patients rarely seek psychiatric help unless forced to do so by their families or by the courts. Even with these limitations, however, the literature does support the contention that delusional disorder, although uncommon, has a relatively steady rate.

The prevalence of delusional disorder in the United States is currently estimated to be 0.025 to 0.03 percent. Thus, delusional disorder is much rarer than schizophrenia, which has a prevalence of about 1 percent, and the mood disorders, which have a prevalence of about 5 percent. The annual incidence of delusional disorder is 1 to 3 new cases per 100,000 people, about 4 percent of all first admissions to psychiatric hospitals for psychoses not due to a general medical condition or a substance. The mean age of onset is about 40 years, but the range for the age of onset runs from 18 to the 90s. There is a slight preponderance of female patients. Many patients are married and employed, but there may be some association with recent immigration and low socioeconomic status.

ETIOLOGY

As with all major psychiatric disorders, the cause of delusional disorder is unknown. Moreover, patients currently classified as having delusional disorder probably have a heterogeneous group of conditions with delusions as the predominant symptom. The central concept about the cause of delusional disorder is its distinctness from schizophrenia and the mood disorders. Delusional disorder is much more rare than either schizophrenia or mood disorders, with a later onset than schizophrenia and a much less pronounced female predominance than that in the mood disorders. The most convincing data come from family studies that report an increased prevalence of delusional disorder and related personality traits (for example, suspiciousness, jealousy, and secretiveness) in the relatives of delusional disorder probands. Family studies have reported neither an increased incidence of schizophrenia and mood disorders in the families of delusional disorder probands nor an increased incidence of delusional disorder in the families of schizophrenic probands. Long-term follow-up of patients with delusional disorder indicates that the diagnosis of delusional disorder is relatively stable, with less than one fourth of the patients eventually being reclassified as having schizophrenia and less than 10 percent of patients eventually being reclassified as having a mood disorder. These data indicate that delusional disorder is not simply an early stage in the development of one or both of these two more common disorders.

Biological Factors

A wide range of nonpsychiatric medical conditions and substances, including clear-cut biological factors, can cause delusions, but not everyone with a brain tumor, for example, has delusions. Unique and as yet not understood factors in a patient's brain and personality are likely to be relevant to the specific pathophysiology of delusional disorder.

The neurological conditions most commonly associated with delusions are conditions that affect the limbic system and the basal ganglia. Patients whose delusions are caused by neurological diseases and who show no intellectual impairment tend to have complex delusions similar to those in patients with delusional disorder. Conversely, patients with neurological disorder with intellectual impairments often have simple delusions unlike those in patients with delusional disorder. Thus, delusional disorder may involve the limbic system or basal ganglia in patients who have intact cerebral cortical functioning.

Delusional disorder may arise as a normal response to abnormal experiences in the environment, the peripheral nervous system, or the central nervous system. Thus, if patients have erroneous sensory experiences of being followed (for example, hearing footsteps), they may come to believe that they are actually being followed. This hypothesis hinges on the presence of hallucinatory-like experiences that need to be explained. The presence of such hallucinatory experiences in delusional disorder has not been proved.

Psychodynamic Factors

Practitioners have a strong clinical impression that many patients with delusional disorder are socially isolated and have attained less than expected levels of achievement. Specific psychodynamic theories about the cause and the evolution of delusional symptoms involve suppositions regarding hypersensitive people and specific ego mechanisms: reaction formation, projection, and denial.

Freud's Contributions. Freud believed that delusions, rather than being symptoms of the disorder, are part of a healing process. In 1896, he described projection as the main defense mechanism in paranoia. Later, Freud read *Memories of My Nervous Illness,* an autobiographical account by Daniel Paul Schreber. Although he never met Schreber, Freud theorized from his review of the autobiography that unconscious homosexual tendencies are defended against by denial and projection. According to classic psychodynamic theory, the dynamics underlying the formation of delusions for a female patient are the same as for a male patient.

According to Freud, because homosexuality is consciously inadmissible to some paranoid patients, male patients deny this feeling of "I love him" and change them by reaction formation into "I do not love him; I hate him." Patients further transform these feelings through projection into "It is not I who hate him; it is he who hates me." In a full-blown paranoid state, the feeling is elaborated into "I am persecuted by him." Patients are then able to rationalize their anger by consciously hating those they perceive to hate them. Instead of being aware of the passive homosexual impulses, patients reject the love of anyone except themselves. In erotomanic delusions, male patients change "I love him" to "I love her," and these feelings, through projection, become "She loves me." In delusional grandiosity "I do not love him" becomes "I love myself."

Freud also believed that unconscious homosexuality causes delusions of jealousy. To ward off threatening impulses, patients become preoccupied by jealous thoughts; thus, male patients assert, "I do not love him; she [a wife, for example] loves him." Freud believed that the man whom a paranoid patient suspects his wife of loving is a man to whom the patient feels sexually attracted. Clinical evidence has not supported Freud's thesis. A significant number of delusional patients do not have demonstrable homosexual inclinations, and most homosexual men do not have symptoms of paranoia or delusions.

Paranoid Pseudocommunity. Norman Cameron described seven situations that favor the development of delusional disorders: an increased expectation of receiving sadistic treatment, situations that increase distrust and suspicion, social isolation, situations that increase envy and jealousy, situations that lower self-esteem, situations that cause people to see their own defects in others, and situations that increase the potential for rumination over probable meanings and motivations. When frustration from any combination of these conditions exceeds the limit that people can tolerate, they become withdrawn and anxious; they realize that something is wrong, seek an explanation for the problem, and crystallize a delusional system as a solution. Elaboration of the delusion to include imagined people and attribution of malevolent motivations to both real and imagined people result in the organization of the pseudocommunity—a perceived community of plotters. This delusional entity hypothetically binds together projected fears and wishes to justify the patient's aggression and to provide a tangible target for the patient's hostilities.

Other Psychodynamic Factors. Clinical observations indicate that some paranoid patients experience a lack of trust in relationships. This distrust has been hypothesized to be related to a consistently hostile family environment, often with an overcontrolling mother and a distant or sadistic father.

Patients with delusional disorder use primarily the defense mechanisms of reaction formation, denial, and projection. They use reaction formation as a defense against aggression, dependence needs, and feelings of affection and transform the need for dependence into staunch independence. Patients use denial to avoid awareness of painful reality. Consumed with anger and hostility and unable to face responsibility for the rage, they project their resentment and anger onto others and use projection to protect themselves from recognizing unacceptable impulses in themselves.

Hypersensitivity and feelings of inferiority have been hypothesized to lead, through reaction formation and projection, to delusions of superiority and grandiosity. Delusions of erotic ideas have been suggested as replacements for feelings of rejection. Some clinicians have noted that children who are expected to perform impeccably and are undeservedly punished when they fail to do so may develop elaborate fantasies as a way of enhancing their injured self-esteem; these secret thoughts may eventually evolve into delusions. Critical and frightening delusions are often described as projections of superego criticism.

The delusions of female patients with paranoia often involve accusations of prostitution. When as young girls they turned to their fathers for the maternal love that they were unable to receive from their mothers, incestuous desires developed. Later heterosexual encounters are an unconscious reminder of the incestuous desires of childhood; these desires are defended against by superego projections accusing the women of prostitution.

Somatic delusions can be psychodynamically explained as a regression to the infantile narcissistic state, in which patients withdraw emotional involvement from other people and fixate on their physical selves. In erotic delusions, the love can be conceptualized as projected narcissistic love used as a defense against low self-esteem and severe narcissistic injury. Delusions of grandeur may be a regression to the omnipotent feelings of childhood, in which feelings of undenied and undiminished powers predominated.

DIAGNOSIS

The conceptual challenge in the diagnosis of delusional disorder rests on the necessity to differentiate it from schizophrenia. The revised third edition of *Diagnostic and Statistical Manual of Mental Disorders* (DSM-III-R) based the differentiation on two criteria. First, the delusions of delusional disorder were defined as nonbizarre; that is, the content of the delusion is at least possible (for example, being followed), even if unlikely. Second, the delusions had to occur in the absence of other symptoms of schizophrenia, including bizarre behavior, catatonia, and flat affect. Practically, the clinical distinction between bizarre and nonbizarre delusions can be difficult. Furthermore, both clinicians and researchers noted that the emphasis in the distinction between delusional disorder and schizophrenia should rest on the mild functional impairment seen in delusional disorder when compared with that seen in schizophrenia. The fourth edition of DSM (DSM-IV) addresses both the nonbizarre nature of the symptoms and the absence of other symptoms of schizophrenia in its diagnostic criteria for delusional disorder (Table 14.4–1).

DSM-IV presents two criteria for describing the clinical symptoms of delusional disorder. Criterion A requires the presence of delusions for at least 1 month (at least 3 months in the 10th revision of *International Statistical Classification of Diseases and Related Health Problems* [ICD-10]) and describes the delusions as nonbizarre in an attempt to assist clinicians in discriminating them from the bizarre delusions seen in patients with schizophrenia. Criterion B requires the absence of other symptoms of schizophrenia at any time during the course of the disorder except for tactile or olfactory halluci-

Table 14.4–1
DSM-IV Diagnostic Criteria for Delusional Disorder

A. Nonbizarre delusions (ie, involving situations that occur in real life, such as being followed, poisoned, infected, loved at a distance, or deceived by spouse or lover, or having a disease) of at least 1 month's duration.

B. Criterion A for schizophrenia has never been met. **Note:** Tactile and olfactory hallucinations may be present in delusion disorder if they are related to the delusional theme.

C. Apart from the impact of the delusion(s) or its ramifications, functioning is not markedly impaired and behavior is not obviously odd or bizarre.

D. If mood episodes have occurred concurrently with delusions, their total duration has been brief relative to the duration of the delusional periods.

E. The disturbance is not due to the direct physiological effects of a substance (eg, a drug of abuse, a medication) or a general medical condition.

Specify type (the following types are assigned based on the predominant delusional theme):

Erotomanic type: delusions that another person, usually of higher status, is in love with the individual

Grandiose type: delusions of inflated worth, power, knowledge, identity, or special relationship to a deity or famous person

Jealous type: delusions that the individual's sexual partner is unfaithful

Persecutory type: delusions that the person (or someone to whom the person is close) is being malevolently treated in some way

Somatic type: delusions that the person has some physical defect or general medical condition

Mixed type: delusions characteristic of more than one of the above types but no one theme predominates

Unspecified type

nations if they are consistent with the delusional system. DSM-IV also specifies that the effects of the disorder on the patient's functioning are limited to the effects that the delusions themselves have on the patient's life. This criterion is meant to exclude patients who are functionally impaired because of characteristic schizophrenic symptoms such as ambivalence.

Types

DSM-IV allows clinicians to specify one of seven types of delusional disorder, based on the predominant content of the delusions (see Table 14.4–1). The types include erotomanic, grandiose, jealous, persecutory, and somatic, as well as mixed, for patients with delusions containing more than one theme, and unspecified, for patients with delusions that do not fit any of the previous categories. Persecutory and jealous types are the most common, grandiose type is not as common, and erotomanic and somatic types are the most unusual.

Other Delusions

Other delusions have been given specific names in the literature. In the absence of an organic explanation, patients with these delusions may be classified according to DSM-IV either as having delusional disorder (unspecified type) or as having a psychotic disorder not otherwise specified. Capgras's syndrome is the delusion that familiar people have been replaced by identical impostors. Fregoli's phenomenon is the delusion that a persecutor is taking on a variety of faces, like an actor. Lycanthropy is the delusion of being a werewolf, and heutoscopy is the false belief that one has a double. Cotard's syndrome was originally called *délire de négation;* those with the syndrome may believe that they have lost everything—possessions, strength, and even bodily organs, such as the heart.

CLINICAL FEATURES

Mental Status

General Description. Patients are usually well groomed and well dressed, without evidence of gross disintegration of personality or of daily activities, yet they may seem eccentric, odd, suspicious, or hostile. They are sometimes litigious and may make this inclination clear to the examiner. What is usually most remarkable about patients with delusional disorder is that the mental status examination shows them to be remarkably normal except for the presence of a markedly abnormal delusional system. Patients may attempt to engage clinicians as allies in their delusions, but a clinician should not pretend to accept the delusion; this collusion further confounds reality and sets the stage for eventual distrust between the patient and the therapist.

Mood, Feelings, and Affect. Patients' moods are consistent with the content of their delusions. A patient with grandiose delusions is euphoric; one with persecutory delusions is suspicious. Whatever the nature of the delusional system, the examiner may sense some mild depressive qualities.

Perceptual Disturbances. By definition, patients with delusional disorder do not have prominent or sustained hallucinations. According to DSM-IV, tactile or olfactory hallucinations may be present if they are consistent with the delusion (for example, somatic delusion of body odor). A few delusional patients have other hallucinatory experiences—virtually always auditory rather than visual.

Thought. Disorder of thought content, in the form of delusions, is the key symptom of the disorder. The delusions are usually systematized and are characterized as being possible, for example, delusions of being persecuted, of having an unfaithful spouse, of being infected with a virus, or of being loved by a famous person. These examples of delusional content contrast with the bizarre and impossible delusional content in some patients with schizophrenia. The delusional system itself may be complex or simple. Patients lack other signs of thought disorder, although some may be verbose, circumstantial, or idiosyncratic in their speech when they talk about their delusions. Clinicians should not assume that all unlikely scenarios are delusional; the veracity of a patient's beliefs should be checked before automatically considering their content to be delusional.

Sensorium and Cognition. ORIENTATION. Patients with delusional disorder usually have no abnormality in orientation unless they have a specific delusion about a person, place, or time.

MEMORY. Memory and other cognitive processes are intact in patients with delusional disorder.

Impulse Control. Clinicians must evaluate patients with delusional disorder for ideation or plans to act on their delusional material by suicide, homicide, or other violence. Although the incidence of these behaviors is not known, therapists should not hesitate to ask patients about their suicidal, homicidal, or other violent plans. Destructive aggression is most common in patients with a history of violence; if aggressive feelings existed in the past, therapists should ask patients how they managed these feelings. If patients are unable to control their impulses, hospitalization is probably necessary. Therapists can sometimes help foster a therapeutic alliance by openly discussing how hospitalization can help patients gain additional control of their impulses.

Judgment and Insight. Patients with delusional disorder have virtually no insight into their condition and are almost always brought to the hospital by the police, family members, or employers. Judgment can best be assessed by evaluating the patient's past, present, and planned behavior.

Reliability. Patients with delusional disorder are usually reliable in their information, except when it impinges on their delusional system.

Types

Erotomanic Type. In the erotomanic type of delusional disorder, the central delusion is that the affected patient is loved intensely by another usually famous person, such as a movie star or a superior at work. Patients with erotic delusions are significant sources of harassment to public figures. The erotomanic type of delusional disorder has also been referred to as erotomania, *psychose passionelle,* and de Clerambault syndrome. The onset of the symptom can be sudden and often becomes the central focus of the affected person's life. Efforts to contact the object of the delusion—through telephone calls, letters, gifts, visits, and even surveillance and stalking—are common, although the person occasionally attempts to keep the delusion secret. The symptom of paradoxical conduct consists of interpreting all verbal and physical denials of love as cryptic proof of love.

Whereas in clinical samples most patients with the erotomanic type are women, in forensic samples most are men. Some people with the disorder, particularly men, come into conflict with the law in their efforts to pursue the objects of their delusions or in misguided efforts to rescue them from imagined dangers. For example, a man with delusional disorder may attempt to murder the husband of a woman whom he believes is really in love with him.

People with the erotomanic type of delusional disorder often have isolated and withdrawn lives. They are usually single, have had limited sexual contacts, and are employed in modest occupations.

A 23-year-old woman came to the walk-in clinic in a state of anxiety with concerns that her true love, a star of a local athletic team, might already be married. The patient explained that she had never really met or talked with the local celebrity but that she had been at a crowded party several months ago, where she had stood approximately 10 feet away from him. She knew within hours after the party that he loved her, and she in turn loved him. She had sent letters, had telephoned repeatedly, and even waited outside the sports arena to meet her love. These attempts to communicate had not been successful, but only confirmed her suspicion that he was having difficulty keeping the relationship and his desires secret.

The patient showed no other symptoms except for mild anxiety and depressed mood, appropriate to her concerns. There was no prior history of psychiatric illness. Antipsychotic medication was not prescribed, and the patient underwent a brief period of supportive psychotherapy. This case remitted briefly, but relapsed later when a new lover was identified. (Courtesy of Theo C. Manschreck, M.D., M.P.H.)

Grandiose Type. The grandiose type of delusion disorder has also been referred to as megalomania. The most common form of grandiose delusion is the belief that a person has a great but unrecognized talent or insight or has made an important discovery, which the patient may submit to various government agencies, such as the Federal Bureau of Investigation (FBI) and the U.S. Patent Office. Less common is the delusion that a person has a special relationship with a prominent figure, such as the president of the United States. Grandiose delusions may have a religious content, and those with such delusions can become leaders of religious cults.

A 49-year-old married woman was taken to the hospital by her family because they feared she would be arrested for disturbing the peace. For several months, the patient had become aware of special abilities for healing the sick and she began to preach in her neighborhood about her powers. The patient was scornful and angry both toward the physician and her family whom she perceived to be railroading her into treatment when in fact she was not at all ill. On admission, the patient calmed considerably and began to discuss her abilities with other patients. Her affect lost much of its intensity and remained entirely appropriate, and there was no other psychopathological evidence, including euphoria. Eventually, the delusional concerns began to increase, and the patient complained that there was a conspiracy to prevent her from using her special powers. At discharge, there was no change in the delusion, but there was a reduction in activity associated with it. (Courtesy of Theo C. Manschreck, M.D., M.P.H.)

Jealous Type. The jealous type of delusional disorder is also known as conjugal paranoia and Othello syndrome when the delusion concerns the fidelity of the spouse. Men are more commonly affected than women, but the jealous type of delusional disorder is rare and affects probably less than 0.2 percent of all psychiatric patients. The onset is often sudden, and the symptoms may resolve only after the couple separates or the spouse dies. A person with a jealous delusion can inflict significant verbal and physical abuse on the spouse and can even kill him or her. In 1891, Richard Freiherr von Krafft-Ebing emphasized the frequent association between alcoholism and jealous delusions.

People affected with the jealous type of delusional disorder may collect bits of "evidence" such as disarrayed clothing and spots on the sheets and use them to justify the delusion. Almost invariably, people with the delusion confront their spouses or lovers and may take extraordinary steps to intervene in the imagined infidelity. These attempts may include restricting autonomy by insisting that the spouse or lover never leave the house unaccompanied, secretly following the spouse or lover, and investigating the other "lover."

A 32-year-old man was taken to the hospital by police after neighbors complained that he was beating his wife. The patient denied psychiatric illness and reported that he was feeling depressed because his wife was having an affair. The patient had spent large amounts of time trying to prove his suspicions about infidelity. He telephoned frequently to see what his wife was doing; laid traps (for example, he placed tape recorders in the bedroom) before he went to work; checked her purse, clothes, and telephone bill frequently for "evidence"; and commented that he was planning to buy a video camera to document his wife's indiscretions. On numerous occasions, he interrogated her about past lovers. This pattern had begun just before his marriage, and the delusions of infidelity had emerged fully formed within 2 months after the wedding.

The patient was admitted to the hospital, but argued vigorously and angrily that he was not ill. He threatened lawsuits, kept extensive notes, and made numerous complaints to the hospital administration. His affect was intense and appropriate. He showed no signs of perceptual, cognitive, or thinking disturbance. The delusion remained unchanged for several months despite a trial of antipsychotic medications. His continued threats to harm his wife led to legal commitment. His wife separated from and then divorced him. This change coincided with reduced activity about the delusions but did not lead to its remission. (Courtesy of Theo C. Manschreck, M.D., M.P.H.)

Persecutory Type. The persecutory type is the most common type of delusional disorder. The persecutory delusion may be simple or elaborate and usually involves a single theme or a series of connected themes, such as being conspired against, cheated, spied on, followed, poisoned or drugged, maliciously maligned, harassed, or obstructed in the pursuit of long-term goals. Small slights may be exaggerated until they become the focus of a delusional system. Sometimes, the focus of the delusion is an injustice that must be remedied by legal action (querulous paranoia), and the affected person often engages in repeated attempts to obtain satisfaction by appeals to courts and other government agencies. Those with persecutory delusions are often resentful and angry and may resort to violence against those they believe to be hurting them.

A seclusive 30-year-old college-educated man was living alone and working as a clerk in a printing supplies store when he became suspicious, apprehensive, and agitated. He claimed that he did not need to be in a psychiatric clinic, but had been referred by an acquaintance because he was so worried. He explained that he was upset because his brother was plotting to keep him out of the family inheritance. There was no evidence of hallucinations or confusion, and the patient's thinking was clear and logical. The brother, a successful businessman, allegedly made remarks that the patient interpreted as unsubtle suggestions that he move away from his parents' hometown. With the patient out of the way, he reasoned, the brother would be able to endear himself to the elderly parents, who had been disappointed by the patient's lack of success in the work world.

The patient's delusional thinking responded initially to antipsychotic medication, in that the agitation, preoccupation, and conviction concerning the delusions diminished. However, the patient had harbored the delusions for more than a decade, despite antipsychotic drug treatment and numerous attempts by the family to present the facts and reassure the patient. The conspiracy has broadened to include various therapists, employers, and neighbors of the patient. (Courtesy of Theo C. Manschreck, M.D., M.P.H.)

Somatic Type. The somatic type of delusional disorder is also known as monosymptomatic hypochondriacal psychosis. The differentiation between hypochondriasis and the somatic type of delusional disorder rests on the degree of conviction that patients with delusional disorder have about their presumed illness. The most common delusional afflictions are infection (for example, with bacteria, viruses, parasites); infestation of insects on or in the skin; dysmorphophobia (for example, misshapen nose or breasts); delusions about body odors coming from the skin, mouth, or vagina; and delusions that certain parts of the body, such as the large intestine, are not functioning. The somatic type affects both sexes equally and is thought to be rare, although most patients probably consult nonpsychiatric physicians. Histories of substance abuse or head injury may be common in patients with the disorder. The frustration caused by the symptom may lead some patients to suicide.

A 38-year-old white, single man went to treatment complaining that his nose was irregular in shape and that he was losing all his hair. His nose was normal in appearance and he had no evidence of premature baldness. He had been reassured about this repeatedly, not only by his family physician but also by a specialist with whom he consulted. He believed all his physicians were "quacks" or were trying to "get rid of him."

He had been mildly depressed and irritable in response to the change in his appearance, which he claimed was due to medicine he had received years before from a physician. He could not explain why he was so troubled, even though his appearance had been altered for a long time. Trained as an upholsterer, he had been able to work at times, but when be became more delusional, he was too fearful to go to his job, was unable to remain in his apartment, and refused to go to his parents' home. There was no evidence of confusion, neurovegetative features of depression, memory impairment, or bizarre delusions. There were no hallucinations and he had no insight into his illness. Family history was negative. He responded gradually to antipsychotic medication, which he reluctantly took. (Courtesy of Theo C. Manschreck, M.D., M.P.H.)

DIFFERENTIAL DIAGNOSIS

Delusion can accompany many medical and neurological illnesses (Table 14.4–2). The most common sites for lesions are the basal ganglia and the limbic system. The medical evaluation should include toxicology screening and routine admission laboratory work. Neuropsychological testing (such as the Bender Gestalt test and the Wechsler Memory Scale) and an electroencephalogram or a computed tomography scan may be indicated at the time of the initial presentation, especially if other signs or symptoms suggest cognitive impairment or electrophysiological or structural lesions.

Delirium, Dementia, and Substance-Related Disorders

Delirium and dementia should be considered in the differential diagnosis of a patient with delusions. Delirium can be differentiated by the presence of a fluctuating level of consciousness or impaired cognitive abilities. Delusions early in the course of a dementing illness, as in dementia of the Alzheimer's type, may give the appearance of a delusional disorder; neuropsychological testing, however, usually detects cognitive impairment. Although alcohol abuse is an associated feature for patients with delusional disorder, delusional disorder should be distinguished from alcohol-induced psychotic disorder with hallucinations. Intoxication with sympathomimetics (including amphetamine), marijuana, or L-dopa is likely to result in delusional symptoms.

Table 14.4–2
Neurological and Medical Conditions That Can Present with Delusions

Basal ganglia disorders—Parkinson's disease, Huntington's disease
Deficiency states—B_{12}, folate, thiamine, niacin
Delirium
Dementia—Alzheimer's disease, Pick's disease
Drug-induced—amphetamines, anticholinergics, antidepressants, antihypertensives, antituberculosis drugs, antiparkinson agents, cimetidine, cocaine, disulfiram (Antabuse), hallucinogens
Endocrinopathies—adrenal, thyroid, parathyroid
Limbic system disorders—epilepsy, cerebrovascular diseases, tumors
Systemic—hepatic encephalopathy, hypercalcemia, hypoglycemia, porphyria, uremia

Other Disorders

The psychiatric differential diagnosis for delusional disorder includes malingering and factitious disorder with predominantly psychological signs and symptoms. The nonfactitious disorders in the differential diagnosis are schizophrenia, mood disorders, obsessive-compulsive disorder, somatoform disorders, and paranoid personality disorder. Delusional disorder is distinguished from schizophrenia by the absence of other schizophrenic symptoms and by the nonbizarre quality of the delusions; patients with delusional disorder also lack the impaired functioning seen in schizophrenia. The somatic type of delusional disorder may resemble a depressive disorder or a somatoform disorder. The somatic type of delusional disorder is differentiated from depressive disorders by the absence of other signs of depression and by the lack of a pervasive quality to the depression. Delusional disorder can be differentiated from somatoform disorders by the degree to which the somatic belief is held by the patient. Patients with somatoform disorders allow for the possibility that their disorder does not exist, whereas patients with delusional disorder have no doubt of its reality. Separating paranoid personality disorder from delusional disorder requires the sometimes difficult clinical distinction between extreme suspiciousness and a frank delusion. In general, if clinicians doubt that a symptom is a delusion, the diagnosis of delusional disorder should not be made.

COURSE AND PROGNOSIS

Some clinicians and some research data indicate that an identifiable psychosocial stressor often accompanies the onset of the disorder. The nature of the stressor may be such that a degree of suspicion or concern on the part of the person is warranted. Examples of such stressors are recent immigration, social conflict with family members or friends, and social isolation. A sudden onset is generally thought to be more common than an insidious onset. Some clinicians believe that a person with delusional disorder is likely to be below average in intelligence and that the premorbid personality of such a person is likely to be extroverted, dominant, and hypersensitive. The person's initial suspicions or concerns gradually become elaborate, consume much of the person's attention, and finally become delusional. People may begin quarreling with coworkers, may seek protection from the FBI or the police, or may begin visiting many medical or surgical physicians to seek consultations, lawyers about suits, or police about delusional suspicions.

Delusional disorder is thought to be a fairly stable diagnosis. Less than 25 percent of all cases of delusional disorder are later diagnosed as schizophrenia, and less than 10 percent of such patients have a mood disorder. About 50 percent of patients have recovered at long-term follow-up, 20 percent show a decrease in symptoms, and 30 percent have no change in symptoms. The following factors correlate with a good prognosis: high levels of occupational, social, and functional adjustments; female sex; onset before age 30; sudden onset; short duration of illness; and the presence of precipitating factors. Although reliable data are limited, patients with persecutory, somatic, and erotic delusions are thought to have a better prognosis than do patients with grandiose and jealous delusions.

TREATMENT

Hospitalization

Patients with delusional disorder can generally undergo treatment as outpatients, but clinicians should consider hospitalization for several reasons. First, patients may need a complete medical and neurological evaluation to determine whether a nonpsychiatric medical condition is causing the delusional symptoms. Second, patients need an assessment of their ability to control violent impulses, such as to commit suicide and homicide, that may be related to the delusional material. Third, patients' behavior about the delusions may have significantly affected their ability to function within their family or occupational settings; they may require professional intervention to stabilize social or occupational relationships.

If a physician is convinced that a patient would receive the best treatment in a hospital, then the physician should attempt to persuade the patient to accept hospitalization; failing that, legal commitment may be indicated. If a physician convinces a patient that hospitalization is inevitable, the patient often voluntarily enters a hospital to avoid legal commitment.

Pharmacotherapy

In an emergency, severely agitated patients should be given an antipsychotic drug intramuscularly. Although adequately conducted clinical trials with large numbers of patients have not been conducted, most clinicians think that antipsychotic drugs are the treatment of choice for delusional disorder. Patients are likely to refuse medication because they can easily incorporate the administration of drugs into their delusional systems; physicians should not insist on medication immediately after hospitalization but, rather, should spend a few days establishing rapport with patients. Physicians should explain potential side effects to patients, so that patients do not later suspect that the physician lied.

A patient's history of medication response is the best guide to choose a drug. A physician should often start with low doses (for example, 2 mg of haloperidol [Haldol]) and increase the dose slowly. If a patient fails to respond to the drug at a reasonable dosage in a 6-week trial, antipsychotic drugs from other classes should be given clinical trials. Some investigators have indicated that pimozide (Orap) may be particularly effective in delusional disorder, especially in patients with somatic delusions. A common cause of drug failure is noncompliance, which should also be evaluated.

If the patient receives no benefit from antipsychotic medication, the drug should be discontinued. In patients who do respond to antipsychotic drugs, some data indicate that maintenance doses can be low. Although essentially no studies evaluate the use of antidepressants, lithium (Eskalith), or anticonvulsants (such as carbamazepine [Tegretol] and valproate [Depakene]) in the treatment of delusional disorder, trials with these drugs may be warranted in patients who are unresponsive to antipsychotic drugs. Trials of these drugs should also be considered when a patient has either the features of a mood disorder or a family history of mood disorders.

Psychotherapy

The essential element in effective psychotherapy is to establish a relationship in which patients begin to trust a therapist. Individual therapy seems to be more effective than group therapy; insight-oriented supportive, cognitive, and behavioral therapies are often effective. A therapist should initially neither agree with nor challenge a patient's delusions. Although therapists must ask about a delusion to establish its extent, persistent questioning about it should probably be avoided. Physicians may stimulate the motivation to receive help by emphasizing a willingness to help patients with their anxiety or irritability, without suggesting that the delusions be treated, but therapists should not actively support the notion that the delusions are real.

The unwavering reliability of therapists is essential in psychotherapy. Therapists should be on time and make appointments as regularly as possible, with the goal of developing a solid and trusting relationship with a patient. Overgratification may actually increase patients' hostility and suspiciousness because ultimately they must realize that not all demands can be met. Therapists can avoid overgratification by not extending the designated appointment period, by not giving extra appointments unless absolutely necessary, and by not being lenient about the fee.

Therapists should avoid making disparaging remarks about a patient's delusions or ideas but can sympathetically indicate to patients that their preoccupation with their delusions is both distressing to themselves and interferes with a constructive life. When patients begin to waver in their delusional beliefs, therapists may increase reality testing by asking the patients to clarify their concerns.

Psychodynamic Factors. The internal experience of patients with delusional disorder is that of victims of a world that persecutes them. Projection is the principal defense mechanism, and all malevolence is projected into people or institutions in the environment. By substituting an external threat for an internal one, delusional patients feel a sense of control. The patients' need for control reflects the low self-esteem at the core of paranoia. Paranoid patients compensate for feelings of weakness and inferiority by assuming that they are so special that governmental agencies, famous people, and a host of others in the environment are all deeply concerned about them and are trying to persecute them.

Clinicians who attempt to treat delusional disorder must respect the patients' need for the defense of projection. Psychotherapists must be willing to serve as a container for all the negative feelings projected by patients; any efforts to turn such feelings prematurely will result in a patient's feeling attacked and blamed. A corollary of this principle is that therapists should not challenge delusions when working psychotherapeutically with delusional patients. Instead, they should simply ask for further elaborations of a patient's perceptions and feelings.

Another approach useful in building a therapeutic alliance is to empathize with the patient's internal experience of being overwhelmed by persecution. It may be helpful to make such comments as, "You must be exhausted, considering what you've been through." Without agreeing with every delusional misperception, a therapist can acknowledge that, from the patient's perspective, such perceptions create much distress. The ultimate goal is to help patients entertain the possibility of a doubt about their perceptions. As they become less rigid, feelings of weakness and inferiority, associated with some depression, may surface. When a patient allows feelings of vulnerability to enter into the therapy, a positive therapeutic alliance has been established, and constructive therapy becomes possible.

Family Therapy. When family members are available, clinicians may decide to involve them in the treatment plan. Without being delusionally seen as siding with the enemy, a clinician should attempt to enlist the family as allies in the treatment process. Consequently, both the patient and the family members need to understand that the therapist maintains physician–patient confidentiality and that communications from relatives are discussed with the patient. The family may benefit from the therapist's support and may thus be supportive of the patient.

A good therapeutic outcome depends on a psychiatrist's ability to respond to the patient's mistrust of others and the resulting interpersonal conflicts, frustrations, and failures. The mark of successful treatment may be a satisfactory social adjustment rather than an abatement of the patient's delusions.

References

Albus M, Strauss A, Stieglitz RD: Schizophrenia, schizotypal and delusional disorders (section F2): Results of the ICD-10 field trial. Pharmacopsychiatry *23* (4, Suppl): 155, 1990.

Bentall RP, Kaney S, Dewey ME: Paranoia and social reasoning: An attribution theory analysis. Br J Clin Psychol *30:* 12, 1991.

Block B, Pristach CA: Diagnosis and management of the paranoid patient. Am Fam Physician *45:* 2634, 1992.

Candido CL, Romney DM: Attributional style in paranoid vs. depressed patients. Br J Med Psychol *63:* 355, 1990.

Gabbard GO: *Psychodynamic Psychiatry in General Practice: The DSM-IV Edition.* American Psychiatric Press, Washington, 1994.

Gabriel E, Schanda H: Why do the results of follow-up studies in delusional disorders differ? Psychopathology *24:* 304, 1991.

Gambini O, Colombo C, Cavallaro R, Scarone S: Smooth pursuit eye movements and saccadic eye movements in patients with delusional disorder. Am J Psychiatry *150:* 1411, 1993.

Garety PA, Hemsley DR, Wessely S: Reasoning in deluded schizophrenic and paranoid patients: Biases in performance on a probabilistic inference task. J Nerv Ment Dis *179:* 194, 1991.

Garfield D, Havens L: Paranoid phenomena and pathological narcissism. Am J Psychother *45:* 160, 1991.

Hart JJ: Paranoid states: Classification and management. Br J Hosp Med *44:* 34, 1990.

Houseman C: The paranoid person: A biopsychosocial perspective. Arch Psychiatr Nurs *4:* 176, 1990.

Kennedy HG, Kemp LI, Dyer DE: Fear and anger delusional (paranoid) disorder: The association with violence. Br J Psychiatry *160:* 488, 1992.

Manschreck TM: Delusional disorder and shared psychotic disorder. In *Comprehensive Textbook of Psychiatry,* ed 6, HI Kaplan, BJ Sadock, editors, p 1031. Williams & Wilkins, Baltimore, 1995.

Marino C, Nobile M, Bellodi L, Smeraldi E: Delusional disorder and mood disorder: Can they coexist? Psychopathology *26:* 53, 1993.

Newhill CE: The role of culture in the development of paranoid symptomatology. Am J Orthopsychiatry *60:* 176, 1990.

Opjordsmoen S, Retterstol N: Delusional disorder: The predictive validity of the concept. Acta Psychiatr Scand *84:* 250, 1991.

Opjordsmoen S, Retterstol N: Outcome in delusional disorder in different periods of time: Possible implications for treatment with neuroleptics. Psychopathology *26:* 90, 1993.

Retterstol N, Opjordsmoen S: Fatherhood, impending or newly established, precipitating delusional disorders: Long-term course and outcome. Psychopathology *24:* 232, 1991.

Rippon G: Paranoid-nonparanoid differences: Psychophysiological parallels. Int J Psychophysiol *13:* 79, 1992.

Rudden M, Sweeney J, Frances A: Diagnosis and clinical course of erotomanic and other delusional patients. Am J Psychiatry *147:* 625, 1990.

Statel SL, Southwick SM, Gawin FH: Clinical features of cocaine-induced paranoia. Am J Psychiatry *148:* 495, 1991.

▲ 14.5 Brief Psychotic Disorder

The fourth edition of *Diagnostic and Statistical Manual of Mental Disorders* (DSM-IV) combines two diagnostic concepts in the diagnosis of brief psychotic disorder. First, the disorder has lasted a short time, defined in DSM-IV as less than 1 month but at least 1 day; the symptoms may or may not meet the diagnostic criteria for schizophrenia. Second, the disorder may have developed in response to a severe psychosocial stressor or group of stressors. The grouping of these two concepts in DSM-IV as brief psychotic disorder acknowledges the practical difficulty of differentiating them in routine clinical practice.

HISTORY

Brief psychotic disorder has been poorly studied in psychiatry in the United States, partly because of the frequent changes in diagnostic criteria that have occurred during the past 15 years. The diagnosis has been better appreciated and more completely studied in Scandinavia and in other Western European countries than in the United States. Patients with disorders similar to brief psychotic disorder have previously been classified as having reactive, hysterical, stress, and psychogenic psychoses.

Reactive psychosis was often used as a synonym for good-prognosis schizophrenia, but the DSM-IV diagnosis of brief psychotic disorder is not meant to imply a relation with schizophrenia. In 1913, Karl Jaspers described several essential features for the diagnosis of reactive psychosis, including the presence of an identifiable and extremely traumatic stressor, a close temporal relation between the stressor and the development of the psychosis, and a generally benign course for the psychotic episode. Jaspers also stated that the content of the psychosis often reflected the nature of the traumatic experience and that the development of the psychosis seemed to serve a purpose for the patient, often as an escape from a traumatic condition.

EPIDEMIOLOGY

Reliable estimates of the incidence, prevalence, sex ratio, and average age of onset for brief psychotic disorder are not available, but it is generally considered uncommon. Another widely held clinical impression is that the disorder is more common among young patients than older patients, although some case histories involve older people.

Some clinicians indicate that the disorder may be seen most frequently in patients from low socioeconomic classes and in those with preexisting personality disorders (most commonly, histrionic, narcissistic, paranoid, schizotypal, and borderline personality disorders). People who have experienced disasters or major cultural changes (such as immigrants) may also be at risk for the disorder following psychosocial stressors. Well-controlled clinical studies, however, have shown that these clinical impressions are inaccurate.

ETIOLOGY

In DSM-IV, brief psychotic disorder belongs to the same category as the many other major psychiatric disorders in which the cause is unknown, and the diagnosis is likely to include a heterogeneous group of disorders. Patients with brief psychotic disorder who have had a personality disorder may have biological or psychological vulnerability toward the development of psychotic symptoms. Although patients with brief psychotic disorder as a group may not have an increased incidence of schizophrenia in their families, some data indicate an increased incidence of mood disorders. Psychodynamic formulations have emphasized the presence of inadequate coping mechanisms and the possibility of secondary gain for those patients with psychotic symptoms. As with the biological theories for the disorder, the psychological theories have not been validated by carefully controlled clinical studies. Additional psychodynamic theories suggest that the psychotic symptoms are a defense against a prohibited fantasy, the fulfillment of an unattained wish, or an escape from a specific psychosocial situation.

DIAGNOSIS

DSM-IV describes a continuum of diagnoses for psychotic disorders, based primarily on the duration of the symptoms. For psychotic symptoms that last at least 1 day but less than 1 month and that are not associated with a mood disorder, a substance-related disorder, or a psychotic disorder due to a general medical condition, a diagnosis of brief psychotic disorder is likely to be appropriate. (By contrast, in the 10th revision of the *International Statistical Classification of Diseases and Related Disorders* [ICD-10], acute psychotic disorders are diagnosed by setting up a ''diagnostic sequence that reflects the order of priority given to selected key features,'' including acute [within 48 hours] or abrupt [more than 48 hours but within 2 weeks] onset, typical syndromes, and associated acute distress.) For psychotic symptoms that last more than 1 month, the appropriate diagnoses to consider are delusional disorder (if delusions are the primary psychotic symptoms), schizophreniform disorder (if the symptoms have lasted less than 6 months), and schizophrenia (if the symptoms have lasted more than 6 months).

Thus, brief psychotic disorder is classified in DSM-IV as being a psychotic disorder of short duration (Table 14.5–1). The diagnostic criteria specify the presence of at least one clearly psychotic symptom lasting from 1 day to 1 month. DSM-IV further allows the specification of two features: the presence or the absence of one or more marked stressors and a postpartum onset.

Table 14.5–1
DSM-IV Diagnostic Criteria for Brief Psychotic Disorder

A. Presence of one (or more) of the following symptoms:
  (1) delusions
  (2) hallucinations
  (3) disorganized speech (eg, frequent derailment or incoherence)
  (4) grossly disorganized or catatonic behavior

  Note: Do not include a symptom if it is a culturally sanctioned response pattern.

B. Duration of an episode of the disturbance is at least 1 day but less than 1 month, with eventual full return to premorbid level of functioning.

C. The disturbance is not better accounted for by a mood disorder with psychotic features, schizoaffective disorder, or schizophrenia and is not due to the direct physiological effects of a substance (eg, a drug of abuse, a medication) or a general medical condition.

Specify if:
  With marked stressor(s) (brief reactive psychosis): if symptoms occur shortly after and apparently in response to events that, singly or together, would be markedly stressful to almost anyone in similar circumstances in the person's culture
  Without marked stressor(s): if psychotic symptoms do *not* occur shortly after, or are not apparently in response to events that, singly or together, would be markedly stressful to almost anyone in similar circumstances in the person's culture
  With postpartum onset: if onset within 4 weeks postpartum

Reprinted with permission from American Psychiatric Association: *Diagnostic and Statistical Manual of Mental Disorders,* ed 4. Copyright, American Psychiatric Association, Washington, 1994.

As with other acutely ill psychiatric patients, the history necessary to make the diagnosis may not be obtainable solely from the patient. Although psychotic symptoms may be obvious, information about prodromal symptoms, previous episodes of a mood disorder, and the recent history of the ingestion of a psychotomimetic substance may not be available from the clinical interview alone. In addition, clinicians may not be able to obtain accurate information about the presence or absence of precipitating stressors. Such information is usually best and most accurately obtained from a relative or a friend.

CLINICAL FEATURES

The symptoms of brief psychotic disorder always include at least one major symptom of psychosis, usually with an abrupt onset, but do not always include the entire symptom pattern seen in schizophrenia. Some clinicians have observed that affective symptoms, confusion, and impaired attention may be more common in brief psychotic disorder than in the chronic psychotic disorders. Characteristic symptoms in brief psychotic disorder include emotional volatility, outlandish dress or behavior, screaming or muteness, and impaired memory for recent events. Some of the symptoms suggest a diagnosis of delirium and warrant a complete organic workup, although the results may be negative.

Scandinavian and other European literature differentiate several characteristic symptom patterns in brief psychotic disorder, although these may differ somewhat in Europe and America. The symptom patterns include acute paranoid reactions, reactive confusions, reactive excitations, and reactive depressions. Some data suggest that in the United States paranoia is often the predominant symptom in the disorder. In French psychiatry, *bouffée délirante* is similar to brief psychotic disorder.

Precipitating Stressors

The clearest examples of precipitating stressors are major life events that would cause any person significant emotional upset. Such events include the loss of a close family member or a severe automobile accident. Some clinicians argue that the severity of the event must be considered in relation to the patient's life. This view, although reasonable, may broaden the definition of precipitating stressor to include events unrelated to the psychotic episode. Others have argued that the stressor may be a series of modestly stressful events rather than a single markedly stressful event, but evaluating the amount of stress caused by a sequence of events calls for an almost impossibly high degree of clinical judgment.

DIFFERENTIAL DIAGNOSIS

Clinicians must not assume that the correct diagnosis for a briefly psychotic patient is brief psychotic disorder, even when a clear precipitating psychosocial factor is identified. Such a factor may be merely coincidental. Other diagnoses to consider in the differential diagnosis include factitious disorder with predominantly psychological signs and symptoms, malingering, psychotic disorder caused by a general medical condition, and substance-induced psychotic disorder. A patient unwilling to admit the use of illicit substances may thereby make the assessment of substance intoxication or substance withdrawal difficult without the use of laboratory testing. Patients with epilepsy or delirium can also show psychotic symptoms that resemble those seen in brief psychotic disorder. Additional psychiatric disorders to be considered in the differential diagnosis include dissociative identity disorder and psychotic episodes associated with borderline and schizotypal personality disorders.

COURSE AND PROGNOSIS

By definition, the course of brief psychotic disorder is less than 1 month. Nonetheless, the development of such a significant psychiatric disorder may signify a patient's mental vulnerability. An unknown percentage of patients who are first classified as having brief psychotic disorder later display chronic psychiatric syndromes such as schizophrenia and mood disorders. Patients with brief psychotic disorder, however, generally have good prognoses, and European studies have indicated that 50 to 80 percent of all patients have no further major psychiatric problems.

The length of the acute and residual symptoms is often just a few days. Occasionally, depressive symptoms follow the resolution of the psychotic symptoms. Suicide is a concern during both the psychotic phase and the postpsychotic depressive phase. Several indicators have been associated with a good prognosis (Table 14.5–2). Patients with these features are unlikely to have subsequent episodes, and schizophrenia or a mood disorder is unlikely to develop later.

Table 14.5–2
Good Prognostic Features for Brief Psychotic Disorder

Good premorbid adjustment
Few premorbid schizoid traits
Severe precipitating stressor
Sudden onset of symptoms
Affective symptoms
Confusion and perplexity during psychosis
Little affective blunting
Short duration of symptoms
Absence of schizophrenic relatives

TREATMENT

Hospitalization

An acutely psychotic patient may need a brief hospitalization for both evaluation and protection. Evaluation requires close monitoring of symptoms and assessment of the patient's level of danger to self and others. In addition, the quiet and structured setting of a hospital may help patients regain their sense of reality. While clinicians wait for the setting or the drugs to have their effects, seclusion, physical restraints, or one-to-one monitoring of the patient may be necessary.

Pharmacotherapy

The two major classes of drugs to be considered in the treatment of brief psychotic disorder are the dopamine receptor antagonist antipsychotic drugs and the benzodiazepines. When an antipsychotic drug is chosen, a high-potency antipsychotic drug such as haloperidol (Haldol) is usually used. Especially in patients who are at high risk for the development of extrapyramidal side effects (for example, young men), an anticholinergic drug should probably be coadministered with the antipsychotic drug as prophylaxis against medication-induced movement disorder symptoms. Alternatively, benzodiazepines can be used in the short-term treatment of psychosis. Although benzodiazepines have limited or no usefulness in the long-term treatment of psychotic disorders, they can be effective for a short time and are associated with fewer side effects than are the antipsychotic drugs. In rare cases, the benzodiazepines are associated with increased agitation and, more rarely still with withdrawal seizures, which usually occur only with the sustained use of high dosages. The use of other drugs in the treatment of brief psychotic disorder, although reported in case studies, has not been supported in any large-scale studies. Hypnotic medications, however, are often useful during the first 2 to 3 weeks after the resolution of the psychotic episode. Clinicians should avoid long-term use of any medication in the treatment of the disorder. If maintenance medication is necessary, a clinician may have to reconsider the diagnosis.

Psychotherapy

Although hospitalization and pharmacotherapy are likely to control short-term situations, the difficult part of treatment is the psychological integration of the experience (and possibly the precipitating trauma, if one was present) into the lives of the patients and their families. Individual, family, and group psychotherapies may be indicated. Discussion of the stressors, the psychotic episode, and the development of coping strategies are the major topics for such therapies. Associated issues include helping patients cope with the loss of self-esteem and self-confidence.

References

Beighley PS, Brown GR, Thompson JW: DSM-III-R brief reactive psychosis among Air Force recruits. J Clin Psychiatry *53:* 283, 1992.

Jablensky A, Sartorius N, Ernberg G, Anker M, Korten A, Cooper JE, Day R, Bertelsen A: Schizophrenia: Manifestations, incidence and course in different cultures; a World Health Organization ten-country study. Psychol Med [Monogr Suppl] *20,* 1992.

Johnson FA: African perspectives on mental disorder. In *Psychiatric Diagnosis: A World Perspective,* JE Mezzich, Y Honda, MC Kastrup, editors. Springer-Verlag, New York, 1994.

Jorge MR, Mezzich JE: Latin American contributions to psychiatric nosology and classification. In *Psychiatric Diagnosis: A World Perspective,* JE Mezzich, Y Honda, MC Kastrup, editors. Springer-Verlag, New York, 1994.

Jorgensen P, Mortensen P: Reactive psychosis and mortality. Acta Psychiatr Scand *81:* 277, 1990.

Karno M, Jenkins JH: Cultural considerations in the diagnosis of schizophrenia and related disorders and psychotic disorders not otherwise classified. In *DSM-IV Source Book,* TA Widiger, A Frances, HA Pincus, MB First, R Ross, W Davis, editors. American Psychiatric Press, Washington, 1994.

Lin K-M: Cultural influences on the diagnosis of psychotic and organic disorders. In *Culture and Psychiatric Diagnosis,* JE Mezzich, A Kleinman, H Fabrega, DL Parron editors. American Psychiatric Press, Washington, 1995.

Mezzich JE, Lin K-M: Acute and transient psychotic disorders and culture-bound syndromes. In *Comprehensive Textbook of Psychiatry,* ed 6, HI Kaplan, BJ Sadock, editors, p 1049. Williams & Wilkins, Baltimore, 1995.

Pull CB, Chaillet G: The nosological views of French-speaking psychiatry. In *Psychiatric Diagnosis: A World Perspective,* JE Mezzich, Y Honda, MC Kastrup, editors. Springer-Verlag, New York, 1994.

Susser E, Wanderling E: Epidemiology of non-affective acute remitting psychosis vs schizophrenia. Arch Gen Psychiatry *51:* 294, 1994.

Vanderhart O, Witztum E, Friedman B: From hysterical psychosis to reactive dissociative psychosis. J Trauma Stress *6:* 43, 1993.

15 Mood Disorders

▲ 15.1 Overview

Mood may be normal, elevated, or depressed. Ordinarily, people experience a wide range of moods and have an equally large repertoire of affective expressions; they feel in control, more or less, of their moods and affects. In mood disorders, the sense of control is lost, and people experience great distress. Patients with an elevated mood (mania) show expansiveness, flight of ideas, decreased sleep, heightened self-esteem, and grandiose ideas. Patients with depressed mood (depression) have a loss of energy and interest, feelings of guilt, difficulty in concentrating, loss of appetite, and thoughts of death or suicide. Other signs and symptoms of mood disorders include changes in activity level, cognitive abilities, speech, and vegetative functions (such as sleep, appetite, sexual activity, and other biological rhythms). These changes almost always result in impaired interpersonal, social, and occupational functioning. Patients with mood disorders often report an ineffable but distinct quality to their pathological state. The concept of a continuum with normal variations in mood may reflect clinicians' overidentification with the pathology and may distort patients' actual experience.

HISTORY

Terms and Definitions

People have recorded instances of depression since antiquity. Descriptions of what are now called mood disorders appear in many ancient documents. The Old Testament story of King Saul describes a depressive syndrome, as does the story of Ajax's suicide in Homer's *Iliad.* About 400 B.C., Hippocrates used the terms *mania* and *melancholia* to describe mental disturbances. Around A.D. 30, the Roman physician Aulus Cornelius Celsus described melancholia from Greek (*melan* [''black''] and *cholé* [''bile'']) in his work *De re medicina* as a depression caused by black bile. The term continued to be used by other medical authors, including Arateus (120–180), Galen (ca. 129–199), and Alexander of Tralles in the sixth century. The 12th century Jewish physician and philosopher Moses Maimonides considered melancholia a discrete disease entity. In 1686, Bonet described a mental illness that he called *maniaco-melancholicus.*

In 1854, Jules Falret described a condition called *folie circulaire,* in which patients experience alternating moods of depression and mania. About the same time, another French psychiatrist, Jules G. F. Baillarger, described the condition for *folie à double forme,* in which patients become deeply depressed and fall into a stuporous state from which they eventually recover. In 1882, the German psychiatrist Karl Kahlbaum, using the term *cyclothymia,* described mania and depression as stages of the same illness.

Emil Kraepelin

In 1899, Emil Kraepelin, building on the knowledge of previous French and German psychiatrists, described a manic-depressive psychosis using most of the criteria that psychiatrists now use to establish a diagnosis of bipolar I disorder. The absence of a dementing and deteriorating course in manic-depressive psychosis differentiated it from dementia precox (as schizophrenia was then called). Kraepelin also described a depression that came to be known as *involutional melancholia* and has since come to be viewed as a form of mood disorder with a late onset; the disorder begins after menopause in women and during late adulthood in men.

EPIDEMIOLOGY

The lifetime prevalence for mood disorders has been variously reported as 2 to 25 percent (Table 15.1–1).

The prevalence of mood disorders does not differ according to race or ethnic group, but clinicians tend to underdiagnose mood disorders and to overdiagnose schizophrenia in patients with racial or cultural backgrounds different from their own. White psychiatrists, for example, tend to underdiagnose mood disorders in blacks and Hispanics.

ETIOLOGY

The causes of mood disorders are unknown. The many attempts to identify a biological or psychosocial cause may have been hampered by the heterogeneity of the patient population that is defined by any of the available, clinically based diagnostic systems, including the fourth edition of *Diagnostic and Statistical Manual of Mental Disorders* (DSM-IV). The causative factors can be artificially divided into biological, genetic, and psychosocial, but this division is artificial because the three realms likely interact among themselves. Psychosocial and genetic factors can affect biological factors, such as concentrations of a certain neurotransmitter. Biological and psychosocial factors can also affect gene expression, and biological and genetic factors can affect a person's response to

Table 15.1–1
Lifetime Prevalence of Some DSM-IV Mood Disorders

Mood Disorder	Lifetime Prevalence
Depressive disorders	
Major depressive disorder (MDD)	10–25% for women; 5–12% for men
Recurrent, with full interepisode recovery, superimposed on dysthymic disorder	Approximately 3% of persons with MDD
Recurrent, without full interepisode recovery, superimposed on dysthymic disorder (double depression)	Approximately 25% of persons with MDD
Dysthymic disorder	Approximately 6%
Bipolar disorders	
Bipolar I disorder	0.4–1.6%
Bipolar II disorder	Approximately 0.5%
Bipolar I disorder or bipolar II disorder, with rapid cycling	5–15% of persons with bipolar disorder
Cyclothymic disorder	0.4–1.0%

Data are from American Psychiatric Association: *Diagnostic and Statistical Manual of Mental Disorders,* ed 4. Copyright, American Psychiatric Association, Washington, 1994.

psychosocial factors. (See Sections 15.2 and 15.3 for further discussions of the etiology of mood disorders.)

DSM-IV

As clinical and biological researchers have studied the mood disorders, previously recognized clinical distinctions among patients have become appreciated and are now officially recognized in DSM-IV. The two major mood disorders are major depressive disorder and bipolar I disorder. Major depressive disorder and bipolar I disorder are often referred to as affective disorder, but the critical pathology in these disorders is one of *mood,* the sustained internal emotional state of a person, and not one of *affect,* the external expression of present emotional content. Patients who are afflicted with depressive episodes alone are said to have major depressive disorder, sometimes called unipolar depression (not a DSM-IV term). Patients with both manic and depressive episodes and patients with manic episodes alone are said to have bipolar I disorder. The terms *unipolar mania* and *pure mania* (not DSM-IV terms) are sometimes used for bipolar I disorder patients who do not have depressive episodes.

According to DSM-IV, a major depressive disorder is defined as one or more major depressive episodes without a history of manic, mixed, or hypomanic episodes. A major depressive episode must last at least 2 weeks; typically, a person is either depressed or loses interest in most activities. A person diagnosed with major depressive episode must also experience at least four symptoms from a list that includes changes in appetite and weight, changes in sleep and activity, lack of energy, feeling of guilt, problems in thinking and making decisions, and recurring thoughts of death or suicide.

A manic episode is a distinct period (at least 1 week, less if a patient must be hospitalized) of an ''abnormally and persistently elevated, expansive, or irritable mood.'' A mixed episode is a period of at least 1 week in which both a manic episode and a major depressive episode occur almost daily. The symptoms of a hypomanic episode, which has a duration of at least 4 days, are similar to those of a manic episode but also include at least three symptoms from among inflated self-esteem, decreased need for sleep, distractibility, great physical and mental activity, and overinvolvement in pleasurable behavior with unpleasant consequences. If a person is irritable instead of elevated in mood, four of these symptoms must be present. According to DSM-IV, bipolar I disorder is defined as having a clinical course of one or more manic episodes or mixed episodes and sometimes of major depressive episodes.

Two additional mood disorders, dysthymic disorder and cyclothymic disorder, have also been appreciated clinically for some time. Dysthymic disorder and cyclothymic disorder are characterized by the presence of symptoms that are less severe than the symptoms of major depressive disorder and of bipolar I disorder, respectively. DSM-IV defines dysthymic disorder as characterized by at least 2 years of depressed mood that occurs more often than not and by additional depressive symptoms that cannot fit the diagnosis of major depressive episode. Cyclothymic disorder is characterized by at least 2 years of frequently occurring hypomanic symptoms that cannot fit the diagnosis of manic episode and of depressive symptoms that cannot fit the diagnosis of major depressive episode.

The authors of DSM-IV codified additional mood disorders, both in the main body of the text and in the appendices. Those disorders include syndromes related to depression (minor depressive disorder, recurrent brief depressive disorder, and premenstrual dysphoric disorder) and disorders related to bipolar I disorder (bipolar II disorder). In minor depressive disorder, the symptoms do not reach the severity necessary for a diagnosis of major depressive disorder; in recurrent brief depressive disorder, the depressive episodes do reach the severity of symptoms required for a diagnosis of major depressive disorder but for only an amount of time that is insufficient to meet the diagnostic criteria for major depressive disorder. Bipolar II disorder is characterized by the presence of major depressive episodes alternating with episodes of hypomania—that is, episodes of manic symptoms that do not meet the full criteria for the manic episodes of bipolar I disorder. Additional mood disorder diagnoses include mood disorder due to a general medical condition, substance-induced mood disorder, and mood disorder not otherwise specified.

DSM-IV introduces one new mood disorder diagnostic category (bipolar II disorder) in the body of the text and three new mood disorder research categories (minor depressive disorder, recurrent brief depressive disorder, and premenstrual dysphoric disorder). Other DSM-IV diagnoses are mood disorder due to a general medical condition and substance-induced mood disorder. These changes are designed to broaden the recognition of mood disorder diagnoses, to describe mood disorder symptoms more specifically than in the past, and to facilitate the differential diagnosis of mood disorders.

Depressive Disorders

Diagnostic Criteria. The diagnostic criteria for major depressive disorder specify a certain level of severity and a certain duration of symptoms as minimum requirements to meet the diagnosis. Although the criteria reflect a great deal of research and discussion, they are, by necessity, arbitrary. Many clinicians, especially primary care physicians, report that they have seen many patients with depressive symptoms that cause them psychosocial impairment but who do not meet the diagnostic criteria for major depressive disorder; usually, their symptoms are not severe enough or have not lasted long enough. DSM-IV addresses the diagnostic problem posed by these patients by including two additional categories.

The diagnostic criteria for minor depressive disorder are derived from the Research Diagnostic Criteria and apply to patients whose depressive symptoms fail to meet the criteria for major depressive disorder in terms of severity but do meet the criteria for duration. The diagnostic criteria for recurrent brief depressive disorder are derived from the 10th revision of *International Statistical Classification of Diseases and Related Health Problems* (ICD-10) and apply to patients who have depressive symptoms that fail to meet the criteria for major depressive disorder in terms of duration but that do meet the criteria for severity.

Minor depressive disorder and recurrent brief depressive disorder differ from dysthymic disorder, which is a chronic depressive disorder. In contrast, both minor depressive disorder and recurrent brief depressive disorder are characterized by discrete episodes.

Depressive Disorder Not Otherwise Specified. If a patient exhibits depressive symptoms as the major feature and does not meet the diagnostic criteria for any other mood disorder or other DSM-IV mental disorder, the most appropriate diagnosis is a depressive disorder not otherwise specified (Table 15.1–2). Examples discussed subsequently and in the appendixes are minor depressive disorder, recurrent brief disorder, and premenstrual dysphoric disorder.

Table 15.1–2
DSM-IV Diagnostic Criteria for Depressive Disorder Not Otherwise Specified

The depressive disorder not otherwise specified category includes disorders with depressive features that do not meet the criteria for major depressive disorder, dysthymic disorder, adjustment disorder with depressed mood, or adjustment disorder with mixed anxiety and depressed mood. Sometimes depressive symptoms can present as part of an anxiety disorder not otherwise specified. Examples of depressive disorder not otherwise specified include:

1. Premenstrual dysphoric disorder: in most menstrual cycles during the past year, symptoms (eg, markedly depressed mood, marked anxiety, marked affective lability, decreased interest in activities) regularly occurred during the last week of the luteal phase (and remitted within a few days of the onset of menses). These symptoms must be severe enough to markedly interfere with work, school, or usual activities and be entirely absent for at least 1 week postmenses.
2. Minor depressive disorder: episodes of at least 2 weeks of depressive symptoms but with fewer than the five items required for major depressive disorder.
3. Recurrent brief depressive disorder: depressive episodes lasting from 2 days up to 2 weeks, occurring at least once a month for 12 months (not associated with the menstrual cycle).
4. Postpsychotic depressive disorder of schizophrenia: a major depressive episode that occurs during the residual phase of schizophrenia.
5. A major depressive episode superimposed on delusional disorder, psychotic disorder not otherwise specified, or the active phase of schizophrenia.
6. Situations in which the clinician has concluded that a depressive disorder is present but is unable to determine whether it is primary, due to a general medical condition, or substance induced.

Reprinted with permission from American Psychiatric Association: *Diagnostic and Statistical Manual of Mental Disorders,* ed 4. Copyright, American Psychiatric Association, Washington, 1994.

MINOR DEPRESSIVE DISORDER. The literature in the United States on minor depressive disorder is limited, in part by the fact that the term minor depression is used to describe a wide range of disorders, including what is called dysthymic disorder in DSM-IV. The European literature on minor depressive disorder is also limited, but it is more extensive than that in the United States. The information about this disorder is supplemented considerably in the appendix of DSM-IV by the introduction of specific diagnostic guidelines that allow researchers to use a single definition of the disorder.

Epidemiology. The epidemiology of minor depressive disorder is unknown, but preliminary data indicate that it may be as common as major depressive disorder—that is, about 5 percent prevalence in the general population. Preliminary data also indicate that the disorder is more common in women than in men. Minor depressive disorder probably affects people of virtually any age, from childhood onward.

Etiology. The cause of minor depressive disorder is unknown. The same causative considerations given major depressive disorder should be considered. Specifically, the biological theories involve the activities of noradrenergic and serotonergic biogenic amine systems and the thyroid and adrenal neuroendocrine axes. The psychological theories center on issues of loss, guilt, and punitive superegos.

Diagnosis. The DSM-IV research criteria for minor depressive disorder include symptoms equal in duration to those of major depressive disorder but of less severity (Table 15.1–3). The category allows for the specific diagnosis of patients whose lives are affected by depressive symptoms but whose symptoms do not meet the severity required for a diagnosis of major depressive disorder.

Clinical Features. Except that they are of less severity, the clinical features of minor depressive disorder are virtually identical to those of major depressive disorder. The central symptom of both disorders is the same—a depressed mood.

Differential Diagnosis. The differential diagnosis for minor depressive disorder is the same as that for major depressive disorder. Of special importance for the differential diagnosis of minor depressive disorder are dysthymic disorder and recurrent brief depressive disorder. Dysthymic disorder is characterized by the presence of chronic depressive symptoms, whereas recurrent brief depressive disorder is characterized by multiple brief episodes of severe depressive symptoms.

Course and Prognosis. No definitive data on the course and the prognosis of minor depressive disorder are available, but minor depressive disorder, probably like major depressive disorder, has a long-term course that may require long-term treatment. A significant proportion of patients with minor depressive disorder are probably at risk for other mood disorders, including dysthymic disorder, bipolar I disorder, bipolar II disorder, and major depressive disorder.

Treatment. The treatment of minor depressive disorder can include psychotherapy, pharmacotherapy, or both. Some psychotherapists advocate using multiple psychotherapeutic approaches, but using the psychotherapy data for major depressive disorder is a more conservative approach. Insight-oriented psychotherapy, cognitive therapy, interpersonal therapy, and behavior therapy are the psychotherapeutic treatments for major depressive disorder and, by implication, for minor depressive disorder. Although the experimental data are limited, patients with minor depressive disorder are probably responsive to pharmacotherapy, particularly serotonin-specific reuptake inhibitors (SSRIs) and bupropion (Wellbutrin).

Table 15.1–3
DSM-IV Research Criteria for Minor Depressive Disorder

A. A mood disturbance, defined as follows:
   (1) At least two (but less than five) of the following symptoms have been present during the same 2-week period and represent a change from previous functioning; at least one of the symptoms is either (a) or (b):
      (a) depressed mood most of the day, nearly every day, as indicated by either subjective report (eg, feels sad or empty) or observation made by others (eg, appears tearful). **Note:** In children and adolescents, can be irritable mood.
      (b) markedly diminished interest or pleasure in all, or almost all, activities most of the day, nearly every day (as indicated by either subjective account or observation made by others)
      (c) significant weight loss when not dieting or weight gain (eg, a change of more than 5% of body weight in a month), or decrease or increase in appetite nearly every day. **Note:** In children, consider failure to make expected weight gains.
      (d) insomnia or hypersomnia nearly every day
      (e) psychomotor agitation or retardation nearly every day (observable by others, not merely subjective feelings of restlessness or being slowed down)
      (f) fatigue or loss of energy nearly every day
      (g) feelings of worthlessness or excessive or inappropriate guilt (which may be delusional) nearly every day (not merely self-reproach or guilt about being sick)
      (h) diminished ability to think or concentrate, or indecisiveness, nearly every day (either by subjective account or as observed by others)
      (i) recurrent thoughts of death (not just fear of dying), recurrent suicidal ideation without a specific plan, or a suicide attempt or a specific plan for committing suicide
   (2) the symptoms cause clinically significant distress or impairment in social, occupational, or other important areas of functioning
   (3) the symptoms are not due to the direct physiological effects of a substance (eg, a drug of abuse, a medication) or a general medical condition (eg, hypothyroidism)
   (4) the symptoms are not better accounted for by bereavement (ie, a normal reaction to the death of a loved one)

B. There has never been a major depressive episode, and criteria are not met for dysthymic disorder.

C. There has never been a manic episode, a mixed episode, or a hypomanic episode, and criteria are not met for cyclothymic disorder. **Note:** This exclusion does not apply if all of the manic-, mixed-, or hypomanic-like episodes are substance or treatment induced.

D. The mood disturbance does not occur exclusively during schizophrenia, schizophreniform disorder, schizoaffective disorder, delusional disorder, or psychotic disorder not otherwise specified.

Reprinted with permission from American Psychiatric Association: *Diagnostic and Statistical Manual of Mental Disorders,* ed 4. Copyright, American Psychiatric Association, Washington, 1994.

RECURRENT BRIEF DEPRESSIVE DISORDER. Recurrent brief depressive disorder is characterized by multiple, relatively brief episodes (of less than 2 weeks) of depressive symptoms that, except for their brief duration, meet the diagnostic criteria for major depressive disorder. Recurrent brief depressive disorder has been written about mostly in the European literature, but with its introduction as research category in the appendix of DSM-IV, the diagnosis is likely to gain rapid acceptance in the United States. This acceptance will likely be further facilitated by clinicians' increasing awareness that recurrent brief depressive disorder is relatively common and associated with significant morbidity.

Epidemiology. Extensive studies of the epidemiology of recurrent brief depressive disorder have not been conducted in the United States. Available data indicate that the 10-year prevalence rate for the disorder is estimated to be 10 percent for people in their 20s; the 1-year prevalence rate for the general population is estimated to be 5 percent. These numbers indicate that recurrent brief depressive disorder is most common among young adults, but many more studies must be conducted to refine the data.

Etiology. One study showed that patients with recurrent brief depressive disorder share several biological abnormalities with patients with major depressive disorder as compared with control subjects who are mentally healthy. The variables include nonsuppression on the dexamethasone-suppression test (DST), a blunt response to thyrotropin-releasing hormone (TRH), and a shortening of rapid eye movement (REM) sleep latency. The data are consistent with the idea that recurrent brief depressive disorder is closely related to major depressive disorder in its cause and pathophysiology. The available data also suggest a close relation between the two disorders, and indicate that family histories of mood disorders are similar for recurrent brief depressive disorder and major depressive disorder.

Diagnosis. The DSM-IV research criteria for recurrent brief depressive disorder specify that the symptom duration for each episode is less than 2 weeks (Table 15.1–4). Otherwise, the diagnostic criteria for recurrent brief depressive disorder and major depressive disorder are essentially identical.

Clinical Features. The clinical features of recurrent brief depressive disorder are almost identical to those of major depressive disorder. One subtle difference is that the lives of patients with recurrent brief depressive disorder may seem more disrupted or chaotic because of the frequent changes in their moods than are the lives of patients with major depressive disorder, whose depressive episodes occur at a measured pace. In one study, the mean length of time between depressive disorder episodes in recurrent brief depressive disorder

Table 15.1–4
DSM-IV Research Criteria for Recurrent Brief Depressive Disorder

A. Criteria, except for duration, are met for a major depressive episode.

B. The depressive periods in criterion A last at least 2 days but less than 2 weeks.

C. The depressive periods occur at least once a month for 12 consecutive months and are not associated with the menstrual cycle.

D. The periods of depressed mood cause clinically significant distress or impairment in social, occupational, or other important areas of functioning.

E. The symptoms are not due to the direct physiological effects of a substance (eg, a drug of abuse, a medication) or a general medical condition (eg, hypothyroidism).

F. There has never been a major depressive episode, and criteria are not met for dysthymic disorder.

G. There has never been a manic episode, a mixed episode, or a hypomanic episode, and criteria are not met for cyclothymic disorder. **Note:** This exclusion does not apply if all of the manic-, mixed-, or hypomanic-like episodes are substance or treatment induced.

H. The mood disturbance does not occur exclusively during schizophrenia, schizophreniform disorder, schizoaffective disorder, delusional disorder, or psychotic disorder not otherwise specified.

Reprinted with permission from American Psychiatric Association: *Diagnostic and Statistical Manual of Mental Disorders,* ed 4. Copyright, American Psychiatric Association, Washington, 1994.

was calculated to be 18 days. Results of another study showed that episodes of sleep disturbances closely coincide with the episodes of depression and thus helping clinicians establish the periodicity of the depressive episodes.

Differential Diagnosis. The differential diagnosis for recurrent brief depressive disorder is the same as that for major depressive disorder. Clinicians should consider bipolar disorders and major depressive disorder with seasonal pattern in the differential diagnosis. Research into recurrent brief depressive disorder may find an association with the rapid cycling type of bipolar disorder. Clinicians should also assess whether there is a seasonal pattern to the recurrence of depressive episodes in a patient being evaluated for a diagnosis of recurrent brief depressive disorder. At least one researcher has proposed that patients with recurrent brief depressive disorder be subtyped according to the relative frequencies of their depressive episodes. This differentiation is not included in DSM-IV, although it may yet prove to have prognostic or treatment implications.

Course and Prognosis. The course and the prognosis for patients with recurrent brief depressive disorder are not well known. On the basis of available data, their course, including age of onset, and their prognosis are similar to those of patients with major depressive disorder.

Treatment. The treatment of patients with recurrent brief depressive disorder should be similar to the treatment of patients with major depressive disorder. The main treatments are psychotherapy (insight-oriented psychotherapy, cognitive therapy, interpersonal therapy, or behavioral therapy) and pharmacotherapy with the standard antidepressant drugs. Some of the treatments for bipolar I disorder—lithium (Eskalith) and anticonvulsants—may be of therapeutic value.

PREMENSTRUAL DYSPHORIC DISORDER. In its appendix, DSM-IV includes suggested diagnostic criteria for premenstrual dysphoric disorder to help researchers and clinicians evaluate the validity of the diagnosis. Premenstrual dysphoric disorder has also been referred to as late luteal phase dysphoric disorder, premenstrual syndrome, and simply PMS. Whether the syndrome warrants an official diagnosis remains controversial. Nevertheless, the generally recognized syndrome involves mood symptoms (for example, lability), behavior symptoms (for example, changes in eating patterns), and physical symptoms (for example, breast tenderness, edema, and headaches). This pattern of symptoms occurs at a specific time during the menstrual cycle, and the symptoms resolve for some period of time between menstrual cycles.

Epidemiology. Because of the absence of generally agreed-on diagnostic criteria, the epidemiology of premenstrual dysphoric disorder is not known with certainty. One study reported that about 40 percent of women have at least mild symptoms of the disorder and that from 2 to 10 percent meet the full diagnostic criteria for the disorder.

Etiology. On the one hand, the cause of premenstrual dysphoric disorder is unknown. On the other hand, because the symptoms are timed to the menstrual cycle, the hormonal changes occurring during the menstrual cycle are probably involved in producing symptoms. A common theory among many proposed theories characterizes the disorder as the result of an abnormally high estrogen-to-progesterone ratio in affected women. Other hypotheses suggest that the biogenic amine neurons of affected women are abnormally affected by changes in the hormones, that the disorder is an example of a chronobiological phase disorder, and that it is the result of abnormal prostaglandin activity. In addition to the biological theories, societal and personal issues about menstruation and womanhood may affect the symptoms of individual patients.

Diagnosis. The appendix of DSM-IV contains suggested diagnostic criteria for premenstrual dysphoric disorder (Table 15.1–5). The criteria include symptoms about abnormal mood, abnormal behavior, and somatic complaints.

Clinical Features. The most common mood and cognitive symptoms are lability of mood, irritability, anxiety, decreased interest in activities, increased fatigability, and difficulty in concentrating. Behavioral symptoms often include changes in appetite and sleep patterns. The most common somatic complaints are headache, breast tenderness, and edema. In affected women, the symptoms appear during most (if not all) menstrual cycles, although they usually remit before the end of the blood flow. Affected women are symptom free for at least 1 week during each menstrual cycle.

Differential Diagnosis. If symptoms are present throughout the menstrual cycle, with no intercycle symptom relief, clinicians should consider one of the nonmenstrual cycle-related mood disorders and anxiety disorders. The presence of especially severe symptoms, even if cyclical, should prompt clinicians to consider other mood disorders and anxiety disorder.

Table 15.1–5
DSM-IV Research Criteria for Premenstrual Dysphoric Disorder

A. In most menstrual cycles during the past year, five (or more) of the following symptoms were present for most of the time during the last week of the luteal phase, began to remit within a few days after the onset of the follicular phase, and were absent in the week postmenses, with at least one of the symptoms being either (1), (2), (3), or (4):
   (1) markedly depressed mood, feelings of hopelessness, or self-deprecating thoughts
   (2) marked anxiety, tension, feelings of being "keyed up" or "on edge"
   (3) marked affective liability (eg, feeling suddenly sad or tearful or increased sensitivity to rejection)
   (4) persistent and marked anger or irritability or increased interpersonal conflicts
   (5) decreased interest in usual activities (eg, work, school, friends, hobbies)
   (6) subjective sense of difficulty in concentrating
   (7) lethargy, easy fatigability, or marked lack of energy
   (8) marked change in appetite, overeating, or specific food cravings
   (9) hypersomnia or insomnia
   (10) a subjective sense of being overwhelmed or out of control
   (11) other physical symptoms, such as breast tenderness or swelling, headaches, joint or muscle pain, a sensation of "bloating," weight gain

Note: In menstruating females, the luteal phase corresponds to the period between ovulation and the onset of menses, and the follicular phase begins with menses. In nonmenstruating females (eg, those who have had a hysterectomy), the timing of luteal and follicular phases may require measurement of circulating reproductive hormones.

B. The disturbance markedly interferes with work or school or with usual social activities and relationships with others (eg, avoidance of social activities, decreased productivity and efficiency at work or school).

C. The disturbance is not merely an exacerbation of the symptoms of another disorder, such as major depressive disorder, panic disorder, dysthymic disorder, or a personality disorder (although it may be superimposed on any of these disorders).

D. Criteria A, B, and C must be confirmed by prospective daily ratings during at least two consecutive symptomatic cycles. (The diagnosis may be made provisionally prior to this confirmation.)

Course and Prognosis. The course and the prognosis of premenstrual dysphoric disorder have not been studied enough to reach any reasonable conclusions. Anecdotally, the symptoms tend to be chronic unless effective treatment is initiated.

Treatment. Treatment of premenstrual dysphoric disorder includes support for the patient about the presence and recognition of the symptoms. In preliminary studies, progesterone supplementation, fluoxetine (Prozac), and alprazolam (Xanax) have all been reported to be effective, although no treatment has been conclusively demonstrated to be effective in multiple, well-controlled trials.

Bipolar Disorders

Clinicians have long reported that some patients have a disorder, the primary symptoms of which are depressive episodes, yet the course of the disorder is interspersed with episodes of mild manic symptoms (that is, hypomanic episodes). Such disorders have been called bipolar II disorder (by those researchers who think that the disorder belongs in the bipolar disorders spectrum) and major depressive disorder with hypomanic episodes (by those researchers who think that the disorder belongs in the depressive disorders spectrum). DSM-IV uses the term *bipolar II disorder.* The distinction between bipolar II disorder and recurrent major depressive episodes with hypomania has important implications for prognostic and treatment assessments and decisions.

Bipolar Disorder Not Otherwise Specified. If patients exhibit depressive and manic symptoms as the major features of their disorder and do not meet the diagnostic criteria for any other mood disorder or other DSM-IV mental disorder, the most appropriate diagnosis is bipolar disorder not otherwise specified (Table 15.1–6). DSM-IV allows for further specifications: with rapid cycling, with seasonal pattern, or with postpartum onset (see Tables 15.2–22, 15.2–24, and 15.2–25).

ATYPICAL CYCLOID PSYCHOSES. These disorders show some features of bipolar I disorder but generally do not meet the complete diagnostic criteria for that category. Some patients with atypical cycloid psychoses may be classified as having bipolar disorder not otherwise specified.

MOTILITY PSYCHOSIS. The two forms of motility psychosis are akinetic and hyperkinetic. The akinetic form of motility psychosis has a clinical presentation similar to that of catatonic stupor. In contrast to the catatonic type of schizophrenia, however, akinetic motility psychosis has a rapidly resolving and favorable course that does not lead to personality deterioration. In its hyperkinetic form, motility psychosis may resemble manic or catatonic excitement.

Table 15.1–6
DSM-IV Diagnostic Criteria for Bipolar Disorder Not Otherwise Specified

The bipolar disorder not otherwise specified category includes disorders with bipolar features that do not meet criteria for any specific bipolar disorder. Examples include:

1. Very rapid alternation (over days) between manic symptoms and depressive symptoms that do not meet minimal duration criteria for a manic episode or major depressive episode
2. Recurrent hypomanic episodes without intercurrent depressive symptoms
3. A manic or mixed episode superimposed on delusional disorder, residual schizophrenia, or psychotic disorder not otherwise specified
4. Situations in which the clinician has concluded that a bipolar disorder is present but is unable to determine whether it is primary, due to a general medical condition, or substance induced

As with the akinetic form, the hyperkinetic form has a rapidly resolving and favorable course.

CONFUSIONAL PSYCHOSIS. As described originally, excited confusional psychosis was differentiated from mania by several characteristics: more anxiety, less distractibility, and a degree of speech incoherence out of proportion to the severity of the flight of ideas. Confusional psychosis is probably a clinical variation of the mania seen in bipolar I disorder.

ANXIETY-BLISSFULNESS PSYCHOSIS. Anxiety-blissfulness psychosis may resemble agitated depression but may also be characterized by so much inhibition that a patient can hardly move. Periodic states of overwhelming anxiety and paranoid ideas of reference are characteristic of the condition, but self-accusation, hypochondriacal preoccupation, other depressive symptoms, and hallucinations may also accompany it. The blissful phase manifests itself most frequently in expansive behavior and grandiose ideas, which are concerned less with self-aggrandizement than with the mission of making others happy and of saving the world.

Other Mood Disorders

Two mood disorder diagnoses to be considered in the differential diagnosis of any patient with mood disorder symptoms are mood disorder due to a general medical condition and substance-induced mood disorder. DSM-IV includes these diagnostic categories within the section on mood disorders to encourage and facilitate the process of differential diagnosis.

It can be difficult to determine whether mood disorder symptoms in a patient with a general medical condition are secondary to the effects on the brain of the general medical condition (classified as a mood disorder caused by a general medical condition); secondary to the effects on the brain of drugs used to treat the general medical condition (classified as a substance-induced mood disorder); reflective of an adjustment disorder caused by the general medical condition (classified as an adjustment disorder); or reflective of a primary mood disorder (for example, major depressive disorder). The difficulty of the clinical differentiation is recognized in DSM-IV by grouping the disorders (except for adjustment disorder) in the mood disorders section.

Mood Disorders Due to a General Medical Condition. When depressive or manic symptoms are present in a patient with a general medical condition, attributing the depressive symptoms either to the general medical condition or to a mood disorder can be difficult. Many general medical conditions present depressive symptoms, such as poor sleep, decreased appetite, and fatigue.

EPIDEMIOLOGY. The epidemiology of mood disorder caused by a general medical condition is unknown, but the disorder is probably common and often undiagnosed.

ETIOLOGY. A wide array of somatic disorders have been implicated as causes of mood disorder symptoms, including endocrine disorders, especially Cushing's syndrome (as a result of high cortisol levels), and neurological disorders, such as brain tumors, encephalitis, and epilepsy. Structural damage to the brain, like that occurring in hemispheric cerebrovascular diseases, is a common cause of mood disorder caused by a general medical condition. Some of the common medical conditions associated with depression are listed in Table 15.1–7, and those associated with mania are listed in Table 15.1–8.

DIAGNOSIS. The DSM-IV diagnostic criteria for mood disorder due to

Table 15.1–7
Neurological and Medical Causes of Depression

Neurological disorders
- Extrapyramidal diseases
  - Parkinson's disease
  - Huntington's disease
  - Progressive supranuclear palsy
- Alzheimer's disease
- Cerebrovascular disease (especially anterior hemispheric lesions)
- Cerebral neoplasms
- Cerebral trauma
- CNS infections
- Dementia
- Migraine
- Multiple sclerosis
- Epilepsy
- Narcolepsy
- Hydrocephalus
- Sleep apnea
- Wilson's disease

Systemic disorders
- Infections
  - Viral
  - Bacterial

Endocrine disorders
- Adrenal (Cushing's, Addison's diseases)
- Hyperaldosteronism
- Menses-related
- Parathyroid disorders (hyper- and hypo-)
- Postpartum

Thyroid disorders (hypothyroidism and apathetic hyperthyroidism)

Inflammmatory disorders
- Systemic lupus erythematosus
- Rheumatoid arthritis
- Temporal arteritis
- Sjögren's syndrome

Vitamin deficiencies
- Folate
- Vitamin B_{12}
- Niacin
- Vitamin C
- Thiamine

Other disorders
- Cancer
- Cardiopulmonary disease
- Renal disease and uremia
- Systemic neoplasms
- Porphyria
- Klinefelter's syndrome
- Acquired immune deficiency syndrome (AIDS)
- Postpartum mood disorders
- Postoperative mood disorders

Adapted from Cummings JL: *Clinical Neuropsychiatry*, p 187. Grune & Stratton, Orlando, 1985.

Table 15.1–8
Neurological, Medical, and Pharmacological Causes of Mania

Neurological disorders
- Extrapyramidal diseases
  - Huntington's disease
  - Postencephalitic Parkinson's disease
  - Wilson's disease
- CNS infections
  - General paresis
  - Viral encephalitis
- Miscellaneous conditions
  - Cerebral neoplasms
  - Cerebral trauma
  - Thalamotomy
  - Cerebrovascular accidents
  - Multiple sclerosis
  - Temporal lobe epilepsy
  - Pick's disease
  - Kleine-Levin syndrome
  - Klinefelter's syndrome

Other disorders
- Uremia and hemodialysis
- Dialysis dementia
- Hyperthyroidism
- Pellagra
- Carcinoid syndrome
- Vitamin B_{12} deficiency
- Postpartum mania

Drugs
- Amphetamines
- Baclofen
- Bromide
- Bromocriptine
- Captopril
- Cimetidine
- Cocaine
- Corticosteroids (including ACTH)
- Cyclosporine
- Disulfiram
- Hallucinogens (intoxication and flashbacks)
- Hydralazine
- Isoniazid
- Levodopa
- Methylphenidate
- Metrizamide (following myelography)
- Opiates and opioids
- Phencyclidine (PCP)
- Procarbazine
- Procyclidine
- Yohimbine

Adapted from Cummings JL: *Clinical Neuropsychiatry*, p 187. Grune & Stratton, Orlando, 1985.

a general medical condition (Table 15.1–9) allow clinicians to specify whether the symptoms are manic (full or partial symptoms), depressive (full or partial symptoms), or mixed.

CLINICAL FEATURES. Disturbances of mood resembling those observed in depressive and manic states are the predominant and essential clinical features, along with a general medical condition that antedates the onset of the mood disorder symptoms. The mood disorder varies in severity from mild to severe or psychotic and may be indistinguishable from the symptoms seen in major depressive disorder and bipolar I disorder. Delusions and hallucinations, as well as mild to moderate cognitive impairment, may be present.

DIFFERENTIAL DIAGNOSIS. The differential diagnosis should include substance-induced mood disorder (produced by substances used to treat the medical condition), the primary mood disorders, and adjustment disorders. In some health delivery systems, malingering must also be considered in the differential diagnosis.

COURSE AND PROGNOSIS. The onset of the symptoms may be sudden or insidious. The course varies, according to the underlying cause, but removing the cause does not necessarily result in a patient's prompt recovery

Table 15.1–9
DSM-IV Diagnostic Criteria for Mood Disorder Due to a General Medical Condition

A. A prominent and persistent disturbance in mood predominates in the clinical picture and is characterized by either (or both) of the following:
   (1) depressed mood or markedly diminished interest or pleasure in all, or almost all, activities
   (2) elevated, expansive, or irritable mood

B. There is evidence from the history, physical examination, or laboratory findings that the disturbance is the direct physiological consequence of a general medical condition.

C. The disturbance is not better accounted for by another mental disorder (eg, adjustment disorder with depressed mood, in response to the stress of having a general medical condition).

D. The disturbance does not occur exclusively during the course of delirium or dementia.

E. The symptoms cause clinically significant distress or impairment in social, occupational, or other important areas of functioning.

Specify type:
- **With depressive features:** if the predominant mood is depressed but the full criteria are not met for a major depressive episode
- **With major depressive-like episode:** if the full criteria are met (except criterion D) for a major depressive episode
- **With manic features:** if the predominant mood is elevated, euphoric, or irritable
- **With mixed features:** if symptoms of both mania and depression are present and neither predominates

from the mood disorder. The disorder may persist for weeks or months after the successful treatment of the underlying physical condition. As with the other mood disorders, suicide is a risk for patients with mood disorder caused by a general medical condition.

TREATMENT. Management of the disorder involves determining the cause and treating the underlying disorder. Psychopharmacological treatment may be indicated and should follow the guidelines applicable to treating depression or mania, with due regard for the coexisting physical condition. Psychotherapy may be useful as an adjunct to other treatments.

Substance-Induced Mood Disorder.

Substance-induced mood disorder must always be considered in the differential diagnosis of mood disorder symptoms. Clinicians should consider three possibilities. First, a patient may be taking drugs for the treatment of nonpsychiatric medical problems. Second, a patient may have been accidentally and perhaps unknowingly exposed to neurotoxic chemicals. Third, the patient may have taken a substance for recreational purposes or may be dependent on such a substance.

EPIDEMIOLOGY. The epidemiology of substance-induced mood disorder is unknown. The prevalence is probably high, however, given the widespread use of so-called recreational drugs, that many prescription drugs can cause depression and mania, and toxic chemicals abound in the environment and the workplace.

ETIOLOGY. Medications, especially antihypertensives, are probably the most frequent cause of substance-induced mood disorder, although a wide range of drugs can produce depression (Table 15.1–10) and mania (see Table 15.1–8). Drugs such as reserpine (Serpasil) and methyldopa (Aldomet), both antihypertensive agents, can precipitate a depressive disorder, presumably by depleting serotonin, as happens in more than 10 percent of all persons who take the drugs.

DIAGNOSIS. The DSM-IV diagnostic criteria for substance-induced mood disorder allow the specification of the substance involved, the time of

Table 15.1–10
Pharmacological Causes of Depression

Cardiac and antihypertensive drugs	
Bethanidine	Digitalis
Clonidine	Prazosin
Guanethidine	Procainamide
Hydralazine	Veratrum
Methyldopa	Lidocaine
Propranolol	Oxprenolol
Reserpine	Methoserpidine
Sedatives and hypnotics	
Barbiturates	Benzodiazepines
Chloral hydrate	Chlormethiazole
Ethanol	Chlorazepate
Steroids and hormones	
Corticosteroids	Triamcinalone
Oral contraceptives	Norethisterone
Prednisone	Danazol
Stimulants and appetite suppressants	
Amphetamine	Diethylpropion
Fenfluramine	Phenmetrazine
Psychotropic drugs	
Butyrophenones	Phenothiazines
Neurological agents	
Amantadine	Baclofen
Bromocriptine	Carbamazepine
Levodopa	Methosuximide
Tetrabenazine	Phenytoin
Analgesics and anti-inflammatory drugs	
Fenoprofen	Phenacetin
Ibuprofen	Phenylbutazone
Indomethacin	Pentazocine
Opiates	Benzydamine
Antibacterial and antifungal drugs	
Ampicillin	Griseofulvin
Sulfamethoxazole	Metronidazole
Clotrimazole	Nitrofurantoin
Cycloserine	Nalidixic acid
Dapsone	Sulfonamides
Ethionamide	Streptomycin
Tetracycline	Thiocarbanilide
Antineoplastic drugs	
C-Asparaginase	6-Azauridine
Mithramycin	Bleomycin
Vincristine	Trimethoprim
	Zidovudine
Miscellaneous drugs	
Acetazolamide	Anticholinesterases
Choline	Cimetidine
Cyproheptadine	Diphenoxylate
Disulfiram	Lysergide
Methysergide	Mebeverine
Meclizine	Metaclopramide
Pizotifen	Salbutamol

Adapted from Cummings JL: *Clinical Neuropsychiatry,* p 187. Grune & Stratton, Orlando, 1985.

Table 15.1–11
DSM-IV Diagnostic Criteria for Substance-Induced Mood Disorder

A. A prominent and persistent disturbance in mood predominates in the clinical picture and is characterized by either (or both) of the following:
(1) depressed mood or markedly diminished interest or pleasure in all, or almost all, activities
(2) elevated, expansive, or irritable mood

B. There is evidence from the history, physical examination, or laboratory findings of substance intoxication or withdrawal, and the symptoms in A developed during, or within a month of, significant substance intoxication or withdrawal.

C. The disturbance is not better accounted for by a mood disorder that is not substance-induced. Evidence that the symptoms are better accounted for by a mood disorder that is not substance-induced might include: the symptoms precede the onset of the substance abuse or dependence; persist for a substantial period of time (eg, about a month) after the cessation of acute withdrawal or severe intoxication; are substantially in excess of what would be expected given the character, duration, or amount of the substance used; or there is other evidence suggesting the existence of an independent non-substance-induced mood disorder (eg, a history of recurrent non-substance-related major depressive episodes).

D. The disturbance does not occur exclusively during the course of delirium.

E. The symptoms cause clinically significant distress or impairment in social, occupational, or other important areas of functioning.

Note: This diagnosis should be made instead of a diagnosis of substance intoxication or substance withdrawal only when the mood symptoms are in excess of those usually associated with the intoxication or withdrawal syndrome and when the symptoms are sufficiently severe to warrant independent clinical attention.

Code: [specific substance] mood disorder: (alcohol; amphetamine [or amphetamine-like substance]; cocaine, hallucinogen; inhalant; opioid; phencyclidine [or phencyclidine-like substance]; sedative, hypnotic, or anxiolytic, other [or unknown] substance)

Specify type:
With depressive features: if the predominant mood is depressed.
With manic features: if the predominant mood is elevated, euphoric, or irritable.
With mixed features: if symptoms of both mania and depression are present and neither predominates.

Specify if:
With onset during intoxication: if the criteria are met for intoxication with the substance and the symptoms develop during the intoxication syndrome
With onset during withdrawal: if criteria are met for withdrawal from the substance and the symptoms develop during, or shortly after, a withdrawal syndrome

onset (during intoxication or withdrawal), and the nature of the symptoms (for example, manic or depressed) (Table 15.1–11). A maximum of 1 month between the use of the substance and the appearance of the symptoms is allowed in DSM-IV, although the usual time frame is probably shorter. In some cases, the diagnosis may be warranted after more than 1 month.

CLINICAL FEATURES. Substance-induced manic and depressive features can be identical to those of bipolar I disorder and major depressive disorder. Substance-induced mood disorder, however, may show more waxing and waning of symptoms and a fluctuation in patients' level of consciousness.

DIFFERENTIAL DIAGNOSIS. The presence of a history of mood disorders in the patient or a patient's family weights toward the diagnosis of a primary mood disorder, although such a history does not rule out the possibility of substance-induced mood disorder. Substances may also trigger an underlying mood disorder in a patient who is biologically vulnerable to mood disorders.

COURSE AND PROGNOSIS. The course and prognosis of substance-induced mood disorder are variable. Shortly after the substance has been cleared from the body, a normal mood usually returns. Sometimes, however, the substance exposure seems to precipitate a long-lasting mood disorder that may take weeks or months to resolve completely.

TREATMENT. The primary treatment of substance-induced mood disorder is the identification of the causally involved substance. Stopping the intake of the substance is usually sufficient to cause the mood disorder symptoms to abate. If the symptoms linger, treatment with appropriate psychiatric drugs may be necessary.

Mood Disorder Not Otherwise Specified. If patients exhibit depressive or manic symptoms or both as the major features of their disorder and do not meet the diagnostic criteria for any other mood disorder or other DSM-IV mental disorder, including depressive disorder not otherwise specified and bipolar disorder not otherwise specified, the most appropriate diagnosis is mood disorder not otherwise specified (Table 15.1–12).

ICD-10

ICD-10 describes mood (affective) disorders as characterized by "a change in mood or affect, usually to depression (with or without associated anxiety) or to elation." A change in activity level accompanies the mood change, and "most other symptoms are either secondary to, or easily understood in the context of, such changes." These disorders are recurrent, and the onset of the episodes may be related to "stressful events or situations." The mood disorders also include those occurring in children.

Table 15.1–12
DSM-IV Diagnostic Criteria for Mood Disorder Not Otherwise Specified

This category includes disorders with mood symptoms that do not meet the criteria for any specific mood disorder and in which it is difficult to choose between depressive disorder not otherwise specified and bipolar disorder not otherwise specified (eg, acute agitation).

Table 15.1–13
ICD-10 Diagnostic Criteria for Mood [Affective] Disorders

Manic episode

Hypomania

A. The mood is elevated or irritable to a degree that is definitely abnormal for the individual concerned and sustained for at least 4 consecutive days.

B. At least three of the following signs must be present, leading to some interference with personal functioning in daily living:
   (1) increased activity or physical restlessness;
   (2) increased talkativeness;
   (3) destractibility or difficulty in concentration;
   (4) decreased need for sleep;
   (5) increased sexual energy;
   (6) mild overspending, or other types of reckless or irresponsible behavior;
   (7) increased sociability or overfamiliarity.

C. The episode does not meet the criteria for mania, bipolar affective disorder, depressive episode, cyclothymia, or anorexia nervosa.

D. *Most commonly used exclusion clause.* The episode is not attributable to psychoactive substance use or to any organic mental disorder.

Mania without psychotic symptoms

A. Mood must be predominantly elevated, expansive, or irritable, and definitely abnormal for the individual concerned. The mood change must be prominent and sustained for at least 1 week (unless it is severe enough to require hospital admission).

B. At least three of the following signs must be present (four if the mood is merely irritable), leading to severe interference with personal functioning in daily living:
   (1) increased activity or physical restlessness;
   (2) increased talkativeness ("pressure of speech");
   (3) flight of ideas or the subjective experience of thoughts racing;
   (4) loss of normal social inhibitions, resulting in behavior that is inappropriate to the circumstances;
   (5) decreased need for sleep;
   (6) inflated self-esteem or grandiosity;
   (7) distractibility or constant changes in activity or plans;
   (8) behavior that is foolhardy or reckless and whose risks the individual does not recognize, eg, spending sprees, foolish enterprises, reckless driving;
   (9) marked sexual energy or sexual indiscretions.

C. There are no hallucinations or delusions, although perceptual disorders may occur (eg, subjective hyperacusis, appreciation of colors as especially vivid).

D. *Most commonly used exclusion clause.* The episode is not attributable to psychoactive substance use or to any organic mental disorder.

Mania with psychotic symptoms

A. The episode meets the criteria for mania without psychotic symptoms with the exception of criterion C.

B. The episode does not simultaneously meet the criteria for schizophrenia or schizoaffective disorder, manic type.

C. Delusions or hallucinations are present, other than those listed as typically schizophrenic in criterion G1(1)b, c and d for schizophrenia (ie, delusions other than those that are completely impossible or culturally inappropriate, and hallucinations that are not in the third person or giving a running commentary). The commonest examples are those with grandiose, self-referential, erotic, or persecutory content.

D. *Most commonly used exclusion clause.* The episode is not attributable to psychoactive substance use or to any organic mental disorder.

Specify whether the hallucinations or delusions are congruent or incongruent with the mood:
With mood-congruent psychotic symptoms
   (such as grandiose delusions or voices telling the individual that he or she has superhuman powers)
With mood-incongruent psychotic symptoms
   (such as voices speaking to the individual about affectively neutral topics, or delusions of reference or persecution)

Other manic episodes

Manic episode, unspecified

Bipolar affective disorder

Note. Episodes are demarcated by a switch to an episode of opposite mixed polarity or by a remission.

Bipolar affective disorder, current episode hypomanic

A. The current episode meets the criteria for hypomania.

B. There has been at least one other affective episode in the past, meeting the criteria for hypomanic or manic episode, depressive episode, or mixed affective episode.

(continued)

Table 15.1–13 *(continued)*

Bipolar affective disorder, current episode manic without psychotic symptoms

A. The current episode meets the criteria for mania without psychotic symptoms.

B. There has been at least one other affective episode in the past, meeting the criteria for hypomanic or manic episode, depressive episode, or mixed affective episode.

Bipolar affective disorder, current episode manic without psychotic symptoms

A. The current episode meets the criteria for mania without psychotic symptoms.

B. There has been at least one other affective episode in the past, meeting the criteria for hypomanic or manic episode, depressive episode, or mixed affective episode.

Specify whether the psychotic symptoms are congruent or incongruent with the mood:
With mood-congruent psychotic symptoms
With mood-incongruent psychotic symptoms

Bipolar affective disorder, current episode moderate or mild depression

A. The current episode meets the criteria for a depressive episode of either mild or moderate severity.

B. There has been at least one other affective episode in the past, meeting the criteria for hypomanic or manic episode, depressive episode, or mixed affective episode.

Specify the presence of the "somatic syndrome" in the current episode of depression:
Without somatic syndrome
With somatic syndrome

Bipolar affective disorder, current episode severe depression without psychotic symptoms

A. The current episode meets the criteria for a severe depressive episode without psychotic symptoms.

B. There has been at least one well-authenticated hypomanic or manic episode or mixed affective episode in the past.

Bipolar affective disorder, current episode severe depression with psychotic symptoms

A. The current episode meets the criteria for a severe depressive episode without psychotic symptoms.

B. There has been at least one well-authenticated hypomanic or manic episode or mixed affective episode in the past.

Specify whether the psychotic symptoms are congruent or incongruent with the mood:
With mood-congruent psychotic symptoms
With mood-incongruent psychotic symptoms

Bipolar affective disorder, current episode mixed

A. The current episode is characterized by either a mixture or a rapid alternation (ie, within a few hours) of hypomanic, manic, and depressive symptoms.

B. Both manic and depressive symptoms must be prominent most of the time during a period of at least 2 weeks.

C. There has been at least one well-authenticated hypomanic or manic episode, depressive episode, or mixed affective episode in the past.

Bipolar affective disorder, currently in remission

A. The current state does not meet the criteria for depressive or manic episode of any severity or for any other mood [affective] disorder (possibly because of treatment to reduce the risk of future episodes).

B. There has been at least one well-authenticated hypomanic or manic episode in the past and in addition at least one other affective episode (hypomanic or manic, depressive, or mixed).

Other bipolar affective disorders

Bipolar affective disorder, unspecified

Depressive episode

G1. The depressive episode should last for at least 2 weeks.

G2. There have been no hypomanic or manic symptoms sufficient to meet the criteria for hypomanic or manic episode at any time in the individual's life.

G3. *Most commonly used exclusion clause.* The episode is not attributable to psychoactive substance use or to any organic mental disorder.

Somatic syndrome

Some depressive symptoms are widely regarded as having special clinical significance and are here called "somatic." (Terms such as biological, vital, melancholic, or endogenomorphic are used for this syndrome in other classifications.)

A fifth character may be used to specify the presence or absence of the somatic syndrome. To qualify for the somatic syndrome, *four* of the following symptoms should be present:

(1) marked loss of interest or pleasure in activities that are normally pleasurable;
(2) lack of emotional reactions to events or activities that normally produce an emotional response;
(3) waking in the morning 2 hours or more before the usual time;
(4) depression worse in the morning;

(continued)

Table 15.1–13 *(continued)*

(5) objective evidence of marked psychomotor retardation or agitation (remarked on or reported by other people);
(6) marked loss of appetite;
(7) weight loss (5% or more of body weight in the past month);
(8) marked loss of libido.

In *The ICD-10 Classification of Mental and Behavioural Disorders: Clinical descriptions and diagnostic guidelines,* the presence or absence of the somatic syndrome is not specified for severe depressive episode, since it is presumed to be present in most cases. For research purposes, however, it may be advisable to allow for the coding of the absence of the somatic syndrome in severe depressive episode.

Mild depressive episode

A. The general criteria for depressive episode must be met.

B. At least two of the following three symptoms must be present:
(1) depressed mood to a degree that is definitely abnormal for the individual, present for most of the day and almost every day, largely uninfluenced by circumstances, and sustained for at least 2 weeks;
(2) loss of interest or pleasure in activities that are normally pleasurable;
(3) decreased energy or increased fatiguability.

C. An additional symptom or symptoms from the following list should be present, to give a total of at least *four:*
(1) loss of confidence or self-esteem;
(2) unreasonable feelings of self-reproach or excessive and inappropriate guilt;
(3) recurrent thoughts of death or suicide, or any suicidal behavior;
(4) complaints or evidence of diminished ability to think or concentrate, such as indecisiveness or vacillation;
(5) change in psychomotor activity, with agitation or retardation (either subjective or objective);
(6) sleep disturbance of any type;
(7) change in appetite (decrease or increase) with corresponding weight change.

A fifth character may be used to specify the presence or absence of the "somatic syndrome":
Without somatic syndrome
With somatic syndrome

Moderate depressive episode

A. The general criteria for depressive episode must be met.

B. At least two of the three symptoms listed for criterion B above must be present.

C. Additional symptoms from depressive episode, criterion C, must be present, to give a total of at leas *six.*

A fifth character may be used to specify the presence or absence of the "somatic syndrome":
Without somatic syndrome
With somatic syndrome

Severe depressive episode without psychotic symptoms

Note: If important symptoms such as agitation or retardation are marked, the patient may be unwilling or unable to describe many symptoms in detail. An overall grading of severe episode may still be justified in such a case.

A. The general criteria for depressive episode must be met.

B. All three of the symptoms in criterion B, depressive episode, must be present.

C. Additional symptoms from depressive episode, criterion C, must be present, to give a total of at least *eight.*

D. There must be no hallucinations, delusions, or depressive stupor.

Severe depressive episode with psychotic symptoms

A. The general criteria for depressive episode must be met.

B. The criteria for severe depressive episode without psychotic symptoms must be met with the exception of criterion D.

C. The criteria for schizophrenia or schizoaffective disorder, depressive type, are not met.

D. Either of the following must be present:
(1) delusions or hallucinations, other than those listed as typically schizophrenic in criterion G1(1)b, c, and d for general criteria for paranoid, hebephrenic, catatonic, and undifferentiated schizophrenia (ie, delusions other than those that are completely impossible or culturally inappropriate and hallucinations that are not in the third person or giving a running commentary); the commonest examples are those with depressive, guilty, hypochondriacal, nihilistic, self-referential, or persecutory content
(2) depressive stupor.

A fifth character may be used to specify whether the psychotic symptoms are congruent or incongruent with mood:
With mood-congruent psychotic symptoms
(ie, delusions of guilt, worthlessness, bodily disease, or impending disaster, derisive or condemnatory auditory hallucinations)
With mood-incongruent psychotic symptoms
(ie, persecutory or self-referential delusions and hallucinations without an affective content)

Other depressive episodes

Episodes should be included here which do not fit the descriptions given for depressive episodes, but for which the overall diagnostic impression indicates that they are depressive in nature. Examples include fluctuating mixtures of depressive symptoms (particularly those of the somatic syndrome) with nondiagnostic symptoms such as tension, worry, and distress, and mixtures of somatic depressive symptoms with persistent pain or fatigue not due to organic causes (as sometimes seen in general hospital services).

(continued)

Table 15.1–13 *(continued)*

Depressive episode, unspecified

Recurrent depressive disorder

G1. There has been at least one previous episode, mild, moderate, or severe, lasting a minimum of 2 weeks and separated from the current episode by at least 2 months free from any significant mood symptoms.

G2. At no time in the past has there been an episode meeting the criteria for hypomanic or manic episode.

G3. *Most commonly used exclusion clause.* The episode is not attributable to psychoactive substance use or to any organic mental disorder.

It is recommended that the predominant type of previous episodes is specified (mild, moderate, severe, uncertain).

Recurrent depressive disorder, current episode mild

A. The general criteria for recurrent depressive disorder are met.

B. The current episode meets the criteria for mild depressive episode.

A fifth character may be used to specify the presence or absence of the "somatic syndrome," in the current episode:
Without somatic syndrome
With somatic syndrome

Recurrent depressive disorder, current episode moderate

A. The general criteria for recurrent depressive disorder are met.

B. The current episode meets the criteria for moderate depressive episode.

A fifth character may be used to specify the presence or absence of the "somatic syndrome," in the current episode:
Without somatic syndrome
With somatic syndrome

Recurrent depressive disorder, current episode without psychotic symptoms

A. The general criteria for recurrent depressive disorder are met.

B. The current episode meets the criteria for severe depressive episode without psychotic symptoms.

Recurrent depressive disorder, current episode severe with psychotic symptoms

A. The general criteria for recurrent depressive disorder are met.

B. The current episode meets the criteria for severe depressive episode with psychotic symptoms.

A fifth character may be used to specify whether the psychotic symptoms are congruent or incongruent with the mood:
With mood-congruent psychotic symptoms
With mood-incongruent psychotic symptoms

Recurrent depressive disorder, currently in remission

A. The general criteria for recurrent depressive disorder have been met in the past.

B. The current state does not meet the criteria for a depressive episode of any severity or for any other disorder in mood [affective] disorders.

Comment

This category can still be used if the patient receives treatment to reduce the risk of further episodes.

Other recurrent depressive disorders

Recurrent depressive disorder, unspecified

Persistent mood [affective] disorders

Cyclothymia

A. There must have been a period of at least 2 years of instability of mood involving several periods of both depression and hypomania, with or without intervening periods of normal mood.

B. None of the manifestations of depression or hypomania during such a 2-year period should be sufficiently severe or long-lasting to meet criteria for manic episode or depressive episode (moderate or severe); however, manic or depressive episode(s) may have occurred before, or may develop after, such a period of persistent mood instability.

C. During at least some of the periods of depression at least three of the following should be present:
   (1) reduced energy or activity;
   (2) insomnia;
   (3) loss of self-confidence or feelings of inadequacy;
   (4) difficulty in concentrating;
   (5) social withdrawal;
   (6) loss of interest in or enjoyment of sex and other pleasurable activities;
   (7) reduced talkativeness;
   (8) pessimism about the future or brooding over the past.

(continued)

Table 15.1–13 ***(continued)***

D. During at least some of the periods of mood elevation at least three of the following should be present:
   (1) increased energy or activity;
   (2) decreased need for sleep;
   (3) inflated self-esteem;
   (4) sharpened or unusually creative thinking;
   (5) increased gregariousness;
   (6) increased talkativeness or wittiness;
   (7) increased interest and involvement in sexual and other pleasurable activities;
   (8) overoptimism or exaggeration of past achievements.

Note. If desired, time of onset may be specified as early (in late teenage or the 20s) or late (usually between age 30 and 50 years, following an affective episode).

Dysthymia

A. There must be a period of at least 2 years of constant or constantly recurring depressed mood. Intervening periods of normal mood rarely last for longer than a few weeks, and there are no episodes of hypomania.

B. None, or very few, of the individual episodes of depression within such a 2-year period should be sufficiently severe or long-lasting to meet the criteria for recurrent mild depressive disorder.

C. During at least some of the periods of depression at least three of the following should be present:
   (1) reduced energy or activity;
   (2) insomnia;
   (3) loss of self-confidence or feelings of inadequacy;
   (4) difficulty in concentrating;
   (5) frequent tearfulness;
   (6) loss of interest in or enjoyment of sex and other pleasurable activities;
   (7) feeling of hopelessness or despair;
   (8) a perceived inability to cope with the routine responsibilities of everyday life;
   (9) pessimism about the future or brooding over the past;
   (10) social withdrawal;
   (11) reduced talkativeness.

Note. If desired, time of onset may be specified as early (in late teenage or the 20s) or late (usually between age 30 and 50 years, following an affective episode).

Other persistent mood [affective] disorders

This is a residual category for persistent affective disorders that are not sufficiently severe or long-lasting to fulfill the criteria for cyclothymia or dysthymia but that are nevertheless clinically significant. Some types of depression previously called "neurotic" are included here, provided that they do not meet the criteria for either cyclothymia or dysthymia or for depressive episode of mild or moderate severity.

Persistent mood [affective] disorder, unspecified

Other mood [affective] disorders

There are so many possible disorders that could be listed that no attempt has been made to specify criteria, except for mixed affective episode and recurrent brief depressive disorder. Investigators requiring criteria more exact than those available in *Clinical descriptions and diagnostic guidelines* should construct them according to the requirements of their studies.

Other single mood [affective] disorders

Mixed affective episode

A. The episode is characterized by either a mixture or a rapid alternation (ie, within a few hours) of hypomanic, manic, and depressive symptoms.

B. Both manic and depressive symptoms must be prominent most of the time during a period of at least 2 weeks.

C. There is no history of previous hypomanic, depressive, or mixed episodes.

Other recurrent mood [affective] disorders

Recurrent brief depressive disorder

A. The disorder meets the symptomatic criteria for mild, moderate, or severe depressive episode.

B. The depressive episodes have occurred about once a month over the past year.

C. The individual episodes last less than 2 weeks (typically 2–3 days).

D. The episodes do not occur solely in relation to the menstrual cycle.

Other specified mood [affective] disorders

This is a residual category for affective disorders that do not meet the criteria for any other categories above.

ICD-10 classifies single episodes as different from multiple-episode disorders; the severity of the disorder is an important characteristic because treatment varies accordingly. The criteria for classifying the mood disorders are meant to allow clinicians to easily identify one or another of them, but the authors stress that their classification is open to discussion.

The ICD-10 categories of classification include a single manic episode; bipolar affective disorder with at least two episodes (including manic-depressive disorder, psychosis or reaction); depressive episode (including single episode and major depression without psychotic symptoms); recurrent depressive disorder; persistent mood (affective) disorders (including cyclothymia and dysthymia); other mood disorders; and unspecified mood disorder, all of which are further subdivided and characterized (Table 15.1–13).

References

Angst J, Dobler-Mikola A: The Zurich study: A prospective epidemiological study of depressive, neurotic and psychosomatic syndromes. IV. Recurrent and nonrecurrent brief depression. Eur Arch Psychiatry Neurol Sci *234:* 408, 1995.

Caplan LR, Ahmed I: Depression and neurological disease: Their distinction and association. Gen Hosp Psychiatry *14:* 177, 1992.

Covinsky KE, Fortinsky RH, Palmer RM, Kresevic DM, Landefeld CS: Relation between symptoms of depression and health status outcomes in acutely ill hospitalized older persons. Ann Intern Med *126:* 417, 1997.

Depue RA, Arbisi P, Krauss S, Iacono WG, Leon A, Muir R, Allen J: Seasonal independence of low prolactin concentration and high spontaneous eye blink rates in unipolar and bipolar II seasonal affective disorder. Arch Gen Psychiatry *47:* 356, 1990.

Fogel BS: Major depression versus organic mood disorder: A questionable distinction. J Clin Psychiatry *51:* 53, 1990.

Freeman EW: Rickels K, Sondheimer SJ: Course of premenstrual syndrome symptom severity after treatment. Am J Psychiatry *149:* 531, 1992.

Harrison WM, Endicott J, Nee J: Treatment of premenstrual dysphoria with alprazolam: A controlled study. Arch Gen Psychiatry *47:* 270, 1990.

Heun R, Maier W: The distinction of bipolar II disorder from bipolar I and recurrent unipolar depression: Results of a controlled family study. Acta Psychiatr Scand *87:* 279, 1993.

Hurt SW, Schnuee PP, Severino SK, Freeman EW, Gise LH, Rivera-Tovar A, Steege JF: Late luteal phase dysphoric disorder in 670 woman evaluated for premenstrual complaints. Am J Psychiatry *149:* 525, 1992.

Kasper S, Ruhrmann S, Hasse T, Moller HJ: Recurrent brief depression and its relationship to seasonal affective disorder. Eur Arch Psychiatry Clin Neurosci *242:* 20, 1992.

Larazue AA: The multimodal approach to the treatment of minor depression. Am J Psychother *46:* 50, 1992.

Moline ML: Pharmacologic strategies for managing premenstrual syndrome. Clin Pharmacol Ther *12:* 181, 1993.

Montgomery SA, Montgomery D, Baldwin D, Green M: The duration, nature and recurrent rate of brief depressions. Prog Neuropsychopharmacol Biol Psychiatry *14:* 729, 1990.

Parry BL, Berga SL, Kripke DF, Klauber MR, Laughlin GA, Yen SSC, Gillin C: Altered waveform of plasma nocturnal melatonin secretion in premenstrual dysphoria. Arch Gen Psychiatry *47:* 1139, 1990.

Paykel E, moderator: Workshop IV: Depression in medical illness. Int Clin Psychopharmacol *7:* 205, 1993.

Phillip M, Delmo CD, Buller R, Schwarze H, Winter P, Maier W, Benkert O: Differentiation between major and minor depression. Psychopharmacology *106* (2, Suppl)*:* S75, 1992.

Rice JP, McDonald-Scott P, Endicott J, Coryell W, Grove WM, Keller MB, Altis D: The stability of diagnosis with an application to bipolar II disorder. Psychiatry Res *19:* 285, 1986.

Rihmer Z, Barsi J, Arato M, Demeter E: Suicide in subtypes of primary major depression. J Affect Disord *18:* 221, 1990.

Simpson SG, Folstein SE, Meyers DA, McMahon FJ, Brusco DM, DePaulo JR Jr: Bipolar II: The most common bipolar phenotype? Am J Psychiatry *150:* 901, 1993.

Staner L, De Fuente JM, Kerkhofs M, Linkowski P, Medlewicz J: Biological and clinical features of recurrent brief depression: A comparison with major depressed and health subjects. J Affect Disord *26:* 241, 1992.

Starkstein SE, Fedoroff P, Berthier ML, Robinson RG: Manic-depressive and pure manic states after brain lesions. Biol Psychiatry *29:* 149, 1991.

Stuart JW, Quitkin FM, Klein DF: The pharmacotherapy of minor depression. Am J Psychother *46:* 23, 1992.

Sunblad C, Hedberg MA, Eriksson E: Clomipramine administered during the lateral-phase reduces the symptoms of premenstrual-syndrome—A placebo-controlled trial. Neuropsychopharmacology *9:* 133, 1993.

▲ 15.2 Major Depressive Disorder, Bipolar I Disorder, and Bipolar II Disorder

There are at least three major theories of the relation between major depressive disorder and bipolar I disorder. According to the most accepted hypothesis, which is supported by several types of genetic and biochemical studies, major depressive disorder and bipolar I disorder are two different disorders. Second, some investigators have suggested that bipolar I disorder is a more severe expression of the same pathophysiological process seen in major depressive disorder. The third hypothesis is that depression and mania are two extremes of a continuum of emotional experience; this conceptualization is not supported by the common clinical observation that many patients have mixed states with both depressed and manic features.

Although classifying bipolar II disorder with the mood disorders, such as major depressive disorder and bipolar II disorder, implies a close association, some investigators have hypothesized that bipolar II disorder is related to borderline personality disorder. Nevertheless, some data indicate that bipolar II disorder tends to be inherited as bipolar II disorder and thus may have its own unique genetic predisposition.

EPIDEMIOLOGY

Major depressive disorder is a common disorder, with a lifetime prevalence of about 15 percent, perhaps as high as 25 percent for women. The incidence of major depressive disorder is also higher in primary care patients, in whom it approaches 10 percent, and in medical inpatients, in whom it approaches 15 percent. Bipolar I disorder is less common than is major depressive disorder, with a lifetime prevalence of about 1 percent, similar to the figure for schizophrenia. Because it is increasingly appreciated that the course of bipolar I disorder is not as favorable as the course for major depressive disorder, the cost of bipolar I disorder to patients, their families, and society is significant.

Whereas most people with bipolar I disorder eventually come to the attention of a physician and receive treatment, by contrast only about half of those with major depressive disorder ever receive specific treatment. Although the National Institute of Mental Health (NIMH) has a program to increase the awareness of depression in the general population and among physicians, the symptoms of depression are often inappropriately dismissed as understandable reactions to stress, evidence of a weakness of will, or simply a conscious attempt to achieve some secondary gain. One estimate of the lifetime prevalence of bipolar II disorder is about 0.5 percent.

Sex

An almost universal observation, independent of country or culture, is the twofold greater prevalence of major depressive disorder in women than in men. Although the reasons for the difference are unknown, research has clearly shown that the difference in Western countries arises not solely because of socially biased diagnostic practices. The reasons for the difference have been hypothesized to involve hormonal differences, the effects of childbirth, differing psychosocial stressors for women and for men, and behavioral models of learned helplessness. In contrast to major depressive disorder, bipolar I disorder has an equal prevalence for men and women.

Age

The onset of bipolar I disorder is generally earlier than that for major depressive disorder. The age of onset for bipolar I disorder ranges from childhood (as early as age 5 or 6) to 50 years or even older in rare cases, with a mean age of 30. The mean age of onset for major depressive disorder is about 40 years; 50 percent of all patients have an onset between the ages of 20 and 50. Although uncommonly, major depressive disorder can also begin in childhood or in old age. Some recent epidemiological data suggest that the incidence of major depressive disorder may be increasing among people less than 20 years old. If true, the observation may be related to the increased use of alcohol and other substances in this age group.

Marital Status

Major depressive disorder occurs most often in people without close interpersonal relationships or in those who are divorced or separated. Bipolar I disorder may be more common in divorced and single people than among married people, but the difference may reflect the early onset and the resulting marital discord characteristic of the disorder.

Socioeconomic and Cultural Considerations

No correlation has been found between socioeconomic status and major depressive disorder. A higher than average incidence of bipolar I disorder does appear among the upper socioeconomic groups, possibly because of biased diagnostic practices. Depression may be more common in rural areas than in urban areas. Bipolar I disorder is more common in people who did not graduate from college than in college graduates, a fact that probably reflects the relatively early age of onset for the disorder.

ETIOLOGY

Biological Factors

Many studies have reported abnormalities in biogenic amine metabolites—such as 5-hydroxyindoleacetic acid (5-HIAA), homovanillic acid (HVA), and 3-methoxy-4-hydroxyphenylglycol (MHPG)—in blood, urine, and cerebrospinal fluid (CSF) of patients with mood disorders (Table 15.2–1). The data reported are most consistent with the hypothesis that mood disorders are associated with heterogeneous dysregulations of the biogenic amines.

Biogenic Amines. Of the biogenic amines, norepinephrine and serotonin are the two neurotransmitters most implicated in the pathophysiology of mood disorders. In animal models, virtually all effective somatic antidepressant treatments that have been tested are associated with a decrease in the sensitivity of postsynaptic β-adrenergic and 5-hydroxytryptamine type 2 (5-HT_2) receptors after long-term treatment, although other changes resulting from long-term treatment with these drugs have also been reported (Table 15.2–2). The temporal response of these receptor changes in animal models

Table 15.2–1
Frequently Reported Neurotransmitter and Metabolite Changes in Some Depressed Patients (Compared with Normal Controls)

	NE	MHPG	NM	VMA	Epi	MET	DA	HVA	5-HT	5-HIAA	GABA	GAD	CRH	Endorphins
CSF	nd	↓ ↑ ↔	nd	nd	nd	nd	nd	↓ ↑ psychotic dep.	nd	↓ ↔	↓	nd	↑	↑ mania ↔ dep.
Plasma	nd	nd	nd	nd	nd	nd	nd	nd	↓	nd	↓	nd	nd	↑ ↔
Uptake into platelets	nd	nd	nd	nd	nd	nd	nd	nd	↓	nd	nd	nd	nd	nd
Urine	↑ ↔	↓	↑ ↔	↑ ↔	↑ ↔	↑ ↔	↑ mania	nd	nd	nd	nd	nd	nd	nd
Brain tissue	nd	nd	nd	nd	nd	nd	nd	nd	↓	↓	nd	↓ ↔	nd	nd

Reprinted with permission from Caldecott-Hazard S, Morgan DG, DeLeon-Jones F, Overstreet DH, Janowsky D: Clinical and biochemical aspects of depressive disorders. II. Transmitter/receptor theories. Synapse *9:* 253, 1991.

nd, no data in this review; ↑, increased levels as compared with controls; ↓, decreased levels as compared with controls; ↔, no change as compared with controls. NE, norepinephrine; MHPG, 3-methoxy-4-hydroxyphenethyleneglycol; NM, normetanephrine; VMA, 3-methoxy-4-hydroxymandelic acid; Epi, epinephrine; MET, metanephrine; DA, dopamine; HVA, homovanillic acid; 5-HT, serotonin; 5-HIAA, 5-hydroxyindoleacetic acid; GABA, γ-aminobutyric acid; GAD, glutamatic acid decarboxylase; CRH, corticotropin-releasing hormone.

Table 15.2–2
Antidepressant-Induced Changes in Neurotransmitters, Metabolites, and Their Receptors in Humans and Animals

What Was Measured	Drugs					
	Tricyclics	MAOIs	SUBs	Iprindole	LI	ECT
Concentrations in brain tissue						
MHPG	↑	nd	nd	nd	nd	nd
Enkephalins	↑	nd	nd	↑	nd	↑
Concentrations in CSF						
MHPG	↓	↓	↓	nd	nd	nd
HVA	nd	↓	nd	nd	nd	nd
5-HIAA	↓	↓	↓	nd	nd	nd
β-Endorphin	nd	nd	nd	nd	nd	↑
Concentrations in urine						
MHPG	↓↑↔	nd	nd	nd	nd	nd
Effects on uptake of						
NE	↓	nd	↔	↔	nd	nd
5-HT	↓	nd	↓	↔	nd	nd
GABA	↓	nd	nd	nd	nd	nd
Number of receptors						
Brain α-2	↓↑↔	nd	nd	nd	nd	nd
Platelet α-2	nd	nd	nd	nd	↓	nd
Brain α-1	↑↔	nd	nd	nd	↑	nd
Brain β	↓	↓	↓↔	↓	nd	↓
Brain 5-HT-2	↓	↓	↓	↓	nd	↑
Brain 5-HT-1	↓↑↔	↓	↓↔	nd	nd	nd
Brain mACh	↑	nd	nd	nd	↑↔	nd
Brain dopamine-1	↓	nd	nd	nd	nd	↓
Brain $GABA_{\beta}$	↑↔	↑	↑	nd	nd	↑
Brain μ and Δ opioid	nd	nd	nd	nd	nd	↑↓
Sensitivity of somatodendritic DA receptors	↓↔	↓	nd	nd	nd	↓
Effect on stimulation of cAMP by NE	↓	↓	↓	↓	nd	↓
Effect on stimulation of PI by muscarinic agonists	nd	nd	nd	nd	↓↔	nd
Amount of glucocorticoid mRNA on receptor sites in brain	↑↓	nd	nd	nd	nd	nd

Reprinted with permission from Caldecott-Hazard S, Morgan DG, DeLeon-Jones F, Overstreet DH, Janowsky D: Clinical and biochemical aspects of depressive disorders. II. Transmitter/receptor theories. Synapse *9:* 254, 1991.

nd, no data in this review; ↑, increased; ↓, decreased; ↔, no change. Arrows represent the most frequently observed (not necessarily all) effects of the drugs in each group. MAOI, monoamine oxidase inhibitor; SUB, serotonin uptake blocker; Li, lithium; ECT, electroconvulsive therapy; CSF, cerebrospinal fluid; MHPG, 3-methoxy-4-hydroxyphenethyleneglycol; HVA, homovanillic acid; 5-HIAA, 5-hydroxyindoleacetic acid; 5-HT, serotonin; NE, norepinephrine; DA, dopamine, GABA, γ-aminobutyric acid; mACh, muscarinic cholinergic; cAMP, cyclic adenosine monophosphate; PI, phosphoinositide; mRNA, messenger ribonucleic acid.

correlates with the 1- to 3-week delay in clinical improvement usually seen in patients. In addition to norepinephrine, serotonin, and dopamine, evidence points to dysregulation of acetylcholine in mood disorders.

NOREPINEPHRINE. The correlation suggested by basic science studies between the down-regulation of β-adrenergic receptors and clinical antidepressant responses is probably the single most compelling piece of data indicating a direct role for the noradrenergic system in depression. Other evidence has also implicated the presynaptic β_2-adrenergic receptors in depression, as activation of these receptors results in a decrease of the amount of norepinephrine released. Presynaptic β_2-adrenergic receptors are also located on serotonergic neurons and regulate the amount of serotonin released. The existence of almost purely noradrenergic, clinically effective antidepressant drugs—for example, desipramine (Norpramin)—is further support of a role for norepinephrine in the pathophysiology of at least the symptoms of depression.

SEROTONIN. With the huge effect that the serotonin-specific reuptake inhibitors (SSRIs)—for example, fluoxetine (Prozac)—have made on the treatment of depression, serotonin has become the biogenic amine neurotransmitter most commonly associated with depression. The identification of multiple serotonin receptor subtypes has also increased the excitement within the research community about the development of even more specific treatments for depression. Besides the fact that SSRIs and other serotonergic antidepressants are effective in the treatment of depression, other data indicate that serotonin is involved in the pathophysiology of depression. Depletion of serotonin may precipitate depression, and some patients with suicidal impulses have low CSF concentrations of serotonin metabolites and low concentrations of serotonin uptake sites on platelets, as measured by imipramine (Tofranil) binding to platelets. Some depressed patients also have abnormal neuroendocrine responses (for example, growth hormone, prolactin, and adrenocorticotropic hormone [ACTH]), to challenges with serotonergic agents. Although current serotonin-active antidepressants act primarily through the blockade of serotonin reuptake, other SSRIs have other effects on the serotonin system, including antagonism of the serotonin type 2 ($5\text{-}HT_2$) receptor (for example, nefazodone [Serzone]) and agonism of the serotonin type 1A ($5\text{-}HT_{1A}$) receptor (for example, ipsapirone).

It is perhaps consistent with the decrease in serotonin receptors after long-term exposure to antidepressants that a decrease in the number of serotonin reuptake sites (assessed by measuring the binding of ^{3}H-imipramine) and an increased concentration of serotonin have been found at postmortem in the brains of people who have committed suicide. Researchers have also found decreased tritiated-imipramine binding to blood platelets in some depressed people.

DOPAMINE. Although norepinephrine and serotonin are the biogenic amines most often associated with the pathophysiology of depression, dopamine has also been theorized to play a role. The data suggest that dopamine activity may be reduced in depression and increased in mania. The discovery of new subtypes of the dopamine receptors and increasing understanding of the presynaptic and postsynaptic regulation of dopamine function have further enriched the research into the relation between dopamine and mood disorders. Drugs that reduce dopamine concentrations—for example, reserpine (Serpasil)—and diseases that reduce dopamine concentrations (such as Parkinson's disease) are associated with depressive symptoms. In contrast, drugs that increase dopamine concentrations such as tyrosine, amphetamine, and bupropion (Wellbutrin), reduce the symptoms of depression. Two recent theories about dopamine and depression are that the mesolimbic dopamine pathway may be dysfunctional in depression and that the dopamine type 1 (D_1) receptor may be hypoactive in depression.

Other Neurochemical Factors. Although the data are not yet conclusive, amino acid neurotransmitters (particularly γ-aminobutyric acid [GABA]) and neuroactive peptides (particularly vasopressin and the endogenous opiates) have been implicated in the pathophysiology of mood disorders. Some investigators have suggested that second-messenger systems—such as adenylate cyclase, phosphatidylinositol, and calcium regulation—may also be of causal relevance.

Neuroendocrine Regulation. The hypothalamus is central to the regulation of the neuroendocrine axes and itself receives many neuronal inputs that use biogenic amine neurotransmitters. Various neuroendocrine dysregulations have been reported in patients with mood disorders, and thus the abnormal regulation of neuroendocrine axes may be a result of abnormal functioning of biogenic amine-containing neurons. Although it is theoretically possible for a particular dysregulation of a neuroendocrine axis (such as the thyroid or adrenal axis) to be involved in the cause of a mood disorder, the dysregulations are more likely reflections of a fundamental underlying brain disorder. The major neuroendocrine axes of interest in mood disorders are the adrenal, thyroid, and growth hormone axes. Other neuroendocrine abnormalities that have been described in patients with mood disorders include decreased nocturnal secretion of melatonin, decreased prolactin release to tryptophan administration, decreased basal levels of follicle-stimulating hormone (FSH) and luteinizing hormone (LH), and decreased testosterone levels in men.

ADRENAL AXIS. *Role of Cortisol.* A correlation between the hypersecretion of cortisol and depression is one of the oldest observations in biological psychiatry. Basic and clinical research of this relation has produced an understanding of how cortisol release is regulated in people with and without depression. Neurons in the paraventricular nucleus (PVN) release corticotropin-releasing hormone (CRH), which stimulates the release of adrenocorticotropic hormone (ACTH) from the anterior pituitary. (ACTH is co-released with β-endorphin and β-lipotropin, two peptides synthesized from the same precursor protein from which ACTH is synthesized.) ACTH, in turn, stimulates the release of cortisol from the adrenal cortex. The cortisol feedback on the loop works through at least two mechanisms. A fast feedback mechanism, sensitive to the rate of cortisol concentration increase, operates through cortisol receptors on the hippocampus and results in a decreased release of ACTH. A slow feedback mechanism, sensitive to the steady-state cortisol concentration, is thought to operate through pituitary and adrenal receptors.

Dexamethasone-Suppression Test. Dexamethasone is a synthetic analogue of cortisol. Many researchers have noted that a significant proportion, perhaps 50 percent, of depressed patients fail to have the normal cortisol suppression response to a single dose of dexamethasone. Although, the dexamethasone-suppression test (DST) was initially thought to be of diagnostic usefulness, many patients with other psychiatric disorders also show a positive result (nonsuppression of cortisol); thus the test is not entirely valid for indicating mood disorders. New data indicate that the DST may, however, correlate with the likelihood of a relapse: Depressed patients whose DSTs do not normalize with clinical responses to treatment are more likely to relapse than are those whose DSTs do normalize.

There are at least two problems with the DST. First, considerable variation in the results of the DST is due to variability in how the dexamethasone is metabolized. Second, as dexamethasone seems to have its major effects only at pituitary receptors, the DST does not effectively assess the functional state of cortisol receptors located elsewhere in the limbic-hypothalamic-pituitary-adrenal (LHPA) axis.

A recent advance in the assessment of the LHPA axis in depression involved infusions of cortisol in people who were and were not depressed. Cortisol, the naturally occurring hormone, is a better test substance than is dexamethasone, which does not reach or activate all the relevant receptors. In one study, depressed patients had impaired function of the fast feedback loop; thus, for at least some of them, the functioning of cortisol receptors in the hippocampus may have been abnormal. As other researchers have found that hypercortisolemia can damage hippocampal neurons, a cycle involving stress, stimulation of cortisol release, and inability to stop cortisol release may result in increasing damage to an already impaired hippocampus.

THYROID AXIS. Thyroid disorders are often associated with affective symptoms, and researchers have described abnormal regulation of the thyroid axis in patients with mood disorders. One direct clinical implication of the association is the critical importance of testing all affectively ill patients to determine their thyroid status. About one third of all patients with major depressive disorder who have an otherwise normal thyroid axis have been found to have a blunted release of thyrotropin, the thyroid-stimulating hormone (TSH), to an infusion of thyrotropin-releasing hormone protirelin (TRH). This same abnormality has been reported in a wide range of other psychiatric diagnoses, however, so that the diagnostic usefulness of the test is limited. Moreover, attempts to subtype depressed patients on the basis of their TRH test results have been contradictory.

Recent research has focused on the possibility that a subset of depressed people have an unrecognized autoimmune disorder that affects their thyroid glands. Several studies have reported that about 10 percent of patients with mood disorders, perhaps particularly bipolar I disorder patients, have detectable concentrations of antithyroid antibodies. Whether the antibodies are in fact associated pathophysiologically with depression has not yet been determined. Another potential association is between hypothyroidism and the development of a rapidly cycling course in bipolar I disorder patients. Available research data indicate that the association is independent of the effects of lithium treatment.

GROWTH HORMONE. Several studies have shown a statistical difference between depressed patients and others in the regulation of growth hormone release. Depressed patients have a blunted sleep-induced stimulation of growth hormone release. Inasmuch as sleep abnormalities are common symptoms of depression, a neuroendocrine marker related to sleep is an avenue for research. Studies have also found that depressed patients have a blunted response to clonidine (Catapres)-induced increases in growth hormone secretion.

Sleep Abnormalities. Problems with sleeping—initial and terminal insomnia, multiple awakenings, hypersomnia—are common and classic symptoms of depression, and perceived decreased need for sleep is a classic symptom of mania.

Researchers have long recognized that the sleep electroencephalograms (EEGs) of many depressed people show abnormalities. Common abnormalities are delayed sleep onset, shortened rapid eye movement (REM) latency (the time between falling asleep and the first REM period), an increased length of the first REM period, and abnormal delta sleep. Some investigators have attempted to use the sleep EEG in the diagnostic assessment of patients with mood disorders.

Kindling. Kindling is the electrophysiological process in which repeated subthreshold stimulation of a neuron eventually generates an action potential. At the organ level, repeated subthreshold stimulation of an area of the brain results in a seizure. The clinical observation that anticonvulsants—for example, carbamazepine (Tegretol) and valproic acid (Depakene)—are useful in the treatment of mood disorders, particularly bipolar I disorder, has given rise to the theory that the pathophysiology of mood disorders may involve kindling in the temporal lobes. Although kindling has been found in laboratory animals, it has never been convincingly demonstrated in humans, and the salutary effects of anticonvulsants in bipolar disorder may also be due to electrochemical alterations unrelated to epilepsy.

Circadian Rhythms. The abnormalities of sleep architecture in depression and the transient clinical improvement associated with sleep deprivation have led to theories that depression reflects an abnormal regulation of circadian rhythms. Some experimental studies with animals indicate that many of the standard antidepressant treatments are effective in changing the setting of internal biological clocks (endogenous *zeitgebers*).

Neuroimmune Regulation. Researchers have reported immunological abnormalities in depressed people and in those grieving the loss of a relative, spouse, or close friend. The dysregulation of the cortisol axis may affect the immune status; there may be abnormal hypothalamic regulation of the immune system. A less likely possibility is that, in some patients, a primary pathophysiological process involving the immune system leads to the psychiatric symptoms of mood disorders.

Brain Imaging. Brain imaging studies of patients with mood disorders have provided several inconclusive clues about abnormal brain function in these disorders. No brain imaging data about mood disorders have been replicated as consistently as has the finding of increased ventricular size in patients with schizophrenia. Nevertheless, structural brain imaging studies with computed tomography (CT) and magnetic resonance imaging (MRI) have produced interesting data. Although the studies have not reported consistent findings, the data indicate the following: A significant set of bipolar I disorder patients, predominantly men, have enlarged cerebral ventricles; ventricular enlargement is less common in patients with major depressive disorder than in those with bipolar I disorder, except that patients with major depressive disorder with psychotic features do tend to have enlarged cerebral ventricles. MRI studies have also indicated that patients with major depressive disorder have smaller caudate nuclei and smaller frontal lobes than do control subjects; the depressed patients also have abnormal hippocampal T1 relaxation times, compared with control subjects. At least one MRI study reported that patients with bipolar I disorder have a significantly increased number of deep white matter lesions, when compared with control subjects.

Many reports in the literature concern cerebral blood flow in mood disorders, usually measured by using single photon emission computed tomography (SPECT) or positron emission tomography (PET). A slight majority of the studies have shown decreased blood flow affecting the cerebral cortex in general and the frontal cortical areas in particular. In contrast, investigators in one study found increases in cerebral blood flow in patients with major depressive disorder. They found state-dependent increases in the cortex, the basal ganglia, and the medial thalamus, with the suggestion of a trait-dependent increase in the amygdala.

Another brain imaging technique that is being applied to a broad range of mental disorders is magnetic resonance spectroscopy (MRS). MRS studies of patients with bipolar I disorder have produced data consistent with the hypothesis that the pathophysiology of the disorder may involve an abnormal regulation of membrane phospholipid metabolism. ^{7}Li MRS is also used to study brain and plasma concentrations of lithium in patients with bipolar I disorder. Results of these studies have demonstrated that the brain concentrations of lithium are about 40 percent of the plasma concentrations after about 1 week of treatment. MRS studies of animals treated with lithium have shown the effects of lithium on phospholipids.

Neuroanatomical Considerations. Both the symptoms of mood disorders and biological research findings support the hypothesis that mood disorders involve pathology of the limbic system, the basal ganglia, and the hypothalamus. People with neurological disorders of the basal ganglia and the limbic system (especially excitatory lesions of the nondominant hemisphere) are likely to show depressive symptoms. The limbic system and the basal ganglia are intimately connected, and the limbic system may well play a major role in the production of emotions. Depressed patients' alterations in sleep, appetite, and sexual behavior and biological changes in endocrine, immunological, and chronobiological measures suggest dysfunction of the hypothalamus. Depressed patients' stooped posture, motor slowness, and minor cognitive impairment are similar to the signs of disorders of the basal ganglia, such as Parkinson's disease and other subcortical dementias.

Genetic Factors

Genetic data strongly indicate that a significant genetic factor is involved in the development of a mood disorder, but the pattern of genetic inheritance occurs by means of complex mechanisms. Not only is it impossible to exclude psychosocial effects, but nongenetic factors probably have causative roles in the development of mood disorders in at least some people. A genetic component plays a more significant role in transmitting bipolar I disorder than in major depressive disorder.

Family Studies. Family studies have repeatedly found that first-degree relatives of bipolar I disorder probands are 8 to 18 times more likely than are the first-degree relatives of control subjects to have bipolar I disorder and 2 to 10 times more likely to have major depressive disorder. Family studies have also found that the first-degree relatives of major depressive disorder probands are 1.5 to 2.5 times more likely to have bipolar I disorder than are the first-degree relatives of normal control subjects and 2 to 3 times more likely to have major depressive disorder. The likelihood of having a mood disorder decreases as the degree of relationship widens. For example, a second-degree relative, such as a cousin, is less likely to be affected than is a first-degree relative, like a brother. The inheritability of bipolar I disorder is also apparent in the fact that about 50 percent of all bipolar I disorder patients have at least one parent with a mood disorder, most often major depressive disorder. If one parent has bipolar I disorder, there is a 25 percent chance that any child has a mood disorder; if both parents have bipolar I disorder, there is a 50 to 75 percent chance that their child has a mood disorder.

Adoption Studies. Adoption studies have also produced data supporting the genetic basis for the inheritance of mood disorders. Two of three adoption studies have found a strong genetic component for the inheritance of major depressive disorder; the only adoption study for bipolar I disorder also indicated a genetic basis. These adoption studies have shown that the biological children of affected parents remain at increased risk of a mood disorder, even if they are reared in nonaffected adoptive families. Such studies have also shown that the biological parents of adopted mood-disordered children have a prevalence of mood disorder similar to that of the parents of nonadopted mood-disordered children. The prevalence of mood disorders in the adoptive parents is similar to the baseline prevalence in the general population.

Twin Studies. Twin studies have shown that the concordance rate for bipolar I disorder in monozygotic twins is 33 to 90 percent, depending on the particular study; for major depressive disorder, the concordance rate in monozygotic twins is about 50 percent. By contrast, the concordance rates in dizygotic twins are about 5 to 25 percent for bipolar I disorder and 10 to 25 percent for major depressive disorder.

Linkage Studies. The availability of modern techniques of molecular biology, including restriction fragment length polymorphisms (RFLPs), has led to many studies that have reported, replicated, or failed to replicate various associations between specific genes or gene markers and a mood disorders. At this time, no genetic association has been consistently replicated. The most reasonable interpretation of the studies is that the particular genes identified in the positive studies may be involved with the genetic inheritance of the mood disorder in the families studies but may not be involved in the genetic inheritance of the mood disorder in other families. Associations between the mood disorders, particularly bipolar I disorder, and genetic markers have been reported for chromosomes 5, 11, and X. The D_2 receptor gene is located on chromosome 5. The gene for tyrosine hydroxylase, the rate-limiting enzyme for catecholamine synthesis, is located on chromosome 11.

CHROMOSOME II AND BIPOLAR I DISORDER. In 1987, a study reported an association between bipolar I disorder among members of an Old Order Amish family and genetic markers on the short arm of chromosome 11. With subsequent extension of the pedigree and the development of bipolar I disorder in previously unaffected family members, the statistical association ceased to apply. That turn of events effectively illustrated the degree of caution that must be used in carrying out and interpreting genetic linkage studies in mental disorders.

X CHROMOSOME AND BIPOLAR I DISORDER. Linkage has long been suggested between bipolar I disorder and a region on the X chromosome that contains genes for color blindness and glucose-6-phosphate dehydrogenase deficiency. As with most linkage studies in psychiatry, the application of molecular genetic techniques has produced contradictory results; some studies find a linkage and others do not. The most conservative interpretation is the possibility that an X-linked gene is a factor in the development of bipolar I disorder in some patients and families.

Psychosocial Factors

Life Events and Environmental Stress. A long-standing clinical observation that has been replicated is that stressful life events more often precede first rather than subsequent episodes of mood disorders. This association has been reported for both patients with major depressive disorder and bipolar I disorder. One theory proposed to explain the observation is that the stress accompanying the first episode results in long-lasting changes in the brain's biology. These long-lasting changes may produce changes in the functional states of various neurotransmitter and intraneuronal signaling systems, changes that may even include the loss of neurons and an excessive reduction in synaptic contacts. As a result, a person has a high risk of undergoing subsequent episodes of a mood disorder, even without an external stressor.

Some clinicians believe that life events play the primary or principal role in depression; others suggest that life events have only a limited role in the onset and timing of depression. The most compelling data indicate that the life event most often associated with a person's later developing of depression is losing a parent before age 11. The environmental stressor most often associated with the onset of an episode of depression is the loss of a spouse.

Family. Several theoretical articles and many anecdotal reports concern the relation between family functioning and the onset and course of mood disorders, particularly major depressive disorder. Several reports have indicated that the psychopathology observed in a family during the time an identified patient is being treated tends to remain even after the patient has recovered. Moreover, the degree of psychopathology in the family may affect the rate of recovery, the return of symptoms, and the patient's postrecovery adjustment. The clinical and anecdotal data support the clinical importance of evaluating the family life of a patient and of addressing any identified family-related stresses.

Premorbid Personality Factors. No single personality trait or type uniquely predisposes a person to depression; all humans, of whatever personality pattern, can and do become depressed under appropriate circumstances. People with certain personality types—oral-dependent, obsessive-compulsive, hysterical—may be at greater risk for depression, however, than are people with antisocial, paranoid, and other personality types, who can use projection and other externalizing defense mechanisms to protect themselves from their inner rage. No evidence indicates that any particular personality disorder is associated with a later development of bipolar I disorder, but those with dysthymic disorder and cyclothymic disorder are at risk of later developing bipolar I disorder.

Carefully designed twin studies have shown that recent stressful events are the most powerful predictors of the onset of a depressive episode. From a psychodynamic perspective, the clinician is always interested in the meaning of the stressor. Research has demonstrated that stressors that are experienced by the patient as reflecting more negatively on the patient's self-esteem are more likely to produce depression. Moreover, what may seem like a relatively mild stressor to outsiders may be devastating to the patient because of the particular idiosyncratic meanings attached to the event.

The psychodynamic clinician is also interested in elucidating the psychodynamic themes associated with the depression. Sigmund Freud spoke of the tendency for depressed patients to direct any hatred and anger originally connected with someone they have lost inward toward themselves.

Melanie Klein understood depression as involving the expression of aggression toward loved ones, much as Freud did, but she connected depression to different developmental experiences. She viewed clinical depression as an inability to successfully work through the depressive position in childhood. She regarded depressed persons as fixated or stuck at a developmental level at which they are extraordinarily concerned that loved good objects have been destroyed by the greed and destructiveness they have directed at them. In the absence of these good objects, depressed persons feel persecuted by the hated bad objects. Hence, in the Klein view, the self-reproach experienced by depressed persons is directed against the self rather than toward an internalized object, as in Freud's view.

Edward Bibring viewed depression as tension arising from within the ego itself rather than between the ego and the superego. He regarded depression as a phenomenon that sets in when a person becomes aware of the discrepancy between extraordinarily high ideals and the reality of his or her situation. Edith Jacobson saw the state of depression as similar to a powerless, helpless child victimized by a tormented parent. The self is experienced as identified with the negative aspects of the tormenting parent, while the sadistic qualities of that parent are transformed into cruel superego. Silvano Arieti observed that many depressed people have lived their lives for someone else rather than for themselves. He referred to this person for whom depressed patients live as the *dominant other,* which may be a principle, an ideal, or an institution, as well as an individual. Depression sets in when patients realize that the person or ideal for whom they have been living is never going to respond in a manner that will meet their expectations. Heinz Kohut's conceptualization of depression, derived from his self psychological theory, rests on the assumption that the developing self has specific needs that must be met by parents to give the child a positive sense of self-esteem and self-cohesion. These needs include admiration, validation, affirmation, and idealization. When others do not perform these functions, there is a massive loss of self-esteem that presents as depression.

Just as biological theories of mood disorder have linked mania and depression, psychodynamic theory also connects the two. Melanie Klein conceptualized mania as a defense against feelings of depression. This formulation is supported by the

Table 15.2–3
DSM-IV Criteria for Major Depressive Episode

A. Five (or more) of the following symptoms have been present during the same 2-week period and represent a change from previous functioning; at least one of the symptoms is either (1) depressed mood or (2) loss of interest or pleasure.

Note: Do not include symptoms that are clearly due to a general medical condition, or mood-incongruent delusions or hallucinations.

(1) depressed mood most of the day, nearly every day, as indicated by either subjective report (eg, feels sad or empty) or observation made by others (eg, appears tearful). **Note:** in children and adolescents, can be irritable mood.
(2) markedly diminished interest or pleasure in all, or almost all, activities most of the day, nearly every day (as indicated either by subjective account or observation made by others)
(3) significant weight loss when not dieting or weight gain (eg, a change of more than 5% of body weight in a month), or decrease or increase in appetite nearly every day. **Note:** in children, consider failure to make expected weight gains.
(4) insomnia or hypersomnia nearly every day
(5) psychomotor agitation or retardation nearly every day (observable by others, not merely subjective feelings of restlessness or being slowed down)
(6) fatigue or loss of energy nearly every day
(7) feelings of worthlessness or excessive or inappropriate guilt (which may be delusional) nearly every day (not merely self-reproach or guilt about being sick)
(8) diminished ability to think or concentrate, or indecisiveness, nearly every day (either by subjective account or as observed by others)
(9) recurrent thoughts of death (not just fear of dying), recurrent suicidal ideation without a specific plan, or a suicide attempt or a specific plan for committing suicide

B. The symptoms do not meet criteria for a mixed episode.

C. The symptoms cause clinically significant distress or impairment in social, occupational, or other important areas of functioning.

D. The symptoms are not due to the direct physiological effects of a substance (eg, a drug of abuse, a medication) or a general medical condition (eg, hypothyroidism).

E. The symptoms are not better accounted for by bereavement, ie, after the loss of a loved one, the symptoms persist for longer than 2 months or are characterized by marked functional impairment, morbid preoccupation with worthlessness, suicidal ideation, psychotic symptoms, or psychomotor retardation.

clinical observation that depression breaks through a manic episode in dysphoric mania. Also, the manic patient can minimize distressing feelings of sorrow or regret that may arise in connection with concerns about having destroyed or hurt loved objects by engaging in excessive euphoria and manic denial.

Learned Helplessness. In experiments in which animals were repeatedly exposed to electric shocks from which they could not escape, the animals eventually gave up and made no attempt at all to escape future shocks. They had learned that they were helpless. Humans who are depressed experience a similar state of helplessness. According to learned-helplessness theory, depression can improve if a clinician instills in a depressed patient a sense of control and mastery of the environment. The clinician uses behavioral techniques of reward and positive reinforcement in such efforts.

Cognitive Theory. According to cognitive theory, common cognitive misinterpretations involve negative distortions of life experience, negative self-evaluation, pessimism, and hopelessness. People who have learned negative views then feel depressed. Cognitive therapists attempt to identify negative cognitions by using behavioral tasks, such as recording and consciously modifying patients' thoughts.

DIAGNOSIS

In addition to the diagnostic criteria for major depressive disorder and bipolar disorders, DSM-IV includes specific criteria for mood episodes (Tables 15.2–3 through 15.2–6) and criteria, such as severity (Tables 15.2–7 through 15.2–9) to qualify the episodes.

Major Depressive Disorder

DSM-IV lists the criteria for a major depressive episode separately from the diagnostic criteria for depression-related diagnoses (see Table 15.2–3) and also lists severity descriptors for a major depressive episode (see Table 15.2–7).

Table 15.2–4
DSM-IV Criteria for Manic Episode

A. A distinct period of abnormally and persistently elevated, expansive, or irritable mood, lasting at least 1 week (or any duration if hospitalization is necessary).

B. During the period of mood disturbance, three (or more) of the following symptoms have persisted (four if the mood is only irritable) and have been present to a significant degree:
(1) inflated self-esteem or grandiosity
(2) decreased need for sleep (eg, feels rested after only 3 hours of sleep)
(3) more talkative than usual or pressure to keep talking
(4) flight of ideas or subjective experience that thoughts are racing
(5) distractibility (ie, attention too easily drawn to unimportant or irrelevant external stimuli)
(6) increase in goal-directed activity (either socially, at work or school, or sexually) or psychomotor agitation
(7) excessive involvement in pleasurable activities that have a high potential for painful consequences (eg, engaging in unrestrained buying sprees, sexual indiscretions, or foolish business investments)

C. The symptoms do not meet criteria for a mixed episode.

D. The mood disturbance is sufficiently severe to cause marked impairment in occupational functioning or in usual social activities or relationships with others, or to necessitate hospitalization to prevent harm to self or others, or there are psychotic features.

E. The symptoms are not due to the direct physiological effects of a substance (eg, a drug of abuse, a medication, or other treatment) or a general medical condition (eg, hyperthyroidism).

Note: Manic-like episodes that are clearly caused by somatic antidepressant treatment (eg, medication, electroconvulsive therapy, light therapy) should not count toward a diagnosis of bipolar I disorder.

Table 15.2–5
DSM-IV Criteria for Hypomanic Episode

A. A distinct period of persistently elevated, expansive, or irritable mood, lasting throughout 4 days, that is clearly different from the usual nondepressed mood.

B. During the period of mood disturbance, three (or more) of the following symptoms have persisted (four if the mood is only irritable) and have been present to a significant degree:
(1) inflated self-esteem or grandiosity
(2) decreased need for sleep (eg, feels rested after only 3 hours of sleep)
(3) more talkative than usual or pressure to keep talking
(4) flight of ideas or subjective experience that thoughts are racing
(5) distractibility (ie, attention too easily drawn to unimportant or irrelevant external stimuli)
(6) increase in goal-directed activity (either socially, at work or school, or sexually) or psychomotor agitation
(7) excessive involvement in pleasurable activities that have a high potential for painful consequences (eg, the person engages in unrestrained buying sprees, sexual indiscretions, or foolish business investments)

C. The episode is associated with an unequivocal change in functioning that is uncharacteristic of the person when not symptomatic.

D. The disturbance in mood and the change in functioning are observable by others.

E. The episode is not severe enough to cause marked impairment in social or occupational functioning, or to necessitate hospitalization, and there are no psychotic features.

F. The symptoms are not due to the direct physiological effects of a substance (eg, a drug of abuse, a medication, or other treatment) or a general medical condition (eg, hyperthyroidism).

Note: Hypomanic-like episodes that are clearly precipitated by somatic antidepressant treatment (eg, medication, electroconvulsive therapy, light therapy) should not count toward a diagnosis of bipolar II disorder.

Table 15.2–6
DSM-IV Criteria for Mixed Episode

A. The criteria are met both for a manic episode and for a major depressive episode (except for duration) nearly every day during at least a 1-week period.
B. The mood disturbance is sufficiently severe to cause marked impairment in occupational functioning or in usual social activities or relationships with others, or to necessitate hospitalization to prevent harm to self or others, or there are psychotic features.
C. The symptoms are not due to the direct physiological effects of a substance (eg, a drug of abuse, a medication, or other treatment) or a general medical condition (eg, hyperthyroidism).

Note: Mixed-like episodes that are clearly caused by somatic antidepressant treatment (eg, medication, electroconvulsive therapy, light therapy) should not count toward a diagnosis of bipolar I disorder.

Reprinted with permission from American Psychiatric Association: *Diagnostic and Statistical Manual of Mental Disorders,* ed 4. Copyright, American Psychiatric Association, Washington, 1994.

Major Depressive Disorder, Single Episode. DSM-IV specifies the diagnostic criteria for the first episode of major depressive disorder (Table 15.2–10). The differentiation between these patients and those who have two or more episodes of major depressive disorder is justified because of the uncertain course of the former patients' disorder. Several studies have reported data consistent with the notion that major depression covers a heterogeneous population of disorders. One type of study assessed the stability of a diagnosis of major depression in a patient over time. The studies found that 25 to 50 percent of the patients were later reclassified as having a different psychiatric condition or a nonpsychiatric medical condition with psychiatric symptoms. A second type of study evaluated first-degree relatives of affectively ill patients to determine the presence and type of psychiatric diagnoses present in these relatives over time. Both types of study found that depressed patients with more depressive symptoms are more likely to have stable diagnoses over time and are more likely to have affectively ill relatives than are depressed patients with fewer depressive symptoms. Also, patients with bipolar I disorder and bipolar II disorder (recurrent major depressive episodes with hypomania) are likely to have stable diagnoses over time.

Major Depressive Disorder, Recurrent. Patients who are experiencing at least a second episode of depression are classified in DSM-IV as having major depressive disorder, recurrent (Table 15.2–11). The major problem with diagnosing recurrent episodes of major depressive disorder is choosing the criteria to designate the resolution of each period. Two variables are the degree of resolution of the symptoms and the length of the resolution. DSM-IV requires that distinct episodes of depression be separated by at least 2 months, during which time a patient has no significant symptoms of depression.

Table 15.2–7
DSM-IV Criteria for Severity/Psychotic/Remission Specifiers for Current (or Most Recent) Major Depressive Episode

Note: Can be applied to the most recent major depressive episode in major depressive disorder and to a major depressive episode in biopolar I or II disorder only if it is the most recent type of mood episode.

Mild: Few, if any, symptoms in excess of those required to make the diagnosis and symptoms result in only minor impairment in occupational functioning or in usual social activities or relationships with others.

Moderate: Symptoms or functional impairment between "mild" and "severe"

Severe without psychotic features: Several symptoms in excess of those required to make the diagnosis, **and** symptoms markedly interfere with occupational functioning or with usual social activities or relationships with others.

With psychotic features: Delusions or hallucinations. If possible, specify whether the psychotic features are mood-congruent or mood-incongruent:

Mood-congruent psychotic features: Delusions or hallucinations whose content is entirely consistent with the typical depressive themes of personal inadequacy, guilt, disease, death, nihilism, or deserved punishment.

Mood-incongruent psychotic features: Delusions or hallucinations whose content does not involve typical depressive themes of personal inadequacy, guilt, disease, death, nihilism, or deserved punishment. Included here are such symptoms as persecutory delusions (not directly related to depressive themes), thought insertion, thought broadcasting, and delusions of control.

In partial remission: Symptoms of a major depressive episode are present but full criteria are not met, or there is a period without any significant symptoms of a major depressive episode lasting less than 2 months following the end of the major depressive episode. (If the major depressive episode was superimposed on dysthymic disorder, the diagnosis of dysthymic disorder alone is given once the full criteria for a major depressive episode are no longer met.)

In full remission: During the past 2 months, no significant signs or symptoms of the disturbance.

Unspecified.

Reprinted with permission from American Psychiatric Association: *Diagnostic and Statistical Manual of Mental Disorders,* ed 4. Copyright, American Psychiatric Association, Washington, 1994.

Bipolar I Disorder

DSM-IV contains a separate list of criteria for a manic episode (see Table 15.2–4). DSM-IV requires the presence of a distinct period of abnormal mood lasting at least 1 week and includes separate bipolar I disorder diagnoses for a single manic episode and a specific type of recurrent episode, based on the symptoms of the most recent episode.

The designation *bipolar I disorder* is synonymous with what was known as bipolar disorder—a syndrome in which a complete set of mania symptoms occurs during the course of the disorder. DSM-IV has formalized the diagnostic criteria for bipolar II disorder; it is characterized by depressive episodes and hypomanic episodes (see Table 15.2–9) during the course of the disorder, but the episodes of manic symptoms do not quite meet the diagnostic criteria for a full manic syndrome.

Table 15.2–8
DSM-IV Criteria for Severity/Psychotic/Remission Specifiers for Current (or Most Recent) Manic Episode

Note: Can be applied to a manic episode in bipolar I disorder only if it is the most recent type of mood episode.

Mild: Minimum symptom criteria are met for a manic episode.

Moderate: Extreme increase in activity or impairment in judgment.

Severe, without psychotic features: Almost continual supervision required to prevent physical harm to others.

Severe, with psychotic features: Delusions or hallucinations. If possible, specify whether the psychotic features are mood-congruent or mood-incongruent:

- **Mood-congruent psychotic features:** Delusions or hallucinations whose content is entirely consistent with the typical manic themes of inflated worth, power, knowledge; identity, or special relationship to a deity or famous person.
- **Mood-incongruent psychotic features:** Delusions or hallucinations whose content does not involve typical manic themes of inflated worth, power, knowledge, identity, or special relationship to a deity or famous person. Included are such symptoms as persecutory delusions (not directly related to grandiose ideas or themes), thought insertion, and delusions of being controlled.

In partial remission: Symptoms of a manic episode are present but full criteria are not met, or there is a period without any significant symptoms of a manic episode lasting less than 2 months following the end of the manic episode.

In full remission: During the past 2 months, no significant signs or symptoms of the disturbance were present.

Unspecified.

Table 15.2–9
DSM-IV Criteria for Severity/Psychotic/Remission Specifiers for Current (or Most Recent) Mixed Episode

Note: Can be applied to a manic episode in bipolar I disorder only if it is the most recent type of mood episode.

Mild: No more than minimum symptom criteria are met for both a manic episode and a major depressive episode.

Moderate: Symptoms or functional impairment between "mild" and "severe."

Severe, without psychotic features: Almost continual supervision required to prevent physical harm to self or others.

Severe, with psychotic features: Delusions or hallucinations. If possible, specify whether the psychotic features are mood-congruent or mood-incongruent:

- **Mood-congruent psychotic features:** Delusions or hallucinations whose content is entirely consistent with the typical manic or depressive themes.
- **Mood-incongruent psychotic features:** Delusions or hallucinations whose content does not involve typical manic or depressive themes. Included are such symptoms as persecutory delusions (not directly related to grandiose or depressive themes), thought insertion, and delusions of being controlled.

In partial remission: Symptoms of a mixed episode are present but full criteria are not met, or there is a period without any significant symptoms of a mixed episode lasting less than 2 months following the end of the mixed episode.

In full remission: During the past 2 months, no significant signs or symptoms of the disturbance were present.

Unspecified.

DSM-IV specifically states that manic episodes clearly precipitated by antidepressant treatment (for example, pharmacotherapy, electroconvulsive therapy) are not indicative of bipolar I disorder.

Bipolar I Disorder, Single Manic Episode. According to DSM-IV, patients must be experiencing their first manic episode to meet the diagnostic criteria for bipolar I disorder, single manic episode (Table 15.2–12). This requirement rests on the fact that patients who are having their first episode of bipolar I disorder depression cannot be distinguished from patients with major depressive disorder.

Bipolar I Disorder, Recurrent. The issues about defining the end of an episode of depression also apply to defining the end of an episode of mania. In DSM-IV, episodes are considered distinct when they are separated by at least 2 months without significant symptoms of mania or hypomania. DSM-IV specifies diagnostic criteria for recurrent bipolar I disorder based on the symptoms of the most recent episode: bipolar I disorder, most recent episode hypomanic (Table 15.2–13); bipolar I disorder, most recent episode manic (Table 15.2–14); bipolar I disorder, most recent episode mixed (Table 15.2–15); bipolar I disorder, most recent episode depressed (Table

Table 15.2–10
DSM-IV Diagnostic Criteria for Major Depressive Disorder, Single Episode

A. Presence of a single major depressive episode.

B. The major depressive episode is not better accounted for by schizoaffective disorder, and is not superimposed on schizophrenia, schizophreniform disorder, delusional disorder, or psychotic disorder not otherwise specified.

C. There has never been a manic episode, a mixed episode, or a hypomanic episode. **Note:** This exclusion does not apply if all of the manic-like, mixed-like, or hypomanic-like episodes are substance or treatment induced or are due to the direct physiological effects of a general medical condition.

Specify (for current or most recent episode):
- **Severity/psychotic/remission specifiers**
- **Chronic**
- **With catatonic features**
- **With melancholic features**
- **With atypical features**
- **With postpartum onset**

Table 15.2–11
DSM-IV Diagnostic Criteria for Major Depressive Disorder, Recurrent

A. Presence of two or more major depressive episodes.
Note: To be considered separate episodes, there must be an interval of at least 2 consecutive months in which criteria are not met for a major depressive episode.
B. The major depressive episodes are not better accounted for by schizoaffective disorder and are not superimposed on schizophrenia, schizophreniform disorder, delusional disorder, or psychotic disorder not otherwise specified.
C. There has never been a manic episode, a mixed episode, or a hypomanic episode. **Note:** This exclusion does not apply if all of the manic-like, mixed-like, or hypomanic-like episodes are substance or treatment induced or are due to the direct physiological effects of a general medical condition.

Specify (for current or most recent episode):
Severity/psychotic/remission specifiers
Chronic
With catatonic features
With melancholic features
With atypical features
With postpartum onset

Specify:
Longitudinal course specifiers (with and without interepisode recovery)
With seasonal pattern

15.2–16); bipolar I disorder, most recent episode unspecified (Table 15.2–17).

Bipolar II Disorder

The diagnostic criteria for bipolar II disorder specify a particular severity, frequency, and duration of the hypomanic symptoms. The diagnostic criteria for a hypomanic episode (see Table 15.2–5) are listed separately from the criteria for bipolar II disorder (Table 15.2–18). The criteria have been established to decrease the overdiagnosis of hypomania episodes and the incorrect classification of patients with major depressive disorder as patients with bipolar II disorder. Clinically, psychiatrists may find it difficult to distinguish euthymia from hypomania in a patient who has been chronically depressed for many months or years. As with bipolar I disorder, antidepressant-induced hypomanic episodes are not diagnostic of bipolar II disorder.

Table 15.2–12
DSM-IV Diagnostic Criteria for Bipolar I Disorder, Single Manic Episode

A. Presence of only one manic episode and no past major depressive episodes.
Note: Recurrence is defined as either a change in polarity from depression or an interval or at least 2 months without manic symptoms.
B. The manic episode is not better accounted for by schizoaffective disorder, and is not superimposed on schizophrenia, schizophreniform disorder, delusional disorder, or psychotic disorder not otherwise specified.

Specify if:
Mixed: if symptoms meet criteria for a mixed episode

Specify (for current or most recent episode):
Severity/psychotic/remission specifiers
With catatonic features
With postpartum onset

Table 15.2–13
DSM-IV Diagnostic Criteria for Bipolar I Disorder, Most Recent Episode Hypomanic

A. Currently (or most recently) in a hypomanic episode.
B. There has previously been at least one manic episode or mixed episode.
C. The mood symptoms cause clinically significant distress or impairment in social, occupational, or other important areas of functioning.
D. The mood episodes in criteria A and B are not better accounted for by schizoaffective disorder and are not superimposed on schizophrenia, schizophreniform disorder, delusional disorder, or psychotic disorder not otherwise specified.

Specify
Longitudinal course specifiers (with and without interepisode recovery)
With seasonal pattern (applies only to the pattern of major depressive episodes)
With rapid cycling

Table 15.2–14
DSM-IV Diagnostic Criteria for Bipolar I Disorder, Most Recent Episode Manic

A. Currently (or most recently) in a manic episode.
B. There has previously been at least one major depressive episode, manic episode, or mixed episode.
C. The mood episodes in criteria A and B are not better accounted for by schizoaffective disorder and are not superimposed on schizophrenia, schizophreniform disorder, delusional disorder, or psychotic disorder not otherwise specified.

Specify (for current or most recent episode):
Severity/psychotic remission specifiers
With catatonic features
With postpartum onset

Specify:
Longitudinal course specifiers (with and without interepisode recovery)
With seasonal pattern (applies only to the pattern of major depressive episodes)
With rapid cycling

Table 15.2–15
DSM-IV Diagnostic Criteria for Bipolar I Disorder, Most Recent Episode Mixed

A. Currently (or most recently) in a mixed episode.
B. There has previously been at least one major depressive episode, manic episode, or mixed episode.
C. The mood episodes in criteria A and B are not better accounted for by schizoaffective disorder and are not superimposed on schizophrenia, schizophreniform disorder, delusional disorder, or psychotic disorder not otherwise specified.

Specify (for current or most recent episode):
Severity/psychotic remission specifiers
With catatonic features
With postpartum onset

Specify:
Longitudinal course specifiers (with and without interepisode recovery)
With seasonal pattern (applies only to the pattern of major depressive episodes)
With rapid cycling

Specifiers Describing Most Recent Episode

In addition to the severity/psychotic/remission specifiers (see Tables 15.2–7 through 15.2–9), DSM-IV defines additional symptom features that can be used to describe patients with various mood disorders. Two of the cross-sectional features (melancholic and atypical) are limited to describing depressive episodes. Two others (catatonic features and with postpartum onset) can be applied to describing depressive and manic episodes.

With Psychotic Features. The presence of psychotic features (see Table 15.2–7) in major depressive disorder reflects severe disease and is a poor prognostic indicator. Clinicians and researchers had dichotomized depressive illness along a psychotic-neurotic continuum. A review of the literature comparing psychotic with nonpsychotic major depressive disorder indicates that the two conditions may be distinct in their pathogenesis. One difference is that bipolar I disorder is more common in the families of probands with psychotic depression than in the families of probands with nonpsychotic depression.

The psychotic symptoms themselves are often categorized as either mood in harmony with the mood disorder ("I deserve to be punished because I am so bad")—or mood incongruent—not in harmony with the mood disorder. Although mood disorder patients with mood-congruent psychoses have a psychotic type of mood disorder, mood disorder patients with mood-incongruent psychotic symptoms have been variously typed as having schizoaffective disorder or a subtype of schizophrenia or a completely distinct diagnostic entity. The classification of these mood-incongruent patients remains controversial, but the weight of the research data and the guidelines in DSM-IV indicate that clinicians should classify such patients as having a psychotic mood disorder.

Table 15.2–16
DSM-IV Diagnostic Criteria for Bipolar I Disorder, Most Recent Episode Depressed

A. Currently (or most recently) in a major depressive episode.
B. There has previously been at least one manic episode or mixed episode.
C. The mood episodes in criteria A and B are not better accounted for by schizoaffective disorder and are not superimposed on schizophrenia, schizophreniform disorder, delusional disorder, or psychotic disorder not otherwise specified.

The following factors have been associated with a poor prognosis for patients with mood disorders: long duration of episodes, temporal dissociation between the mood disorder and the psychotic symptoms, and a poor premorbid history of social adjustment. The presence of psychotic features also has significant treatment implications. These patients typically require antipsychotic drugs in addition to antidepressants and may need electroconvulsive therapy (ECT) to obtain clinical improvement.

With Melancholic Features. In the literature on the melancholic features of depression, about 10 systems have been suggested, with almost 3 times as many specific criteria for symptoms and course specifiers. In view of the lack of

Table 15.2–17
DSM-IV Diagnostic Criteria for Bipolar I Disorder, Most Recent Episode Unspecified

A. Criteria, except for duration, are currently (or most recently) met for a manic, a hypomanic, a mixed, or a major depressive episode.
B. There has previously been at least one manic episode or mixed episode.
C. The mood symptoms cause clinically significant distress or impairment in social, occupational, or other important areas of functioning.
D. The mood symptoms in criteria A and B are not better accounted for by schizoaffective disorder and are not superimposed on schizophrenia, schizophreniform disorder, delusional disorder, or psychotic disorder not otherwise specified.
E. The mood symptoms in criteria A and B are not due to the direct physiological effects of a substance (eg, a drug of abuse, a medication, or other treatment) or a general medical condition (eg, hyperthyroidism).

Specify:
Longitudinal course specifiers (with and without interepisode recovery)
With seasonal pattern (applies only to the pattern of major depressive episodes)
With rapid cycling

Table 15.2–18
DSM-IV Diagnostic Criteria for Bipolar II Disorder

A. Presence (or history) of one or more major depressive episodes.
B. Presence (or history) of at least one hypomanic episode.
C. There has never been a manic episode.
D. The mood symptoms in criteria A and B are not better accounted for by schizoaffective disorder, and are not superimposed on schizophrenia, schizophreniform disorder, delusional disorder, or psychotic disorder not otherwise specified.
E. The symptoms cause clinically significant distress or impairment in social, occupational, or other important areas of functioning.

Specify current or most recent episode:
- **Hypomanic:** if currently (or most recently) in a hypomanic episode
- **Depressed:** if currently (or most recently) in a major depressive episode

Specify (for current or most recent major depressive episode only if it is the most recent type of mood episode):
- **Severity/psychotic/remission specifiers**
- **Chronic**
- **With catatonic features**
- **With melancholic features**
- **With atypical features**
- **With postpartum onset**

Specify:
- **Longitudinal course specifiers (with or without interepisode recovery)**
- **With seasonal pattern** (applies only to the pattern of major depressive episodes)
- **With rapid cycling**

Table 15.2–19
DSM-IV Criteria for Melancholic Features Specifiers

Specify if:
With melancholic features (can be applied to major depressive episodes occurring in major depressive disorder, bipolar I disorder or bipolar II disorder only if it is the most recent type of mood episode)

A. Either of the following, occurring during the most severe period of the current episode:
   (1) loss of pleasure in all, or almost all, activities.
   (2) lack of reactivity to usually pleasurable stimuli (does not feel much better, even temporarily, when something good happens).
B. Three (or more) of the following:
   (1) distinct quality of depressed mood (ie, the depressed mood is perceived as distinctly different from the kind of feeling experienced after the death of a loved one)
   (2) the depression is regularly worse in the morning
   (3) early morning awakening (at least 2 hours before usual time of awakening)
   (4) marked psychomotor retardation or agitation
   (5) significant anorexia or weight loss
   (6) excessive or inappropriate guilt

sufficient data and of adequate comparative studies for any one of these systems, any decision about the specific criteria is essentially arbitrary. Moreover, the arbitrary nature of the decisions has not succeeded in discouraging frequent changes in the officially accepted definition of melancholia. The potential importance of identifying the melancholic features of major depressive episodes is to identify a group of patients who some data indicate are more responsive to pharmacotherapeutic treatment than are nonmelancholic depressed patients.

The DSM-IV melancholic features can be applied to major depressive episodes in major depressive disorder, bipolar I disorder, or bipolar II disorder (Table 15.2–19).

With Atypical Features. The introduction of a formally defined depression with atypical features is a response to research and clinical data indicating that patients with atypical features have specific, predictable characteristics: overeating and oversleeping. These symptoms have sometimes been referred to as reversed vegetative symptoms, and the symptom pattern has sometimes been referred to as hysteroid dysphoria. When patients with major depressive disorder with these features are compared with those patients without the features, the patients with atypical features are found to have a younger age of onset, a more severe degree of psychomotor slowing, and more frequent coexisting diagnoses of panic disorder, substance abuse or dependence, and somatization disorder. The high incidence and severity of anxiety symptoms in patients with atypical features has been correlated in some research with the likelihood of their being misclassified as having an anxiety disorder rather than a mood disorder. Patients with atypical features may also be likely to have a long-term course, a diagnosis of bipolar I disorder, or a seasonal pattern to their disorder. The major treatment implication of patients with atypical features is that they are more likely to respond to monoamine oxidase inhibitors (MAOIs) than to tricyclic drugs. Yet the significance of atypical features remains controversial, as does the preferential treatment response to MAOIs. Moreover, the absence of specific diagnostic criteria has limited researchers' ability to assess the criteria's validity and the disorder's prevalence and to ascertain the existence of any other biological or psychological factors that may differentiate it from other symptom patterns.

The DSM-IV atypical features can be applied to the most recent major depressive episode in major depressive disorder, bipolar I disorder, bipolar II disorder, or dysthymic disorder (Table 15.2–20).

With Catatonic Features. The decision to include a specific classification for catatonic features (Table 15.2–21) in the mood disorders category was motivated by two factors. First, because one intent of DSM-IV's authors was to serve as a guide in the differential diagnosis of mental disorders, the inclusion of a specifically catatonic type of mood disorder helps balance the presence of a catatonic type of schizophrenia.

Table 15.2–20
DSM-IV Criteria for Atypical Features Specifier

Specify if:
With atypical features (can be applied when these features predominate during the most recent 2 weeks of a major depressive episode in major depressive disorder or in bipolar I or bipolar II disorder when the major depressive episode is the most recent type of mood episode, or when these features predominate during the most recent 2 years of dysthymic disorder)

A. Mood reactivity (ie, mood brightens in response to actual or potential positive events).
B. Two (or more) of the following features, present for most of the time, for at least 2 weeks:
   (1) significant weight gain or increase in appetite
   (2) hypersomnia
   (3) leaden paralysis (ie, heavy, leaden feelings in arms or legs)
   (4) long-standing pattern of interpersonal rejection sensitivity (not limited to episodes of mood disturbance) resulting in significant social or occupational impairment
C. Criteria are not met with melancholic features or with catatonic features during the same episode.

As a symptom, catatonia can be present in several mental disorders, most commonly schizophrenia and the mood disorders. Second, although as yet incompletely studied, the presence of catatonic features in patients with mood disorders will probably be shown to have prognostic and treatment significance.

The hallmark symptoms of catatonia—stuporousness, blunted affect, extreme withdrawal, negativism, and marked psychomotor retardation—can be seen in both catatonic and noncatatonic schizophrenia, major depressive disorder (often with psychotic features), and medical and neurological disorders, but catatonic symptoms are probably most commonly associated with bipolar I disorder. Clinicians often do not associate catatonia symptoms with this disorder because of the marked contrast between the symptoms of stuporous catatonia and the classic symptoms of mania. Because catatonic symptoms are a behavioral syndrome appearing in several medical and psychiatric conditions, catatonic symptoms do not imply a single diagnosis.

In DSM-IV, catatonic features can be applied to the most recent manic episode or major depressive episode in major depressive disorder, bipolar I disorder, or bipolar II disorder.

Table 15.2–21
DSM-IV Criteria for Catatonic Features Specifier

Specify if:
With catatonic features (can be applied to the current or most recent major depressive episode, manic episode, or mixed episode in major depressive disorder, bipolar I disorder, or bipolar II disorder)

The clinical picture is dominated by at least two of the following:
   (1) motoric immobility as evidenced by catalepsy (including waxy flexibility) or stupor
   (2) excessive motor activity (that is apparently purposeless and not influenced by external stimuli)
   (3) extreme negativism (an apparently motiveless resistance to all instructions or maintenance of a rigid posture against attempts to be moved) or mutism
   (4) peculiarities of voluntary movement as evidenced by posturing (voluntary assumption of inappropriate or bizarre postures), stereotyped movements, prominent mannerisms, or prominent grimacing
   (5) echolalia or echopraxia

Table 15.2–22
DSM-IV Criteria for Postpartum Onset Specifier

Specify if:
With postpartum onset (can be applied to the current or most recent major depressive, manic, or mixed episode in major depressive disorder, bipolar I disorder, or bipolar II disorder; or to brief psychotic disorder)

Onset of episode within 4 weeks postpartum.

Postpartum Onset. DSM-IV allows for the specification of a postpartum mood disturbance if the onset of symptoms is within 4 weeks postpartum (Table 15.2–22). Postpartum mental disorders commonly include psychotic symptoms (see Table 14.1–6 and Table 14.5–1).

Chronic. DSM-IV allows for the specification of chronic to describe major depressive episodes that occur as a part of major depressive disorder, bipolar I disorder, and bipolar II disorder (Table 15.2–23).

Describing Course of Recurrent Episodes

DSM-IV includes criteria for three distinct course specifiers for mood disorders. One of the course specifiers, *with rapid cycling* (Table 15.2–24), is restricted to bipolar I disorder and

Table 15.2–23
DSM-IV Criteria for Chronic Specifier

Specify if:
Chronic (can be applied to the current or most recent major depressive episode in major depressive disorder and to a major depressive episode in bipolar I or II disorder only if it is the most recent type of mood episode)

Full criteria for a major depressive episode have been met continuously for at least the past 2 years.

Table 15.2–24
DSM-IV Diagnostic Criteria for Rapid Cycling Specifier

Specify if:

With rapid cycling (can be applied to bipolar I disorder or bipolar II disorder)

At least four episodes of a mood disturbance in the previous 12 months that meet criteria for a major depressive, manic, mixed, or hypomanic episode.

Note: Episodes are demarcated either by partial or full remission for at least 2 months or a switch to an episode of opposite polarity (eg, major depressive episode to manic episode).

Reprinted with permission from American Psychiatric Association: *Diagnostic and Statistical Manual of Mental Disorders,* ed 4. Copyright, American Psychiatric Association, Washington, 1994.

bipolar II disorder. Two other course specifiers, *with seasonal pattern* (Table 15.2–25) and *with or without full interepisode recovery* (Table 15.2–26), can be applied to bipolar I disorder, bipolar II disorder, and major depressive disorder, recurrent. The course specifier, *with postpartum onset,* can be applied to major depressive or manic episodes in bipolar I disorder, bipolar II disorder, major depressive disorder, and brief psychotic disorder.

Rapid Cycling. Patients with rapid cycling bipolar I disorder are likely to be female and to have had depressive and hypomanic episodes. No data indicate that rapid cycling has a familial pattern of inheritance, and thus an external factor such as stress or drug treatment may be involved in the pathogenesis of rapid cycling. The DSM-IV criteria specify that the patient must have at least four episodes within a 12-month period (Table 15.2–24).

Seasonal Pattern. Patients with a seasonal pattern to their mood disorders tend to experience depressive episodes during a particular season, most commonly winter. The pattern has become known as seasonal affective disorder (SAD), although this term is not used in DSM-IV (Table 15.2–25). Two types of evidence indicate that the seasonal pattern may represent a separate diagnostic entity. First, the patients are likely to respond to treatment with light therapy, although adequate studies to evaluate light therapy in nonseasonally depressed patients have not been conducted. Second, one PET study showed that patients show decreased metabolic activity in the orbital frontal cortex and in the left inferior parietal lobule. Future studies will probably focus on differentiating depressed people with seasonal pattern from other depressed people.

Longitudinal Course Specifiers. DSM-IV includes specific descriptions of longitudinal courses for major depressive disorder, bipolar I disorder, and bipolar II disorder (Table 15.2–26). These longitudinal course specifiers allow clinicians and researchers to prospectively identify any treatment or prognostic significance in various longitudinal courses. Although preliminary studies of the DSM-IV longitudinal course specifiers indicate that clinicians can assess the longitudinal course, more and larger studies are needed to develop a solid appreciation of the assessment and implications of variations in the longitudinal course.

Table 15.2–25
DSM-IV Criteria for Seasonal Pattern Specifier

Specify if:

With seasonal pattern (can be applied to the pattern of major depressive episodes in bipolar I disorder, bipolar II disorder, or major depressive disorder, recurrent)

A. There has been a regular temporal relationship between the onset of major depressive episodes in bipolar I or bipolar II disorder or major depressive disorder, recurrent, and a particular time of the year (eg, regular appearance of the major depressive episode in the fall or winter)
Note: Do not include cases in which there is an obvious effect of seasonal-related psychosocial stressors (eg, regularly being unemployed every winter).

B. Full remissions (or a change from depression to mania or hypomania) also occur at a characteristic time of the year (eg, depression disappears in the spring).

C. In the last 2 years, two major depressive episodes have occurred that demonstrate the temporal seasonal relationships defined in criteria A and B, and no nonseasonal major depressive episodes have occurred during that same period.

D. Seasonal major depressive episodes (as described above) substantially outnumber any nonseasonal major depressive episodes that may have occurred over the individual's lifetime.

Reprinted with permission from American Psychiatric Association: *Diagnostic and Statistical Manual of Mental Disorders,* ed 4. Copyright, American Psychiatric Association, Washington, 1994.

Non–DSM-IV Types. Other systems that identify types of patients with mood disorders usually separate patients with good and poor prognoses or patients who may respond to one treatment or another. They also differentiate endogenous-reactive and primary-secondary schemes.

The endogenous-reactive continuum is a controversial division. It implies that endogenous depressions are biological and that reactive depressions are psychological, primarily on the basis of the presence or absence of an identifiable precipitating stress. Other symptoms of endogenous depression have been described as diurnal variation, delusions, psychomotor retardation, early morning awakening, and feelings of guilt; thus, endogenous depression is similar to the DSM-IV diag-

Table 15.2–26
DSM-IV Criteria for Longitudinal Course Specifiers

Specify if (can be applied to recurrent major depressive disorder or bipolar I or II disorder):

With full interepisode recovery: if full remission is attained between the two most recent mood episodes

Without full interepisode recovery: if full remission is not attained between the two most recent mood episodes

Reprinted with permission from American Psychiatric Association: *Diagnostic and Statistical Manual of Mental Disorders,* ed 4. Copyright, American Psychiatric Association, Washington, 1994.

nosis of major depressive disorder with psychotic features or melancholic features or both. Symptoms of reactive depression have been described as including initial insomnia, anxiety, emotional lability, and multiple somatic complaints.

Primary depressions are what DSM-IV refers to as mood disorders, except for the diagnoses of mood disorder caused by a general medical condition and substance-induced mood disorder, which are considered secondary depressions. *Double depression* is the condition in which major depressive disorder is superimposed on dysthymic disorder. A *depressive equivalent* is a symptom or syndrome that may be a forme fruste of a depressive episode. For example, a triad of truancy, alcohol abuse, and sexual promiscuity in a formerly well-behaved adolescent may constitute a depressive equivalent.

CLINICAL FEATURES

The two basic symptom patterns in mood disorders are those of depression and mania. Depressive episodes can occur in both major depressive disorder and bipolar I disorder. In many studies, researchers have attempted to find reliable differences between bipolar I disorder depressive episodes and episodes of major depressive disorder, but the differences are elusive. In a clinical situation, only the patient's history, family history, and future course can help differentiate the two conditions. Some patients with bipolar I disorder have mixed states with both manic and depressive features, and some seem to experience brief—minutes to a few hours—episodes of depression during manic episodes.

Depressive Episodes

A depressed mood and a loss of interest or pleasure are the key symptoms of depression. Patients may say that they feel blue, hopeless, in the dumps, or worthless. For a patient, the depressed mood often has a distinct quality that differentiates it from the normal emotion of sadness or grief. Patients often describe the symptom of depression as one of agonizing emotional pain and sometimes complain about being unable to cry, a symptom that resolves as they improve.

About two thirds of all depressed patients contemplate suicide, and 10 to 15 percent commit suicide. Yet depressed patients sometimes seem unaware of their depression and do not complain of a mood disturbance, even though they exhibit withdrawal from family, friends, and activities that previously interested them. Almost all depressed patients (97 percent) complain about reduced energy; they find difficulty in finishing tasks, are impaired at school and work, and have decreased motivation to undertake new projects. About 80 percent of patients complain of trouble in sleeping, especially early morning awakening (that is, terminal insomnia) and multiple awakenings at night, during which they ruminate about their problems. Many patients have decreased appetite and weight loss, but others experience increased appetite and weight gain, and sleep longer than usual. These patients are classified in DSM-IV as having atypical features; this version of depression is also known as having hysteroid dysphoria.

Anxiety is a common symptom of depression and affects as many as 90 percent of all depressed patients. The various changes in food intake and rest can aggravate coexisting medical illnesses, such as diabetes, hypertension, chronic obstructive lung disease, and heart disease. Other vegetative symptoms include abnormal menses and decreased interest and performance in sexual activities. Sexual problems can sometimes lead to inappropriate referrals, such as to marital counseling and sex therapy, when clinicians fail to recognize the underlying depressive disorder. Anxiety (including panic attacks), alcohol abuse, and somatic complaints (such as constipation and headaches) often complicate the treatment of depression. About 50 percent of all patients describe a diurnal variation in their symptoms, with an increased severity in the morning and a lessening of symptoms by evening. Cognitive symptoms include subjective reports of an inability to concentrate (84 percent of patients in one study) and impairments in thinking (67 percent of patients in another study).

Depression in Children and Adolescents. School phobia and excessive clinging to parents may be symptoms of depression in children. Poor academic performance, substance abuse, antisocial behavior, sexual promiscuity, truancy, and running away may be symptoms of depression in adolescents. (This subject is further discussed in Chapter 48.)

Depression in Older People. Depression is more common in older people than it is in the general population. Various studies have reported prevalence rates ranging from 25 to almost 50 percent, although the percentage of these cases that are caused by major depressive disorder is uncertain. Several studies have reported data indicating that depression in older people may be correlated with low socioeconomic status, the loss of a spouse, a concurrent physical illness, and social isolation. Other studies have indicated that depression in older people is underdiagnosed and undertreated, perhaps particularly by general practitioners. The under-recognition of depression in older people may occur because the disorder more often appears with somatic complaints in older than in younger age groups. Further, ageism may influence and cause them to accept more depressive symptoms in older patients than in younger patients.

Manic Episodes

Clinical Signs and Symptoms. An elevated, expansive, or irritable mood is the hallmark of a manic episode. The elevated mood is euphoric and often infectious and can even cause a countertransferential denial of illness by an inexperienced clinician. Although uninvolved people may not recognize the unusual nature of a patient's mood, those who know the patient recognize it as abnormal. Alternatively, the mood may be irritable, especially when a patient's overtly ambitious plans are thwarted. Patients often exhibit a change of predominant mood from euphoria early in the course of the illness to later irritability.

The treatment of manic patients in an inpatient ward can be complicated by their testing of the limits of ward rules, their tendency to shift responsibility for their acts onto others, their exploitation of the weaknesses of others, and their propensity to dividing staffs. Outside the hospital, manic patients often drink alcohol excessively, perhaps in an attempt to self-medicate. Their disinhibited nature is reflected in an excessive use of the telephone, especially in the making of long-distance calls during the early morning hours. Pathological gambling, a tendency to disrobe in public places, wearing clothing and jewelry of bright colors in unusual or outlandish combinations, and an inattention to small details (such as forgetting to hang up the telephone) are also symptomatic of the disorder. Patients act impulsively and at the same time with a sense of conviction and purpose. They are often preoccupied by religious, political, financial, sexual, or persecutory ideas that can evolve into complex delusional systems. Occasionally, manic patients become regressed and play with their urine and feces.

Mr. Z., a 37-year-old engineer, had experienced three manic episodes for which he had been hospitalized; all three episodes were preceded by several weeks of moderate psychomotor retardation. Although each time he had responded to lithium (Eskalith, Lithobid), once outside the hospital, he had been reluctant to take it and eventually refused to do so. Now that he was euthymic, following his third and most disruptive episode during which he had badly beaten his wife, he said that he could better explain how he felt when manic. Mania, he felt, was "like God implanted in him," so he could serve as "testimony to man's communication with God." He elaborated as follows: "Ordinary mortals will never, never understand the supreme manic state which I'm privileged to experience every few years. It is so vivid, so intense, so compelling. When I feel that way, there can be no other explanation: To be manic is, ultimately, to be God. God himself must be supermanic: I can feel it, when mania enters through my left brain like laser beams, transforming my sluggish thoughts, recharging them, galvanizing them. My thoughts acquire such momentum, they rush out of my head, to explain the true nature of mania to psychiatrists and all others concerned. That's why I will never accept lithium—to do so is to obstruct the divinity in me." Although he was on the brink of divorce, he would not yield to his wife's plea to go back on lithium.

DISCUSSION

The vignette illustrates the possibility that even some of the most psychotic experiences in mania represent explanatory delusions, the patient's attempt to make sense of the mania. Mr. Z had bipolar I disorder, most recent episode manic, severe with mood-incongruent psychotic features. (Courtesy of Hagop S. Akiskal, M.D.)

Mania in Adolescents. Mania in adolescents is often misdiagnosed as antisocial personality disorder or schizophrenia. Symptoms of mania in adolescents may include psychosis, alcohol or other substance abuse, suicide attempts, academic problems, philosophical brooding, obsessive-compulsive disorder symptoms, multiple somatic complaints, marked irritability resulting in fights, and other antisocial behaviors. Although many of these symptoms are seen in normal adolescence, severe or persistent symptoms should cause clinicians to consider bipolar I disorder in the differential diagnosis.

Bipolar II Disorder

The clinical features of bipolar II disorder are those of major depressive disorder combined with those of a hypomanic episode. Although the data are limited, a few studies indicate that bipolar II disorder is associated with more marital disruption and with onset at an earlier age than is bipolar I disorder. Evidence also indicates that patients with bipolar II disorder are at greater risk of both attempting and completing suicide than are patients with bipolar I disorder and major depressive disorder.

Coexisting Disorders

Anxiety. In the anxiety disorders, DSM-IV notes the existence of mixed anxiety-depressive disorder. Significant symptoms of anxiety can and often do coexist with significant symptoms of depression. Whether patients who exhibit significant symptoms of both anxiety and depression are affected by two distinct disease processes or by a single disease process that produces both sets of symptoms is not yet resolved. Patients of both types may constitute the group of patients with mixed anxiety-depressive disorder.

Alcohol Dependence. Alcohol dependence frequently coexists with mood disorders. Both patients with major depressive disorder and those with bipolar I disorder are likely to meet the diagnostic criteria for an alcohol use disorder. The available data indicate that alcohol dependence in women is more strongly associated with a coexisting diagnosis of depression than is alcohol dependence in men. In contrast, the genetic and family data about men who have both a mood disorder and alcohol dependence indicate that they are likely to be suffering from two genetically distinct disease processes.

Other Substance-Related Disorders. Substance-related disorders other than alcohol dependence are also commonly associated with mood disorders. The abuse of substances may be involved in precipitating an episode of illness or, conversely, may represent patients' attempts to treat their own illnesses. Although manic patients seldom use sedatives to dampen their euphoria, depressed patients often use stimulants, such as cocaine and amphetamines, to relieve their depression.

Medical Conditions. Depression commonly coexists with medical conditions, especially in older people. When depression and medical conditions coexist, clinicians must try to determine whether the underlying medical condition is pathophysiologically related to the depression or whether any drugs that the patient is taking for the medical condition are causing the depression. Many studies indicate that treatment of a coexisting major depressive disorder can improve the course of the underlying medical disorder, including cancer.

MENTAL STATUS EXAMINATION

Depressive Episodes

General Description. Generalized psychomotor retardation is the most common symptom, although psychomotor agitation is also seen, especially in older patients. Hand wringing and hair pulling are the most common symptoms of agitation. Classically, a depressed patient has a stooped posture, no spontaneous movements, and a downcast, averted gaze (Figs. 15.2–1 and 15.2–2). On clinical examination, depressed patients exhibiting gross symptoms of psychomotor retardation may appear identical to patients with catatonic schizophrenia. This fact is recognized in DSM-IV by the inclusion of the symptom qualifier ''with catatonic features'' for some mood disorders.

Mood, Affect, and Feelings. Depression is the key symptom, although about 50 percent of patients deny depressive feelings and do not appear to be particularly depressed. Family members or employers often bring or send these patients for treatment because of social withdrawal and generally decreased activity.

Speech. Many depressed patients evidence a decreased rate and volume of speech; they respond to questions with single words and exhibit delayed responses to questions. The examiner may literally have to wait 2 or 3 minutes for a response to a question.

Perceptual Disturbances. Depressed patients with delusions or hallucinations are said to have a major depressive episode with psychotic features. Even in the absence of delusions or hallucinations, some clinicians use the term *psychotic depression* for grossly regressed depressed patients—mute, not bathing, soiling. Such patients are probably better described as having catatonic features.

Delusions and hallucinations that are consistent with a depressed mood are said to be mood congruent. Mood-congruent delusions in a depressed person include those of guilt, sinfulness, worthlessness, poverty, failure, persecution, and terminal somatic illnesses (such as cancer and ''rotting'' brain). The content of mood-incongruent delusions or hallucinations is not consistent with a depressed mood. Mood-incongruent delusions in a depressed person involve grandiose themes of exaggerated power, knowledge, and worth—for example, the belief that a person is being persecuted because he or she is the Messiah. Although relatively rare, hallucinations can also occur in major depressive episodes with psychotic features.

Thought. Depressed patients customarily have a negative view of the world and of themselves. Their thought con-

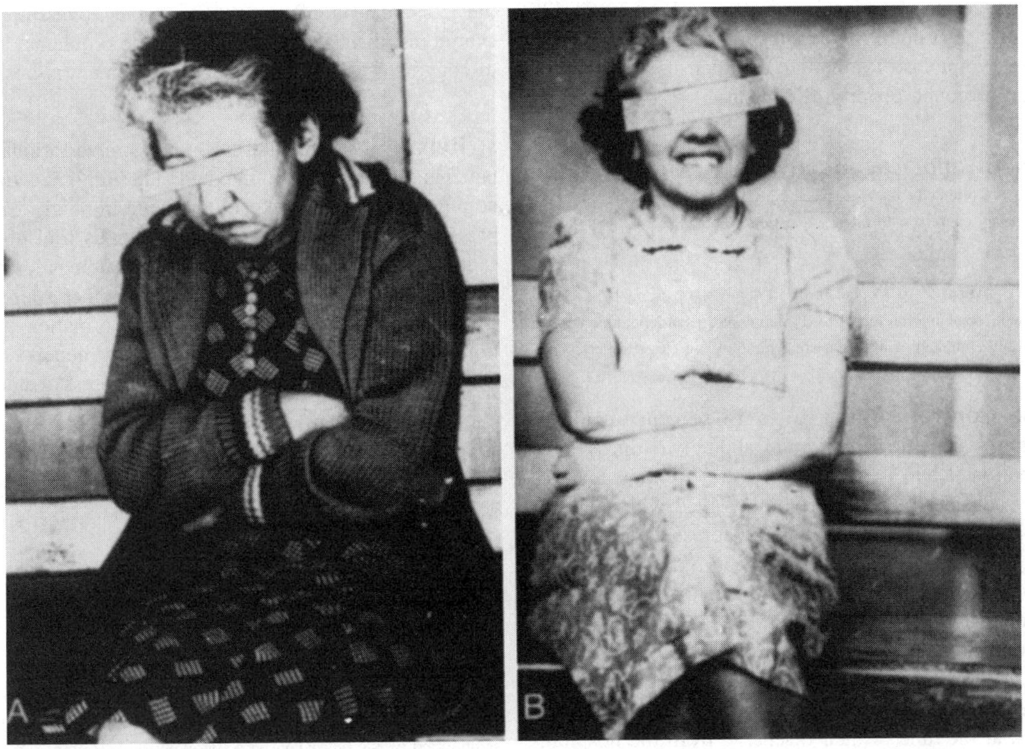
A
B

FIGURE 15.2–1
A 38-year-old woman during a state of deep retarded depression (**A**) and 2 months later, after recovery (**B**). The turned-down corners of her mouth, her stooped posture, her drab clothing, and her hairdo during the depressed episode are noteworthy. (Courtesy of Heinz E. Lehmann, M.D.)

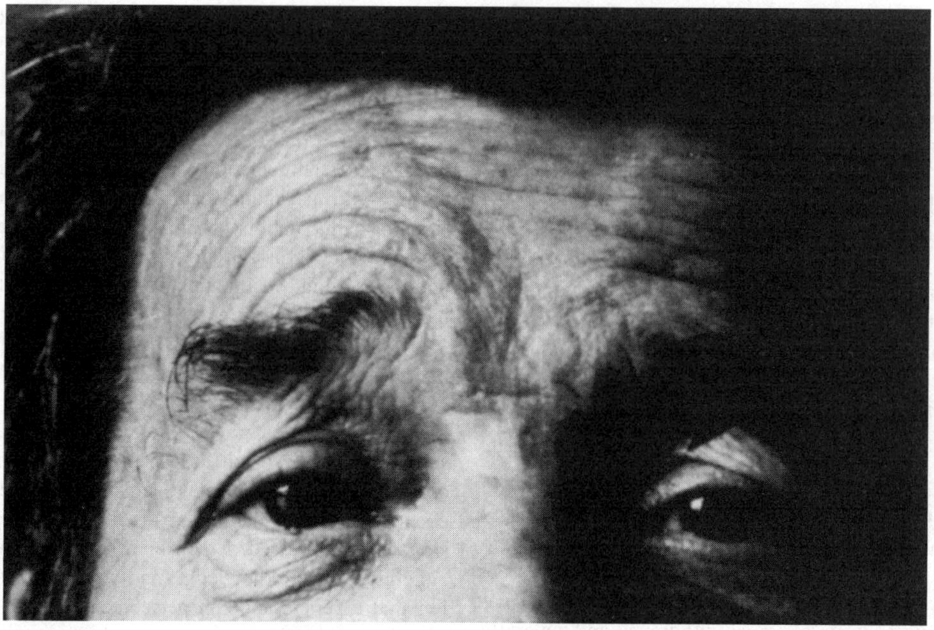

FIGURE 15.2–2
The Swiss neuropsychiatrist Otto Veraguth described a peculiar triangle-shaped fold in the nasal corner of the upper eyelid. The fold is often associated with depression and referred to as Veraguth's fold. The photograph illustrates this physiognomic feature in a 50-year-old man during a major depressive episode. Veraguth's fold may also be seen in persons who are not clinically depressed, usually while they are harboring a mild depressive affect. Distinct changes in the tone of the corrugator and zygomatic facial muscles accompany depression, as shown on electromyograms. (Courtesy of Heinz E. Lehmann, M.D.)

tent often includes nondelusional ruminations about loss, guilt, suicide, and death. About 10 percent of all depressed patients have marked symptoms of a thought disorder, usually thought blocking and profound poverty of content.

Sensorium and Cognition. ORIENTATION. Most depressed patients are oriented to person, place, and time, although some may not have enough energy or interest to answer questions about these subjects during an interview.

MEMORY. About 50 to 75 percent of all depressed patients have a cognitive impairment, sometimes referred to as depressive pseudodementia. Such patients commonly complain of impaired concentration and forgetfulness.

Impulse Control. About 10 to 15 percent of all depressed patients commit suicide, and about two thirds have suicidal ideation. Depressed patients with psychotic features occasionally consider killing a person involved with their delusional systems, but the most severely depressed patients often lack the motivation or the energy to act in an impulsive or violent way. Patients with depressive disorders are at increased risk of suicide as they begin to improve and to regain the energy needed to plan and carry out a suicide (paradoxical suicide). It is usually clinically unwise to give a depressed patient a large prescription for antidepressants, especially tricyclic drugs, at the time of their discharge from the hospital.

Judgment and Insight. Patients' judgment is best assessed by reviewing their actions in the recent past and their behavior during the interview. Depressed patients' insight into their disorder is often excessive; they overemphasize their symptoms, their disorder, and their life problems. It is difficult to convince such patients that improvement is possible.

Reliability. In interviews and conversations, depressed patients overemphasize the bad and minimize the good. A common clinical mistake is to unquestioningly believe a depressed patient who states that a previous trial of antidepressant medications did not work. Such statements may be false, and they require confirmation from another source. Psychiatrists should not view patients' misinformation as an intentional fabrication; the admission of any hopeful information may be impossible for a person in a depressed state of mind.

Objective Rating Scales for Depression. Objective rating scales for depression can be useful in clinical practice for documenting the depressed patient's clinical state.

ZUNG. The Zung Self-Rating Depression Scale is a 20-item report scale. A normal score is 34 or less; a depressed score is 50 or more. The scale provides a global index of the intensity of a patient's depressive symptoms, including the affective expression of depression.

RASKIN. The Raskin Depression Scale is a clinician-rated scale that measures the severity of a patient's depression, as reported by the patient and as observed by the physician, on a five-point scale of three dimensions: verbal report, displayed behavior, and secondary symptoms. The scale has a range of 3 to 13; a normal score is 3, and a depressed score is 7 or more.

HAMILTON. The Hamilton Rating Scale for Depression (HAM-D) is a widely used depression scale with up to 24 items, each of which is rated 0 to 4 or 0 to 2, with a total score of 0 to 76. The clinician evaluates the patient's answers to questions about feelings of guilt, thoughts of suicide, sleep habits, and other symptoms of depression, and the ratings are derived from the clinical interview.

Manic Episodes

General Description. Manic patients are excited, talkative, sometimes amusing, and frequently hyperactive. At times, they are grossly psychotic and disorganized and require physical restraints and the intramuscular injection of sedating drugs.

Mood, Affect, and Feelings. Manic patients classically are euphoric, but they can also be irritable, especially when mania has been present for some time. They also have a low frustration tolerance, which may lead to feelings of anger and hostility. Manic patients may be emotionally labile, switching from laughter to irritability to depression in minutes or hours.

Speech. Manic patients cannot be interrupted while they are speaking, and they are often intrusive nuisances to those around them. Their speech is often disturbed. As the mania gets more intense, speech becomes louder, more rapid, and difficult to interpret, then filled with puns, jokes, rhymes, plays on words, and irrelevancies as the activated state increases. At a still greater activity level, associations become loosened, the ability to concentrate fades, and flight of ideas, word salad, and neologisms appear. In acute manic excitement, speech may be totally incoherent and indistinguishable from that of a person with schizophrenia.

Perceptual Disturbances. Delusions occur in 75 percent of all manic patients. Mood-congruent manic delusions are often concerned with great wealth, extraordinary abilities, or power. Bizarre and mood-incongruent delusions and hallucinations also appear in mania.

Thought. Manic patients' thought content includes themes of self-confidence and self-aggrandizement. Manic patients are often easily distracted, and cognitive functioning in the manic state is characterized by an unrestrained and accelerated flow of ideas.

Sensorium and Cognition. Although the cognitive deficits of patients with schizophrenia have been much discussed, less has been written about similar deficits in patients with bipolar I disorder, who may have similar minor cognitive deficits. The reported cognitive deficits can be interpreted as reflecting diffuse cortical dysfunction; subsequent work may localize the abnormal areas. Grossly, orientation and memory are intact, although some manic patients may be so euphoric that they answer incorrectly. Emil Kraepelin called the symptom "delirious mania."

Impulse Control. About 75 percent of all manic patients are assaultive or threatening. Manic patients do attempt suicide and homicide, but the incidence of these behaviors is unknown. Patients who threaten important people (such as the President of the United States) more often have bipolar I disorder than schizophrenia.

Judgment and Insight. Impaired judgment is a hallmark of manic patients. They may break laws about credit cards, sexual activities, and finances and sometimes involve their families in financial ruin. Manic patients also have little insight into their disorder.

Reliability. Manic patients are notoriously unreliable in their information. Because lying and deceit are common in mania, inexperienced clinicians may treat manic patients with inappropriate disdain.

DIFFERENTIAL DIAGNOSIS

Major Depressive Disorder

Medical Disorders. The DSM-IV diagnosis of mood disorder due to a general medical condition describes a mood disorder caused by a nonpsychiatric medical condition. The DSM-IV diagnosis of substance-induced mood disorder describes a mood disorder caused by a substance. Both these diagnostic categories are discussed in Section 15.1.

Failure to obtain a good clinical history or to consider the context of a patient's current life situation may lead to diagnostic errors. Clinicians should have depressed adolescents tested for mononucleosis, and patients who are markedly overweight or underweight should be tested for adrenal and thyroid dysfunctions. Homosexuals, bisexual men, and people who abuse an intravenous substance should be tested for acquired immune deficiency syndrome (AIDS). Older patients should be evaluated for viral pneumonia and other medical conditions.

Many neurological and medical disorders and pharmacological agents can produce symptoms of depression (see Table 15.1–7). Patients with depressive disorders often first visit their general practitioners with somatic complaints. Most medical causes of depressive disorders can be detected with a comprehensive medical history, a complete physical and neurological examination, and routine blood and urine tests. The workup should include tests for thyroid and adrenal functions, because disorders of both these endocrine systems can appear as depressive disorders. In substance-induced mood disorder, a reasonable rule of thumb is that any drug a depressed patient is taking should be considered a potential factor in the mood disorder. Cardiac drugs, antihypertensives, sedatives, hypnotics, antipsychotics, antiepileptics, antiparkinsonian drugs, analgesics, antibacterials, and antineoplastics are all commonly associated with depressive symptoms.

NEUROLOGICAL CONDITIONS. The most common neurological problems that manifest depressive symptoms are Parkinson's disease, dementing illnesses (including dementia of the Alzheimer's type), epilepsy, cerebrovascular diseases, and tumors. About 50 to 75 percent of all patients with Parkinson's disease have marked symptoms of depressive disorder that do not correlate with the patient's degree of physical disability, age, or duration of illness but do correlate with the presence of abnormalities found on neuropsychological tests. The symptoms of depressive disorder may be masked by the almost identical motor symptoms of Parkinson's disease. Depressive symptoms often respond to antidepressant drugs or electroconvulsive therapy (ECT).

The interictal changes associated with temporal lobe epilepsy can mimic a depressive disorder, especially if the epileptic focus is on the right side. Depression is a common complicating feature of cerebrovascular diseases, particularly in the 2 years after the episode. Depression is more common in anterior brain lesions than in posterior brain lesions and in both cases often respond to antidepressant medications. Tumors of the diencephalic and temporal regions are particularly likely to be associated with depressive disorder symptoms.

PSEUDODEMENTIA. Clinicians can usually differentiate the pseudodementia of major depressive disorder from the dementia of a disease, such as dementia of the Alzheimer's type, on clinical grounds. The cognitive symptoms in major depressive disorder have a sudden onset, and other symptoms of the disorder, such as self-reproach, are also present. A diurnal variation in the cognitive problems, which is not seen in primary dementias, may occur. Depressed patients with cognitive difficulties often do not try to answer questions ("I don't know"), whereas patients with dementia may confabulate. In depressed patients, recent memory is more affected than is remote memory. And, during an interview, depressed patients can sometimes be coached and encouraged into remembering, an ability that demented patients lack.

Mental Disorders.

Depression can be a feature of virtually any mental disorder listed in DSM-IV, but the mental disorders listed in Table 15.2–26 should be particularly considered in the differential diagnosis.

OTHER MOOD DISORDERS. Clinicians must consider the range of DSM-IV diagnosis categories available before arriving at a final diagnosis. First, they must rule out mood disorder caused by a general medical condition and substance-induced mood disorder. Next, clinicians must determine whether a patient has had episodes of mania-like symptoms, indicating bipolar I disorder (complete manic and depressive syndromes), bipolar II disorder (recurrent major depressive episodes with hypomania), or cyclothymic disorder (incomplete depressive and manic syndromes). If a patient's symptoms are limited to those of depression, clinicians must assess the severity and duration of the symptoms to differentiate among major depressive disorder (complete depressive syndrome for 2 weeks), minor depressive disorder (incomplete but episodic depressive syndrome), recurrent brief depressive disorder (complete depressive syndrome but for less than 2 weeks per episode), and dysthymic disorder (incomplete depressive syndrome without clear episodes).

OTHER MENTAL DISORDERS. Substance-related disorders (see Table 14.1–9), psychotic disorders, eating disorders, adjustment disorders, somatoform disorders, and anxiety disorders are all commonly associated with depressive symptoms and must be considered in the differential diagnosis of a patient with depressive symptoms. Perhaps the most difficult differential is that between anxiety disorders with depression and depressive disorders with marked anxiety. The difficulty of making this differentiation is reflected in the inclusion of the diagnosis of mixed anxiety-depressive disorder in DSM-IV. An abnormal result on the dexamethasone-suppression test, the presence of shortened REM latency on a sleep EEG, and a negative lactate infusion test result support a diagnosis of major depressive disorder in particularly troublesome cases.

UNCOMPLICATED BEREAVEMENT. Uncomplicated bereavement is not considered a mental disorder, even though about one third of all bereaved spouses for a time meet the diagnostic criteria for major depressive disorder. Some patients with uncomplicated bereavement do develop major depressive disorder, but the diagnosis is not made unless a resolution of the grief does not occur; the differentiation is based on the symptoms' severity and length. In major depressive disorder, common symptoms that evolve from unresolved bereavement are a morbid preoccupation with worthlessness, suicidal ideation, feelings that the person has committed an act (not just an omission) that caused the spouse's death, mummification (keeping the deceased's belongings exactly as they were), and a particularly severe anniversary reaction, which sometimes includes a suicide attempt.

Bipolar I Disorder

When a patient with bipolar I disorder has a depressive episode, the differential diagnosis is the same as that for a patient being considered for a diagnosis of major depressive disorder. When a patient is manic, however, the differential diagnosis includes bipolar I disorder, bipolar II disorder, cyclothymic disorder, mood disorder caused by a general medical condition, and substance-induced mood disorder. For manic symptoms, borderline, narcissistic, histrionic, and antisocial personality disorders need special consideration.

Schizophrenia.

A great deal has been published about the clinical difficulty of distinguishing a manic episode from schizophrenia. Although difficult, a differential diagnosis is possible with a few clinical guidelines. Merriment, elation, and an infectiousness of mood are much more common in manic episodes than in schizophrenia. The combination of a manic mood, rapid or pressured speech, and hyperactivity weights heavily toward a diagnosis of a manic episode. The onset in a manic episode is often rapid and is perceived as a marked change from a patient's previous behavior. Half of all patients with bipolar I disorder have a family history of mood disorder. Catatonic features may be a depressive phase of bipolar I disorder. When evaluating patients with catatonia, clinicians should carefully look for a past history of manic or depressive episodes and for a family history of mood disorders. Manic symptoms in people from minority groups (particularly blacks and Hispanics) are often misdiagnosed as schizophrenic symptoms.

Medical Conditions.

In contrast to depressive symptoms, which are present in almost all psychiatric disorders, manic symptoms are more distinctive, although they can be caused by a wide range of medical and neurological conditions and substances (see Table 15.1–8). Antidepressant treatment can also be associated with the precipitation of mania in some patients.

Bipolar II Disorder

The differential diagnosis of patients being evaluated for a mood disorder should include the other mood disorders, psychotic disorders, and borderline disorder. The differentiation between major depressive disorder and bipolar I disorder on one hand and bipolar II disorder on the other hand rests on the clinical evaluation of the mania-like episodes. Clinicians should not mistake euthymia in a chronically depressed patient as a hypomanic or manic episode. Patients with borderline personality disorder often have a severely disrupted life, similar to that of patients with bipolar II disorder, because of the multiple episodes of significant mood disorder symptoms.

COURSE AND PROGNOSIS

The many studies of the course and prognosis of mood disorder have generally concluded that mood disorders tend to have long courses and that patients tend to have relapses. Although mood disorders are often considered benign in contrast to schizophrenia, they exact a profound toll on affected pa-

Table 15.2–27
Studies of Association Between Life Events and First Versus Subsequent Episodes of Mood Disorders

				Percentage of Patients for Whom Major Life Event Preceded Episode			
Author	**Disorder**	**Number of Episodes**	**N**	**First Episode**	**Later Episode**	**p**	**Assessment**
Matussek et al.	Depression	1	242	44		—	Stressors (138 psychological; 58 somatic) had to clearly precede onset of episode
		2	135		34	—	
		3	82		24	—	
		4	119		19	—	
Angst	Depression	1	103	60		—	No inventory
		4			38	—	
Okuma and Shimoyama	Bipolar	1	134	45		—	Any event (3 months prior)
		2	134		26	—	
		3	134		13	—	
Glassner et al.	Bipolar	1	25	75		—	Event rated stressful by patient and on Holmes and Rahe Scale (1 year prior; usually 2–24 days); role loss critical in patients and comparison subjects
		1[a]			56		
Ambelas[b]	Mania	1	14	50		0.01	Paykel Life Events Scale (4 weeks prior); one third of cases followed bereavement
		2	67		28		
Gutierrez et al.	Depression	1	43	55.8		0.05	Social and somatic stressors; patients with late onset had more events than did those with early onset
		2	35		40.0		
		3	18		38.8		
		4	47		29.7		
Perris	Depression	1	37	62	50[c]	0.02	Semistructured interview; 56-item inventory (3 months prior)
		2	112	43	19[d]	0.001	
Dolan et al.	Depression	1	21	62		0.05	Bedford College-Life Events and Difficulties Schedule (6 months prior) (Brown, Harris, 1978)
		2	57		29		
Ezquiaga et al.	Depression	3	52	50		0.01	Semistructured interview (Brown, Harris); no effect of chronic stress
		3	45		16		
Ambelas	Mania	1	50	66		0.001	Paykel Life Events Scale (4 weeks prior)
		2	40		20		
Ghaziuddin et al.	Depression	1	33	91		0.05	Paykel Life Events Scale (6 months prior)
		2	40		50		
Cassano et al.	Depression	1	94	66.0		0.05	Paykel Life Events Scale
		2	173		49.4		

Reprinted with permission from Post RM. Transduction of psychosocial stress into the neurobiology of recurrent affective disorder. Am J Psychiatry *149*: 1000, 1992.
[a] For this group, the most recent hospitalization was preceded by a life event resulting in role loss.
[b] Of surgical comparison subjects, 6.6% had experienced recent major life events.
[c] Percentage for negative or undesirable events.
[d] Percentage for events involving psychological conflict.

tients. Another common conclusion from studies is that life stressors more frequently precede the first episode of mood disorders than subsequent episodes (Table 15.2–27). This finding has been interpreted to indicate that psychosocial stress may play a role in the initial cause of mood disorders and that, even though the initial episode may resolve, a long-lasting change in the biology of the brain puts a patient at great risk for subsequent episodes.

Major Depressive Disorder

Course. **ONSET.** About 50 percent of patients undergoing their first episode of major depressive disorder had significant depressive symptoms before the first identified episode. One implication of this observation is that early identification and treatment of early symptoms may prevent the development of a full depressive episode. Although symptoms may have been present, patients with major depressive disorder usually have not had a premorbid personality disorder. The first depressive episode occurs before age 40 in about 50 percent of patients. A later onset is associated with the absence of a family history of mood disorders, antisocial personality disorder, and alcohol abuse.

DURATION. An untreated depressive episode lasts 6 to 13 months; most treated episodes last about 3 months. The withdrawal of antidepressants before 3 months has elapsed almost always results in the return of the symptoms. As the course of the disorder progresses, patients tend to have more frequent episodes that last longer. Over a 20-year period, the mean number of episodes is five or six.

DEVELOPMENT OF MANIC EPISODES. About 5 to 10 percent of

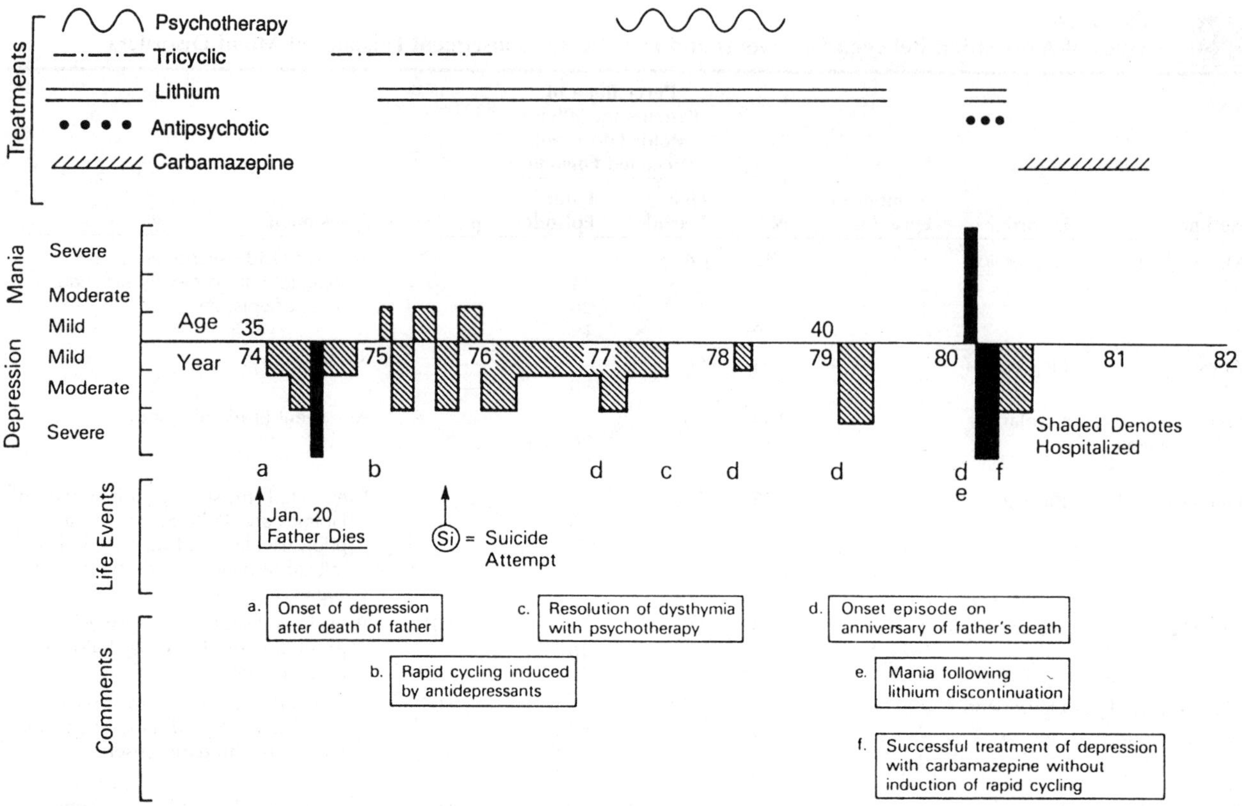
Treatments
Psychotherapy
Tricyclic
Lithium
Antipsychotic
Carbamazepine
Mania
Severe
Moderate
Mild
Depression
Mild
Moderate
Severe
Age 35
40
Year 74 75 76 77 78 79 80 81 82
Shaded Denotes Hospitalized
a b d c d d d f e
Life Events
Jan. 20 Father Dies
Si = Suicide Attempt
Comments
a. Onset of depression after death of father
b. Rapid cycling induced by antidepressants
c. Resolution of dysthymia with psychotherapy
d. Onset episode on anniversary of father's death
e. Mania following lithium discontinuation
f. Successful treatment of depression with carbamazepine without induction of rapid cycling

FIGURE 15.2–3
Graphing the course of a mood disorder. Prototype of a life chart. (Courtesy of Robert M. Post, M.D.)

patients with an initial diagnosis of major depressive disorder have a manic episode 6 to 10 years after the first depressive episode. The mean age for this switch is 32 years, and it often occurs after two to four depressive episodes. Although the data are inconsistent and controversial, some clinicians report that the depression of patients who are later classified as having bipolar I disorder is often characterized by hypersomnia, psychomotor retardation, psychotic symptoms, a history of postpartum episodes, a family history of bipolar I disorder, and a history of antidepressant-induced hypomania.

Prognosis. Major depressive disorder is not a benign disorder. It tends to be chronic, and patients tend to relapse. Patients who have been hospitalized for a first episode of major depressive disorder have about a 50 percent chance of recovering in the first year. The percentage of patients recovering after hospitalization decreases with passing time, and at 5 years posthospitalization, 10 to 15 percent of patients have not recovered. Many unrecovered patients remain affected with dysthymic disorder. Recurrences of major depressive episodes are also common. About 25 percent of patients experience a recurrence in the first 6 months after release from a hospital, about 30 to 50 percent in the first 2 years, and about 50 to 75 percent in 5 years. The incidence of relapse is lower than these figures in patients who continue prophylactic psychopharmacological treatment and in patients who have had only one or two depressive episodes. Generally, as a patient experiences more and more depressive episodes, the time between the episodes decreases, and the severity of each episode increases.

PROGNOSTIC INDICATORS. Many studies have focused on identifying both good and bad prognostic indicators in the course of major depressive disorder. Mild episodes, the absence of psychotic symptoms, and a short hospital stay are good prognostic indicators. Psychosocial indicators of a good course include a history of solid friendships during adolescence, stable family functioning, and a generally sound social functioning for the 5 years preceding the illness. Additional good prognostic signs are the absence of a comorbid psychiatric disorder and of a personality disorder, no more than one previous hospitalization for major depressive disorder, and an advanced age of onset. The possibility of a poor prognosis is increased by coexisting dysthymic disorder, abuse of alcohol and other substances, anxiety disorder symptoms, and a history of more than one previous depressive episode. Men are more likely than women to experience a chronically impaired course.

Bipolar I Disorder

Course. The natural history of bipolar I disorder is such that it is often useful to make a graph of a patient's disorder and to keep it up-to-date as treatment progresses (Fig. 15.2–3). Although cyclothymic disorder is sometimes diagnosed retrospectively in patients with bipolar I disorder, no identified personality traits are specifically associated with bipolar I disorder.

Bipolar I disorder most often starts with depression (75 percent of the time in women, 67 percent in men) and is a recurring disorder. Most patients experience both depressive and manic episodes, although 10 to 20 percent experience only manic episodes. The manic episodes typically have a rapid onset (hours or days) but may evolve over a few weeks. An untreated manic episode lasts about 3 months; therefore, clinicians should not discontinue drugs before that time. As the disorder progresses, the time between episodes often decreases. After about five episodes, however, the interepisode interval often stabilizes at 6 to 9 months. Some patients with bipolar I disorder have rapidly cycling episodes.

BIPOLAR I DISORDER IN CHILDREN AND OLDER PEOPLE. Bipolar I disorder can affect both the very young and older people. The incidence of bipolar I disorder in children and adolescents is about 1 percent, and the onset can be as early as age 8. Common misdiagnoses are schizophrenia and oppositional defiant disorder. Bipolar I disorder with such an early onset is associated with a poor prognosis. Manic symptoms are common in older people, although the range of causes is broad and includes nonpsychiatric medical conditions, dementia, delirium, and bipolar I disorder. Currently available data indicate that the onset of true bipolar I disorder in older people is relatively uncommon.

Prognosis. Patients with bipolar I disorder have a poorer prognosis than do patients with major depressive disorder. About 40 to 50 percent of bipolar I disorder patients may have a second manic episode within 2 years of the first episode. Although lithium (Eskalith) prophylaxis improves the course and prognosis of bipolar I disorder, probably only 50 to 60 percent of patients achieve significant control of their symptoms with lithium. One 4-year follow-up study of patients with bipolar I disorder found that a premorbid poor occupational status, alcohol dependence, psychotic features, depressive features, interepisode depressive features, and male gender were all factors that weighted toward a poor prognosis. Short duration of manic episodes, advanced age of onset, few suicidal thoughts, and few coexisting psychiatric or medical problems weight toward a good prognosis.

About 7 percent of all patients with bipolar I disorder do not have a recurrence of symptoms; 45 percent have more than one episode, and 40 percent have a chronic disorder. Patients may have from 2 to 30 manic episodes, although the mean number is about nine. About 40 percent of all patients have more than 10 episodes. On long-term follow-up, 15 percent of all patients with bipolar I disorder are well, 45 percent are well but have multiple relapses, 30 percent are in partial remission, and 10 percent are chronically ill. One third of all patients with bipolar I disorder have chronic symptoms and evidence of significant social decline.

Bipolar II Disorder

The course and prognosis of bipolar II disorder have just begun to be studied. Preliminary data indicate, however, that the diagnosis is stable, as shown by the high likelihood that patients with bipolar II disorder will have the same diagnosis up to 5 years later. The data thus show that bipolar II disorder is a chronic disease that warrants long-term treatment strategies.

TREATMENT

The treatment of patients with mood disorders must be directed toward several goals. First, the patient's safety must be guaranteed. Second, a complete diagnostic evaluation of the patient must be carried out. Third, a treatment plan that addresses not only the immediate symptoms but also the patient's prospective well-being must be initiated. Although current treatment emphasizes pharmacotherapy and psychotherapy addressed to the individual patient, stressful life events are also associated with increases in relapse rates among patients with mood disorders. Thus, treatment must reduce the number and severity of the stressors in patients' lives.

Overall, the treatment of mood disorders is rewarding for psychiatrists. Specific treatments are now available for both manic and depressive episodes, and available data indicate that prophylactic treatment is also effective. Because the prognosis for each episode is good, optimism is always warranted and is welcomed by both the patient and the patient's family, even if initial treatment results are not promising. Mood disorders are chronic, however, and the psychiatrist must advise the patient and the family about future treatment strategies.

Hospitalization

The first and most critical decision a physician must make is whether to hospitalize a patient or to attempt outpatient treatment. Clear indications for hospitalization are the need for diagnostic procedures, the risk of suicide or homicide, and a patient's grossly reduced ability to get food and shelter. A history of rapidly progressing symptoms and the rupture of a patient's usual support systems are also indications for hospitalization.

A physician may safely treat mild depression or hypomania in the office if he or she evaluates the patient frequently. Clinical signs of impaired judgment, weight loss, or insomnia should be minimal. The patient's support system should be strong, neither overinvolved nor withdrawing from the patient. Any adverse changes in the patient's symptoms or behavior or the attitude of the patient's support system may be sufficient to warrant hospitalization.

Patients with mood disorders are often unwilling to enter a hospital voluntarily, and may have to be involuntarily committed. These patients are often incapable of making decisions because of their slowed thinking, negative *Weltanschauung* (world view), and hopelessness. Manic patients often have such a complete lack of insight into their disorder that hospitalization seems absolutely absurd to them.

Psychosocial Therapy

Although most studies indicate—and most clinicians and researchers believe—that a combination of psychotherapy and pharmacotherapy is the most effective treatment for major depressive disorder, some data suggest another view: Either pharmacotherapy or psychotherapy alone is effective, at least in patients with mild major depressive episodes, and the regular use of combined therapy adds to the cost of treatment and exposes patients to unnecessary side effects.

Three types of short-term psychotherapies—cognitive therapy, interpersonal therapy, and behavior therapy—have been studied to determine their efficacy in the treatment of major depressive disorder. Although its efficacy in treating major depressive disorder is not as well researched as these three therapies, psychoanalytically oriented psychotherapy has long been used for depressive disorders, and many clinicians use the technique as their primary method. What differentiates the three short-term psychotherapy methods from the psychoanalytically oriented approach are the active and directive roles of the therapist, the directly recognizable goals, and the endpoints for short-term therapy.

Although less research has been conducted on psychodynamic theory of depression than on some other forms of psychotherapy, the accumulating evidence is encouraging regarding the efficacy of dynamic therapy. In a randomized controlled trial comparing psychodynamic therapy with cognitive behavior therapy, the outcomes of the depressed patients in the study showed no differences between the two treatments.

Table 15.2–28 summarizes the features of the psychodynamic, cognitive, and interpersonal approaches; Table 15.2–29 summarizes some nonselective and selective patient variables for psychotherapy; Table 15.2–30 summarizes the advantages and the limitations of the three approaches; and Tables 15.2–31 and 15.2–32 summarize features that may affect the choice of pharmacotherapy or psychotherapy or combined therapy. The NIMH Treatment of Depression Collaborative Research Program found the following predictors of response to various treatments: Low social dysfunction suggested a good response to interpersonal therapy; low cognitive dysfunction suggested a good response to cognitive-behavior therapy and pharmacotherapy; high work dysfunction suggested a good response to pharmacotherapy; and high depression severity suggested a good response to interpersonal therapy and pharmacotherapy.

Cognitive Therapy. Cognitive therapy, developed originally by Aaron Beck, focuses on the cognitive distortions postulated to be present in major depressive disorder. Such distortions include selective attention to the negative aspects of circumstances and unrealistically morbid inferences about consequences. For example, apathy and low energy are results of a patient's expectation of failure in all areas. The goal of cognitive therapy is to alleviate depressive episodes and to prevent their recurrence by helping patients identify and test

Table 15.2–28
Major Features of Three Psychotherapeutic Approaches to Depression

Feature	Psychodynamic Approach	Cognitive Approach	Interpersonal Approach
Major theorists	Freud, Abraham, Jacobson, Kohut	Plato, Adler, Beck, Rush	Meyer, Sullivan, Klerman, Weissman
Concepts of pathology and cause	Ego regression: damaged self-esteem and unresolved conflict due to childhood object loss and disappointment	Distorted thinking: dysphoria due to learned negative views of self, others, and the world	Impaired interpersonal relations: absent or unsatisfactory significant social bonds
Major goals and mechanisms of change	To promote personality change through understanding of past conflicts; to achieve insight into defenses, ego distortions, and superego defects; to provide a role model; to permit cathartic release of aggression	To provide symptomatic relief through alteration of target thoughts; to identify self-destructive cognitions; to modify specific erroneous assumptions; to promote self-control over thinking patterns	To provide symptomatic relief through solution of current interpersonal problems; to reduce stress involving family or work; to improve interpersonal communication skills
Primary techniques and practices	Expressive-empathic: fully or partially analyzing transference and resistance; confronting defenses; clarifying ego and superego distortions	Behavioral-cognitive: recording and monitoring cognitions; correcting distorted themes with logic and experimental testing; providing alternative thought content; homework	Communicative-environmental: clarifying and managing maladaptive relationships and learning new ones through communication and social skills training; providing information on illness
Therapist role-therapeutic relationship	Interpreter-reflector: establishment and exploration of transference; therapeutic alliance for benign dependence and empathic understanding	Educator-shaper: positive relationship instead of transference; collaborative empiricism as basis for joint scientific (logical) task	Explorer-prescriber: positive relationship-transference without interpretation; active therapist role for influence and advocacy
Marital-family role	Full individual confidentiality; exclusion of significant others except in life-threatening situations	Use of spouse as objective reporter; couples therapy for disturbed cognitions sustained in marital relationship	Integral role of spouse in treatment; examination of spouse's role in patient's predisposition to depression and effects of illness on marriage

Reprinted with permission from Karasu TB: Toward a clinical model of psychotherapy for depression. I. Systematic comparison of three psychotherapies. Am J Psychiatry *147*: 141, 1990.

Table 15.2–29
Nonselective and Selective Patient Variables for Psychotherapy for Depression

	Selective Patient Variables		
Nonselective Patient Variables	**Psychodynamic Therapy**	**Cognitive Therapy**	**Interpersonal Therapy**
Feelings of hopelessness and helplessness Apathy, decreased enjoyment, diminished desire or gratification Too high ego ideals and expectations Oversleeping, morbid dreams or nightmares Feelings of restlessness or being slowed down Lack of motivation or will Low self-esteem, inappropriate or excessive guilt and self-reproach Distractibility, sluggish thinking or decision making Wish or intention to be dead Social withdrawal, fear of rejection or failure Psychosomatic complaints, hypochondriasis	Long-term sense of emptiness and underestimation of self-worth Loss or long separation in childhood Conflicts in past relationships (eg, with parent, sexual partner) Capacity for insight Ability to modulate regression Access to dreams and fantasy Little need for direction and guidance Stable environment	Obvious distorted thoughts about self, world, and future Pragmatic (logical) thinking Real inadequacies (including poor response to other psychotherapies) Moderate to high need for direction and guidance Responsiveness to behavioral training and self-help (high degree of self-control)	Recent, focused dispute with spouse or significant other Social or communication problems Recent role transition or life change Abnormal grief reaction Modest to moderate need for direction and guidance Responsiveness to environmental manipulation (available support network)

Reprinted with permission from Karasu TB: Toward a clinical model of psychotherapy for depression. II. An integrative and selective treatment approach. Am J Psychiatry *147*: 275, 1990.

negative cognitions; develop alternative, flexible, and positive ways of thinking; and rehearse new cognitive and behavioral responses.

About a dozen studies have shown that cognitive therapy is effective in the treatment of major depressive disorder. Most of the studies found that cognitive therapy is equal in efficacy to pharmacotherapy, and associated with fewer side effects and with better follow-up than is pharmacotherapy. Most of the studies, however, can be criticized for using antidepressant dosages that were too low and for using the antidepressant medications for too short a period. Some of the best controlled studies have indicated that the combination of cognitive therapy and pharmacotherapy is more efficacious than either therapy alone, although other studies have not found that additive effect. At least one study, the NIMH Treatment of Depression Collaborative Research Program, found that pharmacotherapy, either alone or with psychotherapy, may be the treatment of choice for patients with severe major depressive episodes.

Interpersonal Therapy. Interpersonal therapy, developed by Gerald Klerman, focuses on one or two of a patient's current interpersonal problems. This therapy is based on two assumptions. First, current interpersonal problems are likely to have their roots in early dysfunctional relationships. Second, current interpersonal problems are likely to be involved in precipitating or perpetuating the current depressive symptoms. Several controlled trials have compared interpersonal therapy, cognitive therapy, pharmacotherapy, and the combination of pharmacotherapy with psychotherapy. These trials indicated that interpersonal therapy is effective in the treatment of major depressive disorder and may, not surprisingly, be specifically helpful in addressing interpersonal problems. The data about the efficacy of interpersonal therapy in the treatment of severe major depressive episodes are less reliable, although some information indicates that interpersonal therapy may be the most effective method for severe major depressive episodes when the treatment choice is psychotherapy alone.

The interpersonal therapy program usually consists of 12 to 16 weekly sessions and is characterized by an active therapeutic approach. Intrapsychic phenomena, such as defense mechanisms and internal conflicts, are not addressed. Discrete behaviors—such as lack of assertiveness, impaired social skills, and distorted thinking—may be addressed but only in the context of their meaning in or their effect on interpersonal relationships.

Behavior Therapy. Behavior therapy is based on the hypothesis that maladaptive behavioral patterns result in a person's receiving little positive feedback, and perhaps outright rejection, from society. By addressing maladaptive behaviors in therapy, patients learn to function in the world in such a way that they receive positive reinforcement. Although individual and group therapies have been studied, behavior therapy for major depressive disorder has not yet been the subject of many controlled studies. The data to date indicate that behavior therapy is an effective treatment for major depressive disorder.

Psychoanalytically Oriented Therapy. The psychoanalytic approach to mood disorders is based on psychoanalytic theories about depression and mania. The goal of psychoanalytic psychotherapy is to effect a change in a patient's

Table 15.2–30
Advantages and Limitations of Three Psychotherapeutic Approaches to Depression

Feature	Psychodynamic Approach	Cognitive Approach	Interpersonal Approach
Theory			
Advantages	Individual depth approach encourages patient to look inward for solutions, rather than depending on external sources	Cognitive-behavioral orientation is tangible and objective	Interpersonal orientation addresses broader (eg, social, family) context, useful in focusing on man-woman relations
Limitations	Focus on intrapsychic phenomena may obscure other (eg, interpersonal, environmental) factors; aggression-depression theory can be overgeneralized and lead to overreliance on catharsis	Cognitive-behavioral emphasis may neglect whole person, especially affective component; symptom-oriented perspective overlooks past history, complex problem areas, and hidden conflicts	Emphasis on four designated interpersonal problems can bias toward preconceived themes; interpersonal orientation may stress marital/family factors while underplaying intrapsychic forces
Goals			
Advantages	Enduring structural change transcends symptomatic relief; strengthened adaptive capacities can be useful beyond specific depressive pathology	Primary goal of symptom relief is expedient in itself and is first stage in changing cognitive style	Improvement of interpersonal relations is expedient in itself and may also result in relief of symptoms
Limitations	Personality alteration can be too ambitious and may be unnecessary or excessive for most depression diagnoses	Symptom reduction may be insufficient, superficial, or temporary; focus on current problems can preclude enduring modification of personality or prophylactic function of treatment	Symptom relief may be fragile and temporary if it is highly dependent on external factors
Structure			
Advantages	Indefinite duration allows long-term or flexible goals[a]	Brief or fixed duration is cost-effective and can foster results in short period, may heighten expectation of rapid change and encourage optimism	Predetermined duration is cost-effective; approach reengages family and may have preventive effect
Limitations	Long-term or open-ended treatment is uneconomical and difficult to evaluate[a]	Short or predetermined duration may be insufficient or inflexible	Time limitation predetermines the extent of personal growth and independence
Therapist role			
Advantages	Neutral, accepting stance ensures nonjudgmental attitude and objectivity; receptive listening encourages transference formation and ensuing analytic process	Active therapist can directly intervene to interrupt depressive schemata and suggest alternatives to faulty thinking	Therapist position between activity and reactivity can reassure patient and provide supportive person for patient to relate to
Limitations	Transference regression can produce overidealization of therapist and underestimation of patient self-worth; therapist silence may be misconstrued as rejection, which can perpetuate depression and cause premature termination	Active suggestion and direction can undermine patient responsibility and self-esteem by imposing therapist point of view or values	Supportive interpersonal role may encourage dependence and rage at withdrawal of therapist
Techniques			
Advantages	Free association provides verbal catharsis; interpretations provide new understanding of depressogenic conflicts and historical events	Specific approach is directly tailored to depressed population and aims at particular target symptoms; identification of depressogenic assumptions and homework to test new thinking foster cognitive modification	Specific approach is directly tailored to depressed population and can address particular current interpersonal maladaptions
Limitations	No specific techniques developed; focus on past events and spontaneous associations may encourage repetitive litany of depressive complaints at the expense of present therapeutic tasks	Emphasis on specific cognitive schemata may bias toward certain preconceived themes; overt simplicity of techniques may lead to underestimation of technical skill required	Identification of specific interpersonal problem areas may be overly restrictive, yet techniques are relatively nonspecific; legitimation of patient sick role may encourage passivity

(continued)

Table 15.2–30 *(continued)*

Feature	Psychodynamic Approach	Cognitive Approach	Interpersonal Approach
Research status			
Advantages	Longitudinal case study approach useful for detailed examination and follow-up of individual patients	Operational manual allows for replication of treatment and training and empirical establishment of efficacy	Same as for cognitive approach
Limitations	Idiographic approach or anecdotal case history is not amenable to controlled or comparative research	Research-oriented operationalized approach may become oversimplified formula for complex clinical phenomena	Same as for cognitive approach
Relation to other modalities			
Advantages	Integrity of transference is maintained through elimination of outside influences	Competition with pharmacotherapy encourages research on relative efficacy, especially instances when cognitive therapy alone is most effective	Approach designed to be used alone or with drugs; it is especially amenable to combination with marital therapy
Limitations	Need for neutrality may limit use of other helpful treatment approaches (eg, family therapy, drug treatment)	Competition with pharmacotherapy fosters polarization of approaches and partisan resistance to integration with drug treatment	Amenability to additive or eclectic modalities requires integrative theoretical model, clinical expertise in more than one modality, and ability to collaborate with other disciplines, which may lead to role diffusion and insufficient knowledge or training
Patient population			
Advantages	Special patient requisites (eg, verbal orientation, psychological-mindedness) ensure maximal insight	Logical thinking ensures maximal potential to deal with and change depressogenic assumptions and thought patterns	Orientation toward interpersonal relations, especially marital interaction, can address gender issues in marriage, especially important given high prevalence of women among depressed patients
Limitations	Special patient requisites may limit usefulness to verbal, psychological-minded population	Cognitively impaired population may not benefit; sophisticated, introspective patients may find approach too simple-minded or superficial	Interpersonal orientation may overemphasize marriage; primarily female population may bias toward women; conjoint focus may bias against unmarried population

Reprinted with permission from Karasu TB: Toward a clinical model of psychotherapy for depression. I. Systematic comparison of three psychotherapies. Am J Psychiatry *147*: 142–143, 1990.

[a] Advantages and limitations of short-term psychodynamic therapy are similar to those for the cognitive and interpersonal approaches.

personality structure or character, not simply to alleviate symptoms. Improvements in interpersonal trust, intimacy, coping mechanisms, the capacity to grieve, and the ability to experience a wide range of emotions are some of the aims of psychoanalytic therapy. Treatment often requires the patient to experience heightened anxiety and distress during the course of therapy, which may continue for several years.

Family Therapy. Family therapy is not generally viewed as a primary therapy for the treatment of major depressive disorder, but increasing evidence indicates that helping a patient with a mood disorder to reduce and cope with stress can lessen the chance of a relapse. Family therapy is indicated if the disorder jeopardizes a patient's marriage or family functioning or if the mood disorder is promoted or maintained by the family situation. Family therapy examines the role of the mood-disordered member in the overall psychological well-being of the whole family; it also examines the role of the entire family in the maintenance of the patient's symptoms. Patients with mood disorders have a high rate of divorce, and about 50 percent of all spouses report that they would not have married or had children if they had known that the patient was going to develop a mood disorder.

Pharmacotherapy

Although the specific, short-term psychotherapies such as interpersonal therapy and cognitive therapy have influenced the treatment approaches to major depressive disorder, the pharmacotherapeutic approach to mood disorders has revolutionized their treatment and has dramatically affected the courses of mood disorders and reduced their inherent costs to society. Physicians must integrate pharmacotherapy with psychotherapeutic interventions. If physicians view mood disorders as fundamentally evolving from psychodynamic issues,

Table 15.2–31
Indications for Psychotherapy and Pharmacotherapy in the Treatment of Depression

	Indication for Treatment[a]	
Variable	Pharmacotherapy	Psychotherapy
Symptom criteria for major depressive episode		
Depressed mood	Marked vegetative signs; extreme or uncontrolled mood	Mild to moderate situational or characterological depressed mood
Diminished interest or pleasure	Anhedonia; loss of libido; impaired sexual function or performance	Apathy, decreased enjoyment; diminished sexual desire or gratification
Weight loss or gain	Significant weight loss	Insignificant weight gain
Insomnia or hypersomnia	Early morning wakening	Oversleeping, morbid dreams or nightmares
Psychomotor agitation	Hyperactivity or motor retardation	Restlessness or feelings of being slowed down
Fatigue or loss of energy (anergia)	Depressive stupor	Lack of motivation or will
Feelings of worthlessness or excessive guilt	Nihilistic or self-deprecatory delusions, self-berating auditory hallucinations	Low self-esteem, inappropriate guilt feelings, self-reproach
Diminished ability to think or concentrate, indecisiveness	Loss of control over thinking, obsessive rumination, inability to focus or act	Distractibility, sluggish thinking or decision making; negative cognitions
Recurrent thoughts of death or suicide	Acute, episodic, and uncontrolled suicidal acts or plans[b]	Chronic feelings of hopelessness or helplessness[c]
Associated features	Panic (anxiety) attacks or phobias; persecutory delusions; pseudodementia; physical symptoms or somatic delusions	Social withdrawal or fears of rejection or failure; psychosomatic complaints or hypochondriasis
Family history	Genetic loading (bipolar disorder or depressive disorder)	No genetic loading (dysthymic disorder)
Predisposing factors	Other mental disorders, eg, schizophrenia, alcohol dependence, anorexia nervosa	Psychosocial stressors, eg, loss of significant other, change in status or role
Personality disorders	Borderline, histrionic, obsessive-compulsive	Dependent, inadequate, masochistic

Reprinted with permission from Karasu TB: Toward a clinical model of psychotherapy for depression. II. An integrative and selective treatment approach. Am J Psychiatry *147*: 274, 1990.
[a] These are not mutually exclusive categories.
[b] Hospitalization may be required.
[c] Medication may also be useful.

Table 15.2–32
Approach to Pharmacotherapy of Three Psychotherapies for Depression

Feature of Combined Treatment	Psychodynamic Therapy	Cognitive Therapy	Interpersonal Therapy
Basic stance	Medication is avoided except in life-threatening situation, used judiciously for severe vegetative signs	Pharmacotherapy and cognitive therapy alone are in ongoing competition, but drugs are used in case of poor response to cognitive therapy and for breaking psychotherapeutic impasses in severe depression when symptomatic relief is required	Interpersonal therapy and pharmacotherapy are considered having different effects and response timetables (early drug effects on vegetative symptoms, later psychotherapy effects on suicidal ideation, work, and interests)
Techniques	Personal (unconscious and conscious) meanings are explored and interpreted within therapy session	Information and rationale for use is provided; special tasks are assigned to increase adherence, eg, postsession homework (lists of side effects); phone contact with therapist is encouraged	Information and rationale for use is provided, in line with medical model; time is set aside in each session to discuss pharmacological issues

Reprinted with permission from Karasu TB: Toward a clinical model of psychotherapy for depression. II. An integrative and selective treatment approach. Am J Psychiatry *147*: 272, 1990.

their ambivalence about the use of drugs may result in a poor response, noncompliance, and probably inadequate dosages for too short a treatment period. Alternatively, if physicians ignore the psychosocial needs of a patient, the outcome of pharmacotherapy may be compromised.

Major Depressive Disorder. Effective and specific treatments, such as tricyclic drugs, for major depressive disorder have been available for 40 years. The use of specific pharmacotherapy approximately doubles the chance that a depressed patient will recover in 1 month. Nevertheless, problems remain in the treatment of major depressive disorder: Some patients do not respond to the first treatment; all currently available antidepressants may take up to 3 to 4 weeks to exert significant therapeutic effects, although they may begin to show their effects earlier; and, until relatively recently, all available antidepressants have been toxic in overdoses and have had adverse effects. Now, however, the introduction of the serotonin-specific reuptake inhibitors (SSRIs), such as fluoxetine, paroxetine (Paxil), and sertraline (Zoloft), bupropion, venlafaxine (Effexor), nefazodone, and mirtazapine (Remeron), offers clinicians drugs that are equally effective but safer and better tolerated than previous drugs. Recent indications (for example, eating disorders and anxiety disorders) for antidepressant medications make the grouping of these drugs under the single label of antidepressants somewhat confusing.

The principal indication for antidepressants is a major depressive episode. The first symptoms to improve are often poor sleep and appetite patterns, although that may be less true when SSRIs are used than when tricyclic drugs are used. Agitation, anxiety, depressive episodes, and hopelessness are the next symptoms to improve. Other target symptoms include low energy, poor concentration, helplessness, and decreased libido.

PATIENT EDUCATION. Adequate patient education about the use of antidepressants is as critical to treatment success as is choosing the most appropriate drug and dosage. When introducing the topic of a drug trial to a patient, physicians should emphasize that major depressive disorder is a combination of biological and psychological factors, all of which benefit from drug therapy. Physicians should also stress that the patient will not become addicted to antidepressants, because these drugs do not give immediate gratification. Further, it will probably take 3 to 4 weeks for the effects of the antidepressant to be felt, and even if the patient shows no improvement by that time, other medications are available. Some clinicians say that the appearance of side effects shows that the drug is working, but the expected side effects should be explained in detail. For example, some patients taking SSRIs may experience agitation, gastrointestinal upset, or nausea before any reduction in depression. The adverse effects pass with time. With tricyclic drugs and MAOIs, physicians may find it useful to tell the patient that sleep and appetite will improve first, followed by a sense of returned energy, and that the feeling of depression, unfortunately, will be the last symptom to change.

Physicians must always consider the risk of suicide in patients with mood disorder. Most antidepressants are lethal if taken in large amounts. It is unwise to give large prescriptions to most patients with mood disorder when they are discharged from the hospital unless another person monitors the drug's administration.

ALTERNATIVES TO DRUG TREATMENT. Two organic therapies that are alternatives to pharmacotherapy are electroconvulsive therapy (ECT) and phototherapy. ECT is generally used when a patient is unresponsive to pharmacotherapy or cannot tolerate pharmacotherapy, or the clinical situation is so severe that the rapid improvement seen with ECT is needed. Although the use of ECT is often limited to these three situations, it is an effective antidepressant treatment and can be reasonably considered as the treatment of choice in some patients, such as older depressed people. Phototherapy is a novel treatment that has been used with patients with a seasonal pattern to their mood disorder. It can be used alone in mild cases of mood disorder with a seasonal pattern. For severely affected patients, it can be used in combination with pharmacotherapy, although studies of the efficacy of this combination have not yet produced definitive results.

AVAILABLE DRUGS. The SSRIs are the most widely used antidepressant drugs in the United States. They are the agents of choice because of their effectiveness, ease of use, and relative lack of adverse effects, even at high dosages. Because they are well tolerated, they have been prescribed by clinicians in a wide range of specialties. Of the other newer agents, bupropion, venlafaxine, and nefazodone have gained widespread use among psychiatrists. Each of these agents is safer than the tricyclic and tetracyclic drugs and MAOIs, and each has been shown to be as effective for depression in clinical trials. The tricyclic and tetracyclic drugs, trazodone (Desyrel), alprazolam (Xanax), and mirtazapine, may cause sedation. The MAOIs require dietary restrictions. These drugs are less widely used because of their adverse effects. Sympathomimetic drugs, such as dextroamphetamine (Dexedrine) and methylphenidate (Ritalin), may produce a rapid improvement of mood (within 1 week) and are indicated in closely monitored situations.

PHARMACOLOGICAL ACTIONS. In patients who tolerate full therapeutic dosages of the various available antidepressants, no one agent has shown an obvious superiority. There are marked differences, however, in adverse effect profiles, and individual patients may respond to one antidepressant and not to another. Most antidepressants interact with either serotonergic or noradrenergic neurotransmission or with both. Moreover, potentiation of either of these neurotransmitter systems has been shown to stimulate the other system, such that the details of the pharmacodynamics of each drug are difficult to translate into a prediction of efficacy. There is a fairly good correlation between in vitro evidence of interaction with a particular neurotransmitter and clinical evidence of particular adverse effects, which is outlined in Table 15.2–33.

CHOICE OF DRUG. Because of the many antidepressant drugs now available commercially, physicians face many clinical considerations in choosing a first-line drug. In the treatment of all mental disorders, the best reason for choosing a particular drug is a history of a good response to that agent by the patient or a family member. If such information is not available, the choice of a drug is based principally on the adverse effects of the drug (Table 15.2–34). Clinicians must consider both the severity and the frequency of potential adverse effects when using side effects as the basis for choosing among available antidepressants.

Most clinicians choose an SSRI as the first-line treatment of major depressive disorder because of their effectiveness and favorable adverse effect profile. Fluoxetine was the first clinically available SSRI, and many experts continue to consider it the most effective. It may cause transient agitation, insomnia, and anorexia, but it is also the least likely to produce sedation of all the currently available antidepressants. Sertraline is the most associated with transient stomach pain and loose stools, paroxetine is most likely to cause sedation, and fluvoxamine is most likely to cause transient nausea. Patients are more likely to tolerate these adverse effects if the clinicians emphasize the short-term duration of the adverse effects and distinguish them from the persistent beneficial effects. One adverse effect of SSRIs that is likely to persist is sexual dysfunction, most often delayed orgasm in men and women. Despite thorough patient education, 10 to 15 percent of patients discontinue an SSRI because of an adverse effect. For these patients, tricyclic drugs represent a reasonable alternative because they generally lack the serotonergic adverse effects that render SSRIs intolerable. Among tricyclic drugs, secondary amines—nortriptyline (Pamelor), desipramine, and protriptyline (Vivactil)—are generally better tolerated than are tertiary amines—imipramine, amitriptyline (Elavil), and clomipramine (Anafranil).

Bupropion is used because it is generally free of adverse effects, such as nausea, insomnia, and anxiety. Concerns about seizure diathesis can be minimized by limiting the dosage. Venlafaxine is a useful agent for severely depressed patients or patients in whom a rapid response is desired. Venlafaxine is less well tolerated by patients with mild to moderate depression, because of its high rate of nausea and somnolence. Nefazodone is distinguished by its lack of sexual adverse effects and its improvement of sleep continuity.

Table 15.2–33
Antidepressant Effects on CNS Neurotransmitters

	Serotonin	Norepinephrine	Dopamine	MAO Activity	Serotonin Type 2 Blockade
Amitriptyline	+++	++++	0	0	++
Amoxapine	+++	+++	–	0	+++
Bupropion	0	+	++	0	0
Clomipramine	++++	+++	+	0	++
Desipramine[a]	+	++++	0/+	0	+
Doxepin	+++	+	0	0	+
ALL SSRIs	+++++ (or more)	0/+	0/+	0	0/+
Imipramine	+++	++	0/+	0	++
Lithium	0/++[b]	–	–	0	0
Maprotiline	0	++++	0	0	NA
Moclobemide	0	0	0	Reversible type A	0
Nefazodone	+++[a]	0	0	0	++++
Nortriptyline[a]	++	+++	0	0	+
Phenelzine/Tranylcypromine	0	0	0	Irreversible type A/B	0
Protriptyline	+	++++	0	0	NA
Trazodone	++	0	0	0	+++
Trimipramine	++	++	0	0	++
Venlafaxine	++++	+++	0/+	0	0

Reprinted with permission from Prim Psychiatry *2* (6): 41, 1995.
[a] Tertiary amine is demethylated to secondary amine.
[b] Acutely increases; chronically stabilizes.

Table 15.2–34
Adverse Effects of Antidepressant

	Anticholinergic Effects	Arrhythmias	Sedation	Seizures[a]	Orthostasis	GI	Sexual Dysfunction	Toxicity in Overdose
Amitriptyline	5	5	5	2	4	2	3	4
Amoxapine	2	1	3	3	1	1	3	5
Bupropion	0	0	0	4	0	1	0/1	3
Clomipramine	5	5	4	4	4	3	4	5
Desipramine	2	4	2	2	3	1	3	4
Doxepin	3	3	4	2	3	1	3	4
Fluoxetine	0	0	0/1	0	0	4	4	1
Fluvoxamine	1	0	0/1	0	0	5	4	1
Imipramine	3	5	3	2	4	2	3	5
Lithium	0	1	1	1	0	3	1	5
Maprotiline	3	3	3	3	2	1	3	5
Meclobemide	1	0	0	0	2	1	2	2
Nefazodone	1	0	3	0	1	3	1	1
Nortriptyline	3	4	2	2	1	2	3	5
Paroxetine	2	0	1/2	0	0	4	4	1
Protriptyline	3	3	0	2	2	1	3	4
Sertraline	0	0	0/1	0	0	4	4	1
Trazodone	0	1	4	1	3	1	2[b]	2
Trimipramine	4	5	5	2	3	2	4	5
Venlafaxine	1	0	0/1	0	0/1[c]	5	2/3	1

Reprinted with permission from Prim Psychiatry *2* (6): 41, 1995.
0 = none; 1 = minimal; 2 = low; 3 = moderate; 4 = high; 5 = very high.
[a] Although ranked 1–4, "high risk" for seizures is still under 1%.
[b] Priapism.
[c] Slight increase in blood pressure also reported; dose-related.

Table 15.2–35
Drug Interactions and Cytochrome P450 Isoenzyme Systems

	Illustrative Antidepressant Risk Potential (in vitro and in vivo)			
Relative Ranking	**CYP 1A2**	**CYP 2C**	**CYP 2D6**	**CYP 3A3/4**
High	Fluvoxamine	Fluvoxamine Fluoxetine	Paroxetine Fluoxetine	Fluvoxamine Nefazodone TCAs
Moderate to Minimal	Tertiary TCAs Fluoxetine	Tertiary TCAs	Secondary TCAs Sertraline	Sertraline Fluoxetine
Low to Minimal	Paroxetine		Nefazodone Fluvoxamine Venlafaxine (in vitro)	Venlafaxine (in vitro)
	Unknown Risk			
	Nefazodone Sertraline Venlafaxine	Most antidepressants		Paroxetine

Illustrative Drugs That Might Interact with an Antidepressant			
CYP 1A2	**CYP 2C**	**CYP 2D6**	**CYP 3A3/4**
Theophylline Imipramine (minor) Caffeine Phenacetin Acetaminophen Warfarin (minor) Phenothiazines	Mephenytoin Diazepam Hexobarbital Imipramine Phenacetin Warfarin Propranolol Tertiary TCAs	Desipramine, secondary TCAs Flecainide/ecainide Risperidone Phenothiazines Haloperidol (minor) Reduced haloperidol Codeine Propranolol (minor) Quinidine[a]	Terfenadine Astemizole Ketoconazole Alprazolam Triazolam Erythromycin Nifedipine Cyclosporine Corticosteroids

Reprinted with permission from Prim Psychiatry *2* (6): 41, 1995.
[a] Inhibitor at 2D6, not a substrate. Drug can be substrate and/or inhibitor at a given enzyme system.

The MAOIs are less frequently chosen because they may cause a hypertensive crisis if patients ingest foods with a high content of tyramine, which requires strict adherence to a simple set of dietary guidelines. Alprazolam, a benzodiazepine, is FDA approved for treatment of depression, but it is rarely used because of concerns about sedation and because it may be addictive and may be very difficult to discontinue. Sympathomimetics, while among the most effective antidepressants, are rarely used because of concerns for abuse, even though this is unlikely at the low dosages usually necessary for treatment of depression. The use of thioridazine (Mellaril), a dopamine receptor antagonist, for the treatment of depression with marked anxiety or agitation has been approved in the United States, although other drugs with superior efficacy and safety profiles are available.

ADVERSE EFFECTS. One of the most serious concerns about antidepressants is their lethality when taken in overdoses. Tricyclic and tetracyclic drugs are, by far, the most lethal of the antidepressants; the SSRIs, bupropion, trazodone, nefazodone, mirtazapine, venlafaxine, and the MAOIs are safer, although even these drugs can be lethal when taken in overdose in combination with alcohol or other drugs. Another concern about antidepressants is their cardiac safety. Again, tricyclic and tetracyclic drugs are generally the least safe. Hypotension is a potentially serious adverse effect of many antidepressants, particularly in older people. Among the conventional antidepressants, amoxapine (Asendin), maprotiline (Ludiomil), nortriptyline, and trazodone are associated with little hypotension, and bupropion and the SSRIs are associated with the least hypotension. One set of adverse effects that many clinicians inappropriately ignore are the sexual adverse effects of antidepressants. Almost all the antidepressants, except nefazodone and mirtazapine, have been associated with decreased libido, erectile dysfunction, or anorgasmia. The serotonergic drugs are probably more closely associated with sexual adverse effects than are the noradrenergic compounds.

DRUG–DRUG INTERACTIONS. Another increasing concern among clinicians prescribing drugs for depressive disorders and conditions are possible drug–drug interactions, especially in regard to the hepatic cytochrome P450 (CYP) enzyme. The cytochrome P450 isoenzyme system is involved in the metabolism of most drugs, but some people are genetically at risk for developing high blood concentrations of drugs that are metabolized by one of the cytochrome P450 enzymes, such as CYP 2D6 (Table 15.2–35).

TYPE-SPECIFIC TREATMENTS. Some clinical types of major depressive episodes may have varying responses to particular antidepressants. For example, patients with major depressive disorder with atypical features (sometimes called hysteroid dysphoria) may preferentially respond to treatment with MAOIs. Two other specific groups are patients with depressed bipolar I disorder and with major depressive episodes with psychotic features.

Lithium is a potential first-line pharmacological agent in treating depression in patients with bipolar I disorder and in some patients with major depressive disorder with a marked periodicity to their disorder. Patients with bipolar I disorder who are being treated with conventional antidepressants must be observed carefully for the emergence of manic symptoms.

Antidepressants alone are not likely to be effective in the treatment of major depressive episodes with psychotic features. One exception may be amoxapine, an antidepressant closely related to loxapine (Loxitane), an antipsychotic. Clinicians usually, however, use a combination of an antidepressant and an antipsychotic. Several studies have also shown that ECT is effective for this indication—perhaps more effective than pharmacotherapy.

GENERAL CLINICAL GUIDELINES. The most common clinical mistake leading to an unsuccessful trial of an antidepressant drug is the use of too low a dosage for too short a time. Table 15.2–36 lists the dosage ranges and indications for a range of drugs. Unless adverse events prevent it, the dosage of an antidepressant should be raised to the maximum recommended level and maintained at that level for at least 4 or 5 weeks before a drug trial can be considered unsuccessful. Alternatively, if a patient is improving clinically on a low dosage of the drug, this dosage should not be raised unless clinical improve-

Table 15.2–36
Selected Drugs Used to Treat Depression

Drug	Starting Dose (mg)	Dosage[a] (mg/day)	Uses	Therapeutic Plasm Concentration (ng/mL)
Amitriptyline (Elavil, Endep)	25 hs to 25 tid	50–300	Depression, chronic pain, migraine, sleep disorders	60–200[b]
Amoxapine (Asendin)	50 bid[b]–50 tid	100–600	Depression	180–600[b]
Bupropion (Wellbutrin)	50–75 bid	300–450	Depression, attention-deficit disorders	50–100[b]
Clomipramine (Anafranil)	25 tid	100–250	Depression, obsessive-compulsive disorder, panic disorder	200–300[b]
Desipramine (Norpramin, Pertofrane)	25 hs to 25 tid	50–300	Depression, panic and attention-deficit disorders	125–250[c]
Doxepin (Adapin, Sinequan)	25 hs to 25 bid	75–300	Depression, chronic pain, peptic ulcer, irritable bowel syndrome, sleep disorders	110–250
Fluoxetine (Prozac)	20 qam	10–80	Depression, eating and obsessive-compulsive disorders, panic disorder	—
Fluvoxamine (Luvox)	50–100 qam	100–300	Obsessive-compulsive disorders, depression, panic disorder	—
Imipramine (Janimine, Tofranil)	25 hs to 25 tid	50–300	Depression, panic disorder	180[b,c]
Maprotiline (Ludiomil)	25 hs to 25 tid	50–225	Depression	200–400[b]
Nefazodone (Serzone)	100 mg tid	100–600	Depression, obsessive-compulsive disorder[d]	—
Nortriptyline (Aventyl, Pamelor)	25 hs to 25 tid	50–200	Depression, panic disorder	50–150[c]
Paroxetine (Paxil)	20 qam	10–50	Depression, obsessive-compulsive, eating, and panic disorders	—
Phenelzine (Nardil)	15 qam	15–90	Depression, panic disorder, phobia, atypical depression	80% inhibition of platelet MAO activity
Protriptyline (Vivactyl)	10 qam	15–60	Depression	100–200
Sertraline (Zoloft)	50 qam	50–200	Depression, obsessive-compulsive, eating, and panic disorders	—
Trazodone (Desyrel)	50 tid	50–600	Depression, sleep disorders, chronic pain	800–1600
Trimipramine (Surmontil)	25 hs to 25 tid	75–300	Depression, chronic pain	—
Tranylcypromine (Parnate)	10 qam	10–60	Depression, panic disorder, phobia, atypical depression	80% inhibition of platelet MAO activity
Venlafaxine (Effexor)	37.5 bid	75–375	Depression, obsessive-compulsive, panic, and attention deficit disorders[d]	—

Reprinted with permission from Prim Psychiatry *2* (6): 41, 1995.
[a] In geriatric patients, the appropriate dose is widely variable, but in general is one half the young adult dose range for tricyclic antidepressants and for those compounds with significant cardiovascular toxicity.
[b] Parent and metabolite.
[c] Therapeutic drug monitoring well established.
[d] Limited clinical data available.

ment stops before the maximal benefit is obtained. When a patient does not begin to respond to appropriate dosages of a drug after 2 or 3 weeks, clinicians may decide to obtain a plasma concentration of the drug if the test is available for the particular drug being used. The test may indicate either noncompliance or particularly unusual pharmacokinetic disposition of the drug and may thereby suggest an alternative dosage.

DURATION AND PROPHYLAXIS. Antidepressant treatment should be maintained for at least 6 months or the length of a previous episode, whichever is greater. Several studies show that prophylactic treatment with antidepressants is effective in reducing the number and severity of recurrences. Conclusions drawn from one study were that, when episodes are less than 2½ years apart, prophylactic treatment for 5 years is probably indicated. Another factor suggesting prophylactic treatment is the seriousness of previous depressive episodes. Episodes that have involved significant suicidal ideation or impairment of psychosocial functioning may indicate that clinicians should consider prophylactic treatment. When antidepressants are stopped, they should be tapered gradually over 1 to 2 weeks, depending on the half-life of the particular compound. Several studies indicate that maintenance antidepressant medication appears to be safe and effective for the treatment of chronic depression.

FAILURE OF DRUG TRIAL. When the first antidepressant drug has been used for an adequate trial and, if appropriate, clinicians are sure that adequate plasma concentrations were obtained, there are two options if symptoms have not satisfactorily improved: to augment the drug with lithium, liothyronine (Cytomel) (the levorotatory isomer of triiodothyronine [T_3]), or L-tryptophan, or to switch to an alternative primary agent (Fig. 15.2–4). A now rarely used strategy is to combine a tricyclic or tetracyclic drug with an MAOI. When switching agents, clinicians should switch a patient who has been taking a tricyclic or tetracyclic drug to an SSRI (or possibly an MAOI) and should switch a patient who has been taking an SSRI to bupropion, venlafaxine, nefazodone, a tricyclic or tetracyclic drug, mirtazapine, trazodone, or possibly an MAOI. At least 2 weeks should elapse between the use of an SSRI and the use of an MAOI, and the two drugs should never be used concurrently. Clinicians can also consider switching a first-line drug nonresponder to trazodone or bupropion.

Lithium. Lithium (900 to 1,200 mg a day, serum level between 0.6 and 0.8 mEq/L) can be added to the antidepressant dosage for 7 to 14 days. This approach converts a significant number of antidepressant nonresponders to responders. The mechanism of action is unknown, although the lithium may potentiate the serotonergic neuronal system. Some data indicate that pretreatment with the antidepressant alone is necessary for this effect and that beginning treatment with the two drugs simultaneously is not as effective as starting with an antidepressant and then adding lithium.

Liothyronine. The addition of 25 to 50 μg a day of liothyronine to an antidepressant regimen for 7 to 14 days may convert antidepressant nonresponders to responders. The adverse effects of liothyronine are minor but may include headaches and feelings of warmth. The mechanism of action for liothyronine augmentation is not known, although the modulation of β-adrenergic receptors and the presence of undetectable thyroid axis abnormalities in major depressive disorder have been suggested. If liothyronine augmentation is successful, the liothyronine should be continued for 2 months and then tapered at the rate of 12.5 μg a day every 3 to 7 days.

L-Tryptophan. L-Tryptophan, the amino acid precursor to serotonin, has been used as an adjuvant both to antidepressant drugs in major depressive disorder and to lithium in bipolar I disorder. L-Tryptophan has also been used alone as an antidepressant and a hypnotic. L-Tryptophan–containing products have been recalled in the United States because of an outbreak of eosinophilia-myalgia syndrome associated with the use of L-tryptophan. The symptoms of the syndrome include fatigue, myalgia, shortness of breath, rashes, and swelling of the extremities. Congestive heart failure and death can also occur. Although several studies have shown that L-tryptophan is an effective adjuvant in the treatment of mood disorders, the drug should not be used for any purpose until the problem with the syndrome is completely resolved. The syndrome is probably related to a contaminant in a single manufacturing plant, but this hypothesis has yet to be proved.

Tricyclic or Tetracyclic Drug and MAOI Combinations. The combination of a tricyclic or tetracyclic drug and an MAOI is sometimes used for patients who have not responded to several other pharmacological treatments.

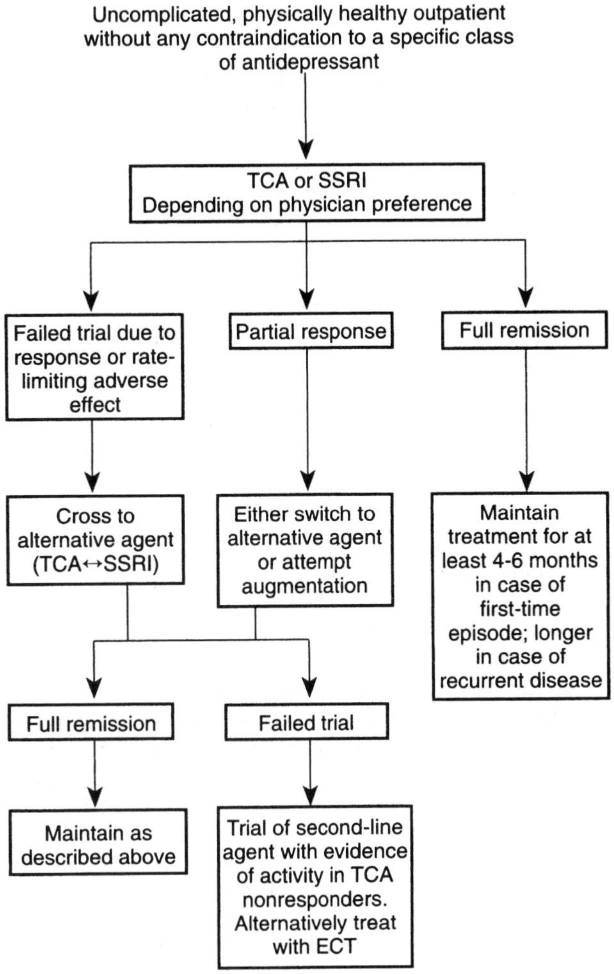
Uncomplicated, physically healthy outpatient without any contraindication to a specific class of antidepressant
TCA or SSRI
Depending on physician preference
Failed trial due to response or rate-limiting adverse effect
Partial response
Full remission
Cross to alternative agent (TCA↔SSRI)
Either switch to alternative agent or attempt augmentation
Maintain treatment for at least 4-6 months in case of first-time episode; longer in case of recurrent disease
Full remission
Failed trial
Maintain as described above
Trial of second-line agent with evidence of activity in TCA nonresponders. Alternatively treat with ECT

FIGURE 15.2–4

Algorithm for treating patient with major depressive disorder. *ECT,* electroconvulsive therapy; *SSRI,* serotonin-specific reuptake inhibitor; *TCA,* tricyclic antidepressant. (Reprinted with permission from Preskorn SH, Burke M: Somatic therapy for major depressive disorder: Selection of an antidepressant. J Clin Psychiatry *53* (9, Suppl): 10, 1992.)

With the availability of a broad range of antidepressants, however, this combination therapy is rarely used. Because of the high incidence of adverse effects, it is not a treatment of first, second, or even third choice. When this combination is used, clinicians should initiate treatment with the two drugs simultaneously at low dosages for each and should then raise the dosages slowly. Imipramine or trimipramine (Surmontil) and an MAOI should not be used in combination because of their high incidence of toxic effects, including restlessness, dizziness, tremulousness, muscle twitching, sweating, convulsions, hyperpyrexia, and sometimes death.

When a patient has been taking a tricyclic or tetracyclic drug, physicians should quarter the dosage of the drug for 5 to 7 days and then slowly add the MAOI to the regimen. When the patient has been taking an MAOI, physicians should stop the drug for 2 weeks and then start the two drugs simultaneously. The reasons for this strategy are that MAOIs irreversibly inhibit monoamine oxidase and it takes about 2 weeks for normal MAO activity levels to be achieved.

Bipolar I Disorder. Whereas the treatment of major depressive disorder has been changed by the introduction of the SSRIs, the treatment of bipolar I disorder has been changed by the many studies that have demonstrated the efficacy of two anticonvulsants—carbamazepine and valproate (Depakene) or divalproex (Depakote)—in the treatment of manic episodes and probably in the prophylaxis of manic and depressive episodes in bipolar I disorder. Although the data in support of the efficacy of lithium are numerous, sufficient data have accumulated to warrant consideration of the two anticonvulsants as first-line treatments of bipolar I disorder. Clinicians should base such a decision primarily on the compatibility between the patient and the relevant side effects of the drugs. The long-term treatment of bipolar I disorder is an indication for these anticonvulsants, but the initial stages of manic episodes often require the addition of drugs with potent sedative effects. Drugs commonly used at the initiation of therapy for bipolar I disorder include clonazepam (Klonopin) (1 mg every 4 to 6 hours), lorazepam (Ativan) (2 mg every 4 to 6 hours), and haloperidol (Haldol) (5 mg every 2 to 4 hours). Physicians should taper these medications and discontinue them as soon as the initial phase of the manic episode has subsided and the effects of the lithium, carbamazepine, or valproate are beginning to be seen clinically.

Lithium, carbamazepine, and valproate are drugs used for the treatment of bipolar I disorder, in addition to other anticonvulsants (clonazepam and gabapentin [Neurontin]), a calcium channel inhibitor (verapamil [Calan]), a β_2-adrenergic receptor agonist (clonidine), antipsychotics (especially risperidone [Risperdal]), and electroconvulsive therapy (ECT).

LITHIUM. Lithium is still a standard treatment for bipolar I disorder. The adverse effects that may limit the use of lithium and cause clinicians to consider using either carbamazepine or valproate include renal effects (thirst, polyuria), nervous system effects (tremor, memory loss), metabolic effects (weight gain), gastrointestinal effects (diarrhea), dermatological effects (acne, psoriasis), and thyroid effects (goiter, myxedema). Of potentially serious concern with lithium treatment are its effects on the kidneys, which can include moderate and occasionally severe impairment of tubular function; uncommon, moderate, and unspecific morphological changes; and rarely, a nephrotic syndrome. These many adverse effects require careful monitoring of patients' renal and thyroid status.

Compliance with lithium treatment is increased with the early initiation of treatment, adequate treatment of concomitant illness, treatment of coexisting substance abuse, early detection and prevention of side effects, and the patients participation in individual and group psychotherapy. Responsiveness to lithium treatment is improved when adequate lithium levels are maintained, adjunctive medication is used as indicated, and laboratory and clinical monitoring is carried out. Nonresponsiveness to lithium treatment is most likely with severe illness, the presence of schizoaffective disorder symptoms, mixed manic and depressive symptoms, somatic symptoms, alcohol and other substance abuse, rapid cycling, and the absence of a family history of bipolar I disorder.

ANTICONVULSANTS. As stated previously, the efficacy data for carbamazepine and valproate are now sufficient to warrant their use as first-line drugs. Carbamazepine is associated with sedation, nausea, blurred vision, rash, blood dyscrasias, and hyponatremia. Valproate has a relatively benign safety profile but is associated with gastrointestinal symptoms, tremor, hair loss, weight gain, and blood dyscrasias. Both valproate and carbamazepine require routine blood monitoring for hepatic and hematological indices of function.

Valproate. A significant number of patients seem to tolerate valproate better than they tolerate lithium and carbamazepine. The initial dosage of valproate in manic patients is usually 20 mg/kg daily, which usually achieves therapeutic blood concentrations of 50 to 125 μg/mL. Patients who respond usually show significant improvements in their symptoms 1 week after reaching these blood concentrations. Outpatients usually tolerate a starting dosage of 500 to 1,000 mg daily, depending on the patient's size. The dosage can then be adjusted upward until therapeutic plasma concentrations are obtained.

The common gastrointestinal problems can usually be minimized by initiating therapy with low dosages, increasing the dosage slowly, and using enteric-coated tablets. Tremor usually responds to treatment with a β-adrenergic antagonist—for example, propranolol (Inderal)—and hair loss can be lessened by the coadministration of a vitamin supplement that contains zinc and selenium. Thrombocytopenia is usually mild and reversible when the dosage is reduced or the drug is discontinued. Although fatal hepatotoxicity has been reported in young children receiving multiple anticonvulsants that include valproate, this adverse effect has not been reported in any patients over 10 years of age.

Carbamazepine. Carbamazepine is usually initiated with daily dosages in the range of 200 to 600 mg. The dosage can be increased every 5 days, as indicated by the patient's therapeutic response and the emergence of adverse effects, to reach serum concentrations of 4 to 12 μg/mL. Once therapeutic serum concentrations are reached, a favorable clinical response is usually observed in 1 to 2 weeks.

The most common dose-related adverse effects of carbamazepine are sedation, nausea, blurred vision, and ataxia. Rash develops in about 10 percent of all patients. Although rash is not an indication to discontinue carbamazepine, other signs of an allergic reaction (for example, bleeding, fever, and joint pain) are important evidence that it may be necessary to discontinue the drug. Exfoliative rashes (such as Stevens-Johnson syndrome), aplastic anemia, agranulocytosis, and thrombocytopenia, although rare, can be potentially fatal.

OTHER AGENTS. Clonazepam, clonidine, clozapine, and verapamil should be considered in the treatment of bipolar I disorder. Although some studies have found these four compounds effective, the database to support their routine use in the treatment of bipolar I disorder is not yet as solid as that for lithium, carbamazepine, and valproate. ECT may be considered in particularly severe or drug-resistant cases as another alternative treatment of bipolar I disorder.

RAPID CYCLING. The development of rapid cycling in patients with bipolar I disorder has been associated with the use of conventional antidepressants, especially tricyclic drugs, and with the presence of hypothyroidism. In addition to the use of thyroid treatments—that is, levothyroxine (T_4) (Levothroid) 0.3 to 0.5 mg a day—some researchers and clinicians have reported preliminary positive results with the use of other psychopharmacological agents, including bupropion and nimodipine (Nimotop).

MAINTENANCE. The decision to maintain a patient on lithium (or other drug) prophylaxis is based on the severity of the patient's disorder, the risk of adverse effects from the particular drug, and the quality of the patient's support systems. Maintenance treatment is generally indicated for the prophylaxis of bipolar I disorder in any patient who has had more than one episode. The rationale for this practice is the relative safety of the available drugs, their demonstrated efficacy, and the significant potential for psychosocial problems if another bipolar I disorder episode occurs.

Bipolar II Disorder

The treatment of bipolar II disorder must be approached cautiously; treatment for depressive episodes with antidepressants can frequently precipitate a manic episode. Whether typical bipolar I disorder medication strategies (for example, lithium and anticonvulsants) are effective in the treatment of patients with bipolar II disorder is still under investigation. A trial of such agents seems warranted, especially when treatment with antidepressants alone has not been successful.

References

Andreasen NC, Swayze V, Flaum M, Alliger R, Cohen G: Ventricular abnormalities in affective disorder: Clinical and demographic correlates. Am J Psychiatry *147:* 893, 1990.

Bauer MS, Whybrow PC: Validity of rapid cycling as a modifier for bipolar disorder in DSM-IV. Depression *1:* 11, 1993.
Cassano GB, Akiskal HS, Savino M, Musetti L, Perugi G: Proposed subtypes of bipolar II and related disorders: With hypomanic episodes (or cyclothymia) and with hyperthymic temperament. J Affect Disord *26:* 127, 1992.
Clayton PJ Guse SB, Cloninger CR, Martin RL: Unipolar depression: Diagnostic inconsistency and its implications. J Affect Disord *26:* 111, 1992.
Coffey CE, Wilkinson WE, Weiner RD, Parashos IA, Djang WT, Webb WC, Figiel GS, Spritzer CF: Quantitative cerebral anatomy in depression: A controlled magnetic resonance imaging study. Arch Gen Psychiatry *50:* 7, 1993.
Coryell W, Endicott J, Keller M: Major depression in a nonclinical sample: Demographic and clinical risk factors for first onset. Arch Gen Psychiatry *49:* 117, 1992.
Coryell W, Endicott J, Keller M: Rapid cycling affective disorder: Demographics, diagnosis, family history, and course. Arch Gen Psychiatry *49:* 126, 1992.
Deakin JFW: Depression and 5HT. Int Clin Psychopharmacol *6:* 23, 1991.
Drevets WC, Videen TO, Price JL, Preskorn SH, Carmichael ST, Raichle ME: A functional anatomical study of unipolar depression. J Neurosci *12:* 3628, 1992.
Emery VO, Oxman TE: Update on the dementia spectrum of depression. Am J Psychiatry *149:* 305, 1992.
Gabbard GO: *Psychodynamic Psychiatry in Clinical Practice: The DSM-IV Edition.* American Psychiatric Press, Washington, 1994.
Gallagher-Thompson D, Steffen AM: Comparative effects of cognitive-behavioral and brief psychodynamic psychotherapies for depressed family caregivers. J Consult Clin Psychol *62:* 543, 1994.
Gastpar M, Gilsdorf U, Abou-Aleh MT, Ngo-Khac T: Clinical correlates of response to CST: The dexamethasone-suppression test in depression: A World Health Organization collaborative study. J Affect Disord *26:* 17, 1992.
Hammen C, Gitlin M: Stress reactivity in bipolar patients and its relation to prior history of disorder. Am J Psychiatry *154:* 856, 1997.
Harrow M, Goldberg JF, Grossman LS, Meltzer HY: Outcome in manic disorders: A naturalistic follow-up study. Arch Gen Psychiatry *47:* 665, 1990.
Horwath E, Johnson J, Weissman MM, Hornig CD: The validity of major depression with atypical features based on a community study. J Affect Disord *26:* 117, 1992.
Hunt N, Bruce-Jones W, Silverstone T: Life events and relapse in bipolar affective disorder. J Affect Disord *25:* 13, 1992.
Jorge RE, Robinson RG, Starkstein SE, Arndt SV, Forrester AW, Geisler FM: Secondary mania following traumatic brain injury. Am J Psychiatry *150:* 916, 1993.
Karasu TB: Toward a clinical model of psychotherapy for depression. II. An integrative and selective treatment approach. Am J Psychiatry *147:* 269, 1990.
Kato T, Takahashi S, Shioiri T, Inubushi T: Alterations in brain phosphorous metabolism in bipolar disorder detected by in vivo ^{31}P and ^{7}Li magnetic resonance spectroscopy. J Affect Disord *27:* 53, 1993.
Katon W, Schulberg H: Epidemiology of depression in primary care. Gen Hosp Psychiatry *14:* 237, 1992.
Keck PE, McElroy SL, Nemeroff CB: Anticonvulsants in the treatment of bipolar disorder. J Neuropsychiatry Clin Neurosci *4:* 395, 1992.
Keck PE Jr, Nabulsi AA, Taylor JL, Henke CJ, et al: A pharmacoeconomic model of divalproex vs. lithium in the acute and prophylactic treatment of bipolar I disorder. J Clin Psychiatry *57* (5): 213, 1996.
Keitner GI, Ryan CE, Miller IW, Norman WH: Recovery and major depression: Factors associated with twelve-month outcome. Am J Psychiatry *149:* 93, 1992.
Keller MB, Lavori PW, Mueller TI, Endicott J, Coryell W, Hirschfield RMA, Shea T: Time to recovery, chronicity, and levels of psychopathology in major depression: A 5-year prospective follow-up of 431 subjects. Arch Gen Psychiatry *49:* 809, 1992.
Kendler KS: Mood-incongruent psychotic affective illness: A historical and empirical review. Arch Gen Psychiatry *48:* 362, 1991.
Kendler KS, Kessler RC, Walters EE, MacLean C, Neale MC, Heath AC, Eaves LJ: Stressful life events, genetics liability, and onset of an episode of major depression in women. Am J Psychiatry *152:* 883, 1995.
Krishnan KRR, McDonald WM, Escalona PR, Doraiswamy PM, Na C, Husain MM, Figiel GS, Boyko OB, Ellinwood EH, Nemeroff CB: Magnetic resonance imaging of the caudate nuclei in depression. Arch Gen Psychiatry *49:* 553, 1992.
Kupfer DJ, Ehlers CL, Frank E, Grochocinski VJ, McEachran AB: EEG sleep profiles and recurrent depression. Biol Psychiatry *30:* 641, 1991.
Kupfer DJ, Frank E, Perel JM, Cornes C, Mallinger AG, Thase ME, McEachran AB, Grochocinski VJ: Five-year outcome for maintenance therapies in recurrent depression. Arch Gen Psychiatry *49:* 769, 1992.
Miller AH, Spencer RL, Pulera M, Kang S, McEwen BS, Stein M: Adrenal steroid receptor activation in rat brain and pituitary following dexamethasone: Implications for the dexamethasone suppression test. Biol Psychiatry *32:* 850, 1992.
Mitchell P, Parker G, Jamieson K, Wilhelm K, Hickie I, Brodaty B, Boyce P, Hadzi-Pavlovic D, Roy K: Are there any differences between bipolar and unipolar melancholia? J Affect Disord *25:* 97, 1992.
Parker G, Roy K, Hadzi-Pavlovic D, Pedic F: Psychotic (delusional) depression: A meta-analysis of physical treatments. J Affect Disord *24:* 17, 1992.
Post RM: Transduction of psychosocial stress into the neurobiology of recurrent affective disorder. Am J Psychiatry *149:* 999, 1992.
Post RM, Ketter TA, Denicoff K, Pazzaglia PJ: The place of anticonvulsant therapy in bipolar illness. Psychopharmacology *128* (2): 115, 1996.
Power AC, Cowen PJ: Neuroendocrine challenge tests: Assessment of 5-HT function in anxiety and depression. Mol Aspects Med *13:* 205, 1992.
Rice J P, Rochberg N, Endicott J, Lavori P W, Miller C: Stability of psychiatric diagnoses: An application to the affective disorder. Arch Gen Psychiatry *49:* 824, 1992.
Roy A: Features associated with suicide attempts in depression: A partial replication. J Affect Disord *27:* 35, 1993.
Schatzberg AF, Rothschild AJ: Psychotic (delusional) major depression: Should it be included as a distinct syndrome in DSM-IV? Am J Psychiatry *149:* 733, 1992.
Schnyder U, Koller-Leiser A: A double-blind, multicentre study of paroxetine and maprotiline in major depression. Can J Psychiatry *41* (4): 239, 1996.
Shamoian CA, editor: Depression in the elderly. Psychiatr Ann *20* (2, Suppl): 2, 1990.
Shelton RC, Winn S, Ekhatore N, Loosen PT: The effects of antidepressants on the thyroid axis in depression. Biol Psychiatry *33:* 120, 1993.
Stephens JH, McHugh PR: Characteristics and long-term follow-up of patients hospitalized for mood disorders in the Phipps Clinic, 1913-1940. J Nerv Ment Dis *179:* 64, 1991.
Stravynski A, Greenberg D: The psychological management of depression. Acta Psychiatr Scand *85:* 407, 1992.
Thomsen PH, Moller LL, Dehlholm B, Brask BH: Manic-depressive psychosis in children younger than 15 years: A register-based investigation of 39 cases in Denmark. Acta Psychiatr Scand *85:* 401, 1992.
Vestergaard P: Treatment and prevention of mania: A Scandinavian perspective. Neuropsychopharmacology *7:* 249, 1992.
Wexler BE, Cicchetti DV: The outpatient treatment of depression: Implications of outcome research for clinical practice. J Nerv Ment Dis *180:* 277, 1992.
Workman EA, Short DD: Atypical antidepressants versus imipramine in the treatment of major depression: A meta-analysis. J Clin Psychiatry *54:* 5, 1993.
Young RC, Klerman GL: Mania in late life: Focus on age at onset. Am J Psychiatry *149:* 867, 1992.

▲ 15.3 Dysthymic Disorder and Cyclothymic Disorder

Dysthymic disorder and cyclothymic disorder are sometimes known in unofficial parlance as subaffective disorders. This term suggests that these two disorders are mild forms of major depressive disorder and bipolar I disorder, respectively. Some research data indicate, however, that although the disorders may be related, they probably have fundamental biological and psychosocial differences. One major difference is that, whereas major depressive disorder is characterized by discrete episodes of symptoms, dysthymic disorder is characterized by chronic, nonepisodic symptoms. The conceptualization of dysthymic disorder and cyclothymic disorder as subaffective disorders must also be considered with respect to other mood disorders, namely bipolar II disorder, minor depressive disorder, and recurrent brief depressive disorder.

Grouping the so-called subaffective disorders with the mood disorders is a controversial classification in the field of psychiatry. Their inclusion with the major mood disorders implies similarities in cause, genetic bases, prognoses, and treatment responses. On the other hand, some psychodynamically oriented psychiatrists believe that dysthymic disorder and cyclothymic disorder are primarily the results of incompletely resolved issues in people's psychodynamic development.

DYSTHYMIC DISORDER

Dysthymic disorder is a chronic disorder characterized by the presence of a depressed (or irritable in children and adolescents) mood that lasts most of the day and is present on most days. According to the fourth edition of *Diagnostic and Statistical Manual of Mental Disorders* (DSM-IV), the most typical features of the disorder are feelings of inadequacy, guilt, irritability, and anger; withdrawal from society; loss of interest; and inactivity and lack of productivity. The term *dysthymia,* which means ''ill humored,'' was introduced in 1980 and changed to *dysthymic disorder* in DSM-IV. Before 1980, most patients now classified as having dysthymic disorder were classified as having depressive neurosis (also called neurotic depression), although some patients were classified as having cyclothymic personality.

The theoretical biases of various diagnostic systems are reflected in the DSM-IV and non–DSM-IV names for the disorder. *Dysthymia* implies a temperamental dysphoria, an inborn tendency to experience a depressed mood. In contrast, *depressive neurosis* implies a maladaptive, repetitive pattern of thinking and behavior resulting in depression. Patients described as having *depressive neurosis* are often anxious, obsessive, and prone to somatization. *Characterological depression* implies a dysphoric mood that is integral to a patient's character. *Hypochondriacal depression* implies a condition characterized by multiple somatic complaints. According to DSM-IV, patients with such complaints may more appropriately be classified as having somatization disorder.

Epidemiology

Dysthymic disorder is common among the general population and affects 3 to 5 percent of all people. It is common among patients in general psychiatric clinics, where it affects between one half and one third of all clinic patients. In at least one study, the reported prevalences of dysthymic disorder among young adolescents were about 8 percent in boys and 5 percent in girls. The disorder is more common in women younger than 64 years of age than in men of any age and is more common among unmarried and young people and in those with low incomes. Moreover, dysthymic disorder frequently coexists with other mental disorders, particularly major depressive disorder, anxiety disorders (especially panic disorder), substance abuse, and, probably, borderline personality disorder. Such patients with dysthymic disorder are likely to be taking a wide range of psychiatric medications, including antidepressants, antimanic agents such as lithium (Eskalith) and carbamazepine (Tegretol), and sedative-hypnotics.

Etiology

A major question about the cause of dysthymic disorder is whether it is related to other psychiatric diagnoses, including major depressive disorder and borderline personality disorder. At this point, it is impossible to arrive at a final conclusion, but as with most psychiatric diagnoses, patients whose disorders are defined by the DSM-IV criteria have a heterogeneous assortment of disease processes—for example, decreased rapid eye movement (REM) sleep and a family history of mood disorders.

Biological Factors. Some studies of biological measures in dysthymic disorder support its classification with the mood disorders; other studies question this association. One hypothesis drawn from the data is that the biological basis for the symptoms of dysthymic disorder and major depressive disorder are similar, but the biological bases for the underlying pathophysiology in the two disorders are different.

SLEEP STUDIES. Decreased rapid eye movement (REM) latency and increased REM density are two state markers of depression in major depressive disorder that also occur in a significant proportion of patients with dysthymic disorder. Some investigators have reported preliminary data indicating that the presence of these sleep abnormalities in patients with dysthymic disorder predicts a response to antidepressant drugs.

NEUROENDOCRINE STUDIES. The two most studied neuroendocrine axes in major depressive disorder and dysthymic disorder are the adrenal axis and the thyroid axis, which have been tested by using the dexamethasone-suppression test (DST) and the thyrotropin-releasing hormone (TRH)-stimulation test, respectively. Although the results of studies are not absolutely consistent, most studies indicate that patients with dysthymic disorder are less likely to have abnormal results on a DST than are patients with major depressive disorder. Fewer studies of the TRH-stimulation test have been conducted, but they have produced preliminary data indicating that abnormalities in the thyroid axis may be a trait variably associated with chronic illness. This hypothesis is supported by a generally increased percentage of patients with dysthymic disorder who have thyroid axis abnormalities when compared with normal controls.

Psychosocial Factors. Psychodynamic theories about the development of dysthymic disorder posit that the disorder results from personality and ego development and culminates in difficulty in adapting to adolescence and young adulthood. Karl Abraham, for example, thought that the conflicts of depression center on oral- and anal-sadistic traits. Anal traits include excessive orderliness, guilt, and concern for others; they are postulated to be a defense against preoccupation with anal matter and with disorganization, hostility, and self-preoccupation. A major defense mechanism used is reaction formation. Low self-esteem, anhedonia, and introversion are often associated with the depressive character.

FREUD. In ''Mourning and Melancholia,'' Sigmund Freud asserted that an interpersonal disappointment early in life can cause a vulnerability to depression that leads to ambivalent love relationships as an adult; real or threatened losses in adult life then trigger depression. People prone to depression are orally dependent and require constant narcissistic gratification. When deprived of love, affection, and care, they become clinically depressed; when they experience a real loss, they internalize or introject the lost object and turn their anger on it and, thus, on themselves.

COGNITIVE THEORY. The cognitive theory of depression also applies to dysthymic disorder. It holds that a disparity between actual and fantasized situations leads to diminished self-esteem and a sense of helplessness. The success of cognitive therapy in the treatment of some patients with dysthymic disorder may provide some support for the theoretical model.

Diagnosis

The DSM-IV diagnosis criteria for dysthymic disorder (Table 15.3–1) stipulate the presence of a depressed mood most of the time for at least 2 years (or 1 year for children and adolescents). To meet the diagnostic criteria, a patient should not have symptoms that are better accounted for as major de-

Table 15.3–1
DSM-IV Diagnostic Criteria for Dysthymic Disorder

A. Depressed mood for most of the day, for more days than not, as indicated either by subjective account or observation by others, for at least 2 years. **Note:** In children and adolescents, mood can be irritable and duration must be at least 1 year.
B. Presence, while depressed, of two (or more) of the following:
(1) poor appetite or overeating
(2) insomnia or hypersomnia
(3) low energy or fatigue
(4) low self-esteem
(5) poor concentration or difficulty making decisions
(6) feelings of hopelessness
C. During the 2-year period (1 year for children or adolescents) of the disturbance, the person has never been without the symptoms in criteria A and B for more than 2 months at a time.
D. No major depressive episode has been present during the first 2 years of the disturbance (1 year for children and adolescents); ie, the disturbance is not better accounted for by chronic major depressive disorder, or major depressive disorder, in partial remission.
Note: There may have been a previous major depressive episode provided there was a full remission (no significant signs or symptoms for 2 months) before development of the dysthymic disorder. In addition, after the initial 2 years (1 year in children or adolescents) of dysthymic disorder, there may be superimposed episodes of major depressive disorder, in which case both diagnoses may be given when the criteria are met for a major depressive episode.
E. There has never been a manic episode, a mixed episode, or a hypomanic episode, and criteria have never been met for cyclothymic disorder.
F. The disturbance does not occur exclusively during the course of a chronic psychotic disorder, such as schizophrenia or delusional disorder.
G. The symptoms are not due to the direct physiological effects of a substance (eg, a drug of abuse, a medication) or a general medical condition (eg, hypothyroidism).
H. The symptoms cause clinically significant distress or impairment in social, occupational, or other important areas of functioning.

Specify if:
Early onset: if onset before age 21 years
Late onset: if onset is age 21 years or older

Specify (for most recent 2 years of dysthymic disorder):
With atypical features

pressive disorder and should never have had a manic or hypomanic episode. DSM-IV allows clinicians to specify whether the onset was early (before age 21) or late (age 21 or older). DSM-IV also allows for the specification of atypical features in dysthymic disorder (see Table 15.3–1).

Clinical Features

Dysthymic disorder is a chronic disorder characterized not by episodes of illness but rather by the steady presence of symptoms. Nevertheless, patients with dysthymic disorder can show some temporal variation in the severity of their symptoms. The symptoms themselves are similar to those for major depressive disorder, and the presence of a depressed mood—characterized by feeling sad, blue, down in the dumps, or low and by a lack of interest usual activities—is central to the disorder. The severity of the depressive symptoms in dysthymic disorder is generally less than in major depressive disorder, but the lack of discrete episodes most weights toward the diagnosis of dysthymic disorder.

Patients with dysthymic disorder can often be sarcastic, nihilistic, brooding, demanding, and complaining. They can be tense, rigid, and resistant to therapeutic interventions, even though they come regularly to appointments. As a result, clinicians may feel angry toward patients and may even disregard their complaints. By definition, dysthymic disorder patients do not have any psychotic symptoms.

Mr. Turm is a German lawyer. He is 36 years old and married, with two children.

Problem. Mr. Turm was admitted to the psychiatric department of a general hospital after he had taken an overdose of diazepam. For some weeks he had felt overwhelmed by his workload. He felt tired and more depressed than usual, had difficulties in concentrating, and experienced feelings of inadequacy. At home he said hardly a word and showed no interest in his family. His wife finally told him that she was thinking about getting a divorce because she could no longer face his recurrent bouts of depression.

Since the age of 26, Mr. Turm had experienced constantly recurring depressed mood, lasting 1–2 months at a time, with only a few weeks in between when his mood would be normal. When depressed, he felt pessimistic and inadequate and often went for long periods during which he exchanged only minimal conversation with his family. He managed to continue working. There were no noticeable changes in his appetite or weight, but sometimes he had trouble falling asleep. He never had periods of elated mood or increased energy. Mr. Turm had occasionally seen his general practitioner, but except for a prescription of diazepam to help him get to sleep, he did not receive any treatment.

History. Mr. Turm was the younger of two brothers. Their father was authoritarian, and the mother appears to have been a sensitive person. Mr. Turm was a student with above average ability at school; he went on to college and finished his studies in law at the age of 28. He opened his own lawyer's office with a partner, and that same year, he married a woman 2 years younger. She was a nurse, but she gave up her job after the birth of their first son, 1 year after their marriage. Two years later a second son was born. Both are in good health. Mr. Turm's business had many clients, he had to work long days, and he felt under great pressure. His relationship with his wife had deteriorated in recent years because of his apparent loss of interest in his family. Never before had she mentioned that she was contemplating divorce, which came as a great shock to him.

Mr. Turm described himself as having always suffered

from low self-confidence, and he had difficulty in making friends. He had worked hard at school to get good results to balance his feelings of inadequacy. He was rather shy and had preferred to stay in his room, where he busied himself with homework and books.

His mother had experienced various somatic complaints. She committed suicide by hanging herself when Mr. Turm was 12 years old. His father, a well-known actor, died of cerebral infarction when Mr. Turm was age 33. Two years before Mr. Turm's own suicide attempt, his brother had spent 2 months in a psychiatric hospital because of depression.

Findings. On his arrival at the psychiatric ward, Mr. Turm appeared tired but gave an adequate account of himself. His mood was depressed, and he reported feelings of hopelessness and inadequacy. There were no delusions or hallucinations. His cognitive abilities were undisturbed, although he reported difficulties in concentrating.

Physical and neurological examinations, including laboratory investigations, were all normal.

DISCUSSION

Mr. Turm presents with a depressive disorder, meeting the criteria for mild severity with more than usually depressed mood, tiredness, difficulty in concentrating, and an attempt at suicide.

For at least 8 years, he had suffered from constantly recurring depressed mood, with only a few weeks of normal mood in between, accompanied by low self-esteem, pessimism, and lack of interest in his family. Only the current episode meets the criteria for a depressive episode, whereas the state of recurring depressed mood meets the criteria of dysthymia, with early onset. The current episode may, therefore, be considered as an exacerbation of his dysthymia, caused by his wife's threat of divorce. (From *ICD-10 Casebook.*)

Associated Symptoms. Associated symptoms include changes in appetite and sleep patterns, low self-esteem, loss of energy, psychomotor retardation, decreased sexual drive, and obsessive preoccupation with health matters. Pessimism, hopelessness, and helplessness may cause these patients to be seen as masochistic, but if their pessimism is directed outward, patients may rant against the world and complain that they have been poorly treated by relatives, children, parents, colleagues, and the system.

Social Impairment. Impairment in social functioning is sometimes the reason that patients with dysthymic disorder seek treatment. In fact, divorce, unemployment, and social problems are common for these patients. They may complain that they have difficulty in concentrating and may report that their school or work performance is suffering. Because of complaints of physical illness, patients may miss workdays and social occasions. Patients with dysthymic disorder may have marital problems resulting from sexual dysfunction (such as impotence) or from an inability to sustain emotional intimacy.

Coexisting Diagnoses. As mentioned previously, the diagnosis of dysthymic disorder is frequently made for people who also have other mental disorders. Data indicate that the comorbidity of dysthymic disorder with other mental disorders is a significant negative predictor of a good prognosis. The presence of a chronic, untreated depressive disorder appears to limit a patient's rate and extent of improvement for other mental disorders. Frequently occurring comorbid disorders are major depressive disorder and substance-related disorders.

DOUBLE DEPRESSION. An estimated 40 percent of patients with major depressive disorder also meet the criteria for dysthymic disorder, a combination often referred to as double depression. Available data support the conclusion that patients with double depression have a poorer prognosis than do patients with only major depressive disorder. The treatment of patients with double depression should be directed toward both disorders, as the resolution of the symptoms of major depressive episode still leaves these patients with significant psychiatric impairment.

ALCOHOL AND OTHER SUBSTANCE ABUSE. Patients with dysthymic disorder commonly meet the diagnostic criteria for a substance-related disorder. This comorbidity can be logical: Patients with dysthymic disorder tend to develop coping methods for their chronically depressed state. Therefore, they are likely to use alcohol or stimulants such as cocaine, or marijuana, the choice perhaps depending primarily on a patient's social context. The presence of a comorbid diagnosis of substance abuse presents a diagnostic dilemma for clinicians; the long-term use of many substances can result in a symptom picture indistinguishable from that of dysthymic disorder.

Differential Diagnosis

The differential diagnosis for dysthymic disorder is essentially identical to that for major depressive disorder. Many substances and medical illnesses can cause chronic depressive symptoms. Two disorders are particularly important to consider in the differential diagnosis of dysthymic disorder—minor depressive disorder and recurrent brief depressive disorder.

Minor Depressive Disorder. Minor depressive disorder (discussed in Section 15.1) is characterized by episodes of depressive symptoms that are less severe than those seen in major depressive disorder. The difference between dysthymic disorder and minor depressive disorder is primarily the episodic nature of the symptoms in the latter. Between episodes, patients with minor depressive disorder have a euthymic mood, whereas patients with dysthymic disorder have virtually no euthymic periods.

Recurrent Brief Depressive Disorder. Recurrent brief depressive disorder (discussed in Section 15.1) is characterized by brief periods (less than 2 weeks) during which depressive episodes are present. Patients with the disorder would meet the diagnostic criteria for major depressive disorder if their episodes lasted longer. Patients with recurrent brief depressive disorder differ from patients with dysthymic disorder on two counts: They have an episodic disorder, and the severity of their symptoms is greater.

Course and Prognosis. About 50 percent of patients with dysthymic disorder experience an insidious onset of symptoms before age 25. Despite the early onset, patients often suffer with the symptoms for a decade before seeking psychiatric help and may consider early-onset dysthymic disorder simply as part of life. Patients with an early onset of symptoms are at risk for either major depressive disorder or bipolar I disorder in the course of their disorder. Studies of patients with the diagnosis of depressive neurosis indicated that about 20 percent progressed to major depressive disorder, 15 percent to bipolar II disorder, and less than 5 percent to bipolar I disorder.

The prognosis for patients with dysthymic disorder is variable. Antidepressive agents (for example, fluoxetine [Prozac] and bupropion [Wellbutrin]), and specific types of psychotherapy (for example, cognitive and behavior therapies) have positive effects on the course and prognosis of dysthymic disorder. The available data about previously available treatments indicate that only 10 to 15 percent of patients are in remission 1 year after the initial diagnosis. About 25 percent of all patients with dysthymic disorder never attain a complete recovery.

Treatment

Historically, patients with dysthymic disorder either received no treatment or were seen as candidates for long-term, insight-oriented psychotherapy. Contemporary data offer the most objective support for cognitive therapy, behavior therapy, and pharmacotherapy. The combination of pharmacotherapy and either cognitive or behavior therapy may be the most effective treatment for the disorder. Other therapies may be beneficial, but the benefit has yet to be proved in well-controlled studies.

Cognitive Therapy. Cognitive therapy is a technique in which patients are taught new ways of thinking and behaving to replace faulty negative attitudes about themselves, the world, and the future. It is a short-term therapy program oriented toward current problems and their resolution.

Behavior Therapy. Behavior therapy for depressive disorders is based on the theory that depression is caused by a loss of positive reinforcement as a result of separation, death, or sudden environmental change. The various treatment methods focus on specific goals to increase activity, to provide pleasant experiences, and to teach patients how to relax. Altering personal behavior in depressed patients is believed to be the most effective way to change the associated depressed thoughts and feelings. Behavior therapy is often used to treat the learned helplessness of some patients who seem to meet every life challenge with a sense of impotence.

Insight-Oriented (Psychoanalytic) Psychotherapy. Individual insight-oriented psychotherapy is the most common treatment method for dysthymic disorder, and many clinicians believe it to be the treatment of choice. The psychotherapeutic approach attempts to relate the development and the maintenance of depressive symptoms and maladaptive personality features to unresolved conflicts from early childhood. Insight into depressive equivalents (such as substance abuse) or into childhood disappointments as antecedents to adult depression can be gained through treatment. Ambivalent current relationships with parents, friends, and others in the patient's current life are examined. Patients' understanding of how they try to gratify an excessive need for outside approval to counter low self-esteem and a harsh superego is an important goal in the therapy.

Dysthymic disorder involves a chronic state of depression that for certain people becomes a way of life. These people consciously experience themselves to be at the mercy of a tormenting internal object that is unrelenting in its persecution. Usually conceptualized as a harsh superego, the internal agency criticizes them, punishes them for not measuring up to expectations, and generally contributes to their feelings of misery and unhappiness. This pattern may be associated with self-defeating tendencies because patients do not feel that they deserve to be successful. They may also have a long-standing sense of despair about ever getting their emotional needs met by important people in their lives. The patients' bleak outlook on life and their pessimism about relationships result in a self-fulfilling prophecy—many people avoid them because their company is unpleasant.

Interpersonal Therapy. In interpersonal therapy for depressive disorders, a patient's current interpersonal experiences and ways of coping with stress are examined to reduce depressive symptoms and to improve self-esteem. Interpersonal therapy lasts for about 12 to 16 weekly sessions and can be combined with antidepressant medication.

Family and Group Therapies. Family therapy may help both the patient and the patient's family deal with the symptoms of the disorder, especially when a biologically based subaffective syndrome seems to be present. Group therapy may help withdrawn patients learn new ways to overcome their interpersonal problems in social situations.

Pharmacotherapy. THERAPEUTIC OPTIONS. Because of long-standing and commonly held theoretical beliefs that dysthymic disorder is primarily a psychologically determined disorder, many clinicians avoid prescribing antidepressants for patients, but many studies have shown therapeutic success with antidepressants. The data generally indicate that monoamine oxidase inhibitors (MAOIs) may be more beneficial than are tricyclic drugs. The well-tolerated serotonin-specific reuptake inhibitors (SSRIs) are of use for patients with dysthymic disorder. Reports indicate that the SSRIs may be the drugs of choice. Similarly, bupropion may also be an effective treatment for patients with dysthymic disorder. Sympathomimetics, such as amphetamines, have also been of use in selected patients.

FAILURE OF THERAPEUTIC TRIAL. A therapeutic trial of an antidepressant in the treatment of dysthymic disorder should include maximal tolerated dosages for a minimum of 8 weeks before clinicians conclude that the trial was not effective. When a drug trial is unsuccessful, clinicians should reconsider the diagnosis, especially the possibility of an underlying medical disorder (especially a thyroid disorder) or adult attention-deficit disorder. When a reconsideration of the differential diagnosis still suggests that dysthymic disorder is the most likely diagnosis, clinicians may follow the same therapeutic strategy as for major depressive disorder and may attempt to augment the first antidepressant by adding lithium or liothyronine (Cytomel), although augmentation strategies for dysthymic disorder have not been studied. As an alternative, clinicians may decide to switch to an antidepressant from a completely different class of drugs. For example, if a trial with an SSRI is unsuccessful, a clinician may switch to bupropion or to an MAOI.

Hospitalization. Hospitalization is usually not indicated for patients with dysthymic disorder, but particularly severe symptoms, marked social or professional incapacitation, the need for extensive diagnostic procedures, and suicidal ideation are all indications for hospitalization.

CYCLOTHYMIC DISORDER

Cyclothymic disorder is symptomatically a mild form of bipolar II disorder, characterized by episodes of hypomania and mild depression. In DSM-IV, cyclothymic disorder is defined as a "chronic, fluctuating disturbance" with many periods of hypomania and of depression. The disorder is differentiated from bipolar II disorder, which is characterized by the presence of major depressive and hypomanic episodes. As with dysthymic disorder, the categorization of cyclothymic disorder with the mood disorders implies a relation, probably biological, to bipolar I disorder. Some psychiatrists, however, consider cyclothymic disorder to be distinct from bipolar I disorder and to result from chaotic object relations early in life.

Contemporary understanding of cyclothymic disorder is based to some extent on the observations of Emil Kraepelin and Kurt Schneider that one third to two thirds of patients with mood disorders exhibit personality disorders. Kraepelin described four types of personality disorders: depressive (gloomy), manic (cheerful and uninhibited), irritable (labile and explosive), and cyclothymic. He described the irritable personality as simultaneously depressive and manic and the cyclothymic personality as the alternation of the depressive and manic personalities.

Epidemiology

Patients with cyclothymic disorder may constitute from 3 to 10 percent of all psychiatric outpatients, perhaps particularly those with significant complaints about marital and interpersonal difficulties. In the general population, the lifetime prevalence of cyclothymic disorder is estimated to be about 1 percent. This figure is probably lower than the actual prevalence, because, as with patients with bipolar I disorder, the patients may not be aware that they have a psychiatric problem. Cyclothymic disorder, like dysthymic disorder, frequently coexists with borderline personality disorder. An estimated 10 percent of outpatients and 20 percent of inpatients with borderline personality disorder have a coexisting diagnosis of cyclothymic disorder. The female-to-male ratio in cyclothymic disorder is about 3 to 2, and 50 to 75 percent of all patients have an onset between ages 15 and 25.

Etiology

As with dysthymic disorder, there is controversy about whether cyclothymic disorder is related to the mood disorders, either biologically or psychologically. Some researchers have postulated that cyclothymic disorder has a closer relation to borderline personality disorder than to the mood disorders. In spite of these controversies, the preponderance of biological and genetic data favors the ideas of cyclothymic disorder as a bona fide mood disorder.

Biological Factors. The strongest evidence for the hypothesis that cyclothymic disorder is a mood disorder is the genetic data. About 30 percent of all patients with cyclothymic disorder have positive family histories for bipolar I disorder; this rate is similar to the rate for patients with bipolar I disorder. Moreover, the pedigrees of families with bipolar I disorder often contain generations of patients with bipolar I disorder linked by a generation with cyclothymic disorder. Conversely, the prevalence of cyclothymic disorder in the relatives of patients with bipolar I disorder is much higher than is the prevalence of cyclothymic disorder either in the relatives of patients with other mental disorders or in people who are mentally healthy. The observations that about one third of patients with cyclothymic disorder subsequently have major mood disorders, that they are particularly sensitive to antidepressant-induced hypomania, and that about 60 percent respond to lithium add further support to the idea of cyclothymic disorder as a mild or attenuated form of bipolar I disorder.

Psychosocial Factors. Most psychodynamic theories postulate that the development of cyclothymic disorder lies in traumas and fixations during the oral stage of infant development. Freud hypothesized that the cyclothymic state is the ego's attempt to overcome a harsh and punitive superego. Hypomania is explained psychodynamically as the lack of self-criticism and an absence of inhibitions occurring when a depressed person throws off the burden of an overly harsh superego. The major defense mechanism in hypomania is denial, by which the patient avoids external problems and internal feelings of depression.

Patients with cyclothymic disorder are characterized by periods of depression alternating with periods of hypomania. Psychoanalytic exploration reveals that such patients defend themselves against underlying depressive themes with their euphoric or hypomanic periods. Hypomania is frequently triggered by a profound interpersonal loss. The false euphoria generated in such instances is a patient's way to deny dependence on love objects while simultaneously disavowing any aggression or destructiveness that may have contributed to the loss of the loved person. Hypomania may also be associated with an unconscious fantasy that the lost object has been restored. This denial is generally short-lived, and the patient soon resumes the preoccupation with suffering and misery characteristic of dysthymic disorder.

Diagnosis

Although many patients seek psychiatric help for depression, their problems are often related to the chaos that their manic episodes have caused. Clinicians must consider a diagnosis of cyclothymic disorder when a patient appears with what may seem to be sociopathic behavioral problems. Marital difficulties and instability in relationships are common complaints because patients with cyclothymic disorder are often promiscuous and irritable while in manic and mixed states. Although there are anecdotal reports of increased productivity and creativity when patients are hypomanic, most clinicians report that their patients become disorganized and ineffective in work and school during these periods.

The DSM-IV diagnostic criteria for cyclothymic disorder (Table 15.3–2) stipulate that a patient has never met the criteria for a major depressive episode and did not meet the criteria for a manic episode during the first 2 years of the disturbance. The criteria also require the more or less constant presence of symptoms for 2 years (or 1 year for children and adolescents).

Clinical Features

Signs and Symptoms. The symptoms of cyclothymic disorder are identical to the symptoms of bipolar I disorder, except that they are generally less severe. On occasion, however, the symptoms may be equal in severity but of shorter duration than those seen in bipolar I disorder. About half of all patients with cyclothymic disorder have depression as their major symptom, and these patients are most likely to seek psychiatric help while depressed. Some patients with cyclothymic disorder have primarily hypomanic symptoms and are less likely to consult a psychiatrist than are primarily depressed patients. Almost all patients with cyclothymic disorder have periods of mixed symptoms with marked irritability.

Most patients with cyclothymic disorder seen by psychiatrists have not succeeded in their professional and social lives as a result of their disorder, but a few have become high achievers who have worked especially long hours and have required little sleep. Some people's ability to successfully control the symptoms of the disorder depends on multiple individual, social, and cultural attributes.

The lives of most patients with cyclothymic disorder are difficult. The cycles of the disorder tend to be much shorter than those in bipolar I disorder. In cyclothymic disorder, the changes in mood are irregular and abrupt and sometimes occur within hours. Occasional periods of normal mood and the unpredictable nature of the mood changes produces great stress. Patients often feel that their moods are out of control. In irritable, mixed periods, they may become involved in unprovoked disagreements with friends, family, and coworkers.

Substance Abuse. Alcohol and other substance abuse are common in cyclothymic disorder patients, who use substances either to self-medicate (with alcohol, benzodiazepines, and marijuana) or to achieve even further stimulation (with cocaine, amphetamines, and hallucinogens) when they are manic. About 5 to 10 percent of all patients with cyclothymic disorder have substance dependence. People with this disorder often have a history of multiple geographical moves, involvements in religious cults, and dilettantism.

Table 15.3–2
DSM-IV Diagnostic Criteria for Cyclothymic Disorder

A. For at least 2 years, the presence of numerous periods with hypomanic symptoms and numerous periods with depressive symptoms that do not meet criteria for a major depressive episode. **Note:** In children and adolescents, the duration must be at least 1 year.

B. During the above 2-year period (1 year in children and adolescents), the person has not been without the symptoms in criterion A for more than 2 months at a time.

C. No major depressive episode, manic episode, or mixed episode has been present during the first 2 years of the disturbance.
Note: After the initial 2 years (1 year in children and adolescents) of cyclothymic disorder, there may be superimposed manic or mixed episodes (in which case both bipolar I disorder and cyclothymic disorder may be diagnosed) or major depressive episodes (in which case both bipolar and cyclothymic disorder may be diagnosed).

D. The symptoms in criterion A are not better accounted for by schizoaffective disorder and are not superimposed on schizophrenia, schizophreniform disorder, delusional disorder, or psychotic disorder not otherwise specified.

E. The symptoms are not due to the direct physiological effects of a substance (eg, a drug of abuse, a medication) or a general medical condition (eg, hyperthyroidism).

F. The symptoms cause clinically significant distress or impairment in social, occupational, or other important areas of functioning.

Reprinted with permission from American Psychiatric Association: *Diagnostic and Statistical Manual of Mental Disorders,* ed 4. Copyright, American Psychiatric Association, Washington, 1994.

Differential Diagnosis

When a diagnosis of cyclothymic disorder is under consideration, all the possible medical and substance-related causes of depression and mania such as seizures and particular substances (cocaine, amphetamine, and steroids) must be considered. Borderline, antisocial, histrionic, and narcissistic personality disorders should also be considered in the differential diagnosis. Attention-deficit/hyperactivity disorder can be difficult to differentiate from cyclothymic disorder in children and adolescents. A trial of stimulants helps most patients with attention-deficit/hyperactivity disorder and exacerbates the symptoms of most patients with cyclothymic disorder. The diagnostic category of bipolar II disorder (discussed in Section 15.2) is characterized by the combination of major depressive and hypomanic episodes.

Course and Prognosis

Some patients with cyclothymic disorder are characterized as having been sensitive, hyperactive, or moody as young children. The onset of frank symptoms of cyclothymic disorder often occurs insidiously in the teens or early 20s. The emergence of symptoms at that time hinder a person's performance in school and the ability to establish friendships with peers. The reactions of patients to such a disorder vary; patients with adaptive coping strategies or ego defenses have better outcomes than do patients with poor coping strategies. About one third of all patients with cyclothymic disorder develop a major mood disorder, most often bipolar II disorder.

Treatment

Biological Therapy. The antimanic drugs are the first line of treatment for patients with cyclothymic disorder. Although the experimental data are limited to studies with lithium, other antimanic agents—for example, carbamazepine and valproate (Depakene)—are reported to be effective. Dosages and plasma concentrations of these agents should be the same as those in bipolar I disorder. Antidepressant treatment of depressed patients with cyclothymic disorder should be done with caution, because these patients have increased susceptibility to antidepressant-induced hypomanic or manic episodes. About 40 to 50 percent of all patients with cyclothymic disorder who are treated with antidepressants experience such episodes.

Psychosocial Therapy. Psychotherapy for patients with cyclothymic disorder is best directed toward increasing patients' awareness of their condition and helping them develop coping mechanisms for their mood swings. Therapists usually need to help patients repair any damage, both work and family related, done during episodes of hypomania. Because of the long-term nature of cyclothymic disorder, patients often require lifelong treatment. Family and group therapies may be supportive, educational, and therapeutic for patients and for those involved in their lives.

References

Akiskal HS: Depression in cyclothymic and related temperaments: Clinical and pharmacologic considerations. J Clin Psychiatry Monogr *10:* 37, 1992.

Bloch AL, Shear MK, Markowitz JC, Leon AC, Perry JC: An empirical study of defense mechanisms in dysthymia. Am J Psychiatry *150:* 1194, 1993.

Gabbard GO: *Psychodynamic Psychiatry in Clinical Practice: The DSM-IV Edition.* American Psychiatric Press, Washington, 1994.

Garrison CZ, Addy CL, Jackson KL, McKeown RE, Waller JL: Major depressive disorder and dysthymia in young adolescence. Am J Epidemiol *135:* 792, 1992.

Hellerstein DJ, Yanowitch P, Rosenthal J, Samstag LW, Maurer M, Kasch K, Burrows L, Poster M, Cantillon M, Winston A: A randomized double-blind study of fluoxetine versus placebo in the treatment of dysthymia. Am J Psychiatry *150:* 1169, 1993.

Howland RH: Pharmacotherapy of dysthymia: A review. J Clin Psychopharmacol *11:* 83, 1991.

Howland RH, Thase ME: Biological studies of dysthymia. Biol Psychiatry *30:* 283, 1991.

Howland RH, Thase ME: A comprehensive review of cyclothymic disorder. J Nerv Ment Dis *181:* 485, 1993.

Kocsis JH, Zisook S, Davidson J, Shelton R, Yonkers K, Hellerstein DJ, Rosenbaum J, Halbreich U: Double-blind comparison of sertraline, imipramine, and placebo in the treatment of dysthymia: Psychosocial outcomes. Am J Psychiatry *154:* 390, 1997.

Levitt AJ, Joffe RT, Ennis J, MacDonald C, Kutcher SP: The prevalence of cyclothymia in borderline personality disorder. J Clin Psychiatry *51:* 335, 1990.

Markowitz JC, Moran ME, Kocsis JH, Francis AJ: Prevalence and comorbidity of dysthymic disorder among psychiatric outpatients. J Affect Disord *24:* 63, 1992.

Osser DN: A systematic approach to the classification and pharmacotherapy of nonpsychotic major depression and dysthymia. J Clin Psychopharmacol *13:* 133, 1993.

Rosenthal J, Hemlock C, Hellerstein DJ, Yanowitch P, Kasch K, Shupak C, Samstag L, Winston A: A preliminary study of serotonergic antidepressants in treatment of dysthymia. Prog Neuropsychopharmacol Biol Psychiatry *16:* 933, 1992.

Stewart JW, McGrath PJ, Quitkin FM: Can mildly depressed outpatients with atypical depression benefit from antidepressants? Am J Psychiatry *149:* 615, 1992.

Wells KB, Burnam MA, Rogers W, Hays R, Camp P: The course of depression in adult outpatients: Results from the medical outcomes study. Arch Gen Psychiatry *49:* 788, 1992.

Zisook S: Treatment of dysthymia and atypical depression. J Clin Psychiatry Monogr *10:* 15, 1992.

16 Anxiety Disorders

16.1 Overview

Of all mental disorders, anxiety disorders are probably the most common as well as the ones most affected by changes in the diagnostic criteria of the fourth edition (and earlier editions) of *Diagnostic and Statistical Manual of Mental Disorders* (DSM-IV). Over the past 20 years, increasing knowledge of the biological factors affecting anxiety has altered the concepts of these disorders by shifting their diagnostic bases from the psychodynamic formulation of neuroses to valid, reliable, and recognizable criteria (Table 16.1–1).

Despite these changes, clinicians assessing patients with anxiety must still distinguish between normal and pathological anxiety. In practical terms, evaluation by patients, their families and friends, and the clinician can help to differentiate pathological from normal anxiety and can determine whether pathological anxiety is present. These evaluations are based on patients' reported internal states, their behaviors, and their abilities to function. Patients with pathological anxiety require complete neuropsychiatric assessments and individually tailored treatment plans. Clinicians must be aware that anxiety can be a symptom of many medical conditions as well as of other mental disorders, especially depressive disorders.

In contrast to pathological anxiety, normal anxiety is an advantageous response to a threatening situation. For example, infants threatened by separation from parents, children on their first day at school, adolescents on their first date, adults contemplating old age and death, and anyone faced with illness all experience normal anxiety. Such anxiety normally accompanies growth, change, new experiences, and finding an identity and meaning in life. By contrast, pathological anxiety, by virtue of its intensity or duration, is an inappropriate response to a given stimulus.

HISTORY

Nearly a century ago, Sigmund Freud coined the term *anxiety neurosis* and identified two forms of anxiety. One type results from dammed-up libido: A physiological increase in sexual tension leads to a corresponding increase in libido, the mental representation of the physiological event. The normal outlet for such tension is, in Freud's view, sexual intercourse, but sexual practices such as abstinence and coitus interruptus prevent tension release and produce neuroses. The conditions of heightened anxiety related to libidinal blockage include neurasthenia, hypochondriasis, and anxiety neuroses, all of which Freud regarded as having a biological basis, that is, actual neuroses.

The other form of anxiety is best described as a diffuse sense of worry or dread that originates in a repressed thought or wish. This form is responsible for the psychoneuroses—hysteria, phobias, and obsessional neuroses. Freud understood these conditions and the anxiety associated with them to be primarily related to psychological rather than physiological factors. Intrapsychic conflict is responsible for anxiety and psychoneuroses, and Freud observed that the anxiety resulting from this conflict is less intense and less dramatic than that which he observed in actual neuroses.

With the publication of "Inhibitions, Symptoms, and Anxiety" in 1926, Freud created a new theory of anxiety that accounted for both real external anxiety and neurotic internal anxiety as a response to a dangerous situation. Freud identified two anxiety-provoking situations, one involving overwhelming instinctual stimulation and another more common one involving anxiety that develops in anticipation of, rather than as the result of, danger. The experience of birth is the prototype of the first situation in which excessive amounts of drive pressure penetrate the protective barriers of the ego and produce a reaction of helplessness and trauma. Either external or internal sources of danger may produce signal anxiety, a warning to the organism, which operates unconsciously and serves to mobilize the specific defense mechanisms of the ego to guard against or to reduce the degree of instinctual excitation.

NORMAL ANXIETY

Everyone experiences anxiety—a diffuse, unpleasant, vague sense of apprehension, often accompanied by autonomic symptoms (Table 16.1–2), such as headache, perspiration, palpitations, tightness in the chest, mild stomach discomfort, and restlessness, as indicated by an inability to sit or stand still for long. The particular constellation of symptoms present during anxiety tends to vary among people.

Fear and Anxiety

Anxiety is an alerting signal; it warns of impending danger and enables a person to take measures to deal with a threat. Fear is a similar alerting signal but should be differentiated from anxiety. Fear is a response to a known, external, definite, or nonconflictual threat; anxiety is a response to a threat that is unknown, internal, vague, or conflictual.

This distinction between fear and anxiety arose accidentally when Freud's early translator mistranslated *angst,* the German

Table 16.1–1
Psychoanalytic Neuroses and Disorders in DSM-IV

Classic Neuroses	DSM-IV Classification
Anxiety	Generalized anxiety disorder
Phobic	Agoraphobia, specific and social phobias
Obsessive-compulsive	Obsessive-compulsive disorder
Depressive	Dysthymic disorder
Hysterical (conversion)	Conversion disorder
Hysterical (dissociative)	Depersonalization disorder
Hypochondriacal	Hypochondriasis
Paraphilic	Sexual disorders

Table 16.1–2
Peripheral Manifestations of Anxiety

Diarrhea
Dizziness, light-headedness
Hyperhidrosis
Hyperreflexia
Hypertension
Palpitations
Pupillary mydriasis
Restlessness (eg, pacing)
Syncope
Tachycardia
Tingling in the extremities
Tremors
Upset stomach ("butterflies")
Urinary frequency, hesitancy, urgency

word for "fear," as anxiety. Freud himself generally ignored the distinction that associates anxiety with a repressed, unconscious object and fear with a known, external object. The distinction may be difficult to make because fear may also be due to an unconscious, repressed, internal object displaced to another object in the external world. For example, a boy may fear barking dogs because he actually fears his father and unconsciously associates his father with barking dogs.

Nevertheless, according to postfreudian psychoanalytic formulations, the separation of fear and anxiety is psychologically justifiable. The emotion caused by a rapidly approaching car as a person crosses the street differs from the vague discomfort a person may experience when meeting new people in a strange setting. The main psychological difference between the two emotional responses is the acuteness of fear and the chronicity of anxiety.

Charles Darwin pointed out that the word *fear* is derived from words meaning "sudden" and "dangerous." Duration also seems to be vital in the neurophysiological phenomena of anxiety and fear. In 1896 Darwin gave the following psychophysiological description of acute fear merging into terror:

> Fear is often preceded by astonishment, and is so far akin to it, that both lead to the senses of sight and learning being instantly aroused. In both cases the eyes and mouth are widely opened, and the eyebrows raised. The frightened man at the first stands like a statue motionless and breathless, or crouches down as if instinctively to escape observation. The heart beats quickly and violently, so that it palpitates or knocks against the ribs; but it is very doubtful whether it then works more efficiently than usual, so as to send a greater supply of blood to all parts of the body; for the skin instantly becomes pale, as during incipient faintness. This paleness of the surface, however, is probably in large part, or exclusively, due to the vasomotor center being affected in such a manner as to cause the contraction of the small arteries of the skin. That the skin is much affected under the sense of great fear, we see in the marvelous and inexplicable manner in which perspiration immediately exudes from it. This exudation is all the more remarkable, as the surface is then cold, and hence the term a cold sweat; whereas, the sudorific glands are properly excited into action when the surface is heated. The hairs also on the skin stand erect; and the superficial muscles shiver. In connection with the disturbed action of the heart, the breathing is hurried. The salivary glands act imperfectly; the mouth becomes dry, and is often opened and shut. I have also noticed that under slight fear there is a strong tendency to yawn. One of the best-marked symptoms is the trembling of all the muscles of the body; and this is often first seen in the lips. From this cause, and from the dryness of the mouth, the voice becomes husky or indistinct, or may altogether fail. . . .
>
> As fear increases into an agony of terror, we behold, as under all violent emotions, diversified results. The heart beats wildly or may fail to act and faintness ensues; there is a deathlike pallor; the breathing is labored; the wings of the nostrils are widely dilated; there is a gasping and convulsive motion on the lips, a tremor on the hollow cheek, a gulping and catching of the throat; the uncovered and protruding eyeballs are fixed on the object of terror; or they may roll restlessly from side to side. The pupils are said to be enormously dilated. All the muscles of the body may become rigid, or may be thrown into convulsive movements. The hands are alternately clenched and opened, often with a twitching movement. The arms may be protruded, as if to avert some dreadful danger, or may be thrown wildly over the head. . . . In other cases there is a sudden and uncontrollable tendency to headlong flight; and so strong is this, that the boldest soldiers may be seized with a sudden panic.

Adaptive Functions of Anxiety

When considered simply as an alerting signal, anxiety seems basically the same emotion as fear. As a warning of an external or internal threat, anxiety has lifesaving qualities. At a lower level, anxiety warns of threats of bodily damage, pain, helplessness, possible punishment, or the frustration of social or bodily needs; of separation from loved ones; of a menace to one's success or status; and ultimately of threats to unity or wholeness. It prompts a person to take the necessary steps to prevent the threat or to lessen its consequences. Examples of a person's warding off threats in daily life include getting down to the hard work of preparing for an examination, dodging a ball thrown at the head, sneaking into the dormitory after curfew to prevent punishment, and running to catch the last commuter train. Thus, anxiety prevents damage by alerting the person to carry out certain acts that forestall the danger.

Stress, Conflict, and Anxiety

Whether an event is perceived as stressful depends on the nature of the event and on the person's resources, psychological defenses, and coping mechanisms. All involve the ego, a collective abstraction for the process by which a person perceives, thinks, and acts on external events or internal drives. A person whose ego is functioning properly is in adaptive balance with both external and internal worlds; if the ego is not functioning properly and the resulting imbalance continues long enough, the person experiences chronic anxiety.

Whether the imbalance is external, between the pressures of the outside world and the person's ego, or internal, between the person's impulses (for example, aggressive, sexual, and dependent impulses) and conscience, the imbalance produces a conflict. Externally caused conflicts are usually interpersonal, whereas those that are internally caused are intrapsychic or intrapersonal. A combination of the two is possible, as in the case of employees whose excessively demanding and critical boss provokes impulses that they must control for fear of losing their jobs. Interpersonal and intrapsychic conflicts are, in fact, usually intertwined. Because human beings are social, their main conflicts are usually with other people.

Psychological and Cognitive Symptoms

The experience of anxiety has two components: the awareness of the physiological sensations (such as palpitations and sweating) and the awareness of being nervous or frightened. A feeling of shame may increase anxiety—"Others will recognize that I am frightened." Many people are astonished to find out that others are not aware of their anxiety or, if they are, do not appreciate its intensity.

In addition to motor and visceral effects, anxiety affects thinking, perception, and learning. It tends to produce confusion and distortions of perception, not only of time and space but of people and the meanings of events. These distortions can interfere with learning by lowering concentration, reducing recall, and impairing the ability to relate one item to another—that is, to make associations.

An important aspect of emotions is their effect on the selectivity of attention. Anxious people are apt to select certain things in their environment and overlook others in their effort to prove that they are justified in considering the situation frightening and in their response. If they falsely justify their fear, they augment their anxieties by the selective response and set up a vicious circle of anxiety, distorted perception, and increased anxiety. If, alternatively, they falsely reassure themselves by selective thinking, appropriate anxiety may be reduced, and they may fail to take necessary precautions.

PATHOLOGICAL ANXIETY

Epidemiology

The anxiety disorders make up one of the most common groups of psychiatric disorders. The National Comorbidity Study reported that one in four people has met the diagnostic criteria for at least one anxiety disorder and that there is a 12-month prevalence rate of 17.7 percent. Women (30.5 percent lifetime prevalence) are more likely to have an anxiety disorder than are men (19.2 percent lifetime prevalence). Finally the prevalence of anxiety disorders decreases with higher socioeconomic status.

Psychological Theories

Three major schools of psychological theory—psychoanalytic, behavioral, and existential—have contributed theories about the causes of anxiety. Each theory has both conceptual and practical usefulness in treating anxiety disorders.

Psychoanalytic Theories. Although Freud originally believed that anxiety stemmed from a physiological buildup of libido, he ultimately redefined anxiety as a signal of the presence of danger in the unconscious. Anxiety was viewed as the result of psychic conflict between unconscious sexual or aggressive wishes and corresponding threats from the superego or external reality. In response to this signal, the ego mobilized defense mechanisms to prevent unacceptable thoughts and feelings from emerging into conscious awareness. In his classic paper, "Inhibitions, Symptoms, and Anxiety," Freud states that "it was anxiety which produced repression and not, as I formerly believed, repression which produced anxiety." One of the unfortunate consequences of regarding the symptom of anxiety as a *disorder* rather than a *signal* is that the underlying sources of the anxiety may be ignored. From a psychodynamic perspective, the goal of therapy is not necessarily to eliminate all anxiety but to increase anxiety tolerance, that is, the capacity to experience anxiety and use it as a signal to investigate the underlying conflict that has created it. Anxiety appears in response to various situations during the life cycle, and an attempt to eradicate it by psychopharmacological means may do nothing to address the life situation or its internal correlates that have induced the state of anxiety.

To fully understand a particular patient's anxiety, it is often useful to think in terms of a developmental hierarchy that links the source of the anxiety to developmental issues. At the earliest level, disintegration anxiety may be present. This anxiety may derive either from the fear of losing the sense of self or of boundedness through merger with an object or from concern that the self will fragment because others are not responding with the needed affirmation and validation. At a somewhat more advanced level, persecutory or paranoid anxiety may be connected with the perception that a person is at risk of being invaded and annihilated by an outside malevolent force. A still more advanced source of anxiety is less of a problem, but a child may be anxious from fear of losing the love or approval of a parent or loved object. Castration anxiety, linked to the oedipal phase of development in boys, concerns the fear of a retaliatory parental figure, usually the father, damaging the little boy's genitals or otherwise causing bodily harm. At the most mature level, superego anxiety is understood as related to guilt feelings about not living up to internalized standards of moral behavior derived from the parents. Often a psychodynamic interview can elucidate the principal level of anxiety with which a patient is dealing. Some anxiety is obviously related to multiple conflicts at various developmental levels.

Behavioral Theories. The behavioral or learning theories of anxiety have spawned some of the most effective treatments for anxiety disorders. According to these theories, anxiety is a conditioned response to specific environmental stimuli. In a model of classic conditioning, people without food allergies may become sick after eating contaminated shellfish in a restaurant. Subsequent exposures to shellfish may cause these people to feel sick. Through generalization, they may come to distrust all food prepared by others. As an alternative causal possibility, they may learn to have an internal response of anxiety by imitating the anxiety responses of their parents (social learning theory). In either case, treatment is usually a form of desensitization by repeated exposure to the anxiogenic stimulus, coupled with cognitive psychotherapeutic approaches.

In recent years, proponents of behavioral theories have shown increasing interest in cognitive approaches to conceptualizing and treating anxiety disorders, and cognitive theorists have proposed alternatives to traditional learning theory causal models of anxiety. According to conceptualizations of nonphobic anxiety states, faulty, distorted, or counterproductive thinking patterns accompany or precede maladaptive behaviors and emotional disorders. According to one model, patients with anxiety disorders tend to overestimate the degree of danger and the probability of harm in a given situation and tend to underestimate their abilities to cope with perceived threats to their physical or psychological well-being. This model asserts that patients with panic disorder often have thoughts of loss of control and fears of dying that follow inexplicable physiological sensations (such as palpitations, tachycardia, and light-headedness) but that precede and then accompany panic attacks.

Existential Theories. Existential theories of anxiety provide models for generalized anxiety disorder, in which there is no specifically identifiable stimulus for a chronically anxious feeling. The central concept of existential theory is that people become aware of feelings of profound nothingness in their lives, feelings that may be even more discomforting than an acceptance of their inevitable death. Anxiety is their response to the vast void in existence and meaning. Such existential concerns may have increased since the development of nuclear weapons.

Biological Theories

Biological theories of anxiety have developed from preclinical studies with animal models of anxiety, the study of patients in whom biological factors were ascertained, the growing knowledge about basic neuroscience, and the actions of psychotherapeutic drugs. One pole of thought posits that measurable biological changes in patients with anxiety disorders reflect the results of psychological conflicts; the opposite pole posits that the biological events precede the psychological conflicts. Both situations may exist in specific persons, and a range of biologically based sensitivities may exist among persons with the symptoms of anxiety disorders.

Autonomic Nervous System. Stimulation of the autonomic nervous system causes certain symptoms—cardiovascular (for example, tachycardia), muscular (for example, headache), gastrointestinal (for example, diarrhea), and respiratory (for example, tachypnea). These peripheral manifestations of anxiety are neither peculiar to anxiety disorders nor necessarily correlated with the subjective experience of anxiety. In the first third of the 20th century, Walter Cannon demonstrated that cats exposed to barking dogs exhibit behavioral and physiological signs of fear that are associated with the adrenal release of epinephrine. The James-Lange theory states that subjective anxiety is a response to peripheral phenomena. It is currently generally thought that central nervous system anxiety precedes the peripheral manifestations of anxiety, except when a specific peripheral cause is present, such as when a patient has a pheochromocytoma. The autonomic nervous systems of some patients with anxiety disorder, especially those with panic disorder, exhibit increased sympathetic tone, adapt slowly to repeated stimuli, and respond excessively to moderate stimuli.

Neurotransmitters. The three major neurotransmitters associated with anxiety on the bases of animal studies and responses to drug treatment are norepinephrine, serotonin, and γ-aminobutyric acid (GABA). Much of the basic neuroscience information about anxiety comes from animal experiments involving behavioral paradigms and psychoactive agents. One such animal model of anxiety is the conflict test, in which the animal is simultaneously presented with stimuli that are positive (for example, food) and negative (for example, electric shock). Anxiolytic drugs (for example, benzodiazepines) tend to facilitate the adaptation of the animal to this situation, whereas other drugs (for example, amphetamines) further disrupt the animal's behavioral responses.

NOREPINEPHRINE. The general theory about the role of norepinephrine in anxiety disorders is that affected patients may have a poorly regulated noradrenergic system with occasional bursts of activity. The cell bodies of the noradrenergic system are primarily localized to the locus ceruleus in the rostral pons, and they project their axons to the cerebral cortex, the limbic system, the brainstem, and the spinal cord. Experiments in primates have demonstrated that stimulation of the locus ceruleus produces a fear response in the animals and that ablation of the same area inhibits or completely blocks the ability of the animals to form a fear response.

Human studies have found that, in patients with panic disorder, β-adrenergic agonists (for example, isoproterenol [Isuprel]) and α_2-adrenergic antagonists (for example, yohimbine [Yocon]) can provoke frequent and severe panic attacks. Conversely, clonidine (Catapres), an α_2-adrenergic agonist, reduces anxiety symptoms in some experimental and therapeutic situations. A less consistent finding is that patients with anxiety disorders, particularly panic disorder, have elevated cerebrospinal fluid (CSF) or urinary levels of the noradrenergic metabolite 3-methoxy-4-hydroxyphenylglycol (MHPG).

SEROTONIN. The identification of many serotonin receptor types has stimulated the search for the role of serotonin in the pathogenesis of anxiety disorders. The interest in this relation was initially motivated by the observation that serotonergic antidepressants have therapeutic effects in some anxiety disorders—for example, clomipramine (Anafranil) in obsessive-compulsive disorder. The effectiveness of buspirone (BuSpar), a serotonergic type 1A ($5\text{-}HT_{1A}$) receptor agonist, in the treatment of anxiety disorders also suggests the possibility of an association between serotonin and anxiety. The cell bodies of most serotonergic neurons are located in the raphe nuclei in the rostral brainstem and project to the cerebral cortex, the limbic system (especially the amygdala and the hippocampus), and the hypothalamus. Although the administration of serotonergic agents to animals results in behavior suggestive of anxiety, the data on similar effects in humans are less robust. Several reports indicate that *m*-chlorophenylpiperazine (mCPP), a drug with multiple serotonergic and nonserotonergic effects, and fenfluramine (Pondimin), which causes the release of serotonin, do cause increased anxiety in patients with anxiety disorders; and many anecdotal reports indicate that serotonergic hallucinogens and stimulants—for example, lysergic acid diethylamide (LSD) and 3,4-methylenedioxymethamphetamine (MDMA)—are associated with the development of both acute and chronic anxiety disorders in people who use these drugs.

γ-AMINOBUTYRIC ACID (GABA). A role of GABA in anxiety disorders is most strongly supported by the undisputed efficacy of benzodiazepines, which enhance the activity of GABA at the $GABA_A$ receptor, in the treatment of some types of anxiety disorders. Although low-potency benzodiazepines are most effective for the symptoms of generalized anxiety disorder, high-potency benzodiazepines, such as alprazolam (Xanax), are effective in the treatment of panic disorder. Studies in primates have found that autonomic nervous system symptoms of anxiety disorders are induced when a benzodiazepine inverse agonist, β-carboline-3-carboxylic acid (BCCE), is administered. BCCE also causes anxiety in normal control volunteers. A benzodiazepine antagonist, flumazenil, causes frequent severe panic attacks in patients with panic disorder. These data have led researchers to hypothesize that some patients with anxiety disorders have abnormal functioning of their $GABA_A$ receptors, although this connection has not been shown directly.

APLYSIA. A neurotransmitter model for anxiety disorders is based on the study of *Aplysia california,* a sea snail that reacts to danger by moving away, withdrawing into its shell, and decreasing its feeding behavior. These behaviors can be classically conditioned, so that the snail responds to a neutral stimulus as if it were a dangerous stimulus. The snail can also be sensitized by random shocks, so that it exhibits a flight response in the absence of real danger. Parallels have previously been drawn between classical conditioning and human phobic anxiety. The classically conditioned aplysia shows measurable changes in presynaptic facilitation, resulting in the release of increased amounts of neurotransmitter. Although the sea snail is a simple animal, this work shows an experimental approach to complex neurochemical processes potentially involved in anxiety disorders in humans.

Brain-Imaging Studies. A range of brain-imaging studies, almost always conducted with a specific anxiety disorder, have produced several possible leads in the understanding of anxiety disorders. Structural studies—for example, computed tomography and magnetic resonance imaging (MRI)—have occasionally shown some increase in the size of cerebral ventricles. In one study, the increase was correlated with the length of time patients had been taking benzodiazepines. In one MRI study, a specific defect in the right temporal lobe was noted in patients with panic disorder. Several other brain-imaging studies have reported abnormal findings in the right hemisphere but not the left hemisphere; this finding suggests that some types of cerebral asymmetry may be important in the development of anxiety disorder symptoms in specific patients. Functional brain-imaging studies—for example, positron emission tomography, single photon emission computed tomography, and electroencephalography—of patients with anxiety disorder have variously reported abnormalities in the frontal cortex, the occipital and temporal areas, and, in a study of panic disorder, the parahippocampal gyrus. Several functional neuroimaging studies have implicated the caudate nucleus in the pathophysiology of obsessive-compulsive disorder. A conservative interpretation of these data is that some patients with anxiety disorders have a demonstrable functional cerebral pathological condition and that the condition may be causally relevant to their anxiety disorder symptoms.

Genetic Studies. Genetic studies have produced solid data that at least some genetic component contributes to the development of anxiety disorders. Almost half of all patients with panic disorder have at least one affected relative. The figures for other anxiety disorders, although not as high, also indicate a higher frequency of the illness in first-degree relatives of affected patients than occurs in the relatives of nonaffected persons. Although adoption studies with anxiety disorders have not been reported, data from twin registers also support the hypothesis that anxiety disorders are at least partially genetically determined. A recent report has attributed about 4 percent of the intrinsic variability of anxiety within the general population to a polymorphic variant of the gene for the serotonin transporter, which is the site of action of many serotonergic drugs. People with the variant produce less transporter and have higher levels of anxiety.

Neuroanatomical Considerations. The locus ceruleus and the raphe nuclei project primarily to the limbic system and the cerebral cortex. In combination with the data from brain-imaging studies, these areas have become the focus of much hypothesis-building about the neuroanatomical substrates of anxiety disorders.

LIMBIC SYSTEM. In addition to receiving noradrenergic and serotonergic innervation, the limbic system also contains a high concentration of $GABA_A$ receptors. Ablation and stimulation studies in nonhuman primates have also implicated the limbic system in the generation of anxiety and fear responses. Two areas of the limbic system have received special attention in the literature: increased activity in the septohippocampal pathway, which may lead to anxiety, and the cingulate gyrus, which has been implicated particularly in the pathophysiology of obsessive-compulsive disorder.

CEREBRAL CORTEX. The frontal cerebral cortex is connected with the parahippocampal region, the cingulate gyrus, and the hypothalamus and therefore may be involved in the production of anxiety disorders. The temporal cortex has also been implicated as a pathophysiological site in anxiety disorders. This association is based in part on the similarity in clinical presentation and electrophysiology between some patients with temporal lobe epilepsy and patients with obsessive-compulsive disorder.

DSM-IV

DSM-IV lists the following anxiety disorders: panic disorder with and without agoraphobia, agoraphobia without a history of panic disorder, specific and social phobias, obsessive-compulsive disorder, posttraumatic stress disorder, acute stress disorder, generalized anxiety disorder (all discussed in other sections in this chapter), anxiety disorder due to a general medical condition, substance-induced anxiety disorder, and anxiety disorder not otherwise specified, including mixed anxiety-depressive disorder (all subsequently discussed in this section).

Virtually everyone who drinks alcohol has, on at least a few occasions, used it to reduce anxiety, most often social anxiety. In contrast, carefully controlled studies have found that the effects of alcohol on anxiety are variable and can be significantly affected by gender, the amount of alcohol ingested, and cultural attitudes. Nevertheless, alcohol use disorders and other substance-related disorders are commonly associated with anxiety disorders. Alcohol use disorders are about 4 times more common among patients with panic disorder than among the general population, about 3.5 times more common among patients with obsessive-compulsive disorder, and about 2.5 times more common among patients with phobias. Several studies have reported data indicating that genetic diatheses for both anxiety disorders and alcohol use disorders may cosegregate in some families.

Anxiety Disorder Due to a General Medical Condition

As with other major syndromes (such as psychosis and mood disorder symptoms), anxiety disorder due to a general medical condition is included within the relevant section to encourage the formulation and consideration of a complete differential diagnosis.

Epidemiology. The occurrence of anxiety symptoms related to general medical conditions is common, although the incidence of the disorder varies for each specific general medical condition.

Etiology. A wide range of medical conditions can cause symptoms similar to those of anxiety disorders (Table 16.1–3). Hyperthyroidism, hypothyroidism, hypoparathyroidism, and vitamin B_{12} deficiency are frequently associated with anxiety symptoms. A pheochromocytoma produces epinephrine, which can cause paroxysmal episodes of anxiety symptoms. Certain lesions of the brain and postencephalitic states reportedly produce symptoms identical to those seen in obsessive-compulsive disorder. Other medical conditions, such as cardiac arrhythmia, can produce physiological symptoms of panic disorder. Hypoglycemia can also mimic the symptoms of an anxiety disorder. The diverse medical conditions that can cause symptoms of anxiety disorder may do so through a common mechanism, the noradrenergic system, although the effects on the serotonergic system are also under study.

Diagnosis. The DSM-IV diagnosis of anxiety disorder due to a general medical condition (Table 16.1–4) requires the presence of symptoms of an anxiety disorder. DSM-IV allows clinicians to specify whether the disorder is characterized by symptoms of generalized anxiety, panic attacks, or obsessive-compulsive symptoms.

Clinicians should have an increased level of suspicion for the diagnosis when chronic or paroxysmal anxiety is associated with a physical disease known to cause such symptoms in some patients. Paroxysmal bouts of hypertension in an anxious patient may indicate that a workup for a pheochromocytoma is appropriate. A general medical workup may reveal diabetes, an adrenal tumor, thyroid disease, or a neurological condition. For example, some patients with complex partial epilepsy have extreme episodes of anxiety or fear as their only manifestation of the epileptic activity.

Clinical Features. The symptoms of anxiety disorder due to a general medical condition can be identical to those of the primary anxiety disorders. A syndrome similar to panic disorder is the most common clinical picture, and a syndrome similar to a phobia is the least common.

PANIC ATTACKS. Patients who have cardiomyopathy may have the highest incidence of panic disorder secondary to a general medical condition. One study reported that 83 percent of patients with cardiomyopathy awaiting cardiac transplantation had panic disorder symptoms. Increased noradrenergic tone in these patients may be the provoking stimulus for the panic attacks. In some studies, about 25 percent of patients with Parkinson's disease and chronic obstructive pulmonary disease have symptoms of panic disorder. Other medical disorders associated with panic disorder include chronic pain, primary biliary cirrhosis, and epilepsy, particularly when the focus is in the right parahippocampal gyrus.

GENERALIZED ANXIETY. A high prevalence of generalized anxiety disorder symptoms in patients with Sjögren's syndrome has been reported, and this rate may be related to the effects of Sjögren's syndrome on cortical and

Table 16.1–3
Disorders Associated with Anxiety

Neurological disorders	Miscellaneous conditions
Cerebral neoplasms	Hypoglycemia
Cerebral trauma and postconcussive syndromes	Carcinoid syndrome
Cerebrovascular disease	Systemic malignancies
Subarachnoid hemorrhage	Premenstrual syndrome
Migraine	Febrile illnesses and chronic infections
Encephalitis	Porphyria
Cerebral syphilis	Infectious mononucleosis
Multiple sclerosis	Posthepatitis syndrome
Wilson's disease	Uremia
Huntington's disease	Toxic conditions
Epilepsy	Alcohol and drug withdrawal
Systemic conditions	Amphetamines
Hypoxia	Sympathomimetic agents
Cardiovascular disease	Vasopressor agents
Cardiac arrhythmias	Caffeine and caffeine withdrawal
Pulmonary insufficiency	Penicillin
Anemia	Sulfonamides
Endocrine disturbances	Cannabis
Pituitary dysfunction	Mercury
Thyroid dysfunction	Arsenic
Parathyroid dysfunction	Phosphorus
Adrenal dysfunction	Organophosphates
Pheochromocytoma	Carbon disulfide
Virilization disorders of females	Benzene
Inflammatory disorders	Aspirin intolerance
Lupus erythematosus	Idiopathic psychiatric disorders
Rheumatoid arthritis	Depression
Polyarteritis nodosa	Mania
Temporal arteritis	Schizophrenia
Deficiency states	Anxiety disorders
Vitamin B_{12} deficiency	Generalized anxiety
Pellagra	Panic attacks
	Phobic disorders
	Posttraumatic stress disorder

Reprinted with permission from Cumming, JL: *Clinical Neuropsychiatry*, p 214. Grune & Stratton, Orlando, 1985.

subcortical functions and on thyroid function. The highest prevalence of generalized anxiety disorder symptoms in a medical disorder seems to be in Graves' disease, in which as many as two thirds of all patients meet the criteria for generalized anxiety disorder.

OBSESSIVE-COMPULSIVE SYMPTOMS. Reports have associated the development of obsessive-compulsive disorder symptoms with Sydenham's chorea and multiple sclerosis.

PHOBIAS. Symptoms of phobias appear to be uncommon, although one study reported a 17 percent prevalence of symptoms of social phobia in patients with Parkinson's disease.

Differential Diagnosis. Anxiety as a symptom can be associated with many psychiatric disorders, in addition to the anxiety disorders themselves. A mental status examination is necessary to determine the presence of mood symptoms or psychotic symptoms that may suggest another psychiatric diagnosis. For a clinician to conclude that a patient has an anxiety disorder due to a general medical condition, the patient should clearly have anxiety as the predominant symptom and should have a specific causative nonpsychiatric medical disorder. To ascertain the degree to which a general medical con-

Table 16.1–4
DSM-IV Diagnostic Criteria for Anxiety Disorder Due to a General Medical Condition

A. Prominent anxiety, panic attacks, or obsessions or compulsions predominate in the clinical picture.
B. There is evidence from the history, physical examination, or laboratory findings that the disturbance is the direct physiological consequence of a general medical condition.
C. The disturbance is not better accounted for by another mental disorder (eg, adjustment disorder with anxiety, in which the stressor is a serious general medical condition).
D. The disturbance does not occur exclusively during the course of a delirium.
E. The disturbance causes clinically significant distress or impairment in social, occupational, or other important areas of functioning.

Specify if:
With generalized anxiety: if excessive anxiety or worry about a number of events or activities predominates in the clinical presentation
With panic attacks: if panic attacks predominate in the clinical presentation
With obsessive-compulsive symptoms: if obsessions or compulsions predominate in the clinical presentation

Reprinted with permission from American Psychiatric Association: *Diagnostic and Statistical Manual of Mental Disorders,* ed 4. Copyright, American Psychiatric Association, Washington, 1994.

dition is causative for the anxiety, the clinician should know whether the medical condition and the anxiety symptoms have been related closely in the literature, the age of onset (primary anxiety disorders usually have their onset before age 35), and the patient's family history of both anxiety disorders and relevant general medical conditions (for example, hyperthyroidism). A diagnosis of adjustment disorder with anxiety must also be considered in the differential diagnosis.

Course and Prognosis. The unremitting experience of anxiety can be disabling and can interfere with every aspect of life, including social, occupational, and psychological functioning. A sudden increase in level of anxiety may prompt an affected person to seek medical or psychiatric help more quickly than when the onset is insidious. The treatment or the removal of the primary medical cause of the anxiety usually initiates a clear course of improvement in the anxiety disorder symptoms. In some cases, however, the anxiety disorder symptoms continue even after the primary medical condition is treated—for example, after an episode of encephalitis. Some symptoms, particularly obsessive-compulsive disorder symptoms, linger for a longer time than do other anxiety disorder symptoms. When anxiety disorder symptoms are present for a significant period after the medical disorder has been treated, the remaining symptoms should probably be treated as if they were primary—that is, with psychotherapy or pharmacotherapy or both.

Treatment. The primary treatment for anxiety disorder due to a general medical condition is the treatment of the underlying medical condition. If a patient also has an alcohol or other substance use disorder, this disorder must also be therapeutically addressed to gain control of the anxiety disorder symptoms. If the removal of the primary medical condition does not reverse the anxiety disorder symptoms, treatment of these symptoms should follow the treatment guidelines for the specific mental disorder. In general, behavioral modification techniques, anxiolytic agents, and serotonergic antidepressants have been the most effective treatment modalities.

Substance-Induced Anxiety Disorder

DSM-IV includes the substance-induced mental disorders in the categories for the relevant mental disorder syndromes. Substance-induced anxiety disorder, therefore, is contained in the category of anxiety disorders.

Epidemiology. Substance-induced anxiety disorder is common, both as the result of the ingestion of so-called recreational drugs and as the result of prescription drug use.

Etiology. A wide range of substances can cause symptoms of anxiety that mimic any of the DSM-IV anxiety disorders. Although sympathomimetics (such as amphetamine, cocaine, and caffeine) have been most associated with the production of anxiety disorder symptoms, many serotonergic drugs (for example, LSD and MDMA) can also cause both acute and chronic anxiety syndromes in users of these drugs. A wide range of prescription medications is also associated with the production of anxiety disorder symptoms in susceptible persons.

Diagnosis. The DSM-IV diagnostic criteria for substance-induced anxiety disorder require the presence of prominent anxiety, panic attacks, obsessions, or compulsions (Table 16.1–5). The DSM-IV guidelines state that the symptoms should have developed during the use of the substance or within a month of the cessation of substance use, but DSM-IV encourages clinicians to use appropriate clinical judgment to assess the relation between substance exposure and anxiety symptoms. The structure of the diagnosis includes specification of the substance (for example, cocaine), specification of the appropriate state during the onset (for example, intoxication), and mention of the specific symptom pattern (for example, panic attacks).

Clinical Features. The associated clinical features of substance-induced anxiety disorder vary with the particular substance involved. Even infrequent use of psychostimulants can result in anxiety disorder symptoms in some persons. Associated with the anxiety disorder symptoms may also be cognitive impairments in comprehension, calculation, and memory. These cognitive deficits are usually reversible when the substance use is stopped.

Differential Diagnosis. The differential diagnosis for substance-induced anxiety disorder includes the primary anxiety disorders, anxiety disorder due to a general medical condition (for which the patient may be receiving an implicated drug), and mood disorders, which are frequently accompanied

Table 16.1–5
DSM-IV Diagnostic Criteria for Substance-Induced Anxiety Disorder

A. Prominent anxiety, panic attacks, obsessions or compulsions predominate in the clinical picture.

B. There is evidence from the history, physical examination, or laboratory findings of either (1) or (2):
 (1) the symptoms in criterion A developed during, or within 1 month of, substance intoxication or withdrawal
 (2) medication use is etiologically related to the disturbance

C. The disturbance is not better accounted for by an anxiety disorder that is not substance induced. Evidence that the symptoms are better accounted for by an anxiety disorder that is not substance induced might include the following: the symptoms precede the onset of the substance use (or medication use); the symptoms persist for a substantial period of time (eg, about a month) after the cessation of acute withdrawal or severe intoxication or are substantially in excess of what would be expected given the type or amount of the substance used or the duration of use; or there is other evidence suggesting the existence of an independent non–substance-induced anxiety disorder (eg, a history of recurrent non–substance-related episodes).

D. The disturbance does not occur exclusively during the course of a delirium.

E. The disturbance causes clinically significant distress or impairment in social, occupational, or other important areas of functioning.

Note: This diagnosis should be made instead of a diagnosis of substance intoxication or substance withdrawal only when the anxiety symptoms are in excess of those usually associated with the intoxication or withdrawal syndrome and when the anxiety symptoms are sufficiently severe to warrant independent clinical attention.

Code [Specific substance-induced anxiety disorder (alcohol; amphetamine (or amphetamine-like substance); caffeine; cannabis; cocaine; hallucinogen; inhalant; phencyclidine (or phencyclidine-like substance); sedative, hypnotic, or anxiolytic; other [or unknown] substance)

Specify if:
 With generalized anxiety: if excessive anxiety or worry about a number of events or activities predominates in the clinical presentation
 With panic attacks: if panic attacks predominate in the clinical presentation
 With obsessive-compulsive symptoms: if obsessions or compulsions predominate in the clinical presentation
 With phobic symptoms: If phobic symptoms predominate in the clinical presentation

Specify if:
 With onset during intoxication: if the criteria are met for intoxication with the substance and the symptoms develop during the intoxication syndrome
 With onset during withdrawal: if criteria are met for withdrawal from the substance and the symptoms develop during, or shortly after, a withdrawal syndrome

by symptoms of anxiety disorders. Personality disorders and malingering must be considered in the differential diagnosis, particularly in some urban emergency rooms.

Course and Prognosis. The course and prognosis generally depend on the removal of the causally involved substance and the long-term ability of the affected person to limit the use of the substance. The anxiogenic effects of most drugs are reversible. When the anxiety does not reverse with the cessation of the drug, clinicians should reconsider the diagnosis of substance-induced anxiety disorder or consider the possibility that the substance causes irreversible brain damage.

Treatment. The primary treatment for substance-induced anxiety disorder is the removal of the causally involved substance. Treatment then must focus on finding an alternative treatment if the substance was a medically indicated drug, on limiting the patient's exposure if the substance was introduced through environmental exposure, or on treating the underlying substance-related disorder. If anxiety disorder symptoms continue even though substance use has stopped, treatment of the anxiety disorder symptoms with appropriate psychotherapeutic or pharmacotherapeutic modalities may be appropriate.

Anxiety Disorder Not Otherwise Specified

Some patients have symptoms of anxiety disorders that do not meet the criteria for any specific DSM-IV anxiety disorder or adjustment disorder with anxiety or mixed anxiety and depressed mood. Such patients are most appropriately classified as having anxiety disorder not otherwise specified. DSM-IV includes four examples of conditions that are appropriate for the diagnosis (Table 16.1–6). One of the examples is mixed anxiety-depressive disorder.

Mixed Anxiety-Depressive Disorder. DSM-IV follows the lead of the 10th revision of *International Statistical Classification of Diseases and Related Health Problems* (ICD-10) by including mixed anxiety-depressive disorder in the DSM-IV appendix and as an example of anxiety disorder not otherwise specified. This disorder describes patients with the condition of both anxiety and depressive symptoms who do not meet the diagnostic criteria for either an anxiety disorder or a mood disorder. The combination of depressive and anxiety symptoms results in a significant functional impairment for the affected person. The condition may be particularly prevalent in primary care practices and outpatient mental health clinics. Opponents have argued that the availability of the diagnosis may discourage clinicians from taking the necessary time to obtain a complete psychiatric history to differentiate true depressive disorders from true anxiety disorders.

Epidemiology. The coexistence of major depressive disorder and panic disorder is common. As many as two thirds of all patients with depressive symptoms have prominent anxiety symptoms, and one third may meet the diagnostic criteria for panic disorder. Researchers have reported that from 20 to

Table 16.1–6
DSM-IV Diagnostic Criteria for Anxiety Disorder Not Otherwise Specified

This category includes disorders with prominent anxiety or phobic avoidance that do not meet criteria for any specific anxiety disorder, adjustment disorder with anxiety, or adjustment disorder with mixed anxiety and depressed mood. Examples include

1. MIxed anxiety-depressive disorder: clinically significant symptoms of anxiety and depression, but the criteria are not met for either a specific mood disorder or a specific anxiety disorder.
2. Clinically significant social phobic symptoms that are related to the social impact of having a general medical condition or mental disorder (eg, Parkinson's disease, dermatological conditions, stuttering, anorexia nervosa, body dysmorphic disorder).
3. Situations in which the clinician has concluded that an anxiety disorder is present but is unable to determine whether it is primary, due to a general medical condition, or substance induced.

90 percent of all patients with panic disorder have episodes of major depressive disorder. These data suggest that the coexistence of depressive and anxiety symptoms, neither of which meet the diagnostic criteria for other depressive or anxiety disorders, may be common. At this time, however, formal epidemiological data on mixed anxiety-depressive disorder are not available. Nevertheless, some clinicians and researchers have estimated that the prevalence of the disorder in the general population is as high as 10 percent and in primary care clinics as high as 50 percent, although conservative estimates suggest a prevalence of about 1 percent in the general population.

Etiology. Four principal lines of evidence suggest that anxiety symptoms and depressive symptoms are causally linked in some affected patients. First, several investigators have reported similar neuroendocrine findings in depressive disorders and anxiety disorders, particularly panic disorder, including blunted cortisol response to adrenocorticotropic hormone, blunted growth hormone response to clonidine, and blunted thyroid-stimulating hormone and prolactin responses to thyrotropin-releasing hormone. Second, several investigators have reported data indicating that hyperactivity of the noradrenergic system is causally relevant to some patients with depressive disorders and with panic disorder. Specifically, these studies have found elevated concentrations of the norepinephrine metabolite MHPG in the urine, the plasma, or the CSF of depressed patients and panic disorder patients who were actively experiencing a panic attack. As with other anxiety and depressive disorders, serotonin and GABA may also be causally involved in mixed anxiety-depressive disorder. Third, many studies have found that serotonergic drugs, such as fluoxetine (Prozac) and clomipramine (Anafranil), are useful in treating both depressive and anxiety disorders. Fourth, a number of family studies have reported data indicating that anxiety and depressive symptoms are genetically linked in at least some families.

Diagnosis. The DSM-IV criteria (Table 16.1–7) require the presence of subsyndromal symptoms of both anxiety and depression and the presence of some autonomic symptoms, such as tremor, palpitations, dry mouth, and the sensation of a churning stomach. Some preliminary studies have indicated that the sensitivity of general practitioners to a syndrome of mixed anxiety-depressive disorder is low, although this lack of recognition may reflect the lack of an appropriate diagnostic label for the patients.

Clinical Features. The clinical features of mixed anxiety-depressive disorder combine symptoms of anxiety disorders and some symptoms of depressive disorders. In addition, symptoms of autonomic nervous system hyperactivity, such as gastrointestinal complaints, are common and contribute to the high frequency with which the patients are seen in outpatient medical clinics.

Differential Diagnosis. The differential diagnosis includes other anxiety and depressive disorders and personality disorders. Among the anxiety disorders, generalized anxiety disorder is most likely to overlap with mixed anxiety-depressive disorder. Among the mood disorders, dysthymic disorder and minor depressive disorder are most likely to overlap with mixed anxiety-depressive disorder. Among the personality dis-

Table 16.1–7
DSM-IV Research Criteria for Mixed Anxiety-Depressive Disorder

A. Persistent or recurrent dysphoric mood lasting at least 1 month.

B. The dysphoric mood is accompanied by at least 1 month of four (or more) of the following symptoms:
 (1) difficulty concentrating or mind going blank
 (2) sleep disturbance (difficulty falling or staying asleep, or restless unsatisfying sleep)
 (3) fatigue or low energy
 (4) irritability
 (5) worry
 (6) being easily moved to tears
 (7) hypervigilance
 (8) anticipating the worst
 (9) hopelessness (pervasive pessimism about the future)
 (10) low self-esteem or feelings of worthlessness

C. The symptoms cause clinically significant distress or impairment in social, occupational, or other important areas of functioning.

D. The symptoms are not due to the direct physiological effects of a substance (e.g., a drug of abuse, a medication) or a general medical condition.

E. All of the following:
 (1) criteria have never been met for major depressive disorder, dysthymic disorder, panic disorder, or generalized anxiety disorder
 (2) criteria are not currently met for any other anxiety or mood disorder (including an anxiety or mood disorder, in partial remission)
 (3) the symptoms are not better accounted for by any other mental disorder

Table 16.1–8
ICD-10 Diagnostic Criteria for Phobic Anxiety Disorders

Agoraphobia

A. There is marked and consistently manifest fear in, or avoidance of, at least two of the following situations:
(1) crowds;
(2) public places;
(3) traveling alone;
(4) traveling away from home.

B. At least two symptoms of anxiety in the feared situation must have been present together, on at least one occasion since the onset of the disorder, and one of the symptoms must have been from items (1) to (4) listed below:

Autonomic arousal symptoms
(1) palpitations or pounding heart, or accelerated heart rate;
(2) sweating;
(3) trembling or shaking;
(4) dry mouth (not due to medication or dehydration);

Symptoms involving chest and abdomen
(5) difficulty in breathing;
(6) feeling of choking;
(7) chest pain or discomfort;
(8) nausea or abdominal distress (eg, churning in stomach);

Symptoms involving mental state
(9) feeling dizzy, unsteady, faint, or light-headed;
(10) feelings that objects are unreal (derealization), or that the self is distant or "not really here" (depersonalization);
(11) fear of losing control, "going crazy," or passing out;
(12) fear of dying;

General symptoms
(13) hot flushes or cold chills;
(14) numbness or tingling sensations.

C. Significant emotional distress is caused by the avoidance or by the anxiety symptoms, and the individual recognizes that these are excessive or unreasonable.

D. Symptoms are restricted to, or predominate in, the feared situations or contemplation of the feared situations.

E. *Most commonly used exclusion clause.* Fear or avoidance of situations (criterion A) is not the result of delusions, hallucinations, or other disorders such as organic mental disorders, schizophrenia and related disorders, mood [affective] disorders, or obsessive-compulsive disorder, and is not secondary to cultural beliefs.

The presence or absence of panic disorder in a majority of agoraphobic situations may be specified by using a fifth character:
Without panic disorder
With panic disorder

Options for rating severity
Severity in agoraphobia may be rated by indicating the degree of avoidance, taking into account the specific cultural setting. Severity in social phobias may be rated by counting the number of panic attacks.

Social phobias

A. Either of the following must be present:
(1) marked fear of being the focus of attention, or fear of behaving in a way that will be embarrassing or humiliating;
(2) marked avoidance of being the focus of attention, or of situations in which there is fear of behaving in an embarrassing or humiliating way.

These fears are manifested in social situations, such as eating or speaking in public, encountering known individuals in public, or entering or enduring small group situations (eg, parties, meetings, classrooms).

B. At least two symptoms of anxiety in the feared situation as defined in agoraphobia, criterion B, must have been manifest at some time since the onset of the disorder, together with at least one of the following symptoms:
(1) blushing or shaking;
(2) fear of vomiting;
(3) urgency or fear of micturition or defecation.

C. Significant emotional distress is caused by the symptoms or by the avoidance, and the individual recognizes that these are excessive or unreasonable.

D. Symptoms are restricted to, or predominate in, the feared situations or contemplation of the feared situations.

E. *Most commonly used exclusion clause.* The symptoms listed in criteria A and B are not the result of delusions, hallucinations, or other disorders such as organic mental disorders, schizophrenia and related disorders, mood [affective] disorders, or obsessive-compulsive disorder, and are not secondary to cultural beliefs.

Specific (isolated) phobias

A. Either of the following must be present:
(1) marked fear of a specific object or situation not included in agoraphobia or social phobia;
(2) marked avoidance of a specific object or situation not included in agoraphobia or social phobia.

Among the most common objects and situations are animals, birds, insects, heights, thunder, flying, small enclosed spaces, the sight of blood or injury, injections, dentists, and hospitals.

B. Symptoms of anxiety in the feared situation as defined in agoraphobia, criterion B, must have been manifest at some time since the onset of the disorder.

C. Significant emotional distress is caused by the symptoms or by the avoidance, and the individual recognizes that these are excessive or unreasonable.

D. Symptoms are restricted to the feared situation or contemplation of the feared situation.

If desired, the specific phobias may be subdivided as follows:
— animal type (eg, insects, dogs)
— nature-forces type (eg, storms, water)
— blood, injection, and injury type
— situational type (eg, elevators, tunnels)
— other type

Other phobic anxiety disorders

Phobic anxiety disorder, unspecified

Table 16.1–9
ICD-10 Diagnostic Criteria for Other Anxiety Disorders

Panic disorder [episodic paroxysmal anxiety]

A. The individual experiences recurrent panic attacks that are not consistently associated with a specific situation or object and that often occur spontaneously (ie, the episodes are unpredictable). The panic attacks are not associated with marked exertion or with exposure to dangerous or life-threatening situations.

B. A panic attack is characterized by all of the following:
(1) it is a discrete episode of intense fear of discomfort;
(2) it starts abruptly;
(3) it reaches a maximum within a few minutes and lasts at least some minutes;
(4) at least four of the symptoms listed below must be present, one of which must be from items (a) to (d):

Autonomic arousal symptoms
(a) palpitations or pounding heart, or accelerated heart rate;
(b) sweating;
(c) trembling or shaking;
(d) dry mouth (not due to medication or dehydration);

Symptoms involving chest and abdomen
(e) difficulty in breathing;
(f) feeling of choking;
(g) chest pain or discomfort;
(h) nausea or abdominal distress (eg, churning in stomach);

Symptoms involving mental state
(i) feeling dizzy, unsteady, faint, or light-headed;
(j) feelings that objects are unreal (derealization), or that the self is distant or "not really here" (depersonalization);
(k) fear of losing control, "going crazy," or passing out;
(l) fear of dying;

General symptoms
(m) hot flushes or cold chills;
(n) numbness or tingling sensations.

C. *Most commonly used exclusion clause.* Panic attacks are not due to a physical disorder, organic mental disorder, or other mental disorders, such as schizophrenia and related disorders, mood [affective] disorders, or somatoform disorders.

The range of individual variation in both content and severity is so great that two grades, moderate and severe, may be specified, if desired, with a fifth character:

Panic disorder, moderate
At least four panic attacks in a 4-week period.

Panic disorder, severe
At least four panic attacks per week over a 4-week period.

Generalized anxiety disorder

Note. In children and adolescents the range of complaints by which the general anxiety is manifest is often more limited than in adults, and the specific symptoms of autonomic arousal are often less prominent. For these individuals, an alternative set of criteria is provided for use in (generalized anxiety disorder of childhood) if preferred.

A. There must have been a period of at least 6 months with prominent tension, worry, and feelings of apprehension about everyday events and problems.

B. At least four of the symptoms listed below must be present, at least one of which must be from items (1) to (4):

Autonomic arousal symptoms
(1) palpitations or pounding heart, or accelerated heart rate;
(2) sweating;
(3) trembling or shaking;
(4) dry mouth (not due to medication or dehydration);

Symptoms involving chest and abdomen
(5) difficulty in breathing;
(6) feeling of chocking;
(7) chest pain or discomfort;
(8) nausea or abdominal distress (eg, churning in stomach);

Symptoms involving mental state
(9) feeling dizzy, unsteady, faint, or light-headed
(10) feelings that objects are unreal (derealization), or that the self is distant or "not really here" (depersonalization);
(11) fear of losing control, "going crazy", or passing out;
(12) fear of dying;

General symptoms
(13) hot flushes or cold chills;
(14) numbness or tingling sensations;

Symptoms of tension
(15) muscle tension or aches and pains;
(16) restlessness and inability to relax;
(17) feeling keyed up, on edge, or mentally tense;
(18) a sensation of a lump in the throat, or difficulty in swallowing;

Other nonspecific symptoms
(19) exaggerated response to minor surprise or being startled;
(20) difficulty in concentrating, or mind "going blank," because of worrying or anxiety;
(21) persistent irritability;
(22) difficulty in getting to sleep because of worrying.

C. The disorder does not meet the criteria for panic disorder, phobic anxiety disorders, obsessive-compulsive disorder, or hypochondriacal disorder.

D. *Most commonly used exclusion clause.* The anxiety disorder is not due to a physical disorder, such as hyperthyroidism, an organic mental disorder, or a psychoactive substance-related disorder, such as excess consumption of amphetamine-like substances or withdrawal from benzodiazepines.

Mixed anxiety and depressive disorder

There are so many possible combinations of comparatively mild symptoms for these disorders that specific criteria are not given, other than those already in *Clinical descriptions and diagnostic guidelines.* It is suggested that researchers wishing to study patients with these disorders should arrive at their own criteria within the guidelines, depending upon the setting and purpose of their studies.

Other mixed anxiety disorders

Other specified anxiety disorders

Anxiety disorder, unspecified

Reprinted with permission from World Health Organization: *The ICD-10 Classification of Mental and Behavourial Disorders: Diagnostic Criteria for Research.* Copyright, World Health Organization, Geneva, 1993.

Table 16.1–10
ICD-10 Diagnostic Criteria for Obsessive-Compulsive Disorder

A. Either obsessions or compulsions (or both) are present on most days for a period of at least 2 weeks.
B. Obsessions (thoughts, ideas, or images) and compulsions (acts) share the following features, all of which must be present:
   (1) They are acknowledged as originating in the mind of the patient and are not imposed by outside persons or influences.
   (2) They are repetitive and unpleasant, and at least one obsession or compulsion that is acknowledged as excessive or unreasonable must be present.
   (3) The patient tries to resist them (but resistance to very long-standing obsessions or compulsions may be minimal). At least one obsession or compulsion that is unsuccessfully resisted must be present.
   (4) Experiencing the obsessive thought or carrying out the compulsive act is not in itself pleasurable. (This should be distinguished from the temporary relief of tension or anxiety.)
C. The obsessions or compulsions cause distress or interfere with the patient's social or individual functioning, usually by wasting time.
D. *Most commonly used exclusion clause.* The obsessions or compulsions are not the result of other mental disorders, such as schizophrenia and related disorders or mood [affective] disorders.

The diagnosis may be further specified by the followign four-character codes:
Predominantly obsessional thoughts and ruminations
Predominantly compulsive acts [obsessional rituals]
Mixed obsessional thoughts and acts
Other obsessive-compulsive disorders
Obsessive-compulsive disorder, unspecified

Reprinted with permission from World Health Organization: *The ICD-10 Classification of Mental and Behavioural Disorders: Diagnostic Criteria for Research.* Copyright, World Health Organization, Geneva, 1993.

orders, avoidant, dependent, and obsessive-compulsive personality disorders may have symptoms that resemble those of mixed anxiety-depressive disorder. A diagnosis of a somatoform disorder should also be considered. Only a psychiatric history, a mental status examination, and a working knowledge of the specific DSM-IV criteria can help clinicians differentiate among these conditions.

Course and Prognosis. On the basis of clinical data to date, patients seem to be equally likely to have prominent anxiety symptoms, prominent depressive symptoms, or an equal mixture of the two symptoms at onset. During the course of the illness, anxiety or depressive symptoms may alternate in their predominance. The prognosis is not known.

Treatment. Because adequate studies comparing treatment modalities for mixed anxiety-depressive disorder are not available, clinicians are probably most likely to provide treatment based on the symptoms present, their severity, and the clinician's own levels of experience with various treatment modalities. Psychotherapeutic approaches may involve time-limited approaches, such as cognitive therapy or behavior modification, although some clinicians use a less structured psychotherapeutic approach, such as insight-oriented psychotherapy. Pharmacotherapy for mixed anxiety-depressive disorder may include antianxiety drugs, antidepressive drugs, or both. Among the anxiolytic drugs, some data indicate that the use of triazolobenzodiazepines (for example, alprazolam) may be indicated because of their effectiveness in treating depression associated with anxiety. A drug that affects the 5-HT_{1A} receptor, such as buspirone, may also be indicated. Among the antidepressants, despite the noradrenergic theories linking anxiety disorders and depressive disorders, the serotonergic antidepressants (for example, fluoxetine) may be most effective in treating mixed anxiety-depressive disorder.

ICD-10

In ICD-10, neurotic (anxiety) disorders are grouped with stress-related and somatoform disorders because of "their historical association with the concept of neurosis and the association of a substantial (though uncertain) proportion of these disorders with psychological causation." In ICD-10, mixtures of symptoms are described as common, especially in less severe varieties of these disorders, and a category for cases that cannot be based on a single main syndrome is provided. Although the idea of neurosis is no longer the organizing principle, "care has been taken to allow the easy identification of disorders that some users still might wish to regard as neurotic in their own usage of the term."

There are three ICD-10 categories for "neurotic" disorders: phobic anxiety disorders (agoraphobia, social phobias, specific phobias, other phobic anxiety disorders, and phobic anxiety disorder, unspecified); other anxiety disorders (panic disorder, generalized anxiety disorder, mixed anxiety and depressive disorder, other mixed anxiety disorders, other specified anxiety disorders, and anxiety disorder, unspecified); and obsessive-compulsive disorder (with predominantly obsessional thoughts, predominantly compulsive acts, or mixed obsessional thoughts and acts); other obsessive-compulsive disorders; and obsessive-compulsive disorder, unspecified (Tables 16.1–8 through 16.1–10).

In ICD-10, reaction to severe stress and adjustment disorders are grouped into one category, which is classed together with neurotic and somatoform disorders. However, the stress-related category differs from the other two categories because it not only can be defined on the basis of symptoms but also on the basis of one of two causative influences: a stressful life event causing an acute stress reaction or a significant life change producing an adjustment disorder. Unlike severe disorders, these disorders are always linked to the acute stress or continuing trauma. Stress-related disorders in all age groups, including children, fall into this category.

In this group, ICD-10 classifies reactions to severe stress (acute stress reaction, posttraumatic distress disorder) and adjustment disorders (see Chapter 26). ICD-10 also includes the dissociative (conversion) disorders in the category of stress-related disorders. (For a discussion of dissociative disorders, see Chapter 20.) The criteria for reactions to severe stress are given in Table 16.1–11.

Table 16.1–11
ICD-10 Diagnostic Criteria for Reactions to Severe Stress

Acute stress reaction

A. The patient must have been exposed to an exceptional mental or physical stressor.

B. Exposure to the stressor is followed by an immediate onset of symptoms (within 1 hour).

C. Two groups of symptoms are given: the acute stress reaction is graded as:
Mild
Only criterion (1) below is fulfilled.
Moderate
Criterion (1) is met, and there are any two symptoms from criterion (2).
Severe
Either criterion (1) is met, and there are any four symptoms from criterion (2); *or* there is dissociative stupor.
(1) Criteria B, C, and D for generalized anxiety disorder are met.
(2) (a) Withdrawal from expected social interaction.
(b) Narrowing of attention.
(c) Apparent disorientation.
(d) Anger or verbal aggression.
(e) Despair or hopelessness.
(f) Inappropriate or purposeless overactivity.
(g) Uncontrollable and excessive grief (judged by local cultural standards).

D. If the stressor is transient or can be relieved, the symptoms must begin to diminish after not more than 8 hours. If exposure to the stressor continues, the symptoms must begin to diminish after not more than 48 hours.

E. *Most commonly used exclusion clause.* The reaction must occur in the absence of any other concurrent mental or behavioral disorder in ICD-10 (except generalized anxiety disorder and personality disorders) and not within 3 months of the end of an episode of any other mental or behavioral disorder.

Posttraumatic stress disorder

A. The patient must have been exposed to a stressful event or situation (either short- or long-lasting) of exceptionally threatening or catastrophic nature, which would be likely to cause pervasive distress in almost anyone.

B. There must be persistent remembering or "reliving" of the stressor in intrusive "flashbacks," vivid memories, or recurring dreams or in experiencing distress when exposed to circumstances resembling or associated with the stressor.

C. The patient must exhibit an actual or preferred avoidance of circumstances resembling or associated with the stressor, which was not present before exposure to the stressor.

D. Either of the following must be present:
(1) inability to recall, either partially or completely, some important aspects of the period of exposure to the stressor;
(2) persistent symptoms of increased psychological sensitivity and arousal (not present before exposure to the stressor), shown by any two of the following:
(a) difficulty in falling or staying asleep;
(b) irritability or outbursts of anger;
(c) difficulty in concentrating;
(d) hypervigilance;
(e) exaggerated startle response.

E. Criteria B, C, and D must all be met within 6 months of the stressful event or of the end of a period of stress. (For some purposes, onset delayed more than 6 months may be included, but this should be clearly specified.)

References

Cassem EH: Depression and anxiety secondary to medical illness. Psychiatr Clin North Am *13:* 597, 1990.

Coryell W, Endicott J, Winokur G: Anxiety syndromes as epiphenomena of primary major depression: Outcome and financial psychopathology. Am J Psychiatry *149:* 100, 1992.

Davis M: The role of the amygdala in fear-potentiated startle: Implications for animal models of anxiety. Trends Pharmacol Sci *13:* 35, 1992.

Dubovsky SL: Approaches to developing new anxiolytics and antidepressants. J Clin Psychiatry *54* (5, Suppl): 75, 1993.

Fawcett J: Targeting treatment in patients with mixed symptoms of anxiety and depression. J Clin Psychiatry *51* (11, Suppl): 40, 1990.

Fick SN, Roy-Byrne PP, Cowley DS, Shores MM, Dunner DL: DSM-III-R personality disorders in a mood and anxiety disorders clinic: Prevalence, comorbidity, and clinical correlates. J Affect Disord *27:* 71, 1993.

Gabbard GO: *Psychodynamics Psychiatry in Clinical Practice: The DSM-IV Edition.* American Psychiatric Press, Washington, 1994.

Gabbard GO: Psychodynamic psychiatry in the "decade of the brain." Am J Psychiatry *149:* 991, 1992.

Gorman JM, Papp LA, editors: Anxiety disorders. In *American Psychiatric Press Review of Psychiatry,* vol 11, A Tasman, MB Riba, editors, p 243. American Psychiatric Press, Washington, 1992.

Hecht H, von Zerssen D, Wittchen HU: Anxiety and depression in a community sample: The influence of comorbidity on social functioning. J Affect Disord *18:* 137, 1990.

Johnson EO, Kamilaris TC, Chrousos GP, Gold PW: Mechanisms of stress: A dynamic overview of hormonal and behavioral homeostases. Neurosci Biobehav Rev *16:* 115, 1992.

Katon W, Roy-Byrne PP: Mixed anxiety and depression. J Abnorm Psychol *100:* 337, 1991.

Kessler RC, McGonagle KA, Zhao S, Nelson CB, Hughes M, Eshleman S,

Wittchen H-U, Kendler KS: Lifetime and 12-month prevalence of DSM-III-R psychiatric disorder in the United States: Results from the National Comorbidity Survey. Arch Gen Psychiatry *51:* 8, 1994.
Lucki I: Serotonin receptor specificity in anxiety disorders. J Clin Psychiatry *57* (Suppl 6): 5, 1996.
Lydiard RB: Coexisting depression and anxiety: Special diagnostic and treatment issues. J Clin Psychiatry *52* (6, Suppl): 48, 1991.
Mathew RJ, Wilson WH: Anxiety and cerebral blood flow. Am J Psychiatry *147:* 838, 1990.
McNally RJ: Automaticity and the anxiety disorders. Behav Res Ther *33:* 747, 1995.
Mixed anxiety and depression: A nosologic reality? J Clin Psychiatry *54* (1, Suppl): 2, 1993.
Papp LA, Gorman JM: Generalized anxiety disorder. In *Comprehensive Textbook of Psychiatry,* ed 6, HI Kaplan, BJ Sadock, editors, p 1236. Williams & Wilkins, Baltimore, 1995.
Wesner RB: Alcohol use and abuse secondary to anxiety. Psychiatr Clin North Am *13:* 699, 1990.

▲ 16.2 Panic Disorder and Agoraphobia

In the fourth edition of *Diagnostic and Statistical Manual of Mental Disorders* (DSM-IV), a panic attack is defined as a ''discrete period of intense fear or discomfort,'' accompanied by at least four somatic or cognitive symptoms such as palpitations, trembling, shortness of breath, sweating, and feelings of choking, among others. Since panic disorder was codified in 1980, a wealth of research data about the disorder as well as clinical experiences with affected patients has been accumulated. Panic disorder is characterized by the spontaneous, unexpected occurrence of panic attacks, which can vary from several attacks during 1 day to only a few attacks during a year. Panic disorder is often accompanied by agoraphobia, the fear of being alone in public places (such as supermarkets), particularly places from which a rapid exit would be difficult in the course of a panic attack.

Agoraphobia can be the most disabling of the phobias, as its presence may significantly interfere with a person's ability to function in work and social situations outside the home. In the United States, most researchers of panic disorder believe that agoraphobia almost always develops as a complication in patients with panic disorder. That is, the fear of having a panic attack in a public place from which escape would be formidable is thought to cause the agoraphobia. Researchers in other countries as well as some U.S. researchers and clinicians disagree with this theory, but DSM-IV establishes panic disorder as the predominant disorder in the dyad. DSM-IV includes diagnoses for panic disorder with and without agoraphobia and also for agoraphobia without panic disorder. Panic attacks can also occur in many mental disorders (such as depressive disorders) and medical conditions (such as substance withdrawal or intoxication), and the presence of a panic attack does not in itself require a diagnosis of panic disorder.

Because patients who have experienced panic attacks often go to medical clinics, the symptoms may be misdiagnosed as a serious medical condition (such as myocardial infarction) or as a so-called hysterical symptom. Nevertheless, since 1980, health care providers have an increased ability to recognize the symptoms of panic disorder, and effective and specific treatments are available. Those who supply health care must be able to recognize the symptoms of panic disorder so that affected patients can receive appropriate therapy, including pharmacotherapeutic agents and psychotherapy.

HISTORY

The idea of panic disorder may have its roots in the concept of irritable heart syndrome, which Jacob Mendes DaCosta noted in soldiers in the American Civil War. DaCosta's syndrome included many psychic and somatic symptoms that have since become included among the diagnostic criteria for panic disorder. In 1895, Sigmund Freud introduced the concept of anxiety neurosis, consisting of acute and chronic psychic and somatic symptoms. Freud's acute anxiety neurosis was similar to panic disorder as defined in DSM-IV, and Freud first noted the relation between panic attacks and agoraphobia. The term *agoraphobia* had been coined in 1871 to describe the condition of patients who were afraid to venture alone into public places. The term is derived from the Greek words *agora* and *phobos,* meaning ''fear of the marketplace.''

EPIDEMIOLOGY

Epidemiological studies have reported lifetime prevalence rates of 1.5 to 5 percent for panic disorder and 3 to 5.6 percent for panic attacks. For example, a recent study of more than 1,600 randomly selected adults in Texas found a lifetime prevalence rate of 3.8 percent for panic disorder, 5.6 percent for panic attacks, and 2.2 percent for panic attacks with limited symptoms that did not meet the full diagnostic criteria.

Women are 2 to 3 times more likely to be affected than are men, although underdiagnosis of panic disorder in men may contribute to the skewed distribution. The differences among Hispanics, whites, and blacks are small. The only social factor identified as contributing to the development of panic disorder is a recent history of divorce or separation. Panic disorder most commonly develops in young adulthood—the mean age of presentation is about 25 years—but both panic disorder and agoraphobia can develop at any age. Panic disorder has been reported to occur in children and adolescents, and it is probably underdiagnosed in these age groups.

The lifetime prevalence of agoraphobia has been reported as ranging from as low as 0.6 percent to as high as 6 percent. The major factor leading to this wide range of estimates is the use of varying diagnostic criteria and assessment methods. Although studies of agoraphobia in psychiatric settings have reported that at least three fourths of the affected patients have panic disorder as well, studies of agoraphobia in community samples have found that as many as half the patients have agoraphobia without panic disorder. The reasons for these divergent findings are unknown but probably involve differences in ascertainment techniques. In many cases, the onset of agoraphobia follows a traumatic event.

Comorbidity

Ninety-one percent of patients with panic disorder and 84 percent of those with agoraphobia have at least one other psychiatric disorder. Common comorbidity conditions are major depressive disorder, other anxiety disorders, personality disorders, and substance-related disorders.

ETIOLOGY

Biological Factors

Research on the biological basis of panic disorder has produced a range of findings; one interpretation is that the symptoms of panic disorder are related to a range of biological abnormalities in brain structure and function. Most work has taken place in the area of using biological stimulants to induce panic attacks in patients with panic disorder. These and other studies have produced hypotheses implicating both peripheral and central nervous system dysregulation in the pathophysiology of panic disorder. The autonomic nervous systems of some patients with panic disorder have been reported to exhibit increased sympathetic tone, to adapt slowly to repeated stimuli, and to respond excessively to moderate stimuli. Studies of the neuroendocrine status of these patients have shown several abnormalities, although the studies have been inconsistent in their findings.

The major neurotransmitter systems that have been implicated are those for norepinephrine, serotonin, and γ-aminobutyric acid (GABA). The totality of the biological data has led to a focus on the brainstem (particularly the noradrenergic neurons of the locus ceruleus and the serotonergic neurons of the median raphe nucleus), the limbic system (possibly responsible for the generation of anticipatory anxiety), and the prefrontal cortex (possibly responsible for the generation of phobic avoidance).

Panic-Inducing Substances. Panic-inducing substances (sometimes called panicogens) induce panic attacks in a majority of patients with panic disorder and in a much smaller proportion of people without panic disorder or a history of panic attacks. (The use of panic-inducing substances is strictly limited to research settings; there are no clinically indicated reasons to stimulate panic attacks in patients.) So-called respiratory panic-inducing substances cause respiratory stimulation and a shift in the acid–base balance. These substances include carbon dioxide (5 to 35 percent mixtures), sodium lactate, and bicarbonate. Neurochemical panic-inducing substances, which act through specific neurotransmitter systems, include yohimbine (Yocon), an α_2-adrenergic receptor antagonist; fenfluramine (Pondimin), a serotonin-releasing agent; *m*-chlorophenylpiperazine (mCPP), an agent with multiple serotonergic effects; μ-carboline drugs; $GABA_B$ receptor inverse agonists; flumazenil, a $GABA_B$ receptor antagonist; cholecystokinin; and caffeine. Isoproterenol (Isuprel) is also a panic-inducing substance, although its mechanism of action in inducing panic attacks is poorly understood. The respiratory panic-inducing substances may act initially at the peripheral cardiovascular baroreceptors and relay their signal by vagal afferents to the nucleus tractus solitarii and then on to the nucleus paragigantocellularis of the medulla. The neurochemical panic-inducing substances are presumed to primarily affect the noradrenergic, serotonergic, and GABA receptors of the central nervous system directly.

Brain Imaging. Structural brain-imaging studies, for example, magnetic resonance imaging (MRI), in patients with panic disorder have implicated pathological involvement in the temporal lobes, particularly the hippocampus. One MRI study reported abnormalities, especially cortical atrophy, in the right temporal lobe of these patients. Functional brain-imaging studies, for example, positron emission tomography (PET), have implicated a dysregulation of cerebral blood flow. Specifically, anxiety disorders and panic attacks are associated with cerebral vasoconstriction, which may result in central nervous system symptoms such as dizziness and in peripheral nervous system symptoms that may be induced by hyperventilation and hypocapnia. Most functional brain-imaging studies have used a specific panic-inducing substance (for example, lactate, caffeine, or yohimbine) in combination with PET or single photon emission computed tomography to assess the effects of the panic-inducing substance and the induced panic attack on cerebral blood flow.

Mitral Valve Prolapse. Although great interest was formerly expressed in an association between mitral valve prolapse and panic disorder, research has almost completely erased any clinical significance or relevance to the association. Mitral valve prolapse is a heterogeneous syndrome consisting of the prolapse of one of the mitral valve leaflets, resulting in a midsystolic click on cardiac auscultation. Research studies have found that the prevalence of panic disorder in patients with mitral valve prolapse is the same as the prevalence of panic disorder in patients without mitral valve prolapse.

Genetic Factors

Although the number of well-controlled studies of the genetic basis of panic disorder and agoraphobia is small, the data to date support the conclusion that the disorders have a distinct genetic component. In addition, some data indicate that panic disorder with agoraphobia is a severe form of panic disorder and is thus more likely to be inherited. Various studies have found a fourfold to eightfold increase in the risk for panic disorder among the first-degree relatives of panic disorder patients compared with first-degree relatives of other psychiatric patients. The twin studies conducted to date have generally reported that monozygotic twins are more likely to be concordant for panic disorder than are dizygotic twins.

Psychosocial Factors

Both cognitive-behavioral and psychoanalytic theories have been developed to explain the pathogenesis of panic disorder and agoraphobia. The success of cognitive-behavioral approaches to the treatment of these disorders may add credence to the cognitive-behavioral theories.

Cognitive-Behavioral Theories. Behavioral theories posit that anxiety is a response learned either from modeling parental behavior or through the process of classic conditioning. In a classic conditioning approach to panic disorder and agoraphobia, a noxious stimulus (such as a panic attack) that occurs with a neutral stimulus (such as a bus ride) can result in the avoidance of the neutral stimulus. Other behavioral theories posit a linkage between the sensation of minor somatic symptoms (such as palpitations) and the generation of a panic attack. Although cognitive-behavioral theories can help explain the development of agoraphobia or an increase in the number or severity of panic attacks, they do not explain the occurrence of the first unprovoked and unexpected panic attack that an affected patient experiences.

Psychoanalytic Theories. Psychoanalytic theories conceptualize panic attacks as arising from an unsuccessful defense against anxiety-provoking impulses. What was previously a mild signal anxiety becomes an overwhelming feeling of apprehension, complete with somatic symptoms. To explain agoraphobia, psychoanalytic theories emphasize the loss of a parent in childhood and a history of separation anxiety. Being alone in public places revives the childhood anxiety about being abandoned. The defense mechanisms used include repression, displacement, avoidance, and symbolization. Traumatic separations during childhood may affect children's developing nervous systems in such a manner that they become susceptible to anxieties in adulthood.

Many patients describe panic attacks as coming out of the blue, as though no psychological factors were involved, but psychodynamic exploration frequently reveals a clear psychological trigger for the panic attack. Although panic attacks are correlated neurophysiologically with the locus ceruleus, the onset of panic is generally related to environmental or psychological factors. Patients with panic disorder have a higher incidence of stressful life events, particularly loss, compared with control subjects in the months before the onset of panic disorder. Moreover, the patients typically experience greater distress about life events than do control subjects.

The hypothesis that stressful psychological events produce neurophysiological changes in panic disorder is supported by a study of female twins. The research findings revealed that panic disorder was strongly associated with both parental separation and parental death before children had reached the age of 17. Separation from the mother early in life was clearly more likely to result in panic disorder than was paternal separation in the cohort of 1,018 pairs of female twins. Further support for psychological mechanisms in panic disorder can be inferred from a study of panic disorder in which patients received successful treatment with cognitive therapy. Before the therapy, the patients responded to panic attack induction with lactate. After successful cognitive therapy, lactate infusion no longer resulted in a panic attack.

The research indicates that the cause of panic attacks is likely to involve the unconscious meaning of stressful events and that the pathogenesis of the panic attacks may be related to neurophysiological factors triggered by the psychological reactions. Psychodynamic clinicians should always do a thorough investigation of possible triggers whenever assessing a patient with panic disorder.

DIAGNOSIS

Panic Attacks

In DSM-IV, the diagnostic criteria for a panic attack are listed as a separate set of criteria (Table 16.2–1). Panic attacks can occur in mental disorders other than panic disorder, particularly in specific phobia, social phobia, and posttraumatic stress disorder. Unexpected panic attacks occur at any time and

Table 16.2–1
DSM-IV Criteria for Panic Attack

Note: A panic attack is not a codable disorder. Code the specific diagnosis in which the panic attack occurs (eg, panic disorder with agoraphobia).

A discrete period of intense fear or discomfort, in which four (or more) of the following symptoms developed abruptly and reached a peak within 10 minutes:

(1) palpitations, pounding heart, or accelerated heart rate
(2) sweating
(3) trembling or shaking
(4) sensations of shortness of breath or smothering
(5) feeling of choking
(6) chest pain or discomfort
(7) nausea or abdominal distress
(8) feeling dizzy, unsteady, lightheaded, or faint
(9) derealization (feelings of unreality) or depersonalization (being detached from oneself)
(10) fear of losing control or going crazy
(11) fear of dying
(12) paresthesias (numbness or tingling sensations)
(13) chills or hot flushes

are not associated with any identifiable situational stimulus, but panic attacks need not be unexpected. Attacks in patients with social and specific phobias are usually expected or cued to a recognized or specific stimulus. Some panic attacks do not fit easily into the distinction between unexpected and expected, and these attacks are referred to as situationally predisposed panic attacks; they may or may not occur when a patient is exposed to a specific trigger, or they may occur either immediately after exposure or after a considerable delay.

Panic Disorder

DSM-IV contains two diagnostic criteria for panic disorder, one without agoraphobia (Table 16.2–2) and the other with agoraphobia (Table 16.2–3), but both require the presence of panic attacks as described in Table 16.2–1. Some community surveys have indicated that panic attacks are common, and a major issue in developing diagnostic criteria for panic disorder was the determination of a threshold number or frequency of panic attacks required to meet the diagnosis. Setting the threshold too low results in the diagnosis of panic disorder in patients who do not have an impairment from an occasional panic attack; setting the threshold too high results in a situation in which patients who are impaired by their panic attacks do not meet the diagnostic criteria. The vagaries of setting a threshold are evidenced by the range of thresholds set in various diagnostic criteria. The Research Diagnostic Criteria require that six panic attacks occur during a 6-week period. The 10th revision of *International Statistical Classification of Diseases and Related Health Problems* (ICD-10) requires that three attacks occur in 3 weeks (for moderate disease) or four attacks in 4 weeks (for severe disease). DSM-IV does not specify a minimum number of panic attacks or a time frame but does require that at least one attack be followed by at least a month-long period of concern about having another panic attack or

Table 16.2–2
DSM-IV Diagnostic Criteria for Panic Disorder Without Agoraphobia

A. Both (1) and (2):
  (1) recurrent unexpected panic attacks
  (2) at least one of the attacks has been followed by at least 1 month (or more) of the following:
    (a) persistent concern about having additional attacks
    (b) worry about the implications of the attack or its consequences (eg, losing control, having a heart attack, "going crazy")
    (c) a significant change in behavior related to the attacks

B. Absence of agoraphobia.

C. The panic attacks are not due to the direct physiological effects of a substance (eg, a drug of abuse, a medication) or a general medical condition (eg, hyperthyroidism).

D. The panic attacks are not better accounted for by another mental disorder, such as social phobia (eg, occurring on exposure to feared social situations), specific phobia (eg, on exposure to a specific phobic situation), obsessive-compulsive disorder (eg, on exposure to dirt in someone with an obsession about contamination), posttraumatic stress disorder (eg, in response to stimuli associated with a severe stressor), or separation anxiety disorder (eg, in response to being away from home or close relatives).

about the implications of the attack or a significant change in behavior. DSM-IV also requires that the panic attacks generally be unexpected but allows for expected or situationally predisposed attacks.

Agoraphobia Without History of Panic Disorder

Table 16.2–4 lists criteria for agoraphobia. The DSM-IV diagnostic criteria for agoraphobia without history of panic disorder (Table 16.2–5) are based on the fear of a sudden incapacitating or embarrassing symptom. In contrast, the ICD-10 criteria require the presence of interrelated or overlapping phobias but do not require that fear of incapacitating or embarrassing symptoms be present.

The DSM-IV criteria also address the avoidance of situations that are based on a concern related to a medical disorder (for example, fear of a myocardial infarction in a patient with severe heart disease).

CLINICAL FEATURES

Panic Disorder

The first panic attack is often completely spontaneous, although panic attacks occasionally follow excitement, physical exertion, sexual activity, or moderate emotional trauma. DSM-

Table 16.2–3
DSM-IV Diagnostic Criteria for Panic Disorder With Agoraphobia

A. Both (1) and (2):
  (1) recurrent unexpected panic attacks
  (2) at least one of the attacks has been followed by 1 month (or more) of the following:
    (a) persistent concern about having additional attacks
    (b) worry about the implications of the attack or its consequences (eg, losing control, having a heart attack, "going crazy")
    (c) a significant change in behavior related to the attacks

B. The presence of agoraphobia.

C. The panic attacks are not due to the direct physiological effects of a substance (eg, a drug of abuse, a medication or a general medical condition (eg, hyperthyroidism).

D. The panic attacks are not better accounted for by another mental disorder, such as social phobia (eg, occurring on exposure to feared social situations), specific phobia (eg, on exposure to a specific phobic situation), obsessive-compulsive disorder (eg, on exposure to dirt in someone with an obsession about contamination), posttraumatic stress disorder (eg, in response to stimuli associated with a severe stressor), or separation anxiety disorder (eg, in response to being away from home or close relatives).

Table 16.2–4
DSM-IV Criteria for Agoraphobia

Note: Agoraphobia is not a codable disorder. Code the specific disorder in which the agoraphobia occurs (eg, panic disorder with agoraphobia or agoraphobia without history of panic disorder).

A. Anxiety about being in places or situations from which escape might be difficult (or embarrassing) or in which help may not be available in the event of having an unexpected or situationally predisposed panic attack or panic-like symptoms. Agoraphobic fears typically involve characteristics clusters of situations that include being outside the home alone; being in a crowd or standing in a line; being on a bridge; and traveling in a bus, train, or automobile.
Note: Consider the diagnosis of specific phobia if the avoidance is limited to one or only a few specific situations, or social phobia if the avoidance is limited to social situations.

B. The situations are avoided (eg, travel is restricted) or else are endured with marked distress or with anxiety about having a panic attack or panic-like symptoms, or require the presence of a companion.

C. The anxiety or phobic avoidance is not better accounted for by another mental disorder, such as social phobia (eg, avoidance limited to social situations because of fear of embarrassment), specific phobia (eg, avoidance limited to a single situation like elevators), obsessive-compulsive disorder (eg, avoidance of dirt in someone with an obsession about contamination), posttraumatic stress disorder (eg, avoidance of stimuli associated with a severe stressor), or separation anxiety disorder (eg, avoidance of leaving home or relatives).

Table 16.2–5
DSM-IV Diagnostic Criteria for Agoraphobia Without History of Panic Disorder

A. The presence of agoraphobia related to fear of developing panic-like symptoms (eg, dizziness or diarrhea).
B. Criteria have never been met for panic disorder.
C. The disturbance is not due to the direct physiological effects of a substance (eg, a drug of abuse, a medication) or a general medical condition.
D. If an associated general medical condition is present, the fear described in criterion A is clearly in excess of that usually associated with the condition.

IV emphasizes that at least the first attacks must be unexpected (uncued) to meet the diagnostic criteria for panic disorder. Clinicians should attempt to ascertain any habit or situation that commonly precedes a patient's panic attacks. Such activities may include the use of caffeine, alcohol, nicotine, or other substances; unusual patterns of sleeping or eating; and specific environmental settings, such as harsh lighting at work.

The attack often begins with a 10-minute period of rapidly increasing symptoms. The major mental symptoms are extreme fear and a sense of impending death and doom. Patients are usually unable to name the source of their fear; they may feel confused and have trouble in concentrating. The physical signs often include tachycardia, palpitations, dyspnea, and sweating. Patients often try to leave whatever situation they are in to seek help. The attack generally lasts 20 to 30 minutes and rarely more than an hour. A formal mental status examination during a panic attack may reveal rumination, difficulty in speaking (for example, stammering), and an impaired memory. Patients may experience depression or depersonalization during an attack. The symptoms may disappear quickly or gradually. Between attacks, patients may have anticipatory anxiety about having another attack. The differentiation between anticipatory anxiety and generalized anxiety disorder can be difficult, although pain disorder patients with anticipatory anxiety are able to name the focus of their anxiety.

Somatic concerns of death from a cardiac or respiratory problem may be the major focus of patients' attention during panic attacks. Patients may believe that the palpitations and chest pain indicate that they are about to die. As many as 20 percent of such patients actually have syncopal episodes during a panic attack. The patients may be seen in emergency rooms as young (20s), physically healthy persons who nevertheless insist that they are about to die from a heart attack. Rather than immediately diagnosing hypochondriasis, the emergency room physician should consider a diagnosis of panic disorder. Hyperventilation may produce respiratory alkalosis and other symptoms. The age-old treatment of breathing into a paper bag sometimes helps.

A 26-year-old woman came to the clinic complaining of waves of terror and the effect they were having on her life. About 1 year earlier, while sitting at home watching television, she had experienced an inexplicable rush of anxiety (''like someone injected me with a large dose of adrenaline'') that was accompanied by a pounding heart, gasping for air, chest pain (''like someone was sitting on top of me''), numbness in her fingers and toes, and violent shaking. Although the attack subsided in minutes, she rushed to the emergency room of a local hospital in the belief that she had experienced a heart attack. All test results were negative.

About 5 months after the first attack she experienced another episode while walking to her job as a legal secretary. Again, the attack seemed to come from nowhere. She took the day off from work and consulted a cardiologist. The results of all examinations were negative. The cardiologist told her that she was suffering from anxiety and prescribed a mild tranquilizer.

A third attack with the same symptoms occurred 3 months later while the patient was in a supermarket. She became terrified, dropped her groceries, and ran home.

The attacks quickly escalated in frequency, from one every few weeks to weekly, then daily. There was no escaping them—they occurred at home, in restaurants, at work. Soon, she became so preoccupied with having the attacks that she could not concentrate on her work. When she was seen at the clinic, she had been experiencing multiple attacks daily for nearly 2 months.

DISCUSSION

The patient's attacks were described by her as ''inexplicable'' and ''seem[ing] to come out of nowhere'' (that is, they were unexpected, uncued, spontaneous). The results of medical examinations were negative; no organic factor could be identified that initiated and maintained the disturbance. The patient's reactions to the attacks (rushing to an emergency room, consulting a cardiologist) are often observed in patients with panic disorder, who (understandably) think they are having a heart attack. Further, the patient became preoccupied with having the attacks. Although functional impairment was minimal (she had difficulty concentrating on her work, but there was no major disruption of occupational, home, or daily routine functioning), the panic attacks were a significant source of distress in her life. (Courtesy of Abby J. Fyer, M.D., Salvatore Mannuzza, Ph.D., and Jeremy D. Coplan, M.D.)

Agoraphobia

Patients with agoraphobia rigidly avoid situations in which it would be difficult to obtain help. They prefer to be accompanied by a friend or a family member in busy streets, crowded stores, closed-in spaces (such as tunnels, bridges, and elevators), and closed-in vehicles (such as subways, buses, and airplanes). The patients may insist that they be accompanied every time they leave the house. The behavior may result in marital discord, which may be misdiagnosed as the primary problem. Severely affected patients may simply refuse to leave the house. Particularly before a correct diagnosis is made, patients may be terrified that they are going crazy.

A 60-year-old widow proprietor of a large manufacturing company came to the clinic escorted by two of her employees. Until 2 years earlier her life had been rewarding and fulfilling. She and her husband had built a small company into a major enterprise. "I made all the decisions and fielded all the criticism and pessimism expressed by others; he supplied the money," she said. The patient continued to develop the business after her husband's death 15 years earlier. However, at age 58, for no known reason, she began to experience sudden spells of dizziness that lasted for 5 to 10 minutes. Tests conducted by her neurologist and otolaryngologist failed to identify any organic cause for the spells.

Although the patient had not experienced an episode for nearly a year before she came to the clinic, the fear of becoming dizzy (and of falling and being injured) continued to have a profound effect on her life. For example, her housekeeper escorted her to the limousine each morning. When she arrived at her company, she was met and escorted to her office by an employee. She could not walk down the hallway to the lavatory without being accompanied. All of her dependency needs revolved around the fear of sudden incapacitation and consequent injury resulting from a fall. Although the fear did not impair her keen business sense or her long-standing social relationships, it clearly pervaded her life.

Recently, her manufacturing company had experienced major financial difficulties beyond her control, and she was concerned about what her life would be like without a staff of housekeepers and business employees to rely on. "I cannot travel, shop, or even leave the house alone. The only time I feel safe is when I'm sitting down. I am even afraid to live at home alone, for fear that I may become dizzy and no one will be there to help me. What will become of me?"

DISCUSSION

If it were not for her relatively unique situation, in all likelihood the patient would have been totally incapacitated. Her entire life was arranged around her fear of sudden dizzy spells and their consequences. She became completely dependent on others, and even the thought of living alone, with no one around to help her in the event of a fall, terrified her. (Courtesy of Abby J. Fyer, M.D., Salvatore Mannuzza, Ph.D., and Jeremy D. Coplan, M.D.)

Associated Symptoms

Depressive symptoms are often present in panic disorder and agoraphobia, and, in some patients, a depressive disorder coexists with the panic disorder. Some studies have found that the lifetime risk of suicide in persons with panic disorder is higher than it is in persons with no mental disorder. Clinicians should be alert to the risk of suicide. In addition to agoraphobia, other phobias and obsessive-compulsive disorder can coexist with panic disorder. The psychosocial consequences of panic disorder and agoraphobia, in addition to marital discord, can include time lost from work, financial difficulties related to the loss of work, and alcohol and other substance abuse.

DIFFERENTIAL DIAGNOSIS

Panic Disorder

The differential diagnosis for a patient with panic disorder includes a large number of medical disorders (Table 16.2–6), as well as many mental disorders.

Medical Disorders. Whenever a patient, regardless of age or risk factors, reports to an emergency room with symptoms of a potentially fatal condition (for example, myocardial infarction), a complete medical history must be obtained and a physical examination performed. Standard laboratory procedures include a complete blood count; studies of electrolytes, fasting glucose, calcium concentrations, liver function, urea, creatinine, and thyroid; a urinalysis; a drug screen; and an ECG. Once the presence of an immediately life-threatening condition is ruled out, the clinical suspicion is panic disorder. The possibility that additional medical diagnostic procedures will reveal a medical condition must be weighed against the potentially adverse effects of the procedure in helping the patient accept a diagnosis of panic disorder. Nevertheless, the presence of atypical symptoms (such as vertigo, loss of bladder control, and unconsciousness) or the late onset of the first panic attack (older than age 45 years) should cause clinicians to reconsider the presence of an underlying nonpsychiatric medical condition.

The standard workup helps clinicians evaluate patients for the presence of thyroid, parathyroid, adrenal, and substance-related causes of panic attacks. Symptoms of chest pain, especially in patients with cardiac risk factors (for example, obesity and hypertension), may warrant further cardiac tests, including a 24-hour ECG, a stress test, a chest X-ray, and the measurement of cardiac enzymes. The presence of atypical neurological symptoms may warrant obtaining an electroencephalogram or an MRI to assess the possibility that the patient has temporal lobe epilepsy, multiple sclerosis, or a space-occupying brain lesion. The rare possibility that a patient has carcinoid syndrome or pheochromocytoma can best be checked by measuring a 24-hour urine sample for serotonin metabolites or catecholamines. Although hypoglycemia was once thought to be associated with panic disorder, especially in the lay literature, available data now indicate that hypoglycemia is rarely a cause of panic attacks in the absence of other symptoms that point to hypoglycemia.

Mental Disorders. The psychiatric differential diagnosis for panic disorder includes malingering, factitious disorders, hypochondriasis, depersonalization disorder, social and specific phobias, posttraumatic stress disorder, depressive disorders, and schizophrenia. In the differential diagnosis, clinicians must determine whether a panic attack was unexpected, situationally bound, or situationally predisposed. Unexpected panic attacks are the hallmark of panic disorder; situationally bound panic attacks generally indicate a different condition, such as social phobia or specific phobia (when exposed to the phobic situation), obsessive-compulsive disorder (when trying to resist a compulsion), or a depressive disorder (when overwhelmed with anxiety). The focus of the anxiety or the fear is also important. Was there no focus (as in panic disorder), or

Table 16.2–6
Organic Differential Diagnosis for Panic Disorder

Cardiovascular diseases
Anemia
Angina
Congestive heart failure
Hyperactive β-adrenergic state
Hypertension
Mitral valve prolapse
Myocardial infarction
Paradoxical atrial tachycardia
Pulmonary diseases
Asthma
Hyperventilation
Pulmonary embolus
Neurological diseases
Cerebrovascular disease
Epilepsy
Huntington's disease
Infection
Ménière's disease
Migraine
Multiple sclerosis
Transient ischemic attack
Tumor
Wilson's disease
Endocrine diseases
Addison's disease
Carcinoid syndrome
Cushing's syndrome
Diabetes
Hyperthryoidism
Hypoglycemia
Hypoparathyroidism
Menopausal disorders
Pheochromocytoma
Premenstrual syndrome
Drug intoxications
Amphetamine
Amyl nitrite
Anticholinergics
Cocaine
Hallucinogens
Marijuana
Nicotine
Theophylline
Drug withdrawal
Alcohol
Antihypertensives
Opiates and opioids
Sedative-hypnotics
Other conditions
Anaphylaxis
B_{12} deficiency
Electrolyte disturbances
Heavy metal poisoning
Systemic infections
Systemic lupus erythematosus
Temporal arteritis
Uremia

was there a specific focus (for example, a person with social phobia who fears becoming tongue-tied)? Somatoform disorders should also be considered in the differential diagnosis, although a patient may meet the criteria for both somatoform disorder and panic disorder.

Specific and Social Phobias. DSM-IV addresses the sometimes difficult diagnostic task of distinguishing between panic disorder with agoraphobia, on the one hand, and specific and social phobias, on the other hand. Some patients who experience a single panic attack in a specific setting (for example, an elevator) may go on to have a long-lasting avoidance of the specific setting, regardless of whether they ever have another panic attack. These patients meet the diagnostic criteria for a specific phobia, and clinicians must use their judgment about what is the most appropriate diagnosis. In another example, a person who experiences one or more panic attacks may then fear speaking in public. Although the clinical picture is almost identical to the clinical picture in social phobia, a diagnosis of social phobia is excluded because the avoidance of the public situation is based on fear of having a panic attack, rather than on fear of the public speaking itself. Because empirical data on the distinctions are limited, DSM-IV advises clinicians to use their clinical judgment to diagnose difficult cases.

Agoraphobia Without History of Panic Disorder

The differential diagnosis for agoraphobia without a history of panic disorder includes all the medical disorders that may cause anxiety or depression. The psychiatric differential diagnosis includes major depressive disorder, schizophrenia, paranoid personality disorder, avoidance personality disorder, and dependent personality disorder.

COURSE AND PROGNOSIS

Panic Disorder

Panic disorder usually has its onset during late adolescence or early adulthood, although onset during childhood, early adolescence, and midlife does occur. Some data implicate increased psychosocial stressors with the onset of panic disorder, although no psychosocial stressor can be definitely identified in most cases.

Panic disorder, in general, is a chronic disorder, although its course is variable both among patients and within a single patient. The available long-term follow-up studies of panic disorder are difficult to interpret because they have not controlled for the effects of treatment. Nevertheless, about 30 to 40 percent of patients seem to be symptom free at long-term follow-up; about 50 percent have symptoms that are mild enough not to affect their lives significantly; and about 10 to 20 percent continue to have significant symptoms.

After the first one or two panic attacks, patients may be relatively unconcerned about their condition; with repeated attacks, however, the symptoms may become a major concern. Patients may attempt to keep the panic attacks secret and thereby cause their families and friends concern about unexplained changes in behavior. The frequency and severity of the attacks may fluctuate. Panic attacks may occur several times in a day or less than once a month. The excessive intake of caffeine or nicotine may exacerbate the symptoms.

Depression may complicate the symptom picture in anywhere from 40 to 80 percent of all patients, as estimated by various studies. Although the patients do not tend to talk about suicidal ideation, they are at increased risk for committing suicide. Alcohol and other substance dependence occurs in about 20 to 40 percent of all patients, and obsessive-compulsive disorder may also develop. Family interactions and performance in school and at work commonly suffer. Patients with good premorbid functioning and a brief duration of symptoms tend to have good prognoses.

Agoraphobia

Most cases of agoraphobia are thought to be due to panic disorder. When the panic disorder is treated, the agoraphobia often improves with time. For a rapid and complete reduction of agoraphobia, behavior therapy is sometimes indicated. Agoraphobia without a history of panic disorder is often incapacitating and chronic, and depressive disorders and alcohol dependence often complicate its course.

TREATMENT

With treatment, most patients have a dramatic improvement in the symptoms of panic disorder and agoraphobia. The two most effective treatments are pharmacotherapy and cognitive-behavioral therapy. Family and group therapy may help affected patients and their families adjust to the fact that the patients have the disorder and to the psychosocial difficulties that the disorder may have precipitated.

Pharmacotherapy

Alprazolam (Xanax), sertraline (Zoloft), and paroxetine (Paxil) are the three drugs approved by the Food and Drug Administration for the treatment of panic disorder. In general, experience is showing superiority of the SSRIs and clomipramine (Anafranil) over the benzodiazepines, MAOIs, and tricyclic and tetracyclic drugs in terms of effectiveness and tolerance of adverse effects. A few reports have suggested a role for nefazodone (Serzone) and venlafaxine (Effexor), and buspirone (BuSpar) has been suggested as an additive medication in some cases. β-Adrenergic receptor antagonists have not been found to be useful for panic disorder. A conservative approach is to begin with paroxetine, sertraline, or fluvoxamine (Luvox) in isolated panic disorder. If rapid control of severe symptoms is desired, a brief course of alprazolam should be initiated concurrently with the SSRI, followed by slowly tapering off the benzodiazepine. In long-term use, fluoxetine (Prozac) is an effective drug for panic with comorbid depression, although its initial activating properties may mimic panic symptoms for the first several weeks and it may be poorly tolerated on this basis.

Serotonin-Specific Reuptake Inhibitors. Although once in long-term use at therapeutic dosages, all SSRIs are effective for panic disorder, significant differences in adverse effects make paroxetine the best tolerated for this indication. Paroxetine has sedative effects and tends to calm patients immediately, which leads to greater compliance and less discontinuation. Fluvoxamine and sertraline are the next best tolerated. Anecdotal reports suggest that patients with panic disorder are particularly sensitive to the activating effects of SSRIs, particularly fluoxetine, which requires that they be started at small doses and titrated up slowly. Once at therapeutic dosages, for example, 20 mg a day of paroxetine, some patients may experience increased sedation. One reasonable approach for patients with panic disorder and comorbid depression is to begin with 5 or 10 mg a day of paroxetine for 1 to 2 weeks, then increase the dosage by 10 mg a day every 1 to 2 weeks. If sedation becomes intolerable, then taper paroxetine down to 10 mg a day and switch to fluoxetine at 10 mg a day and titrate upward slowly. Other strategies can be used based on the experience of the clinician.

Benzodiazepines. Benzodiazepines have the most rapid onset of action against panic, often within the first week, and they can be used for long periods without the development of tolerance to the antipanic effects. Alprazolam has been the most widely used benzodiazepine for panic disorder, but controlled studies have demonstrated equal efficacy for lorazepam (Ativan), and case reports have also indicated that clonazepam (Klonopin) is effective. Some patients use benzodiazepines as needed when faced with a phobic stimulus. Benzodiazepines can reasonably be used as the first agent for treatment of panic disorder while a serotonergic drug is being slowly titrated to a therapeutic dose. After 4 to 12 weeks, the benzodiazepine can be slowly tapered (over 4 to 10 weeks) while the serotonergic drug is continued. The major reservation among clinicians regarding the use of benzodiazepines for panic disorder is the potential for dependence, cognitive impairment, and abuse, especially after long-term use. Patients should be instructed not to drive or operate dangerous equipment while taking benzodiazepines. Benzodiazepines elicit a sense of well-being, whereas discontinuation of benzodiazepines produces a well-documented and unpleasant withdrawal syndrome. Anecdotal reports and small case series have indicated that addiction to alprazolam is one of the most difficult to overcome, and it may require a comprehensive program of detoxification. Benzodiazepines should be tapered slowly, and all anticipated withdrawal effects should be thoroughly explained to the patient.

Tricyclic and Tetracyclic Drugs. The most robust data show that among tricyclic drugs, clomipramine and imipramine (Tofranil) are the most effective in the treatment of panic disorder. Clinical experience indicates that the doses must be titrated slowly upward to avoid overstimulation and that the full clinical benefit requires full dosages and may not be achieved for 8 to 12 weeks. Some data support the efficacy of desipramine (Norpramin), and less evidence suggests a role for maprotiline (Ludiomil), trazodone (Desyrel), nortriptyline (Pamelor), amitriptyline (Elavil), and doxepin (Adapin). Tricyclic drugs are less widely used than SSRIs because the tricyclic drugs generally have more severe adverse effects at the higher dosages required for effective treatment of panic disorder.

Monoamine Oxidase Inhibitors (MAOIs). The most robust data support the effectiveness of phenelzine (Nardil), and some data also support the use of tranylcypromine (Parnate). MAOIs appear less likely to cause overstimulation than either SSRIs or tricyclic drugs, but they may require full dosages for at least 8 to 12 weeks to be effective. The need for dietary restrictions has limited the use of MAOIs, particularly since the appearance of the SSRIs.

Treatment Failures. If patients fail to respond to one class of drugs, another should be tried. Recent data support the effectiveness of nefazodone and venlafaxine. The combination of an SSRI or a tricyclic drug and a benzodiazepine or of an SSRI and lithium or a tricyclic drug can be tried. Case reports have suggested the effectiveness of carbamazepine (Tegretol), valproate (Depakote), and calcium channel inhibitors. Buspirone may have a role in the augmentation of other medications but has little effectiveness by itself. Clinicians should reassess the patient, particularly to establish the presence of comorbid conditions such as depression, alcohol use, or other substance use.

Duration of Pharmacotherapy. Once it becomes effective, pharmacological treatment should generally continue for 8 to 12 months. Data indicate that panic disorder is a chronic, perhaps lifelong condition that recurs when treatment is discontinued. Studies have reported that from 30 to 90 percent of panic disorder patients who have received successful treatment have a relapse when their medication is discontinued. Patients may be likely to relapse if they have been given benzodiazepines and the benzodiazepine therapy is terminated in such a way as to cause withdrawal symptoms.

Cognitive and Behavior Therapies

Cognitive and behavior therapies are effective treatments for panic disorder. Various reports have concluded that cognitive and behavior therapies are superior to pharmacotherapy alone; other reports have concluded the opposite. Several studies and reports have found that the combination of cognitive or behavior therapy with pharmacotherapy is more effective than is either therapeutic approach alone. Several studies that included long-term follow-up of patients who received cognitive or behavior therapy have shown that the therapies are effective in producing long-lasting remission of symptoms.

Cognitive Therapy. The two major foci of cognitive therapy for panic disorder are instruction about a patient's false beliefs and information about panic attacks. The instruction about false beliefs centers on the patient's tendency to misinterpret mild bodily sensations as indicative of impending panic attacks, doom, or death. The information about panic attacks includes explanations that, when panic attacks occur, they are time limited and not life threatening.

Applied Relaxation. The goal of applied relaxation (for example, Herbert Benson's relaxation training) is to instill in patients a sense of control about their levels of anxiety and relaxation. Through the use of standardized techniques for muscle relaxation and the imagining of relaxing situations, patients learn techniques that may help them through a panic attack.

Respiratory Training. Because the hyperventilation associated with panic attacks is probably related to some symptoms such as dizziness and faintness, one direct approach to control panic attacks is to train patients to control the urge to hyperventilate. After such training, patients can use the technique to help control hyperventilation during a panic attack.

In Vivo Exposure. In vivo exposure used to be the primary behavior treatment for panic disorder. The technique involves sequentially greater exposure of a patient to the feared stimulus; over time, the patient becomes desensitized to the experience. Previously, the focus was on external stimuli; recently, the technique has included exposure of the patient to internal feared sensations (for example, tachypnea and fear of having a panic attack).

Other Psychosocial Therapies

Family Therapy. Families of patients with panic disorder and agoraphobia may also have been affected by the family member's disorder. Family therapy directed toward education and support is often beneficial.

Insight-Oriented Psychotherapy. Insight-oriented psychotherapy can be of benefit in the treatment of panic disorder and agoraphobia. Treatment focuses on helping patients understand the hypothesized unconscious meaning of the anxiety, the symbolism of the avoided situation, the need to repress impulses, and the secondary gains of the symptoms. A resolution of early infantile and oedipal conflicts is hypothesized to correlate with the resolution of current stresses.

Combined Psychotherapy and Pharmacotherapy

Even when pharmacotherapy is effective in eliminating the primary symptoms of panic disorder, psychotherapy may be needed to treat secondary symptoms. Glen O. Gabbard wrote:

> Panic-disordered patients frequently require a combination of drug therapy and psychotherapy. . . . Even when patients with panic attacks and agoraphobia have their symptoms pharmacologically controlled, they are often reluctant to venture out into the world again and may require psychotherapeutic interventions to help overcome this fear. . . . Some patients will adamantly refuse any medication because they believe that it stigmatizes them as being mentally ill, so psychotherapeutic intervention is required to help them understand and eliminate their resistance to pharmacotherapy. . . . For a comprehensive and effective treatment plan, these patients require psychotherapeutic approaches in addition to appropriate medications. In all patients with symptoms of panic disorder or agoraphobia, a careful psychodynamic evaluation will help weigh the contributions of biological and dynamic factors.

References

Ballenger JC: Medication discontinuation in panic disorder. J Clin Psychiatry *53* (3, Suppl): 26, 1992.

Barlow DH: Cognitive-behavioral approaches to panic disorder and social phobia. Bull Menninger Clin *56* (2, Suppl): A14, 1992.

Basoglu M, Marks IM, Sengun S: A prospective study of panic and anxiety in agoraphobia with panic disorder. Br J Psychiatry *160:* 57, 1992.

Black DW, Wesner R, Bowers W, Gabel J: A comparison of fluvoxamine, cognitive therapy, and placebo in the treatment of panic disorder. Arch Gen Psychiatry *50:* 44, 1993.

Charney DS, Woods SW, Krystal JH, Nagy LM, Heninger GR: Noradrenergic neuronal dysregulation in panic disorder: The effects of intravenous yohimbine and clonidine in panic disorder patients. Acta Psychiatr Scand *86:* 273, 1992.

Coplan JD, Gorman JM, Klein DF: Serotonin related functions in panic-anxiety: A critical overview. Neuropsychopharmacology *6:* 189, 1992.

Fawcett J: Suicide risk factors in depressive disorders and panic disorder. J Clin Psychiatry *53* (3, Suppl): 9, 1992.

Francis G, Last CG, Strauss CC: Avoidant disorder and social phobia in children and adolescents. J Am Acad Child Adolesc Psychiatry *31:* 1086, 1992.

Fyer AJ, Mannuzza S, Coplan JD: Panic disorders and agoraphobia. In *Comprehensive Textbook of Psychiatry,* ed 6, HI Kaplan, BJ Sadock, editors, p 1191. Williams & Wilkins, Baltimore, 1995.

Gabbard GO: *Psychodynamic Psychiatry in Clinical Practice: The DSM-IV Edition.* American Psychiatric Press, Washington, 1994.

Gabbard GO: Psychodynamic psychiatry in the ''decade of the brain.'' Am J Psychiatry *149:* 991, 1992.

Gelernter CS, Uhde TW, Cimbolic P, Arnkoff DB, Vittone BJ, Tancer ME, Bartko JJ: Cognitive-behavioral and pharmacological treatments of social phobia: A controlled study. Arch Gen Psychiatry *48:* 938, 1991.

Heimberg RG, Barlow DH: New developments in cognitive-behavioral therapy for social phobia. J Clin Psychiatry *52* (11, Suppl): 21, 1991.

Himle JA, Crystal D, Curtis GC, Fluent TE: Mode of onset of simple phobia subtypes: Further evidence of heterogeneity. Psychiatry Res *36:* 37, 1991.

Hollifield M, Katon W, Skipper B, Chapman T, Ballenger JC, Mannuzza S, Fyer AJ: Panic disorder and quality of life: Variables predictive of functional impairment. Am J Psychiatry *154:* 766, 1997.

Horwath E, Herbert JD, Hope DA, Bellack AS: Validity of the distinction between generalized social phobia and avoidant personality disorder. J Abnorm Psychol *101:* 332, 1991.

Jacob RG, Furman JM, Durrant JD, Turner SM: Panic, agoraphobia, and vestibular dysfunction. Am J Psychiatry *153:* 503, 1996.

Johnson J, Hornig CD: Epidemiology of panic disorder in African-Americans. Am J Psychiatry *150:* 465, 1993.

Johnson MR, Lydiard RB, Ballenger JC: Panic disorder. Pathophysiology and drug treatment. Drugs *49:* 328, 1995.

Katerndahl DA, Realini JP: Lifetime prevalence of panic states. Am J Psychiatry *150:* 246, 1993.

Keller MB, Hanks DL: Course and outcome in panic disorder. Prog Neuropsychopharmacol Biol Psychiatry *17:* 551, 1993.

Kenardy J, Fried L, Kraemer HC, Taylor CB: Psychological precursors of panic attacks. Br J Psychiatry *160:* 668, 1992.

Klein DF: Panic disorder and agoraphobia: Hypothesis hothouse. J Clin Psychiatry *57* (6, Suppl): 21, 1996.

Klerman GL: Drug treatment of panic disorder: Reply to comment by Marks and associates. Br J Psychiatry *161:* 465, 1992.

Lydiard RB, Lesser IM, Ballenger JC, Rubin RT, Laraia M, DuPont R: A fixed-dose study of alprazolam 2 mg, alprazolam 6 mg, and placebo in panic disorder. J Clin Psychopharmacol *12:* 96, 1992.

Margraf J, Barlow DH, Clark DM, Telch MJ: Psychological treatment of panic: Work in progress on outcome, active ingredients, and follow-up. Behav Res Ther *31:* 1, 1993.

Modigh K, Westberg P, Eriksson E: Superiority of clomipramine over imipramine in the treatment of panic disorder: A placebo-controlled trial. J Clin Psychopharmacol *12:* 251, 1992.

Moreau D, Weissman MM: Panic disorder in children and adolescents: A review. Am J Psychiatry *149:* 1306, 1992.

Nutt D, Lawson C: Panic attacks: A neurochemical overview of models and mechanisms. Br J Psychiatry *160:* 165, 1992.

Ost LG: Blood and injection phobia: Background and cognitive, physiological, and behavioral variables. J Abnorm Psychol *101:* 68, 1992.

Panic disorder: Strategies for long-term treatment. J Clin Psychiatry *52* (2, Suppl): 2, 1991.

Pollard CA, Tait RC, Meldrum D, Dubinsky IH, Gall JS: Agoraphobia without panic: Case illustrations of an overlooked syndrome. J Nerv Ment Dis *184:* 61, 1996.

Rapee RM, Litwin EM, Barlow DH: Impact on life events on subjects with panic disorder and on comparison subjects. Am J Psychiatry *147:* 640, 1990.

Rickels K, Schweizer E, Weiss S, Zavodnick S: Maintenance drug treatment for panic disorder: II. Short- and long-term outcome after drug taper. Arch Gen Psychiatry *50:* 61, 1993.

Ross J: Social phobia: The Anxiety Disorders Association of America helps raise the veil of ignorance. J Clin Psychiatry *52* (11, Suppl): 43, 1991.

Schneier FR, Johnson J, Hornic CD, Liebowitz MR, Weissman MM: Social phobia: Comorbidity and morbidity in an epidemiologic sample. Arch Gen Psychiatry *49:* 282, 1992.

Schweizer E, Rickels K, Weiss S, Zavodnick S: Maintenance drugs treatment of panic disorder: I. Results of a prospective, placebo-controlled comparison of alprazolam and imipramine. Arch Gen Psychiatry *50:* 51, 1993.

Shear MK: Panic disorder with and without agoraphobia. In *Psychiatry,* A Tasman, J Kay, JA Lieberman, editors, p 1021. Saunders, Philadelphia, 1995.

Shear MK, Cooper AM, Klerman GL, Busch FN, Shapiro T: A psychodynamic model of panic disorder. Am J Psychiatry *150:* 859, 1993.

Spiegel DA, Bruce TJ: Benzodiazepines and exposure-based cognitive behavior therapies for panic disorder: Conclusions from combined treatment trials. Am J Psychiatry *154:* 773, 1997.

▲ 16.3 Specific Phobia and Social Phobia

The fourth edition of *Diagnostic and Statistical Manual of Mental Disorders* (DSM-IV) lists two other phobias in addition to agoraphobia: specific phobia and social phobia. DSM-IV defines specific phobia as a strong, persisting fear of an object or situation, whereas social phobia is a strong, persisting fear of situations in which embarrassment can occur. People with specific phobias may anticipate harm, such as being bitten by a dog, or may panic at the thought of losing control; for instance, if they fear being in an elevator, they may also worry about fainting after the door closes. People with social phobias (also called social anxiety disorder) have excessive fears of humiliation or embarrassment in various social settings, such as in speaking in public, urinating in a public rest room (also called shy bladder), and speaking to a date. A generalized social phobia, which is often a chronic and disabling condition characterized by a phobic avoidance of most social situations, can be difficult to distinguish from avoidant personality disorder.

A phobia is defined as an irrational fear that produces a conscious avoidance of the feared subject, activity, or situation. Either the presence or the anticipation of the phobic entity elicits severe distress in an affected person, who usually recognizes that the reaction is excessive. Phobic reactions usually disrupt people's ability to function in life.

Recent epidemiological studies have shown that phobias are the single most common mental disorder in the United States, where approximately 5 to 10 percent of the population is estimated to be afflicted with these troubling and sometimes disabling disorders. Less conservative estimates have ranged as high as 25 percent of the population. The distress associated with phobias, especially when they are not recognized or acknowledged as mental disorders, can lead to further psychiatric complications, including other anxiety disorders, major depressive disorder, and substance-related disorders, especially alcohol use disorders. Recent research studies have found that phobias are often responsive to treatment with cognitive and behavioral psychotherapies and with specific pharmacotherapies, including tricyclic drugs, monoamine oxidase inhibitors (MAOIs), and β-adrenergic receptor antagonists.

EPIDEMIOLOGY

Although phobias are common mental disorders, a large percentage of people with phobias either do not seek help to overcome their phobias or are misdiagnosed when they do come to psychiatric or medical attention. The lifetime prevalence of specific phobia is about 11 percent, and the lifetime prevalence of social phobia has been reported at 3 to 13 percent.

Specific Phobia

Specific phobia is more common than social phobia. Specific phobia is the most common mental disorder among women and the second most common among men, second only to substance-related disorders. The 6-month prevalence of specific phobia is about 5 to 10 per 100 people. The female-to-male ratio is about 2 to 1, although the ratio is closer to 1 to 1 for the blood-injection-injury type. (Types of phobia are discussed later in this section.) The peak age of onset for the natural environment type and the blood-injection-injury type is in the range of 5 to 9 years, although onset also occurs at older ages. In contrast, the peak age of onset for the situational type (except fear of heights) is higher, in the mid-20s, which is closer to the age of onset for agoraphobia. The feared objects and situations in specific phobia (listed in descending frequency of appearance) are animals, storms, heights, illness, injury, and death.

Social Phobia

The 6-month prevalence for social phobia is about 2 to 3 per 100 people. In epidemiological studies, females are affected more often than males, but in clinical samples, the reverse is often true. The reasons for these varying observations are unknown. The peak age of onset for social phobia is in the teens, although onset is common as young as 5 years of age and as old as 35.

ETIOLOGY

Both specific phobia and social phobia have types, and the precise causes of these types are likely to differ. Even within the types, as in all mental disorders, causative heterogeneity is found. The pathogenesis of the phobias, once it is understood, may prove to be a clear model for interactions between biological and genetic factors, on the one hand, and environmental events, on the other hand. In the blood-injection-injury type of specific phobia, affected people may have inherited a particularly strong vasovagal reflex, which becomes associated with phobic emotions.

General Principles

Behavioral Factors. In 1920, John B. Watson wrote an article called "Conditioned Emotional Reactions," in which he recounted his experiences with Little Albert, an infant with a fear of rats and rabbits. Unlike Sigmund Freud's Little Hans, who had phobic symptoms in the natural course of his maturation, Little Albert's difficulties were the direct result of the scientific experiments of two psychologists who used techniques that had successfully induced conditioned responses in laboratory animals.

Watson's hypothesis invoked the traditional pavlovian stimulus–response model of the conditioned reflex to account for the creation of the phobia: Anxiety is aroused by a naturally frightening stimulus that occurs in contiguity with a second inherently neutral stimulus. As a result of the contiguity, especially when the two stimuli are paired on several successive occasions, the originally neutral stimulus takes on the capacity to arouse anxiety by itself. The neutral stimulus, therefore, becomes a conditioned stimulus for anxiety production.

In the classic stimulus–response theory, the conditioned stimulus gradually loses its potency to arouse a response if it is not reinforced by a periodic repetition of the unconditioned stimulus. In phobias, the attenuation of the response to the phobic or conditioned stimulus does not occur; the symptom may last for years without any apparent external reinforcement. Operant conditioning theory provides a model to explain this phenomenon: Anxiety is a drive that motivates the organism to do whatever it can to obviate a painful affect. In the course of its random behavior, the organism learns that certain actions enable it to avoid the anxiety-provoking stimulus. These avoidance patterns remain stable for long periods as a result of the reinforcement they receive from their capacity to diminish activity. This model is readily applicable to phobias in that avoidance of the anxiety-provoking object or situation plays a central part. Such avoidance behavior becomes fixed as a stable symptom because of its effectiveness in protecting the person from the phobic anxiety.

Learning theory is particularly relevant to phobias and provides simple and intelligible explanations for many aspects of phobic symptoms. Critics contend, however, that learning theory deals mostly with surface mechanisms of symptom formation and is less useful than are psychoanalytic theories in clarifying some of the complex underlying psychic processes involved.

Psychoanalytic Factors. Sigmund Freud's formulation of phobic neurosis is still the analytic explanation of specific phobia and social phobia. Freud hypothesized that the major function of anxiety is to signal the ego that a forbidden unconscious drive is pushing for conscious expression and to alert the ego to strengthen and marshall its defenses against the threatening instinctual force. Freud viewed the phobia—*anxiety hysteria,* as he continued to call it—as a result of conflicts centered on an unresolved childhood oedipal situation. Because sex drives continue to have a strong incestuous coloring in adults, sexual arousal can kindle an anxiety that is characteristically a fear of castration. When repression fails to be entirely successful, the ego must call on auxiliary defenses. In patients with phobias, the defense involves primarily the use of displacement; that is, the sexual conflict is displaced from the person who evokes the conflict to a seemingly unimportant, irrelevant object or situation, which then has the power to arouse the constellation of affects, including signal anxiety. The phobic object or situation may have a direct associative connection with the primary source of the conflict and, thus, symbolizes it (the defense mechanism of symbolization). Furthermore, the situation or the object is usually one that the person is able to keep away from; with this additional defense mechanism of avoidance, the person can escape suffering serious anxiety. Freud first discussed the theoretical formulation of phobia formation in his famous case history of Little Hans, a 5-year-old boy who feared horses.

Although psychiatrists followed Freud's thought that phobias resulted from castration anxiety, recent psychoanalytic theorists have suggested that other types of anxiety may be involved. In agoraphobia, for example, separation anxiety clearly plays a leading role, and in erythrophobia (a fear of red that can be manifested as a fear of blushing), the element of shame implies the involvement of superego anxiety. Clinical observations have led to the view that anxiety associated with phobias has a variety of sources and colorings.

Phobias illustrate the interaction between a genetic constitutional diathesis and environmental stressors. Longitudinal studies suggest that certain children are constitutionally predisposed to phobias because they are born with a specific temperament known as behavioral inhibition to the unfamiliar, but a chronic environmental stress must act on a child's temperamental disposition to create a full-blown phobia. Stressors such as the death of a parent, separation from a parent, criticism or humiliation by an older sibling, and violence in the household may activate the latent diathesis within the child, who then becomes symptomatic.

COUNTERPHOBIC ATTITUDE. Otto Fenichel called attention to the fact that phobic anxiety can be hidden behind attitudes and behavior patterns that represent a denial, either that the dreaded object or situation is dangerous or that the person is afraid of it. Instead of being a passive victim of external circumstances, a person reverses the situation and actively attempts to confront and master whatever is feared. People with counterphobic attitudes seek out situations of danger and rush enthusiastically toward them. Devotees of potentially dangerous sports, such as parachute jumping and rock climbing, may be exhibiting counterphobic behavior. Such patterns may be secondary to phobic anxiety or may be normal means of dealing with a realistically dangerous situation. Children's play may exhibit counterphobic elements, as when children play doctor and give a doll the shot they received earlier that day in the pediatrician's office. This pattern of behavior may involve the related defense mechanism of identifying with the aggressor.

Specific Phobia

The development of specific phobia may result from the pairing of a specific object or situation with the emotions of fear and panic. Various mechanisms for the pairing have been postulated. In general, a nonspecific tendency to experience fear or anxiety forms the backdrop; when a specific event (driving, for example) is paired with an emotional experience (an accident, for example), the person is susceptible to a permanent emotional association between driving or cars and fear or anxiety. The emotional experience itself can be responsive to an external incident, as in a traffic accident, or to an internal incident, most commonly a panic attack. Although a person may never again experience a panic attack and may not meet the diagnostic criteria for panic disorder, he or she may have a generalized fear of driving, not an expressed fear of having a panic attack while driving. Other mechanisms of association between the phobic object and the phobic emotions include modeling, in which a person observes the reaction in another (for example, a parent), and information transfer, in which a person is taught or warned about the dangers of specific objects (for example, venomous snakes).

Genetic Factors. Specific phobia tends to run in families. The blood-injection-injury type has a particularly high familial tendency. Studies have reported that two thirds to three fourths of affected probands have at least one first-degree relative with specific phobia of the same type, but the necessary twin and adoption studies have not been conducted to rule out a significant contribution by nongenetic transmission of specific phobia.

Social Phobia

Several studies have reported that some children possibly have a trait characterized by a consistent pattern of behavioral inhibition. This trait may be particularly common in the children of parents who are affected with panic disorder and may develop into severe shyness as the children grow older. At least some people with social phobia may have exhibited behavioral inhibition during childhood. Perhaps associated with this trait, which is thought to be biologically based, are the psychologically based data indicating that the parents of people with social phobia were, as a group, less caring, more rejecting, and more overprotective of their children than were other parents. Some social phobia research has referred to the spectrum from dominance to submission observed in the animal kingdom. For example, dominant humans may tend to walk with their chins in the air and to make eye contact, whereas submissive humans may tend to walk with their chins down and to avoid eye contact.

Neurochemical Factors. The success of pharmacotherapies in treating social phobia has generated two specific neurochemical hypotheses about two types of social phobia. Specifically, the use of β-adrenergic antagonists—for example, propranolol (Inderal)—for performance phobias (such as public speaking) has led to the development of an adrenergic theory for these phobias. Patients with performance phobias may release more norepinephrine or epinephrine, both centrally and peripherally, than do nonphobic people, or such patients may be sensitive to a normal level of adrenergic stimulation. The observation that MAOIs may be more effective than tricyclic drugs in the treatment of generalized social phobia, in combination with preclinical data, has led some investigators to hypothesize that dopaminergic activity is related to the pathogenesis of the disorder.

Genetic Factors. First-degree relatives of people with social phobia are about 3 times more likely to be affected with social phobia than are first-degree relatives of those without mental disorders. And some preliminary data indicate that monozygotic twins are more often concordant than are dizygotic twins, although in social phobia it is particularly important to study twins reared apart to help control for environmental factors.

DIAGNOSIS

Specific Phobia

DSM-IV uses the term specific phobia to match the nomenclature in the 10th revision of *International Statistical*

Classification of Diseases and Related Health Problems (ICD-10) and to avoid restricting the scope of the diagnosis (Table 16.3–1). Criteria A and B have been carefully worded in DSM-IV to allow for the possibility that exposure to a phobic stimulus results in a panic attack. In contrast to panic disorder, however, in specific phobia, the panic attack is situationally bound to the specific phobic stimulus. Criterion G in DSM-IV includes the words "not better accounted for" to emphasize the need for clinicians' judgment about diagnosing the symptoms. The specific content of the phobia and the strength of the relation (for example, cued or noncued) between the stimulus and a panic attack also need to be considered.

Because a review of the literature indicated that specific phobia is associated with varying ages of onset, sex ratios, family histories, and physiological responses, DSM-IV includes distinctive types of specific phobia: animal type; natural environment type (for example, storms); blood-injection-injury type; situational type (for example, cars); and other type (for specific phobias that do not fit into the previous four types). Preliminary data indicate that the natural environment type is most common in children younger than 10 years old and the situational type most often occurs in people in their early 20s. The blood-injection-injury type is differentiated from the others in that bradycardia and hypotension often follow the initial tachycardia common in all phobias. The blood-injection-injury type of specific phobia is particularly likely to affect many members and generations of a family. One type of recently reported specific phobia is space phobia, in which people are afraid of falling when there is no nearby support like a wall or a chair. Some data indicate that affected people may have abnormal right hemisphere function, possibly resulting in a visual-spatial impairment. Balance disorders should also be ruled out in such cases.

Table 16.3–1
DSM-IV Diagnostic Criteria for Specific Phobia

A. Marked and persistent fear that is excessive or unreasonable, cued by the presence or anticipation of a specific object or situation (eg, flying, heights, animals, receiving an injection, seeing blood).

B. Exposure to the phobic stimulus almost invariably provokes an immediate anxiety response, which may take the form of a situationally bound or situationally predisposed panic attack. **Note:** in children, the anxiety may be expressed by crying, tantrums, freezing, or clinging.

C. The person recognizes that the fear is excessive or unreasonable. **Note:** in children, this feature may be absent.

D. The phobic situation(s) is avoided, or else endured with intense anxiety or distress.

E. The avoidance, anxious anticipation, or distress in the feared situation(s) interferes significantly with the person's normal routine, occupational (or academic) functioning, or social activities or relationships with others, or there is marked distress about having the phobia.

F. In individuals under age 18 years, the duration is at least 6 months.

G. The anxiety, panic attacks, or phobic avoidance associated with the specific object or situation are not better accounted for by another mental disorder, such as obsessive-compulsive disorder (eg, fear of dirt in someone with an obsession about contamination), posttraumatic stress disorder (eg, avoidance of stimuli associated with a severe stressor), separation anxiety disorder (eg, avoidance of school), social phobia (eg, avoidance of social situations because of fear of embarrassment), panic disorder with agoraphobia, or agoraphobia without history of panic disorder.

Specify type:

Animal type
Natural environment type (eg, heights, storms, and water)
Blood-injection-injury type
Situational type (eg, planes, elevators, enclosed places)
Other type (eg, phobic avoidance of situations that may lead to choking, vomiting, or contracting an illness; in children, avoidance of loud sounds or costumed characters)

Social Phobia

The DSM-IV diagnostic criteria for social phobia (Table 16.3–2) acknowledge that the disorder can be associated with panic attacks. DSM-IV also includes a specifier for generalized type, which may be of use in the prediction of course, prognosis, and treatment response. DSM-IV excludes a diagnosis of social phobia when the symptoms are a result of social avoidance stemming from embarrassment about another psychiatric or nonpsychiatric medical condition.

CLINICAL FEATURES

Phobias are characterized by the arousal of severe anxiety when patients are exposed to specific situations or objects or when patients even anticipate exposure to the situations or objects. DSM-IV emphasizes the possibility that panic attacks can and frequently do occur in patients with specific and social phobias, but the panic attacks, except perhaps for the first few, are expected. Exposure to the phobic stimulus or anticipation of it almost invariably results in a panic attack in a person who is susceptible to them.

People with phobias, by definition, try to avoid the phobic stimulus; some go to great trouble to avoid anxiety-provoking situations. For example, a phobic patient may take a bus across the United States, rather than fly, to avoid contact with the object of the patient's phobia, an airplane. Perhaps as another way to avoid the stress of the phobic stimulus, many phobic patients have substance-related disorders, particularly alcohol use disorders. Moreover, an estimated one third of patients with social phobia have major depressive disorder.

The major finding on the mental status examination is the presence of an irrational and ego-dystonic fear of a specific situation, activity, or object; patients are able to describe how they avoid contact with the phobia. Depression is commonly found on the mental status examination and may be present in as many as one third of all phobic patients.

Sheila, a 28-year-old housewife, sought psychiatric treatment for a fear of storms that had become progressively more disturbing to her. Although frightened of storms since she was a child, the fear seemed to abate

Table 16.3–2
DSM-IV Diagnostic Criteria for Social Phobia

A. A marked and persistent fear of one or more social or performance situations in which the person is exposed to unfamiliar people or to possible scrutiny by others. The individual fears that he or she will act in a way (or show anxiety symptoms) that will be humiliating or embarrassing. **Note:** in children, there must be evidence of capacity for age-appropriate social relationships with familiar people and the anxiety must occur in peer settings, not just in interactions with adults.

B. Exposure to the feared social situation almost invariably provokes anxiety, which may take the form of a situationally bound or situationally predisposed panic attack. **Note:** In children, the anxiety may be expressed by crying, tantrums, freezing, or shrinking from social situations with unfamiliar people.

C. The person recognizes that the fear is excessive or unreasonable. **Note:** in children, this feature may be absent.

D. The feared social or performance situations are avoided, or else endured with intense anxiety or distress.

E. The avoidance, anxious anticipation, or distress in the feared social or performance situation(s) interferes significantly with the person's normal routine, occupational (academic) functioning, or social actitivies or relationships with others, or there is marked distress about having the phobia.

F. In individuals under age 18 years, the duration is at least 6 months.

G. The fear or avoidance is not due to the direct physiological effects of a substance (eg, a drug of abuse, a medication) or a general medical condition, and is not better accounted for by another mental disorder (eg, panic disorder with or without agoraphobia, separation anxiety disorder, body dysmorphic disorder, a pervasive developmental disorder, or schizoid personality disorder).

H. If a general medical condition or other mental disorder is present, the fear in criterion A is unrelated to it, eg, the fear is not of stuttering, trembling in Parkinson's disease, or exhibiting abnormal eating behavior in anorexia nervosa or bulimia nervosa.

Specify if:

Generalized: if the fears include most social situations (also consider the additional diagnosis of avoidant personality disorder).

Reprinted with permission from American Psychiatric Association: *Diagnostic and Statistical Manual of Mental Disorders,* ed 4. Copyright, American Psychiatric Association, Washington, 1994.

somewhat during adolescence but had been increasing in severity over the past few years. This gradual exacerbation of her anxiety, plus the fear that she might pass it on to her children, led her to seek treatment.

She is most frightened of lightning but is uncertain about the reason for this. She is only vaguely aware of a fear of being struck by lightning and recognizes that this is an unlikely occurrence. When asked to elaborate on her fears, she imagines that lightning could strike a tree in her yard and the tree might fall and block her driveway, thus trapping her at home. This frightens her, but she is quite aware that her fear is irrational. She also recognizes the irrational nature of her fear of thunder. She begins to feel anxiety long before a storm arrives. A weather report predicting a storm later in the week can cause her anxiety to increase to the point where she worries for days before the storm. Although she does not express a fear of rain, her anxiety increases even when the sky becomes overcast because of the increased likelihood of a storm.

During a storm, she does several things to reduce her anxiety. Because being with another person reduces her fear, she often tries to make plans to visit friends or relatives or go to a store when a storm is threatening. Sometimes, when her husband is away on business, she stays overnight with a close relative if a storm is forecast. During a storm she covers her eyes or moves to a part of the house far from windows where she cannot see lightning should it occur.

Sheila has three young children. She describes her marriage as a happy one and states that her husband has been supportive of her, when she is frightened, and has encouraged her to seek psychiatric treatment. She is in good physical health, and at the time she entered treatment there were no unusually stressful situations in her life or other emotional difficulties. Her parents separated shortly after she began treatment. Although she found this distressing, she felt her personal supports were adequate and that this occurrence did not necessitate psychiatric attention.

She describes her personal history as generally unremarkable in terms of any obvious emotional problems, except for her fear of storms. She feels that she may have "learned" this fear from her grandmother, who also was frightened of storms. She denies panic attacks or any other unusual or incapacitating fears.

DISCUSSION

Many people feel uncomfortable during thunder and lightning storms, but Sheila's persistent fear of this circumscribed stimulus is clearly excessive, causes her considerable distress, and is acknowledged by her to be unreasonable. Furthermore, the fear and the avoidant behavior frequently interfere significantly with her normal routine. These features indicate the presence of a phobia. Although she is afraid of being alone during storms, there is apparently no fear of developing a panic attack or some other incapacitating or embarrassing symptom when alone or in public places away from home, as in agoraphobia without history of panic disorder. Her fear of storms does not involve a fear of humiliation or embarrassment in certain social situations, as in social phobia, and it is not related to the content of the obsessions of obsessive-compulsive disorder. Therefore, by exclusion, the diagnosis is specific phobia, natural environment type. (From *DSM-IV Casebook.*)

DIFFERENTIAL DIAGNOSIS

Specific phobia and social phobia need to be differentiated from appropriate fear and normal shyness, respectively. DSM-IV aids in the differentiation by requiring that the symptoms impair the patient's ability to function appropriately. Nonpsychiatric medical conditions that can result in the development of a phobia include the use of substances (particularly hallucinogens and sympathomimetics), central nervous system tumors, and cerebrovascular diseases. Phobic symptoms in these instances are unlikely in the absence of additional suggestive findings on physical, neurological, and mental status examinations. Schizophrenia is also in the differential diagnosis of both specific phobia and social phobia, as schizophrenic patients can have phobic symptoms as part of their psychoses. Unlike patients with schizophrenia, however, phobic patients have insight into the irrationality of their fears and lack the bizarre quality and other psychotic symptoms that accompany schizophrenia.

In the differential diagnosis of both specific phobia and social phobia, clinicians must consider panic disorder, agoraphobia, and avoidant personality disorder. DSM-IV acknowledges that the differentiation among panic disorder, agoraphobia, social phobia, and specific phobia can be difficult in individual cases, and clinicians are advised to use clinical judgment. In general, however, patients with specific phobia or nongeneralized social phobia tend to experience anxiety immediately when presented with the phobic stimulus. Furthermore, the anxiety or panic is limited to the identified situation; patients are not abnormally anxious when they are neither confronted with the phobic stimulus nor caused to anticipate the stimulus.

A patient with agoraphobia is often comforted by the presence of another person in an anxiety-provoking situation, whereas a patient with social phobia is made more anxious than before by the presence of other people. Whereas breathlessness, dizziness, a sense of suffocation, and a fear of dying are common in panic disorder and agoraphobia, the symptoms associated with social phobia usually involve blushing, muscle twitching, and anxiety about scrutiny. The differentiation between social phobia and avoidant personality disorder can be difficult and can require extensive interviews and psychiatric histories.

Specific Phobia

Other diagnoses to consider in the differential diagnosis of specific phobia are hypochondriasis, obsessive-compulsive disorder, and paranoid personality disorder. Hypochondriasis is the fear of having a disease, whereas specific phobia of the illness type is the fear of contracting the disease. Some patients with obsessive-compulsive disorder manifest behavior indistinguishable from that of a patient with specific phobia. For example, patients with obsessive-compulsive disorder may avoid knives because they have compulsive thoughts about killing their children, whereas patients with specific phobia about knives may avoid them for fear of cutting themselves. Patients with paranoid personality disorder have generalized fear that distinguishes them from those with specific phobia.

Social Phobia

Two additional differential diagnostic considerations for social phobia are major depressive disorder and schizoid personality disorder. The avoidance of social situations can often be a symptom in depression, but a psychiatric interview with the patient is likely to elicit a broad constellation of depressive symptoms. In patients with schizoid personality disorder, the lack of interest in socializing, not the fear of socializing, leads to the avoidant social behavior.

COURSE AND PROGNOSIS

Little is known about the course and the prognosis of specific phobia and social phobia because of their relatively recent recognition as important mental disorders. The introduction of specific psychotherapies and pharmacotherapies to treat phobias will also affect the interpretation of data on course and prognosis unless the studies control for the treatment strategies.

Phobic disorders may be associated with more morbidity than was previously recognized. On the basis of the degree to which phobic behavior interferes with a person's ability to function, affected patients may always be financially dependent on others and may have various impairments in their social lives, occupations and, in the case of young people, school performance. The development of associated substance-related disorders can also adversely affect the course and prognosis of the disorders.

TREATMENT

Insight-Oriented Psychotherapy

Early in the development of psychoanalysis and the dynamically oriented psychotherapies, theorists believed that these methods were the treatments of choice for phobic neurosis, which was then thought to stem from oedipal-genital conflicts. Soon, however, therapists recognized that, despite progress in uncovering and analyzing unconscious conflicts, patients frequently failed to lose their phobic symptoms. Moreover, by continuing to avoid phobic situations, patients excluded a significant degree of anxiety and its related associations from the analytic process. Both Freud and his pupil Sándor Ferenczi recognized that, if progress in analyzing these symptoms was to be made, therapists had to go beyond their analytic roles and actively urge phobic patients to seek the phobic situation and experience the anxiety and resultant insight. Since then, psychiatrists have generally agreed that a measure of activity on the therapist's part is often required to treat phobic anxiety successfully. The decision to apply the techniques of psychodynamic insight-oriented therapy should be based not on the presence of phobic symptoms alone but on positive indications from the patient's ego structure and life patterns for the use of this method of treatment. Insight-oriented therapy enables patients to understand the origin of the phobia, the phenomenon of secondary gain, and the role of resistance and enables them to seek healthy ways of dealing with anxiety-provoking stimuli.

Other Therapies

Hypnosis, supportive therapy, and family therapy may be useful in treating phobias. Hypnosis is used to enhance the therapist's suggestions that the phobic object is not dangerous, and self-hypnosis can be taught to the patient as a method of relaxation when confronted with the phobic object. Supportive psychotherapy and family therapy are often useful in helping the patient actively confront the phobic object during treatment. Not only can family therapy enlist the family's aid in treating the patient but it may also help the family understand the nature of the patient's problem. An additional therapeutic and supportive activity for patients may be involvement in the Anxiety Disorders Association of America.

Specific Phobia

The most commonly used treatment for specific phobia is exposure therapy, a type of behavior therapy originally pioneered by Joseph Wolpe. Therapists desensitize patients by using a series of gradual, self-paced exposures to the phobic stimuli, and they teach patients various techniques to deal with anxiety, including relaxation, breathing control, and cognitive approaches. The cognitive approaches include reinforcing the realization that the phobic situation is, in fact, safe. The key aspects of successful behavior therapy are the patient's commitment to treatment, clearly identified problems and objectives, and alternative strategies for coping with the patient's feelings. In the special situation of blood-injection-injury phobia, some therapists recommend that patients tense their bodies and remain seated during the exposure to help avoid the possibility of fainting from a vasovagal reaction to the phobic stimulation. Some preliminary reports indicate that β-adrenergic antagonists can be useful in the treatment of specific phobia. When specific phobia is associated with panic attacks, pharmacotherapy or psychotherapy directed to the attacks may also be of benefit.

Social Phobia

Both psychotherapy and pharmacotherapy are useful in treating social phobias, and varying approaches are indicated for the generalized type and for performance situations. Some studies indicate that the use of both pharmacotherapy and psychotherapy produces better results than either therapy alone, although the finding may not be applicable to all situations and patients.

Several controlled studies have reported successful treatment of social phobia, especially severe cases, with both irreversible MAOIs, such as phenelzine (Nardil), and reversible inhibitors of monoamine oxidase, such as moclobemide (Aurorix) and brofaromine (Consonar) (which are not available in the United States). Other drugs for which evidence of effectiveness is accruing include the serotonin-specific reuptake inhibitors (SSRIs), the benzodiazepines, venlafaxine (Effexor), and buspirone (BuSpar). Buspirone has shown additive effects when used to augment treatment with SSRIs. β-Adrenergic receptor antagonists have been widely used for situational anxiety, such as performance anxiety, to block tachycardia and perspiration. The benefits of a reduction in the peripheral manifestations of anxiety by β-adrenergic receptor antagonists should be weighed against their possible effects to create lethargy.

Psychotherapy for the generalized type of social phobia usually involves a combination of behavioral and cognitive methods, including cognitive retraining, desensitization, rehearsal during sessions, and a range of homework assignments.

The treatment of social phobia associated with performance situations frequently involves the use of β-adrenergic receptor antagonists shortly before exposure to a phobic stimulus. The two compounds most widely used are atenolol (Tenormin), 50 to 100 mg every morning or 1 hour before the performance, and propranolol (20 to 40 mg). Cognitive, behavioral, and exposure techniques can also be useful in performance situations.

References

Barlow DH, Liebowitz MR: Specific phobia and social phobia. In *Comprehensive Textbook of Psychiatry,* ed 6, HI Kaplan, BJ Sadock, editors, p 1204. Williams & Wilkins, Baltimore, 1995.

Chapman TF, Fyer AJ, Mannuzza S, Klein DF: A comparison of treated and untreated simple phobia. Am J Psychiatry *150:* 816, 1993.

Dilsaver SC, Qamar AB, Del Medico VJ: Secondary social phobia in patients with major depression. Psychiatry Res *44:* 33, 1992.

Francis G, Last CG, Strauss CC: Avoidant disorder and social phobia in children and adolescents. J Am Acad Child Adolesc Psychiatry *31:* 1086, 1992.

Gabbard GO: Psychodynamics of panic disorder and social phobia. Bull Menninger Clin *56* (2, Suppl): A3, 1992.

Greist JH: The diagnosis of social phobia. J Clin Psychiatry *56:* 5, 1995.

Jefferson JW: Social phobia: Everyone's disorder? J Clin Psychiatry *57* (6, Suppl): 28, 1996.

Magee WJ, Eaton WW, Wittchen HU, McGonagle KA, Kessler RC: Agoraphobia, simple phobia, and social phobia in the National Comorbidity Survey. Arch Gen Psychiatry *53:* 159, 1996.

Parker JDA, Taylor GJ, Bagby RM, Acklin MW: Alexithymia in panic disorder and simple phobia: A comparative study. Am J Psychiatry *150:* 1105, 1993.

Potts NLS, Davidson JRT: Social phobia: Biological aspects and pharmacotherapy. Prog Neuropsychopharmacol Biol Psychiatry *16:* 635, 1992.

Schneier FR: Social phobia. Psychiatr Ann *21:* 349, 1991.

Stein MB, Walker JR, Forde DR: Public-speaking fears in a community sample: Prevalence, impact on functioning, and diagnostic classification. Arch Gen Psychiatry *53:* 169, 1995.

Swinson RP, Cox BJ, Woszczyna CB: Use of medical services and treatment for panic disorder with agoraphobia and for social phobia. Can Med J *147:* 878, 1992.

Van Ameringen M, Mancini C, Streiner DL: Fluoxetine efficacy in social phobia. J Clin Psychiatry *54:* 27, 1993.

▲ 16.4 Obsessive-Compulsive Disorder

In the fourth edition of *Diagnostic and Statistical Manual of Mental Disorders* (DSM-IV), obsessive-compulsive disorder is described as recurring obsessions or compulsions "severe enough to be time consuming . . . or cause marked distress or significant impairment." People with the disorder recognize that their reactions are irrational or disproportionate.

An obsession is a recurrent and intrusive thought, feeling, idea, or sensation. A compulsion is a conscious, standardized, recurring pattern of behavior, such as counting, checking, or avoiding. Obsessions increase anxiety, whereas carrying out compulsions reduces it; but when a person resists carrying out a compulsion, anxiety is increased. A person with obsessive-compulsive disorder generally experiences both the obsession and the compulsion as ego-dystonic. Obsessive-compulsive disorder can be disabling: Obsessions are often time consuming and interfere significantly with people's normal routine, occupational functioning, usual social activities, or relationships with friends and family members.

The treatment of obsessive-compulsive disorder exemplifies the positive effects that modern research can produce in a short time. As recently as the 1980s, obsessive-compulsive disorder responded poorly to treatment. It has since become recognized that obsessive-compulsive disorder is more common than previously thought and very responsive to treatment.

EPIDEMIOLOGY

The lifetime prevalence of obsessive-compulsive disorder in the general population is estimated at 2 to 3 percent. Some researchers have estimated that the disorder is found in as many as 10 percent of outpatients in psychiatric clinics. These figures make obsessive-compulsive disorder the fourth most common psychiatric diagnosis after phobias, substance-related disorders, and major depressive disorder. Epidemiological studies in Europe, Asia, and Africa have confirmed these rates across cultural boundaries.

Among adults, men and women are equally likely to be affected, but among adolescents, boys are more commonly affected than are girls. The mean age of onset is about 20 years, although men have a slightly earlier age of onset (mean around 19 years) than do women (mean around 22 years). Overall, the symptoms of about two thirds of affected people have an onset before age 25, and the symptoms of fewer than 15 percent have an onset after age 35. The onset of the disorder can occur in adolescence or childhood, in some cases as early as 2 years of age. Single people are more frequently affected with obsessive-compulsive disorder than are married people, although this finding probably reflects the difficulty that people with the disorder have in maintaining a relationship. Obsessive-compulsive disorder occurs less often among blacks than among whites, although access to health care rather than differences in prevalence may explain the variation.

People with obsessive-compulsive disorder are commonly affected by other mental disorders. The lifetime prevalence for major depressive disorder in people with obsessive-compulsive disorder is about 67 percent and for social phobia about 25 percent. Other common comorbid psychiatric diagnoses in patients with obsessive-compulsive disorder include alcohol use disorders, specific phobia, panic disorder, and eating disorders.

ETIOLOGY

Biological Factors

Neurotransmitters. The many clinical drug trials that have been conducted support the hypothesis that a dysregulation of serotonin is involved in the symptom formation of obsessions and compulsions in the disorder. Data show that serotonergic drugs are more effective than drugs that affect other neurotransmitter systems, but whether serotonin is involved in the cause of obsessive-compulsive disorder is not clear. Clinical studies have assayed cerebrospinal fluid concentrations of serotonin metabolites (for example, 5-hydroxyindoleacetic acid) and affinities and numbers of platelet-binding sites of tritiated imipramine (which binds to serotonin reuptake sites) and have reported variable findings of these measures in patients with obsessive-compulsive disorder. Some researchers have noted that the cholinergic and dopaminergic neurotransmitter systems of such patients are two areas for future research studies.

Brain-Imaging Studies. Various functional brain-imaging studies—for example, positron emission tomography (PET)—have shown increased activity (for example, metabolism and blood flow) in the frontal lobes, the basal ganglia (especially the caudate), and the cingulum of patients with obsessive-compulsive disorder. Pharmacological and behavioral treatments reportedly reverse these abnormalities (Fig. 16.4–1). Data from the functional brain-imaging studies are consistent with data from structural brain-imaging studies. Both computed tomographic and magnetic resonance imaging (MRI) studies have found bilaterally decreased sizes of caudates in patients with obsessive-compulsive disorder. Both functional and structural brain-imaging studies are also compatible with the observation that neurological procedures involving the cingulum are sometimes effective in the treatment of obsessive-compulsive disorder patients. One recent MRI study reported increased T1 relaxation times in the frontal cortex, a finding consistent with the location of abnormalities discovered in PET studies.

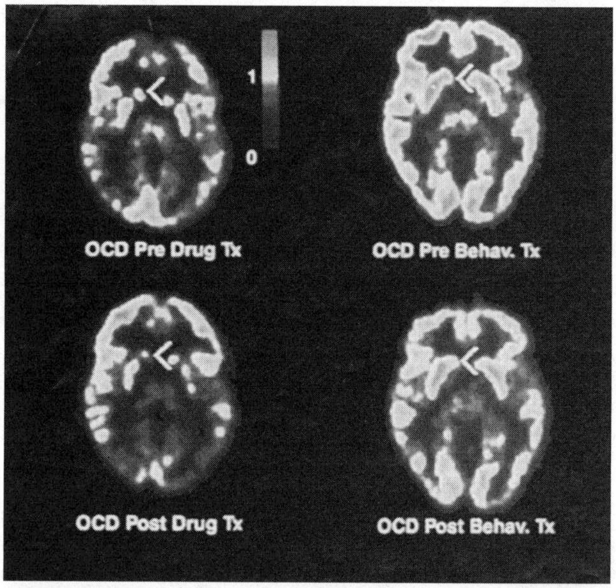
1
0
OCD Pre Drug Tx
OCD Pre Behav. Tx
OCD Post Drug Tx
OCD Post Behav. Tx

FIGURE 16.4–1

[^{18}F]Fluorodeoxyglucose positron emission tomographic scans of representative patients in a horizontal plane at a middle level of the head of the caudate nuclei before and after successful drug treatment *(Drug Tx)* or behavior therapy *(Behav. Tx)* for obsessive-compulsive disorder *(OCD)*. Scans were processed to reflect the ratio of glucose metabolic rate registered by each pixel element, divided by that of the whole brain. *Arrowheads* indicate right head of caudate nucleus. (Display follows radiological and anatomical convention of displaying the right side on the viewer's left.) The examples were chosen for illustration because of exactness of scan repositioning and because they show various degrees of visible left–right asymmetry of caudate nucleus change from before to after treatment. (Reprinted with permission from Baxter LR Jr, Schwartz JM, Bergman KS, Szuba MP, Guze GH, Mazziotta JC, Alazraki A, Selin CE, Ferng H-K, Munford P, Phelps ME: Caudate glucose metabolic rate changes with both drug and behavior therapy for obsessive-compulsive disorder. Arch Gen Psychiatry *49:* 685, 1992.)

Genetics. Available genetic data on obsessive-compulsive disorder support the hypothesis that the disorder has a significant genetic component. The data, however, do not yet distinguish the influence of cultural and behavioral effects on the transmission of the disorder. Studies of concordance for the disorder in twins have consistently found a significantly higher concordance rate for monozygotic twins than for dizygotic twins. Family studies of these patients have shown that 35 percent of the first-degree relatives of obsessive-compulsive disorder patients are also afflicted with the disorder.

Other Biological Data. Electrophysiological studies, sleep electroencephalogram (EEG) studies, and neuroendocrine studies have contributed data that indicate some commonalities between depressive disorders and obsessive-compulsive disorder. A higher than usual incidence of nonspecific EEG abnormalities occurs in patients with obsessive-compulsive disorder. Sleep EEG studies have found abnormalities similar to those in depressive disorders, such as decreased rapid eye movement latency. Neuroendocrine studies have also produced some analogies to depressive disorders, such as nonsuppression on the dexamethasone-suppression test in about one third of patients and decreased growth hormone secretion with clonidine (Catapres) infusions.

Behavioral Factors

According to learning theorists, obsessions are conditioned stimuli. A relatively neutral stimulus becomes associated with fear or anxiety through a process of respondent conditioning by being paired with events that are by nature noxious or anxiety-producing. Thus, previously neutral objects and thoughts become conditioned stimuli capable of provoking anxiety or discomfort.

Compulsions are established in a different way. When a person discovers that a certain action reduces anxiety attached to an obsessional thought, he or she develops active avoidance strategies in the form of compulsions or ritualistic behaviors to control the anxiety. Gradually, because of their efficacy in reducing a painful secondary drive (anxiety), the avoidance strategies become fixed as learned patterns of compulsive behaviors. Learning theory provides useful concepts for explaining certain aspects of obsessive-compulsive phenomena—for example, the anxiety-provoking capacity of ideas not necessarily frightening in themselves and the establishment of compulsive patterns of behavior.

Psychosocial Factors

Personality Factors. Obsessive-compulsive disorder differs from obsessive-compulsive personality disorder. Most people with obsessive-compulsive disorder do not have premorbid compulsive symptoms, and, such personality traits are neither necessary nor sufficient for the development of obsessive-compulsive disorder. Only about 15 to 35 percent of obsessive-compulsive disorder patients have had premorbid obsessional traits.

Psychodynamic Factors. Sigmund Freud described three major psychological defense mechanisms that determine the form and the quality of obsessive-compulsive symptoms and character traits: isolation, undoing, and reaction formation.

ISOLATION. Isolation is a defense mechanism that protects people against anxiety-provoking affects and impulses. Under ordinary circumstances, people consciously experience both the affect and the imagery of an emotion-laden idea, whether it is a fantasy or the memory of an event. With isolation, the affect and the impulse of which it is a derivative are separated from the ideational component and are pushed out of consciousness. If isolation is completely successful, the impulse and its associated affect are totally repressed, and the patient is consciously aware only of the affectless idea related to it.

UNDOING. Because of the constant threat that the impulse may escape the primary defense of isolation and break free, secondary defensive operations must combat the impulse and quiet the anxiety that its imminent eruption into consciousness arouses. The compulsive act constitutes the surface manifestation of a defensive operation aimed at reducing anxiety and at controlling the underlying impulse that has been insufficiently contained by isolation. A particularly important secondary defensive operation is the mechanism of undoing. As the word suggests, undoing is a compulsive act performed in an attempt to prevent or undo the consequences that the patient irrationally anticipates from a frightening obsessional thought or impulse.

REACTION FORMATION. Both isolation and undoing are defensive maneuvers that are intimately involved in the production of clinical symptoms. Reaction formation results in the formation of character traits rather than symptoms. As the term implies, reaction formation involves manifest patterns of behavior and consciously experienced attitudes that are exactly the opposite of the underlying impulses. Often, the patterns seem to an observer to be highly exaggerated and inappropriate.

OTHER PSYCHODYNAMIC FACTORS. In classic psychoanalytic theory, obsessive-compulsive disorder was termed obsessive-compulsive neurosis and was considered a regression from the oedipal phase to the anal psychosexual phase of development. When patients with obsessive-compulsive disorder feel threatened by anxiety about retaliation or by the loss of a significant object's love, they retreat from the oedipal position and regress to an intensely ambivalent emotional stage associated with the anal phase. The ambivalence is connected to the unraveling of the smooth fusion between sexual and aggressive drives characteristic of the oedipal phase. The coexistence of hatred and love toward the same person leaves patients paralyzed with doubt and indecision.

One of the striking features of patients with obsessive-compulsive disorder is the degree to which they are preoccupied with aggression or cleanliness, either overtly in the content of their symptoms or in the associations that lie behind them. Therefore, the psychogenesis of obsessive-compulsive disorder may lie in disturbances in normal growth and development related to the anal-sadistic phase of development.

Ambivalence. Ambivalence is the direct result of a change in the characteristics of the impulse life. It is an important feature of normal children during the anal-sadistic developmental phase; children feel both love and murderous hate toward the same object, sometimes simultaneously. Patients with obsessive-compulsive disorder often consciously experience both love and hate toward an object. This conflict of opposing emotions is evident in a patient's doing–undoing patterns of behavior and in paralyzing doubt in the face of choices.

Magical Thinking. In magical thinking, regression uncovers early modes of thought rather than impulses; that is, ego functions, as well as id functions, are affected by regression. Inherent in magical thinking is omnipotence of thought. People believe that merely by thinking about an event in the external world they can cause the event to occur without intermediate physical actions. This feeling causes them to fear having an aggressive thought.

DIAGNOSIS

As part of the diagnostic criteria for obsessive-compulsive disorder, DSM-IV allows clinicians to specify that patients

Table 16.4–1
DSM-IV Diagnostic Criteria for Obsessive-Compulsive Disorder

A. Either obsessions or compulsions:

Obsessions as defined by (1), (2), (3), and (4):

(1) recurrent and persistent thoughts, impulses, or images that are experienced, at some time during the disturbance, as intrusive and inappropriate and that cause marked anxiety or distress
(2) the thoughts, impulses, or images are not simply excessive worries about real-life problems
(3) the person attempts to ignore or suppress such thoughts, impulses, or images, or to neutralize them with some other thought or action
(4) the person recognizes that the obsessional thoughts, impulses, or images are a product of his or her own mind (not imposed from without as in thought insertion)

Compulsions as defined by (1) and (2):

(1) repetitive behaviors (eg, handwashing, ordering, checking) or mental acts (eg, praying, counting, repeating words silently) that the person feels driven to perform in response to an obsession, or according to rules that must be applied rigidly.
(2) the behaviors or mental acts are aimed at preventing or reducing distress or preventing some dreaded event or situation; however, these behaviors or mental acts either are not connected in a realistic way with what they are designed to neutralize or prevent, or are clearly excessive.

B. At some point during the course of the disorder, the person has recognized that the obsessions or compulsions are excessive or unreasonable. **Note:** this does not apply to children.

C. The obsessions or compulsions cause marked distress; are time-consuming (take more than an hour a day); or significantly interfere with the person's normal routine, occupational (or academic) functioning, or usual social activities or relationships.

D. If another Axis I disorder is present, the content of the obsessions or compulsions is not restricted to it (eg, preoccupation with food in the presence of an eating disorder; hair pulling in the presence of trichotillomania; concern with appearance in the presence of body dysmorphic disorder; preoccupation with drugs in the presence of a substance use disorder; preoccupation with having a serious illness in the presence of hypochondriasis; preoccupation with sexual urges or fantasies in the presence of a paraphilia; or guilty ruminations in the presence of major depressive disorder).

E. The disturbance is not due to the direct effects of a substance (eg, a drug of abuse, a medication) or a general medical condition.

Specify if:

With poor insight: if, for most of the time during the current episode, the person does not recognize that the obsessions and compulsions are excessive or unreasonable.

Reprinted with permission from American Psychiatric Association: *Diagnostic and Statistical Manual of Mental Disorders,* ed 4. Copyright, American Psychiatric Association, Washington, 1994.

Table 16.4–2
Nonpsychiatric Clinical Specialists Likely to See Obsessive-Compulsive Disorder Patients

Specialist	Presenting Problem
Dermatologist	Chapped hands, eczematoid appearance
Family practitioner	Family member washing excessively, may mention counting or checking compulsions
Oncologist, infectious disease internist	Insistent belief that person has acquired immune deficiency syndrome
Neurologist	Obsessive-compulsive disorder associated with Tourette's disorder, head injury, epilepsy, choreas, other basal ganglia lesions or disorders
Neurosurgeon	Severe, intractable obsessive-compulsive disorder
Obstetrician	Postpartum obsessive-compulsive disorder
Pediatrician	Parent's concern about child's behavior, usually excessive washing
Pediatric cardiologist	Obsessive-compulsive disorder secondary to Sydenham's chorea
Plastic surgeon	Repeated consultations for "abnormal" features
Dentist	Gum lesions from excessive teeth cleaning

Reprinted with permission from Rapoport JL: The neurobiology of obsessive-compulsive disorder. JAMA *260:* 2889, 1988.

have the poor insight type of obsessive-compulsive disorder if they generally do not recognize the excessiveness of their obsessions and compulsions (Table 16.4–1).

CLINICAL FEATURES

Patients with obsessive-compulsive disorder often go to physicians other than psychiatrists (Table 16.4–2). People with both obsessions and compulsions constitute at least 75 percent of affected patients. Some researchers and clinicians believe that the number may be much closer to 100 percent if patients are carefully assessed for the presence of mental compulsions in addition to behavioral compulsions. For example, an obsession about hurting a child may be followed by a mental compulsion to repeat a specific prayer a specific number of times. Other researchers and clinicians, however, believe that some patients do have only obsessive thoughts without compulsions. Such patients are likely to have repetitious thoughts of a sexual or aggressive act reprehensible to them. For clarity, it is best to conceptualize obsessions as thoughts and compulsions as behavior.

Obsessions and compulsions have certain features in common: An idea or an impulse intrudes itself insistently and persistently into a person's conscious awareness. A feeling of anxious dread accompanies the central manifestation and frequently leads the person to take countermeasures against the initial idea or impulse. The obsession or the compulsion is ego-alien; that is, it is experienced as being foreign to the person's experience of himself or herself as a psychological being. No matter how vivid and compelling the obsession or compulsion, the person usually recognizes it as absurd and irrational. The person suffering from obsessions and compulsions usually feels a strong desire to resist them. Nevertheless, about half of all patients offer little resistance to compulsions, although about 80 percent of all patients believe that the compulsion is irrational. Sometimes patients overvalue obsessions and compulsions—for example, they may insist that compulsive cleanliness is morally correct, even though they have lost their jobs because of time spent cleaning.

Symptom Patterns

The presentation of obsessions and compulsions is heterogeneous in adults (Table 16.4–3) and in children and adolescents (Table 16.4–4). The symptoms of an individual patient may overlap and change with time, but obsessive-compulsive disorder has four major symptom patterns.

Contamination. The most common pattern is an obsession of contamination, followed by washing or accompanied by compulsive avoidance of the presumably contaminated object. The feared object is often hard to avoid (for example, feces, urine, dust, or germs). Patients may literally rub the skin off their hands by excessive hand washing or may be unable to leave their homes because of fear of germs. Although anxiety is the most common emotional response to the feared object, obsessive shame and disgust are also common. Patients with contamination obsessions usually believe that the contamination is spread from object to object or person to person by the slightest contact.

Table 16.4–3
Obsessive-Compulsive Symptoms in Adults

Variable	%
Obsessions (N = 200)	
Contamination	45
Pathological doubt	42
Somatic	36
Need for symmetry	31
Aggressive	28
Sexual	26
Other	13
Multiple obsessions	60
Compulsions (N = 200)	
Checking	63
Washing	50
Counting	36
Need to ask or confess	31
Symmetry and precision	28
Hoarding	18
Multiple comparisons	48
Course of illness (N = 100)[a]	
Type	
Continuous	85
Deteriorative	10
Episodic	2
Not present	71
Present	29

Reprinted with permission from Rasmussen SA, Eiser JL: The epidemiology and differential diagnosis of obsessive compulsive disorder. J Clin Psychiatry *53* (4, Suppl): 6, 1992.

[a] Age at onset: men, 17.5 ± 6.8 years; women, 20.8 ± 8.5 years.

Table 16.4–4
Reported Obsessions and Compulsions for 70 Consecutive Child and Adolescent Patients

Major Presenting Symptom	No. (%) Reporting Symptom at Initial Interview[a]
Obsession	
Concern or disgust with bodily wastes or secretions (urine, stool, saliva), dirt, germs, environmental toxins	30 (43)
Fear something terrible may happen (fire, death or illness of loved one, self, or others)	18 (24)
Concern or need for symmetry, order, or exactness	12 (17)
Scrupulosity (excessive praying or religious concerns out of keeping with patient's background)	9 (13)
Lucky and unlucky numbers	6 (8)
Forbidden or perverse sexual thoughts, images, or impulses	3 (4)
Intrusive nonsense sounds, words, or music	1 (1)
Compulsion	
Excessive or ritualized hand washing, showering, bathing, toothbrushing, or grooming	60 (85)
Repeating rituals (going in and out of door up and down from chair)	36 (51)
Checking doors, locks, stove, appliances, car brakes	32 (46)
Cleaning and other rituals to remove contact with contaminants	16 (23)
Touching	14 (20)
Ordering and arranging	12 (17)
Measures to prevent harm to self or others (eg, hanging clothes a certain way)	11 (16)
Counting	13 (18)
Hoarding and collecting	8 (11)
Miscellaneous rituals (eg, licking, spitting, special dress pattern)	18 (26)

Reprinted with permission from Rapoport JL: The neurobiology of obsessive-compulsive disorder. JAMA *260:* 2889, 1988.

[a] Multiple symptoms recorded, so total exceeds 70.

Pathological Doubt. The second most common pattern is an obsession of doubt, followed by a compulsion of checking. The obsession often implies some danger of violence (such as forgetting to turn off the stove or not locking a door). The checking may involve multiple trips back into the house to check the stove, for example. The patients have an obsessional self-doubt and always feel guilty about having forgotten or committed something.

Intrusive Thoughts. In the third most common pattern, there are intrusive obsessional thoughts without a compulsion. Such obsessions are usually repetitious thoughts of a sexual or aggressive act that is reprehensible to the patient. Patients obsessed with thoughts of aggressive or sexual acts may report themselves to police or confess to a priest.

Symmetry. The fourth most common pattern is the need for symmetry or precision, which can lead to a compulsion of slowness. Patients can literally take hours to eat a meal or shave their faces.

Other Symptom Patterns. Religious obsessions and compulsive hoarding are common in patients with obsessive-compulsive disorder. Trichotillomania (compulsive hair pulling) and nail biting may be compulsions related to obsessive-compulsive disorder.

Mental Status Examination

On mental status examinations, patients with obsessive-compulsive disorder show symptoms of depressive disorders. Such symptoms are present in about 50 percent of all patients. Some obsessive-compulsive disorder patients have character traits suggestive of obsessive-compulsive personality disorder, but most do not. Patients with obsessive-compulsive disorder, especially men, have a higher than average celibacy rate. Married patients have a greater than usual amount of marital discord.

Jens is German and 18 years old. He stopped going to high school because of his illness.

Problem. When he was almost 15 years old, Jens's parents noticed that after his newspaper and magazine delivery rounds, Jens would wash his hands more and more often and for a longer and longer time. Eventually he ended up spending more than an hour under the shower. When asked about it, Jens told his parents that he felt as if he were being contaminated by a popular women's magazine. He also feared that through contact with boys from less academic schools, he might become like them—"common, slimy, impulsive, aggressive, and stupid." Because he was afraid that he might be touched by such schoolboys in the bus, he insisted that his mother take him to school every day by car. Jens soon came to regard the walls, furniture, and other objects in his parents' home as contaminated by their less educated visitors. Only his own room, where no one else was allowed, seemed uninfected. He soon came to regard entire streets, buildings, shops, and playgrounds as contaminated, and he often went out of his way to avoid passing these places. He gave up his beloved tennis and also stopped playing on the football team. He spent almost all of his spare time in his room with the blinds down, sitting for hours in his chair doing nothing. He even refused to put on his washed and ironed clothing unless his mother had washed and ironed it under his supervision. In the end he could no longer read newspapers and magazines and could no longer touch his school books. He soon became a complete failure at school because he could no longer follow the lessons and no longer did any school work.

Worst of all were his evening rituals in the shower, where he spent hours using several bottles of shower gel. He would clean his fingernails until they bled, and his skin became chapped and sore. When his parents tried to prevent him from showering excessively, he became aggressive. To their desperate attempts to make him realize that his fear of contamination and his endless washing were devoid of any realistic foundation, he constantly responded, "I know it's nonsense, but I just have to do it; I can't help it." He was often quite desperate and unhappy about his situation and kept crying about it.

History. Jens grew up as the second of four children. The father was an architect, and the mother worked as a librarian. His birth and childhood were quite normal. From infancy Jens was always very well behaved, orderly, and helpful. At school he was ambitious, and his grades were above average. He always kept his room clean and tidy and did not want playmates to come and make it untidy. At about the age of 13 he grew a lot in height, and at the age of 14 he was already more than 1.8 m tall, with the physical appearance of a young man. Before his illness he was very keen on sports, especially tennis, football, and cycling.

His 49-year-old father came from a family of professional soldiers, with a very strict and efficiency-oriented upbringing, and his 50-year-old mother came from a similar family and had always made very high demands on herself. A cousin of the father was reported to suffer from a severe compulsion neurosis, but otherwise there was no information about psychiatric disorders in the family.

Findings. On referral Jens appeared shy and reticent, with apparent difficulties in talking about himself and particularly about his emotions. He was aware that his obsessions and compulsions were his own ideas or impulses and that they were nonsensical. Initially he had tried to resist them, but eventually he realized that he simply could not do it. In the beginning giving in to the impulses relieved his tensions, but later on it became a torture. There was no evidence of hallucinatory experiences or delusional ideas. His speech was normal, and no catatonic features were observed. Throughout the interview he appeared mildly depressed. No cognitive deficiencies were detected, and he was fully oriented in all respects.

DISCUSSION

Jens meets the criteria for an obsessive-compulsive disorder with mixed obsessional thoughts and acts. For several years he experienced obsessions of contamination and compulsions of washing that were repetitive and unpleasant, causing severe distress and interference with social and individual functioning. He acknowledged that the obsessions and compulsions originated from his own mind and that they were unreasonable. He had initially tried to resist his compulsions, but eventually he had to give in to them. There is no evidence of primary schizophrenic or affective disorders.

A few depressive symptoms are mentioned, but not enough to meet the criteria of a depressive episode, and such symptoms obviously appear secondary to his obsessive-compulsive disorder. Exaggerated personality traits of an anancastic nature are described, but they are not sufficient to meet the criteria for a personality disorder, which his young age will also hardly allow. (From *ICD-10 Casebook.*)

DIFFERENTIAL DIAGNOSIS

Medical Conditions

The DSM-IV diagnostic requirement of personal distress and functional impairment differentiates obsessive-compulsive disorder from ordinary or mildly excessive thoughts and habits. The major neurological disorders to consider in the differential diagnosis are Tourette's disorder, other tic disorders, temporal lobe epilepsy, and, occasionally, trauma and postencephalitic complications.

Tourette's Disorder

The characteristic symptoms of Tourette's disorder are motor and vocal tics that occur frequently and virtually every day. Tourette's disorder and obsessive-compulsive disorder have a similar age of onset and similar symptoms. About 90 percent of people with Tourette's disorder have compulsive symptoms, and as many as two thirds meet the diagnostic criteria for obsessive-compulsive disorder.

Other Psychiatric Conditions

The major psychiatric considerations in the differential diagnosis of obsessive-compulsive disorder are schizophrenia, obsessive-compulsive personality disorder, phobias, and depressive disorders. Obsessive-compulsive disorder can usually be distinguished from schizophrenia by the absence of other schizophrenic symptoms, by the less bizarre nature of the symptoms, and by the patient's insight into the disorder. Obsessive-compulsive personality disorder does not have the degree of functional impairment associated with obsessive-compulsive disorder. Phobias are distinguished by the absence of a relation between the obsessive thoughts and the compulsions. Major depressive disorder can sometimes be associated with obsessive ideas, but patients with only obsessive-compulsive disorder fail to meet the diagnostic criteria for major depressive disorder.

Other psychiatric conditions that may be closely related to obsessive-compulsive disorder are hypochondriasis, body dysmorphic disorder, and possibly other impulse-control disorders, such as kleptomania and pathological gambling. In all these disorders, patients have either a repetitious thought (for example, concern about the body) or a repetitious behavior (for example, stealing). Several research groups are investigating these disorders and other disorders, such as compulsive sexual behavior, their relations to obsessive-compulsive disorder, and their responses to various treatments.

COURSE AND PROGNOSIS

More than half the patients with obsessive-compulsive disorder have a sudden onset of symptoms. The onset of symptoms for about 50 to 70 percent of patients occurs after a stressful event, such as a pregnancy, a sexual problem, or the death of a relative. Because many people manage to keep their symptoms secret, there is often a delay of 5 to 10 years before patients come to psychiatric attention, although the delay is probably shortening with increased awareness of the disorder. The course is usually long but variable; some patients experience a fluctuating course, and others experience a constant one.

About 20 to 30 percent of patients have significant improvement in their symptoms, and 40 to 50 percent have moderate improvement. The remaining 20 to 40 percent of patients either remain ill or have a worsening of their symptoms.

About one third of patients with obsessive-compulsive disorder have major depressive disorder, and suicide is a risk for all patients with obsessive-compulsive disorder. A poor prognosis is indicated by yielding to (rather than resisting) compulsions, childhood onset, bizarre compulsions, the need for hospitalization, a coexisting major depressive disorder, delusional beliefs, the presence of overvalued ideas (that is, some acceptance of obsessions and compulsions), and the presence of a personality disorder (especially schizotypal personality disorder). A good prognosis is indicated by a good social and occupational adjustment, the presence of a precipitating event, and an episodic nature in the symptoms. The obsessional content does not seem to be related to the prognosis.

TREATMENT

With mounting evidence that obsessive-compulsive disorder is largely determined by biological factors, the classic psychoanalytic theory has fallen out of favor. Moreover, because obsessive-compulsive disorder symptoms appear to be largely refractory to psychodynamic psychotherapy and psychoanalysis, pharmacological and behavioral treatments have become common. But psychodynamic factors may be of considerable benefit in understanding what precipitates exacerbations of the disorder and in treating various forms of resistance to treatment, such as noncompliance with medication.

Many patients with obsessive-compulsive disorder tenaciously resist treatment efforts. They may refuse to take medication and may resist carrying out therapeutic homework assignments and other prescribed activities given by behavior therapists. The obsessive-compulsive symptoms themselves, no matter how biologically based, may have important psychological meanings that make patients reluctant to give them up. A psychodynamic exploration of a patient's resistance to treatment may result in improved compliance.

Well-controlled studies have found that pharmacotherapy, behavior therapy, or a combination of both is effective in significantly reducing the symptoms of patients with obsessive-compulsive disorder. The decision about which therapy to use is based on the clinician's judgment and experience and on the patient's acceptance of the various modalities.

Pharmacotherapy

The efficacy of pharmacotherapy in obsessive-compulsive disorder has been proved in many clinical trials and is enhanced by the observation that the studies find a placebo response rate of about 5 percent. This percentage is low, compared with the 30 to 40 percent placebo response rate often seen in studies of antidepressants and anxiolytic drugs.

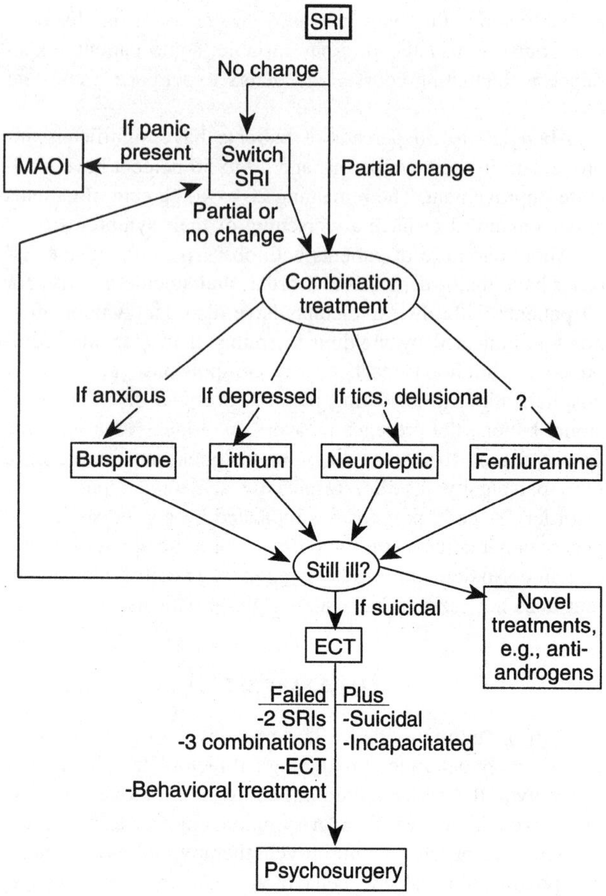
SRI
No change
If panic present
MAOI
Switch SRI
Partial change
Partial or no change
Combination treatment
If anxious
If depressed
If tics, delusional
?
Buspirone
Lithium
Neuroleptic
Fenfluramine
Still ill?
If suicidal
Novel treatments, e.g., anti-androgens
ECT
Failed
-2 SRIs
-3 combinations
-ECT
-Behavioral treatment
Plus
-Suicidal
-Incapacitated
Psychosurgery

FIGURE 16.4–2
Proposed algorithm for biological treatment of obsessive-compulsive disorder. *ECT,* electroconvulsive therapy; *MAOI,* monoamine oxidase inhibitor; *SRI,* potent serotonin reuptake inhibitor (for example, clomipramine, fluvoxamine, fluoxetine, sertraline, paroxetine). (Reprinted with permission from Goodman WK, McDougle CJ, Price LH: Pharmacotherapy of obsessive compulsive disorder. J Clin Psychiatry *53* (4, Suppl): 34, 1992.)

The drugs, all of which are used to treat depressive disorders or other mental disorders, can be used in their usual dosage ranges. Initial effects are generally seen after 4 to 6 weeks of treatment, although 8 to 16 weeks are usually needed to obtain the maximal therapeutic benefit. Treatment with antidepressant drugs is still controversial, and a significant proportion of patients with obsessive-compulsive disorder who respond to treatment with antidepressant drugs seem to relapse if the drug therapy is discontinued.

The standard approach is to start with a serotonin-specific reuptake inhibitor (SSRI) or clomipramine (Anafranil) and then to move to other pharmacological strategies if the serotonin-specific drugs are not effective (Fig. 16.4–2). The serotonergic drugs have increased the percentage of patients with obsessive-compulsive disorder who are likely to respond to treatment to the range of 50 to 70 percent.

Serotonin-Specific Reuptake Inhibitors. Each of the SSRIs available in the United States—fluoxetine (Prozac), fluvoxamine (Luvox), paroxetine (Paxil), sertraline (Zoloft)—has been approved by the Food and Drug Administration (FDA) for the treatment of obsessive-compulsive disorder. Higher doses have often been necessary for a beneficial effect, such as 80 mg a day of fluoxetine. Although the SSRIs may cause sleep disturbance, nausea and diarrhea, headache, anxiety, and restlessness, these adverse effects are often transient and are generally less troubling than the adverse effects associated with tricyclic drugs, such as clomipramine. The best clinical outcomes occur when SSRIs are used in combination with behavioral therapy.

Clomipramine. Of all the tricyclic and tetracyclic drugs, clomipramine is the most selective for serotonin reuptake versus norepinephrine reuptake, exceeded in this respect only by the SSRIs. The potency of serotonin reuptake of clomipramine is exceeded only by sertraline and paroxetine. Clomipramine was the first drug to be FDA approved for the treatment of obsessive-compulsive disorder. Its dosing must be titrated upward over 2 to 3 weeks to avoid gastrointestinal adverse effects and orthostatic hypotension, and like other tricyclic drugs, it causes significant sedation and anticholinergic effects, including dry mouth and constipation. As with SSRIs, the best outcomes result from a combination of drug and behavioral therapy.

Other Drugs. If treatment with clomipramine or an SSRI is unsuccessful, many therapists augment the first drug by the addition of lithium (Eskalith). Other drugs that can be tried in the treatment of obsessive-compulsive disorder are venlafaxine (Effexor) and the monoamine oxidase inhibitors, especially phenelzine (Nardil). Less well-studied pharmacological agents for the treatment of unresponsive patients include buspirone (BuSpar), L-tryptophan, and clonazepam (Klonopin).

Behavior Therapy

Although few head-to-head comparisons have been made, behavior therapy is as effective as pharmacotherapies in obsessive-compulsive disorder, and some data indicate that the beneficial effects are longer lasting with behavior therapy. Therefore, many clinicians consider behavior therapy to be the treatment of choice for obsessive-compulsive disorder. Behavior therapy can be conducted in both outpatient and inpatient settings. The principal behavioral approaches in obsessive-compulsive disorder are exposure and response prevention. Desensitization, thought stopping, flooding, implosion therapy, and aversive conditioning have also been used in patients with obsessive-compulsive disorder. In behavior therapy, patients must be truly committed to improvement.

Psychotherapy

In the absence of adequate studies of insight-oriented psychotherapy for obsessive-compulsive disorder, any valid generalizations about its effectiveness are hard to make, although there are anecdotal reports of successes. Individual analysts have seen striking and lasting changes for the better in patients with obsessive-compulsive personality disorder, especially when they are able to come to terms with the aggressive impulses lying behind their character traits. Likewise, analysts and dynamically oriented psychiatrists have observed marked symptomatic improvement in patients with obsessive-compulsive disorder in the course of analysis or prolonged insight psychotherapy.

Supportive psychotherapy undoubtedly has its place, especially for those obsessive-compulsive disorder patients who, despite symptoms of varying degrees of severity, are able to work and make social adjustments. With continuous and regular contact with an interested, sympathetic, and encouraging professional person, patients may be able to function by virtue of this help, without which their symptoms would incapacitate them. Occasionally, when obsessional rituals and anxiety reach an intolerable intensity, it is necessary to hospitalize patients until the shelter of an institution and the removal from external environmental stresses diminish symptoms to a tolerable level.

A patient's family members are often driven to the verge of despair by the patient's behavior. Any psychotherapeutic endeavors must include attention to the family members through the provision of emotional support, reassurance, explanation, and advice on how to manage and respond to the patient.

Other Therapies

Family therapy is often useful in supporting the family, helping reduce marital discord resulting from the disorder, and building a treatment alliance with the family members for the good of the patient.

Group therapy is useful as a support system for some patients.

For extreme cases in severely treatment-resistant patients, electroconvulsive therapy (ECT) and psychosurgery may be considered. ECT is not as effective as psychosurgery but should be tried before surgery. The most common psychosurgical procedure for obsessive-compulsive disorder is cingulotomy, which is successful in treating 25 to 30 percent of otherwise treatment-unresponsive patients. The most common complication of psychosurgery is the development of seizures, which are almost always controlled by treatment with phenytoin (Dilantin). Some patients who do not respond to psychosurgery alone and who did not respond to pharmacotherapy or behavior therapy before the operation do respond to pharmacotherapy or behavior therapy after psychosurgery.

References

Baxter LR, Schwartz JM, Bergman KS, Szuba MP, Guze BH, Mazziotta JC, Alazraki A, Selin CE, Ferng H-K, Munford P, Phelps ME: Caudate glucose metabolic rate changes with both drug and behavior therapy for obsessive-compulsive disorder. Arch Gen Psychiatry *49:* 681, 1992.

Black DW, Noyes R, Goldstein RB, Blum N: A family study of obsessive-compulsive disorder. Arch Gen Psychiatry *49:* 362, 1992.

Clomipramine Collaborative Study Group: Clomipramine in the treatment of patients with obsessive-compulsive disorder. Arch Gen Psychiatry *48:* 730, 1991.

Fineberg NA, Bullock T, Montgomery DB, Montgomery SA: Serotonin reuptake inhibitors are the treatment of choice in obsessive compulsive disorder. Int Clin Psychopharmacol 7 (1, Suppl): 43, 1992.

Gabbard GO: *Psychodynamic Psychiatry in Clinical Practice: The DSM-IV Edition.* American Psychiatric Press, Washington, 1994.

Gabbard GO: Psychodynamic psychiatry in the "decade of the brain." Am J Psychiatry *149:* 991, 1992.

Hewlett WA, Vinogradov A, Agras WS: Clomipramine, clonazepam, and clonidine treatment of obsessive-compulsive disorder. J Clin Psychopharmacol *12:* 420, 1992.

Hollander E: Obsessive-compulsive spectrum disorders. Psychiatr Ann *23:* 352, 1993.

Insel TR: Toward a neuroanatomy of obsessive-compulsive disorder. Arch Gen Psychiatry *49:* 739, 1992.

Jenike MA: Obsessive-compulsive disorder. In *Comprehensive Textbook of Psychiatry,* ed 6, HI Kaplan, BJ Sadock, editors, p 1218. Williams & Wilkins, Baltimore, 1995.

Jenike MA, editor: Obsessional disorders. Psychiatr Clin North Am *15:* 743, 1992.

Jenike MA, Baer L, Ballantine T, Martuza RL, Tynes S, Giriunas I, Buttolph ML, Cassem NH: Cingulotomy for refractory obsessive-compulsive disorder. Arch Gen Psychiatry *48:* 548, 1991.

McDougle CJ, Gordman WK, Price LH: The pharmacotherapy of obsessive-compulsive disorder. Pharmacopsychiatry *26* (Suppl): 24, 1993.

Nelson E, Rice J: Stability of diagnosis of obsessive-compulsive disorder in the epidemiologic catchment area study. Am J Psychiatry *154:* 826, 1997.

Pigott TA: OCD: where the serotonin selectively story begins. J Clin Psychiatry *57* (6, Suppl): 11, 1996.

▲ 16.5 Posttraumatic Stress Disorder and Acute Stress Disorder

The fourth edition of *Diagnostic and Statistical Manual of Mental Disorder* (DSM-IV) defines posttraumatic stress disorder as a set of typical symptoms that develop after a person sees, is involved in, or hears of an "extreme traumatic stressor." The person reacts to this experience with fear and helplessness, persistently relives the event, and tries to avoid being reminded of it. The symptoms must last for more than a month and must significantly affect important areas of life such as family and work. DSM-IV defines acute stress disorder as largely similar to posttraumatic stress disorder except that the symptoms occur within 4 weeks of the event and last from 2 days to 4 weeks.

The stress causing posttraumatic stress disorder is overwhelming enough to affect almost anyone. It can arise from experiences in war, torture, natural catastrophes, assault, rape, and serious accidents, for example, in cars and in burning buildings. People reexperience the traumatic event in their dreams and their daily thoughts; they are determined to evade anything that would bring the event to mind; and they undergo a numbing of responsiveness along with a state of hyperarousal. Other symptoms are depression, anxiety, and cognitive difficulties such as poor concentration.

HISTORY

Because of the presence of autonomic cardiac symptoms, *soldier's heart* was the name given during the U.S. Civil War to a syndrome similar to posttraumatic stress disorder. Jacob

DaCosta's 1871 paper, "On Irritable Heart," described such soldiers with the syndrome.

In the 1900s the influence of psychoanalysis was strong, particularly in the United States, and clinicians applied the diagnosis of traumatic neurosis to the condition. In World War I, the syndrome was called *shell shock* and was hypothesized to result from brain trauma caused by exploding shells. In 1941, the survivors of a fire in a crowded Boston nightclub, the Coconut Grove, showed increased nervousness, fatigue, and nightmares. World War II veterans, survivors of Nazi concentration camps, and survivors of the atomic bombings in Japan had similar symptoms, sometimes called *combat neurosis* or *operational fatigue.* The psychiatric morbidity associated with Vietnam War veterans finally brought the concept of *posttraumatic stress disorder,* as it is currently known, to fruition. In all these traumatic situations, the appearance of the disorder was roughly correlated with the severity of the stressor; the most severe stresses (for example, incarceration in concentration camps) resulted in the occurrence of the syndrome in more than 75 percent of the victims.

EPIDEMIOLOGY

The lifetime prevalence of posttraumatic stress disorder is estimated to be from 1 to 3 percent of the general population, although an additional 5 to 15 percent may experience subclinical forms or the disorder. Among high-risk groups whose members experienced traumatic events, the lifetime prevalence rates range from 5 to 75 percent. About 30 percent of Vietnam veterans experienced posttraumatic stress disorder, and an additional 25 percent experienced subclinical forms of the disorder.

Although posttraumatic stress disorder can appear at any age, it is most prevalent in young adults, because of the nature of the precipitating situations. Nevertheless, children can have the disorder. Men's trauma is usually combat experience, and women's trauma is most commonly assault or rape. The disorder is most likely to occur in those who are single, divorced, widowed, socially withdrawn, or of low socioeconomic level.

ETIOLOGY

Stressor

By definition, the stressor is the prime causative factor in the development of posttraumatic stress disorder. Yet not everyone experiences the disorder after a traumatic event; although the stressor is necessary, it is not sufficient to cause the disorder. Clinicians must also consider individual preexisting biological and psychosocial factors and events that happened after the trauma. For example, a member of a group who lived through a disaster can sometimes deal with trauma because others shared the experience. Survivor guilt, however, sometimes complicates the management of posttraumatic stress disorder.

Recent research on the disorder has placed greater emphasis on a person's subjective response to trauma than on the severity of the stressor itself. Although posttraumatic stress disorder symptoms were once thought to be directly proportional to the severity of the stressor, empirical studies have shown otherwise. As a result, the growing consensus is that the disorder has a great deal to do with the stressor's subjective meaning to a person.

Even when faced with overwhelming trauma, most people do not experience posttraumatic stress disorder symptoms. Similarly, events that may appear mundane or less than catastrophic to most people may produce posttraumatic stress disorder in some. The predisposing vulnerability factors that appear to play primary roles in determining whether the disorder develops include the presence of childhood trauma; borderline, paranoid, dependent, or antisocial personality disorder traits; an inadequate support system; genetic-constitutional vulnerability to psychiatric illness; recent stressful life changes; perception of an external locus of control rather than an internal one; and recent excessive alcohol intake.

Psychodynamic studies of those who have survived severe traumas have identified alexithymia—the inability to identify or verbalize feeling states—as a common feature. If psychic trauma occurs in childhood, an arrest of emotional development frequently results. If the trauma occurs in adulthood, an emotional regression often occurs. In either case, survivors of trauma usually cannot use internal emotional states as signals and may experience psychosomatic symptoms. They are also incapable of soothing themselves when under stress.

Psychodynamic Factors

The cognitive model of posttraumatic stress disorder posits that affected people are unable to process or rationalize the trauma that precipitated the disorder. They continue to experience the stress and attempt to avoid reexperiencing it by avoidance techniques. Consistent with their partial ability to cope cognitively with the event, people experience alternating periods of acknowledging and blocking the event. The attempt of the brain to process the massive amount of information provoked by the trauma is thought to produce the alternating periods of acknowledging and blocking the event.

The behavioral model of posttraumatic stress disorder emphasizes two phases in its development. First, the trauma (the unconditioned stimulus) is paired, through classical conditioning, with a conditioned stimulus (physical or mental reminders of the trauma). Second, through instrumental learning, people develop a pattern of avoidance of both the conditioned stimulus and the unconditioned stimulus.

The psychoanalytic model of the disorder hypothesizes that the trauma has reactivated a previously quiescent, yet unresolved psychological conflict. The revival of the childhood trauma results in regression and the use of the defense mechanisms of repression, denial, and undoing. The ego relives and thereby tries to master and reduce the anxiety. Some persons also receive secondary gains from the external world, commonly monetary compensation, increased attention or sympathy, and the satisfaction of dependence needs. These gains reinforce the disorder and its persistence.

Biological Factors

The biological theories of posttraumatic stress disorder have developed from both preclinical studies of animal models of stress and from measures of biological variables in clinical populations with the disorder. Many neurotransmitter systems have been implicated by both sets of data. Preclinical models of learned helplessness, kindling, and sensitization in animals have led to theories about norepinephrine, dopamine, endogenous opioids, and benzodiazepine receptors and the hypothalamic-pituitary-adrenal axis. In clinical populations, data have supported hypotheses that the noradrenergic and endogenous opiate systems, as well as the hypothalamic-pituitary-adrenal axis, are hyperactive in at least some patients with posttraumatic stress disorder.

Other major biological findings are increased activity and responsiveness of the autonomic nervous system, as evidenced by elevated heart rates and blood pressure readings and by abnormal sleep architecture (for example, sleep fragmentation and increased sleep latency). Some researchers have suggested a similarity between posttraumatic stress disorder and two other psychiatric disorders, major depressive disorder and panic disorder.

DIAGNOSIS

The DSM-IV diagnostic criteria for posttraumatic stress disorder (Table 16.5–1) specify that the symptoms of reexperiencing, avoidance, and hyperarousal have lasted more than 1 month. For patients in whom symptoms have been present less than 1 month, the appropriate diagnosis may be acute stress disorder (Table 16.5–2). The DSM-IV diagnostic criteria for posttraumatic stress disorder allow clinicians to specify whether the disorder is acute (if the symptoms have lasted less than 3 months) or chronic (if the symptoms have lasted 3 months or more). DSM-IV also allows clinicians to specify that the disorder was with delayed onset if the onset of the symptoms was 6 months or more after the stressful event.

CLINICAL FEATURES

The principal clinical features of posttraumatic stress disorder are the painful reexperiencing of the event, a pattern of avoidance and emotional numbing, and fairly constant hyperarousal. The disorder may not develop until months or even years after the event. The mental status examination often reveals feelings of guilt, rejection, and humiliation. Patients may also describe dissociative states and panic attacks, and illusions and hallucinations may be present. Cognitive testing may reveal that patients have impairments of memory and attention.

Associated symptoms can include aggression, violence, poor impulse control, depression, and substance-related disorders. Patients have elevated Sc, D, F, and Ps scores on the Minnesota Multiphasic Personality Inventory, and the Rorschach test findings often include aggressive and violent material.

Persian Gulf War Syndrome

In the Persian Gulf War against Iraq, which began in 1990 and ended in 1991, 700,000 American soldiers served in the coalition forces. On their return, over 50,000 United States veterans reported a vast array of health problems, including, among other symptoms, chronic fatigue, shortness of breath, muscle and joint pain, migraine headaches, digestive distur-

Table 16.5–1
DSM-IV Diagnostic Criteria for Posttraumatic Stress Disorder

A. The person has been exposed to a traumatic event in which both of the following were present:
  (1) the person experienced, witnessed, or was confronted with an event or events that involved actual or threatened death or serious injury, or a threat to the physical integrity of self or others
  (2) the person's response involved intense fear, helplessness, or horror. **Note:** in children, this may be expressed instead by disorganized or agitated behavior

B. The traumatic event is persistently reexperienced in one (or more) of the following ways:
  (1) recurrent and intrusive distressing recollections of the event, including images, thoughts, or perceptions. **Note:** in young children, repetitive play may occur in which themes or aspects of the trauma are expressed
  (2) recurrent distressing dreams of the event. **Note:** in children, there may be frightening dreams without recognizable content
  (3) acting or feeling as if the traumatic event were recurring (includes a sense of reliving the experience, illusions, hallucinations, and dissociative flashback episodes, including those that occur upon awakening or when intoxicated). **Note:** in young children, trauma-specific reenactment may occur.
  (4) intense psychological distress at exposure to internal or external cues that symbolize or resemble an aspect of the traumatic event
  (5) physiologic reactivity on exposure to internal or external cues that symbolize or resemble an aspect of the traumatic event

C. Persistent avoidance of stimuli associated with the trauma and numbing of general responsiveness (not present before the trauma), as indicated by three (or more) of the following:
  (1) efforts to avoid thoughts, feelings, or conversations associated with the trauma
  (2) efforts to avoid activities, places, or people that arouse recollections of the trauma
  (3) inability to recall an important aspect of the trauma
  (4) markedly diminished interest or participation in significant activities
  (5) feeling of detachment or estrangement from others
  (6) restricted range of affect (eg, unable to have loving feelings)
  (7) sense of a foreshortened future (eg, does not expect to have a career, marriage, children, or a normal life span)

D. Persistent symptoms of increased arousal (not present before the trauma), as indicated by two (or more) of the following:
  (1) difficulty falling or staying asleep
  (2) irritability or outbursts of anger
  (3) difficulty concentrating
  (4) hypervigilance
  (5) exaggerated startle response

E. Duration of the disturbance (symptoms in criteria B, C, and D) is more than 1 month.

F. The disturbance causes clinically significant distress or impairment in social, occupational, or other important areas of functioning.

Specify if:
  Acute: if duration of symptoms is less than 3 months
  Chronic: if duration of symptoms is 3 months or more

Specify if:
  With delayed onset: onset of symptoms at least 6 months after the stressor

Table 16.5–2
DSM-IV Diagnostic Criteria for Acute Stress Disorder

A. The person has been exposed to a traumatic event in which both of the following were present:
 (1) the person experienced, witnessed, or was confronted with an event or events that involved actual or threatened death or serious injury, or a threat to the physical integrity of self or others.
 (2) the person's response involved intense fear, helplessness, or horror
B. Either while experiencing or after experiencing the distressing event, the individual has three (or more) of the following dissociative symptoms:
 (1) a subjective sense of numbing, detachment, or absence of emotional responsiveness
 (2) a reduction in awareness of his or her surroundings (eg, "being in a daze")
 (3) derealization
 (4) depersonalization
 (5) dissociative amnesia (eg, inability to recall an important aspect of the trauma)
C. The traumatic event is persistently reexperienced in at least one of the following ways: recurrent images, thoughts, dreams, illusions, flashback episodes, or a sense of reliving the experience; or distress on exposure to reminders of the traumatic event.
D. Marked avoidance of stimuli that arouse recollections of the trauma (eg, thoughts, feelings, conversations, activities, places, people).
E. Marked symptoms of anxiety or increased arousal (eg, difficulty sleeping, irritability, poor concentration, hypervigilance, exaggerated startle response, and motor restlessness).
F. The disturbance causes clinically significant distress or impairment in social, occupational, or other important areas of functioning, impairs the individual's ability to pursue some necessary tasks, such as obtaining necessary assistance or mobilizing personal resources by telling family members about the traumatic experience.
G. The disturbance lasts for a minimum of 2 days and a maximum of 4 weeks and occurs within 4 weeks of the traumatic event.
H. Not due to the direct physiological effects of a substance (eg, a drug of abuse, a medication) or a general medical condition, is not better accounted for by brief psychotic disorder, and is not merely an exacerbation of a preexisting Axis I or Axis II disorder.

bances, hair loss, forgetfulness, and difficulty in concentrating. Collectively, these symptoms are called Persian Gulf War syndrome, but no government agency has acknowledged the cause of these symptoms. Many veterans believe that their disorders were caused by exposure to biological and chemical agents such as mustard and other nerve gases. The U.S. Department of Defense acknowledges that more than 20,000 troops serving in the combat area may have been exposed to chemical weapons but denies that those complaining of the syndrome are suffering from the effects of chemical exposure. The National Institutes of Health has established a program to evaluate the problem in response to pressure from Persian Gulf War veterans, but to date, no conclusive evidence has shown that U.S. troops were adversely affected by chemical agents. The consensus is that the condition is a disorder that in some cases may have been precipitated by exposure to an unidentified toxin (Table 16.5–3) but that in many cases stems from the psychological stress associated with being in a combat area. Posttraumatic stress disorder is a well-documented condition that occurs in wartime. It was first identified after the Civil War (Table 16.5–4) and has been noted in every war thereafter, although by different names.

Table 16.5–3
Syndromes Associated with Toxic Exposure[a]

Syndrome	Characteristics	Possible Toxins
1	Impaired cognition	Insect repellant containing *N,N'*-diethyl-*m*-toluamide (DEET[b]) absorbed through skin
2	Confusion-ataxia	Exposure to chemical weapons, eg, sarin
3	Arthromyoneuropathy	Insect repellant containing DEET[b] in combination with oral pyridostigmine[c]

[a] The three syndromes involve a relatively small group (N = 249) of veterans and are based on self-reported descriptions and selection. Data are from R. W. Haley and T. L. Kurt.
[b] DEET is a carbomate compound used as an insect repellant. Concentrations above 30 percent DEET are neurotoxic in children. The military repellant contained 75 percent. (DEET is available in 100 percent concentrations as an unregulated over-the-counter preparation usually sold in sports stores.)
[c] Most U.S. troops took low-dose pyridostigmine (Mestinon, 30 mg every 8 hours) for about 5 days in 1991 to protect against exposure to the nerve agent soman.

Table 16.5–4
Eponyms and Symptoms of Posttraumatic Stress Disorders in Various U.S. Wars

War	Disorder
Civil War	"Irritable heart": fatigue, shortness of breath, palpitations, headache, excessive sweating, dizziness, disturbed sleep, fainting
World War I	"Effort syndrome": fatigue, shortness of breath, palpitations, headache, excessive sweating, dizziness, disturbed sleep, fainting, difficulty concentrating
World War II	"Combat stress reaction": fatigue, shortness of breath, palpitations, headache, excessive sweating, dizziness, disturbed sleep, fainting, difficulty concentrating, forgetfulness
Vietnam War	"Posttraumatic stress disorder": fatigue, shortness of breath, palpitations, headache, muscle and joint pain, dizziness, disturbed sleep, difficulty concentrating, forgetfulness
Gulf War	"Gulf War syndrome": fatigue, shortness of breath, headache, muscle and joint pain, disturbed sleep, difficulty concentrating, forgetfulness

Adapted from Hymans KC, Wignall FS, Roswell R: War, syndromes and their evaluation: From the US Civil War to the Persian Gulf War. Ann Intern Med *125:* 1996.

Since July 1995, 4,100 claims have been processed for Gulf War veterans who are seeking disability payments from the Veterans Administration for this syndrome, but 95 percent of claims have been denied. Studies are ongoing to further clarify the situation, but the morale of thousands of afflicted Gulf War veterans has seriously eroded, and confidence in the Department of Defense's concerns for illness among U.S. soldiers has been compromised among the public as a result.

In a 1997 editorial in *Journal of the American Medical Association,* the relationship of the Persian Gulf War syndrome and stress was stated as follows:

> Physicians need to acknowledge that many Gulf War veterans are experiencing stress-related disorders and the physical consequences of stress. These conditions should not be hidden or denied, but rather are well-recognized entities that have been studied extensively in survivors of past wars, most notably the Vietnam conflict. As physicians, we should not accept a diagnosis of stress-related disorder in veterans prior to excluding treatable physical factors, but at the same time, we need to recognize the pervasive presence of stress-related illness such as hypertension, fibromyalgia, and chronic fatigue among Persian Gulf War veterans and manage these illnesses appropriately. As a nation, we need to get beyond the fallacious idea that diseases of the mind either are not real or are shameful and to better recognize that the mind and the body are inextricably linked.

Ayoub was a 32-year-old Egyptian driver who formerly worked in Kuwait. He was brought to the outpatient clinic in a state of acute panic. Ayoub had worked in Kuwait for 5 years to earn a regular income to keep his family and to pay for the education of his children. During the Iraqi invasion of Kuwait, he was exposed to a severe trauma when his sister was raped in front of him. He was imprisoned and was subjected to severe torture during which wooden rods were pushed into his anus. On his release after the Gulf War, he was brought back to Egypt, where he underwent several operations for anal repair. Since then, Ayoub has experienced nightmares and vivid flashbacks of his torture and the rape of his sister; he has also suffered anxiety spells, with screaming and aggressive behavior. The current state of panic came about after he had watched a television documentary about World War II.

The patient's development was fairly normal, and his work record was satisfactory. He completed 9 years of basic schooling, but when his father died during a cardiac operation, Ayoub left school to get a job to help support his sister and two younger brothers. He married at the age of 22 and was divorced when he was age 28. He had three children who had stayed with his mother while he was in Kuwait. Ayoub was known to be sociable, outgoing, and helpful to his neighbors. His brother described him as stubborn and impulsive but very kind and warmhearted. He had been a heavy smoker since age 20 but did not use drugs.

During the interview, Ayoub's mood and behavior fluctuated. At times he was intensely anxious, with bouts of sweating and hyperventilation and outbursts of hostility and aggression manifested in banging the desk or punching the wall. At other times his facial expression became empty; he appeared indifferent and complained of loss of feelings. Ayoub clearly expressed a sense of despair. He said he could not get rid of the horrific memories and the vivid images they had left in his mind. The memories seemed to haunt him all the time and became very distressing whenever anything—a sound, a picture, or a story—reminded him of the original trauma. He did not want to talk about what he had experienced in Kuwait and avoided all that reminded him of the stressing events. He was also troubled because he could not remember certain parts of his torture. "I cannot get the complete story clear in my mind." He felt guilty and ashamed and could not look at the rest of his family in the eyes after he returned home because he had been unable to protect the honor of his sister. Had it not been for his three children and his family, who were dependent on him, he would have tried to end his life.

DISCUSSION

This is a classic case of posttraumatic stress disorder. This diagnosis should not be used unless there is evidence that the disorder arose within 6 months of a traumatic event of exceptional severity. Ayoub had repetitive, intrusive remembering or "reliving" of the stressful events in daytime imagery or in dreams and avoidance of stimuli that reminded him of the trauma, of which he had partial amnesia. The diagnosis therefore is posttraumatic stress disorder. (From *ICD-10 Casebook.*)

DIFFERENTIAL DIAGNOSIS

A major consideration in the diagnosis of posttraumatic stress disorder is the possibility that the patient also incurred a head injury during the trauma. Other organic considerations that can both cause and exacerbate the symptoms are epilepsy, alcohol use disorders, and other substance-related disorders. Acute intoxication or withdrawal from some substances may also present a clinical picture that is difficult to distinguish from the disorder until the effects of the substance have worn off.

Posttraumatic stress disorder is commonly misdiagnosed as another mental disorder and is then inappropriately treated. Clinicians must consider the diagnosis of posttraumatic stress disorder in patients who have pain disorder, substance abuse, other anxiety disorders, and mood disorders. In general, posttraumatic stress disorder can be distinguished from other mental disorders by interviewing a patient about previous traumatic experiences and by the nature of the current symptoms. Borderline personality disorder, dissociative disorders, factitious disorders, and malingering should also be considered. Borderline personality disorder can be difficult to distinguish from posttraumatic stress disorder. The two disorders may coexist or even may be causally related. Patients with dissociative disorders do not usually have the degree of avoidance behavior, the autonomic hyperarousal, or the history of trauma that patients with posttraumatic stress disorder report. Partly because of the publicity that posttraumatic stress disorder has received, clinicians should also consider the possibility of a factitious disorder and malingering.

COURSE AND PROGNOSIS

Posttraumatic stress disorder usually develops some time after the trauma. The delay can be as short as 1 week or as long as 30 years. Symptoms can fluctuate over time and may be most intense during periods of stress. About 30 percent of patients recover completely, 40 percent continue to have mild symptoms, 20 percent continue to have moderate symptoms, and 10 percent remain unchanged or become worse. A good prognosis is predicted by a rapid onset of the symptoms, the short duration of the symptoms (less than 6 months), good premorbid functioning, strong social supports, and the absence of other psychiatric, medical, or substance-related disorders.

In general, the very young and the very old have more difficulty with traumatic events than do those in midlife. For example, about 80 percent of young children who sustain a burn injury show symptoms of posttraumatic stress disorder 1 or 2 years after the initial injury; only 30 percent of adults who suffer such an injury have a posttraumatic stress disorder after 1 year. Presumably, young children do not yet have adequate coping mechanisms to deal with the physical and emotional insults of the trauma. Likewise, older people, when compared with younger adults, are likely to have more rigid coping mechanisms and to be less able to muster a flexible approach to dealing with the effects of trauma. Furthermore, the traumatic effects may be exacerbated by physical disabilities characteristic of late life, particularly disabilities of the nervous system and the cardiovascular system such as reduced cerebral blood flow, failing vision, palpitations, and arrhythmias. Preexisting psychiatric disability, whether a personality disorder or a more serious condition, also increases the effects of particular stressors. The availability of social supports may also influence the development, severity, and duration of posttraumatic stress disorder. In general, patients who have a good network of social support are less likely to have the disorder, are less likely to experience it in its severe forms, and are more likely to recover in less time.

TREATMENT

When a clinician is faced with a patient who has experienced a significant trauma, the major approaches are support, encouragement to discuss the event, and education about a variety of coping mechanisms (for example, relaxation). The use of sedatives and hypnotics can also be helpful. When a clinician is faced with a patient who experienced a traumatic event in the past and now has posttraumatic stress disorder, the emphasis should be on education about the disorder and its treatment, both pharmacological and psychotherapeutic. Additional support for the patient and the family can be obtained through local and national support groups for patients with posttraumatic stress disorder.

Pharmacotherapy

The efficacy of imipramine (Tofranil) and amitriptyline (Elavil), two tricyclic drugs, in the treatment of posttraumatic stress disorder is supported by a number of well-controlled clinical trials. Although some trials of the two drugs have had negative findings, most of these trials had serious design flaws, including too short a duration. Dosages of imipramine and amitriptyline should be the same as those used to treat depressive disorders, and the minimum length of an adequate trial should be 8 weeks. Patients who respond well should probably continue the pharmacotherapy for at least 1 year before an attempt is made to withdraw the drug. Some studies indicate that pharmacotherapy is more effective in treating the depression, anxiety, and hyperarousal than in treating the avoidance, denial, and emotional numbing.

Other drugs that are useful in the treatment of posttraumatic stress disorder include the serotonin-specific reuptake inhibitors, the monoamine oxidase inhibitors, trazodone (Desyrel), and the anticonvulsants (for example, carbamazepine, valproate). Clonidine (Catapres) and propranolol (Inderal) are suggested by the theories about noradrenergic hyperactivity in the disorder. Although some anecdotal reports point to the effectiveness of alprazolam (Xanax) in posttraumatic stress disorder, the use of this drug is complicated by the high association of substance-related disorders in patients with the disorder and by the emergence of withdrawal symptoms on discontinuation of the drug. Almost no positive data concern the use of antipsychotic drugs in the disorder, so the use of these drugs—for example, haloperidol (Haldol)—should be reserved for the short-term control of severe aggression and agitation.

Psychotherapy

Psychodynamic psychotherapy may be useful in the treatment of many patients with posttraumatic stress disorder. In some cases, reconstruction of the traumatic events with associated abreaction and catharsis may be therapeutic, but psychotherapy must be individualized, because some patients are overwhelmed by reexperiencing the traumas.

Psychotherapeutic interventions for posttraumatic stress disorder include behavior therapy, cognitive therapy, and hypnosis. Many clinicians advocate time-limited psychotherapy for the victims of trauma. Such therapy usually takes a cognitive approach and also provides support and security. The short-term nature of the psychotherapy minimizes the risk of dependence and chronicity, but issues of suspicion, paranoia, and trust often adversely affect compliance. Therapists should overcome patients' denial of the traumatic event, encourage them to relax, and remove them from the source of the stress. Patients should be encouraged to sleep, using medication if necessary. Support from people in their environment (such as friends and relatives) should be provided. Patients should be encouraged to review and abreact emotional feelings associated with the traumatic event and to plan for future recovery.

Psychotherapy after a traumatic event should follow a model of crisis intervention with support, education, and the development of coping mechanisms and acceptance of the event. When posttraumatic stress disorder has developed, two major psychotherapeutic approaches can be taken. The first is exposure to the traumatic event through imaginal techniques or in vivo exposure. The exposures can be intense, as in implosive therapy, or graded, as in systematic desensitization. The second approach is to teach the patient methods of stress management, including relaxation techniques and cognitive approaches to coping with stress. Some preliminary data indicate that, although stress management techniques are effective more rapidly than are exposure techniques, the results of exposure techniques are more long lasting.

In addition to individual therapy techniques, group therapy and family therapy have been reported to be effective in cases of posttraumatic stress disorder. The advantages of group therapy include the sharing of multiple traumatic experiences and support from other group members. Group therapy has been particularly successful with Vietnam veterans and survivors of catastrophic disasters, such as earthquakes. Family therapy often helps sustain a marriage through periods of exacerbated symptoms. Hospitalization may be necessary when symptoms are particularly severe or when there is a risk of suicide or other violence.

REFERENCES

Blaustein M, editor: Natural disasters: Psychiatric response. Psychiatr Ann *21:* 2, 1991.

Boudewyns PA: Posttraumatic stress disorder: Conceptualization and treatment. Prog Behav Modif *30:* 165, 1966.

Bremmer JD, Scott TM, Delaney RC, Southwick SM, Mason JW, Johnson DR, Innis RB, McCarthy G, Charney DS: Deficits in short-term memory in posttraumatic stress disorder. Am J Psychiatry *150:* 1015, 1993.

Bremmer JD, Southwick SM, Darnell A, Charney DS: Chronic PTSD in Vietnam combat veterans: Course of illness and substance abuse. Am J Psychiatry *153:* 369, 1996.

Bremmer JD, Steinberg M, Southwick SM, Johnson DR, Charney DS: Use of the structured clinical interview for DSM-IV dissociative disorders for systematic assessment of dissociative symptoms in posttraumatic stress disorder. Am J Psychiatry *150:* 1011, 1993.

Davidson J: Drug therapy of post-traumatic stress disorder. Br J Psychiatry *160:* 309, 1992.

Davidson JRT: Posttraumatic stress disorder and acute stress disorder. In *Comprehensive Textbook of Psychiatry,* ed 6, HI Kaplan, BJ Sadock, editors, p 1227. Williams & Wilkins, Baltimore, 1995.

Davidson JRT, Kudler HS, Saunders WB, Erickson L, Smith RD, Stein RM, Lipper S, Hammett EB, Mahorney SL, Cavenar JO Jr: Predicting response to amitriptyline in posttraumatic stress disorder. Am J Psychiatry *150:* 1024, 1993.

Foa FB, Roghbaum BO, Riggs DS, Murdock TB: Treatment of posttraumatic stress disorder in rape victims: A comparison between cognitive-behavioral procedures and counseling. J Consult Clin Psychol *59:* 715, 1991.

Fones C: Posttraumatic stress disorder occurring after painful childbirth. J Nerv Ment Dis *184:* 195, 1996.

Fontana A, Rosenheck R: Effectiveness and cost of the inpatient treatment of posttraumatic stress disorder: Comparison of three models of treatment. Am J Psychiatry *154:* 758, 1997.

Gabbard GO: *Psychodynamic Psychiatry in Clinical Practice: The DSM-IV edition.* American Psychiatric Press, Washington, 1994.

Gersons BPR, Carlier IVE: Post-traumatic stress disorder: The history of a recent concept. Br J Psychiatry *161:* 742, 1992.

Goenjian AK, Karayan I, Pynoos RS, Minassian D, Najarian LM, Steinberg AM, Fairbanks LA: Outcome of psychotherapy among early adolescents after trauma. Am J Psychiatry *154:* 536, 1997.

Gunderson JG, Sabo AN: The phenomenological and conceptual interface between borderline personality disorder and PTSD. Am J Psychiatry *150:* 19, 1993.

Haley RW, Kurt TL: Self-reported neurotoxic chemical combinations in the Gulf War. JAMA *227:* 232, 1997.

Jordan BK, Schlenger WE, Hough R, Kulka RA, Weiss D, Fairbank JA, Marmar CR: Lifetime and current prevalence of specific psychiatric disorders among Vietnam veterans and controls. Arch Gen Psychiatry *48:* 207, 1991.

Kessler RC, Sonnega A, Bromet E, Hughes M, Nelson CB: Posttraumatic stress disorder in the national comorbidity survey. Arch Gen Psychiatry *52:* 1048, 1995.

Koller P, Marmar CR, Kanas N: Psychodynamic group treatment of posttraumatic stress disorder in Vietnam veterans. Int J Group Psychother *42:* 225, 1992.

Landrigan PJ: Editorial: Illness in Gulf War veterans. JAMA *277:* 260, 1997.

Litz BT, Orsillo SM, Friedman M, Ehlich P, Batres A: Posttraumatic stress disorder associated with peacekeeping duty in Somalia for U.S. military personnel. Am J Psychiatry *154:* 178, 1997.

Mellman TA, Randolph CA, Brawman-Mintzer O, Flores LP, Milanes FJ: Phenomenology and course of psychiatric disorders associated with combat-related stress disorder. Am J Psychiatry *149:* 1568, 1992.

Orsillo SM, Weathers FW, Litz BT, Steinberg HR, Huska JA, Keane TM: Current and lifetime psychiatric disorders among veterans with war zone-related posttraumatic stress disorder. J Nerv Ment Dis *184:* 307, 1996.

Paige SR, Reid GM, Allen MG, Newton JEO: Psychophysiological correlates of posttraumatic stress disorder in Vietnam veterans. Biol Psychiatry *27:* 419, 1990.

Solomon SD, Gerrity ET, Muff AM: Efficacy of treatments for posttraumatic stress disorder: An empirical review. JAMA *268:* 633, 1992.

Yehuda R, Giller EL, Southwick SM, Lowry MT, Mason WT: Hypothalamic-pituitary-adrenal dysfunction in posttraumatic stress disorder. Biol Psychiatry *30:* 1031, 1991.

▲ 16.6 Generalized Anxiety Disorder

The fourth edition of *Diagnostic and Statistical Manual of Mental Disorders* (DSM-IV) defines generalized anxiety disorder as excessive anxiety and worry about several events or activities for a majority of days during at least a 6-month period. The worry is difficult to control and is associated with somatic symptoms such as muscle tension, irritability, difficulty sleeping, and restlessness. The anxiety is not focused on features of another Axis I disorder, is not caused by substance use or a general medical condition, and does not occur only during a mood or psychiatric disorder. The anxiety is difficult to control, is subjectively distressing, and produces impairment in important areas of a person's life.

EPIDEMIOLOGY

Generalized anxiety disorder is a common condition; reasonable estimates for its 1-year prevalence range from 3 to 8 percent. Generalized anxiety disorder is probably the disorder that most often coexists with another mental disorder, usually social phobia, specific phobia, panic disorder, or a depressive disorder. Perhaps 50 to 90 percent of patients with generalized anxiety disorder have another mental disorder.

The ratio of women to men with the disorder is about 2 to 1, but the ratio of women to men who are receiving inpatient treatment for the disorder is about 1 to 1. The age of onset is difficult to specify; most patients with the disorder report that they have been anxious for as long as they can remember. There is a lifetime prevalence of 45 percent. Patients usually come to a clinician's attention in their 20s, although the first contact with a clinician can occur at virtually any age. Only one third of patients who have generalized anxiety disorder seek psychiatric treatment. Many go to general practitioners, internists, cardiologists, pulmonary specialists, or gastroenterologists, seeking treatment for the somatic component of the disorder.

ETIOLOGY

The cause of generalized anxiety disorder is not known. As currently defined, generalized anxiety disorder probably affects a heterogeneous group of people. Perhaps because a certain degree of anxiety is normal and adaptive, differentiating normal anxiety from pathological anxiety and differentiating biological causative factors from psychosocial factors are difficult. Biological and psychological factors probably work together.

Biological Factors

The therapeutic efficacies of benzodiazepines and the azaspirones—for example, buspirone (BuSpar)—have focused biological research efforts on the γ-aminobutyric acid and serotonin (5-hydroxytryptamine [5-HT]) neurotransmitter systems. Benzodiazepines (which are benzodiazepine receptor agonists) are known to reduce anxiety, whereas flumazenil (Rom-

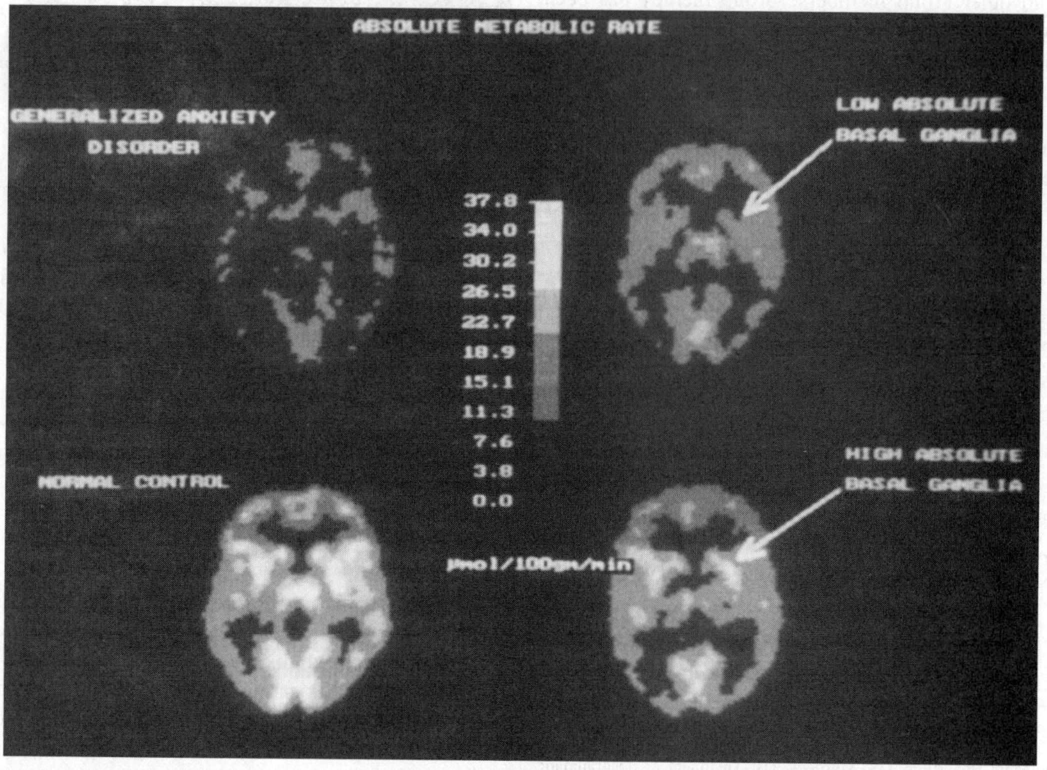
ABSOLUTE METABOLIC RATE
GENERALIZED ANXIETY DISORDER
LOW ABSOLUTE BASAL GANGLIA
37.8
34.0
30.2
26.5
22.7
18.9
15.1
11.3
7.6
3.8
0.0
NORMAL CONTROL
HIGH ABSOLUTE BASAL GANGLIA
μmol/100gm/min

FIGURE 16.6–1

Basal ganglia metabolism. A common glucose scale shows the decrease in absolute glucose metabolic rate in the basal ganglia of two typical subjects with generalized anxiety disorder **(top row)** compared with two normal control subjects **(bottom row)**. (Reprinted with permission from Wu JC, Buchsbaum MS, Hershey TG, Hazlett E, Sicotte N, Johnson JC: PET in generalized anxiety disorder. Biol Psychiatry *29:* 1188, 1991.)

azicon) (a benzodiazepine receptor antagonist) and the β-carbolines (benzodiazepine receptor reverse agonists) are known to induce anxiety. Although no convincing data indicate that the benzodiazepine receptors are abnormal in patients with generalized anxiety disorder, some researchers have focused on the occipital lobe, which has the highest concentrations of benzodiazepine receptors in the brain. Other brain areas that have been hypothesized to be involved in generalized anxiety disorder are the basal ganglia, the limbic system, and the frontal cortex. Because buspirone is an agonist at the 5-HT_{1A} receptor, there is the hypothesis that the regulation of the serotonergic system in generalized anxiety disorder is abnormal. Other neurotransmitter systems that have been the subject of research in generalized anxiety disorder include the norepinephrine, glutamate, and cholecystokinin neurotransmitter systems. Some evidence indicates that patients with generalized anxiety disorder may have a subsensitivity of their α_2-adrenergic receptors, as indicated by a blunted release of growth hormone after clonidine (Catapres) infusion.

Only a limited number of brain-imaging studies of patients with generalized anxiety disorder have been conducted. One positron emission tomography study reported a lower metabolic rate in basal ganglia and white matter in generalized anxiety disorder patients than in normal control subjects (Fig. 16.6–1). A few genetic studies have also been conducted in the field. One study found that a genetic relation may exist between generalized anxiety disorder and major depressive disorder in women. Another study showed a distinct but difficult-to-quantitate genetic component in generalized anxiety disorder. About 25 percent of first-degree relatives of patients with generalized anxiety disorder are also affected. Male relatives are likely to have an alcohol use disorder. Some twin studies report a concordance rate of 50 percent in monozygotic twins and 15 percent in dizygotic twins.

A variety of electroencephalogram (EEG) abnormalities have been noted in alpha rhythm and evoked potentials. Sleep EEG studies have reported increased sleep discontinuity, decreased delta sleep, decreased stage 1 sleep, and reduced rapid eye movement sleep. These changes in sleep architecture are different from the changes seen in depressive disorders.

Psychosocial Factors

The two major schools of thought about psychosocial factors leading to the development of generalized anxiety disorder are the cognitive-behavioral school and the psychoanalytic school. According to the cognitive-behavioral school, patients with generalized anxiety disorder respond to incorrectly and inaccurately perceived dangers. The inaccuracy is generated by selective attention to negative details in the environment, by distortions in information processing, and by an overly negative view of the person's own ability to cope. The psychoanalytic school hypothesizes that anxiety is a symptom of unresolved unconscious conflicts. This psychological theory was first presented by Sigmund Freud in 1909 with his description of Little Hans; before then, Freud had conceptualized anxiety as having a physiological basis.

A hierarchy of anxieties is related to various developmental levels. At the most primitive level, anxiety may relate to the fear of annihilation or of fusion with another person. At a more mature level of development, anxiety is related to separation from a love object. At a still more mature level, anxiety is connected to the loss of love from an important object. Castration anxiety is related to the oedipal phase of development and is considered one of the highest levels of anxiety. Superego anxiety, a person's fear of disappointing his or her own ideals and values (derived from internalized parents), is the most mature form of anxiety.

DIAGNOSIS

The DSM-IV diagnostic criteria (Table 16.6–1) include criteria to help clinicians differentiate among generalized anxiety disorder, normal anxiety, and other mental disorders. The distinction between generalized anxiety disorder and normal anxiety is emphasized by the use of the words ''excessive'' and ''difficult to control'' in the criteria and by the specification that the symptoms cause significant impairment or distress.

Table 16.6–1
DSM-IV Diagnostic Criteria for Generalized Anxiety Disorder

A. Excessive anxiety and worry (apprehensive expectation), occurring more days than not for at least 6 months, about a number of events or activities (such as work or school performance).

B. The person finds it difficult to control the worry.

C. The anxiety and worry are associated with three (or more) of the following six symptoms (with at least some symptoms present for more days than not for the past 6 months). **Note:** Only one item is required in childen.
  (1) restlessness or feeling keyed up or on edge
  (2) being easily fatigued
  (3) difficulty concentrating or mind going blank
  (4) irritability
  (5) muscle tension
  (6) sleep disturbance (difficulty falling or staying asleep, or restless unsatisfying sleep)

D. The focus of the anxiety and worry is not confined to features of an Axis I disorder, eg, the anxiety or worry is not about having a panic attack (as in panic disorder), being embarrassed in public (as in social phobia), being contaminated (as in obsessive-compulsive disorder), being away from home or close relatives (as in separation anxiety disorder), gaining weight (as in anorexia nervosa), having mutliple physical complaints (as in somatization disorder), or having a serious illness (as in hypochondriasis), and the anxiety and worry do not occur exclusively during posttraumatic stress disorder.

E. The anxiety, worry, or physical symptoms cause clinically significant distress or impairment in social, occupational, or other important areas of functioning.

F. The disturbance is not due to the direct physiological effects of a substance (eg, a drug of abuse, a medication) or a general medical condition (eg, hyperthyroidism), and does not occur exclusively during a mood disorder, psychotic disorder, or a pervasive developmental disorder.

Reprinted with permission from American Pscyhiatric Association: *Diagnostic and Statistical Manual of Mental Disorders,* ed 4. Copyright American Psychiatric Association, Washington, 1994.

CLINICAL FEATURES

The primary symptoms of generalized anxiety disorder are anxiety, motor tension, autonomic hyperactivity, and cognitive vigilance. The anxiety is excessive and interferes with other aspects of people's lives. The motor tension is most commonly manifested as shakiness, restlessness, and headaches. The autonomic hyperactivity is commonly manifested by shortness of breath, excessive sweating, palpitations, and various gastrointestinal symptoms. The cognitive vigilance is evidenced by irritability and the ease with which patients are startled.

Patients with generalized anxiety disorder usually seek out a general practitioner or internist for help with a somatic symptom. Alternatively, the patients go to a specialist for a specific symptom—for example, chronic diarrhea. A specific nonpsychiatric medical disorder is rarely found, and patients vary in their doctor-seeking behavior. Some patients accept a diagnosis of generalized anxiety disorder and the appropriate treatment; others seek additional medical consultations for their problems.

A 27-year-old married electrician complained of dizziness, sweating palms, heart palpitations, and ringing in the ears of more than 18 months' duration. He also experienced dry throat, periods of uncontrollable shaking, and a constant edgy and watchful feeling that often interfered with his ability to concentrate. These feelings had been present most of the time over the previous 2 years; they had not been limited to discrete periods.

Because of his symptoms, he had seen a family practitioner, a neurologist, a neurosurgeon, a chiropractor, and an ear, nose, and throat specialist. He had been given a hypoglycemic diet, received physiotherapy for a pinched nerve, and was told that he might have an inner ear problem.

For the past 2 years he had few social contacts because of his nervous symptoms. Although he sometimes had to leave work when the symptoms became intolerable, he continued to work for the same company for which he had worked since his apprenticeship after high school graduation. He tended to hide his symptoms from his wife and children, to whom he wanted to appear perfect, and he reported few problems with them as a result of his nervousness.

DISCUSSION

This man consulted numerous physicians for his symptoms, but the absence of preoccupation with fears of having a specific physical disease precludes a diagnosis of hypochondriasis. He recognized that his worries were often excessive, but they did not have the intrusive and inappropriate quality that characterized the obsessions of obsessive-compulsive disorder.

His predominant symptom was excessive and uncontrollable anxiety and worry for most of the time over the past 2 years. This symptom suggests the diagnosis of generalized anxiety disorder. He also had the characteristic associated symptoms of feeling on edge, difficulty concentrating, and muscle tension. His worries caused him significant distress and impaired his social functioning. The diagnosis of generalized anxiety disorder was made in this case because the worries were not confined to the features of another Axis I disorder (such as worrying about having panic attack, as in panic disorder, or being embarrassed in public, as in social phobia); the symptoms do not occur only during the course of a mood or psychotic disorder; they are not the direct effects of a substance (such as drugs of abuse or medication) or a general medical condition (such as hyperthyroidism); and the disturbance has persisted for more than 6 months. (From *DSM-IV Casebook.*)

DIFFERENTIAL DIAGNOSIS

The differential diagnosis of generalized anxiety disorder includes all the medical disorders that may cause anxiety (see Table 16.1–3). The medical workup should include standard blood chemistry tests, an electrocardiogram, and thyroid function tests. Clinicians must rule out caffeine intoxication, stimulant abuse, alcohol withdrawal, and sedative, hypnotic, or anxiolytic withdrawal. The mental status examination and the history should explore the diagnostic possibilities of panic disorder, phobias, and obsessive-compulsive disorder. In general, patients with panic disorder seek treatment earlier, are more disabled by their disorder, have had a sudden onset of symptoms, and are less troubled by their somatic symptoms than are patients with generalized anxiety disorder. Distinguishing generalized anxiety disorder from major depressive disorder and dysthymic disorder can be difficult; in fact, the disorders frequently coexist. Other diagnostic possibilities are adjustment disorder with anxiety, hypochondriasis, adult attention-deficit/hyperactivity disorder, somatization disorder, and personality disorders.

COURSE AND PROGNOSIS

Because of the high incidence of comorbid mental disorders in patients with generalized anxiety disorder, the clinical course and prognosis of the disorder are difficult to predict. Nonetheless, some data indicate that life events are associated with the onset of generalized anxiety disorder: The occurrence of several negative life events greatly increases the likelihood that the disorder will develop. By definition, generalized anxiety disorder is a chronic condition that may well be lifelong. As many as 25 percent of patients eventually experience panic disorder. An additional high percentage of patients are likely to have major depressive disorder.

TREATMENT

The most effective treatment of generalized anxiety disorder is probably one that combines psychotherapeutic, pharmacotherapeutic, and supportive approaches. The treatment may take a significant amount of time for the involved clinician, whether the clinician is a psychiatrist, a family practitioner, or another specialist.

Psychotherapy

The major psychotherapeutic approaches to generalized anxiety disorder are cognitive behavioral, supportive, and insight oriented. Data are still limited on the relative merits of those approaches, although the most sophisticated studies have examined cognitive-behavioral techniques, which seem to have both short-term and long-term efficacy. Cognitive approaches directly address patients' hypothesized cognitive distortions, and behavioral approaches address somatic symptoms directly. The major techniques used in behavioral approaches are relaxation and biofeedback. Some preliminary data indicate that the combination of cognitive and behavioral approaches is more effective than either technique used alone. Supportive therapy offers patients reassurance and comfort, although its long-term efficacy is doubtful. Insight-oriented psychotherapy focuses on uncovering unconscious conflicts and identifying ego strengths. The efficacy of insight-oriented psychotherapy for generalized anxiety disorder is reported in many anecdotal case reports, but large controlled studies are lacking.

Most patients experience a marked lessening of anxiety when given the opportunity to discuss their difficulties with concerned and sympathetic physicians. If clinicians discover external situations that are anxiety provoking, they may be able—alone or with the help of the patients or their families—to change the environment and thus reduce the stressful pressures. A reduction in symptoms often allows patients to function effectively in their daily work and relationships and thus to gain new rewards and gratification that are in themselves therapeutic.

In the psychoanalytic perspective, anxiety is sometimes a signal of unconscious turmoil that deserves investigation. The anxiety can be normal, adaptive, maladaptive, too intense, or too mild, depending on the circumstances. Anxiety appears in numerous situations over the course of the life cycle; in many cases, symptom relief is not the most appropriate course of action.

For patients who are psychologically minded and motivated to understand the sources of their anxiety, psychotherapy may be the treatment of choice. Psychodynamic therapy proceeds with the assumption that anxiety may increase with effective treatment. The goal of the dynamic approach may be to increase the patient's anxiety tolerance (a capacity to experience anxiety without having to discharge it), rather than to eliminate anxiety. Empirical research indicates that many patients who have successful psychotherapeutic treatment may continue to experience anxiety after termination of the psychotherapy, but their increased ego mastery allows them to use the anxiety symptoms as a signal to reflect on internal struggles and to expand their insight and understanding. A psychodynamic approach to patients with generalized anxiety disorder involves a search for the patient's underlying fears.

Pharmacotherapy

The decision to prescribe an anxiolytic to patients with generalized anxiety disorder should rarely be made on the first visit. Because of the long-term nature of the disorder, a treatment plan must be carefully thought out. The three major drugs to be considered for the treatment of generalized anxiety disorder are buspirone, the benzodiazepines, and the serotonin-specific reuptake inhibitors (SSRIs). Other drugs that may be useful are the tricyclic drugs (for example, imipramine [Tofranil]), antihistamines, and the β-adrenergic antagonists (for example, propranolol [Inderal]).

Although drug treatment of generalized anxiety disorder is sometimes seen as a 6- to 12-month treatment, some evidence indicates that treatment should be long term, perhaps lifelong. About 25 percent of patients relapse in the first month after the discontinuation of therapy, and 60 to 80 percent relapse over the course of the next year. Although some patients become dependent on the benzodiazepines, no tolerance develops to the therapeutic effects of the benzodiazepines, buspirone, or the SSRIs.

Benzodiazepines. Benzodiazepines have been the drugs of choice for generalized anxiety disorder. They can be prescribed on an as-needed basis, so that patients take a rapidly acting benzodiazepine when they feel particularly anxious. The alternative approach is to prescribe benzodiazepines for a limited period, during which psychosocial therapeutic approaches are implemented.

Several problems are associated with the use of benzodiazepines in generalized anxiety disorder. About 25 to 30 percent of all patients fail to respond, and tolerance and dependence may occur. Some patients also experience impaired alertness while taking the drugs and are, therefore, at risk for accidents involving automobiles and machinery.

The clinical decision to initiate treatment with a benzodiazepine should be a considered and specific one. The patient's diagnosis, the specific target symptoms, and the duration of treatment all should be defined, and the information should be shared with patients. Treatment for most anxiety conditions lasts for 2 to 6 weeks, followed by 1 or 2 weeks of tapering the drug before it is discontinued. The most common clinical mistake with benzodiazepine treatment is to continue treatment indefinitely.

For the treatment of anxiety, it is usual to begin a drug at the low end of its therapeutic range and to increase the dosage to achieve a therapeutic response. The use of a benzodiazepine with an intermediate half-life (8 to 15 hours) is likely to avoid some of the adverse effects associated with the use of benzodiazepines with long half-lives, and the use of divided doses prevents the development of adverse effects associated with high peak plasma levels. The improvement produced by benzodiazepines may go beyond a simple antianxiety effect. For example, the drugs may cause patients to regard various occurrences in a positive light. The drugs may also have a mild disinhibiting action, similar to that observed after ingesting modest amounts of alcohol.

Serotonergic Agents. **BUSPIRONE.** Buspirone is a 5-HT_{1A} receptor partial agonist and is most likely effective in 60 to 80 percent of patients with generalized anxiety disorder. Data indicate that buspirone is more effective in reducing the cognitive symptoms of generalized anxiety disorder than in reducing the somatic symptoms. Evidence also indicates that patients who have previously undergone treatment with benzodiazepines are not likely to respond to treatment with buspirone. The lack of response may be due to the absence, with buspirone treatment, of some of the nonanxiolytic effects of benzodiazepines (such as muscle relaxation and the additional sense of well-being). Nonetheless, the improved benefit–risk ratio, the lack of cognitive and psychomotor effects, and the absence of withdrawal symptoms may make buspirone the first-line drug in the treatment of generalized anxiety disorder. The major disadvantage of buspirone is that its effects take 2 to 3 weeks to become evident, in contrast to the almost immediate anxiolytic effects of the benzodiazepines. Buspirone is not an effective treatment for benzodiazepine withdrawal.

One reasonable approach is to initiate a benzodiazepine and buspirone simultaneously, then taper off the benzodiazepine after 2 to 3 weeks, at which point the buspirone should have reached its maximum effects. Some studies have also reported that long-term combined treatment with benzodiazepine and buspirone may be more effective than either drug alone.

SEROTONIN-SPECIFIC REUPTAKE INHIBITORS (SSRIs). SSRIs may be effective, especially for patients with comorbid depression. The prominent disadvantage of SSRIs, especially fluoxetine (Prozac), is that they may transiently increase anxiety. For this reason, the SSRIs sertraline (Zoloft) or paroxetine (Paxil) are better choices. It is reasonable to begin treatment with sertraline or paroxetine plus a benzodiazepine, then to taper the benzodiazepine after 2 to 3 weeks. Controlled studies are needed to determine whether SSRIs are as effective for generalized anxiety disorder as they are for panic disorder and obsessive-compulsive disorder.

Other Drugs. If treatment with buspirone or a benzodiazepine is ineffective or not completely effective, then a clinical reassessment is indicated to rule out comorbid conditions, such as depression, or to better understand the patient's environmental stresses. Other drugs that have proven useful for generalized anxiety disorder include the tricyclic and tetracyclic drugs. The β-adrenergic receptor antagonists may reduce the somatic manifestations of anxiety but not the underlying condition, and their use is usually limited to situational anxieties, such as performance anxiety.

REFERENCES

Astrom M: Generalized anxiety disorder in stroke patients. A 3-year longitudinal study. Stroke *27:* 270, 1996.

Borkovec TD, Roemer L: Perceived functions of worry among generalized anxiety disorder subjects: Distraction from more emotionally distressing topics? J Behav Ther Exp Psychiatry *26:* 25, 1995.

Butler G: Predicting outcome after treatment for generalized anxiety disorder. Behav Res Ther *31:* 211, 1993.

Butler G, Fennell M, Robson P, Gelder M: Comparison of behavior therapy and cognitive-behavior therapy in the treatment of generalized anxiety disorder. J Consult Clin Psychol *59:* 167, 1991.

Dubovsky SL: Generalized anxiety disorder: New concepts and psychopharmacologic therapies. J Clin Psychiatry *51* (1, Suppl): 3, 1990.

Gabbard GO: Psychodynamic psychiatry in the "decade of the brain." Am J Psychiatry *149:* 991, 1992.

Gammans RE, Stringfellow JC, Hvizdos AJ, Seidehamel RJ, Cohn JB, Wilcox CS, Fabre LF, Pecknold JC, Smith WT, Rickels K: Use of buspirone in patients with generalized anxiety disorder and coexisting depressive symptoms: A meta-analysis of eight randomized, controlled studies. Neuropsychobiology *25:* 193, 1992.

Gasperini M, Battaglia M, Diaferia G, Bellodi L: Personality features related to generalized anxiety disorder. Compr Psychiatry *31:* 363, 1990.

Gorman JM, Papp LA: Chronic anxiety: Deciding the length of treatment. J Clin Psychiatry *51* (1, Suppl): 11, 1990.

Kendler KS, Neale MC, Kessler RC, Health AC, Eaves LJ: Generalized anxiety disorder in women: A population-based twin study. Arch Gen Psychiatry *49:* 267, 1992.

Kendler KS, Neale MC, Kessler KC, Health AC, Eaves LJ: Major depression and generalized anxiety disorder: Same genes, (partly) different environments? Arch Gen Psychiatry *49:* 716, 1992.

Kollai M, Kollai B: Cardiac vagal tone in generalized anxiety disorder. Br J Psychiatry *161:* 831, 1992.

Massion AO, Warshaw MG, Keller MB: Quality of life and psychiatric morbidity in panic disorder and generalized anxiety disorder. Am J Psychiatry *150:* 600, 1993.

Mathews A, Mogg K, Kentish J, Eysenck M: Effect of psychological treatment on cognitive bias in generalized anxiety disorder. Behav Res Ther *33:* 293, 1995.

Nisita C, Petracca A, Akiskal HS, Galli L, Gepponi I, Cassano GB: Delimitation of generalized anxiety disorder: Clinical comparisons with panic and major depressive disorders. Compr Psychiatry *31:* 409, 1990.

Noyes R Jr, Woodman C, Garvey MJ, Cook BL, Suelzer M, Clancy J, Anderson DJ: Generalized anxiety disorder vs panic disorder: Distinguishing characteristics and patterns of comorbidity. J Nerv Ment Dis *180:* 369, 1992.

Papp LA, Gorman JM: Generalized anxiety disorder. In *Comprehensive Textbook of Psychiatry,* ed 6, HI Kaplan, BJ Sadock, editors, p 1236. Williams & Wilkins, Baltimore, 1995.

Rickels K, Schweizer E: The clinical course and long-term management of generalized anxiety disorder. J Clin Psychopharmacol *10:* 101S, 1990.

Rickels K, Schweizer E: The treatment of generalized anxiety disorder in patients with depression symptomatology. J Clin Psychiatry *54* (1, Suppl): 20, 1993.

Sanderson WC, Barlow DH: A description of patients diagnosed with DSM-III generalized anxiety disorder. J Nerv Ment Dis *178:* 588, 1990.

Shores MM, Glubin T, Cowley DS, Dager SR, Roy-Byrne PP, Dunner DL: The relationship between anxiety and depression: A clinical comparison of generalized anxiety disorder, dysthymic disorder, panic disorder, and major depressive disorder. Compr Psychiatry *33:* 237, 1992.

Thayer JF, Friedman BH, Borkovec TD: Autonomic characteristics of generalized anxiety disorder and worry. Biol Psychiatry *39:* 255, 1996.

17

Somatoform Disorders

According to the fourth edition of *Diagnostic and Statistical Manual of Mental Disorders* (DSM-IV), the somatoform disorders are distinguished by physical symptoms suggesting a medical condition, yet the symptoms are not fully explained by the medical condition, by substance use, or by another mental disorder. The symptoms are severe enough to cause patients significant distress or impaired social, occupational, or other functioning. The physical symptoms of somatoform disorders are not intentionally produced as are those of factitious disorders and malingering, but no medical condition can fully explain the somatic symptoms. Clinicians must judge that the onset, severity, and duration of symptoms are strongly linked to psychological factors to diagnose a somatoform disorder.

In DSM-IV, five specific somatoform disorders are recognized (Table 17–1): somatization disorder, characterized by many physical complaints affecting many organ systems; conversion disorder, characterized by one or two neurological complaints; hypochondriasis, characterized less by a focus on symptoms than by patients' beliefs that they have a specific disease; body dysmorphic disorder, characterized by a false belief or exaggerated perception that a body part is defective; and pain disorder, characterized by symptoms of pain that are either solely related to or significantly exacerbated by psychological factors. DSM-IV also has two residual diagnostic categories for somatoform disorders: Undifferentiated somatoform disorder includes somatoform disorders not otherwise described that have been present for 6 months or longer; and somatoform disorder not otherwise specified is the category for somatoform symptoms that do not meet any of the previously mentioned somatoform disorder diagnoses.

ICD-10

In the 10th revision of *International Statistical Classification of Diseases and Related Health Problems* (ICD-10), somatoform disorders are described as a "repeated presentation of physical symptoms, together with persistent requests for medical investigation," although patients have been reassured by their physicians that the symptoms have no physical basis. If physical disorders are present, they cannot account for patients' symptoms or for their distress. Although the symptoms may sometimes be linked to unpleasant internal or external experiences, patients refuse to explore possibly psychological causes of their disorders. Both physicians and patients can be frustrated by attempts to understand and alleviate these disorders. Patients who cannot convince physicians that their problems are physical may often behave histrionically.

The categories of somatoform disorders are similar in DSM-IV and ICD-10, except that in ICD-10, body dysmorphic disorder is a subcategory (Table 17–2). ICD-10 also stresses that differential diagnosis of somatoform disorders requires that a clinician know the patient well. A patient's "degree of conviction" may be temporarily lessened by a clinician's assurances and by a physical examination, but the disorders are a culturally accepted way of exhibiting physical illness and explaining physical symptoms.

ICD-10 also includes the diagnosis of neurasthenia, which has many signs and symptoms that overlap with the DSM-IV categories of anxiety, depression, and somatization. (Neurasthenia is discussed in Chapter 18.)

SOMATIZATION DISORDER

According to DSM-IV, somatization disorder is characterized by many somatic symptoms that cannot be explained adequately on the basis of physical and laboratory examinations. It usually begins before the age of 30, may continue for years, and is distinguished by "a combination of pain, gastrointestinal, sexual, and pseudoneurological symptoms." Somatization disorder differs from other somatoform disorders because of the multiplicity of the complaints and the multiple organ systems (for example, gastrointestinal and neurological) that are affected. The disorder is chronic and is associated with significant psychological distress, impairment in social and occupational functioning, and excessive medical-help–seeking behavior.

Somatization disorder has been recognized since the time of ancient Egypt. An early name for somatization disorder was *hysteria,* a condition incorrectly thought to affect only women. (The word *hysteria* is derived from the Greek word for uterus, *hystera.*) In the 17th century, Thomas Sydenham recognized that psychological factors, which he called antecedent sorrows, were involved in the pathogenesis of the symptoms. In 1859, Paul Briquet, a French physician, observed the multiplicity of the symptoms and the affected organ systems and commented on the usually chronic course of the disorder. Because of these astute clinical observations, the disorder was called *Briquet's syndrome* for a time, although the term *somatization disorder* became the standard in the United States when the third edition of DSM (DSM-III) was introduced in 1980.

Epidemiology

The lifetime prevalence of somatization disorder in the general population is estimated to be 0.1 or 0.2 percent, although

Table 17–1
Clinical Features of Somatoform Disorders

Diagnosis	Clinical Presentation	Demographic and Epidemiological Features	Diagnostic Features	Management Strategy	Prognosis	Associated Disturbances	Primary Differential Presentation	Psychological Processes Contributing to Symptoms	Motivation for Symptom Production
Somatization disorder	Polysymptomatic Recurrent and chronic Sickly by history	Young age Female predominance 20 to 1 Familial pattern 5–10% incidence in primary care populations	Review of systems profusely positive Multiple clincal contacts Polysurgical	Therapeutic alliance Regular appointments Crisis intervention	Poor to fair	Histrionic personality disorder Antisocial personality disorder Alcohol and other substance abuse Many life problems Conversion disorder	Physical disease Depression	Unconscious Cultural and developmental	Unconscious psychological factors
Conversion disorder	Monosymptomatic Mostly acute Simulates disease	Highly prevalent Female predominance Young age Rural and low social class Little-educated and psychologically unsophisticated	Simulation incompatible with known physiological mechanisms or anatomy	Suggestion and persuasion Multiple techniques	Excellent except in chronic conversion disorder	Alcohol and other substance dependence Antisocial personality disorder Somatization disorder Histrionic personality disorder	Depression Schizophrenia Neurological disease	Unconscious Psychological stress or conflict may be present	Unconscious psychological factors
Hypochondriasis	Disease concern or preoccupation	Previous physical disease Middle or old age Male-female ratio equal	Disease conviction amplifies symptoms Obsessional	Document symptoms Psychosocial review Psychotherapeutic	Fair to good Waxes and wanes	Obsessive compulsive personality disorder Depressive and anxiety disorders	Depression Physical disease Personality disorder Delusional disorder	Unconscious Stress—bereavement Developmental factors	Unconscious psychological factors
Body dysmorphic disorder	Subjective feelings of ugliness or concern with body defect	Adolescence or young adult ? Female predominance Largely unknown	Pervasive bodily concerns	Therapeutic alliance Stress management Psychotherapies Antidepressant medications	Unknown	Anorexia nervosa Psychosocial distress Avoidant or obsessive-compulsive personality disorder	Delusional disorder Depressive disorders Somatization disorder	Unconscious Self-esteem factors	Unconscious psychological factors
Pain disorder	Pain syndrome simulated	Female predominance 2 to 1 Older: 4th or 5th decade Familial pattern Up to 40% of pain populations	Simulation or intensity incompatible with known physiological mechanisms or anatomy	Therapeutic alliance Redefine goals of treatment Antidepressant medications	Guarded, variable	Depressive disorders Alcohol and other substance abuse Dependent or histrionic personality disorder	Depression Psychophysiological Physical disease Malingering and disability syndrome	Unconscious Acute stressor and developmental Physical trauma may predispose	Unconscious psychological factors

Adapted from Folks DG, Ford CV, Houck CA: Somatoform disorders, factitious disorders, and malingering. In *Clinical Psychiatry for Medical Students,* A Stoudemire, editor, p 233. Lippincott, Philadelphia, 1990.

Table 17–2
ICD-10 Diagnostic Criteria for Somatoform Disorders

Somatization disorder

A. There must be a history of at least 2 years' complaints of multiple and variable physical symptoms that cannot be explained by any detectable physical disorders. (Any physical disorders that are known to be present do not explain the severity, extent, variety, and persistence of the physical complaints, or the associated social disability.) If some symptoms clearly due to autonomic arousal are present, they are not a major feature of the disorder in that they are not particularly persistent or distressing.

B. Preoccupation with the symptoms causes persistent distress and leads the patient to seek repeated (three or more) consultations or sets of investigations with either primary care or specialist doctors. In the absence of medical services within either the financial or physical reach of the patient, there must be persistent self-medication or multiple consultations with local healers.

C. There is persistent refusal to accept medical reassurance that there is no adequate physical cause for the physical symptoms. (Short-term acceptance of such reassurance, ie, for a few weeks during or immediately after investigations, does not exclude this diagnosis.)

D. There must be a total of six or more symptoms from the following list, with symptoms occurring in at least two separate groups:

Gastrointestinal symptoms
(1) abdominal pain;
(2) nausea;
(3) feeling bloated or full of gas;
(4) bad taste in mouth, or excessively coated tongue;
(5) complaints of vomiting or regurgitation of food;
(6) complaints of frequent and loose bowel motions or discharge of fluids from anus;

Cardiovascular symptoms
(7) breathlessness without exertion;
(8) chest pains;

Genitourinary symptoms
(9) dysuria or compliants of frequency of micturition;
(10) unpleasant sensations in or around the genitals;
(11) complaints of unusual or copious vaginal discharge;

Skin and pain symptoms
(12) blotchiness or discoloration of the skin;
(13) pain in the limbs, extremities, or joints;
(14) unpleasant numbness or tingling sensations.

E. *Most commonly used exclusion clause.* Symptoms do not occur only during any of the schizophrenic or related disorders, any of the mood [affective] disorders, or panic disorder.

Undifferentiated somatoform disorder

A. Criteria A, C, and E for somatization disorder are met, except that the duration of the disorder is at least 6 months.

B. One or both of criteria B and D for somatization disorder are incompletely fulfilled.

Hypochondriacal disorder

A. Either of the following must be present:
(1) a persistent belief, of at least 5 months' duration, of the presence of a maximum of two serious physical diseases (of which at least one must be specifically named by the patient);
(2) a persistent preoccupation with a presumed deformity or disfigurement (body dysmorphic disorder).

B. Preoccupation with the belief and the symptoms causes persistent distress or interference with personal functioning in daily living and leads the patient to seek medical treatment or investigations (or equivalent help from local healers).

C. There is persistent refusal to accept medical reassurance that there is no physical cause for the symptoms or physical abnormality. (Short-term acceptance of such reassurance, ie, for a few weeks during or immediately after investigations, does not exclude this diagnosis.)

D. *Most commonly used exclusion clause.* The symptoms do not occur only during any of the schizophrenic and related disorders or any of the mood [affective] disorders.

Somatoform autonomic dysfunction

A. There must be symptoms of autonomic arousal that are attributed by the patient to a physical disorder of one or more of the following systems or organs:
(1) heart and cardiovascular system;
(2) upper gastrointestinal tract (esophagus and stomach);
(3) lower gastrointestinal tract;
(4) respiratory system;
(5) genitourinary system.

B. Two or more of the following autonomic symptoms must be present:
(1) palpitations;
(2) sweating (hot or cold);
(3) dry mouth;
(4) flushing or blushing;
(5) epigastric discomfort, "butterflies", or churning in the stomach.

C. One or more of the following symptoms must be present:
(1) chest pains or discomfort in and around the precordium;
(2) dyspnea or hyperventilation;
(3) excessive tiredness on mild exertion;
(4) aerophagy, hiccough, or burning sensations in chest or epigastrium;
(5) reported frequent bowel movements;
(6) increased frequency of micturition or dysuria;
(7) feeling of being bloated, distended, or heavy

D. There is no evidence of a disturbance of structure or function in the organs or systems about which the patient is concerned.

E. *Most commonly used exclusion clause.* These symptoms do not occur only in the presence of phobic disorders or panic disorder.

A fifth character is to be used to classify the individual disorders in this group, indicating the organ or system regarded by the patient as the origin of the symptoms:

Heart and cardiovascular system
Includes: cardiac neurosis, neurocirculatory asthenia, da Costa's syndrome.

Upper gastrointestinal tract
Includes: psychogenic aerophagy, hiccough, gastric neurosis.

Lower gastrointestinal tract
Includes: psychogenic irritable bowel syndrome, psychogenic diarrhea, gas syndrome.

Respiratory system
Includes: hyperventilation.

Genitourinary system
Includes: psychogenic increase of frequency of micturition and dysuria.

Other organ or system

Persistent somatoform pain disorder

A. There is persistent severe and distressing pain (for at least 6 months, and continously on most days), in any part of the body, which cannot be explained adequately by evidence of a physiological process or a physical disorder and which is consistently the main focus of the patient's attention.

B. *Most commonly used exclusion clause.* This disorder does not occur in the presence of schizophrenia or related disorders, or only during any of the mood [affective] disorders, somatization disorder, undifferentiated somatoform disorder, or hypochondriacal disorder.

Other somatoform disorders

In these disorders the presenting complaints are not mediated through the autonomic nervous system, and are limited to specific systems or parts of the body, such as the skin. This is in contrast to the multiple and often changing complaints of the origin of symptoms and distress found in somatization disorder and undifferentiated somatoform disorder. Tissue damage is not involved.

Any other disorder of sensation not due to physical disorder, which are closely associated in time with stressful events or problems, or which result in significantly increased attention for the patient, either personal or medical, should also be classified here.

Somatoform disorder, unspecified

several research groups believe that the actual figure may be closer to 0.5 percent. Women with somatization disorder outnumber men 5 to 20 times, but the highest estimates may be due to the early tendency not to diagnose somatization disorder in male patients. Nevertheless, it is not an uncommon disorder. With a 5-to-1 female-to-male ratio, the lifetime prevalence of somatization disorder among women in the general population may be 1 or 2 percent. Among patients in the offices of general practitioners and family practitioners, as many as 5 to 10 percent may meet the diagnostic criteria for somatization disorder. The disorder is inversely related to social position and occurs most often among patients who have little education and low income levels. Somatization disorder is defined as beginning before age 30; it most often begins during a person's teenage years.

Several studies have noted that somatization disorder commonly coexists with other mental disorders. About two thirds of all patients with somatization disorder have identifiable psychiatric symptoms, and as many as half have other mental disorders. Commonly associated personality traits or personality disorders are those characterized by avoidant, paranoid, self-defeating, and obsessive-compulsive features. Two disorders that are not more commonly seen in patients with somatization disorder than in the general population are bipolar I disorder and substance abuse.

Etiology

Psychosocial Factors. The cause of somatization disorder is unknown. Psychosocial formulations of the cause involve interpretations of the symptoms as social communication, the result of which is to avoid obligations (for example, going to a job a person does not like), to express emotions (for example, anger at a spouse), or to symbolize a feeling or a belief (for example, a pain in the guts). Strict psychoanalytic interpretations of symptoms rest on the hypothesis that the symptoms substitute for repressed instinctual impulses.

A behavioral perspective on somatization disorder emphasizes that parental teaching, parental example, and ethnic mores may teach some children to somatize more than do others. In addition, some patients with somatization disorder come from unstable homes and have been physically abused. Social, cultural, and ethnic factors may also be involved in the development of symptoms.

Biological Factors. Some studies point to a neuropsychological basis for somatization disorder. These studies propose that the patients have characteristic attention and cognitive impairments that result in the faulty perception and assessment of somatosensory inputs. The reported impairments include excessive distractibility, inability to habituate to repetitive stimuli, the grouping of cognitive constructs on an impressionistic basis, partial and circumstantial associations, and lack of selectivity, as indicated in some studies of evoked potentials. A limited number of brain-imaging studies have reported decreased metabolism in the frontal lobes and in the nondominant hemisphere.

Genetic data indicate that in at least some families the transmission of somatization disorder has genetic components. The data indicate that somatization disorder tends to run in families and occurs in 10 to 20 percent of the first-degree female relatives of patients with somatization disorder. Within these families, first-degree male relatives are prone to substance abuse and antisocial personality disorder. One study also reported a concordance rate of 29 percent in monozygotic twins and 10 percent in dizygotic twins, an indication of a genetic effect.

Research into cytokines, a new area of basic neuroscience study, may be relevant to somatization disorder and other somatoform disorders. Cytokines are messenger molecules that the immune system uses to communicate within itself and with the nervous system, including the brain. Examples of cytokines are interleukins, tumor necrosis factor, and interferons. Some preliminary experiments indicate that cytokines may help cause some of the nonspecific symptoms of disease, especially of infections, such as hypersomnia, anorexia, fatigue, and depression. Although no data yet support the hypothesis, abnormal regulation of the cytokine system may result in some of the symptoms seen in somatoform disorders.

Diagnosis

For the diagnosis of somatoform disorder, DSM-IV requires that the onset of symptoms occurs before age 30 (Table 17–3). During the course of the disorder, patients must have complained of at least four pain symptoms, two gastrointestinal symptoms, one sexual symptom, and one pseudoneurological symptom, none of which are completely explained by physical or laboratory examinations.

Clinical Features

Patients with somatization disorder have many somatic complaints and long, complicated medical histories. Nausea and vomiting (other than during pregnancy), difficulty in swallowing, pain in the arms and legs, shortness of breath unrelated to exertion, amnesia, and complications of pregnancy and menstruation are among the most common symptoms. Patients frequently believe that they have been sickly most of their lives.

Psychological distress and interpersonal problems are prominent; anxiety and depression are the most prevalent psychiatric conditions. Suicide threats are common, but actual suicide is rare. If suicide does occur, it is often associated with substance abuse. Patients' medical histories are often circumstantial, vague, imprecise, inconsistent, and disorganized. Patients classically but not always describe their complaints in a dramatic, emotional, and exaggerated fashion, with vivid and colorful language; they may confuse temporal sequences and cannot clearly distinguish current from past symptoms. Female patients with somatization disorder may dress in an exhibitionistic manner. Patients may be perceived as dependent, self-centered, hungry for admiration or praise, and manipulative.

Somatization disorder is commonly associated with other mental disorders, including major depressive disorder, personality disorders, substance-related disorders, generalized anxiety disorder, and phobias. The combination of these disorders and the chronic symptoms results in an increased incidence of marital, occupational, and social problems.

A 29-year-old mother of two requested medical clearance for impending surgery for cysts in her breasts. She

Table 17–3
DSM-IV Diagnostic Criteria for Somatization Disorder

A. A history of many physical complaints beginning before age 30 years that occur over a period of several years and result in treatment being sought or significant impairment in social, occupational, or other important areas of functioning.

B. Each of the following criteria must have been met, with individual symptoms occurring at any time during the course of the disturbance:
  (1) *four pain symptoms:* a history of pain related to at least four different sites or functions (eg, head, abdomen, back, joints, extremities, chest, rectum, during menstruation, during sexual intercourse, or during urination)
  (2) *two gastrointestinal symptoms:* a history of at least two gastrointestinal symptoms other than pain (eg, nausea, bloating, vomiting other than during pregnancy, diarrhea, or intolerance of several different foods)
  (3) *one sexual symptom:* a history of at least one sexual or reproductive symptom other than pain (eg, sexual indifference, erectile or ejaculatory dysfunction, irregular menses, excessive menstrual bleeding, vomiting throughout pregnancy)
  (4) *one pseudoneurological symptom:* a history of at least one symptom or deficit suggesting a neurological condition not limited to pain (conversion symptoms such as impaired coordination or balance, paralysis or localized weakness, difficulty swallowing or lump in throat, aphonia, urinary retention, hallucinations, loss of touch or pain sensation, double vision, blindness, deafness, seizures; dissociative symptoms such as amnesia; or loss of consciousness other than fainting)

C. Either (1) or (2):
  (1) after appropriate investigation, each of the symptoms in criterion B cannot be fully explained by a known general medical condition or the direct effects of a substance (eg, the effects of injury, medication, drugs, or alcohol)
  (2) when there is a related general medical condition, the physical complaints or resulting social or occupational impairment are in excess of what would be expected from the history, physical examination, or laboratory findings

D. The symptoms are not intentionally feigned or produced (as in factitious disorder or malingering).

Reprinted with permission from American Psychiatric Association: *Diagnostic and Statistical Manual of Mental Disorders,* ed 4. Copyright, American Psychiatric Association, Washington, 1994.

described the cysts as rapidly enlarging and unbearably painful. While drawing attention to her breasts, she noted, "They are so large and so tender to the touch. And I just can't have relations—forget that."

She also had disabling back pain that spread up and down her spine and made her legs give out on her suddenly, causing her to fall. When discussing this symptom, she winced visibly, and added: "Oh, there it goes; my back keeps clicking. The pain is so severe it affects me with my kids. Pain like that will make anyone into a beast." (She had previously been suspected of child abuse.) She also complained of dyspnea and a dry cough that prevented her from walking uphill.

Her medical history began at menarche with dysmenorrhea and menorrhagia. At 18 she had exploratory surgery for a possible ovarian cyst and subsequently underwent another operation for suspected abdominal adhesions. She also had a history of recurrent urinary tract symptoms, although no organisms were ever clearly documented, and she had a normal workup for "an enlarged thyroid." At various times, she had received the diagnoses of spastic colon, migraine, and endometriosis.

Two marriages, both to alcoholic and abusive men who refused to pay child support, had ended in divorce. She had lost several clerical jobs because of excessive absences. During the periods when she felt worst, she spent most of the day at home in a bathrobe while her relatives cared for her children. She had a history of narcotic dependence and claimed that she began using analgesics for her back pain and then, "overdid it."

The physical examination at the time of her visit revealed inconsistencies in the breast tissue but no frank masses, and mammography findings were normal. (Courtesy of Arthur J. Barsky, M.D.)

Differential Diagnosis

Clinicians must always rule out nonpsychiatric medical conditions that may explain a patient's symptoms. Several medical disorders often show nonspecific, transient abnormalities in the same age group. These medical disorders include multiple sclerosis, myasthenia gravis, systemic lupus erythematosus, acquired immune deficiency syndrome (AIDS), acute intermittent porphyria, hyperparathyroidism, hyperthyroidism, and chronic systemic infections. The onset of multiple somatic symptoms in patients older than 40 should be presumed to be caused by a nonpsychiatric medical condition until an exhaustive medical workup has been completed.

Many mental disorders are considered in the differential diagnosis, which is complicated by the observation that at least 50 percent of patients with somatization disorder have a coexisting mental disorder. Patients with major depressive disorder, generalized anxiety disorder, and schizophrenia may all have an initial complaint that focuses on somatic symptoms. In all these disorders, however, the symptoms of depression, anxiety, or psychosis eventually predominate over the somatic complaints. Although patients with panic disorder may complain of many somatic symptoms related to their panic attacks, they are not bothered by somatic symptoms between panic attacks.

Among the other somatoform disorders, hypochondriasis, conversion disorder, and pain somatization disorder, patients with hypochondriasis falsely believe that they have a specific disease, whereas those with somatization disorder are concerned with many symptoms. The symptoms of conversion disorder are limited to one or two neurological symptoms rather than to the wide-ranging symptoms of somatization disorder. Pain disorder is limited to one or two complaints of pain symptoms.

Course and Prognosis

Somatization disorder is chronic and often debilitating. By definition, the symptoms should have begun before age 30 and have been present for several years. Episodes of increased symptom severity and the development of new symptoms are thought to last 6 to 9 months and may be separated by less symptomatic periods lasting 9 to 12 months. Rarely, however, does a patient with somatization disorder go for more than a year without seeking medical attention. There is often an association between periods of increased stress and the exacerbation of somatic symptoms.

Treatment

Somatization disorder is best treated when the patient has a single identified physician as primary caretaker. When more than one clinician is involved, patients have increased opportunities to express somatic complaints. Primary physicians should see patients during regularly scheduled visits, usually at monthly intervals. The visits should be relatively brief, although a partial physical examination should be conducted to respond to each new somatic complaint. Additional laboratory and diagnostic procedures should generally be avoided. Once somatization disorder has been diagnosed, the treating physician should listen to the somatic complaints as emotional expressions rather than as medical complaints. Nevertheless, patients with somatization disorder can also have bona fide physical illnesses; therefore, physicians must always use their judgment about what symptoms to work up and to what extent. A reasonable long-range strategy for a primary care physician who is treating a patient with somatization disorder is to increase the patient's awareness of the possibility that psychological factors are involved in the symptoms until the patient is willing to see a mental health clinician, probably a psychiatrist, on a regular basis.

Psychotherapy, both individual and group, decreases these patients' personal health care expenditures by 50 percent, largely by decreasing their rates of hospitalization. In psychotherapy settings, patients are helped to cope with their symptoms, to express underlying emotions, and to develop alternative strategies for expressing their feelings.

Giving psychotropic medications whenever somatization disorder coexists with a mood or anxiety disorder is always a risk, but psychopharmacological treatment, as well as psychotherapeutic treatment, of the coexisting disorder is indicated. Medication must be monitored, because patients with somatization disorder tend to use drugs erratically and unreliably. In patients without coexisting mental disorders, few available data indicate that pharmacological treatment is effective.

CONVERSION DISORDER

DSM-IV defines conversion disorder as a disorder characterized by the presence of one or more neurological symptoms (for example, paralysis, blindness, and paresthesias) that cannot be explained by a known neurological or medical disorder. In addition, the diagnosis requires that psychological factors be associated with the initiation or the exacerbation of the symptoms.

The syndrome currently known as conversion disorder was originally combined with the syndrome known as somatization disorder and was referred to as hysteria, conversion reaction, or dissociative reaction. Briquet and Jean-Martin Charcot contributed to the development of the concept of conversion disorder by noting the influence of heredity on the symptom and the common association with a traumatic event. The term *conversion* was introduced by Sigmund Freud, who, based on his work with Anna O., hypothesized that the symptoms of conversion disorder reflect unconscious conflicts.

Epidemiology

The prevalence of some symptoms of conversion disorder that are not of sufficient severity to warrant the diagnosis may occur in as many as one third of the general population sometime during their lives. One community reported that the annual incidence of conversion disorder was 22 per 100,000. Among specific populations, the occurrence of conversion disorder may be even higher than that, perhaps making conversion disorder the most common somatoform disorder in some populations. Several studies have reported that 5 to 15 percent of psychiatric consultations in a general hospital and 25 to 30 percent of admissions to a Veterans Administration hospital involve patients with conversion disorder diagnoses.

The ratio of women to men among adult patients is at least 2 to 1 and as much as 5 to 1; among children there is an even higher predominance in girls. Men with conversion disorder have often been involved in occupational or military accidents. Conversion disorder can have its onset at any time, from childhood to old age, but it is most common in adolescents and young adults. Data indicate that conversion disorder is most common among rural populations, people with little education, those with low intelligence quotients, those in low socioeconomic groups, and military personnel who have been exposed to combat situations. Conversion disorder is commonly associated with comorbid diagnoses of major depressive disorder, anxiety disorders, and schizophrenia.

Etiology

Psychoanalytic Factors. According to psychoanalytic theory, conversion disorder is caused by the repression of unconscious intrapsychic conflict and the conversion of anxiety into a physical symptom. The conflict is between an instinctual impulse (for example, aggression or sexuality) and the prohibitions against its expression. The symptoms allow the partial expression of the forbidden wish or urge but disguise it, so that patients can avoid consciously confronting their unacceptable impulses; that is, the conversion disorder symptom has a symbolic relation to the unconscious conflict. Conversion disorder symptoms also enable patients to communicate that they need special consideration and special treatment. Such symptoms may function as a nonverbal means of controlling or manipulating others.

Biological Factors. Increasing data implicate biological and neuropsychological factors in the development of conversion disorder symptoms. Preliminary brain-imaging studies have found hypometabolism of the dominant hemisphere and hypermetabolism of the nondominant hemisphere and have implicated impaired hemispheric communication in the cause of conversion disorder. The symptoms may be caused by an excessive cortical arousal that sets off negative feedback loops between the cerebral cortex and the brainstem reticular formation. Elevated levels of corticofugal output, in turn, inhibit the patient's awareness of bodily sensation, which, in some patients with conversion disorder, may explain the observed sensory deficits. Neuropsychological tests sometimes reveal subtle cerebral impairments in verbal communication, memory, vigilance, affective incongruity, and attention in these patients.

Diagnosis

DSM-IV limits the diagnosis of conversion disorder to those symptoms that affect a voluntary motor or sensory function, that is, neurological symptoms (Table 17–4). Physicians are unable to explain the neurological symptoms solely on the basis of any known neurological condition.

The diagnosis of conversion disorder requires that clinicians find a necessary and critical association between the cause of the neurological symptoms and psychological factors, although the symptoms cannot be the result of malingering or factitious disorder. The diagnosis of conversion disorder also excludes symptoms of pain and sexual dysfunction and symptoms that occur only in somatization disorder. DSM-IV allows the specification of the type of symptom or deficit seen in conversion disorder (see Table 17–4).

Clinical Features

Paralysis, blindness, and mutism are the most common conversion disorder symptoms. Conversion disorder may be most commonly associated with passive-aggressive, dependent, antisocial, and histrionic personality disorders. Depressive and anxiety disorder symptoms can often accompany the symptoms of conversion disorder, and affected patients are at risk for suicide.

Table 17–4
DSM-IV Diagnostic Criteria for Conversion Disorder

A. One or more symptoms or deficits affecting voluntary motor or sensory function that suggest a neurological or other general medical condition.

B. Psychological factors are judged to be associated with the symptom or deficit because the initiation or exacerbation of the symptom or deficit is preceded by conflicts or other stressors.

C. The symptom of deficit is not intentionally produced or feigned (as in factitious disorder or malingering).

D. The symptoms or deficit cannot, after appropriate investigation, be fully explained by a general medical condition, or by the direct effects of a substance, or as a culturally sanctioned behavior or experience.

E. The symptom or deficit causes clinically significant distress or impairment in social, occupational, or other important areas of functioning or warrants medical evaluation.

F. The symptom or deficit is not limited to pain or sexual dysfunction, does not occur exclusively during the course of somatization disorder, and is not better accounted for by another mental disorder.

Specify type of symptom of deficit:
With motor symptom or deficit
With sensory symptom or deficit
With seizures or convulsions
With mixed presentation

Reprinted with permission from American Psychiatric Association: *Diagnostic and Statistical Manual of Mental Disorders,* ed 4. Copyright, American Psychiatric Association, Washington, 1994.

Sensory Symptoms.

In conversion disorder, anesthesia and paresthesia are common, especially of the extremities. All sensory modalities can be involved, and the distribution of the disturbance is usually inconsistent with that of either central or peripheral neurological disease. Thus, clinicians may see the characteristic stocking-and-glove anesthesia of the hands or feet or the hemianesthesia of the body beginning precisely along the midline.

Conversion disorder symptoms may involve the organs of special sense and can produce deafness, blindness, and tunnel vision. These symptoms may be unilateral or bilateral, but neurological evaluation reveals intact sensory pathways. In conversion disorder blindness, for example, patients walk around without collisions or self-injury, their pupils react to light, and their cortical evoked potentials are normal.

Motor Symptoms.

The motor symptoms include abnormal movements, gait disturbance, weakness, and paralysis. Gross rhythmical tremors, choreiform movements, tics, and jerks may be present. The movements generally worsen when attention is called to them. One gait disturbance seen in conversion disorder is astasia-abasia, which is a wildly ataxic, staggering gait accompanied by gross, irregular, jerky truncal movements and thrashing and waving arm movements. Patients with the symptoms rarely fall; if they do, they are generally not injured.

Other common motor disturbances are paralysis and paresis involving one, two, or all four limbs, although the distribution of the involved muscles does not conform to the neural pathways. Reflexes remain normal; the patients have no fasciculations or muscle atrophy (except after longstanding conversion paralysis); electromyography findings are normal.

Seizure Symptoms.

Pseudoseizures are another symptom in conversion disorder. Clinicians may find it difficult to differentiate a pseudoseizure from an actual seizure by clinical observation alone. Moreover, about one third of the patient's pseudoseizures also have a coexisting epileptic disorder. Tongue biting, urinary incontinence, and injuries after falling can occur in pseudoseizures, although these symptoms are generally not present. Pupillary and gag reflexes are retained after pseudoseizure, and patients have no postseizure increase in prolactin concentrations.

Other Associated Features.

Several psychological symptoms have also been associated with conversion disorder.

PRIMARY GAIN. Patients achieve primary gain by keeping internal conflicts outside their awareness. Symptoms have symbolic value in that they represent an unconscious psychological conflict.

SECONDARY GAIN. Patients accrue tangible advantages and benefits as a result of their being sick, such as being excused from obligations and difficult life situations, receiving support and assistance that might not otherwise be forthcoming, and controlling other people's behavior.

LA BELLE INDIFFÉRENCE. *La belle indifférence* is a patient's inappropriately cavalier attitude toward serious symptoms; that is, the patient seems to be unconcerned about what appears to be a major impairment. That bland indifference may be lacking in some patients; it is also seen in some seriously ill medical patients who develop a stoic attitude. The presence or the absence of *la belle indifférence* is an inaccurate measure of whether a patient has conversion disorder.

IDENTIFICATION. Patients with conversion disorder may unconsciously model their symptoms on those of someone important to them. For example, a parent or a person who has recently died may serve as a model for conversion disorder. During pathological grief reaction, bereaved people commonly have symptoms of the deceased.

A 46-year-old housewife was referred by her husband's psychiatrist for consultation. In the course of discussing certain marital conflicts that he was having with his wife, the husband had described ''attacks'' of dizziness that his wife experienced that left her quite incapacitated.

In consultation, the wife described being overcome with feelings of extreme dizziness, accompanied by slight nausea, 4 or 5 nights a week. During these attacks, the room around her would take on a ''shimmering'' appearance, and she would have the feeling that she was ''floating'' and unable to keep her balance. Inexplicably, the attacks almost always occurred at about 4:00 PM. She usually had to lie down on a couch and often did not feel better until 7:00 PM or 8:00 PM. After recovering, she generally spent the rest of the evening watching TV; more often than not, she would fall asleep in the living room, not going to bed in the bedroom until 2:00 AM or 3:00 AM.

The patient had been pronounced physically fit by her internist, a neurologist, and an ear-nose-throat specialist on more than one occasion. Hypoglycemia had been ruled out by glucose tolerance tests.

When asked about her marriage, the patient described her husband as a tyrant, frequently demanding and verbally abusive of her and their four children. She admitted that she dreaded his arrival home from work each day, knowing that he would comment that the house was a mess and the dinner, if prepared, not to his liking. Recently, since the onset of her attacks, when she was unable to make dinner he and the four kids would go to McDonald's or the local pizza parlor. After that, he would settle in to watch a ball game on TV in the bedroom, and their conversation was minimal. In spite of their troubles, the patient claimed that she loved and needed her husband very much.

DISCUSSION

This woman complains of a variety of physical symptoms (dizziness, nausea, visual disturbances, loss of balance) that all suggest a physical disorder; but thorough examinations by a number of medical specialists have failed to detect a general medical condition that could account for the symptoms. Therefore, the differential diagnosis is between undiagnosed physical symptoms and a mental disorder.

The context in which these symptoms occur suggests the role of psychological factors in their development: They recur at virtually the same time each day, closely associated with the husband's arrival home from work; the husband's angry tirades and verbal abuse are undoubtedly very stressful. Because there is no evidence that the patient is conscious of intentionally producing the symptoms (e.g., taking a drug that would induce such symptoms, claiming to have the symptoms when they are not present), the diagnosis of a factitious disorder or malingering is ruled out. Although the symptoms resemble those of a panic attack, there is no evidence that they occur unexpectedly, thus ruling out panic disorder. The disorder, therefore, is a somatoform disorder—a mental disorder with symptoms that suggest a neurological or general medical disorder.

Because the patient's complaints are not part of a long-standing polysymptomatic disturbance involving many organ systems, somatization disorder is excluded. The symptoms are limited to an alteration in sensory functioning; hence, the diagnosis is conversion disorder. (From *DSM-IV Casebook.*)

Differential Diagnosis

One of the major problems in diagnosing conversion disorder is the difficulty of definitively ruling out a medical disorder. Concomitant nonpsychiatric medical disorders are common in hospitalized patients with conversion disorder, and evidence of a current or previous neurological disorder or of a systemic disease affecting the brain has been reported in 18 to 64 percent of such patients. An estimated 25 to 50 percent of patients classified as having conversion disorder eventually receive diagnoses of neurological or nonpsychiatric medical disorders that could have caused their earlier symptoms. Therefore, a thorough medical and neurological workup is essential in all cases. If the symptoms can be resolved by suggestion, hypnosis, or parenteral amobarbital (Amytal) or lorazepam (Ativan), they are probably the result of conversion disorder.

Neurological disorders (such as dementia and other degenerative diseases), brain tumors, and basal ganglia disease must be considered in the differential diagnosis. For example, weakness may be confused with myasthenia gravis, polymyositis, acquired myopathies, or multiple sclerosis. Optic neuritis may be misdiagnosed as conversion disorder blindness. Other diseases that may cause confusing symptoms are Guillain-Barré syndrome, Creutzfeldt-Jakob disease, periodic paralysis, and early neurological manifestations of AIDS. Conversion disorder symptoms occur in schizophrenia, depressive disorders, and anxiety disorders, but these other disorders are associated with their own distinct symptoms that eventually make differential diagnosis possible.

Sensorimotor symptoms also occur in somatization disorder. But somatization disorder is a chronic illness that begins early in life and includes symptoms in many other organ systems. In hypochondriasis, patients have no actual loss or distortion of function; the somatic complaints are chronic and are not limited to neurological symptoms, and the characteristic hypochondriacal attitudes and beliefs are present. If the patient's symptoms are limited to pain, pain disorder can be diagnosed. Patients whose complaints are limited to sexual function are classified as having a sexual dysfunction, rather than conversion disorder.

In both malingering and factitious disorder, the symptoms are under conscious, voluntary control. A malingerer's history is usually more inconsistent and contradictory than is that of a patient with conversion disorder, and a malingerer's fraudulent behavior is clearly goal directed.

Course and Prognosis

The initial symptoms of most patients with conversion disorder, perhaps 90 to 100 percent, resolve in a few days or less than a month. A reported 75 percent of patients may not experience another episode, but 25 percent have additional episodes during periods of stress. Associated with a good prognosis are a sudden onset, an easily identifiable stressor, good premorbid adjustment, no comorbid psychiatric or medical disorders, and no ongoing litigation. The longer the conversion disorder symptoms are present, the worse the prognosis. As discussed previously, 25 to 50 percent of patients may later have neurological disorders or nonpsychiatric medical conditions affecting the nervous system. Therefore, patients with conversion disorder must have complete medical and neurological evaluations at the time of the diagnosis.

Treatment

Resolution of the conversion disorder symptom is usually spontaneous although probably facilitated by insight-oriented supportive or behavior therapy; the most important feature of the therapy is a relationship with a caring and authoritative therapist. With patients who are resistant to the idea of psychotherapy, physicians can suggest that the psychotherapy will focus on issues of stress and coping. Telling such patients that their symptoms are imaginary often makes them worse. Hypnosis, anxiolytics, and behavioral relaxation exercises are effective in some cases. Parenteral amobarbital or lorazepam may be helpful in obtaining additional historic information, especially when a patient has recently experienced a traumatic event. Psychodynamic approaches include psychoanalysis and insight-oriented psychotherapy, in which patients explore intrapsychic conflicts and the symbolism of the conversion disorder symptoms. Brief and direct forms of short-term psychotherapy have also been used to treat conversion disorder. The greater the duration of these patients' sick role and the more they have regressed, the more difficult the treatment.

HYPOCHONDRIASIS

In DSM-IV, hypochondriasis is defined as a person's preoccupation with the fear of contracting, or the belief of having, a serious disease. This fear or belief arises when a person misinterprets bodily symptoms or functions. The term *hypochondriasis* is derived from the old medical term *hypochondrium,* (''below the ribs'') and reflects the common abdominal complaints of many patients with the disorder. Hypochondriasis results from patients' unrealistic or inaccurate interpretations of physical symptoms or sensations, even though no known medical causes can be found. Patients' preoccupations result in significant distress to them and impair their ability to function in their personal, social, and occupational roles.

Epidemiology

One recent study reported a 6-month prevalence of hypochondriasis of 4 to 6 percent in a general medical clinic population. Men and women are equally affected by hypochondriasis. Although the onset of symptoms can occur at any age, the disorder most commonly appears in people 20 to 30 years of age. Some evidence indicates that the diagnosis is more common among blacks than among whites, but social position, education level, and marital status do not appear to affect the diagnosis.

Etiology

In the diagnostic criteria for hypochondriasis, DSM-IV indicates that the symptoms reflect a misinterpretation of bodily symptoms. A reasonable body of data indicates that people with hypochondriasis augment and amplify their somatic sensations; they have lower than usual thresholds for and a lower tolerance of physical discomfort. For example, what people normally perceive as abdominal pressure, people with hypochondriasis experience as abdominal pain. They may focus on bodily sensations, misinterpret them, and become alarmed by them because of a faulty cognitive scheme.

A second theory is that hypochondriasis is understandable in terms of a social learning model. The symptoms of hypochondriasis are viewed as a request for admission to the sick role made by a person facing seemingly insurmountable and insolvable problems. The sick role offers an escape that allows a patient to avoid noxious obligations, to postpone unwelcome challenges, and to be excused from usual duties and obligations.

A third theory about hypochondriasis is that it is a variant form of other mental disorders, among which depressive disorders and anxiety disorders are most frequently included. An estimated 80 percent of patients with hypochondriasis may have coexisting depressive or anxiety disorders. Patients who meet the diagnostic criteria for hypochondriasis may be somatizing subtypes of these other disorders.

The psychodynamic school of thought has produced a fourth theory of hypochondriasis. According to this theory, aggressive and hostile wishes toward others are transferred (through repression and displacement) into physical complaints. The anger of patients with hypochondriasis originates in past disappointments, rejections, and losses, but the patients express their anger in the present by soliciting the help and concern of other people and then rejecting them as ineffective. Hypochondriasis is also viewed as a defense against guilt, a sense of innate badness, an expression of low self-esteem, and a sign of excessive self-concern. Pain and somatic suffering thus become means of atonement and expiation (undoing) and can be experienced as deserved punishment for past wrongdoing (either real or imaginary) and for a person's sense of wickedness and sinfulness.

Diagnosis

The DSM-IV diagnostic criteria for hypochondriasis require that patients be preoccupied with the false belief that they have a serious disease and that the false belief be based on a misinterpretation of physical signs or sensations (Table 17–5). The belief must last at least 6 months, despite the absence of pathological findings on medical and neurological examinations. The diagnostic criteria also stipulate that the belief not have the intensity of a delusion (more appropriately diagnosed as

Table 17–5
DSM-IV Diagnostic Criteria for Hypochondriasis

A. Preoccupation with fears of having, or the idea that one has, a serious disease based on the person's misinterpretation of bodily symptoms.
B. The preoccupation persists despite appropriate medical evaluation and reassurance.
C. The belief in criterion A is not of delusional intensity (as in delusional disorder, somatic type) and is not restricted to a circumscribed concern about appearance (as in body dysmorphic disorder).
D. The preoccupation causes clinically significant distress or impairment in social, occupational, or other important areas of functioning.
E. The duration of the disturbance is at least 6 months.
F. The preoccupation is not better accounted for by generalized anxiety disorder, obsessive-compulsive disorder, panic disorder, a major depressive episode, separation anxiety, or another somatoform disorder.

Specify if:
With poor insight: if, for most of the time during the current episode, the person does not recognize that the concern about having a serious illness is excessive or unreasonable

delusional disorder) and that it not be restricted to distress about appearance (more appropriately diagnosed as body dysmorphic disorder). The symptoms of hypochondriasis must be of an intensity that causes emotional distress or impairs the patient's ability to function in important areas of life. Clinicians may specify the presence of poor insight; patients do not consistently recognize that the concerns about disease are excessive.

Clinical Features

Patients with hypochondriasis believe that they have a serious disease that has not yet been detected, and they cannot be persuaded to the contrary. They may maintain a belief that they have a particular disease; as time progresses, they may transfer their belief to another disease. Their convictions persist despite negative laboratory results, the benign course of the alleged disease over time, and appropriate reassurances from physicians. Yet their beliefs are not so fixed as to be delusions. Hypochondriasis is often accompanied by symptoms of depression and anxiety and commonly coexists with a depressive or anxiety disorder.

Although DSM-IV specifies that the symptoms must be present for at least 6 months, transient hypochondriacal states can occur after major stresses, most commonly the death or serious illness of someone important to the patient, or a serious (perhaps life-threatening) illness that has been resolved but that leaves the patient temporarily hypochondriacal in its wake. Such states that last fewer than 6 months should be diagnosed as somatoform disorder not otherwise specified. Transient hypochondriacal responses to external stress generally remit when the stress is resolved, but they can become chronic if reinforced by people in the patient's social system or by health professionals.

Differential Diagnosis

Hypochondriasis must be differentiated from nonpsychiatric medical conditions, especially disorders that show symptoms that are not necessarily easily diagnosed. Such diseases include AIDS, endocrinopathies, myasthenia gravis, multiple sclerosis, degenerative diseases of the nervous system, systemic lupus erythematosus, and occult neoplastic disorders.

Hypochondriasis is differentiated from somatization disorder by the emphasis in hypochondriasis on fear of having a disease and emphasis in somatization disorder on concern about many symptoms. A subtle distinction is that patients with hypochondriasis usually complain about fewer symptoms than do patients with somatization disorder. Somatization disorder usually has an onset before age 30, whereas hypochondriasis has a less specific age of onset. Patients with somatization disorder are more likely to be women than are those with hypochondriasis, which is equally distributed among men and women.

Hypochondriasis must also be differentiated from the other somatoform disorders. Conversion disorder is acute and generally transient and usually involves a symptom rather than a particular disease. The presence or absence of *la belle indifférence* is an unreliable feature with which to differentiate the two conditions. Pain disorder is chronic, as is hypochondriasis, but the symptoms are limited to complaints of pain. Patients with body dysmorphic disorder wish to appear normal but believe that others notice that they are not, whereas those with hypochondriasis seek out attention for their presumed diseases.

Hypochondriacal symptoms can also occur in patients with depressive disorders and anxiety disorders. If a patient meets the full diagnostic criteria for both hypochondriasis and another major mental disorder, such as major depressive disorder or generalized anxiety disorder, the patient should receive both diagnoses, unless the hypochondriacal symptoms occur only during episodes of the other mental disorder. Patients with panic disorder may initially complain that they are affected by a disease (for example, heart trouble), but careful questioning during the medical history usually uncovers the classic symptoms of a panic attack. Delusional hypochondriacal beliefs occur in schizophrenia and other psychotic disorders but can be differentiated from hypochondriasis by their delusional intensity and by the presence of other psychotic symptoms. In addition, schizophrenic patients' somatic delusions tend to be bizarre, idiosyncratic, and out of keeping with their cultural milieus.

Hypochondriasis is distinguished from factitious disorder with physical symptoms and from malingering in that patients with hypochondriasis actually experience and do not simulate the symptoms they report.

Course and Prognosis

The course of hypochondriasis is usually episodic; the episodes last from months to years and are separated by equally long quiescent periods. There may be an obvious association between exacerbations of hypochondriacal symptoms and psychosocial stressors. Although well-conducted large outcome studies have not yet been reported, an estimated one third to one half of all patients with hypochondriasis eventually improve significantly. A good prognosis is associated with a high socioeconomic status, treatment-responsive anxiety or depression, the sudden onset of symptoms, the absence of a personality disorder, and the absence of a related nonpsychiatric medical condition. Most children with hypochondriasis recover by late adolescence or early adulthood.

Treatment

Patients with hypochondriasis are usually resistant to psychiatric treatment although some accept this treatment if it takes place in a medical setting and focuses on stress reduction and education in coping with chronic illness. Among such patients, group psychotherapy is the modality of choice, in part because it provides the social support and social interaction that seem to reduce their anxiety. Individual insight-oriented psychotherapy may be useful, but is generally unsuccessful.

Frequent, regularly scheduled physical examinations are useful to reassure patients that their physicians are not abandoning them and that their complaints are being taken seriously. Invasive diagnostic and therapeutic procedures should only be undertaken, however, when objective evidence calls for them. When possible, the clinician should refrain from treating equivocal or incidental physical examination findings.

Pharmacotherapy alleviates hypochondriacal symptoms only when a patient has an underlying drug-responsive condition, such as an anxiety disorder or major depressive disorder. When hypochondriasis is secondary to another primary mental disorder, that disorder must be treated in its own right. When hypochondriasis is a transient situational reaction, clinicians must help patients cope with the stress without reinforcing their illness behavior and their use of the sick role as a solution to their problems.

BODY DYSMORPHIC DISORDER

DSM-IV defines body dysmorphic disorder as a preoccupation with an imagined defect (for example, a misshapen nose) or an exaggerated distortion of a minimal or minor defect in physical appearance. To be considered a mental disorder, the preoccupation must cause patients significant distress or be associated with impairment in the patient's personal, social, or occupational life.

The disorder was recognized and named dysmorphophobia more than 100 years ago by Emil Kraepelin, who considered it a compulsive neurosis; Pierre Janet called it *obsession de la honte du corps* (obsession with shame of the body). Freud wrote about the condition in his description of the Wolf-Man, who was excessively concerned about his nose. Although dysmorphophobia was widely recognized and studied in Europe, it was not until the publication of DSM-III in 1980 that dysmorphophobia, as an example of a typical somatoform disorder, was specifically mentioned in the United States diagnostic criteria. In DSM-IV, the condition is known as body dysmorphic disorder, because the DSM editors believed that the term *dysmorphophobia* inaccurately implied the presence of a behavioral pattern of phobic avoidance.

Epidemiology

Body dysmorphic disorder is a poorly studied condition, partly because patients are more likely to go to dermatologists, internists, or plastic surgeons than to psychiatrists. One study of a group of college students found that more than 50 percent had at least some preoccupation with a particular aspect of their appearance and that in about 25 percent of the students the concern had at least some significant effect on their feelings and functioning. Although 25 percent is undoubtedly an overestimate, body dysmorphic disorder or a subsyndromal variant may be common. Another study of patients attending a plastic surgery clinic found that only 2 percent of the patients met the diagnostic criteria for body dysmorphic disorder; thus, patients with all the diagnostic criteria may be rare.

Available data indicate that the most common age of onset is between 15 and 20 years and that women are somewhat more often affected than men. Affected patients are also likely to be unmarried. Body dysmorphic disorder commonly coexists with other mental disorders. One study found that more than 90 percent of patients with body dysmorphic disorder had experienced a major depressive episode in their lifetimes; about 70 percent had experienced an anxiety disorder; and about 30 percent had experienced a psychotic disorder.

Etiology

The cause of body dysmorphic disorder is unknown. The high comorbidity with depressive disorders, a higher-than-expected family history of mood disorders and obsessive-compulsive disorder, and the reported responsiveness of the condition to serotonin-specific drugs indicate that in at least some patients the pathophysiology of the disorder may involve serotonin and may be related to other mental disorders. Stereotyped concepts of beauty emphasized in certain families and within the culture at large may significantly affect patients with body dysmorphic disorder. In psychodynamic models, body dysmorphic disorder is seen as reflecting the displacement of a sexual or emotional conflict onto a nonrelated body part. Such an association occurs through the defense mechanisms of repression, dissociation, distortion, symbolization, and projection.

Table 17–6
DSM-IV Diagnostic Criteria for Body Dysmorphic Disorder

A. Preoccupation with an imagined defect in appearance. If a slight physical anomaly is present, the person's concern is markedly excessive.

B. The preoccupation causes clinically significant distress or impairment in social, occupational, or other important areas of functioning.

C. The preoccupation is not better accounted for by another mental disorder (eg, dissatisfaction with body shape and size in anorexia nervosa).

Diagnosis

The DSM-IV diagnostic criteria for body dysmorphic disorder stipulate a preoccupation with an imagined defect in appearance or an overemphasis of a slight defect (Table 17–6). The preoccupation causes patients significant emotional distress or markedly impairs their ability to function in important areas.

Clinical Features

The most common concerns (Table 17–7) involve facial flaws, particularly those involving specific parts (for example, the nose). Sometimes the concern is vague and difficult to understand, such as extreme concern over a ''scrunchy'' chin. One study found that, on average, patients had concerns about four body regions during the course of the disorder. The specific body part may change during the time a patient is affected with the disorder. Common associated symptoms include ideas or frank delusions of reference (usually about people's noticing the alleged body flaw), either excessive mirror checking or avoidance of reflective surfaces, and attempts to hide the presumed deformity (with makeup or clothing). The effects on a person's life can be significant; almost all affected patients avoid social and occupational exposure. As many as one third of the patients may be housebound because of worry about being ridiculed for the alleged deformities, and as many as one fifth attempt suicide. As previously discussed, comorbid diagnoses of depressive disorders and anxiety disorders are common, and patients may also have traits of obsessive-compulsive, schizoid, and narcissistic personality disorders.

Table 17–7
Location of Imagined Defects in 30 Patients with Body Dysmorphic Disorder[a]

Locaton	N	%
Hair[b]	19	63
Nose	15	50
Skin[c]	15	50
Eyes	8	27
Head, face[d]	6	20
Overall body build, bone structure	6	20
Lips	5	17
Chin	5	17
Stomach, waist	5	17
Teeth	4	13
Legs, knees	4	13
Breasts, pectoral muscles	3	10
Ugly face (general)	3	10
Ears	2	7
Cheeks	2	7
Buttocks	2	7
Penis	2	7
Arms, wrists	2	7
Neck	1	3
Forehead	1	3
Facial muscles	1	3
Shoulders	1	3
Hips	1	3

Reprinted with permission from Phillips KA, McElroy SL, Keck PE Jr, Pope HG, Hudson JI: Body dysmorphic disorder: 30 cases of imagined ugliness. Am J Psychiatry *150:* 303, 1993.

[a] Total is greater than 100% because most patients had ''defects'' in more than one location.

[b] Involved head hair in 15 cases, beard growth in two cases, and other body hair in three cases.

[c] Involved acne in seven cases, facial lines in three cases, and other skin concerns in seven cases.

[d] Involved concerns with shape in five cases and size in one case.

Differential Diagnosis

Distortions of body image occur in anorexia nervosa, gender identity disorders, and some specific types of brain damage (for example, neglect syndromes); body dysmorphic disorder should not be diagnosed in these situations. Body dysmorphic disorder must also be distinguished from a person's normal concern about appearance. In body dysmorphic disorder, however, a person experiences significant emotional distress and functional impairment because of the concern. Although distinguishing between a strongly held idea and a delusion is difficult, if a patient's preoccupation with the perceived body defect is, in fact, of delusional intensity, the appropriate diagnosis is delusional disorder, somatic type. Other diagnostic considerations are narcissistic personality disorder, depressive disorders, obsessive-compulsive disorder, and schizophrenia. In narcissistic personality disorder, concern about a body part is only a minor feature in the general constellation of personality traits. In depressive disorders, schizophrenia, and obsessive-compulsive disorder, the other symptoms of these disorders usually evidence themselves in short order, even when the initial symptom is excessive concern about a body part.

Course and Prognosis

The onset of body dysmorphic disorder is usually gradual. An affected person may experience increasing concern over a particular body part until the person notices that functioning is being affected. Then the person may seek medical or surgical help to address the presumed problem. The level of concern about the problem may wax and wane over time, although the disorder is usually chronic if left untreated.

Treatment

Treatment of patients with body dysmorphic disorder with surgical, dermatological, dental, and other medical procedures to address the alleged defects is almost invariably unsuccessful. Although tricyclic drugs, monoamine oxidase inhibitors, and pimozide (Orap) have been reported to be useful in individual cases, a larger body of data indicate that serotonin-specific drugs—for example, clomipramine (Anafranil) and fluoxetine (Prozac)—are effective in reducing symptoms in at least 50 percent of patients. In any patient with a coexisting mental disorder, such as a depressive disorder or an anxiety disorder, the coexisting disorder should be treated with the appropriate pharmacotherapy and psychotherapy. How long treatment should be continued when the symptoms of body dysmorphic disorder have remitted is unknown.

PAIN DISORDER

In DSM-IV, pain disorder is defined as the presence of pain that is "the predominant focus of clinical attention." Psychological factors play an important role in the disorder. The primary symptom is pain, in one or more sites, which is not *fully* accounted for by a nonpsychiatric medical or neurological condition. The symptoms of pain are associated with emotional distress and functional impairment. The disorder has been called somatoform pain disorder, psychogenic pain disorder, idiopathic pain disorder, and atypical pain disorder.

Epidemiology

Pain is perhaps the most frequent complaint in medical practice, and intractable pain syndromes are common. Low back pain has disabled an estimated 7 million people in the United States and accounts for more than 8 million physician office visits annually. Pain disorder is diagnosed twice as frequently in women as in men. The peak ages of onset are in the fourth and fifth decades, perhaps because the tolerance for pain declines with age. Pain disorder is most common in people with blue-collar occupations, perhaps because of increased likelihood of job-related injuries. First-degree relatives of patients with pain disorder have an increased likelihood of having the same disorder; thus genetic inheritance or behavioral mechanisms are possibly involved in its transmission. Depressive disorders, anxiety disorders, and substance abuse are also more common in the families of patients with pain disorder than they are in the general population.

Etiology

Psychodynamic Factors. Patients who experience bodily aches and pains without identifiable and adequate physical causes may be symbolically expressing an intrapsychic conflict through the body. For patients suffering from alexithymia, in which they are unable to articulate their internal feeling states in words, their bodies express their feelings. Other patients may unconsciously regard emotional pain as weak and somehow lacking in legitimacy. By displacing the problem to the body, they may feel that they have a legitimate claim to the fulfillment of their dependence needs. The symbolic meaning of body disturbances may also relate to atonement for perceived sin, to expiation of guilt, or to suppressed aggression. Many patients have intractable and unresponsive pain because they are convinced that they deserve to suffer.

Pain can function as a method of obtaining love, a punishment for wrongdoing, and a way of expiating guilt and of atoning for an innate sense of badness. Among the defense mechanisms used by patients with pain disorder are displacement, substitution, and repression. Identification plays a part when a patient takes on the role of an ambivalent love object who also has pain, such as a parent.

Behavioral Factors. Pain behaviors are reinforced when rewarded and are inhibited when ignored or punished. For example, moderate pain symptoms may become intense when followed by the solicitous and attentive behavior of others, by monetary gain, or by the successful avoidance of distasteful activities.

Interpersonal Factors. Intractable pain has been conceptualized as a means for manipulation and gaining advantage in interpersonal relationships, for example, to ensure the devotion of a family member or to stabilize a fragile marriage. Such secondary gain is most important to patients with pain disorder.

Biological Factors. The cerebral cortex can inhibit the firing of afferent pain fibers. Serotonin is probably the main neurotransmitter in the descending inhibitory pathways, and endorphins also play a role in the central nervous system modulation of pain. Endorphin deficiency seems to correlate with the augmentation of incoming sensory stimuli. Some patients may have pain disorder, rather than another mental disorder, because of sensory and limbic structural or chemical abnormalities that predispose them to experience pain.

Diagnosis

The DSM-IV diagnostic criteria for pain disorder require the presence of clinically significant complaints of pain (Table 17–8). The complaints of pain must be judged to be significantly affected by psychological factors, and the symptoms must result in a patient's significant emotional distress or functional impairment (for example, social or occupational). DSM-IV requires that the pain disorder be associated primarily with psychological factors or with both psychological factors and a general medical condition. DSM-IV further specifies that pain disorder associated solely with a general medical condition be diagnosed as an Axis III condition and also allows clinicians to specify whether the pain disorder is acute or chronic, depending on whether the duration of symptoms has been 6 months or more.

Clinical Features

Patients with pain disorder do not constitute a uniform group but, instead, are a heterogeneous collection of people with low back pain, headache, atypical facial pain, chronic pelvic pain, and other kinds of pain. A patient's pain may be posttraumatic, neuropathic, neurological, iatrogenic, or musculoskeletal; to meet a diagnosis of pain disorder, however, the disorder must have a psychological factor that is judged to be significantly involved in the pain symptoms and their ramifications.

Patients with pain disorder often have long histories of medical and surgical care. They visit many physicians, request many medications, and may be especially insistent in their desire for surgery. Indeed, they can be completely preoccupied with their pain and cite it as the source of all their misery. Such patients often deny any other sources of emotional dysphoria and insist that their lives are blissful except for their pain. Their clinical picture can be complicated by substance-

Table 17–8
DSM-IV Diagnostic Criteria for Pain Disorder

A. Pain in one or more anatomical sites is the predominant focus of the clinical presentation and is of sufficient severity to warrant clinical attention.

B. The pain causes clinically significant distress or impairment in social, occupational, or other important areas of functioning.

C. Psychological factors are judged to have an important role in the onset, severity, exacerbation, or maintenance of the pain.

D. The symptom or deficit is not intentionally produced or feigned (as in factitious disorder or malingering).

E. The pain is not better accounted for by a mood, anxiety, or psychotic disorder and does not meet criteria for dyspareunia.

Code as follows:

Pain disorder associated with psychological factors: psychological factors are judged to have the major role in the onset, severity, exacerbation, or maintenance of the pain. (If a general medical condition is present, it does not have a major role in the onset, severity, exacerbation, or maintenance of the pain.) This type of pain disorder is not diagnosed if criteria are also met for somatization disorder.

Specify if:
Acute: duration of less than 6 months
Chronic: duration of 6 months or longer

Pain disorder associated with both psychological factors and a general medical condition: both psychological factors and a general medical condition are judged to have important roles in the onset, severity, exacerbation, or maintenance of the pain. The associated general medical condition or anatomical site of the pain (see below) is coded on Axis III.

Specify if:
Acute: duration of less than 6 months
Chronic: duration of 6 months or more

Note: the following is not considered to be a mental disorder and is included here to facilitate differential diagnosis.

Pain disorder associated with a general medical condition: a general medical condition has a major role in the onset, severity, exacerbation, or maintenance of the pain. (If psychological factors are present, they are not judged to have a major role in the onset, severity, exacerbation, or maintenance of the pain.) The diagnostic code for the pain is selected based on the associated general medical condition if one has been established or on the anatomical location of the pain if the underlying general medical condition is not yet clearly established—for example, low back, sciatic, pelvic, headache, facial, chest, joint, bone, abdominal, breast, renal, ear, eye, throat, tooth, and urinary.

Reprinted with permission from American Psychiatric Association: *Diagnostic and Statistical Manual of Mental Disorders,* ed 4. Copyright, American Psychiatric Association, Washington, 1994.

related disorders, because these patients attempt to reduce the pain through the use of alcohol and other substances.

At least one study has correlated the number of pain symptoms to the likelihood and severity of symptoms of somatization disorder, depressive disorders, and anxiety disorders. Major depressive disorder is present in about 25 to 50 percent of all patients with pain disorder, and dysthymic disorder or depressive disorder symptoms are reported in 60 to 100 percent of the patients. Some investigators believe that chronic pain is almost always a variant of a depressive disorder, a masked or somatized form of depression. The most prominent depressive symptoms in patients with pain disorder are anergia, anhedonia, decreased libido, insomnia, and irritability; diurnal variation, weight loss, and psychomotor retardation appear to be less common symptoms.

A 36-year-old London meter maid was referred for psychiatric examination by her solicitor. Six months previously, moments after she had written a ticket and placed it on a windshield of an illegally parked car, a man came dashing out of a barbershop, ran up to her, swearing and shaking his fist, swung, and hit her in the jaw with enough force to knock her down. A fellow worker came to her aid and summoned the police, who caught the man a few blocks away and placed him under arrest.

The patient was taken to the hospital, where a hairline fracture of the jaw was diagnosed by X-ray. The fracture did not require that her jaw be wired, but the patient was placed on a soft diet for 4 weeks. Several different physicians, including her own, found her physically fit to return to work after 1 month. The patient, however, complained of severe pain and muscle tension in her neck and back that virtually immobilized her. She spent most of her days sitting in a chair or lying on a bedboard on her bed. She enlisted the services of a solicitor as the Workmen's Compensation Board was cutting off her payments and her employer was threatening her with suspension if she did not return to work.

The patient shuffled slowly and laboriously into the psychiatrist's office and lowered herself with great care into a chair. She was attractively dressed, well made up, and wore a neck brace. She related her story with vivid detail and considerable anger directed at her assailant (whom she repeatedly referred to as that "bloody foreigner"), her employer, and the compensation board. It was as if the incident had occurred yesterday. Regarding her ability to work, she said that she wanted to return to the job, would soon be severely strapped financially, but was physically not up to even the lightest office work.

She denied any previous psychological problems and initially described her childhood and family life as storybook perfect. In subsequent interviews, however, she admitted that as a child she had frequently been beaten by her alcoholic father and had once had a broken arm as a result and that she had often been locked in a closet for hours at a time as punishment for misbehavior.

DISCUSSION

In this case the first question is: Can this woman's pain be entirely accounted for by the nature of her very real physical injury? Evidently, the answer is no, given the extensive assessment by several physicians. The next question is: Is this woman simply attempting to get continued financial support from Workmen's Compensation so that she will no longer have to earn a living? If the answer is yes, this would be an instance of malingering—that is, the intentional production and presentation of false or grossly exaggerated symptoms in pursuit of external incentives. The apparent genuineness of her suffering and her desire to return to work make this unlikely.

Although the pain was initially caused by her injury, most physicians who examined the patient thought she was sufficiently recovered physically and that her persistent complaints of pain were excessive. In addition, there is evidence of specific psychological factors contributing to the severity and maintenance of the pain. The history of the patient's having been physically abused by her father as a child probably produced psychological conflict that was revived by the assault. This might account for the continuation of the pain beyond what would be accounted for by her injury. This leaves us with the diagnosis of pain disorder associated with both psychological factors and a general medical condition, as both are judged to play an important role in this case. (From *DSM-IV Casebook.*)

Differential Diagnosis

Purely physical pain can be difficult to distinguish from purely psychogenic pain, especially because the two are not mutually exclusive. Physical pain fluctuates in intensity and is highly sensitive to emotional, cognitive, attentional, and situational influences. Pain that does not vary and is insensitive to any of these factors is likely to be psychogenic. When pain does not wax and wane and is not even temporarily relieved by distraction or analgesics, clinicians can suspect an important psychogenic component.

Pain disorder must be distinguished from other somatoform disorders, although some somatoform disorders can coexist. Patients with hypochondriacal preoccupations may complain of pain, and aspects of the clinical presentation of hypochondriasis, such as bodily preoccupation and disease conviction, can also be present in patients with pain disorder. Patients with hypochondriasis tend to have many more symptoms than do patients with pain disorder, and their symptoms tend to fluctuate more than do the symptoms of patients with pain disorder. Conversion disorder is generally short lived, whereas pain disorder is chronic. In addition, pain is, by definition, not a symptom in conversion disorder. Malingering patients consciously provide false reports, and their complaints are usually connected to clearly recognizable goals.

The differential diagnosis can be difficult because patients with pain disorder often receive disability compensation or a litigation award. Muscle contraction (tension) headaches, for example, have a pathophysiological mechanism to account for the pain and so are not diagnosed as pain disorder. Patients with pain disorder are not, however, pretending to be in pain.

Course and Prognosis

The pain in pain disorder generally begins abruptly and increases in severity for a few weeks or months. The prognosis varies, although pain disorder can often be chronic, distressful, and completely disabling. When psychological factors predominate in pain disorder, the pain may subside with treatment or after the elimination of external reinforcement. The patients with the poorest prognoses, with or without treatment, have preexisting characterological problems, especially pronounced passivity; are involved in litigation or receive financial compensation; use addictive substances; and have long histories of pain.

Treatment

Because it may not be possible to reduce the pain, the treatment approach must address rehabilitation. Clinicians should discuss the issue of psychological factors early in treatment and should frankly tell patients that such factors are important in the cause and consequences of both physical and psychogenic pain. Therapists should also explain how various brain circuits that are involved with emotions (such as the limbic system) may influence the sensory pain pathways. For example, if a person hits his or her head while happy at a party, the pain can seem to be less than when a person hits his or her head while angry and at work. Nevertheless, therapists must fully understand that the patient's experiences of pain are real.

Pharmacotherapy. Analgesic medications are not generally helpful for most patients with pain disorder. In addition, substance abuse and dependence are often major problems for patients who receive long-term analgesic treatment. Sedatives and antianxiety agents are not especially beneficial and often become problems in themselves because of their frequent abuse, misuse, and side effects.

Antidepressants, such as tricyclics and serotonin-specific reuptake inhibitors (SSRIs), are useful. Whether antidepressants reduce pain through their antidepressant action or exert an independent, direct analgesic effect (possibly by stimulating efferent inhibitory pain pathways) remains controversial. The success of SSRIs supports the hypothesis that serotonin is important in the pathophysiology of the disorder. In some patients, amphetamine, which has analgesic effects, may be useful, especially when used as an adjunct to SSRIs.

Behavioral Therapy. Biofeedback can be helpful in the treatment of pain disorder, particularly with migraine pain, myofacial pain, and muscle tension states, such as tension headaches. Hypnosis, transcutaneous nerve stimulation, and dorsal column stimulation also have been used. Nerve blocks and surgical ablative procedures are ineffective for most patients with pain disorder; the pain returns after 6 to 18 months.

Psychotherapy. Some outcome data indicate that psychodynamic psychotherapy is helpful to patients with pain disorder. The first step in psychotherapy is to develop a solid therapeutic alliance by empathizing with the patient's suffering. Clinicians should not confront somatizing patients with comments such as, "This is all in your head." For the patient, the pain is real, and clinicians must acknowledge the reality of the pain, even though they suspect that it is largely intrapsychic in origin. A useful entry point into the emotional aspects of the pain is to examine its interpersonal ramifications in the patient's life. By exploring marital problems, for example, the psychotherapist may soon get to the source of the patient's psychological pain and the function of the physical complaints in significant relationships. Cognitive therapy has been used to alter negative thoughts and to foster a positive attitude.

Pain Control Programs. It may sometimes be necessary to remove patients from their usual settings and place them in a comprehensive inpatient pain control program. Multidisciplinary pain units use many modalities, such as cognitive, behavior, and group therapies. They provide extensive physical conditioning through physical therapy and exercise and offer vocational evaluation and rehabilitation. Concurrent mental disorders are diagnosed and treated, and patients dependent on analgesics and hypnotics are detoxified. Inpatient multimodal treatment programs generally report encouraging results.

UNDIFFERENTIATED SOMATOFORM DISORDER

According to DSM-IV, undifferentiated somatoform disorder is defined as unexplained physical effects that last for at least 6 months and that are below the threshold for diagnosing somatization disorder. The DSM-IV diagnosis (Table 17–9) is appropriate for patients with one or more physical complaints that cannot be explained by a known medical condition or that grossly exceed the expected complaints in a medical condition but that do not meet the diagnostic criteria for a specific somatoform disorder. The symptoms must cause patients significant emotional distress or impair their social or occupational functioning.

Table 17–9
DSM-IV Diagnostic Criteria for Undifferentiated Somatoform Disorder

A. One or more phsyical complaints (eg, fatigue, loss of appetite, gastrointestinal or urinary complaints)

B. Either (1) or (2);
 (1) after appropriate investigation, the symptoms cannot be fully explained by a known general medical condition or by the direct effects of a substance (eg, the effects of injury, medication, drugs, or alcohol)
 (2) when there is a related general medical condition, the physical complaints or resulting social or occupational impairment is in excess of what would be expected from the history, physical examination, or laboratory findings

C. The symptoms cause clinically significant distress or impairment in social, occupational, or other important areas of functioning.

D. The duration of the disturbance is at least 6 months

E. The disturbance is not better accounted for by another mental disorder (eg, another somatoform disorder, sexual dysfunction, mood disorder, anxiety disorder, sleep disorder, or psychotic disorder).

F. The symptom is not intentionally produced or feigned (as in factitious disorder or malingering).

Table 17–10
DSM-IV Diagnostic Criteria for Somatoform Disorder Not Otherwise Specified

This category includes disorders with somatoform symptoms that do not meet the criteria for any specific somatoform disorder. Examples include:

1. pseudocyesis: a false belief of being pregnant that is associated with objective signs of pregnancy, which may include abdominal enlargement (although the umbilicus does not become everted), reduced menstrual flow, amenorrhea, subjective sensation of fetal movement, nausea, breast engorgement and secretions, and labor pains at the expected date of delivery. Endocrine changes may be present but the syndrome cannot be explained by a general medical condition that causes endocrine changes (eg, hormone-secreting tumor).
2. a disorder involving nonpsychotic hypochondriacal symptoms of less than 6 months' duration.
3. a disorder involving unexplained physical complaints (eg, fatigue or body weakness) of less than 6 months' duration that are not due to another mental disorder.

Two types of symptom patterns may be seen in patients with undifferentiated somatoform disorder: those involving the autonomic nervous system and those involving sensations of fatigue or weakness. In what is sometimes referred to as autonomic arousal disorder, some patients are affected with somatoform disorder symptoms that are limited to bodily functions innervated by the autonomic nervous system. Such patients have complaints involving the cardiovascular, respiratory, gastrointestinal, urogenital, and dermatological systems. Other patients complain of mental and physical fatigue, physical weakness and exhaustion, and inability to perform many everyday activities because of their symptoms. Clinicians often call this syndrome neurasthenia, a name used in other diagnostic systems as well. The syndrome may overlap chronic fatigue syndrome, which various research reports have hypothesized to involve psychiatric, virological, and immunological factors.

SOMATOFORM DISORDER NOT OTHERWISE SPECIFIED

The DSM-IV diagnostic category of somatoform disorder not otherwise specified (Table 17–10) is a residual category for patients who have symptoms suggestive of a somatoform disorder but who do not meet the specific diagnostic criteria for other somatoform disorders. Such patients may have a symptom not covered in the other somatoform disorders (for example, pseudocyesis) or may not have met the 6-month criterion of the other somatoform disorders.

References

Barsky AJ: Hypochondriasis: Medical management and psychiatric treatment. Psychosomatics *37:* 48, 1996.

Barsky AJ, Cleary PD, Sarnie MK, Klerman GL: The course of transient hypochondriasis. Psychiatry *150:* 484, 1993.

Barsky AJ, Coeytaux RR, Sarnie MK, Cleary PD: Hypochondriacal patients' beliefs about good health. Am J Psychiatry *150:* 1085, 1993.

Barsky AJ, Frank CB, Cleary PD, Wyshak G, Klerman GL: The relation between hypochondriasis and age. Am J Psychiatry *148:* 923, 1991.

Barsky AJ, Wyshak G, Klerman GL: Psychiatric comorbidity in DSM-III-R hypochondriasis. Arch Gen Psychiatry *49:* 101, 1992.

Barsky AJ, Wyshak G, Latham KS, Klerman GL: Hypochondriacal patients, their physicians, and their medical care. J Gen Intern Med *6:* 413, 1991.

Bass C, Murphy M: Somatization disorder in a British teaching hospital. Br J Clin Pract *45:* 237, 1991.

Boffeli TJ, Guze GB: The simulation of neurologic disease. Psychiatr Clin North Am *15:* 301, 1992.

Brown FW, Golding JM, Smith GR Jr: Psychiatric comorbidity in primary care somatization disorder. Psychosom Med *52:* 445, 1990.

Creed F, Guthrie E: Techniques for interviewing the somatising patient. Br J Psychiatry *162:* 467, 1993.

Dwoekin SF, Von Korff M, LeResche L: Multiple pains and psychiatric disturbance: An epidemiologic investigation. Arch Gen Psychiatry *47:* 239, 1990.

Fink P: Surgery and medical treatment in persistent somatizing patients. J Psychosom Res *36:* 439, 1992.

Ford CV: Dimensions of somatization and hypochondriasis. Neuro Clin *13:* 241, 1995.

Goldberg RJ, Novack DH, Gask L: The recognition and management of somatization: What is needed in primary case training. Psychosomatics *33:* 55, 1992.

Golding JM, Smith R Jr, Kashner M: Does somatization disorder occur in men? Clinical characteristics of women and men with multiple unexplained somatic symptoms. Arch Gen Psychiatry *48:* 231, 1991.

Guggenheim FG, Smith GR: Somatoform disorders. In *Comprehensive Textbook of Psychiatry,* ed 6, HI Kaplan, BJ Sadock, editors, p 1251. Williams & Wilkins, Baltimore, 1995.

Hollander E, Neville D, Frenkel M, Josephson S, Liebowitz MR: Body dysmorphic disorder: Diagnostic issues and related disorders. Psychosomatics *33:* 156, 1992.

Kellner R, Hernandez J, Pathak D: Hypochondriacal fears and beliefs, anxiety, and somatization. Br J Psychiatry *160:* 525, 1992.

Kent D, Tomasson K, Coryell W: Course and outcome of conversion and somatization disorders: A four-year follow-up. Psychosomatics *36:* 138, 1995.

Kent S, Bluthe R-M, Kelley KW, Danzer R: Sickness behavior as a new target for drug development. Trends Pharmacol Sci *13:* 24, 1992.

Kirmayer LJ, Robbins JM, Dworkind M, Yaffe MJ: Somatization and the recognition of depression and anxiety in primary care. Am J Psychiatry *150:* 734, 1993.

Krull F, Schifferdecker M: Inpatient treatment of conversion disorder: A clinical investigation outcome. Psychother Psychosom *53:* 161, 1990.

Lempert T, Schmidt D: Natural history and outcome of psychogenic seizures: A clinical study in 50 patients. J Neurol *237:* 35, 1990.

Lesser RP: Psychogenic seizures. Neurology *46:* 1499, 1996.

Mabe PA, Jones RA, Riley WT: Managing somatization phenomenon in primary care. Psychiatr Med *8:* 117, 1990.

Martin RL: Diagnostic issues for conversion disorder. Hosp Community Psychiatry *43:* 771, 1992.

Mayou R: Somatization. Psychother Psychosom *59:* 69, 1993.

National Institutes of Health: Integration of behavioral approaches with the treatment of chronic pain and insomnia. NIH Technical Assessment Statement, 1995.

Phillips KA: Body dysmorphic disorder: The distress of imagined ugliness. Am J Psychiatry *148:* 1138, 1991.

Phillips KA, McElroy SL, Keck PE Jr, Pope HG, Judson JI: Body dysmorphic disorder: 30 cases of imagined ugliness. Am J Psychiatry *150:* 302, 1993.

Rost KM, Akins RN, Brown FW, Smith GR: The comorbidity of DSM-III-R personality disorders in somatization disorder. Gen Hosp Psychiatry *14:* 322, 1992.

Silver FW: Management of conversion disorder. Am J Phys Med Rehab *75:* 134, 1996.

Smith GR: The epidemiology and treatment of depression when it coexists with somatoform disorders, somatization, or pain. Gen Hosp Psychiatry *14:* 265, 1992.

Stern R, Fernandez M: Group cognitive and behavioral treatment for hypochondriasis. Br J Med *303:* 1229, 1991.

Van Kempen GM, Zitman FG, Linssen AC, Edelbroek PM: Biochemical measures in patients with a somatoform pain disorder, before, during, and after treatment with amitriptyline with or without flupentixol. Biol Psychiatry *31:* 670, 1992.

18

Neurasthenia and Chronic Fatigue Syndrome

NEURASTHENIA

The term *neurasthenia* was introduced in the 1860s by the American neuropsychiatrist George Miller Beard, who applied it to a condition characterized by chronic fatigue and disability (Figs. 18–1 and 18–2). The term *neurasthenia* (''nervous exhaustion'') is not now used frequently, but it does appear in psychiatric literature and remains a diagnostic entity in the 10th revision of *International Statistical Classification of Diseases and Related Health Problems* (ICD-10).

In ICD-10, neurasthenia is classified as one of the neurotic disorders. According to current nosology in the United States, the disorder is not considered a distinct diagnosis. In the fourth edition of *Diagnostic and Statistical Manual of Mental Disorders* (DSM-IV), neurasthenia is categorized as *undifferentiated somatoform disorder.*

The disorder is a prime example of cultural differences influencing the classification and manifestations of diseases. Neurasthenia is an accepted condition in Europe and Asia, where it is characterized by fatigue, headache, insomnia, and other vague somatic complaints and is thought to result from chronic stress rather than from unconscious psychological conflicts. In many cultures (especially China), in which people resist being categorized as having a mental disorder, neurasthenia is a preferred diagnosis. Thus, the disorder is most commonly diagnosed in eastern Asia.

Epidemiology

Difficulties in investigating the epidemiology of neurasthenia stem from the fact that it occurs in connection with other conditions, such as anxiety, depression, and somatoform disorders, and it has not been sufficiently studied as an independent disorder. Beard considered neurasthenia one of the most frequently observed conditions in the 19th century United States, although no statistics were available to support his observation. A 1994 study in Switzerland showed a prevalence rate (using ICD-10) of 12 percent in that country.

Studies have indicated that the major symptoms—fatigue and heightened concerns with bodily symptoms—most commonly appear in people who are socially and economically deprived, although the disorder is no more prevalent in this group than in others and may, in fact, occur more frequently in higher socioeconomic groups. Precursors of neurasthenia in the form of ''growing pains,'' fatigue, and sleep disturbances appear in children. Beard believed childhood to be one of the peak periods for the onset of the disorder, the other being middle age (adults 40 to 65 years of age).

Etiology

According to Beard, the cause of neurasthenia was ''nervous exhaustion,'' which referred to the nerve cell's (neuron) being depleted of its ''stored nutrient.'' Such depletion resulted from stress, such as overwork. Beard considered the disorder to have a physiological cause in which (as described by Arthur Noyes) ''the nervous system is drained of its energy in the manner of a partially discharged battery of low voltage.'' Beard postulated a ''nervous diathesis'' theory, in which a person has a specific vulnerability that, when acted on by a stressful environmental influence, allowed the symptoms of neurasthenia to develop. The environmental components could be either biological (infection) or psychological (death of a loved one).

Freud was acquainted with the disorder. He agreed with Beard that stress was involved, but Freud considered neurasthenia to be produced by a disturbance in sexual functioning (one of the neuroses), specifically the inadequate discharge of sexual energy that occurred when masturbation replaced normal intercourse. Psychoanalysts after Freud considered neurasthenia as a reaction to unconscious factors such as feelings of rejection, low self-esteem, a sense of worthlessness, and repressed anger.

Depletion Hypothesis. The present-day depletion hypothesis, which holds that prolonged stress lowers the levels of neurotransmitters in neurons, bears a striking resemblance to Beard's concept of nerve exhaustion. Brain amines, when depleted, cause symptoms of anxiety or depression. Low neuronal dopamine activity occurs in depression; the noradrenergic and adrenergic systems are affected in anxiety disorder and depression; and serotonin levels are low in depressive disorder.

A variety of neuroendocrine dysregulations have been reported in patients with mood and anxiety disorders, the major ones affecting the adrenal, thyroid, and growth hormone axes. Other neuroendocrine abnormalities include decreased nocturnal secretion of melatonin, decreased basal levels of follicle-stimulating hormone (FSH) and luteinizing hormone (LH), and

FIGURE 18–1
George Miller Beard. (Courtesy of New York Academy of Medicine, New York, NY.)

A

PRACTICAL TREATISE

ON

NERVOUS EXHAUSTION

(NEURASTHENIA)

ITS

Symptoms, Nature, Sequences, Treatment

BY

GEORGE M. BEARD, A.M., M.D.

FELLOW OF THE NEW YORK ACADEMY OF MEDICINE; OF THE NEW YORK ACADEMY OF SCIENCES; VICE-PRESIDENT OF THE AMERICAN ACADEMY OF MEDICINE; MEMBER OF THE AMERICAN NEUROLOGICAL ASSOCIATION; OF THE AMERICAN MEDICAL ASSOCIATION; THE NEW YORK NEUROLOGICAL SOCIETY, ETC.

EDITED, WITH NOTES AND ADDITIONS,

BY

A. D. ROCKWELL, A.M., M.D.

PROFESSOR OF ELECTRO THERAPEUTICS IN THE NEW YORK POST GRADUATE MEDICAL SCHOOL AND HOSPITAL; FELLOW OF THE NEW YORK ACADEMY; MEMBER OF THE AMERICAN NEUROLOGICAL ASSOCIATION; OF THE NEW YORK NEUROLOGICAL SOCIETY, ETC.

NEW YORK

E. B. TREAT, 771 BROADWAY

1888

Price $2.75

FIGURE 18–2
Cover page of a late edition of Beard's book on neurasthenia. (Reprinted from Beard GM: *A Practical Treatise on Nervous Exhaustion [Neurasthenia]*. EB Treat, New York, 1888.)

decreased testosterone levels. These hormones are also altered in prolonged stress states and, presumably, in neurasthenia as well.

Diagnosis and Clinical Features

According to ICD-10, neurasthenia is not used as a diagnostic category in all countries. In the United States, for example, many of the cases so diagnosed would meet the criteria for depressive disorder, somatoform disorder, or anxiety disorder. Some patients, however, have such varied symptoms that neurasthenia is the preferred diagnosis. These patients may be diagnosed using the ICD-10 diagnostic criteria (Table 18–1), or they may receive a diagnosis of undifferentiated somatoform disorder according to the DSM-IV criteria (see Table 17–9).

Neurasthenia is characterized by a wide variety of signs and symptoms. The most common findings are chronic weakness and fatigue, aches and pains, and general anxiety or "nervousness." Beard, Freud, and others described a plethora of patients' reported complaints, which are listed in Table 18–2. The symptoms are real to patients. As Beard stated: "They are not imaginary. They have a real objective existence and cannot be willed away."

ICD-10 describes two types of the disorder, with substantial overlap between them. In one type, the main feature is a complaint of increased fatigue after mental effort, often associated with some decrease in occupational performance or coping efficiency in daily tasks. The mental fatigability is typically described as an unpleasant intrusion of distracting associations or recollections, difficulty in concentrating, and generally inefficient thinking. In the other type, the emphasis is on feelings of bodily or physical weakness and exhaustion after only minimal effort, accompanied by muscular aches and pains and inability to relax. In both types, other unpleasant physical feelings, such as dizziness, tension headaches, and a sense of general instability, are common. Worry about decreasing mental and bodily well-being, irritability, anhedonia, and varying degrees of both depression and anxiety may be present. Sleep is frequently disturbed in its initial and middle phases, but hypersomnia may also be prominent.

If the DSM-IV criteria are used, neurasthenia would be associated with one of the two forms of undifferentiated somatoform disorders, that is, with the group of physical complaints including chronic fatigue and loss of appetite.

Table 18–1
ICD-10 Diagnostic Criteria for Neurasthenia

A. Either of the following must be present:
  (1) persistent and distressing complaints of feelings of exhaustion after a minor mental effort (such as performing or attempting to perform everyday tasks that do not require unusual mental effort);
  (2) persistent and distressing complaints of feelings of fatigue and bodily weakness after minor physical effort;

At least one of the following symptoms must be present:
  (1) feelings of muscular aches and pains
  (2) dizziness;
  (3) tension headaches;
  (4) sleep disturbances;
  (5) inability to relax;
  (6) irritability;

The patient is unable to recover from the symptoms in criterion A (1) or (2) by means of rest, relaxation, or entertainment.

The duration of the disorder is at least 3 months.

Most commonly used exclusion clause. The disorder does not occur in the presence of organic emotionally labile disorder, postencephalitic syndrome, postconcussional syndrome, mood disorders, panic disorder, or generalized anxiety disorder.

Reprinted with permission from World Health Organization: *The ICD-10 Classification of Mental and Behavioural Disorders: Diagnostic Criteria for Research.* Copyright, World Health Organization, Geneva, 1993.

Mr. Jorgensen, a Danish social worker, was 51 years old and married. He was referred for a psychiatric disability assessment because for the previous 3 years he had felt increasingly fatigued. He grew tired after minor efforts, and after 1 or 2 hours of work, he felt totally exhausted. He managed to carry out his job for some time because considerate colleagues gave him easy tasks. Eventually, he was allowed to take care of the archives, a job that had previously been given to staff on the verge of retirement. Nevertheless, when he returned home in the evenings, Mr. Jorgensen felt so tired that he had to go straight to bed. Even then, he had difficulty sleeping because of headaches and pains in his neck and back. Most of the time, he felt tense and unable to relax. On weekends, he spent most of his time in bed. He found it hard to concentrate, and he had to give up reading and doing crossword puzzles, both of which he had previously enjoyed. Even looking at plays on television became too much for him. He avoided his colleagues and friends as much as possible because he feared they might ask him to do something or invite him out. In fact, an evening out left him exhausted for several days. He felt increasingly inadequate at work and was scarcely able to carry out everyday activities at home.

Four months before the referral, he took sick leave from his job and applied for a disability pension, but staying away from the responsibilities of work did not improve his condition. He still lacked initiative and sat in his chair most of the day, glancing at the newspaper or looking out the window. He did not feel depressed or unhappy. He seemed to be encouraged when he was told that his children and grandchildren were coming to visit, but the liveliness of the children soon made him tense and irritable. He was able to help his wife with the chores around the house as long as she told him exactly what to do, but everything had to be planned in advance, because sudden change made him perplexed and anxious. He had a constant fear that his application for a disability pension might be refused and that he might have to go back to work, which he felt quite incapable of doing.

Mr. Jorgensen grew up in a provincial town in a rural area of Denmark. He was the second son of a primary school teacher. He finished high school with outstanding marks and trained as a social worker. At age 25, he married a nurse 2 years younger than he. They moved to Copenhagen, the capital, where he got a job as a municipal social worker. He became involved in social care and sheltered workshops for mentally retarded people, and in his spare time he worked for the Association of Relatives of the Mentally Retarded. Mr. Jorgensen also took part in political activities, and for several years he was an elected member of the municipal council. The Jorgensens had three children, who had left home and were apparently managing well. The patient lives with his wife in a rented apartment.

Table 18–2
Signs and Symptoms Reported by Patients with Neurasthenia

General fatigue	Palpitations	Chronic worry
Exhaustion	Extrasystole	Fear of disease
General anxiety	Tachycardia	Irritability
Difficulty concentrating	Excess sweating	Feelings of hopelessness
Physical aches and pains	Flushing of skin	Dry mouth or hypersalivation
Dizziness	Sexual dysfunction, eg, erectile disorder, anorgasmia	Arthralgias
Headache	Dysmenorrhea	Heat insensitivity
Intolerance of noise (hyperacusis) or bright lights	Paresthesia	Dysphagia
Chills	Insomnia	Pruritus
Indigestion	Poor memory	Tremors
Constipation or diarrhea	Pessimism	Back pain
Flatulence		

His economic position had deteriorated because of the reduction in his income when his job situation changed.

Mr. Jorgensen was always an extroverted and active person with plenty of energy and a bright mood. He was interested in his work and concerned for those he was helping. He always felt mentally strong and believed that nothing could bring him down. He was always on good terms with both his colleagues and his clients. He had a good relationship with the members of his family, and his marriage was described as harmonious. He had never suffered mood swings or previous episodes of unexplained fatigue.

His older brother was mentally retarded, but otherwise there was no information about mental disorder in his family. The patient had an appendectomy at the age of 27, but otherwise was healthy. There was no information about cerebral concussion or long-standing viral infection.

DISCUSSION

Mr. Jorgensen met the criteria for neurasthenia, as he had persistent and distressing complaints of feelings of exhaustion after only minor mental efforts, accompanied by accessory symptoms such as tension headaches, muscular aches and pains, inability to relax, sleep disturbances, and irritability. The disorder was long-standing, and rest or sick leave did not lead to any improvement. Organic etiology was not suspected.

A depressive mood disorder should, of course, be taken into consideration. The patient had one of the typical symptoms (decreased energy or increased fatigability) and two or three accessory symptoms (loss of self-confidence, sleep disturbance, lack of concentration). It can be debated whether his reduced interest, which clearly is caused by his inability to cope, should be considered as "loss of interests." If so, he meets the criteria for a mild depressive episode, although this diagnosis does not seem compatible with the severity of his disorder.

The most probable diagnosis therefore is neurasthenia. (From *ICD-10 Casebook.*)

Differential Diagnosis

Neurasthenia must be distinguished from anxiety disorders, depressive disorder, and the somatoform disorders, which include somatization disorder, conversion disorder, hypochondriasis, body dysmorphic disorder, and pain disorder. Because so many signs and symptoms of neurasthenia overlap with and appear in each of these disorders, differential diagnosis may be exceedingly difficult. For example, patients with anxiety disorder do not uncommonly have depressive symptomatology; patients with hypochondriasis often complain of anxiety; and patients with body dysmorphic disorder can have somatic complaints.

Clinicians must rigorously apply the diagnostic criteria for anxiety, depressive, and somatoform disorders before making a diagnosis of neurasthenia. Hallmarks of neurasthenia are a patient's emphasis on fatigability and weakness and concern about lowered mental and physical efficiency (in contrast to the somatoform disorders, in which bodily complaints and preoccupation with physical disease dominate the picture). If the neurasthenic syndrome develops in the aftermath of a physical illness (particularly influenza, viral hepatitis, or infectious mononucleosis), the diagnosis of the illness should also be recorded. Chronic fatigue syndrome, discussed below, must also be considered.

Course and Prognosis

Neurasthenia most often occurs during adolescence or middle age. Untreated, the disorder is usually chronic, and patients may become incapacitated by one or more symptoms so that all areas of functioning become impaired. In childhood, difficulties in school functioning, including poor grades and truancy, are likely. In adulthood, work performance deteriorates, or patients may become so disabled that work is impossible. Similarly, social, marital, and interpersonal relationships suffer.

Beard believed that with treatment (such as it was in the 1860s) "the majority can be relieved or substantially cured." The range of therapeutic options now available is broad, and with treatment the prognosis should be favorable; but the long-term prognosis is unknown. For cases first diagnosed in childhood, the prognosis without treatment is guarded, chronicity of symptoms being the most likely outcome. Sometimes it is difficult to distinguish the prodromal signs of schizophrenia or bipolar disorder from neurasthenia.

A synopsis of a case of neurasthenia reported by Beard in 1888 is presented here.

Mr. O., age 36, consulted me for symptoms that greatly interfered with his happiness and capacity for work for the past 5 to 6 years. These consisted of feelings of depression and severe physical and mental exhaustion. Mr. O. possessed no reserve force and gave out utterly whenever he attempted the most ordinary effort. Other complaints included intermittent bloodshot eyes, local and transient feeling of hotness, and chronic constipation. He had an associated and utterly baseless fear of financial ruin and of developing heart disease. Physical examination was normal except for an irregular pulse, and his weight had not varied for several years. The patient eventually stopped working entirely (he was a mercantile banker) for a period of 18 months, during which time he traveled extensively. His symptoms began to abate during that time; he returned from his travels a well man and has not had a recurrence of symptoms.

Beard attributed the cause of the disorder to chronic stress because the patient had not taken a vacation in 5 years from "the details of an exacting mercantile business." His ability to restore his "impoverished nerve force" occurred as a result of rest and a change of scene. Beard mentioned other patients, not cured by travel or rest, who required a variety of treatments, including doses of cannabis and cocaine (both of which were part of the medical pharmacopeia at the time), bromides, and cathartics, among others. Beard was aware of the abuse potential of these drugs, which he prescribed judiciously and under close supervision.

Treatment

The key concept in the current treatment of neurasthenia is clinicians' understanding that a patient's symptoms are not imaginary. The symptoms are objective and are produced by emotions that influence the autonomic nervous system, which in turn affects body functions. Stress can cause structural change in an organ system, and the result can be life threatening. Therapy must therefore begin with a careful medical workup to determine whether a patient's somatic symptoms are amenable to therapy, and if so, what treatment is likely to produce the best results. Patients should be reassured that the administration of medication (analgesics, laxatives, and so on) to relieve medical symptoms will be successful, but only when combined with concurrent psychotherapeutic intervention. Patients must be helped to recognize the stresses in their lives and the coping mechanisms they use to deal with these stresses, to gain insight into the interaction between mind and body. Without such insight-oriented psychotherapy, the neurasthenic condition is likely to continue unabated.

The availability of psychopharmacological agents has markedly improved therapeutic options. Serotonergic agents (such as fluoxetine [Prozac]), which have both an antidepressant and an antianxiety effect, are the most useful class of drugs. Newer antidepressants, such as nefazodone (Serzone) and mirtazapine (Remeron), are also effective. Mirtazapine is reported to have distinct sedative properties in addition to being an antidepressant and may be especially useful for neurasthenia. Physicians should take care in prescribing drugs with abuse potential, such as benzodiazepines, because of these patients' predilection for self-medication and drug misuse. Such drugs may be useful, for brief periods and under careful supervision, to deal with overwhelming anxiety, phobias, or insomnia. Similarly, small doses of analeptics, such as amphetamine (Dexedrine) or methylphenidate (Ritalin), may help to treat chronic fatigue and anhedonia. Testosterone replacement can be tried in men with demonstrated testosterone deficiency, but long-term treatment with testosterone is associated with serious adverse side effects, such as prostatic cancer.

CHRONIC FATIGUE SYNDROME

In 1988, the U.S. Centers for Disease Control and Prevention (CDC) identified chronic fatigue syndrome, a condition characterized by severe disabling fatigue and disturbances in sleep and concentration. Since then, the disorder has captured the attention of both the medical profession and the general public (Table 18–3). The problems associated with studying chronic fatigue syndrome are of great interest in the United States today. The disorder is classified in ICD-10 as an ill-defined condition of unknown etiology under the heading *Malaise and Fatigue* and is subdivided into asthenia and unspecified disability.

Table 18–3
1994 CDC Criteria for Chronic Fatigue Syndrome

A. Severe unexplained fatigue for over 6 months that is:
  (1) of a new or definite onset
  (2) not due to continuing exertion
  (3) not resolved by rest
  (4) functionally impairing

B. The presence of four or more of the following new symptoms:
  (1) impaired memory or concentration
  (2) sore throat
  (3) tender lymph nodes
  (4) muscle pain
  (5) pain in several joints
  (6) new pattern of headaches
  (7) unrefreshing sleep
  (8) postexertional malaise lasting more than 24 hours

Epidemiology

The exact incidence and prevalence of chronic fatigue syndrome are unknown, but the incidence has been estimated at 1 per 1,000. The illness is observed primarily in young adults (ages 20 to 40). Women are at least twice as likely as men to be affected. In the United States, studies show that about 25 percent of the general adult population experience fatigue lasting 2 weeks or longer. When the fatigue persists beyond 6 months, it is defined as chronic fatigue. A study of patients in primary care clinics found that 24 percent had experienced fatigue lasting over 1 year.

Etiology

The cause of the disorder is unknown. The diagnosis can be made only after all other medical and psychiatric causes of chronic fatiguing illness have been excluded. Scientific studies have validated no pathognomonic signs or diagnostic tests for this condition.

Investigators have tried to implicate the Epstein-Barr herpesvirus (EBV) as the etiological agent in chronic fatigue syndrome. EBV infection, however, is associated with specific antibodies and atypical lymphocytosis, findings that are absent in chronic fatigue syndrome. Results of tests for other viral agents, such as enteroviruses, herpesvirus, and retroviruses, have been negative.

Some investigators have found nonspecific markers of immune abnormalities in patients with chronic fatigue syndrome, for example, reduced proliferation responses of peripheral blood lymphocytes, but these responses are similar to those detected in some patients with major depression.

Diagnosis and Clinical Features

Because chronic fatigue syndrome has no pathognomonic features, diagnosis is difficult. Physicians should attempt to delineate as many signs and symptoms as possible to facilitate the process. Even though chronic fatigue is the most common complaint, most patients have many other symptoms (Table 18–4). As a patient's history unfolds, clinicians are likely to think of a variety of disease states that fall within the range of neurological, metabolic, or psychiatric disorders to account for the patient's distress. In most cases, however, no picture of any disorder emerges with clarity from history-taking alone.

The physical examination is also an unreliable source of diagnostic certainty. In addition to chronic fatigue, for example, patients may complain of feeling warm or having chills

Table 18–4
Signs and Symptoms Reported by Patients with Chronic Fatigue Syndrome

Fatigue or exhaustion	Diarrhea	Insomnia
Headache	Constipation	Fever or sensation of fever
Malaise	Bloating	Chills
Short-term memory loss	Panic attacks	Night sweats
Muscle pain	Eye pain	Weight gain
Difficulty concentrating	Scratchiness in eyes	Allergies
Joint pain	Blurring of vision	Chemical sensitivities
Depression	Double vision	Palpitations
Abdominal pain	Sensitivity to bright lights	Shortness of breath
Lymph node pain	Numbness and/or tingling in extremities	Flushing rash of the face and cheeks
Sore throat	Fainting spells	Swelling of the extremities or eyelids
Lack of restful sleep	Light-headedness	Burning on urination
Muscle weakness	Dizziness	Sexual dysfunction
Bitter or metallic taste	Clumsiness	Hair loss
Balance disturbance		

Adapted from Bell DS: *The Doctor's Guide to Chronic Fatigue Syndrome: Understanding, Treating, and Living with CFIDS,* pp 10–11. Addison-Wesley, Reading, 1995.

with normal body temperature, and others may complain of lymph node tenderness in the absence of node enlargement. These and other equivocal findings neither confirm nor rule out the disorder.

The CDC diagnostic criteria for chronic fatigue syndrome are listed in Table 18–3 and include fatigue for at least 6 months; impaired memory or concentration; sore throat; tender or enlarged lymph nodes; muscle pain; arthralgias; headache; sleep disturbance; and postexertional malaise. Fatigue is the most obvious symptom and is characterized by severe mental and physical exhaustion sufficient to cause a 50 percent reduction in patients' activities. For most patients, the onset is gradual; some have an acute onset that resembles a flulike illness.

Differential Diagnosis

Chronic fatigue must be differentiated from endocrine disorders, such as hypothyroidism; neurological disorders, such as multiple sclerosis; infectious disorders, such as AIDS and infectious mononucleosis; and psychiatric disorders, such as depressive disorders. The evaluation process is complex, and a diagnostic scheme is listed in Table 18–5.

Up to 80 percent of patients with chronic fatigue syndrome meet the diagnostic criteria for major depression. The correlation is so high that many psychiatrists believe all cases of the syndrome to be depressive disorders, yet patients with chronic fatigue syndrome rarely report feelings of guilt, suicidal ideation, or anhedonia and show little or no weight loss. Also, there is usually no family history of depression or other genetic loading for psychiatric disorder and few if any stressful events in patients' lives that might precipitate or account for a depressive illness. In addition, although some patients respond to antidepressant medication, many eventually become refractory to all psychopharmacological agents.

Course and Prognosis

Spontaneous recovery is rare in patients with chronic fatigue syndrome, but improvement does occur. At present, most reports on course and prognosis are based on small samples. In one study, 63 percent of patients with the syndrome followed for up to 4 years reported improvement. Patients with the best prognosis have had no previous or concurrent psychiatric illness, are able to maintain social contacts, and continue to work, even at reduced levels.

Treatment

Treatment of chronic fatigue syndrome is mainly supportive. Physicians must first establish rapport and not dismiss patients' complaints as being without foundation. As with neurasthenia, the complaints are not imaginary. A careful medical examination is necessary, and a psychiatric evaluation is indicated, both of which are geared to rule out other causes for the symptoms.

No effective medical treatment has been identified. Antiviral agents and corticosteroids are not useful, although a few patients have shown a lessening of fatigue with the antiviral drug amantadine. Symptomatic treatment, such as analgesics for arthralgias and muscular pain, is the usual approach, but nonsteroidal anti-inflammatory drugs (NSAIDs) are not effective. It is important to encourage patients to continue their daily activities and to resist their fatigue as much as possible. A reduced workload is far better than absence from work.

Psychiatric treatment is desirable, especially when depression is present. In many cases, symptoms improve markedly when patients are in supportive or insight-oriented psychotherapy. Cognitive behavioral therapy has been reported to be of use. Therapy is geared to help patients overcome and correct mistaken beliefs, such as fear that any activity causing fatigue worsens the disorder. Pharmacological agents, especially antidepressants with nonsedating qualities, such as bupropion (Wellbutrin), may be helpful. Nefazodone was reported to decrease pain and improve sleep and memory in some patients. Analeptics (for instance, amphetamine or methylphenidate) may help to reduce fatigue. Table 18–6 displays recommendations for a general approach to pharmacotherapy.

The following case, described by Hagop S. Akiskal, M.D., is a patient's report that illustrates many of the uncertainties of the interface between chronic fatigue syndrome and mood disorders.

Table 18–5
Approach to the Assessment of Persistent Fatigue

History

- Record the medical and psychosocial circumstances at onset of symptoms.
- Assess previous physical and psychological health.
- Seek clues to an underlying medical disorder (eg, fevers, weight loss, dyspnea).
- Assess the impact of the symptoms on the patient's lifestyle.

Characteristic symptoms of chronic fatigue syndrome (CFS) include fatigue, mylagia, arthralgia, impaired memory and concentration, and unrefreshing sleep.

↓

Physical examination

- Seek abnormalities to suggest an underlying medical disorder:
  - —Hypothyroidism
  - —Chronic hepatitis
  - —Chronic anemia
  - —Neuromuscular disease
  - —Sleep apnea syndrome
  - —Occult malignancy, etc

The physical examination in patients with CFS characteristically shows no abnormalities.

↓

Mental state examination

- Past or family history of psychiatric disorder, notably depression, anxiety
- Past history of frequent episodes of medically unexplained symptoms
- Past history of alcohol or substance abuse
- Current symptoms: depression, anxiety, self-destructive thoughts, and use of over-the-counter medications
- Current signs of psychomotor retardation
- Evaluate psychosocial support system

CFS patients have depressive symptoms, but not guilt, suicidal ideation, or observable psychomotor slowing.

↓

Laboratory investigation

- Screening tests:
  - —Urinalysis
  - —Blood count and differential
  - —Erythrocyte sedimentation rate
  - —Renal function tests
  - —Liver function tests
  - —Calcium, phosphate
  - —Random blood glucose
  - —Thyroid function tests (including thyroid stimulating hormone level)
- Additional investigations as clinically indicated (eg, sleep study)

The diagnosis of CFS is primarily one of exclusion of alternative conditions.

↓

Chronic fatigue syndrome

- *Unexplained, persistent, or relapsing chronic fatigue lasting 6 or more consecutive months* that is of new or definite onset; is not the result of ongoing exertion; is not substantially relieved by rest; and results in substantial reduction in previous levels of occupational, educational, social or personal activities; *and*
- *Four more of the following symptoms occurring concurrently:* (1) impairment of short-term memory or concentration; (2) sore throat; (3) tender cervical or axillary lymph nodes; (4) muscle pain, or multijoint pain; (5) headaches; (6) unrefreshing sleep; and (7) postexertional malaise.

Reprinted with permission from Hickie IB, Lloyd AR, Wakefield D: Chronic fatigue syndrome: Current perspectives on evaluation and management. Med J Aust *163:* 315, 1995.

The patient was a 39-year-old, never married woman, trained as a social worker, but currently on disability. She had experienced extreme lethargy and fatigue for many years, had always felt foggy headed, and had trouble thinking and concentrating. Her complaint was of fatigue, not depression. According to the patient, her body felt like lead and ached all over, as though someone had beaten her up. Her brain felt achy and sore. She felt much worse in the morning and was unable to get out of bed; she felt better at night but nevertheless felt bad every day. When exercise was prescribed, it made her worse. She was very sensitive to hot and cold, and her sexual drive was low.

The patient had a general feeling of anhedonia. As far back as she could remember—in junior high school—she was always exhausted and had always complained about fatigue, not depression, because fatigue was the overwhelming problem. She thought that her depression was secondary to the fatigue. In high school, she had been a compulsive overeater; she was bulimic for a few years, but never severely so, and she was only about 10 pounds overweight. In those days, she would sleep 10 or 12 hours a night on the weekends and still felt exhausted; she could not get up for school on Monday. As an adolescent, she felt inferior and could not make decisions. She felt so insecure that she did not want to go to camp or to leave home for long periods.

The results of a recent sleep study showed a short latency to rapid eye movement (REM) sleep (49 minutes). The patient was diagnosed as having dysthymic disorder and began taking antidepressants. When she took tranylcypromine (Parnate), she stated that she felt like a normal person for the first time in her life. She could play sports, had a sex drive, felt energetic, and was able to think clearly. But the benefits lasted for barely 2 months. Her response was equally short lived to phenelzine (Nardil), imipramine (Tofranil), selegiline (Eldepryl), and bupropion. She did not respond to serotonin-specific reuptake inhibitors (SSRIs) at all.

Table 18–6
Recommendations for a Logical Pharmacotherapy of Chronic Fatigue

- Establish a collaborative patient/physician treatment framework.
- Avoid premature diagnostic closure.
- Determine what self-administered, over-the-counter medications the patient is already taking and assess closely for interaction with the proposed medication.
- Discuss the role of medication and identify clear treatment goals:
  Psychiatric syndromes
  Domains of symptomatic distress (eg, musculoskeletal pain, poor sleep quality, fatigue, subjective cognitive changes, and mood or anxiety symptoms)
- Choice of agent should be based on:
  The predicted side-effect profile
  The patient's preference
  Medical contraindications to the use of a particular medication
- Begin therapy at the lowest possible dose, and increase the dose gradually; observe and discuss side effects during treatment, clarifying issues of significant medical concern.
- Attempt thorough trial to known optimal target dose of drug or until maximum clinical effect is evident.
- Ongoing discussion of the patient's specific response pattern should occur, clarifying the patient's expectations about the treatment.
- Do not continue treatment indefinitely without evidence of clear clinical response; if necessary, discontinue treatment and reassess during medication-free state.
- Avoid polypharmacy; assess treatment response to one agent at a time.
- Frame pharmacotherapy with respect to other aspects of the treatment plan; use medication as setting a context for a multidimensional treatment framework.

Reprinted with permission from Demitrack MA: Psychopharmacological principles in the treatment of chronic fatigue syndrome. In *Chronic Fatigue Syndrome,* MA Demitrack, SE Abbey, editors, p 281. Guilford, New York, 1996.

The patient had never experienced high periods before she took antidepressants. Her main problem had always been one of exhaustion. When she responded to medications, they worked very quickly (within a few days) and she felt great, but all the medications stopped working after a short time. The dosage would be raised, and again she would feel better. Eventually, at a high dose, either she could not tolerate the dose, or the drug would no longer help. She had taken different combinations of drugs for 10 years but had never felt well for more than 6 weeks at a time.

When the patient consulted an immunologist, the immunologist told her that she had an abnormality in regulating antibody production and recommended gammaglobulin shots. They did not help.

When she first started working, she had always felt tired and foggy headed, and it was difficult for her to be sharp at work. At times, she would shut the door to her office, sit at the desk, and put her head down. Working had become increasingly difficult, and the patient had lost two excellent positions. The previous year, she had to go on disability leave. She felt desperate for relief because her condition had drastically affected her life. Disability was a difficult situation for her; she was unmarried and without other financial resources. The patient felt despondent, as though life was passing by without the hope of her ever really improving.

Self-help groups have been of value in patients with chronic fatigue syndrome. They derive benefit from the group dynamic of instilling hope, offering identification, sharing experiences, and imparting information. The cohesion of members in such groups also raises self-esteem, which is usually impaired in these patients, who often feel they are not being taken seriously by their physicians. For this reason, many people with the syndrome rely on vitamins, minerals, and miscellaneous herbal products or treatment methods that fall under the rubric of alternative medicine. None of these or other unidentified general tonics have been peer reviewed in the medical literature and are of little or no benefit.

References

Abbey SE, Garfinkel PE: Neurasthenia and chronic fatigue syndrome: The role of culture in the making of a diagnosis. Am J Psychiatry *148:* 1638, 1991

Jorge CM, Goodnick PJ: Chronic fatigue syndrome and depression: biological differentiation and treatment. Psychiatr Ann *27:* 365, 1997.

Lee S: The vicissitudes of neurasthenia in Chinese societies: Where will it go from the ICD-10? Transcultural Psychiatr Res Rev *31:* 153, 1994.

Lee S, Wong KC: Rethinking neurasthenia: The illness concepts of *shenjing shuairuo* among Chinese undergraduates in Hong Kong. Cult Med Psychiatry *19:* 91, 1995.

Merikangas K, Angst J: Neurasthenia in a longitudinal cohort study of young adults. Psychol Med *24:* 1013, 1994.

Price RK, North CS, Wessely S, Fraser VJ: Estimating the prevalence of chronic fatigue syndrome and associated symptoms in the community. Public Health Rep *107:* 514, 1992.

Vercoulen JH, Swanink CM, Fennis JF, Falama JM, van der Meer JW, Bleijenberg F: Dimensional assessment of chronic fatigue syndrome. J Psychosom Res *38:* 383, 1994.

Walker EA, Katon WJ, Kemelka RP: Psychiatric disorders and medical care among people in the general population who report fatigue. J Gen Intern Med *8:* 436, 1993.

Ware NC, Kleinman A: Culture and somatic experience: The social course of illness in neurasthenia and chronic fatigue syndrome. Psychosom Med *54:* 546, 1992.

Wessely S: Neurasthenia and chronic fatigue: Theory and practice in Britain and America. Transcultural Psychiatr Res Rev *31:* 173, 1994.

Wessely S, Lutz T: Neurasthenia and fatigue syndromes. In *A History of Clinical Psychiatry: The Origin and History of Psychiatric Disorders,* GE Berrios, R Porter, editors, p 509. New York University Press, New York, 1995.

Wilson A, Hickie I, Lloyd A, Wakefield D: The treatment of chronic fatigue syndrome: Science and speculation. Am J Med *96:* 544, 1994.

19 Factitious Disorders

According to the fourth edition of *Diagnostic and Statistical Manual of Mental Disorders* (DSM-IV), factitious disorders are "characterized by physical or psychological symptoms that are intentionally produced or feigned . . . to assume the sick role." Clinicians can assess whether a symptom is intentional "both by direct evidence and by excluding other causes." In these disorders, patients intentionally produce signs of medical or mental disorders and misrepresent their histories and symptoms. The only apparent objective of the behavior is to assume the role of a patient without an external incentive. For many people, hospitalization itself is a primary objective and often a way of life. The disorders have a compulsive quality, but the behaviors are considered voluntary in that they are deliberate and purposeful, even if they cannot be controlled.

EPIDEMIOLOGY

The prevalence of factitious disorders is unknown, although some clinicians believe that they are more common than acknowledged. They appear to occur most frequently in men and among hospital and health care workers. One study reported a 9 percent rate of factitious disorders among all patients admitted to a hospital; another study found factitious fever in 3 percent of all patients. A data bank of people who feign illness has been established to alert hospitals about such patients, many of whom travel from place to place, seek admission under different names, or simulate different illnesses.

ETIOLOGY

The psychodynamic underpinnings of factitious disorders are poorly understood because the patients are difficult to engage in an exploratory psychotherapy process. They may insist that their symptoms are physical and that psychologically oriented treatment is therefore useless. Anecdotal case reports indicate that many of the patients suffered childhood abuse or deprivation, resulting in frequent hospitalizations during early development. In such circumstances, an inpatient stay may have been regarded as an escape from a traumatic home situation, and the patient may have found a series of caretakers (such as doctors, nurses, and hospital workers) to be loving and caring. In contrast, the patients' families of origin included a rejecting mother or an absent father. The usual history reveals that the patient perceives one or both parents as rejecting figures who are unable to form close relationships. The facsimile of genuine illness, therefore, is used to recreate the desired positive parent–child bond. The disorders are a form of repetition compulsion, repeating the basic conflict of needing and seeking acceptance and love while expecting that they will not be forthcoming. Hence, the patient transforms the physicians and staff members into rejecting parents.

Patients who seek out painful procedures, such as surgical operations and invasive diagnostic tests, may have a masochistic personality makeup in which pain serves as punishment for past sins, imagined or real. Some patients may attempt to master the past and the early trauma of serious medical illness or hospitalization by assuming the role of the patient and reliving the painful and frightening experience over and over again through multiple hospitalizations. Patients who feign psychiatric illness may have had a relative who was hospitalized with the illness they are simulating. Through identification, patients hope to reunite with the relative in a magical way.

Many patients have the poor identity formation and disturbed self-image that is characteristic of someone with borderline personality disorder. Some patients are as-if personalities who have assumed the identities of those around them. If these patients are health professionals, they are often unable to differentiate themselves from the patients with whom they come in contact. The cooperation or encouragement of other people in simulating a factitious illness occurs in a rare variant of the disorder and suggests another possible causative factor. Although most patients act alone, friends or relatives participate in fabricating the illness in some instances.

Significant defense mechanisms are repression, identification, identification with the aggressor, regression, and symbolization.

DIAGNOSIS AND CLINICAL FEATURES

The diagnostic criteria for factitious disorder in DSM-IV are given in Table 19–1. The psychiatric examination should emphasize securing information from any available friends, relatives, or other informants, because interviews with reliable outside sources often reveal the false nature of the patient's illness. Although time consuming and tedious, verifying all the facts presented by the patient about previous hospitalizations and medical care is essential.

Psychiatric evaluation is requested on a consultation basis in about 50 percent of the cases, usually after the presence of a simulated illness is suspected. The psychiatrist is often asked to confirm the diagnosis of factitious disorder. Under these circumstances, it is necessary to avoid pointed or accusatory questioning that may provoke truculence, evasion, or flight from the hospital. There may be a danger of provoking frank psychosis if vigorous confrontation is used; in some instances,

Table 19–1
DSM-IV Diagnostic Criteria for Factitious Disorder

A. Intentional production or feigning of physical or psychological signs or symptoms.

B. The motivation for the behavior is to assume the sick role.

C. External incentives for the behavior (such as economic gain, avoiding legal responsibility, or improving physical well-being, as in malingering) are absent.

Code based on type:

With predominantly psychological signs and symptoms: if psychological signs and symptoms predominate in the clinical presentation.

With predominantly physical signs and symptoms: if physical signs and symptoms predominate in the clinical presentation.

With combined psychological and physical signs and symptoms: if both psychological and physical signs and symptoms are present but neither predominate in the clinical presentation.

Reprinted with permission from American Psychiatric Association: *Diagnostic and Statistical Manual of Mental Disorders,* ed 4. Copyright, American Psychiatric Association, Washington, 1994.

the feigned illness serves an adaptive function and is a desperate attempt to ward off further disintegration.

Psychological testing may reveal specific underlying pathology in individual patients. Features that are overrepresented in patients with factitious disorder include normal or above-average intelligence quotient (IQ); absence of a formal thought disorder; poor sense of identity, including confusion over sexual identity; poor sexual adjustment; poor frustration tolerance; strong dependence needs; and narcissism.

Factitious Disorder with Predominantly Psychological Signs and Symptoms

Some patients show psychiatric symptoms that are judged to be feigned. This determination can be difficult and is often made only after a prolonged investigation (see Table 19–1). The feigned symptoms often include depression, hallucinations, dissociative and conversion symptoms, and bizarre behavior. Because the patient does not improve after routine therapeutic measures are administered, he or she may receive large doses of psychoactive drugs and may undergo electroconvulsive therapy.

Factitious psychological symptoms resemble the phenomenon of pseudomalingering, conceptualized as satisfying the need to maintain an intact self-image, which would be marred by admitting psychological problems that are beyond the person's capacity to master through conscious effort. In this case, deception is a transient ego-supporting device.

Recent findings indicate that factitious psychotic symptoms are more common than was previously suspected. The presence of simulated psychosis as a feature of other disorders, such as mood disorders, indicates a poor overall prognosis.

Psychotic inpatients found to have factitious disorder with predominantly psychological signs and symptoms—that is, exclusively simulated psychotic symptoms—generally have a concurrent diagnosis of borderline personality disorder. In these cases, the outcome appears to be worse than that of bipolar I disorder or schizoaffective disorder.

Patients may appear depressed and may explain their depression by offering a false history of the recent death of a significant friend or relative. Elements of the history that may suggest factitious bereavement include a violent or bloody death, a death under dramatic circumstances, and the dead person's being a child or a young adult. Other patients may describe both recent and remote memory loss or both auditory and visual hallucinations.

Other symptoms, which also appear in the physical type of factitious disorder, include pseudologia phantastica and impostorship. In pseudologia phantastica, limited factual material is mixed with extensive and colorful fantasies. The listener's interest pleases the patient and thus reinforces the symptom. The history or the symptoms are not the only distortions of truth. Patients often give false and conflicting accounts about other areas of their lives (for example, they may claim the death of a parent, so as to play on the sympathy of others). Imposture is commonly related to lying in these cases. Many patients assume the identity of a prestigious person. Men, for example, report being war heroes and attribute their surgical scars to wounds received during battle or in other dramatic and dangerous exploits. Similarly, they may say that they have ties to accomplished or renowned figures.

In 1945, at the age of 18, the patient became apprehensive about leaving home to go to an out-of-state college for her freshman year. One day in September, while with her mother shopping for college clothes, she underwent episodes in which she would stop walking and become stiff for a few moments without explanation, then proceed to talk and act appropriately. The next day she became more silent. Sometimes, she made inappropriate remarks; at other times, she acted and talked quite normally. Silences, refusal to eat, and inappropriate comments, such as ''Daddy, kill me,'' precipitated a consultation and then hospitalization, almost on the day that the patient was to have been admitted to college.

In the early days of hospitalization, the patient vaguely suggested that she might be having auditory hallucinations and at times gave ''confused'' or silly answers that were out of keeping with her 121 IQ score on psychological testing. When by herself, she would write coherent letters and short stories that were regarded as publishable. Partly because of the ''lack of progress'' and the bizarreness of her behavior at times, she was diagnosed as having catatonic dementia praecox.

Early in her hospitalization, the patient received individual psychotherapy 4 times a week. She continued to receive psychotherapy in and out of the institution, with a series of nine therapists, for the next 20 years. From the beginning of her hospitalization, she was frequently negativistic, precipitated physical fights, mutilated herself in many minor ways, and induced vomiting. These behaviors contributed to her receiving a great deal of attention in a public institution with limited staff. She stated that she wanted to try every form of therapy, ''even lobotomy,'' and her wishes were carried out, except for the lobotomy. She received a dozen electroconvulsive treatments, four dozen insulin subcoma treatments, dance therapy, occupational therapy, recreational therapy, psychodrama (which she loved), group psychotherapy, and art therapy, in addition to individual psychotherapy and attention from ministers and priests.

After the first 3 stormy years of her hospitalization, the patient was transferred to the care of a woman psychiatrist, became much calmer, registered at a local university, and did well at her studies. Nevertheless, ''hysterical'' vomiting, violence, and other bizarre acts would take place whenever discharge from the institution was mentioned. In 2 more years working primarily with women therapists, she held a job, acted appropriately, and eventually accepted discharge to a female psychotherapist as ''recovered'' at age 24.

One evening, after 6 uneventful years and satisfactory occupational functioning, the patient appeared at the hospital, distraught at being unable to reach her therapist by phone, and asked to be readmitted. She was admitted despite the difficulties in determining the genuineness of her behavior and of her statements about suicide and ''confusion.'' A series of many forms of psychotherapy, including individual psychotherapy, commenced immediately and lasted nearly a decade.

When the patient was 40, a change in the approach to her evaluation and treatment was initiated when it was decided that she had a ''hysterical personality.'' For the next 5 years, continuing efforts to place her in the community were blocked by negativism, threats, minor self-mutilations, self-induced vomiting, occasional inappropriate comments, and other attention-getting behavior, none of which, however, was ''rewarded'' with individual therapy, psychodrama, or other such attentions. Eventually, when she was in her mid-40s, she was discharged, despite complaints that she was not ready. When told that the discharge was being carried out over her objections, the patient vomited, but the therapist stated that she would be discharged nevertheless. She pulled down her pants and defecated in the office but was still discharged. In the decade since she was discharged, she has continued to function outside the institution, usually with the support of a boarding home.

DISCUSSION

This woman was able to engage the attention of countless dedicated mental health professionals over many years. Her remarkable illness persisted despite a trial of almost every known treatment. The pattern of her symptoms, from the start, did not correspond to any recognizable illness, and she seemed able to produce a symptom of a particular behavior at will (such as defecation in public when her discharge was imminent). Over the years, her behavior seemed to have been designed to achieve one goal: continuing to be treated as a psychiatric patient.

In the past, such a case might have been called hysteria because of the exaggerated, self-dramatizing nature of the symptoms. These histrionic features were also noted by the hospital personnel who took care of the patient. In DSM-IV, the intentional production of psychological symptoms for the purpose of assuming the patient role (and the absence of external incentives for the behavior, as in malingering) is called factitious disorder with predominantly psychological signs and symptoms.

In addition to the factitious production of symptoms, this woman's long-term functioning was characterized by excessive emotionality and attention seeking. In her relationships with people, she was vain, demanding, and dependent. These features suggest the additional diagnosis of histrionic personality disorder. There is, however, insufficient information about other symptoms of the disorder, such as inappropriate seductiveness and consistent use of physical appearance to attract attention. We therefore would add the diagnosis of personality disorder not otherwise specified (with histrionic features). (From *DSM-IV Casebook.*)

Factitious Disorder with Predominantly Physical Signs and Symptoms

Factitious disorder with predominantly physical signs and symptoms has been designated by a variety of labels, the best known being Munchausen syndrome, named after the German Baron Karl F. H. von Münchhausen, an 18th century soldier and raconteur. The disorder has also been called hospital addiction, polysurgical addiction, and professional patient syndrome, among other names.

The essential feature of patients with the disorder is their ability to present physical symptoms so well that they are able to gain admission to and stay in a hospital (see Table 19–1). To support their history, the patients may feign symptoms suggestive of a disorder that may involve any organ system. They are familiar with the diagnoses of most disorders that usually require hospital admission or medication and can give excellent histories capable of deceiving even experienced clinicians. Clinical presentations are myriad and include hematoma, hemoptysis, abdominal pain, fever, hypoglycemia, lupuslike syndromes, nausea, vomiting, dizziness, and seizures. Urine is contaminated with blood or feces; anticoagulants are taken to simulate bleeding disorders; insulin is used to produce hypoglycemia; and so on. Such patients often insist on surgery and claim adhesions from previous surgical procedures. They may acquire a gridiron or washboardlike abdomen from multiple procedures. Complaints of pain, especially that simulating renal colic, are common, with the patients wanting narcotics. In about half the reported cases, the patients demand treatment with specific medications, usually analgesics. Once in the hospital, they continue to be demanding and difficult. As each test is returned with a negative result, they may accuse doctors of incompetence, threaten litigation, and become generally abusive. Some may abruptly sign out shortly before they believe they are going to be confronted with their factitious behavior. They then go to another hospital in the same or another city and begin the cycle again. Specific predisposing factors are true physical disorders during childhood leading to extensive medical treatment, a grudge against the medical profession, employment as a medical paraprofessional, and an important relationship with a physician in the past.

Factitious Disorder with Combined Psychological and Physical Signs and Symptoms

In combined forms of factitious disorder, both psychological and physical signs and symptoms are present. If neither

Table 19–2
DSM-IV Diagnostic Criteria for Factitious Disorder Not Otherwise Specified

This category includes disorders with factitious symptoms that do not meet the criteria for factitious disorder. An example is factitious disorder by proxy: the intentional production or feigning of physical or psychological signs or symptoms in another person who is under the individual's care for the purpose of indirectly assuming the sick role.

Reprinted with permission from American Psychiatric Association: *Diagnostic and Statistical Manual of Mental Disorders,* ed 4. Copyright, American Psychiatric Association, Washington, 1994.

type predominates in the clinical presentation, a diagnosis of factitious disorder with combined psychological and physical signs and symptoms should be made (see Table 19–1).

Factitious Disorder Not Otherwise Specified

Some patients with factitious signs and symptoms do not meet the DSM-IV criteria for a specific factitious disorder and should be classified as having factitious disorder not otherwise specified (Table 19–2). The most notable example of the diagnosis is factitious disorder by proxy, which is also included in a DSM-IV appendix (Table 19–3). In this diagnosis, a person intentionally produces physical signs or symptoms in another person who is under the first person's care. The only apparent purpose of the behavior is for the caretaker to indirectly assume the sick role. The most common case of factitious disorder by proxy involves a mother who deceives medical personnel into believing that her child is ill. The deception may involve a false medical history, the contamination of laboratory samples, the alteration of records, or the induction of injury and illness in the child.

ICD-10

The 10th revision of *International Statistical Classification of Diseases and Related Health Problems* (ICD-10) notes that "the condition is best interpreted as a disorder of illness behavior and the sick role. Individuals with this pattern of behavior usually show signs of . . . other marked abnormalities of personality and relationships." ICD-10 also includes a category called elaboration of physical symptoms for psychological reasons. The ICD-10 criteria for both conditions are presented in Table 19–4.

Table 19–3
DSM-IV Research Criteria for Factitious Disorder by Proxy

A. Intentional production or feigning of physical or psychological signs or symptoms in another person who is under the individual's care.
B. The motivation for the perpetrator's behavior is to assume the sick role by proxy.
C. External incentives for the behavior (such as economic gain) are absent.
D. The behavior is not better accounted for by another mental disorder.

Reprinted with permission from American Psychiatric Association: *Diagnostic and Statistical Manual of Mental Disorders,* ed 4. Copyright, American Psychiatric Association, Washington, 1994.

Table 19–4
ICD-10 Diagnostic Criteria for Other Disorders of Adult Personality and Behavior

Elaboration of physical symtpoms for psychological reasons
A. Physical symptoms originally due to a confirmed physical disorder, disease, or disability become exaggerated or prolonged in excess of what can be explained by the physical disorder itself.
B. There is evidence for a psychological causation for the excess symptoms (such as evident fear of disability or death, possible financial compensation, disappointment at the standard of care experienced).

Intentional production or feigning of symptoms or disabilities, either physical or psychological [factitous disorder]
A. The individual exhibits a persistent pattern of intentional production or feigning of symptoms and/or self-infliction of wounds in order to produce symptoms.
B. No evidence can be found for an external motivation such as financial compensation, escape from danger, or more medical care. (If such evidence can be found, the category, malingering, should be used.)
C. *Most commonly used exclusion clause.* There is no confirmed physical or mental disorder that could explain the symptoms.

Other specified disorders of adult personality and behavior
This category should be used for coding any specified disorder of adult personality and behavior that cannot be classified under any one of the preceding headings.

Reprinted with permission from World Health Organization: *The ICD-10 Classification of Mental and Behavioural Disorders: Diagnostic Criteria for Research.* Copyright, World Health Organization, Geneva, 1993.

DIFFERENTIAL DIAGNOSIS

Any disorder in which physical signs and symptoms are prominent should be considered in the differential diagnosis, and the possibility of authentic or concomitant physical illness must always be explored.

Somatoform Disorders

A factitious disorder is differentiated from somatization disorder (Briquet's syndrome) by the voluntary production of factitious symptoms, the extreme course of multiple hospitalizations, and the seeming willingness to undergo an extraordinary number of mutilating procedures in patients with the former disorder. Patients with conversion disorder are not usually conversant with medical terminology and hospital routines, and their symptoms have a direct temporal relation or symbolic reference to specific emotional conflicts.

Hypochondriasis differs from factitious disorder in that the hypochondriacal patient does not voluntarily initiate the production of symptoms and hypochondriasis typically has a later age of onset. As is the case with somatization disorder, patients with hypochondriasis do not usually submit to potentially mutilating procedures. (Somatoform disorders are discussed in Chapter 17.)

Personality Disorders

Because of their pathological lying, lack of close relationships with others, hostile and manipulative manner, and associated substance abuse and criminal history, factitious disorder patients are often classified as having antisocial personality disorder. Antisocial people, however, do not usually volunteer for invasive procedures or resort to a way of life marked by repeated or long-term hospitalization.

Because of attention seeking and an occasional flair for the dramatic, patients with factitious disorder may be classified as having histrionic personality disorder. But not all factitious disorder patients have a dramatic flair; many are withdrawn and bland.

Consideration of the patient's chaotic lifestyle, past history of disturbed interpersonal relationships, identity crisis, substance abuse, self-damaging acts, and manipulative tactics may lead to the diagnosis of borderline personality disorder. People with factitious disorder usually do not have the eccentricities of dress, thought, or communication that characterize schizotypal personality disorder patients. (Personality disorders are discussed in Chapter 27.)

Schizophrenia

The diagnosis of schizophrenia is often based on patients' admittedly bizarre lifestyles, but patients with factitious disorder do not usually meet the diagnostic criteria for schizophrenia unless they have the fixed delusion that they are actually ill and act on this belief by seeking hospitalization. Such a practice seems to be the exception; few patients with factitious disorder show evidence of a severe thought disorder or bizarre delusions.

Malingering

Factitious disorders must be distinguished from malingering. Malingerers have an obvious, recognizable environmental goal in producing signs and symptoms. They may seek hospitalization to secure financial compensation, evade the police, avoid work, or merely obtain free bed and board for the night, but they always have some apparent end for their behavior. Moreover, these patients can usually stop producing their signs and symptoms when they are no longer considered profitable or when the risk becomes too great. (Malingering is discussed in Chapter 32.)

Substance Abuse

Although patients with factitious disorders may have a complicating history of substance abuse, they should be considered not merely as substance abusers but as having coexisting diagnoses.

Ganser's Syndrome

Ganser's syndrome, a controversial condition most typically associated with prison inmates, is characterized by the use of approximate answers. People with the syndrome respond to simple questions with astonishingly incorrect answers. For example, when asked about the color of a blue car, the person answers "red" or answers "*2* plus *2* equals *5*." Ganser's syndrome may be a variant of malingering, in that the patients avoid punishment or responsibility for their actions. Ganser's syndrome is classified in DSM-IV as a dissociative disorder not otherwise specified and in ICD-10 under other dissociative or conversion disorders.

COURSE AND PROGNOSIS

Factitious disorders typically begin in early adult life, although they may appear during childhood or adolescence. The onset of the disorder or of discrete episodes of seeking treatment may follow real illness, loss, rejection, or abandonment. Usually, the patient or a close relative had a hospitalization in childhood or early adolescence for a genuine physical illness. Thereafter, a long pattern of successive hospitalizations begins insidiously and unfolds. As the disorder progresses, the patient becomes knowledgeable about medicine and hospitals. The onset of the disorder in patients who had early hospitalizations for actual illness is earlier than generally reported.

Factitious disorders are incapacitating to the patient and often produce severe traumas or untoward reactions related to treatment. A course of repeated or long-term hospitalization is obviously incompatible with meaningful vocational work and sustained interpersonal relationships. The prognosis in most cases is poor. A few patients occasionally spend time in jail, usually for minor crimes, such as burglary, vagrancy, and disorderly conduct. Patients may also have a history of intermittent psychiatric hospitalization.

Although no adequate data are available about the ultimate outcome for the patients, a few of them probably die as a result of needless medication, instrumentation, or surgery. In view of the patients' often expert simulation and the risks that they take, some may die without the disorder's being suspected. Possible features that indicate a favorable prognosis are (1) the presence of a depressive-masochistic personality; (2) functioning at a borderline, not a continuously psychotic, level; and (3) the attributes of an antisocial personality disorder with minimal symptoms.

TREATMENT

No specific psychiatric therapy has been effective in treating factitious disorders. It is a clinical paradox that patients with the disorders simulate serious illness, and seek and submit to unnecessary treatment while they deny to themselves and others their true illness and thus avoid possible treatment for it. Ultimately, the patients elude meaningful therapy by abruptly leaving the hospital or failing to keep follow-up appointments.

Treatment is thus best focused on management rather than on cure. Perhaps the single most important factor in successful management is a physician's early recognition of the disorder. In this way, physicians can forestall patients' undergoing a multitude of painful and potentially dangerous diagnostic procedures. Good liaison between psychiatrists and the medical or surgical staff is strongly advised.

In cases of factitious disorder by proxy, legal intervention has been obtained in several instances, particularly with children. The senselessness of the disorder and the denial of false action by parents are obstacles to successful court action and often make conclusive proof unobtainable. In such cases, the child welfare services should be notified and arrangements made for the ongoing monitoring of the children's health.

The personal reactions of physicians and staff members are of great significance in treating and establishing a working alliance with the patients, who invariably evoke feelings of futility, bewilderment, betrayal, hostility, and even contempt. In essence, staff members are forced to abandon a basic element of their relationship with patients: acceptance of the truthfulness of the patients' statements. One appropriate psychiatric intervention is to suggest to the staff ways of remaining aware that, even though the patient's illness is factitious, the patient is ill.

Physicians should try not to feel resentment when patients humiliate their diagnostic prowess, and they should avoid any unmasking ceremony that sets up the patients as adversaries and precipitates their flight from the hospital. The staff should not perform unnecessary procedures or discharge patients abruptly, both of which are manifestations of anger.

Clinicians who find themselves involved with patients suffering from factitious disorders often become enraged at the patients for lying and deceiving them. Hence, therapists must be mindful of countertransference whenever they suspect factitious disorder. Often, the diagnosis is unclear because a definitive physical cause cannot be entirely ruled out. Although the use of confrontation is controversial, at some point in the treatment, patients must be made to face reality. Most patients simply leave treatment when their methods of gaining attention are identified and brought out into the open. In some cases, clinicians should reframe the factitious disorder as a cry for help, so that patients do not view clinicians' responses as punitive. A major role for psychiatrists in working with factitious disorder patients is to help other staff members in the hospital deal with their own sense of outrage at having been duped. Education about the disorder and some attempt to understand the patient's motivations may help staff members maintain their professional conduct in the face of extreme frustration.

Although a few cases of individual psychotherapy have been reported in the literature, there is no consensus about the best approach. In general, working in concert with the patient's primary care physician is more effective than working with the patient in isolation.

References

Ballard RS, Stoudemire A: Factitious apraxia. Int J Psychiatry Med *22:* 275, 1992.

Bauer M, Boegner F: Neurological syndromes in factitious disorder. J Nerv Ment Dis *184:* 28, 1996.

Feldman MD, Eisendrath SJ, editors: *The Spectrum of Factitious Disorders.* American Psychiatric Press, Washington, 1996.

Folks DG: Munchausen's syndrome and other factitious disorders. Special Issue: Malingering and conversion reactions. Neurol Clin *13:* 267, 1995.

French J: Pseudoseizers in the era of video-electroencephalogram monitoring. Curr Opin Neurol *8:* 117, 1995.

Heron EA, Kritchevsky M, Delis DC: Neuropsychological presentation of Ganser symptoms. J Clin Exp Neuropsychol *13:* 552, 1991.

Houck CA: Medicolegal aspects of factitious disorder. Psychiatr Med *10:* 105, 1992.

Hyler SE, Sussman N: Chronic factitious disorder with physical symptoms (the Munchausen syndrome). Psychiatr Clin North Am *4:* 365, 1981.

Jones RM: Factitious disorders. In *Comprehensive Textbook of Psychiatry,* ed 6, HI Kaplan, BJ Sadock, editors, p 1271. Williams & Wilkins, Baltimore, 1995.

Jureidini J: Obstetric factitious disorder and Munchausen syndrome by proxy. J Nerv Ment Dis *181:* 135, 1993.

Ludviksson BR, Griffin J, Graziano FM: Munchausen's syndrome: The importance of a comprehensive medical history. Wis Med J *92:* 128, 1993.

Meadow R: Management of Munchausen syndrome by proxy. Arch Dis Child *60:* 385, 1985.

Mountz JM, Parker PE, Liu HG, Bentley TW, Lill DW, Deutsch G: Tc-99m HMPAO brain SPECT scanning in Munchausen syndrome. Psychiatry Neurosci *21:* 49, 1996.

Schmaling KB, Rosenberg SJ, Oppenjeimer J, Moran MG: Factitious disorder with respiratory symptoms. Psychosomatics *32:* 457, 1991.

Schreier HA: The perversion of mothering: Munchausen syndrome by proxy. Bull Menninger Clin *56:* 421, 1992.

Single T, Henry RL: An unusual case of Munchausen syndrome by proxy. Aust NZ J Psychiatry *25:* 442, 1991.

Songer DA: Factitious AIDS. A case reported and literature review. Psychosomatics *36:* 406, 1995.

20

Dissociative Disorders

In the fourth edition of *Diagnostic and Statistical Manual of Mental Disorders* (DSM-IV), the essential feature of the dissociative disorders is defined as a state of disrupted "consciousness, memory, identity, or perception of the environment." DSM-IV offers specific diagnostic criteria for four dissociative disorders: dissociative amnesia (once called psychogenic amnesia), dissociative fugue (once called psychogenic fugue), dissociative identity disorder (once called multiple personality disorder), and depersonalization disorder.

Most people see themselves as human beings with one basic personality; they experience a unitary sense of self. People with dissociative disorders, however, have lost the sense of having one consciousness. They feel as though they have no identity, or they are confused about who they are, or they experience multiple identities. Everything that usually gives people their unique personalities—their integrated thoughts, feelings, and actions—is abnormal in people with dissociative disorders.

Patients with these disorders exhibit a range of dissociative experiences from normal to pathological. The *normal* range of dissociative phenomena can be studied from several perspectives. Many researchers and clinicians consider hypnotizability to be related to these disorders. Normal people vary in their hypnotizability. Patients with dissociative disorders are not necessarily more hypnotizable than are people without the disorder, but hypnosis is an example of a dissociative state in normal people.

Researchers have developed several scales to measure dissociative experiences, one of which is the Dissociative Experience Scale. Using this scale, therapists question interviewees about mild and common dissociative phenomena (such as periods of inattention during conversations) and about pathological dissociative phenomena. Studies using such scales have shown that the scores of about 5 percent of the general population are greater than 3 times the mean score. Other studies of dissociative phenomena have reported that dissociative symptoms decrease with age and that they are about equally common in women and men. Many types of studies have indicated an association between traumatic events, especially childhood physical and sexual abuse, and the development of dissociative symptoms and disorders.

Dissociation arises as a self-defense against trauma. Dissociative defenses perform the dual function of helping people remove themselves from trauma at the time that it occurs and also of delaying the working through needed to place the trauma in perspective within their lives. Unlike the phenomenon of repression, when the repression barrier creates a horizontal split and the material is transferred to the dynamic unconscious, dissociation creates a vertical split so that mental contents coexist in parallel consciousness.

Dissociation and splitting associated with repression are both similar and different. Both involve an active compartmentalization and separation of mental contents. Both are used as defenses to ward off unpleasant affects associated with the integration of contradictory parts of the self. They differ to some extent, however, in the nature of the affected ego function. In splitting, anxiety tolerance and impulse control are specifically impaired. In dissociation, memory and consciousness are affected. Nonetheless, both involve mental cleavages that produce self-representation connected with internal object representations.

In most dissociative states, contradictory representations of the self, which conflict with each other, are kept in separate mental compartments. In the most extreme form of dissociative identity disorder (multiple personality), these separate representations of the self take on the metaphoric existence of separate personalities, known as alters. All these disorders were once known as hysterical neuroses of the dissociative type. Dissociative amnesia is characterized by an inability to remember information, usually related to a stressful or traumatic event, that cannot be explained by ordinary forgetfulness, the ingestion of substances, or a general medical condition. Dissociative fugue is characterized by sudden and unexpected travel away from home or work, associated with an inability to recall the past and with confusion about a person's personal identity or with the adoption of a new identity. Dissociative identity disorder, generally considered the most severe and chronic of the dissociative disorders, is characterized by the presence of two or more distinct personalities within a single person. Depersonalization disorder is characterized by recurrent or persistent feelings of detachment from the body or mind. DSM-IV includes the diagnostic category of dissociative disorder not otherwise specified for dissociative disorders that do not meet the diagnostic criteria of the other dissociative disorders. DSM-IV also includes in its appendix diagnostic guidelines for dissociative trance disorder, which is currently categorized as a dissociative disorder not otherwise specified.

ICD-10

The 10th revision of *International Statistical Classification of Diseases and Related Health Problems* (ICD-10) organizes dissociative (conversion) disorders somewhat differently than does DSM-IV. The dissociative disorders in ICD-10 include dissociative amnesia, dissociative fugue, dissociative stupor, trance and possession disorders, dissociative motor disorders,

Table 20–1
ICD-10 Diagnostic Criteria for Dissociative [Conversion] Disorders

G1. There must be no evidence of a physical disorder that can explain the characteristic symptoms of this disorder (although physical disorders may be present that give rise to other symptoms).

G2. There are convincing associations in time between the onset of symptoms of the disorder and stressful events, problems, or needs.

Dissociative amnesia

A. The general criteria for dissociative disorder must be met.

B. There must be amnesia, either partial or complete, for recent events or problems that were or still are traumatic or stressful.

C. The amnesia is too extensive and persistent to be explained by ordinary forgetfulness (although its depth and extent may vary from one assessment to the next) or by intentional simulation.

Dissociative fugue

A. The general criteria for dissociative disorder must be met.

B. The individual undertakes an unexpected yet organized journey away from home or from the ordinary places of work and social activities, during which self-care is largely maintained.

C. There is amnesia, either partial or complete, for the journey, which also meets criterion C for dissociative amnesia.

Dissociative stupor

A. The general criteria for dissociative disorder must be met.

B. There is profound diminution or absence of voluntary movements and speech and of normal responsiveness to light, noise, and touch.

C. Normal muscle tone, static posture, and breathing (and often limited coordinated eye movements) are maintained.

Trance and possession disorders

A. The general criteria for dissociative disorder must be met.

B. Either of the following must be present:
 (1) *Trance.* There is temporary alteration of the state of consciousness, shown by any two of:
  (a) loss of the usual sense of personal identity;
  (b) narrowing of awareness of immediate surroudings, or unusually narrow and selective focusing on environmental stimuli;
  (c) limitation of movements, postures, and speech to repetition of a small repertoire.
 (2) *Possession disorder.* The individual is convinced that he or she has been taken over by a spirit, power, deity, or other person.

C. Both (1) and (2) of criterion B must be unwanted and troublesome, occurring outside, or being a prolongation of, similar states in religious or other culturally accepted situations.

D. *Most commonly used exclusion clause.* The disorder does not occur at the same time as schizophrenia or related disorders, or mood [affective] disorders with hallucinations or delusions.

Dissociative motor disorders

A. The general criteria for dissociative disorder must be met.

B. Either of the following must be present:
 (1) Complete or partial loss of the ability to perform movements that are normally under voluntary control (including speech);
 (2) Various or variable degrees of incoordination or ataxia, or inability to stand unaided.

Dissociative convulsions

A. The general criteria for dissociative disorder must be met.

B. The individual exhibits sudden and unexpected spasmodic movements, closely resembling any of the varieties of epileptic seizure, but not followed by loss of consciousness.

C. The symptoms in criterion B are not accompanied by tongue-biting, serious bruising or laceration due to falling, or urinary incontinence.

Dissociative anesthesia and sensory loss

A. The general criteria for dissociative disorder must be met.

B. Either of the following must be present:
 (1) Partial or complete loss of any or all of the normal cutaneous sensations over part or all of the body (specify: touch, pinprick, vibration, heat, cold);
 (2) Partial or complete loss of vision, hearing, or smell (specify).

Mixed dissociative [conversion] disorders

Other dissociative [conversion] disorders

This residual code may be used to indicate other dissociative and conversion states that meet criteria G1 and G2 for dissociative [conversion] disorders but do not meet the criteria for the dissociative disorders listed above.

Ganser's syndrome
(approximate answers)

Multiple personality disorder

A. Two or more distinct personalities exist within the individual, only one being evident at a time.

B. Each personality has its own memories, preferences, and behavior patterns, and at some time (and recurrently) takes full control of the individual's behavior.

C. There is inability to recall important personal information which is too extensive to be explained by ordinary forgetfulness.

D. The symptoms are not due to organic mental disorders (eg, in epileptic disorders) or to psychoactive substance-related disorders (eg, intoxication or withdrawal).

Transient dissociative [conversion] disorders occuring in childhood and adolescence

Other specified dissociative [conversion] disorders

Specific research criteria are not given for all disorders mentioned above, since these other dissociative states are rare and not well described. Research workers studying these conditions in detail should specify their own criteria according to the purpose of their studies.

Dissociative [conversion] disorder, unspecified

dissociative convulsions, dissociative anesthesia and sensory loss, mixed dissociative disorders, other dissociative disorders (Ganser's syndrome, multiple personality disorder, transient dissociative disorders occurring in childhood and adolescence, and other specified dissociative disorders), and unspecific dissociative disorders (Table 20–1). All these disorders share a "partial or complete loss of the normal integration between memories of the past, awareness of identity and immediate sensations, and control of bodily movements." A person's ability to choose to remember or to choose to move seems to be impaired. The extent of impairment can change from day to day, and to determine to what extent the loss of ability is under control is difficult.

These disorders usually are connected with trauma, personal conflicts, and poor relationships with others. ICD-10 adds the term *conversion* to indicate that the affects of the unsolvable problems are transformed into symptoms.

According to ICD-10, the sudden onset and terminations of the dissociative states are usually observed only during "contrived interactions or procedures such as hypnosis or abreaction," and any changes in the state usually last no longer than the "procedure" itself. Dissociative states with a traumatic onset remit after a few weeks or months; those produced by insoluble problems may be chronic and slow to develop. People with these disorders tend to see their problems as connected with the dissociative symptoms, not with the disorders themselves.

DISSOCIATIVE AMNESIA

The symptom of amnesia is common to dissociative amnesia, dissociative fugue, and dissociative identity disorder. Dissociative amnesia is the appropriate diagnosis when the dissociative phenomena are limited to amnesia. Its key symptom is the inability to recall information, usually about stressful or traumatic events in people's lives. This inability cannot be explained by ordinary forgetfulness, and there is no evidence of an underlying brain disorder. People retain the capacity to learn new information.

A common form of dissociative amnesia involves amnesia for personal identity but intact memory of general information. This clinical picture is exactly the reverse of the one seen in dementia, in which patients may remember their names but forget general information, such as what they had for lunch. Except for their amnesia, patients with dissociative amnesia appear completely intact and function coherently. By contrast, in most amnesias due to a general medical condition (such as postictal and toxic amnesias), patients may be confused and behave in a disorganized manner. Other types of amnesias (for example, transient global amnesia and postconcussion amnesia) are associated with an ongoing anterograde amnesia, which does not occur in patients with dissociative amnesia.

Epidemiology

Amnesia is the most common dissociative symptom and occurs in almost all the dissociative disorders. Dissociative amnesia is thought to be the most common of the dissociative disorders, although epidemiological data for all the dissociative disorders are limited and uncertain. Dissociative amnesia is thought to occur more often in women than in men and more often in young adults than in older adults. Inasmuch as the disorder is usually associated with stressful and traumatic events, its incidence probably increases during times of wars and natural disasters. Cases of dissociative amnesia related to domestic settings—for example, spouse abuse and child abuse—are probably constant in number.

Etiology

The neuroanatomical, neurophysiological, and neurochemical processes of memory storage and retrieval are much better understood today than they were a decade ago. The differentiation between short-term and long-term memory, the central role of the hippocampus, and the involvement of neurotransmitter systems have been clarified. The newly appreciated complexity of the formation and retrieval of memories may make dissociative amnesia intuitively understandable because of the many potential areas for dysfunction. Most patients with dissociative amnesia are unable to retrieve painful memories of stressful and traumatic events, and thus the emotional content of the memory is clearly related to the pathophysiology and the cause of the disorder.

One relevant observation about people in general is that learning is often state dependent—that is, dependent on the context in which learning occurs. Information learned or experienced during a particular behavior (for example, while driving a car), a pharmacological state (for example, while drinking alcohol), or a neurochemical state (for example, associated with an emotion such as happiness) or in a particular physical setting (for example, in a garden) is often recalled only, or more easily, while reexperiencing the original state. Thus, people can remember where a light switch is located in their car more easily while they are driving than when they are watching television. The theory of state-dependent learning applies to dissociative amnesia in that the memory of a traumatic event is laid down during the event, and the emotional state may be so extraordinary that it is hard for an affected person to remember information learned during that state.

In the psychoanalytic approach to dissociative amnesia, the disorder is considered primarily as a defense mechanism whereby a person alters consciousness as a way of dealing with an emotional conflict or an external stressor. Secondary defenses involved in dissociative amnesia include repression (disturbing impulses are blocked from consciousness) and denial (an aspect of external reality is ignored by the conscious mind).

Diagnosis

The diagnostic criteria for dissociative amnesia in DSM-IV (Table 20–2) emphasize that the forgotten information is usually of a traumatic or stressful nature. Dissociative amnesia

Table 20–2
DSM-IV Diagnostic Criteria for Dissociative Amnesia

A. The predominant disturbance is one or more episodes of inability to recall important personal information, usually of a traumatic or stressful nature, that is too extensive to be explained by ordinary forgetfulness.

B. The disturbance does not occur exclusively as a symptom of dissociative identity disorder, dissociative fugue, posttraumatic stress disorder, acute stress disorder, or somatization disorder and is not due to the direct physiolgoical effects of a substance (eg, a drug of abuse, a medication) or a neurological or other general medical condition (eg, amnestic disorder due to head trauma).

C. The symptoms cause clinically significant distress or impairment in social, occupational, or other important areas of functioning.

can be diagnosed only when the symptoms are not limited to amnesia that occurs in the course of dissociative identity disorder and are not the result of a general medical condition (for example, head trauma) or the ingestion of a substance.

Clinical Features

Although rare episodes of dissociative amnesia occur spontaneously, the history usually reveals a precipitating emotional trauma charged with painful emotions and psychological conflict—for example, a natural disaster in which people witnessed severe injuries or feared for their lives. A fantasized or actual expression of an impulse (sexual or aggressive) with which a person is unable to deal may also act as a precipitant, and amnesia may follow behavior that a person later finds morally reprehensible, for example, violence, an extramarital affair.

Although not necessary for diagnosis, the onset of the amnesia is often abrupt, and patients are usually aware that they have lost their memories. Some patients are upset by the memory loss, but others appear to be unconcerned or indifferent. When patients are not aware of their memory loss but a clinician suspects that they have dissociative amnesia, it is often useful to ask specific questions that may reveal the symptoms (Table 20–3). Amnestic patients are usually alert before and after the amnesia occurs. A few patients, however, report a slight clouding of consciousness during the period immediately surrounding the onset of amnesia. Depression and anxiety are common predisposing factors and frequently appear in a patient's mental status examination. Amnesia may provide a primary or a secondary gain. A woman who is amnestic about the birth of a dead infant achieves a primary gain by protecting herself from painful emotions. A soldier who has a sudden case of amnesia and is then removed from combat as a result exemplifies a secondary gain.

Dissociative amnesia may take one of several forms: *Localized amnesia,* the most common type, is the loss of memory for the events of a short time (a few hours to a few days); *generalized amnesia* is the loss of memory for a whole lifetime of experience; *selective* (also known as *systematized*) *amnesia* is the failure to recall some but not all events that occurred during a short time.

Table 20–3
Questions to Reveal Dissociative Amnesia

If the answers to the mental status questions (below) are positive, the patient should be asked to describe in detail his or her experience of the symptom, including its relation to the use of psychoactive substances.

Blackouts or time loss
 Mental status questions: "Do you lose time?" "Do you have blackouts?"

Reports by others of disremembered behavior
 Mental status questions: "Are you told of things you say and do for which you have no memory? Out of character behavior? Childlike behavior?"

Appearance of unexplained possessions
 Mental status questions: "Do you find things in your possession that you cannot explain? For example, clothes, tools, weapons, artwork, writing, items in your shopping basket, receipts?"

Perplexing changes in relationships
 Mental status questions: "Do you find that your relationships with people seem influenced by factors that you cannot recall? For example, do you find that people are angry with you or act closer to you apparently based on events for which you have no memory?

Fuguelike episodes
 Mental status questions: "Do you find yourself in places with no idea how you got there? Do you set out to go somewhere but find yourself somewhere else without knowing how you got there? What is the longest period of time you have lost during such an experience?"

Evidence of unusual fluctuations in abilities, habits, tastes, knowledge
 Mental status questions: "Does your ability to do things—such as athletics, artistic endeavors, mechanical tasks, work tasks, and intellectual tasks—fluctuate markedly in ways you cannot explain? Are you told that you do things you didn't know you could do?"

Fragmentary recall of the life history
 Mental status questions: "Are you aware of gaps in your memory for your life? Are you missing memories for important events in your life, like a wedding or a graduation? For your childhood? For events in wartime? For other important aspects of your adult life?"

Chronic mistaken identity experiences
 Mental status questions: "Do you find that you are approached by people whom you don't know, who insist they know you? Who say they have met you before? Who say they have done things with you? Who even call you by another name?"

Brief (micro) amnesias during personal interactions
 Mental status questions: "Do you find that you do not remember all or part of your interactions or conversations with people? Like this interview? Do you or will you remember all or part of our conversation today?"

Reprinted with permission from Lowenstein RJ: Psychogenic amnesia and psychogenic fugue: A comprehensive review. In *American Psychiatric Association Review of Psychiatry,* vol 10, A Tasman, SM Goldfinger, editors, p 189. American Psychiatric Press, Washington, 1991.

Barbara was a young unmarried mother of a 3-year-old son. Early one evening, the police took her to the emergency ward of a large general hospital. Although aware of her identity, she could remember nothing of the events of the preceding 8 hours. Pressed to recollect them, she was aware only of a vivid, hallucinatory vision of a parking lot full of cars and "someone running to someone for help," a scene to which she could attach no meaning or relation with herself.

Admitted to the psychiatric unit, she continued to be amnestic, despite all the therapeutic attempts to revive her hidden memories. She could, however, recount in detail the events of a short but troubled life. Some years earlier, her parents had separated because of her mother's flagrant promiscuity. The patient initially lived with her mother. In this situation, she was witness to her mother's many affairs and was on occasion sexually approached by her mother's male visitors. At 17, she gave birth to a boy after being jilted by the infant's father, but the change brought her little peace or security, and her life was punctuated by bitter arguments with both her father and her brother. The 2 weeks before the onset of her amnesia had been particularly quarrelsome, and the patient found herself growing increasingly disturbed. Her only source of comfort was a new boyfriend, Frank, to whom she had become deeply attached.

Despite seeing him daily, she experienced mounting anxiety, headaches, fatigue, insomnia, depression, and despair. On the day her amnesia began, she had been on her way to her doctor because of her increasingly distressing symptoms. Her last memory was of boarding a bus to reach his office.

When her amnesia had not lifted by the end of a week in the hospital, it was decided to use hypnosis to retrieve her lost memories. The patient responded readily to trance induction, and when questioned about the events covered by the amnestic interval, she was able to recount the details with a considerable show of emotion. At her doctor's office, she found to her dismay that he was unavailable. Wondering what to do, she suddenly thought of Frank and impulsively decided to visit him at his place of work. As she approached the parking lot of the factory where he was employed, she saw his car in the distance and Frank himself walking toward it to go home. She ran to catch him but in vain. He did not see her and drove off, leaving her behind in despair. Suddenly, she felt dizzy, frightened, disappointed, angry, abandoned, and confused, and, as she said, "I just gave up." Not knowing where to turn, she wandered in a daze along the street, where the police found her and took her to the hospital.

When the patient was wakened from hypnosis, she retained all the painful memories that she had recovered in the trance state, with no subsequent recurrence of the amnesia. From that point on, she had no further dissociative symptoms, and she was able to confront her emotional difficulties directly in outpatient psychotherapy. (Courtesy of John C. Nemiah, M.D.)

Table 20–4
Differential Diagnostic Considerations in Dissociative Amnesia

Dementia
Delirium
Anoxic amnesia
Cerebral infections (eg, herpes simplex affecting temporal lobes)
Cerebral neoplasms (especially limbic and frontal)
Substance-induced (eg, ethanol, sedative hypnotics, anticholinergics, steroids, lithium carbonate, β-adrenergic antagonists, pentazocine, phencyclidine, hypoglycemic agents, marijuana, hallucinogens, methyldopa)
Electroconvulsive therapy (or other strong electric shock)
Epilepsy
Metabolic disorders (eg, uremia, hypoglycemia, hypertensive encephalopathy, porphyria)
Postconcussion (posttraumatic) amnesia
Sleep-related amnesia (eg, sleepwalking disorder)
Transient global amnesia
Wernicke-Korsakoff syndrome
Postoperative amnesia
Other dissociative disorders
Posttraumatic stress disorder
Acute stress disorder
Somatoform disorders (somatization disorder, conversion disorder)
Malingering (especially when associated with criminal activity)

Differential Diagnosis

The differential diagnosis of dissociative amnesia involves a consideration of both general medical conditions and other mental disorders (Table 20–4). Clinicians should conduct a medical history, a physical examination, a laboratory workup, a psychiatric history, and a mental status examination.

Amnesia associated with dementia and delirium is usually associated with many other easily recognized cognitive symptoms. When a patient has amnesia about personal information in these conditions, the dementia or delirium is usually advanced and easily differentiated from dissociative amnesia. Especially in a case of delirium, the patient may evidence confabulation during the interview. In general, a prompt return of memory usually indicates dissociative amnesia rather than amnestic disorder due to a general medical condition.

In postconcussion amnesia, the memory disturbance follows head trauma, is often retrograde (as opposed to the anterograde disturbance of dissociative amnesia), and usually does not extend beyond 1 week. The clinical evaluation of a patient with postconcussion amnesia may reveal a history of unconsciousness, external evidence of trauma, or other evidence of a brain injury. Some researchers have hypothesized that a history of head trauma may predispose a person to a dissociative disorder. Epilepsy can lead to sudden memory impairment associated with motor and electroencephalogram (EEG) abnormalities. Patients with epilepsy are prone to seizures during periods of stress, and some researchers have hypothesized that an epileptic-like cause may be involved in the dissociative disorders. A history of an aura, head trauma, or incontinence can help clinicians recognize amnesia related to epilepsy.

Transient Global Amnesia. Transient global amnesia is an acute and transient retrograde amnesia that affects recent more than remote memories. Although patients are usually aware of the amnesia, they may still perform highly complex mental and physical acts during the 6 to 24 hours that transient global amnesia episodes usually last. Recovery from the disorder is usually complete. Transient global amnesia is most often caused by transient ischemic attacks (TIAs) that affect limbic midline brain structures. It can also be associated with migraine headaches, seizures, and intoxication with sedative-hypnotic drugs.

Transient global amnesia can be differentiated from dissociative amnesia in several ways. Transient global amnesia is associated with an anterograde amnesia during the episode; dissociative amnesia is not. Patients with transient global amnesia tend to be more upset and concerned about the symptoms than are patients with dissociative amnesia. The personal identity of a patient with dissociative amnesia is lost; that of a patient with transient global amnesia is retained. The memory loss of a patient with dissociative amnesia may be selective for certain areas and usually does not show a temporal gradient; the memory loss of a patient with transient global amnesia is generalized, and remote events are remembered better than recent events. Because of the association of transient global amnesia with vascular problems, the disorder is most common in patients in their 60s and 70s, whereas dissociative amnesia is most common in patients in their 20s to 40s, a period associated with the common psychological stressors seen in these patients.

Other Mental Disorders. Two other dissociative disorders, dissociative fugue and dissociative identity disorder, should be considered in the differential diagnosis. These disorders are distinguished on the basis of their additional symptoms.

In DSM-IV, sleepwalking disorder is classified as a parasomnia, a type of sleep disorder. Patients suffering from sleepwalking disorder behave in a strange manner that resembles the behavior of someone in a dissociative state. They exhibit an altered state of conscious awareness of their surroundings; they often have vivid hallucinatory recollections of an emotionally traumatic event in the past of which there is no memory during the usual waking state. Such patients are out of contact with the environment, appear preoccupied with a private world, and stare into space if their eyes are open. They may appear emotionally upset, speak excitedly in words and sentences that are frequently hard to understand, or engage in a pattern of seemingly meaningful activities repeated every time an episode occurs. The patient has amnesia for the sleepwalking episode once it has ended.

Although amnesia for a period of immediate past experience is found in patients with sleepwalking disorder and with localized and general amnesia, the state of consciousness during the period for which they are amnestic differs in character. Patients with sleepwalking disorder seem out of touch with the environment and appear to be dreaming. Patients with amnesia, by contrast, usually give no indication to observers that anything is amiss and seem entirely alert both before and after the amnesia occurs.

Posttraumatic stress disorder, acute stress disorder, and the somatoform disorders (especially somatization disorder and conversion disorder) should be considered in the differential diagnosis and may coexist with dissociative amnesia. The somatoform disorders may be associated with the same traumatic events that are usually seen in dissociative amnesia. Malingering, in this case a deliberate attempt to mimic amnesia, may be difficult to confirm. Any possible secondary gain, especially in regard to escaping punishment for criminal activity, should increase a clinician's suspicion, although such secondary gain does not rule out the diagnosis of dissociative amnesia.

Course and Prognosis

The symptoms of dissociative amnesia usually terminate abruptly, and recovery is generally complete with few recurrences. In some cases, especially if there is secondary gain, the condition may last a long time. Clinicians should try to restore patients' lost memories to consciousness as soon as possible; otherwise, the repressed memory may form a nucleus in the unconscious mind around which future amnestic episodes may develop.

Treatment

Interviewing may give clinicians clues to the psychologically traumatic precipitant. Intermediate- and short-acting barbiturates, such as thiopental (Pentothal) and sodium amobarbital given intravenously, and benzodiazepines may help patients recover their forgotten memories. Hypnosis can be used primarily as a means of relaxing patients enough for them to recall what has been forgotten. When a patient is placed in a somnolent state, mental inhibitions are diminished and the amnestic material emerges into consciousness and is then recalled. Once the lost memories have been retrieved, psychotherapy is generally recommended to help patients incorporate the memories into their conscious states.

DISSOCIATIVE FUGUE

The behavior of patients with dissociative fugue is more purposefully integrated with their amnesia than is that of patients with dissociative amnesia. Patients with dissociative fugue have physically traveled away from their customary homes or work situations and fail to remember important aspects of their previous identities (name, family, occupation). Such patients often, but not always, take on an entirely new identity and occupation, although the new identity is usually less complete than are the alternate personalities in dissociative identity disorder, and the old and new identities do not alternate, as they do in dissociative identity disorder.

Epidemiology

Dissociative fugue is rare and, like dissociative amnesia, occurs most often during wartime, after natural disasters, and as a result of personal crises with intense internal conflicts.

Etiology

Although heavy alcohol abuse may predispose people to dissociative fugue, the cause of the disorder is thought to be basically psychological. The essential motivating factor seems to be a desire to withdraw from emotionally painful experiences. Patients with mood disorders and certain personality disorders (such as borderline, histrionic, and schizoid personality disorders) are predisposed to develop dissociative fugue.

A variety of stressors and personal factors predispose a person to the development of dissociative fugue. The psychosocial factors include marital, financial, occupational, and war-related stressors. Other associated predisposing features include depression, suicide attempts, organic disorders (especially epilepsy), and a history of substance abuse. A history of head trauma also predisposes a person to dissociative fugue.

Diagnosis

DSM-IV requires that a person either be confused about his or her identity or assume a new identity (Table 20–5). Unlike dissociative amnesia, the diagnosis of dissociative fugue requires that the onset of the symptoms be sudden. The diagnosis is excluded if the symptoms occur only during the course of dissociative identity disorder or are the result of substance in-

Table 20–5
DSM-IV Diagnostic Criteria for Dissociative Fugue

A. The predominant disturbance is sudden, unexpected travel away from home or one's customary place of work, with inability to recall one's past.

B. Confusion about personal identity or assumption of a new identity (partial or complete).

C. The disturbance does not occur exclusively during the course of dissociative identity disorder and is not due to the direct physiological effects of a substance (eg, a drug of abuse, a medication) or a general medical condition (eg, temporal lobe epilepsy).

D. The symptoms cause clinically significant distress or impairment in social, occupational, or other important areas of functioning.

gestion or a general medical condition (such as temporal lobe epilepsy).

Clinical Features

Dissociative fugue has several typical features. Patients wander in a purposeful way, usually far from home and often for days at a time. During this period, they have complete amnesia for their past lives and associations, but, unlike patients with dissociative amnesia, they are generally unaware that they have forgotten anything. Only when they suddenly return to their former selves do they recall the time antedating the onset of fugue, but then they remain amnestic for the period of the fugue itself. Patients with dissociative fugue do not seem to others to be behaving in extraordinary ways, nor do they give evidence of acting out any specific memory of a traumatic event. On the contrary, these patients lead quiet, prosaic, reclusive existences; work at simple occupations; live modestly; and, in general, do nothing to draw attention to themselves.

Differential Diagnosis

The differential diagnosis for dissociative fugue is similar to that for dissociative amnesia (see Table 20–4). The wandering that is seen in dementia or delirium is usually distinguished from the traveling of a patient with dissociative fugue by the aimlessness of the former and the absence of complex and socially adaptive behaviors. Complex partial epilepsy may be associated with episodes of travel, but the patient does not usually assume a new identity, and the episodes are generally not precipitated by psychological stress. In dissociative amnesia, a loss of memory results from psychological stress, but there are no episodes of purposeful travel or of a new identity. Malingering may be difficult to distinguish from dissociative fugue; any evidence of a clear secondary gain should raise the clinicians' suspicions. Hypnosis and amobarbital interviews may be useful in clarifying the clinical diagnosis.

Course and Prognosis

The fugue is usually brief—hours to days. Less commonly, a fugue lasts many months and involves extensive travel covering thousands of miles. Generally, recovery is spontaneous and rapid, and recurrences are rare.

Treatment

Treatment of dissociative fugue is similar to that of dissociative amnesia. Psychiatric interviewing, drug-assisted interviewing, and hypnosis may help reveal to therapists and patients the psychological stressors that precipitated the fugue episode. Psychotherapy is generally indicated to help patients incorporate the precipitating stressors into their psyches in a healthy and integrated manner. The treatment of choice for dissociative fugue is expressive-supportive psychodynamic psychotherapy. The most widely accepted technique requires a mixture of abreaction of the past trauma and integration of the trauma into a cohesive self that no longer requires fragmentation to deal with the trauma.

DISSOCIATIVE IDENTITY DISORDER

Dissociative identity disorder is the name that DSM-IV uses for what has been commonly known as multiple personality disorder. Dissociative identity disorder is a chronic dissociative disorder, and its cause typically involves a traumatic event, usually childhood physical or sexual abuse. The concept of personality conveys the sense of an integration of the way people think, feel, and behave and the appreciation of themselves as a unitary being. People with dissociative identity disorder have two or more distinct personalities, each of which determines behavior and attitudes during any period that it is the dominant personality. Dissociative identity disorder is usually considered the most serious of the dissociative disorders, although some clinicians who diagnose a variety of patients with the disorder have suggested that there may be a wider range of severities than was previously appreciated.

History

Until about 1800, patients with dissociative identity disorder were mainly seen as suffering from various states of possession. In the early 1800s, Benjamin Rush, building on earlier clinical reports, provided a clinical description of the phenomenology of dissociative identity disorder. Subsequently, both Jean-Martin Charcot and Pierre Janet described the symptoms of the disorder and recognized the disease's dissociative nature. Both Sigmund Freud and Eugen Bleuler recognized the symptoms, although Freud attributed psychodynamic mechanisms to the symptoms and Bleuler considered the symptoms to be reflective of schizophrenia. Perhaps because of an increased appreciation of the problem of sexual and physical abuse of children and perhaps because of the cases described in the popular media *(The Three Faces of Eve, Sybil),* awareness of dissociative identity disorder increased. In 1980, with the inclusion of multiple personality disorder in the third edition of DSM (DSM-III), the stage was set for developing of a solid clinical research base of the disorder.

Epidemiology

Anecdotal and research reports about dissociative identity disorder have varied in their estimates of the prevalence of the disorder. At one extreme, some investigators believe that dissociative identity disorder is extremely rare; at the other extreme, some believe that dissociative identity disorder is vastly underrecognized. Well-controlled studies have reported that from 0.5 to 2 percent of general psychiatric hospital admissions meet the diagnostic criteria for dissociative identity disorder, as do perhaps as many as 5 percent of all psychiatric disorders. Patients who receive the diagnosis of dissociative identity disorder are overwhelmingly women—90 to 100 percent of most samples reported. Many clinicians and researchers, however, believe that men are underreported in clinical samples because, they believe, most men with the disorder enter the criminal justice system rather than the mental health system.

The disorder is most common in late adolescence and young adult life, with a mean age of diagnosis of 30 years, although patients have usually had symptoms for 5 to 10 years before the diagnosis. Several studies have found that the disorder is more common in first-degree biological relatives of people with the disorder than in the general population.

Dissociative identity disorder frequently coexists with other mental disorders, including anxiety disorders, mood disorders, somatoform disorders, sexual dysfunctions, substance-related disorders, eating disorders, sleeping disorders, and posttraumatic stress disorder. The symptoms of dissociative identity disorder are similar to those seen in borderline personality disorder, and differentiating the two disorders can be difficult. Suicide attempts are common in patients with dissociative identity disorder; some studies have reported that as many as two thirds of all patients with dissociative identity disorder attempt suicide during the course of their illness.

Etiology

The cause of dissociative identity disorder is unknown, although the histories of the patients invariably (approaching 100 percent) involve a traumatic event, most often in childhood. In general, four types of causative factors have been identified: a traumatic life event, a tendency for the disorder to develop, formulative environmental factors, and the absence of external support. The traumatic event is usually childhood physical or sexual abuse, commonly incestuous. Other traumatic events can include the death of a close relative or friend during childhood and the witnessing of a trauma or a death.

The tendency for the disorder to develop may be biologically or psychologically based. The variable ability of people to be hypnotized may be one example of a risk factor for the development of dissociative identity disorder. Epilepsy has been hypothesized to be involved in the cause of dissociative identity disorder, and a high percentage of abnormal EEG activity has been reported in some studies of affected patients. One study of regional cerebral blood flow revealed temporal hyperperfusion in one of the subpersonalities but not in the main personality. Although several studies have found differences in pain sensitivity and other physiological measures among the personalities, the use of these data as proof of the existence of dissociative identity disorder should be approached with great caution.

The formulative environmental factors involved in the pathogenesis of dissociative identity disorder are nonspecific and are likely to involve such factors as role models and the availability of other mechanisms with which to deal with stress.

In many cases, a factor in the development of dissociative identity seems to have been the absence of support from significant others, such as parents, siblings, other relatives, and nonrelated people, such as teachers.

Diagnosis

In DSM-IV, the name *dissociative identity disorder* replaces the earlier *multiple personality disorder.* As a diagnostic criterion (Table 20–6), DSM-IV requires an amnestic component, which research has found to be essential to the complete clinical picture. The diagnosis also requires the presence of at least two distinct personality states. A diagnosis of dissociative personality disorder is excluded if the symptoms are the result of a substance (such as alcohol) or of a general medical condition (such as complex partial seizures).

Clinical Features

Patients with dissociative identity disorder are often thought to have a personality disorder (commonly borderline personality disorder), schizophrenia, or a rapidly cycling bipolar disorder. Clinicians must be aware of the diagnostic category and must listen for specific suggestive features of dissociative identity disorder in the clinical interview (Table 20–7). The relative frequency of specific symptoms was reported in one study of 102 patients with dissociative identity disorder (Table 20–8).

Table 20–6
DSM-IV Diagnostic Criteria for Dissociative Identity Disorder

A. The presence of two or more distinct identities or personality states (each with its own relatively enduring pattern of perceiving, relating to, and thinking about the environment and self).

B. At least two of these identities or personality states recurrently take control of the person's behavior.

C. Inability to recall important personal information that is too extensive to be explained by ordinary forgetfulness.

D. The disturbance is not due to the direct physiological effects of a substance (eg, blackouts or chaotic behavior during alcohol intoxication) or a general medical condition (eg, complex partial seizures). **Note:** In children, the symptoms are not attributable to imaginary playmates or other fantasy play.

Reprinted with permission from American Psychiatric Association: *Diagnostic and Statistical Manual of Mental Disorders,* ed 4. Copyright, American Psychiatric Association, Washington, 1994.

Table 20–7
Signs of Multiplicity

1. Reports of time distortions, lapses, and discontinuities
2. Being told of behavioral episodes by others that are not remembered by the patient
3. Being recognized by others or called by another name by people whom the patient does not recognize
4. Notable changes in the patient's behavior reported by a reliable observer; the patient may call himself or herself by a different name or refer to himself or herself in the third person
5. Other personalities are elicited under hypnosis or during amobarbital interviews
6. Use of the word "we" in the course of an interview
7. Discovery of writings, drawings, or other productions or objects (identification cards, clothing, etc.) among the patient's personal belongings that are not recognized or cannot be accounted for
8. Headaches
9. Hearing voices originating from within and not identified as separate
10. History of severe emotional or physical trauma as a child (usually before the age of 5 years)

Reprinted with permission from Cummings JL: Dissociative states, depersonalization, multiple personality, episodic memory lapses. In *Clinical Neuropsychiatry*, JL Cummings, editor, p 122. Grune & Stratton, Orlando, 1985.

Table 20–8
Frequency of 16 Secondary Features of Dissociative Identity Disorder in 102 Patients

	Patients	
Item	No.	%
Another person existing inside	92	90.2
Voices talking	89	87.3
Voices coming from inside	84	82.4
Another person taking control	83	81.4
Amnesia for childhood	83	81.4
Referring to self as "we" or "us"	75	73.5
Person inside has a different name	72	70.6
Blank spells	69	67.7
Flashbacks	68	66.7
Being told by others of unremembered events	64	62.8
Feelings of unreality	58	56.9
Strangers know the patient	45	44.1
Noticing that objects are missing	43	42.2
Coming out of blank spell in a strange place	37	36.3
Objects are present that cannot be accounted for	32	31.4
Different handwriting styles	28	27.5

Reprinted with permission from Ross CA, Miller SD, Reagor P, Bjornson L, Fraser GA, Anderson G: Structured interview data from 102 cases of multiple personality disorder from four centers. Am J Psychiatry *147:* 596, 1990.

In spite of stories in the popular press about patients with more than 20 personalities, the median number of personalities in dissociative identity disorder is in the range of 5 to 10. Often, only two or three of the personalities are evident at diagnosis; the others are recognized during the course of treatment.

The transition from one personality to another is often sudden and dramatic. During each personality state, patients generally are amnestic about other states and the events that took place when another personality was dominant. Sometimes, however, one personality state is not bound by such amnesia and retains complete awareness of the existence, qualities, and activities of the other personalities. At other times, the personalities are aware of all or some of the others to varying degrees and may experience the others as friends, companions, or adversaries. In classic cases, each personality has a fully integrated, highly complex set of associated memories and characteristic attitudes, personal relationships, and behavior patterns. Most often, the personalities have proper names; occasionally, one or more is given the name of its function—for example, the protector. Although some clinicians have emphasized that one of the personalities tends to be dominant, this is not always the case. In fact, sometimes one personality masquerades as one of the others, but usually a host personality is the one who comes for treatment and carries the patient's legal name. This host personality is likely to be depressed or anxious, may have masochistic personality traits, and may seem overly moral.

The first appearance of the secondary personality or personalities may be spontaneous or may emerge in relation to what seems to be a precipitant (including hypnosis or a drug-assisted interview). The personalities may be of both sexes, of various races and ages, and from families different from the patient's family of origin. The most common subordinate personality is childlike. The personalities are often disparate and may even be opposites. In the same person, one of the personalities may be extroverted, even sexually promiscuous, and others may be introverted, withdrawn, and sexually inhibited.

On examination, patients frequently show nothing unusual in their mental status, other than a possible amnesia for periods of varying durations. Often, only with prolonged interviews or many contacts with a patient with dissociative identity disorder can a clinician detect the presence of multiple personalities. Sometimes, by asking a patient to keep a diary, the clinician finds the multiple personalities revealed in the diary entries. An estimated 60 percent of patients switch to alternate personalities only occasionally; another 20 percent of patients not only have rare episodes but also are adept at covering the switches.

Martha B., a 35-year-old married woman, was admitted to a hospital because she had been unable to walk for the past 6 months. Three years previously, she had joined an evangelical religious sect and had given up "partying and dancing" because "the Lord didn't like those things." Six months before admission, she had suffered a minor injury to her back in a car accident and had thereafter been confined to her bed—unable to walk and generally feeling chronically tired, sick, cold, and achy. A physical examination revealed no abnormalities whatsoever, save for a loss of all sensation in both legs from her hips down. As she commented: "My legs—there's no legs there. I don't know whether I have legs. I have to keep looking to see that they're there. There's no feeling, you know." Although she could stand with support, she could not take any steps. Otherwise, all her motor functions were intact. A diagnosis of conversion was made.

In addition to her physical symptoms, the patient complained of "hearing a terrible voice" that urged her constantly to "say and do mean things." During an interview shortly after her initial evaluation, the patient complained that the voice was particularly troublesome and threatened "to take me over completely." When the interviewer asked "Why don't you let it take over?" the patient's response was immediate and dramatic. She closed her eyes, threw back her head, clenched her fists, and rocked back and forth, appearing to be momentarily out of contact with her environment. Suddenly, she opened her eyes, looked around with a smile, and, with a brightness and alertness in her manner and tone of voice that had previously been absent, exclaimed, "We got rid of that other one who stays sick all the time!" Her name, she said, was Harriet, and she proceeded to heap scorn on Martha for her chronic physical complaints and for her righteous, pious life. "We like different things," Harriet said bitterly. "I like to go out partying and dancing, and she likes to go to church, and I don't!" When asked if she could dance, she replied, "Sure, I can dance!" and (to the surprise of the observers) stood up and walked back and forth in the office without difficulty.

Shortly thereafter, the interviewer suggested that it was time for Martha to return. After a mild protest, Harriet assented, and once again the patient appeared to lose contact with her environment as she rocked to and fro, clenched her fists, and muttered "No! No!" as if undergoing an internal struggle. On regaining consciousness, the patient remarked, "Oh, I've been asleep on you." It was evident that she had complete amnesia for the period in which Harriet had been in the ascendancy and that she had no awareness of the secondary personality she harbored inside. Furthermore, she once again had all her sensorimotor symptoms and complained in a plaintive, suffering voice, "I'm tired and cold, and my back's aching." Sick Martha had returned. (Courtesy of John C. Nemiah, M.D.)

Differential Diagnosis

The differential diagnosis includes two other dissociative disorders, dissociative amnesia and dissociative fugue. Both of those disorders, however, lack the shifts in identity and the awareness of the original identity that are seen in dissociative identity disorder. Psychotic disorders, notably schizophrenia, may be confused with dissociative identity disorder only because people with schizophrenia may be delusional and believe that they have separate identities or report hearing other personalities' voices. In schizophrenia, a formal thought disorder, chronic social deterioration, and other distinguishing signs are present. Recently, clinicians have increasingly appreciated rapidly cycling bipolar disorders, whose symptoms appear similar to those of dissociative identity disorder; interviewing, however, reveals the presence of *discrete* personalities in patients with dissociative identity disorder. Borderline personality disorder may coexist with dissociative identity disorder, but the alteration of personalities in dissociative identity disorder may be mistakenly interpreted as nothing more than the irritability of mood and self-image problems characteristic of patients with borderline personality disorder. Malingering presents a difficult diagnostic problem. Clear secondary gain raises suspicion, and drug-assisted interviews may be helpful in making the diagnosis. Among the neurological disorders to consider, complex partial epilepsy is the most likely to imitate the symptoms of dissociative identity disorder (see Table 20–4).

Course and Prognosis

Dissociative identity disorder can develop in children as young as 3 years of age. In children, the symptoms may appear trancelike and may be accompanied by depressive disorder symptoms, amnestic periods, hallucinatory voices, disavowal of behaviors, changes in abilities, and suicidal or self-injurious behaviors. Although women are more likely to have the disorder than are men, affected children are more likely to be boys than girls; the female predominance develops only in adolescence. Two symptom patterns in affected female adolescents have been observed. One pattern is that of a chaotic life with promiscuity, drug use, somatic symptoms, and suicide attempts. Such patients may be misclassified as having an impulse control disorder, schizophrenia, rapidly cycling bipolar I disorder, or histrionic or borderline personality disorder. A second pattern is characterized by withdrawal and childlike behaviors. Sometimes, these patients are misclassified as having a mood disorder, a somatoform disorder, or generalized anxiety disorder. In male adolescents with dissociative identity disorder, the symptoms may cause them to have trouble with the law or school officials, and they may eventually end up in prison.

The earlier the onset of dissociative identity disorder, the worse the prognosis. One or more of the personalities may function relatively well while others function marginally. The level of impairment ranges from moderate to severe, the determining variables being the number, the type, and the chronicity of the various personalities. The disorder is considered the most severe and chronic of the dissociative disorders, and recovery is generally incomplete. In addition, individual personalities may have their own separate mental disorders; mood disorders, personality disorders, and other dissociative disorders are the most common.

Treatment

The most efficacious approaches to dissociative identity disorder involve insight-oriented psychotherapy, often in association with hypnotherapy or drug-assisted interviewing techniques. Hypnotherapy or drug-assisted interviewing can be useful in obtaining additional history, identifying previously unrecognized personalities, and fostering abreaction. A psychotherapeutic treatment plan should begin by confirming the diagnosis and by identifying and characterizing the various personalities. If any of the personalities are inclined toward self-destructive or otherwise violent behavior, the therapist should engage the patient and the appropriate personalities in treatment contracts about these dangerous behaviors. Hospitalization may be necessary in some cases.

Several clinicians and researchers have discussed psychotherapy with dissociative identity disorder patients. A summation of the basic principles (Table 20–9) and a description of the stages of therapy (Table 20–10) are useful guides in the difficult therapy for these patients. The initial therapy stage usually fosters communication between the personalities to begin reintegration and to help patients control their overall behavior. The relative benefits of reintegration versus resolution continue to be disputed, and the relative benefits of each approach are not known. Communication among the personalities also helps patients control their overall behavior. Clinicians must attempt to identify the personalities who remember the traumatic childhood events almost invariably associated with the disorder.

The use of antipsychotic medications in the patients is almost never indicated. Some data indicate that antidepressants and antianxiety medications may be useful as adjuvants to psychotherapy. A few uncontrolled studies report that anticonvulsant medications such as carbamazepine (Tegretol) help selected patients.

DEPERSONALIZATION DISORDER

DSM-IV characterizes depersonalization disorder as a persistent or recurrent alteration in the perception of the self to the extent that a person's sense of his or her own reality is temporarily lost. Patients with depersonalization disorder may feel that they are mechanical, in a dream, or detached from their bodies. The episodes are ego-dystonic, and the patients realize the unreality of the symptoms.

Some clinicians distinguish between depersonalization and derealization. *Depersonalization* is the feeling that the body or the personal self is strange and unreal; *derealization* is the perception of objects in the external world as being strange and unreal. The distinction provides a more accurate description of each phenomenon than is achieved by grouping them together under the rubric of depersonalization.

Epidemiology

As an occasional isolated experience in the lives of many people, depersonalization is a common phenomenon and is not necessarily pathological. Studies indicate that transient depersonalization may occur in as many as 70 percent of a given population, with no significant difference between men and women. Children frequently experience depersonalization as they develop the capacity for self-awareness, and adults often undergo a temporary sense of unreality when they travel to new and strange places.

Information about the epidemiology of pathological depersonalization is scanty. In a few recent studies, depersonalization was found to occur in women at least twice as frequently as in men; it is rarely found in people over 40 years of age.

Etiology

Depersonalization may be caused by psychological, neurological, or systemic disease. Systemic causes include endo-

Table 20–9
Principles of Successful Therapy for Dissociative Identity Disorder

- Condition was created by broken boundaries. Therefore, a successful treatment has a secure treatment frame and firm, consistent boundaries.
- Condition is one of subjective dyscontrol and passively endured assaults and changes. Therefore, the focus must be on mastery and the patient's active participation in the treatment process.
- Condition is one of involuntariness. Its sufferers did not elect to be traumatized and find their symptoms are often beyond their control. Therefore, the therapy must be based on a strong therapeutic alliance, and efforts to establish that alliance must be undertaken throughout the process.
- Condition is one of buried traumata and sequestered affect. Therefore, what has been hidden away must be uncovered, and what feeling has been buried must be abreacted.
- Condition is one of perceived separateness and conflict among the alters. Therefore, the therapy must emphasize their collaboration, cooperation, empathy, and identification with one another so that their separateness becomes redundant and their conflicts are muted.
- Condition is one of hypnotic alternate realities. Therefore, the therapist's communication must be clear and straight. There is no room for confusing communication.
- Condition is related to the inconsistency of important others. Therefore, the therapist must be evenhanded with all the alters, avoiding playing favorites or dramatically altering his or her own behavior toward the various personalities. The therapist's consistency across all the alters is one of the most powerful assaults on the patient's dissociative defenses.
- Condition is one of shattered security, self-esteem, and future orientation. Therefore, the therapist must make efforts to restore morale and inculcate realistic hope.
- Condition stems from overwhelming experiences. Therefore, the pacing of the therapy is essential. Most treatment failures occur when the pace of the therapy outstrips the patient's capacity to tolerate the material under discussion. It is wise to adhere to the rule of thirds: if one cannot get into the difficult material one planned to address in the first third of the session, to work on it in the second, and process it and restablize the patient in the third, not approaching the material, lest the patient leave the session in an overwhelmed state. Abreaction cannot be allowed to become retraumatization.
- Condition often results from the irresponsibility of others. Therefore, the therapist must be responsible and hold the patient to a high standard of responsibility once the therapist is confident that the patient, across alters, actually grasps what reasonable responsibility entails.
- Condition often results because people who could have protected a child did nothing. The therapist can anticipate that technical neutrality will be interpreted as uncaring and rejecting and is best served by taking a warm stance that allows for a latitude of affective expression.
- Patient has many cognitive errors. The therapy must address and correct them on an ongoing basis.

Adapted from Kluft RP: Multiple personality disorder. In *American Psychiatric Association Review of Psychiatry,* vol 10, A Tasman, SM Goldfinger, editors, p 161. American Psychiatric Press, Washington, 1991.

Table 20–10
Stages of Therapy for Dissociative Identity Disorder

1. Establishing the psychotherapy involves the creation of an atmosphere of safety in which the diagnosis can be made, the security of the treatment frame can be assured, the patient begins to understand the concept of the treatment alliance in a preliminary way, the nature of the treatment is introduced to the patient, and sufficient hope and confidence are established so that the patient feels prepared to begin what may be a long and difficult process.
2. Preliminary interventions involve gaining access to the most readily reached personalities; establishing agreements or contracts with the alters against terminating treatment abruptly, self-harm, suicide, and as many other dysfunctional behaviors as the patient is able to agree to curtail; fostering communication and cooperation among the alters (a process that is the core of the treatment from here on); expanding the therapeutic alliance by gaining the patient's acceptance of the diagnosis across increasing numbers of the personalities (some deny it to the end); and offering what symptomatic relief is possible. Hypnosis may play a valuable role in facilitating those measures.
3. History gathering and mapping lead to learning more about the personalities, their origins, and their relationships with one another. The patient may be regarded as a system with its own rules of interaction. Here one learns the who, when, why, where, what, and how of the alters; their names (if any); age of onset and self-perceived age; the reasons for their creation and persistence; where they fit in the patient's overall history and in their relationships within the world of the personalities; and their particular problems, functions, and concerns. On that basis, one begins to work with their individual and interactional issues and presses for still more cooperation and collaboration.
4. Metabolism of the trauma refers to the often strenuous efforts needed to access and process the overwhelming events associated with the origins of the disorder. Such work should not be undertaken until one has some idea of the lay of the land in terms of the patient's system of personalities and at least some intellectual insight into what material is likely to be encountered. Negative therapeutic reactions are common. Precipitous or premature entry into this stage before stages 1 through 3 are achieved is a frequent cause of unnecessary crises and interruptions of therapy.
5. Moving toward integration-resolution involves the working through of recovered materials across the alters and facilitating still further cooperation, communication, and mutual awareness with enhanced mutual identification and empathy. Communication is increased, many internal conflicts become muted or resolved, and the alters begin to show some blurring of their once discrete characteristics. Some experience identity diffusion (for example, "for a moment I wasn't sure who I was"; "I guess I am both Sally and Joanie").
6. Integration-resolution consists of the patient's coming to a new and more solid stance toward his or her self and the world. A smooth collaboration among the alters constitutes a resolution; their blending into a unity is an integration.
7. Learning new coping skills is important. The patient may have to face for the first time perspectives on his or her life that were not appreciable before and be helped to negotiate the circumstances that once were handled in a dissociative manner in constructive ways. Many important life decisions and relationships may require renegotiation.
8. Solidification of gains and working through may require as much therapy as reaching integration or resolution. The patient has to relearn how to live in the world. Often working through in the transference what has been learned about the past is valuable. Characterological issues that were inaccessible before or hidden behind a welter of symptoms must be addressed. Often extensive coaching on the management of relationships and intercurrent traumata is necessary.
9. Follow-up is advisable on several grounds. The stability of the outcome should be assessed, especially for those who opt for resolution rather than integration. Also, layers of personalities that had not entered the prior treatment may be encountered, and some apparent good results are flights into health.

Adapted from Kluft RP: Multiple personality disorder. In *American Psychiatric Association Review of Psychiatry,* vol 10, A Tasman, SM Goldfinger, editors, p 161. American Psychiatric Press, Washington, 1991.

crine disorders of the thyroid and the pancreas. Experiences of depersonalization have been associated with epilepsy, brain tumors, sensory deprivation, and emotional trauma, and depersonalization phenomena have been caused by electrical stimulation of the cortex of the temporal lobes during neurosurgery. Depersonalization is associated with an array of substances, including alcohol, barbiturates, benzodiazepines, scopolamine, β-adrenergic antagonists, marijuana, and virtually any phencyclidine (PCP)-like or hallucinogenic substance. Anxiety and depression are predisposing factors, as is severe stress experienced, for example, in combat or in an automobile accident. Depersonalization is a symptom frequently associated with anxiety disorders, depressive disorders, and schizophrenia.

Diagnosis

The DSM-IV diagnostic criteria for depersonalization disorder (Table 20–11) require persistent or recurrent episodes of depersonalization that result in significant distress to patients or in an impairment in their ability to function in social, occupational, or interpersonal relationships. The disorder is

Table 20–11
DSM-IV Diagnostic Criteria for Depersonalization Disorder

A. Persistent or recurrent experiences of feeling detached from, and as if one is an outside observer of, one's mental processes or body (eg, feeling like one is in a dream).
B. During the depersonalizing experience, reality testing remains intact.
C. The depersonalization causes clinically significant distress or impairment in social, occupational, or other important areas of functioning.
D. The depersonalization experience does not occur exclusively during the course of another mental disorder, such as schizophrenia, panic disorder, acute stress disorder, or another dissociative disorder, and is not due to the direct physiological effects of a substance (eg, a drug of abuse, a medication) or a general medical condition (eg, temporal lobe epilepsy).

Reprinted with permission from American Psychiatric Association: *Diagnostic and Statistical Manual of Mental Disorders,* ed 4. Copyright, American Psychiatric Association, Washington, 1994.

largely differentiated from psychotic disorders by the diagnostic requirement that reality testing remains intact in depersonalization disorder. The disorder cannot be diagnosed if the symptoms are better accounted for by another mental disorder, substance ingestion, or general medical condition.

Clinical Features

The central characteristic of depersonalization is the quality of unreality and estrangement. Inner mental processes and external events seem to go on exactly as before, but they feel different and no longer appear to have any relation or significance to the person. Parts of the body or the entire physical being may seem foreign, as may mental operations and accustomed behavior. Particularly common is the sensation of a change in the patient's body; for instance, patients may feel that their extremities are bigger or smaller than usual. Hemidepersonalization, the patient's feeling that half of the body is unreal or does not exist, may be related to contralateral parietal lobe disease. Anxiety often accompanies the disorder, and many patients complain of distortions in their senses of time and space.

An occasional phenomenon is doubling; patients feel that the point of consciousness is outside their bodies, often a few feet overhead; from there they observe themselves, as if they were totally separate people. Sometimes, patients believe that they are in two places at the same time, a condition known as reduplicative paramnesia or double orientation. Most patients are aware of the disturbances in their sense of reality; this awareness is considered one of the salient characteristics of the disorder.

Differential Diagnosis

Depersonalization may occur as a symptom in numerous other disorders (Table 20–12). The common occurrence of depersonalization in patients with depressive disorders and schizophrenia should alert clinicians to the possibility that a patient who initially complains of feelings of unreality and estrangement is suffering from one of these more common disorders. A history and the mental status examination should in most cases disclose the characteristic features of depressive disorders and schizophrenia. Because psychotomimetic drugs often induce long-lasting changes in the experience of the reality of the self and the environment, clinicians must inquire about the use of such substances. The presence of other clinical phenomena in patients complaining of a sense of unreality should usually take precedence in determining the diagnosis. In general, the diagnosis of depersonalization disorder is reserved for those conditions in which depersonalization constitutes the predominating symptom.

The fact that depersonalization phenomena may result from gross disturbances in brain function underlies the necessity for a neurological evaluation, especially when the depersonalization is not accompanied by common and obvious psychiatric symptoms. In particular, the possibility of a brain tumor or epilepsy should be considered. The experience of depersonalization may be the earliest presenting symptom of a neurological disorder.

Table 20–12
Causes of Depersonalization

Neurological disorders	Idiopathic mental disorders
Epilepsy	Schizophrenia
Migraine	Depressive disorders
Brain tumors	Manic episodes
Cerebrovascular disease	Conversion disorder
Cerebral trauma	Anxiety disorders
Encephalitis	Obsessive-compulsive disorder
General paresis	Personality disorders
Dementia of the Alzheimer's type	Phobic-anxiety depersonalization syndrome
Huntington's disease	In normal persons
Spinocerebellar degeneration	Exhaustion
Toxic and metabolic disorders	Boredom; sensory deprivation
Hypoglycemia	Emotional shock
Hypoparathyroidism	In hemidepersonalization
Carbon monoxide poisoning	Lateralized (usually right parietal) focal brain lesion
Mescaline intoxication	
Botulism	
Hyperventilation	
Hypothyroidism	

Adapted from Cummings JL: Dissociative states, depersonalization, multiple personality, episodic memory lapses. In *Clinical Neuropsychiatry,* JL Cummings, editor, p 123. Grune & Stratton, Orlando, 1985.

Course and Prognosis

In most patients, the symptoms of depersonalization disorder first appear suddenly; only a few patients report a gradual onset. The disorder starts most often between the ages of 15 and 30 years, but it has been seen in patients as young as 10 years of age; it occurs less frequently after age 30 and almost never in the late decades of life. A few follow-up studies indicate that, in more than 50 percent of cases, depersonalization tends to be a long-lasting condition. In many patients, the symptoms run a steady course without any significant fluctuation of intensity, or the symptoms may occur episodically, interspersed with symptom-free intervals. Little is known about precipitating factors, although the disorder has been observed to begin during a period of relaxation after a person has experienced fatiguing psychological stress. The disorder is sometimes ushered in by an attack of acute anxiety frequently accompanied by hyperventilation.

Treatment

Little attention has been given to the treatment of patients with depersonalization disorder. At this time, data on which a specific pharmacological treatment may be based are insufficient, but the anxiety usually responds to antianxiety agents. An underlying disorder (for example, schizophrenia) can also be treated pharmacologically. Psychotherapeutic approaches are equally untested. As with all patients with neurotic symptoms, the decision to use psychoanalysis or insight-oriented psychotherapy is determined not by the presence of the symptom itself but by a variety of positive indications derived from an assessment of the patient's personality, human relationships, and life situation.

Table 20–13
DSM-IV Diagnostic Criteria for Dissociative Disorder Not Otherwise Specified

This category is included for disorders in which the predominant feature is a dissociative symptom (ie, a disruption in the usually integrated functions of consciousness, memory, identity, or perception of the environment) that does not meet the criteria for any specific dissociative disorder. Examples include:

1. Clinical presentations similar to dissociative identity disorder that fail to meet full criteria for this disorder. Examples include presentations in which (a) there are not two or more distinct personality states, or (b) amnesia for important personal information does not occur.
2. Derealization unaccompanied by depersonalization in adults.
3. States of dissociation that occur in individuals who have been subjected to periods of prolonged and intense coercive persuasion (eg, brainwashing, thought reform, or indoctrination while captive).
4. Dissociative trance disorder: single or episodic disturbances in the state of consciousness, identity, or memory that are indigenous to particular locations and cultures. Dissociative trance involves narrowing of awareness of immediate surroundings or stereotyped behaviors or movements that are experienced as being beyond one's control. Possession trance involves replacement of the customary sense of personal identity by a new identity, attributed to the influence of a spirit, power, deity, or other person, and associated with stereotyped "involuntary" movements or amnesia. Examples include *amok* (Indonesia), *bebainan* (Indonesia), *latab* (Malaysia), *pibloktoq* (Arctic), *ataque de nervios* (Latin America), and possession (India). The dissociative or trance disorder is not a normal part of a broadly accepted collective cultural or religious practice.
5. Loss of consciousness, stupor, or coma not attributable to a general medical condition.
6. Ganser syndrome: the giving of approximate answers to questions (eg, "2 plus 2 equals 5") when not associated with dissociative amnesia or dissociative fugue.

Reprinted with permission from American Psychiatric Association: *Diagnostic and Statistical Manual of Mental Disorders,* ed 4. Copyright, American Psychiatric Association, Washington, 1994.

DISSOCIATIVE DISORDER NOT OTHERWISE SPECIFIED

The diagnosis of dissociative disorder not otherwise specified is applied to disorders with dissociative features that do not meet the diagnostic criteria for dissociative amnesia, dissociative fugue, dissociative identity disorder, or depersonalization disorder. The DSM-IV examples of dissociative disorder not otherwise specified (Table 20–13) take into account changes in the diagnostic criteria for the other dissociative disorders. Specifically, example 1 (see Table 20–13) describes patients who do not meet the diagnostic criteria for dissociative identity disorder because the second personality is not sufficiently distinct or because the patient has no amnestic period. According to DSM-IV, derealization in the absence of depersonalization is an example of dissociative disorder not otherwise specified.

Dissociative Trance Disorder

DSM-IV adds, as an example of dissociative disorder not otherwise specified, patients with single or episodic alterations in consciousness that are limited to particular locations or cultures. The example states that the "dissociative or trance disorder is not a normal part of a broadly accepted collective cultural or religious practice." DSM-IV includes in its appendixes a suggested set of diagnostic criteria for dissociative trance disorder (Table 20–14). The disorder is similar to the diagnosis of trance and possession disorder in ICD-10. The DSM-IV diagnostic criteria require that the symptoms cause a patient significant distress or an impairment in the ability to function.

Trance states are altered states of consciousness, and patients exhibit diminished responsivity to environmental stimuli. Children may have repeated amnestic periods or trancelike states after physical abuse or trauma. Possession and trance states are curious and imperfectly understood forms of dissociation. Apparently, trance states commonly appear in mediums who preside over seances. Mediums typically enter a dissociative state, during which a person from the so-called spirit world takes over much of the mediums' conscious awareness and influences their thoughts and speech.

Table 20–14
DSM-IV Research Criteria for Dissociative Trance Disorder

A. Either (1) or (2):
   (1) trance, ie, temporary marked alteration in the state of consciousness or loss of customary sense of personal identity without replacement by an alternate identity, associated with at least one of the following:
      (a) narrowing of awareness of immediate surroundings, or unusually narrow and selective focusing on environmental stimuli
      (b) stereotyped behaviors or movements that are experienced as being beyond one's control
   (2) possession trance, a single or episodic alteration in the state of consciousness characterized by the replacement of customary sense of personal identity by a new identity. This is attributed to the influence of a spirit, power, deity, or other person, as evidenced by one (or more) of the following:
      (a) stereotyped and culturally determined behaviors or movements that are experienced as being controlled by the possessing agent
      (b) full or partial amnesia for the event

B. The trance or possession trance state is not accepted as a normal part of a collective cultural or religious practice.

C. The trance or possession trance state causes clinically significant distress or impairment in social, occupational, or other important areas of functioning.

D. The trance or possession trance state does not occur exclusively during the course of a psychotic disorder (including mood disorder with psychotic features and brief psychotic disorder) or dissociative identity disorder and is not due to the direct physiological effects of a substance or a general medical condition.

Reprinted with permission from American Psychiatric Association: *Diagnostic and Statistical Manual of Mental Disorders,* ed 4. Copyright, American Psychiatric Association, Washington, 1994.

Automatic writing and crystal gazing are less common manifestations of possession or trance states. In automatic writing, the dissociation affects only the arm and the hand that write the message, which often discloses mental contents of which the writer was unaware. Crystal gazing results in a trance state in which visual hallucinations are prominent.

Phenomena related to trance states include highway hypnosis and similar mental states experienced by airplane pilots. The monotony of moving at high speeds through environments that provide little in the way of distractions to the operator of the vehicle leads to a fixation on a single object, for example, a dial on the instrument panel or the never-ending horizon of a road running straight ahead for miles. When trancelike state of consciousness results, visual hallucinations may occur, and the danger of a serious accident is always present. Possibly in the same category are the hallucinations and dissociated mental states of patients who have been confined to respirators for long periods without adequate environmental distractions.

The religions of many cultures recognize that the practice of concentration may lead to a variety of dissociative phenomena, such as hallucinations, paralyses, and other sensory disturbances. On occasion, hypnosis may precipitate a self-limited but sometimes prolonged trance state.

A happily married, cheerful businessman, Achille was entirely well until, at the age of 33, his wife noted a striking change in his personality after he returned home from a lengthy business trip. In contrast to his previous demeanor, he was depressed, withdrawn, and uncommunicative. He became increasingly agitated, began to worry that he had a variety of serious bodily illnesses, and finally took to his bed, where he lapsed into a state of apparent unconsciousness so extreme that his family thought he was dying. Suddenly, however, he awoke from that state to exhibit a new pattern of behavior. He was alert and in contact with his surroundings, but he insisted that he was possessed by the Devil, who caused him to utter terrible blasphemies.

From that point on, Achille alternated between two states of consciousness. In one, he entered a trancelike phase in which he appeared to hallucinate and, with great terror, cried out that he was surrounded by the Devil and a host of leering demons, who threatened him with horrible tortures and forced him to curse God and the saints. In the other state, he was subdued and in contact with his family but remained convinced that he was possessed by the Devil, who impelled him from within to utter sacrilegious blasphemies. In that state, Achille had no recollection of the events that had occurred during his business trip or of the early stages of his illness. Pierre Janet gave a graphic description of Achille's behavior in one of the second states: "This poor man, small in stature, with haggard eyes and pitiful appearance murmured blasphemies in a muffled, sober voice. 'Cursed be God,' he would say. 'Damn the Trinity and damn the Virgin.' Then in a shriller voice, with tears in his eyes: 'It's not my fault if my voice utters these horrors. It's not me! It's not me! I tighten my lips so that the words won't escape them and be spoken aloud, but it does no good. The Devil speaks these words inside of me. I can clearly hear him speak them and make my tongue move despite me.'"

Undaunted by the power of his diabolical adversary, Janet induced in Achille a hypnotic trance, during which he recovered the memories of the business trip and its immediate sequelae, for which Achille was amnestic. In a brief moment of indiscretion during the trip, Achille had been unfaithful to his wife, a lapse for which, as Janet commented, "he was cruelly punished." On his return home, Achille was suddenly overcome with remorse for his infidelity and was seized by a fear that, if he talked, he would reveal his peccadillo to his wife—hence his withdrawal into uncommunicative isolation. His guilt became worse with the passing days. He began to have vivid dreams that he had died and was surrounded by a host of demons in hell. Those were initially nightmares but then merged into daytime dissociative trance states in which he vividly hallucinated hellfire and a satanic crew of tormentors. The episodes, as noted earlier, developed into a pattern of alternation with more normal states of consciousness, in which he was in contact with his surroundings but was amnesic for the precipitating events and was convinced that he was possessed by the Devil.

Armed with those new facts, Janet was able to use hypnotic suggestion to allay the patient's anxious guilt with the subsequent relief of all his symptoms—a successful therapeutic result that, as Janet reported 8 years later, had been fully maintained. (Courtesy of John C. Nemiah, M.D.)

Recovered Memory Syndrome

Under hypnosis or during psychotherapy, the patient may recover a memory of a painful experience or conflict—particularly of sexual or physical abuse—that is etiologically significant. When the repressed material is brought back to consciousness, the person not only may recall the experience but may relive it accompanied by the appropriate affective response (a process called *abreaction*). If the event recalled never really happened but the person believes it to be true and reacts accordingly, it is known as *false memory syndrome.*

The recovered memory syndrome has been surrounded by controversy because victims of past abuse have sued perpetrators, many of whom have been convicted upon the recovered memory as the only evidence. Problems arise because memory is subject to distortion, retrospective falsification that may also be influenced by the therapist. In children, the recovery of memories of abuse are often obtained by overzealous prosecuting attorneys or by so-called "recovered memory experts," some of whom have no qualifications whatsoever. Such measures are often contaminated by the suggestibility of children and the prejudices of their adult interrogators.

Thomas E. Gutheil describes memory as a slender reed—insufficiently strong to bear the weight of a court case. Even if the memory of abuse is real, the perpetrator is not the present person, but the person of the past. Gutheil does not believe that litigation usually serves the patient's psychological goals. Clinical attention should probably be directed toward helping patients cast aside the limiting restrictive role of victim and transcend their past traumas, work through them, and get on with their lives.

Ganser's Syndrome

Ganser's syndrome is the voluntary production of severe psychiatric symptoms, sometimes described as the giving of approximate answers or talking past the point (for example, when asked to multiply *4* times *5*, the patient answers *21*). The syndrome may occur in people with other mental disorders, such as schizophrenia, depressive disorders, toxic states, paresis, alcohol use disorders, and factitious disorder. The psychological symptoms generally represent the patient's sense of mental illness rather than any recognized diagnostic category. The syndrome is commonly associated with dissociative phenomena such as amnesia, fugue, perceptual disturbances, and conversion symptoms. Ganser's syndrome is apparently most common in men and in prisoners, although prevalence data and familial patterns are not established. A major predisposing factor is the existence of a severe personality disorder. The differential diagnosis may be extremely difficult. Unless a patient is able to admit the factitious nature of the presenting symptoms or unless conclusive evidence from objective psychological tests indicates that the symptoms are false, clinicians may be unable to determine whether the patient has a true disorder. The syndrome may be recognized by its pansymptomatic nature or by the fact that the symptoms are often worse when patients believe they are being watched. Recovery from the syndrome is sudden; patients claim amnesia for the events. Ganser's syndrome was previously classified as a factitious disorder.

Dissociated States

Certain degrees of dissociation may occur in people subjected to periods of prolonged and intensive coercive persuasion (such as brainwashing, thought reform, and indoctrination while being held captive by terrorists or cultists). Whether the states are truly dissociative disorders is open to question; some evidence, especially in survivors of Nazi concentration camps, indicates that the people are often alexithymic as a result of massive regression rather than of dissociation.

References

Boon S, Draijer N: Multiple personality disorder in The Netherlands: A clinical investigation of 71 patients. Am J Psychiatry *150:* 489, 1993.

Brna TG Jr, Wilson CC: Psychogenic amnesia. Am Fam Physician *41:* 229, 1990.

Ellason JW, Ross CA: Two-year follow-up of inpatients with dissociative identity disorder. Am J Psychiatry *154:* 832, 1997.

Fleisher WP, Anderson G: Dissociative disorders in adolescence. Adolesc Psychiatry *20:* 203, 1995.

Gabbard GO: *Psychodynamic Psychiatry in Clinical Practice: The DSM-IV Edition.* American Psychiatric Press, Washington, 1994.

Hollander E, Liebowitz MR, DeCaria C, Fairbanks J, Fallon B, Klein DF: Treatment of depersonalization with serotonin reuptake blockers. J Clin Psychopharmacol *10:* 200, 1990.

Kapur N: Amnesia in relation to fugue states: Distinguishing a neurological form from a psychogenic basis. Br J Psychiatry *159:* 872, 1991.

Loewenstein RJ: Multiple personality disorder. Psychiatr Clin North Am *14* (3): 489, 1991.

Merskey H: The manufacture of personalities: The production of multiple personality disorder. Br J Psychiatry *160:* 327, 1992.

Nemiah JC: Dissociative disorders. In *Comprehensive Textbook of Psychiatry,* ed 6, HI Kaplan, BJ Sadock, editors, vol 2, p 1281. Williams & Wilkins, 1995.

Putnam PW, Loewenstein RJ: Treatment of multiple personality disorder: A survey of current practices. Am J Psychiatry *150:* 1048, 1993.

Ross CA, Anderson G, Fleischer WP, Norton GR: The frequency of multiple personality disorder among psychiatric inpatients. Am J Psychiatry *148:* 1717, 1991.

Ross CA, Miller SD, Reagor P, Bjornson L, Fraser GA, Anderson G: Structured interview data on 102 cases of multiple personality disorder from four centers. Am J Psychiatry *147:* 596, 1990.

Rossini ED, Schwartz DR, Braun BG: Intellectual functioning of inpatients with dissociative identity disorder and dissociative disorder not otherwise specified. J Nerv Ment Dis *184:* 289, 1996.

Rowan AJ, Soenbaum DH: Ictal amnesia and fugue states. Adv Neurol *55:* 357, 1991.

Sandberg DA, Lynn SJ: Dissociative experiences, psychopathology and adjustment, and child and adolescent maltreatment in female college students. J Abnorm Psychol *101:* 717, 1992.

Saxe GN, van der Kolk BA, Berkowitz R, Chinman G, Hall K, Lieberg G, Schwartz J: Dissociative disorders in psychiatric inpatients. Am J Psychiatry *150:* 1037, 1993.

Simeon D, Hollander E: Depersonalization disorder. Psychiatr Ann *23:* 382, 1993.

Spiegel D, editor: Dissociative disorders. In *American Psychiatric Press Review of Psychiatry,* vol 10, A Tasman, SM Goldfinger, editors, p 141. American Psychiatric Press, Washington, 1991.

Steinberg M: *Handbook for the Assessment of Dissociation: A Clinical Guide.* American Psychiatric Press, Washington, 1995.

Steinberg M, Rounsaville B, Cicchetti D: Detection of dissociative disorder in psychiatric patients by screening instrument and a structured diagnostic interview. Am J Psychiatry *48:* 1050, 1991.

Torch EM: The psychotherapeutic treatment of depersonalization disorder. Hillside J Clin Psychiatry *9:* 133, 1987.

21 Human Sexuality

▲ 21.1 Normal Sexuality

Normal sexuality is difficult to define. It is easier to define abnormal sexuality—sexual behavior that is destructive to a person or people, cannot be directed toward a partner, excludes stimulation of the primary sex organs, is inappropriately associated with guilt and anxiety, or is compulsive. In some contexts, sex outside marriage, masturbation, and various forms of sexual stimulation involving other than the primary sexual organs may fall within normal limits.

Sexual behavior is diverse and determined by a complex interaction of factors. It is affected by relationships with others, by life circumstances, and by the culture in which a person lives. Humans, like other animals, have always been interested in sexuality and have depicted almost every form of sexual behavior. During the Renaissance, Leonardo da Vinci created an anatomical study of human intercourse, which is shown in Figure 21.1–1. Sexuality is enmeshed with other personality factors, with biological makeup, and with a general sense of self. It includes the perception of being male or female and reflects developmental experiences with sex throughout life.

PSYCHOSEXUALITY

Sexuality and total personality are so entwined that to speak of sexuality as a separate entity is virtually impossible. The term *psychosexual* is therefore used to describe personality development and functioning as these are affected by sexuality. The term *psychosexual* applies to more than sexual feelings and behavior, and it is not synonymous with *libido* in the broad freudian sense.

Sigmund Freud's generalization that all pleasurable impulses and activities are originally sexual has given laypeople a somewhat distorted view of sexual concepts and has presented psychiatrists a confused picture of motivation. For example, some oral activities are directed toward obtaining food, and others are directed toward achieving sexual gratification. Both activities are pleasure seeking and use the same organs, but they are not, as Freud contended, both necessarily sexual. Labeling all pleasure-seeking behaviors *sexual* makes it impossible to specify precise motivations. People may also use sexual activities for gratification of nonsexual needs, such as dependency, aggression, power, and status. Although sexual and nonsexual impulses may jointly motivate behavior, the analysis of behavior depends on understanding the underlying individual motivations and their interactions.

SEXUAL LEARNING IN CHILDHOOD

Before Freud described the effects of childhood experiences on adults' personalities, the universality of sexual activity and sexual learning in children was unrecognized. Most sexual learning experiences in childhood occur without the parents' knowledge, but awareness of a child's sex does influence parental behavior. Male infants, for instance, tend to be handled more vigorously and female infants to be cuddled more. Fathers spend more time with their infant sons than with their daughters, and they also tend to be more aware of their sons' adolescent concerns than of their daughters' anxieties. Boys are more likely than are girls to be physically disciplined. A child's sex affects parental tolerance for aggression and reinforcement or extinction of activity and of intellectual, aesthetic, and athletic interests.

Observation of children reveals that genital play in infants is part of normal development. According to Harry Harlow, interaction with mothers and peers is necessary for the development of effective adult sexual behavior in monkeys, a finding that has relevance to the normal socialization of children. During a critical period in development, infants are especially susceptible to certain stimuli; later they may be immune to these stimuli. The detailed relation of critical periods to psychosexual development has yet to be established; Freud's stages of psychosexual development—oral, anal, phallic, latent, and genital—presumably provide a broad framework.

PSYCHOSEXUAL FACTORS

Sexuality depends on four interrelated psychosexual factors: sexual identity, gender identity, sexual orientation, and sexual behavior. These factors affect personality growth, development, and functioning. Sexuality is something more than physical sex, coital or noncoital, and something less than all behaviors directed toward attaining pleasure.

Sexual Identity and Gender Identity

Sexual identity is the pattern of a person's biological sexual characteristics: chromosomes, external genitalia, internal genitalia, hormonal composition, gonads, and secondary sex characteristics. In normal development, these characteristics form

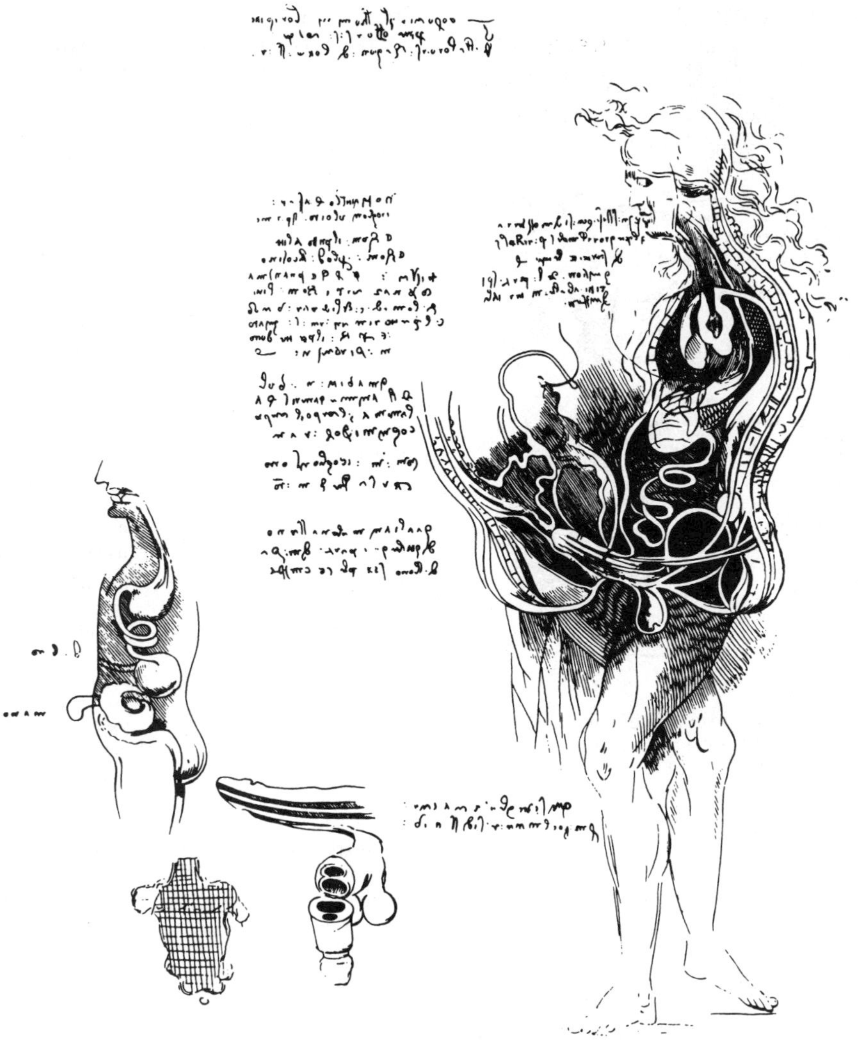

FIGURE 21.1–1
Leonardo da Vinci's anatomical drawing of human intercourse. (Courtesy of Bettmann Archive.)

a cohesive pattern that leaves a person in no doubt about his or her sex. Gender identity is a person's sense of maleness or femaleness.

Sexual Identity. Modern embryological studies have shown that all mammalian embryos, whether genetically male (XY genotype) or genetically female (XX genotype) are anatomically female during the early stages of fetal life. Differentiation of the male from the female results from the action of fetal androgens; the action begins about the sixth week of embryonic life and is completed by the end of the third month (Fig. 21.1–2). Recent studies have explained the effects of fetal hormones on the masculinization or feminization of the brain. In animals, prenatal hormonal stimulation of the brain is necessary for male and female reproductive and copulatory behavior. The fetus is also vulnerable to exogenously administered androgens during that period. For instance, if a pregnant woman receives sufficient exogenous androgens, her female fetus possessing ovaries can develop external genitalia resembling those of a male (Table 21.1–1).

Gender Identity. By the age of 2 to 3 years, almost everyone has a firm conviction that "I am male" or "I am female." Yet even if maleness and femaleness develop normally, people must still develop a sense of masculinity or femininity.

Gender identity, according to Robert Stoller, "connotes psychological aspects of behavior related to masculinity and femininity." He considers gender social and sex biological: "Most often the two are relatively congruent, that is, males tend to be manly and females womanly." But sex and gender may develop in conflicting or even opposite ways. Gender identity results from an almost infinite series of cues derived from experiences with family members, teachers, friends, and coworkers and from cultural phenomena. Physical characteristics derived from a person's biological sex—such as phy-

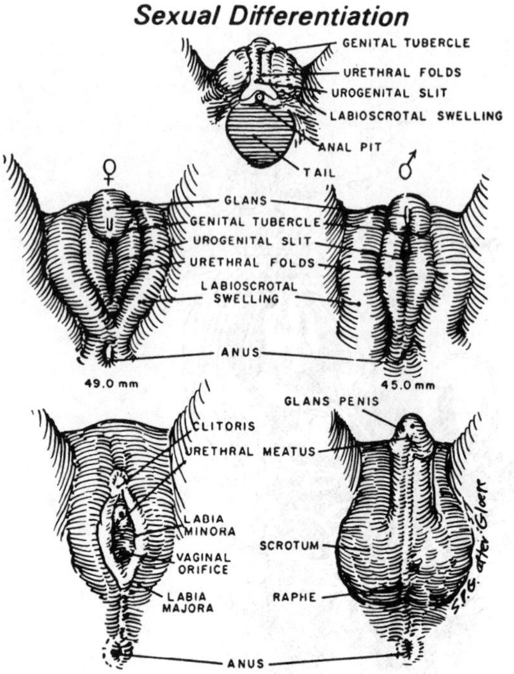
Sexual Differentiation
GENITAL TUBERCLE
URETHRAL FOLDS
UROGENITAL SLIT
LABIOSCROTAL SWELLING
ANAL PIT
TAIL
♀
♂
GLANS
GENITAL TUBERCLE
UROGENITAL SLIT
URETHRAL FOLDS
LABIOSCROTAL SWELLING
ANUS
49.0 mm
45.0 mm
GLANS PENIS
CLITORIS
URETHRAL MEATUS
LABIA MINORA
SCROTUM
VAGINAL ORIFICE
LABIA MAJORA
RAPHE
ANUS

FIGURE 21.1–2

Differentiation of male and female external genitalia from indifferent primordia. Male differentiation occurs only in the presence of androgenic stimulation during the first 12 weeks of fetal life. (Redrawn from Van Wyk and Grumbach, 1968; reprinted with permission from Brobeck JR, editor: *Best & Taylor's Physiological Basis of Medical Practice,* ed 9. Williams & Wilkins, Baltimore, 1973.)

Table 21.1–1
Classification of Intersexual Disorders[a]

Syndrome	Description
Virilizing adrenal hyperplasia (andrenogenital syndrome)	Results from excess androgens in fetus with XX genotype; most common female intersex disorder; associated with enlarged clitoris, fused labia, hirsutism in adolescence
Turner's syndrome	Results from absence of second female sex chromosome (XO); associated with web neck, dwarfism, cubitus valgus; no sex hormones produced; infertile; usually assigned as females because of female-looking genitals
Klinefelter's syndrome	Genotype is XXY; male habitus present with small penis and rudimentary testes because of low androgen production; weak libido; usually assigned as male
Androgen insensitivity syndrome (testicular-feminizing syndrome)	Congenital X-linked recessive disorder that results in inability of tissues to respond to androgens; external genitals look female and cryptorchid testes present; assigned as females, even though they have XY genotype; in extreme form patient has breasts, normal external genitals, short blind vagina, and absence of pubic and axillary hair
Enzymatic defects in XY genotype (eg, 5-α-reductase deficiency, 17-hydroxysteroid deficiency)	Congenital interruption in production of testosterone that produces ambiguous genitals and female habitus; usually assigned as female because of female-looking genitalia
Hermaphroditism	True hermaphrodite is rare and characterized by both testes and ovaries in same person (may be 46 XX or 46 XY)
Pseudohermaphroditism	Usually the result of endocrine or enzymatic defect (eg, adrenal hyperplasia) in persons with normal chromosomes; female pseudohermaphrodites have masculine-looking genitals but are XX; male pseudohermaphrodites have rudimentary testes and external genitals and are XY; assigned as males or females, depending on morphology of genitals

[a] Intersexual disorders include a variety of syndromes that produce persons with gross anatomical or physiological aspects of the opposite sex.

sique, body shape, and physical dimensions—interrelate with an intricate system of stimuli, including rewards and punishment and parental gender labels, to establish gender identity.

Thus formation of gender identity arises from parental and cultural attitudes, the infant's external genitalia, and a genetic influence, which is physiologically active by the sixth week of fetal life. Even though family, cultural, and biological influences may complicate the establishment of a sense of masculinity or femininity, people usually develop a relatively secure sense of identification with their biological sex—a stable gender identity.

GENDER ROLE. Related to, and in part derived from, gender identity is gender role behavior. John Money and Anke Ehrhardt described gender role behavior as all those things that a person says or does to disclose himself or herself as having the status of boy or man, girl or woman, respectively. A gender role is not established at birth but is built up cumulatively through experiences encountered and transacted through casual and unplanned learning, through explicit instruction and inculcation, and through spontaneously putting two and two together to make sometimes four and sometimes five. The usual outcome is a congruence of gender identity and gender role. Although biological attributes are significant, the major factor in achieving the role appropriate to a person's sex is learning.

Research on sex differences in children's behavior reveals more psychological similarities than differences. However, girls are found to be less prone to tantrums after the age of 18 months than are boys, and boys generally are more physically and verbally aggressive than are girls from age 2 onward. Little girls and little boys are similarly active, but boys are more easily stimulated to sudden bursts of activity when they are in groups. Some researchers speculate that although aggression is a learned behavior, male hormones may have sensitized boys' neural organizations to absorb these lessons more easily than do girls.

People's gender roles can seem to be opposed to their gender identities. People may identify with their own sex and yet adopt the dress, hairstyle, or other characteristics of the opposite sex. Or they may identify with the opposite sex and yet for expediency adopt many behavioral characteristics of their own sex. A further discussion of gender issues appears in Chapter 22.

Sexual Orientation

Sexual orientation describes the object of a person's sexual impulses: heterosexual (opposite sex), homosexual (same sex), or bisexual (both sexes).

Sexual Behavior

Physiological Responses. Sexual response is a true psychophysiological experience. Arousal is triggered by both psychological and physical stimuli; levels of tension are experienced both physiologically and emotionally; and with orgasm, there is normally a subjective perception of a peak of physical reaction and release. Psychosexual development, psychological attitudes toward sexuality, and attitudes toward a person's sexual partner are directly involved with and affect the physiology of human sexual response.

Normal men and women experience a sequence of physiological responses to sexual stimulation. In the first detailed description of these responses, William Masters and Virginia Johnson observed that the physiological process involves increasing levels of vasocongestion and myotonia (tumescence) and the subsequent release of the vascular activity and muscle tone as a result of orgasm (detumescence). Tables 21.1–2 and 21.1–3 describe the male and female sexual response cycles. The fourth edition of *Diagnostic and Statistical Manual of Mental Disorders* (DSM-IV) defines a four-phase response cycle: phase 1, desire; phase 2, excitement; phase 3, orgasm; phase 4, resolution.

PHASE 1: DESIRE. The classification of the desire (or appetitive) phase, which is distinct from any phase identified solely through physiology, reflects the psychiatric concern with motivations, drives, and personality. The phase is characterized by sexual fantasies and the desire to have sexual activity.

Table 21.1–2
Male Sexual Response Cycle[a]

Organ	Excitement Phase	Orgasmic Phase	Resolution Phase
	Lasts several minutes to several hours; heightened excitement before orgasm, 30 seconds to 3 minutes	3 to 15 seconds	10 to 15 minutes; if no orgasm, ½ to 1 day
Skin	Just before orgasm: sexual flush inconsistently appears; maculopapular rash originates on abdomen and spreads to anterior chest wall, face, and neck and can include shoulders and forearms	Well-developed flush	Flush disappears in reverse order of appearance; inconsistently appearing film of perspiration on soles of feet and palms of hands
Penis	Erection in 10 to 30 seconds caused by vasocongestion of erectile bodies of corpus cavernosa of shaft; loss of erection may occur with introduction of asexual stimulus, loud noise; with heightened excitement, size of glans and diameter of penile shaft increase further	Ejaculation; emission phase marked by three to four contractions of 0.8 second of vas, seminal vesicles, prostate; ejaculation proper marked by contractions of 0.8 second of urethra and ejaculatory spurt of 12 to 20 inches at age 18, decreasing with age to seepage at 70	Erection: partial involution in 5 to 10 seconds with variable refractory period; full detumescence in 5 to 30 minutes
Scrotum and testes	Tightening and lifting of scrotal sac and elevation of testes; with heightened excitement, 50% increase in size of testes over unstimulated state and flattening against perineum, signaling impending ejaculation	No change	Decrease to baseline size because of loss of vasocongestion; testicular and scrotal descent within 5 to 30 minutes after orgasm; involution may take several hours if no orgasmic release takes place
Cowper's glands	2 to 3 drops of mucoid fluid that contain viable sperm are secreted during heightened excitement	No change	No change
Other	Breasts: inconsistent nipple erection with heightened excitement before orgasm Myotonia: semispastic contractions of facial, abdominal, and intercostal muscles Tachycardia: up to 175 a minute Blood pressure: rise in systolic 20 to 80 mm; in diastolic 10 to 40 mm Respiration: increased	Loss of voluntary muscular control Rectum: rhythmical contractions of sphincter Heart rate: up to 180 beats a minute Blood pressure: up to 40 to 100 mm systolic; 20 to 50 mm diastolic Respiration: up to 40 respirations a minute	Return to baseline state in 5 to 10 minutes

Courtesy of Virginia Sadock, M.D.
[a] A desire phase consisting of sex fantasies and desire to have sex precedes excitement phase.

Table 21.1–3
Female Sexual Response Cycle[a]

Organ	Excitement Phase	Orgasmic Phase	Resolution Phase
	Lasts several minutes to several hours; heightened excitement before orgasm, 30 seconds to 3 minutes	3 to 15 seconds	10 to 15 minutes; if no orgasm, ½ to 1 day
Skin	Just before orgasm: sexual flush inconsistently appears; maculopapular rash originates on abdomen and spreads to anterior chest wall, face, and neck; can include shoulders and forearms	Well-developed flush	Flush disappears in reverse order of appearance; inconsistently appearing film of perspiration on soles of feet and palms of hands
Breasts	Nipple erection in two thirds of women, venous congestion and areolar enlargement; size increases to one fourth over normal	Breasts may become tremulous	Return to normal in about ½ hour
Clitoris	Enlargement in diameter of glans and shaft; just before orgasm, shaft retracts into prepuce	No change	Shaft returns to normal position in 5 to 10 seconds; detumescence in 5 to 30 minutes; if no orgasm, detumescence takes several hours
Labia majora	Nullipara: elevate and flatten against perineum Multipara: congestion and edema	No change	Nullipara: increase to normal size in 1 to 2 minutes Multipara: decrease to normal size in 10 to 15 minutes
Labia minora	Size increased 2 to 3 times over normal; change to pink, red, deep red before orgasm	Contractions of proximal labia minora	Return to normal within 5 minutes
Vagina	Color change to dark purple; vaginal transudate appears 10 to 30 seconds after arousal; elongation and ballooning of vagina; lower third of vagina constricts before orgasm	3 to 15 contractions of lower third of vagina at intervals of 0.8 second	Ejaculate forms seminal pool in upper two thirds of vagina; congestion disappears in seconds or, if no orgasm, in 20 to 30 minutes
Uterus	Ascends into false pelvis; laborlike contractions begin in heightened excitement just before orgasm	Contractions throughout orgasm	Contractions cease, and uterus descends to normal position
Other	Myotonia A few drops of mucoid secretion from Bartholin's glands during heightened excitement Cervix swells slightly and is passively elevated with uterus	Loss of voluntary muscular control Rectum: rhythmical contractions of sphincter Hyperventilation and tachycardia	Return to baseline status in seconds to minutes Cervix color and size return to normal, and cervix descends into seminal pool

Courtesy of Virginia Sadock, M.D.
[a] A desire phase consisting of sex fantasies and desire to have sex precedes excitement phase.

PHASE 2: EXCITEMENT. The excitement phase, brought on by psychological stimulation (fantasy or the presence of a love object) or physiological stimulation (stroking or kissing) or a combination of the two, consists of a subjective sense of pleasure. During this phase, penile tumescence leads to erection in men and vaginal lubrication occurs in women. The nipples of both sexes become erect, although nipple erection is more common in women than in men. A woman's clitoris becomes hard and turgid, and her labia minora become thicker as a result of venous engorgement. Initial excitement may last from several minutes to several hours. With continued stimulation, a man's testes increase 50 percent in size and elevate. A woman's vaginal barrel shows a characteristic constriction along the outer third, known as the orgasmic platform. The clitoris elevates and retracts behind the symphysis pubis, and as a result is not easily accessible. Stimulation of the area, however, causes traction on the labia minora and the prepuce and intrapreputial movement of the clitoral shaft. Women's breast size increases 25 percent. Continued engorgement of the penis and the vagina produces color changes, particularly in the labia minora, which become bright or deep red. Voluntary contractions of large muscle groups occur, the rates of heartbeat and respiration increase, and blood pressure rises. Heightened excitement lasts from 30 seconds to several minutes.

PHASE 3: ORGASM. The orgasm phase consists of a peaking of sexual pleasure, with the release of sexual tension and the rhythmic contraction of the perineal muscles and the pelvic reproductive organs. A subjective sense of ejaculatory inevitability triggers men's orgasms. The forceful emission of semen follows. The male orgasm is also associated with four to five rhythmic spasms of the prostate, seminal vesicles, vas, and urethra. In women, orgasm is characterized by 3 to 15 involuntary contractions of the lower third of the vagina and by strong sustained contractions of the uterus, flowing from the fundus downward to the cervix. Both men and women have involuntary contractions of the internal and external anal sphincters. These and the other contractions during orgasm occur at intervals of 0.8 second. Other manifestations include voluntary and involuntary movements of the large muscle groups, including facial grim-

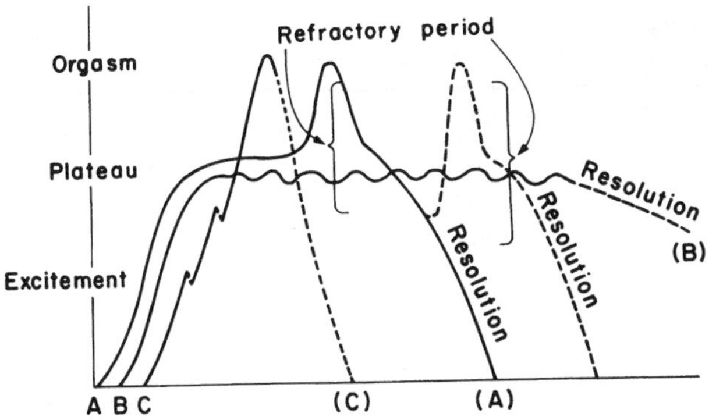
Refractory period
Orgasm
Plateau
Excitement
Resolution
Resolution
Resolution
(B)
A B C
(C)
(A)

FIGURE 21.1–3
Male sexual response. An individual man may experience any of these three patterns (**A, B,** or **C**) during a particular sexual experience. (Reprinted with permission from Walker JI, editor: *Essentials of Clinical Psychiatry,* p 276. Lippincott, Philadelphia, 1985.)

acing and carpopedal spasm. Blood pressure rises 20 to 40 mm (both systolic and diastolic), and the heart rate increases up to 160 beats a minute. Orgasm lasts from 3 to 25 seconds and is associated with a slight clouding of consciousness (Figs. 21.1–3 and 21.1–4).

PHASE 4: RESOLUTION. Resolution consists of the disgorgement of blood from the genitalia (detumescence), which brings the body back to its resting state. If orgasm occurs, resolution is rapid and is characterized by a subjective sense of well-being, general relaxation, and muscular relaxation. If orgasm does not occur, resolution may take from 2 to 6 hours and may be associated with irritability and discomfort. After orgasm, men have a refractory period that may last from several minutes to many hours; in that period they cannot be stimulated to further orgasm. Women do not have a refractory period and are capable of multiple and successive orgasms.

Differences in Erotic Stimuli. Explicit sexual fantasies are common to men and women. The external stimuli for the fantasies frequently differ for the sexes. Many men respond to visual stimuli of nude or barely dressed women, who are depicted as lust driven and interested only in physical satisfaction. Women report responding to romantic stories with tender, demonstrative heroes whose passion for the heroine impels them toward a lifetime commitment to her.

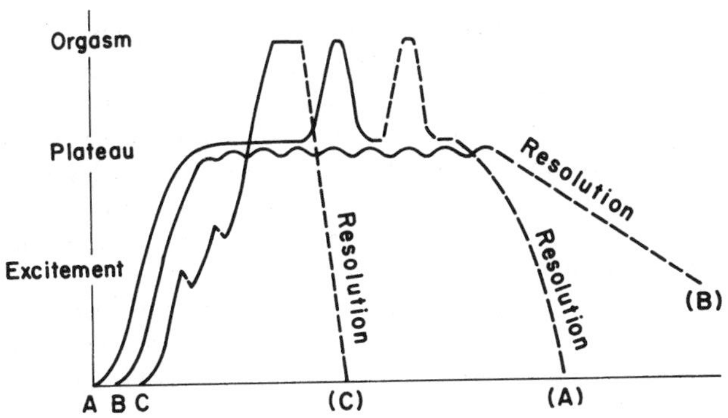
Orgasm
Plateau
Excitement
Resolution
Resolution
Resolution
(B)
A B C
(C)
(A)

FIGURE 21.1–4
Female sexual response. An individual woman may experience any of these three patterns (**A, B,** or **C**) during a particular sexual experience. (Reprinted with permission from Walker JI, editor: *Essentials of Clinical Psychiatry,* p 276. Lippincott, Philadelphia, 1985.)

Masturbation. Masturbation is usually a normal precursor of object-related sexual behavior. No other form of sexual activity has been more frequently discussed, more roundly condemned, and more universally practiced than masturbation. Research by Alfred Kinsey into the prevalence of masturbation indicated that nearly all men and three fourths of all women masturbate sometime during their lives.

Longitudinal studies of development show that sexual self-stimulation is common in infancy and childhood. Just as infants learn to explore the functions of their fingers and mouths, so too do they learn to do the same with their genitalia. At about 15 to 19 months of age, both sexes begin genital self-stimulation. Pleasurable sensations result from any gentle touch to the genital region. Those sensations, coupled with the ordinary desire for exploration of the body, produce a normal interest in masturbatory pleasure at that time. Children also develop an increased interest in the genitalia of others—parents, children, and even animals. As youngsters acquire playmates, the curiosity about their own and others' genitalia motivates episodes of exhibitionism or genital exploration. Such experiences, unless blocked by guilty fear, contribute to continued pleasure from sexual stimulation.

With the approach of puberty, the upsurge of sex hormones, and the development of secondary sex characteristics, sexual curiosity is intensified, and masturbation increases. Adolescents are physically capable of coitus and orgasm but are usually inhibited by social restraints. The dual and often conflicting pressures of establishing their sexual identities and controlling their sexual impulses produce in teenagers a strong physiological sexual tension that demands release, and masturbation is a normal way to reduce sexual tensions. In general, males learn to masturbate to orgasm earlier than females and masturbate more frequently. An important emotional difference between the adolescent and the youngster of earlier years is the presence of coital fantasies during masturbation in the adolescent. These fantasies are an important adjunct to the development of sexual identity; in the comparative safety of the imagination, the adolescent learns to perform the adult sex role. This autoerotic activity is usually maintained into the young adult years, when it is normally replaced by coitus.

Couples in a sexual relationship do not abandon masturbation entirely. When coitus is unsatisfactory or is unavailable because of illness or the absence of the partner, self-stimulation often serves an adaptive purpose, combining sensual pleasure and tension release. Kinsey reported that when women masturbate, most prefer clitoral stimulation. Masters and Johnson stated that women prefer the shaft of the clitoris to the glans because the glans is hypersensitive to intense stimulation. Most men masturbate by vigorously stroking the penile shaft and glans.

Moral taboos against masturbation have generated myths that masturbation causes mental illness or a decrease in sexual potency. No scientific evidence supports such claims. Masturbation is a psychopathological symptom only when it becomes a compulsion beyond a person's willful control. Then it is a symptom of emotional disturbance, not because it is sexual but because it is compulsive. Masturbation is probably a universal and inevitable aspect of psychosexual development, and in most cases it is adaptive.

HOMOSEXUALITY

In 1973, homosexuality was eliminated as a diagnostic category by the American Psychiatric Association and, in 1980, was removed from the DSM. The 10th revision of *International Statistical Classification of Diseases and Related Health Problems* (ICD-10) states: "Sexual orientation alone is not to be regarded as a disorder." This change reflects a change in the understanding of homosexuality, which is now considered an alternative lifestyle occurring with some regularity as a variant of human sexuality, not a pathological disorder. As David Hawkins wrote, "The presence of homosexuality does not appear to be a matter of choice; the expression of it is a matter of choice."

Definition

The term *homosexuality* often describes a person's overt behavior, sexual orientation, and sense of personal or social identity. Many people prefer to identify sexual orientation by using terms like *lesbians* and *gay men,* rather than *homosexual,* which may imply pathology and etiology based on its origin as a medical term, and refer to sexual behavior with terms like *same sex* and *male female.* Hawkins wrote that the terms *gay* and *lesbian* refer to a combination of self-perceived identity and social identity; they reflect a person's sense of belonging to a social group that is similarly labeled. *Homophobia* is a negative attitude toward or fear of homosexuality or homosexuals. *Heterosexism* is the belief that a heterosexual relationship is preferable to all others; it implies discrimination against those practicing other forms of sexuality.

Prevalence

When Alfred C. Kinsey conducted one of the first major studies of the incidence of homosexuality in 1948, he reported that 10 percent of men and 5 percent of women were homosexual. Kinsey also found that 37 percent of all interviewees had had a homosexual experience at some time, including adolescent sexual activities.

Since 1948, these figures have been revised downward in many surveys. A 1988 survey by the U.S. Bureau of the Census concluded that the male prevalence rate for homosexuality is 2 to 3 percent. A 1989 University of Chicago study showed that less than 1 percent of both sexes are exclusively homosexual. The Alan Guttmacher Institute found in 1993 that 1 percent of men reported exclusively same-sex activity in the previous year and that 2 percent reported a lifetime history of homosexual experiences. Because sexual behavior surveys are unreliable, no accurate data are available, but government agencies such as the Centers for Disease Control and Prevention no longer use Kinsey's figures for national projections of homosexual behavior. Table 21.1–4 presents the worldwide estimates of homosexual behavior.

Table 21.1–4
Estimates of Homosexual Behavior

Country	Sample	Findings
Canada	5,514 first-year college students under age 25	98% heterosexual 1% bisexual 1% homosexual
Norway	6,155 adults, ages 18–26	3.5% of males and 3% of females reported past homosexual experience
France	20,055 adults	Lifetime homosexual experience: 4.1% for men and 2.6% for women
Denmark	3,178 adults, ages 18–59	Less than 1% of men exclusively homosexual
Britain	18,876 adults, ages 16–59	6.1% of men reported past homosexual experience

Data reported by *The Wall Street Journal* (March 31, 1993) and *The New York Times* (April 15, 1993) from research studies on homosexual behavior.

Some lesbians and gay men, particularly the latter, report being aware of same-sex romantic attractions before puberty. According to Kinsey's data, about half of all prepubertal boys have had some genital experience with a male partner. These experiences are often exploratory, particularly when shared with a peer, not an adult, and typically lack a strong affective component. Most gay men recall the onset of romantic and erotic attractions to same-sex partners during early adolescence. For women the onset of romantic feelings toward same-sex partners may also be in preadolescence, but the clear recognition of a same-sex partner preference typically occurs in middle to late adolescence or in young adulthood. More lesbians than gay men appear to have engaged in heterosexual experiences. In one study, 56 percent of lesbians had experienced heterosexual intercourse before their first genital homosexual experience, compared with 19 percent of gay men who had sampled heterosexual intercourse first. Nearly 40 percent of the lesbians had had heterosexual intercourse during the year preceding the survey.

Theoretical Issues

Psychological Factors. The determinants of homosexual behavior are enigmatic. Freud viewed homosexuality as an arrest of psychosexual development and mentioned castration fears and fears of maternal engulfment in the preoedipal phase of psychosexual development. According to psychodynamic theory, early-life situations that can result in male homosexual behavior include a strong fixation on the mother; lack of effective fathering; inhibition of masculine development by the parents; fixation at, or regression to, the narcissistic stage of development; and losses when competing with brothers and sisters. Freud's views on the causes of female homosexuality included a lack of resolution of penis envy in association with unresolved oedipal conflicts.

Freud did not consider homosexuality to be a mental illness. In *Three Essays on the Theory of Sexuality,* he wrote that homosexuality "is found in people who exhibit no other serious deviations from normal . . . whose efficiency is unimpaired and who are indeed distinguished by specially high intellectual development and ethical culture.'' In ''Letter to an American Mother,'' Freud wrote, ''Homosexuality is assuredly no advantage, but it is nothing to be ashamed of, no vice, no degradation, it cannot be classified as an illness; we consider it to be a variation of the sexual functions produced by a certain arrest of sexual development.''

New Concepts of Psychoanalytic Factors. Some psychoanalysts have advanced new psychodynamic formulations that contrast with classic psychoanalytic theory. According to Richard Isay, gay men have described same-sex fantasies that occurred when they were 3 to 5 years old, at about the same age that heterosexuals have male-female fantasies.

Isay wrote that same-sex erotic fantasies in gay men center on the father or the father surrogate.

> The child's perception of and exposure to these erotic feelings may account for such ''atypical'' behavior as greater secretiveness than other boys, self-isolation, and excessive emotionality. Some ''feminine'' traits may also be caused by identification with the mother or a mother surrogate. Such characteristics usually develop as a way of attracting the father's love and attention in a manner similar to the way the heterosexual boy may pattern himself after his father to gain his mother's attention.

The psychodynamics of homosexuality in women may be similar. The little girl does not give up her original fixation on the mother as a love object and continues to seek it in adulthood.

Biological Factors. Recent studies indicate that genetic and biological components may contribute to sexual orientation. Gay men reportedly exhibit lower levels of circulatory androgens than do heterosexual men. Prenatal hormones appear to play a role in the organization of the central nervous system: The effective presence of androgens in prenatal life is purported to contribute to a sexual orientation toward females, and a deficiency of prenatal androgens (or a tissue insensitivity to them) may lead to a sexual orientation toward males. Preadolescent girls exposed to large amounts of androgens before birth are uncharacteristically aggressive, and boys exposed to excessive female hormones in utero are less athletic, less assertive, and less aggressive than other boys. Women with hyperadrenocorticalism are lesbian and bisexual in greater proportion than in the general population.

Genetic studies have shown a higher incidence of homosexual concordance among monozygotic twins than among dizygotic twins; these results suggest a genetic predisposition, but chromosome studies have been unable to differentiate homosexuals from heterosexuals. Gay men show a familial distribution; they have more brothers who are gay than do heterosexual men. One study found that 33 of 40 pairs of gay brothers shared a genetic marker on the bottom half of the X chromosome. Another study found that a group of cells in the hypothalamus was smaller in women and in gay men than in heterosexual men. Neither of these studies has been replicated.

Sexual Behavior Patterns. The behavioral features of gay men and lesbian women are as varied as those of heterosexuals. Gay men and lesbians engage in the same sexual practices as do heterosexuals, with the obvious differences imposed by anatomy.

Many ongoing relationship patterns occur among gay men and lesbians. Some same-sex pairs live in a common household in either a monogamous or a primary relationship for decades, and other gay men and lesbians typically have only fleeting sexual contacts. Although many gay men form stable relationships, male–male relationships appear to be less stable and more fleeting than are female–female relationships. Promiscuity among gay men is reported to have diminished since the onset of acquired immune deficiency syndrome (AIDS) and its rapid spread in the gay community through sexual contact.

Gay-male couples are subjected to civil and social discrimination and do not have the legal social support system of marriage or the biological capacity for childbearing that bonds some otherwise incompatible heterosexual couples. Lesbian couples appear to experience less social stigmatization and to have more enduring monogamous or primary relationships.

Psychopathology. The range of psychopathology that may be found among distressed lesbians and gay men parallels that found among heterosexuals; some studies have reported a high suicide rate, however. Distress resulting only from conflict between gay men and lesbians and the societal value structure is not classifiable as a disorder. If the distress is sufficiently severe to warrant a diagnosis, adjustment disorder or a depressive disorder is to be considered. Some gay men and lesbians suffering from major depressive disorder may experience guilt and self-hatred that become directed toward their sexual orientation; then the desire for sexual reorientation is only a symptom of the depressive disorder. ICD-10 describes as *ego-dystonic sexual orientation* a person's desire ''to change gender identity or sexual preference [that] is not in doubt . . . because of associated psychological and behavioural *[sic]* disorders.'' Such a person ''may seek treatment in order to change'' this sexual orientation.

Coming Out. According to Richelle Klinger and Robert Cabaj, coming out is a ''process by which an individual acknowledges his or her sexual orientation in the face of societal stigma and with successful resolution accepts himself or herself.'' The authors wrote:

> Successful coming out involves the individual accepting his or her sexual orientation and integrating it into all spheres (eg, social, vocational, and familial). Another milestone that individuals and couples must eventually confront is the degree of disclosure of sexual orientation to the external world. Some degree of disclosure is probably necessary for successful coming out. . . .
>
> Difficulty in negotiating coming out and disclosure is a common cause of relationship difficulties. For each individual, problems in resolving the coming out process may contribute to poor self-esteem caused by internalized homophobia and lead to deleterious effects on the individual's ability to function in the relationship. Conflict can also arise within a relationship when there is disagreement on the degree of disclosure between partners.

LOVE AND INTIMACY

There are many kinds of love: sexual, parental, filial, fraternal, narcissistic, as well as love for group, school, and country. A desire to maintain closeness to the love object typifies being in love. The development of sexuality and the development of the ability to love have reciprocal effects.

A person able to give and receive love with a minimum of fear and conflict has the capacity to develop genuinely intimate relationships with others. When involved in an intimate relationship, the person actively strives for the growth and the happiness of the loved person. Mature love is marked by the intimacy that is a special attribute of the relationship between two people. The quality of intimacy in a mature sexual relationship is what Rollo May called "active receiving," in which a person, while loving, permits himself or herself to be loved. This capability indicates a profound awareness of love for another and for oneself. In such a loving relationship, sex acts as a catalyst. May described the values of sexual love as an expansion of self-awareness, the experience of tenderness, an increase of self-affirmation and pride, and sometimes, at the moment of orgasm, loss of feelings of separateness. In that setting, sex and love are reciprocally enhancing and healthily fused.

A person is attracted to a potential mate for various reasons. The attraction may be purely physical, and the relationship transient. A person may strive to fulfill a magical desire for the perfect lover, whose qualities are reminiscent of the idealized qualities of parents or other past sources of love and affection. A person's expectations of a partner may or may not be realistic. One neurotic motivation for marrying is an inability to separate from parents. Another neurotic motivation is selecting a partner to compensate for unmet childhood needs. Every person and every marriage probably carry an element of such unrealistic expectations. When these tendencies predominate and the couple act mainly to exchange patterns of exploitations, or when interlocking complementary needs fail to bring sufficient security or happiness, discomfort and anxiety occur, and the relationship may break down.

REFERENCES

Freud S: General theory of the neuroses. In *Standard Edition of the Complete Psychological Works of Sigmund Freud,* vol 16, p 241. Hogarth Press, London, 1966.

Freud S: Letter to an American mother. Am J Psychiatry *102:* 786, 1951.

Freud S: Three essays on the theory of sexuality. In *Standard Edition of the Complete Psychological Works of Sigmund Freud,* vol 7, p 135. Hogarth Press, London, 1953.

Harlow HF: The nature of love. Am Psychol *13:* 673, 1958.

Hawkins DM: Group psychotherapy with gay men and lesbians. In *Comprehensive Group Psychotherapy,* ed 3, HI Kaplan, BJ Sadock, editors, p 506. Williams & Wilkins, Baltimore, 1993.

Kinsey AC, Pomeroy WB, Martin CE: *Sexual Behavior in the Human Male.* Saunders, Philadelphia, 1948.

Kinsey AC, Pomeroy WB, Martin CE, Gebbard PH: *Sexual Behavior in the Human Female.* Saunders, Philadelphia, 1953.

Masters WH, Johnson VE: *Human Sexual Response.* Little, Brown, Boston, 1966.

Money J, Ehrhardt AA: *Man and Woman/Boy and Girl.* Johns Hopkins University Press, Baltimore, 1972.

Sadock VA: Normal human sexuality. In *Comprehensive Textbook of Psychiatry,* ed 6, HI Kaplan, BJ Sadock, editors, p 1295. Williams & Williams, Baltimore, 1995.

Schiavi RC, Segraves RT: The biology of sexual function. Psychiatr Clin North Am *18:* 7, 1995.

Sherfey MJ: *The Nature and Evolution of Female Sexuality.* Random House, New York, 1972.

Stoller RJ: *Sex and Gender.* Science House, New York, 1968.

Tanfer K, Cubbins LA: Coital frequency among single women: Normative constraints and situational opportunities. J Sex Res *29:* 221, 1992.

▲ 21.2 Sexual Dysfunctions

In the fourth edition of *Diagnostic and Statistical Manual of Mental Disorders* (DSM-IV), a sexual dysfunction is defined as a disturbance in the sexual response cycle or as pain with sexual intercourse. Seven major categories of sexual dysfunction are listed in DSM-IV: sexual desire disorders, sexual arousal disorders, orgasm disorders, sexual pain disorders, sexual dysfunction caused by a general medical condition, substance-induced sexual dysfunction, and sexual dysfunction not otherwise specified.

It is useful to think of the sexual dysfunctions as disorders related to a particular phase of the sexual response cycle. Thus, sexual desire disorders are associated with the first phase of the response cycle, known as the desire phase. Table 21.2–1 lists each DSM-IV phase of the sexual response cycle and the sexual dysfunctions usually associated with it.

Sexual dysfunctions can be symptomatic of biological (biogenic) problems or intrapsychic or interpersonal (psychogenic) conflicts or a combination of these factors. Sexual function can be adversely affected by stress of any kind, by emotional disorders, or by ignorance of sexual function and physiology. The dysfunction may be lifelong or acquired—that is, it can develop after a period of normal functioning. The dysfunction may be generalized or limited to a specific partner or a certain situation.

In considering each of the disorders, clinicians need to rule out an acquired medical condition and the use of a pharmacological substance that could account for or contribute to the dysfunction. If the disorder is biogenic, it is coded on Axis III unless there is substantial evidence of dysfunctional episodes apart from the onset of physiological or pharmacological influences. In some cases a patient suffers from more than one dysfunction—for example, premature ejaculation and male erectile disorder.

ICD-10

According to the 10th revision of *International Statistical Classification of Diseases and Related Health Problems* (ICD-10), sexual dysfunction refers to a person's inability to "participate in a sexual relationship as he or she would wish." This dysfunction is expressed in various ways: as a lack of desire or of pleasure or as a physiological inability to begin, maintain, or complete sexual interaction. Because sexual response is psychosomatic, it may be difficult to determine "the relative importance of psychological and/or organic factors."

Sexual dysfunction such as lack of desire can occur in both men and women, but women more often complain of the "subjective quality" of the experience than of the "failure of a specific response." ICD-10 advises looking "beyond the presenting complaint to find the most appropriate diagnostic category." Table 21.1–2 presents the ICD-10 diagnostic criteria.

SEXUAL DESIRE DISORDERS

Sexual desire disorders are divided into two classes: hypoactive sexual desire disorder, characterized by a deficiency

Table 21.2–1
DSM-IV Phases of the Sexual Response Cycle and Associated Sexual Dysfunctions[a]

Phases	Characteristics	Dysfunction
1. Desire	This phase is distinct from any identified solely through physiology and reflects the patient's motivations, drives, and personality. The phase is characterized by sexual fantasies and the desire to have sex.	Hypoactive sexual desire disorder; sexual aversion disorder; hypoactive sexual desire disorder due to a general medical condition (male or female); substance-induced sexual dysfunction with impaired desire
2. Excitement	This phase consists of a subjective sense of sexual pleasure and accompanying physiological changes. All the physiological responses noted in Masters and Johnson's excitement and plateau phases are combined and occur in this phase.	Female sexual arousal disorder; male erectile disorder; male erectile disorder due to a general medical condition; dyspareunia due to a general medical condition (male or female); substance-induced sexual dysfunction with impaired arousal
3. Orgasm	This phase consists of a peaking of sexual pleasure, with release of sexual tension and rhythmic contraction of the perineal muscles and pelvic reproductive organs.	Female orgasmic disorder; male orgasmic disorder; premature ejaculation; other sexual dysfunction due to a general medical condition (male or female); substance-induced sexual dysfunction with impaired orgasm
4. Resolution	This phase entails a sense of general relaxation, well-being, and muscle relaxation. During this phase men are refractory to orgasm for a period of time that increases with age, whereas women are capable of having multiple orgasms without a refractory period.	Postcoital dysphoria; postcoital headache

[a] DSM-IV consolidates the Masters and Johnson excitement and plateau phases into a single excitement phase, which is preceded by the desire (appetitive) phase. The orgasm and resolution phases remain the same as originally described by Masters and Johnson.

or absence of sexual fantasies and desire for sexual activity (Table 21.2–3); and sexual aversion disorder, characterized by an aversion to and avoidance of genital sexual contact with a sexual partner or by masturbation (Table 21.2–4). The former condition is more common than the latter and more common among women than among men. An estimated 20 percent of the population have hypoactive sexual desire disorder.

A variety of causative factors are associated with sexual desire disorders. Patients with desire problems often use inhibition of desire in a defensive way to protect against unconscious fears about sex. Sigmund Freud conceptualized low sexual desire as the result of inhibition during the phallic psychosexual phase of development and of unresolved oedipal conflicts. Some men, fixated at the phallic state of development, are fearful of the vagina and believe that they will be castrated if they approach it. Freud called this concept *vagina dentata;* because men unconsciously believe that the vagina has teeth, they avoid contact with the female genitalia. Equally, women may suffer from unresolved developmental conflicts that inhibit desire. Lack of desire can also be the result of chronic stress, anxiety, or depression.

Abstinence from sex for a prolonged period sometimes results in suppression of sexual impulses. Loss of desire may also be an expression of hostility to a partner or the sign of a deteriorating relationship. In one study of young married couples who ceased having sexual relations for 2 months, marital discord was the reason most frequently given for the cessation or inhibition of sexual activity.

The presence of desire depends on several factors: biological drive, adequate self-esteem, the ability to accept oneself as a sexual person, previous good experiences with sex, the availability of an appropriate partner, and a good relationship in nonsexual areas with a partner. Damage to, or absence of, any of these factors may result in diminished desire.

In making the diagnosis, clinicians must evaluate a patient's age, general health, and life stresses and must attempt to establish a baseline of sexual interest before the disorder began. The need for sexual contact and satisfaction varies among people and over time in any given person. In a group of 100 couples with stable marriages, 8 percent reported having intercourse less than once a month. In another group of couples, one third reported episodic lack of sexual relations for periods averaging 8 weeks. Married couples have coitus 3 times a month, on average. The diagnosis should not be made unless the lack of desire is a source of distress to a patient.

SEXUAL AROUSAL DISORDERS

The sexual arousal disorders are divided by DSM-IV into female sexual arousal disorder, characterized by the persistent or recurrent partial or complete failure to attain or maintain the lubrication-swelling response of sexual excitement until the completion of the sexual act; and male erectile disorder, characterized by the recurrent and persistent partial or complete failure to attain or maintain an erection to perform the sex act. The diagnosis takes into account the focus, the intensity, and the duration of the sexual activity in which patients engage (Tables 21.2–5 and 21.2–6). If sexual stimulation is inadequate in focus, intensity, or duration, the diagnosis should not be made.

Female Sexual Arousal Disorder

The prevalence of female sexual arousal disorder is generally underestimated. Women who have excitement-phase dysfunction often have orgasm problems as well. In one study of relatively happy married couples, 33 percent of the women described difficulty in maintaining sexual excitement. Many psychological factors (for example, anxiety, guilt, and fear) are

Table 21.2–2
ICD-10 Diagnostic Criteria for Sexual Dysfunction, Not Caused by Organic Disorder or Disease

G1. The subject is unable to participate in a sexual relationship as he or she would wish.

G2. The dysfunction occurs frequently, but may be absent on some occasions.

G3. The dysfunction has been present for at least 6 months.

G4. The dysfunction is not entirely attributable to any of the other mental and behavioral disorders in ICD-10, physical disorders (such as endocrine disorder), or drug treatment.

Comments

Measurement of each form of dysfunction can be based on rating scales that assess severity as well as frequency of the problem. More than one type of dysfunction can coexist.

Lack or loss of sexual desire

A. The general criteria for sexual dysfunction must be met.

B. There is a lack or loss of sexual desire, manifest by diminution of seeking out sexual cues, of thinking about sex with associated feelings of desire or appetite, or of sexual fantasies.

C. There is a lack of interest in initiating sexual activity either with a partner or as solitary masturbation, resulting in a frequency of activity clearly lower than expected, taking into account age and context, or in a frequency very clearly reduced from previous much higher levels.

Sexual aversion and lack of sexual enjoyment

Sexual aversion

A. The general criteria for sexual dysfunction must be met.

B. The prospect of sexual interaction with a partner produces sufficient aversion, fear, or anxiety that sexual activity is avoided, or, if it occurs, is associated with strong negative feelings and an inability to experience any pleasure.

C. The aversion is not the result of performance anxiety (reaction to previous failure of sexual response).

Lack of sexual enjoyment

A. The general criteria for sexual dysfunction must be met.

B. Genital response (orgasm and/or ejaculation) occurs during sexual stimulation, but is not accompanied by pleasurable sensations or feelings of pleasant excitement.

C. There is no manifest and persistent fear or anxiety during sexual activity (see sexual aversion).

Failure of genital response

A. The general criteria for sexual dysfunction must be met.

In addition, for men:

B. Erection sufficient for intercourse fails to occur when intercourse is attempted. The dysfunction takes one of the following forms:
   (1) full erection occurs during the early stages of lovemaking but disappears or declines when intercourse is attempted (before ejaculation if it occurs);
   (2) erection does occur, but only at times when intercourse is not being considered;
   (3) partial erection, insufficient for intercourse, occurs, but not full erection;
   (4) no penile tumescence occurs at all.

In addition, for women:

B. There is failure of genital response, experienced as failure of vaginal lubrication, together with inadequate tumescence of the labia. The dysfunction takes one of the following forms:
   (1) general: lubrication fails in all relevant circumstances;
   (2) lubrication may occur initially but fails to persist for long enough to allow comfortable penile entry;
   (3) Situational: lubrication occurs only in some situations (eg, with one partner but not another, or during masturbation, or when vaginal intercourse is not being contemplated).

Orgasmic dysfunction

A. The general criteria for sexual dysfunction must be met.

B. There is orgasmic dysfunction (either absence or marked delay of orgasm), which takes one of the following forms:
   (1) orgasm has never been experienced in any situation;
   (2) orgasmic dysfunction has developed after a period of relatively normal response:
      (a) general: orgasmic dysfunction occurs in all situations and with any partner;
      (b) situational:
         for *women:* orgasm does occur in certain situations (eg, when masturbating or with certain partners);
         for *men,* one of the following can be applied:
         i) orgasm occurs only during sleep, never during the waking state;
         ii) orgasm never occurs in the presence of the partner;
         iii) orgasm occurs in the presence of the partner but not during intercourse.

Premature ejaculation

A. The general criteria for sexual dysfunction must be met.

B. There is an inability to delay ejaculation sufficiently to enjoy lovemaking, manifest as either of the following:
   (1) occurrence of ejaculation before or very soon after the beginning of intercourse (if a time limit is required: before or within 15 seconds of the beginning of intercourse);
   (2) ejaculation occurs in the absence of sufficient erection to make intercourse possible.

C. The problem is not the result of prolonged abstinence from sexual activity.

Nonorganic vaginismus

A. The general criteria for sexual dysfunction must be met.

B. There is spasm of the perivaginal muscles, sufficient to prevent penile entry or make it uncomfortable. The dysfunction takes one of the following forms:
   (1) normal response has never been experienced;
   (2) vaginismus has developed after a period of relatively normal response:
      (a) when vaginal entry is not attempted, a normal sexual response may occur;
      (b) any attempt at sexual contact leads to generalized fear and efforts to avoid vaginal entry (eg, spasm of the adductor muscles of the thighs).

Nonorganic dyspareunia

A. The general criteria for sexual dysfunction must be met.

In addition, for women:

B. Pain is experienced at the entry of the vagina, either throughout sexual intercourse or only when deep thrusting of the penis occurs.

C. The disorder is not attributable to vaginismus or failure of lubrication; dyspareunia of organic origin should be classified according to the underlying disorder.

In addition, for men:

B. Pain or discomfort is experienced during sexual response. (The timing of the pain and the exact localization should be carefully recorded.)

C. The discomfort is not the result of local physical factors. If physical factors are found, the dysfunction should be classified elsewhere.

Excessive sexual drive

No research criteria are attempted for this category. Researchers studying this category are recommended to design their own criteria.

Other sexual dysfunction, not caused by organic disorder or disease

Unspecified sexual dysfunction, not caused by organic disorder or disease

Table 21.2–3
DSM-IV Diagnostic Criteria for Hypoactive Sexual Desire Disorder

A. Persistently or recurrently deficient (or absent) sexual fantasies and desire for sexual activity. The judgment of deficiency of absence is made by the clinician, taking into account factors that affect sexual functioning, such as age and the context of the person's life.
B. The disturbance causes marked distress or interpersonal difficulty.
C. The sexual dysfunction is not better accounted for by another Axis I disorder (except another sexual dysfunction), and is not due exclusively to the direct physiological effects of a substance (eg, a drug of abuse, a medication) or a general medical condition.

Specify type:
Lifelong type
Acquired type
Specify type:
Generalized type
Situational type
Specify:
Due to psychological factors
Due to combined factors

Reprinted with permission from American Psychiatric Association: *Diagnostic and Statistical Manual of Mental Disorders,* ed 4. Copyright, American Psychiatric Association, Washington, 1994.

associated with female sexual arousal disorder. In many women, excitement-phase disorders are associated with dyspareunia and with lack of desire.

Physiological studies of sexual dysfunctions indicate that a hormonal pattern may contribute to responsiveness in women who have excitement-phase dysfunction. William Masters and Virginia Johnson found women to be particularly desirous of sex before the onset of the menses. Other women report that they feel the greatest sexual excitement immediately after the menses or at the time of ovulation. Alterations in testosterone,

Table 21.2–4
DSM-IV Diagnostic Criteria for Sexual Aversion Disorder

A. Persistent or recurrent extreme aversion to, and avoidance of, all (or almost all) genital sexual contact with a sexual partner.
B. The disturbance causes marked distress or interpersonal difficulty.
C. The sexual dysfunction is not better accounted for by another Axis I disorder (except another sexual dysfunction).

Specify type:
Lifelong type
Acquired type
Specify type:
Generalized type
Situational type
Specify:
Due to psychological factors
Due to combined factors

Reprinted with permission from American Psychiatric Association: *Diagnostic and Statistical Manual of Mental Disorders,* ed 4. Copyright, American Psychiatric Association, Washington, 1994.

Table 21.2–5
DSM-IV Diagnostic Criteria for Female Sexual Arousal Disorder

A. Persistent or recurrent inability to attain, or to maintain until completion of the sexual activity, an adequate lubrication-swelling response of sexual excitement.
B. The disturbance causes marked distress or interpersonal difficulty.
C. The sexual dysfunction is not better accounted for by another Axis I disorder (except another sexual dysfunction) and is not due exclusively to the direct physiological effects of a substance (eg, a drug of abuse, a medication) or a general medical condition.

Specify type:
Lifelong type
Acquired type
Specify type:
Generalized type
Situational type
Specify:
Due to psychological factors
Due to combined factors

Reprinted with permission from American Psychiatric Association: *Diagnostic and Statistical Manual of Mental Disorders,* ed 4. Copyright, American Psychiatric Association, Washington, 1994.

estrogen, prolactin, and thyroxin levels have been implicated in female sexual arousal disorder. Also, medications with antihistaminic or anticholinergic properties cause a decrease in vaginal lubrication. Some evidence indicates that women who are dysfunctional are less aware of the physiological arousal of their bodies and experience less warmth or less sensation in the genitalia.

Male Erectile Disorder

Male erectile disorder is also called erectile dysfunction and impotence. A man with lifelong male erectile disorder has never been able to obtain an erection sufficient for vaginal insertion. In acquired male erectile disorder a man has successfully achieved vaginal penetration at some time in his sexual life but is later unable to do so. In situational male erectile disorder a man is able to have coitus in certain circumstances but not in others; for example, he may function effectively with a prostitute but be impotent with his wife.

Acquired male erectile disorder has been reported in 10 to 20 percent of all men. Freud declared it common among his patients. Impotence is the chief complaint of more than 50 percent of all men treated for sexual disorders. Lifelong male erectile disorder is rare; it occurs in about 1 percent of men under age 35, but the incidence increases with age. Among young adults it has been reported in about 8 percent of the population. Alfred Kinsey reported that 75 percent of all men were impotent at age 80. All men over 40, Masters and Johnson reported, have a fear of impotence, which the researchers believe reflects the masculine fear of loss of virility with advancing age. Male erectile disorder, however, is not universal in aging men; having an available sex partner is related to continuing potency, as is a history of consistent sexual activity and the absence of vascular disease.

The causes of male erectile disorder may be organic or

Table 21.2–6
DSM-IV Diagnostic Criteria for Male Erectile Disorder

A. Persistent or recurrent inability to attain, or to maintain until completion of the sexual activity, an adequate erection.

B. The disturbance causes marked distress or interpersonal difficulty.

C. The erectile dysfunction is not better accounted for by another Axis I disorder (other than a sexual dysfunction) and is not due exclusively to the direct physiological effects of a substance (eg, a drug of abuse, a medication) or a general medical condition.

Specify type:
Lifelong type
Acquired type
Specify type:
Generalized type
Situational type
Specify:
Due to psychological factors
Due to combined factors

psychological or a combination of both, but in young and middle-aged men the cause is usually psychological. A good history is of primary importance in determining the cause of the dysfunction. If a man reports having spontaneous erections at times when he does not plan to have intercourse, having morning erections, or having good erections with masturbation or with partners other than his usual one, the organic causes of his impotence can be considered negligible, and costly diagnostic procedures can be avoided. Male erectile disorder caused by a general medical condition or a pharmacological substance is discussed later in this section.

Freud ascribed one type of impotence to an inability to reconcile feelings of affection toward a woman with feelings of desire for her. Men with such conflicting feelings can function only with women whom they see as degraded. Other factors that have been cited as contributing to impotence include a punitive superego, an inability to trust, and feelings of inadequacy or a sense of being undesirable as a partner. A man may be unable to express a sexual impulse because of fear, anxiety, anger, or moral prohibition. In an ongoing relationship, impotence may reflect difficulties between the partners, particularly when a man cannot communicate his needs or his anger in a direct and constructive way. In addition, episodes of impotence are reinforcing, with the man becoming increasingly anxious before each sexual encounter.

ORGASM DISORDERS

Female Orgasmic Disorder

Female orgasmic disorder, sometimes called inhibited female orgasm or anorgasmia, is defined as the recurrent or persistent inhibition of female orgasm, as manifested by the recurrent delay in, or absence of, orgasm after a normal sexual excitement phase that a clinician judges to be adequate in focus, intensity, and duration—in short, a woman's inability to achieve orgasm by masturbation or coitus. Women who can achieve orgasm by one of these methods are not necessarily categorized as anorgasmic, although some degree of sexual inhibition may be postulated (Table 21.2–7).

Research on the physiology of the female sexual response has shown that orgasms caused by clitoral stimulation and those caused by vaginal stimulation are physiologically identical. Freud's theory that women must give up clitoral sensitivity for vaginal sensitivity to achieve sexual maturity is now considered misleading, but some women report that they gain a special sense of satisfaction from an orgasm precipitated by coitus. Some researchers attribute this satisfaction to the psychological feeling of closeness engendered by the act of coitus, but others maintain that the coital orgasm is a physiologically different experience. Many women achieve orgasm during coitus by a combination of manual clitoral stimulation and penile vaginal stimulation.

A woman with lifelong female orgasmic disorder has never experienced orgasm by any kind of stimulation. A woman with acquired orgasmic disorder has previously experienced at least one orgasm, regardless of the circumstances or means of stimulation, whether by masturbation or while dreaming during sleep. Kinsey found that only 5 percent of married women over 35 years of age had never achieved orgasm by any means. The incidence of orgasm increases with age. According to Kinsey, the first orgasm occurs during adolescence in about 50 percent of women as a result of masturbation or genital caressing with a partner; the rest usually experience orgasm as they get older. Lifelong female orgasmic disorder is more common among

Table 21.2–7
DSM-IV Diagnostic Criteria for Female Orgasmic Disorder

A. Persistent or recurrent delay in, or absence of, orgasm following a normal sexual excitement phase. Women exhibit wide variability in the type or intensity of stimulation that triggers orgasm. The diagnosis of female orgasmic disorder should be based on the clinician's judgment that the woman's orgasmic capacity is less than would be reasonable for her age, sexual experience, and the adequacy of sexual stimulation she receives.

B. The disturbance causes marked distress or interpersonal difficulty.

C. The orgasmic dysfunction is not better accounted for by another Axis I disorder (except another sexual dysfunction) and is not due exclusively to the direct physiological effects of a substance (eg, a drug of abuse, a medication) or a general medical condition.

Specify type:
Lifelong type
Acquired type
Specify type:
Generalized type
Situational type
Specify:
Due to psychological factors
Due to combined factors

unmarried than married women. Increased orgasmic potential in women over 35 has been explained on the basis of less psychological inhibition, greater sexual experience, or both.

Acquired female orgasmic disorder is a common complaint in clinical populations. One clinical treatment facility reported having about 4 times as many nonorgasmic women in its practice as patients with all other sexual disorders. In another study, 46 percent of women complained of difficulty in reaching orgasm. The true prevalence of problems in maintaining excitement is not known, but inhibition of excitement and orgasmic problems often occur together. The overall prevalence of female orgasmic disorder from all causes is estimated to be 30 percent.

Numerous psychological factors are associated with female orgasmic disorder. They include fears of impregnation, rejection by a sex partner, damage to the vagina, hostility toward men, and feelings of guilt about sexual impulses. For some women, orgasm is equated with loss of control or with aggressive, destructive, or violent impulses; their fear of these impulses may be expressed through inhibition of excitement or orgasm. Cultural expectations and social restrictions on women are also relevant. Many women have grown up to believe that sexual pleasure is not a natural entitlement for so-called decent women. Nonorgasmic women may be otherwise symptom free or may experience frustration in a variety of ways; they may have such pelvic complaints as lower abdominal pain, itching, and vaginal discharge, as well as increased tension, irritability, and fatigue.

Male Orgasmic Disorder

In male orgasmic disorder, sometimes called inhibited orgasm or retarded ejaculation, a man achieves ejaculation during coitus with great difficulty, if at all. A man with lifelong orgasmic disorder has never been able to ejaculate during coitus. The disorder is diagnosed as acquired if it develops after previously normal functioning (Table 21.2–8). Some researchers think that orgasm and ejaculation should be differentiated, especially in the case of men who ejaculate but complain of a decreased or absent subjective sense of pleasure during the orgasmic experience (orgasmic anhedonia).

Table 21.2–8
DSM-IV Diagnostic Criteria for Male Orgasmic Disorder

A. Persistent or recurrent delay in, or absence of, orgasm following a normal sexual excitement phase during sexual activity that the clinician, taking into account the person's age, judges to be adequate in focus, intensity, and duration.

B. The disturbance causes marked distress or interpersonal difficulty.

C. The orgasmic dysfunction is not better accounted for by another Axis I disorder (except another sexual dysfunction) and is not due exclusively to the direct physiological effects of a substance (eg, a drug of abuse, a medication) or a general medical condition.

Specify type:
Lifelong type
Acquired type
Specify type:
Generalized type
Situational type
Specify:
Due to psychological factors
Due to combined factors

The incidence of male orgasmic disorder is much lower than the incidence of premature ejaculation or impotence. Masters and Johnson reported an incidence of male orgasmic disorder of only 3.8 percent in one group of 447 men with sexual dysfunctions. A general prevalence of 5 percent has been reported.

Lifelong male orgasmic disorder indicates severe psychopathology. A man may come from a rigid, puritanical background; he may perceive sex as sinful and the genitals as dirty; and he may have conscious or unconscious incest wishes and guilt. He usually has difficulties with closeness in areas beyond those of sexual relations. In a few cases the condition is aggravated by an attention-deficit disorder. A man's distractibility prevents arousal sufficient for climax to occur.

In an ongoing relationship, acquired male orgasmic disorder frequently reflects interpersonal difficulties. The disorder may be a man's way of coping with real or fantasized changes in the relationship, such as plans for pregnancy about which the man is ambivalent, the loss of sexual attraction to the partner, or demands by the partner for greater commitment as expressed by sexual performance. In some men the inability to ejaculate reflects unexpressed hostility toward a woman. The problem is more common among men with obsessive-compulsive disorder than among others.

Premature Ejaculation

In premature ejaculation men persistently or recurrently achieve orgasm and ejaculation before they wish to. There is no definite time frame within which to define the dysfunction; the diagnosis is made when a man regularly ejaculates before or immediately after entering the vagina. Clinicians need to consider factors that affect the duration of the excitement phase, such as age, the novelty of the sex partner, and the frequency and duration of coitus (Table 21.2–9). Masters and Johnson conceptualized the disorder in terms of the couple and considered a man a premature ejaculator if he could not control ejaculation for a sufficient time during intravaginal containment to satisfy his partner in at least half their episodes of coitus. This definition assumes that the female partner is capable of an orgasmic response. Like the other dysfunctions, premature ejaculation is not diagnosed when it is caused exclusively by organic factors or when it is not symptomatic of any other clinical psychiatric syndrome.

Premature ejaculation is more commonly reported among college-educated men than among men with less education. The complaint is thought to be related to their concern for partner satisfaction, but the true cause of the increased frequency has not been determined. Premature ejaculation is the chief complaint of about 35 to 40 percent of men treated for sexual disorders. Some researchers divide men who experience premature ejaculation into two groups: those who are physiologically predisposed to climax quickly because of shorter

Table 21.2–9
DSM-IV Diagnostic Criteria for Premature Ejaculation

A. Persistent or recurrent ejaculation with minimal sexual stimulation before, on, or shortly after penetration and before the person wishes it. The clinician must take into account factors that affect duration of the excitement phase, such as age, novelty of the sexual partner or situation, and recent frequency of sexual activity.

B. The disturbance causes marked distress or interpersonal difficulty.

C. The premature ejaculation is not due exclusively to the direct effects of a substance (eg, withdrawal from opioids).

Specify type:
Lifelong type
Acquired type
Specify type:
Generalized type
Situational type
Specify:
Due to psychological factors
Due to combined factors

nerve latency time and those with a psychogenic or behaviorally conditioned etiology. Difficulty in ejaculatory control may be associated with anxiety regarding the sex act, with unconscious fears about the vagina, or with negative cultural conditioning. Men whose early sexual contacts occurred largely with prostitutes who demanded that the sex act proceed quickly or whose sexual contacts took place in situations in which discovery would be embarrassing (such as in the back seat of a car or in the parental home) might have been conditioned to achieve orgasm rapidly. With young, inexperienced men, who are more likely to have the problem, it may resolve in time. In ongoing relationships the partner has a great influence on a premature ejaculator, and a stressful marriage exacerbates the disorder. The developmental background and the psychodynamics found in premature ejaculation and in impotence are similar.

Other Orgasm Disorders

Data on female premature orgasm are lacking; no separate category of premature orgasm for women is included in DSM-IV. A case of multiple spontaneous orgasms without sexual stimulation has been seen in a woman; the cause was an epileptogenic focus in the temporal lobe. Instances have been reported of women on antidepressants (such as fluoxetine [Prozac] and clomipramine [Anafranil]) who experience spontaneous orgasm associated with yawning.

SEXUAL PAIN DISORDERS

Dyspareunia

Dyspareunia is recurrent or persistent genital pain occurring in either men or women before, during, or after intercourse.

Table 21.2–10
DSM-IV Diagnostic Criteria for Dyspareunia

A. Recurrent or persistent genital pain associated with sexual intercourse in either a male or a female.

B. The disturbance causes marked distress or interpersonal difficulty.

C. The disturbance is not caused exclusively by vaginismus or lack of lubrication, is not better accounted for by another Axis I disorder (except another sexual dysfunction) and is not due exclusively to the direct physiological effects of a substance (eg, a drug of abuse, a medication) or a general medical condition.

Specify type:
Lifelong type
Acquired type
Specify type:
Generalized type
Situational type
Specify:
Due to psychological factors
Due to combined factors

Much more common in women than in men, dyspareunia is related to, and often coincides with, vaginismus. Repeated episodes of vaginismus may lead to dyspareunia and vice versa; in either case, somatic causes must be ruled out. Dyspareunia should not be diagnosed when an organic basis for the pain is found or when, in a woman, it is caused exclusively by vaginismus or by a lack of lubrication (Table 21.2–10). The incidence of dyspareunia is unknown.

In most cases, dynamic factors are considered causative. Chronic pelvic pain is a common complaint in women with a history of rape or childhood sexual abuse. Painful coitus may result from tension and anxiety about the sex act that cause women to involuntarily contract their vaginal muscles. The pain is real and makes intercourse unpleasant or unbearable. Anticipation of further pain may cause women to avoid coitus altogether. If a partner proceeds with intercourse regardless of a woman's state of readiness, the condition is aggravated. Dyspareunia can also occur in men, but it is uncommon and is usually associated with an organic condition, such as herpes, prostatitis, or Peyronie's disease, which consists of sclerotic plaques on the penis that cause penile curvature.

Vaginismus

Vaginismus is an involuntary muscle constriction of the outer third of the vagina that interferes with penile insertion and intercourse. This response may occur during a gynecological examination when involuntary vaginal constriction prevents the introduction of the speculum into the vagina. The diagnosis is not made when the dysfunction is caused exclusively by organic factors or when it is symptomatic of another Axis I mental disorder (Table 21.2–11).

Vaginismus is less prevalent than is female orgasmic disorder. It most often afflicts highly educated women and those in high socioeconomic groups. Women with vaginismus may consciously wish to have coitus but unconsciously wish to

Table 21.2–11
DSM-IV Diagnostic Criteria for Vaginismus

A. Recurrent or persistent involuntary spasm of the musculature of the outer third of the vagina that interferes with sexual intercourse.
B. The disturbance causes marked distress or interpersonal difficulty.
C. The disturbance is not better accounted for by another Axis I disorder (eg, somatization disorder) and is not due exclusively to the direct physiological effects of a general medical condition.

Specify type:
Lifelong type
Acquired type
Specify type:
Generalized type
Situational type
Specify:
Due to psychological factors
Due to combined factors

keep a penis from entering their bodies. A sexual trauma such as rape may cause vaginismus; women with psychosexual conflicts may perceive the penis as a weapon. In some cases, pain or the anticipation of pain at the first coital experience causes vaginismus. Clinicians have noted that a strict religious upbringing in which sex is associated with sin is frequent in these patients. Other women have problems in dyadic relationships; if women feel emotionally abused by their partners, they may protest in this nonverbal fashion.

SEXUAL DYSFUNCTION DUE TO A GENERAL MEDICAL CONDITION

The category sexual dysfunction due to a general medical condition covers sexual dysfunction that results in marked distress and interpersonal difficulty; the history, physical examination, or laboratory findings must provide evidence of a general medical condition judged to be causally related to the sexual dysfunction (Table 21.2–12).

Table 21.2–12
DSM-IV Diagnostic Criteria for Sexual Dysfunction Due to a General Medical Condition

A. Clinically significant sexual dysfunction that results in marked distress or interpersonal difficulty predominates in the clinical picture.
B. There is evidence from the history, physical examination, or laboratory findings that the sexual dysfunction is fully explained by the direct physiological effects of a general medical condition.
C. The disturbance is not better accounted for by another mental disorder (eg, major depressive disorder)

Select code and term based on the predominant sexual dysfunction:
Female hypoactive sexual desire disorder due to a general medical condition: if deficient or absent sexual desire is the predominant feature.
Male hypoactive sexual desire disorder due to a general medical condition: if deficient or absent sexual desire is the predominant feature.
Male erectile disorder due to a general medical condition: if male erectile dysfunction is the predominant feature.
Female dyspareunia due to a general medical condition: if pain associated with intercourse is the predominant feature.
Male dyspareunia due to a general medical condition: if pain associated with intercourse is the predominant feature.
Other female sexual dysfunction due to a general medical condition: if some other feature is predominant (eg, orgasmic disorder) or no feature predominates.
Other male sexual dysfunction due to a general medical condition: if some other feature is predominant (eg, orgasmic disorder) or no feature predominates.

Coding note: Include the name of the general medical condition on Axis I, eg, male erectile disorder due to diabetes mellitus; also code the general medical condition on Axis III.

Male Erectile Disorder Due to a General Medical Condition

The incidence of psychological, as opposed to organic, male erectile disorder has been the focus of many studies. Statistics indicate that 20 to 50 percent of men with erectile disorder have an organic basis for the disorder. The organic causes of male erectile disorder are listed in Table 21.2–13. Side effects of medication may impair male sexual functioning in a variety of ways (Table 21.2–14). Castration (removal of the testes) does not always lead to sexual dysfunction, as erection may still occur. A reflex arc, fired when the inner thigh is stimulated, passes through the sacral cord erectile center to account for the phenomenon.

A number of procedures, benign and invasive, are used to help differentiate organically caused impotence from functional impotence. The procedures include monitoring nocturnal penile tumescence (erections that occur during sleep), normally associated with rapid eye movement; monitoring tumescence with a strain gauge; measuring blood pressure in the penis with a penile plethysmograph or an ultrasound (Doppler) flowmeter, both of which assess blood flow in the internal pudendal artery; and measuring pudendal nerve latency time. Other diagnostic tests that delineate organic bases for impotence include glucose tolerance tests, plasma hormone assays, liver and thyroid function tests, prolactin and follicle-stimulating hormone (FSH) determinations, and cystometric examinations. Invasive diagnostic studies include penile arteriography, infusion cavernosography, and radioactive xenon penography. Invasive procedures require expert interpretation and are used only for patients who are candidates for vascular reconstructive procedures.

Dyspareunia Due to a General Medical Condition

An estimated 30 percent of all surgical procedures on the female genital area result in temporary dyspareunia. In addi-

Table 21.2–13
Diseases and Other Medical Conditions Implicated in Male Erectile Disorder

Infectious and parasitic diseases
  Elephantiasis
  Mumps
Cardiovascular disease[a]
  Atherosclerotic disease
  Aortic aneurysm
  Leriche's syndrome
  Cardiac failure
Renal and urological disorders
  Peyronie's disease
  Chronic renal failure
  Hydrocele and varicocele
Hepatic disorders
  Cirrhosis (usually associated with alcohol dependence)
Pulmonary disorders
  Respiratory failure
Genetics
  Klinefelter's syndrome
  Congenital penile vascular and structural abnormalities
Nutritional disorders
  Malnutrition
  Vitamin deficiencies
Endocrine disorders[a]
  Diabetes mellitus
  Dysfunction of the pituitary-adrenal-testis axis
  Acromegaly
  Addison's disease
  Chromophobe adenoma
  Adrenal neoplasia
  Myxedema
  Hyperthyroidism
	Neurological disorders
	  Multiple sclerosis
	  Transverse myelitis
	  Parkinson's disease
	  Temporal lobe epilepsy
	  Traumatic and neoplastic spinal cord diseases[a]
	  Central nervous system tumor
	  Amyotrophic lateral sclerosis
	  Peripheral neuropathy
	  General paresis
	  Tabes dorsalis
	Pharmacological contributants
	  Alcohol and other dependence-inducing substances (heroin, methadone, morphine, cocaine, amphetamines, and barbiturates)
	  Prescribed drugs (psychotropic drugs, antihypertensive drugs, estrogens, and antiandrogens)
	Poisoning
	  Lead (plumbism)
	  Herbicides
	Surgical procedures[a]
	  Perineal prostatectomy
	  Abdominal-perineal colon resection
	  Sympathectomy (frequently interferes with ejaculation)
	  Aortoiliac surgery
	  Radical cystectomy
	  Retroperitoneal lymphadenectomy
	Miscellaneous
	  Radiation therapy
	  Pelvic fracture
	  Any severe systemic disease or debilitating condition

Courtesy of Virginia A. Sadock, M.D.
[a] In the United States an estimated 2 million men are impotent because they suffer from diabetes mellitus; an additional 300,000 are impotent because of other endocrine diseases; 1.5 million are impotent as a result of vascular disease; 180,000 because of multiple sclerosis; 400,000 because of traumas and fractures leading to pelvic fractures or spinal cord injuries; and another 650,000 are impotent as a result of radical surgery, including prostatectomies, colostomies, and cystectomies.

tion, 30 to 40 percent of women with the complaint who are seen in sex therapy clinics have pelvic pathology. Organic abnormalities leading to dyspareunia and vaginismus include irritated or infected hymenal remnants, episiotomy scars, Bartholin's gland infection, various forms of vaginitis and cervicitis, and endometriosis. Postcoital pain has been reported by women with myomata and endometriosis and is attributed to the uterine contractions during orgasm. Postmenopausal women may have dyspareunia resulting from thinning of the vaginal mucosa and reduced lubrication.

Dyspareunia can also occur in men, but it is uncommon and is usually associated with an organic condition, such as Peyronie's disease, which consists of sclerotic plaques on the penis that cause penile curvature.

Hypoactive Sexual Desire Disorder Due to a General Medical Condition

Desire commonly decreases after major illness or surgery, particularly when the body image is affected after such procedures as mastectomy, ileostomy, hysterectomy, and prostatectomy. Illnesses that deplete a person's energy, chronic conditions that require physical and psychological adaptation, and serious illnesses that may cause a person to become depressed can all result in a marked lessening of sexual desire in both men and women.

In some cases, biochemical correlates are associated with hypoactive sexual desire disorder (Table 21.2–15). A recent study found markedly lower levels of serum testosterone in men complaining of low desire than in normal controls in a sleep-laboratory situation. Drugs that depress the central nervous system (CNS) or decrease testosterone production can decrease desire.

Other Male Sexual Dysfunction Due to a General Medical Condition

When another dysfunctional feature is predominant (for example, orgasmic disorder) or when no feature predominates, the category other male sexual dysfunction due to a general medical condition is used.

Male orgasmic disorder may have physiological causes and can occur after surgery on the genitourinary tract, such as prostatectomy. It may also be associated with Parkinson's disease and other neurological disorders involving the lumbar or sacral sections of the spinal cord. The antihypertensive drug gua-

Table 21.2–14
Pharmacological Agents Implicated in Male Sexual Dysfunctions

Drug	Impairs Erection	Impairs Ejaculation
Psychiatric drugs		
Cyclic drugs[a]		
Imipramine (Tofranil)	+	+
Protriptyline (Vivactil)	+	+
Desipramine (Pertofrane)	+	+
Clomipramine (Anafranil)	+	+
Amitriptyline (Elavil)	+	+
Trazodone (Desyrel)[b]	−	−
Monoamine oxidase inhibitors		
Tranylcypromine (Parnate)	+	
Phenelzine (Nardil)	+	+
Pargyline (Eutonyl)	−	+
Isocarboxazid (Marplan)	−	+
Other mood-active drugs		
Lithium (Eskalith)	+	
Amphetamines	+	+
Fluoxetine (Prozac)	−	+
Antipsychotics[c]		
Fluphenazine (Prolixin)	+	
Thioridazine (Mellaril)	+	+
Chlorprothixene (Taractan)	−	+
Mesoridazine (Serentil)	−	+
Perphenazine (Trilafon)	−	+
Trifluoperazine (Stelazine)	−	+
Reserpine (Serpasil)	+	+
Haloperidol (Haldol)	−	+
Antianxiety agent[d]		
Chlordiazepoxide (Librium)	−	+
Antihypertensive drugs		
Clonidine (Catapres)	+	
Methyldopa (Aldomet)	+	+
Spironolactone (Aldactone)	+	−
Hydrochlorothiazide	+	−
Guanethidine (Ismelin)	+	+
Commonly abused substances		
Alcohol	+	+
Barbiturates	+	+
Cannabis	+	−
Cocaine	+	+
Heroin	+	+
Methadone	+	−
Morphine	+	+
Miscellaneous drugs		
Antiparkinsonian agents	+	+
Clofibrate (Atromid-S)	+	−
Digoxin (Lanoxin)	+	−
Glutethimide (Doriden)	+	+
Indomethacin (Indocin)	+	−
Phentolamine (Regitine)	−	+
Propranolol (Inderal)	+	−

Courtesy of Virginia A. Sadock, M.D.

[a] The incidence of male erectile disorder associated with the use of tricyclic drugs is low.

[b] Trazodone has been causative in some cases of priapism.

[c] Impairment of sexual function is not a common complication of the use of antipsychotics. Priapism has occasionally occurred in association with the use of antipsychotics.

[d] Benzodiazepines have been reported to decrease libido, but in some patients the diminution of anxiety caused by those drugs enhances sexual function.

nethidine monosulfate (Ismelin), methyldopa (Aldomet), the phenothiazines, the tricyclic drugs, and the serotonin-specific reuptake inhibitors (SSRIs), among others, have been implicated in retarded ejaculation. Male orgasmic disorder must also be differentiated from retrograde ejaculation, in which ejaculation occurs but the seminal fluid passes backward into the bladder. Retrograde ejaculation always has an organic cause. It can develop after genitourinary surgery and is also associated with medications that have anticholinergic side effects, such as the phenothiazines, especially thioridazine (Mellaril).

Other Female Sexual Dysfunction Due to a General Medical Condition

Some medical conditions—specifically, endocrine diseases such as hypothyroidism, diabetes mellitus, and primary hyperprolactinemia—can affect a woman's ability to have orgasms. Several drugs also affect some women's capacity to have orgasms (Table 21.2–16). Antihypertensive medications, CNS stimulants, tricyclic drugs, SSRIs, and, frequently, monoamine oxidase inhibitors (MAOIs) have interfered with female orgasmic capacity. One study of women taking MAOIs, however, found that after 16 to 18 weeks of pharmacotherapy, the side effect of the medication disappeared and the women were able to reexperience orgasms, although they continued taking an undiminished dosage of the drug.

SUBSTANCE-INDUCED SEXUAL DYSFUNCTION

The diagnosis of substance-induced sexual dysfunction is used when evidence of substance intoxication or withdrawal is apparent from the history, physical examination, or laboratory findings. Distressing sexual dysfunction occurs within a month of significant substance intoxication or withdrawal (Table 21.2–17). Specified substances include alcohol; amphetamines or related substances; cocaine; opioids; sedatives, hypnotics, or anxiolytics; and other or unknown substances.

Abused recreational substances affect sexual function in various ways. In small doses, many substances enhance sexual performance by decreasing inhibition or anxiety or by causing a temporary elation of mood. With continued use, however, erectile engorgement, orgasmic, and ejaculatory capacities become impaired. The abuse of sedatives, anxiolytics, hypnotics, and particularly opiates and opioids nearly always depresses desire. Alcohol may foster the initiation of sexual activity by removing inhibition, but it also impairs performance. Cocaine and amphetamines produce similar effects. Although no direct evidence indicates that sexual drive is enhanced, users initially have feelings of increased energy and may become sexually active. Ultimately, dysfunction occurs. Men usually go through two stages: an experience of prolonged erection without ejaculation, then a gradual loss of erectile capability.

Patients recovering from substance dependency may need therapy to regain sexual function, partly because of psychological readjustment to a nondependent state. Many substance abusers have always had difficulty with intimate interactions. Others who spent their crucial developmental years under the influence of a substance have missed the experiences that would have enabled them to learn social and sexual skills.

Table 21.2–15
Neurophysiology of Sexual Dysfunction

	DA	5-HT	NE	ACh	Clinical Correlation
Erection	↑	O	α, β ↓ ↑	M	Antipsychotics may lead to erectile dysfunction (DA block): DA agonists may lead to enhanced erection and libido; priapism with trazodone (α_1 block); β-blockers may lead to impotence
Ejaculation and orgasm	O	± ↓	α_1 ↑	M	α_1-Blockers (tricyclic drugs, MAOIs, thioridazine) may lead to impaired ejaculation; 5-HT agents may inhibit orgasm

Reprinted with permission from Segraves R: *Psychiatric Times,* 1990.
↑, facilitates; ↓, inhibits or decreases; ±, some; ACh, acetylcholine; DA, dopamine; 5-HT, serotonin; M, modulates; NE, norepinephrine; O, minimal.

PHARMACOLOGICAL AGENTS IMPLICATED IN SEX DYSFUNCTION

Almost every pharmacological agent, particularly those used in psychiatry, has been associated with an effect on sexuality. In men these effects include decreased sex drive, erectile failure (impotence), decreased volume of ejaculate, and delayed or retrograde ejaculation. In women decreased sex drive, decreased vaginal lubrication, inhibited or delayed orgasm, and decreased or absent vaginal contractions may occur. Drugs may also enhance the sexual responses and increase the sex drive, but this is less common than are adverse effects (Table 21.2–18).

Psychoactive Drugs

Antipsychotic Drugs. Most antipsychotic drugs are dopamine receptor antagonists that also block adrenergic and

Table 21.2–16
Some Psychiatric Drugs Implemented in Inhibited Female Orgasm[a]

Tricyclic antidepressants
- Imipramine (Tofranil)
- Clomipramine (Anafranil)
- Nortriptyline (Aventyl)

Monoamine oxidase inhibitors
- Tranylcypromine (Parnate)
- Phenelzine (Nardil)
- Isocarboxazid (Marplan)

Dopamine receptor antagonists
- Thioridazine (Mellaril)
- Trifluoperazine (Stelazine)

Selective serotonergic receptor inhibitors
- Fluoxetine (Prozac)
- Paroxetine (Paxil)
- Sertraline (Zoloft)

Courtesy of Virginia A. Sadock, M.D.
[a] The interrelationship between female sexual dysfunction and pharmacological agents has been less extensively evaluated than have male reactions. Oral contraceptives are reported to decrease libido in some women, and some drugs with anticholinergic side effects may impair arousal as well as orgasm. Benzodiazepines have been reported to decrease libido, but in some patients the diminution of anxiety caused by those drugs enhances sexual function.
Both increase and decrease in libido have been reported with psychoactive agents. It is difficult to separate those effects from the underlying condition or from improvement of the condition. Sexual dysfunction associated with the use of a drug disappears when the drug is discontinued.

Table 21.2–17
DSM-IV Diagnostic Criteria for Substance-Induced Sexual Dysfunction

A. Clinically significant sexual dysfunction that results in marked distress or interpersonal difficulty predominates in the clinical picture.
B. There is evidence from the history, physical examination, or laboratory findings that the sexual dysfunction is fully explained by substance use as manifested by either (1) or (2):
   (1) the symptoms in criterion A developed during, or within a month of, substance intoxication
   (2) medication use is etiologically related to the disturbance
C. The disturbance is not better accounted for by a sexual dysfunction that is not substance induced. Evidence that the symptoms are better accounted for by a sexual dysfunction that is not substance induced might include the following: the symptoms precede the onset of the substance use or dependence (or medication use); the symptoms persist for a substantial period of time (eg, about a month) after the cessation of intoxication, or are substantially in excess of what would be expected given the type or amount of the substance used or the duration of use; or there is other evidence that suggests the existence of an independent non-substance-induced sexual dysfunction (eg, a history of recurrent non–substance-related episodes).

Note: This diagnosis should be made instead of a diagnosis of substance intoxication only when the sexual dysfunction is in excess of that usually associated with the intoxication syndrome and when the dysfunction is sufficiently severe to warrant independent clinical attention.

Code: [Specific substance]-induced sexual dysfunction (alcohol, amphetamine [or amphetamine-like substance]; cocaine; opioid; sedative, hypnotic, or anxiolytic; other [or unknown] substance)

Specify if:
With impaired desire
With impaired arousal
With impaired orgasm
With sexual pain

Specify if:
With onset during intoxication: if the criteria are met for intoxication with the substance and the symptoms develop during the intoxication syndrome

Reprinted with permission from American Psychiatric Association: *Diagnostic and Statistical Manual of Mental Disorders,* ed 4. Copyright, American Psychiatric Association, Washington, 1994.

Table 21.2–18
Diagnostic Issues With Sex and Drugs

Differential diagnosis of drug-induced sexual dysfunction	Problem after drug therapy started or drug overdose Problem not situation or partner-specific Not a lifelong or recurrent problem No obvious nonpharmacological precipitant Dissipates with drug discontinuation
Antipsychotic drugs and ejaculatory problems	Perphenazine Chlorpromazine Trifluoperazine Haloperidol Mesoridazine Thioridazine Chlorprothixene
Antipsychotic drugs and priapism	Perphenazine Mesoridazine Chlorpromazine Thioridazine Fluphenazine Molindone Risperidone Clozapine

Adapted from Seagraves RT: Prim Psychiatry *4:* 46, 1997.

cholinergic receptors, thus accounting for adverse sexual effects. Chlorpromazine (Thorazine), thioridazine, and trifluoperazine (Stelazine) are potent anticholinergics and impair erection and ejaculation, in which the seminal fluid backs up into the bladder rather than being propelled through the penile urethra. Patients still have a pleasurable sensation, but the orgasm is dry. When urinating after orgasm, the urine may be milky white because it contains the ejaculate. The condition is startling but harmless and may occur in up to 50 percent of patients taking the drug. Paradoxically, some rare cases of priapism have been reported with antipsychotics.

Antidepressant Drugs. The tricyclic and tetracyclic antidepressants have anticholinergic effects that interfere with erection and delay ejaculation. Since the anticholinergic effects vary among the cyclic antidepressants, those with the fewest effects (such as desipramine [Norpramin]) produce the fewest sexual side effects. The effects in women of the tricyclics and tetracyclics have not been documented sufficiently; however, few women seem to complain of any effects.

Some men report an increased sensitivity of the glans that is pleasurable and that does not interfere with erection, although it delays ejaculation. In some cases, however, the tricyclic causes a painful ejaculation, perhaps as the result of interference with seminal propulsion caused by interference with, in turn, urethral, prostatic, vas, and epididymal smooth muscle contractions. Clomipramine has been reported to increase sex drive in some persons. Deprenyl (Selegiline), a selective MAO type B (MAO_B) inhibitor, and bupropion (Wellbutrin) have also been reported to increase sex drive, possibly by dopaminergic activity and increased production of norepinephrine.

Venlafaxine (Effexor) and the SSRIs most often have adverse effects because of the rise in serotonin levels. A lowering of the sex drive and a difficulty in reaching orgasm occur in both sexes. Reversal of those negative effects has been achieved with cyproheptadine (Periactin), an antihistamine with antiserotonergic effects, and with methylphenidate (Ritalin), which has adrenergic effects. Trazodone is associated with the rare occurrence of priapism, the symptom of prolonged erection in the absence of sexual stimuli. That symptom appears to result from the α_2-adrenergic antagonism of trazodone.

The MAOIs affect biogenic amines broadly. Accordingly, they produce impaired erection, delayed or retrograde ejaculation, vaginal dryness, and inhibited orgasm. Tranylcypromine (Parnate) has a paradoxical sexually stimulating effect in some persons, possibly as a result of its amphetamine-like properties.

GENERAL EFFECTS. Since depression is associated with a decreased libido, varying levels of sexual dysfunction and anhedonia are part of the disease process. Some patients report improved sexual functioning as their depression improves as a result of antidepressant medication. The phenomenon makes the evaluation of sexual side effects difficult; also, the side effects may disappear with time, perhaps because a biogenic amine homeostatic mechanism comes into play.

Lithium. Lithium regulates mood and in the manic state may reduce hypersexuality, possibly by a dopamine antagonist activity. In some patients, impaired erection has been reported.

Sympathomimetics. Psychostimulants are sometimes used in the treatment of depression and include amphetamines, methylphenidate, and pemoline (Cylert), which raise the plasma levels of norepinephrine and dopamine. Libido is increased; however, with prolonged use, men may experience a loss of desire and erections.

α-Adrenergic and β-Adrenergic Receptor Antagonists. α-Adrenergic and β-adrenergic receptor antagonists are used in the treatment of hypertension, angina, and certain cardiac arrhythmias. They diminish tonic sympathetic nerve outflow from vasomotor centers in the brain. As a result, they can cause impotence, decrease the volume of ejaculate, and produce retrograde ejaculation. Changes in libido have been reported in both sexes.

Suggestions have been made to use the side effects of drugs therapeutically. Thus a drug that delays or interferes with ejaculation (such as fluoxetine) might be used to treat premature ejaculation.

Anticholinergics. The anticholinergics block cholinergic receptors and include such drugs as amantadine (Symmetrel) and benztropine (Cogentin). They produce dryness of the mucous membranes (including that of the vagina) and impotence.

Antihistamines. Drugs such as diphenhydramine (Benadryl) have anticholinergic activity and are mildly hypnotic. They may inhibit sexual function as a result. Cyproheptadine, although an antihistamine, also has potent activity as a serotonin antagonist. It is used to block the serotonergic sexual side effects produced by SSRIs, such as delayed orgasm and impotence.

Antianxiety Agents. The major class of anxiolytics is the benzodiazepines (such as diazepam [Valium]). They act on the γ-aminobutyric acid (GABA) receptors, which are believed to be involved in cognition, memory, and motor control. Because they decrease plasma epinephrine concentrations, they diminish anxiety, and as a result they improve sexual function in people inhibited by anxiety.

Alcohol. Alcohol suppresses CNS activity generally and can produce erectile disorders in men as a result. Alcohol has a direct gonadal effect that decreases testosterone levels in men; paradoxically, it can produce a slight rise in testosterone levels in women. The latter finding may account for women reporting increased libido after drinking small amounts of alcohol. The long-term use of alcohol reduces the ability of the liver to metabolize estrogenic compounds. In men that produces signs of feminization (such as gynecomastia as a result of testicular atrophy).

Opioids. Opioids, such as heroin, have adverse sexual effects, such as erectile failure and decreased libido. The alteration of consciousness may enhance the sexual experience in occasional users.

Hallucinogens. The hallucinogens include lysergic acid diethylamide (LSD), phencyclidine (PCP), psilocybin (from some mushrooms), and mescaline (from peyote cactus). In addition to inducing hallucinations, the drugs cause loss of contact with reality and an expanding and heightening of consciousness. Some users report that the sexual experience is similarly enhanced, but others experience anxiety, delirium, or psychosis, which clearly interferes with sex function.

Cannabis. The altered state of consciousness produced by cannabis may enhance sexual pleasure for some persons. Its prolonged use depresses testosterone levels.

Barbiturates and Similarly Acting Drugs. Barbiturates and similarly acting sedative-hypnotic drugs may enhance sexual responsiveness in people who are sexually unresponsive as a result of anxiety. They have no direct effect on the sex organs; however, they do produce an alteration in consciousness that some people find pleasurable. They are subject to abuse and may be fatal when combined with alcohol or other CNS depressants.

Methaqualone (Quaalude) acquired a reputation as a sexual enhancer, which had no biological basis in fact. It is no longer marketed in the United States.

SEXUAL DYSFUNCTION NOT OTHERWISE SPECIFIED

The category sexual dysfunction not otherwise specified covers sexual dysfunctions that cannot be classified under the categories described above (Table 21.2–19). Examples include people who experience the physiological components of sexual excitement and orgasm but report no erotic sensation or even anesthesia (orgasmic anhedonia). Women with conditions analogous to premature ejaculation in men are classified here. Orgasmic women who desire, but have not experienced, multiple orgasms can be classified under this heading as well. Also, disorders of excessive rather than inhibited dysfunction, such as compulsive masturbation or coitus (sex addiction), or those with genital pain occurring during masturbation may be classified here. Other unspecified disorders are found in people who have one or more sexual fantasies about which they feel guilty or otherwise dysphoric, but the range of common sexual fantasies is broad.

Table 21.2–19
DSM-IV Diagnostic Criteria for Sexual Dysfunction Not Otherwise Specified

This category includes sexual dysfunctions that do not meet criteria for any specific sexual dysfunction. Examples include

1. No (or substantially diminished) subjective erotic feelings despite otherwise normal arousal and orgasm
2. Situations in which the clinician has concluded that a sexual dysfunction is present but is unable to determine whether it is primary, due to a general medical condition, or substance induced.

Postcoital Headache

Postcoital headache, characterized by headache immediately after coitus, may last for several hours. It is usually described as throbbing and is localized in the occipital or frontal area. The cause is unknown. There may be vascular, muscle-contraction (tension), or psychogenic causes. Coitus may precipitate migraine or cluster headaches in predisposed people.

Orgasmic Anhedonia

Orgasmic anhedonia is a condition in which a person has no physical sensation of orgasm, even though the physiological component (for example, ejaculation) remains intact. Organic causes, such as sacral and cephalic lesions that interfere with afferent pathways from the genitalia to the cortex, must be ruled out. Psychic causes usually relate to extreme guilt about experiencing sexual pleasure. These feelings produce a dissociative response that isolates the affective component of the orgasmic experience from consciousness.

Masturbatory Pain

People may experience pain during masturbation. Organic causes should always be ruled out; a small vaginal tear or early Peyronie's disease may produce a painful sensation. The condition should be differentiated from compulsive masturbation. People may masturbate to the extent that they do physical damage to their genitals and eventually experience pain during subsequent masturbatory acts. Such cases constitute a separate sexual disorder and should be so classified.

Certain masturbatory practices have resulted in what has been called autoerotic asphyxiation. The practices involve people masturbating while hanging by the neck to heighten the erotic sensations and the orgasm's intensity through the mechanism of mild hypoxia. Although the people intend to release themselves from the noose after orgasm, an estimated 500 to 1,000 people a year accidentally kill themselves by hanging. Most who indulge in the practice are male; transvestism is often associated with the habit, and most deaths occur among adolescents. Such masochistic practices are usually associated with severe mental disorders, such as schizophrenia and major mood disorders.

TREATMENT

Before 1970 the most common treatment of sexual dysfunctions was individual psychotherapy. Classic psychodynamic theory holds that sexual inadequacy has its roots in early developmental conflicts, and the sexual disorder is treated as part of a pervasive emotional disturbance. Treatment focuses on the exploration of unconscious conflicts, motivation, fantasy, and various interpersonal difficulties. One of the assumptions of therapy is that the removal of the conflicts allows the sexual impulse to become structurally acceptable to the ego and thereby the patient finds appropriate means of satisfaction in the environment. Unfortunately, the symptoms of sexual dysfunctions frequently become secondarily autonomous and continue to persist, even when other problems evolving from the patients' pathology have been resolved. The addition of behavioral techniques is often necessary to cure the sexual problem.

Dual-Sex Therapy

The theoretical basis of dual-sex therapy is the concept of the marital unit or dyad as the object of therapy; the approach represents the major advance in the diagnosis and treatment of sexual disorders in this century. The methodology was originated and developed by William Masters and Virginia Johnson. In dual-sex therapy, treatment is based on a concept that the couple must be treated when a dysfunctional person is in a relationship. Because both are involved in a sexually distressing situation, both must participate in the therapy program.

The sexual problem often reflects other areas of disharmony or misunderstanding in the marriage so that the entire marital relationship is treated, with emphasis on sexual functioning as a part of the relationship. The keystone of the program is the roundtable session in which a male and female therapy team clarifies, discusses, and works through problems with the couple. The four-way sessions require active participation by the patients. Therapists and patients discuss the psychological and physiological aspects of sexual functioning, and therapists have an educative attitude. Therapists suggest specific sexual activities, which the couple follows in the privacy of their home. The aim of the therapy is to establish or reestablish communication within the marital unit. Sex is emphasized as a natural function that flourishes in the appropriate domestic climate, and improved communication is encouraged toward that end. In a variation of this therapy that has proved effective, one therapist may treat the couple.

Treatment is short-term and behaviorally oriented. The therapists attempt to reflect the situation as they see it, rather than to interpret underlying dynamics. An undistorted picture of the relationship presented by the therapists often corrects the myopic, narrow view held by each marriage partner. This new perspective can interrupt the couple's vicious circle of relating and can encourage improved, more effective communication.

Specific exercises are prescribed for the couple to treat their particular problems. Sexual inadequacy often involves lack of information, misinformation, and performance fear. Therefore, the couple are specifically prohibited from any sexual play other than that prescribed by the therapists. Beginning exercises usually focus on heightening sensory awareness to touch, sight, sound, and smell. Initially, intercourse is interdicted, and the couple learn to give and receive bodily pleasure without the pressure of performance or penetration. At the same time, they learn how to communicate nonverbally in a mutually satisfactory way, and they learn that sexual foreplay is an enjoyable alternative to intercourse and orgasm.

During the sensate focus exercises, the couple receive much reinforcement to reduce their anxiety. They are urged to use fantasies to distract them from obsessive concerns about performance (spectatoring). The needs of both the dysfunctional partner and the nondysfunctional partner are considered. If either partner becomes sexually excited by the exercises, the other is encouraged to bring him or her to orgasm by manual or oral means. Open communication between the partners is urged, and the expression of mutual needs is encouraged. Resistances, such as claims of fatigue or not enough time to complete the exercises, are common and must be dealt with by the therapists. Genital stimulation is eventually added to general body stimulation. The couple are instructed sequentially to try various positions for intercourse, without necessarily completing the act, and to use varieties of stimulating techniques before they are instructed to proceed with intercourse.

Psychotherapy sessions follow each new exercise period, and problems and satisfactions, both sexual and in other areas of the couple's lives, are discussed. Specific instructions and the introduction of new exercises geared to the individual couple's progress are reviewed in each session. Gradually, the couple gain confidence and learn to communicate, verbally and sexually. Dual-sex therapy is most effective when the sexual dysfunction exists apart from other psychopathology.

Specific Techniques and Exercises

Various techniques are used to treat the various dysfunctions. In cases of vaginismus, a woman is advised to dilate her vaginal opening with her fingers or with graduated dilators.

In cases of premature ejaculation, an exercise known as the squeeze technique is used to raise the threshold of penile excitability. In this exercise the man or the woman stimulates the erect penis until the earliest sensations of impending ejaculation are felt. At this point, the woman forcefully squeezes the coronal ridge of the glans, the erection is diminished, and ejaculation is inhibited. The exercise program eventually raises the threshold of the sensation of ejaculatory inevitability and allows the man to become aware of his sexual sensations and confident about his sexual performance. A variant of the exercise is the stop-start technique developed by James H. Semans, in which the woman stops all stimulation of the penis when the man first senses an impending ejaculation. No squeeze is used. Research has shown that the presence or absence of circumcision has no bearing on a man's ejaculatory control; the glans is equally sensitive in the two states. Sex therapy has been most successful in the treatment of premature ejaculation.

A man with a sexual desire disorder or male erectile disorder is sometimes told to masturbate to prove that full erection and ejaculation are possible. Male orgasmic disorder is managed initially by extravaginal ejaculation and then by gradual vaginal entry after stimulation to a point near ejaculation.

In cases of lifelong female orgasmic disorder, the woman is directed to masturbate, sometimes using a vibrator. The shaft of the clitoris is the masturbatory site most preferred by women, and orgasm depends on adequate clitoral stimulation. An area on the anterior wall of the vagina has been identified in some women as a site of sexual excitation known as the G-spot; but reports of an ejaculatory phenomenon at orgasm in women following the stimulation of the G-spot have not been satisfactorily verified.

Hypnotherapy

Hypnotherapists focus specifically on the anxiety-producing symptom—that is, the particular sexual dysfunction. The successful use of hypnosis enables patients to gain control over the symptom that has been lowering self-esteem and disrupting psychological homeostasis. The cooperation of the patient is first obtained and encouraged during a series of nonhypnotic sessions with the therapist. Those discussions permit the development of a secure doctor–patient relationship, a sense of physical and psychological comfort on the part of the patient, and the establishment of mutually desired treatment goals. During this time the therapist assesses the patient's capacity for the trance experience. The nonhypnotic sessions also permit the clinician to take a psychiatric history and perform a mental status examination before beginning hypnotherapy. The focus of treatment is on symptom removal and attitude alteration. The patient is instructed in developing alternative means of dealing with the anxiety-provoking situation, the sexual encounter.

Patients are also taught relaxation techniques to use on themselves before sexual relations. With these methods to alleviate anxiety, the physiological responses to sexual stimulation can readily result in pleasurable excitation and discharge. Psychological impediments to vaginal lubrication, erection, and orgasms are removed, and normal sexual functioning ensues. Hypnosis may be added to a basic individual psychotherapy program to accelerate the effects of psychotherapeutic intervention.

Behavior Therapy

Behavioral approaches were initially designed for the treatment of phobias but are now used to treat other dysfunctions as well. Behavior therapists assume that sexual dysfunction is learned maladaptive behavior, which causes patients to be fearful of sexual interaction. Using traditional techniques, therapists set up a hierarchy of anxiety-provoking situations, ranging from least threatening, for instance, the thought of kissing, to most threatening, the thought of penile penetration. The behavior therapist enables the patient to master the anxiety through a standard program of systematic desensitization, which is designed to inhibit the learned anxious response by encouraging behaviors antithetical to anxiety. The patient first deals with the least anxiety-producing situation in fantasy and progresses by steps to the most anxiety-producing situation. Medication, hypnosis, and special training in deep muscle relaxation are sometimes used to help with the initial mastery of anxiety.

Assertiveness training is helpful in teaching patients to express sexual needs openly and without fear. Exercises in assertiveness are given in conjunction with sex therapy; patients are encouraged to make sexual requests and to refuse to comply with requests perceived as unreasonable. Sexual exercises may be prescribed for patients to perform at home, and a hierarchy may be established, starting with those activities that have proved most pleasurable and successful in the past.

One treatment variation involves the participation of the patient's sexual partner in the desensitization program. The partner, rather than the therapist, presents items of increasing stimulation value to the patient. In such situations, a cooperative partner is necessary to help the patient carry gains made during treatment sessions to sexual activity at home.

Group Therapy

Group therapy has been used to examine both intrapsychic and interpersonal problems in patients with sexual disorders. A therapy group provides a strong support system for a patient who feels ashamed, anxious, or guilty about a particular sexual problem. It is a useful forum in which to counteract sexual myths, correct misconceptions, and provide accurate information about sexual anatomy, physiology, and varieties of behavior.

Groups for the treatment of sexual disorders can be organized in several ways. Members may all share the same problem, such as premature ejaculation; members may all be of the same sex with different sexual problems; or groups may be composed of both men and women who are experiencing a variety of sexual problems. Group therapy may be an adjunct to other forms of therapy or the prime mode of treatment. Groups organized to treat a particular dysfunction are usually behavioral in approach.

Groups composed of married couples with sexual dysfunctions have also been effective. A group provides the opportunity to gather accurate information, offers consensual validation of individual preferences, and enhances self-esteem and self-acceptance. Techniques such as role playing and psychodrama may be used in treatment. Such groups are not indicated for couples when one partner is uncooperative, when a patient has a severe depressive disorder or psychosis, when a patient finds explicit sexual audiovisual material repugnant, or when a patient fears or dislikes groups.

Analytically Oriented Sex Therapy

One of the most effective treatment modalities is the use of sex therapy integrated with psychodynamic and psychoanalytically oriented psychotherapy. The sex therapy is conducted over a longer period than usual, which allows learning or relearning of sexual satisfaction under the realities of patients' day-to-day lives. The addition of psychodynamic conceptualizations to behavioral techniques used to treat sexual dysfunctions allows the treatment of patients with sexual disorders associated with other psychopathology.

The material and dynamics that emerge in patients in analytically oriented sex therapy are the same as those in psychoanalytic therapy, such as dreams, fear of punishment, aggressive feelings, difficulty trusting a partner, fear of intimacy, oedipal feelings, and fear of genital mutilation. The combined approach of analytically oriented sex therapy is used by the general psychiatrist who carefully judges the optimal timing of sex therapy and the ability of patients to tolerate the directive approach that focuses on their sexual difficulties.

Biological Treatments

Biological forms of treatment have limited application but are currently receiving more attention. Intravenous methohexital (Brevital) has been used in desensitization therapy. Anxiolytics may have application in tense patients, although these drugs can also interfere with sexual response. Sometimes the side effects of such drugs as thioridazine, SSRIs, and the tricyclic drugs are taken advantage of to prolong sexual response in such conditions as premature ejaculation. The use of tricyclics has also been advocated in the treatment of patients who are phobic about sex. Pharmacological approaches are also appropriate for treating any underlying mental disorder that may be contributing to sexual dysfunction. For example, patients whose sexual functioning is impaired as a result of depression usually show improved performance as their depression responds to antidepressant medication.

Specific medications to deal with sexual dysfunctions have differing rates of success. Testosterone, which affects libido, is beneficial to those patients who have a demonstrated low testosterone level. In some postmenopausal women it may be used to increase desire. In women, however, testosterone may lead to masculinization, such as deep voice, enlarged clitoris, and hirsutism, all of which may not be reversible on discontinuing the medication. Testosterone is contraindicated when fertility must be maintained. Case reports indicate that cyproheptadine and amantadine can reverse drug-induced female orgasmic disorder and male orgasmic disorder in men taking fluoxetine. Clomipramine has been reported to both induce spontaneous orgasms and inhibit orgasms in women. There are no known aphrodisiacs. Although recent studies report improvement in erectile responses in men ingesting yohimbine (Yocon) or amphetamines, these findings remain controversial. Also controversial is the use of gonadotropin-releasing hormone as an inhalant. Such substances as powdered rhinoceros horn, used in Asia for its alleged stimulatory effects, are of benefit only through the power of suggestion in a particular culture.

There are several biological treatments for male erectile dysfunction. They include the use of vacuum pumps, constrictive rings, self-injection or urethral insertion of vasoactive materials into the penis, and surgical treatment.

Patients without vascular diseases can use pumps to obtain erections, which are then maintained by placing a constrictive ring at the base of the penis. The bulkiness of the pump, however, along with the occasional pain and the atypically red color it produces in the penis makes this method unsatisfactory for many men and their partners.

Injection of vasoactive materials into the corporal bodies of the penis produces erections for periods of an hour or longer. The newest pharmacological agent, alprostadil (Caverject), is a type of prostaglandin E_1. Mixtures of prostaglandin, papaverine, and phentolamine (Regitine) have also been used. Alprostadil may be administered by direct injection into the corpora cavernosa or by intraurethral insertion using a cannula.

Treatment consists of introducing alprostadil into the corpora or urethra by the patient before coitus. This technique is easily taught by a urologist and is relatively painless. The drug causes direct smooth muscle relaxation of penile vessels and erectile tissue; this reaction lowers the vascular resistance of the corpora and causes a significant increase in blood flow to the penis. A firm erection is produced by the increased blood flow within 2 to 3 minutes. When coupled with insight-oriented or behavioral sex therapy, the use of alprostadil can reverse psychogenic erectile disorder resistant to psychotherapy alone, the ultimate goal being unassisted erectile function.

Ongoing trials with topical prostaglandin E_1 and oral medication are promising and may offer a less invasive medicinal alternative in the near future.

Surgical treatment is rarely advocated. Improved penile prosthetic devices are available for men with inadequate erectile responses who are resistant to other treatment methods or who have deficiencies of organic origin. The placement of a penile prosthesis in a man who has lost the ability to ejaculate or have an orgasm because of organic causes will not enable him to recover these functions. Men with prosthetic devices have generally reported satisfaction with their subsequent sexual functioning, but their wives report much less satisfaction than do the men. Presurgical counseling is strongly recommended so that the couple have a realistic expectation of what the prosthesis can do for their sex lives. Some physicians are attempting revascularization of the penis as a direct approach to treating erectile dysfunction caused by vascular disorders. In patients with corporal shunts that allow normally entrapped blood to leak from the corporal spaces, a process leading to inadequate erections (steal phenomenon), such surgical procedures are indicated. There are limited reports of prolonged success with the technique. Endarterectomy can be of benefit if aortoiliac occlusive disease is responsible for erectile dysfunction.

Surgical approaches to female sexual dysfunctions include hymenectomy in the case of dyspareunia in an unconsummated marriage, vaginoplasty in multiparous women who complain of reduced vaginal sensation, and the release of clitoral adhesions in women with sexual arousal disorder. Such surgical treatments have not been carefully studied and should be considered with great caution.

References

Dawkins S, Taylor R: Non-consummation of marriage. Lancet *2:* 1029, 1961.

DeWire DM: Evaluation and treatment of erectile dysfunction. Am Fam Physician *53:* 2101, 1996.

Fordney DS: Dyspareunia and vaginismus. Clin Obstet Gynecol *21:* 205, 1978.

Frank E: Frequency of sexual dysfunction in "normal" couples. N Engl J Med *299:* 111, 1978.

Freud S: Three essays on the theory of sexuality. In *Standard Edition of the Complete Psychological Works of Sigmund Freud,* vol 7, p 125. Hogarth Press, London, 1953.

Furlow WL: Male sexual dysfunction. Urol Clin North Am *8:* 1, 1981.

Hawton K, Catalan J, Fagg J: Sex therapy for erectile dysfunction: Characteristics of couples, treatment outcome, and prognostic factors. Arch Sex Behav *21:* 161, 1992.

Herman J, Lo Piccolo J: Clinical outcome of sex therapy. Arch Gen Psychiatry *40:* 443, 1983.

Linet OI, Ogrinc FG: Efficacy and safety of intracavernosal alprostadil in men with erectile dysfunction. The Alprostadil Study Group. N Engl J Med *334:* 873, 1996.

Marmor J, editor: *Homosexual Behavior.* Basic Books, New York, 1980.

Masters WH, Johnson VE: *Human Sexual Inadequacy.* Little, Brown, Boston, 1970.

Moss HB, Panzak GL, Tarter RE: Sexual functioning of male anabolic steroid abusers. Arch Sex Behav *22:* 1, 1993.

Rowland DL, Slob AK: Understanding and diagnosing sexual dysfunction: Re-

cent progress through psychophysiological and psychophysical methods. Neurosci Biobehav Rev *19:* 201, 1995.
Sadock BJ, Kaplan HI, Freedman AM, editors: *The Sexual Experience.* Williams & Wilkins, Baltimore, 1976.
Sadock VA: Normal human sexuality and sexual dysfunction. In *Comprehensive Textbook of Psychiatry,* ed 6, HI Kaplan, BJ Sadock, editors, p 1295. Williams & Wilkins, Baltimore, 1995.
Schiavi RC, Karstaedt A, Schreiner-Engel P, Mandeli J: Psychometric characteristics of individuals with sexual dysfunction and their partners. J Sex Marital Ther *18:* 219, 1992.
Segraves RT: Effects of psychotropic drugs on human erections and ejaculation. Arch Gen Psychiatry *46:* 782, 1989.
Semans JH: Premature ejaculation: A new approach. South Med J *49:* 353, 1956.
Zorgniotto AW, Lefleueck RS: Autoinjection of corpus cavernosum with vasoactive drug combination with vasculogenic impotence. J Urol *133:* 39, 1985.

▲ 21.3 Paraphilias and Sexual Disorder Not Otherwise Specified

PARAPHILIAS

The word *paraphilia* comes from two Greek words meaning "to the side of" and "love." In the fourth edition of *Diagnostic and Statistical Manual of Mental Disorders* (DSM-IV), paraphilia is defined as unusual fantasies or sexual urges or behaviors that are recurrent and sexually arousing. These activities generally focus on a person's humiliating himself or herself or a partner, on children or other nonconsenting people, or on nonhuman objects. The urges and behaviors must occur for at least 6 months and must cause "clinically significant distress or impairment in social, occupational, or other important areas of functioning." Paraphilia can involve illegal activities; criminal sexual offenses belong to this category of disorder.

The specialized sexual fantasies and intense sexual urges and practices of paraphilias are usually repetitive and distressing to those undergoing them. A special fantasy, with its unconscious and conscious components, is the pathognomonic element, with sexual arousal and orgasm being associated phenomena. The influence of fantasies and their behavioral manifestations extend beyond the sexual sphere to pervade people's lives. The major functions of human sexual behavior are to assist in bonding, to express and enhance love between two people, and to procreate. Paraphilias are divergent behaviors in that their participants conceal them, and the acts appear to exclude or harm others and to disrupt the potential for bonding between people. Paraphiliac arousal may be transient in some people who act out their impulses only during periods of stress or conflict. More often they are lifelong problems with paraphiliac imagery starting before or during puberty.

Classification

DSM-IV. The major categories of paraphilias in DSM-IV are exhibitionism, fetishism, frotteurism, pedophilia, sexual masochism, sexual sadism, voyeurism, transvestic fetishism, and a separate category for other paraphilias not otherwise specified—for example, zoophilia. A given person may have multiple paraphiliac disorders.

ICD-10. In the 10th revision of *International Statistical Classification of Diseases and Related Health Problems* (ICD-10), the paraphilias are classified as disorders of sexual preference. In ICD-10, six specific disorders—fetishism, fetishistic transvestism, exhibitionism, voyeurism, pedophilia, and sadomasochism—and three residual categories are listed (Table 21.3–1).

Epidemiology

Paraphilias are practiced by only a small percentage of the population, but the insistent, repetitive nature of the disorders results in a high frequency of such acts. Thus, a large proportion of the population has been victimized by people with paraphilias.

Among legally identified cases of paraphilias, pedophilia is most common. Ten to 20 percent of all children have been molested by age 18. Because a child is the object, the act is taken more seriously, and greater effort is spent tracking down the culprit than in other paraphilias. People with exhibitionism who publicly display themselves to young children are also commonly apprehended. Those with voyeurism may be apprehended, but their risk is not great. Twenty percent of adult females have been the targets of people with exhibitionism and voyeurism. Sexual masochism and sexual sadism are underrepresented in any prevalence estimates. Sexual sadism usually comes to attention only in sensational cases of rape, brutality, and lust murder. The excretory paraphilias are scarcely reported, as any activity usually takes place between consenting adults or between prostitute and client. People with fetishism rarely become entangled in the legal system. Those with transvestic fetishism may be arrested occasionally for disturbing the peace or on other misdemeanor charges if they are obviously men dressed in women's clothes, but arrest is more common among those with gender identity disorders. Zoophilia as a true paraphilia is rare.

As usually defined, the paraphilias seem to be largely male conditions. Fetishism almost always occurs in men. More than 50 percent of all paraphilias have their onset before age 18. Patients with paraphilia frequently have three to five paraphilias, either concurrently or at different times in their lives. This pattern of occurrence is especially the case with exhibitionism, fetishism, sexual masochism, sexual sadism, transvestic fetishism, voyeurism, and zoophilia (Table 21.3–2). The occurrence of paraphiliac behavior peaks between ages 15 and 25 and gradually declines; in men of 50, criminal paraphiliac acts are rare. Those that occur are practiced in isolation or with a cooperative partner.

Etiology

Psychosocial Factors. In the classic psychoanalytic model, people with a paraphilia have failed to complete the normal developmental process toward heterosexual adjustment, but the model has been modified by new psychoanalytic approaches. What distinguishes one paraphilia from another is the method chosen by a person (usually male) to cope with the anxiety caused by the threat of castration by the father and separation from the mother. However bizarre its manifestation, the resulting behavior provides an outlet for the sexual and

Table 21.3–1
ICD-10 Diagnostic Criteria for Disorders of Sexual Preference

G1. The individual experiences recurrent intense sexual urges and fantasies involving unusual objects or activities.

G2. The individual either acts on the urges or is markedly distressed by them.

G3. The preference has been present for at least 6 months.

Fetishism

A. The general criteria for disorders of sexual preference must be met.

B. The fetish (some nonliving object) is the most important source of sexual stimulation or is essential for satisfactory sexual response.

Fetishistic transvestism

A. The general criteria for disorders of sexual preference must be met.

B. The individual wears articles of clothing of the opposite sex in order to create the appearance and feeling of being a member of the opposite sex.

C. The cross-dressing is closely associated with sexual arousal. Once orgasm occurs and sexual arousal declines, there is a strong desire to remove the clothing.

Exhibitionism

A. The general criteria for disorders of sexual preference must be met.

B. There is either a recurrent or a persistent tendency to expose the genitalia to unsuspecting strangers (usually of the opposite sex), which is almost invariably associated with sexual arousal and masturbation.

C. There is no intention or invitation to have sexual intercourse with the "witness(es)."

Voyeurism

A. The general criteria for disorders of sexual preference must be met.

B. There is either a recurrent or a persistent tendency to look at people engaging in sexual or intimate behavior such as undressing, which is associated with sexual excitement and masturbation.

C. There is no intention to reveal one's presence.

D. There is no intention of sexual involvement with the person(s) observed.

Pedophilia

A. The general criteria for disorders of sexual preference must be met.

B. There is a persistent or predominant preference for sexual activity with a prepubescent child or children.

C. The individual is at least 16 years old and at least 5 years older than the child or children in criterion B.

Sadomasochism

A. The general criteria for disorders of sexual preference must be met.

B. There is preference for sexual activity, as recipient (masochism) or provider (sadism), or both, which involves at least one of the following:
(1) pain;
(2) humiliation;
(3) bondage.

C. The sadomasochistic activity is the most important source of stimulation or is necessary for sexual gratification.

Multiple disorders of sexual preference

The likelihood of more than one abnormal sexual preference occurring in one individual is greater than would be expected by chance. For research purposes the different types of preference, and their relative importance to the individual, should be listed. The most common combination is fetishism, transvestism, and sadomasochism.

Other disorders of sexual preference

A variety of other patterns of sexual preference and activity may occur, each being relatively uncommon. These include such activities as making obscene telephone calls, rubbing up against people for sexual stimulation in crowded public places (frotteurism), sexual activity with animals, use of strangulation or anoxia for intensifying sexual excitement, and a preference for partners with some particular anatomical abnormality such as an amputated limb.

Erotic practices are too diverse and many too rare or idiosyncratic to justify a separate term for each. Swallowing urine, smearing feces, or piercing foreskin or nipples may be part of the behavioral repertoire in sadomasochism. Masturbatory rituals of various kinds are common, but the more extreme practices, such as the insertion of objects into the rectum or penile urethra, or partial self-strangulation, when they take the place of ordinary sexual contracts, amount to abnormalities. Necrophilia should also be coded here.

Disorder of sexual preference, unspecified

aggressive drives that would otherwise have been channeled into proper sexual behavior.

Failure to resolve the oedipal crisis by identifying with the father-aggressor (for boys) or mother-aggressor (for girls) results either in improper identification with the opposite-sex parent or in an improper choice of object for libido cathexis. Classic psychoanalytic theory holds that transsexualism and transvestic fetishism are disorders because each involves identification with the opposite-sex parent instead of the same-sex parent; for instance, a man dressing in women's clothes is believed to identify with his mother. Exhibitionism and voyeurism may be an attempt to calm their anxiety about castration. Fetishism is an attempt to avoid anxiety by displacing libidinal impulses to inappropriate objects. A person with a shoe fetish unconsciously denies that women have lost their penises through castration by attaching libido to a phallic object, the shoe, that symbolizes the female penis. People with pedophilia and sexual sadism have a need to dominate and control their victims to compensate for their feelings of powerlessness during the oedipal crisis. Some theorists believe that choosing a child as a love object is a narcissistic act. People with sexual masochism overcome their fear of injury and their sense of powerlessness by showing that they are impervious to harm. Another theory proposes that the masochist directs the aggression inherent in all paraphilias toward herself or himself. Although recent developments in psychoanalysis place more emphasis on treating defense mechanisms than on oedipal traumas, psychoanalytic therapy for patients with a paraphilia remains consistent with Sigmund Freud's theory.

Other theories attribute the development of a paraphilia to

Table 21.3–2
Frequency of Paraphiliac Acts Committed by Paraphilia Patients Seeking Outpatient Treatment

Diagnostic Category	Paraphilia Patients Seeking Outpatient Treatment (%)	Paraphiliac Acts per Paraphilia Patient[a]
Pedophilia	45	5
Exhibitionism	25	50
Voyeurism	12	17
Frotteurism	6	30
Sexual masochism	3	36
Transvestic fetishism	3	25
Sexual sadism	3	3
Fetishism	2	3
Zoophilia	1	2

Courtesy of Gene G. Abel, M.D.
[a] Median number.

early experiences that condition or socialize children into committing a paraphiliac act. The first shared sexual experience can be important in that regard. Molestation as a child can predispose a person to accept continued abuse as an adult or, conversely, to become an abuser of others. Also, early experiences of abuse that is not specifically sexual, such as spanking, enemas, or verbal humiliation, can be sexualized by a child and can form the basis for a paraphilia. Such experiences can result in the development of an *eroticized child*. The onset of paraphiliac acts can result from people's modeling their behavior on the behavior of others who have carried out paraphiliac acts, mimicking sexual behavior depicted in the media, or recalling emotionally laden events from the past, such as their own molestation. Learning theory indicates that because the fantasizing of paraphiliac interests begins at an early age and because personal fantasies and thoughts are not shared with others (who could block or discourage them), the use and misuse of paraphiliac fantasies and urges continue uninhibited until late in life. Only then do people begin to realize that such paraphiliac interests and urges are inconsistent with societal norms. Unfortunately, by that time the repetitive use of such fantasies has become ingrained; people's sexual thoughts and behaviors have become associated with, or conditioned to, paraphiliac fantasies.

Biological Factors. Several studies have identified abnormal organic findings in people with paraphilias. None has used random samples of such people; instead, they have extensively investigated paraphilia patients who were referred to large medical centers. Among these patients, those with positive organic findings included 74 percent with abnormal hormone levels, 27 percent with hard or soft neurological signs, 24 percent with chromosomal abnormalities, 9 percent with seizures, 9 percent with dyslexia, 4 percent with abnormal electroencephalograms (EEGs) without seizures, 4 percent with major mental disorders, and 4 percent with mental handicaps. The question is whether these abnormalities are causally related to paraphiliac interests or are incidental findings that bear no relevance to the development of paraphilia.

Psychophysiological tests have been developed to measure penile volumetric size in response to paraphiliac and nonparaphiliac stimuli. The procedures may be of use in diagnosis and treatment but are of questionable diagnostic validity because some men are able to suppress their erectile responses.

Diagnosis and Clinical Features

In DSM-IV the diagnostic criteria for paraphilias include the presence of a pathognomonic fantasy and an intense urge to act out the fantasy or its behavior elaboration. The fantasy, which may distress a patient, contains unusual sexual material that is relatively fixed and shows only minor variations. Arousal and orgasm depend on the mental elaboration or the behavioral playing out of the fantasy. Sexual activity is ritualized or stereotyped and makes use of degraded, reduced, or dehumanized objects.

Exhibitionism. Exhibitionism is the recurrent urge to expose the genitals to a stranger or to an unsuspecting person (Table 21.3–3). Sexual excitement occurs in anticipation of the exposure, and orgasm is brought about by masturbation during or after the event. In almost 100 percent of cases, those with exhibitionism are men exposing themselves to women. The dynamic of men with exhibitionism is to assert their masculinity by showing their penises and by watching the victims' reactions—fright, surprise, disgust. In this situation, men unconsciously feel castrated and impotent. Wives of men with exhibitionism often substitute for the mothers to whom the men were excessively attached during childhood. In other related paraphilias the central themes involve derivatives of looking or showing.

George was a 22-year-old single man referred following his fourth arrest for exhibitionism. He would usually expose himself from his car to women up to their late 20s. The victim's response was to laugh, to be startled and run away, or to make harsh comments to him. Following his first exposure, he concluded that there was nothing to it, and he did not expose himself again until 4 months later. Since then, he exposed himself 2 or 3 times per month. Exposures occurred in waves, followed by periods of up to a year of no exhibitionism. His four arrests had led to minimal consequences for him. During the year prior to referral, he had

Table 21.3–3
DSM-IV Diagnostic Criteria for Exhibitionism

A. Over a period of at least 6 months, recurrent, intense sexually arousing fantasies, sexual urges, or behaviors involving the exposure of one's genitals to an unsuspecting stranger.
B. The fantasies, sexual urges, or behaviors cause clinically significant distress or impairment in social, occupational, or other important areas of functioning.

a rich, enjoyable sexual relationship with his girlfriend, with frequent intercourse and without sexual dysfunction.

An intelligent student, George logically appreciated the inappropriateness of his exposing himself. Although he hoped for a sexual encounter with one of his victims, it never occurred. Although 15 percent of his masturbatory fantasies involved recalling previous episodes of exposing, his remaining fantasies were of normal heterosexual intercourse. An increased intensity of his urges to expose were provoked by seeing female peers walking or driving by themselves. He would follow a woman in his car while fantasizing her possible positive reaction should he expose himself. These fantasies were soon accompanied by masturbation while driving. His excitement and anxiety intensified as the time of his attempted exposure approached. Exposure was usually to a woman in her car while driving his car, a technically difficult feat fraught with danger.

Typical was his careless disregard for protecting his identity. George made minimal attempts to conceal his appearance, the characteristics of his car, or even his license plate. After a series of exposures, he would be overcome by depression and intense guilt. He would resolve not to expose himself again, but after 1 to 6 weeks, his cycle of recurrent urges and exposures would return. (Courtesy of John K. Meyer, M.D.)

Fetishism. In fetishism the sexual focus is on objects (such as shoes, gloves, pantyhose, and stockings) that are intimately associated with the human body (Table 21.3–4). The particular fetish is linked to someone closely involved with a patient during childhood and has a quality associated with this loved, needed, or even traumatizing person. Usually, the disorder begins by adolescence, although the fetish may have been established in childhood. Once established, the disorder tends to be chronic.

Sexual activity may be directed toward the fetish itself (for example, masturbation with or into a shoe), or the fetish may be incorporated into sexual intercourse (for example, the demand that high-heeled shoes be worn). The disorder is almost exclusively found in men. According to Freud, the fetish serves as a symbol of the phallus to people with unconscious castration fears. Learning theorists believe that the object was associated with sexual stimulation at an early age.

Table 21.3–4
DSM-IV Diagnostic Criteria for Fetishism

A. Over a period of at least 6 months, recurrent, intense sexually arousing fantasies, sexual urges, or behaviors involving the use of nonliving objects (eg, female undergarments).
B. The fantasies, sexual urges, or behaviors cause clinically significant distress or impairment in social, occupational, or other important areas of functioning.
C. The fetish objects are not articles of female clothing used in cross-dressing (as in transvestic fetishism) or devices designed for the purpose of tactile genital stimulation (eg, a vibrator).

Frotteurism. Frotteurism is usually characterized by a man's rubbing his penis against the buttocks or other body part of a fully clothed woman to achieve orgasm (Table 21.3–5). At other times, he may use his hands to rub an unsuspecting victim. The acts usually occur in crowded places, particularly in subways and buses. Those with frotteurism are extremely passive and isolated, and frottage is often their only source of sexual gratification. The expression of aggression in this paraphilia is readily apparent.

James had been a frotteur for 10 years when seen at age 45. His usual pattern was first to decide at home if he had time to carry out frottage while on his way to work. He would then place plastic wrap around his penis while dressing, anticipating that when he ejaculated, the ejaculate would not show through his suit pants. To increase the likelihood of crowding, he would stand in the middle of the subway platform with most passengers waiting to board. He would then select a woman with large buttocks and tight-fitting clothes. After entering the train, pressed to her, he would fantasize a sexual experience with her as he pushed his penis against her buttocks. On 40 percent of occasions, he would ejaculate and go on to work. If he did not ejaculate, he would continue the cycle with a new victim until he ran out of time or was able to ejaculate. By the time he was seen, he had been arrested twice but had carried out frottage on more than a thousand separate occasions.

Referral for treatment was precipitated by his arrest. His guilt following each commission of frottage was usually high, but it was now accompanied by great anxiety as he anticipated that others at work would learn of his deviant behavior and that he would be fired from his white-collar job. (Courtesy of John K. Meyer, M.D.)

Pedophilia. Pedophilia involves recurrent intense sexual urges toward or arousal by children 13 years of age or younger, over a period of at least 6 months. People with pedophilia are at least 16 years of age and at least 5 years older than the victims (Table 21.3–6). When a perpetrator is a late adolescent involved in an ongoing sexual relationship with a 12 or 13 year old, the diagnosis is not warranted.

Table 21.3–5
DSM-IV Diagnostic Criteria for Frotteurism

A. Over a period of at least 6 months, recurrent, intense sexually arousing fantasies, sexual urges, or behaviors involving touching and rubbing against a nonconsenting person.
B. The fantasies, sexual urges, or behaviors cause clinically significant distress or impairment in social, occupational, or other important areas of functioning.

Table 21.3–6
DSM-IV Diagnostic Criteria for Pedophilia

A. Over a period of at least 6 months, recurrent, intense sexually arousing fantasies, sexual urges, or behaviors involving sexual activity with a prepubescent child or children (generally age 13 years or younger).

B. The fantasies, sexual urges, or behaviors cause clinically significant distress or impairment in social, occupational, or other important areas of functioning.

C. The person is at least 16 years and at least 5 years older than the child or children in criterion A.
Note: Do not include an individual in late adolescence involved in an ongoing sexual relationship with a 12- or 13-year-old.

Specify if:
Sexually attracted to males
Sexually attracted to females
Sexually attracted to both

Specify if:
Limited to incest

Specify type:
Exclusive type (attracted only to children)
Nonexclusive type

Most child molestations involve genital fondling or oral sex. Vaginal or anal penetration of children occurs infrequently except in cases of incest. Although most child victims coming to public attention are girls, this finding appears to be a product of the referral process. Offenders report that when they touch a child, most (60 percent) of the victims are boys. This figure is in sharp contrast to the figure for nontouching victimization of children, such as window peeping and exhibitionism; 99 percent of all such cases are perpetrated against girls. Of those with pedophilia, 95 percent are heterosexual, and 50 percent have consumed alcohol to excess at the time of the incident. In addition to their pedophilia, a significant number of the perpetrators are concomitantly, or have previously been, involved in exhibitionism, voyeurism, or rape.

Incest is related to pedophilia by the frequent selection of an immature child as a sex object, the subtle or overt element of coercion, and occasionally the preferential nature of the adult–child liaison.

Sexual Masochism. Masochism takes its name from the activities of Leopold von Sacher-Masoch, a 19th century Austrian novelist whose characters derived sexual pleasure from being abused and dominated by women. According to DSM-IV, people with sexual masochism have a recurrent preoccupation with sexual urges and fantasies involving the act of being humiliated, beaten, bound, or otherwise made to suffer (Table 21.3–7). Sexual masochistic practices are more common among men than among women. Freud believed masochism resulted from destructive fantasies turned against the self. In some cases, people can allow themselves to experience sexual feelings only when punishment for the feelings follows. People with sexual masochism may have had childhood experiences that convinced them that pain is a prerequisite for sexual pleasure. About 30 percent of those with sexual masochism also have sadistic fantasies. Moral masochism involves a need to suffer but is not accompanied by sexual fantasies.

Table 21.3–7
DSM-IV Diagnostic Criteria for Sexual Masochism

A. Over a period of at least 6 months, recurrent, intense sexually arousing fantasies, sexual urges, or behaviors involving the act (real, not simulated) of being humiliated, beaten, bound, or otherwise made to suffer.

B. The fantasies, sexual urges, or behaviors cause clinically significant distress or impairment in social, occupational, or other important areas of functioning.

Denise was 35 when referred for treatment for her anxiety in groups. She described herself as a social isolate with marked difficulties when around others because she never knew how to act or what to say. She came from an exceedingly poor family living in an isolated, primitive mountainous area of the United States. When she was born, her mother refused to bring her home from the hospital, claiming she already had too many children to care for. Denise was bought home after her father agreed to care for her. At age 3, her father died, and she was cared for by her hostile, violent, and physically abusive mother. Denise's only form of entertainment was to read pulp magazines that described how women were exploited by their lovers.

She slept in her mother's bed from childhood until age 19. At age 11, her mother began to fondle her while she lay in bed. If she cried during these molestations, her mother callously told her to "shut up." When one of her sisters attempted to console her after one of these molestations, her mother struck the sister so hard that she was knocked across the room. The mother's molestations continued throughout Denise's adolescence until she left home at age 19. Throughout the years, she realized the inappropriateness of her mother's behavior, but her utter isolation prevented her from getting help. She was most upset that she had no control of her body during the molestations.

At age 13, Denise began using masochistic fantasies during masturbation, recalling the violent scenes that she read about in magazines. These fantasies persisted and became progressively more violent, so that when she was evaluated, 100 percent of her masturbatory fantasies were of being raped and violated by brutalizing men. Although some of the rape fantasies were tolerable (imagining a lover overcome by lust and raping her), others were intolerable (imagining being sadistically raped by strangers while onlookers watched). Her own attempts at dislodging the masochistic fantasies had proved unsuccessful, and she became increasingly concerned because she was unable to achieve orgasm other than by using these fantasies, which were abhorrent to her. (Courtesy of John K. Meyer, M.D.)

Table 21.3–8
DSM-IV Diagnostic Criteria for Sexual Sadism

A. Over a period of at least 6 months, recurrent, intense sexually arousing fantasies, sexual urges, or behaviors involving acts (real, not simulated) in which the psychological or physical suffering (including humiliation) of the victim is sexually exciting to the person.
B. The fantasies, sexual urges, or behaviors cause clinically significant distress or impairment in social, occupational, or other important areas of functioning.

Reprinted with permission from American Psychiatric Association: *Diagnostic and Statistical Manual of Mental Disorders,* ed 4. Copyright, American Psychiatric Association, Washington, 1994.

Table 21.3–9
DSM-IV Diagnostic Criteria for Voyeurism

A. Over a period of at least 6 months, recurrent, intense sexually arousing fantasies, sexual urges, or behaviors involving the act of observing an unsuspecting person who is naked, in the process of disrobing, or engaging in sexual activity.
B. The fantasies, sexual urges, or behaviors cause clinically significant distress or impairment in social, occupational, or other important areas of functioning.

Reprinted with permission from American Psychiatric Association: *Diagnostic and Statistical Manual of Mental Disorders,* ed 4. Copyright, American Psychiatric Association, Washington, 1994.

Sexual Sadism. The DSM-IV diagnostic criteria for sexual sadism are presented in Table 21.3–8. The onset of the disorder is usually before the age of 18 years; most people with sexual sadism are male. According to psychoanalytic theory, sadism is a defense against fears of castration: People with sexual sadism do to others what they fear will happen to them and derive pleasure from expressing their aggressive instincts. The disorder was named after the Marquis de Sade, an 18th century French author and military officer who was repeatedly imprisoned for his violent sexual acts against women. Sexual sadism is related to rape, although rape is more aptly considered an expression of power. Some sadistic rapists, however, kill their victims after having sex (so-called lust murders). In many cases, these people have underlying schizophrenia. John Money believes that lust murderers have dissociative identity disorder and perhaps a history of head trauma. He lists five contributory causes of sexual sadism: hereditary predisposition, hormonal malfunctioning, pathological relationships, a history of sexual abuse, and the presence of other mental disorders.

Charlie was 25 and single when referred because of sadistic arousal. He began voyeuristic activities at age 15, window peeping at a rate in excess of 100 times per year until age 22. Shortly after his voyeurism began, he started fantasizing about transsexuals and men who cross-dressed. He was especially attracted to thoughts of raping them. He subsequently began dating drag queens, whom he would eventually intoxicate with drugs and then rape anally. At age 16, he also engaged in oral and anal intercourse with male homosexuals, but he denied raping them. At age 18, he began accelerating the frequency of his sadistic attacks on intoxicated drag queens and would not only rape them but also beat them in the testicles. He also began raping 10- to 30-year-old women in attacks that did not involve sadistic beatings, but during which he used threats of physical attack with a knife to subdue his victims.

When referred, he described himself as a bisexual, equally attracted to adult males and adult females. Fifty percent of his masturbatory fantasies were of mutually consenting sexual experiences with adults, but 50 percent of his fantasies involved imagining sadistic attacks upon drag queens or transsexuals. In spite of various paraphiliac experiences, he had been arrested only once for a sex crime. (Courtesy of John K. Meyer, M.D.)

Voyeurism. Voyeurism, also known as scopophilia, is the recurrent preoccupation with fantasies and acts that involve observing people who are naked or engaged in grooming or sexual activity (Table 21.3–9). Masturbation to orgasm usually accompanies or follows the event. The first voyeuristic act usually occurs during childhood and is most common in men. When people with voyeurism are apprehended, the charge is usually loitering.

Fred was 31 when referred for treatment of his voyeurism that had culminated in his recent arrest. His interest in voyeurism began at age 15 when he began window peeping approximately twice per month on his 15-year-old neighbor while she dressed. He terminated window-peeping activity because he felt guilty for the behavior and also feared getting caught. At age 24, he separated from his wife for a few months because of a major conflict between them regarding child rearing. Eight months later, while jogging, he began glancing at windows, and 1 month later he began window peeping. After eight episodes of window peeping, he told his wife what he had done. Feeling guilty about his voyeuristic activity, he stopped jogging. Shortly thereafter, he began going to strip joints to watch nude dancing. Just prior to his referral, while between jobs, he found himself with nothing to do, so he began jogging again. His voyeurism returned, and he was subsequently arrested. By the time he was evaluated, he had window peeped on 10 victims for a total of 33 times. He and his wife both confirmed their rich and varied sex life with intercourse 5 to 7 times per week. As a prelude to intercourse, she would often undress in front of him as if he were watching a stranger. (Courtesy of John K. Meyer, M.D.)

Transvestic Fetishism. Transvestic fetishism is described as fantasies and sexual urges to dress in opposite gender clothing as a means of arousal and as an adjunct to masturbation or coitus (Table 21.3–10). Transvestic fetishism typically begins in childhood or early adolescence. As years pass, some men with transvestic fetishism want to dress and live permanently as women. More rarely, women want to dress and live as men. These people are classified in DSM-IV as those with transvestic fetishism and gender dysphoria. Usually

Table 21.3–10
DSM-IV Diagnostic Criteria for Transvestic Fetishism

A. Over a period of at least 6 months, in a heterosexual male, recurrent, intense sexually arousing fantasies, sexual urges, or behaviors involving cross-dressing.

B. The fantasies, sexual urges, or behaviors cause clinically significant distress or impairment in social, occupational, or other important areas of functioning.

Specify if:

With gender dysphoria: if the person has persistent discomfort with gender role or identity.

Reprinted with permission from American Psychiatric Association: *Diagnostic and Statistical Manual of Mental Disorders,* ed 4. Copyright, American Psychiatric Association, Washington, 1994.

a person wears more than one article of opposite sex clothing; frequently, an entire wardrobe is involved. When a man with transvestic fetishism is cross-dressed, the appearance of femininity may be striking, although not usually to the degree found in transsexualism. When not dressed in women's clothes, men with transvestic fetishism may be hypermasculine in appearance and occupation. Cross-dressing can be graded from solitary, depressed, guilt-ridden dressing to ego-syntonic, social membership in a transvestite subculture.

The overt clinical syndrome of transvestic fetishism may begin in latency but is more often seen around pubescence or in adolescence. Frank dressing in opposite sex clothing usually does not begin until mobility and relative independence from parents are well established.

Paraphilia Not Otherwise Specified. The classification of paraphilia not otherwise specified includes varied paraphilias that do not meet the criteria for any of the aforementioned categories (Table 21.3–11).

TELEPHONE AND COMPUTER SCATOLOGIA. Telephone scatologia is characterized by obscene phone calling and involves an unsuspecting partner. Tension and arousal begin in anticipation of phoning; the recipient of the call listens while the telephoner (usually male) verbally exposes his preoccupations or induces her to talk about her sexual activity. The conversation is accompanied by masturbation, which is often completed after the contact is interrupted.

People also use interactive computer networks, sometimes compulsively, to send obscene messages by electronic mail and to transmit sexually explicit messages and video images. Because of the anonymity of the users in chat rooms who use aliases, on-line sex (cybersex) allows some people to play the role of the opposite sex (''genderbending''), which represents an alternative method of expressing transvestite or transsexual fantasies. A danger of on-line cybersex is that pedophiles often make contact with children or adolescents who are lured into meeting and then molested. Many on-line contacts develop into off-line liaisons. While some people report that the off-line encounters develop into meaningful relationships, most such meetings usually are filled with disappointment and disillusionment, as the fantasized person fails to meet unconscious expectations of perfection. In other situations, when adults meet, rape or even homicide may occur.

Table 21.3–11
DSM-IV Diagnostic Criteria for Paraphilia Not Otherwise Specified

This category is included for coding paraphilias that do not meet the criteria for any of the specific categories. Examples include, but are not limited to, telephone scatologia (obscene phone calls), necrophilia (corpses), partialism (exclusive focus on part of body), zoophilia (animals), coprophilia (feces), klismaphilia (enemas), and urophilia (urine).

Reprinted with permission from American Psychiatric Association: *Diagnostic and Statistical Manual of Mental Disorders,* ed 4. Copyright, American Psychiatric Association, Washington, 1994.

NECROPHILIA. Necrophilia is an obsession with obtaining sexual gratification from cadavers. Most people with this disorder find corpses in morgues, but some have been known to rob graves or even to murder to satisfy their sexual urges. In the few cases studied, those with necrophilia believed that they were inflicting the greatest conceivable humiliation on their lifeless victims. According to Richard von Krafft-Ebing, the diagnosis of psychosis is, under all circumstances, justified.

PARTIALISM. People with the disorder of partialism concentrate their sexual activity on one part of the body to the exclusion of all others. Mouth-genital contact—such as cunnilingus (oral contact with a woman's external genitals), fellatio (oral contact with the penis), and anilingus (oral contact with the anus)—is normally associated with foreplay; Freud recognized the mucosal surfaces of the body as erotogenic and capable of producing pleasurable sensation. But when a person uses these activities as the sole source of sexual gratification and cannot have or refuses to have coitus, a paraphilia exists. It is also known as oralism.

ZOOPHILIA. In zoophilia, animals—which may be trained to participate—are preferentially incorporated into arousal fantasies or sexual activities, including intercourse, masturbation, and oral-genital contact. Zoophilia as an organized paraphilia is rare. For many people, animals are the major source of relatedness, so it is not surprising that a broad variety of domestic animals are sensually or sexually used.

Sexual relations with animals may occasionally be an outgrowth of availability or convenience, especially in parts of the world where rigid convention precludes premarital sexuality and in situations of enforced isolation. Because masturbation is also available in such situations, however, a predilection for animal contact is probably present in opportunistic zoophilia.

COPROPHILIA AND KLISMAPHILIA. Coprophilia is attraction to sexual pleasure associated with the desire to defecate on a partner, to be defecated on, or to eat feces (coprophagia). A variant is the compulsive utterance of obscene words (coprolalia). These paraphilias are associated with fixation at the anal stage of psychosexual development. Similarly, klismaphilia, the use of enemas as part of sexual stimulation, is related to anal fixation.

UROPHILIA. Urophilia, a form of urethral eroticism, is interest in sexual pleasure associated with the desire to urinate on a partner or to be urinated on. In both men and women, the disorder may be associated with masturbatory techniques involving the insertion of foreign objects into the urethra for sexual stimulation.

MASTURBATION. Masturbation is a normal activity that is common in all stages of life from infancy to old age, but this viewpoint was not always accepted. Freud believed neurasthenia to be caused by excessive masturbation. In the early 1900s, masturbatory insanity was a common diagnosis in hospitals for the criminally insane in the United States. Masturbation can be defined as a person's achieving sexual pleasure, which usually results in orgasm, by himself or herself (autoeroticism). Alfred Kinsey found it to be more prevalent in males than in females, but this difference may no longer exist. The frequency of masturbation varies from 3 to 4 times a week in adolescence to 1 to 2 times a week in adulthood. It is common among married people; Kinsey reported that it occurred on the average of once a month among married couples.

The techniques of masturbation vary in both sexes and among people. The most common technique is direct stimulation of the clitoris or penis with the hand or the fingers. Indirect stimulation may also be used, such as rubbing against a pillow or squeezing the thighs. Kinsey found that 2 percent of women are capable of achieving orgasm through fantasy alone. Men and women have been known to insert objects into the urethra to achieve orgasm. The hand vibrator is now used as a masturbatory device by both sexes.

Masturbation is abnormal when it is the only type of sexual activity performed in adulthood, when it is done with such frequency as to indicate a compulsion or sexual dysfunction, or when it is consistently preferred to sex with a partner.

HYPOXYPHILIA. Hypoxyphilia is the desire to achieve an altered state of consciousness secondary to hypoxia while experiencing orgasm. People may use a drug (such as a volatile nitrite or nitrous oxide) to produce hypoxia. Autoerotic asphyxiation is also associated with hypoxic states but should be classified as a form of sexual masochism. (A discussion of autoerotic asphyxiation appears in Section 2 of this chapter.)

Differential Diagnosis

Clinicians must differentiate a paraphilia from an experimental act that is not recurrent or compulsive and that is done for its novelty. Paraphiliac activity is most likely to occur during adolescence. Some paraphilias (especially the bizarre types) are associated with other mental disorders, such as schizophrenia. Brain diseases may also release perverse impulses.

Course and Prognosis

A poor prognosis for paraphilias is associated with an early age of onset, a high frequency of acts, no guilt or shame about the act, and substance abuse. The course and the prognosis are good when patients have a history of coitus in addition to the paraphilia, when they have a high motivation for change, and when they are self-referred rather than referred by a legal agency.

Treatment

Insight-oriented psychotherapy is the most common approach to treating the paraphilias. Patients have the opportunity to understand their dynamics and the events that caused the paraphilia to develop. In particular, they become aware of the daily events that cause them to act on their impulses (such as a real or fantasized rejection). Psychotherapy also allows patients to regain self-esteem, to improve their interpersonal skills, and to find acceptable methods for sexual gratification. Group therapy is also useful. Sex therapy is an appropriate adjunct to the treatment of patients who suffer from specific sexual dysfunctions when they attempt nondeviant sexual activities with partners.

Behavior therapy is used to disrupt learned paraphiliac patterns. When the impulses are paired with noxious stimuli, such as electric shocks and bad odors, the impulses diminish. The stimuli can be self-administered and used by patients whenever they feel that they will act on an impulse.

Drug therapy, including antipsychotic or antidepressant medication, is indicated for the treatment of schizophrenia or depressive disorders if the paraphilia is associated with these disorders. Antiandrogens, such as cyproterone acetate in Europe and medroxyprogesterone acetate (Depo-Provera) in the United States, have been used experimentally in hypersexual paraphilias. Some patients have reported decreases in hypersexual behavior. Medroxyprogesterone acetate seems to benefit those patients whose driven hypersexuality (for example, virtually constant masturbation, sexual contact at every opportunity, compulsively assaultive sexuality) is out of control or dangerous. Serotonergic agents such as fluoxetine (Prozac) have been used in some paraphiliac cases with limited success.

SEXUAL DISORDER NOT OTHERWISE SPECIFIED

Many sexual disorders are not classifiable as sexual dysfunctions or as paraphilias. These unclassified disorders are rare, poorly documented, not easily classified, or not specifically described in DSM-IV (Table 21.3–12). ICD-10 has a similar residual category for problems related to sexual development or preference (Table 21.3–13).

Postcoital Dysphoria

Not listed in DSM-IV, postcoital dysphoria occurs during the resolution phase of sexual activity, when people normally experience a sense of general well-being and muscular and psychological relaxation. Some people, however, undergo postcoital dysphoria at this time and, after an otherwise satisfactory sexual experience, become depressed, tense, anxious, and irritable and show psychomotor agitation. They often want to get away from their partners and may become verbally or even physically abusive. The incidence of the disorder is unknown, but it is more common in men than in women. The causes are several and relate to the person's attitude toward sex in general and toward the partner in particular. The disorder may occur in adulterous sex and in contacts with prostitutes. The fear of acquired immune deficiency syndrome (AIDS) causes some people to experience postcoital dysphoria. Treatment requires insight-oriented psychotherapy to help patients understand the unconscious antecedents to their behavior and attitudes.

Couple Problems

At times, a complaint arises from the spousal unit or the couple, rather than from an individual dysfunction. For example, one partner may prefer morning sex, but the other func-

Table 21.3–12
DSM-IV Diagnostic Criteria for Sexual Disorder Not Otherwise Specified

This category is included for coding a sexual disturbance that does not meet the criteria for any specific sexual disorder and is neither a sexual dysfunction nor a paraphilia. Examples include

1. Marked feelings of inadequacy concerning sexual performance or other traits related to self-imposed standards of masculinity or femininity
2. Distress about a pattern of repeated sexual relationships involving a succession of lovers who are experienced by the individual only as things to be used
3. Persistent and marked distress about sexual orientation

Reprinted with permission from American Psychiatric Association: *Diagnostic and Statistical Manual of Mental Disorders,* ed 4. Copyright, American Psychiatric Association, Washington, 1994.

Table 21.3–13
ICD-10 Diagnostic Criteria for Psychological and Behavioral Disorders Associated with Sexual Development and Orientation

This section is intended to cover those types of problem that derive from variations of sexual development or orientation, when the sexual preference per se is not necessarily problematic or abnormal.

Sexual maturation disorder
The patient suffers from uncertainty about his or her gender identity or sexual orientation, which causes anxiety or depression.

Ego-dystonic sexual orientation
The gender identity or sexual preference is not in doubt, but the individual wishes it were different.

Sexual relationship disorder
The abnormality of gender identity or sexual preference is responsible for difficulties in forming or maintaining a relationship with a sexual partner.

Other psychosexual development disorders

Psychosexual development disorder, unspecified

Reprinted with permission from American Psychiatric Association: *Diagnostic and Statistical Manual of Mental Disorders,* ed 4. Copyright, American Psychiatric Association, Washington, 1994.

tions more readily at night, or the partners have unequal frequencies of desire.

Unconsummated Marriage

A couple involved in an unconsummated marriage have never had coitus and are typically uninformed and inhibited about sexuality. Their feelings of guilt, shame, or inadequacy are increased by their problem, and they experience conflict between their need to seek help and their need to conceal their difficulty. Couples may seek help for the problem after having been married several months or several years. William Masters and Virginia Johnson reported one unconsummated marriage of 17 years' duration.

Frequently, the couple do not seek help directly; the woman may reveal the problem to her gynecologist on a visit ostensibly concerned with vague vaginal or other somatic complaints. On examining her, the gynecologist may find an intact hymen. In some cases, however, the wife may have undergone a hymenectomy to resolve the problem, but the surgery usually aggravates the situation without solving the basic problem. The surgical procedure is another stress and often increases the couple's feelings of inadequacy. The wife may feel put upon, abused, or mutilated, and the husband's concern about his manliness may increase. The inquiry of a physician who is comfortable dealing with sexual problems may be the first opening to a frank discussion of the couple's distress. Often, the pretext of the medical visit is a discussion of contraceptive methods or—even more ironically—a request for an infertility workup. Once presented, the complaint can often be successfully treated. The duration of the problem does not significantly affect the prognosis or the outcome of the case.

The causes of unconsummated marriage are varied: lack of sex education, sexual prohibitions overly stressed by parents or society, problems of an oedipal nature, immaturity in both partners, overdependence on primary families, and problems in sexual identification. Religious orthodoxy, with severe control of sexual and social development, and the equation of sexuality with sin or uncleanliness have also been cited as a dominant cause. Many women involved in an unconsummated marriage have distorted concepts about their vaginas. They may fear that it is too small or too soft, or they may confuse the vagina with the rectum, and thereby feel unclean. Men may share these distortions about the vagina and perceive it as dangerous to themselves. Similarly, both partners may have distortions about the man's penis and perceive it as a weapon, as too large, or as too small. Many patients can be helped by simple education about genital anatomy and physiology, by suggestions for self-exploration, and by correct information from a physician. The problem of unconsummated marriage is best treated by seeing both members of the couple. Dual-sex therapy involving a male-female cotherapist team has been markedly effective. Other forms of conjoint therapy, marital counseling, traditional psychotherapy on a one-to-one basis, and counseling from a sensitive family physician, gynecologist, or urologist are also helpful.

Body Image Problems

Some people are ashamed of their bodies and experience feelings of inadequacy related to self-imposed standards of masculinity or femininity. They may insist on sex only during total darkness, not allow certain body parts to be seen or touched, or seek unnecessary operative procedures to deal with their imagined inadequacies. Body dysmorphic disorder should be ruled out.

Sex Addiction

The concept of sex addiction developed over the past 2 decades to refer to persons who compulsively seek out sexual experiences and whose behavior becomes impaired if they are unable to gratify their sexual impulses. The concept of sex addiction derived from the model of addiction to such drugs as heroin or addiction to behavioral patterns, such as gambling. Addiction implies psychological dependence, physical dependence, and the presence of a withdrawal syndrome if the substance (such as the drug) is unavailable or the behavior (such as gambling) is frustrated.

In DSM-IV the term *sex addiction* is not used, nor is it a disorder that is universally recognized or accepted. Nevertheless, the phenomenon of a person whose entire life revolves around sex-seeking behavior and activities, who spends an excessive amount of time in such behavior, and who often tries to stop such behavior but is unable to do so is well known to clinicians. Such people show repeated and increasingly frequent attempts to have a sexual experience, of which deprivation gives rise to symptoms of distress. Sex addiction is a useful concept heuristically, in that it can alert the clinician to seek an underlying cause for the manifest behavior.

Diagnosis. Sex addicts are unable to control their sexual impulses, which can involve the entire spectrum of sexual fantasy or behavior. Eventually, the need for sexual activity in-

Table 21.3–14
Signs of Sexual Addiction

1. Out-of-control behavior
2. Severe adverse consequences (medical, legal, interpersonal) due to sexual behavior
3. Persistent pursuit of self-destructive or high-risk sexual behavior
4. Repeated attempts to limit or stop sexual behavior
5. Sexual obsession and fantasy as a primary coping mechanism
6. The need for increasing amounts of sexual activity
7. Severe mood changes related to sexual activity (eg, depression, euphoria)
8. Inordinate amount of time spent in obtaining sex, being sexual, or recovering from sexual experience
9. Interference of sexual behavior in social, occupational, or recreational activities

Data from Carnes P: *Don't Call It Love.* Bantam Books, New York, 1991.

creases, and the person's behavior is motivated solely by the persistent desire to experience the sex act. The history usually reveals a long-standing pattern of such behavior, which the person repeatedly has tried to stop, but without success. Although there may be feelings of guilt and remorse after the act, they are not sufficient to prevent its recurrence. The patient may report that the need to act out is most severe during stressful periods or when angry, depressed, anxious, or otherwise dysphoric. Most acts culminate in a sexual orgasm, although a sense of excitement (a high) usually accompanies the sex-seeking behavior even in the absence of orgasm. Eventually, the sexual activity interferes with the person's social, vocational, or marital life, which begins to deteriorate.

The signs of sexual addictions are listed in Table 21.3–14.

Types of Behavioral Patterns. The paraphilias constitute the behavioral patterns most often found in the sex addict. As defined in DSM-IV, the essential features of a paraphilia are recurrent intense sexual urges or behaviors, including exhibitionism, fetishism, frotteurism, sadomasochism, cross-dressing, voyeurism, and pedophilia. Paraphilias are associated with clinically significant distress and almost invariably interfere with interpersonal relationships, and they often lead to legal complications. In addition to the paraphilias, however, sex addiction can also include behavior that is considered normal, such as coitus and masturbation, except that it is promiscuous and uncontrolled.

In the 19th century the psychiatrist Richard von Krafft-Ebing reported on several cases of abnormally increased sexual desire. One was that of a 36-year-old married teacher, the father of seven children, who masturbated repeatedly while sitting at his desk in front of his pupils, after which he was "penitent and filled with shame." He indulged in coitus 3 or 4 times a day in addition to his repeated masturbatory acts. In another case a young woman masturbated almost incessantly and was unable to control her impulses. She had frequent coitus with many men, but neither coitus nor masturbation was sufficient, and she eventually was placed in an institution. Krafft-Ebing referred to the condition as "sexual hyperaesthesia," which he believed could occur in otherwise normal people.

In many cases sex addiction is the final common pathway of a variety of other disorders. In addition to the paraphilias that are often present, there may be an associated major mental disorder, or schizophrenia. Antisocial personality disorder and borderline personality disorder are common.

DON JUANISM. Some men who appear to be hypersexual, as manifested by their need to have many sexual encounters or conquests, use their sexual activities to mask deep feelings of inferiority. Some have unconscious homosexual impulses, which they deny by compulsive sexual contacts with women. After having sex, most Don Juans are no longer interested in the woman. The condition is sometimes referred to as satyriasis or sex addiction.

NYMPHOMANIA. Nymphomania signifies a woman's excessive or pathological desire for coitus. There have been few scientific studies of the condition, but those patients who have been studied usually have had one or more sexual disorders, often including female orgasmic disorder. The woman often has an intense fear of losing love and attempts to satisfy her dependence needs, rather than to gratify her sexual impulses, through her actions. This disorder is a form of sex addiction.

Comorbidity. Comorbidity (dual diagnosis) refers to the presence of an addiction that coexists with another psychiatric disorder. For example, about 50 percent of patients with substance-use disorder also have an additional psychiatric disorder. Similarly, many sex addicts have an associated psychiatric disorder. Dual diagnosis implies that the psychiatric illness and the addiction are separate disorders; one does not cause the other. The diagnosis of comorbidity is often difficult to make because addictive behavior (of all types) can produce extreme anxiety and severe disturbances in mood and affect, especially while the addictive behavior is treated. If, after a period of abstinence, symptoms of a psychiatric disorder remain, the comorbid condition is more easily recognized and diagnosed than during the addictive period. Finally, there is a high correlation between sex addiction and substance-use disorders (up to 80 percent in some studies), which not only complicates the task of diagnosis, but also complicates treatment.

Treatment. Self-help groups based on the 12-step concept used in Alcoholics Anonymous (AA) have been employed successfully with many sex addicts. They include such groups as Sexaholics Anonymous (SA), Sex and Love Addicts Anonymous (SLAA), and Sex Addicts Anonymous (SAA). The groups differ in that some are for men or women or for married people or couples. All advocate some degree of abstinence from either the addictive behavior or sex in general. Should a substance-use disorder also be present, the patient often requires referral to AA or Narcotics Anonymous (NA) as well. The patient may enter an inpatient treatment unit when he or she lacks sufficient motivation to control his or her behavior on an outpatient basis or may be a danger to self or others. Additionally, there may be severe medical or psychiatric symptoms that require careful supervision and treatment best carried out in a hospital.

A 42-year-old married businessman with two children was considered to be a model of virtue in his community. He was active in his church and on the boards of several charitable organizations. He was living a secret life, however, in that he would visit a local video store where he would watch pornographic videotapes while masturbating. In addition, he would lie to his wife, telling her that he was at a board meeting when he was actually visiting massage parlors for paid sex. He eventually was engaging in the behavior 4 to 5 times a day, and although he tried to quit many times, he was unable to do so. He knew that he was harming himself by putting his reputation and marriage at risk.

The patient presented himself to the psychiatric emergency room, stating that he would prefer to be dead rather than continue the behavior described. He was admitted with a diagnosis of major depressive disorder and started on a daily dose of 20 mg of fluoxetine. In addition, he received 100 mg of medroxyprogesterone (Provera) intramuscularly once a day. His need to masturbate diminished markedly and ceased entirely on the third hospital day, as did his mental preoccupation with sex. The medroxyprogesterone was discontinued on the sixth day, when he was discharged. He was continued on fluoxetine, enrolled in a local SA group, and entered individual and couples psychotherapy. His addictive behavior eventually stopped, he was having satisfactory sexual relations with his wife, and he was no longer suicidal or depressed.

Psychotherapy. Insight-oriented psychotherapy may help patients understand the dynamics of their behavioral patterns. Supportive psychotherapy can help repair the interpersonal, social, or occupational damage that occurs. Cognitive behavioral therapy helps the patient to recognize dysphoric states that precipitate sexual acting out. Marital therapy or couples therapy can aid the patient in regaining self-esteem, which is severely impaired by the time a treatment program is begun. Finally, psychotherapy may be of help in the treatment of any associated psychiatric disorder.

Pharmacotherapy. Most specialists in general addiction avoid the use of pharmacological agents, especially in the early stages of treatment. Substance-dependent people have a tendency to abuse those agents, especially agents with a high abuse potential, such as the benzodiazepines. Pharmacotherapy is of use in the treatment of associated psychiatric disorders, such as major depressive disorders and schizophrenia.

Certain medications may be of use to the sex addict, however, because of their specific effects on reducing the sex drive. Serotonin-specific reuptake inhibitors (SSRIs) reduce libido in some persons, a side effect that is used therapeutically. Compulsive masturbation is an example of a behavioral pattern that may benefit from such medication. Medroxyprogesterone acetate diminishes libido in men and thus enables the person better to control sexually addictive behavior.

The use of antiandrogens in women to control hypersexuality has not been sufficiently tested, but since androgenic compounds contribute to the sex drive in women, antiandrogens could be of benefit. Antiandrogenic agents (cyproterone acetate) are not available in the United States but are used in Europe with varying success.

Persistent and Marked Distress About Sexual Orientation

Distress about sexual orientation is characterized by a dissatisfaction with sexual arousal patterns and is usually applied to dissatisfaction with homosexual arousal patterns, a desire to increase heterosexual arousal, and strong negative feelings about being homosexual. A person's occasional statements to the effect that life would be easier if the person were not homosexual do not constitute persistent and marked distress about sexual orientation.

Treatment of sexual orientation distress is controversial. One study reported that with a minimum of 350 hours of psychoanalytic therapy, about a third of 100 bisexual and gay men achieved a heterosexual reorientation at a 5-year follow-up; but this study has been challenged. Behavior therapy and avoidance conditioning techniques have also been used, but with these techniques, behavior may be changed in the laboratory setting but not outside. Prognostic factors weighing in favor of heterosexual reorientation for men include being under 35 years of age, having some experience of heterosexual arousal, and feeling highly motivated to reorient.

Another style of intervention is directed at enabling people with persistent and marked distress about sexual orientation to live comfortably with homosexuality without shame, guilt, anxiety, or depression. Gay counseling centers are engaged with patients in such treatment programs. At present, outcome studies of such centers have not been reported in detail.

As for the treatment of women with persistent and marked distress about sexual orientation, few data are available, and these are primarily single-case studies with variable outcomes. (Section 21.1 of this chapter presents a further discussion of sexual orientation, homosexuality, and coming out.)

References

Abel GG, Blanchard EB: The role of fantasy in the treatment of sexual deviation. Arch Gen Psychiatry *30:* 467, 1974.

Abel GG, Osborn C: The paraphilias: The extent and nature of sexually deviant and criminal behavior. Psychiatr Clin North Am *15:* 675, 1992.

Berlin FS, Meinecke CF: Treatment of sex offenders with antiandrogenic medication: Conceptualization, review of treatment modalities, and preliminary findings. Am J Psychiatry *138:* 237, 1981.

Blair CD, Lanyon RI: Exhibitionism: Etiology and treatment. Psychol Bull *89:* 439, 1981.

Cook M, Howells K: *Adult Sexual Interest in Children.* Academic Press, New York, 1981.

Freud S: Three essays on the theory of sexuality. In *Standard Edition of the Complete Psychological Works of Sigmund Freud,* vol 7, p 125. Hogarth Press, London, 1953.

Gange P: Treatment of sex offenders with medroxyprogesterone acetate. Am J Psychiatry *138:* 644, 1981.

Kinsey A, Pomeroy W, Martin CE: *Sexual Behavior in the Human Male.* Saunders, Philadelphia, 1948.

Krafft-Ebing R: *Psychopathia Sexualis.* Stein and Day, New York, 1965.

Langevin R: Biological factors contributing to paraphiliac behavior. Psychiatr Ann *22:* 307, 1992.

Leif H, editor: *Sex Problems in Medical Practice.* American Medical Association, Chicago, 1981.

Levine SM, Stava L: Personality characteristics of sex offenders: A review. Arch Sex Behav *16:* 57, 1987.

Meyer JK: Paraphilias. In *Comprehensive Textbook of Psychiatry,* ed 6, HI Kaplan, BJ Sadock, editors, p 1334. Williams & Wilkins, Baltimore, 1995.

Slag MF: Impotence in medical clinic outpatients. JAMA *249:* 1736, 1983.

Stein DJ, Hollander E, Anthony DT, Schneier FR: Serotonergic medications for sexual obsessions, sexual addictions, and paraphilias. J Clin Psychiatry *53:* 267, 1992.

Travin S: Compulsive sexual behaviors. Psychiatr Clin North Am *18:* 155, 1995.

22

Gender Identity Disorders

The fourth edition of *Diagnostic and Statistical Manual of Mental Disorders* (DSM-IV) defines gender identity disorder as having two components: evidence of a "strong and persistent cross-gender identification" and evidence of "persistent discomfort about one's assigned sex or a sense of inappropriateness in the gender role of that sex." According to DSM-IV, people cannot be diagnosed with gender identity disorder when they have a concurrent physical intersex condition, and the diagnosis can be made only when there is evidence of significant distress or impaired social, occupational, or other areas of functioning.

To understand the disorder and to avoid confusion, the complex and varied terminology used in discussing this condition must be clearly described. Gender identity is a psychological state that reflects the self's sense of being male or female. Gender identity is based on culturally determined sets of attitudes, behavior patterns, and other attributes usually associated with masculinity or femininity. A person with a healthy gender identity is able to say with certainty, "I am male," or "I am female." Gender role is the external behavioral pattern that reflects a person's inner sense of gender identity. It is a public declaration of gender whereby the image of maleness versus femaleness is communicated to others.

Under ideal circumstances, gender identity and gender role are congruent: A woman who has a sense of herself as a woman conveys her view to the rest of the world by acting as a woman; a man who views himself as a man acts like a man. Gender role is everything that people say and do to indicate to others or to themselves the degree to which they are male or female. Gender identity and gender role must be distinguished from sex (also known as biological sex), which is strictly limited to the anatomical and physiological characteristics that indicate whether a person is male or female (for example, a penis or a vagina).

All these terms must be differentiated from sexual orientation, a person's erotic-response tendency (for example, homosexual or heterosexual). Sexual orientation takes into account people's object choices (man or woman) and fantasy life (for example, erotic fantasies about men or women or both).

EPIDEMIOLOGY

Almost no information is available about the prevalence of gender identity disorders among children, teenagers, and adults. Most estimates of prevalence are based on the number of people seeking sex-reassignment surgery, a number that indicates a male preponderance. The ratios of boys to girls reported in three child-gender-identity clinics were 30 to 1, 17 to 1, and 6 to 1; thus these clinics had little experience of girls. This disparity may indicate a greater male vulnerability to gender identity disorders or a greater sensitivity to and worry about cross-gender–identified boys than about cross-gender–identified girls in the United States. Studies of boys referred for outpatient psychiatric treatment revealed that up to about 50 percent had a significant amount of effeminate behavior. The boys were not referred primarily for problems with gender identity. How many met the criteria for gender identity disorders is unclear.

ETIOLOGY

Biological Factors

For mammals, the resting state of tissue is initially female; as the fetus develops, a male is produced only if androgen (set off by the Y chromosome, which is responsible for testicular development) is introduced. Without testes and androgen, female external genitalia develop. Thus, maleness and masculinity depend on fetal and perinatal androgens. Lower animals' sexual behavior is governed by sex steroids; as the evolutionary tree is scaled, this effect diminishes. Sex steroids influence the expression of sexual behavior in mature men or women; that is, testosterone can increase libido and aggressiveness in women, and estrogen can decrease libido and aggressiveness in men. But masculinity, femininity, and gender identity are more the product of postnatal life events than of prenatal hormonal organization.

The same principle of masculinization or feminization has been applied to the brain. Testosterone affects brain neurons that contribute to the masculinization of the brain in such areas as the hypothalamus. Whether testosterone contributes to so-called masculine or feminine behavioral patterns in gender identity disorders remains a controversial issue.

Psychosocial Factors

Children develop a gender identity consonant with their sex of rearing (also known as assigned sex). The formation of gender identity is influenced by the interaction of children's temperament and parents' qualities and attitudes. There are culturally acceptable gender roles: Boys are not expected to be effeminate, and girls are not expected to be tomboys. There are boys' games (such as cops and robbers) and girls' toys (such as dolls and dollhouses). These roles are learned, although some investigators believe that some boys are temperamentally delicate and sensitive and that some girls are aggressive and energized—traits that are stereotypically known in today's culture as feminine and masculine, respectively.

Sigmund Freud believed that gender identity problems resulted from conflicts experienced by children within the oedipal triangle. These conflicts are fueled by both real family events and children's fantasies. Whatever interferes with a child's loving the opposite-sex parent and identifying with the same-sex parent interferes with normal gender identity.

The quality of the mother–child relationship in the first years of life is paramount in establishing gender identity. During this period, mothers normally facilitate their children's awareness of and pride in their gender: Children are valued as little boys and girls, but devaluing, hostile mothering can result in gender problems. At the same time, the separation–individuation process is unfolding. When gender problems become associated with separation–individuation problems, the result can be the use of sexuality to remain in relationships characterized by shifts between a desperate infantile closeness and a hostile, devaluing distance.

Some children are given the message that they would be more valued if they adopted the gender identity of the opposite sex. Rejected or abused children may act on such a belief. Gender identity problems can also be triggered by a mother's death, extended absence, or depression, to which a young boy may react by totally identifying with her—that is, by becoming a mother to replace her.

The father's role is also important in the early years, and his presence normally helps the separation–individuation process. Without a father, mother and child may remain overly close. For a girl, the father is normally the prototype of future love objects; for a boy, the father is a model for male identification.

DIAGNOSIS

According to DSM-IV, the essential feature of gender identity disorders is a person's persistent and intense distress about his or her assigned sex and a desire to be, or an insistence that he or she is of, the other sex. As children, both girls and boys show an aversion to normative, stereotypically feminine or masculine clothing and repudiate their respective anatomical characteristics. Table 22–1 lists the DSM-IV criteria for the disorder.

Table 22–1
DSM-IV Diagnostic Criteria for Gender Identity Disorder

A. A strong and persistent cross-gender identification (not merely a desire for any perceived cultural advantages of being the other sex).

In children, the disturbance is manifested by four (or more) of the following:

(1) repeatedly stated desire to be, or insistence that he or she is, the other sex
(2) in boys, preference for cross-dressing or simulating female attire; in girls, insistence on wearing only stereotypical masculine clothing
(3) strong and persistent preferences for cross-sex roles in make-believe play or persistent fantasies of being the other sex
(4) intense desire to participate in the stereotypical games and pastimes of the other sex
(5) strong preference for playmates of the other sex

In adolescents and adults, the disturbance is manifested by symptoms such as a stated desire to be the other sex, frequent passing as the other sex, desire to live or be treated as the other sex, or the conviction that he or she has the typical feelings and reactions of the other sex.

B. Persistent discomfort with his or her sex or sense of inappropriateness in the gender role of that sex.

In children, the disturbance is manifested by any of the following: in boys, assertion that his penis or testes are disgusting or will disappear or assertion that it would be better not to have a penis, or aversion toward rough-and-tumble play and rejection of male stereotypical toys, games, and activities; in girls, rejection of urinating in a sitting position, assertion that she has or will grow a penis, or assertion that she does not want to grow breasts or menstruate, or marked aversion toward normative feminine clothing.

In adolescents and adults, the disturbance is manifested by symptoms such as preoccupation with getting rid of primary and secondary sex characteristics (eg, request for hormones, surgery, or other procedures to physically alter sexual characteristics to simulate the other sex) or belief that he or she was born the wrong sex.

C. The disturbance is not concurrent with a physical intersex condition.

D. The disturbance causes clinically significant distress or impairment in social, occupational, or other important areas of functioning.

Code based on current age:
Gender Identity Disorder in Children
Gender Identity Disorder in Adolescents or Adults

Specify if (for sexually mature individuals):
Sexually Attracted to Males
Sexually Attracted to Females
Sexually Attracted to Both
Sexually Attracted to Neither

CLINICAL FEATURES

Children

At the extreme of gender identity disorder in children are boys who, by the standards of their cultures, are as feminine as the most feminine of girls and girls who are as masculine as the most masculine of boys. No sharp line can be drawn on the continuum of gender identity disorder between children who should receive a formal diagnosis and those who should not. Girls with the disorder regularly have male companions and an avid interest in sports and rough-and-tumble play; they show no interest in dolls or playing house (unless they play the father or another male role). They may refuse to urinate in a sitting position, claim that they have or will grow a penis, not want to grow breasts or to menstruate, and assert that they will grow up to become a man (not merely to play a man's role). Boys with the disorder are usually preoccupied with stereotypically female activities. They may have a preference for dressing in girls' or women's clothes or may improvise such items from available material when the genuine articles are not available. (The cross-dressing typically does not cause sexual excitement, as in transvestic fetishism.) They often have a compelling desire to participate in the games and pastimes of girls. Female dolls are often their favorite toys, and girls are regularly their preferred playmates. When playing house, they take a girl's role. Their gestures and actions are often judged to be feminine, and they are usually subjected to male peer group teasing and rejection, a phenomenon that rarely occurs with boyish girls until adolescence. Boys with the disorder may assert that they will grow up to become a woman (not merely in role). They may claim that their penis or testes are disgusting or will disappear or that it would be better not to have a penis or testes. Some children refuse to attend school because of teasing or the pressure to dress in attire stereotypical of their assigned sex. Most children deny being disturbed by the disorder, except that it brings them into conflict with the expectations of their families or peers.

A 7-year-old boy was brought for evaluation by his mother because he had been saying intermittently since age 4 that he wanted to be a girl. He was demonstrating a range of girl-type play interests and behaviors and had an extensive interest in dress-up dolls like Barbie since age 2½. The mother had wanted a girl during her second pregnancy but claimed that she quickly became reconciled shortly after his birth to having another son.

When the boy was old enough to draw pictures, they were of princesses with long, flowing gowns. Characters imitated from the media were heroines. When playing mother–father games, he would be the mother. Recently, he had begun to display feminine gestures, particularly with his hands and wrists, and when he spoke he emphasized certain words in a manner that the mother described as effeminate. Although he had no girls' clothing, he would improvise, and at nursery school he preferred girls' and women's dress-up costumes. At a subsequent interview, the father acknowledged some of his son's cross-gender behaviors but felt that they were of little consequence. He reported that he did not spend nearly as much time with this boy as he did with the boy's older brother. The older brother and father had been closer since birth and were involved together in athletic activities.

At initial evaluation the boy confirmed that he wished that he had been born a girl and acknowledged that "I am a boy, but playing with dolls makes me happy." He also expressed the fantasy that he had been a girl before he was born. Toy preferences were decidedly cross-gendered: "It hits me to be a girl every time I go to the toy store." He imagined that he was a girl: "Sometimes I talk to myself and say that I'm a girl." (Courtesy of Richard Green, M.D., J.D., and Ray Blanchard, Ph.D.)

Adolescents and Adults

There are similar signs and symptoms in adolescents and adults. Adolescents and adults with the disorder manifest a stated desire to be the other sex; they frequently try to pass as a member of the other sex; and they desire to live or to be treated as the other sex. In addition, they desire to acquire the sex characteristics of the opposite sex. They may believe that they were born the wrong sex and may make such characteristic statements as, "I feel that I'm a woman trapped in a male body" or vice versa.

Adolescents and adults frequently request medical or surgical procedures to alter their physical appearance. Although the term *transsexual* is not used in DSM-IV, many clinicians find the term useful and will probably continue to use it. In addition, *transsexualism* appears in the 10th revision of *International Statistical Classification of Diseases and Related Health Problems* (ICD-10), and people refer to themselves as transsexuals. Transsexual people have a persistent preoccupation with getting rid of their primary and secondary sex characteristics and with acquiring the sex characteristics of the other sex. The wish to dress and live as a member of the other sex is always present.

Most retrospective studies of transsexuals report gender identity problems during childhood, but prospective studies of children with gender identity disorders indicate that few become transsexuals and want to change their sex. The disorder is much more common in men (1 per 30,000) than in women (1 per 100,000). Adult transsexuals usually complain that they are uncomfortable wearing the clothes of their assigned sex; therefore, they dress like the other sex dresses and engage in activities associated with the other sex. They find their genitals repugnant, a feeling that may lead to persistent requests for surgery. This desire may override all other wishes.

Men take estrogen to create breasts and other feminine contours, have electrolysis to remove their male hair, and have surgery to remove the testes and the penis and to create an artificial vagina. Women bind their breasts or have a double mastectomy, a hysterectomy, and an oophorectomy; take testosterone to build up muscle mass and deepen the voice; and have surgery in which an artificial phallus is created. These procedures may make a person indistinguishable from members of the other sex. Some investigators describe behavior in sex-reassigned people as almost a caricature of the newly assumed male or female role.

A 21-year-old woman complained that she felt uncomfortable with her body, that she should have been a male, and that she wanted to be a male. She appeared in the female role, but all of her clothes (jeans, shoes, shirt, vest) were men's style. Her mannerisms and her voice were convincingly masculine.

The patient recounted a childhood history typical of gender identity disorder in girls. Her dissatisfaction with her sex intensified at puberty. She hated her menses and her developing breasts, which she began hiding with jackets, sweatshirts, and so on. The last time she wore a dress was at her eighth-grade graduation.

The patient had no sexual experience with men. Her first homosexual relationship occurred in high school and lasted about 2 years. Her second was with her current partner, a divorcee 10 years older than she. She was currently cohabiting with her partner and her two young children. Their sexual relationship was reported by both partners to be satisfactory, although it was one-sided; the patient brought her partner to orgasm but would not allow her own breasts or vulva to be touched because it reminded her of her anatomical sex.

The patient regarded herself as gay in high school but eventually came to realize that she was transsexual. Her goal at clinical presentation was to undergo sex reassignment, to marry her partner, and to be a father to her partner's children. (Courtesy of Richard Green, M.D., J.D., and Ray Blanchard, Ph.D.)

Sexual Object Choice

People with gender identity disorder may be sexually attracted to men, sexually attracted to women, sexually attracted to both, or sexually attracted to neither. In almost all cases, they do not consider themselves to be homosexual, even if they have undergone a male-to-female change and are attracted to men. Similarly, persons with a female-to-male change who are attracted to women may not consider themselves to be homosexual. Because they think of themselves as members of the opposite sex, they believe themselves to be heterosexual. According to DSM-IV, once a diagnosis of gender identity disorder is made, the object of sexual attraction should be specified (for example, male, female, both, or neither).

Gender Identity Disorder Not Otherwise Specified

The diagnosis of gender identity disorder not otherwise specified is reserved for people who cannot be classified as having a gender identity disorder with the characteristics just described (Table 22–2). Three examples are listed in DSM-IV: people with intersex conditions and gender dysphoria; adults with transient, stress-related cross-dressing behavior; and people who have a persistent preoccupation with castration or penectomy without a desire to acquire the sex characteristics of the other sex.

Intersex Conditions. Intersex conditions include a variety of syndromes in which people have gross anatomical or physiological aspects of the opposite sex.

Table 22–2
DSM-IV Diagnostic Criteria for Gender Identity Disorder Not Otherwise Specified

This category is included for coding disorders in gender identity that are not classifiable as a specific gender identity disorder. Examples include

1. Intersex conditions (eg, androgen insensitivity syndrome or congenital adrenal hyperplasia) and accompanying gender dysphoria
2. Transient, stress-related cross-dressing behavior
3. Persistent preoccupation with castration or penectomy without a desire to acquire the sex characteristics of the other sex

Reprinted with permission from American Psychiatric Association: *Diagnostic and Statistical Manual of Mental Disorders,* ed 4. Copyright, American Psychiatric Association, Washington, 1994.

TURNER'S SYNDROME. In Turner's syndrome, one sex chromosome is missing (XO). The result is an absence (agenesis) or minimal development (dysgenesis) of the gonads; no significant sex hormones, male or female, are produced in fetal life or postnatally. The sexual tissues remain in a female resting state. Because the second X chromosome, which seems responsible for full femaleness, is missing, girls have an incomplete sexual anatomy and, lacking adequate estrogens, develop no secondary sex characteristics without treatment. They often show other signs, such as web neck, low posterior hairline margin, short stature, and cubitus valgus. Infants are born with normal-appearing female external genitals and so are unequivocally assigned to the female sex and are reared as girls. All the children develop as unremarkably feminine, heterosexually oriented girls; but later medical management is necessary to assist them with their infertility and absence of secondary sex characteristics.

KLINEFELTER'S SYNDROME. People (usually XXY) with Klinefelter's syndrome have a male habitus under the influence of the Y chromosome, but the effect is weakened by the presence of the second X chromosome. Although patients are born with a penis and testes, the testes are small and infertile, and the penis may also be small. Beginning in adolescence, some patients develop gynecomastia and other feminine-appearing contours. Their sexual desire is usually weak. Sex assignment and rearing should lead to a clear sense of maleness, but the patients often have gender disturbances, ranging from a complete reversal, as in transsexualism, to an intermittent desire to put on women's clothes. As a result of lessened androgen production, the fetal hypogonadal state in some patients seems to have interfered with the completion of the central nervous system organization that should underlie masculine behavior. In fact, many patients have a wide variability of psychopathology, ranging from emotional instability to mental retardation.

CONGENITAL VIRILIZING ADRENAL HYPERPLASIA (ADRENOGENITAL SYNDROME). Congenital virilizing adrenal hyperplasia results from an excess of androgen acting on the fetus. When the condition occurs in women, excessive fetal androgens from the adrenal gland have caused androgenization of the external genitals; the androgenization can range from mild clitoral enlargement to external genitals that look like a normal scrotal sac, testes, and a penis; but hidden behind these external genitals are a vagina and a uterus (Fig. 22–1). The patients are otherwise normally female. At birth, if the genitals look male, children are assigned to the male sex and so reared; the result is a clear sense of maleness and unremarkable masculinity. If the children are assigned to the female sex and so reared, a sense of femaleness and femininity results. If the parents are uncertain about the sex of their child, a hermaphroditic identity results. The resultant gender identity thus reflects the rearing practices, but androgens may help determine behavior; children raised unequivocally as girls have a tomboy quality more intense than that found in a control group. The girls nonetheless do have a heterosexual orientation.

PSEUDOHERMAPHRODITISM. Infants born with ambiguous genitals are an obstetrical emergency: Sex assignment, based on the genitals' appearance at birth, determines gender identity, which is male, female, or hermaphroditic, depending on the family's conviction about the child's sex. Male pseudohermaphroditism is incomplete differentiation of the external genitalia even though a Y chromosome is present; testes are present but rudimentary. Female pseudohermaphroditism is the presence of virilized genitals in a person who is XX, the most common cause being the adrenogenital syndrome described above. Figure 22–2 illustrates a phenotypic female with XY karotype.

True hermaphroditism is characterized by the presence of both testes and ovaries in the same person; it is a rare condition (Fig. 22–3).

ANDROGEN INSENSITIVITY SYNDROME. Androgen insensitivity syndrome, a congenital X-linked recessive trait disorder—also known as testicular feminization syndrome—results from the inability of target tissues to respond to androgens. Unable to respond, the fetal tissues remain in their female resting state, and the central nervous system is not organized as masculine. At birth the infant appears unremarkably female, although she is later found to have cryptorchid testes, which produce the testosterone to which the tissues do not respond, and minimal or absent internal sexual organs. Secondary sex characteristics at puberty are female because of the small but sufficient amounts of

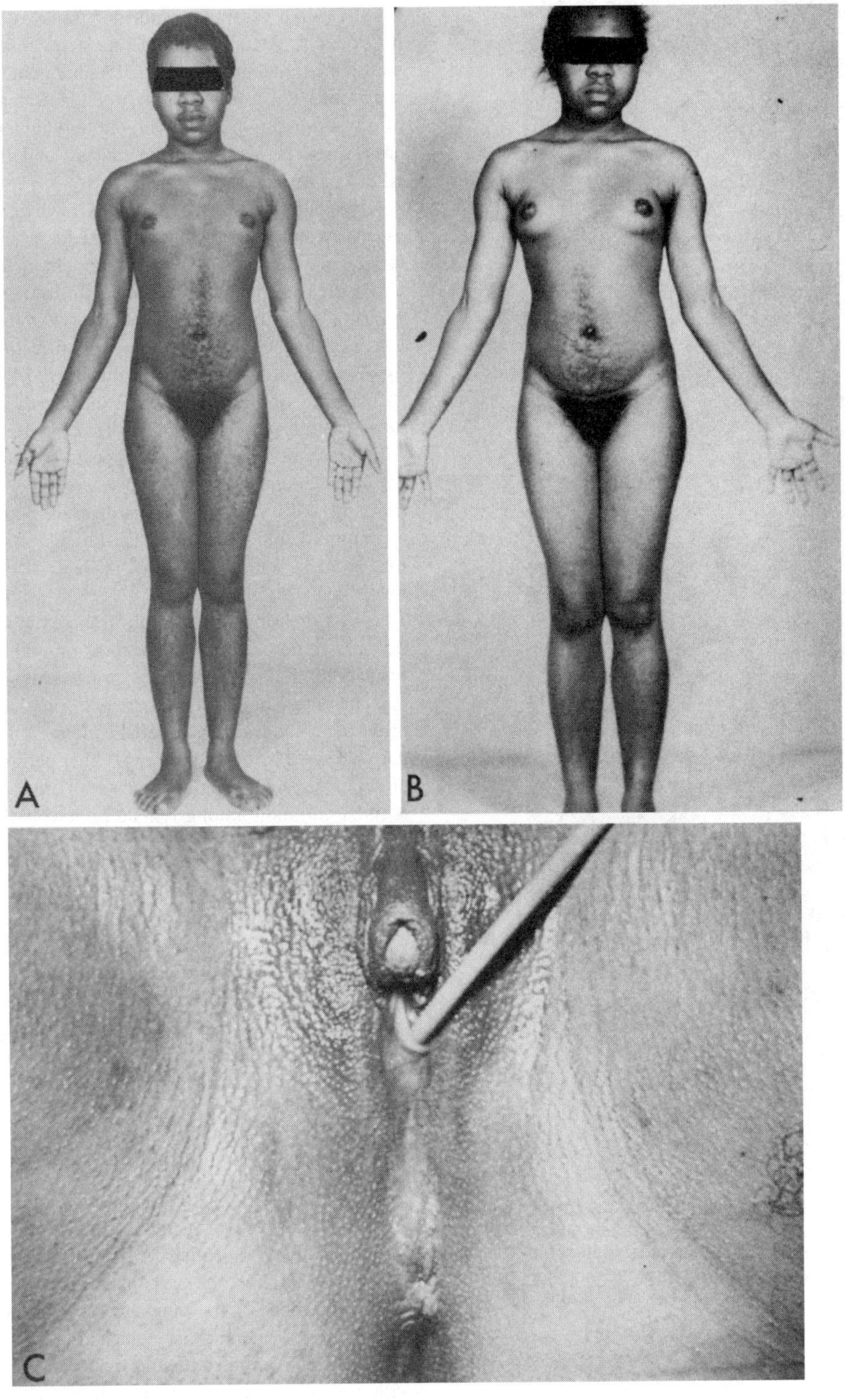
A
B
C

FIGURE 22–1

A. Female pseudohermaphroditism due to congenital adrenal hyperplasia. **B.** Note the breast development after 6 months of cortisone therapy; normal cyclic menses began within a few months. **C.** Note the enlarged clitoris and urogenital sinus. (Courtesy of Robert B. Greenblatt, M.D., and Virginia P. McNamara, M.D.)

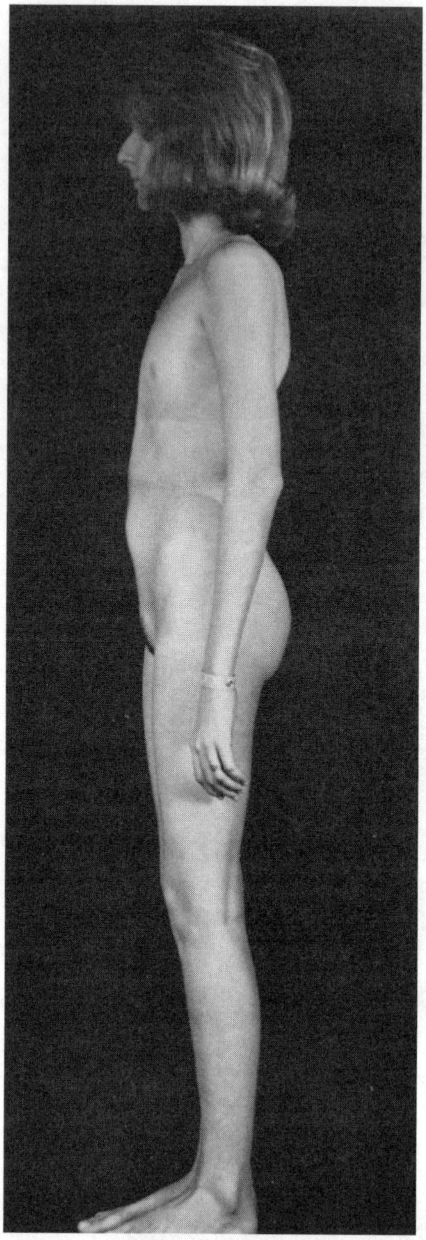

FIGURE 22–2
The vaginal canal was normal with clitoral enlargement. At laparotomy, dysgenetic gonads and a uterus with fallopian tubes were present. On cyclic estrogen-progestogen therapy, menses were induced at regular intervals, and good breast development resulted. (Courtesy of Robert B. Greenblatt, M.D., and Virginia P. McNamara, M.D.)

estrogens typically produced by the testes. The patients invariably sense themselves as females and are feminine.

Cross-Dressing. DSM-IV lists cross-dressing—dressing in clothes of the opposite sex—as a gender identity disorder if it is transient and related to stress. If the disorder is not stress related, people who cross-dress are classified as having transvestic fetishism, which is described as a paraphilia in DSM-IV. An essential feature of transvestic fetishism is that it produces sexual excitement. Stress-related cross-dressing may sometimes produce sexual excitement, but it also reduces a patient's tension and anxiety. Patients may harbor fantasies of cross-dressing but act them out only under stress. Male adult cross-dressers may have the fantasy that they are female, in whole or in part.

Cross-dressing is commonly known as transvestism, and the cross-dresser as a transvestite. Although these terms are no longer used in DSM-IV, they remain in common parlance. Cross-dressing phenomena range from the occasional solitary wearing of clothes of the other sex to extensive feminine identification in men and masculine identification in women, with involvement in a transvestic subculture. More than one article of clothing of the other sex is involved, and a person may dress entirely as a member of the opposite sex. The degree to which a cross-dressed person appears as a member of the other sex varies, depending on mannerisms, body habitus, and cross-dressing skill. When not cross-dressed, people usually appear as unremarkable members of their assigned sex. Cross-dressing may coexist with paraphilias, such as sexual sadism, sexual masochism, and pedophilia.

Cross-dressing differs from transsexualism in that the patients have no persistent preoccupation with getting rid of their primary and secondary sex characteristics and acquiring the sex characteristics of the other sex. Some people with the disorder once had transvestic fetishism but no longer become sexually aroused by cross-dressing. Other people with the disorder are homosexual men and women who cross-dress. The disorder is most common among female impersonators.

Preoccupation with Castration. The category of preoccupation with castration is reserved for men and women who have a persistent preoccupation with castration or penectomy without a desire to acquire the sex characteristics of the opposite sex. They are clearly uncomfortable with their assigned sex and live a life driven by the fantasy of what it would be like to be a different gender. They may be asexual and lack sexual interest in either men or women.

ICD-10

ICD-10 lists five gender identity disorders: transsexualism, dual-role transvestism, gender identity disorder of childhood, other gender identity disorders, and gender identity disorder, unspecified (Table 22–3). Transsexualism, defined as a wish to be a member of the opposite sex, can be diagnosed when the transsexual identity has persisted for at least 2 years, is not a symptom of another mental disorder, and is not associated with intersex, genetic, or sex chromosome abnormality. In dual-role transvestism, a person wears opposite-sex clothing to temporarily change to the other sex but does not want a permanent change of sex and is not sexually excited by cross-dressing.

Childhood gender identity disorder, defined as a ''persistent and intense distress about assigned sex, . . . with a desire to be . . . of the other sex,'' must appear before puberty for a diagnosis to be made.

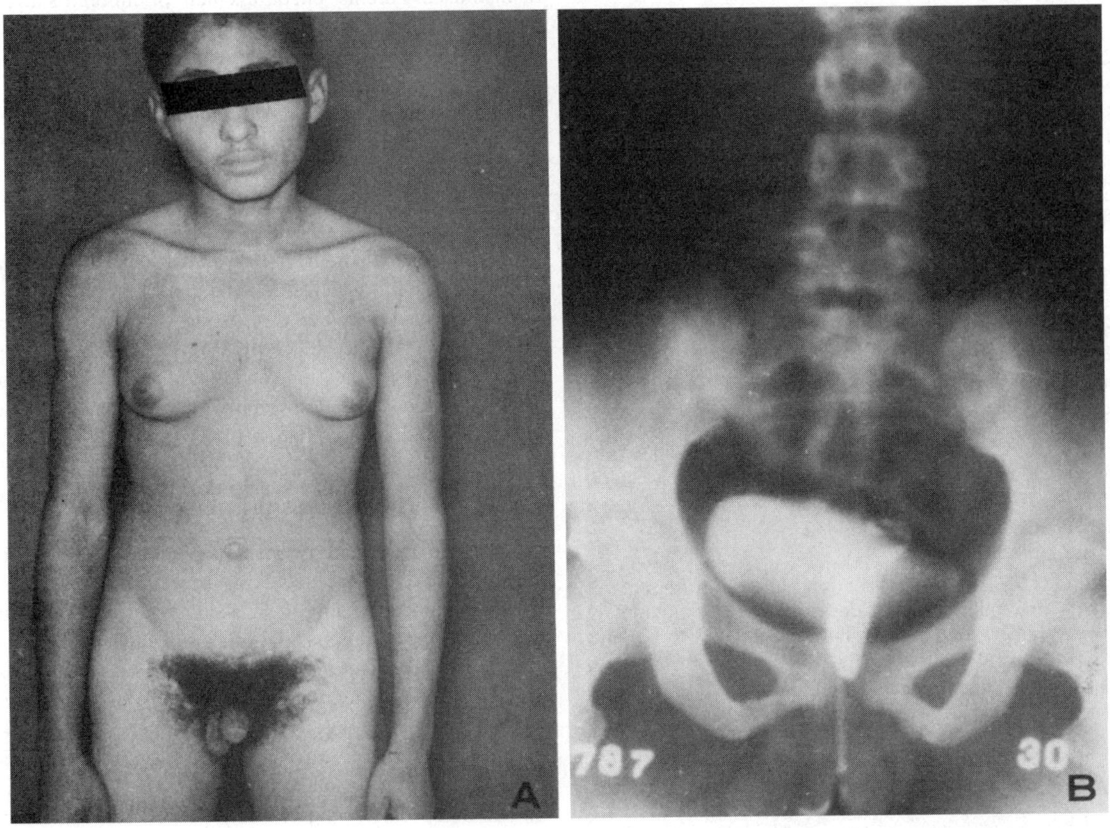
A
787
30
B

FIGURE 22–3
A true hermaphrodite. An abdominal ovary and a scrotal testis were found on biopsy of gonadal structures. Menses occurred each month from the urogenital sinus. **A.** Note gynecomastia. **B.** A cystogram and vaginal-uterosalpingogram revealed separate openings for the urethra and vaginal tract. The unicollis uterus and the fallopian tube are outlined. (Courtesy of Robert B. Greenblatt, M.D., and Virginia P. McNamara, M.D.)

COURSE AND PROGNOSIS

The prognosis for gender identity disorder depends on the age of onset and the intensity of the symptoms. Boys begin to have the disorder before the age of 4 years, and peer conflict develops during the early school years, at about the age of 7 or 8 years. Grossly feminine mannerisms may lessen as boys grow older, especially if attempts are made to discourage such behavior. Cross-dressing may be part of the disorder, and 75 percent of boys who cross-dress begin to do so before age 4. The age of onset is also early for girls, but most give up masculine behavior by adolescence.

In both sexes, homosexuality is likely to develop in one third to two thirds of all cases, although, for reasons that are unclear, fewer girls than boys have a homosexual orientation. Steven Levine reported that follow-up studies of gender-disturbed boys consistently indicated that homosexual orientation was the usual adolescent outcome. Transsexualism—that is, the desire for sex-reassignment surgery—occurs in less than 10 percent of cases. Retrospective data on homosexual men indicate a high frequency of cross-gender identifications and feminine gender role behavior during childhood.

Impaired social and occupational functioning as a result of a person's wanting to participate in the desired (and opposite) gender role is common. Depression is also a common problem, especially if a person feels hopeless about obtaining a sex change with surgery or hormones. Men have been known to castrate themselves, not as a suicide attempt but as a way of forcing a surgeon to deal with their problem.

TREATMENT

Treatment of gender identity disorders is complex and rarely successful when the goal is to reverse the disorder. Most people with gender identity disorders have fixed ideas and values and are unwilling to change. If and when they enter psychotherapy, it is most often because of depression or anxiety that they attribute to their condition. Countertransference problems must be addressed assiduously by therapists, many of whom are uncomfortable with patients who have gender identity disorder.

Parents generally bring children with cross-gender behavior patterns to a psychiatrist. Richard Green developed a treatment program designed to inculcate culturally acceptable behavior patterns in boys. Green uses a one-to-one play relationship with children in which adults or peers role-model masculine behavior. Parental counseling in conjunction with group meetings of parents and their children with gender identity disorder

Table 22–3
ICD-10 Diagnostic Criteria for Gender Identity Disorders

Transsexualism

A. The individual desires to live and be accepted as a member of the opposite sex, usually accompanied by the wish to make his or her body as congruent as possible with the preferred sex through surgery and hormonal treatment.

B. The transsexual identity has been present persistently for at least 2 years.

C. The disorder is not a symptom of another mental disorder, such as schizophrenia, nor is it associated with chromosome abnormality.

Dual-role transvestism

A. The individual wears clothes of the opposite sex in order to experience temporarily membership of the opposite sex.

B. There is no sexual motivation for the cross-dressing.

C. The individual has no desire for a permanent change to the opposite sex.

Gender identity disorder of childhood

For girls:

A. The individual shows persistent and intense distress about being a girl, and has a stated desire to be a boy (not merely a desire for any perceived cultural advantages to being a boy), or insists that she is a boy.

B. Either of the following must be present:
 (1) persistent marked aversion to normative feminine clothing and insistence on wearing stereotypical masculine clothing, eg, boy's underwear and other accessories;
 (2) persistent repudiation of female anatomical structures, as evidenced by at least one of the following:
  (a) an assertion that she has, or will grow, a penis;
  (b) rejection of urinating in a sitting position;
  (c) assertion that she does not want to grow breasts or menstruate.

C. The girl has not yet reached puberty.

D. The disorder must have been present for at least 6 months.

For boys:

A. The individual shows persistent and intense distress about being a boy, and has an intense desire to be a girl or, more rarely, insists that he is a girl.

B. Either of the following must be present:
 (1) preoccupation with stereotypical female activities, as shown by a preference for either cross-dressing or simulating female attire, or by an intense desire to participate in the games and pastimes of girls and rejection of stereotypical male toys, games, and activities;
 (2) persistent repudiation of male anatomical structures, as indicated by at least one of the following repeated assertions:
  (a) that he will grow up to become a woman (not merely in role);
  (b) that his penis or testes are disgusting or will disappear;
  (c) that it would be better not to have a penis or testes.

C. The boy has not yet reached puberty.

D. The disorder must have been present for at least 6 months.

Other gender identity disorders

Gender identity disorder, unspecified

Reprinted with permission from World Health Organization: *The ICD-10 Classification of Mental and Behavioural Disorders: Diagnostic Criteria for Research.* Copyright, World Health Organization, Geneva, 1993.

is also used. Parents' encouragement of children's atypical behavior (such as dressing a boy in girl's clothing or not cutting his hair) is examined when parents are unaware that they are fostering cross-gender behavior.

Adolescent patients are difficult to treat because of the coexistence of normal identity crises and gender identity confusion. Acting out is common, and adolescents rarely have a strong motivation to alter their stereotypical cross-gender roles. Adult patients generally enter psychotherapy to learn how to deal with their disorder, not to alter it. Therapists usually set a goal of helping patients become comfortable with the gender identity they desire, not of creating a person with a conventional sexual identity. Therapy also explores sex-reassignment surgery and the indications and contraindications for such procedures, which are often impulsively decided on by severely distressed and anxious patients.

Sex-Reassignment Surgery

Surgical treatment is definitive, and because there is no turning back, careful standards preceding the surgery have been developed. Among these standards are the following: Patients must go through a trial of cross-gender living for at least 3 months and sometimes up to 1 year. For some transsexuals the real-life test may change their minds, because they find it uncomfortable to relate to friends, workers, and lovers in this role. Patients must receive hormone treatments, with estradiol and progesterone in male-to-female changes and testosterone in female-to-male changes. Many transsexuals like the changes that occur in their bodies a result of this treatment and stop at this point. About 50 percent of transsexuals who meet these criteria go on to sex-reassignment surgery. Outcome studies are highly variable in terms of how success is defined and measured (for example, successful intercourse and body image satisfaction).

About 70 percent of male-to-female and 80 percent of female-to-male sex reassignment surgery patients report satisfactory results. Unsatisfactory results correlate with a preexisting mental disorder. Suicide in postoperative sex-reassignment surgery patients has been reported in up to 2 percent of all cases. Sex-reassignment surgery is a highly controversial measure that is undergoing much scrutiny.

Hormonal Treatment

Both sexes may be treated with hormones in lieu of surgery. Those who are biologically male take estrogen, and those who are biologically female take testosterone. Patients who take estrogen usually report immediate psychological satisfaction, based on a sense of tranquility, less frequent erections, and fewer sexual drive manifestations than before the hormone treatment. Their new sterility is not of concern to them. After several months, bodily contours become rounded, a limited but pleasing breast enlargement develops, and testicular volume decreases. The quality of the voice does not change. Clinicians must monitor patients for hypertension, hyperglycemia, hepatic dysfunction, and thromboembolic phenomena.

Women who take androgens quickly notice an increased sexual drive, clitoral tingling and enlargement, and, after several months, amenorrhea and hoarseness. If patients undertake weight lifting, a pronounced increase in muscle mass may occur. Depending on the hair distribution already present, patients may have a moderate increase in the amount and coarseness of facial and body hair; some develop frontal balding. Thromboembolic phenomena, hepatic dysfunction, and elevations of cholesterol and triglyceride levels are possible.

Treatment of Intersex Conditions

Because intersex conditions are present at birth, treatment must be timely, and some physicians believe the conditions to be true medical emergencies. The appearance of the genitalia in diverse conditions is often ambiguous, and a decision must be made about the assigned sex (boy or girl) and how the child should be reared.

Assignment should be agreed on as early as possible, so that the entire family can regard the child in a consistent, relaxed manner. When surgery is necessary to normalize genital appearance, it is generally undertaken before the age of 3 years. It is easier to assign a child to be female than to assign one to be male, because male-to-female genital surgical procedures are far more advanced than are female-to-male surgical procedures.

Intersex patients may have gender identity problems because of complicated biological influences and familial confusion about their actual sex. When intersex conditions are discovered, a panel of pediatric, urological, and psychiatric experts usually determines the sex of rearing on the basis of clinical examination, urological studies, buccal smears, chromosomal analyses, and assessment of the parental wishes. Some believe that all surgery for intersex conditions is unethical because the infant cannot consent. About 2,000 babies in the United States each year have a surgical procedure performed for ambiguous genitalia. In many cases, a markedly enlarged clitoris or ambiguous penis may be plastically reshaped. Some groups, for example, the Intersex Society of North America, oppose this practice on the grounds that it is only a cosmetic change and may interfere with later sexual functioning. In the view of most experts, however, such intervention is essential to the well-being of both parents and child. To have genitals concordant with chromosomal, biological, physiological, and other genetic determinants allows for the development of a person with a healthier gender identity than if the ambiguity is allowed to persist. To prohibit doctors, by law, from performing such operations, as some congressional lobbying groups advocate, will do more harm than good. Cosmetic surgical techniques for ambiguous genitalia are sufficiently advanced that the risk of deformity or lack of future sexual response is practically nonexistent. Finally, the determination of whether or not to proceed with surgical intervention is ultimately the decision of the parents.

Treatment of Cross-Dressing

A combined approach, using psychotherapy and pharmacotherapy, is often useful in the treatment of cross-dressing. The stress factors that precipitate the behavior are identified in therapy. The goal is to help patients cope with the stressors appropriately and, if possible, eliminate them. Intrapsychic dynamics about attitudes toward men and women are examined, and unconscious conflicts are identified. Medication, such as antianxiety and antidepressant agents, is used to treat the symptoms. Because cross-dressing may occur impulsively, medications that reinforce impulse control may be helpful, such as thioridazine (Mellaril) and fluoxetine (Prozac). Behavior therapy, aversive conditioning, and hypnosis are alternative methods that may be of use in selected cases.

References

Blanchard R, Steiner BW, editors: *Clinical Management of Gender Identity Disorders in Children and Adults.* American Psychiatric Press, Washington, 1990.

Brown GR, Wise TN, Costa PT, Herbat JH, et al: Personality characteristics and sexual functioning of 188 cross-dressing men. J Nerv Ment Dis *184:* 265, 1996.

Coates S, Person ES: Extreme boyhood femininity: Isolated behavior or pervasive disorder. J Am Acad Child Psychiatry *24:* 702, 1985.

Gonzalez T, Angel M: Transsexualism: Some considerations on aggression, transference and countertransference. Int Forum Psychoanal *5:* 11, 1996.

Green R: Gender identity in childhood and later sexual orientation: Followup of 78 males. Am J Psychiatry *142:* 399, 1985.

Green R, Blanchard R: Gender identity disorders. In *Comprehensive Textbook of Psychiatry,* ed 6, HI Kaplan, BJ Sadock, editors, p 1347. Williams & Wilkins, Baltimore, 1995.

Greenblatt RB, McNamara VP: Endocrinology of human sexuality: In *The Sexual Experience*, BJ Sadock, HI Kaplan, editors, p 104. Williams & Wilkins, Baltimore, 1976.

Hirschfield M: *Transvestites: The Erotic Drive to Cross-Dress.* Prometheus, Buffalo, NY, 1991.

Levine SB: Gender-disturbed males. J Sex Marital Ther *19:* 131, 1993.

Lothstein LM: *Female to Male Transsexualism: Historical, Clinical, and Theoretical Issues.* Routledge Kegan Paul, Boston, MA, 1982.

Marantz S, Coates S: Mothers of boys with gender identity disorder: A comparison of matched controls. J Am Acad Child Adolesc Psychiatry *30:* 310, 1991.

Pleak RR, Meyer-Bahlburg HFL, O'Brian JD, Bowen HA, Morganstein A: Cross-gender behavior and psychopathology in boy psychiatric outpatients. J Am Acad Child Adolesc Psychiatry *28:* 385, 1989.

Sherebrin H: Gender dysphoria: The therapist's dilemma—the client's choice. Art Ther *13:* 47, 1996.

Sreenivasan V: Effeminate boys in a child psychiatric clinic: Prevalence and associated factors. J Am Acad Child Psychiatry *24:* 689, 1989.

Stoller RJ: *Presentations of Gender.* Yale University Press, New Haven, 1986.

Sugar M: A clinical approach to childhood gender identity disorder. Am J Psychother *49:* 260, 1995.

Zucker KJ, Wild J, Bradley SJ, Lowry CB: Physical attractiveness of boys with gender identity disorder. Arch Sex Behav *22:* 23, 1993.

23 Eating Disorders

23.1 Anorexia Nervosa

In the fourth edition of *Diagnostic and Statistical Manual of Mental Disorders* (DSM-IV), anorexia nervosa is characterized as a disorder in which people refuse to maintain a minimally normal weight, intensely fear gaining weight, and significantly misinterpret their body and its shape. DSM-IV also notes that the term *anorexia* (''lack of appetite'') is misleading because loss of appetite rarely occurs in the early stage of the disorder. Anorexia nervosa is thus characterized by a profound disturbance of body image and the relentless pursuit of thinness, often to the point of starvation. The disorder has been recognized for many decades and has been described in various people with remarkable uniformity. Anorexia nervosa is much more prevalent in females than in males and usually has its onset in adolescence. Hypotheses of an underlying psychological disturbance in young women with the disorder include conflicts surrounding the transition from girlhood to womanhood. Psychological issues related to feelings of helplessness and to difficulty in establishing autonomy have also been suggested as contributing to the development of the disorder.

The diagnostic criteria for anorexia nervosa in DSM-IV consist of a persistent refusal to maintain body weight at or above a minimum expected weight (for example, loss of weight leading to a weight of less than 85 percent of expected weight) or a failure to gain the expected weight during a period of growth, leading to a body weight less than 85 percent of the expected weight. Patients characteristically fear becoming fat, even when drastically underweight, and exhibit disturbances of body image; they feel fat or misshapen and often deny their emaciation. To meet the diagnostic criteria for anorexia nervosa, postmenarcheal women must have an absence of at least three consecutive menstrual cycles. DSM-IV divides episodes of anorexia nervosa into two types: the restricting type, during which people restrict intake but do not regularly engage in binge eating or purging by vomiting or using laxatives or diuretics, and the binge eating–purging type, during which people regularly engage in binge eating or purging through self-induced vomiting or the use of laxatives or diuretics.

Bulimic symptoms may occur as a separate disorder (bulimia nervosa) or as part of anorexia nervosa. People with either disorder are excessively preoccupied with weight, food, and body shape.

The outcome of anorexia nervosa is variable and ranges from spontaneous recovery to a waxing and waning course to death.

EPIDEMIOLOGY

Eating disorders of various kinds have been reported in up to 4 percent of adolescent and young adult students. Anorexia nervosa has been reported more frequently over the past several decades than in the past, with increasing reports of the disorder in prepubertal girls and in males. The most common ages of onset of anorexia nervosa are the midteens, but up to 5 percent of anorectic patients have the onset of the disorder in their early 20s. Anorexia nervosa is estimated to occur in about 0.5 to 1 percent of adolescent girls. It occurs 10 to 20 times more often in females than in males. The prevalence of young women with some symptoms of anorexia nervosa but who do not meet the diagnostic criteria is estimated to be close to 5 percent. Although the disorder was initially reported most often among the upper classes, recent epidemiological surveys do not show that distribution. It seems to be most frequent in developed countries, and it may be seen with greatest frequency among young women in professions that require thinness, such as modeling and ballet.

ETIOLOGY

Biological, social, and psychological factors are implicated in the causes of anorexia nervosa. Some evidence points to higher concordance rates in monozygotic twins than in dizygotic twins. Sisters of patients with anorexia nervosa are likely to be afflicted, but this association may reflect social influences more than genetic factors. Major mood disorders are more common in family members than in the general population. Neurochemically, diminished norepinephrine turnover and activity are suggested by the reduced 3-methoxy-4-hydroxyphenylglycol (MHPG) in the urine and the cerebrospinal fluid (CSF) of some patients with anorexia nervosa. An inverse relation is seen between MHPG and depression in these patients: An increase in MHPG is associated with a decrease in depression.

Biological Factors

Endogenous opioids may contribute to the denial of hunger in patients with anorexia nervosa. Preliminary studies show dramatic weight gains in some patients who were administered opiate antagonists. Starvation results in many biochemical changes, some of which are also present in depression, such as hypercortisolemia and nonsuppression by dexamethasone. Thyroid function is suppressed as well. These abnormalities are corrected by realimentation. Starvation produces amenorrhea, which reflects lowered hormonal levels (luteinizing, follicle-stimulating, and gonadotropin-releasing hormones). Some anorexia nervosa patients, however, become amenorrheic before significant weight loss. Several computed tomographic (CT) studies reveal enlarged CSF spaces (enlarged sulci and ventricles) in patients with anorexia nervosa during starvation, a finding that is reversed by weight gain. In one positron emission tomographic (PET) scan study, caudate nucleus metabolism was higher in the anorectic state than after realimentation.

Social Factors

Patients with anorexia nervosa find support for their practices in society's emphasis on thinness and exercise. No family constellations are specific to anorexia nervosa, but some evidence indicates that these patients have close but troubled relationships with their parents. A recent review found that in families in which children presented with eating disorders, especially binge eating or purging subtypes, there were high levels of hostility, chaos, and isolation and low levels of nurturance and empathy. An adolescent with a severe eating disorder may tend to draw attention away from strained marital relationships.

Psychological and Psychodynamic Factors

Anorexia nervosa appears to be a reaction to the demands requiring adolescents to behave more independently and to increase their social and sexual functioning. Patients with the disorder substitute their preoccupations, which are similar to obsessions, with eating and weight gain for other, normal adolescent pursuits. These patients typically lack a sense of autonomy and selfhood. Many experience their bodies as somehow under the control of their parents, so that self-starvation may be an effort to gain validation as a unique and special person. Only through acts of extraordinary self-discipline can an anorectic patient develop a sense of autonomy and selfhood.

Psychoanalytic clinicians who treat patients with anorexia nervosa generally agree that these young patients have been unable to separate psychologically from their mothers. The body may be perceived as though it were inhabited by an introject of an intrusive and unempathic mother. Starvation may unconsciously mean arresting the growth of this intrusive internal object and thereby destroying it. Often, a projective identification process is involved in the interactions between the patient and the patient's family. Many anorectic patients feel that oral desires are greedy and unacceptable; therefore, these desires are projectively disavowed. Parents respond to the refusal to eat by becoming frantic about whether the patient is actually eating. The patient can then view the parents as the ones who have unacceptable desires and can projectively disavow them: Others may be voracious and ruled by desire but not the patient.

DIAGNOSIS AND CLINICAL FEATURES

The onset of anorexia nervosa usually occurs between the ages of 10 and 30 years. Patients outside this age range are not typical, and their diagnoses should be questioned. After the age of 13 years, the frequency of onset increases rapidly, with the maximum frequency at 17 to 18 years of age. For about 85 percent of all anorexia nervosa patients, the onset of the illness occurs between the ages of 13 to 20 years. Before age 10, some patients were picky eaters or had frequent digestive problems. The DSM-IV diagnostic criteria for anorexia nervosa are given in Table 23.1–1.

An intense fear of gaining weight and becoming obese is present in all patients with the disorder and undoubtedly contributes to their lack of interest in, and even resistance to, therapy. Most aberrant behavior directed toward losing weight occurs in secret. Patients with anorexia nervosa usually refuse to eat with their families or in public places. They lose weight by a drastic reduction in their total food intake, with a disproportionate decrease in high-carbohydrate and fatty foods.

The term *anorexia* is a misnomer, because loss of appetite is usually rare until late in the disorder. Patients' passions for collecting recipes and for preparing elaborate meals for others are evidence that they are constantly thinking about food. Some patients cannot continuously control their voluntary restriction of food intake and so have eating binges. These binges usually occur secretly and often at night; self-induced vomiting frequently follows an eating binge. Patients abuse laxatives and even diuretics to lose weight, and ritualistic exercising, extensive cycling, walking, jogging, and running are common activities.

Patients with the disorder exhibit peculiar behavior about

Table 23.1–1
DSM-IV Diagnostic Criteria for Anorexia Nervosa

A. Refusal to maintain body weight at or above a minimally normal weight for age and height (eg, weight loss leading to maintenance of body weight less than 85% of that expected; or failure to make expected weight gain during period of growth, leading to body weight less than 85% of that expected).

B. Intense fear of gaining weight or becoming fat, even though underweight.

C. Disturbance in the way in which one's body weight or shape is experienced; undue influence of body weight or shape on self-evaluation, or denial of the seriousness of the current low body weight.

D. In post-menarchal females, amenorrhea, ie, the absence of at least three consecutive menstrual cycles. (A woman is considered to have amenorrhea if her periods occur only following hormone, eg, estrogen, administration.)

Specify type:

Restricting type: During the current episode of anorexia nervosa, the person has not reguarly engaged in binge eating or purging behavior (ie, self-induced vomiting or the misuse of laxatives, diuretics, or enemas)

Binge eating/purging type: During the current episode of anorexia nervosa, the person has regularly engaged in binge eating or purging behavior (ie, self-induced vomiting or the misuse of laxatives, diuretics, or enemas)

food. They hide food all over the house and frequently carry large quantities of candies in their pockets and purses. While eating meals, they try to dispose of food in their napkins or hide it in their pockets. They cut their meat into very small pieces and spend a great deal of time rearranging the pieces on their plates. If the patients are confronted with their peculiar behavior, they often deny that their behavior is unusual or flatly refuse to discuss it.

Obsessive-compulsive behavior, depression, and anxiety are other psychiatric symptoms of anorexia nervosa most frequently noted in the literature. Patients tend to be rigid and perfectionist, and somatic complaints, especially epigastric discomfort, are usual. Compulsive stealing, usually of candies and laxatives but occasionally of clothes and other items, is common.

Poor sexual adjustment is frequently described in patients with the disorder. Many adolescent patients with anorexia nervosa have delayed psychosocial sexual development; in adults, a markedly decreased interest in sex often accompanies the onset of the disorder. An unusual minority of anorexia nervosa patients have a premorbid history of promiscuity, substance abuse, or both and during the disorder do not show a decreased interest in sex.

Patients usually come to medical attention when their weight loss becomes apparent. As the weight loss grows profound, physical signs such as hypothermia (as low as 35 C), dependent edema, bradycardia, hypotension, and lanugo (the appearance of neonatal-like hair) appear, and patients show a variety of metabolic changes (Fig. 23.1–1). Some female patients with anorexia nervosa come to medical attention because of amenorrhea, which often appears before their weight loss is noticeable. Some patients induce vomiting or abuse purgatives and diuretics; such behavior causes concern about hypokalemic alkalosis. Impaired water diuresis may be noted.

Electrocardiographic (ECG) changes, such as flattening or inversion of the T waves, ST segment depression, and lengthening of the QT interval, have been noted in the emaciated stage of anorexia nervosa. ECG changes may also result from potassium loss, which can lead to death. Gastric dilation is a rare complication of anorexia nervosa. In some patients, aortography has shown a superior mesenteric artery syndrome. Other medical complications of eating disorders are listed in Table 23.1–2.

DSM-IV identifies two types of anorexia nervosa—the restricting type and the binge eating–purging type. Binge eating–purging is common among patients with anorexia nervosa and develops in up to 50 percent of them. Each type appears to have distinct historic and clinical features. Those who practice binge eating and purging share many features with people who have bulimia nervosa without anorexia nervosa. Those who binge eat and purge tend to have families in which some members are obese, and they themselves have histories of heavier body weights before the disorder than do people with the restricting type. Binge eating–purging people are likely to be associated with substance abuse, impulse control disorders, and personality disorders. People with restricting anorexia nervosa limit their food selection, take in as few calories as possible, and often have obsessive-compulsive traits with respect to food and other matters. Both types of people are preoccupied with weight and body image, and both may exercise for hours every day and exhibit bizarre eating behaviors. Both may be socially isolated and have depressive disorder symptoms and diminished sexual interest. Some people with anorexia nervosa may purge but not binge.

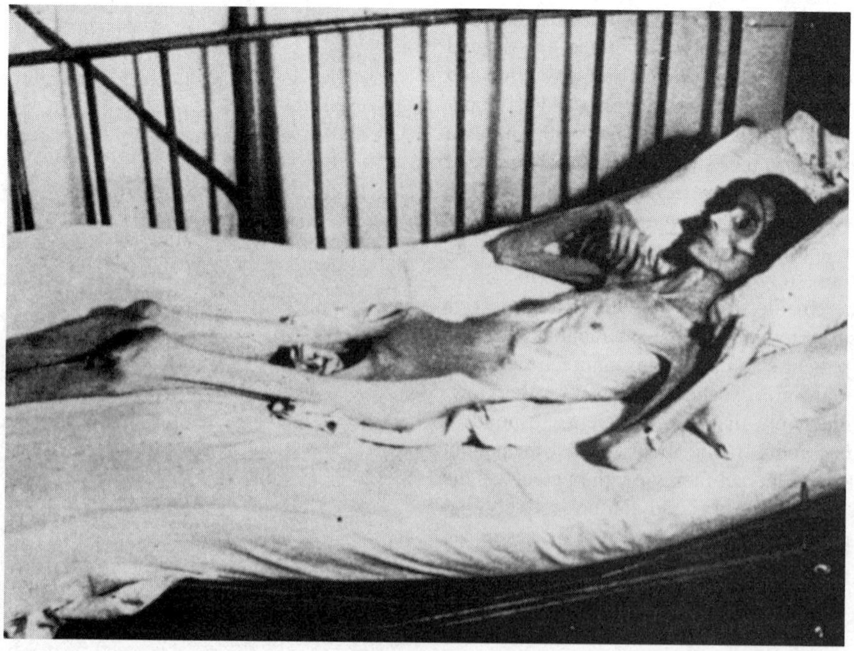

FIGURE 23.1–1
A patient with anorexia nervosa. (Courtesy of Katherine Halmi, M.D.)

Table 23.1–2
Medical Complications of Eating Disorders

Related to weight loss:
Cachexia: Loss of fat, muscle mass, reduced thyroid metabolism (low T_3 syndrome), cold intolerance, and difficulty in maintaining core body temperature
Cardiac: Loss of cardiac muscle; small heart; cardiac arrhythmias, including atrial and ventricular premature contractions, prolonged His' bundle transmission (prolonged QT interval), bradycardia, ventricular tachycardia; sudden death
Digestive-gastrointestinal: Delayed gastric emptying, bloating, constipation, abdominal pain
Reproductive: Amenorrhea, low levels of luteinizing hormone (LH) and follicle-stimulating hormone (FSH)
Dermatological: Lanugo (fine babylike hair over body), edema
Hematological: Leukopenia
Neuropsychiatric: Abnormal taste sensation (?zinc deficiency), apathetic depression, mild cognitive disorder
Skeletal: Osteoporosis

Related to purging (vomiting and laxative abuse):
Metabolic: Electrolyte abnormalities, particularly hypokalemic, hypochloremic alkalosis; hypomagnesemia
Digestive-gastrointestinal: Salivary gland and pancreatic inflammation and enlargement with increase in serum amylase, esophageal and gastric erosion, dysfunctional bowel with haustral dilation
Dental: Erosion of dental enamel, particularly of front teeth, with corresponding decay
Neuropsychiatric: Seizures (related to large fluids shifts and electrolyte disturbances), mild neuropathies, fatigue and weakness, mild cognitive disorder

Reprinted with permission from Yager J: Eating disorders. In *Clinical Psychiatry for Medical Students,* A Stoudemire, editor, p 324. Lippincott, Philadelphia, 1990.

People with anorexia nervosa have high rates of comorbid major depressive disorders: Major depressive disorder or dysthymic disorder has been reported in up to 50 percent of anorexia nervosa patients. The suicide rate is higher in people with the binge eating–purging type of anorexia nervosa than in people with the restricting type.

Patients with anorexia nervosa are often secretive, deny their symptoms, and resist treatment. In almost all cases, relatives or intimate acquaintances must confirm a patient's history. The mental status examination usually shows a patient who is alert and knowledgeable on the subject of nutrition and who is preoccupied with food and weight.

A patient must have a thorough general physical and neurological examination. If the patient is vomiting, a hypokalemic alkalosis may be present. Because most patients are dehydrated, clinicians must obtain serum electrolyte levels initially and periodically during hospitalization.

When Peggy was first evaluated for admission to an inpatient eating disorder program, she was a 20-year-old woman who had difficulty supporting her 5-foot 3-inch body with a weight of only 67 pounds. She had begun to lose weight 4 years earlier, initially dieting to lose an unwanted 6 pounds. Encouraged by compliments on her new body, she proceeded to lose 8 more pounds. Over the next 2 years she continued to lose weight, increased her physical activity until her weight reached a low of 64 pounds, and stopped menstruating. She was admitted to a medical unit, treated for peptic ulcer disease, and discharged, only to be admitted 3 months thereafter to the psychiatric unit of a general hospital. During that 8-week hospitalization, she went from 84 pounds to 100 pounds. She did well until she went off to college, where, with increased academic and social demands, she again began to diet until she weighted only 67 pounds. Her eating habits were ritualized: she cut food into very small pieces, moved them around on the plate, and ate very slowly. She was troubled by the changes in her body and became increasingly anxious as her figure developed. She was forced to drop out of school and to accept another hospitalization.

Peggy was motivated to comply with treatment, but her fears of gaining weight and becoming obese affected her progress. She was expected to gain a minimum of 2 pounds every week, and she was restricted to bed rest if she failed to gain sufficient weight. In psychotherapy, Peggy was gradually guided to discuss her feelings and to actually look at herself in the mirror. She was initially instructed to look at one part of her body for a minimum of 10 seconds, and the time was progressively increased until she could look at her whole body without any anxiety. Her menses returned at a weight of 93 pounds. After 7 months of individual and family treatment, she was discharged at a weight of 100 pounds. Peggy returned to college, worked part time, and lived with her parents.

DISCUSSION

As is usually the case with anorexia nervosa, the characteristic signs and symptoms leave little doubt concerning the correct diagnosis. Peggy has all of the salient features, including refusal to maintain body weight at or above a minimally normal weight for age and height; intense fear of gaining weight or of becoming fat, even though underweight; disturbance in the way in which her body weight or shape is experienced (anxiety when viewing her body); and, in postmenarcheal females, amenorrhea. Because her method of losing weight has never involved purging (self-induced vomiting or use of laxatives or diuretics) or binge eating (consumption of large amounts of food with a sense of loss of control), the subtype is specified as restricting type.

Peggy exhibited compulsive ritualistic behavior with regard to food (e.g., cutting her food into very small pieces and moving it around on her plate before eating it), a feature commonly seen in patients with anorexia nervosa. Although her compulsive eating behavior might suggest the possible additional diagnosis of obsessive-compulsive disorder, a separate diagnosis is not given as the compulsive behavior is accounted for by the diagnosis of anorexia nervosa.

During the course of the anorexia nervosa, Peggy experienced depression and panic attacks. There is insufficient information about these symptoms to make a definitive diagnosis of a mood or anxiety disorder. However, the occurrence of these comorbid disorders is common in patients with anorexia nervosa.

Anorexia nervosa is a serious and often life-threatening disorder. This case illustrates that with expert treatment, a good outcome is possible.

FOLLOW-UP

Over the next 10 years, Peggy graduated from college with a degree in nutrition and was selected to do an internship with a major corporation. She has excelled in her work, receiving several promotions. She married, but the relationship deteriorated as her husband became physically abusive. She moved out, obtained a court order of protection, and eventually a divorce. Her most recent correspondence told of her return to graduate school (all expenses paid and full salary), a new romance, and success in a marathon (third place in a 26-mile race). She has maintained her weight at around 116 pounds and menstruates normally. She did seek counseling to sort out issues related to her broken marriage and her estrangement from her sister, which has since been resolved. She describes her life now as full and satisfying. (From *DSM-IV Casebook.*)

ICD-10

The 10th revision of *International Statistical Classification of Diseases and Related Health Disorders* (ICD-10) describes anorexia nervosa as a deliberate, severe weight loss caused by the patient. According to ICD-10, its causes remain unknown, but a combination of sociocultural and biological factors apparently contributes to the disorder, along with a vulnerable personality and other psychological processes. Undernutrition produces endocrine and metabolic changes and disturbs bodily functions. Whether the endocrine disorder is completely caused by the eating disorder or whether other factors are also at work is uncertain. The ICD-10 criteria for eating disorders are presented in Table 23.1–3.

Pathology and Laboratory Examination

No single laboratory test unconditionally helps to diagnose anorexia nervosa. A multitude of endocrinological and medical problems can develop secondary to the starvation that occurs with the disorder; therefore, a battery of screening laboratory tests is warranted in people who meet the diagnostic criteria for anorexia nervosa. The tests include serum electrolytes with renal function tests; thyroid function tests; glucose, amylase, and hematological tests; an electrocardiogram; cholesterol level; dexamethasone-suppression test; and carotene level. Clinicians may find decreased thyroid hormone and serum glucose levels, nonsuppression of cortisol after dexamethasone, hypokalemia, increased blood urea nitrogen, and hypercholesterolemia. Cardiovascular complications are common and include hypotension and bradycardia.

DIFFERENTIAL DIAGNOSIS

The differential diagnosis of anorexia nervosa is complicated by patients' denial of the symptoms, the secrecy surrounding their bizarre eating rituals, and their resistance to seeking treatment. Thus, it may be difficult to identify the

Table 23.1–3
ICD-10 Diagnostic Criteria for Eating Disorders

Anorexia nervosa

A. There is weight loss or, in children, a lack of weight gain, leading to a body weight at least 15% below the normal or expected weight for age and height.

B. The weight loss is self-induced by avoidance of "fattening foods."

C. There is self-perception of being too fat, with an intrusive dread of fatness, which leads to a self-imposed low weight threshold.

D. A widespread endocrine disorder involving the hypothalamic-pituitary-gonadal axis is manifest in women as amenorrhea and in men as a loss of sexual interest and potency. (An apparent exception is the persistence of vaginal bleeds in anorexic women who are on replacement hormonal therapy, most commonly taken as a contraceptive pill.)

E. The disorder does not meet criteria A and B for bulimia nervosa.

Comments

The following features support the diagnosis but are not essential elements: self-induced vomiting, self-induced purging, excessive exercise, and use of appetite suppressants and/or diuretics.

If onset is prepubertal, the sequence of pubertal events is delayed or even arrested (growth ceases; in girls the breasts do not develop, and there is a primary amenorrhea; in boys the genitals remain juvenile). With recovery, puberty is often completed normally, but the menarche is late.

Atypical anorexia nervosa

Researchers studying atypical forms of anorexia nervosa are recommended to make their own decisions about the number and type of criteria to be fulfilled.

Bulimia nervosa

A. There are recurrent episodes of overeating (at least twice a week over a period of 3 months) in which large amounts of food are consumed in short periods.

B. There is persistent preoccupation with eating and a strong desire or a sense of compulsion to eat (craving).

C. The patient attempts to counteract the "fattening" effects of food by one or more of the following:
   (1) self-induced vomiting;
   (2) self-induced purging;
   (3) alternating periods of starvation;
   (4) use of drugs such as appetite suppressants, thyroid preparations, or diuretics; when bulimia occurs in diabetic patients, they may choose to neglect their insulin treatment.

D. There is self-perception of being too fat, with an intrusive dread of fatness (usually leading to underweight).

Atypical bulimia nervosa

Researchers studying atypical forms of bulimia nervosa, such as those involving normal or excessive body weight, are recommended to make their own decisions about the number and type of criteria to be fulfilled.

Overeating associated with other psychological disturbances

Researchers wishing to use this category are recommended to design their own criteria.

Vomiting associated with other psychological disturbances

Researchers wishing to use this category are recommended to design their own criteria.

Other eating disorders

Eating disorder, unspecified

Adapted from World Health Organization: *The ICD-10 Classification of Mental and Behavioural Disorders: Diagnostic Criteria for Research.* Copyright, World Health Organization, Geneva, 1993.

mechanism of weight loss and the patient's associated ruminative thoughts about distortions of body image.

Clinicians must ascertain that a patient does not have a medical illness that can account for the weight loss (for example, a brain tumor or cancer). Weight loss, peculiar eating behaviors, and vomiting can occur in several mental disorders. Depressive disorders and anorexia nervosa have several features in common, such as depressed feelings, crying spells, sleep disturbance, obsessive ruminations, and occasional suicidal thoughts. The two disorders, however, have several distinguishing features. Generally, a patient with a depressive disorder has a decreased appetite, whereas a patient with anorexia nervosa claims to have a normal appetite and to feel hungry; only in the severe stages of anorexia nervosa do patients actually have a decreased appetite. In contrast to depressive agitation, the hyperactivity seen in anorexia nervosa is planned and ritualistic. The preoccupation with recipes and the caloric content of foods and the preparation of gourmet feasts is typical of patients with anorexia nervosa but is absent in patients with a depressive disorder. And, in depressive disorders patients have no intense fear of obesity or disturbance of body image.

Weight fluctuations, vomiting, and peculiar food handling may occur in somatization disorder. On rare occasions a patient fulfills the diagnostic criteria for both somatization disorder and anorexia nervosa; in such a case both diagnoses should be made. Generally, the weight loss in somatization disorder is not as severe as that in anorexia nervosa, nor does a patient with somatization disorder express a morbid fear of becoming overweight, as is common in the anorexia nervosa patient. Amenorrhea for 3 months or longer is unusual in somatization disorder.

In schizophrenic patients, delusions about food are seldom concerned with caloric content. More likely, they believe the food to be poisoned. Schizophrenic patients are rarely preoccupied with a fear of becoming obese and do not have the hyperactivity that is seen in patients with anorexia nervosa. Schizophrenic patients have bizarre eating habits but not the entire syndrome of anorexia nervosa.

Anorexia nervosa must be differentiated from bulimia nervosa, a disorder in which episodic binge eating, followed by depressive moods, self-deprecating thoughts, and often self-induced vomiting, occurs while patients maintain their weight within a normal range. Patients with bulimia nervosa seldom lose 15 percent of their weight, but the two conditions frequently coexist.

COURSE AND PROGNOSIS

The course of anorexia nervosa varies greatly—spontaneous recovery without treatment, recovery after a variety of treatments, a fluctuating course of weight gains followed by relapses, a gradually deteriorating course resulting in death caused by complications of starvation. A recent study reviewing subtypes of anorexic patients found that restricting-type anorexic patients seemed to be less likely to recover than those who were of the binge eating–purging type. The short-term response of patients to almost all hospital treatment programs is good. In those who have regained sufficient weight, however, preoccupation with food and body weight often continues, social relationships are often poor, and depression is often present. In general, the prognosis is not good. Studies have shown a range of mortality rates from 5 to 18 percent.

Indicators of a favorable outcome are the admission of hunger, a lessening of denial and immaturity, and improved self-esteem. Such factors as childhood neuroticism, parental conflict, bulimia nervosa, vomiting, laxative abuse, and various behavioral manifestations (such as obsessive-compulsive, hysterical, depressive, psychosomatic, neurotic, and denial symptoms) have been related to poor outcome in some studies but have not been significant in affecting the outcome in other studies.

Thirty to 50 percent of patients with anorexia nervosa have symptoms of bulimia nervosa, which usually occur within 1½ years after the beginning of anorexia nervosa. The bulimic symptoms sometimes precede the onset of anorexia nervosa.

TREATMENT

In view of the complicated psychological and medical implications of anorexia nervosa, a comprehensive treatment plan, including hospitalization when necessary and both individual and family therapy, is recommended. Behavioral, interpersonal, and cognitive approaches and, in some cases, medication should be considered.

Hospitalization

The first consideration in the treatment of anorexia nervosa is to restore patients' nutritional state; dehydration, starvation, and electrolyte imbalances can lead to serious health compromises and, in some cases, death. The decision to hospitalize a patient is based on the patient's medical condition and the degree of structure needed to ensure patient cooperation. In general, anorexia nervosa patients who are 20 percent below the expected weight for their height are recommended for inpatient programs, and patients who are 30 percent below their expected weight require psychiatric hospitalization that ranges from 2 to 6 months.

Inpatient psychiatric programs for patients with anorexia nervosa generally use a combination of a behavioral management approach, individual psychotherapy, family education and therapy, and, in some cases, psychotropic medications. Successful treatment is promoted by the ability of staff members to maintain a firm yet supportive approach to patients, often through a combination of positive reinforcers (praise) and negative reinforcers (restriction of exercise and purging behavior). The program must have some flexibility for individualizing treatment to meet patients' needs and cognitive abilities. Patients must become willing participants for treatment to succeed in the long run.

Most patients are uninterested in psychiatric treatment and even resist it; they are brought to a doctor's office unwillingly by agonizing relatives or friends. The patients rarely accept the recommendation of hospitalization without arguing and criticizing the proposed program. Emphasizing the benefits, such as the relief of insomnia and patients' depressive signs and symptoms, may help persuade the patients to admit themselves willingly to the hospital. Relatives' support and confidence in the physicians and treatment team are essential when firm recommendations must be carried out. Patients' families should be warned that the patients will resist admission and, for the several weeks of treatment, will make many dramatic pleas for the family's support to obtain release from the hospital program. Only when the risk of death from the complications of malnutrition is likely should compulsory admission or commitment be obtained. On rare occasions, patients prove that the doctor's statements about the probable failure of outpatient treatment are wrong. Some patients may gain a specified amount of weight by the time of each outpatient visit, but such behavior is uncommon, and a period of inpatient care is usually necessary.

The general management of patients with anorexia nervosa during a hospitalized treatment program should take into account the following: Patients should be weighed daily early in the morning after emptying the bladder. The daily fluid intake and urine output should be recorded. If vomiting is occurring, hospital staff members must monitor serum electrolyte levels regularly and watch for the development of hypokalemia. Because food is often regurgitated after meals, the staff may be able to control vomiting by making the bathroom inaccessible for at least 2 hours after meals or by having an attendant in the bathroom to prevent vomiting. Constipation in these patients is relieved when they begin to eat normally. Stool softeners, but never laxatives, may occasionally be given. If diarrhea occurs, it usually means that patients are surreptitiously taking laxatives. Because of the rare complication of stomach dilation and the possibility of circulatory overload when patients immediately start eating an enormous number of calories, the hospital staff should give patients about 500 calories over the amount required to maintain their present weight (usually 1,500 to 2,000 calories a day). It is wise to give these calories in six equal feedings throughout the day, so that patients need not eat a large amount of food at one sitting. Giving patients a liquid food supplement such as Sustagen may be advisable, because they may be less apprehensive about gaining weight slowly with the formula than by eating food.

After patients are discharged from the hospital, clinicians usually find it necessary to continue outpatient supervision of the problems identified in the patients and their families.

Psychotherapy

Most patients with anorexia nervosa require continued interventions after discharge from the hospital or after they are restored to health through outpatient treatment plans. Because for most patients the onset of the disorder occurs in adolescence, family therapy is part of a comprehensive treatment plan. Although classic psychodynamically oriented therapy has not been useful in the early stages of treatment, especially when patients are in a starvation state, insight-oriented psychotherapies have been helpful to some patients when they have been stabilized.

Dynamic Psychotherapy. Dynamic expressive-supportive psychotherapy is sometimes used in the treatment of patients with anorexia nervosa, but patients' resistances may make the process difficult and painstaking. Because patients view their symptoms as constituting the core of their specialness, therapists must avoid excessive investment in trying to change their eating behaviors. The opening phase of the psychotherapy process must be geared to building a therapeutic alliance. Patients may experience early interpretations as though someone else were telling them what they really feel and thereby minimizing and invalidating their own experiences. Therapists who empathize with patients' points of view and take an active interest in what their patients think and feel, however, convey to patients that their autonomy is respected. Above all, psychotherapists must be flexible, persistent, and durable in the face of patients' tendencies to defeat any efforts to help them.

Many clinicians prefer cognitive-behavioral approaches to monitor weight gain and maintenance and to address eating behaviors. Cognitive or interpersonal strategies have also been recommended to explore other issues related to the disorder. Family therapy has been used to examine interactions among family members and the disorder's possible secondary gain for patients.

Biological Therapy

Pharmacological studies have not yet identified any medication resulting in definitive improvement of the core symptoms of anorexia nervosa. Some reports support the use of cyproheptadine (Periactin), a drug with antihistaminic and antiserotonergic properties, for patients with the restricting type of anorexia nervosa. Amitriptyline (Elavil) has also been reported to have some benefit. Other medications that have been tried by patients with anorexia nervosa with variable results include clomipramine (Anafranil), pimozide (Orap), and chlorpromazine (Thorazine). Trials of fluoxetine (Prozac) have resulted in some reports of weight gain, and serotonergic agents have yielded positive responses. In anorexia nervosa patients with coexisting depressive disorders, the depressive condition should be treated. Concern exists about the use of tricyclic drugs in low-weight, depressed patients with anorexia nervosa, who may be vulnerable to hypotension, cardiac arrhythmia, and dehydration. Once an adequate nutritional status has been attained, the risks of serious side effects from the tricyclic drugs may decrease; in some cases the depression improves with weight gain and normalized nutritional status.

Rarely, electroconvulsive therapy (ECT) may be beneficial in certain cases of anorexia nervosa and major depressive disorder.

References

American Psychiatric Association: Practice guidelines for eating disorders. Am J Psychiatry *150:* 212, 1993.

Brewerton TD, Lydiard RB, Ballenger JC, Herzog DB: Eating disorders and social phobia: Arch Gen Psychiatry *50:* 70, 1993.

Ferguson JM: The use of electroconvulsive therapy in patients with intractable anorexia nervosa. Int Eating Disord *13:* 171, 1993.

Gabbard GO: *Psychodynamic Psychiatry in Clinical Practice: The DSM-IV Edition.* American Psychiatric Press, Washington, 1994.

Garfinkel PE: Eating disorders. In *Comprehensive Textbook of Psychiatry,* ed 6, HI Kaplan, BJ Sadock, editors, p 1361. Williams & Wilkins, Baltimore, 1995.

Garner DM, Garner MV, Rosen LW: Anorexia nervosa "restricters" who purge: Implications for subtyping anorexia nervosa. Int J Eating Disord *13:* 187, 1993.

Gillberg IC, Rastam M, Gillberg C: Anorexia nervosa outcomes: six-year controlled longitudinal study of 51 cases including a population cohort. J Am Acad Child Adolesc Psychiatry *33:* 729, 1994.

Harper-Giuffre H, MacKenzie KR, editors: *Group Psychotherapy for Eating Disorders.* American Psychiatric Press, Washington, 1992.

Herzog DB, Field AE, Keller MB, West JC, Robbins WM, Staley J, Colditz G: Subtyping earing disorders: Is it justified? J Am Acad Child Adolesc Psychiatry *35:* 928, 1996.

Herzog DB, Sacks NR, Keller MB, Lavori PW, von Ranson KB, Gray HM: Patterns and predictors of recovery in anorexia nervosa and bulimia nervosa. J Am Acad Child Adolesc Psychiatry *32:* 835, 1993.
Horesh N, Apter A, Ishai J, Danziger Y, Miculincer M, Stein D, Lepkifker E, Minouni M: Abnormal psychosocial situations and eating disorders in adolescence. J Am Acad Child Adolesc Psychiatry *35:* 921, 1996.
Hsu LKG, Kaye WH, Weltzin T: Are the eating disorders related to obsessive compulsive disorder? Int J Eat Disord *14:* 305, 1993.
Jarry JL, Vaccarine FJ: Eating disorder and obsessive-compulsive disorder: Neurochemical and phenomenological commonalities. J Psychiatry Neurosci *21:* 36, 1996.
Ponton LE: A review of eating disorders in adolescents. Adolesc Psychiatry *20:* 267, 1995.
Stoner SA, Fedoroff IC, Andersen AE, Rolls BJ: Food preferences and desire to eat in anorexia and bulimia nervosa. Int J Eat Disord *19:* 13, 1996.
Vanderlinden J, Vandereycken W, van Dyck R, Vertommen H: Dissociative experiences and trauma in eating disorders. Int J Eating Disord *13:* 195, 1993.
Waller G: Sexual abuse and eating disorders: Borderline personality disorder as a mediating factor? Br J Psychiatry *162:* 771, 1993.
Wilson GT, Fairburn CG: Cognitive treatments for eating disorders. J Consult Clin Psychol *61:* 261, 1993.
Yates A: Current perspectives on the eating disorders: II. Treatment, outcome, and research directions. J Am Acad Child Adolesc Psychiatry *29:* 1, 1990.

▲ 23.2 Bulimia Nervosa and Eating Disorder Not Otherwise Specified

BULIMIA NERVOSA

In the fourth edition of *Diagnostic and Statistical Manual of Mental Disorders* (DSM-IV), bulimia nervosa is defined as binge eating combined with inappropriate ways of stopping weight gain. The recurrent episodes of bulimia nervosa, which is more common than is anorexia nervosa, are accompanied by feelings of being out of control. Social interruption or physical discomfort—that is, abdominal pain or nausea—terminates the binge eating, which is often followed by feelings of guilt, depression, or self-disgust. People with bulimia nervosa also show recurrent compensatory behaviors—such as purging (self-induced vomiting, repeated laxative or diuretic use), fasting, or excessive exercise—to prevent weight gain. Unlike patients with anorexia nervosa, those with bulimia nervosa may maintain a normal body weight. According to the diagnostic criteria for bulimia nervosa in DSM-IV, the binge eating and compensatory behaviors must both occur an average of at least twice a week for 3 months. In addition, people with bulimia nervosa evaluate themselves predominantly on the basis of body shape and weight. DSM-IV adds that bulimia nervosa may not be diagnosed if it occurs exclusively during episodes of anorexia nervosa. DSM-IV also lists several types of bulimia nervosa. People with the purging type of disorder regularly engage in self-induced vomiting or the misuse of laxatives or diuretics. People with the nonpurging type use other inappropriate compensatory behaviors to prevent weight gain, such as fasting and exercise, but do not purge.

Epidemiology

Bulimia nervosa is more prevalent than is anorexia nervosa. Estimates of bulimia nervosa range from 1 to 3 percent of young women. Like anorexia nervosa, bulimia nervosa is significantly more common in women than in men, but its onset is often later in adolescence than is the onset of anorexia nervosa. The onset may even occur in early adulthood. Occasional symptoms of bulimia nervosa, such as isolated episodes of binge eating and purging, have been reported in up to 40 percent of college women. Although bulimia nervosa is often present in normal-weight young women, they sometimes have a history of obesity.

Etiology

Biological Factors. Some investigators have attempted to associate cycles of binging and purging with various neurotransmitters. Because antidepressants often benefit patients with bulimia nervosa, serotonin and norepinephrine have been implicated. Because plasma endorphin levels are raised in some bulimia nervosa patients who vomit, the feelings of well-being after vomiting that some of these patients experience may be mediated by raised endorphin levels.

Social Factors. Patients with bulimia nervosa, like those with anorexia nervosa, tend to be high achievers and to respond to societal pressures to be slender. As with anorexia nervosa patients, many patients with bulimia nervosa are depressed and have increased familial depression, but the families of patients with bulimia nervosa are generally less close and more conflictual than are the families of anorexia nervosa patients. Patients with bulimia nervosa describe their parents as neglectful and rejecting.

Psychological Factors. Patients with bulimia nervosa, like those with anorexia nervosa, have difficulties with adolescent demands, but bulimia nervosa patients are more outgoing, angry, and impulsive than are anorexia nervosa patients. Alcohol dependence, shoplifting, and emotional lability (including suicide attempts) are associated with bulimia nervosa. These patients generally experience their uncontrolled eating as more ego-dystonic than do anorexia nervosa patients and so more readily seek help.

Patients with bulimia nervosa lack superego control and the ego strength of their counterparts with anorexia nervosa. Their difficulties in controlling their impulses are often manifested by substance dependence and self-destructive sexual relationships, in addition to the binge eating and purging that are the hallmarks of the disorder. Many bulimia nervosa patients have histories of difficulties in separating from caretakers, as manifested by the absence of transitional objects during their early childhood years. Some clinicians have observed that patients with bulimia nervosa use their own bodies as transitional objects. The struggle for separation from a maternal figure is played out in the ambivalence toward food; eating may represent a wish to fuse with the caretaker, and regurgitating may unconsciously express a wish for separation.

Diagnosis and Clinical Features

According to DSM-IV, the essential features of bulimia nervosa are recurrent episodes of binge eating; a sense of lack of control over eating during the eating binges; self-induced vomiting, the misuse of laxatives or diuretics, fasting, or ex-

Table 23.2–1
DSM-IV Diagnostic Criteria for Bulimia Nervosa

A. Recurrent episodes of binge eating. An episode of binge eating is characterized by both of the following:
   (1) eating, in a discrete period of time (eg, within any 2 hour period), an amount of food that is definitely larger than most people would eat during a similar period of time and under similar circumstances
   (2) a sense of lack of control over eating during the episode (eg, a feeling that one cannot stop eating or control what or how much one is eating)

B. Recurrent inappropriate compensatory behavior in order to prevent weight gain, such as self-induced vomiting; misuse of laxatives, diuretics, enemas, or other medications; fasting; or excessive exercise.

C. The binge eating and inappropriate compensatory behaviors both occur, on average, at least twice a week for 3 months.

D. Self-evaluation is unduly influenced by body shape and weight.

E. The disturbance does not occur exclusively during episodes of anorexia nervosa.

Specify type:

Purging type: during the current episode of bulimia nervosa, the person has regularly engaged in self-induced vomiting or the misuse of laxatives, diuretics, or enemas

Nonpurging type: during the current episodes of bulimia nervosa, the person has used other inappropriate compensatory behaviors, such as fasting or excessive exercise, but has not regularly engaged in self-induced vomiting or the misuse of laxatives, diuretics, or enemas

cessive exercise to prevent weight gain; and persistent self-evaluation unduly influenced by body shape and weight (Table 23.2–1). Binging usually precedes vomiting by about 1 year.

Vomiting is common and is usually induced by sticking a finger down the throat, although some patients are able to vomit at will. Vomiting decreases the abdominal pain and the feeling of being bloated and allows patients to continue eating without fear of gaining weight. Depression, sometimes called postbinge anguish, often follows the episode. During binges, patients eat food that is sweet, high in calories, and generally soft or of smooth texture, such as cakes and pastry. Some patients prefer bulky foods without regard to taste. The food is eaten secretly and rapidly and is sometimes not even chewed.

Most patients with bulimia nervosa are within their normal weight range, but some may be underweight or overweight. These patients are concerned about their body image and their appearance, worry about how others see them, and are concerned about their sexual attractiveness. Most are sexually active, compared with anorexia nervosa patients, who are not interested in sex. Pica and struggles during meals are sometimes revealed in the histories of patients with bulimia nervosa.

Patients with the purging type of bulimia nervosa may be at risk for certain medical complications, such as hypokalemia from vomiting or laxative abuse and hypochloremic alkalosis. Those who vomit repeatedly are at risk for gastric and esophageal tears, although these complications are rare. Patients who purge may have a different course from that of patients who binge and then diet or exercise.

Bulimia nervosa occurs in people with high rates of mood disorders and impulse control disorders. Bulimia nervosa is also reported to occur in those at risk for substance-related disorders and a variety of personality disorders. Patients with bulimia nervosa also have increased rates of anxiety disorders, bipolar I disorder, and dissociative disorders and histories of sexual abuse.

Abby Thurmond, age 42, had not had a food binge for over 2 years when she flew from Miami to Chicago to attend the wedding of her friend's daughter. Single, independent, and devoted to her work, Abby had just sold her first screenplay. She was pleased but she was also experiencing the "postpartum" letdown that always occurred when she finished a major project.

Despite knowing, from 2 years in Overeaters Anonymous (OA), that she needed to keep a safe distance from food, especially in emotionally hard times, Abby spent the entire day of the wedding rehearsal party in the company of food. She stood in her friend's kitchen for hours—cutting, chopping, sorting, arranging, and, eventually, picking at the food.

When night and the guests came, the flurry of activity made it easy for Abby to disappear—physically and emotionally—into a binge. She started with a plate of what would have been an "abstinent" meal (an OA concept for whatever is included on one's meal plan): pasta salad, green salad, cold cuts, and a roll. Although the portions were generous, Abby wanted more. She spent the next 5 hours eating, at first trying to graze among the guests, but then, when shame set in, retreating to dark corners of the room to take frantic, stolen bites.

Abby stuffed herself with crackers, cheeses, breads, chicken, turkey, pasta, and salads, but all that was a prelude to what she really wanted—sugar. She'd been waiting for the guests to leave the dining room, where the desserts were. When they finally did, she cut herself two pieces of cake, then two more, then ate directly from the serving tray, shoveling the food into her mouth. She reached for cookies, more cake, and cookies again. Heart racing, terrified of being discovered, Abby finally tore herself away and slipped out onto the terrace.

By now, in what she thought of as a "food trance," Abby piled her plate with bread, onto which she smeared some unidentifiable spread. Though the food tasted like mud, Abby kept eating. Soon, other guests came out to the terrace, leaving Abby feeling she had to move again, which she did, stepping into the kitchen—and the light. When Abby glanced down at her plate, she was horrified: ants were crawling all over it. Instead of reflexively spitting out the food, Abby, overcome by shame, could only swallow. Then her eyes began to search the debris on her plate for uncontaminated morsels. Witnessing her own madness, Abby began to cry. She flung the plate into the trash and ran to her room.

That event marked the beginning of a 6-month relapse

into binge eating—Abby's worst experience with binging since the problem began 15 years earlier. During the relapse, she binged on sugar foods and refined carbohydrates, returned to cigarette smoking to control the binging, and once again was driven to "get rid" of the calories by incessant exercise after each binge, walking 4 or 5 hours at a time, dragging her bicycle up and down six flights of stairs, and biking miles after dark in a dangerous city park.

DISCUSSION

The term *eating binge* is often used by people to describe occasions on which they eat more food than they should. However, Abby's description of her eating episode at the wedding rehearsal leaves little doubt that her episodes of binge eating, during which she has no control over how much she eats, represent a serious symptom. In diagnosing a person with recurrent eating binges, the first question is whether or not that person regularly compensates for the overeating by some drastic inappropriate behavior. If the answer is no, the diagnosis is probably binge eating disorder, a nonofficial diagnosis that is included in a DSM-IV appendix of diagnoses requiring further study. If the answer is yes and, as is usually the case, self-evaluation is unduly influenced by body shape and weight, the diagnosis is bulimia nervosa. Most patients with bulimia nervosa compensate for the binge eating by some method of purging—either self-induced vomiting (most common) or the use of diuretics of laxatives. Abby's disorder is an example of the relatively unusual diagnosis of bulimia nervosa, nonpurging type, in which the patient uses methods such as excessive exercise (Abby's method) or fasting.

FOLLOW-UP

Throughout the relapse, Abby went to therapy and to OA. But the bingeing worsened, as did the accompanying isolation and depression, which kept her awake, often crying uncontrollably, until the early morning hours. Finally, her therapist, a social worker, referred her to a psychiatrist, who put her on an antidepressant that has been used to control binge eating and on a structured food plan that excluded refined sugars, breads, crackers, and similar carbohydrates. Within a few weeks, Abby was able to stop bingeing, come out of the depression, and resume her life. After 2 years on the medication, no binges, and the gradual reintroduction of breads and related carbohydrates into her diet, Abby was able to stop taking the antidepressant, without depression or a return to binge eating. She continues to be active in OA. (From *DSM-IV Casebook.*)

ICD-10. In the 10th revision of *International Statistical Classification of Diseases and Related Health Problems* (ICD-10), bulimia nervosa is described as repeated bouts of overeating and a preoccupation about controlling weight that lead to self-induced vomiting; in turn, vomiting produces physical complications, electrolyte disturbances, and severe weight loss (see Table 23.1–3).

Pathology and Laboratory Examinations. Bulimia nervosa can result in electrolyte abnormalities and various degrees of starvation, although it may not be as obvious as in low-weight patients with anorexia nervosa. Thus, even normal-weight patients with bulimia nervosa should have laboratory studies of electrolytes and metabolism. In general, thyroid function remains intact in bulimia nervosa, but patients may show nonsuppression on the dexamethasone-suppression test. Dehydration and electrolyte disturbances are likely to occur in bulimia nervosa patients who regularly purge. These patients commonly exhibit hypomagnesemia and hyperamylasemia. Although not a core diagnostic feature, many patients with bulimia nervosa have menstrual disturbances. Hypotension and bradycardia occur in some patients.

Differential Diagnosis

The diagnosis of bulimia nervosa cannot be made if the binge eating and purging behaviors occur exclusively during episodes of anorexia nervosa. In such cases the diagnosis is anorexia nervosa, binge eating–purging type.

Clinicians must ascertain that patients have no neurological disease, such as epileptic-equivalent seizures, central nervous system tumors, Klüver-Bucy syndrome, or Kleine-Levin syndrome. The pathological features manifested by Klüver-Bucy syndrome are visual agnosia, compulsive licking and biting, examination of objects by the mouth, inability to ignore any stimulus, placidity, altered sexual behavior (hypersexuality), and altered dietary habits, especially hyperphagia. The syndrome is exceedingly rare and is unlikely to cause a problem in differential diagnosis. Kleine-Levin syndrome consists of periodic hypersomnia lasting for 2 to 3 weeks and hyperphagia. As in bulimia nervosa, the onset is usually during adolescence, but the syndrome is more common in men than in women. Patients with borderline personality disorder sometimes binge eat, but the eating is associated with the other signs of the disorder.

Course and Prognosis

Little is known about the long-range course of bulimia nervosa, and the short-term outcome is variable. Overall, bulimia nervosa seems to have a better prognosis than does anorexia nervosa. In the short run, patients with bulimia nervosa who are able to engage in treatment have reported more than 50 percent improvement in binge eating and purging; among outpatients, improvement seems to last more than 5 years. The patients are not symptom free during periods of improvement, however; bulimia nervosa is a chronic disorder with a waxing and waning course. Some patients with mild courses have long-term remissions. Other patients are disabled by the disorder and have been hospitalized; less than one third of them are doing well at 3-year follow-up, more than one third have some improvement in their symptoms, and about one third have a poor outcome, with chronic symptoms, within 3 years. In a recent study, at 5 to 10 years, about half of patients recovered fully from the disorder, while 20 percent continued to meet full diagnostic criteria for bulimia nervosa.

The prognosis depends on the severity of the purging sequelae—that is, whether a patient has electrolyte imbalances and to what degree the frequent vomiting results in esophagitis, amylasemia, salivary gland enlargement, and dental caries. In some cases of untreated bulimia nervosa, spontaneous remission occurs in 1 to 2 years.

Treatment

Treatment of bulimia nervosa consists of various interventions, including individual psychotherapy with a cognitive-behavioral approach, group therapy, family therapy, and pharmacotherapy. Because of the comorbidity of mood disorders, anxiety disorders, and personality disorders with bulimia nervosa, clinicians must factor these additional disorders into the treatment plan.

Most patients with uncomplicated bulimia nervosa do not require hospitalization. In general, patients with bulimia nervosa are not as secretive about their symptoms as are patients with anorexia nervosa. Therefore, outpatient treatment is usually not difficult, but psychotherapy is frequently stormy and may be prolonged. Some obese patients with bulimia nervosa who have had prolonged psychotherapy do surprisingly well. In some cases—when eating binges are out of control, outpatient treatment does not work, or a patient exhibits such additional psychiatric symptoms as suicidality and substance abuse—hospitalization may become necessary. In addition, in cases of severe purging, resulting electrolyte and metabolic disturbances may necessitate hospitalization.

Psychotherapy. Some reports encourage the use of cognitive-behavioral psychotherapy to address the specific behaviors surrounding and leading up to eating binges. Some helpful programs include a behavioral contract and desensitization to the thoughts and feelings that patients with bulimia nervosa have just before binge eating. Many patients with bulimia nervosa, however, have psychopathology that exceeds the binging behaviors; therefore, additional psychotherapeutic approaches—such as psychodynamic, interpersonal, and family therapies—can be useful.

Psychodynamic treatment of patients with bulimia nervosa has revealed a tendency to concretize introjective and projective defense mechanisms. In a manner analogous to splitting, patients divide food into two categories: items that are nutritious and those that are unhealthy. Food that is designated nutritious may be ingested and retained because it unconsciously symbolizes good introjects. But junk food is unconsciously associated with bad introjects and is, therefore, expelled by vomiting, with the unconscious fantasy that all destructiveness, hate, and badness are being evacuated. Patients may temporarily feel good after vomiting because of the fantasized evacuation, but the associated feeling of "being all good" is short-lived because it is based on an unstable combination of splitting and projection.

Pharmacotherapy. Antidepressant medications have been shown to be helpful in bulimia. This includes the serotonin reuptake inhibitors such as fluoxetine. This may be based on elevating central 5-hydroxytryptamine levels. Antidepressant medications can reduce binge eating and purging independent of the presence of a mood disorder. Thus, for particularly difficult binge–purge cycles that are not responsive to psychotherapy alone, antidepressants have been successfully used. Imipramine (Tofranil), desipramine (Norpramin), trazodone (Desyrel), and monoamine oxidase (MAO) inhibitors have been helpful. In general, most of the antidepressants have been effective at dosages usually given in the treatment of depressive disorders. However, dosages of fluoxetine that are effective in decreasing binge eating may be higher (60 to 80 mg a day) than those used for depressive disorders. In cases of comorbid depressive disorders and bulimia nervosa, medication is helpful. Carbamazepine (Tegretol) and lithium (Eskalith) have not shown impressive results as treatments for binge eating, but they have been used in the treatment of bulimia nervosa patients with comorbid mood disorders, such as bipolar I disorder.

EATING DISORDER NOT OTHERWISE SPECIFIED

The DSM-IV diagnostic classification of eating disorder not otherwise specified is a residual category used for eating disorders that do not meet the criteria for a specific eating disorder (Table 23.2–2). Binge-eating disorder—that is, recurrent episodes of binge eating in the absence of the inappropriate compensatory behaviors characteristic of bulimia nervosa (Table 23.2–3)—falls into this category. Such patients are not fixated on body shape and weight.

ICD-10

In the category of eating disorders, ICD-10 also includes atypical anorexia, atypical bulimia nervosa, overeating associated with other psychological disturbances, vomiting associated with other psychological disturbances, other eating disorders, and eating disorders, unspecified (see Table 23.1–3).

Table 23.2–2
DSM-IV Diagnostic Criteria for Eating Disorder Not Otherwise Specified

The eating disorder not otherwise specified category is for disorders of eating that do not meet the criteria for any specific eating disorder. Examples include:

1. for females, all of the criteria for anorexia nervosa are met except the individual has regular menses.
2. all of the criteria for anorexia nervosa are met except that, despite significant weight loss, the individual's current weight is in the normal range.
3. all of the criteria for bulimia nervosa are met except that the binge eating and inappropriate compensatory mechanisms occur at a frequency of less than twice a week or for a duration of less than three months.
4. the regular use of inappropriate compensatory behavior by an individual of normal body weight after eating small amounts of food (eg, self-induced vomiting after the consumption of two cookies).
5. repeatedly chewing and spitting out, but not swallowing, large amounts of food.
6. binge-eating disorder: recurrent episodes of binge eating in the absence of the regular use of inappropriate compensatory behaviors characteristic of bulimia nervosa.

Table 23.2–3
DSM-IV Research Criteria for Binge-Eating Disorder

A. Recurrent episodes of binge eating. An episode of binge eating is characterized by both of the following:
   (1) eating, in a discrete period of time (eg, within any 2-hour period), an amount of food that is definitely larger than most people would eat in a similar period of time under similar circumstances
   (2) a sense of lack of control over eating during the episode (eg, a feeling that one cannot stop eating or control what or how much one is eating)

B. The binge eating episodes are associated with three (or more) of the following:
   (1) eating much more rapidly than normal
   (2) eating until feeling uncomfortably full
   (3) eating large amounts of food when not feeling physically hungry
   (4) eating alone because of being embarrassed by how much one is eating
   (5) feeling disgusted with oneself, depressed, or very guilty after overeating

C. Marked distress regarding binge eating is present.

D. The binge eating occurs, on average, at least 2 days a week for 6 months.
   Note: The method of determining frequency differs from that used for bulimia nervosa; future research should address whether the preferred method of setting a frequency threshold is counting the number of days on which binges occur or counting the number of episodes of binge eating.

E. The binge eating is not associated with the regular use of inappropriate compensatory behaviors (eg, purging, fasting, excessive exercise) and does not occur exclusively during the course of anorexia nervosa or bulimia nervosa.

References

Childress AC, Brewerton TD, Hodges EL, Jarrell MP: The Kids Eating Disorders Survey (KEDS): A study of middle school students. J Am Acad Child Adolesc Psychiatry *32:* 843, 1993.

Cohen P: Seasonal patterns of bulimia nervosa. Am J Psychiatry *150:* 357, 1993.

Fahy TA, Eisler I, Russell GFM: Personality disorder and treatment response in bulimia nervosa. Br J Psychiatry *162:* 765, 1993.

Fairburn CG, Welch SL, Hay PJ: The classification of recurrent overeating: The ''binge eating disorder'' proposal. Int J Eating Disord *13:* 155, 1993.

Fichter MM, Quadflieg N, Brandl B: Recurring overeating: An empirical comparison of binge eating disorder, bulimia nervosa, and obesity. Int J Eating Disord *13:* 1, 1993.

Fluoxetine Bulimia Nervosa Collaborative Group: Fluoxetine in the treatment of bulimia nervosa. Arch Gen Psychiatry *49:* 139, 1992.

Gabbard GO: *Psychodynamic Psychiatry in Clinical Practice: The DSM-IV Edition.* American Psychiatric Press, Washington, 1994.

Garfinkel PE: Eating disorders. In *Comprehensive Textbook of Psychiatry,* ed 6, HI Kaplan, BJ Sadock, editors, p 1361. Williams & Wilkins, Baltimore, 1995.

Garner DM, Rockert W, Davis R, Garner MV: Comparison of cognitive-behavioral and supportive-expressive therapy for bulimia nervosa. Am J Psychiatry *150:* 37, 1993.

Keel PK, Mitchell JE: Outcome in bulimia nervosa. Am J Psychiatry *154:* 313, 1997.

Marchi M, Cohen P: Early childhood eating behaviors and adolescent eating disorders. J Am Acad Child Adolesc Psychiatry *29:* 112, 1990.

Nemeroff CB: The clinical pharmacology and use of paroxetine, a new selective serotonin reuptake inhibitor. Pharmacotherapy *14:* 127, 1994.

Striegel-Moore RH, Silberstein LR, Rodin J: The social self in bulimia nervosa: Public self-consciousness, social anxiety, and perceived fraudulence. J Abnorm Psychol *102:* 297, 1993.

Telch CF, Agras WS: Obesity, binge eating and psychopathology: Are they related? Int J Eating Disord *15:* 53, 1994.

Waller D, Fairburn CG, McPherson A, Kay R, et al: Treating bulimia nervosa in primary care: A pilot study. Int J Eat Disord *19:* 99, 1996.

Walters EE, Neale MC, Eaves LJ, Health AC, Kessler RC, Kendler KS: Bulimia nervosa: A population-based study of purgers versus non-purgers. Int J Eating Disord *13:* 265, 1993.

Wilson G: Treatment of bulimia nervosa: When CUT fails. Behav Res Ther *34:* 197, 1996.

Woodbine DB: A review of anorexia nervosa and bulimia nervosa. Curr Probl Pediatr *25:* 67, 1995.

▲ 23.3 Obesity

DEFINITION

Obesity is a condition characterized by excessive accumulation of fat in the body. By convention, obesity is said to be present when body weight exceeds by 20 percent the standard weight listed in the usual height–weight tables (Table 23.3–1).

Another and more precise measurement of obesity is the amount of fat in the body or the body mass index (BMI), which is calculated by the following formula: BMI equals [body weight in kg] divided by [height in m]^2. The BMI correlates with morbidity and mortality. In general, a normal BMI is in the range of 20 to 25 (Fig. 23.3–1 and Table 23.3–2).

EPIDEMIOLOGY

More than one half of people in the United States are obese. Obesity is 6 times more common among women of lower socioeconomic status than among women of higher socioeconomic status. A similar, although weaker, relationship is found among men. The prevalence of obesity increases threefold between ages 20 and 50. The weights of men stabilize after age 50 and begin to decline around the age of 60. Women continue to gain weight until age 60, at which time their weight begins to decline. Black men and women have a higher prevalence of obesity than do white people. Studies also show that one third or more of children and adolescents in the United States are too heavy. Girls are more likely to be affected than are boys, and an obese child has a greater risk of becoming an obese adult than does a child of normal weight.

ETIOLOGY

People accumulate fat by eating more calories than are expended as energy; thus intake of energy exceeds its dissipation. If fat is to be removed from the body, fewer calories must be put in or more calories must be taken out than are put in. An error of no more than 10 percent in either intake or output would lead to a 30-pound change in body weight in 1 year.

Satiety

Satiety is the feeling that results when hunger is satisfied. People stop eating at the end of a meal because they have replenished nutrients that had been depleted. People become hungry again when nutrients restored by earlier meals are once again depleted. It seems reasonable that a metabolic signal,

Table 23.3–1
Height and Weight Tables (Weights at Ages 25–59)

Men

Height	Small	Medium	Large
5′2″	128–134	131–141	138–150
5′3″	130–136	133–143	140–153
5′4″	132–138	135–145	142–156
5′5″	134–140	137–148	144–160
5′6″	136–142	139–151	146–164
5′7″	138–145	142–154	149–168
5′8″	140–148	145–157	152–172
5′9″	142–151	148–160	155–176
5′10″	144–154	151–163	158–180
5′11″	146–157	154–168	161–184
6′0″	149–160	157–170	164–188
6′1″	152–164	160–174	168–192
6′2″	155–168	164–178	172–197
6′3″	158–172	167–182	176–202
6′4″	162–176	171–187	181–207

Weight in pounds according to frame, wearing 5 pounds indoor clothing and shoes with 1-inch heels.

Women

Height	Small	Medium	Large
4′10″	102–111	109–121	118–131
4′11″	103–113	111–123	120–134
5′0″	104–115	113–126	122–137
5′1″	106–118	115–129	125–140
5′2″	108–121	118–132	128–143
5′3″	111–124	121–135	131–147
5′4″	114–127	124–138	134–151
5′5″	117–130	127–141	137–155
5′6″	120–133	130–144	140–159
5′7″	123–136	133–147	143–163
5′8″	126–139	136–150	146–167
5′9″	129–142	139–153	149–170
5′10″	132–145	142–156	152–173
5′11″	135–148	145–159	155–176
6′0″	138–151	148–162	158–179

Weight in pounds according to frame, wearing 3 pounds indoor clothing and shoes with 1-inch heels.

Reprinted with permission from 1979 Build Study, Society of Actuaries and Association of Life Insurance Medical Directors of America, 1980.

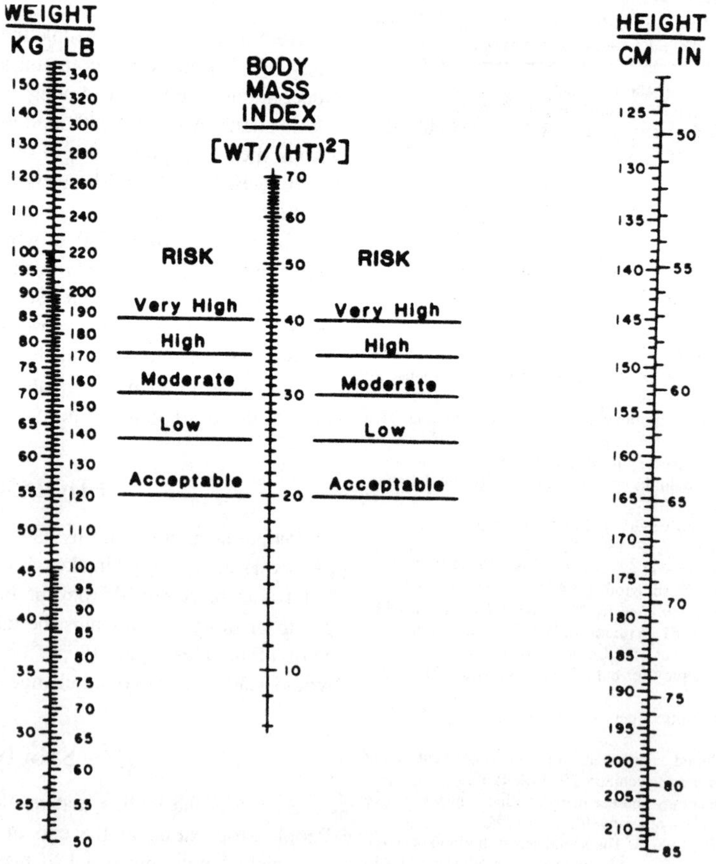
WEIGHT
KG LB
BODY MASS INDEX
[WT/(HT)²]
RISK
Very High
High
Moderate
Low
Acceptable
RISK
Very High
High
Moderate
Low
Acceptable
HEIGHT
CM IN

FIGURE 23.3–1
Nomogram for body mass index (BMI). To determine BMI, place a ruler or other straight edge between the body-weight column on the *left* and the height column on the *right* and read the BMI from the point where it crosses the center. (Reproduced with permission from Bray GA: Definitions, measurements and classification of the syndromes of obesity. Int J Obes *2:* 99, 1978.)

Table 23.3–2
Desirable Body Mass Index (BMI) in Relation to Age

Age (years)	BMI (kg/m^2)
19–24	19–24
25–34	20–25
35–44	21–26
45–54	22–27
55–65	23–28
65	24–29

Reprinted with permission from Committee on Diet on Health, Food and Nutrition Board, National Research Council: Diet and Health: Implications for Reducing Chronic Disease Risk, p 564. Washington, National Academy Press, 1989.

derived from food that has been absorbed, is carried by the blood to the brain, where the signal activates receptor cells, probably in the hypothalamus, to produce satiety. Hunger is the consequence of the decreasing strength of this same metabolic signal, secondary to the depletion of a critical nutrients.

Satiety occurs soon after the beginning of a meal and before the total caloric content of the meal has been absorbed; therefore satiety is only one regulatory mechanism controlling food intake. Appetite, defined as the desire for food, is also involved. A hungry person may eat to full satisfaction when food is available, but appetite can also induce a person to overeat past the point of satiety. Appetite may be increased by psychological factors such as thoughts or feelings, and an abnormal appetite may result in an abnormal increase of food intake.

The olfactory system may play a role in satiety. Experiments have shown that strong stimulation of the olfactory bulbs in the nose with food odors by using an inhaler saturated with a particular smell produces satiety for that food. This may have implications for therapy of obesity.

Genetic Factors

The existence of numerous forms of inherited obesity in animals and the ease with which adiposity can be produced by selective breeding make it clear that genetic factors can play a role in obesity. These factors must also be presumed to be important in human obesity.

About 80 percent of patients who are obese have a family history of obesity. This fact can be accounted for not only by genetic factors but also in part by identification with fat parents and by learned oral methods for coping with anxiety. Nonetheless, studies show that identical twins raised apart can both be obese, an observation that suggests a hereditary role. To date, no specific genetic marker of obesity has been identified.

Developmental Factors

Early in life, adipose tissue grows by increases in both cell number and cell size. Once the number of adipocytes has been established, it does not seem to be susceptible to change. Obesity that begins early in life is characterized by adipose tissue with an increased number and size of adipocytes. Obesity that begins in adult life, on the other hand, results solely from an increase in the size of the adipocytes. In both instances, weight reduction produces a decrease in cell size. The greater number and size of adipocytes in patients with juvenile-onset diabetes may be a factor in their widely recognized difficulties with weight reduction and the persistence of their obesity.

The distribution and amount of fat vary in individuals, and fat in different body areas has different characteristics. Fat cells around the waist, flanks, and abdomen (the so-called potbelly) are more active metabolically than are those in the thighs and buttocks. The former pattern is more common in men and has a higher correlation with cardiovascular disease than does the latter pattern. Women, whose fat distribution is in the thighs and buttocks, may become obsessed with nostrums that are advertised to reduce fat in these areas (so-called cellulite, which is not a medical term); but no externally applied preparation to reduce this fat pattern exists. Men with abdominal fat may attempt to reduce their girth with machines that exercise the abdominal muscles, but exercise has no effect on fat loss.

A hormone called *leptin*, made by fat cells, acts as a fat thermostat. When the blood level of leptin is low, more fat is consumed; when high, less fat is consumed. Further research is needed to determine whether this might lead to new ways of managing obesity.

Physical Activity Factors

The marked decrease in physical activity in affluent societies seems to be the major factor in the rise of obesity as a public health problem. Physical inactivity restricts energy expenditure and may contribute to increased food intake. Although food intake increases with increasing energy expenditure over a wide range of energy demands, intake does not decrease proportionately when physical activity falls below a certain minimum level.

Brain-Damage Factors

Destruction of the ventromedial hypothalamus can produce obesity in animals, but this is probably a very rare cause of obesity in humans. There is evidence that the central nervous system, particularly in the lateral and ventromedial hypothalamic areas, adjusts to food intake in response to changing energy requirements so as to maintain fat stores at a baseline determined by a specific set point. This set point varies from one person to another and depends on height and body build.

Other Clinical Factors

A variety of clinical disorders are associated with obesity. Cushing's disease is associated with a characteristic fat distribution (buffalo adiposity) (Fig. 23.3–2). Myxedema is associated with weight gain, although not invariably. Other neuroendocrine disorders include adiposogenital dystrophy (Fröhlich's syndrome), which is characterized by obesity and sexual and skeletal abnormalities. Some workers have reported that the prolonged use of serotonergic agonists in the treatment of depression is associated with weight gain, but more studies are needed. Depressed patients are known to have fluctuations in weight.

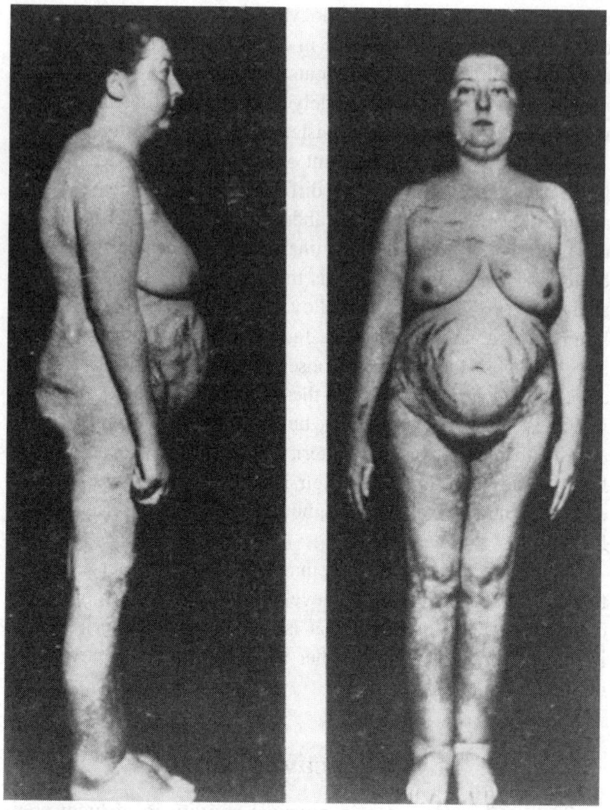

FIGURE 23.3–2
Cushing's syndrome. Obesity and round face are evident. Hirsutism and abdominal striae are noted. (Reproduced with permission from Spillane JD, Spillane JA: *An Atlas of Clinical Neurology,* ed 3, p 365. Oxford University Press, New York, 1982.)

Psychological Factors

Although psychological factors are evidently crucial to the development of obesity, how such psychological factors result in obesity has not yet been explained. The food-regulating mechanism is susceptible to environmental influence, and cultural, family, and psychodynamic factors have all been shown to contribute to the development of obesity. Although many investigators have proposed specific family histories, precipitating factors, personality structures, and unconscious conflicts as causing obesity, people who are overweight may suffer from every conceivable psychiatric disorder and come from a variety of disturbed backgrounds. Thus, obese patients may be characterized as emotionally disturbed persons, who, because of the availability of the overeating mechanism in their environments, have learned to use hyperphagia as a means of coping with psychological problems.

CLINICAL FEATURES

Many obese people report that they overeat when they are emotionally upset, often soon thereafter. But many nonobese people report similar experiences, and it is difficult to ascertain the specificity for obesity of such short-term contingencies. Reports linking emotional factors and obesity over the long range seem more specific: Some obese people lose large amounts of weight when they fall in love and gain weight when they lose a loved one.

The habitual eating patterns of many obese people often seem similar to patterns found in experimental obesity. Impaired satiety is a particularly important problem. Obese people seem inordinately susceptible to food cues in their environment, to the palatability of foods, and to the inability to stop eating if food is available. Obese people are usually susceptible to all kinds of external stimuli to eating, but they remain relatively unresponsive to the usual internal signals of hunger. Some are unable to distinguish between hunger and other kinds of dysphoria.

DIFFERENTIAL DIAGNOSIS

Other Syndromes

The night-eating syndrome, in which people eat excessively after they have had their evening meal, seems to be precipitated by stressful life circumstances and, once present, tends to recur daily until the stress is alleviated. The binge-eating syndrome (bulimia) is characterized by the sudden, compulsive ingestion of very large amounts of food in a very short time, usually with great subsequent agitation and self-condemnation. Binge eating, too, appears to represent a reaction to stress. In contrast to the night-eating syndrome, however, these bouts of overeating are not periodic, and they are far more often linked to specific precipitating circumstances. (See Chapter 23, Section 23.2 for a complete discussion of bulimia.) The *pickwickian syndrome* is said to exist when a person is 100 percent over desirable weight and has associated respiratory and cardiovascular pathology.

Body Dysmorphic Disorder (Dysmorphophobia)

Some obese people feel that their bodies are grotesque and loathsome and that others view them with hostility and contempt. This feeling is closely associated with self-consciousness and impaired social functioning. Emotionally healthy obese people have no body image disturbances, and only a minority of neurotic obese people have such disturbances. The disorder is confined mainly to persons who have been obese since childhood; even among them, less than half suffer it.

COURSE AND PROGNOSIS

Effects on Health

Obesity has adverse effects on health and is associated with a broad range of illnesses (Table 23.3–3). There is a strong correlation between obesity and cardiovascular disorders. Hypertension (blood pressure higher than 160/95) is 3 times higher for people who are overweight, and hypercholesterolemia (blood cholesterol over 250 mg/dL) is twice as common. Studies show that blood pressure and cholesterol levels can be reduced by weight reduction.

Diabetes, which has clear genetic determinations, can often be reversed with weight reduction, especially type II diabetes (mature-onset or non–insulin-dependent diabetes mellitus).

Table 23.3–3
Health Disorders Thought to Be Caused or Exacerbated by Obesity

Heart
Premature coronary heart disease
Left ventricular hypertrophy
Angina pectoris
Sudden death (ventricular arrhythmia)
Congestive heart failure
Vascular system
Hypertension
Cerebrovascular disorder (cerebral infarction or hemorrhage)
Venous stasis (with lower-extremity edema, varicose veins)
Respiratory system
Obstructive sleep apnea
Pickwickian syndrome (alveolar hypoventilation)
Secondary polycythemia
Right ventricular hypertrophy (sometimes leading to failure)
Hepatobiliary system
Cholelithiasis and cholecystitis
Hepatic steatosis
Hormonal and metabolic functions
Diabetes mellitus (insulin independent)
Gout (hyperuricemia)
Hyperlipidemias (hypertriglyceridemia and hypercholesterolemia)
Kidney
Proteinuria and, in very severe obesity, nephrosis
Renal vein thrombosis
Joints, muscles, and connective tissue
Osteoarthritis of knees
Bone spurs of the heel
Osteoarthrosis of spine (in women)
Aggravation of preexisting postural faults
Neoplasia
In woman: increased risk of cancer of endometrium, breast, cervix, ovary, gallbladder, and biliary passages
In men: increased risk of cancer of colon, rectum, and prostate

Reprinted with permission from VanItallie TB: Obesity: Adverse effects on health and longevity. Am J Clin Nutr *32:* 2723, 1979.

According to National Institutes of Health data, obese men, regardless of smoking habits, have a higher mortality from colon, rectal, and prostate cancer than do men of normal weight. Obese women have a higher mortality from cancer of the gallbladder, biliary passages, breast (postmenopause), uterus (including cervix and endometrium), and ovaries than do women of normal weight.

Longevity

Reliable studies indicate that the greater a person's degree of overweight, the higher is the person's risk for death. A person who reduces weight to acceptable levels has a decline in mortality to normal rates. Weight reduction may be lifesaving for patients with extreme obesity, defined as weight that is twice the desirable weight. Such patients may have cardiorespiratory failure, especially when asleep (sleep apnea).

The prognosis for weight reduction is poor, and the course of obesity tends toward inexorable progression. Of patients who lose significant amounts of weight, 90 percent regain it eventually. The prognosis is particularly poor for those who become obese in childhood. Juvenile-onset obesity tends to be more severe, more resistant to treatment, and more likely to be associated with emotional disturbance than is adult obesity.

TREATMENT

As many as half of patients routinely treated for obesity by family physicians may develop mild anxiety and depression. In addition, a high incidence of emotional disturbances has been reported among obese people undergoing long-term, in-hospital treatment by fasting or severe calorie restriction. Obese people with extensive psychopathology, those with a history of emotional disturbance during dieting, and those in the midst of a life crisis should attempt weight reduction, if at all, cautiously and under careful supervision.

Diet

The basis of weight reduction is simple—establish a caloric deficit by bringing intake below output. The simplest way to reduce caloric intake is by means of a low-calorie diet. The best long-term effects are achieved with a balanced diet that contains readily available foods. For most people, the most satisfactory reducing diet consists of their usual foods in amounts determined with the aid of tables of food values that are available in standard works. Such a diet gives the best chance of long-term maintenance of weight loss achieved by dieting. Total unmodified fasts are used for short-term weight loss; but they have associated morbidity including orthostatic hypotension, sodium diuresis, and impaired nitrogen balance.

Ketogenic diets are high-protein, high-fat diets used to promote weight loss. They have a high cholesterol content and produce ketosis, which is associated with nausea, hypotension, and lethargy. Many obese people find it tempting to use a novel or even bizarre diet. Whatever effectiveness these diets may have, in large part results from their monotony. When a dieter stops the diet and returns to the usual fare, the incentives to overeat are multiplied.

In general, the best method of weight loss is a balanced diet of 1100 to 1200 calories. Such a diet can be followed for long periods but should be supplemented with vitamins, particularly iron, folic acid, zinc, and vitamin B_6.

Exercise

Increased physical activity is frequently recommended as part of a weight-reduction regimen. Because caloric expenditure in most forms of physical activity is directly proportional to body weight, obese people expend more calories with the same amount of activity than do people of normal weight. Furthermore, increased physical activity may actually cause a decrease in food intake for formerly sedentary people. This combination of increased caloric expenditure and decreased food intake makes an increase in physical activity a highly desirable feature of any weight-reduction program. Exercise also helps maintain weight loss.

Pharmacotherapy

Various drugs, some more effective than others, are used to treat obesity. Table 23.3–4 lists the drugs currently availa-

Table 23.3–4
Drugs for the Treatment of Obesity

Generic Name	Trade Name(s)	Usual Dosage Range (mg/day)
Amphetamine and dextroamphetamine	Biphetamine	12.5–20
Methamphetamine	Desoxyn	10–15
Benzphetamine	Didrex	75–150
Phendimetrazine	Bontril, Plegine, Prelu-2, X-Trozine	105
Phentermine		
Hydrochloride	Adipex-P, Fastin, Oby-trim	18.75–37.5
Resin	Ionamin	15–30
Diethylpropion hydrochloride	Tenuate	75
Mazindol	Sanorex, Mazanor	3–9
Dexfenfluramine[a]	Redux	30
Fenfluramine[a]	Pondimin	60–120
Phenylpropanolamine	Dexatrim, Acutrim	75

[a] On September 15, 1997, Pondimin and Redux were withdrawn by Wyeth-Ayerst because of heart valve abnormalities in patients using these medications.

ble. Drug treatment is effective because it suppresses appetite; but tolerance to this effect may develop after several weeks of use. An initial trial period of 4 weeks with a specific drug can be used; then, if the patient responds with weight loss the drug can be continued to see whether tolerance develops. If a drug remains effective, it can be dispensed for a longer time until the desired weight is achieved.

The biogenic amines and serotonin are involved in regulating eating behavior. Recent appetite suppressants include dexfenfluramine (Redux) and fenfluramine (Pondimin), but these drugs were withdrawn in 1997 because of reports of aortic and mitral valve regurgitation in patients who used these drugs. Amphetamine (Dexedrine) and its congeners, such as methamphetamine (Desoxyn) and phentermine (Adipex-P, Fastin), work mainly by increasing norepinephrine levels.

Impaired Eating Behavior. Drugs exist that prevent the absorption of certain macronutrients (such as fat or carbohydrate). Perfluoroctyl bromide coats the gastrointestinal tract, inhibiting fat absorption. Other drugs inhibit the hydrolysis of carbohydrates or fats so they cannot be absorbed. A new drug is orlistat (Xenical), a nonsystemic pancreatic lipase inhibitor that has been shown to decrease the amount of fat absorbed by 30 percent. To be effective, drugs in this category must be used in conjunction with a mildly hypocaloric, low-fat diet to avoid uncomfortable adverse gastrointestinal effects such as oily spotting. As such, drugs with this mechanism of action are ideally coadministered with a behavioral modification program.

Surgery

Surgical methods that cause malabsorption of food or reduce gastric volume have been used in people who are markedly obese. *Gastric bypass* is a procedure in which the stomach is made smaller by transecting or stapling one of the stomach curvatures. In *gastroplasty* the size of the stomach stoma is reduced so that the passage of food slows. Results are successful, although vomiting, electrolyte imbalance, and obstruction may occur. The surgical removal of fat (lipectomy) is used for cosmetic reasons and has no effect on weight loss in the long run.

Psychotherapy

The psychological problems of obese people are varied, and there is no particular personality type that is obese. Some patients may respond with weight loss to insight-oriented psychodynamic therapy, but this treatment has not achieved much success. There is little evidence that uncovering the unconscious causes of overeating can alter the symptom choice of people who overeat in response to stress. Years after successful psychotherapy and successful weight reduction, most people who overeat under stress continue to do so. Furthermore, many obese people seem particularly vulnerable to overdependency on a therapist and the inordinate regression that may occur during the uncovering psychotherapies.

Behavior modification has been the most successful of the psychotherapies and is considered the method of choice. Patients are taught to recognize external cues that are associated with eating and to keep diaries of foods consumed in particular circumstances, such as at the movies or while watching television, or during certain emotional states, such as anxiety or depression. Patients are also taught to develop new eating patterns, such as eating slowly, chewing food well, not reading while eating, and not eating between meals or when not seated. Operant conditioning therapies that use rewards such as praise or new clothes to reinforce weight loss have also been successful.

Group therapy helps to maintain motivation, to promote identification among members who have lost weight, and to provide education about nutrition.

References

Bruch H: *Eating Disorders: Obesity and Anorexia Nervosa and the Person Within.* Basic Books, New York, 1973.

Health Implication of Obesity. NIH Consensus Statement Online 1985, Feb 11–13 [cited 1997, Jan 7] *5:* 1, 1997.

Kaplan HI, Kaplan HS: The psychosomatic concept of obesity. J Nerv Ment Dis *125:* 181, 1957.

LeMagnen J: Advances in studies on the psychological control and regulation of food intake. Prog Physiol Psychol *4:* 203, 1971.

Mayer J: *Overweight: Causes, Cost, and Control.* Prentice-Hall, Englewood Cliffs, NJ, 1968.

Pi-Sunyen FX: *Obesity in Modern Nutrition,* ME Shils, JA Olson, M Shike, editors. Lea & Febiger, Malvern, PA, 1994.

Stuart RB, Davis B: *Slim Chance in a Fat World: Behavioral Control of Obesity.* Research Press, Champaign, IL, 1971.

Stunkard AJ: New therapies for the eating disorders: Behavior modification of obesity and anorexia nervosa. Arch Gen Psychiatry *26:* 391, 1972.

Yanovski SZ: Long-term pharmacotherapy in the management of obesity: National Task Force on Obesity. JAMA *276:* 1907, 1996.

24 Normal Sleep and Sleep Disorders

▲ 24.1 Normal Sleep

The ancient Greeks ascribed the need for sleep to the god *Hypnos* (''Sleep''), the child of Darkness and Night and the brother of Death, whose power, as he swept across humanity, was so great that even the gods succumbed to him. Today, although researchers have come to understand the nature of sleep in great detail during the past several decades, they still have not completely clarified the function of sleep. Some workers find evidence that the varieties of sleep have functions that are associated with restoring the brain and the body, perhaps through expediting protein and ribonucleic acid synthesis.

With sleep, many physiological changes occur: in respiration, cardiac function, muscle tone, temperature, hormone secretion, and blood pressure. Currently, research on sleep focuses on two main areas: (1) basic sleep mechanisms and sleep physiology and (2) sleep problems in clinical medicine. Study of sleep functions in mental disorders is directed at describing the underlying biochemical disturbances in these disorders.

SLEEP PATTERNS

Sleep is a regular, recurrent, easily reversible state that is characterized by relative quiescence and by a great increase in the threshold of response to external stimuli relative to the waking state. Close monitoring of sleep is an important part of clinical practice; sleep disturbance is often an early symptom of impending mental illness. Some mental disorders are associated with characteristic changes in sleep physiology.

The waking electroencephalogram (EEG) is characterized by alpha waves of 8 to 12 cycles a second and low-voltage activity of mixed frequency. As people fall asleep, their brain waves go through certain characteristic changes (Fig. 24.1–1), and alpha activity begins to disappear. Stage 1, considered the lightest stage of sleep, is characterized by low-voltage, regular activity at 3 to 7 cycles a second. After a few seconds or minutes, this stage gives way to stage 2, a pattern showing frequent spindle-shaped tracings at 12 to 14 cycles a second (sleep spindles) and slow, triphasic waves known as K complexes. Soon thereafter, delta waves—high-voltage activity at 0.5 to 2.5 cycles a second—make their appearance and occupy less than 50 percent of the tracing (stage 3). Eventually, in stage 4, delta waves occupy more than 50 percent of the record. It is common practice to describe stages 3 and 4 as delta sleep or slow-wave sleep (SWS) because of the characteristic appearance of the EEG record.

POLYSOMNOGRAM REM FINDINGS

Sleep is made up of two physiological states: non–rapid eye movement (NREM) sleep and rapid eye movement (REM) sleep. In NREM sleep, which is composed of stages 1 through 4, most physiological functions are markedly reduced compared with wakefulness. REM sleep is a qualitatively different kind of sleep characterized by a high level of brain activity and physiological activity levels similar to those in wakefulness. About 90 minutes after sleep onset, NREM yields to the first REM episode of the night. This REM latency of 90 minutes is a consistent finding in normal adults: A shortening of REM latency frequently occurs with such disorders as depressive disorders and narcolepsy. The EEG records the rapid conjugate eye movements that are the identifying feature of the sleep state (there are no or few rapid eye movements in NREM sleep); the EEG pattern consists of low-voltage, random fast activity with sawtooth waves; the electromyograph (EMG) shows a marked reduction in muscle tone.

In normal people, NREM sleep is a peaceful state relative to waking. The pulse rate is typically slowed 5 to 10 beats a minute below the level of restful waking and is very regular. Respiration is similarly affected, and blood pressure also tends to be low, with few minute-to-minute variations. The resting muscle potential of the body musculature is lower in REM sleep than in a waking state. Episodic, involuntary body movements are present in NREM sleep. There are few rapid eye movements, if any, and seldom any penile erections in men. Blood flow through most tissues, including cerebral blood flow, is slightly reduced.

The deepest portions of NREM sleep—stages 3 and 4—are sometimes associated with unusual arousal characteristics. When people are aroused ½ to 1 hour after sleep onset—usually in slow-wave sleep—they are disoriented, and their thinking is disorganized. Brief arousals from slow-wave sleep are also associated with amnesia for events that occur during the arousal. The disorganization during arousal from stage 3 or stage 4 may result in specific problems, including enuresis, somnambulism, and stage 4 nightmares or night terrors.

Polygraphic measures during REM sleep show irregular patterns, sometimes close to aroused waking patterns. Otherwise, if researchers were unaware of the behavioral stage and happened to be recording a variety of physiological measures (aside from muscle tone) during REM periods, they would undoubtedly conclude that the person or animal they were studying was in an active waking state. Because of this observation, REM sleep has also been termed *paradoxical sleep.* Pulse, respiration, and blood pressure in humans are all high

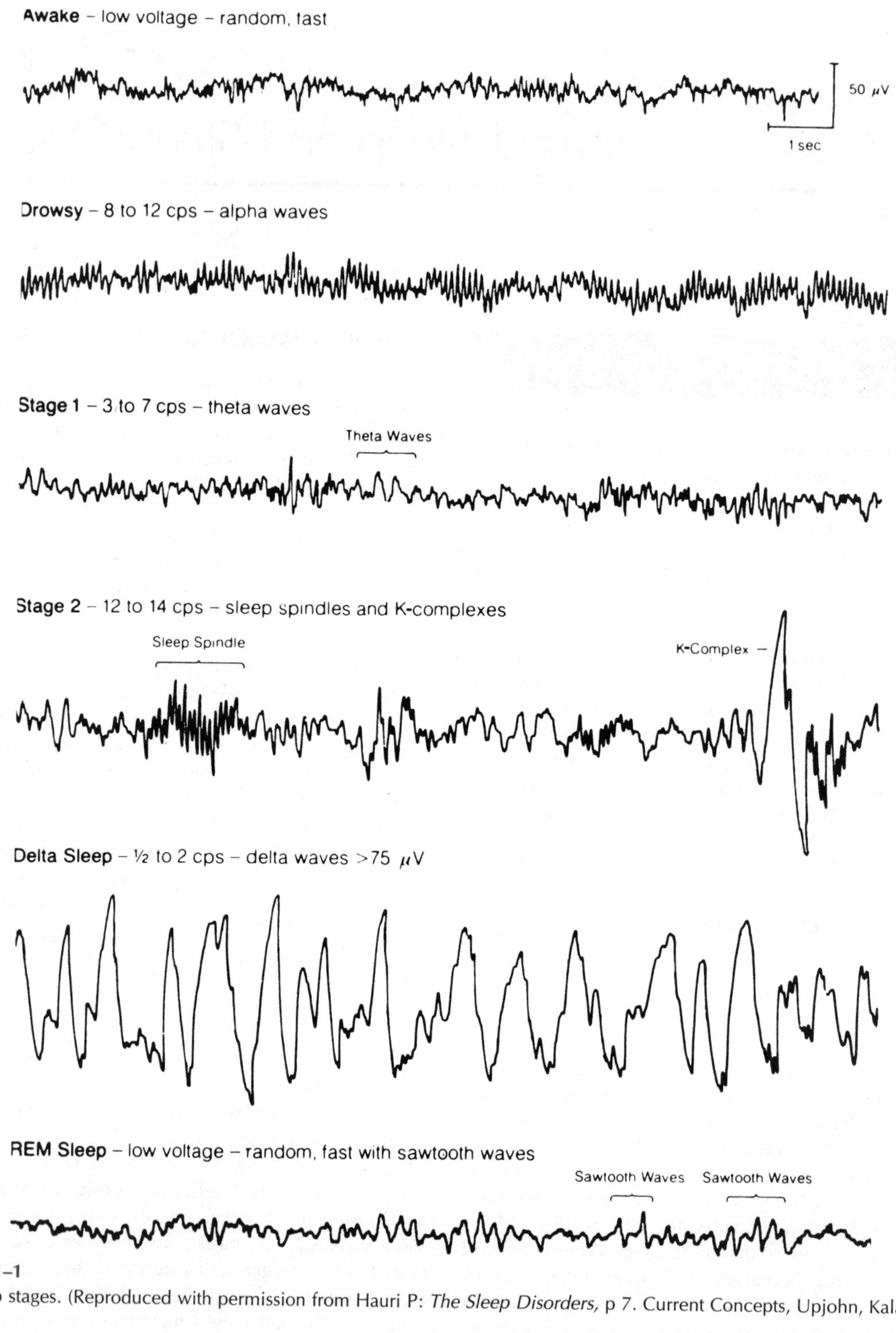
Awake – low voltage – random, fast
50 μV
1 sec
Drowsy – 8 to 12 cps – alpha waves
Stage 1 – 3 to 7 cps – theta waves
Theta Waves
Stage 2 – 12 to 14 cps – sleep spindles and K-complexes
Sleep Spindle
K-Complex
Delta Sleep – ½ to 2 cps – delta waves >75 μV
REM Sleep – low voltage – random, fast with sawtooth waves
Sawtooth Waves
Sawtooth Waves

FIGURE 24.1–1
Human sleep stages. (Reproduced with permission from Hauri P: *The Sleep Disorders,* p 7. Current Concepts, Upjohn, Kalamazoo, MI, 1982.)

during REM sleep—much higher than during NREM sleep and often higher than during waking. Even more striking than the level or rate is the variability from minute to minute. Brain oxygen use increases during REM sleep. The ventilatory response to increased levels of carbon dioxide (CO_2) is depressed during REM sleep, so that there is no increase in tidal volume as the partial pressure of carbon dioxide (pCO_2) increases. Thermoregulation is altered during REM sleep. In contrast to the homeothermic condition of temperature regulation that is present during wakefulness or NREM sleep, a poikilothermic condition (a state in which animal temperature varies with the changes in the temperature of the surrounding medium) prevails during REM sleep. Poikilothermia, which is characteristic of reptiles, results in a failure to respond to changes in ambient temperature with shivering or sweating, whichever is appropriate to maintaining body temperature. Almost every REM period in men is accompanied by a partial or full penile erection. This finding is of significant clinical value in evaluating the cause of impotence; the nocturnal penile tumescence study is one of the most commonly requested sleep laboratory tests. Another physiological change that occurs during REM sleep is the near-total paralysis of the skeletal (postural) muscles. Because of this motor inhibition, body movement is absent during REM sleep. Probably the most distinctive feature of REM sleep is dreaming. People awakened during REM sleep frequently (60 to 90 percent of the time) report that they had been dreaming. Dreams during REM sleep are typically abstract and surreal. Dreaming does occur during NREM sleep, but it is typically lucid and purposeful.

The cyclical nature of sleep is regular and reliable; a REM period occurs about every 90 to 100 minutes during the night (Fig. 24.1–2). The first REM period tends to be the shortest, usually lasting less than 10 minutes; the later REM periods may last 15 to 40 minutes each. Most REM periods occur in the last third of the night, whereas most stage 4 sleep occurs in the first third of the night.

These sleep patterns change over a person's life span. In the neonatal period, REM sleep represents more than 50 percent of total sleep time, and the EEG pattern moves from the alert state directly to the REM state without going through stages 1 through 4. Newborns sleep about 16 hours a day, with brief periods of wakefulness. By 4 months of age, the pattern shifts so that the total percentage of REM sleep drops to less than 40 percent, and entry into sleep occurs with an initial period of NREM sleep. By young adulthood, the distribution of sleep stages is as follows:

NREM (75 percent)
- **Stage 1:** 5 percent
- **Stage 2:** 45 percent
- **Stage 3:** 12 percent
- **Stage 4:** 13 percent

REM (25 percent)

This distribution remains relatively constant into old age, although a reduction occurs in both slow-wave sleep and REM sleep in older people.

SLEEP REGULATION

Most researchers think that there is not one simple sleep control center but a small number of interconnecting systems or centers that are located chiefly in the brainstem and that mutually activate and inhibit one another. Many studies also support the role of serotonin in sleep regulation. Prevention of serotonin synthesis or destruction of the dorsal raphe nucleus of the brainstem, which contains nearly all the brain's serotonergic cell bodies, reduces sleep for a considerable time. Synthesis and release of serotonin by serotonergic neurons are influenced by the availability of amino acid precursors of this neurotransmitter, such as L-tryptophan. Ingestion of large amounts of L-tryptophan (1 to 15 g) reduces sleep latency and nocturnal awakenings. Conversely, L-tryptophan deficiency is associated with less time spent in REM sleep.

Norepinephrine-containing neurons with cell bodies located in the locus ceruleus play an important role in controlling nor-

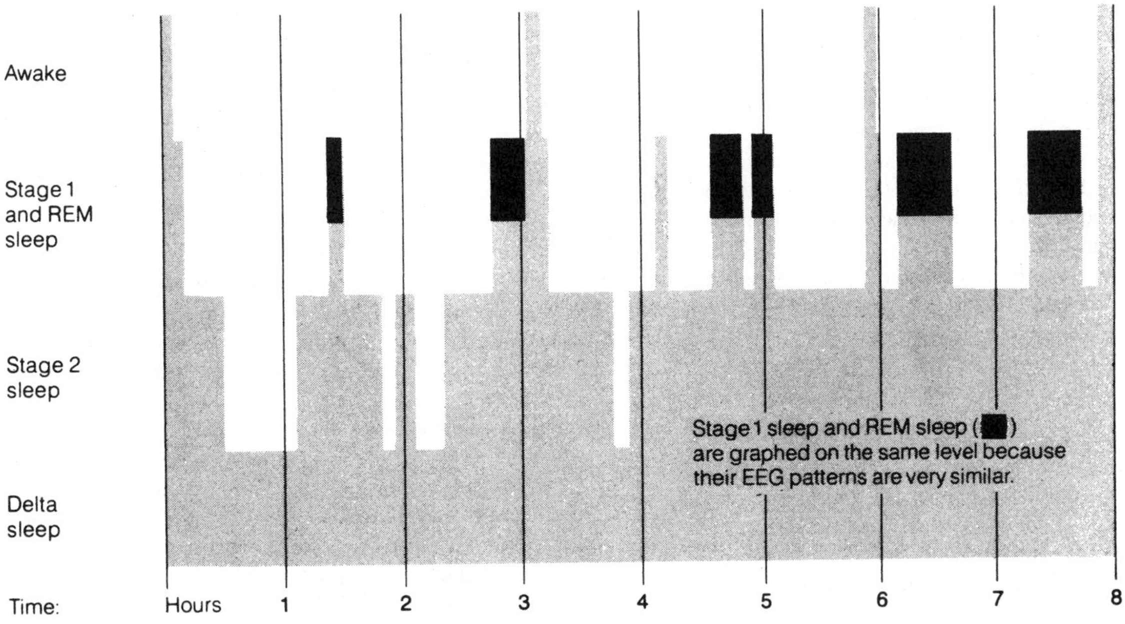

Awake
Stage 1 and REM sleep
Stage 2 sleep
Delta sleep
Time:
Hours
1
2
3
4
5
6
7
8
Stage 1 sleep and REM sleep ( ) are graphed on the same level because their EEG patterns are very similar.

FIGURE 24.1–2
Typical sleep pattern of a young human adult. (Reproduced with permission from Hauri P: *The Sleep Disorders,* p 8. Current Concepts, Upjohn, Kalamazoo, MI, 1982.)

mal sleep patterns. Drugs and manipulations that increase the firing of these noradrenergic neurons produce a marked reduction in REM sleep (REM-off neurons) and an increase in wakefulness. In humans with implanted electrodes (for the control of spasticity), electrical stimulation of the locus ceruleus profoundly disrupts all sleep parameters.

Brain acetylcholine is also involved in sleep, particularly in the production of REM sleep. In animal studies, the injection of cholinergic-muscarinic agonists into pontine reticular formation neurons (REM-on neurons) results in a shift from wakefulness to REM sleep. Disturbances in central cholinergic activity are associated with the sleep changes observed in major depressive disorder. Compared with healthy people and nondepressed psychiatric controls, patients who are depressed have marked disruptions of REM sleep patterns. These disruptions include shortened REM latency (60 minutes or less), an increased percentage of REM sleep, and a shift in REM distribution from the last half to the first half of the night. Administration of a muscarinic agonist, such as arecoline, to depressed patients during the first or second NREM period results in a rapid onset of REM sleep. Depression may be associated with an underlying supersensitivity to acetylcholine.

Drugs that reduce REM sleep, such as antidepressants, produce beneficial effects in depression. Indeed, about half the patients with major depressive disorder experience temporary improvement when they are deprived of sleep or when sleep is restricted. Conversely, reserpine (Serpasil), one of the few drugs that increases REM sleep, also produces depression.

Patients with dementia of the Alzheimer's type have sleep disturbances characterized by reduced REM and slow-wave sleep. The loss of cholinergic neurons in the basal forebrain has been implicated as the cause of these changes. Melatonin secretion from the pineal gland is inhibited by bright light, so the lowest serum melatonin concentrations occur during the day. The suprachiasmatic nucleus of the hypothalamus may act as the anatomical site of a circadian pacemaker that regulates melatonin secretion and the entrainment of the brain to a 24-hour sleep–wake cycle.

Evidence shows that dopamine has an alerting effect. Drugs that increase brain dopamine tend to produce arousal and wakefulness. In contrast, dopamine blockers, such as pimozide (Orap) and the phenothiazines, tend to increase sleep time.

A hypothesized homeostatic drive to sleep, perhaps in the form of an endogenous substance—process S—may accumulate during wakefulness and act to induce sleep. Another compound—process C—may act as a regulator of body temperature and sleep duration.

FUNCTIONS OF SLEEP

The functions of sleep have been examined in a variety of ways. Most investigators conclude that sleep serves a restorative, homeostatic function and appears to be crucial for normal thermoregulation and energy conservation. As NREM sleep increases after exercise and starvation, this stage may be associated with satisfying metabolic needs.

Sleep Deprivation

Prolonged periods of sleep deprivation sometimes lead to ego disorganization, hallucinations, and delusions. Depriving people of REM sleep by awakening them at the beginning of REM cycles produces an increase in the number of REM periods and in the amount of REM sleep (rebound increase) when they are allowed to sleep without interruption. REM-deprived patients may exhibit irritability and lethargy.

In studies with rats, sleep deprivation produces a syndrome that includes a debilitated appearance, skin lesions, increased food intake, weight loss, increased energy expenditure, decreased body temperature, and death. The neuroendocrine changes include increased plasma norepinephrine and decreased plasma thyroxine levels.

Sleep Requirements

Some people are normally short sleepers who require fewer than 6 hours of sleep each night to function adequately. Long sleepers are those who sleep more than 9 hours each night to function adequately. Long sleepers have more REM periods and more rapid eye movements within each period (known as REM density) than do short sleepers. These movements are sometimes considered a measure of the intensity of REM sleep and are related to the vividness of dreaming. Short sleepers are generally efficient, ambitious, socially adept, and content. Long sleepers tend to be mildly depressed, anxious, and socially withdrawn. Increased sleep needs occur with physical work, exercise, illness, pregnancy, general mental stress, and increased mental activity. REM periods increase after strong psychological stimuli, such as difficult learning situations and stress, and after the use of chemicals or drugs that decrease brain catecholamines.

SLEEP–WAKE RHYTHM

Without external clues, the natural body clock follows a 25-hour cycle. The influence of external factors—such as the light–dark cycle, daily routines, meal periods, and other external synchronizers—entrain people to the 24-hour clock. Sleep is also influenced by biological rhythms. Within a 24-hour period, adults sleep once, sometimes twice. This rhythm is not present at birth but develops over the first 2 years of life. In some women, sleep patterns change during the phases of the menstrual cycle.

Naps taken at different times of the day differ greatly in their proportions of REM and NREM sleep. In a normal nighttime sleeper, a nap taken in the morning or at noon includes a great deal of REM sleep, whereas a nap taken in the afternoon or the early evening has much less REM sleep. A circadian cycle apparently affects the tendency to have REM sleep.

Sleep patterns are not physiologically the same when people sleep in the daytime or during the time when they are accustomed to being awake; the psychological and behavioral effects of sleep differ as well. In a world of industry and communications that often functions on a 24-hour-a-day basis, these interactions are becoming increasingly significant.

Even in people who work at night, interference with the various rhythms can produce problems. The best-known example is jet lag, in which, after flying east to west, people try to convince their bodies to go to sleep at a time that is out of phase with some body cycles. Most people adapt within a few days, but some require more time. Conditions in these people's bodies apparently involve long-term cycle disruption and interference.

References

Armitage R: The distribution of EEG frequencies in REM and NREM sleep stages in healthy young adults. Sleep *18:* 334, 1995.

Czeisler CA, Weitzman ED, Moore-Ede MC, Zimmerman JC, Knaner RS: Human sleep: Its duration and organization depend on its circadian phase. Science *210:* 1264, 1980.

Dahl RE: The regulation of sleep and arousal: Development and psychopathology. Dev Psychopathol *8:* 3, 1996.

Dement W, Kleitman N: Cyclic variations in EEG during sleep and their relation to eye movements, body motility, and dreaming. Electroencephalogr Clin Neurophysiol *9:* 673, 1975.

Gillin JC, Zoltoski RK, Salin-Pascual R: Basic science of sleep. In *Comprehensive Textbook of Psychiatry,* ed 6, HI Kaplan, BJ Sadock, editors, p 80. Williams & Wilkins, Baltimore, 1995.

Harrison Y, Bright V, Horne JA: Can normal subjects be motivated to fall asleep faster? Physiol Behav *60:* 681, 1996.

Hobson AJ: Sleep and dreaming. J Neurosci *10:* 371, 1990.

O'Hara BF, Young KA, Watson FL, Heller HC, Kilduff T: Immediate early gene expression in brain during sleep deprivation. Sleep *16:* 1, 1993.

Shapiro CM, Flanigan MJ: Function of sleep. Br Med J *306:* 383, 1993.

Smith A, Pollock J, Thomas M, Llewelyn M, et al: The relationship between subjective ratings of sleep and mental functioning in healthy subjects and patients with chronic fatigue syndrome. Hum Psychopharmacol *11:* 161, 1996.

Waterhouse J: Circadian rhythms. Br Med J *306:* 448, 1993.

Webb WB, editor: *Biological Rhythms, Sleep, and Performance.* Wiley, New York, 1982.

Williams RL, Karacan I, Moore CA, Hirshkowitz M: Sleep disorders. In *Comprehensive Textbook of Psychiatry,* ed 6, HI Kaplan, BJ Sadock, editors, p 1373. Williams & Wilkins, Baltimore, 1995.

▲ 24.2 Sleep Disorders

About a third of all U.S. adults experience some type of sleep disorder during their lifetimes. Over half of persons with sleep problems do not seek medical advice at any time. Insomnia is the most common and the most widely recognized sleep disorder, but many other kinds occur. Careful diagnosis and specific treatment aimed at the cause are essential. Factors associated with the increased prevalence of sleep disorders include female sex, presence of mental and medical disorders, substance abuse, and advanced age. Table 24.2–1 lists the polysomnographic measures commonly used in diagnosing and describing sleep disorders.

Table 24.2–1
Common Polysomnographic Measures

Sleep latency: Period of time from turning out the lights until the appearance of stage 2 sleep

Early morning awakening: Time of being continuously awake from the last stage of the sleep until the end of the sleep record (usually at 7 AM)

Sleep efficiency: Total sleep time/total time of the sleep record × 100

Apnea index: Number of apneas longer than 10 seconds per hour of sleep

Nocturnal myoclonus index: Number of periodic leg movements per hour

REM latency: Period of time from the onset of sleep until the first REM period of the night

Sleep-onset REM period: REM sleep within the first 10 minutes of sleep.

MAJOR SYMPTOMS

Individual sleep requirements vary: Many people are long sleepers and require 9 to 10 hours of sleep a night; but, like short sleepers, they do not have a sleep problem. Four major symptoms characterize most sleep disorders: insomnia, hypersomnia, parasomnia, and sleep–wake schedule disturbance. The symptoms often overlap.

Insomnia

Insomnia is difficulty in initiating or maintaining sleep. It is the most common sleep complaint and may be transient or persistent. Common causes of insomnia are given in Table 24.2–2.

A brief period of insomnia is most often associated with anxiety, either as a sequela to an anxious experience or in anticipation of an anxiety-provoking experience (for example, an examination or an impending job interview). In some people, transient insomnia of this kind may be related to grief, loss, or almost any life change or stress. The condition is not likely to be serious, although a psychotic episode or a severe depression sometimes begins with acute insomnia. Specific treatment for the condition is usually not required. When treatment with hypnotic medication is indicated, the physician and the patient should both be clear that the treatment is of short duration and that some symptoms, including a brief recurrence of the insomnia, may be expected when the medication is discontinued.

Persistent insomnia is a fairly common group of conditions in which the problem is most often difficulty in falling asleep rather than in remaining sleep. This insomnia involves two sometimes separable, but often intertwined, problems: somatized tension and anxiety, and a conditioned associative response. Patients often have no clear complaint other than insomnia. They may not experience anxiety per se but discharge the anxiety through physiological channels; they may complain chiefly of apprehensive feelings or ruminative thoughts that appear to keep them from falling asleep. Sometimes but not always, a patient describes the condition's exacerbation at times of stress at work or at home and its remission during vacations.

Hypersomnia

Hypersomnia manifests as excessive amounts of sleep, excessive daytime sleepiness (somnolence), or sometimes both. The term *somnolence* should be reserved for patients who complain of sleepiness and have a clearly demonstrable tendency to fall asleep suddenly in the waking state, who have sleep attacks, and who cannot remain awake; it should not be used for people who are simply physically tired or weary. The distinction, however, is not always clear. Complaints of hypersomnia are much less frequent than are complaints of insomnia, but they are by no means rare if clinicians are alert to

Table 24.2–2
Common Causes of Insomnia

Symptom	Insomnias Secondary to Medical Conditions	Insomnias Secondary to Psychiatric or Environmental Conditions
Difficulty in falling asleep	Any painful or uncomfortable condition CNS lesions Conditions listed below, at times	Anxiety Tension anxiety, muscular Environmental changes Circadian rhythm sleep disorder
Difficulty in remaining asleep	Sleep apnea syndromes Nocturnal myoclonus and restless legs syndrome Dietary factors (probably) Episodic events (parasomnias) Direct substance effects (including alcohol) Substance withdrawal effects (including alcohol) Substance interactions Endocrine or metabolic diseases Infectious, neoplastic, or other diseases Painful or uncomfortable conditions Brainstem or hypothalamic lesions or diseases Aging	Depression, especially primary depression Environmental changes Circadian rhythm sleep disorder Posttraumatic stress disorder Schizophrenia

Courtesy of Ernest L. Hartmann, M.D.

them. More than 100,000 narcoleptics are estimated to live in the United States. Narcolepsy is just one well-known condition clearly producing hypersomnia. If substance-related conditions are included, hypersomnia is a common symptom.

Table 24.2–3 lists some common causes of hypersomnia. As with insomnia, hypersomnia is associated with borderline conditions, situations that are hard to classify, and idiopathic cases. According to a recent survey, the most common conditions responsible for hypersomnia severe enough to be evaluated by all-night recordings at a sleep disorders center were sleep apnea and narcolepsy.

Transient and situational hypersomnia is a disruption of the normal sleep–wake pattern; it is marked by excessive difficulty in remaining awake and a tendency to remain in bed for unusually long periods or to return to bed to nap frequently during the day. The pattern is experienced suddenly in response to an identifiable recent life change, conflict, or loss and is much less common than insomnia. It is seldom marked by definite sleep attacks or unavoidable sleep but, rather, is characterized by tiredness or by falling asleep sooner than usual and by difficulty in arising in the morning.

Parasomnia

Parasomnia is an unusual or undesirable phenomenon that appears suddenly during sleep or that occurs at the threshold between waking and sleeping. Parasomnia usually occurs in stages 3 and is 4 and is thus associated with poor recall of the disturbance.

Sleep–Wake Schedule Disturbance

Sleep–wake schedule disturbance involves the displacement of sleep from its desired circadian period. Patients commonly

Table 24.2–3
Common Causes of Hypersomnia

Symptom	Chiefly Medical	Chiefly Psychiatric or Environmental
Excessive sleep (hypersomnia)	Kleine-Levin syndrome Menstrual-associated somnolence Metabolic or toxic conditions Encephalitic conditions Alcohol and depressant medications Withdrawal from stimulants	Depression (some) Avoidance reactions
Excessive daytime sleepiness	Narcolepsy and narcolepsy-like syndromes Sleep apneas Hypoventilation syndrome Hyperthryoidism and other metabolic and toxic conditions Alcohol and depressant medications Withdrawal from stimulants Sleep deprivation or insufficient sleep Any condition producing serious insomnia	Depression (some) Avoidance reactions Circadian rhythm sleep disorder

Courtesy of Ernest Hartmann, M.D.

Table 24.2–4
Sleep History Questionnaire

Patient name ______________________________

Date ______________________________

Please check the appropriate box or give short answers for the following:

	Yes	No
1. Do you feel sleepy or have sleep attacks during the day?	☐	☐
2. Do you nap during the day?	☐	☐
3. Do you have trouble concentrating during the day?	☐	☐
4. Do you have trouble falling asleep when you first go to bed?	☐	☐
5. Do you awaken during the night?	☐	☐
6. Do you awaken more than once?	☐	☐
7. Do you awaken too early in the morning?	☐	☐
8. How long have you had trouble sleeping? What do you think precipitated the problem? ______		
9. How would you describe your usual night's sleep (hours of sleep, quality of sleep, etc.)? ______		
10. Does your schedule for sleep and rising on the weekend differ from what it is during the week?	☐	☐
11. Do others live at home who interrupt your sleep?	☐	☐
12. Are you regularly awakened at night by pain or the need to use the bathroom?	☐	☐
13. Does your job require shift changes or travel?	☐	☐
14. Do you drink caffeinated beverages (coffee, tea, or soft drinks)?	☐	☐
15. Apart from difficulty in sleeping, what, if any, other medical problems do you have? ______		
16. What sleep medications, prescription or nonprescription, do you take? (Please include the dosage, how often you take it, and for how many months or years you have taken it.) ______		
17. What other prescription and over-the-counter medications do you regularly use? (Again, please include the dosage, the frequency, and the duration.) ______		
18. Have you ever suffered from depression, anxiety, or similar problems?	☐	☐
19. Do you snore?	☐	☐
Questions for the sleep partner		
1. Does your sleep partner snore?	☐	☐
2. Does your sleep partner seem to stop breathing repeatedly during the night?	☐	☐
3. Does your sleep partner jerk his or her legs or kick you while he or she is sleeping?	☐	☐
4. Have you ever experienced trouble sleeping? Please explain. ______	☐	☐

cannot sleep when they wish to sleep, although they are able to sleep at other times. Correspondingly, they cannot be fully awake when they want to be fully awake, but they are able to be awake at other times. The disturbance does not precisely produce insomnia or somnolence, although the initial complaint is often either insomnia or somnolence; the inabilities to sleep and be awake are elicited only on careful questioning. Sleep–wake schedule disturbance can be considered a misalignment between sleep and wake behaviors. A sleep history questionnaire is helpful in diagnosing a patient's sleep disorder (Table 24.2–4).

CLASSIFICATION

ICD-10

In the 10th revision of *International Statistical Classification of Diseases and Related Health Problems* (ICD-10), the subject of sleep disorders covers only those of nonorganic type. These disorders are classified as *dyssomnias,* psychogenic conditions "in which the predominant disturbances . . . [are] in the amount, quality, or timing of sleep" because of emotional causes; and *parasomnias,* "abnormal episodic events occurring during sleep." The dyssomnias include insomnia, hypersomnia, and disorder of the sleep–wake schedule. The parasomnias in childhood are related to development; those in adulthood are psychogenic and include sleepwalking, sleep terrors, and nightmares. Sleep disorders of organic origin, nonpsychogenic disorders such as narcolepsy and cataplexy, and sleep apnea and episodic movement disorders are discussed under other categories.

ICD-10 notes that sleep disorders are often symptoms of other disorders, but even when they are not, the specific sleep disorder should be diagnosed along with as many other relevant diagnoses as necessary to describe the "psychopathology and/or pathophysiology involved in a given case." Table 24.2–5 presents the ICD-10 criteria for nonorganic sleep disorders.

ICSD

The most detailed classification of sleep disorders appears in the American Sleep Disorders Association's *International Classification of Sleep Disorders: Diagnostic and Coding Manual* (ICSD). ICSD divides sleep disorders into four categories: dyssomnias, parasomnias, sleep disorders associated with medical-psychiatric disorders, and proposed sleep disorders. Table 24.2–6 presents an outline of ICSD.

DSM-IV

The fourth edition of *Diagnostic and Statistical Manual of Mental Disorders* (DSM-IV) classifies sleep disorders on the basis of clinical diagnostic criteria and presumed etiology. The three major categories of sleep disorders in DSM-IV are primary sleep disorders, sleep disorders related to another mental disorder, and other sleep disorders, most notably those due to a general medical condition or substance induced. The disorders described in DSM-IV are only a fraction of the known sleep disorders; they provide a framework for a clinical assessment.

PRIMARY SLEEP DISORDERS

DSM-IV defines primary sleep disorders as those not caused by another mental disorder, a physical condition, or a substance but, rather, caused by an abnormal sleep–wake mechanism and often by conditioning. The two main primary sleep disorders are dyssomnias and parasomnias. Dyssomnias are a heterogeneous group of sleep disorders that includes primary insomnia, primary hypersomnia, narcolepsy, breathing-related sleep disorder, circadian rhythm sleep disorder (sleep–wake schedule disorder), and dyssomnia not otherwise specified. Parasomnias include nightmare disorder (dream anxiety disorder), sleep terror disorder, sleepwalking disorder, and parasomnia, not otherwise specified.

Dyssomnias

Primary Insomnia. Primary insomnia is diagnosed when the chief complaint is nonrestorative sleep or a difficulty in initiating or maintaining sleep and the complaint continues for at least a month (Table 24.2–7). (According to ICD-10, the disturbance must occur at least 3 times a week for a month.) The term *primary* indicates that the insomnia is independent of any known physical or mental condition. Primary insomnia is often characterized by both difficulty falling asleep and by repeated awakenings. Increased nighttime physiological or psychological arousal and negative conditioning for sleep are frequently evident. Patients with primary insomnia are generally preoccupied with getting enough sleep. The more they try to sleep, the greater the sense of frustration and distress and the more elusive sleep becomes.

Treatment of primary insomnia is among the most difficult problems in sleep disorders. When the conditioned component is prominent, a deconditioning technique may be useful. Patients are asked to use their beds for sleeping and for nothing else; if they are not asleep after 5 minutes in bed, they are instructed to simply get up and do something else. Sometimes, changing to another bed or to another room is useful. When somatized tension or muscle tension is prominent, relaxation tapes, transcendental meditation, and practicing the relaxation response and biofeedback are occasionally helpful. Psychotherapy has not been very useful in the treatment of primary insomnia. Satisfying sexual experiences promote sleep, more so in men than in women.

Primary insomnia is commonly treated with benzodiazepines, zolpidem (Ambien), chloral hydrate (Noctec), and other hypnotics. Hypnotic drugs should be used with care. Over-the-counter sleep aids have limited effectiveness. Various nonspecific measures—so-called sleep hygiene—can be helpful in improving sleep (Table 24.2–8). It is important for physicians to reassure patients with insomnia that their health is not at risk if they do not get 6 to 8 hours of sleep. Light therapy is also used. Long-acting sleep medications (for example, flurazepam [Dalmane], quazepam [Doral]) are best for middle-of-the-night insomnia; short-acting drugs (for example, zolpidem [Ambien], triazolam [Halcion]) are useful for persons who have difficulty falling asleep. In general, sleep medications should not be prescribed for more than 2 weeks because tolerance and withdrawal may result.

Table 24.2–5
ICD-10 Diagnostic Criteria for Nonorganic Sleep Disorders

Note: A more comprehensive classification of sleep disorders is available (*International Classification of Sleep Disorders*[a]), but it should be noted that this is organized differently from ICD-10.

For some research purposes, where particularly homogeneous groups of sleep disorders are required, four or more events occurring within a 1-year period may be considered as a criterion for use of categories sleepwalking (somnambulism), sleep terrors (night terrors), and nightmares.

Nonorganic insomnia

A. The individual complains of difficulty falling asleep, difficulty maintaining sleep, or nonrefreshing sleep.
B. The sleep disturbance occurs at least 3 times a week for at least 1 month.
C. The sleep disturbance results in marked personal distress or interference with personal functioning in daily living.
D. There is no known causative organic factor, such as a neurological or other medical condition, psychoactive substance use disorder, or a medication.

Nonorganic hypersomnia

A. The individual complains of excessive daytime sleepiness or sleep attacks or of prolonged transition to the fully aroused state upon awakening (sleep drunkenness), which is not accounted for by an inadequate amount of sleep.
B. This sleep disturbance occurs nearly every day for at least 1 month or recurrently for shorter periods of time and causes either marked distress or interference with personal functioning in daily living.
C. There are no auxiliary symptoms of narcolepsy (cataplexy, sleep paralysis, hypnagogic hallucinations) and no clinical evidence for sleep apnea (nocturnal breath cessation, typical intermittent snorting sounds, etc.).
D. There is no known causative organic factor, such as a neurological or other medical condition, psychoactive substance use disorder, or a medication.

Nonorganic disorder of the sleep–wake schedule

A. The individual's sleep–wake pattern is out of synchrony with the desired sleep–wake schedule, as imposed by societal demands and shared by most people in the individual's environment.
B. As a result of disturbance of the sleep–wake schedule, the individual experiences insomnia during the major sleep period or hypersomnia during the waking period, nearly every day for at least 1 month or recurrently for shorter periods of time.
C. The unsatisfactory quantity, quality, and timing of sleep causes either marked personal distress or interference with personal functioning in daily living.
D. There is no known causative organic factor, such as a neurological or other medical condition, psychoactive substance use disorder, or a medication.

Sleepwalking (somnambulism)

A. The predominant symptom is repeated (two or more) episodes of rising from bed, usually during the first third of nocturnal sleep, and walking about for between several minutes and half an hour.
B. During an episode, the individual has a blank, staring face, is relatively unresponsive to the efforts of others to influence the event or to communicate with him or her, and can be awakened only with considerable difficulty.
C. Upon awakening (either from an episode or the next morning), the individual has amnesia for the episode.
D. Within several minutes for awakening from the episode, there is no impairment of mental activity or behavior, although there may initially be a short period of some confusion and disorientation.
E. There is no evidence of an organic mental disorder, such as dementia, or a physical disorder, such as epilepsy.

Sleep terrors (night terrors)

A. Repeated (two or more) episodes in which the individual gets up from sleep with a panicky scream and intense anxiety, body motility, and autonomic hyperactivity (such as tachycardia, heart pounding, rapid breathing, and sweating).
B. The episodes occur mainly during the first third of sleep.
C. The duration of the episode is less than 10 minutes.
D. If others try to comfort the individual during the episode, there is a lack of response followed by disorientation and perseverative movements.
E. The individual has limited recall of the event.
F. There is no known causative organic factor, such as a neurological or other medical condition, psychoactive substance use disorder, or a medication.

Nightmares

A. The individual wakes from nocturnal sleep or naps with detailed and vivid recall of intensely frightening dreams, usually involving threats to survival, security, or self-esteem. The awakening may occur during any part of the sleep period, but typically during the second half.
B. Upon awakening from the frightening dreams, the individual rapidly becomes oriented and alert.
C. The dream experience itself and the disturbance of sleep resulting from the awakings associated with the episodes cause marked distress to the individual.
D. There is no known causative organic factor, such as a neurological or other medical condition, psychoactive substance use disorder, or a medication.

Other nonorganic sleep disorders

Nonorganic sleep disorder, unspecified

[a] Diagnostic Classification Steering Committee: *International Classification of Sleep Disorders: Diagnostic and Coding Manual.* American Sleep Disorders Association, Rochester, MN, 1990.

Mrs. Dickinson is a 47-year-old Englishwoman. She is married and has two teenage children. Mrs. Dickinson complained that she was having increasing difficulty getting to sleep and was always very tired during the daytime. Apparently the problem had been present almost every night for many years but had recently become so bad that she had given up her job.

Mrs. Dickinson's sleep pattern seemed to have been disturbed since she was a teenager, when she used to read in bed until the early hours of the morning and then found it

Table 24.2–6
International Classification of Sleep Disorders (ICSD)

1. Dyssomnias
   A. Intrinsic sleep disorders
      1. Psychophysiological insomnia
      2. Sleep state misperception
      3. Idiopathic insomnia
      4. Narcolepsy
      5. Recurrent hypersomnia
      6. Idiopathic hypersomnia
      7. Posttraumatic hypersomnia
      8. Obstructive sleep apnea syndrome
      9. Central sleep apnea syndrome
      10. Central alveolar hypoventilation syndrome
      11. Periodic limb movement disorder
      12. Restless legs syndrome
      13. Intrinsic sleep disorder NOS
   B. Extrinsic sleep disorder
      1. Inadequate sleep hygiene
      2. Environmental sleep disorder
      3. Altitude insomnia
      4. Adjustment sleep disorder
      5. Insufficient sleep syndrome
      6. Limit-setting sleep disorder
      7. Sleep-onset association disorder
      8. Food allergy insomnia
      9. Nocturnal eating (drinking) syndrome
      10. Hypnotic-dependent sleep disorder
      11. Stimulant-dependent sleep disorder
      12. Alcohol-dependent sleep disorder
      13. Toxin-induced sleep disorder
      14. Extrinsic sleep disorder NOS
   C. Circadian rhythm sleep disorders
      1. Time zone change (jet lag) syndrome
      2. Shift work sleep disorder
      3. Irregular sleep–wake pattern
      4. Delayed sleep phase syndrome
      5. Advanced sleep phase syndrome
      6. Non–24-hour sleep–wake disorder
      7. Circadian rhythm sleep disorder NOS
2. Parasomnias
   A. Arousal disorders
      1. Confusional arousals
      2. Sleepwalking
      3. Sleep terrors
   B. Sleep-wake transition disorders
      1. Rhythmic movement disorder
      2. Sleep starts
      3. Sleep talking
      4. Nocturnal leg cramps
   C. Parasomnias usually associated with REM sleep
      1. Nightmares
      2. Sleep paralysis
      3. Impaired-sleep–related penile erections
      4. Sleep-related painful erections
      5. REM-sleep–related sinus arrest
      6. REM sleep behavior disorder
   D. Other parasomnias
      1. Sleep bruxism
      2. Sleep enuresis
      3. Sleep-related abnormal swallowing syndrome
      4. Nocturnal paroxysmal dystonia
      5. Sudden unexplained nocturnal death syndrome
      6. Primary snoring
      7. Infant sleep apnea
      8. Congenital central hypoventilation syndrome
      9. Sudden infant death syndrome
      10. Benign neonatal sleep myoclonus
      11. Other parasomnia NOS
3. Sleep disorders associated with medical-psychiatric disorders
   A. Associated with Mental Disorders
      1. Psychoses
      2. Mood disorders
      3. Anxiety disorders
      4. Panic disorders
      5. Alcoholism
   B. Associated with neurological disorders
      1. Cerebral degenerative disorders
      2. Dementia
      3. Parkinsonism
      4. Fatal familial insomnia
      5. Sleep-related epilepsy
      6. Electrical status epilepticus of sleep
      7. Sleep-related headaches
   C. Associated with other medical disorders
      1. Sleeping sickness
      2. Nocturnal cardiac ischemia
      3. Chronic obstructive pulmonary disease
      4. Sleep-related asthma
      5. Sleep-related gastroesophageal reflux
      6. Peptic ulcer disease
      7. Fibrositis syndrome
4. Proposed sleep disorders
   1. Short sleeper
   2. Long sleeper
   3. Subwakefulness syndrome
   4. Fragmentary myoclonus
   5. Sleep hyperhidrosis
   6. Menstrual-associated sleep disorder
   7. Pregnancy-associated sleep disorder
   8. Terrifying hypnagogic hallucinations
   9. Sleep-related neurogenic tachypnea
   10. Sleep-related laryngospasm
   11. Sleep choking syndrome

NOS, not otherwise specified.

difficult to get up for school. This habit of going to sleep late persisted, and she had additional difficulty in getting to sleep because of distress resulting from marital difficulties when she was in her 20s. She remarried at the age of 29, but her sleep was further disrupted, as her new husband had an irregular sleep pattern because he worked shifts at that time. Two years before her referral, Mrs. Dickinson's insomnia worsened still further when a number of family misfortunes occurred in quick succession. Typically, she went to bed between 10:30 PM and 1:30 AM, but lay awake until 2:00 or 3:00 AM. She found it difficult to ''wind down'' and clear her mind of thoughts about her daytime activities. She often felt too hot and ''itchy all over'' and would go to the bathroom 8 or 9 times a night. Often she went downstairs to make a drink or find something to eat or made lists of things to do the next day. When she finally got to sleep, she slept soundly. Getting up for work at 7:30 AM was difficult. She felt fatigued most of the day, although she did not actually fall asleep, and she had difficulty managing her job. She still continued to go to sleep late, and although she was able to sleep until about 9:00 AM, she still felt tired and sleepy during the day.

Table 24.2–7
DSM-IV Diagnostic Criteria for Primary Insomnia

A. The predominant complaint is difficulty initiating or maintaining sleep, or nonrestorative sleep, for at least 1 month.
B. The sleep disturbance (or associated daytime fatigue) causes clinically significant distress or impairment in social, occupational, or other important areas of functioning.
C. The sleep disturbance does not occur exclusively during the course of narcolepsy, breathing-related sleep disorder, a circadian rhythm sleep disorder, or a parasomnia.
D. The disturbance does not occur exclusively during the course of another mental disorder (eg, major depressive disorder, generalized anxiety disorder, a delirium).
E. The disturbance is not due to the direct physiological effects of a substance (eg, a drug of abuse, a medication) or a general medical condition.

Reprinted with permission from American Psychiatric Association: *Diagnostic and Statistical Manual of Mental Disorders,* ed 4. Copyright, American Psychiatric Association, Washington, 1994.

Past treatments with caffeine and alcohol restriction, relaxation tapes, yoga, hypnotherapy, and benzodiazepine hypnotics had all been ineffective. Short-term use of zopiclone was helpful, but Mrs. Dickinson relapsed when this treatment was discontinued on her physician's advice. She claimed that a relaxing social evening with a modest amount of alcohol also usually helped her to get to sleep. Recently she had preferred to sleep on her own to avoid the additional problem of keeping her husband awake.

Mrs. Dickinson was born and grew up in an industrial town in central England, the only child of a skilled worker. After secondary school she trained as a secretary and later had clerical jobs. At the age of 21, she married an accountant who worked in a textile factory. Her husband was 5 years older than she. The marriage was stormy because of her husband's drinking and infidelity and was finally dissolved when she was 27 years of age. She married again 2 years later, this time to a man her own age who worked as a skilled laborer in a major steel company. They had two children, a boy and a girl, ages 16 and 13 at the time of their mother's referral. Her present marriage has been quite harmonious. She had no major difficulties with her parents or her children. There was no history of mental disorders in her family.

Apart from troubles with pain in her neck and back from time to time, her general health was good. She drank alcohol only on social occasions and did not use any medication.

Mrs. Dickinson was neatly and correctly dressed. She was somewhat tense but open minded and cooperative. There was no evidence of a mood disorder or any other psychopathology and no indication of any cognitive impairment. Physical and neurological examinations, including routine laboratory investigations, were all normal.

DISCUSSION

Mrs. Dickinson presented a long-standing difficulty in falling asleep, resulting in marked distress, with fatigue and sleepiness in the daytime. With no evidence of organic etiology, psychopathology, or psychoactive substance use, she meets the criteria for insomnia. (From *ICD-10 Casebook.*)

Table 24.2–8
Nonspecific Measures to Induce Sleep (Sleep Hygiene)

1. Arise at the same time daily.
2. Limit daily in-bed time to the usual amount present before the sleep disturbance.
3. Discontinue CNS-acting drugs (caffeine, nicotine, alcohol, stimulants).
4. Avoid daytime naps (except when sleep chart shows they induce better night sleep).
5. Establish physical fitness by means of a graded program of vigorous exercise early in the day.
6. Avoid evening stimulation; substitute radio or relaxed reading for television.
7. Try very hot, 20-minute, body temperature-raising bath soaks near bedtime.
8. Eat at regular times daily; avoid large meals near bedtime.
9. Practice evening relaxation routines, such as progressive muscle relaxation or meditation.
10. Maintain comfortable sleeping conditions.

Reprinted with permission from Regestein QR: Sleep disorders. In *Clinical Psychiatry for Medical Students,* A Stoudemire, editor, p 578. Lippincott, Philadelphia, 1990.

REPEATED RAPID EYE MOVEMENT (REM) SLEEP INTERRUPTIONS. Repeated REM sleep interruptions are rare but are examples of a primary insomnia. Their cause is unknown. They have been related to psychological difficulties and periods of nightmares or other disturbing dreams. In these instances, they may be a conditioned avoidance response in which a patient's central nervous system (CNS) senses the beginning of a dream period (REM period), associates it with an oncoming unpleasant dream or nightmare, and produces an immediate arousal response.

ATYPICAL POLYSOMNOGRAPHIC FEATURES. Another example of a primary insomnia, atypical polysomnographic features is a condition in which sleep is frequently interrupted and nonrestorative and in which the sleep-stage structure is marked by abnormal physiological features. Most commonly, patients describe the quality of sleep as poor, light, or unrestful.

Primary Hypersomnia. Primary hypersomnia is diagnosed when no other cause for excessive somnolence occurring for at least 1 month can be found. Some people are long sleepers who, like short sleepers, show a normal variation. Their sleep, although long, is normal in architecture and physiology. Sleep efficiency and the sleep–wake schedule are normal. This pattern is without complaints about the quality of sleep, daytime sleepiness, or difficulties with the awake mood, motivation, and performance. Long sleep may be a lifetime pattern, and it appears to have a familial incidence. Many people are variable sleepers and may become long sleepers at certain times in their lives.

Some people have subjective complaints of feeling sleepy but have no objective findings. They do not have a tendency to fall asleep more often than normal and do not have any objective signs. Clinicians should try to rule out clear-cut

Table 24.2–9
DSM-IV Diagnostic Criteria for Primary Hypersomnia

A. The predominant complaint is excessive sleepiness for at least 1 month (or less if recurrent) as evidenced by either prolonged sleep episodes or daytime sleep episodes that occur almost daily.

B. The excessive sleepiness causes clinically significant distress or impairment in social, occupational, or other important areas of functioning.

C. The excessive sleepiness is not better accounted for by insomnia and does not occur exclusively during the course of another sleep disorder (eg, narcolepsy, breathing-related sleep disorder, circadian rhythm sleep disorder, or a parasomnia) and cannot be accounted for by an inadequate amount of sleep.

D. The disturbance does not occur exclusively during the course of another mental disorder.

E. The disturbance is not due to the direct physiological effects of a substance (eg, a drug of abuse, a medication) or a general medical condition.

Specify if:

Recurrent: if there are periods of excessive sleepiness that last at least 3 days occurring several times a year for at least 2 years.

causes of excessive somnolence. According to DSM-IV, the disorder should be coded as recurrent if patients have periods of excessive sleepiness lasting at least 3 days and occurring several times a year for at least 2 years (Table 24.2–9).

The treatment of primary hypersomnia consists mainly of stimulant drugs, such as amphetamines, given in the morning or evening. Nonsedating antidepressant drugs, such as serotonin-specific reuptake inhibitors, may be of value in some patients.

A 55-year-old businessman had had excessive sleepiness since age 21, which he had described to his new family physician, who then referred him to a sleep specialist. Typically, he slept regularly from 10:15 PM to 6:30 AM. He also took ½- to ¾-hour naps irregularly between 9 and 10:15 AM, and 1:30 and 2 PM, and napped irregularly between 4:30 and 8:30 PM. When napping at work, on his office floor, he deferred all calls. He awoke temporarily refreshed. Delaying his naps caused overwhelming fatigue. He had no sudden loss of muscle tone (as in cataplexy) or other symptoms suggesting narcolepsy and neither snored nor had any other symptoms suggesting a breathing-related sleep disorder.

The patient owned a television station in Birmingham, Alabama. He was spared obligatory hard work as his staff could run the operation. Nevertheless, he was an organized, motivated person. He was in good health, and jogged 4 to 5 miles. He lived with his wife and youngest son. He enjoyed socializing with his married children and their families and dabbling in local politics. He would take a longer afternoon nap in anticipation of an evening activity, which he always left early in favor of his regular bedtime.

His father had taken a nap daily after lunch, and his paternal grandfather had been excessively sleepy. During childhood the patient had had some nightmares but no other sleep problem. He had been athletic and spontaneously ran along his paper route.

The patient drank about two beers a week but avoided additional alcohol, caffeine, and other drugs. Previous physical examinations had revealed good health, with a resting heart rate maintained in the 50s, blood pressures of about 100/70 to 105/70 mm Hg, normal thyroid function, and normal fasting blood sugar levels.

When interviewed, the patient was friendly, informative, and self-assured. He denied depressed mood or loss of interest or pleasure. He regarded his sleepiness as a difficulty with which he had come to terms, but would be grateful for further relief.

Tests of daytime vigilance indicated impaired arousal. He had an average interval to sleep onset of 11 minutes, during five polygraphically recorded naps, which is within the normal range. During a nighttime polygraphic recording, he had normal-appearing sleep that continued uninterrupted for 9½ hours until he had to be awakened.

DISCUSSION

In most patients with a chief complaint of excessive daytime sleepiness (hypersomnia) sufficiently severe to cause them to seek help at a sleep disorders center, either a general medical condition or use of a substance or medication is found to cause the disturbance. This case illustrates the relatively uncommon situation in which neither of these factors nor another mental disorder (such as major depressive disorder) can account for the disturbance. The diagnosis is therefore primary hypersomnia. Primary hypersomnia is usually associated, as in this case, with normal sleep latency and patterns as measured by the polysomnogram.

FOLLOW-UP

Treatment with a long-acting stimulant caused severe headaches. Amphetamines and caffeine-containing beverages did not help, as their initial stimulation was followed by increased sleepiness.

Because the patient speculated that psychotherapy might shed light on his problem and pose fewer disadvantages, he began a course of weekly sessions. However, after 2 years of this treatment with a psychoanalyst, his sleep pattern was unchanged, and he continued to manage his sleepiness with regular naps. (From *DSM-IV Casebook.*)

Narcolepsy. Narcolepsy consists of excessive daytime sleepiness and abnormal manifestations of REM sleep occurring daily for at least 3 months (Table 24.2–10). The REM sleep includes hypnagogic and hypnopompic hallucinations, cataplexy, and sleep paralysis. The appearance of REM sleep within 10 minutes of sleep onset (sleep onset REM periods) is also considered evidence of narcolepsy. The disorder can be

Table 24.2–10
DSM-IV Diagnostic Criteria for Narcolepsy

A. Irresistible attacks of refreshing sleep that occur daily over at least 3 months.
B. The presence of one or both of the following:
  (1) Cataplexy (eg, brief episodes of sudden bilateral loss of muscle tone, most often in association with intense emotion).
  (2) Recurrent intrusions of elements of rapid eye movement (REM) sleep into the transition between sleep and wakefulness, as manifested by either hypnopompic or hypnagogic hallucinations or sleep paralysis at the beginning or end of sleep episodes.
C. The disturbance is not due to the direct physiological effects of a substance (eg, a drug of abuse, a medication) or another general medical condition.

Reprinted with permission from American Psychiatric Association: *Diagnostic and Statistical Manual of Mental Disorders,* ed 4. Copyright, American Psychiatric Association, Washington, 1994.

dangerous because it can lead to automobile and industrial accidents.

Narcolepsy is not as rare as was once thought. It is estimated to occur in 0.02 to 0.16 percent of adults and shows some familial incidence. Narcolepsy is neither a type of epilepsy nor a psychogenic disturbance. It is an abnormality of the sleep mechanisms—specifically, REM-inhibiting mechanisms—and it has been studied in dogs, sheep, and humans. Narcolepsy can occur at any age, but it most frequently begins in adolescence or young adulthood, generally before the age of 30. The disorder either progresses slowly or reaches a plateau that is maintained throughout life.

The most common symptom is sleep attacks: Patients cannot avoid falling sleep. Often associated with the problem (close to 50 percent of long-standing cases) is cataplexy, a sudden loss of muscle tone, such as jaw drop, head drop, weakness of the knees, or paralysis of all skeletal muscles with collapse. Patients often remain awake during brief cataplectic episodes; the long episodes usually merge with sleep and show the electroencephalographic (EEG) signs of REM sleep.

Other symptoms include hypnagogic or hypnopompic hallucinations: vivid perceptual experiences, either auditory or visual, occurring at sleep onset or on awakening. Patients are often momentarily frightened, but within a minute or two they return to an entirely normal frame of mind and are aware that nothing was actually there.

Another uncommon symptom is sleep paralysis, most often occurring on awakening in the morning; during the episode patients are apparently awake and conscious but unable to move a muscle. If the symptom persists for more than a few seconds, as it often does in narcolepsy, it can become extremely uncomfortable. (Isolated brief episodes of sleep paralysis occur in many nonnarcoleptic people.) Patients with narcolepsy report falling asleep quickly at night but often experience broken sleep.

When the diagnosis is not clinically clear, a nighttime polysomnographic recording reveals a characteristic sleep-onset REM period. A test of daytime multiple sleep latency (several recorded naps at 2-hour intervals) shows rapid sleep onset and usually one or more sleep-onset REM periods. A type of human leukocyte antigen called HLA-DR2 is found in 90 to 100 percent of patients with narcolepsy and only 10 to 35 percent of unaffected persons.

A regimen of forced naps at a regular time of day occasionally helps patients with narcolepsy, and in some cases, the regimen alone, without medication, can almost cure the patients. When medication is required, stimulants (for example, amphetamines and methylphenidate [Ritalin]) are most useful, sometimes combined with antidepressants (for example, protriptyline [Vivactil]) when cataplexy is prominent.

Modafinil, an experimental α_1 agonist, has been reported to reduce the number of sleep attacks and to improve psychomotor performance in narcolepsy; this observation suggests the involvement of noradrenergic mechanisms in the disorder.

Nora, a 24-year-old graduate student, complained of episodes of severe sleepiness that forced her to take naps. Sometimes when she attempted to stay awake, she was unable to do so; she had fallen asleep at the dinner table and even when walking. She had trouble staying alert enough to get off at the right bus stop. In fact, she was unable to remain seated without becoming sleepy, slept through classes, and failed her courses in graduate school.

Nora is bothered by frequent cataplexy, in which she becomes limp and briefly unable to move after sudden emotional arousal. This occurred, for example, when she discovered that her cat had urinated on her rug and when she had become enraged with her roommate. On another occasion she almost had a car accident when another driver did something that annoyed her and she nearly lost control of her car.

As she falls asleep at night, she sees vivid scenes that seem real and feels that someone else is in the room. She still feels awake, however, and knows that really there is no one there. Her sleep is frequently punctuated by nightmares. She then wakes up feeling very hungry and has a snack.

Extremely bothersome to Nora is her continual automatic behavior, in which she suddenly discovers that she has accomplished very little after a lengthy period of work on a task. For example, she spent 2 hours unsuccessfully trying to fix her glasses and was unaware of this until her roommate interrupted her and pointed it out. The automatic behavior makes it difficult for her to change from one task to another, so it sometimes takes her 2 hours to get out of the house in the morning or to get ready for bed at night. Delays in getting to bed prevent her from getting a good night's sleep, which further aggravates her daytime sleepiness. Her roommates grew weary of her undependability, and she had to move back to her parents' home.

Previous treatment with a drug regimen consisting of an antidepressant, a stimulant, and a bedtime sedative was unsuccessful.

DISCUSSION

Nora's problem of sleep attacks and excessive daytime sleepiness is an example of hypersomnia. Her daytime sleep attacks, cataplexy, hypnogogic (when falling asleep) hallucinations, automatic behavior, nightmares, and disturbed sleep are the characteristic features of narcolepsy. Although traditionally this disorder has been regarded as a neurological disorder, to facilitate the differential diagnosis of hypersomnia, in DSM-IV it is included in the Sleep Disorder section as an Axis I disorder.

Nora was instructed to keep records of her in-bed times, nap times, cataplexy attacks, episodes of night eating, and automatic behavior. Psychotherapy was focused on examining the details of her failure to adhere to prescribed bedtimes, forgetting to take medication, and other behaviors that worsened her situation. She was withdrawn from the sedative, and her treatment with an antidepressant and a stimulant was empirically adjusted on the basis of the record she kept of her behavior.

Nora's symptoms gradually disappeared, and she was able to move out of her patents' house, get a job, reestablish a social life, and return to graduate school. (From *DSM-IV Casebook.*)

Breathing-Related Sleep Disorder. Breathing-related sleep disorder is characterized by sleep disruption leading to excessive sleepiness or insomnia that is due to a sleep-related breathing disturbance (Table 24.2–11). Breathing disturbances that may occur during sleep include apneas, hypopneas, and oxygen desaturations. These disturbances invariably cause hypersomnia. Two disorders of the respiratory system that can produce hypersomnia are sleep apnea and central alveolar hypoventilation. Both disorders can also cause insomnia but more commonly produce hypersomnia.

OBSTRUCTIVE SLEEP APNEA SYNDROME. Many people—older people and obese people, even those without clinical symptoms—are likely to have apneic periods in sleep and, in general, more respiratory problems in sleep than when awake. Sleep apnea refers to the cessation of airflow at the nose or the mouth. By convention, an apneic period is one that lasts 10 seconds or more. Sleep apnea can be of several distinct types. In pure central sleep apnea, both airflow and respiratory effort (abdomen and chest) cease during the apneic episodes and begin again during arousals. In pure obstructive sleep apnea, airflow ceases but respiratory effort increases during apneic periods; this pattern indicates an obstruction in the airway and increasing efforts by the abdominal and thoracic muscles to force air past the obstruction. Again, the episode ceases with an arousal. The mixed types involve elements of both obstructive and central sleep apnea.

Sleep apnea usually is considered pathological if patients have at least five apneic episodes an hour or 30 apneic episodes during the night. In severe cases of obstructive sleep apnea, patients may have as many as 300 apneic episodes, each followed by an arousal. Thus almost no normal sleep occurs, even though patients have been in bed and often assume that they have been sleeping for the entire night.

Sleep apnea can be a dangerous condition. It is thought to account for a number of unexplained deaths and crib deaths of infants and children. It is probably also responsible for many pulmonary and cardiovascular deaths in adults and in older people. Episodes of sleep apnea can produce cardiovascular changes, including arrhythmias, and transient alterations in blood pressure for each apneic episode. Long-standing sleep apnea is associated with an increase in pulmonary blood pressure and eventually an increase in systemic blood pressure as well. These cardiovascular changes in sleep apnea may account for a considerable number of cases in which the diagnosis is essential hypertension.

The prevalence of sleep apnea in the population has not been established, but an increasing number of cases are discovered as awareness of its existence grows. In a recent survey of patients with daytime sleepiness whose disorder was serious enough for them to be evaluated polygraphically at a sleep disorders center, 42 percent were found to be suffering from one of the variants of sleep apnea.

A tentative diagnosis of sleep apnea can be made even without polysomnographic recordings. The most characteristic picture is that of middle-aged or older men who report tiredness and inability to stay awake in the daytime, sometimes associated with depression, mood changes, and daytime sleep attacks. They may or may not complain of anything unusual during sleep. When a history is obtained from a spouse or bed partner, it includes reports of loud, intermittent snoring, at times accompanied by gasping. Observers sometimes recall apneic periods when patients appeared to be trying to breathe but were unable to do so. Such patients almost certainly have obstructive sleep apnea. With central or mixed apnea, the complaints are of repeated awakenings during the night, associated with morning headaches and mood changes, but with no difficulty of falling asleep. At onset, the patients may have no complaints at all, although bed partners or roommates report heavy snoring and restless sleep. Obese patients with the disorder are said to have pickwickian syndrome.

Patients suspected of having sleep apnea should undergo laboratory recordings. The usual all-night sleep recordings including EEG, electromyogram (EMG), electrocardiogram (ECG), and respiratory tracings of various kinds are useful. Recording airflow and respiratory effort is usually necessary to make a diagnosis. The severity of apneic episodes is determined by using oximetry to measure oxygen saturation during the night. Twenty-four-hour ECG monitoring is sometimes useful to monitor cardiac changes.

Nasal continuous positive airway pressure (nCPAP) is the treatment of choice for obstructive sleep apnea. Other procedures include weight loss, nasal surgery, tracheostomy, and uvulopalatoplasty. No medications are consistently effective in normalizing sleep in patients with apnea. When sleep apnea is established or suspected, patients must avoid the use of sedative medication, including alcohol, because it can considerably exacerbate the condition, which may then become life threatening.

Table 24.2–11
DSM-IV Diagnostic Criteria for Breathing-Related Sleep Disorder

A. Sleep disruption, leading to excessive sleepiness or insomnia, that is judged to be due to a sleep-related condition (eg, obstructive or central sleep apnea syndrome or central alveolar hypoventilation syndrome).

B. The disturbance is not better accounted for by another mental disorder and is not due to the direct physiological effects of a substance (eg, a drug of abuse, a medication) or another general medical condition (other than a breathing-related disorder).

Coding note: Also code sleep-related breathing disorder on Axis III.

Mr. Grim is a 46-year-old advertising salesman and writer for a small magazine. During 15 years of marriage, his wife had noticed loud snoring and episodes, lasting 10 to 15 seconds, during which he did not breathe. "Then he takes a giant breath, exhales, inhales 1 to 4 or 5 times, then he stops breathing for another one of these silences." During longer, "not-breathing" periods, as she called them, "He is very restless. He can dish out quite a kick or punch if I haven't moved far enough out of the way." After nights full of such events, Mr. Grim groggily drags himself out of bed, finding he has a headache.

Mr. Grim is usually sleepy during the day, especially while driving the turnpike around New England, which his work requires. To remain vigilant, he munches on coin-machine sandwiches, washed down by gallons of Coca-Cola. Any alcoholic beverages make him want to fall asleep.

As a result of his snacks, Mr. Grim has 280 pounds packed onto his 5-foot 8-inch frame. He is able to diet and lost weight only temporarily. Recently he has developed a hiatus hernia (associated with stomach pains and indigestion), mild diabetes, and high blood pressure, all complications of the obesity.

When he was a child, his mother constantly berated him for being too fat, and he feared she would starve him. It was then that he developed a habit of stopping for food whenever he was out of the house.

Nasal stuffiness during the ragweed season worsened his snoring, the nocturnal ''struggles,'' and the morning headaches. Just before his first interview about his sleep problems, he had cleaned out an old barn and attic, both full of dust and pigeon droppings, and had had a severe allergy attack. It was for this reason that he came for help.

Physical examination disclosed a deviated nasal septum, enlargement and thickening of pharyngeal structures, and collapse of his pharyngeal walls into the airway upon taking a deep breath with his nose blocked.

A daytime continuous performance test was administered. The test involved his pushing a button whenever he saw certain letters, presented at a rate of one per second. He scored 44 percent correct (compared with a normal rate of 66 percent to 78 percent), indicating moderate impairment in concentration, which was worse in the morning. Laboratory sleep monitoring revealed recurrent 15- to 66-second periods of not breathing (sleep apnea), associated with decreased oxygen saturation (frequently below 50 percent) and decreased heart rate (50 to 55 beats a minute), followed by increased rates (to about 90 a minute). No normal periods of deep sleep were recorded on the polysomnograph. These findings indicated severe sleep apnea, which interfered with the quality of his nocturnal sleep and caused his daytime sleepiness and impaired daytime arousal. The clinician decided that Mr. Grim's obesity and the structural and functional impairment of his upper airway were the cause of the apnea.

DISCUSSION

Mr. Grim's primary problem is chronic excessive daytime sleepiness (hypersomnia), which is caused by recurrent periods of sleep apnea, which in turn result in sleep that is adequate in amount but not restful. Breathing-related sleep disorder is noted on Axis I. On Axis III, the associated general medical conditions are noted: sleep apnea associated with obesity, deviated nasal septum, and other upper airway obstructions. We also note the hypertension, hiatus hernia, and diabetes.

The cluster of symptoms that Mr. Grim has—loud snoring, respiratory pauses, upper airway problems, obesity, and hypertension—is commonly seen in people with the chief complaint of hypersomnia who present at sleep disorder centers.

Treatment of the sleep apnea was CPAP, a technique in which the pressure of the inspired air is increased by a machine connected to the patient with a tube and face mask at night, which helps overcome the airway obstruction. The patient's snoring and sleepiness were rapidly relieved, and he was now motivated, for the first time, to stay on a diet. Within 6 months he lost 80 pounds. He said he felt ''like I have gotten my youth back.'' (From *DSM-IV Casebook.*)

CENTRAL ALVEOLAR HYPOVENTILATION. Central alveolar hypoventilation refers to several conditions marked by impaired ventilation in which the respiratory abnormality appears or greatly worsens only during sleep and in which significant apneic episodes are not present. The ventilatory dysfunction is characterized by inadequate tidal volume or respiratory rate during sleep. Death may occur during sleep (Ondine's curse). Central alveolar hypoventilation is treated with some form of mechanical ventilation (for example, nasal ventilation).

Circadian Rhythm Sleep Disorder. Circadian rhythm sleep disorder includes a wide range of conditions involving a misalignment between desired and actual sleep periods. DSM-IV lists four types of circadian rhythm sleep disorder: delayed sleep phase type, jet lag type, shift work type, and unspecified (Table 24.2–12).

DELAYED SLEEP PHASE TYPE. Delayed sleep phase type of circadian rhythm sleep disorder is marked by sleep and wake times that are intractably later than desired, actual sleep times at virtually the same daily clock hour, no

Table 24.2–12
DSM-IV Diagnostic Criteria for Circadian Rhythm Sleep Disorder

A. A persistent or recurrent pattern of sleep disruption leading to excesive sleepiness or insomnia that is due to mismatch between the sleep-wake schedule required by a person's environment and his or her circadian sleep-wake pattern.

B. The sleep disturbance causes clinically significant distress or impairment in social, occupational, or other important areas of functioning.

C. The disturbance does not occur exclusively during the course of another sleep disorder or other mental disorder.

D. The disturbance is not due to the direct effects of a substance (eg, a drug of abuse, a medication) or a general medical condition.

Specify type:

Delayed sleep phase type: a persistent pattern of late sleep onset and late awakening times, with an inability to fall asleep and awaken at a desired earlier time.

Jet lag type: sleepiness and alertness that occur at an inappropriate time of day relative to local time, occurring after repeated travel across more than one time zone.

Shift work type: insomnia during major sleep period or excessive sleepiness during major wake period associated with night-shift work or frequently changing shift work.

Unspecified type

reported difficulty in maintaining sleep once begun, and an inability to advance the sleep phase by enforcing conventional sleep and wake times. The patients' major complaint is often the difficulty of falling asleep at a desired conventional time, and their disorder may appear to be similar to a sleep onset insomnia. Daytime sleepiness often occurs secondary to sleep loss.

Delayed sleep phase type can be treated by gradually delaying the hour of sleep over a period of several days until the desired sleep time is achieved. The strategy works when advancing the sleep time does not work. The process of sleep phase adjustment can be assisted by the brief use of short-half-life hypnotic agents, such as triazolam (Halcion), to enforce sleep. Another approach to treating delayed sleep phase type is the use of light therapy. Evening light therapy tends to delay sleep; regular morning light exposure tends to advance sleep.

JET LAG TYPE. Depending on the length of the east-to-west trip and individual sensitivity, jet lag type usually disappears spontaneously in 2 to 7 days; no specific treatment is required. Some people find that they can prevent the symptoms by altering their mealtimes and sleep times in an appropriate direction before traveling. Others find that what appear to be symptoms of jet lag (fatigue and so on) are actually associated with sleep deprivation and that simply obtaining enough sleep helps. Melatonin taken orally at prescribed times is of use for some persons who respond.

SHIFT WORK TYPE. Shift work type of circadian rhythm sleep disorder occurs in people who repeatedly and rapidly change their work schedules and occasionally in people with self-imposed chaotic sleep schedules. The most frequent symptom is a period of mixed insomnia and somnolence, but many other symptoms and somatic problems, including peptic ulcer, may be associated with the pattern after some time. Some adolescents and young adults appear to withstand such changes remarkably well and show few symptoms, but older people and those with sensitivity to change are clearly affected.

The symptoms are generally worst the first few days after shifting to a new schedule, but in some people the disrupted sleep–wake patterns persist for a long time. Enforcement of new sleep hours and light therapy may help workers adjust to their new schedules. Many people never adapt completely to unusual shift schedules because they maintain the altered pattern only 5 days a week and return to the prevailing pattern of the rest of the population on days off and on vacations.

Shift work schedules are an important area that has not received sufficient study, especially in view of the unusual shifts and changing shift schedules that a large proportion of the population now work. People's sensitivities to shifting schedules vary widely, but the bodies of a fair number of people simply do not adapt to shift work; therefore, these people should not be assigned to work in shifts. Temperamentally, some people are ''owls,'' who like to stay up at night and sleep during the day, and others are ''larks,'' who rise early and retire early.

A particular problem occurs in the training of physicians, who are often required to work 36 to 48 hours without sleeping. This condition is dangerous to both doctors and their patients. It behooves medical educators to develop more shifts for doctors in training.

UNSPECIFIED. *Advanced Sleep Phase Syndrome.* Advanced sleep phase syndrome is characterized by sleep onsets and wake times that are intractably earlier than desired, actual sleep times at virtually the same daily clock hour, no reported difficulty in maintaining sleep once begun, and an inability to delay the sleep phase by enforcing conventional sleep and wake times. Unlike delayed sleep phase type, the condition does not interfere with the work or school day. The major presenting complaint is the inability to stay awake in the evening and to sleep in the morning until desired conventional times.

Disorganized Sleep–Wake Pattern. Disorganized sleep–wake pattern is defined as irregular and variable sleep and waking behavior that disrupts the regular sleep–wake pattern. The condition is associated with frequent daytime naps at irregular times and excessive bed rest. Sleep at night is not of adequate length, and the condition may seem to be insomnia, although the total amount of sleep in 24 hours is normal for the patient's age.

Table 24.2–13
DSM-IV Diagnostic Criteria for Dyssomnia Not Otherwise Specified

The dyssomnia not otherwise specified category is for insomnias, hypersomnias, or circadian rhythm disturbances that do not meet criteria for any specific dyssomnia. Examples include

1. Complaints of clinically significant insomnia or hypersomnia that are attributable to environmental factors (eg, noise, light, frequent interruptions).
2. Excessive sleepiness that is attributable to ongoing sleep deprivation.
3. Idiopathic "restless legs syndrome": uncomfortable sensations (eg, discomfort, crawling sensations, or restlessness) that lead to an intense urge to move the legs. Typically, the sensations begin in the evening before sleep onset and are temporarily relieved by moving the legs or walking, only to begin again when the legs are immobile. The sensations can delay sleep onset or awaken the individual from sleep.
4. Idiopathic periodic limb movements ("nocturnal myoclonus"): repeated low-amplitude brief limb jerks, particularly in the lower extremities. These movements begin near sleep onset and decrease during stage 3 or 4 non–rapid eye movement (NREM) and rapid eye movement (REM) sleep. Movements usually occur rhythmically every 20–60 seconds, leading to repeated, brief arousals. Individuals are typically unaware of the actual movements, but may complain of insomnia, frequent awakenings, or daytime sleepiness if the number of movements is very large.
5. Situations in which the clinician has concluded that a dyssomnia is present but is unable to determine whether it is primary, due to a general medical condition, or substance induced.

Dyssomnia Not Otherwise Specified. According to DSM-IV, dyssomnia not otherwise specified includes insomnias, hypersomnias, and circadian rhythm disturbances that do not meet the criteria for any specific dyssomnia (Table 24.2–13).

NOCTURNAL MYOCLONUS. Nocturnal myoclonus consists of highly stereotyped abrupt contractions of certain leg muscles during sleep. Patients lack any subjective awareness of the leg jerks. The condition may be present in about 40 percent of people over age 65.

The repetitive leg movements occur every 20 to 60 seconds, with extension of the large toe and flexion of the ankle, the knee, and the hips. Frequent awakenings, unrefreshing sleep, and daytime sleepiness are major symptoms. No treatment for nocturnal myoclonus is universally effective. Treatments that may be useful include benzodiazepines, levodopa (Larodopa), quinine, and, in rare cases, opioids.

RESTLESS LEGS SYNDROME. In restless legs syndrome people feel deep sensations of creeping inside the calves whenever sitting or lying down. The dysesthesias are rarely painful but are agonizingly relentless and cause an almost irresistible urge to move the legs; thus this syndrome interferes with sleep and with falling asleep. It peaks in middle age and occurs in 5 percent of the population.

The syndrome has no established treatment. Symptoms of restless legs syndrome are relieved by movement and by leg massage. When pharmacotherapy is required, the benzodiazepines, levodopa, quinine, opioids, propranolol (Inderal), and carbamazepine (Tegretol) are of some benefit.

KLEINE-LEVIN SYNDROME. Kleine-Levin syndrome is a relatively rare condition consisting of recurrent periods of prolonged sleep (from which patients may be aroused) with intervening periods of normal sleep and alert waking. During the hypersomniac episodes, wakeful periods are usually marked by withdrawal from social contacts and return to bed at the first opportunity; patients may also display apathy, irritability, confusion, voracious eating, loss of sexual inhibitions, delusions, hallucinations, frank disorientation, memory impairment, incoherent speech, excitation or depression, and truculence. Unexplained fevers have occurred in a few patients.

Kleine-Levin syndrome is uncommon. About 100 cases with features suggesting the diagnosis have been reported. In most cases, several periods of hypersomnia, each lasting for one or several weeks, are experienced by patients over a year. With few exceptions the first attack occurs between the ages of 10 and 21 years. Rare instances of onset in the fourth and fifth decades of life have been reported. The syndrome appears to be almost invariably self-limited, and enduring remission occurs spontaneously before age 40 in early-onset cases.

MENSTRUAL-ASSOCIATED SYNDROME. Some women experience intermittent marked hypersomnia, altered behavioral patterns, and voracious eating at or shortly before the onset of their menses. Nonspecific EEG abnormalities similar to those associated with Kleine-Levin syndrome have been documented in several instances. Endocrine factors are probably involved, but specific abnormalities in laboratory endocrine measures have not been reported. Increased cerebrospinal fluid (CSF) turnover of 5-hydroxytryptamine (5-HT) was identified in one patient.

INSUFFICIENT SLEEP. Insufficient sleep is defined as an earnest complaint of daytime sleepiness and associated waking symptoms by a person who persistently fails to obtain sufficient daily sleep to support alert wakefulness. The person is voluntarily, but often unwittingly, chronically sleep deprived. The diagnosis can usually be made on the basis of the history, including a sleep log. Some people, especially students and shift workers, who want to maintain an active daytime life and perform their nighttime jobs, may seriously deprive themselves of sleep and thus produce somnolence during waking hours.

SLEEP DRUNKENNESS. Sleep drunkenness is an abnormal form of awakening in which the lack of a clear sensorium in the transition from sleep to full wakefulness is prolonged and exaggerated. A confusion state develops that often leads to individual or social inconvenience and sometimes to criminal acts. Essential to the diagnosis is the absence of sleep deprivation. It is a rare condition, and there may be a familial tendency. Before making the diagnosis, clinicians should examine patients' sleep and rule out such conditions as apnea, nocturnal myoclonus, narcolepsy, and an excessive use of alcohol and other substances.

Parasomnias

Nightmare Disorder. Nightmares are long, frightening dreams from which people awaken frightened (Table 24.2–14). Like other dreams, nightmares almost always occur during REM sleep and usually after a long REM period late in the night. Some people have frequent nightmares as a lifelong condition; others experience them predominantly at times of stress and illness. About 50 percent of the adult population may report occasional nightmares. No specific treatment is usually required for nightmare disorder. Agents that suppress REM sleep, such as tricyclic drugs, may reduce the frequency of nightmares, and benzodiazepines have also been used. Contrary to popular belief, no harm results from awakening a person who is having a nightmare.

Table 24.2–14
DSM-IV Diagnostic Criteria for Nightmare Disorder

A. Repeated awakening from the major sleep period or naps with detailed recall of extended and extremely frightening dreams, usually involving threats to survival, security, or self-esteem. The awakenings generally occur during the second half of the sleep period.

B. On awakening from the frightening dream, the person rapidly becomes oriented and alert (in contrast to the confusion and disorientation seen in sleep terror disorder and some forms of epilepsy).

C. The dream experience, or the sleep disturbance resulting from the awakening, causes clinically significant distress or impairment in social, occupational, or other important areas of functioning.

D. The nightmares do not occur exclusively during the course of another mental disorder (eg, a delirium, posttraumatic stress disorder) and are not due to the direct physiological effects of a substance (eg, a drug of abuse, a medication) or a general medical condition.

Monika is an 18-year-old Austrian woman who lives with her parents. From an early age, she had very vivid dreams. However, at the age of 17 she began to suffer very frightening dreams that caused her to wake up terrified and extremely agitated. Initially the frightening dreams occurred on about one night in three, but over about 9 months their regularity increased until she was having the dreams every night and sometimes repeatedly during the night. The dreams contained several recurrent themes of being pregnant, suffering severe pain during childbirth, or witnessing the violent and bloody deaths of relatives or friends. On waking, Monika was always alert and oriented, but she was often afraid of going back to sleep in case the same dream continued. Typically, the dreams occurred between 4:00 and 6:00 AM. When she got up in the morning, she felt tired and complained of lack of energy during the day. Sometimes even in the daytime, she would briefly relive her frightening dream experiences. Monika was very attached to her brother, and the onset of her frightening dreams coincided with his leaving home for college. At the same time, she was worried about her coming examinations and about the fact that she would probably have to leave home soon herself if she wanted to continue her studies.

Monika's early development was normal except that she often wet her bed at night until she was 8 years old. As a child she went through a time of being afraid to go to bed after seeing frightening television movies. She described herself as a perfectionist and "something of a worrier" who found it hard to cope with changes in her life and who had little self-confidence. She had one close girlfriend and a few friends with whom she was not so close, but she had no boyfriend. She had never had sexual experiences, and she admitted worrying that she might not be able "to find the right person."

Monika had no difficulties in school. She was studious and was generally determined to get good grades. She said she would like to go to college if she could pass the examinations, which would begin in about 1 month. However, she very much feared being without her family, and she doubted whether she had been wise in choosing to study economics, although her choice of this subject was made only after a great deal of deliberation.

Monika's father and mother were both schoolteachers. The young woman described the marriage of her parents as stable, but she said that her relationship with her parents "could be better." She found her mother rather pessimistic and negative, whereas her father tended to overemphasize the important of good school grades. Both parents were very busy and usually had little time for Monika and her brother. The brother, who was 2 years older than Monika, had to repeat a year's studies at school, which represented a great failure in the eyes of her father. Monika had always had a very good relationship with her brother, and they had spent many hours together when their parents were both working. They always supported each other in arguments with other children.

There was no history of neurological or other physical disease and no evidence of alcohol or drug use. Monika had received no medication for her problem.

DISCUSSION

Monika suffered from nightmare disorder—dream experiences that are loaded with anxiety or fear and of which the individual has very detailed recall. Typically, the dreams include recurrent themes that involve threats to survival, security, or self-esteem. Upon awakening, usually during the second half of the sleep period, the individual is alert and oriented. During the episode there is no or only minimal vocalization. These characteristics make the distinction from sleep terrors possible, as sleep terrors occur during the first third of the sleep period and are associated with intense vocalization, body motility, the person's relative lack of response to the efforts of others to influence the event, and the absence of recollection of the episode on awakening. (From *ICD-10 Casebook.*)

Table 24.2–15
DSM-IV Diagnostic Criteria for Sleep Terror Disorder

A. Recurrent episodes of abrupt awakening from sleep, usually occurring during the first third of the major sleep episode and beginning with a panicky scream.
B. Intense fear and signs of autonomic arousal, such as tachycardia, rapid breathing, and sweating, during each episode.
C. Relative unresponsiveness to efforts of others to comfort the person during the episode.
D. No detailed dream is recalled and there is amnesia for the episode.
E. The episodes cause clinically significant distress or impairment in social, occupational, or other important areas of functioning.
F. The disturbance is not due to the direct physiological effects of a substance (eg, a drug of abuse, a medication) or a general medical condition.

Sleep Terror Disorder. A sleep terror is an arousal in the first third of the night during deep non–REM (NREM) (stages 3 and 4) sleep. It is almost invariably inaugurated by a piercing scream or cry and accompanied by behavioral manifestations of intense anxiety bordering on panic (Table 24.2–15).

Typically, patients sit up in bed with a frightened expression, scream loudly, and sometimes awaken immediately with a sense of intense terror. Patients may remain awake in a disoriented state but more often, fall asleep, and, as with sleepwalking, they forget the episodes. A night terror episode after the original scream frequently develops into a sleepwalking episode. Polygraphic recordings of night terrors are somewhat like those of sleepwalking; in fact, the two conditions appear to be closely related. Night terrors, as isolated episodes, are especially frequent in children. About 1 to 6 percent of children have the disorder, which is more common in boys than in girls and which tends to run in families.

Night terrors may reflect a minor neurological abnormality, perhaps in the temporal lobe or underlying structures, because when night terrors begin in adolescence and young adulthood, they turn out to be the first symptom of temporal lobe epilepsy. In a typical case of night terrors, however, no signs of temporal lobe epilepsy or other seizure disorders are seen either clinically or on EEG recordings.

Although night terrors are closely related to sleepwalking and are occasionally related to enuresis, they are different from nightmares. Night terrors are associated with simply awakening in terror: Patients generally have no dream recall but may occasionally recall a single frightening image.

Specific treatment for night terror disorder is seldom required. Investigation of stressful family situations may be important, and individual or family therapy is sometimes useful. In the rare cases in which medication is required, diazepam (Valium) in small doses at bedtime improves the condition and sometimes completely eliminates the attacks.

Sleepwalking Disorder. Sleepwalking, also known as somnambulism, consists of a sequence of complex behaviors that are initiated in the first third of the night during deep NREM (stages 3 and 4) sleep and frequently, although not always, progress—without full consciousness or later memory of the episode—to leaving bed and walking about (Table 24.2–16).

Patients sit up and sometimes perform perseverative motor acts, such as walking, dressing, going to the bathroom, talking, screaming, and even driving. The behavior occasionally terminates in an awakening with several minutes of confusion; more frequently, they return to sleep without any recollection of the sleepwalking event. An artificially induced arousal from stage 4 sleep can sometimes produce the condition. For instance, in children, especially those with a history of sleepwalking, an attack can sometimes be provoked by standing

Table 24.2–16
DSM-IV Diagnostic Criteria for Sleepwalking Disorder

A. Repeated episodes of rising from bed during sleep and walking about, usually occurring during the first third of the major sleep episode.
B. While sleepwalking, the person has a blank, staring face, is relatively unresponsive to the efforts of others to communicate with him or her, and can be awakened only with great difficulty.
C. On awakeninig (either from the sleepwalking episode or the next morning), the person has amnesia for the episode.
D. Within several minutes after awakening from the sleepwalking episode, there is no impairment of mental activity or behavior (although there may initially be a short period of confusion or disorientation).
E. The sleepwalking causes clinically significant distress or impairment in social, occupational, or other important areas of functioning.
F. The disturbance is not due to the direct physiological effects of a substance (eg, a drug of abuse, a medication), or a general medical condition.

them on their feet and thus producing a partial arousal during stage 4 sleep.

Sleepwalking usually begins between ages 4 and 8. Peak prevalence is at about 12 years of age. The disorder is more common in boys than in girls, and about 15 percent of children have an occasional episode. It tends to run in families. A minor neurological abnormality probably underlies the condition; the episodes should not be considered purely psychogenic, although stressful periods are associated with an increase in sleepwalking in affected people. Extreme tiredness or previous sleep deprivation exacerbates attacks. The disorder is occasionally dangerous because of the possibility of accidental injury. Treatment consists of measures to prevent injury and of drugs that suppress stages 3 and 4 sleep. The sleepwalker may be awakened during the episode without ill effects.

An 11-year-old girl asked her mother to take her to a psychiatrist because she feared she might be ''going crazy.'' Several times during the last 2 months she had awakened confused about where she was until she realized she was on the living room couch or in her little sister's bed, even though she went to bed in her own room. When she recently woke up in her older brother's bedroom, she became very concerned and felt quite guilty about it. Her younger sister said that she had seen the patient walking during the night, looking like a ''zombie,'' that she didn't answer when she called her, and that the patient had done that several times, but usually went back to her bed. The patient feared she might have ''amnesia'' because she had no memory of anything happening during the night.

There is no history of seizures or of similar episodes during the day. An EEG and physical examination proved normal. The patient's mental status was unremarkable except for some anxiety about her symptoms and the usual early adolescent concerns. School and family functioning were excellent.

DISCUSSION

This girl was not ''going crazy'' but, rather, was experiencing the characteristic features of sleepwalking disorder: episodes of arising from bed during sleep and walking about, appearing unresponsive during episodes, experiencing amnesia for the episode upon awakening, and exhibiting no evidence of impairment in consciousness several minutes after awakening. Psychomotor epileptic seizures were ruled out by the normal EEG and the absence of any seizurelike behavior during the waking state.

Although the process of dissociation is involved in sleepwalking disorder, because the disturbance begins during sleep, it was classified as sleep disorder rather than as a dissociative disorder. (From *DSM-IV Casebook.*)

Parasomnia Not Otherwise Specified. The diagnostic criteria for parasomnia not otherwise specified are given in Table 24.2–17.

SLEEP-RELATED BRUXISM. Bruxism, tooth grinding, occurs throughout the night, most prominently in stage 2 sleep. According to dentists, 5 to 10 percent of the population suffer from bruxism severe enough to produce noticeable damage to teeth. The condition often goes unnoticed by the sleepers, except for an occasional jaw ache in the morning, but bed partners and roommates are consistently awakened by the sound. Treatment consists of a dental bite plate and corrective orthodontic procedures.

Table 24.2–17
DSM-IV Diagnostic Criteria for Parasomnia Not Otherwise Specified

The parasomnia not otherwise specified category is for disturbances that are characterized by abnormal behavioral or physiological events during sleep or sleep-wake transitions, but that do not meet criteria for a more specific parasomnia. Examples include

1. REM sleep behavior disorder: motor activity, often of violent nature, that arises during rapid eye movement (REM) sleep. Unlike sleepwalking, these episodes tend to occur later in the night and are associated with vivid dream recall.
2. Sleep paralysis: an inability to perform voluntary movement during the transition between wakefulness and sleep. The episodes may occur at sleep onset (hypnagogic) or with awakening (hypnopompic). The episodes are usually associated with extreme anxiety and, in some cases, fear of impending death. Sleep paralysis occurs commonly as an ancillary symptom of narcolepsy and, in such cases, should not be coded separately.
3. Situations in which the clinician has concluded that a parasomnia is present but is unable to determine whether it is primary, due to a general medical condition, or substance induced.

REM SLEEP BEHAVIOR DISORDER. REM sleep behavior disorder is a chronic and progressive condition found mainly in men. It is characterized by the loss of atonia during REM sleep and subsequent emergence of violent and complex behaviors. In essence, patients with the disorder are acting out their dreams. Serious injury to patients or bed partners is a major risk. The development or aggravation of the disorder has been reported in patients with narcolepsy who have been treated with psychostimulants and tricyclic drugs and in patients with depression and obsessive-compulsive disorder who have been treated with fluoxetine (Prozac). REM sleep behavior disorder is treated with clonazepam (Klonopin), 0.5 to 2.0 mg a day. Carbamazepine, 100 mg 3 times a day, is also effective in controlling the disorder.

SLEEPTALKING (SOMNILOQUY). Sleeptalking is common in children and adults. It has been studied extensively in the sleep laboratory and is found to occur in all stages of sleep. The talking usually involves a few words that are difficult to distinguish. Long episodes of talking involve the sleeper's life and concerns, but sleeptalkers do not relate their dreams during sleep, nor do they often reveal deep secrets. Episodes of sleeptalking sometimes accompany night terrors and sleepwalking. Sleeptalking alone requires no treatment.

SLEEP-RELATED HEAD BANGING (JACTATIO CAPITIS NOCTURNA). Sleep-related head banging is the term for a sleep behavior consisting chiefly of rhythmic to-and-fro head rocking, less commonly of total body rocking, occurring just before or during sleep. Usually, it is observed in the immediate presleep period and is sustained into light sleep. It uncommonly persists into or occurs in deep NREM sleep. Treatment consists of measures to prevent injury.

SLEEP PARALYSIS. Familial sleep paralysis is characterized by a sudden inability to execute voluntary movements either just at the onset of sleep or on awakening during the night or in the morning.

SLEEP DISORDERS RELATED TO ANOTHER MENTAL DISORDER

DSM-IV defines a sleep disorder related to another mental disorder as a complaint of sleep disturbance caused by a diagnosable mental disorder but severe enough to merit clinical attention on its own.

Insomnia Related to Axis I or Axis II Disorder

Insomnia that occurs for at least 1 month and that is clearly related to the psychological and behavioral symptoms of the clinically well-known mental disorders is classified here (Table 24.2–18). The category consists of a heterogeneous group of conditions. The sleep problem is usually, but not always, difficulty in falling asleep and is secondary to anxiety that is part of any of the various mental disorders listed. The insomnia is more common in women than in men. In clear-cut cases in which the anxiety has psychological roots, psychiatric treatment of the cause of the anxiety (for example, individual psychotherapy, group psychotherapy, or family therapy) often relieves the insomnia.

The insomnia associated with major depressive disorder involves relatively normal sleep onset but repeated awakenings during the second half of the night and premature morning awakening, usually with an uncomfortable mood in the morning. (Morning is the worst time of day for many patients with major depressive disorder.) Polysomnography shows reduced stages 3 and 4 sleep, often a short REM latency, and a long first REM period. The use of partial or total sleep deprivation can accelerate the response to antidepressant medication.

Table 24.2–18
DSM-IV Diagnostic Criteria for Insomnia Related to Axis I or Axis II Disorder

A. The predominant complaint is difficulty initiating or maintaining sleep, or nonrestorative sleep, for at least one month that is associated with daytime fatigue or impaired daytime functioning.
B. The sleep disturbance (or daytime sequelae) causes clinically significant distress or impairment in social, occupational, or other important areas of functioning.
C. The insomnia is judged to be related to another Axis I or Axis II disorder (eg, major depressive disorder, generalized anxiety disorder, adjustment disorder with anxiety) but is sufficiently severe to warrant independent clinical attention.
D. The disturbance is not better accounted for by another sleep disorder (eg, narcolepsy, breathing-related sleep disorder, a parasomnia).
E. The disturbance is not due to the direct physiological effects of a substance (eg, a drug of abuse, a medication) or a general medical condition.

Panic disorder may be associated with paroxysmal awakenings or with entering stages 3 and 4 sleep. The emotional and cognitive symptoms of a panic attack are present, along with tachycardia and increased respiratory rate. Patients with manic episodes and bipolar II disorder appear to be extreme cases of short sleepers. They sometimes appear to have difficulty in falling asleep but most often do not complain of sleep problems. They awaken refreshed after 2 to 4 hours of sleep and appear to have a true reduction in their need for sleep during the course of the manic or hypomanic episode. In schizophrenia, total sleep time and slow-wave sleep are reduced. REM sleep is often reduced early during an exacerbation. Other conditions associated with insomnia include posttraumatic stress disorder (nightmares), obsessive-compulsive disorder (rituals), and eating disorders.

Hypersomnia Related to Axis I or Axis II Disorder

Hypersomnia that occurs for at least 1 month and that is associated with a mental disorder is found in a variety of conditions, including mood disorders. Excessive daytime sleepiness may be reported in the initial stages of many mild depressive disorders and characteristically in the depressed phase of bipolar I disorder. For a few weeks, hypersomnia may sometimes be associated with uncomplicated grief. Other mental disorders—such as personality disorders, dissociative disorders, somatoform disorders, dissociative fugue, and amnestic disorders—can produce hypersomnia (Table 24.2–19). Treatment of the primary disorder should result in the resolution of the hypersomnia.

Table 24.2–19
DSM-IV Diagnostic Criteria for Hypersomnia Related to Axis I or Axis II Disorder

A. The predominant complaint is excessive sleepiness for at least 1 month as evidenced by either prolonged sleep episodes or daytime sleep episodes that occur almost daily.

B. The excessive sleepiness causes clinically significant distress or impairment in social, occupational, or other important areas of functioning.

C. The hypersomnia is judged to be related to another Axis I or Axis II disorder (eg, major depressive disorder, dysthymic disorder), but is sufficiently severe to warrant independent clinical attention.

D. The disturbance is not better is not better accounted for by another sleep disorder (eg, narcolepsy, breathing-related sleep disorder, a parasomnia) or by an inadequate amount of sleep.

E. The disturbance is not due to the direct physiological effects of a substance (eg, a drug of abuse, a medication) or a general medical condition.

Table 24.2–20
DSM-IV Diagnostic Criteria for Sleep Disorder Due to a General Medical Condition

A. A prominent disturbance in sleep that is sufficiently severe to warrant independent clinical attention.

B. There is evidence from the history, physical examination, or laboratory findings that the sleep disturbance is the direct physiological consequence of a general medical condition.

C. The disturbance is not better accounted for by another mental disorder (eg, an adjustment disorder in which the stressor is a serious medical illness).

D. The disturbance does not occur exclusively during the course of a delirium.

E. The disturbance does not meet criteria for a breathing-related sleep disorder or narcolepsy.

F. The sleep disturbance causes clinically significant distress or impairment in social, occupational, or other important areas of functioning.

Specify type:

Insomnia type: if the predominant sleep disturbance is insomnia

Hypersomnia type: if the prominent sleep disturbance is hypersomnia

Parasomnia type: if the prominent sleep disturbance is a parasomnia

Mixed type: if more than one sleep disturbance is present and none predominates

Coding note: Include the name of the general medical condition on Axis I, eg, sleep disorder due to chronic obstructive pulmonary disease, insomnia type; also code the general medical condition on Axis III.

OTHER SLEEP DISORDERS

DSM-IV defines a sleep disorder caused by a medical condition as a complaint of sleep disturbance produced by a physiological effect of the medical condition on the sleep–wake system. A substance-induced sleep disorder arises from the use, or the recently discontinued use, of a substance.

Sleep Disorder Due to a General Medical Condition

Any sleep disturbance (such as insomnia, hypersomnia, parasomnia, or a combination) can be caused by a general medical condition (Table 24.2–20). Almost any medical condition associated with pain and discomfort (such as arthritis or angina) can produce insomnia. Some conditions are associated with insomnia even when pain and discomfort are not specifically present. These conditions include neoplasms, vascular lesions, infections, and degenerative and traumatic conditions. Other conditions, especially endocrine and metabolic diseases, frequently involve some sleep disturbance.

Being aware of the possibility of such conditions and obtaining a good medical history usually lead to a correct diagnosis; the treatment, whenever possible, is treatment of the underlying medical condition.

Sleep-Related Epileptic Seizures. The relation of sleep and epilepsy is complex. Almost every form of epilepsy either improves or becomes worse at various times in the sleep cycle. When seizures occur almost exclusively during sleep, the condition is called sleep epilepsy.

Sleep-Related Cluster Headaches and Chronic Paroxysmal Hemicrania. Sleep-related cluster headaches are agonizingly severe unilateral headaches that often appear during sleep and are marked by an on-off pattern of attacks. Chronic paroxysmal hemicrania is a similar unilateral headache that occurs every day with more frequent but short-lived onsets that are without a preponderant sleep distribution. Both types of vascular headache are examples of sleep-exacerbated conditions and appear in association with REM sleep periods; paroxysmal hemicrania is virtually REM sleep locked.

Sleep-Related Abnormal Swallowing Syndrome. Abnormal swallowing syndrome is a condition during sleep in which inadequate swallowing results in aspiration of saliva, coughing, and choking. It is intermittently associated with brief arousals or awakenings.

Sleep-Related Asthma. Asthma that is exacerbated by sleep in some people may result in significant sleep disturbances.

Sleep-Related Cardiovascular Symptoms. Sleep-related cardiovascular symptoms derive from disorders of cardiac rhythm, myocardial incompetence, coronary artery insufficiency, and blood pressure variability, which may be induced or exacerbated by sleep-altered or sleep-stage–modified cardiovascular physiology.

Sleep-Related Gastroesophageal Reflux. Sleep-related gastroesophageal reflux is a disorder in which patients awaken from sleep with burning, substernal pain or a feeling of general pain or tightness in the chest or a sour taste in the mouth. Coughing, choking, and vague respiratory discomfort may also occur repeatedly.

Sleep-Related Hemolysis (Paroxysmal Nocturnal Hemoglobinuria). Paroxysmal nocturnal hemoglobinuria is a rare, acquired, chronic hemolytic anemia in which intravascular hemolysis results in hemoglobinemia and hemoglobinuria. The hemolysis and consequent hemoglobinuria are accelerated during sleep, and the morning urine is colored a brownish red. Hemolysis is linked to the sleep period, even when the period is shifted.

Substance-Induced Sleep Disorder

Any sleep disturbance (such as insomnia, hypersomnia, parasomnia, or a combination) can be caused by a substance (Table 24.2–21). According to DSM-IV, clinicians should also specify whether the onset of the disorder occurred during intoxication or withdrawal.

Somnolence related to tolerance or withdrawal from a CNS stimulant is common in people withdrawing from amphetamines, cocaine, caffeine, and related substances. The somnolence may be associated with severe depression, which occasionally reaches suicidal proportions. The sustained use of CNS depressants, such as alcohol, can cause somnolence. Heavy alcohol use in the evening produces sleepiness and difficulty in arising the next day. This reaction may present a diagnostic problem when patients do not admit to alcohol abuse.

Insomnia is associated with tolerance to or withdrawal from sedative-hypnotic drugs, such as benzodiazepines, barbiturates, and chloral hydrate. With the sustained use of such agents—usually undertaken to treat insomnia arising from a different source—tolerance increases, and the drugs lose their sleep-inducing effects; patients then often increase the dosage. On sudden discontinuation of the drug, severe sleeplessness supervenes, often accompanied by the general features of substance withdrawal. Typically patients experience a temporary increase in the severity of the insomnia.

Long-term use (more than 30 days) of a hypnotic agent is well tolerated by some patients, but others begin to complain of sleep disturbance, most often multiple brief awakenings during the night. Recordings show a disruption of sleep architecture, reduced stages 3 and 4 sleep, increased stages 1 and 2 sleep, and a fragmentation of sleep throughout the night.

Clinicians should be aware of CNS stimulants as a possible cause of insomnia and should remember that various medications for weight reduction, beverages containing caffeine, and occasionally adrenergic drugs taken by asthmatic patients may all produce this insomnia. Alcohol may help induce sleep but frequently results in nocturnal awakening. Alcohol use during the cocktail hour can produce difficulty in falling asleep later in the evening.

For reasons that are not always clear, a wide variety of drugs occasionally produce sleep problems as a side effect. These drugs include antimetabolites and other cancer chemo-

Table 24.2–21
DSM-IV Diagnostic Criteria for Substance-Induced Sleep Disorder

A. A prominent disturbance in sleep which is sufficiently severe to warrant independent clinical attention.

B. There is evidence from the history, physical examination, or laboratory findings of either (1) or (2):
  (1) The symptoms in criterion A developing during, or within a month of, substance intoxication or withdrawal
  (2) Medication use is etiologically related to the sleep disturbance

C. The disturbance is not better accounted for by a sleep disorder that is not substance induced. Evidence that the symptoms are better accounted for by a sleep disorder that is not substance induced might include the following: the symptoms precede the onset of the substance abuse (or medication use); the symptoms persist for a substantial period of time (eg, about a month) after the cessation of acute withdrawal or severe intoxication, or are substantially in excess of what would be expected given the type or amount of the substance used or the duration of use; or there is other evidence that suggests the existence of an independent non–substance-induced sleep disorder (eg, a history of recurrent non–substance-related episodes).

D. The disturbance does not occur exclusively during the course of a delirium.

E. The sleep disturbance causes clinically significant distress or impairment in social, occupational, or other important areas of functioning.

Note: This diagnosis should be made instead of a diagnosis of substance intoxication or substance withdrawal only when the sleep symptoms are in excess of those usually associated with the intoxication or withdrawal syndrome and when the symptoms are sufficiently severe to warrant independent clinical attention.

Code: [Specific substance]-induced sleep disorder (alcohol; amphetamine; caffeine; cocaine; opioid; sedative, hypnotic, or anxiolytic; other [or unknown] substance)

Specify type:

Insomnia type: if the predominant sleep disturbance is insomnia

Hypersomnia type: if the predominant sleep disturbance is hypersomnia

Parasomnia type: if the prominent sleep disturbance is a parasomnia

Mixed type: if more than one sleep disturbance is present and none predominates

Specify if:

With onset during intoxication: if the criteria are met for intoxication with the substance and the symptoms develop during the intoxication syndrome

With onset during withdrawal: if criteria are met for withdrawal from the substance and the symptoms develop during, or shortly after, a withdrawal syndrome

therapeutic agents, thyroid preparations, anticonvulsant agents, antidepressant drugs, adrenocorticotropic hormone (ACTH)-like drugs, oral contraceptives, α-methyldopa, and β-adrenergic receptor antagonists.

Other agents do not produce sleep disturbance while being used but may have this effect after withdrawal. Almost any drug with sedating or tranquilizing agents, including at times the benzodiazepines, the phenothiazines, the sedating tricyclic drugs, and various street drugs, including marijuana, opiates, and opioids, can have this effect.

Alcohol is a CNS depressant and produces the serious problems of other CNS depressants, both during administration—perhaps related to the development of tolerance—and after withdrawal. The insomnia after long-term alcohol consumption is sometimes severe and lasts for weeks or longer. Clinicians should not give potentially addicting medications to patients who have just recovered from an addiction; if possible, sleeping medications should be avoided.

Among cigarette smokers, the combination of a relaxing ritual and the tendency of low doses of nicotine to cause sedation may actually help sleep, but high doses of nicotine can interfere with sleep, particularly sleep onset. Cigarette smokers typically sleep less than nonsmokers. Nicotine withdrawal may cause drowsiness or arousal.

References

Aldrich MS: The clinical spectrum of narcolepsy and idiopathic hypersomnia. Neurology *46:* 393, 1996.

Bamford CR: Carbamazepine in REM sleep behavior disorder. Sleep *16:* 33, 1992.

Boivin DB, Montplaisir J, Petit D, Lambert C, Lubin S: Effects of modafinil on symptomatology of human narcolepsy. Clin Neuropharmacol *16:* 46, 1993.

Buysse J, Morin CM, Reynolds CF III: Sleep disorders. In *Synopsis of Treatments of Psychiatric Disorders,* ed 2, Gabbard GO, Atkinson SD, editors, pp 1013–1041. American Psychiatric Press, Washington, 1996.

Czeisler CA, Allan JS, Strogatz SH, Ronda JM, Sanchez R, Rios C, Frietag WO, Richardson GS, Kronauer RE: Bright light resets the human circadian pacemaker independent of the timing of the sleep–wake cycle. Science *233:* 667, 1986.

Farney RJ, Walker JM: Office management of common sleep–wake disorders. Med Clin North Am *79:* 391, 1995.

Hartmann PM: Drug treatment of insomnia: Indications and newer agents. Am Fam Physician *51:* 191, 1995.

Karacan I, editor: *Psychophysiological Aspects of Sleep.* Noyes Medical, Park Ridge, NJ, 1981.

Kryger MH, Roth T, Dement WC, editors: *Principles and Practice of Sleep Medicine,* ed 2. Saunders, Philadelphia, 1993.

Mahowald MW: Diagnostic testing: Sleep disorders. Neurol Clin *14:* 183, 1996.

Morin CM, Woote V: Psychological and pharmacological approaches to treating insomnia: Critical issues in assessing their separate and combined effects. Clin Psychol Rev *16:* 521, 1996.

Neylan TC: Treatment of sleep disturbances in depressed patients. J Clin Psychiatry *56:* 56, 1995.

Papadimitriou GN, Christodoulou GN, Katsouyanni K, Stefanis CN: Therapy and prevention of affective illness by total sleep deprivation. J Affect Disord *27:* 107, 1993.

Prinz PN: Sleep and sleep disorders in older adults. J Clin Neurophysiol *12:* 139, 1995.

Regestein QR, Monk TH: Delayed sleep phase syndrome: A review of its clinical aspects. Am J Psychiatry *152:* 602, 1995.

Schneck CH, Mahowald MW: Long-term, nightly benzodiazepine treatment of injurious parasomnias and other disorders of disrupted nocturnal sleep in 170 adults. Am J Med *100:* 333, 1996.

Schramm E, Hohagen F, Grasshoff U, Riemann D, Hajak G, Weeb H-G, Berger M: Test–retest reliability and validity of the structured interview for sleep disorders according to DSM-III-R. Am J Psychiatry *150:* 867, 1993.

Stradling JR: Recreational drugs and sleep. Br J Med *306:* 573, 1993.

Tyrer P: Withdrawal from hypnotic drugs. Br J Med *306:* 706, 1993.

Williams RL, Karacan I, Moore C, editors: *Sleep Disorders: Diagnosis and Treatment,* ed 2. Wiley, New York, 1988.

Williams RL, Karacan I, Moore CA, Hirshkowitz M: Sleep disorders. In *Comprehensive Textbook of Psychiatry,* ed 6, HI Kaplan, BJ Sadock, editors, p 1373. Williams & Wilkins, Baltimore, 1995.

25

Impulse-Control Disorders Not Elsewhere Classified

The fourth edition of *Diagnostic and Statistical Manual of Mental Disorders* (DSM-IV) lists six categories of impulse-control disorders not classified elsewhere: intermittent explosive disorder, kleptomania, pyromania, pathological gambling, trichotillomania, and impulse-control disorder not otherwise specified. As defined in DSM-IV, the disorders of impulse control share certain features. Patients with these disorders do not resist impulses, drives, or enticements to do something harmful to themselves or to others. Patients may or may not consciously try to resist the impulses, and they may or may not plan their behaviors. Before they act, patients sense increasing tension or arousal; afterward they experience feelings of pleasure, satisfaction, or freedom but may or may not feel sincere remorse, self-reproach, or guilt. Because their behaviors consciously coincide with their desires, however, their acts are ego-syntonic.

ETIOLOGY

The causes of impulse disorders are unknown, but psychodynamic, biological, and psychosocial factors seem to interact to cause the disorders. The disorders may have common underlying neurobiological mechanisms.

Psychodynamic Factors

An impulse is a disposition to act to decrease heightened tension caused by the buildup of instinctual drives or by diminished ego defenses against the drives. The impulse disorders have in common an attempt to bypass the experience of disabling symptoms or painful affects by acting on the environment. In his work with adolescents who were delinquent, August Aichhorn described impulsive behavior as related to a weak superego and weak ego structures associated with psychic trauma produced by childhood deprivation.

Otto Fenichel linked impulsive behavior to attempts to master anxiety, guilt, depression, and other painful affects by means of action. He thought that such actions defend against internal danger and that they produce a distorted aggressive or sexual gratification. To observers, impulsive behaviors may appear to be irrational and motivated by greed, but they may actually be endeavors to find relief from pain.

Heinz Kohut considered many forms of impulse control problems—including gambling, kleptomania, and some paraphiliac behaviors—to be related to an incomplete sense of self. He observed that when patients do not receive the validating and affirming responses that they seek from people in significant relationships with them, the self may fragment. As a way of dealing with this fragmentation and of regaining a sense of wholeness or cohesion in the self, people may engage in impulsive behaviors that to others appear self-destructive. Kohut's formulation has some similarities to Donald Winnicott's view that impulsive or deviant behavior in children is a way for them to try to recapture a primitive maternal relationship. Winnicott saw such behavior as hopeful in that the child searches for affirmation and love from the mother rather than abandoning any attempt to win her affection. Several therapists have stressed patients' fixation at the oral stage of development. Patients attempt to master anxiety, guilt, depression, and other painful affects by means of actions, but such actions aimed at obtaining relief seldom succeed even temporarily.

Biological Factors

Many investigators have focused on possible organic factors in the impulse-control disorders, especially for patients with overtly violent behavior. Experiments have shown that impulsive and violent activity is associated with specific brain regions such as the limbic system and that the inhibition of such behaviors is associated with other brain regions. Certain hormones, especially testosterone, have also been associated with violent and aggressive behavior. Some reports have described a relation between temporal lobe epilepsy and certain impulsive violent behaviors, as well as an association of aggressive behavior in patients who have histories of head trauma with increased numbers of emergency room visits and other potential organic antecedents. A high incidence of mixed cerebral dominance may be found in some violent populations.

Impulse-control disorder symptoms may continue into adulthood in people whose disorder has been diagnosed as childhood attention-deficit/hyperactivity disorder. Lifelong or acquired mental deficiency, epilepsy, and even reversible brain syndromes have long been implicated in lapses of impulse control.

Considerable evidence indicates that the serotonin neurotransmitter system mediates symptoms evident in impulse-control disorders. A relation has been found between cerebrospinal fluid (CSF) levels of 5-hydroxyindoleacetic acid (5-HIAA) and impulsive aggression. Brainstem and CSF levels of 5-HIAA are decreased and 5-hydroxytryptamine (5-HT) binding sites are increased in people who have committed suicide. Involvement of the dopaminergic and noradrenergic systems has also been implicated in impulsivity.

In some disorders of impulse control, the ego defenses are overwhelmed without actual nervous system pathology. Fatigue, incessant stimulation, and psychic trauma can lower resistance and temporarily suspend the ego's control.

Psychosocial Factors

Some workers have stressed the psychosocial aspects of impulse-control disorders, such as early life events, as important causative factors. Improper models for identification and parental figures who themselves have difficulty in controlling impulses have also been implicated: Such parental factors as violence in the home, alcohol abuse, promiscuity, and antisocial tendencies have been thought to be significant.

ICD-10

In the 10th revision of *International Statistical Classification of Diseases and Related Health Problems* (ICD-10), the same categories listed in DSM-IV under impulse control are discussed under habit and impulse disorders (Table 25–1). In this brief category, the authors define habit and impulse disorders as characterized by uncontrollable "repeated acts that have no clear rational motivation and that generally harm the patient's own interests and those of other people." The disorders are grouped together not because they have common causes (the causes are unknown) or share other common features but because of descriptive similarities and because they cannot be otherwise classified.

Table 25–1
ICD-10 Diagnostic Criteria for Habit and Impulse Disorders

Pathological gambling
A. Two or more episodes of gambling occur over a period of at least 1 year.
B. These episodes do not have a profitable outcome for the individual but are continued despite personal distress and interference with personal functioning in daily living.
C. The individual describes an intense urge to gamble which is difficult to control and reports that he or she is unable to stop gambling by an effort of will.
D. The individual is preoccupied with thoughts or mental images of the act of gambling or the cirumstances surrounding the act.

Pathological fire setting (pyromania)
A. There are two or more acts of fire setting without apparent motive.
B. The individual describes an intense urge to set fire to objects, with a feeling of tension before the act and relief afterwards.
C. The individual is preoccupied with thoughts or mental images of fire setting or of the circumstances surrounding the act (eg, abnormal interest in fire engines or in calling out the fire service).

Pathological stealing (kleptomania)
A. There are two or more thefts in which the individual steals without any apparent motive of personal gain or gain for another person.
B. The individual describes an intense urge to steal, with a feeling of tension before the act and relief afterward.

Trichotillomania
A. Noticeable hair loss is caused by the individual's persistent and recurrent failure to resist impulses to pull out hairs.
B. The individual describes an intense urge to pull out hairs, with mounting tension before the act and a sense of relief afterward.
C. There is no preexisting inflammation of the skin, and the hair pulling is not in response to a delusion or hallucination.

Other habit and impulse disorders
This category should be used for other kinds of persistently repeated maladaptive behavior that are not secondary to a recognized psychiatric syndrome and in which it appears that there is repeated failure to resist impulses to carry out the behavior. There is a prodromal period of tension with a feeling of release at the time of the act.

Habit and impulse disorder, unspecified

Reprinted with permission from World Health Organization: *The ICD-10 Classification of Mental and Behavioural Disorders: Diagnostic Criteria for Research.* Copyright, World Health Organization, Geneva, 1993.

INTERMITTENT EXPLOSIVE DISORDER

Intermittent explosive disorder manifests as discrete episodes of losing control of aggressive impulses; these episodes can result in serious assault or the destruction of property. The aggressiveness expressed is grossly out of proportion to any stressors that may have helped elicit the episodes. The symptoms, which patients may describe as spells or attacks, appear within minutes or hours and, regardless of duration, remit spontaneously and quickly. After each episode patients usually show genuine regret or self-reproach, and signs of generalized impulsivity or aggressiveness are absent between episodes. The diagnosis of intermittent explosive disorder should not be made if the loss of control can be accounted for by schizophrenia, antisocial or borderline personality disorder, attention-deficit/hyperactivity disorder, conduct disorder, or substance intoxication.

The term *epileptoid personality* has been used to convey the seizurelike quality of the characteristic outbursts, which are not typical of the patient's usual behavior, and to convey the suspicion of an organic disease process, for example, damage to the central nervous system. Several associated features suggest the possibility of an epileptoid state: the presence of auras; postictal-like changes in the sensorium, including partial or spotty amnesia; and hypersensitivity to photic, aural, or auditory stimuli. People with the disorder have a high incidence of hyperactivity, soft neurological signs, nonspecific electroencephalogram (EEG) findings, and accident proneness.

Epidemiology

Intermittent explosive disorder is underreported but appears to be more common in men than in women. The men are likely to be found in correctional institutions and the women in psychiatric facilities. In one study, about 2 percent of all people admitted to a university hospital psychiatric service had disorders that were diagnosed as intermittent explosive disorder; 80 percent were men.

Evidence indicates that intermittent explosive disorder is more common in first-degree biological relatives of people with the disorder than in the general population. Many factors other than a simple genetic explanation may be responsible.

Etiology

Typical patients have been described as physically large but dependent men whose sense of masculine identity is poor. A sense of being useless and impotent or of being unable to change the environment often precedes an episode of physical violence, and a high level of anxiety, guilt, and depression usually follows an episode. Some investigators suggest that disordered brain physiology, particularly in the limbic system, is involved in most cases of episodic violence, but an unfavorable childhood environment is generally believed to be the major determinant. Predisposing factors in childhood are thought to include perinatal trauma, infantile seizures, head trauma, encephalitis, minimal brain dysfunction, and hyperactivity. Patients' childhood environments are often filled with alcohol dependence, beatings, threats to life, and promiscuity.

Workers who have concentrated on psychogenesis as causing episodic explosiveness have stressed identification with assaultive parental figures as symbols of the target for violence. Early frustration, oppression, and hostility have been noted as predisposing factors. Situations directly or symbolically reminiscent of early deprivations (for example, people who directly or indirectly evoke the image of the frustrating parent) become targets for destructive hostility.

Compelling evidence indicates that serotonergic neurons mediate behavioral inhibition. Decreases in serotonergic transmission, which can be induced by inhibiting serotonin synthesis or by antagonizing its effects, decrease the effect of punishment as a deterrent to behavior. The restoration of serotonin activity—by administering serotonin precursors such as tryptophan or drugs that increase synaptic serotonin levels—restores the behavioral effect of punishment. Low levels of CSF 5-HIAA have been correlated with impulsive aggression.

Diagnosis and Clinical Features

The diagnosis of intermittent explosive disorder should be the result of history-taking that reveals several episodes of loss of control associated with aggressive outbursts (Table 25–2). A single discrete episode does not justify the diagnosis. The histories are typically of a childhood in an atmosphere of alcohol dependence, violence, and emotional instability. Patients' work histories are poor; they report job losses, marital difficulties, and trouble with the law. Most patients have sought psychiatric help in the past but to no avail. Neurological examination sometimes reveals soft neurological signs such as left-right ambivalence and perceptual reversal. EEG findings are frequently normal or show nonspecific changes. Psychological tests for organicity often result in normal findings.

Table 25–2
DSM-IV Diagnostic Criteria for Intermittent Explosive Disorder

A. Several discrete episodes of failure to resist aggressive impulses that result in serious assaultive acts or destruction of property.

B. The degree of aggressiveness expressed during the episodes in grossly out of proportion to any precipitating psychosocial stressors.

C. The aggressive episodes are not better accounted for by another mental disorder (eg, antisocial personality disorder, borderline personality disorder, a psychotic disorder, a manic episode, conduct disorder, or attention-deficit/hyperactivity disorder) and are not due to the direct physiological effects of a substance (eg, a drug of abuse, a medication), or a general medical condition (eg, head trauma, Alzheimer's disease).

Reprinted with permission from American Psychiatric Association: *Diagnostic and Statistical Manual of Mental Disorders,* ed 4. Copyright, American Psychiatric Association, Washington, 1994.

Differential Diagnosis

The diagnosis of intermittent explosive disorder can be made only after disorders associated with the occasional loss of control of aggressive impulses have been ruled out. These other disorders include psychotic disorders, personality change due to a general medical condition, antisocial or borderline personality disorder, conduct disorder, and substance intoxication.

Intermittent explosive disorder differs from the antisocial and borderline personality disorders because, in the personality disorders, aggressiveness and impulsivity are part of patients' characters and thus are present between outbursts. In paranoid and catatonic schizophrenia, patients may display violent behavior in response to delusions and hallucinations, and they show gross impairments in reality testing. Hostile patients with mania may be impulsively aggressive, but the underlying diagnosis is generally apparent from their mental status examinations and clinical presentations. Epilepsy, brain tumors, degenerative diseases, and endocrine disorders must be considered and ruled out, as must acute intoxications with such substances as alcohol, barbiturates, hallucinogens, and amphetamines. Its repetitive and resistant pattern of behavior, as opposed to an episodic pattern, rules out conduct disorder.

Course and Prognosis

Intermittent explosive disorder may begin at any stage of life but usually appears in the second or third decade. In most cases the disorder decreases in severity with the onset of middle age, but heightened organic impairment can lead to frequent and severe episodes.

Treatment

A combined pharmacological and psychotherapeutic approach has the best chance of success. Psychotherapy with patients who have intermittent explosive disorder is difficult, dangerous, and often unrewarding; therapists may have problems with countertransference and limit setting. Group psychotherapy may be of some help, as may family therapy, particularly when the explosive patient is an adolescent or a young adult.

Anticonvulsants have long been used, with mixed results, in treating explosive patients. Phenothiazines and antidepressants have been effective in some cases, but clinicians must then wonder whether schizophrenia or a mood disorder is the true diagnosis. When there is a likelihood of subcortical seizurelike activity, these medications can aggravate the situation. Benzodiazepines have been reported to produce a paradoxical reaction of dyscontrol in some cases. Lithium (Eskalith) has been reported useful in generally lessening aggressive behavior, and carbamazepine (Tegretol) and phenytoin (Dilantin) have been reported helpful. Propranolol (Inderal), buspirone (BuSpar), and trazodone (Desyrel) have also been effective in some cases. Reports increasingly indicate that fluoxetine (Prozac) and other serotonin-specific reuptake inhibitors are useful in reducing impulsivity and aggression. Some neurosurgeons have performed operative treatments for intractable violence and aggression. No evidence indicates that such treatment is effective.

KLEPTOMANIA

The essential feature of kleptomania is a recurrent failure to resist impulses to steal objects not needed for personal use or for monetary value. The objects taken are often given away, returned surreptitiously, or kept and hidden. People with kleptomania usually have the money to pay for the objects they impulsively steal.

Like other impulse-control disorders, kleptomania is characterized by mounting tension before the act, followed by gratification and lessening of tension with or without guilt, remorse, or depression during the act. The stealing is not planned and does not involve others. Although the thefts do not occur when immediate arrest is probable, people with kleptomania do not always consider their chances of being apprehended, even though repeated arrests lead to pain and humiliation. These people may feel guilt and anxiety after the theft, but they do not feel anger or vengeance. Furthermore, when the object stolen is the goal, the diagnosis is not kleptomania: In kleptomania the act of stealing is itself the goal.

Epidemiology

The prevalence of kleptomania is not known. The estimated rate ranges from 3.8 to 24 percent of those arrested for shoplifting. The sex ratio is unknown, but kleptomania appears to be more common among females than among males. DSM-IV reports that it occurs in fewer than 5 percent of identified shoplifters; thus kleptomania as an impulse-control disorder is rare.

Etiology

Psychodynamic Factors. The symptoms of kleptomania tend to appear in times of significant stress—for example, losses, separations, and endings of important relationships. Some psychoanalytic writers have stressed the expression of aggressive impulses in kleptomania; others have discerned a libidinal aspect. Those who focus on symbolism see meaning in the act itself, the object stolen, and the victim of the theft.

Kleptomania is often associated with other disturbances, such as mood disorders, obsessive-compulsive disorder, and eating disorders: It is frequently associated with bulimia nervosa. In some reports, nearly one fourth of patients with bulimia nervosa meet the diagnostic criteria for kleptomania.

Analytic writers have focused on stealing by children and adolescents. Anna Freud pointed out that the first thefts from mother's purse indicate the degree to which all stealing is rooted in the oneness between mother and child. Karl Abraham wrote of the central feeling of being neglected, injured, or unwanted. One theoretician established seven categories of stealing in chronically acting-out children: as a means of restoring the lost mother–child relationship; as an aggressive act; as a defense against fears of being damaged (perhaps a search by girls for a penis or a protection against castration anxiety in boys); as a means of seeking punishment; as a means of restoring or adding to self-esteem; in connection with and as a reaction to a family secret; and as excitement *(lust Angst)* and a substitute for a sexual act. One or more of these categories can also apply to adult kleptomania.

Biological Factors. Brain diseases and mental retardation have been associated with kleptomania, as they have with other disorders of impulse control. Focal neurological signs, cortical atrophy, and enlarged lateral ventricles have been found in some patients. Disturbances in monoamine metabolism, particularly of serotonin, have been postulated.

Diagnosis and Clinical Features

The essential feature of kleptomania consists of recurrent, intrusive, and irresistible urges or impulses to steal unneeded objects (Table 25–3). Patients with kleptomania may also be distressed about the possibility or actuality of being apprehended and may manifest signs of depression and anxiety. Patients feel guilty, ashamed, and embarrassed about their behavior. They often have serious problems with interpersonal relationships and often, but not invariably, show signs of personality disturbance. In one study of patients with kleptomania, the frequency of stealing ranged from less than 1 to 120 episodes a month. Most kleptomaniac patients steal from retail stores, but they may also steal from family members in their own households.

Table 25–3
DSM-IV Diagnostic Criteria for Kleptomania

A. Recurrent failure to resist impulses to steal objects that are not needed for personal use or for their monetary value.
B. Increasing sense of tension immediately before committing the theft.
C. Pleasure, gratification, or relief at the same time of committing the theft.
D. The stealing is not committed to express anger or vengeance, and is not in response to a delusion or a hallucination.
E. The stealing is not better accounted for by conduct disorder, a manic episode, or antisocial personality disorder.

Reprinted with permission from American Psychiatric Association: *Diagnostic and Statistical Manual of Mental Disorders,* ed 4. Copyright, American Psychiatric Association, Washington, 1994.

Differential Diagnosis

Because most patients with kleptomania are referred for examination in connection with legal proceedings after apprehension, the clinical picture may be clouded by subsequent symptoms of depression and anxiety. Clinicians must differentiate between kleptomania and other forms of stealing. For a diagnosis of kleptomania, stealing must always follow a failure to resist the impulse and must be a solitary act, and the stolen articles must be without immediate usefulness or monetary gain. By contrast, ordinary stealing is usually planned, and the objects are stolen for their use or financial value. Malingerers may try to simulate kleptomania to avoid prosecution. Stealing that occurs in association with conduct disorder, antisocial personality disorder, and manic episodes is clearly related to the pervasive, underlying disorder. People with kleptomania do not typically display antisocial behavior other than stealing. Patients with schizophrenia may steal in response to hallucinations and delusions, and patients with cognitive disorders may be accused of stealing when they forget to pay for objects.

Course and Prognosis

Kleptomania may begin in childhood, although most children and adolescents who steal do not become kleptomaniac adults. The course of the disorder waxes and wanes but tends to be chronic. Its spontaneous recovery rate is unknown. Serious impairment and complications are usually secondary to being caught, particularly to being arrested. Many people seem never to have consciously considered the possibility of facing the consequences of their acts, a feature that agrees with some descriptions of patients with kleptomania, sometimes as people who feel wronged and therefore entitled to steal. People sometimes have bouts of being unable to resist the impulse to steal, followed by free periods that last for weeks or months. The prognosis with treatment can be good, but few patients come for help of their own accord. Often, the disorder in no way impairs people's social or work functioning. In quiescent cases, new bouts of the disorder may be precipitated by loss or disappointment.

Treatment

Because true kleptomania is rare, reports of treatment tend to be individual case descriptions or a short series of cases. Insight-oriented psychotherapy and psychoanalysis have been successful but depend on patients' motivations. Those who feel guilt and shame may be helped by insight-oriented psychotherapy because of their increased motivation to change their behavior.

Behavior therapy, including systematic desensitization, aversive conditioning, and a combination of aversive conditioning and altered social contingencies, has been reported successful, even when motivation was lacking. The reports cite follow-up studies of up to 2 years. Serotonin-specific reuptake inhibitors, such as fluoxetine, appear to be effective in some patients with kleptomania. There have also been case reports of successful treatment with tricyclic drugs, trazodone, lithium, valproate (Depakote), and electroconvulsive therapy.

PYROMANIA

The essential features of pyromania are deliberate and purposeful fire setting on more than one occasion; tension or affective arousal before setting the fires; fascination with, interest in, curiosity about, or attraction to fire and the activities and equipment associated with fire fighting; and pleasure, gratification, or relief when setting fires or when witnessing or participating in their aftermath. Patients may make considerable advance preparations before starting a fire.

A diagnosis of pyromania should not be made when fires are set to make money, to express a sociopolitical ideology, to conceal criminal activity, to express anger or vengeance, to improve living circumstances, or to respond to a delusion or a hallucination.

Epidemiology

No information is available on the prevalence of pyromania, but only a small percentage of adults who set fires can be classified as having pyromania. The disorder is found far more often in men than in women, and people who set fires are more likely to be mildly retarded than are the general population. Some studies have noted an increased incidence of alcohol abuse in people who set fires. Fire setters also tend to have a history of antisocial traits, such as truancy, running away from home, and delinquency. Enuresis has been considered a common finding in the history of fire setters, although controlled studies have failed to confirm this. Studies have, however, found an association between cruelty to animals and fire setting.

Etiology

Sigmund Freud saw fire as a symbol of sexuality. The warmth radiated by fire evokes the same sensation that accompanies a state of sexual excitation, and a flame's shape and movements suggest a phallus in activity. Other therapists have associated pyromania with an abnormal craving for power and social prestige. Some patients with pyromania are volunteer firefighters who set fires to prove themselves brave, to force other firefighters into action, or to demonstrate their power to extinguish a blaze. The incendiary act is a way to vent accumulated rage over frustration caused by a sense of social, physical, or sexual inferiority. Several studies have noted that the fathers of patients with pyromania were absent from the home. Thus, one explanation of fire setting is that it represents a wish for absent father to return home as a rescuer, to put out the fire and to save the child from a difficult existence.

Female fire setters, in addition to being much fewer in number than are male fire setters, do not start fires to put firefighters into action as men frequently do. Rather, promiscuity without pleasure and petty stealing, often approaching kleptomania, have been frequently noted delinquent trends in female fire setters.

Significantly low CSF levels of 5-HIAA and 3-methoxy-4-hydroxyphenylglycol (MHPG) were found in one group of male fire setters.

Diagnosis and Clinical Features

People with pyromania often regularly watch fires in their neighborhoods, frequently set off false alarms, and show in-

Table 25–4
DSM-IV Diagnostic Criteria for Pyromania

A. Deliberate and purposeful fire setting on more than one occasion.
B. Tension or affective arousal before the act.
C. Fascination with, interest in, curiosity about, or attraction to fire and its situational contexts (eg, paraphernalia, uses, consequences).
D. Pleasure, gratification, or relief when setting fires, or when witnessing or participating in their aftermath.
E. The fire setting is not done for monetary gain, as an expression of sociopolitical ideology, to conceal criminal activity, to express anger or vengeance, to improve one's living circumstances, in response to a delusion or hallucination, or as a result of impaired judgment (eg, in dementia, mental retardation, substance intoxication).
F. The fire setting is not better accounted for by conduct disorder, a manic episode, or antisocial personality disorder.

Reprinted with permission from American Psychiatric Association: *Diagnostic and Statistical Manual of Mental Disorders,* ed 4. Copyright, American Psychiatric Association, Washington, 1994.

terest in firefighting paraphernalia (Table 25–4). Their curiosity is very evident, but they show no remorse and may be indifferent to the consequences for life or property. Fire setters may gain satisfaction from the resulting destruction; frequently, they leave obvious clues. Commonly associated features include alcohol intoxication, sexual dysfunctions, lower-than-average intelligence quotient (IQ), chronic personal frustrations, and resentment toward authority figures. In some cases, fire setters become sexually aroused by the fire.

Bruce is an attractive 6-year-old boy whose mother brought him to the emergency room because she was frightened that she could not prevent the child from setting fires, which he had done several times in the last year and a half. Although he had so far managed to put out all the fires he set himself, his mother was afraid that he would set the house afire while she and his sister were asleep. She complained that he was sneaky about setting the fires, making it impossible for her to control him or to know how many fires he had actually set.

Bruce says that he has set fires because a "man in my head tells me to." This "man" stays in his room when he is awake and "goes away" when he is asleep. The man makes a noise ("brrr"), which Bruce interprets as a command to "set fires." He is afraid to talk to anyone about the man or not to obey his commands, "because he might beat me up." His mother apparently does not take the voice seriously, stating that Bruce has offered a variety of different reasons for setting fires, depending on to whom he was talking. Both agree that he sets fires in retaliation against his mother when he is angry with her.

Bruce has been fascinated with setting fires for the last 2 years. His mother remembers that he and a friend set the first fire by burning holes in the plastic sheets on his and his sister's beds. His mother found out about the incident later and reacted by hitting him on his hands and telling him how dangerous fires were. During the next fire-setting incident, Bruce used a lighter to try to burn a door frame that his mother had just painted. This time he was not hit, but was forbidden to ride his bicycle for a week. His mother was sleeping during a third episode, in which he set the garbage on fire with a table lighter. He then took a broom and beat out the fire. His mother awoke to a funny smell and remembers that he was running all over the house in a peculiar manner. She related this incident with amusement at the child's antics.

The last two fires had taken place 3 weeks previously, when Bruce first tried to burn a dishtowel on a gas flame. After he burned the fringe, he rolled up the towel and threw it in the garbage. His mother, who was just outside the apartment at the time, sent him to bed and later explained to him again about the dangers of fire setting. During the last incident, he took a stretch monster toy that was kept in a Styrofoam box and burned holes with a lighter on the sides of the box that corresponded to the monster's arms and feet.

Apart from these incidents, his mother remembers that Bruce would often find matches or go into the bathroom with a lighter and try to smoke. His mother has talked to him at length about fires, how they get bigger with alcohol, and can be put out with water. He becomes excited during these discussions but then promises never again to play with fire.

At the present time, his mother reports, Bruce is unhappy in school and misses his former friends from the neighborhood the family moved from 3 months before this evaluation. She says that he has made no new friends outside school and that he and his sister complain frequently of boredom.

Aside from the fire setting, there is no history of any other aggressive or antisocial behavior. His mother reports that Bruce has been difficult to discipline, but mainly because he ignores her. Bruce's schoolteacher was surprised to hear of his fire setting. She described him as a lovely, bright, obedient child who played and worked well with both the teacher and his peers. Upon further inquiry, she could say only that at times he became a "little wild" in play.

Bruce lives with his 10-year-old sister and 26-year-old mother, who herself was hospitalized as an adolescent after she had been truant from school for 7 months in retaliation for her mother's remarriage. In an initial discussion with the interviewer, she acknowledged that at times she becomes violently angry, to the point where she is unable to control herself.

The findings of Bruce's physical examination were within normal limits except for a second-degree burn on his hand, which his mother initially said came from her attempts to "teach him that fire hurts" by insisting that he put his hand in a gas flame. (She later denied this, but Bruce insisted that she had done it.)

When interviewed, Bruce was somewhat guarded and distrustful at first. This seemed to be a manifestation of shyness and fear of what his mother would say or do. Over the course of several evaluation sessions, Bruce's play revolved around themes of fires getting bigger and out of control. He knows that he can get burned and that a big fire could burn his house and "I would die." When talking about fires, his affect was either inappropriate (laughter) or blunted. When discussing the "man" and his command hallucinations, Bruce seemed to be genuinely frightened, as if he regarded the man as real and threatening. He denied suicidal ideation, although his mother reported that he had recently said that he wished to die.

DISCUSSION

Recurrent setting of fires may be a symptom of conduct disorder; Bruce, however, is described by his teacher as a "lovely, bright, obedient child who plays and works well with both the teacher and his peers," and he apparently engages in no antisocial activities other than fire setting. Political extremists may set fires to make a political statement. We doubt this is what Bruce is up to.

It does seem that Bruce has committed deliberate and purposeful fire setting on several occasions, that he derives pleasure form the fire setting, that he is very fascinated with fires, as evidenced by his excitement over his mother's discussions with him about the specifics of fires, and that there is no understandable goal, such as monetary gain from insurance. The diagnosis is therefore pyromania, within the group of impulse-control disorders not elsewhere classified.

Some readers may notice that the DSM-IV diagnostic criteria for this disorder require "tension or affective arousal before the act." This feature can only be inferred from the available information, as this subjective experience is often not easily documented in a very young person.

Other readers may be bothered by the "command hallucination." It is hard to reconcile his mother's evaluation that the "man" in his head is one of a number of stories that he provides to explain his behavior with his behavior during the interview when he seemed genuinely frightened at thoughts of the "man." If the hallucinations were truly genuine, one would certainly expect other signs of disorganized or psychotic behavior, which have not been present. Therefore, we do not add a diagnosis of a psychotic disorder. (From *DSM-IV Casebook.*)

Differential Diagnosis

Clinicians should have little trouble distinguishing between pyromania and the fascination of many young children with matches, lighters, and fire as part of the normal investigation of their environments. Pyromania must also be separated from incendiary acts of sabotage carried out by dissident political extremists or by paid torches, termed *arsonists* in the legal system.

When fire setting occurs in conduct disorder and antisocial personality disorder, it is a deliberate act, not a failure to resist an impulse. Fires may be set for profit, sabotage, or retaliation. Patients with schizophrenia or mania may set fires in response to delusions or hallucinations, and patients with brain dysfunction may set fires because of a failure to appreciate the consequences of the act.

Course and Prognosis

Pyromania usually begins in childhood. When the onset is in adolescence or adulthood, the fire setting tends to be deliberately destructive. The prognosis for treated children is good, and complete remission is a realistic goal. The prognosis for adults is guarded, because they frequently deny their actions, refuse to take responsibility, are dependent on alcohol, and lack insight.

Treatment

Little has been written about the treatment of pyromania, and treating fire setters has been difficult because of their lack of motivation. Incarceration may be the only method of preventing a recurrence. Behavior therapy can then be administered in the institution.

Fire setting by children must be treated with the utmost seriousness. Intensive interventions should be undertaken when possible, but as therapeutic and preventive measures, not as punishment. Because of the recurrent nature of pyromania, any treatment program should include supervision of patients to prevent a repeated episode of fire setting.

PATHOLOGICAL GAMBLING

As defined by DSM-IV, the essential feature of pathological gambling is persistent and recurrent maladaptive gambling behavior. Aspects of the maladaptive behavior include a preoccupation with gambling; the need to gamble with increasing amounts of money to achieve the desired excitement; repeated unsuccessful efforts to control, cut back, or stop gambling; gambling as a way to escape from problems; gambling to recoup losses; lying to conceal the extent of the involvement with gambling; the commission of illegal acts to finance gambling; jeopardizing or losing personal and vocational relationships because of gambling; and a reliance on others for money to pay off debts.

Epidemiology

Estimates place the number of pathological gamblers at 1 to 3 percent of the adult United States population; the disorder is more common in men than in women. Both the fathers of men and the mothers of women with the disorder are more likely to have the disorder than is the population at large. Women with the disorder are more likely than are those not so affected to be married to alcoholic men who are usually absent from the home. Alcohol dependence is generally more common among the parents of pathological gamblers than among the overall population.

Etiology

Several factors may predispose people to develop the disorder: loss of a parent by death, separation, divorce, or desertion before a child is 15 years of age; inappropriate parental discipline (absence, inconsistency, or harshness); exposure to and availability of gambling activities for adolescents; a family emphasis on material and financial symbols; and a lack of family emphasis on saving, planning, and budgeting.

There is an association between pathological gambling and mood disorders, especially major depressive disorder. Other associated disorders include panic disorder, obsessive-compulsive disorder, and agoraphobia. Childhood attention-deficit/hyperactivity disorder may be a predisposing factor for pathological gambling.

Disorders of catecholamine metabolism have been suggested, with gamblers seeking to experience the activating effect of norepinephrine that accompanies the tension associated with gambling. Some researchers have hypothesized that the disorder may be associated with abnormalities in the serotonin system.

Diagnosis and Clinical Features

In addition to the features already described, pathological gamblers often appear overconfident, somewhat abrasive, energetic, and free spending when they have obvious signs of personal stress, anxiety, and depression (Table 25–5). They commonly have the attitude that money is both the cause of, and the solution to, all their problems. As their gambling increases, they are usually forced to lie to obtain money and to continue gambling while hiding the extent of their gambling. They make no serious attempt to budget or save money. When their borrowing resources are strained, they are likely to engage in antisocial behavior to obtain money for gambling. Their criminal behavior is typically nonviolent, such as forgery, embezzlement, or fraud, and they consciously intend to return or repay the money. Complications include alienation from family members and acquaintances, the loss of life accomplishments, suicide attempts, and association with fringe and illegal groups. Arrest for nonviolent crimes may lead to imprisonment.

Table 25–5
DSM-IV Diagnostic Criteria for Pathological Gambling

A. Persistent and recurrent maladaptive gambling behavior as indicated by five (or more) of the following:
   (1) is preoccupied with gambling (e.g., preoccupied with reliving past gambling experiences, handicapping or planning the next venture, or thinking of ways to get money with which to gamble)
   (2) needs to gamble with increasing amounts of money in order to achieve the desired excitement
   (3) has repeated unsuccessful efforts to control, cut back, or stop gambling
   (4) is restless or irritable when attempting to cut down or stop gambling
   (5) gambles as a way of escaping from problems or of relieving a dysphoric mood (e.g., feelings of helplessness, guilt, anxiety, depression)
   (6) after losing money gambling, often returns another day to get even ("chasing" one's losses)
   (7) lies to family members, therapist, or others to conceal the extent of involvement with gambling
   (8) has committed illegal acts such as forgery, fraud, theft, or embezzlement, to finance gambling
   (9) has jeopardized or lost a significant relationship, job, or educational or career opportunity because of gambling
   (10) relies on others to provide money to relieve a desperate financial situation caused by gambling

B. The gambling behavior is not better accounted for by a manic episode.

Reprinted with permission from American Psychiatric Association: *Diagnostic and Statistical Manual of Mental Disorders*, ed 4. Copyright American Psychiatric Association, Washington, 1994.

Differential Diagnosis

Social gambling is distinguished from pathological gambling in that the former occurs with friends, on special occasions, and with predetermined acceptable and tolerable losses. Gambling that is symptomatic of a manic episode can usually be distinguished from pathological gambling by the history of a marked mood change and the loss of judgment preceding the gambling. Maniclike mood changes are common in pathological gambling but always follow winning and are usually succeeded by depressive episodes because of subsequent losses. People with antisocial personality disorder may have problems with gambling. When both disorders are present, both should be diagnosed.

Course and Prognosis

Pathological gambling usually begins in adolescence for men and late in life for women. The disorder waxes and wanes and tends to be chronic. Three phases are seen in pathological gambling: the winning phase, ending with a big win, equal to about a year's salary, which hooks patients; the progressive-loss phase, in which patients structure their lives around gambling and then move from being excellent gamblers to being stupid ones who take considerable risks, cash in securities, borrow money, miss work, and lose jobs; and the desperate phase, with patients frenziedly gambling with large amounts of money, not paying debts, becoming involved with loan sharks, writing bad checks, and possibly embezzling. The disorder may take up to 15 years to reach the third phase, but then, within a year or two, patients are totally deteriorated.

Treatment

Gamblers seldom voluntarily come forward to be treated. Legal difficulties, family pressures, or other psychiatric complaints bring gamblers to treatment. Gamblers Anonymous (GA) was founded in Los Angeles in 1957 and modeled on Alcoholics Anonymous (AA); it is accessible—at least in large cities—and is probably the most effective treatment for gambling. GA is a method of inspirational group therapy, which involves public confession, peer pressure, and the presence of reformed gamblers (like sponsors in AA) available to help members resist the impulse to gamble. In some cases, hospitalization may help by removing patients from their environments. Insight should not be sought until patients have been away from gambling for 3 months. At this point, patients who are pathological gamblers may become excellent candidates for insight-oriented psychotherapy.

Little is known about the efficacy of pharmacotherapies for treating patients with pathological gambling. One study reported that 7 of 10 patients remained completely abstinent over 8 weeks after taking fluvoxamine (Luvox). There have also been case reports of successful treatment with lithium and clomipramine. If gambling is associated with depressive disorders, mania, anxiety, or other mental disorders, pharmacotherapy with antidepressants, lithium, or antianxiety agents is useful.

TRICHOTILLOMANIA

According to DSM-IV, the essential feature of trichotillomania is the recurrent pulling out of hair, which can result in noticeable hair loss. Other clinical symptoms include an increasing sense of tension before pulling the hair and a sense of pleasure, gratification, or relief when pulling out the hair. The diagnosis should not be made if hair pulling is the result of another mental disorder (such as disorders manifesting delusions or hallucinations) or a general medical disorder (such as a preexisting lesion of the skin).

Epidemiology

Trichotillomania is apparently more common in women than in men. No information is available on familial patterns, but one study reported that 5 of 19 children had family histories of some form of alopecia. Prevalence data are unavailable, but some experts contend that the DSM-IV criteria are too restrictive. Trichotillomania may be more common than is now believed, especially if hair pulling without the sense of tension before the pulling and without the sense of relief afterward is considered trichotillomania. Associated disorders are obsessive-compulsive disorder, obsessive-compulsive personality disorder, borderline personality disorder, and depressive disorders.

Etiology

Although trichotillomania is regarded as multidetermined, its onset has been linked to stressful situations in more than one fourth of all cases. Disturbances in mother–child relationships, fear of being left alone, and recent object loss are often cited as critical factors contributing to the condition. Substance abuse may encourage development of the disorder. Depressive dynamics are often cited as predisposing factors, but no particular personality trait or disorder characterizes patients. Some see self-stimulation as the primary goal of hair pulling. Trichotillomania is increasingly being viewed as having a biologically determined substrate that may reflect inappropriately released motor activity or excessive grooming behaviors.

Diagnosis and Clinical Features

Before engaging in the behavior, patients with trichotillomania experience an increasing sense of tension and achieve a sense of release or gratification from pulling out their hair (Table 25–6). All areas of the body may be affected, most commonly the scalp. Other areas involved are eyebrows, eyelashes, and beard; less commonly, trunk, armpits, and pubic area are involved. Hair loss is often characterized by short, broken strands appearing together with long, normal hairs in the affected areas. No abnormalities of the skin or scalp are present. Hair pulling is not reported to be painful, although pruritus and tingling in the involved area may be present. Trichophagy, mouthing of the hair, may follow the hair plucking. Complications of trichophagy include trichobezoars, malnutrition, and intestinal obstruction.

Characteristic histopathological changes in the hair follicle, known as trichomalacia, are demonstrated by biopsy and help distinguish trichotillomania from other causes of alopecia. Patients usually deny the behavior and often try to hide the resultant alopecia. Head banging, nail biting, scratching, gnawing, excoriation, and other acts of self-mutilation may be present.

Table 25–6
DSM-IV Diagnostic Criteria for Trichotillomania

A. Recurrent pulling out of one's hair resulting in noticeable hair loss.
B. An increasing sense of tension immediately before pulling out the hair or when attempting to resist the behavior.
C. Pleasure, gratification, or relief when pulling out the hair.
D. The disturbance is not better accounted for by another mental disorder and not due to a general medical condition (eg, a dermatologic condition).
E. The disturbance causes clinically significant distress or impairment in social, occupational, or other important areas of functioning.

Differential Diagnosis

Hair pulling may be a wholly benign condition, or it may occur in the context of several mental disorders. The phenomenology of trichotillomania and obsessive-compulsive disorder overlap. Like obsessive-compulsive disorder, trichotillomania is often chronic and recognized by patients as undesirable. Unlike obsessive-compulsive disorder, patients with trichotillomania do not experience obsessive thoughts, and the compulsive activity is limited to one act—hair pulling. Patients with factitious disorder with predominantly physical signs and symptoms actively seek medical attention and the patient role and deliberately simulate illness toward these ends. Patients who malinger or who have factitious disorder may mutilate themselves to get medical attention, but they do not acknowledge the self-inflicted nature of the lesions. Patients with stereotypic movement disorder have stereotypical and rhythmic movements, and they usually do not seem distressed by their behavior. A biopsy may be necessary to distinguish trichotillomania from alopecia areata and tinea capitis.

Course and Prognosis

Trichotillomania generally begins in childhood or adolescence, but onsets have been reported much later in life. A late onset may be associated with an increased likelihood of chronicity. The course of the disorder is not well known; both chronic and remitting forms occur. In some cases the disorder has persisted for more than 2 decades. About a third of people presenting for treatment report a duration of 1 year or less.

Treatment

No consensus is available on the best treatment modality for trichotillomania. Treatment usually involves psychiatrists and dermatologists in a joint endeavor. Psychopharmacological methods that have been used to treat psychodermatological disorders include topical steroids and hydroxyzine hydrochloride, an anxiolytic with antihistamine properties; antidepressants; serotonergic agents; and antipsychotics. Whether depression is present or not, antidepressant agents may lead to dermatological improvement. Current evidence strongly points to the efficacy of drugs that alter central serotonin turnover. In patients who respond poorly to serotonin-specific reuptake inhibitors, augmentation with pimozide (Orap), a dopamine blocker, may lead to improvement. A report of successful lithium treatment for trichotillomania cited the possible effect of the drug on aggressivity, impulsivity, and mood instability as an explanation. Lithium also possesses serotonergic activity. There have been case reports of successful treatment with buspirone, clonazepam, and fenfluramine (Pondimin). In one placebo-controlled study, patients taking naltrexone (ReVia) had a reduction in symptom severity.

Successful behavioral treatments, such as biofeedback, have been reported, but most studies have been based on individual cases or small series of cases with relatively short follow-up periods. Further controlled study of the treatments is warranted. Trichotillomania has been treated successfully with insight-oriented psychotherapy. Hypnotherapy and behavior therapy have been mentioned as potentially effective in the treatment of dermatological disorders in which psychological factors may be involved; the skin has been shown to be susceptible to hypnotic suggestion. Most of the work has been research oriented, with little effect as yet on clinical management.

IMPULSE-CONTROL DISORDER NOT OTHERWISE SPECIFIED

The DSM-IV diagnostic category of impulse-control disorder not otherwise specified (Table 25–7) is a residual category for disorders of impulse control that do not meet the criteria for a specific impulse-control disorder. Included in the not otherwise specified disorders are compulsive buying or shopping, addiction to video games, compulsive sexual behavior, and repetitive self-mutilation.

Originally referred to as *oniomania,* compulsive buying is not recognized as a separate diagnostic category in DSM-IV and ICD-10. Compulsive buying is estimated to effect 1.1 to 5.9 percent of the general population. It is more common in women than in men.

The cause of the disorder is unknown. Psychodynamic theories have implicated low self-esteem, anxiety, and the need to reduce stress. Comorbid conditions include other disorders of impulse control (for example, kleptomania), mood disorders, and obsessive-compulsive disorders. A diagnosis of compulsive buying should not be made if the behavior occurs as part of a hypomanic or manic episode.

The onset of the disorder is usually around 18 years of age; however, patients do not seek treatment until their 20s or 30s usually because they have developed serious financial problems. Compulsive buyers usually buy with credit and have many credit cards. Serious financial problems are usual, and some persons must declare bankruptcy. One study reported an average level of debt in compulsive shoppers of $23,000. The disorder may be chronic with urges to buy occurring hourly or as infrequently as once a month. Patients often try to limit their behavior but are unsuccessful.

Treatment of compulsive buying is difficult. Some patients are helped with supportive therapy, insight-oriented therapy, and self-help groups, such as Debtors Anonymous. Pharmacological therapies include antidepressants, antimanic drugs, anxiolytics, and antipsychotics to treat any comorbid conditions. The serotonin-specific reuptake inhibitors have been used to limit compulsive behavior and may be of use in this condition, which has compulsive aspects.

Table 25–7
DSM-IV Diagnostic Criteria for Impulse-Control Disorder Not Otherwise Specified

This category is for disorders of impulse control that do not meet the criteria for any specific impulse-control disorder or for another mental disorder having features involving impulse control described elsewhere in the manual (eg, substance dependence, a paraphilia).

REFERENCES

Aichhorn A: *Wayward Youth.* Viking, New York, 1935.
Allcock CC: Pathological gambling. Aust NZ J Psychiatry *20:* 259, 1986.
Bort VK: Impulse-control disorders not elsewhere classified. In *Comprehensive Textbook of Psychiatry,* ed 6, HI Kaplan, BJ Sadock, editors, p 1409. Williams & Wilkins, Baltimore, 1995.
Chong SA, Low BL: Treatment of kleptomania with fluvoxamine. Acta Psychiatr Scand *93:* 314, 1996.
Christenson GA, Crow SJ: The characterization and treatment of trichotillomania. J Clin Psychiatry *57* (8, Suppl): 42, 1996.
Corrigan PW, Yudofsky SC, Silver JM: Pharmacological and behavioral treatments for aggressive psychiatric inpatients. Hosp Community Psychiatry *44:* 125, 1993.
Cusack JR, Malaney KR, DePry DL: Insights about pathological gamblers: ''Chasing losses'' in spite of the consequences. Postgrad Med *93:* 169, 1993.
Custer RL: Profile of the pathological gambler. J Clin Psychiatry *45:* 35, 1984.
DeCaria CM, Hollander E, Grossman R, Wong CM, Mosovich SA, Cherkasky S: Diagnosis, neurobiology, and treatment of pathological gambling. J Clin Psychiatry *57* (8, Suppl): 80, 1996.
Frosch J: The relation between acting out and disorders of impulse control. Psychiatry *40:* 295, 1977.
Goldman MJ: Kleptomania: Making sense of the nonsensical. Am J Psychiatry *148:* 986, 1991.
Greenberg HR, Sarner CA: Trichotillomania: Symptom and syndrome. Arch Gen Psychiatry *12:* 482, 1965.
Gupta S, Freimer M: Trichotillomania, topical steroids. Am J Psychiatry *150:* 524, 1993.
Jaspers JPC: The diagnosis and psychopharmacological treatment of trichotillomania: A review. Pharmacopsychiatry *29:* 115, 1996.
Jenkins SC, Maruta T: Therapeutic use of propranolol for intermittent explosive disorder. Mayo Clin Proc *62:* 204, 1987.
Kammerer T, Singer L, Michel D: The incendiaries: Criminological, clinical and psychological study of 72 cases. Ann Med Psychol *1:* 687, 1967.
Keuthen NJ, Savage CR, O'Sullivan RL, Brown H: Neuropsychological functioning in trichotillomania. Biol Psychiatry *39:* 747, 1996.
Lion JR: The intermittent explosive disorder. Psychiatr Ann *22:* 64, 1992.
McElroy SL, Keck PE, Phillips KA: Kleptomania, compulsive buying, and binge eating disorder. J Clin Psychiatry *56* (4, Suppl): 14, 1995.
McElroy SL, Pope HG, Hudson JI, Keck PE, White KL: Kleptomania: A report of 20 cases. Am J Psychiatry *148:* 652, 1991.
Rugle L, Melamed L: Neuropsychological assessment of attention problems in pathological gamblers. J Nerv Ment Dis *181:* 107, 1993.
Stein DJ, Hollander E: Impulsive aggression and obsessive-compulsive disorders. Psychiatr Ann *23:* 289, 1993.
Stein DJ, Hollander E, Liebowitz MR: Neurobiology of impulsivity and the impulse control disorders. J Neuropsychiatry *5:* 9, 1993.
Swedo SE: Trichotillomania. Psychiatr Ann *23:* 402, 1993.
Vitulano LA, King RA, Scahill L, Cohen DS: Behavioral treatment of children and adolescents with trichotillomania. J Am Acad Child Adolesc Psychiatry *31:* 109, 1992.

26 Adjustment Disorders

According to the fourth edition of *Diagnostic and Statistical Manual of Mental Disorders* (DSM-IV), adjustment disorders are defined as "clinically significant emotional or behavioral symptoms" that develop "in response to an identifiable psychosocial stressor or stressors." Symptoms must appear within 3 months of a stressor's onset. Either the reaction should be disproportionate to the nature of the stressor, or social or occupational functioning should be significantly impaired. If the reaction meets the criteria for another specific anxiety or mood disorder or if it is merely an aggravation of a preexisting Axis I or II disorder, the diagnosis of an adjustment disorder is not made. The diagnosis is appropriate, however, in the presence of another Axis I or II disorder that does not account for the new symptoms. The symptoms of the disorder usually resolve within 6 months, although they may last longer if produced by a chronic stressor or one with long-lasting consequences. Thus, adjustment disorders are short-term maladaptive reactions to what a layperson would call a personal calamity but in psychiatric terms would be referred to as a psychosocial stressor.

EPIDEMIOLOGY

Adjustment disorders are one of the most common psychiatric diagnoses for disorders of patients hospitalized for medical and surgical problems. In one study, 5 percent of people admitted to a hospital over a 3-year period were classified as having an adjustment disorder. In a survey of psychiatric patients, 10 percent of the sample population were found to have an adjustment disorder. The ratio of females to males was about 2 to 1.

The disorders are most frequently diagnosed in adolescents but may occur at any age. Single women are generally overly represented as being most at risk. Among adolescents of either sex, common precipitating stresses are school problems, parental rejection and divorce, and substance abuse. Among adults, common precipitating stresses are marital problems, divorce, moving to a new environment, and financial problems.

ETIOLOGY

An adjustment disorder is precipitated by one or more stressors. The severity of the stressor or stressors is not always predictive of the severity of the disorder; the stressor severity is a complex function of degree, quantity, duration, reversibility, environment, and personal context. For example, the loss of a parent is different for a 10 year old and a 40 year old. Personality organization and cultural or group norms and values contribute to the disproportionate responses to stressors.

Stressors may be single, such as a divorce or the loss of a job, or multiple, such as the death of a person important to a patient which coincides with the patient's own physical illness and loss of a job. Stressors may be recurrent, such as seasonal business difficulties, or continuous, such as chronic illness or poverty. A discordant intrafamilial relationship may produce an adjustment disorder that affects the entire family system, or the disorder may be limited to a patient who was perhaps the victim of a crime or who has a physical illness. Sometimes adjustment disorders occur in a group or community setting, and the stressors affect several people, as in a natural disaster or in racial, social, or religious persecution. Specific developmental stages—such as beginning school, leaving home, getting married, becoming a parent, failing to achieve occupational goals, having the last child leave home, and retiring—are often associated with adjustment disorders.

Psychoanalytic Factors

Several psychoanalytic researchers have pointed out that the same stress can produce a range of responses in various normal human beings. Throughout his life, Sigmund Freud remained interested in why the stresses of ordinary life produce illness in some and not in others, why an illness takes a particular form, and why some experiences and not others predispose a person to psychopathology. He gave considerable weight to constitutional factors and viewed them as interacting with a person's life experiences to produce fixation.

Psychoanalytic research has emphasized the role of the mother and the rearing environment in a person's later capacity to respond to stress. Particularly important was Donald Winnicott's concept of the good-enough mother, a person who adapts to the infant's needs and provides enough support to enable the growing child to tolerate the frustrations in life.

Psychodynamic Factors

Pivotal to the understanding of adjustment disorders is an understanding of three factors: the nature of the stressor, the conscious and unconscious meanings of the stressor, and the patient's preexisting vulnerability. A concurrent personality disorder or organic impairment may make a person vulnerable to adjustment disorders. Vulnerability is also associated with the loss of a parent during infancy. Actual or perceived support from key relationships may affect behavioral and emotional responses to stressors.

Clinicians must undertake a detailed exploration of a patient's experience of the stressor. Certain patients commonly place all the blame on a particular event when a less obvious event may have been more significant to the patient in terms of the psychological meaning. Current events may reawaken past traumas or disappointments from childhood, so patients should be encouraged to think about how the current situation relates to similar past events.

Throughout early development, each child develops a unique set of defense mechanisms to deal with stressful events. Because of greater amounts of trauma or greater constitutional vulnerability, some children have less mature defensive constellations than do other children. This disadvantage may cause them as adults to react with substantially impaired functioning when they are faced with a loss, a divorce, or a financial setback, but those who have developed mature defense mechanisms are less vulnerable and bounce back more quickly from the stressor. Resilience is also crucially determined by the nature of children's early relationships with their parents. Studies of trauma repeatedly indicate that supportive, nurturant relationships prevent traumatic incidents from causing permanent psychological damage.

Psychodynamic clinicians must take into account the relation between a stressor and the human developmental life cycle. When adolescents leave home for college, for example, they are at high developmental risk for reacting with a temporary symptomatic picture. Similarly, if the young person who leaves home is the last child in the family, the parents may be particularly vulnerable to a reaction of adjustment disorder. Moreover, middle-aged people who are confronting their own mortality may be especially sensitive to the effects of loss or death.

DIAGNOSIS AND CLINICAL FEATURES

Although by definition adjustment disorders follow a stressor, the symptoms do not necessarily begin immediately: According to DSM-IV, up to 3 months may elapse between a stressor and the development of symptoms. Symptoms do not always subside as soon as the stressor ceases; if the stressor continues, the disorder may be chronic. The disorder may occur at any age, and its symptoms vary considerably, with depressive, anxious, and mixed features most common in adults. Physical symptoms are most common in children and the elderly but may occur in any age group. Manifestations may also include assaultive behavior and reckless driving, excessive drinking, defaulting on legal responsibilities, and withdrawal.

The clinical presentations of adjustment disorder can vary widely. DSM-IV lists six adjustment disorders, including an unspecified category (Table 26–1).

Table 26–1
DSM-IV Diagnostic Criteria for Adjustment Disorders

A. The development of emotional or behavioral symptoms in response to an identifiable stressor(s) occuring within 3 months of the onset of the stressor(s).

B. These symptoms or behaviors are clinically significant as evidenced by either of the following:
   (1) marked distress that is in excess of what would be expected from exposure to the stressor
   (2) significant impairment in social or occupational (academic) functioning

C. The stress-related disturbance does not meet the criteria for another specific Axis I disorder and is not merely an exacerbation of a preexisting Axis I or Axis II disorder.

D. The symptoms do not represent bereavement.

E. Once the stressor (or its consequences) has terminated, the symptoms do not persist for more than an additional 6 months.

Specify if:
Acute: if the disturbance lasts for less than 6 months
Chronic: if the disturbance lasts for 6 months or longer

Adjustment disorders are coded based on the subtype, which is selected according to the predominant symptoms. The specific stressor(s) can be specified on Axis IV
With depressed mood
With anxiety
With mixed anxiety and depressed mood
With disturbance of conduct
With mixed disturbance of emotions and conduct
Unspecified

Reprinted with permission from American Psychiatric Association: *Diagnostic and Statistical Manual of Mental Disorders,* ed 4. Copyright, American Psychiatric Association, Washington, 1994.

Adjustment Disorder with Depressed Mood

In adjustment disorder with depressed mood, the predominant manifestations are depressed mood, tearfulness, and hopelessness. This type must be distinguished from major depressive disorder and uncomplicated bereavement.

Dolores is 45 years old and married. She is a teacher in São Paulo, Brazil.

Dolores was admitted to a psychiatric department on an emergency basis because she had a nervous breakdown and threatened to commit suicide. Four days before, she had visited a general practitioner because she had a feeling of constant pressure in her lower abdomen. The physician told her that she was in the second trimester of pregnancy. This was completely unexpected, and she felt both shocked and despairing. Dolores felt that she just could not manage to have another child at her age, that she would have to give up working, and that her life would be utterly disrupted. The thought of this was too much for her. She became tense, and although she was tired, she was unable to sleep. She had excessive and uncontrollable crying spells, became agitated, and had difficulty breathing. Finally, she repeatedly said that she could see no solution other than committing suicide. Her husband called for the general practitioner, who had her immediately admitted to the psychiatric department.

Dolores grew up in the city, where her father was a bank manager. She had two older sisters and a younger brother. After high school she trained as a teacher and started working in the same city. When she was 25 years old, she married a technical assistant of the same age. They had two children, who are now 19 and 20 years old. When the children were young, Dolores gave up her job to take care of them, but 10 years prior to this admission, she resumed her job as a teacher. For a long time she and her husband had had a low income, but they had finally been a little better off in the previous few years and had moved to a better apartment.

Dolores had always seemed strong and in good health. Her menstruations were irregular during the previous 2 years, and when they finally stopped altogether 5 months earlier, she thought she had reached menopause. She visited the general practitioner for uncharacteristic dyspeptic symptoms, and he initially thought these were caused by an irritable colon. On examination, however, he discovered she was pregnant.

On admission, Dolores was crying and agitated but in clear consciousness and fully oriented. No perceptual or delusional features were observed.

Physical examination showed a normal pregnancy of 25 weeks. Laboratory investigations showed no abnormalities except for a slightly decreased hemoglobin concentration as a result of the pregnancy.

During the following 2 days, she gradually quieted down. She began planning for the delivery and started investigating the possibility of obtaining a leave from her job. She was discharged after 5 days, by which time she appeared completely recovered.

DISCUSSION

Dolores meets the criteria for an adjustment disorder with brief depressive reaction occurring immediately after exposure to the psychosocial stressor of an unexpected pregnancy, which may be considered as a life event that is not of an unusual or catastrophic character. Although quite severe, the symptoms were short-lived and did not meet the requirement of 2 weeks for a depressive episode. No other mental disorder was suspected.

She therefore has the diagnosis of adjustment disorder with depressed mood. (From *ICD-10 Casebook.*)

Adjustment Disorder with Anxiety

Symptoms of anxiety, such as palpitations, jitteriness, and agitation, are present in adjustment disorder with anxiety, which must be differentiated from anxiety disorders.

Adjustment Disorder with Mixed Anxiety and Depressed Mood

In adjustment disorder with mixed anxiety and depressed mood, patients exhibit features of both anxiety and depression that do not meet the criteria for an already established anxiety disorder or depressive disorder.

Adjustment Disorder with Disturbance of Conduct

In adjustment disorder with disturbance of conduct, the predominant manifestation involves conduct in which the rights of others are violated or age-appropriate societal norms and rules are disregarded. Examples of behavior in this category are truancy, vandalism, reckless driving, and fighting. The category must be differentiated from conduct disorder and antisocial personality disorder.

Adjustment Disorder with Mixed Disturbance of Emotions and Conduct

A combination of disturbances of emotions and of conduct sometimes occurs. Clinicians are encouraged to try to make one or the other diagnosis in the interest of parsimony.

Adjustment Disorder Unspecified

Adjustment disorder unspecified is a residual category for atypical maladaptive reactions to stress. Examples include inappropriate responses to the diagnosis of physical illness, such as massive denial, severe noncompliance with treatment, and social withdrawal, without significant depressed or anxious mood.

ICD-10

The 10th revision of *International Statistical Classification of Diseases and Related Health Problems* (ICD-10) places adjustment disorders in the same category as reactions to severe stress and thus presents a view of the disorders, their nature, and their diagnosis that is quite different from that of DSM-IV. The authors of ICD-10 state that this category is unlike others in their classification scheme because it includes disorders recognizable not only by their symptoms and course but by their causative influences: "The disorders . . . in this category are thought to arise always as a direct consequence of the acute severe stress or continued trauma," and the authors emphasize the severity of the stress or the continuing unpleasantness of circumstances rather than the possible disproportion between the severity of the response and the severity of the stress.

ICD-10 therefore includes acute stress reaction and posttraumatic stress disorder in this category. In acute stress reaction, an overwhelming physical or mental stress produces a state of "daze" within minutes; the symptoms begin to subside after a day or two and "are usually minimal after about three days." ICD-10 notes that not all people exposed to exceptional stress develop the disorder, so that individual variation plays a role in the disorder's occurrence and severity. Posttraumatic stress disorder is defined as a delayed or protracted response to an especially threatening event or situation that would disturb almost anyone (see Table 16.1–11). The onset may range from a few weeks to months but rarely exceeds 6 months, and most but not all people recover.

Adjustment disorders, according to ICD-10, are more affected by individual variability than are the reactions to severe stress. Nevertheless, the stressor is a necessary feature of the condition, as is the emotional disturbance caused by the stress or life change; to be classified as an adjustment disorder, the emotional disturbance must be severe enough to interfere with social performance (Table 26–2). ICD-10's time pattern for the disorders differs from that of DSM-IV, with an onset usually within a month of the stressful event or life change and a duration usually of no more than 6 months.

Although normal bereavement is not covered in this category, grief reactions of any length that are abnormal in form or content are classified as adjustment disorders. The prominent features of the adjustment disorders are grouped into brief

Table 26–2
ICD-10 Diagnostic Criteria for Adjustment Disorders

A. Onset of symptoms must occur within 1 month of exposure to an identifiable psychosocial stressor, not of an unusual or catastrophic type.

B. The individual manifests symptoms or behavior disturbance of the types found in any of the affective disorders (except for delusions and hallucinations), any disorder in neurotic, stress-related, and somatoform disorders, and conduct disorders, but the criteria for an individual disorder are not fulfilled. Symptoms may be variable in both form and severity.

The predominant feature of the symptoms may be further specified by the use of a fifth character.

Brief depressive reaction
A transient mild depressive state of a duration not exceeding 1 month.

Prolonged depressive reaction
A mild depressive state occurring in response to a prolonged exposure to a stressful situation but of a duration not exceeding 2 years.

Mixed anxiety and depressive reaction
Both anxiety and depressive symptoms are prominent, but at levels no greater than those specified for mixed anxiety and depressive disorder or other mixed anxiety disorders.

With predominant disturbance of other emotions
The symptoms are usually of several types of emotion, such as anxiety, depression, worry, tensions, and anger. Symptoms of anxiety and depression may meet the criteria for mixed anxiety and depressive disorder or for other mixed anxiety disorders, but they are not so predominant that other more specific depressive or anxiety disorders can be diagnosed. This category should also be used for reactions in children in whom regressive behavior such as bed-wetting or thumb-sucking is also present.

With predominant disturbance of conduct
The main disturbance is one involving conduct, eg, an adolescent grief reaction resulting in aggressive or dissocial behavior.

With mixed disturbance of emotions and conduct
Both emotional symptoms and disturbances of conduct are prominent features.

With other specified predominant symptoms

C. Except in prolonged depressive reaction, the symptoms do not persist for more than 6 months after the cessation of the stress or its consequences. However, this should not prevent a provisional diagnosis being made if this criterion is not yet fulfilled.

Reprinted with permission from World Health Organization: *The ICD-10 Classification of Mental and Behavioural Disorders: Diagnostic Criteria for Research.* Copyright, World Health Organization, Geneva, 1993.

depressive reaction (no longer than a month), prolonged depressive reaction (no more than 2 years), mixed anxiety and depressive reaction, reaction with predominant disturbance of emotions and conduct, and reaction with other specified predominant symptoms.

DIFFERENTIAL DIAGNOSIS

Although uncomplicated bereavement can often produce temporarily impaired social and occupational functioning, the person's dysfunctioning remains within the expectable bounds of a reaction to the loss of a loved one and, thus, is not considered adjustment disorder. Other disorders from which adjustment disorder must be differentiated include major depressive disorder, brief psychotic disorder, generalized anxiety disorder, somatization disorder, various substance-related disorders, conduct disorder, academic problem, occupational problem, identity problem, and posttraumatic stress disorder. These diagnoses should be given precedence in all cases that meet their criteria, even in the presence of a stressor or group of stressors that served as a precipitant.

Patients with an adjustment disorder, unlike those with these just-described other conditions, are impaired in social or occupational functioning and show symptoms beyond the normal and expectable reaction to the stressor. Because no absolute criteria help to distinguish an adjustment disorder from another condition, clinical judgment is necessary. Some patients, however, meet the criteria for both an adjustment disorder and a personality disorder.

Posttraumatic Stress Disorder

In posttraumatic stress disorder, the symptoms develop after a psychologically traumatizing event or events outside the range of normal human experience; the stressors producing this syndrome are expected to cause such a reaction in average human beings. People may experience the stressors alone, as in rape or assault, or in groups, as in military combat or death camps. Mass catastrophes—such as hurricanes, floods, airplane crashes, and atomic bombings—have also been identified as stressors. These stressors contain a psychological component and frequently a concomitant physical component that may directly damage people's nervous systems. Clinicians believe that the disorder is more severe and longer lasting when the stressor is of human origin, as in rape, than when it is not, as in floods. In adjustment disorders, the precipitating stress need not be severe or unusual.

COURSE AND PROGNOSIS

With appropriate treatment, the overall prognosis of an adjustment disorder is generally favorable. Most patients return to their previous level of functioning within 3 months. Adolescents usually require a longer time to recover than do adults. Some people (particularly adolescents) who receive a diagnosis of an adjustment disorder later have mood disorders or substance-related disorders.

TREATMENT

Psychotherapy

Psychotherapy remains the treatment of choice for adjustment disorders. Group therapy can be particularly useful for patients who have undergone similar stresses—for example, a group of retired people or patients undergoing renal dialysis. Individual psychotherapy offers the opportunity to explore the meaning of the stressor to the patient so that earlier traumas can be worked through. After successful therapy, patients sometimes emerge from an adjustment disorder stronger than in the premorbid period, although no pathology was evident during that period.

Because a stressor can be clearly delineated in adjustment disorders, it is often believed that psychotherapy is not indicated and that the disorder will remit spontaneously. But this viewpoint ignores the fact that many people exposed to the same stressor experience different symptoms, and in adjustment disorders, the response is pathological. Psychotherapy can help people adapt to stressors if they are not reversible or time limited and can serve as a preventive intervention if the stressor does remit.

Psychiatrists treating adjustment disorders must be particularly aware of problems of secondary gain. The illness role may be rewarding to some normal people who have had little experience with illness's capacity to free them from responsibility. Thus, patients can find therapists' attention, empathy, and understanding—which are necessary for success—rewarding in their own right, and therapists may thereby reinforce patients' symptoms. Such considerations must be weighed before intensive psychotherapy is begun; when a secondary gain has already been established, therapy is difficult.

Patients in whom adjustment disorder includes a conduct disturbance may have difficulties with the law, authorities, or school. Psychiatrists should not attempt to rescue such patients from the consequences of their actions. Too often, such kindness only reinforces socially unacceptable means of tension reduction and hinders the acquisition of insight and subsequent emotional growth. In these cases, family therapy can help.

Crisis Intervention. A brief type of therapy, crisis intervention is aimed at helping people with adjustment disorders resolve their situations quickly by supportive techniques, suggestion, reassurance, environmental modification, and even hospitalization, if necessary. The frequency and length of visits for crisis support vary according to patients' needs; daily sessions may be necessary, sometimes 2 or 3 times each day. Flexibility is essential in this approach.

Pharmacotherapy

The judicious use of medications can help patients with adjustment disorders, but they should be prescribed for brief periods. Depending on the type of adjustment disorder, a patient may respond to an antianxiety agent or to an antidepressant. Patients with severe anxiety bordering on panic or decompensation can benefit from small dosages of antipsychotic medications, and those in withdrawn or inhibited states may be helped by a short course of psychostimulant medication. Few if any cases of adjustment disorder can be adequately treated by medication alone. In most cases, psychotherapy should be added to the treatment regimen.

References

Bronisch T: Adjustment reactions: A long-term prospective and retrospective follow-up of former patients in a crisis intervention ward. Acta Psychiatr Scand *84:* 86, 1991.

Holmes J, Raphe R: The social readjustment rating scale. J Psychosom Res *11:* 213, 1967.

Horowitz MJ: *Stress Response Syndromes.* Aronson, New York, 1976.

Lewis D: *Vulnerability to Delinquency.* Spectrum, New York, 1981.

Newcorn JH, Strain JJ: Adjustment disorder in children and adolescents. J Am Acad Child Adolesc Psychiatry *31:* 318, 1991.

Newcorn JH, Strain JJ: Adjustment disorders. In *Comprehensive Textbook of Psychiatry,* ed 6, HI Kaplan, BJ Sadock, editors, p 1418. Williams & Wilkins, Baltimore, 1995.

Pollock D: Structured ambiguity and the definition of psychiatric illness: Adjustment among medical inpatients. Soc Sci Med *35:* 25, 1992.

Regier DA, Meyers JK, Kramer M, Robins LN, Blazer DG, Hough RL, Eaton WW, Locke BZ: The NIMH Epidemiologic Catchment Area program. Arch Gen Psychiatry *41:* 934, 1984.

Strain JW, Newcorn J, Wolf D, Fulop G, Davis W: Considering changes in adjustment disorder. Hosp Community Psychiatry *44:* 13, 1993.

27

Personality Disorders

The fourth edition of *Diagnostic and Statistical Manual of Mental Disorders* (DSM-IV) defines personality disorders as enduring subjective experiences and behavior that deviate from cultural standards, are rigidly pervasive, have an onset in adolescence or early adulthood, are stable through time, and lead to unhappiness and impairment. *Personality* may be described as a person's characteristic totality of emotional and behavioral traits apparent in ordinary life, a totality that is usually stable and predictable. When this totality appears to differ in a way that exceeds the range of variation found in most people, and when personality traits are rigid, maladaptive, and produce functional impairment of subjective distress, a personality disorder may be diagnosed.

People with personality disorders are far more likely to refuse psychiatric help and to deny their problems than are people with anxiety disorders, depressive disorders, or obsessive-compulsive disorder. Personality disorder symptoms are alloplastic (can adapt to, and alter, the external environment) and ego-syntonic (acceptable to the ego); people with personality disorders do not feel anxiety about their maladaptive behavior. Because they do not routinely acknowledge pain from what others perceive as their symptoms, they often seem disinterested in treatment and impervious to recovery.

CLASSIFICATION

DSM-IV

Personality disorders are grouped into three clusters in DSM-IV. Cluster A covers the paranoid, schizoid, and schizotypal personality disorders; people with these disorders are often perceived as odd and eccentric. Cluster B is made up of the antisocial, borderline, histrionic, and narcissistic personality disorders; people with these disorders often seem dramatic, emotional, and erratic. Cluster C includes the avoidant, dependent, and obsessive-compulsive personality disorders, and a category called personality disorder not otherwise specified (such as passive-aggressive personality disorder and depressive personality disorder); people with those disorders often seem anxious or fearful. Many people exhibit traits that are not limited to a single personality disorder. When a patient meets the criteria for more than one personality disorder, clinicians should diagnose each. Personality disorders are coded on Axis II of DSM-IV.

ICD-10

In the 10th revision of *International Statistical Classification of Diseases and Related Health Problems* (ICD-10), personality disorders are described as severe disturbances of personality and behavior that are pronounced deviations from normal cultural patterns. ICD-10's diagnostic guidelines include disturbances of long-standing duration in several areas of functioning; pervasive and maladaptive behavior; onset in childhood or adolescence; continuation into adulthood; considerable personality distress (although sometimes apparent only late in the disorder's course); and usually, but not always, significant problems in work and in social behavior. ICD-10 also allows for the possibility of criteria developed to describe personality disorders in different cultures. The diagnostic criteria for specific personality disorders appear in Table 27–1.

Other related disorders in ICD-10 are mixed and other personality disorders (Table 27–2); enduring personality changes not attributed to brain damage and disease (Table 27–3); other disorders of adult personality and behavior (see Table 19–4); and a residual category, unspecified disorder of adult personality and behavior.

ETIOLOGY

Genetic Factors

The best evidence that genetic factors contribute to personality disorders comes from investigations of 15,000 pairs of twins in the United States. Among monozygotic twins, the concordance for personality disorders was several times higher than that among dizygotic twins. Moreover, according to one study, monozygotic twins reared apart are about as similar as monozygotic twins reared together. Similarities include multiple measures of personality and temperament, occupational and leisure-time interests, and social attitudes.

Cluster A personality disorders (paranoid, schizoid, and schizotypal) are more common in the biological relatives of patients with schizophrenia than among control groups. More relatives with schizotypal personality disorder occur in the family histories of people with schizophrenia than among control groups. Less correlation exists between paranoid or schizoid personality disorder and schizophrenia.

Cluster B personality disorders (antisocial, borderline, histrionic, and narcissistic) apparently have a genetic base. Antisocial personality disorder is associated with alcohol use disorders. Depression is common in the family backgrounds of patients with borderline personality disorder. These patients have more relatives with mood disorders than do control groups, and people with borderline personality disorder often have mood disorder as well. A strong association is found between histrionic personality disorder and somatization dis-

Table 27–1
ICD-10 Diagnostic Criteria for Specific Personality Disorders

G1. There is evidence that the individual's characteristic and enduring patterns of inner experience and behavior as a whole deviate markedly from the culturally expected and accepted range (or "norm"). Such deviation must be manifest in more than one of the following areas:
  (1) cognition (i.e., ways of perceiving and interpreting things, people, and events; forming attitudes and images of self and others);
  (2) affectivity (range, intensity, and appropriateness of emotional arousal and response);
  (3) control over impulses and gratification of needs;
  (4) manner of relating to others and of handling interpersonal situations.

G2. The deviation must manifest itself pervasively as behavior that is inflexible, maladaptive, or otherwise dysfunctional across a broad range of personal and social situations (ie, not being limited to one specific "triggering" stimulus or situation).

G3. There is personal distress, or adverse impact on the social environment, or both, clearly attributable to the behavior referred to in criterion G2.

G4. There must be evidence that the deviation is stable and of long duration, having its onset in late childhood or adolescence.

G5. The deviation cannot be explained as a manifestation or consequence of other adult mental disorders, although episodic or chronic conditions of this classification may coexist with, or be superimposed upon, the deviation.

G6. Organic brain disease, injury, or dysfunction must be excluded as the possible cause of the deviation. (If an organic causation is demonstrable, the personality and behavioral disorders due to brain disease, damage, and dysfunction category should be used.)

Comments

The assessment of criteria G1–G6 above should be based on as many sources of information as possible. Although it is sometimes possible to obtain sufficient evidence from a single interview with the individual, as a general rule it is recommended to have more than one interview with the person and to collect history data from informants or past records.

It is suggested that subcriteria should be developed to define behavior patterns specific to different cultural settings concerning social norms, rules, and obligations where needed (such as examples of irresponsibility and disregard of social norms in dissocial personality disorder).

The diagnosis of personality disorder for research purposes requires the identification of a subtype. (More than one subtype can be coded if there is compelling evidence that the individual meets multiple sets of criteria.)

Paranoid personality disorder

A. The general criteria for personality disorder must be met.

B. At least four of the following must be present:
  (1) excessive sensitivity to setbacks and rebuffs;
  (2) tendency to bear grudges persistently, eg, refusal to forgive insults, injuries, or slights;
  (3) suspiciousness and a pervasive tendency to distort experience by misconstruing the neutral or friendly actions of others as hostile or contemptuous;
  (4) a combative and tenancious sense of personal rights out of keeping with the actual situation;
  (5) recurrent suspicions, without justification, regarding sexual fidelity of spouse or sexual partner;
  (6) persistent self-referential attitude, associated particularly with excessive self-importance;
  (7) preoccupation with unsubstantiated "conspiratorial" explanations of events either immediate to the patient or in the world at large.

Schizoid personality disorder

A. The general criteria for personality disorder must be met.

B. At least four of the following must be present:
  (1) few, if an, activities provide pleasure;
  (2) display of emotional coldness, detachment, or flattened affectivity;
  (3) limited capacity to express either warm, tender feelings or anger towards others;
  (4) an appearance of indifference to either praise or criticism;
  (5) little interest in having sexual experience with another person (taking into account age);
  (6) consistent choice of solitary activities;
  (7) excessive preoccupation with fantasy and introspection;
  (8) no desire for, or possession of, any close friends or confiding relationships (or only one);
  (9) marked insensitivity to prevailing social norms and conventions; disregard for such norms and conventions is unintentional.

Dissocial personality disorder

A. The general criteria for personality disorder must be met.

B. At least three of the following must be present:
  (1) callous unconcern for the feelings of others;
  (2) gross and persistent attitude of irresponsibility and disregard for social norms, rules, and obligations;
  (3) incapacity to maintain enduring relationships, though with no difficulty in establishing them;
  (4) very low tolerance to frustration and a low threshold for discharge of aggression, including violence;
  (5) incapacity to experience guilt or to profit from adverse experience, particularly punishment;
  (6) marked proneness to blame others or to offer plausible rationalizations for the behavior that has brought the individual into conflict with society.

Comments

Persistent irritability and the presence of conduct disorder during childhood and adolescence complete the clinical picture but are not required for the diagnosis.

It is suggested that subcriteria should be developed to define behavior patterns specific to different cultural settings concerning social norms, rules, and obligations where needed (such as examples of irresponsibility and disregard of social norms).

Emotionally unstable personality disorder

Impulsive type

A. The general criteria for personality disorder must be met.

B. At least three of the following must be present, one of which must be (2):
  (1) marked tendency to act unexpectedly and without consideration of the consequences;
  (2) marked tendency to quarrelsome behavior and to conflicts with others, especially when impulsive acts are thwarted or criticized;
  (3) liability to outbursts of anger or violence, with inability to control the resulting behavioral explosions;
  (4) difficulty in maintaining any course of action that offers no immediate reward;
  (5) unstable and capricious mood.

(continued)

Table 27–1 ***(continued)***

Borderline type

A. The general criteria for personality disorder must be met.

B. At least three of the symptoms mentioned in criterion B for emotionally unstable personality disorder, impulsive type, must be present, with at least two of the following in addition:
   (1) disturbances in and uncertainty about self-image, aims, and internal preferences (including sexual);
   (2) liability to become involved in intense and unstable relationships, often leading to emotional crises;
   (3) excessive efforts to avoid abandonment;
   (4) recurrent threats or acts of self-harm;
   (5) chronic feelings of emptiness.

Histrionic personality disorder

A. The general criteria for personality disorder must be met.

B. At least four of the following must be present:
   (1) self-dramatization, theatricality, or exaggerated expression of emotions;
   (2) suggestibility (the individual is easily influenced by others or by circumstances);
   (3) shallow and labile affectivity;
   (4) continual seeking for excitement and activities in which the individual is the center of attention;
   (5) inappropriate seductiveness in appearance or behavior;
   (6) overconcern with physical attractiveness.

Comments

Egocentricity, self-indulgence, continuous longing for appreciation, lack of consideration for others, feelings that are easily hurt, and persistent manipulative behavior complete the clinical picture, but are not required for the diagnosis.

Anancastic personality disorder

Note. This disorder is often referred to as obsessive-compulsive personality disorder.

A. The general criteria for personality disorder must be met.

B. At least four of the following must be present:
   (1) feelings of excessive doubt and caution;
   (2) preoccupation with details, rules, lists, order, organization, or schedule;
   (3) perfectionism that interferes with task completion;
   (4) excessive conscientiousness and scrupulousness;
   (5) undue preoccupation with productivity to the exclusion of pleasure and interpersonal relationships;
   (6) excessive pedantry and adherence to social conventions;
   (7) rigidity and stubbornness;
   (8) unreasonable insistence by the individual that others submit to exactly his or her way of doing things, or unreasonable reluctance to allow others to do things.

Anxious (avoidant) personality disorder

A. The general criteria for personality disorder must be met.

B. At least four of the following must be present:
   (1) persistent and pervasive feelings of tension and apprehension;
   (2) belief that one is socially inept, personally unappealing, or inferior to others;
   (3) excessive preoccupation with being critized or rejected in social situations;
   (4) unwillingness to become involved with people unless certain of being liked;
   (5) restrictions in lifestyle because of need for physical security;
   (6) avoidance of social or occupational activities that involve significant interpersonal contact, because of fear of criticism, disapproval, or rejection.

Dependent personality disorder

A. The general criteria for personality disorder must be met.

B. At least four of the following must be present:
   (1) encouraging or allowing others to make the most of one's important life decisions;
   (2) subordination of one's own needs to those of others on whom one is dependent, and undue compliance with their wishes;
   (3) unwillingness to make even reasonable demands on the people one depends on;
   (4) feeling uncomfortable or helpless when alone, because of exaggerated fears of inability to care for oneself;
   (5) preoccupation with fears of being left to care for oneself;
   (6) limited capacity to make everyday decisions without an excessive amount of advice and reassurance from others.

Other specific personality disorders

If none of the preceding rubrics is fitting, but a condition meeting the general criteria for specific personality disorders is nevertheless present, this code should be used. An extra character may be added for identifying specific personality disorders not currently in ICD-10. In using other specific personality disorders it is recommended always to record a vignette description of the specific disorder.

Personality disorder, unspecified

order (Briquet's syndrome); patients with each disorder show an overlap of symptoms.

Cluster C personality disorders (avoidant, dependent, obsessive-compulsive, and not otherwise specified) may also have a genetic base. Patients with avoidant personality disorder often have high anxiety levels. Obsessive-compulsive traits are more common in monozygotic twins than in dizygotic twins, and patients with obsessive-compulsive personality disorder show some signs associated with depression—for example, shortened rapid eye movement (REM) latency period, and abnormal dexamethasone-suppression test (DST) results.

Biological Factors

Hormones. People who exhibit impulsive traits also often show increased levels of testosterone, 17-estradiol, and estrone. In nonhuman primates, androgens increase the likelihood of aggression and sexual behavior, but the role of testosterone in human aggression is unclear. Dexamethasone-suppression test (DST) results are abnormal in some patients with borderline personality disorder who also have depressive symptoms.

Platelet Monoamine Oxidase. Low platelet monoamine oxidase (MAO) levels have been associated with activity and sociability in monkeys. College students with low platelet MAO levels report spending more time in social activities than do students with high platelet MAO levels. Low platelet MAO levels have also been noted in some patients with schizotypal disorders.

Table 27–2
ICD-10 Diagnostic Criteria for Mixed and Other Personality Disorders

No attempt has been made to provide standard sets of criteria for these mixed disorders, since those doing research in this field will prefer to state their own criteria depending upon the purpose of their studies.

Mixed personality disorders
Features of several of the specific personality disorders are present, but not to the extent that the criteria for any of the specified personality disorders in that category are met.

Troublesome personality changes
Not classifiable in specific personality disorders or enduring personality changes, not attributable to brain damage and disease, and regarded as secondary to a main diagnosis of a coexisting affective or anxiety disorder.

Reprinted with permission from World Health Organization: *The ICD-10 Classification of Mental and Behavioural Disorders: Diagnostic Criteria for Research.* Copyright, World Health Organization, Geneva, 1993.

Smooth Pursuit Eye Movements. Smooth pursuit eye movements are saccadic (that is, jumpy) in people who are introverted, who have low self-esteem and tend to withdraw, and who have schizotypal personality disorder. These findings have no clinical application, but they do indicate the role of inheritance.

Neurotransmitters. Endorphins have effects similar to those of exogenous morphine, such as analgesia and the suppression of arousal. High endogenous endorphin levels may be associated with people who are phlegmatic. Studies of personality traits and the dopaminergic and serotonergic systems indicate an arousal-activating function for these neurotransmitters. Levels of 5-hydroxyindoleacetic acid (5-HIAA), a metabolite of serotonin, are low in people who attempt suicide and in patients who are impulsive and aggressive.

Raising serotonin levels with serotonergic agents such as fluoxetine (Prozac) may produce dramatic changes in some character traits of personality. In many people, serotonin reduces depression, impulsiveness, and rumination, and can produce a sense of general well-being. Increased dopamine in the central nervous system, produced by certain psychostimulants (such as amphetamines) can induce euphoria. The effects of neurotransmitters on personality traits have generated much interest, and controversy, about whether personality traits are inborn or acquired.

In his book *Listening to Prozac,* Peter Kramer described dramatic personality changes, such as decreased sensitivity to rejection, increased assertiveness, and improved self-esteem and ability to tolerate stress, that can occur when serotonin levels are raised by fluoxetine. These changes in personality traits occur in patients with a wide range of psychiatric conditions.

Electrophysiology. Changes in electrical conductance on the electroencephalogram (EEG) occur in some patients with personality disorders, most commonly antisocial and borderline types; these changes appear as slow-wave activity on EEGs.

Psychoanalytic Factors

Sigmund Freud suggested that personality traits are related to a fixation at one psychosexual stage of development. For example, those with an oral character are passive and dependent because they are fixated at the oral stage, when the dependence on others for food is prominent. Those with an anal character are stubborn, parsimonious, and highly conscientious because of struggles over toilet training during the anal period.

Wilhelm Reich subsequently coined the term *character armor* to describe people's characteristic defensive styles for protecting themselves from internal impulses and from interpersonal anxiety in significant relationships. Reich's theory has had a broad influence on contemporary concepts of personality and of personality disorders. For example, each human being's unique stamp of personality is considered largely determined by his or her characteristic defense mechanisms. Each personality disorder in Axis II has a cluster of defenses that help psychodynamic clinicians recognize the type of character pathology present. People with paranoid personality disorder, for instance, use projection, whereas schizoid personality disorder is associated with withdrawal.

When defenses work effectively, people with personality disorders master feelings of anxiety, depression, anger, shame, guilt, and other affects. They often view their behavior as ego-syntonic: That is, it creates no distress for them, even though it may adversely affect others. They may also be reluctant to engage in a treatment process; because their defenses are important in controlling unpleasant affects, they are not interested in surrendering them.

In addition to characteristic defenses in personality disorders, another central feature is internal object relations. During development, particular patterns of self in relation to others are internalized. Through introjection children internalize a parent or another significant person as an internal presence that continues to feel like an object rather than a self. Through identification children internalize parents and others in such a way that the traits of the external object are incorporated into the self and the child "owns" the traits. These internal self-representations and object representations are crucial in developing the personality and, through externalization and projective identification, are played out in interpersonal scenarios in which others are coerced into playing a role in the person's internal life. Hence, people with personality disorders are also identified by particular patterns of interpersonal relatedness that stem from these internal object relations patterns.

Defense Mechanisms. To help those with personality disorders, psychiatrists must appreciate patients' underlying defenses, the unconscious mental processes that the ego uses to resolve conflicts among the four lodestars of the inner life: instinct (wish or need), reality, important people, and conscience. When defenses are most effective, especially in those with personality disorders, they can abolish anxiety and depression. Thus, abandoning a defense increases conscious anxiety and depression—a major reason that those with personality disorders are reluctant to alter their behavior.

Although patients with personality disorders may be characterized by their most dominant or rigid mechanism, each patient uses several defenses. Therefore, the management of defense mechanisms used by patients with personality disor-

Table 27–3
ICD-10 Diagnostic Criteria for Enduring Personality Changes, Not Attributable to Brain Damage and Disease

Enduring personality change after catastrophic experience

A. There must be evidence (from the personal history or from key informants) of a definite and persistent change in the individual's pattern of perceiving, relating to, and thinking about the environment and the self, following exposure to catastrophic stress (eg, concentration camp experience; torture; disaster; prolonged exposure to life-threatening situations).

B. The personality change should be significant and represent inflexible and maladaptive features as indicated by the presence of at least two of the following:
   (1) a permanent hostile or distrustful attitude toward the world in a person who previously showed no such traits;
   (2) social withdrawal (avoidance of contacts with people other than a few close relatives with whom the individual lives) which is not due to another current mental disorder (such as a mood disorder);
   (3) a constant feeling of emptiness or hopelessness, not limited to a discrete episode of mood disorder, which was not present before the catastrophic stress experience; this may be associated with increased dependency on others, inability to express negative or aggressive feelings, and prolonged depressive mood without any evidence of depressive disorder before exposure to the catastrophic stress;
   (4) an enduring feeling of being "on edge" or of being threatened without any external cause, as evidenced by an increased vigilance and irritability in a person who previously showed no such traits or hyperalertness; this chronic state of inner tension and feeling threatened may be associated with a tendency to excessive drinking or use of drugs;
   (5) a permanent feeling of being changed or of being different from others (estrangement); this feeling may be associated with an experience of emotional numbness.

C. The change should cause significant interference with personal functioning in daily living, personal distress, or adverse impact on the social environment.

D. The personality change should have developed after the catastrophic experience, and there should be no history of a preexisting adult personality disorder or trait accentuation, or of personality or developmental disorders during childhood or adolescence, that could explain the current personality traits.

E. The personality change must have been present for at least 2 years. It is not related to episodes of any other mental disorder (except posttraumatic stress disorder) and cannot be explained by brain damage or disease.

F. The personality change meeting the above criteria is often preceded by a posttraumatic stress disorder. The symptoms of the two conditions can overlap and the personality change may be a chronic outcome of a posttraumatic stress disorder. However, an enduring personality change should not be assumed in such cases unless, in addition to at least 2 years of posttraumatic stress disorder, there has been a further period of no less than 2 years during which the above criteria have been met.

Enduring personality change after psychiatric illness

A. There must be evidence of a definite and enduring change in the individual's pattern of perceiving, relating to, and thinking about the environment and the self, following the experience of suffering from one or several episodes of psychiatric illness from which he or she has recovered clinically without residual symptoms.

B. The personality change should be significant and represent inflexible and maladaptive features as indicated by the presence of at least two of the following:
   (1) dependence on others (the individual passively assumes, or demands, that others take responsibility for his or her own life, and is unwilling to decide on important issues related to his or her actions or future);
   (2) social withdrawal or isolation, which is secondary to a conviction (not delusional) or feeling of being "changed" or stigmatized as a result of the illness; this conviction or feeling may be strengthened by societal attitudes but cannot be completely explained by the objective social circumstances; feeling vulnerable to others' moral opprobrium (narcissistic injury) may also be a factor but such feeling should be ego-syntonic if it is to be considered an enduring personality trait;
   (3) passivitiy, reduced interests, an diminished involvement in previously entertained leisure activities (which may reinforce the social isolation);
   (4) a change in self-perception, leading to a frequent or constant claim of being ill; this may be associated with hypochondriacal behavior and an increased utilization of psychiatric or other medical services;
   (5) a demanding attitude toward other people in which the individual expects special favors or considers himself or herself deserving of special attention or treatment;
   (6) dysphoric or labile mood, not due to a current mental disorder or antecedent mental disorder with residual affective symptoms.

C. The personality change following the psychiatric illness must be understandable in terms of the individual's subjective emotional experience of the situation, his or her previous adjustment, vulnerabilities, and life situation including the attitudes or reactions of significant others following the illness.

D. The personality change should cause significant interference with personal functioning in daily living, personal distress, or adverse impact on the social environment.

E. There should be no history of a preexisting adult personality disorder or trait accentuation or of personality or developmental disorders during childhood or adolescence that could explain the current personality traits.

F. The personality change has been present for at least 2 years and is not a manifestation of another mental disorder or secondary to brain damage or disease.

Other enduring personality changes

Enduring personality change, unspecified

ders is discussed here as a general topic and not as an aspect of the specific disorders. Many formulations presented here in the language of psychoanalytic psychiatry can be translated into principles consistent with cognitive and behavioral approaches.

FANTASY. Many people who are often labeled schizoid—those who are eccentric, lonely, or frightened—seek solace and satisfaction within themselves by creating imaginary lives, especially imaginary friends. In their extensive dependence on fantasy, these people often seem to be strikingly aloof. Therapists must understand that the unsociableness of these patients rests on a fear of intimacy. Rather than criticizing them or feeling rebuffed by their rejection, therapists should maintain a quiet, reassuring, and considerate interest without insisting on reciprocal responses. Recognition of patients' fear of closeness and respect for their eccentric ways are both therapeutic and useful.

DISSOCIATION. Dissociation or denial is a Pollyanna-like replacement of unpleasant affects with pleasant ones. People who frequently dissociate are often seen as dramatizing and emotionally shallow; they may be labeled histrionic personalities. They behave like anxious adolescents who, to erase anxiety, carelessly expose themselves to exciting dangers. Accepting such patients as exuberant and seductive is to overlook their anxiety, but confronting them with their vulnerabilities and defects makes them still more defensive. Because they seek appreciation of their courage and attractiveness, therapists should not behave with inordinate reserve. While remaining calm and firm, clinicians should realize that these patients are often inadvertent liars, but they benefit from ventilating their own anxieties and may in the process "remember" what they "forgot." Often therapists deal best with dissociation and denial by using displacement. Thus, clinicians may talk with patients about an issue of denial in an unthreatening circumstance. Empathizing with the denied affect without directly confronting patients with the facts may allow them to raise the original topic themselves.

ISOLATION. Isolation is characteristic of the orderly, controlled people who are often labeled obsessive-compulsive personalities. Unlike those with histrionic personality, people with obsessive-compulsive personality remember the truth in fine detail but without affect. In a crisis patients may show an intensification of self-restraint, overly formal social behavior, and obstinacy. Patients' quests for control may annoy clinicians or make them anxious. Often, such patients respond well to precise, systematic, and rational explanations and value efficiency, cleanliness, and punctuality as much as they do clinicians' effective responsiveness. Whenever possible, therapists should allow such patients to control their own care and should not engage in a battle of wills.

PROJECTION. In projection, patients attribute their own unacknowledged feelings to others. Patients' excessive faultfinding and sensitivity to criticism may appear to therapists as prejudiced, hypervigilant injustice collecting, but should not be met by defensiveness and argument. Instead, clinicians should frankly acknowledge even minor mistakes on their part and should discuss the possibility of future difficulties. Strict honesty, concern for patients' rights, and maintaining the same formal, concerned distance as with patients who use fantasy defenses are all helpful. Confrontation guarantees a lasting enemy and an early termination of the interview. Therapists need not agree with patients' injustice collecting, but should ask whether both can agree to disagree.

The technique of counterprojection is especially helpful. Clinicians acknowledge and give paranoid patients full credit for their feelings and perceptions; they neither dispute patients' complaints nor reinforce them but agree that the world described by patients is conceivable. Interviewers can then talk about real motives and feelings, misattributed to someone else, and begin to cement an alliance with patients.

SPLITTING. In splitting, people toward whom patients' feelings are or have been ambivalent are divided into good and bad. For example, in an inpatient setting, a patient may idealize some staff members and uniformly disparage others. This defense behavior can be highly disruptive on a hospital ward and can ultimately provoke the staff to turn against the patient. When staff members anticipate the process, discuss it at staff meetings, and gently confront the patient with the fact that no one is all good or all bad, the phenomenon of splitting can be effectively dealt with.

PASSIVE AGGRESSION. People with passive-aggressive defense turn their anger against themselves. In psychoanalytic terms this phenomenon is called masochism and includes failure, procrastination, silly or provocative behavior, self-demeaning clowning, and frankly self-destructive acts. The hostility in such behavior is never entirely concealed. Indeed, in a mechanism such as wrist cutting, others feel as much anger as if they themselves had been assaulted and view the patient as a sadist, not a masochist. Therapists can best deal with passive aggression by helping patients to ventilate their anger.

ACTING OUT. In acting out, patients directly express unconscious wishes or conflicts through action to avoid being conscious of either the accompanying idea or the affect. Tantrums, apparently motiveless assaults, child abuse, and pleasureless promiscuity are common examples. Because the behavior occurs outside reflective awareness, acting out often appears to observers to be unaccompanied by guilt, but when acting out is impossible, the conflict behind the defense may be accessible. Faced with acting out, either aggressive or sexual, in an interview situation, a clinician must recognize that the patient has lost control, that anything the interviewer says will probably be misheard, and that getting the patient's attention is of paramount importance. Depending on the circumstances, a clinician's response may be, "How can I help you if you keep screaming?" or, if the patient's loss of control seems to be escalating, "If you continue screaming, I'll leave." An interviewer who feels genuinely frightened of the patient can simply leave and, if necessary, ask for help from ward attendants or the police.

PROJECTIVE IDENTIFICATION. The defense mechanism of projective identification appears mainly in borderline personality disorder and consists of three steps: An aspect of the self is projected onto someone else; the projector tries to coerce the other person to identify with what has been projected; and the recipient of the projection and the projector feel a sense of oneness or union.

Temperamental, Familial, and Environmental Factors

Temperamental factors identified in childhood may be associated with personality disorders in adulthood. For example, children who are temperamentally fearful may later develop avoidant personality disorder. Childhood central nervous system dysfunctions associated with soft neurological signs are most common in people with antisocial and borderline personality disorders. Children with minimal brain damage are at risk for personality disorders, particularly antisocial personality disorder.

Stella Chess and Alexander Thomas referred to goodness of fit in child rearing, and some personality disorders may arise from poor parental fit: that is, a poor match between temperament and child-rearing practices. For example, anxious children reared by equally anxious mothers are more vulnerable to personality disorders than would be the same children raised by tranquil mothers. Cultural factors may also play a part in personality disorders, as may the physical environment. For example, cultures that encourage aggression may unwittingly reinforce and thereby contribute to paranoid and antisocial personality disorders. And active children may appear hyperactive when they live in a small apartment but may behave normally in a roomy house with a fenced-in yard.

PARANOID PERSONALITY DISORDER

People with paranoid personality disorder are characterized by long-standing suspiciousness and mistrust of people in general. They refuse responsibility for their own feelings and assign responsibility to others. They are often hostile, irritable, and angry. Bigots, injustice collectors, pathologically jealous spouses, and litigious cranks often have paranoid personality disorder.

Epidemiology

The prevalence of paranoid personality disorder is 0.5 to 2.5 percent of the general population. Those with the disorder rarely seek treatment themselves; when referred to treatment by a spouse or an employer, they can often pull themselves together and appear undistressed. Relatives of patients with schizophrenia show a higher incidence of paranoid personality disorder than do controls. The disorder is more common in men than in women and does not appear to have a familial pattern. The prevalence among people who are homosexual is no higher than usual, as was once thought, but is believed to be higher among minority groups, immigrants, and people who are deaf than it is in the general population.

Diagnosis

On psychiatric examination, patients with paranoid personality disorder may be formal in manner and act baffled about having to seek psychiatric help. Muscular tension, an inability to relax, and a need to scan the environment for clues may be evident, and patients' manner is often humorless and serious. Although some premises of their arguments may be false, their speech is goal directed and logical. Their thought content shows evidence of projection, prejudice, and occasional ideas of reference. The DSM-IV diagnostic criteria are listed in Table 27–4.

Table 27–4
DSM-IV Diagnostic Criteria for Paranoid Personality Disorder

A. A pervasive distrust and suspiciousness of others such that their motives are interpreted as malevolent, beginning by early adulthood and present in a variety of contexts, as indicated by four (or more) of the following:
 (1) suspects, without sufficient basis, that others are exploiting, harming, or deceiving him or her
 (2) is preoccupied with unjustified doubts about the loyalty or trustworthiness of friends or associates
 (3) is reluctant to confide in others because of unwarranted fear that the information will be used maliciously against him or her
 (4) reads hidden, demeaning, or threatening meanings into benign remarks or events
 (5) persistently bears grudges, ie, is unforgiving of insults, injuries, or slights
 (6) perceives attacks on his or her character or reputation that are not apparent to others and is quick to react angrily or to counterattack
 (7) has recurrent suspicions, without justification, regarding fidelity of spouse or sexual partner

B. Does not occur exclusively during the course of schizophrenia, a mood disorder with psychotic features, or another psychotic disorder and is not due to the direct physiological effects of a general medical condition.
Note: if criteria are met prior to the onset of schizophrenia, add "premorbid," eg, "paranoid personality disorder (premorbid)."

Reprinted with permission from American Psychiatric Association: *Diagnostic and Statistical Manual of Mental Disorders,* ed. 4. Copyright, American Psychiatric Association, Washington, 1994.

Clinical Features

The essential feature of people with paranoid personality disorder is a pervasive and unwarranted tendency, which begins by early adulthood and appears in a variety of contexts, to interpret other people's actions as deliberately demeaning or threatening. Almost invariably, those with the disorder expect to be exploited or harmed by others in some way. They frequently dispute, without any justification, friends' or associates' loyalty or trustworthiness. Such people are often pathologically jealous and for no reason question the fidelity of their spouses or sexual partners. People with this disorder externalize their own emotions and use the defense of projection: They attribute to others the impulses and thoughts that they are unable to accept in themselves. Ideas of reference and logically defended illusions are common.

People with paranoid personality disorder are affectively restricted and appear to be unemotional. They pride themselves on being rational and objective, but such is not the case. They lack warmth and are impressed with, and pay close attention to, power and rank; they express disdain for those who are seen as weak, sickly, impaired, or in some way defective. In social situations, people with paranoid personality disorder may appear business-like and efficient, but they often generate fear or conflict in others.

Differential Diagnosis

Paranoid personality disorder can usually be differentiated from delusional disorder by the absence of fixed delusions. Unlike people with paranoid schizophrenia, those with personality disorders have no hallucinations or formal thought disorder. Paranoid personality disorder can be distinguished from borderline personality disorder because paranoid patients are rarely capable of overly involved, tumultuous relationships with others. Paranoid patients lack the long history of antisocial behavior of people with antisocial character. People with schizoid personality disorder are withdrawn and aloof and do not have paranoid ideation.

Course and Prognosis

Adequate and systematic long-term studies of paranoid personality disorder have not been conducted. In some, paranoid personality disorder is lifelong; in others it is a harbinger of schizophrenia. In still others, paranoid traits give way to reaction formation, appropriate concern with morality, and altruistic concerns as they mature or as stress diminishes. In general, however, those with paranoid personality disorder have lifelong problems working and living with others. Occupational and marital problems are common.

Treatment

Psychotherapy. Psychotherapy is the treatment of choice. Therapists should be straightforward in all their dealings with these patients. If a therapist is accused of an inconsistency or fault, such as lateness for an appointment, honesty and an apology are preferable to a defensive explanation. Therapists must remember that trust and toleration of intimacy are troubled areas for patients with the disorder. Individual psychotherapy thus requires a professional and not overly warm style from therapists. Clinicians' over zealous use of interpretation—especially interpretation about deep feelings of dependence, sexual concerns, and wishes for intimacy—significantly increase patients' mistrust. Paranoid patients usually do not do well in group psychotherapy, although it can be useful for improving social skills and diminishing suspiciousness through role playing. Many cannot tolerate the intrusiveness of behavior therapy, also used for social skills training.

At times, patients with paranoid personality disorder behave so threateningly that therapists must control or set limits on their actions. Delusional accusations must be dealt with realistically but gently and without humiliating patients. Paranoid patients are profoundly frightened when they feel that those trying to help them are weak and helpless; therefore, therapists should never offer to take control unless they are willing and able to do so.

Pharmacotherapy. Pharmacotherapy is useful in dealing with agitation and anxiety. In most cases an antianxiety agent such as diazepam (Valium) is sufficient. But it may be necessary to use an antipsychotic, such as thioridazine (Mellaril) or haloperidol (Haldol), in small dosages and for brief periods to manage severe agitation or quasi-delusional thinking. The antipsychotic drug pimozide (Orap) has been successfully used to reduce paranoid ideation in some patients.

SCHIZOID PERSONALITY DISORDER

Schizoid personality disorder is diagnosed in patients who display a lifelong pattern of social withdrawal. Their discomfort with human interaction, their introversion, and their bland, constricted affect are noteworthy. People with schizoid personality disorder are often seen by others as eccentric, isolated, or lonely.

Epidemiology

The prevalence of schizoid personality disorder is not clearly established, but the disorder may affect 7.5 percent of the general population. The sex ratio of the disorder is unknown; some studies report a 2-to-1 male-to-female ratio. People with the disorder tend to gravitate toward solitary jobs that involve little or no contact with others. Many prefer night work to day work, so that they need not deal with many people.

Diagnosis

On an initial psychiatric examination, patients with schizoid personality disorder may appear ill at ease. They rarely tolerate eye contact, and interviewers may surmise that such patients are eager for the interview to end. Their affect may be constricted, aloof, or inappropriately serious, but underneath the aloofness, sensitive clinicians can recognize fear. These patients find it difficult to be lighthearted: Their efforts at humor may seem adolescent and off the mark. Their speech is goal-directed, but they are likely to give short answers to questions and to avoid spontaneous conversation. They may occasionally use unusual figures of speech, such as an odd metaphor, and may be fascinated with inanimate objects or metaphysical constructs. Their mental content may reveal an unwarranted sense of intimacy with people they do not know well or whom they have not seen for a long time. Their sensorium is intact, their memory functions well, and their proverb interpretations are abstract. The DSM-IV diagnostic criteria are listed in Table 27–5.

Clinical Features

People with schizoid personality disorder seem to be cold and aloof; they display a remote reserve and show no involvement with everyday events and the concerns of others. They appear quiet, distant, seclusive, and unsociable. They may pursue their own lives with remarkably little need or longing for emotional ties, and are the last to be aware of changes in popular fashion.

The life histories of such people reflect solitary interests and success at noncompetitive, lonely jobs that others find difficult to tolerate. Their sexual lives may exist exclusively in fantasy, and they may postpone mature sexuality indefinitely. Men may not marry because they are unable to achieve intimacy; women may passively agree to marry an aggressive man who wants the marriage. People with schizoid personality disorder usually reveal a lifelong inability to express anger di-

Table 27–5
DSM-IV Diagnostic Criteria for Schizoid Personality Disorder

A. A pervasive pattern of detachment from social relationships and a restricted range of expression of emotions in interpersonal settings, beginning by early adulthood and present in a variety of contexts, as indicated by four (or more) of the following:
   (1) neither desires nor enjoys close relationships, including being part of a family
   (2) almost always chooses solitary activities
   (3) has little, if any, interest in having sexual experiences with another person
   (4) takes pleasure in few, if any, activities
   (5) lacks close friends or confidants other than first-degree relatives
   (6) appears indifferent to the praise or criticism of others
   (7) shows emotional coldness, detachment, or flattened affectivity

B. Does not occur exclusively during the course of schizophrenia, a mood disorder with psychotic features, another psychotic disorder, or a pervasive developmental disorder, and is not due to the direct physiological effects of a general medical condition.
Note: if criteria are met prior to the onset of schizophrenia, add "premorbid," eg, "schizoid personality disorder (premorbid)."

Reprinted with permission from American Psychiatric Association: *Diagnostic and Statistical Manual of Mental Disorders,* ed. 4. Copyright, American Psychiatric Association, Washington, 1994.

rectly. They are able to invest enormous affective energy in nonhuman interests such as mathematics and astronomy, and they may be very attached to animals. Dietary and health fads, philosophical movements, and social improvement schemes, especially those that require no personal involvement, often engross them.

Although people with schizoid personality disorder appear self-absorbed and lost in daydreams, they have a normal capacity to recognize reality. Because aggressive acts are rarely included in their repertoire of usual responses, most threats, real or imagined, are dealt with by fantasied omnipotence or resignation. They are often seen as aloof, yet such people can sometimes conceive, develop, and give to the world genuinely original, creative ideas.

Differential Diagnosis

In contrast to patients with schizophrenia and schizotypal personality disorder, patients with schizoid personality disorder do not have schizophrenic relatives, and they may have successful, if isolated, work histories. They also differ from patients with schizophrenia by exhibiting no thought disorder or delusional thinking. Although patients with paranoid personality disorder share many traits with those with schizoid personality disorder, the former exhibit more social engagement, a history of aggressive verbal behavior, and a greater tendency to project their feelings onto others. If just as emotionally constricted, patients with obsessive-compulsive and avoidant personality disorders experience loneliness as dysphoric, possess a richer history of past object relations, and do not engage as much in autistic reverie. Theoretically, the chief distinction between a patient with schizotypal personality disorder and one with schizoid personality disorder is that a schizotypal patient is more similar to a patient with schizophrenia in oddities of perception, thought, behavior, and communication. Patients with avoidant personality disorder are isolated but strongly wish to participate in activities, a characteristic absent in those with schizoid personality disorder.

Course and Prognosis

The onset of schizoid personality disorder usually occurs in early childhood. Like all personality disorders, schizoid personality disorder is long lasting, but not necessarily lifelong. The proportion of patients who incur schizophrenia is unknown.

Treatment

Psychotherapy. The treatment of patients with schizoid personality disorder is similar to that of those with paranoid personality disorder. Schizoid patients' tendencies toward introspection, however, are consistent with psychotherapists' expectations, and schizoid patients may become devoted, if distant, patients. As trust develops, schizoid patients may, with great trepidation, reveal a plethora of fantasies, imaginary friends, and fears of unbearable dependence—even of merging with the therapist.

In group therapy settings, patients with schizoid personality disorder may be silent for long periods; nonetheless, they do become involved. The patients should be protected against aggressive attack by group members for their proclivity to be silent. With time the group members become important to schizoid patients and may provide the only social contact in their otherwise isolated existence.

Pharmacotherapy. Pharmacotherapy with small dosages of antipsychotics, antidepressants, and psychostimulants has been effective in some patients. Serotonergic agents may make patients less sensitive to rejection.

SCHIZOTYPAL PERSONALITY DISORDER

People with schizotypal personality disorder are strikingly odd or strange, even to laypersons. Magical thinking, peculiar notions, ideas of reference, illusions, and derealization are part of a schizotypal person's everyday world.

Epidemiology

This disorder occurs in about 3 percent of the population. The sex ratio is unknown. There is a greater association of cases among the biological relatives of patients with schizophrenia than among controls, and a higher incidence among monozygotic twins than among dizygotic twins (33 percent versus 4 percent in one study).

Diagnosis

Schizotypal personality disorder is diagnosed on the basis of the patients' peculiarities of thinking, behavior, and appearance. Taking a history may be difficult because of the patients' unusual way of communicating. The DSM-IV diagnostic criteria for schizotypal personality disorder are given in Table 27–6.

Clinical Features

In patients with schizotypal personality disorder, thinking and communicating are disturbed. Although frank thought disorder is absent, their speech may be distinctive or peculiar, may have meaning only to them, and may often need interpretation. Like patients with schizophrenia, those with schizotypal personality disorder may not know their own feelings yet are exquisitely sensitive to, and aware of, the feelings of others, especially negative affects like anger. These patients may be superstitious or claim powers of clairvoyance and may believe that they have other special powers of thought and insight. Their inner world may be filled with vivid imaginary relationships and childlike fears and fantasies. They may admit to perceptual illusions or macropsia and confess that other people seem to them to be wooden and all the same.

Because people with schizotypal personality disorder have poor interpersonal relationships and may act inappropriately, they are isolated and have few, if any, friends. Patients may show features or borderline personality disorder, and indeed, both diagnoses can be made. Under stress, patients with schizotypal personality disorder may decompensate and have psychotic symptoms, but these are usually of brief duration. In

Table 27–6
DSM-IV Diagnostic Criteria for Schizotypal Personality Disorder

A. A pervasive pattern of social and interpersonal deficits marked by acute discomfort with, and reduced capacity for, close relationships as well as by cognitive or perceptual distortions and eccentricities of behavior, beginning by early adulthood and present in a variety of contexts, as indicated by five (or more) of the following:
 (1) ideas of reference (excluding delusions of reference)
 (2) odd beliefs or magical thinking that influence behavior and are inconsistent with subcultural norms (eg, superstitiousness, belief in clairvoyance, telepathy, or "sixth sense;" in children and adolescents, bizarre fantasies or preoccupations)
 (3) unusual perceptual experiences, including bodily illusions
 (4) odd thinking and speech (eg, vague, circumstantial, metaphorical, overelaborate, or stereotyped)
 (5) suspiciousness or paranoid ideation
 (6) inappropriate or constricted affect
 (7) behavior or appearance that is odd, eccentric, or peculiar
 (8) lack of close friends or confidants other than first-degree relatives
 (9) excessive social anxiety that does not diminish with familiarity and tends to be associated with paranoid fears rather than negative judgments about self

B. Does not occur exclusively during the course of schizophrenia, a mood disorder with psychotic features, another psychotic disorder, or a pervasive developmental disorder.
Note: if criteria are met prior to the onset of schizophrenia, add "premorbid," eg, "schizotypal personality disorder (premorbid)."

patients with severe cases of the disorder, anhedonia and severe depression may be present.

Differential Diagnosis

Theoretically, people with schizotypal personality disorder can be distinguished from those with schizoid and avoidant personality disorders by the presence of oddities in their behavior, thinking, perception, and communication, and perhaps by a clear family history of schizophrenia. Patients with schizotypal personality disorder can be distinguished from those with schizophrenia by their absence of psychosis. If psychotic symptoms do appear, they are brief and fragmentary. Some patients meet the criteria for both schizotypal personality disorder and borderline personality disorder. Patients with paranoid personality disorder are characterized by suspiciousness, but lack the odd behavior of patients with schizotypal personality disorder.

Course and Prognosis

A long-term study by Thomas McGlashan reported that 10 percent of those with schizotypal personality disorder eventually committed suicide. Retrospective studies have shown that many patients thought to have had schizophrenia actually had schizotypal personality disorder, and according to current clinical thinking the schizotype is the premorbid personality of the patient with schizophrenia. Some, however, maintain a stable schizotypal personality throughout their lives and marry and work in spite of their oddities.

Treatment

Psychotherapy. The principles of treatment of schizotypal personality disorder are no different from those of schizoid personality disorder, but clinicians must deal sensitively with the former. These patients have peculiar patterns of thinking, and some are involved in cults, strange religious practices, and the occult. Therapists must not ridicule such activities or be judgmental about these beliefs or activities.

Pharmacotherapy. Antipsychotic medication may be useful in dealing with ideas of reference, illusions, and other symptoms of the disorder and can be used in conjunction with psychotherapy. Positive results have been reported with haloperidol (Haldol). Antidepressants are of use when a depressive component of the personality is present.

ANTISOCIAL PERSONALITY DISORDER

Antisocial personality disorder is an inability to conform to the social norms that ordinarily govern many aspects of people's adolescent and adult behavior. Although characterized by continual antisocial or criminal acts, the disorder is not synonymous with criminality (ICD-10 uses the name dissocial personality disorder).

Epidemiology

The prevalence of antisocial personality disorder is 3 percent in men and 1 percent in women. It is most common in poor urban areas and among mobile residents of these areas. Boys with the disorder come from larger families than do girls with the disorders. The onset of the disorder is before the age of 15. Girls usually have symptoms before puberty, and boys even earlier. In prison populations the prevalence of antisocial personality disorder may be as high as 75 percent. A familial pattern is present in that the disorder is 5 times more common among first-degree relatives of men with the disorder than among controls.

Diagnosis

Patients with antisocial personality disorder can fool even the most experienced clinicians. In an interview, patients can appear composed and credible, but beneath the veneer (or, to use Hervey Cleckley's term, the mask of sanity), there is tension, hostility, irritability, and rage. A stress interview, in which patients are vigorously confronted with inconsistencies in their histories, may be necessary to reveal the pathology.

A diagnostic workup should include a thorough neurological examination. Because patients often show abnormal electroencephalogram (EEG) results and soft neurological signs suggestive of minimal brain damage in childhood, these findings can be used to confirm the clinical impression. The DSM-IV diagnostic criteria are listed in Table 27–7.

Table 27–7
DSM-IV Diagnostic Criteria for Antisocial Personality Disorder

A. There is a pervasive pattern of disregard for and violation of the rights of others occurring since age 15 years, as indicated by three (or more) of the following:
  (1) failure to conform to social norms with respect to lawful behaviors as indicated by repeatedly performing acts that are grounds for arrest
  (2) deceitfulness, as indicated by repeated lying, use of aliases, or conning others for personal profit or pleasure
  (3) impulsivity or failure to plan ahead
  (4) irritability and aggressiveness, as indicated by repeated physical fights or assaults
  (5) reckless disregard for safety of self or others
  (6) consistent irresponsibility, as indicated by repeated failure to sustain consistent work behavior or honor financial obligations
  (7) lack of remorse, as indicated by being indifferent to or rationalizing having hurt, mistreated, or stolen from another

B. The individual is at least age 18 years.

C. There is evidence of conduct disorder with onset before age 15 years.

D. The occurrence of antisocial behavior is not exclusively during the course of schizophrenia or a manic episode.

Reprinted with permission from American Psychiatric Association: *Diagnostic and Statistical Manual of Mental Disorders,* ed 4. Copyright, American Psychiatric Association, Washington, 1994.

Clinical Features

Patients with antisocial personality disorder can often seem to be normal and even charming and ingratiating. Their histories, however, reveal many areas of disordered life functioning. Lying, truancy, running away from home, thefts, fights, substance abuse, and illegal activities are typical experiences that patients report as beginning in childhood. These patients often impress opposite-sex clinicians with the colorful, seductive aspects of their personalities, but same-sex clinicians may regard them as manipulative and demanding. Patients with antisocial personality disorder exhibit no anxiety or depression, a lack that may seem grossly incongruous with their situations, although suicide threats and somatic preoccupations may be common. Their own explanations of their antisocial behavior make it seem mindless, but their mental content reveals the complete absence of delusions and other signs of irrational thinking. In fact, they frequently have a heightened sense of reality testing and often impress observers as having good verbal intelligence.

People with antisocial personality disorder are highly represented by so-called con men. They are extremely manipulative and can frequently talk others into participating in schemes for easy ways to make money or to achieve fame or notoriety. These schemes may eventually lead the unwary to financial ruin or social embarrassment or both. Those with this disorder do not tell the truth and cannot be trusted to carry out any task or adhere to any conventional standard of morality. Promiscuity, spouse abuse, child abuse, and drunk driving are common events in their lives. A notable finding is a lack of remorse for these actions; that is, they appear to lack a conscience.

Differential Diagnosis

Antisocial personality disorder can be distinguished from illegal behavior in that antisocial personality disorder involves many areas of a person's life. When antisocial behavior is the only manifestation, patients are classified in the DSM-IV category of additional conditions that may be a focus of clinical attention—specifically, adult antisocial behavior. Dorothy Lewis found that many of these people have a neurological or mental disorder that has been either overlooked or undiagnosed. More difficult is the differentiation of antisocial personality disorder from substance abuse. When both substance abuse and antisocial behavior begin in childhood and continue into adult life, both disorders should be diagnosed. When, however, the antisocial behavior is clearly secondary to premorbid alcohol abuse or other substance abuse, the diagnosis of antisocial personality disorder is not warranted.

In diagnosing antisocial personality disorder, clinicians must adjust for the distorting effects of socioeconomic status, cultural background, and sex. Furthermore, the diagnosis of antisocial personality disorder is not warranted when mental retardation, schizophrenia, or mania can explain the symptoms.

Course and Prognosis

Once an antisocial personality disorder develops, it runs an unremitting course, with the height of antisocial behavior usually occurring in late adolescence. The prognosis is variable. Some reports indicate that symptoms decrease as people grow older. Many patients have somatization disorder and multiple physical complaints. Depressive disorders, alcohol use disorders, and other substance abuse are common.

Treatment

Psychotherapy. If patients with antisocial personality disorder are immobilized (for example, placed in hospitals), they often become amenable to psychotherapy. When patients feel that they are among peers, their lack of motivation for change disappears. Perhaps for this reason self-help groups have been more useful than have jails in alleviating the disorder.

Before treatment can begin, firm limits are essential. Therapists must find ways of dealing with patients' self-destructive behavior. And to overcome patients' fear of intimacy, therapists must frustrate patients' desire to run from honest human encounters. In doing so, a therapist faces the challenge of separating control from punishment and of separating help and confrontation from social isolation and retribution.

Pharmacotherapy. Pharmacotherapy is used to deal with incapacitating symptoms such as anxiety, rage, and depression, but because patients are often substance abusers, drugs must be used judiciously. If a patient shows evidence of attention-deficit/hyperactivity disorder, psychostimulants such as methylphenidate (Ritalin) may be of use. Attempts have been made to alter catecholamine metabolism with drugs and to control impulsive behavior with antiepileptic drugs, for example, valproate (Depakote), especially if abnormal wave forms are noted on an EEG.

BORDERLINE PERSONALITY DISORDER

Patients with borderline personality disorder stand on the border between neurosis and psychosis and are characterized by extraordinarily unstable affect, mood, behavior, object relations, and self-image. The disorder has also been called ambulatory schizophrenia, as-if personality (a term coined by Helene Deutsch), pseudoneurotic schizophrenia (described by Paul Hoch and Phillip Politan), and psychotic character disorder (described by John Frosch). ICD-10 uses the name emotionally unstable personality disorder.

Epidemiology

No definitive prevalence studies are available, but borderline personality disorder is thought to be present in about 1 to 2 percent of the population and is twice as common in women as in men. An increased prevalence of major depressive disorder, alcohol use disorders, and substance abuse is found in first-degree relatives of people with borderline personality disorder.

Diagnosis

According to DSM-IV, the diagnosis of borderline personality disorder can made by early adulthood when patients show at least five of the criteria listed in Table 27–8.

Table 27–8
DSM-IV Diagnostic Criteria for Borderline Personality Disorder

A pervasive pattern of instability of interpersonal relationships, self-image, and affects, and marked impulsivity by early adulthood and present in a variety of contexts, as indicated by five (or more) of the following:

(1) frantic efforts to avoid real or imagined abandonment. **Note:** do not include suicidal or self-mutilating behavior covered in criterion 5.
(2) a pattern of unstable and intense interpersonal relationships characterized by alternating between extremes of idealization and devaluation
(3) identity disturbance: markedly and persistently unstable self-image or sense of self
(4) impulsivity in at least two areas that are potentially self-damaging (eg, spending, sex, substance abuse, reckless driving, binge eating). **Note:** do not include suicidal or self-mutilating behavior covered in criterion 5.
(5) recurrent suicidal behavior, gestures, or threats, or self-mutilating behavior
(6) affective instability due to a marked reactivity of mood (eg, intense episodic dysphoria, irritability, or anxiety usually lasting a few hours and only rarely more than a few days)
(7) chronic feelings of emptiness
(8) inappropriate, intense anger or difficulty controlling anger (eg, frequent displays of temper, constant anger, recurrent physical fights)
(9) transient, stress-related paranoid ideation or severe dissociative symptoms

Reprinted with permission from American Psychiatric Association: *Diagnostic and Statistical Manual of Mental Disorders,* ed 4. Copyright, American Psychiatric Association, Washington, 1994.

Biological studies may aid in the diagnosis; some patients with borderline personality disorder show shortened rapid eye movement (REM) latency and sleep continuity disturbances, abnormal dexamethasone-suppression test results, and abnormal thyrotropin-releasing hormone test results. Those changes, however, are also seen in some cases of depressive disorders.

Clinical Features

People with borderline personality disorder almost always appear to be in a state of crisis. Mood swings are common: Patients can be argumentative at one moment, depressed at the next, and later complain of having no feelings.

Patients may have short-lived psychotic episodes (so-called micropsychotic episodes) rather than full-blown psychotic breaks, and the psychotic symptoms of these patients are almost always circumscribed, fleeting, or doubtful. The behavior of patients with borderline personality disorder is highly unpredictable, and their achievements are rarely at the level of their abilities. The painful nature of their lives is reflected in repetitive self-destructive acts. Such patients may slash their wrists and perform other self-mutilations to elicit help from others, to express anger, or to numb themselves to overwhelming affect.

Because they feel both dependent and hostile, people with this disorder have tumultuous interpersonal relationships. They can be dependent on those to whom they are close and when frustrated can express enormous anger toward their intimate friends. Patients with borderline personality disorder cannot tolerate being alone, and they prefer a frantic search for companionship, no matter how unsatisfactory, to their own company. To assuage loneliness, if only for brief periods, they accept a stranger as a friend or behave promiscuously. They often complain about chronic feelings of emptiness and boredom and the lack of a consistent sense of identify (identity diffusion); when pressed, they often complain about how depressed they usually feel despite the flurry of other affects.

Otto Kernberg described the defense mechanism of projective identification that occurs in patients with borderline personality disorder. In this primitive defense mechanism, intolerable aspects of the self are projected onto another; the other person is induced to play the projected role, and the two people act in unison. Therapists must be aware of this process so that they can act neutrally toward such patients.

Most therapists agree that these patients show ordinary reasoning abilities on structured tests, such as the Wechsler adult intelligence scale, and show deviant processes only on unstructured projective tests, such as the Rorschach test.

Functionally, patients with borderline personality disorder distort their relationships by considering each person to be either all good or all bad. They see people as either nurturing attachment figures or as hateful and sadistic figures who deprive them of security needs and threaten them with abandonment whenever they feel dependent. As a result of this splitting, the good person is idealized, and the bad person devalued. Shifts of allegiance from one person or group to another are frequent.

Some clinicians use the concepts of panphobia, pananxiety,

panambivalence, and chaotic sexuality to delineate these patients' characteristics.

Differential Diagnosis

The disorder is differentiated from schizophrenia on the basis of the borderline patient's lack of prolonged psychotic episodes, thought disorder, and other classic schizophrenic signs. Patients with schizotypal personality disorder show marked peculiarities of thinking, strange ideation, and recurrent ideas of reference. Those with paranoid personality disorder are marked by extreme suspiciousness. Patients with borderline personality disorder generally have chronic feelings of emptiness and short-lived psychotic episodes; they act impulsively and demand extraordinary relationships; they may mutilate themselves and make manipulative suicide attempts.

Course and Prognosis

This disorder is fairly stable; patients change little over time. Longitudinal studies show no progression toward schizophrenia, but patients have a high incidence of major depressive disorder episodes. The diagnosis is usually made before the age of 40, when patients are attempting to make occupational, marital, and other choices and are unable to deal with the normal stages of the life cycle.

Treatment

Psychotherapy. Psychotherapy for patients with borderline personality disorder is an area of intensive investigation and has been the treatment of choice. For best results, pharmacotherapy has been added to the treatment regimen.

Psychotherapy is difficult for patient and therapist alike. Patients regress easily, act out their impulses, and show labile or fixed negative or positive transferences, which are difficult to analyze. Projective identification may also cause countertransference problems when a therapist is unaware that patients are unconsciously trying to coerce him or her to act out a particular behavior. Splitting as a defense mechanism causes patients to alternately love and hate therapists and others in the environment. A reality-oriented approach is more effective than in-depth interpretations of the unconscious.

Therapists have used behavior therapy to control patients' impulses and angry outbursts and to reduce their sensitivity to criticism and rejection. Social skills training, especially with videotape playback, is helpful to enable patients to see how their actions affect others and thereby to improve their interpersonal behavior.

Patients with borderline personality disorder often do well in a hospital setting in which they receive intensive psychotherapy on both an individual basis and a group basis. In a hospital they can also interact with trained staff members from a variety of disciplines and can be provided with occupational, recreational, and vocational therapy. Such programs are especially helpful when the home environment is detrimental to a patient's rehabilitation because of intrafamilial conflicts or other stresses such as parental abuse. Within the protected environment of the hospital, patients who are excessively impulsive, self-destructive, or self-mutilating can be given limits, and their actions can be observed. Under ideal circumstances, patients remain in the hospital until they show marked improvement, up to one year in some cases. Patients can then be discharged to special support systems such as day hospitals, night hospitals, and halfway houses.

Pharmacotherapy. Pharmacotherapy is useful to deal with specific personality features that interfere with patients' overall functioning. Antipsychotics have been used to control anger, hostility, and brief psychotic episodes. Antidepressants improve the depressed mood common in patients with borderline personality disorder. The monoamine oxidase inhibitors (MAOIs) have been effective in modulating impulsive behavior in some patients. Benzodiazepines, particularly alprazolam (Xanax), help anxiety and depression, but other patients show a disinhibition with this class of drugs. Anticonvulsants such as carbamazepine (Tegretol) may improve global functioning for some patients. Serotonergic agents such as fluoxetine (Prozac) have been helpful in some cases.

HISTRIONIC PERSONALITY DISORDER

People with histrionic personality disorder are excitable and emotional and behave in a colorful, dramatic, extroverted fashion. Accompanying their flamboyant aspects, however, is often an inability to maintain deep, long-lasting attachments.

Epidemiology

According to DSM-IV, limited data from general population studies suggest a prevalence of histrionic personality disorder of about 2 to 3 percent. Rates of about 10 to 15 percent have been reported in inpatient and outpatient mental health settings when structured assessment is used. The disorder is diagnosed more frequently in women than in men. Some studies have found an association with somatization disorder and alcohol use disorders.

Diagnosis

In interviews, patients with histrionic personality disorder are generally cooperative and eager to give a detailed history. Gestures and dramatic punctuation in their conversations are common; they may make frequent slips of the tongue, and their language is colorful. Affective display is common, but, when pressed to acknowledge certain feelings (such as anger, sadness, and sexual wishes), they may respond with surprise, indignation, or denial. The results of the cognitive examination are usually normal, although a lack of perseverance may be shown on arithmetic or concentration tasks, and the patients' forgetfulness of affect-laden material may be astonishing. The DSM-IV diagnostic criteria are listed in Table 27–9.

Clinical Features

People with histrionic personality disorder show a high degree of attention-seeking behavior. They tend to exaggerate

Table 27–9
DSM-IV Diagnostic Criteria for Histrionic Personality Disorder

A pervasive pattern of excessive emotionality and attention seeking, beginning by early adulthood and present in a variety of contexts, as indicated by five (or more) of the following:
(1) is uncomfortable in situations in which he or she is not the center of attention
(2) interaction with others is often characterized by inappropriate sexually seductive or provocative behavior
(3) displays rapidly shifting and shallow expression of emotions
(4) consistently uses physical appearance to draw attention to self
(5) has a style of speech that is excessively impressionistic and lacking in detail
(6) shows self-dramatization, theatricality, and exaggerated expression of emotion
(7) is suggestible, ie, easily influenced by others or circumstances
(8) considers relationships to be more intimate than they actually are

Reprinted with permission from American Psychiatric Association: *Diagnostic and Statistical Manual of Mental Disorders,* ed 4. Copyright, American Psychiatric Association, Washington, 1994.

their thoughts and feelings and make everything sound more important than it really is. They display temper tantrums, tears, and accusations when they are not the center of attention or are not receiving praise or approval.

Seductive behavior is common in both sexes. Sexual fantasies about people with whom patients are involved are common, but patients are inconsistent about verbalizing these fantasies and may be coy or flirtatious rather than sexually aggressive. In fact, histrionic patients may have a psychosexual dysfunction: Women may be anorgasmic, and men may be impotent. Their need for reassurance is endless: They may act on their sexual impulses to reassure themselves that they are attractive to the other sex. Their relationships tend to be superficial, however, and they can be vain, self-absorbed, and fickle. Their strong dependence needs make them overly trusting and gullible.

The major defenses of patients with histrionic personality disorder are repression and dissociation. Accordingly, such patients are unaware of their true feelings and are unable to explain their motivations. Under stress, reality testing easily becomes impaired.

Differential Diagnosis

Distinguishing between histrionic personality disorder and borderline personality disorder is difficult, but in borderline personality disorder, suicide attempts, identity diffusion, and brief psychotic episodes are more likely. Although both conditions may be diagnosed in the same patient, clinicians should separate the two. Somatization disorder (Briquet's syndrome) may occur in conjunction with histrionic personality disorder. Patients with brief psychotic disorder and dissociative disorders may warrant a coexisting diagnosis of histrionic personality disorder.

Course and Prognosis

With age, people with histrionic personality disorder show fewer symptoms, but because they lack the energy of earlier years, the difference in number of symptoms may be more apparent than real. People with this disorder are sensation seekers and may get into trouble with the law, abuse substances, and act promiscuously.

Treatment

Psychotherapy. Patients with histrionic personality disorder are often unaware of their own real feelings; clarification of their inner feelings is an important therapeutic process. Psychoanalytically oriented psychotherapy, whether group or individual, is probably the treatment of choice for histrionic personality disorder.

Pharmacotherapy. Pharmacotherapy can be adjunctive when symptoms are targeted (such as the use of antidepressants for depression and somatic complaints, antianxiety agents for anxiety, and antipsychotics for derealization and illusions).

NARCISSISTIC PERSONALITY DISORDER

People with narcissistic personality disorder are characterized by a heightened sense of self-importance and grandiose feelings of uniqueness.

Epidemiology

According to DSM-IV, estimates of the prevalence of narcissistic personality disorder range from 2 to 16 percent in the clinical population and less than 1 percent in the general population. People with the disorder may impart to their children an unrealistic sense of omnipotence, grandiosity, beauty, and talent; thus offspring of such parents may have a higher than usual risk for developing the disorder themselves. The number of cases of narcissistic personality disorder reported is increasing steadily.

Diagnosis

Table 27–10 gives the DSM-IV diagnostic criteria for narcissistic personality disorder.

Clinical Features

People with narcissistic personality disorder have a grandiose sense of self-importance; they consider themselves special and expect special treatment. Their sense of entitlement is striking. They handle criticism poorly and may become enraged when someone dares to criticize them, or they may appear completely indifferent to criticism. People with this disorder want their own way and are frequently ambitious to achieve fame and fortune. Their relationships are fragile, and they can make others furious by their refusal to obey conven-

Table 27–10
DSM-IV Diagnostic Criteria for Narcissistic Personality Disorder

A pervasive pattern of grandiosity (in fantasy or behavior), need for admiration, and lack of empathy, beginning by early adulthood and present in a variety of contexts, as indicated by five (or more) of the following:

(1) has a grandiose sense of self-importance (eg, exaggerates achievements and talents, expects to be recognized as superior without commensurate achievements)
(2) is preoccupied with fantasies of unlimited success, power, brilliance, beauty, or ideal love
(3) believes that he or she is "special" and unique and can only be understood by, or should associate with, other special or high-status people (or institutions)
(4) requires excessive admiration
(5) has a sense of entitlement ie, unreasonable expectations of especially favorable treatment or automatic compliance with his or her expectations
(6) is interpersonally exploitative ie, takes advantage of others to achieve his or her own ends
(7) lacks empathy: is unwilling to recognize or identify with the feelings and needs of others
(8) is often envious of others or believes that others are envious of him or her
(9) shows arrogant, haughty behaviors or attitudes

tional rules of behavior. Interpersonal exploitiveness is commonplace. They are unable to show empathy and feign sympathy only to achieve their selfish ends. Because of their fragile self-esteem, they are prone to depression. Interpersonal difficulties, occupational problems, rejection, and loss are among the stresses that narcissists commonly produce by their behavior—stresses they are least able to handle.

Differential Diagnosis

Borderline, histrionic, and antisocial personality disorders often accompany narcissistic personality disorder so that a differential diagnosis is difficult. Patients with narcissistic personality disorder have less anxiety than do those with borderline personality disorder; their lives tend to be less chaotic, and they are less likely to attempt suicide. Patients with antisocial personality disorder have a history of impulsive behavior, often associated with alcohol or other substance abuse, that frequently gets them into trouble with the law. Patients with histrionic personality disorder show features of exhibitionism and interpersonal manipulativeness that are similar to those of patients with narcissistic personality disorder.

Course and Prognosis

Narcissistic personality disorder is chronic and difficult to treat. Patients with the disorder must constantly deal with blows to their narcissism resulting from their own behavior or from life experience. Aging is handled poorly; patients value beauty, strength, and youthful attributes, to which they cling inappropriately. They may be more vulnerable, therefore, to midlife crises than are other groups.

Treatment

Psychotherapy. Because patients must renounce their narcissism to make progress, the treatment of narcissistic personality disorder is difficult. Psychiatrists such as Otto Kernberg and Heinz Kohut have advocated using psychoanalytic approaches to effect change, but much research is required to validate the diagnosis and to determine the best treatment.

Pharmacotherapy. Lithium (Eskalith) has been used with patients whose clinical picture includes mood swings. Because patients with narcissistic personality disorder tolerate rejection poorly and are prone to depression, antidepressants, especially serotonergic drugs, may also be of use.

AVOIDANT PERSONALITY DISORDER

People with avoidant personality disorder show an extreme sensitivity to rejection and may lead a socially withdrawn life. Although shy, they are not asocial and show a great desire for companionship, but they need unusually strong guarantees of uncritical acceptance. Such people are commonly described as having an inferiority complex. (ICD-10 uses the term anxious personality disorder.)

Epidemiology

Avoidant personality disorder is common: The prevalence of the disorder is 1 to 10 percent of the general population. No information is available on sex ratio or familial pattern. Infants classified as having a timid temperament may be more prone to the disorder than are those high on activity–approach scales.

Diagnosis

In clinical interviews, patients' most striking aspect is anxiety about talking with an interviewer. Their nervous and tense manner appears to wax and wane with their perception of whether an interviewer likes them. They seem vulnerable to the interviewer's comments and suggestions and may regard a clarification or an interpretation as a criticism. The DSM-IV diagnostic criteria for avoidant personality disorder are listed in Table 27–11.

Clinical Features

Hypersensitivity to rejection by others is the central clinical feature of avoidant personality disorder, and their main personality trait is timidity. People with the disorder desire the warmth and security of human companionship but justify their avoidance of relationships by their alleged fear of rejection. When talking with someone, they express uncertainty, show a lack of self-confidence, and may speak in a self-effacing manner. Because they are hypervigilant about rejection, they are

Table 27–11
DSM-IV Diagnostic Criteria for Avoidant Personality Disorder

A pervasive pattern of social inhibition, feelings of inadequacy, and hypersensitivity to negative evaluation, beginning by early adulthood and present in a variety of contexts, as indicated by four (or more) of the following:

(1) avoids occupational activities that involve significant interpersonal contact, because of fears of criticism, disapproval, or rejection
(2) is unwilling to get involved with people unless certain of being liked
(3) shows restraint within intimate relationships because of the fear of being shamed or ridiculed
(4) is preoccupied with being criticized or rejected in social situations
(5) is inhibited in new interpersonal situations because of feelings of inadequacy
(6) views self as socially inept, personally unappealing, or inferior to others
(7) is unusually reluctant to take personal risks or to engage in any new activities because they may prove embarrassing

Reprinted with permission from American Psychiatric Association: *Diagnostic and Statistical Manual of Mental Disorders,* ed 4. Copyright, American Psychiatric Association, Washington, 1994.

afraid to speak up in public or to make requests of others. They are apt to misinterpret other people's comments as derogatory or ridiculing. The refusal of any request leads them to withdraw from others and to feel hurt.

In the vocational sphere, patients with avoidant personality disorder often take jobs on the sidelines. They rarely attain much personal advancement or exercise much authority but seem shy and eager to please. These people are generally unwilling to enter relationships unless they are given an unusually strong guarantee of uncritical acceptance. Consequently, they often have no close friends or confidants.

Differential Diagnosis

Patients with avoidant personality disorder desire social interaction, unlike patients with schizoid personality disorder, who want to be alone. Patients with avoidant personality disorder are not as demanding, irritable, or unpredictable as are those with borderline and histrionic personality disorders. Avoidant personality disorder and dependent personality disorder are similar. Patients with dependent personality disorder are presumed to have a greater fear of being abandoned or unloved than do those with avoidant personality disorder, but the clinical picture may be indistinguishable.

Course and Prognosis

Many people with avoidant personality disorder are able to function in a protected environment. Some marry, have children, and live their lives surrounded only by family members. Should their support system fail, however, they are subject to depression, anxiety, and anger. Phobic avoidance is common, and patients with the disorder may give histories of social phobia or incur social phobia in the course of their illness.

Treatment

Psychotherapy. Psychotherapeutic treatment depends on solidifying an alliance with patients. As trust develops, a therapist must convey an accepting attitude toward the patient's fears, especially the fear of rejection. The therapist eventually encourages a patient to move out into the world to take what are perceived as great risks of humiliation, rejection, and failure. But therapists should be cautious when giving assignments to exercise new social skills outside therapy; failure may reinforce a patient's already poor self-esteem. Group therapy may help patients understand the effects of their sensitivity to rejection on themselves and others. Assertiveness training is a form of behavior therapy that may teach patients to express their needs openly and to enlarge their self-esteem.

Pharmacotherapy. Pharmacotherapy has been used to manage anxiety and depression when they are associated with the disorder. Some patients are helped by β-blockers, such as atenolol (Tenormin), to manage autonomic nervous system hyperactivity, which tends to be high in patients with avoidant personality disorder, especially when they approach feared situations. Serotonergic agents may help rejection sensitivity.

DEPENDENT PERSONALITY DISORDER

People with dependent personality disorder subordinate their own needs to those of others, get others to assume responsibility for major areas of their lives, lack self-confidence, and may experience intense discomfort when alone for more than a brief period. The disorder has been called passive-dependent personality. Freud described an oral-dependent personality dimension characterized by dependence, pessimism, fear of sexuality, self-doubt, passivity, suggestibility, and lack of perseverance; his description is similar to the DSM-IV categorization of dependent personality disorder.

Epidemiology

Dependent personality disorder is more common in women than in men. One study diagnosed 2.5 percent of all personality disorders as falling into this category. It is more common in young children than in older ones. People with chronic physical illness in childhood may be most prone to the disorder.

Diagnosis

In interviews, patients appear to be compliant. They try to cooperate, welcome specific questions, and look for guidance. The DSM-IV diagnostic criteria for dependent personality disorder are listed in Table 27–12.

Clinical Features

Dependent personality disorder is characterized by a pervasive pattern of dependent and submissive behavior. People with the disorder cannot make decisions without an excessive amount of advice and reassurance from others. They avoid

Table 27–12
DSM-IV Diagnostic Criteria for Dependent Personality Disorder

A pervasive and excessive need to be taken care of that leads to submissive and clinging behavior and fears of separation, beginning by early adulthood and present in a variety of contexts, as indicated by five (or more) of the following:

(1) has difficulty making everyday decisions without an excessive amount of advice and reassurance from others
(2) needs others to assume responsibility for most major areas of his or her life
(3) has difficulty expressing disagreement with others because of fear of loss of support or approval. **Note:** do not include realistic fears of retribution.
(4) has difficulty initiating projects or doing things on his or her own (because of a lack of self-confidence in judgment or abilities rather than a lack of motivation or energy)
(5) goes to excessive lengths to obtain nurturance and support from others, to the point of volunteering to do things that are unpleasant
(6) feels uncomfortable or helpless when alone because of exaggerated fears of being unable to care for himself or herself
(7) urgently seeks another relationship as a source of care and support when a close relationship ends
(8) is unrealistically preoccupied with fears of being left to take care of himself or herself

positions of responsibility and become anxious if asked to assume a leadership role. They prefer to be submissive. When on their own, they find it difficult to persevere at tasks but may find it easy to perform these tasks for someone else.

Because people with the disorder do not like to be alone, they seek out others on whom they can depend; their relationships are thus distorted by their need to be attached to another person. In *folie à deux* (shared psychotic disorder), one member of the pair usually suffers from dependent personality disorder; the submissive partner takes on the delusional system of the more aggressive, assertive partner on whom he or she is dependent.

Pessimism, self-doubt, passivity, and fears of expressing sexual and aggressive feelings all typify the behavior of people with dependent personality disorder. An abusive, unfaithful, or alcoholic spouse may be tolerated for long periods in order not to disturb the sense of attachment.

Differential Diagnosis

The traits of dependence are found in many psychiatric disorders so that differential diagnosis is difficult. Dependence is a prominent factor in patients with histrionic and borderline personality disorders, but those with dependent personality disorder usually have a long-term relationship with one person, rather than a series on whom they are dependent, and they do not tend to be overtly manipulative. Patients with schizoid and schizotypal personality disorders may be indistinguishable from those with avoidant personality disorder. Dependent behavior may occur in patients with agoraphobia, but these patients tend to have a high level of overt anxiety or even panic.

Course and Prognosis

Little is known about the course of dependent personality disorder. There tends to be impaired occupational functioning, as people with the disorder lack the ability to act independently and without close supervision. Social relationships are limited to those on whom they can depend, and many suffer physical or mental abuse because they cannot assert themselves. They risk major depressive disorder if they sustain the loss of the person on whom they are dependent, but with treatment the prognosis is favorable.

Treatment

Psychotherapy. The treatment of dependent personality disorder can often be successful. Insight-oriented therapies enable patients to understand the antecedents of their behavior, and, with the support of a therapist, patients can become more independent, assertive, and self-reliant. Behavioral therapy, assertiveness training, family therapy, and group therapy have all been used, with successful outcomes in many cases.

A pitfall in treatment may arise when a therapist encourages a patient to change the dynamics of a pathological relationship (for example, supports a physically abused wife in seeking help from the police). At this point patients may become anxious and unable to cooperate in therapy; they may feel torn between complying with the therapist and losing a pathological external relationship. Therapists must show great respect for these patients' feelings of attachment, no matter how pathological these feelings may seem.

Pharmacotherapy. Pharmacotherapy has been used to deal with specific symptoms such as anxiety and depression, which are common associated features of dependent personality disorder. Patients who experience panic attacks or who have high levels of separation anxiety may be helped by imipramine (Tofranil). Benzodiazepines and serotonergic agents have also been useful. If a patient's depression or withdrawal symptoms respond to pyschostimulants, they may be used.

OBSESSIVE-COMPULSIVE PERSONALITY DISORDER

Obsessive-compulsive personality disorder is characterized by emotional constriction, orderliness, perseverance, stubbornness, and indecisiveness. The essential feature of the disorder is a pervasive pattern of perfectionism and inflexibility. (ICD-10 uses the name anancastic personality disorder.)

Epidemiology

The prevalence of obsessive-compulsive personality disorder is unknown. It is more common in men than in women and is diagnosed most often in oldest children. The disorder also occurs more frequently in first-degree biological relatives of people with the disorder than in the general population. Patients often have backgrounds characterized by harsh discipline. Freud hypothesized that the disorder is associated with difficulties in the anal stage of psychosexual development, generally around the age of 2, but in various studies this theory has not been validated.

Diagnosis

In interviews, patients with obsessive-compulsive personality disorder may have a stiff, formal, and rigid demeanor. Their affect is not blunted or flat but can be described as constricted. They lack spontaneity, and their mood is usually serious. Such patients may be anxious about not being in control of the interview. Their answers to questions are unusually detailed. The defense mechanisms they use are rationalization, isolation, intellectualization, reaction formation, and undoing. The DSM-IV diagnostic criteria for obsessive-compulsive personality disorder are listed in Table 27–13.

Clinical Features

Persons with obsessive-compulsive personality disorder are preoccupied with rules, regulations, orderliness, neatness, details, and the achievement of perfection. These traits account for the general constriction of the entire personality. They insist that rules be followed rigidly and are unable to tolerate what they perceive to be infractions. Accordingly, they lack flexibility and are intolerant. They are capable of prolonged work, provide it is routinized and does not require changes to which they cannot adapt.

People with obsessive-compulsive personality disorder have limited interpersonal skills. They are formal and serious and often lack a sense of humor. They alienate people, are unable to compromise, and insist that others submit to their needs. They are, however, eager to please those whom they see as more powerful than themselves, and they carry out these people's wishes in an authoritarian manner. Because they fear making mistakes, they are indecisive and ruminate about making decisions. Although a stable marriage and occupational adequacy are common, people with obsessive-compulsive personality disorder have few friends. Anything that threatens to upset their perceived stability or the routine of their lives can precipitate a great deal of anxiety otherwise bound up in the rituals that they impose on their lives and try to impose on others.

Table 27–13
DSM-IV Diagnostic Criteria for Obsessive-Compulsive Personality Disorder

A pervasive pattern of preoccupation with orderliness, perfectionism, and mental and interpersonal control, at the expense of flexibility, openness, and efficiency, beginning by early adulthood and present in a variety of contexts, as indicated by four (or more) of the following:

(1) is preoccupied with details, rules, lists, order, organization, or schedules to the extent that the major point of the activity is lost
(2) shows perfectionism that interferes with task completion (eg, is unable to complete a project because his or her own overly strict standards are not met)
(3) is excessively devoted to work and productivity to the exclusion of leisure activities and friendships (not accounted for by obvious economic necessity)
(4) is overconscientious, scrupulous, and inflexible about matters of morality, ethics, or values (not accounted for by cultural or religious identification)
(5) is unable to discard worn-out or worthless objects even when they have no sentimental value
(6) is reluctant to delegate tasks or to work with others unless they submit to exactly his or her way of doing things
(7) adopts a miserly spending style toward both self and others; money is viewed as something to be hoarded for future catastrophes
(8) shows rigidity and stubbornness

Reprinted with permission from American Psychiatric Association: *Diagnostic and Statistical Manual of Mental Disorders,* ed 4. Copyright, American Psychiatric Association, Washington, 1994.

Differential Diagnosis

When recurrent obsessions or compulsions are present, obsessive-compulsive disorder should be noted on Axis I. Perhaps the most difficult distinction is between outpatients with some obsessive-compulsive traits and those with obsessive-compulsive personality disorder. The diagnosis of personality disorder is reserved for those patients with significant impairments in their occupational or social effectiveness. In some cases, delusional disorder coexists with personality disorders and should be noted.

Course and Prognosis

The course of obsessive-compulsive personality disorder is variable and unpredictable. From time to time, people may develop obsessions or compulsions in the course of their disorder. Some adolescents with obsessive-compulsive personality disorder evolve into warm, open, and loving adults; in others, the disorder can be either the harbinger of schizophrenia or—decades later and exacerbated by the aging process—major depressive disorder.

People with obsessive-compulsive personality disorder may flourish in positions demanding methodical, deductive, or detailed work, but they are vulnerable to unexpected changes, and their personal lives may remain barren. Depressive disorders, especially those of late onset, are common.

Treatment

Psychotherapy. Unlike patients with the other personality disorders, those with obsessive-compulsive personality disorder are often aware of their suffering, and they seek treatment on their own. Overtrained and oversocialized, these patients highly value free association and no-directive therapy. Treatment, however, is often long and complex, and countertransference problems are common.

Group therapy and behavior therapy occasionally offer certain advantages. In both contexts it is easy to interrupt the patients in the midst of their maladaptive interactions or explanations. Preventing the completion of their habitual behavior raises patients' anxiety and leaves them susceptible to learning new coping strategies. Patients can also receive direct rewards for change in group therapy, something less often possible in individual psychotherapies.

Pharmacotherapy. Clonazepam (Klonopin), a benzodiazepine with anticonvulsant use, has reduced symptoms in patients with severe obsessive-compulsive disorder. Whether it is of use in the personality disorder is unknown. Clomipramine (Anafranil) and such serotonergic agents as fluoxetine, usually at dosages of 60 to 80 mg a day, may be of use if obsessive-compulsive signs and symptoms break through.

PERSONALITY DISORDER NOT OTHERWISE SPECIFIED

In DSM-IV, this category of personality disorder not otherwise specified is reserved for disorders that do not fit into any of the previously described personality disorder categories. Passive-aggressive personality disorder and depressive personality disorder are now listed as examples of personality disorder not otherwise specified. A narrow spectrum of behavior or a particular trait—such as oppositionalism, sadism, or masochism—can also be classified in this category. A patient with features of more than one personality disorder but without the complete criteria of any one disorder can be assigned this classification. The DSM-IV criteria for personality disorder not otherwise specified are presented in Table 27–14.

Passive-Aggressive Personality Disorder

People with passive-aggressive personality disorder are characterized by covert obstructionism, procrastination, stubbornness, and inefficiency. Such behavior is a manifestation of passively expressed underlying aggression. In DSM-IV the disorder is also called negativistic personality disorder.

Epidemiology. No data are available about the epidemiology of the disorder. Sex ratio, familial patterns, and prevalence have not been adequately studied.

Diagnosis. The criteria for passive-aggressive disorder are presented in Table 27–15.

Table 27–14
DSM-IV Diagnostic Criteria for Personality Disorder Not Otherwise Specified

This category is for disorders of personality functioning that do not meet criteria for any specific personality disorder. An example is the presence of features of more than one specific personality disorder that do not meet the full criteria for any one personality disorder ("mixed personality"), but that together cause clinically significant distress or impairment in one or more important areas of functioning (eg, social or occupational). This category can also be used when the clinician judges that a specific personality disorder that is not included in this classification is appropriate. Examples include passive aggressive personality disorder and depressive personality disorder.

Reprinted with permission from American Psychiatric Association: *Diagnostic and Statistical Manual of Mental Disorders,* ed 4. Copyright, American Psychiatric Association, Washington, 1994.

Table 27–15
DSM-IV Diagnostic Research Criteria for Passive-Aggressive Personality Disorder

A. A pervasive pattern of negativistic attitudes and passive resistance to demands for adequate performance, beginning by early adulthood and present in a variety of contexts, as indicated by four (or more) of the following:
   (1) passively resists fulfilling routine social and occupational tasks
   (2) complains of being misunderstood and unappreciated by others
   (3) is sullen and argumentative
   (4) unreasonably criticizes and scorns authority
   (5) expresses envy and resentment toward those apparently more fortunate
   (6) voices exaggerated and persistent complaints of personal misfortune
   (7) alternates between hostile defiance and contrition
B. Does not occur exclusively during major depressive episodes and is not better accounted for by dysthymic disorder.

Reprinted with permission from American Psychiatric Association: *Diagnostic and Statistical Manual of Mental Disorders,* ed 4. Copyright, American Psychiatric Association, Washington, 1994.

Clinical Features. Passive-aggressive personality disorder patients characteristically procrastinate, resist demands for adequate performance, find excuses for delays, and find fault with those on whom they depend; yet they refuse to extricate themselves from the dependent relationships. They usually lack assertiveness and are not direct about their own needs and wishes. They fail to ask needed questions about what is expected of them and may become anxious when forced to succeed or when their usual defense of turning anger against themselves is removed.

In interpersonal relationships, these people attempt to manipulate themselves into a position of dependence, but others often experience this passive, self-detrimental behavior as punitive and manipulative. People with this disorder expect others to do their errands and to carry out their routine responsibilities. Friends and clinicians may become enmeshed in trying to assuage the patients' many claims of unjust treatment. The close relationships of people with passive-aggressive personality disorder, however, are rarely tranquil or happy. Because they are bound to their resentment more closely than to their satisfaction, they may never even formulate goals for finding enjoyment in life. People with the disorder lack self-confidence and are typically pessimistic about the future.

Differential Diagnosis. Passive-aggressive personality disorders must be differentiated from histrionic and borderline personality disorders. Patients with passive-aggressive personality disorder, however, are less flamboyant, dramatic, affective, and openly aggressive than are those with histrionic and borderline personality disorders.

Course and Prognosis. In a follow-up study averaging 11 years of 100 passive-aggressive inpatients, Ivor Small found that the primary diagnosis in 54 was passive-aggressive personality disorder; 18 were also alcohol abusers, and 30 could be clinically labeled as depressed. Of the 73 former patients located, 58 (79 percent) had persistent psychiatric difficulties, and 9 (12 percent) were considered symptom-free. Most seemed irritable, anxious, and depressed; somatic complaints were numerous. Only 32 (44 percent) were employed full time as workers or homemakers. Although neglect of responsibility and suicide attempts were common, only one patient had committed suicide in the interim. Twenty-eight (38 percent) had been readmitted to a hospital, but the disorders of only three had been diagnosed as schizophrenia.

Treatment. Patients with passive-aggressive personality disorder who receive supportive psychotherapy have good outcomes, but psychotherapy for these patients has many pitfalls. To fulfill their demands is often to support their pathology, but to refuse their demands is to reject them. Therapy sessions can thus become a battleground on which a patient expresses feelings of resentment against a therapist on whom the patient wishes to become dependent. With these patients, clinicians must treat suicide gestures as any covert expression of anger, and not as object loss in major depressive disorder. Therapists must point out the probable consequences of passive-aggression behaviors as they occur. Such confrontations may be more helpful than a correct interpretation in changing patients' behavior.

Antidepressants should be prescribed only when clinical indications of depression and the possibility of suicide exist. Depending on the clinical features, some patients have responded to benzodiazepines and psychostimulants.

Depressive Personality Disorder

People with depressive personality disorder are characterized by lifelong traits that fall along the depressive spectrum. They are pessimistic, anhedonic, duty bound, self-doubting, and chronically unhappy. The disorder is newly classified in DSM-IV, but melancholic personality was described by early 20th century European psychiatrists such as Ernst Kretschmer.

Epidemiology. Because depressive personality disorder is a new category, no epidemiological data are available. On the basis of the prevalence of depressive disorders in the overall population, however, depressive personality disorder seems to be common, to occur equally in men and women, and to occur in families in which depressive disorders are found.

Etiology. The cause of depressive personality disorder is unknown, but the same factors involved in dysthymic disorder and major depressive disorder may be at work. Psychological theories involve early loss, poor parenting, punitive superegos, and extreme feelings of guilt. Biological theories involve the hypothalamic-pituitary-adrenal-thyroid axis, including the noradrenergic and serotonergic amine systems. Genetic predisposition, as indicated by Stella Chess's studies of temperament, may also play a role.

Diagnosis and Clinical Features. A classic description of depressive personality was provided in 1963 by Arthur Noyes and Laurence Kolb:

> They feel but little of the normal joy of living and are inclined to be lonely and solemn, to be gloomy, submissive, pessimistic, and self-depreciatory. They are prone to express regrets and feelings of inadequacy and hopelessness. They are often meticulous, perfectionistic, overconscientious, preoccupied with work, feel responsibility keenly, and are easily discouraged under new conditions. They are fearful of disapproval, tend to suffer in silence and perhaps to cry easily, although usually not in the presence of others. A tendency to hesitation, indecision, and caution betrays an inherent feeling of insecurity.

More recently, Hagop Akiskal described seven groups of depressive traits: quiet, introverted, passive, and nonassertive; gloomy, pessimistic, serious, and incapable of fun; self-critical, self-reproachful, and self-derogatory; skeptical, critical of others, and hard to please; conscientious, responsible, and self-disciplined; brooding and given to worry; preoccupied with negative events, feelings of inadequacy, and personal shortcomings.

Patients with depressive personality disorder complain of chronic feelings of unhappiness. They admit to low self-esteem and find it difficult to find anything in their lives about which they are joyful, hopeful, or optimistic. They are self-critical and derogatory and are likely to denigrate their work, themselves, and their relationships with others. Their physiognomy often reflects their mood—poor posture, depressed facies, hoarse voice, and psychomotor retardation.

Differential Diagnosis. Dysthymic disorder is a mood disorder characterized by greater fluctuation in mood than occurs in depressive personality disorder. The personality disorder is chronic and lifelong, whereas dysthymic disorder is episodic, can occur at any time, and usually has a precipitating stressor. The depressive personality can be conceptualized as part of a spectrum of affective conditions in which dysthymic disorder and major depressive disorder are more severe variants. Patients with avoidant personality disorder are introverted and dependent but tend to be more anxious than depressed, compared with people with depressive personality disorder.

Course and Prognosis. People with depressive personality disorder may be at great risk for dysthymic disorder and major depressive disorder. In a recent study by Donald Klein and Gregory Mills, subjects with depressive personality exhibited significantly higher rates of current mood disorder, lifetime mood disorder, major depression, and dysthymia than did subjects without depressive personality.

Treatment. Psychotherapy is the treatment of choice for depressive personality disorder. Patients respond to insight-oriented psychotherapy, and because their reality testing is good, they are able to gain insight into the psychodynamics of their illness and to appreciate its effects on their interpersonal relationships. Treatment is likely to be long term. Cognitive therapy helps patients understand the cognitive manifestations of their low self-esteem and pessimism. Group psychotherapy and interpersonal therapy are also useful. Some people respond to self-help measures.

Psychopharmacological approaches include the use of antidepressant medications, especially such serotoneric agents as sertraline (Zoloft), 50 mg a day. Some patients respond to small dosages of psychostimulants, such as amphetamine, 5 to 15 mg a day. In all cases, psychopharmacological agents should be combined with psychotherapy to achieve maximum effects.

Sadomasochistic Personality Disorder

Some personality types are characterized by elements of sadism or masochism or a combination of both. Sadomasochistic personality disorder is listed here because it is of major clinical and historical interest in psychiatry. It is not an official diagnostic category in DSM-IV or its appendix, but it can be diagnosed as personality disorder not otherwise classified.

Sadism is the desire to cause others pain by being either sexually abusive or generally physically or psychologically abusive. It is named after the Marquis de Sade, a late 18th century writer of erotica describing people who experienced sexual pleasure while inflicting pain on others. Freud believed that sadists ward off castration anxiety and are able to achieve sexual pleasure only when they can do to others what they fear will be done to them.

Masochism, named after Leopold von Sacher-Masoch, a 19th century German novelist, is the achievement of sexual gratification by inflicting pain on the self. So-called moral masochists generally seek humiliation and failure rather than physical pain. Freud believed that masochists' ability to achieve orgasm is disturbed by anxiety and guilt feelings about sex, which are alleviated by suffering and punishment.

Clinical observations indicate that elements of both sadistic and masochistic behavior are usually present in the same person. Treatment with insight-oriented psychotherapy, including psychoanalysis, has been effective in some cases. As a result of therapy, patients become aware of the need for self-punishment secondary to excessive unconscious guilt, and also come to recognize their repressed aggressive impulses, which originate in early childhood.

Sadistic Personality Disorder

Sadistic personality disorder is not included in DSM-IV, but it still appears in the literature and may be of descriptive use. Beginning in early adulthood, people with sadistic personality disorder show a pervasive pattern of cruel, demeaning, and aggressive behavior that is directed toward others. Physical cruelty or violence is used to inflict pain on others and not to achieve another goal, such as mugging a person in order to steal. People with the disorder like to humiliate or demean people in front of others and have usually treated or disciplined people uncommonly harshly, especially children. In general, people with sadistic personality disorder are fascinated by violence, weapons, injury, or torture. To be included in this category, such people cannot be motivated solely by the desire to derive sexual arousal from their behavior; if they are so motivated, the paraphilia of sexual sadism should be diagnosed.

PERSONALITY CHANGE DUE TO A GENERAL MEDICAL CONDITION

Personality change due to a general medical condition (see Table 10.5–3) deserves some discussion here. ICD-10 includes the category of personality and behavioral disorders due to brain disease, damage, and dysfunction, which includes organic personality disorder (see Table 10.5–5), postencephalitic syndrome, and postconcussional syndrome. Personality change due to a general medical condition is characterized by a marked change in personality style and traits from a previous level of functioning. Patients must show evidence of a causative organic factor antedating the onset of the personality change.

Etiology

Structural damage to the brain is usually the cause of the personality change, and head trauma is probably the most common cause. Cerebral neoplasms and vascular accidents, particularly of the temporal and frontal lobes, are also common causes. The conditions most often associated with personality change are listed in Table 27–16.

Diagnosis and Clinical Features

A change in personality from previous patterns of behavior or an exacerbation of previous personality characteristics is notable. Impaired control of the expression of emotions and impulses is a cardinal feature. Emotions are characteristically labile and shallow, although euphoria or apathy may be prominent. The euphoria may mimic hypomania, but true elation is absent, and patients may admit to not really feeling happy. There is a hollow and silly ring to their excitement and facile jocularity, particularly when the frontal lobes are involved. Also associated with damage to the frontal lobes, the so-called frontal lobe syndrome, is prominent indifference and apathy, characterized by a lack of concern for events in the immediate environment. Temper outbursts with little or no provocation may occur, especially after alcohol ingestion, and may result in violent behavior. The expression of impulses may be man-

Table 27–16
Medical Conditions Associated with Personality Change

Head trauma
Cerebrovascular diseases
Cerebral tumors
Epilepsy (particularly complex partial epilepsy)
Huntington's disease
Multiple sclerosis
Endocrine disorders
Heavy metal poisoning (manganese, mercury)
Neurosyphilis
Acquired immune deficiency syndrome (AIDS)

ifested by inappropriate jokes, a coarse manner, improper sexual advances, and antisocial conduct resulting in conflicts with the law, such as assaults on others, sexual misdemeanors, and shoplifting. Foresight and the ability to anticipate the social or legal consequences of actions are typically diminished. People with temporal lobe epilepsy characteristically show humorlessness, hypergraphia, hyperreligiosity, and marked aggressiveness during seizures.

People with personality change due to a general medical condition have a clear sensorium. Mild disorders of cognitive function often coexist, but do not amount to intellectual deterioration. Patients may be inattentive, which may account for disorders of recent memory. With some prodding, however, patients are likely to recall what they claim to have forgotten. The diagnosis should be suspected in patients who show marked changes in behavior or personality involving emotional lability and impaired impulse control, who have no history of mental disorder, and whose personality changes occur abruptly or over a relatively brief time. The DSM-IV diagnostic criteria appear in Table 10.5–3.

Anabolic Steroids. An increasing number of high school and college athletes and bodybuilders are using anabolic steroids as a shortcut to maximize physical development. Anabolic steroids include oxymetholone (Anadrol), somatropin (Humatrope), stanozolol (Winstrol), and testosterone.

DSM-IV does not include a diagnostic category for substance-induced personality disorder, so it is unclear whether a personality change caused by steroid abuse is better diagnosed as personality change due to a general medical condition or as one of the other (or unknown) substance use disorders. It is mentioned here because anabolic steroids can cause persistent alterations of personality and behavior. Anabolic steroid abuse is discussed in Section 12.13.

Differential Diagnosis

Dementia involves global deterioration in intellectual and behavioral capacities, of which personality change is just one category. A personality change may herald a cognitive disorder that will eventually evolve into dementia. In these cases, as deterioration begins to encompass significant memory and cognitive deficits, the diagnosis of the disorder changes from personality change caused by a general medical condition to dementia. In differentiating the specific syndrome from other disorders in which personality change may occur—such as schizophrenia, delusional disorder, mood disorders, and impulse control disorders—physicians must consider the most important factor, the presence in the personality change disorder of a specific organic causative factor.

Course and Prognosis

Both the course and the prognosis of personality change due to a general medical condition depend on its cause. If the disorder is the result of structural damage to the brain, the disorder tends to persist. The disorder may follow a period of coma and delirium in cases of head trauma or vascular accident and may be permanent. The personality change may evolve into dementia in cases of brain tumor, multiple sclerosis, and Huntington's disease. Personality changes produced by chronic intoxication, medical illness, or drug therapy (such as levodopa [Larodopa] for parkinsonism) may be reversed if the underlying cause is treated. Some patients require custodial care, or at least close supervision, to meet their basic needs, avoid repeated conflicts with the law, and protect themselves and their families from the hostility of others and from destitution resulting from impulsive and ill-considered actions.

Treatment

Management of personality change disorder involves treatment of the underlying organic condition when possible. Psychopharmacological treatment of specific symptoms may be indicated in some cases, such as imipramine or fluoxetine for depression.

Patients with severe cognitive impairment or weakened behavioral controls may need counseling to help avoid difficulties at work or to prevent social embarrassment. As a rule, patients' families need emotional support and concrete advice on how to help minimize patients' undesirable conduct. Alcohol should be avoided, and social engagements should be curtailed when patients have tendencies to act in a grossly offensive manner.

References

Bouchard TJ Jr, Lykken DT, McGue M, Segal NL, Tellegen A: Sources of human psychological differences: The Minnesota study of twins reared apart. Science *250:* 223, 1990.

Deckel AW, Hesselbrock V, Bauer L: Antisocial personality disorder, childhood delinquency, and frontal brain functioning: EEG and neuropsychological findings. J Clin Psychol *52* (6): 639, 1996.

Fabrega H, Ulrich R, Pilkonis P, Mezzich J: Personality disorders diagnosed at intake at a public psychiatric facility. Hosp Community Psychiatry *44:* 159, 1993.

Gabbard GO: *Psychodynamic Psychiatry in Clinical Practice: The DSM-IV Edition.* American Psychiatric Press, Washington, 1994.

Gunderson JG, Phillips KA: Personality disorders. In Comprehensive Textbook of Psychiatry, ed 6, HI Kaplan, BJ Sadock, editors, p 1425. Williams & Wilkins, Baltimore, 1995.

Gunderson JG, Sabo AN: The phenomenological and conceptual interface between borderline personality disorder and PTSD. Am J Psychiatry *150:* 19, 1993.

Kernberg OF: *Borderline Conditions and Pathological Narcissism.* Aronson, New York, 1975.

Klein DN, Miller GA: Depressive personality. Am J Psychiatry *150:* 11, 1993.

Kramer PD: *Listening to Prozac.* Viking, New York, 1993.

Lazare A, Klerman G, Armor D: Oral, obsessive and hysterical personality patterns: An investigation of psychoanalytic concepts by means of factor analysis. Arch Gen Psychiatry *14:* 624, 1966.

Markovitz PJ, Schulz SC: Drug treatment of personality disorders. Br J Psychiatry *162:* 122, 1993.

Meissner WW, Stone MH, Meloy JR, Gunderson JG, et al: Personality disorders. In *Synopsis of Treatments of Psychiatric Disorders,* ed 2, GO Gabbard, SD Atkinson, editors, pp 947–1010. American Psychiatric Press, Washington, 1996.

Perkins DO, Davidson EJ, Leserman J, Liao D: Personality disorder in patients infected with HIV: A controlled study with implications for clinical care. Am J Psychiatry *150:* 309, 1993.

Robins LN: *Deviant Children Grown Up: A Sociological and Psychiatric Study of Sociopathic Personality.* Williams & Wilkins, Baltimore, 1966.

Rost KM, Akins RN, Brown FW, Smith GR: The comorbidity of DSM-III-R personality disorders in somatization disorder. Gen Hosp Psychiatry *14:* 322, 1992.

Silverman JM, Siever LJ, Horvath TB, Coccaro EF: Schizophrenia-related and affective personality disorder traits in relatives of probands with schizophrenia and personality disorders. Am J Psychiatry *150:* 435, 1993.

Sternlicht HC: Obsessive-compulsive disorder, fluoxetine, and buspirone. Am J Psychiatry *150:* 526, 1993.

Thomas A, Chess S: *Temperament and Development.* Brunner/Mazel, New York, 1977.

Vaillant GE: *Adaptation to Life.* Little, Brown, Boston, 1977.

28

Psychological Factors Affecting Medical Condition

▲ 28.1 Overview

The fourth edition of *Diagnostic and Statistical Manual of Mental Disorders* (DSM-IV) describes *psychological factors affecting medical conditions* as one or more psychological or behavioral problems that adversely and significantly affect the course or outcome of a general medical condition, or that significantly increase a person's risk of an adverse outcome. In 1978 the National Academy of Sciences defined behavioral medicine as "the interdisciplinary field concerned with the development and integration of behavioral and biomedical science knowledge and techniques relevant to health and illness and the application of this knowledge and these techniques to prevention, diagnosis, and rehabilitation." Psychosomatic medicine is now part of the larger field of behavioral medicine, and DSM-IV uses the phrase *psychological factors affecting medical condition* in place of the term *psychosomatic.* Nevertheless, few would disagree that psychological or behavioral factors play a role in almost every medical condition.

Psychosomatic medicine emphasizes the unity of mind and body and the interaction between them (this is also the basis of holistic and alternative medicine). Overall, the conviction is that psychological factors are important in the development of all diseases. Whether that role is in the initiation, progression, aggravation, or exacerbation of a disease, or in the predisposition or reaction to a disease, is open to debate and varies from disorder to disorder.

CLASSIFICATION

The DSM-IV diagnostic criteria for psychological factors affecting medical conditions (that is, psychosomatic disorders) specify that psychological factors adversely affect patients' medical conditions in one of several ways. Crucially, however, "the factors have influenced the course of the general medical condition as shown by a close temporal association between the psychological factors and the development or exacerbation of, or delayed recovery from, the general condition." Among the psychological factors are mental disorders (including Axis I disorders such as major depressive disorder), psychological symptoms (such as depressive symptoms and anxiety), personality traits or coping style (such as denial of the need for surgery), and maladaptive health behaviors (such as overeating). Patients' general medical condition is coded on Axis III.

The DSM-IV emphasis on psychological factors permits a wide range of psychological stimuli to be noted, for example, personality traits and maladaptive health behaviors.

Many believe that the deletion of the nosological term *psychophysiological,* an earlier synonym for *psychosomatic,* deemphasizes the interaction of the mind (psyche) and the body (soma). The term *psychosomatic* emphasizes a unitary causative or holistic approach to medicine, as all diseases are

Table 28.1–1
DSM-IV Diagnostic Criteria for Psychological Factors Affecting Medical Condition

A. A general medical condition (coded on Axis III) is present.

B. Psychological factors adversely affect the general medical condition in one of the following ways:
   (1) the factors have influenced the course of the general medical condition as shown by a close temporal association between the psychological factors and the development or exacerbation of, or delayed recovery from, the general medical condition.
   (2) the factors interfere with the treatment of the general medical condition.
   (3) the factors constitute additional health risks for the individual.
   (4) stress-related physiological responses precipitate or exacerbate symptoms of a general medical condition

Choose name based on the nature of the psychological factors (if more than one factor is present, indicate the most prominent):

Mental disorder affecting medical condition (eg, an Axis I disorder such as major depressive disorder delaying recovery from a myocardial infarction)

Psychological symptoms affecting medical condition (eg, depressive symptoms delaying recovery from surgery; anxiety exacerbating asthma)

Personality traits or coping style affecting medical condition (eg, pathological denial of the need for surgery in a patient with cancer; hostile, pressured behavior contributing to cardiovascular disease)

Maladaptive health behaviors affecting medical condition (eg, lack of exercise, unsafe sex, overeating)

Stress-related physiological response affecting general medical condition (eg, stress-related exacerbations of ulcer, hypertension, arrhythmia, or tension headache

Other unspecified psychological factors affecting medical condition (eg, interpersonal, cultural, or religious factors)

Table 28.1–2
ICD-10 Diagnostic Criteria for Psychological and Behavioral Factors Associated with Disorders or Diseases Classified Elsewhere

This category should be used to record the presence of psychological or behavioral factors thought to have influenced the manifestation, or affected the course, of physical disorders that can be classified using other chapters of ICD-10. Any resulting mental disturbances are usually mild and often prolonged (such as worry, emotional conflict, apprehension) and do not of themselves justify the use of any of the categories described in the rest of this book. An additional code should be used to identify the physical disorder. (In the rare instances in which an overt psychiatric disorder is thought to have caused a physical disorder, a second additional code should be used to record the psychiatric disorder.)

Reprinted with permission from World Health Organization: *International Classification of Mental and Behavioural Disorders: Diagnostic Criteria for Research.* Copyright, World Health Organization, Geneva, 1993.

Table 28.1–4
Some Psychosomatic Disorders

Acne	Migraine
Allergic reactions	Mucous colitis
Angina pectoris	Nausea
Angioneurotic edema	Neurodermatitis
Arrhythmia	Obesity
Asthmatic wheezing	Painful menstruation
Bronchial asthma	Pruritus ani
Cardiospasm	Pylorospasm
Chronic pain syndromes	Regional enteritis
Coronary heart disease	Rheumatoid arthritis
Diabetes mellitus	Sacroiliac pain
Duodenal ulcer	Skin diseases, such as psoriasis
Essential hypertension	Spastic colitis
Gastric ulcer	Tachycardia
Headache	Tension headache
Herpes	Tuberculosis
Hyperinsulinism	Ulcerative colitis
Hyperthyroidism	Urticaria
Hypoglycemia	Vomiting
Immune diseases	Warts
Irritable colon	

Table 28.1–3
History of Psychosomatic Medicine

Date	Historical Period	Psychosomatic Orientation
10,000 BC	Primitive society	Disease is caused by spiritual powers and must be fought by spiritual means; the evil spirit that enters and affects the total being must be liberated through exorcism, trepanation, and so on.
2500–500 BC	Babylonian-Assyrian civilization	Medicine is dominated by religion, and suggestion is the major tool of treatment. Sigerist: "Mesopotamian medicine was psychosomatic in all its aspects."
400 BC	Greek civilization	Socrates: "As it is not proper to cure the eyes without the head, nor the head without the body, so neither is it proper to cure the body without the soul." Hippocrates: "In order to cure the human body, it is necessary to have a knowledge of the whole of things."
100 BC–AD 400	Late Greek-early Roman civilization	Galen's humoral theory postulates that disease is caused by disturbances in the fluids of the body. Medicine adopts a holistic approach to disease.
500–1450	Middle Ages	Mysticism and religion dominate medicine. Sinning is the cause of mental and somatic illnesses.
1500–1700	Renaissance	Renewed interest in the natural sciences and their application to medicine; advances in anatomy (Vesalius), autopsy (Morgagni), microscopy (Leeuwenhoek). Psychic influences on the soma are rejected as unscientific; the study of the mind is relegated to religion and philosophy.
1800–1900	19th century	Modern laboratory-based medicine of Pasteur and Virchow. Virchow: "Disease has its origin in disease of the cell." Psychosomatic approach discarded, as all disease must be associated with structural cell change. The disease is treated, not the patient.
1900–present	20th century	Freud's psychoanalytic formulations emphasize the role of psychic determinism in somatic conversion reactions (Dora case). Early concepts are limited to major hysterical conversions; subsequently, Alexander differentiates conversion reactions from psychosomatic disorders and studies psychological factors in a series of diseases.

Table 28.1–5
Social Readjustment Rating Scale

Life Event	Mean Value
1. Death of spouse	100
2. Divorce	73
3. Marital separation from mate	65
4. Detention in jail or other institution	63
5. Death of a close family member	63
6. Major personal injury or illness	53
7. Marriage	50
8. Being fired at work	47
9. Marital reconciliation with mate	45
10. Retirement from work	45
11. Major change in the health or behavior of a family member	44
12. Pregnancy	40
13. Sexual difficulties	39
14. Gaining a new family member (through birth, adoption, oldster moving in, etc.)	39
15. Major business readjustment (merger, reorganization, bankruptcy, etc.)	39
16. Major change in financial state (a lot worse off or a lot better off than usual)	38
17. Death of a close friend	37
18. Changing to a different line of work	36
19. Major change in the number of arguments with spouse (either a lot more or a lot less than usual regarding child rearing, personal habits, etc.)	35
20. Taking on a mortgage greater than $10,000 (purchasing a home, business, etc.)[a]	31
21. Foreclosure on a mortgage or loan	30
22. Major change in responsibilities at work (promotion, demotion, lateral transfer)	29
23. Son or daughter leaving home (marriage, attending college, etc.)	29
24. In-law troubles	29
25. Outstanding personal achievement	28
26. Wife beginning or ceasing work outside the home	26
27. Beginning or ceasing formal schooling	26
28. Major change in living conditions (building a new home, remodeling, deterioration of home or neighborhood)	25
29. Revision of personal habits (dress, manners, associations, etc.)	24
30. Troubles with the boss	23
31. Major change in working hours or conditions	20
32. Change in residence	20
33. Changing to a new school	20
34. Major change in usual type or amount of recreation	19
35. Major change in church activities (a lot more or a lot less than usual)	19
36. Major change in social activities (clubs, dancing, movies, visiting, etc.)	18
37. Taking on a mortgage or loan less than $10,000 (purchasing a car, TV, freezer, etc.)	17
38. Major change in sleeping habits (a lot more or a lot less sleep or change in part of day when asleep)	16
39. Major change in number of family get-togethers (a lot more or a lot less than usual)	15
40. Major change in eating habits (a lot more or a lot less food intake or very different meal hours or surroundings)	15
41. Vacation	15
42. Christmas	12
43. Minor violations of the law (traffic tickets, jaywalking, disturbing the peace, etc.)	11

Reprinted with permission from Holmes T: Life situations, emotions, and disease. Psychosom Med *19*: 747, 1978.
[a] This figure no longer has any relevance in the light of inflation; what is significant is the total amount of debt from all sources.

Table 28.1–6
Some Hypothesized Psychological Correlates of Psychophysiological Disorders

Disorder	Psychogenic Causes, Personality Characteristics, and Coping Aims
Peptic ulcer	Feels deprived of dependence needs; is resentful; represses anger; cannot vent hostility or actively seek dependence security; characterizes self-sufficient and responsible go-getter types who are compensating for dependence desires; has strong regressive wish to be nurtured and fed; revengeful feelings are repressed and kept unconscious
Colitis	Was intimidated in childhood into dependence and conformity; feels conflict over resentment and desire to please; anger restrained for fear of retaliation; is fretful, brooding, and depressive or passive, sweet and bland; seeks to camouflage hostility by symbolic gesture of giving
Essential hypertension	Was forced in childhood to restrain resentments; inhibited rage; is threatened by and guilt-ridden over hostile impulses that may erupt; is a controlled, conforming, and "mature" personality; is hard-driving and conscientious; is guarded and tense; needs to control and direct anger into acceptable channels; wishes to gain approval from authority
Migraine	Is unable to fulfill excessive self-demands; feels intense resentment and envy toward intellectually or financially more successful competitors; has meticulous, scrupulous, perfectionistic, and ambitious personality; failure to attain perfectionist ambitions results in self-punishment
Bronchial asthma	Feels separation anxiety; was given inconsistent maternal affection; has fear and guilt that hostile impulses will be expressed toward loved persons; is demanding, sickly, and cranky or clinging and dependent; symptom expresses suppressed cry for help and protection
Neurodermatitis	Has overprotective but ungiving parents; has craving for affection; has conflict regarding hostility and dependence; shows guilt and self-punishment for inadequacies; is a superficially friendly and oversensitive personality with depressive features and low self-image; symptoms are atonement for inadequacy and guilt by self-excoriation; displays oblique expression of hostility and exhibitionism in need for attention and soothing

Reprinted with permission from Millon T, Millon R. Psychophysiologic disorders. In *Medical Behavioral Science,* T Millon, editor, p 211. Saunders, Philadelphia, 1975.

influenced by psychological factors, a correlation exploited by various schools of alternative medicine.

The DSM-IV diagnostic criteria for psychological factors affecting medical conditions are presented in Table 28.1–1. Excluded are classic mental disorders with physical symptoms as part of the disorder (for example, conversion disorder, in which a physical symptom is produced by psychological conflict); somatization disorder, in which the physical symptoms are not based on organic pathology; hypochondriasis, in which patients have an exaggerated concern about their health; physical complaints frequently associated with mental disorders (for example, dysthymic disorder, which usually has such somatic accompaniments as muscle weakness, asthenia, fatigue, and exhaustion); and physical complaints associated with substance-related disorders (for example, coughing associated with nicotine dependence).

The 10th revision of *International Statistical Classification of Diseases and Related Health Problems* (ICD-10) includes a similar category for psychosomatic conditions—psychological and behavioral factors associated with disorders or diseases classified elsewhere (Table 28.1–2).

HISTORY

The history of psychosomatic medicine parallels the history of humankind. A historical summary of the psyche–soma interaction is presented in Table 28.1–3.

Exactly where and how do the psyche and the soma interact? For more than 150 years, authorities in both psychiatry and medicine have agreed that, in some disorders, emotional and somatic activities overlap. These disorders were first called psychosomatic by Johann Christian Heinroth in 1818, when he used the term regarding insomnia. The word was later popularized by Maximilian Jacobi, a German psychiatrist. The number of disorders identified as psychosomatic grew to include ulcerative colitis, peptic ulcer, migraine headache, bronchial asthma, and rheumatoid arthritis. Table 28.1–4 lists some psychosomatic disorders.

ETIOLOGY

Although most agree that chronic, severe, and perceived stress plays some causative role in the development of many somatic diseases, some researchers have questioned the validity of the concept of psychosomatic medicine by suggesting that the term is too vague or too narrow. The character of the stress, the general underlying psychophysiological factors, patients' genetic and organ vulnerability, the nature of emotional conflicts (whether they are specific or nonspecific), and the way conflicts interact to produce diseases—all are still controversial.

General Stress Factors

A stressful life event or situation—internal or external, acute or chronic—generates challenges to which the organism cannot adequately respond. Thomas Holmes and Richard Rahe constructed a social readjustment rating scale after asking hundreds of people from varying backgrounds to rank the relative degree of adjustment required by changing life events. Holmes and Rahe listed 43 life events associated with varying amounts of disruption and stress in average people's lives: for example,

Table 28.1–7
Modern Concepts of Psychosomatic Medicine

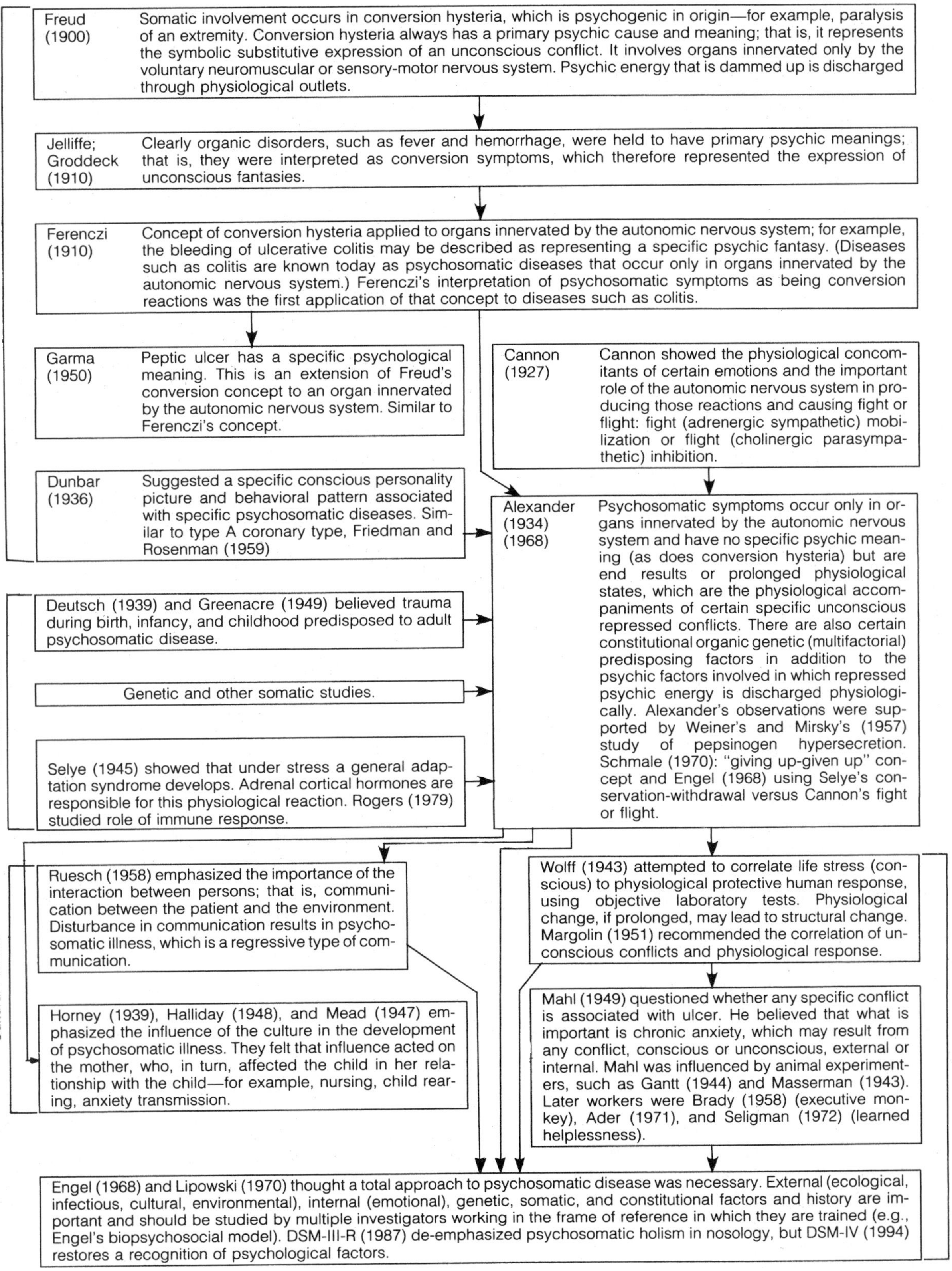
Psychological Factors
Freud (1900) Somatic involvement occurs in conversion hysteria, which is psychogenic in origin—for example, paralysis of an extremity. Conversion hysteria always has a primary psychic cause and meaning; that is, it represents the symbolic substitutive expression of an unconscious conflict. It involves organs innervated only by the voluntary neuromuscular or sensory-motor nervous system. Psychic energy that is dammed up is discharged through physiological outlets.
Jelliffe; Groddeck (1910) Clearly organic disorders, such as fever and hemorrhage, were held to have primary psychic meanings; that is, they were interpreted as conversion symptoms, which therefore represented the expression of unconscious fantasies.
Ferenczi (1910) Concept of conversion hysteria applied to organs innervated by the autonomic nervous system; for example, the bleeding of ulcerative colitis may be described as representing a specific psychic fantasy. (Diseases such as colitis are known today as psychosomatic diseases that occur only in organs innervated by the autonomic nervous system.) Ferenczi's interpretation of psychosomatic symptoms as being conversion reactions was the first application of that concept to diseases such as colitis.
Garma (1950) Peptic ulcer has a specific psychological meaning. This is an extension of Freud's conversion concept to an organ innervated by the autonomic nervous system. Similar to Ferenczi's concept.
Cannon (1927) Cannon showed the physiological concomitants of certain emotions and the important role of the autonomic nervous system in producing those reactions and causing fight or flight: fight (adrenergic sympathetic) mobilization or flight (cholinergic parasympathetic) inhibition.
Dunbar (1936) Suggested a specific conscious personality picture and behavioral pattern associated with specific psychosomatic diseases. Similar to type A coronary type, Friedman and Rosenman (1959)
Alexander (1934) (1968) Psychosomatic symptoms occur only in organs innervated by the autonomic nervous system and have no specific psychic meaning (as does conversion hysteria) but are end results or prolonged physiological states, which are the physiological accompaniments of certain specific unconscious repressed conflicts. There are also certain constitutional organic genetic (multifactorial) predisposing factors in addition to the psychic factors involved in which repressed psychic energy is discharged physiologically. Alexander's observations were supported by Weiner's and Mirsky's (1957) study of pepsinogen hypersecretion. Schmale (1970): "giving up-given up" concept and Engel (1968) using Selye's conservation-withdrawal versus Cannon's fight or flight.
Somatic Factors
Deutsch (1939) and Greenacre (1949) believed trauma during birth, infancy, and childhood predisposed to adult psychosomatic disease.
Genetic and other somatic studies.
Selye (1945) showed that under stress a general adaptation syndrome develops. Adrenal cortical hormones are responsible for this physiological reaction. Rogers (1979) studied role of immune response.
Cultural Factors
Ruesch (1958) emphasized the importance of the interaction between persons; that is, communication between the patient and the environment. Disturbance in communication results in psychosomatic illness, which is a regressive type of communication.
Horney (1939), Halliday (1948), and Mead (1947) emphasized the influence of the culture in the development of psychosomatic illness. They felt that influence acted on the mother, who, in turn, affected the child in her relationship with the child—for example, nursing, child rearing, anxiety transmission.
Laboratory Factors
Wolff (1943) attempted to correlate life stress (conscious) to physiological protective human response, using objective laboratory tests. Physiological change, if prolonged, may lead to structural change. Margolin (1951) recommended the correlation of unconscious conflicts and physiological response.
Mahl (1949) questioned whether any specific conflict is associated with ulcer. He believed that what is important is chronic anxiety, which may result from any conflict, conscious or unconscious, external or internal. Mahl was influenced by animal experimenters, such as Gantt (1944) and Masserman (1943). Later workers were Brady (1958) (executive monkey), Ader (1971), and Seligman (1972) (learned helplessness).
Engel (1968) and Lipowski (1970) thought a total approach to psychosomatic disease was necessary. External (ecological, infectious, cultural, environmental), internal (emotional), genetic, somatic, and constitutional factors and history are important and should be studied by multiple investigators working in the frame of reference in which they are trained (e.g., Engel's biopsychosocial model). DSM-III-R (1987) de-emphasized psychosomatic holism in nosology, but DSM-IV (1994) restores a recognition of psychological factors.

the death of a spouse, 100 life-change units; divorce, 73 units; marital separation, 65 units; and the death of a close family member, 63 units (Table 28.1–5). An accumulation of 200 or more life-change units in a single year increases the incidence of psychosomatic disorders.

Recent studies have found that people who face general stresses optimistically, rather than pessimistically, are not apt to experience psychosomatic disorders; if they do, they are apt to recover easily.

Specific versus Nonspecific Stress Factors

In addition to general stresses such as a divorce or the death of a spouse, some investigators have suggested that specific personalities and conflicts are associated with specific psychosomatic diseases. Other investigators believe that nonspecific generalized anxiety from any conflict may lead to many diseases.

Specific psychic stress may be defined as a specific personality or an unconscious conflict that causes a homeostatic disequilibrium contributing to the development of a psychosomatic disorder. Researchers first identified specific personality types in connection with the coronary disorders (a coronary personality is a hard-driving, aggressive person who experiences myocardial occlusion). The so-called type A personality (similar to the coronary personality) was singled out as one that predisposes a person to coronary disease. Meyer Friedman and Ray Rosenman first defined type A and type B personalities (type A and type B personalities are discussed in Section 28.2.)

Franz Alexander hypothesized that specific unconscious conflicts are associated with specific psychosomatic disorders (for example, unconscious dependence conflict predisposes people to peptic ulcer). Alexander's multifactorial theories were later confirmed by Arthur Mirsky and Herbert Weiner. Both the specific personality type and the unconscious conflicts fall under the rubric of specific causative theories of psychosomatic diseases. Table 28.1–6 gives some psychological correlates of psychophysiological disorders.

Researchers have alternatively suggested that chronic nonspecific stress, usually with the intervening variable of anxiety, has physiological correlates that, combined with genetic organ vulnerability or debility, predisposes certain people to psychosomatic disorders. People with alexithymia have impoverished fantasy lives and are unconscious of their emotional conflicts; psychosomatic disorders may serve as an outlet for their accumulated tensions. Nonspecific causal theories are supported by experimental evidence that, under chronic stress, animals have psychosomatic disorders (such as peptic ulcer).

Physiological Factors

The mediator between cognitively based stress and disease may be hormonal, as in the general-adaption syndrome of Hans Selye, in which hydrocortisone is the intermediary; or the mediator may be changes in the functioning of the anterior pituitary-hypothalamic-adrenal axis, with autonomic effects, adrenal enlargement, and lymphoid shrinkage. In the hormonal linkage, hormones are released from the hypothalamus and travel to the anterior pituitary, where the trophic hormones interact directly or release hormones from other endocrine glands. Alexander pointed to the autonomic nervous system—for example, the parasympathetic nervous system in peptic ulcer and the sympathetic nervous system in hypertension—as the mechanism linking chronic stress and psychosomatic disorders.

Another intervening factor may be the action of the immune system's monocytes. The monocytes interact with brain neuropeptides, which serve as messengers between brain cells. Thus, immunity may influence psychic state and mood. Herbert Benson, in explaining the effects of relaxation therapy on certain psychosomatic disorders, postulated that relaxation decreases the activity of cerebral adrenergic catecholamines and that these substances affect the limbic system—the Papez circuit—which is important in the cause of psychosomatic and mental disorders. A summary of the major theories of psychosomatic medicine is presented in Table 28.1–7.

TREATMENT

Both psychosomatic medicine and behavioral medicine deal with the interaction of the psyche and the soma, and psychosomatic disorders have traditionally been treated with psychoanalysis and psychotherapy. Within the past two decades, interest in using behavior modification (learning theory) techniques to treat these disorders has grown. Among the therapeutic techniques emphasized in behavior modification are muscle relaxation therapy, biofeedback, hypnosis, controlled breathing, yoga, and massage. The goal of both the behavioral techniques and the usual psychotherapeutic modalities is to improve the psychosomatic equation.

REFERENCES

Alexander F: *Psychosomatic Medicine.* Norton, New York, 1950.

Alexander F, French TM, Pollack GH: *Psychosomatic Specificity: Experimental Study and Results.* University of Chicago Press, Chicago, 1968.

Benson H: The relaxation response. In *Mind Body Medicine: How to Use Your Mind for Better Health,* D Goleman, J Gurin, editors, p 233. Consumer Reports, Yonkers, NY, 1993.

Engel GH, Reichsman F, Siegel HL: A study of an infant with a gastric fistula. Psychosom Med *18:* 374, 1956.

Feifel H, Strack S, Nagy VT: Degree of life-threat and differential use of coping modes. J Psychol Res *31:* 91, 1987.

Frasure-Smith N, Lesperance F, Talajic M: Depression and 18-month prognosis after myocardial infarction. Circulation *91:* 999, 1995.

Kiecolt-Glaser JK, Glaser R: Psychoneuroimmunology: Can psychological interventions modulate immunity? J Consult Clin Psychol *60:* 569, 1992.

Nakano K: Application of self-control procedures to modifying type A behavior. Psychol Rec *46* (4): 595, 1996.

Schwartz GE, Weiss SM: Behavioral medicine revisited: An amended definition. J Behav Med *1:* 249, 1978.

Stoudemire A: *Psychological Factors Affecting Medical Conditions.* American Psychiatric Press, Washington, 1995.

Stoudemire A, McDaniel JS: History, classification, and current trends in psychosomatic medicine. In *Comprehensive Textbook of Psychiatry,* ed 6, HI Kaplan, BJ Sadock, editors, p 1463. Williams & Wilkins, Baltimore, 1995.

Whitehead WE: Behavioral medicine approaches to gastrointestinal disorders. J Consult Clin Psychol *60:* 605, 1992.

▲ 28.2 Specific Disorders

CARDIOVASCULAR SYSTEM

Coronary Artery Disease

Coronary artery disease causes a decrease in blood flow to the heart and is characterized by episodic chest and heart pain, discomfort, or pressure. It is usually produced by exertion or stress and is relieved by rest or sublingual nitroglycerine.

Personality Type. Flanders Dunbar first described patients with coronary disease as aggressive and compulsive personalities with a tendency to work long hours and to seize authority. Later, Meyer Friedman and Ray Rosenman defined type A and type B personalities. Type A personalities, strongly associated with the development of coronary heart disease, are action-oriented people who struggle to achieve poorly defined goals by means of competitive hostility. They are aggressive, impatient, upwardly mobile, striving, and angry when frustrated. Type B personalities are the opposite: relaxed, less aggressive, and less concerned with striving vigorously to achieve their goals. Type A personalities have increased amounts of low-density lipoprotein, serum cholesterol, triglycerides, and 17-hydroxycorticosteroids. In these people, sudden loss may cause death by coronary occlusion.

Treatment. When coronary occlusion occurs, clinicians prescribe various medications for patients' cardiac status. To alleviate the psychic distress such as anxiety and depression associated with the disease, physicians use psychotropics such as diazepam (Valium) and fluoxetine (Prozac) and treat pain with analgesics (such as morphine). Medical treatment should be supportive and reassuring, with some psychological emphasis on the alleviation of psychic stress, compulsivity, and tension.

Essential Hypertension

Hypertension is a disease characterized by a blood pressure of 160/95 mm Hg or higher. Twenty percent of the adult population in the United States is hypertensive.

Personality Type. People with hypertension appear to be congenial, compliant, and compulsive. Although their anger is not expressed openly, they have much inhibited rage, which they handle poorly. There may be a familial genetic predisposition to hypertension; that is, when chronic stress occurs in a genetically predisposed compulsive personality who has repressed and suppressed rage, hypertension may result. Hypertension also tends to occur in type A personalities.

Treatment. Supportive psychotherapy and behavioral techniques, for example, biofeedback, meditation, and relaxation therapy, have been reported to be useful in treating hypertension. Medically, patients must comply with the antihypertensive medication regimen.

Congestive Heart Failure

Congestive heart failure is a disorder in which the heart fails to move the blood forward normally, which produces congestion in the lungs and systemic circulation and decreased tissue blood flow with diminished cardiac output. Psychological factors, such as nonspecific emotional stress and conflict, are frequently significant in the initiation or exacerbation of the disorder. Thus, supportive psychotherapy is important in its treatment.

Vasomotor (Vasodepressor) Syncope

Vasomotor (vasodepressor) syncope is characterized by a sudden loss of consciousness (fainting) caused by a vasovagal attack. Sympathetic autonomic activity is inhibited, and parasympathetic vagal nerve activity is augmented; the result is decreased cardiac output, decreased vascular peripheral resistance, vasodilation, and bradycardia. According to Franz Alexander, acute fear or fright inhibits the impulse to fight or flee, causing vasodilation of the blood vessels in the extremities, and thereby pools the blood in the lower extremities. This reaction results in decreased ventricular filling, a drop in the blood supply to the brain, and consequent brain hypoxia and loss of consciousness.

Treatment. Because patients with vasomotor syncope normally put themselves or fall into a prone position, the decreased cardiac output is corrected. Raising their legs also helps correct the physiological imbalance. Psychotherapy should be used to determine the cause of the fright or the trauma associated with syncope. When syncope is related to orthostatic hypotension, patients should be advised to shift slowly from a sitting to a standing position.

Cardiac Arrhythmias

Potentially life-threatening arrhythmias—such as palpitations, ventricular tachycardia, and ventricular fibrillation—sometimes occur in conjunction with an emotional upset. Also associated with emotional trauma are sinus tachycardia, ST-wave and T-wave changes, ventricular ectopy, increased plasma catecholamines, and free fatty acid concentrations. Emotional stress is nonspecific, as is the personality description associated with the disorders.

Treatment. Psychotherapy and β-blocking drugs, such as propranolol (Inderal), help protect against emotionally induced arrhythmias.

Raynaud's Phenomenon

In addition to external stress, such as extreme cold, psychological stress frequently produces idiopathic paroxysmal bilateral cyanosis of the digits, caused by arteriolar contraction.

Treatment. Raynaud's phenomenon may be treated with supportive psychotherapy, progressive relaxation, or biofeedback, and by protecting the body from cold and using a mild sedative. Patients who smoke must stop because nicotine is a vasoconstrictor. β-Adrenergic receptor antagonists, clonidine (Catapres), and ergot preparations also cause vasoconstriction and are contraindicated.

Psychogenic Cardiac Nondisease

Some patients free of heart disease complain of symptoms suggestive of the condition. They often exhibit morbid concerns about their hearts and have exaggerated fears of heart disease. Their fear may range from an anxious concern, manifested by a severe phobia or hypochondriasis, to a delusional conviction that they have cardiac disease. Many patients suffer from an ill-defined syndrome often referred to as neurocirculatory asthenia.

Neurocirculatory asthenia was first described in 1871 by Jacob M. DaCosta, who named it irritable heart. The condition has some 20 names, including effort syndrome, DaCosta's syndrome, cardiac neurosis, vasoregulatory asthenia, hyperkinetic heart syndrome, and hyperdynamic-adrenergic circulatory state. Psychiatrists tend to view it as a clinical variant of anxiety disorders, although it does not appear in the fourth edition of *Diagnostic and Statistical Manual of Mental Disorders* (DSM-IV). According to the 10th revision of *International Statistical Classification of Diseases and Related Health Problems* (ICD-10), a patient with the condition should be diagnosed with somatoform autonomic dysfunction (see Table 17–2).

Diagnosis. The diagnostic criteria for neurocirculatory asthenia are respiratory complaints such as sighing respiration, inability to take a deep breath, smothering and choking, and dyspnea; palpitations, chest pain, or discomfort; nervousness, dizziness, faintness, or discomfort in crowds; undue fatigue or limitation of activities; and excessive sweating, insomnia, and irritability. The symptoms usually start in adolescence or the early 20s but may begin in middle age. Such symptoms are twice as common in women as in men and tend to be chronic, with recurrent acute exacerbations.

Treatment. The management of neurocirculatory asthenia may be difficult, and the prognosis is guarded if the condition is chronic. Phobic elements are prominent, and patients often derive primary or secondary gains from the disability. Psychotherapy aimed at uncovering psychodynamic factors—often relating to hostility, unacceptable sexual impulses, dependence, guilt, and death anxiety—may be effective in some cases, but most patients with the condition tend to shun psychiatric help. Other behavioral techniques may be useful. Physical training programs aimed at correcting faulty breathing habits and gradually increasing patients' effort tolerance may be helpful, especially when the programs are combined with group psychotherapy. Psychopharmacological treatment focuses on the predominant symptoms. The use of propranolol may interrupt the vicious circle of cardiac symptoms and have a positive reinforcement feedback effect on anxiety, which aggravates the symptoms. Antianxiety agents (for example, diazepam) can be used for major anxiety symptoms. If fatigue, lassitude, and weakness are the major complaints, the judicious use of amphetamines or methylphenidate (Ritalin) may be helpful.

RESPIRATORY SYSTEM

Bronchial Asthma

Bronchial asthma is a chronic recurrent obstructive disease of the bronchial airways, which tend to respond to various stimuli by bronchial constriction, edema, and excessive secretion. Genetic factors, allergic factors, infections, and acute and chronic stress all combine to produce the disease. Whereas the rate and depth of a healthy person's breathing can be changed voluntarily to correlate with various emotional states, such changes are aggravated and prolonged in people with asthma.

Psychological Factors. Although patients with asthma are characterized as having excessive dependence needs, no specific personality type has been identified. Alexander pointed to psychodynamic conflictual factors, as he found in many asthmatic patients a strong unconscious wish for protection and for envelopment by the mother or surrogate mother. The mother figures tend to be overprotective and oversolicitous, perfectionistic, dominating, and helpful. When protection is sought but is not received, an asthmatic attack occurs.

Treatment. Some asthmatic children improve when separated from their mothers (so-called parentectomy). All standard psychotherapies are used: individual, group, behavioral (systematic desensitization), and hypnotic. Patients with asthma should be treated jointly by internists, allergists, and psychiatrists. β-Adrenergic receptor antagonists are contraindicated.

Hay Fever

Strong psychological factors combine with allergic elements to produce hay fever. One factor may dominate over the others, or factors may alternate in importance.

Treatment. Psychiatric, medical, and allergic factors must be considered in treating hay fever.

Hyperventilation Syndrome

Normal people can voluntarily change the rate, depth, and regularity of their breathing, which can also be correlated with various emotional states. Patients with hyperventilation syndrome breathe rapidly and deeply for several minutes, feel lightheaded, and then faint because of cerebral vasoconstriction and a respiratory alkalosis. Other symptoms, such as paresthesias and carpopedal spasm, may be present. Specific medical differentials for the syndrome are epilepsy, conversion disorder, vasovagal or hypoglycemic attacks, myocardial attacks, bronchial asthma, acute porphyria, Ménière's disease, and pheochromocytoma. Psychiatric differentials include anxiety attacks, panic attacks, schizophrenia, borderline or histrionic personality disorder, and phobic or obsessive complaints.

Treatment. Patients can consciously avoid precipitating symptoms with instruction or retraining concerning particular symptoms and how they are evoked by hyperventilation. Breathing into a paper bag can abort the attack. Reassurance and supportive psychotherapy are also indicated.

Tuberculosis

The onset and aggravation of tuberculosis are often associated with acute and chronic stress. Psychological factors affect the immune system and may influence patients' resistance to the disease.

Treatment. In the past, treatment was effective with antituberculosis drugs and antibiotics. In the past 5 years there has been a significant resurgence in the incidence of tuberculosis and the development of antibiotic-resistant tubercle bacilli. People with immune-compromised systems readily become hosts to tuberculosis; thus many people with acquired immunodeficiency syndrome (AIDS) and human immunodeficiency virus (HIV) also have tuberculosis, particularly of the miliary type. The role of stress in the incidence of tuberculosis has not been thoroughly studied, but most people with AIDS have psychiatric and neurological complications and are liable to stress. Supportive psychotherapy is valuable because of the role of stress and the complicated psychosocial situation. Patients with tuberculosis are often noncompliant in taking medication.

GASTROINTESTINAL SYSTEM

Peptic Ulcer

Peptic ulcer is a circumscribed ulceration of the mucous membrane of the stomach or the duodenum; the ulceration penetrates to the muscularis mucosae and occurs in areas exposed to gastric acid and pepsin.

Table 28.2–1
Drugs for Peptic Ulcers

Histamine type 2 (H_2)-receptor antagonists
Cimetidine (Tagamet)
Famotidine (Pepcid)
Nizatidine (Axid)
Ranitidine (Zantac)
Proton-pump inhibitors
Lansoprazole (Prevacid)
Omeprazole (Prilosec)
Antacids
Magnesium hydroxide–aluminum hydroxide–simethicone (Extra Strength Maalox antacid, Mylanta Double Strength)
Other drugs
Sucralfate (Carafate)
Misoprostol (Cytotec)

Table 28.2–2
Some Drug Regimens for *H. Pylori*

Drugs	Daily Dosage (mg)	Duration (wk)
Bismuth subsalicylate	1,100	2
and metronidazole	1,000	2
and tetracycline	2,000	2
and ranitidine (Zantac)	300	2
or nizatidine (Axid)	300	2
Clarithromycin (Biaxin)	1,500	2
and omeprazol (Prilosec)	40	2
followed by omeprazole	20	2
Ranitidine bismuth citrate (Tritec)	800	4
and clarithromycin	1,500	2

Etiology. SPECIFIC FACTOR. Alexander hypothesized that chronic frustration of intense dependence needs results in a characteristic unconscious conflict, which pertains to intense dependent oral-receptive longings to be cared for and loved. This conflict causes a chronic regressive unconscious hunger and anger, which is manifested physiologically by persistent vagal hyperactivity leading to gastric acid hypersecretion. This reaction is particularly ominous in those genetically predisposed hypersecretors of acid. With the above equation, ulcer formation may result. Genetic factors and preexisting organ damage or disease (for example, gastritis) are causally important. Such gastritis may result from excessive caffeine, nicotine, or alcohol.

NONSPECIFIC FACTORS. Stress and anxiety caused by various nonspecific conflicts may produce gastric hyperacidity and hypersecretion of pepsin and may result in an ulcer. Because various traumatic occurrences in animals, for example, electric shock in dogs, may produce ulcers, such experimental data support a nonspecific approach. Peptic ulcers have been diagnosed in all personality types.

Most gastric ulcers may be caused by the gram-negative bacillus *Helicobacter pylori.* Duodenal ulcer, on the other hand, should be considered to have a psychosomatic cause and should be treated with psychological and psychosocial management. However, an infectious agent may yet be implicated in duodenal ulcer.

Treatment. Psychotherapy is directed toward patients' dependence conflicts. Biofeedback and relaxation therapy may be useful. Medical treatment with cimetidine (Tagamet), ranitidine (Zantac), sucralfate (Carafate), or famotidine (Pepcid); antacid medications; and dietary control (for example, no alcohol) are indicated in ulcer management (Table 28.2–1). The treatment of gastric ulcer includes antimicrobial drugs (Table 28.2–2).

Ulcerative Colitis

Ulcerative colitis is a chronic inflammatory ulcerative disease of the colon and is usually associated with bloody diarrhea. Familial incidence and genetic factors are significant. Related diseases include regional ileitis and irritable bowel syndrome.

Personality Type. Most studies show that patients have a predominance of compulsive personality traits and are neat, orderly, clean, punctual, hyperintellectual, timid, and inhibited in expressing their anger.

Etiology. SPECIFIC FACTOR. Alexander described a typical specific conflictual constellation in ulcerative colitis. The central issue is an inability to fulfill an obligation (usually of accomplishment) to a key dependency figure. This frustrated dependence stimulates oral-aggressive feelings, produces guilt and anxiety, and results in restitution through the ''gifting'' of diarrhea. In regard to colitis, George Engel described a pathological mother–child relationship, with feelings of hopelessness–helplessness and a giving up–given up complex.

NONSPECIFIC FACTORS. Nonspecific stress of many types may aggravate ulcerative colitis.

Treatment. Nonconfrontational, supportive psychotherapy is indicated during acute ulcerative colitis, with interpretative psychotherapy during the quiescent periods. Medical treatment consists of nonspecific supportive medical measures such as anticholinergics and antidiarrheal agents. Prednisone therapy is useful in severe cases. Bismuth-containing medications, for example, Pepto-Bismol, are useful in managing diarrhea.

Obesity

Obesity is discussed in Chapter 23, Section 23.3.

Anorexia Nervosa

Anorexia nervosa is characterized by behavior directed toward losing weight, peculiar patterns of handling food, weight loss, intense fear of gaining weight, disturbance of body image, and, in women, amenorrhea. It is one of the few psychiatric illnesses that may have a course unremitting until death. (Anorexia nervosa is discussed further in Chapter 23, Section 23.1.)

Neurological Diseases

Most neurological disorders cause psychological reactions that are significant and can affect their prognosis and course. Stroke, brain tumors, degenerative brain diseases (such as Parkinson's disease) invariably are associated with a significant depression. Studies have been carried out on depressed patients with multiple sclerosis, epilepsy, and migraine headaches; serotonin-specific reuptake inhibitors may be of therapeutic value in the management of these conditions.

MUSCULOSKELETAL SYSTEM

Rheumatoid Arthritis

Rheumatoid arthritis is a disease characterized by chronic musculoskeletal pain arising from inflammation of the joints. The disorder's significant causative factors are hereditary, allergic, immunological, and psychological. Psychological stress may predispose people to rheumatoid arthritis and to other autoimmune diseases by producing immune suppression. People with arthritis feel restrained and confined. Because many people with the condition have a history of physical activity (for example, dancers), they often have repressed rage about problems with their muscle function inhibition, and this rage aggravates their stiffness and immobility.

Treatment. Treatment should include psychotherapy, which is usually supportive during chronic (sharp) attacks and interpretive between acute attacks. Rest and exercise should be structured, and patients should be encouraged not to become bed-bound and to return to their usual activities. The rest and exercise program should be coordinated with the medical treatment of the pain and inflammation of the joints.

Low Back Pain

Low back pain affects almost 15 million Americans and is one of the major reasons for days lost from work and for disability claims paid to workers by insurance companies. Signs and symptoms vary from patient to patient, most often consisting of excruciating pain, restriction of movement, paraesthesias, weakness or numbness, all of which may be accompanied by anxiety, fear, or even panic. The areas most affected are the lower lumbar, lumbosacral, and sacroiliac regions. It is often accompanied by sciatica, with pain radiating down one or both buttocks or following the distribution of the sciatic nerve. Although low back pain may be caused by a ruptured intervertebral disk, a fracture of the back, congenital defects of the lower spine, or a ligamentous muscle strain, many instances are psychosomatic. Some reports indicate that 95 percent of cases are psychological in origin. John Sarno, M.D., Professor of Clinical Rehabilitation Medicine at NYU Medical Center, has done extensive work in this area and has termed psychological cases *tension myositis syndrome* (TMS).

Examining physicians should be particularly alert to patients who give a history of minor back trauma followed by severe disabling pain. Patients with low back pain often report that the pain began at a time of psychological trauma or stress, but others (perhaps 50 percent) develop pain gradually over a period of months. Patients' reaction to the pain is disproportionately emotional, with excessive anxiety and depression. Furthermore, the distribution of the pain rarely follows a normal neuroanatomical distribution and may vary in location and intensity.

Treatment. There are two approaches to treatment. In the first or conventional method, treatment is symptomatic. Analgesics such as aspirin (up to 4 grams a day) can be used for pain. Muscle relaxants such as diazepam (2.5 to 5 mg every 4 to 6 hours for 2 or 3 days) are used to reduce muscle spasms and anxiety. Physical therapy is prescribed for the person in severe pain with restrictions in movement. Some patients respond to relaxation therapy and biofeedback. A great many techniques have been proposed to treat low back pain, most of which are untested and unproven as to overall effectiveness. These include various forms of massage, acupressure, acupuncture, injections of anesthetics or steroids, traction, bed rest, electrical stimulation, ultrasound, and hot packs and cold packs.

The second approach, developed by Sarno, is psychoeducational. This treatment is based on the premise that the back is structurally sound without any abnormality to account for symptoms. To assure both patient and doctor, a careful physical examination is recommended, including a neurological examination and magnetic resonance imaging (MRI) if necessary. An MRI study that shows some abnormality does not automatically imply that that is the cause of the pain. To the contrary, changes in spinal morphology that are normal occur with age, and the majority of such patients are asymptomatic. Additionally, many patients who have MRI studies show spinal abnormalities as an incidental finding and have never complained of back pain. These include bulging or herniated intravertebral discs, osteophytes, spinal stenosis, and other osteoarthritic changes, but they are not responsible for pain or any neurological symptom.

According to Sarno, the pathophysiology involved in TMS is vasospasm of blood vessels that supply the involved muscle, nerve, or tendon. Vasospasm is mediated by the autonomic nervous system, which is extraordinarily sensitive to changes in emotional tone, chronic emotional stress, and unconscious affects. The ischemia and oxygen deprivation cause pain in the areas involved. An analogy can be drawn to the vasospasm of coronary arteries that cause angina.

Treatment includes educating patients about the physiological component (vasospasm) and helping them understand the working of the unconscious mind and conflicts that arise from unconscious affects, especially that of rage. The patient understands that the mind is substituting physical pain for emotional pain so that the conscious mind does not have to deal with conflict. Physical activity should be resumed as quickly as possible, and treatments such as spinal manipulation and mandatory physical therapy sessions are not necessary. Sarno has treated over 10,000 patients successfully with this approach. About 10 percent of patients require referral to a psychotherapist for insight-oriented therapy to fully understand the unconscious conflicts.

Choices of Therapy. Those patients who are not psychologically oriented or who are unable to grasp the relationship between mind and body will not respond to a psychoeducational approach. Most patients with psychosomatic back pain have been to many doctors, including chiropractors, and have a fixed idea that there is a structural abnormality to account for their symptoms. Such patients have been subjected to surgery, spinal manipulations, and other therapies without relief. Their prognosis is poor, with remissions and exacerbations that persist throughout life. Many of these patients end up on disability or welfare roles and are permanently impaired. Those patients who are capable of psychological insight and who do not have a severe comorbid psychiatric illness, such as bipolar disorder or schizophrenia, have a good prognosis with psychoeducational treatment.

Fibromyalgia

Fibromyalgia is characterized by pain and stiffness of the soft tissues, such as muscles, ligaments, and tendons. There are local areas of tenderness referred to as "trigger points." The cervical and thoracic areas are affected most often, but the pain may be located in the arms, shoulders, low back, or legs. It is more common in women than in men. The etiology is unknown; however, it is often precipitated by stress that causes localized arterial spasm that interferes with perfusion of oxygen in the affected areas. Pain results with associated symptoms of anxiety, fatigue, and inability to sleep because of the pain.

There are no pathognomonic laboratory findings. The diagnosis is made after excluding rheumatic disease or hypothyroidism. Fibromyalgia is often present in chronic fatigue syndrome and depressive disorders. According to Sarno, fibromyalgia is a variant of TMS.

Treatment. Analgesics such as aspirin and acetaminophen are useful for pain. Narcotics should be avoided. Some patients may respond to nonsteroidal anti-inflammatory drugs. More severe cases may respond to injections of an anesthetic (for example, procaine) into the affected area; steroid injections are usually unwarranted. Explanations of the relationship between stress, spasms, and pain should be provided. Relaxation exercises and massage of the trigger points may also be of use. Antidepressants, especially sertraline (Zoloft), have shown encouraging results. A trial of treatment similar to that for TMS may be warranted in patients who are able to gain insight into the nature of the disorder and who will benefit therefrom. Brief psychotherapy to identify and deal with psychosocial stressors can be of great help in motivated patients.

HEADACHES

Headaches are the most common neurological symptom and one of the most common medical complaints. Every year about 80 percent of the population are estimated to suffer from at least one headache, and 10 to 20 percent of the population go to physicians with headache as their primary complaint. Headaches are also a major cause of absenteeism from work and of avoidance of social and personal activities.

Most headaches are not associated with significant organic disease; many people are susceptible to headaches at times of emotional stress. Moreover, in many psychiatric disorders, including anxiety and depressive disorders, frequently headache is a prominent symptom. Patients with headaches are often referred to psychiatrists by primary care physicians and neurologists after extensive biomedical workups, which often include a computed tomography (CT) scan of the head. Most workups for common headache complaints have negative findings, and such results may be frustrating for both patient and physician. Physicians not well versed in psychological medicine may attempt to reassure such patients by telling them that there is no disease. But this reassurance may have the opposite effect: It may increase patients' anxiety and even escalate into a disagreement about whether the pain is real or imagined.

Psychological stresses usually exacerbate headaches, whether their primary underlying cause is physical or psychological. Psychosomatic headaches are sometimes differentiated from psychogenic (for example, anxiety, depression, hypochondriacal, delusional) headaches. Headaches may be a conversion symptom of inpatients. In these patients, the headache symbolizes unconscious psychological conflicts, and the symptoms are mediated through the voluntary sensorimotor nervous system. In contrast, psychosomatic or unconscious conflicts are not symbolic in nature. Psychiatrists must make this distinction to reach the proper diagnosis, which then allows the most specific treatment to be recommended.

Migraine (Vascular) Headaches

Migraine (vascular) headaches are a paroxysmal disorder characterized by recurrent headaches, with or without related visual and gastrointestinal disturbances. They are probably caused by a functional disturbance in the cranial circulation.

Personality Type. Two thirds of all patients with migraine headaches have family histories of similar disorders. Obsessional personalities who are overly controlled and perfectionistic, who suppress anger, and who are genetically predisposed to migraines may have such headaches in times of severe nonspecific emotional conflict or stress.

Treatment. Migraines are best treated during the prodromal period with ergotamine tartrate (Cafergot) and analgesics. The prophylactic administration of propranolol or phenytoin (Dilantin) is useful when the headaches are frequent. Sumatriptan (Imitrex) is indicated for the short-term treatment of migraine. Serotonin-specific reuptake inhibitors are also useful for prophylaxis. Psychotherapy to diminish the effects of conflict and stress and certain behavioral techniques (for example, biofeedback) have been reported to be useful.

Tension (Muscle Contraction) Headaches

Emotional stress is often associated with the prolonged contraction of head and neck muscles, which over several hours may constrict the blood vessels and result in ischemia. A dull, aching pain, sometimes feeling like a tightening band, often begins suboccipitally and may spread over the head. The scalp may be tender to the touch, and in contrast to a migraine, the headache is usually bilateral and not associated with prodromata, nausea, and vomiting. The onset is often toward the end of the workday or in the early evening, possibly after people leave a stressful job, try to relax, and focus on somatic sensations. But when family or personal pressures are equal to or greater than those at work, the headaches may be worse later in the evening, on weekends, or during vacations.

Tension headaches, frequently associated with anxiety and depression, may occur to some degree in about 80 percent of people during periods of emotional stress. Tense, high-strung, competitive, type A personalities are especially prone to the disorder. In the initial stage people may be treated with antianxiety agents, muscle relaxants, and massage or heat application to the head and the neck; antidepressants may be prescribed when an underlying depression is present. Psychotherapy, however, is usually the treatment of choice for people chronically afflicted by tension headaches. Learning to avoid or better cope with tension is the most effective long-term management approach. Electromyogram (EMG) feedback from the frontal or temporal muscles may help some patients with tension headache. Relaxation associated with practice periods, meditation, or other changes in a pressured lifestyle may provide symptomatic relief for some patients.

ENDOCRINE SYSTEM

Hyperthyroidism

Hyperthyroidism (thyrotoxicosis) is a syndrome characterized by biochemical and psychological changes that occur as the result of a chronic endogenous or exogenous excess of thyroid hormone.

Psychosomatic Factors. In people who are genetically predisposed, stress is often associated with the onset of hyperthyroidism. According to psychoanalytic theory, during childhood, people with hyperthyroidism had an unusual attachment to and dependence on a parent, usually the mother, and so could not tolerate any threat to their mother's approval. As children, such people often lacked adequate support because of economic stress, divorce, death, or multiple siblings. The persistent threat to security in early life led to premature and unsuccessful attempts to identify with an adult object and also caused early stress, overuse of the endocrine system, and further frustration of childhood dependence cravings. These people continuously strive toward premature self-sufficiency and tend to dominate others with smothering attention and affection. As adults they build defenses against a repetition of the unbearable feelings of rejection and isolation that occurred in childhood. Should these mechanisms break down, and require a premature stimulation of the body's psychophysiological defense in genetically predisposed patients, thyrotoxicosis may result.

Treatment. Antithyroid medication, tranquilizers, and supportive psychotherapy are useful. Crisis intervention may be helpful at the onset of the disease.

Diabetes Mellitus

Diabetes mellitus is a disorder of metabolism and of the vascular system manifested by a disturbance of the body's handling of glucose, lipid, and protein.

Etiology. Heredity and family history are important in the onset of diabetes. A sudden onset is often associated with emotional stress, which disturbs the homeostatic balance in people who are predisposed to the disorder. Psychological factors that seem significant are those provoking feelings of frustration, loneliness, and dejection. Patients with diabetes must usually maintain some dietary control over their diabetes. When they are depressed and dejected, they often overeat or overdrink self-destructively and cause their diabetes to get out of control. This reaction is especially common in patients with juvenile diabetes. Terms such as oral, dependent, seeking maternal attention, and excessively passive have been applied to people with this condition.

Treatment. Supportive psychotherapy is necessary to achieve cooperation in the medical management of the complex disease. Therapists should encourage patients to lead as normal a life as possible, with the recognition that they have a chronic but manageable disease.

Female Endocrine Disorders

Premenstrual Dysphoric Disorder. Premenstrual dysphoric disorder and premenstrual syndrome (PMS) are characterized by cyclical subjective changes in mood and general sense of physical and psychological well-being correlated with the menstrual cycle. The symptoms usually begin soon after ovulation, increase gradually, and reach a maximum of intensity about 5 days before the menstrual period begins. Psychological, social, and biological factors have been implicated in the disorder's pathogenesis. In particular, changes in estrogen, progesterone, androgen, and prolactin levels have been hypothesized to be causally important. Excessive exposure to and subsequent abrupt withdrawal from endogenous opiate peptides, which fluctuate under the influence of gonadal steroids, may contribute to premenstrual dysphoric disorder. An increase in prostaglandins secreted by the uterine musculature has been implicated in the pain associated with the disorder. Premenstrual dysphoric disorder and PMS also occur in women past menopause and after hysterectomy, as long as the ovaries remain intact. Seventy to 90 percent of all women of childbearing age report at least some symptoms.

Menopausal Distress. Menopause is a natural physiological event, which is considered to have occurred after a 1-year absence of menstrual periods. The menses usually taper off during a 2- to 5-year span, most often between the ages of 48 and 55; the median age is 51.4 years. Menopause also occurs immediately after the surgical removal of the ovaries. The term *involutional period* refers to advancing age, and *climacteric* refers to involution of the ovaries.

Many psychological symptoms have been attributed to menopause, including anxiety, fatigue, tension, emotional lability, irritability, depression, dizziness, and insomnia. There is no general agreement on the relative contribution of physiological changes and of these accompanying complaints to the psychological and social meanings of menopause and to this developmental period in women's lives.

Physical signs and symptoms include night sweats, flushes and hot flashes, and sudden perceptions of heat within or on the body that may be accompanied by sweating and color change. The cause of hot flashes is unknown; they may be linked to pulsatile luteinizing hormone (LH) secretion. Estrogen-dependent functions are sequentially lost, and women may have atrophic changes in mucosal surfaces, accompanied by vaginitis, pruritus, dyspareunia, and stenosis. There are also changes in calcium and lipid metabolism, probably as secondary effects of the lowered levels of estrogen, and these changes may be associated with medical problems occurring after menopause such as osteoporosis and coronary arteriosclerosis. Physical changes may begin as much as 4 to 8 years before the last menstrual period. During this time, women may have irregular menstrual periods with variations in the menstrual intervals and the quantity of menstrual flow.

Blood levels of ovarian hormones decline gradually during the climacteric period, usually over a period of several years. For many years, decreasing estrogen levels were thought to be of primary importance in relation to the clinical manifestations of menopause. Both estrogen and progesterone bind directly to brain tissue and were believed to act directly on brain function. Recently, however, other hormones, such as androgens and LH, are also considered to be involved, and the effects of estrogen on mood may be indirectly moderated through its influence on androgen production. In any case, the significance of hormonal changes is evidenced by the severe physical and psychological symptoms that follow abrupt (surgical) depletion of ovarian hormones. In studies that have attempted to assess the relations of changing hormonal levels in normal women, one problem is the difficulty in establishing the date of the last menstrual period and of menopause. These events merely mark a point on a curve of changing hormonal function, and the presence or absence of menstrual bleeding is not an exact measure of hormonal status.

The severity of the symptoms at menopause seems to be related to the rate of hormone withdrawal; the amount of hormone depletion; women's constitutional ability to withstand the overall aging process, including their overall health and level of activity; and the psychological meanings of aging to women.

Clinically significant psychiatric difficulties may develop during the life cycle's involutional phase. Women who have previously experienced psychological difficulties, such as low self-esteem and low life satisfaction, are likely to be vulnerable to difficulties during menopause. Women's responses to menopause have been noted to parallel their responses to other crucial developmental events in their lives, such as puberty and pregnancy. Attempts to link the severity of menopausal distress with premenstrual tension syndrome have been inconclusive.

Women who have invested heavily in childbearing and child-rearing activities are most likely to suffer distress during postmenopausal years. Concerns about aging, loss of childbearing capacity, and changes in appearance may all be focused on the social and symbolic significance attached to the physical changes of menopause.

Although in the past it was assumed that the incidence of mental disorders and depression increased during menopause, epidemiological evidence casts some doubt on that assumption as an all-inclusive, complete explanation. Epidemiological studies of mental disorders showed no increase in symptoms of mental disorders or depression during menopausal years, and studies of psychological complaints revealed no greater frequency in menopausal women than in younger women.

Treatment programs must be individualized. Postclimacteric women may be asymptomatic for estrogen deprivation or may manifest estrogen excess (dysfunctional uterine bleeding).

The use of estrogen replacement treatment is still controversial. For women with signs of estrogen depletion, recent studies have been encouraging about long-term combined estrogen and progesterone (Premarin) replacement therapy, both in estrogen depletion syndrome and in prevention of osteoporosis. Topical estrogen cream used to treat mucosal atrophy is readily absorbed systemically. The increased risk of cancer, particularly endometrial cancer, has been implicated in the use of exogenous estrogen, but the addition of a progestational agent to the replacement estrogen regimen is thought to reduce the increased risk. Estrogen therapy has recently been reported to lower the risk of having Alzheimer's disease by 50 percent. It is reported to reduce mortality risk by 37 percent, mostly because of a reduction in heart disease.

Exercise, diet, and symptomatic treatment are all helpful in treating physical discomfort. Psychological distress should be evaluated and treated primarily by appropriate psychotherapeutic and sociotherapeutic measures. Psychotherapy should include an exploration of the life stages and the meanings of aging and reproduction to patients. Therapists should encourage patients to accept the menopause as a natural life event and to develop new activities, interests, and gratifications. Psychotherapy should also attend to family dynamics and should enlist family and other social support systems when necessary.

Idiopathic Amenorrhea. The cessation of normal menstrual cycles in nonpregnant, premenopausal women with no demonstrable structural abnormalities in the brain, the pituitary, or the ovaries is termed idiopathic amenorrhea.

The diagnosis is made first by exclusion and then, if possible, by identifying the primary psychogenic cause. Amenorrhea may occur as one feature of complex clinical psychiatric syndromes, such as anorexia nervosa and pseudocyesis. Other conditions associated with amenorrhea include massive obesity, diseases of the pituitary and the hypothalamus, and, in some cases, excessive amounts of running or jogging. Drugs such as reserpine (Serpasil) and chlorpromazine (Thorazine) can block ovulation and so delay the menses. Drug-induced amenorrhea is almost always accompanied by galactorrhea and elevated levels of prolactin.

The patterns of hormone defect that result in psychogenic amenorrhea are not well understood. Disturbed menstrual function with delayed or precipitate menses is a well-known stress response in healthy women. The stress can be as minor as going away to college or as catastrophic as being imprisoned in a concentration camp.

In most women the menstrual cycling returns without medical intervention, sometimes even in continuing stressful conditions. Psychotherapy should be undertaken for psychological reasons, not just to determine the cause of the symptom of amenorrhea. If the amenorrhea has been protracted and refractory, however, psychotherapy may be helpful in restoring regular menses.

Infertility

Fertility is strongly affected by psychic factors such as the frequency, duration, and timing of sexual intercourse; phobic avoidance of intercourse, and painful intercourse. A relaxed attitude about procreation can facilitate fertilization.

CHRONIC PAIN

Persistent pain is patients' most frequent complaint, yet because of differing causes and individual responses to pain, it is one of the most difficult symptoms to treat.

Pain is affected by a myriad of subjective, unmeasurable factors, including level of attention, emotional state, personality, and past experiences. Pain may simultaneously serve as a symptom of psychological stress and as a defense against it. Psychological factors may cause people to become somatically preoccupied and to magnify even normal sensations to chronic pain. People may also be excessively responsive to pain for personal, social, or financial secondary gain. Chronic pain may be a way to justify failure in establishing relationships with others. Cultural, ethnic, or religious affiliations may influence the degree and manner in which people express pain and the ways in which their families react to the symptoms. Therefore, in evaluating and treating persistent pain, physicians should realize that pain is not a simple stimulus–response phenomenon. Rather, reactions to pain are multifactorial and combine many biopsychosocial variables.

Pain Threshold and Perception

Peripheral sensations are transmitted through the pain pathways (for example, lateral spinothalamic tract, posterior thalamus of the diencephalon) to cortical somatosensory regions of the central nervous system (CNS) for conscious perception. The parietal cortex both localizes pain and perceives intensity, but psychogenic pain may be entirely of central nervous system origin. Complex reactions to pain involve areas of the cortex responsible for memory and for conscious and unconscious elements of people's personalities.

Most people have the same threshold for pain, but biofeedback, positive emotional states, relaxation exercises, physical therapy or other physical activity, medication, guided imagery, suggestion, hypnosis, placebos, and analgesics may increase the threshold by about 40 percent. The beneficial response to placebos is sometimes falsely thought to differentiate organic from functional causes. In fact, about one third of normal people whose pain is organically caused have at least a transient positive response to a placebo.

Variations in the effectiveness and responsiveness of people's endorphin or other neurotransmitter systems may modulate pain perception and tolerance. A proposed gate-control theory suggests that large peripheral afferent nerve fibers modulate sensory input by inhibiting hypothetical sensory transmitting neurons (gateway cells) in the substantia gelatinosa of the spinal cord. Relief of pain by transcutaneous or dorsal column electrical stimulators may result from this system's activation.

Classification

DSM-IV classifies pain disorder under somatoform disorders. If patients have multiple recurrent pains of at least several years' duration and beginning before age 30, they are considered to have a somatization disorder. When patients' pain suggests a physical illness but may be attributed to psychological factors alone, the diagnosis is conversion disorder or pain disorder (when pain is the only symptom). Patients with somatization disorder, major depressive disorder, or schizophrenia complain of various aches and pains, but pain is not the major complaint. In conversion disorder the distribution and the referral of pain are inconsistent.

Treatment

Psychotherapy with pain patients is summarized in Table 28.2–3.

Table 28.2–3
Psychotherapy with Pain Patients

Explain the nature of the pain signal.

Explain realistic expectations about the degree and the course of the pain.

Explain realistic expectations of analgesic, and, as much as possible, reframe side effects positively.

Maximize placebo effect by making the initial doses large rather than small, by supporting belief in efficacy, and by using suggestion through the attitude of the physician and the staff administering the analgesic.

Relieve concomitant anxiety, if necessary.

Chronic pain requires special arrangements:
- Eliminate doubts about the availability of medication.
- Do not make medication availability contingent on proof of need, leading to subjective struggles.
- Focus therapeutic encounters on healthy material; do not reinforce obsession with pain.
- Do not make contact with the care system contingent on pain; remove that contingency.

Courtesy of Barry Blackwell, M.D.

Clinicians often undermedicate patients with pain disorder because they lack knowledge about the pharmacology of analgesics, unrealistically fear causing addiction (even in patients who are terminal), and make the ethical judgment that only bad physicians prescribe large dosages of narcotics. Clinicians must separate patients with chronic benign pain (who tend to profit from psychotherapy and psychotropic drugs) from those with chronic pain caused by cancer or other chronic medical disorders. Patients with chronic benign pain often respond to the combination of an antidepressant and a phenothiazine. Those with chronic pain caused by medical disorders usually react favorably to analgesics or nerve blocks. Many patients with cancer may remain relatively active, alert, and comfortable with the judicious use of large amounts of morphine and other opioids; they thereby avoid costly and partially effective surgical procedures such as peripheral nerve section, cordotomy, and stereotaxic thalamic ablations. Addiction in these patients is rare, and the medical establishment is increasingly prescribing larger doses of opioids.

A program of behavior modification and deconditioning may also be useful. Analgesics should be prescribed at regular intervals rather than only as needed. Otherwise, patients must suffer before receiving relief, an experience that only increases their anxiety and sensitivity to pain. Standing orders can dissociate experiencing pain from receiving medication. The deconditioning of needed care from experiencing increased pain should also extend to patients' interpersonal relationships. Patients should receive as much or more attention for displaying active and healthy behavior as they receive for passive, dependent, pain-related behaviors. Spouses, bosses, friends, physicians, and health care or social agencies should not reinforce chronic pain and penalize patients (for instance, with threats to discontinue disability payments) when patients begin to relinquish the sick role. Patients should be assured of regular and supportive appointments that are not contingent on pain. Hospitalization should be avoided, if possible, to prevent further regression.

Pain clinics with a multispecialty staff evaluate and treat patients with complex pain disorders. Psychiatrists are involved early, not after the organic causes of pain have been ruled out and patients and physicians are frustrated. Patients are treated without addictive drugs, although many patients commence treatment already addicted. Exploratory or neurodestructive surgery is not encouraged, especially for patients with hysterical personality or a history of multiple surgical procedures. The pain clinic staffs also recognize that most patients with chronic pain experience a vicious cycle of biological and psychosocial factors, so that the most effective treatment involves a systems approach addressing each biopsychosocial component relevant to patients.

IMMUNE DISORDERS

Considerable evidence points to a relationship among psychosocial factors, immune function, and health and illness. Psychosocial processes—including the range of people's life experiences, stresses, and traits—seem to influence the CNS and thereby encourage the suppression of immune activity. In 1968, George Solomon suggested that emotional stress affects the immune system, especially through a decrease in T lymphocytes; he named the new field psychoimmunology. S. E. Keller later found a decrease in lymphocytes in rats that were helpless to escape or to stop electric shocks. In 1975, Robert Ader found a conditioned suppression of the immune response in rats and renamed the field psychoneuroimmunology.

Transposing the stress research to humans, other investigators found a decrease in lymphocytic response in bereavement (both conjugal and anticipatory), in the caretakers of patients with dementia of the Alzheimer's type, in nonpsychotic inpatients, in resident physicians, in medical and graduate students during final examinations, in women who were separated or divorced, in older people with a lack of social support, and in people who were unemployed. A decrease in lymphatic activity parallels a decrease in immunity and an increased incidence of infections and malignancy, probably correlated with increased psychic stress. Table 28.2–4 gives a summary of psychoneuroimmunological factors in health and disease.

Most studies have shown the negative effects of psychic stress on psychoimmunity and lymphatic activity and related diseases. A study by David Phillips and Daniel Smith indicates that positive psychological events may have beneficial effects on certain people in certain areas. The investigators found that important symbolic events have a positive significant short-time effect on mortality and potentially on health in general. Symbolic events that they studied—such as Passover for Jewish men and the Chinese harvest moon festival for Chinese women—often prolong the lives of patients dying from malignant neoplasms and cerebrovascular diseases. This effect points to an additional parameter, not previously considered, that should be evaluated in the psychosomatic equation.

Recent investigations have revealed that the interaction between neuroendocrines and the CNS is reciprocal, that is, immune responses affect the CNS and vice versa. For example, a monokine released by macrophages and monocytes, interleukin-1 (IL-1), activates the hypothalamus-pituitary-adrenal axis at the hypothalamus and pituitary level and stimulates the release of the potent adrenocorticotropic hormone (ACTH). Lymphocytes also synthesize peptides, such as ACTH and endorphins, which have numerous behavioral effects. Regulation of the immune system can be learned and conditioned, a fact that further indicates the potential effect of the immune system in the brain.

Infectious Diseases

Research indicates that the primary immune response is cell-mediated. Clinical studies have indicated that psychological variables influence the rate of recovery from infectious mononucleosis and influenza, and the susceptibility to rhinovirus-induced common cold symptoms and tularemia. Recurrent herpes simplex and genital herpes lesions occur most frequently in patients who have a clinical depression or who experience unusual stress. Stressful life events and a poor psychological state decrease resistance to tuberculosis and influence the course of the illness. Social supports play a role in recovery from tuberculosis. Life experiences that induce anger alter the intestine's bacterial composition. College students who respond to upsetting events (such as examination taking) with maladaptive aggression or affective changes have a high incidence of subsequent upper respiratory infections, as do women, of Alzheimer's disease. In AIDS, transmitted by HIV, psychiatric symptoms are common, and many think that the progress of the disease is influenced by psychological state.

Table 28.2–4
Summary of Psychoneuroimmunology Factors by Robert Ader

Nerve endings have been found in the tissues of the immune system. The central nervous system is linked both to the bone marrow and the thymus, where immune system cells are produced and developed, and to the spleen and the lymph nodes, where those cells are stored.

Changes in the central nervous system (the brain and the spinal cord) alter immune responses, and triggering an immune response alters central nervous system activity. Animal experiments dating back to the 1960s show that damage to different parts of the brain's hypothalamus can either suppress or enhance the allergic-type response. Recently, researchers have found that inducing an immune response causes nerve cells in the hypothalamus to become more active and that the brain cell anxiety peaks at precisely the same time that levels of antibodies are at their highest. Apparently, the brain monitors immunological changes closely.

Changes in hormones and neurotransmitter levels alter immune responses, and vice versa. The stress hormones generally suppress immune responses. But other hormones, such as growth hormone, also seem to affect immunity. Conversely, when experimental animals are immunized, they show changes in various hormone levels.

Lymphocytes are chemically responsive to hormones and neurotransmitters. Immune system cells have receptors—molecular structures on the surface of their cells—that are responsive to endorphins, stress hormones, and a wide range of other hormones.

Lymphocytes can produce hormones and neurotransmitters. When an animal is infected with a virus, lymphocytes produce minuscule amounts of many of the same substances produced by the pituitary gland.

Activated lymphocytes—cells actively involved in an immune response—produce substances that can be perceived by the central nervous system. The interleukins and interferons—chemicals that immune system cells use to talk to each other—can also trigger receptors on cells in the brain, more evidence that the immune system and the nervous system speak the same chemical language.

Psychosocial factors may alter the susceptibility to or the progression of autoimmune disease, infectious disease, and cancer. Evidence for those connections comes from many researchers.

Immunological reactivity may be influenced by stress. Chronic or intense stress, in particular, generally makes immune system cells less responsive to a challenge.

Immunological reactivity can be influenced by hypnosis. In a typical study, both of a subject's arms are exposed to a chemical that normally causes an allergic reaction. But the subject is told, under hypnosis, that only one arm will show the response—and that, in fact, is often what happens.

Immunological reactivity can be modified by classical conditioning. As Ader's own key experiments showed, the immune system can learn to react in certain ways as a conditioned response.

Psychoactive drugs and substances of abuse influence immune function. A range of substances that affect the nervous system—including alcohol, marijuana, cocaine, heroin, and nicotine—have all been shown to affect the immune response, generally suppressing it. Some psychiatric drugs, such as lithium (prescribed for bipolar I disorder), also modulate the immune system.

Adapted from Goleman D, Guerin J: *Mind Body Medicine.* Consumer Reports, Yonkers, NY, 1993.

Allergic Disorders

Considerable clinical evidence indicates that psychological factors are related to the precipitation of many allergic disorders. Bronchial asthma is a prime example of a pathological process involving immediate hypersensitivity associated with psychosocial processes. Emotional reactions to life experience, personality patterns, and conditioning have been reported to contribute to the onset and course of asthma.

Organ Transplantation

Psychosocial factors appear to play a role in organ transplantation. Several clinical studies have shown that stressful life events, anxiety, and depression precede some cases of graft rejection. Psychosocial effects on the immune system may contribute to the mechanisms involved in such rejections.

Autoimmune Diseases

A prime function of the immune system is to distinguish between self and nonself and to reject foreign antigens (nonself). Occasionally, for reasons that are presently unclear, a cell-mediated or humoral immune response develops against a person's own cells. This reaction produces a variety of pathological effects known clinically as autoimmune diseases. Disorders in which an autoimmune component has been implicated include Graves' disease, Hashimoto's disease, rheumatoid arthritis, ulcerative colitis, regional ileitis, systemic lupus erythematosus, psoriasis, myasthenia gravis, pernicious anemia, and multiple sclerosis.

Mental Disorders

Although several investigators have found evidence suggesting altered immunity and autoimmunity in patients with schizophrenia, the specific findings have been difficult to replicate. Whether the immune abnormalities are involved in the pathogenesis of some or all types of schizophrenia, or whether such abnormalities are related to a wide range of factors including long-term institutionalization and antipsychotic agents, remains to be determined.

Immune phenomena in mental disorders other than schizophrenia have been less extensively studied. Research indicates that psychiatric patients show increased immunoglobulin M (IgM) and immunoglobulin A (IgA) levels, and these findings indicate the need for further study. The notion that patients with depressive disorders have an increased incidence of autoimmune antibodies has sparked some controversy. Marvin Stein concluded that the effect of depression on the modulation of immunity is complex and may involve a range of neurobiological mechanisms.

Table 28.2–5
Areas of Assessment in Cancer Patients

Psychiatric
- Past history
- Current mental state
- Understanding of the illness
- Meaning of the illness

Medical
- Cancer
- Cancer treatment
- Associated medical conditions and treatments

Environmental
- Interface with the family
- Interface with the medical team
- Other social supports
- Financial issues

Courtesy of Marguerite S. Lederberg, M.D., and Jimmie C. Holland, M.D.

Table 28.2–6
Medical Conditions Associated with Delirium in Cancer Patients

Metabolic encephalopathy
Vital organ failure
Electrolyte imbalance (such as hypercalcemia in patients with bony metastases or those receiving tamoxifen, diethylstilbestrol, or chlorotrianisene)
Hypoxia, especially in patients with pulmonary involvement or severe anemia
Nutritional deficiencies, such as thiamine, folic acid, and B_{12}
Infections, especially in immunosuppressed hosts
Vascular disorders, especially in patients with coagulopathies
Endocrine and hormonal abnormalities

Courtesy of Marguerite S. Lederberg, M.D., and Jimmie C. Holland, M.D.

Psychosocial and Psychotherapeutic Implications.

Various research groups have reported positive effects on immunological functioning from biofeedback, relaxation therapy, aerobic exercise training, and group therapy support.

CANCER

Because new treatment protocols have in many cases transformed cancer from an incurable to a frequently chronic and often curable disease, the psychiatric aspects of cancer—the reactions to both the diagnosis and the treatment—are increasingly important. At least half of the 1 million people who contracted cancer in the United States in 1987 were alive 5 years later. Currently, an estimated 3 million cancer survivors have no evidence of the disease.

Patient Problems

When people learn that they have cancer, their psychological reactions include fear of death, disfigurement, and disability; fear of abandonment and loss of independence; fear of disruption in relationships, role functioning, and financial standing; and denial, anxiety, anger, and guilt.

Table 28.2–7
Causes of Mood Disorders Common in Cancer Patients

Drugs
Chemotherapeutic agents such as prednisone, dexamethasone, procarbazine, vincristine, vinblastine, L-asparaginase, tamoxifen, interferon
Additive effect of narcotics and many other drugs known to cause depression, such as antihypertensives, benzodiazepines, antiparkinson agents, and β-blockers
Tumor effects
Hormone-secreting tumors
Central nervous system tumors
Associated medical conditions
Uremia
Viral encephalopathies
Electrolyte imbalances

Courtesy of Marguerite S. Lederberg, M.D., and Jimmie C. Holland, M.D.

Table 28.2–8
Suicide Vulnerability Factors in Cancer Patients

Depression and hopelessness
Poorly controlled pain
Mild delirium (disinhibition)
Feeling of loss of control
Exhaustion
Anxiety
Preexisting psychopathology (substance abuse, character pathology, major psychiatric disorder)
Family problems
Threats and history of prior attempts of suicide
Positive family history of suicide
Other usually described risk factors in psychiatric patients

Adapted from Breitbart W: Suicide in cancer patients. Oncology *1*: 49, 1987.

About half of all cancer patients have mental disorders. The largest group have adjustment disorder (68 percent), with major depressive disorder (13 percent) and delirium (8 percent) being the next most common diagnoses. Most of these disorders are thought to be reactive to the knowledge of having cancer. The psychiatric, medical, and environmental factors that should be explored in people with cancer are listed in Table 28.2–5. Some of the most common causes of delirium are listed in Table 28.2–6, and some of the medical conditions associated with mood disorders in cancer patients are listed in Table 28.2–7. David Spiegel, M.D., reported on the value of group therapy in patients with breast cancer, who lived 18 months longer than cancer patients who did not receive group therapy.

Suicide. Although suicidal thoughts and wishes are frequent in people with cancer, the actual incidence of suicide is only 1.4 to 1.9 times that of the general population. Factors that signal a vulnerability to suicide in people with cancer are listed in Table 28.2–8.

Table 28.2–9
Emetogenic Potential of Some Commonly Used Anticancer Agents

Highly emetogenic	Cisplatin Dacarbazine Streptozocin Actinomycin Nitrogen mustard
Moderately emetogenic	Doxorubicin Daunorubicin Cyclosphosphamide Nitrosoureas Mitomycin-C Procarbazine
Minimally emetogenic	Vincristine Vinblastine 5-Fluorouracil Bleomycin

Courtesy of Marguerite S. Lederberg, M.D., and Jimmie C. Holland, M.D.

Table 28.2–10
Current Chemotherapy Antiemetic Regimens

Neurotransmitter blocking agent	Metoclopramide[a] 3 mg/kg intravenous piggyback (IVPB) 30 min before therapy, and 1½ hours after therapy or Ondansetron 0.15 mg/kg IVPB 30 min before therapy and 1½ and 3 hours after therapy
plus	
Steroid	Dexamethasone[a] 20 mg IVPB 20 min before therapy
plus	
Benzodiazepine	Lorazepam 1.5 mg/m^2 (max 3 mg) IVPB before therapy
or	or
Antihistamine	Diphenhydramine[a] 50 mg—oral, IV, or IM—every 4 hours as needed for restlessness or acute dystonic reaction

Courtesy of Marguerite S. Lederberg, M.D., and Jimmie C. Holland, M.D.
[a] Should also be used in oral form for delayed nausea and vomiting, starting 24 hours after cisplatin therapy.

Treatment-Related Factors

The most common medical treatments of cancer are radiation and drugs (chemotherapy). Drugs are toxic when given in tumoricidal dosages, and patients undergoing long courses of treatment may become much sicker symptomatically from the treatment than from their disease.

Radiation Therapy. The side effects of radiation therapy include encephalopathy associated with increased intracranial pressure (nausea, vomiting, dizziness), headache, somnolence, personality changes, cognitive disturbances, and reactive psychic symptoms of fear and depression.

Table 28.2–11
Neurological Complications of Chemotherapy

- Encepholopathy
  - Methotrexate with radiotherapy
  - Hexamethylmelamine
  - 5-Fluorouracil
  - Procarbazine
  - Carmustine (BCNU) (intracarotid)
  - Cisplatin (intracarotid)
  - Cyclophosphamide
  - 5-Azacytidine
  - Spirogermanium
  - Misonidazole
  - Cytarabine (high dose)
  - L-Asparaginase
- Acute cerebellar syndrome, ataxia
  - 5-Fluorouracil
  - Cytarabine
  - Procarbazine
  - Hexamethylmelamine
- Myelopathy
  - Intrathecal methotrexate
  - Intrathecal cytarabine
  - Intrathecal thiotepa
- Neuropathy
  - Vinca alkaloids[a]
  - Cisplatin[a]
  - Procarbazine
  - 5-Azacytidine
  - Vasopressin 16
  - VM-26
  - Misonidazole
  - Methyl-G
  - Cytarabine
- Ototoxicity
  - Cisplatin
  - Misonidazole

Adapted from Patchell RA, Posner JB: Neurologic complications of systemic cancer. In *Symposium on Neuro-oncology Neurologic Clinics,* NA Vick, DD Bigner, editors, vol 3, p 729. Saunders, Philadelphia, 1985.
[a] Also involve cranial nerves.

Table 28.2–12
Chemotherapy Agents with Mood and Psychotic Symptoms

Dacarbazine: depression and suicide reported, especially when used with hexamethylamine

Vinblastine: frequent reversible depression

Vincristine: 5 percent incidence of hallucinations; depression noted

L-Asparaginase: reversible depression noted

Procarbazine: MAOI; concurrent tricyclics are contraindicated; associated with mania and depression; potentiates alcohol, barbiturates, phenothiazines

Hydroxyurea: hallucinations reported

Interferon: anxiety, depression with suicidal ideation common at doses above 40 million units

Steroids: frequent alterations of mental state ranging from emotional lability through mania or severe, suicidal depression to frank psychosis

Courtesy of Marguerite S. Lederberg, M.D., and Jimmie C. Holland, M.D.

Chemotherapy. The most common side effects of chemotherapy are nausea and vomiting. In Table 28.2–9 the emetogenic problems with various chemotherapeutic agents are summarized. Table 28.2–10 shows antiemetic treatments for these complications; the neurological complications of che-

Table 28.2–13
Pain Syndromes in Patients with Cancer

- Pain syndromes associated with direct tumor involvement
  - Tumor infiltration of the bone
    - Metastases to the cranial vault
      - Metastases to the base of the skull
        - Jugular foramen syndrome
        - Clivus metastases
        - Sphenoid sinus metastases
    - Vertebral body syndromes
      - Fracture of the odontoid vertebra
      - C7-T1 metastases
      - L1 metastases
      - Sacral syndrome
  - Tumor infiltration of nerve
    - Peripheral nerve
      - Peripheral neuropathy
      - Intercostal neuropathy
    - Plexus
      - Brachial plexopathy
      - Lumbosacral plexopathy
      - Celiac plexopathy
    - Root
      - Radiculopathy
      - Leptomeningeal metastases
    - Spinal cord
      - Epidural spinal cord compression
      - Intramedullary mestastases
    - Brain
      - Intracranial metastases
  - Tumor infiltration of viscera
    - Infiltration of the pleura
    - Small and large bowel obstruction
    - Infiltration of the pelvis and the bladder wall

Courtesy of Marguerite S. Lederberg, M.D., and Jimmie C. Holland, M.D.

motherapy are listed in Table 28.2–11, and mood and psychotic symptoms in Table 28.2–12.

Pain. Pain in patients with cancer should not be underestimated or undermedicated (Tables 28.2–13 through 28.2–16). Because cancer patients with pain have a significantly higher incidence of depression and anxiety than those without pain, proper and adequate treatment is essential for their psychological well-being. Cancer patients with acute pain respond well to treatment with antipain medications such as opiates and opioids; but their tolerance levels rise, and they require additional medication when the pain lasts more than a few days. This need is often inappropriately viewed as addiction; studies have shown that cancer patients easily and voluntarily wean themselves when pain eases. Cancer patients with acute pain require sympathetic and supportive treatment from medical personnel, as do those with chronic pain whose addictive problems are common, and who nevertheless may require additional medication. As tolerance levels inevitably rise, patients require increased dosages of narcotics, and there may be no dosage ceiling. In patients with cancer, however, tolerance to opiates and opioids does not imply addiction. Adjuvants to opiate and opioid medications, which potentiate their effects, are antidepressants, anticonvulsants, phenothiazines, and butyrophenones. Physicians should be cautious about drug–drug interactions such as meperidine (Demerol) and monoamine oxidase inhibitors (MAOIs), which can be fatal.

Table 28.2–14
Nonopioid and Adjuvant Analgesic Drugs in the Management of Cancer Pain

Class or Drug	Indications	Starting Oral Dose (mg range, 24/hr)	Comments
Nonsteroidal anti-inflammatory drugs			
Aspirin	Soft tissue and metastatic bone	650 650–1,000	Used in combination with opioids, GI and hematological effects; avoid combination with steroids
Acetaminophen	Like aspirin	650 650–1,000	Fewer GI effects, no effects on platelet function, no significant anti-inflammatory effects
Ibuprofen		400 200–800	Higher analgesic potential than aspirin, fewer GI and hematological effects than aspirin
Choline magnesium trisalicylate	Like aspirin	1,500 1,000–4,000	Anti-inflammatory and analgesic effects; similar to aspirin without hematological effects
Fenoprofen	Like aspirin	200 200–400	Higher analgesic potential than aspirin, fewer GI and hematological effects than aspirin
Diflunisal	Like aspirin	500 500–1,000	Longer duration of action than ibuprofen, higher analgesic potential than aspirin
Naproxen	Like aspirin	250 250–500	Longer duration of action than ibuprofen, higher analgesic potential than aspirin
Anticonvulsants			
Phenytoin	Neuropathic pain, acute lancinating type (tic)	100 200–800	Useful in paroxysmal nerve pain
Antidepressants			
Amitriptyline Imipramine	Neuropathic pain, eg, postherpetic neuralgia	10 10–150	Start at low dose and titrate slowly; has analgesic properties
Antihistamines			
Hydroxyzine	Somatic and visceral pain	25 25–100	Additive analgesia in combination with opioids, antiemetic, antianxiety properties
Phenothiazines			
Methotrimeprazine	Somatic and visceral pain; useful in opioid-tolerant patients with GI obstruction and pain	5–16 IM	Has anxiolytic and antiemetic effects; available only in IM preparation
Steroids			
Prednisone	Somatic and neuropathic pain, eg, inflammatory bone pain	5 5–60	Anti-inflammatory, antiemetic, analgesic effects
Dexamethasone	Reflex sympathetic dystrophy; brachial, lumbar plexopathy	0.5–16	
Neurostimulants			
Dextroamphetamine	Somatic and visceral pain, eg, postoperative pain	2.5 2.5–10	Additive analgesia in combination with opioids; reduces sedative effects
Methylphenidate	Opioid-induced sedation	5 5–15	Additive analgesia in combination with opioids; reduces sedative effects
Caffeine		300 300–600	Additive analgesia in combination with opioids; reduces sedative effects

Adapted from Foley K: Management of cancer pain. In *Cancer: Principles and Practice of Oncology,* ed 4, VT DeVita, S Hellman, SA Rosenberg, editors, p 2430. Lippincott, Philadelphia, 1993.

Table 28.2–15
Opioid Analgesics for Management of Cancer Pain

Drug and Equianalgesic Dose Relative Potency	Dose (mg IM or oral)	Plasma Half-life (hr)	Starting Oral Dose[a] (mg)	Available Commercial Preparations
Opioid agonists				
Morphine	10 IM 60 oral	3–4	30–60	Oral: tablet, liquid, slow-release tablet Rectal: 5–30 mg Injectable: SC, IM, IV, epidural, intrathecal
Hydromorphone	1.5 IM 7.5 oral	2–3	2–48	Oral: tablets: 1, 2, 4 mg Injectable: SC, IM, IV 2 mg/mL, 3 mg/mL, and 10 mg/mL
Methadone	10 IM 20 oral	12–24	5–10	Oral: tablets, liquid Injectable: SC, IM, IV
Levorphanol	2 IM 4 oral	12–16	2–4	Oral: tablets Injectable: SC, IM, IV
Oxymorphone	1	2–3	NA	Rectal: 10 mg Injectable: SC, IM, IV
Heroin	5 IM 60 oral	3–4	NA	NA
Meperidine	75 IM 300 oral	3–4 (normeperidine 12–16)	75	Oral: tablets Injectable: SC, IM, IV
Codeine	130 oral 200 oral	3–4	60	Oral: tablets and combination with acetylsalicylic acid, acetaminophen, liquid
Oxycodone	15 oral 30 oral	—	5	Oral: tablets, liquid, oral formulation in combination with acetaminophen (tablet and liquid) and aspirin (tablet)

The times of peak analgesia in nontolerant patients ranges form ½ hour to 1 hour, and the duration from 4 to 6 hours. The peak analgesic effect is delayed, and the duration is prolonged after oral administrations.

Adapted from Foley K: Management of cancer pain. In *Cancer: Principles and Practice of Oncology,* ed 4, VT DeVita, S Hellman, SA Rosenberg, editors, p 22. Lippincott, Philadelphia, 1993.

[a] Recommended starting IM doses; the optimal dose for each patient is determined by titration, and the maximal dose is limited by adverse effects.

Palliative Care. For the medical staff, palliation should be an active and involved process, with no hint of withdrawal or abandonment. Psychotherapy is useful in pain management (Table 28.2–17).

Ethical Issues. Included among the ethical issues of treating patients with cancer are questions of informed consent for both traditional and experimental treatments, and third-party consent (for example, insurance companies, which may not pay for such treatments in certain cases).

Staff Factors

The care of patients with cancer causes special stresses for caretakers. Table 28.2–18 presents a summary of these stresses.

Family Factors

Because cancer strikes not only the patient but also the family, caretakers in the family must provide care for the patient and also respond to the increased demands of other family members. Anxiety and depression in family members require active intervention. Family problems requiring treatment are preexisting intrafamily conflicts, family abandonment, and family exhaustion.

Cancer in Children

Fewer children than adults have cancer. Of about 7,000 new cases of cancer in children in the United States in 1986, more than 60 percent had leukemia, lymphoma, and CNS tumors, and they received a combination of chemotherapy and radiation therapy. Five-year survival rates for children with fibrosarcomas, retinoblastomas, Hodgkin's disease, and gonadal and germ cell tumors have passed the 80 percent mark, and the survival rate for most other childhood cancers is between 40 and 60 percent.

SKIN DISORDERS

Psychosomatic skin disorders include a great variety of abnormal skin sensations. Emotional factors are important in every aspect of skin disorders: manifestations, aggravations, responses, causes, and prognoses.

Generalized Pruritus

The same afferent fibers convey itch, tickle, and pain, which are differentiated only by the frequency of electrical impulses.

Table 28.2–16
Guidelines for the Rational Use of Analgesics in the Management of Cancer Pain

Start with a specific drug for a specific type of pain
Know the phamacology of the drug prescribed
- Know the relative potency of the drug
- Know the duration of the analgesic effect
- Know the pharmacokinetics of the drug
- Know the equianalgesic doses for the drug and its route of administration

Administer analgesic on a regular basis
Gear the route of administration to the patient's needs

Oral	Sublingual
Buccal	Transmucosal
Rectal	Transdermal
Subcutaneous	Intravenous
Intrathecal	Intraventricular

Use a combination of drugs to provide additive analgesia
- Narcotic plus nonnarcotic (aspirin, acetaminophen, nonsteroidal anti-inflammatory drug)
- Narcotic plus adjuvants

Anticipate and treat side effects
- Sedation
- Respiratory depression
- Nausea and vomiting
- Constipation
- Multifocal myoclonus and seizures

Treat the drug-tolerant patient
- Use combinations of nonopioid and opioid drugs
- Use combinations of drug therapy and anesthetic and neurosurgical procedures
- Switch to an alternative opioid analgesic, starting with one half the equianalgesic dose
- Use epidural local anesthetics
- Reassess the nature of the pain

Prevent and treat acute withdrawal
- Taper drugs slowly

Anticipate complications
- Overdose
- Physiological dependence

Adapted from Foley K: Management of cancer pain. In *Cancer: Principles and Practice of Oncology,* ed 4, VT DeVita, S Hellman, SA Rosenberg, editors, p 2428. Lippincott, Philadelphia, 1993.

The itching dermatoses include scabies, pediculosis, bites of insects, urticaria, atopic dermatitis, contact dermatitis, lichen ruber planus, and miliaria. Internal disorders that frequently cause itching are diabetes mellitus, nephritis, diseases of the liver, gout, diseases of the thyroid gland, food allergies, Hodgkin's disease, leukemia, and cancer. Itching can also occur during pregnancy and senility.

The term *generalized psychogenic pruritus* denotes that no organic cause for the itching exists or, at least, no longer exists and that, on psychiatric examination, emotional conflicts are seen to account for its occurrence. The emotions that most frequently lead to generalized psychogenic pruritus are repressed anger and repressed anxiety. When people consciously or unconsciously experience anger or anxiety, they scratch themselves, often violently. An inordinate need for affection is a common characteristic of patients. Frustrations of this need elicit aggressiveness that is inhibited. Rubbing the skin provides a substitute gratification of the frustrated need, and the scratching represents aggression turned against the self.

Localized Pruritus

Pruritus Ani. The investigation of pruritus ani commonly yields a history of local irritation (for example, threadworms, irritant discharge, fungal infection) or general systemic factors (for example, nutritional deficiencies, drug intoxication). After running a conventional course, however, pruritus ani often fails to respond to therapeutic measures and acquires a life of its own, apparently perpetuated by scratching and superimposed inflammation. It is a distressing complaint that often interferes with work and social activity. Investigation of large numbers of patients with the disorder has revealed that personality deviations often precede the condition and that emotional disturbances often precipitate and maintain it.

Pruritus Vulvae. As in pruritus ani, specific physical causes, either localized or generalized, may be demonstrable in pruritus vulvae, and the presence of glaring psychopathology in no way lessens the need for adequate medical investigation. In some patients, pleasure derived from rubbing and scratching is conscious—they realize that it is a symbolic form of masturbation—but more often than not the pleasure element is repressed. Most patients studied gave a long history of sexual frustration, which was frequently intensified at the time of the onset of the pruritus.

Hyperhidrosis

States of fear, rage, and tension can induce increased sweat secretion. Perspiration in humans has two distinct forms: thermal and emotional. Emotional sweating appears primarily on

Table 28.2–17
Cognitive-Behavior Therapy Techniques for Cancer Patients

Cognitive therapy
- Preparatory information
- Cognitive restructuring
- Focusing
  - Controlled mental imagery
- Distraction
  - Controlled attention
  - Mental, behavioral
  - Music therapy
  - Hypnosis
  - Biofeedback

Behavior therapy
- Self-monitoring
- Systematic desensitization
- Graded task management
- Contigency management
- Modeling
- Behavioral rehearsal
- Relaxation
  - Passive, progressive
- Meditation
- Music therapy
- Hypnosis
- Biofeedback

Reprinted with permission from Breitbart W: Psychiatric management of cancer pain. Cancer *63*: 2336, 1989.

Table 28.2–18
Staff Stresses Common to Special Care Settings

High morbidity, high mortality
Complex technology used under high pressure
High frequency of life-death decisions
Terminal care issues
Third-party conflicts
Interstaff conflicts
Response to severe debilitation and disfigurement
Response to difficult patients (excessive dependence, anger, uncooperativeness)
Response to suicidal ideation
Issue of inflicting pain as part of treatment

Courtesy of Marguerite S. Lederberg, M.D., and Jimmie C. Holland, M.D.

the palms, the soles, and the axillae; thermal sweating is most evident on the forehead, the neck, the trunk, and the dorsum of the hands and the forearms. The sensitivity of the emotional sweating response serves as the basis for the measurement of sweat by the galvanic skin response (an important tool of psychosomatic research), biofeedback, and the polygraph (lie detector test).

Under conditions of prolonged emotional stress, excessive sweating (hyperhidrosis) may lead to secondary skin changes, rashes, blisters, and infections; therefore, hyperhidrosis may underlie several other dermatological conditions that are not primarily related to emotions. Basically, hyperhidrosis may be viewed as an anxiety phenomenon mediated by the autonomic nervous system; it must be differentiated from drug-induced states of hyperhidrosis.

References

Ader R, Cohen N: Behaviorally conditioned immunosuppression. Psychosom Med *37:* 333, 1995.

Ader R, Cohen N, Felten D: Brain, behavior, and immunity. Brain Behav Immun *1:* 1, 1987.

Asthma, health behaviors, social adjustment, and psychosomatic symptoms in adolescence. J Asthma *33:* 157, 1996.

Berman WH, Berman ER, Heymsfield S, Fauci M, et al: The incidence and comorbidity of psychiatric disorders in obesity. J Pers Disord *6:* 168, 1992.

Borbjerg DH: Psychoneuroimmunology implications for oncology. Cancer *67:* 828, 1991.

Breitbart W: Psychiatric management of cancer pain. Cancer *63* (11, Suppl): 2336, 1989.

Byrne DG: Personality, life events and cardiovascular disease. J Psychosom Res *31:* 661, 1987.

Case RB, Heller SS, Case NB: Type A behavior and survival after acute myocardial infarction. N Engl J Med *311:* 737, 1984.

Cassileth BR, Lusk EJ, Miller DS, Brown LL, Miller R: Psychosocial correlates of survival in advanced malignant disease. N Engl J Med *312:* 1551, 1985.

Dimsdale JE, Young D, Moore L, Strauss HW: Do plasma norepinephrine levels reflect behavioral stress? Psychosom Med *49:* 375, 1987.

Drossman DA, Powell DW, Sessions JT Jr: The irritable bowel syndrome. Gastroenterology *73:* 811, 1977.

Engel GL: *Psychological Development in Health and Disease.* Saunders, Philadelphia, 1962.

Engel GL: Studies of ulcerative colitis: III. The nature of the psychological processes. Am J Med *19:* 231, 1955.

Fernandez E, Turk DC: The utility of cognitive coping strategies for altering pain perception: A meta-analysis. Pain *38:* 123, 1989.

Goldstein MG, Niaura R: Psychological factors affecting physical condition: Cardiovascular disease literature review. Psychosomatics *33:* 134, 1992.

Kiecolt-Glaser JK, Glaser R: Psychological influences on immunity: Making sense of the relationship between stressful life events and health. Adv Exp Med Biol *245:* 237, 1988.

Lederberg MS, Holland JC: Psycho-oncology. In *Comprehensive Textbook of Psychiatry,* ed 6, HI Kaplan, BJ Sadock, editors, p 1570. Williams & Wilkins, Baltimore, 1995.

Massie MJ, Holland JC: The cancer patient with pain: Psychiatric complications and their management. J Pain Symptom Manage *7:* 99, 1992.

Miller TW: Advances in understanding the impact of stressful life events on health. Hosp Community Psychiatry *39:* 615, 1988.

Niaura R, Goldstein MG: Psychological factors affecting physical condition: Cardiovascular disease literature review: II. Coronary artery disease and sudden death and hypertension. Psychosomatics *33:* 146, 1992.

Norton CS, Clouse RE, Spitznagel EL, Alpers DH: The relation of ulcerative colitis to psychiatric factors: A review of findings and methods. Am J Psychiatry *147:* 974, 1990.

Phillips DP, Smith DG: Postponement of death until symbolically meaningful occasions. JAMA *263:* 1947, 1990.

Price DD: *Psychological and Neural Mechanisms of Pain.* Raven, New York, 1988.

Shekelle RB, Gale M, Ostfeld AM, Paul O: Hostility, risk of coronary heart disease and mortality: Psychosom Med *45:* 109, 1983.

Solomon GF: Psychoneuroimmunology: Interactions between central nervous system and immune system. J Neurosci Res *18:* 1, 1987.

Stein M, Miller AH, Restman T: Depression and the immune system, and health and illness. Arch Gen Psychiatry *8:* 171, 1991.

▲ 28.3 Consultation-Liaison Psychiatry

In consultation-liaison (C-L) psychiatry, a rapidly growing area of expertise and an expanding field of concentration, psychiatrists serve as consultants to medical colleagues (either another psychiatrist or, more commonly, a nonpsychiatric physician) or to other mental health professionals (psychologist, social worker, or psychiatric nurse). In addition, C-L psychiatrists consult regarding patients in medical or surgical settings and provide follow-up psychiatric treatment as needed. C-L psychiatry is associated with all the diagnostic, therapeutic, research, and teaching services that psychiatrists perform in the general hospital and serves as a bridge between psychiatry and other specialties.

In the medical wards of the hospital, C-L psychiatrists must play many roles: skillful and brief interviewer, good psychiatrist and psychotherapist, teacher, and knowledgeable physician who understands the medical aspects of the case. The C-L psychiatrist must be viewed as a part of the medical team who makes a unique contribution to the patient's total medical treatment.

DIAGNOSIS

Knowledge of psychiatric diagnosis is essential to C-L psychiatrists. Both dementia and delirium frequently complicate organic medical illness, especially among hospital patients. Psychoses and other mental disorders often complicate the treatment of medical illness, and deviant illness behavior, such as suicide, is a common problem in patients who are organically ill. C-L psychiatrists must be aware of the many medical illnesses that can have psychiatric symptoms. (A list of such medical problems is presented in Table 28.3–1.) Interviews and serial clinical observations are the C-L psychiatrist's tools for diagnosis. The purposes of the diagnosis are to identify mental disorders and psychological responses to physical ill-

Table 28.3–1
Medical Conditions That Present with Psychiatric Symptoms

Disease	Common Medical Symptoms	Psychiatric Symptoms and Complaints	Impaired Performance and Behavior	Laboratory Tests and Findings	Diagnostic Problems
Hyperthyroidism (thyrotoxicosis)	Heat intolerance Excessive sweating Diarrhea Weight loss Tachycardia Palpitations Vomiting	Nervousness Excitability Irritability Pressured speech Insomnia May express fear of impending death Psychosis	Fine tremor Impaired cognition Decreased concentration Hyperactivity Intrusiveness	Free T_4 increased T_3 increased TSH decreased T_3 uptake decreased ECG: Tachycardia Atrial fibrillation P and T wave changes	Full range of symptoms may not be present Hyperthyroidism and anxiety states may coexist Rule out occult malignancy, cardiovascular disease, amphetamine intoxication, cocaine intoxication, anxiety states, mania
Hypothyroidism (myxedema)	Cold intolerance Dry skin Constipation Weight gain Brittle hair Goiter	Lethargy Depressed affect Personality change Maniclike psychosis Paranoia Hallucinations	Muscle weakness Decreased concentration Psychomotor slowing Apathy Unusual sensitivity to barbiturates	TSH increased TSH low if pituitary disease Free T_4 decreased ECG: Bradycardia	More common in women Associated with lithium carbonate therapy Rule our pituitary disease, hypothalamic disease, major depressive disorder, bipolar I disorder
Hypoglycemia	Sweating Drowsiness Stupor Coma Tachycardia	Anxiety Confusion Agitation	Tremor Restlessness Seizures	Hypoglycemia Tachycardia	Excess insulin often complicated by exercise, alcohol, decreased food intake Rule out insulinoma, postictal states, agitated depression, paranoid psychosis
Hyperglycemia	Polyuria Anorexia Nausea Vomiting Dehydration Abdominal complaints	Anxiety Agitation Delirium	Acetone breath Seizures	Hyperglycemia Serum ketones Urine ketones Anion gap acidosis	Almost always associated with brittle diabetes in young juvenile diabetics and elderly non-insulin-dependent diabetics Rule out depressive disorders, anxiety disorders
Brain neoplasms	Headache Vomiting Papilledema Focal findings on neurology examination	Personality changes		Lumbar puncture: increased CSF pressure, skull X-ray, CT scan, EEG	40–50% gliomas most common in 40–50-year age group Cerebellar tumors most common in children
Frontal lobe tumor		Mood changes Irritability Facetiousness Impaired judgment Impaired memory Delirium	Seizures Loss of speech Loss of smell	Angiogram: space-occupying lesion	Rule out intracranial abscess, aneurysm, subdural hematoma, seizure disorder, cerebrovascular disease, reactive depression, mania, schizophreniform disorder, dementia
Parietal lobe tumor	Hyperreflexia Babinski's sign Astereognosis		Sensory and motor abnormalities Contralateral hemiparesis Focal seizures		
Occipital lobe tumor	Headache Papilledema Homonymous hemianopsia	Aura Visual hallucinations	Visual problems Seizures		
Temporal lobe tumor	Contralateral homonymous field cut		Psychomotor seizures Aphasia		
Cerebellar tumor	Early evidence of increased intracranial pressure		Disturbed equilibrium Disturbed coordination		
Head trauma	History or evidence of head trauma Headache Dizziness Bleeding from ear Altered level of consciousness Loss of consciousness Focal neurological findings	Confusion Personality changes Memory impairment	Seizures Paralysis	Lumbar puncture, skull X-rays, CT scan show evidence of bleeding or increased intracranial pressure Cerebral angiogram EEG	History of blow to head or bleeding confirms cause of ALS Rule out cerebrovascular disease, seizure disorder, alcohol dependence, diabetes mellitus, hepatic encephalopathy, depression, dementia

(continued)

Table 28.3–1 ***(continued)***

Disease	Common Medical Symptoms	Psychiatric Symptoms and Complaints	Impaired Performance and Behavior	Laboratory Tests and Findings	Diagnostic Problems
AIDS	Fever Weight loss Ataxia Incontinence Focal findings on neurological examination	Progressive dementia Personality changes Depression Loss of libido Psychosis Mutism	Impaired memory Decreased concentration Seizures	HIV testing CT, MRI, lumbar puncture, CSF, and blood cultures	60% of patients have neuropsychiatric symptoms; always consider in high-risk populations and young patients with signs of dementia Rule out other infections, brain neoplasms, dementia, depression, schizophreniform disorder
Injuries requiring ambulatory surgical evaluation and treatment (for example, wrist slashing)	Alcohol abuse and other substance abuse Recent surgery Chronic pain Chronic illness Terminal illness	90% have major psychiatric disease History of prior suicide attempts Depressed mood Postpartum psychosis in women	Frequent accidents Repeated emergency room visits Eager to leave emergency room before full evaluation		Suicidal behavior is a symptom of underlying psychiatric illness Knowledge of risk factors is helpful but not a substitute for good clinical judgment Prediction is best done through assessment of current risk projected into the immediate future
Hyponatremia	Excessive thirst Polydipsia Stupor Coma	Confusion Lethargy Personality changes	Seizures Speech abnormalities	Decreased serum Na^+ Serum Na^+ and osmolalities to document syndrome of inappropriate secretion of antidiuretic hormone (SIADH)	Caused by excessive free water for level of total body Na^+ Often abnormal SIADH May be psychogenic Rule out nephrotic syndrome, liver disease, congestive heart failure, schizophreniform disorder, schizotypal personality disorder
Pancreatic carcinoma	Weight loss Abdominal pain	Depression Lethargy Anhedonia	Apathy Decreased energy	Elevated amylase	Always consider in depressed middle-aged patients Rule out other GI illness, major depressive disorder
Cushing's syndrome	Central obesity Purple striae Easy bruising Osteoporosis Proximal muscle weakness Hirsutism	Depression Insomnia Emotional lability Suicidality Euphoria Mania Psychosis Delirium	Disturbed sleep Decreased energy Agitation Difficulty in concentrating	Elevated blood pressure Poor glucose tolerance Dexamethasone-suppression test (may be falsely positive)	Must distinguish other causes—for example, cancer from exogenous steroid excess Suicide rate in untreated cases is about 10% Rule out major depressive disorder, bipolar I disorder
Adrenocortical insufficiency (Addison's disease)	Nausea Vomiting Anorexia Stupor Coma Hyperpigmentation	Lethargy Depression Psychosis Delirium	Fatigue	Decreased blood pressure Decreased Na^+ Increased K^+ Eosinophilia	May be primary (Addison's disease) or secondary Rule out eating disorders, mood disorders
Seizure disorder	Sensory distortions Aura	Confusion Psychosis Dissociative states Catatonic-like state	Violence Motor automatisms Belligerence Bizarre behavior	EEG, including NP leads	Consider complex partial seizures in all dissociative states Rule out postictal states, catatonic schizophrenia
Hyperparathyroidism	Constipation Polydipsia Nausea	Depression Paranoia Confusion		Increased Ca^{2+} PTH variable ECG: shortened QT interval	Causes hypercalcemia Rule out major depressive disorder, schizoaffective disorder
Hypoparathyroidism	Headache Paresthesias Tetany Carpopedal spasm Laryngeal spasm Abdominal pain	Anxiety Agitation Depression Confusion	Impaired memory	Low Ca^{2+}, normal albumin Low blood pressure ECG: QT prolongation, ventricular arrhythmias	Causes hypocalcemia Rule out anxiety disorders, mood disorders

(continued)

Table 28.3–1 *(continued)*

Disease	Common Medical Symptoms	Psychiatric Symptoms and Complaints	Impaired Performance and Behavior	Laboratory Tests and Findings	Diagnostic Problems
Systemic lupus erythematosus	Fever Photosensitivity Butterfly rash Joint pains Headache	Depression Mood disturbances Psychosis Delusions Hallucinations	Fatigue	Positive ANA Positive lupus erythematosus test Anemia Thrombocytopenia Chest X-ray: pleural effusion, pericarditis	Multisystemic autoimmune disease most frequent in women Psychiatric symptoms are present in 50% of cases Steroid treatment can cause psychiatric symptoms Rule out depressive disorders, paranoid psychosis psychotic mood disorder
Multiple sclerosis	Sudden transient motor and sensory disturbances Impaired vision Diffuse neurological signs with remissions and exacerbations	Anxiety Euphoria Mania	Slurred speech Incontinence	CSF may show increased gamma globulin CT: degenerative patches in brain and spinal cord	Onset usually in young adults Rule out tertiary syphillis, other degenerative diseases, hysteria, mania (late)
Acute intermittent porphyria	Abdominal pain Fever Nausea Vomiting Constipation Peripheral neuropathy Paralysis	Acute depression Agitation Paranoia Visual hallucinations	Restlessness Diaphoresis Weakness	Leukocytosis Elevated δ-aminolevulinic acid Elevated porphobilinogen Tachycardia	Autosomal dominant More common in women in the 20–40 age group May be precipitated by a variety of drugs Rule out acute abdominal disease, acute psychiatric episode, schizophreniform disorder, major depressive disorder
Hepatic encephalopathy	Asterixis Hyperreflexia Spider angiomata Palmar erythema Ecchymoses Liver enlargement and atrophy	Euphoria Disinhibition Psychosis Depression	Restlessness Decreased activities of daily living (ADL) Impaired cognition Impaired concentration Ataxia Dysarthria	Abnormal liver function test results Abnormal albumin EEG: diffuse slowing	May be acute or chronic depending on cause Rule out substance intoxication, mania, depressive disorder, dementia
Injuries requiring inpatient surgical evaluation and treatment (for example, suicide attempts, self-mutilation)	Alcohol abuse and other substance abuse Serious injury Major blood loss Damage to genitals, eyes, face, etc.	99% have severe psychiatric disease associated with psychosis, psychotic depression Impaired mental status secondary to substance intoxication Bizarre, inappropriate affect	Remain at great risk for suicide		Must assess and treat the underlying psychiatric condition on a priority basis Maintain a high index of suspicion for suicide risk
Pheochromocytoma	Paroxysmal hypertension Headache	Anxiety Apprehension Feeling of impending doom	Panic Diaphoresis Tremor	Hypertension Elevated VMA in 24-hr. urine Tachycardia	Adrenal medulla secreting catecholamines Rule out anxiety disorders
Wilson's disease	Kayser-Fleischer corneal ring Hepatitis-like picture	Mood disturbances Delusions Hallucinations	Choreoathetoid movements Gait disturbance Clumsiness Rigidity	Decreased serum ceruloplasmin Increased copper in urine	Hepatolenticular degeneration Autosomal recessive disorder of copper metabolism Often presents in adolescence, early adulthood Rule out extrapyramidal reactions, schizophreniform disorder, mood disorders
Huntington's disease	Family history	Depression Euphoria	Rigidity Choreoathetoid movements		Autosomal dominant Rule out mood disorders, mania, schizophrenia
Vitamin deficiencies Thiamine	Neuropathy Cardiomyopathy Wernicke-Korsakoff syndrome Nystagmus Headache Amnesia	Confusion Confabulation	General malaise Inability to sustain a conversation Poor concentration	Low thiamine level	Most common in alcoholic persons Rule out hypomania, depressive disorder, dementia

(continued)

Table 28.3–1 *(continued)*

Disease	Common Medical Symptoms	Psychiatric Symptoms and Complaints	Impaired Performance and Behavior	Laboratory Tests and Findings	Diagnostic Problems
Vitamin deficiencies—*continued*					
Nicotinamide	Diarrhea Stocking-glove dermatitis	Confusion Irritability Insomnia Depression Psychosis Dementia	Memory disturbances		Rule out mood disorders, mania, schizophreniform disorder, dementia
Pyridoxine		Apathy Irritability	Memory disturbance Muscle weakness Seizures		Often caused by medication: isoniazid Rule out mood disorders, dementia
Vitamin B_{12}	Pallor Dizziness Peripheral neuropathy Dorsal column signs	Irritability Inattentiveness Psychosis Dementia	Fatigue Ataxia	Low B_{12} level Schilling test Megaloblastic anemia	Often due to pernicious anemia Rule out dementia, mania, mood disorders
Tertiary syphilis	Skin lesions Leukoplakia Periostitis Arthritis Respiratory distress Progressive cardiovascular distress	Personality changes Irritability Confusion Psychosis	Irresponsible behavior Decreased attention to activities of daily living (ADL)	VDRL, Treponema antibody test CSF abnormal	General paresis Rule out neoplasias, meningitis, dementia, psychotic mood disorder, schizophrenia

ness, identify patients' personality features, and identify patients' characteristic coping techniques to recommend the most appropriate therapeutic intervention for patients' needs.

TREATMENT

C-L psychiatrists' principal contribution to medical treatment is a comprehensive analysis of a patients' response to illness, psychological and social resources, coping style, and psychiatric illness, if any.

This assessment is the basis of the patient treatment plan. In discussing the plan, C-L psychiatrists provide their patient assessment to nonpsychiatric health professionals. Psychiatrists' recommendations should be clear, concrete guidelines for action. A C-L psychiatrist may recommend a specific therapy, suggest areas for further medical inquiry, inform doctors and nurses of their roles in the patient's psychosocial care, recommend a transfer to a psychiatric facility for long-term psychiatric treatment, or suggest or undertake brief psychotherapy with the patient on the medical ward.

C-L psychiatrists must deal with a broad range of problems. Studies show that up to 65 percent of medical inpatients have psychiatric disorders, the most common symptoms being anxiety, depression, and disorientation. Treatment problems account for 50 percent of the consultation requests made of psychiatrists. (Table 28.3–2 covers the most common C-L problems.)

SPECIAL SETTINGS

Intensive Care Units

The central psychological aspect of patients in intensive care units (ICUs) is that they are suffering life-threatening illnesses with psychological responses that are predictable and that, if untreated, may threaten life or recovery. Coronary and medical ICU staff members see patients' reactions to acute unexpected illnesses. Patients first show fear and anxiety, followed by the psychological behaviors associated with denial, such as acting out, signing out, hostility, and excessive dependence. Staff members working in burn units encounter patients going through the problems of acute unexpected illness and, later, depression, grief, and dissociation related to pain and disfigurement. Staff members in surgical ICUs see patients recovering from major surgery with the expected disorientation of delirium, depression, and adjustment reactions to surgery.

Treatment of the psychological problems in ICUs requires close attention to diagnostic possibilities and details of the environment, as well as careful team communication. Clinicians are clearly helped by familiarity with patients' premorbid character, because the reactions to disease and illness are influenced by previous conditioning. The most common initial reactions to medical disasters include shock, fear, and anxiety. In many patients these reactions respond to treatment by the care team, especially succinct, authoritative, and consistent reassurance. When these measures are insufficient, benzodiazepines—preferably the short-acting forms—should be considered and used cautiously. When fear leads to panic or psychotic loss of control, fast-acting antipsychotics—for example, haloperidol (Haldol)—should be used.

Denial and associated behaviors of acting out, hostility, dependence, and demanding behavior must be dealt with individually on the basis of knowledge of patients and the reasons for their reactions. Several general points are pertinent. Direct communication with patients, which allows but does not force a discussion of feelings, often eliminates disruptive behaviors without dealing with them directly. Allowing patients as much mastery as they want and can handle is the most reassuring

Table 28.3–2
Common Consultation-Liaison Problems

Reason for Consultation	Comments
Suicide attempt or threat	High-risk factors are men over 45, no social support, alcohol dependence, previous attempt, incapacitating medical illness with pain, and suicidal ideation. If risk is present, transfer to psychiatric unit or start 24-hour nursing care.
Depression	Suicidal risks must be assessed in every depressed patient (see above); presence of cognitive defects in depression may cause diagnostic dilemma with dementia; check for history of substance abuse or depressant drugs (eg, reserpine, propranolol); use antidepressants cautiously in cardiac patients because of conduction side effects, orthostatic hypotension.
Agitation	Often related to cognitive disorder, withdrawal from drugs, (eg, opioids, alcohol, sedative-hypnotics); haloperidol most useful drug for excessive agitation; use physical restraints with great caution; examine for command hallucinations or paranoid ideation to which patient is responding in agitated manner; rule out toxic reaction to medication.
Hallucinations	Most common cause in hospital is delirium tremens; onset three to four days after hospitalization. In intensive care units, check for sensory isolation; rule out brief psychotic disorder, schizophrenia, cognitive disorder. Treat with antipsychotic medication.
Sleep disorder	Common cause is pain; early morning awakening associated with depression; difficulty in falling asleep associated with anxiety. Use antianxiety or antidepressant agent, depending on cause. Those drugs have no analgesic effect, so prescribe adequate painkillers. Rule out early substance withdrawal.
No organic basis for symptoms	Rule out conversion disorder, somatization disorder, factitious disorder, and malingering; glove and stocking anesthesia with autonomic nervous system symptoms seen in conversion disorder; multiple body complaints seen in somatization disorder; wish to be hospitalized seen in factitious disorder; obvious secondary gain in malingering (eg, compensation case).
Disorientation	Delirium versus dementia; review metabolic status, neurological findings, substance history. Prescribe small dose of antipsychotics for major agitation; benzodiazepines may worsen condition and cause sundowner syndrome (ataxia, confusion); modify environment so patient does not experience sensory deprivation.
Noncompliance or refusal to consent to procedure	Explore relationship of patient and treating doctor; negative transference is most common cause of noncompliance; fears of medication or of procedure require education and reassurance. Refusal to give consent is issue of judgment; if impaired, patient can be declared incompetent, but only by a judge; cognitive disorder is main cause of impaired judgment in hospitalized patients.

approach. Permitting patients to make small choices restores some sense of control over the self and the future, gives them a symbolic sense of progress, and calms them far beyond the meaning of the specific choices. For example, allowing patients to control pain medications, the level of lighting, or the place where they sit reassures and relaxes them. Whether the disruptive behavior is hostility, dependence, or panic, allowing some behavior to be shown while setting limits of their extremes reassures patients. Thus, an independent patient can be allowed to move around but not too far; a dependent patient can make a limited number of interactions, such as using the call button; and a hostile patient can be permitted some disagreement and ventilation but be limited in disruptive acts.

All ICUs deal mainly with anxiety, depression, and delirium. ICUs also impose extraordinarily high stress, on staff and patients, related to the intensity of the problems. Patients and staff members alike frequently observe cardiac arrests, deaths, and medical disasters, which leave all autonomically aroused and psychologically defensive. ICU nurses and their patients experience particularly high levels of anxiety and depression. As a result, nurse burnout and high turnover rates are very common.

Much attention is paid to the problem of stress among ICU staff, especially in nursing literature. Much less attention is given to the house staff, especially those on the surgical services. All people in ICUs must to be able to deal directly with their feelings about their extraordinary experiences and difficult emotional and physical circumstances. Regular support groups in which people can discuss their feelings are important to the ICU staff and the house staff. Such support groups protect staff members from the otherwise predictable psychiatric morbidity that some may experience, and protect their patients from the loss of concentration, decreased energy, and psychomotor-retarded communications that some staff members otherwise exhibit.

Hemodialysis Units

Hemodialysis units present a paradigm of complex modern medical treatment settings. Patients are coping with lifelong, debilitating, and limiting disease; they are totally dependent on a multiplex group of caretakers for access to a machine controlling their well-being. Dialysis is scheduled 3 times a week and takes 4 to 6 hours; thus, it disrupts patients' previous living routines.

In this context, patients first and foremost fight the disease. Invariably, however, they also have to come to terms with a level of dependence on others, a dependence probably not experienced since childhood. Predictably, patients entering dialysis struggle for their independence; regress to childhood

Table 28.3–3
Transplantation and Surgical Problems

Organ	Biological Factors	Psychological Factors
Kidney	50% to 90% success rate; may not be done if patient is over age 55; increasing use of cadaver kidneys, rather than those from living donors	Living donors must be emotionally stable; parents are best donors, siblings may be ambivalent; donors are subject to depression. Patients who panic before surgery may have poor prognoses; altered body image with fear of organ rejection is common. Group therapy for patients is helpful.
Bone marrow	Used in aplastic anemias and immune system disease	Patients are usually ill and must deal with death and dying; compliance is important. The procedure is commonly done in children who present problems of prolonged dependence; siblings are often donors and may be angry or ambivalent about procedure.
Heart	End-stage coronary artery disease and cardiomyopathy	Donor is legally dead; relatives of the deceased may refuse permission or be ambivalent. No fall-back position is available if the organ is rejected; kidney rejection patient can go on hemodialysis. Some patients seek transplantation hoping to die. Postcardiotomy delirium is seen in 25% of patients.
Breast	Radical mastectomy versus lumpectomy	Reconstruction of breast at time of surgery leads to postoperative adaptation; veteran patients are used to counsel new patients; lumpectomy patients are more open about surgery and sex than are mastectomy patients; group support is helpful.
Uterus	Hysterectomy performed on 10% of women over 20	Fear of loss of sexual attractiveness with sexual dysfunction may occur in a small percentage of women; loss of childbearing capacity is upsetting.
Brain	Anatomical location of lesion determines behavioral change	Environmental dependence syndrome in frontal lobe tumors is characterized by inability to show initiative; memory disturbances are involved to periventricular surgery; hallucinations are involved in parieto-occipital area.
Prostate	Cancer surgery has more negative psychobiological effects and is more technically difficult than is surgery for benign hypertrophy	Sexual dysfunction is common except in transurethral prostatectomy. Perineal prostatectomy produces the absence of emission, ejaculation, and erection; penile implant may be of use.
Colon and rectum	Colostomy and ostomy are common outcomes, especially for cancer	One third of patients with colostomies feel worse about themselves than before bowel surgery; shame and self-consciousness about the stoma can be alleviated by self-help groups that deal with those issues.
Limbs	Amputation performed for massive injury, diabetes, or cancer	Phantom-limb phenomenon occurs in 98% of cases; the experience may last for years; sometimes the sensation is painful, and neuroma at the stump should be ruled out; the condition has no known cause or treatment; it may stop spontaneously.

states; show denial by acting out against doctor's orders, by breaking their diet, or by missing sessions; show anger directed against staff members; bargain and plead or become infantilized and obsequious; but most often are accepting and courageous. The determinants of patients' responses to entering dialysis include personality styles and previous experiences with this or another chronic illness. Patients who have had time to react and adapt to their chronic renal failure face less new psychological work of adaptation than do those with recent renal failure and machine dependence.

Although little has been written about social factors, the effect of cultural factors in reaction to dialysis and the management of the dialysis unit are known to be important. Units run with a firm hand, that are consistent in dealing with patients, have clear contingencies for behavioral failures, and have adequate psychological support for staff members tend to produce the best results.

Complications of dialysis treatment can include psychiatric problems such as depression, and suicide is not rare. Sexual problems can be neurogenic, psychogenic, or related to gonadal dysfunction and testicular atrophy. Dialysis dementia is a rare condition that evidences loss of memory, disorientation, dystonias, and seizures. The disorder occurs in patients who have been receiving dialysis treatment for many years. The cause is unknown.

The psychological treatment of dialysis patients falls into two areas. First, careful preparation before dialysis, including the work of adaptation to chronic illness, is important, especially in dealing with denial and unrealistic expectations. All predialysis patients should have a psychosocial evaluation.

Second, once in a dialysis program, patients need periodic specific inquiries about adaptation that do not encourage dependence or the sick role. Staff members should be sensitive to the likelihood of depression and sexual problems. Group sessions function well for support, and patient self-help groups restore a useful social network, self-esteem, and self-mastery. When needed, tricyclic drugs or phenothiazines can be used for dialysis patients. Psychiatric care is most effective when brief and problem-oriented.

The use of home dialysis units has improved treatment attitude. Compared with hospital-treated patients, home-treated patients are better able to integrate the treatment into their daily lives and feel more autonomous and less dependent on others for their care.

Surgical Units

Some surgeons believe that patients who expect to die during surgery will do so. This belief now seems less superstitious than it once did. Chase Patterson Kimball and others have studied the premorbid psychological adjustment of patients scheduled for surgery and have shown that those who show evident depression or anxiety and deny it have a higher risk for morbidity and mortality than do those who, given similar depression or anxiety, can express it. Even better results occur in those with a positive attitude toward impending surgery. The factors that contribute to an improved outcome for surgery are informed consent, the education of patients so that they know what they can expect to feel, where they will be (for example, it is useful to show patients the recovery room), what loss of function to expect, what tubes and gadgets will be in place, and how to cope with the anticipated pain. In cases in which the patients will not be able to talk or see, it is helpful to explain before surgery what they can do to compensate for these losses. If postoperative states such as confusion, delirium, and pain can be predicted, they should be discussed with patients in advance to avoid their experiencing them as unwarranted or as signs of danger. Constructive family support members can help both before and after surgery. Table 28.3–3 lists various surgical conditions with which C-L psychiatrists must deal.

References

Burns BS, Scott J, Burke J, Kessler L: Mental health training of primary care residents: A review of recent literature (1974–1984). Gen Hosp Psychiatry *5:* 157, 1983.

Cohen-Cole SA, Pincus HA, Stoudemire A, Fiester S, Houpt JL: Recent research developments in consultation-liaison psychiatry. Gen Hosp Psychiatry *8:* 316, 1986.

Engle GL: The need for a new medical model: A challenge for biomedical science. Science *196:* 129, 1977.

Feifel H, Strack S, Nagy VT: Coping strategies and associated features of medically ill patients. Psychosom Med *49:* 545, 1987.

Fulop G, Strain J, Hammer JS, Lyons JS: Psychiatric and medical comorbidity: Length of stay. Am J Psychiatry *44:* 878, 1987.

Greenhill MB: The development of liaison programs. In *Psychiatric Medicine,* G Usdin, editor, p 103. Brunner/Mazel, New York, 1977.

Hall RCW, Frankel BL: The value of consultation-liaison interventions to the general hospital. Psychiatr Serv *47* (4): 418, 1996.

Hammer JS, Lyons J, Strain JJ: Microcomputers and consultation psychiatry in the general hospital. Gen Hosp Psychiatry *7:* 119, 1985.

Houpt JL: Introduction: Psychosomatic medicine, consultation-liaison psychiatry, and behavioral medicine. In *Psychiatry,* R Michael, AM Cooper, SB Guze, LL Judd, GL Klerman, AJ Solnit, AJ Stunkard, PJ Wilner, editors. Lippincott, Philadelphia, 1991.

Jacobs J, Bernhard MR, Delgado A, Strain J: Screening for organic mental syndrome in medically ill. Ann Intern Med *86:* 40, 177.

Lamdan RM, Ramchandani D, Schindler B: Constant observation in a medical-surgical setting: The role of consultation-liaison psychiatry. Psychosomatics *37* (4): 368, 1996.

Levenson JL, Mishra A, Hammer R, Hastillo A: Denial and medical outcome in unstable angina. Psychosom Med *51:* 27, 1989.

Levitan S, Kornfeld D: Clinical and costs benefits of liaison psychiatry. Am J Psychiatry *138:* 790, 1981.

Lipowski ZJ: Consultation-liaison psychiatry at century's end. Psychosomatics *33:* 128, 1992.

Lipowski ZJ: Consultation-liaison psychiatry: The first century. Gen Hosp Psychiatry *8:* 305, 1986.

Lipowski ZJ: *Psychosomatic Medicine and Liaison Psychiatry: Selected Papers.* Plenum, New York, 1985.

Mumford E, Schlesinger HJ, Glass GV, Patrick C, Cuerdon T: A new look at evidence about reduced cost of medical utilization following mental health treatment. Am J Psychiatry *141:* 1145, 1984.

Olfson M: Depressed patients who do and do not receive psychiatric consultation in general hospitals. Gen Hosp Psychiatry *13:* 39, 1991.

Pincus HA: Linking health and mental health systems of care: Conceptual models of implementation. Am J Psychiatry *137:* 315, 1980.

Popkin M, MacKenzie T, Callies A: Consultation liaison outcome evaluation system. Arch Gen Psychiatry *40:* 215, 1983.

Popkin MK: Consultation-liaison psychiatry. In *Comprehensive Textbook of Psychiatry,* ed 6, HI Kaplan, BJ Sadock, editors, p 1592. Williams & Wilkins, Baltimore, 1995.

Regier DA, Myers JK, Kramer M, Robins LN, Blazer DG, Hough RL, Eaton WW, Locke BZ: The NIMH Epidemiologic Catchment Area (ECA) programs: Historical context, major objectives, and study population characteristics. Arch Psychiatry *41:* 934, 1984.

Rundell JR, Wise MG, editors: *The American Psychiatric Press Textbook of Consultation-Liaison Psychiatry.* American Psychiatric Press, Washington, 1996.

Schwab JJ: Consultation-liaison psychiatry: A historical overview. Psychosomatics *30:* 245, 1989.

Strain J: Diagnostic considerations in the medical setting. Psychiatr Clin North Am *4:* 287, 1981.

Strain J: *Psychological Interventions in Medical Practice.* Appleton-Century-Crofts, New York, 1978.

Strain J, Hammer JS, Huertas D, Lam HC, et al: The problem of coping as a reason for psychiatric consultation. Gen Hosp Psychiatry *15:* 1, 1993.

Strain J, Pincus HA, Houpt JL, Gise LH, Taintor Z: Model of mental health training for primary care physicians. Psychosom Med *47:* 95, 1985.

Uhlenhuth EH, Balter MB, Mellinger GD, Cisin IH, Clinthorne J: Symptom checklist syndromes in the general population: Correlations with psychotherapeutic drug use. Arch Gen Psychiatry *40:* 1167, 1983.

Vaz FJ, Salcedo M: A model for evaluating the impact of consultation-liaison psychiatry activities on referral patterns. Psychosomatics *37* (3): 289, 1996.

Wallen J, Pincus HA, Goldman HA, Marcus SE: Psychiatric consultations in short-term general hospital. Arch Gen Psychiatry *44:* 163, 1987.

Weiner H: *Psychobiology of Health and Disease.* Elsevier, New York, 1977.

▲ 28.4 Treatment

The concept of combined psychotherapeutic and medical treatment—that is, the approach that emphasizes the interrelation of mind and body in the genesis of symptom and disorder—calls for a greatly expanded sharing of responsibility among various professions. From a multicausal point of view, every disease can be considered to be caused by or to be associated with emotional factors. The evaluation of all these factors is usually carried out by the primary care physician, who may need the participation of the psychiatrist to explain fully the psychological factors.

Hostility, rage, guilt, depression, and anxiety in varying proportions are at the root of most psychosomatic disorders. Psychosomatic medicine is principally concerned with illnesses that present primarily somatic manifestations. The presenting complaint is usually physical; patients rarely complain of their anxiety or depression or tension but, rather, of their vomiting or diarrhea or anorexia.

TYPES OF PATIENTS

A special evaluation of the psychological and somatic factors of three major groups of medical patients is required.

Psychosomatic Illness Group

Patients in the psychosomatic illness group have classic psychosomatic disorders, such as peptic ulcer and ulcerative colitis. In these disease processes clinicians cannot posit a strictly psychogenic explanation; the particular set of emotional factors found, for example, in the typical ulcer cases may also appear in patients with no history of ulcer. There are changes in the autonomic nervous system, however, that cause pathophysiology to occur (for example, vasospasm causing muscle pain).

Psychiatric Group

Patients in the psychiatric group experience physical disturbances caused by psychological rather than physical illness. As mentioned above, when the illness is real, the disability involves the autonomic nervous system, which causes pathophysiological changes. There are no pathophysiological signs in hypochondriasis and delusional preoccupation with physical functioning. Patients in this group suffer primarily from a psychological disturbance that requires psychiatric treatment, but auxiliary medical therapy may be necessary. Patients with conversion disorders (for example, paralysis) show no objective changes consistent with a known disease. In conversion disorder the voluntary nervous system is involved, not the autonomic nervous system.

Reactive Group

Patients in the reactive group have actual organic disorders, but they also suffer from an associated psychological disturbance. For example, a patient with heart disease or one with renal disease who requires dialysis may have anxiety and depression in response to the life-threatening condition. This anxiety, in turn, may produce physical manifestations that complicate the somatic situation.

COMBINED TREATMENT

The combined treatment approach, in which a psychiatrist handles the psychiatric aspects of the case and internist or other specialist treats the somatic aspects, requires the closest collaboration between the two physicians. The purpose of the medical therapy is to build up the patient's physical state so that the patient can successfully participate in psychotherapy for a total cure.

Disorders such as bronchial asthma, in which psychosocial processes play a distinct role in the development and course, may respond well to the combined treatment approach. Although the asthmatic attacks themselves may be treated successfully by the internist, psychiatric treatment can be useful in the short run by helping to alleviate the anxiety associated with the attacks and in the long run by helping to uncover the causes of the interdependence involved in the disorder.

In an acute somatic illness, such as an acute attack of ulcerative colitis, medical therapy is the primary form of treatment; at this stage, psychotherapy, with its long-range goals, consists of reassurance and support. As the pendulum of disease activity shifts and the illness becomes chronic, psychotherapy assumes the primary role, and medical therapy takes the less active position.

Sometimes, reassurance is all that is needed in the treatment of psychosomatic syndromes. Patients must participate in the process of improving their life situations. The symptoms themselves may be treated by the internist, if necessary. Usually, the psychiatrist can help patients focus on their feelings about the symptoms and gain understanding of the unconscious processes involved with symptom improvement. If patients are handled insensitively or if their illnesses are regarded unsympathetically, the results can be grave.

Indications for Combined Treatment

If during an initial attack of a psychosomatic disorder patients respond to active medical therapy in association with the superficial support, ventilation, reassurance, and environmental manipulation provided by an internist, additional psychotherapy by a psychiatrist may not be required. Psychosomatic illness that is chronic or does not respond to medical treatment should receive psychosomatic evaluation by a psychiatrist, and combined therapy as indicated.

Goal of Treatment

It is useful to set up a tentative, flexible spectrum of therapeutic goals in the treatment of psychosomatic disorders. The desired end is a cure, which means resolution of any structural impairment and reorganization of the personality so that needs and tensions no longer produce pathophysiological results. Treatment should aim at a mature general life adjustment, increased capacity for physical and occupational activity, amelioration of the progression of the disease, reversal of the pathology, avoidance of complications of the basic disease process, decreased use of secondary gain associated with the illness, and increased capacity to adjust to the presence of the disease.

PSYCHIATRIC ASPECTS

Treatment of psychosomatic disorders from a psychiatric viewpoint is a difficult task. Psychiatrists must focus therapy on understanding the motivations and mechanisms of disturbed functioning and helping patients realize the nature of their illness and the implications of its costly adaptive patterns. These insights should produce changed and healthier patterns of behavior.

Psychotherapy based on analytic principles is effective in treating psychosomatic disorders mainly in terms of the patients' experiences in the treatment, particularly their relationships with the therapist. Patients with psychosomatic disorders are usually even more reluctant to deal with their emotional problems than are patients with other psychiatric problems. Psychosomatic patients try to avoid responsibility for their illness by isolating the diseased organ and presenting it to the doctor for diagnosis and cure. They may be satisfying an infantile need to be cared for passively, while denying that they are adults, with all the attendant stresses and conflicts.

Resistance to Entering Psychotherapy

When psychosomatic patients first become ill, they are usually convinced that the illness is purely organic in origin. They reject psychotherapy as treatment for their sickness; in fact, the very idea of emotional illness may be repugnant because of personal prejudices about psychiatry.

In the initial phase, physical treatment and psychotherapeutic procedures must be combined subtly. In this stage, treatment by a psychologically oriented physician who is sensitive to unconscious and transference phenomena can be therapeutic.

Development of Relationship and Transference

Psychotherapy with psychosomatic patients must often proceed more slowly and cautiously than with other psychiatric patients. Positive transference should be developed gradually, and psychiatrists must be supportive and reassuring during the acute illness. As disorders become chronic, a psychiatrist may make exploratory interpretations, but a strong patient–physician relationship must precede any such exploration. As psychosomatic patients are dependent, this characteristic can be used supportively and interpretatively at crucial periods in the treatment. Much hostility surfaces during therapy—first in the form of overt ventilation and then in the framework of the transference. Therapists must encourage free and appropriate expression of patients' hostility.

Interpretation

Therapists must pay particular attention to current problems in patients' immediate life situation and must deal with patients' reaction to the therapist and to treatment. Therapists should increasingly emphasize evaluation of patients' characterological difficulties and habitual reactions, particularly reactions to themselves (self-esteem, guilt) and reactions to his or her environment (dependence, submission, need for affection). Psychiatrists should also analyze patients' anxieties and coping mechanisms for stress situations, such as requests for complete care, the need to always be right, lack of self-assertion, and suppression of all forbidden impulses.

Some psychoanalytic investigators have reported dramatic results when unconscious material was interpreted as a drastic measure during an acute illness. Although most freudian psychoanalysts seem to think that genetic material must eventually be interpreted for a complete cure, new approaches have shown that adequate results can be obtained when psychotherapy is limited to the analysis of characterological and ego defenses associated with disturbed interpersonal relationships.

Patients with psychosomatic disorders are often involved in a repetitious pattern of stress in their interpersonal relationships. Because such patients are usually unaware of the pattern, it is helpful to show them that it is not accidental but is determined by factors of which they are unaware. It is essential to show patients how to change the disturbing pattern and act in a new and healthier manner.

Psychosomatic patients tend to drive toward psychologically regressed mental and physical behavior and usually regress to a traumatic or highly conflictual period. By reenacting certain specific attitudes of childhood or infancy, they are attempting to master the anxiety and illness first manifested during these earlier stages.

In the treatment of psychosomatic disorders, the key concept is flexibility in technique. Because of patients' lack of motivation and poor physical condition, it may be necessary to make frequent changes in the psychotherapeutic approach.

Resistance During Therapy

Because patients with psychosomatic disorders often strongly resist entering psychotherapy, resistance frequently continues unabated during therapy. Many patients' motivations for entering treatment are so poor that they frequently drop out of therapy for minor reasons.

Interruption of Psychotherapy for a Medical Emergency

During a course of psychotherapy, a patient with a psychosomatic disorder may require medical or surgical treatment for the organic disorder. The psychiatrist should cooperate closely with the surgeon or medical personnel and should maintain contact with the patient—in person or by telephone—during the emergency. Such interest offers valuable emotional support in a time of crisis.

If a patient is hospitalized, the psychiatrist should help other hospital personnel recognize and learn to tolerate the frequently difficult and provocative behavior of some psychosomatic patients. The preparation can be of use to the patients as well; when they see their demands being met considerately, they may be less inclined to view their world as hostile and formidable.

Danger of Psychosis

There are no simple relations between psychosomatic disorders and psychoses. Some people in whom physiological and psychological processes are poorly integrated manifest both psychosomatic disorders and psychoses. In other people, the ego integration is such that stress produces a breakdown of bodily function rather than a psychotic maladjustment. Some nonpsychotic psychosomatic patients can become psychotic or exhibit psychotic symptoms as a result of too active an interpretation and with the removal of defensive elements in the personality structure.

MEDICAL ASPECTS

Internists' treatment of psychosomatic disorders should follow the established rules for medical management. Generally, internists should spend as much time as possible with a patient and listen sympathetically to the many complaints; they must be reassuring and supportive. Before performing a physically manipulative procedure—particularly if it is painful, such as a colonoscopy—the internist should explain to a patient just what to expect. The explanation allays the patient's anxiety, makes the patient more cooperative, and actually facilitates the examination.

Patients' attitudes toward taking drugs may also affect the outcome of the psychosomatic treatment. For example, patients with diabetes who do not accept their illness and who have self-destructive impulses of which they are unaware may purposely not control their diet and, as a result, end up in a hyperglycemic coma. Some cardiac patients refuse to curtail their physical activity after a myocardial infarction because of a reluctance to admit weakness or because of a fear that they will somehow be considered unsuccessful. Others use their illness as a welcome punishment for guilt or as a way to avoid responsibility. Therapy in such cases must strive to help patients minimize their fears and focus on self-care and reestablishment of a healthy body image.

ACCEPTANCE OF PSYCHOMEDICAL TREATMENT

An advantage of the collaborative approach is that patients benefit from the efforts of specialists trained in various medical disciplines, each working in the area in which they are best equipped to function. Some physicians, however, have resisted a psychiatric approach because of inadequate psychiatric training in medical school, unfamiliarity with the specialized language of psychiatry, and a general prejudice based on the cost of psychotherapy and the alleged unscientific and subjective aspects of psychiatry.

OTHER TYPES OF THERAPY

Other types of treatment have been introduced for psychosomatic disorders. The first category includes psychotherapies based on psychological insight and change, such as group and family psychotherapy; the second category is composed of behavior therapy techniques based on pavlovian principles of learning new behavior, such as biofeedback and relaxation therapy.

Group Psychotherapy and Family Therapy

Because of the psychopathological significance of the mother–child relationship in developing psychosomatic disorders, modification of this relationship has been suggested as a likely focus of emphasis in the psychotherapy of psychosomatic disorders. Toksoz Byram Karasu wrote that the group approach should also offer greater interpersonal contact and provide increased ego support for the weak egos of psychosomatic patients who fear the threat of isolation and parental separation. Family therapy offers hope of a change in the relationship between the family and the child. Both therapies have had excellent initial clinical results.

The long-term evaluation of the results of the various psychotherapies, individual and group, for psychosomatic disorders remains to be carried out. After an exhaustive study of psychosomatic psychotherapeutic treatment, Karasu concluded that some patients with medical disorders may respond positively to psychological treatment, either physically or psychologically. Some medical disorders seem more amenable to psychotherapy than others, and some therapeutic modalities appear to be more effective than others. Some people may be more responsive to psychotherapy than others, especially in relation to the nature of their psychopathology rather than their physical pathology.

Behavior Therapy

Biofeedback. The application of biofeedback techniques to patients with hypertension, cardiac arrhythmias, epilepsy, and tension headaches has been successful in many, but not all, instances. Some patients do not respond.

Relaxation Techniques. The treatment of hypertension may include the use of the relaxation techniques. Positive results have been published about the treatment of alcohol and other substance abuse by using transcendental meditation. Workers have also used meditation in the treatment of headaches.

REFERENCES

Alexander F: *Psychosomatic Medicine.* Norton, New York, 1950.

Book HE: Empathy: Misconceptions and misuses in psychotherapy. Am J Psychiatry *145:* 4, 1988.

Dolinar LJ: Obstacles to the care of patients with medical-psychiatric illness on general hospital psychiatry units. Gen Hosp Psychiatry *15:* 14, 1993.

Fink P: Surgery and medical treatment in persistent somatizing patients. J Psychosom Res *36:* 439, 1992.

Karasu TB: Psychotherapy of the medically ill. Am J Psychiatry *136:* 1, 1979.

Karush A, Daniels GE, Flood C, O'Connor JF: *Psychotherapy in Chronic Ulcerative Colitis.* Saunders, Philadelphia. 1977.

Kyle J: *Crohn's Disease.* Heinemann, London, 1972.

Matheny KB, Brack GL, McCarthy CJ, Penick JM: The effectiveness of cognitively-based approaches in treating stress-related symptoms. Psychotherapy *33* (2): 305, 1996.

Sanders D: Counselling for psychosomatic problems. In *Counselling in Practice.* Sage Publications, London, 1996.

Temple N, Walker J, Evans M: Group psychotherapy with psychosomatic and somatizing patients in a general hospital. Psychoanal Psychother *10* (3): 251, 1996.

Wolman T, Thompson TL II: Psychoanalytic approach to the psychosomatic interface. In *Textbook of Psychoanalysis,* E Nersessian, RG Kopff Jr, editors. American Psychiatric Press, Washington, 1996.

29

Alternative Medicine and Psychiatry

Traditional medicine, as it is practiced in the United States and elsewhere in the Western world, is based on scientific method: the use of experiments to validate a hypothesis or to determine the probability of a theory. Traditional medicine presumes that the body is a biological and physiological system and that disorders have a cause that can be treated with medications, surgery, and complex technological methods to produce a cure. Traditional medicine is thus also referred to as biomedicine or technomedicine.

The term *alternative medicine* refers to the various disease-treating or disease-preventing practices whose methods and efficacy differ from traditional or conventional biomedical knowledge. Other terms used to describe these therapeutic approaches are complementary and holistic medicine. In complementary medicine, some approaches can be used in conjunction with traditional therapeutic methods. In holistic medicine, a doctor treats a patient as a whole rather than focusing on a specific disease or disorder. The idea of emphasizing the whole patient and the need to evaluate psychosocial, environmental, and lifestyle factors in health and disease have been subsumed under the psychosomatic approach in previous years and are not new concepts in psychiatry; of all the alternative therapies, however, only hypnosis and biofeedback have entered the mainstream of psychiatry.

Traditional medicine is also known as allopathic medicine. The term *allopathy,* derived from the Greek word *allos* (''other''), refers to the use of medication to counteract the signs and symptoms of disease. Allopathy is the type of medicine taught in U.S. medical schools. Samuel Hahnemann, M.D. (1755–1843), a German physician, coined the term to distinguish this form of medicine from homeopathy (derived from the Greek word *homos* [''same'']), in which special medicinal remedies, different from allopathic medicine, are used. Allopathy is the most prevalent form of medicine practiced in the Western world. (Homeopathy is discussed more fully later in this chapter.)

Alternative medical therapy is increasingly popular: It is estimated that one person in three at some time uses these therapies for common ailments such as back problems, headaches, anxiety, and depression. These therapies are also sought by people with acquired immune deficiency syndrome (AIDS), cancer, and other life-threatening medical illnesses. More than $15 billion a year is spent on alternative medical therapies in the United States.

In 1991, the National Institutes of Health (NIH) established the Office of Alternative Medicine (OAM) to evaluate a broad range of unrelated, nonorthodox therapeutic systems to evaluate their usefulness and to provide scientific explanations for their effectiveness. In 1995, the OAM compiled a classification of alternative medical practices (Table 29–1), which was designed to support research to investigate the effectiveness of these therapies. The OAM was careful to point out that including a treatment in the classification did not imply an endorsement of the method. Indeed, many methods in the OAM classification are based on no known scientific principles and are considered quackery. Some health maintenance organizations (HMOs) have recently approved alternative medical therapies for reimbursement. The HMOs claim to be responding to public pressure, but many health experts believe that these HMOs are motivated solely by financial consideration: People who visit alternative practitioners are reimbursed at lower fees than are those who visit traditional practitioners. Some HMOs allow their members to be self-referred to these practitioners. In contrast, referral to a traditional medical specialist can only be initiated by the patient's primary care physician. The practice of self-referral may endanger the health of the general public by encouraging people to seek alternative treatment that may not help them.

Following are some methods listed in the OAM classification of alternative medical practices. They are briefly described and listed in alphabetical order. The discussion of therapies should not be considered definitive, and new therapies continue to emerge.

ACUPRESSURE AND ACUPUNCTURE

Acupressure and acupuncture are Chinese healing techniques that are mentioned in ancient medical texts dating back to 3000 B.C. A basic tenet of Chinese medicine is the belief that vital energy (qi or chi) flows along specific pathways (meridians), which have about 350 points (acupoints), whose manipulation corrects imbalances by stimulating or removing blockages to energy flow. Another fundamental concept is the idea of two opposing energy fields (yin and yang), which must be in balance for health to be sustained. In acupressure the acupoints are manipulated by the fingers; in acupuncture sterilized silver or gold needles (some the diameter of a human hair) are inserted into the skin to varying depths (0.5 mm to 1.5 cm) and are rotated or left in place for varying periods to correct any imbalance of qi.

In the West, acupressure and acupuncture are explained on the basis of nerve stimulation that releases endogenous neurotransmitters and endorphins to help cure illness. Some of the conditions for which these techniques are applied are asthma, headaches, dysmenorrhea, cervical pain, insomnia, anxiety, de-

Table 29–1
Classification of Alternative Medical Practices from the NIH Office of Alternative Medicine

Diet, Nutrition, Lifestyle Changes	**Manual Healing**
Changes in lifestyle	Acupressure
Diet	Alexander technique
Nutritional supplements	Aromatherapy
Gerson therapy	Biofield therapeutics
Macrobiotics	Chiropractic medicine
Megavitamin	Feldenkrais method
Mind/Body Control	Massage therapy
Art therapy, relaxation techniques	Osteopathy
Biofeedback	Reflexology
Counseling and prayer therapies	Rolfing
Dance therapy	Therapeutic touch
Guided imagery	Trager method
Humor therapy	Zone therapy
Psychotherapy	**Pharmacological and Biological Treatments**
Sound, music therapy	Antioxidizing agents
Support groups	Cell treatment
Yoga, meditation	Chelation therapy
Alternative Systems of Medical Practice	Metabolic therapy
Acupuncture	Oxidizing agents (ozone, hydrogen peroxide)
Anthroposophically extended medicine	**Bioelectromagnetic Applications**
Ayurveda	Blue light treatment and artificial lighting
Community-based health care practices	Electroacupuncture
Environmental medicine	Electromagnetic fields
Homeopathic medicine	Electrostimulation and neuromagnetic stimulation devices
Latin American rural practices	Magnetoresonance spectroscopy
Native American	**Herbal Medicine**
Natural products	*Echinacea* (purple coneflower)
Naturopathic medicine	*Ginkgo biloba* extract
Past life therapy	Ginger rhizome
Shamanism	Ginseng root
Tibetan medicine	Wild chrysanthemum flower
Traditional oriental medicine	Witch hazel
	Yellowdock

This classification was developed by the ad hoc Advisory Panel to the Office of Alternative Medicine (OAM), National Institutes of Health (NIH), and further refined by the Workshop on Alternative Medicine as described in the report *Alternative Medicine: Expanding Medical Horizons.* This classification was designed to facilitate the grant review process and should not be considered definitive.

pression, and substance abuse. (See the later description of moxibustion.)

ALEXANDER TECHNIQUE

Alexander technique was developed by F. M. Alexander (1869–1955), who was born in Tasmania and eventually became a well-known stage actor. After developing aphonia, he experimented on himself by changing his body posture and eventually regained his voice. Alexander developed a theory of the proper use of body musculature to help alleviate somatic and mental illness. Techniques involve corrective manipulation of the muscles involving the head and neck, torso, pelvis, and extremities to improve posture. With treatment, there is improvement in cardiovascular, respiratory, and gastrointestinal functioning as well as in mood. A small and devoted group of Alexander practitioners is found throughout the world, including the United States. The Alexander technique deserves consideration, if for no other reason than that so many people in the United States have poor posture (Fig. 29–1).

ANTHROPOSOPHICALLY EXTENDED MEDICINE

This form of healing was developed by the Austrian philosopher Rudolf Steiner (1861–1925). The healing process involves the use of conscious understanding, which Steiner called *anthroposophy,* or the ''wisdom of life.'' Anthroposophy focuses on mental exercises that enable people to find a balance between mind and body to ensure health maintenance. Steiner founded a school represented in this country by the Rudolf Steiner School, which teaches children these concepts as they apply to civilization, besides a standard educational curriculum.

AROMATHERAPY

Aromatherapy is the therapeutic use of plant oils. Named by the French chemist René-Maurice Gattefosse in 1928, aromatherapy is one of the fastest growing alternative therapies in the United States and Europe. The essential oils of plants

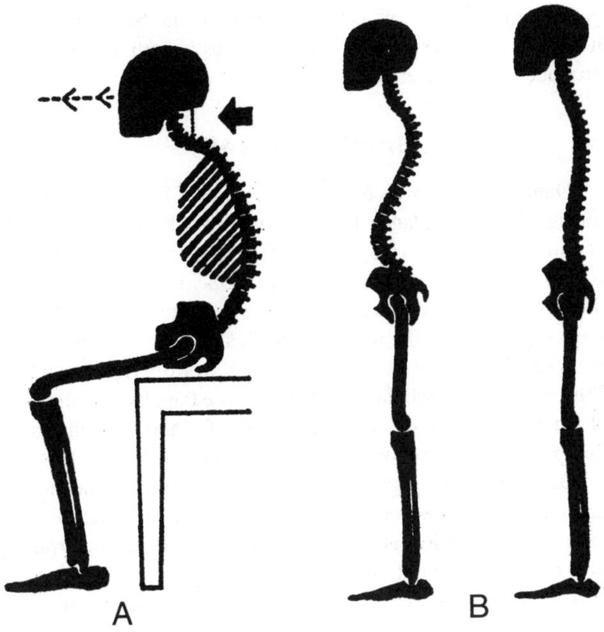
A
B

FIGURE 29–1
A. Position of pelvis, back, neck, and head in slumped position. **B.** Standing in hunched position *(left)* and well balanced *(right)*. (Reprinted with permission from Barlow W: *The Alexander Principle.* Gollancz, London, 1973.)

are organic compounds that are benzene derivatives. Aromatic substances were used in ancient civilization for both medicine and perfume. Today, plant oils are inhaled using atomizers or absorbed through the skin using massage (aromatherapy massage). Plant oils have many therapeutic effects—analgesic, psychological, antimicrobial—some of which have been demonstrated scientifically. Aromatherapy is used to reduce stress and anxiety and to alleviate gastrointestinal and musculoskeletal disorders, among others. In psychiatry, olfactory stimulation has been used to elicit feeling tones, memories, and emotions during psychotherapy. Aromatherapy can cause skin irritation or allergic reactions in some people. Table 29–2 lists essential oils and their effects.

AYURVEDA

Ayurveda means "knowledge of life." The technique originated in India around 3000 B.C. and is believed to be the oldest and most comprehensive medical system in the world. Ayurveda is similar to Chinese medicine in the beliefs about energy points on the body and a vital force (*prana*) that must be in balance to maintain health. Ayurveda practitioners diagnose illness by examining the pulse, the urine, and the heat or coldness of the body. Treatment relies on diet, medicines, purification, enemas, and bloodletting. (See also Tibetan medicine.)

BATES METHOD

The Bates method, designed to treat vision problems, was devised by William H. Bates. It is aimed at naturally strengthening the eye muscles and includes the following basic exercises: splashing closed eyes 20 times with warm water, then 20 times with cold water; alternating focusing on near and distant objects; focusing on an object while gently swaying the body; remembering objects in the mind's eye to facilitate the actual perception of these objects in reality; and closing the eyes, cupping them with the palms of both hands (without touching the eyes), and focusing on pleasant thoughts.

Bates practitioners claim that people who need glasses to correct refraction errors will not need them if these methods are followed rigorously.

BIOENERGETICS

Bioenergetics, based on the belief that damned-up energy produces maladaptive behavioral patterns, evolved from the work of the Austrian psychoanalyst Wilhelm Reich (1897–1957), who studied with Sigmund Freud. Reich believed that energy fields were propelled by sexual impulses called ergs and that satisfactory orgasms were an indication of healthy bodily functioning. Modern-day practitioners look for areas of muscular tension in the body that are thought to be associated with repressed memories and emotions. Therapists try to bring these repressions to consciousness through a variety of relaxation techniques, including massage.

CHELATION

Chelation therapy is a traditional medical procedure used to treat accidental poisoning with heavy metals, such as lead, arsenic, and mercury. A chelating agent (ethylenediaminetetraacetic acid [EDTA]) is infused into the bloodstream and binds to the metal, which is then excreted from the body. As an alternative medical practice, chelation therapy is used as a form of preventive medicine to remove lead, cadmium, and aluminum from the body. These substances are believed to be associated with premature aging, memory loss, and the symptoms of Alzheimer's disease. Chelation therapy has also been used to treat atherosclerosis.

Table 29–2
Essentials Oils in Aromatherapy and Their Effects

Oil	Effect
Chamomile	Tranquilizing
Eucalyptus	Antiseptic
Geranium	Astringent
Jasmine	Stimulant
Lavender	Analgesic, tranquilizing
Neroli	Sedative-hypnotic
Peppermint	Stimulant
Rosemary	Stimulant
Sandalwood	Antiseptic, stimulant

FIGURE 29–2

Daniel David Palmer (1845–1913), the founder of chiropractic. (Reprinted with permission from Shealy CN, editor: *The Complete Family Guide to Alternative Medicine: An Illustrated Encyclopedia of Natural Healing,* p 39. Barnes & Noble Books, New York, 1996. Credited to British Chiropractic Association.)

CHIROPRACTIC

Chiropractic is concerned with the diagnosis and treatment of disorders of the musculoskeletal system, especially those of the spine. It was developed by a Canadian, Daniel David Palmer (1845–1913), who moved to the United States in 1895 and who believed that spinal misalignment leading to abnormal nerve transmission is the cause of all illness (Fig. 29–2).

Chiropractors diagnose illness by clinical examination and X-ray. Treatment involves manual manipulation of bones, joints, and musculature to restore biomechanical function. Chiropractic is the largest independent alternative health profession in the Western world, and the United States is home to 52,000 of the world's approximately 56,000 chiropractors. Chiropractors are recognized by government and insurance agencies, and treat approximately 20 million people in the United States annually.

COLOR THERAPY

In color therapy, different colors are thought to affect mood, and monocolor therapy has been used to address specific health problems. For example, blue is believed to be sedating, and red, excitatory. A Swiss psychologist, Max Luscher, devised a color test in which a subject's mood at a particular time is determined by exposing the subject to various colors. Luscher also experimented with the effect of color on the autonomic nervous system and found that pure red is sympathomimetic and can cause an increase in blood pressure, heart rate, and respiration. Blue is parasympathomimetic and produces opposite effects.

DANCE THERAPY

Dance therapy was formally recognized in 1942, with the hiring of pioneer dance therapist Marian Chace (1896–1990) at St. Elizabeth's Hospital in Washington, DC. Although within the profession *dance* and *movement* are used synonymously, each term actually describes a point of view: Movement encompasses the world of physical motion, whereasdance is a specific creative act within that world. The American Dance Therapy Association defines dance therapy as ''the psychotherapeutic use of movement which furthers the emotional and physical integration of the individual.''

Dance therapy sessions have four basic goals: the development of body awareness; the expression of feelings; the fostering of interaction and communication; and the integration of the physical, emotional, and social experiences that result in a sense of increased self-confidence and contentment.

Table 29–3
Common Nutritional Supplements and Their Effects

Substance	Comment
Calcium	Most Americans do not get the RDA of 1 to 2 grams, particularly women who are subject to osteoporosis, especially after menopause
Iron	20% of low-income children are anemic due to iron deficiency
Magnesium	Supplementation causes decrease in LDL and increase in HDL; may be protective against cardiovascular disease; has anticoagulant activity
Vitamin C	Supplementation associated with reduced risk of cataracts, cancer
Vitamin D	Synthesized by exposure to sun and obtained in fortified milk; necessary for calcium metabolism
Vitamin E	Supplementation decreases risk of coronary artery disease, oral cancer, cataracts; useful in treating tardive dyskinesia
β-Carotene	May be protective against certain cancers, cardiovascular disease
Folic acid (folate)	Supplementation in pregnant women reduces risk of neural tube defects, infectious disease, and cardiovascular disease
Coenzyme Q_{10}	Associated with increased levels of immunoglobulin G and T_4 lymphocytes
Selenium	Deficiency associated with depression; supplementation for prostate, colon, and lung cancer
Garlic	Supplement associated with decreased cholesterol; may be protective against cardiovascular disease and cancer
Glucosamine–chondroitin sulfate	Used to reduce pain in osteoarthritis and stimulate cartilage growth

DIET AND NUTRITION

Nutritional methods to prevent or cure disease have an important place in modern medicine, and their efficacy has been proved by scientific evidence. The federal government has established recommended daily allowances (RDA) to meet the nutritional needs of average people in the United States, as illustrated in Figure 29–3, the food guide pyramid. There are many alternative diets, and specific vitamin and mineral supplementation programs have been developed to deal with specific diseases or bodily processes (Table 29–3). Diets low in fat have been recommended for the treatment of cardiovascular disease and diabetes. The Pritikin diet developed by Nathan Pritikin is extremely low in fat (less than 10 percent of daily calories), high in complex carbohydrates, and high in fiber. The Ornish diet, developed by Dean Ornish, M.D., is vegetarian: No meat, poultry, or fish is allowed, and only 10 percent of calories are obtained from fat. Both diets include an exercise program. Studies have shown that these diets can produce a reduction in cholesterol, decreased blood pressure, and increased cardiac performance. They have also been effective in eliminating the need for drugs in newly diagnosed cases of adult-onset diabetes.

Diets from other cultures have certain health benefits. In Asia, diets are low in fat, and there is a low incidence of cardiac disease; diets in Mediterranean countries are high in the use of olive oil, garlic, and grains, and are associated with a low incidence of colon cancer and cardiac disease. Food allergies have been implicated in many conditions: arthritis, asthma, hyperactivity, and ulcerative colitis, among others. According to the OAM, alternative dietary practices may have possible benefits in view of the evidence now available, and the OAM is conducting extensive and rigorous scientific evaluations of these potentially beneficial practices. (See also macrobiotics.)

ENVIRONMENTAL MEDICINE

The field of environmental medicine began to emerge in the 1950s when physicians such as Theron Randolf, M.D., professor of allergy and immunology at Northwestern University School of Medicine, began to examine some people's allergic reactions to various foods. Other workers studied the effects on the body of pollutants in water and air, and eventually the field expanded to include the total environment in which humans exist. As a result, environmental medicine now concerns itself with issues such as food additives, electromagnetic fields from electric utility wires, fertilizers and hormones used in food production, microwaves from appliances such as microwave ovens, television sets, and cellular telephones, and nuclear radiation. Practitioners of environmental medicine believe that many people are extraordinarily sensitive to environmental contaminants that can trigger a disease process. Some issues are highly controversial. For instance, studies fail to demonstrate a higher incidence of cancer in people exposed to electromagnetic fields; however, a correlation exists between higher cancer rates and living near oil refineries and chemical plants. Environmental medicine is a form of preventative medicine that focuses on increased individual awareness to environmental hazards and the control or elimination of these hazards. (See also naturopathic medicine.)

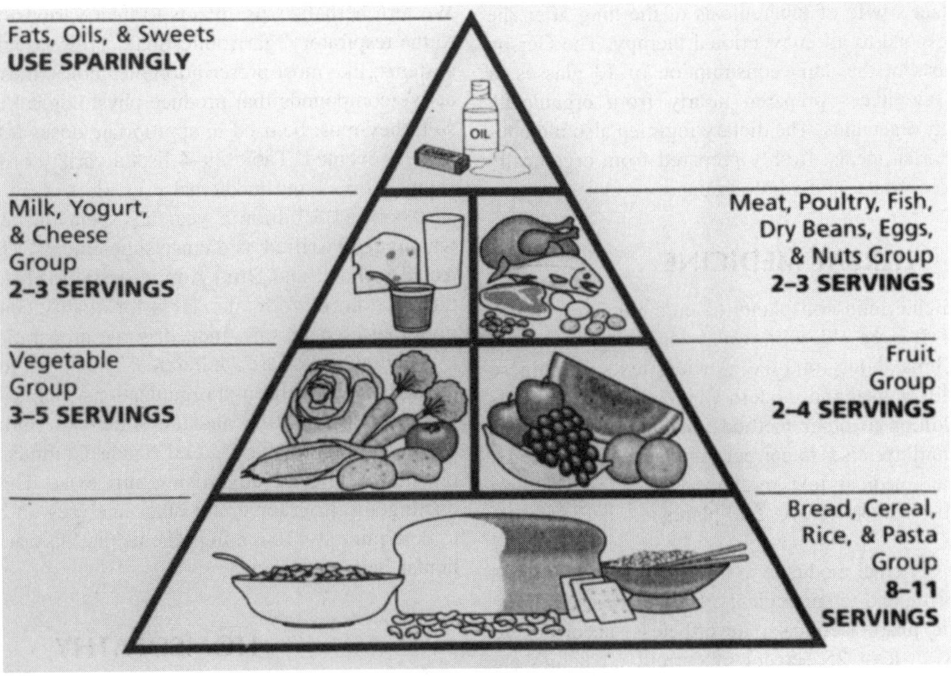
Fats, Oils, & Sweets
USE SPARINGLY
OIL
Milk, Yogurt, & Cheese Group
2–3 SERVINGS
Meat, Poultry, Fish, Dry Beans, Eggs, & Nuts Group
2–3 SERVINGS
Vegetable Group
3–5 SERVINGS
Fruit Group
2–4 SERVINGS
Bread, Cereal, Rice, & Pasta Group
8–11 SERVINGS

FIGURE 29–3
Food guide pyramid.

FELDENKRAIS METHOD

The Feldenkrais method was developed by Moshe Feldenkrais (1904–1982), a Russian-born physicist who in the 1940s developed a theory evolved from Freud's theory of human development. Feldenkrais concluded that the body should be emphasized as much as the mind and that proprioception (somatic sensations from muscles and other organs) can influence behavior. He believed that posture and the positions of the body reflected conflict; therefore, retraining the body was part of his treatment program (Fig. 29–4). Practitioners of the Feldenkrais method are active throughout the world. Those learning the Feldenkrais method are referred to as students rather than patients to reinforce the view that the work is primarily an educational process. Lessons generally last from 30 to 60 minutes and consist of structured movement that involves thinking, sensing, moving, and imagining. The method has been used in central nervous system disorders, such as multiple sclerosis, cerebral palsy, and stroke. Older people who use the method claim that they retain or regain their ability to move without strain or discomfort.

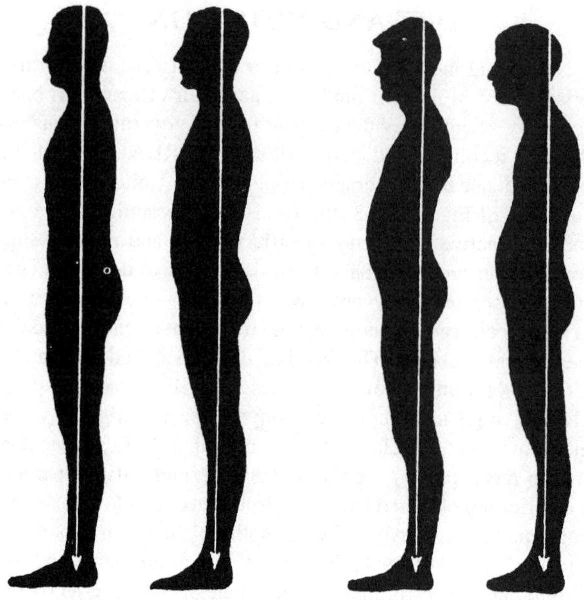
A
B
C
D

FIGURE 29–4
The Harvard University chart for grading body mechanics. The four figures represent (from *left* to *right*) excellent **(A)**, good **(B)**, poor **(C)**, and very poor **(D)** mechanical use of the body, determined by positions of head, chest, abdomen, and back. (Reprinted with permission from Feldenkrais M: *Body and Mature Behavior*, p 104. International Universities Press, New York, 1949.)

GERSON THERAPY

Gerson therapy is an intensive, nutrition-based medical treatment. It works closely with nature to help the sick body rid itself of disease through the supportive effects of simple foods, juices, and nontoxic medication. Gerson therapy is named after the German physician Max Gerson (1881–1959), who cured himself of severe migraine headaches by avoiding salt, fats, and pickled and smoked foods and by eating fresh fruits and vegetables. He began to prescribe this new "migraine diet" to his patients. Gerson gained support for his methods from Nobel Prize winner Albert Schweitzer, M.D., by curing Schweitzer's wife of tuberculosis of the lung after she had failed to respond to all conventional therapy. The Gerson treatment consists of the daily consumption of 13 glasses of various fresh raw juices prepared hourly from organically grown fruits and vegetables. The dietary regimen also includes three full vegetarian meals, freshly prepared from organically grown vegetables, fruits, and whole grains.

HERBAL MEDICINE

Herbal medicine relies on plants to cure illnesses and to maintain health. It is the oldest known system of medicine and originated in China about 4000 B.C. Ancient texts of Chinese medicine are still in use, and modern Chinese medicine relies on herbs in addition to other methods, such as acupuncture, massage, diet, and exercise, to correct imbalances in the body. A Greco-Roman medical text by Dioscorides, *De Materia Medica,* describes the use of over 500 plants and herbs to cure disease.

The decline of herbal medicine in the late 20th century was related to scientific and technological advances that led to the use of synthetic pharmaceuticals; nevertheless, according to some estimates, at least 25 percent of current medicines are devised from the active ingredients of plants. The examples are many: digitalis from foxglove; ephedrine from ephedra; morphine from the opium poppy; taxol from the yew tree; quinine from the bark of the chinchona tree.

Herbal medicine is becoming more and more popular. Western herbalists use plants to treat various disorders related to the respiratory, gastrointestinal, cardiovascular, and nervous systems; like most prescription medicines, these plants contain active compounds that produce physiological effects. As a result, they must be used in appropriate doses if toxic results are to be prevented. Table 29–4 lists a variety of herbs with their safety profiles and medicinal uses.

About $1.5 billion a year are spent on herbal medicines, which are classified as dietary supplements. They are not subjected to Food and Drug Administration (FDA) approval, and there are no uniform standards for quality control or potency in herbal preparations. Indeed, some preparations have no active ingredients or are adulterated. The herbal industry attempts to regulate itself through organizations such as the Council for Responsible Nutrition and the American Herbal Association, but according to the Federal Trade Commission, fraudulent practices and false advertising still exist. The OAM is conducting spectrographic and other analyses on herbal medicine to determine the active ingredients that may account for a particular herb's efficacy.

HOMEOPATHY

Homeopathic healing was developed in the early 1800s by Samuel Hahnemann, M.D., a German physician (Fig. 29–5). It

Table 29–4
FDA Profile of Herbs Used in Tea[a]

Common Names	Botanical Name	Remarks
Arnica Arnica flowers Wolfsbane Leopard's bane Mountain tobacco	*Arnica montana*	Aqueous and alcoholic extracts of the plant contain, besides choline, two unidentified substances which affect the heart and vascular systems. Arnica is an active irritant which can produce violent toxic gastroenteritis, nervous disturbances, change in pulse rate, intense muscular weakness, collapse, and death.
Belladonna Deadly nightshade	*Atropa belladonna*	Poisonous plant which contains the toxic alkaloids, hyoscyamine, atropine, and hyoscine.
Bittersweet twigs Dulcamara Bittersweet Woody nightshade Climbing nightshade	*Solanum dulcamara*	Poisonous. Contains the toxic glycoalkaloid solanine, also solanidine and dulcamarin.
Bloodroot Sanguinaria Red puccoon	*Sanguinaris canadensis*	Contains the poisonous alkaloid sanguinarine, and other alkaloids
Broom-tops Scoparius Spartium Scotch broom Irish broom Broom	*Cystisus scoparius*	Contains toxic sparteine, isosparteine and other alkaloids, also hydroxytyramine.
Buckeyes Aesculus Horse chestnut	*Aesculus hippocastanum*	Contains a toxic coumarin glycoside, aesculin (esculin). A poisonous plant. Buckeyes have caused cattle death. Ingestion of horse chestnut has killed children.
Calamus Sweet flag Sweet root Sweet cinnamon Sweet cane	*Acorus calamus*	Oil of calamus. Jammu variety is a carcinogen.
Adam and Eve Puttyroot	*Aplectrum hyemale*	An American orchid. Has a sticky substance in its bulbs.
Areca Areca nut Betel nut	*Areca catechu*	Immense quantities of areca nut are consumed in the East. Areca nut is powerfully astringent and tends to contract the intestines. Owes its therapeutic uses almost entirely to the alkaloid arecoline.
Arrowroot Arrowroot starch Maranta	*Maranta arundinacea*	Mild; easily digested. Used for bowel complaints because of its demulcent properties.
Black cohosh Cimicifuga Black snakeroot Marocrotys Bugbane	*Cimicifuga racemosa*	No pharmacologic evidence of any therapeutic value.
Boneset Eupatorium Thoroughwort Vegetable antimony Feverwort Sweating plant Indian sage	*Eupatorium perfoliatum*	Has diaphoretic effect. Emetic and laxative in large doses.
Burdock Burdock root Lappa Beggar's buttons Hareburr	*Arctium lappa; Arctium minus*	No medicinal value.
Catnip Cataria Catnep Catmint	*Nepeta cataria*	Has been used as a sudorific.
Coltsfoot Farfara Coltsfoot leaves Tussilago leaves	*Tussilago farfara*	The only therapeutic value the leaves possess is a demulcent effect due to their musilage.

(continued)

Table 29–4 *(continued)*

Common Names	Botanical Name	Remarks
Echinacea Purple cornflower	*Echinacea angustifolia*	Colds and flu, stimulates immune system.
Hibiscus Musk mallow Musk okra	*Hibiscus abelmoschus*	Has showy flowers. Seeds were formerly considered stimulant and antispasmodic, but are now used only in perfumery. The Arabs flavor their coffee with them. *Hibiscus esculentus* is okra, bendee, or gumbo whose fruit is used for thickening soup.
Holy herb Cypress herb Lavender cotton	*Santolina chamaecyparissus*	Reputed anthelmintic. Stated to have long been used popularly against round worm in Scotland.
Holy-herb European vervain Blue vervain Enchanter's herb Enchanter's plant Herb-of-grace Herb-of-the-cross Juno's tears Pigeon grass Simpler's joy	*Verbena officinalis*	Herb is an astringent vulnerary. Leaves a substitute for Chinese tea.
Heliotrope	*Heliotropium europaeum*	A poisonous plant. It contains alkaloids which produce liver damage. Not to be confused with garden heliotrope (*Valeriana officinalis*).
Hemlock Conium poison hemlock Spotted hemlock Spotted parsley St. Bennet's herb Spotted cowbane Fool's parsley	*Conium maculatum*	Contains poisonous alkaloid, coniine, and four other closely related alkaloids. Often confused with water hemlock (*Cicuta maculata*). Not to be confused with Hemlock, Hemlock Spruce, etc. (*suga canadensis*)
Henbane Hyoscyamus Black henbane Hog's bean Poison tobacco Devil's eye	*Hyoscyamus niger*	Contains alkaloids, hyoscyamine, hyoscine (scopolamine), and atropine. A poisonous plant.
White snakeroot Snakeroot Richweed	*Eupatorium rugosum* (also called *W. ogeratoides* and *E. urticaefolium)*	Poisonous plant. Contains a toxic, unsaturated alcohol called tremetol combined with a resin acid. Causes the associated diseases of "trembles" in cattle and other livestock and of "milksickness" in human beings. Milksickness is produced by ingestion of milk, butter, or possibly meat from animals poisoned by ingestion of this plant.
Wormwood Absinthium Absinth Absinthe Madderwort Wermuch Mugwort Mingwort warmot Magenkraut Herba absinthii	*Artemisia absinthium*	Contains a volatile oil that alters mood and is a poison. Oil of wormwood is in absinthe.
Yohimbine Yohimbi	*Corynanthe yohimbe:* Pausinystali a Yohimbe	Contains the toxic alkaloid, yohimbine, and other alkaloids.
Horsetail Equisetum Scouring rush	*Equisetum hyemale*	Infusion of whole plant used sometimes in renal diseases but the diuretic action is very weak.
Hydrangea Seven-barks Wild hydrangea root Smooth hydrangea Mountain hydrangea	*Hydrangea arborescens*	Contains hydrangin, an alkaloid. At one time used in medicine in treatment of calculus in the bladder and cystitis but has been abandoned. Overdose is said to cause vertigo and feeling of oppression of the chest.
Hydrangea	*Hydrangea thunbergi*	Leaves used for tea called Ama-tsja or "Tea of Heaven" or Amacha (Sweet Tea) in Japan

Table 29–4 *(continued)*

Common Names	Botanical Name	Remarks
Job's tears Coix lacryma Semen lacrymae jobi	*Coix lacryma-jobi*	The seeds have been used in medicine either as a tincture or decoction in catarrhal infections in inflammation of the urinary passages. The seeds are reputed diuretic and lithontriptic. These seeds are used in some parts of the world, e.g., in China, for food under the name of adlay.
Kava-kava Kava methysticum	*Piper methysticum*	Natives of Sandwich Islands have used a beverage prepared from kava rhizome as an intoxicant. The intoxication is wholly unlike that caused by alcohol. Kava resin acts upon the spinal cord. Kava root, as long ago as 1857, was employed in treatment of gonorrhea and other conditions of the genitourinary tract.
Kinninkinnic Arbutus uva ursi Bearberry Red bearberry Barren myrtle Mountain box Rockberry	*Arctostaphylos uva-ursi*	The leaves contain two glycosides, arbutin (ursin) and ericolin, among other constituents. Has been used in treatment of acute cystitis probably acting as a mild antiseptic by yielding hydroquinine in the urine. Also has been employed as a diuretic.
Knotgrass Knotweed Prostate knotweed	*Polygonum aviculare*	Contains the glycosides, quercetin 3-arabinoside and avicularin. A mild astringent. Used in some countries of Europe as a home remedy for lung complaints, hemorrhoids, and rheumatism. Toward end of 19th century, Hernero Tea derived from it, was esteemed for treatment of asthma and bronchitis in Germany and Austria.
Life-everlasting Gnaphalium Pearl everlasting Cudweed	*Gnaphalium margaritaceum; Anaphilis margaritacea*	It is sometimes used as a tea in intestinal and pulmonary infection and externally in bruises, but it probably possesses little medicinal virtue.
Mastic gum Mastic Mastich Mastiche Mastix Pistacia galls	*Pistacia lentiscus*	Scarcely ever given internally except in certain cathartic pills. Varnish is made from it.
Mormon tea Brigham tea Teamaster's tea Mexican tea Mountain tea Whorehouse tea Desert tea Mormon plant Brigham weed Joint fir Mountain rush Shrubby horsetail Herb of the sun Popotillo	*Ephedra antisyphilitica* and other species of *Ephedra* of the western U.S. such as *Ephedra nevadensis*	Once used as an antisyphilitic. Also used as an astringent. A Chinese species, *Ephedra sinica,* called mahuang in China, contains the alkaloid ephedrine, a powerful decongestant.
Motherwort Leonurus	*Leonurus cardiaca*	An infusion is sometimes used in amenorrhea.
Nettles Urtica Nettle Common nettle Dwarf nettle Stinging nettle	*Urtica dioica; Urtica urens*	Were at one time used medicinally as local irritants and to arrest uterine hemorrhage.
Plantain	*Plantago major*	*The Dispensary of the United States of America,* 21st edition, p. 1432 (1926), stated, "The common plantain weed was formerly considered refrigerant, diuretic, and somewhat astringent. The ancients esteemed it highly, but it is at present never used, except externally in domestic practice as a stimulant application to sores. The leaves are applied whole or bruised in the form of a poultice."

(continued)

Table 29–4 *(continued)*

Common Names	Botanical Name	Remarks
Poke berries Pokeroot Phytolacca Poke Pocan Scoke American nightshade root	*Phytolacca americana; Phytolacca decandra*	Contains steroid saponin. Has slow emetic action of long duration. Narcotic effects have been observed. Has been employed internally in chronic rheumatism but is not therapeutically useful. Overdoses have sometimes been fatal.
Queen of the meadow Spiraea Meadow-sweet Meadow-queen	*Filipendula ulmaria: Spirae ulmaria*	Contains salicylic aldehyde, methyl salicylate, salicylic acid. Decoction of flowers was at one time used as a diuretic. The roots are astringent and have been used in treatment of diarrhea.
Rose of Jericho	*Anastatica heirochuntica*	There is no data for determining safety of this herb.
Saw palmetto Serenoa Saw palmetto berries Sabal	*Serenoa repens: Serenoa serrulata*	Saw Palmetto berries yield about 1.5% of oil composed of free fatty acids and ethyl esters of these acids. Claimed to exert a stimulant action upon mucous membrane of the genitourinary tract. Has been used in chronic and subacute cystitis and in cases of enlarged prostate.
Scullcap Scutellaria Skullcap Quaker bonnet Madweed Hoodwort Helmet flower	*Scutellaria lateriflora*	No medicinal properties. At one time used as a remedy in hydrophobia and in nervous diseases.
Senna Senna leaves Alexandria senna Tinnevelly senna India senna	*Cassia acutifolia; Cassia augustifolia*	Laxative. The usual dose of senna leaf is 2 grams. Used as a drug.

[a] In November 1975, the FDA completed a toxicological review of 171 herbs being offered for sale in brewing teas. In the FDS's opinion, 27 were unsafe, 53 were classified as being of undefined safety, and the remaining 91 were called safe.

is based on the concept that self-healing is a basic characteristic of human life and that special medications can aid this inherent process. The homeopathic pharmacopoeia is unique in several ways. First, there are over 2,000 medications, including plants, such as aconite, ergot, and hellebore; minerals, such as copper, gold, and iodine; and animals, such as snake and jellyfish venom and tissue extracts. Second, medications are prepared as tinctures, that is, mixed with 95 percent grain alcohol, or as pills with lactose fillers. Last, medications are dispersed in infinitesimally dilute solutions, such as $1{:}10^{20,000}$, which prevents the medication from being detected by conventional chemical methods. Homeopaths claim the therapeutic effect is based on "molecular medicine." Hahnemann based his drug treatment on the following assumptions: Medical substances elicit a standard array of signs and symptoms in healthy people; the medicine whose effect in normal people most closely resembles the illness being treated is the one most likely to initiate a curative response. This law of similars—*Similia similibus curantur* ("Let likes be cured by likes")—led to the coining of the word *homeopathy* ("similar experiences"). In traditional medicine, such highly dilute substances can have no effect, and no pharmacological research studies demonstrate the contrary. In the United States there are no longer any homeopathic medical schools (the last one was Hahnemann University Medical School, which closed in 1994); nevertheless, the practice of homeopathy is increasing in this country and around the world. In Europe, homeopathy has been popular throughout the 20th century.

Homeopathic medicines are sold over the counter in the United States; in 1992, sales were $200 million and have increased each year since then.

LIGHT AND MELATONIN THERAPY

Light therapy is based on the concept that humans are subject to circadian rhythms [from the Latin words *circa* ("around") and *dies* ("day")] that affect physiological processes in predictable ways. There are 24-hour cycles of rest and activity that include changing levels of corticosteroids, electrolyte excretion, and physiological processes; for instance, blood pressure is higher during the day than at night. By varying light exposure, circadian rhythms can be altered. The hormone melatonin, produced by the pineal gland, is highest in the bloodstream at night and low or absent during the daylight. Melatonin is believed to regulate sleep, and exogenous melatonin (available over the counter) produces drowsiness in normal people. Artificial bright-light therapy (over 2,500 lux) is a proven method used to treat depressive disorder with seasonal pattern (see Section 15.2), which is seen during the winter months when daylight hours are reduced.

FIGURE 29–5
Samuel Hahnemann. (Reprinted with permission from the New York Academy of Medicine, New York, NY.)

MACROBIOTICS

Macrobiotics [from the Greek words *makros* (''long'') and *bios* (''life'')] is a health practice that focuses on living in harmony with nature, using mainly a balanced diet. Macrobiotics became associated with the biblical patriarchs, the Chinese sages, and the Ethiopians of Africa, who were said to live 120 years or more. In 1797, a German physician and philosopher, Christoph W. Hufeland, M.D., wrote an influential book on diet and health titled *Macrobiotics or the Art of Prolonging Life.*

Macrobiotic foods are classified as yin (cold and wet) and yang (hot and dry); the goal is to keep yin and yang in balance. The diet consists of 50 percent grain products, 25 percent cooked or raw vegetables, 10 percent protein, 10 percent vegetable or fish soup, and 5 percent teas and fruits. Prolonged use of the diet may result in vitamin and mineral deficiencies.

MASSAGE

Massage is a treatment that involves manipulation of the soft tissues and the surfaces of the body. It was prescribed for the treatment of diseases over 5,000 years ago by Chinese physicians, and Hippocrates believed it to be a method of maintaining health.

Massage is believed to affect the body in several ways: It increases blood circulation, improves the flow of lymph through the lymphatic vessels, improves the tone of the musculoskeletal system, and has a tranquilizing effect on the mind.

Massage techniques have been described in various ways: stroking, kneading, pinching, rubbing, knuckling, tapping, or applying friction. Massage is most often done with the hands and fingers, but vibrating machines and electrical stimulation are also used. The different types of massage therapy that have evolved over the years are more similar than different. These include Swedish, Oriental, Shiatsu, and Esalen massages. Most people who experience massage find it physically and mentally restorative.

MEDITATION

Meditation is a technique that involves entering a trance state by focusing thought on a word or sound (a mantra), on an object, such as a burning candle, or on a movement, such as an oscillating disc. During the trance, the person experiences a state of calm. A meditative trance has physiological effects, all associated with decreased anxiety: Heart and respiratory rates slow, blood pressure decreases, and alpha brain waves increase.

Transcendental meditation (TM), developed by the Indian mystic Maharishi Majesh Yogi, was introduced into the United States in the 1950s. TM uses mantras based on personal characteristics to induce a trance state. In the 1960s, Herbert Benson, M.D., developed the *relaxation response,* which used mantras and breath control as a treatment for stress and stress-related disorders.

MOXIBUSTION

Moxibustion is based on theories of Oriental medicine in which energy forces are balanced by applying heat to stimulate specific acupoints. The heat is generated by burning dry *mugwort* leaves (*Artemisia vulgaris,* known as moxa). Heat is applied either directly or indirectly. In the direct method, dried moxa wool is rolled into small cones and placed on the skin. The tops of the cones are lit, but they are extinguished as soon as heat is felt. In the indirect method, a burning cigarlike moxa is held near the skin at acupoints.

Moxibustion is used in musculoskeletal disorder, arthritis, asthma, and eczema. As with many other alternative therapies, however, scientific clinical trials are not available as to its effectiveness.

NATUROPATHY

Naturopathy is a health care system intended to ensure a healthy mind and body based on three principles: maintaining pollution-free air and water supplies; eating healthy foods; and exercising regularly. The treatment is based on the belief that the body has the power to heal itself; it requires the patient's active participation in the health maintenance program.

Naturopathy developed in Germany in the later 19th century under the guidance of Benedict Lusz, who prescribed hydrotherapy as a form of natural healing. Lusz came to the United States, became an osteopathic physician, and founded the American School of Naturopathy in 1902. Since then, naturopathic medicine has grown into a major form of health care, which uses an eclectic group of methods in addition to hydrotherapy. These methods include eating specialized diets, breathing ionized air, using fomentations (the application of hot and cold compresses), taking colonic irrigations and enemas, drinking pollution-free water, eating foods grown organically, and using massage therapy, herbs, and rest therapy. Naturopaths are licensed in several states (Alaska, Connecticut, New Hampshire, among others), but because there is no standard regulation of the field, people with minimal or no educational background may call themselves naturopaths. This fact has contributed to the widespread belief that the field has many charlatans and quacks.

ORIENTAL MEDICINE

Oriental medicine is a broad term covering the traditional medicines of China, Korea, Japan, Vietnam, Tibet, and other Asian countries. In general, the techniques of Oriental medicine were first developed in China and include acupuncture, moxibustion, herbology, massage, cupping, gwa sha, breath work (qi gong), and exercise (tai chi). Chinese medicine is a coherent and independent system of thought and practice based on ancient texts. It is the result of a continuous process of critical thinking, extensive clinical observation, and testing and represents a thorough exposition of material by respected clinicians and theoreticians. It is rooted in philosophy, logic, sensibility, and habits of civilization foreign to Western civilization and is therefore difficult for Western physicians to understand. The basic theory is that there is a life force, called chi energy, and that this life force flows in us in a harmonious, balanced way. This harmony and balance signify health. When the life force is not flowing properly, disharmony and imbalance, or illness, is present.

OSTEOPATHY

The scope of osteopathy or osteopathic medicine is best indicated by the fact that doctors of osteopathy (D.O.s) are licensed to practice in every state, are accepted into medical, surgical, and psychiatric residency programs and the military on the same basis as M.D.s, are qualified to practice in every branch of clinical medicine, and take the same licensure examinations as M.D.s. Their medical education is identical to that of medical doctors, except that they have additional training in disorders of the musculoskeletal system, in which D.O.s consider themselves more knowledgeable than M.D.s. Fifteen osteopathic medical schools exist in the United States. Approximately 35,000 osteopaths treat about 20 million patients each year. Osteopathy was developed by Andrew Taylor Sill, M.D. (1828–1899), who founded the American School of Osteopathy in Kuksville, Ohio, in 1892. Disease is viewed in the same way as in allopathic medicine; however, special emphasis on proper musculoskeletal alignment is a prerequisite for health maintenance. Osteopaths may rely on the manipulation of body parts, particularly the craniosacral spinal axis, as part of a treatment plan. Osteopathic manipulation therapy is perceived as an adjunct, not a substitute, to traditional medical, surgical, and pharmacological intervention.

OZONE THERAPY

Ozone acts as an antioxidant and disinfectant and is used conventionally for water purification, odor control, and air purification. Ozone therapy is based on the assumption that most illness is caused by viral and bacterial infection; ozone is used to treat medical conditions that range from influenza to cancer and AIDS. The first ozone generators were developed by Werner von Siemens in Germany in 1857, and ozone was used therapeutically to purify blood shortly thereafter in Germany and other European countries.

Ozone therapy introduces ozone into the body in various ways. Some of these include drinking ozonated water; ozone limb bagging, in which ozone is pumped into an airtight bag that covers an arm or leg; breathing ozone bubbled through olive oil or topically applying ozonated olive oil; insufflations, in which a catheter is inserted into the rectum or vagina with ozone administered at a slow flow rate; and autohemotherapy, in which a person's own ozonized blood is reintroduced into the body.

PAST LIFE MEDICINE

In past life medicine, the healing process is aided by contact with spiritual beings who are believed to have the ability to reverse illness and maintain health. The spirits are approached through the use of altered states of consciousness, channeling, higher states of awareness, and transmissions from spiritually evolved beings.

REFLEXOLOGY

Reflexology is the gentle massaging of the feet, hands, and ears to stimulate the body's natural healing power. It is used to alleviate tension by clearing crystalline deposits under the skin that may interfere with the natural flow of the body's energy. Reflexologists believe that all body parts can be mapped out on the soles or sides of the feet; for instance, the tip of the second toe represents the eye. By applying pressure to a particular area of the foot, disorders related to the represented body parts can be relieved (Fig. 29–6).

REIKI

Reiki is a Japanese word with the general meaning of "healing." (*Rei* means "universal" or "spiritual," and *Ki* is "life force energy.") This energy is used during Reiki healing; but the actual methodology employed is known as the Usui natural healing system (sometimes written as Usui Shiki Ryoho), from the name of the individual who developed the healing system that uses Reiki energy.

In a Reiki healing session, the practitioner places his or her hands onto the patient's body at several strategic points. The patient feels the energy begin to flow as heat, cold, or a strange "flow" through the body, often in places remote from the point at which it is needed; it flows to the point where it can do most good. Reiki is used to help all types of ailments, both physical and mental, but its most profound effect is an almost immediate feeling of relaxation, resulting in a deep reduction of stress. Some practitioners claim that they can even send

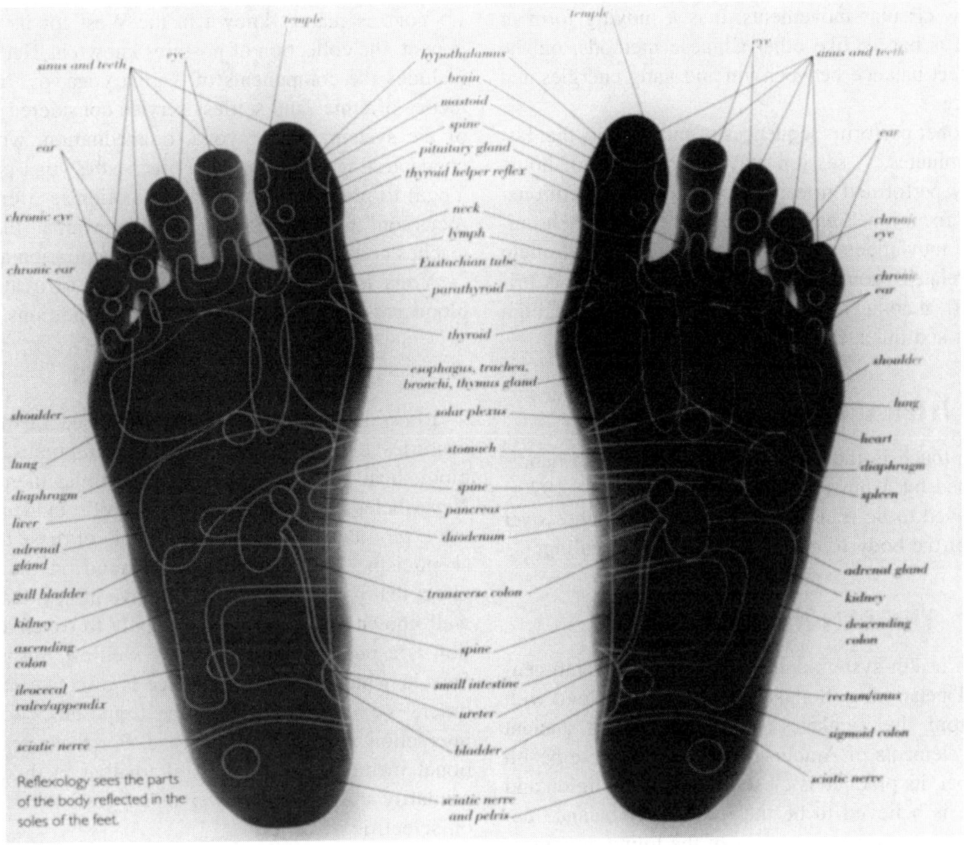
temple
eye
sinus and teeth
ear
chronic eye
chronic ear
shoulder
lung
diaphragm
liver
adrenal gland
gall bladder
kidney
ascending colon
ileocecal valve/appendix
sciatic nerve
Reflexology sees the parts of the body reflected in the soles of the feet.
temple
hypothalamus
brain
mastoid
spine
pituitary gland
thyroid helper reflex
neck
lymph
Eustachian tube
parathyroid
thyroid
esophagus, trachea, bronchi, thymus gland
solar plexus
stomach
spine
pancreas
duodenum
transverse colon
spine
small intestine
ureter
bladder
sciatic nerve and pelvis
temple
eye
sinus and teeth
ear
chronic eye
chronic ear
shoulder
lung
heart
diaphragm
spleen
adrenal gland
kidney
descending colon
rectum/anus
sigmoid colon
sciatic nerve

FIGURE 29–6
Reflexology points of the feet. (Reprinted with permission from Shealy CN, editor: *The Complete Family Guide to Alternative Medicine: An Illustrated Encyclopedia of Natural Healing,* p 52. Barnes & Noble Books, New York, 1996.)

Reiki over a distance—sometimes thousands of miles—to achieve a healing effect.

ROLFING

Rolfing is a type of massage that was developed by an American biochemist, Ida Rolf (1896–1979), to relieve tension in muscle, connective tissue, and fascia, which is the cause of musculoskeletal diseases such as arthritis and fibromyalgia. Therapy consists of deep, sometimes painful, massage to produce flexible planes between muscle groups throughout the body. Rolf discovered that she could achieve remarkable changes in posture and structure by manipulating the body's myofascial system; as various parts of the body are massaged, past memories and emotional states are often released. In this sense rolfing is a psychophysiological experience.

SHAMANISM

Shamanism refers to a practice of spiritual healing that has been used in some primitive societies. Illness is believed to be caused by spirits either stealing or possessing the soul of the sick person. The shaman intervenes by entering a trance, traveling to the spirit world, and consulting with the spirits. The shaman negotiates with spirits for the return of the sufferer's soul or exorcises the evil spirit that has possessed the patient. In some cases, a shamanic seance may last for many hours; the smoke-laden air, rhythmic drumbeats, and voices of animal helpers in the tent (produced by the shaman who may be an expert ventriloquist) can have a potent psychological affect on a suggestible person who accepts the situation as reality.

SOUND THERAPY

Sound therapy is an ancient technique in which sounds, such as chants, bell rings, or drum beats, are used to create vibrations in the body and believed to have healing powers. Practitioners claim that a sense of relaxation can also be achieved. Sound therapy is used in Ayurveda to promote health, with claims of reducing tumor growth by using certain sounds known as Sama Veda.

Music therapy uses the sound of musical instruments such as the flute, to achieve similar results. In the Bible, David attempted to treat King Saul's depression by playing the harp.

TAI CHI CHUAN

Tai chi chuan, or Tai chi, is one of the most popular Asian movement arts used in the West. This ancient Chinese technique is designed to increase the life force in the body through a series of slow circular movements. It is a moving form of meditation and is based, like other Chinese methods, on the search for perfect balance between yin and yang energies and chi, or life force.

The practitioner performs sequences of movements that last from 5 to 30 minutes. A session may last a couple of hours and is typically performed in early morning. The practitioner is expected to focus on breathing and its precise synchronization with the movements. Tai chi chuan is believed to help mainly stress-related problems and conditions and so is primarily used to treat anxiety, depression, muscular tension, high blood pressure, and other cardiovascular conditions.

THERAPEUTIC TOUCH

Therapeutic touch is the technique of healing with hands. It was developed by a nurse, Dolores Krieger, in the 1970s. Energy is believed to be transferred by laying the hands over specific parts of the body to aid in the process of healing.

TIBETAN MEDICINE

The Tibetan health system dates to about the seventh century A.D. The Tibetan king, Songsten Gampo, is credited with its creation from the synthesis of various, more ancient sources. It has elements of Arabic, Indian, and Chinese health systems. In Tibet, its practice is closely related to religion and magic. Disease is believed to be the result of imbalance between the three components or humors of the living organism: wind (breathing and movement in general), bile (related to digestion and temperament), and phlegm (related to sleep, joint mobility, and skin elasticity). Imbalance can be caused by ignorance of health principles, environmental assaults, or improper diet. Treatment consists of restoring the balance between the different humors through the use of herbal medicine and accessory therapies, such as massage, moxibustion, acupuncture, appropriate diet, religious rituals, and purification techniques.

TRAGER METHOD

The Trager method, developed by Milton Trager, M.D., in Chicago, is a technique of movement reduction to aid individuals suffering from polio and other neuromuscular disorders. The client, in typical 60- to 90-minute sessions, is instructed to relax all conscious muscles and to allow the unconscious to choose natural, less restrictive body movements, as guided by the practitioner. This method is particularly suitable to individuals with back pain and severe restrictions of movement.

YOGA

Yoga (''yoking'' or ''union'' in Sanskrit) is a comprehensive philosophical system that has the goal of preparing an individual to unite with the supreme being. The technique of early Yoga seeks to bring into balance all the disparate aspects of body, mind, and personality. Early evidence of yoga practice dates back to 5,000 years ago in India and has been practiced as a religion and health system ever since.

Yoga is mainly known in the West for its physical component, the collection of postures known as Hatha Yoga. Yoga includes the components of Karma yoga, or ''dos,'' with the theory of ethics and selfless service considered the foundation of the system; Bhakti yoga, or meditation, with the goal of concentrating on the spirit by using the yoga postures (Hatha Yoga) to prepare the body to sit motionless, remain alert, and focus on the meditation; and Pranayama, the system that teaches correct breathing to help concentration and meditation.

Yoga is used to reduce stress and to treat anxiety, high blood pressure, and musculoskeletal conditions.

CONCLUSION

Many systems of treatment discussed in this chapter are centuries old, and it would be presumptuous for traditional biomedical practitioners to lightly dismiss them as worthless. Nevertheless, without rigorous scientific evidence to the contrary, physicians must approach many of these treatments with skepticism. The influence of the mind on the body and the effect that psychological factors have in health and disease are well known to physicians, especially to psychiatrists. Suggestion is a potent remedy, and the well-established placebo effect, in which an inert substance is effective in curing a disorder, serves to confirm the importance of mind–body interaction in health and disease. For these reasons, conventional medicine views most alternative methods as effective primarily through the power of suggestion rather than based on scientific evidence.

A new era, however, may be emerging. OAM is now funding studies on mind–body techniques and on each of the alternative systems discussed (as well as many others not mentioned) to see whether they can withstand the rigors of controlled clinical trials, including precise measures of outcome.

Currently, more than 35 medical schools in the United States offer courses in alternative therapies. Many have developed centers for alternative medicine research, with professors of mind–body medicine drawn largely from the ranks of such traditional specialities as internal medicine and psychiatry. This trend is likely to continue with the goal of determining which of the many existing alternative medical systems have scientific merit. Only when and if they can withstand rigorous clinical trials can certain of these techniques be integrated into medicine. At present, physicians should be informed of these various techniques, even though most are not acceptable methods of treatment.

REFERENCES

Anderson S, Lundeberg T: Acupuncture—from empiricism to science: Functional background to acupuncture effects in pain and disease. Med Hypotheses *45:* 271, 1995.

Aular JJ: Alternative cancer treatments. Sci Am *275:* 162, 1996.

Chan K: Progress in traditional Chinese medicine. Trends Pharmacol Sci *16:* 182, 1995.

Consumer Reports staff: Herbal roulette. Consumer Rep *60:* 698, 1995.

Der Marderosian AH: Understanding homeopathy. Am J Pharm Assoc *NS36:* 317, 1996.

Field T: Massage therapy for infants and children. J Dev Behav Pediatr *16:* 105, 1995.

Tyler VE: *Herbs of Choice: The Therapeutic Use of Phytomedicinals.* Pharmaceutical Products Press, New York, 1994.

Zhu YP, Woergenbag HJ: Traditional Chinese herbal medicine. Pharm World Sci *17:* 103, 1995.

30

Relational Problems

The fourth edition of *Diagnostic and Statistical Manual of Mental Disorders* (DSM-IV) defines relational problems as ''patterns of interaction between or among members of a relational unit.'' These patterns may be associated with significantly impaired functioning in one or more members of the group or in the entire unit. The problems may complicate the treatment of a mental disorder or medical condition in one or more members of the unit, or they may be the result of a mental disorder or medical condition. They may be independent of other conditions or may occur in the absence of other conditions. Most people live in a matrix of relationships. In relationships people find sources of comfort, connection, and happiness but also of obligation, responsibility, and friction. The ability to function in a variety of relationships can be stressed by psychological problems as well as by external events such as illnesses, wars, natural disasters, economic crises, and social changes. People can feel isolated and depressed at the loss or lack of relationships.

No reliable figures are available on the prevalence of relational problems. One can assume they are ubiquitous; however, most relational problems resolve without professional intervention. The nature, frequency, and effects of the problem on those involved are elements that need to be taken into account before a diagnosis of relational problem is made. For example, divorce, which occurs in just under 50 percent of marriages, is a problem between partners that is resolved though the legal remedy of divorce and need not be diagnosed as a relational problem. However, if the persons are unable to resolve the disputation between them and continue to live together in a sadomasochistic or pathologically depressed relationship with unhappiness and abuse, then they should be so labeled. Relationship problems that cannot be resolved by friends, family, or clergy of the persons involved will need professional intervention by psychiatrists, clinical psychologists, social workers, and other mental health professionals.

RELATIONAL PROBLEM RELATED TO A MENTAL DISORDER OR GENERAL MEDICAL CONDITION

According to DSM-IV, clinicians should use the category of relational problems related to a mental disorder or general medical condition when the focus of clinical attention is a pattern of impaired interaction associated with a mental disorder or a general medical condition in a family member.

Adults must often assume the responsibility of caring for aging parents while they are still caring for their own children, and this dual obligation can create stress. When adults take care of their parents, both parties must adapt to a reversal of their former roles, and the caretakers not only face the potential loss of their parents, but must cope with evidence of their own mortality.

Some caretakers abuse their aging parents—a problem that is now receiving attention. Abuse is most likely to occur when the caretaking offspring have substance abuse problems, are under economic stress, and have no relief from their caretaking duties or when the parent is bedridden or has a chronic illness requiring constant nursing attention. More women are abused than are men, and most abuse occurs in people over age 75.

The development of a chronic illness in a family member stresses the family system and requires adaptation on the part of the sick person and the other family members. The person who has become sick must frequently face a loss of autonomy, an increased sense of vulnerability, and sometimes a taxing medical regimen. The other family members must experience the loss of the person as he or she was before the illness, and they usually have substantial caretaking responsibility—for example, in debilitating neurological diseases, including dementia of the Alzheimer's type, and in diseases such as acquired immune deficiency syndrome (AIDS) and cancer. In these cases, the whole family must deal with the stress of prospective death as well as the current illness. Some families use the anger engendered by such situations to create support organizations, increase public awareness of the disease, and rally around the sick member. But chronic illness frequently produces depression in family members and may cause them to withdraw from or to attack one another. The burden of caring for ill family members falls disproportionately on the women in a family—mothers, daughters, and daughters-in-law.

Chronic emotional illness also requires major adaptations by families. For instance, family members may react with chaos or fear to the psychotic productions of a family member with schizophrenia. The schizophrenic person's regression, exaggerated emotions, frequent hospitalizations, and economic and social dependence can stress the family system. Family members may react with hostile feelings (referred to as expressed emotion) that are associated with a poor prognosis for the person who is sick. Similarly, a family member with bipolar I disorder can disrupt a family, particularly during manic episodes.

Family devastation can occur when illness suddenly strikes a previously healthy person, when illness occurs earlier than expected in the life cycle (some impairment of physical capacities is expected in old age, although many older people are healthy), when illness affects the economic stability of the family, and when little can be done to improve or ease the condition of the sick family member.

PARENT–CHILD RELATIONAL PROBLEM

Parent–child problems may refer to those of a parent or a child or both; these conflicts often fall within the range of the normal developmental stages or crises of each person. According to DSM-IV, this category applies to cases in which the focus of clinical attention is a pattern of interaction between parent and child associated with clinically significant impairment in individual or family functioning or with clinically significant symptoms. Examples include impaired communication, overprotection, and inadequate discipline.

Difficulties in many situations stress the usual parent–child interaction. In a family in which the parents are divorced, parent–child problems may arise in the relationship with either the custodial or the noncustodial parent. The remarriage of a divorced or widowed parent can also lead to a parent–child problem. The resentment of a stepparent and the favoring of a natural child are usual reactions in a new family's initial phases of adjustment. When a second child is born, both familial stress and happiness may result. The birth of a child can also be troublesome when parents had adopted a child in the belief that they were infertile.

Other situations that may produce a parent–child problem are the development of fatal, crippling, or chronic illness, such as leukemia, epilepsy, sickle-cell anemia, or spinal cord injury, in either a parent or a child. The birth of a child with congenital defects, such as cerebral palsy, blindness, and deafness, may also produce parent–child problems. These situations, which are not rare, challenge the emotional resources of those involved. Parents and child must face present and potential loss and must adjust their day-to-day lives physically, economically, and emotionally. These situations can strain the healthiest families and produce parent–child problems not just with the sick person but also with the unaffected family members. In a family with a severely sick child, parents may resent, prefer, or neglect the other children because the ill child requires so much time and attention.

Parents with children who have emotional disorders face particular problems, depending on the child's illness. In families with a schizophrenic child, family treatment is beneficial and improves the social adjustment of the patient. Similarly, family therapy is of use if there is a child with mood disorder. In families with a substance-abusing child or adolescent, involvement of the family is crucial to help provide control of the drug-seeking behavior and to allow family members to verbalize feelings of frustration and anger that are invariably present.

Day Care Centers

Quality of care during the first 3 years of life is crucial to neuropsychological development. A 1997 study from the National Institute of Child Health and Human Development indicated that day care was not harmful to children, provided that the caregivers and day care teachers provided consistent, empathetic, nurturing care. Unfortunately, not all day care centers can meet that level of care, especially those located in poor urban areas. Children receiving less than optimal caring show decreased intellectual and verbal skills that indicate delayed neurocognitive development. They may also become irritable, anxious, or depressed, which interferes with the parent-child bonding experience, and as mentioned earlier, they are less assertive and less effectively toilet trained by the age of 5.

Currently, over 55 percent of women are in the work force, many of whom have no choice but to place their children in day care centers. Approximately 40 percent of entering medical students are women; unfortunately, very few medical centers make adequate provisions for on-site day care centers for their students or staff. Similarly, corporations need to provide on-site, high-quality care for the children of their employees. Not only will that approach benefit the children, but corporate economic benefits will accrue as a result of reduced absenteeism, increased productivity, and happier working mothers. Such programs have the added benefit of decreasing stresses on marriages.

PARTNER RELATIONAL PROBLEM

According to DSM-IV, clinicians should use this category when the focus of clinical attention is a pattern of interaction between the spouses or partners. These patterns are characterized by negative communication (such as criticisms), distorted communication (such as unrealistic expectations), or noncommunication (such as withdrawal), associated with clinically significant impairment in individual or family functioning or symptoms in one or both partners.

When people have partner relational problems, psychiatrists must assess whether a patient's distress arises from the relationship or from a mental disorder. Mental disorders are more common in single people—those who never married or who are widowed, separated, or divorced—than among married people. Clinicians should evaluate developmental, sexual, and occupational and relationship histories, for purposes of diagnosis.

(Divorce is discussed in Chapter 2, Section 2.5, and couples therapy is discussed in Chapter 34, Section 34.4.)

Marriage demands a sustained level of adaptation from both partners. In a troubled marriage, a therapist can encourage the partners to explore areas such as the extent of communication between the partners, their ways of solving disputes, their attitudes toward childbearing and child rearing, their relationships with their in-laws, their attitudes toward social life, their handling of finances, and the couple's sexual interaction. The birth of a child, an abortion or miscarriage, economic stresses, moves to new areas, episodes of illness, major career changes, and any situations that involve a significant change in marital roles can precipitate stressful periods in a relationship. Illness in a child exerts the greatest strain on a marriage, and marriages in which a child has died through illness or accident more often than not end in divorce. Complaints of life-long anorgasmia or impotence by marital partners are usually indicative of intrapsychic problems, although sexual dissatisfaction is involved in many cases of marital maladjustment.

Adjustment to marital roles can be a problem when partners are of different backgrounds and have grown up with different value systems. For example, members of low socioeconomic status groups perceive a wife as making most of the decisions in the family, and they accept physical punishment as a way to discipline children. Middle-class people perceive family decision-making processes as shared, with the husband often being the final arbiter, and they prefer to discipline children verbally.

Problems involving conflicts in values, adjustment to new roles, and poor communication are most effectively handled when therapist and partners examine the couple's relationship, as in marital therapy.

A 30-year-old male chemist was referred to a psychiatrist by his internist because the patient wanted to talk to someone about his shaky marriage. During 5 years of courtship and 2 years of marriage, the couple had had numerous separations, usually precipitated by the patient's dissatisfaction. Although he and his wife shared many interests and, until recently, had had a satisfactory sexual relationship, he thought that his wife was basically cold and self-centered with no real concern about his career or his feelings. His dissatisfactions periodically exploded into fights, which often ended in temporary separations. He then felt lonely and came "crawling back" to her. Their relationship was currently one of "icy separateness," and the patient seemed to be seeking support to make a permanent break. Although he was in distress because of his marital situation and frequently choked back tears, he showed no evidence of difficulties with his other interpersonal relationships. He had many good friends, functioned well in his job, and denied symptoms other than distress about his marital situation.

Physician Marriages

Physicians have a higher risk of divorce than other occupational groups. A study reported in the *New England Journal of Medicine* (March 13, 1997) showed that the incidence of divorce among physicians was 29 percent. Specialty choice influenced divorce. The highest rate of divorce occurred in psychiatrists (50 percent), followed by surgeons (33 percent) and internists, pediatricians, and pathologists (31 percent). The average age of first marriages was 26 years among all groups.

It is not clear why physicians (including psychiatrists) are at high risk for divorce. Factors implicated include the stresses of dealing with dying patients, making life and death decisions, working long hours, and the constant risk of malpractice litigation. Such stressors may predispose physicians to a variety of emotional ills, with the most common being depression and substance abuse, including alcoholism. Such persons are unable, generally, to deal with the complex interactions required to maintain successful long-term relationships of any kind, with marriage requiring the most interpersonal skills of all.

SIBLING RELATIONAL PROBLEM

According to DSM-IV, clinicians should use this category when the focus of clinical attention is a pattern of sibling interaction associated with clinically significant impairment in individual or family functioning or symptoms in one or more siblings.

Problems arising from sibling rivalry can occur with the birth of a child and can recur as the children grow up. Competition among children for the attention, affection, and esteem of their parents is a fact of family life. This rivalry can extend to others who are not siblings and can remain a factor in normal and abnormal competitiveness throughout life. In some families, children receive labels early in life, such as "the good child" or "the black sheep," and they may turn these labels into self-fulfilling prophesies. In good sibling relationships, the pleasures of companionship and the bonds created by kinship and shared experiences outweigh feelings of rivalry.

RELATIONAL PROBLEM NOT OTHERWISE SPECIFIED

According to DSM-IV, clinicians should use this category when clinical attention is focused on relational problems not classifiable by any of the specific problems previously noted. Problems may arise in relationships with romantic partners, coworkers, neighbors, teachers, students, friends, and social groups, causing enough strain to bring a person into contact with the mental health care system.

Racial and religious prejudices can cause problems in interpersonal relationships. Some social scientists believe that racism and religious bigotry have only a weak psychological base, and they emphasize social and class factors as causative. Other investigators view prejudice as a learned attitude and consider it a cultural variant. Several psychiatrists think that people are motivated to change their prejudices only if they see them as part of a mental disorder. When prejudice is a maladaptive defense built to protect the prejudiced person from profound feelings of inadequacy, it involves the projection of unwanted and devalued attributes onto the blamed group.

REFERENCES

Arrby G, Giota J: Parental conceptions of quality in daycare centers in relation to quality measured by the ECERS. Early Child Dev Care *110:* 1, 1995.

Barth JM, Parke RD: Parent–child relationship influences on children's transition to school. Merrill Palmer Q *39:* 173, 1993.

Brody GH, Stoneman Z, Gauger K: Parent–child relationships, family problem-solving behavior, and sibling relationship quality: The moderating role of sibling temperaments. Child Dev *67* (3): 1289, 1996.

Cook WL: Interdependence and the interpersonal sense of control: An analysis of family relationships. J Pers Soc Psychol *64:* 587, 1993.

Galambos NL: Parent–adolescent relations. Curr Direct Psychol Sci *1:* 146, 1992.

Gonzales NA, Cauce AM, Friedman RJ, Mason CA: Family, peer, and neighborhood influences on academic achievement among African-American adolescents: One-year prospective effects. Am J Community Psychol *24* (3): 365, 1996.

Hetherington EM, Clingempeel WG: Coping with marital transitions: A family system perspective. Monogr Soc Res Child Dev *57:* 1, 1992.

Hibbs ED, Hamburger SD, Kruesi MJ, Lenane M: Factors affecting expressed emotion in parents of ill and normal children. Am J Orthopsychiatry *63:* 103, 1993.

Jacob T, Leonard K: Sequential analysis of marital interactions involving alcoholic, depressed, and nondistressed men. J Abnorm Psychol *101:* 647, 1992.

Jouriles EN, Farris AM: Effects of marital conflict on subsequent parent–son interactions. Behav Ther *23:* 355, 1992.

Krauss MW: Child-related and parenting stress: Similarities and differences between mothers and fathers of children with disabilities. Am J Ment Retard *97:* 393, 1993.

Leach P, Eyer DE: Women's behavior: Do mothers harm their children when they work outside the home? In *Women, Men, & Gender: Ongoing Debates,* MR Walsh, editor, p 383. Yale University Press, New Haven, CT, 1997.

Legazpi-Blair MC, Blair SL: Choice of child care and mother–child interaction: Racial/ethnic distinctions in the maternal experience. In *American Families: Issues in Race and Ethnicity*. CK Jacobson, editor, p 261. Garland Publishing, New York, 1995.

Manne SL, Jacobsen PB, Gorfinkle K, Gerstein F: Treatment adherence difficulties among children with cancer: The role of parenting style. J Pediatr Psychol *18:* 47, 1993.

Newman J: The more the merrier? Effects of family size and sibling spacing on sibling relationships. Child Care Health Dev *22* (5): 285, 1996.

Oliver JM, Berger LS: Depression, parent–offspring relationships, and cognitive vulnerability. J Soc Behav Pers *7:* 415, 1992.

Pruchno R, Kleban MH: Caring for an institutionalized parent: The role of coping strategies. Psychol Aging *8:* 18, 1993.

Robinson BE: Relationship between work addiction and family functioning: Clinical implications for marriage and family therapists. J Fam Psychother *7* (3): 13, 1996.

Sternberg KJ, Lamb ME, Greenbaum C, Cicchetti D: Effects of domestic violence on children's behavior problems and depression. Dev Psychol *29:* 44, 1993.

Takigiku SK, Brubaker TH, Hennon CB: A contextual model of stress among parent caregivers of gay sons with AIDS. AIDS Educ Prev *5:* 25, 1993.

Tuttle DH, Cornell DG: Maternal labeling of gifted children: Effects on the sibling relationship. Except Child *59:* 402, 1993.

31

Problems Related to Abuse or Neglect

The fourth edition of *Diagnostic and Statistical Manual of Mental Disorders* (DSM-IV) describes problems related to abuse or neglect as categories that clinicians should use to focus on the ''mistreatment of one individual by another through physical abuse, sexual abuse, or child neglect.'' Because problems of abuse and neglect beset people whom health professionals frequently see, these categories are coded according to whether the person under treatment is the perpetrator, the victim, or a member of the family unit. The specific problems described in DSM-IV are physical abuse of child, sexual abuse of child, neglect of child, physical abuse of adult, and sexual abuse of adult (Table 31–1). A general term used by many child psychiatrists to describe abuse of children is child maltreatment.

CHILD ABUSE AND NEGLECT

Girls and boys of all ages, ethnic groups, and socioeconomic levels experience alarmingly high rates of child abuse and neglect, which are associated with a wide range of emotional problems and psychiatric symptoms. Children who are beaten or burned, repeatedly sexually assaulted, or deprived of food, clothing, and shelter may perish or may survive to struggle with the consequences. In most cases of persistent incest, sexually abused children are threatened with further abuse or abandonment if they disclose the family secrets; such treatment leaves them in the irreconcilable position of silently enduring continued abuse or risking the total loss of their families.

Children who have been physically or sexually abused exhibit many psychiatric disturbances, including anxiety, aggressive behavior, paranoid ideation, posttraumatic stress disorder, depressive disorders, and an increased risk of suicidal behavior. Abuse seems to increase the risk of psychiatric disturbances in already vulnerable children, and abused children of parents with psychopathology are more likely to experience a mental disorder than are children of psychiatrically disturbed parents who are not abused. Children who have been sexually abused reportedly have an increased frequency of poor self-esteem, depression, dissociative disorders, and substance abuse. Chronic maltreatment appears to promote aggressive and violent behavior in vulnerable children.

Epidemiology

According to the National Committee for the Prevention of Child Abuse, about 3 million cases of child abuse and neglect were reported to public social service agencies in 1994; of this number, about 1 million cases were substantiated. Each year in the United States, child abuse and neglect cause 2,000 to 4,000 deaths, and each year 150,000 to 200,000 new cases of sexual abuse are reported. An estimated one of every three to four girls and an estimated one of every seven to eight boys will be sexually assaulted by the age of 18 years. The actual occurrence rates are likely to be higher than these estimates, because many maltreated children go unrecognized, and many are reluctant to report the abuse. Of these children who are physically abused, 32 percent are less than 5 years of age; 27 percent are between 5 and 9 years; 27 percent are between 10 and 14 years; and 14 percent are between 15 and 18 years. More than 50 percent of all abused and neglected children were born prematurely or had low birth weights. Most child maltreatment is at the hands of parents (75 percent), other relatives (15 percent), or an unrelated caretaker (10 percent).

Sexual attacks on children by groups of other children have recently increased. Of 1,600 young offenders whose cases of sexual abuse of other children were analyzed by a university abuse-prevention center, more than 25 percent had started before the age of 12 years. Group leaders had often been abused themselves. However, followers seemed to succumb to peer pressure and to a society that glamorizes violence and links violence with sex.

Etiology

Many factors contribute to child abuse and neglect. Abusive parents have themselves often been victims of physical and sexual abuse and of long-term exposure to violent home lives of pain and physical torment, which are powerful promoters of aggression. Thus, parents brought up with harsh corporal punishment and cruel treatment by their own families may continue the abuse tradition with their children. In some cases, adults believe that their methods are acceptable ways of teaching discipline. In other cases, parents are ambivalent about their methods of abusive parenting but find themselves without coping mechanisms and so fall into behaviors similar to those of their own parents.

Stressful living conditions, such as overcrowding and poverty, can contribute to aggressive behavior and may contribute to physical abuse toward children. Social isolation, the lack of a support system, and parental substance abuse increase the potential for abusive and neglectful treatment of children. When such environmental crises as unemployment, housing problems, and lack of finances heighten stress levels in vulnerable families, neglect or abuse may ensue. Mental disorders can play a role in child abuse and neglect insofar as a parent's judgment and thought processes may be impaired. Parents who

Table 31–1
DSM-IV Problems Related to Abuse or Neglect

Physical Abuse of Child
This category should be used when the focus of clinical attention is physical abuse of a child.

Sexual Abuse of Child
This category should be used when the focus of clinical attention is sexual abuse of a child.

Neglect of Child
This category should be used when the focus of clinical attention is child neglect.

Physical Abuse of Adult
This category should be used when the focus of clinical attention is physical abuse of an adult (eg, spouse beating, abuse of elderly parent).

Sexual Abuse of Adult
This category should be used when the focus of clinical attention is sexual abuse of an adult (eg, sexual coercion, rape).

are depressed or psychotic or who have severe personality disorders may view their children as bad or as trying to drive them crazy.

Certain characteristics may increase a child's vulnerability to neglect and physical and sexual abuse. Children who are premature, mentally retarded, or physically disabled and those who cry excessively or are unusually demanding—the so-called difficult child—may be at high risk for abuse or neglect. Many abused children are perceived by their parents as being different, slow in development, bad, selfish, or hard to discipline. Children who are hyperactive are particularly vulnerable to abuse, especially when they are born to parents with limited capacities for nurturant behavior. The child who is the object of physical abuse is also known as the battered child.

The perpetrator of physical abuse is more often the mother than the father. One parent is usually the active batterer, and the other passively accepts the battering. Of a group of perpetrators studied, 80 percent were regularly living in the homes of the children they abused. More than 80 percent of the children studied were living with married parents, and about 20 percent were living with a single parent. The average age of a mother who abuses her children is reported to be around 26 years; the father's average age is 30 years. Many abused children come from poor homes, and the families tend to be socially isolated.

Abusive parents have inappropriate expectations of their children, with a reversal of dependence needs. Parents treat an abused child as if the child were older than the parents. A parent often turns to the child for reassurance, nurturing, comfort, and protection and expects a loving response. Ninety percent of such parents were severely physically abused by their own mothers or fathers.

Men usually perpetrate sexual abuse, although women acting in concert with men or alone are also involved, especially in child pornography. Men are the perpetrators in about 95 percent of cases of sexual abuse of girls and about 80 percent of cases of sexual abuse of boys. Perpetrators of sexual abuse are usually known to the child and in many cases have been victims of physical or sexual abuse. In some circumstances, pedophilia is a factor: The adult perpetrator is more aroused by children than by adult partners. Many times, however, the perpetrator has no preference for child sexual partners. In some cases sexual abuse is mixed with physical abuse.

Diagnosis and Clinical Features

Physical Abuse of Child. Clinicians must always consider physical abuse when a child shows bruises or injuries that cannot be adequately explained or that are incompatible with the history that the parent gives. Suspicious physical indicators are bruises and marks that form symmetrical patterns, such as injuries to both sides of the face and regular patterns on the back, buttocks, and thighs; accidental injuries are unlikely to result in symmetrical patterns. Bruises may have the shape of the instrument used to make them, such as a belt buckle or a cord. Burns by cigarettes result in symmetrical, round scars, and immersions in boiling water produce burns that look like socks or gloves or that are doughnut-shaped. Physical aggression can cause multiple and spiral fractures, especially in a young baby; retinal hemorrhages in an infant may be due to shaking.

Children repeatedly brought to hospitals for treatment of

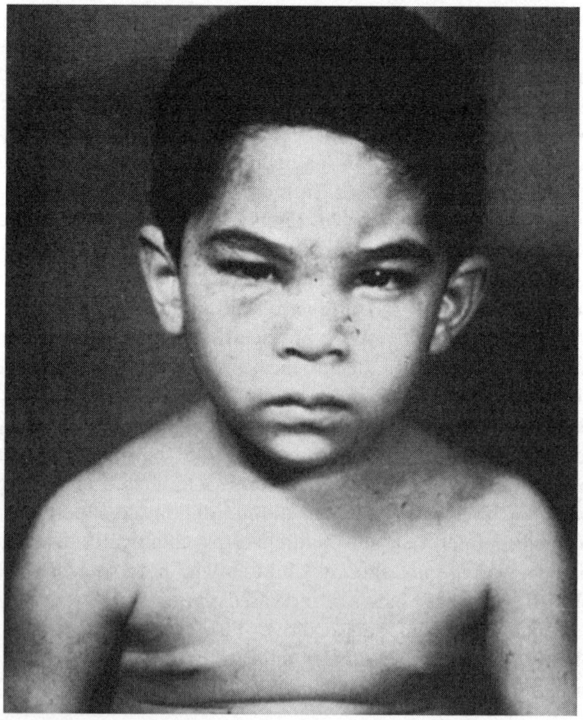

FIGURE 31–1
A 5-year-old boy was admitted with abrasions and bruises in various stages of healing and with evidence of recent trauma to his right eye and face. A history of periodic beatings by his sadistic, mentally retarded mother facilitated the diagnosis of physical abuse of child. (Courtesy of Vincent J. Fontana, M.D.)

peculiar or puzzling problems by overly cooperative parents may be victims of Munchausen syndrome by proxy, that is, factitious disorder: In this abuse scenario, a parent repeatedly inflicts illness on or causes injury to a child—by injecting toxins or by inducing the child to ingest drugs or toxins so as to cause diarrhea, dehydration, or other symptoms—and then eagerly seeks medical attention. Because the pathological parents are stealthy and superficially compliant, this diagnosis is difficult to make.

In hospital emergency rooms, severely abused children show external evidence of body trauma, bruises, abrasions, cuts, lacerations, burns, soft tissue swellings, and hematomas (Figs. 31–1 and 31–2). Hypernatremic dehydration, after periodic water deprivation of their children by mothers who are usually psychotic, is another form of child abuse. Inability to move certain extremities because of dislocations and fractures associated with neurological signs of intracranial damage can also indicate inflicted trauma. Other clinical signs and symptoms attributed to inflicted abuse may include injury to the viscera. Abdominal trauma may result in unexplained ruptures of the stomach, the bowel, the liver, or the pancreas, with manifestations of an injured abdomen. Those children with the most severe maltreatment injuries arrive at the hospital or physician's office in a coma or in convulsions; some arrive dead.

Behaviorally, abused children may appear withdrawn and frightened or may show aggressive behavior and labile mood. They often exhibit depression, poor self-esteem, and anxiety. They may try to physically cover up injuries and are usually reticent to disclose the abuse for fear of retaliation. Abused children often show some delay in developmental milestones, may have difficulties with peer relationships, and may engage in self-destructive or suicidal behaviors.

Sexual Abuse of Child. Adults within the immediate or extended family of a child perpetrate most child sexual abuse. Thus, children commonly know the sexual abuser, who is often a highly trusted family member with a position of authority and with wide access to the child (Table 31–2). Most cases of sexual abuse involving children are never revealed because of the victim's feelings of guilt, shame, ignorance, and tolerance, compounded by some physicians' reluctance to recognize and report sexual abuse, the court's insistence on strict rules of evidence, and families' fears of dissolution if the sexual abuse is discovered. Despite their familial roles, sexual abusers often threaten to hurt, kill, or abandon the children if the events are disclosed.

The incidence of sexual abuse and of child pornography,

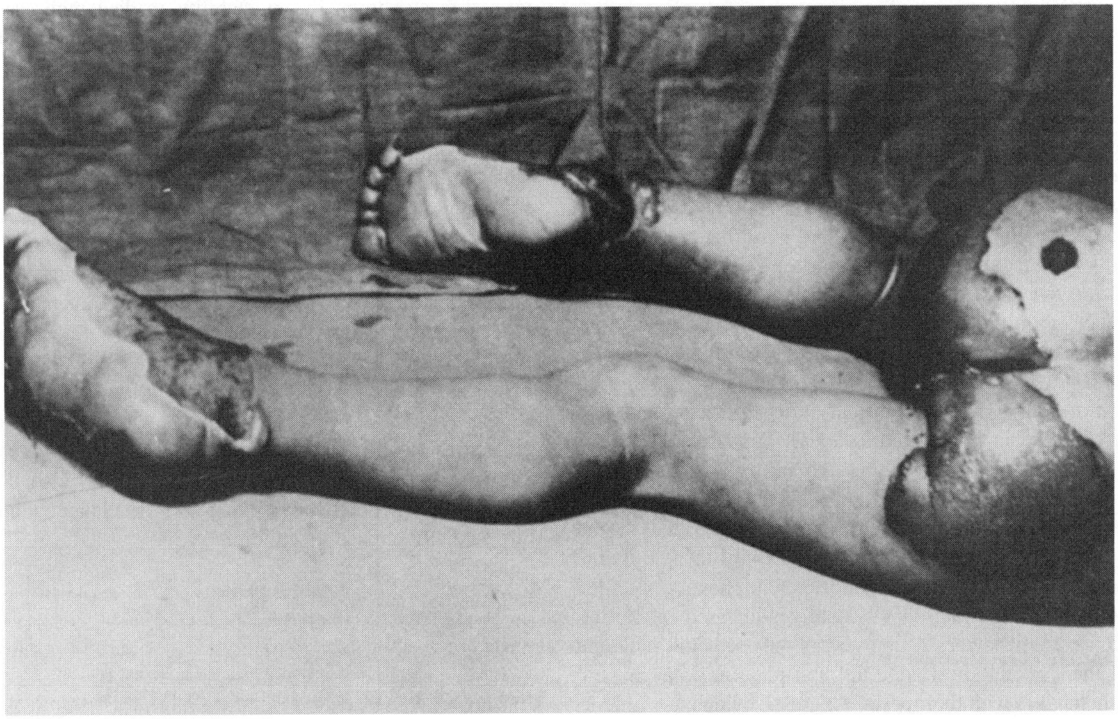

FIGURE 31–2

A 3½-year-old boy, brought into an emergency room by his mother, had second-degree burns of his buttocks, perineum, hands, and feet. His mother related that the child accidentally fell into a tub of hot water while preparing to take a bath. Physical examination revealed no evidence of burns along the body area. The location of the burns led physicians to suspect that the child's buttocks were forced into boiling water, and, in an attempt to keep himself from being submerged, he extended his feet and hands into the water. Scalding injury to his feet, perineum, and buttocks caused burn areas corresponding to the child's posture on dunking. His mother later admitted that a boyfriend had placed the child into a tub of hot water while she was out shopping. (Courtesy of Vincent J. Fontana, M.D.)

Table 31–2
Sexual Abuse of Children

Reported cases in U.S., 1985[a]	123,000
Prevalence of male abuse	3–31 percent
Prevalence of female abuse	6–62 percent
Perpetrators	
Father or stepfather	7–8 percent
Uncles or older siblings	16–42 percent
Friends	32–60 percent
Strangers	1 percent
Sexual activity	
Coitus	16–29 percent
Oral sex and intercourse	3–11 percent
Touching genitals	13–33 percent
Age	Peak between ages 9 and 12 25 percent below age 8
High-risk factors	Child living in single-parent home Marital conflict History of physical abuse Increase in sexual abuse
Reported motivation of abuser	Pedophilic impulses No other sexual object Inability to delay gratification

Data are from Finklehor D: The sexual abuse of children: Current research reviewed. Psychiatr Ann *17*: 4, 1987. Percentages may total more than 100 percent because of overlapping studies.

[a] Current estimates are 150,000 to 200,000 new cases each year.

which is a form of sexual abuse, is much higher than was previously assumed. Children may be sexually abused as early as infancy and as late as adolescence. Sexual abuse has been reported in schools, day care centers, and group homes, where adult caretakers are the major offenders.

The overwhelming fear, shame, and guilt that contribute to a child's reticence to disclose sexual abuse also complicate identifying the abuse. Most often, no definitive physical evidence can prove the occurrence of sexual abuse. Physical indicators of sexual abuse include bruises, pain, and itching in the genital region. Genital or rectal bleeding may be a sign of sexual molestation. Recurrent urinary tract infections and vaginal discharges may be related to abuse. Sexually transmitted diseases and difficulty in walking and sitting raise suspicions of sexual abuse.

No specific behavioral manifestations prove that sexual abuse has taken place, but children may exhibit many possible significant behaviors. Young children who have a detailed knowledge of sexual acts have usually witnessed or participated in sexual behavior. Young sexually abused children often exhibit their sexual knowledge through play and may initiate sexual behaviors with their peers. Aggressive behavior is common among abused children. Children who are extremely fearful of adults, particularly men, may have been subjected to sexual abuse. Clinicians should listen carefully to children who report sexual assaults even when parts of their stories are not consistent. When a child begins to disclose information about sexual assaults, retractions and contradictions are typical, and anxiety may prevent full disclosure.

The diagnosis of sexual abuse in children is full of pitfalls. An estimated 2 to 8 percent of allegations of sexual abuse are false. A much higher percentage of reports cannot be substantiated. Many investigations are hastily done or carried out by inexperienced evaluators. In custody cases, an allegation of sexual abuse can be a maneuver to limit a parent's visitation rights. Alleged sexual abuse of a preschool-age child is particularly difficult to evaluate because of the child's immature cognitive and language development. The use of anatomically correct dolls has grown in popularity, but the use of such dolls is controversial. Patient and careful evaluations by experienced, objective professionals are necessary, and leading questions must be avoided. Children under the age of 3 years are unlikely to produce a verbal memory of past trauma or abuses, but their experience may be reflected in play or fantasies. Some abused children meet the DSM-IV diagnostic criteria for posttraumatic stress disorder.

No specific psychiatric symptom universally results from sexual abuse. Vulnerability to the sequelae of sexual abuse depends on the type of abuse, its chronicity, the age of the child, and the overall relationship of the victim and the abuser. The psychological and physical effects of sexual abuse can be devastating and long lasting. Children who are sexually stimulated by an adult feel anxiety and overexcitement, lose confidence in themselves, and become mistrustful of adults. Seduction, incest, and rape are important predisposing factors to later symptom formations such as phobias, anxiety, and depression. Abused children tend to be hyperalert to external aggression as shown by an inability to deal with their own aggressive impulses toward others or with others' hostility directed toward them.

Depressive feelings, usually combined with shame, guilt, and a sense of permanent damage, are commonly reported among children who have been sexually abused. Adolescents who have undergone sexual abuse are said to show high rates of poor impulse control and self-destructive and suicidal behaviors. Posttraumatic stress disorder and dissociative disorders are common in adults who have been sexually abused as children. Sexual abuse is a common preexisting factor in the development of dissociative identity disorder (also known as multiple personality disorder). Signs of dissociation are described as periods in which the children are amnestic, do not feel the pain, or feel that they are somewhere else. Borderline personality disorder has been reported in some patients with histories of sexual abuse. Substance abuse has also been reported with high frequency among adolescents and adults who were sexually abused as children.

INCEST. Incest is defined as the occurrence of sexual relations between close blood relatives. A broader definition describes incest as sexual intercourse between participants who are related to each other by a formal or informal kinship bond that is culturally regarded as a bar to sexual relations. For example, sexual relations between stepparents and stepchildren or among stepsiblings are usually considered incestuous, even though no blood relationships exist.

Sociologists have underlined the role of incest prohibitions as socialization factors, and biological factors also support the taboo. Inbreeding groups risk unmasking lethal or detrimental recessive genes and the progeny of inbred groups are generally less fit than are less closely related offspring. Anthropologists have observed that different cultures have different types of incest taboos. In *Totem and Taboo*, Sigmund Freud developed the concept of the primal horde, in which young men collectively murdered the group's patriarch, who had kept all the women to himself. According to Freud, the incest taboo arose both from guilt about the murder and from a group's desire to prevent a repetition of the act, further rivalry after the murder, and subsequent disintegration of the horde.

Fathers, stepfathers, uncles, and older siblings most commonly abuse children. A passive, sick or absent, or somehow incapacitated mother, a daughter who takes on a maternal role in the family, a father who abuses alcohol, and overcrowding are features of father–daughter incest common in many homes. Mother–son incest is the strongest and most nearly universal taboo, and this form of incest is rarer than any other. Such behavior usually indicates a more severe psychopathology in the participants than is the case in father–daughter and sibling incest.

Accurate figures on the incidence of incest are difficult to obtain because of families' shame and embarrassment. Girls are victims more often than are boys; in the United States, about 15 million women have been the objects of incestuous attention, and one third of all sexually abused people have been molested before the age of 9.

Incestuous behavior is reported much more frequently among families of low socioeconomic status than among other families. This difference may be caused by greater contact with reporting officials such as welfare workers, public health personnel, and law enforcement agents and does not truly reflect a higher incidence in these families. Incest is more easily hidden by economically stable families than by those of low socioeconomic status.

Social, cultural, physiological, and psychological factors all contribute to the breakdown of the incest taboo. Incestuous behavior has been associated with alcohol abuse, overcrowding, increased physical proximity, and rural isolation that prevents adequate extrafamilial contacts. Some communities tolerate incestuous behavior more than does the whole of society. Major mental disorders and intellectual deficiencies can contribute to clinical incest. Some family therapists view incest as a defense designed to maintain a dysfunctional family unit. The older and stronger participant in incestuous behavior is usually male. Thus, incest may be viewed as a form of child abuse, as a pedophilia, or as a variant of rape.

About 75 percent of reported cases involve father–daughter incest, but parents often deny the occurrence of sibling incest. Other instances of sibling incest involve nearly normal interaction of prepubertal sexual play and exploration. In many cases of father–daughter incest, the daughter has had a close relationship with her father throughout her childhood and may appear to be pleased when he approaches her sexually. The incestuous behavior usually begins when the daughter is 10 years old. As the behavior continues, however, the abused daughter becomes bewildered, confused, and frightened, and when she nears adolescence, she undergoes physiological changes that add to her confusion. She never knows whether her father is a parent or sexual partner. Her mother may be alternately caring and competitive and may often refuse to believe her daughter's reports or to confront her husband with her suspicion. The daughter's relationships with her siblings are also affected; they sense her special position with her father and treat her as an outsider. The father, fearing that his daughter may expose their relationship and often jealously possessive of her, interferes with her development of normal peer relationships.

Physicians must be aware that intrafamilial sexual abuse can cause a wide variety of emotional and physical symptoms, including abdominal pain, genital irritations, separation anxiety disorder, phobias, nightmares, and school problems. When incest is suspected, clinicians must interview the child apart from the rest of the family.

Homosexual Incest. Father–son and mother–daughter incest are rarely reported, but a family in which same-sex incest occurs is usually highly disturbed, with a violent, alcohol-dependent, or antisocial father; a dependent or disabled mother who is unable to protect her children; and an absence of the usual family roles and individual identities. A son involved in father–son incest is frequently the eldest child, and, if there is a daughter, the father often sexually abuses her as well. Fathers in this situation do not necessarily have any other history of homosexual behavior. Sons may experience homicidal or suicidal ideation and may first consult or be sent to a psychiatrist because of self-destructive behavior.

STATUTORY RAPE. Intercourse is unlawful between a man more than 16 years of age and a woman under the age of consent, which varies from 14 to 21 years, depending on the jurisdiction. Thus, a man of 18 and a girl of 15 may have consensual intercourse, yet the man may be held for statutory rape. Statutory rape may vary dramatically from other types of rape in being nonassaultive and nonviolent, and it is not a deviant act unless the age discrepancy is sufficient for the man to be defined as a pedophile—that is, when the girl is less than 13 years old. Parents of a consenting girl, rather than the girl herself, usually press charges of statutory rape.

Neglect of Child. A maltreated child often shows no obvious signs of being battered but has multiple minor physical evidences of emotional and, at times, nutritional deprivation, neglect, and abuse. A maltreated child, often brought to a hospital or to a private physician, has a history of failure to thrive, malnutrition, poor skin hygiene, irritability, withdrawal, and other signs of psychological and physical neglect.

Children who have been neglected may show overt failure to thrive at less than 1 year of age. Their physical and emotional development is drastically impaired; they may be physically small and unable to display appropriate social interaction. Hunger, chronic infections, poor hygiene, inappropriate dress, and eventual malnutrition may all be evident. Behaviorally, children who are chronically neglected can be indiscriminately affectionate, even with strangers, or socially unresponsive, even in familiar situations. Neglected children may be runaways or exhibit conduct disorder.

An extreme form of failure to thrive in children of 5 years or older is psychosocial dwarfism, in which a chronically deprived child does not grow and develop, even when offered adequate amounts of food. Such children have normal proportions but are exceedingly small for their age. They often have reversible endocrinological changes resulting in decreased growth hormone, and they cease to grow for a time. Behaviorally, children with this disorder exhibit bizarre eating behaviors and disturbed social relationships. Binge eating, the ingestion of garbage or inedible substances, the drinking of toilet water, and induced vomiting have been reported.

Parents who neglect their children are often overwhelmed, depressed, isolated, and impoverished. Unemployment, the absence of a two-parent family, and substance abuse may exacerbate the situation. There are several possible prototypes of neglectful mothers. Some young, inexperienced, socially isolated, and ignorant mothers may temporarily be unable to care for their children. Other neglectful mothers are chronically passive and withdrawn women who may have been raised in chaotic, abusive, and neglectful homes. In these cases, once the situation comes to the attention of a child protective agency, the mother often accepts help. Mothers with major mental disorders who view their children as evil or as purposely driving them crazy are difficult to help.

Pathology and Laboratory Examination. Although no definitive laboratory tests are available to help clinicians diagnose child physical or sexual abuse or neglect, a physical examination to identify physical stigma is indicated when abuse is suspected. In cases of failure to thrive, endocrinological screening is indicated. An external genital examination is indicated in cases of suspected child sexual abuse to identify scars, tears, and genital infections. X-ray evidence of fractures may be present in various stages of reparative changes, but when no fractures or dislocations are apparent on examination, bone repair may become evident within weeks after the specific bone trauma.

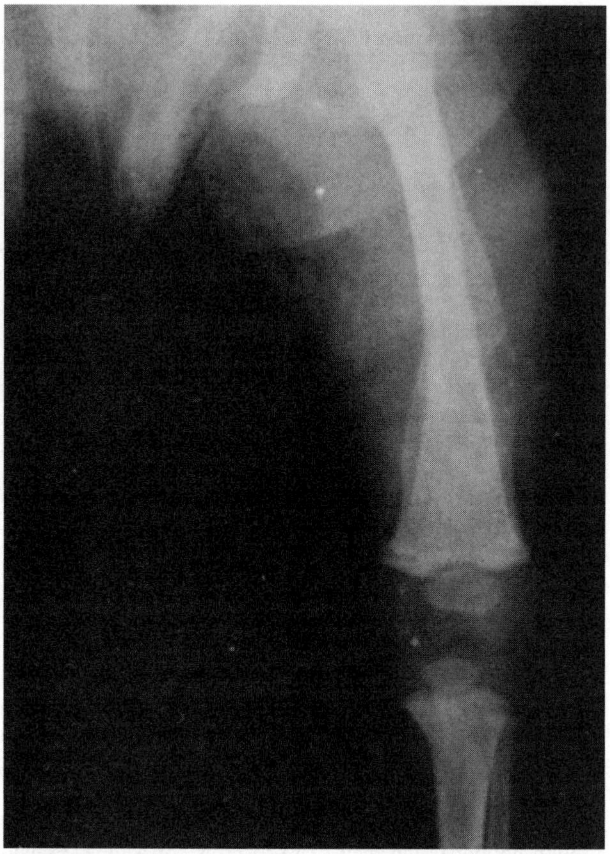

FIGURE 31–3
Follow-up X-ray of a maltreated 6-month-old infant taken 4 weeks after inflicted trauma to the upper thigh. Extensive reparative changes are noted in association with new bone formation, external cortical thickening, and squaring of the metaphysis—diagnostic evidence of bone changes after trauma. The layer of calcification around the shaft of the bone and the presence of bone fragments at the ends of the bone should be evidence for suspicion of inflicted trauma and should prompt further investigations into the causes of the X-ray findings. The X-ray changes may be diagnostic when correlated with other manifestations of physical abuse of child. (Courtesy of Vincent J. Fontana, M.D.)

Roentgenological examinations of unrecognized traumatic fractures reveal several unusual bone changes (Fig. 31–3). Metaphyseal fragmentation is caused by twisting or pulling of the afflicted extremity. There may be squaring of the long bones secondary to the new bone formation on the metaphyseal fragments. Periosteal hemorrhages are frequently noted because the periosteum of infants is not securely attached to the underlying bone. Periosteal calcification follows this hemorrhaging and begins to become apparent from 5 to 7 days after the inflicted trauma. A layer of calcification around the shaft of the bone should cause suspicion of inflicted abuse. Epiphyseal separations and periosteal shearing usually result from traction and torsion of the affected extremity. The X-ray findings of reparative changes involving excessive new bone formation or previously healed fractures with periosteal reactions may be diagnostic when correlated with other manifestations of child abuse.

Differential Diagnosis

Parental feuding and custody disputes are among the factors that complicate identifying and substantiating of abuse and neglect situations. When marital discord is severe, children are often caught in the line of fire. A mother who is overwhelmingly hostile toward a separated father may be convinced and may convince a child that the father is abusive. In some cases, parents have gone so far as to fabricate entire abuse scenarios and to coach children to repeat them. In other instances, parents may refuse to accept the possibility that a spouse or close relative is the perpetrator of abuse, may repeatedly insist that a child stop telling lies, and may coerce a child into retracting the disclosures. In either scenario, the child suffers profoundly, and the alleged abuse situation is never disentangled.

When a child speaks in a manner consistent with his or her language development stage and does not use rehearsed sounding, adultlike phrasing, the abuse allegations may be true. Distress, the display of precocious sexual behavior, and a knowledge of or preoccupation with sexual material also support the possibility of sexual abuse. A child who has not been abused but who is coached to report sexual or physical abuse is also placed under unbearable duress. Therefore, clinicians must recognize that severe chronic parental conflict discord in which a child is caught can be as destructive as physical and sexual abuse.

Controversies are now arising in the courts because children are accusing caretakers and teachers of sexual abuse and the children's veracity is being challenged. See Chapter 20 for a discussion of the recovered or false memory syndrome.

Course and Prognosis

The outcome of cases of child physical and sexual abuse and neglect is multifactorial, depending on the severity, duration, and nature of the abuse, and on the child's vulnerabilities. Children who already suffer from mental retardation, pervasive developmental disorders, physical disabilities, disruptive behavior, and attention-deficit disorders are likely to have a poorer outcome than are children unhampered by mental or physical disorders. Children who are abused for long periods, from the time they are babies or toddlers into adolescence, are likely to be more profoundly damaged than are those who have experienced only brief episodes of abuse. The development of mental disorders—such as major depressive disorder, suicidal behavior, posttraumatic stress disorder, dissociative identity disorder, and substance abuse—further complicates the long-term prognosis, as does the nature of the relationship between victim and abuser and the adult support figures available to children after disclosure. The best outcomes occur when children are cognitively intact, the abuse is recognized and interrupted in an early phase, and the entire family is capable of participating in treatment.

Treatment

Child. The first part of treating child abuse and neglect is to ensure the child's safety and well-being. Children may need to be removed from abusive or neglectful families to ensure their protection; yet, on an emotional level, a child may feel additionally vulnerable in an unfamiliar setting. Because of the high risk for psychiatric symptoms in abused and neglected children, a comprehensive psychiatric evaluation is in order. Next, along with providing specific treatments for any mental disorders present, a therapist may have to deal with the immediate situation and the long-term implications of the abuse or neglect. Therapists must address several psychotherapeutic issues: dealing with the child's fears, anxieties, and self-esteem; building a trusting adult relationship in which the child is not exploited or betrayed; and ultimately gaining a helpful perspective of the factors contributing to the child's victimization at home.

Ideally, each abused and neglected child should receive an intervention plan based on the assessment of the factors responsible for parents' psychopathology. The plan should include an overall prognosis for parents' achieving adequate parenting skills; the time estimated to achieve meaningful change in parents' ability to parent; an estimate of whether the parent's dysfunction is confined to this child or involves other children, whether the parents' overall malfunctioning, if that is the case, is short term or long term, and whether a mother's malfunctioning is confined to infants as opposed to older children (that is, when the incidence of abuse is inversely related to a child's age); willingness of those involved to participate in the intervention plan; the availability of personnel and physical resources to implement the various intervention strategies; and the risk of the child sustaining additional physical or sexual abuse by remaining in the home.

Parents. On the basis of the information obtained, several options can be selected to improve parents' functioning: eliminate or diminish the social or environmental stresses; lessen the adverse psychological effects of social factors on the parents; reduce the demands on the mother to a level within her capacity through day care placement of the child or the provision of a housekeeper or baby-sitter; provide emotional support, encouragement, sympathy, stimulation, instruction in maternal care, and aid in learning to plan for, assess, and meet the needs of the infant (supportive casework); and resolve or diminish the parents' inner psychic conflicts (psychotherapy).

INCESTUOUS BEHAVIOR. The first step in the treatment of incestuous behavior is its disclosure. Once a breakthrough of family members' denial, collusion, and fear has been achieved, incest is unlikely to recur. When the participants suffer from severe psychopathology, treatment must be directed toward the underlying illness. Family therapy is useful to reestablish the group as a functioning unit and to develop healthier role definitions for each member. While the participants are learning to develop internal restraints and appropriate ways to gratify their needs, the external control provided by therapy helps prevent further incestuous behavior. At times, legal agencies must help enforce external controls.

Reporting. In cases of suspected child abuse and neglect, physicians should diagnose the suspected maltreatment; secure the child's safety by admitting the child to a hospital or by arranging out-of-home placement; report the case to the appropriate social service department, child protection unit, or central registry; make an assessment with the help of a history, a physical examination, a skeletal survey, and photographs; request a social worker's report and appropriate surgical and medical consultations; confer with members of a child abuse committee within 72 hours; arrange a program of care for the child and the parents; and arrange for social service follow-up. Among those generally included as mandated child-abuse reporters are physicians, psychologists, school officials, police officers, hospital personnel engaged in the treatment of patients, district attorneys, and providers of child day care and foster care.

Prevention. To prevent child abuse and neglect, clinicians must identify those families at high risk and intervene before a child becomes a victim. Once high-risk families have been identified, a comprehensive program should include psychiatric monitoring of the families, including the identified high-risk child. Families can be educated to recognize when they are being neglectful or abusive, and alternative coping strategies can be suggested.

In general, child abuse and neglect prevention and treatment programs should try to prevent the separation of parents and children if possible, prevent the placement of children in institutions, encourage the parents' attainment of self-care status, and encourage the family's attainment of self-sufficiency. As a last resort and to prevent further abuse and neglect, children may have to be removed from families who are unwilling or unable to profit from the treatment program. In cases of sexual abuse, the licensing of day care centers and the psychological screening of people who work in them should be mandatory to prevent further abuses. Education of the medical profession, members of allied health fields, and all who come in contact with children aid in early detection. And providing support services to stressed families aids in preventing the problem in the first place.

PHYSICAL ABUSE OF ADULT

Spouse Abuse

Spouse abuse is estimated to occur in 2 to 12 million families in the United States. This aspect of domestic violence has been recognized as a severe problem, largely because of recent cultural emphasis on civil rights and the work of feminist groups, but the problem itself is long standing.

The major problem in spouse abuse is wife abuse. One study estimated that there are 1.8 million battered wives in the United States, excluding divorced women and women battered on dates. Wife beating occurs in families of every racial and religious background and in all socioeconomic strata. It is most frequent in families with problems of substance abuse, particularly alcohol and crack abuse. Behavioral, cultural, intrapsychic, and interpersonal factors all contribute to the problem. Abusive men are likely to have come from violent homes where they witnessed wife beating or were abused themselves as children. The act itself is reinforcing; once a man has beaten his wife, he is likely to do so again. Abusive husbands tend to be immature, dependent, nonassertive, and to suffer from strong feelings of inadequacy.

The husbands' aggression is bullying behavior designed to humiliate their wives and to build up their own low self-esteem. Impatient, impulsive, abusive husbands physically displace aggression provoked by others onto their wives. The abuse is most likely to occur when a man feels threatened or frustrated at home, at work, or with his peers. The dynamics include identification with an aggressor (father, boss), testing behavior (Will she stay with me, no matter how I treat her?), distorted desires to express manhood, and dehumanization of women. As in rape, aggression is deemed permissible when a woman is perceived as property. About 50 percent of battered wives grew up in violent homes, and their most common trait is dependence.

The Surgeon General's office has identified pregnancy as a high-risk period for battering; 15 to 25 percent of pregnant women are physically abused while pregnant, and the abuse often results in birth defects. Hot lines, emergency shelters for women, and other organizations (such as the National Coalition Against Domestic Violence) have been established to aid battered wives and to educate the public. One major problem of abused women has been finding a place to go when they leave home, frequently in fear of their lives.

Battering is often severe, involving broken limbs, broken ribs, internal bleeding, and brain damage. When an abused wife tries to leave her husband, he often becomes doubly intimidating and threatens to ''get'' her. If the woman has small children to care for, her problem is compounded. The abusive husband wages a conscious campaign to isolate his wife and make her feel worthless. Women face risks when they leave an abusive husband; they have a 75 percent greater chance of being killed by their batterers than do women who stay. In 1990, California passed the first antistalking law, making stalking a crime. By 1992, a total of 28 states passed similar laws.

Some men feel remorse and guilt after an episode of violent behavior and so become particularly loving. If this behavior gives the wife hope, she remains until the next, inevitable occurring cycle of violence.

When a man is convinced that a woman will no longer tolerate the situation and when she begins to exert control over his behavior, change is initiated. By leaving for a prolonged period, if she is physically and economically able to do so, and by making therapy for the man a condition of return, a woman can begin a cycle of improvement. Family therapy is effective in treating the problem, usually in conjunction with social and legal agencies. With men who are relatively less impulsive, external controls, such as calling the neighbors or the police, may be sufficient to stop the behavior.

Some husband-beating wives have been also reported. Husbands complain of fear of ridicule if they expose the problem; they fear charges of counterassault and often feel unable to leave the situation because of financial difficulties. Husband abuse has also been reported when a frail, elderly man is married to a much younger woman.

Elder Abuse

Elder abuse is discussed in Chapter 54.

SEXUAL ABUSE OF ADULT

Rape

The conventional definition of rape is the perpetration of an act of sexual intercourse with a woman against her will and consent, whether her will is overcome by force or fear resulting from the threat of force or by drugs or intoxicants; or when, because of mental deficiency, she is incapable of exercising rational judgment, or when she is below an arbitrary age of consent. Rape, however, can occur between married partners and between people of the same sex. The crime of rape requires only slight penile penetration of the victim's outer vulva; full erection and ejaculation are unnecessary for defining the crime. Forced acts of fellatio and anal penetration, although they frequently accompany rape, are legally considered sodomy.

The problem of rape is most appropriately discussed under the heading of aggression. Rape is an act of violence and humiliation that happens to be expressed through sexual means. Rape expresses power or anger; sex is rarely the dominant issue because sexuality is used in the service of nonsexual needs.

Rape of Women. In recent research, male rapists are categorized into separate groups: sexual sadists, who are aroused by the pain of their victims; exploitive predators, who use their victims as objects for their gratification in an impulsive way; inadequate men, who believe that no woman would voluntarily sleep with them and who are obsessed with fantasies about sex; and men for whom rape is a displaced expression of anger and rage. Some believe that the anger was originally directed toward a wife or mother, but feminist theory proposes that a woman serves as an object for the displacement of aggression that a rapist cannot express directly toward other men. Women are considered men's property or vulnerable possessions, a rapist's instrument for revenge against other men.

Rape often occurs as an accompaniment to another crime. Rapists always threaten their victims, with fists, a knife, or a gun, and frequently harm them in nonsexual ways as well. Victims may be beaten, wounded, and killed.

Statistics show that most men who commit rapes are between 25 and 44 years of age; 51 percent are white and tend to rape white victims, 47 percent are black and tend to rape black victims, and the remaining 2 percent come from all other races. Alcohol is involved in 34 percent of all forcible rapes. A composite characterization of the archetypical rapist drawn from police statistics portrays a single 19-year-old man from a low socioeconomic group who has a police record of acquisitive offenses.

According to the Federal Bureau of Investigation, 97,464 forcible rapes were reported to law enforcement in the United States in 1995. Rape, however, is a highly underreported crime: An estimated 4 to 5 out of 10 rapes is reported. The underreporting is attributed to victims' feelings of shame and to the belief that there is no recourse through the legal system. According to the FBI Uniform Crime Reporting program, in 1995, 72 of every 100,000 females in the United States were reported rape victims.

People who are raped can be of any age. Cases have been reported in which the victims were as young as 15 months and as old as 82 years, but women age 16 to 24 are at highest risk. Rape most commonly occurs in a woman's own neighborhood, frequently inside or near her own home. Most rapes are premeditated; about half are committed by strangers and half by men known, to varying degrees, by the victims. Seven percent of all rapes are perpetrated by close relatives of the victim; ten percent of rapes involve more than one attacker.

A woman being raped is frequently in a life-threatening situation. During the rape, she experiences shock and fright approaching panic; her prime motivation is to stay alive. In most cases, rapists choose victims slightly smaller than themselves. Rapists may urinate or defecate on their victims, ejaculate into their faces and hair, force anal intercourse, and insert foreign objects into their vaginas and rectums.

After a rape, a woman often experiences shame, humiliation, confusion, fear, and rage. The type and duration of the reaction are variable, but women report that the effects last for a year or longer. Many women experience the symptoms of posttraumatic stress disorder. Some women, particularly those who have always felt sexually adequate, are able to resume sexual relations with men; but others become phobic about sexual interaction or have such symptoms as vaginismus. Few women emerge from the assault completely unscathed. The manifestations and the degree of damage depend on the violence of the attack itself, the vulnerability of the woman, and the support system available to her immediately after the attack.

A rape victim fares best when she receives immediate support and is able to ventilate her fear and rage to loving family members, sympathetic physicians, and law enforcement officials. Knowing that she has socially acceptable means of recourse, such as the arrest and conviction of the rapist, can help a rape victim.

Unless a woman has a severe underlying disorder, therapy is usually supportive in approach and focuses on restoring a victim's sense of adequacy and control over her life; it also aims to relieve the feelings of helplessness, dependence, and obsession with the assault that frequently follow rape. Group therapy with homogeneous groups of people who have been raped is a particularly effective form of treatment.

In addition to the physical and psychological trauma experienced when they are assaulted, rape victims until recently also faced skepticism from those to whom they reported the crime (if they had sufficient strength to do so) or accusations of having provoked or desired the assault. In reality, the National Commission on the Causes and Prevention of Violence found discernible victim participation in rape in only 4.4 percent of all cases. This statistic is lower than that of any other crime of violence. The education of police officers and the assignment of policewomen to deal with rape victims have helped increase reporting the crime. Rape crisis centers and telephone hot lines are available for immediate aid and information for victims. Volunteer groups work in emergency rooms in hospitals and with physician education programs to assist in the treatment of victims.

Legally, women no longer must prove in court that they actively struggled against a rapist, and testimony about a victim's previous sexual history has been declared inadmissible as evidence in several states. Because penalties for first-time rapists have been reduced, juries are likely to consider a conviction. In some states, wives can now prosecute husbands for rape.

DATE RAPE. Date or acquaintance rape is a term applied to rapes in which the rapist is known to the victim. The assault can occur on a first date or after the man and woman have known each other for many months. Considerable data on date rape have been gathered from college populations. In one study, 38 percent of male students said that they would commit rape if they thought they could get away with it, and 11 percent stated that they had committed rape; 16 percent of female students said that they had been raped by men they knew or were dating. In addition to suffering the symptoms of all rape survivors, victims of date rape berate themselves for exercising poor judgment in their choice of male friends and are more likely to blame themselves for provoking the rapist than are other victims. Many colleges and universities have set up programs for rape prevention and for counseling those who have been assaulted.

Rape of Men. In some states the definition of rape is being changed to substitute the word *person* for *female.* In most states, male rape is legally defined as sodomy. Homosexual rape is much more frequent among men than among women and occurs frequently in closed institutions such as prisons and maximum-security hospitals.

The dynamics are identical to those of heterosexual rape. The crime enables the rapist to discharge aggression and to aggrandize himself. The victim is usually smaller than the rapist, is always perceived as passive and unmanly (weaker), and is used as an object. A rapist selecting a male victim may be heterosexual, bisexual, or homosexual. The most common act is anal penetration of the victim; the second most common is fellatio.

Homosexual-rape victims often feel, as do raped women, that they have been ruined, and some also fear that they will become homosexual because of the attack.

Sexual Coercion

Sexual coercion is a term used in DSM-IV for incidents in which one person dominates another by force or compels the other person to perform a sexual act.

References

Brownmiller S: *Against Our Will: Men, Women and Rape.* Simon & Schuster, New York, 1975.

Campbell JC, Poland ML, Waller JB, Ager J: Correlates of battering during pregnancy. Res Nurs Health *15:* 219, 1992.

Carter-Lourensz JH, Johnson-Powell G: Physical abuse, sexual abuse, and neglect of child. In *Comprehensive Textbook of Psychiatry,* ed 6, HI Kaplan, BJ Sadock, editors, p 2455. Williams & Wilkins, Baltimore, 1995.

Cosentino CE, Collins M: Sexual abuse of children: Prevalence, effects, and treatment. Ann NY Acad Sci *789:* 45, 1996.

Donald T, Jureidini J: Munchausen syndrome by proxy. Child abuse in the medical system. Arch Pediatr Adolesc Med *150:* 753, 1996.

Everson MD, Boat BW: False allegations of sexual abuse by children and adolescents. Am J Psychiatry *28:* 230, 1989.

Fitzpatrick KM, Boldizar JP: The prevalence and consequences of exposure to violence among African-American youth. J Am Acad Child Adolesc Psychiatry *32:* 424, 1993.

Foa EB, Rothbaum BO, Steketee GS: Treatment of rape victims. J Interpers Violence *8:* 256, 1993.

Follette VM, Polusny MA, Bechtle AE, Naugle AE: Cumulative trauma: The impact of child sexual abuse, adult sexual assault, and spouse abuse. J Trauma Stress *9:* 25, 1996.

Frazier PA: A comparative study of male and female rape victims seen at a hospital-based rape crisis program. J Interpers Violence *8:* 64, 1993.

Henderson DJ: Incest. In *The Sexual Experience,* BJ Sadock, HI Kaplan, AM Freedman, editors, p 415. Williams & Wilkins, Baltimore, 1976.

Herman JL, Perry C, Van der Kolk BA: Childhood trauma in borderline personality disorder. Am J Psychiatry *146:* 490, 1989.

Hymel KP, Jenny C: Child sexual abuse. Pediatr Rev *17:* 236, 1996.

Lewis DO: From abuse to violence: Psychophysiological consequences of maltreatment. J Am Acad Child Adolesc Psychiatry *31:* 383, 1992.

McCall GJ: Risk factors and sexual assault prevention. J Interpers Violence *8:* 277, 1993.

McCoy M: Domestic violence: Clues to victimization. Ann Emerg Med *27:* 764, 1996.

Ogletree RJ: Sexual coercion experience and help-seeking behavior of college women. J Am Coll Health *41:* 149, 1993.

Resick PA: The psychological impact of rape. J Interpers Violence *8:* 223, 1993.

Rubinstein M, Yeager CA, Goodstein C, Lewis DO: Sexually assaultive male juveniles: A follow-up. Am J Psychiatry *150:* 262, 1993.

Sadock VA: Physical and sexual abuse of adult. In *Comprehensive Textbook of Psychiatry,* ed 6, HI Kaplan, BJ Sadock, editors, p 1729. Williams & Wilkins, Baltimore, 1995.

Salzinger S, Feldman, RS, Hammer M, Rosario M: The effects of physical abuse on children's social relationships. Child Dev *64:* 169, 1993.

Schafran LH: Rape is a major public health issue. Am J Public Health *86:* 15, 1996.

Sternberg KJ, Lamb ME, Greenbaum C, Cicchetti D, et al: Effects of domestic violence on children's behavior problems and depression. Dev Psychol *29:* 44, 1993.

True WR, Rice J, Eisen SA, Heath AC, Goldberg J, Lyons MJ, Nowak J: A twin study of genetic and environmental contributions to liability for post-traumatic stress symptoms. Arch Gen Psychiatry *50:* 257, 1993.

Ullman SE, Knight RA: The efficacy of women's resistance strategies in rape situations. Psychol Women *17:* 23, 1993.

Vazquez CI: Spousal abuse and violence against women: The significance of understanding attachment. Ann NY Acad Sci *789:* 119, 1996.

Wilt S, Olson S: Prevalence of domestic violence in the United States. J Am Med Wom Assoc *51:* 77, 1996.

Zlotnick C, Zakriski AL, Shea MT, Costello E, Begin A, Pearlstein T, Simpson E: The long-term sequelae of sexual abuse: Support for a complex posttraumatic stress disorder. J Trauma Stress *9:* 195, 1996.

32

Additional Conditions That May Be a Focus of Clinical Attention

There are 13 conditions that make up the diagnostic category of additional disorders that may be a focus of clinical attention. Nine of these conditions are discussed in this chapter: bereavement, occupational problems, adult antisocial behavior, malingering, phase of life problem, noncompliance with treatment for a mental disorder, religious or spiritual problem, acculturation problem, and age-associated memory decline. (Four other conditions included in the fourth edition of *Diagnostic and Statistical Manual of Mental Disorders* (DSM-IV) are discussed in Chapter 51: borderline intellectual functioning, academic problem, childhood or adolescent antisocial behavior, and identity problem.)

In DSM-IV, these conditions are not considered true mental disorders, but are problems that have led people to come into contact with the mental health care system. Once in the system, people with an additional condition that may be a focus of clinical attention should have a thorough neuropsychiatric evaluation, which may or may not uncover a mental disorder. The above listed categories are of clinical interest to psychiatrists because they may accompany mental illness or may be early harbingers of underlying mental disorders. For recording purposes in DSM-IV, the conditions are coded on Axis I.

As mentioned in DSM-IV, a person with a mental disorder may be treated for a condition that is not due to the mental disorder. For example, the treatment of a person with social phobia who has an occupational problem not directly related to the phobia may focus on the occupational problem. At times, however, the distinction is not clear-cut, and clinicians must do as thorough a workup as possible not to overlook a diagnosable mental disorder.

BEREAVEMENT

Normal bereavement begins immediately after or within a few months of the loss of a loved one. Feelings of sadness, preoccupation with thoughts about the deceased, tearfulness, irritability, insomnia, and difficulties in concentrating and carrying out daily activities are some typical signs and symptoms. On the basis of cultural group, bereavement is limited to a varying time, usually no longer than 6 months. Normal bereavement, however, can lead to a full depressive disorder that requires treatment. (Chapter 2, Section 2.7, presents a further discussion of bereavement.)

DSM-IV includes the following description of bereavement:

> This category can be used when the focus of clinical attention is a reaction to the death of a loved one. As part of their reaction to the loss, some grieving individuals present with symptoms characteristic of a Major Depressive Episode (e.g., feelings of sadness and associated symptoms such as insomnia, poor appetite, and weight loss). The bereaved individual typically regards the depressed mood as ''normal,'' although the person may seek professional help for relief of associated symptoms such as insomnia or anorexia. The duration and expression of ''normal'' bereavement vary considerably among different cultural groups. The diagnosis of Major Depressive Disorder is generally not given unless the symptoms are still present 2 months after the loss. However, the presence of certain symptoms that are not characteristic of a ''normal'' grief reaction may be helpful in differentiating bereavement from a Major Depressive Episode. These include 1) guilt about things other than actions taken or not taken by the survivor at the time of the death; 2) thoughts of death other than the survivor feeling that he or she would be better off dead or should have died with the deceased person; 3) morbid preoccupation with worthlessness; 4) marked psychomotor retardation; 5) prolonged and marked functional impairment; and 6) hallucinatory experiences other than thinking that he or she hears the voice of, or transiently sees the image of, the deceased person.

OCCUPATIONAL PROBLEM

Occupational or industrial psychiatry is that area of psychiatry specifically concerned with vocational maladjustment and the psychiatric aspects of problems at work. The practical symptoms of job dissatisfaction are mistakes at work, accident-proneness, absenteeism, and sabotage. The psychiatric symptoms include insecurity, reduced self-esteem, anger, and resentment at having to work.

DSM-IV includes the following statement about occupational problem:

> This category can be used when the focus of clinical attention is an occupational problem that is not due to a mental disorder or, if it is due to a mental disorder, is sufficiently severe to warrant independent clinical attention. Examples include job dissatisfaction and uncertainty about career choices.

People are particularly vulnerable to occupational problems at several points in their working lives—on entry into the working world, at times of promotion or transfer, during periods of unemployment, and at retirement. Specific situations—such as having too much or too little to do, being subjected to conflicting demands, feeling distracted by family problems, having responsibility without authority, and working for demanding and unhelpful managers—also create occupational distress.

Career Choices and Changes

The choice of a career is a major life decision. A significant number of young people follow in their parents' footsteps, but many others are unsure of what to do and try several jobs before settling on an occupation. Disadvantaged youngsters frequently have little choice about a career. When young adults have a poor education and lack training and skills, even overwhelming ambition rarely leads them out of poverty or into occupational satisfaction. When the disadvantaged are women or members of minority groups, they have even less chance of occupational success. In discussing career choices with a patient, a psychiatrist should explore special talents and interests, childhood goals, the patient's models, family influences, future expectations, work and academic histories, and motivation to work.

Distress about work is readily understood when an employee has been fired, demoted, or passed over for promotion. Minorities and those in low socioeconomic groups are particularly vulnerable to losing their jobs. In one 5-year period, 11.5 million people in the United States age 20 or over lost their jobs as a result of industrial plant closings and cutbacks. Some left the labor force altogether. Others moved to lower-paying, low-skill jobs with fewer benefits than their former jobs. Some worked intermittently.

Women are specifically at risk when they leave outside employment for homemaking, a transition that researchers have found to be extremely stressful.

Some people experience problems after they win professional advancement. Anxiety about assuming new responsibilities and the fact that people may be promoted to jobs that are beyond their capacities are among the reasons for this reaction.

Adjusting to retirement is most difficult for those unprepared for it. Adverse reactions occur when a person is forced to retire prematurely or because of illness. Retirement is also a problem for people whose identity is based primarily on occupational status and income. Women are reported to adjust faster to retirement than do men. Some researchers, however, think that retirement poses a greater hardship for women than for men; women face a longer retirement period owing to their greater life expectancy, are more likely to be alone (widowed) during their retirement years, and are usually poorer and have lower retirement incomes than do men.

Psychological Problems and the Workplace

Maladaptation at work may arise from psychodynamic conflicts, which can reflect unfulfilled infantile needs. People with unresolved conflicts about their competitive and aggressive impulses may experience great difficulties in the work area. They may suffer from a pathological envy of others' success, or may fear their own success because they cannot tolerate envy from others. These conflicts are also manifest in other areas and are not limited to work.

Career Problems of Women

During the past 25 years, the U.S. business world has undergone many changes. A significant number of women have entered the workforce; many corporations now employ a husband and a wife in the same organization; and teenagers have entered the labor force on a part-time basis, on a large scale.

Ninety percent of all women alive today in the United States will have to work to support themselves and probably one or two others. Economic necessity now prompts homemakers to work, and rejection by employers on the basis of age, lack of recent experience, or insufficient training can cause dysphoria and depression. This is particularly true for recently divorced women in their 40s or 50s who have spent most of their adult lives as wives and mothers.

Young women have different stresses, primarily related to the conflicting demands of work and family responsibilities: More than 50 percent of all mothers in the workforce have children 1 year old or younger. But women's organizations and other critics charge that few corporations are removing barriers to women's advancement or are concerned about reducing the tension that arises when job and family demands conflict. Specific issues that need to be addressed are provisions for child care or for the care of elderly parents, the option of flexible work hours, and the availability and use of unpaid parental leaves. Studies reveal that, when these leaves are made available to both parents, fathers rarely take them; that managers are more sensitive to crises in men's lives than to crises in the lives of female employees; and that managers respond to such major events as divorce and the death of a family member but ignore the stress placed on a worker by the illness of a child or a school closing because of a snow day. A few socially conscious corporations hold workshops to address the changes arising from the influx of women into the workforce and the issues of family responsibilities, sexual harassment in the workplace, personal safety during business travel, and rape prevention. Day care facilities have been established on site in some organizations and have proved successful.

Dual-career families (in which both husband and wife have jobs) now constitute more than 40 percent of all families. Problems can arise when an employer wants one partner to make a geographic move to a new post. Even if the transfer is a promotion, the transfer can result in lower total income for the family because of the spouse's loss of job or career disruption. Some corporations offer new jobs to both spouses when one is asked to relocate, but such approaches are rare. A more common advance is the acceptance of couples, married or unmarried, as employees of the same corporation. Couples employed by the same company seem to cause problems for themselves and others only when they are competitive with each other. Those couples who fare best treat their spouses differently at the office than they do at home. Resentment from co-workers occurs when one spouse reports directly to the other. Otherwise, no adverse responses from other employees have been noted.

Vocational Rehabilitation

Rehabilitation is often necessary for those traumatized by stresses in the workplace, or who have had to take a leave of absence because of medical or psychiatric reasons, or who have been fired. Individual or group counseling enables people to improve personal relationships, raise self-esteem, or learn new work skills. Patients with schizophrenia may benefit from sheltered workshops in which they perform work that is geared to their level of function. Some patients with schizophrenia do well in tasks that are repetitive or require obsessive concern with details.

ADULT ANTISOCIAL BEHAVIOR

Characterized by activities that are illegal or immoral or both, antisocial behavior usually begins in childhood and often persists throughout life.

DSM-IV includes the following statements about adult antisocial behavior:

> This category can be used when the focus of clinical attention is adult antisocial behavior that is not due to a mental disorder (e.g., Conduct Disorder, Antisocial Personality Disorder, or an Impulse-Control Disorder). Examples include the behavior of some professional thieves, racketeers, or dealers in illegal substances.

The term *antisocial behavior* somewhat confusingly applies both to people's actions not due to a mental disorder, and to behavior by those who have never received an adequate neuropsychiatric workup to determine the presence or absence of a mental disorder. As Dorothy Lewis noted, the term can apply to behavior by normal people who "struggle to make a dishonest living."

Epidemiology

Depending on the criteria and the sampling, estimates of the prevalence of adult antisocial behavior range from 5 to 15 percent of the population. Within prison populations, investigators report prevalence figures of between 20 and 80 percent. Men account for more adult antisocial behavior than do women.

Etiology

Antisocial behaviors in adulthood are characteristic of a variety of people, ranging from those with no demonstrable psychopathology to those who are severely impaired and suffer from psychotic disorders, cognitive disorders, and retardation, among other conditions. A comprehensive neuropsychiatric assessment of antisocial adults is indicated and may reveal potentially treatable psychiatric and neurological impairments that can easily be overlooked. Only in the absence of mental disorders can patients be categorized as displaying adult antisocial behavior. Adult antisocial behavior may be influenced by genetic and social factors.

Genetic Factors. Data supporting the genetic transmission of antisocial behavior are based on studies that find a 60 percent concordance rate in monozygotic twins and about a 30 percent concordance rate in dizygotic twins. Adoption studies show a high rate of antisocial behavior in the biological relatives of adoptees identified with antisocial behavior and a high incidence of antisocial behavior in the adopted-away offspring of those with antisocial behavior. The prenatal and perinatal periods of those who subsequently display antisocial behavior often are associated with low birth weight, mental retardation, and prenatal exposure to alcohol and other drugs of abuse.

Social Factors. Studies showed that in neighborhoods in which families with low socioeconomic status (SES) predominate, the sons of unskilled workers are more likely to commit more offenses, and more serious criminal offenses, than are the sons of middle-class and skilled workers, at least during adolescence and early adulthood. These data are not as clear for women, but the findings are generally similar in studies from many countries. Areas of family training differ by SES group. Middle-SES parents' use love-oriented techniques in discipline, the withdrawal of affection versus physical punishment, negative parental attitudes toward aggressive behavior, attempts to curb aggressive behavior, and the verbal ability to communicate the various reasons for the parents' values and proscriptions of such behavior. Adult antisocial behavior is associated with the use and abuse of alcohol and other substances and also with the easy availability of handguns.

Diagnosis and Clinical Features

The diagnosis of adult antisocial behavior is one of exclusion. Substance dependence in such behavior often makes it difficult to separate the antisocial behavior related primarily to substance dependence from disordered behaviors that occurred either before substance use or during episodes unrelated to substance dependence.

During the manic phases of bipolar I disorder, certain aspects of behavior, such as wanderlust, sexual promiscuity, and financial difficulties, can be similar to adult antisocial behavior. Patients with schizophrenia may have episodes of adult antisocial behavior, but the symptom picture is usually clear, especially regarding thought disorder, delusions, and hallucinations on the mental status examination.

Neurological conditions may be associated with adult antisocial behavior, and electroencephalograms (EEGs), computed tomography (CT) scans, magnetic resonance imaging (MRI), and complete neurological examinations are indicated. Temporal lobe epilepsy should be considered in the differential diagnosis. When a clear-cut diagnosis of temporal lobe epilepsy or encephalitis can be made, the disorder may be considered to contribute to the adult antisocial behavior. Abnormal EEG findings are prevalent among violent offenders: An estimated 50 percent of aggressive criminals have abnormal EEG findings.

People with adult antisocial behavior have difficulties in work, marriage, and money matters, and conflicts with various authorities. The symptoms of adult antisocial behavior are summarized in Table 32–1. (Antisocial personality disorder is discussed in Chapter 27.)

Treatment

In general, therapists are pessimistic about treating adult antisocial behavior. They have little hope of changing a pattern that has been present almost continuously throughout a person's life. Psychotherapy has not been effective, and no major breakthroughs with biological treatments, including medications, have occurred.

Therapists show more enthusiasm for the use of therapeutic communities and other forms of group treatment, even though

Table 32–1
Symptoms of Adult Antisocial Behavior

Life Area	Antisocial Patients with Significant Problems in Area (%)
Work problems	85
Marital problems	81
Financial dependence	79
Arrests	75
Alcohol abuse	72
School problems	71
Impulsiveness	67
Sexual behavior	64
Wild adolescence	62
Vagrancy	60
Belligerence	58
Social isolation	56
Military record (of those serving)	53
Lack of guilt	40
Somatic complaints	31
Use of aliases	29
Pathological lying	16
Drug abuse	15
Suicide attempts	11

Data are from Robins L: *Deviant Children Grown Up: A Sociological and Psychiatric Study of Sociopathic Personality.* Williams & Wilkins, Baltimore, 1966.

the data provide little basis for optimism. Many adult criminals who are incarcerated and in institutional settings have shown some response to group therapy approaches. The history of violence, criminality, and antisocial behavior has shown that such behaviors seem to decrease after age 40. Recidivism in criminals, which can reach 90 percent in some studies, also decreases in middle age.

Prevention. Because antisocial behavior often begins during childhood, the major focus must be on delinquency prevention. Any measures that improve the physical and mental health of socioeconomically disadvantaged children and their families are likely to reduce delinquency and violent crime. Often, recurrently violent people have sustained many insults to the central nervous system (CNS), prenatally and throughout childhood and adolescence. Consequently, programs must be developed to educate parents about the dangers to their children of CNS injury from maltreatment, including the effects of psychoactive substances on the brain of the growing fetus. Public education about the releasing effect of alcohol on violent behaviors (not to mention its contribution to vehicular homicide) may also reduce crime.

In a Surgeon General's Report on Violence and Public Health issued over 10 years ago, the committee on the prevention of assault and homicide emphasized the importance of discouraging corporal punishment in the home, forbidding it in the schools, and even abolishing capital punishment by the state, saying that all are models and sanctions for violence. Since that time, capitol punishment has been instituted in states that did not have it, such as New York.

Although people disagree about the contribution of violence in the media to violent crime, there is universal recognition that the media have propaganda potential. The extent to which the media, such as television, can be used to transmit positive social values has not yet been realized. The guidelines issued by the television industry to indicate the amount of sex and violence in programs is an attempt to deal with the issue; however, program content that espouses traditional societal values would be beneficial.

The most successful preventive measures within the field of medicine have come from community-wide public health programs (such as campaigns against smoking) and from programs that detect individual vulnerabilities (such as individual monitoring of blood pressure). Studies of adult antisocial behavior reveal the contribution of broad cultural factors and constellations of individual biopsychosocial vulnerabilities. Prevention programs must recognize and address both kinds of factors.

MALINGERING

Malingering is characterized by the voluntary production and presentation of false or grossly exaggerated physical or psychological symptoms. Patients always have an external motivation that falls into one of three categories: to avoid difficult or dangerous situations, responsibilities, or punishment; to receive compensation, free hospital room and board, a source of drugs, or haven from the police; and to retaliate when the patient feels guilt or suffers a financial loss, legal penalty, or job loss. The presence of a clearly definable goal is the main factor that differentiates malingering from factitious disorders.

Epidemiology

The incidence of malingering is unknown, but it is common and occurs most frequently in settings with a preponderance of men—the military, prisons, factories, and other industrial settings—although the condition also occurs in women.

Diagnosis and Clinical Features

DSM-IV includes the following remarks about malingering:

> The essential feature of Malingering is the intentional production of false or grossly exaggerated physical or psychological symptoms, motivated by external incentives such as avoiding military duty, avoiding work, obtaining financial compensation, evading criminal prosecution, or obtaining drugs. Under some circumstances, malingering may represent adaptive behavior—for example, feigning illness while a captive of the enemy during wartime.
>
> Malingering should be strongly suspected if any combination of the following is noted:
>
> 1. Medicolegal context of presentation (e.g., the person is referred by an attorney to the clinician for examination)
> 2. Marked discrepancy between the person's claimed stress or disability and the objective findings

3. Lack of cooperation during the diagnostic evaluation and in complying with the prescribed treatment regimen
4. The presence of Antisocial Personality Disorder

Many malingerers express mostly subjective, vague, ill-defined symptoms—for example, headache; pains in the neck, lower back, chest, or abdomen; dizziness; vertigo; amnesia; anxiety; and depression—and the symptoms often have a family history, in all likelihood not medically caused but incredibly difficult to refute. Malingerers may complain bitterly and describe how much the symptoms impair their normal function and how much they dislike the symptoms. The patients may use the best doctors who are the most trusted (and perhaps most gullible) and promptly and willingly pay all their bills, even if excessive, to impress the doctors with their integrity. To seem credible, malingerers must report the symptoms but tell their physicians as little as possible. But often they complain of misery without objective signs or other symptoms congruent with recognized diseases and syndromes; if they do describe all the symptoms of a disease, the symptoms are said to come and go. Malingerers are often preoccupied with compensation rather than cure and have a knowledge of the law and precedents relative to their claims.

Objective tests—such as audiometry, brainstem audiometry, auditory and visually evoked potentials, galvanic skin response, electromyography, and nerve conduction studies—may be helpful in sorting out auditory, labyrinthine, ophthalmological, neurological, and other problems.

Differential Diagnosis

As DSM-IV notes:

> Malingering differs from Factitious Disorder in that the motivation for the symptom production in Malingering is an external incentive, whereas in Factitious Disorder external incentives are absent. Evidence of an intrapsychic need to maintain the sick role suggests Factitious Disorder. Malingering is differentiated from Conversion Disorder and other Somatoform Disorders by the intentional production of symptoms and by the obvious, external incentives associated with it. In Malingering (in contrast to Conversion Disorder), symptom relief is not often obtained by suggestion or hypnosis.

Table 32–2 lists features that differentiate malingering from genuine illness.

Treatment

A patient suspected of malingering should be thoroughly and objectively evaluated, and the physician should refrain from showing any suspicion. If a clinician becomes angry (a common response to malingerers) a confrontation may occur, with two consequences: The doctor–patient relationship is disrupted, and no further positive intervention is possible; the patient will be even more guarded, and proof of deception may become virtually impossible. If the patient is accepted and not discredited, subsequent patient hospital or outpatient observation may reveal the versatility of the symptoms, which are consistently present only when patients know that they are being observed. Preserving the doctor–patient relationship is often essential to diagnosis and long-term treatment. Careful evaluation usually reveals the relevant issue without the need for a confrontation. It is usually best to use an intensive treatment approach as though the symptoms were real. The symptoms can then be given up in response to treatment, without the patient's losing face.

Table 32–2
Malingering Features Usually Not Found in Genuine Illness

Symptoms are vague, ill-defined, overdramatized, and not in conformity with known clinical conditions.
The patient seeks addicting drugs, financial gain, the avoidance of onerous (eg, jail) or other unwanted conditions.
History, examination, and evaluative data do not elucidate complaints.
The patient is uncooperative and refuses to accept a clean bill of health or an encouraging prognosis.
The findings appear compatible with self-inflicted injuries.
History or records reveal multiple past episodes of injury or undiagnosed illness.
Records or test data appear to have been tampered with (eg, erasures, unprescribed substances in urine).

Courtesy of Arthur T. Meyerson, M.D.

PHASE OF LIFE PROBLEM

DSM-IV includes the following description of phase of life problem:

> This category can be used when the focus of clinical attention is a problem associated with a particular developmental phase or some other life circumstance that is not due to a mental disorder or, if it is due to a mental disorder, is sufficiently severe to warrant independent clinical attention. Examples include problems associated with entering school, leaving parental control, starting a new career, and changes involved in marriage, divorce, and retirement.

External events are most likely to overwhelm people's adaptive capacities when they are unexpected or numerous—that is, a number of stresses occurring within a short time—when the strain is chronic and unremitting, or when one loss heralds a myriad of concomitant adjustments that strain people's recuperative powers.

The strains most likely to produce anxiety and depression relate to major life-cycle changes: marriage, occupation, and parenthood changes. These events affect both men and women, but women, those in low socioeconomic groups, and minorities seem particularly vulnerable to adverse reactions. Again, the change creates significant strain when it is unexpected and when it involves not only adjustment to a loss (a spouse or a job) but also the need to adjust to a new status that entails further hardships and problems.

In general, people are able to adjust to life changes if they have mature defense mechanisms such as altruism, humor, and capacity for sublimation. Flexibility, reliability, strong family ties, regular employment, adequate income, job satisfaction, a pattern of regular recreation and social participation, realistic goals, and a history of adequate performance—in short, a full and satisfying life—create resilience to deal with life changes.

NONCOMPLIANCE WITH TREATMENT

In DSM-IV the following statement appears:

> This category can be used when the focus of clinical attention is noncompliance with an important aspect of the treatment for a mental disorder or a general medical condition. The reasons for noncompliance may include discomfort resulting from treatment (e.g., medication side effects), expense of treatment, decisions based on personal value judgments of religious or cultural beliefs about the advantages and disadvantages of the proposed treatment, maladaptive personality traits or coping styles (e.g., denial of illness), or the presence of a mental disorder (e.g., Schizophrenia, Avoidant Personality Disorder). This category should be used only when the problem is sufficiently severe to warrant independent clinical attention.

(Further discussion of noncompliance and compliance appears in Chapter 1.)

RELIGIOUS AND SPIRITUAL PROBLEM

In DSM-IV the following statement appears:

> This category can be used when the focus of clinical attention is a religious or spiritual problem. Examples include distressing experiences that involve loss or questioning of faith, problems associated with conversion to a new faith, or questioning other spiritual values which may not necessarily be related to an organized church or religious institution.

From the psychological point of view, perhaps the most striking feature of religion is its universality. There are few societies in which religion plays no significant role, and there are relatively few people who, at one time or another, have not experienced some religious stirring. From this universality one must infer that religion performs some adaptive function, that it is invoked to satisfy one or more universal human needs.

Pastoral Counseling

The pastoral function of the clergy in the United States extends to assisting the individual members of the religious congregation to deal with serious problems that they cannot resolve alone and that may cause anguish and damage. The pastoral function includes visiting the ill, comforting the mourner, encouraging the widow, and helping the orphan. The term *counseling* involves consultation for the purpose of helping the troubled person solve a specific presenting problem. It may be a marital problem, a parent–child problem, a problem of conflict among siblings, or a complaint of feeling guilt or anxiety.

CULTS

Cults are charismatic groups that can affect participants in adverse ways, which may eventually bring them into contact with the mental health care system. Cults are characterized by an intensely held belief system and ideology imposed on members, by a high level of group cohesion serving to prevent members' freedom of choice to leave the group, and by a profound influence on the members' behavior, possibly inducing psychiatric symptoms, producing overt psychotic disorders.

Most potential cult members are in their adolescence or otherwise struggling with establishing their own identities. They are drawn to a cult, which holds out the false promise of emotional well-being and purports to offer the sense of direction for which the people are searching. Cult members are encouraged to proselytize and to draw new members into the group. They are often encouraged to break with family members and friends and to socialize only with other group members. Cults are invariably led by charismatic personalities, who are often ruthless in their quest for financial, sexual, and power gains. Cult leaders usually demand conformity to the cult's ideological belief system, which may have strong religious or quasi-religious overtones. Exit therapy has been developed to guide cult members out of the group in cases where lingering emotional ties to people outside the cult can be mobilized.

On March 28, 1997, the biggest group of suicides recorded in the United States was found in Rancho Santa Fe, California. Thirty-nine men and women who were members of a millennialist cult called Heaven's Gate killed themselves with lethal doses of phenobarbital combined with alcohol. Some suffocated themselves with plastic bags. Cult members believed that their human bodies were physical containers that had to be discarded so that their souls could be transported to a new level of being. Their souls were to rendezvous with an unidentified flying object that was trailing the Hale-Bopp comet passing Earth at that time and was a signal for them to kill themselves. In their new plane of existence, they would inhabit new bodies and travel through different galaxies. The cult was made up primarily of young persons in their 20s who had left their parental homes for various reasons and who were seeking a sense of spiritual identity. The cult leader was an ex-minister who called himself Bo after Bo-peep who shepherded sheep and, like most cult leaders, was charismatic and convincing to a group of psychologically vulnerable people seeking an omnipotent godlike authority figure to diminish their sense of anxiety, depression, and alienation. The cult recruited its members through personal contacts and advertising on the internet where they had a site called Heaven's Gate.

ACCULTURATION PROBLEM

In DSM-IV the following statement about the acculturation problem appears:

> This category can be used when the focus of clinical attention is a problem involving adjustment to a different culture (e.g., following migration).

Periods of cultural transition, with changing mores and fluidity of role definition, may increase people's vulnerability to life strain. Extreme cultural transition can create a condition of severe distress, also called culture shock, which occurs when a person is suddenly thrust into an alien culture or has divided loyalties to two different cultures. In a less extreme form, culture shock occurs when young men and women enter the army, when people change jobs, when families move or undergo a significant change in income, when children first go to school, and when black inner-city children are bused to white middle-class schools. (Further discussion of culture change and culture shock appears in Chapter 4, Section 4.6.)

Brainwashing

First practiced by the Chinese Communists on U.S. prisoners during the Korean War, brainwashing is the deliberate creation of cultural shock. A condition of isolation, alienation, and intimidation is developed for the express purpose of assaulting ego strengths and leaving the person to be brainwashed vulnerable to the imposition of alien ideas and behavior that would usually be rejected. Brainwashing relies on both mental and physical coercion. All people are vulnerable to brainwashing if they are exposed to it for a long enough time, if they are alone and without support, and if they are without hope of escape from the situation. Help from the mental health care system, in the form of deprogramming, is usually necessary to help brainwashed persons readjust to their usual environments after the brainwashing experience. Supportive therapy is offered, with emphasis on re-education, restitution of ego strengths that existed before the trauma, and alleviation of the guilt and depression that are remnants of the frightening experience and of the lost confidence and confusion in identity that result from it.

AGE-RELATED COGNITIVE DECLINE

DSM-IV includes the following comment:

> This category can be used when the focus of clinical attention is an objectively identified decline in cognitive functioning consequent to the aging process that is within normal limits given the person's age. Individuals with this condition may report problems remembering names or appointments or may experience difficulty in solving complex problems. This category should be considered only after it has been determined that the cognitive impairment is not attributable to a specific mental disorder or neurological condition.

Daily intake of vitamin E (200 to 600 mg) has been reported to delay age-related cognitive loss.

References

Bernard LC, Houston W, Natoli L: Malingering on neuropsychological memory tests: Potential objective indicators. J Clin Psychol *49:* 45, 1993.

Buckalew LW, Buckalew NM: Survey of the nature and prevalence of patients' noncompliance and implications for intervention. Psychol Rep *76:* 315, 1995.

Caine ED: Should aging-associated cognitive decline be included in DSM-IV? J Neuropsychiatry Clin Neurosci *5:* 1, 1993.

Holmes T: Life situations, emotions, and disease. Psychosomatics *19:* 747, 1978.

Hutri M: When careers reach a dead end: Identification of occupational crisis states. J Psychol *130:* 383, 1996.

Keck PE Jr, McElroy SL, Strakowski SM, Stanton SP, Kizer DL, Balistreri TM, Bennet JA, Tugrul KC, West SA: Factors associated with pharmacologic noncompliance in patients with mania. J Clin Psychiatry *57:* 292, 1996.

Kissane DW, Bloch S, Dowe DL, Snyder RD, Onghena P, McKenzie DP, Wallace CS: The Melbourne Family Grief Study, I: Perceptions of family functioning in bereavement. Am J Psychiatry *153:* 650, 1996.

Kissane DW, Bloch S, Onghena P, McKenzie DP, Snyder RD, Dowe DL: The Melbourne Family Grief Study, II: Psychosocial morbidity and grief in bereaved families. Am J Psychiatry *153:* 659, 1996.

Lehman DR, Davis CG, DeLongis A, Wortman CB: Positive and negative life changes following bereavement and their relations to adjustment. J Soc Clin Psychol *12:* 90, 1993.

Lewis DO, Pincus JH, Feldman M, Jackson L, Bard B: Psychiatric, neurological, and psychoeducational characteristics of 15 death row inmates in the United States. Am J Psychiatry *143:* 7, 1986.

Lukoff D, Lu FG, Turner R: Cultural considerations in the assessment and treatment of religious and spiritual problems. Psychiatr Clin North Am *18:* 467, 1995.

Mills MJ, Lipian MS: Malingering. In *Comprehensive Textbook of Psychiatry,* ed 6, HI Kaplan, BJ Sadock, editors, p 1614. Williams & Wilkins, Baltimore, 1995.

Pawliuk N, Grizenko N, Chan-Yip A, Gantous P, Mathew J, Nguyen D: Acculturation style and psychological functioning in children of immigrants. Am J Orthopsychiatry *66:* 111, 1996.

Repetti RL: Short-term effects of occupational stressors on daily mood and health complaints. Health Psychol *12:* 125, 1993.

Rogler LH, Cortes DE, Malgady RG: Acculturation and mental health status among Hispanics: Convergence and new directions for research. Am Psychol *46:* 585, 1991.

Sadock VA: Other additional conditions that may be a focus of clinical attention. In *Comprehensive Textbook of Psychiatry,* ed 6, HI Kaplan, BJ Sadock, editors, p 1633. Williams & Wilkins, Baltimore, 1995.

33 Psychiatric Emergencies

33.1 Suicide

Although suicide has occurred in many societies at least as early as Roman times, attitudes toward it have varied. The Stoics saw suicide as a free person's last act; to the Roman Catholic Church it is a sin. At the end of the 19th century, Émile Durkheim suggested that suicide is more a social than a moral deed.

Today, most workers in Western societies consider suicide as a complex phenomenon associated with psychological, biological, and social factors. Suicide may result from a desire to escape from a difficult situation or to hurt a person or an institution. Some have speculated that a genetic factor predisposes certain people to depression and to suicide.

Most commonly, however, suicide seems to arise from a depressed person's feeling that life is so unbearable that death is the only escape from great pain, terminal illness, financial losses, and other such circumstances. A suicidal person experiences hopelessness and helplessness, ambivalent conflicts between life and unending stress, and no apparent possibilities for change or improvement. These feelings and attitudes are distress signals. The next step is intentional self-inflicted death.

Edwin Shneidman defined suicide as ''the conscious act of self-induced annihilation, best understood as a multidimensional malaise in a needful individual who defines an issue for which the act is perceived as the best solution.'' Thus suicide is not random or pointless, but a release from a problem or crisis inevitably producing intense suffering. (Suicide in children and adolescents is discussed in Chapter 48.)

EPIDEMIOLOGY

Incidence and Prevalence

Each year about 30,000 people die by suicide in the United States. This figure refers to successful suicides; estimates for the number of attempted suicides are 8 to 10 times as high. Lost in the reporting are intentional misclassifications of the cause of death, accidents of undetermined cause, and so-called chronic suicides—for example, deaths through alcohol and other substance abuse, and consciously poor adherence to medical regimens for diabetes, obesity, and hypertension. There are about 75 suicides a day in this country—about 1 every 20 minutes.

The total suicide rate has remained fairly constant over the years and is currently 12.0 per 100,000. In 1977 the rate peaked at 13.3 suicide deaths per 100,000 and has slightly declined since then. Suicide is currently ranked as the ninth overall cause of death in this country, after heart disease, cancer, cerebrovascular disease, chronic obstructive pulmonary diseases, accidents, pneumonia and influenza, diabetes mellitus, and human immunodeficiency virus (HIV) virus.

U.S. suicide rates are at the midpoint of the national rates for industrialized countries as reported to the United Nations. Internationally, suicide rates range from highs of more than 25 per 100,000 people in Scandinavia, Switzerland, Germany, Austria, the eastern European countries (the so-called suicide belt), and Japan, to fewer than 10 per 100,000 in Spain, Italy, Ireland, Egypt, and the Netherlands.

A state-by-state analysis of suicides in the last decade among people between the ages of 15 to 44 revealed that New Jersey had the nation's lowest suicide rates for both sexes. Nevada and New Mexico had the highest rates for men, and Nevada and Wyoming had the highest rates for women. Women in Nevada killed themselves at a higher frequency than did men in New Jersey. The prime suicide site of the world is the Golden Gate Bridge in San Francisco, with more than 800 suicides since the bridge opened in 1937.

Associated Factors

Sex. Men commit suicide more than 3 times as often as do women, a rate that is stable over all ages. Women, however, are 4 times more likely to *attempt* suicide than are men.

Methods. Men's higher rate of successful suicide is related to the methods they use: firearms, hanging, or jumping from high places. Women more commonly take an overdose of psychoactive substances or a poison, but they are beginning to use firearms more often than previously. In states with gun control laws, the use of guns has decreased as a method of suicide.

Age. Suicide rates increase with age and underscore the significance of the midlife crisis. Among men, suicides peak after age 45; among women, the greatest number of completed suicides occurs after age 55. Rates of 40 per 100,000 population occur in men age 65 and older. Older people attempt suicide less often than do younger people, but are more often successful. Although they are only 10 percent of the total population, older people account for 25 percent of suicides. The rate for those 75 or older is more than 3 times the rate among young people.

The suicide rate, however, is rising most rapidly among young people, particularly for males 15 to 24 years old, and the rate is still rising. The suicide rate for females in the same age group is increasing at a lesser rate than males. Among men 25 to 34 years old, the suicide rate increased almost 30 percent over the past decade. Suicide is the third leading cause of death in the 15- to 24-year-old age group after accidents and homicides, and attempted suicides in this age group number between 1 million and 2 million annually. The majority of suicides now occur among those aged 15 to 44.

Race. Two of every three suicides are white males. The rate of suicide among whites is nearly twice that among all other groups; these figures, however, are now questionable as the suicide rate among blacks is rising. The suicide rate for white males (19.6 per 100,000 people) is 1.6 times that for black males (12.5), 4 times that for white women (4.8), and 8.2 times that for black women (2.4) (Fig. 33.1–1). Among young people who live in inner cities and certain Native American and Inuit groups, suicide rates have greatly exceeded the national rate. Suicide rates among immigrants are higher than in the native-born population.

Religion. Historically, suicide rates among Roman Catholic populations have been lower than the rates among Protestants and Jews. One's degree of orthodoxy and integration may be a more accurate measure of risk in this category than is simple institutional religious affiliation.

Marital Status. Marriage reinforced by children seems to significantly lessen the risk of suicide: Among married people the suicide rate is 11 per 100,000. Single, never-married people register an overall rate of nearly double that for married people. Previously married people, however, show sharply higher rates than do those who never married: 24 per 100,000 among people who are widowed; 40 per 100,000 among those who are divorced, with divorced men registering 69 suicides per 100,000, compared with 18 per 100,000 for divorced women. Suicide occurs more frequently than usual in people who are socially isolated and have a family history of suicide (attempted or real). People who commit so-called anniversary suicides take their lives on the same day as did a member of their family.

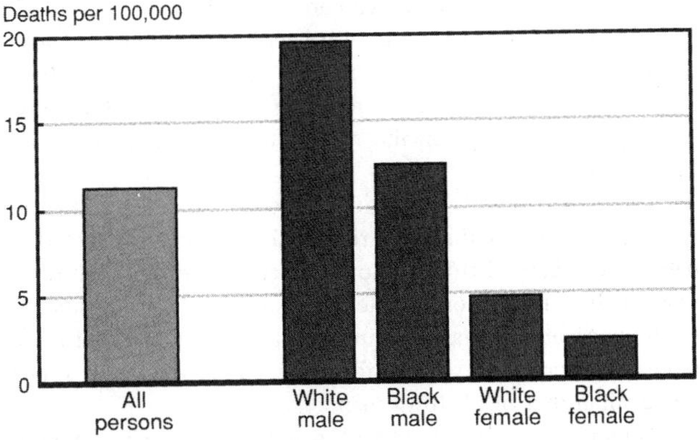
Deaths per 100,000
20
15
10
5
0
All persons
White male
Black male
White female
Black female

FIGURE 33.1–1

Death rates for suicide, according to race and sex: United States, 1989. Death rates are age adjusted. (Reprinted with permission from National Center for Health Statistics: *Health, United States, 1991*. Public Health Service, Hyattsville, MD, 1992.)

Occupation. The higher a person's social status, the greater the risk of suicide, but a fall in social status also increases the risk. Work, in general, protects against suicide. Among occupational rankings, professionals, particularly physicians, have traditionally been considered to be at the greatest risk of suicide, but the best recent studies have found no increased suicide risk for male physicians in the United States. Their annual suicide rate is about 36 per 100,000, which is the same as that for white men over 25 years of age. Recent U.K. and Scandinavian data, by contrast, show that the suicide rate for male physicians is 2 to 3 times the rate found in the general male population of the same age.

Studies agree that female physicians have a higher risk of suicide than do other women. In the United States the annual suicide rate for female physicians is about 41 per 100,000, compared with the rate of 12 per 100,000 among all white women over 25 years of age. Similarly, in England and Wales the suicide rate for unmarried female physicians is 2.5 times greater than the rate among unmarried women in the general population, although it is comparable to that of other groups of professional women.

Studies show that physicians who commit suicide have a mental disorder. The most common mental disorders among physicians and among physician suicide victims are depressive disorders and substance dependence. Often, a physician who commits suicide has experienced recent professional, personal, or family difficulties. Both male and female physicians commit suicide significantly more often by substance overdoses and less often by firearms than do people in the general population; drug availability and knowledge about toxicity are important factors in physician suicides. Some evidence indicates that female physicians have an unusually high lifetime risk for mood disorders, which may be the major determinant of the elevated suicide risk.

Among physicians, psychiatrists are considered to be at greatest risk, followed by ophthalmologists and anesthesiologists, but the trend is toward an equalization among all specialties. Special at-risk populations are musicians, dentists, law enforcement officers, lawyers, and insurance agents. Suicide is higher among unemployed than among employed people. The suicide rate increases during economic recessions and depressions and times of high unemployment and decreases during times of high employment and during wars.

Climate. No significant seasonal correlation with suicide has been found. Suicides increase slightly in Spring and Fall, but contrary to popular belief, not during December and holiday periods.

Physical Health. The relation of physical health and illness to suicide is significant. Previous medical care appears to be a positively correlated risk indicator of suicide: 32 percent of all people who commit suicide have had medical attention within 6 months of death. Postmortem studies show that a physical illness is present in some 25 to 75 percent of all suicide victims; a physical illness is estimated to be an important contributing factor in 11 to 51 percent of all suicides. In each instance the percentage increases with age. For example, 50 percent of men with cancer who commit suicide do so within a year of receiving the diagnosis. Cancer of the breast or the genitals is found in 70 percent of all women with cancer who commit suicide. Seven diseases of the central nervous system (CNS) increase the risk of suicide: epilepsy, multiple sclerosis, head injury, cardiovascular disease, Huntington's disease, dementia, and acquired immune deficiency syndrome (AIDS). All these diseases are associated with mood disorders, and patients with epilepsy have available barbiturates and other medications with which to kill themselves.

Some endocrine conditions are associated with increased suicide risk: Cushing's disease, Klinefelter's syndrome, and porphyria. Mood disorders also attend these disorders. Two gastrointestinal disorders with an increased suicide risk are peptic ulcer and cirrhosis, both physical disorders found among people who are alcohol dependent. Two urogenital problems with an increased suicide risk are prostatic hypertrophy treated with prostatectomy and renal disease treated with hemodialysis; mood changes may occur in both conditions.

Factors associated with illness and contributing to both suicides and suicide attempts are: loss of mobility, especially when physical activity is important to occupation or recreation; disfigurement, particularly among women; and chronic, intractable pain. In addition to the direct effects of illness, the secondary effects—for example, disruption of relationships and loss of occupational status—are prognostic factors.

Certain drugs can produce depression, which may lead to suicide in some cases. Among these drugs are reserpine (Serpasil), corticosteroids, antihypertensives, and some anticancer agents.

Mental Health. Highly significant psychiatric factors in suicide include substance abuse, depressive disorders, schizophrenia, and other mental disorders. Almost 95 percent of all people who commit or attempt suicide have a diagnosed mental disorder. Depressive disorders account for 80 percent of this figure, schizophrenia accounts for 10 percent, and dementia or delirium for 5 percent. Among all people with mental disorders, 25 percent are also alcohol-dependent and have dual diagnoses. People with delusional depression are at the highest risk of suicide. The suicide risk in people with depressive disorders is about 15 percent, and 25 percent of all those with a history of impulsive behavior or violent acts are also at high risk of suicide. Previous psychiatric hospitalization for any reason increases the risk of suicide.

Among adults who commit suicide, significant differences between young and old exist for both psychiatric diagnoses and antecedent stressors. A study in San Diego, California, showed that diagnoses of substance abuse and antisocial personality disorder occurred most often among suicides under 30 years of age, and diagnoses of mood disorders and cognitive disorders most often among suicides ages 30 and over. Stressors associated with suicide in those under 30 were separation, rejection, unemployment, and legal troubles; illness stressors most often occurred among suicide victims over 30.

Psychiatric Patients. Psychiatric patients' risk for suicide is 3 to 12 times greater than that of nonpatients. The degree of risk varies according to age, sex, diagnosis, and inpatient or outpatient status. After adjustment for age, male and female psychiatric patients who have at some time been inpatients have 5 and 10 times higher suicide risks, respectively, than do their counterparts in the general population. For male and female outpatients who have never been admitted to a hospital for psychiatric treatment, the suicide risks are 3 and 4 times greater, respectively, than are those of their counterparts in the general population. The higher suicide risk for psychiatric patients who have been inpatients reflects the fact that patients with severe mental disorders tend to be hospitalized—for example, patients with depressive disorder who require electroconvulsive therapy (ECT). The psychiatric diagnosis with greatest risk of suicide in both sexes is a mood disorder.

Those in the general population who commit suicide tend to be middle aged or older, but studies increasingly report that psychiatric patients who commit suicide tend to be relatively young. In one study the mean age of male suicides was 29.5 years and that of women 38.4 years. The relative youthfulness of these suicide cases was due partly to the fact that two early-onset, chronic mental disorders—schizophrenia and recurrent major depressive disorder—accounted for just over half of all these suicides, and so reflected an age and diagnostic pattern found in most studies of psychiatric patient suicides.

A small but significant percentage of psychiatric patients who commit suicide do so while they are inpatients. Most of these do not kill themselves in the psychiatric ward itself but on the hospital grounds, while on a pass or weekend leave, or when absent without leave.

For both sexes, the suicide risk is highest in the first week of the psychiatric admission; after three to five weeks, inpatients have a risk no greater than the general population. The inpatient rates of suicide do not rise uniformly with age, as in the general population; in fact, the rates for female psychiatric patients fall with advancing age. This difference is due mainly to the fact that older people who are suicidal do not seek medical aid. Times of staff rotation, particularly of the psychiatric residents, are periods associated with inpatient suicides. Epidemics of inpatient suicides tend to be associated with periods of ideological change on the ward, staff disorganization, and staff demoralization.

Among psychiatric outpatients, the period after discharge is a time of increased suicide risk. A follow-up study of 5,000 patients discharged from an Iowa psychiatric hospital showed that, in the first 3 months after discharge, the rate of suicide for female patients was 275 times higher than that of all Iowa women; the rate of suicide for male patients was 70 times higher than that of all Iowa men.

Patients, especially those with panic disorder, who frequent emergency services, also have an increased suicide risk. One study reported that such patients have a suicide rate more than 7 times the age-adjusted and sex-adjusted rate for the general population (but the rate is similar to that of other clinical psychiatric populations). The two main risk groups are patients with depressive disorders, schizophrenia, and substance abuse, and patients who make repeated visits to the emergency room. Thus, mental health professionals working in emergency services must be well trained in taking patients' psychiatric histories, examining their mental states, assessing suicidal risk, and making appropriate dispositions. They must also be aware of the need to contact patients at risk who fail to keep follow-up appointments.

DEPRESSIVE DISORDERS. Mood disorders are the diagnoses most commonly associated with suicide. As the suicide risk in depressive disorders rises mainly when patients are depressed, the psychopharmacological advances of the past 25 years may have reduced the suicide risk among patients with depressive disorder. Nevertheless, the age-adjusted suicide rates for patients with mood disorders have been estimated to be 400 per 100,000 for male patients and 180 per 100,000 for female patients.

More patients with depressive disorders commit suicide early in the illness rather than later; more men than women commit suicide; and the chance of depressed persons' killing themselves is increased by their being single, separated, divorced, widowed, or recently bereaved. Depressive disorder patients in the community who commit suicide tend to be middle aged or older.

A few studies have investigated which patients with mood disorders have an increased suicide risk. These studies indicate that social isolation enhances suicidal tendencies among depressed patients. This finding is in accord with the data from epidemiological studies showing that people who commit suicide may be poorly integrated into society. Suicide among depressed patients is likely at the onset or the end of a depressive episode. As among other psychiatric patients, the months after discharge from a hospital are a time of high risk. Studies show that one third or more of depressed patients who commit suicide do so within 6 months of leaving a hospital; presumably they have relapsed.

Regarding outpatient treatment, most depressed suicidal patients had a history of therapy; however, less than half were receiving psychiatric treatment at the time of suicide. Of those who were in treatment, studies have shown that it was less than adequate. For example, most patients who received antidepressants were prescribed subtherapeutic doses of the medication.

SCHIZOPHRENIA. The suicide risk is high among patients with schizophrenia: Up to 10 percent die by committing suicide. In the United States an estimated 4,000 schizophrenic patients commit suicide each year. The onset of schizophrenia is typically in adolescence or early adulthood, and most of these patients who commit suicide do so during the first few years of their illness; therefore, schizophrenic patients who commit suicide are young.

About 75 percent of all schizophrenic suicides are committed by unmarried men, and about 50 percent have made a previous suicide attempt. Depressive symptoms are closely associated with their suicides. Hospital-based studies have reported that depressive symptoms were present during the last period of contact in at least two thirds of all the patients with schizophrenia who committed suicide; only a small percentage committed suicide because of hallucinated instructions or of a need to escape persecutory delusions. Up to 50 percent of suicides among patients with schizophrenia occur during the first few weeks and months after discharge from a hospital; only a minority commit suicide while inpatients.

Thus, the risk factors for suicide among patients with schizophrenia are young age, male gender, single marital status, a previous suicide attempt, a vulnerability to depressive symptoms, and a recent discharge from a hospital. Having three or four hospitalizations during their 20s probably undermines the social, occupational, and sexual adjustment of possibly suicidal schizophrenic patients. Consequently, potential suicide victims are likely to be male, unmarried, unemployed, socially isolated, and living alone—perhaps in a single room. After discharge from their last hospitalization, they may experience a new adversity or return to ongoing difficulties. As a result, they become dejected, experience feelings of helplessness and hopelessness, reach a depressed state, and have, and eventually act on, suicidal ideas.

ALCOHOL DEPENDENCE. Up to 15 percent of all alcohol-dependent people commit suicide. The suicide rate for those who are alcoholic is estimated to be about 270 per 100,000 a year; in the United States, between 7,000 and 13,000 alcohol-dependent people commit suicide each year.

About 80 percent of all alcohol-dependent suicide victims are male, a percentage that largely reflects the sex ratio for alcohol dependence. Alcohol-dependent suicide victims tend to be white, middle aged, unmarried, friendless, socially isolated, and currently drinking. Up to 40 percent have made a previous suicide attempt. Up to 40 percent of all suicides by people who are alcohol-dependent occur within a year of the patient's last hospitalization; older alcohol-dependent patients are at particular risk during the postdischarge period.

Studies show that many alcohol-dependent patients who eventually commit suicide are rated as being depressed during hospitalization and that up to two thirds are assessed as having mood disorder symptoms during the period in which they commit suicide. As many as 50 percent of all alcohol-dependent suicide victims have experienced the loss of a close affectionate relationship during the previous year. Such interpersonal losses and other types of undesirable life events are probably brought about by the alcohol dependence and contribute to the development of the mood disorder symptoms, which are often present in the weeks and months before the suicide.

The largest group of male alcohol-dependent patients are those with an associated antisocial personality disorder. Studies show that such patients are particularly likely to attempt suicide; to abuse other substances; to exhibit impulsive, aggressive, and criminal behaviors; and to be found among alcohol-dependent suicide victims.

OTHER SUBSTANCE DEPENDENCE. Studies in various countries have found an increased suicide risk among those who abuse substances. The suicide rate for people who are heroin-dependent is about 20 times greater than the rate for the general population. Adolescent girls who use intravenous substances also have a high suicide rate. The availability of a lethal amount of substances, intravenous use, associated antisocial personality disorder, a chaotic lifestyle, and impulsivity are some of the factors that predispose substance-dependent people to suicidal behavior, particularly when they are dysphoric, depressed, or intoxicated.

PERSONALITY DISORDERS. A high proportion of those who commit suicide have various associated personality difficulties or disorders. Having a personality disorder may be a determinant of suicidal behavior in several ways: by predisposing to major mental disorders like depressive disorders or alcohol dependence; by leading to difficulties in relationships and social adjustment; by precipitating undesirable life events; by impairing the ability to cope with a mental or physical disorder; and by drawing people into conflicts with those around them, including family members, physicians, and hospital staff members.

An estimated 5 percent of patients with antisocial personality disorder commit suicide. Suicide is 3 times more common among prisoners than among the general population. More than one third of prisoner suicides have had past psychiatric treatment, and half have made a previous suicide threat or attempt, often in the previous 6 months.

ANXIETY DISORDER. Unsuccessful suicide attempts are made by almost 20 percent of patients with a panic disorder and social phobia. If depression is an associated feature, however, the risk of success rises.

Previous Suicidal Behavior. A past suicide attempt is perhaps the best indicator that a patient is at increased risk of suicide. Studies show that about 40 percent of depressed patients who commit suicide have made a previous attempt. The risk of a second suicide attempt is highest within 3 months of the first attempt. The relation between a mood disorder, completed suicide, and attempts at suicide is shown in Figure 33.1–2.

Depression is associated not only with completed suicide, but also with serious attempts at suicide. The clinical feature most often associated with the seriousness of the intent to die is a diagnosis of a depressive disorder. This is shown by studies that relate the clinical characteristics of suicidal patients

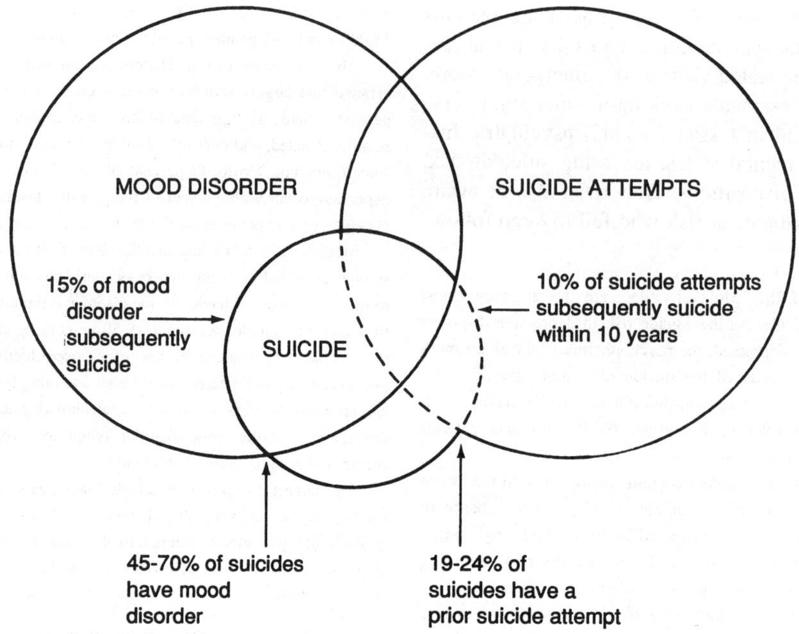
MOOD DISORDER
SUICIDE ATTEMPTS
15% of mood disorder subsequently suicide
SUICIDE
10% of suicide attempts subsequently suicide within 10 years
45-70% of suicides have mood disorder
19-24% of suicides have a prior suicide attempt

FIGURE 33.1–2
Venn diagram summarizing suicide data and its relation to mood disorder and suicide attempts. (Courtesy of Alec Roy, M.D.)

with various measures of the medical seriousness of the attempt, or of the intent to die. Also, intent-to-die scores correlate significantly with both suicide risk scores and the number and severity of depressive symptoms. When the attempters rated as having high suicide intent are compared with those with low intent, they are more often male, older, single or separated, and living alone. In other words, depressed patients who seriously attempt suicide more closely resemble suicide victims than they do suicide attempters.

ETIOLOGY

Sociological Factors

Durkheim's Theory. The first major contribution to the study of the social and cultural influences on suicide was made at the end of the 19th century by the French sociologist Émile Durkheim. In an attempt to explain statistical patterns, Durkheim divided suicides into three social categories: egoistic, altruistic, and anomic. Egoistic suicide applies to those who are not strongly integrated into any social group. The lack of family integration explains why unmarried persons are more vulnerable to suicide than married, and why couples with children are the best-protected group. Rural communities have more social integration than urban areas and, thus, less suicide. Protestantism is a less-cohesive religion than Roman Catholicism, and so Protestants have a higher suicide rate than Catholics.

Altruistic suicide applies to those prone to suicide stemming from their excessive integration into a group, with suicide being the outgrowth of the integration—for example, a Japanese soldier who sacrifices his life in battle. Anomic suicide applies to people whose integration into society is disturbed so that they cannot follow customary norms of behavior. Anomie explains why a drastic change in economic situation makes people more vulnerable than they were before their change in fortune. In Durkheim's theory, anomie also refers to social instability, and a general breakdown of society's standards and values.

Psychological Factors

Freud's Theory. Sigmund Freud offered the first important psychological insight into suicide. He described only one patient who made a suicide attempt, but he saw many depressed patients. In his paper "Mourning and Melancholia," Freud stated his belief that suicide represents aggression turned inward against an introjected, ambivalently cathected love object. Freud doubted that there would be a suicide without an earlier repressed desire to kill someone else.

Menninger's Theory. Building on Freud's ideas, Karl Menninger in *Man Against Himself* conceived of suicide as inverted homicide because of a patient's anger toward another person. This retroflexed murder is either turned inward or used as an excuse for punishment. He also described a self-directed death instinct (Freud's concept of Thanatos) plus three components of hostility in suicide: the wish to kill, the wish to be killed, and the wish to die.

Recent Theories. Contemporary suicidologists are not persuaded that a specific psychodynamic or personality structure is associated with suicide. They believe that much can be learned about the psychodynamics of suicidal patients from their fantasies about what would happen and what the consequences would be if they commit suicide. Such fantasies often include wishes for revenge, power, control, or punishment; atonement, sacrifice, or restitution; escape or sleep; rescue, rebirth, reunion with the dead; or a new life. The suicidal patients most likely to act out suicidal fantasies may have lost a love object or received a narcissistic injury, experience overwhelming affects like rage and guilt, or identify with a suicide victim. Group dynamics underlie mass suicides like those at Masada, Jonestown, and the Heaven's Gate cult.

Depressed people may attempt suicide just as they appear to be recovering from their depression. A suicide attempt can cause a long-standing depression to disappear, especially if it fulfills a patient's need for punishment. Of equal relevance, many suicide patients use a preoccupation with suicide as a way of fighting off intolerable depression and a sense of hopelessness. In fact, a study by Aaron Beck showed that hopelessness was one of the most accurate indicators of long-term suicidal risk.

Physiological Factors

Genetics. Researchers have suggested a genetic factor in suicide, and studies show that suicide runs in families. For example, at all stages of the life cycle, a family history of suicide has been noted to be present significantly more often among people who have attempted suicide than among those who have not. One major study found that the suicide risk for first-degree relatives of psychiatric patients was almost 8 times greater than that for the relatives of controls. Furthermore, the suicide risk among the first-degree relatives of psychiatric patients who had committed suicide was 4 times greater than that found among the relatives of patients who had not committed suicide. In some situations, particularly among adolescents, the family member who has committed suicide may serve as a role model with whom to identify when the option of committing suicide becomes one possible solution to intolerable psychological pain.

One study of 51 monozygotic twin pairs found nine cases of suicide; no dizygotic twins were concordant for suicide. A longitudinal study of an Amish community found 26 suicides committed in just four families, all of whom exhibited heavy genetic loading for major depressive disorder, bipolar I disorder, and other mood disorders.

The genetic factors in suicide may be those involved in the transmission of bipolar I disorder, schizophrenia, and alcohol dependence—the mental disorders most commonly associated with suicide—but a genetic factor for suicide may be independent of, or in addition to, the genetic transmission of a mental disorder. For instance, a genetic factor for impulsivity, which may be associated with an abnormality in the central serotonin system, could produce an increased suicide risk.

Neurochemistry. A serotonin deficiency, measured as a decrease in the metabolism of 5-hydroxyindoleacetic acid (5-HIAA), appeared in a group of depressed patients who attempted suicide. Those patients who attempted suicide by violent means (for example, with guns or by jumping) had a lower 5-HIAA level in the cerebrospinal fluid (CSF) than did those depressed patients who were not suicidal or who attempted suicide in a less violent manner (for example, by a substance overdose).

Some animal and human studies have indicated an association between a deficiency in the central serotonin system and poor impulse control, and some workers have viewed suicide as one type of impulsive behavior. Furthermore, a significant negative correlation between CSF 5-HIAA levels and lifetime aggression scores has been reported among patients with personality disorders. Other patient groups thought to have problems with impulse control include violent offenders, arsonists, and those with alcohol dependence, groups who have also been noted to have lower CSF 5-HIAA levels than do controls.

Researchers have also studied possible peripheral markers of suicidal behavior. High outputs of urinary free cortisol, nonsuppression of plasma cortisol after the administration of dexamethasone, an exaggerated plasma cortisol response to the infusion of 5-hydroxytryptophan, a blunted plasma thyroid-stimulating hormone (TSH) response to the infusion of thyrotropin-releasing hormone (TRH), skin conductance abnormalities, altered urinary catechol ratios, decreases in platelet serotonin uptake or titrated imipramine (Tofranil) binding number have all been reported to be associated with suicidal behavior among depressed patients.

Blood samples analyzed for platelet monoamine oxidase (MAO) from a group of normal volunteers revealed that those with the lowest level of the enzyme in their platelets had 8 times the prevalence of suicide in their families, compared with people with high levels of the enzyme. There is strong evidence for an alteration of platelet MAO activity in depressive disorders.

A few studies have shown ventricular enlargement and abnormal electroencephalograms (EEGs) in some suicidal patients.

SELF-INJURY

Studies show that about 4 percent of all patients in psychiatric hospitals have cut themselves; the female-to-male ratio is almost 3 to 1. The incidence of self-injury in psychiatric patients is estimated to be more than 50 times greater than that in the general population. Psychiatrists note that cutters have cut themselves chronically over several years. Self-injury is found in about 30 percent of all abusers of oral substances and 10 percent of all intravenous users admitted to substance-treatment units.

These patients are usually in their 20s and may be single or married. Most cut delicately, not coarsely, usually in private with a razor blade, knife, broken glass, or mirror. The wrists, arms, thighs, and legs are most commonly cut; the face, breasts, and abdomen are cut infrequently. Most people who cut themselves claim to experience no pain and give reasons such as anger at themselves or others, relief of tension, and the wish to die. The great majority are classified as having personality disorders and are significantly more introverted, neurotic, and hostile than are controls. Alcohol abuse and other substance abuse are common, and the majority of cutters have attempted suicide.

Self-mutilation has been viewed as localized self-destruction, with mishandling of aggressive impulses caused by a person's unconscious wish to punish either himself or herself or an introjected object. Some have referred to people who cut themselves as pseudosuicidal.

PREDICTION

Clinicians must assess an individual patient's risk for suicide on the basis of a clinical examination. The most predictive items associated with suicide risk are listed in Table 33.1–1. High-risk characteristics include more than 45 years of age, male gender, alcohol dependence (the suicide rate is 50 times higher in alcohol-dependent persons than in those who are not alcohol dependent), violent behavior, previous suicidal behavior, and previous psychiatric hospitalization. Suicide is grouped into high-risk–related and low-risk–related factors (Table 33.1–2).

Clinicians should always ask about suicide ideation as part of every mental status examination, especially when a patient is depressed. The patient should be asked directly: "Are you or have you ever been suicidal? Do you want to die?" Eight of 10 people who eventually kill themselves give warnings of their intent. Fifty percent say openly that they want to die. A patient's admitting to a plan of action is a particularly dangerous sign; as is a patient's becoming quiet and less agitated than in the past, when he or she had threatened suicide. Clinicians should be especially concerned with the factors listed in Table 33.1–3.

Table 33.1–1
Factors Associated with Suicide Risk

Rank Order	Factor
1	Age (45 and older)
2	Alcohol dependence
3	Irritation, rage, violence
4	Prior suicidal behavior
5	Male
6	Unwilling to accept help
7	Longer than usual duration of current episode of depression
8	Prior inpatient psychiatric treatment
9	Recent loss or separation
10	Depression
11	Loss of physical health
12	Unemployed or retired
13	Single, widowed, or divorced

Modified from Litman RE, Faberow NL, Wold CI, Brown TR: Prediction models of suicidal behaviors. In *The Prediction of Suicide,* H Beck, LP Resnik, DJ Lettieri, editors, p 141. Charles Press, Bowie, MD, 1974.

TREATMENT

Most suicides among psychiatric patients are preventable, as indicated by the evidence that inadequate assessment or treatment is associated with suicide. Some patients experience suffering so great and intense, or so chronic and unresponsive to treatment, that their eventual suicides may be perceived as inevitable. Fortunately, such patients are relatively uncommon. Other patients have severe personality disorders, are highly impulsive, and commit suicide spontaneously, often when dysphoric or intoxicated or both.

The evaluation for suicide potential involves a complete psychiatric history; a thorough examination of a patient's mental state; and an inquiry about depressive symptoms, suicidal thoughts, intents, plans, and attempts. Taken together, a lack of future plans, giving away personal property, making a will, and having recently experienced a loss imply increased risk of suicide. The decision to hospitalize a patient depends on diagnosis, severity of the depression and suicidal ideation, the patient's and the family's coping abilities, the patient's living situation, availability of social support, and the absence or presence of risk factors for suicide.

Inpatient versus Outpatient Treatment

Whether to hospitalize patients with suicidal ideation is the most important clinical decision to be made. Not all such patients require hospitalization; some may be treated on an outpatient basis. But the absence of a strong social support system, a history of impulsive behavior, and a suicidal plan of action are indications for hospitalization. To decide whether outpatient treatment is feasible, clinicians should use a straightforward clinical approach: They should ask patients considered suicidal to agree to call when reaching the point of uncertainty about to their ability to control suicidal impulses. Patients who can make such an agreement with a doctor with whom they have a relationship reaffirm the belief that they have sufficient strength to control such impulses and to seek help.

In return for a patient's commitment, clinicians should be available to the patient 24 hours a day. If a patient who is considered seriously suicidal cannot make the commitment, immediate emergency hospitalization is indicated; both the patient and the patient's family should be so advised. If, however, the patient is to be treated on an outpatient basis, the therapist should note the patient's home and work telephone numbers for emergency reference; occasionally, a patient hangs up unexpectedly during a late night call or gives only a name to the answering service. If the patient refuses hospitalization, the family must take the responsibility to be with the patient 24 hours a day.

According to Shneidman, a clinician has several practical preventive measures for dealing with a suicidal person: Reduce the psychological pain by modifying the patient's stressful environment, enlisting the aid of the spouse, the employer, or a friend; build realistic support by recognizing that the patient may have a legitimate complaint; and offer alternatives to suicide.

Many psychiatrists believe that any patient who has attempted suicide, despite its lethality, should be hospitalized. Although most of these patients voluntarily enter a hospital, the danger to self is one of the few clear-cut indications currently acceptable in all states for involuntary hospitalization. In a hospital, patients can receive antidepressant or antipsychotic medications as indicated; individual therapy, group therapy, and family therapy are available, and patients receive the hospital's social support and sense of security. Other therapeutic measures depend on patients' underlying diagnoses. For

Table 33.1–2
Evaluation of Suicide Risk

Variable	High Risk	Low Risk
Demographic and social profile		
Age	Over 45 years	Below 45 years
Sex	Male	Female
Marital status	Divorced or widowed	Married
Employment	Unemployed	Employed
Interpersonal relationship	Conflictual	Stable
Family background	Chaotic or conflictual	Stable
Health		
Physical	Chronic illness	Good health
	Hypochondriac	Feels healthy
	Excessive substance intake	Low substance use
Mental	Severe depression	Mild depression
	Psychosis	Neurosis
	Severe personality disorder	Normal personality
	Substance abuse	Social drinker
	Hopelessness	Optimism
Suicidal activity		
Suicidal ideation	Frequent, intense, prolonged	Infrequent, low intensity, transient
Suicide attempt	Multiple attempts	First attempt
	Planned	Impulsive
	Rescue unlikely	Rescue inevitable
	Unambiguous wish to die	Primary wish for change
	Communication internalized (self-blame)	Communication externalized (anger)
	Method lethal and available	Method of low lethality or not readily available
Resources		
Personal	Poor achievement	Good achievement
	Poor insight	Insightful
	Affect unavailable or poorly controlled	Affect available and appropriately controlled
Social	Poor rapport	Good rapport
	Socially isolated	Socially integrated
	Unresponsive family	Concerned family

Reprinted with permission from Adam K: Attempted suicide. Pscyhiatr Clin North Am *8*: 183, 1985.

example, if alcohol dependence is an associated problem, treatment must be directed toward alleviating that condition.

Although patients classified as acutely suicidal may have favorable prognoses, chronically suicidal patients are difficult to treat, and they exhaust the caretakers. Constant observation by special nurses, seclusion, and restraints cannot prevent suicide when a patient is resolute. Electroconvulsive therapy (ECT) may be necessary for some severely depressed patients, who may require several treatment courses.

Useful measures for the treatment of depressed suicidal inpatients include searching patients' belongings and person on arrival in the ward for objects that may be used for suicide, and repeating the search at times of exacerbation of the suicidal ideation. Ideally, suicidal depressed inpatients should be treated on a locked ward where the windows are shatterproof, and the patient's room should be located near the nursing station to maximize observation by the nursing staff. The treatment team has to assess how much to restrict the patient and whether to make regular checks or continuous direct observation. Vigorous treatment with antidepressant medication should be initiated.

Table 33.1–3
History, Signs, and Symptoms of Suicidal Risk

1. Previous attempt or fantasized suicide
2. Anxiety, depression, exhaustion
3. Availability of means of suicide
4. Concern for effect of suicide on family members
5. Verbalized suicidal ideation
6. Preparation of a will, resignation after agitated depression
7. Proximal life crisis, such as mourning or impending surgery
8. Family history of suicide
9. Pervasive pessimism or hopelessness

Supportive psychotherapy by a psychiatrist shows concern and may alleviate some of a patient's intense suffering. Some patients may be able to accept the idea that they are suffering from a recognized illness and that they will probably make a complete recovery. Patients should be dissuaded from making major life decisions while they are suicidally depressed, because such decisions are often morbidly determined and may be irrevocable. The consequences of such bad decisions can cause further anguish and misery when the patient has recovered.

Patients recovering from a suicidal depression are at particular risk. As the depression lifts, patients become energized and are thus able to put their suicidal plans into action (paradoxical suicide). Sometimes, depressed patients, with or without treatment, suddenly appear to be at peace with themselves because they have reached a secret decision to commit suicide. Clinicians should be especially suspicious of such a dramatic clinical change, which may portend a suicidal attempt.

A patient may commit suicide even when in the hospital. According to one survey, about 1 percent of all suicides were committed by patients who were being treated in general medical-surgical or psychiatric hospitals, but the annual suicide rate in psychiatric hospitals is only 0.003 percent.

Legal and Ethical Factors. Liability issues stemming from suicides in psychiatric hospitals frequently involve questions about a patient's rate of deterioration, the presence during hospitalization of clinical signs indicating risk, and psychiatrists' and staff members' awareness of and response to these clinical signs.

In about half the cases in which suicides occur while patients are on a psychiatric unit, a lawsuit results. Courts do not require zero suicide rates, but periodic patient evaluation for suicidal risk, formulation of a treatment plan with a high level of security, and that the staff members follow the treatment plan.

Currently, suicide and attempted suicide are variously viewed as a felony and a misdemeanor, respectively; in some states the acts are considered not crimes but unlawful under common law and statutes. Aiding and abetting a suicide adds another dimension to the legal morass; some court decisions have held that, although neither suicide nor attempted suicide is punishable, anyone who assists in the act may be punished. (Doctor-assisted suicide is discussed in Chapter 2, Section 2.7.)

Community Organizations

Community organizations seem to have fewer problems than do individual therapists with the ethics and legalities of helping suicidal people. Prevention centers, crisis listening posts, and so-called suicide telephone hot lines are clear attempts to intervene and diminish the isolation, withdrawal, and loneliness of suicidal patients. Outreach programs enable highly motivated laypeople to respond to cries for help in many ways. But such responses only diminish an acute crisis; highly suicidal people place fewer than 10 percent of such calls. Two studies in the United States have failed to find that suicide prevention centers had an effect on suicide rates. Nevertheless, suicide prevention centers are important mental health resources for people in distress.

References

Asnis GM, Friedman TA, Sanderson WC, Kaplan ML: Suicidal behaviors in adult psychiatric outpatients: I. Description and prevalence. Am J Psychiatry *150:* 108, 1993.

Barraclough B, Bunch J, Nelson B, Sainsbury P: A hundred cases of suicide. Br J Psychiatry *125:* 355, 1974.

Beskow J: Depression and suicide. Pharmacopsychiatry *23* (1, Suppl): 3, 1990.

Duberstein PR, Conwell Y, Caine ED: Interpersonal stressors, substance abuse, and suicide. J Nerv Ment Dis *181:* 80, 1993.

Durkheim É: *Suicide.* Free Press, Glencoe, IL, 1951.

Farmer R, Hirsch S, editors: *The Suicide Syndrome.* Croom Helm, London, 1980.

Griffith EE, Bell CC: Recent trends in suicide and homicide among blacks. JAMA *262:* 2265, 1989.

Henry JA: Suicide risk and antidepressant treatment. J Psychopharmacol *10* (1, Suppl): 39, 1996.

Kastenbaum R: Death, suicide and the older adult. Suicide Life Threat Behav *22:* 1, 1992.

Kreitman N, editor: *Parasuicide.* Wiley, New York, 1977.

Mann J, Stanley M, editors: *Psychobiology of Suicidal Behavior.* New York Academy of Sciences, New York, 1986.

Murphy GE, Wetzel RD, Robins E, McEvoy L: Multiple risk factors predict suicide in alcoholism. Arch Gen Psychiatry *49:* 459, 1992.

Osgood NJ: Suicide in the elderly: Etiology and assessment. Int Rev Psychiatry *4:* 217, 1992.

Robins E: *The Final Months: A Study of the Lives of 134 Persons Who Committed Suicide.* Oxford University Press, New York, 1981.

Roy A: Are there genetic factors in suicide? Int Rev Psychiatry *4:* 169, 1992.

Roy A, editor: *Suicide.* Williams & Wilkins, Baltimore, 1986.

Roy A: Suicide. In *Comprehensive Textbook of Psychiatry,* ed 6, HI Kaplan, BJ Sadock, editors, p 1739. Williams & Wilkins, Baltimore, 1995.

Roy A, Segal N, Centerwall B, Robinette D: Suicide in twins. Arch Gen Psychiatry *48:* 29, 1991.

Shneidman E: *Definition of Suicide.* Wiley, New York, 1985.

Shneidman ES: *The Suicidal Mind.* Oxford University Press, New York, 1996.

Spirito A, Francis G. Overholser J, Frank N: Coping, depression, and adolescent suicide attempts. J Clin Child Psychol *25* (2): 147, 1996.

Tsuang MT, Simpson JC, Fleming JA: Epidemiology of suicide. Int Rev Psychiatry *4:* 117, 1992.

van Poppel F, Day LH: A test of Durkheim's theory of suicide—without committing the "ecological fallacy." Am Sociol Rev *61* (3): 500, 1996.

Weishaar ME, Beck AT: Hopelessness and suicide. Int Rev Psychiatry *4:* 177, 1992.

▲ 33.2 Other Psychiatric Emergencies

A psychiatric emergency is any disturbance in thoughts, feelings, or actions for which immediate therapeutic intervention is necessary. For a variety of reasons—such as the growing incidence of violence, the increased appreciation of the role of medical disease in altered mental status, and the epidemic of alcohol dependence and other substance-related disorders—the number of emergency patients is on the rise. Physicians, including psychiatrists, are performing an expanded role as a primary clinician or as a consultant in integrated emergency medicine services. The widening scope of emergency psychiatry goes beyond general psychiatric practice to include such specialized problems as the abuse of substances, children, and spouses; the violence of suicide, homicide, and rape; and such social issues as homelessness, aging, competence, and acquired immune deficiency syndrome (AIDS). Emergency psychiatrists must be up-to-date on medicolegal issues and managed care.

EPIDEMIOLOGY

Psychiatric emergency rooms are used equally by men and women and more by single than married people. About 20 percent of these patients are suicidal, and about 10 percent are violent. The most common diagnoses are mood disorders (including depressive disorders and manic episodes), schizophrenia, and alcohol dependence. About 40 percent of all patients seen in psychiatric emergency rooms require hospitalization. Most visits occur during the night hours, but there is no usage difference based on the day of the week or the month of the year. Contrary to popular belief, studies have not found a higher than usual use of psychiatric emergency rooms during a full moon or during the Christmas season.

EMERGENCY PSYCHIATRIC INTERVIEW

An emergency interview is similar to a standard psychiatric interview except for the time limitation imposed by the other patients waiting to be seen and by the potential sense of urgency in assessing the risk to the patient or others. Usually, a physician focuses on the presenting complaint and the reasons that the patient has come to the emergency room. The time constraint requires that a clinician structure the interview, particularly with patients who may respond with long, rambling accounts of their illnesses. If friends, relatives, or the police accompany the patient, a supplemental history should be obtained from them, especially if the patient is mute, negativistic, uncooperative, or otherwise unable to give a coherent history.

Patients may be highly motivated to reveal themselves to gain relief from suffering, but they may also be both consciously and unconsciously motivated to conceal innermost feelings that they perceive to be shameful or threatening. If a patient has been brought to the hospital involuntarily, willingness or ability to cooperate may be impaired. A psychiatrist's relationship with a patient strongly influences what the patient does and does not say, even within the context of a first interview in an emergency room; therefore, a large portion of the psychiatric emergency interview involves the specific and sophisticated techniques of listening, observation, and interpretation that provide the foundation of psychiatric training overall. Being straightforward, honest, calm, and nonthreatening is very important, as is the ability to convey to patients the idea that the clinician is in control and will act decisively to protect them from hurting themselves or others. Table 33.2–1 summarizes a number of necessary initial factors in the evaluation of a psychiatric emergency.

Table 33.2–1
General Strategy in Evaluating Patients

I. Self-protection
- A. Know as much as possible about the patients before meeting them.
- B. Leave physical restraint procedures to those who are trained to handle them.
- C. Be alert to risks for impending violence.
- D. Attend to the safety of the physical surroundings (eg, door access, room objects).
- E. Have others present during the assessment if needed.
- F. Have others in the vicinity.
- G. Attend to developing an alliance with the patient (eg, do not confront or threaten patients with paranoid psychoses).

II. Prevent harm
- A. Prevent self-injury and suicide. Use whatever methods are necessary to prevent patients from hurting themselves during the evaluation.
- B. Prevent violence toward others. During the evaluation, briefly assess the patient for the risk of violence. If the risk is deemed significant, consider the following options:
  1. Inform the patient that violence is not acceptable.
  2. Approach the patient in a nonthreatening manner.
  3. Reassure and calm the patient or assist in reality testing.
  4. Offer medication.
  5. Inform the patient that restraint or seclusion will be used if necessary.
  6. Have teams ready to restrain the patient.
  7. When patients are restrained, always closely observe them, and frequently check their vital signs. Isolate restrained patients from agitating stimuli. Immediately plan a further approach—medication, reassurance, medical evaluation.

III. Rule out cognitive disorders caused by a general medical condition.

IV. Rule out impending psychosis.

Sometimes people contact the emergency room by telephone. In such cases a psychiatrist should obtain the number from which the call is made and the exact address. If the call is interrupted, the psychiatrist can direct help to the patient. If the patient is alone and the psychiatrist ascertains that the patient is in danger, the police should be alerted. If possible, an assistant should call the police on another line while the psychiatrist keeps the patient engaged until help arrives. The patient should not be told to drive alone to the hospital, but an emergency medical team should be dispatched to bring the patient to the hospital.

The greatest potential error in emergency room psychiatry is overlooking a physical illness as the cause of an emotional illness. Head traumas, medical illnesses, substance abuse (including alcohol), cerebrovascular diseases, metabolic abnormalities, and medications may all cause abnormal behavior, and psychiatrists should take concise medical histories that concentrate on these areas.

Violence and Assaultive Behavior

The first task in evaluating violent behavior is to ascertain its cause: Cause directs treatment. Patients with thought disorders characterized by hallucinations commanding them to kill someone require psychiatric hospitalization and antipsychotic medication. If they are unwilling to accept treatment, certification is necessary to protect the intended victim and the patient. Those who take an extreme civil libertarian perspective fail to recognize that medical certification has evolved legally not only to protect society from violent patients, but also to protect patients from the consequences of their uncontrollable behavior. Psychotic patients who, while psychotic, destroy families' and friends' property, or threaten to commit violent assaults destroy social supports that they need to help them function after the aberrant mood or delusional ideation is corrected.

Violence and assaultive behavior are difficult to predict (Table 33.2–2), but the fear with which some people regard all psychiatric patients is completely out of proportion to the few who are an authentic danger to others. The best predictors of potential violent behavior are excessive alcohol intake, a history of violent acts with arrests or criminal activity, and a history of childhood abuse. Although violent patients can arouse a realistic fear in psychiatrists, they can also touch off irrational fears that impair clinical judgment and that may lead to premature and excessive use of sedation or physical restraint. Violent patients are usually frightened by their own hostile impulses and desperately seek help to prevent loss of

Table 33.2–2
Assessing and Predicting Violent Behavior

Signs of impending violence
- Recent acts of violence, including property violence
- Verbal or physical threats (menacing)
- Carrying weapons or other objects that may be used as weapons (eg, forks, ashtrays)
- Progressive psychomotor agitation
- Alcohol or other substance intoxication
- Paranoid features in a psychotic patient
- Command violent auditory hallucinations—some but not all patients are at high risk
- Brain diseases, global or with frontal lobe findings; less commonly with temporal lobe findings (controversial)
- Catatonic excitement
- Certain manic episodes
- Certain agitated depressive episodes
- Personality disorders (rage, violence, or impulse dyscontrol)

Assess the risk for violence
- Consider violent ideation, wish, intention, plan, availability of means, implementation of plan, wish for help
- Consider demographics—sex (male), age (15–24), socioeconomic status (low), social supports (few)
- Consider the patient's history: violence, nonviolent antisocial acts, impulse dyscontrol (eg, gambling, substance abuse, suicide or self-injury, psychosis)
- Consider overt stressors (eg, marital conflict, real or symbolic loss)

control. Nevertheless, restraints should be applied if there is a reasonable risk of violence.

DIFFERENTIAL DIAGNOSIS

Emergency psychiatrists must consider a wide range of conditions that may account for the presenting signs and symptoms. The most common complaints fall within the categories of anxiety, depression, mania, and thought disorder. These conditions may overlap and have multiple causes.

The differential diagnoses of anxiety, depressive episodes, manic episodes, and thought disorders are listed in Tables 33.2–3 through 33.2–6. Anxiety is different from depression, mania, and thought disorder in that many illnesses that can cause anxiety are life-threatening. Incipient myocardial infarctions, pulmonary emboli, cardiac arrhythmias, and internal hemorrhages can cause acute anxiety to the degree of panic. Untreated congestive heart failure secondary to a silent myocardial infarction or malignant cardiac arrhythmia may be fatal. Older people and those who have just suffered a loss may be perceived as having depressive or nihilistic ideation when, in fact, age or stress has propelled them into a life-threatening illness manifested by anxiety and a sense of impending doom. People who experience depression as a side effect of antihypertensive medications may perceive spouses, children, friends, or work in a negative light that changes on cessation of the medication.

Table 33.2–7 outlines features that should make emergency room clinicians consider an organic condition as the cause of the complaint. Table 33.2–8 lists the central nervous system (CNS) disorders that require immediate treatment. Table 33.2–9 lists the CNS disorders with behavioral features that may cause patients to be brought to a psychiatric emergency room.

The differential diagnosis of violent behavior includes substance-induced persisting dementia, antisocial personality disorder, catatonic schizophrenia, cerebral infection, cerebral neoplasm, obsessive-compulsive personality disorder, dissociative disorders, impulse-control disorders, sexual disorders, idiosyncratic alcohol intoxication, delusional disorder, paranoid personality disorder, schizophrenia, social maladjustment without mental disorder, temporal lobe epilepsy, bipolar I disorder, and uncontrollable violence secondary to interpersonal stress.

TREATMENT

Patients in the grip of a violent episode pay no attention to the rational intercessions of others and probably do not even

Table 33.2–3
Differential Diagnosis of Anxiety

Alcohol delirium and withdrawal
Amphetamine (or related substance) intoxication and withdrawal
Anxiety disorders
Bipolar I disorder
Borderline personality disorder
Caffeine intoxication
Cerebral arteriosclerosis
Cocaine intoxication
Encephalitis
Essential hypertension
Hyperthyroidism
Hyperventilation syndrome
Hypocalcemia
Hypoglycemia
Hypokalemia
Impending myocardial infarction
Internal hemorrhage
Major depressive disorder
Mitral valve prolapse
Normal anxiety
Other temporal lobe diseases
Panic disorder
Paroxysmal atrial tachycardia and other cardiac arrhythmias
Pheochromocytoma
Phobias
Postconcussion syndrome
Psychomotor epilepsy
Psychotic disorders
Pulmonary embolism
Schizophrenia
Sedative, hypnotic, or anxiolytic withdrawal and delirium
Sexual disorders
Subacute bacterial endocarditis

Adapted from Andrew Edmund Slaby, M.D., Ph.D.

Table 33.2–4
Differential Diagnosis of Depressive Episodes

Adjustment disorder with depressed mood
Dysthymic disorder
Schizoaffective disorder
Schizophrenia
Major depressive disorder
Bipolar I disorder
Borderline personality disorder
Hypokalemia
Brief psychotic disorder
Cyclothymic disorder
Antihypertensive toxicity
Steroid psychotic disorder
Hypothyroidism
Cerebral neoplasm
General paresis
Amphetamine use disorders
Cocaine use disorders
Carcinoma of pancreas
Hepatitis
Postviral infection syndrome
Dementia of the Alzheimer's type
Vascular dementia
Dementia of the Alzheimer's type with late onset
Dementia of the Alzheimer's type with early onset
Cirrhosis of the liver
Arteriosclerosis
Infectious mononucleosis
Hyperthyroidism
Occult malignancy
AIDS
Schizoid personality disorder
Schizotypal personality disorder

Adapted from Andrew Edmund Slaby, M.D., Ph.D.

hear them. When armed, they are particularly dangerous and capable of murder. Such patients should be disarmed by trained law enforcement personnel without harming the patients, if at all possible. If unarmed, such patients should be approached with sufficient help and with overwhelming strength, so that there is, in effect, no contest. In the emergency room, armed police should always remove bullets from their weapons. In numerous instances, disturbed patients have grabbed a loaded gun and randomly killed others.

Patients must be placed in a safe setting. Some need to be transferred to a forensic unit because of the magnitude of their violent potential. Medication specific to a disorder is administered when indicated, unless a nonspecific measure is required to modify behavior until the cause is ascertained and specific therapy can be initiated.

The use of medication is contraindicated in acutely agitated patients who have suffered a head injury, because medication

Table 33.2–5
Differential Diagnosis of Manic Episodes

Bipolar I disorder
Schizoaffective disorder
Alcohol intoxication
Catatonic schizophrenia
Delirium
Hyperthyroidism
Postencephalitic syndrome
Steroid-induced mania
Antidepressant-induced mania
Decongestant-induced mania
Amphetamine-induced mania
Cocaine-induced mania
L-Dopa-induced mania
Brochodilator-induced mania
Phencyclidine-induced mania
AIDS
Atypical psychosis

Courtesy of Andrew Edmund Slaby, M.D., Ph.D.

Table 33.2–6
Differential Diagnosis of Thought Disorders

Schizophrenia
Bipolar I disorder
Major depressive disorder
Alcohol psychotic disorder with hallucinations
Dementia of the Alzheimer's type with early onset
Frontal lobe neoplasm
Alcohol intoxication
Adjustment disorder
Dissociative disorders
Delusional disorder
Substance-induced (eg, PCP, amphetamine) psychotic disorder
Steroid psychotic disorder
Syphilis
Endocrine diseases
Pernicious anemia
Temporal lobe epilepsy
Migraine equivalent
Cimetidine psychotic disorder
AIDS
Brief psychotic disorder
Schizophreniform disorder
Shared psychotic disorder
Atypical psychosis
Dementia of the Alzheimer's type
Vascular dementia
Dementia of the Alzheimer's type with late onset

Adapted from Andrew Edmund Slaby, M.D., Ph.D.

Table 33.2–7
Features That Point to a Medical Cause of a Mental Disorder

Acute onset (within hours or minutes, with prevailing symptoms)
First episode
Geriatric age
Current medical illness or injury
Significant substance abuse
Nonauditory disturbances of perception
Neurological symptoms—loss of consciousness, seizures, head injury, change in headache pattern, change in vision
Classic mental status signs—diminished alertness, disorientation, memory impairment, impairment in concentration and attention, dyscalculia, concreteness
Other mental status signs—speech, movement, or gait disorders
Constructional apraxia—difficulties in drawing clock, cube, intersecting pentagons, Bender gestalt design
Catatonic features—nudity, negativism, combativeness, rigidity, posturing, waxy flexibility, echopraxia, echolalia, grimacing, muteness

can confuse the clinical picture. In general, intramuscular (IM) haloperidol (Haldol) is one of the most useful emergency treatments for violent psychotic patients.

Psychotherapy

In an emergency psychiatric intervention, all attempts are made to help patients' self-esteem. Empathy is critical to healing in a psychiatric emergency. The acquired knowledge of how biogenetic, situational, developmental, and existential forces converge at one point in history to create a psychiatric emergency is tantamount to the maturation of skill in emergency psychiatry.

Adjustment disorder in all age groups may result in tantrumlike outbursts of rage. These outbursts are particularly common in marital quarrels, and police are often summoned by neighbors distressed by the sounds of a violent altercation. Such family quarrels should be approached with caution, because they may be complicated by the use of alcohol and the presence of dangerous weapons. The warring couple frequently turn their combined fury on an unwary outsider. Wounded self-esteem is a major issue, and clinicians must avoid patronizing or contemptuous attitudes and must make an effort to communicate an attitude of respect and an authentic peacemaking concern.

In family violence, psychiatrists should note the special vulnerability of selected close relatives. A wife or husband may have a curious masochistic attachment to the spouse and can provoke violence by taunting and otherwise undermining a partner's self-esteem. Such relationships often end in the murder of the provoking partner and sometimes in the suicide of the other partner, the dynamics behind most so-called suicide pacts. As in the case of many suicidal patients, many violent patients require hospitalization and usually accept the offer of inpatient care with a sense of relief.

Table 33.2–8
Common Global Central Nervous System Disorders That Require Immediate Treatment

Hypoglycemia—dextrose 50% IV or juice orally, immediately; give to all diabetics
Wernicke's encephalopathy—thiamine, 100 mg IV, immediately
Opioid intoxication—naloxone (Narcan), 4 mg IV, immediately

More than one psychotherapist or psychotherapy is frequently used in emergency therapy. For example, a 28-year-old man, depressed and suicidal after a colostomy for intractable colitis, whose wife was threatening to leave him because of his irritability and their constant altercations, may be referred to a psychiatrist for supportive psychotherapy and antidepressant medication, to a marital therapist with his wife to improve their marital functioning, and to a colostomy support group to learn ways of coping with a colostomy. Emergency psychiatric clinicians are pragmatic; they use every necessary mode of therapeutic intervention available to enhance the resolution of the crisis and to facilitate value exploration and growth, with less concern than usual about the dilution of a therapeutic relationship. Emergency therapy emphasizes how various psychiatric modalities act synergistically to enhance recovery.

No one word is appropriate for all people in similar situations. What does a doctor say to a patient and a family experiencing a psychiatric emergency such as a suicide attempt or a schizophrenic break? For some, a genetic rationale helps: The information that an illness has a strong biological component relieves some people. For others, however, this approach underlines lack of control and increases depression and anxiety; all feel helpless because neither the family nor the patient can alter the behavior to minimize the likelihood of recurrence. Some people may benefit from an explanation of family or individual dynamics. Others only want someone to listen to them; in time, they reach their own understanding.

In the emergency situation as in any other psychiatric situation, when a clinician does not know what to say, the best approach is to listen. People in crisis reveal how much they need support, denial, ventilation, and words to conceptualize the meaning of their crisis and to discover paths to resolution.

Table 33.2–9
Common Focal Central Nervous System Disorders with Behavioral Features

Aphasias—fluent or receptive aphasia results in patients' not understanding spoken word, although they have fluent but incoherent speech
Frontal lobe syndromes—changes in motor behavior, ability to concentrate, reasoning, thinking, social judgment, and impulse control
Temporal lobe syndromes—psychosis, seizure, personality and Klüver-Bucy features
Parietal lobe syndromes—right lesion with denial and hypomania
Occipital lobe syndromes—Anton's syndrome (cortical blindness with denial)

Pharmacotherapy

The major indications for the use of psychotropic medication in an emergency room include violent or assaultive behavior, massive anxiety or panic, and extrapyramidal reactions, such as dystonia and akathisia as side effects of psychiatric drugs. A rare form of dystonia is laryngospasm, and psychiatrists should be prepared to maintain an open airway with intubation if necessary.

People who are paranoid or in a state of catatonic excitement require tranquilization. Episodic outbursts of violence respond to haloperidol (Haldol), β-blockers, carbamazepine (Tegretol), and lithium (Eskalith). If a history suggests a seizure disorder, clinical studies should confirm the diagnosis, and an evaluation is performed to ascertain the cause. If the findings are positive, anticonvulsants are commenced, or appropriate surgery is provided (for example, in the case of a cerebral mass). For intoxication from recreational substances or drugs of abuse, conservative measures may be adequate. In some instances, drugs such as thiothixene (Navane) and haloperidol, 5 to 10 mg every half hour to an hour, are needed until a patient is stabilized. Benzodiazepines are used instead of, or in addition to, antipsychotics (to reduce the antipsychotic dosage). When a recreational drug has strong anticholinergic properties, benzodiazepines are more appropriate than are antipsychotics. People with allergic or aberrant responses to antipsychotics and benzodiazepines are treated with amobarbital (Amytal [for example, 130 mg orally or IM]), paraldehyde, or diphenhydramine (Benadryl [50 to 100 mg orally or IM]).

Violent, struggling patients are most effectively subdued with an appropriate sedative or antipsychotic. Diazepam (Valium), 5 to 10 mg, or lorazepam (Ativan), 2 to 4 mg, may be given slowly intravenously (IV) over two minutes. Clinicians must give IV medication with great care so that respiratory arrest does not occur. Patients who require IM medication can be sedated with haloperidol, 5 to 10 mg IM, or with chlorpromazine (Thorazine), 25 mg IM. If the furor is due to alcohol or is part of a postseizure psychomotor disturbance, the sleep produced by a relatively small amount of an IV medication may go on for hours. On awakening, patients are often entirely alert and rational and typically have a complete amnesia about the violent episode.

If the disturbance is part of an ongoing psychotic process, and returns as soon as the IV medication wears off, continuous medication may be given. It is sometimes better to use small IM or oral doses at half-hour to one-hour intervals—for example, haloperidol, 2 to 5 mg, or diazepam, 20 mg—until the patient is controlled, than to use large dosages initially and end up with an overmedicated patient. As a patient's disturbed behavior is brought under control, successively smaller and less frequent doses should be used. During the preliminary treatment, a patient's blood pressure and other vital signs should be monitored.

Rapid Tranquilization. Antipsychotic medication can be given rapidly at 30- to 60-minute intervals to achieve the quickest therapeutic result possible. The procedure is useful for agitated patients and for those in excited states. The drugs of choice for rapid tranquilization are haloperidol and other high-potency antipsychotics. In adults, 5 to 10 mg of haloperidol can be given orally or IM and repeated in 20- to 30-minute intervals until a patient becomes calm. Some patients may experience mild extrapyramidal symptoms within the first 24 hours after rapid tranquilization; although the side effects are rare, psychiatrists should not overlook them. In general, most patients respond before a total dose of 50 mg is given. The goal is not to produce sedation or somnolescence; rather, a patient should be able to cooperate in the assessment process and, ideally, be able to provide some explanation of the agitated behavior. Agitated or panic-stricken patients can be treated with small doses of lorazepam, 2 to 4 mg IV or IM, which can be repeated if necessary in 20 to 30 minutes until quieted down. Extrapyramidal emergencies respond to benztropine (Cogentin), 2 mg orally or IM, or diphenhydramine, 50 mg IM or IV. Some patients respond to diazepam, 5 to 10 mg orally or IV.

Restraints

Restraints are used when patients are so dangerous to themselves or others that they pose a severe threat that cannot be controlled in any other way. Patients may be restrained temporarily to receive medication, or for long periods if medication cannot be used. Most often, patients in restraints quiet down after a time. On a psychodynamic level, such patients may even welcome the control of their impulses provided by

Table 33.2–10
Use of Restraints

Preferably five or a minimum of four persons should be used to restrain the patient. Leather restraints are the safest and surest type of restraints.

Explain to the patient why he or she is going into restraints.

A staff member should always be visible and reassuring the patient who is being restrained. Reassurance helps alleviate the patient's fear of helplessness, impotence, and loss of control.

Patients should be restrained with legs spread-eagled and one arm restrained to one side and the other arm restrained over the patient's head.

Restraints should be placed so that intravenous fluids can be given if necessary.

The patient's head is raised slightly to decrease the patient's feelings of vulnerability and to reduce the possibility of aspiration.

The restraints should be checked periodically for safety and comfort.

After the patient is in restraints, the clinician begins treatment, using verbal intervention.

Even in restraints, a majority of patients still take antipsychotic medication in concentrated form.

After the patient is under control, one restraint at a time should be removed at 5-minute intervals until the patient has only two restraints on. Both of the remaining restraints should be removed at the same time, because it is inadvisable to keep a patient in only one restraint.

Always thoroughly document the reason for the restraints, the course of treatment, and the patient's response to treatment while in restraints.

Data are from Dubin WR, Weiss KJ: Emergency psychiatry. In *Psychiatry*, R Michaels, A Cooper, SB Guze, LL Judd, GL Klerman, AJ Solnit, AJ Sunkard, PJ Wilner, editors, vol 2. Lippincott, Philadelphia, 1991.

Table 33.2–11
Common Psychiatric Emergencies

Syndrome	Emergency Manifestations	Treatment Issues
Abuse of child or adult	Signs of physical trauma	Management of medical problems; psychiatric evaluation; report to authorities
Acquired immune deficiency syndrome (AIDS)	Changes in behavior secondary to organic causes; changes in behavior secondary to fear and anxiety; suicidal behavior	Management of neurological illness; management of psychological concomitants; reinforcement of social support
Adolescent crises	Suicidal attempts and ideation; substance abuse, truancy, trouble with law, pregnancy, running away; eating disorders; psychosis	Evaluation of suicidal potential, extent of substance abuse, family dynamics; crisis-oriented family and individual therapy; hospitalization if necessary; consultation with appropriate extrafamilial authorities
Agoraphobia	Panic; depression	Alprazolam (Xanax), 0.25 mg to 2 mg; propranolol (Inderal); antidepressant medication
Agranulocytosis (Clozapine [Clozaril]-induced)	High fever, pharyngitis, oral and perianal ulcerations	Discontinue medication immediately; administer granulocyte-colony stimulating factor
Akathisia	Agitation, restlessness, muscle discomfort; dysphoria	Reduce antipsychotic dosage; propranolol (30 to 120 mg a day); benzodiazepines; diphenhydramine (Benadryl) orally or IV; benztropine (Cogentin) IM
Alcohol-related emergencies		
Alcohol delirium	Confusion, disorientation, fluctuating consciousness and perception, autonomic hyperactivity; may be fatal	Chlordiazepoxide; haloperidol (Haldol) for psychotic symptoms may be added if necessary
Alcohol intoxication	Disinhibited behavior, sedation at high doses	With time and protective environment, symptoms abate
Alcohol persisting amnestic disorder	Confusion, loss of memory even for all personal identification data	Hospitalization; hypnosis; amobarbital (Amytal) interview; rule out organic cause
Alchohol persisting dementia	Confusion, agitation, impulsivity	Rule out other causes for dementia; no effective treatment; hospitalization if necessary
Alcohol psychotic disorder with hallucinations	Vivid auditory (at times visual) hallucinations with affect appropriate to content (often fearful); clear sensorium	Haloperidol for psychotic symptoms
Alcohol seizures	Grand mal seizures; rarely status epilepticus	Diazepam (Valium), phenytoin (Dilantin); prevent by using chlordiazepoxide (Librium) during detoxification
Alcohol withdrawal	Irritability, nausea, vomiting, insomnia, malaise, autonomic hyperactivity, shakiness	Fluid and electrolytes maintained; sedation with benzodiazepines; restraints; monitoring of vital signs; 100 mg thiamine IM
Idiosyncratic alcohol intoxication	Marked aggressive or assaultive behavior	Generally no treatment required other than protective environment
Korsakoff's syndrome	Alcohol stigmata, amnesia, confabulation	No effective treatment; institutionalization often needed
Wernicke's encephalopathy	Oculomotor disturbances, cerebellar ataxia; mental confusion	Thiamine, 100 mg IV or IM, with $MgSO_4$ given before glucose loading
Amphetamine (or related substance) intoxication	Delusions, paranoia; violence; depression (from withdrawal); anxiety, delirium	Antipsychotics; restraints; hospitalization if necessary; no need for gradual withdrawal; antidepressants may be necessary
Anorexia nervosa	Loss of 25% of body weight of the norm for age and sex	Hospitalization; electrocardiogram (ECG), fluid and electrolytes; neuroendocrine evaluation
Anticholinergic intoxication	Psychotic symptoms, dry skin and mouth, hyperpyrexia, midriasis, tachycardia, restlessness, visual hallucinations	Discontinue drug, IV physostigmine (Antilirium), 0.5 to 2 mg, for severe agitation or fever, benzodiazepines; antipsychotics contraindicated
Anticonvulsant intoxication	Psychosis; delirium	Dosage of anticonvulsant is reduced
Benzodiazepine intoxication	Sedation, somnolence, and ataxia	Supportive measures; flumazenil (Romazicon), 7.5 to 45 mg a day, titrated as needed, should be used only by skilled personnel with resuscitative equipment available
Bereavement	Guilt feelings, irritability; insomnia; somatic complaints	Must be differentiated from major depressive disorder; antidepressants not indicated; benzodiazepines for sleep; encouragement of ventilation

(continued)

Table 33.2–11 *(continued)*

Syndrome	Emergency Manifestations	Treatment Issues
Borderline personality disorder	Suicidal ideation and gestures; homicidal ideations and gestures; substance abuse; micropsychotic episodes; burns, cut marks on body	Suicidal and homicidal evaluation (if great, hospitalization); small dosages of antipsychotics; clear follow-up plan
Brief psychotic disorder	Emotional turmoil, extreme lability; acutely impaired reality testing after obvious psychosocial stress	Hospitalization often necessary; low dosage of antipsychotics may be necessary but often resolves spontaneously
Bromide intoxication	Delirium; mania; depression; psychosis	Serum levels obtained (50 mg a day); bromide intake discontinued; large quantities of sodium chloride IV or orally; if agitation, paraldehyde or antipsychotic is used
Caffeine intoxication	Severe anxiety, resembling panic disorder; mania; delirium; agitated depression; sleep disturbance	Cessation of caffeine-containing substances; benzodiazepines
Cannabis intoxication	Delusions; panic; dysphoria; cognitive impairment	Benzodiazepines and antipsychotics as needed; evaluation of suicidal or homicidal risk; symptoms usually abate with time and reassurance
Catatonic schizophrenia	Marked psychomotor disturbance (either excitement or stupor); exhaustion; can be fatal	Rapid tranquilization with antipsychotics; monitor vital signs; amobarbital may release patient from catatonic mutism or stupor but can precipitate violent behavior
Cimetidine psychotic disorder	Delirium; delusions	Reduce dosage or discontinue drug
Clonidine withdrawal	Irritability; psychosis; violence; seizures	Symptoms abate with time, but antipsychotics may be necessary; gradual lowering of dosage
Cocaine intoxication and withdrawal	Paranoia and violence; severe anxiety; manic state; delirium; schizophreniform psychosis; tachycardia, hypertension, myocardial infarction, cerebrovascular disease; depression and suicidal ideation	Antipsychotics and benzodiazepines; antidepressants or ECT for withdrawal depression if persistent; hospitalization
Delirium	Fluctuating sensorium; suicidal and homicidal risk; cognitive clouding; visual, tactile, and auditory hallucinations; paranoia	Evaluate all potential contributing factors and treat each accordingly; reassurance, structure, clues to orientation; benzodiazepines and low-dosage, high-potency antipsychotics must be used with extreme care because of their potential to act paradoxically and increase agitation
Delusional disorder	Most often brought in to emergency room involuntarily; threats directed toward others	Antipsychotics if patient will comply (IM if necessary); intensive family intervention; hospitalization if necessary
Dementia	Unable to care for self; violent outbursts; psychosis; depression and suicidal ideation; confusion	Small dosages of high-potency antipsychotics; clues to orientation; organic evaluation, including medication use; family intervention
Depressive disorders	Suicidal ideation and attempts; self-neglect; substance abuse	Assessment of danger to self; hospitalization if necessary; nonpsychiatric causes of depression must be evaluated
L-Dopa intoxication	Mania; depression; schizophreniform disorder; may induce rapid cycling in patients with bipolar I disorder	Lower dosage or discontinue drug
Dystonia, acute	Intense involuntary spasm of muscles of neck, tongue, face, jaw, eyes, or trunk	Decrease dosage of antipsychotic; benztropine or diphenhydramine IM
Group hysteria	Groups of people exhibit extremes of grief or other disruptive behavior	Group is dispersed with help of other health care workers; ventilation, crisis-oriented therapy; if necessary, small dosages of benzodiazepines
Hallucinogen-induced psychotic disorder with hallucinations	Symptom picture is result of interaction of type of substance, dose taken, duration of action, user's premorbid personality, setting; panic; agitation; atropine psychosis	Serum and urine screens; rule out underlying medical or mental disorder; benzodiazepines (2 to 20 mg) orally; reassurance and orientation; rapid tranquilization; often responds spontaneously

(continued)

Table 33.2–11 *(continued)*

Syndrome	Emergency Manifestations	Treatment Issues
Homicidal and assaultive behavior	Marked agitation with verbal threats	Seclusion, restraints, medication
Homosexual panic	Not seen with men or women who are comfortable with their sexual orientation; occurs in those who adamantly deny having any homoerotic impulses; impulses are aroused by talk, a physical overture, or play among same-sex friends, such as wrestling, sleeping together, or touching each other in a shower or hot tub; panicked person sees others as sexually interested in him or her and defends against them	Ventilation, environmental structuring, and, in some instances, medication for acute panic (eg, alprazolam, 0.25 to 2 mg) or antipsychotics may be required; opposite-sex clinician should evaluate the patient whenever possible, and the patient should not be touched save for the routine examination; patients have attacked physicians who were examining an abdomen or performing a rectal examination (eg, on a man who harbors thinly veiled unintegrated homosexual impulses)
Hypertensive crisis	Life-threatening hypertensive reaction secondary to ingestion of tyramine-containing foods in combination with MAOIs; headache, stiff neck, sweating, nausea, vomiting	α-Adrenergic blockers (eg, phentolamine [Regitine]); nifedipine (Procardia) 10 mg orally; chlorpromazine (Thorazine); make sure symptoms are not secondary to hypotension (side effect of monoamine oxidase inhibitors [MAOIs] alone)
Hyperthermia	Extreme excitement or catatonic stupor or both; extremely elevated temperature; violent hyperagitation	Hydrate and cool; may be drug reaction, so discontinue any drug; rule out infection
Hyperventilation	Anxiety, terror, clouded consciousness; giddiness, faintness; blurring vision	Shift alkalosis by having patient breathe into paper bag; patient education; antianxiety agents
Hypothermia	Confusion; lethargy; combativeness; low body temperature and shivering; paradoxical feeling of warmth	IV fluids and rewarming; cardiac status must be carefully monitored; avoidance of alcohol
Incest and sexual abuse of child	Suicidal behavior; adolescent crises; substance abuse	Corroboration of charge; protection of victim; contact social sevices; medical and psychiatric evaluation; crisis intervention
Insomnia	Depression and irritability; early morning agitation; frightening dreams; fatigue	Hypnotics only in short term; eg, triazolam (Halcion), 0.25 to 0.5 mg, at bedtime; treat any underlying mental disorder; rules of sleep hygiene (Table 24.2–8)
Intermittent explosive disorder	Brief outbursts of violence; periodic episodes of suicide attempts	Benzodiazepines or antipsychotics for short term; long-term evaluation with computed tomography (CT) scan, sleep-deprived electroencephalogram (EEG), glucose tolerance curve
Jaundice	Uncommon complication of low-potency phenothiazine use (eg, chlorpromazine)	Change drug to low dosage of a low-potency agent in a different class
Leukopenia and agranulocytosis	Side effects within the first two months of treatment with antipsychotics	Patient should call immediately for sore throat, fever, etc., and obtain immediate blood count; discontinue drug; hospitalize if necessary
Lithium toxicity	Vomiting; abdominal pain; profuse diarrhea; severe tremor, ataxia; coma; seizures; confusion; dysarthria; focal neurological signs	Lavage with wide-bore tube; osmotic diuresis; medical consultation; may require ICU treatment
Major depressive episode with psychotic features	Major depressive episode symptoms with delusions; agitation, severe guilt; ideas of reference; suicide and homicide risk	Antipsychotics plus antidepressants; evaluation of suicide and homicide risk; hospitalization and ECT if necessary
Manic episode	Violent, impulsive behavior; indiscriminate sexual or spending behavior; psychosis; substance abuse	Hospitalization; restraints if necessary; rapid tranquilization with antipsychotics; restoration of lithium levels

(continued)

Table 33.2–11 *(continued)*

Syndrome	Emergency Manifestations	Treatment Issues
Marital crises	Precipitant may be discovery of an extramarital affair, onset of serious illness, announcement of intent to divorce, or problems with children or work; one or both members of the couple may be in therapy or may be psychiatrically ill; one spouse may be seeking hospitalization for the other	Each should be questioned alone regarding extramarital affairs, consultations with lawyers regarding divorce, and willingness to work in crisis-oriented or long-term therapy to resolve the problem; sexual, financial, and psychiatric treatment histories from both, psychiatric evaluation at the time of presentation; may be precipitated by onset of untreated mood disorder or affective symptoms caused by medical illness or insidious-onset dementia; referral for management of the illness reduces immediate stress and enhances the healthier spouse's coping capacity; children may give insights available only to someone intimately involved in the social system
Migraine	Throbbing, unilateral headache	Sumatriptan (Imitrex) 6 mg IM
Mitral valve prolapse	Associated with panic disorder; dyspnea and palpitations; fear and anxiety	Echocardiogram; alprazolam or propranolol
Neuroleptic malignant syndrome	Hyperthermia; muscle rigidity; autonomic instability; parkinsonian symptoms; catatonic stupor; neurological signs; 10% to 30% fatality; elevated creatine phosphokinase	Discontinue antipsychotic; IV dantrolene (Dantrium); bromocriptine (Parlodel) orally; hydration and cooling; monitor CPK levels
Nitrous oxide toxicity	Euphoria and light-headedness	Symptoms abate without treatment within hours of use
Nutmeg intoxication	Agitation; hallucinations; severe headaches; numbness in extremities	Symptoms abate within hours of use without treatment
Opioid intoxication and withdrawal	Intoxication can lead to coma and death; withdrawal is not life-threatening	IV naloxone, narcotic antagonist; urine and serum screens; psychiatric and medical illnesses (eg, AIDS) may complicate picture
Panic disorder	Panic, terror; acute onset	Must differentiate from other anxiety-producing disorders, both medical and psychiatric; ECG to rule out mitral valve prolapse; propranolol (10 to 30 mg); alprazolam (0.25 to 2.0 mg); long-term management may include an antidepressant
Paranoid schizophrenia	Command hallucinations; threat to others or themselves	Rapid tranquilization; hospitalization; long-acting depot medication; threatened persons must be notified and protected
Parkinsonism	Stiffness, tremor, bradykinesia, flattened affect, shuffling gait, salivation, secondary to antipsychotic medication	Oral antiparkinsonian drug for four weeks to three months; decrease dosage of the antipsychotic
Perioral (rabbit) tremor	Perioral tumor (rabbitlike facial grimacing) usually appearing after long-term therapy with antipsychotics	Decrease dosage or change to a medication in another class
Phencyclidine (or phencyclidine-like) intoxication	Paranoid psychosis; can lead to death; acute danger to self and others	Serum and urine assay; benzodiazepines may interfere with excretion; antipsychotics may worsen symptoms because of anticholinergic side effects; medical monitoring and hospitalization for severe intoxication
Phenelzine-induced psychotic disorder	Psychosis and mania in predisposed people	Reduce dosage or discontinue drug
Phenylpropanolamine toxicity	Psychosis; paranoia; insomnia; restlessness; nervousness; headache	Symptoms abate with dosage reduction or discontinuation (found in over-the-counter diet aids and oral and nasal decongestants)
Phobias	Panic, anxiety; fear	Treatment same as for panic disorder
Photosensitivity	Easy sunburning secondary to use of antipsychotic medication	Patient should avoid strong sunlight and use high-level sunscreens
Pigmentary retinopathy	Reported with dosages of thioridazine (Mellaril) equal to or greater than 800 mg a day	Remain below 800 mg a day of thioridazine

(continued)

Table 33.2–11 ***(continued)***

Syndrome	Emergency Manifestations	Treatment Issues
Postpartum psychosis	Childbirth can precipitate schizophrenia, depression, reactive psychoses, mania, and depression; affective symptoms are most common; suicide risk is reduced during pregnancy but increased in the postpartum period	Danger to self and others (including infant) must be evaluated and proper precautions taken; medical illness presenting with behavioral aberrations is included in the differential diagnosis and must be sought and treated; care must be paid to the effects on father, infant, grandparents, and other children
Posttraumatic stress disorder	Panic, terror; suicidal ideation; flashbacks	Reassurance; encouragement of return to responsibilities; avoid hospitalization if possible to prevent chronic invalidism; monitor suicidal ideation
Priapism (trazodone [Desyrel]-induced)	Persistent penile erection accompanied by severe pain	Intracorporeal epinephrine; mechanical or surgical drainage
Propranolol toxicity	Profound depression; confusional states	Reduce dosage or discontinue drug; monitor suicidality
Rape	Not all sexual violations are reported; silent rape reaction is characterized by loss of appetite, sleep disturbance, anxiety, and, sometimes, agoraphobia; long periods of silence, mounting anxiety, stuttering, blocking, and physical symptoms during the interview when the sexual history is taken; fear of violence and death and of contracting a sexually transmitted disease or being pregnant	Rape is a major psychiatric emergency; victim may have enduring patterns of sexual dysfunction; crisis-oriented therapy, social support, ventilation, reinforcement of healthy traits, and encouragement to return to the previous level of functioning as rapidly as possible; legal counsel; thorough medical examination and tests to identify the assailant (eg, obtaining samples of pubic hairs with a pubic hair comb, vaginal smear to identify blood antigens in semen); if a woman, methoxyprogesterone or diethylstilbestrol orally for five days to prevent pregnancy; if menstruation does not commence within one week of cessation of the estrogen, all alternatives to pregnancy, including abortion, should be offered; if the victim has contracted a venereal disease, appropriate antibiotics; witnessed written permission is required for the physician to examine, photograph, collect specimens, and release information to the authorities; obtain consent, record the history in the patient's own words, obtain required tests, record the results of the examination, save all clothing, defer diagnosis, and provide protection against disease, psychic trauma, and pregnancy; men's and women's responses to rape affectively are reported similarly, although men are more hesitant to talk about homosexual assault for fear they will be assumed to have consented
Reserpine intoxication	Major depressive episodes; suicidal ideation; nightmares	Evaluation of suicidal ideation; lower dosage or change drug; antidepressants or ECT may be indicated
Schizoaffective disorder	Severe depression; manic symptoms; paranoia	Evaluation of dangerousness to self or others; rapid tranquilization if necessary; treatment of depression (antidepressants alone can enhance schizophrenic symptoms); use of antimanic agents
Schizophrenia	Extreme self-neglect; severe paranoia; suicidal ideation or assaultiveness; extreme psychotic symptoms	Evaluation of suicidal and homicidal potential; identification of any illness other than schizophrenia; rapid tranquilization
Schizophrenia in exacerbation	Withdrawn; agitation; suicidal and homicidal risk	Suicide and homicide evaluation; screen for medical illness; restraints and rapid tranquilization if necessary; hospitalization if necessary; reevaluation of medication regimen

(continued)

Table 33.2–11 ***(continued)***

Syndrome	Emergency Manifestations	Treatment Issues
Sedative, hypnotic, or anxiolytic intoxication and withdrawal	Alterations in mood, behavior, thought—delirium; derealization and depersonalization; untreated, can be fatal; seizures	Naloxone (Narcan) to differentiate from opioid intoxication; slow withdrawal with phenobarbital (Luminal) or sodium thiopental or benzodiazepine; hospitalization
Seizure disorder	Confusion; anxiety; derealization and depersonalization; feelings of impending doom; gustatory or olfactory hallucinations; fugue-like state	Immediate EEG; admission and sleep-deprived and 24-hour EEG; rule out pseudoseizures; anticonvulsants
Substance withdrawal	Abdominal pain; insomnia, drowsiness; delirium; seizures; symptoms of tardive dyskinesia may emerge; eruption of manic or schizophrenic symptoms	Symptoms of psychotropic drug withdrawal disappear with time or disappear with reinstitution of the substance; symptoms of antidepressant withdrawal can be successfully treated with anticholinergic agents, such as atropine; gradual withdrawal of psychotropic substances over two to four weeks generally obviates development of symptoms
Sudden death associated with antipsychotic medication	Seizures; asphyxiation; cardiovascular causes; postural hypotension; laryngeal-pharyngeal dystonia; suppression of gag reflex	Specific medical treatments
Sudden death of psychogenic origin	Myocardial infarction after sudden psychic stress; voodoo and hexes; hopelessness, especially associated with serious physical illness	Specific medical treatments; folk healers
Suicide	Suicidal ideation; hopelessness	Hospitalization, antidepressants
Sympathomimetic withdrawal	Paranoia; confusional states; depression	Most symptoms abate without treatment; antipsychotics; antidepressants if necessary
Tardive dyskinesia	Dyskinesia of mouth, tongue, face, neck, and trunk; choreoathetoid movements of extremities; usually but not always appearing after long-term treatment with antipsychotics, especially after a reduction in dosage; incidence highest in the elderly and brain-damaged; symptoms are intensified by antiparkinsonian drugs and masked but not cured by increased dosages of antipsychotic	No effective treatment reported; may be prevented by prescribing the least amount of drug possible for as little time as is clinically feasible and using drug-free holidays for patients who need to continue taking the drug; decrease or discontinue drug at first sign of dyskinetic movements
Thyrotoxicosis	Tachycardia; gastrointestinal dysfunction; hyperthermia; panic, anxiety, agitation; mania; dementia; psychosis	Thyroid function test (T_3, T_4, thyroid-stimulating hormone [TSH]); medical consultation
Toluene abuse	Anxiety; confusion; cognitive impairment	Neurological damage is nonprogressive and reversible if toluene use is discontinued early
Vitamin B_{12} deficiency	Confusion; mood and behavior changes; ataxia	Treatment with vitamin B_{12}
Volatile nitrates	Alternations of mood and behavior; light-headedness; pulsating headache	Symptoms abate with cessation of use

restraints. Table 33.2–10 lists the guidelines for the use of restraints.

SPECIFIC PSYCHIATRIC EMERGENCIES

Table 33.2–11 outlines in alphabetical order common psychiatric emergencies. Readers are referred to the index and to specific chapters of this textbook for a thorough discussion of each disorder.

References

Brown GL, Linnoila MI: CSF serotonin metabolite (5-HIAA) studies in depression, impulsivity, and violence. J Clin Psychiatry *51* (4, Suppl): 31, 1990.

Fauman BJ: Other psychiatric emergencies. In *Comprehensive Textbook of Psychiatry,* ed 6, HI Kaplan, BJ Sadock, editors, p 1752. Williams & Wilkins, Baltimore, 1995.

Hillard JR, editor: *Manual of Clinical Emergency Psychiatry.* American Psychiatric Press, Washington, 1990.

Hyman SE, editor: *Manual of Psychiatric Emergencies,* ed 2. Little, Brown, Boston, 1988.

Kaplan HI, Sadock BJ: *Pocket Handbook of Primary Care Psychiatry.* Williams & Wilkins, Baltimore, 1996.

Marson DC, McGovern MP, Pomp HC: Psychiatric decision making in the emergency room: A research overview. Am J Psychiatry *145:* 918, 1988.
Puryear DA, Lovitt R, Miller DA: Characteristics of elderly persons seen in an urban psychiatric emergency room. Hosp Community Psychiatry *42:* 802, 1991.
Rosenberg RC, Kesselman M: The therapeutic alliance and the psychiatric emergency room. Hosp Community Psychiatry *44:* 78, 1993.
Sanguineti VR, Brooks MO: Factors related to emergency commitment of chronically mentally ill patients who are substance abusers. Hosp Community Psychiatry *43:* 237, 1992.
Segal SP, Bola JR, Watson MA: Race, quality of care, and antipsychotic prescribing practices in psychiatric emergency services. Psychiatr Serv *47* (3): 282, 1996.
Szuster RR, Schanbacher BL, McCann SC: Characteristics of psychiatric emergency room patients with alcohol- or drug-induced disorders. Hosp Community Psychiatry *41:* 1342, 1990.
Thienhaus OJ: Rational physical evaluation in the emergency room. Hosp Community Psychiatry *43:* 311, 1992.
Waller FS: Hospital and room security: The next decade. J Health Protect Manage *7:* 43, 1991.
Weissberg M: Chained in the emergency department. The new asylum for the poor. Hosp Community Psychiatry *42:* 317, 1991.

34 Psychotherapies

34.1 Psychoanalysis and Psychoanalytic Psychotherapy

Psychoanalysis and psychoanalytic psychotherapy are treatments derived from psychoanalytic theory (discussed in Chapter 6, Section 6.1). Psychoanalytic psychotherapy is sometimes referred to as psychodynamic psychotherapy, insight-oriented psychotherapy, intensive psychotherapy, exploratory psychotherapy, or uncovering psychotherapy. Although a form of brief psychotherapy based on psychoanalytic or psychodynamic principles has been highly developed in both clinical practice and studies in various investigations, this discussion is confined to long-term, or extended, psychoanalytic psychotherapy, which is usually considered to be more than 6 months in duration.

Psychoanalytic psychotherapy is often subdivided into expressive and supportive subtypes. The expressive variety, which emphasizes interpreting unconscious conflict and gaining insight, is much closer to psychoanalysis proper. Psychodynamically informed supportive psychotherapy is geared to restoring and strengthening patients' defenses and directing them toward adaptive and healthy ways of problem solving. In practice, psychoanalytic psychotherapy often shifts flexibly along an expressive-supportive continuum, but for purposes of clarity, the two are discussed separately.

The choice of psychoanalysis, expressive psychotherapy, or supportive psychotherapy rests primarily on a careful psychodynamic assessment of each patient. Although the descriptive DSM-IV diagnosis may be useful in making a decision, the information provided by such diagnoses is limited. A patient's motivation to understand, the characteristic strengths and weaknesses of the ego, the quality of the patient's object relations, and the cohesiveness of the self are all psychodynamic characteristics that must be taken into account. Table 34.1–1 provides an outline of the different types of psychotherapies.

PSYCHOANALYSIS

When Sigmund Freud first developed psychoanalysis at the end of the 19th century, he was treating hysterical patients under the assumption that the de-repression of childhood memories through a cathartic approach would relieve symptoms. When he recognized that symptoms did not disappear with abreaction, he evolved the technique of free association, by which patients were instructed to say whatever came to mind without censoring. Hence the focus of analysis shifted from deeply buried memories to the defenses and conflicts among ego, id, superego, and external reality.

Since Freud's time, object relations theory has been in the ascendancy under the influence of Melanie Klein, Donald W. Winnicott, Ronald Fairbairn, Michael Balint, and others. As a result, emphasis on analyzing the manifestations of patients' internal object relations in the unfolding of transference and countertransference in the analytic relationship has increased. Heinz Kohut's self psychology has also prompted more attention to the needs of patients' selves and to the fragmentations of the self that occurs when analysts fail to meet patients' needs for mirroring, twinship, and idealization.

Goals and Therapeutic Action

The goals of psychoanalysis are intimately linked to conceptualizations of the therapeutic action in psychoanalytic treatment. Freud initially regarded the therapeutic action of psychoanalysis as involving a redistribution of the interrelationships among the three intrapsychic agencies. In Freud's words, "Where id was, there ego shall be." Transference interpretation was considered crucial to the accomplishment of this goal. Through interpretation of patients' transference, the superego is modified, the id is tamed, and the ego is expanded. Patients recognize that their hostile impulses toward the analyst are really directed toward internal parental objects. They also recognize that the analyst is not dangerous and threatening; the danger and the threat come from patients' own superegos. This change involves a slow process of integrating previously unconscious material into patients' conscious awareness and expanding their capacity to deal with this material. Much of this process is accomplished through analysis of patients' defense mechanisms that fend off the awareness of unconscious conflicts.

Object relations theorists conceptualized the mechanism of therapeutic action differently. They stressed the need for change in mental representation of self and object and in the affect linkage between these representations. They believed that such changes are brought about partly through interpretation but also through the analytic relationship, which provides a holding environment. They emphasized the process of containment in producing change. Through projective identification, the analyst becomes a container of patients' self-representations and object-representations, often in association with powerful affective states. Before these projected contents are returned to patients by the process of reintrojection, the

Table 34.1–1
Scope of Psychoanalytic Practice: A Clinical Continuum[a]

Feature	Psychoanalysis	Psychoanalytic Psychotherapy: Expressive Mode	Psychoanalytic Psychotherapy: Supportive Mode
Frequency	Regular 4 to 5 times a week: 50-minute hour	Regular one to three times a week: half to full hour	Flexible once a week or less; or as needed, half to full hour
Duration	Long-term: usually 3 to 5+ years	Short-term or long-term: several sessions to months or years	Short-term or intermittent long-term; single session to lifetime
Setting	Patient primarily on couch with analyst out of view	Patient and therapist face to face; occasional use of couch	Patient and therapist face to face; couch contraindicated
Modus operandi	Systematic analysis of all (positive and negative) transference and resistance; primary focus on analyst and intrasession events; transference neurosis facilitated; regression encouraged	Partial analysis of dynamics and defenses; focus on current interpersonal events and transference to others outside sessions; analysis of negative transference; positive transference left unexplored unless it impedes progress; limited regression encouraged	Formation of therapeutic alliance and real object relationship; analysis of transference contraindicated with rare exceptions; focus on conscious external events; regression discouraged
Analyst-therapist role	Absolute neutrality; frustration of patient; reflector-mirror role	Modified neutrality; implicit gratification of patient and great activity	Neutrality suspended; limited explicit gratification, direction, and disclosure
Putative change agents	Insight predominates within relatively deprived environment	Insight within empathic environment; identification with benevolent object	Auxiliary or surrogate ego as temporary substitute; holding environment; insight to degree possible
Patient population	Neuroses; mild character psychopathology	Neuroses; mild to moderate character psychopathology, especially narcissistic and borderline personality disorders	Severe character disorders; latent or manifest psychoses; acute crises; physical illness
Patient requisites	High motivation; psychological-mindedness; good previous object relationships; ability to maintain transference neurosis; good frustration tolerance	High to moderate motivation and psychological-mindedness; ability to form therapeutic alliance; some frustration tolerance	Some degree of motivation and ability to form therapeutic alliance
Basic goals	Structural reorganization of personality; resolution of unconscious conflicts; insight into intrapsychic events; symptom relief an indirect result	Partial reorganization of personality and defenses; resolution of preconscious and conscious derivatives of conflicts; insight into current interpersonal events; improved object relations; symptom relief a goal or prelude to further exploration	Reintegration of self and ability to cope; stabilization or restoration of preexisting equilibrium; strengthening of defenses; better adjustment or acceptance of pathology; symptom relief and environmental restructuring as primary goals
Major techniques	Free association method predominates; fully dynamic interpretation (including confrontation, clarification, and working through), with emphasis on genetic reconstruction	Limited free association; confrontation, clarification, and partial interpretation predominate, with emphasis on here-and-now interpretation and limited genetic interpretation	Free association method contraindicated; suggestion (advice) predominates; abreaction useful; confrontation, clarification, and interpretation in the here and now secondary; genetic interpretation contraindicated
Adjunct treatment	Primarily avoided; if applied, all negative and positive meanings and implications thoroughly analyzed	May be necessary (eg, psychotropic drugs as temporary measure); if applied, negative implications explored and diffused	Often necessary (eg, psychotropic drugs, family therapy, rehabilitative therapy, or hospitalization); if applied, positive implications are emphasized

Courtesy of Toksoz Byram Karasu, M.D.
[a] This division is not categorical; all practice resides on a clinical continuum.

analyst psychologically processes and thereby modifies patients' representations.

In self psychology, the goal of psychoanalytic treatment is to strengthen a weakened self so that it can move from dependence on archaic selfobject experiences to a position of greater self-cohesion that allows for reliance on more mature selfobjects. Kohut asserted that the goal was accomplished by laying down psychic structure through optimal frustration and by transmuting internalizations. The essential curative aspect of the analytic process is the establishment of empathic attunement between the self and the selfobject on a mature level.

Analytic Setting

In the usual analytic setting, patients lie on a couch or sofa, and the analyst sits behind, partially or totally outside a patient's field of vision. The couch helps the analyst produce the controlled regression that favors the emergence of repressed material. The patient's reclining position in the presence of an attentive analyst almost recreates symbolically the early parent–child situation, which varies from patient to patient. The position also helps the patient focus on inner thoughts, feelings, and fantasies, which can then become the focus of free associations. Moreover, the use of the couch introduces an element of sensory deprivation; the patient's visual stimuli are limited, and the analyst's verbalizations are relatively few. This state promotes regression. There has been some disagreement, however, about the necessary use of the couch in psychoanalysis. Otto Fenichel stated that whether the patient lies down or sits and whether certain rituals of procedure are used do not matter. The best condition is the one most appropriate to the analytic task.

Duration of Treatment

The patient and the psychoanalyst must be prepared to persevere in the process indefinitely. Psychoanalysis takes time—between 3 and 6 years, sometimes even longer. Sessions are usually held 4 or more times a week for 45 to 50 minutes each.

Treatment Methods

Fundamental Rule of Psychoanalysis. According to the fundamental or basic rule, patients agree to be completely honest with their analysts and to tell everything without selection. Freud referred to the technique that allowed for such honesty as free association.

Free Association. In free association, patients attempt to comply with the fundamental rule by saying whatever comes to mind. Inevitably, they cannot accomplish this task because of embarrassment, concerns about what the analyst thinks, and the evaluations of whether an association is relevant. These resistances to the process of saying whatever comes to mind becomes a primary focus of analytic work. The analyst does not become more authoritarian in response to a patient's difficulties with free association but instead tries to understand the patient's obstacles in complying with the fundamental rule.

Free-Floating Attention. The analyst's counterpart to patients' free association is a particular way of listening, often referred to as free-floating or evenly suspended attention. An analyst avoids an intense focus on a patient's comments and instead allows the patient's associations to stimulate associations in the analyst. Similarly, analysts strive to attain a state of free-floating responsiveness, in which they allow themselves to be drawn into a patient's internal object world by identifying with the roles cast upon them by the patient's unconscious.

Analytic Process

Transference. Transference is a term that refers to the displacement of attitudes and feelings originally experienced in relationships with people from the past onto the analyst. Modern analysts recognize that transference is also influenced by an analyst's *real* characteristics; thus transference is always to some extent an amalgam of old relationships and the new relationships with the analyst. Although Freud initially encouraged analysts to be opaque to their patients (the principal of anonymity), the contemporary view is that analysts' subjectivity is an ongoing influence to help shape the transference. Most analysts attempt to use restraint and avoid excessive self-disclosure, but they also recognize that the stereotype of the blank-screen analyst is no longer useful.

A major criterion by which psychoanalysis can, in principle, be differentiated from other forms of psychotherapy is its intensive focus on transference. To a considerable extent, psychoanalysis is defined by a much more systematic analysis of the transference than occurs in psychotherapy. In Freud's original formulation, a patient's infantile neurosis was revealed in the form of a transference neurosis to the analyst, in which a patient struggles to gratify unconscious infantile wishes through the analyst. The term *transference neurosis* is now controversial, and many analysts refer simply to *transference.* Transference is best understood as the repetition of a patient's habitual modes of object relatedness in the analytic dyad. Transference may be idealizing, erotic, or highly negative. With some narcissistic patients, there is an apparent absence of transference attachment. Freud believed that such patients could not be analyzed. Analysts today disagree with Freud and simply regard the apparent absence of transference as the nature of a narcissistic patient's object relations transferred to the analytic setting.

The analyst's role is to help a patient gain insight into the underlying wishes and conflicts inherent in transference and therefore make the unconscious conscious. By systematically understanding the nature of the relationship with the analyst, a patient also gains insight about characteristic patterns of relationships with others outside analysis.

Interpretation. In psychoanalysis, the analyst provides patients with interpretations about psychological events that were neither previously understood by, nor meaningful to the patients. The transference constitutes a major frame of reference for interpretation. A complete psychoanalytic interpretation includes meaningful statements of current conflicts and the historical factors that influenced them. Such complete interpretations, however, constitute a relatively small part of analysis; most interpretations are limited in scope and deal with matters of immediate concern.

Interpretations must be well timed. An analyst may have a formulation in mind, but a patient may not be prepared to deal with it directly because of factors such as anxiety level, negative transference, and external life stress. The analyst may decide to wait until the patient can fully understand the interpretation. The proper timing of interpretation requires great clinical skill.

DREAM INTERPRETATION. In his classic work, *The Interpretation of Dreams,* Freud referred to the dream as the "royal road to the unconscious." The manifest content of a dream is what a dreamer reports. The latent content is a dream's unconscious meaning after the condensations, substitutions, and symbols are analyzed. Dreams arise from what Freud referred to as the day residue (the events of the preceding day, which stimulated the patient's unconscious mind). Dreaming may serve as a wish-fulfillment mechanism and as a way of mastering anxiety about a life event.

Freud outlined several technical procedures to use in dream interpretation: Have a patient associate to elements of the dream in the order in which they occurred; have the patient associate to a particular dream element that the patient or the therapist chooses; disregard the content of the dream, and ask the patient what events of the previous day can be associated with the dream (the day residue); and avoid giving any instructions, and leave it to the dreamer to begin. Analysts use patients' associations to find a clue to the workings of the unconscious mind.

Countertransference. Freud originally understood countertransference as an analyst's transference to a patient. He viewed it as an obstacle, based on the analyst's own personal conflicts, that had to be removed so as not to interfere with the patient's analysis. This narrow or classical view has been superseded by the broad view of countertransference as an analyst's feelings that are thought to be related to what the patient is projecting onto the analyst. This formulation underscores the value of countertransference as a therapeutic tool: It provides the analyst with clues about the nature of the patient's internal object world. The most widely held view of countertransference today is that it is a joint creation involving contributions from the analyst's past and the patient's internal world.

Therapeutic Alliance. In addition to transferential and countertransferential issues, the relationship between the analyst and the patient involves two adults entering into a joint venture, referred to as the therapeutic or working alliance. Both commit themselves to exploring the patient's problems, to establishing mutual trust, and to cooperating with each other to achieve a realistic goal of a cure or the amelioration of symptoms.

Resistance. Freud believed that unconscious ideas or impulses are repressed and prevented from reaching awareness because they are unacceptable to consciousness for some reason. He referred to this phenomenon as resistance, which must be overcome if the analysis is to proceed. Resistance may sometimes be a conscious process manifested by a patient's withholding relevant information. Other examples of patients' resistance are remaining silent for a long time, being late or missing appointments, and paying bills late or not at all. The signs of resistance are legion, and almost any feature of the analytic situation can be used in resistance. Freud once said that psychoanalysis is any treatment that works by undoing resistance and interpreting transferences.

Indications for Psychoanalytic Treatment

The indications for psychoanalysis must consider generalized criteria for analyzability, which apply regardless of the diagnosis. There must be significant suffering so that patients are motivated to make the sacrifices of time and financial resources required for psychoanalysis. Patients who enter analysis must have a genuine wish to understand themselves, not a desperate hunger for symptomatic relief. They must be able to withstand frustration, anxiety, and other strong affects that emerge in analysis without fleeing or acting out their feelings in a self-destructive manner. They must also have a reasonable mature superego that allows them to be honest with the analyst. Intelligence must be at least average, and above all, they must be psychologically minded in the sense that they can think abstractly and symbolically about the unconscious meanings of their behavior.

A 1994 survey of 580 analytic patients offers a basis for a general statement about indications for psychoanalysis. This survey found that 82 percent of patients currently in psychoanalysis had in the past undergone other forms of psychotherapy that had failed to address their problems. Hence, a common indication for psychoanalysis is failure of brief therapies or psychopharmacologic interventions.

Contraindications for Treatment

Many contraindications for psychoanalysis are the flip side of the indications. The absence of suffering, poor impulse control, inability to tolerate frustration and anxiety, and low motivation to understand are all contraindications. The presence of extreme dishonesty or antisocial personality disorder contraindicates analytic treatment. Concrete thinking or the absence of psychological mindedness is another contraindication. Some patients who might ordinarily be psychologically minded are not suitable for analysis because they are in the midst of a major upheaval or life crisis, such as a job loss or a divorce. Serious physical illness may also interfere with a person's ability to invest in a long-term treatment process. Patients of low intelligence generally do not understand the procedure or cooperate in the process. An age older than 40 was once considered a contraindication, but today analysts recognize that patients are malleable and analyzable in their 60s or 70s. One final contraindication is a close relationship with the analyst. Analysts should avoid analyzing friends, relatives, or people with whom they have other involvements.

PSYCHOANALYTIC PSYCHOTHERAPY

Psychoanalytic psychotherapy is based on psychoanalytic formulations that have been modified conceptually and technically. In highly expressive therapy, interpretation is still a commonly used intervention, but there is a less systematic analysis of the transference, there is only a partial analysis of dynamics, and the couch is not generally used. More typically, patient and therapist sit opposite each other, a situation that

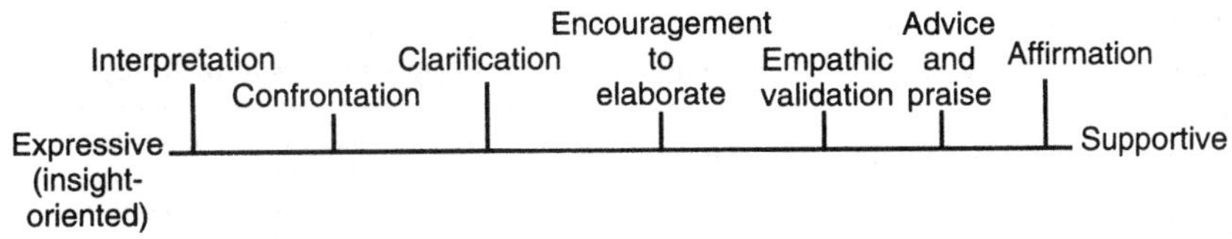
Interpretation
Confrontation
Clarification
Encouragement to elaborate
Empathic validation
Advice and praise
Affirmation
Expressive (insight-oriented)
Supportive

FIGURE 34.1–1
An expressive (insight-oriented)-supportive continuum of interventions. (Reproduced with permission from Gabbard GO: *Psychodynamic Psychiatry in Clinical Practice,* p 78. American Psychiatric Press, Washington, 1990.)

can lend a greater degree of reality to the therapist compared to a situation in which the therapist is out of view. Expressive psychotherapy is often conducted between 1 and 3 times a week for 45- or 50-minute sessions; sometimes 30-minute sessions are used as well. Supportive therapy is generally no more frequent than once a week and often even less frequently; sessions may be anywhere from 30 to 50 minutes in length.

Types

Many clinicians and researchers have conceptualized the types of psychotherapies as falling along a spectrum, with expressive (insight-oriented) therapies (such as psychoanalysis) and analytically oriented therapies at one end of the spectrum and supportive therapies at the other end. The Menninger Clinic Treatment Intervention Project has suggested that therapist intervention can be placed in seven categories along an expressive (insight-oriented)-supportive continuum, summarized in Figure 34.1–1. Table 34.1–2 summarizes the Menninger group's definitions of the terms.

Expressive Psychotherapy. In expressive or insight-oriented therapy, therapists attempt to provide insight into the patients' unconscious processes. By systematically examining

Table 34.1–2
Psychotherapeutic Interventions Defined

1. *Interpretation.* In the most expressive forms of treatment, interpretation is regarded as the therapist's ultimate decisive instrument. In its simplest form, interpretation involves making something conscious that was previously unconscious. An interpretation is an explanatory statement that links a feeling, thought, behavior, or symptom to its unconscious meaning or origin. For example, the therapist might say to a patient who is late, "Perhaps the reason you are late is that you were afraid I would react to the success you are now having the way your father reacted." Depending on the point in therapy and the patient's readiness to hear the interpretation, interpretations may focus on the transference (as in that example), extratransference issues, the patient's past or present situation, or the patient's resistances or fantasies. As a general rule, the therapist does not address unconscious content by interpretation until the material is almost conscious and, therefore, relatively accessible to the patient's awareness.
2. *Confrontation.* The next most expressive intervention is confrontation, which addresses something the patient does not want to accept or identifies the patient's avoidance or minimization. A confrontation may be geared to clarifying how the patient's behavior affects others or to reflecting back to the patient a denied or suppressed feeling. Confrontation, which is often gentle, carries the unfortunate connotation in common parlance of being aggressive or blunt. The following example illustrates that confrontration is not necessarily forceful or hostile. In the last session of a long-term therapy process, one patient talked at great length about car problems he encountered on the way to the session. The therapist commented, "I think you'd rather talk about your car than face the sadness you're feeling about our last session."
3. *Clarification.* Further along the continuum from expressive to supportive interventions, clarification involves a reformulation or pulling together of the patient's verbalizations to convey a coherent view of what is being communicated. Clarification differs from confrontation because it lacks the element of denial or minimization. A clarification is aimed at helping the patient articulate something that is difficult to put into words.
4. *Encouragement to elaborate.* Closer to the center of the continuum come interventions that are neither supportive nor expressive in and of themselves. Encouragement to elaborate may be broadly defined as a request for information about a topic brought up by the patient. It may be an open-ended question, such as, "What comes to mind about that?" or a more specific request, as in. "Tell me more about your father." Such interventions are commonly used in both the most expressive and the most supportive treatments.
5. *Empathic validation.* This intervention is a demonstration of the therapist's empathic attunement with the patient's internal state. A typically validating comment is, "I can understand why you feel depressed about that," or "It hurts when you're treated that way." In the view of the self psychologists, empathic immersion in the patient's internal experience is essential, regardless of the location of the therapy on the expressive-supportive continuum. When patients feel that the therapist understands their subjective experiences, they are likely to accept interpretations.
6. *Advice and praise.* This category really includes two interventions that are linked by the fact that they both prescribe and reinforce certain activities. Advice involves direct suggestions to the patient regarding how to behave; praise reinforces certain patient behaviors by expressing overt approval of them. An example of the former is, "I think you should stop going out with that man immediately." An example of the latter is, "I'm very pleased that you were able to tell him that you would not see him anymore." Those comments are on the opposite end of the continuum from traditional psychoanalytic interventions because they are departures from neutrality and to some extent compromise the patient's autonomy in making decisions.
7. *Affirmation.* This simple intervention involves succinct comments in support of the patient's comments or behaviors, such as "Uh-huh," and "Yes, I see what you mean."

Adapted from Gabbard GO: *Psychodynamic Psychiatry in Clinical Practice,* p 78. American Psychiatric Press, Washington, 1990.

patterns of behavior, both in transference and in outside relationships, patients become progressively aware of unconscious determinants of behavior.

Therapists rely on a range of interventions along the expressive-supportive continuum but emphasize interpretation, confrontation, and clarification much more than advice and praise. Interpretations often focus on linkages between relationships in childhood and the present. There is less emphasis on reconstructing childhood events in expressive psychotherapy than occurs in psychoanalysis and more focus on current functioning.

Therapists create a nonjudgmental environment in which patients can talk about a wide range of issues. On the other hand, therapists might also set limits if self-destructive or aggressive behavior becomes a major issue.

Therapists also have the more limited goals of partially reorganizing patients' personality and defenses without completely resolving major conflicts. Object relations may improve based partly on insight gained from interpretation and also on internalizing the therapeutic relationship. Much like psychoanalysts, expressive therapists point out how a patient's unconscious is observable through various behaviors and actions that go on outside the patient's awareness. The indications for expressive versus supportive emphasis in psychotherapy are outlined in Table 34.1–3.

Supportive Psychotherapy. Supportive psychotherapy offers patients the support of an authority figure during a period of illness, turmoil, or temporary decompensation. This treatment has the goal of restoring and strengthening patients' impaired defenses and integrating capacities. It provides a period of acceptance and dependence for a patient who needs help to deal with guilt, shame, and anxiety and to meet frustrations or external pressures that may be too great to handle.

Table 34.1–3
Indications for Expressive or Supportive Emphasis in Psychotherapy

Insight-Oriented (Expressive)	Supportive
Strong motivation to understand	Significant ego defects of a long-term nature
Significant suffering	Severe life crisis
Ability to regress in the service of the ego	
Tolerance for frustration	Poor frustration tolerance
Capacity for insight (psychological-mindedness)	Lack of psychological-mindedness
Intact reality testing	Poor reality testing
Meaningful object relations	Severely impaired object relations
Good impulse control	Poor impulse control
Ability to sustain work	Low intelligence
Capacity to think in terms of analogy and metaphor	Little capacity for self-observation
Reflective responses to trial interpretations	Organically based cognitive dysfunction
	Tenuous ability to form a therapeutic alliance

Reprinted with permission from Gabbard GO: *Psychodynamic Psychotherapy in Clinical Practice,* p 88. American Psychiatric Press, Washington, 1990.

Table 34.1–4
Supportive Psychotherapy

Goal	Support reality testing Provide ego support Maintain or reestablish usual level of functioning
Selection criteria	Very healthy patient faced with overwhelming crises Patient with ego deficits
Duration	Days, months, or years—as needed
Technique	Therapist predictably available Interpretation used to strengthen defenses Therapist maintains working, reality-based relationship based on support, concern, and problem solving Suggestion, reinforcement, advice, reality testing, cognitive restructuring, and reassurance Psychodynamic life narrative Medication

Reprinted with permission from Ursano RJ, Silberman EK: Individual psychotherapies. In *The American Psychiatric Press Textbook of Psychiatry,* JA Talbott, RE Hales, SC Yudofsky, editors, p 878. American Psychiatric Press, Washington, 1988.

Supportive therapy uses several methods, either singly or in combination, including warm, friendly, strong leadership; partial gratification of dependency needs; support in the ultimate development of legitimate independence; help in developing pleasurable activities (such as hobbies); adequate rest and diversion; removal of excessive strain when possible; hospitalization when indicated; medication to alleviate symptoms; and guidance and advice in dealing with current issues. This therapy uses techniques to help patients feel secure, accepted, protected, encouraged, safe, and not anxious.

One of the greatest dangers of supportive therapy is the possibility of an analyst's fostering too great a regression and too strong a dependence. From the beginning, psychiatrists must plan to work persistently to enable patients to assume independence. Some patients, however, require supportive therapy indefinitely, often with the goal of maintaining a marginal adjustment that enables them to function in society.

The expression of emotion is an important part of supportive psychotherapy and verbalizing unexpressed strong emotions may bring considerable relief. Talking things out is not primarily meant to gain insight into unconscious dynamic patterns that may be intensifying current responses. Rather, reduced inner tension and anxiety may result from expressing emotion, and subsequent discussion may lead to insight into a current problem and objectivity in evaluating it.

CORRECTIVE EMOTIONAL EXPERIENCE. The relationship between therapist and patient gives a therapist an opportunity to display behavior different from the destructive or unproductive behavior of a patient's parent. At times, such experiences seem to neutralize or reverse some effects of the parents' mistakes. If the patient had overly authoritarian parents, the therapist's friendly, flexible, nonjudgmental, nonauthoritarian—but at times firm and limit-setting—attitude gives the patient an opportunity to adjust to, be led by, and identify with a new parent figure. Franz Alexander described this process as a corrective emotional experience.

Supportive psychotherapy is suitable for various psychogenic illnesses, for example, when a patient resists an expressive psychotherapy or is considered too emotionally disturbed for such a procedure. Supportive therapy may be chosen when a diagnostic assessment indicates that a gradual maturing process, based on elaborating new foci for identification, is the most promising path toward improvement. Table 34.1–3 summarizes indications for insight-oriented (expressive) therapy versus supportive therapy. Table 34.1–4 outlines supportive psychotherapy.

REFERRAL BY A NONPSYCHIATRIC PHYSICIAN

Nonpsychiatric physicians often treat psychiatric patients who may require referral to a psychiatrist for in-depth evaluation and treatment that cannot be provided in a nonpsychiatric setting. Sometimes a nonpsychiatric physician may think that a patient would benefit from psychotherapy. Such a patient may or may not carry an Axis I or Axis II diagnosis. Table 34.1–5 summarizes a few key features involved in effectively referring a patient for psychotherapy.

CURRENT PROBLEMS

With the advent of managed care, increasing pressure is put on psychiatrists to provide psychotherapy that is short term and, theoretically, low cost. Short-term therapies—enthusiastically promoted by private insurance companies, health maintenance organizations, and several psychiatric residency programs—have explicitly delineated parameters about the number of sessions, concrete goals, and outcome evaluation criteria. The therapies are largely designed so that the techniques involved can be learned quickly and performed with the aid of instructional manuals by various practitioners other than psychiatrists.

The pressure to develop therapies that are less expensive, less training intensive, and less time consuming than is psychoanalysis stems from some legitimate concerns about the accessibility of traditional insight-oriented approaches of psychoanalysis and analytically oriented psychotherapy. Nevertheless, the rush to relegate such powerfully effective treatments to the periphery seems shortsighted and is ultimately impoverishing to the field of psychiatry and to those patients who respond only to extended treatment. The American Psychiatric Association attended to some of these issues in its APA Position Statement on Medical Psychotherapy (Table 34.1–6). A 1995 survey by *Consumer Reports* magazine found that over 85 percent of their subscribers who received psychotherapy found it of value and of help.

Table 34.1–5
Guidelines for Patient Referral

It is important to exhibit confidence and enthusiasm when making a referral for psychiatric evaluation or psychotherapy. Patients will detect ambivalence and skepticism on the physician's part about the need for such treatment. It is usually helpful to recommend a psychiatrist or other mental health professional who is known *personally* by the physician.

Always present the psychiatric referral as part of the patient's ongoing medical care. Some patents view a psychiatric referral as a means to dump them onto another doctor or as a rejection. Patients should be reassured that any psychiatric treatment will be in parallel with their ongoing medical care.

Have the name and telephone number of your referral source readily available to give to the patient.

Call the psychiatrist to personally explain the reason and need for the referral and what role you would like to continue to play in the patient's care.

Make the appointment for the psychiatric evaluation while the patient is still in the office or clinic.

Be sure to schedule a follow-up appointment after the date of the psychiatric evaluation to check on the patient's reaction to the referral and his or her response to the initial treatment.

Reprinted with permission from Stoudemire A: *Clinical Psychiatry for Medical Students,* p 457. Lippincott, Philadelphia, 1990.

Gender Issues in Psychotherapy

Little data are available about the influence of therapist gender on the therapeutic process. Most studies show a higher correlation between the therapist's experience and the outcome of psychotherapy or patient satisfaction with the therapist than between the patient's gender and the outcome. In general, patients of more experienced physicians fared better than did those of less experienced clinicians regardless of gender.

Nevertheless, the literature on gender issues in psychiatric treatment is growing. Carol Nadelson has pointed out that a patient's choosing to be treated by a woman may represent a search for the idealized mother whether the patient is a man or a woman. Similarly, choosing a male therapist may represent a search for a father figure. If a patient has had traumatic experiences with people of one gender, he or she may wish to avoid entering into a therapeutic relationship with someone who can evoke these experiences. It is not uncommon, for example, for women who have been sexually abused by men to request a female therapist. Women therapists are less likely to become sexually involved with their patients than are men, but such involvement does occur.

In a psychoanalytic situation, analysis of the transference is a basic issue. As the analytic process unfolds, patients can often perceive a psychotherapist as a member of the opposite sex: A woman may see a male therapist as a mother figure, and a man may perceive a female analyst as a father figure. These unconscious perceptions may shift as the analysis proceeds. These transference issues are analyzed in psychoanalysis. In supportive therapies, similar transference distortions may occur, but if they are discussed at all, they are not interpreted in the same way as in psychoanalysis. In any case, it is important to note that patients can view therapists as male or female regardless of the therapists' actual gender.

When patients identify with their therapists and rely on them as role models, as they often do, patients identify with therapists' value systems, not with their gender assignment. Under ideal circumstances, female therapists have worked through negative cultural stereotypes of the female role and so can facilitate the same process in their female patients and can raise the consciousness of their male patients about prejudice toward females.

Gender identification is defined as a sense of being a man or woman. Ideally, gender identity and gender role—what is expected of men and women in society—are congruent. For example, women procreate and men inseminate; but to do neither is not indicative of mental illness. Therapists are expected to have flexible attitudes toward gender identity and gender role, especially about sexual orientation. Gay and lesbian psy-

Table 34.1–6
American Psychiatric Association (APA) Position Statement on Medical Psychotherapy

Medical psychotherapy is fundamental to American psychiatry and essential to the skills of the psychiatrist. Medical psychotherapy relies on the unique relationship between psychiatrist and patient. It employs verbal communication to treat a broad spectrum of mental disorders, dysfunction, and distress. The psychiatrist brings to this work specialized knowledge and experience, grounded in the physician's expertise and professional standards. Most forms of medical psychotherapy are derived from one of two theoretical models: psychoanalytic theory and learning theory. Often the two approaches are integrated to meet the needs of particular patients. Various adaptations, taking biological and social factors into account, are frequently used for children and youth, the elderly, people with dual diagnoses of addictive and mental disorders, and people with severe nonpsychiatric illness. Medical psychotherapy takes place through individual, family, and group modalities, depending on medical necessity.

The special education, training, and medical experience of a psychiatric physician provide the differentiating variables that define medical psychotherapy. As physicians, psychiatrists add unique and vital dimensions to psychotherapy that limited licensed practitioners do not have: medical standards of ethics and professional responsibility for life-and-death decisions, comprehensive grounding in medical diagnosis and treatment, the capacity to integrate complex psychopharmacology with psychotherapy and social rehabilitation, and in-depth knowledge of human biology, general medical conditions, and their interaction with psychiatric illness and mental phenomena. Psychiatrists are thoroughly grounded in human emotional development and the life cycle. Provision of both psychotherapy and medication management by the same treating psychiatrist provides high-quality, comprehensive, and accountable care. However, psychiatrists are also in an optimal position to prescribe and perform psychotherapy as the sole treatment modality. Psychiatrists in organized systems must be free to conduct psychotherapy with their patients without financial or other disincentives.

Psychiatrists have extensive training in the conduct of medical psychotherapy. Because of the expanded role of neurobiology in psychiatry and marked constriction of services allowed in managed systems, academic departments must struggle to preserve the quality of medical psychotherapy training in psychiatric residencies. These training experiences must be maintained for psychiatrists to retain expertise in the full range of core skills needed to treat the psychiatrically ill.

Conditions necessary for effective medical psychotherapy are (1) a setting of confidentiality and privacy, (2) active participation by the patient in treatment decisions, and (3) continuity of therapist so that a doctor-patient working alliance can develop and work begun can be properly concluded.

The aforementioned conditions necessary for effective medical psychotherapy must be maintained in any system of health care delivery. Intrusive micromanagement and central data-collecting systems create special challenges to these conditions that call for active negotiation by APA. Psychiatrists should vigorously expose inadequacies in managed health care systems that restrict or deny medically necessary treatment, including medical psychotherapy, and endeavor to rectify such inadequacies. Superficial advice or referral to self-help groups, as often advocated in managed behavioral health care organizations, does not substitute for needed specific treatments, including medical psychotherapy.

Affordable point-of-service options or other similar measures must be available to allow patients the choice of continuing with essential doctor–patient relationships when health plan contracts or conditions are changed and to seek consultation or treatment from psychiatrists with special qualifications for their treatment needs. Psychiatrists and patients must be free to contract privately and independently for services if they so choose, with no third-party interference or requirements for reporting to external entities. These concerns apply to all patients but are especially compelling for those in medical psychotherapy.

There is abundant scientific evidence that medical psychotherapy is effective for a wide variety of psychiatric illnesses and that it reduces utilization of more expensive medical services and improves compliance with treatment regimens. Data on pervasive mind–body interactions are rapidly accumulating, requiring psychiatrists familiar with both brain and mind. The cost of medical psychotherapy is a modest and predictable segment of overall medical expenditures in a large-scale system, and utilization is self-limiting even when benefits are generous.

Many patients' psychiatric disorders respond to short-term psychotherapeutic treatments. Some patients gain much more from intensive and/or long-term medical psychotherapy and should have access to it; such patients commonly have long-standing conditions that cause significant dysfunction and distress in their family, work, and social relationships. Development of evidence-based practice guidelines has reinforced the critical role of medical psychotherapy in the treatment of patients with mental disorders.

Patients in need of medical psychotherapy should have the same respect and access to care as any other persons needing medical treatment. APA strongly objects to stereotyping or caricaturing patients who utilize medical psychotherapy, especially in ways that minimize the seriousness of their illness.

Reprinted with permission from *Psychiatric News*, June 7, 1996.

chiatrists treat patients of both sexes, and heterosexual psychiatrists treat gay and lesbian patients. In general, however, gay and lesbian patients feel more comfortable with therapists who share their orientation. The range of backgrounds of psychiatrists, psychologists, and other providers of psychotherapy is expanding rapidly. Gender identity, gender role, sexual orientation, country of origin, and languages spoken are all issues that require further study. Patients who like their therapists and who in turn are liked by their therapists establish a positive therapeutic alliance, and patients with good therapeutic alliances, regardless of the therapeutic technique used, have the best outcomes. Thus far, research indicates that psychiatrists treat patients who are more like them than they are different. The similarities and differences between therapist and patient represent a frontier area of psychotherapy research.

References

Abend SM: Countertransference and psychoanalytic technique. Psychoanal Q *58;* 374, 1989.

Blechner J: Psychoanalysis and HIV disease. Contemp Psychoanal *29:* 61, 1993.

Bowden CL: Implications of psychopharmacological studies for the practice of psychoanalysis. J Am Acad Psychoanal *20:* 477, 1992.

Brenner C: *Psychoanalytic Technique and Psychic Conflict.* International Universities Press, New York, 1976.

Etchegoyen A: Psychoanalysis of the child: Psychic reality of the patient and the analyst. Int J Psychoanal *77:* 353, 1996.

Fenichel O: Problems of psychoanalytic technique. Psychoanal Q *10:* 84, 1941.

Freud A: *The Ego and Mechanisms of Defense.* International Universities Press, New York, 1966.

Gabbard GO: Countertransference: The emerging common ground. Int J Psychoanal *76:* 475, 1995.

Gabbard GO: *Psychodynamic Psychiatry in Clinical Practice: The DSM-IV Edition.* American Psychiatric Press, Washington, 1994.

Gill MM: *Psychoanalysis in Transition: A Personal View.* Analytic Press, Hillsdale, NJ. 1994.

Hartmann H: *Ego Psychology and the Problem of Adaption.* International Universities Press, New York, 1959.
Hirsch I: An interpersonal perspective: The analyst's unwitting participation in the patient's change. Psychoanal Psychol *9:* 299, 1992.
Holinser PC: A developmental perspective on psychotherapy and psychoanalysis. Am J Psychiatry *146:* 1494, 1989.
Jones E: *The Life and Work of Sigmund Freud,* vols 1–3. Basic Books, New York, 1953–1957.
Karasu TB: Psychoanalysis and psychoanalytic psychotherapy. In *Comprehensive Textbook of Psychiatry,* ed 6, HI Kaplan, BJ Sadock, editors, p 1767. Williams & Wilkins, Baltimore, 1995.
Kay J, Gabbard GO, Greist J: Is psychoanalytic psychotherapy relevant to the treatment of OCD? J Psychother Pract Res *5:* 341, 1996.
Kernberg OF: *Object Relations Therapy and Clinical Psychoanalysis.* Aronson, New York, 1976.
Kernberg OF: The current status of psychoanalysis. J Am Psychoanal Assoc *41:* 45, 1993.
Klein M: *Contributions of Psychoanalysis.* Hogarth, London, 1948.
Kohut HH: *The Analysis of the Self.* International Universities Press, New York, 1984.
Lazar R: Psychotherapy and psychoanalysis: Relations between the two modalities. Contemp Psychoanal *32:* 135, 1996.
Mahler M: *On Human Symbiosis and the Vicissitudes of Individuation.* International Universities Press, New York, 1968.
May R, Angel E, Ellenberger H: *Existence: A New Dimension in Psychiatry and Psychology.* Basic Books, New York, 1958.
Oremland JD: Interactive interventions in psychoanalytic psychotherapy and psychoanalysis: A critical review. Psychoanal Inq *16:* 67, 1996.
Reich W: *Character Analysis.* Touchstone, New York, 1974.
Schwaber EA: The conceptualization and communication of clinical facts in psychoanalysis: A discussion. Int J Psychoanal *77:* 235, 1996.
Shafer R: *A New Language for Psychoanalysis.* Yale University Press, New Haven, 1976.
Sullivan HS: *Interpersonal Theory of Psychiatry.* Norton, New York, 1953.
Wallerstein RS: Follow-up in psychoanalysis: What happens to treatment gains? J Am Psychoanal Assoc *40:* 665, 1992.
Yorke V: Boundaries, psychic structure, and time. J Anal Psychol *38:* 57, 1993.

▲ 34.2 Brief Psychotherapy and Crisis Intervention

A recent trend in psychotherapy is the use of short-term treatment methods (also called time-limited psychotherapy) to help people deal with current problems and crises. Derived from psychoanalytic and learning theories, these therapies have their own treatment techniques and specific criteria for selecting patients. Short-term therapies have aroused great interest and gained widespread popularity, partly because of the great pressure on health care professionals to contain treatment costs: It is simpler to evaluate treatment efficacy by comparing groups of people who have undergone a particular therapy for the same psychological problem with control groups than it is to measure the results of long-term psychotherapy.

Although the short-term therapies are obviously of limited duration, the proponents of these therapies express no consensus about the exact meaning of the concept *short term.* Thus, the categories of *brief psychotherapies* and *crisis intervention* as discussed here include several different treatment types.

BRIEF PSYCHOTHERAPY

History

In 1946, Franz Alexander and Thomas French identified most of the basic characteristics of brief psychotherapy. They described a therapeutic experience designed to put patients at ease, to manipulate the transference, and to flexibly use trial interpretations. Alexander and French emphasize developing a corrective emotional experience capable of repairing traumatic events of the past and convincing patients that new ways of thinking, feeling, and behaving are possible.

At about the same time, Eric Lindemann established a consultation service at the Massachusetts General Hospital in Boston for people experiencing a crisis. He developed new treatment methods to deal with these situations and eventually applied these techniques to people who were not in crisis but who were experiencing various kinds of emotional distress.

Selection Criteria

The most valuable predictor of a successful outcome in brief psychotherapy is a patient's motivation for treatment. Patients must also be able to deal with psychological concepts, to respond to interpretation, and to concentrate on and resolve the conflict around the central issue or focus that underlies their basic problems. They must be able to develop a therapeutic alliance and work with a therapist toward achieving emotional health.

Types

Brief Focal Psychotherapy (Tavistock-Malan). Brief focal psychotherapy was originally developed in the 1950s by the Michael Balint team at the Tavistock Clinic in London. Daniel Malan, a member of the team, reported the results of the therapy. Malan's selection criteria for treatment included eliminating absolute contraindications, rejecting patients for whom certain dangers seemed inevitable, clearly assessing patients' psychopathology, and determining patients' capacities to consider problems in emotional terms, face disturbing material, respond to interpretations, and endure the stress of the treatment. Malan found that high motivation invariably correlated with successful outcome. Contraindications to treatment were serious suicidal attempts, substance dependence, chronic alcohol abuse, incapacitating chronic obsessional symptoms, incapacitating chronic phobic symptoms, and gross destructive or self-destructive acting out.

REQUIREMENTS AND TECHNIQUES. In Malan's routine, therapists should identify the transference early and interpret it and the negative transference. They should then link the transferences to patients' relationships to their parents. Both patients and therapists should be willing to become deeply involved and to bear the ensuing tension. Therapists should formulate circumscribed focus and set a termination date in advance, and patients should work through grief and anger about termination. An experienced therapist should allow about 20 sessions as an average length for the therapy; a trainee should allow about 30 sessions. Malan himself did not exceed 40 interviews with his patients. Tables 34.2–1 and 34.2–2 summarize Malan's techniques and exclusion criteria.

Time-Limited Psychotherapy (Boston University-Mann). A psychotherapeutic model of exactly 12 interviews focusing on a specified central issue was developed at Boston University by James Mann and his colleagues in the early 1970s. In contrast with Malan's emphasis on clear-cut selection and rejection criteria, Mann has not been as explicit about the appropriate candidates for time-limited psychotherapy.

Table 34.2–1
Malan and the Tavistock Group: Brief Focal Psychotherapy

Goal	Clarify the nature of the defense, the anxiety, and the impulse Link the present, the past, and the transference
Selection criteria	Patient able to think in feeling terms High motivation Good response to trial interpretation
Duration	Up to one year Mean, 20 sessions
Focus	Internal conflict present since childhood
Termination	Set definite date at beginning of treatment

Reprinted with permission from Ursano RJ, Silberman EK: Individual psychotherapies. In *The American Psychiatric Press Textbook of Psychiatry*, JA Talbott, RE Hales, SC Yudofsky, editors, p 861. American Psychiatric Press, Washington, 1988.

Mann considered determining a patient's central conflict reasonably correctly and exploring young people's maturational crises with many psychological and somatic complaints to be the major emphases of his theory.

Mann's exceptions, similar to his rejection criteria, include people with major depressive disorder that interferes with the treatment agreement, those with acute psychotic states and desperate patients who need, but cannot tolerate, object relations.

REQUIREMENTS AND TECHNIQUES. Mann's technical requirements included strict limitation to 12 sessions, positive transference predominating early, specification and strict adherence to a central issue involving transference, positive identification, making separation a maturational event for patients, absolute prospect of termination to avoid development of dependence, clarification of present and past experiences and resistances, active therapists who support and encourage patients, and education of patients through direct information, reeducation, and manipulation. The conflicts likely to be encountered included independence versus dependence, activity versus passivity, unresolved or delayed grief, and adequate verses inadequate self-esteem. Table 34.2–3 summarizes the features of Mann's time-limited psychotherapy.

Short-Term Dynamic Psychotherapy (McGill University-Davanloo). As conducted by Habib Davanloo at McGill University, short-term dynamic psychotherapy encompasses nearly all varieties of brief psychotherapy and crisis intervention. Patients treated in Davanloo's series are classified as those whose psychological conflicts are predominantly oedipal, those whose conflicts are not oedipal, and those whose conflicts have more than one focus. Davanloo also devised a specific psychotherapeutic technique for patients with severe, long-standing neurotic problems, specifically those with incapacitating obsessive-compulsive disorders and phobias.

Davanloo's selection criteria emphasize the evaluation of those ego functions of primary importance to psychotherapeutic work: the establishment of a psychotherapeutic focus, the psychodynamic formulation of patients' psychological problems, the ability to have emotional interaction with evaluators, the history of give-and-take relationships with a significant person in patients' life, patients' ability to experience and tolerate anxiety, guilt, and depression; patients' motivations for

Table 34.2–2
Malan and the Tavistock Group's Exclusion Criteria for Brief Focal Psychotherapy

1. Patient is unavailable to therapeutic contact.
2. Therapist anticipates that prolonged work will be needed to
   - generate motivation
   - penetrate rigid defenses
   - deal with complex or deep-seated issues
   - resolve unfavorable, intense transference, dependent or other, that may develop
3. Depressive or psychotic disturbance may intensify

Reprinted with permission from Ursano RJ, Silberman EK: Individual psychotherapies. In *The American Psychiatric Press Textbook of Psychiatry*, JA Talbott, RE Hales, SC Yudofsky, editors, p 861. American Psychiatric Press, Washington, 1988.

Table 34.2–3
Mann: Time-Limited Psychotherapy

Goal	Resolution of the present and chronically endured pain and the patient's negative self-image
Selection criteria	High ego strength Able to engage and disengage Therapist quickly able to identify a central issue Excludes major depressive disorder, acute psychosis, and borderline personality disorder
Duration	12 treatment hours
Focus	Present and chronically endured pain Particular image of the self
Termination	Specific last session set at beginning of treatment Termination a major focus of the therapy work

Reprinted with permission from Ursano RJ, Silberman EK: Individual psychotherapies. In *The American Psychiatric Press Textbook of Psychiatry*, JA Talbott, RE Hales, SC Yudofsky, editors, p 864. American Psychiatric Press, Washington, 1988.

Table 34.2–4
Davanloo: Short-Term Dynamic Psychotherapy

Goal	Resolution of oedipal conflict, loss focus, or multiple foci
Selection criteria	Psychological-mindedness At least one past meaningful relationship Able to tolerate affect Good response to trial transference interpretation High motivation Flexible defenses Lack of projection, splitting, and denial
Duration	5–40 sessions, usually 5–25 Longer durations for seriously ill
Termination	No specific termination date Patient is told that treatment will be short

Reprinted with permission from Ursano RJ, Silberman EK: Individual psychotherapies. In *The American Psychiatric Press Textbook of Psychiatry*, JA Talbott, RE Hales, SC Yudofsky, editors, p 865. American Psychiatric Press, Washington, 1988.

change, patients' psychological-mindedness, and the patient's ability to respond to interpretation and to link evaluators with people in the present and past. Both Malan and Davanloo emphasized patients' responses to interpretation as an important selection and prognostic criterion.

REQUIREMENTS AND TECHNIQUES. The highlights of Davanloo's psychotherapeutic approach are flexibility (therapists should adapt the technique to patients' needs), control of patients' regressive tendencies, active intervention so as not to allow patients to develop overdependence on a therapist, and patients' intellectual insight and emotional experiences in the transference. These emotional experiences become corrective as a result of the interpretation. Table 34.2–4 summarizes the features of Davanloo's short-term dynamic psychotherapy.

Short-Term Anxiety-Provoking Psychotherapy (Harvard University-Sifneos).

Peter Sifneos developed short-term anxiety-provoking psychotherapy at the Massachusetts General Hospital in Boston during the 1950s. He used the following criteria for selection: a circumscribed chief complaint (implying a patient's ability to select one of a variety of problems to be given top priority and the patient's desire to resolve the problem in treatment), one meaningful or give-and-take relationship during early childhood, the ability to interact flexibly with an evaluator and to express feelings appropriately, above-average psychological sophistication (implying not only above-average intelligence but also an ability to respond to interpretations), a specific psychodynamic formulation (usually a set of psychological conflicts underlying a patient's difficulties and centering on an oedipal focus), a contract between therapist and patient to work on the specified focus and the formulation of minimal expectations of outcome, and good-to-excellent motivation for change and not just for symptom relief.

REQUIREMENTS AND TECHNIQUES. Treatment can be divided into four major phases: patient–therapist encounter, early therapy, height of treatment, and evidence of change and termination. Therapists use the following techniques during the four phases.

Patient–Therapist Encounter. A therapist establishes a working alliance by using the patient's quick rapport with and positive feelings for the therapist that appear in this phase. Judicious use of open-ended and forced-choice questions enables the therapist to outline and concentrate on a therapeutic focus. The therapist specifies the minimum expectations of outcome to be achieved by the therapy.

Early Therapy. In transference, feelings for the therapist are clarified as soon as they appear, a technique that leads to the establishment of a true therapeutic alliance.

Height of the Treatment. This phase emphasizes active concentration on the oedipal conflicts that have been chosen as the therapeutic focus for the therapy; repeated use of anxiety-provoking questions and confrontations; avoidance of pregenital characterological issues, which the patient uses defensively to avoid dealing with the therapist's anxiety-provoking techniques; avoidance at all costs of a transference neurosis; repetitive demonstration of the patient's neurotic ways or maladaptive patterns of behavior; concentration on the anxiety-laden material, even before the defense mechanisms have been clarified; repeated demonstrations of parent-transference links by the use of properly timed interpretations based on material given by the patient; establishment of a corrective emotional experience; encouragement and support of the patient, who becomes anxious while struggling to understand the conflicts; new learning and problem-solving patterns; and repeated presentations and recapitulations of the patient's psychodynamics until the defense mechanisms used in dealing with oedipal conflicts are understood.

Evidence of Change and Termination of Psychotherapy. This phase emphasizes the tangible demonstration of change in the patient's behavior outside therapy, evidence that adaptive patterns of behavior are being used, and initiation of talk about terminating the treatment. Table 34.2–5 summarizes features of the Sifneos short-term anxiety-provoking psychotherapy.

Table 34.2–5
Illness: Short-Term Anxiety-Provoking Psychotherapy

Goal	Resolution of oedipal conflict
Selection criteria	Above-average intelligence At least one past meaningful relationship High motivation Specific chief complaint Able to interact with evaluator Able to express feelings Flexible
Duration	A few months Average 12–16 sessions
Focus	Oedipal (triangular) conflict
Termination	No specific date given

Reprinted with permission from Ursano RJ, Silberman EK: Individual psychotherapies. In *The American Psychiatric Press Textbook of Psychiatry*, JA Talbott, RE Hales, SC Yudofsky, editor, p 863. American Psychiatric Press, Washington, 1988.

Interpersonal Psychotherapy.

A specific type of short-term psychotherapy called interpersonal psychotherapy (IPT), described by Myrna Weissman and Gerald Klerman, is used to treat depressive disorders. Therapy consists of 45- to 50-minute sessions held weekly over a 3- to 4-month period. Interpersonal behavior is emphasized as a cause of depressive disorders and as a method of cure. Patients are taught to realistically evaluate their interactions with others and to become aware of their deliberate self-isolation, which contributes to or aggravates the depression they complain about. The therapist offers direct advice, aids the patient in making decisions, and helps clarify areas of conflict. Little or no attention is given to the transference. The therapist attempts to be consistently supportive, empathic, and flexible. Studies have shown that, in selected cases of depressive disorders, interpersonal psychotherapy compares favorably with drug therapy that uses antidepressant agents. IPT has also been used successfully in other mental disorders such as bulimia nervosa and substance abuse. Table 34.2–6 summarizes the features of interpersonal psychotherapy.

Dialectical Therapy.

Dialectical therapy combines aspects of cognitive and behavior therapy. The therapist is supportive and directive. Specific exercises are performed to help solve problems and to improve interpersonal skills. It was developed by M. Linehan as a training manual for treating borderline personality disorder (BPD) and has been effective in diminishing suicidal acts that are often associated with BPD.

Outcome

The shared techniques of all these brief psychotherapies, which outdistance their differences, include the therapeutic alliance or dynamic interaction between therapist and patient, the use of transference, the active interpretation of a therapeutic focus or central issue, the repetitive links between parental and transference issues, and the early termination of therapy.

Table 34.2–6
Interpersonal Psychotherapy

Goal	Improvement in current interpersonal skills
Selection criteria	Outpatient, nonbipolar disorder, nonpsychotic depressive disorder
Duration	12–16 weeks, usually once-weekly meetings
Technique	Reassurance Clarification of feeling states Improvement of interpersonal communication Testing perceptions Development of interpersonal skills Medication

Reprinted with permission from Ursano RJ, Silberman EK: Individual psychotherapies. In *The American Psychiatric Press Textbook of Psychiatry*, JA Talbott, RE Hales, SC Yudofsky, editors, p 868. American Psychiatric Press, Washington, 1988.

The outcomes of these brief treatments have been investigated more extensively than has any other form of psychotherapy. Contrary to prevailing ideas that the therapeutic factors in psychotherapy are nonspecific, controlled studies and other assessment methods (for example, interviews with unbiased evaluators, patients' self-evaluations) point to the importance of the specific techniques used. Malan summarized the results in five major generalizations: The capacity for genuine recovery in certain patients is far greater than was thought. A certain type of patient receiving brief psychotherapy can benefit greatly from a practical working through of his or her nuclear conflict in the transference. Such patients can be recognized in advance through a process of dynamic interaction, because they are responsive and motivated and able to face disturbing feelings and because a circumscribed focus can be formulated for them. The more radical the technique in terms of transference, depth of interpretation, and the link to childhood, the more radical the therapeutic effects will be. For some disturbed patients, a carefully chosen partial focus can be therapeutically effective.

CRISIS INTERVENTION

Theory

Crisis intervention, by definition, is a therapy limited by the parameters of the crisis causing a patient to consult a therapist. Crisis intervention is based on crisis theory, which emphasizes not only immediate responses to an immediate situation but also long-term development of psychological adaption aimed at preventing future problems. A crisis is a response to hazardous events, which people experience as a painful state. A crisis is self-limited and can last from a few hours to weeks. It is characterized by an initial phase in which anxiety and tension rise, followed by a phase in which problem-solving mechanisms are set in motion. These mechanisms may be successful, depending on whether they are adaptive or maladaptive.

Crisis tends to mobilize powerful reactions to help people alleviate the discomfort and return to their former state of emotional equilibrium. If a person regains emotional equilibrium, the crisis can be overcome, and the person also learns how to use adaptive reactions. Furthermore, by resolving the crisis, the person's state of mind may be superior to the state preceding the onset of psychological difficulties. When, however, a patient reacts maladaptively the painful state intensifies, the crisis deepens, and a regressive deterioration occurs producing psychiatric symptoms. These symptoms, in turn, may crystallize into a neurotic pattern of behavior that restricts a patient's ability to function freely. At times when the situation cannot be stabilized, new maladaptive reactions are introduced, and the consequences can be of catastrophic proportions, even leading to death by suicide. In this sense, psychological crises are painful and may be viewed as turning points for better or for worse.

During a period of turmoil, patients are receptive to almost any help they are offered and get meaningful results from minimal assistance. All sorts of services, therefore, have been devised to help people in crisis. Some services are open ended while others limit the number of sessions or the time available. Crisis theory lets therapists understand healthy normal people in crisis and allows them to develop therapeutic tools aimed at preventing future psychological difficulties.

Criteria for Selection

The criteria used to select patients are a history of a recent, specific hazardous situation that produced the anxiety, a precipitating event that intensified the anxiety, clear-cut evidence of the patient's psychological incapacitation from a severe disturbance, high motivation to overcome the crisis, a potential for making a psychological adjustment equal or superior to the one that existed before the development of the crisis, and a certain degree of psychological sophistication—an ability to recognize psychological reasons for the present predicament.

Requirements and Techniques

Crisis intervention deals with people amid a crisis in which speed is of the essence. Therapy requires a joint understanding of the psychodynamics involved and an awareness of how the people concerned are responsible for the crisis. The participants work together and aim to resolve the crisis. Patients as well as the therapists actively participate in the treatment.

Techniques include reassurance, suggestion, environmental manipulation, and psychotropic medications. Brief hospitalization may be added as part of the treatment plan. All these therapeutic maneuvers are aimed at decreasing the patient's anxiety. The length of crisis intervention varies from 1 or 2 sessions to several interviews over a period of 1 or 2 months. The technical requirements for crisis intervention include rapidly establishing a rapport with the patient to create a therapeutic alliance, reviewing the steps that have led to the crisis, understanding the maladaptive reactions the patient is using to deal with the crisis, focusing only on the crisis, learning to use adaptive ways to deal with crises, avoiding the development of symptoms, using the predominating positive transference feelings for the therapist to transform the work into a learning experience, teaching the patient how to avoid hazardous situations that are likely to produce future crises, and ending the intervention as soon as evidence indicates that the crisis has been resolved and the patient clearly understands all the steps in its development and resolution.

Outcome

The most striking result of crisis therapy is a patient's ability to become better equipped to avoid or, if necessary, to deal with future hazards. In addition, on the basis of some patients' objective observations, the therapeutic experience enables them to attain a level of emotional functioning that is superior to that before the onset of the crisis. In this sense, therefore, crisis intervention is not only therapeutic but also preventive.

References

Brom D, Kleber RJ, Defares PB: Brief psychotherapy for posttraumatic stress disorders. J Consult Clin Psychol *57:* 607, 1989.

Davanloo H: *Basic Principles and Technique of Short Term Dynamic Psychotherapy.* Spectrum, New York, 1978.

Flesenheimer WV, Pollack J: The time limit in brief psychotherapy. Bull Menninger Clin *53:* 44, 1989.

Horowitz M: *Personality Styles and Brief Psychotherapy.* Basic Books, New York, 1984.

Hughes KH, Ashby C: Essential components of the short-term psychiatric unit. Perspect Psychiatr Care *32:* 20, 1996.

Jayaram G, Tien AY, Sullivan P, Gwon H: Elements of a successful short-stay inpatient psychiatric service. Psychiatr Serv *47:* 407, 1996.

MacKenzie KR: Recent developments in brief psychotherapy. Hosp Community Psychiatry *39:* 742, 1988.

Mann J: *Time Limited Psychotherapy.* Harvard University Press, Cambridge, 1973.

Maxim RE, Hunt DD: Appraisal and coping in the process of patient change during short-term psychotherapy. J Nerv Ment Dis *178:* 235, 1990.

Mohl PC: Brief psychotherapy. In *Comprehensive Textbook of Psychiatry,* ed 6, HI Kaplan, BJ Sadock, editors, p 1873. Williams & Wilkins, Baltimore, 1995.

Pinkerton R: The interaction between brief and very brief psychotherapy: Allowing for flexible time limits on individual counseling services. Prof Psychol Res Pract *27:* 315, 1996.

Piper WE, Joyce AS: A consideration of factors influencing the utilization of time-limited, short-term group therapy. Int J Group Psychother *46:* 331, 1996.

Porter R: *The Role of Learning in Psychotherapy.* Churchill, London, 1968.

Schram PC, Burti L: Crisis intervention techniques designed to prevent hospitalization. Bull Menninger Clin *50:* 194, 1986.

Sifneos PE: *Short-Term Dynamic Psychotherapy Evaluation and Technique,* ed 2. Plenum, New York, 1987.

Sifneos PE: *Short-Term Psychotherapy and Emotional Crisis.* Harvard University Press, Cambridge, 1972.

Sifneos PE, Greenberg WE: Patient management. In *The New Harvard Guide to Psychiatry,* p 589. Harvard University Press, Cambridge, 1988.

Swinson RP, Soulios C, Cox BJ, Kuch K: Brief treatment of emergency room patients with panic attacks. Am J Psychiatry *149:* 944, 1992.

Werner MJ: Principles of brief intervention for adolescent alcohol, tobacco, and other drug use. Pediatr Clin North Am *42:* 335, 1995.

Wilborg IM, Dahl AA: Does brief dynamic psychotherapy reduce the relapse rate of panic disorder? Arch Gen Psychiatry *53:* 689, 1996.

▲ 34.3 Group Psychotherapy, Combined Individual and Group Psychotherapy, and Psychodrama

In group therapy, the interactions of group members offer possibilities for change and growth, while therapists serve to support and regulate group behavior. Participants are carefully selected for their ability to profit from group encounters, and therapists are specially trained to conduct these procedures by using various techniques drawn from different theoretical sources. In addition to being less expensive than individual therapy, group therapy offers people the opportunity to realize that others share their problems. Group therapy can take the form of a psychodrama, in which people enact their problems to become more aware of them. Patients may also work in groups and meet individually with their therapists.

GROUP PSYCHOTHERAPY

Group psychotherapy is a treatment in which carefully selected people who are emotionally ill meet in a group guided by a trained therapist and help one another effect personality change. By using a variety of technical maneuvers and theoretical constructs, the leader directs group members' interactions to bring about changes.

Group psychotherapy encompasses the theoretical spectrum of therapies in psychiatry: supportive, structured, limit-setting (for example, groups with chronically psychotic people), cognitive-behavior, interpersonal, family, and analytically oriented groups. Compared with individual therapies, two of the main strengths of group therapy are the opportunity for immediate feedback from a patient's peers and the chance for both patient and therapist to observe a patient's psychological, emotional, and behavioral responses to a variety of people, who elicit a variety of transferences. Table 34.3–1 outlines some of the key features of group therapies.

Classification

Group therapy at present has many approaches. Some clinicians work within a psychoanalytic frame of reference. Others use therapy techniques such as transactional group therapy, which was devised by Eric Berne and emphasizes the here-and-now interactions among group members; behavioral group therapy, which relies on conditioning techniques based on learning theory; Gestalt group therapy, which was created from the theories of Frederick Perls and enables patients to abreact and express themselves fully; and client-centered group psychotherapy, which was developed by Carl Rogers and is based

Table 34.3–1
Group Therapies

Goal	Alleviation of symptoms Change interpersonal relations Alter specific family-couple dynamics
Selection	Varies greatly based on type of group Homogeneous groups target specific disorders Adolescents and patients with personality disorders may especially benefit Families and couples where the system needs change Contraindications: substantial suicide risk, sadomasochistic acting out in family or couple
Types	Directive-supportive group psychotherapy Psychodynamic-interpersonal group psychotherapy Psychoanalytic group psychotherapy Family therapy Couples therapy
Duration	Weeks to years; time limited and open-ended

Reprinted with permission from Stoudemire A: *Clinical Psychiatry for Medical Students,* p 449. Lippincott, Philadelphia, 1990.

on the nonjudgmental expression of feelings among group members. Table 34.3–2 outlines the major group psychotherapy approaches.

Patient Selection

To determine a patient's suitability for group psychotherapy, a therapist needs a great deal of information, which is gathered in a screening interview. The psychiatrist should take a psychiatric history and perform a mental status examination to obtain certain dynamic, behavioral, and diagnostic information. Table 34.3–3 outlines the general criteria for the selection of patients for group therapy.

Authority Anxiety. Those patients whose primary problem is their relationship to authority and who are ex-

Table 34.3–2
Comparison of Types of Group Psychotherapy

Parameters	Supportive Group Therapy	Analytically Oriented Group Therapy	Psychoanalysis of Groups	Transactional Group Therapy	Behavioral Group Therapy
Frequency	Once a week	1–3 times a week	1–5 times a week	1–3 times a week	1–3 times a week
Duration	Up to 6 months	1–3+ years	1–3+ years	1–3 years	Up to 6 months
Primary indications	Psychotic and anxiety disorders	Anxiety disorders, borderline states, personality disorders	Anxiety disorders, personality disorders	Anxiety and psychotic disorders	Phobias, passivity, sexual problems
Individual screening interview	Usually	Always	Always	Usually	Usually
Communication content	Primarily environmental factors	Present and past life situations, intragroup and extragroup relationships	Primarily past life experiences, intragroup relationships	Primarily intragroup relationships; rarely, history; here and now stressed	Specific symptoms without focus on causality
Transference	Positive transference encouraged to promote improved functioning	Positive and negative transference evoked and analyzed	Transference neurosis evoked and analyzed	Positive relationships fostered, negative feelings analyzed	Positive relationships fostered, no examination of transference
Dreams	Not analyzed	Analyzed frequently	Always analyzed and encouraged	Analyzed rarely	Not used
Dependence	Intragroup dependence encouraged, members rely on leader to great extent	Intragroup dependence encouraged, dependence on leader variable	Intragroup dependence not encouraged, dependence on leader variable	Intragroup dependence encouraged, dependence on leader not encouraged	Intragroup dependence not encouraged; reliance on leader is high
Therapist activity	Strengthen existing defenses, active, give advice	Challenge defenses, active, give advice or personal response	Challenge defenses, passive, give no advice or personal response	Challenge defenses, active, give personal response, rather than advice	Create new defenses, active and directive
Interpretation	No interpretation of unconscious conflict	Interpretation of unconscious conflict	Interpretation of unconscious conflict extensive	Interpretation of current behavioral patterns in the here and now	Not used
Major group processes	Universalization, reality testing	Cohesion, transference, reality testing	Transference, ventilation, catharsis, reality testing	Abreaction, reality testing	Cohesion, reinforcement, conditioning
Socialization outside of group	Encouraged	Generally discouraged	Discouraged	Variable	Discouraged
Goals	Improved adaptation to environment	Moderate reconstruction of personality dynamics	Extensive reconstruction of personality dynamics	Alteration of behavior through mechanism of conscious control	Relief of specific psychiatric symptoms

Table 34.3–3
General Membership Criteria for Group Therapy

Inclusion criteria
Ability to perform the group task
Problem areas compatible with goals of group
Motivation to change
Exclusion criteria
Marked incompatibility with group norms for acceptable behavior
Inability to tolerate group setting
Severe incompatibility with one or more of the other members
Tendency to assume deviant role

Reprinted with permission from Vinogradov S, Yalom ID: Group therapy. In *The American Psychiatric Press Textbook of Psychiatry*, JA Talbott, RE Hales, SC Yudofsky, editors, p 956. American Psychiatric Press, Washington, 1988.

tremely anxious in the presence of authority figures may or may not do well in group therapy because they are more comfortable in a group. But they are more likely to do better in a group than in a dyadic (one-to-one) setting. Patients with a great deal of authority anxiety may be blocked, anxious, resistant, and unwilling to verbalize thought and feelings in an individual setting, generally for fear of the therapist's censure or disapproval. Thus, they may welcome the suggestion of group psychotherapy to avoid the scrutiny of the dyadic situation. Conversely, if a patient reacts negatively to the suggestion of group psychotherapy or openly resists the idea, the therapist should consider the possibility that the patient has a high degree of peer anxiety.

Peer Anxiety. Patients with conditions such as borderline and schizoid personality disorders who have destructive relationships with their peer groups or who have been extremely isolated from peer group contact, generally react negatively or anxiously when placed in a group setting. When such patients can work through their anxiety, however, group therapy can be beneficial.

Diagnosis. The diagnosis of patients' disorders is important in determining the best therapeutic approach and in evaluating patients' motivations for treatment, capacities for change, and personality structure strengths and weaknesses.

There are few contraindications to group therapy. Antisocial patients generally do poorly in a heterogeneous group setting because they cannot adhere to group standards; but, if the group is composed of other antisocial patients, they may respond better to peers than to perceived authority figures. Depressed patients profit from group therapy after they have established a trusting relationship with the therapist. Patients who are actively suicidal or severely depressed should not be treated solely in a group setting. Manic patients are disruptive but, once under pharmacological control, do well in the group setting. Patients who are delusional and who may incorporate the group into their delusional system should be excluded, as should patients who pose a physical threat to other members because of uncontrollable aggressive outbursts.

Preparation

Patients prepared by a therapist for a group experience tend to continue in treatment longer and report less initial anxiety than do those who are not so prepared. The preparation consists of a therapist's explaining, before the first session, the procedure in as much detail as possible and answering the patient's questions.

Structural Organization

Table 34.3–4 summarizes some of the critical tasks that a group therapist must face when organizing a group.

Size. Group therapy has been successful with as few as 3 members and as many as 15, but most therapists consider 8 to 10 members the optimal size. There may be insufficient interaction with fewer members unless they are especially verbal, and with more than 10 members the interaction may be too great for the members or the therapist to follow.

Frequency and Length of Sessions. Most group psychotherapists conduct group sessions once a week. Maintaining continuity in sessions is important. When there are alternate sessions, the group meets twice a week, once with and once without the therapist. Group sessions generally last anywhere from one to two hours, but the time limit set should be constant.

Marathon groups were most popular in the 1970s but are much less common today. In time-extended therapy (marathon group therapy), the group meets continuously for 12 to 72 hours. Enforced interactional proximity and, during the longest time-extended sessions, sleep deprivation break down certain ego defenses, release affective processes, and theoretically promote open communication. Time-extended sessions, however, can be dangerous for patients with weak ego structures, such as people with schizophrenia and borderline personality disorder.

Table 34.3–4
Therapist's Basic Tasks in Group Therapy

1. Decision to establish a therapy group:
   - Determine setting and size of the group
   - Choose frequency and length of group sessions
   - Decide on open versus closed group
   - Select a cotherapist for the group
   - Formulate policy on group therapy with other therapeutic modalities
2. Act of creating a therapy group:
   - Formulate appropriate goals
   - Select patients who can perform the group task
   - Prepare patients for group therapy
3. Construction and maintenance of a therapeutic environment:
   - Build the culture of the group explicitly and implicitly identify and resolve common problems (membership turnover, subgrouping, conflict)

Reprinted with permission from Vinogradov S, Yalom ID: Group therapy. In *The American Psychiatric Press Textbook of Psychiatry*, JA Talbott, RE Hales, SC Yudofsky, editors, p 964. American Psychiatric Press, Washington, 1988.

Table 34.3–5
Twenty Therapeutic Factors in Group Psychotherapy

Factor	Definition
Abreaction	A process by which repressed material, particularly a painful experience or conflict, is brought back to consciousness. In the process, the person not only recalls but relives the material, which is accompanied by the appropriate emotional response; insight usually results from the experience.
Acceptance	The feeling of being accepted by other members of the group; differences of opinion are tolerated, and there is an absence of censure.
Altruism	The act of one member's being of help to another; putting another person's need before one's own and learning that there is value in giving to others. The term was originated by Auguste Comte (1798–1857), and Sigmund Freud believed it was a major factor in establishing group cohesion and community feeling.
Catharsis	The expression of ideas, thoughts, and suppressed material that is accompanied by an emotional response that produces a state of relief in the patient.
Cohesion	The sense that the group is working together toward a common goal; also referred to as a sense of "weness"; believed to be the most important factor related to positive therapeutic effects.
Consensual validation	Confirmation of reality by comparing one's own conceptualizations with those of other group members; interpersonal distortions are thereby corrected. The term was introduced by Harry Stack Sullivan; Trigant Burrow had used the phrase "consensual observation" to refer to the same phenomenon.
Contagion	The process in which the expression of emotion by one member stimulates the awareness of a similar emotion in another member.
Corrective familial experience	The group re-creates the family of origin for some members who can work through original conflicts psychologically through group interaction (e.g., sibling rivalry, anger toward parents).
Empathy	The capacity of a group member to put himself or herself into the psychological frame of reference of another group member and thereby understand his or her thinking, feeling, or behavior.
Identification	An unconscious defense mechanism in which the person incorporates the characteristics and the qualities of another person or object into his or her ego system
Imitation	The conscious emulation or modeling of one's behavior after that of another (also called role modeling); also known as spectator therapy, as one patient learns from another.
Insight	Conscious awareness and understanding of one's own psychodynamics and symptoms of maladaptive behavior. Most therapists distinguish two types: (1) intellectual insight—knowledge and awareness without any changes in maladaptive behavior; (2) emotional insight—awareness and understanding leading to positive changes in personality and behavior.
Inspiration	The process of imparting a sense of optimism to group members; the ability to recognize that one has the capacity to overcome problems; also known as instillation of hope.
Interaction	The free and open exchange of ideas and feelings among group members; effective interaction is emotionally charged.
Interpretation	The process during which the group leader formulates the meaning or significance of a patient's resistance, defenses, and symbols; the result is that the patient has a cognitive framework within which to understand his or her behavior.
Learning	Patients acquire knowledge about new areas, such as social skills and sexual behavior; they receive advice, obtain guidance, and attempt to influence and are influenced by other group members.
Reality testing	Ability of the person to evaluate objectively the world outside the self; includes the capacity to perceive oneself and other group members accurately. *See also* Consensual validation.
Transference	Projection of feelings, thoughts, and wishes onto the therapist, who has come to represent an object from the patient's past. Such reactions, while perhaps appropriate for the condition prevailing in the patient's earlier life, are inappropriate and anachronistic when applied to the therapist in the present. Patients in the group may also direct such feelings toward one another, a process called multiple transferences.
Universalization	The awareness of the patient that he or she is not alone in having problems; others share similar complaints or difficulties in learning; the patient is not unique.
Ventilation	The expression of suppressed feelings, ideas, or events to other group members; the sharing of personal secrets that ameliorate a sense of sin or guilt (also referred to as self-disclosure).

Homogeneous versus Heterogeneous Groups. Most therapists believe that groups should be as heterogeneous as possible to ensure maximum interaction. Members with different diagnostic categories and varied behavioral patterns, from all races, social levels, and educational backgrounds, and of varying ages and both sexes should be brought together. Patients between ages 20 and 65 can be effectively included in the same group. Age differences aid in developing of parent–child and brother–sister models, and patients have the opportunity to relive and rectify interpersonal difficulties that may have appeared insurmountable.

Both children and adolescents are best treated in groups composed mostly of people in their own age groups. Some adolescent patients are capable of assimilating the material of an adult group, regardless of content, but they should not be deprived of a constructive peer experience that they may otherwise not have.

Open versus Closed Groups. Closed groups have a set number and composition of patients. If members leave, no new members are accepted. In open groups membership is more fluid, and new members are taken on whenever old members leave.

Mechanisms

Group Formation. Each patient approaches group therapy differently, and in this sense groups are microcosms. Patients use typical adaptive abilities, defense mechanisms, and ways of relating, and when these tactics are ultimately reflected back to them by the group, patients learn to be introspective about their personality functioning. A process inherent in group formation requires that patients suspend their previous ways of coping. In entering the group, they allow their executive ego functions—reality testing, adaptation to and mastery of the environment, and perception—to be assumed to some degree by the collective assessment provided by the total membership, including the leader.

Therapeutic Factors. Table 34.3–5 outlines 20 significant therapeutic factors that account for change in group psychotherapy. Table 34.3–6 summarizes the forces that shape learning and change secondary to the nature of the group as a social microcosm.

Role of the Therapist

Although opinions differ about how active or passive a group therapist should be, the consensus is that the therapist's role is primarily facilitative. Ideally, the group members themselves are the primary source of cure and change. The climate produced by the therapist's personality is a potent agent of change. The therapist is more than an expert applying techniques; he or she exerts a personal influence that taps such variables as empathy, warmth, and respect.

Table 34.3–6
Learning from Behavioral Patterns in the Social Microcosm of the Therapy Group

Display of interpersonal pathology
↓
Feedback and self-observation
↓
Sharing reactions
↓
Examining the results of sharing reactions
↓
Understanding one's opinion of self
↓
Developing a sense of responsibility
↓
Realizing one's power to effect change
↓
High affect potentiates change

Reprinted with permission from Vinogradov S, Yalom ID: Group therapy. In *The American Psychiatric Press Textbook of Psychiatry*, JA Talbott, RE Hales, SC Yudofsky, editors, p 982. American Psychiatric Press, Washington, 1988.

Inpatient Group Psychotherapy

Group therapy is an important part of hospitalized patients' therapeutic experiences. Groups may be organized in many ways on a ward. In a community meeting, an entire inpatient unit meets with all the staff members (for example, psychiatrists, psychologists, and nurses). In team meetings, 15 to 20 patients and staff members meet; a regular or small group composed of 8 to 10 patients may meet with one or two therapists, as in traditional group therapy. Although the goals of each group vary, they all have common purposes: to increase patients' awareness of themselves through their interactions with the other group members, who provide feedback about their behavior; to provide patients with improved interpersonal and social skills; to help the members adapt to an inpatient setting; and to improve communication between patients and staff. In addition, one type of group meeting is attended only by inpatient hospital staff and is meant to improve communication among the staff members and to provide mutual support and encouragement in their day-to-day work with patients. Community meetings and team meetings are more helpful for dealing with patient treatment problems than they are for providing insight-oriented therapy, which is the province of the small-group therapy meeting. Tables 34.3–7 and 34.3–8 summarize the goals and techniques for short-term inpatient therapy groups.

Group Composition. Two key factors of inpatient groups common to all short-term therapies are the heterogeneity of the members and the rapid turnover of patients. Outside the hospital, therapists have large caseloads from which to select patients for group therapy. On the ward, therapists have a limited number of patients to choose from and are further restricted to those patients who are both willing to participate in and suitable for a small-group experience. In certain settings, group participation may be mandatory (for example, in substance abuse and alcohol dependence units). But man-

Table 34.3–7
Goals for Short-Term Inpatient Therapy Groups

Engaging patients in the therapeutic process
Teaching patients that talking helps
Problem spotting
Decreasing isolation
Allowing patients to be helpful
Alleviating hospital-related anxiety

Reprinted with permission from Vinogradov S, Yalom ID: Group therapy. In *The American Psychiatric Press Textbook of Psychiatry*, JA Talbott, RE Hales, SC Yudofsky, editors, p 980. American Psychiatric Press, Washington, 1988.

Table 34.3–8
Techniques for Short-Term Inpatient Therapy Groups

Use a shortened time frame.
Show direct support.
Emphasize the here and now.
Provide structure.

Reprinted with permission from Vinogradov S, Yalom ID: Group therapy. In *The American Psychiatric Press Textbook of Psychiatry,* JA Talbott, RE Hales, SC Yudofsky, editors, p 981. American Psychiatric Press, Washington, 1988.

datory attendance does not usually apply in a general psychiatry unit. In fact, most group experiences are more productive when the patients themselves choose to enter them.

More sessions are preferable to fewer. During patients' hospital stays, groups may meet daily and allow for interactional continuity and the carryover of themes from one session to the next. A new member of a group can quickly be brought up to date, either by the therapist in an orientation meeting or by one of the members. A newly admitted patient has often learned many details about the small-group program from another patient before actually attending the first session. The less frequently the group sessions are held, the greater the need for a therapist to structure the group and be active in it.

Inpatient versus Outpatient Groups. Although the therapeutic factors that account for change in small inpatient groups are similar to those in the outpatient settings, there are qualitative differences. For example, the relatively high turnover of patients in inpatient groups complicates the process of cohesion. But the fact that all the group members are together in the hospital aids cohesion, as do the therapists' efforts to foster the process. Sharing of information, universalization, and catharsis are the main therapeutic factors at work in inpatient groups. Although insight is more likely to occur in outpatient groups because of their long-term nature, some patients can obtain a new understanding of their psychological makeup within the confines of a single group session. A unique quality of inpatient groups is the patients' extragroup contacts, which are extensive because they live together on the same ward. Verbalizing their thoughts and feelings about such contacts in the therapy sessions encourages interpersonal learning. In addition, conflicts between patients or between patients and staff members can be anticipated and resolved. Table 34.3–9 lists the differences between inpatient and outpatient groups.

Self-Help Groups

Self-help groups are composed of people who are trying to cope with a specific problem or life crisis. Usually organized with a particular task in mind, such groups do not attempt to explore individual psychodynamics in great depth or to change personality functioning significantly. But self-help groups have improved the emotional health and well-being of many people.

A distinguishing characteristic of the self-help groups is their homogeneity. The members have the same disorders and share their experiences—good and bad, successful and unsuccessful—with one another. By so doing, they educate each other, provide mutual support, and alleviate the sense of alienation usually felt by people drawn to this kind of group.

Self-help groups emphasize cohesion, which is exceptionally strong in these groups. Because of the group members' similar problems and symptoms, they develop a strong emotional bond. Each group may have its unique characteristics, to which the members can attribute magical qualities of healing. Examples of self-help groups are Alcoholics Anonymous (AA), Gamblers Anonymous (GA), and Overeaters Anonymous (OA).

The self-help group movement is presently in its ascendency. These groups meet their members' needs by providing acceptance, mutual support, and help in overcoming maladaptive patterns of behavior or states of feeling with which traditional mental health and medical professionals have not generally dealt successfully. Self-help groups and therapy groups have begun to converge: Self-help groups have enabled their members to give up patterns of unwanted behavior; therapy groups have helped their members understand why and how they got to be the way they were or are.

Table 34.3–9
Differences Between Outpatient Groups and Inpatient Groups

Outpatient Groups	Inpatient Groups
Stable composition	Rarely the same group for more than one or two meetings
Patients well selected and prepared	Patients admitted to the group with little prior selection or preparation
Group is homogeneous regarding ego function, although conflicts and issues differ	Heterogeneous level of ego functioning
Motivated, self-referred patients; growth-oriented	Ambivalent, often compulsory patients in crisis; relief-oriented
Treatment proceeds as long as required; 1 to 2 years; 50 to 100 meetings	Treatment limited to the hospitalization period; 1 to 3 weeks, with rapid patient turnover
Boundary of group well maintained with few external influences	Continuous boundary interface with the milieu
Group cohesion develops normally, given sufficient time in treatment	No time for cohesion to develop spontaneously; group development aborted in early phases
Therapy is private and unexposed	Exposed, open to observation and scrutiny by the milieu
Leader allows the process to unfold; there is ample time to set group norms	Group leader's structuring of the group is critical; passive analytic approaches lead to group disintegration
No extra group contact encouraged	Patients sleep, eat, and live together outside the group; extragroup contact endorsed

Reprinted with permission from Leszcz M: Inpatient groups. Ann Rev Psychiatry *5*: 729, 1986.

COMBINED INDIVIDUAL AND GROUP PSYCHOTHERAPY

In combined individual and group psychotherapy, patients individually see a therapist and also take part in group sessions. The therapist for the group and individual sessions is usually the same person. Groups can vary in size from 3 to 15 members, but the most helpful size is 8 to 10. Patients must attend all group sessions. Attendance at individual sessions is also important, and the failure to attend either group or individual sessions should be examined as part of the therapeutic process.

Combined therapy is a particular treatment modality, not a system by which individual therapy is augmented by an occasional group session or a group therapy in which a participant meets alone with a therapist from time to time. Rather, it is an ongoing plan in which the group experience interacts meaningfully with the individual sessions and in which reciprocal feedback helps form an integrated therapeutic experience. Although the one-to-one doctor–patient relationship makes possible a deep examination of the transference reaction for some patients, it may not provide the corrective emotional experiences necessary for therapeutic change for other patients. The group gives patients a variety of people with whom they can have transferential reactions. In the microcosm of the group, patients can relive and work through familial and other important influences.

Techniques

Differing techniques based on varying theoretical frameworks have been used in the combined therapy format. Some clinicians increase the frequency of individual sessions to encourage the emergence of the transference neurosis. In the behavioral model, individual sessions are regularly scheduled but tend to be less frequent than in other approaches. Whether patients use a couch or a chair during individual sessions depends on a therapist's orientation. Techniques such as alternate meetings may be used in the group setting. Harold Kaplan and Benjamin Sadock developed a combined therapy approach called structured interactional group psychotherapy in which a different group member is the focus of each weekly group session and is discussed in some depth by the other members.

Results

Most workers in the field believe that combined therapy has the advantages of both dyadic and group settings, without sacrificing the qualities of either. Generally, the dropout rate in combined therapy is lower than that in group therapy alone. In many cases, combined therapy appears to bring problems to the surface and to resolve them more quickly than may be possible with either method alone.

PSYCHODRAMA

Psychodrama is a method of group psychotherapy originated by the Viennese-born psychiatrist Jacob Moreno in which personality makeup, interpersonal relationships, conflicts, and emotional problems are explored by means of special dramatic methods. Therapeutic dramatization of emotional problems includes the protagonist or patient, the person who acts out problems with the help of auxiliary egos, people who enact varying aspects of the patient, and the director, psychodramatist, or therapist, the person who guides those in the drama toward the acquisition of insight.

Roles

Director. The director is the leader or therapist and so must be an active participant. He or she has a catalytic function by encouraging the members of the group to be spontaneous. The director must also be available to meet the group's needs without superimposing his or her values. Of all the group psychotherapies, psychodrama requires the most participation from the therapist and the greatest ability to lead.

Protagonist. The protagonist is the patient in conflict. The patient chooses the situation to portray in the dramatic scene, or the therapist chooses it if the patient so desires.

Auxiliary Ego. An auxiliary ego is another group member who represents something or someone in the protagonist's experience. The auxiliary egos help account for the great range of therapeutic effects available in psychodrama.

Group. The members of the psychodrama and the audience make up the group. Some are participants, and others are observers, but all benefit from the experience to the extent that they can identify with the ongoing events. The concept of spontaneity in psychodrama refers to the ability of each member of the group, especially the protagonist, to experience the thoughts and feelings of the moment and to communicate emotion as authentically as possible.

Techniques

The psychodrama may focus on any special area of functioning (a dream, a family, or a community situation), a symbolic role, an unconscious attitude, or an imagined future situation. Such symptoms as delusions and hallucinations can also be acted out in the group. Techniques to advance the therapeutic process and to increase productivity and creativity include the soliloquy (a recital of overt and hidden thoughts and feelings), role reversal (the exchange of the patient's role for the role of a significant person), the double (an auxiliary ego acting as the patient), the multiple double (several egos acting as the patient did on varying occasions), and the mirror technique (an ego imitating the patient and speaking for him or her). Other techniques include the use of hypnosis and psychoactive drugs to modify the acting behavior in various ways.

References

Amaranto EA, Bender SS: Individual psychotherapy as an adjunct to group psychotherapy. Int J Group Psychother *40:* 91, 1990.

Carlin ME: Large group treatment of severely disturbed/conduct-disordered adolescents. Int J Group Psychother *46:* 379, 1996.

Cartwright D, Zander A, editors: *Group Dynamics and Research Theory.* Harper & Row, New York, 1960.

Dies RR: The future of group therapy. Psychotherapy *29:* 58, 1992.

Erickson RC: *Inpatient Small Group Psychotherapy.* Thomas, Springfield, IL, 1984.

Frank JD: Some determinants, manifestations, and effects of cohesiveness in therapy groups. J Psychother Pract Res *6* (1): 59, 1997.

Freud S: Group psychology and analysis of the ego. In *Standard Edition of the Complete Psychological Works of Sigmund Freud,* vol 18, p 67. Hogarth Press, London, 1962.

Kaplan HI, Sadock BJ, editors: *Comprehensive Group Psychotherapy,* ed 3. Williams & Wilkins, Baltimore, 1993.

Karterud SW: Reflections on group-analytic research. Group Analysis *25:* 353, 1992.

Leszcz M: The interpersonal approach to group psychotherapy. Int J Group Psychother *42:* 37, 1992.

Lieberman MA, Yalom I: Brief group psychotherapy for the spousally bereaved: A controlled study. Int J Group Psychother *42:* 117, 1992.

Moreno JL: *Psychodrama.* Beacon Press, Beacon, New York, 1947.

Najavits LM, Weiss RD, Liese BS: Group cognitive-behavioral therapy for women with PTSD and substance use disorder. J Subst Abuse Treat *13:* 13, 1996.

Ormont LR: Subjective countertransference in the group setting: The modern analytic experience. Mod Psychoanal *17:* 3, 1992.

Pilkonis PA, Imber SD, Lewis P, Rubinsky P: A comparative outcome study of individual, group and conjoint psychotherapy. Arch Gen Psychiatry *41:* 431, 1984.

Rosenthal L: Phenomena of resistance in modern group analysis. Am J Psychother *50:* 75, 1996.

Rutan JS: Psychodynamic group psychotherapy. Int J Group Psychother *42:* 19, 1992.

Sadock BJ: Group psychotherapy, combined individual and group psychotherapy, and psychodrama. In *Comprehensive Textbook of Psychiatry,* ed 5, HI Kaplan, BJ Sadock, editors, p 1517. Williams & Wilkins, Baltimore, 1989.

Scheidlinger S: The concept of identification in group psychotherapy. Am J Psychother *50* (4): 529, 1996.

Sigrell B: The long-term effects of group psychotherapy: A thirteen-year follow-up study. Group Analysis *25:* 333, 1992.

Soldz S, Budman S, Demby A, Feldstein M: Patient activity and outcome in group psychotherapy: New findings. Int J Group Psychother *40:* 53, 1990.

Stone WN: The place of self psychology in group psychotherapy: A status report. Int J Group Psychother *42:* 335, 1992.

Steengarger BN, Budman SH: Group psychotherapy and managed behavioral health care: Current trends and future challenges. Int J Group Psychother *46:* 297, 1996.

Weiner MF: Group therapy reduces medical and psychiatric hospitalization. Int J Group Psychother *42:* 267, 1992.

Wolf A, Schwartz M: *Psychoanalysis in Groups.* Grune & Stratton, New York, 1962.

Wolk DJ: The psychodramatic reenactment of a dream. J Group Psychother Psychodrama Sociometry *49* (1): 3, 1996.

Wong N: Group psychotherapy, combined individual and group psychotherapy and psychodrama. In *Comprehensive Textbook of Psychiatry,* ed 6, HI Kaplan, BJ Sadock, editors, p 1821. Williams & Wilkins, Baltimore, 1995.

Yalom ID: *The Theory and Practice of Group Psychotherapy,* ed 3. Basic Books, New York, 1985.

▲ 34.4 Family Therapy and Couples Therapy

Family and couples (marital) therapy are special forms of group therapy that came into common use in the 1950s. Instead of focusing on individual family members' psychological difficulties, family and couples therapists work toward improving group interactions and thereby helping each member to function better. According to family systems theory, family units act as though each has its own homeostasis of interacting that must be maintained at any cost. Family therapy aims to bring to light the often hidden patterns that maintain the group's balance and to help the group understand the purposes of the pattern. Similarly, the goal of couples therapy is to improve, if possible, the functioning of the two-person group and to encourage individual change and growth.

Family therapists generally think that one family member has been labeled as the patient whom the family identifies as "the one who is the problem, is to blame, and needs help." A family therapist's goal is to help a family understand that the identified patient's symptoms in fact serve the crucial function of maintaining the family's homeostasis. The process of family therapy helps reveal a family's repetitious and ultimately predictable communication patterns that sustain and reflect the identified patient's behavior.

Inherent in family systems theory is the belief, to one degree or another, that a marital relationship strongly influences the nature of a family's system of homeostasis. One influential family therapist has expressed this concept by describing the marital dyad as the "architects of the family."

FAMILY THERAPY

Initial Consultation

Family therapy is familiar enough to the general public for families with a high level of conflict to request it specifically. When the initial complaint is about an individual family mem-

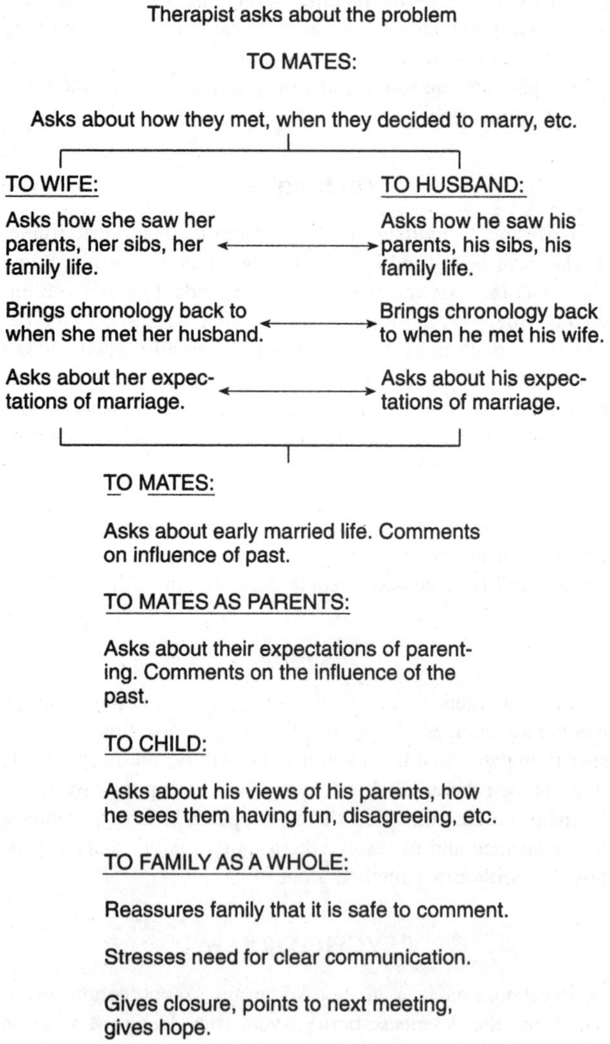

Therapist asks about the problem
TO MATES:
Asks about how they met, when they decided to marry, etc.
TO WIFE:
Asks how she saw her parents, her sibs, her family life.
Brings chronology back to when she met her husband.
Asks about her expectations of marriage.
TO HUSBAND:
Asks how he saw his parents, his sibs, his family life.
Brings chronology back to when he met his wife.
Asks about his expectations of marriage.
TO MATES:
Asks about early married life. Comments on influence of past.
TO MATES AS PARENTS:
Asks about their expectations of parenting. Comments on the influence of the past.
TO CHILD:
Asks about his views of his parents, how he sees them having fun, disagreeing, etc.
TO FAMILY AS A WHOLE:
Reassures family that it is safe to comment.
Stresses need for clear communication.
Gives closure, points to next meeting, gives hope.

FIGURE 34.4–1
Main flow of family-life chronology to family as a whole. (Reproduced with permission from Satir V: *Conjoint Family Therapy,* p 55. Science and Behavior, Palo Alto, CA, 1967.)

Table 34.4–1
Rationale for Family-Life Chronology

The family therapist enters a session knowing little or nothing about the family.
- The therapist may know who the identified patient is and what symptoms the patient manifests, but that is usually all. So the therapist must get clues about the meaning of the symptom.
- The therapist may know that pain exists in the marital relationship but needs to get clues about how the pain shows itself.
- The therapist needs to get clues about how the pain shows itself.
- The therapist needs to know how the mates have tried to cope with their problems.
- The therapist may know that the mates both operate from models (from what they saw going on between their own parents) but needs to find out how those models have influenced each mate's expectations about how to be a mate and how to be a parent.

The family therapist enters a session knowing that the family has, in fact, had a history, but that is usually all.
- Every family, as a group, has gone through or jointly experienced many events. Certain events (such as deaths, childbirth, sickness, geographical moves, and job changes) occur in almost all families.
- Certain events primarily affected the mates and only indirectly the children. (Maybe the children were not born yet or were too young to fully comprehend the nature of an event as it affected their parents. They may have only sensed periods of parental remoteness, distraction, anxiety, or annoyance.)
- The therapist can profit from answers to just about every question asked.

Family members enter therapy with a great deal of fear.
- Therapist structuring helps decrease the threats. It says: "I am in charge of what will happen here. I will see to it that nothing catastrophic happens here."
- All members are covertly feeling to blame for the fact that nothing seems to have turned out right (even though they may overtly blame the identified patient or the other mate).
- Parents, especially, need to feel that they did the best they could as parents. They need to tell the therapist: "This is why I did what I did. This is what happened to me."
- A family-life chronology that deals with such facts as names, dates, labeled relationships, and moves seems to appeal to the family. It asks questions that members can answer, questions that are relatively nonthreatening. It deals with life as the family understands it.

Family members enter therapy with a great deal of despair.
- Therapist structuring helps stimulate hope.
- As far as family members are concerned, past events are part of them. They now can tell the therapist, "I existed." And they can also say: "I am not just a big blob of pathology. I succeeded in overcoming many handicaps."
- If the family knew what questions needed asking, they would not need to be in therapy. So the therapist does not say, "Tell me what you want to tell me." Family members will simply tell the therapist what they have been telling themselves for years. The therapist's questions say: "I know what to ask. I take responsibility for understanding you. We are going to go somewhere."

The family therapist also knows that, to some degree, the family has focused on the identified patient to relieve marital pain. The therapist also knows that, to some degree, the family will resist any effort to change that focus. A family-life chronology is an effective, nonthreatening way to change from an emphasis on the "sick" or "bad" family member to an emphasis on the marital relationship.

The family-life chronology serves other useful therapy purposes, such as providing the framework within which a reeducation process can take place. The therapist serves as a model in checking out information or correcting communication techniques and placing questions and eliciting answers to begin the process. In addition, when taking the chronology, the therapist can introduce in a relatively nonfrightening way some of the crucial concepts to induce change.

Adapted from Satir V: *Conjoint Family Therapy,* p 57. Science and Behavior, Palo Alto, CA, 1967.

ber, however, pretreatment work may be needed. Underlying resistance to a family approach typically includes fears by parents that they will be blamed for their child's difficulties, that the entire family will be pronounced sick, that a spouse will object, and that open discussion of one child's misbehavior will have a negative influence on siblings. Refusal by an adolescent or young adult patient to participate in family therapy is frequently a disguised collusion with the fears of one or both parents.

Interview Technique

The special quality of a family interview springs from two important facts: A family comes to treatment with its history and dynamics firmly in place. To a family therapist, the established nature of the group, more than the symptoms, constitutes the clinical problem. Family members usually live together and, at some level, depend on one another for their physical and emotional well-being. Whatever transpires in the therapy session is known to all. Central principles of technique also derive from these facts. For example, the therapist must carefully channel the catharsis of anger by one family member toward another. The person who is the object of the anger will react to the attack, and the anger may escalate into violence and fracture relationships, with one or more member withdrawing from therapy. For another example, free association is inappropriate in family therapy because it can encourage one person to dominate a session. Thus therapists must always control and direct the family interview.

Virginia Satir recommended initiating at least the first two sessions of family therapy with a family-life chronology. The technique reflects many family therapy paradigms. Figure 34.4–1 summarizes the key features of the family-life chronology, and Table 34.4–1 summarizes Satir's reasoning behind its use.

Frequency and Length of Treatment

Unless an emergency arises, sessions are usually held no more than once a week. Each session, however, may require as much as two hours. Long sessions can include an intermission to give the therapist time to organize the material and plan a response. A flexible schedule is necessary when geography or personal circumstances make it physically difficult for the family to get together. The length of treatment depends not only on the nature of the problem but also on the therapeutic model. Therapists who exclusively use problem-solving models may accomplish their goals in a few sessions while therapists using growth-oriented models may work with a family for years and may schedule sessions at long intervals. Table 34.4–2 summarizes one model for treatment termination.

Models of Intervention

An overview of family therapy models, techniques, and goals appears in Table 34.4–3.

Psychodynamic-Experiential Models. Psychodynamic-experiential models emphasize individual maturation in the context of the family system and are free from unconscious patterns of anxiety and projection rooted in the past. Therapists seek to establish an intimate bond with each family member, and sessions alternate between the therapist's exchanges with the members and the members' exchanges with one another. Clarity of communication and honestly admitted feelings are given high priority. Toward this end, family members may be encouraged to change their seats, to touch each other, and to make direct eye contact. Their use of metaphor, body language, and parapraxes helps reveal the unconscious pattern of family relationships. The therapist may also employ *family sculpting,* in which family members physically arrange one another in tableaus depicting their personal view of relationships, past or present. The therapist both interprets the living sculpture and modifies it in a way to suggest new relationships. In addition, the therapist's subjective responses to the family are given great importance. At appropriate moments, the therapist expresses these responses to the family to form yet another feedback loop of self-observation and change.

Table 34.4–2
Criteria for Treatment Termination

Treatment is completed:
- When family members can complete transactions, check, ask.
- When they can interpret hostility.
- When they can see how others see them.
- When they can see how they see themselves.
- When one member can tell others how they manifest themselves.
- When one member can tell others what is hoped, feared, and expected from them.
- When they can disagree.
- When they can make choices.
- When they can learn through practice.
- When they can free themselves from the harmful effects of past models.
- When they can give a clear message—that is, be congruent in their behavior—with a minimum of difference between feelings and communication and with a minimum of hidden messages.

Adapted from Satir V: *Conjoint Family Therapy,* p 133. Science and Behavior, Palo Alto, CA, 1967.

Bowen Model. Murray Bowen called his model family systems, but in the family therapy field it rightfully carries the name of its originator. The hallmark of the Bowen model is people's differentiation from their family of origin, their ability to be their true selves in the face of familial or other pressures that threaten the loss of love or social position. Problem families are assessed on two levels: the degree of their enmeshment versus the degree of their ability to differentiate and the analysis of emotional triangles in the problem for which they seek help.

An emotional triangle is defined as a three-party system (and there can be many of these within a family) arranged so that the closeness of two members expressed as either love or repetitive conflict, tends to exclude a third. When the excluded third person attempts to join with one of the other two or when one of the involved parties shifts in the direction of the excluded one, emotional cross-currents are activated. The therapist's role is, first, to stabilize or shift the ''hot'' triangle—the one producing the presenting symptoms—and, second, to work with the most psychologically available family members, individually if necessary, to achieve enough personal differentiation so that the hot triangle does not recur. To preserve his or her neutrality in the family's triangles, the therapist minimizes emotional contact with family members.

Bowen also originated the *genogram,* a theoretical tool that is a historical survey of the family going back several generations.

Structural Model. In a structural model families are viewed as single interrelated systems assessed in terms of significant alliances and splits among family members, hierarchy of power (parents in charge of children), clarity and firmness of boundaries between the generations, and family tolerance for each other. The structural model uses concurrent individual and family therapy.

General Systems Model. Based on general systems theory, a general systems model holds that families are systems and that every action in a family produces a reaction in one or more of its members. Families have external boundaries and internal rules. Every member is presumed to play a role (for example, spokesperson, persecutor, victim, rescuer, symptom bearer, nurturer), which is relatively stable, but the member who fills each role may change. Some families try to scapegoat one member by blaming him or her for the family's problems (the identified patient). If the identified patient improves, another family member may become the scapegoat. The family is defined as having external boundaries and internal rules. The general systems model overlaps with some of the other models presented, particularly the Bowen and structural models.

Techniques

Family Group Therapy. Family group therapy combines several families into a single group. Families share mu-

Table 34.4–3
Major Models of Family Therapy: Normality, Dysfunction, and Therapeutic Goals

Model of Family Therapy	View of Normal Family Functioning	View of Dysfunction and Symptoms	Goals of Therapy
Structural Minuchcin Montaivo Aponte	Boundaries clear and firm Hierarchy with strong parental subsystem Flexibility of system for autonomy and interdependence, individual growth and system maintenance, continuity and adaptive restructuring in response to changing internal (developmental) and external (environmental) demands	Symptoms result from current family structural imbalance: malfunctioning hierarchical arrangement, boundaries maladaptive reaction to changing requirements (developmental, environmental)	Reorganize family structure: shift members' relative positions to disrupt malfunctioning pattern and strengthen parental hierarchy create clear, flexible boundaries mobilize more adaptive alternative patterns
Strategic Haley Milan team Palo Alto group	Flexibility Large behavioral repertoire for problem resolution and life-cycle passage Clear rules governing hierarchy (Haley)	Multiple origins of problems; symptoms maintained by family's unsuccessful problem-solving attempts; inability to adjust the life-cycle transitions (Haley), malfunctioning hierarchy: triangle or coalition across hierarchy (Haley) Symptom is a communicative act embedded in interaction pattern	Resolve presenting problem only: specific behaviorally defined objectives Interrupt rigid feedback cycle: change symptom-maintaining sequence to new outcome Define clearer hierarchy (Haley)
Behavioral-social exchange Liberman Patterson Alexander	Maladaptive behavior is not reinforced Adaptive behavior is rewarded Exchange of benefits outweighs costs Long-term reciprocity	Maladaptive symptomatic behavior reinforced by family attention and reward, deficient reward exchanges (e.g., coercive), and communication deficit	Concrete, observable behavioral goals: change contingencies of social reinforcement (interpersonal consequences of behavior): rewards for adaptive behavior no rewards for maladaptive behavior
Psychodynamic Ackerman Boszormenyl-Nagy Framo Lidz Meissner Paul Stierlin	Parental personalities and relationships well-differentiated Relationship perceptions based on current realities, not projections from past Boszormenyl-Nagy: relational equitability Lidz: family task requisites: parenteral coalition; generation boundaries, and sex-linked parental roles	Symptoms caused by family projection process stemming from unresolved conflicts and losses in family of origin	Insight and resolution of family of origin conflict and losses Family projection processes Relationship reconstruction and reunion Individual and family growth
Family systems therapy Bowen	Differentiation of self Intellectual-emotional balance	Functioning impaired by relationships with family of origin: poor differentiation, anxiety (reactivity), family projection process, and triangulation	Differentiation Cognitive functioning Emotional reactivity Modification of relationships in family system: detriangulation repair cutoffs
Experiential Satir Whitaker	Satir: Self-worth: high Communication: clear, specific, honest Family rules: flexible, human, appropriate Linkage to society: open, hopeful Whitaker: multiple aspects of family structure and shared experience	Symptoms are nonverbal messages in reaction to current communication dysfunction in system	Direct, clear communication Individual and family growth through immediate shared experience

Reprinted with permission from Walsh F: Conceptualizations of normal family functioning. In *Normal Family Processes*, F Walsh, editor, p 133. Guilford, New York, 1982.

tual problems, and compare their interactions with those of the other families in the group. Treatment of schizophrenia has been effective in multiple family groups. Parents of disturbed children may also meet together to share their situations.

Social Network Therapy. In social network therapy, the social community or network of a disturbed patient meet in group sessions with the patient. The network includes those with whom the patient comes into contact in daily life, not only the immediate family but also relatives, friends, tradespeople, teachers, and co-workers.

Paradoxical Therapy. In this approach, which evolved from the work of Gregory Bateson, a therapist suggests that the patient intentionally engage in the unwanted behavior (called the paradoxical injunction), and, for example, avoid a phobic object or perform a compulsive ritual. Although paradoxical therapy and the use of paradoxical injunctions are relatively new, the therapy can create new insights for some patients. When used in an arbitrary or routine fashion, however, this technique may be dangerous.

Positive Connotation. Positive connotation or reframing is a relabeling of all negatively expressed feelings or behavior as positive. When the therapist attempts to get family members to view behavior from a new frame of reference, "This child is impossible" becomes "This child is desperately trying to distract and protect you from what he or she perceives as an unhappy marriage."

Goals

Family therapy has several goals: to resolve or reduce pathogenic conflict and anxiety within the matrix of interpersonal relationships; to enhance the perception and fulfillment by family members of one another's emotional needs; to promote appropriate role relationships between the sexes and generations; to strengthen the capacity of individual members and the family as a whole to cope with destructive forces inside and outside the surrounding environment; and to influence family identity and values so that members are oriented toward health and growth.

The therapy ultimately aims to integrate families into the large systems of society, extended family, community groups, and social systems such as schools, medical facilities, and social, recreational, and welfare agencies.

COUPLES (MARITAL) THERAPY

Couples or marital therapy is a form of psychotherapy designed to psychologically modify the interaction of two people who are in conflict with each other over one parameter or a variety of parameters—social, emotional, sexual, economic. In couples therapy a trained person establishes a therapeutic contract with a patient-couple and, through definite types of communication, attempts to alleviate the disturbance, to reverse or change maladaptive patterns of behavior, and to encourage personality growth and development.

Marriage counseling may be considered more limited in scope than marriage therapy: Only a particular familial conflict is discussed, and the counseling is primarily task oriented, geared to solving a specific problem such as child rearing. Marriage therapy, by contrast, emphasizes restructuring a couple's interaction and sometimes explores the psychodynamics of each partner. Both therapy and counseling stress helping marital partners to cope effectively with their problems. Most important is the definition of appropriate and realistic goals, which may involve extensive reconstruction of the union or problem-solving approaches or a combination of both.

Types of Therapy

Individual Therapy. In individual therapy, the marital partners may consult different therapists, who do not necessarily communicate with each other and indeed may not even know each other. The goal of treatment is to strengthen each partner's adaptive capacities. At times, only one of the partners is in treatment; and in such cases, it is often helpful for the spouse who is not in treatment to visit the therapist. The visiting partner may give the therapist data about the patient that may otherwise be overlooked, overt or covert anxiety in the visiting partner as a result of change in the patient can be identified and dealt with, irrational beliefs about treatment events can be corrected, and conscious or unconscious attempts by the partner to sabotage the patient's treatment can be examined.

Individual Couples Therapy. In individual couples therapy each marriage partner is in therapy, which is either concurrent, with the same therapist, or collaborative, with each partner seeing a different therapist.

Conjoint Therapy. Conjoint therapy is the most common treatment method in couples therapy, in which either one or two therapists treat the partners in joint sessions. Cotherapy with therapists of both sexes prevents a particular patient from feeling ganged up on when confronted by two members of the opposite sex.

Four-Way Session. In a four-way session each partner is seen by a different therapist, with regular joint sessions in which all four people participate. A variation of the four-way session is the roundtable interview, developed by William Masters and Virginia Johnson for the rapid treatment of sexually dysfunctional couples. Two patients and two opposite-sex therapists meet regularly.

Group Psychotherapy. Group therapy for married couples allows a variety of group dynamics to affect the couples. Groups usually consist of three to four couples and one or two therapists. The couples identify with one another and recognize that others have similar problems, each gains support and empathy from fellow group members of the same or opposite sex, they explore sexual attitudes and have an opportunity to gain new information from their peer groups, and each receives specific feedback about his or her behavior, either negative or positive, that may have more meaning and be better assimilated coming from a neutral nonspouse member than from the spouse or the therapist.

When only one partner is in a therapy group, the spouse may occasionally visit the group to allow the members to test reality. At times, a group may be so organized that only one married couple is part of the large group.

Combined Therapy. Combined therapy refers to all or any of the preceding techniques used concurrently or in combination. Thus, a particular patient-couple may begin treatment with one or both partners in individual psychotherapy, continue in conjoint therapy with the partner, and terminate therapy after a course of treatment in a married couples group. The rationale for combined therapy is that no single approach to marital problems has been shown to be superior to another. A familiarity with a variety of approaches thus allows therapists a degree of flexibility that provides maximum benefit for couples in distress.

Indications

Whatever the specific therapeutic technique, initiation of couples therapy is indicated when individual therapy has failed to resolve the relationship difficulties, when the onset of distress in one or both partners is clearly a relational problem, and when couples therapy is requested by a couple in conflict. Problems in communication between partners are a prime indication for couples therapy. In such instances one spouse may be intimidated by the other, may become anxious when attempting to tell the other about thoughts or feelings, or may project unconscious expectations onto the other. The therapy is geared toward enabling each partner to see the other realistically.

Conflicts in one or several areas, such as the partners' sexual life, are also indications for treatment. Similarly, difficulty in establishing satisfactory social, economic, parental, or emotional roles implies that a couple needs help. Clinicians should evaluate all aspects of the marital relationship before attempting to treat only one problem, which could be a symptom of a pervasive marital disorder.

Contraindications

Contraindications for couples therapy include patients with severe forms of psychosis, particularly patients with paranoid elements and those in whom the marriage's homeostatic mechanism is a protection against psychosis, marriages in which one or both partners really want to divorce, and marriages in which one spouse refuses to participate because of anxiety or fear.

Goals

Nathan Ackerman defined the aims of couples therapy as follows: The goals of therapy for partner relational problems are to alleviate emotional distress and disability and to promote the levels of well-being of both partners together and of each as an individual. Ideally, therapists move toward these goals by strengthening the shared resources for problem solving, by encouraging the substitution of adequate controls and defenses for pathogenic ones, by enhancing both the immunity against the disintegrative effects of emotional upset and the complementarity of the relationship, and by promoting the growth of the relationship and of each partner.

Part of a therapist's task is to persuade each partner in the relationship to take responsibility in understanding the psychodynamic makeup of personality. Each person's accountability for the effects of behavior on his or her own life, the life of the partner, and the lives of others in the environment is emphasized, and the result is often a deep understanding of the problems that created the marital discord.

Couples therapy does not ensure the maintenance of any marriage or relationship. Indeed, in certain instances it may show the partners that they are in a nonviable union that should be dissolved. In these cases couples may continue to meet with therapists to work through the difficulties of separating and obtaining a divorce, a process that has been called divorce therapy.

References

Babcock JC, Waltz J, Jacobson NS, Gottman JM: Power and violence: The relation between communication patterns, power discrepancies, and domestic violence. J Consult Clin Psychol *61:* 40, 1993.

Bowen M: *Family Theory in Clinical Practice.* Aronson, New York, 1978.

Coyne JC: Strategic therapy with married depressed persons: Initial agenda, themes and interventions. J Marital Fam Ther *10:* 153, 1984.

Diamond G, Liddle HA: Resolving a therapeutic impasse between parents and adolescents in multidimensional family therapy. J Consult Clin Psychol *64:* 481, 1996.

Diamond GS, Serrano AC, Dickey M, Sonis WA: Current status of family-based outcome and process research [Review]. J Am Acad Child Adolesc Psychiatry *35:* 6, 1996.

Green RJ, Framo JL, editors: *Family Therapy: Major Contributions.* International Universities Press, New York, 1981.

Guerin PJ, Pendagast E: Evaluation of family systems and genogram. In *Family Therapy Theory and Practice,* PJ Guerin, editor, p 450. Gardner, New York, 1976.

Houlihan MM, Jackson J, Rogers TR: Decision making of satisfied and dissatisfied married couples. J Soc Psychol *130:* 89, 1990.

Kadis LB, McClendon RA: Couples and marital therapy. In *Comprehensive Textbook of Psychiatry,* ed 6, HI Kaplan, BJ Sadock, editors, p 1857. Williams & Wilkins, Baltimore, 1995.

Lidz T, Fleck S, Cornelison A: *Schizophrenia and the Family.* International Universities Press, New York, 1965.

Markman HJ, Hahlweg K: The prediction and prevention of marital distress: An international perspective. Clin Psychol Rev *13:* 29, 1993.

Minuchin S: *Families and Family Therapy.* Harvard University Press, Cambridge, 1974.

Mittleman B: Complementary neurotic reactions in intimate relationships. Psychoanal Q *13:* 479, 1944.

Nadelson CC, Polonsky DC, Mathews MA: Marriage as a developmental process. In *Marriage and Divorce: A Contemporary Perspective,* CC Nadelson, DC Polonsky, editors, p 137. Guilford, New York, 1983.

O'Leary KD, Beach SR: Marital therapy: A viable treatment for depression and marital discord. Am J Psychiatry *147:* 183, 1990.

Pinsof WM: A conceptual framework and methodological criteria for family therapy process research. J Consult Clin Psychol *57:* 53, 1989.

Satir V: *Conjoint Family Therapy.* Science & Behavior, Palo Alto, CA, 1967.

Scharff D, Scharff J: *Object Relations Family Therapy.* Aronson, New York, 1987.

Solomon P, Draine J, Mannion E, Meisel M: Impact of brief family psychoeducation on self-efficacy. Schizophr Bull *22:* 41, 1996.

Steinglass P: Family therapy. In *Comprehensive Textbook of Psychiatry,* ed 6, HI Kaplan, BJ Sadock, editors, p 1838. Williams & Wilkins, Baltimore, 1995.

Tarrier N: Effect of treating the family to reduce relapse in schizophrenia: A review. J R Soc Med *82:* 423, 1989.

Tatum DW, DelCampo RL: Selective mutism in children: A structural family therapy approach to treatment. Comtemp Fam Ther *17:* 177, 1995.

Vansteenwegen A: Who benefits from couple therapy? A comparison of successful and failed couples. J Sex Marital Ther *22:* 63, 1996.

▲ 34.5 Biofeedback

Biofeedback helps people control usually involuntary physiological functions so as to change them. People learn to control these functions by hearing or seeing signals from instruments that produce information about various measures such as muscle tension. This feedback of information about the body helps people try to change a function, for instance, by relaxing. Biofeedback is based on the idea that the autonomic nervous system can come under voluntary control through operant conditioning. In fact, the benefits of biofeedback may be produced by the relaxation that patients are trained to facilitate.

THEORY

Neal Miller demonstrated the medical potential of biofeedback by showing that the normally involuntary autonomic nervous system can be operantly conditioned, by using appropriate feedback. By means of instruments, patients acquire information about the status of involuntary biological functions, such as skin temperature and electrical conductivity, muscle tension, blood pressure, heart rate, and brain wave activity. Patients then learn to regulate one or more of these biological states that affect symptoms. For example, a person can learn to raise the temperature of his or her hands to reduce the frequency of migraines, palpitations, or angina pectoris. Presum-

Table 34.5–1
Biofeedback Applications

Condition	Effects
Asthma	Both frontal EMG and airway resistance biofeedback have been reported as producing relaxation from the panic associated with asthma, as well as improving air flow rate.
Cardiac arrhythmias	Specific biofeedback of the electrocardiogram has permitted patients to lower the frequency of premature ventricular contractions.
Fecal incontinence and enuresis	The timing sequence of internal and external anal sphincters has been measured, using triple lumen rectal catheters providing feedback to incontinent patients in order for them to reestablish normal bowel habits in a relatively small number of biofeedback sessions. An actual precursor of biofeedback dating to 1938 was the sounding of a buzzer for sleeping enuretic children at the first sign of moisture (the pad and bell).
Grand mal epilepsy	A number of EEG biofeedback procedures have been used experimentally to suppress seizure activity prophylactically in patients not responsive to anticonvulsant medication. The procedures permit patients to enhance the sensorimotor brain wave rhythm or to normalize brain activity as computed in real-time power spectrum displays.
Hyperactivity	EEG biofeedback procedures have been used on children with attention-deficit/hyperactivity disorder to train them to reduce their motor restlessness.
Idiopathic hypertension and orthostatic hypotension	A variety of specific (direct) and nonspecific biofeedback procedures—including blood pressure feedback, galvanic skin response, and foot-hand thermal feedback combined with relaxation procedures—have been used to teach patients to increase or decrease their blood pressure. Some follow-up data indicate that the changes may persist for years and often permit the reduction or elimination of antihypertensive medications.
Migraine	The most common biofeedback strategy with classic or common vascular headaches has been thermal biofeedback from a digit accompanied by autogenic self-suggestive phrases encouraging hand warming and head cooling. The mechanism is thought to help prevent excessive cerebral artery vasoconstriction, often accompanied by an ischemic prodromal symptom, such as scintillating scotomata, followed by rebound engorgement of arteries and stretching of vessel wall pain receptors.
Myofacial and temporomandibular joint (TMJ) pain	High levels of EMG activity over the powerful muscles associated with bilateral temporomandibular joints have been decreased, using biofeedback in patients who are jaw clenchers or have bruxism.
Neuromuscular rehabilitation	Mechanical devices or an EMG measurement of muscle activity displayed to a patient increases the effectiveness of traditional therapies, as documented by relatively long clinical histories in peripheral nerve-muscle damage, spasmodic torticollis, selected cases of tardive dyskinesia, cerebral palsy, and upper motor neuron hemiplegias.
Raynaud's syndrome	Cold hands and cold feet are frequent concomitants of anxiety and also occur in Raynaud's syndrome, caused by vasospasm of arterial smooth muscle. A number of studies report that thermal feedback from the hand, an inexpensive and benign procedure compared with surgical sympathectomy, is effective in about 70 percent of cases of Raynaud's syndrome.
Tension headaches	Muscle contraction headaches are most frequently treated with two large active electrodes spaced on the forehead to provide visual or auditory information about the levels of muscle tension. The frontal electrode placement is sensitive to EMG activity regarding the frontalis and occipital muscles, which the patient learns to relax.

ably, patients lower the sympathetic activation and voluntarily self-regulate arterial smooth muscle vasoconstrictive tendencies. (Biofeedback is further discussed in Chapter 28, Sections 28.2 and 28.4.).

METHODS

The feedback instrument used depends on the patient and the specific problem. The most effective instruments are the electromyogram (EMG), which measures the electrical potentials of muscle fibers; the electroencephalogram (EEG), which measures alpha waves that occur in relaxed states; the galvanic skin response gauge (GSR), which shows decreased skin conductivity during a relaxed state; and the thermistor, which measures skin temperature (which drops during tension because of peripheral vasoconstriction). Patients are attached to one of the measuring instruments to measure a physiological function and translate the measurement into an audible or visual signal that patients use to gauge their responses. For example, in the treatment of bruxism, an EMG is attached to the masseter muscle. The EMG emits a high tone when the muscle is contracted and a low tone when at rest. Patients can learn to alter the tone to indicate relaxation. Patients receive feedback about the masseter muscle, the tone reinforces the learning, and the condition ameliorates—all these events interacting synergistically.

Table 34.5–1 outlines some important clinical applications of biofeedback and shows that a wide variety of biofeedback modalities have been used to treat numerous conditions. Many less specific clinical applications—such as treating insomnia, dysmenorrhea, and speech problems, improving athletic performance, treating volitional disorders, achieving altered states of consciousness, managing stress, and supplementing psychotherapy for anxiety associated with somatoform disorders—use a model in which frontalis muscle EMG biofeedback is combined with thermal biofeedback and verbal instructions in progressive relaxation.

REFERENCES

Berghmans LC, Frederiks CM, de Bie RA, Weil EH, Smeets LW, van Waalwijk, van Doorn ES, Janknegt RA: Efficacy of biofeedback, when included with pelvic floor muscle exercise treatment, for genuine stress incontinence. Neurol Urodynam *15:* 37, 1996.

Burgio KL, Engel BT: Biofeedback-assisted behavioral training for elderly men and women. J Am Geriatr Soc *38:* 338, 1990.

Burish TG, Jenkins RA: Effectiveness of biofeedback and relaxation training in reducing the side effects of cancer chemotherapy. Health Psychol *11:* 17, 1992.

Elton D: Combined use of hypnosis and EMG biofeedback in the treatment of stress-induced conditions. Stress Med *9:* 25, 1993.

Gaarder KR, Montgomery S: *Clinical Biofeedback: A Procedural Manual for Behavioral Medicine.* Williams & Wilkins, Baltimore, 1981.

Linden M, Habib T, Radojevic V: A controlled study of the effects of EEG biofeedback on cognition and behavior of children with attention deficit disorder and learning disabilities. Biofeedback Self Regul *21:* 35, 1996.

Lisspers J, Ost LG: BVP-biofeedback in the treatment of migraine: The effects of constriction and dilatation during different phases of the migraine attack. Behav Modif *14:* 200, 1990.

McGrady A, Conran P, Dickey D, Garman D, et al: The effects of biofeedback-assisted relaxation on cell-mediated immunity, cortisol, and white blood cell count in healthy and adult subjects. J Behav Med *15:* 343, 1992.

Orne MT, editor: *Task Force Report No. 19: Biofeedback.* American Psychiatric Association, Washington, 1980.

Runck B: *Biofeedback: Issues and Treatment Assessment.* National Institute of Mental Health (DDHS Pub. No. ADM 80-1032), Rockville, MD, 1980.

Wehck L, Leu PW, D'Amato RC: Evaluating the efficacy of a biofeedback intervention to reduce children's anxiety. J Clin Psychol *52:* 469, 1996.

Whitehead WE: Biofeedback treatment of gastrointestinal disorders. Biofeedback Self Regul *17:* 59, 1992.

Whitehead WE, Drossman DA: Biofeedback for disorders of elimination: Fecal incontinence and pelvic floor dyssynergia. Prof Psychol Res Pract *27:* 234, 1996.

▲ 34.6 Behavior Therapy

Unlike other psychotherapies, behavior therapy focuses on ameliorating people's maladaptive behavior without theorizing about their inner conflicts. Behaviorists look for observable factors that have been learned or conditioned and can therefore be unlearned or unconditioned and replaced by new and adaptive behavior. Because all behavior has been learned, according to behavior therapists, undesirable behavior can be unlearned and desirable behavior relearned in its place.

Behavior therapy is based on the principles of learning theory, particularly operant and classical conditioning. This therapy is most often directed at specific, delineated habits of reacting with anxiety to objectively nondangerous stimuli such as phobias, compulsions, psychophysiological reactions, and sexual dysfunctions. Clinicians who wish to apply a behavioral approach must answer the four questions in Table 34.6–1 in conjunction with the patient, relatives, and other caretakers. The questions are raised repeatedly throughout the course of

Table 34.6–1
Behavior Analysis of Clinical Problems Requires Answers to These Questions

1. What are the problems and goals for therapy?
   This question addresses the patient's assets, as well as deficits of adaptive behavior and the excesses of maladaptive behavior. Often, the patient's problems are related to inappropriate timing or context of behavioral responses. The assessment of problems and the formulation of goals must consider the full range of objective, subjective, affective, social, and cognitive responses.
2. How can progress be measured and monitored?
   Each problem and goal requires behavioral specification and ongoing monitoring in terms of frequency, duration, form, latency, or context of occurrence. Operationalizing the goals of therapy enables the therapist to determine whether selected interventions are effective and provides the empirical basis for behavior therapy.
3. What environmental contingencies are maintaining the problem?
   A behavior analysis considers the functional relations between clinical problems and their environmental antecedents (precipitants or triggering stimuli) and consequences (reinforcers). Before formulating a treatment plan, the therapist must understand the current social and instrumental contingencies that may have to be modified for a successful outcome.
4. Which interventions are likely to be effective?
   This final question addresses the specific techniques that can be used in the treatment plan. Only after the first three questions are answered can a rational selection of interventions be made. Often, a combination of learning principles is packaged to maximize treatment effects.

Courtesy of Robert Paul Liberman, M.D., and Jeffrey Bedell, Ph.D.

treatment in recurring cycles—first tentatively and later definitively as information accrues and progress occurs.

HISTORY

As early as the 1920s, scattered reports about the application of learning principles to the treatment of behavioral disorders began to appear but had little effect on the mainstream of psychiatry and clinical psychology. Not until the 1960s did behavior therapy emerge as a systematic and comprehensive approach to psychiatric (behavioral) disorders, and at that time it arose independently on three continents. Joseph Wolpe and his colleagues in Johannesburg, South Africa, used large pavlovian techniques to produce and eliminate experimental neuroses in cats. From this research Wolpe developed systematic desensitization, the prototype of many current behavioral procedures for the treatment of maladaptive anxiety produced by identifiable stimuli in the environment. At about the same time a group at the Institute of Psychiatry of the University of London, particularly Hans Jurgen Eysenck and M. B. Shapiro, stressed the importance of an empirical, experimental approach to understanding and treating individual patients using own-control, single-case experimental paradigms and modern learning theory. The third origin of behavior therapy was work inspired by the research of Harvard psychologist B. F. Skinner. Skinner's students began to apply his operant-conditioning technology developed in animal-conditioning laboratories, and to human beings in clinical settings.

SYSTEMATIC DESENSITIZATION

Developed by Joseph Wolpe, systematic desensitization is based on the behavioral principle of counterconditioning, whereby a person overcomes maladaptive anxiety elicited by a situation or an object by approaching the feared situation gradually and in a psychophysiological state that inhibits anxiety. In systematic desensitization, patients attain a state of complete relaxation and are then exposed to the stimulus that elicits the anxiety response. The negative reaction of anxiety is inhibited by the relaxed state, a process called reciprocal inhibition. Rather than use actual situations or objects that elicit fear, patients and therapists prepare a graded list or hierarchy of anxiety-provoking scenes associated with a patient's fears. The learned relaxation state and the anxiety-provoking scenes are systematically paired in treatment. Thus, systematic desensitization consists of three steps: relaxation training, hierarchy construction, and desensitization of the stimulus.

Relaxation Training

Relaxation produces physiological effects opposite those of anxiety: slow heart rate, increased peripheral blood flow, and neuromuscular stability. A variety of relaxation methods have been developed. Some, such as yoga and Zen, have been known for centuries. Most methods use so-called progressive relaxation. Patients relax major muscle groups in a fixed order, beginning with the small muscle groups of the feet and working cephalad or vice versa. Some clinicians employ hypnosis to facilitate relaxation or use tape-recorded exercise to allow patients to practice relaxation on their own. Mental imagery is a relaxation method in which patients are instructed to imagine themselves in a place associated with pleasant relaxed memories. Such images allow patients to enter a relaxed state or experience or, as H. Benson termed it, the relaxation response.

Hierarchy Construction

When constructing a hierarchy, clinicians determine all the conditions that elicit anxiety, and then patients create a hierarchy list of 10 to 12 scenes in order of increasing anxiety. For example, an acrophobic hierarchy may begin with a patient's imagining standing near a window on the second floor and end with being on the roof of a 20-story building, leaning on a guard rail and looking straight down. Table 34.6–2 provides two examples of hierarchy constructions described by the British psychiatrist Thomas Kraft.

Desensitization of the Stimulus

In desensitization patients proceed systematically through the list from the least to the most anxiety-provoking scene while in a deeply relaxed state. The rate at which patients progress through the list is determined by their responses to the stimuli. When patients can vividly imagine the most anxiety-provoking scene of the hierarchy with equanimity, they experience little anxiety in the corresponding real-life situation.

Adjunctive Use of Drugs

Clinicians have used various drugs to hasten desensitization, but drugs should be used cautiously and only by clinicians trained and experienced in potential adverse effects. The widest experience is with the ultrarapidly acting barbiturate sodium methohexital (Brevital), which is given intravenously in subanesthetic doses. Usually, up to 60 mg of the drug is given in divided doses in a session. Intravenous diazepam (Valium) may also be used cautiously. If the procedural details are carefully followed, almost all patients find the procedure pleasant, with few unpleasant side effects. The advantages of pharmacological desensitization are that preliminary training in relaxation can be shortened, almost all patients are able to become adequately relaxed, and the treatment itself seems to proceed more rapidly than without the drugs.

Indications

Systematic desensitization works best when there is a clearly identifiable anxiety-provoking stimulus. Phobias, obsessions, compulsions, and certain sexual disorders have been successfully treated with the technique.

GRADED EXPOSURE

Graded exposure is similar to systematic desensitization except that relaxation training is not involved and treatment is usually carried out in a real-life context.

FLOODING

Flooding is based on the premise that escaping from an anxiety-provoking experience reinforces the anxiety through conditioning. Thus, clinicians can extinguish the anxiety and

Table 34.6–2
Two Examples of Hierarchy Constructions (Least Anxious to Most Anxious)

Dog Phobia

1. Looking at a picture of a dog in a children's picture book.
2. Cuddling the children's toy dog.
3. Seeing a poodle on a lead
   (a) 10 yards away.
   (b) 5 yards away.
   (c) passing by.
4. Touching a puppy behind a wire mesh in the market.
5. Looking at the neighbor's spaniel, Kim, held in the arms of its mistress.
6. Touching Kim when the dog is quiet and held in the arms of its mistress.
7. Touching Kim when the dog is quiet.
8. Stroking Kim.
9. Kim putting up her paws.
10. Looking at an Alsatian dog.
11. Watching Kim jumping on the road when the patient is indoors and the windows are closed.
12. Watching Kim walk around the room.
13. Feeding Kim a biscuit.
14. Kim held by its mistress and then jumping onto the ground.
15. Kim running.
16. Kim jumping from a chair onto the floor.
17. Kim jumping onto the floor and then putting up her paw.
18. Kim wagging her tail.
19. Kim wagging her tail and then putting her paw up.
20. Kim running down the corridor.
21. Kim running away from the patient.
22. Kim running toward the patient.
23. Kim roaming around the house without a lead.
24. Knocking on the door of the neighbor, and Kim running toward her, barking.
25. Dogs fighting.

Fear of Water and Heights

1. Taking a bath at home.
2. Taking a shower at home.
3. Going into the shallow end of the swimming pool.
4. Starting to swim at the shallow end of the swimming pool, breaststroke only.
5. Swimming at the shallow end, doing the crawl.
6. Jumping into the swimming pool at the shallow end.
7. Jumping into the pool and then doing the crawl.
8. Swimming at the shallow end, first breaststroke, then the crawl.
9. Pushing away from the bars and causing a splash.
10. Swimming in the middle of the pool at a depth of 5 feet 3 inches.
11. Swimming at the shallow end and then at the deep end (10 feet 3 inches).
12. Going into the deep end of the swimming pool.
13. Watching people jump from the diving boards.
14. Standing on a step at the deep end of the pool and making a little jump into the water.
15. Backstroke at the shallow end of the pool.
16. Jumping into the water at the shallow end of the pool (belly-flop dive).
17. Belly-flop dive at the deep end of the pool.
18. Racing dive at the shallow end of the pool.
19. Racing dive at the deep end of the pool.
20. Swimming three times across the deep end of the pool without stopping
    (a) breaststroke
    (b) crawl
    (c) backstroke
21. Jumping into the pool at a depth of:
    (a) 5 feet 3 inches
    (b) 6 feet
    (c) 7 feet
22. Several jumps at 6 feet and 7 feet, alternating them, and then remaining at the 7-foot depth.
23. Going onto the first diving board and jumping into the water.
24. Jumping off the first diving board, then diving from the first board.
25. Diving off the first board.
26. Jumping from the first diving board, jumping from the second diving board, then diving from the first diving board.
27. Jumping off the first, second, and third diving boards, then diving from the first diving board.
28. Jumping off the first, second, and third diving boards, then diving from the first and then the second diving board.
29. Jumping off the fourth diving board, then diving off the second diving board.
30. Jumping off the fifth diving board, then diving off the third diving board.
31. Jumping off the fifth diving board, then diving off the fourth diving board.
32. Jumping off the top board, then diving off the fourth diving board.
33. Jumping off the top board, then diving off the fifth diving board.
34. Diving off the top diving board.
35. Random stimuli.
36. Looking around before jumping off the third diving board.
37. Looking around before jumping off the fourth diving board.
38. Looking around before jumping off the fifth diving board.
39. Diving from the fifth diving board and looking around before diving.
40. Diving from the top board and looking around before diving.

Reprinted with permission from Kraft T. The use of behavior therapy in a psychotherapeutic context. In *Clinical Behavior Therapy,* AA Lazarus, editor, p 222. Brunner/Mazel, New York, 1972.

prevent the conditioned avoidance behavior by not allowing patients to escape the situation. Clinicians encourage patients to confront feared situations directly, without a gradual buildup as in systematic desensitization or graded exposure. No relaxation exercises are used, as in systematic desensitization. Patients experience fear, which gradually subsides after a time. The success of the procedure depends on patients' remaining in the fear-generating situation until they are calm and feeling a sense of mastery. Prematurely withdrawing from the situation or prematurely terminating the fantasized scene is equivalent to an escape, which then reinforces both the conditioned anxiety and the avoidance behavior and produces the opposite of the desired effect. In a variant of flooding, called implosion, the feared object or situation is confronted only in the imagination rather than in real life. Many patients refuse flooding because of the psychological discomfort involved. It is also contraindicated in patients for whom intense anxiety would be hazardous (for example, patients with heart disease or fragile psychological adaptation). The technique works best with specific phobias.

PARTICIPANT MODELING

In participant modeling, patients learn a new behavior by imitation, primarily by observation, without having to perform the behavior until they feel ready. Just as irrational fears may be acquired by learning, they can be unlearned by observing a fearless model confront the feared object. The technique has been useful with phobic children who are placed with other children of their own age and sex who approach the feared object or situation. With adults, a therapist may describe the feared activity in a calm manner that a patient can identify. Or the therapist may act out the process of mastering the feared activity with a patient. Sometimes a hierarchy of activities is established, with the least anxiety-provoking activity being dealt with first. The participant-modeling technique has been used successfully with agoraphobia by having a therapist accompany a patient into the feared situation. In a variant of the procedure called behavior rehearsal, real-life problems are acted out under a therapist's observation or direction. The technique is useful for complex behavioral patterns, such as job interviews and shyness.

ASSERTIVENESS AND SOCIAL SKILLS TRAINING

To be assertive requires that people have confidence in their judgment and sufficient self-esteem to express their opinions. Assertiveness and social skills training teach people how to respond appropriately in social situations, to express their opinions in acceptable ways, and to achieve their goals. A variety of techniques—including role modeling, desensitization, and positive reinforcement (reward of desired behavior)—are used to increase assertiveness. Social skills training deals with assertiveness but also attends to a variety of real-life tasks, such as food shopping, looking for work, interacting with other people, and overcoming shyness.

AVERSION THERAPY

When a noxious stimulus (punishment) is presented immediately after a specific behavioral response, theoretically the response is eventually inhibited and extinguished. Many types of noxious stimuli are used: electric shocks, substances that induce vomiting, corporal punishment, and social disapproval. The negative stimulus is paired with the behavior, which is thereby suppressed. The unwanted behavior may disappear after a series of such sequences. Aversion therapy has been used for alcohol abuse, paraphilias, and other behaviors with impulsive or compulsive qualities; but this therapy is controversial for many reasons. For example, punishment does not always lead to the expected decrease in response and can sometimes be positively reinforcing.

EYE MOVEMENT DESENSITIZATION AND REPROCESSING (EMDR)

Saccadic eye movements are rapid oscillations of the eyes that occur when a person tracks an object that is moved back and forth across the line of vision. If saccades are induced while the person is imagining or thinking about an anxiety-producing event, a few studies have demonstrated that a positive thought or image can be induced that results in decreased anxiety. EMDR has been used in posttraumatic stress disorders and phobias; however, results have not been replicated in other studies, and the method requires further validation.

POSITIVE REINFORCEMENT

When a behavioral response is followed by a generally rewarding event such as food, avoidance of pain, or praise, it tends to be strengthened and to occur more frequently than before the reward. This principle has been applied in a variety of situations. On inpatient hospital wards, patients with mental disorder receive a reward for performing a desired behavior, such as tokens that they may use to purchase luxury items or certain privileges. The process, known as token economy, has been successful in altering behavior.

Some workers have suggested that psychotherapy is effective, in part, because patients want to please the therapist and so change their behavior to receive the therapist's praise. Sigmund Freud stated that, in treating phobias, doctors must encourage patients to face their phobias at some point determined by the positive relationship between doctor and patient.

RESULTS

Behavior therapy has been successful in a variety of disorders (Table 34.6–3) and can be easily taught (Table 34.6–4). It requires less time than other therapies and is less expensive to administer. Although useful for circumscribed behavioral symptoms, the method cannot treat global areas of dysfunction (for example, neurotic conflicts, personality disorders).

One interpretation of behavior theory is epitomized by Eysenck's controversial statement: "Learning theory regards neurotic symptoms as simply learned habits; there is no neurosis underlying the symptoms, but merely the symptom itself. Get rid of the symptom and you have eliminated the neurosis." Analytically oriented theorists have criticized behavior therapy by noting that simple symptom removal may lead to symptom

Table 34.6–3
Some Common Clinical Applications of Behavior Therapy

Disorder	Comments
Agoraphobia	Graded exposure and flooding can reduce the fear of being in crowded places. About 60 percent of patients so treated are improved. In some cases the spouse can serve as the model while accompanying the patient into the fear situation; however, the patient cannot get a secondary gain by keeping the spouse nearby and displaying symptoms.
Alcohol dependence	Aversion therapy in which the alcohol-dependent patient is made to vomit (by adding an emetic to the alcohol) every time a drink is ingested is effective in treating alcohol dependence. Disulfiram (Antabuse) can be given to alcohol-dependent patients when they are alcohol free. Such patients are warned of the severe physiological consequences of drinking (eg, nausea, vomiting, hypotension, collapse) with disulfiram in the system.
Anorexia nervosa	Observe eating behavior; contingency management; record weight.
Bulimia nervosa	Record bulimic episodes; log moods
Hyperventilation	Hyperventilation test; controlled breathing; direct observation.
Other phobias	Systematic desensitization has been effective in treating phobias, such as fears of heights, animals, and flying. Social skills training has also been used for shyness and fear of other people.
Paraphilias	Electric shocks or other noxious stimuli can be applied at the time of a paraphilic impulse, and eventually the impulse subsides. Shocks can be administered by either the therapist or the patient. The results are satisfactory but must be reinforced at regular intervals.
Schizophrenia	The token economy procedure, in which tokens are awarded for desirable behavior and can be used to buy ward privileges, has been useful in treating inpatient schizophrenic patients. Social skills training teaches schizophrenic patients how to interact with others in a socially acceptable way so that negative feedback is eliminated. In addition, the aggressive behavior of some schizophrenic patients can be diminished through those methods.
Sexual dysfunctions	Sex therapy, developed by William Masters and Virginia Johnson, is a behavior therapy technique used for various sexual dysfunctions, especially male erectile disorder, orgasm disorders, and premature ejaculation. It uses relaxation, desensitization, and graded exposure as the primary techniques.
Shy bladder	Inability to void in a public bathroom; relaxation exercises.
Type A behavior	Physiological assessment; muscle relaxation, biofeedback (on EMG)

Table 34.6–4
Social Skills Competence Checklist of Therapist-Trainer Behaviors

1. Actively helps the patient in setting and eliciting specific interpersonal goals.
2. Promotes favorable expectations, a therapeutic orientation, and motivation before role playing begins.
3. Assists the patient in building possible scenes in terms of: "What emotion or communication?" "Who is the interpersonal target?" "Where and when?"
4. Structures the role playing by setting the scene and assigning roles to the patient and surrogates.
5. Engages the patient in behavioral rehearsal—getting the patient to role-play with others.
6. Uses self or other group members in modeling appropriate alternatives for the patient.
7. Prompts and cues the patient during the role playing.
8. Uses an active style of training through coaching, shadowing, being physically out of a seat, and closely monitoring and supporting the patient.
9. Gives the patient positive feedback for specific verbal and nonverbal behavioral skills.
10. Identifies the patient's specific verbal and nonverbal behavioral deficits or excesses and suggests constructive alternatives.
11. Ignores or suppresses inappropriate and interfering behavior.
12. Shapes behavioral improvements in small, attainable increments.
13. Solicits from the patient or suggests an alternative behavior for a problem situation that can be used and practiced during the behavioral rehearsal or role playing.
14. Evaluates deficits in social perception and problem solving and remedies them.
15. Gives specific attainable and functional homework assignments.

Courtesy of Robert Paul Liberman, M.D., and Jeffrey Bedell, Ph.D.

Table 34.6–5
Behavior Therapy

Goal	Modify learned maladaptive behavior patterns that lead to pathological symptoms
Selection criteria	Specific, well-delineated, circumscribed, easily identified maladaptive behaviors (eg, phobias, overeating, sexual dysfunctions) Psychophysiological disorders in which manifestations of symptoms are affected by stress (eg, asthma, pain, hypertension)
Duration	Generally time-limited, specific to specific behavior
Techniques	Based on learning theory principles (eg, operant and classical conditioning) Relaxation training Reinforcements Aversive therapy Systematic desensitization Flooding Participant modeling Token economies

Courtesy of Rebecca Jones, M.D.

substitution. In other words, when symptoms are not viewed as consequences of inner conflicts and the core cause of the symptoms is not addressed or altered, the result is the production of new symptoms. Some therapists consider behavior therapy to be an oversimplified approach to psychopathology and to the complex interaction between therapist and patient. Symptom substitution may not be inevitable, but its possibility is an important consideration in evaluating behavior therapy's efficacy.

As with other forms of treatment, clinicians should evaluate a patients' problems, motivation, and psychological strengths before instituting any behavior therapy approach. Table 34.6–5 gives a summary of behavior therapy.

REFERENCES

Achenbach TM: Implications of multiaxial empirically based assessment for behavior therapy with children. Behav Ther *24:* 91, 1993.

Agras WS: Behavior therapy. In *Comprehensive Textbook of Psychiatry,* ed 6, HI Kaplan, BJ Sadock, editors, p 1788. Williams & Wilkins, Baltimore, 1995.

Barlow D, editor: *Clinical Handbook of Psychological Disorders.* Guilford, New York, 1985.

Baum M: Contributions of animal studies of response prevention (flooding) to human exposure therapy. Psychol Rep *63:* 421, 1988.

Becker RE, Heimberg RG, Bellack AS: *Social Skills Training Treatment for Depression.* Pergamon, New York, 1987.

Carr JE, Bailey JS: A brief behavior therapy protocol for Tourette syndrome. J Behav Ther Exp Psychiatry *27:* 33, 1996.

Ciminero AR, Calhoun KS, Adams HE, editors: *Handbook of Behavioral Assessment,* ed 2. Wiley, New York, 1986.

Cinciripini PM, Cinciripini LG, Wallfisch A, Haque B, Waheedul C, et al: Behavior therapy and the transdermal nicotine patch: Effects on cessation outcome, affect, and coping. J Consult Clin Psychol *64:* 314, 1996.

Collins FL, Thompson JK: The integration of empirically derived personality assessment data into behavioral conceptualization and treatment plan: Rationale, guidelines, and caveats. Behav Modif *17:* 58, 1993.

Council on Scientific Affairs: Aversion therapy. JAMA *13:* 2562, 1987.

Forehand R, Wierson M: The role of developmental factors in planning behavioral interventions for children: Disruptive behavior as an example. Behav Ther *24:* 117, 1993.

Frawley PJ, Smith JW: Chemical aversion therapy in the treatment of cocaine dependence as part of multimodal treatment program: Treatment outcome. J Subst Abuse Treat *7:* 21, 1990.

Herbert JD, Mueser KT: Eye movement desensitization: A critique of the evidence. J Behav Ther Exp Psychiatry *23:* 169, 1992.

Kellner R, Neidhardt J, Krakow B, Pathak D: Changes in chronic nightmares after one session of desensitization or rehearsal instructions. Am J Psychiatry *149:* 659, 1992.

Kohlenberg RJ, Tsai M, Kohlenberg BS: Functional analysis in behavior therapy. Prog Behav Modif *30:* 1, 1996.

Liberman RP: *A Guide to Behavioral Analysis and Therapy.* Pergamon, New York, 1972.

Marks IM: *Fears, Phobias and Rituals.* Oxford University Press, New York, 1987.

McKee MG: Behavioral techniques in pain modification. Cleve Clin J Med *56:* 502, 1989.

Mohr B, Muller V, Mattes R, Rosin R, Et al: Behavioral treatment of Parkinson's disease leads to improvement of motor skills and to tremor reduction. Behav Ther *27:* 235, 1996.

Muris P, Merckelbach H: Defense style and behavior therapy outcome in a specific phobia. Psychol Med *26:* 635, 1996.

Stanley MA, Beck JG, Averill PM, Baldwin LE, Deagle EA III, Stadler JG: Patterns of change during cognitive behavioral treatment for panic disorder. J Nerv Ment Dis *184:* 567, 1996.

Thase ME, Dube S, Bowler K, Howland RH, Myers JE, Friedman E, Jarrett DB: Hypothalamic-pituitary-adrenocortical activity and response to cognitive behavior therapy in unmedicated, hospitalized depressed patients. Am J Psychiatry *153:* 886, 1996.

Wadden TA, Foster GD, Letizia KA: Response of obese binge eaters to treatment by behavior therapy combined with very low calorie diet. J Consult Clin Psychol *60:* 808, 1992.

▲ 34.7 Hypnosis

Hypnosis is a complex mental phenomenon that has been defined as a state of heightened focal concentration and receptivity to the suggestions of another person who brings about the condition by focusing the person's attention on a monotonous routine. People may hypnotize themselves by practicing similar monotonous routines. Hypnosis has also been described as an altered state of consciousness, a dissociated state, and a state of regression. Nevertheless, unlike sleep, in which typical electroencephalogram (EEG) changes are evident, hypnosis has no known psychophysiological basis.

Martin Orne defined hypnosis as a state or condition in which a person can respond to appropriate suggestions by experiencing alterations of perceptions, memory, or mood. The essential feature of hypnosis is the subjective experimental change. A pioneer in clinical hypnotic induction, Milton Erickson, described the process of a clinical trance as "a free period in which individuality can flourish."

Hypnotherapists perceive clinical hypnosis and therapeutic trance as extensions of common processes in everyday life. Daydreaming and inner preoccupation, during which people seemingly automatically go through the motions of a daily routine, are typical examples. During such periods, people spontaneously focus attention inward, just as in a trance state a patient is induced to be receptive to inner experiences. The primary view shared by hypnotherapists and other psychotherapists is an appreciation and understanding of the dynamics of unconscious processes in behavior.

HISTORY

The Austrian physician Friedrich Anton Mesmer (1734–1815) originated the phenomenon of hypnosis, which he called mesmerism and believed to be the result of "animal magnetism" or an invisible fluid passing between subject and mesmerizer. A Scottish physician, James Braid (1795–1860), first used the term hypnosis (from *hypnos,* the Greek word for "sleep") in the 1840s to refer to what he thought was a specific state of sleep. In the late 19th century the French neurologist Jean-Martin Charcot (1825–1893) considered hypnotism a special physiological state. His contemporary Hippolyte-Marie Bernheim (1840–1919) believed it to be a psychological state of heightened suggestibility.

Sigmund Freud, who had studied with Charcot, used hypnosis early in his career to help patients recover repressed memories. Freud noted that patients relived traumatic events while under hypnosis, a process known as abreaction. Freud later replaced hypnosis with the technique of free association.

Today, hypnosis is used as a form of therapy (hypnotherapy), a method of investigation to recover lost memories, and a research tool.

HYPNOTIC CAPACITY AND INDUCTION

Therapists can use several specific procedures to help patients be hypnotized and respond to suggestion. These procedures capitalize on naturally occurring hypnosis-like phenomena that most people have probably experienced. But because these experiences are rarely talked about patients find them fascinating. For example, when discussing hypnosis with a patient, a therapist may ask: "Have you ever had the experience of driving home while thinking about an issue that preoccupies you and suddenly realize that, although you have arrived safe and sound, you can't recall having driven past familiar landmarks? It's as if you had been asleep, and yet you stopped at all the red lights, and you avoided collisions. You were somehow traveling on automatic pilot." Most people resonate to this experience and are usually happy to describe similar personal experiences.

When patients realize that they have probably undergone hypnosis-like episodes, they can understand that they have the capacity to use the hypnotic mode, which is merely an extension of such states. Although the episodes were not necessarily hypnotic states, the extent to which a person experiences them is correlated with hypnotizability. Table 34.7–1 lists a variety of naturally occurring trancelike experiences that can be discussed with patients and that point to the capacity to be hypnotized. Table 34.7–2 summarizes the three key purposes of trance induction, as set forth by Erickson.

The following is a typical induction protocol (courtesy of William Holt, M.D.) used to induce the trance state. There are many variations of the protocol, some less direct than this one. The one presented here is most likely to be effective in people with a high hypnotizability potential.

Take a long, deep, breath—inhale and exhale; now close your eyes and relax. Pay particular attention to the muscles in and about your eyes—relax them to the point that they just won't work. Are you trying to do that? Good. If you really have them relaxed, right at this very moment, no matter how hard you try, they just won't open. Test them. The harder you try, the faster they stick together, just as if they were glued together. That's fine!

Now you can open your eyes; that's good. When I tell you to and not before, open and close your eyes once more, and, when you close them this time, you will be 10 times as relaxed as you are right now. Go ahead, open and close, and feel that surge of relaxation go through your whole body, from the top of your head to the tip of your toes. Very good!

Now once again, open and close your eyes, and this time, when you close them, you will double the relaxation that you now have. Fine.

If you have followed my suggestions, right at this very moment, when I lift your hand and let it drop into your lap, it will drop like a wet cloth, heavy and limp. That's very, very good.

You now have good physical relaxation, but medical relaxation consists of two phases: physical, which you now have, and mental, which I will now show you how to achieve.

When I ask you to and not before, I want you to start counting backward from 100. I know you can count; that is not what we're after. I just want you to relax mentally. As you say each number, pause momentarily until you feel a wave of relaxation cover your whole body, from the top of your head to the tip of your toes. When you feel this wave of relaxation, then say the next number, and each time you say a number, you will double the relaxation you had before you said the number. If you do this properly, an interesting thing will happen—as you say the numbers and relax, the succeeding numbers will start to disappear and vanish from your mind. Command your mind to dispel these numbers. Now, aloud and slowly, start counting backward from 100.

Patient: One hundred.

Doctor: Very good.

Patient: Ninety-nine.

Doctor: Make them start to disappear now.

Patient: Ninety-eight.

Doctor: Now they're fading away, and after the next number they'll all be gone. Make them disappear. Let the numbers go.

Table 34.7–1
Naturally Occurring Hypnotic-like Experiences and the Percentage of Persons Indicating That They Have Had Such Experiences

Have you ever been in a room full of people, ostensibly taking part in the group yet mentally being far away from it?	90%
Have you ever been unsure whether you did something or just thought about having to do it (eg, not knowing whether you either mailed a certain letter or just thought about mailing it)?	87%
Have you ever been able to block out sounds from your mind so that they were no longer important to you? Or so that they seemed very far away? Or so that you no longer understood them? Or so that you did not hear them at all?	87%
Have you ever been so lost in thought that you did not understand what people said to you, even when they were talking directly to you and even when you nodded token agreement?	84%
Have you ever been staring off into space, actually thinking of nothing and hardly been aware of the passage of time?	81%
Have you ever had the experience of recollecting a past experience in your life with such clarity and vitality that it was almost like living it again? Or so that it actually seemed identical with living it again?	78%
Have you ever been able to shut out your surroundings from your mind by concentrating very hard on something else?	77%
Have you ever had the experience of reading a novel (or watching a play) and, while doing so, actually forget yourself, your surroundings, and live the story with such great reality and vividness that it became temporarily almost reality for you? Or actually seemed to become reality for you?	75%
Have you ever been lulled into a groggy state or put to sleep by a lecture or a concert, even though you were not otherwise fatigued or tired?	73%
Have you ever wandered off in your own thoughts while doing a routine task so that you actually forgot you were doing the task and then found, a few minutes later, that you had completed it without even being aware that you were doing it?	70%

Courtesy of Martin Orne, M.D., Ph.D., and David Dinges, Ph.D.

Table 34.7–2
Purposes of Trance Induction

- To reduce the foci of attention (usually to a few inner realities)
- To facilitate alterations in the habitual patterns of direction and control
- To facilitate patients' receptivity to their own inner associations and mental skills that can be integrated into therapeutic responses

Reprinted with permission from Erickson M, Rossi EL, Rossi SI: *Hypnotic Realities: The Induction of Clinical Hypnosis and Forms of Indirect Suggestion,* p 97. Irvington, New York, 1976.

Patient: Ninety-seven.

Doctor: And now they're all gone. Are they gone? Fine. If there are any numbers still lurking in your mind, when I lift your hand and drop it, they will all disappear.

TRANCE STATE

People under hypnosis are said to be in a trance state, which may be light, medium, or heavy (deep). In a light trance there are changes in motor activity: People's muscles can feel relaxed, the hands can levitate, and paresthesia can be induced. A medium trance is characterized by diminished pain sensation and partial or complete amnesia. A deep trance is associated with induced visual or auditory experiences and deep anesthesia. Time distortion occurs at all trance levels but is most profound in the deep trance. Table 34.7–3 summarizes a number of the indicators of a developing and deepening trance state. Patients manifest the indications in differing degrees and combinations.

In posthypnotic suggestion a person is instructed to perform a simple act or to experience a particular sensation after awakening from the trance state. The suggestion may cause a person to perceive a bad taste to cigarettes or to a particular food and thus can aid in treating nicotine dependence or obesity. Posthypnotic suggestions are associated with deep trance states.

HYPNOTHERAPY

Patients in hypnotic trances can recall memories that are unavailable to consciousness in the nonhypnotic state. In therapy such memories can corroborate psychoanalytic hypotheses about a patient's dynamics or can enable a patient to use such memories as a catalyst for new associations. Some patients can induce age regression, during which they reexperience events that occurred earlier in life. Whether the patient experiences the events as they actually occurred is controversial, but the material elicited can be used to further the therapy. Patients in a trance state may describe an event with an intensity similar to its original occurrence (abreaction) and can feel a sense of relief as a result. Trance states play a role in treating of amnestic disorders and dissociative fugue, although clinicians should be aware that quickly bringing repressed memory into consciousness may be hazardous and may overwhelm the patient with anxiety.

Indications and Uses

Hypnosis has been used, with varying degrees of success, to control obesity and substance-related disorders such as alcohol abuse and nicotine dependence. Major surgery has been performed with no anesthetic except hypnosis. Hypnosis has also been applied to managing chronic pain disorder, asthma, warts, pruritus, aphonia, and conversion disorder. Patients can easily achieve relaxation with hypnosis, so that they can deal with phobias by controlling their anxiety. Hypnosis can also induce relaxation in systematic desensitization.

Contraindication

Hypnotized patients are in a state of atypical dependence on a therapist; they may develop a strong transference, characterized by a positive attachment that must be respected and interpreted. In other instances a negative transference may erupt in patients who are fragile or who have difficulty in testing reality. Patients who have problems about basic trust, such as those with paranoia or patients who dislike giving up control, such as those who are obsessive-compulsive, are not good candidates for hypnosis. A secure ethical value system is important to all therapy and particularly to hypnotherapy, in which patients (especially those in a deep trance) are extremely suggestible and malleable. There is controversy about whether patients can perform acts during a trance state that they otherwise find repugnant or that run contrary to their moral code.

Table 34.7–3
Indicators of Trance Development

Autonomous ideation	Retardation of reflexes:
Balanced tonicity (catalepsy)	Swallowing
	Blinking
Changed voice quality	Sensory, muscular, and body changes
Comfort, relaxation	
Economy of movement	Slowing and loss of blink reflex
Eye changes and closure	
Facial features ironed out	Slowing pulse
	Slowing respiration
Feeling distant	Spontaneous hypnotic phenomena:
Feeling good after trance	
Lack of body movement	Amnesia
Lack of startle response	Anesthesia
Literalism	Catalepsy
Objective and impersonal ideation	Regression
	Time distortion
Pupillary changes	Time lag in motor and conceptual behavior
Response attentiveness	

Reprinted with permission from Erickson M, Rossi EL, Rossi SI: *Hypnotic Realities: The Induction of Clinical Hypnosis and Forms of Indirect Suggestion,* p. 98. Irvington, New York, 1976.

References

Allison DB, Faith MS: Hypnosis as an adjunct to cognitive-behavioral psychotherapy for obesity: A meta-analytic reappraisal. J Consult Clin Psychol *64:* 513, 1996.

Barnier AJ, McConkey KM: Reports of real and false memories: The relevance of hypnosis, hypnotizability, and context of memory test. J Abnorm Psychol *101:* 521, 1992.

Benson H: Hypnosis and the relaxation response. Gastroenterology *96:* 1609, 1989.

Erickson M, Rossi EL, Rossi SI: *Hypnotic Realities: The Induction of Clinical Hypnosis and Forms of Indirect Suggestion.* Irvington, New York, 1976.

Gabel S: The right hemisphere in imagery, hypnosis, rapid eye movement sleep and dreaming: Empirical studies and tentative conclusions. J Nerv Ment Dis *176:* 323, 1988.

Gruzelier J: The state of hypnosis: Evidence and applications. QJM *89:* 313, 1996.

Hilgard E: *The Experience of Hypnosis: A Shorter Version of Hypnotic Susceptibility.* Harcourt, Brace & World, New York, 1968.

Hilgard E, Hilgard J: *Hypnosis in the Relief of Pain.* Kaufmann, Los Altos, CA, 1983.

Kingsbury SJ: Brief hypnotic treatment of repetitive nightmares. Am J Clin Hypn *35:* 161, 1993.

MacHovec F: Hypnosis complications, risk factors, and prevention. Am J Clin Hypn *31:* 40, 1988.

Miller ME, Bowers KS: Hypnotic analgesia: Dissociated experience or dissociated control? J Abnorm Psychol *102:* 29, 1993.

McNeilly RB: Individualizing stress and the benefits of hypnosis. Aust Fam Physician *25:* 1261, 1996.

Orne MT, Dinges DF: Hypnosis. In *Comprehensive Textbook of Psychiatry,* ed 6, HI Kaplan, BJ Sadock, editors, p 1807. Williams & Wilkins, Baltimore, 1996.

Patterson DR, Everett JJ, Burns GL, Marvin JA: Hypnosis for the treatment of burn pain. J Consult Clin Psychol *60:* 713, 1992.

Silva CE, Kirsch I: Interpretive sets, expectancy, fantasy proneness, and dissociation as predictors of hypnotic response. J Pers Soc Psychol *63:* 847, 1992.

Syrjala KL, Cummings C, Donaldson GW: Hypnosis or cognitive behavioral training for the reduction of pain and nausea during cancer treatment: A controlled clinical trial. Pain *48:* 137, 1992.

Valbo A, Eide T: Smoking cessation in pregnancy: The effect of hypnosis in a randomized study. Addict Behav *21:* 29, 1996.

▲ 34.8 Cognitive Therapy

Cognitive therapy—according to its originator, Aaron Beck—is "based on an underlying theoretical rationale that an individual's affect and behavior are largely determined by the way in which he structures the world." A person's structuring of the world is based on cognitions (verbal or pictorial ideas available to consciousness), which are based on assumptions (schemas developed from previous experiences). According to Beck,

> [i]f a person interprets all his experiences in terms of whether he is competent and adequate, his thinking may be dominated by the schema, "Unless I do everything perfectly, I'm a failure." Consequently, he reacts to situations in terms of adequacy even when they are unrelated to whether or not he is personally competent.

Table 34.8–1 summarizes the general assumptions underlying cognitive therapy.

GENERAL CONSIDERATIONS

Cognitive therapy is a short-term structure therapy that uses active collaboration between patient and therapist to achieve its therapeutic goals, which are oriented toward current problems and their resolution. Therapy is usually conducted on an individual basis, although group methods are sometimes helpful. A therapist may also prescribe drugs in conjunction with therapy.

Depressive disorders (with or without suicidal ideation) have been the main focus of cognitive therapy; however, cognitive therapy is also used with other conditions, such as panic disorder, obsessive-compulsive disorder, paranoid personality disorder, and somatoform disorders. The treatment of depression can serve as a paradigm of the cognitive approach.

Table 34.8–1
General Assumptions of Cognitive Therapy

Perception and experiencing in general are active processes that involve both inspective and introspective data.

The patient's cognitions represent a synthesis of internal and external stimuli.

How persons appraise a situation is generally evident in their cognitions (thoughts and visual images).

Those cognitions constitute their stream of consciousness or phenomenal field, which reflects their configuration of themselves, their world, their past and future.

Alterations in the content of their underlying cognitive structures affect their affective state and behavioral pattern.

Through psychological therapy, patients can become aware of their cognitive distortions.

Correction of those faulty dysfunctional constructs can lead to clinical improvement.

Adapted from Beck AT, Rush AJ, Shaw BF, Emery G: *Cognitive Therapy of Depression,* p 47. Guilford, New York, 1979.

COGNITIVE THEORY OF DEPRESSION

According to the cognitive theory of depression, cognitive dysfunctions are the core of depression, and affective and physical changes and other associated features of depression are consequences of cognitive dysfunctions. For example, apathy and low energy are results of a person's expectation of failure in all areas. Similarly, paralysis of will stems from a person's pessimism and feelings of hopelessness. The cognitive triad of depression is a negative self-perception whereby people see themselves as defective, inadequate, deprived, worthless, and undesirable; they have a tendency to experience the world as negative, demanding, and self-defeating and to expect failure and punishment; and they have an expectation of continued hardship, suffering, deprivation, and failure.

The goal of therapy is to alleviate depression and to prevent its recurrence by helping patients to identify and test negative cognitions, to develop alternative and more flexible schemas, and to rehearse both new cognitive and behavioral responses. By changing the way people think, the depressive disorder can be alleviated. Table 34.8–2 gives examples of typical depressive thinking (termed primitive thinking by Beck), contrasted with the adaptive (mature) thinking that cognitive therapy attempts to foster.

Table 34.8–2
Primitive versus Mature Thinking

Primitive Thinking	Mature Thinking
Nondimensional and global: I am fearful.	Multidimensional: I am moderately fearful, quite generous, and fairly intelligent.
Absolutistic and moralistic: I am a despicable coward.	Relativistic and nonjudgmental: I am more fearful than most people I know.
Invariant: I always have been and always will be a coward.	Variable: My fears vary from time to time and from situation to situation.
Character diagnosis: I have a defect in my character.	Behavioral diagnosis: I avoid situations too much, and I have many fears.
Irreversibility: Since I am basically weak, there's nothing that can be done about it.	Reversibility: I can learn ways of facing situations and fighting my fears.

Reprinted with permission from Beck AT, Rush AJ, Shaw BF, Emery G: *Cognitive Therapy of Depression,* p 31. Gullford, New York, 1979.

STRATEGIES AND TECHNIQUES

Therapy is relatively short and lasts up to about 25 weeks. If a patient does not improve in this time, the diagnosis should be reevaluated. Maintenance therapy can be carried out over years. As with other psychotherapies, therapists' attributes are important to successful therapy. They must exude warmth, understand the life experience of each patient. and be truly genuine and honest with themselves and with their patients. Therapists must be able to relate skillfully and interactively with their patients. Cognitive therapists set the agenda at the beginning of each session, assign homework to be performed between sessions, and teach new skills. Therapist and patient actively collaborate (Table 34.8–3). The three components of cognitive therapy are didactic aspects, cognitive techniques, and behavioral techniques.

Table 34.8–3
Cognitive Psychotherapy

Goal	Identify and alter cognitive distortions that maintain symptoms
Selection criteria	Primarily used in dysthymic disorder Nonendogenous depressive disorders Symptoms not sustained by pathological family
Duration	Time-limited, usually 15–25 weeks, once-weekly meetings
Techniques	Collaborative empiricism Structured and directive Assigned readings Homework and behavioral techniques Identification of irrational beliefs and automatic thoughts Identification of attitudes and assumptions underlying negatively biased thoughts

Reprinted with permission from Ursano RJ, Silberman EK: Individual psychotherapies. In *The American Psychiatric Press Textbook of Psychiatry*. JA Talbott, RE Hales, SC Yudofsky, editors, p 872. American Psychiatric Press, Washington, 1988.

Didactic Aspects

The therapy's didactic aspects include explaining to patients the cognitive triad, schemas, and faulty logic. Therapists must tell patients that they will formulate hypotheses together and test them over the course of the treatment. Cognitive therapy requires a full explanation of the relationship between depression and thinking, affect, and behavior, as well as the rationale for all aspects of treatment. This explanation contrasts with psychoanalytically oriented therapies, which require little explanation.

Cognitive Techniques

The therapy's cognitive approach includes four processes: eliciting automatic thoughts, testing automatic thoughts, identifying maladaptive underlying assumptions, and testing the validity of maladaptive assumptions.

Eliciting Automatic Thoughts. Automatic thoughts, also called cognitive distortions, are cognitions that intervene between external events and a person's emotional reaction to the event. As an example, the belief that ''people will laugh at me when they see how badly I bowl'' is an automatic thought that occurs to someone who has been asked to go bowling and responds negatively. Another example is a person's thinking that ''she doesn't like me'' when someone passes the person in the hall without saying hello. Every psychopathological disorder has its own specific cognitive profile of distorted thought, which, if known, provides a framework for specific cognitive interventions (Table 34.8–4).

Testing Automatic Thoughts. Acting as a teacher, a therapist helps a patient test the validity of automatic thoughts. The goal is to encourage the patient to reject inaccurate or exaggerated automatic thoughts after careful examination. Patients often blame themselves when things that may well have been outside their control go awry. The therapist reviews the entire situation with the patient and helps reattribute the blame or cause of the unpleasant events. Generating alternative explanations for events is another way of undermining inaccurate and distorted automatic thoughts.

Identifying Maladaptive Assumptions. As patient and therapist continue to identify automatic thoughts, patterns usually become apparent. The patterns represent rules or maladaptive general assumptions that guide a patient's life. Samples of such rules are ''In order to be happy, I must be perfect'' and ''If anyone doesn't like me, I'm not lovable.'' Such rules

Table 34.8–4
Cognitive Profile of Psychiatric Disorders

Disorder	Specific Cognitive Content
Depressive disorder	Negative view of self, experience, and future
Hypomanic episode	Inflated view of self, experience, and future
Anxiety disorders	Fear of physical or psychological danger
Panic disorder	Catastrophic misinterpretation of bodily and mental experiences
Phobias	Danger in specific, avoidable situations
Paranoid personality disorder	Negative bias, interference, and so forth by others
Conversion disorder	Concept of motor or sensory abnormality
Obsessive-compulsive disorder	Repeated warning or doubting about safety and repetitive acts to ward off threat
Suicidal behavior	Hopelessness and deficit in problem solving
Anorexia nervosa	Fear of being fat or unshapely
Hypochondriasis	Attribution of serious medical disorder

Courtesy of Aaron Beck, M.D., and A. John Rush, M.D.

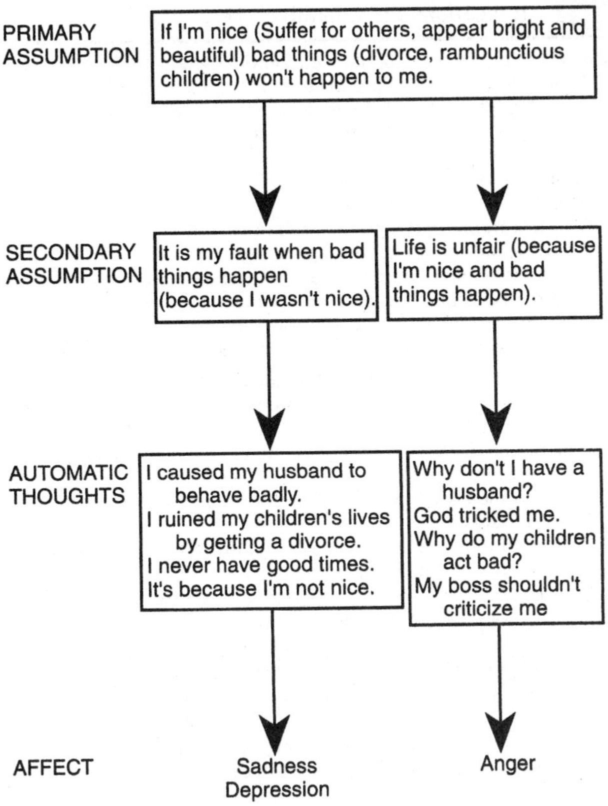
PRIMARY ASSUMPTION
If I'm nice (Suffer for others, appear bright and beautiful) bad things (divorce, rambunctious children) won't happen to me.
SECONDARY ASSUMPTION
It is my fault when bad things happen (because I wasn't nice).
Life is unfair (because I'm nice and bad things happen).
AUTOMATIC THOUGHTS
I caused my husband to behave badly.
I ruined my children's lives by getting a divorce.
I never have good times.
It's because I'm not nice.
Why don't I have a husband?
God tricked me.
Why do my children act bad?
My boss shouldn't criticize me
AFFECT
Sadness Depression
Anger

FIGURE 34.8–1.
Cognition-affect flowchart. (Reproduced with permission from Beck AT, Rush AJ, Shaw BF, Emery G: *Cognitive Therapy of Depression,* p 33. Guilford, New York, 1979.)

Table 34.8–6
Key Features of Graded Task Assignment

Problem definition—eg, patients' beliefs that they are not capable of attaining goals that are important to them.

Formulation of a project. Stepwise assignment of tasks (or activities) from simple to complex.

Immediate and direct observation by patients that they are successful in reaching a specific objective (carrying out an assigned task). The continual concrete feedback provides patients with new corrective information regarding their functional capacity.

Ventilation of patients' doubts, cynical reactions, and belittling of their achievements.

Encouragement of realistic evaluation by patients of their actual performance.

Emphasis on the fact that patients reached goals as a result of their own efforts and skill.

Devising new, complex assignments in collaboration with the patients.

Adapted from Beck AT, Rush AJ, Shaw BF, Emery G: *Cognitive Therapy of Depression,* p 39. Guilford, New York, 1979.

inevitably lead to disappointments and failure and ultimately to depression (Fig. 34.8–1).

Testing the Validity of Maladaptive Assumptions. Similar to testing the validity of automatic thoughts is testing the accuracy of maladaptive assumptions. In a particularly effective test, therapists ask patients to defend the validity of their assumptions. For example, patients may state that they should always work up to their potential, and a therapist may ask, "Why is that so important to you?" Table 34.8–5 gives examples of some interventions designed to elicit, identify, test, and correct the cognitive distortions that lead to depressive and other painful affects.

Table 34.8–5
Cognitive Errors Derived from Assumptions

Cognitive Error	Assumption	Intervention
Overgeneralizing	If it's true in one case, it applies to any case that is even slightly similar.	Exposure of faulty logic. Establish criteria of which cases are similar and to what degree.
Selective abstraction	The only events that matter are failures, deprivation, etc. Should measure self by errors, weaknesses, etc.	Use log to identify successes patient forgot.
Excessive responsibility (assuming personal causality)	I am responsible for all bad things, failures, etc.	Disattribution technique.
Assuming temporal causality (predicting without sufficient evidence)	If it has been true in the past, it's always going to be true.	Expose faulty logic. Specify factors that could influence outcome other than past events.
Self-references	I am the center of everyone's attention—especially my bad performances. I am the cause of misfortunes.	Establish criteria to determine when patient is the focus of attention and also the probable facts that cause bad experiences.
Catastrophizing	Always think of the worst. It's most likely to happen to you.	Calculate real probabilities. Focus on evidence that the worst did not happen.
Dichotomous thinking	Everything is either one extreme or another (black or white, good or bad).	Demonstrate that events may be evaluated on a continuum.

Reprinted with permission from Beck AT, Rush AJ, Shaw BF, Emery G: *Cognitive Therapy of Depression,* p 48. Guilford, New York, 1979.

Behavioral Techniques

Behavioral and cognitive techniques go hand in hand: Behavioral techniques test and change maladaptive and inaccurate cognitions. The overall purposes of such techniques are to help patients understand the inaccuracy of their cognitive assumptions and learn new strategies and ways of dealing with issues.

Among the behavioral techniques in cognitive therapy are scheduling activities, mastery and pleasure, graded task assignments, cognitive rehearsal, self-reliance training, role playing, and diversion techniques. Scheduling activities on an hourly basis is one of the first things done in therapy. Patients keep records of the activities and review them with the therapist. In addition to scheduling activities, patients are asked to rate the amount of mastery and pleasure their activities bring them. Patients are often surprised to learn that they have much more mastery of activities and enjoy them more than they had thought.

To simplify the situation and to allow for miniaccomplishments, therapists often break tasks into subtasks, as in graded task assignments, so as to demonstrate to patients that they can succeed. Table 34.8–6 outlines the key features of a graded task assignment as described by Beck. In cognitive rehearsal, patients imagine and rehearse the various steps in meeting and mastering a challenge.

Patients, especially inpatients, are encouraged to become self-reliant by doing such simple things as making their own beds, doing their own shopping, and preparing their own meals. This process is called self-reliance training. Role playing is a particularly powerful and useful technique to elicit automatic thoughts and to learn new behaviors. Diversion techniques are useful in helping patients get through difficult times and include physical activity, social contact, work, play, and visual imagery.

Table 34.8–7
Cognitions Contributing to Poor Adherence to Medication Prescription

Cognitions about the medication (before taking it):
- It's addicting.
- I am stronger if I don't need medicine.
- I am weak to need it (a crutch).
- It won't work for me.
- If I don't take medication, I'm not crazy.
- I can't stand side effects.
- I'll never get off medication once I start.
- There's nothing I need to do except take medicine.
- I only need to take medication on bad days.

Cognitions about medication (while taking it):
- Since I'm not perfectly well (any better) after days or weeks, the medicine isn't working.
- I should feel good right away.
- The medicine will solve all my problems.
- The medicine won't solve problems, so how can it help?
- I can't stand the dizziness (or fuzziness) or other side effects.
- It makes me into a zombie.

Cognitions about depression:
- I am not ill (I don't need help).
- Only weak people get depressed.
- I deserve to be depressed, since I am a burden to everybody.
- Isn't depression a normal reaction to the bad state of things?
- Depression is incurable.
- I am one of the small percentage who do not respond to any treatment.
- Life isn't worth living, so why should I try to get over my depression?

Reprinted with permission from Beck AT, Rush AJ, Shaw BF, Emery G: *Cognitive Therapy of Depression,* p 72. Guilford, New York, 1979.

Table 34.8–8
Indications for Cognitive Therapy

Criteria that justify the administration of cognitive therapy alone:
- Failure to respond to adequate trials of two antidepressants
- Partial response to adequate dosages of antidepressants
- Failure to respond or only a partial response to other psychotherapies
- Diagnosis of dysthymic disorder
- Variable mood reactive to environmental events
- Variable mood that correlates with negative cognitions
- Mild somatoform disorders (sleep, appetite, weight, libidinal)
- Adequate reality testing (ie, no hallucinations or delusions), span of concentration, and memory function
- Inability to tolerate medication side effects or evidence that excessive risk is associated with pharmacotherapy

Features that suggest cognitive therapy alone is not indicated:
- Evidence of coexisting schizophrenia, dementia, substance-related disorders, mental retardation
- Patient has medical illness or is taking medication that is likely to cause depression
- Obvious memory impairment or poor reality testing (hallucinations, delusions)
- History of manic episode (bipolar 1 disorder)
- History of family member who responded to antidepressant
- History of family member with bipolar 1 disorder
- Absence of precipitating or exacerbating environmental stresses
- Little evidence of cognitive distortions
- Presence of severe somatoform disorders (eg, pain disorder)

Indications for combined therapies (medication plus cognitive therapy):
- Partial or no response to trial of cognitive therapy alone
- Partial but incomplete response to adequate pharmacotherapy alone
- Poor compliance with medication regimen
- Historical evidence of chronic maladaptive functioning with depressive syndrome on intermittent basis
- Presence of severe somatoform disorders and marked cognitive distortions (eg, hopelessness)
- Impaired memory and concentration and marked psychomotor difficulty
- Major depressive disorder with suicidal danger
- History of first-degree relative who responded to antidepressants
- History of manic episode in relative or patient

Adapted from Beck AT, Rush AJ, Shaw BF, Emery G: *Cognitive Therapy of Depression,* p 42. Guilford, New York, 1979.

Imagery. The effect of imagery on behavior was first discussed by Paul Schilder in his book, *The Image and Appearance of the Human Body.* Schilder described images as having physiological components: When people visualize themselves running, they subliminally activate the same muscles used in running and this reaction can be measured with electromyography. This phenomenon is used in sports training, in which athletes visualize every conceivable event in a performance and develop a muscle memory for each activity. A combination of behavioral and cognitive theories can help to master anxiety or to deal with feared situations.

Table 34.8–9
Major Features of Three Psychotherapeutic Approaches to Depression

Feature	Psychodynamic Approach	Cognitive Approach	Interpersonal Approach
Major theorists	Freud, Abraham, Jacobson, Kohut	Plato, Adler, Beck, Rush	Meyer, Sullivan, Klerman, Weissman
Concepts of pathology and causes	Ego regression: damaged self-esteem and unresolved conflict caused by childhood object loss and disappointment	Distorted thinking: dysphoria caused by learned negative views of self, others, and the world	Impaired interpersonal relationships: absent or unsatisfactory significant social bonds
Major goals and mechanisms of change	To promote personality change through understanding of past conflicts; to achieve insight into defenses, ego distortions, and superego defects; to provide a role model; to permit cathartic release of aggression	To provide symptomatic relief through alteration of target thoughts; to identify self-destructive cognitions; to modify specific erroneous assumptions; to promote self-control over thinking patterns	To provide symptomatic relief through solution of current interpersonal problems; to reduce stress involving family or work; to improve interpersonal communication skills
Primary techniques and practices	Expressive, empathic; fully or partially analyzing transference and resistance; confronting defenses; clarifying ego and superego distortions	Behavioral cognitive: recording and monitoring cognitions; correcting distorted themes with logic and experimental testing; providing alternative thought content; homework	Communicative, environmental: clarifying and managing maladaptive relationships and learning new ones through communication and social skills training; providing information on illness
Therapist role, therapeutic relationship	Interpreter, reflector: establishment and exploration of transference; therapeutic alliance for benign dependence and empathic understanding	Educator, shaper: positive relationship instead of transference; collaborative empiricism as basis for joint scientific (logical) task	Explorer, prescriber: positive relationship, transference without interpretation; active therapist role for influence and advocacy
Marital, family role	Full individual confidentiality; exclusion of significant others except in life-threatening situations	Use of spouse as objective reporter; couples therapy for disturbed cognitions sustained in marital relationship	Integral role of spouse in treatment: examination of spouse's role in patient's predisposition to depression and effect of illness on marriage

Reprinted with permission from Karasu TB: Psychotherapy for depression. Am J Psychiatry *147*: 141, 1990.

Thought stoppage can treat impulsive or obsessive behavior. For instance, patients imagine a stop sign with a police officer nearby or another image that evokes inhibition at the same time that they recognize an impulse or obsession that is alien to the ego. Similarly, obesity can be treated by having patients visualize themselves as thin, athletic, trim, and well muscled and then training them to evoke this image whenever they have an urge to eat. Hypnosis or autogenic training can enhance such imagery. In a technique called guided imagery, therapists encourage patients to have fantasies that can be interpreted as wish fulfillments or attempts to master disturbing affects or impulses.

EFFICACY

Cognitive therapy can be used alone in the treatment of mild to moderate depressive disorders or in conjunction with antidepressant medication for major depressive disorder. Studies have clearly shown that cognitive therapy is effective and in some cases is superior or equal to medication alone. It is one of the most useful psychotherapeutic interventions currently available for depressive disorders and shows promise in the treatment of other disorders.

Cognitive therapy has also been studied as a way of increasing compliance with lithium (Eskalith) in patients with bipolar I disorder and as an adjunct in treating withdrawal from heroin. Table 34.8–7 summarizes a number of negative cognitions that are common in producing noncompliance with medications. Table 34.8–8 outlines Beck's criteria for determining when cognitive therapy is and is not indicated. Table 34.8–9 summarizes and contrasts the major features of three of the most commonly used psychotherapeutic approaches to the treatment of depression, including the cognitive approach.

REFERENCES

Arntz A, van den Hout M: Psychological treatments of panic disorder without agoraphobia: Cognitive therapy versus applied relaxation. Behav Res Ther *34:* 113, 1996.

Barlow DH: Cognitive-behavioral approaches to panic disorder and social phobia. Bull Menninger Clin *56* (2, Suppl A): *14,* 1992.

Beck AT: *Cognitive Therapy and the Emotional Disorders.* International Universities Press, New York, 1976.

Beck AT, Rush AJ: Cognitive therapy. In *Comprehensive Textbook of Psychiatry,* ed 6, HI Kaplan, BJ Sadock, editors, p 1847. Williams & Wilkins, Baltimore, 1996.

Beck AT, Rush AJ, Shaw BF, Emery G: *Cognitive Therapy of Depression.* Guilford, New York, 1979.

Elliott CH, Adams RL, Hodge GK: Cognitive therapy: Possible strategies for optimizing outcome. Psychiatr Ann *22:* 459, 1992.

Epstein N, Baucom DH, Rankin LA: Treatment of marital conflict: A cognitive-behavioral approach. Clin Psychol Rev *13:* 45, 1993.

Garner DM, Rockert W, Davis R, Garner MV, et al: Comparison of cognitive-behavioral and supportive-expressive therapy for bulimia nervosa. Am J Psychiatry *150:* 37, 1993.

Hoffart A: Cognitive treatments of agoraphobia: A critical evaluation of theoretical basis and outcome evidence. J Anxiety Disord *7:* 75, 1993.
Juster HR, Heimberg RG, Holt CS: Social phobia: Diagnostic issues and review of cognitive behavioral treatment strategies. Prog Behav Modif *30:* 74, 1996.
Liberman RP, Green MF: Whither cognitive-behavioral therapy for schizophrenia? Schizophr Bull *18:* 27, 1992.
Pruitt D: Cognitive therapy: Efficacy of current applications. Psychiatr Ann *22:* 474, 1992.
Rush AJ: Cognitive therapy in combination with antidepressant medication. In *Combining Psychotherapy and Drug Therapy in Clinical Practice,* BD Beitman, GL Klerman, editors, p 121. Spectrum, New York, 1984.
Salkovskis PM, editor: *Frontiers of Cognitive Therapy.* Guilford, New York, 1996.
Scott J: Cognitive therapy of affective disorders: A review. J Affect Disord *37:* 1, 1996.
Thompson LW: Cognitive-behavioral therapy and treatment for late-life depression. J Clin Psychiatry *5:* 29, 1996.

▲ 34.9 Psychosocial Treatment and Rehabilitation

Psychosocial treatment and rehabilitation refer to the use of various methods to enable people who are severely mentally ill to develop social and vocational skills for independent living. Such treatment is carried out at many sites: hospitals, outpatient clinics, mental health centers, day hospitals, and home or social clubs.

SOCIAL SKILLS TRAINING

Social skills are interpersonal behaviors required for community survival, for independence, and for establishing, maintaining, and deepening supportive, socially rewarding relationships. Severe mental disorders such as schizophrenia disrupt one or more affective, cognitive, verbal, and behavioral domains of functioning and impair people's potential for enjoying and sustaining interpersonal relationships, which are the essence of social life. Clinicians have developed treatment packages termed *social skills training,* which have proved effective for patients with schizophrenia to remediate deficits in social behaviors (Table 34.9–1).

Table 34.9–1
Social Skills Training in Schizophrenia

Skills	Component Behaviors
Initiating positive comments	
Listening empathically	
Making positive requests for action	
Expressing negative feelings directly	
Coping with unexpected hostility and withdrawal	
Acknowledging pleasing events	Look at the other person Pleasant facial expression Warm tone of voice Say what the other person did or said and how that pleased you
Problem solving	Pinpoint the problem Share ownership of the problem Generate alternatives Weigh pros and cons of each alternative Choose a reasonable alternative Plan how to implement Review and reward progress and efforts

Courtesy of Robert Paul Liberman, M.D.

Methods

Role playing is the vehicle used to assess a patient's pretreatment social competence and to train targeted behavioral excesses or deficits during treatment. Training scenes are selected either on the basis of an individual's past difficulties or of problems that apply to most of the psychiatric population to which the patient belongs. Training sessions vary in length from 15 to 20 minutes, depending on the number of patients participating and on their levels of functioning. Although the group format provides vicarious learning opportunities through observation of other patients' behavior as well as through reinforcement by peers, the group experience is sometimes supplemented by individual training; such training allows more intensive focus on a single patient's behavior and provides an opportunity for more practice in sessions.

Results

In a treatment setting, positive results of social skills training include the following: Patients with schizophrenia can be trained to improve social skills in specific situations; moderate generalization of acquired skills to similar situations can be expected from training; most patients with schizophrenia can acquire or relearn social and conversational skills; and participants in training consistently report decreases in social anxiety after training. Learning, however, occurs tediously or little at all when patients are still floridly ill with positive symptoms and high levels of distractibility.

Some findings limit the applicability of social skills training. It is more difficult to teach complex conversational skills than to teach briefer, more discrete verbal and nonverbal responses in social situations. Because complex behaviors are more critical for generating social support in the community, methods have been developed to improve the learning and durability of conversational skills. These training methods focus on problem-solving, perceptual, and information-processing skills.

MILIEU THERAPY

The locus of milieu is a living, learning, or working environment. The defining characteristics of treatment are the use of a team to provide treatment and the time the patient spends in the environment. Recent adaptations of milieu therapy have included 24-hour-a-day programs that are situated in community locales frequented by patients and that provide in vivo support, case management, and training in living skills.

Most milieu therapy programs emphasize group and social interaction; rules and expectations are mediated by peer pressure for normalization of adaptation. When patients are viewed as responsible human beings, the patient role becomes blurred. Milieu therapy stresses a patient's rights to goals and to have freedom of movement and informal relationship with staff; it also emphasizes interdisciplinary participation and goal-oriented, clear communications.

PSYCHOSOCIAL REHABILITATION

Psychosocial rehabilitation emerged during the late 1940s when ex-patients began to meet together in so-called social clubs to satisfy their needs for acceptance and emotional support. Emphasizing self-help, mutual interdependence, and reliance on assets, the movement led to the establishment of Fountain House and hundreds of cloned offspring throughout the United States. Instead of thinking of themselves as patients, they became members and formed groups and teams to accomplish tasks, plan activities, and solve problems; and in so doing, the quality of their lives improved. Creating their own social support network, members of psychosocial clubs design activities that build experiences of mutual ownership and needs. Staff members, primarily nonprofessionals or those trained in vocational rehabilitation, provide positive, accepting reactions and require members to obtain psychiatric treatment, such as medication, elsewhere. Thus, the club has rehabilitation goals, not clinical goals. During the day, members of the club spend time engaging in activities such as chores, operating a snack bar, assisting each other in banking and budgeting, visiting friends who are hospitalized, printing a newspaper, helping each other with entitlements from social agencies, manning a thrift shop, working the switchboard, or refurbishing cooperative apartments.

Vocational Training

An important part of psychosocial rehabilitation is enabling people to work. Job placements are located in normal places of business, from large corporations to small businesses; they are at the entry level, and require minimal training or skills. These transitional jobs are opportunities to work temporarily en route to full-time employment elsewhere or to longer term employment in the entry level position.

Results

The number of transitional employment programs in the United States has grown to over 100, with over 500 employers involved in providing wages in excess of $4 million. An 18-month follow-up evaluation of people working in transitional jobs revealed that 16 percent were employed independently on a full-time basis, and an additional 45 percent continued part-time work in the transitional program or were attending school or other training programs. Only 2 percent were in psychiatric hospitals at the time of the 18-month follow-up.

COMBINING PSYCHOSOCIAL AND DRUG THERAPIES

In a disorder such as schizophrenia, where the biological diathesis runs deep, it is important to combine drug and psychosocial treatments for most patients. Evidence from many studies supports the conclusion that, when combined with rationally prescribed neuroleptic drugs, properly designed psychosocial treatments offer greater protection against relapse and higher levels of social adjustment than do drugs or psychosocial treatment alone. The overall consensus of these studies is that drugs have a primary effect on cognitive disorganization and positive symptoms of schizophrenia and have less impact on psychosocial functioning. The opposite seems to be the case with social and psychosocial therapies. In combination, their beneficial impact on the comprehensive needs of patients with schizophrenia is additive. A therapist, therefore, must be capable of providing both biological and psychosocial care to be professionally responsive to the needs of schizophrenic patients. If a therapist is not a psychiatrist, close collaboration with a psychiatrist is necessary so that medication may be appropriately managed.

REFERENCES

Baker F, Intagliata J: Case management. In *Handbook of Psychiatric Rehabilitation,* RP Liberman, editor, p 213. Macmillan, New York, 1992.

Beitchman PD: Psychosocial rehabilitation in residential programs for adults. Int J Ment Health *24:* 52, 1996.

Dobson DJ, McDougall G, Busheikin J, Aldous J: Effects of social skills training and social milieu treatment on symptoms of schizophrenia. Psychiatr Serv *46:* 376, 1995.

Dowdy A: Vocational rehabilitation and special education: Partners in transition for individuals with learning disabilities. J Learn Disabil *29:* 137, 1996.

Fisher DB: Health care reform based on an empowerment model of recovery of people with psychiatric disabilities. Hosp Community Psychiatry *45:* 913, 1994.

Green MF: Cognitive remediation in schizophrenia: Is it time yet? Am J Psychiatry *150:* 178, 1993.

Lehman AF: Schizophrenia: Psychosocial treatment. In *Comprehensive Textbook of Psychiatry.* ed 6, HI Kaplan, BJ Sadock, editors, p 998. Williams & Wilkins, Baltimore, 1995.

Reddon JR, Pope GA, Dorias S, Pullan MD: Improvement in psychosocial adjustment for psychiatric patients after a 16-week life skills education program. J Clin Psychol *52:* 169, 1996.

Starrfield JH, Avnon M, Starrfield W, Rabinowitz J, et al: Effects of psychosocial rehabilitation for hospitalized mentally ill homeless persons. Psychiatr Serv *46:* 948, 1995.

Weiden P, Havens L: Psychotherapeutic management techniques in the treatment of outpatients with schizophrenia. Hosp Community Psychiatry *45:* 549, 1994.

▲ 34.10 Combined Psychotherapy and Pharmacotherapy

Psychiatry is the medical speciality that integrates the biological and psychosocial perspectives in both diagnosis and treatment. To provide optimal clinical care, psychiatrists must avoid either biological or psychological reductionism. The best psychiatric treatment plan for a given patient often involves a combination of medication and psychotherapy. Among all medical specialists and mental health professionals, psychiatrists are uniquely positioned to administer both treatments.

The challenge of integrating psychosocial and biological understandings of patients is formidable. If psychiatry were reduced to the prescription of medication, other medical specialists could replace psychiatrists, and if psychiatry were confined to psychotherapeutic interventions, other mental health professionals could perform similar functions. The breadth of psychiatry as a specialty, however, requires psychiatrists to be knowledgeable about neurotransmitters, the latest psychopharmacologic agents, and the interface between genetics and environment. At the same time, psychiatry requires psychiatrists to be familiar with intrapsychic conflicts, patterns of relationships, and psychological meanings of symptoms. This interface between mind and brain makes psychiatry one of the most intellectually stimulating pursuits.

Psychotherapy and medication often work synergistically to provide the best possible treatment for patients. In the ensuing discussion, many ways in which psychotherapy and pharmacotherapy interact are discussed, with the full recognition that aspects of this interaction remain unknown.

PSYCHOTHERAPEUTIC MANAGEMENT

In conceptualizing how psychotherapeutic intervention and medication work together, two general strategies can be delineated. One is the psychotherapeutic management inherent in skilled pharmacotherapy practice. The other is the combination of formal psychotherapy and the prescription of medication.

In considering the former, a good starting point is the *American Psychiatric Association Practice Guidelines on Depression,* which points out that "psychotherapeutic management" is an essential component of every medication-based treatment plan. In fact, one way of understanding that good clinical management has psychotherapeutic effects is the recurrent finding that a placebo condition in a controlled trial is often an effective treatment for a significant number of patients. Simply by asking about symptoms and taking a history, clinicians often help patients to become aware of connections among external events, the meaning of these events, and symptoms that lead them to insight about their illness. In addition, the fact that a caring physician is listening and providing help may be a powerful corrective emotional experience for some patients. Another mechanism of action may involve the so-called transference cure, in which a patient gets better to please the physician.

Many psychodynamic principles derived from psychotherapy apply equally to pharmacotherapy practice. A *pharmacotherapeutic* alliance is essential to assure that a patient understands the reason for medication and complies with the treatment plan, just as a psychotherapeutic alliance is essential to enlist a patient as a collaborator in psychotherapy. Other dynamic principles, such as transference, resistance, and countertransference, are also integral parts of the pharmacotherapy practice. Many problems with noncompliance can be traced to these principles. The application of psychodynamic constructs to compliance problems in pharmacotherapy is often referred to as dynamic pharmacotherapy.

The phenomenon of transference is not limited to psychotherapy. Attributing qualities that stem from figures in patients' past to the prescribing physician occurs routinely in clinical practice. Patients may perceive a psychiatrist as authoritarian and refuse to cooperate with the prescribed treatment plan because it reminds them of a father barking orders and trying to control them. If the psychiatrist feels irritated at patients for not cooperating and becomes more insistent, the problem may worsen because the clinician is behaving in the authoritarian manner that the patient fears. In this case, the psychiatrist's countertransference has entered into the equation and has affected the patient's capacity to collaborate in a good alliance.

Resistance to taking medication can often relate to issues of transference and countertransference or to a fundamental ambivalence about getting better. In particular with cases of depression, some patients may feel that they have committed such sinful and evil acts that they deserve to be punished by remaining depressed. For such patients, an antidepressant medication may have a specific meaning, such as the potential to relieve suffering, and they may not fill their prescription or take the tablets as prescribed.

Medication may be imbued with a myriad of other meanings. To many patients, the idea of needing medication is represented in their own minds as a crutch. They may make no distinction between being addicted to a narcotic and taking a maintenance dose of antidepressant medication. Needing the medication may be interpreted by some patients as a sign of weakness, so they will often discontinue it on their own as soon as their symptoms start to lift. In still other cases, the medication has meaning connected with a family member.

Optimal psychotherapeutic management of a pharmacotherapy patient involves attention to these psychological dimensions of the relationship and to the medication itself. In addition, clinicians must empathize with patients' perceptions of medication and try to appreciate its meaning for each patient. Good listening skills, attention to rapport, and a systematic effort to establish a good alliance based on careful explanations are all integral parts of this approach to pharmacotherapy.

MEDICATION IN COMBINATION WITH FORMAL PSYCHOTHERAPY

In clinical practice today, there is a widespread acceptance of the combined use of medication and psychotherapy. Even among psychoanalysts, who were once the most vocal critics of combined treatment, prescribing is commonplace. In a survey of members of the American Academy of Psychoanalysts, 90 percent of respondents said they were prescribing medications. In a study of psychoanalytic candidates training cases at the Columbia University Center for Psychoanalytic Training and Research, medication was combined with psychoanalysis in 29 percent of cases. This fact indicates that medication is no longer seen as a contaminant that interferes with certification or graduation.

Many analysts and other therapists have noted that medication and psychotherapy work synergistically to improve outcomes in a wide variety of illnesses. Investigations of outcome geared to specific disorders consistently demonstrate advantages to combined approaches.

Specific Diagnostic Categories

Schizophrenia. An extensive series of studies has examined the rate of relapse when a specific form of psychoeducational family therapy is combined with antipsychotic medication. This intervention is based on the observation that high levels of expressed emotion (EE) in the families of patients with schizophrenia predicted a relapse following hospital discharge. High EE families have been characterized as excessively intrusive, critical, and overinvolved with the patient who suffers from schizophrenia. Psychoeducational family therapy is aimed at helping the family reduce the factors that constitute expressed emotion and at educating the family about the disease of schizophrenia and the need to continue antipsychotic medication indefinitely.

In a follow-up study by a team of investigators led by Gerald Hogarty, the impact of family therapy on relapse prevention was just as significant as the impact of antipsychotic medication. In other words, the relapse rate was cut in half by the addition of antipsychotic drugs, and was reduced by half again when family psychoeducational therapy was combined with drugs. The relapse rate was even further reduced at 1-year follow-up when social skills training was added to family therapy and medication. Recent research has suggested that group treatment involving families is also successful in reducing relapse rates and is even more cost effective than single-family therapy.

Major Depressive Disorder. A study of interpersonal therapy as well as medication included comparison groups of medication alone and the therapy alone. After 16 weeks, there was a clear advantage for combined treatments over either single modality. As predicted, the two approaches appeared to target different symptoms preferentially. Medication seemed most useful for vegetative symptoms, and psychotherapy had a greater impact on interest and mood. Medication also acted more rapidly than did psychotherapy.

Studies of cognitive therapy have also provided some modest evidence of advantages for combined treatment. The addition of cognitive therapy to antidepressants appears to be more effective in preventing relapse than medication alone. Studies combining behavior therapy with antidepressants have methodological problems, but the combined treatment does appear to work more rapidly than does behavior therapy alone. Combinations of psychodynamic therapy and antidepressants have not been tested in randomized, controlled trials.

Investigations that combined couples-family therapy with medication suggests that combined treatment produces improvement in the overall quality of marital and family relationships while medication produces rapid symptom change. Hence the combination enhances the breadth of the response; both sets of target symptoms are improved when the combination modalities are part of the treatment plan.

In studies where medication and psychotherapy were combined during the continuation and maintenance phases of recurrent unipolar depression, there was again a trend toward the superiority of combined treatment in that social functioning is maintained at improved levels with the addition of psychotherapy while medication suppresses relapse. The combination also has been shown to reduce the number of patient dropouts from studies during the maintenance phase.

In summary, psychotherapy and medication work on different target symptoms in patients with recurrent major depressive disorder and therefore combine to enhance the overall breadth of response. Medication works more rapidly than psychotherapy and may provide more reliable relief from acute distress while psychotherapeutic modalities enhance social functioning and appear to extend the relapse-free period.

Bipolar I Disorder. Much less controlled research has been conducted on combined treatments of bipolar I disorder, although there is a growing consensus that psychosocial interventions are essential in treating most patients. A German study looked at the relapse rates in 20 cases of bipolar disorder and in 10 cases of schizoaffective disorder before and after treatment with systemic family therapy in conjunction with medication. The average duration of treatment was 14.7 months with a range of 0 to 35 months, and the average number of sessions was 6.60 with a range of 1 to 19. The relapse rate was measured by the number of hospitalizations during the observation period. Following family therapy, there was a 77.6 percent reduction of relapse in the total sample (67.8 percent for patients with bipolar disorder and 89.8 percent for patients with schizoaffective disorder).

This statistically significant reduction in relapse rate was accompanied by a low rate of hospitalization. Before family therapy, only 1 of 30 cases required no hospitalization whatsoever. After family therapy, 14 of 30 cases required no hospitalization. Because only an average 6.6 sessions of family therapy was required, this intervention was also highly effective in reducing hospital costs.

Several characteristics were noted in the families with improved relapse rates. Most significantly, patients were no longer viewed by themselves or by their family members as victims of an illness beyond their control. Both family members and patients felt empowered and gained a sense of mastery over the illness.

Although this study did not utilize random assignment or control groups, the results nevertheless suggest that some family interventions that have proven so effective in preventing relapse in schizophrenia may also be useful in treating bipolar disorder. A study at Cornell University Medical Center, utilizing both random assignment and a control group, has lent further support to the value of combining family therapy and medication. In this study 60 patients with major affective disorder were randomly assigned to an inpatient family intervention and medication in the context of standard hospital treatment or to medication and standard hospital treatment without family intervention. Twelve patients who received the family therapy and nine in the control group were diagnosed as having bipolar affective disorder. At 18-month follow-up, significantly fewer patients from the family intervention group had been rehospitalized as compared with the group who did not receive family treatment. Similarly, on measures of global outcome and work or primary role functioning, patients who received the family intervention were doing significantly better than those who did not.

With the increasing awareness that lithium alone does not constitute effective prophylaxis for many patients with bipolar disorders, individual psychotherapy has been added to increase occupational and social functioning, encourage compliance with lithium or other mood stabilizers, and cut through the denial that is so common in bipolar patients. Many patients deny that their mania or hypomania is part of their illness and insist that it is simply part of who they are. Others manifest a form of psychic discontinuity in which the manic "self" is split from the euthymic "self," as though the two are in no way connected. Some clinicians use video or audiotapes of patients during a manic episode to help them integrate this aspect of themselves as part of the illness and overcome their denial. Bipolar disorder patients may also need assistance in mourning losses they have incurred through their erratic behavior during manic episodes.

At least one controlled study has demonstrated that the addition of cognitive therapy to lithium treatment improves compliance with the treatment and prevents relapse. Many patients have acknowledged that psychotherapy has been an important adjunct in their overall treatment.

Panic Disorder. Meta-analyses of the existing studies on the combination of behavior therapy and imipramine have consistently shown that greater improvement occurs when the treatments are combined than when either is used alone. The combined treatments show superior efficacy for reducing phobic anxiety, phobic avoidance, and functional impairment. The combined treatments are roughly equivalent to medication in terms of reducing the frequency of panic attacks.

The same advantage of combined treatments does not hold when a combination of benzodiazepines and behavior therapy is compared to either modality alone. Benzodiazepines may even impede the efficacy of behavior therapies.

A Scandinavian study compared clomipramine alone for patients with panic disorder with clomipramine and 15 weekly sessions of dynamic psychotherapy. All patients in both treatment groups were panic free within 26 weeks. On termination of clomipramine after 9 months, the relapse rate was significantly lower in the clomipramine-psychotherapy group. The investigators concluded that dynamic therapy reduces psychosocial vulnerability associated with panic disorder.

In selected cases, couples or family therapy may be necessary in combination with medication, behavior therapy, or both.

> A middle-aged woman was virtually housebound because of her anxiety about having a panic attack in the shopping mall. Her husband had adapted to her disorder to a large extent, and he frequently performed routine tasks like grocery shopping for her. When she was successfully treated with exposure plus imipramine, she described deterioration in her marital relationship. The treating psychiatrist asked her to bring her husband with her to the sessions. It soon became apparent that her husband was highly ambivalent about her improvement because he was convinced that she would be attracted to another man when she went out shopping and would have an extramarital affair. His jealous rage had led him to become extremely controlling of his wife at home, and she was wondering whether it would be better if she just returned to being housebound again.

This case vignette reflects how a couple can reach an equilibrium around an illness. Without attention to the marital issues that support and maintain a disorder, there is little likelihood that improvement will be lasting.

Obsessive-Compulsive Disorder. Treatment of obsessive-compulsive disorder usually takes one of two directions. Selective serotonin reuptake inhibitors (SSRIs) often make significant symptomatic improvements in patients. Clomipramine is also useful, but troublesome side effects make SSRIs the preferred agents. About three quarters of patients who comply with behavior therapy and who consciously apply the techniques show sustained improvement in symptoms.

Because the improvements effected by SSRIs are limited in terms of overall symptom reduction in patients who relapse rapidly when the agents are discontinued, there is a strong case to be made for combining behavior therapy and SSRIs. Some studies suggest both short-term and long-term improvements as well as more rapid response when both treatments are used. Behavior therapy, of course, also holds out the possibility of stopping the medication without relapsing.

Despite some suggestive data, however, the reports published so far are not entirely convincing about the advantages of combined medication and behavior therapy. Overall, combining treatments appear to improve the outcome as compared to medication alone but not necessarily for behavior therapy alone. Nevertheless, for behavior therapy to maintain robust results, there is a cost to the patient of time, energy, and money. Daily therapy sessions are usually conducted for several weeks. When the sessions are over, patients are expected to devote a good deal of their day to exposure work. Hence, it may not always be practical to provide behavior therapy at this intensity, and many patients may benefit with less intense exposure accompanied by the use of SSRIs.

Substance Dependence. Both psychotherapy and methadone have shown encouraging success with opiate-dependent patients. Data are also accumulating that the combination of the two approaches may achieve even better outcomes. In a randomized, controlled trial comparing treatments, opiate-dependent patients were assigned to one of three groups. One group had only methadone and virtually no psychotherapy. The second group had methadone along with meetings with a counselor that were oriented toward behavioral interventions. The third group had enhanced services involving the same dose of methadone and the same form of counseling, but patients also received additional resources, including a half-time employment counselor, a full-time psychiatrist, and a half-time family therapist.

Analysis of the results of this trial showed that the groups receiving psychotherapy had greater earning power, less welfare income, and strikingly lower hospital rates as compared to the group that did not receive psychotherapy. In addition, a beneficial impact on costs could be inferred because of the reduced rate of hospitalization when psychotherapy was added. The investigators also noted that the incremental value of enhanced services over simple counseling in the second group indicated that family therapy, the presence of a psychiatrist, and employment counseling were highly useful interventions.

Borderline Personality Disorder. Although both psychotherapy and pharmacotherapy have been shown to be effective in the treatment of symptoms associated with borderline personality disorder, the combination of the two approaches has not been systematically investigated. Nevertheless, an evolving clinical literature suggests that the optimal strategy with such patients is to combine psychotherapy and medication.

Psychopharmacologic intervention with borderline personality disorder is a new field of study with some preliminary data indicating that certain medications may serve as valuable adjuncts to psychotherapy. Because the symptoms of the disorder are varied, a target-symptom approach is generally recommended. Problems of cognitive dyscontrol, such as brief paranoid states, often respond well to low-dose neuroleptics. Problems related to impulsivity and behavioral dyscontrol may respond well to carbamazepine or perhaps lithium carbonate.

Many patients with borderline personality disorder are comorbid for major depressive disorder on Axis I. Tricyclic antidepressants have not been shown to be effective with these patients, but monamine oxidase inhibitors have shown some promise, particularly for patients with atypical depression involving so-called paradoxical symptoms, such as hyperphagia and hypersomnia. In addition, recent double-blind controlled studies are highly encouraging about the use of SSRIs. In one study, patients receiving fluoxetine (Prozac) showed improvement in a wide range of areas, including depression, anxiety, paranoia, psychoticism, interpersonal sensitivity, obsessionality, hostility, and global functioning when compared with the placebo group.

A second study using fluoxetine indicated that the intense anger of patients with borderline personality disorder appears to be positively affected by the medication. Hence, when SSRIs are used in conjunction with psychotherapy, patients may be able to reflect and think more clearly because the anger and other intense affects are toned down by the medication. This improvement in affective regulation may allow patients to collaborate with therapists more effectively.

One of the central features of borderline psychopathology is difficulty tolerating aloneness. During a therapist's vacations, some borderline patients begin to deteriorate: Because of a lack of object constancy, they develop anxieties that their therapist has disappeared and will never come back. Pills prescribed by the psychotherapist may serve as a transitional object that represents the therapist during his or her absence. Some patients will look at the pill or the name of the therapist on the label and experience a soothing effect from this substance for the therapist's actual presence.

Finally, the literature suggests that at least half of borderline patients misuse prescription drugs. Psychotherapy in combination with medication may be effective in uncovering the meanings of the medication misuse and in exploring the transference manifestations of these forms of acting-out behavior. Because suicidality is a frequent problem with these patients, a therapist's psychotherapeutic understanding may also help prevent overdoses with prescribed medication.

CLINICAL CONSIDERATIONS

In considering various combinations of pharmacotherapy and psychotherapy, two models are commonly used in clinical practice today. The one-person model involves a psychiatrist conducting the psychotherapy and prescribing medication for the same patient at the same time. The two-person model divides the functions so that the clinician conducting psychotherapy and the physician prescribing medication are separate individuals. There are, of course, practical considerations in deciding which model to use. If a psychotherapist does not feel competent in prescribing certain medications, a psychopharmacology consultant must be involved. Conversely, if a psychopharmacologist does not feel sufficiently skilled to provide the psychotherapy, the patient must be referred to a separate psychotherapist. A managed care company may stipulate for economic reasons that a psychotherapist can see the patient for only 15 minutes to prescribe while psychotherapy is carried out with a less expensive nonmedical therapist. Another common situation occurs when psychotherapy begins with a nonmedical therapist and the patient becomes depressed. A consultation by a psychopharmacologist is then requested. Assuming, however, for purpose of discussion that a psychiatrist is the primary treater and is competent at both treatment modalities, there are several factors that must be taken into account in deciding which approach to recommend.

One-Person Model

Just like a physicist who simultaneously thinks in terms of particles and waves, a psychiatrist must think about a dysfunctional brain and a distressed mind as part of a unified whole. In practice, this may require a flexible shifting back and forth between an empathic and introspective subjective approach on the one hand and an objective descriptive approach on the other. Although psychotherapy often encourages verbalization as opposed to action, prescription of medication requires clear action on the part of the clinician (and the patient). Moreover, direct questions designed to elicit information about symptoms and side effects must be asked in contrast to a more open-ended approach of allowing the patient to set the agenda in a dynamic therapy process.

In addition, whereas a dynamic therapist may eschew an authoritarian posture vis-à-vis a patient, this position may shift when discussing medication and citing the literature on such things as maintenance doses and prevention of relapse. Both patient and clinician alike may need to shift mental sets in the course of a session.

One strategy for managing these difficulties is to set aside a few minutes at the beginning or end of each session to review how the medication is affecting the symptoms and to write a prescription, if necessary. During the remainder of the session, the medication may be discussed from the standpoint of its meaning to the patient. Indeed, one of the advantages in this arrangement is that the prescribing and the psychotherapy do not get split from one another in a way that fragments treatment. All transferences and resistances are dealt with by one clinician. Compliance problems may be readily linked to specific transference paradigms because of the clinician's intimate knowledge of the patient's internal object relations.

Two-Person Model

Surveys have shown that approximately 65 percent of psychiatrists have provided medication for patients who are in psychotherapy with other clinicians. In some cases, of course, two clinicians must be involved because one is a nonmedical therapist. In other cases, however, psychiatrists who are conducting psychotherapy do not feel comfortable with the kind of bimodal thinking necessary to prescribe medication as well. They may prefer to keep the transference uncontaminated by feelings about the medication, and they may also not feel qualified to prescribe because they have not kept up with psychopharmacology data.

The two-person model may be effective for some patients, but it also runs the risk of serving as a nidus for splitting, particularly, although not exclusively, with borderline patients.

A 27-year-old woman with a diagnosis of borderline personality disorder had been seeing a psychotherapist once weekly for 1 year. She and her therapist had felt that they were at an impasse, and the therapist suggested that she might seek consultation with a local psychopharmacologist. She saw the psychopharmacologist for 30 minutes, and he diagnosed her disorder as major depression. He explained the illness to her and prescribed fluoxetine.

The patient felt an almost immediate positive response to the medication, and at her next psychotherapy appointment, she blasted her psychotherapist with a long tirade about her inadequacies: "You sit there for 1 year, just listening and trying to understand me. All this time I had a depression that needed drug treatment. Dr. A. (her psychopharmacologist) was so helpful. He took my complaints seriously, and for God's sake, he took some action! All you do is talk, talk, talk. Why didn't it occur to you sooner that something needed to be done?"

In this brief vignette, the psychopharmacologist becomes the idealized object who was responsive to the patient's needs, in contrast to the psychotherapist, who is seen as the bad object, almost sadistic in her perceived refusal to "do something." The individual prescribing the medication may contribute to the split by implying either directly or indirectly that the psychotherapist has been derelict in her duty by not sending the patient for medication sooner.

The cleavage may occur along opposite lines as well. Some borderline patients feel that the prescribing psychiatrist is eager to get rid of them because the appointment is scheduled for only 15 minutes. They may object to being "thrown out" of the doctor's office without the opportunity to talk more about what they are experiencing. In this case, the prescriber becomes the bad object, while the therapist is idealized because he or she takes the time to listen and to express great concern about the patient's internal experiences.

Splitting of this nature cannot be entirely prevented, but steps can be taken to minimize the potential destructiveness of such behavior. From the beginning, a patient should understand that the psychotherapist and the prescribing psychiatrist must be given permission to communicate about diagnosis and treatment. They should consider themselves as part of a treatment team rather than as isolated individuals. Often, discussing the patient's perceptions about the other clinician openly and honestly reduces a great deal of the tension created by such splits. In addition, the two clinicians should have an agreement about which one has responsibility for making decisions about hospitalization, vacation coverage, changes in medication, and the investigation of any potential medical problems.

Although the frequency and duration of communication between clinicians cannot be arbitrarily established, it must take place often enough so that each has a clear understanding of the other's treatment approach. Often a critical factor in the evolution of splitting is that the patient distorts to one clinician what the other is saying or doing. If the clinician hearing this report simply takes it at face value without calling and checking the veracity of the account with the other clinician, the situation may rapidly deteriorate. The clinician hearing the report may subsequently collude with the patient's feeling of being victimized by the other clinician. When communication finally occurs, the colluding clinician may confront the colleague in an accusatory tone that creates greater defensiveness. A tactful inquiry about whether the patient's account is accurate is generally much more productive.

COST EFFECTIVENESS

Many managed care companies insist that psychiatrists do not need to conduct psychotherapy because nonmedical therapists can do just as well at a cheaper price. Hence, they allow a psychiatrist to see a patient for a 15-minute medication check while referring the psychotherapy to someone whose time is much less expensive, often a counselor with a bachelor's degree, who is not well trained in psychotherapy. Although this approach seems to be cost effective, the treatment may become fragmented to the point where the patient's condition deteriorates and hospitalization is necessary. In this event, the hospital costs far outweigh the added expense of one clinician who serves both functions. Moreover, the division of labor between two clinicians requires extremely close collaboration. The time spent in communication between the two is often a hidden cost, not generally reimbursed, which must ultimately be factored into a comprehensive consideration of cost effectiveness. Meanwhile, data need to be collected on the two alternative arrangements to systematically study whether one is ultimately more cost effective than the other.

In the absence of definitive data, clinical experiences suggest that in many situations there are advantages when a psychiatrist performs both roles. Patients with severe psychotic disorders who are not compliant with prescribed medication, patients with bipolar affective disorder who deny illness, those with schizoaffective disorder, and patients with schizophrenia all may require one central clinician who works with them around the issue of medication as well as psychological and family issues to ensure adherence to the treatment plan. Patients with severe or unstable medical conditions may also require a combined approach in which a psychiatrist's medical knowledge is important in the overall management. Because of the potential for splitting, many patients with borderline personality disorder will also do better with one central clinician performing both roles. Finally, patients who are likely to require hospitalization because of severe suicidality and impulse control problems may be treated most beneficially by a psychiatrist attentive to both psychotherapeutic and pharmacotherapeutic issues.

In many discussions of the value of combined psychotherapy and pharmacotherapy, dissenters argue that the combination of the two treatments may be unduly expensive and without benefits commensurate with the additional cost. This perspective has left some to suggest innovative means of gaining benefit from both modalities. For example, for patients with agoraphobia, some have suggested that the prescription of imipramine with the provision of instructions for systematic self-directed exposure may be a cost-efficient way to derive benefits from both treatments. Similar efforts have been made to assist patients with obsessive-compulsive disorder with self-administered exposure in vivo practice.

Generalizations about the expense of combined treatments must be made with caution however. In a well-designed study of the delivery of treatment for depression in primary care settings, the Rand Corporation found that in the general practitioner's office, where the average appointment lasted 8 minutes, the diagnosis of depression was frequently missed. Also, when medication was prescribed, either benzodiazepines or suboptimal doses of antidepressants were frequently prescribed. When mental health professionals became involved with the patients, they frequently delivered a combination of psychotherapy and appropriate doses of antidepressant medication. The specialist treatment was somewhat more expensive to deliver, but the small increase in money quadrupled the effectiveness of the overall treatment in terms of vastly improved functional outcomes for the patients. The investigators pointed out that too often the emphasis is only on cost rather than on effectiveness and cost. The concept of cost effectiveness should not be synonymous with cheap but with high value.

In the treatment of some disorders, a beneficial economic impact has been clearly demonstrated. For example, the combination of antipsychotic medication and family therapy in the treatment of people with schizophrenia prevents relapse and the need for further inpatient care to the extent that the additional cost of the combined treatments is more than offset by the savings in fewer inpatient days. Similarly, in patients with bipolar and schizoaffective disorder, an average of six family therapy sessions significantly reduced the need for hospitalization and thus more than paid for itself. When cost effectiveness is considered from the standpoint of all costs, including the direct costs of treatment and the indirect costs of work disability and absenteeism, the combined use of pharmacotherapy and psychotherapy is often the most cost-efficient intervention available.

References

American Psychiatric Association: Practice guidelines for major depressive disorder in adults. Am J Psychiatry *150* (4, Suppl): 1993.

Beitman BD: Pharmacotherapy and the stages of psychotherapeutic change. In *American Psychiatric Press Review of Psychiatric,* vol 12, JM Oldham, MB Riba, A Tasman, editors, p 521. American Psychiatric Press, Washington, 1993.

Cowdry RW, Gardner DL: Pharmacotherapy of borderline personality disorder: Alprazolam, carbamazepine, trifluoperazine, and tranylcypromine. Arch Gen Psychiatry *45:* 111, 1988.

Elin I, Shea T, Watkins JT, Imber SD, Collins JF, Glass DR, Pilkonis PA, Leber WR, Docherty JP, Fiester SJ, Parloff MB: National Institute of Mental Health Treatment of Depression Collaborative Research Program: General effectiveness of treatments. Arch Gen Psychiatry *46:* 971, 1989.

Faloon IR, Boyd JL, McGill CW, Williamson M, Razani J, Moss HB, Gilderman AM, Simpson GM: Family management in the prevention of morbidity of schizophrenia: Clinical outcome of a two-year longitudinal study. Arch Gen Psychiatry *42:* 887, 1985.

Gabbard GO: Mind and brain in psychiatric treatment. Bull Menninger Clin *58:* 427, 1994.

Gabbard GO: *Psychodynamic Psychiatry in Clinical Practice: The DSM-IV Edition.* American Psychiatric Press, Washington, 1994.

Gabbard GO, Goodwin FK: Integrating biological and psychosocial perspectives. In *American Psychiatric Press Review of Psychiatry,* vol 15, LJ Dickstein, MB Riba, JM Oldham, editors, p 527. American Psychiatric Press, Washington, 1996.

Gabbard GO, Lazar SG, Hornberger J, Spiegel D: The economic impact of psychotherapy: A review. Am J Psychiatry *154:* 147, 1997.

Glick ID, Clarkin JF, Goldsmith SJ: Combining medications with family psychotherapy. In *American Psychiatric Press Review of Psychiatry,* vol 12, JM Oldham, MB Riba, A Tasman, editors, p 585. American Psychiatric Press, Washington, 1993.

Greist JH, Jefferson JW: Obsessive-compulsive disorder. In *Treatment of Psychiatric Disorders: The Second Edition,* vol 2, GO Gabbard, editor, p 1477. American Psychiatric Press, Washington, 1995.

Gutheil TG: The psychology of psychopharmacology. Bull Menninger Clin *46:* 231, 1982.

Gunderson J, Links P: Borderline personality disorder. In *Treatments of Psychiatric Disorders: The Second Edition,* vol 2, GO Gabbard, editor, p 2291. American Psychiatric Press, Washington, 1995.

Hogarty GE, Anderson CM, Reiss DJ, Kornblith SJ, Greenwald DP, Ulrich RF, Carter M: The Environmental-personal indicators in the Course of Schizophrenia (EPICS) Research Group: Family psychoeducation, social skills training, and maintenance chemotherapy in the aftercare treatment of schizophrenia: II. Two-year effects of a controlled study on relapse and adjustment. Arch Gen Psychiatry *48:* 340, 1991.

Hollon SD, Fawcett J: Combined medication and psychotherapy. In *Treatments of Psychiatric Disorders: The Second Edition,* vol 2, GO Gabbard, editor, p 1221. American Psychiatric Press, Washington, 1995.

Koenigsberg HW: Combining psychotherapy and pharmacotherapy in the treatment of borderline patients. In *American Psychiatric Press Review of Psychiatry,* vol 12, JM Oldham, MB Riba, A Tasman, editors, p 541. American Psychiatric Press, Washington, 1993.

Leff JP, Kuipers L, Berkowitz R, Sturgeon D: A controlled trial of social intervention in the families of schizophrenic patients: A two-year follow-up and issues in treatment. Br J Psychiatric *146:* 594, 1985.

Linehan MM, Armstrong HE, Suarez A, Allmon D, Heard HL: Cognitive-behavioral treatment of chronically parasuicidal borderline patients. Arch Gen Psychiatry *48:* 1060, 1991.

Links PS, Steiner M, Boiago I, Irwin D: Lithium therapy for borderline patients: Preliminary findings. J Pers Disord *4:* 173, 1990.

Mavissakalian MR: Combined behavioral and pharmacological treatment of anxiety disorders. In *American Psychiatric Press Review of Psychiatry,* vol 12, JM Oldham, MB Riba, A Tasman, editors, p 565. American Psychiatric Press, Washington, 1993.

McLellan AT, Arndt IO, Metzger DS, Woody GE, O'Brien CP: The effects of psychosocial services in substance abuse treatment. JAMA *269:* 1953, 1993.

Retzer A, Simon FG, Webber G, Stierlin H, Schmidt G: A follow-up study of manic-depressive and schizoaffective psychoses after systemic family therapy. Family Process *30:* 139, 1991.

Wiborg IM, Dahl AA: Does brief dynamic psychotherapy reduce the relapse rate of panic disorder? Family Process *30:* 139, 1991.

Woodward B, Duckworth KS, Gutheil TG: The pharmacotherapist–psychotherapist collaboration. In *American Psychiatric Press Review of Psychiatry,* vol 12, JM Oldham, MB Riba, A Tasman, editors, p 631. American Psychiatric Press, Washington, 1993.

35 Biological Therapies

▲ 35.1 GENERAL PRINCIPLES OF PSYCHOPHARMACOLOGY

Psychopharmacology is one of the most active areas of research and development in clinical medicine. The biological basis of behavior is coming ever more clearly into focus, in large part because of the use of pharmacological agents that modify behavior and mood. Clinical psychiatry continues to be revolutionized by both new drugs and new indications for existing drugs. Physicians must have a thorough underpinning in the uses of the wide spectrum of available agents. The art of astute clinical observation to arrive at the appropriate diagnosis, the formulation of a treatment plan based on physicians' knowledge and preferences, the sensitive and straightforward presentation of the risks and benefits of a particular therapy, and close monitoring of the outcome form the essential skills of a successful psychopharmacologist.

The biological therapies mainly employed in psychiatry are pharmacological agents, but electroconvulsive therapy (ECT) and many other nonpharmacological treatments are used in specialized settings. Psychiatric drugs are the first-line treatments for disorders, such as thought disorders, mania, or attention-deficit/hyperactivity disorder; in other disorders, such as depression or anxiety, drugs provide a valuable addition to psychologically based therapies. For many patients, psychiatric drugs offer a degree of stability that enables them to remain in relationships, to participate in the workplace, or to tolerate insight-oriented psychotherapy. Psychoactive drugs have also been widely applied in nonpsychiatric indications, such as pain control and management of obesity.

After several decades from 1960 to the late 1980s in which the psychiatric pharmacopoeia remained little changed, there has recently been a welcome expansion in the number of available drugs. Many of these new agents define novel mechanisms of action through which psychological states may be treated. Because of incomplete knowledge of the relation between the brain and behavior, the drug treatment of psychiatric disorders is empirical. As scientists begin to make inroads into the biological regulation of thought and mood, however, many drugs are being identified by their pharmacological profiles before being tested on patients. This strategy of drug development has greatly accelerated the introduction of novel chemical classes of drugs into clinical practice. With the growing availability of safer and more effective agents, the practice of psychopharmacology will increase among health care providers at all levels, although failure to recognize a treatable psychiatric condition and prejudices against mental illness continue to deprive many patients of potentially beneficial treatments.

Clinicians should not oversimplify the practice of pharmacotherapy in psychiatry—for example, by practicing a one diagnosis–one pill approach. Many variables impinge on the practice of psychopharmacology, including drug selection, prescription, administration, psychodynamic meaning to patients, and family and environmental influences. Some patients may view a drug as a panacea, and others may view it as an assault. Nursing staffs and relatives, as well as patients, must be instructed about the reasons for, expected benefits of, and potential risks of pharmacotherapy. In addition, clinicians often find it useful to explain the theoretical basis for pharmacotherapy to patients, their caretakers, and psychiatric staff members. Moreover, the theoretical biases of the treating psychiatrists are critical in the success of drug treatment: Psychiatrists prescribe pharmacotherapeutic drugs as a function of their theories and beliefs about such treatments.

Drugs must be used in effective dosages for sufficient times, as determined by previous clinical investigations and personal experience. Subtherapeutic dosages and incomplete trials should not be given to a patient because a psychiatrist is excessively concerned about the development of adverse effects. The prescription of drugs for mental disorders requires continuous clinical observation and must be made by qualified practitioners. Treatment response and the emergence of adverse effects must be monitored closely. Drug dosages must be adjusted accordingly, and appropriate treatments for emergent adverse effects must be instituted as quickly as possible.

HISTORY

Although the historical development of biological therapies in psychiatry extends from the mid-1800s to the present, by 1960 the psychiatric drug armamentarium included treatments for most major classes of psychiatric illness (Table 35.1–1). Organic therapies such as ECT (pioneered by Ugo Cerletti and Lucio Bini), insulin coma therapy (developed by Manfred Sakel), and psychosurgery (introduced by Antonio Egas Moniz) all began in the first half of the 20th century and heralded the biological revolution in psychiatry. In 1917 Julius Wagner-Jauregg introduced malaria toxin to treat syphilis; he is the only psychiatrist to have won a Nobel prize.

In the second half of the 20th century, chemotherapy as a

Table 35.1–1
Some Historical Events in Psychopharmacology, 1845–1960

1845—Hashish intoxication proposed as a model of insanity (Moreau)
1869—Chloral hydrate introduced as a treatment for melancholia and mania
1875—Cocaine proposed as a treatment in psychiatry (Freud)
1882—Paraldehyde introduced
1892—Research with morphine, alcohol, ether, and paraldehyde in normal persons (Kraeplin)
1903—Barbiturates introduced
1917—Psychosis of syphilis treated with malaria fever therapy (Julius Wagner-Jauregg)
1922—Barbiturate-induced coma (Jaboe Klaesi)
1927—Insulin shock for schizophrenia (Manfred Sakel)
1931—*Rauwolfia serpentina* (reserpine) introduced (Sen and Bose) (confirmed as a treatment for schizophrenia in 1953 by Nathan Kline)
1934—Pentylenetetrazol-induced convulsions (Ladislas von Meduna)
1936—Frontal lobotomies (Egas Moniz)
1938—Electroconvulsive therapy (Ugo Cerletti and Lucio Bini)
1940—Phenytoin introduced as anticonvulsant (Tracy Putnam)
1943—Lysergic acid diethylamide (LSD) synthesized (Albert Hofmann)
1949—Lithium introduced
1952—Chlorpromazine introduced
1955–1958—Tricyclic drugs and monoamine oxidase inhibitors introduced
1960—Chlordiazepoxide introduced

treatment for mental disorders became a major field of research and practice. Almost immediately after the introduction of chlorpromazine (Thorazine) in the early 1950s, psychotherapeutic drugs became a mainstay of psychiatric treatment, particularly for seriously mentally ill patients.

In 1949 the Australian psychiatrist John Cade had described the treatment of manic excitement with lithium (Eskalith). While conducting animal experiments, Cade noted that lithium carbonate made animals lethargic. He was thus prompted to administer the drug to several agitated psychiatric patients, who received therapeutic benefits from it.

In 1950 Charpentier synthesized chlorpromazine (an aliphatic phenothiazine antipsychotic) in an attempt to develop a histaminergic drug that would serve as an adjuvant to anesthetics. Laborit reported the drug's ability to induce an artificial hibernation. Reports by Paraire and Sigwald, John Delay and Pierre Deniker, and Heinz Lehmann and Hanrahan described the effectiveness of chlorpromazine in treating severe agitation and psychosis. The drug was quickly introduced into psychiatry in the United States, and many similarly effective drugs have since been synthesized, including haloperidol (Haldol) (a butyrophenone antipsychotic) in 1958 by Paul Janssen.

Imipramine (Tofranil), a tricyclic drug, is structurally related to the phenothiazine antipsychotics. While carrying out clinical research on chlorpromazine-like drugs, Thomas Kuhn found that, although imipramine was not effective in reducing agitation, it did seem to reduce depression in some patients. The introduction of monoamine oxidase inhibitors (MAOIs) to treat depression evolved from the observation that the antituberculosis agent iproniazid had mood-elevating effects in some patients. In 1958 Nathan Kline was one of the first investigators to report the efficacy of MAOI treatment in depressed psychiatric patients.

By 1960, with the introduction of chlordiazepoxide (Librium), a benzodiazepine antianxiety agent synthesized by Richard Sternbach at Roche Laboratories in the late 1950s, the psychiatric armamentarium of drugs included antipsychotics (for example, chlorpromazine), tricyclic drugs for depression (for example, imipramine), MAOIs for depression (for example, tranylcypromine [Parnate]), lithium for the treatment of mania, and the benzodiazepines as well as the barbiturates for the treatment of anxiety and insomnia. The next 30 years were devoted primarily to clinical studies demonstrating the efficacy of these drugs and to the development of related drugs in each category. The efficacy of each class of drugs for treating relatively specific psychiatric syndromes and the elucidation of their pharmacodynamic effects provided the impetus to develop the various neurotransmitter hypotheses of mental disorders (for example, the dopamine hypothesis of schizophrenia and the biogenic amine hypothesis of mood disorders).

Since 1960 the major additions to the psychotherapeutic drugs have been the anticonvulsants, particularly carbamazepine (Tegretol) and valproate (Depakote), which are effective in the treatment of bipolar I disorder. Buspirone (BuSpar), a nonbenzodiazepine anxiolytic, was introduced for clinical use in the United States in 1986. Several serotonin-specific reuptake inhibitors (SSRIs)—for example, fluoxetine (Prozac)—have become the most widely used agents in the United States for treating depression, and, together with the serotonin-specific tricyclic drug clomipramine (Anafranil), for treating obsessive-compulsive disorder. A new class of antipsychotic agents, the serotonin-dopamine antagonists—for example, clozapine (Clozaril) and risperidone (Risperdal)—is effective against both positive and negative symptoms of schizophrenia while causing few if any neurological adverse effects. Two new drugs for the treatment of cognitive decline in dementia of the Alzheimer's type have become available, tacrine (Cognex) and donepezil (Aricept), and more such agents appear to be nearing approval. Four new chemical classes of antidepressants, venlafaxine (Effexor), nefazodone (Serzone), bupropion (Wellbutrin), and mirtazapine (Remeron), which variously affect serotonergic and noradrenergic neurotransmission, have some therapeutic advantages over currently available drugs. The pure opioid antagonist naltrexone (ReVia) has been approved for the treatment of opiate and alcohol addiction. A reversible class of MAOIs, the reversible inhibitors of monoamine oxidase type A (RIMAs)—for example, moclobemide (Aurorix)—may rekindle interest in this mechanism of action as a treatment for depression. Dozens of other agents under development or currently available in other countries may become available in the United States in the next several years.

PHARMACOLOGICAL ACTIONS

Pharmacokinetic interactions concern how the body handles a drug; pharmacodynamic interactions concern the effects of the drug on the body. In a parallel fashion, pharmacokinetic drug interactions concern the effects of drugs on the plasma concentrations of each other, and pharmacodynamic drug interactions concern the effects of drugs on the receptor activities of each other.

Pharmacokinetics

Absorption. A psychotherapeutic drug must first reach the blood on its way to the brain, unless it is directly administered into the cerebrospinal fluid or the brain. Orally administered drugs must dissolve in the fluid of the gastrointestinal (GI) tract before the body can absorb them. Drug tablets can be designed to disintegrate quickly or slowly; the absorption depends on the drug's concentration and lipid solubility and the GI tract's local pH, motility, and surface area. Depending on the drug's pK_a and the GI tract's pH, the drug may be present in an ionized form that limits its lipid solubility. Omeprazole (Prilosec), histamine type 2 (H_2) receptor blockers such as cimetidine (Tagamet) or ranitidine (Zantac), or antacids may reduce stomach acidity and interfere with drug solubility. Gastric and intestinal motility may be slowed by anticholinergic drugs or may be increased by dopamine receptor antagonists, such as metoclopramide (Reglan), which may influence the rate of drug absorption. An extremely rapid rate of absorption may lead to toxic peak concentrations, whereas slow absorption may delay the onset of therapeutic effects. If the pharmacokinetic absorption factors are favorable, the drug may reach therapeutic blood concentrations quickly when it is administered intramuscularly. If a drug is coupled with an appropriate carrier molecule, intramuscular administration can sustain the drug's release over a long period. Some antipsychotic drugs are available in depot forms that allow the drug to be administered only once every 1 to 4 weeks. Although intravenous administration is the quickest route to achieve therapeutic blood concentrations, it also carries the highest risk of sudden life-threatening adverse effects.

Distribution. Drugs can be freely dissolved in the blood plasma, bound to dissolved plasma proteins (primarily albumin), or dissolved in the blood cells. If a drug is bound too tightly to plasma proteins, it may have to be metabolized before it can leave the bloodstream; thus, the amount of active drug reaching the brain is greatly reduced. The lithium ion is an example of a water-soluble drug that is not bound to plasma proteins. The distribution of a drug to the brain is determined by the blood–brain barrier, the brain's regional blood flow, and the drug's affinity with its receptors in the brain. Both high blood flow and high affinity favor the distribution of the drug to the brain. Drugs may also reach the brain after passively diffusing into the cerebrospinal fluid from the bloodstream. Most psychotherapeutic drugs are highly lipophilic, which enables them to cross the blood–brain barrier readily. The volume of distribution is a measure of the body's apparent space available to contain the drug. The volume distribution can also vary with a patient's age, sex, and disease state. The net efficiency of absorption from the site of administration to the neuronal site of action determines the *bioavailability.* The Food and Drug Administration (FDA) requires the bioavailability of generic formulations of a drug to deviate from the bioavailability of the brand name formulation by no more than 30 percent. This may mean, however, that two separate generic formulations may vary in bioavailability by as much as 60 percent.

Metabolism and Excretion. Metabolism is synonymous with the term *biotransformation.* The four major metabolic routes for drugs are oxidation, reduction, hydrolysis, and conjugation. In general, the lipophilic drugs are transformed into more polar, hydrophilic compounds, which may be more readily excreted in urine or feces. Although the usual result of metabolism is to produce inactive metabolites that are more readily excreted than are the parent compounds, many examples of active metabolites are produced from psychoactive drugs. The liver is the principal site of metabolism, and bile, feces, and urine are the major routes of excretion. Psychoactive drugs are also excreted in sweat, saliva, tears, and breast milk; therefore, mothers who are taking psychotherapeutic drugs should not breast-feed their children. Disease states and coadministered drugs can both raise and lower the blood concentrations of a psychoactive drug.

Four concepts relevant to metabolism and excretion are time of peak plasma concentration, half-life, first-pass effect, and clearance. The time between the administration of a drug and the appearance of peak concentrations of the drug in the plasma varies primarily according to the route of administration and absorption. A drug's half-life is defined as the amount of time it takes for half of the drug's peak plasma level to be metabolized and excreted from the body. A general guideline is that, if a drug is administered repeatedly in doses separated by time intervals shorter than its half-life, the drug reaches 97 percent of its steady-state plasma concentrations in a time equal to 5 times its half-life. The first-pass effects concern the extensive initial metabolism of some drugs within the portal circulation of the liver, a reaction that thereby reduces the amount of unmetabolized drug reaching the systemic circulation. Clearance is a measure of the amount of the drug excreted in each unit of time. If a disease process or other drug interferes with the clearance of a psychoactive drug, the drug accumulates in a patient and may reach toxic plasma concentrations.

For a chemical to act as a drug it must be metabolized by the body. Most psychotherapeutic drugs are oxidized by the hepatic cytochrome P450 (CYP) enzyme system. This family of enzymes, named for its ability to absorb light at the wavelength of 450 nm, is phylogenetically very old and arose at the time of evolutionary divergence of plants and animals. The xenobiotic system, which oxidizes and inactivates foreign compounds such as toxins and carcinogens, evolved from an even older system, the steroidogenic enzymes, which synthesize components of the cellular membranes. The xenobiotic enzymes are responsible for the inactivation of plant toxins, and these are the enzymes that metabolize most psychiatric drugs, many of which were originally isolated from plants. Although these enzymes are distributed widely throughout the body, they act primarily in the endoplasmic reticulum of the hepatocytes and the cells of the intestine. In the past 10 years, a large family of human CYP enzymes has been molecularly cloned, and the gene sequences are known. This knowledge

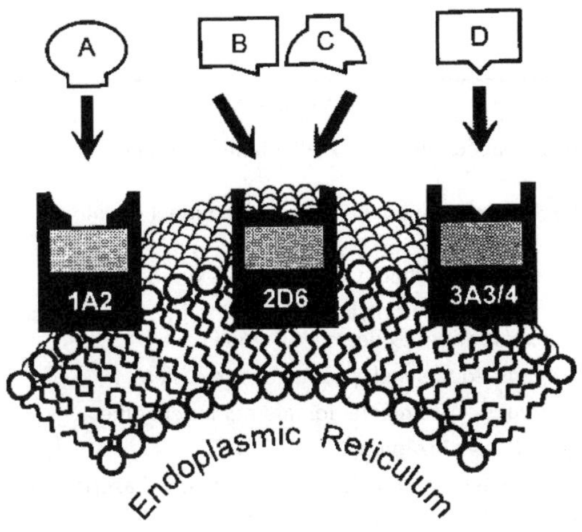
A
B
C
D
1A2
2D6
3A3/4
Endoplasmic Reticulum

FIGURE 35.1–1
Drug metabolism by cytochrome P450 (CYP) enzymes. Drugs *A* and *C* contain the chemical moiety recognized by CYP 1A2, drugs *B* and *C* contain the moiety metabolized by CYP 2D6, and drug *D* contains the moiety metabolized by CYP 3A3/4. The order in which the drugs interact with the CYP enzymes is determined by the binding affinities: High-affinity reactions occur first, but if these are blocked by drug–drug interactions, then drug concentrations build to the point at which lower affinity reactions occur. (Reprinted with permission from Preskorn SH: *Clinical Pharmacology of Selective Serotonin Reuptake Inhibitors,* p 136. Professional Communications, Caddo, OK, 1996.)

has permitted the categorization of the CYP enzymes into families and subfamilies. Members of separate families share at least 40 percent identity of the primary amino acid sequence, whereas members of a specific family share at least 55 percent amino acid identity. At least 27 families are recognized, but clinically relevant drug metabolic interactions have been attributed to members of only three families. A nomenclature has been established, in which the family is denoted by a numeral, the subfamily by a capital letter, and the individual member of the subfamily by a second number (for example, 2D6 or, with a roman numeral, IID6.)

The CYP gene expression may be induced by alcohol, by certain drugs (barbiturates, anticonvulsants), or by smoking, which has the effect of increasing the metabolism of certain drugs and procarcinogens. Other agents may directly inhibit the enzymes and slow the metabolism of other drugs. In some cases, if one CYP enzyme is inhibited, then, once the precursor accumulates to a sufficiently high level in the cell, another CYP enzyme may begin to act (Fig. 35.1–1). Cellular pathophysiology, such as that caused by viral hepatitis or cirrhosis, may also affect the efficiency of the CYP system. With the gene sequence data available, several polymorphisms in the CYP genes are now recognized, some of which are manifested in a decreased rate of metabolism. Patients with an inefficient version of a specific CYP enzyme are considered poor metabolizers. Although the blossoming of knowledge about the CYP system has provided a clearer understanding of the metabolism of psychotropic drugs and has provided investigators with an additional in vitro screen for potential new drugs, there are relatively few important examples of CYP interactions with clinical relevance.

With respect to CYP 2D6, for which 7 percent of whites are poor metabolizers, tricyclic antidepressants, antipsychotics, and type 1C antiarrhythmics should be used cautiously or avoided together with SSRIs. Because of inhibition of the CYP 3A4 enzyme, fluvoxamine (Luvox), nefazodone, and fluoxetine should not be used with terfenadine (Seldane), astemizole (Hismanal), alprazolam (Xanax), triazolam (Halcion), or carbamazepine (Tegretol). Because of interactions with CYP 1A2, fluvoxamine should not be used with theophylline (Slo-Bid, Theo-Dur) or clozapine. Inhibition of CYP 2C9/10 and CYP 2C19 warrants caution for the following combinations: fluoxetine plus phenytoin (Dilantin), sertraline (Zoloft) plus tolbutamide (Orinase), and fluvoxamine plus warfarin (Coumadin). It is also important to consider the long half-lives of certain psychiatric drugs, especially fluoxetine, which may prolong their inhibition of the CYP enzymes (Table 35.1–2).

Pharmacodynamics

The major pharmacodynamic considerations include receptor mechanisms; the dose–response curve; the therapeutic index; and the development of tolerance, dependence, and withdrawal phenomena. The receptor for a drug can be generally defined as the cellular component that binds to the drug and initiates the drug's pharmacodynamic effects. A drug can be an agonist for its receptor and can thereby stimulate a physiological effect. Agonists are recognized either as full agonists, which cause maximal stimulation of the receptor, or as partial agonists, which are only partially capable of activating the receptor even at concentrations that saturate the binding site. Conversely, a drug can be an antagonist for the receptor, most often by blocking the receptor so that an endogenous agonist

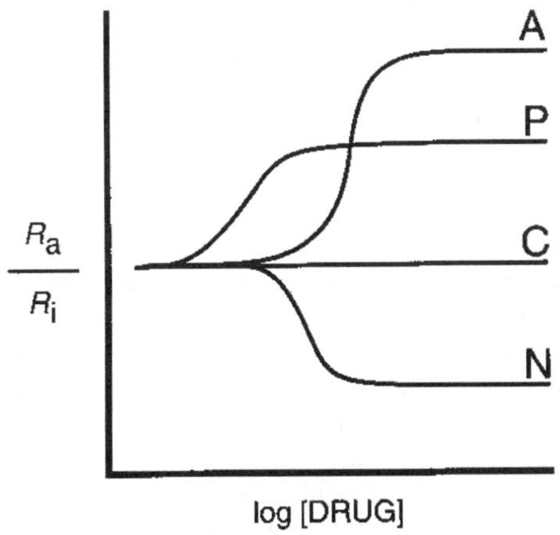
A
P
C
N
R_a / R_i
log [DRUG]

FIGURE 35.1–2
A working model for receptor-mediated response. Effects of drugs on the relative concentrations of two hypothetical forms of a receptor, R_a (active) and R_i (inactive), which are in equilibrium, $R_a \rightleftharpoons R_i$. The relative distribution of the receptor between these two forms is differentially influenced by agonists *(A),* partial agonists *(P),* competitive antagonists *(C),* and negative antagonists *(N),* also known as inverse agonists. (Reprinted with permission from Ross EM: Pharmacodynamics. In *Goodman & Gilman's The Pharmacological Basis of Therapeutics,* ed 9, JG Hardman, LE Limbird, PB Molinoff, RW Ruddon, editors, p 40. McGraw-Hill, New York, 1996.)

Table 35.1–2
Drugs Metabolized by CYP Enzymes[a,b]

CYP 1A2

Antidepressants—amitriptyline, clomipramine, imipramine
Antipsychotics—clozapine
β-Blockers—propranolol
Miscellaneous—caffeine, paracetamol, theophylline, *R*-warfarin

CYP 2C9/10

Phenytoin, *S*-warfarin, tolbutamide

CYP 2C19

Antidepressants—citalopram, clomipramine, imipramine
Barbiturates—hexobarbital, mephobarbital, *S*-mephenytoin
β-Blockers—propranolol

CYP 2D6

Antiarrhythmics—encainide, flecainide, mexiletine, propafenone
Antipsychotics—haloperidol, perphenazine, risperidone, thioridazine
β-Blockers—alprenolol, bufarolol, metoprolol, propranolol, timolol
Miscellaneous—debrisoquin, 4-hydroamphetamine, perhexiline, phenformin, sparteine
Opiates—codeine, dextromethorphan, ethylmorphine
SSRIs—fluoxetine, *N*-desmethylcitalopram, paroxetine
TCAs—amitriptyline, clomipramine, desipramine, imipramine, *N*-desmethylclomipramine, clomipramine, nortriptyline, trimipramine
Other antidepressants—venlafaxine, the mCPP metabolite of nefazodone and trazodone

CYP 3A3/4

Analgesics—acetaminophen, alfentanil, codeine, dextromethorphan
Antiarrhythmics—amiodarone, disopyramide, lidocaine, propafenone, quinidine
Anticonvulsants—carbamazepine, ethosuximide
Antidepressants—amitriptyline, clomipramine, imipramine, nefazodone, sertraline, *O*-desmethylvenlafaxine
Antiestrogens—docetaxel, paclitaxel, tamoxifen
Antihistamines—astemizole, loratadine, terfenadine
Antipsychotics—clozapine
Benzodiazepines—alprazolam, clonazepam, diazepam, midazolam, triazolam
Calcium channel blockers—diltiazem, felodipine, nicardipine, nifedipine, niludipine, minodipine, nisoldipine, nitrendipine, verapamil
Immunosuppressants—cyclosporine, tacrolimus (FK506—macrolide)
Local anesthetics—cocaine, lidocaine
Macrolide antibiotics—clarithromycin, erythromycin, triacetyloleandomycin
Steroids—androstendione, cortisol, dihydroepiandrosterone 3-sulfate, dexamethasone, estradiol, ethinylestradiol, progesterone, testosterone
Miscellaneous—benzphetamine, cisapride, dapsone, lovastatin, omeprazole (sulfonation)

Reprinted with permission from Preskorn SH: *Clinical Pharmacology of Selective Serotonin Reuptake Inhibitors.* Professional Communications, Caddo, OK, 1996.
[a] Major pathway for elimination of tricyclic antidepressants is ring hydroxylation; *N*-desmethylation, a minor pathway, is mediated by several CYP enzymes.
[b] Tables such as this are limited by current knowledge. The CYP enzymes responsible for biotransformation have been determined for only approximately 20% of marketed drugs. Many drugs were developed before the necessary knowledge and technology existed. Hence these lists are first attempts but will become more comprehensive as more data accumulate. Also note that some drugs are listed under more than one CYP enzyme, since different enzymes mediate either the same or different metabolic pathways. That does not necessarily mean that each of these enzymes contributes equally to the elimination of the drug. One enzyme may be principally responsible based on the substrate affinity and the capacity and abundance of the enzyme.

cannot affect the receptor. Two types of receptor antagonists are recognized. Competitive antagonists displace other ligands from the receptor but do not influence the receptor's cellular actions, Negative antagonists, also called inverse agonists, not only block the binding of agonist ligands but also reduce receptor activation (Fig. 35.1–2). The receptor site for most psychotherapeutic drugs is also a receptor site for an endogenous neurotransmitter. For example, the primary receptor site for chlorpromazine is the dopamine type 2 receptor. For some psychotherapeutic drugs, this may not be the case. The receptor for lithium may be the enzyme inositol-1-phosphatase, and the receptor for verapamil (Calan) is a calcium channel. Figure 35.1–3 illustrates 12 steps in the process of synaptic transmission, and Figure 35.1–4 shows 8 sites at which drugs have been shown to act.

The dose–response curve plots the drug concentration against the effects of the drug (Fig. 35.1–5). The potency of a drug is the relative dose required to achieve a certain effect. Haloperidol, for example, is more potent than is chlorpromazine because approximately 5 mg of haloperidol is required to achieve the same therapeutic effect as 100 mg of chlorpromazine. Haloperidol and chlorpromazine, however, are equal in their clinical efficacy—the maximum clinical response achievable by the administration of a drug.

The adverse effects of most drugs are often direct results of their primary pharmacodynamic effects. The therapeutic index, a relative measure of a drug's toxicity or safety, is defined as the ratio of the median toxic dose (TD_{50}) to the median effective dose (ED_{50}). The TD_{50} is the dose at which 50 percent of patients experience toxic effects, and the ED_{50} is the dose at which 50 percent of patients experience therapeutic effects. Haloperidol, for example, has a high therapeutic index, as evidenced by the wide range of dosages in which it is prescribed. Conversely, lithium has a low therapeutic index, and this necessitates the monitoring of serum lithium concentrations. Both interindividual and intraindividual variation can appear in the response to a specific drug. An individual patient may be hyporeactive, normally reactive, or hyper-reactive to a

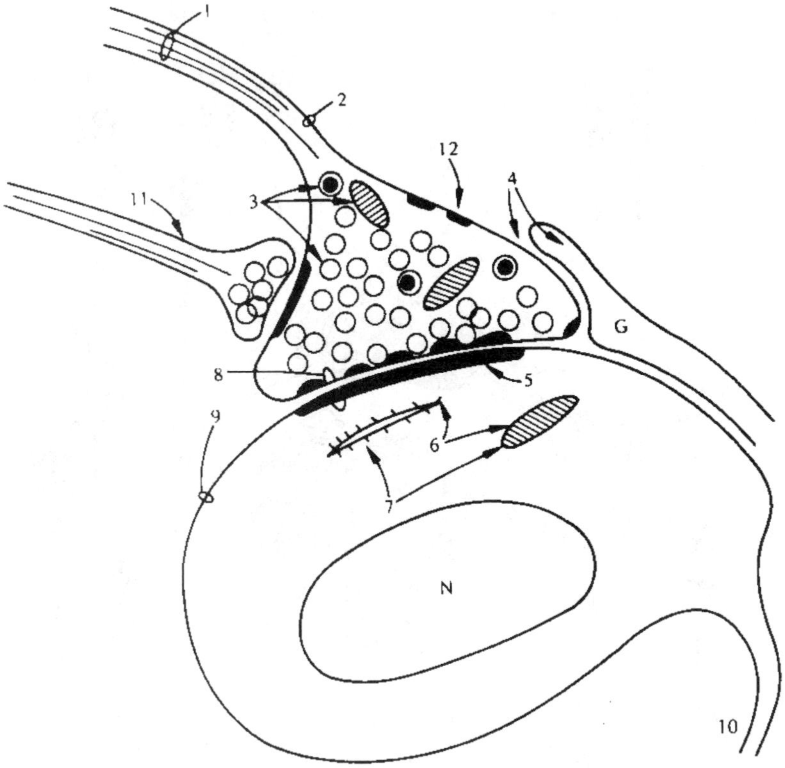
1
2
12
4
11
3
G
8
5
9
6
7
N
10

FIGURE 35.1–3

Twelve steps in the synaptic transmission process are indicated in this idealized synaptic connection. *Step 1* is transport down the axon. *Step 2* is the electrically excitable membrane of the axon. *Step 3* involves the organelles and enzymes present in the nerve terminal for synthesizing, storing, and releasing the transmitter, as well as for the process of active reuptake. *Step 4* includes the enzymes present in the extracellular space and within the glia *(G)* for catabolizing excess transmitter released from nerve terminals. *Step 5* is the postsynaptic receptor that triggers the response of the postsynaptic cell to the transmitter. *Step 6* shows the organelles within the postsynaptic cells, which respond to the receptor trigger. *Step 7* is the interaction between genetic expression of the postsynaptic nerve cell and its influences on the cytoplasmic organelles that respond to transmitter action. *Step 8* includes the possible "plastic" steps modifiable by events at the specialized synaptic contact zone. *Step 9* includes the electrical portion of the nerve cell membrane that, in response to the various transmitters, is able to integrate the postsynaptic potentials and produce an action potential. *Step 10* is the continuation of the information transmission by which the postsynaptic cell sends an action potential down its axon. *Step 11,* release of transmitter, is subjected to modification by a presynaptic (axoaxonic) synapse; in some cases an analogous control can be achieved between dendritic elements. *Step 12,* release of the transmitter from a nerve terminal or secreting dendritic site, may be further subject to modulation through autoreceptors that respond to the transmitter that the same secreting structure has released. Glia *(G)* can accumulate *(4)* released transmitters. (Reprinted with permission from Cooper JR, Bloom FE, Roth RH: *The Biochemical Basis of Neuropharmacology,* ed 7, p 46. Oxford University Press, New York, 1996.)

particular drug. For example, some patients require 50 mg a day of sertraline, whereas other patients require 200 mg a day. Idiosyncratic drug responses occur when a patient experiences a particularly unusual effect from a drug. For example, some patients become agitated when given benzodiazepines, such as diazepam (Valium).

Pharmacodynamic drug–drug interactions may lead to toxic adverse effects, if two or more drugs cause additive biochemical changes. For example, MAOIs, when coadministered with either tricyclic antidepressants or SSRIs, may precipitate a serotonin syndrome in which serotonin is produced normally but only very slowly metabolized and thus accumulates in excessive concentrations. The interaction of disulfiram (Antabuse) and alcohol is another example of toxicity caused by inhibition of a degradative pathway.

A patient may become less responsive to a particular drug as it is administered over time, a reaction referred to as tolerance. The development of tolerance can be associated with the appearance of physical dependence, which may be defined as psychological craving for the drug and the necessity to continue administering the drug to prevent the appearance of withdrawal symptoms.

A number of drugs that do not elicit dependence, nevertheless, may be associated in a minority of patients with the emergence of symptoms upon discontinuation or reduction of dosage. The first such discontinuation reaction was described in 1959 with imipramine, but this phenomenon has gained new significance with the serotonergic agents, venlafaxine and the SSRIs. Because the serotonergic agents are generally free of major adverse effects at therapeutic doses, the emergence of symptoms upon discontinuation may be quite noticeable. There is a spectrum of severity of the serotonin discontinuation syndrome, which consists of agitation, nausea, dysequilibrium, and dysphoria. The syndrome is more likely to occur if the

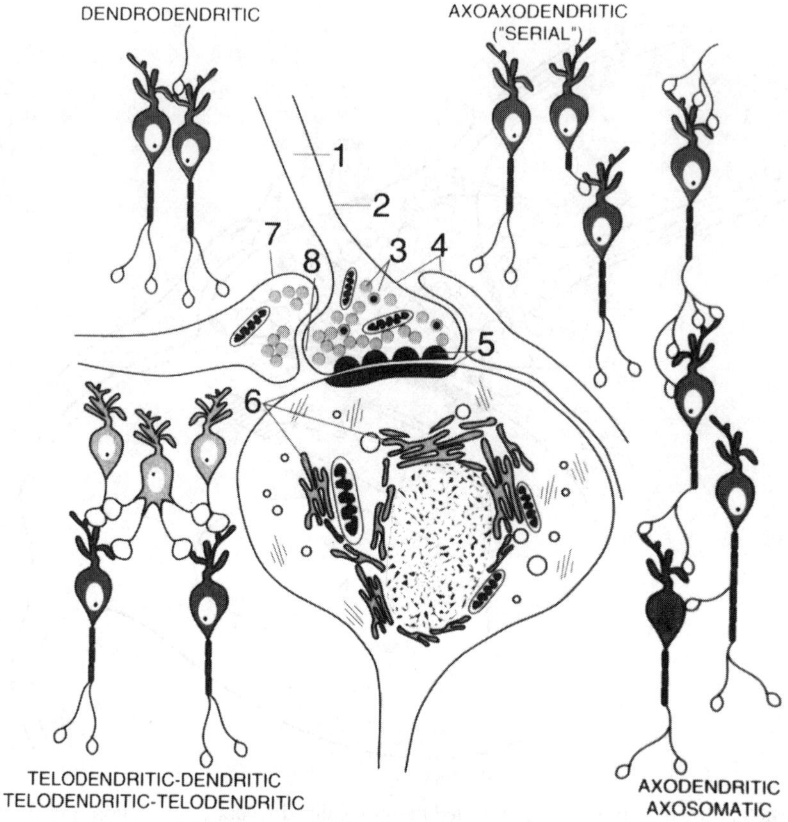
DENDRODENDRITIC
AXOAXODENDRITIC
("SERIAL")
1
2
3
4
5
6
7
8
TELODENDRITIC-DENDRITIC
TELODENDRITIC-TELODENDRITIC
AXODENDRITIC
AXOSOMATIC

FIGURE 35.1–4

Drug-sensitive sites in synaptic transmission. Schematic view of the drug-sensitive sites in prototypical synaptic complexes. In the center, a postsynaptic neuron receives a somatic synapse (shown greatly oversized) from an axonic terminal; an axoaxonic terminal is shown in contact with this presynaptic nerve terminal. Drug-sensitive sites include: *(1)* microtubules responsible for bidirectional transport of macromolecules between the neuronal cell body and distal processes; *(2)* electrically conductive membranes; *(3)* sites for the synthesis and storage of transmitters; *(4)* sites for the active uptake of transmitters by nerve terminals or glia; *(5)* sites for the release of transmitter; *(6)* postsynaptic receptors, cytoplasmic organelles, and postsynaptic proteins for expression of synaptic activity and for long-term mediation of altered physiological states; and *(7)* presynaptic receptors on adjacent presynaptic processes and *(8)* on nerve terminals (autoreceptors). Around the central neuron are schematic illustrations of the more common synaptic relationships in the central nervous system. (Reprinted with permission from Bloom FE: Neurotransmission and the central nervous system. In *Goodman & Gilman's The Pharmacological Basis of Therapeutics,* ed 9, JG Hardman, LE Limbird, PB Molinoff, RW Ruddon, editors, p 270. McGraw-Hill, New York, 1996.)

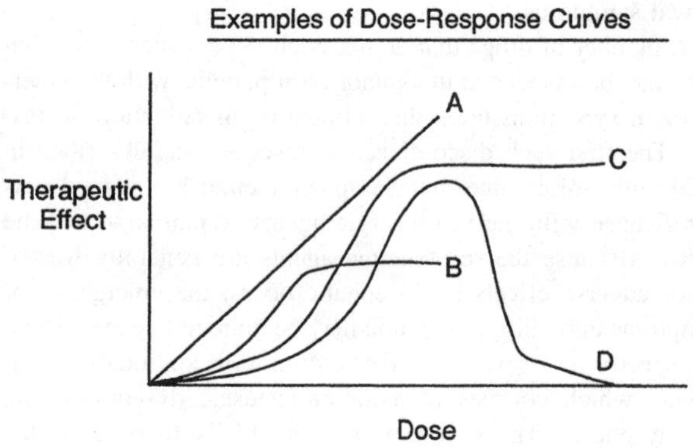
Examples of Dose-Response Curves
Therapeutic Effect
A
B
C
D
Dose

FIGURE 35.1–5

These dose–response curves plot the therapeutic effect as a function of increasing the dose, often calculated as the log of the dose. Drug *A* has a linear dose response; drugs *B* and *C* have sigmoidal curves; and drug *D* has a curvilinear dose–response curve. Although doses of drug *B* are more potent than are equal doses of drug *C,* drug *C* has a higher maximum efficacy than does drug *B.* Drug *D* has a therapeutic window, such that both low and high doses are less effective than are midrange doses.

plasma half-life of the agent is brief, if the drug is taken for at least 2 months, or if higher doses are used. The symptoms are time-limited and can be minimized by a slow tapering of the dosage.

CLINICAL GUIDELINES

Physicians who practice clinical psychopharmacology require skill as both diagnosticians and psychotherapists, knowledge of the available drugs, and the ability to plan a pharmacotherapeutic regimen. The selection and initiation of drug treatment should be based on patients' history, current clinical state, and the treatment plan. Psychiatrists should know the purpose or the goal of a drug trial, the length of time that the drug needs to be administered to assess its efficacy, the approach to be taken to reduce any adverse effects that may occur, alternative drug strategies should the current one fail, and indications for long-term maintenance of the patient on the drug. In almost all cases psychiatrists should explain the treatment plan to patients and often to families and other caretakers. A patient's reaction to and ideas about a proposed drug trial should be considered, but if a psychiatrist thinks that accommodating the patient's wishes would hinder treatment, this fact should also be explained to the patient.

Choice of Drug

The first two steps in selecting drug treatment, diagnosis and identification of the target symptoms, should ideally be carried out when patient has been in a drug-free state for 1 to 2 weeks. The drug-free state should include the absence of medications for sleep, such as hypnotics, as the quality of sleep can be both an important diagnostic guide and a target symptom. If a patient is hospitalized, however, insurance guidelines may make a drug-free period difficult or even impossible to obtain. Psychiatrists often evaluate symptomatic patients who are already receiving one or more psychoactive medications, and it is usually necessary to wean patients from the current medication and then to make an assessment. It is essential to note not only the current drugs but also those recently discontinued, which could be producing symptoms of withdrawal. An exception to this practice occurs when a patient is taking a suboptimal dosage of an otherwise appropriate drug. In such cases a psychiatrist may decide to continue the drug at a higher dosage to complete a full therapeutic trial. The importance of an accurate and complete diagnostic evaluation cannot be overstated. It is no longer reasonable to try all available agents. Rather, the choice of drug and nondrug interventions should be based on careful and thorough review of all the patient's problems and resources. Failure to diagnose a treatable condition accurately is a common reason for unsatisfactory clinical outcomes.

From among the drugs appropriate to a particular diagnosis, a specific drug should be selected according to a patient's history of drug response (compliance, therapeutic response, and adverse effects), the patient's family history of drug response, the profile of adverse effects for the drug with regard to the particular patient, and the psychiatrist's usual practice. If a drug has previously been effective in treating a patient or a family member, the same drug should be used again unless there is a specific reason not to use the drug. A history of severe adverse effects from a specific drug is a strong indicator that the patient would not be compliant with this drug regimen. Patients and their families are often ignorant about what drugs have been used before, in what dosages, and for how long. This ignorance may reflect the tendency of psychiatrists not to explain drug trials to their patients. Psychiatrists should consider giving their patients written records of drug trials for their personal medical records. A caveat in obtaining a history of drug response from patients is that, because of their mental disorders, they may inaccurately report the effects of a previous drug trial. If possible, therefore, the patients' medical records should be obtained to confirm their reports. Most psychotherapeutic drugs of a single class are equally efficacious; but drugs do differ in their adverse effects on individual patients. A selected drug should minimally exacerbate any preexisting medical problems of the patient.

Nonapproved Dosages and Uses. Under the federal Food, Drug, and Cosmetic (FDC) Act, the FDA has authority to control the initial availability of a drug by approving only those new drugs that demonstrate both safety and effectiveness and then to ensure that the drug's proposed labeling is truthful and contains all pertinent information for the safe and effective use of the drug. An additional level of government regulation is directed by the Drug Enforcement Agency, which has classified drugs according to their abuse potential (Table 35.1–3). Clinicians are advised to exercise extra caution when prescribing controlled substances.

Before a new drug can be approved by the FDA, it must be studied in humans. For the drug ultimately to be approved for commercial use, the sponsor must justify its safety and effectiveness by submitting a New Drug Application (NDA) to the FDA. The NDA is approved or disapproved, on the basis of the clinical data accumulated. For approval, the FDA requires that adequate tests be conducted showing that the drug is "safe for use under the conditions prescribed, recommended, or suggested." There must also be substantial evidence that the drug will have the effect it purports under the conditions of use prescribed, recommended, or suggested in the proposed labeling.

According to the Medical Liability Mutual Insurance Company, a malpractice insurance company in New York State, once a drug is approved for commercial use, physicians may, as part of the practice of medicine, lawfully prescribe a different dosage for a patient or otherwise vary the conditions of use from those approved in the package labeling without notifying the FDA or obtaining its approval. Specifically, the FDC Act does not limit the manner in which physicians may use an approved drug. Although physicians may treat patients with an approved drug for unapproved purposes—that is, indications not included on the drug's official labeling—without violating the FDC Act, patients may have a right to redress for possible medical malpractice. Patients' rights are a significant concern, because the failure to follow the FDA-approved label may allow an inference that a physician was departing from the prevailing standard of care. Although the failure to follow the contents of the drug label does not impose liability per se and should not preclude physicians from using good

Table 35.1–3
Characteristics of Drugs at Each DEA Level

DEA Control Level (Schedule)	Characteristics of Drug at Each Control Level	Examples of Drugs at Each Control Level
I	High abuse potential No accepted use in medical treatment in the United States at the present time and, therefore, not for prescription use Can be used for research	LSD, heroin, marijuana, peyote, PCP, mescaline, psilocybin, tetrahydrocannabinols, nicocodeine, nicomorphine
II	High abuse potential Severe physical dependence liability Severe psychological dependence liability No refills; no telephone prescriptions	Amphetamine, opium, morphine, codeine, hydromorphine, phenmetrazine, amobarbital, secobarbital, pentobarbital, methylphenidate
III	Abuse potential less than levels I and II Moderate or low physical dependence liability High psychological liability Prescriptions must be rewritten after 6 months or five refills	Glutethimide, methyprylon, nalorphine, sulfonmethane, benzphetamine, phendimetrazine, mazindol, chlorphentermine; compounds containing codeine, morphine, opium, hydrocodone, dihydrocodeine, naltrexone, diethylpropion
IV	Low abuse potential Limited physical dependence liability Limited psychological dependence liability Prescriptions must be rewritten after 6 months or five refills	Phenobarbital, benzodiazepines,[a] chloral hydrate, ethchlorvynol, ethinamate, meprobamate, paraldehyde
V	Lowest abuse potential of all controlled substances	Narcotic preparations containing limited amounts of nonnarcotic active medicinal ingredients

DEA, Drug Enforcement Agency; LSD, lysergic acid diethylamide; and PCP, phencyclidine.
[a] In New York State, benzodiazepines are treated as schedule II substances, which require a triplicate prescription for a maximum of 1 month's supply.

clinical judgment in patients' interest, physicians should be aware that the drug label presents important information about the safe and effective use of the drug.

Psychiatrists may thus prescribe medication for any reason that they believe is medically indicated for patients' welfare. This clarification is important in view of the increasing regulation of physicians by federal, state, and local government agencies and the intimidation experienced by many physicians in exercising their best medical judgment. When using a drug for an unapproved indication or in a dosage outside the usual range, physicians should document the reasons for their treatment decisions in patients' charts. If clinicians are in doubt about a treatment plan, they should consult a colleague or suggest that the patient obtain a second opinion.

Therapeutic Trials. A drug's therapeutic trial with a particular patient should last for a previously determined time. Because behavioral symptoms are more difficult to assess than are other physiological symptoms such as hypertension, it is particularly important for specific target symptoms to be identified at the initiation of a drug trial. The psychiatrist and the patient can then assess the target symptom over the course of the drug trial to help determine whether the drug has been effective. Several objective rating scales, such as the Brief Psychiatric Rating Scale and the Hamilton Rating Scale for Depression, are available to help assess a patient's progress over the course of a drug trial. If a drug has not been effective in reducing target symptoms in the specified time and if other reasons for the lack of response can be eliminated, the drug should be tapered and stopped. The brain is not a group of on-off neurochemical switches; rather, it is an interactive network of neurons in a complex homeostasis. Thus, the abrupt discontinuation of virtually any psychoactive drug is likely to disrupt the brain's functioning. For example, lithium discontinuation may lead to rebound mania; dopamine receptor antagonist discontinuation may lead to tardive dyskinesias; serotonergic drug discontinuation may lead to agitation, nausea, dysequilibrium, and dysphoria; and benzodiazepine discontinuation may lead to anxiety and insomnia. Another common clinical mistake is the routine addition of medications without discontinuing a previously prescribed drug. Although this practice is indicated in specific circumstances, such as lithium potentiation of an unsuccessful trial of antidepressants, it often results in increased noncompliance and adverse effects. A clinician may also not know whether the second drug alone or the combination of drugs resulted in a therapeutic success or adverse effect.

Therapeutic Failures. The failure of a specific drug trial should prompt clinicians to reconsider several possibilities. First, was the original diagnosis correct? This reconsideration should include the possibility of an undiagnosed cognitive disorder, including illicit drug abuse. Second, are the observed remaining symptoms the drug's adverse effects and not related to the original disease? Antipsychotic drugs, for example, can produce akinesia, which resembles psychotic withdrawal; akathisia and neuroleptic malignant syndrome resemble increased psychotic agitation. Third, was the drug administered in sufficient dosage for an appropriate time? Patients can have varying drug absorption and metabolic rates

Table 35.1–4
Conditions That May Reduce Adherence to Recommended Treatment

Excessively complex regimen (multiple agents, multiple small doses)
Early onset and persistence of side effects
Slow onset of beneficial effects
Low apparent relapse risk experienced if treatment is interrupted
Psychosis, confusion, dementia, pseudodementia, low intelligence, impaired hearing or vision, illiteracy
Simple lack of information, need for patient education
Financial hardship, conflicting obligations of time or money
Resentment, lack of confidence or trust
Specific psychopathology: paranoid delusions, hopelessness, masochism, anxiety and fear, ambivalence, control, splitting, passive aggression, passive dependence, denial, sociopathy, substance abuse
Involvement of multiple clinicians
Poor clinician-patient relationship
Inevitable human error

Adapted from Baldessarini RJ, Cole JO: Chemotherapy. In *The New Harvard Guide to Psychiatry*, AM Nicholi, editor, p 530. Belknap, Cambridge, MA, 1988.

for the same drug, and plasma drug concentrations should be obtained to assess this variable. Fourth, did a pharmacokinetic or pharmacodynamic interaction with another drug the patient was taking reduce the efficacy of the psychotherapeutic drug? Fifth, did the patient take the drug as directed? Drug noncompliance is a common clinical problem. The reasons for drug noncompliance include complicated drug regimens (more than one drug in more than one daily dose), adverse effects (especially if unnoticed by a clinician), and poor patient education about the drug treatment plan (Table 35.1–4). Drug compliance is improved if the clinician explains the use of the drug and the expected responses fully, if the patient has a positive transference toward the clinician, and if the patient does not have to wait in the waiting room to see the clinician. Patients should be warned in particular about the potential adverse consequences of missing even one dose of medication.

COMBINED PSYCHOTHERAPY AND PHARMACOTHERAPY

Using drugs that affect the brain in combination with psychotherapy is one of the fastest growing practices in contemporary psychiatry. In this therapeutic approach, individual or group therapy is combined with pharmacological therapy. The therapist does not meet with the patient on an occasional or irregular basis to monitor the effects of medication or to make notations on a rating scale to assess progress and side effects; rather, both therapies are integrated and synergistic (Table 35.1–5). In many cases the results of combined therapy are superior to either therapy used alone. The term *pharmacotherapy-oriented psychotherapy* is used by some practitioners for this combined approach. The methods of psychotherapy used can vary, and all can be combined with pharmacotherapy.

Countertransference

As in all types of psychotherapy, psychiatrists must be aware of countertransference: their conscious and unconscious feelings toward their patients. Similarly, psychiatrists must be aware of their own psychological attitudes toward drugs. Medications cannot replace the therapeutic alliance; they are not a shortcut to cure and are no substitute for the intense concentration and involvement on the part of the psychiatrist who is conducting psychotherapy. Therapists who are pessimistic about the value of psychotherapy or who misjudge a patient's motivation may prescribe medications on the basis of their own nihilism. Others may withhold medication if they overvalue psychotherapy or devalue pharmacological agents. Withholding medication is most likely to occur with patients who have borderline personality disorder, suicidal behavior, or a history of substance abuse. Each patient must be evaluated individually, and the risk–benefit ratio must be carefully assessed so that the patient is not punished, deprived, or mistreated.

Combined Therapy in Specific Disorders

Depressive Disorders. Some patients and clinicians fear that medications act to cover depression and that psychotherapy is impeded. Medications should be viewed as facilitators in overcoming the anergia that may inhibit a communication process between doctor and patient. Psychiatrists should explain to patients that depression interferes with interpersonal activity in many ways. For example, depression produces withdrawal and irritability, which alienate significant others who may otherwise gratify the patient's strong dependence needs that make up much of depressive disorders' psychodynamics.

Psychiatrists should be alert for signs and symptoms of recurrent major depressive disorder. Medication may have to be reinstituted, but before doing so, psychiatrists should review any stress, especially rejections, that may have precipitated the disorder. A major depressive episode may occur because a patient is in a stage of negative transference, and the psychiatrist must try to elicit the negative feelings. In many cases ventilating angry feelings toward the therapist without an angry response can serve as a corrective emotional experience, and a major depressive episode necessitating medication can thereby be forestalled.

Depressed patients are generally maintained on their medication for 6 months or longer after clinical improvement. The cessation of pharmacotherapy before this time is likely to result in a relapse.

The availability of newer antidepressant agents, such as the SSRIs, venlafaxine, bupropion, nefazodone, and mirtazapine, which have few adverse effects and relatively little toxicity in overdosage, has invited prescriptions from a broader spectrum of physicians. In the era of managed health care, some practitioners may not have the skills or time to perform a thorough psychiatric diagnostic evaluation prior to recommending antidepressant medications. Short batteries of questions, such as the Beck Depression Inventory or the Primary Care Evaluation of Mental Disorders (PRIME-MD), may indicate a tendency toward depression based on 5 to 10 minutes of evaluation.

Table 35.1–5
Stages of Individual Psychotherapy: A Medication Emphasis

Stage	Engagement	Pattern Search	Change	Termination
Goals	Trust Credibility Self-observer alliance	To define problem patterns that, if changed, would lead to a desirable outcome	1. Relinquish old pattern(s) 2. Initiate new pattern(s) 3. Practice new pattern(s)	To separate efficiently
Techniques	Convey empathic understanding Effective suggestions Effective medications	Questionnaires Homework—idiosyncratic meanings ascribed to medication	Interpretation Reframing Behavioral suggestion Medication-induced change	Mutually agreed Patient initiates Therapist initiates Medication-influenced
Content	Medication responsive Diagnosis	Does response to medication reflect a problem pattern?	Medication effects or insight around medication use accelerates change	Medications may prolong termination
Resistance	Are excessive side effects resistance to treatment?	Does pattern of nonadherence to medication regimen reflect a problem pattern?	Do new side effects suggest resistance to change?	Symptom reoccurrence not necessarily indication for medication change
Transference	Physician seen as malevolent or all-powerful	Is key interpersonal pattern reflected in meaning of medication?	Unresolved distortions may be signaled by a new medication issue inhibiting change	Desire for new or more medication reflects desire to hold therapist
Countertransference	Physician failure to prescribe appropriately	Medication prescription reflects distorted response to patient	Sudden change in regimen reflects an attempt to undermine change	New medication reflects desire to keep contact

Reprinted with permission from Beitman BD. In *Integrating Pharmacotherapy and Psychotherapy,* BD Beitman, GL Klerman, editors, p 22. American Psychiatric Press, Washington, 1991.

Because of economic pressures, many patients with depression are likely to be treated only with drugs. Training in the use of antidepressants is therefore critically important for all physicians.

Suicidal Behavior. The possibility of suicide must be considered in treating patients who have schizophrenia, bipolar I disorder, depressive disorders, and anxiety disorders (especially those patients who have panic attacks). If a psychiatrist decides that a patient is in imminent risk of suicidal behavior, hospitalization is always indicated. If the patient can be managed outside a hospital, medication should be given to a responsible family member who can monitor its dosage and frequency. As a further precaution, the psychiatrist may treat the patient with a drug known to have little or no lethal potential when taken in an overdose attempt. Medication is almost always indicated in suicidally depressed patients.

Bipolar I Disorder. Patients taking lithium or other treatments for bipolar I disorder are usually medicated for an indefinite period of time for recent episodes of either mania or depression. Most psychotherapists insist that patients with bipolar I disorder be medicated before starting any insight-oriented therapy. Without such premedication, most patients with the disorder are unable to make the necessary therapeutic alliance. When these patients are depressed, their abulia seriously disrupts their flow of thoughts, and the sessions are nonproductive. When they are manic, their flow of associations can be rapid and their speech so pressured that a therapist may be flooded with material and unable to make appropriate interpretations or to assimilate the material into the patient's disrupted cognitive framework.

Anxiety Disorders. Anxiety disorders encompass obsessive-compulsive disorder, posttraumatic stress disorder, generalized anxiety disorder, phobias, and panic disorder with or without agoraphobia. Many drugs are effective in managing distressing signs and symptoms associated with these disorders, and over 60 percent of persons with obsessive-compulsive disorder respond to SSRIs. As the symptoms are controlled by medication, patients are reassured and develop confidence that they will not be incapacitated by the disorder. This effect is particularly strong in panic disorder, which is often associated with anticipatory anxiety about the attack. Depression may complicate the symptom picture in patients with anxiety disorders and must be addressed both pharmacologically and psychotherapeutically.

Schizophrenia and Other Psychotic Disorders. Included in this group of disorders are schizophrenia, delusional disorder, schizoaffective disorder, schizophreniform disorder, and brief psychotic disorder. Drug treatment for these disorders is always indicated, and hospitalization is often necessary for diagnostic purposes, to stabilize medication, to prevent danger to self or others, and to establish a psychosocial treatment program that may include individual psychotherapy. Several studies have reported remarkable cost-effectiveness of serotonin-dopamine antagonists for severely ill patients because of the reduced need for hospitalization. In attempting individual psychotherapy, therapists must establish a treatment relationship and a therapeutic alliance with patients. Schizophrenic patients defend against closeness and trust and often become suspicious, anxious, hostile, or regressed in therapy.

Substance Abuse. Patients who abuse alcohol or other substances offer the most difficult challenge in combined therapy. They are often impulsive, and even though they promise not to abuse a substance, they may do so repeatedly. In addition, they frequently withhold information from the psychiatrist about episodes of abuse. For this reason, some psychiatrists do not prescribe medications to such patients, especially not medications with a high abuse potential, such as benzodiazepines, barbiturates, and amphetamines. Drugs with no abuse potential—such as thioridazine (Mellaril), amitriptyline (Elavil), and fluoxetine—have an important role in the treatment of anxiety, depression, or both that almost always accompany substance-related disorders. Psychiatrists conducting psychotherapy with such patients should have no reservations about sending them to a laboratory for random urine toxicological testing. As in all forms of insight-oriented psychotherapy, the psychological significance of such tests should be examined.

SPECIAL TREATMENT CONSIDERATIONS

Children

Special care must be given when administering psychotherapeutic drugs to children. Although the small volume of distribution suggests the use of lower dosages than in adults, children's higher rate of metabolism indicates that higher ratios of milligrams of drug to kilograms of body weight should be used. In practice, it is best to begin with a small dose and to increase the dosage until clinical effects are observed. Clinicians should not hesitate to use adult dosages in children, however, if the dosages are effective and the adverse effects are acceptable.

Geriatric Patients

The two major concerns when treating geriatric patients with psychotherapeutic drugs are that older persons may be especially susceptible to adverse effects (particularly cardiac effects) and may metabolize drugs slowly (Table 35.1–6). Thus, geriatric patients may require low dosages of medication. Another concern is that geriatric patients are often taking other medications, and psychiatrists must consider possible drug interactions. In practice, psychiatrists should begin treating geriatric patients with a small dose, usually approximately one half the usual dose. The dosage should be raised in small amounts more slowly than in younger adults until either a clinical benefit is achieved or unacceptable adverse effects appear. Although many geriatric patients require a small dosage of medication, others require the usual adult dosage.

Table 35.1–6
Pharmacokinetics and Aging

Phase	Change	Effect
Absorption	Gastric pH increases Decreased surface villi Decreased gastric motility and delayed gastric emptying Intestinal perfusion decreases	Little overall change Absorption is slowed but just as complete
Distribution	Total body water and lean body mass decrease Increased total body fat, more marked in women than in men Albumin decreases, gamma globulin increases, alpha, acid glycoprotein unchanged	V_d increases for lipid-soluble drugs, decreases for water-soluble drugs The free or unbound percentage of albumin-bound drugs increases
Metabolism	Renal: renal blood flow and glomerular filtration rates decrease Hepatic: decreased enzyme activity and perfusion	Decreased metabolism leads to prolonged half-lives, if V_d remains the same
Total body weight	Decreases	Think on a mg/kg basis
Receptor sensitivity	May increase	Increased effect

Reprinted with permission from Guttmacher LB. *Concise Guide to Somatic Therapies in Psychiatry,* p 126. American Psychiatric Press, Washington, 1988.
V_d, volume of distribution.

Pregnant and Nursing Women

The basic rule is to avoid administering any drug to a woman who is pregnant (particularly during the first trimester) or breast-feeding a child. This rule, however, occasionally is broken when a women's mental disorder is severe. If psychotherapeutic medications need to be administered during a pregnancy, the possibility of therapeutic abortion should be discussed. The two most teratogenic drugs in the psychopharmacopoeia are lithium and the anticonvulsants. Lithium administration during pregnancy is associated with a high incidence of birth abnormalities, including Ebstein's anomaly, a serious abnormality in cardiac development. Anticonvulsants used during pregnancy are associated with fetal craniofacial and neural tube abnormalities in less than 10 percent of infants. The risk of teratogenicity can be reduced by the administration of folic acid. Other psychoactive drugs (antidepressants, antipsychotics, and anxiolytics), although less clearly associated with birth defects, should also be avoided during pregnancy if at all possible. The most common clinical situation is a pregnant woman's becoming psychotic. If a decision is made not to terminate the pregnancy, ECT or antipsychotics are preferable to lithium.

The administration of psychotherapeutic drugs at or near delivery may cause a baby to be overly sedated at delivery, to need a respirator or to be physically dependent on the drug, and to require detoxification and treatment of a withdrawal syndrome. Virtually all psychotropic drugs are secreted in the milk of a nursing women; therefore, mothers taking these agents should not breast-feed their infants.

Medically Ill Patients

Considerations in administering psychotropic drugs to medically ill patients include a potentially increased sensitivity to a drug's side effects, either increased or decreased metabolism and excretion of the drug, and interactions with other medications. As with children and geriatric patients, the most reasonable clinical practice is to begin with a small dose, increase it slowly, and watch for both clinical and adverse effects. The testing of plasma drug concentrations may be particularly helpful in these patients.

ADVERSE EFFECTS

Most psychotherapeutic drugs do not affect a single neurotransmitter system, and their effects are not solely localized to the brain. Psychotherapeutic drugs produce a wide range of adverse effects on neurotransmitter systems. For example, some of the most common adverse effects of psychotherapeutic drugs are caused by the blockade of muscarinic acetylcholine receptors (Table 35.1–7). Many psychotherapeutic drugs antagonize dopaminergic, histaminergic, and adrenergic neurons or excessively activate serotonergic neurons, resulting in the adverse effects listed in Table 35.1–8. There are also several commonly observed adverse effects for which the neurotransmitters involved have not been specifically identified.

Table 35.1–7
Potential Adverse Effects Caused by Blockade of Muscarinic Acetylcholine Receptors

Blurred vision
Constipation
Decreased salivation
Decreased sweating
Delayed or retrograde ejaculation
Delirium
Exacerbation of asthma (through decreased bronchial secretions)
Hyperthermia (through decreased sweating)
Memory problems
Narrow-angle glaucoma
Photophobia
Sinus tachycardia
Urinary retention

Table 35.1–8
Potential Adverse Effects of Psychotherapeutic Drugs and Associated Neurotransmitter Systems

Antidopaminergic
- Endocrine dysfunction
  - Hyperprolactinemia
  - Menstrual dysfunction
  - Sexual dysfunction
- Movement disorders
  - Akathisia
  - Dystonia
  - Parkinsonism
  - Tardive dyskinesia

Antiadrenergic (primarily α_1)
- Dizziness
- Postural hypotension
- Reflex tachycardia

Antihistaminergic
- Hypotension
- Sedation
- Weight gain

Excessive serotonergic
- Akathisia and agitation
- Anxiety
- GI upset and diarrhea
- Headache
- Insomnia or somnolence
- Nausea and vomiting
- Sexual dysfunction

Multiple neurotransmitter systems
- Agranulocytosis (and other blood dyscrasias)
- Allergic reactions
- Anorexia
- Cardiac conduction abnormalities
- Nausea and vomiting
- Seizures

Patients generally have decreased trouble with adverse effects if they have been told to expect them. Psychiatrists can explain the appearance of adverse effects as evidence that the drug is working. But clinicians should distinguish between probable or expected adverse effects and rare or unexpected adverse effects.

Treatment of Common Adverse Effects

Many adverse effects occur with psychotherapeutic drugs. The management of the adverse effects is similar, regardless of which psychotherapeutic drug a patient is taking. If possible, another drug with similar benefits but fewer or less undesirable adverse effects should be substituted. For example, common adverse effects of antidepressant drugs are listed in Table 35.1–9. In addition to those listed here, common antidopaminergic effects are discussed in Section 35.2, Medication-Induced Movement Disorders.

Anxiety, Akathisia, Agitation, and Insomnia. Serotonergic antidepressants, especially fluoxetine, can transiently increase psychomotor activation in the first 2 to 3 weeks of use. Although these adverse effects usually subside spon-

Table 35.1–9
Adverse Effects of Antidepressants

Drugs	Sedation	Anticholinergic	Orthostatic Hypotension	Cardiac Conduction Effects
Heterocyclics				
Amitriptyline	High	High	Moderate	High
Imipramine	Moderate	Moderate	High	High
Doxepin	High	Moderate	Moderate	Moderate
Desipramine	Low	Low	Low	Moderate
Nortriptyline	Moderate	Moderate	Low	Moderate
Trimipramine	High	High	Moderate	High
Protriptyline	Low	Moderate	Low	Moderate
Clomipramine	High	High	Low	Moderate
Maprotiline	Moderate	Moderate	Low	Moderate
Serotonin Reuptake Inhibitors				
Fluoxetine	Very low	None	Very low	Very low
Sertraline	Low	None	None	Very low
Paroxetine	Low	Low	None	Very low
Fluvoxamine	Low	None	None	Very low
Phenylethylamine				
Venlafaxine	Low	None	Very low	Very low
Dibenzoxazepines				
Amoxapine	Low	Low	Low	Low
Triazolopyridines				
Trazodone	High	Very low	Moderate	Low
Phenylpiperazines				
Nefazodone	Moderate	None	Low	Low
Piperazinoazepines				
Mirtazapine	High	Moderate	Low	Low
Aminoketones				
Bupropion	Low	Very low	Very low	0
Triazolobenzodiazepines				
Alprazolam	High	Very low	Very low	0
Monoamine Oxidase Inhibitors				
Phenelzine Tranylcypromine Isocarboxazid	As a class, orthostatic hypotension, dizziness, headache, drowsiness, overstimulation (hypomania, insomnia, anxiety), constipation, nausea, diarrhea, abdominal pain			

Adapted from Janicak PG, Davis JM, Preskorn SH, Ayd FJ: *Principles and Practice of Psychopharmacology,* p 272. Williams & Wilkins, Baltimore, 1993.

taneously if the drugs are continued, they may elicit an aversive response from a patient, who vividly experiences a worsening of the symptoms of depression with only the promise of improvement at some point in the future. It is usually not possible to predict which patients will not tolerate a serotonergic agent. A history of poor tolerance of a previous antidepressant or paranoid features may predict a poor response to a serotonergic drug. Particular caution is warranted in suicidal patients, for whom the agitating effect of fluoxetine has been suggested to increase the risk of acting out suicidal impulses. Frequent clinician–patient contact, or hospitalization, during the initial period of SSRI treatment is advisable in the management of such patients, depending on the clinician's assessment of the risk for suicide. The anxiogenic effects of serotonergic drugs may be counteracted by addition of a sedating antidepressant, such as trazodone or a tricyclic drug, or a benzodiazepine. A small number of patients will experience persistent increased anxiety beyond the initial 3-week period, and these patients may require a different agent, such as paroxetine (Paxil), sertraline, or a non-SSRI.

Gastrointestinal Upset and Diarrhea. Most of the body's serotonin is in the gastrointestinal tract, and increasing levels of serotonin due to reuptake blockade may produce prominent stomach pain, nausea, and diarrhea for the first few weeks of therapy. Sertraline is most likely to cause loose stools, and fluvoxamine is most likely to cause nausea. These symptoms may be minimized by starting with a very small dose for the first 3 weeks, then increasing to the standard dose. Taking the drugs after a meal may also reduce discomfort. Dietary alteration may reduce loose stools, such as the so-called BRAT diet: bananas, rice, apples, and toast. These symptoms usually abate over time, but some patients never accommodate and must be switched to another drug.

Anorexia. This adverse effect is more pronounced in obese patients and patients with carbohydrate craving and therefore may be desirable. At the other end of the spectrum, it may dangerously worsen tendencies toward anorexia nervosa or bulimia in patients with these disorders. Although high-dose fluoxetine in the context of a comprehensive program of behavioral management is an FDA-approved treatment for the bulimia and is also useful for anorexia nervosa, fluoxetine may be abused by patients with eating disorders if used in an unmonitored fashion. Unless such combination therapy is available, SSRIs should be used cautiously by patients with eating disorders.

Headache. The relationship between serotonin and headache is under active study, yet remains elusive. Although one of the most effective antimigraine drugs, sumatriptan (Imitrex), is a serotonin type 1D receptor agonist, the increased synaptic serotonin due to SSRIs may cause headache. Fluoxetine is most likely to cause this adverse effect. In general, however, SSRIs are an effective treatment for chronic tension-type headache and for migraine headache. Although some patients with treatment-emergent headaches may get relief from over-the-counter analgesics, it may be necessary to switch to another antidepressant.

Somnolence. Many psychotropic drugs cause sedation in a high percentage of patients. Some patients may self-medicate this adverse effect with caffeine, but this practice may worsen orthostatic hypotension. Although sympathomimetic drugs are a highly effective treatment for somnolence, long-term use of even low doses of sympathomimetics for this indication is a questionable practice. It is important for the clinician to alert the patient to the possibility of sedation and to document that the patient was advised not to drive or operate dangerous equipment if sedated by medications. Fortunately, newer generations of antidepressant and antipsychotic drugs are much less likely to cause sedation than their predecessors, and these drugs should be substituted for the sedating medications where possible.

Dry Mouth. Dry mouth is caused by the blockade of muscarinic acetylcholine receptors. When patients attempt to relieve the dry mouth by constantly sucking on sugar-containing hard candies, they increase their risk for dental caries. They can avoid the problem by chewing sugarless gum or sucking on sugarless hard candies. Some clinicians recommend the use of a 1 percent solution of pilocarpine, a cholinergic agonist, as a mouthwash 3 times daily. Other clinicians suggest bethanechol (Urecholine) tablets, another cholinergic agonist, 10 to 30 mg, once or twice daily. It is best to start with 10 mg once a day and to increase the dosage slowly. Adverse effects of cholinomimetic drugs such as bethanechol include tremor, diarrhea, abdominal cramps, and excessive eye watering.

Blurred Vision. The blockage of muscarinic acetylcholine receptors causes mydriasis (pupillary dilation) and cycloplegia (ciliary muscle paresis) and results in presbyopia (blurred near vision). The symptom can be relieved by cholinomimetic eye drops. A 1 percent solution of pilocarpine can be prescribed as 1 drop 4 times daily. As an alternative, bethanechol can be used as it is used for dry mouth.

Urinary Retention. The anticholinergic activity of many psychotropic drugs can lead to urinary hesitation, dribbling, urinary retention, and increased urinary tract infections. Elderly men with enlarged prostates are at increased risk for these adverse effects. Ten to 30 mg of bethanechol 3 to 4 times daily is usually effective in the treatment of the adverse effects.

Constipation. The anticholinergic activity of psychotropic drugs can result in the particularly disturbing adverse effect of constipation. The first line of treatment involves prescribing bulk laxatives, such as Metamucil and Fiberall. If this treatment fails, cathartic laxatives such as milk of magnesia can be tried. Prolonged use of cathartic laxatives can result in a loss of effectiveness. Bethanechol, 10 to 30 mg 3 to 4 times daily, can also be used.

Orthostatic Hypotension. Orthostatic hypotension is caused by the blockade of α_1-adrenergic receptors. Psychiatrists should warn patients of this possible adverse effect, particularly if a patient is elderly. The risk of hip fractures from falls is significantly elevated in patients who are taking psychotropic drugs. With patients at high risk for orthostatic hypotension, clinicians should choose a drug with low α_1-adrenergic activity. Patients can be instructed to get up slowly and to sit down immediately if dizziness is experienced. Caffeine should be avoided, at least 2 liters of fluid should be consumed each day, and salt supplements may be given if hypertension is not present. Aerobic exercise to augment cardiac contractility may also be of benefit. Patients can also try support hose to help reduce venous pooling. Specific adjuvant medications have been recommended for specific pharmacotherapeutic drugs.

Sexual Dysfunction. Psychotropic drug use, particularly of serotonergic agents, can be associated with sexual dysfunctions—decreased libido, impaired ejaculation and erection, and inhibition of female orgasm. Warning a patient about these adverse effects may increase the patient's concern. Alternatively, patients are not likely to report adverse sexual effects spontaneously to a physician. Some sexual dysfunctions may be related to the primary mental disorder; but if sexual dysfunctions emerge after pharmacotherapy has begun, it may be worthwhile to treat them. Neostigmine (Prostigmin), 7.5 to 15 mg orally 30 minutes before sexual intercourse, may help alleviate impaired ejaculation. Impaired erectile function may be helped with bethanechol given regularly or possibly bromocriptine (Parlodel), amantadine (Symmetrel), or yohimbine (Yocon). Cyproheptadine (Periactin), 4 mg every morning, can be used for the treatment of inhibited female orgasm; 4 to 8 mg orally can be taken 1 to 2 hours before anticipated sexual activity for the treatment of inhibited male orgasm secondary to use of serotonergic agents.

Weight Gain. Weight gain accompanies the use of many psychotropic drugs and results from retained fluid, increased caloric intake, or decreased exercise. Edema can be treated by elevating the affected body parts or by administering a thiazide diuretic. If patients are taking lithium or cardiac medications, clinicians must monitor drug blood concentrations, blood chemistries, and vital signs. Patients should also be instructed to minimize the intake of fats and carbohydrates and to exercise regularly. But if a patient has not been exercising, the clinician should recommend that the patient start an exercise program at a modest level of exertion.

Overdoses

An extreme adverse effect of drug treatment is an attempt by a patient to commit suicide by overdosing on a psychotherapeutic drug. One psychodynamic theory of such behavior is that the patients are angry at their therapists for not having been able to help them. Whatever the motivation, psychiatrists should be aware of the risk and attempt to prescribe the safest possible drugs. It is good clinical practice to write nonrefillable prescriptions for small quantities of drugs when suicide is a consideration. In extreme cases, an attempt should be made to verify that patients are taking the medication and not hoarding the pills for a later overdose attempt. Patients may attempt suicide just as they are beginning to get better. Clinicians, therefore, should continue to be careful about prescribing large quantities of medication until patients are almost completely recovered. Another consideration for psychiatrists is the possibility of an accidental overdose, particularly by children in the household. Patients should be advised to keep psychotherapeutic medications in a safe place. A guide to the signs and symptoms and the treatment of overdoses with psychotherapeutic drugs is contained in Table 35.1–10.

DRUG INTERACTIONS

Drug interactions may increase or decrease the activity of both the psychiatric drug and any other medications the patient may be taking. In some cases, this may increase the risk of adverse reactions, and clinicians should be fully aware of all of the possible interactions before exposing patients to more than one drug at a time. Drug interactions are frequently used to augment the desired therapeutic benefit by influencing distinct pharmacodynamic sites of action. For example, in the treatment of depression, SSRIs, which raise synaptic serotonin levels, may be mixed with bupropion, which has little serotonergic activity but is highly active on the norepinephrine and dopamine systems. The resulting mixture of activities may be a more powerful antidepressant than either drug alone. Augmentation strategies should avoid duplication of pharmacodynamic activity, should not pair an agonist with an antagonist of the same receptor, and should be approached with caution to avoid potentially dangerous adverse effects. For example, mixing of a tricyclic drug and an MAOI is conceivable, in that each drug affects distinct cellular sites, but it is also perilous, in that it may cause a hypertensive crisis. In general, drugs with few adverse effects make the best candidates for augmentation strategies.

Drug interactions may be either pharmacokinetic or pharmacodynamic, and they vary greatly in their potential to cause serious problems. An additional consideration is that of phantom drug interactions. A patient who was taking only drug A may later receive both drug A and drug B. The clinician may notice some effect and attribute it to the induction of metabolism. What may have happened is that the patient was more compliant at one point in the observation period than in another, or there may have been some other effect of which the clinician was unaware. The clinical literature can contain reports of phantom drug interactions that are rare or nonexistent.

Other interactions are true but unproved, although reasonably plausible. Still other interactions have some modest effects and are well documented, and some clinically important drug interactions are well studied and well proved. But clinicians must remember that animal pharmacokinetic data are not always readily generalizable to humans; in vitro data do not necessarily replicate the results obtained under in vivo conditions; single-case reports can contain misleading information; and studies of acute conditions should not be uncritically regarded as relevant to chronic, steady-state conditions.

Informed clinicians need to keep these considerations in mind and to focus on clinically important interactions, not on those that may be mild, unproved, or entirely phantom. At the same time, clinicians should maintain an open and receptive attitude toward the possibility of pharmacokinetic and pharmacodynamic drug interactions.

DEVELOPMENT OF NEW DRUGS

The first stage in the development of a new drug involves the identification of a compound that for theoretical reasons may be effective in treating a disorder. Techniques under development, called combinatorial chemistry, promise to generate several times the existing number of drugs for testing in the near future. The compound is then studied in a wide variety of in vitro and in vivo tests that may predict the clinical drug effects. Compounds found to be of potential importance in these tests then undergo studies of their toxicity and pharmacokinetics in animals. If these preliminary preclinical tests are thought to merit the costs of further drug development, a pharmaceutical company in the United States can file an Investigational New Drug application with the FDA. If the application is granted, the compound can then be used in humans for research purposes. Only 1 in 1,000 compounds examined in preclinical testing proceeds to human testing.

The first such experiments are called phase I experiments, in which the drug is administered to 20 to 80 normal persons to assess its pharmacokinetic effects and its potential for adverse effects. Phase I studies are conducted primarily to determine the safety and tolerability of a new compound. The information from the phase I trials is then used to help decide on a dosage of the new drug in phase II trials, which involve the use of the new compound in a patient population of 100 to 300 volunteers. The primary purpose of phase II trials is to assess the efficacy of the new drug in the treatment of specific disorders. If the phase II trials indicate that a drug is efficacious, safe, and well tolerated, much larger phase III trials are conducted on 1,000 to 3,000 patients to validate the findings of the phase II studies. Phase III studies also require gathering detailed information about optimum dosage schedules and the use of the drug in elderly and young populations and in persons with impaired hepatic or renal function. After the com-

Table 35.1–10
Intoxication and Overdose with Psychotherapeutic Drugs

Drug	Toxic or Lethal Dose[a]	Signs and Symptoms	Treatment[b]
β-Adrenergic receptor antagonists	Propranolol 1 g	Hypotension, bradycardia, seizures, loss of consciousness, bronchospasm, cardiac failure	Supportive care; emesis or gastric lavage after ingestion. If needed (comatose, seizures, absent gag), lavage with endotracheal tube with inflated cuff in place; intravenous (IV) atropine for symptomatic bradycardia. IV isoproterenol for persistent cases, a pacemaker if refractory; norepinephrine or dopamine for severe hypotension; IV diazepam for seizures, glucagon may be useful for hypotension and myocardial depression, theophylline or β_2 agonist for bronchospasm, a diuretic or cardiac glycoside for heart failure
Amantadine	2.5 g	Disorientation, visual hallucinations, confusion, aggressive behavior, minimally reactive and slightly dilated pupils, urinary retention, acid-base disturbances, coma	Induce emesis or use gastric lavage in recent overdose; supportive measures including airway maintainance, cardiovascular monitoring, control of respiration and oxygen administration; monitoring urine pH, urinary output, serum electrolytes; acidifying agents can increase the rate of excretion, force fluids (IV if needed); observe for hypotension, seizures, psychosis, urinary retention, arrhythmias, hyperactivity, which should be treated appropriately; physostigmine may be useful in treating central nervous system (CNS) toxicity; chlorpromazine may be useful for toxic psychosis; adrenergic agents may predispose the patient to ventricular arrhythmias
Amphetamine	100 mg	Elation, irritability, hyperactivity, rapid speech, anorexia, hyperreflexia, insomnia, dry mouth, chest pain, arrhythmia, heart block, poor concentration, restlessness, psychotic symptoms	Emesis or lavage can be effective long after ingestion because of recycling through gastric mucosa; reduce external stimuli; treat cerebral edema and hyperthermia; peritoneal dialysis; sedate with chlorpromazine 0.5–1 mg/kg intramuscular (IM) or by mouth every 30 minutes as needed; use 1/2 the dose for mixed amphetamine-barbiturate overdose
Anticholinergics	700 mg–7 g (doses vary, depending on agent involved)	Hot, dry, flushed skin; unreactive dilated pupils; blurred vision; dry mucous membranes; foul breath; difficulty in swallowing; urinary retention; decreased bowel sounds; tachycardia; nausea; vomiting; rash; anticholinergic delirium with delusions, hallucinations, disorientation	Supportive and symptomatic therapy; continuous electrocardiograph (ECG) monitoring; empty stomach immediately by inducing emesis if patient is conscious, has gag reflex and no seizures; otherwise, gastric lavage and activated charcoal can be used with endotracheal tube with inflated cuff in place; saline cathartics may be used; exchange transfusions can be considered in extreme cases; fluid therapy should be used for shock; cold packs, mechanical cooling devices, or sponging with tepid water can be used for hyperthermia; diazepam can be used for agitation; 1 mg can reverse adverse effects of physostigmine; IV propranolol may be useful for supraventricular tachyarrhythmias; avoid dopamine receptor antagonists

(continued)

Table 35.1–10 *(continued)*

Drug	Toxic or Lethal Dose[a]	Signs and Symptoms	Treatment[b]
Antihistamines	2.8 g (diphenhydramine), 1,750–17,500 mg (hydroxyzine)	Disorientation, drowsiness, excitation or depression, hallucinations, anxiety, delirium, hyperthermia, tachycardia, arrhythmias, seizures	Empty stomach with ipecac emesis or gastric lavage; support cardiorespiratory function; physostigmine may be useful for anticholinergic effects, diazepam for seizures; sponge baths with tepid water (not alcohol) or cold packs for hyperthermia
Barbiturates	10 times the daily therapeutic dose (eg, 1–2 g of secobarbital)	Delirium, confusion, excitement, headache, CNS and respiratory depression from somnolence to coma, areflexia, circulatory collapse	Supportive treatment, including maintaining airway and respiration and treating shock as needed; within 30 minutes of ingestion, use activated charcoal; gastric lavage and aspiration can be used within 4 hours of ingestion; nasogastric administration of charcoal in multiple doses can shorten coma; maintain vital signs, fluid balance; alkalinizing the urine increases the excretion of mephobarbital, aprobarbital, phenobarbital; forced diuresis may be of use if renal function is normal; hemodialysis or peritoneal dialysis may be useful in severe cases
Benzodiazepines	Toxic dose: diazepam, 2 g; chlordiazepoxide, 6 g	Slurred speech, incoordination, somnolence, confusion, coma, hyporeflexia, hypotension	General supportive care; induce emesis for recent ingestions in fully conscious patients; gastric lavage with endotracheal tube with inflated cuff if comatose; after above, use a saline cathartic and activated charcoal; maintain airway, monitor vital signs, give IV fluids; norepinephrine or metaraminol can be used for hypotension; flumazenil can be used with extreme caution
Bromocriptine	Survival of 225 mg dose reported	Severe hypotension, nausea, vomiting, psychosis	Empty stomach by lavage and aspiration; IV fluids for hypotension
Bupropion	Ingestions of 850–4,200 mg have been survived; deaths have been reported in massive overdoses	Seizures, loss of consciousness, hallucinations, tachycardia	Ipecac emesis if conscious; gastric lavage with endotracheal tube in place with inflated cuff if there are seizures or a decreased level of consciousness; during first 12 hours after ingestion, use activated charcoal every 6 hours, provide fluids; electroencephalogram (EEG) and ECG monitoring for 48 hours; seizures can be treated with IV benzodiazepines
Buspirone	Toxic dose of 375 mg (used in studies); lethal dose unknown	Dizziness, drowsiness, nausea, vomiting, miosis, gastric distention	Symptomatic and supportive care; empty stomach with emesis or lavage in large ingestions; if needed, perform lavage with endotracheal tube in place with cuff inflated; monitor vital signs
Calcium channel inhibitors	9.6 g of verapamil has resulted in death; patients have survived ingestion of 8–10 g of diltiazem and 9 g of nifedipine (case reports)	Confusion, headache, nausea, vomiting, seizures, flushing, constipation, bradycardia, hypotension, atrioventricular block, hyperglycemia, metabolic acidosis	Emesis followed by gastric lavage with activated charcoal; calcium gluconate or calcium chloride 10–20 mg/kg in 10% solution with normal saline IV given over 30 minutes and repeated as needed; atropine or isoproterenol for atrioventricular block; a pacemaker may be needed

(continued)

Table 35.1–10 *(continued)*

Drug	Toxic or Lethal Dose[a]	Signs and Symptoms	Treatment[b]
Carbamazepine	Lowest known lethal dose in adults: 60 g; highest doses survived: children 10 g, adults 30 g	Drowsiness, stupor, dizziness, restlessness, ataxia, agitation, nausea, vomiting, involuntary movements, abnormal reflexes, adiadochokinesis, nystagmus, mydriasis, flushing, cyanosis, urinary retention, hypotension or hypertension, coma, cardiac arrhythmias	Induce emesis or gastric lavage; supportive measures; ECG monitoring
Carisoprodol	Patients have recovered from 3.4 g and 9.45 g ingestions	Stupor, shock, coma, respiratory depression, headache, diplopia, dizziness, drowsiness, nystagmus	Supportive treatment; induce emesis or use gastric lavage with endotracheal tube in place with cuff inflated if clinically indicated; activated charcoal after emptying stomach; maintain airway, respiration, and blood pressure; pressor agents can be used with caution if necessary; elimination may be enhanced by forced diuresis with hemodialysis, peritoneal dialysis, or osmotic diuresis; avoid overhydration; monitor neurological status, electrolytes, and vital signs; continue monitoring for relapse secondary to delayed absorption and incomplete gastric emptying
Chloral hydrate	4–10 g	Coma, confusion, drowsiness, respiratory depression, hypotension, hypothermia, vomiting, miosis, gastric necrosis and perforation, esophageal stricture, hepatic injury, renal injury	General supportive measures; gastric lavage with endotracheal tube with inflated cuff in place; maintain airway, oxygenation, cardiorespiratory function, and body temperature; hemodialysis or peritoneal dialysis may be of use; saline enema if drug was administered rectally
Clonidine	No known deaths from overdoses of clonidine alone; 100 mg is the largest known overdose survived; two known deaths from mixed overdoses that included clonidine	Hypotension, hyporeflexia or areflexia, vomiting, weakness, irritability, sedation, coma, lethargy, hypothermia, constricted pupils, dry mouth, hypoventilation, seizures, arrhythmia, cardiac conduction defects	Induce emesis or lavage followed by activated charcoal and a saline cathartic; lavage is preferred in patients with decreased levels of consciousness and should be used with endotracheal tube with inflated cuff in place if patient is comatose, has seizures, or lacks gag reflex; supportive and symptomatic measures; establish airway, IV fluids, and Trendelenburg's position for hypotension; if persistent, use dopamine; atropine IV for symptomatic bradycardia; tolazoline 10 mg IV every 30 minutes may reverse cardiovascular effects of clonidine; IV furosemide, α-blockers, or diazoxide for hypertension; IV benzodiazepines can be used for seizures
Clozapine	Lethal dose: 2.5 g, although patients have survived ingestions of 4 g	Delirium, drowsiness, coma, respiratory depression, tachycardia, arrhythmias, hypotension, hypersalivation, seizures	Symptomatic and supportive care; establish and maintain airway, ventilation, and oxygenation; activated charcoal with sorbitol (may be as effective as or more effective than lavage or emesis); monitor and adjust acid-base and electrolyte balance; physostigmine may be a useful adjunct for anticholinergic toxicity but is not for routine use; epinephrine, quinidine, procainamide are to be avoided; patient should be observed for several days for delayed effects
Dantrolene	No data available	Speech and visual disturbances, gastrointestinal (GI) upset or bleeding, liver damage, nausea, vomiting, CNS depression	Supportive measures; immediate gastric lavage; ECG monitoring; large quantities of IV fluids; maintain airway; have artificial respiratory measures available; observe patient

(continued)

Table 35.1–10 *(continued)*

Drug	Toxic or Lethal Dose[a]	Signs and Symptoms	Treatment[b]
Dextroamphetamine	500 mg has been survived	Restlessness, tremor, hyperreflexia, rhabdomyolysis, rapid respiration, hyperpyrexia, confusion, assaultiveness, hallucinations, panic states, fatigue, depression, arrhythmias, hypertension, hypotension, circulatory collapse, nausea, vomiting, diarrhea, abdominal cramps, convulsions, coma	Supportive care; gastric lavage; sedation with a barbiturate; acidification of the urine; phentolamine for hypertension; chlorpromazine; continue measures until all of the sustained release drug is thought to be released
Disulfiram	Six or more fatalities have occurred with ingestions of 0.5–1 g of disulfiram; with blood alcohol levels of 1 mg/mL; a 30 g ingestion would produce serious toxicity	Headache, rash, peripheral or optic neuropathy, mucous membrane injury, psychotic behavior	Supportive treatment, gastric lavage or aspiration
Dopamine receptor antagonists	Fatal doses reported: chlorpromazine: 26 g (in an adult), 350 mg in a child; thiothixene: 2.5–4 g; phenothiazines: 1,050 mg–10.5 g	Sedation, hypotension, severe extrapyramidal symptoms, confusion, excitement, CNS depression, coma, arrhythmias, miosis, tremor, spasm, rigidity, seizures, dry mouth, ileus, difficulty in swallowing, muscular hypotonia, difficulty in breathing, hypothermia, vasomotor or respiratory collapse, sudden apnea	Symptomatic and supportive care; if clinically indicated, lavage may be performed with endotracheal tube with inflated cuff in place; emesis should not be induced; saline cathartic may be helpful; hypotension should be treated as necessary (avoid epinephrine): anticholinergics may be useful for extrapyramidal symptoms; exchange transfusions may be useful; oversedation and hypothermia should be treated as appropriate
Ethchlorvynol	6 g has been lethal; overdoses of 50 g and in one case 100 g have been survived	Hypotension, hypothermia, severe respiratory depression, apnea, deep coma (can last days to weeks), areflexia, mydriasis, bradycardia	Supportive treatment; gastric lavage with endotracheal tube with inflated cuff in place; maintain airway; give oxygen; maintain cardiorespiratory function and body temperature; monitor blood gases; provide pulmonary care; hemoperfusion with Amberlite XAD-4 resin hastens drug elimination; hemodialysis or peritoneal dialysis may be beneficial
Fenfluramine	2 g (460 mg in a child) was lowest reported fatal dose; 1.8 g in an adult is the highest reported nonfatal dose	Drowsiness, agitation, flushing, tremor, confusion, shivering, hyperventilation, dilated nonreactive pupils, tachycardia, hyperpyrexia, coma, seizures, cardiac arrest	Symptomatic and supportive care; gastric lavage; activated charcoal; endotracheal tube placement in consultation with an anesthesiologist is needed if trismus is present and lavage is to be performed; maintain cardiorespiratory function; cardiac monitoring; defibrillation, cardioversion, ventilatory support if needed; phenobarbital or diazepam for seizures or muscle hyperactivity; propranolol for severe tachycardia; lidocaine for ventricular extrasystoles; chlorpromazine may be useful for hyperthermia; forced acid diuresis with ammonium chloride may increase excretion rate
Fluoxetine	Lethal dose unknown (one death reported)	Restlessness, insomnia, agitation, tremor, hypomania, tachycardia, seizures, nausea, vomiting, hypertension, drowsiness, coma, nystagmus	Supportive and symptomatic care; keep airway open; maintain oxygenation and ventilation; monitor ECG and vital signs; gastric lavage (if clinically indicated, have endotracheal tube with cuff inflated during lavage) or emesis in recent ingestion, or use activated charcoal; IV diazepam for ongoing seizures; consider phenobarbital or phenytoin if refractory to diazepam

(continued)

Table 35.1–10 *(continued)*

Drug	Toxic or Lethal Dose[a]	Signs and Symptoms	Treatment[b]
Fluvoxamine	Two deaths solely due to fluvoxamine (dose not reported); 10 g has been survived	Drowsiness, vomiting, diarrhea, dizziness, coma, tachycardia, bradycardia, hypotension, ECG abnormalities, liver function abnormalities, convulsions	Establish and maintain airway; gastric lavage; activated charcoal 20–30 g every 4–6 hours for 24 hours; monitor ECG and vital signs
Glutethimide	5 g, severe intoxication; 10–20 g, often lethal	Hypotension, prolonged coma (up to days), shock, respiratory depression, hypothermia, fever, inadequate ventilation, apnea, cyanosis, fixed and dilated pupils, ileus, bladder atony, dry mouth, hyporeflexia, areflexia, intermittent spasticity or flaccidity	Supportive treatment; gastric lavage using 1 to 1 mixture of castor oil and water (may be more effective than aqueous lavage); perform with endotracheal tube in place with inflated cuff; leave 50 mL castor oil in stomach as a cathartic; activated charcoal may be of use; maintain airway and cardiorespiratory function; hemodialysis may be useful in severe cases (particularly with activated charcoal or soybean dialysate); hemoperfusion with Amberlite XAD-2 resin may be more effective than hemodialysis; charcoal hemoperfusion may be useful; continue drug removal procedures for at least 2 hours after the patient regains consciousness; maintain urinary output but avoid overhydration
Levodopa	Dose should not exceed 8 g a day in therapeutic use	Palpitations, arrhythmias, spasm or closing of eyes, psychosis	Symptomatic treatment; maintain airway, lavage; ECG monitoring; IV fluids; treat arrhythmias as necessary
Lithium	Lethal dose produces serum levels of 3.5 mEq/L 12 hours after ingestion	Diarrhea, vomiting, confusion, drowsiness, tremor, apathy, giddiness, nausea, ataxia, muscle rigidity, vertical nystagmus, impaired consciousness, cogwheel rigidity, coma, seizures, cardiovascular collapse	Induce emesis or lavage (lavage with endotracheal tube in place with cuff inflated if indicated); infuse 0.9% sodium chloride IV if toxicity is due to sodium depletion; hemodialysis for 8–12 hours if fluid and electrolyte imbalance does not respond to supportive measures; if level is 3 mEq/L or if level is 2–3 mEq/L and patient is deteriorating or if level has not decreased 20% in 6 hours, repeated courses of dialysis are often needed; goal is level of 1 mEq/L 8 hours after dialysis is completed
Meprobamate	12 g is usually lethal; 40 g overdoses have been survived	Stupor, drowsiness, lethargy, ataxia, coma, respiratory depression, hypotension	Supportive treatment; induce emesis or use gastric lavage with endotracheal tube in place with cuff inflated if clinically indicated; use activated charcoal after emptying stomach; maintain airway, respiration, and blood pressure; pressor agents can be used with caution if necessary; elimination may be enhanced by forced diuresis with hemodialysis, peritoneal dialysis, or osmotic diuresis
Methadone	Lethal dose: 40–60 mg in nontolerant persons	CNS depression (stupor to coma), pinpoint pupils, shallow respiration, bradycardia, hypotension, hypothermia, cold and clammy skin, apnea, cardiac arrest, mydriasis in severe hypoxia or terminal narcosis	Establish and maintain airway and respiration; gastric lavage; supportive care with IV fluids; naloxone may be used to treat respiratory depression; initial adult dose is 0.4–2 mg IV every 2–3 minutes if needed; if there is no response after a total of 10 mg has been given, other diagnoses should be considered; repeated doses of naloxone may be needed, as narcotic-induced respiratory depression may return as the effects of naloxone diminish; dosage regimens for continuous naloxone infusions are not well established and should be titrated to the patient's response; patients should be observed for sustained improvement after treatment

(continued)

Table 35.1–10 *(continued)*

Drug	Toxic or Lethal Dose[a]	Signs and Symptoms	Treatment[b]
Methylphenidate hydrochloride	2 g	Delirium, confusion, psychosis, agitation, hallucinations, palpitations, arrhythmias, hypertension, vomiting, hyperpyrexia, mydriasis, sweating, tremors, muscle twitching, seizures, coma	Emesis or lavage in mild cases; if patient is conscious, careful use of a short-acting barbiturate may be required before lavage in severe cases; supportive measures, including maintenance of respiratory and circulatory function; isolation to reduce external stimuli; protection against self-harm; external cooling procedures for hyperpyrexia
Methyprylon	Toxic blood concentration: 30 μg/mL	Confusion, somnolence, hypotension, tachycardia, edema, coma, shock, respiratory depression	Induce emesis or gastric lavage with endotracheal tube in place with cuff inflated if clinically indicated; support cardiorespiratory function; barbiturates can be used with caution to control seizures and agitation
Mirtazapine	Lethal dose unknown (no deaths reported solely due to mirtazapine)	Disorientation, drowsiness, impaired memory, tachycardia	Supportive measures; induce emesis or use gastric lavage with cuffed endotracheal tube in place, with cuff inflated if clinically indicated; activated charcoal
Monoamine oxidase inhibitors (MAOIs)	Single doses of 1.75–7 g have been fatal	Dizziness, drowsiness, irritability, ataxia, restlessness, insomnia, headache, tachycardia, hypotension, arrhythmia, confusion, fever, diaphoresis, hyporeflexia or hyperreflexia, respiratory depression, chest pain, shock, hypertension (rare)	Symptomatic and supportive care; induce emesis or use gastric lavage with endotracheal tube in place with inflated cuff if clinically indicated; maintain normal vital signs; correct fluid and electrolyte abnormalities with conservative measures; volume expansion for hypotension (pressor amines may be potentiated by MAOIs and may be of limited value); evaluate liver function immediately and 4–6 weeks later; barbiturates may relieve myoclonic reactions, but MAOIs may prolong their effect; phenothiazines can be used for agitation; hypertensive crisis mainly occurs in conjunction with tyramine; discontinue MAOIs and treat with phentolamine (5 to 10 mg by slow IV injection)
Naltrexone	Estimated 50–100 g	Unknown in humans; convulsions and respiratory failure in animals	Supportive care
Nefazodone	1–11 g have all been survived	Nausea, vomiting, somnolence	Supportive care; use gastric lavage with cuffed endotracheal tube in place, with cuff inflated if clinically indicated
Olanzapine	300 mg have been survived	Drowsiness, slurred speech	Establish and maintain airway; gastric lavage; activated charcoal; continuous cardiovascular monitoring; fluid management of hypotension; avoid epinephrine and dopamine in the presence of α-adrenergic blockade
Paroxetine	850 mg has been survived	Nausea, vomiting, drowsiness, tachycardia, mydriasis	Establish and maintain airway; gastric lavage; activated charcoal 20–30 g every 4–6 hours; monitor ECG and vital signs
Pemoline	2 g; hepatic effects not due to overdose	Excitement, agitation, restlessness, hallucinations, tachycardia, rhabdomyolysis, choreoathetosis, fulminant liver failure	Gastric lavage in mild cases; symptomatic treatment, maintain respiratory and circulatory function; monitor cardiac function; reduce stimulation; haloperidol or chlorpromazine for psychosis and agitation; IV benzodiazepines can control choreoathetosis; hemodialysis may be of value; liver transplantation for liver failure

(continued)

Table 35.1–10 *(continued)*

Drug	Toxic or Lethal Dose[a]	Signs and Symptoms	Treatment[b]
Risperidone	20–300 mg have all been survived	Drowsiness, sedation, tachycardia, hypotension, extrapyramidal symptoms, hyponatremia, hypokalemia, prolonged QT interval, widened QRS complex convulsions	Establish and maintain airway; gastric lavage; activated charcoal; continuous cardiovascular monitoring; disopyramide, procainamide, and quinidine should be avoided in the presence of arrhythmias; fluid management of hypotension; avoid epinephrine and dopamine in the presence of α-adrenergic blockade; anticholinergics for extrapyramidal symptoms
Sertraline	Three known overdoses at 750–2,100 mg; no deaths reported	Possible symptoms include confusion, ataxia, incoordination, hypotension, hypertension, seizures, arrhythmias, serotonin syndrome, coma, mydriasis	General symptomatic and supportive measures; establish and maintain airway; ensure adequate oxygenation and ventilation; use activated charcoal with sorbitol; monitor vital signs and cardiac function
Tacrine	2 g	Cholinergic crisis: nausea, vomiting, salivation, perspiration, bradycardia, hypotension, collapse, convulsions	Supportive care; tertiary anticholinergics such as atropine 1–2 mg IV (0.05 mg/kg IV), repeated every 10–30 minutes based on the clinical response; CPR for cardiovascular failure
Thyroid hormones	0.3 g/kg desiccated thyroid has caused severe toxicity (with recovery)	Nervousness, sweating, palpitations, abdominal cramps, diarrhea, tachycardia, hypertension, headache, arrhythmias, tremors, cardiac failure	Symptomatic and supportive treatment; induce emesis or use gastric lavage with endotracheal tube in place with cuff inflated if clinically indicated; control fluid loss, fever, hypoglycemia; give oxygen and maintain ventilation; β-adrenergic receptor antagonists can be used to counteract increased sympathetic activity
Trazodone	Patients have survived overdoses of 7.5 g and 9.2 g	Lethargy, vomiting, drowsiness, headache, orthostasis, dizziness, dyspnea, tinnitus, myalgias, tachycardia, incontinence, shivering, coma	Symptomatic and supportive treatment; induce emesis or use gastric lavage; forced diuresis may enhance elimination; treat hypotension and sedation as appropriate
Tricyclics and tetracyclics	700–1,400 mg: moderate to severe toxicity; 2.1–2.8 g: often fatal; one patient survived ingestion of 10 g amitriptyline; lowest known fatal dose of amitriptyline: 500 mg; average lethal dose of imipramine: 30 mg/kg (fatalities occurred with 500 mg)	Initial CNS stimulation, confusion, agitation, hallucinations, hyperpyrexia, hypertension, nystagmus, hyperreflexia, parkinsonian symptoms, mydriasis, ileus, constipation, seizures, CNS depression (follows stimulation), hyperthermia, areflexia, respiratory depression, cyanosis, hypotension, coma, cardiac conduction abnormalities, tachycardia, quinidinelike effects (QRS prolongation, the degree of which may be the best indication of the severity of the overdose)	Symptomatic and supportive care; monitor ECG and vital signs; support vital functions; establish and maintain airway; treat and correct fluid, electrolyte, acid-base, and temperature abnormalities; minimize stimulation; gastric lavage with activated charcoal or ipecac emesis if gag reflex is present and patient is awake; treat hypotension supportively; IV diazepam (with caution) for seizures; lidocaine, phenytoin, propranolol for life-threatening arrhythmias, sodium bicarbonate IV to achieve pH of 7.4–7.5 to help treat arrhythmias and hypotension; use of multiple antiarrhythmics or pacemaker may be needed in some cases; physostigmine has been used for anticholinergic symptoms, but its use is controversial because of serious adverse effects, and it should be used only for life-threatening treatment-refractory anticholinergic toxicity

(continued)

Table 35.1–10 *(continued)*

Drug	Toxic or Lethal Dose[a]	Signs and Symptoms	Treatment[b]
Valproic acid	One adult survived an ingestion of 36 g valproic acid as part of a polydrug overdose	Somnolence, coma	Supportive measures; lavage may be of limited value because of drug's rapid absorption; the value of emesis or lavage varies with time since ingestion if delayed-release preparations are ingested; maintain adequate urinary output; naloxone may reverse CNS depressant effects of overdose but may also reverse anticonvulsant effects and should be used with caution
Venlafaxine	6.75 g have been survived	Somnolence, convulsions, prolonged QT interval, mild tachycardia	Establish and maintain airway; gastric lavage; activated charcoal; continuous cardiovascular monitoring

[a] The toxic dose is the amount of the drug capable of producing signs and symptoms of an overdose. The same dose may also have lethal effects, depending on such factors as the rate of administration, the rate of absorption, and the age and general health of the patient. A toxic dose for one patient may be lethal for another. The ranges given in this table are approximate, based on available scientific literature.
The clinician should always consult Physician's Desk Reference *(PDR) or contact the manufacturer of the drug for the latest information on toxicity and lethality.*

[b] A patient may have ingested more than one substance, and the signs and symptoms may represent polysubstance abuse or overdose. Treatment must be adjusted accordingly, and a history (from other persons, if necessary) and an inspection of all drugs should be obtained.

pletion of the phase III trials, the pharmaceutical company can apply to the FDA for a NDA, which, if granted, allows the drug company to market the drug commercially. On average, only one in five agents subjected to clinical trials generates an NDA. The total elapsed time from initial identification of a drug to FDA approval is usually 15 years, and the cost averages $500 million per approved drug. In 1997, the FDA proposed a New Use Initiative, which will permit approval of new drugs or new indications for existing drugs based on fewer trials or on existing data that was collected for other reasons. Once marketed, a drug enters phase IV, in which postmarketing experience on a far larger patient population is monitored for the emergence of adverse effects. On occasion, the FDA has withdrawn approval of a drug for a certain indication based on severe toxicity.

Drugs under Development

Ten years from now the psychopharmacotherapy armamentarium will probably be very different from that available today. For a variety of reasons, however, it is difficult to predict which new drugs will come to market in the United States. First, for commercial reasons, pharmaceutical companies are secretive about their drugs under development. Second, a candidate drug may be well into phase III development before its association with a particularly severe adverse effect is noted, and the compound's development is terminated. Third, a candidate drug may be well into phase II or even phase III development before an assessment of its efficacy results in a determination that it is not significantly superior to competing compounds and does not merit the cost of introducing it commercially.

References

Beitman BD, Klerman GL, editors: *Integrating Pharmacotherapy and Psychotherapy.* American Psychiatric Press, Washington, 1991.

Dahl ML, Bertilsson L: Genetically variable metabolism of antidepressants and neuroleptic drugs in man. Pharmacogenetics *3:* 61, 1993.

Fisher S, Greenburg RP: How sound is the double-blind design for evaluating psychotropic drugs? J Nerv Ment Dis *181:* 345, 1993.

Hardman JG, Limbird LE, editors: *Goodman and Gilman's The Pharmacological Basis of Therapeutics,* ed 9. McGraw-Hill, New York, 1996.

Hyman SE, Arana GW, Rosenbaum JF: *Handbook of Psychiatric Drug Therapy,* ed 3. Little, Brown, Boston, 1996.

Janicak PG, Davis JM, Preskorn SH, Ayd FJ Jr: *Principles and Practice of Psychopharmacology,* ed 2. Williams & Wilkins, Baltimore, 1997.

Preskorn SH: *Clinical Pharmacology of Selective Serotonin Reuptake Inhibitors.* Professional Communications, Caddo, OK, 1996.

Rowland M, Tozer TN: *Clinical Pharmacokinetics: Concepts and Applications,* ed 2. Lea & Febiger, Philadelphia, 1990.

Welling PG, Tse FLS, Dighe SV, editors: *Pharmaceutical Bioequivalence.* Dekker, New York, 1991.

▲ 35.2 MEDICATION-INDUCED MOVEMENT DISORDERS

The psychopharmacological ideal of medications that improve patients' mood and thought processes while causing no unwanted adverse effects is approximated more closely with every generation of drugs. For example, in the past 5 to 10 years, new drugs have been approved for mood disorders (such as the serotonin-specific reuptake inhibitors [SSRIs], mirtazapine, nefazodone, and venlafaxine) and for psychotic disorders (such as the serotonin-dopamine antagonists). Each of these drugs represents a significant advance, in terms of adverse effects, over the main drugs available for these indications for the past 30 years. Nevertheless, reality falls short of the ideal for patients who require intensive psychopharmacological treatment and who may experience unwanted neurological adverse effects from their medications. Clinicians who pointedly alter the brain's chemistry in an effort to treat illness must be aware of the possible unintended consequences of this pharmacological approach. Adverse drug effects must be distinguished from features of the underlying disease, and effects ascribed to the drugs must be skillfully managed through changes in dosing, addition of adjunct medications, or substitutions of other agents. Clinicians should use the lowest effective dosage of any psychotropic medication, to reduce the risk of adverse effects, but this desire should be tempered by the need to prevent relapse of illness.

The most common medication-induced movement disorders in psychiatry are those attributed to the dopamine receptor antagonist antipsychotic drugs. These drugs act by blocking the binding of dopamine to the dopamine type 2 (D_2) receptors, some of which are located in the caudate nucleus and other nuclei in the basal ganglia that belong to the extrapyramidal motor system. It is thought that D_2 receptor blockade disables crucial neural pathways in the basal ganglia that are involved in the control of movements, both voluntary and involuntary; it also disinhibits primitive circuits that coarsely determine ''extrapyramidal'' abnormalities of muscle tone and movement. The clinical expression of the disarrayed loops of feedback and feed-forward regulation in the basal ganglia may include dystonic posturing, features of parkinsonism (tremor, rigidity, and bradykinesia), akathisia (restlessness), and choreiform (''dancing'') or athetoid (writhing) movements. The association between D_2 blockade and the extrapyramidal system is not straightforward: There is no immediate and direct temporal association between the administration of the drugs and the appearance of the various symptom patterns, which occur at different times after the administration of dopamine receptor antagonists (Fig. 35.2–1).

The newer antipsychotics, the serotonin-dopamine antagonists, produce much less D_2 receptor blockade and are much less likely to produce movement disorders; in preclinical trials, these drugs are significantly associated only with an increased risk of akathisia. Nonetheless, there have been a few case reports of more severe movement disorders even in patients on these newer agents. Because the natural history of psychotic disorders may include features of parkinsonism, dystonia, akathisia, and tardive dyskinesia, the contribution of specified drugs to movement disorders must be carefully assessed by withdrawing and rechallenging with the agent presumed responsible. Other psychotherapeutic agents, including antidepressants and antianxiety agents, have been occasionally reported to be associated with movement disorders. For example, SSRIs may cause akathisia.

The fourth edition of *Diagnostic and Statistical Manual of Mental Disorders* (DSM-IV) includes in the category of ''medication-induced movement disorders'' not only such disorders but also any medication-induced adverse effect that becomes a focus of clinical attention. When one of these diagnoses is made and included as a focus of treatment, the movement disorder or adverse effect diagnosis should be listed on Axis I of the DSM-IV multiaxial diagnostic formulation. When faced with a patient on medication who develops a movement disorder, clinicians should consider the differential diagnosis for these symptoms. For example, anxiety needs to be distinguished from akathisia, catatonia from neuroleptic malignant syndrome, parkinsonism from depression, and tardive dyskinesia from other basal ganglia-related movement disorders.

NEUROLEPTIC-INDUCED MOVEMENT DISORDERS

The most common neuroleptic-related movement disorders are parkinsonism, acute dystonia, and acute akathisia. The gen-

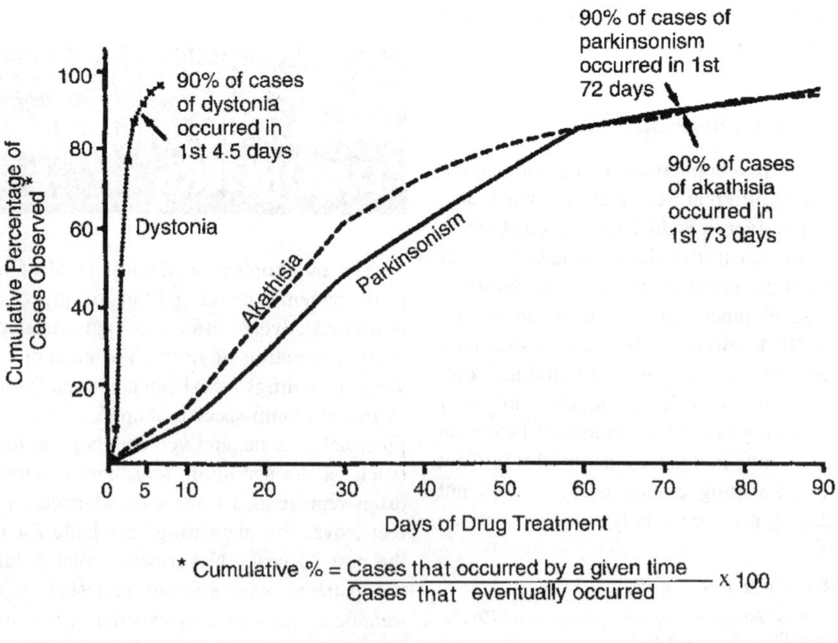
90% of cases of parkinsonism occurred in 1st 72 days
90% of cases of dystonia occurred in 1st 4.5 days
90% of cases of akathisia occurred in 1st 73 days
Dystonia
Akathisia
Parkinsonism
Cumulative Percentage of Cases Observed*
100
80
60
40
20
0
5
10
20
30
40
50
60
70
80
90
Days of Drug Treatment
* Cumulative % = Cases that occurred by a given time / Cases that eventually occurred x 100

FIGURE 35.2–1
Drug-induced extrapyramidal reactions: time for onset. (Reprinted with permission from Friedman JH: Drug-induced parkinsonism. In *Drug-Induced Movement Disorders,* AF Lang, WJ Weiner, editors, p 49. Futura, Mount Kisco, NY, 1992.)

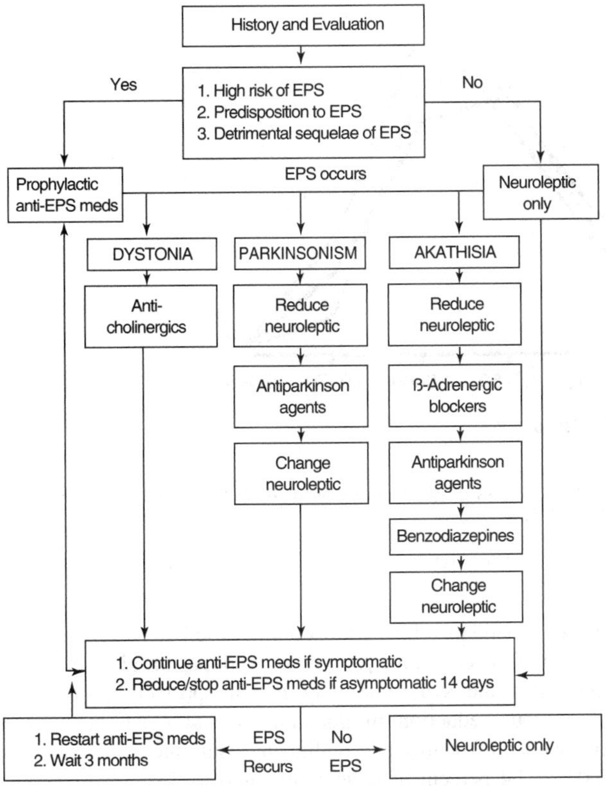
History and Evaluation
Yes
No
1. High risk of EPS
2. Predisposition to EPS
3. Detrimental sequelae of EPS
Prophylactic anti-EPS meds
EPS occurs
Neuroleptic only
DYSTONIA
PARKINSONISM
AKATHISIA
Anti-cholinergics
Reduce neuroleptic
Reduce neuroleptic
Antiparkinson agents
ß-Adrenergic blockers
Change neuroleptic
Antiparkinson agents
Benzodiazepines
Change neuroleptic
1. Continue anti-EPS meds if symptomatic
2. Reduce/stop anti-EPS meds if asymptomatic 14 days
1. Restart anti-EPS meds
2. Wait 3 months
EPS
Recurs
No
EPS
Neuroleptic only

FIGURE 35.2–2
Outline of the treatment approach for major extrapyramidal system *(EPS)* disorders. (Reprinted with permission from Casey DE: Neuroleptic drug-induced extrapyramidal syndromes and tardive dyskinesia. Schizophr Res *4:* 109, 1991.)

eral outline of the treatment approach for these three disorders is shown in Figure 35.2–2. Neuroleptic malignant syndrome is a life-threatening and often misdiagnosed condition. Neuroleptic-induced tardive dyskinesia is a late-appearing adverse effect of neuroleptic drugs and can be irreversible; but recent data indicate that the syndrome, although still serious and potentially disabling, is less pernicious than was previously thought in patients taking dopamine receptor antagonists and occurs only rarely in patients taking serotonin-dopamine antagonists.

Neuroleptic-Induced Parkinsonism

Neuroleptic-induced parkinsonism is characterized principally by the triad of resting tremor, rigidity, and bradykinesia (referred to in DSM-IV as akinesia) (Table 35.2–1). The typical parkinsonian tremor oscillates at a steady rate of 3 to 6 cycles per second, and it may be suppressed by intended movement. Rigidity is a disorder of muscle tone—that is, the degree of underlying tension involuntarily present in the muscles. Disorders of tone can result in either hypertonia (rigidity) or hypotonia. The hypertonia associated with neuroleptic-induced parkinsonism is of either the lead-pipe type, in which tone is continuously elevated, or the cogwheel type, in which a tremor is superimposed on rigidity. Cogwheel rigidity is revealed when an examiner rotates the hand around the axis of the wrist and encounters a regular rhythmical, ratchetlike resistance. The syndrome of bradykinesia can include a patient's masklike facial appearance, decreased accessory arm movements when the patient walks, and a characteristic difficulty in initiating movement. The so-called rabbit syndrome is a tremor affecting the lips and perioral muscles; it is most commonly thought to be part of the syndrome of neuroleptic-induced parkinsonism, although it often appears later in treatment than do other symptoms. Other parkinsonian features include slowed thinking, worsening of negative symptoms, excessive salivation, drooling, shuffling gait, micrographia, seborrhea, and dysphoria. The pathophysiology of neuroleptic-induced parkinsonism involves the blockade of D_2 receptors in the caudate at the termination of the nigrostriatal dopamine neurons, the same neurons that degenerate in idiopathic Parkinson's disease. Patients who are elderly (Fig. 35.2–3) and female are at the highest risk for neuroleptic-induced parkinsonism. More than 50 percent of patients treated with long-term, high-potency dopamine receptor antagonists may develop neuroleptic-induced parkinsonism at some point in their course of medication. Functional

Table 35.2–1
DSM-IV Diagnostic and Research Criteria for Neuroleptic-Induced Parkinsonism

Parkinsonian tremor, muscular rigidity or akinesia developing within a few weeks of starting or raising the dose of a neuroleptic medication (or after reducing a medication used to treat extrapyramidal symptoms).

A. One (or more) of the following signs or symptoms has developed in association with the use of neuroleptic medication:
   (1) parkinsonian tremor (ie, a coarse, rhythmic, resting tremor with a frequency between 3 and 6 cycles per second, affecting the limbs, head, mouth, or tongue)
   (2) parkinsonian muscular rigidity (ie, cogwheel rigidity or continuous "lead-pipe" rigidity)
   (3) akinesia (ie, a decrease in spontaneous facial expression, gestures, speech, or body movements)
B. The symptoms in criterion A developed within a few weeks of starting or raising the dose of a neuroleptic medication, or of reducing medication used to treat (or prevent) acute extrapyramidal symptoms (eg, anticholinergic agents).
C. The symptoms in criterion A are not better accounted for by a mental disorder (eg, catatonic or negative symptoms in schizophrenia, psychomotor retardation in a major depressive episode). Evidence that the symptoms are better accounted for by a mental disorder might include the following: the symptoms precede the exposure to neuroleptic medication or are not compatible with the pattern of pharmacologic intervention (eg, no improvement after lowering the neuroleptic dose or administering anticholinergic medication).
D. The symptoms in criterion A are not due to a nonneuroleptic substance or to a neurological or other general medical condition (eg, Parkinson's disease, Wilson's disease). Evidence that the symptoms are due to a general medical condition might include the following: the symptoms precede exposure to neuroleptic medication, unexplained focal neurological signs are present, or the symptoms progress despite a stable medication regimen.

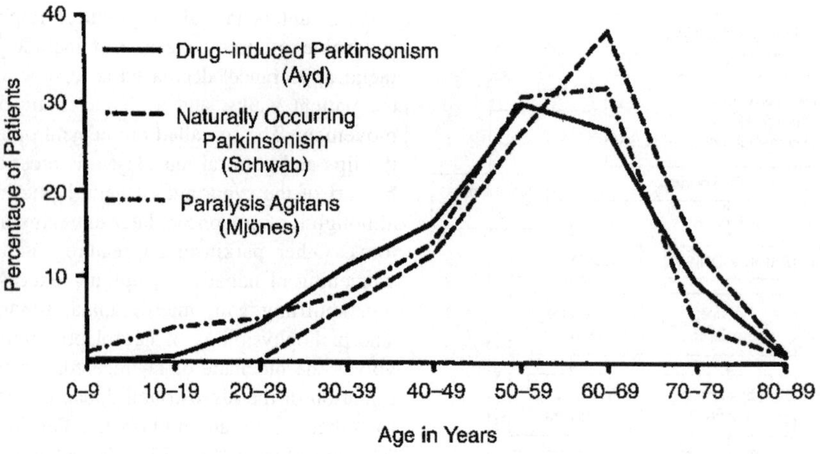
Percentage of Patients
40
30
20
10
Drug-induced Parkinsonism
(Ayd)
Naturally Occurring
Parkinsonism
(Schwab)
Paralysis Agitans
(Mjönes)
0–9
10–19
20–29
30–39
40–49
50–59
60–69
70–79
80–89
Age in Years

FIGURE 35.2–3

Parkinsonism: age distribution. (Reprinted with permission from Friedman JH: Drug-induced parkinsonism. In *Drug-Induced Movement Disorders,* AF Lang, WJ Weiner, editors, p 54. Futura, Mount Kisco, NY, 1992.)

neuroimaging studies have shown that parkinsonism is seen with 80 percent or higher occupancy of D_2 receptors in the caudate. By the same method, antipsychotic efficacy was seen with only 50 to 75 percent D_2 receptor occupancy.

Treatment. The benefits and the risks of prophylactic treatment with antiextrapyramidal system medications—for example, anticholinergics and amantadine (Symmetrel) or antihistamines—continue to be debated. Once parkinsonian symptoms appear, the three steps in treatment are to reduce the dosage of the neuroleptic, to institute antiextrapyramidal system medications, and possibly to change the neuroleptic. The serotonin-dopamine antagonists are a recommended alternative to the dopamine receptor antagonists for patients with neuroleptic-induced movement disorders. Studies have shown that the incidence of drug-induced parkinsonism is low for the serotonin-dopamine antagonists and for low-potency dopamine receptor antagonists, such as thioridazine (Mellaril). Extrapyramidal symptoms are associated with dosages of risperidone (Risperdal) in excess of the recommended maximum dose of 4 to 6 mg a day. A poorly understood phenomenon is the common development of tolerance to the parkinsonian adverse effects of these drugs. Once treatment is initiated, therefore, clinicians should attempt to reduce or stop the antiextrapyramidal system medications after 14 to 21 days of treatment to assess whether the medications are still necessary.

Neuroleptic Malignant Syndrome

Neuroleptic malignant syndrome is a life-threatening complication of antipsychotic treatment and can occur anytime during the course of treatment (Table 35.2–2). The symptoms include muscular rigidity and dystonia (hence the classification of the disorder as a movement disorder), akinesia, mutism, obtundation, and agitation. The autonomic symptoms include high fever, sweating, and increased blood pressure and heart rate. The neuroleptic malignant syndrome may also be precipitated in patients with Parkinson's disease by the abrupt withdrawal of the dopamine precursor levodopa, a finding that suggests that the syndrome may be one possible result of a precipitous reduction in dopamine receptor activation. The prevalence of neuroleptic malignant syndrome is estimated at 0.02 to 2.4 percent of patients exposed to dopamine receptor antagonists. In addition to supportive medical treatment, the most commonly used medications for the condition are dantrolene (Dantrium) and bromocriptine (Parlodel), although

Table 35.2–2
DSM-IV Research Criteria for Neuroleptic Malignant Syndrome

A. The development of severe muscle rigidity and elevated temperature associated with the use of neuroleptic medication.

B. Two (or more) of the following:
- (1) diaphoresis
- (2) dysphagia
- (3) tremor
- (4) incontinence
- (5) changes in level of consciousness ranging from confusion to coma
- (6) mutism
- (7) tachycardia
- (8) elevated or labile blood pressure
- (9) leukocytosis
- (10) laboratory evidence of muscle injury (eg, elevated CPK)

C. The symptoms in criteria A and B are not due to another substance (eg, phencyclidine) or a neurological or other general medical condition (eg, viral encephalitis).

D. The symptoms in criteria A and B are not better accounted for by a mental disorder (eg, mood disorder with catatonic features).

Reprinted with permission from American Psychiatric Association, *Diagnostic and Statistical Manual of Mental Disorders,* ed 4. Copyright, American Psychiatric Association, Washington, 1994.
CPK, creatine phosphokinase.

amantadine is sometimes used. Bromocriptine and amantadine possess direct dopamine receptor agonist effects and may serve to overcome the antipsychotic-induced dopamine receptor blockade. Mortality rates are reported to be 10 to 20 percent. The lowest effective dosage of antipsychotic drug should be used to reduce the chance of neuroleptic malignant syndrome. Antipsychotic drugs with anticholinergic effects appear less likely to cause neuroleptic malignant syndrome.

Neuroleptic-Induced Acute Dystonia

Dystonias are brief or prolonged contractions of muscles that result in obviously abnormal movements or postures, including oculogyric crises, tongue protrusion, trismus, torticollis, laryngeal-pharyngeal dystonias, and dystonic postures of the limbs and the trunk (Table 35.2–3). The development of dystonic symptoms is characterized by their early onset during the course of treatment with neuroleptics (see Fig. 35.2–1) and their high incidence in men, in patients under age 30, and in patients given high dosages of high-potency medications. The pathophysiological mechanism for dystonias is not clearly understood, although changes in neuroleptic concentrations and the resulting changes in homeostatic mechanisms within the basal ganglia may be the major causes of dystonias.

Treatment. Treatment of dystonias should be immediate; the most common agents are anticholinergic or antihistaminergic drugs. If a patient fails to respond to three doses of these drugs within 2 hours, the clinician should consider a cause of the dystonic movements other than neuroleptic medications. After resolution of the acute episode, oral anticholinergic agents should be given, and their effects reassessed every 2 weeks.

Neuroleptic-Induced Acute Akathisia

Akathisia is characterized by subjective feelings of restlessness, objective signs of restlessness, or both. Examples include a sense of anxiety, an inability to relax, jitteriness, pacing, rocking motions while sitting, and the rapid alternation of sitting and standing (Table 35.2–4). Akathisia can often be misdiagnosed as anxiety or as increased psychotic agitation, and it may result in an increase in the dosage of antipsychotic medication, which actually exacerbates the condition. Middle-aged women are at increased risk of akathisia, and the time

Table 35.2–3
DSM-IV Research Criteria for Neuroleptic-Induced Acute Dystonia

A. One (or more) of the following signs or symptoms has developed in association with the use of neuroleptic medication:
   (1) abnormal positioning of the head and neck in relation to the body (eg, retrocollis, torticollis)
   (2) spasms of the jaw muscles (trismus, gaping, grimacing)
   (3) impaired swallowing (dysphagia), speaking, or breathing (laryngeal-pharyngeal spasm, dysphonia)
   (4) thickened or slurred speech due to hypertonic or enlarged tongue (dysarthria, macroglossia)
   (5) tongue protrusion or tongue dysfunction
   (6) eyes deviated up, down, or sideward (oculogyric crisis)
   (7) abnormal positioning of the distal limbs or trunk

B. The signs or symptoms in criterion A developed within seven days of starting or rapidly raising the dose of neuroleptic medication; or of reducing a medication used to treat (or prevent) acute extrapyramidal symptoms (eg, anticholinergic agents).

C. The symptoms in criterion A are not better accounted for by a mental disorder (eg, catatonic symptoms in schizophrenia). Evidence that the symptoms are better accounted for by a mental disorder might include the following: the symptoms precede the exposure to neuroleptic medication or are not compatible with the pattern of pharmacological intervention (eg, no improvement after neuroleptic lowering of anticholinergic administration).

D. The symptoms in criterion A are not due to a nonneuroleptic substance or to a neurological or other general medical condition. Evidence that the symptoms are due to a general medical condition might include the following: the symptoms precede the exposure to the neuroleptic medication, unexplained focal neurological signs are present, or the symptoms progress in the absence of change in medication.

Table 35.2–4
DSM-IV Research Criteria for Neuroleptic-Induced Acute Akathisia

A. The development of subjective complaints of restlessness after exposure to a neuroleptic medication.

B. At least one of the following is observed:
   (1) fidgety movements or swinging of the legs
   (2) rocking from foot to foot while standing
   (3) pacing to relieve restlessness
   (4) inability to sit or stand for at least several minutes

C. The onset of the symptoms in criteria A and B occur within four weeks of initiating or increasing the dose of the neuroleptic, or of reducing medication used to treat (or prevent) acute extrapyramidal symptoms (eg, anticholinergic agents).

D. The symptoms in criterion A are not better accounted for by a mental disorder (eg, schizophrenia, substance withdrawal, agitation from a major depressive or manic episode, hyperactivity in attention-deficit/hyperactivity disorder). Evidence that symptoms may be better accounted for by a mental disorder might include the following: the onset of symptoms preceding the exposure to the neuroleptics, the absence of increasing restlessness with increasing neuroleptic doses, and the absence of relief with pharmacological interventions (eg, no improvement after decreasing the neuroleptic dose or treatment with medication intended to treat the akathisia).

E. The symptoms in criterion A are not due to a nonneuroleptic substance or to a neurological or other general medical condition. Evidence that symptoms are due to a general medical condition might include the onset of the symptoms preceding the exposure to neuroleptics or the progression of symptoms in the absence of a change in medication.

course is similar to that for neuroleptic-induced parkinsonism (see Fig. 35.2–1). Akathisia has been associated with the use of a wide range of psychiatric drugs, including antipsychotics, antidepressants, and sympathomimetics. It has recently been reported to be associated with a poor treatment outcome.

Treatment. The three basic steps in the treatment of akathisia are to reduce neuroleptic medication dosage, to attempt treatment with appropriate drugs, and to consider changing the neuroleptic. The most efficacious drugs in the treatment of akathisia are the β-adrenergic receptor antagonists, although anticholinergic drugs, benzodiazepines, and cyproheptadine may also be useful in some cases. Patients may be less likely to experience akathisia while receiving low-potency neuroleptics—for example, thioridazine—than while receiving high-potency neuroleptics—for example, haloperidol (Haldol); the serotonin-dopamine antagonists are associated with a low incidence of akathisia.

Neuroleptic-Induced Tardive Dyskinesia

Neuroleptic-induced tardive dyskinesia is a late-appearing disorder of involuntary, choreoathetoid movements (Table 35.2–5). The most common movements involve the orofacial region along with choreoathetoid movements of the fingers and toes. Athetoid movements of the head, neck, and hips also occur in seriously affected patients. In the most serious cases, patients may have irregularities in breathing and swallowing that result in aerophagia, belching, and grunting. The Abnormal Involuntary Movement Scale (AIMS), administered every 3 to 6 months to patients who are taking antipsychotic drugs, is an effective diagnostic tool for tardive dyskinesia (Table 35.2–6). The risk factors for tardive dyskinesia, which occurs in up to 25 percent of patients treated with dopamine receptor

Table 35.2–5
DSM-IV Research Criteria for Neuroleptic-Induced Tardive Dyskinesia

A. Involuntary movements of the tongue, jaw, trunk, or extremities have developed in association with the use of neuroleptic medication.

B. The involuntary movements are present over a period of at least four weeks, and occur in any of the following patterns:
(1) choreiform movements (ie, rapid, jerky, nonrepetitive)
(2) athetoid movements (ie, slow, sinuous, continual)
(3) rhythmic movements (ie, stereotypies)

C. The signs or symptoms in criteria A and B develop during exposure to a neuroleptic medication or within 4 weeks of withdrawal from an oral (or within 8 weeks of withdrawal from a depot) neuroleptic medication.

D. There has been exposure to neuroleptic medication for at least three months (one month if age 60 or older).

E. The symptoms are not due to a neurological or general medical condition (eg, Huntington's disease, Sydenham's chorea, spontaneous dyskinesia, hyperthyroidism, Wilson's disease); ill-fitting dentures; or exposure to other medications that cause acute reversible dyskinesia (eg, L-dopa, bromocriptine). Evidence that the symptoms are due to one of these etiologies might include the following: the symptoms precede the exposure to the neuroleptic medication or unexplained focal neurological signs are present.

F. The symptoms are not better accounted for by a neuroleptic-induced acute movement disorder (eg, neuroleptic-induced acute dystonia, neuroleptic-induced acute akathisia).

Reprinted with permission from American Psychiatric Association: *Diagnostic and Statistical Manual of Mental Disorders*, ed 4. Copyright, American Psychiatric Association, Washington, 1994.

Table 35.2–6
Abnormal Involuntary Movement Scale (AIMS) Examination Procedure

Patient identification: ______________ Date ________
Rated by:

Either before or after completing the examination procedure, observe the patient unobtrusively at rest (eg, in waiting room).

The chair to be used in this examination should be a hard, firm one without arms.

After observing the patient, he or she may be rated on a scale of 0 (none), 1 (minimal), 2 (mild), 3 (moderate), and 4 (severe) according to the severity of symptoms.

Ask the patient whether there is anything in his/her mouth (ie, gum, candy, etc.) and if there is to remove it.

Ask patient about the current condition of his/her teeth. Ask patient if he/she wears dentures. Do teeth or dentures bother patient now?

Ask patient whether he/she notices any movement in mouth, face, hands, or feet. If yes, ask to describe and to what extent they currently bother patient or interfere with his/her activities.

0 1 2 3 4	Have patient sit in chair with hands on knees, legs slightly apart, and feet flat on floor. (Look at entire body for movements while in this position.)
0 1 2 3 4	Ask patient to sit with hands hanging unsupported. If male, between legs; if female and wearing a dress, hanging over knees. (Observe hands and other body areas.)
0 1 2 3 4	Ask patient to open mouth. (Observe tongue at rest within mouth.) Do this twice.
0 1 2 3 4	Ask patient to protrude tongue. (Observe abnormalities of tongue movement.) Do this twice.
0 1 2 3 4	Ask the patient to tap thumb, with each finger, as rapidly as possible for 10–15 seconds; separately with right hand, then with left hand. (Observe facial and leg movements.)
0 1 2 3 4	Flex and extend patient's left and right arms. (One at a time.)
0 1 2 3 4	Ask patient to stand up. (Observe in profile. Observe all body areas again, hips included.)
0 1 2 3 4	Ask patient to extend both arms outstretched in front with palms down. (Observe trunk, legs, and mouth.)[a]
0 1 2 3 4	Have patient walk a few paces, turn and walk back to chair. (Observe hands and gait.) Do this twice.[a]

[a] Activated movements.

antagonists for over 4 years, include long-term treatment with neuroleptics, increasing age, female sex, the presence of a mood disorder, and the presence of a cognitive disorder. Tardive dystonia may appear after several years of exposure to neuroleptics, is more common in younger patients, and may coexist with tardive dyskinesia. It is characterized by sustained or slow involuntary movements of the neck, trunk, face, or limbs. Although various treatments for tardive dyskinesia have been unsuccessful, the course of tardive dyskinesia is considered less relentless than was previously thought. The serotonin-dopamine antagonists are associated with an extremely low risk of developing tardive dyskinesia and therefore present an effective treatment approach. Patients with tardive dyskinesia frequently experience an exacerbation of their symptoms when the dopamine receptor antagonist is withheld, whereas substitution of a serotonin-dopamine antagonist may limit the abnormal movements without worsening the progression of the dyskinesia. Before the appearance of the antipsychotics in the 1950s, clinicians noted that 1 to 5 percent of psychiatric inpatients with schizophrenia developed movements resembling tardive dyskinesia. This observation suggests that not all cases of tardive dyskinesia need necessarily be attributed to antipsychotics. Nevertheless, the treatment is the same whatever the cause.

MEDICATION-INDUCED POSTURAL TREMOR

Tremor is defined as a rhythmical alteration in movement that is usually faster than 1 beat per second (Table 35.2–7). Typically, tremors decrease during periods of relaxation and sleep and increase during periods of anger and increased tension. These characteristics sometimes mistakenly lead inexperienced clinicians to assume that a patient is faking the tremor. Whereas all the DSM-IV diagnoses previously discussed specifically include an association with neuroleptics, DSM-IV acknowledges that a range of psychiatric medications can produce tremor—most notably lithium (Eskalith), antidepressants, and valproate (Depakene)—and still other psychiatric medications are associated with the induction of tremor.

The treatment of tremor involves four general steps. First, the lowest possible dosage of the psychiatric drug should be used. Second, patients should minimize their caffeine and alcohol consumption. Third, the psychiatric drug should be taken at bedtime to minimize the amount of daytime tremor. Fourth, β-adrenergic receptor antagonists can be given to treat drug-induced tremors.

Table 35.2–7
DSM-IV Research Criteria for Medication-Induced Postural Tremor

A. A fine postural tremor that has developed in association with the use of a medication (eg, lithium, antidepressants, valproic acid).

B. The tremor (ie, a regular, rhythmic oscillation of the limbs, head, mouth, or tongue) has a frequency between 8 and 12 cycles per second.

C. The symptoms are not due to a preexisting nonpharmacologically induced tremor. Evidence that the symptoms are due to a preexisting tremor might include the following: the tremor was present before the introduction of the medication, the tremor does not correlate with serum levels of the medication, and the tremor persists after discontinuation of the medication.

D. The symptoms are not better accounted for by neuroleptic-induced parkinsonism.

Reprinted with permission from American Psychiatric Association: *Diagnostic and Statistical Manual of Mental Disorders,* ed 4. Copyright, American Psychiatric Association, Washington, 1994.

MEDICATION-INDUCED MOVEMENT DISORDER NOT OTHERWISE SPECIFIED

Although neuroleptics are the psychiatric drugs most commonly associated with movement disorders, almost all the most commonly used psychiatric drugs can produce movement disorders in some patients (Table 35.2–8). Furthermore, many nonpsychiatric drugs can produce movement disorders, and patients who are treated with both psychiatric and nonpsychiatric drugs may experience the additive effects of these medications on their movement disorders. DSM-IV also defines the diagnostic category as including movement disorders other than those already specified. Such movement disorders include tardive dystonia, tardive Tourette's syndrome, tardive myoclonus, tardive akathisia, and tardive parkinsonism. Table 35.2–9 lists several movement disorders and the drugs that induce them.

Table 35.2–8
DSM-IV Diagnostic Criteria for Medication-Induced Movement Disorder Not Otherwise Specified

This category is for medication-induced movement disorders not classified by any of the specific disorders listed above. Examples include: (1) parkinsonism, acute akathisia, acute dystonia, or dyskinetic movement that is associated with a medication other than a neuroleptic; (2) a presentation that resembles neuroleptic malignant syndrome that is associated with a medication other than a neuroleptic; or (3) tardive dystonia.

Reprinted with permission from American Psychiatric Association: *Diagnostic and Statistical Manual of Mental Disorders,* ed 4. Copyright, American Psychiatric Association, Washington, 1994.

ADVERSE EFFECTS OF MEDICATION NOT OTHERWISE SPECIFIED

This category allows clinicians to record the adverse effects of medications, other than movement symptoms, that become a focus of treatment (Table 35.2–10). Examples of such adverse effects include priapism, severe hypotension, and cardiac abnormalities.

Table 35.2–9
Drug-Induced Movement Disorders

Syndrome	Drugs Responsible	Degree
Postural tremor	Sympathomimetics	+ +
	Levodopa	+ +
	Amphetamines	+ +
	Bronchodilators	+ +
	Tricyclic drugs	+ +
	Lithium carbonate	+ +
	Caffeine	+ +
	Thyroid hormone	+ +
	Sodium valproate	+ +
	APDs	+ +
	Hypoglycemic agents	+ +
	Adrenocorticosteroids	+ +
	Alcohol withdrawal	+ +
	Amiodarone	+
	Cyclosporine A	+
	MAOIs	+ +
Acute dystonic reactions	APDs	+ +
	Metoclopramide	+ +
	Antimalarial agents	+
	Tetrabenazine	+/−
	Diphenhydramine	+/−
	Mefenamic acid	+/−
	Oxatomide	+/−
	Tricyclic drugs	+/−
	Flunarizone and cinnarizine	+/−
Akathisia	APDs	+ +
	Metoclopramide	+ +
	Reserpine	+ +
	Tetrabenazine	+ +
	Levodopa and dopamine agonists[a,b]	+
	Flunarizine and cinnarizine	+/−
	Ethosuximide	+/−
	Methysergide	+/−
	Amoxapine	+/−
Parkinsonism, including rabbit syndrome	APDs	+ +
	Metoclopramide	+ +
	Reserpine	+ +
	Tetrabenazine	+ +
	Methyldopa	+
	Flunarizine and cinnarizine	+/−
	Fluoxetine	+/−
	Lithium	+/−
	Phenelzine	+/−
	Phenytoin	+/−
	Captopril	+/−
	Alcohol withdrawal	+
	MPTP	+
	Other toxins (manganese, carbon disulfide, cyanide)	+
	Cytosine arabinoside	+/−
Chorea, including tardive dyskinesia and orofacial dyskinesia	APDs	+ +
	Metoclopramide	+ +
	Levodopa	+ +
	Direct dopamine agonists	+ +
	Indirect dopamine agonists and other catecholaminergic drugs[a]	+ +
	Anticholinergics	+
	Antihistaminics	+
	Oral contraceptives	+
	Phenytoin (T)	+
	Carbamazepine (T)	+/−
	Ethosuximide	+/−
	Phenobarbital (T)	+/−
	Lithium carbonate (T)	+/−
	Benzodiazepines	+/−
	MAOIs	+/−
	Tricyclic drugs	+/−
	Methyldopa	+/−
	Methadone	+/−
	Digoxin	+/−
	Alcohol withdrawal	+/−
	Toluene (glue-sniffing)	+/−
	Flunarizine and cinnarizine	+/−
Dystonia, including tardive dystonia (excluding acute dystonic reactions)	APDs	+ +
	Metoclopramide	+ +
	Levodopa	+ +
	Direct dopamide agonists[a]	+
	Phenytoin (T)	+
	Carbamazepine (T)	+/−
	Flunarizine and cinnarizine	+/−
	Trazodone	+/−
	Lithium	+/−
Neuroleptic malignant syndrome	APDs	+
	Tetrabenazine with AMPT	+/−
Tics (simple and complex), including aggravation of preexisting tic disorders	Withdrawal of antiparkinsonian drugs in Parkinson's disease	+/−
	Levodopa	+
	Direct dopamine agonists	+
	Indirect dopamine agonists	+ +
	APDs	+
	Carbamazepine	+/−
Myoclonus	Levodopa	+ +
	Anticonvulsants[c] (T)	+ +
	MAOIs	+ +
	Lithium	+ +
	Tricyclic drugs	+ +
	APDs	+/−
Asterixis	Anticonvulsants[c] (T)	+ +
	Levodopa	+/−
	Hepatotoxins (T)	+ +
	Respiratory depressants (T)	+ +

Adapted from Gershanil OS: Drug-induced movement disorders. Curr Opin Neurol Neurosurg *6:* 369, 1993.
+ +, well documented; common or not infrequent; +, relatively well documented; uncommon; +/−, not well documented or only small number of cases in literature; AMPT, α-methyl-paratyrosine; APD, antipsychotic drug; MAOI, monoamine oxidase inhibitor; MPTP, 1-methyl-4-phenyl-1,2,3,6-tetrahydropyridine; T, usually evidence of drug toxicity present (including serum drug levels).
[a] Includes apomorphine, bromocriptine, lisuride, pergolide.
[b] Includes amphetamines, methylphenidate, amantadine, pemoline, fenfluramine.
[c] Includes most categories of anticonvulsant drugs.

Table 35.2–10
DSM-IV Diagnostic Criteria for Adverse Effects of Medication Not Otherwise Specified

This category is available for optional use by clinicians to code side effects of medication (other than movement symptoms) when these adverse effects become a main focus of clinical attention. Examples include severe hypotension, cardiac arrhythmias, and priapism.

Reprinted with permission from American Psychiatric Association: *Diagnostic and Statistical Manual of Mental Disorders*, ed 4. Copyright, American Psychiatric Association, Washington, 1994.

References

Arya DK: Extrapyramidal symptoms with selective serotonin reuptake inhibitors. Br J Psychiatry *165* (6): 728, 1994.

Casey DE: Neuroleptic drug-induced extrapyramidal syndromes and tardive dyskinesia. Schizophr Res *4:* 109, 1991.

Dursun SM, Burke JG, Reveley MA: Toxic serotonin syndrome or extrapyramidal side-effects? Br J Psychiatry *166* (3): 401, 1995.

Gershanik OS: Drug-induced movement disorders. Curr Opin Neurol Neurosurg *6:* 369, 1993.

Glazer WM, Morgenstern H, Doucette JT: Predicting long-term risk of tardive dyskinesia in outpatients maintained on neuroleptic medications. J Clin Psychiatry *54:* 133, 1993.

Lang AE, Weiner WJ: *Drug-Induced Movement Disorders.* Futura, Mount Kisco, NY, 1992.

Meltzer HY: Pre-clinical pharmacology of atypical antipsychotic drugs: A selective review. Br J Psychiatry *168* (29, Suppl): 23, 1996.

McGreadie RG, Thara R: Abnormal movements in never-medicated Indian patients with schizophrenia. Br J Psychiatry *168:* 221, 1996.

van Harten PN, Kamphuis DJ, Matroos GE: Use of clozapine in tardive dystonia. Prog Neuropsychopharmacol Biol Psychiatry *20:* 263, 1996.

van Harten PN, Matroos GE, Kahn RS: The prevalence of tardive dystonia, tardive dyskinesia, parkinsonism and akathisia. The Curacao extrapyramidal syndromes study: I. Schizophr Res *19* (2–3): 195, 1996.

▲ 35.3 PSYCHOTHERAPEUTIC DRUGS

The treatment of psychiatric disorders has increasingly relied on pharmacological agents. Astute clinicians of earlier generations added drugs to their management, often as a result of a serendipitous observation of the effect of a drug intended for an unrelated medical condition. In the 1950s and 1960s, investigators built on observations of the benefits of chlorpromazine

Table 35.3–1
Index to Chapter: Alphabetic List of Generic Drugs

Generic Name	Trade Name	Subsection Title	Subsection Number
Acetophenazine	Tindal	Dopamine Receptor Antagonists	16
Alprazolam	Xanax	Benzodiazepine Receptor Agonists and Antagonists	6
Amantadine	Symadine, Symmetrel	Anticholinergics and Amantadine	3
Amitriptyline	Endep, Elavil	Tricyclics and Tetracyclics	31
Amobarbital	Amytal	Barbiturates and Other Similarly Acting Drugs	5
Amoxapine	Asendin	Tricyclics and Tetracyclics	31
Atenolol	Tenormin	β-Adrenergic Receptor Antagonists	2
Benztropine	Cogentin	Anticholinergics and Amantadine	3
Biperiden	Akineton	Anticholinergics and Amantadine	3
Brofaromine	Consonar	Monoamine Oxidase Inhibitor	22
Bromocriptine	Parlodel	Bromocriptine	7
Bupropion	Wellbutrin, Zyban	Bupropion	8
Buspirone	BuSpar	Buspirone	9
Butabarbital	Butisol	Barbiturates and Other Similarly Acting Drugs	5
Carbamazepine	Tegretol	Carbamazepine	11
Carisoprodol	Soma	Barbiturates and Other Similarly Acting Drugs	5
Carphenazine	Proketazine	Dopamine Receptor Antagonists	16
Chloral hydrate	Noctec	Chloral Hydrate	12
Chlordiazepoxide	Librium	Benzodiazepine Receptor Agonists and Antagonists	6
Chlorpromazine	Thorazine	Dopamine Receptor Antagonists	16
Chlorprothixene	Taractan	Dopamine Receptor Antagonists	16
Citalopram	No trade name	Serotonin-Specific Reuptake Inhibitors	27
Clomipramine	Anafranil	Tricyclics and Tetracyclics	31
Clonazepam	Klonopin	Benzodiazepine Receptor Agonists and Antagonists	6

(continued)

Table 35.3–1 ***(continued)***

Generic Name	Trade Name	Subsection Title	Subsection Number
Clonidine	Catapres	Clonidine	13
Clorazepate	Tranxene	Benzodiazepine Receptor Agonists and Antagonists	6
Clorgyline	No trade name	Monoamine Oxidase Inhibitors	22
Clozapine	Clozaril	Serotonin-Dopamine Antagonists	25
Cyproheptadine	Periactin	Antihistamines	4
Dantrolene	Dantrium	Dantrolene	14
Desipramine	Norpramin, Pertofrane	Tricyclics and Tetracyclics	31
Dextroamphetamine	Dexedrine	Sympathomimetics	28
Dexfenfluramine	Redux	Fenfluramine and Dexfenfluramine	17
Diazepam	Valium	Benzodiazepine Receptor Agonists and Antagonists	6
Diltiazem	Cardizem	Calcium Channel Inhibitors	10
Diphenhydramine	Benadryl	Antihistamines	4
Disulfiram	Antabuse	Disulfiram	15
Divalproex	Depakote	Valproate	33
Donepezil	Aricept	Acetylcholinesterase Inhibitors	1
L-Dopa	Larodopa	Levodopa	18
Doxepin	Adapin, Sinequan	Tricyclics and Tetracyclics	31
Droperidol	Inapsine	Dopamine Receptor Antagonists	16
Estazolam	ProSom	Benzodiazepine Receptor Agonists and Antagonists	6
Ethchlorvynol	Placidyl	Barbiturates and Other Similarly Acting Drugs	5
Fenfluramine	Pondimin	Fenfluramine and Dexfenfluramine	17
Flumazenil	Romazicon	Benzodiazepine Receptor Agonists and Antagonists	6
Fluoxetine	Prozac	Serotonin-Specific Reuptake Inhibitors	27
Fluphenazine	Permitil, Prolixin	Dopamine Receptor Antagonists	16
Flurazepam	Dalmane	Benzodiazepine Receptor Agonists and Antagonists	6
Fluvoxamine	Luvox	Serotonin-Specific Reuptake Inhibitors	27
Glutethimide	No trade name	Barbiturates and Other Similarly Acting Drugs	6
Halazepam	Paxipam	Benzodiazepine Receptor Agonists and Antagonists	6
Haloperidol	Haldol	Dopamine Receptor Antagonists	16
Hydroxyzine	Atarax, Vistaril	Antihistamines	4
Imipramine	Tofranil	Tricyclics and Tetracyclics	31
Isocarboxazid	Marplan	Monoamine Oxidase Inhibitors	22
Levodopa	Larodopa	Levodopa	18
Levothyroxine	Levoxyl, Levothroid, Synthroid	Thyroid Hormones	29
Liothyronine	Cytomel	Thyroid Hormones	29
Lithium	Eskalith, Lithobid	Lithium	19
Lorazepam	Ativan	Benzodiazepine Receptor Agonists and Antagonists	6
Loxapine	Loxitane	Dopamine Receptor Antagonists	16
Maprotiline	Ludiomil	Tricyclics and Tetracyclics	31
Mephobarbital	Mebaral	Barbiturates and Other Similarly Acting Drugs	5
Meprobamate	Miltown, Equanil	Barbiturates and Other Similarly Acting Drugs	5
Mesoridazine	Serentil	Dopamine Receptor Antagonists	16
Methadone	Dolophine	Methadone	20
Methylphenidate	Ritalin	Sympathomimetics	28
Methyprylon	Noludar	Barbiturates and Other Similarly Acting Drugs	5
Metoprolol	Lopressor	β-Adrenergic Receptor Antagonists	2
Midazolam	Versed	Benzodiazepines	6
Mirtazapine	Remeron	Mirtazapine	21
Moclobemide	Aurorix	Monoamine Oxidase Inhibitors	22
Molindone	Moban, Lidone	Dopamine Receptor Antagonists	16
Nadolol	Corgard	β-Adrenergic Receptor Antagonists	2

(continued)

Table 35.3–1 *(continued)*

Generic Name	Trade Name	Subsection Title	Subsection Number
Naltrexone	ReVia	Naltrexone	23
Nefazodone	Serzone	Nefazodone	24
Nifedipine	Procardia	Calcium Channel Inhibitors	10
Nimodipine	Nimotop	Calcium Channel Inhibitors	10
Nortriptyline	Pamelor	Tricyclics and Tetracyclics	31
Olanzapine	Zyprexa	Serotonin-Dopamine Antagonists	25
Orphenadrine	Dispal	Anticholinergics and Amantadine	3
Oxazepam	Serax	Benzodiazepines	6
Paraldehyde	Paral	Barbiturates and Other Similarly Acting Drugs	5
Paroxetine	Paxil	Serotonin-Specific Reuptake Inhibitors	27
Pemoline	Cylert	Sympathomimetics	28
Pentobarbital	Nembutal	Barbiturates and Other Similarly Acting Drugs	5
Perphenazine	Trilafon	Dopamine Receptor Antagonists	16
Phenelzine	Nardil	Monoamine Oxidase Inhibitors	22
Phenobarbital	Solfoton	Barbiturates and Other Similarly Acting Drugs	5
Pimozide	Orap	Dopamine Receptor Antagonists	16
Pindolol	Visken	β-Adrenergic Receptor Antagonists	2
Piperacetazine	No trade name	Dopamine Receptor Antagonists	16
Prazepam	Centrax	Benzodiazepine Receptor Agonists and Antagonists	6
Prochlorperazine	Compazine	Dopamine Receptor Antagonists	16
Procyclidine	Kemadrin	Anticholinergics and Amantadine	3
Promazine	Sparine	Dopamine Receptor Antagonists	16
Propranolol	Inderal	β-Adrenergic Receptor Antagonists	2
Protriptyline	Vivactil	Tricyclics and Tetracyclics	31
Quazepam	Doral	Benzodiazepine Receptor Agonists and Antagonists	6
Quetiapine	Seroquel	Serotonin-Dopamine Antagonists	25
Reserpine	Diupres	Dopamine Receptor Antagonists	16
Risperidone	Risperdal	Serotonin-Dopamine Antagonists	25
Secobarbital	Seconal	Barbiturates and Other Similarly Acting Drugs	5
Selegiline	Eldepryl, Deprenyl	Monoamine Oxidase Inhibitors	22
Sertindole	Serlect	Serotonin-Dopamine Antagonists	25
Sertraline	Zoloft	Serotonin-Specific Reuptake Inhibitors	27
Tacrine	Cognex	Acetylcholinesterase Inhibitors	1
Temazepam	Restoril	Benzodiazepine Receptor Agonists and Antagonists	6
Thioridazine	Mellaril	Dopamine Receptor Antagonists	16
Thiothixene	Navane	Dopamine Receptor Antagonists	16
L-Thyroxine	Levoxyl, Levothroid, Synthroid	Thyroid Hormones	29
Tranylcypromine	Parnate	Monoamine Oxidase Inhibitors	22
Trazodone	Desyrel	Trazodone	30
Triazolam	Halcion	Benzodiazepine Receptor Agonists and Antagonists	6
Trifluoperazine	Stelazine	Dopamine Receptor Antagonists	16
Triflupromazine	Vesprin	Dopamine Receptor Antagonists	16
Trihexyphenidyl	Artane	Anticholinergics and Amantadine	3
L-Triiodothyronine	Cytomel	Thyroid Hormones	29
Trimipramine	Surmontil	Tricyclics and Tetracyclics	31
L-Tryptophan	No trade name	L-Tryptophan	32
Valproate	Depakene	Valproate	33
Venlafaxine	Effexor	Serotonin-Norepinephrine Reuptake Inhibitors	34
Verapamil	Calan, Isoptin	Calcium Channel Inhibitors	10
Yohimbine	Yocon	Yohimbine	34
Ziprasidone	Zeldox	Serotonin-Dopamine Antagonists	25
Zolpidem	Ambien	Benzodiazepine Receptor Agonists and Antagonists	6

for psychosis, imipramine and iproniazid for depression, and chlordiazepoxide for anxiety to synthesize chemically related compounds to test on patients who had the respective disorders. This period marked the heyday of empirical development of psychotherapeutic drugs. Subsequent neurobiological investigations of the mechanism of actions of these agents led to the dopamine hypothesis of schizophrenia, the serotonin and norepinephrine hypothesis of affective disorders, and the serotonin and γ-aminobutyric acid (GABA) hypothesis of anxiety disorders. The neurochemical insights in turn have allowed investigators to develop assays not for clinical efficacy, but specifically for the ability of a novel chemical compound to influence one or more of these ligand-receptor systems in an in vitro model system. This approach, called rational drug design, has yielded agents that are highly specific for the desired neurotransmitter systems, yet lack interactions with other receptors that are normally associated with adverse effects. One potential pitfall of such a "rational" approach is the possibility that drug screens based on an incomplete understanding of the biological basis of psychopathology might exclude potentially valuable agents. For example, clozapine (Clozaril) might never have emerged from rational screens for antipsychotic drugs. Any drug identified in an in vitro screen must be thoroughly tested in a series of preclinical and clinical trials, as supervised by the Food and Drug Administration. Such rational drug design is likely to yield many interesting and safe new agents in the coming years; psychopharmacology will probably become ever more widely practiced by nonspecialists, who will be less reliant on expert advice about adverse effects and drug–drug interactions than has been necessary with the classical drugs.

A parallel trend in psychopharmacology is the trial of a particular class of medications in a wide variety of clinical conditions to broaden the array of useful indications. Therefore, it is no longer practical to discuss psychopharmacological drugs according to therapeutic indication, and in this book, each drug is discussed according to its pharmacological category. Moreover, this organization anticipates the development of newer agents through rational drug design, which is grounded in established and emerging insights into the neurobiological basis of mental illness.

GUIDE TO USE

The table of contents to this chapter section lists the 34 groups into which drugs used in psychiatry have been divided for discussion in this textbook. An alphabetical list of generic drug names discussed in this book is presented in Table 35.3–1, with cross-references to the subsections in which they are discussed. A list of therapeutic indications and the drugs commonly used for these indications is presented in Table 35.3–2, with cross-references to the appropriate subsections.

COMBINATION DRUGS

In addition to the drugs that contain a single active component, a few combination drugs are available in the United States (Table 35.3–3). The use of such drugs may increase patient compliance by simplifying the drug regimen. A problem with combination drugs, however, is that clinicians have little flexibility in adjusting the dosage of one of the components; that is, the use of combination drugs may cause two drugs to be administered when only one drug continues to be necessary for therapeutic efficacy.

Table 35.3–2
Major Mental Disorders and the Drugs and Classes of Drugs Used in Their Treatment

Indication/Drug (Drug Class)	Subsection Number
Aggression and agitation (see Intermittent explosive disorder)	
Akathisia (see Medication-induced movement disorders)	
Alcohol-related disorders	
β-Adrenergic receptor antagonists	2
Benzodiazepines	6
Carbamazepine	11
Disulfiram	15
Lithium	19
Naltrexone	23
Anorexia nervosa (see Eating disorders)	
Anxiety (see also specific anxiety disorders)	
Antihistamines	4
Barbiturates and similarly acting drugs	5
Benzodiazepines	6
Buspirone	9
Serotonin-specific reuptake inhibitors	27
Attention-deficit/hyperactivity disorder (in children or adults)	
Clonidine	13
Sympathomimetics	28
Tricyclics and tetracyclics	31
Bupropion	8
Bipolar disorders	
Benzodiazepines (especially clonazepam)	6
Calcium channel inhibitors	10
Carbamazepine	11
Dopamine receptor antagonists	16
Lithium	19
Serotonin-Dopamine Agonists	25
L-Tryptophan	32
Valproate	33
Bulimia nervosa (see Eating disorders)	
Cyclothymic disorder (see Bipolar disorders)	
Delusional disorder (see Schizophrenia)	
Dementia of the Alzheimer's type (cognitive symptoms)	
Acetylcholinesterase Inhibitors	1

(continued)

Table 35.3–2 *(continued)*

Indication/Drug (Drug Class)	Subsection Number
Depressive disorders	
Benzodiazepines (especially alprazolam)	6
Bromocriptine	7
Bupropion	8
Carbamazepine	11
Lithium	19
Mirtazapine	21
Monoamine oxidase inhibitors	22
Nefazodone	24
Serotonin-specific reuptake inhibitors	27
Sympathomimetics	28
Thyroid hormones	29
Trazodone	30
Tricyclics and tetracyclics	31
L-Tryptophan	32
Serotonin-norepinephrine reuptake inhibitors	26
Dysthymic disorder (see Depressive disorders)	
Dystonia (see Medication-induced movement disorders)	
Eating disorders	
Fenfluramine and dexfenfluramine	17
Lithium	19
Monoamine oxidase inhibitors	22
Serotonin-specific reuptake inhibitors	27
Sympathomimetics	28
Tricyclics and tetracyclics	31
Generalized anxiety disorder	
β-Adrenergic receptor antagonists	2
Barbiturates and similarly acting drugs	5
Benzodiazepines	6
Buspirone	9
Serotonin-specific reuptake inhibitors	27
Tricyclics and tetracyclics	31
Intermittent explosive disorder	
β-Adrenergic receptor antagonists	2
Barbiturates (primarily for acute agitation)	5
Buspirone	9
Carbamazepine	11
Dopamine receptor antagonists	16
Lithium	19
Valproate	33
Medication-induced movement disorders (see also Neuroleptic malignant syndrome)	
β-Adrenergic receptor antagonists	2
Amantadine	3
Anticholinergics	3
Antihistamines	4
Benzodiazepines	6
Levodopa	18
Neuroleptic malignant syndrome	
Bromocriptine	7
Dantrolene	14
Obsessive-compulsive disorder	
Serotonin-specific reuptake inhibitors	27
Tricyclics and tetracyclics (especially clomipramine)	31
Opioid-related disorders	
Clonidine	13
Methadone	20
Naltrexone	23
Panic disorder (with and without agoraphobia)	
β-Adrenergic receptor antagonists	2
Benzodiazepines (especially alprazolam and clonazepam)	6
Monoamine oxidase inhibitors	22
Serotonin-specific reuptake inhibitors	27
Tricyclics and tetracyclics	31
Parkinsonism (see Medication-induced movement disorders)	
Phobias (see also Panic disorder)	
β-Adrenergic receptor antagonists	2
Benzodiazepines	6
Monoamine oxidase inhibitors	22
Posttraumatic stress disorder	
Monoamine oxidase inhibitors	22
Trazodone	27
Serotonin-specific reuptake inhibitors	
Tricyclics and tetracyclics	31
Psychosis (see Schizophrenia)	
Rabbit syndrome (see Medication-induced movement disorders)	
Schizoaffective disorder (see Depressive disorders, Bipolar disorders, and Schizophrenia)	
Schizophrenia	
Benzodiazepines	6
Carbamazepine	11
Dopamine receptor antagonists	16
Lithium	19
Serotonin-dopamine antagonists	25
Sexual dysfunctions	
Antihistamines (cyproheptadine)	4
Yohimbine	34
Sleep disorders	
Antihistamines	4
Barbiturates and similarly acting drugs	5
Benzodiazepines	6
Chloral hydrate	12
Sympathomimetics	28
Trazodone	30
L-Tryptophan	32
Tic disorders	
Clonidine	13
Dopamine receptor antagonists (especially pimozide)	16
Serotonin-dopamine antagonists (especially risperidone)	16
Tricyclics and tetracyclics	31
Tourette's disorder (see Tic disorders)	
Violence (see Intermittent explosive disorder)	

Table 35.3–3
Combination Drugs Used in Psychiatry

Ingredients	Preparation	Manufacturer	Amount of Each Ingredient	Recommended Dosage	Indications	DEA Control
Perphenazine and amitriptyline	Triavil	Merck, Sharp & Dohme	Tablet—2:25, 4:25, 4:50, 2:10, 4:10	Initial therapy: tablet of 2:25 or 4:25 qid	Depression and associated anxiety	0
	Etrafon	Schering		Maintenance therapy: tablet 2:25 or 4:25 bid or qid		
Meprobamate and benactyzine	Deprol	Wallace	Tablet—400:1	Initial therapy: one tablet qid. Maintenance therapy: initial dosage may be increased to six tablets a day, then gradually reduced to the lowest levels that provide relief	Depression and associated anxiety	IV
Dextroamphetamine and amphetamine	Biphetamine[a]	Fisons	Sustained release capsule—6.25:6.24	One capsule in the morning	Exogenous obesity ADHD	II
	Adderal	Richwood	Tablet—5:5, 10:10	3–5 years: 2.5 mg/d 6 years and older: 5 mg/d		
Chlordiazepoxide and clidinium bromide	Librax	Roche	Capsule—5:25	One or two capsules tid or qid, before meals and at bedtime	Peptic ulcer, gastritis, duodenitis, irritable bowel syndrome, spastic colitis, and mild ulcerative colitis	0
Chlordiazepoxide and amitriptyline	Limbitrol	Roche	Tablet—5:12.5, 10:25	Tablet of 5:12.5 tid or qid. Tablet of 10:25 tid or qid, initially, then may increase to six tablets daily as required	Depression and associated anxiety	IV

ADHD, attention-deficit/hyperactivity disorder; DEA, Drug Enforcement Administration (see Table 35.1–3).
[a] The US Food and Drug Administration recommends the use of amphetamine only for weight reduction and ADHD.

▲ 35.3.1 ACETYLCHOLINESTERASE INHIBITORS

Alzheimer's disease has proved the most intractable behavioral disorder to treat pharmacologically. It is one of the most active areas of basic neurobiological research and of drug development, because it is a public health concern of increasing significance. Yet, so far only two drugs have been approved by the Federal Drug Administration (FDA) for treatment of cognitive deficits, tacrine (Cognex) and donepezil (Aricept). Both of these drugs are acetylcholinesterase inhibitors, which reduce intrasynaptic cleavage and inactivation of acetylcholine and thus potentiate cholinergic neurotransmission, which in turn tends to produce a modest improvement in memory and goal-directed thought. The hippocampus is thought to be a major site of action of acetylcholinesterase inhibitors (Fig. 35.3.1–1). The beneficial effects of acetylcholinesterase inhibitors on memory and mood may be noticed by patients in 1 to 3 days, but objective slowing of the decline in memory function that typifies Alzheimer's disease may not be apparent for several months. Preliminary studies suggested the efficacy of physostigmine, a long-known acetylcholinesterase inhibitor, but tacrine has a longer half-life and a wider therapeutic window than does physostigmine, which has not entered widespread use for this indication.

From 1993 until November 1996 tacrine was the only drug available, and several untoward effects rendered it useful to only a minority of patients who have Alzheimer's disease. Do-

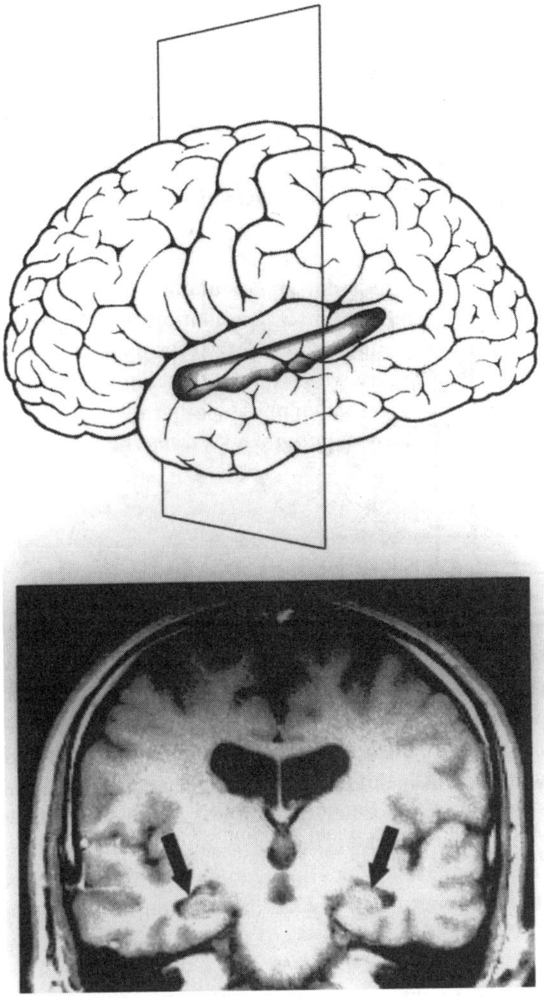

FIGURE 35.3.1–1

The hippocampus is a major site of action of memory-enhancing acetylcholinesterase inhibitors. **Upper.** Schematic depiction of the hippocampus in the temporal lobe. **Lower.** Magnetic resonance image in the coronal plane at the level indicated in the upper drawing. *Arrows* denote the hippocampi at the inner border of the temporal lobes. (Reprinted with permission from Spitzer M: *Geist im Netz,* p 215. Spektrum Akademischer Verlag, Heidelberg, 1996.)

nepezil, which was approved in November 1996, has a simpler dosage regimen, has fewer adverse effects, and does not require weekly blood tests; it is therefore likely to become more widely used. Other similar agents are in the investigational stages of development but are not yet available for use in the United States, including sustained-release physostigmine salicylate (Synapton), ENA 713 (Exelon), galantamine, suronacrine, eptastigmine, and metrifonate. These drugs are considered most useful for patients who have mild-to-moderate memory loss but who nevertheless have preservation of enough of their basal forebrain cholinergic neurons to benefit from augmentation of cholinergic neurotransmission. Cognitive enhancers, such as the acetylcholinesterase inhibitors, are best used as part of a multifaceted approach to the relentless diminution in the basic skills of daily living that affects Alzheimer's patients and their families. Some data show that acetylcholinesterase inhibitors may allow patients to maintain nearly the same scores on cognition scales over several months, whereas control groups would be expected to worsen over the same time. Neurobiologists speculate that preserved cognition maintains existing synaptic connections and that the acetylcholinesterase inhibitors may therefore preserve interneuronal pathways (Fig. 35.3.1–2). Unfortunately, the effect is always temporary, as these drugs have no impact on the underlying neurodegenerative condition.

The approval of tacrine was an important first step in indicating that clinically important treatment effects can be attained through the manipulation of the central nervous system (CNS) cholinergic system. Second-generation anticholinesterases and selective muscarinic and nicotinic receptor agonists will receive increasing attention as potential therapeutic approaches over the next decade. The oldest putative cognition-enhancing drug is dihydroergotoxine (Hydergine), which was introduced in the 1940s. A mixture of four ergotoxine derivatives, the drug has diverse effects on the central α-adrenergic, dopaminergic, and serotonergic systems. Several clinical trials of variable rigor have failed to demonstrate a clear benefit of Hydergine.

Other treatment approaches are also beginning to be evaluated. These approaches fall under six broad categories: agents affecting amyloid deposition directly; agents that may stabilize neuronal membranes and therefore prolong neuronal life span; estrogens and nerve growth factors, which provide trophic support to neurons, especially those in the basal forebrain; antioxidants (such as vitamin E), *N*-methyl-D-aspartate glutamate receptor antagonists, calcium channel blockers (for example, nimodipine), monoamine oxidase type B inhibitors (for example, selegiline), and other agents that may reduce excitotoxic or free-radical–mediated cell death; angiotensin-converting enzyme inhibitors; and phosphodiesterase inhibitors (Fig. 35.3.1–3).

TACRINE

Tacrine was first synthesized in 1945 although its inhibition of acetylcholinesterase was not recognized and demonstrated until 1953. In the late 1940s, tacrine was found to antagonize morphine-induced narcosis in dogs, and this finding led to its use as an adjuvant to morphine treatment of severe pain in cancer patients. The first small pilot studies of the use of tacrine in the treatment of dementia of the Alzheimer's type were conducted in the early 1980s.

Chemistry

The molecular structure of tacrine is shown in Figure 35.3.1–4.

Pharmacological Actions

Pharmacokinetics. Tacrine is absorbed rapidly from the gastrointestinal tract. Peak plasma concentrations are reached about 90 minutes after oral dosing. Tacrine is rapidly metabolized and is cleared by the hepatic route. The half-life

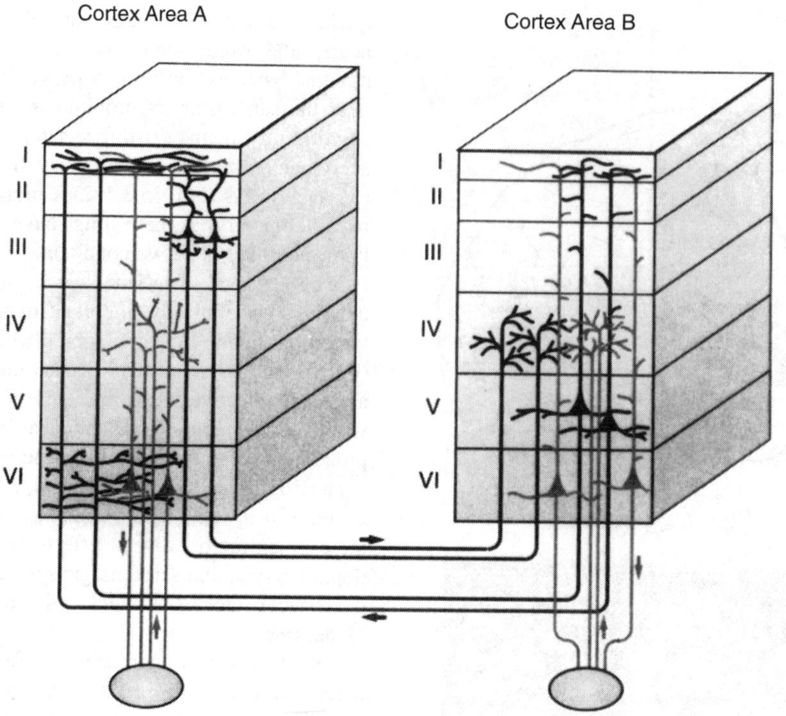
Cortex Area A
Cortex Area B
I
II
III
IV
V
VI
I
II
III
IV
V
VI

FIGURE 35.3.1–2
The loss of intracortical connections *(small arrows)* is strongly associated with dementia. Experts speculate that acetylcholinesterase inhibitors may preserve intracortical fibers, which would otherwise atrophy from disuse. The drugs potentiate cholinergic neurotransmission, which serves to strengthen existing synaptic connections. It may therefore be important to administer the drugs early in the disease to slow the process of degeneration of interneuronal connections. (Reprinted with permission from Spitzer M: *Geist im Netz,* p 137. Spektrum Akademischer Verlag, Heidelberg, 1996.)

of tacrine is about 3 to 4 hours, thereby necessitating 4-times-daily dosing.

Pharmacodynamics. Tacrine's primary mechanism of action is reversible, nonacetylating inhibition of acetylcholinesterase, the enzyme that catabolizes acetylcholine. The inhibition of the enzyme results in high concentrations of acetylcholine in the synaptic clefts. Some data indicate that tacrine also affects excitatory amino acids (for example, glutamate and aspartate), potassium channels, and biogenic amine systems, although the contribution of these pharmacodynamic effects to the clinical effects of tacrine is unknown.

Effects on Specific Organs and Systems

In addition to its effects on cognitive performance, tacrine affects the liver and the parasympathetic nervous system. Tacrine is associated with an increase in hepatic enzymes—serum glutamic–oxaloacetic transaminase (SGOT) and serum glutamic–pyruvic transaminase (SGPT)—in 25 to 30 percent of all patients. Because of its cholinomimetic properties, tacrine causes activation of the parasympathetic nervous system and results in all the usual signs and symptoms of muscarinic activity: nausea, vomiting, diarrhea, and other autonomic symptoms.

Therapeutic Indications

The only indication for tacrine at present is the treatment of mildly to moderately demented patients who have dementia of the Alzheimer's type. The efficacy of tacrine in mildly demented patients and in patients who have other forms of dementia has not as yet been studied. Tacrine was approved for clinical use primarily on the basis of two large multicenter placebo-controlled studies, although a number of other studies with various designs have also demonstrated the clinical efficacy of tacrine. The two basic studies demonstrated tacrine's beneficial effect as measured both by a specific cognitive rating scale and by a clinically based global impression scale. Recent data show that tacrine may delay or reduce the need for nursing home placement.

Precautions and Adverse Reactions

On the basis of the available studies, researchers believe that about 70 percent of all patients started on tacrine will be able to tolerate long-term treatment with the drug. The most troublesome and common side effects are potentially significant elevations in hepatic transaminase levels in 25 to 30 percent of the patients, nausea and vomiting in about 20 percent of the patients, and diarrhea and other cholinergic symptoms in about 11 percent of the patients. Aside from elevations in

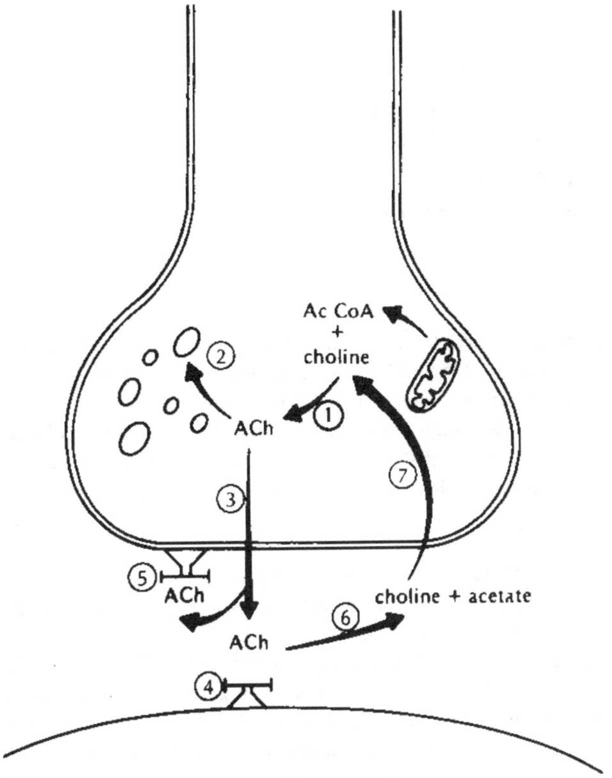
Ac CoA
+
choline
ACh
1
2
3
ACh
5
ACh
4
6
7
choline + acetate

FIGURE 35.3.1–3

Potential sites of drug action at cholinergic synapses. Acetylcholinesterase inhibitors, such as donepezil and tacrine, block the hydrolysis of acetylcholine *(ACh)* in the synaptic cleft *(6)* and therefore prolong the action of secreted ACh. Anticholinergic drugs, such as benztropine and trihexyphenidyl, block presynaptic *(5)* and postsynaptic *(4)* muscarinic receptors and therefore reduce the action of intrasynaptic ACh. Other sites of potential drug action for which no clinical agents are yet available include synthesis of ACh *(1)*, transport of ACh into vesicles *(2)*, secretion of ACh into the synaptic cleft *(3)*, and reuptake of choline *(7)*. (Reprinted with permission from Cooper JR, Bloom FE, Roth RH: *The Biochemical Basis of Neuropharmacology*, ed 7, p 221. Oxford University Press, New York, 1996.)

transaminase levels, the most common specific adverse effects associated with tacrine treatment are nausea, vomiting, myalgia, anorexia, and rash, but only nausea, vomiting, and anorexia have been found to have a clear relationship to the dosage. Decreases in weight, eructation, and increased sweating may also be caused by tacrine treatment, but these effects occur in less than 2 percent of tacrine-treated patients. Transaminase elevations, if present, will characteristically develop during the first 6 to 12 weeks of treatment, and cholinergically mediated events are dosage related. For this reason, weekly transaminase determinations are recommended for the first 18 weeks of treatment. No significant effects of tacrine treatment have been seen in vital signs, in cardiac function as indicated by electrocardiograms or in laboratory measures of anything other than transaminases. Although a low incidence of white blood cell dyscrasias (for example, neutropenia, leukopenia, and agranulocytosis) has been associated with a metabolite of tacrine (1-hydroxytacrine, velnacrine), there is no evidence at this time that such blood dyscrasias are associated with tacrine treatment.

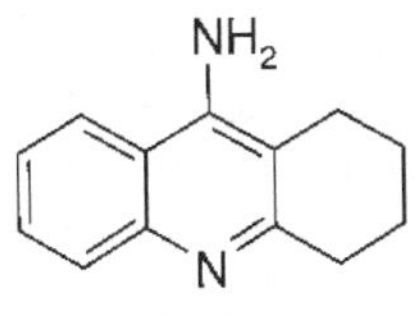
NH_2
N

Tacrine

FIGURE 35.3.1–4

Molecular structure of tacrine.

Hepatotoxicity. Tacrine is clearly associated with increases in the plasma levels of alanine aminotransferase (ALT, formerly SGPT) and aspartate aminotransferase (AST, formerly SGOT). The ALT measurement is the more sensitive indicator for the hepatic effects of tacrine. About 50 percent of tacrine-treated patients show ALT levels higher than the upper limit of normal (ULN); about 25 to 30 percent of the patients show ALT levels higher than 3 times the upper limit of normal (3 × ULN); and about 2 percent of the patients have ALT levels higher than 20 times the upper limit of normal (20 × ULN). Women are more likely than men to have elevated ALT levels, as evidenced by 54 percent of women who have ALT values ULN, compared with 43 percent of men who have ALT values ULN. The development of elevated ALT levels is not correlated with age or weight. About 95 percent of tacrine-treated patients who have elevated ALT levels show this effect in the first 18 weeks of treatment. The mean time to the development of ALT levels 3 × ULN is 9 weeks, but patients with higher elevations show these elevations sooner than do patients with lower elevations. For example, the mean time to the development of ALT levels 10 × ULN is 6 weeks. The average length of time for elevated ALT levels to return to normal after stopping tacrine treatment is 4 weeks.

The development of elevated ALT levels does not necessarily indicate that tacrine treatment must be stopped or, if stopped, that tacrine treatment cannot be restarted once the ALT levels have returned to normal. Specific guidelines for the treatment of patients who have elevated ALT levels are suggested in the discussion of dosage and administration. Virtually all tacrine-treated patients who have elevations in ALT levels have been asymptomatic, although jaundice has been associated with rare cases. Currently available clinical data indicate that all patients have recovered from their tacrine-associated ALT level elevations, and no cases of hepatic failure or death have been reported. The possibility of such extreme outcomes remains possible, thus warranting monitoring of the hepatic enzymes during tacrine treatment.

Drug Interactions

Data on drug interactions with tacrine are not available at this time, but tacrine should be used cautiously with drugs that also possess cholinomimetic activity. The coadministration of tacrine and drugs that have cholinergic antagonist activity (for example, tricyclic drugs) is probably counterproductive.

Laboratory Interferences

No laboratory interferences have been associated with tacrine administration.

Dosage and Administration

Before the initiation of tacrine treatment, a complete physical and laboratory examination should be conducted, with special attention to liver function tests and baseline hematological indexes. Treatment should be initiated at 10 mg 4 times a day and then raised by 10 mg per dose increments every 6 weeks up to 160 mg a day; the patient's tolerance of each dosage is indicated by the absence of unacceptable side effects and elevated ALT levels. Some small studies and case reports have used dosages up to 200 mg a day, but these higher dosages should probably be avoided at this time. Tacrine should be given 3 or 4 times daily—ideally 1 hour before meals, because the absorption of tacrine is reduced by about 25 percent when it is taken with meals or within 2 hours after meals.

Management of ALT Level Elevations

Specific guidelines have been proposed for the management of ALT level elevations. For routine monitoring of hepatic enzymes, AST and ALT level levels should be measured weekly for the first 18 weeks, every month for the second 4 months, and every 3 months thereafter. Weekly assessments of the AST and ALT levels should be performed for at least 6 weeks after any increase in dosage. For patients who have elevated ALT levels between 3 × ULN and 5 × ULN, their ALT levels should be monitored weekly, and the tacrine dosage should not be increased until the ALT level drops to below 3 × ULN. For patients with ALT levels greater than 5 × ULN, the clinician should stop tacrine immediately, monitor ALT levels weekly, and not rechallenge the patients with tacrine until the ALT levels return to the normal range. When tacrine treatment is reinitiated, the same upward titration schedule can be followed, but ALT levels should be assessed weekly. For patients who have ALT levels greater than 10 × ULN, the clinician should stop tacrine and monitor the patients until their ALT levels return to normal; the decision to rechallenge the patients should be based on a careful assessment of the risk–benefit ratio for each patient. For any patient who has elevated ALT levels and jaundice, tacrine treatment should be stopped, and the patients should not be given the drug again.

DONEPEZIL

Chemistry

The molecular structure of donepezil, a piperidine, is shown in Figure 35.3.1–5.

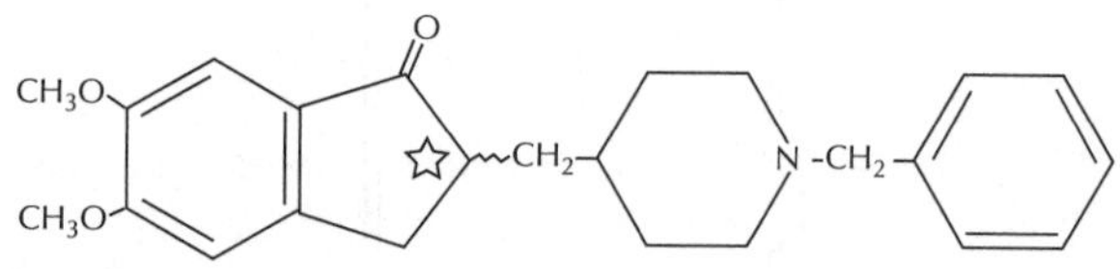
CH₃O
CH₃O
O
CH₂
N -CH₂

FIGURE 35.3.1–5
Molecular structure of donepezil.

Pharmacological Actions

Pharmacokinetics. Donepezil is absorbed completely from the gastrointestinal tract. Peak plasma concentrations are reached about 3 to 4 hours after oral dosing. Donepezil is hepatically metabolized via the cytochrome P450 (CYP) isoenzymes CYP 2D6 and CYP 3A4 and cleared primarily via urine. The half-life of donepezil is 70 hours in older persons, and it needs to be taken only once a day. Steady-state levels are achieved in about 2 weeks. Presence of stable alcoholic cirrhosis reduces clearance of donepezil by 20 percent.

Pharmacodynamics. The primary mechanism of action of donepezil is reversible, nonacetylating inhibition of acetylcholinesterase and, secondarily, butyrylcholinesterase, the enzymes that catabolize acetylcholine in the CNS. The inhibition of the enzymes results in higher concentrations of acetylcholine in the synaptic clefts. Unlike tacrine and physostigmine, which are nonselective for all forms of acetylcholinesterase, donepezil appears to be selectively active in the CNS and to have little activity in the periphery. This fact may account for its favorable side effect profile, because it does not significantly increase acetylcholine in the gastrointestinal tract.

Effects on Specific Organs and Systems

In addition to its effects on cognitive performance, donepezil affects the cardiovascular and parasympathetic nervous system. Because of its cholinomimetic properties, donepezil may cause activation of the parasympathetic nervous system in up to 3 percent of patients and may result in all the usual signs and symptoms of muscarinic activity: nausea, vomiting, diarrhea, and other autonomic symptoms.

Therapeutic Indications

The only indication for donepezil at this time is the treatment of mild-to-moderate dementia of the Alzheimer's type. The efficacy of donepezil in mildly demented patients and in patients who have other forms of dementia has not been studied as yet. Donepezil was approved for clinical use primarily on the basis of two large multicenter placebo-controlled studies, lasting 15 and 30 weeks, respectively. On the Alzheimer's Disease Assessment Scale, a cognitive rating scale on which untreated patients are expected to gain 6 to 12 units a year, donepezil-treated patients, in contrast, gained only approximately 2 to 4 units a year. On the Clinician's Interview-Based Impression of Change, donepezil showed a modest but statistically significant effect. Efforts to use donepezil to improve memory in nondemented persons should be discouraged.

Precautions and Adverse Reactions

Donepezil is generally well tolerated when used by patients with dementia of the Alzheimer's type. Its adverse effects in patients with other causes of dementia are unknown. The most troublesome and common adverse effects of donepezil are nausea, diarrhea, and vomiting in about 3 percent of the patients taking the 10-mg daily dosage. The effects were not seen at the 5-mg dosage, and when present, they tended to resolve after 3 weeks of continued use of donepezil. Donepezil treatment has been frequently associated with bradyarrhythmias, especially in patients who have underlying cardiac disease. A small number of patients have experienced syncope. Unlike tacrine, donepezil has not been associated with hepatotoxicity. Increases in gastric acetylcholine may increase secretion of gastric acid and may therefore cause gastrointestinal bleeding or the development of peptic ulcer disease. This effect indicates a need for caution about the concomitant use of steroids or nonsteroidal anti-inflammatory agents, but neither of these complications was reported in clinical trials with donepezil. Although also not seen in clinical trials, cholinomimetic drugs such as donepezil in theory can cause bladder outflow obstruction, seizures, or bronchoconstriction.

Carcinogenicity studies have not been completed for donepezil. There were minor mutagenic tendencies, but there was no effect on fertility in laboratory animals. At doses equivalent to 10 times the highest recommended human dose, when given in the last third of pregnancy, donepezil caused some increased fetal and neonatal death. Therefore, although there are no data for humans, donepezil should be avoided during pregnancy and lactation; in any case, this limitation would not be expected to affect patients who have Alzheimer's disease.

Drug Interactions

Donepezil is highly protein bound, but it does not displace other protein-bound drugs, such as furosemide, digoxin, or warfarin. Ketoconazole and quinidine inhibit donepezil metabolism in vitro, but the clinical significance of this observation is unclear. Although donepezil is not known to induce hepatic enzymes, its metabolism, because of the induction of cytochrome P450 isoenzymes CYP 2D6 and CYP 3A4, may be increased by phenytoin, carbamazepine, dexamethasone, rifampin, or phenobarbital. Donepezil should be used cautiously with drugs that also possess cholinomimetic activity, such as succinylcholine or bethanechol. The coadministration of donepezil and drugs that have cholinergic antagonist activity (for example, tricyclic drugs) is probably counterproductive.

Laboratory Interferences

No laboratory interferences have been associated with donepezil administration.

Dosage and Administration

Before the initiation of donepezil treatment, the diagnosis of dementia of the Alzheimer's type should be established by a thorough neurological evaluation to rule out other, potentially treatable causes of dementia. Treatment should be initiated at 5 mg each day, given at night, and additional benefit may accrue from an increase to 10 mg per day, after 6 weeks at the starting dose. Donepezil absorption is unaffected by meals. Donepezil is available in 5 mg and 10 mg tablets.

References

Davis KL, Thal LJ, Gamzu ER, Davis CS, Woolson RF, Gracon SI, Drachman DA, Schneider LS, Whitehouse PJ, Hoover TM, Morris JC, Kawas CH, Knopman DS, Earl NI, Kumar V, Doody RS, Tacrine Collaborative Study Group: Tacrine Collaborative Study Group: A double-blind, placebo-controlled multicenter study of tacrine for Alzheimer's disease. N Engl J Med *327:* 1253, 1992.

Doraiswamy PM: Current cholinergic therapy for symptoms of Alzheimer's disease. Prim Psychiatry *3:* 56, 1996.

Eager S, Levy R, Sahakian BJ: Tacrine in Alzheimer's disease. Lancet *337:* 989, 1991.

Farlow M, Gracon SI, Hershey LA, Lewis KW, Sadowsky CH, Dolan-Ureno J: Tacrine Study Group: A controlled trial of tacrine in Alzheimer's disease. JAMA *268:* 2523, 1992.

Lyketsos CG, Corazzini K, Steele CD, Kraus MF: Guidelines for the use of tacrine in Alzheimer's disease: Clinical application and effectiveness. J Neuropsychiatry Clin Neurosci *8* (1): 67, 1996.

Pacheco G, Palacios-Esquivel R, Moss DE: Cholinesterase inhibitors proposed for treating dementia in Alzheimer's disease: Selectivity toward human brain acetylcholinesterase compared with butyrylcholinesterase. J Pharmacol Exp Ther *274* (2): 767, 1995.

Rogers SL, Doody R, Mohs R, Friedhoff LT: E2020 produces both clinical global and cognitive test improvement in patients with mild to moderately severe Alzheimer's disease (AD): Results of a 30-week Phase III trial. Neurology *46:* A217, 1996.

Rogers SL, Friedhoff LT: The efficacy and safety of donepezil in patients with Alzheimer's disease: Results of a US multi-center, randomized, double blind, placebo-controlled trial. Dementia *7:* 293, 1996.

Williams M: Tacrine—recommendation for approval. Curr Opin Invest Drugs *2:* 541, 1993.

▲ 35.3.2 β-ADRENERGIC RECEPTOR ANTAGONISTS

In psychiatry, the most salient modification of the adrenergic ligand-receptor system is the potentiation of norepinephrine neurotransmission by reuptake inhibitors or monoamine oxidase inhibitors, in the treatment of mood and anxiety disorders. The β-adrenergic receptor antagonists, which are variously referred to as β-blockers and β-antagonists, represent a second important pharmacological intervention—the reduction of adrenergic receptor activation. β-Adrenergic receptor antagonists are commonly used in medical practice for their peripheral effects in the treatment of hypertension, angina, and certain cardiac arrhythmias, and the symptoms of hyperthyroidism, but the drugs are also used for their central actions in the treatment of migraine. Their effectiveness as peripherally and centrally acting agents has been well demonstrated for social phobia (for example, performance anxiety), lithium-induced postural tremor, control of aggressive behavior, and neuroleptic-induced acute akathisia. Preliminary research about their use in other psychiatric conditions has also been reported.

CHEMISTRY

The seven β-adrenergic receptor antagonists most commonly studied for psychiatric indications in the United States are atenolol (Tenormin), metoprolol (Lopressor), labetalol (Normodyne, Trandate), acebutolol (Sectral), nadolol (Corgard), propranolol (Inderal), and pindolol (Visken). The molecular structures of these drugs are shown in Figure 35.3.2–1.

PHARMACOLOGICAL ACTIONS

Pharmacokinetics

The seven β-adrenergic receptor antagonists listed in Table 35.3.2–1 differ with regard to lipophilicities, metabolic routes, β-adrenergic receptor selectivity, and half-lives. The absorption of the β-adrenergic receptor antagonists from the gastrointestinal tract varies, but the absorption is good enough to permit oral formulations of all seven drugs. The agents that are most soluble in lipids (that is, those that are lipophilic) are likely to cross the blood–brain barrier and enter the brain; those agents that are least lipophilic are not likely to enter the brain in significant concentrations. The solubility of a particular agent determines the ratio of its peripheral to central activity. For a comparison of the properties of these seven drugs, see Table 35.3.2–1.

Pharmacodynamics

Three subtypes of the β-adrenergic receptor have been reported. Significant data are available regarding the β_1 and β_2 receptors, which regulate the function of nearly every organ in the body, often in antagonism to the effects of the α-adrenergic receptors. The β_3 receptors have recently been found to regulate energy metabolism. They are expressed in adipocytes, and their activation by antagonists reduces the amount of body fat. Antagonist activity of peripheral β-adrenergic receptors blocks the activation of the β_1 and β_2 receptors by peripheral epinephrine and norepinephrine, the primary neurotransmitters of the sympathetic nervous system. Thus, when acting peripherally, the β-adrenergic receptor antagonists act as sympatholytic drugs. In the central nervous system (CNS), the locus ceruleus contains the majority of the noradrenergic and adrenergic neurons, which project widely throughout the brain. In the brain, β-adrenergic receptors are located primarily postsynaptically, and these receptors are blocked by the β-adrenergic receptor antagonists.

Some of the available β-adrenergic receptor antagonists (for example, nadolol, propranolol, pindolol, and labetalol) have

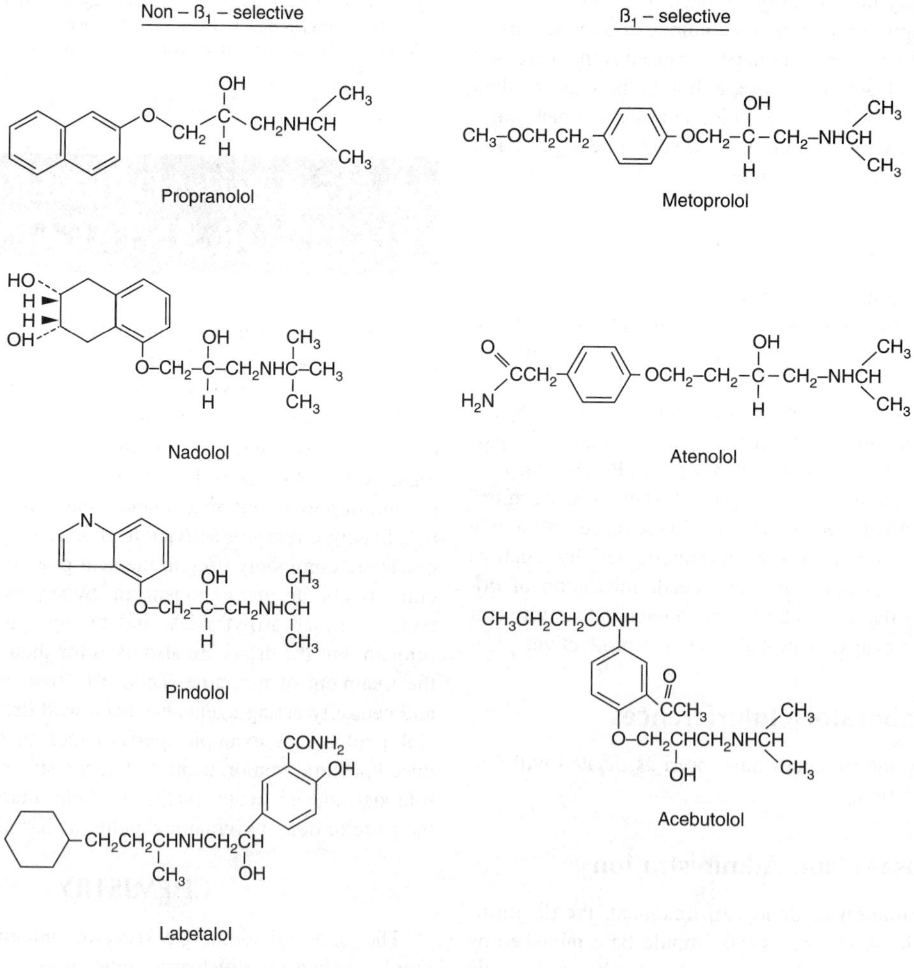
Non – β1 – selective
β1 – selective
Propranolol
Metoprolol
Nadolol
Atenolol
Pindolol
Acebutolol
Labetalol

FIGURE 35.3.2–1
Molecular structures of β-adrenergic receptor antagonists.

Table 35.3.2–1
β-Adrenergic Drugs Used in Psychiatry

Generic Name	Trade Name	Lipophilic	Metabolism	Receptor Selectivity	Half-Life (h)	Usual Starting Dosage (mg)	Usual Maximum Dosage (mg)
Propranolol	Inderal	Yes	Hepatic	$\beta_1 = \beta_2$	3–6	10–20 bid or tid	80–140 tid
Nadolol	Corgard	No	Renal	$\beta_1 = \beta_2$	14–24	40 od	80–240 od
Pindolol	Visken	Intermediate	Hepatic	$\beta_1 = \beta_2$	3–4	5 bid	30 bid
Labetalol	Normodyne, Trandate	Intermediate	Hepatic	$\beta_1 = \beta_2$	4–6	100 bid	400–800 tid
Metoprolol	Lopressor	Yes	Hepatic	$\beta_1 \quad \beta_2$	3–4	50 bid	75–150 bid
Atenolol	Tenormin	No	Renal	$\beta_1 \quad \beta_2$	5–8	50 od	50–100 od
Acebutolol	Sectral	No	Hepatic	$\beta_1 \quad \beta_2$	3–4	400 od	600 bid

essentially equal potency at both the β_1 and β_2 receptors, whereas other β-adrenergic receptor antagonists (for example, atenolol, acebutolol, and metoprolol) have greater affinity for the β_1 receptor than for the β_2 receptor. This relative β_1 selectivity confers few pulmonary and vascular effects on those drugs, although their use in asthmatic patients must be undertaken with caution, because the drugs contain some activity at the β_2 receptors.

Pindolol has intrinsic sympathomimetic effects in addition to its β-antagonist effects, which has permitted its use for augmentation of antidepressant drugs. Pindolol, propranolol, and nadolol possess some antagonist activity at the serotonin type 1A ($5\text{-}HT_{1A}$) receptors.

EFFECTS ON SPECIFIC ORGANS AND SYSTEMS

The relative importance of β_1 and β_2 receptor activity in the central nervous system is uncertain in reference to the effects of β-adrenergic receptor antagonists in the treatment of mental disorders (for example, social phobia) and medication-induced movement disorders (for example, lithium-induced postural tremor). Studies of the least lipophilic β-adrenergic receptor drugs, which are not likely to cross the blood–brain barrier, indicate that blocking peripheral β_1 receptors may be enough to obtain certain desired clinical benefits in psychiatry (for example, the reduction of lithium-induced postural tremor), although whether central β-adrenergic receptor activity or peripheral β_2-adrenergic receptor activity increases the efficacy of these drugs for these indications is uncertain.

With regard to nonneural organs and systems, peripheral β_1-adrenergic receptors modulate chronotropic and inotropic cardiac functions. Peripheral β_2-adrenergic receptors modulate bronchodilatation and vasodilation. For this reason, β_1-selective drugs are preferable in the treatment of patients with asthma and other obstructive pulmonary diseases; the blockade of the pulmonary β_2 receptors blocks the bronchodilating effects of epinephrine. Some experts, however, would never use β-adrenergic receptor antagonists in patients with asthma but might substitute a benzodiazepine for the same indication.

THERAPEUTIC INDICATIONS

Although the β-adrenergic receptor antagonists have been studied for use in many mental disorders and medication-induced movement disorders (Table 35.3.2–2), use of the β-adrenergic receptor antagonists is best supported for social phobia, lithium-induced postural tremor, and neuroleptic-induced acute akathisia. The data on the use of these drugs as adjuncts to benzodiazepines for alcohol withdrawal and for the control of impulsive aggression or violence are also promising.

Anxiety Disorders

Propranolol has been well studied for the treatment of social phobia, primarily of the performance type (for example, disabling anxiety before a musical performance). Data are also available for propranolol's treatment of panic disorder, posttraumatic stress disorder and generalized anxiety disorder. Although the beneficial effects probably result primarily from the reduction of the sympathetic peripheral manifestations of anxiety (for example, tremor, sweating, and tachycardia), the blocking of central nervous system β-adrenergic receptors may be of some additional benefit. Studies of the least lipophilic β-adrenergic receptor antagonists have also shown the drugs to be of benefit for this indication. A common treatment approach is to have the patient take 10 to 40 mg propranolol 20 to 30 minutes before the anxiety-provoking situation. Patients may try a test run of the β-adrenergic antagonist before using it in an anxiety-provoking situation to be sure that they do not experience any adverse effects from the drug or the dosage. Consideration should be given, for example, to the fact that β-

Table 35.3.2–2
Indications for β-Adrenergic Receptor Antagonists in Psychiatric Practice

Effective
- Social phobia (especially of the performance type)
- Lithium-induced postural tremor
- Neuroleptic-induced acute akathisia

Probably effective
- Control of impulsive aggression or violence
- Adjunct to benzodiazepines in the treatment of alcohol withdrawal

Possibly effective
- Generalized anxiety disorder
- Schizophrenia
- Depression

adrenergic receptor antagonists may blunt cognition in some people and thus may undermine the goal of improving performance. Use of β-receptor antagonists for treating panic disorder is less efficacious than either the use of the benzodiazepines or the serotonin-specific reuptake inhibitors (SSRIs).

Lithium-Induced Postural Tremor

Lithium-induced postural tremor is perhaps the most common of the medication-induced postural tremors. Although most studies of the β-adrenergic receptor antagonists for medication-induced postural tremor have been conducted for lithium-induced postural tremor, a β-adrenergic receptor antagonist would probably also be beneficial in other medication-induced postural tremors—for example, those induced by tricyclic drugs and valproate (Depakene). The initial approach to this movement disorder includes lowering the dose of lithium, eliminating aggravating factors such as caffeine, and the administration of lithium at bedtime. However, if these interventions are inadequate, propranolol in the range of 20 to 160 mg a day, given 2 or 3 times daily, is generally effective for the treatment of lithium-induced postural tremor. Some studies have found that the least lipophilic β-adrenergic receptor antagonists are also effective, although other studies have reported that these drugs are not as effective as propranolol.

Neuroleptic-Induced Acute Akathisia

Neuroleptic-induced acute akathisia is recognized in the fourth edition of *Diagnostic and Statistical Manual of Mental Disorders* (DSM-IV) as one of the medication-induced movement disorders. Many studies have shown that β-adrenergic receptor antagonists can be effective in the treatment of neuroleptic-induced acute akathisia. The majority of clinicians and researchers believe that β-adrenergic receptor antagonists are more effective for this indication than are anticholinergics and benzodiazepines, although the relative efficacy of these agents may vary among patients. Clinicians must realize, however, that the β-adrenergic receptor antagonists are not effective in the treatment of such neuroleptic-induced movement disorders as acute dystonia and parkinsonism. Propranolol is the drug that has been most studied for treating neuroleptic-induced acute akathisia, and at least one study has reported that a less lipophilic compound was not effective in the treatment of the disorder. There does not appear to be a clear superiority of β_1-selective versus nonselective agents for this indication.

Aggression and Violent Behavior

Several studies have shown that β-adrenergic receptor antagonists may be effective in reducing the number of aggressive and violent outbursts in patients who have impulse disorders, schizophrenia, and aggression associated with brain injuries such as trauma, tumors, anoxic injury, encephalitis, alcohol dependence, and degenerative disorders (for example, Huntington's disease). Many of these studies have added a β-adrenergic receptor antagonist to the ongoing therapy (for example, antipsychotics, anticonvulsants, lithium); therefore, it is difficult to distinguish additive effects from independent effects. Nevertheless, about 50 percent of all patients studied in various trials showed a clinically significant reduction in their aggressive and violent symptoms after the addition of a β-adrenergic receptor antagonist. Many controlled and anecdotal reports indicate that high doses of β-adrenergic receptor antagonists, sometimes up to a gram of propranolol, were used. The lipophilic β-adrenergic receptor antagonists, pindolol and metoprolol, have also been shown to be beneficial in case reports and open trials. Some experts speculate that serotonin type 1A (5-HT_{1A}) receptor antagonism of certain β-adrenergic receptor antagonists may contribute to these drugs' suppression of aggressive behavior.

Alcohol Withdrawal

Propranolol has been reported to be useful as an adjuvant to benzodiazepines, but not as a sole agent, in the treatment of alcohol withdrawal. One study used the following dose schedule: no propranolol for a pulse rate less than 50, 50 mg propranolol for a pulse rate between 50 and 79, and 100 mg propranolol for a pulse rate equal to or greater than 80. The patients who received propranolol and benzodiazepines had less severe withdrawal symptoms, more stable vital signs, and a shorter hospital stay than did the patients who received only benzodiazepines.

Depression

Pindolol has been used to augment the antidepressant effects of SSRIs and the reversible inhibitor of monoamine oxidase type A moclobemide in case reports. Experts speculate that pindolol's inhibition of the 5-HT_{1A} receptors, as well as its sympathomimetic activity, may contribute to this effect. However, a recent double-blind, controlled study of fluoxetine plus either pindolol or placebo failed to show any benefit to augmentation with pindolol. Because of the possibility that the β-adrenergic receptor antagonists induce depression in some patients, the use of augmentation strategies should be further clarified in controlled trials.

Other Disorders

A number of case reports and controlled studies have reported data indicating that β-adrenergic receptor antagonists may be of clinical benefit for treating patients who have schizophrenia and those patients who have manic symptoms. The data about the effectiveness of β-adrenergic receptor antagonists in schizophrenia and mania are not robust, although a trial of the medications may be warranted under extreme or research situations. One report described the use of 1 gram propranolol a day for mania with severe adverse effects.

PRECAUTIONS AND ADVERSE REACTIONS

The β-adrenergic receptor antagonists are contraindicated for use in patients who have asthma, insulin-dependent diabetes, congestive heart failure, significant vascular disease, persistent angina, and hypothyroidism. The contraindication in diabetic patients is due to the fact that these drugs antagonize the normal physiological response to hypoglycemia. The β-adrenergic receptor antagonists can worsen atrioventricular

(A-V) conduction defects and lead to complete A-V heart block and death. If a clinician decides that the risk–benefit ratio warrants a trial of a β-adrenergic receptor antagonist in a patient with one of these coexisting medical conditions, a β_1-selective agent should probably be the first choice.

The most common adverse effects of β-adrenergic receptor antagonists are hypotension and bradycardia (Table 35.3.2–3). In patients who are at risk for these adverse effects, a test dosage of 20 mg a day of propranolol can be given to assess the patient's reaction to the drug. Depression has been associated with lipophilic β-adrenergic receptor antagonists, such as propranolol, but it is probably rare and less than previously reported in the literature. Nausea, vomiting, diarrhea, and constipation may also be caused by treatment with these agents. Serious CNS adverse effects (for example, agitation, confusion, and hallucinations) are rare.

DRUG INTERACTIONS

Several studies have found that concomitant administration of propranolol has resulted in increases in plasma concentrations of antipsychotics, theophylline (Slo-Bid, Theo-Dur), and thyroxine. The plasma concentrations of antiepileptics would probably be affected similarly, and other β-adrenergic receptor antagonists possibly have similar effects. The β-adrenergic receptor antagonists that are eliminated by the kidneys may have similar effects on drugs that are also eliminated by the renal route. When there is a possibility of a drug–drug interaction, the plasma concentrations of the involved drugs should be monitored whenever possible. Barbiturates, phenytoin, and nicotine increase the elimination of β-adrenergic receptor antagonists that are metabolized by the liver. Several reports have associated hypertensive crises and bradycardia with the coadministration of β-adrenergic receptor antagonists and monoamine oxidase inhibitors. Patients on these two types of drugs should be treated with low dosages of both drugs and should have their blood pressure and pulse rates monitored regularly. Depressed myocardial contractility and A-V nodal conduction may occur from concomitant administration of a β-adrenergic receptor antagonist and a calcium channel inhibitor.

Table 35.3.2–3
Adverse Effects and Toxicity of β-Blockers

Cardiovascular
Hypotension
Bradycardia
Dizziness
Congestive failure (in patients with compromised myocardial function)
Respiratory
Asthma (less risk with β_1-selective drugs)
Metabolic
Worsened hypoglycemia in diabetics receiving insulin or oral agents
Gastrointestinal
Nausea
Diarrhea
Abdominal pain
Sexual function
Impotence
Neuropsychiatric
Lassitude
Fatigue
Dysphoria
Insomnia
Vivid nightmares
Depression (possible)
Psychosis (rare)
Other (rare)
Raynaud's phenomenon
Peyronie's disease
Withdrawal syndrome
Rebound worsening of preexisting angina pectoris when β blockers are discontinued

Reproduced with permission from Arana GW, Hyman SE: *Handbook of Psychiatric Drug Therapy*, ed 2, p 176. Little, Brown, Boston, 1991.

LABORATORY INTERFERENCES

The β-adrenergic receptor antagonists have no known interferences with standard laboratory tests.

DOSAGE AND ADMINISTRATION

The β-adrenergic receptor antagonists act within 1 hour of administration. Because some β-adrenergic receptor antagonists act peripherally and others act both peripherally and centrally, peripherally acting drugs may be safer than the drugs that act both centrally and peripherally, especially with regard to such CNS side effects as depression, lassitude, and changes in sleep patterns. The problem with the data is that for most indications it remains unclear whether the peripherally acting drugs (that is, those that are least lipophilic) are as effective as the most lipophilic drugs.

Propranolol is available in 10, 20, 40, 60, 80, and 90 mg tablets; 4, 8, and 80 mg/mL solutions; and 60, 80, 120, and 160 mg sustained-released capsules. Nadolol is available in 20, 40, 80, 120, and 160 mg tablets. Pindolol is available in 5 and 10 mg tablets. Labetalol is available in 100, 200, and 300 mg tablets. Metoprolol is available in 50 and 100 mg tablets and in 50, 100, and 200 mg sustained-release tablets. Atenolol is available in 25, 50, and 100 mg tablets. Acebutolol is available in 200 and 400 mg capsules.

For the treatment of chronic disorders, propranolol is usually initiated at 10 mg by mouth 3 times a day or 20 mg by mouth twice daily. The dosage can be raised by 20 to 30 mg a day until a therapeutic effect begins to emerge. The dosage should be leveled off at the appropriate range for the disorder under treatment. The treatment of aggressive behavior sometimes requires dosages up to 800 mg a day, and therapeutic effects may not be seen until the patient has been receiving the maximal dosage for 4 to 8 weeks.

The patient's pulse and blood pressure readings should be taken regularly, and the drug should be withheld if the patient's pulse rate is less than 50 or the patient's systolic blood pressure is less than 90. The drug should be temporarily withheld if the patient has severe dizziness, ataxia, or wheezing. Treatment with β-adrenergic receptor antagonists should never be discontinued abruptly. Propranolol should be tapered by 60 mg a day until a dosage of 60 mg a day is reached, after which the drug should be tapered by 10 to 20 mg a day every 3 or 4 days.

References

Adler LA, Peselow E: A controlled comparison of the effects of propranolol, benztropine, and placebo on akathisia: An interim analysis. Psychopharmacol Bull *29:* 283, 1993.

Arana GW, Santos AN: β-Adrenergic receptor antagonists. In *Comprehensive Textbook of Psychiatry,* ed 6, HI Kaplan, BJ Sadock, editors, p 1915. Williams & Wilkins, Baltimore, 1995.

Baldassano CF, Truman CJ, Nierenberg A, Ghaemi SN, et al: Akathisia: A review and case report following paroxetine treatment. Comp Psychiatry *37* (2): 122, 1996.

Bright RA, Everitt DE: β-Blockers and depression. JAMA *267:* 1783, 1992.

Carpentier AF, Bonnet AM, Vidailhet M, Agid Y. Improvement of levodopa-induced dyskinesia by propranolol in Parkinson's disease. Neurology *46* (6): 1548, 1996.

Dave M, Langbart MM: Nadolol for lithium tremor in the presence of liver damage. Ann Clin Psychiatry *6:* 51, 1994.

Duman JP, Catteau J, Lanvin F, Dupuis BA: Randomized, double-blind, cross-over, placebo-controlled comparison of propranolol and betaxolol in the treatment of neuroleptic induced akathisia. Am J Psychiatry *149:* 647, 1992.

Giancola PR, Zeichner A: Aggressive behavior in the elderly: A critical review. Clin Gerontol *13* (2): 3, 1993.

Liebowitz MR, Schneier F, Campeas R, Hollander E: Phenelzine vs atenolol in social phobia: A placebo-controlled comparison. Arch Gen Psychiatry *49:* 290, 1992.

Ratey JJ, Sorgi P, O'Driscoll GA, Sands S, Daehler ML, Fletcher JR, Kadish W, Spruiell G, Polakoff S, Lindem KJ, Bemporad JR, Richardson L, Rosenfeld B: Nadolol to treat aggression and psychiatric symptomatology in chronic psychiatric inpatients: A double-blind, placebo-controlled study. J Clin Psychiatry *53:* 41, 1992.

Sachdev P, Loneragan C: Intravenous benztropine and propranolol challenges in tardive akathisia. Psychopharmacology *113:* 119, 1993.

Sorgi P, Ratey J, Knoedler D, Arnold W, Cole L: Depression during treatment with beta-blockers: Results from a double-blind placebo-controlled study. J Neuropsychiatry Clin Neurosci *4:* 187, 1992.

Ziegler MG, Wilner KD: Sertraline does not alter the beta-adrenergic blocking activity of atenolol in healthy male volunteers. J Clin Psychiatry *57* (1, Suppl): 12, 1996.

▲ 35.3.3 Anticholinergics and Amantadine

In the clinical practice of psychiatry, the anticholinergic drugs and amantadine (Symmetrel), like the antihistamines, have their primary use as treatments for medication-induced movement disorders, particularly neuroleptic-induced parkinsonism, neuroleptic-induced acute dystonia, and medication-induced postural tremor. The anticholinergic drugs and amantadine may also be of limited use in the treatment of neuroleptic-induced acute akathisia. Before the introduction of levodopa (Larodopa), the anticholinergic drugs were commonly used in the treatment of idiopathic Parkinson's disease. The antiparkinsonian effects of amantadine, which was initially developed as an antiviral compound, were initially discovered when the drug improved the parkinsonian symptoms of a patient who was being treated with amantadine for influenza A2.

The common use of the term *anticholinergic drugs* is misleading. There are two general types of acetylcholine receptors, the muscarinic receptors and the nicotinic receptors. The muscarinic receptors are G protein-linked receptors, and the nicotinic receptors are ligand-gated ion channels. The anticholinergic drugs discussed in this section are specific for the muscarinic receptors and, therefore, are also referred to as antimuscarinic drugs.

CHEMISTRY

The molecular structures of representative anticholinergic drugs and amantadine are shown in Figures 35.3.3–1 and 35.3.3–2, respectively. The two most commonly used anticholinergic drugs, benztropine (Cogentin) and trihexyphenidyl (Artane), are tertiary amines. Benztropine is similar to both atropine, the classic anticholinergic compound, and to diphenhydramine (Benadryl), the classic antihistaminergic compound, and, in fact, possesses antihistaminergic activity.

PHARMACOLOGICAL ACTIONS

Pharmacokinetics

Five anticholinergic drugs and amantadine are available in the United States (Table 35.3.3–1). The pharmacokinetics of the anticholinergics are not well studied, but all are well ab-

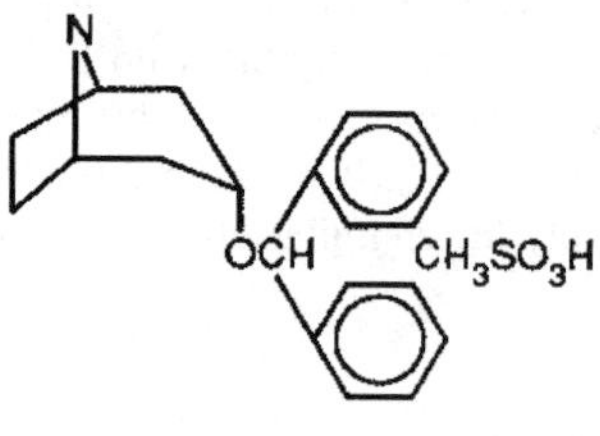
N
OCH
CH_3SO_3H

Benztropine mesylate

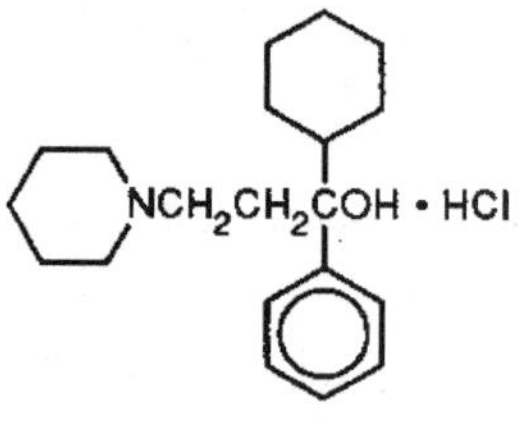
$NCH_2CH_2COH \cdot HCl$

Trihexyphenidyl hydrochloride

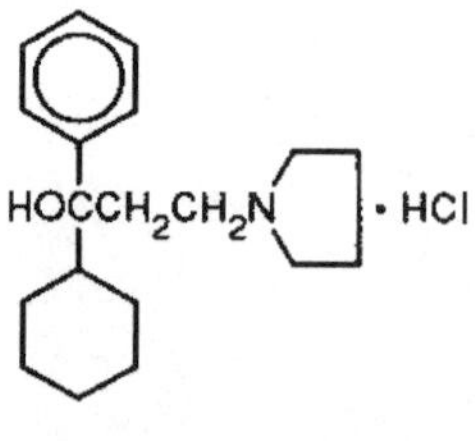
$HOCCH_2CH_2N$
• HCl

Procyclidine hydrochloride

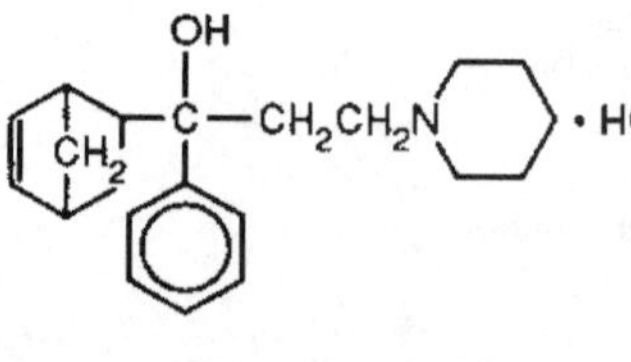
OH
C
CH_2
CH_2CH_2N
• HCl

Biperiden hydrochloride

FIGURE 35.3.3–1
Molecular structures of selected anticholinergic drugs.

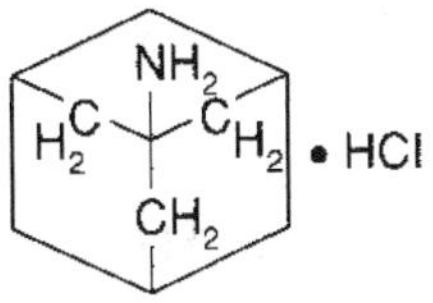
NH2
H2C
CH2
CH2
• HCl

FIGURE 35.3.3–2
Molecular structure of amantadine.

sorbed from the gastrointestinal (GI) tract after oral administration, and all are lipophilic enough to enter the central nervous system (CNS). Trihexyphenidyl reaches peak plasma concentrations in 2 to 3 hours after oral administration and has a duration of action of 1 to 12 hours. Benztropine probably has similar pharmacokinetic properties. Only three of the marketed anticholinergics are available in parenteral forms. Benztropine is probably the most commonly used parenteral anticholinergic. Benztropine is absorbed equally rapidly by intramuscular (IM) and intravenous (IV) administration; therefore, IM is preferred because of its low risk of adverse effects.

Amantadine is well absorbed from the GI tract, reaches peak plasma levels in about 2 to 3 hours, has a half-life of 16 to 24 hours, and attains steady-state plasma levels after about 4 or 5 days of administration. Amantadine is excreted unmetabolized in urine. Because of decreased renal function, amantadine plasma concentrations can be as much as twice as high in older persons as in non-elderly adults although other patients who have renal failure accumulate administered amantadine in their bodies.

Pharmacodynamics

Although all five available anticholinergics have their primary effects through the blockade of muscarinic acetylcholine receptors, benztropine also has some antihistaminergic effects. None of the available anticholinergic drugs discussed in this section has any effects on the nicotinic acetylcholine receptors. Of the six drugs, trihexyphenidyl is the most stimulating agent, perhaps acting through dopaminergic neurons, and benztropine may be the least stimulating and thus is least associated with abuse potential.

In addition to antagonizing muscarinic receptors, amantadine augments dopaminergic neurotransmission in the CNS, but the precise mechanism for this effect is unknown. The mechanism may involve increasing the release of dopamine from presynaptic vesicles, blocking the reuptake of dopamine into presynaptic nerve terminals, or exerting an agonist effect on postsynaptic dopamine receptors. For this reason, it has also been used extensively to treat idiopathic Parkinson's disease.

EFFECTS ON SPECIFIC ORGANS AND SYSTEMS

The antimuscarinic activity of the anticholinergic drugs discussed here affects the functioning of the autonomic ganglia and most commonly affects the gastrointestinal tract, the heart, the bladder, and other parasympathetic functions. Amantadine is generally better tolerated than are the anticholinergics, although it is associated with CNS adverse effects at high dosages, as are the anticholinergic compounds.

THERAPEUTIC INDICATIONS

Neuroleptic-Induced Parkinsonism

The primary indication for the use of anticholinergics or amantadine in psychiatric practice is to treat neuroleptic-induced parkinsonism, which, in the full clinical syndrome, is characterized by tremor, rigidity, cogwheeling, bradykinesia, sialorrhea, stooped posture, and festination. Akinesia and the so-called rabbit syndrome may be related to the characteristic parkinsonian symptoms. Neuroleptic-induced akinesia can sometimes be confused clinically with catatonic symptoms. Rabbit syndrome is characterized by a rhythmic, involuntary, approximately 5-Hz perioral tremor that resembles the masti-

Table 35.3.3–1
Anticholinergic Drugs and Amantadine

Generic Name	Brand Name	Tablet Size	Injectable	Usual Daily Oral Dose	Short-Term IM or IV Dose
Amantadine	Symmetrel	100 mg, elixir 50 mg/5 mL	—	100–200 mg 2 times (max. 300 mg/day)	—
Benztropine mesylate	Cogentin	0.5, 1, 2 mg	1 mg/mL	1–4 mg 1 to 2 times	1–2 mg
Biperiden hydrochloride (tab) lactate (inj)	Akineton	2 mg	5 mg/mL	2 mg 1 to 3 times	2 mg
Procyclidine hydrochloride	Kemadrin	5 mg	—	2.5–5 mg 3 times	—
Trihexyphenidyl hydrochloride	Artane, Trihexane, Trihexy-5	2.5 mg elixir 2 mg/5 mL	—	2–5 mg 2 to 3 times	—
Orphenadrine citrate	Norflex, Dispal	100 mg	30 mg/mL	50–100 mg 3 times/ (max. 250 mg/day)	60 mg IV given over 5 min

IM, intramuscular; IV, intravenous; —, not available.

catory movements of a rabbit. Neuroleptic-induced parkinsonism is most common in older persons and is most frequently seen with high-potency antipsychotics—for example, haloperidol (Haldol). The onset of symptoms usually occurs after 2 or 3 weeks of treatment. The incidence of neuroleptic-induced parkinsonism is significantly less with the newer antipsychotic drugs of the serotonin-dopamine antagonist class.

All the available anticholinergics and amantadine are equally effective in the treatment of parkinsonian symptoms, although the efficacy of amantadine may diminish in some patients in the first month of treatment. Amantadine may be more effective than are the anticholinergics in the treatment of rigidity and tremor. Amantadine may also be the drug of choice if a clinician does not want to add additional anticholinergic drugs to a patient's treatment regimen, particularly if a patient is taking an antipsychotic or an antidepressant with high anticholinergic activity—for example, chlorpromazine (Thorazine) or amitriptyline (Elavil)—or is elderly and therefore at risk for anticholinergic adverse effects.

Neuroleptic-Induced Acute Dystonia

Neuroleptic-induced acute dystonia is most common in young men. The syndrome often occurs early in the course of treatment and is commonly associated with high-potency antipsychotics (for example, haloperidol). The dystonia most commonly affects the muscles of the neck, tongue, face, and back. Opisthotonos (involving the entire body) and oculogyric crises (involving the muscles of the eyes) are examples of specific dystonias. Dystonias are uncomfortable, sometimes painful, and often frightening to patients. Although the onset is frequently sudden, the syndrome may develop in 3 to 6 hours and often results in patients' complaining about having a thick tongue or difficulty in swallowing. Dystonic contractions can be powerful enough to dislocate joints, and laryngeal dystonias can result in suffocation if the patient is not treated immediately.

Anticholinergic drugs are effective both in the short-term treatment of dystonias and in prophylaxis against neuroleptic-induced acute dystonias. Prophylactic treatment may, in fact, be indicated in the treatment of young patients, particularly men. Prophylactic treatment should be continued for only a few weeks, after which it should be gradually tapered. It should be restarted only if dystonias recur. If anticholinergics are not effective or if a patient cannot tolerate anticholinergics, treatment with antihistamines (for example, diphenhydramine—50 mg IV) or benzodiazepines (for example, lorazepam [Ativan]) may be effective. Amantadine is not generally considered as effective as the anticholinergics for the treatment of acute dystonias.

Neuroleptic-Induced Acute Akathisia

Akathisia is characterized by a subjective and objective sense of restlessness, anxiety, and agitation. Although a trial of anticholinergics or amantadine for the treatment of neuroleptic-induced acute akathisia is reasonable, these drugs are not generally considered the first drugs of choice for the syndrome. The β-adrenergic receptor antagonists and perhaps the benzodiazepines and clonidine (Catapres) are preferable drugs to try initially.

PRECAUTIONS AND ADVERSE REACTIONS

The adverse effects of the anticholinergic drugs are those resulting from the blockade of muscarinic acetylcholine receptors (Table 35.3.3–2). Older patients are prone to memory loss or even the development of delirium with relatively modest doses of anticholinergic drugs. Anticholinergic drugs should be given cautiously, if at all, to patients who have prostatic hypertrophy, urinary retention, narrow-angle glaucoma, and poorly compensated heart disease because the antimuscarinic activity exacerbates these problems. The anticholinergics, especially trihexyphenidyl, are occasionally used as drugs of abuse on the street and by patients. Their abuse potential is related to their mild mood-elevating properties.

Amantadine is generally well tolerated, especially in dosages below 200 mg a day; dosages above 300 mg a day should be avoided. Amantadine is generally better tolerated than are the anticholinergics, and preliminary data indicate that amantadine is associated with less memory impairment than are the anticholinergics. The most common CNS effects of amantadine are mild dizziness, insomnia, and impaired concentration, which occur in 5 to 10 percent of all patients. Irritability, depression, anxiety, and ataxia occur in 1 to 5 percent of all patients. Severe CNS adverse effects, including seizures, have been reported. Nausea is the most common peripheral adverse effect of amantadine. Livedo reticularis, usually affecting the lower extremities, occurs in a few patients who are treated with amantadine for a long time. Amantadine is relatively contraindicated in patients who have renal disease and seizure disorders. Some evidence indicates that amantadine is teratogenic and, therefore, should not be given to pregnant women. Because amantadine is excreted in breast milk, women who are breast-feeding should not be given the drug. Suicide attempts with amantadine overdoses are life threatening. The symptoms

Table 35.3.3–2
Potential Adverse Effects Caused by Blockade of Muscarinic Acetylcholine Receptors

Blurred vision
Constipation
Decreased salivation
Decreased sweating
Delayed or retrograde ejaculation
Delirium
Exacerbation of asthma (because of decreased bronchial secretions)
Exacerbation of narrow-angle glaucoma
Hyperthermia (through decreased sweating)
Memory problems
Photophobia
Sinus tachycardia
Urinary retention

can include toxic psychoses (confusion, hallucinations, and aggressiveness) and cardiopulmonary arrest. Emergency treatment beginning with gastric lavage or the induction of emesis is indicated.

Anticholinergic Intoxication

The most serious adverse effect associated with anticholinergic toxicity is anticholinergic intoxication, which can be characterized by delirium, coma, seizures, agitation, hallucinations, severe hypotension, supraventricular tachycardia, and the usual peripheral manifestations—flushing, mydriasis, dry skin, hyperthermia, and decreased bowel sounds. Treatment should begin with the immediate discontinuation of all anticholinergic drugs. The syndrome of anticholinergic intoxication can be diagnosed and treated with physostigmine (Antilirium, Eserine), an inhibitor of anticholinesterase, 1 to 2 mg IV (1 mg every 2 minutes) or IM every 30 to 60 minutes, although the absorption of IM physostigmine can be erratic. The first dose should be repeated in 15 to 20 minutes if no improvement is seen. Benzodiazepines can be used to treat agitation. Treatment with physostigmine should be used only when emergency cardiac monitoring and life-support services are available, because physostigmine can lead to severe hypotension and bronchial constriction. These effects of physostigmine can be reversed with rapid IV administration of atropine, 0.5 mg for each milligram of physostigmine administered. Physostigmine is also contraindicated in patients with unstable vital signs, asthma, or a history of cardiac abnormalities. In general, physostigmine should be used only to confirm a diagnosis of anticholinergic activity or to treat the most serious symptoms of anticholinergic intoxication—seizures, severe hypotension, and delirium.

Table 35.3.3–3
Anticholinergic Drug Levels in 25 Medications Ranked by the Frequency of Their Prescription for Elderly Patients

Medication[a]	Anticholinergic Drug Level (ng/mL of Atropine Equivalents)[b]
1. Furosemide	0.22
2. Digoxin	0.25
3. Dyazide[c]	0.08
4. Lanoxin	0.25
5. Hydrochlorothiazide	0.00
6. Propranolol	0.00
7. Salicylic acid	0.00
8. Dipyridamole	0.11
9. Theophylline anhydrous	0.44
10. Nitroglycerin	0.00
11. Insulin	0.00
12. Warfarin	0.12
13. Prednisolone	0.55
14. α-Methyldopa	0.00
15. Nifedipine	0.22
16. Isosorbide dinitrate	0.15
17. Ibuprofen	0.00
18. Codeine	0.11
19. Cimetidine	0.86
20. Diltiazem hydrochloride	0.00
21. Captopril	0.02
22. Atenolol	0.00
23. Metoprolol	0.00
24. Timolol	0.00
25. Ranitidine	0.22

Reprinted with permission from Tune L, Carr S, Hoag E, Cooper T: Anticholinergic effects of drugs commonly prescribed for the elderly: Potential means for assessing risk of delirium. Am J Psychiatry *149:* 1393, 1992.
[a] At a 10^{-8} M concentration.
[b] Drugs above 0.1 can contribute significant anticholinergic effects in patients.
[c] A digoxin compound.

DRUG INTERACTIONS

The most common drug–drug interactions with the anticholinergics occur when they are coadministered with psychotropics that also have high anticholinergic activity, such as most antipsychotics, tricyclic and tetracyclic drugs, and monoamine oxidase inhibitors. Older patients may be taking other medications that may also contribute significant anticholinergic activity (Table 35.3.3–3). Many over-the-counter cold preparations also induce significant anticholinergic activity. The coadministration of these drugs can result in a life-threatening anticholinergic intoxication syndrome. Anticholinergic drugs can also delay gastric emptying and thereby decrease the absorption of drugs that are broken down in the stomach and usually absorbed in the duodenum (for example, levodopa and antipsychotics). Coadministration of amantadine with anticholinergics may result in an increased incidence of cognitive impairment, confusion, nightmares, and psychotic symptoms (for example, hallucinations). This combination of drugs, therefore, should be used cautiously, especially with older persons.

In one case report, amantadine coadministered with phenelzine (Nardil) resulted in a significant increase in resting blood pressure. Because of the dopaminergic activity of amantadine, the drug may augment the stimulatory effects of CNS stimulant substances such as cocaine and other sympathomimetics (for example, amphetamine).

LABORATORY INTERFERENCES

No known laboratory interferences have been associated with either anticholinergics or amantadine.

DOSAGE AND ADMINISTRATION

Although the anticholinergic drugs and amantadine are the most commonly used drugs for the treatment of neuroleptic-induced parkinsonism and neuroleptic-induced acute dystonia, antihistamines and benzodiazepines are also effective. Amantadine and the five anticholinergic drugs discussed in this subsection are available in a range of preparations (see Table 35.3.3–1). Anticholinergics and amantadine act in 1 to 3 hours after administration.

Neuroleptic-Induced Parkinsonism

In addition to the use of antiparkinsonian drugs, the treatment of neuroleptic-induced parkinsonism can involve reducing the antipsychotic dosage or switching from a dopamine receptor antagonist to a serotonin-dopamine antagonist. Both anticholinergics and amantadine are effective, as are antihistaminergic drugs. For the treatment of neuroleptic-induced parkinsonism, the equivalent of 1 to 4 mg benztropine should be given 1 to 4 times daily. Patients usually respond to this dosage of benztropine in 1 or 2 days. When amantadine is used for the treatment of neuroleptic-induced parkinsonism, the starting dosage is usually 100 mg orally twice a day, although the dosage can be cautiously increased up to 200 mg orally in the morning and 100 mg orally at night if indicated. The anticholinergic drug or amantadine should be administered for 4 to 8 weeks; then it should be discontinued to assess whether the patient still requires the drug. Anticholinergic drugs and amantadine should be tapered over a period of 1 to 2 weeks.

Treatment with anticholinergics or amantadine as prophylaxis against the development of neuroleptic-induced parkinsonism is usually not indicated, as the symptoms of neuroleptic-induced parkinsonism are usually mild and gradual enough in onset to allow a clinician to initiate treatment only after it is clearly indicated. In young men, however, prophylaxis may be indicated, especially if a high-potency dopamine receptor antagonist is being used. A clinician should attempt to discontinue the antiparkinsonian agent in 4 to 6 weeks to assess whether its continued use is necessary.

Neuroleptic-Induced Acute Dystonia

Although anticholinergics are indicated for short-term treatment and prophylaxis of neuroleptic-induced acute dystonia, amantadine is not considered effective. For the treatment of neuroleptic-induced acute dystonia, 1 to 2 mg benztropine or its equivalent in another drug should be given IM. If this dose is not effective in 20 to 30 minutes, the drug should be administered again. If the patient still does not improve in another 20 to 30 minutes, a benzodiazepine (for example, 1 mg IM or IV lorazepam) should be given. Laryngeal dystonia is a medical emergency and should be treated with benztropine, up to 4 mg in a 10-minute period, followed by 1 to 2 mg of lorazepam, administered slowly IV.

Prophylaxis against dystonias is indicated in patients who have had one episode or in patients at high risk (young men taking high-potency antipsychotics). A clinician should continue prophylactic treatment for 4 to 8 weeks and then gradually taper the drug over a period of 1 to 2 weeks to allow an assessment of the continued need for prophylactic treatment. Whether prophylaxis with anticholinergics is indicated when first giving a patient an antipsychotic continues to be debated. Clinicians who are in favor of prophylaxis argue that patient compliance is hindered if uncomfortable neurological adverse effects occur. Clinicians opposed to prophylactic treatment cite the increased risk of anticholinergic toxicity. Studies have shown that prophylactic treatment with anticholinergic drugs does reduce the incidence of acute dystonias. The prophylactic use of anticholinergics in patients requiring antipsychotic drugs may become a moot issue as serotonin-dopamine antagonists, which are relatively free of parkinsonian effects, become more widely used.

References

Arana GW, Santos AB: Anticholinergics and amantadine. In *Comprehensive Textbook of Psychiatry,* ed 6, HI Kaplan, BJ Sadock, editors, p 1919. Williams & Wilkins, Baltimore, 1995.

Avorn J, Bohn RL, Mogun H, Gurwitz JH: Neuroleptic drug exposure and treatment of parkinsonism in the elderly: A case-control study. Am J Med *99:* 48, 1995.

Blaisdell GD: Akathisia: A comprehensive review and treatment summary. Pharmacopsychiatry *27:* 139, 1994.

Calne DB: Early idiopathic parkinsonism: Initiation and optimization of treatment. Clin Neuropharmacol *17* (2, Suppl): S14, 1994.

Goff DC, et al: The effect of benztropine on haloperidol-induced dystonia, clinical efficacy and pharmacokinetics: A prospective, double-blind trial. J Clin Psychopharmacol *11:* 106, 1991.

Gratz SS, Levinson DF, Simpson GM: The treatment and management of neuroleptic malignant syndrome. Prog Neuropsychopharmacol Biol Psychiatry *16:* 425, 1992.

Grauer E, Kapon J: Differential effects of anticholinergic drugs on paired discrimination performance. Pharmacol Biochem Behav *53* (2): 463, 1996.

Konig P, Chwatal K, Havelec L, Riedl F, Schubert H, Schultes H: Amantadine versus biperiden: a double-blind study of treatment efficacy in neuroleptic extrapyramidal movement disorders. Neuropsychobiology *33:* 80, 1996.

Noveske FG: Breakthrough panic after amantadine treatment in a Parkinson's disease patient. J Clin Psychiatry *57* (8): 374, 1996.

Pranzatelli MR, Mott SH, Pavlakis SG, Conry JA: Clinical spectrum of secondary parkinsonism in childhood: A reversible disorder. Pediatr Neurol *10:* 131, 1994.

Spina E, et al: Prevalence of acute dystonic reactions associated with neuroleptic treatment with and without anticholinergic prophylaxis. Int Clin Psychopharmacol *8:* 21, 1993.

Stroe AE, Hall J, Amin F: Psychotic episode related to phenylpropanolamine and amantadine in a healthy female. Gen Hosp Psychiatry *17* (6): 457, 1995.

Tonda ME, Guthrie SK: Treatment of acute neuroleptic-induced movement disorders. Pharmacotherapy *14:* 543, 1994.

Tune L, Carr S, Hoag E, Cooper T: Anticholinergic effects of drugs commonly prescribed for the elderly: Potential means for assessing risk of delirium. Am J Psychiatry *149:* 1393, 1992.

Uitti RJ, et al: Amantadine treatment is an independent predictor of improved survival in Parkinson's disease. Neurology *46:* 1551, 1996.

▲ 35.3.4 Antihistamines

Histamine, like serotonin, is a biogenic amine that is predominantly active outside the central nervous system (CNS), but it also serves as a CNS neurotransmitter. Histamine exerts its effects by binding to one of at least three known receptor types. The first histamine receptor antagonists, also called *antihistamines,* were synthesized in the 1930s and were first used in clinical medicine in the 1940s. Efforts to synthesize related compounds with similar sedative effects to the first antihistamines lead to the discovery of the antipsychotic drug chlorpromazine (Thorazine), which signaled the beginning of the modern era of psychopharmacology. Antagonists of the histamine type 1 (H_1) receptors are used in clinical psychiatry to treat neuroleptic-induced parkinsonism and neuroleptic-induced acute dystonia and are also used as hypnotics and anxiolytics. Diphenhydramine (Benadryl) is used to treat neuroleptic-induced parkinsonism and neuroleptic-induced acute dystonia and is sometimes used as a hypnotic. Hydroxyzine hydrochloride (Atarax) and hydroxyzine pamoate (Vistaril) are used as anxiolytics. Promethazine (Phenergan) is used for its sedative and anxiolytic effects. Cyproheptadine (Periactin) has been used to treat inhibited male and female orgasm caused by serotonergic agents, such as fluoxetine (Prozac). Second-generation histamine type 1 (H_1) receptor antagonists—for example, loratadine (Claritin)—which are much less sedating than the first-generation antihistamines, have recently become widely used for allergic conditions but are not used for psychiatric indications. Antagonists of the histamine type 2 (H_2) receptors—for example, cimetidine (Tagamet)—are used for the treatment of gastric ulcer but may also produce adverse psychiatric effects of clinical significance. Agonists and antagonists of the histamine type 3 (H_3) receptor have been synthesized but have not yet entered clinical use.

Histamine H_1 antagonists are found in a variety of over-the-counter hypnotic drugs. Because the antihistamines have been in clinical use for a long time, their use in specific clinical situations has not been well studied in well-controlled, double-blind clinical trials. Therefore, comparative data about the use of antihistamines are limited.

CHEMISTRY

The molecular structures of representative antihistamines used in psychiatry are shown in Figure 35.3.4–1.

PHARMACOLOGICAL ACTIONS

Pharmacokinetics

H_1 antagonists are well absorbed from the gastrointestinal tract. About 50 percent of diphenhydramine is metabolized in a first-pass effect by the liver, and the metabolites are excreted in urine. The antiparkinsonian effects of intramuscular (IM) diphenhydramine have their onset in 15 to 30 minutes; the sedative effects of diphenhydramine peak in 1 to 3 hours. Hydroxyzine is also metabolized by the liver, but its metabolites are excreted in the feces. The sedative effects begin between 30 to 60 minutes after administration and last 4 to 6 hours. The sedative effects of promethazine begin after 20 to 60 minutes and last for 4 to 6 hours. Because all three drugs are metabolized in the liver, patients with hepatic disease, such as cirrhosis, may attain high plasma concentrations with long-term administration. Cyproheptadine is well absorbed after oral administration, and its metabolites are excreted in urine.

Pharmacodynamics

All the above drugs share the blockade of H_1 receptors as a common mechanism of action. H_1 receptors are widely distributed in the CNS and are particularly dense in the hypothalamus. Activation of H_1 receptors stimulates wakefulness; therefore, receptor antagonism causes sedation. All four agents also possess some antimuscarinic cholinergic activity. Cyproheptadine is unique among the drugs, since it has potent activity both as a serotonin type 2 ($5\text{-}HT_2$) receptor antagonist and as a histamine antagonist.

EFFECTS ON SPECIFIC ORGANS AND SYSTEMS

The effects of the antihistamines on the CNS include sedation and antagonism of dopamine type 2 (D_2) receptor blockade-induced movement disorders. The antihistamines may also reduce the symptoms of motion sickness in some patients. Peripherally, histamine triggers capillary permeability and stimulates the release of mediators of inflammation. The peripheral

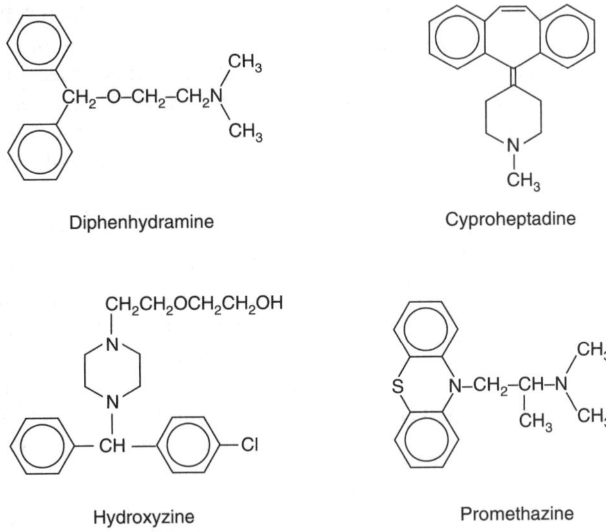
CH2-O-CH2-CH2N
CH3
CH3
Diphenhydramine
N
CH3
Cyproheptadine
CH2CH2OCH2CH2OH
N
N
CH
Cl
Hydroxyzine
S
N-CH2-CH-N
CH3
CH3
CH3
Promethazine

FIGURE 35.3.4–1
Molecular structure of antihistamines used in psychiatry.

effects of the antihistamines are mediated by the autonomic nervous system and include effects on the respiratory system (for example, bronchodilation, though not in asthmatic patients) and the cardiovascular system (for example, tachycardia).

THERAPEUTIC INDICATIONS

The most justified indication for the use of antihistamines is as a treatment for neuroleptic-induced parkinsonism and neuroleptic-induced acute dystonia. The use of cyproheptadine for impaired orgasms is also reasonable; however, some patients do not respond. Benzodiazepines are more effective as short-acting hypnotics and anxiolytics than are antihistamines.

Neuroleptic-Induced Parkinsonism and Neuroleptic-Induced Acute Dystonia

The use of diphenhydramine is a reasonable alternative to anticholinergics and amantadine for neuroleptic-induced parkinsonism and neuroleptic-induced acute dystonia, especially in patients who are particularly sensitive to the adverse effects of the other drugs.

Hypnotic and Anxiolytic Applications

The antihistamines are relatively safe hypnotics, but they are not superior to the benzodiazepines, which are a much better studied class of drugs in terms of efficacy and safety. The antihistamines have not been proved to be effective as long-term anxiolytic therapy; therefore, either the benzodiazepines or buspirone (BuSpar) or the serotonin-specific reuptake inhibitors (SSRIs) are preferable for such treatment.

Other Indications

Several case reports have asserted that cyproheptadine (4 to 8 mg before coitus) is efficacious in treating abnormal orgasm, especially abnormal orgasm resulting from treatment with serotonergic drugs (for example, fluoxetine). A number of case reports and small studies have also reported that cyproheptadine may be of some use in the treatment of eating disorders, such as anorexia nervosa. Cyproheptadine has been shown in an open trial to reduce neuroleptic-induced akathisia, and it has been reported to be effective for recurrent nightmares with posttraumatic themes. The antiserotonergic activity of cyproheptadine may counteract the serotonin syndrome caused by concomitant use of multiple serotonin-activating drugs, such as SSRIs and monoamine oxidase inhibitors. Hydroxyzine has been used in management of chronic pain.

PRECAUTIONS AND ADVERSE REACTIONS

Antihistamines are commonly associated with sedation, dizziness, and hypotension, all of which can be severe in elderly patients, who are also likely to suffer from the anticholinergic effects of these drugs. Paradoxical excitement and agitation is an adverse effect seen in a small proportion of patients. Poor motor coordination can result in accidents; therefore, patients should be warned about driving and operating dangerous machinery. Other common adverse effects include epigastric distress, nausea, vomiting, diarrhea, and constipation. Because of the drugs' mild anticholinergic activity, some patients experience dry mouth, urinary retention, blurred vision, and constipation. For this reason also, antihistamines should be used with caution in patients with narrow-angle glaucoma and obstructive gastrointestinal, prostate, or bladder conditions. A central anticholinergic syndrome with psychosis may be induced by either cyproheptadine or diphenhydramine. The use of cyproheptadine in some patients has been associated with weight gain, which may contribute to its reported efficacy in some patients with anorexia nervosa.

H_2 antagonist toxicity may reversibly produce psychiatric symptoms, including psychosis, agitation, hallucinations, delirium, disorientation, confusion, irritability, and hostility.

In addition to the adverse effects, antihistamines have some potential for abuse by susceptible patients. The coadministration of antihistamines and opioids can increase the rush experienced by persons with substance dependence. Also, overdoses of antihistamines can be fatal. Antihistamines are excreted in breast milk, so their use should be avoided by nursing mothers. Because of some potential for teratogenicity, the use of antihistamines should also be avoided by pregnant women.

DRUG INTERACTIONS

The sedative property of antihistamines can be additive with other CNS depressants, such as alcohol, other sedative-hypnotic drugs, and many psychotropic drugs, including tricyclic drugs and monoamine oxidase inhibitors. The anticholinergic activity can also be additive with other drugs producing anticholinergic effects, sometimes resulting in severe anticholinergic symptoms or intoxication. In some cases, the antidepressant and antibulimic benefits of fluoxetine are antagonized by cyproheptadine.

Because the nonsedating H_1 antagonists terfenadine (Seldane) and astemizole (Hismanal) are metabolized by the hepatic cytochrome P450 (CYP) enzyme CYP 3A4, they may reach cardiotoxic levels in patients who also use the antidepressant nefazodone (Serzone) or fluvoxamine (Luvox). In such patients, loratadine, cetirizine (Zyrtec) and fexofenadine (Allegra) are safer nonsedating H_1 antagonists, which are not metabolized by CYP 3A4.

LABORATORY INTERFERENCES

H_1 antagonists may eliminate the wheal and induration that form the basis of allergy skin tests. Promethazine may interfere with pregnancy testing and may increase blood glucose levels. Diphenhydramine may yield a false-positive urine test for phencyclidine. Hydroxyzine has been reported to falsely elevate the values of urinary 17-hydroxycorticosteroids when assayed with either the Poster-Silber chromogens test or the Glenn-Nelson test.

DOSAGE AND ADMINISTRATION

The antihistamines are available in a variety of preparations (Table 35.3.4–1). Antihistamines act within 30 minutes when

Table 35.3.4–1
Antihistamine Preparations

	Tablets (mg)	Capsules (mg)	Elixir[a] (mg/5 mL)	Solution[b] (mg/5 mL)	Parenteral (mg/mL)	Suspension[c] (mg/5 mL)	Suppository (mg)
Diphenhydramine	25, 50	25, 50	12.5	8.3, 12.5	10, 50	—	—
Hydroxyzine	10, 25, 50, 100	25, 50, 100	—	10	25, 50	25	—
Cyproheptadine	4	—	—	2	—	—	—
Promethazine	12.5, 25, 50	—	—	6.25, 25	25, 50	—	50

[a] A sweetened hydroalcoholic liquid intended for oral use.
[b] A drug incorporated into an aqueous or alcoholic solution.
[c] Undissolved drug dispersed in a liquid for oral or parenteral use.

taken orally and within 1 to 5 minutes when administered intravenously. Diphenhydramine is used in the short-term and long-term treatment of neuroleptic-induced parkinsonism and neuroleptic-induced acute dystonia. When the drug is used for IM injections, it should be given deep because superficial administration can cause local irritation. Short-term intravenous administration of 25 to 50 mg is an effective treatment for neuroleptic-induced acute dystonia. Clinicians can use 25 mg 3 times a day—up to 50 mg 4 times a day if necessary—to treat neuroleptic-induced parkinsonism, akinesia, and rabbit syndrome. When used as a hypnotic, doses of 50 mg are recommended, as doses of 100 mg have not been shown to be superior to 50 mg.

Hydroxyzine is most commonly used as a short-term anxiolytic, although the data supporting this indication are limited. Dosages of 50 to 100 mg orally 4 times a day for long-term treatment or 50 to 100 mg every 4 to 6 hours for short-term treatment are usually recommended. Recent studies, however, have indicated that 150 mg a day is ineffective as an anxiolytic, although 400 mg a day may be as effective as chlordiazepoxide (Librium). Other studies have indicated that hydroxyzine is not useful as an anxiolytic in children and that it should be used for this indication with some caution.

References

Avorn J, Soumerai SB, Everitt DE, Ross-Degnan D, Beers MH, Sherman D, Salem-Schatz SR, Fields D: A randomized trial of a program to reduce the use of psychoactive drugs in nursing homes. N Engl J Med *327:* 168, 1992.

Blaustein BS, Gaeta TJ, Balentine JR, Gindi M: Cyproheptadine-induced central anticholinergic syndrome in a child: A case report. Pediatr Emerg Care *11:* 235, 1995.

Goldbloom DS, Kennedy SH: Adverse interaction of fluoxetine and cyproheptadine in two patients with bulimia nervosa. J Clin Psychiatry *52:* 261, 1991.

Harvey KV, Balon R: Clinical implications of antidepressant drug effects on sexual function. Ann Clin Psychiatry *7:* 189, 1995.

Kutcher SP, Reiter S, Gardner DM, Klein RG: The pharmacotherapy of anxiety disorders in children and adolescents. Psychiatr Clin North Am *15:* 41, 1992.

Lee HS, Song DH: Cyproheptadine augmentation of haloperidol in chronic schizophrenic patients: A double-blind placebo-controlled study. Int Clin Psychopharmacol *10:* 67, 1995.

Metzer HY, Lee MA, Ranjan R, Mason EA, et al: Relapse following clozapine withdrawal: Effect of neuroleptic drugs and cyproheptadine. Psychopharmacology *124:* 176, 1996.

Mills KC: Serotonin syndrome. Am Fam Physician *52:* 1475, 1995.

Mumford GK, Silverman K, Griffiths RR: Reinforcing, subjective, and performance effects of lorazepam and diphenhydramine in humans. Exp Clin Psychopharmacol *4* (4): 421, 1996.

Uhde TW, Tancer ME: Antihistamines. In *Comprehensive Textbook of Psychiatry,* ed 6, HI Kaplan, BJ Sadock, editors, p 1923. Williams & Wilkins, Baltimore, 1995.

Wiess D, Aizenberg D, Hermesh H, Zemishlany Z, Munitz H, Radwan M, Weizman A: Cyproheptadine treatment in neuroleptic-induced akathisia. Br J Psychiatry *167:* 483, 1995.

▲ 35.3.5 Barbiturates and Similarly Acting Drugs

BARBITURATES

The barbiturates, first introduced into clinical psychiatry in 1903, were the sedative-hypnotic drugs of first choice until chlordiazepoxide (Librium) and other benzodiazepines were introduced in the early 1960s. The introduction of the benzodiazepines and other anxiolytics (for example, buspirone [BuSpar]) and hypnotics (for example, zolpidem [Ambien]) has practically eliminated the use of barbiturates and other pre–benzodiazepine-era compounds, such as meprobamate (Miltown), because of the lower abuse potential, higher therapeutic index, and lack of hepatic enzyme induction by the new compounds.

Chemistry

The various clinically available barbiturates are derived from the same barbituric acid substrate and differ primarily in their substitutions at the C_5 position of the parent molecule (Fig. 35.3.5–1). These C_5 molecular substitutions are the primary basis for the differing lipid solubilities and half-lives of the various resulting molecules.

Pharmacological Actions

Pharmacokinetics. The barbiturates vary in their degree of absorption after oral administration, and their absorption is delayed when taken with food. The binding of the barbiturates to plasma proteins ranges from 20 to 70 percent, and their degree of lipid solubility varies, although all are lipophilic enough to cross the blood–brain barrier. The barbiturates are metabolized by the hepatic microsomal enzyme P450 system, and the metabolites are largely excreted by the kidneys. Barbiturates are associated with an induction of hepatic enzymes and can thereby reduce the levels of both barbiturates and other concurrently administered drugs that are also metabolized by the liver. The half-lives of the various barbiturates range from 1 to 120 hours. Increasing age, hepatic disease, and renal disease (in the case of phenobarbital [Luminal]) can be associated with an increase in the half-lives of barbiturates.

General Formula:

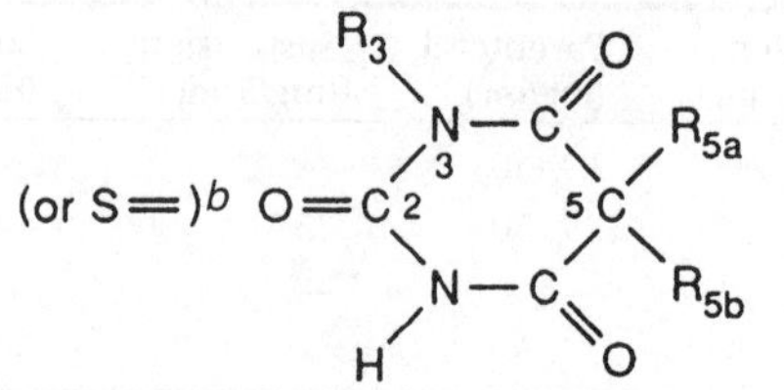
R3
O
N—C
R5a
3
(or S=)b O=C 2
5 C
N—C
R5b
H
O

Barbiturate	R_{5a}	R_{5b}
Amobarbital	Ethyl	Isopentyl
Aprobarbital	Allyl	Isopropyl
Butabarbital	Ethyl	*Sec*-Butyl
Butalbital	Allyl	Isobutyl
Mephobarbital[a]	Ethyl	Phenyl
Methohexital[a]	Allyl	1-Methyl-2-Pentynyl
Pentobarbital	Ethyl	1-Methylbutyl
Phenobarbital	Ethyl	Phenyl
Secobarbital	Allyl	1-Methylbutyl
Thiamylal[b]	Allyl	1-Methylbutyl
Thiopental[b]	Ethyl	1-Methylbutyl

[a] R_3 = H_1 except in mephobarbital and methohexital, where it is replaced by CH_3.
[b] O, except in thiamylal and thiopental, where it is replaced by S.

FIGURE 35.3.5–1.
Molecular structures and names of barbiturates currently available in the United States. (Reprinted with permission from Rall TW: Hypnotics and sedatives: Ethanol. In *Goodman and Gilman's The Pharmacological Basis of Therapeutics,* ed 8, A Goodman, AG Gilman, TW Rall, AS Nies, P Taylor, editors, p 358. McGraw-Hill, New York, 1990.)

Pharmacodynamics. The mechanism of action for the barbiturates appears to involve the γ-aminobutyric acid (GABA) receptor–benzodiazepine receptor–chloride ion channel complex. Current data are consistent with the hypothesis that barbiturates enhance the activity of GABA on the $GABA_A$ receptor complex and thus increase the inhibitory actions of this neurotransmitter. Some preliminary data indicate that barbiturates may reduce glutamate-mediated excitatory neurotransmission and may also inhibit the entry of calcium ions into presynaptic nerve terminals and thus potentially reduce neurotransmitter release.

Effects on Specific Organs and Systems

The barbiturates have their major effects on the central nervous system (CNS), although significant effects also occur in the liver and can occur in the cardiovascular system. In the CNS, barbiturates are associated with the inhibition of the reticular activating system. Respiratory depression can arise, and this effect can be additive with other respiratory depressants (for example, alcohol). In the liver, barbiturate use can cause a twofold induction of metabolic liver enzymes and thus can produce a lowering of the plasma levels of both the barbiturates and other drugs metabolized in the liver. Although at low dosages barbiturates have a relatively safe cardiovascular profile, at high dosages they may impair cardiac contractility or result in cardiac arrhythmias. Barbiturate administration rarely causes potentially fatal laryngospasm, a potential adverse event that may guide clinicians to use benzodiazepines, rather than barbiturates, in most situations (for example, drug-assisted interviewing).

Therapeutic Indications

All the barbiturates were approved by the Food and Drug Administration (FDA) before the current rigorous guidelines for drug approval were instituted. Therefore, the FDA-approved indications for these drugs should be viewed with some caution. Nevertheless, the FDA has approved the use of amobarbital (Amytal), aprobarbital (Alurate), butabarbital (Butisol), mephobarbital (Mebaral), pentobarbital (Nembutal), phenobarbital, and secobarbital (Seconal) for the treatment of anxiety and apprehension. But there have been no carefully conducted clinical trials of these agents for diagnoses of anxiety specified by the revised third edition of *Diagnostic and Statistical Manual of Mental Disorders* (DSM-III-R) or the fourth edition (DSM-IV). The FDA has approved the use of amobarbital, aprobarbital, butabarbital, pentobarbital, phenobarbital, and secobarbital for the treatment of insomnia. Methohexital (Brevital) is approved for use as an anesthetic agent with electroconvulsive therapy (ECT), and amobarbital is approved for use in narcoanalysis, which includes the concept of drug-assisted interviewing.

Although the FDA guidelines approve of the wide application of the barbiturates, the availability of newer, safer, better-studied drugs reduced the number of reasonable applications of the barbiturates to nine circumstances: (1) Amobarbital (50 to 250 mg intramuscular [IM]) may be used in emergency settings to control agitation. The use of IM lorazepam (Ativan) or intravenous (IV) diazepam (Valium), however, is replacing barbiturate usage because of the risk of laryngospasm and respiratory depression associated with the barbiturates. (2) Amobarbital interviews are sometimes used for diagnostic purposes, but several studies have reported that other sedative drugs, particularly the benzodiazepines, are as effective as the barbiturates. (3) Several reports indicate that barbiturates can activate some catatonic patients, although benzodiazepines may also have this effect. (4) Barbiturate use may be indicated for patients who have serious adverse effects associated with the use of benzodiazepines or buspirone. (5) Some patients who do not respond adequately to benzodiazepines or buspirone may respond to barbiturates. (6) Some patients, particularly elderly patients, may have received barbiturates in the past and may insist on taking barbiturates currently, rather than switching to a benzodiazepine or buspirone. (7) Methohexital is a safe and effective anesthetic agent to use during ECT. (8) The pentobarbital challenge test (Table 35.3.5–1) is a safe and effective way to assess the degree of CNS tolerance for barbiturates once a patient's period of initial barbiturate intoxication has resolved. This test is particularly useful when a patient's history of the previously used daily dosage of barbiturates is unreliable. (9) Phenobarbital is the barbiturate of choice to be used when detoxifying a patient from barbiturate dependence.

Precautions and Adverse Reactions

Some adverse effects of barbiturates are similar to those of benzodiazepines, including paradoxical dysphoria, hyperactiv-

Table 35.3.5–1
Pentobarbital Challenge Test

1. Give pentobarbital 200 mg orally.
2. Observe for intoxication after 1 hour (eg, sleepiness, slurred speech, or nystagmus).
3. If patient is not intoxicated, give another 100 mg of pentobarbital every 2 hours (maximum 500 mg over 6 hours).
4. Total dose given to produce mild intoxication is equivalent to daily abuse level of barbiturates.
5. Substitute phenobarbital 30 mg (longer half-life) for each 100 mg of pentobarbital.
6. Decrease by about 10% a day.
7. Adjust rate if signs of intoxication or withdrawal are present.

ity, and cognitive disorganization. Rare adverse effects associated with barbiturate use include the development of Stevens-Johnson syndrome, megaloblastic anemia, and osteopenia.

A major difference between the barbiturates and the benzodiazepines is the low therapeutic index of the barbiturates, an overdose of which can easily prove fatal. In addition to narrow therapeutic indexes, the barbiturates are associated with a significant risk of abuse potential and the development of tolerance and dependence. This increased risk is reflected by the fact that the U.S. Drug Enforcement Agency (DEA) has classified most of the barbiturates as schedule II drugs; the benzodiazepines are classified as schedule IV drugs. Barbiturate intoxication is manifested by confusion, drowsiness, irritability, hyporeflexia or areflexia, ataxia, and nystagmus. The symptoms of barbiturate withdrawal are similar to but more marked than those of benzodiazepine withdrawal.

Because of some evidence of teratogenicity, barbiturates should not be used by pregnant women or women who are breast-feeding. Barbiturates should be used with caution by patients with a history of substance abuse, depression, diabetes, hepatic impairment, renal disease, severe anemia, pain, hyperthyroidism, or hypoadrenalism. Barbiturates are also contraindicated in patients with acute intermittent porphyria, impaired respiratory drive, or limited respiratory reserve.

Drug Interactions

The primary area for concern about drug interactions is the potentially additive effects of respiratory depression. Barbiturates should be used with great caution with other prescribed CNS drugs (including antipsychotic and antidepressant drugs) and nonprescribed CNS agents (for example, alcohol). Caution must also be exercised when prescribing barbiturates to patients who are taking other drugs that are metabolized in the liver, especially cardiac drugs and anticonvulsants. Because individual patients have a wide range of sensitivities to barbiturate-induced enzyme induction, it is not possible to predict the degree to which the metabolism of concurrently administered medications are affected. Drugs that may have their metabolism enhanced by barbiturate administration include narcotic analgesics, antiarrhythmic agents, antibiotics, anticoagulants, anticonvulsants, antidepressants, β-adrenergic receptor antagonists, dopamine receptor antagonists, contraceptives, and immunosuppressants.

Laboratory Interferences

No known laboratory interferences are associated with the administration of barbiturates.

Dosage and Administration

Barbiturates and the other drugs described in this subsection begin to act within 1 to 2 hours of administration. The dosages of barbiturates vary (Table 35.3.5–2), and treatment should begin with low dosages that are increased to achieve a clinical effect. Children and older people are more sensitive to the effects of the barbiturates than are young adults. The most commonly used barbiturates are available in a variety of dose forms (Table 35.3.5–3). Barbiturates with half-lives in the 15- to 40-hour range are preferable, because long-acting drugs tend to accumulate in the body. Clinicians should clearly instruct patients about the adverse effects and the potential for dependence associated with barbiturates.

Although plasma levels of barbiturates are rarely necessary in psychiatry, plasma monitoring of phenobarbital levels is standard practice when the drug is used as an anticonvulsant. The therapeutic blood concentrations for phenobarbital in this indication range from 15 to 40 mg/L, although some patients may experience significant adverse effects in that range.

OTHER SEDATIVE-HYPNOTICS

Four other classes of drugs—carbamates, piperidinediones, cyclic ethers, and tertiary carbinols—are still available for use

Table 35.3.5–2
Selected Barbiturates

Generic Name	DEA Control Level	Trade Name	Half-Life (hr)	Sedative: Adult Dosage Range (mg/day)	Sedative: Adult Single Dose Range (mg)	Hypnotic: Dose Range (mg)
Amobarbital	II	Amytal	8–42	65–400	65–100	100–200
Butabarbital	III	Butisol	34–42	15–120	15–30	50–100
Mephobarbital	IV	Mebaral	11–67	32–400	32–100	—
Pentobarbital	II	Nembutal	15–48	32–120	30–40	100–200
Phenobarbital	IV	Luminal	80–120	15–600	15–60	100–200
Secobarbital	II	Seconal	15–40	—	—	100–300

Table 35.3.5–3
Barbiturate Preparations

	Tablets	Capsules	Elixir	Parenteral	Rectal Suppositories
Amobarbital	—	—	—	250, 500 mg	—
Butabarbital	15, 30, 50, 100 mg	—	30 mg/5 mL, 33.3 mg/5 mL	—	—
Mephobarbital	32, 50, 100 mg	—	—	—	—
Pentobarbital	—	50, 100 mg	18.2 mg/5 mL	50 mg/mL	30, 60, 120, 200 mg
Phenobarbital	15, 16, 30, 32, 60, 65, 100 mg	16 mg	15 mg/5 mL, 20 mg/5 mL	30 mg/mL, 60 mg/mL, 65 mg/mL, 130 mg/mL	—
Secobarbital	—	50, 100 mg	—	50 mg/mL	—

as sedatives and hypnotics (Fig. 35.3.5–2). These drugs are even more rarely used than are barbiturates, because of their high abuse potential and additional toxic effects. Chloral hydrate is discussed in Section 35.3.12.

Carbamates

Meprobamate (Miltown, Equanil) and carisoprodol (Soma) are carbamates that are effective as anxiolytics, sedatives, hypnotics, and muscle relaxants. These drugs have a lower therapeutic index and a higher abuse potential than do the benzodiazepines, and their use is indicated only if the previously described drugs are not options. The carbamates have even more abuse potential and may be more dependence-inducing than the barbiturates.

The usual dosage of meprobamate is 400 mg 3 or 4 times daily. Meprobamate is available in 200, 400, and 600 mg tablets and 200 and 400 mg extended-release capsules. Drowsiness is a common adverse effect, and patients should be warned about the additive effects of sedative drugs. Sudden withdrawal may cause anxiety, restlessness, weakness, delirium, and seizures. Adverse effects can include urticarial or erythematous rashes, anaphylactoid and other allergic reactions, angioneurotic edema, dermatitis, blood dyscrasias, gastrointestinal distress, and extraocular muscular paralysis. Fatal overdoses can occur with meprobamate in doses as low as 12 grams (thirty 400 mg tablets) without the ingestion of other sedatives.

Carisoprodol is available in 350 mg tablets. The usual adult dosage is 350 mg 4 times daily.

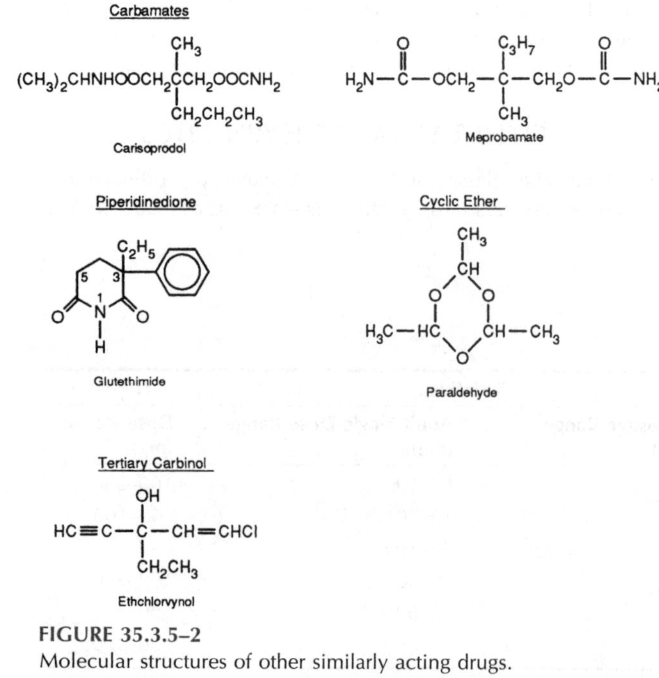
Carbamates
Carisoprodol
Meprobamate
Piperidinedione
Glutethimide
Cyclic Ether
Paraldehyde
Tertiary Carbinol
Ethchlorvynol

FIGURE 35.3.5–2
Molecular structures of other similarly acting drugs.

Piperidinediones

Glutethimide (Doriden) is a piperidinedione that is effective as a hypnotic, sedative, and anxiolytic but is even more subject to abuse and more lethal in overdose than are the barbiturates and carbamates. Glutethimide has a slow and unpredictable absorption after oral administration. Seizures, shock, and anticholinergic toxicity are more common in glutethimide overdoses than in barbiturate overdoses. Treatment with a piperidinedione is rarely indicated. The usual dose of glutethimide is 250 to 500 mg at bedtime. Glutethimide is available in 250 mg tablets.

Cyclic Ethers

Paraldehyde (Paral) was introduced in 1882 as a hypnotic. A 5 mL dose given IM or a 5 to 10 mL dose administered orally is an effective, albeit old-fashioned, treatment for alcohol withdrawal symptoms, anxiety, and insomnia. Paraldehyde is almost completely metabolized, but its excretion in unmetabolized form by the lungs limits its usefulness because of its offensive taste and ubiquitous odor.

Tertiary Carbinols

Ethchlorvynol (Placidyl) is a tertiary carbinol, another nonbarbiturate sedative-hypnotic. It was marketed for use as a short-term treatment for insomnia. The drug is rapidly absorbed and has a fast onset and a relatively short duration of action. The liver is the major site for the drug's metabolism. Ethchlorvynol has sedative-hypnotic, muscle relaxant, and anticonvulsant properties. The usual hypnotic dose is 500 mg at bedtime. It is available in 200, 500, and 750 mg capsules.

The drug has significant potential for abuse, physical dependence, and tolerance. It is particularly dangerous in overdose. The lethal dose range is 10 to 25 grams, although death has been reported from doses as low as 3 grams. There is little to recommend the drug, especially in view of the much safer alternatives. It is cross-tolerant with other sedative-hypnotics, and detoxification can be achieved with barbiturates by using the pentobarbital challenge tests (Table 35.3.5–1) to establish an appropriate dose of barbiturates.

REFERENCES

Agmo A, Galvan A, Heredia A, Morales M: Naloxone blocks the antianxiety but not the motor effects of benzodiazepines and pentobarbital: Experimental studies and literature review. Psychopharmacology *120* (2): 186, 1995.

Baxendale SA, Thompson PJ, Savy L, Bhattacharya J, et al: Dose effects on intracarotid amobarbital test performance. J Epilepsy *9* (2): 135, 1996.

Chermack S, Taylor SP: Barbiturates and human physical aggression. J Res Pers *27* (4): 315, 1993.

Gonzales JJ, Emmerich AD, Rauch SL, Stern TA: Management of the prescription-drug-dependent adult: Case of meprobamate abuse and its treatment. J Geriatr Psychiatry Neurol *9*:91, 1996.

Harris RA: Distinct actions of alcohols, barbiturates and benzodiazepines on GABA-activated chloride channels. Alcohol *7:* 273, 1990.

Hayes SG: Barbiturate anticonvulsants in refractory affective disorders. Ann Clin Psychiatry *5*:35, 1993.

Jensen CF, Cowley DS, Walker RD: Drug preferences of alcoholic polydrug abusers with and without panic. J Clin Psychiatry *51:* 189, 1990.

Marcum J: The use of midazolam with pulse oximetry in the drug-assisted interview. J Clin Psychiatry *57* (3): 111, 1996.

McCall WV, Shelp FE, McDonald WM: Controlled investigation of the amobarbital interview for catatonic mutism. Am J Psychiatry *149:* 202, 1992.

McMillan DE, Hardwick WC: Pentobarbital discrimination and generalization to other drugs under multiple fixed-ratio fixed-interval schedules. Behav Pharmacol *7* (3): 285, 1996.

Uhde TW, Tancer ME: Barbiturates. In *Comprehensive Textbook of Psychiatry,* ed 6, HI Kaplan, BJ Sadock, editors, p 1926. Williams & Wilkins, Baltimore, 1995.

Yu S, Ho IK: Effects of acute barbiturate administration, tolerance and dependence on brain GABA system: Comparison to alcohol and benzodiazepines. Alcohol *7:* 261, 1990.

▲ 35.3.6 Benzodiazepine Receptor Agonists and Antagonists

The benzodiazepine receptor agonists and antagonists have a common site of action on the γ-aminobutyric acid type A ($GABA_A$) receptor complex, which consists of a binding site for the neurotransmitter GABA, a binding site for benzodiazepines, and a chloride ion channel. This section covers the benzodiazepines, a group of compounds that enhance the activity of the $GABA_A$ receptor by binding to the benzodiazepine receptor site; zolpidem (Ambien), a nonbenzodiazepine agonist at the benzodiazepine site; and flumazenil (Romazicon), a benzodiazepine receptor antagonist. The benzodiazepines, zolpidem, and other benzodiazepine receptor agonists that are under development are primarily indicated for treating anxiety and insomnia; flumazenil is primarily indicated for treating benzodiazepine overdose.

The recent subtyping of benzodiazepine receptors and the development of nonbenzodiazepine agonists for these receptors have led to the hope of developing an even safer generation of benzodiazepine receptor agonists. Ideally, the new class of drugs would have an efficacy and safety equal to that of the benzodiazepines but would have even less abuse potential and less rebound anxiety or insomnia. Zolpidem is the first benzodiazepine receptor agonist available in the United States that is a nonbenzodiazepine, and data indicate that it has limited benefits over some benzodiazepine hypnotics. Because benzodiazepines can be fatal in overdoses when combined with other central nervous system (CNS) depressants, the introduction of flumazenil has greatly improved physicians' ability to treat such a medical emergency.

BENZODIAZEPINES

The benzodiazepine-type benzodiazepine receptor agonists are commonly referred to simply as benzodiazepines. Benzodiazepines are also variously referred to as antianxiety agents, anxiolytics, and minor tranquilizers. All these terms are misleading, as benzodiazepines have multiple non–anxiety-related indications. Furthermore, the use of the term *minor tranquilizer* may cause confusion between this class of drugs and the major tranquilizers, another faulty but commonly used term for the antipsychotic drugs.

Benzodiazepines are sometimes classified as sedative-hypnotics, although other drugs can also be classified in this group (for example, barbiturates). A sedative drug reduces daytime anxiety, tempers excessive excitement, and generally quiets or calms patients. Although a distinction that is sometimes drawn between sedatives and anxiolytics is that sedatives treat less pathological conditions than do anxiolytics, this poorly defined distinction should be avoided. A hypnotic drug produces drowsiness and facilitates the onset and maintenance of sleep. In general, benzodiazepines act as hypnotics in high doses and as anxiolytics or sedatives in low doses.

In addition to their use as sedatives and hypnotics, some benzodiazepines are useful in other psychiatric indications, including panic disorder, phobias, and agitation associated with bipolar I disorder. The benzodiazepines are also used as anesthetics, anticonvulsants, and muscle relaxants.

The benzodiazepines have become the sedative-hypnotic drugs of first choice because they have a higher therapeutic index and significantly less abuse potential than do many of the other sedative hypnotics (for example, barbiturates) with the exception of buspirone (BuSpar), which is also a safe and effective drug.

Chemistry

The benzodiazepine nucleus consists of a benzene ring fused to the seven-sided diazepine ring (Fig. 35.3.6–1). All clinically important benzodiazepines also have a second benzene ring attached to the carbon atom at position 5 on the diazepine ring (Table 35.3.6–1). The benzodiazepines can be classified according to the substitution on the diazepine ring. The 2-keto benzodiazepines have a keto group off the carbon atom in position 2 on the diazepine ring. Although chlordiazepoxide (Librium) has a different substitution at the C_2 site, a —$NHCH_3$ group, it is useful to classify it along with the 2-keto derivatives. The 3-hydroxy benzodiazepines have a hydroxy (OH) group on the carbon atom at position 3 of the

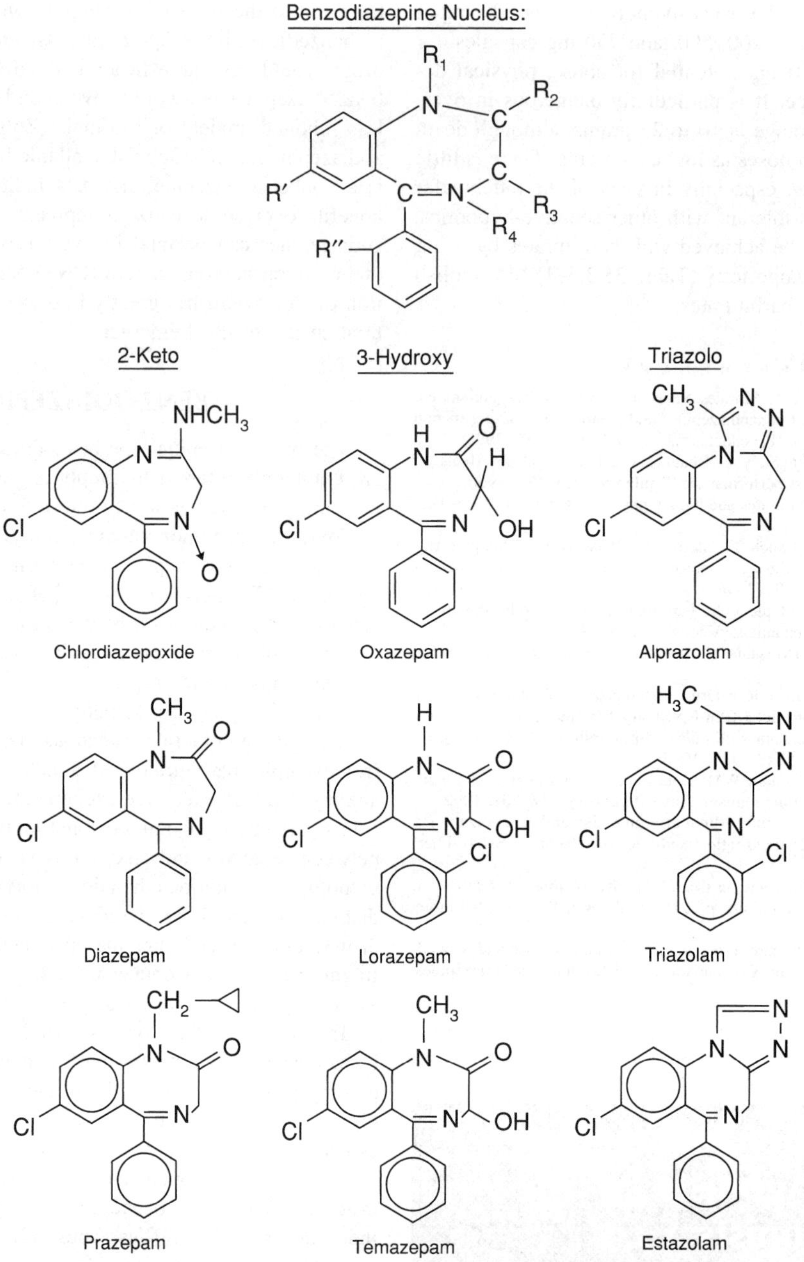
Benzodiazepine Nucleus:
R₁
R₂
R₃
R₄
R′
R″
2-Keto
3-Hydroxy
Triazolo
Chlordiazepoxide
Oxazepam
Alprazolam
Diazepam
Lorazepam
Triazolam
Prazepam
Temazepam
Estazolam

FIGURE 35.3.6–1
Molecular structures of benzodiazepines.

diazepine ring. The triazolobenzodiazepines have a triazolo ring fused to the nitrogen atom at position 1 and to the carbon atom at position 2 of the diazepine ring. Although clonazepam (Klonopin) has a 2-keto group, it is classified separately as a nitro derivative because of the nitrous group (NO_2) off the benzene ring. Quazepam (Doral) is also classified separately as a 2-thione derivative because of the sulfur atom at the C_2 site of the diazepine ring.

Pharmacological Actions

Pharmacokinetics. With the exception of clorazepate (Tranxene), all the benzodiazepines are completely absorbed unchanged from the gastrointestinal (GI) tract. Clorazepate is converted to desmethyldiazepam (Nordazepam) in the GI tract and is absorbed in this form. Absorption, the attainment of peak levels, and the onset of action are quickest for diazepam (Valium), lorazepam (Ativan), alprazolam (Xanax), triazolam (Halcion), and estazolam (ProSom). The rapid onset of effects is important for patients who take a single dose of a benzodiazepine to calm an episodic burst of anxiety or to fall asleep rapidly. The drugs' rapid onset of effects can be partly attributed to their high lipid solubility, a characteristic that varies fivefold among the benzodiazepines. The range of time to peak plasma level is 1 to 3 hours, although prazepam (Centrax) may take up to 6 hours. There may also be a secondary peak plasma

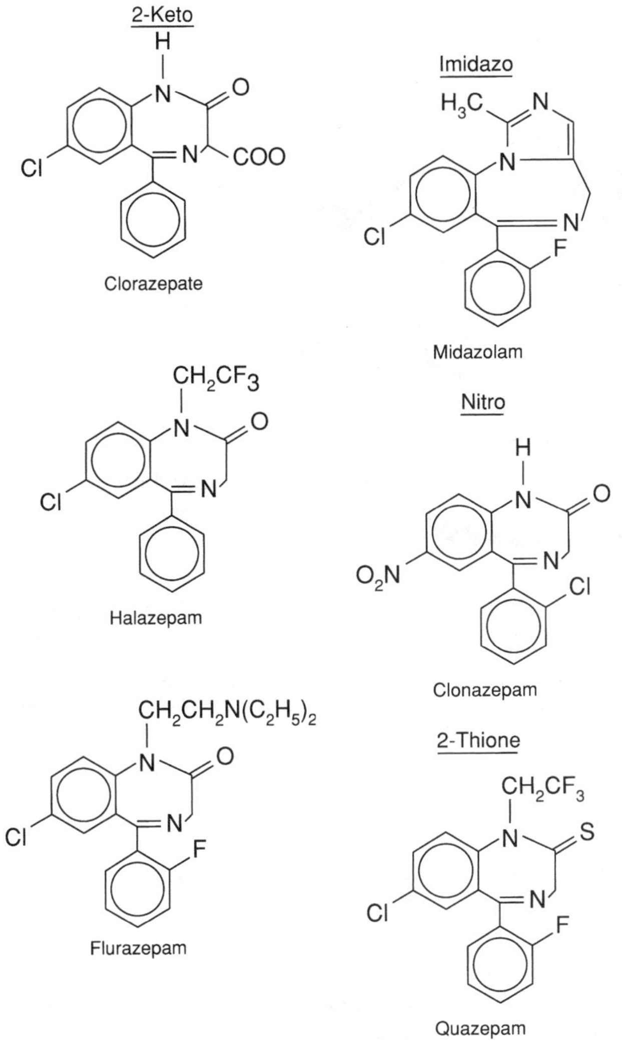
2-Keto
Clorazepate
Halazepam
Flurazepam
Imidazo
Midazolam
Nitro
Clonazepam
2-Thione
Quazepam

FIGURE 35.3.6–1—*continued*

level at 6 to 10 hours because of enterohepatic recirculation. Although several benzodiazepines are available in parenteral forms for intramuscular (IM) administration, only lorazepam has rapid and reliable absorption from this route, a fact that is behind the gradual replacement of intravenous (IV) diazepam by IM lorazepam in psychiatric emergency settings.

The metabolism of the benzodiazepines differs according to the drugs' various classes. Chlordiazepoxide is metabolized to diazepam, then to desmethyldiazepam, then to oxazepam, and finally to a glucuronide form; all these metabolites have some degree of agonist activity at the benzodiazepine receptor. Diazepam, clorazepate, prazepam, and halazepam (Paxipam) are metabolized first to desmethyldiazepam and then follow the same route that chlordiazepoxide takes. Flurazepam (Dalmane) follows similar biochemical steps. As a result of the slow metabolism of desmethyldiazepam, all the 2-keto benzodiazepines have plasma half-lives of 30 to more than 100 hours and are, therefore, the longest-acting benzodiazepines. The plasma half-life can be as high as 200 hours in people who are genetically slow metabolizers of these compounds. Quazepam, a 2-thione benzodiazepine, follows the same metabolic pathways as 2-keto benzodiazepines and, thus, has metabolites with long half-lives. Because the attainment of steady-state plasma levels of the drugs can take up to 2 weeks, patients may experience symptoms and signs of toxicity after only 7 to 10 days of treatment with a dosage that may have seemed to be in the therapeutic range at the initiation of treatment.

The 3-hydroxy benzodiazepines have short half-lives (10 to 30 hours) because they are directly metabolized by glucuronidation and thus have no active metabolites. The triazolo benzodiazepines are hydroxylated before they undergo glucuronidation. Alprazolam has a half-life of 10 to 15 hours; estazolam has a half-life of 10 to 24 hours; and triazolam has the shortest half-life of all the orally administered benzodiazepines (2 to 3 hours).

Midazolam (Versed), an imidazobenzodiazepine, is available only in an injectable form. It is used for sedation during medical procedures and has no clinical use in psychiatry. It produces significant amnestic effects and can suppress respiration.

Pharmacodynamics. Benzodiazepines bind to specific sites on the $GABA_A$ receptors and result in an increase in the affinity of the $GABA_A$ receptor for its neurotransmitter, GABA (Fig. 35.3.6–2). The increased affinity for GABA results in sustained activation of the ion channel and, thus, the passage of increased chloride ions into the neuron. One preliminary study on the other effects of alprazolam reported a global decrease in cerebral blood flow and decreases in plasma epinephrine concentrations. Recently, basic neuroscience research found evidence for two subtypes of CNS benzodiazepine (BZ) receptors (also called ω receptors)—BZ_1 (also called ω_1) re-

Table 35.3.6–1
Classification of Benzodiazepines

2-Keto	3-Hydroxy	Triazolo	Imidazo	Nitro	2-Thione
Chlordiazepoxide	Oxazepam	Alprazolam	Midazolam	Clonazepam	Quazepam
Diazepam	Lorazepam	Triazolam			
Prazepam	Temazepam	Estazolam			
Clorazepate					
Halazepam					
Flurazepam					

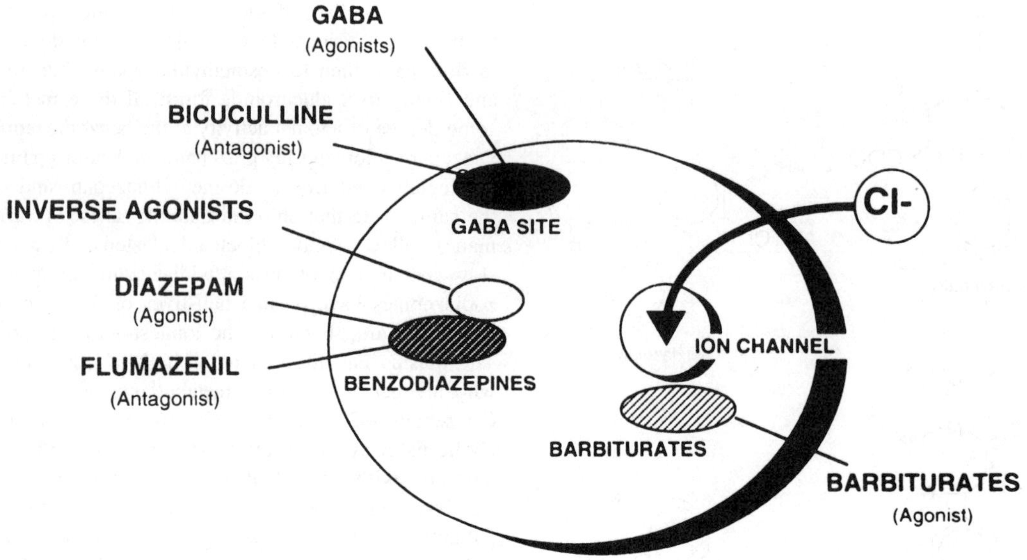
GABA
(Agonists)
BICUCULLINE
(Antagonist)
INVERSE AGONISTS
GABA SITE
Cl-
DIAZEPAM
(Agonist)
FLUMAZENIL
(Antagonist)
BENZODIAZEPINES
ION CHANNEL
BARBITURATES
BARBITURATES
(Agonist)

FIGURE 35.3.6–2
Schematic representation of the $GABA_A$ receptor. This diagram illustrates three of the major binding sites on the $GABA_A$ receptor and the chloride channel but does not represent the actual subunit structure of the receptor. The chloride channel opens when two molecules of GABA bind to their site on the receptor. The proconvulsant compound bicuculline blocks the binding of GABA to its site. The benzodiazepine and barbiturate binding sites are physically separate from the GABA site and from each other. Compounds such as flumazenil, with no intrinsic activity, compete with benzodiazepines such as diazepam for binding and thus serve as benzodiazepine antagonists. (Reprinted with permission from Hyman SE, Arana GW, Rosenbaum JF: *Handbook of Psychiatric Drug Therapy,* ed 3, p 157. Little, Brown, Boston, 1996.)

ceptors and BZ_2 (also called ω_2) receptors. BZ_1 receptors are believed to be involved in the mediation of sleep. BZ_2 receptors are believed to be involved in cognition, memory, and motor control. Theoretically, a benzodiazepine agonist that affects only BZ_1 receptors has few adverse cognitive effects. Quazepam and halazepam are more specific for the BZ_1 receptor than for the BZ_2 receptor and, therefore, may be associated with less amnesia and other cognitive impairments than are other currently available benzodiazepines.

Effects on Specific Organs and Systems

In addition to the CNS effects on anxiety and sleep, benzodiazepines are effective anticonvulsants. In addition to these CNS effects, benzodiazepines are effective as skeletal muscle relaxants, primarily through their ability to inhibit spinal polysynaptic afferent pathways, although monosynaptic afferent pathways may also be affected.

Therapeutic Indications

Anxiety. Generalized anxiety disorder, adjustment disorder with anxiety, but not necessarily pathological anxiety associated with life events (for example, after an accident) are the major clinical applications for benzodiazepines in psychiatry and general medical practice. Most patients should be treated for a predetermined, specific, and relatively brief period. Some patients with generalized anxiety disorder may warrant maintenance treatment with benzodiazepines. The serotonin-specific reuptake inhibitors are effective antianxiety agents that lack abuse potential, although their antianxiety effects require 2 to 4 weeks to develop.

Insomnia. Flurazepam, temazepam (Restoril), quazepam, estazolam, and triazolam are the benzodiazepines approved for use as hypnotics. The benzodiazepine hypnotics differ principally in their half-lives; flurazepam has the longest half-life, and triazolam has the shortest half-life. Flurazepam may be associated with minor cognitive impairment on the day after its administration, and triazolam may be associated with mild rebound anxiety. Temazepam or estazolam may be a reasonable compromise for the average adult patient. Because of its high specificity for the BZ_1 receptor, quazepam may be associated with few adverse cognitive effects, but quazepam shares the final metabolite with flurazepam—desalkylflurazepam (half-life of about 100 hours)—and, therefore, may be associated with daytime impairment when used for a long time. Estazolam produces a rapid onset of sleep and a hypnotic effect for 6 to 8 hours. All the benzodiazepines produce a moderate decrease in rapid eye movement (REM) sleep, although their use is not associated with REM rebound. The benzodiazepines are also associated with a decrease in stage 3 and stage 4 sleep, although the significance of this is not known. Benzodiazepines alone generally should not be taken for more than 3 consecutive weeks, to limit the risk of development of dependence. Longer term treatment of insomnia should include behavioral modification, relaxation techniques, and exploration of the underlying causes of insomnia, such as anxiety or depression. Trazodone's sedating qualities make it a nonaddictive alternative to benzodiazepines for treatment of insomnia.

Depression. Unique among the benzodiazepines, alprazolam has antidepressant effects equal to those of the tricyclic drugs, but alprazolam is not effective with seriously depressed inpatients. The efficacy of alprazolam in depressive disorders may be a reflection of its potency; the antidepressant effects of other benzodiazepines may be evident only at doses that also induce sedation or sleep. The starting dosage of alprazolam for the treatment of depression should be 1 to 1.5 mg a day and should be raised in 0.5 mg a day intervals every 3 or 4 days. The maximal dosage is usually 4 mg a day, although some investigators and clinicians have used dosages as high as 10 mg a day. The use of high dosage is controversial because of the possibility of withdrawal symptoms. Clinicians must taper, rather than abruptly stop, alprazolam, usually at the rate of 0.5 mg a day every 3 to 4 days.

Panic Disorder and Social Phobia. For two anxiety disorders, panic disorder with or without agoraphobia and social phobia, the two high-potency benzodiazepines, alprazolam and clonazepam, are effective. The Food and Drug Administration (FDA) has approved the use of alprazolam for the treatment of panic disorder. The dosage guidelines for the use of alprazolam in panic disorder are similar to those for depression, as already discussed. Paroxetine (Paxil) and sertraline (Zoloft) have also been approved by the FDA for treatment of panic disorder. Because paroxetine and sertraline may not be fully effective for 2 to 4 weeks after initiation, coadministration of a high-potency benzodiazepine for the first 2 to 4 weeks of use of paroxetine or sertraline can provide rapid control of anxiety, before the long-term benefits of paroxetine or sertraline emerge.

Obsessive-Compulsive Disorder and Posttraumatic Stress Disorder. Benzodiazepines, especially clonazepam, which has serotonergic properties, may treat the anxiety component of obsessive-compulsive disorder. Clonazepam may be effective for certain patients who do not respond to clomipramine. Benzodiazepines may also be used to augment clomipramine or the serotonin-specific reuptake inhibitors. Benzodiazepines may help reduce hyperarousal in posttraumatic stress disorder.

Bipolar I Disorder. Clonazepam is effective in the management of manic episodes and as an adjuvant to lithium (Eskalith) therapy in lieu of antipsychotics. As an adjuvant to lithium, clonazepam may result in an increased time between cycles and fewer than usual depressive episodes. The other high-potency benzodiazepine, alprazolam, may be as effective as clonazepam for this indication, which is not recognized by the FDA, and alprazolam should be considered a second-line treatment.

Akathisia. Standard anticholinergic drugs—for example, benztropine (Cogentin)—are often ineffective in treating neuroleptic-induced acute akathisia. The first-line drug for akathisia is most commonly a β-adrenergic receptor antagonist—for example, propranolol (Inderal). Several studies have found, however, that benzodiazepines are also effective in treating some cases of akathisia.

Other Psychiatric Indications. Chlordiazepoxide is used to manage the symptoms of alcohol withdrawal. The benzodiazepines (especially IM lorazepam) are used to manage both substance-induced (except amphetamine) and psychotic agitation in the emergency room. A few studies report the use of high dosages of benzodiazepines in patients with schizophrenia who had not responded to antipsychotics or who were unable to take the traditional drugs because of adverse effects. The successful use of IM lorazepam for the treatment of catatonia has been reported. Benzodiazepines have also been used instead of amobarbital (Amytal) for drug-assisted interviewing.

Precautions and Adverse Reactions

The most common adverse effect of benzodiazepines is drowsiness, which occurs in about 10 percent of all patients. Because of this adverse effect, patients should be advised to be careful while driving or using dangerous machinery when taking the drugs. Drowsiness can be present during the day after the use of a benzodiazepine for insomnia the previous night, so-called residual daytime sedation. Some patients also experience dizziness (less than 1 percent) and ataxia (less than 2 percent). These symptoms can result in falls and hip fractures, especially in elderly patients. The most serious adverse effects of benzodiazepines occur when other sedative substances, such as alcohol, are taken concurrently. The combinations can result in marked drowsiness, disinhibition, or even respiratory depression. Other relatively rare adverse effects have been mild cognitive deficits that may impair job performance in patients who are taking benzodiazepines. Anterograde amnesia has also been associated with benzodiazepines, particularly high-potency benzodiazepines. A rare, paradoxical increase in aggression has been reported in patients given benzodiazepines, although this effect may be most common in patients with brain damage. Allergic reactions to the drugs are also rare, but a few studies report maculopapular rashes and generalized itching. The symptoms of benzodiazepine intoxication include confusion, slurred speech, ataxia, drowsiness, dyspnea, and hyporeflexia.

Triazolam has received significant attention in the media because of an alleged association with serious aggressive behavioral manifestations, which were associated with doses greater than 1 mg, a dose that is twice the recommended maximum dose. Although little evidence supports the association, the Upjohn Company, which manufactures triazolam, has issued a statement emphasizing that the drug is best used as a short-term (fewer than 10 days) treatment of insomnia, that physicians should carefully evaluate the emergence of any abnormal thinking or behavioral changes in patients treated with triazolam, and that they should consider all appropriate potential causes. Triazolam was banned in Great Britain in 1991.

Patients with hepatic disease and elderly patients are particularly likely to have adverse effects and toxicity from the benzodiazepines, especially when the drugs are administered in repeated or high doses, because of the patient's impaired metabolism of the compounds. Benzodiazepines can produce clinically significant impairment of respiration in patients with chronic obstructive pulmonary disease and sleep apnea. Benzodiazepines should be used with caution in patients with a history of substance abuse, cognitive disorders, renal disease, hepatic disease, porphyria, CNS depression, and myasthenia gravis.

Some data indicate that benzodiazepines are teratogenic; therefore, their use during pregnancy is not advised. Moreover, the use of benzodiazepines in the third trimester can precipitate a withdrawal syndrome in newborns. The drugs are secreted in the breast milk in sufficient concentrations to affect neonates. Benzodiazepines may cause dyspnea, bradycardia, and drowsiness in nursing babies.

Tolerance, Dependence, and Withdrawal. When benzodiazepines are used for short periods (1 to 2 weeks) in moderate dosages, they usually cause no significant tolerance, dependence, or withdrawal effects. The short-acting benzodiazepines (for example, triazolam) may be an exception to this rule, as some patients have reported increased anxiety the day after taking a single dose of the drug. Some patients also report a tolerance for the anxiolytic effects of benzodiazepines and require increased dosages to maintain the clinical remission of symptoms. There is also a cross-tolerance among most of the classes of antianxiety drugs, with the notable exception of buspirone and the serotonin-specific reuptake inhibitors.

The appearance of a withdrawal syndrome, also called a discontinuation syndrome (Table 35.3.6–2), depends on the length of time a patient has taken a benzodiazepine, the dosage the patient has been taking, the rate at which the drug is tapered, and the half-life of the compound. Abrupt discontinuation of benzodiazepines, particularly those with short half-lives, is associated with severe withdrawal symptoms. Serious symptoms may include depression, paranoia, delirium, and seizures. The incidence of the syndrome is controversial, but some features of the syndrome may occur in as many as 50 percent of patients treated with the drugs. The development of a severe withdrawal syndrome is seen only in patients who have taken high dosages for long periods. The appearance of the syndrome may be delayed for 1 or 2 weeks in patients who had been taking 2-keto benzodiazepines with long half-lives. Alprazolam seems to be particularly associated with an immediate and severe withdrawal syndrome and should be tapered gradually. A recent study comparing simple tapering of alprazolam with tapering plus cognitive, anticipatory guidance regarding the alprazolam discontinuation effects found that patients were much more likely to remain off of alprazolam indefinitely if they have been fully warned to expect the signs and symptoms of discontinuation. This is important because a significant percentage of patients who use alprazolam for long periods are unable successfully to discontinue taking it.

Overdoses. Overdoses with benzodiazepines alone have a predictably favorable outcome. When the overdose involves drugs in addition to the benzodiazepines, however, respiratory depression, coma, seizures, and death are likely. Drugs that are commonly taken with benzodiazepines in fatal overdoses include alcohol, antipsychotics, and antidepressants. The availability of flumazenil has facilitated the medical management of benzodiazepine overdoses.

Drug Interactions

Because benzodiazepines are widely used, clinicians must be aware of the possible interactions of benzodiazepines and other drugs (Table 35.3.6–3). Cimetidine (Tagamet), disulfiram (Antabuse), isoniazid (Nydrazid), and estrogen increase the plasma levels of 2-keto benzodiazepines. Antacids and food may decrease the plasma levels of benzodiazepines, and smoking may increase the metabolism of benzodiazepines. The benzodiazepines may increase the plasma levels of phenytoin (Dilantin) and digoxin (Lanoxin). All benzodiazepines have additive CNS effects with other sedative drugs. Ataxia and dysarthria may occur when lithium, antipsychotics, and clo-

Table 35.3.6–2
Commonly Observed Withdrawal Symptoms (Benzodiazepine Withdrawal Syndrome)

Anxiety
Irritability
Insomnia
Fatigue
Headache
Muscle twitching or aching
Tremor, shakiness
Sweating
Dizziness
Concentration difficulties
Nausea, loss of appetite[a]
Observable depression[a]
Depersonalization, derealization[a]
Increased sensory perception (smell, sight, taste, touch)[a]
Abnormal perception or sensation of movement[a]

Reprinted with permission from Roy-Byrne, PP, Hommer D: Benzodiazepine withdrawal: Overview and implications for the treatment of anxiety. Am J Med *84:* 1041, 1988.

[a] Symptoms likely to represent true withdrawal, rather than an exacerbation or return of original anxiety.

Table 35.3.6–3
Interactions of Benzodiazepines with Other Drugs

Decrease absorption		
Antacids		
Increase CNS depression		
Antihistamines		
Barbiturates and similarly acting drugs		
Cyclic antidepressants		
Ethanol		
Increase benzodiazepine levels (compete for microsomal enzymes; probably little or no effect on lorazepam, oxazepam, temazepam)		
Cimetidine	Erythromycin	Fluoxetine
Disulfiram	Estrogens	Isoniazid
Decrease benzodiazepine levels		
Carbamazepine (possibly other anticonvulsants)		

Reprinted with permission from Arana GW, Hyman SE: *Handbook of Psychiatric Drug Therapy,* ed 2, p 159. Little, Brown, Boston, 1991.

nazepam are combined. The combination of benzodiazepines and clozapine (Clozaril) has been reported to cause delirium and should be avoided. Because of inhibition of the hepatic cytochrome P450 (CYP) enzyme CYP 3A4, benzodiazepines, especially triazolobenzodiazepines (triazolam and alprazolam), should not be administered concomitantly with nefazodone (Serzone), fluvoxamine (Luvox), cisapride (Propulsid), or grapefruit juice.

Laboratory Interferences

No known laboratory interferences are associated with the use of benzodiazepines.

Dosage and Administration

Benzodiazepines are categorized as short-, intermediate-, or long-acting drugs. Their sedative and anxiolytic effects appear within 30 to 60 minutes of administration and terminate as soon as the drugs are excreted. This is in contrast to the antianxiety effects of the serotonergic drugs, which may take 2 to 4 weeks to develop.

The clinical decision to treat an anxious patient with a benzodiazepine should be carefully considered. Medical causes of anxiety (for example, thyroid dysfunction, caffeinism, and medications) should be ruled out. The benzodiazepine should be started at a low dosage, and the patient should be instructed about the drug's sedative properties and abuse potential. An estimated length of therapy should be decided at the beginning of therapy, and the need for continued therapy should be reevaluated at least monthly because of the problems associated with long-term use.

Duration of Treatment. Benzodiazepines can be used to treat illnesses other than anxiety disorders. In such cases the duration of treatment should generally be similar to that for the standard drugs used to treat these disorders. The use of benzodiazepines over a long period for chronically anxious patients is often valuable although controversial. In his 1980 textbook on drug treatment in psychiatry, Donald Klein stated, "There are many reports of patients maintained on benzodiazepines for years with apparent benefit and without the development of tolerance. Nonetheless, it is dubious practice to prescribe such medications indefinitely without accompanying psychotherapy."

Discontinuation of Therapy. Benzodiazepine withdrawal syndrome occurs when patients discontinue benzodiazepines abruptly; 90 percent of patients after long-term use experience some symptoms of withdrawal on discontinuation, less if the drug is tapered slowly. Benzodiazepine withdrawal syndrome consists of anxiety, nervousness, diaphoresis, restlessness, irritability, fatigue, light-headedness, tremor, insomnia, and weakness. The higher the dose and the shorter the half-life, the more severe the withdrawal symptoms can be.

When the medication is to be discontinued, the drug must be tapered slowly (25 percent a week); otherwise, recurrence or rebound of symptoms is likely to occur. Monitoring of any withdrawal symptoms (possibly with a standardized rating scale) and psychological support for the patient are helpful in the successful accomplishment of benzodiazepine discontinuation. Concurrent use of carbamazepine (Tegretol) during benzodiazepine discontinuation reportedly permits a more rapid and better-tolerated withdrawal than does a gradual taper alone. The dosage range of carbamazepine used to facilitate withdrawal is 400 to 500 mg a day. Some clinicians report particular difficulty in tapering and discontinuing alprazolam, particularly with patients who have been receiving high dosages for long periods. There have been reports of successful discontinuation of alprazolam by switching to clonazepam, which is then gradually withdrawn.

Choice of Drug and Potency. The wide range of benzodiazepines are available in an equally wide range of formulations (Table 35.3.6–4). The drugs differ primarily in their half-lives. Another difference is in the rate of onset of their potency and anxiolytic effects. Potency is a general term used to express the pharmacological activity of a drug. Some benzodiazepines are more potent than others, in that one compound requires a relatively smaller dose than another compound to achieve the same effect. For example, clonazepam requires 0.25 mg to achieve the same effect as 5 mg of diazepam; thus, clonazepam is considered a high-potency benzodiazepine. Conversely, oxazepam (Serax) has an approximate dose equivalence of 15 mg and is a low-potency drug. The four high-potency benzodiazepines—alprazolam, triazolam, estazolam, and clonazepam—are the drugs most likely to be effective for new applications such as depression, bipolar I disorder, panic disorder, and the phobias.

The advantages of the long-half-life drugs over the short-half-life drugs include less frequent dosing, less variation in plasma concentration, and less severe withdrawal phenomena. The disadvantages include drug accumulation, increased risk of daytime psychomotor impairment, and increased daytime sedation. The advantages of the short-half-life drugs over the long-half-life drugs include no drug accumulation and less daytime sedation. The disadvantages include more frequent dosing and earlier and more severe withdrawal syndromes. Rebound insomnia and anterograde amnesia are thought to be more of a problem with the short-half-life drugs than with the long-half-life drugs.

Drug Combinations. The most common drug combinations with benzodiazepines involve antipsychotics and antidepressants, in addition to the benzodiazepines' obvious use as adjuvant hypnotics. The combination of a benzodiazepine and an antidepressant may be indicated in the treatment of markedly anxious depressed patients and patients with panic disorder. Several reports indicate that the combined use of alprazolam and an antipsychotic may further reduce psychotic symptoms for patients who did not respond adequately to the antipsychotic alone. The combined use of benzodiazepines and tricyclic drugs may improve compliance by reducing the subjective side effects and producing an immediate reduction in anxiety and insomnia. The combination, however, may also cause excessive sedation, cognitive impairment, and even exacerbation of the depression, and it significantly adds to the lethality of an overdose.

Table 35.3.6–4
Benzodiazepines

Drug	Approximate Dose Equivalents[a]	Dosage Forms	Benzodiazepines Rate of Absorption	Major Active Metabolites	Average Half-Life of Metabolites (hr)	Short-Acting/ Long-Acting[b]	Usual Adult Dosage Range (mg per day)
Alprazolam (Xanax)	0.25	0.25, 0.5, 1, 2 mg tablets	Medium	α-Hydroxyalprazolam, 4-hydroxyalprazolam	12	Short	0.5–4
Chlordiazepoxide (Librium)	10	5, 10, 25 mg tablets; 5, 10, 25 mg capsules; 100 mg parenteral	Medium	Desmethylchlordiazepoxide, demoxepam, desmethyldiazepam, oxazepam	100	Long	15–100
Clonazepam (Klonopin)	0.5	0.5, 1, 2 mg tablets	Rapid	None	34	Long	0.5–10
Clorazepate (Tranxene)	7.5	3.75, 7.5, 11.25, 15, 22.5 mg tablets; 3.75, 7.5, 15 mg capsules	Rapid	Desmethyldiazepam, oxazepam	100	Long	7.5–60
Diazepam (Valium)	5	2, 5, 10 mg tablets; 15 mg capsules (extended release); 5 mg/mL parenteral	Rapid	Desmethyldiazepam, oxazepam	100	Long	2–40
Estazolam (ProSom)	0.33	1, 2 mg tablets	Rapid	4-Hydroxy estazolam, *l*-oxo-estazolam	17	Short	1–2
Flurazepam (Dalmane)	5	15, 30 mg tablets	Rapid	Desalkylflurazepam, *N*-1-hydroxyethylflurazepam	100	Long	15–30
Halazepam (Paxipam)	20	20, 40 mg tablets	Medium	Desmethyldiazepam, oxazepam	100	Long	60–160
Lorazepam (Ativan)	1	0.5, 1, 2 mg tablets; 2 mg/mL, 4 mg/mL parenteral	Medium	None	15	Short	2–4
Midazolam (Versed)[c]	1.25–1.7	1 mg/mL, 5 mg/mL parenteral	N/A	1-Hydroxymethylmidazolam	2.5	Short	1–5
Oxazepam (Serax)	15	15 mg tablets; 10, 15, 30 mg capsules	Slow	None	8	Short	30–120
Prazepam (Centrax)	10	10 mg tablets; 5, 10, 20 mg capsules	Slow	Desmethyldiazepam, oxazepam	100	Long	20–60
Quazepam (Doral)	5	7.5, 15 mg tablets	Rapid	2-oxoquazepam, *N*-desalkyl-2-oxoquazepam, and 3-hydroxy-2-oxoquazepam glucuronide	100	Long	7.5–30
Temazepam (Restoril)	5	15, 30 mg tablets	Medium	None	11	Short	15–30
Triazolam (Halcion)	0.1–0.03	0.125, 0.25 mg tablets	Rapid	None	2	Short	0.125–0.25

[a] High-potency drugs have an approximate dose equivalent of under 1.0; 1.0–10, medium potency, over 10, low potency.
[b] Short-acting benzodiazepines have a half-life of under 25 hours.
[c] Used only by anesthesiologists.

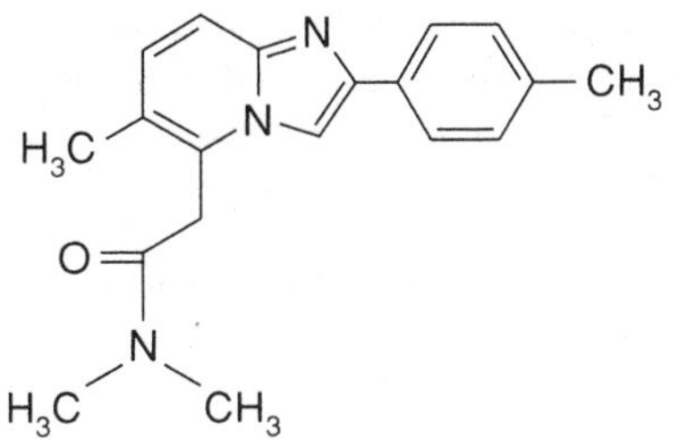

FIGURE 35.3.6–3
Molecular structure of zolpidem.

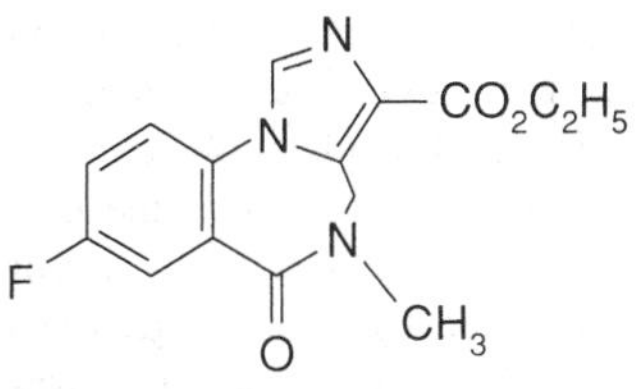

FIGURE 35.3.6–4
Molecular structure of flumazenil.

ZOLPIDEM

Zolpidem (Ambien) is a new hypnotic that acts at the γ-aminobutyric acid (GABA)–benzodiazepine complex as the benzodiazepines do, but it is not itself a benzodiazepine. The only indication for zolpidem at this time is as a hypnotic. The drug lacks the muscle-relaxant effects that are common to the benzodiazepines.

Chemistry

Zolpidem is an imidazopyridine, and its chemical structure is shown in Figure 35.3.6–3.

Pharmacological Actions

Pharmacokinetics. Zolpidem is rapidly and well absorbed after oral administration, and it reaches peak plasma levels in about 2 to 3 hours. Zolpidem has a half-life of about 2 to 3 hours and is metabolized primarily by conjugation. Zolpidem does not have any active metabolites.

Pharmacodynamics. Zolpidem has a much higher affinity for BZ_1 receptors than for BZ_2 receptors. Zolpidem is also more specific for the CNS benzodiazepine receptors than for the peripheral benzodiazepine receptors. These pharmacodynamic properties are consistent with the drug's efficacy as a hypnotic in the absence of significant anticonvulsant or muscle-relaxant properties. The binding site of zolpidem is likely to be similar to that of the benzodiazepines, as the effects of zolpidem can be prevented or reversed by the benzodiazepine receptor antagonist flumazenil.

Therapeutic Indications

The sole indication at this time for zolpidem is as a hypnotic. Several studies have found an absence of rebound REM after the use of the compound for the induction of sleep. The comparatively few data available indicate that zolpidem may not be associated with rebound insomnia after the discontinuation of its use for short periods.

Precautions and Adverse Reactions

Because of the short half-life of zolpidem, clinicians may reasonably evaluate a patient for the possibility of anterograde amnesia and anxiety the day after its administration, although neither of these adverse effects has been reported. Emesis and dysphoric reactions have been reported as adverse effects. Tolerance and dependence have been reported in less than 1 percent of patients, and the withdrawal symptoms are similar to those described for benzodiazepines. Patients taking zolpidem should be advised to exercise additional caution when driving or operating dangerous machinery. Zolpidem is secreted in breast milk and is, therefore, contraindicated for use by nursing mothers. The dosage of zolpidem should be reduced in patients with renal and hepatic impairment. Preliminary data indicate that zolpidem has a longer than usual half-life in older people and a shorter than usual half-life in children.

Drug Interactions and Laboratory Interferences

Information on drug interactions and laboratory interferences is limited. Therefore, clinicians should consider the possibility of such an interaction or interference in a patient who is being treated with zolpidem.

Dosage and Administration

Zolpidem is available in 5, 10, 15, and 20 mg tablets, and a single 10 mg dose is usual for the treatment of insomnia. For patients under age 65, the initial dose of 10 mg can be increased to 15 or 20 mg if necessary. For patients over age 65, an initial dose of 5 mg may be advised. Prolonged use of zolpidem or any hypnotic is not recommended.

FLUMAZENIL

Flumazenil (Mazicon, Romazicon) is a benzodiazepine receptor antagonist. It reverses the psychophysiological effects of the benzodiazepine agonists (for example, diazepam). The use of flumazenil is limited to emergency rooms and other emergency settings.

Chemistry

The molecular structure of flumazenil is based on a benzodiazepine nucleus (Fig. 35.3.6–4).

Pharmacological Actions

Pharmacokinetics. After IV administration, flumazenil has a half-life of 7 to 15 minutes. Protein binding is about

50 percent. Clearance of flumazenil occurs primarily by hepatic metabolism. The major metabolites of flumazenil are the deethylated free acid and its glucuronide conjugate, which are excreted in the urine. Elimination of the drug is essentially complete in 72 hours. The pharmacokinetics of flumazenil are not significantly affected by gender, age, renal failure, or hemodialysis but are affected by hepatic impairment, which prolongs the half-life.

Pharmacodynamics. Flumazenil can both block and reverse the CNS effects of currently available benzodiazepine receptor agonists (for example, diazepam and zolpidem). Specifically, IV flumazenil antagonizes sedation, impairment of recall, and psychomotor retardation produced by benzodiazepine receptor agonists. But flumazenil does not reverse the effects of other CNS depressants, even if they also act partly on the $GABA_A$ receptor (for example, ethanol and barbiturates). Flumazenil is also ineffective in reversing the effects of opioids and opiates (Fig. 35.3.6–2).

Therapeutic Indications

Flumazenil is used to reverse the effects of benzodiazepine receptor agonists that have been used for clinical indications (for example, sedation and anesthesia) or in overdose. Interest has followed early reports that flumazenil may alleviate some of the cognitive and anxiety impairment in cases of hepatic encephalopathy, cirrhosis, and alcoholism, possibly by blocking endogenous benzodiazepine receptor ligands. This therapeutic indication needs further substantiation, however, before widespread acceptance. Candidate endogenous benzodiazepine receptor ligands, including two related peptide neurotransmitters, are under active study.

Precautions and Adverse Reactions

The most common adverse effects of flumazenil are nausea, vomiting, dizziness, agitation, emotional lability, cutaneous vasodilation, injection-site pain, fatigue, impaired vision, and headache. The most common serious adverse effect of the use of flumazenil to reverse benzodiazepine overdose is the precipitation of seizures, which is especially likely to occur in patients with seizure disorders, those who are physically dependent on benzodiazepines, or those who have ingested very large quantities of benzodiazepines. Flumazenil alone may impair memory retrieval.

Drug Interactions and Laboratory Interferences

No deleterious drug interactions have been noted when flumazenil is administered after narcotics, inhalation anesthetics, muscle relaxants, and muscle-relaxant antagonists administered in conjunction with sedation or anesthesia. In mixed-drug overdose the toxic effects (for example, seizures and cardiac arrhythmias) of other drugs (for example, tricyclic drugs) may emerge with the reversal of the benzodiazepine effects of flumazenil. For example, seizures caused by an overdose of tricyclic drugs may have been partially treated in a patient who had also taken an overdose of benzodiazepines. With flumazenil treatment, the tricyclic-induced seizures or cardiac arrhythmias may appear and may result in a fatal outcome.

No laboratory interferences have been associated with the use of flumazenil.

Dosage and Administration

For the initial management of a known or suspected benzodiazepine overdose, the recommended initial dose of flumazenil is 0.2 mg (2 mL) administered IV over 30 seconds. If the desired level of consciousness is not obtained after waiting 30 seconds, a further dose of 0.3 (3 mL) can be administered over 30 seconds. Further doses of 0.5 mg (5 mL) can be administered over 30 seconds at 1-minute intervals up to a cumulative dose of 3.0 mg. Clinicians should not rush the administration of flumazenil. A secure airway and IV access should be established before the administration of the drug. Patients should be awakened gradually.

Most patients with a benzodiazepine overdose respond to a cumulative dose of 1 to 3 mg of flumazenil; doses beyond 3 mg of flumazenil do not reliably produce additional effects. If a patient has not responded 5 minutes after receiving a cumulative dose of 5 mg flumazenil, the major cause of sedation is probably not due to benzodiazepine receptor agonists, and additional flumazenil is likely to have no effect.

Return of Sedation. The return of sedation can occur in 1 to 3 percent of patients. It can be prevented or treated by giving repeated doses of flumazenil at 20-minute intervals. For repeat treatment, no more than 1 mg (given as 0.5 mg a minute) should be given at any one time, and no more than 3 mg should be given in any 1 hour.

References

Ananth J, Swartz R, Burgoyne K, Gadasally R: Hepatic disease and psychiatric illness: Relationships and treatment. Psychother Psychosom *62:* 146, 1994.

Balkin TJ, O'Donnell VM, Wesenten N, McCann U, Belenky G: Comparison of the daytime sleep and performance effects of zolpidem versus triazolam. Psychopharmacology *107:* 83, 1992.

Bishop KI, Curran HV: Psychopharmacological analysis of implicit and explicit memory: A study with lorazepam and the benzodiazepine antagonist flumazenil. Psychopharmacology *121:* 267, 1995.

Curran HV, Birch B: Differentiating the sedative, psychomotor and amnesic effects of benzodiazepines: A study with midazolam and the benzodiazepine antagonist flumazenil. Psychopharmacology *103:* 519, 1991.

Doble A, Martin IL: Multiple benzodiazepine receptors: No reason for anxiety. Trends Pharmacol Sci *13:* 76, 1992.

Kapczinski F, Curran HV, Gray J, Lader M: Flumazenil has an anxiolytic effect in simulated stress. Psychopharmacology *114:* 187, 1994.

Kapczinski F, Sherman D, Williams R, Lader M: Differential effects of flumazenil in alcoholic and nonalcoholic cirrhotic patients. *120:* 220, 1995.

Klein D: *Diagnostic and Drug Treatment for Psychiatry,* ed 2. Williams & Wilkins, Baltimore, 1980.

Kryger MH, Steljes D, Pouliot Z, Neufeld H, Odynski T: Subjective versus objective evaluation of hypnotic efficacy: Experience with zolpidem. Sleep *14:* 399, 1991.

Kunovac JL, Stahl SM: Future directions in anxiolytic pharmacotherapy. *18:* 895, 1995.

Lader M: Rebound insomnia and newer hypnotics. Psychopharmacology *108:* 248, 1992.

Laurijssens BE, Greenblatt DJ: Pharmacokinetic-pharmacodynamic relationships for benzodiazepines. Clin Pharmacokinet *30:* 52, 1996.

Lenox RH, Newhouse PA, Creelman WL, Whitaker TM: Adjunctive treatment of manic agitation with lorazepam versus haloperidol: A double-blind study. J Clin Psychiatry *53:* 47, 1992.
Mumford GK, Rush CR, Griffiths RR: Abecarnil and alprazolam in humans: Behavioral, subjective and reinforcing effects. J Pharmacol Exp Ther *272:* 570, 1995.
Noyes R Jr, Burrows GD, Reich JH, Judd FK, Garvey MJ, Norman TR, Cook BL, Marriott P: Diazepam versus alprazolam for the treatment of panic disorder. J Clin Psychiatry *57:* 349, 1996.
Romach MK, Somer GR, Sobell LC, Sobell MB, Kaplan HL, Seller EM: Characteristics of long-term alprazolam users in the community. J Clin Psychopharmacol *12:* 316, 1992.
Roth T, Roehrs TA: The use of benzodiazepine hypnotics: A scientific examination of a clinical controversy. J Clin Psychiatry *53* (12, Suppl): 2, 1992.
Roy-Byrne P, Fleishaker J, Arnett C, Dubach M, Steward J, Radant A, Veith R, Graham M: Effects of acute and chronic alprazolam treatment on cerebral blood flow, memory, sedation, and plasma catecholamines. Neuropsychopharmacology *8:* 161, 1993.
Roy-Byrne P, Wingerson DK, Radant A, Greenblatt DJ, Cowley DS: Reduced benzodiazepine sensitivity in patients with panic disorder: comparison with patients with obsessive-compulsive disorder and normal subjects. Am J Psychiatry. *153:* 1444, 1996.
Schlich D, L'Heritier C, Coquelin JP, Attali P: Long-term treatment of insomnia with zolpidem. A multicentre general practitioner study of 107 patients. J Int Med Res *19:* 271, 1991.
Shaw SH, Curson H, Coquelin JP: A double-blind, comparative study of zolpidem and placebo in the treatment of insomnia in elderly psychiatric in-patients. J Int Med Res *20:* 150, 1992.
Sutherland SM, Davidson JR: Pharmacotherapy for post-traumatic stress disorder. Psychiatr Clin North Am *17:* 409, 1994.
Tiller JWG, Schweitzer I: Benzodiazepines: Depressants or antidepressants? Drugs *44:* 165, 1992.
Uhde TW, Tancer ME: Benzodiazepine receptor agonists and antagonists. In *Comprehensive Textbook of Psychiatry,* ed 6, HI Kaplan, BJ Sadock, editors, p 1933. Williams & Wilkins, Baltimore, 1995.
Warot D, Danjou P, Douillet P, Keane P, Puech AJ: Cognitive impairments induced by triazolam in healthy volunteers: Antagonism by a partial inverse agonist of benzodiazepine receptor. Therapie *49:* 23, 1994.
Williams JG, Amrein R: Pharmacology of flumazenil. Acta Anaesthesiol Scand Suppl *108:* 3, 1995.

▲ 35.3.7 Bromocriptine

Bromocriptine (Parlodel) has been studied as a potential therapeutic agent in several psychiatric conditions. These studies have been conducted because of interest in the mixed dopamine agonist-antagonist properties of bromocriptine, which is available in the United States as an approved treatment for Parkinson's disease. The most robust data are in support of the therapeutic benefit of bromocriptine to treat antipsychotic-induced hyperprolactinemia and galactorrhea and to treat neuroleptic malignant syndrome. Increasing data also support the use of bromocriptine for the treatment of cocaine withdrawal and depression, although the latter indication should be considered only after standard therapies have failed. The use of bromocriptine for any psychiatric indication should be undertaken only after a review of recent literature about these novel applications, which remain controversial.

CHEMISTRY

Bromocriptine is an ergotamine derivative. The molecular structure of bromocriptine is shown in Figure 35.3.7–1.

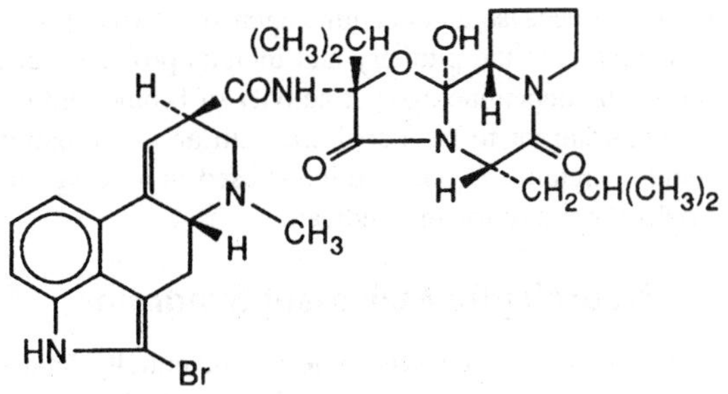
(CH3)2CH
OH
H
CONH
O
N
H
N
O
O
H
CH2CH(CH3)2
N
CH3
H
HN
Br

FIGURE 35.3.7–1
Molecular structure of bromocriptine.

PHARMACOLOGICAL ACTIONS

Pharmacokinetics

Bromocriptine is rapidly, but only partially, absorbed (about 30 percent) from the gastrointestinal (GI) tract. Peak concentrations are achieved 1½ to 3 hours after oral administration. Bromocriptine is metabolized in the liver and is excreted in the bile. No active metabolites have been identified.

Pharmacodynamics

Depending on dosage, bromocriptine has two effects on dopamine function. At low dosages, bromocriptine affects primarily presynaptic dopamine type 2 (D_2) receptors as an agonist, and thus inhibits the release of dopamine and effectively acts as an antagonist to the dopamine system. At high dosages, bromocriptine acts directly on postsynaptic dopamine receptors, as a direct dopamine agonist. This differential activity is due to the increased sensitivity of presynaptic D_2 receptors to dopamine agonist compounds.

EFFECTS ON SPECIFIC ORGANS AND SYSTEMS

Its dopaminergic activity causes bromocriptine to have effects on many organ systems in addition to the central nervous system (CNS). Because of the role of dopamine in the maintenance of blood pressure, bromocriptine use is commonly associated with hypotension, although hypertension has also been reported in some patients treated with the drug. The dopaminergic activity of bromocriptine can also affect heart rate and rhythm. The GI system is also sensitive to dopaminergic drugs, and bromocriptine administration is frequently associated with symptoms of GI distress, especially nausea.

THERAPEUTIC INDICATIONS

Antipsychotic-Induced Hyperprolactinemia

Because most antipsychotic drugs act as potent antagonists of D_2 receptors, they cause an increase in prolactin release by blocking the inhibitory effects of endogenous dopamine in the pituitary. The increase in serum prolactin can result in amenorrhea and galactorrhea in women. Bromocriptine is an effective treatment because its dopamine agonist activity stimulates the D_2 receptors in the pituitary and inhibits prolactin release. In spite of the dopamine agonist activity of bromocriptine, its use does not appear to be associated with an exacerbation of psychotic symptoms. Bromocriptine is used in a dosage range of 5 to 15 mg a day for this indication.

Neuroleptic Malignant Syndrome

Neuroleptic malignant syndrome is a potentially fatal syndrome of autonomic instability associated with the use of antipsychotics—for example, haloperidol (Haldol). Because of the sporadic, unpredictable nature of neuroleptic malignant syndrome, most data on the effectiveness of bromocriptine in the condition come from case reports. Bromocriptine may be effective in neuroleptic malignant syndrome because its dopamine agonist activity reverses the effects of the dopamine antagonists on hypothalamic thermoregulatory function and peripheral muscle contraction. Bromocriptine is effective in neuroleptic malignant syndrome because of its direct dopamine agonist effects. The syndrome is associated with use of dopamine receptor antagonists and occasionally with sudden withdrawal of levodopa, and it therefore appears to represent the consequence of sudden loss of activation of dopamine receptors.

The first and most crucial step in the treatment of neuroleptic malignant syndrome is the recognition that the syndrome is present in a patient. The first steps in the management of the syndrome are discontinuation of the antipsychotic drug and the initiation of supportive care. If bromocriptine or other drugs are used to treat neuroleptic malignant syndrome, the earlier they are begun, the greater their likely benefit. Amantadine (Symmetrel), another dopamine agonist, and dantrolene (Dantrium), a direct-acting skeletal muscle relaxant, are also of benefit in treating neuroleptic malignant syndrome.

Treatment usually begins with 2.5 to 5.0 mg orally 3 times daily. The dosage can then be increased gradually up to 45 mg a day in divided doses to control fever, rigidity, and autonomic instability. In the available case reports published in the literature, the length of treatment has ranged from less than 1 week to 2 months.

Cocaine Withdrawal

The data in support of the use of bromocriptine in cocaine withdrawal come primarily from case reports and not from well-controlled studies. Nevertheless, as there is no clearly superior treatment for cocaine withdrawal, a clinical trial of bromocriptine may be warranted with some patients. Bromocriptine has been used to treat both the withdrawal symptoms of cocaine and the long-term craving for cocaine. Dosages for the treatment of cocaine use disorders have ranged from 0.625 to 12.5 mg a day.

Depressive Disorders

The data in support of the use of bromocriptine in depressive disorders come primarily from case reports that have described its use in patients who have not responded to conventional antidepressant drugs. Although the serotonin and norepinephrine neurotransmitters have been emphasized in theories of depressive disorders, dopamine has also been hypothesized to be involved in the pathophysiology of mood disorders. Specifically, mania may be associated with dopaminergic hyperactivity, and depression may be associated with dopaminergic hypoactivity. In the studies of bromocriptine in depressive disorders, the daily dosages have ranged from 10 to 200 mg, with a mean dosage around 15 mg a day. Response to bromocriptine treatment has been reported to occur usually within 2 weeks, although it may take up to 4 weeks. Some investigators have suggested that bromocriptine is especially effective in treating depressed patients with bipolar I disorder and is particularly safe in elderly depressed patients because of its low sedative and anticholinergic activities. The use of bromocriptine in depressive disorders, however, should be considered an experimental treatment to be used only after other treatments have failed.

Other Psychiatric Indications

Some reports support the use of bromocriptine for treating antipsychotic-induced parkinsonism, antipsychotic-induced tardive dyskinesia, and alcohol withdrawal. As bromocriptine is used to treat idiopathic Parkinson's disease, it may be effective in the treatment of antipsychotic-induced parkinsonism; but, the availability of other, probably safer, drugs—for example, benztropine (Cogentin)—should limit the use of bromocriptine for this indication. In several studies, bromocriptine, in dosages ranging from 0.75 to 7.5 mg a day, has been reported to be effective in reducing tardive dyskinesia symptoms by about 50 percent in about 20 percent of the patients treated. Several case studies have reported that bromocriptine may be effective in the treatment of alcohol withdrawal.

On an experimental basis, bromocriptine has been reported to be effective in the treatment of anxiety disorders (including obsessive-compulsive disorder), mania, and schizophrenia. Anecdotal reports indicate that bromocriptine has also been used to augment antidepressant drugs, especially to counteract the lethargy sometimes induced by the serotonin-specific reuptake inhibitors. Bromocriptine should not be used for the treatment of these disorders unless many other drug trials have failed and the clinician has undertaken a complete review of the available literature on the use of bromocriptine in the particular disorder.

PRECAUTIONS AND ADVERSE REACTIONS

The side effects of bromocriptine tend to be severe at the initiation of treatment and with dosages of more than 20 mg a day. The most common side effects are nausea, headache, and dizziness. Less common GI side effects include vomiting, abdominal cramps, and constipation. About 1 percent of patients have syncopal episodes 15 to 60 minutes after the first dose of the drug, although they can tolerate subsequent doses and dosage increases without syncope. Other patients, however, experience symptomatic orthostatic hypotension and cannot tolerate continued treatment. Other cardiovascular symptoms can include cardiac arrhythmias and an exacerbation of underlying angina. Rare psychiatric side effects can include hallucinations, delusions, confusion, and other behavioral changes, although these symptoms are most common after long-term usage and in elderly patients. Bromocriptine should be used with caution in patients with hypertension, cardiovascular disease, and hepatic disease. Bromocriptine is not recommended for pregnant women or for women who are breast-feeding.

DRUG INTERACTIONS

Although the concurrent use of bromocriptine and drugs that have dopamine antagonist activity (for example, phenothiazines) may theoretically decrease the activity of each of the drugs, the interaction has not proved to be of major clinical importance. The use of bromocriptine in conjunction with antihypertensive agents may produce additive hypotensive effects. Ergot alkaloids and bromocriptine should not be used concurrently, as they may cause hypertension and myocardial infarction. Progestins, estrogens, and oral contraceptives may interfere with the effects of bromocriptine.

LABORATORY INTERFERENCES

No laboratory interferences are known to be associated with the administration of bromocriptine.

DOSAGE AND ADMINISTRATION

Bromocriptine is available in 2.5 mg scored tablets and 5 mg capsules. The dosage of bromocriptine for mental disorders in uncertain, although it seems prudent to begin with low dosages (1.25 mg twice daily) and to increase the dosage gradually. Bromocriptine is usually taken with meals to help reduce the likelihood of nausea. Six to 12 weeks of bromocriptine therapy may be required for suppression of galactorrhea, whereas mitigation of neuroleptic malignant syndrome may occur in 1 to 60 days when bromocriptine is used as part of a multimodal treatment plan.

REFERENCES

Anton RF: Neurobehavioural basis for the pharmacotherapy of alcoholism: Current and future directions. Alcohol Alcohol *31* (1, Suppl): 43, 1996.

Boyd A: Bromocriptine and psychosis: A literature review. Psychiatr Q *66:* 87, 1995.

Cohen AJ: Bromocriptine for prolactinoma-related dissociative disorder and depression. J Clin Psychopharmacol *15* (2): 144, 1995.

Guay AT: Erectile dysfunction: Are you prepared to discuss it? Postgrad Med *97:* 127, 133, 139, 1995.

Inoue T, Tsuchiya K, Miura J, Sakakibara S, et al: Bromocriptine treatment of tricyclic and heterocyclic antidepressant-resistant depression. Biol Psychiatry *40* (2): 151, 1996.

Inzelberg R, Nisipeanu P, Rabey JM, Orlov E, Catz T, Kippervasser S, Schechtman E, Korczyn AD: Double-blind comparison of cabergoline and bromocriptine in Parkinson's disease with motor fluctuations. Neurology *47:* 785, 1996.

Kaplan HI, Sadock BJ: Other pharmacological therapies. In *Comprehensive Textbook of Psychiatry,* ed 6, HI Kaplan, BJ Sadock, editors, p 2122. Williams & Wilkins, Baltimore, 1995.

Montoya ID, Preston KL, Cone EJ, Rothman R, et al: Safety and efficacy of bupropion combined with bromocriptine for treatment of cocaine dependence. Am J Addict *5* (1): 69, 1996.

Penick EC, Powell BJ, Campbell J, Liskow BI, Nickel EJ, Dale TM, Thomas HM, Laster LJ, Noble E: Pharmacological treatment for antisocial personality disorder alcoholics: A preliminary study. Alcohol Clin Exp Res *20:* 477, 1996.

Powell BJ, Campbell JL, Landon JF, Liskow BI, et al: A double-blind, placebo-controlled study of nortriptyline and bromocriptine in male alcoholics subtyped by comorbid psychiatric disorders. Alcohol Clin Exp Res *19* (2): 462, 1995.

Rao S, Ziedonis D, Kosten T: The pharmacotherapy of cocaine dependence. Psychiatr Ann *25* (6): 363, 1995.

Sitland-Marken PA, Wells BG, Froemming JH, Chu CC, Brown CS: Psychiatric applications of bromocriptine therapy. J Clin Psychiatry *51:* 68, 1990.

Weddell RA, Weiser R: A double-blind cross-over placebo-controlled trial of the effects of bromocriptine on psychomotor function, cognition, and mood in de novo patients with Parkinson's disease. Behav Pharmacol *6* (1): 81, 1995.

▲ 35.3.8 Bupropion

Bupropion (Wellbutrin) was first synthesized in 1966, soon after tricyclic antidepressants entered widespread use. It emerged from pharmacological studies designed to identify antidepressants without anticholinergic or cardiac effects—two of the major adverse effects of the tricyclic drugs. Bupropion was approved by the Food and Drug Administration (FDA) for use in depression in 1985. Shortly after its approval, however, a study of bupropion in nondepressed bulimic patients found an increased incidence of drug-induced seizures. The drug company thus suspended marketing activities while the incidence of seizures was reevaluated. Subsequent studies of depressed patients found that the incidence of drug-induced seizures did not differ from that for classic antidepressants when bupropion was used in its usual therapeutic dosage range (300 to 450 mg a day), and the drug was reintroduced into the United States in 1989. A series of recent studies has shown that bupropion is effective for smoking cessation in many patients who had previously tried unsuccessfully to stop smoking. In 1996, bupropion (Zyban) was approved by the FDA for use in combination with behavioral modification techniques for smoking cessation.

Bupropion is a unique antidepressant in the available armamentarium of drugs, with a reduced profile of adverse effects. Of particular note among antidepressants, it is associated with little psychosexual inhibition. It possesses some dopaminergic effects, and may serve as a mild psychostimulant as well as an antidepressant. Bupropion has been shown to be as effective as any other antidepressant and has been proved to be safe and well tolerated. The established safety and efficacy of bupropion should make it an option for a first-line treatment of depressive disorders.

CHEMISTRY

Bupropion is a unicyclic aminoketone that resembles amphetamine and the anorectic diethylpropion (Tenuate) in its molecular structure (Fig. 35.3.8–1). It is structurally unrelated to any other antidepressant available in the United States.

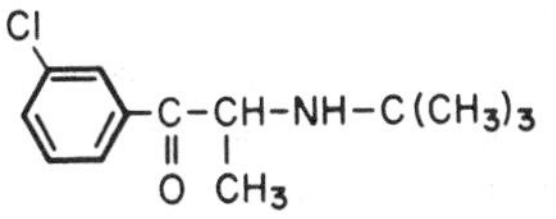

Cl
C–CH–NH–C(CH3)3
O CH3

FIGURE 35.3.8–1
Molecular structure of bupropion.

PHARMACOLOGICAL ACTIONS

Pharmacokinetics

Bupropion is well absorbed from the gastrointestinal (GI) tract and is metabolized by the liver, with its metabolites excreted by the kidneys. Peak plasma levels of the immediate-release version of bupropion are usually reached within 2 hours of oral administration, and peak levels of the sustained release version are seen after 3 hours. The mean half-life of the compound during the postdistributional phase is 12 hours, although its half-life ranges from 8 to 40 hours. Bupropion undergoes extensive hepatic first-pass metabolism and has three major active metabolites, hydroxybupropion, erythrohydrobupropion, and threohydrobupropion, which may be associated with the drug's therapeutic adverse effects. Each of these metabolites has about a twofold longer half-life than does the parent compound; therefore, it may take up to 10 days to reach steady-state concentrations of these metabolites. The rate of metabolism is regulated by the liver, and about 90 percent of the drug and its metabolites are excreted in the urine.

Pharmacodynamics

The mechanism of action for the antidepressant effects of bupropion are unknown. Although bupropion was originally thought to act through the blockade of dopamine reuptake, one study found that an increase in homovanillic acid (a metabolite of dopamine) was associated with a lack of clinical response. Furthermore, central nervous system (CNS) concentrations of bupropion are probably insufficient to result in significant dopamine reuptake inhibition. Bupropion is also associated with low activity either as an uptake inhibitor of norepinephrine and serotonin or as an agonist or an antagonist of biogenic amine receptors. Nonetheless, some data indicate that bupropion exerts its antidepressant effects by acting on the noradrenergic system. These data include the observation that bupropion can reduce the firing rate of noradrenergic neurons in the locus ceruleus of animals that are being studied in animal behavioral models of depression.

EFFECTS ON SPECIFIC ORGANS AND SYSTEMS

Except for its CNS effects, bupropion is nearly devoid of activity in human organs. No evidence has been found for significant effects of bupropion on liver, cardiac, or renal function, although the dosage of bupropion should be adjusted downward in patients with liver and renal impairment. It may increase blood pressure in previously hypertensive patients. Rare cases of lymphadenopathy, anemia, and pancytopenia have been reported, although their association with bupropion use is uncertain, and routine monitoring of blood is not indicated. Bupropion does not affect sexual functioning. It has been associated with changes in weight, more often with weight loss than with weight gain. There have been reports of rashes and pruritus in a few patients.

THERAPEUTIC INDICATIONS

The therapeutic efficacy of bupropion in depression has been established in well-controlled trials with depressed in patients and outpatients. In comparison studies, bupropion has shown efficacy equal to fluoxetine (Prozac), nortriptyline (Pamelor), trazodone (Desyrel), doxepin (Adapin), amitriptyline (Elavil), and imipramine (Tofranil), although patients treated with bupropion may have less improvement in their sleep early in the course of treatment because of the lack of sedative effects. Recent data showed that about half of patients who had failed to respond to tricyclic antidepressants responded well to bupropion. A recent small study of patients who responded only partially to either bupropion or serotonin-specific reuptake inhibitors (SSRIs) found that 70 percent improved with a combination of bupropion and an SSRI. Dosing was increased gradually, and adverse effect profiles appeared to be additive. The combination of bupropion and SSRIs may be especially efficacious because each agent is relatively free of adverse effects, yet their individual pharmacodynamic profiles interlace so that together they influence a wider range of neurotransmitter systems than can either alone. Bupropion has been shown in some, but not all, studies to be less likely to precipitate mania in bipolar patients than tricyclics, and it may be especially effective for patients with rapid-cycling bipolar disorder.

Bupropion has been shown in controlled studies to be equally efficacious to methylphenidate for childhood attention-deficit/hyperactive disorder (ADHD), and in an open study also to be effective for adults with ADHD. Single reports have appeared about the use of bupropion in winter depression (recurrent major depressive disorder with seasonal pattern). Additional open trials of bupropion in the treatment of cocaine abuse have been encouraging. Bupropion has been effective in treatment of bulimia, but it was in this setting that its propensity for triggering of seizures was first seen, such that caution is advised concerning this indication.

PRECAUTIONS AND ADVERSE REACTIONS

The side effect profile of bupropion in placebo-controlled studies did not differ significantly from that for placebo-treated patients (Table 35.3.8–1). No significant cardiovascular or clinical laboratory changes were reported in these placebo-controlled studies. A major advantage of bupropion over serotonin-specific reuptake inhibitors (SSRIs) is that bupropion is virtually devoid of any adverse effects on sexual functioning, whereas the SSRIs are associated with the occurrence of such effects in perhaps 25 to 75 percent of all patients.

The most common adverse effects are headache, insomnia, upper respiratory complaints, and nausea. Restlessness, agitation, and irritability may also occur. Most likely because of its potentiating effects on dopaminergic neurotransmission, bupropion has been associated with psychotic symptoms, including hallucinations, delusions, and catatonia, as well as delirium. Most notable about bupropion is the absence of significant drug-induced orthostatic hypotension, weight gain, daytime drowsiness, and anticholinergic effects. Some patients, however, may experience dry mouth or constipation, and weight loss may occur in about 25 percent of patients. Bu-

Table 35.3.8–1
Adverse Events Associated with Treatment[a]

		Bupropion (N = 110)		Placebo (N = 109)	
Body System	**Adverse Event**	N	%	N	%
Cardiovascular	Palpitations	5	4.6	7	6.4
Gastrointestinal	Abdominal pain	6	5.5	3	2.8
	Anorexia	6	5.5	5	4.6
	Constipation	11	10.0	6	5.5
	Dyspepsia	7	6.4	8	7.3
	Nausea	14	12.7	11	10.1
Genitourinary	Dysmenorrhea[b]	3	4.2	6	8.5
	Impotence[c]	2	5.1	0	0.0
Musculoskeletal	Back pain	9	8.2	8	7.3
	Muscle spasms	2	1.8	6	5.5
Neurological	Dizziness	16	14.6	6	5.5
	Headache	42	38.2	28	25.7
	Insomnia	25	22.7	8	7.3
	Tremor	8	7.3	3	2.8
Psychiatric	Agitation	12	10.9	8	7.3
	Anxiety	10	9.1	5	4.6
	Irritability	6	5.5	6	5.5
Nonspecific	Fatigue	6	5.5	2	1.8
	Flulike symptoms	7	6.4	3	2.8
Oral complaints	Dry mouth	8	7.3	9	8.3
Respiratory	Upper respiratory complaints	21	19.1	36	33.0
Special senses	Blurred vision	6	5.5	1	0.9
	Tinnitus	7	6.4	2	1.8

Reprinted with permission from Lineberry CG, Johnston JA, Raymond RN, Samara B, Feighner JP, Harto NE, Granacher RP, Weisler RH, Carman JS, Boyer WF: A fixed-dose (300 mg) efficacy study of bupropion and placebo in depressed outpatients. J Clin Psychiatry *51*: 194, 1990.

[a] Those events reported at greater than a 5 percent incidence in either group.

[b] Percentages are based on number of female patients only (placebo, N = 71; bupropion, N = 71).

[c] Percentages are based on number of male patients only (placebo, N = 38; bupropion, N = 38).

propion may be a drug to consider early in the treatment of depressed patients with preexisting cardiovascular disease.

At dosages of less than 450 mg a day, the incidence of seizures is about 0.4 percent, which is comparable to the incidence of seizures with tricyclic drugs. The risk of seizures increases to about 5 percent in dosages from 450 to 600 mg a day. Bupropion may be less likely than tricyclic drugs to cause a switch into mania or rapid cycling in bipolar I disorder patients, but the drug can cause mania in some patients.

Overdoses with bupropion are associated with a generally favorable outcome, except in the cases of huge doses and mixed-drug overdoses. Seizures occur in about one third of all overdoses, and fatalities can involve uncontrollable seizures, bradycardia, and cardiac arrest. In general, however, bupropion is safer in overdose cases than are other antidepressants, except perhaps the SSRIs.

The use of bupropion is contraindicated in patients with histories of head trauma, brain tumors, and other organic brain diseases because the drug may reduce a patient's seizure threshold. The presence of electroencephalographic abnormalities and the recent withdrawal of a patient from alcohol or a sedative-hypnotic may also increase the risk of a bupropion-induced seizure. Because high dosages (more than 450 mg a day) of bupropion may be associated with a euphoric feeling, bupropion may be relatively contraindicated in patients with histories of substance abuse. The use of bupropion by pregnant women has not been studied and is not recommended. Because bupropion is secreted in breast milk, the use of bupropion in nursing women is not recommended.

DRUG INTERACTIONS

Bupropion should not be used concurrently with monoamine oxidase inhibitors (MAOIs) because of the possibility of inducing a hypertensive crisis, and at least 14 days should pass after the discontinuation of an MAOI before initiating treatment with bupropion. Delirium, psychotic symptoms, and dyskinetic movements may be associated with the coadministration of bupropion and dopamine agonists, such as amantadine (Symmetrel), levodopa (Larodopa), and bromocriptine (Parlodel). There have also been case reports of CNS toxicity, including seizures, with the combination of lithium (Eskalith) and bupropion. However, there have also been case reports that the combination is effective and well tolerated in some patients with refractory depression. A few case reports indicate that delirium or seizures are associated with the combination of bupropion and fluoxetine. When bupropion is coadministered with drugs that are also metabolized in the liver, particular clinical attention should be given to the possibility of affecting the blood levels of the other drugs. Examples of other drugs metabolized in the liver are carbamazepine (Tegretol), cimetidine (Tagamet), barbiturates, and phenytoin (Dilantin).

LABORATORY INTERFERENCES

A report has indicated that bupropion may give a false-positive result on urinary amphetamine screens. No other reports have appeared of laboratory interferences clearly associated with bupropion treatment. Clinically nonsignificant changes in the electrocardiogram (ECG) (premature beats and nonspecific ST-T changes) and decreases in the white blood cell count (by about 10 percent) have been reported in a few patients.

DOSAGE AND ADMINISTRATION

The clinical benefit of bupropion usually occurs 2 to 4 weeks after the first dose. Immediate-release bupropion (Wellbutrin IR) is available in 75 and 100 mg tablets, and sustained-release bupropion (Wellbutrin SR) is available in 100 and 150 mg tablets. Zyban is a 150-mg sustained-release formulation of bupropion. Initiation of treatment in the average adult patient should be at 100 mg of the IR version orally twice a day or 150 mg of the SR version once a day. On the fourth day of treatment, the dosage can be raised to 100 mg IR orally 3 times a day or 150 mg SR orally twice a day, respectively. As 300 mg is the recommended dosage, the patient should be maintained on this dosage for several weeks before increasing the dosage further. Because of the risk of seizures, increases in dosage should never exceed 100 mg in a 3-day period; a single dose of bupropion IR should never exceed 150 mg, and a single dose of bupropion SR should never exceed 200 mg; and the total daily dose should not exceed 450 mg IR or 400 mg SR.

References

Ambrosini PJ, Emslie GJ, Greenhill LL, Kutcher S: Selecting a sequence of antidepressants for treating depression in youth. J Child Adolesc Psychopharmacol *5* (4): 233, 1995.

Ascher JA, Cole JO, Colin JN, Feighner JP, Ferris RM, Fibiger HC: Bupropion: A review of its mechanism of antidepressant activity. J Clin Psychiatry *56:* 395, 1995.

Feighner JP, Gardner EA, Johnston JA, Batey SR, Khayrallah MA, Ascher JA, Lineberry CG: Double-blind comparison of bupropion and fluoxetine in depressed outpatients. J Clin Psychiatry *52:* 329, 1991.

Goodnick PJ: Blood levels and acute response to bupropion. Am J Psychiatry *149:* 399, 1992.

Goodnick PJ: Pharmacokinetics of second generation antidepressants: Bupropion. Psychopharmacol Bull *27:* 513, 1991.

Johnston JA, Lineberry CG, Ascher JA, Davidson J, Khayrallah MA, Feighner JP, Stark P: A 102-center prospective study of seizure in association with bupropion. J Clin Psychiatry *52:* 450, 1991.

Levinson JL: Priapism associated with bupropion treatment. Am J Psychiatry *152:* 813, 1995.

Lineberry CG, Johnston JA, Raymond RN, Samara B, Feighner JP, Harto NE, Granacher RP, Weisler RH, Carman JS, Boyer WF: A fixed-dose (300 mg) efficacy study of bupropion and placebo in depressed outpatients. J Clin Psychiatry *51:* 194, 1990.

Nixon AL, Long WH, Puopolo PR, Flood JG: Bupropion metabolites produce false-positive urine amphetamine results [Letter]. Clin Chem *41:* 955, 1995.

Roose SP, Dalack GW, Glassman AH, Woodring S, Walsh BT, Giardina EGV: Cardiovascular effects of bupropion in depressed patients with heart disease. Am J Psychiatry *148:* 512, 1991.

Sussman N: Bupropion. In *Comprehensive Textbook of Psychiatry,* ed 6, HI Kaplan, BJ Sadock, editors, p 1951. Williams & Wilkins, Baltimore, 1995.

Young SJ: Panic associated with combining fluoxetine and bupropion. J Clin Psychiatry *57:* 177, 1996.

▲ 35.3.9 Buspirone

Buspirone (BuSpar) is the first clinically available azaspirone drug in the United States, and is approved for the treatment of anxiety disorders. Buspirone is unrelated to the benzodiazepines or the barbiturates, and it does not directly affect the γ-aminobutyric acid (GABA) neurotransmitter system. Also, unlike the benzodiazepines and the barbiturates, buspirone does not have sedative, hypnotic, muscle-relaxant, or anticonvulsant effects. In further contrast to these other drugs, buspirone carries a low potential for abuse and is not associated with withdrawal phenomena or cognitive impairment.

CHEMISTRY

The molecular structure of buspirone is shown in Figure 35.3.9–1. It is chemically distinct from currently available benzodiazepines, barbiturates, and antidepressants.

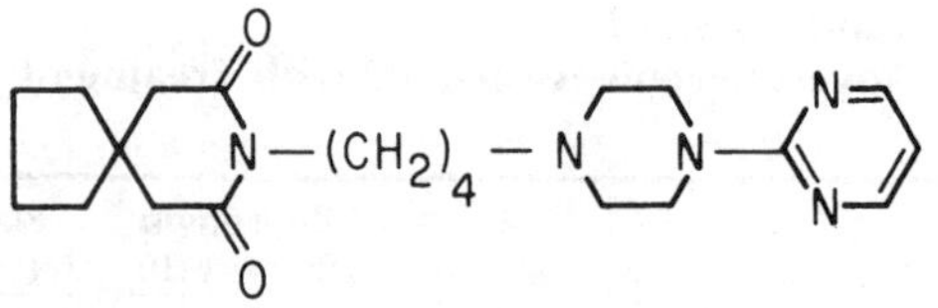

FIGURE 35.3.9–1
Molecular structure of buspirone.

PHARMACOLOGICAL ACTIONS

Pharmacokinetics

Buspirone is well absorbed from the gastrointestinal (GI) tract and is unaffected by food intake. Buspirone is metabolized by the liver and excreted by the kidneys. Oxidative dealkylation produces an active metabolite, which, although less potent than the parent compound, is present in higher concentrations. The drug reaches peak plasma levels in 60 to 90 minutes after oral administration. The short half-life (2 to 11 hours) necessitates 3-times-daily dosing, although the active metabolite has a twofold longer half-life than does the parent compound.

Pharmacodynamics

In contrast to benzodiazepines and barbiturates, which act on the GABA-associated chloride ion channel, buspirone has no effect on this receptor mechanism. Rather, buspirone acts as an agonist or partial agonist on serotonin type 1A ($5\text{-}HT_{1A}$) receptors. In animal models, buspirone decreases the firing rates of serotonergic neurons located in the median raphe nuclei and reduces the release of serotonin in the hippocampus, which has a high concentration of $5\text{-}HT_{1A}$ receptors. Buspirone also has activity at $5\text{-}HT_{2A}$ and dopamine type 2 (D_2) receptors, although the significance of the effects at these receptors is unknown. At D_2 receptors, it has properties of both an agonist and an antagonist, and buspirone treatment may lead to a decrease in the firing rate of the mesolimbic dopaminergic neurons. The mechanism of action for buspirone is not completely understood at this time. The fact that buspirone takes 2 to 3 weeks to exert its therapeutic effects implies that, whatever its initial effects, the therapeutic effects may involve the modulation of several neurotransmitters and intraneuronal mechanisms.

EFFECTS ON SPECIFIC ORGANS AND SYSTEMS

The effects of buspirone on organs other than the brain are minimal. The drug has no significant effects on the respiratory system, heart, vascular system, blood, smooth muscles, or autonomic nervous system.

THERAPEUTIC INDICATIONS

The efficacy and safety of buspirone in the treatment of generalized anxiety disorder have been demonstrated in at least 10 placebo-controlled trials. Most of these trials have found that the efficacy of buspirone did not differ from the efficacy of the benzodiazepines tested—diazepam (Valium), lorazepam (Ativan), clorazepate (Tranxene), and alprazolam (Xanax). All these studies however, used criteria in the third edition of *Diagnostic and Statistical Manual of Mental Disorders* (DSM-III) for generalized anxiety disorder, which differ from the criteria in the fourth edition (DSM-IV) by requiring only 1 month of symptoms, compared with the 6 months required in DSM-IV. Many clinicians are not convinced of the efficacy of buspirone, probably because of its delayed onset of action in comparison with the benzodiazepines and its lack of the mild euphoric effect or sense of well-being that can be associated with benzodiazepine use. Buspirone and the serotonin-specific reuptake inhibitors (SSRIs) share serotonergic properties, and their time-courses for the treatment of anxiety are similar.

Both the benzodiazepines and buspirone have advantages and disadvantages. The beneficial effects of benzodiazepines are felt the same day the drug is started, and the full clinical response takes only days; buspirone has very mild immediate effects, and the full clinical response may take 2 to 4 weeks. Sometimes, the sedative effects of benzodiazepines, which do not occur with buspirone, are desirable, but these sedative effects are also associated with impaired motor performance and cognitive deficits. The major disadvantages of benzodiazepine treatment are its addictive potential and the development of withdrawal phenomena on its discontinuation. Buspirone is not associated with any abuse potential, even in groups of patients who are at high risk for addictive behavior. A comparison of benzodiazepines and buspirone is presented in Table 35.3.9–1.

Buspirone has been studied in patient populations with symptoms in addition to anxiety. A recent preliminary open-label study in which buspirone was administered in a daily transdermal patch formulation to children with attention-deficit/hyperactivity disorder showed a marked, dosage-dependent improvement in symptoms, with a much smoother pharmacokinetic profile than is usually seen with sympathomimetic drugs, such as methylphenidate (Ritalin). These findings will need to be confirmed in a double-blind, controlled trial. Studies have produced mixed results on the efficacy of buspirone in depressive disorders and obsessive-compulsive disorder. The use of buspirone for these disorders should be considered experimental and should be undertaken only after traditional therapies have proved to be ineffective. The data indicate that buspirone is not effective in the treatment of panic disorder or social phobia of the performance type. Because buspirone does not act on the GABA–chloride ion channel complex, the drug is not recommended for the treatment of withdrawal from benzodiazepines, alcohol, or sedative-hypnotic drugs. Buspirone has been used to control agitation and behavioral problems in older people. A few case reports have described treatment with buspirone of anxiety in children.

Table 35.3.9–1
Comparison of Benzodiazepines and Buspirone

	BZD	Buspirone
Effect of single dose	Yes	No
Full therapeutic action	Days	Weeks
Sedating	Yes	No
Dependence liability	Yes	No
Impair performance	Yes	No
Suppress sedative withdrawal symptoms	Yes	No
History of previous BZD response	Good response	Poor response
Side effects	Sedation, memory impairment	Restlessness, nervousness

Reprinted with permission from Silver JM, Yudofsky SC, Hurowitz GI: Psychopharmacology and electroconvulsive therapy. In *The American Psychiatric Press Textbook of Psychiatry*, RE Hales, SC Yudofsky, JA Talbott, editors, ed 2, p 953. American Psychiatric Press, Washington, 1994.

PRECAUTIONS AND ADVERSE REACTIONS

The most common adverse effects of buspirone are headache, nausea, dizziness, and, rarely, insomnia. No sedation is associated with buspirone. Some patients may report a minor feeling of restlessness, although this symptom may reflect an incompletely treated anxiety disorder. No deaths have been reported from overdoses of buspirone, and the median lethal dose (LD_{50}) is estimated to be 160 to 550 times the recommended daily dose. Buspirone should be used with caution in patients with hepatic and renal impairment, in pregnant women, and in nursing mothers. Buspirone can be used safely with older people and children.

DRUG INTERACTIONS

One study reported that the coadministration of buspirone and haloperidol (Haldol) resulted in increased blood concentrations of haloperidol. Buspirone should not be used with monoamine oxidase inhibitors (MAOIs), and a 2-week washout period should pass between the discontinuation of an MAOI and the initiation of treatment with buspirone.

LABORATORY INTERFERENCES

Single doses of buspirone can cause transient elevations in growth hormone, prolactin, and cortisol concentrations, although the effects are not clinically significant.

DOSAGE AND ADMINISTRATION

Buspirone is available in 5 and 10 mg tablets, and treatment is usually initiated with 5 mg orally 3 times daily. The dosage can be raised 5 mg every 2 to 3 days to the usual dosage range of 15 to 30 mg a day. The maximum dosage is 60 mg a day.

Although not common, some patients may note some reduction in anxiety within 1 to 2 hours of administration of a single dose of buspirone, but appearance of the full benefits requires 2 to 3 weeks of continuous use. Buspirone is as effective as the benzodiazepines in the treatment of anxiety in patients who have not received benzodiazepines in the past, but buspirone does not cause the same response in patients who have previously received benzodiazepines. The reason is probably buspirone's lack of the immediate mildly euphoric and sedative effects of the benzodiazepines. The most common clinical problem, therefore, is how to initiate buspirone therapy in a patient who is currently taking benzodiazepines. There are two alternatives: First, the clinician can start buspirone treatment gradually while the benzodiazepine is being withdrawn. Second, the clinician can start buspirone treatment and bring the patient up to a therapeutic dosage for 2 to 3 weeks while the patient is still receiving the regular dosage of the benzodiazepine; at this point the benzodiazepine can be slowly tapered. A few initial reports indicate that the coadministration of buspirone and benzodiazepines may be effective in the treatment of anxiety disorders that have not responded to treatment with either drug alone.

References

Allman BJC, Domantay A, Schoeman HS: Antidepressant activity of buspirone in anxiety. Curr Ther Res *52:* 406, 1992.

Cadieux RJ: Azaspirones: An alternative to benzodiazepines for anxiety. Am Fam Physician *53:* 2349, 1996.

Farid BT, Bulto M: Buspirone in obsessional compulsive disorder. A prospective case study. Pharmacopsychiatry *27:* 207, 1994.

Gammans RE, Stringfellow JC, Hvizdos AJ, Seidehamel RJ, Cohn JB, Wilcox CS, Fabre LF, Pecknold JC, Smith WT, Rickels K: Use of buspirone in patients with generalized anxiety disorder and coexisting depressive symptoms. Pharmacopsychiatry *25:* 193, 1992.

Gonzales JJ, Emmerich AD, Rauch SL, Stern TA: Management of the prescription-drug–dependent adult: Case of meprobamate abuse and its treatment. J Geriatr Psychiatry Neurol *9* (2): 91, 1996.

Harvey KV, Balon R: Augmentation with buspirone: A review. Ann Clin Psychiatry *7:* 143, 1995.

Jacobson FM: Possible augmentation of antidepressant response by buspirone, J Clin Psychiatry *52:* 217, 1991.

Joffe RT, Schuller DR: An open study of buspirone augmentation of serotonin reuptake inhibitors in refractory depression. J Clin Psychiatry *54:* 269, 1993.

Kranzler HR: Evaluation and treatment of anxiety symptoms and disorders in alcoholics. J Clin Psychiatry *57* (7, Suppl): 15, 1996.

Kranzler HR, Burleson JA, Del Boca FK, Babor TF, Korner P, Brown J, Bohn MJ: Buspirone treatment of anxious alcoholics: A placebo-controlled trial. Arch Gen Psychiatry *51:* 720, 1994.

Mitsukini M, Miura S: The future of 5-HT_{1A} receptor agonists (arylpiperazine derivatives). Prog Neuropsychopharmacol Biol Psychiatry *16:* 833, 1992.

Schuckit MA: Recent developments in the pharmacotherapy of alcohol dependence. J Consult Clin Psychol *64:* 669, 1996.

Sramek JJ, Tansman M, Suri A, Hornig-Rohan M, Amsterdam JD, Stahl SM, Weisler RH, Cutler NR: Efficacy of buspirone in generalized anxiety disorder with coexisting mild depressive symptoms. J Clin Psychiatry. *57:* 287, 1996.

Stoudemire A: Epidemiology and psychopharmacology of anxiety in medical patients. J Clin Psychiatry *57* (7, Suppl): 64, 1996.

Uhde TW, Tancer ME: Buspirone. In *Comprehensive Textbook of Psychiatry,* ed 6, HI Kaplan, BJ Sadock, editors, p 1957. Williams & Wilkins, Baltimore, 1995.

▲ 35.3.10 Calcium Channel Inhibitors

The calcium channel inhibitors are variously referred to as the calcium channel antagonists, calcium channel blockers, and organic calcium channel inhibitors. The calcium channel inhibitors were first developed as cardiac drugs to treat hypertension, angina, and specific types of cardiac arrhythmias. About a dozen calcium channel inhibitors are now available in the United States, but most studies of calcium channel inhibitors in psychiatric disorders have been conducted with verapamil (Calan, Isoptin) and, recently, nimodipine (Nimotop). Diltiazem (Cardizem) and nifedipine (Adalat, Procardia) have also been used in a few clinical trials of psychiatric patients. The major psychiatric indications are bipolar disorder and possibly dementia of the Alzheimer's type.

CHEMISTRY

The molecular structures of the four calcium channel inhibitors that are most relevant to psychiatry are shown in Figure 35.3.10–1. Three chemical classes are represented by the four compounds. Nifedipine and nimodipine are dihydropyridine calcium channel inhibitors; verapamil and diltiazem are referred to as nondihydropyridines, but they are chemically distinct from each other.

PHARMACOLOGICAL ACTIONS

Pharmacokinetics

The calcium channel inhibitors are well absorbed from the gastrointestinal (GI) tract, but all four drugs are substantially metabolized by the liver in a first-pass effect. Considerable intraindividual and interindividual variations are seen in the plasma concentrations of the drugs after a single dose. The half-life of verapamil after the first dose is 2 to 8 hours; the half-life increases to 5 to 12 hours after the first few days of therapy. According to some studies, verapamil does pass the blood–brain barrier and reaches the cerebrospinal fluid in concentrations about 0.05 percent of the plasma concentrations.

Pharmacodynamics

The calcium ion is a major intracellular second messenger. Intraneuronal calcium has many functions, including the activation of calcium-dependent protein kinases. Calcium influx may be one step in the cascade of molecular events that trigger excitotoxic cellular damage, of the type postulated to lead to neuronal death, for example, in Alzheimer's disease. The calcium channel inhibitors inhibit the influx of calcium into neurons through one type of voltage-dependent calcium channel called the L-type calcium channel. The calcium channel inhibitors bind to the channel and inhibit its opening. Nifedipine and nimodipine bind to a different part of the channel than do verapamil and diltiazem.

EFFECTS ON SPECIFIC ORGANS AND SYSTEMS

The major effects of calcium channel inhibitors are on the vasculature, which responds with vasodilation to the calcium channel inhibitors. Diuresis has also been associated with the use of calcium channel inhibitors. The calcium channel inhibitors interfere with atrioventricular (AV) conduction and can lead to AV heart block, especially in elderly patients. Calcium channel blockers may also regulate ion flux directly in neurons.

THERAPEUTIC INDICATIONS

Bipolar I Disorder

Case reports describing the efficacy of verapamil in bipolar I disorder first appeared in the early 1980s, and subsequent placebo-controlled and lithium-controlled studies have generally supported the initial finding of efficacy for that indication. Available data support the use of verapamil for both short-term and maintenance treatment of bipolar I disorder, although verapamil should be considered a fourth-line drug, to be used after trials of lithium (Eskalith), carbamazepine (Tegretol), and

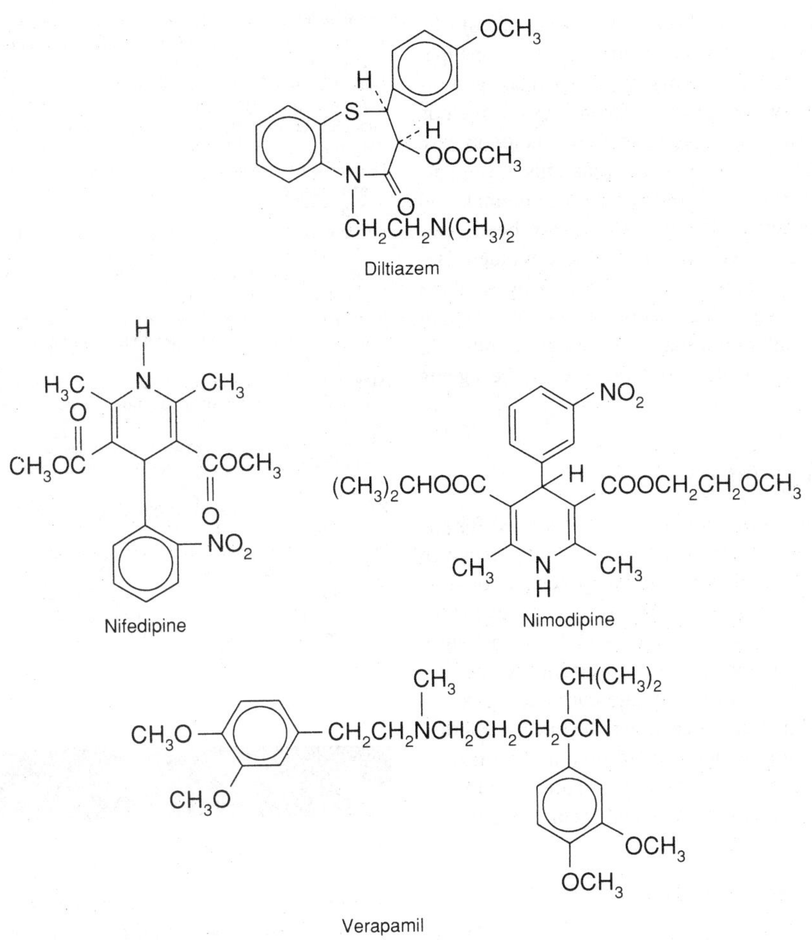

OCH3
H
S
H
OOCCH3
N
O
CH2CH2N(CH3)2
Diltiazem
H
N
H3C
CH3
O
CH3OC
COCH3
O
NO2
Nifedipine
NO2
(CH3)2CHOOC
H
COOCH2CH2OCH3
CH3
N
CH3
H
Nimodipine
CH3
CH(CH3)2
CH3O
CH2CH2NCH2CH2CH2CCN
CH3O
OCH3
OCH3
Verapamil

FIGURE 35.3.10–1
Molecular structures of calcium channel inhibitors.

valproate (Depakene). Because of potential drug interactions, verapamil should cautiously be coadministered with lithium or carbamazepine. Some patients who are treated with lithium and calcium channel inhibitors concurrently may be at increased risk for the signs and symptoms of neurotoxicity, and at least one patient has died from this combination.

Preliminary data indicate that nimodipine may be particularly effective in the treatment of rapid-cycling bipolar I disorder. The requirement of every-4-hours dosing, however, may limit its clinical applicability.

Hypertensive Crisis Associated with Monoamine Oxidase Inhibitors

One controversial use of a calcium channel inhibitor in psychiatry has been in the treatment of monoamine oxidase inhibitor (MAOI)-induced hypertensive crises. In 1996, postmarketing experience with the use of nifedipine for treatment of hypertensive emergencies documented several adverse outcomes, and the Food and Drug Administration has now required the manufacturer to include in the product labeling that nifedipine should no longer be used for acute reduction of blood pressure.

Other Psychiatric Indications

Perhaps the most hopeful of the other indications studied with calcium channel inhibitors is the use of nimodipine for dementia. Nimodipine is thought to reduce the calcium influx that triggers excitotoxic cell death and therefore to limit the loss of neurons in Alzheimer's disease. Two small uncontrolled clinical trials have shown less deterioration on memory tests in demented patients taking nimodipine, and larger trials will be needed to evaluate this indication more fully. Case reports and small studies provide preliminary evidence of the efficacy of calcium channel inhibitors in Tourette's disorder, Huntington's disease, panic disorder, premenstrual dysphoric disorder, and intermittent explosive disorder. Well-controlled studies have found a lack of efficacy for calcium channel inhibitors in schizophrenia, tardive dyskinesia, and depressive disorders.

PRECAUTIONS AND ADVERSE REACTIONS

The most common adverse effects associated with calcium channel inhibitors are hypotension, bradycardia, and AV heart block, which sometimes necessitate discontinuing the drug. In all patients with cardiovascular disease, the drugs should be used with caution. Common GI symptoms include constipation, nausea, and occasionally dry mouth, GI distress, and diarrhea. Adverse effects on the central nervous system include dizziness, headache, and fatigue. Adverse effects noted in case reports with diltiazem include hyperactivity, akathisia, and parkinsonism; with verapamil, delirium, hyperprolactinemia, and galactorrhea have been noted. The drugs have not been evaluated for safety in pregnant women and are best avoided. Because the drugs are secreted in breast milk, nursing mothers should also avoid the drugs. Older people are more sensitive to the calcium channel inhibitors than are younger adults. No specific information is available about the use of the agents for children.

Drug Interactions

Calcium channel inhibitors should not be prescribed for patients taking β-adrenergic receptor antagonists, hypotensives (for example, diuretics, vasodilators, and angiotensin-converting enzyme inhibitors), or antiarrhythmic drugs (for example, quinidine and digoxin) without consulting with the patient's internist or cardiologist. Verapamil and diltiazem, but not nifedipine, have been reported to precipitate carbamazepine-induced neurotoxicity. Cimetidine (Tagamet) has been reported to increase plasma concentrations of nifedipine and diltiazem. The combination of lithium and calcium channel inhibitors may produce significant, and possibly fatal, neurotoxicity.

LABORATORY INTERFERENCES

No known laboratory interferences are associated with the use of calcium channel inhibitors.

DOSAGE AND ADMINISTRATION

Verapamil is available in 40, 80, and 120 mg tablets; 120, 180, and 240 mg extended-release tablets; and 120 and 240 mg capsules. The starting dosage is 40 mg orally 3 times a day and can be raised in increments every 4 to 5 days up to 80 to 120 mg 3 times a day. The patient's blood pressure, pulse, and electrocardiogram (in patients more than 40 years old or with a history of cardiac illness) should be routinely monitored. Diltiazem is available in 30, 60, 90, and 120 mg tablets, 60, 90, and 120 mg capsules, and 120, 180, 240, and 300 mg extended-release capsules. It should be started at 30 mg orally 4 times a day and can be increased up to a maximum of 360 mg a day. Nifedipine is available in 10 and 20 mg capsules and 30, 60, and 90 mg extended-release tablets. It should be started at 10 mg orally 3 or 4 times a day and can be increased up to a maximum dosage of 180 mg a day. Nimodipine is available in 30 mg capsules. It has been used at 60 mg every 4 hours for brief periods of time for ultrarapid-cycling bipolar disorder, but its expense makes it unsuitable for long treatment courses.

REFERENCES

Arana GW, Santos AB: Calcium channel inhibitors. In *Comprehensive Textbook of Psychiatry,* ed 6, HI Kaplan, BJ Sadock, editors, p 1961. Williams & Wilkins, Baltimore, 1995.

Freeman TW, Clothier JL, Pazzaglia P, Lesem MD, Swann AC: A double-blind comparison of valproate and lithium in the treatment of acute mania. Am J Psychiatry *149:* 108, 1992.

Garza-Trevino ES, Overall JE, Hollister LE: Verapamil versus lithium in acute mania. Am J Psychiatry *149:* 121, 1992.

Giannini AJ, Loiselle RH: Verapamil maintenance therapy in bipolar patients. J Clin Psychiatry *57:* 136, 1996.

Goodnick PJ: Treatment of mania: Relationship between response to verapamil and changes in plasma calcium and magnesium levels. South Med J *89* (2): 225, 1996.

Loonen AJ, Verwey HA, Roels PR, van Bavel LP, Doorschot CH: Is diltiazem effective in treating the symptoms of (tardive) dyskinesia in chronic psychiatric inpatients? A negative, double-blind, placebo-controlled trial. J Clin Psychopharmacol *12:* 39, 1992.

Marazziti D, Rotondo A, Lenzi A, Presta S, et al: Effects of mood-stabilizing drugs on the peripheral serotonin transporter. Hum Psychopharmacol 7 (6): 397, 1992.

Meyer FP: Central effects of nifedipine versus placebo following repeated application: Influence of motivation and personality. Hum Psychopharmacol *10* (2): 137, 1995.

Parnetti L: Mental deterioration in old age: Results of two multicenter, clinical trials with nimodipine. The Nimodipine Study Group. Clin Ther *15:* 394, 1993.

Pepeu G: Memory disorders: Novel treatments, clinical perspective. Life Sci *55* (25–26): 2189, 1994.

Pucilowski O: Psychopharmacological properties of calcium channel inhibitors. Psychopharmacology *109:* 12, 1992.

Sharp FR: Neuronal injury produced by NMDA antagonists can be detected using heat shock proteins and can be blocked with antipsychotics. Psychopharmacol Bull *30:* 555, 1994.

▲ 35.3.11 Carbamazepine

Carbamazepine (Tegretol) is an iminodibenzyl drug that is structurally similar to imipramine (Tofranil) and is approved for use in the United States to treat temporal lobe epilepsy, general epilepsy, and trigeminal neuralgia. A beneficial effect on mood was noted by the first investigators in the early 1960s, and a large body of data now supports the use of carbamazepine in treating manic episodes and for prophylactic treatment of bipolar I disorder. Carbamazepine and valproate are the first two of what is likely to be a series of anticonvulsant drugs useful for mania. Among the commercially available anticonvulsants that are under evaluation for this indication are clonazepam (Klonopin), gabapentin (Neurontin), lamotrigine (Lamictal), tiagabine (Gabitril), topiramate (Topamax), and vigabatrin (Sabril). Among the investigational anticonvulsants that may eventually be considered for use in bipolar disorder are oxcarbazepine (which is chemically related to carbamazepine), losigamone, progabide, remacemide, stiripentol, and zonisamide.

CHEMISTRY

The iminostilbene structure of carbamazepine, shown in Figure 35.3.11–1, is similar to the tricyclic structure of imipramine.

PHARMACOLOGICAL ACTIONS

Pharmacokinetics

Carbamazepine is absorbed slowly and erratically from the gastrointestinal (GI) tract, but when the drug is taken with

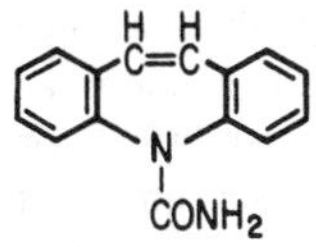

FIGURE 35.3.11–1
Molecular structure of carbamazepine.

meals, absorption is enhanced. Peak plasma levels are reached 2 to 8 hours after a single dose, and steady-state levels are reached after 2 to 4 days on a steady dosage. The half-life of carbamazepine at the initiation of treatment has a wide range (18 to 54 hours); during long-term administration the half-life decreases to a range from 12 to 17 hours because of the induction of hepatic enzymes, which reaches its maximum level after about 1 month of therapy. Carbamazepine is metabolized in the liver and is excreted by the kidneys. The major reactions are catalyzed by the cytochrome P450 (CYP) isoenzymes CYP 1A2, CYP 2C8, and CYP 3A4. The 10-,11-epoxide metabolite is active as an anticonvulsant. Its activity in the treatment of bipolar I disorder is unknown. Recent reports have indicated that carbamazepine can lose one third of its potency when stored in a humid environment. Manufacturers are now advising consumers not to store the drug in environments such as bathrooms.

Pharmacodynamics

The anticonvulsant effects of carbamazepine are thought to be mediated mainly by binding to voltage-dependent sodium channels in the inactive state and prolonging their inactivation. This binding secondarily reduces voltage-dependent calcium channel activation and therefore synaptic transmission. Additional effects include reduction of currents through *N*-methyl-D-aspartate–glutamate receptor channels, competitive antagonism of adenosine A_1 receptors, and potentiation of central nervous system (CNS) catecholamine neurotransmission. Whether each of these mechanisms also results in the stabilization of mood swings is unknown. Arguing against this parsimonious hypothesis is the observation that, although the anticonvulsant and antinociceptive effects of carbamazepine have a rapid onset, the antimanic effects take longer to develop. The potential effect of carbamazepine on calcium channels is interesting theoretically in the light of the increasing use of calcium channel inhibitors for the treatment of bipolar I disorder.

Theoretically, another basis for the antimanic effect of carbamazepine involves the concept of kindling. Kindling is the electrophysiological process in which repeated subthreshold stimulations of a neuron eventually generate an action potential. Countering this argument is the fact that kindling has been observed in laboratory animals but has not been convincingly demonstrated in humans. Although the anticonvulsant effects of carbamazepine have led to the circular argument that bipolar I disorder may present a covert form of limbic epilepsy, the majority of bipolar I disorder patients who respond to carbamazepine demonstrate no evidence of epileptiform activity on electroencephalograms. Carbamazepine has been shown to decrease both basal and induced levels of intracellular cyclic adenosine monophosphate (cAMP). This, in turn, may affect cAMP-regulated gene expression.

EFFECTS ON SPECIFIC ORGANS AND SYSTEMS

Besides the effects on the CNS, carbamazepine has its most significant effects on the hematopoietic system. Carbamazepine is associated with a benign and often transient decrease in the white blood cell count, with values usually remaining above 3,000. The decrease is thought to be due to the inhibition of colony-stimulating factor in bone marrow, an effect that can be reversed by the coadministration of lithium (Eskalith), which stimulates the colony-stimulating factor. The benign suppression of white blood cell production must be differentiated from the potentially fatal adverse effects of agranulocytosis, pancytopenia, and aplastic anemia.

As reflected by its use in treating diabetes insipidus, carbamazepine apparently has a vasopressin-like effect on the vasopressin receptor and sometimes causes the development of water intoxication or hyponatremia, particularly in elderly patients. This side effect can be treated with demeclocycline (Declomycin) or lithium. Another endocrine effect associated with carbamazepine is an increase in urinary free cortisol.

Carbamazepine induces several hepatic enzymes and may thus interfere with the metabolism of various other drugs. The effects of carbamazepine on the cardiovascular system are minimal. It does decrease atrioventricular (A-V) conduction, and thus the use of carbamazepine is contraindicated in patients with A-V heart blocks.

Carbamazepine may cause a rash, which may be transient even if the drug is continued, but may lead to serious and potentially life-threatening dermatological conditions on rare occasions. Other system-specific allergic reactions have been reported, and rarely, a lupuslike disorder has been associated with use of carbamazepine.

THERAPEUTIC INDICATIONS

Bipolar I Disorder

Well-controlled studies have shown that carbamazepine is effective in the treatment of acute mania, with efficacy comparable to lithium and antipsychotics. About 10 studies have also shown that carbamazepine is effective in the prophylaxis of both manic and depressive episodes in bipolar I disorder. Carbamazepine is an effective antimanic agent in 50 to 70 percent of all patients. The antimanic effects of carbamazepine may be augmented by addition of lithium, valproate, neuroleptics, or antidepressants. Additional evidence from these studies indicates that carbamazepine may be effective in some patients who are not responsive to lithium, such as patients with dysphoric mania, rapid cycling, or a negative family history of mood disorders. A few clinical and basic science data, however, indicate that some patients may experience a tolerance for the antimanic effects of carbamazepine.

Schizophrenia and Schizoaffective Disorder

Several well-controlled studies have produced data indicating that carbamazepine is effective in the treatment of schizophrenia and schizoaffective disorder. Patients with positive symptoms (for example, hallucinations) and few negative symptoms (for example, anhedonia) may be likely to respond, as are patients who have impulsive aggressive outbursts as a symptom.

Depressive Disorders

The available data indicate that carbamazepine is an effective treatment for depression in some patients. About 25 to 33 percent of depressed patients respond to carbamazepine. This percentage is significantly smaller than the 60 to 70 percent response rate for standard antidepressants. Nevertheless, carbamazepine is an alternative drug for depressed patients who have not responded to conventional treatments, including electroconvulsive therapy, or who have a marked or rapid periodicity in their depressive episodes.

Impulse-Control Disorders

Several studies have reported that carbamazepine is effective in controlling impulsive, aggressive behavior in nonpsychotic patients of all ages from children to older adults. Other drugs for impulse-control disorders, particularly intermittent explosive disorder, include lithium, propranolol (Inderal), and antipsychotics. Because of the risk of serious adverse effects with carbamazepine, treatment with these other agents is warranted before a trial with carbamazepine is begun.

Carbamazepine is also effective in controlling nonacute agitation and aggressive behavior in patients with schizophrenia. Diagnoses to be ruled out before treatment with carbamazepine is begun include akathisia and neuroleptic malignant syndrome. Lorazepam (Ativan) is more effective than is carbamazepine for the control of acute agitation.

Posttraumatic Stress Disorder

Carbamazepine has been suggested, along with antidepressants, benzodiazepines, lithium, and antihypertensives, as a treatment for posttraumatic stress disorder. This indication has not yet been studied in a placebo-controlled trial.

Alcohol and Benzodiazepine Withdrawal

According to several studies, carbamazepine is as effective as the benzodiazepines in controlling symptoms associated with alcohol withdrawal. It may also assist in withdrawal from chronic benzodiazepine use, especially in seizure-prone patients. The lack of any advantage of carbamazepine over the benzodiazepines for alcohol withdrawal and the potential risk of adverse effects with carbamazepine, however, limit the clinical usefulness of this application. The lack of abuse potential may make carbamazepine preferable to benzodiazepines.

PRECAUTIONS AND ADVERSE REACTIONS

Carbamazepine produces predictable, dose-dependent cerebellar signs and symptoms and GI distress if doses are increased rapidly or toxic levels are reached. The drug also may produce serious, idiosyncratic reactions for which laboratory monitoring is of little predictive value (Table 35.3.11–1). Although the drug's benign hematological effects are not dose related, most of the adverse effects of carbamazepine are correlated with plasma concentrations above 9 μg/mL. A comparison of the adverse effects of lithium and carbamazepine is presented in Table 35.3.11–2. Ataxia, diplopia, sedation, and dizziness are common at plasma concentrations above 12 μg/mL. The rarest but most serious adverse effects of carbamazepine are blood dyscrasias, hepatitis, and exfoliative dermatitis. Carbamazepine otherwise is relatively well tolerated by patients except for mild GI and CNS effects that can be significantly reduced if the dosage is increased slowly and minimal effective plasma concentrations are maintained.

Blood Dyscrasias

Severe blood dyscrasias (aplastic anemia, agranulocytosis) occur in about 1 in 125,000 patients treated with carbamazepine. There does not appear to be a correlation between the degree of benign white blood cell suppression, which is due to inhibition of colony-stimulating factors in the bone marrow, and the emergence of life-threatening blood dyscrasias. Patients should be warned that fever, sore throat, rash, petechiae, bruising, and easy bleeding are potentially symptoms of a serious dyscrasia and should cause the patient to seek medical evaluation immediately. Routine hematological monitoring in carbamazepine-treated patients is recommended at 3, 6, 9, and 12 months. If there is no significant evidence of bone marrow suppression by then, many experts would reduce the interval

Table 35.3.11–1
Adverse Effects and Toxicity of Carbamazepine

Common dosage-related side effects
- Dizziness
- Ataxia
- Clumsiness
- Sedation
- Dysarthria
- Diplopia
- Nausea and gastrointestinal upset
- Reversible mild leukopenia
- Reversible mild increases in liver function tests

Less common dosage-related side effects
- Tremor
- Memory disturbance
- Confusional states (more common in elderly and in combination treatments with lithium or neuroleptics)
- Cardiac conduction delay
- Syndrome of inappropriate antidiuretic hormone (SIADH) secretion

Idiosyncratic toxicities
- Rash (including cases of exfoliation)
- Lenticular opacities
- Hepatitis
- Blood dyscrasias
  - Aplastic anemia
  - Leukopenia
  - Thrombocytopenia

Reprinted with permission from Hyman SE, Arana GW, Rosenbaum JF: *Handbook of Psychiatric Drug Therapy*, ed 3, p 138. Little, Brown, Boston, 1996.

Table 35.3.11–2
Comparative and Differential Side Effects Profiles of Lithium Carbonate and Carbamazepine

Side Effects	Lithium Carbonate	Carba-mazepine	Lithium and Carba-mazepine Combination
White blood count	↑	↓	↑, −, Li*
Diabetes insipidus	↑	↓	↑, Li*
Thyroid hormones T_3, T_4	↓	↓	↓↓
TSH	↑	(−)	↑, Li*
Serum calcium	(↑)	↓	(↑), (Li*)
Weight gain	(↑)	(−)	
Tremor	(↑)	(−)	
Memory disturbances	(↑)	?	
Diarrhea	(↑)	−	
Teratogenic effects	(↑)	−	
Psoriasis	(↑)	(−)	
Pruritic rash (allergy)	−	↑	
Agranulocytosis	−	(↑)	
Hepatitis	−	(↑)	
Hyponatremia, water intoxication	−	(↑)	
Dizziness, ataxia, diplopia	−	↑	
Hypercortisolism, escape from dexamethasone suppression	−	↑	

Courtesy of Robert M. Post, M.D.
↑, increase; ↓, decrease; ( ), inconsistent or rare; −, absent; ↓↓, potentiation; Li*, effect of lithium predominates.

of monitoring, but even assiduous monitoring may fail to presage severe blood dyscrasias.

Hepatitis

In the first few weeks of therapy, carbamazepine can cause both a hypersensitivity hepatitis associated with increases in liver enzymes and a cholestasis associated with elevated bilirubin and alkaline phosphatase. If the drug is reintroduced to the patient, hepatitis will recur, and the death of the patient can result.

Exfoliative Dermatitis

A benign pruritic rash occurs in 10 to 15 percent of patients treated with carbamazepine. It usually occurs in the first few weeks of treatment, but unfortunately a small percentage of these patients may then experience life-threatening dermatological syndromes, including exfoliative dermatitis, erythema multiforme, Stevens-Johnson syndrome, and toxic epidermal necrolysis. The possible emergence of these serious dermatological problems causes most clinicians to discontinue carbamazepine use if any rash develops in a patient. If carbamazepine seems to be the only effective drug for a patient who incurs a benign rash with carbamazepine treatment, a retrial of the drug can be undertaken; the patient can be pretreated with prednisone (40 mg a day) in an attempt to treat the rash, although other symptoms of an allergic reaction (for example, fever and pneumonitis) may develop, even with steroid pretreatment. The duration of steroid treatment should not exceed 2 weeks, and it should be gradually tapered off over 5 to 7 days.

Gastrointestinal Effects

The most common adverse effects of carbamazepine are nausea, vomiting, gastric distress, constipation, diarrhea, and anorexia. The severity of the adverse effects is reduced if the dosage of carbamazepine is increased slowly and kept at the minimal effective plasma concentration.

Central Nervous System Effects

Acute confusional states can occur with carbamazepine alone but occur most often in combination with lithium or antipsychotic drugs. The symptoms of CNS toxicity include drowsiness, confusion, ataxia, hyperreflexia, clonus, and tremor. Elderly patients and patients with cognitive disorders are at increased risk for CNS toxicity from carbamazepine. The common CNS effects of dizziness, ataxia, clumsiness, and sedation are often associated with carbamazepine treatment, although they are reduced by a slow upward titration of the dosage.

Other Adverse Effects

Carbamazepine decreases cardiac conduction (although less than the tricyclic drugs do) and can thus exacerbate preexisting cardiac disease. Carbamazepine should be used with caution in patients with glaucoma, prostatic hypertrophy, diabetes, or a history of alcohol abuse. Carbamazepine may enhance the water-sparing, antidiuretic effects of vasopressin, by activating vasopressin type 2 receptors, and it may therefore produce hyponatremia. This is in contrast to the vasopressin-inhibiting effects of lithium, which remains the dominant effect if the two drugs are coadministered. If a patient taking carbamazepine becomes confused, therefore, serum electrolytes should be checked. Some evidence indicates that minor cranial facial abnormalities and spina bifida in infants may be associated with the maternal use of carbamazepine during pregnancy. This risk can be reduced by addition of folate 1 to 4 mg a day at least 1 month prior to conception and continuing throughout pregnancy. Therefore, pregnant women should not use carbamazepine unless absolutely necessary. However, carbamazepine may pose less of a threat to the fetus than does lithium. Carbamazepine is secreted in breast milk, so women taking carbamazepine should not nurse their babies.

Overdoses

Overdoses of carbamazepine, when taken alone, have a generally favorable outcome. Symptoms associated with an overdose include drowsiness, stupor, coma, sinus tachycardia, hypotension, or hypertension, A-V conduction block, seizures, nystagmus, hypothermia, facial dyskinesias, and respiratory depression. Gastric lavage and the use of activated charcoal (50 to 100 grams, followed by 12.5 grams per hour until the patient has recovered) early in the course of emergency treatment are recommended. Some investigators have recommended the use of flumazenil (Romazicon) to block the effects of carbamazepine on central-type benzodiazepine receptors.

DRUG INTERACTIONS

The mechanisms for drug interactions with carbamazepine are many (Table 33.3.11–3) and result in many potentially relevant drug interactions (Table 35.3.11–4). Carbamazepine induces the cytochrome P450 3A subfamily and specifically the 3A3 and 3A4 isoforms (CYP 3A3/4). Coadministration with lithium, antipsychotic drugs, erythromycin (E-Mycin), verapamil (Calan), nifedipine (Procardia), or diltiazem (Cardizem) can precipitate carbamazepine-induced CNS adverse effects. Carbamazepine can decrease the blood concentrations of oral contraceptives, which results in breakthrough bleeding and uncertain prophylaxis against pregnancy. Carbamazepine should not be administered with monoamine oxidase inhibitors (MAOIs), which should be discontinued for at least 2 weeks before initiating treatment with carbamazepine. Carbamazepine may significantly induce the metabolism of bupropion (Wellbutrin) and haloperidol (Haldol). Concomitant administration of carbamazepine and clozapine (Clozaril) increases the risk of bone marrow suppression.

Table 35.3.11–3
Carbamazepine (CBZ) Properties Relevant to Pharmacokinetics and Drug Interactions

Property	Relevance
Induces catabolic enzymes	↓ Levels of CBZ and other drugs ↓ Thyroid hormones[a], and androgens[a] ↓ Effects of mild inducers on CBZ (induction ceiling ?) ↑ 6-β-Hydroxycortisol excretion ↑ Pseudocholinesterase
Exclusively hepatic metabolism	↑ CBZ levels with certain enzyme inhibitors ↓ CBZ levels with certain robust inducers (phenytoin, phenobarbital, primidone) No kinetic interactions with lithium
Active (CBZ-E) metabolite	Occult ↑ therapeutic and side effects with inducers of CBZ metabolism and inhibitors of CBZ-E metabolism
Induces anabolic enzymes	↑ HDL cholesterol, ↑ cortisol[a] ↑ Sex hormone binding globulin ↑ α_1-Acid glycoprotein
Antidiuretic hormone agonist	Hyponatremia (↑ with diuretics)[a] ↑ Antidiuretic drug effects[a] ↓ Diuretic drug effects[a]
Plasma protein binding not extensive	Few binding interactions in general
Primary albumin binding	↑ Free CBZ with valproate (displaced)
Secondary α_1-acid glycoprotein binding	↑ Bound CBZ and other drugs (in CBZ induction and acute disease) Interindividual variations in free CBZ

Reprinted with permission from Ketter TA, Post RM, Worthington K: Principles of clinically important drug interactions with carbamazepine: Part I. J Clin Psychopharmacol *11:* 199, 1991.
[a] Entirely or partially pharmacodynamic mechanism hypothesized.

Table 35.3.11–4
Clinically Important Interactions Between Carbamazepine and Other Drugs

Influences of Other Drugs on Carbamazepine	
Increased carbamazepine levels and toxicity produced by Danazol Diltiazem (not nifedipine) Erythromycin (and analogues) Influenza vaccine Isoniazid (not tranylcypromine) Nafimidone Triacetyloleandomycin Verapamil Viloxazine	Increased carbamazepine levels not associated with marked toxicity Cimetidine (mild acute increases; none after one week) Josamycin Nicotinamide Propoxyphene Valproate (increases epoxide only)
Decreased carbamazepine levels produced by Phenobarbital Phenytoin Primidone Theophylline Tricyclic drugs	
Influences of Carbamazepine on Other Drugs	
Carbamazepine decreases levels or effects of Clonazepam Cyclosporine Dexamethasone Dicoumarol Doxycycline Ethosuximide	Haloperidol Pregnancy tests Theophylline Tricyclic drugs Valproate Warfarin

LABORATORY INTERFERENCES

Carbamazepine treatment is associated with a decrease in thyroid hormones (thyroxine [T_4], free T_4, and triiodothyronine [T_3]) without an associated increase in thyroid-stimulating hormone (TSH). Carbamazepine is also associated with an increase in total serum cholesterol, primarily by increasing high-density lipoproteins. The thyroid and cholesterol effects are not clinically significant. Carbamazepine may also interfere with the dexamethasone suppression test and may cause a false-positive result in a pregnancy test.

DOSAGE AND ADMINISTRATION

The mood-stabilizing effects of carbamazepine occur between 3 and 15 days after onset of treatment. Carbamazepine can be used alone or with an antipsychotic drug for the treatment of manic episodes, although carbamazepine-induced CNS adverse effects (drowsiness, dizziness, ataxia) are likely to occur with this combination of drugs. Patients who do not respond to lithium alone may respond when carbamazepine is added to the lithium treatment. If patients then respond, an attempt should be made to withdraw the lithium to assess whether the patient can be treated successfully with carbamazepine alone. When lithium and carbamazepine are used together, the clinician should minimize or discontinue any antipsychotics, sedatives, or anticholinergic drugs the patient may be taking to reduce the risks for adverse effects associated with taking multiple drugs. The combination of lithium and carbamazepine must be monitored closely for CNS toxicity, which may escalate to fatality if not properly modulated. The lithium and the carbamazepine should both be used at standard therapeutic plasma concentrations before a trial of combined therapy is considered to have been a therapeutic failure. A 3-week trial of carbamazepine at therapeutic plasma concentrations is usually sufficient to determine whether the drug is effective in the treatment of acute mania; a longer trial is necessary to assess efficacy in treating depression. Carbamazepine is also used in combination with valproate (Depakene), another anticonvulsant that is effective in bipolar I disorder. When carbamazepine and valproate are used in combination, the dosage of carbamazepine should be decreased; valproate displaces carbamazepine binding on proteins, and the dosage of valproate may need to be increased.

Pretreatment Medical Evaluation

A patient's medical history should include information about preexisting hematological, hepatic, and cardiac diseases, because all three can be relative contraindications for carbamazepine treatment. Patients with hepatic disease require only one third to one half the usual dosage; clinicians should be cautious about raising the dosage in such patients and should do so only slowly and gradually. The laboratory examination should include a complete blood count with platelet count, liver function tests, serum electrolytes, and an electrocardiogram in patients more than 40 years of age or with a preexisting cardiac disease. An electroencephalogram is unnecessary before the initiation of treatment but may be helpful in some cases for documenting objective changes correlated with clinical improvement.

Initiation of Treatment

Carbamazepine is available in 100 and 200 mg tablets and as a 100 mg/5 mL suspension. The usual starting dosage is 200 mg orally 2 times a day, but with titration, 3-times-a-day dosing is optimal. An extended-release version suitable for twice-a-day dosing has been approved, in 100, 200, and 400 mg tablets. Carbamazepine should be taken with meals, and the drug should be stored in a cool, dry place. Carbamazepine stored in a bathroom medicine cabinet can lose up to one third of its activity. In an inpatient setting with seriously ill patients, the dosage can be raised by not more than 200 mg a day until a dosage of 600 to 1,000 mg a day is reached. This relatively rapid titration, however, is often associated with adverse effects and may adversely affect compliance with the drug. In less ill patients and in outpatients, the dosage should not be raised more quickly than 200 mg every 2 to 4 days so that the occurrence of minor adverse effects, such as nausea, vomiting, drowsiness, and dizziness, is minimized. When discontinuing treatment with carbamazepine, clinicians should taper the dosage rapidly.

Blood Levels

The anticonvulsant blood level range for carbamazepine is 4 to 12 μg/mL, and this range should be reached before determining that carbamazepine is not effective in treating a mood disorder. It is clinically prudent to come up to this range gradually, as patients are likely to tolerate a gradual increase of carbamazepine better than a rapid increase. Clinicians should titrate carbamazepine up to the highest well-tolerated dosage before deciding that the drug is ineffective. Plasma concentrations should be obtained when a patient has been receiving a steady dosage for at least 5 days. Blood for the determination of plasma levels is drawn in the morning before the first daily dose of carbamazepine is given. The total daily dosage necessary to achieve plasma concentrations in the usual therapeutic range varies from 400 to 1,600 mg a day, with a mean around 1,000 mg a day.

Routine Laboratory Monitoring

The most serious potential effects of carbamazepine are agranulocytosis and aplastic anemia. Although it has been suggested that complete laboratory blood assessments be performed every 2 weeks for the first 2 months of treatment and quarterly thereafter, this conservative approach may not be justified by a cost–benefit analysis and may not detect a serious blood dyscrasia before it occurs. The Food and Drug Administration (FDA) has revised the package insert for carbamazepine to suggest that blood monitoring be performed at the physician's discretion. Patient education about the signs and symptoms of a developing hematological problem is probably more effective than frequent blood monitoring in protecting against this adverse event. It has also been suggested that liver and renal function tests be conducted quarterly, although the benefit of conducting these tests so frequently has been questioned. It seems reasonable, however, to assess hematological status, along with liver and renal functions, whenever a routine examination of the patient is conducted.

The following laboratory values should prompt physicians to discontinue carbamazepine treatment and to consult a hematologist: total white blood cell count less than 3,000 per mm^3, erythrocytes less than 4.0×10^6 per mm^3, neutrophils less than 1,500 per mm^3, hematocrit less than 32 percent, hemoglobin less than 11 g/100 mL, platelet count less than 100,000 per mm^3, reticulocyte count less than 0.3 percent, and a serum iron level less than 150 mg/100 mL.

References

Bowden CL: Role of newer medications for bipolar disorder. J Clin Psychopharmacol *16* (1, Suppl): 48S, 1996.

Calabrese JR, Woyshville MJ: Lithium therapy: Limitations and alternatives in the treatment of bipolar disorders. Ann Clin Psychiatry *7* (2): 103, 1995.

Chatham-Showalter PE: Carbamazepine for combativeness in acute traumatic brain injury. J Neuropsychiatry Clin Neurosci *8:* 96, 1996.

Cueva JE, Overall JE, Small AM, Armenteros JL, et al: Carbamazepine in aggressive children with conduct disorder: A double-blind and placebo-controlled study. J Am Acad Child Adolesc Psychiatry *35* (4): 480, 1996.

Cullen M, Mitchell P, Brodaty H, Boyce P, Parker G, Hickie I, Wilhelm K: Carbamazepine for treatment-resistant melancholia. J Clin Psychiatry *52:* 472, 1991.

Frye MA, Altshuler LL, Szuba MP, Finch NN, et al: The relationship between antimanic agent for treatment of classic or dysphoric mania and length of hospital stay. J Clin Psychiatry *57* (1): 17, 1996.
Johns CA, Thompson JW: Adjunctive treatments in schizophrenia: Pharmacotherapies and electroconvulsive therapy. Schizophr Bull *21* (4): 607, 1995.
Keck PE, McElroy SL: Outcome in the pharmacologic treatment of bipolar disorder. J Clin Psychopharmacol *16* (1, Suppl): 15S, 1996.
Ketter TA, Flockhart DA, Post RM, Denicoff K, Pazzaglia PJ, Marangell LB: The emerging role of cytochrome P450 3A in psychopharmacology. J Clin Psychopharmacol *15:* 387, 1995.
Ketter TA, Jenkins JB, Schroeder DH, Pazzaglia PJ, Marangell LB, George MS, Callahan AM, Hinton ML, Chao J, Post RM: Carbamazepine but not valproate induces bupropion metabolism. J Clin Psychopharmacol *15:* 327, 1995.
Ketter TA, Post RM, Worthington K: Principles of clinically important drug interactions with carbamazepine: Part I. J Clin Psychopharmacol *11:* 198, 1991.
Ketter TA, Post RM, Worthington K: Principles of clinically important drug interactions with carbamazepine: Part II. J Clin Psychopharmacol *11:* 306, 1991.
Leinonen E, Lillsunde P, Laukkanen V, Ylitalo P: Effects of carbamazepine on serum antidepressant concentrations in psychiatric patients. J Clin Psychopharmacol *11:* 313, 1991.
Pantelis C, Barnes TRE: Drug strategies and treatment-resistant schizophrenia. Aust NZ J Psychiatry *30* (1): 20, 1996.
Post RM: Carbamazepine. In *Comprehensive Textbook of Psychiatry,* ed 6, HI Kaplan, BJ Sadock, editors, p 1919, Williams & Wilkins, Baltimore, 1995.
Silva RR, Munoz DM, Alpert M: Carbamazepine use in children and adolescents with features of attention-deficit hyperactivity disorder: a meta-analysis. J Am Acad Child Adolesc Psychiatry *35:* 352, 1996.
Simhandl C, Meszaros K, Denk E, Thau K, et al: Adjunctive carbamazepine or lithium carbonate in therapy-resistant chronic schizophrenia. Can J Psychiatry *41* (5): 317, 1996.
Tohen M, Castillo J, Cole JO, Miller MG, de los Heros R, Farrer RJ: Thrombocytopenia associated with carbamazepine: A case series. J Clin Psychiatry *52:* 494, 1991.
Van Valkenburg C, Kluznik JC, Merrill R: New uses of anticonvulsant drugs in psychosis. Drugs *44:* 326, 1992.

▲ 35.3.12 Chloral Hydrate

Chloral hydrate, in use since 1869, is one of the oldest sedative-hypnotic drugs. Because many compounds were later introduced, chloral hydrate is now prescribed only as a short-term (2- or 3-day) hypnotic.

CHEMISTRY

Chloral hydrate's chemical formula is $CCl^3CH(OH)_2$.

PHARMACOLOGICAL ACTIONS

Pharmacokinetics

Chloral hydrate is well absorbed from the gastrointestinal (GI) tract. The parent compound is metabolized within minutes by the liver and red blood cells and is excreted by the kidneys. An active metabolite, trichloroethanol, has a half-life of 8 to 11 hours. A dose of chloral hydrate induces sleep in about 30 to 60 minutes and maintains sleep for 4 to 8 hours.

Pharmacodynamics

The pharmacodynamic basis for chloral hydrate's hypnotic effect is unknown, although some investigators have hypothesized that the metabolite trichloroethanol is the active agent producing hypnosis.

EFFECTS ON SPECIFIC ORGANS AND SYSTEMS

In addition to its central nervous system (CNS) effects, chloral hydrate has effects on the GI system and the skin. The GI effects include nonspecific irritation, nausea, vomiting, flatulence, and an unpleasant taste. The dermatological effects, although uncommon, include rashes, urticaria, purpura, eczema, and erythema multiforme. The dermatological lesions are sometimes accompanied by fever.

THERAPEUTIC INDICATIONS

The major indication for chloral hydrate is insomnia. Whether chloral hydrate affects rapid eye movement (REM) sleep is controversial, but patients experience no REM rebound after discontinuation of chloral hydrate therapy. Long-term treatment with chloral hydrate is associated with an increased incidence and severity of adverse effects. Tolerance develops to the hypnotic effects of chloral hydrate after 2 weeks of treatment.

PRECAUTIONS AND ADVERSE REACTIONS

The most common GI adverse effects are nausea, vomiting, and diarrhea. Patients should be warned that they may experience residual daytime sedation and impaired motor coordination. Chloral hydrate should be avoided in patients with severe renal, cardiac, or hepatic disease or with porphyria. The drug may aggravate GI inflammatory conditions. Chloral hydrate should not be used during pregnancy or by nursing women. It is not expected to cause particular difficulties in children or older adults. It may be used as a sedative for diagnostic procedures in children weighing up to 25 kg.

In addition to the development of tolerance, chloral hydrate dependence can occur, with symptoms similar to those of alcohol dependence. The symptoms of intoxication include confusion, ataxia, dysarthria, bradycardia, arrhythmia, and severe drowsiness. The lethal adult dose of chloral hydrate has ranged between 5 and 40 grams; thus the drug is a particularly poor choice for potentially suicidal patients. The lethality of the drug is potentiated by other CNS depressants, including alcohol. With long-term use and overdose, gastritis and gastric ulceration can develop. Hepatic and renal damage can follow overdose attempts, which may result in jaundice and albuminuria.

DRUG INTERACTIONS

Patients who have received chloral hydrate less than 24 hours before receiving intravenous furosemide (Lasix) can have diaphoresis, flushes, and an unsteady blood pressure. Reports are somewhat controversial about the potentiation of warfarin (Coumadin) when coadministered with chloral hydrate.

LABORATORY INTERFERENCES

Chloral hydrate administration can lead to false-positive results for urine glucose determinations that use cupric sulfate in the determination (for example, Clinitest) but not in tests that use glucose oxidase (for example, Clinistix and Tes-Tape).

Chloral hydrate may also interfere with the determination of urinary catecholamines and 17-hydroxycorticosteroids.

DOSAGE AND ADMINISTRATION

Chloral hydrate is available in 250 and 500 mg capsules, 250 and 500 mg/5 mL solutions, and 325, 500, and 650 mg rectal suppositories. The standard dose of chloral hydrate is 500 to 2,000 mg at bedtime. Because the drug is a GI irritant, it should be administered with excess water, milk, other liquids, or antacids to decrease the gastric irritation.

REFERENCES

Graham SR, Day RO, Lee R, Fulde GW: Overdose with chloral hydrate: A pharmacological and therapeutic review. Med J Aust *149:* 686, 1988.

Keeter S, Benator RM, Weinberg SM, Hartenburg MA: Sedation in pediatric CT: National survey of current practice. Radiology *175:* 745, 1990.

Schuler ME: Augmentation of chloral hydrate induced sleep by centrally acting hypertensive agents. Proc West Pharmacol Soc *25:* 347, 1982.

▲ 35.3.13 Clonidine

Clonidine (Catapres) is an α_2-adrenergic receptor agonist used primarily as a hypotensive agent. Its major indications in psychiatry are the control of withdrawal symptoms from opiates and opioids, the treatment of Tourette's disorder, and the control of aggressive or hyperactive behavior in children, especially those with autistic features.

CHEMISTRY

The imidazoline molecular structure of clonidine is shown in Figure 35.3.13–1.

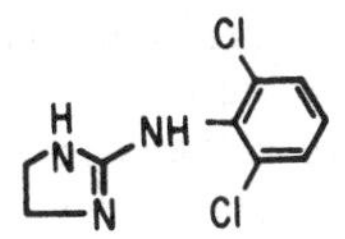
Cl
H
NH
N
N
Cl

FIGURE 35.3.13–1
Molecular structure of clonidine.

PHARMACOLOGICAL ACTIONS

Pharmacokinetics

Clonidine is well absorbed from the gastrointestinal (GI) tract and reaches peak plasma levels 1 to 3 hours after oral administration. About 35 percent of the drug is metabolized by the liver, and 65 percent is excreted in both unchanged and metabolized forms by the kidneys. The half-life of the parent compound is 6 to 20 hours, and there are no active metabolites.

Pharmacodynamics

The agonist effects of clonidine on presynaptic α_2-adrenergic receptors result in a decrease in the amount of neurotransmitter released from the presynaptic nerve terminals. This decrease serves generally to reset the sympathetic tone at a lower level and to decrease arousal. Both the hypotensive and the psychiatric effects of clonidine are mediated by central nervous system (CNS) α_2-adrenergic receptors, rather than by peripheral receptors.

EFFECTS ON SPECIFIC ORGANS AND SYSTEMS

Clonidine exerts its hypotensive effects by stimulating α_2-adrenergic receptors in the medulla oblongata and thus causes the inhibition of sympathetic vasomotor centers. These central effects result in reduced peripheral sympathetic tone, the reduction of diastolic and systolic blood pressure, and bradycardia. Clonidine administration also results in sedation and the release of growth hormone. The effects of clonidine on the GI tract and the kidneys are minimal.

THERAPEUTIC INDICATIONS

The adverse effects and often temporary benefits of clonidine have limited its applicability in psychiatry. It is useful in short-term treatment of opioid withdrawal and in long-term treatment of Tourette's disorder and attention-deficit/hyperactivity disorder (ADHD).

Opiate and Opioid Withdrawal

Clonidine is effective in reducing the autonomic symptoms of opiate and opioid withdrawal (for example, hypertension, tachycardia, dilated pupils, sweating, lacrimation, and rhinorrhea) but not the associated subjective sensations. Clonidine can be used to withdraw patients from methadone, and it has been used to treat opiate withdrawal in newborns. Usually, dosages of 0.15 mg twice a day are sufficient for methadone withdrawal, while dosages of 3 to 4 μg/kg are used in neonatal opioid withdrawal. The efficacy of clonidine in treating opiate and opioid withdrawal may reflect its activity on the noradrenergic neurons of the locus ceruleus.

Tourette's Disorder

Some clinicians use clonidine as a first-line drug to treat Tourette's disorder instead of the standard drugs, haloperidol (Haldol) and pimozide (Orap), because of the serious adverse effects associated with these antipsychotics. The starting child dosage is 0.05 mg a day, and it can be raised to 0.3 mg a day in divided doses. Three months are needed before the beneficial effects of clonidine can be seen in Tourette's disorder. Recent data have suggested that serotonin-dopamine antagonists, such as risperidone (Risperdal), are effective drugs for treatment of Tourette's disorder.

Hyperactivity and Aggression in Children

Clonidine is a third-line agent for treating pure ADHD, after the sympathomimetics and the antidepressants. However, these latter agents may be less effective or may produce paradoxical worsening of hyperactivity in children with mental retardation, aggression, or features on the spectrum of autism. Some multiply-impaired children may respond favorably to clonidine; others may simply become sedated. The starting dose is 0.05 mg a day; the dosage can be raised to 0.3 mg a day in divided doses. Although some clinicians have combined clonidine with sympathomimetics to treat ADHD, this combination has caused at least 5 deaths and should be used only with great caution and with cardiac monitoring. Results of a double-blind, placebo-controlled trial examining the effect of clonidine on hyperactive behavior in children with Tourette's disorder showed statistically significant improvement with desipramine but not with clonidine.

Other Disorders

Other potential indications for clonidine include the anxiety disorders (panic disorder, phobias, obsessive-compulsive disorder, posttraumatic stress disorder, and generalized anxiety disorder) and mania, in which it may be synergistic with lithium (Eskalith) or carbamazepine (Tegretol). Anecdotal reports have noted the efficacy of clonidine in schizophrenia, tardive dyskinesia, and smoking and alcohol cessation. It has also been used to treat pains associated with surgery and labor. The sympatholytic action of clonidine has been used to reduce perspiration caused by certain antidepressant drugs.

PRECAUTIONS AND ADVERSE REACTIONS

The most common adverse effects associated with clonidine are dry mouth and eyes, fatigue, irritability, sedation, dizziness, nausea, hypotension, and constipation, which result in the discontinuation from therapy of about 10 percent of all patients taking the drug. Some patients also experience sexual dysfunction. Uncommon CNS adverse effects include insomnia, anxiety, and depression. Rare CNS adverse effects include vivid dreams, nightmares, and hallucinations. Fluid retention associated with clonidine treatment can be treated with diuretics. When administered in epidural anesthesia, it may cause sedation, bradycardia, and hypotension, and its abrupt withdrawal may cause rebound hypertension and tachycardia. Withdrawal symptoms caused by abrupt cessation of oral clonidine may include headache, anxiety, tachycardia, perspiration, and abdominal pain. Hypertension may also be seen.

Patients who overdose on clonidine can have coma and constricted pupils, symptoms similar to an opioid overdose. Other symptoms of overdose are decreased blood pressure, pulse, and respiratory rates. Clonidine should be used with caution in patients with heart disease, renal disease, Raynaud's syndrome, or a history of depression. Clonidine should be avoided during pregnancy and by nursing mothers. Older adults are more sensitive to the drug than are younger adults. Children are susceptible to the same side effects as adults.

DRUG INTERACTIONS

The most relevant drug interaction is that the coadministration of clonidine and tricyclic drugs can inhibit the hypotensive effects of clonidine. Clonidine may also enhance the CNS depressive effects of barbiturates, alcohol, and other sedative-hypnotics. The concomitant use of β-adrenergic receptor antagonists can increase the severity of rebound phenomena when clonidine is discontinued. At least two patients have developed atrioventricular block and profound hypotension when clonidine was added to verapamil. The α_2-adrenergic antagonist yohimbine (Yocon) can decrease the effects of clonidine. At least 5 deaths have been attributed to the combined use of clonidine and methylphenidate (Ritalin).

LABORATORY INTERFERENCES

No known laboratory interferences are associated with the use of clonidine.

DOSAGE AND ADMINISTRATION

Clonidine is available in 0.1, 0.2, and 0.3 mg tablets. The usual starting dosage is 0.1 mg orally twice a day; the dosage can be raised by 0.1 mg a day to an appropriate level. Clonidine begins to act within 1 hour of administration and, once it is metabolized, has no lingering effects. Clonidine must always be tapered when it is discontinued to avoid rebound hypertension, which occurs about 20 hours after the last clonidine dose. Regardless of the indication for which clonidine is being used, the drug should be withheld if a patient becomes hypotensive (blood pressure less than 90/60 in adults). Clonidine is also available as a transdermal patch that delivers either 0.1, 0.2, or 0.3 mg a day and is replaced every 7 days. Because of its possible variations in transdermal absorption, the patch system should be used with close monitoring during the first weeks.

References

Bohn MJ: Alcoholism. Psychiatr Clin North Am *16:* 679, 1993.

Cuthill JD, Baroniada V, Salvatori VA, Viguie F: Evaluation of clonidine suppression of opiate withdrawal reactions: A multidisciplinary approach. Can J Psychiatry *35:* 377, 1990.

Fankhauser MP, Karumanchi VC, German ML, Yates A, Karumanchi SD: A double-blind, placebo-controlled study of the efficacy of transdermal clonidine in autism. J Clin Psychiatry *53:* 77, 1992.

Harmon RJ, Riggs PD: Clonidine for post-traumatic stress disorder in preschool children. J Am Acad Child Adolesc Psychiatry *35:* 1247, 1996.

Heidemann SM, Sarnaik AP: Clonidine poisoning in children. Crit Care Med *18:* 618, 1990.

Jenike MA: Pharmacologic treatment of obsessive compulsive disorders. Psychiatr Clin North Am *15:* 895, 1992.

Leckman JF, Hardin MT, Riddle MA, Stevenson J, Ort SI, Cohen DJ: Clonidine treatment of Gilles de la Tourette's syndrome. Arch Gen Psychiatry *48:* 324, 1991.

Prince JB, Wilens TE, Biederman J, Spencer TJ, et al: Clonidine for sleep disturbances associated with attention-deficit hyperactivity disorder: A systematic chart review of 62 cases. J Am Acad Child Adolesc Psychiatry *35* (5): 599, 1996.

Rosen MI, McMahan TJ, Hameedi FA, Pearsall HR, Woods SW, Kreek MJ, Kosten TR: Effect of clonidine pretreatment on naloxone-precipitated opiate withdrawal. J Pharmacol Exp Ther *276:* 1128, 1996.

Sandor P: Clinical management or Tourette's syndrome and associated disorders. Can J Psychiatry *40:* 577, 1995.

Tulen JHM, van de Wetering BJM, Kruijk MPCW, von Saher RA, Moleman P, Boomsma F, van Steenis HG, Man in't Veld AJ: Cardiovascular, neuroendocrine, and sedative responses to four graded doses of clonidine in a placebo-controlled study. Biol Psychiatry *32:* 485, 1992.

Uhde TW, Tancer ME: Clonidine. In *Comprehensive Textbook of Psychiatry,* ed 6, HI Kaplan, BJ Sadock, editors, p 1975. Williams & Wilkins, Baltimore, 1995.

Vanelle JM, Leigh TH, Loo H, Priest RG: Resistance to lithium: What alternatives exist? Hum Psychopharmacol *9:* 321, 1994.

Zavodnick JM: Pharmacotherapy. In *Conduct Disorders in Children and Adolescents,* GP Sholevar, editor, p 269. American Psychiatric Press, Washington, 1995.

▲ 35.3.14 Dantrolene

Dantrolene (Dantrium) is a direct-acting skeletal muscle relaxant. In contemporary clinical psychiatry, dantrolene is one of the potentially effective treatments for neuroleptic malignant syndrome, catatonia, and serotonin syndrome.

CHEMISTRY

Dantrolene is derived from hydantoin, as indicated in its molecular structure (Fig. 35.3.14–1). Dantrolene is structurally and pharmacologically unrelated to other skeletal muscle relaxants.

PHARMACOLOGICAL ACTIONS

Pharmacokinetics

About one third of orally administered dantrolene is slowly absorbed from the gastrointestinal (GI) tract. At sufficient dosages, consistent plasma concentrations can be maintained. Peak blood concentrations are seen about 5 hours after oral administration. The elimination half-life of dantrolene is about 9 hours. Dantrolene is largely protein bound, metabolized by the liver, and excreted in the urine.

Pharmacodynamics

Dantrolene produces skeletal muscle relaxation by directly affecting the contractile response of the muscles at the site beyond the myoneural junction. Specifically, dantrolene dissociates excitation–contraction coupling by interfering with the release of calcium from the sarcoplasmic reticulum. The skeletal muscle relaxant effect is the basis of its efficacy in reducing the muscle destruction and hyperthermia associated with neuroleptic malignant syndrome.

EFFECTS ON SPECIFIC ORGANS AND SYSTEMS

The skeletal muscle relaxant effect of dantrolene can cause muscle weakness and such symptoms as slurring of speech and drooling. Dantrolene also has effects on the GI system (for example, diarrhea) and the nervous system (for example, headache and depression) and possibly toxic effects on hepatocytes, as indicated by an association with elevated liver function test results.

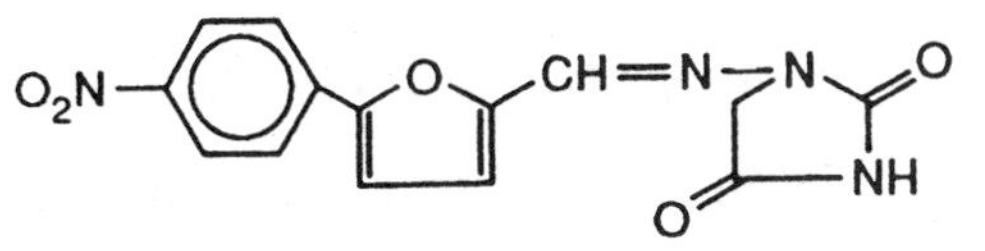
O_2N
O
CH=N
N
O
NH
O

FIGURE 35.3.14–1
Molecular structure of dantrolene.

THERAPEUTIC INDICATIONS

The primary psychiatric indication for intravenous (IV) dantrolene is muscle rigidity in neuroleptic malignant syndrome. Dantrolene is almost always used in conjunction with appropriate supportive measures and a dopamine receptor agonist—for example, bromocriptine (Parlodel). If all available case reports and studies are summarized, about 80 percent of all patients with neuroleptic malignant syndrome who received dantrolene apparently benefited clinically from the drug. Muscle relaxation and a general and dramatic improvement in symptoms can appear within minutes of IV administration, although in most cases the beneficial effects can take several hours to appear. Some evidence indicates that dantrolene treatment must be continued for some time, perhaps days to a week or more, to minimize the risk of symptoms recurring, although the data for this clinical opinion are limited. Dantrolene has been used in efforts to treat other psychiatric conditions characterized by life-threatening muscle rigidity, such as catatonia and serotonin syndrome.

PRECAUTIONS AND ADVERSE REACTIONS

Muscle weakness, drowsiness, dizziness, light-headedness, nausea, diarrhea, malaise, and fatigue are the most common adverse effects of dantrolene. These effects are generally transient. The central nervous system (CNS) effects of dantrolene can include speech disturbances (which may also reflect its effects on the muscles of speech), headaches, visual disturbances, alterations of taste, depression, confusion, hallucinations, nervousness, and insomnia. Many serious adverse effects of dantrolene are associated with long-term treatment, rather than with its short-term use in treating neuroleptic malignant syndrome. The potential serious side effects include hepatitis, seizures, and pleural effusion with pericarditis. Because of its potential for severe adverse effects, dantrolene should not be used by psychiatric patients for any long-term treatment. Dantrolene should be used with caution by patients with hepatic, renal, and chronic lung diseases. Dantrolene can cross the placenta and is thus contraindicated for pregnant women and should not be used by nursing mothers except in emergency situations, such as neuroleptic malignant syndrome. Data are not available about the use of dantrolene by older patients, and no unique problems have been associated with its use by children.

DRUG INTERACTIONS

The risk of liver toxicity may be increased for patients also taking estrogens. Dantrolene should be used with caution by patients who are using other drugs that produce drowsiness, most notably the benzodiazepines. In the case of neuroleptic malignant syndrome, however, the general guidelines for dantrolene must be weighed against the severity of the syndrome. Dantrolene should not be given intravenously in combination with calcium channel inhibitors. Concomitant administration of dantrolene and theophylline in animals has caused seizures and death.

LABORATORY INTERFERENCES

No known laboratory interferences are associated with dantrolene, although experience with its use in patients with neuroleptic malignant syndrome is still limited.

DOSAGE AND ADMINISTRATION

In addition to the immediate discontinuation of antipsychotic drugs, medical support to cool the patient, and the monitoring of vital signs and renal output, dantrolene can be given in dosages of 1 mg/kg orally 4 times daily or 1 to 5 mg/kg IV to reduce muscle spasms in patients with neuroleptic malignant syndrome. Although some clinicians have recommended low dosages because of the adverse effects, other clinicians indicate that dosages of 10 mg/kg a day are most likely to be effective. Intravenous administration of dantrolene provides relaxation of muscle tension within several minutes. Dantrolene is supplied as 25, 50, and 100 mg capsules and in a 20 mg parenteral preparation for reconstitution with 60 mL sterile water.

REFERENCES

Kaplan HI, Sadock BJ: Other pharmacological therapies. In *Comprehensive Textbook of Psychiatry,* ed 6, HI Kaplan, BJ Sadock, editors, p 2122. Williams & Wilkins, Baltimore, 1995.

Mercadante S: Dantrolene treatment of opioid-induced myoclonus. Anesth Analg *18:* 1307, 1995.

Nisijima K, Ishigura T: Does dantrolene influence central dopamine and serotonin metabolism in the neuroleptic malignant syndrome? A retrospective study. Biol Psychiatry *33:* 45, 1993.

Otani K, Mihara K, Kondo T, Okada M, et al: Treatment of neuroleptic malignant syndrome with Levodopa. Hum Psychopharmacol *7:* 217, 1992.

Rice J, Lebowitz PW, Bailine SH, Mowerman A: Malignant hyperthermia and electroconvulsive therapy. Convuls Ther *9:* 45, 1993.

Scheftner WA, Shulman RB: Treatment choice in neuroleptic malignant syndrome. Convuls Ther *8:* 267, 1992.

Tsai G, Crisostomo G, Rosenblatt ML, Stern TA: Neuroleptic malignant syndrome associated with clozapine treatment. Ann Clin Psychiatry *7* (2): 91, 1995.

Waldman HJ: Centrally acting skeletal muscle relaxants and associated drugs. J Pain Symptom Manage *9:* 434, 1994.

▲ 35.3.15 Disulfiram

Disulfiram (Antabuse) is used to ensure abstinence in the treatment of alcohol dependence. Its main effect is to produce a rapid and violently unpleasant reaction in a person who ingests even a small amount of alcohol while taking disulfiram. Because of the risk of severe and even fatal disulfiram–alcohol reactions, disulfiram therapy is used less often today than previously.

CHEMISTRY

The molecular structure of disulfiram is presented in Figure 35.3.15–1.

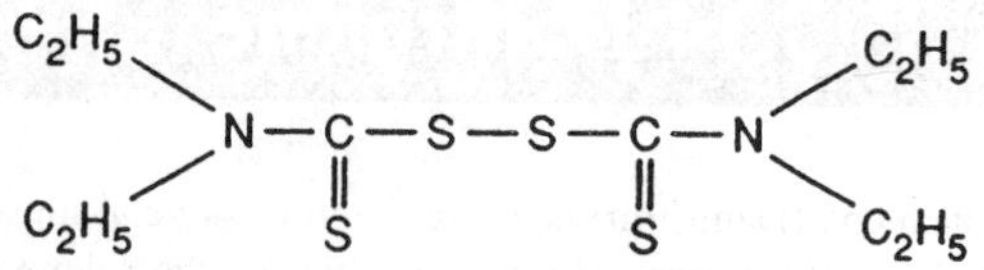

FIGURE 35.3.15–1
Molecular structure of disulfiram.

PHARMACOLOGICAL ACTIONS

Pharmacokinetics

Disulfiram is almost completely absorbed from the gastrointestinal tract after oral administration. It is metabolized in the liver and excreted in the urine. It is lipid soluble and has a half-life estimated at 60 to 120 hours. One or 2 weeks may be needed before disulfiram is totally eliminated from the body after the last dose has been taken.

Pharmacodynamics

The metabolism of ethanol proceeds through oxidation via alcohol dehydrogenase to the formation of acetaldehyde, which is further metabolized to acetylcoenzyme A (acetyl-CoA) by aldehyde dehydrogenase. Acetyl-CoA proceeds down the citric acid cycle and other metabolic pathways. Disulfiram is an aldehyde dehydrogenase inhibitor that interferes with the metabolism of alcohol and produces a marked increase in blood acetaldehyde levels. The accumulation of acetaldehyde (to a level up to 10 times higher than occurs in the normal metabolism of alcohol) produces a wide array of unpleasant reactions called the disulfiram–alcohol reaction, characterized by the following signs and symptoms: nausea, throbbing headache, vomiting, hypotension, flushing, sweating, thirst, dyspnea, tachycardia, chest pain, vertigo, and blurred vision. The reaction occurs almost immediately after the ingestion of one alcoholic drink and may last up to 30 minutes.

THERAPEUTIC INDICATIONS

The primary indication for disulfiram use is as an aversive conditioning treatment for alcohol dependence. Either the fear of having a disulfiram–alcohol reaction or the memory of having had one is meant to condition the patient not to use alcohol. Some clinicians induce a disulfiram–alcohol reaction in patients at the beginning of therapy to convince the patients of the severe unpleasantness of the symptoms. This practice is not recommended, however, as a disulfiram–alcohol reaction can lead to cardiovascular collapse. It is usually sufficient to describe graphically the severity and unpleasantness of the disulfiram–alcohol reaction to discourage patients from imbibing alcohol. Disulfiram treatment should be combined with such treatments as psychotherapy, group therapy, and support groups like Alcoholics Anonymous. The treatment of alcohol dependence requires careful monitoring, since a patient can simply decide not to take the disulfiram; compliance with the medication should be checked if possible.

PRECAUTIONS AND ADVERSE REACTIONS

With Alcohol Consumption

The intensity of the disulfiram–alcohol reaction varies with each patient. In extreme cases it is marked by respiratory depression, cardiovascular collapse, myocardial infarction, convulsions, and death. Therefore, disulfiram is contraindicated for patients with a significant pulmonary or cardiovascular disease. In addition, disulfiram should be used with caution, if at all, by patients with nephritis, brain damage, hypothyroidism, diabetes, hepatic disease, seizures, polydrug dependence, or an abnormal electroencephalogram. Most fatal reactions occur in patients who are taking more than 500 mg a day of disulfiram and who consume more than 3 ounces of alcohol. The treatment of a severe disulfiram–alcohol reaction is primarily supportive to prevent shock.

Without Alcohol Consumption

The adverse effects of disulfiram in the absence of alcohol consumption include fatigue, dermatitis, impotence, optic neuritis, a variety of mental changes, acute polyneuropathy, and hepatic damage. A metabolite of disulfiram inhibits dopamine hydroxylase and thus potentially exacerbates psychosis in patients with psychotic disorders.

DRUG INTERACTIONS

Disulfiram increases the blood concentration of diazepam (Valium), chlordiazepoxide (Librium), paraldehyde (Paral), phenytoin (Dilantin), caffeine, theophylline (Theo-Dur, Slo-Bid), tetrahydrocannabinol (the active ingredient in marijuana), barbiturates, anticoagulants, isoniazid, and tricyclic drugs. Concomitant administration of disulfiram and tranylcypromine (Parnate) causes seizures and death in animals.

LABORATORY INTERFERENCES

In rare instances, disulfiram has been reported to decrease the uptake of iodine-131 (^{131}I) and protein-bound iodine test results. In research settings, disulfiram may reduce urinary concentrations of homovanillic acid, the major metabolite of dopamine, because of its inhibition of dopamine hydroxylase.

DOSAGE AND ADMINISTRATION

Disulfiram is supplied in tablets of 250 and 500 mg. The usual initial dosage is 500 mg a day taken by mouth for the first 1 or 2 weeks, followed by a maintenance dosage of 250 mg a day. The dosage should not exceed 500 mg a day. The maintenance dosage range is 125 to 500 mg a day.

Patients must be instructed that the ingestion of even the smallest amount of alcohol brings on a disulfiram–alcohol reaction, with all its unpleasant effects. Patients should also be warned against ingesting any alcohol-containing preparations, such as cough drops, tonics of any kind, and alcohol-containing foods and sauces. Some reactions have occurred in men who used alcohol-based aftershave lotions and inhaled the fumes; therefore, precautions must be explicit and should include any topically applied preparations containing alcohol, such as perfume.

Disulfiram should not be administered until patients have abstained from alcohol for at least 12 hours. Disulfiram can cause an unpleasant reaction within 15 minutes after the first dose in a person who has even tiny serum concentrations of unmetabolized alcohol. Patients should be warned that the disulfiram–alcohol reaction may occur as long as 1 or 2 weeks after the last dose of disulfiram. Patients should carry identification cards describing the disulfiram–alcohol reaction and listing the name and the telephone number of the physician to be called.

REFERENCES

Fuller RK: Antidipsotrophic medications. In *Handbook of Alcoholism Treatment Approaches: Effective Alternatives,* ed 2, RK Hester, WR Miller, editors, p 123. Allyn & Bacon, Boston, 1995.

Hameedi FA, Rosen MI, McCance-Katz EF, McMahon TJ, et al: Behavioral, physiological, and pharmacological interaction of cocaine and disulfiram in humans. Biol Psychiatry *37* (8): 560, 1995.

Kaminer Y: Disulfiram in adolescents? J Am Acad Child Adolesc Psychiatry *34:* 2, 1995.

Miller NS: Pharmacotherapy in alcoholism. Alcohol Treat Q *12:* 129, 1995.

Miller NS: Pharmacotherapy in alcoholism. J Addict Dis *14* (1): 23, 1995.

Schuckit MA: Recent developments in the pharmacotherapy of alcohol dependence. J Consult Clin Psychology *64:* 669, 1996.

Smith JE, Meyers RJ: The community reinforcement approach. In *Handbook of Alcoholism Treatment Approaches: Effective Alternatives,* ed 2, RK Hester, WR Miller, editors, p 251. Allyn & Bacon, Boston, 1995.

▲ 35.3.16 Dopamine Receptor Antagonists

In 1952, the beginning of the modern era in psychopharmacology was heralded by the recognition of chlorpromazine's calming effects for agitated and psychotic patients. The subsequent development of a diverse group of antipsychotic drugs, which act by blockade of the dopamine type 2 (D_2) receptor, revolutionized psychiatry. The major indication for the use of these drugs is the treatment of schizophrenia and other psychotic disorders. The dopamine receptor antagonist drug class includes, most prominently, chlorpromazine (Thorazine), thioridazine (Mellaril), fluphenazine (Prolixin), and haloperidol (Haldol). For nearly 4 decades after their discovery, the dopamine receptor antagonists were the major antipsychotic drugs, and they continue to be widely used. The presence of sometimes irreversible neurological adverse effects, however, prompted a search for newer agents lacking these consequences. In the past few years, a new class of antipsychotic agents, the serotonin-dopamine antagonists, has appeared. These drugs not only have fewer adverse neurological effects but also act against a fuller range of psychotic symptoms, both positive and negative. Although the dopamine receptor antagonists remain more widely used, the balance is expected to tip toward the newer agents in coming years. The drugs of the serotonin-dopamine antagonist class—clozapine (Clozaril), risperidone (Risperdal), olanzapine (Zyprexa), and sertindole (Serlect) are discussed in Section 35.3.25.

Antipsychotics and *dopamine receptor antagonists* are not necessarily synonymous. Clozapine (Clozaril) is an effective antipsychotic but differs from all the drugs discussed here in that it has comparatively little activity at D_2 receptors. The drugs discussed here have also been referred to as neuroleptics and major tranquilizers. The term *neuroleptic* translates loosely as ''grasping the neuron'' and denotes the neurological or motor effects of most dopamine receptor antagonists. The development of new compounds, such as the serotonin-dopamine antagonists, that are associated with few neurological effects makes the continued use of the term *neuroleptic* inaccurate as an overall label for these compounds. The term *major tranquilizer* inaccurately implies that the primary effect of the drugs is to sedate patients and confounds the drugs with the so-called minor tranquilizers (also a dubious term), such as the benzodiazepines. An additional confusion in the nomenclature of the drugs is the common misuse of the term *phenothiazine* as a synonym for the term *antipsychotic.* This use is inaccurate: The phenothiazines, such as chlorpromazine, are only one type of antipsychotic drug.

HISTORY

Reserpine (Serpasil) is not a dopamine receptor antagonist; rather, it depletes presynaptic biogenic amine neurotransmitter stores, including those of dopamine. Reserpine was historically the first effective antipsychotic drug and is a constituent of the shrub rauwolfia, which is native to areas of India, Africa, and South America and has been used as an ingredient in folk medicines for centuries. In 1931, Sen and Bose published the first paper reporting the effectiveness of rauwolfia in hypertension and mania. In 1953, the active ingredient, reserpine, was identified and quickly entered into the then limited pharmacological approaches to psychosis.

Chlorpromazine, a phenothiazine derivative that was later shown to be a dopamine receptor antagonist, was the first so-called classic or typical antipsychotic to be synthesized in the early 1950s and to enter widespread clinical use. Chlorpromazine was an antihistamine that was initially used as an adjuvant to anesthetics, but two clinically astute French anesthesiologists, Henri Laborit and Jean Huguenard, observed the unusual psychic properties of the compound. Two French psychiatrists, Jean Delay and Pierre Deniker, tried the drug in patients with schizophrenia and reported their success in 1952. Compared with reserpine, chlorpromazine was more effective and had a more rapid onset. In addition, the use of reserpine was associated with a high incidence of depression and suicide, side effects that are now understood to be consistent with reserpine's generalized depletion of biogenic amine neurotransmitters. Word of the clinical results with chlorpromazine quickly spread throughout Europe and then to North America, where a number of investigators were instrumental in its rapid introduction in U.S. psychiatry.

The clinical introduction of chlorpromazine was quickly followed by the introduction of other phenothiazine compounds, such as perphenazine (Trilafon) and fluphenazine. Subsequently, various antipsychotic compounds that differed structurally but not pharmacodynamically from the phenothiazines were introduced into clinical practice. The laboratory of one Belgian researcher in particular, Paul Janssen, was responsible for the introduction of haloperidol, a butyrophenone; pimozide (Orap), a diphenylbutylpiperidine; and, most recently, risperidone, a benzisoxasole. Risperidone and the other serotonin-dopamine antagonists reflect the continuing efforts of clinicians, researchers, and pharmaceutical companies to develop effective antipsychotic drugs that are associated with few adverse effects, particularly neurological adverse effects, such as parkinsonism, dystonias, akathisia, and tardive dyskinesia.

In contrast to the so-called typical antipsychotics (for example, chlorpromazine and haloperidol), the four most extensively studied new antipsychotic drugs—clozapine, risperidone, olanzapine, and sertindole—are often referred to as atypical antipsychotics, although there is no generally agreed-on definition of the distinctions between typical and atypical antipsychotics. The label *atypical* is variably meant to imply any or all of the following characteristics: having less risk of adverse neurological effects; causing less potent increases in prolactin secretion; lacking dopamine antagonism as a primary mechanism of action; possessing significant activity at specific, nondopaminergic receptors (for example, serotonin receptors); and possessing greater efficacy in the treatment of schizophrenia's negative symptoms (for example, anhedonia). In time, it is likely that the serotonin-dopamine antagonists will become the typical antipsychotics. An alternative to the vague subtyping of antipsychotics into typical and atypical drugs is to recognize antipsychotic drugs as being structurally or pharmacologically distinct from one another and not to generalize about their distinctions.

The introduction of antipsychotic drugs revolutionized the treatment of those with schizophrenia and other serious psychotic disorders. Psychiatrists recognize that patients with schizophrenia exhibit positive symptoms such as hallucinations, delusions, disordered thoughts, and agitation and negative symptoms such as withdrawal, flat effect, anhedonia, and catatonia. The use of the typical antipsychotics results in significant clinical improvement in 50 to 75 percent of psychotic patients, and almost 90 percent of these patients receive some clinical benefit from the drugs. These drugs generally are most effective on positive symptoms and often have little or no impact on the negative symptoms.

Nevertheless, the introduction of the antipsychotics, in combination with a poorly planned and executed program of deinstitutionalization, has led to a situation over the past 40 years in which many patients with schizophrenia receive inadequate treatment that does not address the full extent of their illness-related problems. Among the issues poorly addressed by many mental health care delivery systems are community and family support, adequate living arrangements, quality-of-life factors, the reduction of environmental and family stressors, and compliance with medication regimens. Even the most appropriate and effective use of typical antipsychotics is not consistently applied in treatment programs, especially in the use of the lowest effective dosage, the appropriate monitoring of blood levels, the recognition and treatment of adverse effects, and the treatment of residual and negative symptoms. Despite the general trend toward the use of high-potency antipsychotics, which may have few adverse effects, and the reduction in unwarranted simultaneous use of many antipsychotic drugs (polypharmacy), some evidence indicates that there is also a trend toward using unnecessarily high dosages of antipsychotics and thus causing more frequent and more severe adverse effects in patients than is necessary to obtain the optimal clinical benefits.

Workers eventually appreciated that all of the typical antipsychotic drugs act by blocking the effects of dopamine at D_2 receptors. Specifically, high- and low-affinity drugs are recognized, and there is an impressive relation between the affinities of these drugs for D_2 receptors and their clinical potency (Fig. 35.3.16–1). Thus, haloperidol, which has a high affinity for D_2 receptors, is clinically used in low dosages; but chlorpromazine, which has a comparatively low affinity for D_2 receptors, is clinically used in high dosages. This observation—

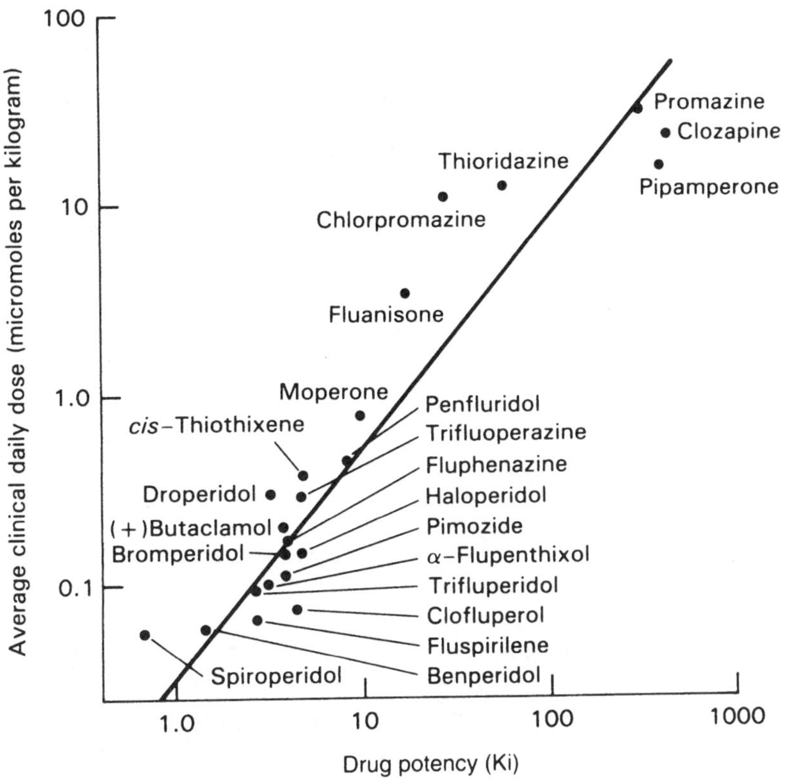
100
10
1.0
0.1
Average clinical daily dose (micromoles per kilogram)
1.0
10
100
1000
Drug potency (Ki)
Promazine
Clozapine
Pipamperone
Thioridazine
Chlorpromazine
Fluanisone
Moperone
cis-Thiothixene
Droperidol
(+)Butaclamol
Bromperidol
Spiroperidol
Penfluridol
Trifluoperazine
Fluphenazine
Haloperidol
Pimozide
α-Flupenthixol
Trifluperidol
Clofluperol
Fluspirilene
Benperidol

FIGURE 35.3.16–1
There is a strong correlation between the clinical potencies of dopamine receptor antagonist drugs and the ability of the drugs to block dopamine D_2 receptors. On the *vertical axis* is the average daily dose required to achieve the same clinical effect. On the *horizontal axis* is the concentration of drug required to bind half the receptors. The higher the concentration required, the lower the affinity for the receptor. (Reprinted with permission from Kandel ER: Disorders of thought: Schizophrenia. In *Principles of Neural Science,* ed 3, ER Kandel, JH Schwartz, TM Jessell, editors, p 861. Elsevier, New York, 1991. Copyright ©1996 by Appleton and Lange.)

in addition to the observation that dopamine agonists, such as amphetamine, can induce psychotic symptoms—led to the development of the dopamine hypothesis of schizophrenia. The introduction of new antipsychotic drugs—such as serotonin-dopamine antagonists—has continued to provide basic and clinical data that have allowed for the steady evolution of the dopamine hypothesis from one involving only dopamine receptors to one that includes interactions with many dopamine receptor subtypes (for example, D_3 and D_4) and other neurotransmitter receptors (for example, serotonin receptors). The serotonin-dopamine antagonists, for example, have much lower affinity for the D_2 receptors than do typical antipsychotics, and they also have a high affinity for serotonin (5-hydroxytryptamine [5-HT]) type 2 (5-HT_2) receptors. A high affinity blockade of the dopamine D_2 receptors is associated with the parkinsonian side effects.

CLASSIFICATION AND CHEMISTRY

Not counting reserpine (which is only historically relevant), seven classes of drugs are generally grouped together as the dopamine receptor antagonist antipsychotics: phenothiazine, thioxanthene, dibenzoxazepine, dihydroindole, butyrophenone, diphenylbutylpiperidine, and benzamide (Fig. 35.3.16–2). Some clinicians and researchers also consider thioridazine, a piperidine phenothiazine, to be atypical because it may be associated with fewer adverse neurological effects than are other antipsychotics.

Phenothiazine

All the phenothiazines have the same three-ring phenothiazine nucleus but differ in the side chains joined to the nitrogen atom of the middle ring. The phenothiazines are typed according to the nature of the side chain: aliphatic (for example, chlorpromazine), piperazine (for example, fluphenazine), or piperidine (for example, thioridazine).

Thioxanthene

The thioxanthene three-ring nucleus differs from the phenothiazine nucleus by the substitution of a carbon atom for the nitrogen atom in the middle ring. The available thioxanthene (thiothixene [Navane]) has a piperazine side chain.

Dibenzoxazepine

The dibenzoxazepines are based on another modification of the three-ring phenothiazine nucleus. The only dibenzoxazepine available in the United States is loxapine (Loxitane), which has a piperazine side chain. Although loxapine is similar in structure to clozapine, the two compounds have dramatically

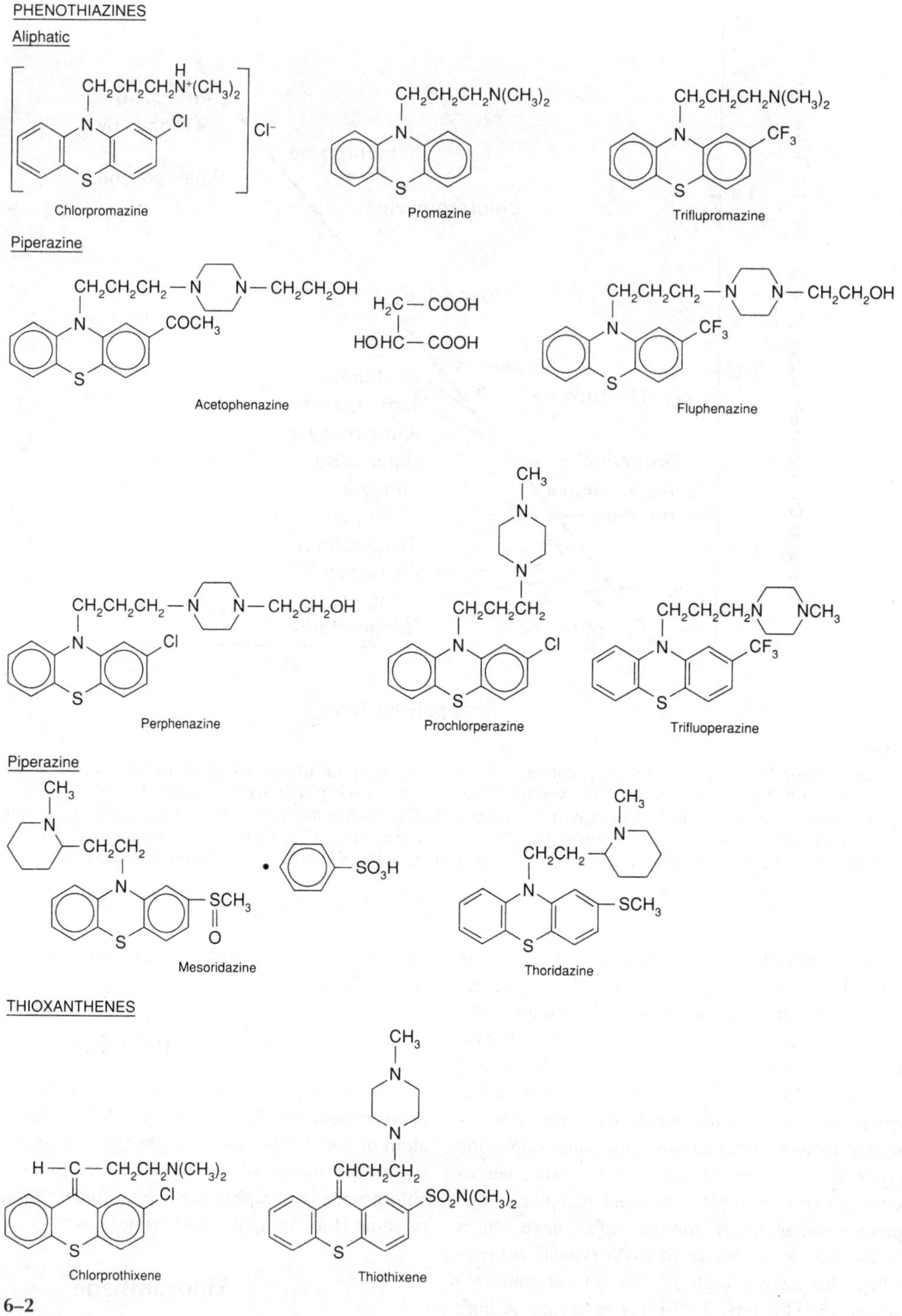
PHENOTHIAZINES
Aliphatic
Chlorpromazine
Promazine
Triflupromazine
Piperazine
Acetophenazine
Fluphenazine
Perphenazine
Prochlorperazine
Trifluoperazine
Piperazine
Mesoridazine
Thoridazine
THIOXANTHENES
Chlorprothixene
Thiothixene

FIGURE 35.3.16–2
Molecular structure of dopamine receptor antagonists and reserpine.

different pharmacodynamic properties, and loxapine is clearly classifiable with the dopamine receptor antagonists, whereas clozapine is not.

Dihydroindole

The only dihydroindole available in the United States, molindone (Moban, Lidone), has unusual clinical properties, such as not inducing weight gain and perhaps being less epileptogenic than are the other dopamine receptor antagonist antipsychotics.

Butyrophenone

The two butyrophenones available in the United States are haloperidol and droperidol (Inapsine). Haloperidol is perhaps

Dibenzoxazepine

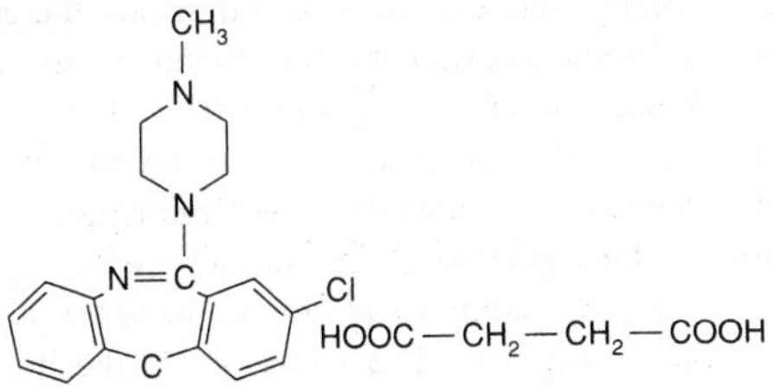

Loxapine

Dihydroindole

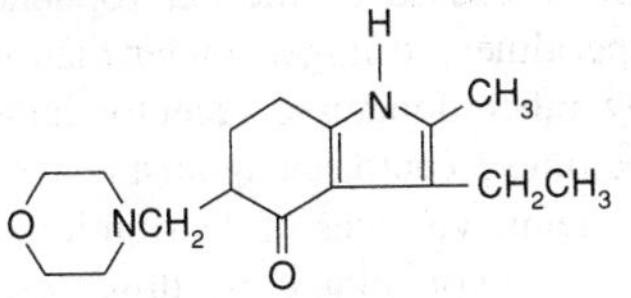

Molindone

Butyrophenones

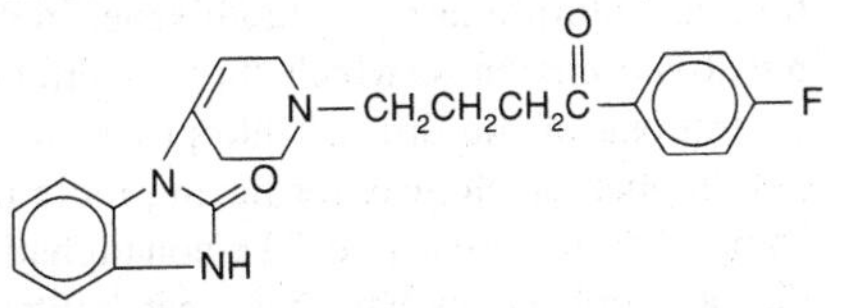

Droperidol

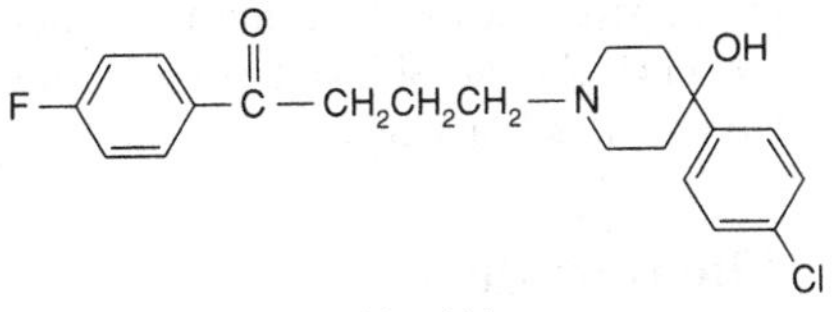

Haloperidol

Diphenylbutylpiperidine

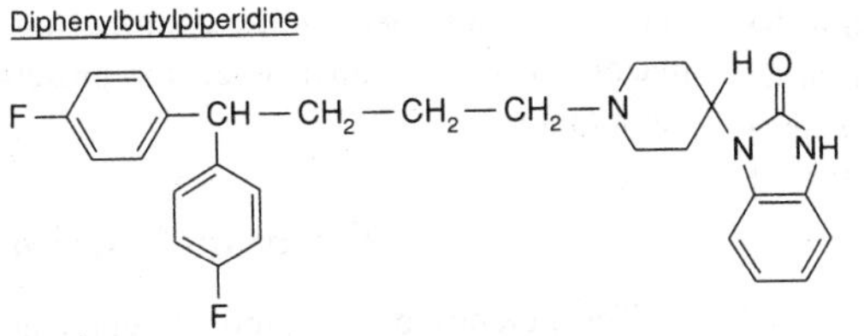

Pimozide

Benzamide

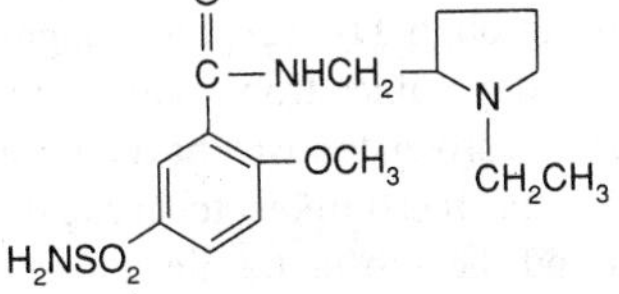

Sulpiride (not available in U.S.)

Rauwolfia Alkaloid

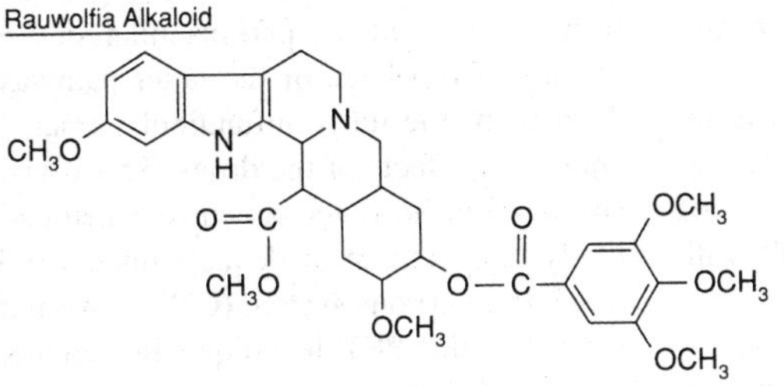

Reserpine

FIGURE 35.3.16–2—*continued*

the most widely used antipsychotic. Although droperidol is approved only for use as an adjuvant to anesthetics, some researchers and clinicians have used droperidol as an intravenous (IV) antipsychotic drug in emergency settings. Spiroperidol, also called spiperone, is a butyrophenone compound that can be labeled with a radioactive atom and is used in basic and clinical research studies (for example, positron emission tomography [PET]) to mark dopamine receptors.

Diphenylbutylpiperidine

Diphenylbutylpiperidines are structurally similar to the butyrophenones. Only one diphenylbutylpiperidine, pimozide, is available in the United States; it is approved for the treatment of Tourette's disorder, although haloperidol is also widely used for this indication, and the other agents are probably equally effective. In Europe, however, pimozide has been shown to be an effective antipsychotic agent. A controversial clinical and research observation about pimozide is that it may be more effective than the other antipsychotics in reducing the deficit or negative symptoms of schizophrenia, although strongly supportive data for this impression are lacking.

Benzamide

Sulpiride (Dogmatil) and raclopride are available in some countries outside the United States and have been found to be effective antipsychotic drugs. Similar to spiperone, raclopride has been used as a radiolabeled ligand in research studies, particularly in PET studies of schizophrenic patients, because of its specificity for D_2 receptors.

PHARMACOLOGICAL ACTIONS

Pharmacokinetics

Although the pharmacokinetic properties of the dopamine receptor antagonists vary widely with their half-lives ranging from 10 to 20 hours, the most important clinical generalization is that all the antipsychotics currently available in the United States (with the exception of clozapine) can be given in one daily oral dose once the patient is in a stable condition and has adjusted to any adverse effects. Most dopamine receptor antagonists are incompletely absorbed after oral administration, although liquid preparations are absorbed more efficiently than are other forms. Many dopamine receptor antagonists are also available in parenteral forms that can be given intramuscularly in emergency situations to attain therapeutic plasma concentrations more rapidly and reliably than is possible with oral administration.

In the United States, two dopamine receptor antagonists, haloperidol and fluphenazine, are available in long-acting depot parenteral formulations that can be given once every 1 to 4 weeks, depending on the dose and the patient. The depot formulations of haloperidol and fluphenazine consist of esters of the parent compound mixed in sesame seed oil. The drug's rate of entry into the body is determined by the rate at which the esterified drug diffuses out of the oil into the body; then the esterified drug is rapidly hydrolyzed and the active compound is released. Because of the long half-life of this formulation, it can take up to 6 months of treatment to reach steady-state plasma levels; thus oral therapy should perhaps be continued during the first month or so of depot antipsychotic treatment. The long half-life of the depot formulation also means that detectable concentrations of the antipsychotic are present long after the last administration of the drug.

Peak plasma concentrations are usually reached 1 to 4 hours after oral administration and 30 to 60 minutes after parenteral administration. The half-lives of the butyrophenones and diphenylbutylpiperidines are longer than those of the phenothiazines, and the clinical effects are seen in the tendency for parkinsonism, caused by the butyrophenones and the diphenylbutylpiperidines, to linger longer than when parkinsonism is caused by other dopamine receptor antagonists. In addition, most dopamine receptor antagonist drugs have high binding to plasma proteins, volumes of distribution, and lipid solubilities. Dopamine receptor antagonist drugs are metabolized in the liver and reach steady-state plasma levels in 5 to 10 days. Some evidence indicates that, after a few weeks of administration, chlorpromazine, thiothixene, and thioridazine induce metabolic enzymes, which thereby produce low plasma concentrations of the drugs. Chlorpromazine is notorious among psychopharmacologists for having more than 150 metabolites, some of which are active. The nonaliphatic phenothiazines and the butyrophenones have few metabolites; whether these metabolites are active remains controversial. The potential presence of active metabolites complicates the interpretation of plasma drug levels that report the presence of only the parent compound.

Pharmacodynamics

The potency of dopamine receptor antagonist drugs to reduce psychotic symptoms is most closely correlated with these drugs' affinity with D_2 receptors. The mechanism of therapeutic action for dopamine receptor antagonist drugs is hypothesized to be through D_2 receptor antagonism, which prevents endogenous dopamine from activating the receptors (Fig. 35.3.16–3). Neuroanatomists have defined two major dopamine tracts, the mesolimbic to cortical (mostly frontal lobe) projection and the substantia nigra to striatum projection. Researchers have hypothesized that the antipsychotic effects derive from inhibition of dopaminergic neurotransmission in the former tract and the parkinsonian side effects are the consequence of blockage of the latter pathway. Interference with a third tract, the tuberoinfundibular tract, is responsible for the endocrine effects of the drugs. This division is little more than speculation, however, as current neuroscientific notions quite likely represent an inadequate understanding of the intricacies of central nervous system (CNS) information processing. Studies using the PET technique in patients who were taking a variety of dopamine receptor antagonists in different dosages have produced data indicating that occupancy of about 60 percent of the D_2 receptors in the caudate-putamen is correlated with clinical response and that occupancy of more than 70 percent of the D_2 receptors is correlated with the development of extrapyramidal symptoms (EPS). Other investigators have reported that theoretically adequate occupancy of D_2 receptors can be found in patients who are still nonresponsive to dopamine receptor antagonist drugs. This finding indicates that oc-

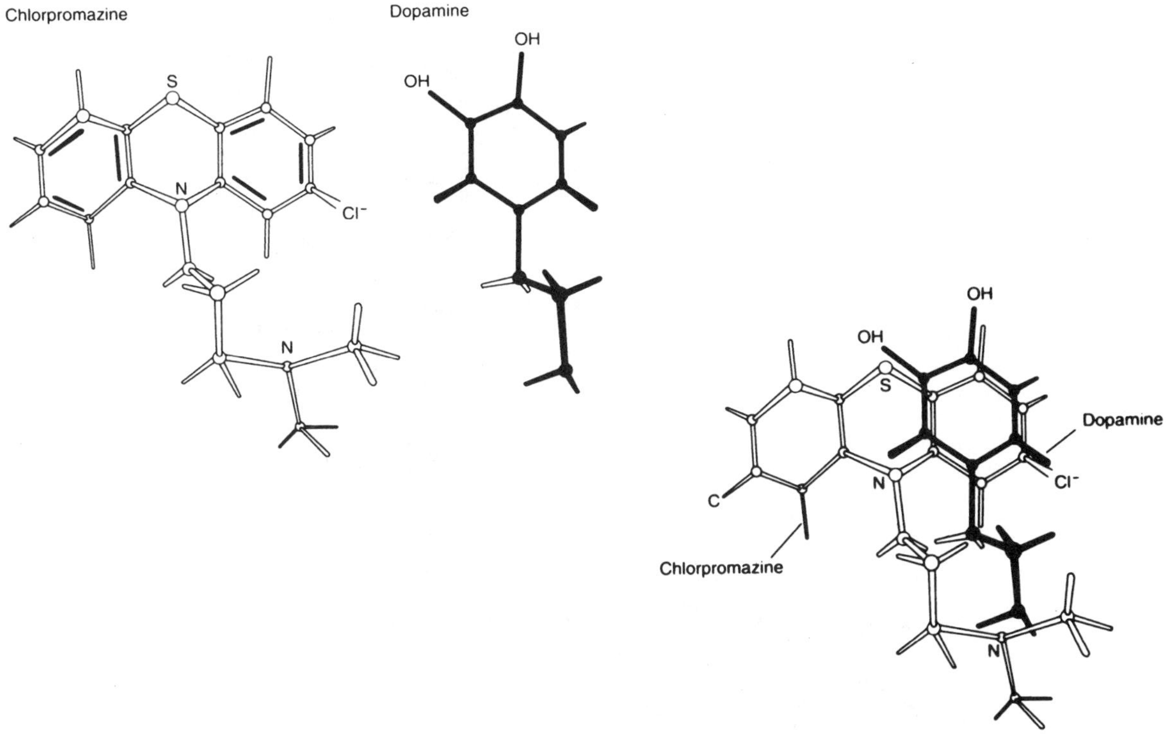
Chlorpromazine
Dopamine
OH
OH
S
N
Cl⁻
N
OH
OH
S
Dopamine
N
Cl⁻
C
Chlorpromazine
N

FIGURE 35.3.16–3
A comparison of the molecular structure of dopamine and chlorpromazine demonstrates why the latter acts on dopamine receptors. It has a similar shape and therefore fits the receptor. Because of differences in structure, however, chlorpromazine simply binds to the receptor without triggering a response. (Reprinted with permission from Kandel ER: Disorders of thought: Schizophrenia. In *Principles of Neural Science,* ed 3, ER Kandel, JH Schwartz, TM Jessell, editors, p 860. Elsevier, New York, 1991. Copyright ©1996 by Appleton and Lange.)

cupancy of D_2 receptors is not the only variable in clinical response. Although the dopamine hypothesis holds for all drugs discussed here, it does not hold for clozapine, which apparently has a different mechanism of action that perhaps involves the D_4 receptor, the 5-HT_2 receptor, or both. Clozapine at active concentrations, for example, may cause only 40 to 60 percent D_2 receptor occupancy.

There are two major caveats to the dopamine hypothesis of schizophrenia as it evolved out of the mechanism of action for the dopamine receptor antagonists: First, although the dopamine receptor blocking effect occurs immediately, the full antipsychotic effects of the drugs may take weeks to develop. This observation indicates that a slowly developing, still unknown homeostatic change in the brain is the mechanism of action for the drug's antipsychotic effects. An example of such a delayed effect is the observation that dopaminergic neurons significantly decrease their firing rates after long-term administration, but not after short-term administration, of D_2 antagonist drugs, an effect referred to as depolarization blockade. Investigators propose that the negative symptoms of schizophrenia are associated with decreased prefrontal dopamine activity and the positive symptoms are associated with increased subcortical dopamine activity. Effective antipsychotic drugs normalize both these trends (Fig. 35.3.16–4). Second, although the correlation of dopamine blocking effects and clinical potency has led to the dopamine hypothesis of schizophrenia, it is also true that the dopamine receptor antagonist drugs reduce psychotic symptoms regardless of diagnosis. There is a strong correlation between D_2 receptor affinity and antipsychotic potency (Fig. 35.3.16–1). The therapeutic effects of dopamine receptor blockade, therefore, are not unique to the pathophysiology of schizophrenia. Another positive association between the clinical efficacy of dopamine receptor antagonists and their dopamine receptor activity is suggested by the effects of the drugs on the plasma concentrations of homovanillic acid, the major metabolite of dopamine. Several studies have reported that high pretreatment concentrations of plasma homovanillic acid are positively correlated with an increased likelihood of a favorable clinical response. Furthermore, a decrease in plasma homovanillic acid concentrations early in the course of treatment is correlated with a favorable clinical response.

Most neurological and endocrinological adverse effects of dopamine receptor antagonists can also be explained by their blockade of dopamine receptors. Various dopamine receptor antagonists, however, also block noradrenergic, cholinergic, and histaminergic receptors, an observation that accounts for the variation in adverse effect profiles among the drugs.

EFFECTS ON SPECIFIC ORGANS AND SYSTEMS

Most dopamine receptor antagonists have significant effect on other receptors, including adrenergic, cholinergic, and histaminergic receptors. The other receptor effects result in varied

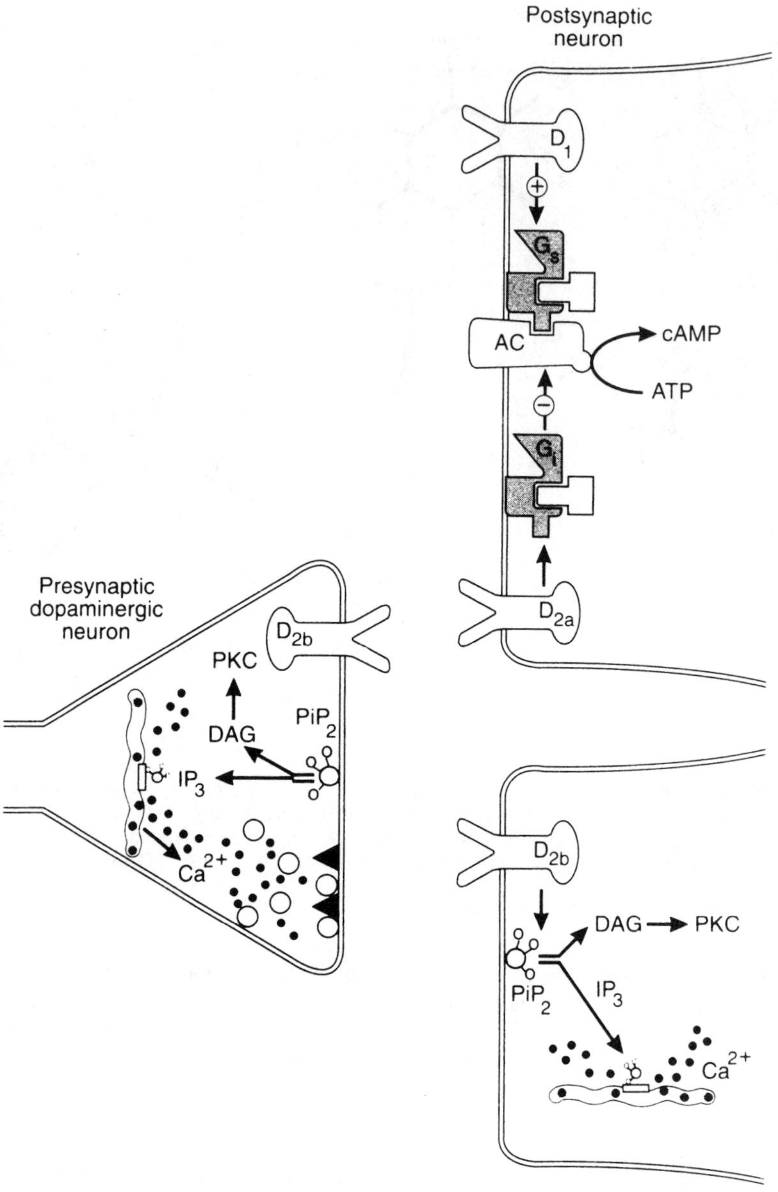
Postsynaptic neuron
D_1
G_s
AC
cAMP
ATP
G_i
Presynaptic dopaminergic neuron
D_{2b}
PKC
DAG
PiP_2
IP_3
Ca^{2+}
D_{2a}
D_{2b}
DAG → PKC
PiP_2
IP_3
Ca^{2+}

FIGURE 35.3.16–4

Location and signaling mechanisms of dopamine D_1, D_{2a}, and D_{2b} receptors. D_{2b} receptors are located on the presynaptic terminal, where they regulate dopamine release through a phosphoinositide second-messenger system. D_{2a} receptors are located in the postsynaptic membrane, where they inhibit adenyl cyclase through an inhibitory G protein. D_1 receptors are also located in the postsynaptic membrane, where they stimulate adenyl cyclase. Dopamine receptor antagonists have a high affinity for the D_{2a} and D_{2b} receptors. In contrast, the serotonin-dopamine antagonists have a relatively lower affinity for D_2 receptors and variously higher affinities for D_1, D_3, and D_4 receptors. *AC,* adenyl cyclase; *ATP,* adenosine triphosphate; *Ca^{2+}*, calcium ion; *cAMP,* cyclic adenosine monophosphate; *DAG,* diacylglycerol; *IP_3,* inositol triphosphate; *PiP_2,* phosphoinositide diphosphate; *PKC,* protein kinase C. (Reprinted with permission from Kandel ER: Disorders of thought: Schizophrenia. In *Principles of Neural Science,* ed 3, ER Kandel, JH Schwartz, TM Jessell, editors, p 861. Elsevier, New York, 1991. Copyright ©1996 by Appleton and Lange.)

effects on organs and systems in addition to the effect on the brain. Perhaps the most significant effects involve the heart and the vascular system. Many dopamine receptor antagonist drugs, particularly the low-potency drugs, decrease cardiac contractility, increase atrial and ventricular conduction times, and increase the length of refractory periods. The α_1-adrenergic antagonist activity can result in vasodilation and orthostatic (postural) hypotension. The major effect on the gastrointestinal system is mediated by the drugs' blockade of muscarinic cholinergic receptors, which results in dry mouth and constipation, especially for clozapine and the low-potency drugs. The dopamine receptor antagonist drugs as a class can have various effects on the skin (for example, rashes, photosensitivities, and discoloring), although these effects are uncommon. A transient decrease in leukopoiesis occurs as a common result of dopamine receptor antagonist treatment. Chlorpromazine has weak diuretic effects, but the predominant genitourinary effects are those affecting sexual function. The effects on sexual function are mediated primarily through the resulting imbalances in adrenergic and cholinergic activities, decreases in catecholamine activity, and endocrine effects of the dopamine receptor antagonists (for example, increased prolactin).

THERAPEUTIC INDICATIONS

The controlled clinical trials that were conducted to demonstrate the efficacy of antipsychotic drugs set a high standard of design for clinical trials in general. Beginning in the 1950s and the 1960s, the trials were conducted by using double-blind, placebo-controlled, parallel-group, randomized designs. These design features usually result in the most compelling data about the efficacy or the lack of efficacy of a compound, and literally hundreds of such well-controlled studies have demonstrated the efficacy of antipsychotic compounds for the treatment of schizophrenia and other psychotic conditions.

Idiopathic Psychoses

The idiopathic psychoses include those in the fourth edition of *Diagnostic and Statistical Manual of Mental Disorders* (DSM-IV) that have no known cause. These disorders include schizophrenia, schizophreniform disorder, schizoaffective disorder, delusional disorder, brief psychotic disorder, manic episodes, and major depressive disorder with psychotic features. Antipsychotic drugs are effective in both short-term and long-term management of these conditions; that is, antipsychotics both reduce acute symptoms and prevent future exacerbations.

Schizophrenia. The short-term efficacy of dopamine receptor antagonists in the treatment of schizophrenia has been demonstrated in hundreds of trials. The comparatively small number of trials that failed to demonstrate the superiority of the dopamine receptor antagonists over a placebo almost always used dosages of a dopamine receptor antagonist that were too low (less than 300 mg chlorpromazine equivalence), or the studies were not rigorously designed in the first place. Similarly, dozens of well-controlled studies have demonstrated the efficacy of dopamine receptor antagonist drugs in the maintenance treatment of psychotic patients. One survey of these studies found that about 75 percent of all patients with schizophrenia had a relapse over the course of 1 year if treated with a placebo, in comparison with only 15 to 25 percent of patients who had a relapse after being treated with dopamine receptor antagonist drugs. Furthermore, the severity of the symptoms during the relapses were less severe in patients receiving maintenance treatment than in those not receiving antipsychotic treatment.

In general, the dopamine receptor antagonists are thought to be more effective in the treatment of positive symptoms (for example, hallucinations, delusions, and agitation) than in the treatment of negative symptoms (for example, emotional withdrawal and ambivalence). A debate continues about this belief, because the dopamine receptor antagonist drugs themselves may contribute to the negative symptoms. It is also generally believed that paranoid patients are more responsive than nonparanoid patients, that so-called reactive psychoses are more responsive than so-called process psychoses, and that female patients are more responsive than male patients. Some patients do not respond to any dopamine receptor antagonist drugs, and these patients are often referred to as treatment resistant. Clozapine has been approved by the Food and Drug Administration (FDA) for the treatment of such patients, and all the serotonin-dopamine antagonists may improve such patients. The latter drugs also have been demonstrated to improve negative as well as positive symptoms.

Other Idiopathic Psychoses. Dopamine receptor antagonists are often used in combination with antimanic drugs to treat psychosis or manic excitement in bipolar I disorder. Although lithium (Eskalith), carbamazepine (Tegretol), and valproate (Depakene) are the drugs of choice for this condition, these drugs generally have a slower onset of action than do dopamine receptor antagonists in the treatment of acute symptoms. Thus, the general practice is to use combination therapy at the initiation of treatment and to gradually withdraw the dopamine receptor antagonist after the antimanic agent has reached its onset of activity.

Combination treatment with an antipsychotic and an antidepressant is the treatment of choice for major depressive disorder with psychotic features, although electroconvulsive therapy is also likely to be effective. Because of the potential adverse effects of long-term administration of the dopamine receptor antagonists (for example, tardive dyskinesia with long-term treatment), maintenance treatment with these drugs is indicated primarily for schizophrenia and not for the mood disorders.

Patients with schizoaffective disorder and delusional disorder often respond favorably to treatment with dopamine receptor antagonist drugs. Some patients with borderline personality disorder who have marked psychotic symptoms as part of their disorder are also at least partially responsive to dopamine receptor antagonist drugs, although these patients in particular also require psychotherapeutic treatment.

Secondary Psychoses

Secondary psychoses are psychotic syndromes that are associated with an identified organic cause, such as a brain tumor, a dementing disorder (for example, dementia of the Alzheimer's type), Huntington's disease, or substance abuse. The dopamine receptor antagonist drugs are generally effective in the treatment of psychotic symptoms that are associated with these syndromes. The high-potency dopamine receptor antagonists are usually safer than the low-potency dopamine receptor antagonists for such patients because of the high-potency drugs' lower cardiotoxic, epileptogenic, and anticholinergic activities. Dopamine receptor antagonist drugs should not be used to treat withdrawal symptoms associated with ethanol or barbiturates because of the risk that such treatment will facilitate the development of withdrawal seizures. The drug of choice in such cases is usually a benzodiazepine. Agitation and psychosis associated with such neurological conditions as dementia of the Alzheimer's type are responsive to antipsychotic treatment; high-potency drugs and low dosages are generally preferable. Even with high-potency drugs, as many as 25 percent of elderly patients may experience episodes of hypotension. Low dosages of high-potency drugs, such as 0.5 to 5 mg a day of haloperidol, are usually sufficient for the treatment of these patients, although thioridazine 10 to 50 mg a day is also used because of its particularly potent sedative properties.

Severe Agitation and Violent Behavior

Antipsychotic drugs are commonly used to treat patients who are severely agitated and violent, although other drugs, such as benzodiazepines and barbiturates, are also usually effective for the immediate control of such behavior. Symptoms such as extreme irritability, lack of impulse control, severe hostility, gross hyperactivity, and agitation are responsive to short-term antipsychotic treatment. The long-term use of dopamine receptor antagonist drugs for these indications must be weighed against the risk for adverse neurological effects (for example, tardive dyskinesia), although the advent of new antipsychotic drugs, such as the serotonin-dopamine antagonists, may affect the risk–benefit consideration in some instances. Mentally handicapped children, especially those with profound mental retardation and autistic disorder, often have associated episodes of violence, aggression, and agitation, which are responsive to treatment with antipsychotic drugs. Again, the risk of the dopamine receptor antagonist drugs must be considered before instituting long-term treatment, and the potentially low risk of the new antipsychotic drugs will have to be evaluated in subsequent clinical trials. In general, the use of the high-potency dopamine receptor antagonists, which cause little sedation, is preferred to the use of the more sedating low-potency drugs. Also, especially for long-term treatment, drugs such as lithium, the anticonvulsants (carbamazepine and valproate), the β-adrenergic receptor antagonists, and even serotonergic drugs should be considered before long-term treatment with dopamine receptor antagonist drugs is undertaken.

Movement Disorders

Both the psychosis and the movement disorder of Huntington's disease are responsive to treatment with dopamine receptor antagonists such as haloperidol. Clinical trials of serotonin-dopamine antagonists in patients with Huntington's disease have not yet been conducted, although such trials may show these drugs' superior efficacy, safety, or tolerability in the condition.

One dopamine receptor antagonist drug, pimozide, is specifically approved in the United States for the treatment of the motor and vocal tics of Tourette's disorder, although haloperidol is probably as frequently used, and other dopamine receptor antagonists are likely to be equally effective. Many experts prefer clonidine for this indication because of the lower risk of adverse neurological effects. Early clinical experience with the use of serotonin-dopamine antagonists for Tourette's disorder is promising, and controlled trials are needed. Pimozide is used for Tourette's disorder because of its alleged association with few EPS, although pimozide has its own adverse effects, such as marked prolongation of the QT interval of the electrocardiogram (ECG) in dosages over 10 mg a day and an increased risk for drug-induced seizures in dosages of 20 mg a day. Because of its prolongation of the QT interval, pimozide is not used as a first-line agent for Tourette's disorder, and it has recently been contraindicated by the FDA for concomitant use with macrolide antibiotics, such as erythromycin (E-Mycin), clarithromycin (Biaxin), azithromycin (Zithromax), and dirithromycin (Dynabac).

The rare neurological disorders ballismus and hemiballismus (which affects only one side of the body) are characterized by propulsive movements of the limbs away from the body. They are also responsive to treatment with dopamine receptor antagonists.

Other Psychiatric and Nonpsychiatric Indications

The use of thioridazine for the treatment of depression with marked anxiety or agitation has been approved in the United States, although this indication is outdated because of the availability of drugs with superior efficacy and safety profiles. Nevertheless, some clinicians use small dosages of dopamine receptor antagonist drugs (0.5 mg of haloperidol or 25 mg of chlorpromazine 2 or 3 times daily) to treat severe anxiety. The risk of inducing adverse neurological effects must be carefully weighed against the potential therapeutic benefits in such cases. The agitated behavior of people with autism may respond to high-potency dopamine receptor antagonists. The dopamine receptor antagonists are also sometimes used as adjuvants to treatment regimens for chronic pain disorder, although the use of the drugs for this indication should generally be done only by specialists in the treatment of chronic pain. Miscellaneous indications for the use of dopamine receptor antagonists include the treatment of nausea, emesis, hiccups, and pruritus.

PRECAUTIONS AND ADVERSE REACTIONS

One generalization about the adverse effects of dopamine receptor antagonists is that low-potency drugs cause most nonneurological adverse effects and high-potency drugs cause most neurological extrapyramidal adverse events (Table 35.3.16–1).

Nonneurological Adverse Effects

Cardiac Effects. Low-potency dopamine receptor antagonists are more cardiotoxic than are high-potency dopamine receptor antagonists. Chlorpromazine causes prolongation of the QT and PR intervals, blunting of the T waves, and depression of the ST segment. Thioridazine, in particular, has marked effects on the T wave and is associated with malignant arrhythmias, such as torsade de pointes, perhaps explaining why overdoses of piperidine phenothiazines may be the most lethal of this group of drugs. When QT intervals exceed 0.44 ms, there is some correlation with an increased risk for sudden death, possibly secondary to ventricular tachycardia or ventricular fibrillation.

Sudden Death. The cardiac effects of dopamine receptor antagonists have been hypothesized to be related to sudden

Table 35.3.16–1
Antipsychotic Drugs: Potencies and Adverse Effect Profiles

Drug	Potency (Approximate dose equivalent [mg])	Sedative Effect	Hypotensive Effect	Anticholinergic Effect	Extrapyramidal Effect
Phenothiazines					
Aliphatic					
Chlorpromazine (Thorazine)	100–low	High	High	Medium	Low
Piperidines					
Mesoridazine (Serentil)	50–low	Medium	Medium	Medium	Medium
Thioridazine (Mellaril)	95–low	High	High	High	Low
Piperazines					
Fluphenazine (Prolixin, Permitil)	2–high	Medium	Low	Low	High
Perphenazine (Trilafon)	8–medium	Low	Low	Low	High
Trifluoperazine (Stelazine)	5–high	Medium	Low	Low	High
Thioxanthene					
Thiothixene (Navane)	5–high	Low	Low	Low	High
Dibenzodiazepines					
Loxapine (Loxitane)	10–medium	Medium	Medium	Medium	High
Butyrophenones					
Droperidol (Inapsine—injection only)	10–medium	Low	Low	Low	High
Haloperidol (Haldol)	2–high	Low	Low	Low	High
Indolone					
Molindone (Moban)	10–medium	Medium	Low	Medium	High
Diphenylbutylpiperidine					
Pimozide (Orap)	1–high	Low	Low	Low	High
Benzamide					
Sulpiride (Dogmatil)	60–low	Medium	Low	Low	Medium

Adapted from Hyman SE, Arana GW, Rosenbaum JF: *Handbook of Psychiatric Drug Therapy*, ed 3, p 8. Little, Brown, Boston, 1996.

death in patients treated with the drugs. But careful evaluation of the literature indicates that it is premature to attribute the sudden deaths to the dopamine receptor antagonist drugs used alone. Supporting this view is the observation that the introduction of dopamine receptor antagonists had no effect on the incidence of sudden death in patients with schizophrenia. In addition, both low-potency and high-potency drugs were involved in the reported cases. Furthermore, many reports were of patients with other medical problems who were also treated with several other drugs. Pimozide prolongs the QT interval, an effect that is potentiated during concomitant administration of macrolide antibiotics, which inhibit the metabolism of pimozide by the hepatic enzyme CYP 3A3/4. At least 2 deaths have been attributed to cardiotoxicity as a result of simultaneous administration of pimozide and clarithromycin. The FDA has therefore recently contraindicated the use of pimozide with clarithromycin, erythromycin, azithromycin, and dirithromycin.

Orthostatic (Postural) Hypotension. Orthostatic (postural) hypotension is mediated by adrenergic blockade and is most common with low-potency dopamine receptor antagonists, particularly chlorpromazine, thioridazine, chlorprothixene, and clozapine. It occurs most frequently during the first few days of treatment, and tolerance is rapidly developed for the adverse effects. The chief dangers of orthostatic hypotension are that the patients may faint, fall, and injure themselves, although such occurrences are uncommon.

When using intramuscular (IM) low-potency dopamine receptor antagonists, clinicians should measure patients' blood pressure (lying and standing) before and after the first dose and during the first few days of treatment. When appropriate, patients should be warned of the possibility of fainting and should be given the usual instructions to rise from bed gradually, sit at first with their legs dangling, wait for a minute, and sit or lie down if they feel faint. Support hose may help some patients. Patients with orthostatic hypotension should avoid caffeine, drink at least 2 liters of fluid per day, and add salt to food, if they are not already hypertensive.

If hypotension does occur in patients receiving the medications, the symptoms can usually be managed by having the patients lie down with the feet higher than the head. On rare occasions, volume expansion or vasopressor agents, such as norepinephrine (Levophed), may be indicated. Because hypotension is produced by α-adrenergic blockade, the drugs also block the α-adrenergic stimulating properties of epinephrine and leave the β-adrenergic stimulating effects untouched. Therefore, the administration of epinephrine results in a paradoxical worsening of hypotension and is contraindicated in cases of dopamine receptor antagonist-induced hypotension. Pure α-adrenergic pressor agents, such as metaraminol (Aramine) and norepinephrine, are the drugs of choice in the treatment of the disorder.

Hematological Effects. An often transient leukopenia with a white blood cell (WBC) count around 3,500 is a common but not serious problem. A life-threatening hematological problem is agranulocytosis, which occurs most often with chlorpromazine and thioridazine use, but is seen with almost all dopamine receptor antagonists. Agranulocytosis occurs most frequently during the first 3 months of treatment and with an incidence of around 1 in 10,000 patients treated with dopamine receptor antagonists. Routine complete blood counts (CBCs) are not indicated, but if a patient reports a sore throat and fever, a CBC should be done immediately to check for the possibility. If the blood indexes are low, the dopamine receptor antagonist should be stopped, and the patient should be transferred to a medical facility. The mortality rate for the complication may be as high as 30 percent. Thrombocytopenic or nonthrombocytopenic purpura, hemolytic anemias, and pancytopenia may occur rarely in patients treated with dopamine receptor antagonists.

Peripheral Anticholinergic Effects. Peripheral anticholinergic effects are common and consist of dry mouth and nose, blurred vision, constipation, urinary retention, and mydriasis. Some patients also have nausea and vomiting. Chlorpromazine, thioridazine, mesoridazine (Serentil), and loxapine (Loxitane) are potent anticholinergics (see Table 35.3.16–1). Anticholinergic effects can be particularly severe if a low-potency dopamine receptor antagonist is used with a tricyclic drug and an anticholinergic drug; such a practice is seldom warranted.

Dry mouth can be a troubling symptom for some patients and can endanger continued compliance. Patients can be advised to rinse out their mouths frequently with water and not to chew gum or candy containing sugar, which can result in fungal infections of the mouth or an increased incidence of dental caries. Constipation should be treated with the usual laxative preparations, but the condition can still progress to paralytic ileus in some patients. A decrease in the dopamine receptor antagonist dosage or a change to another less anticholinergic drug is warranted in such a case. Pilocarpine may be used to treat paralytic ileus, although the relief is only transitory. Bethanechol (Urecholine) (20 to 40 mg a day) may be useful in some patients with urinary retention.

Endocrine Effects. Blockade of the dopamine receptors in the tuberoinfundibular tract results in the increased secretion of prolactin, which can result in breast enlargement, galactorrhea, impotence in men, and amenorrhea and inhibited orgasm in women. The serotonin-dopamine antagonists, in contrast, are not particularly associated with an increase in prolactin levels and may be the drug of choice for patients in whom increased prolactin release results in disturbing effects.

Sexual Side Effects. Psychiatrists may not find out about the disturbing sexual effects of a dopamine receptor antagonist if they do not specifically ask about the effects. The incidence of these effects is believed to be significantly underestimated. As many as 50 percent of men taking dopamine receptor antagonists may experience impotence. Several reports have stated that treatment of the condition with bromocriptine (Parlodel) or yohimbine (Yocon) is successful in some patients, although the risk of exacerbating the underlying psychosis must be considered with both drugs. Both men and women taking dopamine receptor antagonists can experience anorgasmia and decreased libido. Thioridazine is particularly associated with decreased libido and retrograde ejaculation in men. The latter is harmless, but patients should be advised that voiding after orgasm may be characterized by milky-white urine. Other dopamine receptor antagonists have been associated with both delayed and retrograde ejaculation, although some therapeutic success has been reported after treatment with brompheniramine, ephedrine, phenylpropanolamine, and imipramine (Tofranil) for the condition. Priapism and reports of painful orgasms have also been described, both of which possibly result from α_1-adrenergic antagonist activity.

Weight Gain. A common adverse effect of treatment with dopamine receptor antagonists is weight gain, which can be significant in some cases. Molindone and, perhaps, loxapine are not associated with the symptom and may be indicated with patients for whom weight gain is a serious health hazard or a reason for noncompliance.

Dermatological Effects. Allergic dermatitis and photosensitivity occur in a small percentage of patients, most commonly in those taking low-potency drugs, particularly chlorpromazine. A variety of skin eruptions—urticarial, maculopapular, petechial, and edematous—have been reported. The eruptions occur early in treatment, generally in the first few weeks, and remit spontaneously. A photosensitivity reaction that resembles a severe sunburn also occurs in some patients taking chlorpromazine. Patients should be warned of this adverse effect, should spend no more that 30 to 60 minutes in the sun, and should use sunscreens. Chlorpromazine is also associated with some cases of a blue-gray discoloration of the skin over areas exposed to sunlight. The skin changes often begin with a tan or golden brown color and progress to such colors as slate gray, metallic blue, and purple.

Ophthalmological Effects. Thioridazine is associated with irreversible pigmentation of the retina when given in dosages of more than 800 mg a day. An early symptom of this effect can sometimes be nocturnal confusion related to difficulty with night vision. The pigmentation is similar to that seen in retinitis pigmentosa; it can progress even after the thioridazine is stopped and can finally result in blindness. The pigmentation is not reversible.

In contrast, chlorpromazine is associated with a relatively benign pigmentation of the eyes, characterized by whitish-brown granular deposits concentrated in the anterior lens and posterior cornea and visible only by slit-lens examination. The deposits can progress to opaque white and yellow-brown granules, often stellate. Occasionally, the conjunctiva is discolored by a brown pigment. Retinal damage does not occur in the patients, and their vision is almost never impaired. Most patients who show the deposits are those who have ingested 1 to 3 kg of chlorpromazine throughout their lives.

Jaundice. Obstructive or cholestatic jaundice is associated as a rare adverse effect with dopamine receptor antagonist treatment. The adverse effect usually occurs in the first month of treatment and is heralded by symptoms of upper abdominal pain, nausea and vomiting, a flulike syndrome, fever, rash, eosinophilia, bilirubin in the urine, and increase in serum bil-

pain, nausea and vomiting, a flulike syndrome, fever, rash, eosinophilia, bilirubin in the urine, and increase in serum bilirubin, alkaline phosphatase, and hepatic transaminases. In the early days of chlorpromazine treatment, jaundice was not unusual, and occurred in about 1 of every 100 patients treated. For the past decade, the incidence has hovered around 1 in 1,000. The drop in the incidence is perhaps caused by a reduction in impurities in the manufacturing of the compound, although the definitive reason for the drop in incidence is unknown.

If jaundice occurs, clinicians generally discontinue the medication, although the value of this practice has never been proved. Indeed, patients have continued to receive chlorpromazine throughout the illness without adverse effects, although this approach seems unwarranted in view of the wide range of alternative treatments available. Jaundice has also been reported to occur with promazine, thioridazine, and prochlorperazine (Compazine) and very rarely with fluphenazine and trifluoperazine. No convincing evidence indicates that haloperidol or many of the other nonphenothiazine dopamine receptor antagonists can produce jaundice.

Overdoses of Antipsychotics. The symptoms of dopamine receptor antagonist overdose include EPS, mydriasis, decreased deep tendon reflexes, tachycardia, and hypotension. With the exception of overdoses of thioridazine and mesoridazine, the outcome of dopamine receptor antagonist overdose is generally favorable unless a patient has also ingested other CNS depressants, such as alcohol and benzodiazepines. The severe symptoms of overdose include delirium, coma, respiratory depression, and seizures. Haloperidol may be among the safest dopamine receptor antagonists in overdose. After an overdose, the electroencephalogram (EEG) shows diffuse slowing and low voltage. The piperazine phenothiazines (for example, thioridazine) can lead to heart block and ventricular fibrillation and can result in death.

The treatment of dopamine receptor antagonist overdose should include the use of activated charcoal, if possible, and gastric lavage. The use of emetics is not indicated, as the antiemetic actions of the dopamine receptor antagonists inhibit their efficacy. Seizures can be treated with IV diazepam (Valium) or phenytoin (Dilantin). Hypotension can be treated with either norepinephrine or dopamine (Dopastat) but not epinephrine (Adrenalin).

Neurological Adverse Effects

The dopamine receptor antagonist drugs, especially the typical or old ones, are associated with a number of uncomfortable neurological adverse effects and several potentially serious neurological adverse effects. Many of the neurological adverse effects are severe enough to warrant attention as separate problems that require their own treatment plans. The recognition that the treatment-emergent adverse effects are of significant clinical importance is reflected in DSM-IV by the inclusion of a separate group of medication-induced movement disorders (Table 35.3.16–2). The common occurrence of uncomfortable neurological adverse effects—particularly parkinsonism, tremor, akathisia, and dystonia—prompted the search for new antipsychotic drugs that are not likely to cause medication-induced movement disorders. The serotonin-dopamine antagonists are less likely than the dopamine receptor antagonists drugs to cause these movement disorders. Of the side effects next described, for example, only akathisia is significantly more common in patients treated with serotonin-dopamine antagonists than in patients treated with placebo.

Table 35.3.16–2
DSM-IV Medication-Induced Movement Disorders

Neuroleptic-induced parkinsonism
Neuroleptic malignant syndrome
Neuroleptic-induced acute dystonia
Neuroleptic-induced acute akathisia
Neuroleptic-induced tardive dyskinesia
Medication-induced postural tremor
Medication-induced movement disorder not otherwise specified

Neuroleptic-Induced Parkinsonism. Parkinsonian adverse effects occur in about 15 percent of patients who are treated with dopamine receptor antagonists, usually in 5 to 90 days of the initiation of treatment. Symptoms include muscle stiffness (lead-pipe rigidity), cogwheel rigidity, shuffling gait, stooped posture, and drooling. The pill-rolling tremor of idiopathic parkinsonism is rare, but a regular, coarse tremor similar to essential tremor may be present and is referred to as medication-induced postural tremor in DSM-IV. A focal, perioral tremor, sometimes referred to as rabbit syndrome (a term that is best avoided because of its insensitive comparison between the movement disorder and the masticatory movements of a rabbit), is another parkinsonian effect of dopamine receptor antagonists, although perioral tremor is more likely than other tremors to occur late in the course of treatment. A physical sign of parkinsonism is a positive glabella tap reflex, elicited by tapping the forehead between the eyebrows. Normal subjects habituate to the tap to the extent that they no longer blink after a couple of taps. A positive glabellar sign consists of continuous blinking in response to repeated taps. The mask-like facies, bradykinesia, akinesia (lack of initiative), and ataraxia (indifference toward the environment) that are also symptoms of the parkinsonian syndrome are often misdiagnosed as being part of the negative or deficit symptom picture of schizophrenia. This misdiagnosis results in the incorrect clinical decision not to attempt to treat the symptoms with anticholinergic drugs or similarly effective drugs for the treatment of neuroleptic-induced movement disorders.

Women are affected by neuroleptic-induced parkinsonism about twice as often as men; the disorder can occur at all ages, although it is most common after age 40. All dopamine receptor antagonists can cause the symptoms, especially high-potency drugs with low anticholinergic activity. Chlorpromazine and thioridazine are not likely to be involved. The blockade of dopaminergic transmission in the nigrostriatal tract is the cause of neuroleptic-induced parkinsonism. The differential diagnosis of the parkinsonian symptoms should include idio-

Table 35.3.16–3
Drug Treatment of Extrapyramidal Disorders

Generic Name	Trade Name	Usual Daily Dosage	Indications
Anticholinergic			
Benztropine	Cogentin	PO 1–4 mg bid; IM or IV 1–2 mg	Acute dystonic reaction, parkinsonism, akinesia, akathisia
Biperiden	Akineton	PO 2–6 mg tid; IM or IV 2 mg	
Procyclidine	Kemadrin	PO 2.5–5 mg bid-qid	
Trihexyphenidyl	Artane, Tremin, Pipanol	PO 2–5 mg tid	
Orphenadrine	Norflex	PO 50–100 mg bid; IV 60 mg	
Antihistaminergic			
Diphenhydramine	Benadryl	PO 25 mg qid; IM or IV 25 mg	Acute dystonic reaction, parkinsonism, akinesia, rabbit syndrome
Dopamine agonists			
Amantadine	Symmetrel	PO 100–200 mg bid (max 300 mg)	Parkinsonism, akinesia, rabbit syndrome
β-Adrenergic antagonists			
Propranolol	Inderal	PO 20–40 mg tid	Akathisia, tremor
α-Adrenergic antagonists			
Clonidine	Catapres	PO 0.1 mg tid	Akathisia
Benzodiazepines			
Clonazepam	Klonopin	PO 1 mg bid	Akathisia, acute dystonic reactions
Lorazepam	Ativan	PO 1 mg tid	

pathic parkinsonism, other organic causes of parkinsonism, and depression, which can also be associated with parkinsonian symptoms.

The disorder can be treated with anticholinergic agents such as benztropine (Cogentin), amantadine (Symmetrel), or diphenhydramine (Benadryl). Although amantadine may have fewer adverse effects than do anticholinergics, it may be less effective at reducing muscular rigidity. Anticholinergics should be withdrawn after 4 to 6 weeks to assess whether a patient has developed a tolerance for the parkinsonian effects; about 50 percent of patients with neuroleptic-induced parkinsonism need continued treatment. Even after the dopamine receptor antagonists are withdrawn, parkinsonian symptoms may last up to 2 weeks and even up to 3 months in elderly patients. With such patients, clinicians may continue the anticholinergic drug after stopping the dopamine receptor antagonist until the parkinsonian symptoms have completely resolved.

Neuroleptic-Induced Acute Dystonia. About 10 percent of all patients experience dystonia as an adverse effect of dopamine receptor antagonists, usually in the first few hours or days of treatment. Dystonic movements result from a slow, sustained muscular contraction or spasm that can result in an involuntary movement. Dystonia can involve the neck (spasmodic torticollis or retrocollis), the jaw (forced opening resulting in a dislocation of the jaw or trismus), the tongue (protrusions, twisting), and the entire body (opisthotonos). Involvement of the eyes can result in an oculogyric crisis, characterized by the eyes' upward lateral movement. Unlike other types of dystonia, an oculogyric crisis may also occur late in treatment. Other dystonias include blepharospasm and glossopharyngeal dystonia, which can result in dysarthria, dysphagia, and even trouble in breathing, which can cause cyanosis. Children are particularly likely to evidence opisthotonos, scoliosis, lordosis, and writhing movements. Dystonia can be painful and frightening and often results in noncompliance with the drug treatment regimen.

Dystonia is most common in young men (less than 40 years old) but can occur at any age in either sex. Although it is most common with IM dosages of high-potency dopamine receptor antagonists, dystonia can occur with any dopamine receptor antagonist. The mechanism of action is thought to be the dopaminergic hyperactivity in the basal ganglia that occurs when the CNS levels of the dopamine receptor antagonist drug begin to fall between doses. Dystonia can fluctuate spontaneously, can respond to reassurance, and can result in a clinician's false impression that the movement is hysterical or completely under conscious control. The differential diagnosis of a dystonic movement should include seizures and tardive dyskinesia.

Prophylaxis with anticholinergics or related drugs (Table 35.3.16–3) usually prevents the development of dystonia, although the risks of prophylactic treatment weigh against this benefit. Treatment with IM anticholinergics or IV or IM diphenhydramine (50 mg) almost always relieves the symptoms. Diazepam (10 mg IV), amobarbital (Amytal), caffeine sodium benzoate, and hypnosis have also been reported to be effective. Although tolerance for the adverse effect usually develops, it is sometimes prudent to change the dopamine receptor antagonist if a patient is particularly concerned that the reaction may recur.

Neuroleptic-Induced Acute Akathisia. Akathisia is a subjective feeling of muscular discomfort that can cause patients to be agitated, pace relentlessly, alternately sit and stand in rapid succession, and feel generally dysphoric. The symptoms are primarily motor and cannot be controlled by a patient's will. Akathisia can appear at any time during treatment. The disorder is probably underdiagnosed because the symptoms are mistakenly attributed to psychosis, agitation, or lack of cooperation. The mechanism underlying akathisia is poorly understood, although the disorder may represent an imbalance between the noradrenergic and dopaminergic systems caused by the dopamine receptor antagonists.

Once akathisia is recognized and diagnosed, the dopamine receptor antagonist dosage should be reduced to the minimal effective level. Treatment can be attempted with anticholinergics or amantadine, although these drugs are not particularly effective for akathisia. Drugs that may be more effective include propranolol (Inderal, 30 to 120 mg a day), benzodiazepines, and clonidine (Catapres). In some cases of akathisia, no treatment seems to be effective.

Neuroleptic-Induced Tardive Dyskinesia. The word *tardive,* like *tardy,* refers to *late.* Tardive dyskinesia is a delayed effect of antipsychotics; it rarely occurs until after 6 months of treatment. The disorder consists of abnormal, involuntary, irregular choreoathetoid movements of the muscles of the head, the limbs, and the trunk. The severity of the movements ranges from minimal—often missed by patients and their families—to grossly incapacitating. Perioral movements are the most common and include darting, twisting, and protruding movements of the tongue; chewing and lateral jaw movements; lip puckering; and facial grimacing. Finger movements and hand clenching are also common. Torticollis, retrocollis, trunk twisting, and pelvic thrusting occur in severe cases. Respiratory dyskinesia has also been reported. Dyskinesia is exacerbated by stress and disappears during sleep. Other late-appearing movement disorders have been noted and have been referred to, depending on the symptoms, as tardive dystonia, tardive parkinsonism, and tardive Tourette's disorder.

All of the dopamine receptor antagonists have been associated with tardive dyskinesia. Some data indicate that thioridazine is less associated with tardive dyskinesia than are the other dopamine receptor antagonists. The longer that patients take dopamine receptor antagonists, the more likely they are to experience tardive dyskinesia. About 10 to 20 percent of patients who are treated for more than 1 year have tardive dyskinesia. About 15 to 20 percent of long-term hospital patients have tardive dyskinesia. Women are more likely to be affected than are men, and patients more than 50 years of age, patients with brain damage, children, and patients with mood disorders are also at high risk. Before the introduction of antipsychotics in the early 1950s, 1 to 5 percent of patients with schizophrenia had similar abnormal movements. Thus the pattern of movement disorders can be related to the underlying pathophysiology of schizophrenia itself. Tardive dyskinesia may be caused by dopaminergic receptor supersensitivity in the basal ganglia resulting from chronic blockade of dopamine receptors by dopamine receptor antagonists.

The three basic approaches to tardive dyskinesia are prevention, diagnosis, and management. Prevention is best achieved by using dopamine receptor antagonist medications only when clearly indicated and in the lowest effective dosages. Early experience suggests that the serotonin-dopamine antagonists are associated with a lower risk for development of tardive dyskinesias than are the dopamine receptor antagonists. Patients who are receiving dopamine receptor antagonists should be examined regularly for the appearance of abnormal movements, preferably by using a standardized rating scale. When abnormal movements are detected, a differential diagnosis should be considered (Table 35.3.16–4).

Once a diagnosis of tardive dyskinesia is made, clinicians must regularly conduct objective ratings of the movement disorder. Although tardive dyskinesia often emerges while patients are taking a steady dosage of medication, it is even more likely to emerge when the dosage is reduced. Some investigators have referred to this effect as withdrawal dyskinesia, although differentiating withdrawal dyskinesia from tardive dyskinesia is impossible. Once tardive dyskinesia is recognized, clinicians should consider reducing the dosage of the dopamine receptor antagonist or even stopping the medication altogether. The serotonin-dopamine antagonists may be used in patients with tardive dyskinesias, since they reduce the movements and have the lowest risk of exacerbating the condition. Controlled trials to assess whether serotonin-dopamine antagonists are an effective treatment of tardive dyskinesia have not yet been reported.

When tardive dyskinesia was first recognized and until recently, the movement disorder was believed to be chronic and progressive. Recent surveys conclude that tardive dyskinesia develops rapidly, stabilizes, and then often remits, sometimes even when the patient continues the same drug treatment. Nonetheless, continuing the same drug does not seem necessary when potentially better drugs are available. Between 5 and 40 percent of all cases of tardive dyskinesia eventually remit, and between 50 and 90 percent of all mild cases remit; but tardive dyskinesia is less likely to remit in elderly patients than in young patients.

Tardive dyskinesia has no single effective treatment. Low-

Table 35.3.16–4
Differential Diagnosis for Tardive Dyskinesia-like Movements

Common: Schizophrenic mannerisms and stereotypies
- Dental problems (eg, ill-fitting dentures)
- Meige's syndrome and other senile dyskinesias

Drug-induced: Antidepressants
- Antihistamines
- Antimalarials
- Antipsychotics
- Diphenylhydantoin
- Heavy metals
- Levodopa
- Sympathomimetics

CNS: Anoxia-induced
- Hepatic failure
- Huntington's disease
- Parathyroid hypoactivity
- Postencephalitic
- Pregnancy (chorea gravidarum)
- Renal failure
- Sydenham's chorea
- Systemic lupus erythematosus
- Thyroid hyperactivity
- Torsion dystonia
- Tumors
- Wilson's disease

ering the dosage of the dopamine receptor antagonist and switching to a serotonin-dopamine antagonist are the primary treatment strategies. In patients who cannot continue taking any dopamine receptor antagonist medication, lithium, carbamazepine, or benzodiazepines may be effective in reducing both the movement disorder symptoms and the psychotic symptoms, although these drugs are less effective than are the dopamine receptor antagonists in treating the psychiatric symptoms. Various small studies have reported that cholinergic agonists and antagonists, dopaminergic agonists, and γ-aminobutyric acid (GABA)-ergic drugs—for example, valproic acid (Depakene)—may be helpful, although the use of these drugs should be considered experimental and should be started only after a review of the most recent literature.

Neuroleptic Malignant Syndrome. Neuroleptic malignant syndrome is a life-threatening complication that can occur any time during the course of dopamine receptor antagonist treatment. The motor and behavioral symptoms include muscular rigidity and dystonia, akinesia, mutism, obtundation, and agitation. The autonomic symptoms include hyperpyrexia (up to 107 F), sweating, and increased pulse and blood pressure. Laboratory findings include increased WBC count, creatinine phosphokinase, liver enzymes, plasma myoglobin, and myoglobinuria, occasionally associated with renal failure. The symptoms usually evolve over 24 to 72 hours, and the untreated syndrome lasts 10 to 14 days. The diagnosis is often missed in the early stages, and the withdrawal or agitation may mistakenly be considered to reflect increased psychosis. Men are affected more frequently than are women, and young patients are affected more commonly than elderly patients. The mortality rate can reach 20 to 30 percent or even higher when depot dopamine receptor antagonist medications are involved. The pathophysiology is unknown.

The first steps in treatment are the immediate discontinuation of dopamine receptor antagonist drugs, medical support to cool the patient, and the monitoring of vital signs, electrolytes, fluid balance, and renal output and the symptomatic treatment of fevers. Antiparkinsonian medications may reduce some of the muscle rigidity. Intravenous dantrolene (Dantrium), a skeletal muscle relaxant (0.8 to 2.5 mg/kg every 6 hours, up to a total dosage of 10 mg a day), may be useful in the treatment of the disorder. Once the patient can take oral medications, the dantrolene can be given in doses of 100 to 200 mg a day. Bromocriptine (20 to 30 mg a day in four divided doses) or perhaps amantadine can be added to the regimen. Treatment should usually be continued for 5 to 10 days. When dopamine receptor antagonist treatment is restarted, clinicians should consider switching to a low-potency drug or to a serotonin-dopamine antagonist, although neuroleptic malignant syndrome has also been reported to be associated with both clozapine and risperidone.

Epileptogenic Effects. Dopamine receptor antagonist administration is associated with a slowing and an increased synchronization of the EEG. This effect may be the mechanism by which some dopamine receptor antagonists decrease the seizure threshold. Chlorpromazine, loxapine, and other low-potency dopamine receptor antagonists are thought to be more epileptogenic than are high-potency drugs. Animal data and in vitro experimental data indicate that molindone may be the least epileptogenic of the dopamine receptor antagonist drugs. The risk of inducing a seizure by drug administration warrants consideration when a patient already has a seizure disorder or an organic brain lesion.

Sedation. Sedation is primarily a result of the blockade of histamine type 1 receptors. Chlorpromazine is the most sedating dopamine receptor antagonist; thioridazine, chlorprothixene, and loxapine are also sedating; the high-potency dopamine receptor antagonists are much less sedating than are these drugs (Table 35.3.16–1). When first treated with dopamine receptor antagonists, patients should be warned about driving and operating machinery. Giving the entire daily dopamine receptor antagonist dose at bedtime usually eliminates any problems with sedation, and tolerance for this adverse effect often develops.

Central Anticholinergic Effects. The symptoms of central anticholinergic activity include severe agitation; disorientation to time, person, and place; hallucinations; seizures; high fever; and dilated pupils. Stupor and coma may ensue. The treatment of anticholinergic toxicity consists of discontinuing the causal agent or agents, close medical supervision, and physostigmine (Antilirium, Eserine), 2 mg by slow IV infusion, repeated within 1 hour as necessary. Too much physostigmine is dangerous, and symptoms of physostigmine toxicity include hypersalivation and sweating. Atropine sulfate (0.5 mg) can reverse the effects of physostigmine toxicity.

Prevention and Treatment of Some Neuroleptic-Induced Movement Disorders. A variety of drugs (Table 35.3.16–3) may be used to prevent and treat medication-induced movement disorders, particularly neuroleptic-induced parkinsonism and neuroleptic-induced acute dystonia. The drugs include anticholinergics, amantadine, antihistamines, benzodiazepines, β-adrenergic receptor antagonists, and clonidine. Most acute dystonia and parkinsonism symptoms are effectively treated by these drugs, and acute akathisia may also respond in some cases.

It remains controversial whether prophylactic treatment with these drugs is warranted when starting a patient on dopamine receptor antagonist medications. The proponents of prophylactic treatment argue that the increased likelihood of avoiding adverse neurological effects is humane to the patient and increases the possibility of future compliance. The opponents of the practice argue that a large proportion (30 to 50 percent) of patients do not need antiparkinsonian drugs, that their use may increase the likelihood of tardive dyskinesia, autonomic side effects, cognitive impairment, hyperthermia, and anticholinergic toxicity. Many drugs used to treat parkinsonian symptoms also have some abuse liability and may be associated with changes in the plasma concentrations of the dopamine receptor antagonists. A reasonable compromise is to use the drugs prophylactically in patients under the age of 45 who are at risk for adverse effects, particularly dystonia, and not to use the drugs prophylactically in patients over 45 who are at increased risk for anticholinergic toxicity.

Once patients start taking drugs to treat a movement disorder, they should be treated for 4 to 6 weeks. Then clinicians should attempt to taper and stop the medication over a 1-month period. Many patients become tolerant for the neurological adverse effects and no longer require treatment for the neuroleptic-induced movement disorder. Some patients experience the return of neurological symptoms and should be restarted on the appropriate drugs.

Most clinicians use one of the anticholinergic drugs (such as benztropine) or diphenhydramine to provide prophylaxis or treatment of neurological adverse effects. Of these drugs, diphenhydramine is the most sedating; biperiden (Akineton) is neither sedating nor stimulating; and trihexyphenidyl (Artane) may be slightly stimulating. Amantadine is most often used when one of the anticholinergic drugs is ineffective. Although amantadine does not typically exacerbate the psychosis of schizophrenia, some patients become tolerant for its antiparkinsonian effects. Amantadine is also a sedating drug for some patients.

Pregnancy and Lactation

If possible, dopamine receptor antagonists should be avoided during pregnancy, particularly in the first trimester, unless the benefit outweighs the risk. In fact, however, very few data indicate a correlation between the presence of congenital malformations in infants and the use of dopamine receptor antagonists during pregnancy, except perhaps for chlorpromazine. Some data do indicate that the use of dopamine receptor antagonists during pregnancy may result in decreased dopamine receptors in the neonate, increased cholesterol, and perhaps behavioral disturbances. Nevertheless, dopamine receptor antagonist use in the second and third trimesters is probably relatively safe. High-potency dopamine receptor antagonists are preferable to low-potency drugs, as the low-potency drugs are associated with hypotension.

Haloperidol and phenothiazines pass into breast milk. Whether loxapine, molindone, and pimozide pass into breast milk is not known, although they probably do. Women who are taking dopamine receptor antagonists should not breastfeed their infants, as the available data do not prove that the practice is safe.

DRUG INTERACTIONS

Because of their many receptor effects and because of the metabolism of most of the dopamine receptor antagonists in the liver, many pharmacokinetic and pharmacodynamic drug interactions are associated with the drugs (Table 35.3.16–5).

Antacids

Antacids, cimetidine (Tagamet), ranitidine (Zantac), famotidine (Pepcid), and nizatidine (Axid), administered within 2 hours of dopamine receptor antagonist administration, can reduce the absorption of dopamine receptor antagonist drugs.

Anticholinergics

Anticholinergics may decrease the absorption of dopamine receptor antagonists. The additive anticholinergic activity of dopamine receptor antagonists, anticholinergics, and tricyclic drugs may result in anticholinergic toxicity.

Anticonvulsants

Phenothiazines, especially thioridazine, may decrease the metabolism of diphenylhydantoin and can result in toxic levels of diphenylhydantoin. Barbiturates may increase the metabolism of dopamine receptor antagonists, and the dopamine receptor antagonists may lower a patient's seizure threshold.

Antidepressants

Tricyclic drugs and dopamine receptor antagonists may decrease each other's metabolism and result in increased plasma concentrations of both drugs. The anticholinergic, sedative, and hypotensive effects of the drugs may also be additive. Haloperidol, perphenazine, thioridazine, and other dopamine receptor antagonists are metabolized by the hepatic enzyme CYP 2D6. Drugs that inhibit CYP 2D6, such as fluoxetine and paroxetine, may increase antipsychotic levels when administered concomitantly.

Antihypertensives

Dopamine receptor antagonists may inhibit the uptake of guanethidine (Esimil, Ismelin) in the synapse and may also inhibit the hypotensive effects of clonidine and methyldopa (Aldomet). Conversely, dopamine receptor antagonists may have an additive effect on some hypotensive drugs. Dopamine receptor antagonist drugs have a variable effect on the hypotensive effects of clonidine. Propranolol coadministration with dopamine receptor antagonists increases the blood concentrations of both drugs. Coadministration of captopril, hydralazine, minoxidil, opioids, trazodone, and tricyclics can worsen hypotension.

Central Nervous System Depressants

Dopamine receptor antagonists potentiate the CNS depressant effects of sedatives, antihistamines, opiates, opioids, and alcohol, particularly in patients with impaired respiratory status. When these agents are taken with alcohol, the risk for heat stroke may be increased.

Other Substances

Cigarette smoking may decrease the plasma levels of dopamine receptor antagonist drugs. Epinephrine has a paradoxical hypotensive effect in patients taking dopamine receptor antagonists. Dopamine receptor antagonist drugs may decrease the blood concentration of warfarin (Coumadin) and result in decreased bleeding time. Phenothiazines and pimozide should not be coadministered with other agents that prolong the QT interval, particularly macrolide antibiotics (for example, erythromycin, clarithromycin, azithromycin, and dirithromycin). Hydroxyzine may potentiate mesoridazine and thioridazine toxicity.

Table 35.3.16–5
Antipsychotic Drug Interactions

Interacting Medication	Mechanism	Clinical Effect
Drug interactions assessed to have major severity		
Anticholinergics	Pharmacodynamic effects Additive anticholinergic effect	Decreased antipsychotic effect Anticholinergic toxicity
Barbiturates	Phenobarbital induces antipsychotic metabolism	Decreased antipsychotic concentrations
β-Blockers	Synergistic pharmacologic effect; antipsychotic inhibits metabolism of propranolol; antipsychotic increases plasma concentrations	Severe hypotension
Carbamazepine	Induces antipsychotic metabolism	Up to 50% reduction in antipsychotic concentrations
Charcoal	Reduces GI absorption of antipsychotic and adsorbs drug during enterohepatic circulation	May reduce antipsychotic effect or cause toxicity when used during overdose or for GI disturbances
Cigarette smoking	Induction of microsomal enzymes	Reduced plasma concentrations of antipsychotic agents
Epinephrine, norepinephrine	Antipsychotic antagonizes pressor effect	Hypotension
Ethanol	Additive CNS depression	Impaired psychomotor skills
Fluvoxamine	Fluvoxamine inhibits metabolism of haloperidol and clozapine	Increased concentrations of haloperidol and clozapine
Guanethidine	Antipsychotic antagonizes guanethidine reuptake	Impaired antihypertensive effect
Lithium	Unknown	Rare reports of neurotoxicity
Meperidine	Additive CNS depression	Hypotension and sedation
Drug interactions assessed to have minor or moderate severity		
Amphetamines, anorexiants	Decreased pharmacologic effect of amphetamine; drug-disease state interaction	Diminished weight loss effect; amphetamines may exacerbate psychosis; treatment-refractory schizophrenics may improve
Angiotensin-converting enzyme inhibitors	Additive hypotensive crisis	Hypotension, postural intolerance
Antacids containing aluminum	Insoluble complex in GI tract formed	Possible reduced antipsychotic effect
Antidepressants (AD, nonspecific)	Decreased metabolism of AD through competitive inhibition	Increased AD concentration
Benzodiazepines	Increased pharmacological effect of the benzodiazepine	Respiratory depression, stupor, hypotension
Bromocriptine	Antipsychotic antagonizes dopamine receptor stimulation	Increased prolactin
Caffeinated beverages	Form precipitate with antipsychotic solutions	Possible diminished antipsychotic effect
Cimetidine	Reduced antipsychotic absorption and clearance	Decreased antipsychotic effect
Clonidine	Antipsychotic potentiates α-adrenergic hypotensive effect	Hypotension or hypertension
Disulfiram	Impairs antipsychotic metabolism	Increased antipsychotic concentrations
Methyldopa	Unknown	Blood pressure elevations
Phenytoin	Induction of antipsychotic metabolism; decreased phenytoin metabolism	Decreased antipsychotic concentrations; increased phenytoin levels
Serotonin-specific reuptake inhibitors	Impair antipsychotic metabolism; pharmacodynamic interaction	Sudden onset of extrapyramidal symptoms
Valproic acid	Antipsychotic inhibits valproic acid metabolism	Increased valproic acid half-life and levels

Adapted from Ereshefsky L, Overman GP, Karp JK: Current psychotropic dosing and monitoring guidelines. Prim Psychiatry *3:* 21, 1996.

LABORATORY INTERFERENCES

Dopamine receptor antagonist drugs have been reported to interfere with some laboratory tests. Chlorpromazine and perphenazine have been reported to cause both false-positive and false-negative results in immunological pregnancy tests and falsely elevated bilirubin (with reagent test strips) and urobilinogen (with Ehrlich's reagent test) values. Dopamine receptor antagonist drugs have also been associated with an abnormal shift in the glucose tolerance test, although this shift may reflect the effects of the drugs on the glucose-regulating system. Phenothiazines have been reported to interfere with the measurement of 17-ketosteroids (with the Haltorff-Koch modification of the Zimmerman reaction) and 17-hydroxycorticosteroids (with the modified Glenn-Nelson reaction).

DOSAGE AND ADMINISTRATION

Dopamine receptor antagonists may have a calming and sedating effect within 1 hour of administration, but improvement in the full range of positive psychotic symptoms usually appears within 1 to 2 weeks of onset of treatment, and a therapeutic trial in severely or chronically ill patients requires 6 weeks. Continuing improvement in symptoms is seen over the first 3 to 12 months of use. These drugs are remarkably safe in short-term use, and, if necessary, clinicians can administer

Table 35.3.16–6
Dopamine Receptor Antagonist Drugs, Trade Names, and Dosages

Generic Name	Trade Name	Usual Adult Dosage Range (mg per day)	Usual Single IM Dose (mg)
Phenothiazines			
Aliphatic			
Chlorpromazine	Thorazine	300–800	25–50
Triflupromazine	Vesprin	100–150	20–60
Promazine		40–800	50–150
Piperazine			
Prochlorperazine	Compazine	40–150	10–20
Perphenazine	Trilafon	8–40	5–10
Trifluoperazine	Stelazine	6–20	1–2
Fluphenazine	Prolixin, Permitil	1–20	2–5
Acetophenazine	Tindal	60–120	—
Butaperazine	Repoise (not sold in U.S.)	—	—
Carphenazine	Proketazine (not sold in U.S.)	—	—
Piperidine			
Thioridazine	Mellaril	200–700[a]	—
Mesoridazine	Serentil	75–300	25
Piperacetazine	Quide (not sold in U.S.)	—	—
Thioxanthene			
Thiothixene	Navane	6–30	2–4
Dibenzoxazepine			
Loxapine	Loxitane	60–100	—
Dihydroindole			
Molindone	Moban, Lidone	50–100	—
Butyrophenones			
Haloperidol	Haldol	6–20	2–5
Droperidol	Inapsine	—	—
Diphenylbutylpiperidine			
Pimozide	Orap	1–10[b]	—
Benzamide			
Sulpiride[c]	Dogmatil	60–low	600–1200

[a] Maximum 800 mg.
[b] Second-line drug because of cardiotoxicity.
[c] Not currently available in the United States; possible association with hematological toxicity.

the drugs without conducting a physical or laboratory examination of the patient. The major contraindications for dopamine receptor antagonists are a history of a serious allergic response, the possibility that the patient has ingested a substance that will interact with the antipsychotic to induce CNS depression (for example, alcohol, opiates, opioids, barbiturates, and benzodiazepines) or anticholinergic delirium (for example, scopolamine and possibly phencyclidine [PCP]), the presence of a severe cardiac abnormality, a high risk for seizures from organic and idiopathic causes, the presence of narrow-angle glaucoma or prostatic hypertrophy if dopamine receptor antagonist with high anticholinergic activity is to be used, and the presence or a history of tardive dyskinesia. Dopamine receptor antagonists should be administered with caution in patients with hepatic disease, as impaired hepatic metabolism may result in high plasma concentrations of the dopamine receptor antagonists. In the usual assessment, clinicians should obtain a CBC with white blood cell indexes, liver function tests, and an ECG, especially in women over 40 and men over 30. Older adults and children are more sensitive to adverse effects than are young adults; therefore, the dosage of the drug should be adjusted accordingly.

Choice of Drug

Although the potencies of the dopamine receptor antagonists vary widely (Table 35.3.16–6), all available typical dopamine receptor antagonists are equally efficacious in the treatment of schizophrenia. The dopamine receptor antagonists are available in a wide range of formulations and dose sizes (Table 35.3.16–7). Data support the conclusion that serotonin-dopamine antagonists may be more effective than other antipsychotic drugs for the treatment of the negative symptoms of schizophrenia. With the dopamine receptor antagonist drugs, no type of schizophrenia and no particular symptoms are most effectively treated by any single class of dopamine receptor

Table 35.3.16–7
Dopamine Receptor Antagonist Preparations

	Tablets	Capsules	Solution	Parenteral	Rectal Suppositories
Acetophenazine	20 mg	—	—	—	—
Chlorpromazine	10, 25, 50, 100, 200 mg	30, 75, 150, 200, 300 mg	10 mg/5 mL, 30 mg/mL, 100 mg/mL	25 mg/mL	25, 100 mg
Droperidol	—	—	—	2.5 mg/mL	—
Fluphenazine	1, 2.5, 5, 10 mg	—	2.5 mg/5 mL, 5 mg/mL	2.5 mg/mL (IM only)	—
Fluphenazine decanoate	—	—	—	25 mg/mL	—
Fluphenazine enanthate	—	—	—	25 mg/mL	—
Haloperidol	0.5, 1, 2, 10, 20 mg	—	2 mg/mL	5 mg/mL (IM only)	—
Haloperidol decanoate	—	—	—	50 mg/mL, 100 mg/mL (IM only)	—
Loxapine	—	5, 10, 25, 50 mg	25 mg/mL	50 mg/mL	—
Mesoridazine	10, 25, 50, 100 mg	—	25 mg/mL	25 mg/mL	—
Molindone	5, 10, 25, 50, 100 mg	—	20 mg/mL	—	—
Perphenazine	2, 4, 8, 16 mg	—	16 mg/5 mL	5 mg/mL	—
Pimozide	2 mg	—	—	—	—
Prochlorperazine	5, 10, 25 mg	10, 15, 30 mg (SR)	5 mg/5 mL	5 mg/mL	2.5, 5, 25 mg
Promazine	25, 50, 100 mg	—	—	25 mg/mL, 50 mg/mL	—
Thioridazine	10, 15, 25, 50, 100, 150, 200 mg	—	25 mg/5 mL, 100 mg/5 mL, 30 mg/mL, 100 mg/mL	—	—
Thiothixene	—	1, 2, 5, 10, 20 mg	5 mg/mL	10 mg (IM only), 2 mg/mL (IM only)	—
Trifluoperazine	1, 2, 5, 10 mg	—	10 mg/mL	2 mg/mL	—
Triflupromazine	—	—	—	10 mg/mL, 20 mg/mL	—

antagonists. The serotonin-dopamine antagonists may become the drug of first choice in the treatment of schizophrenia if their possibly superior efficacies with negative symptoms and their superior safety profiles are confirmed in wide clinical testing.

The general guidelines for choosing a particular psychotherapeutic drug should be followed when choosing a dopamine receptor antagonist drug (see Section 35.1). If no other rationale prevails, the choice should be based on adverse effect profiles and the clinician's preference. Although high-potency dopamine receptor antagonists are associated with increased neurological adverse effects, current clinical practice favors using them because of the high incidence of other adverse effects (for example, cardiac, hypotensive, epileptogenic, sexual, and allergic) with the low-potency drugs. A myth in psychiatry is that hyperexcitable patients respond best to chlorpromazine because it is highly sedating, whereas withdrawn patients respond best to high-potency dopamine receptor antagonists, such as fluphenazine. This myth has never been proved; if sedation is a desired goal, either the dopamine receptor antagonist can be given in divided doses or a sedative drug, such as a benzodiazepine, can also be administered.

The serotonin-dopamine antagonists offer many advantages over the dopamine receptor antagonists and have been increasingly chosen as first-line agents. The most prominent advantages of the serotonin-dopamine antagonists are their low risk of extrapyramidal symptoms and the therapeutic benefit for both positive and negative symptoms. Clozapine, olanzapine, and sertindole are less likely to raise prolactin levels than are dopamine receptor antagonists. Clozapine and olanzapine have significant anticholinergic effects, however, and may cause sedation. In the future, the dopamine receptor antagonists may be reserved for those patients who tolerate them with minimal adverse effects, for economic reasons, or for the fact that they are available in depot forms.

A clinical observation supported by some research is that a patient's unpleasant reaction to the first dose of a dopamine receptor antagonist drug correlates highly with future poor response and noncompliance. Such experiences include a subjective negative feeling, oversedation, and acute dystonia. If a patient reports such a reaction, the clinician may be well advised to switch the patient to a different antipsychotic. Similarly, if patients have reported that they did not feel well while taking a particular drug in the past, clinicians are well advised not to initiate treatment with this drug again.

Dosage and Schedule

The therapeutic index for dopamine receptor antagonists is favorable and has contributed to the unfortunate practice of routinely using high dosages of the drugs. Because of this common practice, physicians may be pressured by staff members to use very high dosages. Recent investigations of the dose–response curve for dopamine receptor antagonists indicate that the equivalent of 10 to 20 mg of haloperidol is usually efficacious for either short-term or long-term treatment of schizophrenia. Some clinicians and researchers recommend that dosages equivalent to 5 to 10 mg of haloperidol be used before going to higher dosages. Dopamine receptor antagonist drugs may have a bell-shaped dose–response curve. In general, the dosage of a dopamine receptor antagonist drug should be evaluated over a 6-week period before increasing the dosage or switching to another antipsychotic drug. Overly high dosages of dopamine receptor antagonists may lead to adverse neurological effects, such as akinesia and akathisia, which are difficult to distinguish from exacerbations of psychosis.

Although patients can build up a tolerance for most adverse effects caused by dopamine receptor antagonists, they do not build up a tolerance for the antipsychotic effect. Nevertheless, clinicians should taper the dosage when a drug is being discontinued, as patients may experience rebound effects from the other neurotransmitter systems that the drug may have blocked. Cholinergic rebound, for example, can produce a flulike syndrome in patients.

Short-Term Treatment. The equivalent of 5 to 10 mg of haloperidol is a reasonable dose for an adult patient in an acute state. A geriatric patient may benefit from as little as 1 mg of haloperidol. The administration of more than 50 mg of chlorpromazine in one injection may result in serious hypotension. IM administration of the dopamine receptor antagonists results in peak plasma levels in about 30 minutes versus 90 minutes with the oral route. Doses of dopamine receptor antagonists for IM administration are about half the doses given by the oral route. In a short-term treatment setting, patients should be observed for 1 hour after the first dose of dopamine receptor antagonist medication. After that time, most clinicians administer a second dose of a dopamine receptor antagonist or a sedative agent (for example, a benzodiazepine) to achieve effective behavioral control. Possible sedatives include lorazepam (Ativan, 2 mg IM) and amobarbital (50 to 250 mg IM).

RAPID NEUROLEPTIZATION. Rapid neuroleptization (also called psychotolysis) is the practice of administering hourly IM doses of dopamine receptor antagonist medications until marked sedation of a patient is achieved. Several research studies have shown, however, that merely waiting several more hours after one dose of a dopamine receptor antagonist results in the same clinical improvement as that occurring with repeated doses of dopamine receptor antagonists. Nevertheless, clinicians must be careful to keep patients from becoming violent while they are psychotic. Clinicians can help prevent violent episodes by the use of adjuvant sedatives or by temporarily using physical restraints until patients can control their behavior.

Early Treatment. Agitation and excitement are usually the first symptoms to improve with dopamine receptor antagonist treatment. In patients with a short history of illness, about 75 percent of them have significant improvement in their psychosis. In patients with a long history of illness, a full 6 weeks may be necessary to evaluate the extent of the improvement in psychotic symptoms. Data indicate that psychotic symptoms, both positive and negative, continue to improve 3 to 12 months after the initiation of treatment.

The equivalent of 10 to 20 mg of haloperidol or 400 mg of chlorpromazine a day is adequate treatment for most patients with schizophrenia. Some research studies indicate that, in a significant proportion of patients, 5 mg of haloperidol or 200 mg of chlorpromazine may, in fact, be just as effective as higher doses. It is a reasonable practice to give dopamine receptor antagonist drugs in divided doses when initiating treatment to minimize the peak plasma levels and to reduce the incidence of adverse effects. The total daily dose can subsequently be consolidated into a single daily dose after the first or second week of treatment. The single daily dose is usually given at bedtime to help induce sleep and to reduce the incidence of adverse effects. In elderly patients this practice may increase the risk of their falling if they get out of bed during the night. The sedative effects of dopamine receptor antagonists last only a few hours, in contrast to the antipsychotic effects, which last for 1 to 3 days.

GIVEN AS NEEDED MEDICATIONS. It is common clinical practice to order medications to be given as needed (PRN). Although this practice may be reasonable during the first few days that a patient is hospitalized, the amount of time the patient takes antipsychotic drugs, not an increase in dosage, is what produces therapeutic improvement. Clinicians may feel pressured by their staff members to write PRN antipsychotic orders. Such orders for PRN medications should include specific symptoms, how often the drugs should be given, and how many doses can be given each day. Clinicians may choose to use small doses for the PRN doses (for example, 2 mg haloperidol) or to use a benzodiazepine instead (for example, 2 mg lorazepam IM). If PRN doses of a dopamine receptor antagonist are necessary after the first week of treatment, the clinician may want to consider increasing the standing daily dosage of the drug.

Maintenance Treatment. The first 3 to 6 months after a psychotic episode are usually considered a period of stabilization for the patient. After that time, the dosage of the dopamine receptor antagonist can be decreased about 20 percent every 6 months until the minimum effective dosage is found. A patient is usually maintained on antipsychotic medications for 1 to 2 years after the first psychotic episode. Antipsychotic treatment is often continued for 5 years after a second psychotic episode, and lifetime maintenance is considered after the third psychotic episode, although attempts to reduce the daily dosage can be made every 6 to 12 months.

Dopamine receptor antagonist drugs are effective in controlling psychotic symptoms, but patients may report that they prefer being off the drugs, because they feel better without them. This problem may be less common with the new antipsychotic drugs, such as clozapine, risperidone, and olanzapine. Normal people who have taken dopamine receptor antagonist drugs report a sense of dysphoria. Clinicians must discuss maintenance medication with patients and take into account the patients' wishes, the severity of their illnesses, and the quality of their support systems.

Alternative Maintenance Regimens. Alternative maintenance regimens have been designed to reduce both the risk of long-term adverse effects and any unpleasantness associated with taking dopamine receptor antagonist medications. Intermittent medication is the use of antipsychotics only when patients require them. This arrangement requires that patients or their caretakers be both willing and able to watch carefully for early signs of clinical exacerbations. At the earliest signs of such problems, antipsychotic medications should be reinstituted for a reasonable period, usually 1 to 3 months. Although this treatment approach is not indicated for most patients, it is a safe and effective treatment approach for some.

Drug holidays are regular 2- to 7-day periods during which a patient is not given antipsychotic medications. Currently, no evidence indicates that drug holidays reduce the risk of long-term adverse effects from antipsychotics, and drug holidays may increase the incidence of noncompliance.

Long-Acting Depot Medications. Because some patients with schizophrenia do not comply with oral dopamine receptor antagonist regimens, long-acting depot preparations may be needed (Table 35.3.16–8). A clinician usually administers the IM preparations once every 1 to 4 weeks, and therefore immediately knows whether a patient has missed a dose of medication. Depot dopamine receptor antagonists may be associated with increased adverse effects, including tardive dyskinesia, although the data for this increased association are controversial. Some researchers and clinicians limit their use of depot dopamine receptor antagonists to those patients who are not compliant with oral medications; other researchers and clinicians, particularly in Europe, consider depot dopamine receptor antagonists the formulation of choice for the treatment of schizophrenia.

Two depot preparations (a decanoate and an enanthate) of fluphenazine and a decanoate preparation of haloperidol are available in the United States. The preparations are injected IM into an area of large muscle tissue, from which they are absorbed slowly into the blood. Decanoate preparations can be given less frequently than are enanthate preparations because they are absorbed more slowly. Although stabilizing a patient on the oral preparation of the specific drugs is not necessary before initiating the depot form, it is good practice to give at least one oral dose of the drug to assess the possibility of an adverse effect, such as severe EPS or an allergic reaction.

The correct dosage and the time interval for depot preparations are difficult to predict. It is reasonable to begin with 12.5 mg (0.5 mL) of fluphenazine preparation or 25 mg (0.5 mL) of haloperidol decanoate. If symptoms emerge in the next 2 to 4 weeks, a patient can be treated temporarily with additional oral medications or with additional small depot injections. After 3 to 4 weeks the depot injection can be increased to include the supplemental doses given during the initial period.

A good reason to initiate depot treatment with low doses is that the absorption of the preparations may be faster than usual at the onset of treatment and can result in frightening episodes of dystonia that eventually discourage compliance with the medication. Some clinicians keep patients drug free for 3 to 7 days before initiating depot treatment and then give very small doses of the depot preparations (3.125 mg fluphenazine or 6.25 mg haloperidol) every few days to avoid these initial problems. Because the major indication for depot medication is poor compliance with oral forms, clinicians should go slowly with what is practically the last method of achieving compliance.

Table 35.3.16–8
Use of Long-Acting Dopamine Receptor Antagonists

Dosage

a. Stabilize patient on lowest effective dose of oral preparation.
b. Usual dosage conversion:
   10 mg/day oral fluphenazine = 12.5–25 mg/2 weeks fluphenazine decanoate
   10 mg/day oral haloperidol = 100–200 mg/4 weeks haloperidol decanoate
c. As with all other antipsychotic medications, the lowest effective dose should be used. Note that patients with long-term schizophrenia have been adequately maintained on dosages of fluphenazine decanoate as low as 5 mg/2 weeks.
d. Supplementation with oral medication may be necessary for the first several months until the optimum dosage regimen has been determined.

Techniques of Injection

a. Using a 2-inch needle, inject no more than 3 cc of medication per injection into upper quadrant of buttock (to inject more than 3 cc, use alternate buttocks and vary injection sites).
b. After drawing up medication, draw a small air bubble of 0.1 cc into syringe and change needle for injection.
c. Wipe injection site with alcohol swab and allow to dry before giving injection, otherwise alcohol may infiltrate subcutaneous tissue and cause local irritation.
d. Stretch the skin over the injection site to one side and hold firmly.
e. Inject medication slowly, including air bubble, which forces last drop from needle into the muscle and prevents any medication from being deposited in subcutaneous tissue as needle is withdrawn.
f. Wait about 10 seconds before withdrawing needle, then do so quickly and release skin.
g. Do not massage injection site, as this may force medication to ooze from muscle and infiltrate subcutaneous tissue.
h. Precautions should also be taken with glass ampules to avoid injection of glass particles.

Reprinted with permission from Silver JM, Yudofsky SC, Hurowitz GI: Psychopharmacology and electroconvulsive therapy. In *The American Psychiatric Press Textbook of Psychiatry*, RE Hales, SC Yudofsky, JA Talbott, ed 2, p 909. American Psychiatric Press, Washington, 1994.

Plasma Concentrations. Interindividual variation in the metabolism of the antipsychotics is significant and arises in part from genetic differences among patients and from pharmacokinetic interactions with other drugs. In patients who have not improved after 4 to 6 weeks of dopamine receptor antagonist treatment, a plasma concentration of the drug should be obtained if such a test is available. Other possible indications for obtaining a plasma concentration are questions regarding compliance, concern about pharmacokinetic interactions, and the development of significant akathisia or akinesia.

The blood sample must be obtained after a patient has been taking a particular dosage for at least 5 times the half-life of the drug, so as to approach steady-state concentrations. It is also standard practice to obtain plasma samples at trough levels—that is, just before the daily dose is given, usually at least 12 hours after the previous dose and most commonly 20 to 24 hours after the previous dose. Unfortunately, the quality of the laboratories that perform the analyses varies significantly; therefore, clinicians must obtain the normal ranges for a particular laboratory and must test the laboratory with multiple plasma samples from well-controlled patients. Having taken all these precautions, clinicians are still left with the reality that most dopamine receptor antagonists have no well-defined dose–response curve. The best-studied drug is haloperidol, which may have a therapeutic window ranging from 2 to 15 ng/mL. Other therapeutic ranges that have been reasonably well documented are 30 to 100 ng/mL for chlorpromazine and 0.8 to 2.4 ng/mL for perphenazine.

Treatment-Resistant Patients and Adjuvant Medications. Various estimates have ranged from 10 to 35 percent for the proportion of schizophrenic patients who fail to obtain significant benefit from the dopamine receptor antagonist drugs. Patients are often defined as being treatment resistant if they have failed at least two adequate trials of dopamine receptor antagonists from two classes. Adequate trials are usually defined as lasting at least 6 weeks, and using daily dosages equivalent to 20 mg of haloperidol or 1,000 mg of chlorpromazine. It is useful to obtain plasma concentrations for such patients, as one possibility is that they are slow metabolizers and are grossly overmedicated with the dopamine receptor antagonist drugs. More likely, however, they are simply nonresponsive to those typical dopamine receptor antagonist drugs. Studies have shown that up to two thirds of nonresponders to dopamine receptor antagonist drugs may respond to clozapine, and the frequency of response to the other serotonin-dopamine antagonists may turn out to be similar.

ADJUVANT TREATMENTS. Before the introduction of the new antipsychotics, the only approach to treatment-resistant schizophrenic patients was the use of adjuvant medications. Medications that have been reported to be useful as adjuvants to dopamine receptor antagonists include lithium, carbamazepine, β-adrenergic receptor antagonists, antidepressants, and benzodiazepines. Of these medications, the most robust data support the use of lithium as an adjuvant to dopamine receptor antagonist medications. When using the combination of lithium and dopamine receptor antagonists, clinicians may want to use slightly lower dosages of each initially to avoid the development of delirium or neurotoxicity that has been reported with the drug combination in a few cases. The use of carbamazepine has also been reported to be effective as an addition to dopamine receptor antagonist drugs, although the coadministration of carbamazepine and a dopamine receptor antagonist can lower the plasma concentrations of the dopamine receptor antagonist as much as 50 percent because of the induction of hepatic enzymes. Although benzodiazepines have been reported to be effective as adjuvant treatments, their withdrawal can precipitate a significant worsening of symptoms. An increasing body of data supports the use of antidepressants in patients with schizophrenia who have significant depressive symptoms.

REFERENCES

Aymard N, Viala A, Stein I, Caroli F: Pharmacoclinical correlations in schizophrenic patients treated with haloperidol decanoate: Clinical evaluations, concentrations of plasma and red blood cell haloperidol and its reduced metabolite, and plasma homovanillic acid. Prog Neuropsychopharmacol Biol Psychiatry *19* (7): 1119, 1995.

Barbhaiya RH, Shukla UA, Greene DS, Breuel HP, et al: Investigation of pharmacokinetic and pharmacodynamic interactions after coadministration of nefazodone and haloperidol. J Clin Psychopharmacol *16* (1): 26, 1996.

Blin O, Azorin JM, Bouhours P: Antipsychotic and anxiolytic properties of risperidone, haloperidol and methotrimeprazine in schizophrenic patients. J Clin Psychopharmacol *16* (1): 38, 1996.

Brauer LH, de Wit H: Subjective responses to *d*-amphetamine alone and after pimozide pretreatment in normal, healthy volunteers. Biol Psychiatry *39* (1): 26, 1996.

Czobor P, Volavka J: Dimensions of the Brief Psychiatric Rating Scale: An examination of stability during haloperidol treatment. Comp Psychiatry *37* (3): 205, 1996.

Deleu D, Hanssens Y: Aging and neuroleptic-induced acute dystonia. Am J Psychiatry *153* (3): 447, 1996.

Dilsaver SC: Antipsychotic agents: A review. Am Fam Physician *47:* 199, 1993.

Druckenbrod RW, Rosen J, Cluxton RJ: As-needed dosing of antipsychotic drugs: Limitations and guidelines for use in the elderly agitated patient. Ann Pharmacotherapy *27:* 645, 1993.

Finlay WML, Bernal SJ: Tourette's syndrome and challenging behaviour: A case study. Ment Handicap *24* (2): 80, 1996.

Glazer WM, Morgenstern H, Doucette JT: Predicting the long-term risk of tardive dyskinesia in outpatients maintained on neuroleptic medications. J Clin Psychiatry *54:* 133, 1993.

Huang H-F, Jann MW, Tseng Y-T, Chung M-C, et al: Ketone reductase activity and reduced haloperidol/haloperidol ratios in haloperidol-treated schizophrenic patients. Psychiatry Res *57* (2): 101, 1995.

Huttunen MO, Tuhkanen H, Haavisto E, Nyholm R, et al: Low- and standard-dose depot haloperidol combined with targeted oral neuroleptics. Psychiatr Serv *47* (1): 83, 1996.

Jann MW, Wei F-C, Lin H-N, Piao-Chien C, et al: Haloperidol and reduced haloperidol plasma concentrations after a loading dose regimen with haloperidol decanoate. Prog Neuropsychopharmacol Biol Psychiatry *20* (1): 73, 1996.

Kapur S, Remington G, Jones C, Wilson A, et al: High levels of dopamine D_2 receptor occupancy with low-dose haloperidol treatment: A PET study. Am J Psychiatry *153* (7): 948, 1996.

Keshavan MS, Aguilar EJ: Aging and neuroleptic-induced acute dystonia: Reply. Am J Psychiatry *153* (3): 448, 1996.

Lader M: Use of sedative and anxiolytic agents in the field of acute aggressiveness. Am J Forensic Psychiatry *16* (4): 7, 1995.

Levy F, Hobbes G: Does haloperidol block methylphenidate? Psychopharmacology *126* (1): 70, 1996.

Mazurek MF, Rosebush PI: Circadian pattern of acute, neuroleptic-induced dystonic reactions. Am J Psychiatry *153* (5): 708, 1996.

McSwain ML, Forman LM: Severe parkinsonian symptom development on combination treatment with tacrine and haloperidol. J Clin Psychopharmacol *15* (4): 284, 1995.

Meltzer HY: Serotonin-dopamine interactions and atypical antipsychotic drugs. Psychiatr Ann *23:* 193, 1993.

Quigley N, Morgan D, Idzikowski C, King DJ: The effect of chlorpromazine and benzhexol on memory and psychomotor function in healthy volunteers. J Psychopharmacol *10* (2): 146, 1996.

Reveley MA, Dursun SM, Andrews H: A comparative trial use of sulpiride and risperidone in Huntington's disease: A pilot study. J Psychopharmacol *10* (2): 162, 1996.

Sanchez LE, Adams PB, Yusal S, Hallin A, et al: A comparison of live and videotape ratings: Clomipramine and haloperidol in autism. Psychopharmacol Bull *31* (2): 371, 1995.

Silva RR, Munoz DM, Daniel W, Barickman J, et al: Causes of haloperidol discontinuation in patients with Tourette's disorder: Management and alternatives. J Clin Psychiatry *57* (3): 129, 1996.

Stern RG, Kahn RS, Harvey PD, Amin F, Apter SH, Hirschowitz J: Early response to haloperidol treatment in chronic schizophrenia. Schizophr Res *10:* 165, 1993.

Szymanski S, Munne R, Gordon MF, Lieberman J: A selective review of recent advances in the management of tardive dyskinesia. Psychiatr Ann *23:* 209, 1993.

Taylor D, Lader M: Cytochromes and psychotropic drug interactions. Br J Psychiatry *168* (5): 529, 1996.

Teicher MH, Barber NI, Gelbard HA, Gallitano AL, Campbell A, Marsh E, Baldessarini RJ: Developmental differences in acute nigrostriatal and mesocorticolimbic system response to haloperidol. Neuropsychopharmacology *9:* 147, 1993.

Thacker S: The use of depot neuroleptics in the elderly: A survey. Int J Geriatr Psychiatry *11* (5): 423, 1996.
Volavka J: Haloperidol dosing strategies. Am J Psychiatry *153* (8): 1108, 1996.
Volavka J, Cooper TB, Czobor P, Meisner M: Effect of varying haloperidol plasma levels on negative symptoms in schizophrenia and schizoaffective disorder. Psychopharmacol Bull *32* (1): 75, 1996.
Woerner MG, Alvir J, Ma J, Kane JM, Saltz BL, et al: Neuroleptic treatment of elderly patients. Psychopharmacol Bull *31* (2): 333, 1995.
Wolkin A, Sanfilipo M, Duncan E, Angrist B, et al: Blunted change in cerebral glucose utilization after haloperidol treatment in schizophrenic patients with prominent negative symptoms. Am J Psychiatry *153* (3): 346, 1996.

▲ 35.3.17 Fenfluramine and Dexfenfluramine

The pharmacological treatment of obesity has long been a controversial subject, and the manufacturer's recall of flenfluramine (Pondimin) and dexfenfluramine (Redux) in September 1997, because of their association with serious heart and lung diseases, promises to fuel the debate regarding whether any diet pills are safe. The experience of fenfluramine and dexfenfluramine should be taken as a cautionary tale regarding the perils of using drugs strictly to alter appearance. Fenfluramine and its contemporary anorexigenic agent phentermine (Adipex-P, Fastin) were introduced into clinical use about 20 years ago as separate agents to be used singly for no more than 3 months at a time. However, they were soon combined in off-label use as ''fen-phen'' and were used by millions of people, mostly women, in many cases for several consecutive months. It appears that a large number of patients used fen-phen primarily to alter their appearance rather than for a clearly defined medical purpose. The upsurge in the use of fen-phen in the early 1990s, in fact, coincided with the widespread promotion of a very thin feminine ideal in the mass media. The dextrorotatory enantiomer of fenfluramine, dexfenfluramine, was approved in 1995, and its sales rapidly approached those of fen-phen. In 1997, reports emerged documenting an increased association of fenfluramine and dexfenfluramine with fatal pulmonary hypertension and with serious heart valve disease, and the U.S. Food and Drug Administration (FDA) directed the manufacturer to recall the drugs.

CHEMISTRY

Fenfluramine and its dextrorotatory enantiomer, dexfenfluramine, are congeners of amphetamine and phentermine, with which they share some effects. They are also structurally related to aminorex (Menocil), an anorexigenic agent that was used in Europe in the late 1960s and early 1970s. The molecular structure is shown in Figure 35.3.17–1.

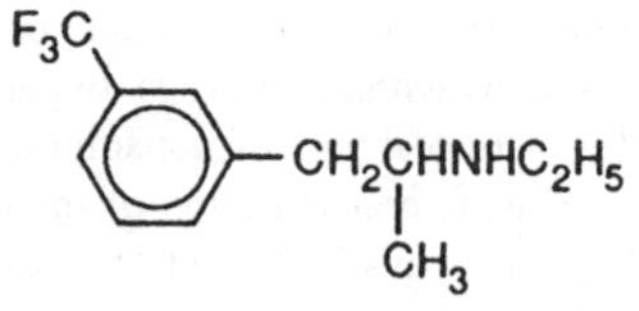

FIGURE 33.3.17–1
Molecular structure of fenfluramine.

PHARMACOLOGICAL ACTIONS

Pharmacokinetics

The major short-term effect of fenfluramine and dexfenfluramine is to release neuronal stores of serotonin. Some data indicate that fenfluramine and dexfenfluramine are also inhibitors of serotonin reuptake. Unlike its relatives amphetamine and racemic fenfluramine, dexfenfluramine does not appear to be associated with a facilitation of dopamine release from neurons. It is possible that stimulation of serotonin 5-HT_{2C} receptors may reduce the appetite.

EFFECTS ON SPECIFIC ORGANS AND SYSTEMS

Fenfluramine and dexfenfluramine potentiate serotonergic neurotransmission and may transiently elicit the full spectrum of serotonergic effects, including diarrhea, dry mouth, and somnolence. Some data indicate that fenfluramine and dexfenfluramine have a stimulatory effect on the ventromedial nucleus of the hypothalamus, perhaps explaining the appetite suppressive effects of the drug. Fenfluramine and dexfenfluramine may also decrease the absorption of dietary fat, increase fat mobilization, and increase cellular glucose uptake. The immediate cardiovascular and autonomic effects of fenfluramine and dexfenfluramine are similar to those of amphetamine, although fenfluramine and dexfenfluramine are much less potent pressor agents than is amphetamine.

Fenfluramine and dexfenfluramine have been linked to three potentially serious delayed outcomes: permanent depletion of serotonergic axons in the brain, fatal pulmonary hypertension, and serious heart valve disease (discussed in Precautions and Adverse Reactions).

THERAPETIC INDICATIONS

FDA approval for dexfenfluramine for use in obese patients who were more than 30 percent heavier than their desired weight, which corresponds to a body mass index of 30 kg/m^2, or who were more than 20 percent heavier than their desired weight, which corresponds to a body mass index of 27 kg/m^2, if the patient also had a risk factor for atherosclerosis, such as hypertension, diabetes, or hyperlipidemia (Table 35.3.17–1), was justified by the assumption that weight loss would provide medical benefits. The drug was to be used as part of a comprehensive weight loss program including a reduced calorie diet and psychological support with behavioral modification. In a 1-year clinical trial, 64 percent of patients taking dexfenfluramine lost 5 percent of their initial body weight, 40 percent lost at least 10 percent of their initial body weight, and 21 percent lost at least 15 percent of their initial body weight. In the FDA appproval process, the benefit of weight loss in terms of reduced incidence of diabetes, heart disease, hypertension, hyperlipidemia, and therefore the complications of atherosclerosis, such as heart attack, stroke, blindness, renal failure, and nerve injury, was assumed to outweigh the known risks of pulmonary hypertension and depletion of brain serotonin stores caused by fenfluramine and dex-

Table 35.3.17–1
Body Mass Index (BMI) (kg/m^2)[a]

Weight (pounds)	Height (feet, inches) 5′0″	5′3″	5′6″	5′9″	6′0″	6′3″
140	27	25	23	21	19	18
150	29	27	24	22	20	19
160	31	28	26	24	22	20
170	33	30	28	25	23	21
180	35	32	29	27	25	23
190	37	34	31	28	26	24
200	39	36	32	30	27	25
210	41	37	34	31	29	26
220	43	39	36	33	30	28
230	45	41	37	34	31	29
240	47	43	39	36	33	30
250	49	44	40	37	34	31

Reprinted with permission from Wyeth-Ayerst Laboratories, Philadelphia, 1997.

[a] Patients with BMI values of 30 may be candidates for dexfenfluramine therapy. Patients with BMI values of 27–29 may be candidates for dexfenfluramine therapy if they also have a concomitant risk factor (eg, hypertension, diabetes, hyperlipidemia).

fenfluramine. This assessment was not supported by any controlled trials of clinical outcome indicating that diet pills reduced any type of morbidity and mortality. At the first review, the FDA advisory committee did not approve dexfenfluramine, but after a second hearing the drug was approved by a margin of 6 votes to 5. The adverse effects on heart valves had not been reported at that time. Once approved, off-label use for patients desiring to lose weight for cosmetic reasons rapidly became the major market for the drug.

ADVERSE REACTIONS

Permanent Depletion of Brain Serotonin

A number of studies in rodents and apes have clearly demonstrated a permanent loss of serotonin-containing axon endings in the cerebral cortex after administration of fenfluramine at doses sufficient to cause weight loss. By a complex calculation these doses were determined to be equivalent to the doses usually used in humans attempting to lose weight. The effects were dose related, but permanent neuronal damage was seen even after brief exposure to fenfluramine. In one study, monkeys given fenfluramine showed no recovery of serotonergic axon endings in the cortex even 17 months after the last dose. No comparative data are available to assess whether neuronal loss occurs in humans who take fenfluramine or dexfenfluramine. Despite use of fenfluramine or dexfenfluramine by an estimated 50 million patients, no prospective controlled trials have been done to examine the effects of diet pills on cognition, memory, mood, anxiety, impulsivity, aggression, sleep, or neuroendocrine function. By analogy, however, the consistent of loss of serotonergic fibers in the brains of several mammalian species, including apes, suggest that all human patients who take fenfluramine or dexfenfluramine at doses sufficient to promote weight loss will very likely suffer irreversible loss of serotonergic nerve fibers. This mechanism may underlie the clinical observation that patients may eventually lose their responsiveness to fenfluramine and dexfenfluramine. In this model, once these drugs have eliminated serotonergic fibers, they are no longer able to promote the release of serotonin from neuronal stores.

Fatal Pulmonary Hypertension

Primary (idiopathic) pulmonary hypertension (PPH), an exceedingly rare (1 to 2 cases per year per 1 million in the general population), potentially fatal disorder, is characterized by a change in exercise tolerance and the appearance of dyspnea, angina pectoris, syncope, or leg edema. PPH causes a characteristics thickening of the walls of the pulmonary artery and is fatal in the majority of cases. Pulmonary hypertension with similar pathological findings appeared in 10-fold increased frequency among users of the diet pill aminorex in the late 1960s and early 1970s. Of those patients, half died, with an average survival time of 3½ years after the onset of symptoms. Of the survivors, half had persistent pulmonary hypertension and half had resolution of the disorder. After the introduction of fenfluramine, a registry was initiated in Europe in the early 1990s that showed a 10- to 40-fold increase in pulmonary hypertension among users of fenfluramine. The risk of pulmonary hypertension was related to duration of therapy and was 23-fold higher among patients using fenfluramine more than 3 months. Although the symptoms sometimes appeared during the course of fenfluramine, many patients first developed respiratory distress several months after stopping the drug. One recent case report documented the classical syndrome of pulmonary hypertension ina 29-year-old woman appearing 5 months after she took fen-phen for only 23 days.

Thickening of Heart Valves

In August and September 1997, at least 100 cases of symptomatic heart valvular insufficiency were reported in patients taking fenfluramine or dexfenfluramine, either alone or in combination with phentermine. The leaflets and chordal structures of the heart valves of 5 of these patients who came to valve replacement surgery were encased in a thick fibrous plaque that impeded the movement of the valves, causing regurgitation or stenosis. Many patients in these reports also had pulmonary hypertension. An initial report of 24 patients led the FDA to insert a waning into the product literature. Additional echocardiographic data of 291 patients who took fenfluramine or dexfenfluramine showed heart valve abnormalities in 92 patients. Twenty-four of the 291 patients had had prior normal echocardiograms, and 8 of these patients were shown to have developed heart valve abnormalities while taking fenfluramine or dexfenfluramine. These data suggested, therefore, that as many as one third of patients taking fenfluramine or dexfenfluramine would be expected to develop heart valve thickening, i.e., potentially several million people. On the basis of these new data, the FDA directed the manufacturer to recall both drugs. This represented only the 12th recall of an FDA-approved drug in the past 17 years. The extent of the injuries caused by fenfluramine and dexfenfluramine will not be fully known for several years. Early evidence suggests that many if not most of the patients with heart valve thickening due to fenfluramine or dexfenfluramine were women who took fen-phen or dexfenfluramine for cosmetic reasons.

Role of Serotonin in Pulmonary Hypertension and Heart Valve Thickening

The pathological changes to the heart valves and pulmonary arteries attributed to fenfluramine and dexfenfluramine resemble those seen in carcinoid syndrome and in prolonged treatment with the migraine drugs ergotamine (Cafergot, Wigraine) and methysergide (Sansert). Each of these conditions is characterized by high plasma concentrations of serotonin or serotonin agonist activity. Serotonin causes shrinkage of endothelial cells and arterial constriction, either by a direct receptor-mediated mechanism or through the blockade of potassium channels. This cellular distortion appears to promote the deposition on the valves and arteries of a fibrous plaque consisting of myofibroblasts and endothelial cells in a thick extracellular stroma. In addition, an unusually extensive plexogenic arteriopathy, consisting of a meshwork of channels that creates shunts between the pulmonary artery and pulmonary vein, is seen in diet pill-associated pulmonary hypertension. It is a characteristic pathological finding that is distinct from rheumatic or inflammatory vegetations.

Carcinoid syndrome occurs when metastatic carcinoid tumor cells embedded in the liver release serotonin into the right side of the heart. This surge of serotonin stimulates the production of plaque before the serotonin can be inactivated in the lungs. The valves most commonly involved in carcinoid syndrome therefore are the right-sided valves, the tricuspid and pulmonary valves. In contrast, fenfluramine and dexfenfluramine caused fibrosis of primarily the left-sided valves, the mitral and aortic valves, with less involvement of the right-sided valves. This is probably because high plasma concentrations of serotonin caused by the drugs overwhelmed the pulmonary clearance mechanisms and acted on all heart valves.

Methysergide, when used for serveral months, may cause fibrosis in many areas of the body, including the heart valves. The fibrosis usually regresses once the drug is stopped, but heart valve damage has been reported to persist indefinitely. For this reason, it is recommened that methysergide be stopped for at least 3 weeks every 6 months.

The fact that serotonin-specific reuptake inhibitors (SSRIs) and other antidipressant drugs potentiate serotonin synaptic activity has raised the question of whether they may also lead to fibrotic changes in the heart valves and lung. These drugs have been used by many millions of patients and have been subjected to a more rigorous analysis than was the case for the diet pills, and no evidence of such an association has been reported. The mechanism of action of SSRIs is to extend the effective life span of the serotonin secreted naturally into the synaptic cleft, which is a tiny compartment of the body. In contrast, fenfluramine and dexfenfluramine promote the excessive release of serotonin from cellular stores throughout the body and result in many times higher plasma concentrations of serotonin than do antidepressants.

At this time, it is not know whether the heart valve and pulmonary artery fibrosis caused by fenfluramine and dexfenfluramine are reversible. Early anecdotal reports suggest progression of the lesions in many cases, though at least two patients in the echocardiography study were subsequently reported to have regression of the valvular lesions after stopping the drugs. It is not known whether phentermine alone causes similar lesions in the heart valves and pulmonary arteries. In the well-documented experience of pulmonary hypertension caused by aminorex, only one fourth of patients recovered to the point of being asymptomatic.

References

Brauer LH, Johanson CE, Schuster CR, Rothman RB, et al: Evaluation of phentermine and fenfluramine, alone and in combination, in normal, healthy volunteers. Neuropsychopharmacology *14* (4): 233, 1996.

Cacoub P, Dorent R, Nataf P, Houppe JP, Piette JC, Godeau P, Gandjbakhch I: Pulmonary hypertension and dexfenfluramine. Eur J Clin Pharmacol *48:* 81, 1995.

Connolly HM, Crary JL, McGoon MD, Hensrud DD, Edwards BS, Edwards WD, Schaff HV: Valvular heart disease associated with fenfluramine-phentermine. N Engl J Med *337* (9): 581, 1997.

Curfman GD: Diet pills redux. N Engl J Med *337* (9): 629, 1997.

Drent ML, Ader HJ, van der Veen EA: The influence of chronic administration of the serotonin agonist dexfenfluramine on responsiveness to corticotrophin releasing hormone. J Endocrinol Invest *18:* 780, 1995.

Galletly C, Clark A, Tomlinson L: Evaluation of dexfenfluramine in a weight loss program for obese infertile women. Int J Eating Disord *19* (2): 209, 1996.

Holdaway IM, Wallace E, Westbrooke L, Gamble G: Effect of dexfenfluramine on body weight, blood pressure, insulin resistance and serum cholesterol in obese individuals. Int J Obes Relat Metab Disord *19:* 749, 1995.

Malone KM, Corbitt EM, Li S, Mann JJ: Prolactin response to fenfluramine and suicide attempt lethality in major depression. Br J Psychiatry *168* (3): 324, 1996.

Mark EJ, Patalas ED, Chang HT, Evans RJ, Kessler SC: Fatal pulmonary hypertension associated with short-term use of fenfluramine and phentermine. N Engl J Med *337* (9): 602, 1997.

Marks SJ, Moore NR, Clark ML, Strauss BJ, Hockaday TD: Reduction of visceral adipose tissue and improvement of metabolic indices: Effect of dexfenfluramine in NIDDM. Obesity Research *4:* 1, 1996.

McCann UD, Seiden LS, Rubin LJ, Ricaurte GA: Brain serotonin neurotoxicity and primary pulmonary hypertension from fenfluramine and dexfenfluramine. JAMA *278* (8): 666, 1997.

O'Conner HT, Richman RM, Steinbeck KS, Caterson ID: Dexfenfluramine treatment of obesity: A double blind trial with post trial follow up. Int J Obe Relat Metab Disord *19:* 181, 1995.

Park SBG, Williamson DJ, Cowen PJ: Do the endocrine and subjective effects of *d*-fenfluramine predict response to selective serotonin reuptake inhibitors? Int Clin Psychopharmacol *10* (4): 215, 1995.

▲ 35.3.18 Levodopa

Dopamine is generally associated in psychiatry with psychosis, and all antipsychotic agents include dopamine receptor antagonism as a prime mechanism of action. Although an excess of dopamine activity may cause psychosis, a deficiency of dopamine activity may cause parkinsonism and depression. As a means of achieving a proper balance of dopamine activity, levodopa (Larodopa, Dopar), also known as L-Dopa, is available as an indirectly acting dopamine agonist. Levodopa, given in combination with a peripheral inhibitor of levodopa decarboxylase (for example, carbidopa), is the most commonly used treatment for idiopathic Parkinson's disease, as well as several other movement disorders. A commonly used commercially available combination of levodopa and carbidopa is Sinemet. In the field of clinical psychiatry, levodopa is not a primary therapy for any single indication; rather, levodopa is used as a second-line or third-line treatment for antipsychotic-induced parkinsonism, for neuroleptic malignant syndrome, and, in experimental use, for cocaine abuse. Skillful use of

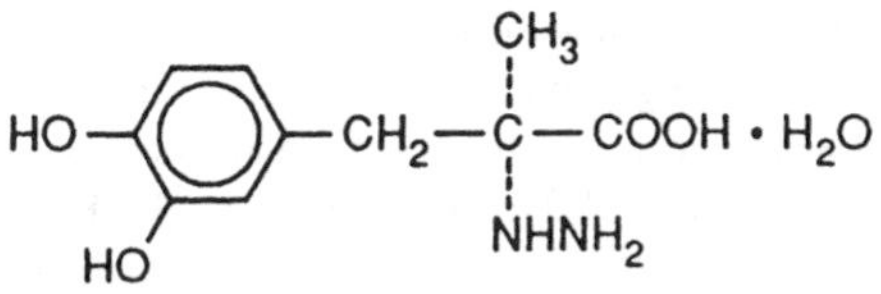

FIGURE 35.3.18–1
Molecular structure of levodopa.

levodopa together with serotonin-dopamine antagonists, such as clozapine, has permitted more effective treatment of Parkinson's disease than with levodopa alone.

CHEMISTRY

The molecular structure of levodopa is shown in Figure 35.3.18–1. Levodopa is the naturally occurring levorotatory enantiomer of dihydroxyphenylalanine (DOPA), a derivative of L-tyrosine that is a precursor to the neurotransmitter dopamine.

PHARMACOLOGICAL ACTIONS

Pharmacokinetics

Levodopa is rapidly absorbed after oral administration, and peak plasma levels are reached after 30 to 120 minutes. The half-life of levodopa is 1 to 3 hours. Absorption of levodopa can be significantly reduced by changes in gastric pH and by ingestion with meals. Levodopa is almost entirely decarboxylated in the periphery by L-amino acid decarboxylase. Dopamine, the decarboxylated form of levodopa, is pharmacologically active and, in contrast to levodopa, cannot cross the blood–brain barrier. In the 1970s, large doses (several grams) of levodopa were originally given so that enough entered the central nervous system (CNS) to be pharmacologically active, but this regimen was accompanied by prominent gastrointestinal and cardiovascular side effects. The efficient delivery of levodopa into the CNS was significantly improved with the addition of the peripherally active inhibitor of levodopa decarboxylase, carbidopa, which also improved the tolerability of levodopa. Sinemet contains an appropriate combination of levodopa and carbidopa in a single tablet.

Pharmacodynamics

Once levodopa enters the CNS, it is available to be rapidly converted into dopamine by CNS L-amino acid decarboxylase. The dopamine can then act as a neurotransmitter at dopamine receptor sites.

THERAPEUTIC INDICATIONS

In psychiatry, levodopa is used to treat antipsychotic-induced parkinsonism, although anticholinergics, amantadine (Symmetrel), antihistamines, and bromocriptine (Parlodel) are more frequently used because these drugs are equally effective and are associated with fewer side effects. Nonetheless, levodopa can be used to treat extrapyramidal symptoms, akinesia, and focal perioral tremors (sometimes called rabbit syndrome). Additional evidence, based on case reports and small studies, indicates that levodopa may be effective in treating restless legs syndrome and tardive dyskinesia. Preliminary data also suggest that levodopa may be effective in treating the negative symptoms of schizophrenia, although this indication should be considered only in research settings. Levodopa has been used as one component to treat neuroleptic malignant syndrome and as part of a multimodal cocaine detoxification program.

PRECAUTIONS AND ADVERSE REACTIONS

Levodopa therapy commonly produces side effects, which limits the drug's usefulness in general psychiatric practice. Most side effects are dose related or associated with withdrawal from the drug. Some side effects that appear early in treatment include nausea, vomiting, orthostatic hypotension, and cardiac arrhythmias. After long-term use, patients may experience abnormal involuntary movements, such as dyskinesias, and psychiatric disturbances, including psychosis, depression, and mania. Anecdotal reports indicate that the abrupt discontinuation of levodopa can precipitate a syndrome similar to neuroleptic malignant syndrome, especially if the patient is concomitantly receiving an antipsychotic. Levodopa is contraindicated during pregnancy and is contraindicated for nursing mothers, especially as the drug inhibits lactation.

DRUG INTERACTIONS

Drugs that block dopamine type 2 (D_2) receptors—for example, haloperidol (Haldol)—are capable of reversing the effects of levodopa. The concurrent use of tricyclic drugs and levodopa has been reported to cause postural hypotension and symptoms of neurotoxicity, such as rigidity, agitation, and tremor. Levodopa is also capable of potentiating the hypotensive effects of diuretics and other antihypertensive medications. Levodopa should not be used in conjunction with monoamine oxidase inhibitors (MAOIs), including selegiline (Eldepryl), because of the possible development of a hypertensive crisis. MAOIs should be discontinued at least 2 weeks before the initiation of levodopa therapy. Benzodiazepines, phenytoin (Dilantin), papaverine, and pyridoxine may interfere with the therapeutic effects of levodopa. Levodopa and halogenated inhalation anesthetics may interact to produce cardiac arrhythmia.

LABORATORY INTERFERENCES

Levodopa administration has been associated with false-positive reports of elevated serum and urinary uric acid concentrations, urinary glucose tests, urinary ketone tests, urinary phenylketonuria tests and urinary catecholamine concentrations. Whether levodopa results in a false-positive result in these tests depends on the specific test method used; some test methods are not affected by levodopa.

DOSAGE AND ADMINISTRATION

Levodopa acts within 30 to 60 minutes after administration. Dosages of levodopa for the treatment of antipsychotic-induced parkinsonism should be similar to the dosages used for idiopathic parkinsonism. Starting dosages of 100 mg 3 times a day may be increased until the patient is functionally improved. The maximum dose of levodopa is 2000 mg a day, but most patients respond to doses of less than 1000 mg a day. The dose of carbidopa should total at least 75 mg a day if Sinemet is used. Hyperkinesias, in the form of choreiform and dystonic movements, are dose-related side effects. Particularly after prolonged therapy, periods of profound bradykinesia may alternate with periods during which the patient can move well or is hyperkinetic (on-off phenomenon). The addition of other antiparkinsonian medications, usually such dopamine agonists as bromocriptine, may ameliorate the problem, although the on-off phenomenon may eventually require the cessation of levodopa therapy. Levodopa is available in 100 mg, 250 mg, and 500 mg tablets and capsules.

REFERENCES

Cummings JL: Behavioral complications of drug treatment of Parkinson's disease. J Am Geriatr Soc *39:* 708, 1991.

Davis JM, Janicak PG, Sakkas P: Electroconvulsive therapy in the treatment of the neuroleptic malignant syndrome. Convuls Ther *7:* 111, 1991.

Dooneief G, Mirabello E: An estimate of the incidence of depression in idiopathic Parkinson's disease. Arch Neurol *49:* 305, 1992.

Doraiswamy M, Martin W, Metz A: Psychosis of Parkinson's disease: Diagnosis and treatment. Prog Neuropsychopharmacol Biol Psychiatry *19:* 835, 1995.

Geminiani G, Cesana BM, Scigliano G, Soliveri P: Variation of therapeutic response in Parkinson's disease: A retrospective study. Acta Neurol Scand *81:* 397, 1990.

Kaplan B, Mason NA: Levodopa in restless legs syndrome. Ann Pharmacother *26:* 214, 1992.

Kaplan HI, Sadock BJ: Other pharmacological therapies. In *Comprehensive Textbook of Psychiatry,* ed 6, HI Kaplan, BJ Sadock, editors, p 2122. Williams & Wilkins, Baltimore, 1995.

Pahwa R, Koller WC: Treatment of Parkinson's disease with controlled-release carbidopa/L-DOPA. Adv Neurol *69:* 487, 1996.

Tutton CS, Crayton JW: Current pharmacotherapies for cocaine abuse: A review. J Addict Dis *12:* 109, 1993.

Wagner ML, Defilippi JL, Menzo MA, Sage JI: Clozapine for the treatment of psychosis in Parkinson's disease: Chart review of 49 patients. J Neuropsychiatry Clin Neurosci *8:* 276, 1996.

▲ 35.3.19 Lithium

Lithium (Eskalith, Lithonate, Lithobid) is the most commonly used short-term and prophylactic treatment for bipolar I disorder. It has recently been used as an adjunctive medication in therapy-resistant chronic schizophrenia, for agitation in both aggressive children and demented adults, in refractory insomnia, and in the treatment of anorexia nervosa and bulimia nervosa. Lithium can be highly effective in long-term use, and its predictable pharmacokinetics allow its serum levels to be readily maintained in a relatively narrow therapeutic window.

HISTORY

Building on the discoveries of others, Humphry Davy isolated the lithium metal in 1818. Lithium was introduced into medicine in the 1840s by Alexander Ure for the treatment of bladder stones and by Alfred Garrod for the treatment of gout. In 1873, in the United States, William Hammond described the use of lithium bromide to treat manic episodes, although the bromide was considered the active ingredient. In 1886 in Denmark, Carl Lange and Fritz Lange described the prophylactic and short-term effects of lithium for depression. In the late 1880s and early 1900s, the general public in the United States was enthusiastically endorsing the taking of the waters, the use of mineral spring waters that supposedly contained lithium. The waters, in which only vanishingly small concentrations of lithium were dissolved, were misleadingly advertised as being beneficial for a wide variety of aches, pains, and ills. In the United States in the 1940s, lithium chloride was used as a replacement for sodium chloride in hypertensive patients with low-salt diets; this practice resulted in lithium toxicity and death for some patients, and lithium-related products were withdrawn from the marketplace. In 1949, an Australian, John F. J. Cade, noticed that lithium urate caused lethargy when injected into animals. He later reported the successful therapeutic effects of lithium in a patient with manic episodes. In the 1950s and the 1960s, Mogens Schou conducted the critical experiments demonstrating the short-term prophylactic efficacy of lithium for bipolar I disorder. Eventually, the U.S. Food and Drug Administration (FDA) approved lithium for the treatment of bipolar I disorder.

CHEMISTRY

Lithium (Li), a monovalent ion, is an element and the lightest of the alkali metals (group IA of the periodic table), and is similar to sodium, potassium, and rubidium. Lithium exists as both ^{6}Li and ^{7}Li. The latter isotope allows the imaging of lithium by magnetic resonance spectroscopy.

PHARMACOLOGICAL ACTIONS

Pharmacokinetics

After ingestion, lithium is completely absorbed by the gastrointestinal tract. Serum levels peak in 1 to 1½ hours for standard preparations and in 4 to 4½ hours for controlled-released preparations. Lithium does not bind to plasma proteins, is not metabolized, and is distributed nonuniformly throughout body water. Lithium does not cross the blood–brain barrier rapidly, a fact that perhaps explains why an overdose is not usually a problem and why long-term lithium intoxication takes time to resolve completely. The half-life of lithium is about 20 hours, and equilibrium is reached after 5 to 7 hours of regular intake. Lithium is almost entirely eliminated by the kidneys. Because lithium is absorbed by the proximal tubules, lithium clearance is about one fifth of creatinine clearance. Renal clearance of lithium is decreased with renal insufficiency (common in older people) and in the puerperium and is increased during pregnancy. Lithium is excreted in breast milk and in insignificant amounts in the feces and perspiration.

Pharmacodynamics

The therapeutic mechanism of action for lithium remains uncertain. The similarity of the lithium ion to the sodium, potassium, calcium, and magnesium ions may be related to its therapeutic effects. The mechanism of action for lithium may involve various neurotransmitter systems and the membrane

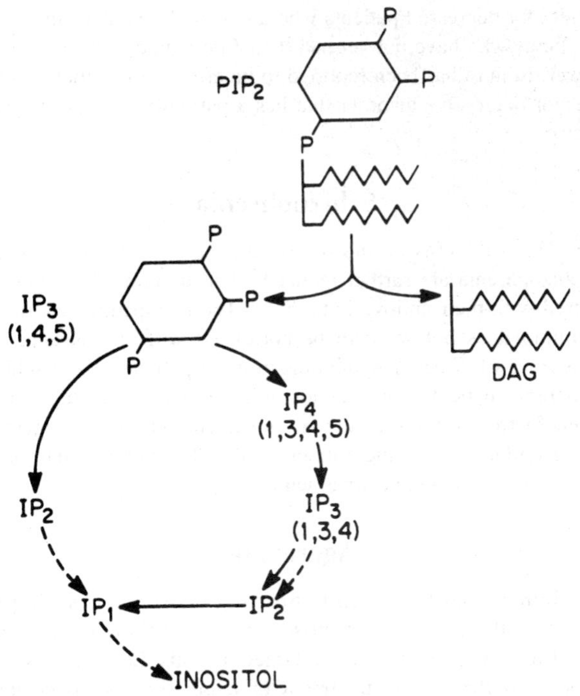
PIP$_2$
P
P
P
P
P
IP$_3$ (1,4,5)
P
DAG
IP$_4$ (1,3,4,5)
IP$_2$
IP$_3$ (1,3,4)
IP$_1$
IP$_2$
INOSITOL

FIGURE 35.3.19–1

Inositol phosphate metabolism. Phosphatidylinositol–bisphosphate (PIP_2) is hydrolyzed by phospholipase C, generating diacylglycerol (DAG), and inositol 1,4,5-triphosphate (IP $_3$[1,4,5]). IP_3(1,4,5) is acted on by either a kinase or a phosphatase, generating 1,3,4,5-tetrabisphosphate (IP_3[1,3,4,5]) or inositol 1,4-bisphosphate (IP_3[1,4]), respectively. IP_3(1,3,4,5) is hydrolyzed to IP_3(1,3,4) and then to IP_2. Specific phosphatases hydrolyze the various IP_2 isomers to inositol. Several inositol phosphatases are inhibited by lithium. Those are shown as *dotted arrows.* In some steps, both lithium-sensitive and lithium-insensitive enzymes are involved, so both *solid* and *dotted arrows* are shown. (Reprinted with permission from Baraban JM, Worley PF, Snyder SH: Second messenger systems and psychoactive drug action: Focus on the phosphoinositide system and lithium. Am J Psychiatry *146:* 1254, 1989.)

structure. One theory, which has mixed support in the literature, is that lithium works by blocking inositol phosphatases within the neurons. This inhibition results in decreased cellular responses to neurotransmitters that are linked to the phosphatidylinositol second-messenger system (Fig. 35.3.19–1).

EFFECTS ON SPECIFIC ORGANS AND SYSTEMS

Lithium most commonly affects the thyroid, heart, kidneys, and hematopoietic system. Lithium impedes the release of thyroid hormones from the thyroid and can result in hypothyroidism or goiter; the disorder affects women more than men. Lithium also impairs sinus node function, which can result in heart block in susceptible people. Lithium reduces the ability of the kidneys to concentrate urine. Although this effect is usually not clinically significant, it is not always reversible after discontinuing lithium. Pathological nonspecific interstitial fibrosis has been reported as a postmortem finding in some persons who were treated with lithium for a long time, but this is an unusual outcome. The major effect of lithium on the hematopoietic system is a clinically nonsignificant increase in leukocyte production.

THERAPEUTIC INDICATIONS

Bipolar I Disorder

Lithium has proved to be effective in both the short-term treatment and the prophylaxis of bipolar I disorder in about 70 to 80 percent of patients. Both manic and depressive episodes respond to lithium treatment alone. Lithium should also be considered as a potential treatment for patients with severe cyclothymic disorder.

Manic Episodes. About 80 percent of manic patients respond to lithium treatment, although the response to lithium alone can take 1 to 3 weeks of treatment at therapeutic concentrations. Because of the delay in response to lithium alone, benzodiazepines—for example, clonazepam (Klonopin) and lorazepam (Ativan)—or antipsychotics are used for the first 1 to 3 weeks to obtain immediate relief from the mania. Predictors of a poor response to lithium in the treatment of manic episodes include mixed and dysphoric manic episodes (which may occur in as many as 40 percent of patients), rapid cycling, and coexisting substance-related disorders (Table 35.3.19–1).

Depressive Episodes. Although not approved by the FDA, lithium is effective in the treatment of bipolar I disorder depression. About 80 percent of bipolar I disorder depressive patients respond to lithium treatment alone, a response that can eliminate the risk of an antidepressant-induced manic episode. When a depressive episode occurs in a patient already receiving maintenance lithium, the differential diagnosis should include lithium-induced hypothyroidism, substance abuse, and the lack of compliance with the lithium therapy. Possible treat-

Table 35.3.19–1
Factors Hypothesized to Predict Response to Lithium

Negative or Unfavorable Response	Positive or Favorable Response
Borderline features	Prior long-term response to lithium
Neuroticism	Classic euphoric or pure mania
Rapid cycling	Family history of bipolar disorder
Mixed manic/depressive symptoms	Secondary mania
Substance abuse	Family history of response to lithium
Psychosis	Obsessional features
Depression is followed by mania	Mania is followed by depression

Reprinted with permission from Krishnan KRR, Davidson JRT, Doraiswamy PM: Pharmacotherapy of depression in bipolar disorder. Prim Psychiatry *3:* 45, 1996.

ment approaches include increasing the lithium concentration (up to 1.2 mEq/L), adding supplemental thyroid hormone (for example, 25 μg a day of levothyroxine) even in the presence of normal findings on thyroid function tests, the judicious use of antidepressants, and electroconvulsive therapy (before which lithium should be discontinued to avoid complicating a patient's cognitive assessment).

Maintenance. Maintenance treatment with lithium markedly decreases the frequency, severity, and duration of manic and depressive episodes in patients with bipolar I disorder. Compared with placebo treatment, during which about 80 percent of bipolar I disorder patients relapse, only about 35 percent of lithium-treated patients relapse. Lithium maintenance is almost always indicated after the second episode of bipolar I disorder depression or mania. Lithium maintenance should be seriously considered after the first episode in patients who are adolescents, have a family history of bipolar I disorder, have poor support systems, had no precipitating factors for the first episode, had a serious first episode, have a high suicide risk, are 30 years old or older, had a sudden onset of their first episode, had a first episode of mania, or are male. Increased interest in initiating maintenance after the first episode is motivated by several observations: First, subsequent episodes may be increasingly likely after each additional episode. Second, some data indicate that relapses increase after lithium is discontinued. Third, case reports describe patients who were initially responsive to lithium but who lost their lithium responsiveness with subsequent episodes. The treatment response of lithium is such that continued maintenance treatment may be associated with increasing efficacy. It is not necessarily representative of treatment failure, therefore, when an episode of depression or mania occurs after a relatively short time of lithium maintenance. If lithium treatment alone loses its effectiveness, a clinician should consider supplemental treatment with carbamazepine (Tegretol) or valproate (Depakene).

Schizophrenic Disorder

The use of lithium for schizoaffective disorder (bipolar type) is certainly indicated. If a patient has schizoaffective disorder (depressive type) with a particularly cyclic nature, a lithium trial may be warranted. In general, the more a schizoaffective disorder patient resembles a patient with a mood disorder, the more likely lithium is to be effective; the more a schizoaffective disorder patient resembles a patient with schizophrenia, the less likely lithium is to be effective.

Major Depressive Disorder

The primary indication for lithium in major depressive disorder is as an adjuvant treatment to antidepressants in patients who have failed to respond to the antidepressants alone. Many studies have shown that about 50 percent of antidepressant nonresponders do respond when lithium is added to the antidepressant regimen (300 mg given 3 times daily). In some patients the response is dramatically rapid and occurs in days; in most patients, several weeks are required to assess the efficacy of the regimen. Lithium alone may be an effective treatment for depressed patients who are actually bipolar I disorder patients who have not yet had their first manic episode. Moreover, lithium has been reported to be effective in patients with major depressive disorder that has a particularly marked cyclicity.

Schizophrenia

The symptoms of one fifth to one half of all patients with schizophrenia are further reduced when lithium is coadministered with their antipsychotic drug. The therapeutic benefit of lithium does not seem to be correlated with the absence or presence of affective symptoms in these patients. Some schizophrenic patients who cannot take antipsychotic drugs may benefit from lithium treatment alone. The intermittent aggressive outbursts of some patients with schizophrenia may also be reduced by lithium treatment.

Aggression

Lithium has been used to treat aggressive outbursts in patients with schizophrenia, prison inmates, children with conduct disorder, and mentally retarded patients. Less success has been reported in the treatment of aggressiveness associated with head trauma and epilepsy. Other drugs for the treatment of aggression include anticonvulsants, β-adrenergic receptor antagonists, and antipsychotics. The treatment of aggressive patients requires a flexible approach in the use of these drugs along with psychosocial and behavioral treatment strategies.

Other Disorders

A few studies have reported that the episodic disorder characterizing premenstrual dysphoric disorder, the intermittent behaviors of borderline personality disorder, bulimia nervosa, and episodes of binge drinking respond to lithium treatment. Animal models of alcohol dependence have shown that lithium intake can reduce the intake of alcohol. In spite of these basic data, at least one large study has shown no benefit of lithium treatment in alcohol dependence, although anecdotal case reports and small studies in the literature are hopeful. Alcohol use disorder partly caused by an underlying bipolar disorder, for example, may be particularly amenable to lithium treatment. The same treatment may be appropriate for a patient with bipolar disorder who abuses cocaine.

Lithium has been used for treatment-refractory obsessive-compulsive disorder, trichotillomania, and posttraumatic stress disorder. Each of these indications, however, remains to be tested in a placebo-controlled trial. Lithium is particularly effective for the short-term treatment of cluster headaches.

PRECAUTIONS AND ADVERSE REACTIONS

The most common adverse effects of lithium treatment are gastric distress, weight gain, tremor, fatigue, and mild cognitive impairment (Table 35.3.19–2). Gastrointestinal symptoms, which can include nausea, decreased appetite, vomiting, and diarrhea, can often be reduced by dividing the dosage, administering the lithium with food, or switching to another lithium preparation. Weight gain results from a poorly understood effect of lithium on carbohydrate metabolism and can also result

Table 35.3.19–2
Side Effects of Lithium and Their Management

Side Effect	Management
Gastrointestinal complaints	Give lithium after meals, give smaller doses more often, try slow-release preparation, lower the dosage
Tremor	Lower the dosage, give propranolol (40–100 mg/day), consider adding a benzodiazepine
Polyuria-diabetes insipidus	Try slow-release preparation, lower the dosage, add amiloride (5–10 mg/day), careful monitoring of lithium levels
Acne	Benzoyl peroxide (5–10%) topical solution, erythromycin (1.5–2%) topical solution
Muscular weakness, fasciculations, headaches	Usually resolve with first few weeks of treatment
Hypothyroidism	Levothyroxine (0.05 mg qd), follow TSH level and increase to 0.2 mg qd as needed
T wave inversion	Benign, no treatment needed
Cardiac dysrhythmias	Usually must discontinue lithium
Psoriasis, alopecia areata	Dermatology consult, reversible if lithium stopped
Weight gain	Difficult to treat, diet, may be partially reversible if lithium stopped
Edema	Consider spironolactone (50 mg orally qd); if severe, monitor lithium levels; resolves when lithium stopped
Leukocytosis	Benign, no treatment needed

Reprinted with permission from Doupe A, Szuba M: Lithium and other antimanic agents. In *The Handbook of Psychiatry*, Residents of the UCLA Department of Psychiatry, p 386. Year Book Medical, Chicago, 1990.
qd, every day.

from lithium-induced edema. The only reasonable approach to weight gain is to encourage the patient to eat wisely and to engage in moderate exercise.

Tremor

The significance of drug-induced tremors is recognized in the fourth edition of *Diagnostic and Statistical Manual of Mental Disorders* (DSM-IV) by the inclusion of the diagnosis of medication-induced postural tremor. The tremor is usually an 8- to 10-Hz tremor and is most notable in outstretched hands, especially in the fingers. The tremor sometimes worsens during times of peak drug levels and can be reduced by dividing the daily dosage and by reducing caffeine intake. Propranolol (Inderal) (30 to 160 mg a day in divided doses) is usually effective in reducing the tremor in most patients. When a lithium-treated patient has a severe tremor, the possibility of lithium toxicity should be suspected and evaluated.

Cognitive Effects

Lithium use has been associated with dysphoria, lack of spontaneity, slowed reaction times, and impaired memory. The differential diagnosis for such symptoms should include depressive disorders, hypothyroidism, other illnesses, and other drugs. Some patients have reported that fatigue and mild cognitive impairment decrease with time.

Renal Effects

The most common adverse renal effect of lithium is polyuria with secondary polydipsia. The symptom is particularly a problem in 25 to 35 percent of patients who may have a urine output of 3 liters a day (normal output is 1 to 2 liters a day). The polyuria results from the lithium antagonism to the effects of antidiuretic hormone, the net result of which is to decrease resorption of fluid from the distal tubules of the kidneys. Polyuria may be significant enough to result in problems at work and in social settings and may be associated with insomnia, weight gain, and dehydration. When polyuria is a significant problem, the patient's renal function should be evaluated and followed up with 24-hour urine collections for creatinine clearance and with consultation with a nephrologist. Treatment consists of fluid replacement, the use of the lowest effective dosage of lithium, and single daily dosing of lithium. Treatment can also involve the use of a thiazide or potassium-sparing diuretic—for example, amiloride (Midamor), spironolactone (Aldactone), triamterene (Dyrenium), or amiloride–hydrochlorothiazide (Moduretic). If treatment with a diuretic is initiated, the lithium dosage should be halved, and the diuretic, because it is likely to increase the retention of lithium, should not be started for 5 days.

The most serious renal adverse effects, which are rarely associated with lithium administration, are minimal change glomerulonephritis, interstitial nephritis, and renal failure. The incidence of these severe renal complications is now thought to be lower than was originally supposed, but clinicians should consider such complications if the clinical picture warrants it.

Thyroid Effects

Lithium affects thyroid function and causes a generally benign and often transient diminution in the concentrations of circulating thyroid hormones. Reports have attributed goiter (5 percent of patients), benign reversible exophthalmos, and hypothyroidism (7 to 9 percent of patients) to lithium treatment. About 50 percent of patients receiving long-term lithium treatment have an abnormal thyrotropin-releasing hormone (TRH) response, and about 30 percent have elevated levels of thyroid-stimulating hormone (TSH). If symptoms of hypothyroidism are present, treatment with levothyroxine (Synthroid) is indicated. Even in the absence of hypothyroid symptoms, some clinicians treat patients with elevated TSH levels with levothyroxine. In lithium-treated patients, TSH levels should be measured every 6 to 12 months. Lithium-induced hypothyroidism should be considered when evaluating depressive episodes that emerge during lithium therapy.

Cardiac Effects

The cardiac effects of lithium, which resemble those of hypokalemia on the electrocardiogram (ECG), are caused by the displacement of intracellular potassium by the lithium ion. The most common changes on the ECG are T wave flattening or inversion. The changes are benign and disappear after the lithium is excreted from the body. Nevertheless, baseline ECGs are essential and should be repeated annually.

Because lithium also depresses the pacemaking activity of the sinus node, lithium treatment can result in sinus dysrhythmias and episodes of syncope. Lithium treatment, therefore, is contraindicated in patients with sick sinus syndrome. In rare cases, ventricular arrhythmias and congestive heart failure have been associated with lithium therapy.

Dermatological Effects

Several cutaneous adverse effects, which may be dose dependent, have been associated with lithium treatment. The most prevalent effects include acneiform, follicular, and maculopapular eruptions; pretibial ulcerations; and worsening of psoriasis. Alopecia has also been reported. Many of these conditions respond favorably to changing to another lithium preparation and to the usual dermatological measures. Lithium levels should be monitored if tetracycline is used to treat acne because of several reports of its increasing the retention of lithium. Occasionally, aggravated psoriasis or acneiform eruptions may force the discontinuation of lithium treatment.

Lithium Toxicity and Overdoses

The early signs and symptoms of lithium toxicity include coarse tremor, dysarthria, and ataxia; the later signs and symptoms include impaired consciousness, muscular fasciculations, myoclonus, seizures, and coma (Table 35.3.19–3). The higher the lithium levels and the longer the lithium levels have been high, the worse the symptoms of lithium toxicity. Lithium toxicity is a medical emergency and can result in permanent neuronal damage and death. The treatment of lithium toxicity involves discontinuing the lithium and treating the dehydration. The value of forced diuresis has been disputed. In the most serious cases, hemodialysis is an effective means by which lithium can be removed from the body (Table 35.3.19–4).

Overdose. Overdose of lithium results in symptoms of severe lithium toxicity. Treatment should be similar to that for lithium toxicity in general but can also include gastric lavage with a wide-bore tube because of the tendency of the drug to form large clumps in the stomach.

Adolescents

The serum lithium levels for adolescents are similar to those for adults. Although the side effect profile is similar in adolescents and adults, the weight gain and acne associated with lithium use can be particularly troublesome to an adolescent.

Geriatric Patients

Lithium is a safe and effective drug for older people. Lithium treatment of elderly patients, however, is complicated by the presence of other medical illnesses, decreased renal function, special diets that affect lithium clearance, and generally increased sensitivity to lithium-induced side effects. Because of this increased sensitivity, many elderly patients must be maintained on lower lithium concentrations than are younger adults. Elderly patients should be started on low dosages, their dosages should be switched less frequently than are dosages in younger patients, and a longer time must be allowed before

Table 35.3.19–3
Adverse Effects of Lithium

Early Onset (lithium level, 1.5–2.0 mEq/L)	Late Onset (lithium level, 2.0–2.5 mEq/L)	Toxicity (lithium level, 2.5 mEq/L)
Dry mouth	Dry mouth	Ataxia
Fine tremor (hand)	Fine tremor (hand)	Coarse tremor (hand)
GI disturbances	Cogwheel rigidity	GI disturbances (incl N/V)
Impaired concentration	Acne	Impaired concentration
Impaired memory	Psoriasis	Impaired memory
Leukocytosis	Leukocytosis	Nephrotoxicity
Muscle weakness	Alopecia	Muscle weakness
Polydipsia	Polydipsia	Convulsions
Polyuria	Polyuria	Coarse tremor
	Rash	Muscle twitches
	Weight gain	Dysarthria
	Metallic taste	Lethargy
	Nonspecific T-wave changes	Coma
	Decreased libido	Confusion
	Hypothyroidism	Hyperreflexia
		Nystagmus

Reprinted with permission from Ereshefsky L, Overman GP, Karp JK: Current psychotropic dosing and monitoring guidelines. Prim Psychiatry *3:* 21, 1996.
GI, gastrointestinal; N/V, nausea and vomiting.

Table 35.3.19–4
Management of Lithium Toxicity

1. The patient should immediately contact his or her personal physician or go to a hospital emergency room.
2. Lithium should be discontinued and the patient instructed to ingest fluids, if possible.
3. Physical examination, including vital signs, and a neurological examination with complete formal mental status examination should be completed.
4. Lithium level, serum electrolytes, renal function tests, and electrocardiogram should be obtained as soon as possible.
5. For significant short-term ingestions, residual gastric contents should be removed by induction of emesis, gastric lavage, and absorption with activated charcoal.
6. Vigorous hydration and maintenance of electrolyte balance are essential.
7. For any patient with a serum lithium level greater than 4.0 mEq per L within six hours of ingestion or for any patient with serious manifestations of lithium toxicity, hemodialysis should be initiated.
8. Repeat dialysis may be required every 6 to 10 hours until the lithium level is within nontoxic range and the patient has no signs or symptoms of lithium toxicity.

Reprinted with permission from Silver JM, Yudofsky SC, Hurowitz GI: Psychopharmacology and electroconvulsive therapy. In *The American Psychiatric Press Textbook of Psychiatry*, ed 2, RE Hales, SC Yudofsky, JA Talbott, editors. p 970. American Psychiatric Association Press, Washington, 1994.

assuming that their lithium concentrations are at steady-state levels because of possibly decreased renal function.

Pregnant Women

Early studies reported that about 10 percent of newborns who were exposed to lithium in the first trimester of pregnancy had major congenital malformations. The most common malformations involve the cardiovascular system, most commonly Ebstein's anomaly of the tricuspid valves. Recent epidemiological studies have found that the early studies may have significantly overestimated the risk. Although, ideally, a woman should not take any drug during pregnancy, the continuation of lithium therapy by a pregnant woman should not be considered out of the question. The possibility of fetal anomalies can be evaluated with fetal echocardiography. If a woman continues taking lithium during pregnancy, the lowest effective dosage should be used. Also, the maternal lithium level must be monitored closely during pregnancy and especially after delivery because of the significant change in renal function that occurs over that time period. Lithium should be discontinued shortly before delivery, and the drug should be restarted after an assessment of the usually high risk of a postpartum mood disorder and the mother's desire to breast-feed her infant. Lithium should not be administered to a woman who is breast-feeding. Signs of lithium toxicity in infants include lethargy, cyanosis, abnormal reflexes, and sometimes hepatomegaly.

Miscellaneous Effects

Rare neurological adverse effects include symptoms of mild parkinsonism, ataxia, and dysarthria, although these last two symptoms are usually symptoms of lithium intoxication. Lithium should be used with caution in patients with diabetes, who should monitor their blood glucose levels carefully to avoid diabetic ketoacidosis. Leukocytosis is a common benign effect of lithium treatment. Dehydrated, debilitated, and mentally ill patients are susceptible to side effects and toxicity.

Drug Interactions

Because of the possibility of lithium toxicity, on the one hand, and the need to maintain therapeutic lithium concentrations, on the other hand, clinicians must be aware of the many drug interactions that can involve lithium (Table 35.3.19–5). In lithium-treated patients who are about to undergo electroconvulsive therapy (ECT), lithium should be discontinued 2 days before beginning ECT, to reduce the risk of delirium resulting from the coadministration of the two treatments.

Most diuretics (for example, thiazide, potassium sparing, and loop) can increase lithium levels; when treatment with such a diuretic is stopped, a clinician may need to increase a patient's daily lithium dosage. Osmotic diuretics, carbonic anhydrase inhibitors, and xanthines (including caffeine) may reduce lithium levels to below therapeutic levels. Increasing reports indicate that angiotensin-converting enzyme inhibitors may cause an increase in lithium concentrations. A wide range of nonsteroidal anti-inflammatory drugs can decrease lithium clearance and thereby increase lithium concentrations; these drugs include diclofenac (Cataflam, Voltaren), diflunisal (Dolobid), etodolac (Lodine), fenoprofen (Nalfon), ibuprofen (Motrin), indomethacin (Indocin), ketoprofen (Orudis), ketorolac (Toradol), mefenamic acid (Ponstel), nabumetone (Relafen), naproxen (Aleve, Anaprox, Naprelan, Naprosyn), oxaprozin (Daypro), piroxicam (Feldene), and tolmetin (Tolectin). Aspirin and sulindac (Clinoril) do not affect lithium concentrations.

When coadministered, antipsychotics and lithium may result in a synergistic increase in the symptoms of lithium-induced neurological adverse effects. This interaction is not, as was initially thought, specifically associated with the coadministration of lithium and haloperidol (Haldol). Although the validity of the clinical observation has been questioned, clinicians should probably avoid the coadministration of high dosages of antipsychotics in the presence of high serum concentrations of lithium.

The coadministration of lithium and anticonvulsants—including carbamazepine, valproate, and clonazepam—may increase lithium levels and aggravate lithium-induced neurological adverse effects. As with antipsychotic medications, the clinician should probably avoid the administration of high dosages of anticonvulsants in patients with high lithium concentrations, but the coadministration of lithium and anticonvulsants can be therapeutically beneficial to some patients. Treatment with the combination should be initiated at slightly lower dosages than usual, and the dosages should be increased gradually. Lithium may have some protective effect against the granulocytopenia induced by carbamazepine, although no data indicate that the lithium reduces the risk of the serious carbamazepine-induced problems with agranulocytosis.

The coadministration of lithium and calcium channel inhibitors may cause neurotoxicity that can be fatal. Changes from

Table 35.3.19–5
Drug Interactions with Lithium

Class and Generic Name	Effect on Plasma Lithium Concentration	Significance
Antibiotics		
Tetracycline	Possible increase	Case reports; possibly from nephrotoxic effect of antibiotics; tetracycline may be safe
Spectinomycin	Possible increase	
Tricyclic drugs	Unknown	May cause switch to mania; increase in tremors
Nonsteroidal anti-inflammatory agents		
Ibuprofen	Increase	Case reports of piroxicam and diclofenac sodium increasing lithium concentrations; sulindac may have minimal effect
Indomethacin	Increase	
Naproxen	Increase	
Phenylbutazone	Increase	
Antipsychotics		
Chlorpromazine	Possibly increase in red blood cell (RBC) lithium	All antipsychotics may increase lithium's neurotoxicity
Fluphenazine	Possibly increase RBC lithium	
Haloperidol	Possibly increase plasma lithium	
Perphenazine	Possibly increase RBC lithium	
Thioridazine	Possibly increase RBC lithium	
Cardiovascular drugs		
Digoxin	Unknown	Case report of CNS confusion and bradycardia
ACE inhibitors	Increase	Case reports of toxicity, renal insufficiency
Methyldopa	Unknown	Case reports of neurological toxicity
Diltiazem	Unknown	Case report of neurological toxicity
Verapamil	Unknown	Case report of neurological toxicity
Diuretics		
Carbonic anhydrase inhibitors	Decrease	Increase lithium excretion
Acetazolamide	Decrease	
Loop diuretics		
Furosemide	Unclear	May increase lithium concentrations
Ethacrynic acid	Unclear	
Distal tubule diuretics		
Thiazides	Increase	Well-documented interaction with increase in lithium concentrations
Metolazone	Increase	
Chlorthalidone	Increase	
Osmotic diuretics		
Mannitol	Decrease	Increase lithium excretion
Urea	Decrease	
Potassium-sparing diuretics		
Triamterene	Increase	May increase lithium concentrations
Spironolactone	Increase	
Amiloride	Unclear	May be used to treat lithium-induced polyuria
Xanthines		
Theophylline	Decrease	Increase lithium excretion
Caffeine	Decrease	
Neuromuscular blocking drugs		
Succinylcholine	Unknown	May prolong neuromuscular blockade
Pancuronium bromide	Unknown	
Miscellaneous		
Sodium chloride	Decrease	Increase lithium excretion
Sodium bicarbonate	Decrease	Alkalinization of urine increases lithium excretion
Metronidazole	Increase	Reports of toxicity, renal damage
Metoclopramide	Unknown	Case report of extrapyramidal symptoms
Carbamazepine	Unknown	May have synergistic effect in treating mania and depression; case reports of neurotoxicity
Iodides	Unknown	May have additive or synergistic hypothyroid effect
Alcohol	Unknown	Increased lithium toxicity in animals; acute alcohol ingestion may increase peak lithium concentration
Phenytoin	Possible increase	Case reports of lithium toxicity and changes in phenytoin concentrations
Quinidine	Unknown	Altered sinus node conduction
Digoxin	Unknown	Altered sinus node conduction

Adapted from Kinney-Parker JL, Fankhauser MP: Bipolar disorder. In *Pharmacotherapy: A Pathophysiologic Approach*, JT DiPiro, RL Talbert, PE Hayes, GC Yee, LM Posey, editors, p 741. Elsevier, New York, 1989.

one to the other treatment for mania should be made carefully, with as little temporal overlap between the drugs as possible.

LABORATORY INTERFERENCES

Lithium is not known to interfere with any laboratory tests, but lithium treatment does affect a number of commonly obtained laboratory values (Table 35.3.19–6).

DOSAGE AND ADMINISTRATION

The mood-stabilizing effects of lithium appear between 5 and 14 days after initiation of therapy. Lithium is a monovalent ion and is available as a carbonate (for example, Lithane [Li_2CO_3]) for oral use in both rapidly acting and slow-release tablets and capsules. Lithium citrate (Cibalith-S) is available in a liquid form for oral administration (Table 35.3.19–7). Regular-release capsules or tablets are usually used first, and the syrup or slow-release preparations are used if noncompliance, nausea, or other adverse effects occur. These effects may improve with a different formulation.

Initial Medical Workup

Before a clinician administers lithium, a physician other than a psychiatrist should conduct a routine laboratory and physical examination. The laboratory examination should include a serum creatinine level (or a 24-hour urine creatinine if the clinician has any reason to be concerned about renal function), an electrolyte screen, thyroid function tests (T_4, T_3RU, FT_4I, and TSH), a complete blood count (CBC), ECG, and a pregnancy test if there is any possibility that the patient is pregnant (Table 35.3.19–8).

Table 35.3.19–6
Possible Effects of Lithium on Laboratory Values

Laboratory Value	Possible Effect
White blood cells (WBCs)	Increased count
Serum glucose	Increased level
Serum magnesium	Increased level
Serum potassium	Decreased level
Serum uric acid	Decreased level
Serum thyroxine	Decreased level
Serum cortisol	Decreased AM levels
Serum parathyroid hormone	Increased level due to adenoma
Serum calcium	Increased level due to increased parathyroid hormone level
Serum phosphorus	Decreased level due to increased parathyroid hormone level

Reprinted with permission from Doupe A, Szuba M: Lithium and other antimanic agents. In *The Handbook of Psychiatry*, Residents of the UCLA Department of Psychiatry, p 366. Year Book Medical, Chicago, 1990.

Table 35.3.19–7
Lithium Preparations

Lithium carbonate capsules 150, 300, 600 (Eskalith, Lithonate, generic)
Lithium carbonate tablets 300 (Eskalith, Lithane, Lithotabs, generic)
Lithium carbonate controlled-release tablets 450 mg (Eskalith CR)
Lithium carbonate slow-release tablets 300 mg (Lithobid)
Lithium citrate syrup 8 mEq/5 mL, 16 mEq/mL, (Cibalith-S, generic)

Plasma Concentrations

Serum and plasma concentrations of lithium are the standard methods of assessing lithium concentrations, and they serve as the basis by which to titrate the dosages. Although reports have noted the measurement of lithium concentrations in saliva, tears, and red blood cells, these methods have no clinical superiority to the standard methods. The patient must be at steady state (usually after 5 days of constant dosing), and the blood sample must be drawn 12 hours (plus or minus 30 minutes) after the last dose in a twice- or thrice-daily dosing regimen. Because available data are based on these standards, clinicians should initiate lithium treatment with regular-release formulations of lithium given at least twice daily. Once the dosage has been adjusted, changing the formulation of the dosing schedule is reasonable. Lithium levels in patients treated with slow-release preparations are about 30 percent higher than the levels obtained with normal-release preparations.

The most common guidelines are 1.0 to 1.5 mEq/L to treat acute mania and 0.6 to 1.2 mEq/L for maintenance treatment.

Table 35.3.19–8
Summary: Method of Lithium Use

Before beginning lithium
- Medical history
- Physical examination
- Blood urea nitrogen, creatinine
- T_4, T_3 resin uptake, TSH
- Electrocardiogram (ECG) with rhythm strip recommended if patient is over age 50 or has history of cardiac disease
- CBC (optional)
- Human chorionic gonadotropin (pregnancy test), if appropriate

Initial dosing
- Usually 300 mg tid
- Lower doses in elderly or with renal disease (150–300 bid)

Blood levels
- Draw approximately 12 hours after the last oral dose
- At start of therapy, every 5 days to adjust dose
- Draw less frequently as levels stabilize
- For stable long-term patients, draw every 3–6 months
- Draw immediately if toxicity suspected

Follow-up monitoring (stable patients)
- Creatinine, TSH every 6 months
- For patients over age 40 or with cardiac disease, follow-up ECGs as indicated

Reprinted with permission from Hyman SE, Arana GW, Rosenbaum JF: *Handbook of Psychiatric Drug Therapy*, ed 3, p 106. Little, Brown, Boston, 1996.

It is almost never necessary to exceed 1.5 mEq/L, as patients with higher lithium levels are at much higher risk for lithium toxicity. If, in a very few patients, maximal therapeutic benefit has not been obtained and if side effects are absent, titration of the patient above 1.5 mEq/L may be warranted. One recent study found that patients with lithium concentrations in the range of 0.8 to 1.0 mEq/L are 2.6 times less likely to relapse than are patients with lithium concentrations in the range of 0.4 to 0.6 mEq/L. This study led some researchers and clinicians to consider 0.8 to 1.0 mEq/L as the most effective range for maintenance lithium concentrations.

Lithium Dosage Prediction. Several researchers and clinicians have proposed various lithium dose prediction protocols. The protocols are generally based on the administration of a single dose of lithium, followed by the assessment of lithium concentrations at 12- or 24-hour time points. These concentrations are then used to predict the final dosage of lithium that a patient will require. Most clinicians and researchers have not adopted lithium dosage prediction protocols for two reasons: First, the upward titration of lithium in patients is relatively straightforward and quick without the use of such a protocol. Second, the rapid dose increase associated with the use of a dosage prediction protocol often results in adverse effects, especially gastrointestinal effects, that may adversely affect the patient's subsequent compliance with the medication regimen.

Dosage

If a patient has previously been treated with lithium and the previous dosage is known, a clinician should probably use this dosage for the current episode unless changes in the patient's pharmacokinetic parameters have affected lithium clearance. For most adult patients, the clinician should start lithium at 300 mg 3 times daily. The starting dosage in patients who are elderly or who have renal impairment should be 300 mg once or twice daily. The usual eventual dosage is between 900 and 1,800 mg a day, given in two or three divided doses.

The use of divided doses reduces gastric upset and avoids single high-peak lithium levels. A current debate concerns whether multiple small daily peaks are less likely than a single high daily peak to cause adverse effects. Single daily dosing is not considered standard practice at this time. Slow-release lithium preparations can be given 2 or 3 times daily and result in low peak levels of lithium, but this procedure has not been proved to be of special value. Magnetic resonance spectroscopy studies have suggested that the clinical response to lithium correlates better with the brain concentrations than with the serum concentrations. These findings further complicate efforts to establish a generalizable, optimal dosing regimen.

Patient Education

Clinicians should advise patients that changes in the body's water and salt content can affect the amount of lithium excreted and can result in either increases or decreases in lithium levels. Excessive sodium intake (for example, a dramatic dietary change) lowers lithium levels. Conversely, too little sodium (for example, fad diets) can lead to potentially toxic levels of lithium. Decreases in body fluid (for example, excessive perspiration) can lead to dehydration and lithium intoxication.

Failure of Drug Treatment

If the drug produces no clinical response after 4 weeks at therapeutic levels, slightly higher serum levels (up to 1.5 mEq/L) may be tried if there are no limiting adverse effects. If, after 2 weeks at a high serum concentration, the drug is still ineffective, the patient should be tapered off the drug over 1 to 2 weeks. Other drugs should be given therapeutic trials at this point.

Rapid Cycling. Rapid cycling is defined as the presence of four or more episodes of illness during the year; some patients experience many more than four episodes. Rapid-cycling bipolar I disorder is present in as many as 20 percent of all patients and is associated with antidepressant treatment, thyroid abnormalities, and neurological disorders. If lithium treatment is ineffective in a rapid-cycling patient, thyroid hormones, carbamazepine, valproate, other anticonvulsants, electroconvulsive therapy, bupropion (Wellbutrin), calcium channel inhibitors, clonazepam, monoamine oxidase inhibitors, and clozapine are all potential treatment options for clinicians to consider.

References

Bouman TK, de Vries J, Koopmans IH: Lithium prophylaxis and inter-episode mood: A prospective longitudinal comparison of euthymic bipolars and non-patient controls. J Affect Disord *24:* 199, 1992.

Campbell M, Katantaris V, Cueva JE: An update on the use of lithium carbonate in aggressive children and adolescents with conduct disorder. Psychopharmacol Bull *31:* 93, 1995.

Granneman GR, Schneck DW, Cavanaugh JH, Witt GF: Pharmacokinetic interactions and side effects resulting from concomitant administration of lithium and divalproex sodium. J Clin Psychiatry *57:* 204, 1996.

Greil W, Ludwig-Mayerhofer W, Erazo N, Engel RR, et al: Comparative efficacy of lithium and amitriptyline in the maintenance treatment of recurrent unipolar depression: A randomized study. J Affect Disord *40* (3): 179, 1996.

Hoffman L, Halmi KA: Psychopharmacology in the treatment of anorexia nervosa and bulimia nervosa. Psychiatr Clin North Am *16:* 767, 1993.

Jefferson JW, Greist JH: Lithium. In *Comprehensive Textbook of Psychiatry,* ed 6, HI Kaplan, BJ Sadock, editors, p 2022. Williams & Wilkins, Baltimore, 1995.

Kane JM: Drug therapy: Schizophrenia. N Engl J Med *334:* 34, 1996.

Katona CLE: Refractory depression: A review with particular reference to the use of lithium augmentation. Eur Neuropsychopharmacol *5* (Suppl): 109, 1995.

Keck PE, McElroy SL: Outcome in the pharmacologic treatment of bipolar disorder. J Clin Psychopharmacol *16* (1, Suppl): 15S, 1996.

Markoff RA, King M Jr: Does lithium dose prediction improve treatment efficiency? Prospective evaluation of a mathematical method. J Clin Psychopharmacol *12:* 305, 1992.

Müller-Oerlinghausen B, Ahrens B, Grof E, Grof P, Lenz G, Schou M, Simhandl C, Thau K, Volk J, Wolf R, Wolf T: The effect of long-term lithium treatment on the mortality of patients with manic-depressive and schizoaffective illness. Acta Psychiatr Scand *86:* 218, 1992.

O'Brien G: Treatment of patients with learning disabilities and schizoaffective illness. Hum Psychopharmacol *10:* 491, 1995.

Pantelis C, Barnes TRE: Drug strategies and treatment-resistant schizophrenia. Aust NZ J Psychiatry *30* (1): 20, 1996.

Pert M, Pratt JP: Lithium: Current status in psychiatric disorders. Drugs *46:* 7, 1993.

Reischer H, Pfeffer CR: Lithium pharmacokinetics. Am Acad Child Adolesc Psychiatry *35* (2): 130, 1996.

Schou M: Forty years of lithium treatment. Arch Gen Psychiatry *54:* 9, 1997.

Sharpley AL, Walsh AES, Cowen PJ: Effect of nefazodone and lithium on sleep architecture in healthy men. J Psychopharmacol *10* (1, Suppl): 26, 1996.
Simhandl C, Meszaros K: Adjunctive carbamazepine or lithium carbonate in therapy-resistant chronic schizophrenia. Can J Psychiatry *41:* 317, 1996.
Solomon DA, Ristow WR, Keller JM, Goldberg AJ, Rosenbaum JF, Warshaw MG: Serum lithium levels and psychosocial function in patients with bipolar I disorder. Am J Psychiatry *153:* 1301, 1996.
Stein G, Bernadt M: Lithium augmentation therapy in tricyclic-resistant depression: A controlled trial using lithium in low and normal doses. Br J Psychiatry *162:* 634, 1993.
Stoll AL, Locke CA, Vuckovic A, Mayer PV: Lithium-associated cognitive and functional deficits reduced by a switch to divalproex sodium: A case series. J Clin Psychiatry *57* (8): 356, 1996.
Swanson CL, Price WA, McEvoy JP: Effects of concomitant risperidone and lithium treatment. Am J Psychiatry *152:* 1096, 1995.
Tariot PN, Schneider LS: Anticonvulsant and other non-neuroleptic treatment of agitation in dementia. J Geriatr Psychiatry Neurol *8* (1, Suppl): S28, 1995.

▲ 35.3.20 Methadone

Methadone (Dolophine) is used in psychiatry primarily for detoxification and maintenance therapy with patients who are addicted to opiates and opioids. The treatment was introduced by Vincent Dole and Marie Nyswander in 1965. Treatment with methadone effectively substitutes a controllable, less harmful addiction for an addiction to illicit drugs. Methadone treatment causes an unpleasant withdrawal reaction if suddenly stopped and requires less adjunctive psychological support than does the treatment of opioid dependence with the pure opioid antagonist naltrexone (ReVia). Methadone has also been used for the chronic management of pain. The mixed opioid agonist-antagonist buprenorphine (Buprenex) and levomethadyl acetate (ORLAAM), a congener of methadone, are two other agents used in the treatment of opioid dependence.

CHEMISTRY

Methadone is a synthetic diphenylheptane derivative. Its molecular structure is shown in Figure 35.3.20–1.

PHARMACOLOGICAL ACTIONS

Pharmacokinetics

Methadone is well absorbed from the gastrointestinal tract and has an initial duration of action of 4 to 6 hours. The duration of action increases to 22 to 48 hours with repeated administration and is elevated in people who have been abusing opiate agonists. Methadone is metabolized by the liver and is excreted by the kidneys. The long half-life of methadone provides a smooth curve of bioavailability and contrasts with the rapid subjective high and subsequent crash associated with heroin use (Fig. 35.3.20–2).

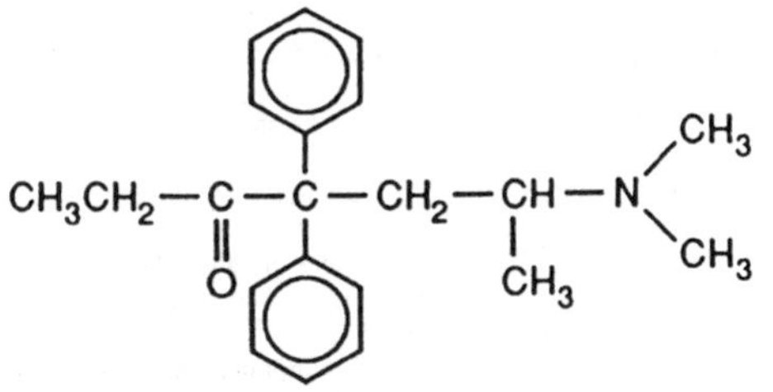

FIGURE 35.3.20–1
Molecular structure of methadone.

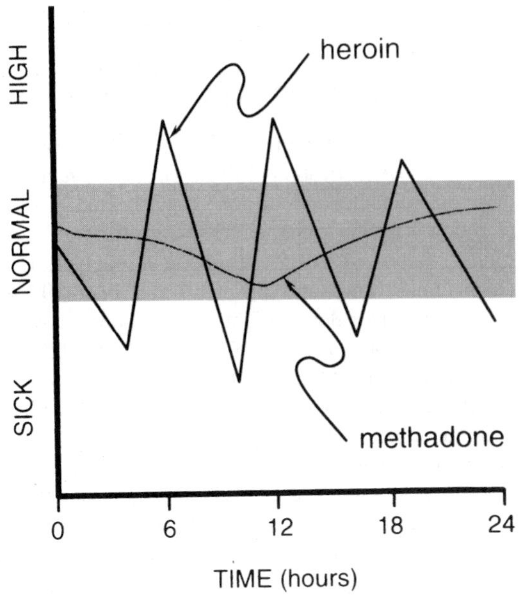
HIGH
NORMAL
SICK
heroin
methadone
0
6
12
18
24
TIME (hours)

FIGURE 35.3.20–2
Differences in responses to heroin and methadone. A person who injects heroin several times a day oscillates between being sick and being high. In contrast, the typical methadone patient remains in the "normal" range (indicated in *gray*) with little fluctuation after dosing once a day. *Curves* represent the subject's mental and physical state, not plasma levels of the drug. (Reprinted with permission from O'Brien CP: Drug addiction and drug abuse. In *Goodman & Gilman's The Pharmacological Basis of Therapeutics,* ed 9, JG Hardman, LE Limbird, PB Molinoff, RW Ruddon, editors, p 568. McGraw-Hill, New York, 1996.)

Pharmacodynamics

Methadone is an opiate receptor agonist. It has activity at μ, κ, and, probably, δ opiate receptors. The agonist effects of methadone on these receptors block the withdrawal symptoms caused by the cessation of heroin abuse. Methadone has its own analgesic effects but does not cause the same euphoria as heroin.

EFFECTS ON SPECIFIC ORGANS AND SYSTEMS

Besides the central nervous system (CNS) effects, the most significant effects of methadone are on the gastrointestinal, genitourinary, and autonomic systems. In the gastrointestinal system, methadone can cause biliary spasm, colic, and constipation. In the genitourinary system, methadone is associated with urinary retention and oliguria. Autonomic activation by methadone can cause sweating, flushing, pruritus, and urticaria.

THERAPEUTIC INDICATIONS

Methadone is used for the short-term detoxification (30 days), long-term detoxification (180 days), and maintenance of opiate and opioid addicts. Methadone is a schedule II drug; its administration is tightly governed by specific federal laws and regulations. Methadone is only available through designated methadone clinics, and some patients travel over 100 miles each way to take their doses. Eight states do not allow methadone clinics, and only 115,000 of the estimated 600,000 heroin users in the United States are enrolled in a methadone program. It is estimated that only 5 to 20 percent of methadone users continue to take the drug for more than 10 years. Various reasons for this fact may include drug abstinence, relapse into heroin use, frustration at the cumbersome and petty bureaucracy that supplies the drug, the incorrect belief that methadone is harmful to one's health, and fears of the social stigma associating methadone with illicit drug use. A small number of well-organized and well-motivated patients are able to use methadone indefinitely while holding down steady employment, but many opioid addicts lack sufficient education and job skills or are addicted to multiple drugs and, therefore, cannot persist with methadone. The regulations are currently in a state of flux because of the increase in efforts to place intravenous drug abusers in methadone programs. The aim of such renewed efforts is to reduce the spread of acquired immune deficiency syndrome (AIDS), which can be contracted by the use of contaminated needles.

The highly effective analgesic effects of methadone are utilized in the management of chronic pain when less potentially addictive agents are inadequate.

PRECAUTIONS AND ADVERSE REACTIONS

An overdose of methadone can cause respiratory and circulatory depression, leading to respiratory arrest, cardiac arrest, and death. Methadone is also capable of inducing tolerance, psychological dependence, and physical dependence. Other adverse effects on the CNS include dizziness, depression, sedation, euphoria, dysphoria, agitation, and seizures. Delirium and insomnia have also been reported in rare cases. Methadone should be used with caution in patients with respiratory disease, hepatic or renal dysfunction, and seizure disorders.

Pregnancy

Methadone should be administered to pregnant women only if the potential benefits outweigh the possible risks. Because detoxification is not recommended for pregnant women, maintenance methadone may be appropriate in some circumstances. Whether methadone treatment is harmful to the fetus is unknown. A significant number of infants born to mothers receiving methadone show withdrawal symptoms, which may be mitigated with use of clonidine. Women should not breast-feed their babies if they are taking methadone.

DRUG INTERACTIONS

Methadone can potentiate CNS depressant effects of other opiate agonists, barbiturates, benzodiazepines, and alcohol. Antipsychotics, especially low-potency agents, tricyclic and tetracyclic drugs, and monoamine oxidase inhibitors (MAOIs) should be used cautiously with methadone. Two other opiate agonists, meperidine (Demerol) and fentanyl (Duragesic), have been associated with fatal drug–drug interactions with the MAOIs. The opiate antagonists naltrexone and naloxone may precipitate an acute methadone withdrawal reaction consisting of drug craving, feeling of temperature change, musculoskeletal pain, gastrointestinal distress, confusion, drowsiness, vomiting, and diarrhea. Therefore, patients should be fully detoxified of methadone, as proven by a naloxone challenge test, before the initiation of naltrexone.

LABORATORY INTERFERENCES

No known laboratory interferences are associated with methadone treatment.

DOSAGE AND ADMINISTRATION

Methadone is supplied in dispersible tablets of 5, 10, and 40 mg; in oral solutions of 5 mg/5 mL, 10 mg/5 mL, and 10 mg/mL; and in a parenteral form of 10 mg/mL.

Methadone acts within 30 to 60 minutes of administration. In maintenance programs, methadone is usually administered dissolved in water or fruit juice. For short-term detoxification, an initial dose of 15 to 20 mg usually suppresses withdrawal symptoms; additional doses can be given if the initial dose is insufficient. A dosage of 40 mg a day in single or divided doses is usually sufficient to control withdrawal symptoms in most patients. After stabilization, the methadone dosage is tapered at a rate that depends on the type of program, whether the patient is an inpatient or an outpatient, and the patient's level of tolerance for the withdrawal symptoms. If withdrawal takes more than 180 days, the treatment program is officially described as methadone maintenance. Maintenance should be at the lowest possible dosage of methadone, and, generally, patients should eventually be withdrawn completely from methadone. The administration of methadone for both withdrawal and maintenance must follow strict federal guidelines, which generally require that patients receive the methadone in person to avoid its abuse by people other than the patient.

References

Cacciola JS, Rutherford MJ, Alterman AI, McKay JR, Snider EC: Personality disorders and treatment outcome in methadone maintenance patients. J Nerv Ment Dis *184:* 234, 1996.

Desmond DP, Maddux JF: Compulsory supervision and methadone maintenance. J Subst Abuse Treat *13* (1): 79, 1996.

Farrell M, Strang J: Compressed opiate withdrawal syndrome and naltrexone. J Psychopharmacol *9:* 383, 1995.

Goehl L, Nunes E, Quitkin F, Hilton L: Social networks and methadone treatment outcome: The costs and benefits of social ties. Am J Drug Alcohol Abuse *19:* 251, 1993.

Gossop M, Strang J: A comparison of the withdrawal responses of heroin and methadone addicts during detoxification. Br J Psychiatry *158:* 697, 1991.

Greif GL, Drechsler M: Common issues for parents in a methadone maintenance group. J Subst Abuse Treat *10:* 339, 1993.

Ling W, Wesson DR: A controlled trial comparing buprenorphine and methadone maintenance in opioid dependence. Arch Gen Psychiatry *53:* 401, 1996.
Loimer N, Lenz K, Schmid R, Presslich O: Technique for greatly shortening the transition from methadone to naltrexone maintenance of patients addicted to opiates. Am J Psychiatry *148:* 933, 1991.
Longshore D, Hsieh SC, Danila B, Anglin MD: Methadone maintenance and needle/syringe sharing. Int J Addict *28:* 983, 1993.
Maddux JF, Desmong DP: Methadone maintenance and recovery from opioid dependence. Am Drug Alcohol Abuse *18:* 63, 1992.
Milby JB, Sims MK, Khuder S, Schumacher JE, Huggins N, McLellan AT, Woody G, Haas N: Psychiatric comorbidity: Prevalence in methadone maintenance treatment. Am J Drug Alcohol Abuse *22:* 95, 1996.
Nunes EV, Quitkin FM, Brady R, Stewart JW: Imipramine treatment of methadone maintenance patients with affective disorder and illicit drug use. Am J Psychiatry *148:* 667, 1991.
Prendergast ML, Grella C, Perry SM, Anglin MD: Levo-alpha-acetylmethadol (LAAM): Clinical, research, and policy issues of a new pharmacotherapy for opioid addiction. J Psychoactive Drugs *27:* 239, 1995.
Schottenfeld RS, Kleber HD: Methadone. In *Comprehensive Textbook of Psychiatry,* ed 6, HI Kaplan, BJ Sadock, editors, p 2031. Williams & Wilkins, Baltimore, 1995.
Strain EC, Stitzer ML, Liebson IA, Bigelow GE: Buprenorphine versus methadone in the treatment of opioid dependence: Self-reports, urinalysis and addiction severity index. J Clin Psychopharmacol *16* (1): 58, 1996.
Walsh SL, June HL, Schuh KJ: Effects of buprenorphine and methadone in methadone-maintained subjects. Psychopharmacology *119:* 268, 1995.
Wolff K, Hay A, Raistrick D, Calvert R, Feely M: Measuring compliance in methadone maintenance patients: Use of a pharmacologic indicator to estimate methadone plasma levels. Clin Pharmacol Ther *50:* 199, 1991.

▲ 35.3.21 Mirtazapine

Mirtazapine (Remeron) is an antidepressant with a novel mechanism of action, specifically the antagonism of central presynaptic α_2-adrenergic receptors, which results in potentiation of central noradrenergic and serotonergic neurotransmission. It appears to be as effective as amitriptyline in lifting mood, yet it lacks the anticholinergic effects of the tricyclic class of antidepressants and the anxiogenic effects of the serotonin-specific reuptake inhibitors (SSRIs). Mirtazapine caused somnolence in over 50 percent of patients in preclinical trials, however, which led to discontinuance in 10 percent of patients. Mirtazapine also potently blocks serotonin 5-hydroxytryptamine type 2 (5-HT_2) and type 3 (5-HT_3) receptors and apparently causes a net activation of primarily the serotonin type 1A (5-HT_{1A}) receptors. For this reason, it has been classified as a noradrenergic and specific serotonergic antidepressant (NaSSA). Only one small clinical trial directly comparing mirtazapine with the SSRIs has been reported, although mirtazapine has been available in Europe since 1994.

CHEMISTRY

Mirtazapine is a tetracyclic antidepressant of the piperazinoazepine class. It is the 6-aza derivative of mianserin, a tetracyclic compound not available in the United States. Its molecular structure is shown in Figure 35.3.21–1.

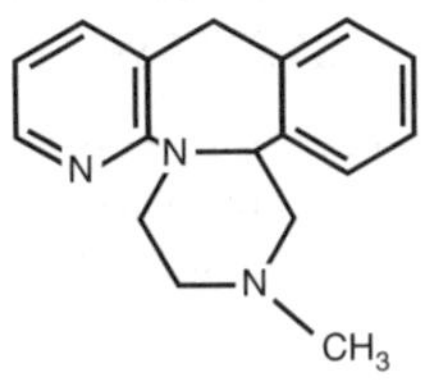
N
N
N
CH3

FIGURE 35.3.21–1
The molecular structure of mirtazapine.

PHARMACOLOGICAL ACTIONS

Pharmacokinetics

Mirtazapine is rapidly and completely absorbed from the gastrointestinal tract, but because of significant first-pass hepatic metabolism, the bioavailability is about 50 percent. Peak concentration of mirtazapine is achieved within 2 hours of ingestion. There are no active metabolites. Plasma levels are linearly related to dose over a range of 15 to 80 mg, and the drug is approximately 85 percent protein bound over a wide range of plasma concentrations. Plasma clearance may be up to 30 percent slower in patients with impaired hepatic function and up to 50 percent slower in patients with impaired renal function. Clearance may be up to 40 percent slower in elderly men and up to 10 percent slower in elderly women. It is not known whether it is distributed into maternal milk.

The mean elimination half-life is 20 to 40 hours. Thus, steady-state levels are achieved in about 5 days. The metabolism consists mainly of hepatic glucuronidation, followed by excretion that is mostly renal.

A clinical response may be seen as early as 1 week after onset of use or may require from 2 to 4 weeks of therapy.

Pharmacodynamics

Mirtazapine acts as an antagonist of central presynaptic α_2-adrenergic receptors in the central nervous system (CNS). This action is thought to potentiate the release of serotonin and noradrenaline and secondarily to increase serotonergic cell firing in the dorsal raphe nucleus, through a noradrenergic mechanism. Thus, like the tricyclics and SSRIs, the drug has a net effect of increasing synaptic levels of noradrenaline and serotonin, albeit by a novel mechanism. It is also a potent antagonist of 5-HT_2 and 5-HT_3 receptors but has little effect on 5-HT_{1A} receptors. The direct serotonergic receptor antagonism appears to bias the activation of serotonin receptors in favor of the 5-HT_1 family, activation of which is thought to treat anxiety and depression, and against the 5-HT_2 and 5-HT_3 families, antagonism of which is also thought to treat anxiety and depression and activation of which may cause unwanted anxiety, insomnia, nausea, and sexual dysfunction. Conclusions about the roles of the various subtypes of serotonin receptors in complex behaviors and emotions are, however, preliminary at best. This area of research is active, and as associations of specific receptors with specific behaviors emerge, mirtazapine will come to be viewed as a prototype for ever more specific psychopharmacological agents.

Mirtazapine is a potent antagonist of histamine H_1 receptors, is a moderate antagonist at α_1-adrenergic and muscarinic cholinergic receptors, and has a low affinity for dopamine D_1 and D_2 receptors.

EFFECTS ON SPECIFIC ORGANS AND SYSTEMS

Mirtazapine exerts most of its effects in the CNS, and the principal non-CNS effects are in the gastrointestinal system (discussed in Precautions and Adverse Reactions).

THERAPEUTIC INDICATIONS

The U.S. Food and Drug Administration (FDA) has approved mirtazapine for the treatment of depression. The drug also appears to reduce anxiety and to induce sleep. In placebo-controlled, double-blind studies, 56 percent of patients taking mirtazapine had significant improvement on two depression rating scales, as opposed to 36 percent of patients taking placebo. The dropout rates for mirtazapine have been relatively high in most studies. There is presently little evidence from direct comparisons of mirtazapine and first-line antidepressants for mildly to moderately depressed patients. In direct comparison with amitriptyline, mirtazapine was equally efficacious and caused equal amounts of somnolence and weight gain, but mirtazapine was associated with fewer anticholinergic and cardiovascular adverse effects than was amitriptyline. In direct comparison with fluoxetine in severely depressed patients, both drugs were effective. Mirtazapine has been shown in direct comparisons to be as efficacious for depression, depression with anxiety, and depression with cognitive disturbances as trazodone, doxepin, and clomipramine, yet to have fewer adverse effects. With the exception of fluoxetine, in which the comparison was in a patient population for which fluoxetine may not be the drug of first choice, each of the drugs with which mirtazapine has been directly compared in controlled studies is distinguished by high degrees of sedation. Mirtazapine's sedating qualities make it as effective for insomnia as amitriptyline and trazodone. Pilot studies have shown mirtazapine to be superior to placebo for anxiety disorders, but more studies will be needed to establish mirtazapine as a first-line agent for treatment of anxiety. Because of unanswered questions regarding whether mirtazapine causes neutropenia and because of its profile of adverse effects, mirtazapine should probably be reserved at this time for use in patients who are unresponsive to first-line antidepressants.

PRECAUTIONS AND ADVERSE REACTIONS

In preclinical trials, 16 percent of patients discontinued mirtazapine because of an adverse event, compared with 7 percent of patients taking placebo. The most common reasons for discontinuance were somnolence (10.4 percent) and nausea (1.5 percent). The adverse reactions reported with mirtazapine are listed in Table 35.3.21–1. Mirtazapine and bupropion (Wellbutrin) are notable among antidepressants for their lack of sexual adverse effects.

Table 35.3.21–1
Adverse Reactions Reported with Mirtazapine

	%
Somnolence	54
Dry mouth	25
Increased appetite	17
Constipation	13
Weight gain	12
Dizziness	7
Myalgias	5
Abnormal dreams	4

Central Nervous System Effects

The most common adverse effect of mirtazapine is somnolence, which may occur in over 50 percent of patients, a rate roughly comparable to that of amitriptyline. Therefore, patients who take mirtazapine should exercise caution when driving or operating dangerous machinery. This side effect is minimized by giving the dose before sleep. Mirtazapine also caused dizziness in 7 percent of patients. It does not appear to increase the risk of seizures. Mania or hypomania occurred in 0.2 percent of patients in clinical trials, a finding that indicates a need for caution in patients with a history of mania or hypomania. Mirtazapine potentiated the sedative effects of alcohol.

Gastrointestinal Effects

Mirtazapine caused increased appetite in 17 percent of patients studied, compared with 2 percent of placebo-treated patients, and 7.5 percent of patients increased their weight more than 7 percent. Eight percent of patients discontinued mirtazapine for this reason. Mirtazapine also caused increases of serum cholesterol to 20 percent above the upper limit of normal in 15 percent of patients and increases of triglycerides to 500 mg/dL in 6 percent of patients. Roughly twice as many mirtazapine patients as placebo or amitriptyline patients showed these dyslipidemias. Elevations of alanine aminotransferase (ALT [SGPT]) levels to more than 3 times the upper limit of normal were seen in 2 percent of mirtazapine patients as opposed to 0.3 percent of placebo controls.

Agranulocytosis and Neutropenia

On the basis of limited premarketing experience, up to 0.3 percent of patients taking mirtazapine may be expected to develop an absolute neutrophil count of 500 per mm^3 within 2 months of onset of use and may develop symptomatic infections. This hematological condition was reversible in all cases. The manufacturer recommends that all patients be instructed to seek medical attention if they develop fever, chills, sore throat, mucous membrane ulceration, or other signs of infection. If a low white blood cell count is found, mirtazapine should be immediately discontinued, and the patient should be followed closely. Although 3 of 2,796 patients in premarketing studies developed this complication, no cases were reported in 13,500 patients who took the drug in the Netherlands, and the true incidence of bone marrow suppression may not be much different from that of other antidepressants.

Other Adverse Reactions

A few patients experienced orthostatic hypotension while on mirtazapine. Therefore it should be used with caution by patients with a history of cardiac conditions or autonomic instability.

Carcinogenicity and Mutagenesis

Possibly incomplete animal experiments have shown an increased incidence of hepatocellular and thyroid follicular adenoma and carcinoma at doses equivalent to 2 to 20 times the maximum recommended human dose (MRHD) of 45 mg a day. The significance of these data for humans is unknown. No direct DNA damaging mutagenetic effects were seen in several standard assays, and teratogenicity was also not seen. Doses 3 times the MRHD disrupted estrus cycles, and doses 20 times the MRHD caused preimplantation losses. Although there are no human data about effects on fetal development, mirtazapine should be used with caution during pregnancy.

Precautions

Mirtazapine use by pregnant women has not yet been studied, and because the drug may be excreted in breast milk, it should not be taken by nursing mothers. Because of the small risk of agranulocytosis associated with mirtazapine use, patients should be attuned to signs of infection as earlier discussed. Whether the risk of agranulocytosis to mirtazapine is higher than for other antidepressants remains a question. Because the antihistamine effects of mirtazapine may impair judgment, thinking, and, above all, motor skills, patients should determine the degree to which they are affected before engaging in driving or other potentially dangerous activities. Other potentially sedating prescription or over-the-counter drugs and alcohol should be avoided during use of mirtazapine.

DRUG INTERACTIONS

Because of its extensive hepatic metabolism, mirtazapine may affect or be affected by other drugs that influence hepatic enzyme levels. The clinical importance of these potential interactions is unknown. Mirtazapine is metabolized by the hepatic enzymes CYP 2D6, CYP 1A2, and CYP 3A4, yet it apparently does not inhibit or potentiate any members of the hepatic cytochrome P450 system. Mirtazapine has been reported to potentiate the sedation of alcohol and benzodiazepines. Mirtazapine should not be used within 14 days of beginning or stopping a monoamine oxidase inhibitor.

LABORATORY INTERFERENCES

No laboratory interferences have yet been described for mirtazapine.

DOSAGE AND ADMINISTRATION

Like the tricyclic drugs and the SSRIs, mirtazapine's antidepressant effects usually appear within 2 to 4 weeks after initiation of treatment. Mirtazapine is administered orally and is currently available in 15 and 30 mg tablets. If patients fail to respond to the initial dose of mirtazapine of 15 mg a day, the dose may be increased in 15-mg increments every 2 weeks to a maximum of 45 mg a day. The manufacturer does not recommend periodic monitoring of the absolute neutrophil count at present.

References

Claghorn JL, Lesem MD: A double-blind placebo-controlled study of Org 3770 in depressed outpatients. J Affect Disord *34:* 165, 1995.

Davis R, Wilde MI: Mirtazapine: A review of its pharmacology and therapeutic potential in the management of major depression. CNS Drugs *5:* 389, 1996.

de Boer T: The effects of mirtazapine on central noradrenergic and serotonergic neurotransmission. Int Clin Psychopharmacol *10* (4, Suppl): 19, 1995.

Kasper S: Clinical efficacy of mirtazapine: A review of meta-analyses of pooled data. Int Clin Psychopharmacol *10* (4, Suppl): 25, 1995.

Kehoe WA, Schorr RB: Focus on mirtazapine: A new antidepressant with noradrenergic and specific serotonergic activity. Formulary *31:* 455, 1996.

Montgomery SA: Safety of mirtazapine: A review. Int Clin Psychopharmacol *10* (4, Suppl): 37, 1995.

▲ 35.3.22 Monoamine Oxidase Inhibitors

Monoamine oxidase inhibitors (MAOIs) increase biogenic amine neurotransmitter levels by inhibiting their degradation. The degradation of the biogenic amines, serotonin, norepinephrine, and dopamine, occurs by only two mechanisms. The more important pathway involves the presynaptic reuptake of these neurotransmitters through specific transporter molecules, followed by deamination in mitochondria by monoamine oxidase (MAO). The transporters may be inhibited by, for example, the tricyclic antidepressant and the serotonin-specific reuptake inhibitors (SSRIs), which form the mainstay of current antidepressant drug therapy. MAOIs, however, are generally accepted as being equal in efficacy to other antidepressant drugs. The less important pathway involves binding to postsynaptic receptors and internalization, where catechol-*O*-methyltransferase (COMT) rapidly degrades dopamine and norepinephrine. Two pharmacologically relevant inhibitors of COMT, tolcapone and entacapone, have been evaluated extensively to potentiate dopamine neurotransmission in Parkinson's disease and have also been suggested as antidepressants, although with little evidence yet in humans. The MAOIs are currently used less frequently than other antidepressants because of the dietary precautions that must be followed to avoid tyramine-induced hypertensive crisis. Newer MAOIs that are significantly less likely to cause tyramine-induced hypertensive crises are not yet available in the United States.

Two types of the MAO enzyme have been characterized, MAO_A, which metabolizes serotonin, norepinephrine, and dopamine, and MAO_B, which metabolizes dopamine. Only MAO_A inhibition is thought to relieve depression, although no selective MAO_A inhibitors are in clinical use. Currently available MAOIs irreversibly and nonselectively inactivate and destroy the MAO present in a patient, and a period of at least 2 weeks must follow the last dose of an MAOI before a patient can safely ingest tyramine-containing foods. A new class of MAOIs are the reversible inhibitors of monoamine oxidase (RIMAs). Drugs of the RIMA class have a reversible binding to MAO and only weakly potentiate the pressor effects of tyramine. Therefore, they do not require strict dietary restrictions.

HISTORY

Iproniazid (Marsilid), a derivative of the antituberculosis drug isoniazid, was abandoned as a potential treatment for tuberculosis and introduced as a treatment for depression in 1952, when its stimulatory effects in tubercular patients were noted. This discovery led to the development of several MAOIs that were effective in treating depression. In 1962, however, a case report described a patient's death from a hypertensive crisis. The patient, who was being treated with an MAOI, had ingested a tyramine-rich cheese. This report led to the brief withdrawal in the United States of the MAOIs. After the drugs were reintroduced, they had a negative image and were minimally used for a long time. The lack of MAOI use was further driven by the introduction of the tricyclic drugs, which were judged to have a more favorable side effect profile, a judgment that many clinicians and researchers think is not entirely accurate. The use of MAOIs has decreased in the past decade because of the appearance of several safer alternatives. Several research groups observed that MAOIs may have superior efficacy in the treatment of specific groups of patients—for example, depressed patients with marked anxiety or phobic symptoms. In addition, clinicians now realize that the dietary restrictions that must be followed by patients taking MAOIs are not as difficult or as extensive as was previously thought and that large amounts of tyramine-containing foods must generally be consumed to induce a serious hypertensive crisis. The use of classic MAOIs and tricyclic drugs has declined, as they have been replaced by the SSRIs and other, new antidepressants, which have significantly more favorable adverse effect profiles. A newer class of reversible inhibitors of MAO_A (RIMAs) is used in Europe and may become available in the United States. This class of drugs includes moclobemide (Aurorix), befloxatone, brofaromine (Consonar), tetrindole, pyrasidol, and E2011.

CHEMISTRY

Three MAOIs are commonly used in the United States (Fig. 35.3.22–1). Phenelzine (Nardil) is a derivative of hydrazine (—$NHNH_2$ is the hydrazine moiety). Tranylcypromine (Parnate) is a cyclopropylamine that is structurally related to amphetamine. Whereas these two drugs are nonspecific inhibitors of MAO_A and MAO_B and are approved for the treatment of depression in the United States, selegiline (Eldepryl, Deprenyl), which is also a cyclopropylamine, is a specific inhibitor of MAO_B and is approved for use only in the treatment of Parkinson's disease. Clorgyline is a specific inhibitor of

Generic	Trade	Usual Adult Dose Range (mg)	How Supplied (mg)
Phenelzine	Nardil	15–90	15
Tranylcypromine	Parnate	10–30	10
Selegiline	Eldepryl, Deprenyl	10[a]	5
Moclobemide[b]	Aurorix	—	—
Brofaromine[b]	Consonar	—	—

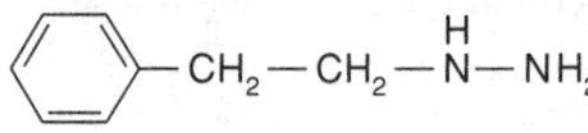
H
CH2 — CH2 — N — NH2

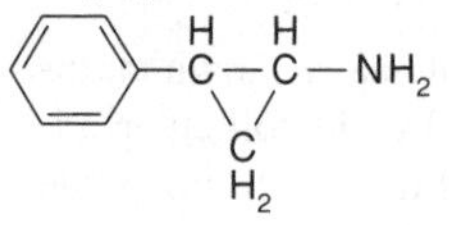
H H
C — C — NH2
C
H2

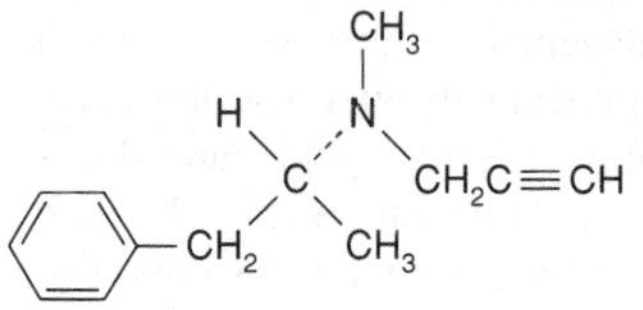
CH3
N
H
C
CH2C≡CH
CH2
CH3

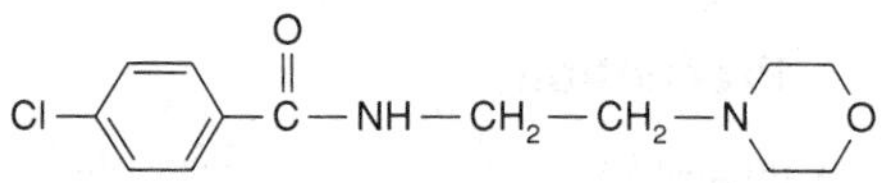
O
Cl
C — NH — CH2 — CH2 — N
O

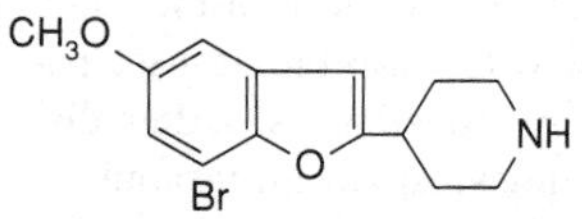
CH3O
O
NH
Br

FIGURE 35.3.22–1

Molecular structures of the monoamine oxidase inhibitors. *a* indicates therapeutic dosage for the treatment of parkinsonism. *b* indicates drug is not available in the United States (RIMAs).

MAO_A and has been reported to be useful in the treatment of rapid-cycling bipolar I disorder, but it is not available for clinical use in the United States. Two RIMAs that are currently under development for the treatment of depressive disorders are moclobemide and brofaromine (Fig. 35.3.22–1).

PHARMACOLOGICAL ACTIONS

Pharmacokinetics

The currently available MAOIs are readily absorbed when administered orally. The hydrazine MAOIs are metabolized by acetylation. About half of all North Americans and Europeans and an even higher proportion of Asians are slow acetylators, which may explain why, when given a hydrazine MAOI, some patients have more adverse effects than do others. Tranylcypromine reaches peak plasma concentrations in about 2 hours and has a half-life of 2 to 3 hours. Unlike the hydrazine MAOIs, the plasma concentrations of tranylcypromine are correlated with its hypotensive effects. Therefore, a clinician can administer tranylcypromine in multiple small daily doses to reduce its hypotensive effects. This approach to administration does not reduce the hypotensive effects of the hydrazine MAOIs. The

RIMA moclobemide has a half-life of 0.5 to 3.5 hours and reaches a steady state in 2 weeks.

Pharmacodynamics

MAO is a widely distributed enzyme in the body and is located primarily intracellularly, where it is usually bound to the external side of the mitochondrial membrane. MAO concentrations are highest in the liver, the gastrointestinal tract, the central nervous system (CNS), and the sympathetic nervous system. The MAO_A in the gastrointestinal tract is responsible for the metabolism of dietary tyramine. When MAO_A is inhibited by an MAOI, dietary tyramine can enter the circulation directly and unmetabolized, can then act as a pressor, and can produce a hypertensive crisis.

As previously mentioned, MAO has two types (Table 35.3.22–1). MAO_A is relatively specific for the metabolism of norepinephrine and serotonin; MAO_B is relatively specific for the metabolism of phenylethylamine; both MAO_A and MAO_B are involved in the metabolism of dopamine. Phenelzine and tranylcypromine are nonselective in their effects on the MAO types. Selegiline is selective (at low doses) for MAO_B, and clorgyline is selective for MAO_A. Moclobemide and brofaromine are known to inhibit MAO_A, and their effects on MAO_B have not yet been fully characterized. Moclobemide and brofaromine differ from the other MAOIs mentioned, in that their interaction with MAO is reversible. Specifically, the binding of these two drugs to MAO can be displaced by tyramine, a fact that contributes significantly to the safety profile of the new drugs.

The measurement of MAO activity in platelets has been used in research and in some clinical settings to assess the degree of MAO inhibition that has been obtained. Platelets contain only MAO_B and, therefore, are not necessarily accurate indicators of the degree of inhibition of MAO_A, which is perhaps more closely associated with antidepressant effects in the brain. Nevertheless, platelet MAO activity needs to be reduced to at least 80 percent to achieve a therapeutic response when phenelzine is used. The measurement of platelet MAO activity is not useful when treating a patient with tranylcypromine, which is more potent at inhibiting MAO_A than at inhibiting MAO_B. When the irreversible MAOIs are used to treat a patient, a period of at least 2 weeks must pass after the last dose of the drug before the patient can safely eat tyramine-containing foods, because the body takes about 2 weeks to resynthesize enough MAO to replace the MAO that had been irreversibly inhibited and destroyed by the irreversible MAOI. In contrast, MAO_A activity returns to normal within 16 hours of the last dose of the RIMA moclobemide, and the tyramine-induced pressor response normalizes within 3 days of cessation of moclobemide.

Although inhibition of MAO is hypothesized to be the primary mechanism of action for the drugs, the MAOIs have additional neurochemical effects. Tranylcypromine, in particular, has significant activity as an inhibitor of catecholamine and serotonin reuptake. Tranylcypromine—because of its similarity to amphetamine, to which it may be metabolized in part—also has some activity on receptors as an indirectly acting sympathomimetic. Brofaromine is active as an inhibitor of serotonin reuptake. Recent neuroscience studies have shown additional roles for MAO in the CNS. One of the additional roles is as an enzymatic pathway for the production of so-called free radicals, a molecular species that may be involved in cell death. The inhibition of free radical production has been hypothesized to be a factor in the efficacy of selegiline in the treatment of Parkinson's disease, although controlled trials have failed to demonstrate a slowing of the progression of Parkinson's disease in patients on long-term treatment with selegiline. Moclobemide has no affinity for adrenergic, dopaminergic, serotonergic, muscarinic, histaminergic, benzodiazepine, or opioid receptors.

EFFECTS ON SPECIFIC ORGANS AND SYSTEMS

The primary effects of the MAOIs in psychiatry are on the CNS. In addition to their effects on depressed mood, the MAOIs are associated with potentially clinically significant disturbances in sleep and sleep architecture. Use of the MAOIs is frequently associated with decreased sleep and insomnia and sometimes results in daytime drowsiness. Furthermore, the sleep of MAOI-treated patients is characterized by significantly decreased amounts of rapid eye movement (REM) sleep. RIMAs lack an effect on, or may improve, sleep.

The other principal concerns when treating patients with MAOIs are the cardiovascular system and the liver. MAOIs are commonly associated with hypotension because of their effects on vascular tone, which may be mediated both centrally

Table 35.3.22–1
Comparison of Monoamine Oxidase A and B

Type	Location	Preferred Substrates	Selective Inhibitors
A	CNS, sympathetic terminals, liver, gut, skin	Norepinephrine, serotonin, dopamine, tyramine, octopamine, tryptamine	Clorgyline
B	CNS, liver, platelets	Dopamine, tyramine, tryptamine, phenylethylamine, benzylamine, *N*-methylhistamine	Selegiline (Eldepryl)[a]

Reprinted with permission from Hyman SE, Arana GW, Rosenbaum JF: *Handbook of Psychiatric Drug Therapy*, ed 3, p 81. Little, Brown, Boston, 1996.
[a] Selectivity lost at higher doses (10 mg a day).

and peripherally. In rare cases, MAOI use alone (without tyramine) is associated with episodes of acute hypertension. With regard to the liver, phenelzine and isocarboxazid are associated with a significant liability for hepatotoxicity.

THERAPEUTIC INDICATIONS

The indications for MAOIs are similar to those for tricyclic and tetracyclic drugs. MAOIs may be particularly effective in panic disorder with agoraphobia, posttraumatic stress disorder, eating disorders, social phobia, and pain disorder. Some investigators have reported that MAOIs may be preferable to tricyclic drugs in the treatment of atypical depression characterized by hypersomnia, hyperphagia, anxiety, and the absence of vegetative symptoms. Patients with this symptom pattern are often less severely depressed than are patients with classic symptoms of depression, which is often evidenced by less functional impairment. The failure of a patient to improve after treatment with an SSRI and a tricyclic or tetracyclic drug may be the most common reason that a patient is given a therapeutic trial of an MAOI.

Although depression is not an approved indication for selegiline, some positive results have been reported. A possible advantage of selegiline is that its primary effect in low dosages is on MAO_B, thus the risk of an MAO_A-associated tyramine-induced hypertensive crisis is lessened. Unfortunately, many of the positive results with selegiline for depression have been at higher dosages (20 to 60 mg a day) than the dosages used to treat Parkinson's disease (10 mg a day). At these higher dosages, selegiline loses a significant amount of its specificity for MAO_B and requires that patients follow the guidelines for a restricted tyramine diet.

PRECAUTIONS AND ADVERSE REACTIONS

The most frequent adverse effects of MAOIs are orthostatic hypotension, weight gain, edema, sexual dysfunction, and insomnia. If the orthostatic hypotension associated with phenelzine or isocarboxazid use is severe, it may respond to support stockings, hydration, and increased salt intake. Orthostatic hypotension associated with tranylcypromine use can usually be relieved by dividing the daily dose. A rare adverse effect of MAOIs, most commonly of tranylcypromine, is a spontaneous hypertensive crisis that occurs after the first exposure to the drug and that is not associated with tyramine ingestion. The mechanism for this rare event is not understood, but tolerance for the hypertensive response does not develop, and patients should not be rechallenged with the drug. Weight gain, edema, and sexual dysfunction are often unresponsive to any treatment and may warrant switching from a hydrazine to a nonhydrazine MAOI or from a nonhydrazine to a hydrazine MAOI. When switching from one MAOI to another, clinicians should taper and stop the first drug for 10 to 14 days before beginning the second drug. Insomnia and behavioral activation can be treated by dividing the dose, not giving the medication after dinner, and using a benzodiazepine hypnotic if necessary.

Myoclonus, muscle pains, and paresthesias occasionally occur in patients treated with MAOIs. Paresthesias may be secondary to MAOI-induced pyridoxine deficiency, which may respond to supplementation with pyridoxine, 50 to 150 mg orally each day. Occasionally, patients complain of feeling drunk or confused, perhaps an indication that the dosage should be reduced and then increased gradually. Reports that the hydrazine MAOIs are associated with hepatotoxic effects are relatively uncommon. MAOIs are less cardiotoxic and less epileptogenic than are the tricyclic and tetracyclic drugs.

The RIMA moclobemide may be generally better tolerated than the SSRIs, with fewer gastrointestinal side effects. Moclobemide does not have adverse anticholinergic or cardiovascular effects and has not been reported to interfere with sexual function. The most common side effects of moclobemide are dizziness and insomnia or sleep disturbance.

MAOIs should be used with caution by patients with renal disease, seizure disorders, cardiovascular disease, or hyperthyroidism. MAOIs may alter the dosage of a hypoglycemic agent required by diabetic patients. MAOIs have been particularly associated with causing depressed bipolar I disorder patients to have manic episodes and causing schizophrenic patients to have a psychotic decompensation. MAOIs are contraindicated during pregnancy, although data on their teratogenic risk are minimal. MAOIs should not be taken by nursing women because the drugs can pass into the breast milk.

Tyramine-Induced Hypertensive Crisis

When patients who are taking nonselective MAOIs ingest foods rich in tyramine (Table 35.3.22–2), they are likely to have a hypertensive reaction that can be life threatening (for example, an intracranial hemorrhage). Patients should also be warned that bee stings may cause a hypertensive crisis. The mechanism involves MAO_A inhibition in the gastrointestinal tract, which results in the increased absorption of tyramine, which then acts as a pressor in the general circulation.

Patients should be warned about the dangers of ingesting tyramine-rich foods while taking MAOIs, and they should be advised to continue the dietary restrictions for 2 weeks after they stop MAOI treatment to allow the body to resynthesize the enzyme. The risk of tyramine-induced hypertensive crises is significantly decreased in patients who are taking RIMAs, such as moclobemide and brofaromine. The prodromal signs and symptoms of a hypertensive crisis may include headache, stiff neck, sweating, nausea, and vomiting. If these signs and symptoms occur, a patient should seek immediate medical treatment. Treatment can include the use of α-adrenergic antagonists—for example, phentolamine (Regitine) or chlorpromazine (Thorazine). MAOIs should not be used for patients with thyrotoxicosis or pheochromocytoma.

Overdose Attempts

In general, intoxication caused by MAOIs is characterized by agitation that progresses to coma with hyperthermia, hypertension, tachypnea, tachycardia, dilated pupils, and hyperactive deep tendon reflexes. Involuntary movements may be present, particularly in the face and the jaw. There is often an asymptomatic period of 1 to 6 hours after the ingestion of the drugs before the occurrence of toxic symptoms. Acidification of the urine markedly hastens the excretion of MAOIs, and dialysis can be of some use. Phentolamine or chlorpromazine may be useful if hypertension is a problem. Moclobemide

Table 35.3.22–2
Sample Instructions for Patients Taking Monoamine Oxidase Inhibitors (MAOIs)

1. Certain foods and beverages must be avoided:
   All cheese except for fresh cottage cheese or cream cheese
   Meat
   - Beef liver
   - Chicken liver
   - Fermented sausages
     - Pepperoni
     - Salami
     - Bologna
     - Other fermented sausages
   - Other cured, unrefrigerated meats

   Fish
   - Caviar
   - Cured, unrefrigerated fish
   - Herring (dried or pickled)
   - Dried fish, shrimp paste

   Vegetables
   - Overripe avocados
   - Fava beans
   - Sauerkraut

   Fruits
   - Overripe fruits, canned figs

   Other foods
   - Yeast extracts (eg, Marmite, Bovril)

   Beverages
   - Chianti wine
   - Beers containing yeast (unfiltered)

   Some foods and beverages should be used only in moderation:
   - Chocolate
   - Coffee
   - Beer
   - Wine
2. If you visit other physicians or dentists, inform them that you are taking an MAOI. This precaution is especially important if other medications are to be prescribed or if you are to have dental work or surgery.
3. Take no medication without a doctor's approval.
   Avoid all over-the-counter pain medications except plain aspirin, acetaminophen (Tylenol), and ibuprofen.
   Avoid all cold or allergy medications except plain chlorpheniramine (Chlor-Trimeton) or brompheniramine (Dimetane).
   Avoid all nasal decongestants and inhalers.
   Avoid all cough medications except plain guaifenesin elixir (plain Robitussin).
   Avoid all stimulants and diet pills.
4. Report promptly any severe headaches, nausea, vomiting, chest pain, or other unusual symptoms. If your doctor is not available, go directly to an emergency room.

Reprinted with permission from Hyman SE, Arana GW, Rosenbaum JF: *Handbook of Psychiatric Drug Therapy*, ed 3, p 85. Little, Brown, Boston, 1996.

alone in overdose causes relatively mild and reversible symptoms. The toxicity of all MAOIs is potentially fatally increased in multidrug overdoses, especially with serotonergic agents.

DRUG INTERACTIONS

The inhibition of MAO can cause severe and even fatal interactions with various other drugs (Table 35.3.22–3). In particular, because MAOIs serve to increase intrasynaptic levels of biogenic amine neurotransmitters, they should never be administered simultaneously with drugs with a similar effect on these neurotransmitters. Such drugs would include any other type of antidepressant, as well as pressor agents. Meperidine (Demerol) has caused death when given to patients on MAOIs. Patients should be instructed to tell any other physicians who are treating them that they are taking an MAOI. MAOIs may potentiate the action or be additive with CNS depressants, including alcohol and barbiturates. A serotonergic syndrome has been described when MAOIs are coadministered with serotonergic drugs, such as SSRIs and clomipramine (Anafranil); thus these combinations should be avoided. The initial symptoms of a serotonin syndrome can include tremor, hypertonicity, myoclonus, and autonomic signs, which can then progress to hallucinosis, hyperthermia, and even death. Cimetidine significantly reduces the elimination of moclobemide.

LABORATORY INTERFERENCES

The MAOIs are associated with the lowering of blood glucose levels, which are accurately reflected by laboratory analysis. MAOIs, however, have been reported to be associated with a minimal false elevation in thyroid function tests.

Dosage and Administration

The antidepressant effects of monoamine oxidase inhibitors usually appear 2 to 4 weeks after the onset of treatment. There is no definitive rationale for choosing one of the current available irreversible MAOIs over another, although some clinicians recommend tranylcypromine because of its activating qualities, possibly associated with a fast onset of action, and its low hepatotoxic potential. Phenelzine should be started with

Table 35.3.22–3
Drugs to Be Avoided During MAOI Treatment

Never use

Anesthetic—never spinal anesthetic or local anesthetic containing epinephrine (lidocaine and procaine are safe)

Antiasthmatic medications

Antihypertensives (α-methyldopa, guanethidine, reserpine, pargyline)

Levodopa; L-tryptophan

Narcotics (especially meperidine [Demerol]; morphine or codeine may be less dangerous)

Over-the-counter cold, hay fever, and sinus medications, especially those containing dextromethorphan (aspirin, acetaminophen, and menthol lozenges are safe)

Sympathomimetics (amphetamine, cocaine, methylphenidate, dopamine, metaraminol, epinephrine, norepinephrine, isoproterenol)

Serotonin-specific reuptake inhibitors, clomipramine

Use carefully

Antihistamines

Hydralazine (Apresoline)

Propranolol (Inderal)

Terpin hydrate with codeine

Tricyclic and tetracyclic drugs

a test dose of 15 mg on the first day. On an outpatient basis, the dosage can be increased to 45 mg a day during the first week and increased by 15 mg a day each week thereafter until the dosage of 90 mg a day is reached by the end of the fourth week. Tranylcypromine should begin with a test dose of 10 mg and may be increased to 30 mg a day by the end of the first week. Many clinicians and researchers have recommended upper limits of 40 mg a day for tranylcypromine. If an MAOI trial is not successful after 6 weeks, lithium (Eskalith) or levothyroxine augmentation is warranted. This combination would probably no longer be indicated, as there are many highly effective newer agents that are much safer. RIMAs may be used in combination with other antidepressants with possibly somewhat less concern for hypertensive crises, but still with great caution.

Liver functions tests should be monitored periodically because of the potential of hepatotoxicity, especially with phenelzine and isocarboxazid. Older adults may be more sensitive to MAOI side effects than younger adults, although, because MAO activity increases with age, the usual dosages of MAOIs are required to treat elderly patients. The use of MAOIs for children has been minimally studied.

Moclobemide is initiated at 300 to 450 mg a day, divided 3 times per day, and it may be increased to a maximum of 600 mg a day after several weeks. Dietary restrictions consist of avoidance of only large quantities of tyramine-containing foods and the administration of moclobemide after, rather than before, tyramine-containing meals. Unlike the irreversible MAOIs, there is no need to wait for regeneration of MAO following use of RIMAs; therefore the obligatory washout period in only 2 days, before administration of a non-RIMA antidepressant.

References

Amrein R, Hetzel W, Stabl M, Schmid-Burgk W: RIMA: A new concept in the treatment of depression with moclobemide. Int Clin Psychopharmacol *7:* 123, 1993.

Baker DG, Diamond BI, Gillette G, Hamner M, et al: A double-blind, randomized, placebo-controlled, multi-center study of brofaromine in the treatment of post-traumatic stress disorder. Psychopharmacology *122* (4): 386, 1995.

Bodkin JA, Cohen BM, Salomon MS, Cannon SE, et al: Treatment of negative symptoms in schizophrenia and schizoaffective disorder by selegiline augmentation of antipsychotic medication. J Nerv Ment Dis *184* (5): 295, 1996.

Coupland NJ, Wilson SJ, Potokar JP, Bell CE, et al: A comparison of the effects of phenelzine treatment with moclobemide treatment on cardiovascular reflexes. Int Clin Psychopharmacol *10* (4): 229, 1995.

Fischer P: Serotonin syndrome in the elderly after antidepressive monotherapy. J Clin Psychopharmacol *15* (6): 440, 1995.

Fitton A, Faulds D, Goa KL: Moclobemide: A review of its pharmacological properties and therapeutic use in depressive illness. Drugs *43:* 561, 1992.

Flint AJ, Rifat SL: The effect of sequential antidepressant treatment on geriatric depression. J Affect Disord *36* (3): 95, 1996.

Hawley CJ, Ratnam S, Pattinson HA, Quick SJ, et al: Safety and tolerability of combined treatment with moclobemide and SSRIs: A preliminary study of 19 patients. J Psychopharmacology *10* (3): 241, 1996.

Merikangas KR, Merikangas JR: Combination monoamine oxidase inhibitor and β-blocker treatment of migraine, with anxiety and depression. Biol Psychiatry *38* (9): 603, 1995.

Reynaert C, Parent M, Mirel J, Janne P, et al: Moclobemide versus fluoxetine for a major depressive episode. Psychopharmacology *118* (2): 183, 1995.

Thase ME, Mallinger AG, McKnight D, Himmelhoch JM: Treatment of imipramine-resistant recurrent depression: IV. A double-blind cross-over study of tranylcypromine for anergic bipolar depression. Am J Psychiatry *149:* 195, 1992.

Thase ME, Trivedi MH, Rush AJ: MAOIs in the contemporary treatment of depression. Neuropsychopharmacology *12* (3): 185, 1995.

Todd KG, Baker GB: GABA-elevating effects of the antidepressant/antipanic drug phenelzine in brain: Effects of pretreatment with tranylcypromine, (-)-deprenyl and clorgyline. J Affect Disord *35* (3): 125, 1995.

▲ 35.3.23 Naltrexone

Naltrexone (ReVia) is a pure opioid antagonist, effective in a once-a-day dosage, that has improved the success of existing behavioral approaches to the treatment of opiate, opioid, and alcohol dependence. The drug appears to reduce or eliminate the craving of people dependent on opioids or alcohol. Unlike disulfiram (Antabuse), which causes violent illness when used with alcohol, naltrexone simply eliminates the subjective high associated with a return to drug abuse. Naltrexone must be initiated cautiously in people who may still be abusing opiates or opioids, because it may induce an acute withdrawal reaction, which may include life-threatening dehydration caused by vomiting and diarrhea. Once in use, however, it may usually be started and stopped without physical consequence. This feature has unfortunately allowed many poorly motivated former addicts to withdraw from naltrexone treatment programs, an outcome perhaps less commonly seen in methadone programs, where stopping the drug precipitates an unpleasant withdrawal syndrome. The success of naltrexone drug and alcohol abstinence programs is therefore more closely associated with psychosocial factors, such as educational level, motivation, family support, and continued behavioral therapy, than with use of naltrexone per se.

CHEMISTRY

Naltrexone is a thebaine derivative, more similar structurally to the pure opioid agonist oxymorphone (Numorphan) than to the pharmacologically similar opioid antagonist naloxone (Narcan). The molecular structure of naltrexone is shown in Figure 35.3.23–1.

PHARMACOLOGICAL ACTIONS

Pharmacokinetics

About 96 percent of ingested naltrexone is rapidly absorbed from the gastrointestinal tract, but the drug undergoes significant first-pass hepatic metabolism, such that only 5 to 40 percent reaches the systemic circulation unchanged. Peak concentrations of naltrexone and its major metabolite, 6-β-naltrexol, are achieved within 1 hour of ingestion. The drug is widely distributed in the body and is approximately 21 to 28 percent

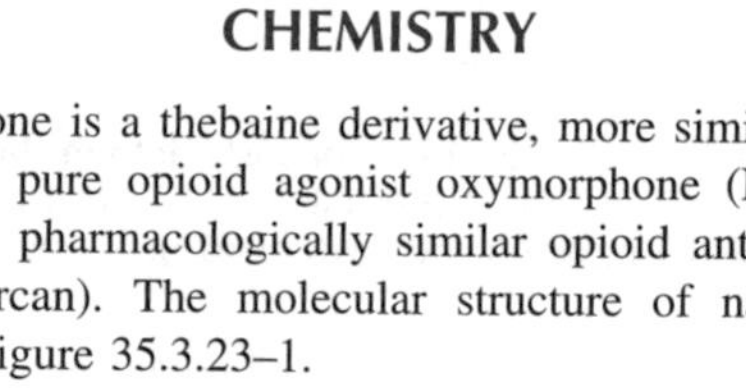

HO
O
OH
H
N—CH2—
O

FIGURE 35.3.23–1
Molecular structure of naltrexone.

protein bound. In rats, it appears in the cerebrospinal fluid (CSF) within 30 minutes of subcutaneous injection and eventually reaches a CSF concentration that is 30 percent of the serum concentration. It is unknown whether it is distributed into maternal milk. Animal studies suggest that doses 100 to 150 times the usual human dose may be embryotoxic. Therefore, although there are no human data about effects on fetal development, naltrexone should be used during pregnancy only if absolutely needed.

Elimination of the parent compound and the major metabolite begins rapidly, with a half-life of 1 to 3 hours, then slows to a rate with a half-life of 10 to 15 hours. Traces of naltrexone may linger for up to 96 hours from a single dose. The metabolism consists mainly of hepatic glucuronidation, followed by renal excretion primarily via filtration.

Pharmacodynamics

Naltrexone, like its intravenous counterpart naloxone, acts as a pure competitive antagonist principally of μ, but also of κ and δ, opioid receptors in the central nervous system (CNS). A daily oral dose of 50 mg of naltrexone antagonizes most of the subjective and objective effects of opioids, such as respiratory depression, miosis, euphoria, and drug craving. A 100-mg dose produces a plasma level of 44 ng/mL in an hour, which decays to a level of 2.1 ng/mL after 24 hours. A plasma level of 1.7 ng/mL may be sufficient to antagonize a 25-mg intravenous dose of heroin. The competitive blockade may be overcome with sufficiently high doses of opioid agonists and may lead to hazardous and unpredictable levels of receptor activation. The effect of naltrexone on alcohol dependence is not well understood but presumably involves antagonism of endogenous opioid agonists, which may be released on alcohol ingestion and which may contribute to the subjective high.

Naltrexone has minor, clinically insignificant effects on several hypothalamic and pituitary hormones but is otherwise free of pharmacological effects in humans.

EFFECTS ON SPECIFIC ORGANS AND SYSTEMS

Naltrexone is generally well tolerated, and its side effects are reversible. Naltrexone may cause dose-related hepatocellular injury, generally at higher doses (such as 300 mg a day). Serum aminotranferase levels may increase 3 to 19 times in 20 percent of patients on such doses. The hepatocellular injury appears to be a direct toxic effect rather than an idiosyncratic reaction. At the lowest doses required for effective opioid antagonism, hepatocellular injury has not typically been observed, but the relatively low ceiling for hepatotoxicity necessitates concern about patients with other causes of liver injury, such as chronic alcoholics.

A set of adverse effects, which may be a vestigial withdrawal syndrome, tends to affect up to 10 percent of patients. The major non-CNS effects of naltrexone are gastrointestinal. Up to 10 percent of patients may experience abdominal pain and cramps, nausea, and vomiting, which occasionally may be so severe as to require discontinuance. Adverse CNS effects, experienced in up to 10 percent of patients, include headache, low energy, insomnia, anxiety, and nervousness. Other psychiatric events, such as paranoia, depression, suicide, and suicidal ideation, which occur in less than 1 percent of patients, must be interpreted in light of the population for which naltrexone is indicated; this population may have a high incidence of underlying psychopathology. Joint and muscle pains and rash may occur in up to 10 percent of patients.

A syndrome of opioid withdrawal affecting several organ systems is described in Adverse Reactions.

THERAPEUTIC INDICATIONS

Naltrexone is used for its opioid antagonistic effects as part of medically supervised behavioral modification programs aimed at the maintenance of an opioid-free state in former opioid addicts. This usage is based on the theory that blocking the reward arm of the opioid effects may reduce the appetitive behavior of the individual toward the opioid drugs of abuse. No data unequivocally demonstrate that naltrexone reduces the risk of a return to opioid abuse, but studies have suggested that a behavioral program plus naltrexone is more successful than either naltrexone or the behavioral program alone. Studies have not compared naltrexone-based opioid-related therapy with traditional methadone or levomethadyl acetate (ORLAAM) maintenance therapy. Because of the absence of adverse consequences of noncompliance with naltrexone treatment, an important factor in the success rate of naltrexone-based programs is encouraging patient compliance because of the social setting of the treatment. Early multicenter, double-blind therapeutic trials were so frequently derailed by high rates of dropout that efficacy was not clearly demonstrated. Open label studies have demonstrated efficacy, although people may undergo several relapses and remissions before achieving long-term abstinence. Factors that increase the chances of success include a high degree of motivation, employment, marriage, and strong family or social support.

Naltrexone is also used as an adjunctive agent in behavioral management programs for alcohol dependence. In this area, compliance with the medication has generally been better than in opioid addicts. Studies have reported that naltrexone reduces alcohol craving and alcohol consumption and ameliorates the severity of relapses. As with opioid dependence, the naltrexone effect is modest and highly dependent on the effectiveness of the associated behavioral modification program. The National Institute of Alcohol Abuse and Alcoholism (NIAAA) has sponsored studies to determine which alcoholic patients are most likely to benefit from naltrexone in connection with behavioral modification. At present, naltrexone is not recommended for routine use in treatment of alcoholism.

On the basis of the hypothesis that endogenous opioids may mediate the reward component of other types of addiction, such as overeating, naltrexone has been suggested to assist in weight loss programs. Indeed, at very high doses, naltrexone reduced caloric intake in animals, but no convincing appetite suppression has been seen in humans. Early therapeutic trials have suggested a beneficial adjunct role for naltrexone in the treatment of bulimia and self-injurious behavior.

PRECAUTIONS AND ADVERSE REACTIONS

Because naltrexone is used to maintain a drug-free state after detoxification, great care must be taken to ensure that at least 7 to 10 days elapse after the last dose of opioids before the first dose of naltrexone. Because the pharmacological effects of naltrexone may persist for more than 24 hours, some experts recommend a test dose of naloxone in cases where the drug-free interval is uncertain (see Dosage and Administration). Naloxone challenge is used because its opioid antagonism lasts less than 1 hour. Symptoms of acute opioid withdrawal include drug craving, feeling of temperature change, musculoskeletal pain, or gastrointestinal distress. Signs of opioid withdrawal include confusion, drowsiness, vomiting, and diarrhea. If any of these reactions follows naloxone infusion, then persistent opioid dependence must be assumed to be present, and naltrexone should not be given.

As discussed earlier, naltrexone may cause dose-related hepatic toxicity at doses in excess of 50 mg a day. Even these doses may be toxic in patients with underlying liver disease. Naltrexone-induced hepatocellular injury may be reflected in increased serum aminotransferases, which should be monitored monthly for the first 6 months of therapy and, thereafter, based on clinical suspicion.

If analgesia is required while a dose of naltrexone is pharmacologically active, opioids should be avoided in favor of benzodiazepines or other nonopioid analgesics. Patients on naltrexone therapy should be instructed that low doses of opioids will have no effects, but larger doses could overcome the receptor blockade and suddenly produce opioid overdose, with sedation possibly progressing to coma or death. Naltrexone is contraindicated in patients who are taking opioid agonists, in patients with acute hepatitis or hepatic failure, and in patients who are hypersensitive to the drug.

A small number, but certainly not all, in vitro and animal mutagenicity and carcinogenicity assays have shown some evidence of naltrexone-induced genetic damage at extremely high doses, but no linkage has been established between naltrexone and human cancers. Similarly, embryotoxicity assays in animals have shown adverse effects only at doses far in excess of the highest doses used in humans. Nonetheless, clinical guidelines for use in pregnant females should reserve the use of naltrexone only for patients whose compelling need outweighs the potential risks to the fetus.

Naltrexone is a relatively safe drug, based on animal studies, which suggest that lethal doses may be several hundred times the usual dose. There is little experience with overdosage in humans. Ingestion of high doses of naltrexone should be treated with supportive measures combined with efforts to decrease gastrointestinal absorption.

DRUG INTERACTIONS

The antagonism of opioid agonists has already been discussed. As many cold preparations containing opioids may be rendered inactive by naltrexone, they should not be given to patients using the drug. Because of its extensive hepatic metabolism, naltrexone may affect or be affected by other drugs that influence hepatic enzyme levels. The clinical importance of these potential interactions is unknown. Naltrexone apparently does not induce its own metabolism. One potentially hepatotoxic drug that has been used in some cases with naltrexone is disulfiram. Although no adverse effects were observed, caution is indicated when such combination therapy is contemplated. Naltrexone has been reported to potentiate the sedation of phenothiazines. The acute withdrawal syndrome induced by naltrexone, which resembles sympathetic overflow, may be mitigated by clonidine, a centrally acting attenuator of sympathetic activity.

LABORATORY INTERFERENCES

No laboratory interferences have yet been described for naltrexone.

DOSAGE AND ADMINISTRATION

Naltrexone antagonizes opioid activity within 15 to 30 minutes of administration. Naltrexone is administered orally and is currently available only in tablet form. The gastrointestinal disturbances may be minimized by taking naltrexone with or after food. Naltrexone should be used only as part of a comprehensive, supervised behavioral modification program for the maintenance of abstinence.

To avoid the possibility of precipitating an acute opioid withdrawal syndrome, several steps should be taken to ensure that a patient is opioid free. In a supervised detoxification setting, at least 7 days should elapse after the last dose of short-acting opioids, such as heroin, hydroxymorphone, meperidine, or morphine, and at least 14 days should elapse after the last dose of longer-acting opioids, such as methadone, before opioid antagonists are initiated. Briefer periods off opioids have been used in certain protocols aimed at particularly relapse-prone patients. To confirm that opioid detoxification is complete, urine toxicological screens should fail to demonstrate opioid metabolites. A person may, however, have a negative urine opioid screen, yet still be physically dependent on opioids and thus be susceptible to antagonist-induced withdrawal effects. Therefore, once the urine screen is negative, a naloxone challenge test is recommended (Table 35.3.23–1).

For the naloxone challenge test, 0.8 mg of intravenous naloxone is used. Initially, 0.2 mg is injected intravenously, and the patient is observed for 30 seconds for evidence of opioid withdrawal. Some authorities extend this period of observation to 15 minutes. The signs and symptoms of opioid withdrawal include, but are not limited to, rhinorrhea, nasal stuffiness, lacrimation, yawning, perspiration, tremor, abdominal cramps, vomiting, piloerection, myalgias, and skin crawling. If none of these features arises, then the remaining 0.6 mg of naloxone should be injected, and the patient should be observed for an additional 20 minutes. Some authorities recommend a total dose of naloxone of 2 mg, to increase the chance of detecting residual opioid dependence. Even mild evidence of gastrointestinal distress should be considered positive evidence of opioid dependence, because it may be a marker for more prolonged and intense distress if naltrexone is given. In such cases, the naloxone challenge test should be readministered in 24 hours. If no evidence of opioid withdrawal is seen, then naltrexone may be safely initiated.

The initial dose of naltrexone of 50 mg a day should be achieved through gradual introduction, even in the presence of a negative naloxone challenge test. Various authorities begin with 5, 10, 12.5, or 25 mg and titrate up to the 50-mg dose over a period ranging from 1 hour to 4 days, while constantly monitoring for evidence of opioid withdrawal. Once a daily dose of 50 mg is well tolerated, it may be averaged over a

Table 35.3.23–1
Naloxone (Narcan) Challenge Test

The naloxone challenge test should not be performed in a patient showing clinical signs or symptoms of opioid withdrawal or in a patient whose urine contains opioid. The naloxone challenge test may be administered by either the intravenous or subcutaneous routes.

Intravenous challenge: Following appropriate screening of the patient, 0.8 mg of naloxone should be drawn into a sterile syringe. If the intravenous route of administration is selected, 0.2 mg of naloxone should be injected, and while the needle is still in the patient's vein, the patient should be observed for 30 seconds for evidence of withdrawal signs or symptoms. If there is no evidence of withdrawal, the remaining 0.6 mg of naloxone should be injected, and the patient should be observed for an additional period of 20 minutes for signs and symptoms of withdrawal.

Subcutaneous challenge: If the subcutaneous route is selected, 0.8 mg should be administered subcutaneously, and the patient should be observed for signs and symptoms of withdrawal for 20 minutes.

Conditions and technique for observation of patient: During the appropriate period of observation, the patient's vital signs should be monitored, and the patient should be monitored for signs of withdrawal. It is also important to question the patient carefully. The signs and symptoms of opioid withdrawal include, but are not limited to the following:

Withdrawal signs: stuffiness or running nose, tearing, yawning, sweating, tremor, vomiting, or piloerection.

Withdrawal symptoms: feeling of temperature change, joint or bone and muscle pain, abdominal cramps, and formication (feeling of bugs crawling under the skin).

Interpretation of the challenge: Warning—the elicitation of the enumerated signs or symptoms indicates a potential risk for the subject, and naltrexone should not be administered. If no signs or symptoms of withdrawal are observed, elicited, or reported, naltrexone may be administered. If there is any doubt in the observer's mind that the patient is not in an opioid free state or is in continuing withdrawal, naltrexone should be withheld for 24 hours and the challenge should be repeated.

week by giving 100 mg on alternate days or 150 mg every third day. Such schedules may increase compliance. To maximize compliance, it is recommended that ingestion of each dose be directly observed either in a facility or by family members and that random urine tests for naltrexone, 6-β-naltrexol, and opioid metabolites be taken. Naltrexone should be continued until such time as the patient is psychologically no longer at risk for relapse into opioid abuse. This generally requires at least 6 months but may take longer, particularly if there are external stresses.

For alcohol dependence, the optimum schedule and dosage of naltrexone remains to be established. It is essential that the same precautions be taken to ensure that a physical dependence on opioids is absent before initiation of naltrexone maintenance therapy. Five to 15 percent of former alcoholics may not tolerate the usual 50-mg daily dosage because of adverse gastrointestinal effects.

References

Jaffe JH: Cocaine-related disorders. In *Comprehensive Textbook of Psychiatry,* ed 6, HI Kaplan, BJ Sadock, editors, p 817. Williams & Wilkins, Baltimore, 1995.

Jaffe JH: Opioid-related disorders. In *Comprehensive Textbook of Psychiatry,* ed 6, HI Kaplan, BJ Sadock, editors, p 842. Williams & Wilkins, Baltimore, 1995.

O'Mara NB, Wesley LC: Naltrexone in the treatment of alcohol dependence. Ann Pharmacother *28:* 210, 1994.

Sax DS, Kornetsky C, Kim A: Lack of hepatotoxicity with naltrexone treatment. J Clin Pharmacol *34:* 898, 1994.

Shufman EN, Porat S, Witztum E, Gandaeu D, Bar-Hamburger R, Ginath Y: The efficacy of naltrexone in preventing reabuse of heroin after detoxification. Biol Psychiatry *35:* 935, 1994.

Volpicelli JR, Watson NT, King AC, Sherman CE, et al: Effects of naltrexone on alcohol ''high'' in alcoholics. Am J Psychiatry *152:* 613, 1995.

▲ 35.3.24 Nefazodone

Nefazodone (Serzone) is an antidepressant medication structurally related to trazodone (Desyrel) and unrelated to the classical tricyclic and tetracyclic drugs, the monoamine oxidase inhibitors (MAOIs), serotonin-specific reuptake inhibitors (SSRIs), and other available antidepressant drugs. Although trazodone is distinctive in having more marked sedative effects than those found with most other antidepressants, nefazodone is relatively free of this adverse effect and generally well tolerated. Nefazodone is less likely than the SSRIs to adversely affect sexual functioning.

CHEMISTRY

Nefazodone is a phenylpiperazine analogue of trazodone. Its molecular structure is shown in Figure 35.3.24–1.

PHARMACOLOGICAL ACTIONS

Pharmacokinetics

Nefazodone is rapidly and completely absorbed, but it is then extensively and variably metabolized so that the bioavailability of active compounds is about 20 percent of the oral dose. Its half-life is 2 to 4 hours, and dosing must be twice daily. Steady-state concentrations of nefazodone and its principal active metabolite, hydroxynefazodone, are achieved within 4 to 5 days. Metabolism in older people, especially women, is about half that seen in younger patients; thus lower doses are recommended in elderly patients.

Pharmacodynamics

Nefazodone is an inhibitor of serotonin uptake and, more weakly, of norepinephrine reuptake. It also acts as an antagonist of the serotonin type 2 ($5\text{-}HT_2$) receptor, antagonism of

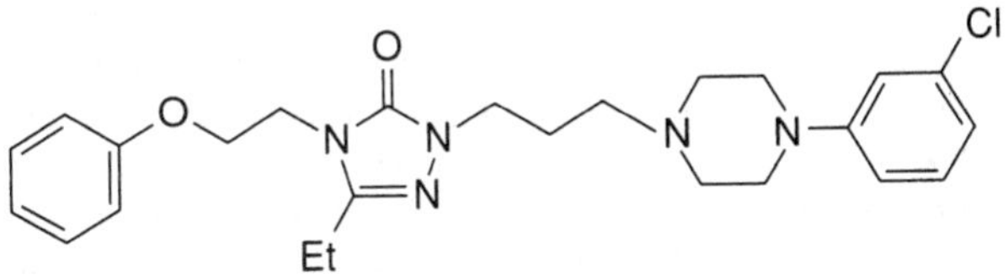
O
O
N
N
N
N
N
N
Et
Cl

FIGURE 35.3.24–1
Molecular structure of nefazodone.

which is thought to treat anxiety and depression. The net effect of serotonin reuptake inhibition and 5-HT_2 receptor blockade is thought to be selective activation of serotonin type 1 (5-HT_1) receptor, which has been suggested to improve both anxiety and depression. Nefazodone causes mild antagonism of the α_1-adrenergic receptors and can predispose some patients to orthostatic hypotension. There is no significant activity at α_2- and β-adrenergic, serotonin type 1A (5-HT_{1A}), cholinergic, dopaminergic, or benzodiazepine receptors.

EFFECTS ON SPECIFIC ORGANS AND SYSTEMS

The main effects of nefazodone are on the central nervous system (CNS). The main extra-CNS effects are related to α_1-adrenergic antagonism, which may cause orthostatic hypotension. Unlike its structural relative trazodone, nefazodone has not been reported to cause priapism.

Cardiovascular Effects

In premarketing trials, 5.1 percent of patients taking nefazodone experienced a significant drop in blood pressure, compared with 2.5 percent of placebo patients. Although there was no increase in true syncopal events, symptoms of postural hypotension were experienced by 2.8 percent of patients treated with nefazodone. This rate compares with postural hypotension in 0.8 percent of placebo-treated, 1.1 percent of SSRI-treated, and 10.8 percent of tricyclic antidepressant-treated patients. Sinus bradycardia was seen in 1.5 percent of nefazodone-treated patients compared with 0.4 percent of placebo-treated patients. Nefazodone should therefore be used with caution in patients with underlying cardiac conditions, history of stroke or heart attack, dehydration, and hypovolemia and in patients under treatment with antihypertensive medications.

Activation of Mania

In patients with known bipolar illness, 1.6 percent of those treated with nefazodone experienced mania, compared with 5.1 percent of tricyclic-treated patients and 0 percent of placebo-treated patients. The activation of mania in unipolar patients was no higher with nefazodone than with placebo. Therefore, nefazodone may be a drug to try earlier in the treatment of patients with a history of manic episodes. Electroconvulsive therapy and the antidepressant lithium are least likely to activate mania.

THERAPEUTIC INDICATIONS

Nefazodone has been approved for the treatment of depression on the basis of data from at least two large clinical trials. Nefazodone has been shown to be equally as efficacious as imipramine, fluoxetine, and paroxetine for treatment of moderate, severe, melancholic, nonmelancholic, chronic, and recurrent depression. Preliminary clinical reports indicate that nefazodone may also be an effective treatment for depression accompanied by anxiety, such as for panic disorder and panic with comorbid depression or depressive symptoms, for obsessive-compulsive disorder, for premenstrual dysphoric disorder, and for the management of chronic pain of neuropathic or non-neuropathic origin. Although small studies report that nefazodone was associated with a trend toward a reduction in obsessive thoughts, a case report documents the initial appearance of obsessive thoughts during nefazodone treatment, which ceased when the drug was discontinued. More data are needed to establish whether nefazodone is as effective for obsessive-compulsive disorder as are the SSRIs and clomipramine.

PRECAUTIONS AND ADVERSE REACTIONS

In preclinical trials, 16 percent of patients discontinued nefazodone because of an adverse event. The most common reasons for discontinuance were nausea (3.5 percent), dizziness (1.9 percent), insomnia (1.5 percent), and agitation (1.2 percent). The adverse reactions reported with nefazodone are listed in Table 35.3.24–1. The adverse events were dose dependent and tended to appear at significant levels only in the dosing range of 300 to 600 mg a day. Nefazodone causes little sexual dysfunction, weight gain, or cardiotoxicity. Nefazodone and trazodone are unusual among antidepressants, in that they do not decrease but, rather, increase REM sleep and improve sleep continuity. However, nefazodone is much less likely than trazodone to produce daytime sedation.

Nefazodone was not shown to cause cancer in laboratory animals or to cause mutagenesis in several common assays. It caused mild loss of fertility at doses comparable to 3 times the highest recommended human dose. Although no teratogenic effects were noted, early neonatal mortality of laboratory animal offspring occurred with doses in the mothers comparable to 5 times the highest recommended human dose. There are no data on the effects of nefazodone on human mothers. Nefazodone should therefore be used during pregnancy only if the potential benefit to the mother outweighs the potential risk to the fetus. It is not known whether nefazodone is excreted

Table 35.3.24–1
Adverse Reactions Reported with Nefazodone (300–600 mg a day)

	%
Headache	36
Dry mouth	25
Somnolence	25
Nausea	22
Dizziness	17
Constipation	14
Insomnia	11
Weakness	11
Lightheadedness	10
Blurred vision	9
Dyspepsia	9
Infection	8
Confusion	7
Scotomata	7

in human breast milk. Therefore, it should not be used by women who are breast-feeding.

DRUG INTERACTIONS

As is true for all antidepressant medications, nefazodone should not be given concomitantly with MAOIs. In addition, nefazodone has particular drug–drug interactions with the triazolobenzodiazepines, triazolam (Halcion) and alprazolam (Xanax), with so-called third-generation antihistamines, terfenadine (Seldane) and astemizole (Hismanal), and with cisapride (Propulsid) because of the inhibition of cytochrome P450 (CYP) isoenzyme CYP 3A4 by nefazodone. Potentially toxic levels of each of these drugs can develop after administration of nefazodone, whereas the levels of nefazodone are generally not affected. The manufacturer recommends that the dose of triazolam be lowered by 75 percent, the dose of alprazolam be lowered by 50 percent when given concomitantly with nefazodone, and terfenadine and astemizole not be used at all with nefazodone.

Nefazodone may modestly increase levels of concomitantly administered haloperidol (Haldol). Nefazodone may slow the metabolism of digoxin; therefore, digoxin levels should be followed carefully in patients taking both medications. Conversely, nefazodone appears to reduce the bioavailability of propranolol (Inderal), and concomitant use of these two drugs should prompt a reevaluation of the dose of propranolol on clinical grounds. Nefazodone should not be given within 14 days of beginning or stopping an MAOI.

LABORATORY INTERFERENCES

No laboratory interferences have been reported for nefazodone.

DOSAGE AND ADMINISTRATION

Like other antidepressant drugs, nefazodone begins to improve mood between 2 and 4 weeks of initiation of therapy. The recommended starting dose of nefazodone is 100 mg 2 times a day. To limit the development of adverse effects, the dosage should be slowly tapered up to increments of 100 to 200 mg a day at intervals of no less than 1 week per increase. Older patients should receive doses about two thirds of the usual nongeriatric doses, with a maximum of 400 mg a day. Dosages should be lowered in patients with hepatic impairment. In common with other antidepressants, clinical benefit of nefazodone usually appears after 2 to 4 weeks of treatment. Nefazodone is available in 100, 150, 200, and 250 mg tablets.

References

Baldwin DS, Hawley CJ, Abed RT, Maragakis BP, et al: A multicenter double-blind comparison of nefazodone and paroxetine in the treatment of outpatients with moderate-to-severe depression. J Clin Psychiatry *57* (2, Suppl): 46, 1996.

Ellingrod VL, Perry PJ: Nefazodone: A new antidepressant. Am J Health System Pharm *52:* 2799, 1995.

DeMartinis NA, Schweizer E, Rickels K: An open-label trial of nefazodone in high comorbidity panic disorder. J Clin Psychiatry *57:* 245, 1996.

Feiger A, Kiev A, Shrivastava RK, Wisselink PG, Wilcox CS: Nefazodone versus sertraline in outpatients with major depression: Focus on efficacy, tolerability, and effects on sexual function and satisfaction. J Clin Psychiatry *57* (2, Suppl): 53, 1996.

Lader MH: Tolerability and safety: Essentials in antidepressant pharmacotherapy. J Clin Psychiatry *57* (2, Suppl): 39, 1996.

Marcus RN, Mendels J: Nefazodone in the treatment of severe, melancholic, and recurrent depression. J Clin Psychiatry *57* (2, Suppl): 19, 1996.

Nemeroff CB, DeVane CL, Pollock BG: Newer antidepressants and the cytochrome P450 system. Am J Psychiatry *153:* 311, 1996.

Robinson DS, Marcus RN, Archibald DG, Hardy SA: Therapeutic dose range of nefazodone in the treatment of major depression. J Clin Psychiatry *57* (2, Suppl): 6, 1996.

▲ 35.3.25 Serotonin-Dopamine Antagonists

Clinical experience has shown that 20 to 30 percent of patients with schizophrenia do not respond to typical antipsychotic drugs (that is, dopamine receptor antagonists such as haloperidol [Haldol] and chlorpromazine [Thorazine]) and that these drugs frequently cause unwanted extrapyramidal side effects such as parkinsonism, dystonia, and akathisia. For about two thirds of such nonresponders, the success of the first atypical antipsychotic agent clozapine (Clozaril), which treats both the positive and negative symptoms of schizophrenia while causing a minimum of extrapyramidal adverse effects, has stimulated efforts to improve on this atypical antipsychotic drug. The significant pharmacological actions of clozapine appear to be the antagonism not only of dopamine receptors but also of serotonin type 2A (5-HT_{2A}) receptors. Therefore, drugs of this class, formerly called atypical antipsychotic agents, are now referred to as serotonin-dopamine antagonists. In addition to clozapine, this group includes risperidone (Risperdal), olanzapine (Zyprexa), sertindole (Serlect), quetiapine (Seroquel), and ziprasidone (Zeldox). Although referred to as serotonin-dopamine antagonists, each agent of this class has a unique combination of receptor affinities, and the relative contribution of each receptor interaction to the clinical effects is unknown (Table 35.3.25–1). A schematic representation of current conceptions of neurotransmitter dysregulation in schizophrenia is presented in Figure 35.3.25–1).

The ability of these agents to reduce the negative features of psychosis (withdrawal, flat affect, anhedonia, catatonia) as well as all positive symptoms (hallucinations, delusions, disordered thoughts, agitation) has led to the use of these drugs with a wide variety of patients, including those refractory to typical antipsychotics. The success of the serotonin-dopamine antagonists has been so dramatic that clinicians have had to deal with the patients' disappointment after they begin to realize the full extent of their disability. The use of serotonin-dopamine antagonists has permitted more patients to be drawn into insight-oriented therapy. The newer agents share extrapyramidal profiles nearly as favorable as that of clozapine, which is essentially devoid of extrapyramidal adverse effects. Moreover, the principal drawbacks of clozapine, specifically the need to monitor closely for agranulocytosis and the relatively high risks of seizure and orthostatic hypotension, have not yet been seen with risperidone, olanzapine, sertindole, quetiapine, or ziprasidone. Although risperidone has shown great clinical promise in its first 2 years of use, olanzapine has only begun to be used, and sertindole, quetiapine, and ziprasidone

Table 35.3.25–1
Receptor Pharmacology of Serotonin-Dopamine Antagonists and Haloperidol

	D_1	D_2	D_3	D_4	5-HT_1	5-HT_2	5-HT_3	Musc.	α_1	α_2	Hist.	NE
Haloperidol	++	+++	?	+	0	++	0	0	++	+	0	0
Olanzapine	++	++	++	++	0	+++	++	++	++	+	+++	+
Clozapine	++	+	?	+	+	++	++	+++	+++	+++	+++	?
Risperidone	++	+++	?	+	+	+++	0	0	+++	+++	+	0
Sertindole	++	+++	?	?	?	+++	?	+	+++	+	+	?
Quetiapine	+	+	+	?	0	+	+	0	+++	++	++	?
Ziprasidone	++	+++	+++	++	+++	+++	?	0	++	0	+	+++

Modified from Gupta S, Masand PS: Olanzapine: Review of its pharmacology and indications in clinical practice. Prim Psychiatry *4:* 73, 1997.
+++, 10 nM; ++, 100 nM; and +, 1000 nM; D_1, dopamine receptor type 1; D_2, dopamine receptor type 2; D_3, dopamine receptor type 3; D_4, dopamine receptor type 4; 5-HT_1, serotonin receptor type 1; 5-HT_2, serotonin receptor type 2; 5-HT_3, serotonin receptor type 3; Musc., muscarinic cholinergic receptor; α_1, α-adrenergic receptor type 1; α_2, α-adrenergic receptor type 2; Hist., histamine receptor; NE, β-adrenergic receptor.

await approval by the Food and Drug Administration (FDA). The antipsychotic effects of serotonin-dopamine antagonists usually appear within the first 2 weeks of use, although severely ill patients may require up to 6 weeks for a beneficial response. Because these agents are relatively new, they are discussed separately.

CLOZAPINE

Chemistry

Clozapine is a dibenzodiazepine. Its molecular structure is shown in Figure 35.3.25–2. It is chemically related to the dopamine receptor antagonist loxapine (Loxitane) and the serotonin-dopamine antagonists olanzapine and quetiapine.

Pharmacological Actions

Pharmacokinetics. Clozapine is rapidly absorbed from the gastrointestinal (GI) tract, and peak plasma levels are reached in 1 to 4 hours (mean, 2 hours). The drug is completely metabolized, with a half-life between 10 and 16 hours (mean, 12 hours); steady-state levels are usually reached in 3 to 4 days if twice-daily dosing is used. The two major metabolites have minimal pharmacological activity and have a shorter half-life than does the parent compound. The metabolites are excreted in both the urine and the feces.

Pharmacodynamics. Clozapine has relatively low potency as a dopamine type 2 (D_2) receptor antagonist. Clozapine has a much higher potency as an antagonist at dopamine type 1 (D_1), type 3 (D_3), and type 4 (D_4), serotonin type 2 (5-HT_2), and noradrenergic α (especially α_1) receptors. Clozapine also has intermediate antagonist activity at muscarinic and histamine type 1 (H_1) receptors. In animal models, clozapine appears more active in the dopaminergic mesolimbic system than in the striatonigral system, an observation that correlates with the absence of parkinsonian effects. Data from positron emission tomography (PET) scanning show that a dose of 10 mg haloperidol produces 80 percent occupancy of striatal D_2 receptors, whereas clinically effective doses of clozapine occupy only 40 to 50 percent of striatal D_2 receptors. Although antagonism of serotonin and dopamine receptors is emphasized in the name, ''serotonin-dopamine antagonists,'' it is not known which particular combination of receptor affinities is responsible for the effects of clozapine and other serotonin-dopamine antagonists.

Effects on Specific Organs and Systems

In addition to its antipsychotic effects, clozapine is associated with an increased risk for seizures. The most significant effects outside the central nervous system (CNS) are on the hematopoietic system and the cardiovascular system (see Precautions and Adverse Reactions).

Therapeutic Indications

Treatment-Resistant Schizophrenia. The only FDA-approved indication for clozapine is as a therapy for treatment-resistant schizophrenia—that is, for people who failed to improve during at least three adequate trials of various typical antipsychotic drugs. In one 6-week study, only 4 percent of such patients showed significant improvement when treated with chlorpromazine and benztropine, compared with 30 percent of those treated with clozapine. After 6 months, 60 percent of those treated with clozapine improved. Clozapine has not formally been compared with placebo. Compared with haloperidol, clozapine was clearly more effective for severely ill and treatment-refractory patients. Compared with risperidone, clozapine was equally efficacious and caused fewer extrapyramidal symptoms for non–treatment-refractory patients. In practical terms, the definition of ''treatment-resistant'' with respect to clozapine has had to be weighed against the necessity of hematological monitoring for agranulocytosis. This potential impediment to treatment does not appear with other serotonin-dopamine antagonists, which should be tried first in all patients except those with severe extrapyramidal symptoms. Treatment with clozapine has been suggested to decrease suicidality, smoking, and water intoxication; to allow continued improvement over at least 2 years; and to avoid tardive dyskinesias, when compared with the dopamine receptor antagonists. Nonrandomized and uncontrolled trials have shown that patients treated with clozapine for 13 years were more likely

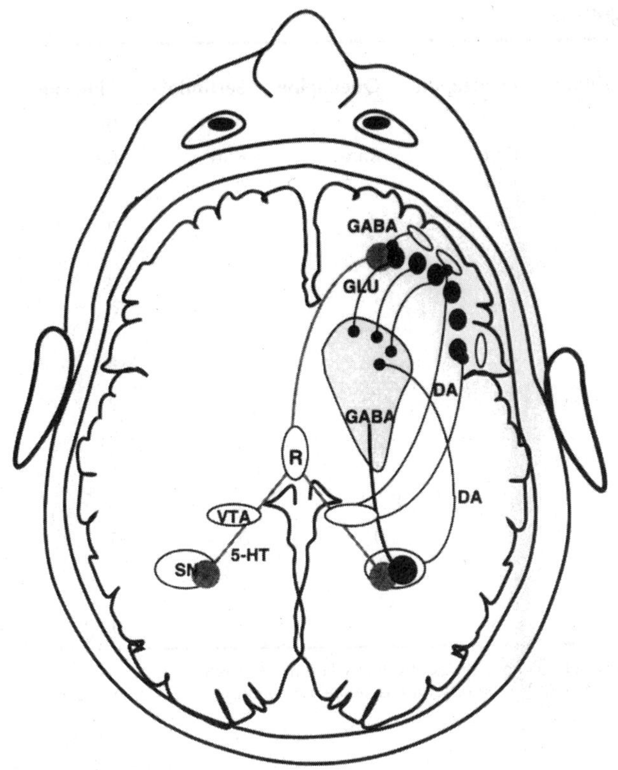
GABA
GLU
DA
GABA
R
DA
VTA
5-HT
SN

FIGURE 35.3.25–1

Schematic diagram of the main neuronal circuits and transmitters dysregulated in schizophrenia. The frontal neocortical projections to the striatum and other subcortical structures are primarily glutamatergic (*GLU*) efferents. Within the cortex, these units are regulated by γ-aminobutyric acid *(GABA)*-containing interneurons (neuropeptides of those GABA neurons not shown) and by dopamine *(DA)* projections from the ventral tegmental area *(VTA)* and serotonergic *(5-HT)* projections from the raphe *(R)* nuclei. The latter monoaminergic neurons may project to either the cortical interneurons or to the cortical efferent neurons. The raphe also projects to the substantia nigra *(SN)*, whose DA axons innervate the basal ganglia but not the cortex. Current evidence favors decreased levels of operation in the nigrostriatal projections but overactivity in the mesolimbic DA systems. Serotonin-dopamine antagonist drugs may work in part through their capacity to inhibit cortically enriched DA receptors (such as the D_4) as well as $5\text{-}HT_2$ receptors. (Reprinted with permission from Cooper JR, Bloom FE, Roth RH: *The Biochemical Basis of Neuropharmacology*, ed 7, p 496. Oxford University Press, New York, 1996.)

to avoid hospitalization and that patients treated with clozapine for 2 years increased their rate of employment from 3 to 40 percent. These observations will need to be replicated and evaluated critically.

Other Indications. Many clinicians use clozapine with patients who are seriously ill or who have severe tardive dyskinesia or a particular sensitivity to the extrapyramidal effects of standard antipsychotic drugs. Clozapine treatment suppresses the abnormal movements of tardive dyskinesia, as does treatment with conventional antipsychotics; in contrast to conventional antipsychotics, however, clozapine may treat the movement disorder. Anecdotal reports and small, uncontrolled studies note the use of clozapine for patients with schizoaffective disorder, severe bipolar I disorder, borderline personality disorder, severe psychotic depression, and Parkinson's disease, in cases where levodopa therapy has induced psychotic symptoms. Anecdotal reports suggest a role for clozapine in the treatment of the tremors of Parkinson's disease, alcoholism, and benign essential tremor and in the rigidity and psychosis of Huntington's disease. Treatment-resistant patients with pervasive developmental disorder, autism, and obsessive-compulsive disorder have responded to clozapine. However, 19 case reports of patients treated with clozapine have noted treatment-emergent symptoms of obsessive-compulsive disorder.

Precautions and Adverse Reactions

The feature of clozapine that distinguishes it from standard antipsychotics is its absence of extrapyramidal adverse effects (Table 35.3.25–2). Clozapine does not cause acute dystonia, and it is associated with low incidences of parkinsonism (less than 5 percent), rabbit syndrome, and akinesia, although there are reports that clozapine may be associated with akathisia. Clozapine may be associated with a much lower incidence of tardive dyskinesia than are other antipsychotics, although a few unconfirmed case reports do note an association. Because of its weak effects on D_2 receptors, clozapine does not affect prolactin secretion; thus, clozapine does not cause galactorrhea. The two most serious adverse effects associated with clozapine are agranulocytosis and seizures.

Agranulocytosis. *Agranulocytosis* is defined as a decrease in the number of polymorphonuclear leukocytes associated with infectious disease. The erythrocyte and platelet concentrations are unaffected. Agranulocytosis occurs in 1 to 2 percent of all patients treated with clozapine; this percentage contrasts with an incidence of 0.04 to 0.5 percent of patients treated with standard antipsychotics. Early studies showed that a third of the patients who experienced agranulocytosis from clozapine died, but careful clinical monitoring of the hematological status of clozapine-treated patients can virtually prevent fatalities by the early recognition of hematological problems and the permanent cessation of clozapine use. Agranulocytosis can appear precipitously or gradually, and it most often develops in the first 6 months of treatment, although it can appear much later. Increased age and female sex are additional risk factors for the development of clozapine-induced agranulocytosis. An undetermined genetic factor probably puts specific

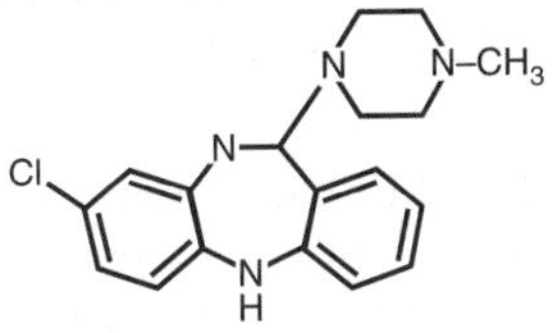
N
N–CH3
N
Cl
N
H

FIGURE 35.3.25–2

Molecular structure of clozapine.

Table 35.3.25–2
Adverse Effect Profiles of Serotonin-Dopamine Antagonists

	Typical Neuroleptic	Clozapine	Risperidone	Olanzapine	Quetiapine	Sertindole	Ziprasidone
Agitation	+ to + +	0	+ +	+	+	0	0
Agranulocytosis	Rare	+ + +	Rare	Rare	Rare	Rare	Rare
Anticholinergic effects	+ to + + +	+ + +	±	+ +	+	0	+
AST/ALT-level elevation	+	+	0	+	+	0	+
EPS	+ to + + +	0	+	0	0	0	+
Dose-related increase in EPS	Yes	No	Yes	Yes	?	No	?
Nausea/dyspepsia	+	0	±	+	0	+	+
Orthostatic hypotension	+ to + + +	+ + +	+	+ +	+ +	+	+
Elevation of prolactin levels	+ to + +	0	+ +	+	0	0	+
Sedation	+ + to + + +	+ + +	+	+ +	+ +	0	+
Seizures	+	+ + + dose related	0	+	0	0	0
Tardive dyskinesia	+ + +	0	±	?	?	?	?
Weight gain	+ to + +	+ + +	+	+ +	+	+ +	0

Modified from Jibson MD, Tandon R: A summary of research findings on the new antipsychotic drugs. Psychiatry Forum *16:* 1996.
+, mild; + +, moderate; + + +, severe; ±, minimal; ?, uncertain; and 0, none; AST/ALT, ratio of serum aspartate aminotransferase to serum alanine aminotransferase; EPS, extrapyramidal symptoms.

patients at risk for agranulocytosis. For example, a high rate of clozapine-induced agranulocytosis is seen in Ashkenazi Jewish patients with human lymphocyte antigens (HLA) B38, DR4, and DQw3, whereas a similar association in non–Ashkenazi Jewish patients occurs with HLA-DR2. Clozapine is also associated with the development of benign cases of leukocytosis (0.6 percent of patients), leukopenia (3 percent), eosinophilia (1 percent), and elevated erythrocyte sedimentation rates.

Seizures. About 5 percent of patients taking more than 600 mg a day of clozapine, 3 to 4 percent of patients taking 300 to 600 mg a day, and 1 to 2 percent of patients taking less than 300 mg a day have clozapine-associated seizures. These percentages are higher than those associated with the use of standard antipsychotic drugs. If seizures develop in a patient, clozapine should be temporarily stopped. Phenobarbital (Luminal) treatment can be initiated, and clozapine can be restarted at about 50 percent of the previous dosage, then gradually raised again. Carbamazepine (Tegretol) should not be used in combination with clozapine because of its association with agranulocytosis. The plasma concentrations of other antiepileptics must be monitored carefully because of the possibility of pharmacokinetic interactions with clozapine.

Cardiovascular Effects. Tachycardia, hypotension, and electrocardiographic (ECG) changes are associated with clozapine treatment. The tachycardia is due to vagal inhibition and can be treated with peripherally acting β-adrenergic antagonists such as atenolol (Tenormin), although this treatment can aggravate the hypotensive effects of clozapine. These hypotensive effects may be severe enough to result in syncopal episodes, especially whenever the initial dosage exceeds 75 mg a day. Syncopal episodes can usually be avoided if the starting dosage is low (25 mg a day) and the dosage is raised gradually, to allow tolerance for the hypotensive effects of the drug to develop. Additional treatment measures for hypotension include avoidance of caffeine, intake of at least 2 liters of fluid a day, support stockings, increased sodium intake, and, possibly, fludrocortisone treatment. In addition to tachycardia, potential ECG changes with clozapine include nonspecific ST-T wave changes, T wave flattening, or T wave inversions, although these changes are usually not clinically significant. Paradoxical hypertension has been observed in 4 percent of patients.

Other Adverse Effects. The most common other adverse effects associated with clozapine treatment are sedation, fatigue, sialorrhea, weight gain, various GI symptoms (most commonly constipation), anticholinergic effects, and fever. Sedation and sialorrhea can often be the most troubling adverse effects to patients. Sedation is most common early in the course of treatment, and the effects of daytime sedation can be reduced by giving most of the clozapine dosage at night. Sialorrhea can be a disturbing adverse effect. It is often most severe at night and results in patients' complaints that their pillows are wet when they awake in the morning. Because of the potentially additive effects of anticholinergic drugs and the anticholinergic activity of clozapine, treatment of sialorrhea with anticholinergic drugs is not advised; there have been reports of successful treatment, however, with clonidine (Catapres) patches (0.1 mg weekly) and low doses of amitriptyline (Elavil) at bedtime. Although mild hypothermia is commonly associated with clozapine, fevers of 1 to 2 F above normal may develop, usually during the first month of treatment; such fevers often cause concern about the development of an infection because of agranulocytosis. The differential diagnosis of fever includes drug fever, dehydration, catatonia, and neuroleptic malignant syndrome. Clozapine should be withheld in these cases; if the white blood cell count (WBC) is normal, clozapine can be reinstituted slowly and at a low dosage. Neuroleptic malignant syndrome is more likely to occur if clozapine is given together with lithium. Enuresis, urinary frequency or urgency, urinary hesitancy or retention, and impotence have been seen with use of clozapine. These problems may respond to desmopressin acetate (DDAVP), oxybutynin (Ditropan), or timed interruption of sleep.

Precautions. Clozapine use by pregnant women has not been studied, and because the drug can be excreted in breast milk, it should not be used by nursing mothers. Clozapine should also not be used by patients with WBCs below 3,500, a history of a bone marrow disorder, or a history of clozapine-induced agranulocytosis. Because of the variety of cardiovascular changes associated with clozapine use, the drug should be used with caution by patients with preexisting cardiac disease. Patients with preexisting seizure disorders or histories of significant head trauma are at greater risk for seizures while taking clozapine.

Drug Interactions

Clozapine should not be used with any other drug that is associated with the development of agranulocytosis or bone marrow suppression. Such drugs include carbamazepine, propylthiouracil, sulfonamides, and captopril (Capoten). CNS depressants, alcohol, or tricyclic drugs coadministered with clozapine may increase the risk for seizures, sedation, and cardiac effects. The coadministration of benzodiazepines and clozapine may be associated with an increased incidence of orthostasis and syncope. There have been rare case reports of respiratory depression after the coadministration of benzodiazepines and clozapine at the initiation of clozapine treatment. Lithium (Eskalith) combined with clozapine may increase the risk of neuroleptic malignant syndrome, seizures, confusion, and movement disorders. A few case reports suggest that lithium not be used in combination with clozapine by patients who have experienced an episode of neuroleptic malignant syndrome. Clozapine clearance is increased by phenytoin (Dilantin) and carbamazepine and is decreased by cimetidine (Tagamet), serotonin-specific reuptake inhibitors, tricyclic and tetracyclic drugs, valproate (Depakote), erythromycin, and ketoconazole.

Laboratory Interferences

No known laboratory interferences are associated with clozapine use.

Dosage and Administration

Pretreatment Assessment. Once a physician has determined that a trial of clozapine is warranted for a particular patient, the risks and benefits of clozapine treatment must be explained to the patient and the family (Table 35.3.25–3). The informed consent procedure should be documented in the patient's chart. The patient's history should include information about blood disorders, epilepsy, cardiovascular disease, and hepatic and renal diseases. The presence of a hepatic or renal

Table 35.3.25–3
Guidelines for the Management of Patients on Clozapine[a]

1. Patients should have a thorough medical history and physical examination prior to initiation of treatment.
2. Testing for tuberculosis should be performed and testing for HIV offered to any patient with risks for either disease. Risk factors include prolonged residence in an institutional facility, group home, shelter, etc. Treatment with clozapine may begin before test results are available if the patient lacks physical signs or symptoms of illness. If either condition is diagnosed, appropriate consultation should be obtained regarding the risks and benefits of continuing clozapine.
3. It is advisable to begin clozapine therapy with a small dose (eg, 25 mg) and build up gradually, over a 30-day period, to a therapeutic level of 500 mg or more per day.
4. The physician must complete a three-part National Registry WBC Reporting Form (provided by Sandoz). The physician keeps one copy and forwards the remaining two copies to the patient's pharmacist.
5. The pharmacist may dispense a maximum of 7 days' supply of medication, provided three criteria are met:
   a. The patient's current WBC is recorded.
   b. The initial WBC is at least 3,500 per mm^3.
   c. Subsequent WBCs, obtained weekly, are at least 3,000 per mm^3.
6. Benign neutropenia is not typical with clozapine. The following thresholds must be observed in monitoring WBC levels:
   a. Treatment should not be initiated if the WBC is less than 3,500 per mm^3.
   b. If subsequent WBCs are between 3,000 and 3,500 per mm^3, twice-weekly WBCs with differentials should be obtained.
   c. If the total WBC falls below 3,000 per mm^3, therapy should be interrupted and the patient closely monitored.
   d. If the total WBC falls below 2,000 per mm^3, therapy should be discontinued, and the patient should never be rechallenged with clozapine.
   e. If a weekly WBC falls 30% from the previous level, the WBC should be repeated. If the repeat level shows the WBC continuing to fall significantly, appropriate consultation from Sandoz and/or another expert (ie, psychiatrist, hematologist, or infectious disease specialist) should be obtained.
   f. A gradual progressive decrease in the WBC from the time of initiation of therapy with clozapine should be monitored closely, and consideration should be given to obtaining consultation as above.

Reprinted with permission from Silver JM, Yudofsky SC, Hurowitz GI: Psychopharmacology and electroconvulsive therapy. In *The American Psychiatric Press Textbook of Psychiatry*, ed 2, RE Hales, SC Yudofsky, JA Talbott, editors, p 920. American Psychiatric Press, Washington, 1994.

[a] These guidelines are based on the requirements set forth by Sandoz (through items 6a, b, and c) and the procedures of the Psychiatry Department of Columbia–Presbyterian Medical Center (items 6d and e).

disease necessitates the use of low starting dosages of the drug. The laboratory examination should include an ECG, several complete blood counts (CBCs) with WBCs, which can then be averaged, and liver and renal function tests.

Switching from and to Another Antipsychotic Drug. Although the transition from a dopamine receptor antagonist to clozapine may be done abruptly, it is probably wiser to taper off the dopamine receptor antagonist slowly while titrating up clozapine. Clozapine and olanzapine have anticholinergic effects, and the transition from one to the other can be accomplished without risk of cholinergic rebound. Risperidone and sertindole lack anticholinergic effects, and the abrupt transition from clozapine to one of these agents may cause cholinergic rebound, which consists of excessive salivation, nausea, vomiting, and diarrhea. The risk of cholinergic rebound can be mitigated by initially augmenting risperidone with an anticholinergic drug, which is then tapered off slowly. Any initiation and termination of clozapine should be accomplished gradually.

Titration and Dosage. Clozapine is available in 25 and 100 mg tablets; 1 mg of clozapine is equivalent to about 1½ to 2 mg of chlorpromazine. The initial dosage is usually 25 mg 1 or 2 times daily, although a conservative initial dosage is 12.5 mg twice daily. The dosage can then be raised gradually (25 mg a day every 2 or 3 days) to 300 mg a day in divided doses, usually 2 or 3 times daily. The gradual increase in dosage is necessitated by the potential development of hypotension, syncope, and sedation, which are adverse effects for which the patient can usually develop tolerance if the dose titration is gradual enough. The usual effective treatment range is 400 to 500 mg a day, although dosages up to 600 mg a day can be used. If a patient stops taking clozapine for more than a 36-hour period, the clinician should restart the drug at 12.5 to 25 mg twice daily and then titrate the dosage upward to the previous dosage level. After the decision to terminate the drug, clozapine treatment should be tapered whenever possible to avoid cholinergic rebound symptoms, such as diaphoresis, flushing, diarrhea, and hyperactivity.

Plasma Concentrations. Data on the relation between plasma concentrations of clozapine and clinical efficacy are still limited, and many of the available data indicate a lack of any clear correlation. For example, the same dose of clozapine may produce up to a 45-fold variation in plasma levels between different individuals. Nevertheless, for cases in which it seems indicated and possible to check plasma concentrations, the average range of plasma concentrations is 200 to 400 ng/mL, with concentrations below 100 ng/mL considered low and those above 500 ng/mL considered high. Studies have indicated that maximum response may require plasma concentrations of 350 mg/mL, with little additional benefit at higher concentrations.

Laboratory Monitoring. Weekly WBCs are indicated to monitor patients for the development of agranulocytosis. Although monitoring is expensive, early indication of agranulocytosis can prevent a fatal outcome. If the WBC is less than 2,000 cells per mm^3 or the granulocyte count is less than 1,000 per mm^3, clozapine should be discontinued, a hematological consultation should be obtained, and obtaining of a bone marrow sample should be considered. Patients with agranulocytosis should not be reexposed to the drug. Physicians can monitor the WBC through any laboratory. Proof of monitoring must be presented to the pharmacist to obtain the medication.

RISPERIDONE

Chemistry

Risperidone is a benzisoxazole. Its molecular structure is shown in Figure 35.3.25–3.

Pharmacological Actions

Pharmacokinetics. Between 70 percent and 85 percent of risperidone is absorbed from the GI tract, and it undergoes extensive first-pass hepatic metabolism by cytochrome P450 (CYP) isoenzyme CYP 2D6 to a metabolite with comparable biological activity. Although genetic polymorphisms in cytochrome CYP 2D6 may lead to differing ratios of risperidone and its metabolite in different people, this result has little bearing on the clinical effects. Both compounds are highly protein bound in plasma. Because the half-lives of both risperidone and its active metabolic are about 20 to 24 hours, risperidone may be taken either once or twice daily.

Pharmacodynamics. Risperidone has a high affinity for the serotonin 5-HT_2, D_2, α_1- and α_2-adrenergic, and H_1 receptors. It has a low affinity for β-adrenergic and muscarinic cholinergic receptors. Although it is as potent an antagonist of D_2 receptors as is haloperidol, risperidone is much less likely than haloperidol to cause catalepsy in laboratory animals and extrapyramidal symptoms in humans.

Effects on Specific Organs and Systems

Risperidone exerts most of its effects in the CNS, and the principal non-CNS effects are in the cardiovascular system (see Precautions and Adverse Reactions).

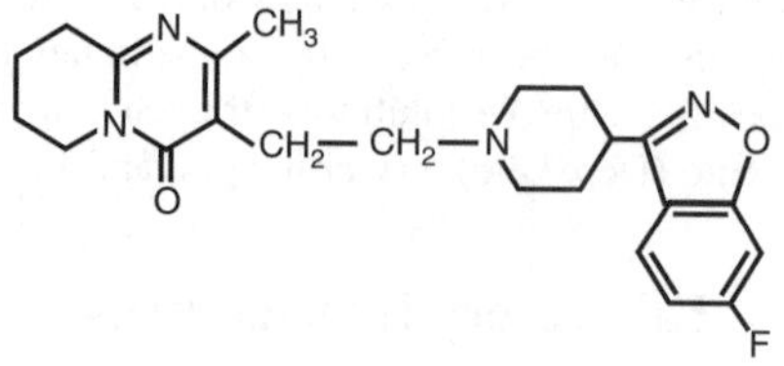
N
CH3
N
CH2— CH2—N
N
O
O
F

FIGURE 35.3.25–3
Molecular structure of risperidone.

Therapeutic Indications

Risperidone is FDA approved for treatment of psychotic disorders. With clinical scales such as the Brief Psychiatric Rating Scale (BPRS) and the Clinical Global Impression (CGI), risperidone was demonstrated to reduce the positive manifestation of schizophrenia and to have more modest benefits on the negative symptoms. It is effective for both first and later episodes of psychosis in schizophrenia and schizoaffective disorders. Uncontrolled studies have suggested that risperidone prevents relapses, even at low doses. Over several years of premarketing and postmarketing experience, the beneficial effects of risperidone have recently been found at lower doses than were initially used, with concomitant reduction in adverse effects. In the first direct comparison of risperidone (12 mg a day) and haloperidol (10 mg a day), both drugs were equally effective for both positive and negative symptoms, and risperidone caused fewer extrapyramidal symptoms. A direct comparison of risperidone (8.5 mg a day) and perphenazine (28 mg a day) found equal effectiveness for positive symptoms and superiority of risperidone for negative symptoms but no difference in extrapyramidal symptoms. A comparison of several doses of risperidone to haloperidol (10 mg a day) found that 1 mg a day of risperidone was subtherapeutic, that 4 and 8 mg a day were most effective, and that there were fewer extrapyramidal symptoms due to risperidone at all doses below 16 mg a day. A larger direct comparison of several doses of risperidone with haloperidol (20 mg a day) or placebo in acutely ill patients found that risperidone at dosages above 2 mg a day and haloperidol at dosages above 20 mg a day were significantly more effective than placebo for positive symptoms. A dosage of 6 mg a day of risperidone was significantly more effective than haloperidol for positive symptoms, and dosages of 6 and 16 mg a day of risperidone, but not haloperidol or placebo, resulted in improvement in negative symptoms. Extrapyramidal symptoms due to risperidone were seen more often than with placebo only at dosages in excess of 6 mg a day. Treatment-refractory patients benefitted the most from risperidone compared with haloperidol. In direct comparison with moderate dosages of clozapine (300 to 400 mg/day), dosages of 4 to 8 mg a day of risperidone were equally effective, with fewer adverse effects such as somnolence, in both acutely ill and treatment-refractory patients.

As experience builds, patients treated with risperidone seem less likely to relapse and require hospitalization, though this observation must be confirmed in a controlled trial. Postmarketing experience noted that the average dosage of risperidone in clinical use was 4.7 mg a day as of the end of 1996, and the optimal dosage may be adjusted further as more experience is gained over the long term with lower doses. The therapeutic dosage of risperidone therefore is significantly below the dosage at which extrapyramidal symptoms are seen. Direct comparisons of risperidone with olanzapine or with low-potency dopamine receptor antagonists such as chlorpromazine or thioridazine have not yet been reported.

Other Indications. Many clinicians use risperidone for patients who are seriously ill or who have severe tardive dyskinesia or a particular sensitivity to the extrapyramidal adverse effects of standard antipsychotic drugs. Risperidone treatment suppresses the abnormal movements of tardive dyskinesia, as does treatment with conventional antipsychotics; but in contrast to conventional antipsychotics, risperidone generally does not appear to worsen the movement disorder. In a few case reports, however, risperidone appeared to cause tardive dyskinesias. Anecdotal reports and small, uncontrolled studies note the use of risperidone in patients with schizoaffective disorder, severe bipolar I disorder, borderline personality disorder, obsessive-compulsive disorder, depressive disorder with psychotic features, psychotic disorder due to head trauma, AIDS encephalopathy, and substance-induced psychosis. Other case reports suggest that risperidone may be beneficial in Tourette's disorder, Huntington's disease, Parkinson's disease in which levodopa treatment has produced hallucinations, and Lesch-Nyhan syndrome.

Precautions and Adverse Reactions

In preclinical trials, 9 percent of patients discontinued risperidone because of an adverse event, which compared favorably to those discontinuing placebo (7 percent) or active control drugs (10 percent). The most common reasons for discontinuance were extrapyramidal symptoms (2.1 percent), dizziness (0.7 percent), hyperkinesia (0.6 percent), somnolence (0.5 percent), and nausea (0.3 percent). The adverse reactions reported with risperidone are listed in Table 35.3.25–2. There is evidence that the extrapyramidal effects may be dose dependent. Dosages below 6 mg a day have generally not been associated with extrapyramidal symptoms, but dystonic reactions have been seen at dosages from 4 to 16 mg a day. Although more rare with serotonin-dopamine antagonists, all antipsychotic drugs may cause neuroleptic malignant syndrome and tardive dyskinesia.

Central Nervous System Effects. The most common adverse effect of risperidone is somnolence, which may occur in over 40 percent of patients on a dose higher than usually necessary for therapeutic response (16 mg a day). Therefore, patients who take risperidone should exercise caution when driving or operating dangerous machinery. This adverse effect is minimized by giving the dose before sleep. Risperidone-associated seizures are seen in less than 1 percent of patients. The D_2 receptor antagonism of risperidone causes a rise in prolactin levels for the duration of the therapy. This is of theoretical concern in patients with a history of breast cancer, a tumor that may be dependent on prolactin for growth, although there are no human data establishing such a connection. Galactorrhea and menstrual disturbances have not yet been seen.

Cardiovascular Effects. If the initial dose of risperidone is titrated up rapidly, less than 1 percent of patients may develop signs and symptoms of orthostatic hypotension, such as dizziness, tachycardia, and syncope. The risk of these effects may be minimized by limiting the starting dose to 1 mg once a day in normal adults and 0.5 mg once a day in older patients, then increasing to the therapeutic range of 4 to 6 mg a day over a few weeks. Approximately 2 percent of patients may experience a prolongation of the QT_c interval to more than 450 ms. A prolonged QT_c interval may lead to cardiac arrhythmias or heart block.

Other Adverse Reactions. Weight gain, constipation, erectile dysfunction, orgastic dysfunction, and increased pigmentation are associated with risperidone use at higher frequencies than with placebo in preclinical trials. A number of cases of neuroleptic malignant syndrome have been reported in patients taking risperidone. Three case reports have noted the emergence of obsessive-compulsive symptoms in patients taking risperidone.

Precautions. Risperidone use by pregnant women has not yet been studied, and because the drug can be excreted in breast milk, it should not be taken by nursing mothers. Because of the variety of cardiovascular changes associated with risperidone use, the drug should be used with caution in patients with a history of cardiovascular disease or cerebrovascular disease or in those with conditions or on therapy that may predispose to hypotension. Alcohol should be avoided during use of risperidone.

Drug Interactions

CNS depressants, alcohol, or tricyclic drugs coadministered with risperidone may increase the risk for seizures, sedation, and cardiac effects. Antihypertensive medications may potentiate the orthostatic hypotension caused by risperidone. The coadministration of benzodiazepines and risperidone may be associated with an increased incidence of orthostasis and syncope. Chronic use of carbamazepine concomitantly with risperidone may increase the clearance of risperidone.

Laboratory Interferences

No known laboratory interferences are associated with risperidone use.

Dosage and Administration

Titration and Dosage. Risperidone is available in 1, 2, 3, and 4 mg tablets. The initial dosage is usually 1 mg once daily. The dosage can then be raised gradually (1 mg daily every 2 or 3 days) to 4 to 6 mg a day. The gradual increase in dosage is necessitated by the potential development of hypotension, syncope, and sedation, adverse effects for which patients can usually develop tolerance if the dose titration is gradual enough. Dosages from 1 to 16 mg a day have been tested, but no therapeutic advantage has been assigned to dosages over 6 mg a day, whereas the higher dosages were associated with increased adverse effects. Recent evidence has shown that lower dosages are effective. Postmarketing surveys have noted that the mean dose for the treatment of schizophrenia is 4.7 mg a day. In the elderly and in children, dosages as low as 0.5 to 1 mg a day are effective. If a patient stops taking risperidone for more than a 36-hour period, the clinician should restart the drug according to the initial titration schedule. There is no correlation between plasma levels and clinical efficacy. An oral solution has recently been approved by the FDA. A long-acting depot formulation is not available. Risperidone is less likely than clozapine, olanzapine, and the dopamine receptor antagonists to produce a calming effect in the first few days of use, and addition of a benzodiazepine or a high-potency dopamine receptor antagonist may be necessary in the first 1 to 2 weeks. The benefit of risperidone is usually noted within 4 weeks.

OLANZAPINE

Chemistry

Olanzapine is a thienobenzodiazepine derivative. Its molecular structure is shown in Figure 35.3.25–4. It is chemically related to clozapine and quetiapine.

Pharmacological Actions

Pharmacokinetics. Approximately 85 percent of olanzapine is absorbed from the GI tract, and about 40 percent of the dose is inactivated by first-pass hepatic metabolism. Peak concentrations are achieved in 6 hours, and the half-life averages 31 hours. Therefore, it is effective in once-a-day dosing. It is highly protein bound in the plasma.

Pharmacodynamics. Olanzapine has a high affinity for the $5\text{-}HT_2$, dopamine types 1 to 4 (D_1, D_2, D_3, D_4), α_1-adrenergic, muscarinic types 1 to 5 (M_1 to M_5), and H_1 receptors. It has little antagonism of α_2- or β-adrenergic receptors. Its antipsychotic activities are thought to be mediated by its antagonism of the serotonin and dopamine receptors.

Effects on Specific Organs and Systems

Olanzapine exerts most of its effects in the CNS, and the principal non-CNS effects are in the cardiovascular system and in the liver (see Precautions and Adverse Reactions).

Therapeutic Indications

Olanzapine is approved by the FDA for the treatment of psychotic disorders. The BPRS and the CGI suggest that olanzapine reduces both the positive and negative manifestations of schizophrenia. In direct comparisons between olanzapine and haloperidol (10 to 20 mg a day) in double-blinded studies,

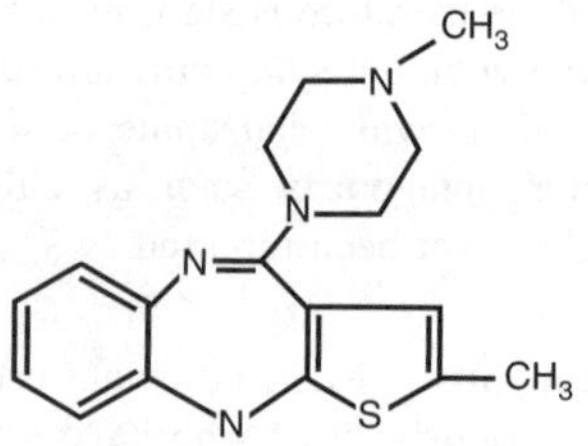
CH3
N
N
N
N
S
CH3

FIGURE 35.3.25–4
Molecular structure of olanzapine.

olanzapine was comparable to haloperidol for the treatment of positive symptoms at doses of 7.5 to 17.5 mg a day and was superior to haloperidol for negative symptoms. Data from controlled trials for the use of olanzapine in treatment-refractory patients have not yet been reported. A year-long maintenance study found a lower rate of relapse and rehospitalization with olanzapine than with haloperidol or placebo. Olanzapine is effective for 65 percent of patients with a first psychotic break and for 40 percent of patients with chronic schizophrenia, according to early studies. Direct comparisons between olanzapine and clozapine or risperidone have not been completed. The relative lack of extrapyramidal effects suggests that olanzapine, like clozapine and risperidone, may become a favored drug for patients who begin to exhibit tardive dyskinesias. Preliminary data suggest that olanzapine has an antidepressant effect in patients with schizophrenia. It is expected that olanzapine will be used for the full range of disorders for which clozapine and risperidone have been tried.

Precautions and Adverse Reactions

In preclinical trials, 5 percent of patients discontinued olanzapine because of an adverse event. This rate compared favorably to those discontinuing placebo (6 percent). One percent discontinued olanzapine because of elevations of transaminases. The adverse reactions reported with olanzapine are listed in Table 35.3.25–2. There is evidence that extrapyramidal effects may be dose dependent, appearing at doses in excess of 15 mg a day. Although more rare with serotonin-dopamine antagonists, all antipsychotic drugs may cause neuroleptic malignant syndrome. No cases of tardive dyskinesia have yet been reported in patients taking olanzapine, although experience is limited. No agranulocytosis was reported in over 3,100 patients taking olanzapine, including 29 who previously experienced clozapine-induced agranulocytosis.

Central Nervous System Effects. The most common adverse effect of olanzapine is somnolence, which may occur in 30 percent of patients on the usual maintenance dose (10 to 15 mg a day). Therefore, patients who take olanzapine should exercise caution when driving or operating dangerous machinery. This adverse effect is minimized by taking the dose before sleep. Olanzapine-associated seizures occurred in less than 1 percent of patients, many of whom had confounding risk factors for seizures. The D_2 receptor antagonism of olanzapine causes a modest rise in prolactin levels for the duration of therapy. This fact is of theoretical concern in patients with a history of breast cancer, a tumor that may be dependent on prolactin for growth, although there are no human data establishing such a connection. Dizziness, acute dystonic reactions, neuroleptic malignant syndrome, akathisia, and nonaggressive objectionable behavior have also been reported at frequencies higher than those seen in placebo controls.

Cardiovascular Effects. If the initial dose of olanzapine is titrated up rapidly, less than 1 percent of patients may develop signs and symptoms of orthostatic hypotension, such as dizziness, tachycardia, and syncope. The risk of these effects may be minimized by limiting the starting dose to 5 mg a day, then increasing to the therapeutic range of 10 to 15 mg a day over a few weeks. Olanzapine should be used with caution by patients with a history of myocardial infarction or unstable angina.

Hepatic Effects. In 2 percent of patients taking olanzapine, serum alanine aminotransferase (SGPT) elevations more than 3 times normal were seen. None of these patients developed jaundice. The levels returned to normal in different patients whether or not the drug was discontinued. These data suggest that olanzapine should be used with caution by patients with underlying liver disease.

Other Adverse Reactions. Weight gain and constipation have been significantly associated with olanzapine use. In long-term use (average 238 days), olanzapine caused an average weight gain of 12 pounds in 56 percent of patients. Because of its anticholinergic effects, olanzapine should be used with caution in patients with narrow-angle glaucoma, paralytic ileus, or urinary outflow obstruction.

Precautions. Olanzapine use by pregnant women has not been studied, and because the drug can be excreted in breast milk, it should not be taken by nursing mothers. Olanzapine should not be used with other drugs that may cause orthostatic hypotension, such as benzodiazepines, antihypertensives, or alcohol.

Drug Interactions

CNS depressants, alcohol, or tricyclic drugs coadministered with olanzapine may increase the risk of seizures, sedation, and cardiac effects. Antihypertensive medications may potentiate the orthostatic hypotension caused by olanzapine. The coadministration of benzodiazepines and olanzapine may be associated with an increased incidence of orthostasis and syncope. Chronic use of carbamazepine concomitantly with olanzapine may increase the clearance of olanzapine by 50 percent or more. Concomitant use of cimetidine may increase olanzapine concentrations.

Laboratory Interferences

No known laboratory interferences are associated with olanzapine use. Olanzapine causes little, if any, inhibition of hepatic cytochrome P450 enzymes.

Dosage and Administration

Titration and Dosage. Olanzapine is available in 5, 7.5, and 10 mg tablets. The initial dosage is usually 5 mg once daily. The dosage can then be raised after 1 week to 10 mg a day. Because of the long half-life, 1 week must be allowed for achievement of each new steady-state blood concentration. Dosages from 5 to 30 mg a day have been tested, but no therapeutic advantage has been noted with dosages over 20 mg a day, whereas the higher dosages were associated with increased adverse effects. Many patients will respond to 10 mg a day, but severely ill or treatment-refractory patients may need 20 mg a day. The manufacturer recommends ''periodic'' assessment of transaminases during treatment with olanzapine. There is no association between plasma concentrations and therapeutic efficacy.

SERTINDOLE

Chemistry

Sertindole is an arylpiperidylindole. The molecular structure is shown in Figure 35.3.25–5.

Pharmacological Actions

Pharmacokinetics. Detailed pharmacokinetic data for sertindole are not yet available. The half-life of sertindole is 27 hours, and it is effective in once-a-day dosing. The long plasma half-life of sertindole requires that the drug be taken for a least 2 weeks before a steady-state level is achieved.

Pharmacodynamics. Sertindole is a potent antagonist of serotonin types 2A and 2C (5-HT_{2A} and 5-HT_{2C}), dopamine type 2 (D_2), and α_1-adrenergic receptors, whereas it has little antagonism at muscarinic, α_2-adrenergic, and histamine type 1 (H_1) receptors. Its antipsychotic activities are thought to be mediated by its antagonism of the serotonin and dopamine receptors. Sertindole is said to be selectively active in the limbic system and the ventral tegmental area but to be nearly devoid of activity in the striatonigral area. This dichotomy is thought to underlie its absence of extrapyramidal adverse effects.

Effects on Specific Organs and Systems

Sertindole exerts most of its effects in the CNS, and the principal non-CNS effects are in the cardiovascular system and in the liver (see Precautions and Adverse Reactions).

Therapeutic Indications

Sertindole is used for the treatment of psychotic disorders. As of mid-1997, sertindole had not yet been approved by the FDA for use in the United States. It had received a letter of approvability and was expected to be approved for the treatment of schizophrenia on the basis of controlled studies. The Positive and Negative Symptoms Scale (PANSS) and the CGI suggest that sertindole reduces the positive manifestations of schizophrenia. At higher doses, it has a modest effect on the negative features of schizophrenia. In a placebo-controlled comparison of sertindole (12, 20, and 24 mg a day) and haloperidol (4, 8, 16 mg a day), sertindole and haloperidol were equally effective for positive symptoms at all doses, whereas only sertindole at 20 mg a day was more effective than placebo for negative symptoms. Extrapyramidal symptoms were no more frequent for sertindole than for placebo. As expected for a drug with a long half-life, the full benefit of a particular dose was not realized for several months. Controlled trials of sertindole for treatment-refractory patients have not yet been reported. The relative lack of extrapyramidal adverse effects suggests that sertindole may be a favored drug for patients who have begun to exhibit tardive dyskinesias. Studies of animal models of drug abuse suggest that sertindole may abrogate certain reward effects of opiates, cocaine, and amphetamines. It is expected that sertindole will be used in the same spectrum of disorders for which clozapine and risperidone are now used.

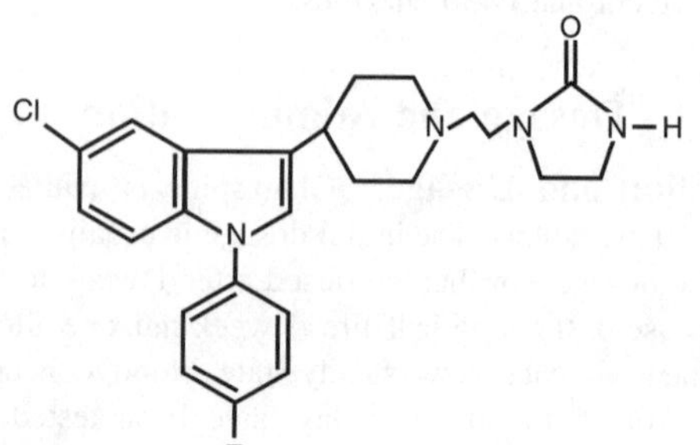
Cl
N
N
N
N–H
O
F

FIGURE 35.3.25–5
Molecular structure of sertindole.

Precautions and Adverse Reactions

The most common side effects of sertindole are tachycardia, nasal congestion, postural hypotension, dizziness, weight gain, nausea, reduced volume of ejaculation, and prolongation of the QT_c interval (Table 35.3.23–2). There is evidence that sertindole causes little, if any, extrapyramidal effects. Although more rare with serotonin-dopamine antagonists, all antipsychotic drugs may cause neuroleptic malignant syndrome.

Central Nervous System Effects. Sertindole is not associated with sedation, cognitive adverse effects, or increases in prolactin levels.

Cardiovascular Effects. If the initial dose of sertindole of 4 mg a day is titrated up by 4 mg each day to the target dose of 20 to 24 mg a day, tachycardia and postural hypotension limit tolerability, whereas 4-mg increases every other day are well tolerated. Approximately 3 percent of patients in early preclinical trials experienced a prolongation of the QT_c interval to more than 500 ms. Although a prolonged QT_c interval may lead to cardiac arrhythmias or heart block, no ventricular arrhythmias, such as torsade de pointes, were seen in premarketing trials involving 600 patients or in 7 months of postmarketing experience with 2,000 patients in Great Britain.

Other Adverse Reactions. Decreased ejaculatory volume is the most common reason for discontinuance of sertindole, but this effect has not been accompanied by retrograde ejaculation, by decreased libido, erection, or orgasm, or by irreversible effects. Of the 20 percent of patients reporting this effect, 16 percent experienced a return of normal volume on continued therapy. Weight gain and constipation have been significantly associated with sertindole use.

Precautions. Sertindole use by pregnant women has not been studied, and because the drug can be excreted in breast milk, it should not be taken by nursing mothers. Sertindole should not be used with other drugs that may cause orthostatic hypotension, such as benzodiazepines, antihypertensives, or alcohol. Because of the effects on the QT_c interval, sertindole should be used with caution in patients with a history of cardiac disease.

Drug Interactions

Coadministration of sertindole and either fluoxetine or paroxetine may decrease the clearance of sertindole by 50 percent and may necessitate a lowering of the dose of sertindole. Conversely, chronic use of carbamazepine or phenytoin concomitantly with sertindole may increase the clearance of sertindole by 50 percent or more and may require an increase in the dose of sertindole.

Laboratory Interferences

No known laboratory interferences are associated with sertindole use.

Dosage and Administration

Titration and Dosage. The initial dosage is usually 4 mg once daily. The dosage can be then raised every 2 to 3 days in 4-mg increments to 12 to 24 mg a day. Because of the lack of sedation, sertindole may not rapidly calm acutely psychotic patients, and addition of a benzodiazepine or a high-potency dopamine receptor antagonist may be needed for the first several weeks.

QUETIAPINE

Chemistry

Quetiapine is a benzothiazepine that is structurally related to clozapine and olanzapine. The molecular structure is shown in Figure 35.3.25–6.

Pharmacological Actions

Pharmacokinetics. Detailed pharmacokinetic data for quetiapine are not yet available. Peak plasma concentrations are reached in 1 to 2 hours. Steady-state half-life is about 7 hours, but receptor occupancy lingers for at least 12 hours, and twice-per-day dosing is optimal. Quetiapine has many metabolites, most of which are inactive. Quetiapine is principally metabolized by the hepatic enzyme CYP 3A4, with a minor contribution from CPY 2D6.

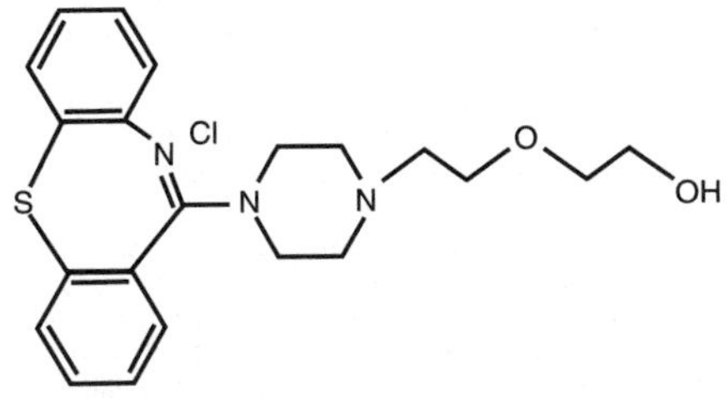

Cl
N
S
N
N
O
OH

FIGURE 35.3.25–6
Molecular structure of quetiapine.

Pharmacodynamics. Quetiapine has high affinity for serotonin types 2 and 6 ($5\text{-}HT_2$ and $5\text{-}HT_6$), histamine type 1 (H_1), and α_1- and α_2-adrenergic receptors; moderate affinity for dopamine type 2 (D_2) receptors; low affinity for dopamine type 1 (D_1) receptors; and very low affinity for dopamine type 4 (D_4) and muscarinic type 1 (M_1) receptors. However, the degree of receptor antagonism for quetiapine is lower than that for other antipsychotic drugs, and it is not associated with extrapyramidal symptoms.

Effects on Specific Organs and Systems

Quetiapine's few effects outside the CNS occur in the cardiovascular system (postural hypotension, small increases in heart rate) and the GI system (constipation).

Therapeutic Indications

Quetiapine has been evaluated for safety and effectiveness in patients with acute schizophrenia, schizoaffective disorder, secondary psychoses, and other psychotic disorders. Quetiapine was as effective as haloperidol and chlorpromazine for positive symptoms and was more effective than placebo for negative symptoms. Quetiapine has not yet been shown to be superior to dopamine receptor antagonists for negative symptoms. Use of quetiapine in treatment-refractory patients and long-term use of quetiapine have not yet been reported. It is expected that quetiapine will be used in the same spectrum of disorders for which clozapine and risperidone are now used.

Precautions and Adverse Reactions

The most common adverse effects of quetiapine are somnolence, postural hypotension, and dizziness, which are usually transient and are best managed with initial upward titration of the dosage. Quetiapine appears no more likely to cause extrapyramidal symptoms than does placebo. Quetiapine is associated with modest transient weight gain and transient rise in liver transaminases. Bone marrow suppression has not been seen, and prolongation of the QT_c interval is no more likely than with dopamine receptor antagonists (Table 35.3.25–2).

Drug Interactions

Phenytoin increases quetiapine clearance fivefold, and thioridazine increases quetiapine clearance by 60 percent.

Laboratory Interferences

No laboratory interferences have been reported for quetiapine.

Dosage and Administration

Quetiapine should be titrated up to 300 mg a day divided into twice-daily dosing. Studies have shown efficacy in the range of 300 to 800 mg a day, most frequently at the dose of 225 to 250 mg twice-a-day.

ZIPRASIDONE

Chemistry

Ziprasidone is a benzisothiazolyl piperazine. The molecular structure is shown in Figure 35.3.25–7.

Pharmacological Actions

Pharmacokinetics. Detailed pharmacokinetic data for ziprasidone are not yet available. Peak plasma concentrations are reached in 2 to 6 hours. Steady-state half-life is 5 to 10 hours, which is reached by the third day, and twice-a-day dosing is optimal. Ziprasidone has many metabolites, most of which are inactive. Ziprasidone is principally metabolized by the hepatic enzyme CYP 3A4.

Pharmacodynamics. Ziprasidone is a potent antagonist of serotonin types 1D, 2A, and 2C (5-HT_{1D}, 5-HT_{2A}, and 5-HT_{2C}) and dopamine types 2 (D_2), and 3 (D_3) receptors. It has moderate affinity for dopamine type 4 (D_4) and α_1-adrenergic receptors; low affinity for histamine type 1 (H_1) receptors; and very low affinity for dopamine type 1 (D_1), α_2-adrenergic receptors, and muscarinic type 1 (M_1) receptors. Data from PET scanning show that the 5-HT_{2A} receptor occupancy (80 to 90 percent) significantly exceeds the D_2 receptor occupancy (45 to 75 percent), which correlates clinically with a low incidence of extrapyramidal symptoms. Ziprasidone is unique among the serotonin-dopamine antagonists, in that it has agonist activity at the serotonin type 1A (5-HT_{1A}) receptors and is an inhibitor of reuptake of both serotonin and norepinephrine. These features suggest it may treat not only psychosis but also anxiety and depression.

Effects on Specific Organs and Systems

Ziprasidone has almost no significant effects outside of the CNS.

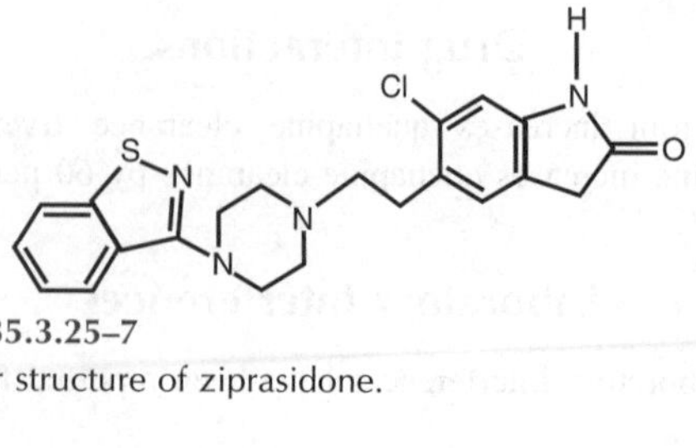

FIGURE 35.3.25–7
Molecular structure of ziprasidone.

Therapeutic Indications

Ziprasidone has been evaluated for safety and effectiveness in patients with acute schizophrenia and schizoaffective disorder. Ziprasidone was as effective as haloperidol for positive symptoms and was more effective than placebo for negative symptoms. Ziprasidone has not yet been shown to be superior to dopamine receptor antagonists for negative symptoms. Long-term use of ziprasidone has been shown to reduce the rate of relapse and to lead to continuing improvement over time. Use of ziprasidone in treatment-refractory patients has not yet been reported. It is expected that ziprasidone will be used in the same spectrum of disorders for which clozapine and risperidone are now used, and it may be particularly useful for patients with features of anxiety and depression.

Precautions and Adverse Reactions

In three clinical trails involving 524 patients with schizophrenia or schizoaffective disorder, no adverse effects were more frequently reported by patients taking ziprasidone than by those taking placebo. The most common adverse effects of ziprasidone are somnolence, dizziness, nausea, and light-headedness. Ziprasidone appears no more likely to cause extrapyramidal symptoms or orthostatic hypotension than placebo. Ziprasidone is associated with almost no weight gain. Bone marrow suppression has not been seen (Table 35.3.25–2).

Drug Interactions and Laboratory Interferences

No significant drug interactions or laboratory interferences have been reported for ziprasidone.

Dosage and Administration

Ziprasidone should be initiated at 40 mg a day twice daily. Studies have shown efficacy in the dosage range of 80 to 160 mg a day, divided twice daily. Ziprasidone is expected to be the first serotonin-dopamine antagonist to be available in a long-acting injectable formulation.

REFERENCES

Antonacci DJ, Swartz CM: Clozapine treatment of euphoric mania. Ann Clin Psychiatry *7* (4); 203, 1995.

Bennett JA, Keck PE Jr: A target-dose finding study of clozapine in patients with schizophrenia. Ann Clin Psychiatry *8* (1): 19, 1996.

Blin O, Azorin JM, Bouhours P: Antipsychotic and anxiolytic properties of risperidone, haloperidol and methotrimeprazine in schizophrenic patients. J Clin Psychopharmacol *16* (1): 38, 1996.

Borison RL: Clinical efficacy of serotonin-dopamine antagonists relative to classic neuroleptics. J Clin Psychopharmacol *15* (1, Suppl): 24S, 1995.

Bruun RD, Budman CL: Risperidone as a treatment for Tourette's syndrome. J Clin Psychiatry *57* (1): 29, 1996.

Carpenter WT: The treatment of negative symptoms: Pharmacological and methodological issues. Br J Psychiatry *168* (29, Suppl): 17, 1996.

de Boer T: The pharmacologic profile of mirtazapine. J Clin Psychiatry *57* (4, Suppl): 19, 1996.

Diantoniis MR, Henry KM, Partridge PAH, Soucar E: Risperidone for negative symptoms. J Am Acad Child Adolesc Psychiatry *35* (7); 838, 1996.

Duffy JD, Kant R: Clinical utility of clozapine in 16 patients with neurological disease. J Neuropsychiatry Clin Neurosci *8* (1): 92, 1996.

Frye MA, Altshuler LL, Bitran JA: Clozapine in rapid cycling bipolar disorder. J Clin Psychopharmacol *16* (1): 87, 1996.

Honigfield G: Effects of the clozapine national registry system on incidence of deaths related to agranulocytosis. Psychiatr Serv *47* (1): 52, 1996.
Janicak PG, Davis JM: Antipsychotic dosing strategies in acute schizophrenia. Int Clin Psychopharmacol *11* (2, Suppl): 35, 1996.
McDougle CJ. Brodkin ES, Yeung PP, Naylor ST: Risperidone in adults with autism or pervasive developmental disorder. J Child Adolesc Psychopharmacol *5* (4): 273, 1995.
Marder SR: Clinical experience with risperidone. J Clin Psychiatry *57* (9, Suppl): 57, 1996.
Meltzer HY: Pre-clinical pharmacology of atypical antipsychotic drugs: A selective review. Br J Psychiatry *168* (29, Suppl): 23, 1996.
Meltzer HY, Maes M, Lee MA: The cimetidine-induced increase in prolactin secretion in schizophrenia: Effect of clozapine. Psychopharmacology *112* (1, Suppl): S95, 1993.
Menditto AA, Beck NC, Stuve P, Fisher JA, et al: Effectiveness of clozapine and a social learning program for severely disabled psychiatric inpatients. Psychiatr Serv *47* (1): 46, 1996.
Musser WS, Akil M: Clozapine as a treatment for psychosis in Parkinson's disease: A review. J Neuropsychiatry Clin Neurosci *8* (1): 1, 1996.
Needham PL, Atkinson J, Skill MJ, Heal DJ: Zotepine: Preclinical tests predict antipsychotic efficacy and an atypical profile. Psychopharmacol Bull *32:* 123, 1996.
Peacock L, Solgaard T, Lublin H, Gerlach J: Clozapine versus typical antipsychotics: A retro- and prospective study of extrapyramidal side effects. Psychopharmacology *124* (1): 188, 1996.
Petit M, Raniwalla J, Tweed J, Leutenegger E, Dollfus S, Kelly F: A comparison of an atypical and typical antipsychotic, zotepine versus haloperidol in patients with acute exacerbation of schizophrenia: A parallel-group double-blind trial. Psychopharmacol Bull *32:* 81, 1996.
Rangwani SR, Gupta S, Burke WJ, Potter J: Improvement of debilitating tardive dyskinesia with risperidone. Ann Clin Psychiatry *8:* 27, 1996.
Reveley MA, Dursun SM, Andrews H: A comparative trial use of sulpiride and risperidone in Huntington's disease: A pilot study. J Psychopharmacol *10* (2): 162, 1996.
Sajatovic M, DiGiovanni SK, Bastani B, Hattab H, Ramirez LF: Risperidone therapy in treatment refractory acute bipolar and schizoaffective mania. Psychopharmacol Bull *32:* 55, 1996.
Seeger TF, Seymour PA, Schmidt AW, Zorn SH, Schulz DW, Lebel LA, McLean S, Guanowsky V, Howard HR, Lowe JA III, et al: Ziprasidone (CP-88, 059): A new antipsychotic with combined dopamine and serotonin receptor antagonist activity. J Pharmacol Exp Ther *275:* 101, 1995.
Tamminga CA, Lahti AC: The new generation of antipsychotic drugs. Int Clin Psychopharmacol *11* (2, Suppl): 73, 1996.
Umbricht D, Kane JM: Risperidone: Efficacy and safety. Schizophr Bull *21* (4): 593, 1995.
Van Kammen DP, Marder SR: Clozapine. In *Comprehensive Textbook of Psychiatry,* ed 6, HI Kaplan, BJ Sadock, editors, p 1979. Williams & Wilkins, Baltimore, 1995.
Van Kammen DP, McEvoy JP, Targum SD, Kardatzke D, et al: A randomized, controlled, dose-ranging trial of sertindole in patients with schizophrenia. Psychopharmacology *124* (1): 168, 1996.
van Moffaert M, de Wilde J, Vereecken A, Dierick M, Evrard JL, Wilmotte J, Mendlewicz J: Mirtazapine is more effective than trazodone: A double-blind controlled study in hospitalized patients with major depression. Int Clin Psychopharmacol *10:* 3, 1995.
Wolters EC, Jansen EN, Tuynman-Qua HG, Bergmans PL: Olanzapine in the treatment of dopaminomimetic psychosis in patients with Parkinson's disease. Neurology *47:* 1085, 1996.

▲ 35.3.26 Serotonin-Norepinephrine Reuptake Inhibitors

The classical tricyclic and tetracyclic antidepressants are thought to exert their antidepressant effects by raising the synaptic concentrations of serotonin and norepinephrine through inhibition of the reuptake of both neurotransmitters. But these older drugs also activate other receptor systems that may produce undesirable effects such as somnolence, constipation, weight gain, and cardiotoxicity. Several novel drugs are more selective for the desirable serotonin and norepinephrine reuptake inhibition but have fewer of the undesirable effects of the older generation of drugs. The first of these, venlafaxine (Effexor), has been approved by the Food and Drug Administration (FDA) for the treatment of depression. Two additional investigational drugs under evaluation for this indication are duloxetine, which is chemically related to fluoxetine (Prozac), and milnacipran. Another serotonin-norepinephrine reuptake inhibitor, sibutramine, has shown promising results in early trials as a treatment for obesity. The principal adverse action of these compounds is their tendency to raise blood pressure, but this consequence of potentiation of the catecholamine system is not a major drawback for most patients.

VENLAFAXINE

Venlafaxine is an effective antidepressant drug that is chemically distinct from other antidepressants, possesses a slightly different mechanism of action, and may have unique efficacy properties. These efficacy properties may include a faster-than-usual onset of action and demonstrated efficacy in seriously depressed patients (for example, patients with melancholic features).

Chemistry

Venlafaxine is a novel phenylethylamine that is structurally distinct from existing antidepressant drugs (Fig. 35.3.26–1).

Pharmacological Actions

Pharmacokinetics. Venlafaxine is absorbed from the gastrointestinal tract and has a half-life of about 5 hours, thereby necessitating 2- to 3-times-daily doses of the drug. Venlafaxine is extensively metabolized in the liver by cytochrome P450 (CYP) isoenzyme CYP 2D6 and possesses at least one active metabolite, *O*-desmethylvenlafaxine.

Pharmacodynamics. Venlafaxine is a nonselective inhibitor of the reuptake of three biogenic amines—serotonin, norepinephrine, and dopamine. It is most potent as a reuptake inhibitor of serotonin (IC_{50} of 0.21 mmol), but its potency as a norepinephrine reuptake inhibitor is also high (IC_{50} of 0.64 mmol), and its potency as a dopamine reuptake inhibitor is significant (IC_{50} of 2.8 mmol). Venlafaxine does not have ac-

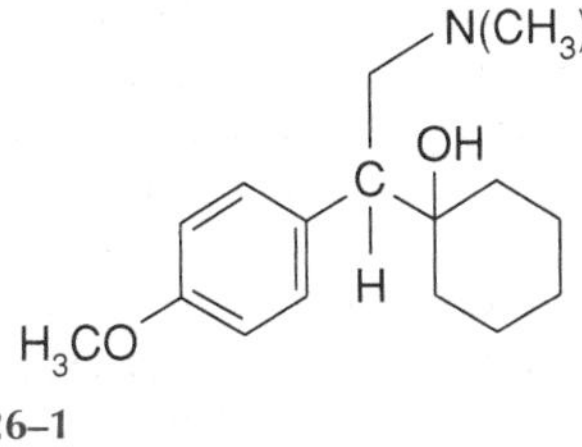
N(CH3)2
OH
C
H
H3CO

FIGURE 35.3.26–1
Molecular structure of venlafaxine.

tivity at muscarinic, nicotinic, histaminergic, or adrenergic receptors, and it is not active as a monoamine oxidase inhibitor.

Effects on Specific Organs and Systems

In addition to its effects on the central nervous system (CNS), venlafaxine may influence the peripheral autonomic nervous system to some degree, possibly by raising catecholamine levels.

Therapeutic Indications

Venlafaxine is approved for the treatment of major depressive disorder. Several well-controlled studies with a sufficient number of patients have shown the efficacy of venlafaxine for this indication. Early studies showed that venlafaxine was superior to placebo for patients with major depressive disorder: 68 percent of patients taking venlafaxine improved, as opposed to 31 percent of patients taking placebo. Higher doses of venlafaxine (150 mg a day) were more effective than lower doses. In direct comparison, venlafaxine was more effective with fewer adverse effects than was imipramine, and venlafaxine was equally as effective as trazodone. In direct comparison with fluoxetine in severely depressed patients with melancholia, venlafaxine showed a significant superiority. Some data from these studies have indicated that venlafaxine may be associated with a faster onset of action of antidepressant effects than currently available antidepressants. Another study with venlafaxine included 93 depressed inpatients with melancholic features. Many patients also responded to venlafaxine within 2 weeks, which is somewhat sooner than the 2- to 4-week period usually seen with other antidepressant drugs, such as the classical tricyclics or the serotonin-specific reuptake inhibitors. Therefore, venlafaxine may become a preferred drug to use for seriously ill patients in whom a rapid response is desired. Sympathomimetics such as dextroamphetamine, however, appear to have the most rapid onset of antidepressant action, usually within 1 week. Electroconvulsive therapy (ECT) also may begin to relieve severe depression within 1 hour, with increasing benefit over the first week. Venlafaxine appears to be effective for many depressed patients refractory to other antidepressants.

Case reports and uncontrolled studies have suggested that venlafaxine may be beneficial in obsessive-compulsive disorder, panic disorder, chronic pain, neuropathic pain, and attention-deficit/hyperactivity disorder in adults. Controlled trials are needed to confirm these possibilities.

Precautions and Adverse Reactions

In published clinical reports, venlafaxine has generally been reported to be well tolerated. The following were the most common adverse reactions reported in the placebo-controlled studies: nausea (37 percent of all patients treated), somnolence (23 percent), dry mouth (22 percent), dizziness (19 percent), nervousness (13 percent), constipation (15 percent), asthenia (12 percent), anxiety (6 percent), anorexia (11 percent), blurred vision (6 percent), abnormal ejaculation or orgasm (12 percent), and impotence (6 percent). The gastrointestinal effects may be limited by taking venlafaxine with food and have been mitigated by some experts through augmentation with a 3- to 4-week course of cisapride (Propulsid), 5 to 10 mg twice daily. Nausea, somnolence, and insomnia were the three most common adverse reactions associated with patient discontinuation of venlafaxine. A withdrawal syndrome is more likely seen with abrupt discontinuation than with a gradual tapering over a few weeks.

The most potentially worrisome adverse effect associated with venlafaxine is an increase in blood pressure in some patients, particularly in patients who are treated with more than 300 mg a day. In clinical trials, a mean increase of 7.2 mm Hg was observed in the diastolic blood pressure of patients receiving 375 mg a day of venlafaxine, in contrast to no significant change in patients receiving 75 or 225 mg a day and a mean decrease of 2.2 mm Hg in patients receiving a placebo. In one study, sustained elevations of blood pressure above 140/90 were experienced by 2 percent of patients who received a placebo, by 3 percent of patients who received less than 100 mg of venlafaxine a day, by 5 percent of patients who received 101 to 200 mg of venlafaxine a day, by 7 percent of patients who received 201 to 300 mg of venlafaxine a day, and by 13 percent of patients who received more than 300 mg of venlafaxine a day. This adverse effect has lead the FDA to recommend that the drug be used cautiously in patients with preexisting hypertension. The clinical significance of the side effect may be less worrisome if low dosages of venlafaxine are used.

Information about use of venlafaxine by pregnant and nursing women is not available at this time, but clinicians should avoid the use of all newly introduced drugs by pregnant and nursing women until more clinical experience has been gained.

Drug Interactions

Cimetidine appears to inhibit the first-pass hepatic metabolism of venlafaxine and to raise the levels of the unmetabolized drug. Because the metabolite is mainly responsible for the therapeutic effect, however, this interaction is of concern only in patients with preexisting hypertension or hepatic disease, in whom this combination should be avoided. As is true of all antidepressant medications, venlafaxine should not be used within 14 days of the use of monoamine oxidase inhibitors, and it may potentiate the sedative effects of other drugs that act on the CNS. Venlafaxine has minimal inhibitory effects on CYP 3A4.

Laboratory Interferences

Data are not currently available on laboratory interferences with venlafaxine.

Dosage and Administration

The antidepressant effects of venlafaxine frequently appear in the first 1 to 2 weeks of treatment, which is less time than is usually required for most other available antidepressants. Venlafaxine is available in 25, 37.5, 50, 75, and 100 mg tablets. The usual starting dose in depressed outpatients is 75 mg a day, given in two to three divided doses. Venlafaxine is also available in 37.5, 75, and 150 mg extended-release capsules, which can be given once a day. In this patient population the dose can be raised to 150 mg a day, given in two or three divided doses after an appropriate period of clinical assessment at the lower dose (usually 2 to 3 weeks). The dose can be raised in increments of 75 mg a day. Doses of venlafaxine over 300 mg a day should be given in three divided doses. The maximum dose of venlafaxine is 375 mg a day. The dose of venlafaxine should be halved in patients with significantly diminished hepatic or renal function. If discontinued, venlafaxine should be tapered off over 1 week.

SIBUTRAMINE

Sibutramine inhibits the reuptake of serotonin and, to a lesser extent, of norepinephrine and dopamine. Although this drug failed to demonstrate efficacy as an antidepressant in early trials, subjects taking it consistently lost weight, a finding that led to trials designed to test efficacy for weight reduction. Early results indicate promise for this indication and additionally demonstrate that it may improve glucose tolerance in patients with non–insulin-dependent diabetes mellitus. At a dose of 15 to 20 mg a day, sibutramine produced significantly greater weight loss than did placebo in patients who were 130 to 180 percent of their ideal body weight. Seven percent of trial participants, however, experienced a rise in systolic and diastolic blood pressures of more than 30 percent. Other adverse effects included headache and insomnia. The manufacturer must create and test effective clinical guidelines to identify and exclude patients who may incur dangerous elevations in blood pressure from sibutramine, before its approval for clinical use. This finding is of particular concern because of the likelihood of widespread use for weight loss for strictly cosmetic reasons, if the drug is approved.

REFERENCES

Ansseau M, Papart P, Troisfontaines B, Bartholome F, et al: Controlled comparison of milnacipran and fluoxetine in major depression. Psychopharmacology *114:* 131, 1994.

Ansseau M, von Frenckell R, Gerard MA, Mertens C, et al: Interest of a loading dose of milnacipran in endogenous depressive inpatients: Comparison with the standard regimen and with fluvoxamine. Eur Neuropsychopharmacol *1:* 113, 1991.

Ansseau M, von Frenckell R, Serre C: Pilot study of milnacipran in panic disorder. Eur Psychiatry *6:* 103, 1991.

Bray GA, Ryan DH, Gordon D, Heidingsfelder S, Cerise F, Wilson K: A double-blind randomized placebo-controlled trial of sibutramine. Obes Res *4:* 263, 1996.

Caron J, Libersa C, Hazard JR, Lacroix D: Acute electrophysiological effects of intravenous milnacipran, a new antidepressant agent. Eur Neuropsychopharmacol *3:* 493, 1993.

Feighner JP: Cardiovascular safety in depressed patients: Focus on venlafaxine. J Clin Psychiatry *56:* 574, 1995.

Findling RL, Schwartz MA, Flannery DJ, Manos MJ: Venlafaxine in adults with attention-deficit/hyperactivity disorder: An open clinical trial. J Clin Psychiatry *57:* 184, 1996.

Kasahara T, Ishigooka J: Long-lasting inhibition of 5-HT uptake of platelets in subjects treated by duloxetine, a potential antidepressant. Nihon Shinkei Seishin Yakurigaku Zasshi *16:* 25, 1996.

Montgomery SA (chairperson): Venlafaxine: A new dimension in anti-depressant pharmacotherapy. J Clin Psychiatry *54:* 119, 1993.

Russell JL: Relatively low doses of cisapride in the treatment of nausea in patients with venlafaxine for treatment-refractory depression. J Clin Psychopharmacol *16:* 35, 1996.

Ryan DH, Kaiser O, Bray GA: Sibutramine: A novel new agent for obesity treatment. Obes Res *3:* 553S, 1995.

Saletu B, Grunberger J, Anderer P, Linzmayer L, Semlitsch HV, Magni G: Pharmacodynamics of venlafaxine evaluated by EEG brain mapping, psychometry, and psychophysiology. Br J Clin Pharmacol *33:* 589, 1992.

Schweizer E, Weise C, Clary C, Fox I, Rickels K: Placebo-controlled trial of venlafaxine for the treatment of major depression. J Clin Psychopharmacol *11:* 233, 1991.

Scott MA, Shelton PS, Gattis W: Therapeutic options for treating major depression, and the role of venlafaxine. Pharmacotherapy *16:* 352, 1996.

Weintraub M, Rubio A, Golik A, Byrne L, Scheinbaum ML: Sibutramine in weight control: A dose-ranging, efficacy study. Clin Pharmacol Ther *50:* 330, 1991.

▲ 35.3.27 Serotonin-Specific Reuptake Inhibitors

All successful pharmacological treatments for depression have raised the synaptic activity of serotonin and norepinephrine by inhibition of reuptake, by inhibition of degradation, or by stimulation of secretion. For poorly understood biological reasons, potentiation of only the serotonin or the norepinephrine system results in efficient activation of the other system; thus, no one site of action is immediately preferable to another. In clinical practice, drugs acting at each site are roughly equivalent in antidepressant efficacy, and clinical preference is largely based on the profile of adverse effects. The toxicity of the tricyclic drugs and the monoamine oxidase inhibitors (MAOIs) limited their use to some degree. The introduction of fluoxetine (Prozac) in 1988, followed by other serotonin-specific reuptake inhibitors (SSRIs)—also called selective serotonin reuptake inhibitors—which have a much more favorable profile of adverse effects, has significantly broadened the horizon for pharmacological treatment of disorders of mood and anxiety. Although depressive disorders were the initial indications for these drugs, they are effective in a wide range of disorders, including eating disorders, panic disorder, obsessive-compulsive disorder, and borderline personality disorder. These drugs are called SSRIs because they share the pharmacodynamic property of specifically inhibiting serotonin reuptake by presynaptic neurons, with relatively little effect on the reuptake of norepinephrine and almost no effect on the reuptake of dopamine.

Fluoxetine, the SSRI first introduced for clinical use in the United States in 1988, was discovered in the early 1970s. Currently, three SSRIs are available in the United States and approved for the treatment of depression: fluoxetine (Prozac), paroxetine (Paxil), and sertraline (Zoloft). All three of these agents, plus a fourth SSRI, fluvoxamine (Luvox), have been approved by the Food and Drug Administration (FDA) for the treatment of obsessive-compulsive disorder. Paroxetine and sertraline have been approved for the treatment of panic disorder, and fluoxetine has additionally been approved for treatment of bulimia. All four United States-approved drugs and a fifth SSRI, citalopram, are in widespread clinical use in Europe. Clomipramine (Anafranil) is another drug that is specific in its actions as an inhibitor of serotonin reuptake, but because it is structurally similar to the tricyclic drugs used to treat depression, it is classified along with the tricyclic and tetracyclic drugs (antidepressants). Since its introduction in 1988, fluoxetine has become the most widely prescribed antidepressant in the United States, and it is taken by more than 12

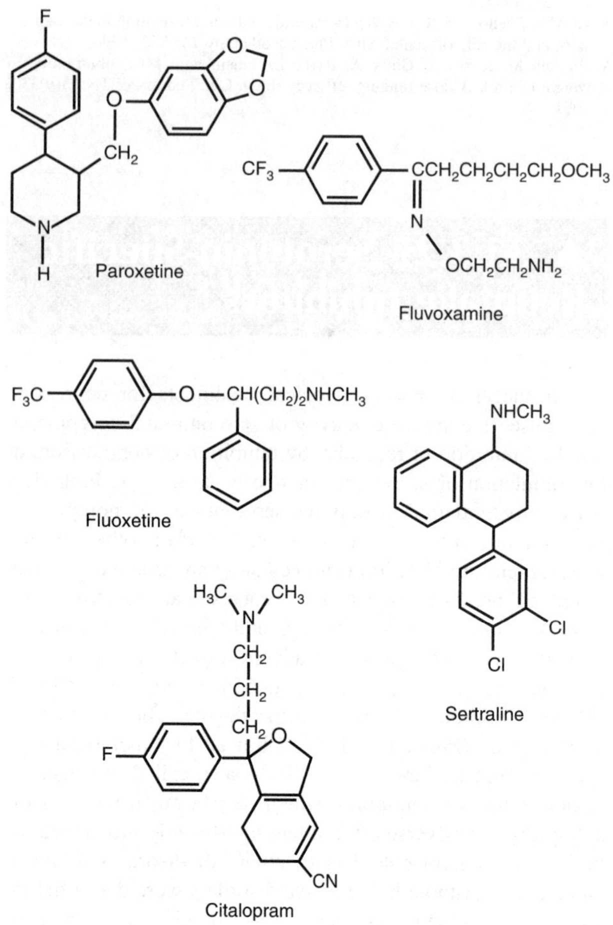
Paroxetine
Fluvoxamine
Fluoxetine
Sertraline
Citalopram

FIGURE 35.3.27–1
Molecular structures of SSRIs.

million people worldwide. At present, SSRIs account for about 50 percent of all prescriptions of antidepressants in the United States. In a 1995 study of the 25 most frequently prescribed drugs of all types in the United States, fluoxetine ranked 9th and sertraline ranked 13th.

CHEMISTRY

The molecular structures of fluoxetine, fluvoxamine, sertraline, paroxetine and citalopram are shown in Figure 35.3.27–1.

PHARMACOLOGICAL ACTIONS

Pharmacokinetics

The major differences among the available SSRIs lie primarily in their pharmacokinetic profiles (Table 35.3.27–1), specifically their half-lives. Fluoxetine has the longest half-life, 2 to 3 days; its active metabolite has a half-life of 7 to 9 days. Full, steady-state brain concentrations of fluoxetine appear after 6 months of use. The half-lives of the other SSRIs are much shorter, about 20 hours, and these SSRIs have no major active metabolites. All SSRIs are well absorbed after oral administration and reach their peak concentrations in the range of 4 to 8 hours. All SSRIs are metabolized in the liver. Paroxetine and fluoxetine are metabolized in the liver by cytochrome P450 (CYP) isoenzyme CYP 2D6, a specific subtype of the enzyme, which may indicate that clinicians should be careful in the coadministration of other drugs that are also metabolized by CYP 2D6. Fluvoxamine inhibits the CYP 3A4 enzyme, which also metabolizes terfenadine (Seldane) and astemizole (Hismanal) and has led the FDA to recommend the fluvoxamine not to be given with these agents. In general, food does not have a large effect on the absorption of SSRIs; in fact, the administration of SSRIs with food often reduces the incidence of the common symptoms of nausea and diarrhea associated with SSRI use.

Pharmacodynamics

SSRIs share two common features: First, they have specific activity in the inhibition of serotonin reuptake without effects

Table 35.3.27–1
Mean (Range) Pharmacokinetic Parameters of 5-HT Reuptake Inhibitors Estimated in Healthy Subjects

Parameter	FLX	FLV	PAR	SERT
Time of peak plasma concentration from initial dose (hours)	4–8	2–8	3–8	6–10
Elimination half-life (hours)	84[a] (26–220)	15 (13–19)	21 (4–65)	26 (NA)
Protein binding (%)	95	77	95	97[b]
Time for steady-state plasma concentration (days)	14–28	10	4–14	10–14
Volume of distribution (L/kg)	25 (12–42)	5 (NA)	13 (3–28)	25[b] (NA)
Plasma clearance (L/hr/kg)	0.29 (0.09–0.53)	NA	0.76 (0.21–1.31)	NA
Active metabolites	NORFLX	None	None	DMSERT

Reprinted with permission from DeVane CL: Pharmacokinetics of the selective serotonin reuptake inhibitors. J Clin Psychiatry *53* (2, Suppl): 14, 1992.
DMSERT, dexmethylsertraline; FLV, fluvoxamine; FLX, fluoxetine; NA, not available; NORFLX, nonfluoxetine; PAR, paroxetine; SERT, sertraline.
[a] Elimination half-life for nonfluoxetine is 146 hours (range 77–235).
[b] Value from animal studies.

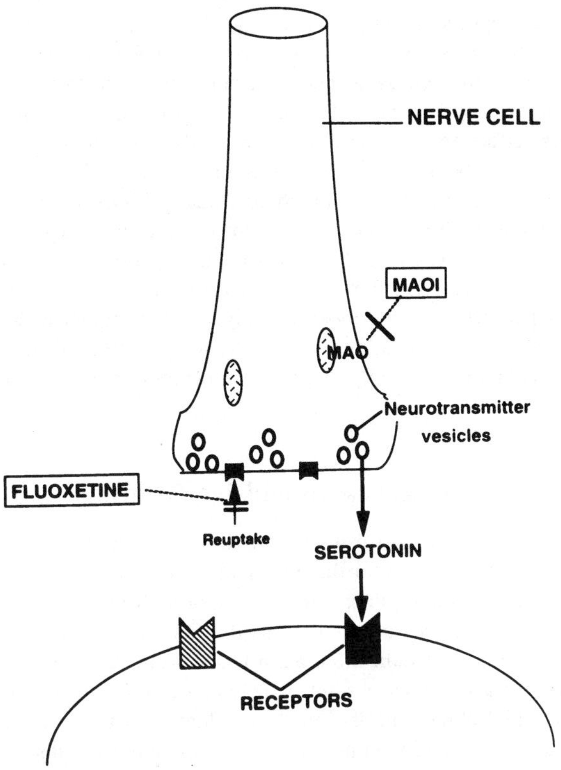
NERVE CELL
MAOI
MAO
Neurotransmitter
vesicles
FLUOXETINE
Reuptake
SEROTONIN
RECEPTORS

FIGURE 35.3.27–2

SSRIs, such as fluoxetine, block the reuptake of serotonin into the presynaptic nerve terminal. This increases the synaptic concentrations of serotonin, which permits increased activation of receptors, and it also prevents serotonin from being metabolized by MAO. MAOIs also prevent the degradation of serotonin. When MAOIs are used in conjunction with SSRIs, the massive excess of synaptic serotonin may produce a toxic serotonin syndrome. (Reprinted with permission from Hyman SE, Arana GW, Rosenbaum JF: *Handbook of Psychiatric Drug Therapy,* ed 3, p 45. Little, Brown, Boston, 1996.)

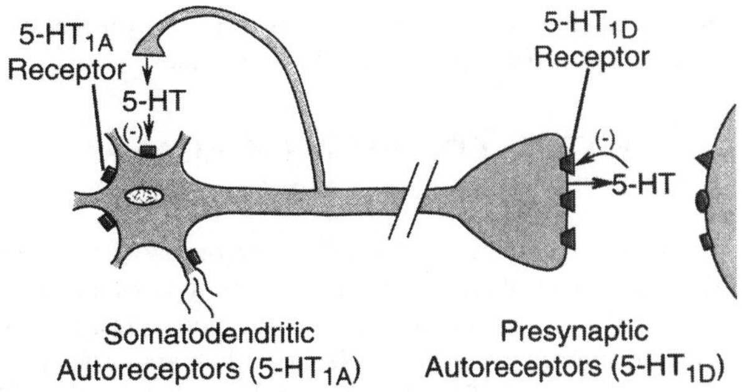
5-HT1A
Receptor
5-HT
(-)
5-HT1D
Receptor
(-)
5-HT
Somatodendritic
Autoreceptors (5-HT1A)
Presynaptic
Autoreceptors (5-HT1D)

FIGURE 35.3.27–3

Two classes of 5-hydroxytryptamine (5-HT) autoreceptors with differential localizations. Somatodendritic 5-HT_{1A} autoreceptors decrease raphe cell firing when activated by 5-HT released from axon collaterals of the same or adjacent neurons. The receptor subtype of the presynaptic autoreceptor on axon terminals in the forebrain has different pharmacological properties and has been classified as 5-HT_{1D} (in human beings) or 5-HT_{1B} (in rodents). This receptor modulates the release of 5-HT. Postsynaptic 5-HT_1 receptors are also indicated. (Reprinted with permission from Sanders-Bush E, Mayer SE: 5-Hydroxytryptamine (serotonin) receptor agonists and antagonists. In *Goodman & Gilman's The Pharmacological Basis of Therapeutics,* ed 9, JG Hardman, LE Limbird, PB Molinoff, RW Ruddon, editors, p 253. McGraw-Hill, New York, 1996.)

on norepinephrine and dopamine reuptake (Fig. 35.3.27–2). Clinical efficacy is associated with 70 to 80 percent occupancy of the serotonin transporters. Inhibition of reuptake raises synaptic concentrations of serotonin, which binds to and activates at least 14 distinct receptors (Fig. 35.3.27–3). It is tempting to assume, as is true of the tricyclic antidepressants, that there is a linear dose–response curve with SSRIs and, therefore, that higher dosages will yield increased clinical effectiveness. In fact, however, at least 90 percent of clinical response occurs at the starting doses, and higher doses tend mainly to increase adverse effects without much additional clinical benefit. In clinical use, sertraline is most commonly raised above its usual starting dosage (50 mg a day, raised to 150 to 200 mg a day), followed by fluoxetine (starting dosage 20 mg a day, raised to 40 to 80 mg a day). Paroxetine is the most likely to be continued at its starting dosage (20 mg a day), and although it may be raised to 30 to 60 mg a day, anticholinergic effects may predominate at higher dosages. Although the available compounds differ in their specific potencies (Table 35.3.27–2), the differences do not result in any meaningful clinical differences. Second, SSRIs are essentially devoid of agonist and antagonist activities on any neurotransmitter receptor. The lack of antihistaminergic and anti–α_1-adrenergic receptor activities is the pharmacodynamic basis for the low incidence of adverse effects with SSRI administration. Paroxetine, fluvox-

Table 35.3.27–2
Approximate Potency of Inhibition of ^{3}H Biogenic Amine Uptake[a]

Compound	Serotonin	K_i (nM) Norepinephrine	Dopamine
Citalopram	4	6,000	20,000
Fluoxetine	6	1,000	10,000
Fluvoxamine	25	500	4,200
Paroxetine	1	350	2,000
Sertraline	7	1,400	230

[a] In vitro rat brain tissue preparation. Lower K_i values indicate higher potency. All five compounds are potent inhibitors of serotonin reuptake.

amine, and, to a lesser extent, sertraline have mild anticholinergic effects, but these effects are significantly lower than the anticholinergic effects of the tricyclic and tetracyclic drugs.

EFFECTS ON SPECIFIC ORGANS AND SYSTEMS

Besides their effects on the central nervous system (CNS), SSRIs have minimal effects on other organs and systems. Specifically, SSRIs have minimal effects on blood pressure and cardiac function, as reflected by electrocardiograms. The major system affected by SSRIs is the gastrointestinal (GI) tract, and symptoms of nausea, anorexia, and diarrhea are common with SSRI administration. Sexual dysfunction is not always addressed by clinicians, but some estimates of the incidence of sexual dysfunction attributable to SSRIs reach up to 80 percent of patients. Weight loss has also been reported to be associated with fluoxetine, whereas weight gain may be seen with paroxetine and occasionally with sertraline and fluvoxamine.

THERAPEUTIC INDICATIONS

Depression

The primary indication for SSRI use is major depressive disorder; fluoxetine, sertraline, and paroxetine have been approved for this indication. Studies with fluoxetine have also shown that it is effective for the treatment of depressive episodes in bipolar I disorder. For the majority of patients whose depression is mild to moderate, SSRIs have become the agents of first choice. Their ease of use and benign adverse effect profile have made them attractive to both specialists and generalists, and they are expected eventually to reach a large percentage of currently untreated depressed patients. For the most severely depressed patients, SSRIs are not necessarily the most effective drugs, but many such patients will also respond favorably. In a controlled trial of severely depressed patients who responded only partially to fluoxetine (20 mg a day), increasing the dose of fluoxetine was superior to augmentation with desipramine or lithium. Another clinical trial found that for severely depressed patients with melancholia, fluoxetine was not as effective as nortriptyline. Patients with this diagnosis may also respond to venlafaxine or electroconvulsive therapy. A recent small study in patients who were not fully improved with SSRI monotherapy showed that augmentation with bupropion (Wellbutrin) led to improvement in 70 percent of the patients. The adverse effects were additive and consisted primarily of sexual dysfunction, insomnia, reduced energy level, and tremor. The patients in this study were not stratified by severity of depression, and the reasons for the incomplete SSRI response were varied. Controlled trials of SSRI and bupropion combination therapy in defined patient populations have not been reported. SSRIs and bupropion may be especially well suited to combination therapy for patients who are refractory to either drug alone, because the agents are relatively free of adverse effects and they act on different neurotransmitter systems. Specifically, bupropion is thought to act on the norepinephrine and dopamine systems, and it may therefore complement the effects of SSRIs on the serotonin system. An uncontrolled trial showed a benefit of fluvoxamine in delusional depression. Most studies and data support the conclusions that SSRIs are equal in efficacy to tricyclic drugs in the treatment of depression and that, compared with these other antidepressant drugs, SSRIs have a significantly superior adverse effect profile. These studies have also consistently shown that some degree of nervousness or agitation, sleep disturbances, GI symptoms, and perhaps sexual side effects are more common in SSRI-treated patients than in tricyclic drug-treated patients. Fluoxetine is the most stimulating and least sedating SSRI, sertraline is the most likely to cause nausea and diarrhea, and paroxetine is the most sedating SSRI, although none of the SSRIs is as sedating as the tricyclic and tetracyclic drugs. Paroxetine is especially effective for depression with features of anxiety.

Obsessive-Compulsive Disorder

Fluvoxamine, paroxetine, sertraline, and fluoxetine have been FDA approved for the treatment of obsessive-compulsive disorder. Clomipramine, a tricyclic drug with high selectivity for the serotonin transporter, was the first agent approved as effective for this indication, but it is a tricyclic drug and therefore has a more serious set of potential adverse effects. Uncontrolled clinical trials found no difference between fluvoxamine and clomipramine for obsessive-compulsive disorder, but a meta-analysis of four controlled trials showed clomipramine to be superior. A controlled trial of paroxetine and clomipramine for obsessive-compulsive disorder found no difference in efficacy and fewer adverse reactions and treatment withdrawals for paroxetine. The fourth edition of *Diagnostic and Statistical Manual of Mental Disorder* (DSM-IV) classifies obsessive-compulsive disorder as one of the anxiety disorders. Although all the SSRIs, especially fluoxetine, may raise anxiety levels in the first 2 to 3 weeks of use, this adverse effect gives way with longer use to a reduction in anxiety, obsessions, and compulsive behaviors, usually by the third or fourth week.

Panic Disorder and Other Anxiety Disorders

Paroxetine and sertraline have been FDA approved for the treatment of panic disorder with or without agoraphobia, on the basis of relatively short clinical trials. Among SSRIs, paroxetine is most likely initially to reduce anxiety and agitation and is also somewhat more likely to produce sedation. Fluoxetine is the most activating, the most likely initially to generate anxiety, especially in the first 3 weeks, and the least sedating. Sertraline is intermediate with respect to control of anxiety and sedation. When patients are followed for several months, a reduction in panic attacks may be seen with each of the SSRIs. For all SSRIs, but especially for fluoxetine, treatment of panic disorder should begin with very small doses, which are then inched up slowly. Fluoxetine has been shown in a small study to be effective in children and adolescents with overanxious disorder, social phobia, or separation anxiety disorder who were refractory to other treatments.

Bulimia

The FDA has recently approved fluoxetine for the treatment of bulimia. Although cognitive-behavioral therapy by itself is highly effective as treatment of bulimia, addition of fluoxetine has been shown to provide added benefit. Fluoxetine was effective for treatment of bulimia at 60 mg a day, whereas it was only marginally effective at 20 mg a day. In multicenter trials, fluoxetine (60 mg a day) for 8 to 16 weeks was superior to placebo in reducing the symptoms of bulimia, including binge eating and induced vomiting. The benefit of longer term therapy or the permanence of the benefit if fluoxetine is discontinued has not yet been determined in controlled trials, but anecdotal evidence suggests that the benefit may persist beyond the course of fluoxetine in many patients. Experts recommend an initial course of cognitive-behavioral therapy, but if no response is seen in 3 to 6 weeks, then fluoxetine should be added. Preliminary data have shown that behavioral therapy plus fluoxetine (60 mg a day) is also an effective treatment for anorexia nervosa. The anorexigenic effects of high-dose fluoxetine create a risk of abuse for patients with eating disorders who take it in the absence of a comprehensive program of behavioral modification, which must be the mainstay of treatment for patients with bulimia or anorexia nervosa.

Other Indications

Because fluoxetine has been clinically available the longest, most studies about other indications have been based on fluoxetine, although it is likely that the other SSRIs are similar to fluoxetine in their efficacies for these additional indications. In several well-controlled studies, fluoxetine (60 mg a day) has been effective in promoting weight loss in overweight people. Fluoxetine and sertraline at low doses have been shown to reduce the tension, irritability, and dysphoria of premenstrual syndrome. Fluoxetine and sertraline have been shown to be useful for postpartum depression, which may affect 10 percent of new mothers. Fluoxetine may improve mood and also help weight loss in the puerperium. The average dose of fluoxetine or sertraline in breast milk is 5 to 9 percent of the weight-adjusted maternal dose, and the doses of SSRIs available in breast milk do not appear to alter platelet serotonin levels (a model for SSRI inhibition of serotonin reuptake in the brain). It is, however, theoretically possible that such small doses may influence the infant's brain. For example, serotonin is known to influence synaptogenesis and other aspects of neonatal brain development, and the long-term effects of intrauterine or early postnatal exposure to SSRIs are unknown.

Other indications for which there is preliminary evidence of efficacy for SSRIs are dysthymic disorder, borderline personality disorder, hypochondriasis, trichotillomania, elective mutism, attention-deficit/hyperactivity disorder, obsessional jealousy, premature ejaculation, body dysmorphic disorder, autistic disorder in children and adults, Asperger's syndrome, augmentation of anticonvulsants for bipolar disorder, Tourette's disorder, self-injurious behavior, paraphilias, aggression in schizophrenia, syncope, neuropathic (diabetic, postherpetic) and nonneuropathic chronic pain, migraine and tension-type headache, and fibromyalgia. There have been case reports of fluoxetine monotherapy for schizophrenia, although SSRIs are generally not considered effective for the treatment of psychotic symptoms.

PRECAUTIONS AND ADVERSE REACTIONS

Over one half of patients do not report an adverse effect, and discontinuation of therapy due to adverse events is much lower with SSRIs than with tricyclic and tetracyclic drugs. Three fourths of patients experience no adverse effects at low starting doses, and doses may be increased relatively rapidly (on the order of an increase every 1 to 2 weeks) in this group. In the remaining one fourth of patients, most of the SSRIs adverse effects appear within the first 1 to 2 weeks, and they generally subside or resolve spontaneously if the drugs are continued at the same dose. But 10 to 15 percent of patients cannot tolerate even a low dose of a particular SSRI and may discontinue taking the drug after only a few doses. One approach to such patients is to average a fractional dose of fluoxetine over a week, with one dose every 2, 3, or 4 days. Some of these patients may tolerate a different SSRI or another class of antidepressant, such as a tricyclic drug or another newer agent; some patients appear unable to tolerate even tiny doses of any antidepressant drug. Because of the unfortunate sequence of effects of SSRIs in some patients in whom adverse effects come and go before the desired benefit occurs, some clinicians begin with a very low dose for the first 3 to 6 weeks, then increase gradually after a therapeutic benefit is seen. Because of the long half-life of the SSRIs, especially fluoxetine, and the even longer time it may take for the full benefit of a particular dose to be appreciated, steep increases in dose are to be avoided. The lowest dose may provide over 90 percent of the benefit of the highest dose, for example, if enough time is allowed for the neurochemical alterations to be completed. On the other hand, adverse effects are much more predictably dose dependent, and too rapid an increase in dose may invite an aversive response in a sensitive patient.

Fluoxetine

A comparison of the adverse event profiles of each SSRI is presented in Table 35.3.27–3). The adverse effect profile of fluoxetine shows that it is a well-tolerated drug. The most common adverse effects of fluoxetine involve the CNS and the GI system (Table 35.3.27–4). The most common CNS effects include headache, nervousness, insomnia, drowsiness, and anxiety. Seizures have been reported in 0.2 percent of all patients treated with the drug, an incidence that is comparable to the incidence reported with other antidepressants. Seizures are more frequent at doses of 100 mg a day or higher. Rarer CNS effects that may be especially troubling in older patients include extrapyramidal symptoms (dystonia, akathisia, tremor), apathy, anorexia, and the secretion of inappropriate antidiuretic hormone (SIADH). Fluoxetine, sertraline, and paroxetine reduce rapid eye movement (REM) sleep, and fluoxetine and paroxetine, but not sertraline, disrupt sleep continuity. For patients with insomnia, some experts recommend the addition of trazodone, a highly sedating antidepressant, for the first several weeks of treatment with fluoxetine, until the full antidepressant

Table 35.3.27–3
Adverse Events for Each SSRI That Occurred 1 Percent More Often Than with Other SSRIs

Fluoxetine	Fluvoxamine	Paroxetine	Sertraline
Nervousness/agitation/anxiety	Nausea	Sexual dysfunction	Loose stools
Respiratory complaints	Drowsiness	Frequent micturition	Tremors
Headache	Constipation Anorexia	Asthenia/fatigue Dizziness Sweating	Dry mouth

Reprinted with permission from Preskorn SH: *Clinical Pharmacology of Selective Serotonin Reuptake Inhibitors,* p 86. Professional Communications, Caddo, OK, 1996.

and antianxiety effects appear. Use of other benzodiazepine or nonbenzodiazepine sedatives is another approach to insomnia in patients with depression. The most common GI complaints are anorexia, nausea, diarrhea, and dyspepsia. Data indicate that the nausea is dose related and is an adverse effect for which patients apparently develop tolerance over the course of a few weeks.

Other adverse effects involve sexual functioning and the skin. Anorgasmia, delayed ejaculation, and impotence affect at least 20 to 50 percent of all patients treated. These adverse sexual effects may respond to combined therapy, including yohimbine (Yocon), bromocriptine (Parlodel), amantadine (Symmetrel), or cyproheptadine (Periactin). Alternatively, bupropion, mirtazapine (Remeron), or nefazodone (Serzone) may be substituted for the SSRI. Various rashes may appear in about 4 percent of all patients; in a small subset of these patients, the allergic reaction may generalize and involve the pulmonary system and may rarely result in fibrotic damage and dyspnea. Fluoxetine treatment may have to be discontinued in patients with drug-related rashes. Fluoxetine is associated with a decrease in glucose concentrations, and, therefore, diabetic patients should be carefully monitored for the possibility of decreasing the dosage of their hypoglycemic drug. Rare cases of fluoxetine-associated hyponatremia and SIADH have occurred in patients treated with diuretics who are also water deprived. There have been case reports of easy bruising in patients taking fluoxetine, sertraline, paroxetine, and fluvoxamine.

SSRI, compared with non-SSRI antidepressants, are safe drugs when taken in overdoses. Only one report has noted a lethal overdose of fluoxetine taken by itself and only a small number of lethal overdoses when fluoxetine was taken with other drugs. The symptoms of overdose include agitation, restlessness, insomnia, tremor, nausea, vomiting, tachycardia, and seizures. Clinicians should ascertain whether other drugs were taken with the fluoxetine. The first steps in the treatment of overdose are gastric lavage and emesis. In the late 1980s a widely publicized report suggested an association between fluoxetine administration and violent acts, including suicide, but many subsequent reviews have clearly proved no increased likelihood of such an association with fluoxetine. A few patients, however, become especially anxious and agitated, almost in an akathisia-like fashion, when given fluoxetine, and the appearance of these symptoms in an already-suicidal patient may aggravate the seriousness of the suicidal ideation. There have been case reports of suicidality and antisocial acts in patients taking fluoxetine, sertraline, and fluvoxamine, but a causal relation is not clear. In a number of sensational criminal trials, defendants have argued unsuccessfully that use of fluoxetine drove them to desperate acts. The negative publicity regarding the association of fluoxetine with agitated behavior has so strongly indoctrinated large sectors of the population against the drug that they flatly refuse even to consider using it under any circumstances. Clinicians may therefore find more ready acceptance of less well-known, albeit less well-tolerated, antidepressants.

Because of the large number of patients who have taken fluoxetine, it is possible to state that the number of birth defects and birth complications when pregnant women took fluoxetine is not significantly different from that seen when mothers did not take fluoxetine during pregnancy. At least seven large studies have addressed the issue of whether fluoxetine is teratogenic, of which only one raised any significant concerns, specifically, that delivery might be premature and that newborns might experience minor morbidity. This particular study, however, contained methodological flaws, particularly in ascertaining a truly comparable control group, and the study could not rigorously exclude that the complications were actually due to the underlying disease and not to the drug. Therefore, the bulk of the evidence is reassuring, in that it suggests that fluoxetine does not harm the development of the fetus in measurable ways. Nevertheless, the general rule of avoiding all drugs during pregnancy should be adhered to unless there is a compelling reason to treat a pregnant woman with an antidepressant drug. All SSRIs are excreted in breast milk; therefore, nursing mothers should not take these drugs. SSRIs should also be used with caution by patients with hepatic disease. Case reports suggest that fluoxetine in the breast milk may produce high concentrations in the infant with symptomatic ''colic,'' but another case report found undetectable levels of sertraline in the breast-fed baby of a mother taking sertraline 100 mg a day. In this latter study, concentrations of sertraline's long-acting metabolite were not measured.

Sertraline

The most common adverse effects of sertraline are GI, including stomach pain, loose stools or diarrhea, and nausea (Table 35.3.27–4). Minor sleep disturbances, either sedation or, less commonly, insomnia, may also occur. Other common side effects of sertraline include tremor, dizziness, increased perspiration, dry mouth, and male sexual dysfunction (primarily delayed ejaculation). Fifteen percent of patients discontinued sertraline in premarketing trials because of adverse effects.

Table 35.3.27–4
Side Effects with an Incidence of 19 Percent Reported for Selected Serotonin Reuptake Inhibitors, Imipramine, and Placebo

Side Effect	Sertraline N = 1,568	Placebo N = 861	Fluoxetine N = 1,378	Fluvoxamine N = 222	Paroxetine N = 1,387	Imipramine N = 599
Nausea and vomiting	21%	—	—	37%	29%	—
Headache	—	20%	—	22%	20%	19%
Dry mouth	—	—	—	26%	20%	76%
Sedation	—	—	—	26%	24%	30%
Nervousness, restlessness, and anxiety	—	—	21%	—	—	—
Dizziness	—	—	—	—	—	27%
Insomnia	—	—	19%	—	—	—
Sweating	—	—	—	—	—	21%

Adapted from Rickels K, Schweizer E: Clinical overview of serotonin reuptake inhibitors. J Clin Psychiatry *51:* 10, 1990.

There have been case reports of akathisia and dystonia in patients taking sertraline. Other case reports have described symmetrical or asymmetrical pupillary dilation in patients taking sertraline and paroxetine.

Paroxetine

The most common adverse effects of paroxetine are anticholinergic, GI, especially nausea and constipation, and somnolence. Sexual dysfunction and weakness may also occur with paroxetine. Paroxetine has been reported to exacerbate extrapyramidal symptoms, and there is one case report of narcolepsy associated with use of paroxetine.

Fluvoxamine

The most common adverse effects of fluvoxamine are nausea and dyspepsia, sexual dysfunction, and sleep disturbances consisting of somnolence or insomnia. Headache may also appear at mildly increased frequency in patients taking fluvoxamine.

SSRI Discontinuation Syndrome

The abrupt discontinuation of an SSRI, especially one with a shorter half-life such as paroxetine, sertraline, or fluvoxamine, has been associated with a syndrome that may include somatic and psychological symptoms. The somatic symptoms may include dysequilibrium (for example, dizziness, vertigo, and ataxia), nausea and vomiting, fatigue, lethargy, myalgia, paresthesias, tremor, insomnia, and migrainelike auras. The psychological symptoms may include anxiety, agitation, crying spells, irritability, overactivity, depersonalization, poor concentration, lowered mood, confusion, memory problems, and vivid dreams. This cluster of symptoms is more common in drugs with a short plasma half-life. The two drugs most likely to be associated with a discontinuation syndrome are venlafaxine, which is not protein bound and is rapidly metabolized, and paroxetine, which has a half-life of 21 hours and the most anticholinergic effects. The syndrome may occur in up to one third of patients who stop these medications abruptly, and it has been noted even over a weekend during which the doses were not taken. If a patient taking either venlafaxine or paroxetine is to be taken off these medicines, the doses should be tapered slowly. In the case of paroxetine, the dose should be lowered by 10 mg each week until 10 mg a day is reached, then patients should take 5 mg a day for a week before stopping. Sertraline has a longer half-life and is much less likely to cause discontinuation of symptoms. Fluoxetine is the least likely to be associated with this syndrome, because the half-life of its metabolite is considerably longer. Fluoxetine has therefore been used in some cases to treat the discontinuation syndrome, although the syndrome is self-limited and usually resolves after 2 to 3 weeks without treatment.

DRUG INTERACTIONS

Clinicians must be informed about many potential drug interactions with SSRIs (Table 35.3.27–5). No SSRI should be administered with L-tryptophan or an MAOI because of the possibility of inducing a potentially fatal serotonin syndrome. A small series of patients tolerated simultaneous use of an SSRI and the MAO_B inhibitor selegiline (Eldepryl), which does not affect metabolism of serotonin. The combination of lithium and all serotonergic drugs should be used with caution because of the possibility of precipitating seizures and serotonin syndrome. One small clinical trial reported that low doses of lithium, producing a serum concentration of 0.2 to 0.6 mEq/mL, improved 7 of 11 treatment-resistant patients who were taking sertraline. Fluoxetine can be administered with tricyclic drugs, but clinicians should use low dosages of the tricyclic drug. This combination may increase the risk of adverse effects. For example, SSRIs may increase concentrations of desipramine threefold to fourfold. The combination of fluoxetine and phentermine may produce tremor, jitters, and akathisia. Because it is metabolized by CYP 2D6, fluoxetine may interfere with the metabolism of other drugs in the 7 percent of the population who have an inefficient isoform of this enzyme, the so-called poor metabolizers. Fluoxetine may slow the metabolism of carbamazepine (Tegretol), antineoplastic

Table 35.3.27–5
Interactions of Drugs with the SSRIs Fluoxetine, Fluvoxamine, Paroxetine, and Sertraline

SSRI	Other Drugs	Effect	Clinical Importance
Fluoxetine	Desipramine	Inhibits metabolism	Possible
	Carbamazepine	Inhibits metabolism	Possible
	Diazepam	Inhibits metabolism	Not important
	Haloperidol	Inhibits metabolism	Possible
	Warfarin	No interaction	
	Tolbutamide	No interaction	
Fluvoxamine	Antipyrine	Inhibits metabolism	Not important
	Propranolol	Inhibits metabolism	Unlikely
	Tricyclics	Inhibits metabolism	Unlikely
	Warfarin	Inhibits metabolism	Possible
	Atenolol	No interaction	
	Digoxin	No interaction	
Paroxetine	Phenytoin	AUC increases by 12%	Possible
	Procyclidine	AUC increases by 39%	Possible
	Cimetidine	Paroxetine AUC increased by 50%	Possible
	Antipyrine	No interaction	
	Digoxin	No interaction	
	Propranolol	No interaction	
	Tranylcypromine	No interaction	Caution with combined treatment
	Warfarin	No interaction	
Sertraline	Antipyrine	Increased clearance	Not important
	Diazepam	13% decreased clearance	Not important
	Tolbutamide	16% decreased clearance	Not important
	Digoxin	No interaction	
	Lithium	No pharmacokinetic interaction	Caution with combined treatment
	Desipramine	No interaction	
	Atenolol	No pharmacodynamic interaction	

Reprinted with permission from Warrington SJ: Clinical implications of the pharmacology of serotonin reuptake inhibitors. Int Clin Psychopharmacol *7* (2, Suppl):13, 1982.

agents, diazepam (Valium), and phenytoin (Dilantin). Possibly significant drug interactions have been described for fluoxetine with benzodiazepines, antipsychotics, benztropine (Cogentin), and lithium (Eskalith). Fluoxetine has no interactions with warfarin (Coumadin), tolbutamide (Orinase), or chlorothiazide (Diuril).

Sertraline may displace warfarin from plasma proteins and may increase the prothrombin time. The drug interaction data on sertraline support a generally similar profile, although sertraline does not interact with the hepatic CYP 2D6 enzyme. Paroxetine has a higher risk for drug interactions than does either fluoxetine or sertraline because of its metabolic pathway through the CYP 2D6 hepatic enzyme. Cimetidine (Tagamet) can increase the concentrations of sertraline and paroxetine, and phenobarbital (Luminal) and phenytoin (Dilantin) can decrease the concentration of paroxetine. Because of the potential for interference with the CYP 2D6 hepatic enzyme, the coadministration of paroxetine with other antidepressants, phenothiazines, and antiarrhythmic drugs should be undertaken with caution. Paroxetine may increase the anticoagulant effect of warfarin. Sertraline and paroxetine have been associated in case reports with induction of flashbacks in adolescents with a history of lysergic acid diethylamide (LSD) abuse. In a case report, concomitant use of paroxetine and zolpidem was associated with hallucinations and disorientation.

Among the SSRIs, fluvoxamine appears to present the most risk of drug–drug interactions. Fluvoxamine is metabolized by CYP 3A4, which also metabolizes terfenadine (Seldane) and astemizole (Hismanal), and may be further inhibited by ketoconazole (Nizoral). Administration of terfenadine to patients in whom the CYP 3A4 enzyme is inhibited may produce cardiotoxicity, which has been fatal in several cases. Fluvoxamine may increase the half-lives of alprazolam (Xanax) and diazepam and should not be coadministered with these agents. Fluvoxamine may increase theophylline (Slo-Bid, Theo-Dur) concentrations threefold and warfarin concentrations twofold, with important clinical consequences. Therefore, the serum concentrations of the later drugs should be closely monitored, and the doses should be adjusted accordingly after the administration of fluvoxamine. Fluvoxamine raises concentrations and may increase the activity of clozapine (Clozaril), carbamazepine, methadone (Dolophine), propranolol (Inderal), and diltiazem (Cardizem). Fluvoxamine has no significant interactions with lorazepam (Ativan) or digoxin (Lanoxin).

LABORATORY INTERFERENCES

No laboratory interferences have been shown as yet with the available SSRI drugs.

DOSAGE AND ADMINISTRATION

The antidepressant effects of the SSRIs appear between 2 and 4 weeks after treatment is begun, although the mildly stimulating effects of fluoxetine may be seen in 1 to 3 days after onset of treatment.

Fluoxetine

Fluoxetine is available in 10 mg and 20 mg pulvules (that is, capsules) and as a liquid (20 mg/5 mL). For depression, the initial dosage is usually 20 mg orally each day, usually given in the morning, because insomnia is a potential adverse effect of the drug. Fluoxetine should be taken with food to minimize possible nausea. The long half-lives of the drug and its metabolite contribute to a 4- to 8-week period to reach steady-state concentrations. As with all available antidepressants, the antidepressant effects of fluoxetine may appear in the first 1 to 3 weeks, but clinicians should wait until the patients have taken the drug for 4 to 6 weeks before evaluating its antidepressant activity. Several studies indicate that 20 mg is as effective as higher doses. The maximum daily dosage recommended by the manufacturer is 80 mg a day, and higher doses may cause seizures. A reasonable strategy is to maintain a patient with 20 mg a day for 3 weeks. If the patient shows no signs of clinical improvement at the end of this time, an increase to 20 mg twice a day may be warranted, although at least one study has found that keeping a patient on the 20-mg-a-day dosage longer is as effective as increasing the dosage.

To minimize the early adverse effects of anxiety and restlessness, some clinicians initiate fluoxetine at 5 to 10 mg a day either by instructing a patient to dissolve the contents of a capsule in water or juice or by using the liquid preparation. If a patient mixes the contents of a capsule with a liquid, the mixture should be kept refrigerated. Alternatively, because of the long half-life of fluoxetine, the drug can be initiated with an every-other-day administration schedule.

With depressed patients who do not respond to fluoxetine treatment, clinicians can augment fluoxetine with other drugs, including tricyclic drugs (for example, desipramine [Norpramin]), sympathomimetics (for example, dextroamphetamine [Dexedrine]), buspirone (BuSpar), bupropion, and lithium. Adding these drugs when a patient has been nonresponsive to fluoxetine alone has resulted in a significant proportion of these patients responding to treatment. Because these adjuvant medications act on the same neurotransmitter systems as SSRIs, only low doses of each drug should be used in combination, to avoid adverse effects. At least 2 weeks should elapse between the discontinuation of MAOIs and the initiation of fluoxetine. Fluoxetine must be discontinued for at least 5 weeks before the initiation of MAOI treatment.

The dosage of fluoxetine that is effective in other indications may differ from the 20 mg a day that is generally used for depression. A dosage of 60 mg a day has been reported to be the most efficacious dosage for obsessive-compulsive disorder, obesity, and bulimia nervosa. In contrast, a starting dosage of 5 mg a day with minimal increases has been reported to be effective in the treatment of panic disorder.

Sertraline

For the treatment of depression, sertraline should be initiated with a dosage of 50 mg once daily. To limit the GI effects, some clinicians begin at 25 mg a day, and increase to 50 mg a day after 3 weeks. Patients who do not respond after 1 to 3 weeks may benefit from dosage increases of 50 mg every week up to a maximum of 200 mg once daily. Sertraline generally is given in the evening because it is more likely to cause sedation than insomnia, but it can be administered in the morning or evening without regard for meals.

Similar guidelines for the logic of dose increases apply to sertraline as well. Several studies suggest that maintaining the 50-mg-a-day dose for many weeks may be nearly as beneficial as rapidly increasing the dose, but many clinicians maintain their patients on doses of 100 to 200 mg a day. The shorter half-life of sertraline and the lack of a long-acting metabolite however, render assessment at closer intervals more reasonable with this drug than with fluoxetine.

Paroxetine

Paroxetine is available in scored 20 mg and unscored 10, 30, and 40 mg tablets. Paroxetine is usually initiated for the treatment of depression at a dosage of 10 or 20 mg a day. An increase in the dosage should be considered when patients do not show an adequate response in 1 to 3 weeks. Clinicians can then initiate upward dose titration in 10-mg increments at weekly intervals to a maximum of 60 mg a day. Patients who experience GI upsets may benefit by taking the drug with food. Paroxetine should be taken as a single daily dose in the morning, whereas higher doses may be divided into two doses per day. Patients with melancholic features may require dosages greater than 20 mg a day. The suggested therapeutic dosage range for elderly patients is 20 to 40 mg a day, as older adults have been found to have higher mean plasma concentrations than younger adults.

Fluvoxamine

Fluvoxamine is available in 50 and 100 mg tablets. The effective daily dosage range is from 50 to 300 mg a day. A usual starting dosage is 50 mg once a day at bedtime for the first week, after which the dosage can be adjusted according to the adverse effects and the patient's response. Doses greater than 100 mg a day may be divided into twice daily dosing. A tapered reduction of the dosage may be necessary if nausea develops over the first 2 weeks of therapy. Fluvoxamine can be administered as a single evening dose to minimize its adverse effects. Tablets should be swallowed with water and, preferably, food without chewing the tablet.

References

American College of Neuropsychopharmacology Council: Suicidal behavior and psychotropic medication. Neuropsychopharmacology *8:* 177, 1993.

Black DW, Monahan P, Wesner R, Gabel J, et al. The effect of fluvoxamine, cognitive therapy, and placebo on abnormal personality traits in 44 patients with panic disorder. J Pers Disord *10:* 185, 1996.

Bodkin JA, Lasser RA, Wines JD, Gardner DM, Baldessarini RJ: Combining serotonin reuptake inhibitors and bupropion in partial responders to antidepressant monotherapy. J Clin Psychiatry *58:* 137, 1997.

Bogenschutz MP, Nurnberg HG: Effects of sertraline in the treatment of alcoholism. Am J Addictions *5:* 91, 1996.

Burke D, Fanker S: Fluoxetine and the syndrome of inappropriate secretion of antidiuretic hormone (SIADH). Aust NZ J Psychiatry *30:* 295, 1996.

De Wilde J, Spieres R, Mertens C, Bartholomé F, Schotte G, Leyman S: A

double-blind, comparative, multicentre study comparing paroxetine with fluoxetine in depressed patients. Acta Psychiatr Scand *87:* 141, 1993.
Den Boer JA, Westenberg HGM: Serotonergic compounds in panic disorder, obsessive-compulsive disorder and anxious depression: A concise review. Hum Psychopharmacol *10* (3, Suppl): S173, 1995.
Hellings JA, Kelley LA, Gabrielli WF, Kilgore E, et al: Sertraline response in adults with mental retardation and autistic disorder. J Clin Psychiatry *57* (8): 333, 1996.
Judd FK, Mijch AM, Cockram A: Fluoxetine treatment of depressed patients with HIV infection. Aust NZ J Psychiatry *29* (3): 433, 1995.
Kosten TR, McCance E: A review of pharmacotherapies for substance abuse. Am J Addict *5* (1): 58, 1996.
Laird LK, Lydiard RB, Morton WA, Steede TE, Kellner C, Thompson NM, Ballenger JC: Cardiovascular effects of imipramine, fluvoxamine, and placebo in depressed outpatients. J Clin Psychiatry *54:* 224, 1993.
Lejoyeux M: Use of serotonin (5-hydroxytryptamine) reuptake inhibitors in the treatment of alcoholism. Alcohol Alcohol *31* (1, Suppl): 69, 1996.
Patel RM, Grossberg GT: The use of selective serotonin reuptake inhibitors in geriatric depression: A review of the literature. Rev Clin Gerontology *5:* 442, 1995.
Reist C, Helmeste D, Albers L, Chhay H, et al: Serotonin indices and impulsivity in normal volunteers. Psychiatry Res *60* (2–3): 177, 1996.
Sandor P: Clinical management of Tourette's syndrome and associated disorders. Can J Psychiatry *40* (10): 577, 1995.
Schatzberg AF: Fluoxetine in the treatment of comorbid anxiety and depression. J Clin Psychiatry *13:* 2, 1995.
Song F, Freemantle N, Sheldon TA, House A, Watson P, Long A, Mason J: Selective serotonin reuptake inhibitors: Meta-analysis of efficacy and acceptability. Br J Med *306:* 683, 1993.
Tam EM, Lam RW, Levitt AJ: Treatment of seasonal affective disorder: A review. Can J Psychiatry *40* (8): 457, 1995.
Tollefson GD, Holman SL, Sayler ME, Potvin JH: Fluoxetine, placebo, and tricyclic antidepressants in major depression with and without anxious features. J Clin Psychiatry Monogr Ser *13* (2): 13, 1995.

▲ 35.3.28 Sympathomimetics

Sympathomimetics cause the stimulation of α- and β-adrenergic receptors directly, as agonists, and, indirectly, by stimulating the release of dopamine and norepinephrine from presynaptic terminals. The drugs are also referred to as stimulants, psychostimulants, and analeptics. The first sympathomimetic, amphetamine (Benzedrine), was synthesized in 1935 and shortly thereafter was recognized as efficacious in treating narcolepsy, depressive disorders, and hyperactivity in children. The use of amphetamine was soon replaced by the use of dextroamphetamine (Dexedrine), which was then joined by two other currently available sympathomimetics, methylphenidate (Ritalin) and pemoline (Cylert). The Food and Drug Administration (FDA)-approved indications for dextroamphetamine and methylphenidate are narcolepsy and attention-deficit/hyperactivity disorder (ADHD), and the approved indication for pemoline is ADHD. Methamphetamine (Desoxyn) is approved for ADHD and as a short-term adjunctive for weight loss. Because of its high addiction potential, methamphetamine, which as a street drug is called speed, crank, uppers, meth, or ice, has fallen from favor for medical indications. The drugs are also effective in the treatment of depressive disorders in special populations (for example, the medically ill). A recent review of postmarketing experience with pemoline, from 1975 to December 1996, reported the accumulation of 13 cases of hepatic failure, 10 of which were in children and 11 of which resulted in death or liver transplantation. The rate was 4 to 17 times the expected rate, and it prompted the FDA to change the package insert to recommend that pemoline no longer be considered as first-line therapy for ADHD.

CHEMISTRY

Dextroamphetamine and methylphenidate are structurally similar to each other and to amphetamine, and all three drugs are similar in structure to the catecholamines (for example, dopamine) (Fig. 35.3.28–1). Pemoline has a different structure from the other three compounds and differs in its speed of onset.

PHARMACOLOGICAL ACTIONS

Pharmacokinetics

All three sympathomimetics are well absorbed from the gastrointestinal tract. Dextroamphetamine begins to act clinically within 1 hour, reaches peak plasma concentrations in 2 to 3 hours, and has a half-life of about 6 hours; multiple daily dosing is necessary. Dextroamphetamine is partially metabolized in the liver and is partially excreted unchanged by the kidneys. Methylphenidate begins to act clinically in 30 minutes, reaches peak plasma levels in 1 to 2 hours, and has a short half-life of 2 to 3 hours, thus it is given in multiple daily dosages. A sustained release formulation essentially doubles the effective half-life. Methylphenidate is completely metabolized by the liver. Pemoline reaches peak plasma concentrations in 2 to 4 hours and has a half-life of about 12 hours; thereby the drug can be used in once-daily doses. Pemoline is metabolized by the liver and is excreted unchanged by the kidneys.

Pharmacodynamics

Dextroamphetamine and methylphenidate are indirectly acting sympathomimetics whose primary effect is the release of catecholamines from presynaptic neurons. Dextroamphetamine

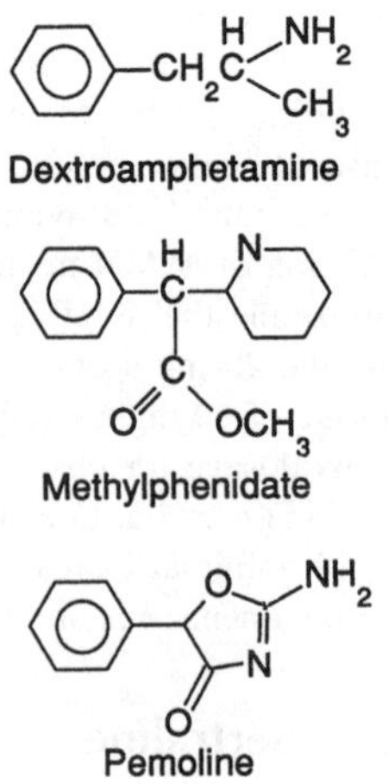
Dextroamphetamine
Methylphenidate
Pemoline

FIGURE 35.3.28–1
Molecular structures of sympathomimetics.

stimulates release of a cytoplasmic store of dopamine, whereas methylphenidate releases dopamine from long-term vesicular stores. Pemoline's strong central nervous system (CNS) dopamine effects have not been fully characterized. Current data place equal emphasis on the role of dopamine and norepinephrine in the clinical effects of sympathomimetics. More recently, dysregulation of serotonin has been implicated in ADHD, and interest has increased for the development of serotonergic drugs for ADHD. Dextroamphetamine and methylphenidate are also inhibitors of catecholamine reuptake, especially dopamine reuptake, and inhibitors of monoamine oxidase. The net result of these activities is believed to be the stimulation of several brain regions, particularly the ascending reticular activating system and areas of the striatum, that have recently been implicated in the pathophysiology of ADHD. Methylphenidate binding in rat brain is highest in the striatum. The pharmacodynamics of pemoline are less well understood than are the pharmacodynamics of dextroamphetamine and methylphenidate.

The short-term use of sympathomimetics induces a euphoric feeling, but tolerance develops for both the euphoric feeling and the sympathomimetic activity. Tolerance does not develop for the therapeutic effects in ADHD.

EFFECTS ON SPECIFIC ORGANS AND SYSTEMS

In addition to the effects of the sympathomimetics on the CNS, the drugs have significant effects on the cardiovascular and endocrine systems. At regular clinical dosages the cardiovascular effects are minimal, but at high dosages the sympathomimetics can cause increases in blood pressure, either increases or reflex decreases in the heart rate, and cardiac arrhythmias at still higher dosages. Studies have indicated that sympathomimetics, particularly amphetamine, affect the endocrine system, as indicated by a decreased growth rate in children during the first year of treatment. This adverse effect can be mitigated by giving the drugs only on school days, not on weekends, and by giving a 3-month holiday over the summer, when studies have shown that catch-up growth eliminates any disparities in stature caused by the drugs.

THERAPEUTIC INDICATIONS

Attention-Deficit/Hyperactivity Disorder

The major indication for the sympathomimetics is ADHD in children. ADHD is one of several types of disruptive behaviors that may be exhibited by children and should be differentiated from oppositional-defiant disorder, conduct disorder, antisocial personality, anxiety, and agitated depression prior to the use of sympathomimetics. The sympathomimetics are effective in about 75 percent of these patients. Many well-controlled studies have shown that the drugs increase the attention span and the ability to concentrate and that they decrease hyperactivity, impulsivity, and oppositional behaviors. Although these were once thought of as paradoxical effects for psychostimulants, subsequent studies found that normal children also display decreased activity and increased cognitive performance when given the drugs. Sympathomimetics appear to boost the influence of the organizing centers of the brain to allow a more efficient flow of information between the various cognitive centers. Sympathomimetics should be given as part of a multifaceted approach, including school and family interventions. Sympathomimetics improve classroom behavior, academic performance and productivity, interactions with peers and adults, and other social interactions. Although methylphenidate is the most commonly used drug for the indication, dextroamphetamine is equally effective. The data on the efficacy of pemoline are less robust, and the onset of action for pemoline is said by some researchers to be slower (3 to 4 weeks) than the onset for the other drugs. Some clinicians, nevertheless, prefer pemoline because of its low abuse potential. In light of the new data connecting pemoline with potentially fatal hepatic failure, this agent may be used only with significant caution in the future.

A syndrome of affective lability, inability to complete tasks, explosive temper, impulsivity, and stress intolerance has been described in adults who often have a history of childhood ADHD. Data indicate that the sympathomimetics are effective in treatment of these adults. Amphetamines (5 to 60 mg a day) or methylphenidate (5 to 60 mg a day) may be efficacious, and psychopharmacological therapy may need to be continued indefinitely. Clinical experience suggests that these drugs are safe and well tolerated by most patients over the course of many years. Other agents used for this indication are bupropion (Wellbutrin), clonidine (Catapres), guanfacine (Tenex), phentermine (Fastin), tricyclic drugs, buspirone (BuSpar), and serotonin-specific reuptake inhibitors.

Narcolepsy

Narcolepsy is the second approved use of sympathomimetics in the United States. The symptoms of narcolepsy include excessive daytime sleepiness and transient, irresistible attacks of daytime sleep (cataplexy), sleep paralysis, and hypnagogic hallucinations. Sympathomimetics should be used as part of a multimodal approach including timed naps and counseling. Because early-onset rapid eye movement (REM) sleep is a key feature of narcolepsy, drugs that delay REM onset, such as most antidepressants except trazodone and nefazodone, are also used. Unfortunately, patients with narcolepsy, unlike patients with ADHD, may develop tolerance for the therapeutic effects of the sympathomimetics.

Depressive Disorders

Sympathomimetics may be used to treat depressive disorders. Possible indications for their use include treatment-resistant depressive disorders; depression in older people who are at increased risk for adverse effects from tricyclic and tetracyclic drugs and monoamine oxidase inhibitors; depression in medically ill patients, especially acquired immune deficiency (AIDS) patients; and clinical situations in which a rapid response is important but for which electroconvulsive therapy (ECT) is contraindicated. Both sympathomimetics and ECT may relieve severe depression in the first week of administration. Sympathomimetics improve alertness and help to focus attention within an hour of administration, which may enable the patient to mobilize resources toward a gratifying goal. An improvement in mood may appear toward the end of the first week.

Dextroamphetamine may be useful in differentiating pseudodementia of depression from dementia. A depressed patient generally responds to a 5-mg dose with increased alertness and improved cognition. Sympathomimetics are thought to provide only short-term benefit (2 to 4 weeks) for depression because tolerance for the antidepressant effects of the drugs develops rapidly in most patients. Some research data and some clinicians, however, report that long-term treatment of patients with sympathomimetics can be of benefit in some cases. Long-term treatment must be monitored to assess the continuing benefit of the drugs and to assess whether the patient is abusing the drugs.

Obesity

Sympathomimetics were previously used in the treatment of obesity because of their anorexia-inducing effects. Because tolerance develops for the anorectic effects and because of the drugs' high abuse potential, this indication is no longer considered justified by many clinicians.

PRECAUTIONS AND ADVERSE REACTIONS

The most common adverse effects associated with sympathomimetics are anxiety, irritability, insomnia, headache, and dysphoria. When taken by children with developmental delays, sympathomimetics may cause an idiosyncratic increase in hyperactivity. Sympathomimetics cause a decreased appetite, although tolerance develops for this effect. The treatment of

Table 35.3.28–1
Management of Side Effects of Sympathomimetic Drugs

Side Effect	Management
For all side effects	Unless severe, allow 7–10 days for tolerance to develop. Evaluate dose–response relationships. Evaluate time-action effects and then adjust dosing intervals or switch to sustained-release preparation. Evaluate for concurrent conditions, including comorbidities and environment stressors. Consider switching stimulant drug.
Anorexia or dyspepsia	Administer before, during, or after meals. With pemoline, consider drug-induced hepatitis.
Weight loss	Give drug after breakfast and after lunch. Implement calorie enhancement strategies. Give brief drug holidays.
Slowed growth	Apply weight loss remedies. Give weekend and vacation (longer) drug holidays. Consider another stimulant or nonstimulant drug.
Dizziness	Monitor blood pressure and pulse. Encourage adequate hydration. If associated with only T_{max}, change to sustained-release preparation.
Insomnia or nightmares	Administer earlier in day. Omit or reduce last dose. If giving sustained preparation, switch to tablet drug. Consider adjunctive antihistamine or clonidine.
Dysphoric mood or emotional constriction	Reduce dose or switch to long-acting preparation. Switch stimulants. Consider comorbidity requiring alternative or adjunctive treatment.
Rebound	Switch to stained-release preparation. Combined long- and short-acting preparations.
Tics	Firmly establish correlation between tics and pharmacotherapy by examining dose–response relationship, including no-medication condition. If tics are mild and abate after 7–10 days with medications, reconsider risks and benefits of continued stimulant treatment and renew informed consent. Switch stimulants. Consider nonstimulant treatment (eg, clonidine or tricyclic antidepressant). If tic disorder and ADHD are severe, consider combining stimulant with a high-potency neuroleptic.
Psychosis	Discontinue stimulant treatment. Assess for comorbid thought disorder. Consider alternative treatments.

Reprinted with permission from Greenhill LL, Halperin JM, March JS: Psychostimulants. In *Psychiatry*, A Tasman, J Kay, JA Lieberman, editors, p 1672. Saunders, Philadelphia, 1997.

common adverse effects in children with ADHD is usually straightforward (Table 35.3.28–1). The drugs can also cause increases in the heart rate and blood pressure and may cause palpitations. Less common adverse effects include the induction of movement disorders, such as tics, Tourette's disorder-like symptoms, and dyskinesia. In children, sympathomimetics have been reported to cause a transient suppression of growth, which is thought to be due to perturbation of the growth hormone axis. This effect may be minimized by administration of sympathomimetics only on school days, with a 3-month break in the summer, during which catch-up growth is said to compensate for any prior stunting of growth. The most limiting adverse effect of sympathomimetics is their association with psychological and physical dependence. Sympathomimetics may exacerbate glaucoma, hypertension, cardiovascular disorders, hyperthyroidism, anxiety disorders, and psychotic disorders, and seizure disorders. In animal models, the seizure threshold is reduced by sympathomimetics; however, many experts would nevertheless consider a trial of sympathomimetics in patients with well-controlled seizure disorders.

High dosages of sympathomimetics can cause dry mouth, pupillary dilation, bruxism, formication, and emotional lability. Long-term use of high dosages can cause a delusional disorder that is indistinguishable from paranoid schizophrenia. Overdosages of sympathomimetics produce hypertension, tachycardia, hyperthermia, toxic psychosis, delirium, and occasionally seizures. Overdosages of sympathomimetics can also result in death, often from cardiac arrhythmias. Seizures can be treated with benzodiazepines, cardiac effects with β-adrenergic receptor antagonists, fever with cooling blankets, and delirium with dopamine receptor antagonists.

There is virtually no justifiable indication for the use of sympathomimetics during pregnancy. Dextroamphetamine and methylphenidate pass into the breast milk, and it is not known whether pemoline does.

DRUG INTERACTIONS

The coadministration of sympathomimetics and tricyclic or tetracyclic drugs used for the treatment of depressive disorders, warfarin (Coumadin), primidone (Mysoline), phenobarbital (Luminal), phenytoin (Dilantin), or phenylbutazone (Butazolidin) decreases the metabolism of these compounds and results in increased plasma levels. Sympathomimetics decrease the therapeutic efficacy of many hypertensives, especially guanethidine (Esimil, Ismelin). The sympathomimetics should be used with extreme caution with monoamine oxidase inhibitors. Because sympathomimetics act to potentiate dopaminergic neurotransmission, their effect may be blocked by antipsychotic drugs such as dopamine receptor antagonists and serotonin-dopamine antagonists. Nevertheless, combination therapy with a sympathomimetic and a serotonin-dopamine antagonist is often used to control hyperactive children with aggressive features.

LABORATORY INTERFERENCES

Dextroamphetamine may elevate plasma corticosteroid levels and interfere falsely with some assay methods for urinary corticosteroids.

DOSAGE AND ADMINISTRATION

The dosage ranges and the available preparations for sympathomimetics are presented in Table 35.3.28–2. Sympathomimetics are schedule II drugs and in some states require triplicate prescriptions. Pretreatment evaluation should include an evaluation of patients' cardiac function, with particular attention to the presence of hypertension or tachyarrhythmias. Clinicians should also examine patients for the presence of movement disorders, such as tics and dyskinesia, because these conditions can be exacerbated by the administration of sympathomimetics. If tics are present, many experts will not use sympathomimetics; instead, they will choose clonidine or antidepressants. Recent data indicate, however, that sympathomimetics may cause only a mild increase in motor tics and may actually suppress vocal tics. Liver function and renal function should be assessed, and dosages of sympathomimetics should be reduced when a patient's metabolism is impaired. In the case of pemoline, any elevation of liver enzymes is a compelling reason to discontinue the medication.

Sympathomimetics act within 30 minutes of ingestion, and their antidepressant effects develop over the first week. When treating children for ADHD, clinicians can give dextroamphetamine or methylphenidate at 8 AM and 12 noon. The sustained-release methylphenidate may be given once at 8 AM. Pemoline is given at 8 AM. The starting dosage of methylphenidate ranges from 2.5 mg a day for regular to 20 mg a

Table 35.3.28–2
Sympathomimetics

Generic Name	Trade Name	Preparations	Adult Starting Dose (mg a day)	Adult Average Daily Dose (mg)	Adult Maximum Daily Dose (mg)
Dextroamphetamine	Dexedrine	5, 10 mg tablets 5 mg per 5 mL elixir 5, 10, 15 mg sustained-release capsules	2.5–10	10–20	60
Methylphenidate	Ritalin	5, 10, 20 mg tablets 20 mg sustained-release tablets	5–10	20–30	60–80
Pemoline	Cylert	18.75, 37.5, 75 mg tablets	18.75–37.5	56.25–75	112.5

day for sustained release. If this dosage is inadequate, it may be increased to a maximum of 60 mg a day. Some clinicians will increase the dosage to a maximum of 90 mg a day. The dosage of dextroamphetamine is 0.5 mg/kg a day, up to a maximum of 40 mg a day. Pemoline is given in dosages of 18.75 to 112.5 mg a day. Liver function tests should be monitored when using pemoline. Although it is not clear that the routine liver screening can predict acute liver failure caused by pemoline, it is certainly necessary to stop pemoline if there is any hint of hepatic dysfunction on screening tests. Children are generally more sensitive to adverse effects than are adults.

Many psychiatrists believe that amphetamine use has been overly regulated by governmental authorities. Amphetamines and narcotics are listed as schedule II drugs by the U.S. Drug Enforcement Agency (DEA). In addition, in New York State, for example, physicians must use triplicate prescriptions for such drugs; one copy is filed with a state government agency. Such mandates worry both patients and physicians about breaches in confidentiality, and physicians are concerned that their prescribing practices may be misinterpreted by official agencies. Consequently, some physicians may withhold sympathomimetics, even from patients who may benefit from the medications.

The outstanding psychopharmacologist Donald Klein and associates in their 1980 book *Diagnosis and Drug Treatment of Psychiatric Disorders* (and reaffirmed in a personal communication [1990]) summarized the use of stimulant medication in the practice of psychiatry as follows:

> The use of stimulant medication, e.g., dextroamphetamine, methylphenidate, and magnesium pemoline, has been energetically discouraged in our present social climate, the reason being that such drugs may be abused, in common with cocaine, their illegal relative. In addition, there is the frightening possibility that prolonged use of stimulants in high doses may result in a paranoid psychosis or the exacerbation of a schizophrenic disorder. In view of these two considerations, it is not surprising that the prescription of these agents is attended by considerable anxiety and that many doctors simply refuse to use them. In certain jurisdictions, e.g., Sweden, they are outlawed.
>
> Short-term use of stimulant medication is often of marked value in helping demoralized people to get going by overcoming their hampering appetitive inhibition. A daily dosage of dextroamphetamine (5 to 15 mg) may enable a patient to start constructive activity, such as searching for a job or becoming socially active. A much more difficult question is whether chronic administration of stimulant medication is ever justified, in view of the risks of addiction and psychosis.
>
> We have treated a number of patients who seem in chronically "low gear," have difficulty mustering energy and initiative, have a variety of neurasthenic complaints, and, despite high intelligence, are underachievers, with chronic small doses of dextroamphetamine (5 to 15 mg) daily. The potential development of tolerance and dependence and the conceivable psychotogenic effects are thoroughly discussed with these patients, and the utilization of the medication is closely monitored. Strikingly, some have been able to maintain the use of amphetamines, at a level that has never exceeded 15 mg daily, for years. During this period their mood has remained consistently improved and their ability to muster energy and function effectively has been clearly benefited. They have been able to cease taking the medication on numerous occasions, such as during vacations, when a high level of focused attention was not necessary and the circumstances were rewarding, so that the mood-elevating effects were superfluous. Several of these patients have been switched from dextroamphetamine to a MAOI with good results.

The controversial use of triplicate prescriptions is discussed further in Section 12.12.

References

Berkovitch M, Pope E, Phillips J, Koren G: Pemoline-associated fulminant liver failure: Testing the evidence for causation. Clin Pharmacol Ther *57:* 696, 1995.

Casat CD, Pearson DA, Van Davelaar MJ, Cherek DR: Methylphenidate effects on a laboratory aggression measure in children with ADHD. Psychopharmacol Bull *31* (2): 353, 1995.

Klein RG: The role of methylphenidate in psychiatry. Arch Gen Psychiatry *52:* 429, 1995.

Levy F, Hobbes G: Does haloperidol block methylphenidate? Psychopharmacology *126* (1): 70, 1996.

Masand P, Murray GB, Pickett P: Psychostimulants in post-stroke depression. J Neuropsychiatry Clin Neurosci *3:* 23, 1991.

Mattay VS, Berman KF, Ostrem JL, Esposito G, et al: Dextroamphetamine enhances "neural network-specific" physiological signals: A positron-emission tomography rCBF study. J Neurosci *16* (15): 4816, 1996.

Olin J, Masand P: Psychostimulants for depression in hospitalized cancer patients. Psychosomatics *37* (1): 57, 1996.

Pelham WE, Swanson JM, Furman MB, Schwindt H: Pemoline effects on children with ADHD: A time-response by dose-response analysis on classroom measures. J Am Acad Child Adolesc Psychiatry *34* (11): 1504, 1995.

Perez-Reyes M, White WR, McDonald SA: Interaction between ethanol and dextroamphetamine: Effects on psychomotor performance. Alcohol Clin Exp Res *16:* 75, 1992.

Spiga R, Pearson DA, Broitman M, Santos CW: Effects of methylphenidate on cooperative responding in children with attention deficit-hyperactivity disorder. Exp Clin Psychopharmacol *4* (4): 451, 1996.

Stoll AL, Pillay SS, Diamond L, Workum A: Methylphenidate augmentation of serotonin selective reuptake inhibitors: A case series. J Clin Psychiatry *57:* 72, 1996.

Wallace AE, Kofoed LL, West AN: Double-blind, placebo-controlled trial of methylphenidate in older, depressed, medically ill patients. Am J Psychiatry *152:* 929, 1995.

Weitzer MA, Meyers CA, Valentine AD: Methylphenidate in the treatment of neurobehavioral slowing associated with cancer and cancer treatment. J Neuropsychiatry Clin Nerosci *7* (3): 347, 1995.

Yee JD, Berde CB: Dextroamphetamine or methylphenidate as adjuvants to opioid analgesia for adolescents with cancer. J Pain Symptom Manage *9:* 122, 1994.

Zeiner P: Body growth and cardiovascular function after extended treatment (1.75 years) with methylphenidate in boys with attention-deficit hyperactivity disorder. J Child Adolesc Psychopharmacol *5* (2): 129, 1995.

▲ 35.3.29 Thyroid Hormones

Thyroid hormones are used in psychiatry as adjuvants to antidepressants, often in an attempt to convert an antidepressant-nonresponsive patient into an antidepressant-responsive patient. Thyroid hormones have also been used in the treatment rapid-cycling bipolar I disorder patients, particularly for lithium-treated patients in whom lithium has created a hypothyroid state. Lithium may prevent the release of thyroid hormones and may inhibit iodine uptake and the iodination of tyrosine by the thyroid gland. A clinically significant hypothyroidism, with or without goiter, may develop in 5 percent of patients who take lithium for more than 18 months, and it may appear as depression. The most commonly used thyroid hormone is liothyronine (Cytomel), the levorotatory isomer of triiodothyronine (T_3). Levothyroxine (Levoxyl, Levothroid, Synthroid), the levorotatory isomer of thyroxine (T_4), is sometimes used for the same indications.

CHEMISTRY

The molecular structures of levothyroxine and liothyronine are shown in Figure 35.3.29–1. Both endogenous levothyrox-

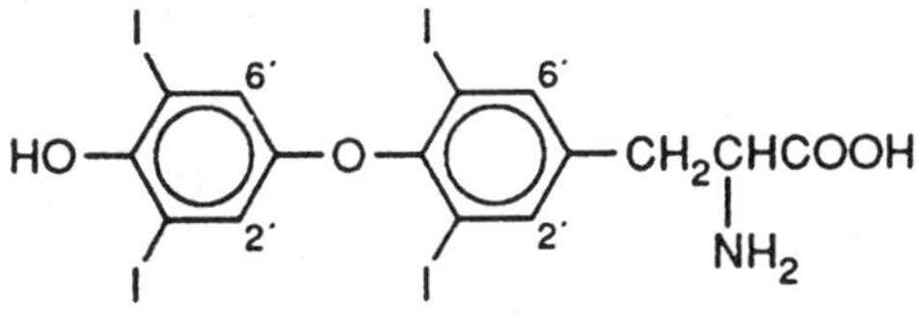

Thyroxine (T_4)

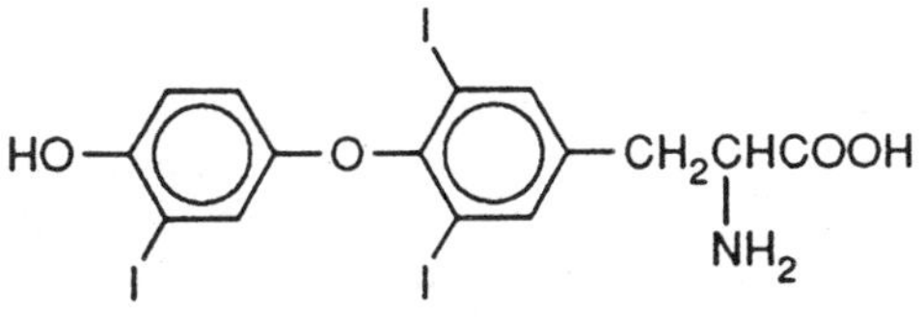

L-Triiodothyronine (T_3)

FIGURE 35.3.29–1
Molecular structures of the thyroid hormones.

ine and exogenous liothyronine are converted into triiodothyronine in the body.

PHARMACOLOGICAL ACTIONS

Pharmacokinetics

Thyroid hormones are administered orally, and their absorption from the gastrointestinal tract is variable. Absorption is increased if the drug is administered while the patient's stomach is empty. The half-life of levothyroxine is 6 to 7 days, and the half-life of liothyronine is 1 to 2 days.

Pharmacodynamics

The mechanism of action for thyroid hormone effects on antidepressant efficacy is unknown, but interactions with the β-adrenergic receptors may be involved. Thyroid hormone is essential to the proper functioning of all neurons. It binds to intracellular receptors that regulate the transcription of a wide range of genes, including several receptors for neurotransmitters.

EFFECTS ON SPECIFIC ORGANS AND SYSTEMS

The effects of the drugs levothyroxine and liothyronine on specific organs and systems are the same as the effects of endogenous thyroid hormones, and the symptoms of toxicity and overdose are the symptoms of hyperthyroidism. Thyroid hormones affect most of the body's organs and systems, especially the cardiovascular system.

THERAPEUTIC INDICATIONS

The major indication for thyroid hormones in psychiatry is as adjuvants to antidepressants. There is no correlation between the laboratory measures of thyroid function and the response to thyroid hormone supplementation of antidepressants. The lithium-induced hypothyroid state, however, is reflected in abnormal thyroid indices (thyroid-stimulating hormone [TSH], T_3, T_4, T_3 resin uptake), and this condition may respond favorably to thyroid supplements. If a patient has been nonresponsive to a 6-week course of an antidepressant at an appropriate dosage, adjuvant therapy with either lithium (Eskalith) or a thyroid hormone is an alternative. Most clinicians use adjuvant lithium before trying a thyroid hormone. The available clinical data indicate that liothyronine is more effective than levothyroxine. Although several controlled trials have indicated that the use of liothyronine converts 33 to 75 percent of antidepressant nonresponders to responders, several other studies have failed to support this finding. Several case reports and small trials have reported successful treatment of rapid-cycling bipolar disorder with high dosages of levothyroxine (125 μg a day), either alone or in combination with valproate (Depakote).

PRECAUTIONS AND ADVERSE REACTIONS

The most common adverse effects associated with thyroid hormones are weight loss, palpitations, nervousness, diarrhea, abdominal cramps, sweating, tachycardia, increased blood pressure, tremors, headache, and insomnia. Osteoporosis may also occur with long-term treatment. Overdoses of thyroid hormones can lead to cardiac failure and death.

Thyroid hormones should not be administered to patients with cardiac disease, angina, or hypertension. The hormones are contraindicated in thyrotoxicosis and uncorrected adrenal insufficiency and in patients with acute myocardial infarctions. Because thyroid hormones do not cross the placenta, they can be administered safely to pregnant women. Thyroid hormones are minimally excreted in the breast milk and have not been shown to cause problems to women who are nursing infants.

DRUG INTERACTIONS

Thyroid hormones can potentiate the effects of warfarin (Coumadin) and other anticoagulants by increasing the catabolism of clotting factors. Thyroid hormones may increase the insulin requirement for patients with diabetes. Sympathomimetics and thyroid hormones should not be coadministered because of the risk of cardiac decompensation.

LABORATORY INTERFERENCES

Levothyroxine has not been reported to interfere with any laboratory test. Liothyronine, however, causes a suppression in the release of endogenous T_4, thereby lowering the value of any thyroid function test dependent on the measure of T_4. The value for TSH is not affected by either levothyroxine or liothyronine administration.

DOSAGE AND ADMINISTRATION

Liothyronine is available in 5, 25, and 50 mg tablets. Levothyroxine is available in 12.5, 25, 50, 75, 88, 100, 112, 125, 137, 150, 175, 200, and 300 μg tablets; it is also available in a 200 and 500 μg parenteral form. The dosage of liothyronine is 25 or 50 μg a day added to the patient's antidepressant regimen. Liothyronine has been used as an adjuvant for all the available antidepressant drugs. An adequate trial of liothyronine supplementation should last 7 to 14 days. If liothyronine supplementation is successful, it should be continued for 2 months and then tapered at the rate of 12.5 μg a day every 3 to 7 days.

References

Aronson R, Offman HJ, Joffe RT, Naylor CD: Triiodothyronine augmentation in the treatment of refractory depression: A meta-analysis. Arch Gen Psychiatry *53* (9): 842, 1996.

Baumgartner A, Bauer M, Hellweg R: Treatment of intractable non–rapid cycling bipolar affective disorder with high-dose thyroxine: An open clinical trial. Neuropsychopharmacology *10:* 183, 1994.

Harris B: Hormonal aspects of postnatal depression. Int Rev Psychiatry *8:* 27, 1996.

Hopkins HS, Gelenberg AJ: Treatment of bipolar disorder: How far have we come?. Psychopharmacol Bull *30:* 27, 1994.

Prohaska ML: Thyroid, lithium, and cognition: The use of thyroid hormone augmentation in the reduction of cognitive side effects associated with lithium maintenance. Diss Abstr Int B Sci Eng *55* (2B): 603, 1994.

Prohaska ML, Stern RA, Nevels CT, Mason GA, et al: The relationship between thyroid status and neuropsychological performance in psychiatric outpatients maintained on lithium. Neuropsychiatry Neuropsychol Behav Neurol *9* (1): 30, 1996.

Suzuki K, Kusumi I, Inoue T, Tsuchiya K, et al: Effect of thyroxine for treatment-resistant affective disorder [Japanese]. Seishin Igaku (Clin Psychiatry) *37* (5): 477, 1995.

Terao T, Oga T, Nozaki S, Ohta A, et al: Possible inhibitory effect of lithium on peripheral conversion of thyroxine to triiodothyronine: A prospective study. Int Clin Psychopharmacol *10* (1): 103, 1995.

Verdoux H, Mury M, Bourgeois M: Comorbidity of bipolar disorder and bulimia nervosa. Eur Psychiatry *9:* 315, 1994.

▲ 35.3.30 Trazodone

Trazodone (Desyrel) is effective in the treatment of depressive disorders. Trazodone is structurally unrelated to the tricyclic and tetracyclic drugs used to treat depressive disorders, the monoamine oxidase inhibitors (MAOIs), serotonin-specific reuptake inhibitors (SSRIs), and other currently available antidepressant drugs. Trazodone may have benefit in anxiety disorders such as panic disorder and obsessive-compulsive disorder. It is chemically related to nefazodone (Serzone).

Trazodone differs from tricyclic and tetracyclic drugs and from MAOIs in having almost no anticholinergic adverse effects. Trazodone is also distinctive in having more marked sedative effects than those found with other antidepressants. For this reason it is used to treat insomnia.

CHEMISTRY

Trazodone is a triazolopyridine derivative that shares the triazolo ring structure with alprazolam (Xanax), a benzodiazepine with possible antidepressant effects (Fig. 35.3.30–1).

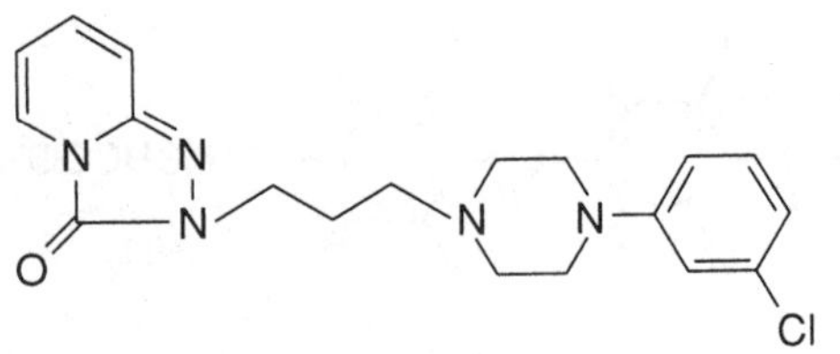
N
N
N
N
N
O
Cl

FIGURE 35.3.30–1
Molecular structure of trazodone.

PHARMACOLOGICAL ACTIONS

Pharmacokinetics

Trazodone is readily absorbed from the gastrointestinal tract, reaches peak plasma levels in 1 to 2 hours, and has a half-life of 6 to 11 hours. Trazodone is metabolized in the liver, and 75 percent of its metabolites are excreted in the urine. The active metabolite of trazodone is *m*-chlorophenylpiperazine (mCPP).

Pharmacodynamics

Trazodone has its therapeutic effects as a relatively specific inhibitor of serotonin reuptake. One active metabolite of trazodone, mCPP, also possesses some postsynaptic serotonin activity. The adverse effects of trazodone are partially mediated by α_1-adrenergic antagonisms and antihistaminergic activity. Long-term administration of trazodone appears to decrease the number of postsynaptic serotonin type 2A (5-HT_{2A}) and β-adrenergic receptors.

EFFECTS ON SPECIFIC ORGANS AND SYSTEMS

Besides its effects on the central nervous system (CNS), trazodone has relatively few effects on organs and systems. The effects it does have are primarily the result of its α_1-adrenergic antagonism, which can affect vascular tone and result in orthostatic hypotension. The drug is also associated with gastric irritation. Relatively rare among the antidepressants is trazodone's association with priapism, which is also probably a result of its α_1-adrenergic antagonist activity. Trazodone has weak activity as a relaxer of skeletal muscles.

THERAPEUTIC INDICATIONS

Depressive Disorders

The primary indication for the use of trazodone is major depressive disorder. Trazodone is as effective as the standard antidepressants in short-term and long-term treatment of major depressive disorder. The drug is particularly effective at improving sleep quality—increasing total sleep time, decreasing the number and duration of nighttime awakenings, and decreasing the amount of rapid eye movement (REM) sleep. Unlike tricyclic drugs, trazodone does not decrease stage 4 sleep. Trazodone may be less likely than tricyclic drugs to precipitate mania.

Insomnia

The marked sedative qualities of trazodone and its favorable effects on sleep architecture have suggested to many clinicians that it would be effective as a hypnotic, and a number of clinicians have used trazodone effectively for this purpose. A recent controlled study confirmed that trazodone is superior to placebo for treatment of insomnia. It has also been used effectively as a hypnotic in combination with less sedating psychotropic drugs. Trazodone has been reported to be useful in treating fluoxetine (Prozac)-induced insomnia. The usual dosage is 50 to 100 mg at bedtime.

Other Indications

Some data indicate that trazodone may be useful in low dosages (50 mg a day) for controlling severe agitation in elderly patients, particularly those with personality change due to a general medical condition. A few case reports and uncontrolled trials of trazodone have indicated its usefulness in the treatment of depression with marked anxiety symptoms, of posttraumatic stress disorder, and of panic disorder with agoraphobia. Because it does not worsen psychotic symptoms, trazodone is preferable to tricyclic drugs as adjunctive treatment for schizophrenia. Limited data support an adjunctive role for trazodone in treatment of alcohol-induced tremor, alcohol-induced depressive disorder, and alcohol-induced anxiety disorder; and anxiety; obsessive-compulsive disorder; eating disorders; chronic pain; autistic disorder; male erectile disorder; and paraphilias. The final evaluation of the use of trazodone in the treatment of these disorders requires further research.

PRECAUTIONS AND ADVERSE REACTIONS

The most common adverse effects associated with trazodone are sedation, orthostatic hypotension, dizziness, headache, and nausea. As a result of α_1-adrenergic blockade, dry mouth is present in some patients. Trazodone may also cause gastric irritation. The drug is not associated with the usual anticholinergic adverse effects, such as urinary retention and constipation. A few case reports have noted an association between trazodone and arrhythmias in patients with preexisting premature ventricular contractions or mitral valve prolapse. Neutropenia, usually not of clinical significance, may develop and should be considered if patients have fever or sore throat.

Trazodone is relatively safe in overdose attempts. No fatalities from trazodone overdoses have been reported when the drug was taken alone, but there have been fatalities when trazodone was taken with other drugs. The symptoms of an overdose include priapism, the loss of muscle coordination, nausea and vomiting, and drowsiness. Trazodone does not have the quinidine-like antiarrhythmic effects of imipramine (Tofranil).

Trazodone is associated with the rare occurrence of priapism, prolonged erection in the absence of sexual stimuli. Patients should be advised to tell their clinicians if erections are gradually becoming frequent or prolonged. In such cases, physicians should strongly consider switching the patients to another antidepressant medication. Untreated priapism can lead to impotence. A patient who experiences priapism while taking trazodone should stop taking the drug and consult a physician immediately. One effective treatment for priapism involves the intracavernosal injection of a 1 μg/mL solution of epinephrine (an α_1-adrenergic agonist). Other forms of sexual dysfunction may also occur with trazodone treatment.

The use of trazodone is contraindicated in pregnant and nursing women. Trazodone should be used with caution in patients with hepatic and renal diseases.

DRUG INTERACTIONS

Trazodone potentiates the CNS depressant effects of other centrally acting drugs and alcohol. The combination of MAOIs and trazodone should be avoided. Trazodone concentrations are increased by fluoxetine, and trazodone increases concentrations of digoxin and phenytoin (Dilantin). Concurrent use of trazodone and antihypertensives may cause hypotension. Electroconvulsive therapy concurrent with trazodone administration should also be avoided.

LABORATORY INTERFERENCES

No known laboratory interferences are associated with the administration of trazodone.

DOSAGE AND ADMINISTRATION

The sedative effects of trazodone appear within 1 hour of administration, whereas the antidepressant effects usually appear after 2 to 4 weeks of treatment. Trazodone is available in tablets that can be divided into 50, 100, 150, and 300 mg amounts. The usual starting dose is 50 mg orally the first day. The dosage can be increased to 50 mg orally twice daily on the second day and possibly 50 mg orally 3 times daily on the third and fourth days if sedation or orthostatic hypotension does not become a problem. The therapeutic range for trazodone is 200 to 600 mg a day in divided doses. Some reports indicate that dosages of 400 to 600 mg a day are required for maximal therapeutic effects; other reports indicate that 300 to 400 mg a day is sufficient. The dosage may be titrated up to 300 mg a day; then the patient can be evaluated for the need for further dosage increases on the basis of the presence or the absence of signs of clinical improvement.

References

Balon R: Sleep terror disorder and insomnia treated with trazodone: A case report. Ann Clin Psychiatry *6:* 161, 1994.

Cunningham LA, Borison RL, Carman JS, Choinard G, et al: A comparison of venlafaxine, trazodone, and placebo in major depression. J Clin Psychopharmacol *14:* 99, 1994.

Halikas JA: Org 3770 (mirtazapine) versus trazodone: A placebo controlled trial in depressed elderly patients. Hum Psychopharmacol *10* (2, Suppl): S125, 1995.

Hellerstein DJ, Yanowitch P, Rosenthal J, Hemlock, et al: Long-term treatment of double depression: A preliminary study with serotonergic antidepressants. Prog Neuropsychopharmacol Biol Psychiatry *18:* 139, 1994.

Khouzam HR, Mayo-Smith MF, Bernard DR, Mahdasian JA, et al: Treatment of crack-cocaine-induced compulsive behavior with trazodone. J Subst Abuse Treat *12* (2): 85, 1995.

Otani K, Yasui N, Kaneko S, Ishida M, et al: Trazodone treatment increases plasma prolactin concentrations in depressed patients. Int Clin Psychopharmacol *10* (2): 115, 1995.

Reeves RR, Bullen JA: Serotonin syndrome produced by paroxetine and low-dose trazodone. Psychosomatics *36:* 159, 1995.

Swinkels JA, de Jonghe F: Safety of antidepressants. Int Clin Psychopharmacol *9* (4, Suppl): 19, 1995.

Tejera CS, Saravay SM: Treatment of organic personality syndrome with low-dose trazodone. J Clin Psychiatry *56* (8): 374, 1995.

Van Bemmel AL, Beersma DGM, Van den Hoofdakker RH: Changes in EEG power density of non–REM sleep in depressed patients during treatment with trazodone. J Affect Disord *35* (1–2: 11, 1995.

van Moffaert M, de Wilde J, Vereecken A, Dierick M, et al: Mirtazapine is more

effective than trazodone: A double-blind controlled study in hospitalized patients with major depression. Int Clin Psychopharmacol *10:* 3, 1995.
Ware JC, Rose FV, McBrayer RH: The acute effects of nefazodone, trazodone and buspirone on sleep and sleep-related penile tumescence in normal subjects. Sleep *17* (6): 544, 1994.
Zarate CA, Tohen M, Baraibar G: Prescribing trends of antidepressants in bipolar depression. J Clin Psychiatry *56:* 260, 1995.

▲ 35.3.31 Tricyclics and Tetracyclics

The group of drugs discussed here are widely known as the tricyclic antidepressants and the tetracyclic antidepressants (both commonly abbreviated as TCAs). Although depressive disorders were the initial indications for these drugs, they are effective in a wide range of disorders including panic disorder, generalized anxiety disorder, posttraumatic stress disorder, obsessive-compulsive disorder, eating disorders, and pain disorder.

The tricyclic drugs share many pharmacokinetic and pharmacodynamic properties and possess similar adverse reaction profiles. Three tetracyclic drugs were initially introduced as being significantly different from the tricyclics, but further study and clinical use have shown that the tetracyclic and tricyclic can best be conceptualized as constituting one large family of drugs. In the past few years the serotonin-specific reuptake inhibitors (SSRIs) have overtaken the tricyclics and tetracyclics as the most frequently prescribed antidepressants in the United States.

CHEMISTRY

All tricyclics have a three-ring nucleus in their molecular structures (Fig. 35.3.31–1). Imipramine (Tofranil), amitriptyline (Elavil), clomipramine (Anafranil), trimipramine (Surmontil), and doxepin (Adapin, Sinequan) are called tertiary amines because two methyl groups are on the nitrogen atom of the side chain. Desipramine (Norpramin), nortriptyline (Pamelor, Aventyl), and protriptyline (Vivactil) are called secondary amines because only one methyl group is in the position. The tertiary amines are metabolized into their corresponding secondary amines in the body.

The arbitrary classification of tetracyclic drugs is based on a gross count of the number of rings in their molecular structures. Amoxapine (Asendin), a dibenzoxazepine, is a derivative of the antipsychotic drug loxapine (Loxitane) and has a cyclic side chain off the three-ring nucleus, for a total of four rings. Maprotiline (Ludiomil) is a tetracyclic with the same side chain as desipramine; its fourth ring bridges the center of the standard tricyclic nucleus. Mianserin is a tetracyclic drug whose side chain has been cyclized to form a fourth ring. Mianserin is not currently available for clinical use in the United States.

PHARMACOLOGICAL ACTIONS

Pharmacokinetics

Absorption from oral administration of most tricyclics and tetracyclics is incomplete, and there is significant metabolism from the first-pass effect. Imipramine pamoate is a depot form of the drug for intramuscular administration, and indications for the use of this preparation are limited. Protein binding is usually

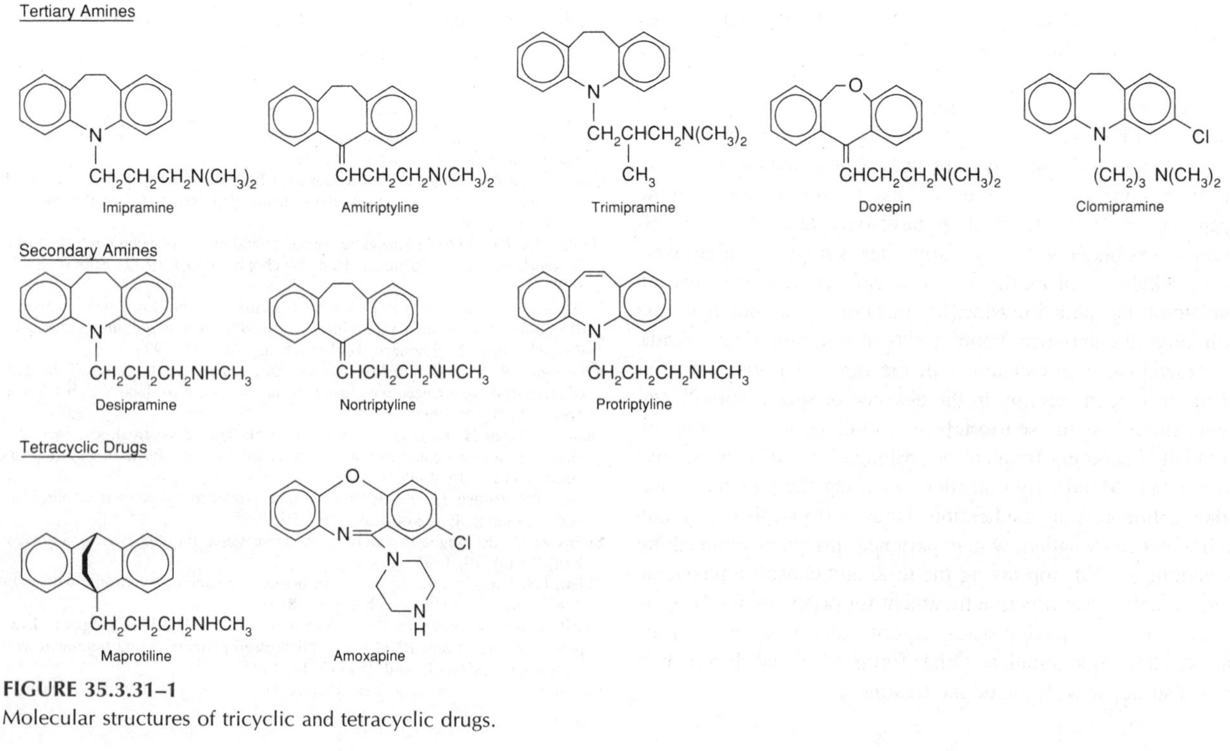
Tertiary Amines
Imipramine
Amitriptyline
Trimipramine
Doxepin
Clomipramine
Secondary Amines
Desipramine
Nortriptyline
Protriptyline
Tetracyclic Drugs
Maprotiline
Amoxapine

FIGURE 35.3.31–1
Molecular structures of tricyclic and tetracyclic drugs.

more than 75 percent, the lipid solubility is high, and the volume of distribution ranges from 10 to 30 L/kg for tertiary amines to 20 to 60 L/kg for secondary amines. The tertiary amines are demethylated to form the related secondary amines. The ratio of methylated to demethylated forms varies widely from person to person. The tricyclic nucleus is oxidized in the liver, conjugated with glucuronic acid, and excreted. The 7-hydroxymetabolite of amoxapine has potent dopamine-blocking activity, which causes the antipsychotic-like neurological and endocrinological adverse effects that are seen with the drug. The half-lives of the tricyclic and tetracyclic drugs vary from 10 to 70 hours, but nortriptyline, maprotiline, and particularly protriptyline can have longer half-lives. The long half-lives allow all the compounds to be given once daily; 5 to 7 days are needed to reach steady-state plasma concentrations.

Because it has been recognized that many tricyclic drugs are metabolized by the hepatic enzyme CYP 2D6, the Food and Drug Administration (FDA) has recommended including the following precaution for prescribing physicians:

> The biochemical activity of the drug metabolizing enzyme CYP 2D6 (debrisoquin hydroxylase) is reduced in a subset of the white population (about 7 to 10 percent of whites are so called poor metabolizers); reliable estimates of the prevalence of reduced CYP 2D6 enzyme activity among Asian, African, and other populations are not yet available. Poor metabolizers have higher than expected plasma concentrations of tricyclic antidepressants when given usual doses. Depending on the fraction of drug metabolized by CYP 2D6, the increase in plasma concentration may be small or quite large (eightfold increase in plasma area under the curve [AUC] of the tricyclic). In addition, certain drugs inhibit the activity of this enzyme and make normal metabolizers resemble poor metabolizers. An individual who is stable on a given dose of tricyclic may become abruptly toxic when given one of these inhibiting drugs as concomitant therapy. The drugs that inhibit cytochrome CYP 2D6 include some that are not metabolized by the enzyme (quinidine, cimetidine) and many that are substrates for CYP 2D6 (most other antidepressants, including fluoxetine, sertraline, and paroxetine; phenothiazines; carbamazepine; and the type IC antiarrhythmics propafenone and flecainide).
>
> Concomitant use of tricyclic antidepressants with drugs that can inhibit CYP 2D6 may require lower doses than usually prescribed for either the tricyclic antidepressant or the other drug. Furthermore, whenever one of these other drugs is withdrawn from cotherapy, an increased dose of tricyclic antidepressants may be required.

Pharmacodynamics

The short-term effects of tricyclics and tetracyclics act to reduce the reuptake of norepinephrine and serotonin and to block the muscarinic acetylcholine and histamine receptors (Fig. 35.3.31–2). The tricyclics and tetracyclics vary in their pharmacodynamic effects (Table 35.3.31–1). Amoxapine, nortriptyline, desipramine, and maprotiline have the least anticholinergic activity; doxepin has the most antihistaminergic activity; clomipramine is the most serotonin selective of the tricyclics and tetracyclics and is often included with the SSRIs, such as fluoxetine (Prozac).

The reuptake blockade of norepinephrine and serotonin by the drugs and monoamine oxidase inhibition by the monoamine oxidase inhibitors (MAOIs) led to the development of the monoamine hypothesis of mood disorders. Long-term administration of tricyclic and tetracyclic drugs results in a decrease in the number of β-adrenergic receptors and, perhaps, a similar decrease in the number of serotonin type 2 ($5\text{-}HT_2$) receptors. The downregulation of receptors after repeated administration most closely correlates with the time needed for clinical effects to appear in patients. The downregulation of β-adrenergic receptors occurs whether the initial effect is blocking of noradrenergic or serotonergic receptors. Research with animal models has shown that intact noradrenergic and serotonergic systems are both required for the β-adrenergic receptor downregulation to occur.

EFFECTS ON SPECIFIC ORGANS AND SYSTEMS

The major effects of the tricyclic and tetracyclic drugs are on the central nervous system (CNS), although the anticholinergic effects of the drugs produce a diverse range of adverse effects mediated by the autonomic nervous system. In addition to these effects, the tricyclic and tetracyclic drugs have significant effects on the cardiovascular system. In therapeutic dosages, the drugs are classified as type 1A antiarrhythmic drugs, as they terminate ventricular fibrillation and can increase the collateral blood supply to an ischemic heart. In overdoses, however, the drugs are highly cardiotoxic and cause decreased contractility, increased myocardial irritability, hypotension, and tachycardia.

THERAPEUTIC INDICATIONS

Major Depressive Disorder

The treatment of a major depressive episode and the prophylactic treatment of major depressive disorder are the principal indications for using tricyclic and tetracyclic drugs. The drugs are also effective in treating depression in patients with bipolar I disorder. Melancholic features, previous major depressive episodes, and a family history of depressive disorders increase the likelihood of a therapeutic response. The treatment of a major depressive episode with psychotic features almost always requires the coadministration of an antipsychotic drug and an antidepressant.

Mood Disorder Due to a General Medical Condition with Depressive Features

Depression associated with a general medical condition (secondary depression) may respond to tricyclic and tetracyclic drug treatment. Depression is associated with dementias and with movement disorders such as Parkinson's disease. Depression associated with acquired immune deficiency syndrome (AIDS) may respond to the drugs.

Panic Disorder with Agoraphobia

Imipramine is the tricyclic most studied for panic disorder with agoraphobia, but other tricyclic and tetracyclics are also effective. Early reports indicated that small dosages of imipramine (50 mg a day) were often effective; recent studies, however, indicate that the usual antidepressant dosages are usually required. In the past few years, SSRIs, especially paroxetine (Paxil), have become additional agents for treatment of panic disorder.

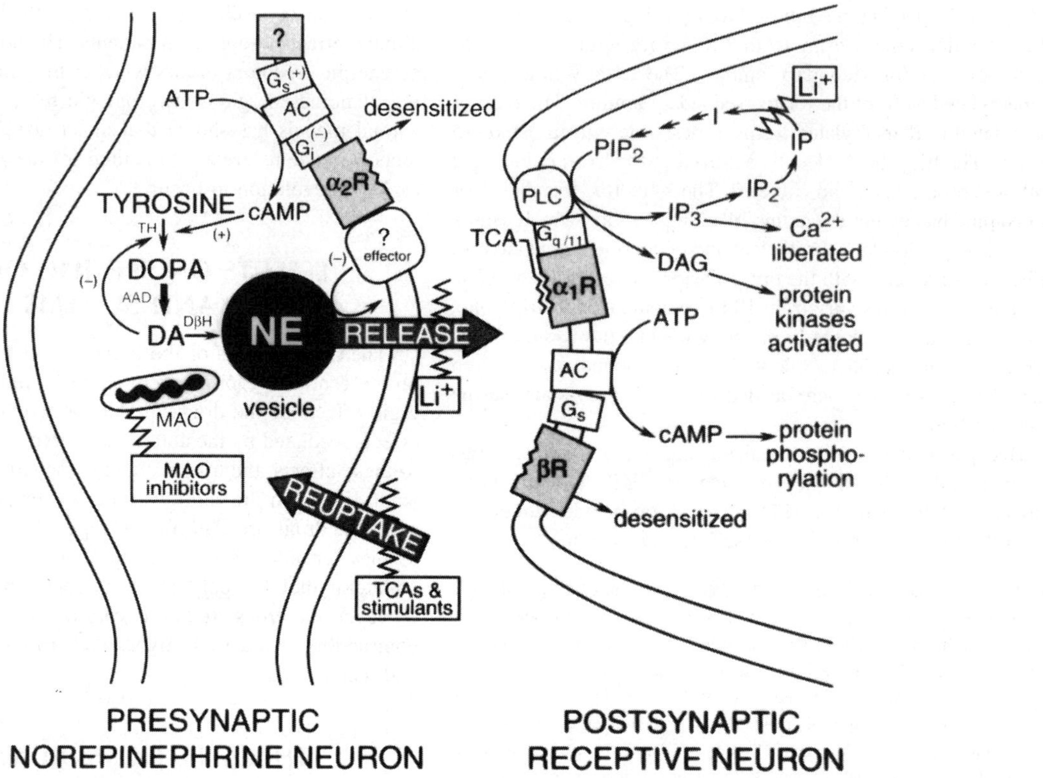
?
Gs (+)
ATP
AC
desensitized
Gi (−)
α2R
TYROSINE
cAMP
TH
(+)
?
effector
(−)
DOPA
(−)
AAD
DβH
DA
NE
RELEASE
Li+
vesicle
MAO
MAO inhibitors
REUPTAKE
TCAs & stimulants
Li+
I
PIP2
IP
PLC
IP2
TCA
Gq/11
IP3
Ca2+ liberated
DAG
α1R
protein kinases activated
ATP
AC
Gs
cAMP
protein phosphorylation
βR
desensitized
PRESYNAPTIC NOREPINEPHRINE NEURON
POSTSYNAPTIC RECEPTIVE NEURON

FIGURE 35.3.31–2

Sites of action of tricyclic and tetracyclic drugs, sympathomimetics, monoamine oxidase (*MAO*) inhibitors, and lithium. In varicosities ("terminals") along terminal arborizations of norepinephrine (*NE*) neurons projecting from brainstem to forebrain, tyrosine is oxidized to dihydrophenylalanine (*DOPA*) by tyrosine hydroxylase (*TH*), then decarboxylated to dopamine (*DA*) by aromatic L-amino acid decarboxylase (*AAD*) and stored in vesicles, where β-oxidation by dopamine β-hydroxylase (*DβH*) converts DA to NE. Following exocytotic release (inhibited by lithium) by depolarization in the presence of Ca^{2+}, NE interacts with postsynaptic α- and β-adrenergic receptor (*R*) subtypes, as well as presynaptic α_2 autoreceptors. Inactivation occurs primarily by active transport ("reuptake") into presynaptic terminals (inhibited by most tricyclic and tetracyclic antidepressants [*TCAs*] and sympathomimetics [stimulants]), with secondary deamination (by mitochondrial MAO, blocked by MAO inhibitors). β-Adrenergic receptors activate adenylyl cyclase (*AC*) through G_s proteins to convert adenosine triphosphate (*ATP*) to cyclic AMP (*cAMP*). α_1-Adrenergic (and other) receptors activate phospholipase C (*PLC*) via additional G proteins to convert phosphatidyl bisphosphate (*PIP_2*) to inositol trisphosphate (*IP_3*) and diacylglycerol (*DAG*), with secondary modulation of intracellular Ca^{2+} and protein kinases; α_2 autoreceptors modulate synthesis and release of NE through effector mechanisms not well defined. Lithium inhibits the phosphatase that liberates inositol (*I*) from inositol phosphate (*IP_2*) and may have other action to modify the abundance or function of G proteins and effectors. Initially, blockade of inactivation of NE by TCAs leads to α_2-receptor–mediated inhibition of firing rates, metabolic activity, and transmitter release from NE neurons; gradually, however, abundance and sensitivity of α_2 autoreceptors are lost, and presynaptic activity returns. Postsynaptic β receptors also desensitize, but α_1 receptors do not. Serotonin-specific reuptake inhibitors have analogous actions to TCAs at serotonin-containing neurons, and TCAs can interact with serotonin (5-HT) neurons and receptors. (Reprinted with permission from Baldessarini RJ: Drugs and the treatment of psychiatric disorders: depression and mania. In *Goodman & Gilman's The Pharmacological Basis of Therapeutics,* ed 9, JG Hardman, LE Limbird, PB Molinoff, RW Ruddon, editors, p 438. McGraw-Hill, New York, 1996.)

Generalized Anxiety Disorder

The use of doxepin to treat anxiety disorders is approved by the FDA. Some research data show that imipramine may also be useful, and some clinicians use a drug containing a combination of chlordiazepoxide and amitriptyline (Limbitrol) for mixed anxiety and depressive disorders.

Obsessive-Compulsive Disorder

Obsessive-compulsive disorder is classified as an anxiety disorder. The disorder appears to respond specifically to clomipramine and SSRIs. None of the other tricyclic and tetracyclic drugs appears to be nearly as effective as clomipramine for the disorder. Multicenter, placebo-controlled trials found clomipramine to be superior to SSRIs, and another controlled trial found paroxetine to be of equal efficacy to clomipramine, for treatment of obsessive-compulsive disorder.

Eating Disorders

Both anorexia nervosa and bulimia nervosa have been successfully treated with imipramine and desipramine, although other tricyclics and tetracyclics may also be effective.

Pain Disorder

Chronic pain disorder, including headache (such as migraine), is often treated with tricyclics and tetracyclics.

Table 35.3.31–1
Neurotransmitter Effects of Tricyclic and Tetracyclic Drugs

	Reuptake Blockade		Receptor Blockade		
Drug	**NE**	**5-HT**	**Muscarinic ACh**	**H_1**	**H_2**
Imipramine	+	+	+ +	±	±
Desipramine	+ + +	±	±	–	–
Trimipramine	±	±	+ +	+ +	?
Amitriptyline	±	+ +	+ + +	+ +	+ +
Nortriptyline	+ +	±	+	±	±
Protriptyline	+ + +	±	+	+ + +	–
Amoxapine	+ +	±	+	±	?
Doxepin	+	±	+ +	+ + +	+
Maprotiline	+ + +	–	+	±	?
Clomipramine	±	+ +	+	?	?

NE, norepinephrine; 5-HT, serotonin; ACh, acetylcholine; H_1, histamine type 1; and H_2, histamine type 2.

Other Disorders

Childhood enuresis is often treated with imipramine. Peptic ulcer disease can be treated with doxepin, which has marked antihistaminergic effects. Other indications for tricyclics and tetracyclics are narcolepsy, nightmare disorder, and posttraumatic stress disorder. The drugs are sometimes used for children and adolescents with attention-deficit/hyperactivity disorder, sleepwalking disorder, separation anxiety disorder, and sleep terror disorder. Clomipramine has been used to treat premature ejaculation, movement disorders, and compulsive behavior in children with autistic disorder.

PRECAUTIONS AND ADVERSE REACTIONS

The relative concentrations at which therapeutic and adverse effects appear for tricyclic drugs is presented in Figure 35.3.31–3).

Psychiatric Effects

A major adverse effect of all tricyclic and tetracyclic drugs and other antidepressants is the possibility of inducing a manic episode in patients with and without a history of bipolar I disorder. Clinicians should watch for this effect in patients with bipolar I disorder, especially if substance-induced mania has been a problem in the past. It is prudent to use low dosages of tricyclic and tetracyclic drugs in such patients or to use an agent such as fluoxetine (Prozac) or bupropion (Wellbutrin), which may be less likely to induce a manic episode. Tricyclic and tetracyclic drugs have also been reported to exacerbate psychotic disorders in susceptible patients.

Anticholinergic Effects

Clinicians should warn patients that anticholinergic effects are common but that patients may develop a tolerance for these

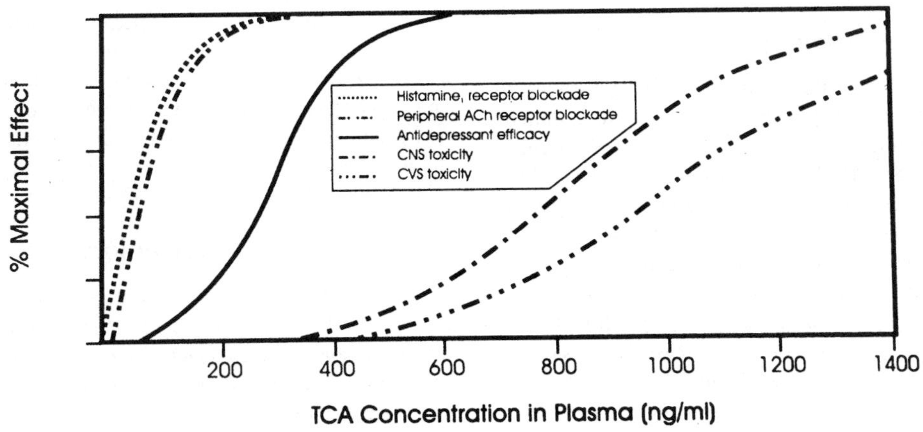

% Maximal Effect
Histamine, receptor blockade
Peripheral ACh receptor blockade
Antidepressant efficacy
CNS toxicity
CVS toxicity
200
400
600
800
1000
1200
1400
TCA Concentration in Plasma (ng/ml)

FIGURE 35.3.31–3
Multiple concentration: response curves of tertiary amine tricyclic drugs. *ACh,* acetylcholine; *CNS,* central nervous system; *CVS,* cardiovascular system. (Reprinted with permission from Preskorn SH: *Clinical Pharmacology of Selective Serotonin Reuptake Inhibitors,* p 154. Professional Communications, Caddo, OK, 1996.)

effects with continued treatment. Amitriptyline, imipramine, trimipramine, and doxepin are the most anticholinergic drugs; amoxapine, nortriptyline, and maprotiline are less anticholinergic; and desipramine may be the least anticholinergic. Anticholinergic effects include dry mouth, constipation, blurred vision, and urinary retention. Sugarless gum, candy, or fluoride lozenges can alleviate the dry mouth. Bethanechol (Urecholine), 25 to 50 mg 3 or 4 times a day, may reduce urinary hesitancy and may be helpful in cases of impotence when the drug is taken 30 minutes before sexual intercourse. Narrow-angle glaucoma can also be aggravated by anticholinergic drugs, and the precipitation of glaucoma requires emergency treatment with a miotic agent. Tricyclic and tetracyclic drugs can be used in patients with narrow-angle glaucoma, provided pilocarpine eye drops are administered concurrently. Severe anticholinergic effects can lead to a CNS anticholinergic syndrome with confusion and delirium, especially if tricyclic and tetracyclic drugs are administered with antipsychotics or anticholinergic drugs. Some clinicians have used intramuscular or intravenous physostigmine (Antilirium) as a diagnostic tool to confirm the presence of anticholinergic delirium.

Sedation

Sedation is a common effect of tricyclic and tetracyclic drugs and may be welcomed if sleeplessness has been a problem. The sedative effect of tricyclic and tetracyclic drugs is a result of serotonergic, cholinergic, and histaminergic activities. Amitriptyline, trimipramine, and doxepin are the most sedating agents; imipramine, amoxapine, nortriptyline, and maprotiline have some sedating effects; and desipramine and protriptyline are the least sedating agents.

Autonomic Effects

The most common autonomic effect, partly because of α_1-adrenergic blockade, is orthostatic hypotension, which can result in falls and injuries in affected patients. Nortriptyline may be the drug least likely to cause the problem, and some patients respond to fludrocortisone (Florinef), 0.05 mg twice a day. Other possible autonomic effects are profuse sweating, palpitations, and increased blood pressure.

Cardiac Effects

When administered in their usual therapeutic dosages, the tricyclic and tetracyclic drugs may cause tachycardia, flattened T waves, prolonged QT intervals, and depressed ST segments on electrocardiograms (ECGs). Imipramine has a quinidine-like effect at therapeutic plasma concentrations and may reduce the number of premature ventricular contractions. Because the drugs prolong conduction time, their use in patients with preexisting conduction defects is contraindicated. In patients with cardiac histories, tricyclic and tetracyclic drugs should be initiated at low dosages, with gradual increases in dosage and monitoring of cardiac functions. At high plasma concentrations, as occur in overdoses, the drugs become arrhythmogenic. The agents should be discontinued several days before elective surgery because of the occurrence of hypertensive episodes during surgery in patients receiving tricyclic and tetracyclic drugs.

Neurological Effects

In addition to the sedation induced by tricyclics and tetracyclics and the possibility of anticholinergic-induced delirium, two tricyclics—desipramine and protriptyline—are associated with psychomotor stimulation. Myoclonic twitches and tremors of the tongue and the upper extremities are common. Rare effects include speech blockage, paresthesia, peroneal palsies, and ataxia.

Amoxapine is unique in causing parkinsonian symptoms, akathisia, and even dyskinesia because of the dopaminergic blocking activity of one of its metabolites. Amoxapine may also cause neuroleptic malignant syndrome in rare cases. Maprotiline may cause seizures when the dosage is increased too quickly or is kept at high levels for too long. Clomipramine and amoxapine may lower the seizure threshold more than do other drugs in the class. As a class, however, the tricyclic and tetracyclic drugs have a relatively low risk for inducing seizures, except in patients who are at risk for seizures (for example, patients with epilepsy or brain lesions). Although tricyclics and tetracyclics can still be used in such patients, the initial dosages should be lower than usual, and subsequent dosage increases should be gradual.

Allergic and Hematological Effects

Exanthematous skin rashes are seen in 4 to 5 percent of all patients treated with maprotiline. Jaundice is rare. Agranulocytosis, leukocytosis, leukopenia, and eosinophilia are rare complications of tetracyclic drug treatment. A patient who has a sore throat or a fever during the first few months of tricyclic and tetracyclic drug treatment, however, should have a complete blood count (CBC) done immediately.

Other Adverse Effects

Weight gain, primarily an effect of the blockade of histamine type 1 (H_1) receptors, is common. If weight gain is a major problem, changing to a different class of antidepressants may help. Impotence, an occasional problem, is perhaps most often associated with amoxapine because of the drug's blockade of dopamine receptors in the tuberoinfundibular tract. Amoxapine can also cause hyperprolactinemia, galactorrhea, anorgasmia, and ejaculatory disturbances. Other tricyclic and tetracyclic drugs have also been associated with gynecomastia and amenorrhea. Inappropriate secretion of antidiuretic hormone has also been reported with tricyclic and tetracyclic drugs. Other effects include nausea, vomiting, and hepatitis.

Precautions

The tricyclic and tetracyclic drugs should be avoided during pregnancy. The drugs pass into breast milk and have the potential to cause serious adverse reactions in nursing infants. A case series suggested, however, that clomipramine at therapeutic concentrations in women who are breast-feeding does not produce detectable concentrations in the infant. The drugs should be used with caution in patients with hepatic and renal diseases.

Tricyclics and tetracyclics should not be administered during a course of electroconvulsive therapy, primarily because of the risk of serious adverse cardiac effects.

Overdoses

Overdoses with tricyclic and tetracyclic drugs are serious and can often be fatal. Prescriptions for the drugs should be nonrefillable and for no longer than 1 week at a time for patients who are at risk for suicide attempts. Amoxapine may be more likely than are other tricyclic and tetracyclic drugs to result in death when taken in an overdose, but all drugs in the class can be lethal in an overdose.

Symptoms of an overdose include agitation, delirium, convulsions, hyperactive deep tendon reflexes, bowel and bladder paralysis, dysregulation of blood pressure and temperature, and mydriasis. The patient then progresses to coma and perhaps respiratory depression. Cardiac arrhythmias may not respond to treatment. Because of the long half-lives of tricyclic and tetracyclic drugs, patients are at risk for cardiac arrhythmias for 3 to 4 days after the overdose, so they should be monitored in an intensive care medical setting.

DRUG INTERACTIONS

Antihypertensives

Tricyclic and tetracyclic drugs block the neuronal reuptake of guanethidine (Ismelin), which is required for antihypertensive activity. The antihypertensive effects of β-adrenergic receptor antagonists (for example, propranolol [Inderal]) and clonidine [Catapres] may also be blocked by tricyclic and tetracyclic drugs. The coadministration of a tricyclic or tetracyclic drug and methyldopa (Aldomet) may cause behavioral agitation.

Antipsychotics

The plasma concentrations of tricyclic and tetracyclic drugs and antipsychotics are increased by their coadministration. Antipsychotics also add to the anticholinergic and sedative effects of the tricyclic and tetracyclic drugs.

Central Nervous System Depressants

Opiates, opioids, alcohol, anxiolytics, hypnotics, and over-the-counter cold medications have additive effects by causing CNS depression when coadministered with tricyclic or tetracyclic drugs.

Sympathomimetics

Tricyclic drug use with sympathomimetic drugs may cause serious cardiovascular effects.

Oral Contraceptives

Birth control pills may decrease tricyclic and tetracyclic drug plasma concentrations through the induction of hepatic enzymes.

Other Interactions

Tricyclic and tetracyclic drug plasma concentrations may also be increased by acetazolamide (Diamox), aspirin, cimetidine (Tagamet), thiazide diuretics, fluoxetine, and sodium bicarbonate. Decreased plasma concentrations may be caused by ascorbic acid, ammonium chloride, barbiturates, cigarette smoking, chloral hydrate, lithium (Eskalith), and primidone (Mysoline). Tricyclic drugs that are metabolized by CYP 2D6 may interfere with the metabolism of other drugs metabolized by the hepatic enzyme.

LABORATORY INTERFERENCES

Laboratory interferences with the tricyclic and tetracyclic drugs have not been reported.

DOSAGE AND ADMINISTRATION

The antidepressant effects of the tricyclic and tetracyclic drugs appear after 2 to 4 weeks of treatment.

Choice of Drug

The choice of which tricyclic or tetracyclic drug to use should be based on the general guidelines outlined in Section 35.3.1. All available tricyclic and tetracyclic drugs are equally effective in the treatment of depressive disorders. In the case of an individual patient, however, one tricyclic or tetracyclic drug may be effective, whereas another may be ineffective. The adverse effects among the tricyclic and tetracyclic drugs differ (Table 35.3.31–2). The tertiary amine tricyclics tend to produce more adverse effects—including sedation, orthostatic hypotension, and such anticholinergic effects as dry mouth—than do the secondary amines. Among the secondary amine tricyclics, nortriptyline is associated with the least orthostatic hypotension, and desipramine is associated with the least anticholinergic activity. Among the tetracyclic drugs, amoxapine is sometimes recommended for the treatment of a major depressive episode with psychotic features because of the drug's antidopaminergic activity.

Researchers have found differences among the tricyclics and the tetracyclics in their relative abilities to block either serotonin or norepinephrine reuptake. No study has found that the serotonin-to-norepinephrine ratio for each of the drugs can be used to help choose a specific drug to treat a particular patient. Switching from a strongly serotonergic drug to a strongly noradrenergic drug or from a strongly noradrenergic drug to a strongly serotonergic drug may be reasonable if the first drug is ineffective in relieving a patient's symptoms.

Clomipramine. Clomipramine is an effective antidepressant that is also useful in the treatment of obsessive-compulsive disorder and, therefore, may be a drug of choice for depressed patients with marked obsessive features. Clomipramine has its major effect as an inhibitor of serotonin reuptake but may also affect dopaminergic neurotransmission. Clomipramine is more effective than a placebo, amitriptyline, imipramine, and doxepin in the treatment of obsessive-compulsive disorder, although SSRIs are equally as effective, with fewer

Table 35.3.31–2
Side Effect Profile of Tricyclic and Tetracyclic Drugs

Drug	Anticholinergic Effects	Sedation	Orthostatic Hypotension	Seizures	Conduction Abnormalities
Tertiary amines					
Amitriptyline	++++	++++	+++	+++	++++
Doxepin	+++	++++	++	+++	++
Imipramine	+++	+++	++++	+++	++++
Trimipramine	++++	++++	+++	+++	++++
Secondary amines					
Desipramine	++	++	+++	++	+++
Nortriptyline	+++	+++	+	++	+++
Protriptyline	+++	+	++	++	++++
Tetracyclics					
Amoxapine	+++	++	+	+++	++
Maprotiline	+++	+++	++	++++	+++

++++, high; +++, moderate; ++, low; and +, very low.

adverse effects. Improvement is usually seen in 2 to 4 weeks, but a gradual improvement may continue for the first 4 to 5 months of treatment. Like the standard tricyclic and tetracyclic drugs, clomipramine may also be effective in the treatment of panic disorder, phobias, and pain disorder.

Initiation of Treatment

A routine physical and laboratory examination should be conducted for patients receiving a tricyclic or a tetracyclic. The routine laboratory tests should include a CBC, a white blood cell count with differential, and serum electrolytes (sequential multichannel autoanalyzer [SMA]-6) with liver function tests (SMA-12). An ECG should probably be obtained for all patients, especially women over 40 and men over 30. The initial dose of the drug should be low and gradually raised. Clinicians can more quickly raise the dosage for inpatients who have close clinical supervision than for outpatients.

Clinicians should explain to patients that although sleep patterns and appetite may improve in 1 to 2 weeks, tricyclics and tetracyclics usually take 3 to 4 weeks to have significant antidepressant effects and a complete trial should last 6 weeks. Clinicians may also explain to patients the exact drug treatment plan if no clinical response is seen after 6 weeks.

Older adults and children are more sensitive to antidepressant side effects than are younger adults. In children, ECG monitoring is needed. A baseline electroencephalogram (EEG) is recommended, as children are sensitive to the epileptogenic effects of antidepressants and are prone to medication-induced constipation.

Dosage

The available preparations of tricyclic and tetracyclic drugs are presented in Table 35.3.31–3.

Depressive Disorders. The dosage schedule for the tricyclics and tetracyclics varies among the drugs (Table 35.3.31–4). Imipramine, amitriptyline, doxepin, desipramine, clomipramine, and trimipramine can be started at 75 mg a day. Divided doses at first reduce the severity of adverse effects, although most of the dosage should be given at night to help induce sleep if a sedating drug, such as amitriptyline, is used. Eventually, the entire daily dose can be given at bedtime. Protriptyline and less-sedating drugs should be given at least 2 to 3 hours before a patient goes to sleep. For outpatients the dosage can be raised to 150 mg a day the second week, 225 mg

Table 35.3.31–3
Tricyclic and Tetracyclic Drug Preparations

Drug	Tablets	Capsules	Parenteral	Solution
Imipramine	10, 25, 50 mg	75, 100, 125, 150 mg	12.5 mg/mL	—
Desipramine	10, 25, 50, 75, 100, 150 mg	—	—	—
Trimipramine	—	25, 50, 100 mg	—	—
Amitriptyline	10, 25, 50, 75, 100, 150 mg	—	10 mg/mL	—
Nortriptyline	—	10, 25, 50, 75 mg	—	10 mg/5 mL
Protriptyline	5, 10 mg	—	—	—
Amoxapine	25, 50, 100, 150 mg	—	—	—
Doxepin	—	10, 25, 50, 75, 100, 150 mg	—	10 mg/mL
Maprotiline	25, 50, 75 mg	—	—	—
Clomipramine	—	25, 50, 75 mg	—	—

Table 35.3.31–4
Clinical Information for the Tricyclic and Tetracyclic Drugs

Generic Name	Trade Name	Usual Adult Dosage Range (mg a day)	Therapeutic Plasma Concentrations[a] (ng/mL)
Imipramine	Tofranil	150–300[b]	150–300
Desipramine	Norpramin	150–300[b]	150–300
Trimipramine	Surmontil	150–200	?[c]
Amitriptyline	Elavil	150–300[b]	100–250[b]
Nortriptyline	Pamelor, Aventyl	50–150	50–150 (maximum)
Protriptyline	Vivactil	15–60	75–250
Amoxapine	Asendin	150–400	?[c]
Doxepin	Adapin, Sinequan	150–300[b]	100–250
Maprotiline	Ludiomil	150–225	150–300
Clomipramine	Anafranil	150–250	?[a]

[a] Exact range may vary among laboratories.
[b] Includes parent compound and desmethyl metabolite.
[c] ?, not clinically useful.

a day the third week, and 300 mg a day the fourth week. A common clinical mistake is to stop increasing the dosage when a patient is taking less than 250 mg a day and does not show clinical improvement. Doing so can result in a further delay in obtaining a therapeutic response, disenchantment with the treatment, and premature discontinuation of the drug. A clinician should routinely assess the patient's pulse and orthostatic changes in blood pressure while the dosage is being increased.

Nortriptyline should be started at 50 mg a day and raised to 150 mg a day over 3 or 4 weeks unless a response occurs at a lower dosage, such as at 100 mg a day. Amoxapine should be started at 150 mg a day and raised to 400 mg a day. Protriptyline should be started at 15 mg a day and raised to 60 mg a day. Maprotiline has been associated with an increased incidence of seizures if the dosage is raised too quickly or is maintained at too high a level; the drug should, therefore, be started at 75 mg a day and maintained at this level for 2 weeks. The dosage can be increased over 4 weeks to 225 mg a day but should be kept at this level for only 6 weeks and then reduced to 175 to 200 mg a day.

Pain Disorder. Patients with pain disorder may be particularly sensitive to adverse effects when tricyclics or tetracyclics are started. Therefore, it may be prudent to begin with low dosages that are raised in small increments. Some clinicians coadminister benzodiazepines until patients are stabilized on an antidepressant.

Children. In children, imipramine can be initiated at 1.5 mg/kg a day. The dosage can be titrated to no more than 5 mg/kg a day. In enuresis the dosage is usually 50 to 100 mg a day taken at bedtime. Clomipramine can be initiated at 50 mg a day and increased to no more than 3 mg/kg a day or 200 mg a day.

Failure of Drug Trial and Treatment-Resistant Depression

If a tricyclic or a tetracyclic has been used for 4 weeks at maximal dosages without a therapeutic effect, the clinician should obtain a plasma concentration and adjust the dosage accordingly. If plasma concentrations are adequate, supplementation with lithium or liothyronine (T_3) (Cytomel) should be considered. Alternatively, an SSRI or other antidepressant can be substituted.

Lithium. Lithium (900 to 1,200 mg a day, serum concentration between 0.6 and 0.8 mEq/L) can be added to the tricyclic or tetracyclic dosage for 7 to 14 days. This approach converts a significant number of nonresponders into responders. The mechanism of action is unknown, but the lithium may potentiate the serotonergic neuronal system.

Liothyronine. The addition of 25 to 50 mg a day of T_3 to the regimen for 7 to 14 days may convert a tricyclic or tetracyclic nonresponder into a responder. The mechanism of action for T_3 augmentation is unknown. Empirical data indicate that T_3 is more effective than thyroxine (T_4) as an adjunct to tricyclic and tetracyclic drugs. If T_3 augmentation is successful, the T_3 should be continued for 2 months and then tapered at the rate of 12.5 μg a day every 3 to 7 days.

Monoamine Oxidase Inhibitors (MAOIs). MAOIs should be discontinued for 2 weeks before initiating treatment with a tricyclic or a tetracyclic. A minimum of a 1-week washout is needed when switching from a tricyclic or tetracyclic to an MAOI.

Termination of Short-Term Treatment

Tricyclics and tetracyclics effectively resolve the acute symptoms of depression. If treatment is stopped prematurely, symptom reemergence is likely to occur. To minimize the risk for recurrence or relapse, clinicians should continue the tricyclic or the tetracyclic at the same treatment dosage throughout the course of treatment. When treatment is discontinued, clinicians may reasonably reduce the dosage to three-fourths maximal dosage for another month. At this time, if no symptoms are present, the drug can be tapered by 25 mg (5 mg for protriptyline) every 2 to 3 days. The slow tapering process is indicated for most psychotherapeutic drugs; in the case of most tricyclics and tetracyclics, slow tapering avoids a cholinergic rebound syndrome, consisting of nausea, upset stomach, sweating, headache, neck pain, and vomiting. The appearance of this syndrome can be treated by reinstituting a small dosage of the drug and tapering more slowly than before. Several case reports note the appearance of rebound mania or hypomania after the abrupt discontinuation of tricyclic and tetracyclic drugs. If a patient has been treated with lithium augmentation, the clinician should probably taper and stop the lithium first and then the tricyclic or tetracyclic drug. But clinical studies supporting this approach are lacking, and the guidelines may change as more physicians report their experience with the drug combination.

Maintenance

Tricyclics and tetracyclics are effective in preventing the recurrence of major depressive episodes. The decision to institute prophylactic treatment is based on the severity and nature of the disorder in a particular patient, but increasing data argue for prophylactic treatment in patients with major depressive disorder. Conversely, some data indicate that the long-term use of antidepressants may induce a rapid-cycling bipolar I disorder. Lithium prophylaxis, therefore, has been suggested as an alternative treatment in selected patients who have frequent, episodic, and serious depressive episodes.

Several investigators have noted that neuroendocrine tests may be a guide for deciding when to maintain the use of tricyclics, tetracyclics, and other antidepressant drugs. Specifically, investigators note that the normalization of a previously abnormal result in a dexamethasone-suppression test or a thyrotropin-releasing hormone (TRH) stimulation test may indicate that a patient can safely discontinue drug treatment. This use of neuroendocrine testing and monitoring is still in the research phases of development.

Plasma Concentrations

Research has defined the dose–response curves for several tricyclic and tetracyclic drugs when they are given to treat depressive disorders. Clinical determinations of plasma concentrations should be conducted 8 to 12 hours after the last dose and after 5 to 7 days on the same dosage of medication. Because of variations in absorption and metabolism, there is a 30- to 50-fold difference in the plasma concentrations in humans given the same dosage of a tricyclic or tetracyclic drug. The therapeutic ranges for plasma concentrations have been determined (Table 35.3.31–4). Nortriptyline is unique in its association with a therapeutic window; that is, plasma concentrations of more than 150 ng/mL may reduce its efficacy. Clinicians must follow the directions for collection from the testing laboratory and have confidence in the assay procedure used at a particular laboratory.

The use of plasma concentrations in clinical practice is still an evolving skill. Plasma concentrations may be useful in confirming compliance, assessing reasons for drug failures, and documenting effective plasma concentrations for future treatment. Clinicians should always treat the patient and never the plasma concentration. Some patients have adequate clinical responses with seemingly subtherapeutic plasma concentrations, and other patients have responses only at supratherapeutic plasma concentrations without experiencing adverse effects. The latter situation, however, should alert clinicians to monitor patients' condition with, for example, serial ECGs.

References

Albers LJ, Reist C, Helmeste D, Vu R, et al: Paroxetine shifts imipramine metabolism. Psychiatry Res *59* (3): 189, 1995.

Buysee DJ, Reynolds CF III, Hoch CG, Houck PR, et al: Longitudinal effects of nortriptyline on EEG sleep and the likelihood of recurrence in elderly depressed patients. Neuropsychopharmacology *14* (4): 243, 1996.

Dahl M-L, Bertilsson L, Nordin C: Steady-state plasma levels of nortriptyline and its 10-hydroxy metabolite: Relationship to the CYP2D6 genotype. Psychopharmacology *123* (4): 315, 1996.

Freeman EW, Rickels K, Sondheimer SJ, Wittmaack FM: Sertraline versus desipramine in the treatment of premenstrual syndrome: An open-label trial. J Clin Psychiatry *57* (1): 7, 1996.

Greil W, Ludwig-Mayerhofer W, Erazo N, Engel RR, et al: Comparative efficacy of lithium and amitriptyline in the maintenance treatment of recurrent unipolar depression: A randomized study. J Affect Disord *40* (3): 179, 1996.

Hotopf M, Lewis G, Normand C: Are SSRIs a cost-effective alternative to tricyclics? Br J Psychiatry *168* (4): 404, 1996.

Johnson A, Giuffre RM, O'Malley K: ECG changes in pediatric patients on tricyclic antidepressants, desipramine, and imipramine. Can J Psychiatry *41* (2): 102, 1996.

Kamath M, Finkel SI, Moran B: A retrospective chart review of antidepressant use, effectiveness, and adverse effects in adults age 70 and older. Am J Geriatr Psychiatry *4:* 167, 1996.

Keller MB, Harrison W, Fawcett JA, Gelenberg A, et al: Mood disorders. Psychopharmacol Bull *31:* 205, 1995.

Kin NMK, Ng Y, Klitgaard N, Nair NPV, Amin M, et al: Clinical relevance of serum nortriptyline and 10-hydroxy-nortriptyline measurements in the depressed elderly: A multicenter pharmacokinetic and pharmacodynamic study. Neuropsychopharmacology *15* (1): 1, 1996.

Kocsis JH, Friedman RA, Markowitz JC, Leon AC, et al: Maintenance therapy for chronic depression: A controlled clinical trial of desipramine. Arch Gen Psychiatry *53* (9) 769, 1996.

Kocsis JH, Friedman RA, Markowitz JC, Miller N, et al: Stability of remission during tricyclic antidepressant continuation therapy for dysthymia. Psychopharmacol Bull *31:* 213, 1995.

Kuhs H, Farber D, Borgstadt S, Mrosek S, et al: Amitriptyline in combination with repeated late sleep deprivation versus amitriptyline alone in major depression. A randomized study. J Affect Disord *37* (1): 31, 1996.

Kye CH, Waterman GS, Ryan ND, Birmaher B, et al: A randomized, controlled trial of amitriptyline in the acute treatment of adolescent major depression. J Am Acad Child Adolesc Psychiatry *35* (9): 1139, 1996.

Leonard BE: Tricyclic antidepressants: Effective, cheap but are they safe? J Psychopharmacol *10* (1, Suppl): 35, 1996.

McGrath PJ, Nunes EV, Steward JW, Goldman D, et al: Imipramine treatment of alcoholics with primary depression: A placebo-controlled clinical trial. Arch Gen Psychiatry *53* (3): 232, 1996.

Miller FT, Freilicher J: Comparison of TCAs and SSRIs in the treatment of major depression in hospitalized geriatric patients. J Geriat Psychiatry Neurol *8:* 173, 1995.

Moller H-J, Kasper S, Muller H, Kissling W, et al: A controlled study of the efficacy and safety of mianserin and Amitriptyline in depressive inpatients. Pharmacopsychiatry *28* (6): 249, 1995.

Mullin J, Lodge A, Bennie E, McCreadie R, et al: A multicentre, double-blind, amitriptyline controlled study of mirtazapine in patients with major depression. J Psychopharmacol *10* (3): 235, 1996.

Oesterheld J: TCA cardiotoxicity: The latest. J Am Acad Child Adolesc Psychiatry *35* (6): 701, 1996.

Popper CW, Zimnitzky B: Sudden death putatively related to desipramine treatment in youth: A fifth case and a review of speculative mechanisms. J Child Adolesc Psychopharmacol *5* (4): 283, 1995.

Sanchez LE, Campbell M, Small AM, Cueva JE, et al: A pilot study of clomipramine in young autistic children. J Am Acad Child Adolesc Psychiatry *35* (4): 537, 1996.

Thase ME, Fava M, Halbreich U, Kocsis JH, et al: A placebo-controlled, randomized clinical trial comparing sertraline and imipramine for the treatment of dysthymia. Arch Gen Psychiatry *53* (9): 777, 1996.

Tollefson GD, Holman SL, Sayler ME, Potvin JH: Fluoxetine, placebo, and tricyclic antidepressants in major depression with and without anxious features. J Clin Psychiatry Monog Ser *13* (2): 13, 1995.

▲ 35.3.32 L-Tryptophan

L-Tryptophan is an essential amino acid and the amino acid precursor of the neurotransmitter serotonin. L-Tryptophan administration to humans results in increased concentrations of serotonin in the central nervous system (CNS). This pharmacological effect led to the use of orally administered L-tryptophan as a hypnotic and as an adjuvant to antidepressant treatment. Several experimental paradigms in animals and certain patient populations have shown that dietary depletion of tryptophan creates hunger and exacerbates hostile and agitated behavior, whereas tryptophan supplementations may relieve anxiety and increase the sense of well-being.

In 1989, L-tryptophan and L-tryptophan-containing products were recalled in the United States because of an outbreak of eosinophilia-myalgia syndrome associated with these products.

CHEMISTRY

The molecular structure of L-tryptophan is shown in Figure 35.3.32–1.

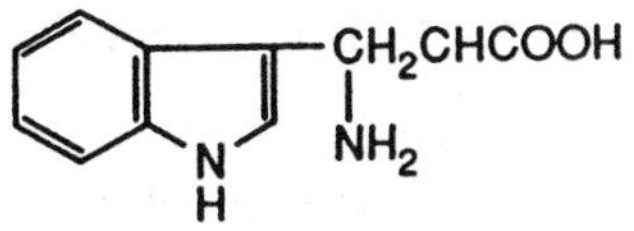

CH2CHCOOH
NH2
N
H

FIGURE 35.3.32–1
Molecular structure of L-tryptophan.

PHARMACOLOGICAL ACTIONS

Pharmacokinetics

L-Tryptophan is erratically absorbed from the gastrointestinal (GI) tract. A significant portion of the drug is metabolized by the liver in a first-pass effect. Absorption of L-tryptophan can be enhanced by taking the drug at least 3 hours after ingestion of food. The half-life of L-tryptophan may be as little as 1 to 2 hours; therefore, unless the drug is used as a hypnotic, 4-times-daily dosing is necessary to maintain plasma levels.

Pharmacodynamics

L-Tryptophan has its effects because a portion of the ingested dose crosses the blood–brain barrier, is taken up by serotonergic neurons, is converted into serotonin, and thus raises serotonin concentrations in the CNS.

EFFECTS ON SPECIFIC ORGANS AND SYSTEMS

Other than the CNS, the major organ system affected by L-tryptophan is the GI system, which contains a high concentration of serotonin. The effects of L-tryptophan on the GI system are usually limited to mild GI distress.

THERAPEUTIC INDICATIONS

Primary Insomnia

The most common indication for L-tryptophan is insomnia. Whether the hypnotic effects of L-tryptophan persist with long-term treatment is uncertain. L-Tryptophan is not associated with visuospatial, cognitive, or memory deficits the day after drug ingestion, as are many of the standard hypnotic agents. Low doses of L-tryptophan are not associated with any change in the sleep electroencephalogram other than earlier-than-usual sleep onset; high doses of L-tryptophan are associated with increases in slow-wave sleep.

Antidepressant Adjuvant Treatment

L-Tryptophan has been used as an adjuvant to tricyclic and tetracyclic drug administration for depressed patients who have not responded to a tricyclic or tetracyclic drug alone. The use of either lithium (Eskalith) or liothyronine (Cytomel) adjuvant therapy with antidepressant nonresponders was more commonly used than was L-tryptophan supplementation when L-tryptophan was still available. L-Tryptophan has also been used as an adjuvant to lithium treatment for patients with bipolar I disorder who had incomplete symptom remission with lithium treatment alone.

Other Indications

L-Tryptophan has been studied as a treatment for obesity, aggression, and obsessive-compulsive disorder. Dietary depletion of L-tryptophan has been proposed as a treatment for anorexia nervosa and bulimia nervosa, but the adverse behavioral complications of this diet, with no obvious benefit, have indicated that such interventions have no role in these disorders.

PRECAUTIONS AND ADVERSE REACTIONS

Except for experiencing eosinophilia-myalgia syndrome, most patients tolerate moderate doses of L-tryptophan. The only significant adverse effect reported is nausea, which is sometimes compared to the nausea associated with pregnancy. L-Tryptophan has also been associated with hepatotoxicity in rare cases. Other adverse effects include muscle pain, dry mouth, ataxia, and tremor.

Eosinophilia-Myalgia Syndrome

The symptoms of eosinophilia-myalgia syndrome include fatigue, myalgia, arthralgia, shortness of breath, rashes, fever, neuropathy, and swelling of the extremities. Congestive heart failure and death can occur. The syndrome was related to a contaminant in a single manufacturing plant. This compound, 1,1′-ethylidene-*bis*-tryptophan, stimulated an acute phase reaction, including the release of cytokines. Although no other manufacturers of L-tryptophan failed to purify the drug and eliminate this contaminant, remaining concerns about protecting against the contaminant have slowed the reintroduction of L-tryptophan in the United States market. Recent reports have raised the possibility that eosinophilia-myalgia syndrome may be due to L-tryptophan itself.

DRUG INTERACTIONS

L-Tryptophan should not be coadministered with serotonin reuptake inhibitors (for example, fluoxetine [Prozac] and clomipramine [Anafranil]) or monoamine oxidase inhibitors. These combinations can result in a syndrome related to serotonin excess and characterized by diarrhea, insomnia, nausea, headaches, chills, agitation, and poor concentration.

LABORATORY INTERFERENCES

No laboratory interferences have been associated with the administration of L-tryptophan.

DOSAGE AND ADMINISTRATION

L-Tryptophan is currently not available in the United States. When it was used as a hypnotic, the dosage ranged from 1 to 7.5 grams taken at bedtime. The use of L-tryptophan as an adjuvant to antidepressant treatment was often in the range of 3 to 6 grams a day in divided doses.

REFERENCES

Adachi J, Naito T, Ueno Y, Ogawa Y, Ninomiya I, Tatsuno Y: Metabolism and distribution in the rat of peak-E substance, a constituent in L-tryptophan product implicated in eosinophilia-myalgia syndrome. Arch Toxicol *67:* 284, 1993.

Cleare AJ, Bond AJ: Effects of alterations in plasma tryptophan levels on aggressive feelings. Arch Gen Psychiatry *51:* 1004, 1994.

Cleare AJ, Bond AJ: The effect of tryptophan depletion and enhancement on subjective and behavioural aggression in normal male subjects. Psychopharmacology *118:* 72, 1995.

Cowen PJ: The effect of tryptophan on brain 5-HT function: A review. Hum Psychopharmacol *9:* 371, 1994.

Flannery MT, Wallach PM, Espinoza LR, Dohrenwend MP, Moscisnski LC: A case of eosinophilia-myalgia syndrome associated with the use of an L-tryptophan product. Ann Intern Med *112:* 300, 1990.

Hajak G, Huenther G, Blanket J, Blomer M, Freyer C, Poeggeler B, Reimer A, Rodenbeck A, Schulz-Varszegi M, Ruther E: The influence of intravenous L-tryptophan on plasma melatonin and sleep in men. Pharmacopsychiatry *24:* 17, 1991.

Kamb ML, Murphy JJ, Jones JL, Caston JL: Eosinophilia-myalgia syndrome in L-tryptophan-exposed patients. JAMA *267:* 77, 1992.

Lam RW, Zis AP, Grewal A, Delgado PL, et al: Effects of rapid tryptophan depletion in patients with seasonal affective disorder in remission after light therapy. Arch Gen Psychiatry *53* (1): 41, 1996.

Lucini V, Lucca A, Catalano M, Smeraldi E: Predictive value of tryptophan/large neutral amino acids ration to antidepressant response. J Affect Disord *36* (3): 129, 1996.

Maes M, Scharpe S, Verkerk R, D'Hondt P, et al: Seasonal variation in plasma L-tryptophan availability in healthy volunteers: Relationships to violent suicide occurrence. Arch Gen Psychiatry *52* (11): 937, 1995.

Maes M, Vandewoude M, Schotte C, Martin M, D'Hondt P, Scharpe S, Block P: The decreased availability of L-tryptophan in depressed females: Clinical and biological correlates. Prog Neuropsychopharmacol Biol Psychiatry *14:* 903, 1990.

Satel SL, Krystal JH, Delgado P: Tryptophan depletion and attenuation of cue-induced craving for cocaine. Am J Psychiatry *152:* 778, 1995.

Steinberg S, Annable L, Young SN, Belanger M-C, et al: Tryptophan in the treatment of late luteal phase dysphoric disorder: A pilot study. J Psychiatry Neurosci *19* (2): 114, 1994.

Villanova M, Declerck LS, Cras P, Ceuterick C, Vanmarck E, Guazzi GC, Martin JJ: Eosinophilia-myalgia syndrome—a clinicopathological study of 4 patients. Clin Neuropathol *12:* 201, 1993.

Zajecka JM, Fawcett J: Antidepressant combination and potentiation. Psychiatr Med *9:* 55, 1991.

▲ 35.3.33 Valproate

Valproate (Depakene), also called valproic acid (because it is rapidly converted to the acid form in the stomach) and divalproex (Depakote), was first recognized as an effective antiepileptic drug in 1963 in France and was approved for use in certain types of epilepsy in the United States in 1978. Since then, valproate has been shown to be effective for absence seizures, generalized epilepsy, and partial epilepsy with or without secondary generalization, and for prophylaxis against migraine headaches. In addition, valproate and two other anticonvulsant drugs, carbamazepine (Tegretol) and clonazepam (Klonopin), have been shown to be effective in treating bipolar I disorder. Commercially available antiepileptic drugs that are being studied for treatment of rapid-cycling bipolar disorder include gabapentin (Neurontin), lamotrigine (Lamictal), vigabatrin (Sabril), tiagabine (Gabitril), and topiramate (Topamax). Among the investigational anticonvulsants that may eventually be studied for use in bipolar disorder are oxcarbazepine, losigamone, progabide, remacemide, stiripentol, and zonisamide. Although lithium (Eskalith) is still the most widely used drug in the treatment of bipolar I disorder, many clinicians consider valproate equal in efficacy and safety.

CHEMISTRY

The molecular structure of valproic acid is shown in Figure 35.3.33–1. Valproic acid is a simple, branched-chain, carboxylic *n*-dipropylacetic acid.

PHARMACOLOGICAL ACTIONS

Pharmacokinetics

When a formulation containing sodium valproate is ingested, the drug is converted into valproic acid in the stomach. Some formulations contain valproic acid itself, which is readily and almost completely absorbed from the gastrointestinal (GI) tract. Peak plasma concentrations vary, depending on the preparation (Table 35.3.33–1) and whether food is ingested with the drug. The ingestion of food with the drug delays the drug's absorption but does not affect the ultimate amount of drug absorbed. The half-life of valproate is about 8 to 17 hours; 3-times-daily dosing is necessary to maintain stable plasma concentrations, although sustained-release preparations are now available (for example, divalproex sodium). Valproate is metabolized by the liver, and some of its metabolites are also effective as antiepileptic agents. When given concurrently with phenobarbital in certain pediatric patients with otherwise subclinical inborn variants of metabolism, some valproate metabolites may cause metabolic encephalopathy or coma.

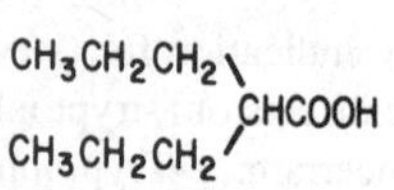

CH3CH2CH2
CHCOOH
CH3CH2CH2

FIGURE 35.3.33–1
Molecular structure of valproic acid.

Table 35.3.33–1
Valproate Preparations Available in the United States

Generic Name	Trade Name, Form (doses)	Time to Peak Serum Concentration
Valproic acid	Depakene, capsules (250 mg)	1–2 hr
Sodium valproate	Depakene, syrup (250 mg/5 mL)	1–2 hr
Divalproex sodium	Depakote, delayed-release tablets (125, 250, 500 mg)	3–8 hr
Divalproex sodium coated particles in capsules	Depakote, sprinkle capsules (125 mg)	Compared with divalproex tablets, divalproex sprinkle has earlier onset and slower rate of absorption, with slightly lower peak plasma concentrations
Valproate sodium injection	Depacon, IV (100 mg/mL)	Immediate

Pharmacodynamics

The therapeutic effects of valproate in both epilepsy and bipolar I disorder may be mediated by the effects of the drug on γ-aminobutyric acid (GABA), an inhibitory amino acid neurotransmitter. GABA receptor activation serves to reduce neuronal excitability, and the GABA system is a site of action of many antiepileptic drugs. In preclinical studies, valproate has both increased and decreased the synthesis of GABA. Valproate may also enhance the postsynaptic effects of GABA through poorly understood mechanisms. Although a precise role for GABA in the pathophysiology of mood disorders has not been defined, GABA may act directly or by regulating the activities of the biogenic amine neurotransmitters (for example, serotonin) or by affecting other central nervous system (CNS) mechanisms (for example, the control of circadian rhythms).

EFFECTS ON SPECIFIC ORGANS AND SYSTEMS

Although the principal effects of valproate are on the CNS, the drug also affects the GI and hematopoietic systems. The effects on the GI system lead both to common adverse effects (for example, nausea) and to serious but rare effects (for example, fatal hepatotoxicity).

THERAPEUTIC INDICATIONS

Bipolar I Disorder

About seven well-controlled but small studies have shown that valproate is effective in the treatment of acute mania. The benefit may appear within 1 to 2 weeks. Case reports suggest that the acute antimanic effects may be augmented by lithium, carbamazepine, dopamine receptor antagonists, clozapine (Clozaril), and gabapentin. Data from uncontrolled studies support the hypothesis that valproate is effective in the prophylactic treatment of bipolar I disorder. Specifically, patients who were treated with valproate had fewer, less severe, and shorter manic episodes while taking valproate than when they were not taking the drug prophylactically. Some available data from both uncontrolled and controlled studies have reported that valproate may be particularly effective in patients with rapid-cycling bipolar I disorder, dysphoric or mixed mania, and mania due to a general medical condition and in patients who have not had completely favorable responses to lithium treatment. Additional data from case reports indicate that valproate can be used effectively in combination with lithium or carbamazepine in patients who do not respond sufficiently to a treatment regimen with a single drug. The data are less supportive of the use of valproate alone for the short-term treatment of depressive episodes in bipolar I disorder, although the data from open-label studies support the conclusion that valproate is effective in the prophylactic treatment of depressive episodes in patients with bipolar I disorder. Many authorities consider valproate to be a first-line antimanic agent for all ages, except children below the age of 10 years, because of its potential hepatotoxicity in this age group. A comparison of the use of lithium, valproate, and carbamazepine in bipolar disorder is presented in Table 35.3.33–2.

Schizoaffective Disorder

Although no controlled studies of valproate in schizoaffective disorder have been conducted, data from uncontrolled studies and case reports support the conclusion that valproate is effective in treating the short-term phase of the bipolar type of schizoaffective disorder. Some data, however, indicate that valproate is less effective in schizoaffective disorder than in bipolar I disorder. The efficacy of valproate for schizoaffective disorder may be increased by augmentation with lithium, carbamazepine, dopamine receptor antagonists, or serotonin-dopamine antagonists.

Panic Disorder

Case reports and one of two controlled trials have shown valproate to be superior to placebo for treatment of panic disorder. Further studies are needed for this indication.

Other Mental Disorders

Preliminary reports note the therapeutic efficacy of valproate in other mental disorders, including major depressive disorder, posttraumatic stress disorder, bulimia nervosa, obses-

Table 35.3.33–2
Comparison of Lithium, Valproic Acid, and Carbamazepine for Bipolar I Disorder

	Lithium (Cibalith-S, Eskalith, Lithane, Lithobid, Lithonate, Lithotabs)	Valproic Acid (Depakene, Depakote)	Carbamazepine (Epitol, Tegretol)
Serum plasma levels	0.6–1.2 mEq/L (acute)	50–100 μg/mL	4–12 μg/mL
Usual adult daily dosage	600–1800 mg/day	750–4200 mg/day	400–1600 mg/day
Onset of action	5–14 days	5–15 days	3–15 days
Protein binding	Not bound to plasma proteins	90% concentration dependent ↓ with high concentration (variable due to saturation)	76%
$t_{1/2}$	24 h (average) Increases with age and/or with decreased renal function	6–16 hours (average) Increases with age and/or decreased hepatic function	Initial range 25–65 hours; with repeated dosing, 12–17 hours; 10,11-epoxide (active), approximately 5–8 hours
Metabolic pathway(s)	Not metabolized, primarily excreted unchanged in urine	Hepatic (glucuronidation, mitochondrial B oxidation, microsomal oxidation)	Hepatic: CYP 3A, possibly 2D6
Route(s) of elimination	Renal	Renal, glucuronidation	Renal (72%), fecal (28%)
Common drug interactions	↑ Lithium serum concentrations (fluoxetine, ACE inhibitors, diuretics, NSAIDs) ↓ Lithium serum concentrations (acetazolamide, osmotic diuretics, theophylline, urinary alkalinizers) Antipsychotics may increase lithium neurotoxicity	Interacts with many drugs that are hepatically metabolized; enzyme inducers can decrease concentrations of valproic acid; valproic acid can increase phenobarbital by impairment of nonrenal clearance (severe CNS depression)	Interacts with drugs that are hepatically metabolized; shortens the half-life of certain drugs that are hepatically metabolized (eg, phenytoin, warfarin, doxycycline, theophylline); carbamazepine levels can be markedly decreased by phenobarbital, phenytoin, or primidone; valproic acid can cause an increase in 10,11-epoxide: parent drug ratio; carbamazepine reduces plasma levels of haloperidol and valproic acid
Common adverse effects	Nausea, vomiting, diarrhea, polyuria, polydipsia, tremor, hypothyroidism	GI distress, diplopia, sedation, tremor, edema, weight gain, alopecia, and thrombocytopenia	Dizziness, drowsiness, unsteadiness
Indication(s)	Manic episodes of bipolar disorder Bipolar disorder maintenance	Bipolar disorder, acute mania (and seizure disorders)	Bipolar disorder (and seizure disorders)

Reprinted with permission from Ereshefsky L, Overman GP, Karp JK: Current psychotropic dosing and monitoring guidelines. Prim Psychiatry *3:* 21, 1996.
ACE, angiotensin-converting enzyme; and NSAIDs, nonsteroidal anti-inflammatory drugs.

sive-compulsive disorder, chronic pain, movement disorders, behavioral agitation in children and in adults with dementia, borderline personality disorder, intermittent explosive disorder, and alcohol, sedative, hypnotic, or anxiolytic withdrawal. Although the data for these indications are limited, the use of valproate for patients who have not responded to other treatments may be indicated, although its use should be undertaken only after a thorough review of the most recent literature. The available data have led many researchers to conclude that valproate is not effective in the treatment of schizophrenia.

PRECAUTIONS AND ADVERSE REACTIONS

Valproate treatment is generally well tolerated and safe, although a range of common mild adverse effects and serious and rare adverse effects have been associated with valproate treatment. The common adverse effects associated with valproate are those affecting the GI system, such as nausea (25 percent of all patients treated), vomiting (5 percent of patients), and diarrhea. The GI effects are generally most common in the first month of treatment but are also common when the treatment is with valproic acid or sodium valproate rather than enteric-coated divalproex sodium, especially the sprinkle formulation. Some clinicians have also treated GI symptoms with histamine type 2 (H_2) receptor antagonists such as cimetidine (Tagamet). Other common adverse effects involve the nervous system, such as sedation, ataxia, dysarthria, and tremor. Valproate-induced tremor has been reported to respond well to treatment with β-adrenergic receptor antagonists. Treatment of the other neurological adverse effects usually requires lowering of the valproate dosage. Weight gain is a common adverse effect, especially in long-term treatment, and can best be addressed by recommending a combination of a reasonable diet and moderate exercise. Hair loss has been reported to occur in 5 to 10 percent of all patients treated; rare cases of complete loss of body hair have been reported. Some clinicians have recommended treatment of valproate-associated hair loss with vitamin supplements that contain zinc and selenium. Another adverse effect that may occur in 5 to 40 percent of patients is a persistent elevation in liver transaminases to 3 times the upper limit of normal. This effect is usually asymptomatic and resolves after discontinuation of the drug. Other rare adverse events include effects on the hematopoietic system, including thrombocytopenia and platelet dysfunction, occurring most commonly at high dosages and resulting in the prolongation of bleeding times. Overdoses of valproate can lead to coma and death. There are reports that valproate-induced coma can be successfully treated with naloxone (Narcan) and that hemodialysis and hemoperfusion can be useful in the treatment of valproate overdoses.

The two most serious adverse effects of valproate treatment involve the pancreas and the liver. Rare cases of pancreatitis have been reported; they occur most often in the first 6 months of treatment, and the condition occasionally results in death. The most attention has been paid to an association between valproate and fatal hepatotoxicity. A result of this focus has been the identification of risk factors, including young age (less than 2 years), the use of multiple anticonvulsants, and the presence of neurological disorders, especially inborn errors of metabolism, in addition to epilepsy. The rate of fatal hepatotoxicity in patients who have been treated with only valproate is 1.0 per 100,000 patients; only one patient over the age of 10 years has been reported to have died from fatal hepatotoxicity, and in this case, confounding factors may have contributed. Therefore, the risk of this adverse reaction in adult psychiatric patients seems to be extremely low. Nevertheless, if symptoms of malaise, anorexia, nausea and vomiting, edema, and abdominal pain occur in a patient treated with valproate, clinicians must consider the possibility of severe hepatotoxicity. A modest increase in liver function test results, however, does not correlate with the development of serious hepatotoxicity.

Valproate should not be used by pregnant or nursing women. The drug has been associated with neural tube defects (for example, spinal bifida) in about 1 to 2 percent of all women who took valproate during the first trimester of the pregnancy. If valproate must be continued throughout conception and pregnancy, the risk of neural tube defects can be minimized by the addition of folic acid of 1 to 4 mg a day. Valproate is contraindicated in nursing mothers because it is excreted in breast milk. Clinicians should not administer the drug to patients with hepatic diseases.

DRUG INTERACTIONS

Valproate is commonly coadministered with lithium, carbamazepine, and the antipsychotics. The only consistent drug interaction with lithium is the exacerbation of drug-induced tremors, which can usually be treated with β-adrenergic receptor antagonists or gabapentin. The combination of valproate and antipsychotics may result in increased sedation, as can be seen when valproate is added to any CNS depressant (for example, alcohol), and increased severity of extrapyramidal symptoms, which generally respond to treatment with the usual antiparkinsonian drugs. Early experience suggests that the combination of valproate and serotonin-dopamine antagonists is well tolerated, although coadministration of valproate and clozapine has been reported to increase sedation. The plasma concentrations of diazepam (Valium), amitriptyline (Elavil), nortriptyline (Pamelor), and phenobarbital (Luminal) may be increased when these drugs are coadministered with valproate; plasma concentrations of phenytoin (Dilantin) and desipramine (Norpramin) may be decreased when these drugs are combined with valproate. The plasma concentrations of valproate may be decreased when the drug is coadministered with carbamazepine and may be increased when coadministered with amitriptyline (Elavil) or fluoxetine (Prozac). Patients who are treated with anticoagulants (for example, aspirin and warfarin [Coumadin]) should also be monitored when valproate is initiated to assess the development of any undesired augmentation of the anticoagulation and antiplatelet effects.

LABORATORY INTERFERENCES

Valproate has been reported to cause an overestimation of serum free fatty acids in almost half of the patients tested. Valproate has also been reported to elevate urinary ketone estimations falsely and to result in falsely abnormal thyroid function test results.

DOSAGE AND ADMINISTRATION

Prior to administration of valproate, hepatic and pancreatic disease should be ruled out by a combination of clinical and laboratory evaluations. Valproate is available in a number of formulations and dosages (Table 35.3.33–1). It is best to initiate drug treatment gradually, so as to minimize the common adverse effects of nausea, vomiting, and sedation. The dose on the first day should be 250 mg administered with a meal. The dosage can be raised up to 250 mg orally 3 times daily over the course of 3 to 6 days. Plasma concentrations can be assessed in the morning before the first daily dose of the drug is administered. Therapeutic plasma concentrations for the control of seizures range between 50 to 100 μg/mL, although some physicians use 125 or even 150 μg/mL if the drug is well tolerated. It is reasonable to use the same range for the treatment of mental disorders; most of the controlled studies have used 50 to 100 μg/mL. Most patients attain therapeutic plasma concentrations on a dosage between 1,200 and 1,500 mg a day in divided doses. The mood-stabilizing effects of valproate appear between 5 and 15 days after initiation of treatment.

References

Bowden CL, Janicak PG, Orsulak P: Relation of serum valproate concentration to response in mania. Am J Psychiatry *153:* 765, 1996.

Bowden CL, Janicak PG, Orsulak P, Swann AC, et al: Relation of serum valproate concentration to response in mania. Am J Psychiatry *153* (6): 765, 1996.

Horne M, Lindley SE: Divalproex sodium in the treatment of aggressive behavior and dysphoria in patients with organic brain syndromes. J Clin Psychiatry *56:* 430, 1995.

Jacobsen FM: Low-dose valproate: A new treatment for cyclothymia, mild rapid cycling disorders, and premenstrual syndrome. J Clin Psychiatry *54:* 229, 1993.

Kando JC, Tohen M, Castillo J, Zarate CA Jr: The use of valproate in an elderly population with affective symptoms. J Clin Psychiatry *57* (6): 238, 1996.

Keck PE, McElroy SL, Tugrul KC, Bennett JA: Valproate oral loading in the treatment of acute mania. J Clin Psychiatric *54:* 305, 1993.

Lott AD, McElroy SL, Keys MA: Valproate in the treatment of behavioral agitation in elderly patients with dementia. J Neuropsychiatry Clin Neurosci 7 (3): 314, 1995.

Minuk GY, Rockman GE, German GB, Duerksen DR, et al: The use of sodium valproate in the treatment of alcoholism. J Addict Dis *14:* 67, 1995.

Stoll AL, Locke CA, Vuckovic A, Mayer PV: Lithium-associated cognitive and functional deficits reduced by a switch to divalproex sodium: A case series. J Clin Psychiatry *57* (8): 356, 1996.

West SA, Keck PE, McElroy SL, Strakowski SM, et al: Open trial of valproate in the treatment of adolescent mania. J Child Adolesc Psychopharmacol *4:* 263, 1994.

▲ 35.3.34 Yohimbine

Yohimbine (Yocon) is an α_2-adrenergic receptor antagonist that has been used as a treatment for both idiopathic and drug-induced male sexual dysfunction. The efficacy of the drug for this indication remains controversial.

CHEMISTRY

The molecular structure of the indoleaklylamine alkaloid yohimbine is shown in Figure 35.3.34–1. Yohimbine is derived from an alkaloid found in *Rubaceae* and related trees and in the *Rauwolfia serpentina* plant.

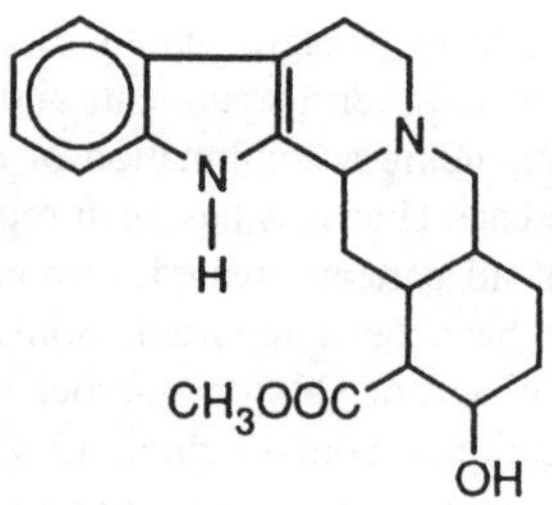
N
N
H
CH_3OOC
OH

FIGURE 35.3.34–1
Molecular structure of yohimbine.

PHARMACOLOGICAL ACTIONS

Pharmacokinetics

Yohimbine is erratically absorbed following oral administration, with bioavailability ranging from 7 to 87 percent. There is extensive hepatic first-pass metabolism. Reflecting yohimbine's effects on the sympathetic autonomic nervous system, one study found that the venous plasma concentration of norepinephrine increased threefold within 15 minutes of intravenous administration of yohimbine. The half-life of yohimbine is 0.5 to 2 hours, which necessitates multiple daily doses.

Pharmacodynamics

Yohimbine is an antagonist of α_2-adrenergic receptors located both presynaptically and postsynaptically on noradrenergic neurons. α_2-Adrenergic receptors are also located on the synaptic terminals of some serotonergic neurons. Stimulation of presynaptic α_2-adrenergic receptors results in a decrease in the release of neurotransmitters from the neuron; therefore, blockade of the receptors results in an increase in the release of neurotransmitters. Both norepinephrine and serotonin are involved in the physiology of the male sexual response.

EFFECTS ON SPECIFIC ORGANS AND SYSTEMS

Yohimbine primarily affects the peripheral nervous system through its effects on adrenergic neurotransmission. The peripheral nervous system effects influence vascular, cardiac, and gastrointestinal functions.

THERAPEUTIC INDICATIONS

In psychiatry, yohimbine has been used experimentally as a possible treatment for organic, psychogenic, and substance-induced erectile impotence and other male sexual dysfunctions. Its effects on male sexual performance are possibly related to its peripheral autonomic nervous system effects, although it is impossible to rule out central nervous system effects completely. Yohimbine, along with amantadine (Symmetrel) and cyproheptadine (Periactin), have been suggested as adjunct medications to counter the loss of libido often caused by antidepressant medications, especially those with potent serotonergic effects, such as the serotonin-specific reuptake inhibitors. Urologists have also used yohimbine for the diagnostic classification of certain types of male impotence.

PRECAUTIONS AND ADVERSE REACTIONS

The adverse effects of yohimbine include elevated blood pressure and heart rate, increased psychomotor activity, irritability, tremor, headache, skin flushing, dizziness, urinary frequency, nausea, vomiting, and perspiration. Patients with panic disorder show heightened sensitivity to yohimbine; they experience increased anxiety, a rise in blood pressure, and increased plasma 3-methoxy-4-hydroxyphenylglycol (MHPG), the major metabolite of norepinephrine. Yohimbine should not be used by female patients or by patients with renal disease, cardiac disease, glaucoma, or a history of gastric or duodenal ulcers.

DRUG INTERACTIONS

Yohimbine should not be used with clonidine (Catapres), an α_2-adrenergic receptor agonist, because the two drugs have mutually canceling pharmacodynamic effects.

LABORATORY INTERFERENCES

No known laboratory interferences are associated with the use of yohimbine.

DOSAGE AND ADMINISTRATION

Yohimbine acts within 15 minutes of oral administration. The dosage of yohimbine in the treatment of impotence is 2.7

to 5.4 mg 3 times a day. In the event of significant adverse effects, the dosage should first be reduced and then gradually increased. Yohimbine is available in 5.4 mg tablets.

References

Ashton AK: Yohimbine in the treatment of male erectile dysfunction. Am J Psychiatry *151* (9): 1397, 1994.

Cappiello A, McDougle CJ, Malison RT, Heninger GR, et al: Yohimbine augmentation of fluvoxamine in refractory depression: A single-blind study. Biol Psychiatry *38* (11): 765, 1995.

Gitlin MJ: Psychotropic medications and their effects on sexual function: Diagnosis, biology, and treatment approaches. J Clin Psychiatry *55:* 406, 1994.

Goddard AW, Charney DS, Germine M, Woods SW, et al: Effects of tryptophan depletion on responses to yohimbine in healthy human subjects. Biol Psychiatry *38* (2): 74, 1995.

Knoll LD, Benson RC Jr, Bilhartz DL, Minich PJ, Furlow WL: A randomized crossover study using yohimbine and isoxsuprine versus pentoxifylline in the management of vasculogenic impotence. J Urol *155:* 144, 1996.

Mann K, Klingler T, Noe S, Roschke J, et al: Effects of yohimbine on sexual experiences and nocturnal penile tumescence and rigidity in erectile dysfunction. Arch Sex Behav *25* (1): 1, 1996.

McDougle CJ, Krystal JH, Price LH, Heninger GR, et al: Noradrenergic response to acute ethanol administration in healthy subjects: Comparison with intravenous yohimbine. Psychopharmacology *118* (2): 127, 1995.

Morgan CA, Grillon C, Southwick SM, Nagy LM, et al: Yohimbine facilitated acoustic startle in combat veterans with post-traumatic stress disorder. Psychopharmacology *117:* 466, 1995.

Morgan CA, Southwick SM, Grillon C, Davis M, et al: Yohimbine—facilitated acoustic startle reflex in humans. Psychopharmacology *110* (3): 342, 1993.

Peskind ER, Wingerson D, Murray S, Pascualy M, et al: Effects of Alzheimer's disease and normal aging on cerebrospinal fluid norepinephrine response to yohimbine and clonidine. Arch Gen Psychiatry *52* (9): 774, 1995.

▲ 35.4 Electroconvulsive Therapy

Electroconvulsive therapy (ECT) is one of the most effective and least understood treatments in psychiatry. The technique and the associated anesthesiological interventions have been highly refined, so that ECT is considered a safe and effective treatment of patients with major depressive disorder, manic episodes, schizophrenia, and other serious mental disorders. In contrast to drug therapies, however, the convulsion-induced neurobiological modulations that are critical to the therapeutic success of ECT have not been isolated. Many clinicians and researchers believe that ECT is grossly underused as a treatment. The major reason for the underuse is hypothesized to be misconceptions and biases about ECT, at least partly fueled by widespread misinformation and inflammatory information in the media. Because ECT requires the use of electricity and the production of a seizure, many laypeople, patients, and patients' families are understandably frightened by the procedure. Many inaccurate reports have appeared in both professional and lay literature about alleged permanent brain damage resulting from ECT. Although these reports have largely been disproved, the specter of ECT-induced brain damage remains. ECT may relieve severe depression within 1 week, but the full benefit requires several treatments over a few weeks.

The decision to suggest ECT to a patient, like all treatment recommendations, should be based on both the treatment options available to the patient and the risk–benefit considerations. The major alternatives to ECT are usually pharmacotherapy and psychotherapy; both have their own risks and benefits. ECT has been shown to be a safe and effective treatment.

HISTORY

Although camphor-induced seizures were used as early as the 16th century to treat psychosis, most histories of ECT start in 1934, when Ladislas J. von Meduna reported the successful treatment of catatonia and other schizophrenic symptoms with pharmacologically induced seizures. Von Meduna began by using intramuscular injections of camphor suspended in oil but quickly switched to intravenously administered pentylenetetrazol. Von Meduna attempted the treatment method on the basis of two observations: First, schizophrenic symptoms often decrease after a seizure; seizures were often accidentally or iatrogenically induced in psychiatric patients secondary to withdrawal from medications (for example, barbiturates). Second, schizophrenia and epilepsy, it was incorrectly believed, cannot coexist in the same patient; therefore, the induction of seizures might rid patients of schizophrenia. Pentylenetetrazol-induced seizures were used as an effective treatment for 4 years before the introduction of electrically induced seizures. Primarily on the basis of the work of von Meduna, Ugo Cerletti and Lucio Bini administered the first electroconvulsive treatment in Rome in April 1938. Initially, the treatment was referred to as electroshock therapy (EST), but it later became known as electroconvulsive therapy.

The major problems associated with ECT were patients' discomfort caused by the procedure and the bone fractures resulting from the motor activity of the seizure. These problems were eventually eliminated by the use of general anesthetics and pharmacological muscle relaxation during treatment. An American psychiatrist, Abram E. Bennett, helped develop the method for extracting pure curare from plant material. Bennett suggested the use of spinal anesthetics and the use of curare (to paralyze the muscles to prevent fractures) during ECT. In 1951, succinylcholine (Anectine) was introduced and became the most widely used muscle relaxant for ECT. In 1957, hexafluorodiethyl ether (Indoklon) was introduced as a new pharmacological means of inducing seizures by administering the compound as a gas. The lack of its superiority to ECT, together with the introduction of antidepressant drugs in the 1950s, led to the removal of hexafluorodiethyl ether from the market and to a decline in the number of patients who were given ECT. Currently, about 50,000 to 100,000 patients annually receive ECT in the United States.

ELECTROPHYSIOLOGICAL PRINCIPLES

Neurons maintain a resting potential across the plasma membrane and may propagate an action potential, which is a transient reversal of the membrane potential. Normal brain activity is desynchronized; that is, neurons fire action potentials asynchronously. A convulsion, or seizure, occurs when a large percentage of neurons fire in unison. Such rhythmical changes in the extracellular potential entrain neighboring neurons, propagate the seizure activity across the cortex and into deeper structures, and eventually engulf the entire brain in high-voltage synchronous neuronal firing. Cellular mechanisms work to contain the seizure activity and to maintain cellular homeostasis, and the seizure eventually ends. In epilepsy, any of possibly several hundred genetic defects can alter the balance in favor of unrestrained activity. In ECT, seizures are triggered in normal neurons by the application through the scalp of pulses of current, the conditions of which are carefully controlled to create a seizure of a particular duration over the entire brain.

OHM'S LAW

The qualities of the electricity used in ECT can be described by Ohm's law, $E = IR$ or $I = E/R$, in which E is voltage, I is current, and R is resistance. The intensity or dose of electricity in ECT is measured in terms of charge (milliampere-seconds or millicoulombs) or energy (watt-seconds or joules). Resistance is synonymous with impedance, and, in the case of ECT, the electrode's contact with the body and the nature of the bodily tissues are the major determinants of resistance. The skull has a high impedance; the brain has a low impedance. Because scalp tissues are much better conductors of electricity than is bone, only about 20 percent of the applied charge actually enters the skull to excite neurons. The ECT machines that are now widely used can be adjusted to administer the electricity under conditions of constant current, voltage, or energy.

MECHANISM OF ACTION

The induction of a bilateral generalized seizure is necessary for both the beneficial and the adverse effects of ECT. Although a seizure superficially seems like an all-or-none event, some data indicate that not all generalized seizures involve all the neurons in deep brain structures (for example, the basal ganglia and the thalamus); recruitment of these deep neurons may be necessary for full therapeutic benefit. After the generalized seizure, the electroencephalogram (EEG) shows a period of about 60 to 90 seconds of postictal suppression. This period is followed by the appearance of high-voltage delta and theta waves and a return of the EEG to preseizure appearances in about 30 minutes. During the course of a series of ECT treatments, the interictal EEG is generally slower and of greater amplitude that usual, but the EEG returns to pretreatment appearances between 1 month and 1 year after the end of the course of treatment.

One research approach to the mechanism of action for ECT has been to study the neurophysiological effects of treatment. Positron emission tomography (PET) studies of both cerebral blood flow and glucose use have been reported. These studies have shown that during seizures, cerebral blood flow, use of glucose and oxygen, and permeability of the blood–brain barrier increase. After the seizure, blood flow and glucose metabolism are decreased, perhaps most markedly in the frontal lobes. Some research indicates that the degree of decrease in cerebral metabolism is correlated with therapeutic response. Seizure foci in idiopathic epilepsy are hypometabolic during interictal periods; ECT itself acts as an anticonvulsant because its administration is associated with an increase in the seizure threshold as treatment progresses. Recent data suggest that for 1 to 2 months following a session of ECT, EEGs record a large increase in slow-wave activity located over the prefrontal cortex in patients who responded well to the ECT. High-intensity bilateral stimulation produced the best response, whereas low-intensity unilateral stimulation produced the weakest response. These data are of unclear significance, however, as the specific EEG correlate disappeared 2 months after ECT, whereas the clinical benefit persisted.

ECT affects the cellular mechanisms of memory and mood regulation and raises the seizure threshold. The latter effect may be blocked by the opiate antagonist naloxone.

Neurochemical research into the mechanisms of action of ECT has focused on changes in neurotransmitter receptors and, recently, changes in second-messenger systems. Virtually every neurotransmitter system is affected by ECT, but a series of ECT sessions results in a downregulation of postsynaptic β-adrenergic receptors, the same receptor change observed with virtually all antidepressant treatments. The effects of ECT on serotonergic neurons remain a controversial area of research. Various research reports have found an increase in postsynaptic serotonin receptors, no change in serotonin receptors, and a change in the presynaptic regulation of serotonin release. ECT has also been reported to affect changes in the muscarinic, cholinergic, and dopaminergic neuronal systems. In second-messenger systems, ECT has been reported to affect the coupling of G proteins to receptors, the activity of adenylyl cyclase and phospholipase C, and the regulation of calcium entry into neurons.

INDICATIONS

Patients with bipolar I disorder account for about 70 percent of those who receive ECT; patients with schizophrenia account for about 17 percent. The three clearest indications for ECT are major depressive disorder, manic episodes, and, in some instances, schizophrenia. The role of ECT in treatment of psychiatric disorders is outlined in Figure 35.4–1.

Major Depressive Disorder

The most common indication for ECT is major depressive disorder, for which ECT is the fastest and most effective available therapy. ECT should be considered as a treatment for patients who have failed medication trials, have not tolerated medications, have severe or psychotic symptoms, are acutely suicidal or homicidal, or have marked symptoms of agitation or stupor. Most clinicians believe that ECT results in at least the same degree of clinical improvement as does standard treatment with antidepressant drugs. Recently, the old studies that reported these comparisons have been questioned because of their use of low dosages of antidepressant drugs. Controlled studies have shown that up to 70 percent of patients who fail to respond to antidepressant medications may respond positively to ECT.

ECT is effective for depression in both major depressive disorder and bipolar I disorder. Delusional or psychotic depression has long been thought to be particularly responsive to ECT; but recent studies have indicated that major depressive episodes with psychotic features are no more responsive to ECT than are nonpsychotic depressive disorders. Nevertheless, because major depressive episodes with psychotic features are poorly responsive to antidepressant pharmacotherapy alone,

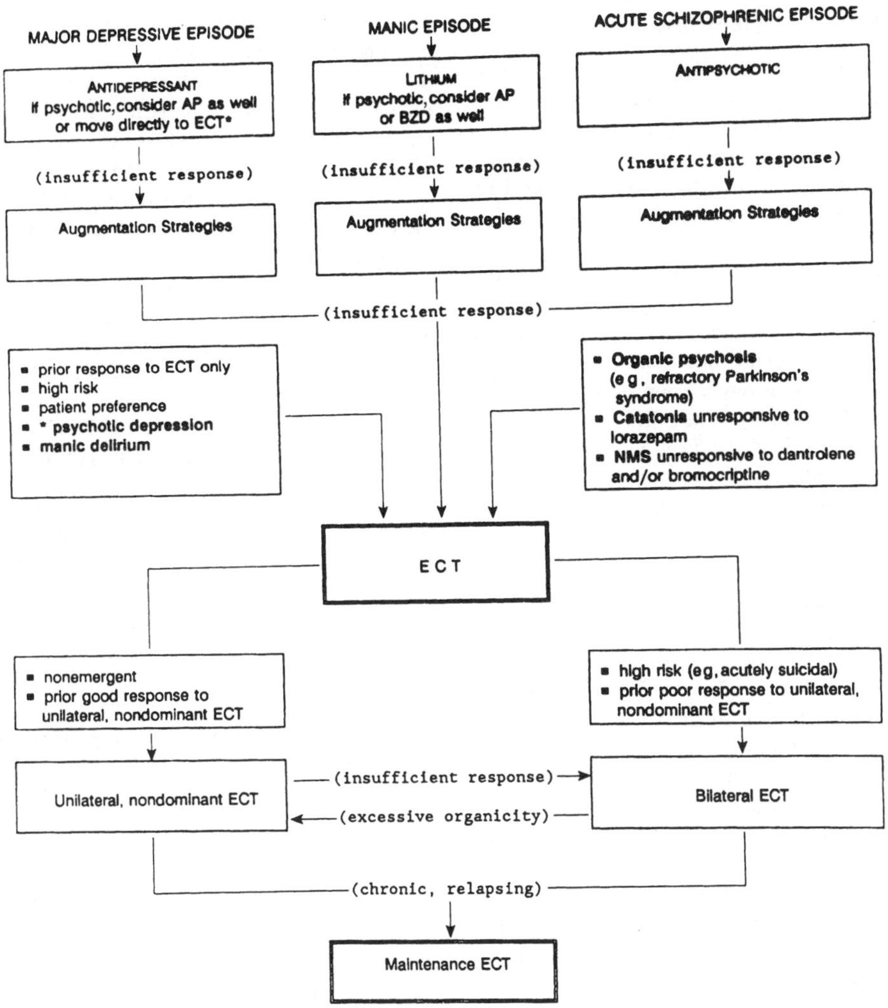

MAJOR DEPRESSIVE EPISODE
ANTIDEPRESSANT
If psychotic, consider AP as well or move directly to ECT*
(insufficient response)
Augmentation Strategies
MANIC EPISODE
LITHIUM
If psychotic, consider AP or BZD as well
(insufficient response)
Augmentation Strategies
ACUTE SCHIZOPHRENIC EPISODE
ANTIPSYCHOTIC
(insufficient response)
Augmentation Strategies
(insufficient response)
▪ prior response to ECT only
▪ high risk
▪ patient preference
▪ * psychotic depression
▪ manic delirium
▪ Organic psychosis (e g, refractory Parkinson's syndrome)
▪ Catatonia unresponsive to lorazepam
▪ NMS unresponsive to dantrolene and/or bromocriptine
ECT
▪ nonemergent
▪ prior good response to unilateral, nondominant ECT
▪ high risk (eg, acutely suicidal)
▪ prior poor response to unilateral, nondominant ECT
Unilateral, nondominant ECT
(insufficient response)
(excessive organicity)
Bilateral ECT
(chronic, relapsing)
Maintenance ECT

FIGURE 35.4–1
Role of ECT in the treatment of psychiatric disorders. (Reprinted with permission from Janicak PG, Davis JM, Preskorn SH, Ayd FJ Jr: *Principles and Practice of Psychopharmacology,* p 294. Williams & Wilkins, Baltimore, 1993.)

ECT should be considered much more often as the first-line treatment for patients with the disorder. Major depressive disorder with melancholic features (such as markedly severe symptoms, psychomotor retardation, early morning awakening, diurnal variation, decreased appetite and weight, and agitation) is thought to be likely to respond to ECT. Patients for whom ECT is particularly indicated include people who are severely depressed, who have psychotic symptoms, who show suicidal intent, or who refuse to eat. Depressed patients who are less likely to respond to ECT include those with somatization disorder. Elderly patients tend to respond to ECT more slowly than do young patients. ECT is a treatment for major depressive episode and does not provide prophylaxis unless it is administered on a long-term maintenance basis.

Manic Episodes

ECT is at least equal to lithium (Eskalith) in the treatment of acute manic episodes. Some data indicate that bilateral placement of electrodes during ECT is more effective than unilateral placement in the treatment of manic episodes. The pharmacological treatment of manic episodes, however, is so effective in the short term and for prophylaxis that the use of ECT to treat manic episodes is generally limited to situations with specific contraindications to all available pharmacological approaches. The relative rapidity of the ECT response indicates its usefulness for patients whose manic behavior has produced dangerous levels of exhaustion. It is important not to use ECT for a patient who is receiving lithium, because lithium may lower the seizure threshold and cause a prolonged seizure.

Schizophrenia

ECT is an effective treatment for the symptoms of acute schizophrenia but not for the symptoms of chronic schizophrenia. Patients with schizophrenia who have marked positive symptoms, catatonia, or affective symptoms are thought to be most likely to respond to ECT. In such patients, the efficacy of ECT is about equal to that of antipsychotics but may occur within a briefer time.

Other Indications

Small studies have found ECT to be effective in the treatment of catatonia, a symptom associated with mood disorders, schizophrenia, and medical and neurological disorders. ECT has also been reported to be useful to treat episodic psychoses, atypical psychoses, obsessive-compulsive disorder, and delirium and such medical conditions as neuroleptic malignant syndrome, hypopituitarism, intractable seizure disorders, and the on-off phenomenon of Parkinson's disease. ECT may also be the treatment of choice for depressed pregnant women who require treatment and cannot take medication, for geriatric and medically ill patients who cannot take antidepressant drugs safely, and perhaps even for severely depressed and suicidal children and adolescents who may be less likely to respond to antidepressant drugs than are adults. ECT is not effective in somatization disorder (unless accompanied by depression), personality disorders, obsessive-compulsive disorder, and anxiety disorders.

CLINICAL GUIDELINES

Patients and their families are often apprehensive about ECT; therefore, clinicians must explain the beneficial as well as adverse effects and alternative treatment approaches. The informed-consent process should be documented in the patients' medical records. The informed-consent process should include a discussion of the disorder, its natural course, and the option of receiving no treatment. Printed literature and videotapes about ECT may be useful in attempting to obtain a truly informed consent. The use of involuntary ECT is rare today and should be reserved for patients who urgently need treatment and with whom a legally appointed guardian has agreed to its use. Clinicians must know local, state, and federal laws about the use of ECT.

Pretreatment Evaluation

Pretreatment evaluation should include standard physical, neurological, and preanesthesia examinations and a complete medical history. Laboratory evaluations should include blood and urine chemistries, a chest X-ray, and an electrocardiogram (ECG). A dental examination to assess the state of patients' dentition is advisable for elderly patients and patients who have had inadequate dental care. An X-ray of the spine is needed if there is other evidence of a spinal disorder. Computed tomography (CT) or magnetic resonance imaging (MRI) should be performed if a clinician suspects the presence of a seizure disorder or a space-occupying lesion. Practitioners of ECT no longer consider even a space-occupying lesion to be an absolute contraindication to ECT, but with such patients the procedure should be performed only by experts.

Concomitant Medications. Patients' ongoing medications should be assessed for effects, both positive and negative, on the seizure threshold, and for drug interactions with the medications used during ECT. The use of tricyclic and tetracyclic drugs, monoamine oxidase inhibitors, and antipsychotics are generally thought to be acceptable. Benzodiazepines used for anxiety should be withdrawn because of their anticonvulsant activity; lithium should be withdrawn because it can result in increased postictal delirium and can prolong seizure activity; clozapine (Clozaril) and bupropion (Wellbutrin) should be withdrawn because they are associated with the development of late-appearing seizures. Lidocaine (Xylocaine) should not be administered during ECT because it markedly increases the seizure threshold; theophylline (Theo-Dur) is contraindicated because it increases the duration of seizures. Reserpine (Serpasil) is also contraindicated because it is associated with further compromise of the respiratory and cardiovascular systems during ECT.

Premedications, Anesthetics, and Muscle Relaxants

Patients should not be given anything orally for 6 hours before treatment. Just before the procedure, the patient's mouth should be checked for dentures and other foreign objects, and an intravenous (IV) line should be established. A bite block is inserted in the mouth just before the treatment is administered to protect the patient's teeth and tongue during the seizure. Except for the brief interval of electrical stimulation, 100 percent oxygen is administered at a rate of 5 L a minute during the procedure until spontaneous respiration returns. Emergency equipment for the establishment of an airway should be immediately available in case it is needed.

Muscarinic Anticholinergic Drugs. Muscarinic anticholinergic drugs are administered before ECT to minimize oral and respiratory secretions and to block bradycardias and asystoles, unless the resting heart rate is above 90 beats a minute. Some ECT centers have stopped the routine use of anticholinergics as premedications, although their use is still indicated for patients taking β-adrenergic receptor antagonist and for those with ventricular ectopic beats. The most commonly used drug is atropine, which can be administered 0.3 to 0.6 mg intramuscularly (IM) or subcutaneously (SC) 30 to 60 minutes before the anesthetic or 0.4 to 1.0 mg IV 2 or 3 minutes before the anesthetic. An option is to use glycopyrrolate (Robinul) (0.2 to 0.4 mg IM, IV, or SC), which is less likely to cross the blood–brain barrier and less likely to cause cognitive dysfunction and nausea, although it is thought to have less cardiovascular protective activity than does atropine.

General Anesthetics. The administration of ECT requires general anesthesia and oxygenation. The depth of anesthesia should be as light as possible, not only to minimize adverse effects but also to avoid elevating the seizure threshold associated with many anesthetics. Methohexital (Brevital) (0.75 to 1.0 mg/kg IV bolus) is the most commonly used anesthetic because of its short duration of action and lower association with postictal arrhythmias than is thiopental (Pentothal) (usual dose 2 to 3 mg/kg IV), although this difference in cardiac effects is not universally accepted. Four other anesthetic alternatives are etomidate (Amidate), ketamine (Ketalar), alfentanil (Alfenta), and propofol (Diprivan). Etomidate (0.15 to 0.3 mg/kg IV) is sometimes used because it does not increase the seizure threshold; this effect is particularly useful for elderly patients because the seizure threshold increases with age. Ketamine (6 to 10 mg/kg IM) is sometimes used because it does not increase the seizure threshold, although its use is limited by the frequent association of psychotic symptoms with emergence from anesthesia with the drug. Alfentanil (2 to 9 mg/kg IV) is sometimes coadministered with barbiturates to allow the use of low doses of the barbiturate anesthetics and thus to reduce the seizure threshold less than usual, although its use may be associated with an increased incidence of nausea. Propofol (0.5 to 3.5 mg/kg IV) is less useful because of its strong anticonvulsant properties.

Muscle Relaxants. After the onset of the anesthetic effect, usually within a minute, a muscle relaxant is administered to minimize the risk of bone fractures and other injuries resulting from motor activity during the seizure. The goal is to produce a profound relaxation of the muscles, not necessarily to paralyze them, unless the patient has a history of osteoporosis or spinal injury or has a pacemaker and is, therefore, at risk for injury related to motor activity during the seizure. Succinylcholine (Anectine), an ultrafast-acting depolarizing blocking agent, has gained virtually universal acceptance for the purpose. Succinylcholine is usually administered in a dose of 0.5 to 1 mg/kg as an IV bolus or drip. Because succinylcholine is a depolarizing agent, its action is marked by the presence of muscle fasciculations, which move in a rostrocaudal progression. The disappearance of these movements in the feet or the absence of muscle contractions after peripheral nerve stimulation indicates that maximal muscle relaxation has been achieved. In some patients, tubocurare (3 mg IV) is administered to prevent myoclonus and increases in potassium and muscle enzymes; these reactions may be a problem in patients with musculoskeletal or cardiac disease. To monitor the duration of the convulsion, a blood pressure cuff may be inflated at the ankle to a pressure in excess of the systolic pressure before infusion of the muscle relaxant, to allow observation of relatively innocuous seizure activity in the foot muscles.

If a patient has a known history of pseudocholinesterase deficiency, atracurium (Tracrium) (0.5 to 1 mg/kg IV) or curare can be used instead of succinylcholine. In such a patient, the metabolism of succinylcholine is disrupted, and a prolonged apnea may necessitate emergency airway management. In general, however, because of the short half-life of succinylcholine, the duration of apnea after its administration is generally shorter than the delay in regaining consciousness caused by the anesthetic and the postictal state.

Stimulus Electrode Placement

ECT can be conducted with either bilaterally or unilaterally placed electrodes. Bilateral placement usually results in a more rapid therapeutic response, and unilateral placement results in less marked cognitive adverse effects in the first week or weeks after treatment, although this difference between placements is absent 2 months after treatment. In bilateral placement, which was introduced first, one stimulating electrode is placed several centimeters apart over each hemisphere of the brain. In unilateral ECT, both electrodes are placed several centimeters apart over the nondominant hemisphere, almost always the right hemisphere. Some attempts have been made to vary the location of the electrodes in unilateral ECT, but these attempts have not been successful in obtaining the rapidity of response seen with bilateral ECT or in further reducing the cognitive adverse effects. The most common approach is to initiate treatment with unilateral ECT because of its more favorable side effect profile. If a patient does not improve after four to six unilateral treatments, the technique is switched to the bilateral placement. Initial bilateral placement of the electrodes may be indicated in the following situations: severe depressive symptoms, marked agitation, immediate suicide risk, manic symptoms, catatonic stupor, and treatment-resistant schizophrenia. Some patients are particularly at risk for anesthetic-related adverse effects, and these patients may also be treated with bilateral placement from the beginning to minimize the number of treatments and exposures to anesthetics.

In traditional bilateral ECT, the electrodes are placed bifrontotemporally with the center of each electrode about 1 inch above the midpoint of an imaginary line drawn from the tragus to the external canthus. With unilateral ECT, one stimulus electrode is typically placed over the nondominant frontotemporal area. Although several locations for the second stimulus electrode have been proposed, placement on the nondominant centroparietal scalp, just lateral to the midline vertex, appears to provide the most effective configuration.

Which cerebral hemisphere is dominant can generally be determined by a simple series of performance tasks (for example, for handedness and footedness) and stated preference. Right body responses correlate highly with left brain dominance. If the responses are mixed or if they clearly indicate left body dominance, clinicians should alternate the polarity of unilateral stimulation during successive treatments. Clinicians should also monitor the time that it takes for patients to recover consciousness and to answer simple orientation and naming questions. The side of stimulation associated with less rapid recovery and return of function is considered dominant. The left hemisphere is dominant in most people; therefore, unilateral electrode placement is almost always over the right hemisphere.

Electrical Stimulus

The electrical stimulus must be sufficiently strong to produce a seizure. The electrical stimulus is given in cycles, and each cycle contains a positive and a negative wave. Old machines use a sine wave; however, this type of machine is now considered obsolete because of the inefficiency of that wave shape. When a sine wave is delivered, the electrical stimulus in the sine wave before the seizure threshold is reached and after the seizure is activated is unnecessary and excessive. Modern ECT machines use a brief square wave pulse form that administers the electrical stimulus usually in a 1- to 2-ms time period at a rate of 30 to 100 pulses a second. Machines that use an ultrabrief pulse (0.5 ms) are not as effective as brief pulse machines.

The establishment of a patient's seizure threshold is not straightforward. A 40-fold variability in seizure thresholds occurs among patients. In addition, during the course of ECT treatment, a patient's seizure threshold may increase 25 to 200 percent. The seizure threshold is also higher in men than in women and higher in older than in younger adults. A common technique is to initiate treatment at an electrical stimulus that is thought to be lower than the seizure threshold for a particular patient and then to increase this intensity by 100 percent for unilateral placement and by 50 percent for bilateral placement until the seizure threshold is reached. A debate in the literature concerns the question of whether a minimally superthreshold dose, a moderately superthreshold dose (1½ times the threshold), or a high superthreshold dose (3 times the threshold) is preferable. The debate about stimulus intensity resembles the debate about electrode placement. Essentially, the data support the conclusion that doses of 3 times the threshold are the most rapidly effective and that minimal superthreshold doses are associated with the fewest and least severe cognitive adverse effects.

Induced Seizures

A brief muscular contraction, usually strongest in a patient's jaw and facial muscles, is seen concurrently with the flow of stimulus current, regardless of whether a seizure occurs. The first behavioral sign of the seizure is often a plantar extension, which lasts 10 to 20 seconds and marks the tonic phase. This phase is followed by rhythmic (that is, clonic) contractions that decrease in frequency and finally disappear. The tonic phase is marked by high-frequency, sharp EEG activity on which may be superimposed a higher-frequency muscle artifact. During the clonic phase, bursts of polyspike activity occur simultaneously with the muscular contractions but usually persist for at least a few seconds after the clonic movements stop.

Monitoring Seizures. A physician must have an objective measure that a bilateral generalized seizure has occurred after the stimulation. The physician should be able to observe either some evidence of tonic-clonic movements or electrophysiological evidence of seizure activity from the EEG or electromyogram (EMG). Seizures with unilateral ECT are asymmetrical, with higher ictal EEG amplitudes over the stimulated hemisphere than over the nonstimulated hemisphere. Occasionally, unilateral seizures are induced; for this reason, at least a single pair of EEG electrodes should be placed over the contralateral hemisphere when using unilateral ECT. For a seizure to be effective in the course of ECT, the seizure should have a duration of at least 25 seconds.

Failure to Induce Seizures. If a particular stimulus fails to cause a seizure of sufficient duration, up to four attempts at seizure induction can be tried during a course of treatment. The onset of seizure activity is sometimes delayed as long as 20 to 40 seconds after the stimulus administration. If a stimulus fails to result in a seizure, the contact between the electrodes and the skin should be checked, and the intensity of the stimulus should be increased by 25 to 100 percent. The clinician can also change the anesthetic agent to minimize increases in the seizure threshold caused by the anesthetic. Additional procedures to lower the seizure threshold include hyperventilation and the administration of 500 to 2000 mg IV of caffeine sodium benzoate 5 to 10 minutes before the stimulus.

Prolonged and Tardive Seizures. Prolonged seizures (seizures lasting more than 180 seconds) and status epilepticus can be terminated either with additional doses of the barbiturate anesthetic agent or with intravenous diazepam (Valium) (5 to 10 mg). Management of such complications should be accompanied by intubation, because the oral airway is insufficient to maintain adequate ventilation over an extended apneic period. Tardive seizures—that is, additional seizures appearing some time after the ECT treatment—may develop in patients with preexisting seizure disorders. In rare patients, ECT precipitates the development of an epileptic disorder. Such situations should be managed clinically as if they were pure epileptic disorders.

Number and Spacing of ECT Treatments

ECT treatments are usually administered 2 to 3 times a week; 2-times-weekly treatments are associated with less memory impairment than are 3-times-weekly treatments. In general, the course of treatment of major depressive disorder can take 6 to 12 treatments (although up to 20 sessions is possible); the treatment of manic episodes can take 8 to 20 treatments; the treatment of schizophrenia can take more than 15 treatments; and the treatment of catatonia and delirium can take as few as 1 to 4 treatments. Treatment should continue until the patient achieves what is thought to be the maximum therapeutic response. Treatment past that point does not result in any therapeutic benefit but increases the severity and duration of the adverse effects. The point of maximal improvement is usually thought to occur when a patient fails to continue to improve after two consecutive treatments. If a patient is not improving after 6 to 10 sessions, bilateral placement and high-density treatment (3 times the seizure threshold) should be attempted before ECT is abandoned.

Multiple Monitored ECT. Multiple monitored ECT (MMECT) involves giving multiple ECT stimuli during a single session, most commonly two bilateral stimuli within 2 minutes. This approach may be warranted in severely ill patients and in patients who are at especially high risk from the anesthetic procedures. MMECT is associated with the most frequent occurrences of serious cognitive adverse effects.

Maintenance Treatment

A short-term course of ECT induces a remission in symptoms but does not, of itself, prevent a relapse. Post-ECT maintenance treatment should always be considered. Maintenance therapy is generally pharmacological, but maintenance ECT treatments (weekly, biweekly, or monthly) have been reported to be effective relapse prevention treatments, although data from large studies are lacking. Indications for maintenance ECT treatments may include a rapid relapse after initial ECT, severe symptoms, psychotic symptoms, and the inability to tolerate medications. If ECT was used because a patient was unresponsive to a specific medication, then, following ECT, the patient either should return to the original medication or should be given a trial of a different medication.

Failure of ECT Trial

If a patient fails to improve after a trial of ECT, the patient may again be treated with the pharmacological agents that failed in the past. Although the data are primarily anecdotal, many reports indicate that patients who had previously failed to improve while taking an antidepressant drug do improve while taking the same drug after receiving a course of ECT treatments, even if the ECT seemed to be a therapeutic failure. Nonetheless, with the increased availability of drugs that act at diverse receptor sites, it is less often necessary to return to a drug that has failed than was formerly true.

ADVERSE EFFECTS

Contraindications

ECT has no absolute contraindications, only situations in which a patient is at increased risk and has an increased need for close monitoring. Pregnancy is not a contraindication for ECT, and fetal monitoring is generally thought to be unnecessary unless the pregnancy is high risk or complicated. Patients with space-occupying central nervous system lesions are at increased risk for edema and brain herniation after ECT. But if the lesion is small, pretreatment with dexamethasone is given, and hypertension is controlled during the seizure, the risk of serious complications can be minimized for these patients. Patients who have increased intracerebral pressure or are at risk for cerebral bleeding (for example, those with cerebrovascular diseases and aneurysms) are at risk during ECT because of the increased cerebral blood flow during the seizure. This risk can be lessened, although not eliminated, by control of the patient's blood pressure during the treatment. Patients with recent myocardial infarctions are another high-risk group, although the risk is greatly diminished 2 weeks after the myocardial infarction and is even further reduced 3 months after the infarction. Patients with hypertension should be stabilized on their antihypertensive medications before ECT is administered. Propranolol (Inderal) and sublingual nitroglycerin can also be used to protect such patients during treatment.

Mortality

The mortality rate with ECT is about 0.002 percent per treatment and 0.01 percent for each patient. These numbers compare favorably with the risks associated with general anesthesia and childbirth. ECT death is usually from cardiovascular complications and is most likely to occur in patients whose cardiac status is already compromised.

Central Nervous System Effects

Common side effects associated with ECT are headache, confusion, and delirium shortly after the seizure while the patient is coming out of anesthesia. Marked confusion may occur in up to 10 percent of patients within 30 minutes of the seizure and can be treated with barbiturates and benzodiazepines. Delirium is usually most pronounced after the first few treatments and in patients who receive bilateral ECT or who have coexisting neurological disorders. The delirium characteristically clears within days or a few weeks at the longest.

Memory. The greatest concern about ECT is the association between ECT and memory loss. About 75 percent of all patients given ECT say that the memory impairment is the worst adverse effect. Although memory impairment during a course of treatment is almost the rule, follow-up data indicate that almost all patients are back to their cognitive baselines after 6 months. Some patients, however, complain of persistent memory difficulties. For example, a patient may not remember the events leading up to the hospitalization and ECT, and such autobiographical memories may never be recalled. The degree of cognitive impairment during treatment and the time it takes to return to baseline are related in part to the amount of electrical stimulation used during treatment. Memory impairment is most often reported by patients who have experienced little improvement with ECT. In spite of the memory impairment, which usually resolves, there is no evidence of brain damage caused by ECT. This subject has been the focus of several brain-imaging studies, using a variety of modalities; virtually all concluded that permanent brain damage is not an adverse effect of ECT. It is generally agreed by neurologists and epileptologists that seizures that last less than 30 minutes do not cause permanent neuronal damage.

Systemic Effects

Occasional, usually mild transient cardiac arrhythmias occur during ECT, particularly in patients with existing cardiac disease. The arrhythmias are usually a by-product of the brief postictal bradycardia and, therefore, can often be prevented by increasing the dosage of anticholinergic premedication. Other arrhythmias are secondary to a tachycardia during the seizure and may occur as a patient returns to consciousness. The prophylactic administration of a β-adrenergic receptor antagonist can be useful in such cases. As already mentioned, an apneic state may be prolonged if the metabolism of succinylcholine is impaired. Toxic and allergic reactions to the pharmacological agents used in ECT have rarely been reported. Sore muscles resulting from the seizure motor activity can generally be alleviated by pretreatment with curare or atracurium or by increasing the succinylcholine dose by 10 to 25 percent.

References

Abrams R: *Electroconvulsive Therapy,* ed 2. Oxford University Press, Oxford, England, 1992.

Beale MD, Bernstein HJ, Kellner CH: Maintenance electroconvulsive therapy for geriatric depression: A one year follow-up. Clin Gerontol *16* (4): 86, 1996.

Colenda CC, McCall WV: A statistical model predicting the seizure threshold for right unilateral ECT in 106 patients. Convuls Ther *12* (1): 3, 1996.

Curran S, Wallace D: Seizure threshold in bilateral and unilateral ECT. Br J Psychiatry *167* (6): 821, 1995.

Devanand DP, Dwork AJ, Hutchinson ER, Bolwig TG, Sackeim HA: Does ECT alter brain structure? Am J Psychiatry *151:* 957, 1994.

Hamner M, Huber M: Discontinuation of antidepressant medications before ECT. Convuls Ther *12* (2): 125, 1996.

Jha AK, Stein GS, Fenwick P: Negative interaction between lithium and electroconvulsive therapy: A case-control study. Br J Psychiatry *168* (2): 241, 1996.

Johns CA, Thompson JW: Adjunctive treatments in schizophrenia: Pharmacotherapies and electroconvulsive therapy. Schizophr Bull *21* (4): 607, 1995.
Krystal AD, Weiner RC, Gassert D, McCall WV, et al: The relative ability of three ictal EEG frequency bands to differentiate ECT seizures on the basis of electrode placement, stimulus intensity, and therapeutic response. Convuls Ther *12* (1): 13, 1996.
McCall WV, Weiner RD, Carroll BJ, Shelp FE, et al: Serum prolactin, electrode placement, and the convulsive threshold during ECT. Convuls Ther *12* (2): 81, 1996.
Mukherjee S, Sackeim HA, Schnur DB: Electroconvulsive therapy of acute manic episodes: A review of 50 years' experience. Am J Psychiatry *151:* 169, 1994.
O'Connor MK, Rummans TA, editors: Updating ECT. Psychiatr Ann *23* (1): 2, 1993.
Potter WZ, Rudorfer MV: Electroconvulsive therapy: A modern medical procedure. N Engl J Med *328:* 882, 1993.
Prudic J, Sackeim HA, Devanand DP, Kiersky JE: The efficacy of ECT in double depression. Depression *1:* 38, 1993.
Sackeim HA, Luber B, Katzman GP, Moeller JR, et al: The effects of electroconvulsive therapy on quantitative electroencephalograms: Relationship to clinical outcome. Arch Gen Psychiatry *53* (9): 814, 1996.
Sackeim HA, Prudic J. Devanand DP, Kiersky JE, Fitzsimmons L, Moody BJ, McElhiney MC, Coleman EA, Settembrino JM: Effects of stimulus intensity and electrode placement on the efficacy and cognitive effects of electroconvulsive therapy. N Engl J Med *328:* 839, 1993.
Swartz CM: Generalization, duration, and low-frequency electroencephalographic persistence of bilateral electroconvulsive therapy seizure. Biol Psychiatry *38* (12): 837, 1995.
Weiner RD, Sibert TE: Use of ECT in treatment of depression in patients with diabetes mellitus. J Clin Psychiatry *57* (3): 138, 1996.
Yeung PP, Milstein RM, Daniels DC, Bowers MB Jr: ECT for lorazepam-refractory catatonia. Convuls Ther *12* (1): 31, 1996.
Zielinski RJ, Roose SP, Devanand DP, Woodring S, Sackeim HA: Cardiovascular complications of ECT in depressed patients with cardiac disease. Am J Psychiatry *150:* 904, 1993.

▲ 35.5 Other Biological Therapies

TRANSCRANIAL MAGNETIC STIMULATION

The electrical activity of the brain, which is registered by electroencephalography and is altered by electroconvulsive therapy (ECT), is exactly paralleled by the magnetic activity of the brain. Magnetic brain activity is registered by magnetoencephalography, and it can be altered by transcranial magnetic stimulation (TMS), a technique with several interesting capabilities. Whereas sufficient electrical stimulation to cause a generalized seizure is required for a therapeutic benefit with ECT, TMS can selectively inactivate or potentiate activity in discrete brain regions at subconvulsive doses. A small number of depressed patients have experienced an improvement in mood following TMS treatments. TMS has also been used to map the location of specific higher cortical functions and to explore the cortical localization of mood and anxiety.

Technique of Stimulation

In TMS, a figure-eight- or teardrop-shaped coil a few inches in diameter is placed on the subject's head to generate a localized magnetic field of 1.5 to 2.5 teslas. When oriented orthogonally to the surface of the head, the field penetrates the skull and excites the most superficial 1 to 2 cm of brain tissue. An important difference between electrical and magnetic stimulation is that, because of the high resistance of bone, most electrical energy fails to enter the cranial vault but, rather, is conducted between the two electrodes through the scalp tissues. In contrast, the skull is relatively transparent to magnetic energy. In addition, generation of an electrical field requires both an anode and a cathode, whereas a magnetic field is generated as a monopole. These features allow a much more focused application of magnetic energy than is possible with electrical energy and enable the stimulation of sectors as limited as 5 mm in diameter, such as the cortical representations of specific muscles.

Initial stimulators fired at a rate of 1 cycle a second (Hertz [Hz]), but later models discharge at 10 to 60 Hz. Use of the faster frequencies is called rapid TMS (rTMS): The stimulator creates a loud noise that necessitates the use of earplugs by patients and investigators. Sham treatments are effected by aiming the stimulator at a 45-degree angle to the surface of the head. Stimulation is typically given several times in a session, in several sessions a week.

Seizures. The intensity of TMS is limited by the possible induction of seizure activity. In one study aimed at determining the range of useful energy levels, 4 of 250 subjects had seizures following TMS at the upper end of the energy range. The investigators subsequently lowered the upper boundary of energy doses, and no further seizures occurred. Another patient who had a post-TMS seizure had begun to take amitriptyline and haloperidol, which lower the seizure threshold. Investigators work to avoid induction of seizures, which are not necessary for the clinical effects of TMS.

Indications

Depression. Several lines of evidence suggest this simplistic model, namely, that the left hemisphere generates positive emotions and the right hemisphere generates negative emotions. TMS pulses that inactivate brain regions, when directed toward the left frontal lobe, suppress positive thoughts and elicit sadness. When the right frontal lobe is suppressed by TMS, in contrast, subjects feel happier and more energetic. These mood changes generally last for only a few hours. But in a recent study, when TMS pulses were applied repeatedly over the left dorsolateral prefrontal cortex on successive days (for example, intensity 90 percent of the seizure threshold, 10-Hz stimulation for 10 seconds, 20 times a day, that is, 2000 stimuli a day), 11 of 17 patients with severe major depression experienced improvement in their mood. Similar treatment over the right dorsolateral prefrontal cortex failed to produce benefit. The definition of the optimal stimulation parameters for TMS in mood disorders is an area of active research. TMS as a research tool, in combination with functional neuroimaging, may provide valuable insights into the functional neuroanatomy of mood regulation.

Anxiety Disorders. A handful of case reports suggests that TMS may eventually be of benefit in obsessive-compulsive disorder, posttraumatic stress disorder, and panic disorder. In one report, TMS to the right orbitofrontal cortex of a patient with obsessive-compulsive disorder reduced compulsive urges for about 8 hours, without, however, reducing anxiety in general. In two other reports, in which TMS was aimed at a slightly different area of the right prefrontal cortex of patients with panic disorder and generalized anxiety disorder, respectively, stimulation produced a marked increase in anxiety, lasting less than 8 hours. Another patient with posttraumatic stress disorder received four consecutive daily TMS treatments to the left prefrontal cortex, which elicited panic lasting 7 days, followed immediately by a 2-week period of unusual calm. The varied effects of TMS in anxiety states suggest that the technique may allow investigators to assign psychological functions to subsections of the prefrontal cortex.

Parkinson's Disease. Magnetic stimulation of the motor cortex in patients with idiopathic Parkinson's disease results transiently in increased speed and dexterity on manual tasks. Investigators hypothesize that the TMS substitutes for the deficient basal activation of the motor cortex by the ventral thalamus in patients with parkinsonian symptoms.

Clinical Guidelines

TMS is an interesting technique with potential as both a research tool and a therapeutic modality. At present, however, there are no established guidelines for its use outside research settings.

LIGHT THERAPY

The major indication for light therapy is major depressive disorder with seasonal pattern, a disorder characterized by symptoms that appear on a seasonal basis, usually in fall and winter. In light therapy, also called phototherapy, patients are exposed to a bright artificial light source on a daily basis during the treatment.

Mechanism of Action

Phase–Response Curves. Human circadian rhythms result from the entrainment of endogenous pacemakers by exogenous zeitgebers. The suprachiasmatic nucleus of the hypothalamus is thought to be the major endogenous pacemaker; the light-dark cycle is thought to be the major exogenous zeitgeber. The body's rhythms exhibit a biological feature called a phase–response curve, which is based on a 24-hour unit. Perturbations such as exposure to light have a differential effect on bodily rhythms (for example, sleep and hormone secretion), depending on the time of day, and hence affect their locations on the phase–response curve. Exposure to light in the morning results in a phase advance—that is, rhythms are shifted to an earlier time; exposure to light in the evening results in a phase delay—that is, rhythms are shifted to a later time. Therefore, the entrainment of endogenous pacemakers by light is the result of a phase advance at dawn and a phase delay at dusk. Melatonin is secreted by the pineal gland during the night. Secretion is stopped by exposure to light during the night but is not stimulated by exposure to darkness during the day.

Effects of Light Exposure. More than 50 controlled studies have shown that light therapy is effective, although its mechanism of action is still uncertain. The most accepted theory is that exposure to bright artificial light in the morning causes a phase advance of biological rhythms, which effectively treats the delayed circadian rhythms associated with major depressive disorder with seasonal pattern. This hypothesis is supported by the observations of several investigators that other depressive disorders do not respond to phototherapy. The initial theory that light exposure works by affecting melatonin secretion has not been supported by subsequent experiments. A high intensity of light was thought to be required for therapeutic effects, but this hypothesis has been disputed by recent studies. Most studies support the idea that 2 hours is more effective than 30 minutes of exposure. Whether light should be administered in the morning or evening or at both times to obtain maximal benefit is undetermined, but most studies support the administration of light in the morning. Full-spectrum light is effective, and some studies have found that narrow-spectrum light is ineffective. Whether an intermediate spectrum of light would be effective is unknown.

Indications

The major indication for light therapy is major depressive disorder with seasonal pattern, which occurs predominantly (80 percent) in women. The mean age of presentation is 40, although the mean age may decrease with better recognition of the disorder. The symptoms usually appear during winter and remit spontaneously in spring, but sometimes the symptoms appear in summer. The most common symptoms include depression, fatigue, hypersomnia, hyperphagia, carbohydrate craving, irritability, and interpersonal difficulties. One third to one half of all patients with the disorder have not previously sought psychiatric help. The remainder have most often been previously classified as having a mood disorder. More than 50 percent of patients with the disorder have a first-degree relative with a mood disorder. Some recent evidence indicates that people with mild, subsyndromal symptoms of a seasonal pattern disorder may also experience some relief with phototherapy.

Clinical Guidelines

The treatment requires exposure to bright light (2,500 lux) that is about 200 times brighter than the usual indoor lighting. The initial experiments exposed patients to the light for 2 to 3 hours before dawn and sometimes an additional 2 to 3 hours after dusk every day. Patients were instructed not to look directly into the light but to glance at it only occasionally. Patients usually responded after 2 to 4 days of treatment and relapsed 2 to 4 days after the treatment was stopped. Recent studies have indicated that only morning exposure may be necessary and that 1 hour of daily exposure may be sufficient. A debate remains about the required intensity of the light.

The most commonly reported adverse effects are headache, eyestrain, and feeling ''wired'' or irritable. These adverse effects can usually be managed by reducing the length of time that the patient is exposed to the light.

SLEEP DEPRIVATION AND ALTERATIONS OF SLEEP SCHEDULES

Sleep deprivation has been suggested as a short-term treatment of depressive disorder, as an adjuvant to antidepressant drugs to facilitate improvement, and as a treatment for premenstrual dysphoric disorder. One night's sleep deprivation results in a dramatic reduction of depressive symptoms in about 60 percent of all patients with depressive disorders. Unfortunately, the beneficial effects last only 1 day. The depressive disorder symptoms are often brought back quickly if a patient takes even a short nap after a night of sleep deprivation. This finding caused some researchers to hypothesize that sleep-related depressogenic process may be temporarily aborted by sleep deprivation. Studies have reported that preventing only rapid eye movement (REM) sleep has the same effects as preventing all sleep; researchers hypothesize that a REM-related process may be related to maintaining or even causing depressive disorders.

Phase-advancing the sleep cycle—that is, going to bed early and waking up early—may have antidepressant effects in some depressed patients, especially when used as an adjuvant to pharmacotherapy. In contrast to the single-day improvement associated with sleep deprivation, the beneficial effects of sleep phase advance sometimes last for a week.

MELATONIN

Mechanism of Action

Melatonin is a metabolite of serotonin produced only in the pineal gland. It is secreted into the bloodstream and binds to receptors, called Mel_{1a}, Mel_{1b}, Mel_{1c}, and Mel_2, located, among other places, in the suprachiasmatic nucleus (SCN) of the hypothalamus. The SCN is thought to regulate circadian rhythms. Melatonin is produced during darkness. When light is perceived by the eyes, retinal fibers carry this information to the SCN, which in turn inhibits the paraventricular nucleus. The paraventricular nucleus, when active, stimulates melatonin production in the pineal gland through sympathetic nerve fibers. Melatonin is therefore involved in a feedback loop that varies melatonin concentrations according to the amount of environmental light. Different concentrations of melatonin may synchronize the body's internal clock and therefore may ensure that the body's sleep–wake cycle remains synchronized with the environment.

Melatonin is implicated in the regulation of seasonal and circadian fluctuations of concentrations of other hormones and in the adjustment of the body to changes in time zones. The sensitivity of the SCN to exogenous melatonin is greatest at night, and the effects of melatonin administration vary widely, depending on the time of day it is given. Melatonin concentrations have been used as a biological marker for the effects of light therapy in mood disorder with seasonal pattern. The production of melatonin declines with age. Concurrent administration of fluoxetine (Prozac) decreases melatonin concentrations, whereas coadministration of fluvoxamine (Luvox) or tricyclic drugs increases melatonin concentrations. Beside its hormonal signaling roles, melatonin also appears to scavenge toxic cellular free radicals and may therefore reduce damage to cellular organelles in times of metabolic stress. Melatonin reduces seizures in animals, possibly by potentiating the γ-aminobutyric acid (GABA)–benzodiazepine receptor complex.

Indications

There are no indications for which melatonin has been proved effective in placebo-controlled, double-blind clinical trials, and most of the claims made for its effects are based on anecdotal reports. Melatonin is said to increase sleep time, sleep efficiency, non–rapid eye movement (non-REM) sleep, and REM latency in both children and adults. The indication for which melatonin has been most vigorously advocated is the management of jet lag. When given in the morning, melatonin is said to cause phase delays, which is the equivalent of traveling westward to a later time zone. Conversely, when given in the afternoon, melatonin is said to cause phase advances, which is the equivalent of traveling eastward to an earlier time zone. Melatonin is claimed to synchronize and equalize advances in wake-up times and bedtimes to maintain 7 to 8 hours of sleep. Uncontrolled case series have shown that administration of melatonin to airplane pilots traveling across time zones can improve their scores on tasks requiring sustained vigilance. Because of the obvious benefits of improving the performance of pilots, the armed forces have initiated several studies of the effects of melatonin. More research is needed before the claims of a salutary effect of melatonin in jet lag can be accepted.

Another work-related indication for melatonin is to facilitate the adjustment of shift workers who switch from one shift to another. A recent study found, however, that timed exposure to bright light is more effective than administration of melatonin. This finding suggests that melatonin may be only one of several biochemical regulators of circadian rhythms and that a broader range of regulatory factors is entrained by exposure to bright light.

Melatonin has been trumpeted in the lay press as useful in treating infectious diseases, AIDS, chronic pain, mood disorders, heart disease, and a growing list of significant public health problems. The data that support these claims are very shaky, and it may be through its emotional appeal to the inner resources tapped by the placebo effect that melatonin has any benefit for these disorders.

Precautions and Adverse Effects

The therapeutic dose of melatonin has not yet been determined. Early evidence indicates that melatonin may constrict blood vessels, which would be of theoretical concern for people with a history of atherosclerosis, heart disease, and stroke. Other reports raise the question of whether melatonin inhibits fertility. Because the manufacture of melatonin is not regulated by governmental agencies, preparations are not standardized, and there is no assurance of purity.

DRUG-ASSISTED INTERVIEWING

To facilitate gathering information during a psychiatric interview, some psychiatrists advocate drug-assisted interviewing. The common use of an intravenous injection of sodium amobarbital (Amytal) led to the popular name *Amytal interview* for the technique. Narcotherapy or narcoanalysis consists of a series of drug-assisted psychotherapy sessions. Both sedatives (for example, barbiturates and benzodiazepines) and stimulants (for example, methylphenidate [Ritalin]) have been used. Narcotherapy was thought to benefit patients by allowing them to experience the catharsis of having a repressed memory or thought brought to conscious awareness. Although narcotherapy is rarely used in modern psychiatry, there has been some renewed interest in it. Some noted psychiatrists have proposed that 3,4-methylenedioxymethamphetamine (MDMA, ecstasy) may be beneficial when used as an agent for drug-assisted psychotherapy. This suggestion has been regarded as extremely controversial.

Indications

Although much has been written about drug-assisted interviewing, the literature consists mainly of uncontrolled studies and anecdotal reports, which make it difficult to determine a definite statement about its indications. Furthermore, several controlled trials have shown that the use of drugs does not guarantee that patients tell the truth, in spite of the popular misconception that sodium amobarbital is a truth serum. A few studies have shown, in fact, that drug-assisted interviews are no better at eliciting information than an empathic interviewer, hypnosis, or the administration of a placebo.

The most common reasons for drug-assisted interviews in modern practice are uninformative or mute patients and the presence of catatonia or supposed conversion disorder. Although drug-assisted interviews often elicit information sooner than interviews without the drug, no evidence indicates that the technique has a positive effect on the therapeutic outcome. Patients may be silent because of excessive anxiety about recounting a traumatic event (for example, a rape or an accident), and drug-assisted interviews have been used successfully in such cases. But hypnosis, daytime sedation, empathic and supportive approaches, and time also help elicit information and do not have the risks of drug-assisted interviewing.

Mute patients with a mental disorder may have catatonic schizophrenia or conversion disorder, or they may be malingering. Barbiturates or benzodiazepines help to activate catatonic patients temporarily; therefore, catatonic schizophrenia may be a reasonable indication for using drug-assisted interviewing. Patients with conversion disorder or malingering may or may not improve during a drug-assisted interview. The commonly held but controversial belief is that a functional or psychological disorder improves during a drug-assisted interview, whereas an organic or medical disorder does not improve or even worsens. If patients do improve, however, there is no indication that the drug-assisted interview facilitated their improvement; if they do not improve or even worsen, the information gained from the interview is of little help in guiding their treatment.

Another indication for drug-assisted interviewing is the differential diagnosis of confusion; the assumption is that functional confusion clears during the procedure and that organic confusion does not. False-positive results occur when a confused patient is withdrawing from alcohol or barbiturates and when a patient has an epileptic disorder. False-negative results occur when the interviewer uses too much drug and sometimes when the patient has conversion disorder or is a malingerer. Another proposed indication for drug-assisted interviewing is to differentiate between schizophrenia and a depressive disorder. It was once thought that when given sodium amobarbital, patients with schizophrenia would recall bizarre material and depressed patients would recall depressive material. This hypothesis has not been confirmed in controlled studies. Sodium amobarbital has also been suggested as an adjuvant in supportive therapy, and the drug is used to reinforce a therapeutic suggestion (for example, to stop smoking).

Clinical Guidelines

A 10 percent solution of sodium amobarbital is administered at a rate of about 0.5 to 1.0 mL a minute. The rate and total dose should be adjusted for each patient. The total dose may vary between 0.25 and 0.5 grams, although some patients need up to 1 gram. The end point is a state of mild sedation but not sleep. The benzodiazepines—for example, diazepam (Valium)—are just as effective as the barbiturates and are less dangerous.

Barbiturates should not be given to patients with liver, renal, or cardiopulmonary diseases or to patients with porphyria or a history of sedative abuse. Patients may have allergic reactions or respiratory suppression during barbiturate interviews, and clinicians must be prepared for both possibilities. Furthermore, the use of what patients may perceive as a truth serum may increase their paranoia and interfere with the development of a psychotherapeutic transference.

PSYCHOSURGERY

Psychosurgery involves surgical modification of the brain with the goal of reducing the symptoms of the most severely ill psychiatric patients who have not responded adequately to less radical treatments. Psychosurgical procedures focus on lesion-specific brain regions (for example, lobotomies and cingulotomies) or their connecting tracts (for example, tractotomies and leukotomies). Psychosurgical techniques are also used in the treatment of neurological disorders such as epilepsy and chronic pain disorder.

The interest in psychosurgical approaches to mental disorders has only recently been rekindled. The renewed interest is based on several factors, including much-improved techniques that allow neurosurgeons to make exact stereotactically placed lesions, improved preoperative diagnoses, and comprehensive preoperative and postoperative psychological assessments. New techniques also facilitate gathering complete follow-up data and enable a growing understanding of the neuroanatomical basis of some mental disorders.

History

In 1935, after C. F. Jacobsen and John F. Fulton at Yale University in New Haven, Connecticut, demonstrated that frontal lobe ablation in a monkey had a calming effect, Antonio Egas Moniz, working in Portugal, severed frontal lobe white matter in 20 psychotic patients and reported a decrease in their tension and psychotic symptoms. In 1936, Walter Freeman and James Watts at George Washington University in Washington, DC, introduced the psychosurgical technique of prefrontal lobotomy to the United States. Although early procedures required burr holes or other exposure of the brain, Freeman eventually developed the technique of transorbital leukotomy, which involved the introduction and lateral movement of a sharp instrument (actually an ice pick) through the eye socket as a method of sectioning the white matter of the frontal lobes. By the late 1940s, psychosurgery was being performed worldwide, and an estimated 5,000 patients were being operated on each year. In 1949, Egas Moniz won the Nobel prize for his work in developing psychosurgical techniques. Shortly thereafter, the introduction of antipsychotic drugs and the increasing public concern about the ethics of psychosurgery led to a near abandonment of these techniques for the treatment of psychiatric patients, although psychosurgical procedures for pain control and epilepsy continued to be used.

Modern Psychosurgical Techniques

Stereotactic neurosurgical equipment now allows neurosurgeons to place discrete lesions in the brain. Radioactive implants, cryoprobes, electrical coagulation, proton beams, and ultrasonic waves are used to make the actual lesions.

Indications

The major indication for psychosurgery is the presence of a debilitating, chronic mental disorder that has not responded to any other treatment. A reasonable guideline is that the disorder should have been present for 5 years, during which a wide variety of alternative treatment approaches was attempted. Chronic intractable major depressive disorder and obsessive-compulsive disorder are the two disorders reportedly most responsive to psychosurgery. The presence of vegetative symptoms and marked anxiety further increases the likelihood of a successful therapeutic outcome. Whether psychosurgery is a reasonable treatment for intractable and extreme aggression is still controversial. Psychosurgery is not indicated for the treatment of schizophrenia, and data about manic episodes are controversial.

Therapeutic and Adverse Effects

When patients are carefully selected, between 50 and 70 percent have significant therapeutic improvement with psychosurgery. Fewer than 3 percent become worse. Continued improvement is often noted from 1 to 2 years after surgery, and patients are often more responsive than they were before psychosurgery to traditional pharmacological and behavioral treatment approaches. Postoperative seizures are present in fewer than 1 percent of patients, and these seizures are usually controlled with phenytoin (Dilantin). As measured by intelligence quotient (IQ) scores, cognitive abilities improve after surgery, probably because of patients' increased ability to attend to cognitive tasks. Undesired changes in personality have not been noted with modern limited procedures.

PLACEBOS

Placebos are substances with no known pharmacological activity. The word *placebo* originated in the Latin word *placere* ("to please"). Although it is usually thought that placebos act through suggestion rather than biological action, this idea is based on the artificial distinction between mind and body. Virtually every treatment modality is accompanied by poorly understood factors affecting its outcome (for example, the taste of a medicine and a patient's emotional response to a physician). Indeed, these poorly understood factors and the effects of placebos are better called nonspecific therapeutic factors. For example, at least one study has shown that naloxone (Narcan), an opioid antagonist, can block the analgesic effects of a placebo; thus a release of an endogenous opioid may explain some placebo effects.

Long-term treatment with placebos should never be undertaken when patients have clearly stated an objection to such a treatment. Furthermore, deceptive treatment with placebos seriously undermines patients' confidence in their physicians. Placebos should never be used when an effective therapy is available, as placebos can lead to both a dependence on pills and various adverse effects.

ACUPUNCTURE AND ACUPRESSURE

An ancient Chinese treatment, acupuncture is the stimulation of specific points of the body with electrical stimulation or the twisting of a needle. Acupressure is the stimulation of these same points with pressure, but acupressure was not a part of traditional Chinese medicine. The stimulation of specific points is associated with the relief of certain symptoms and is identified with particular organs. Many Chinese doctors have reported therapeutic success with these treatments in combination with herbal treatment (given orally, topically, or intradermally) for a variety of disorders, including mental disorders. Several U.S. investigators have reported that acupuncture is an effective treatment for some patients with depressive disorders and substance dependence (for example, to nicotine, caffeine, cocaine, and heroin). Although it is difficult to approach Eastern treatments with a Western mind, it is also true that history has shown that many ancient remedies have a firm biological basis.

ORTHOMOLECULAR THERAPY

Megavitamin therapy is treatment with large dosages of niacin, ascorbic acid, pyridoxine, folic acid, vitamin B_{12}, and various minerals. Special diets and hormone treatments are often part of these treatment protocols. Uncontrolled reports of the successful treatment of schizophrenia with niacin have not been replicated in controlled collaborative studies. Despite claims to the contrary, megavitamin and diet therapies currently have no proved clinical use in psychiatry; however, a balanced diet reasonably supplemented with vitamins is a good prescription for all patients and physicians.

PLANT EXTRACTS

Health foods and herbal medicines constitute a huge industry that offers a wide array of treatments, some of which have been studied in well-designed trials. A full listing of herbal therapies is beyond the scope of this book, but one example serves to illustrate the promise and limitations of such therapies. *Hypericum perforatum,* also called St. John's wort, has been shown in several trials of variable rigor to be superior to placebo and comparable to tricyclic drugs in effectiveness for treatment of mild and moderate depression. It has not been shown to be effective for severe depression. The active pharmacological ingredients have not been isolated, although several dozen distinct compounds called hypericins have been detected in the stem and flowers of the herb. The pharmacodynamic mechanism of the apparent antidepressant and its antianxiety effects also have not been determined. The extracts are widely used in Europe and are generating interest in the United States. At this time, clinical guidelines for use of St. John's wort have not been established by the Food and Drug Administration (FDA).

HISTORICAL TREATMENTS

In psychiatry, various treatments were used before the introduction of effective pharmacological agents. Although most treatments never underwent controlled therapeutic trials, many clinicians reported that the treatments were, in fact, effective. But because most of them were associated with unpleasant or dangerous adverse effects, they have been virtually supplanted by pharmacotherapy.

Subcoma Insulin Therapy

Psychiatrists used to inject small doses of insulin to induce mild hypoglycemia and the resultant sedative effects. Because of the possible complications of the treatment and the introduction of sedating drugs, the treatment has been abandoned.

Coma Therapy

Insulin coma therapy was introduced in 1933 by Manfred Sakel after his observation that patients with schizophrenia who went into coma appeared to have decreased psychiatric symptoms after the coma. Insulin was used to induce a comatose state lasting 15 to 60 minutes. The risk of death or cognitive impairment and the introduction of antipsychotic drugs led to the abandonment of the treatment in the United States.

Atropine sulfate was first used in 1950 to induce coma in psychiatric patients. The atropine-induced comas lasted 6 to 8 hours, and patients took warm and cold showers after awakening. Atropine coma is no longer used in the United States.

Carbon Dioxide Therapy

Carbon dioxide therapy, first used in 1929, involved having patients inhale carbon dioxide; an abreaction with severe motor excitement occurred after the breathing mask was removed. The treatment was used principally for neurotic patients, and there was doubt, even when it was in use, that the treatment was effective. Carbon dioxide therapy is no longer used in the United States.

Electrosleep Therapy

Electrosleep therapy involves applying a low level of current through electrodes applied to a patient's head. Patients usually feel a tingling sensation at the sites of the electrodes, but sleep is not necessarily induced. The treatment is applied to a wide variety of disorders, with mixed reports of efficacy, but it is not used in the United States.

Continuous Sleep Treatment

Continuous sleep treatment is a symptomatic method of treatment in which patients are sedated with any of a variety of drugs to induce 20 hours of sleep a day, sometimes for as long as 3 weeks in severely agitated patients. Klaesi introduced the name in 1922 and used barbiturates to obtain deep narcosis. The treatment is not used in the United States.

REFERENCES

Abarbanel JM, Lemberg T, Yaroslavski U, Grisaru N, et al: Electrophysiological responses to transcranial magnetic stimulation in depression and schizophrenia. Biol Psychiatry *40* (2): 148, 1996.

Avants SK, Margolin A, Chang P, Kosten TR, at al: Acupuncture for the treatment of cocaine addiction: Investigation of a needle puncture control. J Subst Abuse Treat *12* (3): 195, 1995.

Baischer W: Acupuncture in migraine: Long-term outcome and predicting factors. Headache *35* (8): 472, 1995.

Craig AR, Kearns M: Results of a traditional acupuncture intervention for stuttering. J Speech Hear Res *38* (3): 572, 1995.

Cumming S, Hay P, Lee T, Sachdev P: Neuropsychological outcome from psychosurgery for obsessive-compulsive disorder. Aust NZ J Psychiatry *29* (2): 293, 1995.

Duzel E, Hufnagel A, Helmstaedter C, Elger C: Verbal working memory components can be selectively influenced by transcranial magnetic stimulation in patients with left temporal lobe epilepsy. Neuropsychologia *34* (8): 775, 1996.

George MS, editor: Transcranial magnetic stimulation. CNS Spectrums *2:* 17, 1997.

George MS, Wassermann EM, Williams WA, Callahan A, et al: Daily repetitive transcranial magnetic stimulation (rTMS) improves mood in depression. Neurorep Int J Rapid Communication Res Neurosci *6* (14): 1853, 1995.

Hay P, Sachdev P, Cumming S, Smith JS, Lee T, Kitchener P, Matheson J: Treatment of obsessive-compulsive disorder by psychosurgery. Acta Psychiatr Scand *87:* 197, 1993.

Ishimaru K, Kawakita K, Sakita M: Analgesic effects induced by TENS and electroacupuncture with different types of stimulating electrodes on deep tissues in human subjects. Pain *63* (2): 181, 1995.

Leibenluft E, Turner EH, Feldman-Naim S, Schwartz PJ, et al: Light therapy in patients with rapid cycling bipolar disorder: Preliminary results. Psychopharmacol Bull *31* (4): 705, 1995.

Levitt AJ, Joffe RT, Moul DE, Lam RW, Teicher MH, Lebegue B, Murray MG, Oren DA, Schwartz P, Buchanan A, Glod CA, Brown J: Side effects of light therapy in seasonal affective disorder. Am J Psychiatry *150:* 650, 1993.

Neumeister A, Goessler R, Lucht M, Kapitany T, et al: Bright light therapy stabilizes the antidepressant effect of partial sleep deprivation. Biol Psychiatry *39* (1): 16, 1996.

Pascual-Leone A, Dang N, Cohen LG, Brasil-Neto JP, et al: Modulation of muscle responses evoked by transcranial magnetic stimulation during the acquisition of new fine motor skills. J Neurophysiol *74* (3): 1037, 1995.

Riemann D, Vollmann J, Hohagen F, Lohner H, et al: Treatment of depression with sleep deprivation and sleep phase advance. Fortschr Neurol Psychiatr *63* (7): 270, 1995.

Rosenthal NE, Moul DE, Hellekson CJ, Oren DA, Frank A, Brainard GC, Murray MG, Wehr TA: A multicenter study of the light visor for seasonal affective disorder: No difference in efficacy found between two different intensities. Neuropsychopharmacology *8:* 151, 1993.

Turner EH, Leibenluft E, Albert PS, Wehr TA, et al: Effect of season and light treatment upon hot flashes in a perimenopausal SAD patient. Chronobiol Int *12* (4): 290, 1995.

Vincent C, Furnham A: Why do patients turn to complementary medicine? An empirical study. Br J Clin Psychol *35* (1): 37, 1996.

Wirz-Justice A, Graw P, Krauchi K, Sarrafzadeh A: ''Natural'' light treatment of seasonal affective disorder. J Affect Disord *37* (2): 109, 1996.

36

Child Psychiatry: Assessment, Examination, and Psychological Testing

A comprehensive evaluation of a child or adolescent is intended to develop a formulation of the child's overall functioning based on genetic contributions, maturational pattern, environmental factors, and adaptation to the environment. As developmental level and age increase, the evaluation increasingly focuses on the psychiatrist's direct interaction with the child. Thus, with adolescents, it is appropriate to include the adolescent in the initial interview, either alone or with parents or caregivers. Psychiatrists do not usually see young children alone in the first contact; it is difficult for a young child to synthesize his or her history.

A comprehensive evaluation of a child includes clinical interviews with the parents, the child, and the family; information regarding the child's current school functioning; and a standardized assessment of the child's intellectual level and academic achievement. In some cases, developmental tests and neuropsychological assessments are useful. Because psychiatric evaluations of children are rarely initiated by the child, clinicians must obtain information from the family, the school, and any involved community agencies to understand the reasons for the referral. Although children can be excellent informants about symptoms related to mood and inner experiences such as psychotic phenomena, sadness, fears, and anxiety, they often have difficulty with the chronology of symptoms and are sometimes reticent to report behaviors that have got them into trouble. Very young children often cannot articulate their experiences verbally and are better at showing their feelings and preoccupations in a play situation.

The first step in the comprehensive evaluation of a child or adolescent is to obtain a full description of the current concerns, and a history of the child's psychiatric and medical status. The interview and observation of the child are the next steps, followed by psychological testing.

Clinical interviews offer the most flexibility in understanding the evolution of problems and in establishing the role of environmental stressors, but clinical interviews may not systematically cover every clinical area. To increase the information generated, the clinician may use semistructured or structured interviews such as the Kiddie Schedule for Affective Disorders and Schizophrenia (K–SADS), the Diagnostic Interview Schedule for Children–Revised (DISC-R), and rating scales, such as the Child Behavior Checklist and the Teacher Questionnaire.

Disagreement often exists about many symptoms and behaviors found during a child's comprehensive assessment. When faced with contradictory information, the clinician must realize that these differences may reflect an accurate picture of the child in different settings. Once a full history is obtained from the parents, the child is examined, the child's current functioning at home and at school is assessed, and psychological testing is completed, the clinician can make a best-estimate diagnosis by using all the available information and then can make recommendations.

CLINICAL INTERVIEWS

To conduct a useful interview with a child of any age, clinicians must be familiar with normal development to put the child's responses in the proper perspective. For example, a young child's discomfort on separation from a parent and a school-age child's lack of clarity about the purpose of the interview are both perfectly normal and should not be misconstrued as psychiatric symptoms. Furthermore, behavior that is normal in a child at one age, such as temper tantrums in a 2 year old, takes on a different meaning, for example, in a 17 year old.

The interviewer's first task is to engage the child and to develop a rapport, so that the child is comfortable. The interviewer should learn what is the child's concept of the purpose of the interview and should ask what parents have told the child. The interviewer can then briefly describe the reason for the interview in a way that the child understands and that supports the child. During the interview, the clinician should learn about the child's relationships with family members and peers, the child's academic and behavior functioning in school, and the child's pleasurable activities. A general sense of the child's cognitive functioning is a part of the mental status examination.

The confidentiality level in child assessment is correlated with the age of the child. Just about all specific information is shared with the parents of a very young child, whereas more privacy is reasonable with an adolescent. School-age and older children may be told that if the clinician becomes concerned that a child is dangerous to himself or herself or to others, this information must be shared with other adults. The clinician must determine whether the child is safe in his or her environment and must make clinical judgments about whether the child is a victim of abuse or neglect.

Toward the end of the interview, the child may be asked in an open-ended manner whether he or she would like to bring up anything else. Every child should be complimented for his or her cooperation and thanked for participating in the interview, and the interview should end on a positive note.

Infants and Young Children

Assessments of infants usually begin with the parents present, as very young children may be frightened by the interview situation; the interview with the parents present provides the clinician with best way to assess the parent–infant interaction. Infants may be referred for a variety of reasons, including high levels of irritability, difficulty in being consoled, eating disturbances, poor weight gain, sleep disturbances, withdrawn behavior, lack of engagement in play, and developmental delay. The clinician assesses areas of functioning that include motor development, activity level, verbal communication, ability to engage in play, problem-solving skills, adaptation to daily routines, relationships, and social responsiveness. The parents' ability to provide a nurturing, safe, and stimulating environment for the child is assessed through observation and discussions with them. The child's developmental level of functioning is determined by combining observations made during the interview with standardized developmental measures. Observations of play reveal a child's developmental level and reflect the child's emotional state and preoccupations. The examiner can interact with an infant age 18 months or less in a playful manner by using such games as peekaboo. Children between the ages of 18 months and 3 years can be observed in a playroom. Children ages 2 years or older may exhibit symbolic play with toys, revealing more in this mode than through conversation. The use of puppets and dolls with children less than 6 years of age is often an effective way to elicit information, especially if questions are directed to the dolls, rather than to the child.

School-Age Children

Some school-age children are at ease when conversing with an adult; others are hampered by fear, anxiety, poor verbal skills, or oppositionalism. School-age children can usually tolerate a 45-minute session. The room should be spacious enough for the child to move around in, but not large enough to reduce intimate contact between the examiner and the child. Part of the interview can be reserved for unstructured play, and various toys can be made available to capture the child's interest and to elicit themes and feelings.

The initial part of the interview explores the child's understanding of the reasons for the meeting. The clinician should confirm the fact that the interview was not set up because the child did something wrong. Techniques that can facilitate the disclosure of feelings include asking the child to draw a person, family members, and a house and then questioning the child about the drawings. Children may be asked to reveal three wishes, to describe the best and worst events of their lives, and to name a favorite person to be stranded with on a desert island. Games such as Donald Winnicott's squiggle, in which the examiner draws a curved line and then the examiner and the child take turns continuing the drawing, may open lines of communication.

Questions that are partially open-ended with some multiple choices may elicit the most complete answers in school-age children. Simple, closed (yes–no) questions may not elicit enough information, and completely open-ended questions can overwhelm a school-age child who is not able to construct a chronological narrative. These reactions can result in a shrugging of the child's shoulders. The use of indirect commentary—such as, "I once knew a child who felt very sad when he moved away from all his friends"—is helpful, although the clinician must be careful not to lead the child into confirming what the child thinks the clinician wants to hear. School-age children respond well to clinicians who help them compare moods or feelings by asking them to rate feelings on a scale of 1 to 10.

Adolescents

Adolescents can usually give a chronological account of the events leading to the evaluation, although some may disagree with the need for the evaluation. The clinician should communicate the value of hearing the story from an adolescent's point of view and must be careful to reserve judgment and not assign blame. Adolescents may be concerned about confidentiality, and clinicians can assure them that permission will be requested from them before any specific information is shared with parents, except situations involving danger to the adolescent or others, in which case confidentiality must be sacrificed. Adolescents can be approached in an open-ended manner; however, when silences occur during the interview, the clinician should attempt to reengage the patient. Clinicians can explore what the adolescent believes the outcome of the evaluation will be (change of school, hospitalization, removal from home, removal of privileges).

Some adolescents approach the interview with apprehension or outright hostility, but they open up when a clinician is neither punitive nor judgmental. Clinicians must be aware of their own responses to adolescents' behavior (countertransference), and must remain therapeutic, even in the face of defiant, angry, or difficult teenagers. Clinicians should set appropriate limits and should postpone or discontinue an interview if they feel threatened or if patients become destructive to property or to themselves. Interviews should always include an exploration of suicidal thoughts, assaultive behavior, psychotic phenomena, substance use, and sexual relationships. Once rapport has been established, many adolescents appreciate the opportunity to tell their side of the story and may reveal things that they have not disclosed to anyone else.

Family Interview

An interview in which both the parents and the patient are present may take place first or may occur later in the evaluation. Sometimes an interview with the entire family, including other children, can be enlightening. The purpose is to observe the attitudes of the parents toward the patient and the affective responses of the children to their parents. The clinician's job is to maintain a nonthreatening atmosphere in which each member of the family can speak freely without feeling that the clinician is taking sides with any particular member. Although child psychiatrists generally function as advocates for the child, the clinician must validate each family member's feelings in the setting, because lack of communication often contributes to the patient's problems.

Parents

The interview with the patient's parents or caretakers is necessary to get a chronological picture of the child's growth and development. A thorough developmental history and details of any stressors or important events that have influenced the child's development must be elicited. The parents' view of the family dynamics, their marital history, and their own emotional adjustment are also elicited. The family's psychiatric history and the parenting styles of the grandparents are pertinent. Parents can be the best informants about the child's previous psychiatric and medical illnesses, evaluations, and treatments, and the time frame and severity of any preexisting problems. Clinicians should question parents about their understanding of the causes and nature of their child's problems and about their expectations about the assessment and potential treatments.

STRUCTURED AND SEMISTRUCTURED INTERVIEWS

In a structured interview, information that might otherwise be overlooked or minimized is collected in a comprehensive way. Structured interviews, however, cannot replace clinical interviews, because structured interviews do not adequately address the chronology of symptoms, the interplay between environmental stressors and emotional responses, and developmental issues. Nevertheless, clinicians may find it helpful to combine the data from a structured interview with other materials in a comprehensive evaluation.

Kiddie Schedule for Affective Disorders and Schizophrenia (K–SADS)

This semistructured interview presents multiple items with some space for further clarification of symptoms that are keyed to many diagnoses in the third edition of *Diagnostic and Statistical Manual of Mental Disorders* (DSM-III). The schedule comes in a form for parents to give information about their child and in a version for use directly with the child. The schedule takes about 1 to 1½ hours to administer and is applicable to children between the ages of 6 and 17 years. The interviewer should have some training in the field of child psychiatry, but need not be a psychiatrist.

Diagnostic Interview Schedule for Children–Revised (DISC-R)

The Diagnostic Interview Schedule for Children–Revised structured interview was designed to be administered by trained laypersons. It is available in parallel child and parent forms, and it is applicable for a multitude of diagnoses keyed to the revised third edition of DSM (DSM-III-R); a computer scoring algorithm is available. As it is a fully structured interview, the instructions serve as a complete guide for the questions, and the examiner need not have any knowledge of child psychiatry to administer the interview correctly. It is applicable to children between the ages of 8 and 17 years. The interview assesses symptoms over the previous 6 months and, thus, may be useful adjunctively in the evaluation process.

RATING SCALES

Child Behavior Checklist

The parent and teacher versions of the Child Behavior Checklist were developed to cover a broad range of symptoms and several positive attributes related to academic and social competence. The checklist presents items related to mood, frustration tolerance, hyperactivity, oppositional behavior, anxiety, and various other behaviors. The parent version consists of 118 items rated on a scale of 0 (not true), 1 (sometimes true), and 2 (very true). The teacher version is similar but without the items that apply only to home life. Profiles were developed that are based on normal children of three different age groups (4 to 5, 6 to 11, and 12 to 16).

Such a checklist identifies specific problem areas that may otherwise be overlooked, and it may point out areas in which the child's behavior is deviant, compared with normal children of the same age group. The checklist is not used specifically to make diagnoses.

Revised Behavior Problem Checklist

Consisting of 150 items that cover a variety of childhood behavioral and emotional symptoms, the Revised Behavior Problem Checklist discriminates between clinic-referred and nonreferred children. Separate subscales have been found to correlate in the appropriate direction with other measures of intelligence, academic achievement, clinical observations, and peer popularity. As with the other broad rating scales, such an instrument can be helpful in gaining a comprehensive view of a multitude of behavioral areas, yet it is not designed to make psychiatric diagnoses.

CHILD PSYCHIATRIC EVALUATION

Psychiatric evaluation for a child should include a description of the reason for the referral, the child's past and present functioning, and any test results. An outline of the evaluation is given in Table 36–1.

Identifying Data

To understand the clinical problems to be evaluated, the clinician must first identify the patient and keep in mind the family constellation surrounding the child. The clinician must also pay attention to the source of the referral—that is, whether it is the child's family, school, or another agency, as this fact influences the family's attitude toward the evaluation. Finally, many informants contribute to the child's evaluation, and identifying each of them is important in gaining insight into the child's functioning in different settings.

Table 36–1
Child Psychiatric Evaluation

Identifying data
- Identified patient and family members
- Source of referral
- Informants

History
- Chief complaint
- History of present illness
- Developmental history and milestones
- Psychiatric history
- Medical history, including immunizations
- Family social history and parents' marital status
- Educational history and current school functioning
- Peer relationship history
- Current family functioning
- Family psychiatric and medical histories
- Current physical examination

Mental status examination

Neuropsychiatric examination (when applicable)

Developmental, psychological, and educational testing

Formulation and summary

DSM-IV diagnosis

Recommendations and treatment plan

History

A comprehensive history contains information about the child's current and past functioning, based on parents' reports in clinical and structured interviews and from those of teachers and previous medical and psychiatric physicians and therapists. The chief complaint, the history of the present illness, and the child's developmental history are usually obtained from the parents. Psychiatric and medical histories, current physical examination findings, and immunization histories are usually obtained from the psychiatrists and pediatricians who have treated the child in the past. The child is helpful in reporting the current situation regarding peer relationships, adjustment to school, and family functioning. The family's psychiatric and social histories are best obtained from the parents.

Mental Status Examination

A detailed description of the child's current mental functioning can be obtained through observation and specific questioning. An outline of the mental status examination is presented in Table 36–2.

Physical Appearances. The examiner should note and document the child's size, grooming, nutritional state, bruising, head circumference, physical signs of anxiety, facial expressions, and mannerisms.

Parent–Child Interaction. The examiner can observe the interactions between parents and child in the waiting area before the interview and in the family session. The manner in which parents and child converse and the emotional overtones are pertinent.

Separation and Reunion. The examiner should note both the manner in which the child responds to the separation from a parent for an individual interview and the reunion behavior. Either lack of affect at separation and reunion or severe distress on separation or reunion can indicate the presence of problems in the parent–child relationship or other psychiatric disturbances.

Orientation to Time, Place, and People. Impairments in orientation can reflect organic damage, low intelligence, or a thought disorder. The age of the child must be kept in mind, however, because very young children are not expected to know the date, other chronological information, or the name of the interview site.

Speech and Language. The examiner should note the presence of a level of speech and language acquisition appropriate for the child's age. An observable disparity between expressive language usage and receptive language is notable. The examiner should also note the child's rate of speech, rhythm, latency to answer, spontaneity of speech, intonation, articulation of words, and prosody. Echolalia, repetitive stereotypical phrases, and unusual syntax are important psychiatric findings. Children who do not use words by age 18 months or who do not use phrases by age 2½ to 3 years, but who have a history of normal babbling and responding appropriately to nonverbal cues are probably developing normally. The examiner should consider the possibility that a hearing loss is contributing to a speech and language deficit.

Mood. A child's sad expression, lack of appropriate smiling, tearfulness, anxiety, euphoria, and anger are valid indicators of mood, as are verbal admissions of feelings. Persistent themes in play and fantasy also reflect the child's mood.

Table 36–2
Mental Status Examination for Children

1. Physical appearance
2. Parent–child interaction
3. Separation and reunion
4. Orientation to time, place, and person
5. Speech and language
6. Mood
7. Affect
8. Thought process and content
9. Social relatedness
10. Motor behavior
11. Cognition
12. Memory
13. Judgment and insight

Affect. The examiner should note the child's range of emotional expressivity, appropriateness of affect to thought content, ability to move smoothly from one affect to another, and sudden labile emotional shifts.

Thought Process and Content. In evaluating a thought disorder in a child, the clinician must always consider what is developmentally expected for the child's age and what is deviant for any age group. The evaluation of the form of thought considers loosening of associations, excessive magical thinking, perseveration, echolalia, the child's ability to distinguish fantasy from reality, sentence coherence, and the ability to reason logically. The evaluation of the content of thought considers delusions, obsessions, themes, fears, wishes, preoccupations, and interests.

Suicidal ideation is always a part of the mental status examination for children who are sufficiently verbal to understand the questions and old enough to understand the concept. Children of average intelligence more than 4 years of age usually have some understanding of what is real and what is make-believe and may be asked about suicidal ideation, although a firm concept of the permanence of death may not be present until several years later.

Aggressive thoughts and homicidal ideation are assessed here. Perceptual disturbances, such as hallucinations, are also assessed. Very young children are expected to have short attention spans and may change the topic and conversation abruptly without exhibiting a symptomatic flight of ideas. Transient visual and auditory hallucinations in very young children do not necessarily represent major psychotic illnesses, but they do deserve further investigation.

Social Relatedness. The examiner assesses the appropriateness of the child's response to the interviewer, general level of social skills, eye contact, and degree of familiarity or withdrawal in the interview process. Overly friendly or familiar behavior may be as troublesome as extremely retiring and withdrawn responses. The examiner assesses the child's self-esteem, general and specific areas of confidence, and success with family and peer relationships.

Motor Behavior. This part of the mental status examination includes observations of the child's activity level, ability to pay attention and to carry out developmentally appropriate tasks, coordination, involuntary movements, tremors, motor overflow, and any unusual focal asymmetries of muscle movement.

Cognition. The examiner assesses the child's intellectual functioning, problem-solving abilities, and memory. An approximate level of intelligence can be estimated by the child's general information, vocabulary, and comprehension. For a specific assessment of the child's cognitive abilities, the examiner can use a standardized test.

Memory. School-age children should be able to remember three objects after 5 minutes and to repeat five digits forward and three digits backward. Anxiety may interfere with the child's performance, but an obvious inability to repeat digits or to add simple numbers together may reflect brain damage, mental retardation, or learning disabilities.

Judgment and Insight. The child's view of the problems, reactions to them, and potential solutions suggested by the child may give the clinician a good idea of the child's judgment and insight. In addition, the child's understanding of what he or she can realistically do to help and what the clinician can do adds to the assessment of the child's judgment.

Neuropsychiatric Assessment

A neuropsychiatric assessment is appropriate for children who are suspected of having a neurological disorder, a psychiatric impairment that coexists with neurological signs, or psychiatric symptoms that may be due to neuropathology. The neuropsychiatric evaluation combines information from neurological, physical, and mental status examinations. The neurological examination can identify asymmetrical abnormal signs (hard signs) that may indicate lesions in the brain. A physical examination can evaluate the presence of physical stigmata of particular syndromes in which neuropsychiatric symptoms or developmental aberrations play a role (for example, fetal alcohol syndrome, Down's syndrome).

Part of the neuropsychiatric examination is the assessment of neurological soft signs and minor physical anomalies. The term *neurological soft signs* was first noted by Lauretta Bender in the 1940s in reference to nondiagnostic abnormalities in the neurological examinations of children with schizophrenia. Soft signs are not indicative of focal neurological disorders, but they are associated with a wide variety of developmental disabilities and occur frequently in children with low intelligence, learning disabilities, and behavioral disturbances. Soft signs may refer to both behavioral symptoms (which are sometimes associated with brain damage, such as severe impulsivity and hyperactivity), physical findings (including contralateral overflow movements), and a variety of nonfocal signs (such as mild choreiform movements, poor balance, mild incoordination, asymmetry of gait, nystagmus, and the persistence of infantile reflexes). Soft signs can be divided into those that are normal in a young child but become abnormal when they persist in an older child and those that are abnormal at any age. The Physical and Neurological Examination for Soft Signs (PANESS) is an instrument used with children up to the age of 15 years. It consists of 15 questions about general physical status and medical history and 43 physical tasks (for example, touch your finger to your nose, hop on one foot to the end of the line, tap quickly with your finger). Neurological soft signs are important to note, but they are not specific in making a psychiatric diagnosis.

Minor physical anomalies or dysmorphic features occur with a higher than usual frequency in children with developmental disabilities, learning disabilities, speech and language disorders, and hyperactivity. As with soft signs, the documentation of minor physical anomalies is part of the neuropsychiatric assessment, but it is rarely helpful in the diagnostic process and does not imply a good or bad prognosis. Minor physical anomalies include a high-arched palate, epicanthus folds, hypertelorism, low-set ears, transverse palmar creases, multiple hair whorls, a large head, a furrowed tongue, and partial syndactyly of several toes.

When a seizure disorder is being considered in the differential diagnosis or a structural abnormality in the brain is suspected, an electroencephalogram (EEG), computed tomography (CT), or magnetic resonance imaging (MRI) may be indicated.

Developmental, Psychological, and Educational Testing

Psychological tests are not always required to assess psychiatric symptoms, but they are valuable in determining a child's developmental level, intellectual functioning, and academic difficulties. A measure of adaptive functioning (including the child's competence in communication, daily living skills, socialization, and motor skills) is a prerequisite when a diagnosis of mental retardation is being considered. Table 36–3 outlines the general categories of psychological tests.

Development Tests for Infants and Preschoolers. The Gesell Infant Scale, the Cattell Infant Intelligence Scale, Bayley Scales of Infant Development, and the Denver Developmental Screening Test include developmental assessments of infants as young as 2 months of age. When used with very young infants, the tests focus on sensorimotor and social responses to a variety of objects and interactions. When these instruments are used with older infants and preschoolers, emphasis is placed on language acquisition. The Gesell Infant Scale measures development in four areas: motor, adaptive functioning, language, and social. The Cattell Infant Intelligence Scale was developed as a downward extension of the Stanford-Binet Intelligence Scale and is administered in a test-oriented fashion.

An infant's score on one of these developmental assessments is not a reliable way to predict a child's future intelligence quotient (IQ) in most cases. Infant assessments are valuable, however, in detecting developmental deviation and mental retardation and in raising suspicions of a developmental disorder. Whereas infant assessments rely heavily on sensorimotor functions, intelligence testing in older children and adolescents includes later-developing functions, including verbal, social, and abstract cognitive abilities.

Intelligence Tests for School-Age Children and Adolescents. The most widely used test of intelligence for school-age children and adolescents is the third edition of the Wechsler Intelligence Scale for Children (WISC-III). It can be given to children from 6 to 17 years old, yields a verbal IQ, a performance IQ, and a combined full-scale IQ. The verbal subtests consist of vocabulary, information, arithmetic, similarities, comprehension, and digit span (supplemental) categories. The performance subtests include block design, picture completion, picture arrangement, object assembly, coding, mazes (supplemental), and symbol search (supplemental). The scores of the supplemental subtests are not included in the computation of IQ.

Each subcategory is scored from 1 to 19, with 10 being the average score. An average full-scale IQ is 100; 70 to 80 represents borderline intellectual function; 80 to 90 is in the low average range; 90 to 109 is average; 110 to 119 is high average; and above 120 is in the superior or very superior range. The multiple breakdowns of the performance and verbal subscales allow a great flexibility in identifying specific areas of deficit and scatter in intellectual abilities. Because a large part of intelligence testing measures abilities used in academic settings, the breakdown of the WISC-III can also be helpful in pointing out skills in which a child is weak and may benefit from remedial education.

The Stanford-Binet Intelligence Scale covers an age range from 2 to 24 years. It relies on pictures, drawings, and objects for very young children and on verbal performance for older children and adolescents. This intelligence scale, the earliest version of an intelligence test of its kind, leads to a mental age score as well as an intelligence quotient.

The McCarthy Scales of Children's Abilities and the Kaufman Assessment Battery for Children are two other intelligence tests that are available for preschool and school-age children. They do not cover the adolescent age group.

LONG-TERM STABILITY OF INTELLIGENCE. Although a child's intelligence is relatively stable throughout the school-age years and adolescence, some factors can influence intelligence and a child's score on an intelligence test. The intellectual functions of children with severe mental illnesses and of those from low socioeconomic levels may decrease over time, whereas the IQs of children whose environments have been enriched may increase over time. Factors that influence a child's score on a given test of intellectual functioning and thus affect the accuracy of the test are motivation, emotional state, anxiety, and cultural milieu.

Perceptual and Perceptual Motor Tests. The Bender Visual Motor Gestalt test can be given to children between the ages of 4 and 12 years. The test consists of a set of spatially related figures that child is asked to copy. The scores are based on the number of errors. Although not a diagnostic test, it is useful in identifying developmentally age-inappropriate perceptual performances.

Personality Tests. Personality tests are not of much use in making diagnoses, and they are less satisfactory than intelligence tests in regard to norms, reliability, and validity, but they can be helpful in eliciting themes and fantasies.

The Rorschach test is a projective technique in which ambiguous stimuli—a set of bilaterally symmetrical inkblots—are shown to a child, who is then asked to describe what he or she sees in each. The hypothesis is that the child's interpretation of the vague stimuli reflects basic characteristics of personality. The examiner notes the themes and patterns. Two sets of norms have been established for the Rorschach test, one for children between 2 and 10 years and one for adolescents between 10 and 17 years.

A more structured projective test is the Children's Apperception Test (CAT), which is an adaptation of the Thematic Apperception Test (TAT). The CAT consists of cards with pictures of animals in scenes that are somewhat ambiguous but are related to parent–child and sibling issues, caretaking, and other relationships. The child is asked to describe what is hap-

Table 36–3
Commonly Used Child and Adolescent Psychological Assessment Instruments

Test	Ages or Grades	Comments and Data Generated
Intellectual Ability		
Wechsler Intelligence Scale for Children, 3rd edition (WISC-III) (Psychological Corporation)	6–16	Standard scores: verbal, performance, and full-scale IQ; scaled subtest scores permitting specific skill assessment
Wechsler Adult Intelligence Scale–Revised (WAIS-R) (Psychological Corporation)	16–adult	Same as WISC-R
Wechsler Preschool and Primary Scale of Intelligence (WPPSI) (Psychological Corporation)	4–6	Same as WISC-R
McCarthy Scales of Children's Abilities (MSCA) (Psychological Corporation)	2.6–8	Scores: general cognitive index (IQ equivalent), language, perceptual performance, quantitative memory and motor domain scores; percentiles
Kaufman Assessment Battery for Children (K–ABC) (American Guidance Service)	2.6–12.6	Well grounded in theories of cognitive psychology and neuropsychology. Allows immediate comparison of intellectual capacity with acquired knowledge. Scores: mental processing composite (IQ equivalent); sequential and simultaneous processing and achievement standard scores; scaled mental processing and achievement subtest scores; age equivalents, percentiles
Stanford-Binet Intelligence Scale, 4th edition (SB:FE) (Riverside Publishing Company)	2–23	Scores: IQ verbal, abstract-visual, and quantitative reasoning; short-term memory; standard age
Peabody Picture Vocabulary Test–Revised (PPVT-R) (American Guidance Service)	4–adult	Measures receptive vocabulary acquisition. Standard scores, percentiles, age equivalents
Development		
Gesell Infant Scale	8 wk–3 1/2 yr	Mostly motor development in the first year, with some social and language assessment
Bayley Scales of Infant Development	8 wk–2 1/2 yr	Motor and social
Denver Developmental Screening Test	2 mo–6 yr	Screening
Yale Revised Developmental Schedule	4 wk–6 yr	Gross motor, fine motor, adaptive, personal social, language
Achievement		
Woodcock-Johnson Psycho-Educational Battery (DLM/Teaching Resources)	K–12	Scores: reading and mathematics (mechanics and comprehension), written language, other academic achievement; grade and age scores, standard scores, percentiles
Wide-Range Achievement Test–Revised, Levels 1 and 2 (WRAT-R) (Jastak Associates)	Level 1: 5–11 Level 2: 12–75	Permits screening for deficits in reading, spelling, and arithmetic; grade levels, percentiles, stanines, standard scores
Kaufman Test of Educational Achievement, Brief and Comprehensive Forms (K–TEA) (American Guidance Service)	1–12	Standard scores: reading, mathematics, and spelling; grade and age equivalents, percentiles, stanines. Brief form sufficient for most clinical applications; comprehensive form allows error analysis and more detailed curriculum planning
Adaptive Behavior		
Vineland Adaptive Behavior Scales (American Guidance Service)	Normal: 0–19 Retarded: all ages	Standard scores: adaptive behavior composite and communication daily living skills, socialization and motor domains; percentiles, age equivalents, developmental age scores. Separate standardization groups for normal, visually handicapped, hearing impaired, emotionally disturbed, and retarded
Scales of Independent Behavior (DLM Teaching Resources)	Newborn–adult	Standard scores: four adaptive (motor, social interaction and communication, personal living, community living) and three maladaptive (internalized, asocial, and externalized) areas; general maladaptive index and broad independence cluster
Projective		
Rorschach Inkblots (Huber, Haus; U.S. Distrib.: Grune & Stratton)	3–adult	Special scoring systems. Most recently developed and increasingly universally accepted is Exner's (1974) Comprehensive System. Assesses perceptual accuracy, integration of affective and intellectual functioning, reality testing, and other psychological processes
Thematic Apperception Test (TAT) (Harvard University Press)	6–adult	Generates stories that are analyzed qualitatively. Assumed to provide especially rich data regarding interpersonal functioning

(continued)

Table 36–3 *(Continued)*

Test	Ages or Grades	Comments and Data Generated
Machover Draw-A-Person (DAP) test (Charles C Thomas)	3–adult	Qualitative analysis and hypothesis generation, especially regarding subject's feelings about self and significant others
Kinetic Family Drawing (KFD) (Brunner/Mazel)	3–adult	Qualitative analysis and hypothesis generation regarding a person's perception of family structure and sentient environment. Some objective scoring systems in existence
Rotter Incomplete Sentences Blank (Psychological Corporation)	Child, adolescent and adult forms	Primarily qualitative analysis, although some objective scoring systems have been developed
Personality		
Minnesota Multiphasic Personality Inventory (MMPI) (University of Minnesota Press)	16–adult	Most widely used personality inventory. Standard scores: 3 validity scales and 14 clinical scales
Millon Adolescent Personality Inventory (MAPI) (National Computer Systems)	13–18	Standard scores for 20 scales grouped into three categories: personality styles, expressed concerns, behavioral correlates. Normed on adolescent population. Focuses on broad functional spectrum, not just problem areas
Children's Personality Questionnaire (Institute for Personality and Ability Testing)	8–12	Measures 14 primary personality traits, including emotional stability, self-concept level, excitability, and self-assurance. Generates combined broad trait patterns, including extraversion and anxiety
Neuropsychological		
Beery-Buktenika Developmental Test of Visual-Motor Integration (VMI) (Modern Curriculum Press)	2–16	Screening instrument for visual-motor deficits. Standard scores, age equivalents, percentiles
Benton Visual Retention Test (Psychological Corporation)	6–adult	Assesses presence of deficits in visual-figural memory. Mean scores by age
Bender Visual Motor Gestalt test (American Orthopsychiatric Association)	5–adult	Assesses visual-motor deficits and visual-figural retention. Age equivalents
Reitan-Indiana Neuropsychological Test Battery for Children (Neuropsychology Press)	5–8	Cognitive and perceptual-motor tests for children with suspected brain damage
Halstead-Reitan Neuropsychological Test Battery for Older Children (Neuropsychology Press)	9–14	Same as Reitan-Indiana
Luria-Nebraska Neuropsychological Battery: Children's Revision (LNNB-C) (Western Psychological Services)	8–12	Sensory-motor, perceptual, and cognitive tests measuring 11 clinical and 2 additional domains of neuropsychological functioning. Provides standard scores

Reprinted with permission from Racusin GR, Moss NE: Psychological assessment of children and adolescents. In *Child and Adolescent Psychiatry: A Comprehensive Textbook,* M Lewis, editor, p 475. Williams & Wilkins, Baltimore, 1991. Adapted by Melvin Lewis, M.B.

pening and to tell a story about the scene. Animals are used because it was hypothesized that children may respond more readily to animal images than to human figures.

Drawings, toys, and play are also applications of projective techniques that can be used during the evaluation of children. Doll houses, dolls, and puppets have been especially helpful in allowing a child a nonconversational mode in which to express a variety of attitudes and feelings. Play materials that reflect household situations are likely to elicit a child's fears, hopes, and conflicts about the family.

Projective techniques have not fared well as standardized instruments. Rather than being considered tests, projective techniques are best considered as additional clinical modalities.

Educational Tests. Achievement tests measure the attainment of knowledge and skills in a particular academic curriculum. The Wide-Range Achievement Test–Revised (WRAT-R) consists of tests of knowledge and skills and timed performances of reading, spelling, and mathematics. It is used with children ranging from 5 years to adulthood. The test yields a score that is compared with the average expected score for the child's chronological age and grade level.

The Peabody Individual Achievement Test (PIAT) includes word identification, spelling, mathematics, and reading comprehension.

The Kaufman Test of Educational Achievement, the Gray Oral Reading Test–Revised (GORT-R), and the Sequential Tests of Educational Progress (STEP) are achievement tests that determine whether a child has achieved the educational level expected for the child's grade level. Children with an average IQ, whose achievement is significantly lower than expected for their grade level in one or more subjects, are considered to be learning disabled. Thus, achievement testing, combined with a measure of intellectual function, can identify specific learning disabilities for which remediation is recommended. Children who do not reach their grade level according to their chronological age, but who function intellectually in the borderline range or lower, are not necessarily learning disabled unless a disparity exists between their IQs and their levels of achievement.

Formulation and Summary

Once all the information is available, the clinician must put together all the pieces in a formulation that includes the psychodynamic summary, family environmental stressors, the psychiatric symptoms and any disorders that they constitute, and the specific physical, neuromotor, or developmental abnormalities causing the impairment. The clinician should also use the information from standardized psychological and developmental assessments in the summary. Because children are pervasively influenced by their environments, the psychiatric formulation includes not only a child's impairments but also the manner in which the family functions and affects the child's impairments. The clinician should also comment on the appropriateness of the child's educational setting and the issue of the child's general well-being with respect to abuse and neglect.

Diagnosis

At the close of the evaluation process, the clinician should make a diagnosis. A child whose daily function is significantly impaired either in a school setting or at home is likely to meet the criteria for one or more psychiatric disorders. DSM-IV provides a guideline for psychiatric diagnosis that reflects a consensus of current expertise in the field; other clinical situations may not fall into DSM-IV's categories, but they require psychiatric attention and treatment. When dealing with children who are an integral part of a family and who are vulnerable to environmental stressors, the clinician must consider interventions that go beyond the DSM-IV diagnoses.

Recommendations and Treatment Plan

Along with recommending appropriate courses of treatment for psychiatric disorders, clinicians must consider the family's level of functioning and the need for family and environmental interventions that are likely to ameliorate the child's condition. The clinician's decisions in these areas may range from determining that a child's entire family is in need of psychotherapy to recommending that a child's school setting be changed to recommending that the child live outside the family setting. The clinician must communicate the recommendations and proposed treatment plan to both the parents and the child; without the parents' cooperation, treatment may not be obtained.

In many cases, a child is referred by an outside agency, such as a school, therapist, or protective service agency. Therefore, with the family's permission, the clinician must communicate the recommendations to the referring source.

References

Bender L: Childhood schizophrenia: Clinical study of 100 schizophrenic children. Am J Orthopsychiatry *17:* 40, 1947.

Cantwell DP: Introduction and overview. In *Comprehensive Textbook of Psychiatry,* ed 6 HI Kaplan, BJ Sadock, editors, p 2151. Williams & Wilkins, Baltimore, 1995.

Caplan R, Guthrie D, Fish B, Tanguay PE, David-Lando G: The kiddie formal thought disorder rating scale: Clinical assessment, reliability, and validity. J Am Acad Child Adolesc Psychiatry *28:* 408, 1989.

Chandler MC, Gualtieri CT, Barnhill LJ: The neuropsychiatric examination of the child. In *Handbook of Studies on Child Psychiatry,* BJ Tonge, GD Burrows, JC Werry, editors, p 91. Elsevier, Amsterdam, 1990.

Gittleman R: The role of psychological tests for differential diagnosis in child psychiatry. J Am Acad Child Adolesc Psychiatry *19:* 413, 1980.

Gutterman EM, O'Brien JD, Young JG: Structured diagnostic interviews for children and adolescents: Current status and future directions. J Am Acad Child Psychiatry *26:* 621, 1987.

Herjanic B, Reich W: Development of a structured psychiatric interview for children: Agreement between child and parent on individual symptoms. J Abnorm Child Psychol *10:* 307, 1982.

Kaufman AS, Kaufman NL: *Kaufman Assessment Battery for Children: Interpretive Manual.* American Guidance Service, Circle Pines, MN, 1983.

Lewis M: Psychiatric examination of the infant, child, and adolescent. In *Comprehensive Textbook of Psychiatry,* ed 5, HI Kaplan, BJ Sadock, editors, p 1716. Williams & Wilkins, Baltimore, 1989.

Ollendick TH, Hersen M, editors: *Handbook of Child and Adolescent Assessment.* Allyn & Bacon, Boston, 1993.

Parrott R, Burgoon M, Ross C: Parents and pediatricians talk: Compliance-gaining strategies use during well-child exams. Health Commun *4:* 57, 1992.

Puig-Antich J, Chambers WJ, Tabrizi MA: The clinical assessment of current depressive episodes in children and adolescents: Interviews with parents and children. In *Affective Disorders in Childhood and Adolescence: An Update,* DP Cantwell, GA Carlson, editors, p 157. SP Medical & Scientific, New York, 1983.

Rating scales and assessment instruments for use in pediatric psychopharmacology research. Psychopharmacol Bull *21:* 205, 1985.

Wiener JM, editor: *Textbook of Child & Adolescent Psychiatry,* ed 2. American Psychiatric Press, Washington, 1997.

Winnicott DW: *Therapeutic Consultations in Child Psychiatry.* Hogarth Press, London, 1971.

Young JG, O'Brien JB, Gutterman EM, Cohen P: Research on the clinical interview. J Am Acad Child Adolesc Psychiatry *26:* 613, 1987.

37

Mental Retardation

In the fourth edition of *Diagnostic and Statistical Manual of Mental Disorders* (DSM-IV), mental retardation is defined as ''significantly subaverage general intellectual functioning'' accompanied by ''significant limitations in adaptive functioning,'' with an onset before the age of 18. Impaired functioning must accompany intellectual functioning, as assessed by a standard intelligence test, at an IQ of around 70; but environmental, physical, and other factors influencing both adaptive and intellectual functioning must be taken into account. DSM-IV allows for four grades of severity: mild, moderate, severe, and profound mental retardation. Mental retardation consists of a combination of below-average intellectual functioning and impairment in adaptive skills that manifest itself prior to the age of 18 years.

The *American Association of Mental Deficiency* (AAMD), like DSM-IV, defines mental retardation as a significantly subaverage general intellectual functioning resulting in or associated with concurrent impairments in adaptive behavior and manifested during the developmental period, before the age of 18. The diagnosis is made regardless of whether the person has a coexisting physical disorder or other mental disorder. Table 37–1 presents an overview of developmental levels in communication, academic functioning, and vocational skills expected of people with various degrees of mental retardation.

General intellectual functioning is determined by the use of standardized tests of intelligence, and the term *significantly subaverage* is defined as an intelligence quotient (IQ) of approximately 70 or below or two standard deviations below the mean for the particular test. Adaptive functioning can be measured by using a standardized scale, such as the Vineland Adaptive Behavior Scale. In this scale, communications, daily living skills, socialization, and motor skills (up to 4 years, 11 months) are scored and generate an adaptive behavior composite that is correlated with the expected skills at a given age.

Approximately 85 percent of people who are mentally retarded fall within the mild mental retardation category (IQ between 50 and 70). The adaptive functions of mildly retarded people are effective in several areas such as communications, self-care, social skills, work, leisure, and safety. Mental retardation is influenced by genetic, environmental, and psychosocial factors, and in past years, the development of mild retardation has often been attributed to severe psychosocial deprivation. More recently, however, researchers have increasingly recognized the likely contribution of a host of subtle biological factors including chromosomal abnormalities, subclinical lead intoxications, and prenatal exposure to drugs, alcohol, and other toxins. Furthermore, there is increasing evidence that subgroups of people who are mentally retarded, such as those with fragile X syndrome, Down's syndrome, and Prader-Willi syndrome, have characteristic patterns of social, linguistic, and cognitive development and typical behavior manifestations.

ICD-10

The 10th revision of *International Statistical Classification of Diseases and Related Health Problems* (ICD-10) approaches the diagnosis of mental retardation from a somewhat different viewpoint compared to DSM-IV. According to ICD-10, mental retardation is a condition of ''arrested or incomplete development of the mind'' characterized by impaired developmental skills that ''contribute to the overall level of intelligence.'' Language, motor, social, and cognitive abilities are thus affected. ICD-10 notes that retardation need not be accompanied by another mental or physical disorder but that the prevalence of other mental disorders among people who are retarded is 3 to 4 times higher than it is in the general population.

Adaptive behavior is almost always impaired in people who are retarded, but this fact may not be apparent in ''protected social environments.'' ICD-10 offers categories for specifying the extent of behavior impairment: none or minimal; significant, requiring treatment or attention; other impairments; no mention of impairments.

For a definite diagnosis of mental retardation, ICD-10 stipulates ''a reduced level of intellectual functioning resulting in diminished ability to adapt to the daily demands of the normal social environment.'' Global ability, not specific impairments, should be the basis of the diagnosis. In the view of ICD-10's editors, levels of intelligence should not be rigidly applied because of problems of cross-cultural validity. Intelligence tests and scales of social maturity and adaptation should be standardized according to local cultural norms. ''Without the use of standardized procedure, the diagnosis must be regarded as . . . provisional.''

People who are mildly retarded, according to ICD-10, acquire language somewhat late but speak well enough to manage in life. Most are able to take care of themselves although their skills may develop at a slower than usual rate. Their disabilities are evident when they learn reading and writing, but they can learn the basic skills and are capable of earning a living. Developmental disabilities may sometimes interfere with cultural expectations such as coping with marriage.

Moderately mentally retarded people may slowly gain limited language use and are impaired in caring for themselves. Some learn basic school skills, do simple work, and engage in social activities, but they probably achieve their full capacity

Table 37–1
Developmental Characteristics of Mentally Retarded Persons

Degree of Mental Retardation	Preschool Age (0–5) Maturation and Development	School Age (6–20) Training and Education	Adult (21 and Over) Social and Vocational Adequacy
Profound	Gross retardation; minimal capacity for functioning in sensorimotor areas; needs nursing care; constant aid and supervision required	Some motor development present; may respond to minimal or limited training in self-help	Some motor and speech development; may achieve very limited self-care; needs nursing care
Severe	Poor motor development; speech minimal; generally unable to profit from training in self-help; little or no communication skills	Can talk or learn to communicate; can be trained in elemental health habits; profits from systematic habit training; unable to profit from vocational training	May contribute partially to self-maintenance under complete supervision; can develop self-protection skills to a minimal useful level in controlled environment
Moderate	Can talk or learn to communicate; poor social awareness; fair motor development; profits from training in self-help; can be managed with moderate supervision	Can profit from training in social and occupational skills; unlikely to progress beyond second-grade level in academic subjects; may learn to travel alone in familiar places	May achieve self-maintenance in unskilled or semiskilled work under sheltered conditions; needs supervision and guidance when under mild social or economic stress
Mild	Can develop social and communication skills; minimal retardation in sensorimotor areas; often not distinguished from normal until later age	Can learn academic skills up to approximately sixth-grade level by late teens; can be guided toward social conformity	Can usually achieve social and vocational skills adequate to minimum self-support but may need guidance and assistance when under unusual social or economic stress

Adapted from *Mental Retarded Activities of the U.S. Department of Health, Education and Welfare,* p 2. US Government Printing Office, Washington, 1989. Used with permission. DSM-IV criteria are adapted essentially from this chart.

only in a structured, supervised setting. For most people with moderate mental retardation, an organic etiology is present.

Severe mental retardation, according to ICD-10, resembles the moderate category in clinical picture and organic causes. Limited or no language ability and marked motor or other impairments indicate central nervous system damage or maldevelopment. Those with profound mental retardation are severely limited in cognitive abilities, immobile or restrictedly mobile, incontinent, and incapable of providing for their most basic needs. Again, biological cause is usually present.

ICD-10 also includes the categories of other mental retardation, when assessment is extremely difficult or impossible, and unspecified mental retardation, when the information is insufficient to classify a person in one or another category.

The ICD-10 criteria are presented in Table 37–2.

NOMENCLATURE

DSM-IV specifies that a diagnosis of mental retardation can be made only when both the IQ, as measured by a standardized test, is subaverage and a measure of adaptive function reveals deficits in at least two of the following areas: communication, self-care, home living, social, community resources, self-direction, functional academic skills, work leisure, health, and safety. Mental retardation diagnosis care coded on Axis II in the DSM-IV. The term *mental deficiency* was used interchangeably with *mental retardation* until recently, when the AAMD chose *mental retardation* as the preferred term. The World Health Organization (WHO) has recommended the term *mental subnormality,* which includes two categories: mental retardation (subnormal functioning secondary to identifiable underlying pathological causes) and mental deficiency (IQ of less than 70), which is often used as a legal term.

CLASSIFICATION

The degrees or levels of mental retardation are expressed in various terms. DSM-IV presents four types of mental retardation, reflecting the degree of intellectual impairment: mild, moderate, severe, and profound. The degrees of mental retardation by IQ range are indicated in Tables 37–2 and 37–3. The category of borderline mental retardation (between one and two standard deviations below the test mean) was eliminated in 1973. Borderline intellectual functioning, according to DSM-IV, is not within the category of mental retardation but refers to an IQ in the 71 to 84 range and may be a focus of psychiatric attention. In addition, DSM-IV lists mental retardation, severity unspecified, as a type reserved for persons who are strongly suspected of having mental retardation but cannot be tested by standard intelligence tests or are too impaired or uncooperative to be tested. This type may be applicable to infants whose significantly subaverage intellectual functioning is clinically judged but for whom the available tests (for example, Bayley Scales of Infant Development and Cattell Infant Scale) do not yield numerical IQ values. This type should not be used when the intellectual level is presumed to be above 70.

EPIDEMIOLOGY

The prevalence of mental retardation at any one time is estimated to be about 1 percent of the population. The inci-

Table 37–2
ICD-10 Diagnostic Criteria for Mental Retardation

Detailed clinical diagnostic criteria that can be used internationally for research cannot be specified for mental retardation in the same way as they can for most of the other disorders in Chapter V(F) of ICD-10. This is because manifestations of the two main components of mental retardation, namely low cognitive ability and diminished social competence, are profoundly affected by social and cultural influences. Only general guidance can be given here about the most appropriate methods of assessment to use.

Level of cognitive abilities

Depending upon the cultural norms and expectations of the individuals being studied, research workers must make their own judgments as to how best to estimate intelligence quotient (IQ) or mental age according to the bands given below:

Category	*Mental retardation*	*IQ range*	*Mental age (years)*
F70	Mild	50–69	9 to under 12
F71	Moderate	35–49	6 to under 9
F72	Severe	20–34	3 to under 6
F73	Profound	Below 20	Less than 3

Level of social competence

Within most European and north American cultures, the Vineland Social Maturity Scale[a] is recommended for use, if it is judged to be appropriate. Modified versions or equivalent scales should be developed for use in other cultures.

A fourth character may be used to specify the extent of associated impairment of behaviour:

No, or minimal, impairment of behavior
Significant impairment of behavior requiring attention or treatment
Other impairments of behavior
Without mention of impairment of behavior

Comments

A specially designed multi-axial system is required to do justice to the variety of personal, clinical, and social statements needed for the comprehensive assessment of the causes and consequences of mental retardation. One such system is now in preparation for this section of Chapter V(F) of ICD-10.

[a] Doll EA: *Vineland Social Maturity Scale, Condensed Manual of Directions.* American Guidance Service Inc., Circle Pines MN. 1965.

Table 37–3
DSM-IV Diagnostic Criteria for Mental Retardation

A. Significantly subaverage intellectual functioning: an IQ of approximately 70 or below on an individually administered IQ test (for infants, a clinical judgment of significantly subaverage intellectual functioning).

B. Concurrent deficits or impairments in present adaptive functioning (ie, the person's effectiveness in meeting the standards expected for his or her age by his or her cultural group) in at least two of the following areas: communication, self-care, home living, social/interpersonal skills, use of community resources, self-direction, functional academic skills, work, leisure, health and safety.

C. The onset is before age 18 years.

Code based on degree of severity reflecting level of intellectual impairment:

Mild mental retardation: IQ level 50–55 to approximately 70
Moderate retardation: IQ level 35–40 to 50–55
Severe mental retardation: IQ level 20–25 to 35–40
Profound mental retardation: IQ level below 20 or 25
Mental retardation, severity unspecified: when there is a strong presumption of mental retardation but the person's intelligence is untestable by standard tests

dence of mental retardation is difficult to calculate because of the difficulty of identifying the onset. In many cases, retardation may be latent for a long time before a person's limitations are recognized. Because of good adaptation, a formal diagnosis sometimes cannot be made at a particular point in a person's life. The highest incidence is in school-age children, with the peak at ages 10 to 14. Mental retardation is about 1 + times more common among men than among women. In older people, prevalence is less; those with severe or profound mental retardation have high mortality rates resulting from the complications of associated physical disorders.

ETIOLOGY

Causative factors in mental retardation include genetic (chromosomal and inherited) conditions, prenatal exposure to infections and toxins, perinatal trauma (such as prematurity), acquired conditions, and sociocultural factors. The severity of the resulting mental retardation is related to the timing and duration of the trauma or its exposure to the central nervous system. The more severe the mental retardation, the more likely it is that the cause is evident. In about three fourths of people with severe mental retardation, the cause is known, whereas the cause is apparent in only half of those with mild mental retardation. No cause is known for three fourths of people with borderline intellectual functioning. Overall, in up to two thirds of all mentally retarded people, the probable cause can be identified. Among chromosomal and metabolic disorders, Down's syndrome, fragile X syndrome, and phenylketonuria (PKU) are the most common disorders that usually produce at least moderate mental retardation. Those with mild mental retardation sometimes have a familial pattern apparent in parents and siblings. Low socioeconomic groups seem to be overrepresented in cases of mild mental retardation, the significance of which is unclear. Current knowledge suggests that genetic, environmental, biological, and psychosocial factors work additively in mental retardation.

Genetic Factors

Abnormalities in autosomal chromosomes are associated with mental retardation, although aberrations in sex chromosomes are not always associated with mental retardation (such as Turner's syndrome with XO and Klinefelter's syndrome with XXY, XXXY, and XXYY variations). Some children with Turner's syndrome have normal to superior intelligence. There is agreement on a few predisposing factors for chromosomal disorders—among them, the older than usual age of the mother, possibly the increased age of the father, and X-ray radiation.

Down's Syndrome. The description of Down's syndrome, first made by the English physician Langdon Down in 1866, was based on the physical characteristics associated with subnormal mental functioning. Since then, Down's syndrome has remained the most investigated and the most discussed syndrome in mental retardation. The children with the syndrome were originally called mongoloid because of their physical characteristics of slanted eyes, epicanthal folds, and flat nose. Despite a plethora of theories and hypotheses advanced in the past 100 years, the cause of Down's syndrome is still unknown.

The problem of cause is complicated even further by the recent recognition of three types of chromosomal aberrations in Down's syndrome:

1. Patients with trisomy 21 (three of chromosome 21, instead of the usual two) represent the overwhelming majority; they have 47 chromosomes, with an extra chromosome 21. The mothers' karyotypes are normal. A nondisjunction during meiosis, occurring for unknown reasons, is held responsible for the disorder.
2. Nondisjunction occurring after fertilization in any cell division results in mosaicism, a condition in which both normal and trisomic cells are found in various tissues.
3. In translocation there is a fusion of two chromosomes, mostly 21 and 15, resulting in a total of 46 chromosomes, despite the presence of an extra chromosome 21. The disorder, unlike trisomy 21, is usually inherited, and the translocated chromosome may be found in unaffected parents and siblings. Those asymptomatic carriers have only 45 chromosomes.

The incidence of Down's syndrome in the United States is about 1 in every 700 births. In his original description, Down mentioned the frequency of 10 percent among all mentally retarded patients. Today, around 10 percent of patients with Down's syndrome are in institutions for people who are mentally retarded. For a middle-aged mother (more than 32 years old), the risk of having a child with Down's syndrome with trisomy 21 is about 1 in 100 births, but when translocation is present, the risk is about one in three. These facts assume special importance in genetic counseling.

Mental retardation is the overriding feature of Down's syndrome. Most people with the syndrome are moderately and severely retarded, with only a minority having an IQ above 50. Mental development seems to progress normally from birth to 6 months of age; IQ scores gradually decrease from near normal at 1 year of age to about 30 at older ages. The decline in intelligence may be real or apparent: Infantile tests may not reveal the full extent of the defect, which may become manifest when sophisticated tests are used in early childhood. According to many sources, children with Down's syndrome are placid, cheerful, and cooperative and adapt easily at home. With adolescence, the picture changes: Youngsters may experience various emotional difficulties, behavior disorders, and (rarely) psychotic disorders.

The diagnosis of Down's syndrome is made with relative ease in an older child but is often difficult in newborn infants. The most important signs in a newborn include general hypotonia, oblique palpebral fissures, abundant neck skin, a small, flattened skull, high cheekbones, and a protruding tongue. The hands are broad and thick, with a single palmar transversal crease, and the little fingers are short and curved inward. Moro reflex is weak or absent. More than 100 signs or stigmata are described in Down's syndrome, but rarely are all found in one person. Life expectancy was once about 12 years; with the advent of antibiotics, few young patients succumb to infections, but many do not live beyond the age of 40.

People with Down's syndrome tend to show a marked deterioration in language, memory, self-care skills, and problem solving in their 30s. Postmortem studies of those with Down's syndrome over the age of 40 have shown a high incidence of senile plaques and neurofibrillary tangles, as seen in Alzheimer's disease. Neurofibrillary tangles are known to occur in a variety of degenerative diseases, whereas senile plaques seem to be found most often in Alzheimer's disease and in Down's syndrome. Thus the two disorders may share some degree of pathophysiology.

Fragile X Syndrome. Fragile X syndrome is the second most common single cause of mental retardation. The syndrome results from a mutation on the X chromosome at what is known as the fragile site (Xq27.3). The fragile site is expressed in only some cells, and it may be absent in asymptomatic males and female carriers. Much variability is present in both genetic and phenotypic expression. Fragile X syndrome is believed to occur in about 1 in every 1,000 males and 1 in every 2,000 females. The typical phenotype includes a large, long head and ears, short stature, hyperextensible joints, and postpubertal macro-orchidism. The degree of mental retardation ranges from mild to severe. The behavioral profile of people with the syndrome includes a high rate of attention-deficit/hyperactivity disorder, learning disorders, and pervasive developmental disorders, such as autism. Deficits in language function include rapid perseverative speech with abnormalities in combining words into phrases and sentences. People with fragile X syndrome seem to have relatively strong skills in communications and socialization; their intellectual functions seem to decline in the pubertal period. Female carriers are often less impaired than are males with fragile X syndrome, but females can manifest the typical physical characteristics and can be mildly retarded.

Prader-Willi Syndrome. Prader-Willi syndrome is postulated to be the result of a small deletion involving chromosome 15, usually occurring sporadically. Its prevalence is less than 1 in 10,000. Persons with the syndrome exhibit compulsive eating behavior and often obesity, mental retardation, hypogonadism, small stature, hypotonia, and small hands and feet. Children with the syndrome often have oppositional and defiant behavior.

Cat's Cry (Cri-du-Chat) Syndrome. Children with cat's cry syndrome lack part of chromosome 5. They are severely retarded and show many signs often associated with chromosomal aberrations, such as microcephaly, low-set ears, oblique palpebral fissures, hypertelorism, and micrognathia. The characteristic catlike cry caused by laryngeal abnormalities which gave the syndrome its name gradually changes and disappears with increasing age.

Other Chromosomal Abnormalities. Other syndromes of autosomal aberrations associated with mental retardation are much less prevalent than is Down's syndrome. Various types of autosomal and sex chromosome aberration syndromes are included in Table 37–4.

Phenylketonuria. Phenylketonuria (PKU) was first described by Ivar Asbjörn Fölling in 1934 as the paradigmatic inborn error of metabolism. PKU is transmitted as a simple recessive autosomal Mendelian trait and occurs in about 1 in every 10,000 to 15,000 live births. For the parents who have already had a child with PKU, the chance of having another child with PKU is 1 in every 4 to 5 successive pregnancies. Although the disease is reported predominantly in people of North European origin, a few cases have been described in Blacks, Yemenite Jews, and Asians. The frequency among institutionalized retarded patients is about 1 percent. The basic metabolic defect in PKU is an inability to convert phenylalanine, an essential amino acid, to paratyrosine because of the absence or inactivity of the liver enzyme phenylalanine hydroxylase, which catalyzes the conversion. Two other types of hyperphenylalaninemia have recently been described. One is due to a deficiency of an enzyme, dihydroperidine reductase, and the other to a deficiency of a cofactor, biopterin. The first defect can be detected in fibroblasts, and biopterin can be measured in body fluids. Both these rare disorders carry a high risk of fatality.

Most patients with PKU are severely retarded, but some are reported to have borderline or normal intelligence. Eczema, vomiting, and convulsions are present in about a third of all cases. Although the clinical picture varies, typical children with PKU are hyperactive; they exhibit erratic, unpredictable behavior, and are difficult to manage. They frequently have temper tantrums and often display bizarre movements of their bodies and upper extremities and twisting hand mannerisms; their behavior sometimes resembles that of children with autism or schizophrenia. Verbal and nonverbal communication is usually severely impaired or nonexistent. The children's coordination is poor, and they have many perceptual difficulties.

The disease was previously diagnosed on the basis of a urine test: Phenylpyruvic acid in the urine reacts with ferric chloride solution to yield a vivid green color. The test, however, has its limitations; it may not detect the presence of phenylpyruvic acid in urine before a baby is 5 or 6 weeks old, and it may give positive responses with other aminoacidurias. Currently, a more reliable and widely used screening test is the Guthrie inhibition assay, which employs a bacteriological procedure to detect blood phenylalanine.

In the United States, newborn infants are now routinely screened for PKU. Early diagnosis is important, as a low phenylalanine diet, in use since 1955, significantly improves both behavior and developmental progress. The best results seem to be obtained with early diagnosis and the start of dietary treatment before the child is 6 months of age. Dietary treatment, however, is not without risk. Phenylalanine is an essential amino acid, and its omission from the diet may lead to such severe complications as anemia, hypoglycemia, edema, and even death. Dietary treatment of PKU should be continued

Table 37–4
Thirty-five Important Syndromes with Multiple Handicaps

Syndrome	Diagnostic Manifestations: Craniofacial	Diagnostic Manifestations: Skeletal	Diagnostic Manifestations: Other	Mental Retardation	Short Stature	Genetic Transmission
Aerskog-Scott syndrome	Hypertelorism; broad nasal bridge, anteverted nostrils, long philtrum	Small hands and feet; mild interdigital webbing; short stature	Scrotal shawl above penis		+	X-linked semidominant
Apert's syndrome (acrocephalosyndactyly)	Craniosynostosis; irregular midfacial hypoplasia; hypertelorism	Syndactyly; broad distal thumb and toe		±		Autosomal dominant
Cerebral gigantism (Sotos syndrome)	Large head; prominent forehead; narrow anterior mandible	Large hands and feet	Large size in early life; poor coordination	±		?

(continued)

Table 37–4 *(Continued)*

Syndrome	Diagnostic Manifestations: Craniofacial	Skeletal	Other	Mental Retardation	Short Stature	Genetic Transmission
Cockayne's syndrome	Pinched facies; sunken eyes; thin nose; prognathism; retinal degeneration	Long limbs, with large hands and feet; flexion deformities	Hypotrichosis; photosensitivity; thin skin; diminished subcutaneous fat; impaired hearing	+	+	Autosomal recessive
Cohen syndrome	Maxillary hypoplasia with prominent central incisors	Narrow hands and feet	Hypotonia; obesity	+	±	? Autosomal recessive
Cornelia de Lange syndrome	Synophrys (continuous eyebrows); thin downturning upper lip; long philtrum; anteverted nostrils; microcephaly.	Small or malformed hands and feet; proximal thumb	Hirsutism	+	+	?
Cri-du-chat syndrome	Epicanthic folds, slanting palpebral fissures; round facial contour; hypertelorism; microcephaly	Short metacarpals or metatarsals; four-finger line in palm	Catlike cry in infancy	+	+	?
Crouzon's syndrome (craniofacial dysostosis)	Proptosis with shallow orbits; maxillary hypoplasia; craniosynostosis					Autosomal dominant
Down's syndrome	Upward slant to palpebral fissures; midface depression; epicanthic folds; Brushfield spots; brachycephaly	Short hands; clinodactyly of fifth finger; four-finger line in palm	Hypotonia; loose skin on back of neck	+	+	Trisomy 21
Dubowitz syndrome	Small facies; lateral displacement of inner canthi; ptosis; broad nasal bridge; sparse hair; microcephaly		Infantile eczema; high-pitched hoarse voice	±	++	? Autosomal recessive
Fetal alcohol syndrome	Short palpebral fissures; mid-facial hypoplasia; microcephaly		± Cardiac defect; fine motor dysfunction	+	+	
Fetal hydantoin syndrome (phenytoin)	Hypertelorism; short nose; occasional cleft lip	Hypoplastic nails, especially fifth	Cardiac defect	±	±	
Goldenhar's syndrome	Malar hypoplasia; macrostomia; micrognathia; epibulbar dermoid, lipodermoid; malformed ear with preauricular tags	± Vertebral anomalies				?
Incontinentia pigmenti	± Dental defect; deformities of ears; ± patchy alopecia		Irregular skin pigmentation in fleck, whorf, or spidery form	±		? Dominant, X-linked ? Lethal in males
Laurence-Moon-Bardet-Biedl syndrome	Retinal pigmentation	Polydactyly; syndactyly	Obesity; seizures; hypogenitalism	+	±	Autosomal recessive
Linear nevus sebaceus syndrome	Nevus sebaceus, face or neck		± Seizures	+	±	?
Lowe's syndrome (oculocerebrorenal syndrome)	Cataract	Renal tubular dysfunction	Hypotonia	+	+	X-linked recessive
Möbius' syndrome (congenital facial diplegia)	Expressionless facies; ocular palsy	± Clubfoot; syndactyly		±	±	?
Neurofibromatosis	± Optic gliomas; acoustic neuromas	± Bone lesions; pseudarthroses	Neurofibromas; café-au-lait spots; seizures	±		Autosomal dominant
Noonan's syndrome	Webbing of posterior neck; malformed ears; hypertelorism	Pectus excavatum; cubitus valgus	Cryptorchidism; pulmonic stenosis	±	+	?

Table 37–4 *(Continued)*

Syndrome	Diagnostic Manifestations: Craniofacial	Diagnostic Manifestations: Skeletal	Diagnostic Manifestations: Other	Mental Retardation	Short Stature	Genetic Transmission
Prader-Willi syndrome	± Upward slant to palpebral fissures	Small hands and feet	Hypotonia, especially in early infancy; then polyphagia and obesity; hypogenitalism	+	+	?
Robin's syndrome	Micrognathia; glossoptosis; cleft palate, U-shaped		± Cardiac anomalies			?
Rubella	Cataract; retinal pigmentation; ocular malformations		Sensorineural deafness; patent ductus arteriosus	±	±	
Rubinstein-Taybi syndrome	Slanting palpebral fissures; maxillary hypoplasia; microcephaly	Broad thumbs and toes	Abnormal gait	+	+	?
Sackel syndrome	Facial hypoplasia; prominent nose; microcephaly	Multiple minor joint and skeletal abnormalities		+	+	Autosomal recessive
Sjögren-Larsson syndrome		Spasticity, especially of legs	Ichthyosis	+	+	Autosomal recessive
Smith-Lemli-Opitz syndrome	Anteverted nostrils, ptosis of eyelid	Syndactyly of second and third toes	Hypospadias; cryptorchidism	+	+	Autosomal recessive
Sturge-Weber syndrome	Flat hemangioma of face, most commonly trigeminal in distribution		Hemangiomas of meninges with seizures	±		?
Treacher Collins syndrome, (mandibulofacial dysostosis)	Malar and mandibular hypoplasia; downslanting palpebral fissures; defect of lower eyelid; malformed ears					Autosomal dominant
Trisomy 18	Microstomia; short palpebral fissures; malformed ears; elongated skull	Clenched hand, second finger over third; low arches on fingertips; short sternum	Cryptorchidism; congenital heart disease	+	+	Trisomy 18
Trisomy 13	Defects of eyes, nose, lips, ears, and forebrain of holoprosencephaly type	Polydactyly; narrow hyperconvex fingernails	Skin defects, posterior scalp	+	+	Trisomy 13
Tuberous sclerosis	Hamartomatous pink to brownish facial skin nodules	± Bone lesions	Seizures; intracranial calcification	±		Autosomal dominant
Waardenburg syndrome	Lateral displacement of inner canthi and puncta		Partial albinism; white forelock; heterochromia of iris; vitiligo; +/− deafness		Autosomal dominant	
Williams syndrome	Full lips; small nose with anteverted nostrils; iris dysplasia	Mild hypoplasia of nails	± Hypercalcemia in infancy; supravalvular aortic stenosis	+	+	?
Zellweger syndrome (cerebrohepatorenal syndrome)	High forehead; flat facies		Hypotonia; hepatomegaly; death in early infancy			

Adapted from Smith DW: Patterns of malformation. In *Nelson Textbook of Pediatrics*, ed 11, VC Vaughn III, RJ McKay, RE Behrman, editors, p 2035. Saunders, Philadelphia, 1979.

indefinitely. Children who receive a diagnosis before the age of 3 months and are placed on an optimal dietary regimen may have normal intelligence. For untreated older children and adolescents with PKU, a low phenylalanine diet does not influence the level of mental retardation. But the diet does decrease irritability and abnormal electroencephalogram (EEG) changes and does increase social responsiveness and attention span. The parents of children with PKU and some of the children's normal siblings are heterozygous carriers. The disease can be detected by a phenylalanine tolerance test, which may be important in genetic counseling of the people.

Rett's Disorder. Rett's disorder is hypothesized to be an X-linked dominant mental retardation syndrome that is degenerative and affects only females. In 1966, Andreas Rett reported on 22 girls with a serious progressive neurological disability. Deterioration in communications skills, motor behavior, and social functioning starts at 1 + years of age. Autistic-like symptoms are common, as are ataxia, facial grimacing, teeth grinding, and loss of speech. Intermittent hyperventilation and a disorganized breathing pattern are characteristic while the child is awake. Stereotypical hand movements, including handwringing, are typical. Progressive gait disturbance, scoliosis, and seizures occur. Severe spasticity is usually present by middle childhood. Cerebral atrophy occurs with decreased pigmentation of the substantia nigra, which suggests abnormalities of the dopaminergic nigrostriatal system. (The disorder is further discussed in Chapter 41.)

Neurofibromatosis. Also called von Recklinghausen's disease, neurofibromatosis is the most common of the neurocutaneous syndromes caused by a single dominant gene, which may be inherited or may be a new mutation. The disorder occurs in about 1 in 5,000 births and is characterized by café au lait spots on the skin and by neurofibromas, including optic gliomas and acoustic neuromas, caused by abnormal cell migration. Mild mental retardation is present in up to one third of those with the disease.

Tuberous Sclerosis. Tuberous sclerosis is the second most common of the neurocutaneous syndromes; a progressive mental retardation is present in up to two thirds of all affected people. It occurs in about 1 in 15,000 persons and is caused by autosomal dominant transmission. Seizures are present in all those who are mentally retarded and in two thirds of those who are not mentally retarded. Infantile spasms may occur as early as 6 months. The phenotypic presentation includes adenoma sebaceum and ash-leaf spots that can be identified with a slit lamp. The rate of autism is higher than the intellectual impairment would lead one to expect.

Lesch-Nyhan Syndrome. Lesch-Nyhan syndrome is a rare disorder caused by a deficiency of an enzyme involved in purine metabolism. The disorder is X linked; patients have mental retardation, microcephaly, seizures, choreoathetosis, and spasticity. The syndrome is also associated with severe compulsive self-mutilation by biting of the mouth and the fingers. Lesch-Nyhan syndrome is another example of a genetically determined syndrome in which a specific behavioral pattern is predictable.

Adrenoleukodystrophy. The most common of several disorders of sudanophilic cerebral sclerosis, adrenoleukodystrophy is characterized by diffuse demyelination of the cerebral white matter resulting in visual and intellectual impairment, seizures, spasticity, and progression to death. The cerebral degeneration in adrenoleukodystrophy is accompanied by adrenocortical insufficiency. The disorder is transmitted by a sex-linked gene located on the distal end of the long arm of the X chromosome. The clinical onset is generally between 5 and 8 years, with early seizures, disturbances in gait, and mild intellectual impairment. Abnormal pigmentation reflecting adrenal insufficiency sometimes precedes the neurological symptoms, and attacks of crying are common. Spastic contractures, ataxia, and disturbances of swallowing are also frequent. Although the course is often rapidly progressive, some patients may have a relapsing and remitting course. The story of a child with the disorder was presented in the 1992 film *Lorenzo's Oil.*

Maple Syrup Urine Disease. The clinical symptoms of maple syrup urine disease appear during the first week of life. The infant deteriorates rapidly and has decerebrate rigidity, seizures, respiratory irregularity, and hypoglycemia. If untreated, most patients die in the first months of life, and the survivors are severely retarded. Some variants have been reported with transient ataxia and only mild retardation. Treatment follows the general principles established for PKU and consists of a diet very low in the three involved amino acids—leucine, isoleucine, and valine.

Other Enzyme Deficiency Disorders. Several enzyme deficiency disorders associated with mental retardation have been identified, and still more diseases are being added as new discoveries are made, including Hartnup disease, galactosemia, and glycogen-storage disease. Thirty important disorders with inborn errors of metabolism, hereditary transmission patterns, defective enzymes, clinical signs, and relation to mental retardation are listed in Table 37–5.

Prenatal Factors

Important prerequisites for the overall development of the fetus include the mother's physical, psychological, and nutritional health during pregnancy. Maternal chronic illnesses and conditions affecting the normal development of the fetus's central nervous system include uncontrolled diabetes, anemia, emphysema, hypertension, and long-term use of alcohol and narcotic substances. Maternal infections during pregnancy, especially viral infections, have been known to cause fetal damage and mental retardation. The degree of fetal damage depends on such variables as the type of viral infection, the gestational age of the fetus, and the severity of the illness. Although numerous infectious diseases have been reported to affect the fetus's central nervous system, the following medical disorders have been definitely identified as high-risk conditions for mental retardation.

Table 37–5
Thirty Impairment Disorders with Inborn Errors of Metabolism

Disorder	Hereditary Transmission[a]	Enzyme Defect	Prenatal Diagnosis	Mental Retardation	Clinical Signs
I. LIPID METABOLISM					
Niemann-Pick disease					
Group A, infantile					
Group B, adult	A.R.	Sphingomyelinase	+	±	Hepatosplenomegaly
Groups C and D, intermediate		Unknown	−	+	Pulmonary infiltration
Infantile Gaucher's disease	A.R.	β-Glucosidase	+	±	Hepatosplenomegaly, pseudobulbar palsy
Tay-Sachs disease	A.R.	Hexosaminidase A	+	+	Macular changes, seizures, spasticity
Generalized gangliosidosis	A.R.	β-Galactosidase	+	+	Hepatosplanomegaly, bone changes
Krabbe's disease	A.R.	Galactocerebroside β-Galactosidase	+	+	Stiffness, seizures
Metachromatic leukodystrophy	A.R.	Cerebroside sulfatase	+	+	Stiffness, developmental failure
Wolman's disease	A.R.	Acid lipase	+	−	Hepatosplenomegaly, adrenal calcification, vomiting, diarrhea
Farber's lipogranulomatosis	A.R.	Acid ceramidase	+	+	Hoarseness, arthropathy, subcutaneous nodules
Fabry's disease	X.R.	α-Galactosidase	+	−	Angiokeratomas, renal failure
II. MUCOPOLYSACCHARIDE METABOLISM					
Hurler's syndrome MPS I	A.R.	Iduronidase	+	+	
Hurler's disease II	X.R.	Iduronate sulfatase	+	+	
Sanfilippo's syndrome III	A.R.	Various sulfatases (types A–D)	+	+	Varying degrees of bone changes, hepatosplenomegaly, joint restriction, etc.
Morquio's disease IV	A.R.	*N*-Acetylgalactosamine-6-sulfate sulfatase	+	−	
Maroteaux-Lamy syndrome VI	A.R.	Arylsulfatase B	+	±	
III. OLIGOSACCHARIDE AND GLYCOPROTEIN METABOLISM					
I-cell disease	A.R.	Glycoprotein *N*-acetylglucosaminyl-phosphotransferase	+	+	Hepatomegaly, bone changes, swollen gingivae
Mannosidosis	A.R.	Mannosidase	+	+	Hepatomegaly, bone changes, facial coarsening
Fucosidosis	A.R.	Fucosidase	+	+	Same as above
IV. AMINO ACID METABOLISM					
Phenylketonuria	A.R.	Phenylalanine hydroxylase	−	+	Eczema, blonde hair, musty odor
Hemocystinuria	A.R.	Cystathionine β-synthetase	+	+	Ectopia lentis, Marfanlike phenotype, cardiovascular anomalies
Tyrosinosis	A.R.	Tyrosine amine transaminase	−	+	Hyperkeratotic skin lesions, conjunctivitis
Maple syrup urine disease	A.R.	Branched-chain ketoacid decarboxylase	+	+	Recurrent ketoacidosis

(continued)

Table 37–5 *(continued)*

Disorder	Hereditary Transmission[a]	Enzyme Defect	Prenatal Diagnosis	Mental Retardation	Clinical Signs
Methylmalonic acidemia	A.R.	Methylmalonyl-CoA mutase	+	+	Recurrent ketoacidosis, hepatomegaly, growth retardation
Propionic acidemia	A.R.	Propionyl-CoA carboxylase	+	+	Same as above
Nonketotic hyperglycinemia	A.R.	Glycine cleavage enzyme	+	+	Seizures
Urea cycle disorders	Mostly A.R.	Urea cycle enzymes	+	+	Recurrent acute encephalopathy, vomiting
Hartnup disease	A.R.	Renal transport disorder	–	–	None consistent
V. OTHERS					
Galactosemia	A.R.	Galactose-1-phosphate uridyltransferase	+	+	Hepatomegaly, cataracts, ovarian failure
Wilson's hepatolenticular degeneration	A.R.	Unknown factor in copper metabolism	–	±	Liver disease, Kayser-Fleischer ring, neurological problems
Menkes' kinky-hair disease	X.R.	Same as above	+	–	Abnormal hair, cerebral degeneration
Lesch-Nyhan syndrome	X.R.	Hypoxanthine guanine phosphotibosyltransferase	+	+	Behavioral abnormalities

Adapted from Leroy JG: Hereditary, development, and behavior. In *Developmental-Behavioral Pediatrics,* MD Levine, WB Carey, AC Crocker, editors, p 315. Saunders, Philadelphia, 1983.

A.R., autosomal recessive transmission; X.R., X-linked recessive transmission.

Rubella (German Measles). Rubella has replaced syphilis as the major cause of congenital malformations and mental retardation caused by maternal infection. The children of affected mothers may show several abnormalities, including congenital heart disease, mental retardation, cataracts, deafness, microcephaly, and microphthalmia. Timing is crucial, as the extent and the frequency of the complications are inversely related to the duration of the pregnancy at the time of the maternal infection. When mothers are infected in the first trimester of pregnancy, 10 to 15 percent of the children are affected, but the incidence rises to almost 50 percent when the infection occurs in the first month of pregnancy. The situation is often complicated by subclinical forms of maternal infection which often go undetected. Maternal rubella can be prevented by immunization.

Cytomegalic Inclusion Disease. In many cases, cytomegalic inclusion disease remains dormant in the mother. Some children are stillborn, and others have jaundice, microcephaly, hepatosplenomegaly, and radiographic findings of intracerebral calcification. Children with mental retardation from the disease frequently have cerebral calcification, microcephaly, or hydrocephalus. The diagnosis is confirmed by positive findings of the virus in throat and urine cultures and by the recovery of inclusion-bearing cells in the urine.

Syphilis. Syphilis in pregnant women was once the main cause of various neuropathological changes in their offspring, including mental retardation. Today, the incidence of syphilitic complications of pregnancy fluctuates with the incidence of syphilis in the general population. Some recent alarming statistics from several major cities in the United States indicate that there is still no room for complacency.

Toxoplasmosis. Toxoplasmosis can be transmitted by the mother to the fetus. It causes mild or severe mental retardation and, in severe cases, hydrocephalus, seizures, microcephaly, and chorioretinitis.

Herpes Simplex. The herpes simplex virus can be transmitted transplacentally, although the most common mode of infection is during birth. Microcephaly, mental retardation, intracranial calcification, and ocular abnormalities may result.

Acquired Immune Deficiency Syndrome (AIDS). Many fetuses of mothers with AIDS never come to term because of stillbirth or spontaneous abortion. In those who are born infected with the human immunodeficiency virus (HIV), up to half have progressive encephalopathy, mental retardation, and seizures within the first year of life. Children born infected with HIV often live only a few years.

Fetal Alcohol Syndrome. Fetal alcohol syndrome results in mental retardation and a typical phenotypic picture of facial dysmorphism that includes hypertelorism, microcephaly, short palpebral fissures, inner epicanthal folds, and a short, turned-up nose. Often, the affected children have learning disorders and attention-deficit/hyperactivity disorder. Cardiac defects are also frequent. The entire syndrome occurs in up to 15 percent of babies born to women who regularly ingest large amounts of alcohol. Babies born to women who consume alcohol regularly during pregnancy have a high incidence of attention-deficit/hyperactivity disorder, learning disorders, and mental retardation without the facial dysmorphism.

Prenatal Substance Exposure. Prenatal exposure to opiates, such as heroin, often results in infants who are small for their gestational age, with a head circumference below the 10th percentile and withdrawal symptoms that are manifest within the first two days of life. The withdrawal symptoms of infants include irritability, hypertonia, tremor, vomiting, a high-pitched cry, and an abnormal sleep pattern. Seizures are unusual, but the withdrawal syndrome can be life threatening to infants if it is untreated. Diazepam (Valium), phenobarbital (Luminal), chlorpromazine (Thorazine), and paregoric have been used to treat neonatal opiate withdrawal. The long-term sequelae of prenatal opiate exposure are not fully known; the children's developmental milestones and intellectual functions may be within the normal range, but they have an increased risk for impulsivity and behavioral problems. Infants prenatally exposed to cocaine are at high risk for low birth weight and premature delivery. In the early neonatal period, they may have transient neurological and behavioral abnormalities, including abnormal results on EEGs, tachycardia, poor feeding patterns, irritability, and excessive drowsiness. Rather than a withdrawal reaction, the physiological and behavioral abnormalities are a response to the cocaine, which may be excreted for up to a week postnatally.

Complications of Pregnancy. Toxemia of pregnancy and uncontrolled maternal diabetes present hazards to the fetus and sometimes result in mental retardation. Maternal malnutrition during pregnancy often results in prematurity and other obstetrical complications. Vaginal hemorrhage, placenta previa, premature separation of the placenta, and prolapse of the cord may damage the fetal brain by causing anoxia. The potential teratogenic effect of pharmacological agents administered during pregnancy was widely publicized after the thalidomide tragedy (the drug produced a high percentage of deformed babies when given to pregnant women). So far, with the exception of metabolites used in cancer chemotherapy, no usual dosages are known to damage the fetus's central nervous system, but caution and restraint in prescribing drugs to pregnant women are certainly indicated. The use of lithium during pregnancy was recently implicated in some congenital malformations, especially of the cardiovascular system (for example, Ebstein's anomaly).

Perinatal Factors

Some evidence indicates that premature infants and infants with low birth weight are at high risk for neurological and intellectual impairments that are manifest during their school years. Infants who sustain intracranial hemorrhages or show evidence of cerebral ischemia are especially vulnerable to cognitive abnormalities. The degree of neurodevelopmental impairment generally correlates to the severity of the intracranial hemorrhage. Recent studies have documented that among children with very low birth weight (less than 1,000 grams), 20 percent were found to have significant disabilities including cerebral palsy, mental retardation, autism, and low intelligence with severe learning problems. Very premature children and those who suffered intrauterine growth retardation were found to be at high risk for developing both social problems and academic difficulties. Socioeconomic deprivation can also affect the adaptive function of these vulnerable infants. Early intervention may improve their cognitive, language, and perceptual abilities.

Acquired Childhood Disorders

Occasionally, a child's developmental status changes dramatically as a result of a specific disease or physical trauma. In retrospect, it is sometimes difficult to ascertain the full picture of the child's developmental progress before the insult, but the adverse effects on the child's development or skills are apparent afterward.

Infection. The most serious infections affecting cerebral integrity are encephalitis and meningitis. Measles encephalitis has been virtually eliminated by the universal use of measles vaccine, and the incidences of other bacterial infections of the central nervous system have been markedly reduced with antibacterial agents. Most episodes of encephalitis are caused by viral organisms. Sometimes a clinician must retrospectively consider a probable encephalitic component in a past obscure illness with high fever and lasting encephalopathy. Meningitis that was diagnosed late, even when followed by antibiotic treatment, can seriously affect a child's cognitive development. Thrombotic and purulent intracranial phenomena secondary to septicemia are rarely seen today except in small infants.

Head Trauma. The best-known causes of head injury in children which produce developmental handicaps, including seizures, are motor vehicle accidents, but more head injuries are caused by household accidents, such as falls from tables, from open windows, and on stairways. Child abuse is also a cause of head injury.

Other Issues. Brain damage from cardiac arrest during anesthesia is rare. One cause of complete or partial brain damage is asphyxia associated with near drowning. Long-term exposure to lead is a well-established cause of compromised intelligence and learning skills. Intracranial tumors of various types and origins, surgery, and chemotherapy can also adversely affect brain function.

Environmental and Sociocultural Factors

Mild retardation is significantly prevalent among people of culturally deprived, low socioeconomic groups, and many of their relatives are affected with similar degrees of mental retardation. No biological causes have been identified in these cases. Children in poor, socioculturally deprived families are subjected to potentially pathogenic and developmentally adverse conditions. The prenatal environment is compromised by poor medical care and poor maternal nutrition. Teenage pregnancies are frequent and are associated with obstetrical complications, prematurity, and low birth weight. Poor postnatal medical care, malnutrition, exposure to such toxic substances as lead, and physical trauma are frequent. Family instability, frequent moves, and multiple but inadequate caretakers are common. Furthermore, mothers in such families may often be poorly educated and ill equipped to give children appropriate stimulation.

Another unresolved issue is the influence of severe parental mental disorders. Such disorders may adversely affect children's care and stimulation and other aspects of the environment and may thus put the children at developmental risk. Children of parents with mood disorders and schizophrenia are known to be at risk for these and related disorders. Recent studies indicate a high prevalence of motor skills disorder and other developmental disorders, but not necessarily mental retardation, among the children of parents with mental disorders.

DIAGNOSIS

The diagnosis of mental retardation can be made after the history, a standardized intellectual assessment, and a measure of adaptive function indicate that a child's current behavior is significantly below the expected level (Tables 37–2 and 37–3). The diagnosis itself does not specify either the cause or the prognosis. A history and a psychiatric interview are useful in obtaining a longitudinal picture of the child's development and functioning, and examination of physical signs, neurological abnormalities, and laboratory tests can be used to ascertain the cause and prognosis.

History

The history is most often taken from the parents or the caretaker, with particular attention to the mother's pregnancy, labor, and delivery; the presence of a family history of mental retardation; consanguinity of the parents; and hereditary disorders. As part of the history, the clinician assesses the parents' sociocultural background, the home's emotional climate, and the parents' intellectual functioning.

Psychiatric Interview

Two factors are of paramount importance when interviewing the patient: the interviewer's attitude and the manner of communicating with the patient. The interviewer should not be guided by the patient's mental age, which cannot fully characterize the person. A mildly retarded adult with a mental age of 10 is not a 10-year-old child. When addressed as if they were children, some retarded people become justifiably insulted, angry, and uncooperative. Passive and dependent people, alternatively, may assume the child's role that they think is expected of them. In both cases, no valid diagnostic data can be obtained.

The patient's verbal abilities, including receptive and expressive language, should be assessed as soon as possible by observing the verbal and nonverbal communication between the caretakers and the patient and by taking the history. The clinician often finds it helpful to see the patient and the caretakers together. If the patient uses sign language, the caretaker may have to stay during the interview as an interpreter. Retarded people often have the lifelong experience of failing in many areas, and they may be anxious about seeing an interviewer. The interviewer and the caretaker should attempt to give such patients a clear, supportive, and concrete explanation of the diagnostic process, particularly those patients with sufficient receptive language. Giving patients the impression that their bad behavior is the cause of the referral should be avoided. Support and praise should be offered in language appropriate to the patient's age and understanding. Leading questions should be avoided, as retarded people may be suggestible and wish to please others. Subtle directiveness, structure, and reinforcements may be necessary to keep them on the task or topic.

The patient's control over motility patterns should be ascertained, and clinical evidence of distractibility and distortions in perception and memory may be evaluated. The use of speech, reality testing, and the ability to generalize from experiences are important to note. The nature and maturity of the patient's defenses—particularly exaggerated or self-defeating uses of avoidance, repression, denial, introjection, and isolation—should be observed. Sublimation potential, frustration tolerance, and impulse control—especially over motor, aggressive, and sexual drives—should be assessed. Also important are self-image and its role in the development of self-confidence, as well as an assessment of tenacity, persistence, curiosity, and willingness to explore the unknown. In general, the psychiatric examination of a retarded person should reveal how the patient has coped with the stages of development. In regard to failure or regression, the clinician can develop a personality profile that allows the logical planning of management and remedial approaches.

Physical Examination

Various parts of the body may have certain characteristics that have prenatal causes and are commonly found in people who are mentally retarded. For example, the configuration and the size of the head offer clues to a variety of conditions, such as microcephaly, hydrocephalus, and Down's syndrome. The patient's face may have some signs of mental retardation which greatly facilitate the diagnosis, such as hypertelorism, a flat nasal bridge, prominent eyebrows, epicanthal folds, corneal opacities, retinal changes, low-set and small or misshapen ears, a protruding tongue, and a disturbance in dentition. Facial expression, such as a dull appearance, may be misleading and should not be relied on without other supporting evidence. The color and texture of the skin and the hair, a high-arched palate, the size of the thyroid gland, and the size of the child and his or her trunk and extremities are further areas to be explored. The circumference of the head should be measured as part of the clinical investigation. Dermatoglyphics may offer another diagnostic tool, as uncommon ridge patterns and flexion creases are often found in people who are retarded. Abnormal dermatoglyphics occur in chromosomal disorders and in people who were prenatally infected with rubella. Table 37–4 lists the multiple handicaps associated with the syndromes discussed. The clinician should bear in mind during the examination that mentally retarded children, particularly those with associated behavioral problems, are at increased risk for child abuse.

Neurological Examination

Sensory impairments occur frequently among people who are mentally retarded; for example, up to 10 percent are hearing impaired, a rate that is four times that of the general population. Various other neurological impairments are also frequent in mentally retarded people; seizure disorders occur in about 10 percent of all mentally retarded people and in one third of those with severe retardation. When neurological abnormalities are present, their incidence and severity generally rise in direct proportion to the degree of retardation. Many severely retarded children, however, have no neurological abnormalities; conversely, about 25 percent of all children with cerebral palsy have normal intelligence. Disturbances in motor areas are manifested in abnormalities of muscle tone (spasticity or hypotonia), reflexes (hyperreflexia), and involuntary movements (choreoathetosis). A smaller degree of disability is revealed in clumsiness and poor coordination. Sensory disturbances may include hearing difficulties, ranging from cortical deafness to mild hearing deficits. Visual disturbances may range from blindness to disturbances of spatial concepts, design recognition, and concepts of body image.

The infants with the poorest prognoses are those who manifest a combination of inactivity, general hypotonia, and exaggerated response to stimuli. In older children, hyperactivity, short attention span, distractibility, and a low frustration tolerance are often signs of brain damage. In general, the younger the child at the time of investigation, the more caution is indicated in predicting future ability, as the recovery potential of the infantile brain is very good. Observing the child's development at regular intervals is probably the most reliable approach.

Skull X-rays are usually taken routinely but are illuminating in only a relatively few conditions, such as craniosynostosis, hydrocephalus, and other disorders that result in intracranial calcifications (for example, toxoplasmosis, tuberous sclerosis, cerebral angiomatosis, and hypoparathyroidism). Computed tomography (CT) scans and magnetic resonance imaging (MRI) have become important tools for uncovering central nervous system pathology associated with mental retardation. The occasional findings of internal hydrocephalus, cortical atrophy, or porencephaly in a severely retarded, brain-damaged child are not considered important to the general picture. An EEG is best interpreted with caution in cases of mental retardation. The exceptions are patients with hypsarhythmia and grand mal seizures, in whom the EEG may help establish the diagnosis and suggest treatment. In most other conditions, a diffuse cerebral disorder produces nonspecific EEG changes, characterized by slow frequencies with bursts of spikes and sharp or blunt wave complexes. The confusion over the significance of the EEG in the diagnosis of mental retardation is best illustrated by the reports of frequent EEG abnormalities in Down's syndrome, which range from 25 percent to the majority of patients examined.

Laboratory Tests

Laboratory tests used in diagnosing mental retardation include examination of the urine and the blood for metabolic disorders. Enzymatic abnormalities in chromosomal disorders, particularly Down's syndrome, promise to become useful diagnostic tools. The determination of the karyotype in a suitable genetic laboratory is indicated whenever a chromosomal disorder is suspected.

Amniocentesis, in which a small amount of amniotic fluid is removed from the amniotic cavity transabdominally between the 14th and the 16th weeks of gestation, has been useful in diagnosing various infant chromosomal abnormalities, especially Down's syndrome. Amniotic fluid cells, mostly fetal in origin, are cultured for cytogenetic and biochemical studies. Many serious hereditary disorders can be predicted with amniocentesis; therapeutic abortion is the only method of prevention. Amniocentesis is recommended for all pregnant women over the age of 35.

Fortunately, most chromosomal anomalies occur only once in a family. Chorionic villi sampling (CVS) is a new screening technique to determine fetal abnormalities. It is done at 8 to 10 weeks of gestation, 6 weeks earlier than amniocentesis is done. The results are available in a short time (hours or days), and, if the result is abnormal, the decision to terminate the pregnancy can be made within the first trimester. The procedure has a miscarriage risk of between 2 and 5 percent.

Hearing and Speech Evaluations

Hearing and speech evaluations should be done routinely. The development of speech may be the most reliable criterion in investigating mental retardation. Various hearing impairments are often present in people who are mentally retarded, but in some instances impairments can simulate mental retardation. Unfortunately, the commonly used methods of hearing and speech evaluation require the patient's cooperation and, thus, are often unreliable in severely retarded people.

Psychological Assessment

Examining clinicians may use several screening instruments for infants and toddlers. As in many areas of mental retardation, the controversy over the predictive value of infant psychological tests is heated. Some report the correlation of abnormalities during infancy with later abnormal functioning as very low, and others report it as very high. The correlation rises in direct proportion to the age of the child at the time of the developmental examination, however, copying geometric figures, the Goodenough Draw-a-Person test, the Kohs Block Test, and geometric puzzles—all may be used as quick screening tests of visual-motor coordination. Psychological testing, performed by an experienced psychologist, is a standard part of an evaluation for mental retardation. The Gesell and Bayley scales and the Cattell Infant Intelligence Scale are most commonly used with infants. For children, the Stanford-Binet Intelligence Scale and the third edition of the Wechsler Intelligence Scale for Children (WISC-III) are the most widely used in the United States. Both tests have been criticized for penalizing culturally deprived children, for being culturally biased, for testing mainly the potential for academic achievement and not for adequate social functioning, and for their unreliability in children with IQs of less than 50. Some people have tried to overcome the language barrier of people who are mentally retarded by devising picture vocabulary tests, of which the Peabody Vocabulary Test is the most widely used. The tests often found useful in detecting brain damage are the Bender Gestalt test and the Benton Visual Retention Test (see Figs. 5.2–1 and 5.2–3). These tests are also useful for mildly retarded children. In addition, a psychological evaluation should assess perceptual, motor, linguistic, and cognitive abilities. Information about motivational, emotional, and interpersonal factors is also important.

CLINICAL FEATURES

Mild Mental Retardation

Mild mental retardation may not be diagnosed until the affected children enter school; their social skills and communication may be adequate in the preschool years. As they get older, however, such cognitive deficits as poor ability to abstract and egocentric thinking may distinguish them from others of their age. Although mildly retarded people are capable of academic functions at the high elementary level and their vocational skills are sufficient to support themselves in some cases, social assimilation may be difficult. Communication deficits, poor self-esteem, and dependence may contribute to their relative lack of social spontaneity. Some people who are mildly retarded may fall into relationships with peers who exploit their shortcomings. In most cases, people with mild mental retardation can achieve some degree of social and vocational success in a supportive environment.

Moderate Mental Retardation

Moderate mental retardation is likely to be diagnosed at a younger age than is mild mental retardation; communication skills develop more slowly in people who are moderately retarded , and their social isolation may begin in the elementary school years. Although academic achievement is usually limited to the middle-elementary level, moderately retarded children benefit from individual attention focused on the development of self-help skills. Children with moderate mental retardation are aware of their deficits and often feel alienated from their peers and frustrated by their limitations. They continue to require a relatively high level of supervision but can become competent at occupational tasks in supportive settings.

Severe Mental Retardation

Severe mental retardation is generally obvious in the preschool years; affected children's speech is minimal, and their motor development is poor. Some language development may occur in the school-age years. By adolescence, if language is poor, nonverbal forms of communication may have evolved; the inability to fully articulate needs may reinforce the physical means of communicating. Behavioral approaches can help promote some degree of self-care, although those with severe mental retardation generally need extensive supervision.

Profound Mental Retardation

Children with profound mental retardation require constant supervision and are severely limited in communication and motor skills. By adulthood, some speech development may be present, and simple self-help skills may be acquired. Even in adulthood, nursing care is needed.

Other Features

Surveys have identified several clinical features that occur with greater frequency in people who are mentally retarded than in the general population. These features, which may occur in isolation or as part of a mental disorder, include hyperactivity, low frustration tolerance, aggression, affective instability, repetitive, stereotypic motor behaviors, and various self-injurious behaviors. Self-injurious behaviors seem to be more frequent and more intense with increasingly severe mental retardation. It is often difficult to decide whether these clinical features are comorbid mental disorders or direct sequelae of the developmental limitations imposed by mental retardation.

COMORBID PSYCHOPATHOLOGY

Prevalence

Over the past decade, several epidemiological surveys indicated that the rates of other mental disorders in children and adults with mental retardation range between one third and two thirds, rates that are several times higher than those in nonmentally retarded community samples. The prevalence of psychopathology seems to be correlated with the degree of mental retardation; the more severe the mental retardation, the higher the risk for other mental disorders. A recent epidemiological study found that 40.7 percent of intellectually disabled children between 4 and 18 years met criteria for at least one psychiatric disorder. The severity of retardation affected the type of psychiatric disorder: Disruptive and conduct-disorder behaviors occurred more commonly in the mildly retarded group; the more severely retarded group exhibited psychiatric problems more often associated with autism such as self-stimulation and self-mutilation. In contrast to the epidemiology of psychopathology in children in general, age and sex did not affect the prevalence of psychiatric disorders in this study. Those with profound mental retardation were less likely to exhibit psychiatric symptoms.

The mental disorders that occur among people who are mentally retarded appear to run the gamut of those seen in nonmentally retarded people, including mood disorders, schizophrenia, attention-deficit/hyperactivity disorder, and conduct disorder. Those with severe mental retardation have a particularly high rate of autistic disorder and pervasive developmental disorders. About 2 to 3 percent of mentally retarded people meet the criteria for schizophrenia; this percentage is several times higher than the rate for the general population. Up to 50 percent of mentally retarded children and adults had a mood disorder when such instruments as the Kiddie Schedule for Affective Disorders and Schizophrenia, the Beck Depression Inventory, and the Children's Depression Inventory were used in pilot studies, but as these instruments have not been standardized within the mentally retarded population, these findings must be considered preliminary.

Highly prevalent psychiatric symptoms that can occur in mentally retarded people outside the context of a mental disorder include hyperactivity and short attention span, self-injurious behaviors (for example, head banging and self-biting), and repetitive stereotypical behaviors (hand flapping and toe walking). Personality styles and traits in mentally retarded people are not unique to them, but negative self-image, low self-esteem, poor frustration tolerance, interpersonal dependence, and a rigid problem-solving style are overrepresented. Specific causal syndromes seen in mental retardation may also predispose affected people to various types of psychopathology.

Risk Factors

Neurological Impairment. Reports indicate that the risk for psychopathology increases in a variety of neurological conditions, such as seizure disorders. Rates of psychopathology increase with the severity of mental retardation; thus neurological impairment increases as intellectual impairment increases. In a recent review of psychiatric disorders in children and adolescents with mental retardation and epilepsy, approximately one third also had autistic disorder or an autistic-like condition. The combination of mental retardation, active epilepsy, and autism or an autistic-like condition occurs at a rate of 0.07 percent in the general population.

Genetic Syndromes. Some evidence indicates that genetically based syndromes—such as fragile X syndrome, Prader-Willi syndrome, and Down's syndrome—are associated with specific behavioral manifestations. People with fragile X syndrome are known to have extremely high rates (up to three fourths of those studied) of attention-deficit/hyperactivity disorders. High rates of aberrant interpersonal behavior and language function often meet the criteria for autistic disorder and avoidant personality disorder. Prader-Willi syndrome is almost always associated with compulsive eating disturbances, hyperphagia, and obesity. Children with the syndrome have been described as oppositional and defiant. Socialization is an area of weakness, especially in coping skills. Externalizing behavior problems—such as temper tantrums, irritability, and arguing—seem to be heightened in adolescence.

In Down's syndrome, language function is a relative weakness, whereas sociability and social skills, such as interpersonal cooperation and conformity with social conventions, are relative strengths. Most studies have noted muted affect in children with Down's syndrome relative to nonretarded children of the same mental age. Those with Down's syndrome also manifest deficiencies in scanning the environment; they are likely to focus on a single stimulus and have difficulty noticing environmental changes and communicating. A variety of mental disorders occur in people with Down's syndrome, but the rates appear to be lower than those of other mental retardation syndromes, especially autistic disorder.

Psychosocial Factors. A negative self-image and poor self-esteem are common features of mildly and moderately mentally retarded people, who are well aware of being different from others. They experience repeated failure and disappointment in not meeting their parents' and society's expectations and in progressively falling behind their peers and even their younger siblings. Communication difficulties further increase their vulnerability to feelings of ineptness and frustration. Inappropriate behaviors, such as withdrawal, are common. The perpetual sense of isolation and inadequacy has been linked to feelings of anxiety, anger, dysphoria, and depression.

DIFFERENTIAL DIAGNOSIS

By definition, mental retardation must begin before the age of 18. A mentally retarded child has to cope with so many difficult social and academic situations that maladaptive patterns often complicate the diagnostic process. On the other hand, vulnerable children who are exposed to perpetual environmental stressors may not develop at the expected rate. Children whose family life provides inadequate stimulation may manifest motor and mental retardation that can be reversed if an enriched, stimulating environment is provided in early childhood. Several sensory disabilities, especially deafness and blindness, may be mistaken for mental retardation if, during testing, no compensation is allowed. Speech deficits and cerebral palsy often make a child seem retarded, even in the presence of borderline or normal intelligence. Chronic, debilitating diseases of any kind may depress s child's functioning in all areas. Convulsive disorders may give an impression of mental retardation, especially in the presence of uncontrolled seizures. Chronic brain syndromes may result in isolated handicaps—failure to read (alexia), failure to write (agraphia), failure to communicate (aphasia), and several other handicaps—that may exist in a person of normal and even superior intelligence. Children with learning disorders, which can coexist with mental retardation, experience a delay or a failure of development in a specific area, such as reading or mathematics, but the children develop normally in other areas. In contrast, children with mental retardation show general delays in most areas of development.

Mental retardation and pervasive developmental disorders often coexist; 70 to 75 percent of those with pervasive developmental disorders have an IQ of less than 70. A pervasive developmental disorder results in distortion of the timing, rate, and sequence of many basic psychological functions necessary for social development. Because of their general level of functioning, children with pervasive developmental disorders have more problems with social relatedness and more deviant language than do those with mental retardation. In mental retardation, generalized delays in development are present, and mentally retarded children behave in some ways as though they were passing through an earlier normal developmental stage, rather than one with completely aberrant behavior.

A most difficult differential diagnostic problem concerns

children with severe mental retardation, brain damage, autistic disorder, schizophrenia with childhood onset, or, according to some, Heller's disease. The confusion stems from the fact that details of the child's early history are often unavailable or unreliable. In addition, when the children are evaluated, many with these conditions display similar bizarre and stereotyped behavior—mutism, echolalia, or functioning on a retarded level. By the time the children are usually seen, it does not matter from a practical point of view whether their retardation is secondary to a primary early infantile autistic disorder or schizophrenia or whether the personality and behavioral distortions are secondary to brain damage or mental retardation. In a recent epidemiological study, pervasive developmental disorders (such as autistic disorder) were found in 19.8 percent of children with mental retardation.

Children under the age of 18 years who meet the diagnostic criteria for dementia and who manifest an IQ of less than 70 are given the diagnoses of dementia and mental retardation. Those whose IQs drop to less than 70 after the age of 18 years and who have new onsets of cognitive disorders are not given the diagnosis of mental retardation but only the diagnosis of dementia.

COURSE AND PROGNOSIS

In most cases of mental retardation, the underlying intellectual impairment does not improve, yet the affected person's level of adaptation can be positively influenced by an enriched and supportive environment. In general, people with mild and moderate mental retardation have the most flexibility in adapting to various environmental conditions. As in those who are not mentally retarded, the more comorbid mental disorders occur, the more guarded is the overall prognosis. When clear-cut mental disorders are superimposed on mental retardation, standard treatments for the comorbid mental disorders are often beneficial. Yet there is still a lack of clarity about the classification of such aberrant behaviors as hyperactivity, emotional lability, and social dysfunction. Are they additional psychiatric symptoms or direct sequelae of the mental retardation?

TREATMENT

Mental retardation is associated with several heterogeneous groups of disorders and a multitude of psychosocial factors. The best treatment of mental retardation is primary, secondary, and tertiary prevention.

Primary Prevention

Primary prevention concerns actions taken to eliminate or reduce the conditions that lead to developing of the disorders associated with mental retardation. Such measures include education to increase the general public's knowledge and awareness of mental retardation; continuing efforts of health professionals to ensure and upgrade public health policies; legislation to provide optimal maternal and child health care; and eradication of the known disorders associated with central nervous system damage. Family and genetic counseling helps reduce the incidence of mental retardation in a family with a history of a genetic disorder associated with mental retardation. For the children and the mothers of low socioeconomic status, proper prenatal and postnatal medical care and various supplementary enrichment programs and social service assistance may help minimize the medical and psychosocial complications.

Secondary and Tertiary Prevention

Once a disorder associated with mental retardation has been identified, the disorder should be treated to shorten the course of the illness (secondary prevention) and to minimize the sequelae or consequent disabilities (tertiary prevention). Hereditary metabolic and endocrine disorders, such as PKU and hypothyroidism, can be effectively treated in an early stage by dietary control or hormone replacement therapy. Mentally retarded children frequently have emotional and behavioral difficulties requiring psychiatric treatment. Their limited cognitive and social capabilities require modified psychiatric treatment modalities based on the children's level of intelligence.

Education for the Child. Educational settings for children who are mentally retarded should include a comprehensive program that addresses adaptive skills training, social skills training, and vocational training. Particular attention should be focused on communication and efforts to improve the quality of life. Group therapy has often been a successful format in which mentally retarded children can learn and practice hypothetical real-life situations and receive supportive feedback.

Behavior, Cognitive, and Psychodynamic Therapies. The difficulties in adaptation among mentally retarded people are widespread and so varied that several interventions alone or in combination may be beneficial. Behavior therapy has been used for many years to shape and enhance social behaviors and to control and minimize people's aggressive and destructive behaviors. Positive reinforcement for desired behaviors and benign punishment (such as loss of privileges) for objectionable behaviors have been helpful. Cognitive therapy, such as dispelling false beliefs and relaxation exercises with self-instruction, has also been recommended for those mentally retarded people who are able to follow the instructions. Psychodynamic therapy has been used with patients and their families to decrease conflicts about expectations that result in persistent anxiety, rage, and depression.

Family Education. One of the most important areas that a clinician can address is that of educating the family of a mentally retarded patient about ways to enhance competence and self-esteem while maintaining realistic expectations for the patient. The family often finds it difficult to balance the fostering of independence and the providing of a nurturing and supportive environment for a mentally retarded child, who is likely to experience a degree of rejection and failure outside the family context. The parents may benefit from continuous counseling or family therapy and should be allowed opportunities to express their feelings of guilt, despair, anguish, recurring denial, and anger about their child's disorder and future. The psychiatrist should be prepared to give the parents all the basic and current medical information regarding causes, treatment, and other pertinent areas (such as special training and the correction of sensory defects).

Social Intervention. One of the most widely occurring problems among people who are mentally retarded is a sense of social isolation and social skills deficits. Thus, improving the quantity and quality of social competence is a critical part of their care. Special Olympics International is the largest recreational sports program geared for this population. In addition to providing a forum to develop physical fitness, Special Olympics also enhances social interactions, friendships, and it is hoped, an increase in general self-esteem. A recent study confirmed positive effects of the Special Olympics on the social competence of those mentally retarded adults who participated.

Pharmacological Intervention. Pharmacological approaches to the treatment of comorbid mental disorders in mentally retarded patients is much the same as it is for patients who are not mentally retarded. Increasing data support the use of a variety of medications for patients with mental disorders who are not mentally retarded, and some studies have focused on the use of medications for the following behavioral syndromes that are frequent among people who are mentally retarded.

AGGRESSION AND SELF-INJURIOUS BEHAVIOR. Some evidence from controlled and uncontrolled studies indicate that lithium (Eskalith) has been useful in decreasing aggression and self-injurious behavior. Narcotic antagonists such as naltrexone (Trexan) have been reported to decrease self-injurious behaviors in mentally retarded patients who also meet the diagnostic criteria for infantile autistic disorder. One hypothesis proposed as the mechanism of naltrexone treatment is that it interferes with the release of endogenous opioids that are presumed to be associated with self-injury. Carbamazepine (Tegretol) and valproic acid (Depakene) are medications that have also been beneficial in some cases of self-injurious behavior. Double-blind placebo-controlled studies in mentally retarded adults and open clinical trials in mentally retarded children and adolescents have indicated that risperidone (Risperdal), an antipsychotic with potent dopamine type 2 (D_2) and serotonin type 2 ($5\text{-}HT_2$), is efficacious in decreasing aggression and self-injurious behavior.

STEREOTYPICAL MOTOR MOVEMENTS. Antipsychotic medications, such as haloperidol (Haldol) and chlorpromazine (Thorazine), decrease repetitive self-stimulatory behaviors in mentally retarded patients, but these medications have not increased adaptive behavior. Some mentally retarded children and adults (up to one third) face a high risk for tardive dyskinesia with the continued use of antipsychotic medications. Obsessive-compulsive symptoms often overlap with the repetitive stereotypical behaviors seen in mentally retarded children and adolescents and in those with mental retardation and a pervasive developmental disorder. Serotonin reuptake inhibitors, such as clomipramine, fluoxetine, fluvoxamine, paroxetine, and sertraline, are likely to be effective in treating obsessive-compulsive symptoms in children and adolescents.

EXPLOSIVE RAGE BEHAVIOR. Beta blockers, such as propranolol and buspirone (BuSpar), have been reported to result in a decrease in explosive rages among patients with mental retardation and autistic disorder. Systematic study is necessary before these drugs can be confirmed as efficacious.

ATTENTION-DEFICIT/HYPERACTIVITY DISORDER. Studies of methylphenidate treatment in mildly retarded patients with attention-deficit/hyperactivity disorder have shown a significant improvement in the ability to maintain attention and to stay focused on tasks. Methylphenidate treatment studies have not shown evidence of long-term improvement in social skills or learning.

Jerry, a 14-year-old boy, was referred to a psychiatrist by his special education teacher because he was posing a danger to himself by hitting himself when he was frustrated. Jerry's increasingly longer and sudden physical outbursts also threatened his classmates. Although he had always had a short attention span and occasional temper tantrums in school and at home, his recent behavior was becoming increasingly difficult to control. Jerry's mild mental retardation was diagnosed in the first grade, and his significantly poor attention span and hyperactivity had been apparent since age 6. He had been placed in a self-contained special education setting in the middle of the first grade, after he was unable to focus on tasks and exhibited poor frustration tolerance leading to aggressive behavior. At that time, placement in a small, structured classroom with increased individual attention had been sufficient to control his behavior problems. At 7 years of age, Jerry was congenial, although he had a tendency to get frustrated easily. He was socially adaptable and had no problem seeking the attention of the teacher when he needed help. Beginning in the third grade, he was treated with methylphenidate (Ritalin), 20 mg in the morning and at noon, which seemed to help him pay attention and remain focused on tasks in the classroom. At home, he had never been considered a behavior problem until the present time.

Jerry's family history was remarkable, for two first cousins on his father's side who were mildly retarded; his two older brothers had attention-deficit/hyperactivity disorder, but they and his younger sister were of average intelligence. Jerry's father had a history consistent with attention-deficit/hyperactivity disorder and a reading disability when he was a child. Interviews with Jerry's parents revealed that Jerry had always played rough with his two brothers, but only recently had he become irritable and intermittently physically aggressive toward his 10-year-old sister. Over the past two months, since school began, Jerry had become increasingly defiant and explosive with minimal provocation. Jerry was remorseful after he hit his sister or threw a chair at school, but he could not control his intermittent rage. He knew that what he had done was wrong and that he was much too old for such behavior, and he always apologized after the incidents. Nevertheless, his sister was frightened of him, and he was in danger or being expelled from school.

During his interview with the psychiatrist, Jerry was able to admit that he felt "stupid" and believed that he should continue to hit himself when he was frustrated because he deserved punishment. He also felt that he would never be able to match his brothers socially or academically. He was aware that he was losing his temper, but he could not seem to interrupt the process. Although Jerry was sometimes destructive to property when he lost his temper, he did not possess other characteristic behaviors of conduct disorder.

A physical examination revealed no remarkable results, and a laboratory examination also revealed a healthy profile. Jerry's regimen of methylphenidate was continued, and the psychiatrist added risperidone, 1 mg in the morning and at night. Jerry was slightly sedated over the first week, but his aggressive outbursts diminished somewhat. Jerry's dose of risperidone was increased to 2 mg in the morning and at night. His aggression seemed to be reduced, but he began to experience some muscle tightness and a restless feeling. Cogentin, 1 mg twice daily, was added. On this dosage of risperidone and cogentin, Jerry became calmer and less threatening and was able to be managed in the classroom. He was hitting himself much less often, and he was willing to consider other ways of responding to frustrations. The psychiatrist recommended that Jerry become involved with the Special Olympics International to exercise regularly and to increase his social competence. Jerry's parents were counseled to work with him to gradually increase his responsibilities and privileges at home, and to encourage him to socialize with other boys and with girls.

References

Bregman JD: Current developments in the understanding of mental retardation. Part II. Psychopathology. J Am Acad Child Adolesc Psychiatry *30:* 861, 1991.

Bregman JD, Hodapp RM: Current developments in the understanding of mental retardation. Part I. Biological and phenomenological perspectives. J Am Acad Child Adolesc Psychiatry *30:* 707, 1991.

Brown WT: The fragile X syndrome. Neurol Clin *7:* 107, 1989.

Burd L, Martsolf JT: Fetal alcohol syndrome: Diagnosis and syndromal variability. Physiol Behav *46:* 39, 1989.

Campbell MG, Anderson LT, Small AM, Locasio JJ, Lynch NS, Choroco MC: Naltrexone in autistic children: A double blind and placebo-controlled study. Psychopharmacol Bull *26:* 130, 1990.

Craft MJ, Ismail IA, Krishnamurti D, Matthew J, Regan A, Seth RV, North PM: Lithium in the treatment of aggression in mentally handicapped patients: A double blind trial, B J Psychiatry *150:* 685, 1987.

Davis E, Fennoy I: Growth and development in infants of cocaine abusing mothers. Am J Dis Child *144:* 426, 1990.

Diamond GW: Developmental problems in children with HIV infection. Ment Retard *27:* 213, 1989.

Dosen A: Diagnosis and treatment of mental illness in mentally retarded children: A developmental model. Child Psychiatry Hum Dev *20:* 73, 1989.

Dykens EM, Hodapp RM, Walsh K, Nash LJ: Adaptive and maladaptive behavior in Prader-Willi syndrome. J Am Acad Child Adolesc Psychiatry *31:* 1131, 1992.

Dykens EM, Cohen DJ: Effects of Special Olympics International on social competence in persons of mental retardation. J Am Acad Child Adolesc Psychiatry *35:* 223, 1996.

Einfeld SL, Tonge BJ: Population prevalence of psychopathology in children and adolescents with intellectual disability: II. Epidemiological findings. J Intellect Disabil Res *40:* 99, 1996.

Hagerman RJ: Biomedical advances in developmental psychology: The case of fragile X syndrome. Dev Psychol *32* (3): 416, 1996.

Halsey CL, Collins ME, Anderson CL: Extremely low-birth-weight children and their peers: A comparison of school-age outcomes. Arch Pediatr Adolesc Med *150:* 790, 1996.

Handen BL, Breaux AM, Janosky J, McAuliffe S, Feldman H, Gosling A: Effects and noneffects of methylphenidate in children with mental retardation and ADHD. J Am Acad Child Adolesc Psychiatry *31:* 455, 1992.

Hardan A, Johnson K, Johnson C, Hreczny J: Case study: Risperidone treatment of children and adolescents with developmental disorders. J Am Acad Child Adolesc Psychiatry *35:*, 1996.

Hodapp RM, Dykens EM: Mental retardation. In *Child Psychopathology,* EJ Mash, RA Barkley, editors, p 362. Guilford, New York, 1996.

March JS, Leonard HL: Obsessive-compulsive disorder in children and adolescents: A review of the past 10 years. J Am Acad Child Adolesc Psychiatry *35:* 1265, 1996.

Menkes JH: Heredodegenerative disease: In *Textbook of Child Neurology,* JH Menkes, editor, p 139. Lea & Febiger, Philadelphia, 1990.

Nordin V, Gillberg C: Autism spectrum disorders in children with physical or mental disability or both. I. Clinical and epidemiological aspects. Dev Med Child Neurol *38:* 297, 1996.

Perry R, Pataki C, Munoz-Silva DM, Armenteros J, Silva R: Pilot trial of risperidone in pervasive developmental disorders. In Scientific Proceedings of the 149th. American Psychiatric Association Meeting, 1996.

Pulsifer MB: The neuropsychology of mental retardation. J Int Neuropsychol Soc *2* (2): 159, 1996.

Pumpian I, Fisher D, Certo NJ, Smalley KA: Changing jobs: An essential part of career development. Ment Retard *35* (1): 39, 1997.

Ratey J, Sovner R. Mikkelsen E, Chmielinski HE: Buspirone therapy for maladaptive behavior and anxiety in developmentally disabled persons. J Clin Psychiatry *50:* 382, 1989.

Schothorst PF, van Engeland W: Long-term behavioral sequelaw of prematurity. J Am Acad Child Adolesc Psychaitry *35:* 175, 1996.

Simon EW, Blubaugh KM, Pippidis M: Substituting traditional antipsychotics with risperidone for individuals with mental retardation. Ment Retard *34* (6): 359, 1996.

Steffenburg S, Gillberg C, Steffenburg U: Psychiatric disorders in children and adolescents with mental retardation and active epilepsy. Arch Neurol *53:* 904, 1996.

Stevenson R, Massey P, Schroer R, McDermott S, Richter B: Preventable fraction of mental retardation: Analysis based on individuals with severe mental retardation. Ment Retard *34:* 182, 1996.

Sturmey P: The use of DSM and ICD diagnostic criteria in people with mental retardation: A review of empirical studies. J Nerv Ment Dis *181:* 38, 1993.

Szymanski LS, Crocker AC: Mental retardation. In *Comprehensive Textbook of Psychiatry,* ed 5, HI Kaplan, BJ Sadock, editors, p 1728. Williams & Wilkins, Baltimore, 1989.

38

Learning Disorders

According to *Diagnostic and Statistical Manual of Mental Disorders* (DSM-IV), "learning disorders are diagnosed when . . . achievement on . . . standardized tests in reading, mathematics, or written expression is substantially below that expected for age, schooling, and level of intelligence." The learning problems significantly interfere with academic achievement or everyday activities.

In DSM-IV, demoralization, low self-esteem, and deficits in social skills are said to be associated with learning disorders. Approximately 5 percent of students in public schools in the United States have a learning disorder. The school drop-out rate for children or adolescents with these disorders is said to be almost 40 percent—one and a half times the average. Adults with learning disorders may have difficulties in employment and in social adjustment. Learning disorders can be associated with other developmental disorders, with major depressive disorders, and with dysthymic disorder.

People with learning disorders may have abnormal cognitive processing such as deficits in visual perception, speaking, attention, and memory. Genetic predisposition, perinatal injury, and neurological and other medical conditions may contribute to developing learning disorders, but many people with learning disorders have no history. Learning disorders are, nevertheless, frequently found in association with a variety of medical conditions (for example, lead poisoning, fetal alcohol syndrome).

DSM-IV emphasizes that learning disorders must be distinguished from "normal variations in cultural attainment" and from academic difficulties arising from lack of opportunity, poor teaching, cultural factors, and vision and hearing problems.

ICD-10

The 10th revision of *International Statistical Classification of Diseases and Related Health Problems* (ICD-10) classifies specific developmental disorders of scholastic skills learning disorders under the category of disorders of psychological development, which must have an onset during infancy or childhood; must show a delay or impairment in developing functions strongly related to the biological maturation of the central nervous system; and must undergo a steady course without remissions and relapses typical of many mental disorders.

Development disorders are usually of unknown cause, but there is often a family history of similar or related disorders, with some evidence of the influence of genetic factors. Environmental factors may play a part but are often not of major importance.

Specific developmental disorders of scholastic skills include specific reading disorder; specific spelling disorder; specific disorder of arithmetic skills; mixed disorder of scholastic skills; other developmental disorders of scholastic skills; and developmental disorder of scholastic skills, unspecified (Table 38–1).

Normal patterns of skill acquisition are disturbed because of abnormalities in cognitive processing that derive largely from biological dysfunction. Diagnostic difficulties can arise from the need to differentiate the disorders from normal variations; the need to take into account developmental course; the fact that these skills must be taught and learned and are not simply a function of biological maturation; and the difficulty in distinguishing between cognitive abnormalities that cause reading problems and those that arise from reading problems.

READING DISORDER

In DSM-IV, reading disorder is defined as reading achievement that is below the expected level for a child's age, education, and intelligence; the impairment significantly interferes with academic success or the daily activities that involve reading. According to DSM-IV, if a neurological condition or sensory disturbance is present, the degree of reading disability exhibited exceeds that usually associated with the other condition.

The DSM-IV definition of reading disorder differs from that in ICD-10. According to ICD-10, children with specific reading disorder frequently have a history of impaired speech, language, and spelling.

Reading disorder is a relatively common occurrence affecting about 4 percent of school-age children; it results in reading achievement below the expected level for a child's age, intelligence, and education. Reading disorder is characterized by an impaired ability to recognize words, slow and inaccurate reading, and poor comprehension. In addition, children with attention-deficit/hyperactivity disorders are at high risk for reading disorder. Historically, several labels have been used to describe reading disabilities including *dyslexia, reading backward, learning disability, alexia,* and *developmental word blindness.* The term *dyslexia* was used extensively for many years to describe a reading disability syndrome that often included speech and language deficits and right–left confusion. Reading disorder is frequently accompanied by disabilities in other academic skills, and the use of the term *dyslexia* has been replaced by broader terms, such as *learning disorder.*

Table 38–1
ICD-10 Diagnostic Criteria for Specific Developmental Disorders of Scholastic Skills

Specific reading disorder

A. Either of the following must be present:
  (1) A score on reading accuracy and/or comprehension that is at least 2 standard errors of prediction below the level expected on the basis of the child's chronological age and general intelligence, with both reading skills and IQ assessed on an individually administered test standardized for the child's culture and educational system.
  (2) A history of serious reading difficulties, or test scores that met criterion A(1) at an earlier age, plus a score on a spelling test that is at least 2 standard errors of prediction below the level expected on the basis of the child's chronological age and IQ.

B. The disturbance described in criterion A significantly interferes with academic achievement or with activities of daily living that require reading skills.

C. The disorder is not the direct result of a defect in visual or hearing acuity, or of a neurological disorder.

D. School experiences are within the average expectable range (i.e. there have been no extreme inadequacies in educational experiences).

E. *Most commonly used exclusion clause.* IQ is below 70 on an individually administered standardized test.

Possible additional inclusion criterion

For some research purposes, investigators may wish to specify a history of some level of impairment during the preschool years in speech, language, sound categorization, motor coordination, visual processing, attention, or control or modulation of activity.

Comments

The above criteria would not include general reading backwardness of a type that would fall within the clinical guidelines. The research diagnostic criteria for general reading backwardness would be the same as for specific reading disorder except that criterion A(1) would specify reading skills 2 standard errors of prediction below the level expected on the basis of chronological age (ie, not taking IQ into account), and criterion A(2) would follow the same principle for spelling. The validity of the differentiation between these two varieties of reading problem is not unequivocally established, but it seems that the specific type has a more specific association with language retardation (whereas general reading backwardness is associated with a wider range of developmental disabilities), and is more prevalent in boys than in girls.

There are further research differentiations that are based on analyses of the types of spelling error.

Specific spelling disorder

A. The score on a standardized spelling test is at least 2 standard errors of prediction below the level expected on the basis of the child's chronological age and general intelligence.

B. Scores on reading accuracy and comprehension and on arithmetic are within the normal range (±2 standard deviations from the mean).

C. There is no history of significant reading difficulties.

D. School experience is within the average expectable range (ie, there have been no extreme inadequacies in educational experiences).

E. Spelling difficulties have been present from the early stages of learning to spell.

F. The disturbance described in criterion A significantly interferes with academic achievement or with activities of daily living that require spelling skills.

G. *Most commonly used exclusion clause.* IQ is below 70 on an individually administered standardized test.

Specific disorder of arithmetical skills

A. The score on a standardized arithmetic test is at least 2 standard errors of prediction below the level expected on the basis of the child's chronological age and general intelligence.

B. Scores on reading accuracy and comprehension and on spelling are within the normal range (±2 standard deviations from the mean).

C. There is no history of significant reading or spelling difficulties.

D. School experience is within the average expectable range (ie, there have been no extreme inadequacies in educational experiences).

E. Arithmetical difficulties have been present from the early stages of learning arithmetic.

F. The disturbance described in criterion A significantly interferes with academic achievement or with activities of daily living that require arithmetical skills.

G. *Most commonly used exclusion clause.* IQ is below 70 on an individually administered standardized test.

Mixed disorder of scholastic skills

This is an ill-defined, inadequately conceptualized (but necessary) residual category of disorders in which both arithmetical and reading or spelling skills are significantly impaired, but in which the disorder is not solely explicable in terms of general mental retardation or inadequate schooling. It should be used for disorders meeting the criteria for specific disorder arithmetical skills and either specific reading disorder or specific spelling disorder.

Other developmental disorders of scholastic skills

Developmental disorder of scholastic skills, unspecified

This category should be avoided as far as possible and should be used only for unspecified disorders in which there is a significant disability of learning that cannot be solely accounted for by mental retardation, visual acuity problems, or inadequate schooling.

Epidemiology

An estimated 4 percent of school-age children in the United States have reading disorder; prevalence studies find rates ranging between 2 and 8 percent. Three to four times as many boys as girls are reported to have reading disability in school and in clinically referred samples. The rate for boys may be inflated: Boys with reading disorder are apt to be noticed because of their behavioral difficulties. Adults with reading backwardness or reading retardation reportedly show no sex difference in the frequency of the disorder.

Etiology

No unitary cause is known for reading disorder; in view of the many associated learning disorders and language difficulties, reading disorder probably has multifactorial causes. Recent research in the fields of cognitive neuroscience and neuropsychology suggests that encoding processes and working memory, rather than attention or long-term memory, may be areas of weakness for children with reading disorder. One recent study found an association between dyslexia and birth in the months of May, June, and July, a finding suggesting that prenatal exposure to a maternal infectious illness, such as influenza, in the winter months may contribute to reading disorder.

Reading disorder tends to be more prevalent among family members of people affected by the disorder than in the general population. This fact has led to the speculation that the disorder may have a genetic origin, but family and twin studies have not supplied definitive evidence to support this theory. Extremely low birth weight and severely premature children are at higher risk for reading disorder and other learning disorders than are children who are born full term and have normal birth weight.

Studies in the 1930s attempted to explain reading disorder according to the cerebral hemispheric function model, which suggested positive correlations of reading disorder with left-handedness, left-eyedness, or mixed laterality. Subsequent epidemiological studies did not find any consistent association between reading disorder and laterality of handedness or eyedness, but right–left confusion has been shown to be associated with reading difficulties. The reversal of cerebral asymmetry may result in the transference of language lateralization to the less differentiated hemisphere to accommodate language function, a factor that may lead to reading disorder. A few recent studies (computed tomography [CT] scan, magnetic resonance imaging [MRI], and on autopsy) have shown abnormal symmetries in the temporal or parietal lobes of people with reading disorder.

Many workers attribute reading disorder to subtle visual or verbal (auditory) deficits. There is more evidence for the effect of verbal deficits than of visual deficits; thus, reading disorder is considered to be part of an oral language disorder. Reading requires a brain that is mature enough and sufficiently intact to integrate information arriving through various processing systems and to relegate disturbing stimuli to the background. Reading also requires sufficient freedom from conflict to permit the investment of energy in the task and a sociocultural value system that views reading as a vital skill.

A high incidence of reading disorder tends to occur among children of normal intelligence who have cerebral palsy. A slightly increased incidence of reading disorder appears among epileptic children. Complications during pregnancy; prenatal and perinatal difficulties, including prematurity; and low birth weight are common in the histories of children with reading disorder. Children with postnatal brain lesions in the left occipital lobe, which results in right visual-field blindness, may have secondary reading disorder, as may children with lesions in the splenium of the corpus callosum that block the transmission of visual information from the intact right hemisphere to the language areas of the left hemisphere.

Reading disorder may be one manifestation of developmental delay or maturational lag. Temperamental attributes have been reported to be closely associated with reading disorder. Compared with non–reading-disordered children, children with reading disorder often have more difficulty in concentrating and a shorter attention span. Some studies suggest an association between malnutrition and cognitive function. Children who were malnourished for a long time during early childhood show subaverage performances in various cognitive tests. Their cognitive performances are lower than those of their siblings who grew up in the same family environment but who were not subjected to the same degree of malnutrition.

Severe reading disorder is often associated with psychiatric problems. Reading disorder may be the result of a preexisting psychiatric disorder or the cause of emotional and behavior disorders; however, it is not always easy to ascertain the causal relation between reading disorder and a coexisting psychiatric disorder.

Diagnosis

Reading disorder is mainly diagnosed when a child's reading achievement is markedly below intellectual capacity (Table 38–2). Other characteristic diagnostic features include difficulties with recalling, evoking, and sequencing printed letters and words; processing sophisticated grammatical constructions; and making inferences. Clinically, a child may become demoralized or experience symptoms of depression related to

Table 38–2
DSM-IV Diagnostic Criteria for Reading Disorder

A. Reading achievement, as measured by individually administered standardized tests of reading accuracy or comprehension, is substantially below that expected given the person's chronological age, measured intelligence, and age-appropriate education.

B. The disturbance in criterion A significantly interferes with academic achievement or activities of daily living that require reading skills.

C. If a sensory deficit is present, the reading difficulties are in excess of those usually associated with it.

Coding note: if a general medical (eg, neurological) condition or sensory deficit is present, code the condition on Axis III.

the experience of being unable to succeed in school. School failure seems to reinforce some children's preexisting doubts; their energy may be so bound to poor self-esteem that they are unable to apply themselves to academic work. Students who are suspected of having reading disorders are generally evaluated through the facilities of a school district to determine their eligibility for special education services. Special education classification, however, is not uniform across states or regions, and students with identical difficulties in reading may be deemed eligible for services in one region but ineligible in another. Sometimes an evaluation is requested based on disruptive behavioral problems that occur in conjunction with the reading disorder. A psychiatric evaluation should both assess the need for psychiatric intervention and suggest appropriate treatment.

The diagnosis of reading disorder must be confirmed by a standardized reading achievement test. Pervasive developmental disorders, attention-deficit/hyperactivity disorder, and mental retardation must be ruled out.

Psychoeducational Tests. In addition to standardized intelligence tests, psychoeducational diagnostic tests should be administered. The diagnostic battery may include a standardized spelling test, written composition, processing and using oral language, and design copying, a judgment of the adequacy of pencil use. The reading subtests of the Woodcock-Johnson Psycho-Educational Battery–Revised, and the Peabody Individual Achievement Test–Revised are useful in identifying reading disability. A screening projective battery may include human-figure drawings, picture-story tests, and sentence completion. The evaluation should also include a systematic observation of behavior variables.

Clinical Features

Children who have reading disorder can usually be evaluated by the age of 7 years (second grade). Reading difficulty may be apparent among students in classrooms where reading skills are expected as early as the first grade. Children can sometimes compensate for reading disorder in the early elementary grades by the use of memory and inference, particularly when the disorder is associated with high intelligence. In such instances, the disorder may not be apparent until age 9 (fourth grade) or later.

Children with reading disorder make many errors in their oral reading. The errors are characterized by omissions, additions, and distortions of words. Such children have difficulty in distinguishing between printed letter characters and sizes, especially those that differ only in spatial orientation and length of line. The problems in managing printed or written language may pertain to individual letters, sentences, and even a page. The child's reading speed is slow, often with minimal comprehension. Most children with reading disorder have an age-appropriate ability to copy from a written or printed text, but nearly all are poor spellers.

Associated problems include language difficulties, shown often as impaired sound discrimination and difficulties in properly sequencing words. A child with disorders may start a word either in the middle or at the end of a printed or written sentence. At times, such children transpose letters that are to be read because of a poorly established left–right tracking sequence. Failures in both memory recall and sustained elicitation result in the poor recall of letter names and sounds.

Most children with reading disorder dislike and avoid reading and writing. Their anxiety is heightened when they are confronted with demands that involve printed language. Many children with the disorder who do not receive remedial education have a sense of shame and humiliation because of their continuing failure and subsequent frustration. These feelings grow more intense as time progresses. Older children tend to be angry and depressed, and they exhibit poor self-esteem.

Differential Diagnosis

Reading disorder is often accompanied by additional disorders, such as expressive language disorder, disorder of written expression, or attention-deficit/hyperactivity disorder. Deficits in expressive language and speech discrimination are often present in reading disorder and may be severe enough to warrant the additional diagnosis of expressive language disorder or mixed receptive-expressive language disorder. In some cases there is a discrepancy between scores on verbal and performance intelligence. Visual perceptual deficits occur in only about 10 percent of cases. Reading disorder must be differentiated from mental retardation syndromes in which reading, along with other skills, are below the achievement expected for a child's chronological age. Intellectual testing helps to differentiate global deficits from more specific reading difficulties.

Inadequate schooling resulting in poor reading skills can be determined by finding out whether other children in the same school have similarly poor reading performances on standardized reading tests. Hearing and visual impairments should be ruled out with screening tests.

Reading disorder often accompanies other emotional and behavioral disorders, especially attention-deficit/hyperactivity disorder, conduct disorder, and depressive disorders, particularly in older children and adolescents.

Course and Prognosis

Many children with reading disorder acquire a little information about printed language during their first 2 years in grade school, even without any remedial assistance. By the end of the first grade, some have learned how to read a few words, but if no remedial educational intervention is given by the third grade, children remain reading impaired. Under the best circumstances, a child is classified as being at risk for a reading disorder during the kindergarten year or early in the first grade.

When remediation is instituted early, it can sometimes be discontinued by the end of the first or second grade. In severe cases and depending on the pattern of deficits and strengths, remediation may be continued into the middle and high school years. Children who have either compensated satisfactorily or recovered from early reading disorder are over-represented in families with socioeconomically advantaged backgrounds.

Treatment

The treatment of choice for reading disorder is, first, an accurate assessment of a child's specific deficits and weaknesses and, second, a well-matched educational approach. Positive coping strategies include small, structured reading groups that offer individual attention and a child's ease in asking for help.

A specific method developed by Samuel Orton urges therapeutic attention to the mastery of simple phonetic units, followed by the blending of these units into words and sentences. An approach that systematically engages several senses is recommended. The rationale for this and similar methods is that children's difficulties in managing letters and syllables are basic to their failures to learn to read; therefore, if they are taught to cope with graphemes, they will learn to read.

As in psychotherapy, the therapist–patient relationship is important to a successful treatment outcome in remedial educational therapy. Children should be placed in a grade as close as possible to their social functional level and given special remedial work in reading. Coexisting emotional and behavioral problems should be treated by appropriate psychotherapeutic means. Parental counseling may also be helpful.

Approximately 75 percent of children with learning disorders can be differentiated from comparison samples through lower measures of social competence. Therefore, it is important to include social skills improvement as a therapeutic component of a treatment program for children with reading disorders.

MATHEMATICS DISORDER

According to DSM-IV, mathematics disorder is one of the learning disorders. Impairments in four groups of skills have been identified in mathematics disorder: linguistic skills (those related to understanding mathematical terms and to converting written problems into mathematical symbols), perceptual skills (the ability to recognize and understand symbols and to order clusters of numbers), mathematical skills (basic addition, subtraction, multiplication, division, and following sequencing of basic operations), and attentional skills (copying figures correctly and observing operational symbols correctly).

Other disorders often accompany mathematics disorder, include reading disorder, developmental coordination disorder, and mixed receptive-expressive language disorder. Unlike DSM-IV, the equivalent disorder in ICD-10 excludes reading and spelling disabilities.

Mathematic disorder is not new, but it was not recognized as a psychiatric disorder until 1980 in DSM-III. Many terms have been applied to it: *Gerstmann syndrome, dyscalculia, congenital arithmetic disorder, acalculia,* and *developmental arithmetic disorder.*

Mathematics disorder can occur in isolation or in conjunction with language and reading disorders. The disorder is essentially a disability in performing the arithmetic skills expected for a child's intellectual capacity and educational level, as measured by standardized, individually administered tests. The lack of expected mathematics ability interferes with school performance or daily life activities, and the difficulties are in excess of impairments associated with any existing neurological or sensory deficits.

Epidemiology

Because the prevalence of mathematics disorder has not been well studied, it can be only roughly estimated to be 5 percent of school-age children who are not mentally retarded. The extent to which educational limitations influence this number is not clear, but data suggest that children with mathematics disorder are likely to exhibit another learning disorder or language disability. The sex ratio for mathematics disorder is still under investigation; the disorder may be more common in girls than in boys.

Etiology

The cause of mathematics disorder is unknown. An early theory proposed a neurological deficit in the right cerebral hemisphere, particularly in the occipital lobe areas. These regions are responsible for processing visual-spatial stimuli that, in turn, are responsible for mathematical skills. The validity of this theory, however, has received little support in subsequent neuropsychiatric studies.

Currently the cause is thought to be multifactorial, so that maturational, cognitive, emotional, educational, and socioeconomic factors account in varying degrees and combinations for mathematics disorder. Compared with reading, arithmetic abilities seem to be more dependent on the amount and quality of instruction.

Diagnosis

A careful inquiry into a child's school performance history usually reveals early difficulties with arithmetic subjects, in a typical case of mathematics disorder. A child with a mathematics disorder may feel shame and get further and further behind without receiving help. A definitive diagnosis can be made only after a child takes an individually administered standardized arithmetic test and scores markedly below the level expected, in view of the child's schooling and intellectual capacity as measured by a standardized intelligence test. A pervasive developmental disorder and mental retardation should also be ruled out before confirming the diagnosis of mathematics disorder. The diagnosis criteria for mathematics disorder are given in Table 38–3.

Clinical Features

Most children with mathematics disorder can be classified during the second and third grades in elementary school. An affected child's performance in handling basic number concepts, such as counting and adding even one-digit numbers, is significantly below the age-expected norms, but the child shows normal intellectual skills in other areas. During the first 2 or 3 years of elementary school, a child with mathematics disorder may appear to make some progress in mathematics by relying on rote memory. But soon, as arithmetic progresses to complex levels requiring discrimination and manipulation

Table 38–3
DSM-IV Diagnostic Criteria for Mathematics Disorder

A. Mathematical ability, as measured by individually administered standardized tests, is substantially below that expected given the person's chronological age, measured intelligence, and age-appropriate education.

B. The disturbance in criterion A significantly interferes with academic achievement or activities of daily living that require mathematical ability.

C. If a sensory deficit is present, the difficulties in mathematical ability are in excess of those usually associated with it.

Coding note: if a general medical (eg, neurological) condition or sensory deficit is present, code the condition on Axis III.

of spatial and numerical relations, the presence of the disorder becomes conspicuous.

Some investigators have classified mathematics disorder into several categories: difficulty in learning to count meaningfully; difficulty in mastering cardinal and ordinal systems; difficulty in performing arithmetic operations; and difficulty in envisioning clusters of objects as groups. Children with the disorder may have difficulties in associating auditory and visual symbols, understanding the conservation of quantity, remembering sequences of arithmetic steps, and choosing principles for problem-solving activities. Children with these problems are presumed to have good auditory and verbal abilities.

Mathematics disorder often coexists with other disorders affecting reading, expressive writing, coordination, and expressive and receptive language. Spelling problems, deficits in memory or attention, and emotional or behavioral problems may be present. Young grade-school children often first show other learning disorders and should be checked for mathematics disorder. Children with cerebral palsy may have mathematics disorder with normal overall intelligence.

The relation between mathematics disorder and other communication and learning disorders it not yet clear. Although children with mixed receptive-expressive language disorder and expressive language disorder are not necessarily affected by mathematics disorder, the conditions often coexist, as they are associated with impairments in both decoding and encoding processes.

Differential Diagnosis

Mathematics disorder must be differentiated from global causes of impaired functioning such as mental retardation syndromes. Arithmetic difficulties in mental retardation are accompanied by a generalized impairment in overall intellectual functioning. In unusual cases of mild mental retardation, arithmetic skills may be significantly below the level expected, on the basis of a person's schooling and level of mental retardation. In such cases, an additional diagnosis of mathematics disorder should be made; treatment of the arithmetic difficulties can be particularly helpful for a child's chances for employment in adulthood.

Inadequate schooling can often affect a child's poor arithmetic performance on a standardized arithmetic test. If so, most of the other children in the same class probably have similarly poor arithmetic performances. Conduct disorder and attention-deficit/hyperactivity disorder may occur with mathematics disorder, and in these cases both diagnoses should be made.

Course and Prognosis

A child usually shows mathematics disorder by the age of 8 years (third grade). In some children the disorder is apparent as early as 6 years (first grade); in others it may not occur until age 10 (fifth grade) or later. Thus far, few longitudinal study data are available to predict clear patterns of developmental and academic progress of children classified as having mathematics disorder in early school grades. Nevertheless, untreated children with a moderate mathematics disorder and those children whose arithmetic difficulties cannot be resolved by intensive remedial interventions may have complications, including continuing academic difficulties, poor self-concept, depression, and frustration. These complications may lead to reluctance to attend school, truancy, or conduct disturbance.

Treatment

Currently, the most effective treatment for mathematics disorder is remedial education, although controversy continues to the comparative effectiveness of various remedial educational treatments. The consensus is that the treatment methods and materials are useful only when they fit the particular child, the disorder and its severity, and the feasibility of the teaching plans. A recent report indicates that math instruction is most helpful when the focus is on problem-solving activities, including word problems, rather than on only computation. This same approach is useful to those without, as well as with, mathematics disorder. Project MATH, a multimedia self-instructional or group-instructional in-service training program, has been successful for some children with mathematics disorder. Computer programs can be helpful and can increase compliance with remediation efforts. Social skills deficits may contribute to a child's resistance to asking for help, so that once a child is identified with a mathematics disorder, positive problem-solving skills in a social arena as well as in mathematics may be beneficial. Poor coordination may accompany the disorder, and physical therapy and sensory integration activities may be helpful.

DISORDER OF WRITTEN EXPRESSION

Writing skills that are significantly below the expected level for a person's age, intellectual capacity, and education as measured by a standardized test are characteristic of disorder of written expression. The impairment interferes with the person's school performance and with the demands for writing in everyday life, and the disorder is not due to a neurological or sensory deficit. The components of writing disability include poor spelling, errors in grammar and punctuation, and poor handwriting.

Several decades ago the prevailing view was that dysgraphia did not develop in the absence of a reading disorder, but it is now known that disorder of written expression can occur on its own. Terms once used to describe writing disability included *spelling disorder* and *spelling dyslexia.* Writing disabilities are often associated with other learning disorders, but they may be diagnosed later because expressive writing is acquired later than are language and reading.

In addition to a disorder similar to DSM-IV disorder of written expression, ICD-10 also includes a separate specific spelling disorder.

Epidemiology

The prevalence of disorder of written expression is unknown but has been estimated at 3 to 10 percent of school-age children. The male-to-female ratio is also unknown. Some evidence indicates that affected children are frequently from families with a history of the disorder.

Etiology

According to one hypothesis, disorder of written expression results from the combined effects of one or more of the following: expressive language disorder, mixed receptive-expressive language disorder, and reading disorder. This view implies the possible existence of neurological and cognitive defects or malfunctions somewhere in the central information-processing areas of the brain.

Hereditary predisposition to the disorder has been suggested by empirical findings that most children with disorder of written expression have relatives with the disorder. Temperamental characteristics may also play some role in disorder of written expression, especially such characteristics as short attention span and easy distractibility.

Diagnosis

Diagnosing disorder of written expression is based on a person's consistently poor performance on composing written text, including handwriting and impaired ability to spell and to place words sequentially in coherent sentences. Performance is markedly below the person's intellectual capacity, as confirmed by an individually administered standardized expressive writing test (Table 38–4). Tests of written language that are now available include the Test of Written Language (TOWL), the Diagnostic Evaluation of Writing Skills (DEWS), and Test of Early Written Language (TEWL). The presence of a major disorder, such as a pervasive developmental disorder or mental retardation, may obviate the diagnosis of disorder of written expression. Other disorders to be differentiated from disorder of written expression are communication disorders, reading disorder, and impaired vision and hearing.

Any person suspected of having disorder of written expression should first be given a standardized intelligence test, such as the third edition of THE Wechsler Intelligence Scale for Children (WISC-III) or the revised Wechsler Adult Intelligence Scale (WAIS-R) to determine the person's intellectual capacity before administering a standardized expressive writing test.

Table 38–4
DSM-IV Diagnostic Criteria for Disorder of Written Expression

A. Writing skills, as measured by individually administered standardized tests (or functional assessments of writing skills), are substantially below those expected given the person's chronological age, measured intelligence, and age-appropriate education.

B. The disturbance in criterion A significantly interferes with academic achievement or activities of daily living that require the composition of written texts (eg, writing grammatically correct sentences and organized paragraphs).

C. If a sensory deficit is present, the difficulties in writing skills are in excess of those usually associated with it.

Coding note: if a general medical (eg, neurological) condition or sensory deficit is present, code the condition on Axis III.

Reprinted with permission from American Psychiatric Association: *Diagnostic and Statistical Manual of Mental Disorders,* ed 4. Copyright, American Psychiatric Association, Washington, 1994.

Clinical Features

Children with disorder of written expression have difficulties early in grade school in spelling words and in expressing their thoughts according to age-appropriate grammatical norms. Their spoken and written sentences contain an unusually large number of grammatical errors and poor paragraph organization. During and after the second grade, the children commonly make simple grammatical errors in writing a short sentence. For example, they frequently fail, despite constant reminders, to start the first letter of the first word in a sentence with a capital letter and to end a sentence with a period. Common features of the disorder of written expression are spelling errors, grammatical errors, punctuation errors, poor paragraph organization, and poor handwriting.

As they grow older and progress into higher grades in school, such children's spoken and written sentences become more conspicuously primitive, odd, and inferior to what is expected of students at their grade level. Their word choices are erroneous and inappropriate; their paragraphs are disorganized and not in proper sequence; and spelling correctly becomes increasingly difficult as their vocabulary becomes more abstract and larger. Associated features of disorder of written expression include refusal or reluctance to go to school and to do assigned written homework, poor academic performance in other areas (such as mathematics), general disinterest in school work, truancy, attention deficit, and conduct disturbance.

Most children with disorder of written expression become frustrated and angry because of their feelings of inadequacy and failure in their academic performance. They may have a chronic depressive disorder as a result of their growing sense of isolation, estrangement, and despair.

Adults with disorder of written expression who do not receive remedial intervention continue to have difficulties in social adaptation involving writing skills and a continuing sense of incompetence, inferiority, isolation, and estrangement. Some even try to avoid writing a response letter or a simple greeting card for fear that their writing incompetence will be exposed. When their coping mechanisms fail, the severity of their psychopathology is likely to increase. Most adults with the disorder choose occupations that require minimal writing skills, such as trade, custodianship, and other menial work; seldom do they achieve or hold a socially desirable occupational position requiring a high level of expressive writing. Common associated disorders are reading disorder, mixed receptive-expressive language disorder, expressive language disorder, mathematics disorder, developmental coordination disorder, and disruptive behavior and attention-deficit disorders.

K. A. was a 17-year-old female student who presented for reevaluation of problems in school. She attended a nonacademic preschool and was first evaluated when in fourth grade in a regular class at a public school she had attended since kindergarten. Since that time she had attended special schools for children with learning disabilities, and was currently in the 11th grade.

Current evaluation revealed no history of neurological, visual, or hearing problems that could explain her school difficulties. Intelligence testing revealed low average scores in both the verbal and performance subtests of the WISC-III. Reading and mathematical scores on standardized tests of academic performance were consistent with her intelligence and chronological age. However, spelling scores were significantly below the predicted level of performance. Multiple misspellings occurred. The tester noted poor handwriting in the form of rotation and inversion of letters and a mixture of printing and cursive writing. K. A. appeared unable to express thoughts in a complete sentence. Her sentences seemed to run on to three or four sentences that did not clearly state the point. Careful study of K. A.'s written paragraphs revealed grammatical and syntactic errors and errors in punctuation and capitalization. Although in the classroom K. A. was often described as having a short attention span, she did not demonstrate that in one-to-one testing or in nonacademic settings.

The clinical picture of the inability to compose a written text, poor spelling, poor writing, and grammatical errors in the absence of low intelligence; of problems with reading or mathematics; and of pervasive attentional problems led to a diagnosis of a disorder of written expression.

Course and Prognosis

Because writing, language, and reading disorders often coexist and because a child normally speaks well before learning to read and learns to read well before writing well, a child with all these disorders has expressive language disorder diagnosed first and disorder of written expression diagnosed last. In severe cases, a disorder of written expression is apparent by age 7 (second grade); in less severe cases, the disorder may not be apparent until age 10 (fifth grade) or later. Most people with mild and moderate disorder of written expression fare well if they receive timely remedial education early in grade school. Severe disorder of written expression requires continual, extensive remedial treatment through the late part of high school and even into college.

The prognosis depends on the severity of the disorder, the age or grade when the remedial intervention is started, the length and continuity of treatment, and presence or the absence of associated or secondary emotional or behavioral problems. Those who later become well compensated or who recover from disorder of written expression are often from families with high socioeconomic backgrounds.

Treatment

Although controversy continues to the effectiveness of various remedial expressive writing modalities, disorder of written expression responds to remedial treatment. Intensive and continuous administration of individually tailored, one-to-one expressive and creative writing therapy appears to effect the most favorable treatment outcome. Teachers in some special schools devote as much as 2 hours a day to such writing instruction. The treatment of the disorder requires an optimal patient–therapist relationship, as in psychotherapy. Success or failure in sustaining the patient's motivation greatly affects the treatment's long-term efficacy. Associated and secondary emotional and behavioral problems should be given prompt attention, with appropriate psychiatric treatment and parental counseling.

LEARNING DISORDER NOT OTHERWISE SPECIFIED

Learning disorder not otherwise specified is a new category in DSM-IV for disorders that do not meet the criteria for any specific learning disorder but that cause impairment and reflect learning abilities below those expected for a person's intelligence, education, and age. An example of a disability that could be placed in this category is a spelling skills deficit (Table 38–5).

The DSM-III-R category of specific developmental disorder not otherwise specified covered residual disorders of language,

Table 38–5
DSM-IV Diagnostic Criteria for Learning Disorder Not Otherwise Specified

This category is for disorders in learning that do not meet criteria for any specific learning disorder. This category might include problems in all three areas (reading, mathematics, written expression) that together significantly interfere with academic achievement even though performance on tests measuring each individual skill is not substantially below that expected given the person's chronological age, measured intelligence, and age-appropriate education.

speech, academic, and motor skills; the category has been divided in DSM-IV into learning disorder not otherwise specified and communication disorder not otherwise specified.

References

Badian NA: Dyscalculia and nonverbal disorders of learning. In *Progress in Learning Disabilities,* HR Myklebust, editor, vol 5, p 235. Grune & Stratton, New York, 1983.

Badian NA: The prediction of good and poor reading before kindergarten entry: A nine-year follow-up. J Learn Disabil *21:* 88, 1988.

Baker L, Cantwell DP: Disorder of written expression. In *Comprehensive Textbook of Psychiatry,* ed 6, HI Kaplan, BJ Sadock, editors, p 2253. Williams & Wilkins, Baltimore, 1995.

Baker L, Cantwell DP: Mathematics disorder. In *Comprehensive Textbook of Psychiatry,* ed 6, HI Kaplan, BJ Sadock, editors, p 7251. Williams & Wilkins, Baltimore, 1995.

Duane DD: Neurobiological correlates of learning disorders. J Am Acad Child Adolesc Psychiatry *28:* 314, 1989.

Duffy FH, Geschwind N: *Dyslexia: A Neuroscientific Approach to Clinical Evaluation.* Little, Brown, Boston, 1985.

Fellon RH, Wood FB: Cognitive deficits in reading disability and attention deficit disorder. J Learn Disabil *22:* 3, 1989.

Friedland J: Development and breakdown of written language. J Commun Disord *23:* 171, 1990.

Geschwind N: Asymmetries of the brain: New development. Bull Orton Soc *29:* 67, 1979.

Goldstein S: *Managing Attention and Learning Disorders in Late Adolescence and Adulthood: A Guide for Practitioners.* John Wiley & Sons, New York, 1997.

Grant ML, Ilai D, Nussbaum NL, Bigler ED: The relationship between continuous performance tasks and neuropsychological tests in children with attention-deficit/hyperactivity disorder. Percept Mot Skills *70:* 435, 1990.

Hyrid GW, Semrod-Clikeman E: Dyslexia and neurodevelopmental pathology: Relationships to cognition, intelligence, and reading skill acquisition. J Learn Disabil *22:* 204, 1989.

Kose L: Neuropsychological implications of diagnoses and treatment of mathematical learning disabilities. Top Lang Learn Disord *1:* 19, 1981.

LaBuda MC, DeFries JC: Cognitive abilities in children with reading disabilities and controls: A follow-up study. J Learn Disabil *21:* 562, 1988.

Livingston R, Adam BS, Bracha HS: Season of birth and neurodevelopmental disorder: Summer birth is associated with dyslexia. J Am Acad Child Adolesc Psychiatry *32:* 612, 1993.

Mayer R: Understanding individual differences in mathematical problem solving. Learn Disabil Q *16:* 2, 1993.

Nussbaum NL, Grant ML, Roman MJ, Poole JH, Bigler ED: Attention-deficit disorder and the mediating effect of age on academic and behavioral variables. J Dev Behav Pediatr *11:* 22, 1990.

Oliver CE: A sensorimotor program for improving writing readiness skills in elementary-age children. Am J Occup Ther *44:* 111, 1990.

Orton S: *Reading, Writing, and Speech Problems in Children.* Norton, New York, 1937.

Persell CH: *Education and Inequality: A Theoretical and Empirical Synthesis.* Free Press, New York, 1977.

Rourke BP, Strang JD: Subtypes of reading and arithmetic disabilities: A neuropsychological analysis. In *Developmental Neuropsychiatry,* M Rutter, editor, p 473. Guilford, New York, 1983.

Semrod-Clikeman E, Biederman J, Sprich-Buckminster S, Lehman BK, Faraone SV, Norman D: Comorbidity between ADDH and learning disability: A review and report in a clinically referred sample. J Am Acad Child Adolesc Psychiatry *31:* 439, 1992.

Share DL, Moffitt TE, Silva PA: Factors associated with arithmetic and reading disability and specific arithmetic disability. J Learn Disabil *21:* 313, 1988.

Silver AA, Hagin RA: *A Scanning Instrument for the Identification of Learning Disability.* Walker Educational, New York, 1980.

Smith SD, Pennington BF, Kimberling WJ, Ing PS: Familial dyslexia: Use of genetic linkage data to define subtypes. J Am Acad Child Adolesc Psychiatry *29:* 204, 1990.

Vaughn S, Elbaum BE, Schumm JS: The effects of inclusion on the social functioning of students with learning disabilities. J Learn Disabil *29* (6): 598, 1996.

Vogel SA: Gender differences in intelligence, language, visual motor abilities, and academic achievement in students with learning disabilities: A review of the literature. J Learn Disabil *23:* 44, 1990.

39 Motor Skills Disorder

DEVELOPMENTAL COORDINATION DISORDER

According to the fourth edition of *Diagnostic and Statistical Manual of Mental Disorders* (DSM-IV), the essential characteristic of developmental coordination disorder is a "marked impairment in the development of motor coordination." The diagnosis is made only when the impairment significantly interferes with "academic achievement or activities of daily living."

Developmental coordination disorder is a syndrome characterized by imprecise or clumsy gross motor skills. Although their motor skills are not actually grossly impaired, children with this disorder not infrequently also exhibit language and other learning disorders as well as problems with peer relationships. It is currently the only disorder in the category of motor skills disorder, according to DSM-IV.

The disorder is characterized by markedly lower than expected performance in activities requiring motor coordination. Children may have delays in achieving motor milestones, such as sitting up, crawling, and walking. They are usually clumsy in gross and fine motor skills but are not globally impaired. Developmental coordination disorder may also include deficits in handwriting and in the frequency of dropping things. Children with the disorder may resemble children of a younger age in terms of their motor skills. The deficits are significantly poor for a child's chronological and mental age and interfere with daily functioning or school performance. Motor impairment in the disorder cannot be explained on the basis of a medical condition, such as cerebral palsy, muscular dystrophy, or any other neuromuscular disorder.

Clumsiness in children has been associated with learning disorders, communication disorders, disruptive behavior, and attention-deficit disorders, such as attention-deficit/hyperactivity disorder. Children who are clumsy are often poor in sports and may be socially ostracized. DSM-IV makes no provision for motor coordination deficits that do not meet the criteria for developmental coordination disorder.

Epidemiology

The prevalence of developmental coordination disorder is unknown, but it has been estimated at about 5 percent of school-age children. The male-to-female ratio is also unknown, but more boys than girls have the disorder. Reports in the literature of the male-to-female ratio have ranged from 2 to 1 to as much as 4 to 1.

Etiology

The causes of developmental coordination disorder are unknown, but hypotheses include both organic and developmental causes. Risk factors postulated in the disorder include prematurity, hypoxia, perinatal malnutrition, and low birth weight. Neurochemical abnormalities and parietal lobe lesions have also been suggested as contributors to coordination deficits. Developmental coordination disorder and communication disorders have strong associations, although the specific causative agents are unknown for both. Coordination problems are also more frequently found in children who have impulsive behavior and a learning disorder. Developmental coordination disorder probably has a multifactorial cause.

Diagnosis

The diagnosis of developmental coordination disorder requires a history of the child's early motor behavior, including the direct observation of motor activities. Informal screening for developmental coordination disorder can be done by asking the child to perform tasks involving gross motor coordination (for example, hopping, jumping, and standing on one foot); fine motor coordination (for example, finger tapping and shoelace tying); and hand–eye coordination (for example, catching a ball and copying letters). The diagnosis is supported by below-normal scores on performance subtests of standardized intelligence tests and by normal or above-normal scores on verbal subtests. Specialized tests of motor coordination can be useful, such as the Bender Visual Motor Gestalt test, the Frostig Movement Skills Test Battery, and the Bruininks-Oseretsky Test of Motor Development. The child's chronological age and intellectual capacity must be taken into account, and the disorder cannot be caused by a neurological or neuromuscular condition. Slight reflex abnormalities and other soft neurological signs, however, may occasionally be found on examination. The DSM-IV diagnostic criteria are given in Table 39–1.

ICD-10

According to the 10th revision of *International Statistical Classification of Diseases and Related Health Problems* (ICD-10), the main feature of specific developmental disorder of motor function (sometimes called clumsy child syndrome) is a "serious impairment in the development of motor coordination that is not solely explicable in terms of general intellectual retardation or of any specific congenital or acquired

Table 39–1
DSM-IV Diagnostic Criteria for Developmental Coordination Disorder

A. Performance in daily activities that require motor coordination is substantially below that expected given the person's chronological age and measured intelligence. This may be manifested by marked delays in achieving motor milestones (eg, walking, crawling, sitting), dropping things, "clumsiness," poor performance in sports, or poor handwriting.

B. The disturbance in criterion A significantly interferes with academic achievement or activities of daily living.

C. The disturbance is not due to a general medical condition (eg, cerebral palsy, hemiplegia, or muscular dystrophy) and does not meet criteria for a pervasive developmental disorder.

D. If mental retardation is present, the motor difficulties are in excess of those usually associated with it.

Coding note: if a general medical (eg, neurological) condition or sensory deficit is present, code the condition on Axis III.

Reprinted with permission from American Psychiatric Association: *Diagnostic and Statistical Manual of Mental Disorders*, ed 4. American Psychiatric Association, Washington, 1994.

neurological disorder (other than the one that may be implicit in the coordination abnormality)." The motor clumsiness is usually associated with "impaired performance on visuo-spatial cognitive tasks."

A child's motor coordination is significantly lower than that expected on the basis of age and intelligence. These coordination problems must not have been an acquired deficit or the result of any defects in vision or hearing or of a diagnosable neurological disorder.

The pattern of disability varies with age, and developmental milestones may be delayed. Children may be awkward and clumsy, slow to learn motion activities, and poor at drawing. Children with the disorder may also have associated speech problems, "especially involving articulation." Scholastic difficulties can occur with the disorder.

Although no neurological disorder can be diagnosed, some children have a history of very low birth weight or marked prematurity.

The ICD-10 diagnostic criteria are presented in Table 39–2.

Clinical Features

The clinical signs suggesting the existence of developmental coordination disorder are evident as early as infancy, when an affected child begins to attempt tasks requiring motor coordination. The essential clinical feature is markedly impaired performance in motor coordination. The difficulties in motor coordination may vary with a child's age and developmental stage.

In infancy and early childhood the disorder may be manifested by delays in normal developmental milestones, such as turning over, crawling, sitting, standing, walking, buttoning shirts, and zipping up pants. Between the ages of 2 and 4 years clumsiness appears in almost all activities requiring motor coordination. Affected children cannot hold objects, and they drop them easily; their gait is unsteady; they often trip over their own feet; and they may bump into other children while attempting to go around them. In older children the impaired motor coordination may be shown in table games, such as putting together puzzles or building blocks, and in any type of ball game. Although no specific features are pathognomonic of developmental coordination disorder, developmental milestones are frequently delayed. Many children with the disorder also have a speech disorder. Older children may have secondary problems of school difficulties, including behavioral and emotional problems, that require appropriate therapeutic interventions.

Differential Diagnosis

The differential diagnosis includes medical disorders that produce coordination difficulties (such as cerebral palsy and muscular dystrophy), pervasive developmental disorders, and mental retardation. In mental retardation and in the pervasive developmental disorders, coordination usually does not stand out as a deficit compared with other skills. Children with neuromuscular disorders may exhibit more global muscle impairment than they do clumsiness and delayed motor milestones. In these cases, neurological workups usually reveal more extensive deficits than are present in developmental coordination disorder. Extremely hyperactive and impulsive children may be physically careless because of their high levels of motor activity. Clumsy motor behavior and attention-deficit/hyperactivity disorder seem to be associated.

Course and Prognosis

No reliable data are available on the prospective longitudinal outcomes of both treated and untreated children with developmental coordination disorder. Some studies suggest a favorable outcome for those children who have an average or above-average intellectual capacity, because they can learn to compensate for their coordination deficits. The clumsiness generally persists into adolescence and adult life. In severe cases that remain untreated, patients may have secondary com-

Table 39–2
ICD-10 Diagnostic Criteria for Specific Developmental Disorder of Motor Function

A. The score on a standardized test of fine or gross motor coordination is at least 2 standard deviations below the level expected for the child's chronological age.

B. The disturbance described in criterion A significantly interferes with academic achievement or with activities of daily living.

C. There is no diagnosable neurological disorder.

D. *Most commonly used exclusion clause.* IQ is below 70 on an individually administered standardized test.

Reprinted with permission from World Health Organization: *The ICD-10 Classification of Mental and Behavioural Disorders: Diagnostic Criteria for Research.* Copyright, World Health Organization, Geneva, 1993.

plications, such as repeated failures in both nonacademic and academic school tasks, repeated problems in attempting to integrate with a peer group, and inability to play games and sports. These problems may lead to low self-esteem, unhappiness, withdrawal, and, in some cases, increasingly severe behavioral problems as a reaction to the frustration engendered by the disorder. All levels of adaptive functioning can be expected in the children. Commonly associated features include delays in nonmotor milestones, expressive language disorder, and mixed receptive-expressive language disorder.

Treatment

The treatments of developmental coordination disorder include perceptual motor training, neurophysiological techniques of exercise for motor dysfunction, and modified physical education. Because the disorder may be comorbid with other learning and communication disorders, it is wise to address treatment in a global way: Children with coordination disorder may thus benefit from social skill groups and other prosocial interventions. A communication disorder, if present, must be addressed as well.

The Montessori technique (developed by Maria Montessori) may be useful with many preschool children; the technique emphasizes the development of motor skills. No single exercise or training method seems to be more advantageous or effective than another. Secondary behavioral or emotional problems and coexisting communication disorders must be managed by appropriate treatment methods. No large-scale controlled studies have reported on the effects of treatment, although small studies have suggested that exercise in rhythmic coordination, practicing motor movements, and learning to use typewriters are all helpful. Parental counseling helps reduce parents' anxiety and guilt about their child's impairment, increases their awareness, and gives them confidence to cope with the child.

References

Arnheim DD, Sinclair WA: *The Clumsy Child.* Mosby, St. Louis, 1975.

Baker L, Cantwell DP: Developmental coordination disorder. In *Comprehensive Textbook of Psychiatry,* ed 6, HI Kaplan, BJ Sadock, editors, p 2257, Williams & Wilkins, Baltimore, 1995.

Blandis TA, Snow JH, Accardo PJ: Integration of soft signs in academically normal and academically at risk children. Pediatrics *85:* 421, 1990.

Henderson L, Rose P, Henderson S: Reaction time and movement time in children with a developmental coordination disorder. J Child Psychol Psychiatry *33* (5): 895, 1992.

Losse A, Henderson SE, Elliman D, Hall D, Knight E, Jongmans M: Clumsiness in children: Do they grow out of it? A ten-year follow-up study. Dev Med Child Neurol *33:* 55, 1991.

Pine DS, Scott MR, Busner C, Davies M, Fried JA, Parides M, Shaffer D: Psychometrics of neurological soft signs. J Am Acad Child Adoles Psych *35:* 509, 1996.

Prechtl HF, Stemmer CJ: The choreiform syndrome in children. Dev Med Child Neurol *4:* 119, 1962.

Robinson RJ: Causes and associations of severe and persistent specific speech and language disorders in children. Dev Med Child Neurol *33:* 943, 1991.

Roussonis SH, Gaussen TH, Stratton R: A 2-year follow-up study of children with motor coordination problems identified at school entry age. Child Care Health Dev *13:* 377, 1987.

Smyth TR: Abnormal clumsiness in children: A defect of motor programming? Child Care Health Dev *17:* 283, 1991.

Willoughby C, Polatajko HJ: Motor problems in children with developmental coordination disorder: Review of the literature. Am J Occup Ther *49* (8): 787, 1995.

Wright HC, Sugden DA: The nature of developmental coordination disorder: Inter- and intragroup differences. Adapted Phys Activity Q *13* (4): 357, 1996.

40

Communication Disorders

The fourth edition of *Diagnostic and Statistical Manual of Mental Disorders* (DSM-IV) lists four specific communication disorders and one residual category. DSM-IV defines expressive language disorder as an ''impairment in expressive language development . . . demonstrated by scores on standardized individually administered measures of expressive language development substantially below those obtained from standardized measures of both nonverbal intellectual capacity and receptive language development.'' The difficulties interfere with academic or work achievement or with social communication, but the symptoms do not meet criteria for mixed receptive-expressive language disorder or a pervasive developmental disorder. When there is mental retardation, a speech-motor or sensory deficit, or environmental deprivation, language difficulties exceed those usually associated with these problems.

DSM-IV mixed receptive-expressive language disorder is described as an impairment in receptive and expressive language development shown by scores on standardized, individually administered measures of receptive and expressive language development that are significantly lower than those on standardized measures of nonverbal intellectual capacity. The difficulties interfere with academic, work, and social accomplishments, but the symptoms do not meet criteria for a pervasive developmental disorder. Language difficulties exceed the usual level when mental retardation, speech-motor or sensory deficit, or environment deprivation is present.

According to DSM-IV, phonological disorder is a ''failure to use developmentally expected speech sounds that are appropriate for the individual's age and dialect.'' The difficulties interfere with academic, work, and social achievements, and they exceed those usually associated with mental retardation, speech-motor or sensory defect, or environmental deprivation, when these problems are present.

DSM-IV defines stuttering as a ''disturbance in the normal fluency and time patterning of speech'' inappropriate for a person's age. The disturbance interferes with the person's academic, work, and social functioning. If a speech-motor or sensory deficit is present, the difficulties exceed those usual for the problem. The extent of stuttering varies and may be worse in stressful situations than in ordinary life. DSM-IV describes communication disorder not otherwise specified as a category for disorders that do not meet criteria for a specific communication disorder. DSM-IV's examples for this disorder include abnormalities of vocal pitch or loudness. The 10th revision of *International Statistical Classification of Diseases and Related Health Problems* (ICD-10) defines stuttering as speech ''characterized by frequent repetition or prolongation of sounds or syllables or words, or by frequent hesitations or pauses that disrupt the rhythmic flow of speech.'' Minor stuttering is common throughout life, but persistent, severe stuttering that destroys the fluency of speech must be present for stuttering to be diagnosed. The disorder may be accompanied by movements of the face or body which coincide with speech.

ICD-10

The ICD-10 includes four disorders of speech and language, as well as two residual categories (Table 40–1). ICD-10 defines cluttering as a ''rapid rate of speech with breakdown in fluency, but no repetitions or hesitations, of a severity to give rise to reduced speech intelligibility. Speech is erratic and dysrhythmic, with rapid, jerky spurts that usually involve faulty phrasing patterns.'' The faulty speech patterns may include using groups of words unrelated to the sentence's grammar. According to ICD-10, cluttering must be distinguished from stuttering.

EXPRESSIVE LANGUAGE DISORDER

Expressive language disorder is present when a child's skills are below the expected level in vocabulary, the use of correct tenses, the production of complex sentences, and the recall of words. Language disability can be acquired at any time during childhood (for example, secondary to a trauma or a neurological disorder), or it can be developmental; it is usually congenital and without an obvious cause. Most childhood language disorders fall in the developmental category. In either case, deficits in receptive skills (language comprehension) or in expressive skills (ability to express language) can occur. Expressive language disturbance often appears in the absence of comprehension difficulties, whereas receptive dysfunction generally also affects the expression of language.

Children with only expressive language disorder have courses, prognoses, and comorbid diagnoses different from those of children with mixed receptive-expressive language disorder.

In DSM-IV, the diagnosis of expressive language disorder can be made in the absence of receptive language disorder, but DSM-IV allows no diagnosis of receptive language disorder alone. Mixed receptive-expressive language disorder is diagnosed in DSM-IV when both receptive and expressive language syndromes are present, and mixed receptive-expressive language disorder is an exclusionary criterion for expressive language disorder. In general, whenever receptive skills are impaired enough to warrant a diagnosis, expressive skills are

Table 40–1
ICD-10 Diagnostic Criteria for Specific Developmental Disorders of Speech and Language

Specific speech articulation disorder

Note. This disorder is also referred to as specific speech phonological disorder.

A. Articulation (phonological) skills, as assessed on standardized tests, are below the 2 standard deviations limit for the child's age.

B. Articulation (phonological) skills are at least 1 standard deviation below nonverbal IQ as assessed on standardized tests.

C. Language expression and comprehension, as assessed on standardized tests, are within the 2 standard deviations limit for the child's age.

D. There are no neurological, sensory, or physical impairments that directly affect speech sound production, nor is there a pervasive developmental disorder.

E. *Most commonly used exclusion clause.* Nonverbal IQ is below 70 on a standardized test.

Expressive language disorder

A. Expressive language skills, as assessed on standardized tests, are below the 2 standard deviations limit for the child's age.

B. Expressive language skills are at least 1 standard deviation below nonverbal IQ as assessed on standardized tests.

C. Receptive language skills, as assessed on standardized tests, are within the 2 standard deviations limit for the child's age.

D. Use and understanding of nonverbal communication and imaginative language functions are within the normal range.

E. There are no neurological, sensory, or physical impairments that directly affect use of spoken language, nor is there a pervasive developmental disorder.

F. *Most commonly used exclusion clause.* Nonverbal IQ is below 70 on a standardized test.

Receptive language disorder

Note. This disorder is also referred to as mixed receptive/expressive disorder.

A. Language comprehension, as assessed on standardized tests, is below the 2 standard deviations limit for the child's age.

B. Receptive language skills are at least 1 standard deviation below nonverbal IQ as assessed on standardized tests.

C. There are no neurological, sensory, or physical impairments that directly affect receptive language, nor is there a pervasive developmental disorder.

D. *Most commonly used exclusion clause.* Nonverbal IQ is below 70 on a standardized test.

Acquired aphasia with epilepsy [Landau-Kleffner syndrome]

A. Severe loss of expressive and receptive language skills occurs over a period of time not exceeding 6 months.

B. Language development was normal before the loss.

C. Paroxysmal EEG abnormalities affecting one or both temporal lobes become apparent within a time span extending from 2 years before to 2 years after the initial loss of language.

D. Hearing is within the normal range.

E. A level of nonverbal intelligence within the normal range is retained.

F. There is no diagnosable neurological condition other than that implicit in the abnormal EEG and presence of epileptic seizures (when they occur).

G. The disorder does not meet the criteria for a pervasive developmental disorder.

Other developmental disorders of speech and language

Developmental disorder of speech and language, unspecified

This category should be avoided as far as possible and should be used only for unspecified disorders in which there is significant impairment in the development of speech or language that cannot be accounted for by mental retardation, or by neurological, sensory, or physical impairments that directly affect speech or language.

also impaired. Thus, in DSM-IV, receptive language disorder can be diagnosed only if the full syndrome of expressive disorder is also present. In DSM-IV, expressive language disorder and mixed receptive-expressive language disorder are not limited to developmental language disabilities; acquired forms of language disturbances are included. To meet the criteria for expressive language disorder, patient's must have scores on standardized measures of expressive language markedly below those of standardized nonverbal intelligence quotient (IQ) subtests and standardized tests of receptive language.

Epidemiology

The prevalence of expressive language disorder ranges from 3 to 10 percent of all school-age children, with most estimates between 3 and 5 percent. The disorder is 2 to 3 times more common in boys than in girls and is most prevalent among children whose relatives have a family history of phonological disorder or other communication disorders.

Etiology

The cause of expressive language disorder is unknown. Subtle cerebral damage and maturational lags in cerebral development have been postulated as underlying causes, but no evidence supports these theories. Left-handedness or ambilaterality appears to increase the risk. Unknown genetic factors have been suspected to play a role, because the relatives of children with learning disorders have a relatively high incidence of expressive language disorder.

Diagnosis

Markedly below-age-level verbal or sign language, accompanied by a low score on standardized expressive verbal tests, is diagnostic of expressive language disorder (Table 40–2). The disorder is not caused by a pervasive developmental disorder, as children with the disorder show a desire to communicate. If a child uses any language, it is severely retarded, vocabulary is limited, grammar is simple, and articulation is

Table 40–2
DSM-IV Diagnostic Criteria for Expressive Language Disorder

A. The scores obtained from standardized individually administered measures of expressive language development are substantially below those obtained from standardized measures of both nonverbal intellectual capacity and receptive language development. The disturbance may be manifest clinically by symptoms that include having a markedly limited vocabulary, making errors in tense, or having difficulty recalling words or producing sentences with developmentally appropriate length or complexity.

B. The difficulties with expressive language interfere with academic or occupational achievement or with social communication.

C. Criteria are not met for mixed receptive-expressive language disorder or a pervasive developmental disorder.

D. If mental retardation, a speech–motor or sensory deficit, or environmental deprivation is present, the language difficulties are in excess of those usually associated with these problems.

Coding note: if a speech–motor or sensory deficit or a neurological condition is present, code the condition on Axis III.

variable. Inner language or the appropriate use of toys and household objects is present.

To confirm the diagnosis, clinicians should have children tested with standardized expressive language and nonverbal intellectual tests. Observations of children's verbal and sign language patterns in various settings (for example, in the school yard, classroom, home, and playroom) and during interactions with other children help ascertain the severity and the specific areas of a child's impairment and aid in early detection of behavioral and emotional complications.

Family history should include the presence or absence of expressive language disorder among relatives.

An audiogram is indicated for very young children and for those children whose hearing acuity appears to be impaired.

Clinical Features

Children with expressive language disorders may be ostracized by and isolated from other children their age. Neurodevelopmental delays may accompany expressive language impairments, as may motor skills deficits and perceptual difficulties. Severe forms of the disorder are evident before the age of 3 years, but less severe forms may not occur until early adolescence, when language ordinarily becomes complex.

The essential feature of children with expressive language disorder is a marked impairment in the development of age-appropriate expressive language that results in the use of verbal or sign language markedly below the expected level in view of a child's nonverbal intellectual capacity. Language understanding (decoding) skills remain relatively intact. When severe, the disorder becomes recognizable by about the age of 18 months, when the child fails to utter spontaneously or even to echo single words or sounds. Even simple words, such as Mama and Dada, are absent from the child's active vocabulary, and the child points or uses gestures to indicate desires. The child seems to want to communicate, maintains eye contact, relates well to the mother, and enjoys games such as pat-a-cake and peekaboo. The child's repertoire of vocabulary is severely limited. At 18 months the child can, at most, comprehend simple commands and can point to common objects when they are named.

When the child finally begins to speak, the language deficit becomes apparent. Articulation is usually immature; numerous articulation errors occur but are inconsistent, particularly with such sounds as *th, r, s, z, y,* and *l,* which are either omitted or are substituted for other sounds.

By the age of 4 years, most children with expressive language disorder can speak in short phrases, but they appear to forget old words as they learn new ones. After beginning to speak, they acquire language more slowly than do normal children. Their use of various grammatical structures is also markedly lower than the age-expected level, and their developmental milestones may be slightly delayed. Phonological disorder is often present, and developmental coordination disorder and enuresis are common associated disorders.

Associated Features. Emotional problems involving poor self-image, frustration, and depression may develop in school-age children. Children with expressive language disorder may also have a learning disorder, manifested by reading retardation, that may result in serious difficulties in academic subjects. Major learning difficulties in perceptual skills and skills of recognizing and processing symbols in the proper sequence are present.

Other behavioral symptoms and problems that may appear in children with expressive language disorder include hyperactivity, short attention span. withdrawing behavior, thumb sucking, temper tantrums, bed-wetting, disobedience, accident-proneness, and conduct disorder. Neurological abnormalities have been reported in a number of children, including soft neurological signs, depressed vestibular responses, and electroencephalogram (EEG) abnormalities.

Many disorders—such as reading disorder, developmental coordination disorder, and other communication disorders—are associated with expressive language disorder. Children with expressive language disorder often have some degree of receptive impairment, although not always significant enough for the diagnosis of mixed receptive-expressive language disorder. Delayed motor milestones and a history of enuresis are common in children with expressive language disorder. Phonological disorder is commonly found in young children with the disorder.

A large study of children at a community speech and language clinic found that half of those with expressive language disorder met the criteria for another mental disorder, most commonly attention-deficit/hyperactivity disorder. Another recent study found that more than one third of the children referred to a psychiatric outpatient clinic had a language impairment.

Differential Diagnosis

Language disorders are associated with many other psychiatric disorders, and thus the language disorder itself may be difficult to separate from other difficulties. In mental retardation, patients have an overall impairment in intellectual functioning, as shown by below-normal intelligence test scores in all areas, but the nonverbal intellectual capacity and functioning of children with expressive language disorder are within normal limits.

In mixed receptive-expressive language disorder, comprehension of language (decoding) is markedly below the expected age-appropriate level, whereas in expressive language disorder, language comprehension remains within normal limits.

In pervasive developmental disorders, affected children have, in addition to the cardinal cognitive characteristics, no inner language, symbolic or imagery play, appropriate use of gesture, or capacity to form warm and meaningful social relationships. Moreover, children show little or no frustration with the inability to communicate verbally. In contrast, all these characteristics are present in children with expressive language disorder.

Children with acquired aphasia or dysphasia have a history of early normal language development; the disordered language had its onset after a head trauma or other neurological disorder (for example, a seizure disorder). Children with selective mutism have a history of normal language development. Often these children will speak only in front of family members (for example, mother, father, and siblings). More girls than boys are affected by selective mutism, and the affected children are mostly shy and withdrawn outside the family.

Course and Prognosis

In general, the prognosis for expressive language disorder is influenced by other comorbid disorders. In children who do not develop mood disorders or disruptive behavior problems, the prognosis is improved. The rapidity and degree of recovery depend on the severity of the disorder, the child's motivation to participate in therapies, and the timely institution of speech and other therapeutic interventions. The presence or absence of other factors—such as moderate to severe hearing loss, mild mental retardation, and severe emotional problems—also affects the prognosis for recovery. As many as 50 percent of children with mild expressive language disorder recover spontaneously without any sign of language impairment, but children with severe expressive language disorder may later display features of mild to moderate language impairment.

Recent literature has shown that children who demonstrate poor comprehension, poor articulation, or poor academic performance seem to continue to have problems in these areas at follow-up 7 years later. There is also an association between particular language impairment profiles and persistent mood and behavior problems. Children who have poor comprehension associated with expressive difficulties seem to be the most socially isolated and impaired with respect to peer relationships.

Strong relationships occur between expressive language level and many nonverbal and communication skills in children with language impairment. Expressive language may be seen as an index of general development or as a marker of social and other communication skills. Especially in preschool age groups, expressive language appears to be related to social and nonverbal communication skills as much as it is simply a measure of knowledge of words.

Treatment

In view of the marked association between social competence and expressive language skills, therapy should be aimed at improving communication strategies and social interactions as well as at using words. Language therapy should be started immediately after the diagnosis of expressive language disorder. Such therapy consists of behaviorally reinforced exercises and practice with phonemes (sound units), vocabulary, and sentence construction. The goal is to increase the number of phrases by using block-building methods and conventional speech therapies.

Psychotherapy may be useful support insofar as it can be used as a positive model for more effective communication and broadening social skills. Supportive parental counseling may be indicated in some cases. Parents may need help to reduce intrafamilial tensions arising from difficulties in rearing language-disordered children and to increase their awareness and understanding of the disorder.

MIXED RECEPTIVE-EXPRESSIVE LANGUAGE DISORDER

In mixed receptive-expressive language disorder children are impaired in both understanding and expressing language. DSM-IV is the first diagnostic manual to combine receptive and expressive language disorder. The implication is that clinically significant receptive language impairment is always accompanied by expressive language dysfunction. With DSM-IV, it is impossible to code receptive language disorder in the absence of expressive language disorder. DSM-IV allows for receptive and expressive disorders that are acquired, as well as those that are congenital or developmental.

The essential features of mixed receptive-expressive language disorder require that scores on standardized tests of both receptive (comprehension) and expressive language development fall substantially below those obtained from standardized measures of nonverbal intellectual capacity. Language difficulties must be severe enough to impair academic achievement or daily social communication. A patient may not meet the criteria for a pervasive developmental disorder, and the language dysfunctions must be in excess of those usually associated with mental retardation and other neurological and sensory-deficit syndromes.

Epidemiology

Prevalence estimates range from 1 to 13 percent for either receptive or expressive language disorder. Expressive language disorder alone is thought to be much more common than receptive language disorder alone. Both disorders are believed to be more common in boys than in girls.

No studies have examined the prevalence of the DSM-IV category of mixed receptive-expressive language disorder, but prevalence estimates of children who possess both receptive and expressive language disorders are in the 3 to 5 percent range.

Etiology

The cause of mixed receptive-expressive language disorder is unknown. There is some evidence to suggest familial aggregation of language disorder, and a genetic cause is implicated in a significant number of families. Early theories listed perceptual dysfunction, subtle cerebral damage, maturational lag, and genetic factors as probable causative factors, but no definitive evidence supports these theories. As with reading disorder, a number of cognitive deficits have been postulated to exist in mixed receptive-expressive language disorder. Several studies suggest the presence of underlying impairment of auditory discrimination, as most children with the disorder are more responsive to environmental sounds than to speech sounds. As with expressive language disorder, left-handedness and ambilaterality seem to increase the risk.

Diagnosis

A markedly below-age-appropriate level of comprehension of verbal or sign language with intact age-appropriate nonverbal intellectual capacity, the confirmation of language difficulties by standardized receptive language tests, and the absence of pervasive developmental disorders confirm the diagnosis of mixed receptive-expressive language disorder (Table 40–3).

In mixed receptive-expressive language disorder, receptive dysfunction coexists with expressive dysfunction. Therefore, standardized tests for both receptive and expressive language abilities must be given to anyone suspected of having mixed receptive-expressive language disorder.

An audiogram is indicated for all children thought to have mixed receptive-expressive language disorder to rule out or to confirm the presence of deafness and to determine the types of auditory deficits. A history of children and families and observation of children in various settings help clarify the diagnosis.

Table 40–3
DSM-IV Diagnostic Criteria for Mixed Receptive-Expressive Language Disorder

A. The scores obtained from a battery of standardized individually administered measures of both receptive and expressive language development are substantially below those obtained from standardized measures of nonverbal intellectual capacity. Symptoms include those for expressive language disorder as well as difficulty understanding words, sentences, or specific types of words, such as spatial terms.

B. The difficulties with receptive and expressive language significantly interfere with academic or occupational achievement or with social communication.

C. Criteria are not met for a pervasive developmental disorder.

D. If mental retardation, a speech–motor or sensory deficit, or environmental deprivation is present, the language difficulties are in excess of those usually associated with these problems.

Coding note: if a speech–motor or sensory deficit or a neurological condition is present, code the condition on Axis III.

Reprinted with permission from American Psychiatric Association: *Diagnostic and Statistical Manual of Mental Disorders*, ed 4. Copyright, American Psychiatric Association, Washington, 1994.

Clinical Features

The essential clinical feature of the disorder is significant impairment in both language comprehension and language expression. In the mixed disorder, the expressive impairments are similar to those of expressive language disorder but can be more severe. The clinical features of the receptive component of the disorder typically appear before the age of 4 years. Severe forms are apparent by the age of 2; mild forms may not become evident until the age of 7 (second grade) or older, when language becomes complex. Children with mixed receptive-expressive language disorder show markedly delayed and below-normal ability to comprehend (decode) verbal or sign language, although they have age-appropriate nonverbal intellectual capacity. In most cases of receptive dysfunction, verbal or sign expression (encoding) of language is also impaired. The clinical features of mixed receptive-expressive language disorder in children between the ages of 18 and 24 months are the results of a child's failure to make spontaneous utterances of a single phoneme or to mimic another person's words.

Many children with mixed receptive-expressive language disorder have auditory sensory difficulties or are unable to process visual symbols, such as the meaning of a picture. They have deficits in integrating both auditory and visual symbols—for example, recognizing the basic common attributes of a toy truck and a toy passenger car. Whereas a child with expressive language disorder only at 18 months can comprehend simple commands and can point to familiar household objects when told to do so, a child of the same age with mixed receptive-expressive language disorder is unable either to point to common objects or to obey simple commands. A child with mixed receptive-expressive language disorder usually appears to be deaf, but, the child does hear. He or she responds normally to nonlanguage sounds from the environment but not to spoken language. If the child later starts to speak, the speech contains numerous articulation errors, such as omissions, distortions, and substitutions of phonemes. Language acquisition is much slower for children with mixed receptive-expressive language disorder than for normal children.

Children with mixed receptive-expressive language disorder have difficulty in recalling early visual and auditory memories and recognizing and reproducing symbols in proper sequence. In some cases bilateral EEG abnormalities are seen. Some children with mixed receptive-expressive language disorder have a partial hearing defect for true tones, an increased threshold of auditory arousal, and an inability to localize sound sources. Seizure disorders and reading disorder are more common among the relatives of children with mixed receptive-expressive language disorder than they are in the general population.

Most children with mixed receptive-expressive language

disorder are impaired socially and in terms of nonverbal communication. This impairment causes a variety of additional difficulties and often results in poor self-esteem and feelings of inferiority that, in turn, can continue to further alienate the child from succeeding in the usual developmental tasks.

Associated comorbid disorders with mixed receptive-expressive language disorder include reading disorder, mathematics disorder, and disorder of written expression. In a large study of children with communication disorders, more than half the children who met the criteria for mixed receptive-expressive language disorder also had a learning disorder. More than 70 percent in the same study had other mental disorders, especially attention-deficit/hyperactivity disorder, anxiety disorders, and depressive disorders.

Differential Diagnosis

Children with significant mixed receptive-expressive language disorder have a deficit in language comprehension. This deficit may at first be missed, as the expressive language deficit may be more obvious. In expressive language disorder alone, comprehension of spoken language (decoding) remains within age norms. Children with phonological disorder or stuttering have normal expressive and receptive language competence, despite their having speech impairments. Hearing impairment should be ruled out.

Most children with mixed receptive-expressive language disorder have a history of variable and inconsistent responses to sounds; they respond more often to environmental sounds than to speech sounds (Table 40–4). Mental retardation, acquired aphasia, and pervasive developmental disorders should also be ruled out. Hearing impairment, pervasive developmental disorders, and severe environmental deprivation may contribute significantly to language impairment.

Course and Prognosis

The overall prognosis for mixed receptive-expressive language disorder is less favorable than for expressive language disorder alone. When the mixed disorder is identified in a young child, it is usually severe, and the short-term prognosis is poor. Early childhood is a time when language develops at a rapid rate, and young children with the disorder may appear to be falling behind. In view of the likelihood of comorbid learning disorders and other mental disorders, the prognosis is guarded. Young children with severe mixed receptive-expressive language disorder are likely to have learning disorders in the future. In children with mild versions, mixed disorder may not be identified for several years, and the disruption in everyday life may be less overwhelming than that in severe forms of the disorder. Over the long run, some children with mixed receptive-expressive language disorder achieve close to normal language functions. The prognosis for children who acquire mixed receptive-expressive language disorder is widely variable and depends on the nature and severity of the damage.

Treatment

A comprehensive speech and language evaluation, leading to speech and language therapy, is usually recommended for children with mixed receptive-expressive language disorder, despite the lack of controlled treatment studies for the disorder.

Table 40–4
Differential Diagnosis of Language Disorders

	Hearing Impairment	Mental Retardation	Infantile Autism	Expressive Language Disorder	Mixed Receptive-Expressive Language Disorder	Selective Mutism	Phonological Disorder
Language comprehension	−	−	−	+	−	+	+
Expressive language	−	−	−	−	−	Variable	+
Audiogram	−	+	+	+	Variable	+	+
Articulation	−	−	− (Variable)	− (Variable)	− (Variable)	+	−
Inner language	+	+ (Limited)	−	+	+ (Slightly limited)	+	+
Uses gestures	+	+ (Limited)	−	+	+	+ (Variable)	+
Echoes	−	+	+ (Inappropriate)	+	+	+	+
Attends to sounds	Loud or low frequency only	+	−	+	Variable	+	+
Watches faces	+	+	−	+	+	+	+
Performance	+	−	+	+	+	+	+

Courtesy of Lorian Baker, Ph.D., and Dennis Cantwell, M.D.
+, normal; −, abnormal.

Some language therapists favor a low-stimuli setting, in which children are given individual linguistic instruction. Others recommend that speech and language instruction be integrated into a varied setting with several children who are taught several language structures simultaneously. Many symptoms are involved in the disorder, so a small, specialized educational setting may be beneficial in maximizing the results.

Psychotherapy is often necessary because children with mixed receptive-expressive language disorder frequently have emotional and behavioral problems. Particular attention should be paid to improving the child's self-image and social skills. Family counseling in which parents are taught appropriate patterns of interaction with the child can also be helpful.

PHONOLOGICAL DISORDER

Phonological disorders are manifested by inappropriate or poor sound production or articulation. The determination of a phonological disorder is made by comparison with the developmentally expected speech sounds for a patient's age and intelligence. The disorder can consist of errors in sound production, substitutions of one sound for another, and omissions of such sounds as final consonants. According to DSM-IV, if mental retardation, a speech-motor or sensory deficit, or environmental deprivation is present, the language dysfunction is in excess of that associated with those problems.

Phonological disorder is a broader category than a disorder of articulation. Developmental articulation disorder is the most common phonological disorder in children, and it is the prototype of the disorders defined by the DSM-IV category of phonological disorder. Phonological disorder is characterized by frequent misarticulations, sound substitutions, and speech sound omissions, that give the impression of baby talk. The disorder is not caused by anatomical, structural, physiological, auditory, or neurological abnormalities. It varies from mild to severe and results in speech that ranges from completely intelligible to unintelligible.

Epidemiology

The prevalence of all phonological dysfunctions in children is unknown, and estimates vary widely with the diagnostic criteria used. The prevalence of phonological disorder is conservatively estimated to be 10 percent of children below 8 years of age and 5 percent of children 8 years of age and older. The disorder is 2 to 3 times more common in boys than in girls. It is also more common among first-degree relatives of patients with the disorder than in the general population. DSM-IV reports 2 to 3 percent of 6 to 7 year olds have the disorder.

Etiology

The causes of phonological disturbance are variable and range from perinatal problems to hearing impairment to structural abnormalities related to speech. The cause of phonological disorder in children is unknown. A simple developmental lag or maturational delay in the neurological process underlying speech, rather than an organic dysfunction, is at fault.

Articulation disorders caused by structural or mechanical problems are quite rare. Phonological disorders caused by neurological impairment can be divided into dysarthria (poor articulation) and apraxia (loss of movement). Dysarthria results from an impairment in the neural mechanisms regulating the muscular control of speech; apraxia is an impairment in the muscle function itself.

Often present in children with phonological disorder are clusters of additional speech and language symptoms, such as poor comprehension, auditory memory problems, and word-finding problems. A disproportionately high frequency of phonological disorder occurs among children from large families of low socioeconomic status, a finding that suggests the possible causal effects of inadequate speech stimulation and reinforcement in these families.

Constitutional factors, rather than environmental factors, seem to be of major importance in determining whether a child has a phonological disorder. The high proportion of children with the disorder who have relatives with a similar disorder suggests that the disorder may have a genetic component. Poor motor coordination, laterality, and handedness do not contribute to phonological disorder.

Diagnosis

The essential feature of phonological disorder is an articulation defect characterized by a child's consistent failure to use developmentally expected speech sounds of certain consonants, including omissions, substitutions, and distortions of phonemes, which are generally learned late. The disorder cannot be attributed to structural or neurological abnormalities, and it is accompanied by normal language development. The DSM-IV diagnostic criteria for phonological disorder are given in Table 40–5.

Clinical Features

The essential clinical feature of phonological disorder is a variety of developmentally inappropriate speech sounds. The sounds are often substitutions—for example, the use of *t* instead of *k*—and omissions, such as leaving off the final consonants of words. Phonological disorder is recognized in early

Table 40–5
DSM-IV Diagnostic Criteria for Phonological Disorder

A. Failure to use developmentally expected speech sounds that are appropriate for age and dialect (eg, errors in sound production, use representation or organization, such as, but not limited to, substitutions of one sound for another [use of /t/ for target /k/ sound] or omissions of sounds such as final consonants).

B. The difficulties in speech sound production interfere with academic or occupational achievement or with social communication.

C. If mental retardation, a speech–motor or sensory deficit, environmental deprivation is present, the speech difficult are in excess of those usually associated with these problems.

Coding note: if a speech–motor or sensory deficit or a neurological condition is present, code the condition on Axis III.

Reprinted with permission from American Psychiatric Association: *Diagnostic and Statistical Manual of Mental Disorders*, ed 4. Copyright, American Psychiatric Association, Washington, 1994.

childhood. In severe cases the disorder is first recognized at about 3 years of age. In less severe cases the disorder may not be apparent until the age of 6 years. Articulation is judged to be defective when compared with the speech of children at the same age level, and the differences cannot be attributed to abnormalities in intelligence, hearing, or the physiology of a child's speech mechanism.

In very mild cases only one phoneme may be affected. Single phonemes are usually affected, most commonly those acquired late in the normal language acquisition process. The speech sounds most frequently misarticulated, those acquired late in the developmental sequence, are *r, sh, th, f, z, l,* and *ch.* But in severe cases and in young children, sounds such as *b, m, t, d, n,* and *h* may be mispronounced. One or many speech sounds may be affected, but vowel sounds are not among them.

Children with phonological disorder are unable to articulate certain phonemes correctly and may distort, substitute, or even omit the affected phonemes. With omissions, the phonemes are absent entirely—for example, *bu* for *blue, ca* for *car,* or *whaa*? for *what's that*? With substitutions, difficult phonemes are replaced with incorrect ones—for example, *wabbit* for *rabbit, fum* for *thumb,* or *whath dat*? for *what's that*? With distortions, the correct phoneme is approximated but is articulated incorrectly. Rarely, additions, usually of the vowel *uh,* occur—for example, *puhretty* for *pretty, what's uh that uh*? for *what's that*?

Omissions are thought to be the most serious type of misarticulation, with substitutions the next most serious type, and distortions the least serious type. Omissions are most frequently found in the speech of young children and usually occur at the ends of words or in clusters of consonants (*ka* for *car, scisso* for *scissors*). Distortions, which are found mainly in the speech of older children, result in a sound that is not part of the speaker's dialect. Distortions may be the last type of misarticulation remaining in the speech of children whose articulation problems have mostly remitted. The most common types of distortions are the *lateral slip*—in which a child pronounces *s* sounds with the airstream going across the tongue, producing a whistling effect—and the palatal lisp—in which the *s* sound formed with the tongue too close to the palate produces a *ssh* sound effect.

The misarticulations of children with phonological disorder are often inconsistent and random. A phoneme may be pronounced correctly one time and incorrectly another time. Misarticulations are most common at the ends of words, in long and syntactically complex sentences, and during rapid speech.

Omissions, distortions, and substitutions also occur normally in the speech of young children learning to talk. But, whereas young, normally speaking children soon replace these misarticulations, children with phonological disorder do not. Even as children with phonological disorder grow and finally acquire the correct phoneme, they may use it only in newly acquired words and may not correct the words learned earlier that they have been mispronouncing for some time.

Most children eventually outgrow phonological disorder, usually by the third grade. After the fourth grade, however, spontaneous recovery is unlikely, and so it is important to try to remediate the disorder before the development of complications. In cases when recovery from phonological disorder is spontaneous, a child's beginning kindergarten or school often precipitates the improvement. Speech therapy is clearly indicated for children who have not shown a spontaneous improvement by the third or fourth grade. For children whose articulation is significantly unintelligible and who are clearly troubled by their inability to speak clearly, speech therapy should be initiated at an early age.

Other disorders commonly present with phonological disorder are expressive language disorder, mixed receptive-expressive language disorder, reading disorder, and developmental coordination disorder. Enuresis may also accompany the disorder. A delay in reaching speech milestones (such as first word and first sentence) has been reported in some children with phonological disorder, but most children with the disorder begin speaking at the appropriate age.

Children with phonological disorder may have various concomitant social, emotional, and behavioral problems. About one third of the children with the condition have a psychiatric disorder, such as attention-deficit/hyperactivity disorder, separation anxiety disorder, adjustment disorders, and depressive disorders. Children with a severe degree of articulation impairment or whose disorder is chronic and nonremitting are the ones most likely to suffer from psychiatric problems.

Differential Diagnosis

The differential diagnostic process for phonological disorder involves three steps: First, the clinician must determine that the misarticulations are severe enough to be considered abnormal and must rule out the normal misarticulations of young children. Second, the clinician must determine that no physical abnormalities account for the articulation errors and must rule out dysarthria, hearing impairment, and mental retardation. Third, the clinician must establish that expressive language is within normal limits and must rule out expressive language disorder, mixed receptive-expressive language disorder, and pervasive developmental disorders.

A rough guideline for clinical assessment of children's articulation is that normal 3-year-olds correctly articulate *m, n, ng, b, p, h, t, k, q,* and *d;* normal 4-year-olds correctly articulate *f, y, ch, sh,* and *z;* and normal 5-years-olds correctly articulate *th, s,* and *r.*

Neurological, oral structural, and audiometric examinations may be necessary to rule out physical factors that cause certain types of articulation abnormalities. Children with dysarthria, a disorder caused by structural or neurological abnormalities, differ from children with phonological disorder in that dysarthria is difficult and sometimes impossible to remedy. Drooling, slow, or uncoordinated motor behavior, abnormal chewing or swallowing, and awkward or slow protrusion and retraction of the tongue are indications of dysarthria. A slow rate of speech is another indication of dysarthria (Table 40–6).

Course and Prognosis

Recovery is frequently spontaneous, particularly in children whose misarticulations involve only a few phonemes. Children who persist in exhibiting articulation problems after the age of 5 years may be experiencing a myriad of other speech and language impairments, so that a comprehensive evaluation may

Table 40–6
Differential Diagnosis of Phonological Dysfunctions

Criteria	Phonological Dysfunction Due to Structural or Neurological Abnormalities (Dysarthria)	Phonological Dysfunction Due to Hearing Impairment	Phonological Disorder	Phonological Dysfunction Associated with Mental Retardation, Infantile Autism, Developmental Dysphasia, Acquired Aphasia, or Deafness
Language development	Within normal limits	Within normal limits unless hearing impairment is serious	Within normal limits	Not within normal limits
Examination	Possible abnormalities of lips, tongue, or palate; muscular weakness, incoordination, or disturbance of vegetative functions, such as sucking or chewing	Hearing impairment shown on audiometric testing	Normal	
Rate of speech	Slow; marked deterioration of articulation with increased rate	Normal	Normal; possible deterioration of articulation with increased rate	
Phonemes affected	Any phonemes, even vowels	*F, th, sh,* and *s*	*R, sh, th, ch, dg, j, f, v, s,* and *z* are most commonly affected	

Courtesy of Lorian Baker, Ph.D., and Dennis Cantwell, M.D.

be indicated at this time. Children over the age of 5 with articulation problems are at higher risk for auditory perceptual problems. Spontaneous recovery is rare after the age of 8 years.

Treatment

Speech therapy is considered the most successful treatment for most phonological errors. Speech therapy is indicated when a child's articulation intelligibility is poor; when an affected child is over 8 years of age; when a speech problem apparently causes problems with peers, learning, and self-image; when the disorder is so severe that many consonants are misarticulated; and when errors involve omissions and substitutions of phonemes, rather than distortions.

Children with persistent articulation problems are likely to be teased or ostracized by peers, and may become isolated and demoralized. Therefore, it is important to give support to children with phonological disorders and whenever possible to support prosocial activities and social interactions with peers.

Parental counseling and monitoring of child–peer relationships and school behavior can be useful in minimizing the social impairment with speech and language disorder.

STUTTERING

According to DSM-IV, stuttering is defined by a disturbance in the fluency and time patterning of speech that is inappropriate for the patient's age. Stuttering consists of one or more of the following: sound repetitions, prolongations, interjections, pauses within words, observable word substitutions to avoid blocking, and audible or silent blocking. In most cases the disorder originates in childhood. ICD-10 defines stuttering as speech "characterized by frequent repetition or prolongation of sounds or syllables or words, or by frequent hesitations or pauses that disrupt the rhythmic flow of speech." The term *stammering* has been used synonymously with *stuttering.*

Epidemiology

In the general population the prevalence of stuttering is about 1 percent. Stuttering tends to be most common in young children and usually resolves in older children and in adults. Stuttering affects about three to four males for every female. The disorder is more common among family members of affected children than in the general population.

Etiology

The precise cause of stuttering is unknown, but a variety of theories have been proposed. Previously, it was hypothesized that stuttering occurs as a response to conflicts, fears, or neurosis. No evidence indicates that anxiety or conflicts cause stuttering or that people who stutter have more psychiatric disturbances than do those with other forms of speech and language disorders. Stuttering however, may be exacerbated by certain stressful situations.

Other theories about the cause of stuttering include organic models and learning models. Organic models include those that focus on incomplete lateralization or abnormal cerebral dominance. Several studies using electroencephalography found that stuttering males had right-hemispheric alpha suppression across stimulus words and tasks; nonstutters had left-hemispheric suppression. An over-representation of left-handedness and ambidexterity occurs in stutterers. The theory of abnormal cerebral dominance essentially hypothesizes a conflict between the two halves of the cerebrum for control of language functions. Twin studies and striking gender differences in stuttering indicate that stuttering has some genetic basis.

Learning theories about the cause of stuttering include the semantogenic theory, in which stuttering is basically a learned response to normative early childhood dysfluencies. Another learning model focuses on classical conditioning, in which the stuttering becomes conditioned to environmental factors. In the cybernetic model, speech is viewed as a process that depends on appropriate feedback for regulation; stuttering is hypothesized to occur because of a breakdown in the feedback loop. The observations that stuttering is reduced by white noise and that delayed auditory feedback produces stuttering in normal speakers increase the potential validity of the feedback theory.

The motor functioning of some stutterers appears to be delayed or slightly abnormal. The observation of difficulties in speech planning exhibited by some stutterers suggests that stuttering may involve a higher-level cognitive dysfunction. A higher than average family history for a wide range of speech and language disorders appears to be present in probands who stutter. Stuttering is probably caused by a set of interacting variables that include genetic and environmental factors.

Diagnosis

The diagnosis of stuttering is not difficult when the clinical features are apparent and well-developed and each of the four phases, as described in the next section, can be readily recognized. Diagnostic difficulties may arise when trying to determine the existence of stuttering in young children, as some preschool children experience of transient dysfluency. It may not be clear whether the nonfluent pattern is part of normal speech and language development or whether it represents the initial stage in the development of stuttering. If incipient stuttering is suspected, referral to a speech pathologist is indicated. Table 40–7 presents the DSM-IV diagnostic criteria for stuttering.

Table 40–7
DSM-IV Diagnostic Criteria for Stuttering

A. Disturbance in the normal fluency and time patterning of speech (inappropriate for the individual's age), characterized by frequent occurrences of one or more of the following:
   (1) sound and syllable repetitions
   (2) sound prolongations
   (3) interjections
   (4) broken words (eg, pauses within a word)
   (5) audible or silent blocking (filled or unfilled pauses in speech)
   (6) circumlocutions (word substitutions to avoid problematic words)
   (7) words produced with an excess of physical tension
   (8) monosyllabic whole-word repetitions (eg, "I-I-I-I- see him.")

B. The disturbance in fluency interferes with academic or occupational achievement or with social communication.

C. If a speech–motor or sensory deficit is present, the speech difficulties are in excess of those usually associated with these problems.

Coding note: if a speech–motor or sensory deficit or a neurological condition is present, code the condition on Axis III.

Clinical Features

Stuttering usually appears before the age of 12 years, and in most cases it appears between 18 months and 9 years, with two sharp peaks of onset between the ages of 2 to 3½ years and 5 to 7 years. Some but not all stutterers have other speech and language problems, such as phonological disorder and expressive language disorder. Stuttering does not suddenly begin; it typically occurs over a period of weeks or months with a repetition of initial consonants, whole words that are usually the first words of a phrase, or long words. As the disorder progresses, the repetitions become more frequent, with consistent stuttering on the most important words or phrases. Even after it develops, stuttering may be absent during oral readings, singing, and talking to pets or inanimate objects.

Four gradually evolving phases in the development of stuttering have been identified:

- Phase 1 occurs during the preschool period. Initially, the difficulty tends to be episodic and appears for weeks or months between long interludes of normal speech. A high percentage of recovery from these periods of stuttering occurs. During this phase, children stutter most often when excited or upset, when they seem to have a great deal to say, and under other conditions of communicative pressure.
- Phase 2 usually occurs in the elementary school years. The disorder is chronic, with few if any intervals of normal speech. Affected children become aware of their speech difficulties and regard themselves as stutterers. In phase 2, the stuttering occurs mainly with the major parts of speech—nouns, verbs, adjectives, and adverbs.
- Phase 3 usually appears after the age of 8 and up to adulthood, most often in late childhood and early adolescence. During phase 3 stuttering comes and goes largely in response to specific situations, such as reciting in class, speaking to strangers, making purchases in stores, and using the telephone. Some words and sounds are regarded as more difficult than others.
- Phase 4 typically appears in late adolescence and adulthood.

Stutterers show a vivid, fearful anticipation of stuttering. They fear words, sounds, and situations. Word substitutions and circumlocutions are common. Stutterers avoid situations requiring speech and show other evidence of fear and embarrassment.

Stutterers may have associated clinical features: vivid, fearful anticipation of stuttering, with avoidance of particular words, sounds, or situations in which stuttering is anticipated; eye blinks; tics; and tremors of the lips or jaw. Frustration, anxiety, and depression are common among those with chronic stuttering. Other disorders that coexist with stuttering include phonological disorder, expressive language disorder, mixed receptive-expressive language disorder, and attention-deficit/hyperactivity disorder.

Differential Diagnosis

Normal speech dysfluency in preschool years is difficult to differentiate from incipient stuttering. In stuttering there are more nonfluencies, part-word repetitions, sound prolongations, and disruptions in voice airflow through the vocal track. Children who stutter can be observed to be tense and uncomfortable with their speech pattern in contrast to young children who are nonfluent in their speech but seem to be at ease. Spastic dysphonia is a stuttering-like speech disorder, and is distinguished from stuttering by the presence of an abnormal breathing pattern.

Cluttering is a speech disorder characterized by erratic and dysrhythmic speech patterns of rapid and jerky spurts of words and phrases. In cluttering, those affected are usually unaware of the disturbance, whereas, after the initial phase of the disorder, stutterers are aware of their speech difficulties. Cluttering is often an associated feature of expressive language disorder.

Course and Prognosis

The course of stuttering is usually long term, with some periods of partial remission lasting for weeks or months and exacerbations occurring most frequently when a stutterer is under pressure to communicate. Fifty to eighty percent of all children who stutter, mostly those with mild cases, recover spontaneously. School-age children who stutter chronically may have impaired peer relationships as a result of testing and social ostracism. The children may face academic difficulties if they avoid speaking in class. Later major complications include an affected person's limitations in occupational choice and advancement.

Treatment

Treatment entails breathing exercises, relaxation techniques, and speech therapy to help children slow the rate of speaking and modulate speech volume. Until the end of the 19th century, the most common treatments for stuttering were distraction, suggestion, and relaxation. Recent approaches using distraction include teaching stutterers to talk in time to rhythmic movements of the arm, hand, or fingers. Stutterers are also advised to speak slowly in a sing-song or monotone manner. These approaches, however, remove stuttering only temporarily. Suggestion techniques, such as hypnosis, also stop stuttering but, again, only temporarily. Relaxation techniques are based on the premise that it is almost impossible to be relaxed and at the same time to stutter in the usual manner. Because of their lack of long-term benefits, distraction, suggestion, and relaxation approaches as such are not currently used.

Classic psychoanalysis, insight-oriented psychotherapy, group therapy, and other psychotherapeutic modalities have not been successful in treating stuttering. But if stutterers have a poor self-image, are anxious or depressed, or show evidence of an established emotional disorder, individual psychotherapy is indicated and effective for the associated condition. In one study, the reaction of nonstuttering listeners to stutterers who acknowledged their stuttering was much more positive than to stutterers who did not acknowledge their stuttering. Family therapy should also be considered if there is evidence of family dysfunction, family contribution to a stutterer's symptoms, or family stress caused by trying to cope with or help the stutterer.

Most modern treatments of stuttering are based on the view that stuttering is essentially a learned form of behavior not necessarily associated with a basic mental disorder or neurological abnormality. The approaches work directly with the speech difficulty to minimize the issues that maintain and strengthen stuttering, to modify or decrease the severity of stuttering by eliminating the secondary symptoms, and to encourage stutterers to speak, even when stuttering, in a relatively easy and effortless fashion that thereby avoids fears and blocks.

One example of this approach is the self-therapy proposed by the Speech Foundation of America. Self-therapy is based on the premise that stuttering is not a symptom but a behavior that can be modified. Stutterers are told that they can learn to control their difficulty partly by modifying their feelings about stuttering and attitudes toward it and partly by modifying the deviant behaviors associated with their stuttering blocks. The approach includes desensitizing, reducing the emotional reaction to and fears of stuttering, and substituting positive action to control the moment of stuttering.

Recently developed therapies focus on restructuring fluency. The entire speech production pattern is reshaped, with emphasis on a variety of target behaviors, including rate reduction, easy or gentle onset of voicing, and smooth transitions between sounds, syllables, and words. With adults, the approaches have met with substantial success in establishing perceptually fluent speech, but fluency maintenance over long periods and relapses remain problems for all involved in adult-stuttering treatment.

Psychopharmacologic intervention such as treatment with haloperidol (Haldol) has been used in an attempt to induce increased relaxation. There are no data to accurately assess the efficacy of this approach. Whichever therapeutic approach is used, individual and family assessments and supportive interventions may be helpful. A team assessment of a child or adolescent and his or her family should be made before any approaches to treatment are begun.

COMMUNICATION DISORDER NOT OTHERWISE SPECIFIED

Disorders that do not meet the diagnostic criteria for any specific communication disorder fall into the category of communication disorder not otherwise specified. An example is voice disorder, in which the patient has an abnormality in pitch, loudness, quality, tone, or resonance. To be coded as a disorder, the voice abnormality must be severe enough to cause an impairment in academic achievement or social communication (Table 40–8).

Cluttering is not listed as a disorder in DSM-IV, but it is an associated speech abnormality in which the disturbed rate and rhythm of speech result in impaired speech intelligibility.

Table 40–8
DSM-IV Diagnostic Criteria for Communication Disorder Not Otherwise Specified

This category is for disorders in communication that do not meet criteria for any specific communication disorder; for example, a voice disorder (ie, an abnormality of vocal pitch loudness, quality, tone, or resonance).

Speech is erratic and dysrhythmic and consists of rapid, jerky spurts that are inconsistent with normal phrasing patterns. The disorder usually occurs in children between 2 and 8 years of age; in two thirds of the cases, the patient spontaneously recovers by early adolescence. Cluttering is associated with learning disorders and other communication disorders.

References

Aram DM, Morris R, Hall NE: Clinical and research congruence in identifying children with specific language impairment. J Speech Hear Res *36:* 580, 1993.

Baker L, Cantwell DP: The association between emotional/behavioral disorders and learning disorders in a sample of speech/language impaired children. Adv Learn Behav Disord *6:* 27, 1990.

Baker L, Cantwell DP: Specific language and learning disorders. In *Handbook of Child Psychopathology,* ed 2, TH Ollendick, M Herson, editors, p 93. Plenum, New York, 1989.

Beitchman JH, Brownlie EB, Inglis A: Seven-year follow-up of speech/language stability and outcome. J Am Acad Child Adolesc Psychiatry *33:* 1322, 1994.

Beitchman JH, Cohen NJ, Konstantareas MM, Tannock R, editors: *Language, Learning, and Behavior Disorders: Developmental, Biological, and Clinical Perspectives.* Cambridge University Press, New York, 1996.

Beitchman JH, Wilson B, Brownlie EB, Walters H, Inglis A, Lancee W: Long-term consistency in speech/language profiles. II. Behavioral, emotional, and social outcomes. J Am Acad Child Adolesc Psychiatry *35:* 815, 1996.

Beitchman JH, Wilson B, Brownlie EB, Walters H, Lancee W: Long-term consistency in speech/language profiles: Developmental and Academic outcomes. J Am Acad Child Adolesc Psych *35:* 804, 1996.

Benaisich AA, Curtiss S, Tallal P: Language, learning and behavioral disturbances in childhood: A longitudinal perspective: J Am Acad Child Adolesc Psychiatry *32:* 585, 1993.

Campbell TF, Dollaghan CA: Expressive language recovery in severely brain-injured children and adolescents. J Speech Hear Disord *55:* 567, 1990.

Cantwell DP, Baker L: Communication disorder not otherwise specified. In *Comprehensive Textbook of Psychiatry,* ed 6, HI Kaplan, BJ Sadock, editors, p 2275. Williams & Wilkins, Baltimore, 1995.

Caulfield MB, Fischel JE, DeBaryshe BD, Whitehurst GJ: Behavioral correlates of developmental expressive language disorder. J Abnorm Child Psychol *17:* 187, 1989.

Cohen NJ, Davine M, Horodezky N, Lipsett L, Isaacson L: Unsuspected language impairment in psychiatrically disturbed children: Prevalence and language and behavioral characteristics. J Am Acad Child Adolesc Psychiatry *32:* 595, 1993.

Collins CR, Blood GW: Acknowledgement and severity of stuttering as factors influencing nonstutterers' perceptions of stutterers. J Speech Hear Disord *55:* 75, 1990.

Conture EG: *Stuttering,* ed 2. Prentice-Hall, Englewood Cliffs, NJ, 1990.

Coplan J, Gleason JR: Unclear speech: Recognition and significance of unintelligible speech in preschool children. Pediatrics *82:* 447, 1988.

Cordes AK, Ingham RJ: The reliability of observational data. II. Issues in the identification and measurement of stuttering events. J Speech Hear Res *37:* 2, 1994.

Duchan JF: A situated pragmatics approach for supporting children with severe communication disorders. Top Lang Disord *17* (2): 1, 1997.

Fenson L, Dale P, Reznick J, Bates E, Thal D, Pethick S: Variability in early communicative development. Monogr Soc Res Child Dev *59:* 242, 1994.

Fey ME, Cleave PL, Ravida AI, Long SH, Dejami AE, Easton DL: Language impairments. J Speech Hear Res *37:* 3, 1994.

Finn P, Ingham RJ: Stutterers' self-ratings of how natural speech sounds and feels. J Speech Hear Res *37:* 2, 1994.

Gow ML, Ingham RJ: Stuttering modification and changes in phonation: Observations of findings from recent reports. J Speech Hear Res *37:* 2, 1994.

Hoit J, Watson P, Hixon K, McMahon P, Johnson C: Age and velopharyngeal function during speech production. J Speech Hear Res *37:* 295, 1994.

Leung PWL, Connolly KJ: Attentional difficulties in hyperactive and conduct-disordered children: Processing deficit. J Child Psychol Psychiatry *35:* 1229, 1994.

Lord C, Pickles A: Language level and nonverbal social-communicative behaviors in autistic and language delayed children. J Am Acad Child Adolesc Psychiatry *35:* 1542, 1996.

Njiokiktjien C: Developmental dysphasia: Clinical importance and underlying neurological causes. Acta Paedopsychiatr *53:* 126, 1990.

O'Donnell JP, Romero JJ, Leicht DJ: A comparison of language deficits in learning-disabled, head-injured, and nondisabled young adults. J Clin Psychol *46:* 310, 1990.

Perkins WH: What is stuttering. J Speech Disord *55:* 370, 1990.

Plante E, Swisher L, Vance R: Anatomical correlates of normal and impaired language in a set of dizygotic twins. Brain Lang *37:* 643, 1989.

Pool KD, Devous MD, Freeman FJ, Watson B, Flinitzo T: Regional cerebral blood flow in developmental stutterers. Arch Neurol *48:* 509, 1991.

Robinson RJ: Causes and associations of severe and persistent specific speech and language disorders in children. Dev Med Child Neurol *33:* 943, 1991.

Rosenfield DB, Derman HS: Physician referral patterns for stutterers. J Otolaryngol *19:* 19, 1990.

Rvachew S: Speech perception training can facilitate sound production learning. J Speech Hear Res *37:*347, 1994.

Smit AB: Phonologic error distributions in the Iowa-Nebraska articulation norms project: Consonant singletons. J Speech Hear Res *36:* 533, 1993.

Throneburg RN, Yairi E, Paden E: Relation between phonological difficulty and the occurrence of dysfluencies in the early stage of stuttering. J Speech Hear Res *37:* 504, 1994.

Tomblin JB, Hardy JC, Hein HA: Predicting poor communication status in preschool children using risk factors present at birth. J Speech Hear Res *34:* 1096, 1991.

Whitehurst GJ, Fischel JE: Early developmental language delay: What, if anything, should the clinician do about it? J Child Psychol Psychiatry *35:* 613, 1994.

Young MA: Evaluating differences between stuttering and nonstuttering speakers: The group difference design. J Speech Hear Res *37:* 3, 1994.

41

Pervasive Developmental Disorders

The fourth edition of *Diagnostic and Statistical Manual of Mental Disorders* (DSM-IV) describes pervasive developmental disorders as severe, pervasive impairment in developmental areas, such as social interaction and communication, or stereotyped behavior, interests, and activities. The impairments are deviant in comparison to a person's mental or developmental level. The disorders include autistic disorder, Rett's disorder, childhood disintegrative disorder, Asperger's disorder, and pervasive developmental disorder not otherwise specified.

The pervasive developmental disorders include a group of psychiatric conditions in which there is impairment in reciprocal social skills, language development, and range of behavioral repertoire. These areas generally do not develop appropriately, and in some cases skills that have developed diminish or are lost over time. The disorders generally affect multiple areas of development, are manifested early in life, and cause persistent dysfunction. Autistic disorder (also know as infantile autism), best-known of the disorders, is characterized by sustained impairments in reciprocal social interactions, communication deviance, and restricted, stereotypical behavioral patterns. According to DSM-IV, abnormal functioning in at least one of these areas must be present by age 3. More than two thirds of people with autistic disorder have mental retardation, but that is not required for the diagnosis.

DSM-IV maintains the category of pervasive developmental disorder not otherwise specified for patients who show a qualitative impairment in reciprocal social interactions and verbal and nonverbal communication but who do not meet the full criteria for autistic disorder.

Several other DSM-IV disorders are included in the category of pervasive developmental disorders: Rett's disorder, childhood disintegrative disorder, and Asperger's disorder. Rett's disorder appears to occur exclusively in girls; it is characterized by normal development for at least 6 months, stereotyped hand movements, a loss of purposeful motions, diminishing social engagement, poor coordination, and decreasing language use. In childhood disintegrative disorder, development progresses normally for the first 2 years, after which the child shows a loss of previously acquired skills in two or more of the following areas: language use, social responsiveness, play, motor skills, and bladder or bowl control. Asperger's disorder is a condition in which the child shows marked impairment in social relatedness and repetitive and stereotyped patterns of behavior without a delay in language development. The child's cognitive abilities and adaptive skills are normal.

ICD-10

Similar to the description of pervasive developmental disorders in DSM-IV, in the 10th revision of *International Statistical Classification of Diseases and Related Health Problems* (ICD-10), these disorders are characterized by "qualitative abnormalities in reciprocal social interactions and in patterns of communications, and by restricted, stereotyped, repetitive repertoire of interests and activities." Although the abnormalities can vary in degree, they pervade the person's functioning in all situations. The abnormalities are usually apparent in infancy and generally become obvious during the first 5 years. Although cognitive impairment is frequently present, the disorders are defined in terms of behavior "that is deviant in relation to mental age (whether the individual is retarded or not)."

Among these disorders, ICD-10 includes childhood autism, atypical autism, Rett's syndrome, other childhood disintegrative disorder, overactive disorder associated with mental retardation and stereotyped movements, Asperger's syndrome, other pervasive developmental disorders, and pervasive developmental disorder, unspecified. The ICD-10 childhood autism category corresponds to autistic disorder in DSM-IV. According to ICD-10, however, atypical autism differs from childhood autism in age or onset or in failure to fulfill all three sets of diagnostic criteria. It first becomes apparent only after the age of 3 years, shows fewer abnormalities in the areas required for diagnosing autism, and generally occurs in children who are profoundly retarded or who have a severe "specific developmental disorder of receptive language."

According to ICD-10, overactive disorder associated with mental retardation and stereotyped movements is "an ill-defined disorder of uncertain nosological validity." ICD-10 includes this diagnosis because children with severe mental retardation who have hyperactivity and inattention problems also frequently show stereotyped behaviors. Their overactivity tends not to benefit from stimulant drugs, as do children with a normal IQ; in adolescents, these children tend toward underactivity. They may also display developmental delays. (In ICD-10, cases of mild retardation with hyperkinetic syndrome are classified in the category of hyperkinetic disorders.) The ICD-10 criteria are presented in Table 41–1.

AUTISTIC DISORDER

According to DSM-IV, autistic disorder (sometimes called early infantile autism, childhood autism, or Kanner's autism)

Table 41–1
ICD-10 Diagnostic Criteria for Pervasive Developmental Disorders

Childhood autism

A. Abnormal or impaired development is evident before the age of 3 years in at least one of the following areas:
  (1) receptive or expressive language as used in social communication;
  (2) the development of selective social attachments or of reciprocal social interaction;
  (3) functional or symbolic play.

B. A total of at least six symptoms from (1), (2), and (3) must be present, with at least two from (1) and at least one from each of (2) and (3):
  (1) Qualitative abnormalities in reciprocal social interaction are manifest in at least two of the following areas:
    (a) failure adequately to use eye-to-eye gaze, facial expression, body posture, and gesture to regulate social interaction;
    (b) failure to develop (in a manner appropriate to mental age, and despite ample opportunities) peer relationships that involve a mutual sharing of interests, activities, and emotions;
    (c) lack of socioemotional reciprocity as shown by an impaired or deviant response to other people's emotions; or lack of modulation of behavior according to social context; or a weak integration of social, emotional, and communicative behaviors;
    (d) lack of spontaneous seeking to share enjoyment, interests, or achievements with other people (eg, a lack of showing, bringing, or pointing out to other people objects of interest to the individual).
  (2) Qualitative abnormalities in communication are manifest in at least one of the following areas:
    (a) a delay in, or total lack of, development of spoken language that is *not* accompanied by an attempt to compensate through the use of gesture or mime as an alternative mode of communication (often preceded by a lack of communicative babbling);
    (b) relative failure to initiate or sustain conversational interchange (at whatever level of language skills is present), in which there is reciprocal responsiveness to the communications of the other person;
    (c) stereotyped and repetitive use of language or idiosyncratic use of words or phrases;
    (d) lack of varied spontaneous make-believe or (when young) social imitative play.
  (3) Restricted, repetitive, and stereotyped patterns of behavior, interests, and activities are manifest in at least one of the following areas:
    (a) an encompassing preoccupation with one or more stereotyped and restricted patterns of interest that are abnormal in content or focus; or one or more interests that are abnormal in their intensity and circumscribed nature though not in their content or focus;
    (b) apparently compulsive adherence to specific, nonfunctional routines or rituals;
    (c) stereotyped and repetitive motor mannerisms that involve either hand or finger flapping or twisting, or complex whole body movements;
    (d) preoccupations with part-objects or nonfunctional elements of play materials (such as their odor, the feel of their surface, or the noise or vibration that they generate).

C. The clinical picture is not attributable to the other varieties of pervasive developmental disorder: specific developmental disorder of receptive language with secondary socio-emotional problems; reactive attachment disorder or disinhibited attachment disorder, mental retardation with some associated emotional or behavioral disorder; schizophrenia of unusually early onset; and Rett's syndrome.

Atypical autism

A. Abnormal or impaired development is evident at or after the age of 3 years (criteria as for autism except for age of manifestation).

B. There are qualitative abnormalities in reciprocal social interaction or in communication, or restricted, repetitive, and stereotyped patterns of behavior, interests, and activities. (Criteria as for autism except that it is unnecessary to meet the criteria for number of areas of abnormality.)

C. The disorder does not meet the diagnostic criteria for autism.

Autism may be atypical in either age of onset or symptomatology; the two types are differentiated with a fifth character for research purposes. Syndromes that are atypical in both respects should be coded. Atypicality in both ages of onset and symptomatology.

Atypicality in age of onset

A. The disorder does not meet criterion A for autism; that is, abnormal or impaired development is evident only at or after the age of 3 years.

B. The disorder meets criteria B and C for autism.

Atypicality in symptomatology

A. The disorder meets criterion A for autism; that is abnormal or impaired development is evident before the age of 3 years.

B. There are qualitative abnormalities in reciprocal social interactions or in communication, or restricted, repetitive, and stereotyped patterns of behavior, interests, and activities. (Criteria as for autism except that it is unnecessary to meet the criteria for number of areas of abnormality.)

C. The disorder meets criterion C for autism.

D. The disorder does not fully meet criterion B for autism.

Atypicality in both age of onset and symptomatology

A. The disorder does not meet criterion A for autism; that is, abnormal or impaired development is evident only at or after the age of 3 years.

B. There are qualitative abnormalities in reciprocal social interactions or in communication, or restricted, repetitive, and stereotyped patterns of behavior, interests, and activities. (Criteria as for autism except that it is unnecessary to meet the criteria for number of areas of abnormality.)

C. The disorder meets criterion C for autism.

D. The disorder does not fully meet criterion B for autism.

Rett's syndrome

A. There is an apparently normal prenatal and perinatal period *and* apparently normal psychomotor development through the first 5 months *and* normal head circumference at birth.

B. There is deceleration of head growth between 5 months and 4 years *and* loss of acquired purposeful hand skills between 5 and 30 months of age that is associated with concurrent communication dysfunction and impaired social interactions *and* the appearance of poorly coordinated/unstable gait and/or trunk movements.

C. There is severe impairment of expressive and receptive language, together with severe psychomotor retardation.

D. There are stereotyped midline hand movements (such as hand-wringing or "hand-washing") with an onset at or after the time when purposeful hand movements are lost.

(continued)

Table 41–1 (continued)

Other childhood disintegrative disorder

A. Development is apparently normal up to the age of at least 2 years. The presence of normal age-appropriate skills in communication, social relationships, play, and adaptive behavior at age 2 years or later is required for diagnosis.

B. There is a definite loss of previously acquired skills at about the time of onset of the disorder. The diagnosis requires a clinically significant loss of skills (not just a failure to use them in certain situations) in at least two of the following areas:
   (1) expressive or receptive language;
   (2) play;
   (3) social skills or adaptive behavior;
   (4) bowel or bladder control;
   (5) motor skills.

C. Qualitatively abnormal social functioning is manifest in at least two of the following areas:
   (1) qualitative abnormalities in reciprocal social interaction (of the type defined for autism);
   (2) qualitative abnormalities in communication (of the type defined for autism);
   (3) restricted, repetitive, and stereotyped patterns of behavior, interests, and activities, including motor stereotypics and mannerisms;
   (4) a general loss of interest in objects and in the environment.

D. The disorder is not attributable to the other varieties of pervasive developmental disorder; acquired aphasia with epilepsy; elective mutism; Rett's syndrome; or schizophrenia.

Overactive disorder associated with mental retardation and stereotyped movements

A. Severe motor hyperactivity is manifest by at least two of the following problems in activity and attention:
   (1) continuous motor restlessness, manifest in running, jumping, and other movements of the whole body;
   (2) marked difficulty in remaining seated: the child will ordinarily remain seated for a few seconds at most except when engaged in a stereotypic activity (see criterion B);
   (3) grossly excessive activity in situations where relative stillness is expected;
   (4) very rapid changes of activity, so that activities generally last for less than a minute (occasional longer periods spent in highly favored activities do not exclude this, and very long periods spent in stereotypic activities can also be compatible with the presence of this problem at other times).

B. Repetitive and stereotyped patterns of behavior and activity are manifest by at least one of the following:
   (1) fixed and frequently repeated motor mannerisms: these may involve either complex movements of the whole body or partial movements such as hand-flapping;
   (2) excessive and nonfunctional repetition of activities that are constant in form: this may be play with a single object (eg, running water) or a ritual of activities (either alone or involving other people);
   (3) repetitive self-injury.

C. IQ is less than 50.

D. There is no social impairment of the autistic type, ie, the child must show at least three of the following:
   (1) developmentally appropriate use of eye gaze, expression, and posture to regulate social interaction;
   (2) developmentally appropriate peer relationships that include sharing of interests, activities, etc.;
   (3) approaches to other people, at least sometimes, for comfort and affection;
   (4) ability to share other people's enjoyment at times; other forms of social impairment, eg, a disinhibited approach to strangers, are compatible with the diagnosis.

E. The disorder does not meet diagnostic criteria for autism, childhood disintegrative disorder, or hyperkinetic disorders.

Asperger's syndrome

A. There is no clinically significant general delay in spoken or receptive language or cognitive development. Diagnosis requires that single words should have developed by 2 years of age or earlier and that communicative phrases be used by 3 years of age or earlier. Self-help skills, adaptive behavior, and curiosity about the environment during the first 3 years should be at a level consistent with normal intellectual development. However, motor milestones may be somewhat delayed and motor clumsiness is usual (although not a necessary diagnostic feature). Isolated special skills, often related to abnormal preoccupations, are common, but are not required for diagnosis.

B. There are qualitative abnormalities in reciprocal social interaction (criteria as for autism).

C. The individual exhibits an unusually intense, circumscribed interest or restricted, repetitive, and stereotyped patterns of behavior, interests, and activities (criteria as for autism; however it would be less usual for these to include either motor mannerisms or preoccupations with part-objects or nonfunctional elements of play materials).

D. The disorder is not attributable to the other varieties of pervasive developmental disorder: simple schizophrenia; schizotypal disorder; obsessive-compulsive disorder; anankastic personality disorder; reactive and disinhibited attachment disorders of childhood.

Other pervasive developmental disorders

Pervasive developmental disorder, unspecified

This is a residual diagnostic category that should be used for disorders which fit the general description for pervasive developmental disorders but in which contradictory findings or a lack of adequate information mean that the criteria for any of the other Pervasive developmental disorders codes cannot be met.

is characterized by marked abnormal development in social interaction and communication and restricted repertoire of activities and interests.

History

In 1867 Henry Maudsley was the first psychiatrist to pay serious attention to very young children with severe mental disorders involving a marked deviation, delay, and distortion in the developmental processes. Initially, all such disorders were considered psychoses. In 1943 Leo Kanner, in his classic paper ''Autistic Disturbances of Affective Contact,'' coined the term *infantile autism* and provided a clear, comprehensive account of the early childhood syndrome. He described children who exhibited extreme autistic aloneness; failure to assume an anticipatory posture; delayed or deviant language development with echolalia and pronominal reversal (using you for I; monotonous repetitions of noises or verbal utterances; excellent rote memory; limited range of spontaneous activities, stereotypies, and mannerisms; anxiously obsessive desire for the maintenance of sameness and a dread of change; poor eye contact; abnormal relationships with people; and a preference for pictures and inanimate objects. Kanner suspected the syndrome to be more frequent than it seemed and suggested that some children had been misclassified as mentally retarded or schizophrenic. Before 1980, children with any pervasive developmental disorders were classified as having a type of childhood schizophrenia. Evidence shows autistic disorder and schizophrenia represent two distinct psychiatric entities, but sometimes a child with autistic disorder develops a comorbid schizophrenic disorder.

Epidemiology

Prevalence. Autistic disorder occurs at a rate of 2 to 5 cases per 10,000 children (0.02 to 0.05 percent) under age 12. If severe mental retardation with some autistic features is included, the rate can rise as high as 20 per 10,000. In most cases, autism begins before the age of 36 months. Parents, depending on their awareness and the severity of the disorder, however, may not notice any symptoms.

Sex Distribution. Autistic disorder is found more frequently in boys than in girls: Three to five times more boys than girls have the disorder. But autistic girls tend to be more seriously affected and more likely to have family histories of cognitive impairment than do boys.

Socioeconomic Status. Early studies suggested that a high socioeconomic status was common in families with autistic children; however, these findings were probably based on referral biases. Over the past 25 years, an increasing proportion of cases have been seen in low socioeconomic groups. That finding may well be due to an increased awareness of the disorder and the increased availability of child mental health workers for children from low socioeconomic status families.

Etiology and Pathogenesis

Autistic disorder is a developmental behavioral disorder. Although the disorder was first considered to be psychosocial or psychodynamic in origin, much evidence has accumulated to support a biological substrate.

Psychodynamic and Family Factors. In his initial report, Kanner noted that few parents of autistic children were warmhearted and that, for the most part, parents and other family members were preoccupied with intellectual abstractions and tended to express little genuine interest in their children. This finding, however, has not been replicated over the past 50 years. Other theories, such as parental rage and rejection and parental reinforcement of autistic symptoms, have also not been substantiated. Recent studies comparing parents of autistic children with parents of normal children have not shown significant differences in child-rearing skills. No satisfactory evidence indicates that any particular deviant family functioning or psychodynamic constellation of factors leads to the development of autistic disorder. Children with autism, as with children with other disorders, can respond with an exacerbation of symptoms to psychosocial stressors including family discord, the birth of a new sibling, or a family move. In fact, children with autistic disorder may be excruciatingly sensitive to a host of changes in their families and environment.

Neurological and Biological Factors. Autistic disorder and autistic symptoms are associated with conditions with neurological lesions, notably congenital rubella, phenylketonuria (PKU), tuberous sclerosis, and Rett's disorder. Autistic children show more evidence of perinatal complications than do comparison groups of normal children and those with other disorders. The finding that autistic children have significantly more minor congenital physical anomalies than do their siblings and normal controls suggests that complications of pregnancy in the first trimester are significant.

Four to 32 percent of people with autism have grand mal seizures at some time, and about 20 to 25 percent show ventricular enlargement on computed tomography (CT) scans. Various electroencephalogram (EEG) abnormalities are found in 10 to 83 percent of autistic children, and, although no EEG finding is specific to autistic disorder, there is some indication of failed cerebral lateralization. Recently, one magnetic resonance imaging (MRI) study revealed hypoplasia of cerebellar vermal lobules VI and VII, and another MRI study revealed cortical abnormalities, particularly polymicrogyria, in some autistic patients. Those abnormalities may reflect abnormal cell migrations in the first 6 months of gestation. An autopsy study revealed decreased Purkinje's cell counts, and another study found increased diffuse cortical metabolism during positron emission tomography (PET) scanning.

Genetic Factors. In several surveys, between 2 and 4 percent of siblings of those with autism also had autistic disorder, a rate 50 times greater than in the general population. The concordance rate of autistic disorder in the two largest twin studies was 36 percent in monozygotic pairs versus 0 percent in dizygotic pairs in one study and about 96 percent in monozygotic pairs versus about 27 percent in dizygotic pairs in the second study. In the second study, however, zygosity was confirmed in only about half of the sample.

Clinical reports and studies suggest that the nonautistic members of families with autistic members have various language or other cognitive problems but less severely than does the person with autism. Fragile X syndrome appears to be associated with autistic disorder, but the number of persons with both autistic disorder and fragile X syndrome is unclear.

Immunological Factors. Some evidence indicates that immunological incompatibility between the mother and the embryo or fetus may contribute to autistic disorder. The lymphocytes of some autistic children react with maternal antibodies, a fact that raises the possibility that embryonic neural or extraembryonic tissues may be damaged during gestation.

Perinatal Factors. A high incidence of various perinatal complications seems to occur in children with autistic disorder, although no complication has been directly implicated as causative. During gestation, maternal bleeding after the first trimester and meconium in the amniotic fluid have been reported in the histories of autistic children more often than in the general population. In the neonatal period, autistic children have a high incidence of respiratory distress syndrome and neonatal anemia. Some evidence indicates a high incidence of medication usage during pregnancy in the mothers of autistic children.

Neuroanatomical Factors. Recent MRI studies comparing autistic subjects and normal controls found that the total brain volume was increased in those with autism. The greatest average percentage increase in size occurred in the occipital lobe, parietal lobe, and temporal lobe. No differences occurred in the frontal lobes. Although the specific implications and etiology of this enlargement are unknown, the increased volume can arise from three different possible mechanisms: increased neurogenesis, decreased neuronal death, and increased production of non-neuronal brain tissue such as glial cells or blood vessels. Although these data do not specifically identify a neuroanatomical deficit in autism, they suggest that brain enlargement itself may be a biological marker in autistic disorder.

The temporal lobe has been suggested to be a critical area of brain abnormality in autistic disorder. This suggestion is based on reports of autistic-like syndromes in some people with temporal lobe damage. When the temporal region of animals is damaged, expected social behavior is lost, and restlessness, repetitive motor behavior, and a limited behavioral repertoire are seen. Another finding in autistic disorder is a decrease in Purkinje's cells in the cerebellum, a decrease potentially resulting in abnormalities of attention, arousal, and sensory processes.

Biochemical Factors. At least one third of patients with autistic disorder have elevated plasma serotonin. This finding is not specific to autistic disorder: People with mental retardation without autistic disorder also display this trait.

Patients with autistic disorder without mental retardation have a high incidence of hyperserotonemia. In some autistic children, increased cerebrospinal fluid (CSF) homovanillic acid (the major dopamine metabolite) is associated with increased withdrawal and stereotypies. Some evidence indicates that symptom severity decreases as the ratio of CSF 5-hydroxyindoleacetic acid (5-HIAA, metabolite of serotonin) to CSF homovanillic acid increases. CSF 5-HIAA may be inversely proportional to blood serotonin levels; these levels are increased in one third of autistic disorder patients, a nonspecific finding that also occurs in mentally retarded persons.

Diagnosis and Clinical Features

The DSM-IV diagnostic criteria for autistic disorder are given in Table 41–2.

Physical Characteristics. HANDEDNESS. Many autistic children have a failure of lateralization and remain ambidextrous at an age when cerebral dominance is established in normal children. Autistic children also have a higher incidence of abnormal dermatoglyphics (for example, fingerprints) than do the general population. This finding may suggest a disturbance in neuroectodermal development.

INTERCURRENT PHYSICAL ILLNESS. Young children with autistic disorder have a higher incidence of upper respiratory infections, excessive burping, febrile seizures, constipation, and loose bowel movements than do controls. Many autistic children react differently to illness than do normal children, a fact that may reflect an immature or abnormal autonomic nervous system. Autistic children may not have elevated temperatures with infectious illnesses, may not complain of pain either verbally or by gesture, and may not show the malaise of ill children. Their behavior and relatedness may improve to a noticeable degree when they are ill, and in some cases such changes are a clue to physical illness.

Behavioral Characteristics. QUALITATIVE IMPAIRMENTS IN SOCIAL INTERACTION. All autistic children fail to show the usual relatedness to their parents and other people. As infants, many lack a social smile and anticipatory posture for being picked up as an adult approaches. Abnormal eye contact is a common finding. The social development of autistic children is characterized by a lack (but not always a total absence) of attachment behavior and a relatively early failure of person-specific bonding. Autistic children often do not seem to recognize or differentiate the most important people in their lives—parents, siblings, and teachers—and may show virtually no separation anxiety on being left in an unfamiliar environment with strangers. When autistic children have reached school age, their withdrawal may have diminished or not be as obvious, particularly in better-functioning children. Instead, their failure to play with peers and to make friends, their social awkwardness and inappropriateness, and, particularly, their failure to develop empathy are observed. In late adolescence, those autistic persons who make the most progress often have a desire for friendships, but their ineptness of approach and their inability to respond to another's interests, emotions, and feelings are major obstacles in developing friendships. Autistic adolescents and adults have sexual feelings, but their lack of social competence and skills prevents most of them from developing a sexual relationship. It is extremely rare for autistic persons to marry.

DISTURBANCES OF COMMUNICATION AND LANGUAGE. Gross deficits and deviances in language development are among the principal criteria for diagnosing autistic disorder. Autistic children are not

Table 41–2
DSM-IV Diagnostic Criteria for Autistic Disorder

A. A total of six (or more) items from (1), (2), and (3), with at least two from (1), and one each from (2) and (3):
  (1) Qualitative impairment in social interaction, as manifested by at least two of the following:
    (a) marked impairment in the use of multiple nonverbal behaviors such as eye-to-eye gaze, facial expression, body postures, and gestures to regulate social interaction
    (b) failure to develop peer relationships appropriate to developmental level
    (c) a lack of spontaneous seeking to share enjoyment, interests, or achievements with other people (e.g., by a lack of showing, bringing, or pointing out objects of interest)
    (d) lack of social or emotional reciprocity
  (2) Qualitative impairments in communication as manifested by at least one of the following:
    (a) delay in, or total lack of, the development of spoken language (not accompanied by an attempt to compensate through alternative modes of communication such as gesture or mime)
    (b) in individuals with adequate speech, marked impairment in the ability to initiate or sustain a conversation with others
    (c) stereotyped and repetitive use of language or idiosyncratic language
    (d) lack of varied spontaneous make-believe play or social imitative play appropriate to developmental level
  (3) Restricted repetitive and stereotyped patterns of behavior, interests, and activities, as manifested by at least one of the following:
    (a) encompassing preoccupation with one or more stereotyped and restricted patterns of interest that is abnormal either in intensity or focus
    (b) apparently inflexible adherence to specific, nonfunctional routines or rituals
    (c) stereotyped and repetitive motor mannerisms (e.g., hand or finger flapping or twisting, or complex whole body movements)
    (d) persistent preoccupation with parts of objects

B. Delays or abnormal functioning in at least one of the following areas, with onset prior to age 3 years: (1) social interaction, (2) language as used in social communication, or (3) symbolic or imaginative play.

C. The disturbance is not better accounted for by Rett's disorder or childhood disintegrative disorder.

Reprinted with permission from American Psychiatric Association: *Diagnostic and Statistical Manual of Mental Disorders,* ed 4. Copyright, American Psychiatric Association, Washington, 1994.

simply reluctant to speak, and their speech abnormalities are not due to lack of motivation. Language deviance, as much as language delay, is characteristic of autistic disorder. In contrast to normal and mentally retarded children, autistic children make little use of meaning in their memory and thought processes. When autistic persons do learn to converse fluently, they lack social competence and their conversations are not characterized by reciprocal responsive interchanges. In children with autism and also nonautistic children with language impairment, many nonverbal and communication skills seem to be correlated with the degree of impaired expressive language.

In the first year of life, an autistic child's amount and pattern of babbling may be reduced or abnormal. Some children emit noises—clicks, sounds, screeches, and nonsense syllables—in a stereotyped fashion with no seeming intent of communication. Unlike normal young children, who always have better receptive language skills and understand much before they can speak, verbal autistic children may say more than they understand. Words and even entire sentences may drop in and out of a child's vocabulary. Autistic children may use a word once and then not use it again for a week, a month, or years. Their speech contains echolalia, both immediate and delayed, or stereotyped phrases out of context. These abnormalities are often associated with pronominal reversal: A girl asks, "Do you want the toy?" when she means that she wants it. Difficulties in articulation are also noted. The use of peculiar voice quality and rhythm is observed clinically in many cases. About 50 percent of all autistic children never have useful speech. Some of the brightest children show a particular fascination with letters and numbers. A few literally teach themselves to read at a preschool age (hyperlexia), often astonishingly well. In virtually all cases, however, the children read without any comprehension whatsoever.

STEREOTYPED BEHAVIOR. In the first years of an autistic child's life, much of normal children's exploratory play is absent or minimal. Toys and objects are often manipulated in an unintended way, with little variety, creativity, and imagination and few symbolic features. Autistic children cannot imitate or use abstract pantomime. The activities and play, if any, of these children are rigid, repetitive, and monotonous. Ritualistic and compulsive phenomena are common in early and middle childhood. Children often spin, bang, line up objects, and become attached to inanimate objects. In addition, many autistic children, particularly those who are the most intellectually impaired, exhibit various movement abnormalities. Stereotypies, mannerisms, and grimacing are most frequent when a child is left alone, and they may decrease in a structured situation. Autistic children are resistant to transition and change. Moving to a new house, moving furniture in a room, and having breakfast before a bath when the reverse was the routine may result in panic or temper tantrums.

INSTABILITY OF MOOD AND AFFECT. Some children with autistic disorder exhibit sudden mood changes, with bursts of laughing or crying for no apparent reason and without expressing thoughts congruent to the affect.

RESPONSE TO SENSORY STIMULI. Autistic children may be overresponsive or underresponsive to sensory stimuli (for example, to sound and pain). They may selectively ignore spoken language directed at them and so are often thought to be deaf, but they may show unusual interest in the sound of a wristwatch. Many have a heightened pain threshold or an altered response to pain. Indeed, autistic children may injure themselves severely and not cry. Many autistic children seem to enjoy music. They frequently hum a tune or sing a song or commercial jingle before saying words or using speech. Some particularly enjoy vestibular stimulation—spinning, swinging, and up-and-down movements.

OTHER BEHAVIORAL SYMPTOMS. Hyperkinesis is a common behavior problem in young autistic children. Hypokinesis is less frequent; when present, it often alternates with hyperactivity. Aggressiveness and temper tantrums are observed, often for no apparent reason or are prompted by change or demands. Self-injurious behavior includes head banging, biting, scratching, and hair pulling. Short attention span, a complete inability to focus on a task, insomnia, feeding and eating problems, and enuresis are also common among children with autism.

Ian, a 5-year-old boy, was referred for a psychiatric evaluation by his kindergarten teacher who reported that Ian was unable to follow directions, did not communicate well with his classmates, and was hyperactive and aggressive. Ian had already undergone several psychiatric evaluations starting at the age of 3, at which time he was diagnosed with attention-deficit/hyperactivity disorder. Ian has had trouble following directions since he started preschool at age 3½, and he has never been able to play with another child without either becoming aggressive or having a long, inconsolable tantrum. Ian has been taking methylphenidate (Ritalin), 10 mg 3 times a day, since he was 4 years old, and this medication seemed to be helpful until now.

Ian was the product of a normal pregnancy, but he was born 5 weeks early because of his mother's premature labor, at a birth weight of 4 pounds, 1 ounce. He seemed to do well as a neonate, but his parents became increasingly worried about his development when he did not develop any language by 18 months. The pediatrician was unconcerned and assured his parents that some babies, especially low-birth-weight and premature babies, tend to develop more slowly. Not only did Ian not appear to be acquiring language appropriately, but he did not seem to be socially related. He usually did not turn his head when his name was called, and he did not spontaneously seek his mother's comfort when he fell and hurt himself. He was rather clumsy and liked to do the same things over and over. He was fascinated by running water and seemed to be excessively attached to the vacuum cleaner. Nevertheless, Ian's parents, believing that his prematurity accounted for all these peculiarities, were satisfied to wait and see.

When Ian started preschool, it became clear that he was markedly different from most others of his age. He had acquired many words by now, but his sentences were often incomprehensible. He often said "You" when he meant "I," and repeated verbatim phrases that he had heard earlier in the day. He was unable to share toys and never joined in group activities that required the class to sit in a circle. Instead, he stayed in the corner of the room playing by himself. He would not let the teacher know when he was thirsty or had to go to the bathroom. He would not answer questions; sometimes he became overly excited and hyperactive and ran around the room with no apparent goal. At these times, when the teacher tried to stop him, Ian would become combative and required physical restraining. At other times he would hit other children for no apparent reason. Most of the time, however, he did not make eye contact and was isolated from others.

On evaluation and with specific questioning, it became clear that Ian's language skills were poor for his age, and they were characterized by pronoun reversals, echolalia, and unusual syntax. On intellectual testing, Ian's full-scale intelligence quotient (IQ) was 105, with decidedly more difficulty on the verbal items than the performance subtests. Ian's social skills were marked by deficits in responding facially to the affect of the examiner or in playing reciprocally. He appeared to be preoccupied with a pendulum clock hanging in the office. Ian spoke tersely and did not offer to put away the many toys he had superficially examined.

DISCUSSION

A diagnosis of autistic disorder was made, with a normal IQ. It was recommended that Ian be placed in a smaller, more structured special education classroom and a behavioral program be used to reinforce both appropriate social and task-oriented behaviors. Methylphenidate was to be continued because it seemed to help Ian to stay on task more of the time.

Intellectual Functioning. About 40 percent of the children with infantile autism have IQ scores below 50 to 55 (moderate, severe, or profound mental retardation); 30 percent have scores of 50 to approximately 70 (mild mental retardation); and 30 percent have scores of 70 or more. Epidemiological and clinical studies show that the risk for autistic disorder increases as the IQ decreases. About one fifth of all autistic children have a normal nonverbal intelligence. The IQ scores of autistic children tend to reflect problems with verbal sequencing and abstraction skills, rather than with visuospatial or rote memory skills. This finding suggests the importance of defects in language-related functions.

Unusual or precocious cognitive or visuomotor abilities occur in some autistic children. The abilities, which may exist even in the overall retarded functioning, are referred to as *splinter functions* or *islets of precocity*. Perhaps the most striking examples are idiot or autistic savants, who have prodigious rote memories or calculating abilities, usually beyond the capabilities of normal peers. Other precocious abilities in young autistic children include hyperlexia, an early ability to read well (although they are not able to understand what they read), memorizing and reciting, and musical abilities (singing or playing tunes or recognizing musical pieces).

Differential Diagnosis

The major differential diagnoses are schizophrenia with childhood onset, mental retardation with behavioral symptoms, mixed receptive-expressive language disorder, congenital deafness or severe hearing disorder, psychosocial deprivation, and disintegrative (regressive) psychoses. Because children with a pervasive developmental disorder usually have many concurrent problems, Michael Rutter and Lionel Hersov suggested a stepwise approach to use in the differential diagnosis (Table 41–3).

Schizophrenia with Childhood Onset. Whereas a wealth of literature on autistic disorder is available, there are few data on children under age 12 who meet the diagnostic criteria for schizophrenia. Schizophrenia is rare in children un-

Table 41–3
Procedure for Differential Diagnosis on a Multiaxial System

1. Determine intellectual level.
2. Determine level of language development
3. Consider whether child's behavior is appropriate for
   (i) chronological age
   (ii) mental age
   (iii) language age
4. If not appropriate, consider differential diagnosis of psychiatric disorder according to
   (i) pattern of social interaction
   (ii) pattern of language
   (iii) pattern of play
   (iv) other behaviors
5. Identify any relevant medical conditions
6. Consider whether there are any relevant psychosocial factors.

Reprinted with permission from Rutter M, Hersov L: *Child and Adolescent Psychiatry: Modern Approaches*, ed 2, p 73. Blackwell, Oxford, 1985.

der the age of 5. It is accompanied by hallucinations or delusions, with a lower incidence of seizures and mental retardation and a more even IQ than in autistic children. Table 41–4 compares autistic disorder and schizophrenia with childhood onset.

Mental Retardation with Behavioral Symptoms. About 40 percent of autistic children are moderately, severely, or profoundly retarded, and retarded children may have behavior symptoms that include autistic features. When both disorders are present, both should be diagnosed. The main differentiating features between autistic disorder and mental retardation are: Mentally retarded children usually relate to adults and other children in accordance with their mental age; they use the language they do have to communicate with others; and they have a relatively even profile of impairments without splinter functions.

Mixed Receptive-Expressive Language Disorder. A group of children with mixed receptive-expressive language disorder have autistic-like features and may present a diagnostic problem. Table 41–5 summarizes the major differences between autistic disorder and mixed receptive-expressive language disorder.

Acquired Aphasia with Convulsion. Acquired aphasia with convulsion is a rare condition that is sometimes difficult to differentiate from autistic disorder and childhood disintegrative disorder. Children with the condition are normal for several years before losing both their receptive and their expressive language over a period of weeks or months. Most have a few seizures and generalized EEG abnormalities at the onset, but these signs usually do not persist. A profound language comprehension disorder then follows, characterized by a deviant speech pattern and speech impairment. Some children recover but with considerable residual language impairment.

Congenital Deafness or Severe Hearing Impairment. Because autistic children are often mute or show a selective disinterest in spoken language, they are often thought to be deaf. Differentiating factors include the following: Autistic infants may babble only infrequently, whereas deaf infants have a history of relatively normal babbling that then gradually tapers off and may stop from 6 months to 1 year of age. Deaf children respond only to loud sounds, whereas autistic children may ignore loud or normal sounds and respond to soft or low sounds. Most important, audiogram or auditory-evoked potentials indicate significant hearing loss in deaf children. Unlike autistic children, deaf children usually relate to their parents, seek their affection, and, as infants, enjoy being held.

Psychosocial Deprivation. Severe disturbances in the physical and emotional environment (such as maternal deprivation, psychosocial dwarfism, hospitalism, and failure to thrive) can cause children to appear apathetic, withdrawn, and alienated. Language and motor skills can be delayed. Children with these signs almost always rapidly improve when placed in a favorable and enriched psychosocial environment, but such improvement is not the case with autistic children.

Course and Prognosis

Autistic disorder has a long course and a guarded prognosis. As a general rule, autistic children with IQs above 70 and those who use communicative language by ages 5 to 7 have

Table 41–4
Autistic Disorder versus Schizophrenia with Childhood Onset

Criteria	Autistic Disorder	Schizophrenia (with Onset before Puberty)
Age of onset	Before 38 months	Not under 5 years of age
Incidence	2–5 in 10,000	Unknown, possibly same or even rarer
Sex ratio (M:F)	3–4:1	1.67:1 (nearly equal, or slight preponderance of males)
Family history of schizophrenia	Not raised or probably not raised	Raised
Socioeconomic status (SES)	Overrepresentation of upper SES groups (artifact)	More common in lower SES groups
Prenatal and perinatal complications and cerebral dysfunction	More common in autistic disorder	Less common in schizophrenia
Behavioral characteristics	Failure to develop relatedness; absence of speech or echolalia; stereotyped phrases; language comprehension absent or poor; insistence on sameness and stereotypies	Hallucinations and delusions; thought disorder
Adaptive functioning	Usually always impaired	Deterioration in functioning
Level of intelligence	In majority of cases subnormal, frequently severely impaired (70% 70)	Usually within normal range, mostly dull normal (15% 70)
Pattern of IQ	Marked unevenness	More even
Grand mal seizures	4–32%	Absent or lower incidence

Courtesy of Magda Campbell, M.D., and Wayne Green, M.D.

Table 41–5
Autistic Disorder versus Mixed Receptive-Expressive Language Disorder

Criteria	Autistic Disorder	Mixed Receptive-Expressive Language Disorder
Incidence	2–5 in 10,000	5 in 10,000
Sex ratio (M:F)	3–4:1	Equal or almost equal sex ratio
Family history of speech delay or language problems	Present in about 25 percent of cases	Present in about 25 percent of cases
Associated deafness	Very infrequent	Not infrequent
Nonverbal communication (gestures, etc.)	Absent or rudimentary	Present
Language abnormalities (eg, echolalia, stereotyped phrases out of context)	More common	Less common
Articulatory problems	Less frequent	More frequent
Level of intelligence	Often severely impaired	Though may be impaired, less frequently severe
Patterns of IQ tests	Uneven, lower on verbal scores than dysphasic patients, lower on comprehension subtest than dysphasic patients	More even, though verbal IQ lower than performance IQ
Autistic behaviors, impaired social life, stereotypies and ritualistic activities	More common and more severe	Absent or, if present, less severe
Imaginative play	Absent or rudimentary	Usually present

Adapted from Campbell M, Green WH: Pervasive developmental disorders of childhood. In *Comprehensive Textbook of Psychiatry,* ed 4, HI Kaplan, BJ Sanlock, editors. p 1981. Williams & Wilkins, Baltimore, 1995.

the best prognoses. Recent follow-up data comparing high-IQ autistic children at the age of 5 years with their current symptomatology at ages 13 through young adulthood indicate that a small proportion no longer met criteria for autism, although they still exhibited some features of the disorder. Most demonstrated positive changes in communication and social domains over time. The symptom areas that did not seem to improve over time were those related to ritualistic and repetitive behaviors. In general, adult-outcome studies indicate that about two thirds of autistic adults remain severely handicapped and live in complete dependence or semidependence, either with their relatives or in long-term institutions. Only 1 to 2 percent acquire a normal and independent status with gainful employment, and 5 to 20 percent achieve a borderline normal status. The prognosis is improved if the environment or the home is supportive and capable of meeting the extensive needs of such a child. Although a decrease of symptoms is noted in many cases, severe self-mutilation or aggressiveness and regression may develop in others. About 4 to 32 percent have grand mal seizures in late childhood or adolescence, and the seizures adversely affect the prognosis.

Treatment

The goals of treatment are to increase socially acceptable and prosocial behavior, to decrease odd behavioral symptoms, and to aid in the development of verbal and nonverbal communication. Language remediation as well as remediation in academic areas is often required. Children with mental retardation often need more simplistic behavioral interventions to help reinforce socially acceptable behaviors and encourage self-care skills. In addition, parents, often distraught, need support and counseling. Insight-oriented individual psychotherapy has proved to be ineffective. Educational and behavioral methods are currently considered the treatments of choice. Structured classroom training in combination with behavioral methods is the most effective treatment method for many autistic children and is superior to other types of behavioral approaches.

Well-controlled studies indicate that gains in the areas of language and cognition and decreases in maladaptive behaviors are achieved by consistent behavioral programs. Careful training of parents in the concepts and skills of behavior modification and the resolution of the parents' concerns may yield considerable gains in children's language, cognitive, and social areas of behavior. These training programs, however, are rigorous and require much of parents' time. An autistic child requires as much structure as possible, and a daily program for as many hours as feasible is desirable.

With the introduction of facilitated communication, a technique whereby an autistic or a mentally retarded child supposedly communicates with the aid of a teacher who helps the child pick out letters on a computer or letter board, autistic children were thought to be able to produce messages that showed their ability to read and write, to do mathematics, to express their feelings, and even to write poetry. Some messages contained stories of parental abuse and other imaginative accusations, which were occasionally accepted as legal evidence in trials of accused perpetrators. Experiments have demonstrated that the technique conveys the teacher's, not the child's messages; for instance, when the child was shown one picture and the teacher another, in an arrangement where neither could see the other's picture but both were able to see and use the computer, the picture named was invariably the one shown to the teacher. Nevertheless, many families of autistic children and some therapists still have confidence in the technique and continue to use it.

Although no drug has been found to be specific for autistic disorder, psychopharmacotherapy is a valuable adjunct in comprehensive treatment programs to ameliorate a variety of associated symptoms, including aggression and severe temper tantrums, self-injurious behaviors, hyperactivity, and obsessive-compulsive symptomatology and stereotypies. The administration of haloperidol (Haldol) both reduces behavioral symptoms and accelerates learning. The drug decreases hyperactivity, stereotypies, withdrawal, fidgetiness, abnormal object relations, irritability, and labile affect. Supportive evidence indicates that, when used judiciously, haloperidol remains an effective long-term drug. Although tardive and withdrawal dyskinesias can occur with haloperidol treatment in autistic children, evidence indicates that these dyskinesias can resolve when haloperidol is discontinued.

Recently, risperidone (Risperdal), a high-potency antipsychotic with combined dopamine type 2 (D_2) and serotonin (5-hydroxytryptamine [5-HT]) type 2 ($5\text{-}HT_2$) receptor antagonist properties, has been used successfully to diminish aggressiveness, hyperactivity, and self-injurious behavior. In some cases it is reported to encourage socially acceptable behaviors. The serotonin-specific reuptake inhibitors (SSRIs) have been used as adjunctive treatments to diminish and modify obsessive-compulsive and stereotypical behaviors. It remains to be seen whether data will support the use of these medications in autistic disorder.

Clomipramine (Anafranil) has been used in autistic disorders, but without positive results. Fenfluramine (Pondimin), which reduces blood serotonin levels, is effective in a few autistic children. Improvement does not seem to be associated with a reduction in blood serotonin level. Naltrexone (ReVia), an opioid antagonist, is currently being investigated in the hope that blocking endogenous opioids will reduce autistic symptoms. Lithium (Eskalith) can be tried for aggressive or self-injurious behaviors when other medications fail.

RETT'S DISORDER

Rett's disorder is described by DSM-IV as a development of several specific deficits following a period of normal functioning after birth. In 1965 Andreas Rett, an Australian physician, identified a syndrome in 22 girls who appeared to have had normal development for a period of at least 6 months, followed by devastating developmental deterioration. Although few surveys have been done, those available indicate a prevalence of 6 to 7 cases of Rett's disorder per 100,000 girls.

Etiology

The cause of Rett's disorder is unknown, although the progressive deteriorating course after an initial normal period is compatible with a metabolic disorder. In some patients with Rett's disorder, the presence of hyperammonemia has led to postulation that an enzyme metabolizing ammonia is deficient, but hyperammonemia has not been found in most patients with Rett's disorder. It is likely that Rett's disorder has a genetic basis. It has been seen only in girls, and case reports so far indicate complete concordance in monozygotic twins.

Diagnosis and Clinical Features

During the first 5 months after birth, infants have age-appropriate motor skills, normal head circumference, and normal growth. Social interactions show the expected reciprocal quality. At 6 months to 2 years of age, however, children develop a progressive encephalopathy with a number of characteristic features. The signs often include the loss of purposeful hand movements, which are replaced by stereotypic motions such as hand-wringing, the loss of previously acquired speech, psychomotor retardation, and ataxia. Other stereotypical hand movements may occur, such as licking or biting the fingers and tapping or slapping. The head-circumference growth decelerates, and produces microcephaly. All language skills are lost, and both receptive and expressive communicative and social skills seem to plateau at developmental levels between 6 months and 1 year. Poor muscle coordination and an apraxic gait develop; the gait has an unsteady and stiff quality. All these clinical features are diagnostic criteria for the disorder (Table 41–6).

Associated features include seizures in up to 75 percent of affected children and disorganized EEGs with some epileptiform discharges in almost all young children with Rett's disorder, even in the absence of clinical seizures. An additional associated feature is irregular respiration, with episodes of hyperventilation, apnea, and breath holding. The disorganized breathing occurs in most patients while they are awake; during sleep the breathing usually normalizes. Many patients with Rett's disorder also have scoliosis. As the disorder progresses, muscle tone seems to increase from an initial hypotonic condition to spasticity to rigidity.

Although children with Rett's disorder may live for well over a decade after the onset of the disorder, after 10 years, many patients are wheelchair-bound, with muscle wasting, rigidity, and virtually no language ability. Long-term receptive

Table 41–6
DSM-IV Diagnostic Criteria for Rett's Disorder

A. All of the following:
   (1) apparently normal prenatal and perinatal development
   (2) apparently normal psychomotor development through the first 5 months after birth
   (3) normal head circumference at birth
B. Onset of all of the following after the period of normal development:
   (1) deceleration of head growth between ages 5 and 48 months
   (2) loss of previously acquired purposeful hand skills between ages 5 and 30 months with the subsequent development of stereotyped hand movements (eg, hand-wringing or hand-washing)
   (3) loss of social engagement early in the course (although often social interaction develops later)
   (4) appearance of poorly coordinated gait or trunk movements
   (5) severely impaired expressive and receptive language development with severe psychomotor retardation

and expressive communication and socialization abilities remain at a developmental level of less than 1 year.

Differential Diagnosis

Some children with Rett's disorder receive initial diagnoses of autistic disorder because of the marked disability in social interactions in both disorders, but the two disorders have some predictable differences. In Rett's disorder, a child shows a deterioration of developmental milestones, head circumference, and overall growth; in autistic disorder, aberrant development in most cases is present from early on. In Rett's disorder, specific and characteristic hand motions are always present; in autistic disorder, hand mannerisms may or may not appear. Poor coordination, ataxia, and apraxia are predictably part of Rett's disorder; many persons with autistic disorder have unremarkable gross motor function. In Rett's disorder, verbal abilities are usually lost completely; in autistic disorder, patients use characteristically aberrant language. Respiratory irregularity is characteristic of Rett's disorder, and seizures often appear early on; in autistic disorder, no respiratory disorganization is seen, and seizures do not develop in most patients; when seizures do develop, they are more likely in adolescence than in childhood.

Course and Prognosis

Rett's disorder is progressive. The prognosis is not fully known, but those patients who live into adulthood remain at a cognitive and social level equivalent to that in the first year of life.

Treatment

Treatment is aimed at symptomatic intervention. Physiotherapy has been beneficial for the muscular dysfunction, and anticonvulsant treatment is usually necessary to control the seizures. Behavior therapy is useful to control self-injurious behaviors, as it is in the treatment of autistic disorder, and it may help regulate the breathing disorganization.

CHILDHOOD DISINTEGRATIVE DISORDER

According to DSM-IV, childhood disintegrative disorder is characterized by marked regression in several areas of functioning after at least 2 years of apparently normal development. Childhood disintegrative disorder, also known as Heller's syndrome and disintegrative psychosis, was described in 1908 as a deterioration over several months of intellectual, social, and language function occurring in 3 and 4 year olds with previously normal functions. After the deterioration, the children closely resembled children with autistic disorder.

Epidemiology

Epidemiological data have been complicated by the variable diagnostic criteria used, but childhood disintegrative disorder is estimated to be at least one tenth as common as autistic disorder, and the prevalence has been estimated to be about one case in 100,000 boys. The ratio of boys to girls seems to be between 4 and 8 boys to 1 girl.

Etiology

The cause of childhood disintegrative disorder is unknown, but it has been associated with other neurological conditions, including seizure disorders, tuberous sclerosis, and various metabolic disorders.

Diagnosis and Clinical Features

The diagnosis is made on the basis of features that fit a characteristic age of onset, clinical picture, and course. Cases reported have ranged in onset from ages 1 to 9 years, but in the vast majority the onset is between 3 and 4 years; according to DSM-IV, the minimal age of onset is 2 years (Table 41–7). The onset may be insidious over several months, or it may be relatively abrupt, with diminishing abilities occurring in days or weeks. In some cases, a child displays restlessness, increased activity level, and anxiety before the loss of function. The core features of the disorder include a loss of communication skills, marked regression of reciprocal interactions, and the onset of stereotyped movements and compulsive behavior. Affective symptoms are common, particularly anxiety, as is the regression of self-help skills, such as bowel and bladder control.

To receive the diagnosis, a child must exhibit a loss of skills in two of the following areas: language, social or adap-

Table 41–7
DSM-IV Diagnostic Criteria for Childhood Disintegrative Disorder

A. Apparently normal development for at least the first two years after birth as manifested by the presence of age-appropriate verbal and nonverbal communication, social relationships, play, and adaptive behavior.
B. Clinically significant loss of previously acquired skills (before age 10 years) in at least two of the following areas:
   (1) expressive or receptive language
   (2) social skills or adaptive behavior
   (3) bowel or bladder control
   (4) play
   (5) motor skills
C. Abnormalities of functioning in at least two of the following areas:
   (1) qualitative impairment in social interaction (eg, impairment in nonverbal behaviors, failure to develop peer relationships, lack of social or emotional reciprocity)
   (2) qualitative impairments in communication (eg, delay or lack of spoken language, inability to initiate or sustain a conversation, stereotyped and repetitive use of language, lack of varied make-believe play)
   (3) restricted, repetitive, and stereotyped patterns of behavior, interests, and activities, including motor stereotypes and mannerisms
D. The disturbance is not better accounted for by another specific pervasive developmental disorder or by schizophrenia.

Reprinted with permission from American Psychiatric Association: *Diagnostic and Statistical Manual of Mental Disorders,* ed 4. Copyright, American Psychiatric Association, Washington, 1994.

tive behavior, bowel or bladder control, play, and motor skills. Abnormalities must be present in at least two of the following categories: reciprocal social interaction, communication skills, and stereotyped or restricted behavior. The main neurological associated feature is seizure disorder.

Differential Diagnosis

The differential diagnosis of childhood disintegrative disorder includes autistic disorder and Rett's disorder. In many cases the clinical features overlap with autistic disorder, but childhood disintegrative disorder is distinguished from autistic disorder by the loss of previously acquired development. Before the onset of childhood disintegrative disorder (occurring at 2 years or older), language has usually progressed to sentence formation. This skill is strikingly different from the premorbid history of even high-functioning autistic disorder patients, in whom language generally does not exceed single words or phrases before the diagnosis of the disorder. Once the disorder occurs, however, those with childhood disintegrative disorder are more likely to have no language abilities than are high-functioning autistic disorder patients. In Rett's disorder, the deterioration occurs much earlier than in childhood disintegrative disorder, and the characteristic hand stereotypies of Rett's disorder do not occur in childhood disintegrative disorder.

Course and Prognosis

The course of childhood disintegrative disorder is variable, with a plateau reached in most cases, a progressive deteriorating course in rare cases, and some improvement in occasional cases to the point of regaining the ability to speak in sentences. Most patients are left with at least moderate mental retardation.

Treatment

Because of the clinical similarity to autistic disorder, the treatment of childhood disintegrative disorder is the same as that for autistic disorder.

ASPERGER'S DISORDER

According to DSM-IV, those with Asperger's disorder show severe, sustained impairment in social interaction and restricted, repetitive patterns of behavior, interests, and activities. Unlike autistic disorder, in Asperger's disorder there are no significant delays in language, cognitive development, or age-appropriate self-help skills. In 1944 Hans Asperger, an Austrian physician, described a syndrome that he named *autistic psychopathy.* His original description of the syndrome applied to people with normal intelligence who exhibit a qualitative impairment in reciprocal social interaction and behavioral oddities without delays in language development. Since that time, a person with mental retardation but without language delay has received a diagnosis of Asperger's disorder, and a person with language delay but without mental retardation has also been given that diagnosis.

In ICD-10, Asperger's disorder is called *Asperger's syndrome* and is characterized by qualitative social impairment, a lack of significant language and cognitive delays, and the presence of restricted interests and behavior. Assessing the prevalence of the disorder is difficult because of the lack of stability in the diagnostic criteria.

Etiology

The cause of Asperger's disorder is unknown, but family studies suggest a possible relation to autistic disorder. The similarity of Asperger's disorder to autistic disorder leads to genetic, metabolic, infectious, and perinatal hypotheses.

Diagnosis and Clinical Features

The clinical features include at least two of the following indications of qualitative social impairment: markedly abnormal nonverbal communicative gestures, the failure to develop peer relationships, the lack of social or emotional reciprocity, and an impaired ability to express pleasure in other people's happiness. Restricted interests and patterns of behavior are always present. According to DSM-IV, the patient shows no language delay, clinically significant cognitive delay, or adaptive impairment (Table 41–8).

Differential Diagnosis

The differential diagnosis includes autistic disorder, pervasive development disorder not otherwise specified, and, in patients approaching adulthood, schizoid personality disorder. According to DSM-IV, the most obvious distinctions between Asperger's disorder and autistic disorder are the criteria about language delay and dysfunction. The lack of language delay is a requirement for Asperger's disorder, but language impairment is a core feature in autistic disorder. Recent studies comparing children with Asperger's disorder and autistic disorder find that those children with Asperger's disorder were more likely to look for social interaction and sought more vigorously to make friends. More efforts seem to be made on the part of those with Asperger's disorder to engage in an activity with another child. Although significant general delay in language is an exclusionary criterion in the diagnosis of Asperger's disorder, some delay in the acquisition of language has been seen in over one third of clinical samples.

Course and Prognosis

Although little is known about the cohort described by the DSM-IV diagnostic criteria, past case reports have shown variable courses and prognoses for patients who have received diagnoses of Asperger's disorder. The factors associated with a good prognosis are a normal IQ and high-level social skills. Anecdotal reports of some adults diagnosed with Asperger's disorder as children show them to be verbal and intelligent; however, they relate in an awkward way to other adults, appear socially uncomfortable and shy, and often have illogical thinking.

Treatment

Treatment depends on the patient's level of adaptive functioning. For those patients with severe social impairment, some of the same techniques used for autistic disorder are likely to be beneficial in the treatment of Asperger's disorder.

PERVASIVE DEVELOPMENTAL DISORDER NOT OTHERWISE SPECIFIED

DSM-IV defines pervasive disorder not otherwise specified as severe, pervasive impairment in social interaction or communication skills or the presence of stereotyped behavior, interests, and activities; however, the criteria for a specific pervasive developmental disorder, schizophrenia, and schizotypal and avoidant personality disorders are not met (Table 41–9). Some children who receive the diagnosis exhibit a markedly restricted repertoire of activities and interest. The condition usually shows a better outcome than does autistic disorder.

Treatment

The treatment approach is basically the same as in autistic disorder. Mainstreaming in school may be possible. Compared with autistic children, those with pervasive developmental disorder not otherwise specified generally have better language skills and more self-awareness, so they are better candidates for psychotherapy.

Table 41–8
DSM-IV Diagnostic Criteria for Asperger's Disorder

A. Qualitative impairment in social interaction, as manifested by at least two of the following:
  (1) marked impairment in the use of multiple nonverbal behaviors such as eye-to-eye gaze, facial expression, body postures, and gestures to regulate social interaction
  (2) failure to develop peer relationships appropriate to developmental level
  (3) a lack of spontaneous seeking to share enjoyment, interests, or achievements with other people (eg, by a lack of showing, bringing, or pointing out objects of interest to other people)
  (4) lack of social or emotional reciprocity
B. Restricted, repetitive, and stereotyped patterns of behavior, interests, and activities, as manifested by at least one of the following:
  (1) encompassing preoccupation with one or more stereotyped and restricted patterns of interest that is abnormal either in intensity or focus
  (2) apparently inflexible adherence to specific, nonfunctional routines or rituals
  (3) stereotyped and repetitive motor mannerisms (eg, hand or finger flapping or twisting, or complex wholebody movements)
  (4) persistent preoccupation with parts of objects
C. The disturbance causes clinically significant impairment in social, occupational, or other important areas of functioning.
D. There is no clinically significant general delay in language (eg, single words used by age 2 years, communicative phrases used by age 3 years).
E. There is no clinically significant delay in cognitive development or in the development of age-appropriate self-help skills, adaptive behavior (other than in social interaction), and curiosity about the environment in childhood.
F. Criteria are not met for another specific pervasive developmental disorder or schizophrenia.

Table 41–9
DSM-IV Diagnostic Criteria for Pervasive Developmental Disorder Not Otherwise Specified

This category should be used when there is a severe and pervasive impairment in the development of reciprocal social interaction or verbal and nonverbal communication skills, or when stereotyped behavior, interests, and activities are present, but the criteria are not met for a specific pervasive developmental disorder, schizophrenia, schizotypal personality disorder, or avoidant personality disorder. For example, this category includes "atypical autism"—presentations that do not meet the criteria for autistic disorder because of late age at onset, atypical symptomatology, or subthreshold symptomatology, or all of these.

REFERENCES

Anderson LT, Campbell M, Adams P, Small AM, Perry R Shell J: The effects of haloperidol on discrimination learning, and behavioral symptoms in autistic children. J Autism Dev Disord *19:* 227, 1989.

Balottin V, Bejor M, Cecchini A, Martelli A, Polazzi S, Lanzi G: Infantile autism and CT brain-scan findings: Specific versus nonspecific abnormalities. J Autism Dev Discord *19:* 109, 1989.

Campbell M, Schopler E, Cueva JE, Hallin A: Treatment of autistic disorder. J Am Acad Child Adolesc Psychiatry *35:* 134, 1996.

Campbell M, Shay J: Pervasive development disorders. In *Comprehensive Textbook of Psychiatry,* ed 6, HI Kaplan, BJ Sadock, editors, p 2277. Williams & Wilkins, Baltimore, 1995.

Cook EH: Autism: Review of neurochemical investigation. Synapse *6:* 292, 1990.

Ghaziuddin M, Tsai LY, Ghaziuddin N: Brief report: A comparison of the diagnostic criteria for Asperger's syndrome. J Autism Dev Disord *22:* 643, 1992.

Hardan A, Johnson K, Johnson C, Hrecznyi B: Case study: Risperidone treatment of children and adolescents with developmental disorders. J Am Acad Child Adolesc Psychiatry *35:* 1551, 1996.

Kazdin AE: Replication and extension of behavioral treatment of autistic disorder. Am J Ment Retard *97:* 377, 1993.

Lord C, Pickles A: Language level and nonverbal social-communicative behaviors in autistic and language delayed children. J Am Acad Child Adolesc Psychiatry *35:*1542, 1996.

McEachin JJ, Smith T, Lovaas OI: Long-term outcome for children with autism who received early intensive behavioral treatment. Am J Ment Retard *97:* 359, 1993.

Mundy P: Normal versus high-functioning status in children with autism. Am J Ment Retard *97:* 381, 1993.

Ozonoff S, Strayer DL: Inhibitory function in nonretarded children with autism. J Autism Dev Disord *27* (1): 59, 1997.

Payton JB, Steele MW, Wenger SL, Minshew NJ: The fragile X marker and autism in perspective. J Am Acad Child Adolesc Psychiatry *28:* 417, 1989.

Perry A: Rett's syndrome: A comprehensive review of the literature. Am J Ment Retard *96:* 275, 1991.

Perry RI, Pataki CS, Munoz DM, Armenteros JL, Silva RR: Pilot trial of risperidone in children with pervasive developmental disorder. Abstract, Proceedings of the American Psychiatric Association Annual Meeting, 1996.

Petty L, Ornitz EM, Michelman JD, Zimmerman EG: Autistic children who become schizophrenic. Arch Gen Psychiatry *41:* 129, 1984.

Pisen J, Berthier ML, Sharkstein SE, Nehme E, Pearlson G, Folstein S: Magnetic resonance imaging: Evidence for a defect of cerebral cortical development in autism. Am J Psychiatry *147:* 734, 1990.

Piven J, Arndt S, Baily J, Andreasen N: Regional brain enlargement in autism: A magnetic resonance imaging study. J Am Acad Child Adolesc Psychiatry *35:* 530, 1996.

Piven J, Harper, Palmer P, Arndt S: Course of behavioral change in autism: A retrospective study of high-IQ adolescents and adults. J Am Acad Child Adolesc Psychiatry *35:* 523, 1996.

Reiss AL, Freund L: Fragile X syndrome, DSM-III-R, and autism. J Am Acad Child Adolesc Psychiatry *29:* 885, 1990.

Rogers SJ, Di Lalla DL: Age of symptom onset in young children with pervasive developmental disorders. J Am Acad Child Adolesc Psychiatry *29:* 863, 1990.

Rutter M: Infantile autism and other pervasive developmental disorders. In *Child and Adolescent Psychiatry: Modern Approaches,* ed 2. M Rutter, L Hersov, editors, p 545. Blackwell, Oxford, England, 1985.

Sanchez LE, Campbell M, Small AM, Cueva JE, Armenteros JL, Adams PB: A pilot study of clomipramine in young autistic children. J Am Acad Child Adolesc Psychiatry *35:* 537, 1996.

Sponheim E: Changing criteria of autistic disorders: A comparison of the ICD-10 research criteria and DSM-IV with DSM-III–R, CARS, and ABC. J Autism Dev Disord *26* (5): 513, 1996.

Tsai LY: Is Rett's syndrome a subtype of pervasive development disorders? J Autism Dev Disord *22:* 551, 1992.

Volkmar FR: Childhood disintegrative disorder: Issues for DSM-IV. J Autism Dev Disord *22:* 625, 1992.

Volkmar FR, Cooke E, Lord C, Leventhal B, et al: Autism and related conditions. J Am Acad Child Adolesc Psychiatry *35* (4): 401, 1996.

Warren RP, Cole P, Odell D, Pingree CB, Warren WL, White E, Yonk J, Singh VK: Detection of maternal antibodies in infantile autism. J Am Acad Child Adolesc Psychiatry *29:* 873, 1990.

Waterhouse L, Morris R, Allen D, Dunn M, et al: Diagnosis and classification in autism. J Autism Dev Disord *26* (1): 59, 1996.

42

Attention-Deficit Disorders

ATTENTION-DEFICIT/ HYPERACTIVITY DISORDER

According to the fourth edition of *Diagnostic and Statistical Manual of Mental Disorders* (DSM-IV), attention-deficit/hyperactivity disorder (ADHD) is a ''persistent pattern of inattention and/or hyperactivity'' more frequent and severe than is typical of children at a similar level of development. Some symptoms must have been apparent before the age of 7 years, although many children are diagnosed after the symptoms have been obvious for several years. Impairment must be present in at least two settings, and interference with developmentally appropriate functioning must occur in social, academic, or work settings. The disorder must not take place in the course of a pervasive developmental disorder, schizophrenia, or other psychotic disorder and must not be better accounted for by another mental disorder.

The disorder is common, appears more often in boys than in girls, and causes disruption in school and at home. It is characterized by a developmentally inappropriate poor attention span, age-inappropriate features of hyperactivity and impulsivity, or both. To meet the diagnostic criteria, the disorder must be present for at least 6 months, cause impairment in academic or social functioning, and occur before the age of 7 years. According to (DSM-IV), the diagnosis is made by confirming numerous symptoms in the inattention domain, the hyperactivity-impulsivity domain, or both. Thus, a child may qualify for the disorder with symptoms of inattention only or with symptoms of hyperactivity and impulsivity but not inattention. Some children exhibit multiple symptoms along both dimensions. Accordingly, DSM-IV lists three subtypes of ADHD—predominantly inattentive type, predominantly hyperactive-impulsive type, and combined type. To meet DSM-IV criteria, there must be a presence of symptoms in two or more situations, such as at school, home, and work. The disorder has been identified in the literature for many years under a variety of terms. In the early 1900s, impulsive, disinhibited, and hyperactive children—many of whom had neurological damage caused by encephalitis—were grouped under the label *hyperactive syndrome.* In the 1960s, a heterogeneous group of children with poor coordination, learning disabilities, and emotional lability, but without specific neurological damage, were described as having minimal brain damage. Since then, other hypotheses have been put forth to explain the origin of the disorder, such as a genetically based condition reflecting an abnormal level of arousal and poor ability to modulate emotions. This theory was initially supported by the observation that stimulant medications help produce sustained attention and improve these children's ability to focus on a given task. Currently, no single factor is believed to cause the disorder, although many environmental variables may contribute to it and many predictable clinical features are associated with it.

Epidemiology

Reports on the incidence of ADHD in the United States have varied from 2 to 20 percent of grade-school children. A conservative figure is about 3 to 5 percent of prepubertal elementary school children. In Great Britain the incidence is reported to be lower than in the United States, less than 1 percent. ADHD is more prevalent in boys than in girls, with the ratio ranging from 3 to 1 to as much as 5 to 1. The disorder is most common in firstborn boys. Siblings of probands with ADHD are at high risk to develop it, as well as to develop other disorders, including disruptive behavior disorders, anxiety disorders, and depressive disorders. Siblings of children with ADHD are also more likely than others to score more poorly on tests of academic achievement and to show evidence of school failures. The parents of children with ADHD show an increased incidence of hyperkinesis, sociopathy, alcohol use disorders, and conversion disorder. Although the onset is usually by the age of 3, the diagnosis is generally not made until the child is in elementary school and the formal learning situation requires structured behavioral patterns, including developmentally appropriate attention span and concentration.

Etiology

The causes of ADHD are unknown. Most children with ADHD do not show evidence of gross structural damage in the central nervous system (CNS). Conversely, most children with known neurological disorders caused by brain injuries do not display attention deficits and hyperactivity. Despite the lack of a specific neurophysiological or neurochemical basis for the disorder, it is predictably associated with a variety of other disorders that affect brain function, such as learning disorders. The suggested contributory factors for ADHD include prenatal toxic exposures, prematurity, and prenatal mechanical insult to the fetal nervous system.

Food additives, colorings, preservatives, and sugar have also been suggested as possible causes of hyperactive behavior. No scientific evidence indicates that these factors cause ADHD.

Genetic Factors. Evidence for a genetic basis for ADHD includes the greater concordance in monozygotic than in dizygotic twins. Also, siblings of hyperactive children have about twice the risk of having the disorder as does the general population. One sibling may predominantly have hyperactivity symptoms, and others may predominantly have inattention symptoms. Biological parents of children with the disorder have a higher risk for ADHD than do adoptive parents. When ADHD coexists with conduct disorder in a child, alcohol use disorders and antisocial personality disorder are more common in the parents than in the general population.

Developmental Factors. There is some evidence that September is the peak month for births of ADHD children with and without comorbid learning disorders. The implication is that prenatal exposure to winter infections during the first trimester may contribute to the emergence of ADHD symptoms in some susceptible children.

BRAIN DAMAGE. It has long been speculated that some children affected by ADHD received minimal and subtle brain damage to the CNS during their fetal and perinatal periods. The brain damage may also have been caused by adverse circulatory, toxic, metabolic, mechanical, and other effects, and by stress and physical insult to the brain during early infancy caused by infection, inflammation, and trauma. Nonfocal (soft) neurological signs are frequent.

Neurochemical Factors. Many neurotransmitters have been associated with ADHD symptoms. It is well known from animal studies that the locus ceruleus, consisting of mainly noradrenergic neurons, plays a major role in attention. The noradrenergic system consists of the central system (originating in the locus ceruleus), and the peripheral sympathetic system. The peripheral noradrenergic system may be of more importance in ADHD. Thus, a dysfunction in peripheral epinephrine, which causes the hormone to accumulate peripherally, could potentially feed back to the central system and ''reset'' the locus ceruleus to a lower level. In part, hypotheses about the neurochemistry of the disorder have arisen from the impact of many medications that exert a positive effect on it. The most widely studied drugs in the treatment of ADHD, the stimulants, affect both dopamine and norepinephrine, leading to neurotransmitter hypotheses that include possible dysfunction in both the adrenergic and the dopaminergic systems. Stimulants increase catecholamines by promoting their release and by blocking their uptake. Stimulants and some tricyclic drugs—for example, desipramine (Norpramin)—reduce urinary 3-methoxy-4-hydroxyphenylglycol (MHPG), which is a metabolite of norepinephrine. Clonidine (Catapres), a norepinephrine agonist, has been helpful in treating hyperactivity. Other drugs that have reduced hyperactivity include tricyclic drugs and monoamine oxidase inhibitors (MAOIs). Overall, no clear-cut evidence implicates a single neurotransmitter in the development ADHD, but many neurotransmitters may be involved in the process.

Neurophysiological Factors. The human brain normally undergoes major growth spurts at several ages: 3 to 10 months, 2 to 4 years, 6 to 8 years, 10 to 12 years, and 14 to 16 years. Some children have a maturational delay in the sequence and manifest symptoms of ADHD which appear to normalize by about age 5. A physiological correlate is the presence of a variety of nonspecific abnormal electroencephalogram (EEG) patterns that are disorganized and characteristic of young children. In some cases the EEG findings normalize over time. A recent study of quantitative EEGs in children with ADHD, in children with undifferentiated attentional problems, and in normal controls indicates that both groups with attentional problems evidence increased beta band relative percentages and decreased rare tone P3000 amplitudes. Increased beta band percentage or decreased delta band percentage is associated with increased arousal.

Computed tomographic (CT) head scans in children with ADHD show no consistent findings. Studies using positron emission tomography (PET) have found decreased cerebral blood flow and metabolic rates in the frontal lobe areas of children with ADHD compared with controls. PET scans have also shown that adolescent females with the disorder have globally reduced glucose metabolism compared both with normal control females and males and with males with the disorder. One theory explains these findings by supposing that the frontal lobes in children with ADHD are not adequately performing their inhibitory mechanism on lower structures, an effect leading to disinhibition.

Psychosocial Factors. Children in institutions are frequently overactive and have poor attention spans. These signs result from prolonged emotional deprivation, and they disappear when deprivational factors are removed, such as through adoption or placement in a foster home. Stressful psychic events, a disruption of family equilibrium, and other anxiety-inducing factors contribute to the initiation or perpetuation of ADHD. Predisposing factors may include the child's temperament, genetic-familial factors, and the demands of society to adhere to a routinized way of behaving and performing. Socioeconomic status does not seem to be a predisposing factor.

Diagnosis

The principal sign of hyperactivity should alert clinicians to the possibility of ADHD. A detailed prenatal history of a child's early developmental patterns and direct observation usually reveal excessive motor activity. Hyperactivity may occur in some situations (for example, school) but not in others (for example, one-to-one interviews and television watching), and it may be less obvious in structured than in unstructured situations. To diagnose the disorder, however, the hyperactivity should not be an isolated, brief, and transient behavioral manifestation under stress but should have been present over a long time. According to DSM-IV, symptoms must be present in at least two settings (for example, school and home) to meet the diagnostic criteria for ADHD (Table 42–1).

Other distinguishing features of ADHD are short attention span and easy distractibility. In school, children with ADHD cannot follow instructions and often demand extra attention from their teachers. At home, they often do not comply with their parents' requests. They act impulsively, show emotional lability, and are explosive and irritable.

Children who have hyperactivity as a predominant feature are more likely to be referred for treatment than are children with primarily symptoms of attention deficit. Children with the

Table 42–1
DSM-IV Diagnostic Criteria for Attention-Deficit/Hyperactivity Disorder

A. Either (1) or (2):
  (1) six (or more) of the following symptoms of **inattention** have persisted for at least 6 months to a degree that is maladaptive and inconsistent with developmental level:

  Inattention
  (a) often fails to give close attention to details or makes careless mistakes in schoolwork, work, or other activities
  (b) often has difficulty sustaining attention in tasks or play activities
  (c) often does not seem to listen when spoken to directly
  (d) often does not follow through on instructions and fails to finish schoolwork, chores, or duties in the workplace (and due to oppositional behavior or failure to understand instructions)
  (e) often has difficulty organizing tasks and activities
  (f) often avoids, dislikes, or is reluctant to engage in tasks that require sustained mental effort (such as schoolwork or homework)
  (g) often loses things necessary for tasks or activities (eg, toys, school assignments, pencils, books, or tools)
  (h) is often easily distracted by extraneous stimuli
  (i) is often forgetful in daily activities

  (2) six (or more) of the following symptoms of **hyperactivity-impulsivity** have persisted for at least 6 months to a degree that is maladaptive and inconsistent with developmental level:
  Hyperactivity
  (a) often fidgets with hands or feet or squirms in seat
  (b) often leaves seat in classroom or in other situations in which remaining seated is expected
  (c) often runs about or climbs excessively in situations in which it is inappropriate (in adolescents or adults, may be linked to subjective feelings of restlessness)
  (d) often has difficulty playing or engaging in leisure activities quietly
  (e) is often "on the go" or often acts as if "driven by a motor"
  (f) often talks excessively
  Impulsivity
  (g) often blurts out answers before questions have been completed
  (h) often has difficulty awaiting turn
  (i) often interrupts or intrudes on others (eg, butts into conversations or games)

B. Some hyperactive-impulsive or inattentive symptoms that caused impairment were present before age 7 years.

C. Some impairment from the symptoms is present in two or more settings (eg, at school [or work] and at home).

D. There must be clear evidence of clinically significant impairment in social, academic, or occupational functioning.

E. The symptoms do not occur exclusively during the course of a pervasive developmental disorder, schizophrenia, or other psychotic disorder and are not better accounted for by another mental disorder (eg, mood disorder, anxiety disorder, dissociative disorder, or a personality disorder).

Code based on type:
Attention-deficit/hyperactivity disorder, combined type: if the criteria A1 and A2 are met for the past 6 months
Attention-deficit/hyperactivity disorder, predominantly inattentive type: if criterion A1 is met but criterion A2 is not met for the past 6 months
Attention-deficit/hyperactivity disorder, predominantly by active-impulsive type: if criterion A2 is met but criterion A1 is not met for the past 6 months
Coding note: For individuals (especially adolescents and adults) who currently have symptoms that no longer meet full criteria, "in partial remission" should be specified.

Reprinted with permission from American Psychiatric Association: *Diagnostic and Statistical Manual of Mental Disorders,* ed 4. Copyright, American Psychiatric Association, Washington, 1994.

predominantly hyperactive-impulsive type are more likely to have a stable diagnosis over time and are more likely to have concurrent conduct disorder than are children with the predominantly inattentive type without hyperactivity. Disorders involving reading, arithmetic, language, and coordination may occur in association with ADHD. A child's history may give clues to prenatal (including genetic), natal, and postnatal factors that may have affected the CNS structure or function. Rates of development, deviations in development, and parental reactions to significant or stressful behavioral transitions should be ascertained, as they may help clinicians determine the degree to which parents have contributed to or reacted to a child's inefficiencies and dysfunctions.

School history and teachers' reports are important in evaluating whether a child's difficulties in learning and school behavior are primarily due to the child's attitudinal or maturational problems or to poor self-image because of felt inadequacies. These reports may also reveal how the child has handled these problems. How the child has related to siblings, to peers, to adults, and to free and structured activities gives valuable diagnostic clues to the presence of ADHD and helps identify the complications of the disorder.

The mental status examination may show a secondarily depressed mood but no thought disturbance, impaired reality testing, or inappropriate affect. A child may show great distractibility, perseveration, and a concrete and literal mode of thinking. Indications of visual-perceptual, auditory-perceptual, language, or cognition problems may be present. Occasionally, evidence appears of a basic, pervasive, organically based anxiety, often referred to as *body anxiety.* A neurological examination may reveal visual, motor, perceptual, or auditory discriminatory immaturity or impairments without overt signs of visual or auditory acuity disorders. Children may have problems with motor coordination and difficulties in copying age-appropriate figures, rapid alternating movements, right-left discrimination, ambidexterity, reflex asymmetries, and a variety of subtle nonfocal neurological signs (soft signs).

Clinician's should obtain an EEG to recognize the child with frequent bilaterally synchronous discharges resulting in short absence spells. Such a child may react in school with hyperactivity out of sheer frustration. The child with an unrecognized temporal lobe seizure focus can have a secondary behavior disorder. In these instances, several features of

ADHD are often present. Identification of the focus requires an EEG obtained during drowsiness and during sleep.

Clinical Features

ADHD may have its onset in infancy. Infants with the disorder are unduly sensitive to stimuli and are easily upset by noise, light, temperature, and other environmental changes. At times, the reverse occurs, and the children are placid and limp, sleep much of the time, and appear to develop slowly in the first months of life. More commonly, however, infants with ADHD are active in the crib, sleep little, and cry a great deal. They are far less likely than are normal children to reduce their locomotor activity when their environment is structured by social limits.

In school, ADHD children may rapidly attack a test but may answer only the first two questions. They may be unable to wait to be called on in school and may respond before everyone else. At home, they cannot be put off for even a minute. Children with ADHD are often explosive or irritable. The irritability may be set off by relatively minor stimuli, which may puzzle and dismay the children. They are frequently emotionally labile and easily set off to laughter or to tears; their mood and performance are apt to be variable and unpredictable. Impulsiveness and an inability to delay gratification are characteristic. Children are often accident-prone.

Concomitant emotional difficulties are frequent. The fact that other children grow out of this behavior but children with ADHD do not grow out of it at the same time and rate may lead to adults' dissatisfaction and pressure. The resulting negative self-concept and reactive hostility are worsened by the children's recognition that they have problems.

The characteristics of children with the disorder that are most often cited are, in order of frequency, hyperactivity, perceptual motor impairment, emotional lability, general coordination deficit, attention deficit (short attention span, distractibility, perseveration, failure to finish tasks, inattention, poor concentration), impulsivity (action before thought, abrupt shifts in activity, lack of organization, jumping up in class), memory and thinking deficits, specific learning disabilities, speech and hearing deficits, and equivocal neurological signs and EEG irregularities. About 75 percent of children with ADHD fairly consistently show behavioral symptoms of aggression and defiance. But, whereas defiance and aggression are generally associated with adverse intrafamily relationships, hyperactivity is more closely related to impaired performance on cognitive tests requiring concentration.

Some studies claim that some relatives of hyperactive children show features of antisocial personality disorder. School difficulties, both learning and behavioral, are common; they sometimes come from concomitant communication disorders or learning disorders, or from the child's distractibility and fluctuating attention, which hampers the acquisition, retention, and display of knowledge. These difficulties are noted especially on group tests. The adverse reactions of school personnel to the behavior characteristics of ADHD and the lowering of self-regard because of felt inadequacies may combine with the adverse comments of peers to make school a place of unhappy defeat. This situation may lead to acting-out antisocial behavior and self-defeating, self-punitive behaviors.

Tony was a 7-year-old boy who was referred for evaluation when his teacher could no longer manage him in her second grade class. Tony was not only oppositional and unable to sit in his seat, but he was constantly arguing and fighting with his peers. Tony was a verbal and active child who seemed to be learning in spite of his lack of attention and his apparent lack of motivation. Although his teacher thought that Tony started most of the fights that he got into at school, his parents knew that Tony felt disliked by his peers and "picked on" by his teacher. At home, Tony was the most difficult of three brothers. He was the middle child with one brother 2 years older and one brother 2 years younger.

When questioned about the pregnancy and Tony's neonatal history, his mother only mentioned a severe viral infection that she had undergone during her second month of pregnancy. Tony had been born in September, 1 month earlier than planned. He was healthy throughout the neonatal period, but had been a poor sleeper, never sleeping more than 6 hours without waking. He was usually awake between 5 and 6 in the morning, and he was just not tired. In the first grade Tony had undergone some of the same problems that he was experiencing in the second grade, but his teacher had always made special efforts to seat him in the front of the room and to give him more individual attention than some other students. This strategy had seemed to help tremendously in the first grade. In spite of the extra attention, however, even in the first grade Tony had exhibited several areas of weakness, such as reading and writing letters. His letters were often backwards or misformed. On intellectual testing, Tony had a full scale intelligence quotient (IQ) of 105 with little scatter across verbal and performance subtests. Tony was evaluated psychiatrically and by his school psychologist, who thought that he showed signs of having poor self-esteem. Tony met the DSM-IV criteria for ADHD, oppositional-defiant disorder, and reading disorder. After requiring an advocate to attend the Individualized Educational Plan meeting, the school district agreed to place Tony in a smaller, self-contained classroom with a student-to-teacher ratio of 12 to 1. Tony was started on methylphenidate (Ritalin) 10 mg in the morning and 10 mg at noon, titrated to 15 mg in the morning and 15 mg at noon. The medication was very helpful in keeping Tony in his seat for longer periods, and he was even able to get along with peers more comfortably. A social skills group therapy recommended for Tony included boys his age who exhibited attentional problems and disturbances of conduct. Finally, his family was referred for short-term family therapy with the goals of helping Tony and his brothers to relate more supportively and to help the parents to model appropriate problem-solving behavior.

Pathology and Laboratory Examination. No specific laboratory measures are pathognomonic of ADHD. Several laboratory measures often yield nonspecific abnormal results in hyperactive children, such as a disorganized, immature result on an EEG, and PET may show decreased cerebral blood flow in the frontal regions. Cognitive testing helping to confirm a child's inattention and impulsivity includes the continuous performance task, in which a child is asked to press a button each time a particular sequence of letters or numbers is flashed on a screen. Children with poor attention make errors of omission—that is, they fail to press the button, even when the sequence has flashed. Impulsivity is manifested by errors of commission, in which children are unable to resist pushing the button, even though the desired sequence has not yet appeared on the screen.

Differential Diagnosis

A temperamental constellation consisting of high activity level and short attention span, but in the normal range of expectation for a child's age, should be first considered. Differentiating these temperamental characteristics from the cardinal symptoms of ADHD before the age of 3 is difficult, mainly because of the overlapping features of a normally immature nervous system and the emerging signs of visual-motor-perceptual impairments frequently seen in ADHD. Anxiety in a child needs to be evaluated. Anxiety may accompany ADHD as a secondary feature, and anxiety alone may be manifested by overactivity and easy distractibility.

Many children with ADHD have secondary depression in reaction to their continuing frustration over their failure to learn and their consequent low self-esteem. This condition must be distinguished from a primary depressive disorder, which is likely to be distinguished by hypoactivity and withdrawal. Mania and ADHD share many core features such as excessive verbalization, motoric hyperactivity, and high levels of distractibility. Additionally, in children with mania, irritability seems to be more common than is euphoria. Although mania and ADHD can coexist, in children with bipolar I disorder there is more waxing and waning of symptoms than in ADHD. Recent follow-up data for children who met the criteria for ADHD and subsequently developed bipolar disorder suggest that certain clinical features occurring during the course of ADHD are predictive of future mania. ADHD in children with developed bipolar I disorder at a 4-year follow-up had a greater co-occurrence of additional disorders and a greater family history of bipolar disorders and other mood disorders than did children without bipolar disorder.

Frequently, conduct disorder and ADHD coexist, and both must be diagnosed. Learning disorders of various kinds must also be distinguished from ADHD; a child may be unable to read or to do mathematics because of a learning disorder, rather than because of inattention. ADHD often coexists with one or more learning disorders, including reading disorder, mathematics disorder, and disorder of written expression.

Course and Prognosis

The course of ADHD is highly variable. Symptoms may persist into adolescence or adult life; they may remit at puberty; or the hyperactivity may disappear, but the decreased attention span and impulse-control problems may persist. Overactivity is usually the first symptom to remit, and distractibility is the last. In a recent 4-year follow-up study, ADHD was generally persistent. Persistence was predicted by a family history of the disorder, negative life events, and comorbidity with conduct symptoms, depression, and anxiety disorders. Remission is unlikely before the age of 12. When remission does occur, it is usually between the ages of 12 and 20. Remission may be accompanied by a productive adolescence and adult life, satisfying interpersonal relationships, and few significant sequelae. Most patients with the disorder, however, undergo partial remission and are vulnerable to antisocial behavior, substance use disorders, and mood disorders. Learning problems often continue throughout life.

In about 15 to 20 percent of cases, symptoms persist into adulthood. Those with the disorder may show diminished hyperactivity but remain impulsive and accident-prone. Although their educational attainments are lower than those of people without ADHD, their early employment histories are not different from those of people with similar educations.

Children with the disorder whose symptoms persist into adolescence are at high risk for developing conduct disorder. Approximately 50 percent of children with conduct disorder develop antisocial personality disorder in adulthood. Children with both ADHD and conduct disorder are also at risk for developing a substance-related disorder. The development of substance abuse disorders during adolescence appears to be related to the presence of conduct disorder rather than to the ADHD alone.

Most children with ADHD have some social difficulties. Socially dysfunctional children with ADHD have significantly higher rates of comorbid psychiatric disorders and experience more problems with behavior in school as well as with peers and family members. Overall, the outcome of ADHD in childhood seems to be related to the amount of persistent comorbid psychopathology, especially conduct disorder, social disability, and chaotic family factors. Optimal outcomes may be promoted by ameliorating children's social functioning, diminishing aggression, and improving family situations as early as possible.

Treatment

Pharmacotherapy. The pharmacological agents most often used for ADHD are the CNS stimulants, primarily dextroamphetamine (Dexedrine), methylphenidate, and pemoline (Cylert). Other classes of medications that have been used for the disorder include tricyclic antidepressants, antipsychotics, clonidine, serotonin-specific reuptake inhibitors (SSRIs), and bupropion (Wellbutrin). The Food and Drug Administration (FDA) approves the use of dextroamphetamine in children 3 years old and older and methylphenidate in those 6 years old and older; these are the two most commonly used drugs.

The precise mechanism of the stimulant's action remains unknown. The idea of paradoxical response by hyperactive children is no longer accepted. Methylphenidate has been shown to be highly effective in up to three quarters of all children with ADHD and to have relatively few side effects. Methylphenidate is a short-acting medication that is generally used to be effective during school hours, so that children with the disorder can attend to tasks and remain in the classroom. The drug's most common side effects include headaches, stomachaches, nausea, and insomnia. Some children experience a rebound effect, in which they become mildly irritable and appear to be slightly hyperactive for a brief period when the medication wears off. In children with a history of motor tics, some caution must be used; in some cases, methylphenidate may cause an exacerbation of the tic disorder. Another common concern about methylphenidate is whether it causes some growth suppression. During periods of use, methylphenidate is associated with growth suppression, but children tend to make up the growth when they are given drug holidays in the summer or on weekends. An important question about using methylphenidate is how much it normalizes school performance. A recent study found that about 75 percent of a group of hyperactive children exhibited a significant improvement in their ability to pay attention in class and on measures of academic efficiency when treated with methylphenidate. The drug has been shown to improve hyperactive children's scores on tasks of vigilance, such as the continuous performance task and paired associations.

Dextroamphetamine is usually the second line of pharmacological treatment when methylphenidate is not effective. Pemoline has the advantage of a longer half-life and thereby allows less frequent dosing and round-the-clock effects, but there have been some recent reports of serious liver failure in patients being treated with pemoline.

Antidepressants—including imipramine (Tofranil), desipramine, and nortriptyline (Pamelor)—have been used to treat the disorder with some success. In children with comorbid anxiety disorders or depressive disorders and in children in whom tic disorders preclude the use of stimulants, antidepressants may be beneficial, although, for hyperactivity, stimulants are more efficacious. Antidepressants require careful cardiac function monitoring. The report of sudden death in at least four children with ADHD who were being treated with desipramine has made the tricyclic antidepressants a less likely choice. The reasons that the deaths occurred is unclear, but they reinforce the need for close follow-up of any child receiving a tricyclic drug. A recent study of children with the disorder and depressive symptoms who were taking methylphenidate and desipramine simultaneously found that the combination enhanced the children's abilities to use visual search strategies on such cognitive tasks as comparing several pictures with subtle differences—for example, the matching familiar faces task.

Clonidine has also been used in the treatment of ADHD with some degree of success. It may be especially helpful in cases in which patients also have tic disorders. Antipsychotics may be efficacious for some children with the disorder, but with the alternative medications available and the risk for tardive dyskinesia, withdrawal dyskinesia, and neuroleptic malignant syndrome, antipsychotics are less desirable. There are little data to confirm the efficacy of SSRIs in the treatment of ADHD, but because of the comorbidity of depression and anxiety with the disorder, these drugs are often considered.

Bupropion has been used as both an antidepressant and in the treatment of the disorder. A recent multisite, double-blind, placebo-controlled study confirmed the efficacy of bupropion compared with placebo. Further studies comparing bupropion with other stimulants have not yet been done. Although there was initial concern about the risk for seizures, such risks are not significantly different from other antidepressants when the drug is used in dosages of less than 450 mg per day. Overall, stimulants remain the first drug of choice in the pharmacological treatment of ADHD.

EVALUATION OF THERAPEUTIC PROGRESS. Monitoring starts with the initiation of medication. Because school performance is most markedly affected, special attention and effort should be given to establishing and maintaining a close collaborative working relation with a child's school. In most patients, stimulants reduce overactivity, distractibility, impulsiveness, explosiveness, and irritability. No evidence indicates that medications directly improve any existing impairments in learning, although, when the attention deficits diminish, children can learn more effectively than in the past. In addition, medication can improve self-esteem when children are no longer constantly reprimanded for their behavior.

Psychotherapy. Medication alone is often not enough to satisfy the comprehensive therapeutic needs of children with the disorder and is usually but one facet of a multimodality regimen. Individual psychotherapy, behavior modification, parental counseling, and the treatment of any coexisting learning disorder may be necessary. When taking medication, children should be given the opportunity to explore the meaning of the medication. Doing so helps dispel misconceptions (such as, "I'm crazy") about medication use and makes it clear that the medication helps the child handle situations better than before. When children are helped to structure their environment, their anxiety diminishes. Therefore, parents and teachers should set up a predictable structure of reward and punishment; they should use a behavior therapy model and apply it to the physical, temporal, and interpersonal environment.

An almost universal requirement of therapy is to help parents recognize that permissiveness based on a default attitude about the child's inability to take responsibility is not helpful. Parents should also be aided to recognize that, in spite of their children's deficiencies in some areas, they face the normal tasks of maturation, including the need to take responsibility and to develop a sense of mastery. Therefore, children with ADHD do not benefit from being exempted from the requirements, expectations, and planning applicable to other children. Parental training is an integral part of the psychotherapeutic interventions applicable to ADHD. The basis of most parental training is to help parents develop usable behavioral interventions with positive reinforcement, which targets both social and academic behaviors.

Group therapy aimed at refining social skills as well as increasing self-esteem and a sense of success may be very useful for children with ADHD who have great difficulties functioning in group settings, especially in school. A recent year-long group therapy intervention in a clinical setting for

Table 42–2
DSM-IV Diagnostic Criteria for Attention-Deficit/Hyperactivity Disorder Not Otherwise Specified

Category is for disorders with prominent symptoms of inattention or hyperactivity-impulsivity that do not meet criteria for attention-deficit/hyperactivity disorder.

boys with the disorder described the goals as helping the boys improve skills in game playing and feeling a sense of mastery with peers. The boys were first asked to do a fun task in pairs and then were gradually asked to do projects in a group. They were directed about following instructions, waiting, and paying attention, while being praised for successful cooperation. This level of highly structured group therapeutic ''play'' is developmentally appropriate for these children, who benefit from increased ability to participate in any group activities.

ATTENTION-DEFICIT/HYPERACTIVITY DISORDER NOT OTHERWISE SPECIFIED

DSM-IV includes attention-deficit/hyperactivity disorder not otherwise specified as a residual category for disturbances with prominent symptoms of inattention or hyperactivity that do not meet the criteria for ADHD (Table 42–2).

The incidence of adult manifestations of ADHD is unknown, but there are many more cases than were previously

Table 42–3
ICD-10 Diagnostic Criteria for Hyperkinetic Disorders

Note: The research diagnosis of hyperkinetic disorder requires the definite presence of abnormal levels of inattention, hyperactivity, and restlessness that are pervasive across situations and persistent over time and that are not caused by other disorders such as autism or affective disorders.

G1. *Inattention.* At least six of the following symptoms of inattention have persisted for at least 6 months, to a degree that is maladaptive and inconsistent with the developmental level of the child:
(1) often fails to give close attention to details, or makes careless errors in schoolwork, work, or other activities;
(2) often fails to sustain attention in tasks or play activities;
(3) often appears not to listen to what is being said to him or her;
(4) often fails to follow through on instructions or to finish schoolwork, chores, or duties in the workplace (not because of oppositional behavior or failure to understand instructions);
(5) is often impaired in organizing tasks and activities;
(6) often avoids or strongly dislikes tasks, such as homework, that require sustained mental effort;
(7) often loses things necessary for certain tasks or activities, such as school assignments, pencils, books, toys, or tools;
(8) is often easily distracted by external stimuli;
(9) is often forgetful in the course of daily activities.

G2. *Hyperactivity.* At least three of the following symptoms of hyperactivity have persisted for at least 6 months, to a degree that is maladaptive and inconsistent with the developmental level of the child:
(1) often fidgets with hands or feet or squirms on seat;
(2) leaves seat in classroom or in other situations in which remaining seated is expected;
(3) often runs about or climbs excessively in situations in which it is inappropriate (in adolescents or adults, only feelings of restlessness may be present);
(4) is often unduly noisy in playing or has difficulty in engaging quietly in leisure activities;
(5) exhibits a persistent pattern of excessive motor activity that is not substantially modified by social context or demands.

G3. *Impulsivity.* At least one of the following symptoms of impulsivity has persisted for at least 6 months, to a degree that is maladaptive and inconsistent with the developmental level of the child:
(1) often blurts out answers before questions have been completed;
(2) often fails to wait in lines or await turns in games or group situations;
(3) often interrupts or intrudes on others (eg, butts into others' conversations or games);
(4) often talks excessively without appropriate response to social constraints.

G4. Onset of the disorder is no later than the age of 7 years.

G5. *Pervasiveness.* The criteria should be met for more than a single situation, eg, the combination of inattention and hyperactivity should be present both at home and at school, or at both school and another setting where children are observed, such as a clinic. (Evidence for cross-situationality will ordinarily require information from more than one source; parental reports about classroom behavior, for instance, are unlikely to be sufficient.)

G6. The symptoms in G1–G3 cause clinically significant distress or impairment in social, academic, or occupational functioning.

G7. The disorder does not meet the criteria for pervasive developmental disorders, manic episode, depressive episode, or anxiety disorders.

Comments
Many authorities also recognize conditions that are subthreshold for hyperkinetic disorder. Children who meet criteria in other ways but do not show abnormalities of hyperactivity-impulsiveness may be recognized as showing *attention deficit*; conversely, children who fall short of criteria for attention problems but meet criteria in other respects may be recognized as showing *activity disorder.* In the same way, children who meet criteria for only one situation (eg, only the home or only the classroom) may be regarded as showing a *home-specific* or *classroom-specific disorder.* These conditions are not yet included in the main classification because of insufficient empirical predictive validation, and because many children with subthreshold disorders show other syndromes (such as oppositional defiant disorder) and should be classified in the appropriate category.

Disturbance of activity and attention
The general criteria for hyperkinetic disorder must be met, but not those for conduct disorders.

Hyperkinetic conduct disorder
The general criteria for both hyperkinetic disorder and conduct disorders must be met.

Other hyperkinetic disorders

Hyperkinetic disorder, unspecified
This residual category is not recommended and should be used only when there is a lack of differentiation between disturbance of activity and attention and hyperkinetic conduct disorder but the overall criteria for hyperkinetic disorders are fulfilled.

Reprinted with permission from World Health Organization: *The ICD-10 Classification of Mental and Behavioural Disorders: Diagnostic Criteria for Research.* Copyright, World Health Organization, Geneva, 1993.

thought or diagnosed. This category of illness is being more frequently diagnosed and requires much greater attention and study. In adults, residual signs of the disorder include impulsivity and attention deficit (for example, difficulty in organizing and completing work, inability to concentrate, increased distractibility, and sudden decision making without a thought of the consequences). Many people with the disorder suffer from a secondary depressive disorder that is associated with low self-esteem related to their impaired performance and that affects both occupational and social functioning. The treatment of the disorder involves the use of amphetamines (5 to 60 mg a day) or methylphenidate (5 to 60 mg a day). Signs of a positive response are an increased attention span, decreased impulsiveness, and improved mood. Psychopharmacological therapy may need to be continued indefinitely. Because of the abuse potential of the drugs, clinicians should monitor drug response and patient compliance.

ICD-10

The 10th revision of *International Statistical Classification of Diseases and Related Health Problems* (ICD-10), the category of hyperkinetic disorders includes disturbance of activity and attention (which in turn encompasses attention-deficit disorder or syndrome with hyperactivity, ADHD), hyperkinetic conduct disorder, other hyperkinetic disorders, and hyperkinetic disorder, unspecified. According to ICD-10, hyperkinetic disorders are characterized by ''early onset; a combination of overactive, poorly modulated behavior with marked inattention and lack of persistent task involvement; and pervasiveness over situations and persistence over time.''

Hyperkinetic disorders typically feature impaired attention and overactivity, both of which must be present for the diagnosis to be made and both of which should occur in more than one situation. The associated features of hyperkinetic disorders include ''disinhibition in social relationships, recklessness in situations involving some danger, and impulsive flouting of social rules.'' These features are neither necessary nor sufficient for the diagnosis of hyperkinetic disorders, but they help to sustain the diagnosis. The disorders can be diagnosed in adulthood. Acute onset of hyperactive behavior in a school-age child is probably caused by a reactive disorder, manic state, schizophrenia, or neurological disease, not by hyperkinetic disorders.

Subdivisions of hyperkinetic disorders are uncertain, according to ICD-10, but ''follow-up studies show that the outcome in adolescence and adult life is much influenced by whether . . . there is associated aggression, delinquency, or dissocial behavior.'' Therefore, the hyperkinetic disorders are determined by the presence or absence of these associated features. The ICD-10 criteria for hyperkinetic disorders are given in Table 42–3.

REFERENCES

Arnold LE, Jensen PS: Attention-deficit hyperactivity disorders: Adult manifestations. In *Comprehensive Textbook of Psychiatry,* ed 6, HI Kaplan, BJ Sadock, editors, p 2295. Williams & Wilkins, Baltimore, 1995.

Biederman J, Baldessarini RJ, Wright V, Keenan K, Faraone S: A double-blind placebo controlled study of desipramine in the treatment of ADD. III. Lack of impact of comorbidity and family history factors on clinical response. J Am Acad Child Adolesc Psychiatry *32:* 199, 1993.

Biederman J, Faraone S, Mick E, Wozniak J, Chen L, Oullette C, Marrs A, Moore P, Garcia J, Mennin D, Lelon E: Attention-deficit hyperactivity disorder and juvenile mania: An overlooked comorbidity? Am Acad Child Adolesc Psychiatry *35:* 997, 1996.

Biederman J, Munir K, Knee D, Armentano M, Auter S, Waternaux C, Tsuang M: High rate of affective disorders in probands with attention deficit disorder and in their relatives: A controlled family study. Am J Psychiatry *144:* 330, 1987.

Biederman J, Wilens T, Mick E, Faraone SV, Weber W, Curtis T, Thornell A, Pfister K, Jetton JG: Is ADHD a risk factor for psychoactive substance use disorders? Findings from a four-year prospective follow-up study. Am Acad Child Adolesc Psychiatry *36:* 21, 1997.

Cantwell DP: Attention deficit disorder: A review of the past 10 years. Am Acad Child Adolesc Psychiatry *35:* 978, 1996.

Cantwell DP, Baker L: Attention deficit disorder with and without hyperactivity: A review and comparison of matched controls. J Am Acad Child Adolesc Psychiatry *31:* 432, 1992.

Conners CK, Casat CD, Gualtieri CT, Weller E, Reader M, Reiss A, Weller RA, Khayrallah M, Ascher J: Bupropion hydrochloride in attention deficit hyperactivity disorder. Am Acad Child Adolesc Psychiatry *35:* 1314, 1996.

DuPaul GJ, Rapport MD: Does methylphenidate normalize the classroom performance of children with attention deficit disorders? J Am Acad Child Adolesc Psychiatry *32:* 190, 1993.

Fischer M, Barkley RA, Fletcher KE, Smallish L: The adolescent outcome of hyperactive children: Predictors of psychiatric, academic, social and emotional adjustment. J Am Acad Child Adolesc Psychiatry *32:* 324, 1993.

Garfinkel BD, Wender PH: Attention-deficit hyperactivity disorder. In *Comprehensive Textbook of Psychiatry,* ed 5, HI Kaplan, BJ Sadock, editors, p 1828. Williams & Wilkins, Baltimore, 1989.

Hechtman L: Attention-deficit hyperactivity disorder in adolescence and adulthood: An updated follow-up. Psychiatr Ann *19:* 597, 1989.

Horner BR, Scheibe K: Prevalence and implications of attention-deficit hyperactivity disorder among adolescents in treatment for substance abuse. Am Acad Child Adolesc Psychiatry *36:* 30, 1997.

Jacobvitz D, Sroufe LA, Stewart M, Leffert N: Treatment of attentional and hyperactivity problems in children with sympathicomimetic drugs: A comprehensive review. J Am Acad Child Adolesc Psychiatry *29:* 677, 1990.

Klein RG, Landa B, Mattes JA, Klein D: Methylphenidate and growth in hyperactive children. Arch Gen Psychiatry *45:* 1127, 1988.

Klorman R, Brumaghim JT, Fitzpatrick PA, Borgstedt AD: Clinical effects of a controlled trial of methylphenidate on adolescents with attention deficit disorder. J Am Acad Child Adolesc Psychiatry *29:* 702, 1990.

Kuperman S, Johnson B, Arndt A, Lindgren A, Wolraich M: Quantitative EEG differences in a nonclinical sample of children with ADHD and undifferentiated ADD. Am Acad Child Adolesc Psychiatry *35:* 1009, 1996.

Loge DV, Staton D, Beatty WW: Performance of children with ADHD on tests sensitive to frontal lobe dysfunction. J Am Acad Child Adolesc Psychiatry *29:* 540, 1990.

Pataki C, Carlson G, Kelly K, Rapport M, Biancaniello T: Side effects of methylphenidate and desipramine alone and in combination in children. Am Acad Child Adolesc Psychiatry *32:* 1065, 1993.

Pliszka SR, McCracken JT, Mass JW: Catecholamines in attention-deficit hyperactivity disorder: Current perspectives. Am Acad Child Adolesc Psychiatry *35:* 264, 1996.

Rapport MD, Carlson GA, Kelly KL, Pataki C: Methylphenidate and desipramine in hospitalized children. I. Separate and combined effects on cognitive function. J Am Acad Child Adolesc Psychiatry *32:* 333, 1993.

Spencer T, Biederman J, Wilens T, Harding M, O'Donnell D, Griffin S: Pharmacotherapy of attention-deficit hyperactivity disorder across the life cycle. J Am Acad Child Adolesc Psychiatry *35:* 409, 1996.

Steingard R, Biederman J, Spender T, Wilens T, Gonzales A: Comparison of clonidine response in the treatment of attention-deficit hyperactivity disorder with and without comorbid tic disorders. J Am Acad Child Adolesc Psychiatry *3:* 350, 1993.

Vincent J, Varley CK, Leger P: Effects of methylphenidate on early adolescent growth. Am J Psychiatry *147:* 501, 1990.

Wilens TE, Biederman J, Geist DE, Steingard R, Spencer T: Nortriptyline in the treatment of ADHD: A chart review of 58 cases. J Am Acad Child Adolesc Psychiatry *32:* 343, 1993.

43

Disruptive Behavior Disorders

The fourth edition of *Diagnostic and Statistical Manual of Mental Disorders* (DSM-IV) describes two specific disruptive behavior disorders—oppositional defiant disorder and conduct disorder—and one residual category. Oppositional defiant disorder is described as a recurrent pattern of negativistic, defiant, disobedient, and hostile behavior toward authority figures. The behavior lasts for at least 6 months and is characterized by frequent occurrence of at least four of the following: loss of temper, arguments with adults, defiance of or refusal to comply with adults' request or rules, deliberately doing things that annoy people, blaming others for personal failings, touchiness, anger and resentment, and spite. The behavior must occur more frequently than usual for a person's age and developmental level and must cause significant impairment in social, academic, and work settings. The disorder is not diagnosed when it occurs only during a psychotic or mood disorder or when the criteria are met for conduct disorder or antisocial personality disorder in a person over 18 years of age.

Conduct disorder is described as a "repetitive and persistent pattern of behavior in which the basic rights of others or major age-appropriate societal norms or rules are violated." The four groups of behaviors characteristic of the disorder include aggressive conduct that can cause physical harm to people and animals, destruction of property, deceit or theft, and serious violations of rules. For the diagnosis of conduct disorder, three or more characteristic behaviors must have been present for at least 3 months, and at least one behavior must have been present for 6 months. The behavioral disturbance causes significant impairment in social, academic, and work settings. The disorder can be diagnosed in people older than 18 years if the criteria for antisocial personality disorder are not met.

There are two subtypes: childhood onset type—with one typical behavioral characteristic appearing before 10 years of age; and adolescent-onset type—with no behavioral characteristic appearing before 10 years of age. The disorder has three degrees of severity: mild, moderate, and severe.

OPPOSITIONAL DEFIANT DISORDER

In oppositional defiant disorder, a child's temper outbursts, active refusal to comply with rules, and annoying behaviors exceed the expectations for these behaviors compared with others of the same age. The disorder is an enduring pattern of negativistic, hostile, and defiant behaviors in the absence of serious violations of social norms or of the rights of others.

Epidemiology

Oppositional, negativistic behavior may be developmentally normal in early childhood. Epidemiological studies of negativistic traits in nonclinical populations found such behavior in between 16 and 22 percent of school-age children. Although oppositional defiant disorder can begin as early as 3 years of age, it typically begins by 8 years of age and usually not later than adolescence. The disorder is more prevalent in boys than in girls before puberty, and the sex ratio is probably equal after puberty. One authority suggests that girls are classified as having oppositional disorder more frequently than are boys, as boys more often receive the diagnosis of conduct disorder. There are no distinct family patterns, but almost all parents of children with the disorder are themselves overly concerned with issues of power, control, and autonomy. Some families have several obstinate children, controlling and depressed mothers, and passive-aggressive fathers. In many cases the children were unwanted.

Etiology

A person's asserting his or her own will and opposing others' will is crucial to normal development and is related to establishing autonomy, forming an identity, and setting inner standards and controls. The most dramatic example of normal oppositional behavior peaks between 18 and 24 months, the "terrible twos," when toddlers behave negativistically as an expression of growing autonomy. Pathology begins when this developmental phase persists abnormally, authority figures overreact, or oppositional behavior recurs considerably more frequently than in most children of the same mental age.

Children may have constitutional or temperamental predispositions to strong will, strong preferences, or great assertiveness. If power and control are issues for the parents or if they exercise authority for their own needs, the ensuing struggle can set the stage for the development of oppositional defiant disorder. What begins for an infant as an effort to establish self-determination is transformed into a defense against overdependence on the mother and a protective device against intrusion into the ego's autonomy. In late childhood, environmental trauma, illness, or chronic incapacity, such as mental retardation, may trigger oppositionalism as a defense against helplessness, anxiety, and loss of self-esteem. Another normative oppositional stage occurs in adolescence as an expression of the need to separate from the parents and to establish an autonomous identity.

Classic psychoanalytic theory implicates unresolved conflicts that developed during the anal period. Behaviorists have suggested that oppositionalism is a reinforced, learned behavior through which a child exerts control over authority figures; for example, by having a temper tantrum when an undesired act is requested, a child coerces the parents to withdraw their request. In addition, increased parental attention—for example, long discussions about the behavior—many reinforce the behavior.

Diagnosis and Clinical Features

Children with oppositional defiant disorder often argue with adults, lose their temper, and are angry, resentful, and easily annoyed by others. They frequently actively defy adults' requests or rules and deliberately annoy other people. They tend to blame others for their own mistakes and misbehavior. Manifestations of the disorder are almost invariably present in the home, but they may not be present at school or with other adults or peers. In some cases, features of the disorder from the beginning of the disturbance are displayed outside the home; in other cases, the behavior starts in the home but is later displayed outside. Typically, symptoms of the disorder are most evident in interactions with adults or peers whom the child knows well. Thus, the child with the disorder is likely to show little or no sign of the disorder when examined clinically. Usually, these children do not regard themselves as oppositional or defiant but justify their behavior as a response to unreasonable circumstances. The disorder appears to cause more distress to those around the child than to the child personally. The DSM-IV diagnostic criteria for oppositional defiant disorder are given in Table 43–1.

Table 43–1
DSM-IV Diagnostic Criteria for Oppositional Defiant Disorder

A. A pattern of negativistic, hostile, and defiant behavior lasting at least 6 months, during which four (or more) of the following are present:
(1) often loses temper
(2) often argues with adults
(3) often actively defies or refuses to comply with adults' requests or rules
(4) often deliberately annoys people
(5) often blames others for his or her mistakes or misbehavior
(6) is often touchy or easily annoyed by others
(7) is often angry and resentful
(8) is often spiteful or vindictive

Note: Consider a criterion met only if the behavior occurs more frequently than is typically observed in individuals of comparable age and developmental level.

B. The disturbance in behavior causes significant impairment in social, academic or occupational functioning.

C. The behaviors do not occur exclusively during the course of a psychotic or mood disorder.

D. Criteria are not met for conduct disorder and, if individual is age 18 years or older, criteria are not met for antisocial personality disorder.

Chronic oppositional defiant disorder almost always interferes with interpersonal relationships and school performance. The children are often friendless and perceive human relationships as unsatisfactory. Despite adequate intelligence, they do poorly or fail in school, as they withhold participation, resist external demands, and insist on solving problems without others' help. Secondary to these difficulties are low self-esteem, poor frustration tolerance, depressed mood, and temper outbursts. Adolescents may abuse alcohol and illegal substances. Often, the disturbance evolves into a conduct disorder or a mood disorder.

ICD-10

In the 10th revision of *International Statistical Classification of Diseases and Related Health Problems* (ICD-10), conduct disorder include disorder confined to the family context, unsocialized conduct disorder, socialized conduct disorder, oppositional defiant behavior, other conduct disorders, and conduct disorder, unspecified. ICD-10 characterizes conduct disorders as repetitive and persistent patterns of "dissocial, aggressive, or defiant conduct." The behavior can be a major violation of "age-appropriate social expectations" and, thus, is more excessive than is ordinary mischief or rebelliousness. Symptoms of conduct disorder may also indicate other psychiatric conditions, which should instead be diagnosed. Conduct disorders sometimes lead to dissocial personality disorder. The disorders often arise in hostile environments, such as rancorous family life and failure at school, and occur more often in boys than in girls. The disorders can overlap with hyperactivity.

Conduct disorder confined to the family context involves aggressive behavior in the home, with family members, or both. The behavior must be aggressive and dissocial, accompanied by deliberately destructive behavior, all of which is focused on one or two family or household members. Relationships outside the family settings are within normal range, and there are no major conduct disturbances outside the home.

Unsocialized conduct disorder combines persistent dissocial or aggressive behavior with major pervasive deficit in a person's relationship with other children. The absence of peer group functioning distinguishes this disorder from the socialized conduct disorders.

Socialized conduct disorder describes persistent dyssocial or aggressive behavior in people who have adequate social skills and have a peer group with whom they enact the antisocial behavior.

Oppositional defiant disorder, which appear in children younger than 9 or 10 years, is the "*presence* of markedly defiant, disobedient, provocative behavior and . . . the *absence* of more severe acts that violate the law or the rights of others." The behavior must fit the overall criteria of conduct disorders and thus must be aggressive, dissocial, or defiant rather than just naughty. The behavior is most obvious in interactions with familiar adults and peers and may not occur during an interview.

Oppositional defiant disorder is sometimes considered to be a less severe variant of conduct disorder rather than a distinct type. Although, according to ICD-10, it is uncertain whether the distinction is qualitative or quantitative, findings suggest that it is distinctive ''mainly or only in younger children.'' In older children, conduct disorders generally include behavior that is aggressive or dissocial beyond defiance, even when it was preceded by oppositional defiant behaviors. Thus, this disorder accommodates ''common diagnostic practice'' and facilitates ''the classification of disorders occurring in younger children.''

The ICD-10 criteria for conduct disorders are listed in Table 43–2. The criteria for mixed disorders of conduct and emotions are listed in Table 43–3.

Table 43–2
ICD-10 Diagnostic Criteria for Conduct Disorders

G1. There is a repetitive and persistent pattern of behavior, in which either the basic rights of others or major age-appropriate societal norms or rules are violated, lasting at least 6 months, during which some of the following symptoms are present (see individual subcategories for rules or numbers of symptoms).

Note: The symptoms in 11, 13, 15, 16, 20, 21, and 23 need only have occurred once for the criterion to be fulfilled.

The individual:

(1) has unusually frequent or severe temper tantrums for his or her developmental level;

(2) often argues with adults;

(3) often actively refuses adults' requests or defies rules;

(4) often, apparently deliberately, does things that annoy other people;

(5) often blames others for his or her own mistakes or misbehavior;

(6) is often "touchy" or easily annoyed by others;

(7) is often angry or resentful;

(8) is often spiteful or vindictive;

(9) often lies or breaks promises to obtain goods or favors or to avoid obligations;

(10) frequently initiates physical fights (this does not include fights with siblings);

(11) has used a weapon that can cause serious physical harm to others (eg, bat, brick, broken bottle, knife, gun);

(12) often stays out after dark despite parental prohibition (beginning before 13 years of age);

(13) exhibits physical cruelty to other people (eg, ties up, cuts, or burns a victim);

(14) exhibits physical cruelty to animals;

(15) deliberately destroys the property of others (other than by fire-setting);

(16) deliberately sets fires with a risk or intention of causing serious damage;

(17) steals objects of nontrivial value without confronting the victim, either within the home or outside (eg, shoplifting, burglary, forgery);

(18) is frequently truant from school, beginning before 13 years of age;

(19) has run away from parental or parental surrogate home at least twice or has run away once for more than a single night (this does not include leaving to avoid physical or sexual abuse);

(20) commits a crime involving confrontation with the victim (including purse-snatching, extortion, mugging);

(21) forces another person into sexual activity;

(22) frequently bullies others (eg, deliberate infliction of pain or hurt, including persistent intimidation, tormenting, or molestation);

(23) breaks into someone else's house, building, or car.

G2. The disorder does not meet the criteria for dissocial personality disorder, schizophrenia, manic episode, depressive episode, pervasive developmental disorders, or hyperkinetic disorder. (If criteria for emotional disorder are met, the diagnosis should be mixed disorder of conduct and emotions.)

It is recommended that the age of onset be specified:

— *childhood onset type*: onset of at least one conduct problem before the age of 10 years;

— *adolescent onset type*: no conduct problems before the age of 10 years.

Specification for possible subdivisions

Authorities differ on the best way of subdividing the conduct disorders, although most agree that the disorders are heterogeneous. For determining prognosis, the severity (indexed by number of symptoms) is a better guide than the precise type of symptomatology. The best-validated distinction is that between *socialized* and *unsocialized* disorders, defined by the presence or absence of lasting peer friendships. However, it seems that disorders confined to the family context may also constitute an important variety, and a category is provided for this purpose. It is clear that further research is needed to test the validity of all proposed subdivisions of conduct disorder.

In addition to these categorizations, it is recommended that cases be described in terms of their scores on three dimensions of disturbance:

(1) hyperactivity (inattentive, restless behavior);

(2) emotional disturbance (anxiety, depression, obsessionality, hypochondriasis); and

(3) severity of conduct disorder:
 (a) *mild*: few if any conduct problems are in excess of those required to make the diagnosis, *and* conduct problems cause only minor harm to others;
 (b) *moderate*: the number of conduct problems and the effects on others are intermediate between "mild" and "severe";
 (c) *severe*: there are many conduct problems in excess of those required to make the diagnosis, *or* the conduct problems cause considerable harm to others, eg, severe physical injury, vandalism, or theft.

Conduct disorder confined to the family context

A. The general criteria for conduct disorder must be met.

B. Three or more of the symptoms listed for criterion G1 must be present, with at least three from items (9)–(23).

C. At least one of the symptoms from items (9)–(23) must have been present for at least 6 months.

D. Conduct disturbance must be limited to the family context.

(*continued*)

Table 43–2 (*continued*)

Unsocialized conduct disorder
A. The general criteria for conduct disorder must be met.
B. Three or more of the symptoms listed for conduct disorder criterion G1 must be present, with at least three from items (9)–(23).
C. At least one of the symptoms from items (9)–(23) must have been present for at least 6 months.
D. There must be definitely poor relationships with the individual's peer group, as shown by isolation, rejection, or unpopularity, and by a lack of lasting close reciprocal friendships.

Socialized conduct disorder
A. The general criteria for conduct disorder must be met.
B. Three or more of the symptoms listed for criterion G1 must be present, with at least three from items (9)–(23).
C. At least one of the symptoms from items (9)–(23) must have been present for at least 6 months.
D. Conduct disturbance must include settings outside the home or family context.
E. Peer relationships are within normal limits.

Operational defiant disorder
A. The general criteria for conduct disorder must be met.
B. Four or more of the symptoms listed for criterion G1 must be present, but with no more than two symptoms from items (9)–(23).
C. The symptoms in criterion B must be maladaptive and inconsistent with the developmental level.
D. At least four of the symptoms must have been present for at least 6 months.

Other conduct disorders

Conduct disorder, unspecified
This residual category is not recommended and should be used only for disorders that meet the general criteria for conduct disorder but that have not been specified as to subtype or that do not fulfill the criteria for any of the specified subtypes.

Table 43–3
ICD-10 Diagnostic Criteria for Mixed Disorders of Conduct and Emotions

Depressive conduct disorder
A. The general criteria for conduct disorders must be met.
B. Criteria for one of the mood (affective) disorders must be met.

Other mixed disorders of conduct and emotions
A. The general criteria for conduct disorders must be met.
B. Criteria for one of the neurotic, stress-related, and somatoform disorders or childhood emotional disorders must be met.

Mixed disorder of conduct and emotions, unspecified

Pathology and Laboratory Examination. No specific laboratory tests or pathological findings help diagnose oppositional defiant disorder. Because some children with the disorder become physically aggressive and violate the rights of others as they get older, they may share some of the same characteristics under investigation in violent people, such as decreased central nervous system (CNS) serotonin.

Differential Diagnosis

Because oppositional behavior is both normal and adaptive at specific developmental stages, these periods of negativism must be distinguished from oppositional defiant disorder. Developmental-stage oppositional behavior, which is of shorter duration than oppositional defiant disorder, is not considerably more frequent or more intense than that seen in other children of the same mental age.

Oppositional defiant behavior occurring temporarily in reaction to a stress should be diagnosed as an adjustment disorder. When features of oppositional defiant disorder appear during the course of conduct disorder, schizophrenia, or a mood disorder, the diagnosis of oppositional defiant disorder should not be made. Oppositional and negativistic behaviors may also be present in attention-deficit/hyperactivity disorder, cognitive disorders, and mental retardation. Whether a concomitant diagnosis of oppositional defiant disorder should be made depends on the severity, pervasiveness, and duration of such behavior. Some young children who receive a diagnosis of oppositional defiant disorder go on in several years to meet the criteria for conduct disorder. Some investigators believe that the two disorders may be developmental variants of each other, with conduct disorder being the natural progression of oppositional defiant behavior when a child matures. Most children with oppositional defiant disorder, however, do not later meet the criteria for conduct disorder, and up to one quarter of children with oppositional defiant disorder may not meet the diagnosis several years later.

The subtype of oppositional defiant disorder that tends to progress to conduct disorder is one in which aggression is prominent. Most children who have attention-deficit/hyperactivity disorder and conduct disorder develop conduct disorder before the age of 12. Most children who develop conduct disorder have a previous history of oppositional defiant disorder. Overall, the current consensus indicates that there may be two subtypes of oppositional defiant disorder. One type is likely to progress to conduct disorder and includes certain symptoms of conduct disorder (for example, fighting, bullying). The other type is characterized by less aggression and less antisocial traits and does not progress to conduct disorder.

Course and Prognosis

The course and prognosis of oppositional defiant disorder depend on many variables, including the severity of the disorder, its stability over time, the likelihood of comorbid disorders (such as conduct disorder, learning disorders, mood disorders, and substance use disorders), and the degree of the family's intactness.

About one quarter of all the children who receive the diagnosis of oppositional defiant disorder may not qualify for it within the next several years. It is not clear in these cases whether the criteria captured children whose behavior was not developmentally abnormal or whether the disorder spontaneously remitted. Such patients have the best prognosis. Patients in whom the diagnosis persists may remain stable or may go on to violate the rights of others, and thus develop conduct disorder. Such patients should receive guarded prognoses.

It is well known that there is an association between conduct disorder and later substance use disorders, as well as elevated rates of mood disorders, in children with oppositional defiant disorder, conduct disorder, and attention-deficit/hyperactivity disorder. Parental psychopathology, such as antisocial personality disorder and substance abuse, appear to be more common in families with children who have oppositional defiant disorder than in the general population, a finding that creates additional risks for chaotic and troubled home environments. The prognosis for oppositional defiant disorder in a child depends somewhat on the degree of functioning in the family and on the development of comorbid psychopathology.

Treatment

The primary treatment of oppositional defiant disorder is individual psychotherapy for the child with counseling and direct training of the parents in child management skills. Behavior therapists emphasize teaching parents how to alter their behavior to discourage the child's oppositional behavior and to encourage appropriate behavior. Behavior therapy focuses on selectively reinforcing and praising appropriate behavior and ignoring or not reinforcing undesired behavior.

Clinicians who treat patients with individual psychotherapy note that family patterns are rigid and difficult to alter unless the child has a new type of object relationship with the therapist. In the therapeutic relationship, the child can learn new strategies to develop a sense of mastery and success in social situations with peers and families. In the safety of a noncontrolling relationship, children can understand the self-destructive nature of their behavior and risk expressing themselves directly. Their self-esteem must be restored before they can make more positive responses to necessary external control. Parent–child conflict is a strong predictor of conduct problems; patterns of harsh physical and verbal punishment particularly lead to the emergence of aggression and deviance in children. Thus, it is likely that eliminating harsh, punitive parenting and increasing positive parent–child interactions may positively influence the course of oppositional and defiant behaviors. Additionally, the level of parental involvement in a child's life is associated with social skills deficits.

CONDUCT DISORDER

Conduct disorder is an enduring set of behaviors that evolves over time; it is characterized most often by aggression and violations of the rights of others. Conduct disorder is associated with many other psychiatric disorders including attention-deficit/hyperactivity disorder, depression, and learning disorders, and it is also associated with several psychosocial factors such as low socioeconomic level; harsh, punitive parenting; family discord; lack of appropriate parental supervision; and lack of social competence. The DSM-IV criteria state that three specific behaviors are required of the 15 listed behaviors, which include bullying, threatening, or intimidating others and staying out at night despite parental prohibitions, beginning before 13 years of age. DSM-IV also specifies that truancy from school must begin before 13 years of age to be considered a symptom of conduct disorder. The disorder can be diagnosed in a person older than 18 years only if the criteria for antisocial personality disorder are not met. DSM-IV describes a mild level of the disorder as showing few if any conduct problems in excess of those needed to make the diagnosis and conduct problems that cause only minor harm to others. According to DSM-IV, the severe level shows many conduct problems in excess of the minimal diagnostic criteria or conduct problems that cause considerable harm to others.

Epidemiology

Conduct disorder is common during childhood and adolescence. An estimated 6 to 16 percent of boys and 2 to 9 percent of girls under the age of 18 years have the disorder. The disorder is more common among boys than among girls, and the ratio ranges from 4 to 1 to as much as 12 to 1. Conduct disorder is more common in the children of parents with antisocial personality disorder and alcohol dependence than it is in the general population. The prevalence of conduct disorder and antisocial behavior is significantly related to socioeconomic factors.

Etiology

No single factor can account for a child's antisocial behavior and conduct disorder. Rather, many biopsychosocial factors contribute to the development of the disorder.

Parental Factors. Harsh, punitive parenting characterized by severe physical and verbal aggression is associated with the development of children's maladaptive aggressive behaviors. Chaotic home conditions are associated with conduct disorder and delinquency. Divorce itself is considered a risk factor, but the persistence of hostility, resentment, and bitterness between divorced parents may be the more important contributor to maladaptive behavior children. Parental psychopathology, child abuse, and negligence often contribute to conduct disorder. Sociopathy, alcohol dependence, and substance abuse in the parents are associated with conduct disorder in their children. Parents may be so negligent that a child's care is shared by relatives or assumed by foster parents. Many such parents were scarred by their own upbringing and tend to be abusive, negligent, or engrossed in getting their own personal needs met.

In the 1980s, particularly in urban areas, cocaine abuse and acquired immune deficiency syndrome (AIDS) increased family dysfunction. Recent studies suggest that many parents of children with conduct disorder have serious psychopathology, including psychotic disorders. Psychodynamic hypotheses suggest that children with conduct disorder unconsciously act out their parent's antisocial wishes.

Sociocultural Factors. Socioeconomically deprived children are at higher risk for the development of conduct disorder, as are children and adolescents who grow up in urban environments. Unemployment among parents, lack of supportive social network, and lack of positive participation in community activities seem to predict conduct disorder. Other associated findings that may influence the development of conduct disorder in urban areas are increased rates and prevalence of substance use. Although drug and alcohol use does not contribute to the onset of conduct disorder, it possibly makes it more difficult to reach remission from conduct disturbance. Drug use may also aggravate the symptoms. Thus, factors that increase the likelihood of regular substance use may in fact prolong the disorder.

Psychological Factors. Children brought up in chaotic, negligent conditions generally become angry, disruptive, demanding, and unable to progressively develop the tolerance for frustration necessary for mature relationships. As their role models are poor and often frequently changing, the basis for developing both an ego-ideal and a conscience is lacking. The children are left with little motivation to follow societal norms and are relatively remorseless.

Neurobiological Factors. Neurobiological factors in conduct disorder have been little studied, but research in attention-deficit/hyperactivity disorder yields some important findings, and this disorder often coexists with conduct disorder. In some children with conduct disorder, a low level of plasma dopamine β-hydroxylase, an enzyme that converts dopamine to norepinephrine, has been found. This finding supports a theory of decreased noradrenergic functioning in conduct disorder. Some conduct-disordered juvenile offenders have increased blood serotonin (5-hydroxytryptamine [5-HT]) levels. Evidence indicates that blood 5-HT levels correlate negatively with levels of the 5-HT metabolite 5-hydroxyindoleacetic acid (5-HIAA) in the cerebrospinal fluid (CSF) and that low CSF 5-HIAA correlates with aggression and violence.

Child Abuse and Maltreatment. Children who are exposed to violence for long periods, especially those who endure physically abusive treatment, often behave aggressively. Such children may have difficulty in verbalizing their feelings, and this difficulty increases their tendency to express themselves physically. In addition, severely abused children and adolescents tend to be hypervigilant; in some cases they misperceive benign situations and respond with violence. Not all physical behavior is synonymous with conduct disorder, but children with a pattern of hypervigilance and violent responses are likely to violate the rights of others.

Other Factors. Attention-deficit/hyperactivity disorder, central nervous system (CNS) dysfunction or damage, and early extremes of temperament can predispose a child to conduct disorder. Propensity to violence correlates with CNS dysfunction and signs of severe psychopathology, such as delusional tendencies. Longitudinal temperament studies suggest that many behavioral deviations are initially a straightforward response to a poor fit between a child's temperament and emotional needs, on one hand, and parental attitudes and child-rearing practices, on the other.

Diagnosis and Clinical Features

Conduct disorder does not develop overnight; instead, many symptoms evolve over time until a consistent pattern develops that involves violating the rights of others. Very young children are unlikely to meet the criteria for the disorder, as they are not developmentally able to exhibit the symptoms typical of older children with conduct disorder. A 3-year-old does not break into someone's home, steal with confrontation, force someone into sexual activity, or deliberately use a weapon that can cause serious harm. School-age children, however, may become bullies, initiate physical fights, destroy property, or set fires. The DSM-IV diagnostic criteria for conduct disorder are given in Table 43–4.

The average age of onset of conduct disorder is younger in boys than in girls. Boys most commonly meet the diagnostic criteria by 10 to 12 years of age, whereas girls often reach 14 to 16 years of age before the criteria are met.

Children who meet the criteria for conduct disorder express their overt aggressive behavior in various forms. Aggressive antisocial behavior may take the form of bullying, physical aggression, and cruel behavior toward peers. Children may be hostile, verbally abusive, impudent, defiant, and negativistic toward adults. Persistent lying, frequent truancy, and vandalism are common. In severe cases, destructiveness, stealing, and physical violence are often present. Children usually make little attempt to conceal their antisocial behavior. Sexual behavior and the regular use of tobacco, liquor, or nonprescribed psychoactive substances begin unusually early for such children and adolescents. Suicidal thoughts, gestures, and acts are frequent.

Many children with aggressive behaviors fail to develop social attachments, as manifested by their difficulties with peer relationships or their lack of sustained normal peer relationships. Such children are often socially withdrawn or isolated. Some may befriend a much older or younger person or have superficial relationships with other antisocial youngsters. Most have low self-esteem, although they may project an image of toughness. Characteristically, they do not put themselves out for others, even if doing so would bring an obvious, immediate advantage. Their egocentrism is shown by their readily manipulating others for favors without any effort to reciprocate. They lack concern for the feelings, wishes, and welfare of others. They seldom feel guilt or remorse for their callous behavior and try to blame others.

Not only have these children frequently encountered unusual frustrations, particularly of their dependency needs, but they have also escaped any consistent pattern of discipline. Their deficient socialization is revealed in their excessive aggressiveness and their lack of sexual inhibition. Their general behavior is unacceptable in almost any social setting. Unfor-

Table 43–4
DSM-IV Diagnostic Criteria for Conduct Disorder

A. A repetitive and persistent pattern of behavior in which either the basic rights of others or major age-appropriate societal norms or rules are violated, as manifested by the presence of three (or more) of the following criteria in the past 12 months, with at least one criterion present in the past 6 months:

Aggression to people and animals

(1) often bullies, threatens, or intimidates others
(2) often initiates physical fights
(3) has used a weapon that can cause serious physical harm to others (eg, a bat, brick, broken bottle, knife, gun)
(4) has been physically cruel to people
(5) has been physically cruel to animals
(6) has stolen while confronting a victim (eg, mugging, purse snatching, extortion, armed robbery)
(7) has forced someone into sexual activity

Destruction of property

(8) has deliberately engaged in fire setting with the intention of causing serious damage
(9) has deliberately destroyed others' property (other than by fire setting)

Deceitfulness or theft

(10) has broken into someone else's house, building, or car
(11) often lies to obtain goods or favors or to avoid obligations (ie, "cons" others)
(12) has stolen items of nontrivial value without confronting a victim (eg, shoplifting, but without breaking and entering; forgery)

Serious violations of rules

(13) often stays out at night despite parental prohibitions, beginning before 13 years
(14) has run away from home overnight at least twice while living in parental or parental surrogate home (or once without returning for a lengthy period)
(15) often truant from school, beginning before age 13 years

B. The disturbance in behavior causes clinically significant impairment in social, academic, or occupational functioning.

C. If the individual is age 18 years or older, criteria are not met for antisocial personality disorder.

Specify type based on age of onset:
Childhood-onset type: onset of at least one criterion characteristic of conduct disorder prior to age 10 years
Adolescent-onset type: absence of any criteria characteristic of conduct disorder prior to age 10 years

Unspecified type

Specify severity:
Mild: few if any conduct problems in excess of those required to make the diagnosis **and** conduct problems cause only minor harm to others
Moderate: number of conduct problems and effect on others intermediate between "mild" and "severe"
Severe: many conduct problems in excess of those required to make the diagnosis **or** conduct problems cause considerable harm to others

Reprinted with permission from American Psychiatric Association: *Diagnostic and Statistical Manual of Mental Disorders,* ed 4. Copyright, American Psychiatric Association, Washington, 1994.

tunately, severe punishment almost invariably increases their maladaptive expression of rage and frustration, rather than ameliorating the problem.

In evaluation interviews, children with aggressive conduct disordered are typically uncooperative, hostile, and provocative. Some have a superficial charm and compliance until they are urged to talk about their problem behaviors. Then they may angrily deny any problems. If the interviewer persists, the child may attempt to justify misbehavior or become suspicious and angry about the source of the examiner's information and perhaps bolt from the room. Most often, the child becomes angry at the examiner and expresses resentment of the examination with open belligerence or sullen withdrawal. Their hostility is not limited to adult authority figures but is expressed with equal venom toward their age-mates and younger children. In fact, they often bully those who are smaller and weaker than they. By boasting, lying, and expressing little interest in listener's responses, such children reveal their profoundly narcissistic orientation.

Evaluation of the family situation often reveals severe marital disharmony, which initially may center on disagreements about management of the child. Because of a tendency toward family instability, parent surrogates are often in the picture. Many children with conduct disorder are only children of unplanned or unwanted pregnancies. The parents, especially the father, often have antisocial personality disorder or alcohol dependence. Aggressive children and their family show a stereotyped pattern of impulsive and unpredictable verbal and physical hostility. A child's aggressive behavior rarely seems directed toward any definable goal and offers little pleasure, success, or even sustained advantages with peers or authority figures.

In other cases, conduct disorder includes repeated truancy, vandalism, and serious physical aggression or assault against others by a gang, such as mugging, gang fighting, and beating. Children who become part of a gang usually have age-appropriate friendships. They are likely to show concern for the welfare of their friends or their own gang members and are unlikely to blame them or inform on them. In most cases, gang members have a history of adequate or even excessive conformity during early childhood that ended when the youngster became a member of the delinquent peer group, usually in preadolescence or during adolescence. Also present in the history is some evidence of early problems, such as marginal or poor school performance, mild behavior problems, anxiety, and depressive symptoms. Some degree of family social or psychological pathology is usually evident. Patterns of paternal discipline are rarely ideal and may vary from harshness and excessive strictness to inconsistency or relative absence of supervision and control. The mother has often protected the child from the consequences of early mild misbehavior but does not seem to actively encourage delinquency. Delinquency, also called juvenile delinquency, is most often associated with conduct disorder but may also be the result of other psychological or neurological disorders.

Pathology and Laboratory Examination. No specific laboratory test or neurological pathology helps make the diagnosis of conduct disorder. Some evidence indicates that amounts of certain neurotransmitters, such as serotonin in the CNS, are low in some persons with a history of violent or aggressive behavior toward others or themselves. Whether this association is related to the cause or is the effect of violence or is unrelated to the violence is not clear.

Differential Diagnosis

Disturbances of conduct may be part of many childhood psychiatric conditions, ranging from mood disorders to psychotic disorders to learning disorders. Therefore, clinicians must obtain a history of the chronology of the symptoms to determine whether the conduct disturbance is a transient or reactive phenomenon or an enduring pattern. Isolated acts of antisocial behavior do not justify a diagnosis of conduct disorder; an enduring pattern must be present. The relation of conduct disorder to oppositional defiant disorder is still under debate. Historically, oppositional defiant disorder has been conceptualized as a mild precursor of conduct disorder, which is likely to be diagnosed in young children at risk for conduct disorder. Children who progress from oppositional defiant disorder to conduct disorder do maintain their oppositional characteristics, but some evidence indicates that the two disorders are independent. Many children with oppositional defiant disorder never go on to have conduct disorder and, when conduct disorder first appears in adolescence, it may be unrelated to oppositional defiant disorder. The main distinguishing clinical feature of the two disorders is that, in conduct disorder, the basic rights of others are violated, whereas, in oppositional defiant disorder, hostility and negativism fall short of seriously violating the rights of others.

Mood disorders are often present in children who have some degree of irritability and aggressive behavior. Both major depressive disorder and bipolar disorders must be ruled out, but the full syndrome of conduct disorder may occur and be diagnosed during the onset of a mood disorder. There is a substantial comorbidity of conduct disorder and depressive disorders. A recent report concludes that the high correlation between the two disorders arises from shared risk factors for both disorders, rather than one disorder causing the other. Thus, a series of factors including family conflict, negative life events, early history of conduct disturbance, level of parental involvement, and affiliation with delinquent peers contribute to the development of affective disorders and conduct disorder. This is not the case with oppositional defiant disorder, which cannot be diagnosed if it occurs exclusively during a mood disorder.

Attention-deficit/hyperactivity disorder and learning disorders are commonly associated with conduct disorder. Usually, the symptoms of these disorders predate the diagnosis of conduct disorder. Substance abuse disorders are also more common in adolescents with conduct disorder than in the general population. There is evidence of an association between fighting behaviors as a child and substance use as an adolescent. Once a pattern of drug use is formed, this pattern may interfere with the development of positive mediators, such as social skills and problem solving, that could enhance remission of the conduct disorder. Thus, once substance abuse develops, it may promote continuation of the conduct disorder. Obsessive compulsive disorder also frequently seems to coexist with disruptive behavior disorders. All the disorders described here should be noted when they co-occur. Children with attention-deficit/hyperactivity disorder often exhibit impulsive and aggressive behaviors that may not meet the full criteria for conduct disorder.

Course and Prognosis

In general, the poorest prognosis is found for conduct disorder in children who have symptoms at a young age, exhibit the greatest number of symptoms, and express them most frequently. This finding is true partly because those with severe conduct disorder seem to be most vulnerable to another disorder later in life, such as a mood disorder. Conduct disorder is also associated with substance-related disorders later in life. It stands to reason that the more concurrent mental disorders a person has, the more troublesome life will be. A recent report found that, although assaultive behavior in childhood and parental criminality predict a high risk for incarceration later in life, the diagnosis of conduct disorder per se was not correlated with imprisonment. A good prognosis is predicted for mild conduct disorder in the absence of coexisting psychopathology, and normal intellectual functioning.

Treatment

Although assessing treatment strategies is difficult because of the many symptoms involved in conduct disorder, it appears to be more difficult to design effective treatment programs for the covert symptoms of conduct disorder than for overt aggression. Multimodality treatment programs that use all the available family and community resources are likely to bring about the best results in efforts to control conduct-disordered behavior. No treatment is considered curative for the entire spectrum of behaviors that contribute to conduct disorder, but a variety of treatments may be helpful for certain components of the chronic disorder.

An environmental structure with consistent rules and expected consequences can help control a variety of problem behaviors. The structure can be applied to family life in some cases, so that parents become aware of behavioral techniques and grow proficient at using them to foster appropriate behaviors. Families in which psychopathology or environmental stressors prevent parent's grasping the techniques may require parental psychiatric evaluation and treatment before making such an endeavor. When a family is abusive or chaotic, the child may have to be removed from the home to benefit from a consistent and structured environment. School settings can also use behavioral techniques to promote socially acceptable behavior toward peers and to discourage covert antisocial incidents.

Individual psychotherapy oriented toward improving problem-solving skills can be useful, as children with conduct disorder may have a long-standing pattern of maladaptive responses to daily situations. The age at which treatment begins is important, because the longer the maladaptive behaviors continue, the more entrenched they become.

Medication can be a useful adjunctive treatment for symptoms that often contribute to conduct disorder. Overt explosive aggression responds to several medications. Antipsychotics, most notably haloperidol (Haldol), decrease aggressive and as-

Table 43–5
DSM-IV Diagnostic Criteria for Disruptive Behavior Disorder Not Otherwise Specified

This category is for disorders characterized by conduct or oppositional-defiant behaviors that do not meet the criteria for conduct disorder or oppositional defiant disorder. For example, include clinical presentations that do not meet full criteria either for oppositional defiant disorder or conduct disorder, but in which there is clinically significant impairment.

saultive behaviors that may be present in various disorders. Lithium (Eskalith) also has some benefit in the treatment of aggression in or outside the context of bipolar disorders. Some trials suggest that carbamazepine (Tegretol) may help control aggression, but a recent double-blind, placebo-controlled study did not show the superiority of carbamazepine over placebo in decreasing aggression. A recent pilot study found that clonidine (Catapres) may decrease aggression. The serotonin-specific reuptake inhibitors (SSRIs), such as fluoxetine (Prozac), sertraline (Zoloft), and paroxetine (Paxil), have been used in an attempt to diminish impulsivity, irritability, and lability of mood, which often occur with conduct disorder. Conduct disorder frequently coexists with attention-deficit/hyperactivity disorder, learning disorders, and, over time, mood disorders, and substance-related disorders; thus, the treatment of any concurrent disorders must also be addressed.

DISRUPTIVE BEHAVIOR DISORDER NOT OTHERWISE SPECIFIED

According to DSM-IV, the category of disruptive behavior disorder not otherwise specified can be used for disorders of conduct or oppositional-defiant behaviors that do not meet the diagnostic criteria for either conduct disorder or oppositional defiant disorder but in which there is notable impairment (Table 43–5).

REFERENCES

Angold A, Costello EJ: Toward establishing an empirical basis for the diagnosis of oppositional defiant disorder. J Am Acad Child Adolesc Psychiatry *35:* 1205, 1996.

Biederman J, Faraone SV, Milberger S, Jetton JG, Chen L, Mick E, Greene RW, Russell RL: Is childhood oppositional defiant disorder a precursor to adolescent conduct disorder? J Am Acad Child Adolesc Psychiatry *35:* 1193, 1996.

Brooks JS, Whiteman M, Finch SJ, Cohen P: Young adult drug use and delinquency: Childhood antecedents and adolescent mediators. J Am Acad Child Adolesc Psychiatry *35:* 1584, 1996.

Cueva JE, Overall JE, Small AM, Armenteros JL, Perry R, Campbell M: Carbamazepine in aggressive children with conduct disorder: A double-blind and placebo-controlled study. J Am Acad Child Adolesc Psychiatry *35:* 480, 1996.

Gerguson DM, Lynsky MT, Horwood LJ: Origins of comorbidity between conduct and affective disorders. J Am Acad Child Adolesc Psychiatry *35:* 451, 1996.

Geller DA, Biederman J, Griffin S, Jones J, Lefkowitz TR: Co-morbidity of juvenile obsessive-compulsive disorder with disruptive behavior disorders. J Am Acad Child Adolesc Psychiatry *35:* 1637, 1996.

Kemph JP, DeVane CL, Levin GM, Jarecke R, Miller RL: Treatment of aggressive children with clonidine: Results of an open pilot study. J Am Acad Child Adolesc Psychiatry *32:* 577, 1993.

Lahey BB, Applegate B, Barkley RA, et al: DSM-IV field trials for oppositional defiant disorder and conduct disorder in children and adolescents. Am J Psychiatry *151:* 1163, 1994.

Lahey BB, Loeber R, Quay HC, Frick PJ, Grimm J: Oppositional defiant disorder and conduct disorders: Issues to be resolved for DSM-IV. J Am Acad Child Adolesc Psychiatry *31:* 539, 1992.

Lewis DO: From abuse to violence: Psychophysiological consequences of maltreatment. J Am Acad Child Adolesc Psychiatry *31:* 383, 1992.

Lewis DO, Lovely R, Yeager C, Ferguson G, Friedman M, Sloane G, Friedman H, Pincus JH: Intrinsic and environmental characteristics of juvenile murderers. J Am Acad Child Adolesc Psychiatry *27:* 582, 1988.

Lewis DO, Shanok SS, Lewis ML, Unger L, Goldman C: Conduct disorder and its synonyms: Diagnosis of dubious validity and usefulness. Am J Psychiatry *141:* 514, 1984.

Lundy MS, Pfohl BM, Kuperman S: Adult criminality among formerly hospitalized psychiatric patients. J Am Acad Child Adolesc Psychiatry *32:* 568, 1993.

Maziade M, Caron C, Côté R, Boutin P, Thivierge J: Extreme temperament and diagnoses. Arch Gen Psychiatry *47:* 477, 1990.

Robins L: *Deviant Children Grown Up.* Williams & Wilkins, Baltimore, 1966.

Steward JT, Myers WC, Burket RC, Lyles WB: A review of the pharmacotherapy of aggression in children and adolescents. J Am Acad Child Adolesc Psychiatry *29:* 269, 1990.

Vitiello B, Jensen PS: Disruptive behavior disorders. In *Comprehensive Textbook of Psychiatry,* ed 6, HI Kaplan, BJ Sadock, editors, p 2311. Williams & Wilkins, Baltimore, 1995.

Wasserman GA, Miller LS, Pinner E, Jaramillo B: Parenting predictors of early conduct problems in urban, high-risk boys. J Am Acad Child Adolesc Psychiatry *35:* 1227, 1996.

Wichtrom L, Skogen K, Oia T: Increased rate of conduct problems in urban areas: What is the mechanism? J Am Acad Child Adolesc Psychiatry *35:* 471, 1996.

44

Feeding and Eating Disorders of Infancy or Early Childhood

In the fourth edition of *Diagnostic and Statistical Manual of Mental Disorders* (DSM-IV), feeding and eating disorders of infancy or early childhood are described as characterized by persistent feeding and eating disturbances, which include pica, rumination disorder, and feeding disorder of infancy or early childhood.

ICD-10

In the 10th revision of *International Statistical Classification of Diseases and Related Health Problems* (ICD-10), feeding disorder of infancy and childhood (which also includes rumination disorder) and pica are included under the category of other emotional and behavioral disorders with onset usually occurring in childhood and adolescence.

According to ICD-10, feeding disorder of infancy and childhood is "a feeding disorder of varying manifestations, usually specific to infancy and early childhood. It generally involves refusal of food and extreme faddiness in the presence of an adequate food supply and a competent caregiver, and the absence of organic disease. There may or may not be associated rumination (repeated regurgitation without nausea or gastrointestinal illness)." The disorder should be diagnosed only when the difficulties are beyond normal, when the nature of the eating problem is qualitatively abnormal, or when a child fails to gain weight or loses weight over at least 1 month (Table 44–1).

Pica of infancy and childhood is persistent eating of nonnutritive substances such as soil or paint chips, according to ICD-10. The disorder should be diagnosed only when it is an isolated behavior, not one of many symptoms of a wider psychiatric disorder (Table 44–2). Pica is common among children with mental retardation, but it may also occur among children with normal intelligence.

PICA

In DSM-IV, pica is described as the persistent eating of nonnutritive substances for at least 1 month. The behavior must be developmentally inappropriate, not culturally sanctioned, and sufficiently severe to merit clinical attention. Pica is diagnosed even when these symptoms occur in the context of another disorder such as autistic disorder, schizophrenia, or Klein-Levin syndrome.

Pica appears much more frequently in young children than in adults; it also occurs in people who are mentally retarded. Among adults, certain forms of pica, including geophagia (clay eating) and amylophagia (starch eating), have been reported to occur in pregnant women. In certain regions of the world and among certain cultures, such as the Australian aborigines, rates of pica in pregnant women have been reported to be high. According to DSM-IV, however, if such practices are culturally accepted, the diagnostic criteria for pica are not met.

Epidemiology

Pica is estimated to occur in 10 to 32 percent of children between 1 and 6 years of age. In children older than 10 years, reports of pica have indicated a rate of less than 10 percent. In older children and adolescents with normal intelligence, the frequency of pica diminishes. Among institutionalized children and adolescents who are mentally retarded, pica has been reported to occur in up to one fourth of older school-age children and adolescents. The presence of pica appears to affect both sexes equally.

Etiology

Several theories have been proposed to explain the phenomenon of pica, but none has been universally accepted. A higher than expected incidence of pica seems to occur in the relatives of people with the symptoms. Nutritional deficiencies have been postulated as causes of pica; in particular circumstances, cravings for nonedible substances have been produced by dietary insufficiencies. For example, cravings for dirt and ice are sometimes associated with iron and zinc deficiencies, which are eliminated by their administration.

A high incidence of parental neglect and deprivation has been associated with cases of pica. Theories relating children's psychological deprivation and subsequent ingestion of inedible substances have been suggested as compensatory mechanisms to satisfy oral needs. An important contributing factor is the influence of widely accepted cultural rituals and practices in promoting such behaviors as geophagia and the eating of starch. These influences can be compelling, and they disqualify the diagnosis of pica, according to DSM-IV.

Diagnosis and Clinical Features

Eating nonedible substances after 18 months of age is usually considered abnormal. The onset of pica is usually between

Table 44–1
ICD-10 Diagnostic Criteria for Feeding Disorder of Infancy and Childhood

A. There is persistent failure to eat adequately, or persistent rumination or regurgitation of food.
B. The child fails to gain weight, loses weight, or exhibits some other significant health problem over a period of at least 1 month. (In view of the frequency of transient eating difficulties, researchers may prefer a minimum duration of 3 months for some purposes.)
C. Onset of the disorder is before the age of 6 years.
D. The child exhibits no other mental or behavioral disorder in the ICD-10 classification (other than mental retardation).
E. There is no evidence of organic disease sufficient to account for the failure to eat.

Table 44–2
ICD-10 Diagnostic Criteria for Pica of Infancy and Childhood

A. There is persistent or recurrent eating of nonnutritive substances, at least twice a week.
B. Duration of the disorder is at least 1 month. (For some purposes, researchers may prefer a minimum period of 3 months.)
C. The child exhibits no other mental or behavioral disorder in the ICD-10 classification (other than mental retardation).
D. The child's chronological and mental age is at least 2 years.
E. The eating behavior is not part of a culturally sanctioned practice.

ages 12 and 24 months, and the incidence declines with age. The specific substances ingested vary with their accessibility, and they increase with a child's mastery of locomotion and the resultant increased independence and decreased parental supervision. Typically, young children ingest paint, plaster, string, hair, and cloth; older children have access to dirt, animal feces, stones, and paper. The clinical implications can be benign or life-threatening, according to the objects ingested. Among the most serious complications are lead poisoning, usually from lead-based paint; intestinal parasites after the ingestion of soil or feces; anemia and zinc deficiency after the ingestion of clay; severe iron deficiency after the ingestion of large quantities of starch; and intestinal obstruction from the ingestion of hair balls, stones, or gravel. Except with people who are mentally retarded, pica usually remits by adolescence. Pica associated with pregnancy is usually limited to the pregnancy itself. The DSM-IV diagnostic criteria for pica are given in Table 44–3.

Pathology and Laboratory Examination. No single laboratory test confirms or rules out a diagnosis of pica, but several laboratory tests are useful because pica has frequently been associated with abnormal indexes. Serum levels of iron and zinc should always be obtained; in many cases of pica, these levels are low and may contribute to the development of pica. Pica may disappear when oral iron and zinc are administered. Patient's hemoglobin level should be obtained; if the level is reduced, anemia can result. In children with pica, the serum lead level should be obtained when a physician is concerned about a child; lead poisoning can result from ingesting lead. When a child's lead level is increased, this condition must be treated.

Differential Diagnosis

The differential diagnosis of pica includes iron and zinc deficiencies. Pica also may occur in conjunction with failure to thrive and several other mental and medical disorders, including schizophrenia, autistic disorder, anorexia nervosa, and Kleine-Levin syndrome. In psychosocial dwarfism, a dramatic but reversible endocrinological and behavioral form of failure to thrive, children often show bizarre behaviors, including ingesting toilet water, garbage, and other nonnutritive substances. A recent case report presented an association of pica with hypersomnolence, lead intoxication, and precocious puberty. Precocious puberty implicates the hypothalamus as a site for at least a part of the dysfunction. Lead intoxication is known to be associated with pica as well as several other neuropsychiatric abnormalities in memory and cognitive performance. A small minority of children with autistic disorder and schizophrenia may have pica. In children who exhibit pica along with another medical disorder, both disorders should be coded, according to DSM-IV.

Course and Prognosis

The prognosis for pica is variable. In children, pica usually resolves with increasing age; in pregnant women, pica is usually limited to the term of the pregnancy. In some adults, however, especially those who are mentally retarded, pica may

Table 44–3
DSM-IV Diagnostic Criteria for Pica

A. Persistent eating of nonnutritive substances for a period of at least 1 month.
B. The eating of nonnutritive substances is inappropriate to developmental level.
C. The eating behavior is not part of a culturally sanctioned practice.
D. If the eating behavior occurs exclusively during the course of another mental disorder (eg, mental retardation, pervasive developmental disorder, schizophrenia), it is sufficiently severe to warrant independent clinical attention.

continue for years. Follow-up data on these populations are too limited to permit conclusions.

Treatment

The first step in the treatment of pica is to determine the cause whenever possible. When pica is associated with situations of neglect or maltreatment, these circumstances naturally need to be altered. Exposure to toxic substances, such as lead, must also be eliminated. No definitive treatment exists for pica; most treatment is aimed at education and behavior modification. Treatments emphasize psychosocial, environmental, behavioral, and family guidance approaches. An effort should be made to ameliorate any significant psychosocial stressors. When lead is present in the surroundings, it must be eliminated or rendered inaccessible, or the child must be moved to new surroundings.

Several behavioral techniques have been used with some effect. The most rapidly successful technique seems to be mild aversion therapy or negative reinforcement (for example, a mild electric shock, an unpleasant noise, or an emetic drug). Positive reinforcement, modeling, behavioral shaping, and overcorrection treatment have also been used. Increasing parental attention, stimulation, and emotional nurturance may have positive results. One study found that pica was negatively correlated with involvement with play materials and occurred most frequently in impoverished environments. In some patients, correcting an iron or zinc deficiency has resulted in the elimination of pica. Medical complications (for example, lead poisoning) that develop secondarily to the pica must also be treated.

RUMINATION DISORDER

In DSM-IV rumination disorder is described as an infant's or a child's repeated regurgitation and rechewing of food, after a period of normal functioning. The symptoms last for at least 1 month, are not caused by a medical condition, and are severe enough to merit clinical attention. The onset of the disorder generally occurs after 3 months of age; once the regurgitation occurs, the food may be swallowed or spit out. Infants who ruminate are observed to strain in order to bring the food back into their mouths and appear to find the experience pleasurable. The infants are often brought for evaluation because of failure to thrive. The disorder is rare in older children, adolescents, and adults. It varies in its severity, and it is sometimes associated with medical conditions, such as hiatal hernia, that result in esophageal reflux. In its most severe form, the disorder can be fatal.

The diagnosis of rumination disorder can be made whether or not an infant has attained a normal weight for his or her age. Failure to thrive, therefore, is not a necessary criterion of this disorder, but it is sometimes a sequela. According to DSM-IV, the disorder must be present for at least 1 month after a period of normal functioning, and it is not associated with gastrointestinal illness or other general medical conditions.

Rumination has been recognized for hundreds of years. An awareness of the disorder is important, so that it is correctly diagnosed and so that unnecessary surgical procedures and inappropriate treatment are avoided.

Rumination is derived from the Latin word *ruminare,* meaning "to chew the cud." The Greek equivalent is *merycism,* the act of regurgitating food from the stomach into the mouth, rechewing the food, and reswallowing it.

Epidemiology

Rumination is a rare disorder. It seems to be most common among infants between 3 months and 1 year of age and among children and adults who are mentally retarded. Adults with rumination usually maintain a normal weight. The disorder is apparently equally common in boys and girls. No reliable figures on predisposing factors or familial patterns are available. The disorder may appear in up to 10 percent of people with bulimia nervosa.

Etiology

Several causes of rumination have been proposed. In those who are mentally retarded, the disorder may simply be self-stimulatory behavior. In those who are nonretarded, psychodynamic theories hypothesize various disturbances in the mother–child relationship. The mothers of infants with the disorder are usually immature, involved in a marital conflict, and unable to give much attention to the baby. These factors result in insufficient emotional gratification and stimulation for the infant, who seeks gratification from within. The rumination is interpreted as the infant's attempt to recreate the feeding process and to provide gratification that the mother does not provide.

Overstimulation and tension have also been suggested as causes of rumination. A dysfunctional autonomic nervous system may be implicated. As sophisticated and accurate investigative techniques are refined, a substantial number of children classified as ruminators are shown to have gastroesophageal reflux or hiatal hernia.

Behaviorists attribute rumination to the positive reinforcement of pleasurable self-stimulation and to the attention the baby receives from others as a consequence of the disorder.

Diagnosis and Clinical Features

The DSM-IV diagnostic criteria for rumination disorder are given in Table 44–4. DSM-IV notes that the essential feature of the disorder is repeated regurgitation and rechewing of food for a period of at least 1 month after a period of normal functioning. Partially digested food is brought up into the mouth without nausea, retching, disgust, or associated gastrointestinal disorder. This activity can be distinguished from vomiting by the clear, purposeful movements the infant makes to induce it. The food is then ejected from the mouth or reswallowed. A characteristic position of straining and arching of the back, with the head held back, is observed. The infant makes sucking movements with the tongue and gives the impression of gaining considerable satisfaction from the activity. A usually present associated feature is the infant's irritability and hunger between episodes of rumination.

Initially, rumination may be difficult to distinguish from the regurgitation that frequently occurs in normal infants. In fully developed cases, however, the diagnosis is obvious. Food or milk is regurgitated without nausea, retching, or disgust and is subjected to what appears to be innumerable pleasurable sucking and chewing movements. The food is then reswallowed or ejected from the mouth.

Although spontaneous remissions are common, severe secondary complications may develop, such as progressive malnutrition, dehydration, and lowered resistance to disease. Failure to thrive, with absence of growth and developmental delays in all areas, may occur. Mortality as high as 25 percent has been reported in severe cases.

An additional complication is that the mother or caretaker is often discouraged by the failure to feed the infant successfully and may become alienated, if she is not already so. Further alienation often occurs as the noxious odor of the regurgitated material leads to avoidance of the infant.

Table 44–4
DSM-IV Diagnostic Criteria for Rumination Disorder

A. Repeated regurgitation and rechewing of food for a period of at least 1 month following a period of normal functioning.

B. The behavior is not due to an associated gastrointestinal or other general medical condition (eg, esophageal reflux).

C. The behavior does not occur exclusively during the course of anorexia nervosa or bulimia nervosa. If the symptoms occur exclusively during the course of mental retardation or a pervasive developmental disorder, they are sufficiently severe to warrant independent clinical attention.

Reprinted with permission from American Psychiatric Association: *Diagnostic and Statistical Manual of Mental Disorders*, ed 4. Copyright, American Psychiatric Association, Washington, 1994.

Pathology and Laboratory Examination. No specific laboratory examination is pathognomonic of rumination disorder. Clinicians must rule out physical causes of vomiting, such as pyloric stenosis and hiatal hernia, before making the diagnosis of rumination disorder. Rumination disorder can be associated with failure to thrive and varying degrees of starvation. Thus, laboratory measures of endocrinological function (thyroid function tests, dexamethasone-suppression test), serum electrolytes, and a hematological workup help determine the severity of the effects of rumination disorder.

Differential Diagnosis

To make the diagnosis of rumination disorder, clinicians must rule out gastrointestinal congenital anomalies, infections, and other medical illnesses. Pyloric stenosis is usually associated with projectile vomiting and is generally evident before 3 months of age, when rumination has its onset. Rumination has been associated with various mental retardation syndromes in which other stereotypic behaviors and eating disturbances, such as pica, are present. Rumination disorder may occur in patients with other eating disorders, such as bulimia nervosa.

Course and Prognosis

Rumination disorder is believed to have a high rate of spontaneous remission. Indeed, many cases of rumination disorder may develop and remit without ever being diagnosed. Only limited data are available about the prognosis of rumination disorder in adults.

Treatment

The treatment of rumination disorder is often a combination of education and behavioral techniques. Sometimes an evaluation of the mother–child relationship reveals deficits that can be influenced by offering guidance to the mother. Behavioral interventions, such as squirting lemon juice into the infant's mouth whenever rumination occurs, can be effective in diminishing the behavior. This practice appears to be the most rapidly effective treatment; rumination is eliminated in 3 to 5 days. In the aversive-conditioning reports on rumination disorder, infants were doing well at 9- or 12-month follow-ups, with no recurrence of the rumination and with weight gains, increased activity levels, and increased responsiveness to people. Rumination may be decreased by the technique of withdrawing attention from the child whenever this behavior occurs. The effectiveness of treatments is difficult to evaluate. Most reported are single-case studies; patients are not randomly assigned to controlled studies.

Any concomitant medical complications must also be treated. Treatments include improvement of the child's psychosocial environment, increased tender loving care from the mother or caretakers, and psychotherapy for the mother or for both parents. When anatomical abnormalities such as hiatal hernia are present, surgical repair may be necessary. Medications including metoclopramide (Reglan), cimetidine (Tagamet), and antipsychotics, such as haloperidol (Haldol) and thioridazine (Mellaril) have been tried and reported to be successful in anecdotal reports. One study showed that when infants were allowed to eat as much as they wanted, the rate of rumination decreased.

Table 44–5
DSM-IV Diagnostic Criteria for Feeding Disorder of Infancy or Early Childhood

A. Feeding disturbance as manifested by persistent failure to eat adequately with significant failure to gain weight or significant loss of weight over at least 1 month.

B. The disturbance is not due to an associated gastrointestinal or other general medical condition (eg, esophageal reflux).

C. The disturbance is not better accounted for by another mental disorder (eg, rumination disorder) or by lack of available food.

D. The onset is before age 6 years.

Reprinted with permission from American Psychiatric Association: *Diagnostic and Statistical Manual of Mental Disorders*, ed 4. Copyright, American Psychiatric Association, Washington, 1994.

FEEDING DISORDER OF INFANCY OR EARLY CHILDHOOD

According to DSM-IV, feeding disorder of infancy or early childhood is a persistent failure to eat adequately, reflected in significant failure to gain weight or in significant weight loss over 1 month. The symptoms are not better accounted for by a medical condition or by another mental disorder and are not caused by lack of food (Table 44–5). The disorder has its onset before the age of 6 years.

References

Benoit D: Phenomenology and treatment of failure to thrive. Child Adolesc Psychiatry Clin North Am *2:* 61, 1993.

Boris NW, Hagino OR, Steiner GP: Case study: Hypersomnolence and precocious puberty in a child with pica and chronic lead intoxication. J Am Acad Adolesc Psychiatry *35:* 1050, 1996.

Connors ME, Morse W: Sexual abuse and eating disorders: A review. Int J Eat Disord *13:* 1, 1993.

Davis PK, Cuvo AJ: Chronic vomiting and rumination in intellectually normal and retarded individuals: Review and evaluation of behavioral research. Behav Res Severe Dev Disabil *1:* 31, 1980.

Franco K, Campbell N, Tamburrino M, Evans C: Rumination: The eating disorder of infancy. Child Psychiatry Hum Dev *24:* 91, 1993.

Hodes M, Le Grange D: Expressed emotion in the investigation of eating disorders: A review. Int J Eat Disord *13:* 279, 1993.

Kramer SS, Eicher PM: The evaluation of pediatric feeding abnormalities. Dysphagia *8:* 215, 1993.

Mayes SD, Humphrey FJ, Handford HA, Mitchell JF: Rumination disorder: Differential diagnosis. J Am Acad Child Adolesc Psychiatry *27:* 300, 1988.

Millican FK, Lourie RS, Laymen EM: Emotional factors in the etiology and treatment of lead poisoning. Am J Dis Child *91:* 144, 1956.

Nasser M: A prescription of vomiting: Historical footnotes. Int J Eat Disord *13:* 129, 1993.

Parry-Jones B, Parry-Jones WLL: Pica: Symptom or eating disorder? A h

Provence S, Lipton RC: *Infants and Institutions.* International Universities Press, New York, 1962.

Rast J, Johnston JM, Drum C, Conrin J: The relation of food quantity to rumination behavior. J Appl Behav Anal *14:* 221, 1981.

Stunkard AJ, Stellar E, editors: *Eating and Its Disorders.* Raven, New York, 1984.

Vanderlinden J, Vanderecycken W, van Dyck R, Vertommen H: Dissociative experience and trauma in eating disorders. Int J Eat Disord *13:* 187, 1993.

45

Tic Disorders

The fourth edition of *Diagnostic and Statistical Manual of Mental Disorders* (DSM-IV), in the section on tic disorders, includes Tourette's disorder, chronic motor or vocal tic disorder, transient tic disorder, and tic disorder not otherwise specified. DSM-IV defines a tic as a "sudden rapid, recurrent, nonrhythmic, stereotyped motor movement or vocalization." Tics are experienced as irresistible, but they can be suppressed for varying periods, exacerbated by stress, and diminished during times of concentration.

Motor and vocal tics are divided into simple and complex. Simple motor tics are those composed of repetitive, rapid contractions of functionally similar muscle groups—for example, eye blinking, neck jerking, shoulder shrugging, and facial grimacing. Common simple vocal tics include coughing, throat clearing, grunting, sniffing, snorting, and barking. Complex motor tics appear to be more purposeful and ritualistic than are simple tics. Common complex motor tics include grooming behaviors, the smelling of objects, jumping, touching behaviors, echopraxia (the imitation of observed behavior), and copropraxia (the display of obscene gestures). Complex vocal tics include repeating words or phrases out of context, coprolalia (the use of obscene words or phrases), palilalia (a person's repeating his or her words), and echolalia (the repetition of the last-heard words of others).

Some people with tic disorders have the ability to suppress the tics for minutes or hours, but others, especially young children, either are not cognizant of their tics or experience their tics as irresistible. Tics may be attenuated by sleep, relaxation, or absorption in an activity. Tics often, but not always, disappear during sleep.

TOURETTE'S DISORDER

According to DSM-IV, tics in Tourette's disorder are multiple motor tics and one or more vocal tics. The tics occur many times a day for more than 1 year. Tourette's disorder causes distress or significant impairment in important areas of functioning. The disorder has an onset before the age of 18 years, and it is not caused by a substance or by a general medical condition.

Georges Gilles de la Tourette first described a patient with what was later known as Tourette's disorder in 1885, while he was studying with Jean-Martin Charcot in France. De la Tourette noted a syndrome among several patients that included multiple motor tics, coprolalia, and echolalia.

Epidemiology

The lifetime prevalence of Tourette's disorder is estimated to be 4 to 5 per 10,000. The onset of the motor component of the disorder generally occurs by the age of 7 years; vocal tics emerge on average by the age of 11 years. Tourette's disorder occurs about 3 times more often in boys than in girls.

Etiology

Genetic Factors. Twin studies, adoption studies, and segregation analysis studies have all supported a genetic etiology for Tourette's disorder. Twin studies have indicated that concordance for the disorder in monozygotic twins is significantly greater than in dizygotic twins. The fact that Tourette's disorder and chronic motor or vocal tic disorder are likely to occur in the same families lends support to the view that the disorders are part of a genetically determined spectrum. The sons of mothers with Tourette's disorder seem to be at the highest risk for the disorder. Evidence in some families indicates that Tourette's disorder is transmitted in an autosomal dominant fashion. Recent studies of a long family pedigree suggest that Tourette's disorder may be transmitted in a bilinear mode. That is, Tourette's disorder appears to be inherited through an autosomal pattern intermediate between dominant and recessive.

A relation is found between Tourette's disorder and attention-deficit/hyperactivity disorder; up to half of all Tourette's disorder patients also have attention-deficit/hyperactivity disorder. A relation also appears between Tourette's disorder and obsessive-compulsive disorder; up to 40 percent of all those with Tourette's disorder also have obsessive-compulsive disorder. In addition, first-degree relatives of people with Tourette's disorder are at high risk for the development of the disorder, of chronic motor or vocal tic disorder, and of obsessive-compulsive disorder. In view of the presence of symptoms of attention-deficit/hyperactivity disorder in more than half of the people with Tourette's disorder, questions arise about a genetic relation between these two disorders.

Neurochemical and Neuroanatomical Factors. Compelling evidence of dopamine system involvement in tic disorders includes the observations that pharmacological agents that antagonize dopamine—haloperidol (Haldol), pimozide (Orap), and fluphenazine (Prolixin)—suppress tics and that agents that increase central dopaminergic activity—meth-

Table 45–1
ICD-10 Diagnostic Criteria for Tic Disorders

Note: A tic is an involuntary, sudden, rapid, recurrent, nonrythmic, stereotyped motor movement or vocalization.

Transient tic disorder

A. Single or multiple motor or vocal tic(s) or both occur many times a day, on most days, over a period of at least 4 weeks.

B. Duration of the disorder is 12 months or less.

C. There is no history of Tourette's syndrome, and the disorder is not the result of physical conditions or side effects of medication.

D. Onset is before the age of 18 years.

Chronic motor or vocal tic disorder

A. Motor or vocal tics, but not both, occur many times per day, on most days, over a period of at least 12 months.

B. No period of remission during that year lasts longer than 2 months.

C. There is no history of Tourette's syndrome, and the disorder is not the result of physical conditions or side effects of medication.

D. Onset is before the age of 18 years.

Combined vocal and multiple motor tic disorder (de la Tourette's syndrome)

A. Multiple motor tics and one or more vocal tics have been present at some time during the disorder, but not necessarily concurrently.

B. The frequency of tics must be many times a day, nearly every day, for more than 1 year, with no period of remission during that year lasting longer than 2 months.

C. Onset is before the age of 18 years.

Other tic disorders

Tic disorder, unspecified

A nonrecommended residual category for a disorder that fulfills the general criteria for a tic disorder but in which the specific subcategory is not specified or in which the features do not fulfill the criteria for Transient tic disorders, Chronic motor or vocal tic disorder, Combined vocal and multiple motor tic disorder (de la Tourette's syndrome).

Reprinted with permission from World Health Organization: *The ICD-10 Classification of Mental and Behavioural Disorders: Diagnostic Criteria for Research.* Copyright, World Health Organization, Geneva, 1993.

ylphenidate (Ritalin), amphetamines, pemoline (Cylert), and cocaine—tend to exacerbate tics. The relation of tics to the dopamine system is not simple, because in some cases antipsychotic medications, such as haloperidol, are not effective in reducing tics and the effect of stimulants on tic disorders has been reported as variable. In some cases, Tourette's disorder has emerged during treatment with antipsychotic medications. Thus, the term *tardive Tourette's disorder* refers to the disorder's similarity to tardive dyskinesia.

Endogenous opiates may be involved in tic disorders and obsessive-compulsive disorder. Some evidence indicates that pharmacological agents that antagonize endogenous opiates—for example, naltrexone (ReVia)—reduce tics and attention deficits in Tourette's disorder patients. Abnormalities in the noradrenergic system have been implicated in some cases by the reduction of tics with clonidine (Catapres), This adrenergic agonist reduces the release of norepinephrine in the central nervous system, and thus may reduce activity in the dopaminergic system. Abnormalities in the basal ganglia result in various movement disorders, such as in Huntington's disease, and are implicated as possible sites of disturbance in Tourette's disorder, obsessive-compulsive disorder, and attention-deficit/hyperactivity disorder.

Immunological Factors and Postinfection. An autoimmune process that is secondary to streptococcal infections has been identified as a potential mechanism causing Tourette's disorder. Such a process could act synergistically with a genetic vulnerability for this disorder. The poststreptococcal syndromes have also been associated with one potential causative factor in the development of obsessive-compulsive disorder, which occurs in up to 40 percent of people with Tourette's disorder.

Diagnosis and Clinical Features

To make a diagnosis of Tourette's disorder, clinicians must obtain a history of multiple motor tics and the emergence of at least one vocal tic at some point in the disorder. According to both the 10th revision of *International Statistical Classification of Diseases and Related Health Problems* (ICD-10) and DSM-IV, the tics must occur many times a day nearly every day or intermittently for more than 1 year. The average age of onset of tics is 7 years, but tics may occur as early as the age of 2 years. The onset must occur before the age of 18 years (Tables 45–1 and 45–2).

In Tourette's disorder, the initial tics are in the face and neck. Over time, the tics tend to occur in a downward progression.

The most commonly described tics are those affecting the face and head, the arms and hands, the body and lower extremities, and the respiratory and alimentary systems. In these areas, the tics take the form of grimacing; puckering the forehead; raising eyebrows; blinking eyelids; winking; wrinkling the nose; trembling nostrils; twitching mouth; displaying the teeth; biting the lips and other parts; extruding the tongue;

Table 45–2
DSM-IV Diagnostic Criteria for Tourette's Disorder

A. Both multiple motor and one or more vocal tics have been present at some time during the illness, although not necessarily concurrently. (A *tic* is a sudden, rapid, recurrent, nonrhythmic, stereotyped motor movement or vocalization.)

B. The tics occur many times a day (usually in bouts), nearly every day or intermittently throughout a period of more than 1 year, and during this period there was never a tic-free period of more than 3 consecutive months.

C. The onset is before age 18 years.

D. The disturbance is not due to the direct physiological effects of a substance (eg, stimulants) or a general medical condition (eg, Huntington's disease or postviral encephalitis).

Reprinted with permission from American Psychiatric Association: *Diagnostic and Statistical Manual of Mental Disorders,* ed 4. Copyright, American Psychiatric Association, Washington, 1994.

protracting the lower jaw; nodding, jerking, or shaking the head; twisting the neck; looking sideways; head rolling; jerking the hands; jerking the arms; plucking fingers; writhing fingers; clenching fists; shrugging the shoulders; shaking a foot, knee, or toe; walking peculiarly; body writhing; jumping; hiccuping; sighing; yawning; snuffing; blowing through the nostrils; whistling inspiration; breathing exaggeratedly; belching; making sucking or smacking sounds; and clearing the throat.

Typically, prodromal behavioral symptoms—such as irritability, attention difficulties, and poor frustration tolerance—are evident before or coincide with the onset of tics. More than 25 percent of people in some studies received stimulants for a diagnosis of attention-deficit/hyperactivity disorder before receiving a diagnosis of Tourette's disorder. The most frequent initial symptom is an eye-blink tic, followed by a head tic or a facial grimace. Most complex motor and vocal symptoms emerge several years after the initial symptoms. Coprolalia usually begins in early adolescence and occurs in about one third of all cases. Mental coprolalia—in which a patient thinks a sudden, intrusive, socially unacceptable thought or obscene word—may also occur. In some severe cases, physical injuries, including retinal detachment and orthopedic problems, have resulted from severe tics.

Obsessions, compulsions, attention difficulties, impulsivity, and personality problems have been associated with Tourette's disorder. Attention difficulties often precede the onset of tics, whereas obsessive-compulsive symptoms often occur after their onset. It is still being debated whether these problems usually develop secondarily to a patient's tics or are caused primarily by the same underlying pathological condition. Many tics have an aggressive or sexual component that may result in serious social consequences for the patient. Phenomenologically, tics resemble a failure of censorship, both conscious and unconscious, with increased impulsivity and inability to inhibit a thought from being put into action.

David is a 16-year-old adolescent who was psychiatrically hospitalized because of a severe physical altercation with a peer at school. David had been in special education since the second grade, mainly as a result of his hyperactive behavior, aggressive outbursts, and disruptive vocal outbursts. David experienced his first eye-blinking tic at 5 years of age; it went virtually unnoticed for at least 1 year, as his most obvious traits were hyperactivity and short attention span. David went through a series of waxing and waning tics over the next 3 years. These ranged from eye deviations, to head jerking, to facial grimacing, and arm jerks. These tics did not seem to interfere with his peer or family interactions. At the age of 9 years, however, he began to clear his throat very loudly and repeatedly for periods of several months; then this symptom seemed to disappear. At this time, David grew increasingly more impulsive and aggressive in several ways. He often could not wait his turn in games and would push others out of the way to get a turn sooner. Peers often found him to be too rough and a sore loser.

David was started on a trial of methylphenidate at the age of 9 years, to deal with his inability to pay attention to his tasks in school. He benefited from the trial for several months, but when he began to make repeated loud, grunting noises at school, the medication was discontinued because, as in some cases, tics can be exacerbated by stimulants.

When David was 13 years of age, his aggression and tics became more severe. He began to compulsively do things that he could not seem to control, such as grabbing people. His motor tics would come and go, but when he was having an exacerbation, he was particularly upset by his sniffing, coughing, and throat clearing. He had never had coprolalia. He continued in his special education class and was given a trial of clonidine, which seemed to help both his hyperactivity and his tics somewhat. During his hospitalization at age 16, David was finally able to talk about how depressed he was feeling. He was started on a trial of sertraline (Zoloft,) and the clonidine was discontinued. He was also given a small dose of risperidone at night which was well tolerated. The combination seemed to improve his dysphoria and aggression and appeared to slightly diminish the frequency of his tics. The only disturbing side effect he experienced with this combination was occasional enuresis. Although this was unpleasant, his daytime functioning was so much improved that the decision was made to retain this combination.

Pathology and Laboratory Examination. There is no specific laboratory diagnostic test for Tourette's disorder, but many patients with Tourette's disorder have nonspecific abnormal electroencephalogram findings. Computed tomography (CT) and magnetic resonance imaging scans have not revealed specific structural lesions, although about 10 percent of all patients with Tourette's disorder show some nonspecific abnormality on CT scans.

Differential Diagnosis

Tics must be differentiated from other disordered movements (for example, dystonic, choreiform, athetoid, myoclonic, and hemiballismic movements) and the neurological diseases of which they are characteristic (for example, Huntington's disease, parkinsonism, Sydenham's chorea, and Wilson's disease), as listed in Table 45–3. Tremors, mannerisms, and stereotypic movement disorder (for example, head banging or body rocking) must also be distinguished from tic disorders. Stereotypic movement disorders, including movements such as rocking, hand gazing, and other self-stimulatory behaviors, seem to be voluntary and often produce a sense of comfort, in contrast to tic disorders. Although tics in children and adolescents may or may not feel controllable, they rarely produce a sense of well-being. Compulsions are sometimes difficult to distinguish from complex tics and may be on the same continuum biologically. Tic disorders also occur comorbidly with multiple behavioral and mood disturbances. In a recent survey, the greater the severity of tics, the higher the probability of both aggressive and depressive symptoms in children. Even in a given child with Tourette's disorder, it has been reported that when there is an exacerbation of tic symptoms, behavior and mood also seem to deteriorate. This phenomenon occurs with children who have Tourette's disorder and attention-deficit/hy-

Table 45–3
Differential Diagnosis of Tic Disorders

Disease or Syndrome	Age at Onset	Associated Features	Course	Predominant Type of Movement
Hallervorden-Spatz	Childhood–adolescence	May be associated with optic atrophy, club feet, retinitis pigmentosa, dysarthria, dementia, ataxia, emotional lability, spasticity, autosomal recessive inheritance	Progressive to death in 5 to 20 years	Choreic, athetoid, myoclonic
Dystonia musculorum deformans	Childhood–adolescence	Autosomal recessive inheritance commonly, primarily among Ashkenazi Jews; a more benign autosomal dominant form also occurs	Variable course, often progressive but with rare remissions	Dystonia
Sydenham's chorea	Childhood, usually 5–15 years	More common in females, usually associated with rheumatic fever (carditis elevated ASLO titers)	Usually self-limited	Choreiform
Huntington's disease	Usually 30–50 years, but childhood forms are known	Autosomal dominant inheritance, dementia, caudate atrophy on CT scan	Progressive to death in 10 to 15 years after onset	Choreiform
Wilson's disease (hepatolenticular degeneration)	Usually 10–25 years	Kayser-Fleischer rings, liver dysfunction, inborn error of copper metabolism; autosomal recessive inheritance	Progressive to death without chelating therapy	Wing-beating tremor, dystonia
Hyperreflexias (including latah, myriachit, jumper disease of Maine)	Generally in childhood (dominant inheritance)	Familial; may have generalized rigidity and autosomal inheritance	Nonprogressive	Excessive startle response; may have echolalia, coprolalia, and forced obedience
Myoclonic disorders	Any age	Numerous causes, some familial, usually no vocalizations	Variable, depending on cause	Myoclonus
Myoclonic dystonia	5–47 years	Nonfamilial, no vocalizations	Nonprogressive	Torsion dystonia with myoclonic jerks
Paroxysmal myoclonic dystonia with vocalization	Childhood	Attention, hyperactive, and learning disorders; movements interfere with ongoing activity	Nonprogressive	Bursts of regular, repetitive clonic (less tonic) movements and vocalizations
Tardive Tourette's disorder syndromes	Variable (after antipsychotic medication use)	Reported to be precipitated by discontinuation or reduction of medication	May terminate after increase or decrease of dosage	Orofacial dyskinesias, choreoathetosis, tics, vocalization
Neuroacanthocytosis	Third or fourth decade	Acanthocytosis, muscle wasting, parkinsonism, autosomal recessive inheritance	Variable	Orofacial dyskinesia and limb chorea, tics, vocalization

(continued)

Table 45–3 *(continued)*

Disease or Syndrome	Age at Onset	Associated Features	Course	Predominant Type of Movement
Encephalitis lethargica	Variable	Shouting fits, bizarre behavior, psychosis, Parkinson's disease	Variable	Simple and complex motor and vocal tics, coprolalia, echolalia, echopraxia, palilalia
Gasoline inhalation	Variable	Abnormal EEG; symmetrical theta and theta bursts frontocentrally	Variable	Simple motor and vocal tics
Postangiographic complications	Variable	Emotional lability, amnestic syndrome	Variable	Simple motor and complex vocal tics, palilalia
Postinfectious	Variable	EEG: occasional asymmetrical theta bursts before movements, elevated ASLO titers	Variable	Simple motor and vocal tics, echopraxia
Posttraumatic	Variable	Asymmetrical tic distribution	Variable	Complex motor tics
Carbon monoxide poisoning	Variable	Inappropriate sexual behavior	Variable	Simple and complex motor and vocal tics, coprolalia, echolalia, palilalia
XYY genetic disorder	Infancy	Aggressive behavior	Static	Simple motor and vocal tics
XXY and 9_p mosaicism	Infancy	Multiple physical anomalies, mental retardation	Static	Simple motor and vocal tics
Duchenne's muscular dystrophy (X-linked recessive)	Childhood	Mild mental retardation	Progressive	Motor and vocal tics
Fragile X syndrome	Childhood	Mental retardation, facial dysmorphism, seizures, autistic features	Static	Simple motor and vocal tics, coprolalia
Developmental and perinatal disorders	Infancy, childhood	Seizures, EEG and CT abnormalities, psychosis, aggressivity, hyperactivity, Ganser's syndrome, compulsivity, torticollis	Variable	Motor and vocal tics, echolalia

peractivity disorder, and also with those who have depression or oppositional-defiant disorders. In children with Tourette's disorder and attention-deficit/hyperactivity disorder, even when the tic disorder had always been mild, a high frequency of disruptive behavior problems and mood disorder still exist. Both autistic and mentally retarded children may exhibit symptoms similar to those seen in tic disorders, including Tourette's disorder. A greater than expected occurrence of Tourette's disorder, autistic disorder, and bipolar disorder also is present.

Before instituting antipsychotic medication, clinicians must make a baseline evaluation of preexisting abnormal movements; such medication can mask abnormal movements, and if the movements occur later, they can be mistaken for tardive dyskinesia. Stimulant medications (such as methylphenidate, amphetamines, and pemoline) have been reported to exacerbate preexisting tics in some cases. These effects have been reported primarily in some children and adolescents being treated for attention-deficit/hyperactivity disorder. In most but not all cases, after the drug was discontinued, the tics remitted or returned to premedication levels. Most experts suggest that children and adolescents who experience tics while receiving stimulants are probably genetically predisposed and would have experienced tics regardless of their treatment with stimulants. Until the situation is clarified, clinicians should use great caution and should frequently monitor children at risk for tics who are given stimulants.

Course and Prognosis

Untreated, Tourette's disorder is usually a chronic, lifelong disease with relative remissions and exacerbations. Initial symptoms may decrease, persist, or increase, and old symptoms may be replaced by new ones. Severely afflicted people may have serious emotional problems, including major depressive disorder. Some of these difficulties appear to be associated with Tourette's disorder, whereas others result from severe social, academic, and vocational consequences, which are frequent sequelae of the disorder. In some cases, despair over the disruption of social and occupational functioning is so severe that people contemplate and attempt suicide. But some children with Tourette's disorder have satisfactory peer relationships, function well in school, and have adequate self-esteem; they may need no treatment and can be monitored by their pediatricians.

Treatment

Pharmacological treatments are most effective for Tourette's disorder, but patients with mild cases may not require medication. Psychotherapy is usually ineffective as a primary treatment modality, although it may help a patient cope with the disorder's symptoms and any concomitant personality and behavioral difficulties. Several behavioral techniques—including massed (negative) practice, self-monitoring, incompatible response training, presentation and removal of positive reinforcement, and habit reversal treatment—were reviewed by Stanley A. Hobbs. He reported that tic frequency was reduced in many cases, particularly with habit reversal treatment, but relatively few studies have reported clinically significant changes. In general, behavioral treatments were most effective in treating transient and chronic motor or vocal tic disorders, but relatively few cases of Tourette's disorder responded favorably. Behavior therapy currently seems to be most useful in reducing stresses that may aggravate Tourette's disorder. Whether behavior therapy and pharmacotherapy together have a synergistic effect has not been sufficiently investigated.

Pharmacotherapy. Haloperidol is the most frequently prescribed drug for Tourette's disorder. Up to 80 percent of patients have a favorable response; their symptoms decrease by as much as 70 to 90 percent of baseline frequency. Follow-up studies, however, indicate that only 20 to 30 percent of these patients continue to take long-term maintenance therapy. Discontinuation is often based on the drug's adverse effects. Haloperidol appears to be most effective at relatively low dosages. The initial daily dosage for adolescents and adults is usually between 0.25 and 0.5 mg of haloperidol. Haloperidol is not approved for use in children under 3 years of age. For children between 3 and 12 years of age, the recommended total daily dosage is between 0.05 and 0.075 mg/kg, administered in divided doses either 2 or 3 times a day. This dosage imposes a daily limit of 3 mg of haloperidol for a 40-kg child. The dosage for all patients should be increased slowly, to minimize the likelihood of an acute dystonic reaction. The maximal effective dosage in adolescents and adults is often in the range of 3 to 4 mg a day, but some patients require dosages of up to 10 to 15 mg a day.

Patients and their parents, when appropriate, must be made aware of the drug's possible immediate and long-term adverse effects. Clinicians must forewarn them of the possibilities of acute dystonic reactions and parkinsonian symptoms. Although the prophylactic use of an anticholinergic agent is not recommended, it is appropriate to prescribe diphenhydramine (Benadryl) or benztropine (Cogentin) to the patient, so that it is available should an acute dystonic reaction or parkinsonian effects occur at home or on vacation. Other effects of special concern are cognitive dulling, which can impair school performance and learning, and the risk of tardive dyskinesia. School phobias in children and disabling social phobias in adults have been reported during the early phase of treatment, but the phobias usually remit in a few weeks after discontinuing haloperidol.

Pimozide, an inhibitor of postsynaptic dopamine receptors, is also effective in treating Tourette's disorder. In a recent large study, haloperidol was found to be more effective than pimozide. Pimozide, as with haloperidol, should not be used to treat simple tics. Pimozide is an antipsychotic with adverse effects similar to those of other antipsychotics. Furthermore, adverse cardiac effects are unusually frequent, and deaths have occurred at high dosages. Nevertheless, pimozide appears to be safe at recommended dosages, with cardiotoxicity limited to prolonged QT wave intervals. Electrocardiograms must be performed at baseline and periodically during treatment. There is little experience in administering pimozide to children under 12 years of age. The initial dosage of pimozide is usually 1 to 2 mg daily in divided doses; the dosage may be increased every other day. Most patients are maintained at less than 0.2 mg/kg a day or 10 mg a day, whichever is less. A dosage of 0.3 mg/ kg a day or 20 mg a day should never be exceeded.

Although not presently approved for use in Tourette's disorder, clonidine, a noradrenergic antagonist, has been reported to be efficacious in several studies; 40 to 70 percent of patients benefited from the medication. Some clinicians have used clonidine after they have considered its risks and benefits and have fully informed the patient and, when appropriate, the parents. Clonidine has a slower onset of action than does haloperidol, and improvement may continue for more than 1 year in some cases. In addition to the improvement in tic symptoms, patients may experience less tension and a longer attention span, although the drug may also be quite sedating. A newer antipsychotic, risperidone, has been used in open trials for controlling tic behaviors. Although no data are currently available from double-blind placebo-controlled trials, anecdotal reports suggest that risperidone is relatively safe in the short run, and may be helpful in controlling tics.

In view of the frequent comorbidity of tic behaviors and obsessive-compulsive symptoms or disorders, the serotonin-specific reuptake inhibitor drugs (SSRIs) have been used alone or in combination with antipsychotics in the treatment of Tourette's disorder. Some data suggest that SSRIs, such as fluoxetine, may be helpful. Children suffering from tics and severe attention-deficit/hyperactivity disorder can be treated with tricyclic antidepressants, but because of the report of at least four deaths of children treated with desipramine, this class of medication is often not considered.

Although clinicians must weigh the risks versus the benefits of using stimulants in cases of severe hyperactivity and comorbid tics, a recent study reported that methylphenidate reduced vocal tics in some children with hyperactivity and tic disorders. Another recent case report indicated that bupropion (Wellbutrin), an antidepressant of the aminoketone class, resulted in increased tic behavior in several children being treated for Tourette's disorder and attention-deficit/hyperactivity disorder.

CHRONIC MOTOR OR VOCAL TIC DISORDER

In DSM-IV, chronic motor or vocal tic disorder is defined as the presence of either motor tics or vocal tics, but not both. The other features are the same as those of Tourette's disorder, but chronic motor or vocal tic disorder cannot be diagnosed if the criteria for Tourette's disorder have ever been met. According to DSM-IV criteria, the disorder must have its onset before the age of 18 years.

Epidemiology

The rate of chronic motor or vocal tic disorder has been estimated to be from 100 to 1,000 times greater than that of

Tourette's disorder. School-age boys are at highest risk, but the incidence is unknown. Although the disorder was once believed to be rare, current estimates of the prevalence of chronic motor or vocal tic disorder range from 1 to 2 percent.

Etiology

Both Tourette's disorder and chronic motor or vocal tic disorder aggregate in the same families. Twin studies have found a high concordance for either Tourette's disorder or chronic motor tics in monozygotic twins. This finding supports the importance of hereditary factors in the transmission of at least some tic disorders.

Diagnosis and Clinical Features

The onset of chronic motor or vocal tic disorder appears to be in early childhood. The types of tics and their locations are similar to those in transient tic disorder. Chronic vocal tics are considerably rarer than are chronic motor tics. The chronic vocal tics are usually much less conspicuous than those in Tourette's disorder. The vocal tics are usually not loud or intense and are not primarily produced by the vocal cords; they consist of grunts or other noises caused by thoracic, abdominal, or diaphragmatic contractions. The DSM-IV diagnostic criteria are given in Table 45–4.

Differential Diagnosis

Chronic motor tics must be differentiated from a variety of other motor movements, including choreiform movements, myoclonus, restless legs syndrome, akathisia, and dystonias. Involuntary vocal utterances can occur in certain neurological disorders, such as Huntington's disease and Parkinson's disease.

Table 45–4
DSM-IV Diagnostic Criteria for Chronic Motor or Vocal Tic Disorder

A. Single or multiple motor or vocal tics (ie, sudden, rapid, recurrent, nonrhythmic, stereotyped motor movements or vocalizations), but not both, have been present at some time during the illness.
B. The tics occur many times a day nearly every day or intermittently throughout a period of more than 1 year, and during this period there was never a tic-free period of more than 3 consecutive months.
C. The disturbance causes marked distress or significant impairment in social, occupational, or other important areas of functioning.
D. The onset is before 18 years.
E. The disturbance is not due to the direct physiological effects of a substance (eg, Huntington's disease or postviral encephalitis).
F. Criteria have never been met for Tourette's disorder.

Reprinted with permission from American Psychiatric Association: *Diagnostic and Statistical Manual of Mental Disorders,* ed 4. Copyright, American Psychiatric Association, Washington, 1994.

Course and Prognosis

Children whose tics start between the ages of 6 and 8 years seem to have the best outcomes. Symptoms usually last for 4 to 6 years and stop in early adolescence. Children whose tics involve the limbs or trunk tend to do less well than those with only facial tics.

Treatment

The treatment of chronic motor or vocal tic disorder depends on the severity and the frequency of the tics; the patient's subjective distress; the effects of the tics on school or work, job performance, and socialization; and the presence of any other concomitant mental disorder. Psychotherapy may be indicated to minimize the secondary emotional problems caused by the tics. Several studies have found that behavioral techniques, particularly habit reversal treatments, have been effective in treating chronic motor or vocal tic disorder. Antianxiety agents have been unsuccessful. Haloperidol has been helpful in some cases, but the risks must be weighed against the possible clinical benefits because of the drug's adverse effects, including the development of tardive dyskinesia.

TRANSIENT TIC DISORDER

DSM-IV defines transient tic disorder as the presence of a single tic or multiple motor or vocal tics or both. The tics occur many times a day for at least 4 weeks but for no longer than 12 months. The other features are the same as those for Tourette's disorder, but transient tic disorder cannot be diagnosed if the criteria for Tourette's disorder or chronic motor or vocal tic disorder have ever been met. According to DSM-IV, the disorder must have its onset before the age of 18 years.

Epidemiology

Transient, ticlike movements and nervous muscular twitches are common in children. From 5 to 24 percent of all school-age children have a history of tics. The prevalence of tics as defined here is unknown.

Etiology

Transient tic disorder probably has either organic or psychogenic origins, with some tics combining elements of both. Organic tics, which are probably most likely to progress to Tourette's disorder, have an increased family history of tics, whereas psychogenic tics are most likely to remit spontaneously. Tics that progress to chronic motor or vocal tic disorder are most likely to have components of both organic and psychogenic origins. Tics of all sorts are exacerbated by stress and anxiety, but no evidence is available that tics are caused by stress or anxiety.

Diagnosis and Clinical Features

The DSM-IV criteria for establishing the diagnosis of transient tic disorder are as follows: The tics are single or multiple motor or vocal tics. The tics occur many times a day nearly every day for at least 4 weeks but for no longer than 12 consecutive months. The patient has no history of Tourette's disorder or chronic motor or vocal tic disorder. The onset is before age 18. The tics do not occur exclusively during substance intoxication, and they are not caused by a general medical condition. The diagnosis should specify whether a single episode or recurrent episodes are present (Table 45–5). Transient tic disorder can be distinguished from chronic motor or vocal tic disorder and Tourette's disorder only by observing the symptoms' progression over time.

Course and Prognosis

Most people with transient tic disorder do not progress to a more serious tic disorder. Their tics either disappear permanently or recur during periods of special stress. Only a small percentage develop chronic motor or vocal tic disorder or Tourette's disorder.

Treatment

Whether the tics will disappear spontaneously, progress, or become chronic is unclear at the beginning of treatment. Focusing attention on tics may exacerbate them; thus, clinicians often recommend that, at first, the family disregard the tics as much as possible. But if the tics are so severe that they impair the patient or if they are accompanied by significant emotional disturbances, complete psychiatric and pediatric neurological examinations are recommended. Treatment depends on the results of the evaluations. Psychopharmacology is not recommended unless the symptoms are unusually severe and disabling. Several studies have found that behavioral techniques, particularly habit reversal treatment, have been effective in treating transient tics.

TIC DISORDER NOT OTHERWISE SPECIFIED

According to DSM-IV, tic disorder not otherwise specified refers to disorders characterized by tics but not otherwise meeting the criteria for a specific tic disorder (Table 45-6).

Table 45–5
DSM-IV Diagnostic Criteria for Transient Tic Disorder

A. Single or multiple motor and/or vocal tics (ie, sudden, rapid, recurrent, nonrhythmic, stereotyped motor movements or vocalizations)
B. The tics occur many times a day, nearly every day for at least 4 weeks but for no longer than 12 consecutive months.
C. The disturbance causes marked distress or significant impairment in social, occupational, or other important areas of functioning.
D. The onset is before age 18 years.
E. The disturbance is not due to the direct physiological effects of a substance (eg, stimulants) or a general medical condition (eg, Huntington's disease or postviral encephalitis).
F. Criteria have never been met for Tourette's disorder or chronic motor or vocal tic disorder.

Specify if: Single episode or recurrent.

Reprinted with permission from American Psychiatric Association: *Diagnostic and Statistical Manual of Mental Disorders,* ed 4. Copyright, American Psychiatric Association, Washington, 1994.

Table 45–6
DSM-IV Diagnostic Criteria for Tic Disorder Not Otherwise Specified

This category is for disorders characterized by tics that do not meet criteria for a specific tic disorder. Examples include tics lasting less than 4 weeks or tics with an onset after age 18 years.

Reprinted with permission from American Psychiatric Association: *Diagnostic and Statistical Manual of Mental Disorders,* ed 4. Copyright, American Psychiatric Association, Washington, 1994.

ICD-10

In the ICD-10, tic disorders form a category under disorders of childhood and adolescence. ICD-10 includes the same tic disorders as does DSM-IV and adds another, other tic disorders. Tics—motor movements or vocal productions that serve no apparent purpose and are of sudden onset—are described as the predominant manifestation in these syndromes. The severity of tics varies greatly, from near normal, with 1 in 5 or 1 in 10 children occasionally manifesting tics, to Tourette's syndrome, which is rare, severe, and incapacitating. Tic disorders are more common in boys than in girls, and a family history of tics is frequent.

REFERENCES

Caine ED, McBride MC, Chiverton P, Bamford KA, Rediess S, Shiao J: Tourette's syndrome in Monroe County school children. Neurology *38:* 472, 1988.

Cohen DJ, Leckman JF, Shaywitz BA: The Tourette's syndrome and other tics. In *The Clinical Guide to Child Psychiatry,* D Shaffer, AA Ehrandt, LL Greenhill, editors, p 3. Free Press, New York, 1985.

Friedhoff AJ, Chase TN, editors: *Gilles de la Tourette Syndrome.* Raven Press, New York, 1982.

Gadow KD, Nolan EE, Sverd J: Methylphenidate in hyperactive boys with comorbid tic disorder. II. Short-term behavioral effects in school settings. J Am Acad Child Adolesc Psychiatry *31:* 462, 1992.

Hanna GL: Tic disorders. In *Comprehensive Textbook of Psychiatry,* ed 6, HI Kaplan, BJ Sadock, editors, p 2325. Williams & Wilkins, Baltimore, 1995

Hawkridge S, Stein DJ, Bouwer C: Combined pharmacotherapy for TS and OCD. J Am Acad Child Adolesc Psychiatry *35:* 703, 1996.

Hobbs SA, Dorsett PG, Dahlquist LM: Tic disorders. In *Behavior Therapy with Children and Adolescents: A Clinical Approach,* M Hersen, VB Van Hasselt, editors, p 241. Wiley, New York, 1987.

Kerbeshian J, Burd L: Case Study: Comorbidity among Tourette's syndrome, autistic disorder, and bipolar disorder. J Am Acad Child Adolesc Psychiatry *35:* 681, 1996.

Lombroso PJ, Scahill L, King RA: Risperidone treatment of children and adolescents with chronic tic disorders: A preliminary report. J Am Acad Child Adolesc Psychiatry *34:* 147, 1995.

McMahon WM, van de Weterin BJM, Filloux F, Betit K, Coon H, Leppert M: Bilineal transmission and phenotypic variation of Tourette's disorder in a large pedigree. J Am Acad Child Adolesc Psychiatry *35:* 672, 1996.

Nolan EE, Sverd J, Gadow KD, Sprafkin J, Ezor SN: Associated psychopathology in children with both ADHD and chronic tic disorder. J Am Acad Child Adolesc Psychiatry *35:* 1622, 1996.

Price RA, Kidd KK, Cohen DJ, Pauls DL, Leckman JF: A twin study of Tourette's syndrome Arch Gen Psychiatry *43:* 815, 1985.

Segal NL, Dysken MW, Bouchard TJ, Petersen NL, Eckert ED, Heston LL: Tourette's disorder in a set of reared-apart triplets: Genetic and environmental influences. Am J Psychiatry *147:* 196, 1990.

Shapiro E, Shapiro AK, Fulop G, Hubbard M, Mendell J, Nordie J, Phillips R: Controlled study of haloperidol, pimozide and placebo for the treatment of Gilles de la Tourette's syndrome. Arch Gen Psychiatry *46:* 722, 1989.

Spencer T, Biederman J, Steingard R, Wilens T: Bupropion exacerbates tics in children with attention-deficit hyperactivity disorder and Tourette's syndrome. J Am Acad Child Adolesc Psychiatry *32:* 211, 1993.

Spencer T, Biederman J, Wilens T, Steingard R, Geist D: Nortriptyline treatment of children with attention-deficit hyperactivity disorder and tic disorder or

Tourette's syndrome. J Am Acad Child Adolesc Psychiatry *32:* 205, 1993.

Steingard R, Biederman J, Spencer T, Wilens T, Gonzalez A: Comparison of clonidine response in the treatment of attention-deficit hyperactivity disorder with and without comorbid tic disorders. J Am Acad Child Adolesc Psychiatry *32:* 350, 1993.

Tucker DM, Leckman JF, Scahill L, Wilf GE, LaCamera R, Cardona L, Cohen P, Heidmann S, Goldstein J, Judge J, Snyder E, Bult A, Peterson BS, King R, Lombroso P: A putative poststreptococcal case of OCD with chronic tic disorder, not otherwise specified. J Am Acad Child Adolesc Psychiatry *35:* 1684, 1996.

46 Elimination Disorders

The fourth edition of *Diagnostic and Statistical Manual of Mental Disorders* (DSM-IV) includes two elimination disorders, encopresis and enuresis. *Encopresis* is defined in DSM-IV as a pattern of passing feces into inappropriate places, whether the passage is involuntary or intentional. The pattern must be present for at least 3 months; the child's chronological age must be at least 4 years, or the child must have the developmental level of a 4 year old. *Enuresis* is defined in DSM-IV as the repeated voiding of urine into clothes or bed, whether the voiding is involuntary or intentional. The behavior must occur twice weekly for at least 3 months or must cause clinically significant distress or impairment socially or academically. The child's chronological or developmental age must be at least 5 years.

Elimination disorders are thus characterized by passage of feces or urine into inappropriate places by a child whose developmental level implies the ability to have control. Bowel and bladder control develops gradually over time. Toilet training is affected by many factors, such as a child's intellectual capacity and social maturity, cultural determinants, and the psychological interactions between child and parents.

The normal sequence of developing control over bowel and bladder functions is the development of nocturnal fecal continence, diurnal fecal continence, diurnal bladder control, and nocturnal bladder control.

ENCOPRESIS

Epidemiology

In Western cultures, bowel control is established in more than 95 percent of children by the fourth birthday and in 99 percent by the fifth birthday. Thereafter, frequency decreases to virtual absence by the age of 16. After the age of 4, encopresis at all ages is 3 to 4 times as common in boys as in girls. At the ages of 7 to 8, frequency is about 1.5 percent in boys and about 0.5 percent in girls. By the ages of 10 to 12, once-a-month soiling occurs in 1.3 percent of boys and in 0.3 percent of girls. There is a significant relation between encopresis and enuresis.

Etiology

Encopresis involves an often complicated interplay between physiological and psychological factors. Inadequate training or the lack of appropriate toilet training may delay a child's attainment of continence. Evidence indicates that some encopretic children suffer from lifelong inefficient and ineffective sphincter control. Thus, encopresis may occur in children with adequate bowel control who, for a variety of emotional reasons, including anger, anxiety, fear, or some combination of these, do not deposit the feces appropriately. Other children may soil involuntarily, either because of an inability to control the sphincter adequately or because of excessive fluid caused by a retentive overflow. Up to 75 percent of children with encopresis are constipated and have excessive fluid overflow.

Any combination of these factors may promote a power struggle between child and parent over issues of autonomy and control. Perpetual battles often aggravate the disorder and frequently cause secondary behavioral difficulties. Many encopretic children, however, do not have behavioral problems. When behavioral problems do occur, they are the social consequences of soiling. Encopretic children who are clearly able to control their bowel function adequately and who deposit feces of relatively normal consistency in abnormal places usually have a psychiatric difficulty. Encopresis may be associated with other neurodevelopmental problems, including easy distractibility, short attention span, low frustration tolerance, hyperactivity, and poor coordination. Occasionally, the child has a special fear of using the toilet. Encopresis may also be precipitated by life events, such as the birth of a sibling or a move to a new home. Encopresis after a long period of fecal continence sometimes appears to be a regression after such stresses as a parental separation, a change in domicile, or the start of school.

Psychogenic Megacolon. Many encopretic children also retain feces and become constipated, either voluntarily or secondarily to painful defecation. In these cases, no clear evidence indicates that preexisting anorectal dysfunction contributes to the constipation. The resulting chronic rectal distention from large, hard fecal masses may cause loss of tone in the rectal wall and desensitization to pressure. Thus, many children become unaware of the need to defecate, and overflow encopresis occurs, usually with relatively small amounts of liquid or soft stool leaking out.

Olfactory accommodation may diminish or eliminate sensory cues. Children whose parenting has been harsh and punitive and who have been severely punished for "accidents" during toilet training may also develop encopresis.

Diagnosis and Clinical Features

According to the DSM-IV, encopresis is diagnosed when feces are passed into inappropriate places on a regular basis

Table 46–1
DSM-IV Diagnostic Criteria for Encopresis

A. Repeated passage of feces into inappropriate places (eg, clothing or floor) whether involuntary or intentional.
B. At least one such event a month for at least 3 months.
C. Chronological age of at least 4 years (or equivalent developmental level).
D. The behavior is not due exclusively to the direct physiological effects of a substance (eg, laxatives) or a general medical condition except through a mechanism involving constipation.

Code as follows:
With constipation and overflow incontinence
Without constipation and overflow incontinence

(at least once a month) for 3 months (Table 46–1). Encopresis may be present in children who have bowel control and intentionally deposit feces in their clothes or other places for a variety of emotional reasons. Some children engage in the inappropriate behavior when angry at parental figures or as part of a pattern of oppositional defiant disorder. The children often develop repetitive behaviors that seem to seek negative attention. In other children, sporadic episodes of encopresis may occur during times of stress—for example, proximal to the birth of a new sibling—but in such cases the behavior is usually transient and does not fulfill the diagnostic criteria for the disorder.

Encopresis may also be present on an involuntary basis in the absence of physiological abnormalities. In these cases, a child may not exhibit adequate control over the sphincter muscles, either because the child is absorbed in another activity or because he or she is unaware of the process. The feces may be of normal, near-normal, or liquid consistency. Some involuntary soiling is due to the chronic retaining of stool, which results in liquid overflow. In rare cases, the involuntary overflow of stool results from psychological causes of diarrhea or anxiety disorder symptoms.

DSM-IV breaks down the types of encopresis into with constipation and overflow incontinence and without constipation and overflow incontinence. To receive a diagnosis of encopresis, a child must have a development at, or chronological level of at least, 4 years. If the fecal incontinence is directly related to a medical condition, encopresis is not diagnosed.

Studies have indicated that children with encopresis who do not have gastrointestinal illnesses have high rates of abnormal anal sphincter contractions. This finding is particularly prevalent among children with encopresis with constipation and overflow incontinence who have difficulty in relaxing their anal sphincter muscles when trying to defecate. Children with constipation who have difficulties with sphincter relaxation are not likely to be good responders to laxatives in the treatment of their encopresis. Encopretic children without abnormal sphincter tone are likely to improve over a short period.

The criteria for encopresis from the 10th revision of *International Statistical Classification of Diseases and Related Health Problems* (ICD-10) are listed in Table 46–2.

Pathology and Laboratory Examination. Although no specific test indicates a diagnosis of encopresis, clinicians must rule out medical illnesses, such as Hirschsprung's disease, before making a diagnosis. If it is unclear whether fecal retention is responsible for encopresis with constipation and overflow incontinence, a physical examination of the abdomen is indicated, and an abdominal X-ray can be helpful in determining the degree of constipation present. Sophisticated tests to determine whether sphincter tone is abnormal are generally not conducted in simple cases of encopresis.

Differential Diagnosis

In encopresis with constipation and overflow incontinence, constipation can begin as early as the child's first year and can peak between the second and fourth years. Soiling usually begins at the age of 4. Frequent liquid stools and hard fecal masses are found in the colon and the rectum on abdominal palpation and rectal examination. Complications include impaction, megacolon, and anal fissures.

Encopresis with constipation and overflow incontinence can be caused by faulty nutrition; structural disease of the anus, rectum, and colon; medicinal side effects; or nongastrointestinal medical (endocrine or neurological) disorders. The chief differential problem is aganglionic megacolon or Hirschsprung's disease, in which a patient may have an empty rectum and no desire to defecate but may still have an overflow of feces. The disorder occurs in 1 in 5,000 children; signs appear shortly after birth.

Course and Prognosis

The outcome of encopresis depends on the cause, the chronicity of the symptoms, and coexisting behavioral problems. In many cases, encopresis is self-limiting, and it rarely continues beyond middle adolescence. Children who have contributing physiological factors, such as poor gastric motility and an inability to relax the anal sphincter muscles, are more difficult to treat than are those with constipation but normal sphincter tone.

Encopresis is a particularly repugnant disorder to most peo-

Table 46–2
ICD-10 Diagnostic Criteria for Nonorganic Encopresis

A. The child repeatedly passes feces in places that are inappropriate for the purpose (eg, clothing, floor), either involuntarily or intentionally. (The disorder may involve overflow incontinence secondary to functional fecal retention.)
B. The child's chronological and mental age is at least 4 years.
C. There is at least one encopretic event per month.
D. Duration of the disorder is at least 6 months.
E. There is no organic condition that constitutes a sufficient cause for the encopretic events.

ple, including family members; thus, family tension is often high. The child's peers are also sensitive to the developmentally inappropriate behavior and often ostracize the child. An encopretic child is often scapegoated by peers and shunned by adults. Many encopretic children have abysmally low self-esteem and are aware of their constant rejection. Psychologically, the child may appear blunted toward the symptoms or may be entrenched in a pattern of encopresis as a mode of expressing anger. The outcome of cases of encopresis is affected by the family's willingness and ability to participate in treatment without being overly punitive and by the child's awareness of when the passage of feces is about to occur.

Treatment

By the time a child is brought for treatment, considerable family discord and distress are common. Family tensions about the symptom must be reduced, and a nonpunitive atmosphere established. Similar efforts should be made to reduce the child's embarrassment at school. Many changes of underwear with a minimum of fuss should be arranged. Education to the family and correction of misperceptions that a family may have about soiling must occur before treatment. A useful physiological approach involves a combination of daily laxatives or mineral oil along with a behavioral intervention by which the child sits on the toilet for timed intervals daily and is regarded for successful defecation. For children who are not constipated and do have good bowel control, laxatives are not necessary, but regular timed intervals on the toilet may be useful with these children as well.

Supportive psychotherapy and relaxation techniques may be useful in treating encopretic children's anxieties and other sequelae, such as low self-esteem and social isolation. In children who have bowel control but continue to deposit their feces in inappropriate locations, family interventions can be helpful. A good outcome occurs when a child feels in control of life events. Coexisting behavior problems predict a poorer outcome. In all cases, proper bowel habits may need to be taught. In some cases biofeedback techniques have been of help.

ENURESIS

Epidemiology

The prevalence of enuresis decreases with increasing age. Thus, 82 percent of 2 year olds, 49 percent of 3 year olds, 26 percent of 4 year olds, and 7 percent of 5 year olds have been reported to be enuretic on a regular basis. Prevalence rates vary, however, on the basis of the population studied and the tolerance for the symptoms in various cultures and socioeconomic groups.

The Isle of Wight study reported that 15.2 percent of 7-year-old boys were enuretic occasionally and that 6.7 percent of them were enuretic at least once a week. The study reported that 3.3 percent of girls at the age of 7 years were enuretic at least once a week. By age 10, the overall prevalence of enuresis has been reported to be 3 percent. The rate drops drastically for teenagers, in whom a prevalence of 1.5 percent has been reported for 14 year olds. Enuresis affects about 1 percent of adults.

Mental disorders are present in only about 20 percent of enuretic children; they are most common in enuretic girls, in children with symptoms during the day and night, and in children who maintain the symptoms into older childhood.

Etiology

Most children are not enuretic with intention or even with awareness until after they are wet. Physiological factors are likely to play a major role in most cases of enuresis. Normal bladder control, which is acquired gradually, is influenced by neuromuscular and cognitive development, socioemotional factors, toilet training, and possible genetic factors. Difficulties in one or more of these areas may delay urinary continence.

Although a specific organic cause precludes a diagnosis of enuresis, the correction of an anatomical defect or the cure of an infection does not always cure the enuresis. In a longitudinal study of child development, children who were enuretic were about twice as likely to have concomitant developmental delays as were nonenuretic children. About 75 percent of enuretic children have a first-degree relative who is or was enuretic. A child's risk for enuresis has been found to be more than 7 times greater if the father was enuretic. The concordance rate is higher in monozygotic twins than in dizygotic twins. There is a strong suggestion of a genetic component; much can be accounted for by tolerance for enuresis in some families and by other psychosocial factors.

Some studies report that enuretic children have a bladder with a normal anatomical capacity when anesthetized but a functionally small bladder, so that the child feels an urge to void with little urine in the bladder. Other studies report that bed-wetting occurs because the bladder is full and there is a lack of high levels of nighttime antidiuretic hormone. These factors allow for a higher than usual urine output. Enuresis does not appear to be related to a specific stage of sleep or time of night; rather, bed-wetting appears randomly. In most cases, the quality of sleep is normal. Little evidence indicates that enuretic children sleep more soundly than do other children.

Psychosocial stressors appear to precipitate some cases of enuresis. In young children, the disorder has been particularly associated with the birth of a sibling, hospitalization between the ages of 2 and 4, the start of school, the breakup of a family because of divorce or death, and a move to a new domicile.

Diagnosis and Clinical Features

Enuresis is the repeated voiding of urine into a child's clothes or bed; the voiding may be involuntary or intentional. For the diagnosis to be made, a child must exhibit a developmental or chronological age of at least 5 years. According to DSM-IV, the behavior must occur twice weekly for a period of at least 3 months or must cause distress and impairment in functioning to meet the diagnostic criteria. Enuresis is diagnosed only if the behavior is not due to a medical condition. DSM-IV and ICD-10 break down the disorder into three types: nocturnal only, diurnal only, and nocturnal and diurnal (Tables 46–3 and 46–4).

Pathology and Laboratory Examination. No single laboratory finding is pathognomonic of enuresis; but clinicians

Table 46–3
DSM-IV Diagnostic Criteria for Enuresis

A. Repeated voiding of urine into bed or clothes (whether involuntary or intentional).
B. The behavior is clinically significant as manifested by either a frequency of twice a week for at least 3 consecutive months or the presence of clinically significant distress or impairment in social, academic (occupational), or other important areas of functioning.
C. Chronological age is at least 5 years (or equivalent developmental level).
D. The behavior is not due to the direct physiological effect of a substance (eg, a diuretic) or a general medical condition (eg, diabetes, spina bifida, a seizure disorder).

Specify type:
Nocturnal only
Diurnal only
Nocturnal and diurnal

must rule out organic factors, such as the presence of urinary tract infections, that may predispose a child to enuresis. Structural obstructive abnormalities may be present in up to 3 percent of children with apparent enuresis. Sophisticated radiographic studies are usually deferred in simple cases of enuresis with no signs of repeated infections or other medical problems.

Differential Diagnosis

Possible organic causes of bed-wetting must be ruled out. Organic features occur most often in children with both nocturnal and diurnal enuresis combined with urinary frequency and urgency. The organic features include genitourinary pathology—structural, neurological, and infectious—such as obstructive uropathy, spina bifida occulta, and cystitis; other organic disorders that may cause polyuria and enuresis, such as diabetes mellitus and diabetes insipidus; disturbances of consciousness and sleep, such as seizures, intoxication, and sleepwalking disorder, during which a child urinates; and side effects from treatment with antipsychotics—for example, thioridazine (Mellaril).

Course and Prognosis

Enuresis is usually self-limited, and a child can eventually remain dry without psychiatric sequelae. Most enuretic children find their symptoms ego-dystonic and enjoy enhanced self-esteem and improved social confidence when they become continent. About 80 percent of affected children have never achieved a year-long period of dryness. Enuresis after at least 1 dry year usually begins between the ages of 5 and 8 years; if it occurs much later, especially during adulthood, organic causes must be investigated. Some evidence indicates that late onset of enuresis in children is more frequently associated with a concomitant psychiatric difficulty than is enuresis without at least 1 dry year. Relapses occur in enuretic children who are becoming dry spontaneously and in those who are being treated. The significant emotional and social difficulties of enuretic children usually include poor self-image, decreased self-esteem, social embarrassment and restriction, and intrafamilial conflict.

Treatment

Treatment modalities that have been used successfully for enuresis include behavioral and pharmacological interventions. A relatively high rate of spontaneous remission over long periods also occurs. The first step in any treatment plan is to review appropriate toilet training. If toilet training was not attempted, the parents and the patient should be guided in this undertaking. Record keeping is helpful in determining a baseline and following the child's progress and may itself be a reinforcer. A star chart may be particularly helpful. Other useful techniques include restricting fluids before bed and night lifting to toilet train the child.

Behavioral Therapy. Classic conditioning with the bell (or buzzer) and pad apparatus is generally the most effective treatment for enuresis, with dryness resulting in more than 50 percent of all cases. The treatment is equally effective in children with and without concomitant mental disorders, and there is no evidence of symptom substitution. Difficulties may include child and family noncompliance, improper use of the apparatus, and relapse. Bladder training—encouragement or reward for delaying micturition for increasing times during waking hours—has also been used. Although sometimes effective, this method is decidedly inferior to the bell and pad.

Pharmacotherapy. Medication is not the first line of treatment for enuresis and is often not warranted at all. When the problem is so troubling as to significantly interfere with a child's functioning, several medications can be considered, although the problem often recurs as soon as medications are withdrawn. Imipramine (Tofranil) is efficacious and has been approved for use in treating childhood enuresis, primarily on a short-term basis. Initially, up to 30 percent of enuretic pa-

Table 46–4
ICD-10 Diagnostic Criteria for Nonorganic Enuresis

A. The child's chronological and mental age is at least 5 years.
B. Involuntary or intentional voiding of urine into bed or clothes occurs at least twice a month in children aged under 7 years, and at least once a month in children aged 7 years or more.
C. The enuresis is not a consequence of epileptic attacks or of neurological incontinence, and not a direct consequence of structural abnormalities of the urinary tract or any other nonpsychiatric medical condition.
D. There is no evidence of any other psychiatric disorder that meets the criteria for other ICD-10 categories.
E. Duration of the disorder is at least 3 months.

tients stay dry, and up to 85 percent wet less frequently than before treatment. The success often does not last, however, and tolerance can develop after 6 weeks of therapy. Once the drug is discontinued, relapse and enuresis at former frequencies usually occur within a few months. A serious problem is the drug's adverse effects, which include cardiotoxicity.

The tricyclic antidepressants are not currently used very frequently for enuresis because of the risks and the reports of sudden death in several children with attention-deficit/hyperactivity disorder on desipramine. Desmopressin (DDAVP), an antidiuretic compound that is available as an intranasal spray, has shown some initial success in reducing enuresis. Reduction of enuresis has varied from 10 percent to 90 percent with the use of desmopressin. In most studies, enuresis recurred shortly after discontinuation of this medication. Side effects that can occur with DDVAP include headache, nasal congestion, epistaxis, and stomachache. The most serious side effect reported with the use of DDVAP to treat enuresis was a hyponatremic seizure experienced by a child.

Psychotherapy. Although many psychological and psychoanalytic theories regarding enuresis have been advanced, controlled studies have found that psychotherapy alone is not an effective treatment of enuresis. Psychotherapy, however, may be useful in dealing with the coexisting psychiatric problems and the emotional and family difficulties that arise secondary to the disorder.

References

Beach PS, Beach RE, Smith LR: Hyponatremic seizures in a child treated with desmopressin to control enuresis: A rational approach to fluid intake. Clin Pediatr *31:* 566, 1992.

Fournier JBP, Garfinkel BD, Bond A, Becuchesne H, Shapiro SK: Pharmacological and behavioral management of enuresis. J Am Acad Child Adolesc Psychiatry *26:* 849, 1987.

Fritz GK, Rockney RM, Yeung AS: Plasma levels and efficacy of imipramine treatment for enuresis. J Am Acad Child Adolesc Psychiatry *33:* 60, 1994.

Hersov L: Faecal soiling. In *Child and Adolescent Psychiatry: Modern Approaches,* ed 2, M Rutter, L Hersov, editors, p 482. Blackwell, Oxford, England, 1985.

Kisch EH, Pfeffer CR: Functional encopresis: Psychiatric inpatient treatment. Am J Psychother *38:* 264, 1984.

Landman GB: Locus of control and self-esteem in children with encopresis. J Dev Behav Pediatr *7:* 11, 1986.

Loening-Baucke V: Modulation of abnormal defecation dynamics by biofeedback treatment in chronically constipated children with encopresis. J Pediatr *116:* 214, 1990.

Mikkelsen EJ: Elimination disorders. In *Comprehensive Textbook of Psychiatry,* ed 6, HI Kaplan, BJ Sadock, editors, p 2337. Williams & Wilkins, Baltimore, 1995.

Norgaard JP, Rittig S, Djurkuus JC: Nocturnal enuresis: An approach to treatment based on pathogenesis, J Pediatr *114:* 705, 1989.

Rushton HG: Nocturnal enuresis: Epidemiology, evaluation, and currently available treatment options. J Pediatr *114:* 691, 1989.

Rutter M: Isle of Wight revisited: Twenty-five years of child psychiatric epidemiology. J Am Acad Child Adolesc Psychiatry *28:* 633, 1989.

Steinhausen H-C, Göbel D: Enuresis in child psychiatric clinic patients. J Am Acad Child Adolesc Psychiatry *28:* 279, 1989.

Thompson S, Rey JM: Functional enuresis: Is desmopressin the answer? J Am Acad Child Adolesc Psychiatry *34:* 266, 1995.

Von Gontard A, Lehmkuh A: Desmopressin side effects. J Am Acad Child Adolesc Psychiatry *35:* 129, 1996.

47 Other Disorders of Infancy, Childhood, or Adolescence

▲ 47.1 Separation Anxiety Disorder

The fourth edition of *Diagnostic and Statistical Manual of Mental Disorders* (DSM-IV) describes *separation anxiety* as an excessive anxiety about separation from home or from those to whom a person is attached. This disorder must last for at least 4 weeks, must begin before 18 years of age, and must cause significant distress or impairment in important areas of functioning.

Separation anxiety is a universal developmental phenomenon, an expected part of children's normal experiences. Infants exhibit separation anxiety in the form of stranger anxiety at less than 1 year of age when infant and mother are separated. Some separation anxiety is also normal in young children who are entering school for the first time. Separation anxiety disorder, however, occurs when developmentally inappropriate and excessive anxiety emerges over separation from the major attachment figure. According to DSM-IV, separation anxiety disorder requires the presence of at least three symptoms related to excessive worry about separation from the major attachment figures. The worries may take the form of refusal to go to school, fears and distress upon separation, repeated complaints of such physical symptoms as headaches and stomachaches when separation is anticipated, and nightmares related to separation issues.

Separation anxiety disorder is the only anxiety disorder currently found in the child and adolescent section of DSM-IV. Children who are overanxious usually meet the DSM-IV adult category of generalized anxiety disorder. Children with avoidant symptoms meet the DSM-IV diagnostic criteria for social phobia, which is also used for adults. Children and adolescents may also have other anxiety disorders described among the adult disorders of DSM-IV, including specific phobia, panic disorder, obsessive-compulsive disorder, and posttraumatic stress disorder.

EPIDEMIOLOGY

Separation anxiety disorder is more common in young children than in adolescents and has been reported to occur equally in boys and girls. The onset may occur during preschool years but is most common in 7 to 8 year olds. The prevalence of separation anxiety disorder has been estimated to be 3 to 4 percent of all school-age children and 1 percent of all adolescents. The rate of generalized anxiety disorder in school-age children is estimated to be approximately 3 percent, the rate of social phobia is 1 percent, and the rate of simple phobias is 2.4 percent. In adolescents, a lifetime prevalence for panic disorder was found to be 0.6 percent; the prevalence for generalized anxiety disorder was 3.7 percent.

ETIOLOGY

Biopsychosocial Factors

Young children, immature and dependent on a mothering figure, are particularly prone to excessive anxiety related to separation. The relation between temperamental traits and the predisposition to develop anxiety symptoms has been investigated. The temperamental tendency to be unusually shy or to withdraw in unfamiliar situations seems to be an enduring response pattern, and young children with this propensity are at higher risk of developing anxiety disorders during their next few years of life.

There is neurophysiological correlation of *behavioral inhibition* (extreme shyness): Children with this constellation are shown to have higher resting heart rate and acceleration of heart rate with tasks requiring cognitive concentration. Additional physiological correlates of behavioral inhibition include elevated salivary cortisol levels, elevated urinary catecholamines, and larger papillary dilation during cognitive tasks. The quality of maternal attachment also appears to play a role in the development of anxiety disorder in children. Mothers with anxiety disorders who are observed to show insecure attachment to their children tend to have children with higher rates of anxiety disorders. It is difficult to separate the contribution of the relationship between mother and child from the mother's potential genetic contribution toward anxiety. Families in which a child manifests separation anxiety disorder may be close-knit and caring, and the children often seem to be the objects of parental overconcern. External life stresses often coincide with the development of the disorder. The death of a relative, a child's illness, a change in a child's environment, or a move to a new neighborhood or school is frequently noted in the histories of children with separation anxiety disorder. In a vulnerable child, these changes probably intensify anxiety.

Learning Factors

Phobic anxiety may be communicated from parents to children by direct modeling. If a parent is fearful, the child will probably have a phobic adaptation to new situations, especially to a school environment. Some parents appear to teach their children to be anxious by overprotecting them from expected dangers or by exaggerating the dangers. For example, a parent who cringes in a room during a lightning storm teaches a child to do the same. A parent who is frightened of mice or insects conveys the affect of fright to a child. Conversely, a parent who becomes angry at a child during an incipient phobic concern about animals may inculcate a phobic concern in the child by the very intensity of the anger expressed.

Genetic Factors

The temperamental constellation of behavioral inhibition, excessive shyness, the tendency to withdraw from unfamiliar situations, and separation anxiety are all likely to have a genetic contribution. Family studies have shown that the biological offspring of adults with anxiety disorders are prone to suffer from separation anxiety disorder in childhood. Parents who have panic disorder with agoraphobia appear to have an increased risk of having a child with separation anxiety disorder. Separation anxiety disorder and depression in children overlap, and some clinicians view separation anxiety disorder as a feature of a depressive disorder.

DIAGNOSIS AND CLINICAL FEATURES

Separation anxiety disorder is the most common anxiety disorder in childhood. To meet the diagnostic criteria, according to DSM-IV, the disorder must be characterized by three of the following symptoms for at least 4 weeks: persistent and excessive worry about losing, or possible harm befalling, major attachment figures; persistent and excessive worry that an untoward event can lead to separation from a major attachment figure; persistent reluctance or refusal to go to school or elsewhere because of fear of separation; persistent and excessive fear or reluctance to be alone or without major attachment figures at home or without significant adults in other settings; persistent reluctance or refusal to go to sleep without being near a major attachment figure or to sleep away from home; repeated nightmares involving the theme of separation; repeated complaints of physical symptoms, including headaches and stomachaches, when separation from major attachment figures is anticipated; and recurrent excessive distress when separation from home or major attachment figures is anticipated or involved. According to DSM-IV, the disturbance must also cause significant distress or impairment in functioning (Table 47.1–1).

A patient's history may reveal important episodes of separation in the child's life, particularly because of illness and hospitalization, illness or loss of a parent, or geographic relocation. Clinicians should scrutinize the period of infancy for evidence of separation-individuation disorders or lack of an adequate mothering figure. Using fantasies, dreams, and play materials and observing the child are of great help in making the diagnosis. Clinicians should examine not only the content of thought but also the way in which thoughts are expressed. For example, children may express fears that their parents will die, even when their behavior does not show evidence of anxiety. Similarly, a child's difficulty in describing events or bland denial of obviously anxiety-provoking events may indicate the presence of separation anxiety disorder. Difficulty with memory in expressing separation themes and patent distortions in the recital of such themes may give clues to the disorder's presence.

The essential feature of separation anxiety disorder is extreme anxiety precipitated by separation from parents, home, or other familiar surroundings. A child's anxiety may approach terror or panic. The distress is greater than that normally expected for the child's developmental level and cannot be explained by any other disorder. Morbid fears, preoccupations, and ruminations are characteristic of separation anxiety disorder. Children with the disorder become fearful that someone close to them will be hurt or that something terrible will happen to them when they are away from important caring figures.

Table 47.1–1
DSM-IV Diagnostic Criteria for Separation Anxiety Disorder

A. Developmentally inappropriate and excessive anxiety concerning separation from home or from those to whom the individual is attached, as evidenced by three (or more) of the following:
   (1) recurrent excessive distress when separation from home or major attachment figures occurs or is anticipated
   (2) persistent and excessive worry about losing, or about possible harm befalling, major attachment figures
   (3) persistent and excessive worry that an untoward event will lead to separation from a major attachment figure (eg, getting lost or being kidnapped)
   (4) persistent reluctance or refusal to go to school or elsewhere because of fear of separation
   (5) persistently and excessively fearful or reluctant to be alone or without major attachment figures at home or without significant adults in other settings
   (6) persistent reluctance or refusal to go to sleep without being near a major attachment figure or to sleep away from home
   (7) repeated nightmares involving the theme of separation
   (8) repeated complaints of physical symptoms (such as headaches, stomach aches, nausea, or vomiting) when separation from major attachment figures occurs or is anticipated

B. The duration of the disturbance is at least 4 weeks.

C. The onset is before age 18 years.

D. The disturbance causes clinically significant distress or impairment in social, academic (occupational), or other important areas of functioning.

E. The disturbance does not occur exclusively during the course of a pervasive developmental disorder, schizophrenia, or other psychotic disorder and, in adolescents and adults, is not better accounted for by panic disorder with agoraphobia.

Specify if:
Early onset: if onset occurs before age 6 years

Reprinted with permission from American Psychiatric Association: *Diagnostic and Statistical Manual of Mental Disorders,* ed 4. Copyright, American Psychiatric Association: Washington, 1994.

Many children worry that they or their parents will have an accident or become ill. Fears about getting lost and about being kidnapped and never again finding their parents are common.

Adolescents may not directly express any anxious concern about separation from mothering figures. However, their behavior patterns often reflect a separation anxiety in that they express discomfort about leaving home, engage in solitary activities, and continue to use mothering figures as helpers in buying clothes and entering social and recreational activities. Separation anxiety disorder in children is often manifested at the thought of travel or in the course of travel away from home. Children may refuse to go to camp, a new school, or even a friend's house. Frequently, there is a continuum between mild anticipatory anxiety before separation from an important figure and pervasive anxiety after the separation has occurred. Premonitory signs include irritability, difficulty in eating, whining, staying in a room alone, clinging to parents, and following a parent everywhere. Often, when a family moves, a child displays separation anxiety by intense clinging to the mother figure. Sometimes, geographic relocation anxiety is expressed in feelings of acute homesickness or psychophysiological symptoms that break out when the child is away from home or is going to a new country. The child yearns to return home and becomes preoccupied with fantasies of how much better the old home was. Integration into the new life situation may become extremely difficult.

Sleep difficulties are frequent and may require that someone remain with a child until he or she falls asleep. A child often goes to the parent's bed or even sleeps at the parents' door when the bedroom is barred to him or her. Nightmares and morbid fears are other expressions of anxiety.

Associated features include fear of the dark and imaginary, bizarre worries. Children may see eyes staring at them and become preoccupied with mythical figures or monsters reaching out for them in their bedrooms. Many children are demanding and intrusive in adult affairs and require constant attention to allay their anxieties. Symptoms emerge when separation from an important parent figure becomes necessary. If separation is threatened, many children with the disorder do not experience interpersonal difficulties. They may, however, look sad and may cry easily. They sometimes complain that they are not loved, express a wish to die, or complain that siblings are favored over them. They frequently experience gastrointestinal symptoms of nausea, vomiting, and stomachaches and have pains in various parts of the body, sore throats, and flulike symptoms. In older children, typical cardiovascular and respiratory symptoms of palpitations, dizziness, faintness, and strangulation are reported. The most common anxiety disorder that coexists with separation anxiety disorder is specific phobia, which occurs in about one third of all referred cases of separation anxiety disorder.

Pathology and Laboratory Examination

No specific laboratory measures are helpful in the diagnosis of separation anxiety disorder.

ICD-10

The 10th revision of *International Statistical Classification of Diseases and Related Health Problems* (ICD-10) includes a category for emotional disorders with onset specific to childhood. This category contains five specific childhood-onset anxiety disorders and one residual diagnosis (Table 47.1–2). According to ICD-10, there have been several reasons for traditionally differentiating emotional disorders specific to childhood and adolescence from those of adulthood. First, research has consistently shown that most children with emotional disorders become normal adults and that many adult emotional disorders have an onset in adult life and lack precursors in childhood. Second, many emotional disorders of childhood appear to be exaggerations of normal developmental trends rather than abnormalities. Third, the mental mechanisms of childhood emotional disorders are often believed to be different from those of adult disorders; this point, however, has not been verified empirically. Finally, childhood emotional disorders are less clearly separated into specific categories such as phobic or obsessional disorders, but epidemiological data suggest that this distinction is only relative because it is often difficult to differentiate adult disorders as well. Thus, the second feature, developmental appropriateness, is the key factor in diagnosing differences between disorders with specific childhood onset and the neurotic disorders in general; some empirical evidence supports this hypothesis.

ICD-10 states that separation anxiety disorder (similar to DSM-IV's separation anxiety) is diagnosed only when fear of separation is the focus of anxiety and when the anxiety arises during the early years of life. This disorder must persist abnormally beyond the usual age level and must be associated with major problems in social functioning. There should be no generalized disturbance of personality development or functioning, and if the anxiety arises at a developmentally inappropriate age, it should not be coded under this disorder unless the anxiety is an abnormal continuation of developmentally appropriate separation anxiety.

According to the ICD-10, *phobic anxiety disorder of childhood* refers to fears that show a marked developmental phase specificity and arise, to some extent, in most children. Like all disorders organized under emotional disorders with onset specific to childhood, the onset of phobic disorder must occur during the developmentally appropriate age, the degree of anxiety must be clinically abnormal, and the anxiety must not form part of a more generalized disorder.

Social anxiety disorder of childhood, in ICD-10, is applied only to disorders that arise before 6 years of age, are unusual in degree, are accompanied by problems in social functioning, and are not part of a more generalized emotional disorder.

Sibling rivalry disorder is characterized by a combination of evidence of sibling rivalry, an onset during the months after the birth of a younger sibling, and evidence of abnormal emotional disturbance that is associated with psychosocial problems.

The ICD-10 category of other childhood emotional disorders includes identity disorder, overanxious disorder, and peer rivalries. The final subtype in the category is childhood emotional disorder, unspecified.

DIFFERENTIAL DIAGNOSIS

Some degree of separation anxiety is a normal phenomenon, and clinical judgment must be used in distinguishing that

Table 47.1–2
ICD-10 Diagnostic Criteria for Emotional Disorders with Onset Specific to Childhood

Note. Phobic anxiety disorder of childhood, social anxiety disorder of childhood, and general anxiety disorder of childhood have obvious similarities to some of the disorders in neurotic, stress-related and somatoform disorders, but current evidence and opinion suggest that there are sufficient differences in the ways that anxiety disorders present in children for additional categories to be provided. Further studies should show whether descriptions and definitions can be developed that can be used satisfactorily for both adults and children, or whether the present distinction should be preserved.

Separation anxiety disorder of childhood

A. At least three of the following must be present:
   (1) unrealistic and persistent worry about possible harm befalling major attachment figures or about the loss of such figures (eg, fear that they will leave and not return or that the child will not see them again), or persistent concerns about the death of attachment figures;
   (2) unrealistic and persistent worry that some untoward event will separate the child from a major attachment figure (eg, the child getting lost, being kidnapped, admitted to hospital, or killed);
   (3) persistent reluctance or refusal to go to school because of fear over separation from a major attachment figure or in order to stay at home (rather than for other reasons such as fear over events at school);
   (4) difficulty in separating at night, as manifested by any of the following:
      (a) persistent reluctance or refusal to go to sleep without being near an attachment figure;
      (b) getting up frequently during the night to check on, or to sleep near, an attachment figure;
      (c) persistent reluctance or refusal to sleep away from home
   (5) persistent inappropriate fear of being alone, or otherwise without the major attachment figure, at home during the day;
   (6) repeated nightmares involving themes of separation;
   (7) repeated occurrence of physical symptoms (such as nausea, stomachache, headache, or vomiting) on occasions that involve separation from a major attachment figure, such as leaving home to go to school or on other occasions involving separation (holidays, camps, etc.).
   (8) excessive, recurrent distress in anticipation of, during, or immediately after separation from a major attachment figure (as shown by: anxiety, crying, tantrums; persistent reluctance to go away from home; excessive need to talk with parents or desire to return home; misery, apathy, or social withdrawal).

B. The criteria for generalized anxiety disorder of childhood are not met.

C. Onset is before the age of 6 years.

D. The disorder does not occur as part of a broader disturbance of emotions, conduct, or personality or of a pervasive developmental disorder, psychotic disorder, or psychoactive substance use disorder.

E. Duration of the disorder is at least *4 weeks.*

Phobic anxiety disorder of childhood

A. The individual manifests a persistent or recurrent fear (phobia) that is developmentally phase-appropriate (or was so at the time of onset) but that is abnormal in degree and is associated with significant social impairment.

B. The criteria for generalized anxiety disorder of childhood are not met.

C. The disorder does not occur as part of a broader disturbance of emotions, conduct, or personality or of a pervasive developmental disorder, psychotic disorder, or psychoactive substance use disorder.

D. Duration of the disorder is at least 4 weeks.

Social anxiety disorder of childhood

A. Persistent anxiety in social situations in which the child is exposed to unfamiliar people, including peers, is manifested by socially avoidant behavior.

B. The child exhibits self-consciousness, embarrassment, or overconcern about the appropriateness of his or her behavior when interacting with unfamiliar figures.

C. There is significant interference with social (including peer) relationships, which are consequently restricted; when new or forced social situations are experienced, they cause marked distress and discomfort as manifested by crying, lack of spontaneous speech, or withdrawal from the social situation.

D. The child has satisfying social relationships with familiar figures (family members or peers that he or she knows well).

E. Onset of the disorder generally coincides with a developmental phase in which these anxiety reactions are considered appropriate. The abnormal degree, persistence over time, and associated impairment must be manifest before the age of 6 years.

F. The criteria for generalized anxiety disorder of childhood are not met.

G. The disorder does not occur as part of broader disturbances of emotions, conduct, or personality or of a pervasive developmental disorder, psychotic disorder, or psychoactive substance use disorder.

H. Duration of the disorder is at least 4 weeks.

Sibling rivalry disorder

A. The child has abnormally intense negative feelings toward an immediately younger sibling.

B. Emotional disturbance is shown by regression, tantrums, dysphoria, sleep difficulties, oppositional behavior, or attention-seeking behavior with one or both parents (two or more of these must be present).

C. Onset is within 6 months of the birth of an immediately younger sibling.

D. Duration of the disorder is at least 4 weeks.

(continued)

Table 47.1–2 (*continued*)

Other childhood emotional disorders

Generalized anxiety disorder of childhood

Note: In children and adolescents, the range of complaints by which the general anxiety is manifest is often more limited than in adults (see Generalized anxiety disorder), and the specific symptoms of autonomic arousal are often less prominent. For these individuals, the following alternative set of criteria can be used if preferred:

A. Extensive anxiety and worry (apprehensive expectation) occur on at least half of the total number of days over a period of at least 6 months, the anxiety and worry referring to at least several events or activities (such as work or school performance).

B. The individual finds it difficult to control the worry.

C. The anxiety and worry are associated with at least three of the following symptoms (with at least two symptoms present on at least half of the total number of days):
   (1) restlessness, feeling "keyed up" or "on edge" (as shown, for example, by feelings of mental tension combined with an inability to relax);
   (2) feeling tired, "worn out," or easily fatigued because of worry or anxiety;
   (3) difficulty in concentrating, or mind "going blank";
   (4) irritability;
   (5) muscle tension;
   (6) sleep disturbance (difficulty in falling or staying asleep, or restless, unsatisfying sleep) because of worry or anxiety.

D. The multiple anxieties and worries occur across at least two situations, activities, contexts, or circumstances. Generalized anxiety does not present as discrete paroxysmal episodes (as in panic disorder), nor are the main worries confined to a single, major theme (as in separation anxiety disorder or phobic disorder of childhood). (When more focused anxiety is identified in the broader context of a generalized anxiety, generalized anxiety disorder takes precedence over other anxiety disorders.)

E. Onset occurs in childhood or adolescence (before the age of 18 years).

F. The anxiety, worry, or physical symptoms cause clinically significant distress or impairment in social, occupational, or other important areas of functioning.

G. The disorder is not due to the direct effects of a substance (eg, psychoactive substances, medication) or a general medical condition (eg, hyperthyroidism) and does not occur exclusively during a mood disorder, psychotic disorder, or pervasive developmental disorder.

Childhood emotional disorder, unspecified

normal anxiety from separation anxiety disorder. In generalized anxiety disorder, anxiety is not focused on separation. In pervasive developmental disorders and schizophrenia, anxiety about separation may occur but is viewed as caused by these conditions rather than as a separate disorder. In depressive disorders occurring in children, the diagnosis of separation anxiety disorder should also be made when the criteria for both disorders are met; the two diagnoses often coexist. Panic disorder with agoraphobia is uncommon before 18 years of age; the fear is of being incapacitated by a panic attack rather than of separation from parental figures. In some adult cases, however, many symptoms of separation anxiety disorder may be present. In conduct disorder, truancy is common, but children stay away from home and do not have anxiety about separation. School refusal is a frequent symptom in separation anxiety disorder but is not pathognomonic of it. Children with other diagnoses, such as phobias, also show evidence of school refusal; in these disorders, the age of onset may be later and the school refusal may be more severe than in separation anxiety disorder. Common characteristics of selected anxiety disorders that occur in children are presented in Table 47.1–3.

COURSE AND PROGNOSIS

The course and the prognosis of separation anxiety disorder are variable and are related to the age of onset, the duration of the symptoms, and the development of comorbid anxiety and depressive disorders. Young children who experience the disorder but are able to maintain attendance in school generally have a better prognosis than adolescents with the disorder who refuse to attend school for long periods. A follow-up study of children and adolescents with anxiety disorders over a 3-year period reported that up to 82 percent no longer met criteria for the anxiety disorder at the follow-up time. Of the group followed, 96 percent of those with separation anxiety disorder had a remission at follow-up. Most children who recovered did so within the first year. Early age of onset and later age at diagnosis were factors that predicted slower recovery. Close to one third of the group studied, however, had developed another psychiatric disorder within the follow-up period, and 50 percent of these children developed another anxiety disorder. Reports have indicated a significant overlap of separation anxiety disorder and depressive disorders. In these complicated cases, the prognosis is guarded. Most follow-up studies have methodological problems and are limited to hospitalized, school-phobic children and not children with separation anxiety disorder per se. Little is reported about the outcome of mild cases, whether children are seen in outpatient treatment or receive no treatment. Notwithstanding the limitations of the studies, reports indicate that some children with severe school phobia continue to resist attending school for many years.

During the 1970s, it was reported that many adult women with agoraphobia had suffered from separation anxiety disorder in childhood. Although research indicates that many children with an anxiety disorder are at increased risk for an adult anxiety disorder, the specific link between separation anxiety disorder in childhood and agoraphobia in adulthood has not been established clearly. Studies do indicate that anxious parents are at increased risk of having children with anxiety disorders. In addition, in recent years, some cases of children with

Table 47.1–3
Common Characteristics of Selected Anxiety Disorders That Occur in Children

Criteria	Separation Anxiety Disorder	Social Phobia	Generalized Anxiety Disorder
Minimum duration to establish diagnosis	At least 4 weeks	No minimum	At least 6 months
Age of onset	Preschool to 18 years	Not specified	Not specified
Precipitating stresses	Separation from significant parental figures, other losses, travel	Pressure for social participation with peers	Unusual pressure for performance, damage to self-esteem, feelings of lack of competence
Peer relationships	Good when no separation is involved	Tentative, overly inhibited	Overly eager to please, peers sought out and dependent relationships established
Sleep	Reluctance or refusal to go to sleep, fear of dark, nightmares	Difficulty in falling asleep at times	Difficulty in falling asleep
Psychophysiological symptoms	Complaints of stomachaches, nausea, vomiting, flulike symptoms, headaches, palpitations, dizziness, faintness	Blushing, body tension	Stomachaches, nausea, vomiting, lump in the throat, shortness of breath, dizziness, palpitations
Differential diagnosis	Generalized anxiety disorder, schizophrenia, depressive disorders, conduct disorder, pervasive developmental disorders, major depressive disorder, panic disorder with agoraphobia	Adjustment disorder with depressed mood, generalized anxiety disorder, separation anxiety disorder, major depressive disorder, dysthymic disorder, avoidant personality disorder, borderline personality disorder	Separation anxiety disorder, attention deficit/hyperactivity disorder, social phobia, adjustment disorder with anxiety, obsessive-compulsive disorder, psychotic disorders, mood disorders

Adapted from Sidney Werkman, M.D.

both panic disorder and separation anxiety disorder have been reported.

TREATMENT

A multimodal treatment approach—including individual psychotherapy, psychopharmacological approaches, family education, and family therapy—is recommended for separation anxiety disorder. Family therapy helps parents understand the need for consistent support for children while maintaining firm boundaries about children's avoidance behaviors toward anxiety-provoking activities, such as school.

Specific cognitive strategies and relaxation exercises may help children control their anxiety. Pharmacotherapy is also useful when psychotherapy alone is not sufficient. School refusal associated with separation anxiety disorder may be viewed as a psychiatric emergency. A comprehensive treatment plan involves the child, the parents, and the child's peers and school. The child should be encouraged to attend school, but when a return to a full school day is overwhelming, a program should be arranged for the child to progressively increase his or her time spent at school. Graded contact with an object of anxiety is a form of behavior modification that can be applied to any type of separation anxiety. In some severe cases of school refusal, hospitalization is required. Cognitive behavioral modalities can be used in psychotherapy, including exposure to feared separations and cognitive strategies such as coping self-statements aimed at increasing a sense of autonomy and mastery.

Pharmacotherapeutic agents that have been used to treat anxiety symptoms include tricyclic antidepressants, benzodiazepines, and more recently, serotonin-specific reuptake inhibitors (SSRIs). β-Adrenergic receptor antagonists, such as propranolol, and buspirone have also been used. With the advent of the SSRIs, the tricyclic antidepressants, with their risks of cardiotoxicity, are no longer used as frequently. Diphenhydramine (Benadryl) can be used to break a dangerous cycle of sleep disturbances. Open trials and one double-blind, placebo-controlled study suggested that alprazolam may be helpful in controlling anxiety symptoms in separation anxiety disorder. Clonazepam, a benzodiazepine, has been studied in open trials and may be useful in controlling symptoms of panic and other anxiety symptoms. Fluoxetine (Prozac), an SSRI, has been used for children with separation anxiety, social phobia, and generalized anxiety disorder. There is some evidence that this medication helped to control a variety of anxiety symptoms.

References

Alessi NE, Magen DR: Panic disorder in psychiatrically hospitalized children. Am J Psychiatry *145:* 1450, 1988.

Allen AJ, Leonard H, Swedo SE: Current knowledge of medications for the treatment of childhood anxiety disorders. J Am Acad Child Adolesc Psychiatry *34:* 976, 1995.

Bell-Dolan DJ, Last CG, Strauss CC: Symptoms of anxiety disorders in normal children. J Am Acad Child Adolesc Psychiatry *29:* 759, 1990.

Bernstein GA, Borchardt CM, Perwien AR: Anxiety disorders in children and adolescents: A review of the past 10 years. J Am Acad Child Adolesc Psychiatry *35:* 1110, 1996.

Bernstein GA, Garfinkel BD, Borchardt CM: Comparative studies of pharmacotherapy for school refusal. J Am Acad Child Adolesc Psychiatry *29:* 773, 1990.

Birmaher B, Waterman GS, Ryan N: Fluoxetine for childhood anxiety disorders. J Am Acad Child Adolesc Psychiatry *33:* 993, 1994.

Black B, Robbins DR: Case study: Panic disorder in children and adolescents. J Am Acad Child Adolesc Psychiatry *29:* 36, 1990.
Bradley SJ, Hood L: Psychiatrically referred adolescents with panic attacks: Presenting symptoms, stressors, and comorbidity. J Am Acad Child Adolesc Psychiatry *32:* 826, 1993.
Caspi A, Henry B, McGee RO, Moffitt TE, Silva PA: Temperamental origins of child and adolescent behavior problem: From age three to age fifteen. Child Dev *66:* 55, 1995.
Francis G, Last CG, Strauss CC: Avoidant disorder and social phobia in children and adolescents. J Am Acad Child Adolesc Psychiatry *31:* 1086, 1992.
Gittelman R, editor: *Anxiety Disorders of Children.* Guilford, New York, 1986.
Kashani JH, Orveschel H: A community study of anxiety in children and adolescents. Am J Psychiatry *147:* 313, 1990.
Kranzler HR: Use of buspirone in an adolescent with overanxious disorder. J Am Acad Child Adolesc Psychiatry *27:* 789, 1988.
Last CG, Perrin S, Hersen M, Krazdin AE: DSM-III-R anxiety disorders in children: Sociodemographic and clinical characteristics. J Am Acad Child Adolesc Psychiatry *31:* 1070, 1992.
Last CG, Strauss CC: School refusal in anxiety-disordered children and adolescents. J Am Acad Child Adolesc Psychiatry *29:* 31, 1990.
Manassis K, Bradley S, Goldberg S, Hood J, Swinson RP: Behavioral inhibition, attachment and anxiety in children of mothers with anxiety disorders. Can J Psychiatry *40:* 87, 1995.

▲ 47.2 Selective Mutism

The *Diagnostic and Statistical Manual of Mental Disorder* (DSM-IV) describes *selective mutism* as a person's persistent failure to speak in certain situations in which speaking is expected although the person speaks in other situations. The disorder interferes with educational, occupational, or social situations. It must last for at least 1 month and is not limited to the first month of school. Selective mutism is not diagnosed when a person's failure to speak arises from ignorance of, or unease at using, the spoken language required in the particular situation; the disorder is also not diagnosed when the resistance to speaking is associated with embarrassment about a communication disorder, such as stuttering, with a pervasive developmental disorder, with schizophrenia, or with another psychotic disorder.

Selective mutism is an uncommon childhood condition. Most children with the disorder are completely silent during the situations that elicit muteness, but some whisper or use single-syllable words. Despite the absence of speech, some children communicate with eye contact or nonverbal gestures. These children speak fluently in other situations, such as at home and in certain familiar settings. Selective mutism recently was hypothesized to be a form of social phobia, because the lack of speaking occurs only in specific social settings.

EPIDEMIOLOGY

The prevalence of selective mutism is estimated to range between 3 and 8 per 10,000 children. Young children are more vulnerable to the disorder than older children. Although still under investigation, selective mutism appears to be more common in girls than in boys.

ETIOLOGY

Although selective mutism is a psychologically determined inhibition or refusal to speak, many children with the disorder have histories of delayed onset of speech or speech abnormalities that may be contributory. In a recent survey, 90 percent of children with selective mutism met diagnostic criteria for social phobia. These children showed high levels of social anxiety without notable psychopathology in other areas, according to parent and teacher ratings. Thus, selective mutism may not represent a distinct disorder but may be better conceptualized as a subtype of social phobia. Similar to families with children who exhibit other anxiety disorders, maternal anxiety, depression, and heightened dependence needs are often noted in families of children with selective mutism. These factors may result in maternal overprotection and an overly close but ambivalent relationship between a mother and her selectively mute child. Children with selective mutism usually speak freely at home; they have no significant biological disability. Some children seem predisposed to selective mutism after early emotional or physical trauma; therefore, some clinicians refer to the phenomenon as traumatic mutism rather than selective mutism.

DIAGNOSIS AND CLINICAL FEATURES

The diagnosis of selective mutism is not difficult to make after it is clear that a child has adequate language skills in some environments but not in others (Table 47.2–1). The mutism may have developed gradually or suddenly after a disturbing experience. The age of onset can range from 4 to 8 years. Mute periods are most commonly manifested in school or outside the home; in rare cases, a child is mute at home but not in school. Children who exhibit selective mutism may also have symptoms of separation anxiety disorder, school refusal, and delayed language acquisition. Because social anxiety is almost always present in children with selective mutism, behavioral disturbances, such as temper tantrums and oppositional behaviors, may also occur in the home.

ICD-10

The 10th revision of *International Statistical Classification of Diseases and Related Health Problems* (ICD-10) contains

Table 47.2–1
DSM-IV Diagnostic Criteria for Selective Mutism

A. Consistent failure to speak in specific social situations (in which there is an expectation for speaking, eg, at school) despite speaking in other situations.
B. The disturbance interferes with educational or occupational achievement or with social communication.
C. The duration of the disturbance is at least 1 month (not limited to the first month of school).
D. The failure to speak is not due to a lack of knowledge of or comfort with, the spoken language required in the social situation.
E. The disturbance is not better accounted for by a communication disorder (eg, stuttering) and does not occur exclusively during the course of a pervasive developmental disorder, schizophrenia, or other psychotic disorder.

the diagnosis *elective mutism* for children who fail to speak in specific situations. In ICD-10, elective mutism is classified with the attachment disorders (see Table 47.3–2).

Pathology and Laboratory Examination

No specific laboratory measures are useful in the diagnosis or treatment of selective mutism.

DIFFERENTIAL DIAGNOSIS

Shy children may exhibit a transient muteness in new, anxiety-provoking situations. These children often have histories of not speaking in the presence of strangers and of clinging to their mothers. Most children who are mute upon entering school improve spontaneously and may be described as having transient adaptational shyness.

Selective mutism must also be distinguished from mental retardation, pervasive developmental disorders, and expressive language disorder. In these disorders, the symptoms are widespread, and there is not one situation in which the child communicates normally; the child may have an inability, rather than a refusal, to speak. In mutism secondary to conversion disorder, the mutism is pervasive. Children introduced into an environment in which a different language is spoken may be reticent to begin using the new language. Selective mutism should be diagnosed only when children also refuse to converse in their native language and when they have gained communicative competence in the new language but refuse to speak it.

COURSE AND PROGNOSIS

Although children with selective mutism are often abnormally shy during preschool years, the onset of the disorder is usually at age 5 or 6. The most common pattern is that children speak almost exclusively at home with the nuclear family but not elsewhere, especially not at school. Consequently, they may have academic difficulties and even failure. Children with selective mutism are generally shy, anxious, and vulnerable to the development of depression.

Most children with mild forms of anxiety disorder, including selective mutism, remit with or without treatment. With recent data suggesting that fluoxetine (Prozac) may influence the course of selective mutism, recovery may be enhanced. Children in whom the disorder persists often have difficulties in forming social relationships. Teasing and scapegoating by peers may induce them to refuse to go to school. Some children with this degree of severe social phobia are characterized by rigidity, compulsive traits, negativism, temper tantrums, and oppositional and aggressive behavior at home. Other children with the disorder better tolerate the feared situation by communicating with gestures, such as nodding, shaking the head, and saying "Um-hum" or "No."

Most cases last for only a few weeks or months, but some cases persist for years. In one follow-up study, about one half of the children improved within 5 to 10 years. Children who do not improve by age 10 appear to have a long-term course and a worse prognosis than those who do improve by age 10. As many as one third of children with selective mutism, with or without treatment, may develop other psychiatric disorders, particularly other anxiety disorders and depression.

TREATMENT

A multimodal approach using individual, behavioral, and family interventions as well as pharmacological interventions is most likely to be successful. During preschool years, counseling or psychotherapy for the parents may be indicated. Preschool children may also benefit from a therapeutic nursery. For school-age children, individual psychotherapy or behavior therapy may be indicated. When a child's independence is being thwarted, marital counseling or psychotherapy for the parents is paramount.

A recent report of 21 children with selective mutism treated in an open trial with fluoxetine suggested that this medication may be effective for childhood selective mutism. There have been reports confirming the utility of fluoxetine in the treatment of adult social phobia and at least one double-blind, placebo-controlled study using fluoxetine with children with mutism. Other medications such as phenelzine (Nardil) have also been reported to improve symptoms of social phobia in individual case reports. Additional investigation is needed to determine the usefulness of pharmacological interventions for selective mutism.

References

Black B, Uhde TW: Elective mutism as a variant of social phobia. J Am Acad Child Adolesc Psychiatry *31:* 1090, 1991.

Black B, Uhde TW: Psychiatric characteristics of children with selective mutism: A pilot study. J Am Acad Adolesc Psychiatry *34:* 847, 1995.

Black B, Uhde TW: Treatment of elective mutism with fluoxetine: A double-blind placebo controlled study. J Am Acad Adolesc Psychiatry *33:* 1000, 1994.

Dummit ES III, Klein RG, Tancer NK, Asche B, Martin J: Fluoxetine treatment of children with selective mutism: An open trial. J Am Acad Adolesc Psychiatry *35:* 615, 1996.

Golwyn DH, Weinstock RC: Phenelzine treatment of elective mutism: A case report. J Clin Psychiatry *51:* 384, 1990.

Klin A, Volkmar FR: Elective mutism and mental retardation. J Am Acad Child Adolesc Psychiatry *32:* 860, 1993.

Last CG, Perrin S, Hersen M, Kazdin A: A prospective study of childhood anxiety disorders. J Am Acad Adolesc Psychiatry *35:* 1502, 1996.

Mancini C, Van Amerigen M, Szatmari P, Fugere C, Boyle M: A high-risk pilot study of the children of adults with social phobia. J Am Acad Adolesc Psychiatry *35:* 11, 1996.

Schill MT, Kratochwill TR, Gardner WI: An assessment protocol for selective mutism: Analogue assessment using parents as facilitators. J School Psychol *34* (1): 1, 1996.

▲ 47.3 Reactive Attachment Disorder of Infancy or Early Childhood

According to the fourth edition of *Diagnostic and Statistical Manual of Mental Disorders* (DSM-IV), *reactive attachment disorder of infancy or early childhood* is marked by an inappropriate social relatedness that occurs in most contexts. The disorder appears before the age of 5 and is associated with "grossly pathological care." It is not accounted for solely by a developmental delay and does not meet the criteria for pervasive developmental disorder. The pattern of care may exhibit lasting disregard for a child's emotional or physical needs or repeated changes of caregivers as when a child is frequently relocated during foster care. The pathological care pattern is believed to cause the disturbance in social relatedness.

The disorder has two subtypes: the inhibited type, in which the disturbance takes the form of constantly failing to initiate and respond to most social interactions in a developmentally normal way; and the disinhibited type, in which the disturbance takes the form of undifferentiated, unselective social relatedness. These developmentally inappropriate behaviors are presumed to be due to a large degree to pathogenic caregiving, but less severe disturbances in parenting may also be associated with infants who exhibit the disorder.

The disorder may result in a picture of failure to thrive, in which an infant shows physical signs of malnourishment and does not exhibit the expected developmental motor and verbal milestones. When this is the case, the failure to thrive is coded on Axis III.

EPIDEMIOLOGY

No specific data on the prevalence, sex ratio, or familial pattern are currently available. Although patients with reactive attachment disorder of infancy or early childhood come from all socioeconomic groups, studies of some patients (such as infants with failure to thrive) indicate an increased vulnerability among those from low socioeconomic levels. This finding is congruent with the likelihood of psychosocial deprivation, single-parent households, family disorganization, and economic difficulties. A caregiver may be fully satisfactory for one child, but another child under the same care may have a reactive attachment disorder of infancy or early childhood.

ETIOLOGY

The cause of reactive attachment disorder of infancy or early childhood is included in the disorder's definition. Reactive attachment disorder is linked to maltreatment including neglect and possible physical abuse as well. Grossly pathogenic care of an infant or young child by the caregiver presumably causes the markedly disturbed social relatedness that is usually evident. The emphasis is on the unidirectional cause; that is, the caregiver does something inimical or neglects to do something essential for the infant or child. In evaluating a patient for whom such a diagnosis is appropriate, however, clinicians should consider the contributions of each member of the caregiver–child dyad and their interactions. Clinicians should weigh such things as infant or child temperament, deficient or defective bonding, a developmentally disabled or sensorially impaired child, and a particular caregiver–child mismatch. The likelihood of neglect increases with parental mental retardation; lack of parenting skills because of personal upbringing, social isolation, or deprivation and lack of opportunities to learn about caregiving behavior; and premature parenthood (during early and middle adolescence), in which parents are unable to respond to and care for an infant's needs and in which the parents' own needs take precedence over their infant's or child's needs. Frequent changes of the primary caregiver—as may occur in institutionalization, repeated lengthy hospitalizations, and multiple foster care placements—may also cause a reactive attachment disorder of infancy or early childhood.

DIAGNOSIS AND CLINICAL FEATURES

Children with reactive attachment disorder of infancy or early childhood often first come to the attention of a pediatrician. The clinical picture varies greatly according to a child's chronological and mental ages, but expected social interaction and liveliness are not present. Often, a child is developmentally not progressing or is frankly malnourished. Perhaps the most typical clinical picture of an infant with the disorder is the nonorganic failure to thrive. In such infants, hypokinesis, dullness, listlessness, and apathy with a poverty of spontaneous activity usually appear. Infants look sad, joyless, and miserable. Some infants also appear frightened and watchful, with a radar-like gaze. Nevertheless, they may exhibit delayed responsiveness to a stimulus that would elicit fright or withdrawal from a normal infant (Table 47.3–1). Most infants appear significantly malnourished, and many have protruding abdomens (Figs. 47.3–1 and 47.3–2). Occasionally, foul-smelling, celiac-like stools are reported. In unusually severe cases, a clinical picture of marasmus appears.

An infant's weight is often below the third percentile and markedly below the appropriate weight for his or her height. If serial weights are available, the weight percentiles may have decreased progressively because of an actual weight loss or a failure to gain weight as height increases. Head circumference is usually normal for the infant's age. Muscle tone may be poor. The skin may be colder and paler or more mottled than skin of a normal child. Laboratory findings are usually within normal limits, except for abnormal findings coincident with any malnutrition, dehydration, or concurrent illness. Bone age is usually retarded. Growth hormone levels are usually normal or elevated, a finding suggesting that growth failure in these children is secondary to caloric deprivation and malnutrition. The children improve physically and gain weight rapidly after they are hospitalized.

Socially, the infants usually show little spontaneous activity and a marked diminution of both initiative toward others and reciprocity in response to the caregiving adult or examiner. Both mother and infant may be indifferent to separation on hospitalization or to termination of subsequent hospital visits. The infants frequently show none of the normal upset, fretting, or protest about hospitalization. Older infants usually show little interest in their environment. They may not play with toys, even if encouraged; however, they rapidly or gradually take an interest in and relate to their caregivers in the hospital.

Classic psychosocial dwarfism or psychosocially determined short stature is a syndrome that usually is first manifest in children 2 to 3 years of age. The children are typically unusually short and have frequent growth hormone abnormalities and severe behavioral disturbances. All of these symptoms are the result of an inimical caregiver–child relationship. The affectionless character may appear when there is a failure or lack of opportunity to form attachments before the ages of 2 to 3 years. Children are unable to form lasting relationships, and their inability is sometimes accompanied by a lack of guilt,

Table 47.3–1
DSM-IV Diagnostic Criteria for Reactive Attachment Disorder of Infancy or Early Childhood

A. Markedly disturbed and developmentally inappropriate social relatedness in most contexts, beginning before age 5 years, as evidenced by either (1) or (2):
   (1) persistent failure to initiate or respond in a developmentally appropriate fashion to most social interactions, as manifest by excessively inhibited, hypervigilant, or highly ambivalent and contradictory responses (eg, the child may respond to caregiver with a mixture of approach, avoidance, and resistance to comforting, or may exhibit frozen watchfulness)
   (2) diffuse attachments as manifest by indiscriminate sociability with marked inability to exhibit appropriate selective attachments (eg, excessive familiarity with relative strangers or lack of selectivity in choice of attachment figures)

B. The disturbance in criterion A is not accounted for solely by developmental delay (as in mental retardation) and does not meet criteria for a pervasive developmental disorder.

C. Pathogenic care as evidenced by at least one of the following:
   (1) persistent disregard of the child's basic emotional needs for comfort, stimulation, and affection
   (2) persistent disregard of the child's basic physical needs
   (3) repeated changes of primary caregiver that prevent formation of stable attachments (eg, frequent change in foster care)

D. There is a presumption that the care in criterion C is responsible for the disturbed behavior in A (eg, the disturbances in criterion A began following the pathogenic care in criterion C).

Specify type:
Inhibited Type: If criterion A1 predominates in the clinical presentation.
Disinhibited Type: If criterion A2 predominates in the clinical presentation.

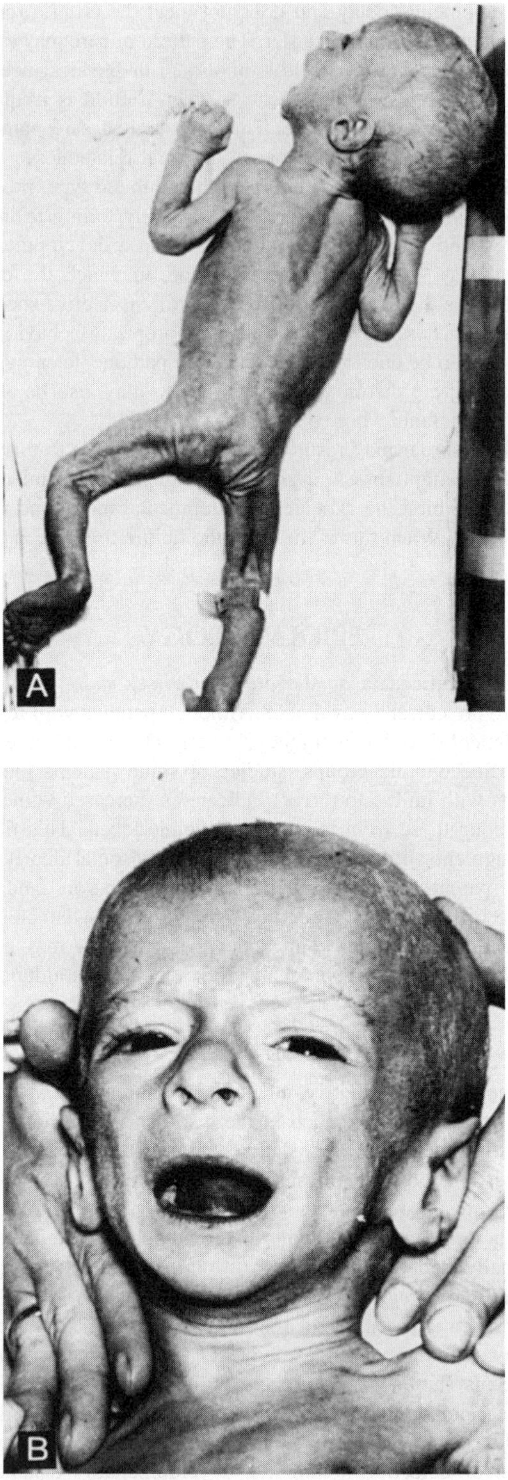
A
B

FIGURE 47.3–1
Three-month-old baby boy suffering from failure to thrive secondary to caloric deprivation. Weight is only 1 ounce over birth weight. (Courtesy of Barton Schmitt, M.D., Children's Hospital, Denver, CO.)

an inability to obey rules, and a need for attention and affection. Some children are indiscriminately friendly.

ICD-10

The 10th revision of *International Statistical Classification of Diseases and Related Health Problems* (ICD-10) includes a category for disorders of social functioning. This category includes reactive attachment disorders of childhood, disinhibited attachment disorder of childhood, elective mutism, and two residual categories (Table 47.3–2).

ICD-10 describes the disorders of social functioning with onset specific to childhood and adolescence as a rather heterogeneous group that shares common abnormalities in social functioning arising during the developmental period but that is not mainly characterized by social incapacity or deficit impairing all areas of functioning. Severe environmental "distortions or privations are commonly associated and are thought to play a crucial etiological role in many instances." Although the disorders are well known, they are not clearly defined di-

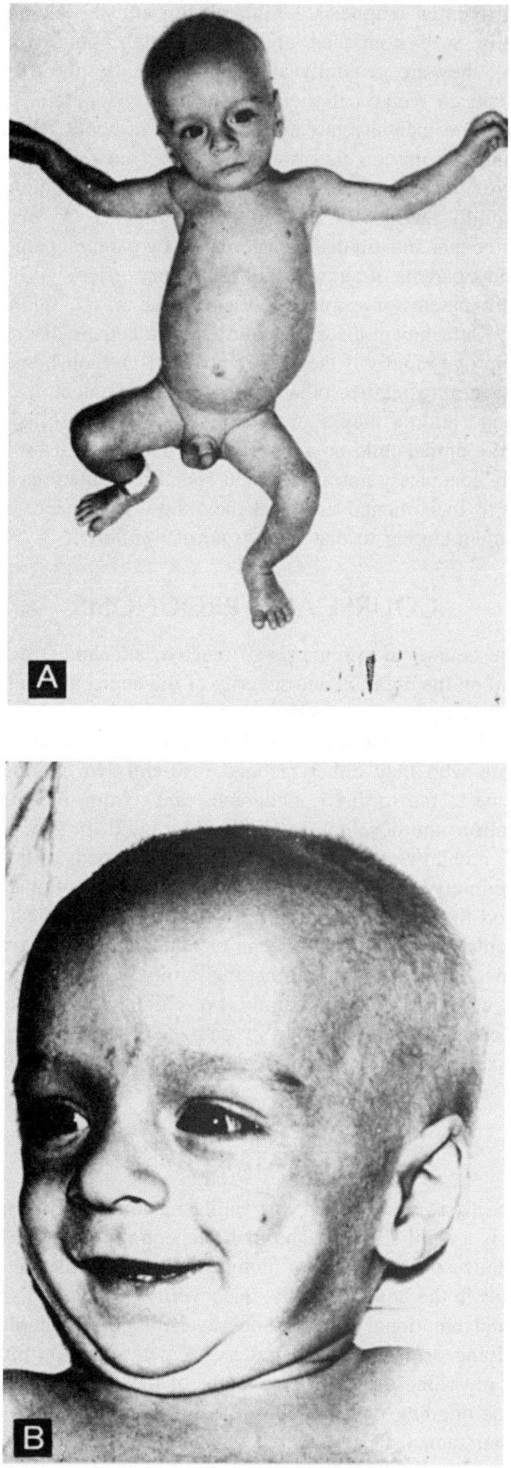
A
B

FIGURE 47.3–2
The same infant as in Figure 47.3–1, 3 weeks later, after hospitalization. (Courtesy of Barton Schmitt, M.D., Children's Hospital, Denver, CO.)

Table 47.3–2
ICD-10 Diagnostic Criteria for Disorders of Social Functioning with Onset Specific to Childhood or Adolescence

Elective mutism

Note. This disorder is also referred to as selective mutism.

A. Language expression and comprehension, as assessed on individually administered standardized tests, is within the 2 standard deviations limit for the child's age.

B. There is demonstrable evidence of a consistent failure to speak in specific social situations in which the child would be expected to speak (eg, in school), despite speaking in other situations.

C. Duration of the elective mutism exceeds 4 weeks.

D. There is no pervasive developmental disorder.

E. The disorder is not accounted for by a lack of knowledge of the spoken language required in the social situation in which there is a failure to speak.

Reactive attachment disorder of childhood

A. Onset is before the age of 5 years.

B. The child exhibits strongly contradictory or ambivalent social responses that extend across social situations (but that may show variability from relationship to relationship).

C. Emotional disturbance is shown by lack of emotional responsiveness, withdrawal reactions, aggressive responses to the child's own or other's distress, and/or fearful hypervigilance.

D. Some capacity for social reciprocity and responsiveness is evident in interactions with normal adults.

E. The criteria for pervasive developmental disorders are not met.

Disinhibited attachment disorder of childhood

A. Diffuse attachments are a persistent feature during the first 5 years of life (but do not necessarily persist into middle childhood). Diagnosis requires a relative failure to show selective social attachments manifest by:
   (1) a normal tendency to seek comfort from others when distressed and
   (2) an abnormal (relative) lack of selectivity in the people from whom comfort is sought

B. Social interactions with unfamiliar people are poorly modulated.

C. At least one of the following must be present:
   (1) generally clinging behavior in infancy
   (2) attention-seeking and indiscriminately friendly behavior in early or middle childhood

D. The general lack of situation-specificity in the above features must be clear. Diagnosis requires that the symptoms in criteria A and B above are manifest across the range of social contacts experienced by the child.

Other childhood disorders of social functioning

Childhood disorder of social functioning, unspecified

Reprinted with permission from World Health Organization: *The ICD-10 Classification of Mental and Behavioural Disorders: Diagnostic Criteria for Research.* Copyright, World Health Organization, Geneva, 1993.

agnostically, and workers disagree about the appropriate classifications.

Elective mutism (similar to DSM-IV's selective mutism) is a marked, emotionally determined selectivity in speaking. Children can speak competently in some situations but not in others. The disorder often appears during early childhood and is usually associated with personality features involving social anxiety, withdrawal, sensitivity, or resistance. There is a normal or nearly normal level of language comprehension, a sufficient competence for social communication, and evidence that the child speaks normally or nearly normally in some situations. A significant minority of children with elective mutism have a history of some speech delay or articulation problem. The diagnosis requires that "failure to speak is persistent over time" and that the periods when speech does and does not occur are consistent.

Reactive attachment disorder of childhood (similar to DSM-IV's reactive attachment disorder of infancy or early childhood), which occurs in infants and young children, is described in ICD-10 as persistent abnormalities in social relationships, associated with emotional disturbance and reactive to environmental changes. A fearful, hypervigilant child may not be helped by comforting. Children interact poorly with peers and show aggression toward themselves and others. They are usually miserable and may even fail to grow. "The syndrome probably occurs as a direct result of severe parental neglect, abuse, or serious mishandling." Its key feature is an "abnormal pattern of relationships with caregivers" that develops before the age of 5 years, a maladaptive pattern that is not present in normal children, and behavior that is persistent but that reacts to marked change in child-rearing practices. This disorder is recognized and accepted, but its diagnostic criteria, boundaries, and even its existence as a valid entity are uncertain. ICD-10 includes the disorder because it exists and is important and because its behavioral pattern does not fit with other diagnostic categories.

Disinhibited attachment disorder of childhood (similar to DSM-IV's reactive attachment disorder of infancy or early childhood) is abnormal social functioning that arises during the first 5 years of life and that persists despite marked environmental changes. At about 2 years of age, children are clinging and show attachment to almost anyone. By 4 years of age, these diffuse attachments are still present, but clinging has been replaced by indiscriminate friendliness and attention-seeking behavior. In later years, attention-seeking behavior continues, and children often have problems with their peers. The disorder has usually been identified among institutionalized children but also occurs whenever there is a lack of opportunity to "develop selective attachments as a consequence of extremely frequent changes in care-givers."

Pathology and Laboratory Examination

Although no single specific laboratory test is used to make a diagnosis, many children with the disorder have disturbances of growth and development. Therefore, establishing a growth curve and examining the progression of developmental milestones may be helpful in determining whether associated phenomena, such as failure to thrive, are present.

DIFFERENTIAL DIAGNOSIS

Metabolic disorders, pervasive developmental disorders, mental retardation, various severe neurological abnormalities, and psychosocial dwarfism are the primary considerations in the differential diagnosis. Children with autistic disorder are typically well nourished and of age-appropriate size and weight; they are generally alert and active, despite their impairments in reciprocal social interactions. Moderate, severe, or profound mental retardation is present in about 50 percent of children with autistic disorder, whereas most children with reactive attachment disorder of infancy or early childhood are only mildly retarded or have normal intelligence. No evidence indicates that autistic disorder is caused by parental pathology, and most parents of autistic children do not differ significantly from the parents of normal children. Unlike most children with reactive attachment disorder, children with autistic disorder do not improve rapidly if they are removed from their homes and placed in a hospital or other favorable environment. Mentally retarded children may show delays in all social skills. Such children, unlike children with reactive attachment disorder, are usually adequately nourished, their social relatedness is appropriate to their mental age, and they show a sequence of development similar to that seen in normal children.

COURSE AND PROGNOSIS

The course and prognosis of reactive attachment disorder depend on the duration and severity of the neglectful and pathogenic parenting and on associated complications such as failure to thrive. Constitutional and nutritional factors interact in children who may either respond resiliently to treatment or continue to fail to thrive. Outcomes range from the extremes of death to the developmentally healthy child. In general, the longer a child remains in the adverse environment without adequate intervention, the more the physical and emotional damage and the worse the prognosis. After the pathological environmental situation has been recognized, the degree of treatment and rehabilitation that the family receives affects the child, who returns to this family. For children who have multiple problems stemming from pathogenic caregiving, their physical recovery may be faster and more complete than their emotional well-being.

TREATMENT

The first consideration in treating reactive attachment disorder is a child's safety. The first decision is often whether to hospitalize the child or to attempt treatment while the child remains in the home. Usually, the severity of the child's physical and emotional state or the severity of the pathological caregiving determines the strategy. A determination must be made regarding the nutritional status of the child and whether there is ongoing physical abuse or threat. For cases in which malnourishment has occurred, hospitalization is necessary. Along with an assessment of the child's physical well-being, an evaluation of the child's emotional condition is important. Immediate intervention must address the parents' awareness and capacity to participate in altering the injurious patterns that have ensued. The treatment team must begin to alter the unsatisfactory relationship between the caregiver and the child. Doing so usually requires extensive and intensive intervention and education with the mother or with both parents when possible. Possible interventions include, but are not limited to, the following: psychosocial support services, including hiring a homemaker, improving the physical condition of the apartment or obtaining more adequate housing, improving the family's financial status, and decreasing the family's isolation; psychotherapeutic interventions, including individual psychotherapy, psychotropic medications, and family or marital therapy; educational counseling services, including mother–infant or mother–toddler groups, and counseling to increase awareness and understanding of the child's needs and to increase parenting skills; and provisions for close monitoring of the progression of the patient's emotional and physical well-being. Sometimes, separating a child from the stressful home environment for a temporary period, such as in a hospitalization, allows the child to break out of the accustomed pattern. A neutral setting, such as the hospital, is the best place to start for families who are genuinely available emotionally and physically for intervention. If those interventions are unfeasible or inadequate or if they fail, placement with relatives or in foster care, adoption, or a group home or residential treatment facility must be considered.

References

Ainsworth MDS: The development of infant–mother attachment. In *Review of Child Development Research,* BM Caldwen, HN Ricciuhi, editors, vol 3, p 1. University of Chicago Press, Chicago, 1973.

Benedersky M, Lewis M: Environmental risks, biological risks, and developmental outcome. Dev Psychol *30:* 484, 1994.

Campbell M, Green WH, Caplon R, David R: Psychiatry and endocrinology in children: Early infantile autism and psychosocial dwarfism. In *Handbook of Psychiatry and Endocrinology,* PJV Beumont, GD Burrows, editors, p 15. Elsevier, Amsterdam, 1982.

Cicetti D, Toth S: A developmental psychology perspective on child abuse and neglect. J Am Acad Child Adolesc Psychiatry *34:* 541, 1995.

Ferholt JB: A psychodynamic study of psychosomatic dwarfism. J Am Acad Child Adolesc Psychiatry *14:* 49, 1985.

Klaus MH, Kennell JM: *Parent–Infant Bonding,* ed 2. Mosby, St. Louis, 1982.

Lamb ME: Social development. Pediatr Ann *18:* 292, 1989.

Nachmias M, Gunnar MR, Mangelsdorf S, Paritz RH, Buss K: Behavioral inhibition and stress reactivity: Moderating role of attachment security. Child Dev *67:* 508, 1996.

Rutter M: *Maternal Deprivation Reassessed,* ed 2. Penguin, Middlesex, England, 1981.

Shaw DS, Vondra JI: Infant attachment security and maternal predictors of early behavior problems: A longitudinal study of low income families. J Child Psychol Psychiatry *23:* 355, 1995.

Terwogt MM, Schene J, Koops W: Concepts of motion in institutionalized children. J Child Psychol Psychiatry *31:* 1131, 1990.

Zeanah CH, Larrieu JA: Infant development and developmental risk: A review of the past 10 years. J Am Acad Child Adolesc Psychiatry *36:* 165, 1997.

▲ 47.4 Stereotypic Movement Disorder and Disorder of Infancy, Childhood, or Adolescence Not Otherwise Specified

STEREOTYPIC MOVEMENT DISORDER

According to the fourth edition of *Diagnostic and Statistical Manual of Mental Disorders* (DSM-IV), *stereotypic movement disorder* is repetitive, nonfunctional motor behavior that seems to be compulsive. The behavior significantly interferes with normal activities or produces self-inflicted bodily injuries severe enough to need medical care unless the child is protected. For children with mental retardation, the injurious behavior is dangerous enough to become the focus of treatment. The disorder is not better diagnosed as a compulsion, tic, stereotypy in pervasive developmental disorder, or hair pulling. The disorder is not caused by a substance or a medical condition and must persist for at least 4 weeks.

According to DSM-IV, stereotypic movement disorder can be diagnosed with mental retardation or a pervasive developmental disorder when the stereotypic behaviors are severe enough to warrant treatment. Stereotypic behaviors are not specified as intentional in DSM-IV.

Epidemiology

The prevalence of stereotypic movement disorder is unknown. Behaviors such as nail biting are common and affect as many as one half of all school-age children; behaviors such as thumb sucking and rocking are normal in young children but are often maladaptive in older children and adolescents. These behaviors usually do not constitute a stereotypic movement disorder; most children who bite their nails function in daily activities without impairment or self-injury. In one pediatric clinic, as many as 20 percent of children had a history of rocking, head banging, or swaying in one form or another.

Deciding which cases are severe enough to confirm a diagnosis of stereotypic movement disorder may be difficult.

The diagnosis is a compilation of many symptoms, and various behaviors must be studied separately to obtain data about prevalence, sex ratio, and familial patterns. It is clear, however, that stereotypic movement disorder is more prevalent in boys than in girls. Stereotypic behaviors are common among children who are mentally retarded; 10 to 20 percent are affected. Self-injurious behaviors occur in some genetic syndromes, such as Lesch-Nyhan syndrome, and are also present in some patients with Tourette's disorder. Self-injurious stereotypic behaviors are increasingly common in people with severe mental retardation. Stereotypic behaviors are also common in children with sensory impairments such as blindness and deafness.

Etiology

The etiology of stereotypic movements is unknown and is likely to be multidetermined because of the wide range of behaviors that fall under this category. Many stereotypic behaviors may be associated with normal development. For example, as many as 80 percent of all normal children show rhythmic activities that phase out by 4 years of age. These rhythmic patterns seem to be purposeful, to provide sensorimotor stimulation and tension release, and to be satisfying and pleasurable to the children. The movements may increase at times of frustration, boredom, and tension.

The progression from what are perhaps vicissitudes of normal development to stereotypic movement disorder is believed to reflect disordered development, as in mental retardation or a pervasive developmental disorder. Genetic factors are likely to play a role in some stereotypic movements such as in the

X-linked recessive deficiency of enzymes leading to Lesch-Nyhan syndrome. In this syndrome, there are predictable features, including mental retardation, hyperuricemia, spasticity, and self-injurious behaviors. Other stereotypic movements (such as nail biting), although often causing minimal or no impairment, seem to run in the families. Some stereotypic behaviors seem to emerge or become exaggerated in situations of neglect or deprivation. Such behaviors as head banging have been associated with psychosocial deprivation.

Stereotypic movements seem to be associated with dopamine activity. Neurobiological factors may be contributory in the development of stereotypic movement disorders. Dopamine agonists induce or increase stereotypic behaviors, whereas dopamine antagonists decrease them. In one report, four children with attention-deficit/hyperactivity disorder who were treated with a stimulant medication began to bite their nails and fingertips. The nail biting ceased when the medication was eliminated. Endogenous opioids also have been implicated in the production of self-injurious behaviors.

Table 47.4–1
DSM-IV Diagnostic Criteria for Stereotypic Movement Disorder

A. Repetitive, seemingly driven, and nonfunctional motor behavior (eg, hand shaking or waving, body rocking, head banging, mouthing of objects, self-biting, picking at skin or bodily orifices, hitting own body).

B. The behavior markedly interferes with normal activities or results in self-inflicted bodily injury that requires medical treatment (or would result in an injury if preventive measures were not used).

C. If mental retardation is present, the stereotypic or self-injurious behavior is of sufficient severity to become a focus of treatment.

D. The behavior is not better accounted for by a compulsion (as in obsessive-compulsive disorder), a tic (as in tic disorder), a stereotypy that is part of a pervasive developmental disorder, or hair pulling (as in trichotillomania).

E. The behavior is not due to the direct physiological effects of a substance or a general medical condition.

F. The behavior persists for 4 weeks or longer.

Specify if:

With self-injurious behavior: if the behavior results in bodily damage that requires specific treatment (or that would result in bodily damage if protective measures were not used).

Reprinted with permission from American Psychiatric Association: *Diagnostic and Statistical Manual of Mental Disorders,* ed 4. Copyright, American Psychiatric Association, Washington, 1994.

Diagnosis and Clinical Features

Affected people may suffer from one or more symptoms of stereotypic movement disorder; thus, the clinical picture varies considerably. Most commonly, one symptom predominates. The presence of several severe symptoms tends to occur among those most severely afflicted with mental retardation or a pervasive development disorder. Patients frequently have other significant mental disorders, especially disruptive behavior disorders.

In extreme cases, severe mutilation and life-threatening injuries may result, and secondary infection and septicemia may follow self-inflicted trauma. The DSM-IV diagnostic criteria for stereotypic movement disorder are listed in Table 47.4–1. The criteria from the 10th revision of *International Statistical Classification of Diseases and Related Health Problems* (ICD-10) are listed in Table 47.4–2.

Head Banging. Head banging is an example of a stereotypic movement disorder that can result in functional impairment. The reported incidence varies between 3.3 and 19 percent. Typically, head banging begins during infancy, between 6 and 12 months of age. Infants strike their heads with a definite rhythmic and monotonous continuity against the crib or other hard surface. They seem to be absorbed in the activity, which may persist until they become exhausted and fall asleep. The head banging is often transitory but sometimes persists into middle childhood.

Head banging that is a component of temper tantrums is different from stereotypic head banging and ceases after the tantrums and their secondary gains have been controlled.

Nail Biting. Nail biting begins as early as 1 year of age and increases in incidence until 12 years of age. All of the nails are usually bitten. Most cases are not sufficiently severe to meet the DSM-IV diagnostic criteria. In other cases, children cause physical damage to the fingers themselves, usually by associated biting of the cuticles, which leads to secondary infections of the fingers and nail beds. Nail biting seems to occur or increase in intensity when a person is either anxious or bored. Some of the most severe nail biting occurs in those who are severely and profoundly mentally retarded and in some patients with paranoid schizophrenia. Some nail biters, however, have no obvious emotional disturbance.

Pathology and Laboratory Examination. No specific laboratory measures are helpful in the diagnosis of stereotypic movement disorder.

Differential Diagnosis

The differential diagnosis of stereotypic movement disorder includes obsessive-compulsive disorder and tic disorders, both

Table 47.4–2
ICD-10 Diagnostic Criteria for Stereotyped Movement Disorders

A. The child exhibits stereotyped movements to an extent that either causes physical injury or markedly interferes with normal activities.

B. Duration of the disorder is at least 1 month.

C. The child exhibits no other mental or behavioral disorder in the ICD-10 classification (other than mental retardation).

Reprinted with permission from World Health Organization: *The ICD-10 Classification of Mental and Behavioural Disorders: Diagnostic Criteria for Research,* Copyright, World Health Organization, Geneva, 1993.

of which are exclusionary criteria in DSM-IV. Although stereotypic movements are voluntary and not spasmodic, it is difficult to differentiate these features from tics in all cases. Stereotypic movements are likely to be comforting, whereas tics are often associated with distress. In obsessive-compulsive disorder, the compulsions must be ego-dystonic, although it, too, is difficult to discern in young children.

Differentiating dyskinetic movements from stereotypic movements can be difficult. Because antipsychotic medications can suppress stereotypic movements, clinicians must note any stereotypic movements before initiating treatment with an antipsychotic agent. Stereotypic movement disorder may be diagnosed concurrently with substance-related disorders (for example, amphetamine use disorders), severe sensory impairments, central nervous system and degenerative disorders (for example, Lesch-Nyhan syndrome), and severe schizophrenia.

Course and Prognosis

The duration and course of stereotypic movement disorder are variable, and the symptoms may wax and wane. As many as 80 percent of normal children show rhythmic activities that seem to be purposeful and comforting and tend to disappear by 4 years of age. When stereotypic movements are present or emerge more severely later in childhood or in a noncomforting manner, they range from brief episodes occurring under stress to an ongoing pattern in the context of a chronic condition such as mental retardation or a pervasive developmental disorder. Even in chronic conditions, the emergence of stereotypic behaviors may come and go. In some cases, stereotypic movements are prominent in early childhood and diminish as a child gets older.

The severity of the dysfunction caused by stereotypic movements also varies with the associated frequency, amounts, and degree of self-injury. Children who exhibit frequent, severe, self-injurious stereotypic behaviors have the poorest prognosis. Repetitive episodes of head banging, self-biting, and eye poking may be difficult to control without physical restraints. Most nail biting is benign and often does not meet the diagnostic criteria for stereotypic movement disorder. In severe cases in which the nail beds are repetitively damaged, bacterial and fungal infections can occur. Although chronic stereotypic movement disorders can severely impair daily functioning, several treatments help control the symptoms.

Treatment

Treatment should be related to the specific symptom or symptoms being treated, their causes, and the patient's mental age. Treatment modalities yielding the most promising effects have been behavioral and pharmacological, sometimes used in combination. In extreme situations in which environmental deprivation is deemed a factor, the psychosocial environment must be adjusted. Behavioral techniques, including reinforcement and behavioral shaping, are successful in some cases. For instances in which severe physical damage occurs, especially in people who are severely retarded, psychopharmacology must be considered.

The dopamine antagonists are the most commonly used medications for treating stereotypic movements and self-injurious behavior. Phenothiazines have been the most frequently used drugs. Opiate antagonists have reduced self-injurious behaviors in some patients without exposing them to tardive dyskinesia or impaired cognition.

Additional pharmacological agents that have been tried in the treatment of stereotypic movement disorder include fenfluramine (Pondimin), clomipramine (Anafranil), and fluoxetine (Prozac). In some reports, fenfluramine diminished stereotypic behaviors in children with autistic disorder; in other studies, the results were less encouraging. Open trials indicate that both clomipramine and fluoxetine may decrease self-injurious behaviors and other stereotypic movements in some patients. Trazodone and buspirone have also been tried with unclear results.

Table 47.4–3
DSM-IV Diagnostic Criteria for Disorder of Infancy, Childhood, or Adolescence Not Otherwise Specified

This category is a residual category for disorders with onset in infancy, childhood, or adolescence that do not meet criteria for any specific disorder in the classification.

DISORDER OF INFANCY, CHILDHOOD, OR ADOLESCENCE NOT OTHERWISE SPECIFIED

DSM-IV describes *disorder of infancy, childhood, or adolescence not otherwise specified* as a category including disorders with onset in infancy, childhood, or adolescence that do not meet the criteria for any specific disorder.

The DSM-IV diagnostic criteria are shown in Table 47.4–3.

The ICD-10 included two residual categories for childhood mental disorders: (1) other specified behavioral and emotional disorders with onset usually occurring in childhood and adolescence, and (2) unspecified behavioral and emotional disorders with onset usually occurring in childhood and adolescence.

References

Buitelaar K: Self-injurious behavior in retarded children: Clinical phenomena and biological mechanisms. Acta Paedopsychiatr *56:* 105, 1993.

Hanna GL: Stereotypic movement disorder of infancy, childhood, or adolescence NOS. In *Comprehensive Textbook of Psychiatry,* ed 6, HI Kaplan, BJ Sadock, editors, p 2359. Williams & Wilkins, Baltimore, 1995.

Kaplan, BJ Sadock, editors, p 2359. Williams & Wilkins, Baltimore, 1995.

King BH: Self-injury by people with mental retardation: A compulsive behavior hypothesis. Am J Ment Retard *98:* 93, 1993.

Leonard HL, Lenane MC, Swedo SE, Rettew DC, Rapoport JL: A double-blind comparison of clomipramine and desipramine treatment of severe onychophagia (nail biting). Arch Gen Psychiatry *48:* 821, 1992.

Linsceid TR, Pejeau C, Cohen S, Footo-Lenz M: Positive side effects in the treatment of SIB using the Self-Injurious Behavior Inhibiting System (SIBIS): Implications for operant and biochemical explanations of SIB. Res Dev Disabil *15:* 81, 1994.

Meiselas KD, Spencer EK, Oberfield R, Peselow ED, Angrist B, Campbell M: Differentiation of stereotypies from neuroleptic-related dyskinesias in autistic children. J Clin Psychopharmacol *9:* 207, 1989.

Ratey JJ: *Mental Retardation: Developing Pharmacotherapies.* American Psychiatric Press, Washington, 1991.

Ricketts RW, Goza AB, Ellis CR, Singh YN, Singh NN, Cooke JC III: Fluoxetine treatment of severe self-injury in young adults with mental retardation. J Am Acad Child Adolesc Psychiatry *32:* 865, 1993.

Silberstein RM, Blackman S, Mandell W: Autoerotic head banging: A reflection of the opportunism of infants. J Am Acad Child Adolesc Psychiatry *5:* 235, 1966.

Sokol MS, Campbell M, Goldstein M, Kriechman AM: Attention deficit disorder with hyperactivity and the dopamine hypothesis: Case presentations with theoretical background. J Am Acad Child Adolesc Psychiatry *26:* 428, 1987.

Troster H: Prevalence and functions of stereotyped behaviors in nonhandicapped children in residential care. J Abnorm Child Psychol *22:* 79, 1994.

48

Mood Disorders and Suicide

MOOD DISORDERS

The diagnostic criteria in the fourth edition of *Diagnostic and Statistical Manual of Mental Disorders* (DSM-IV) for major depressive disorder, dysthymic disorder, and bipolar I disorder are the same for children and adolescents as they are for adults, with some minor modifications. The modifications in the criteria for childhood and adolescent *major depressive disorder* include irritable rather than depressed mood and failure to make expected weight gains instead of significant weight loss or weight gain. In *dysthymic disorder,* irritable mood may replace depressed mood, and the duration criterion in children and adolescents has been modified to 1 year rather than the obligatory 2 years in adults. The criteria for *bipolar I disorder* are the same for children and adolescents as for adults.

Recently, mood disorders among children and adolescents have been increasingly recognized and treated. Although people have always realized that children and adolescents undergo sadness and despair, it has become clear that enduring disorders of mood occur in children of all ages and under many different circumstances. Two criteria for mood disorders in childhood and adolescence are a disturbance of mood, such as depression or elation, and irritability. (Mood disorders in adults are reviewed in detail in Chapter 15). Only those issues that pertain specifically to children and adolescents are discussed here.)

Although the DSM-IV diagnostic criteria for mood disorders are almost identical across all age groups, the expression of disturbed mood varies in children according to their ages. Young, depressed children commonly show symptoms that appear less often as they grow older, including mood-congruent auditory hallucinations, somatic complaints, withdrawn, sad appearance, and poor self-esteem. Symptoms that are more common among depressed youngsters in late adolescence than in young childhood are pervasive anhedonia, severe psychomotor retardation, delusions, and a sense of hopelessness. Symptoms that appear with the same frequency regardless of age and developmental status include suicidal ideation, depressed or irritable mood, insomnia, and diminished ability to concentrate.

Developmental issues, however, influence the expression of all symptoms. For example, unhappy young children who exhibit recurrent suicidal ideation are generally unable to think of a realistic suicide plan or to put their ideas into action. Children's moods are especially vulnerable to the influences of severe social stressors, such as chronic family discord, abuse and neglect, and academic failure. Most young children with major depressive disorder have histories of abuse or neglect. Children with depressive disorders in the midst of toxic environments may have remission of some or many depressive symptoms when the stressors diminish or when the children are removed from the stressful environment. Bereavement often becomes a focus of psychiatric treatment when children have lost a loved one, even when a depressive disorder is not present.

Depressive disorders and bipolar I disorder are generally episodic, although their onset may be insidious. Manic episodes are rare in prepubertal children but fairly common in adolescents. Attention-deficit/hyperactivity disorder, oppositional defiant disorder, and conduct disorder may occur among children who later experience depression. In some cases, conduct disturbances or disorders may occur in the context of a major depressive episode and resolve with the resolution of the depressive episode. Clinicians must clarify the chronology of the symptoms to determine whether a given behavior (such as poor concentration, defiance, or temper tantrums) was present before the depressive episode and is unrelated to it or whether the behavior is occurring for the first time and is related to the depressive episode.

Epidemiology

Mood disorders increase with increasing age, and prevalence in any age group is drastically higher in psychiatrically referred groups than in the general population. Mood disorders in preschool-age children are extremely rare. The rate of major depressive disorder in preschoolers has been estimated to be about 0.3 percent in the community, compared with 0.9 percent in a clinic setting. Among school-age children in the community, about 2 percent have major depressive disorder. Depression is more common in boys than in girls among school-age children. Some bias may be present in the clinic reports, as boys outnumber girls in psychiatric clinics. Among adolescents, about 5 percent in the community have major depressive disorder. Among hospitalized children and adolescents, the rates of major depressive disorder are much higher than in the general community: as many as 20 percent of children and 40 percent of adolescents are depressed. Dysthymic disorder is estimated to be more common than major depressive disorder among school-age children, with rates up to 2.5 percent, compared with 2 percent for major depressive disorder. For school-age children with dysthymic disorder, there is a high likelihood that major depressive disorder will develop at some point after 1 year of the dysthymic disorder. In adolescents, as in adults, dysthymic disorder is less common than major depressive disorder; the prevalence rate for dysthymic disorder is about 3.3

percent, compared with about 5 percent for major depressive disorder.

The rate of bipolar I disorder is exceedingly low in prepubertal children and may take years to be diagnosed, because mania typically appears for the first time in adolescence. The lifetime rate of bipolar I disorder has been estimated to be 0.6 percent in a community study of adolescents. Adolescents with clinical variants of mania (some manic symptoms but without the full diagnostic criteria: *bipolar II disorder*) have rates of up to about 10 percent, according to some studies.

Etiology

Considerable evidence indicates that the mood disorders in childhood are the same fundamental diseases experienced by adults.

Genetic Factors. Mood disorders in children, adolescents, and adult patients tend to cluster in the same families. An increased incidence of mood disorders is generally found among children of parents with mood disorders and relatives of children with mood disorders. In one study, however, depression was equally increased in the parents of both depressed and nondepressed children and adolescent inpatients and outpatients, but having one depressed parent probably doubles the risk for offspring. Having two depressed parents probably quadruples the risk of a child's having a mood disorder before age 18 when compared with the risk for children with two unaffected parents. Some evidence indicates that the number of recurrences of parental depression does increase the likelihood that the children will be affected, but this increase may be at least partly related to the affective loading of the parent's own family tree. Similarly, children with the most severe episodes of major depressive disorder have shown much evidence of dense and deep familial aggregation for major depressive disorder.

Other Biological Factors. Studies of prepubertal major depressive disorder and adolescent mood disorder have revealed biological abnormalities. Prepubertal children in an episode of depressive disorder secrete significantly more growth hormone during sleep than normal children and those with nondepressed mental disorders. These children also secrete significantly less growth hormone in response to insulin-induced hypoglycemia than nondepressed patients. Both abnormalities have been found to persist for at least 4 months of full, sustained clinical response, the last month in a drug-free state. In contrast, the data conflict regarding cortisol hypersecretion during major depressive disorder. Some workers report hypersecretion, and some report normal secretion.

The dexamethasone-suppression test is used in childhood and adolescence but not as frequently or as reliably as in adults. Sleep studies are inconclusive in depressed children and adolescents. Polysomnography shows either no change or changes characteristic of adults with major depressive disorder: reduced rapid eye movement (REM) latency and an increased number of REM periods. A recent study evaluating magnetic resonance imaging (MRI) scans in more than 100 psychiatrically hospitalized children with mood disturbances showed a decrease in frontal lobe volume and an increase in ventricular volume. These results are consistent with MRI findings in adults with major depression insofar as postmortem studies of depressed adults have demonstrated selective loss of frontal lobe cells and frontal lobe serotonin. Damage to the frontal lobes has also been associated with depressive symptoms in poststroke patients. The frontal lobes seem to have multiple connections with the basal ganglia and the limbic system and are also believed to be involved in the neuropathology of depressive symptomatology.

Thyroid hormone studies have found lower free total thyroxine (FT_4) in depressed adolescents compared with a matched control group. These values were associated with normal thyroid-stimulating hormone (TSH) and FT_4 values that were still in the normal range for both groups. This finding suggests that although values of thyroid function remain in the normative range, FT_4 has been shifted downward. These downward shifts in thyroid hormone possibly contribute to the clinical manifestations of depression. Some data suggest that in adults with depression, the addition of exogenous thyroid hormone can potentiate the effects of antidepressant medication. It has also been shown that mood and cognitive function can be impaired in adults with subclinical hypothyroidism and that the impairment can be corrected with exogenous thyroid hormone. The evidence for adolescents is still only speculative, but dysfunction of the hypothalamic pituitary axis may also contribute to the development and maintenance of depression in certain teenagers.

Social Factors. The finding that identical twins do not have a 100 percent concordance rate suggests a role for nongenetic factors. So far, little evidence indicates that parental marital status, number of siblings, family's socioeconomic status, parental separation, divorce, marital functioning, or familial constellation or structure plays much of a role in causing depressive disorders in children. However, some evidence indicates that boys whose fathers died before they were 13 years of age are more likely than controls to have depression.

The psychosocial deficits in depressed children improve after sustained recovery from the depression. These deficits seem to be secondary to the depression itself and may be compounded by the long duration of most dysthymic or depressive episodes, during which poorly accomplished or unaccomplished developmental tasks accumulate. Among preschoolers in whom depressive clinical presentations are described, the role of environmental influences probably will receive experimental support in the future.

Diagnosis and Clinical Features

Major Depressive Disorder. Major depressive disorder in children is diagnosed most easily when it is acute and occurs in a child without previous psychiatric symptoms. In many cases, however, the onset is insidious, and the disorder occurs in a child who has had several years of difficulties with hyperactivity, separation anxiety disorder, or intermittent depressive symptoms.

According to the DSM-IV diagnostic criteria for major depressive episode, at least five symptoms must be present for a period of 2 weeks, and there must be a change from previous functioning (see Table 15.2–3). Among the necessary symptoms is either a depressed or irritable mood or a loss of interest or pleasure. Other symptoms from which the other four diagnostic criteria are drawn include a child's failure to make expected weight gains, daily insomnia or hypersomnia, psychomotor agitation or retardation, daily fatigue or loss of energy, feelings of worthlessness or inappropriate guilt, diminished ability to think or concentrate, and recurrent thoughts of death. These symptoms must produce social or academic impairment. To meet the diagnostic criteria for major depressive disorder, the symptoms cannot be the direct effects of a substance (for example, alcohol) or a general medical condition. A diagnosis of major depressive disorder is not made within 2 months of the loss of a loved one, except when marked functional impairment, morbid preoccupation with worthlessness, suicidal ideation, psychotic symptoms, or psychomotor retardation is present.

A major depressive episode in a prepubertal child is likely to be manifest by somatic complaints, psychomotor agitation, and mood-congruent hallucinations. Anhedonia is also frequent, but anhedonia, as well as hopelessness, psychomotor retardation, and delusions, are more common in adolescent and adult major depressive episodes than in those of young children. Adults have more problems with sleep and appetite than do depressed children and adolescents. In adolescence, negativistic or frankly antisocial behavior and the use of alcohol or illicit substances may occur and may justify the additional diagnoses of oppositional defiant disorder, conduct disorder, and substance abuse or dependence. Feelings of restlessness, grouchiness, aggression, sulkiness, reluctance to cooperate in family ventures, withdrawal from social activities, and a desire to leave home are all common in adolescent depression. School difficulties are likely. Adolescents may be inattentive to personal appearance and show increased emotionality, with particular sensitivity to rejection in love relationships.

Children can be reliable reporters about their own behavior, emotions, relationships, and difficulties in psychosocial functions. They may, however, refer to their feelings by many names. Therefore, clinicians must ask children about feeling sad, empty, low, down, blue, or very unhappy, about feeling like crying, or about having a bad feeling that is present most of the time. Depressed children usually identify one or more of these terms as their persistent feeling. Clinicians should assess the duration and periodicity of the depressive mood to differentiate relatively universal, short-lived, and sometimes frequent periods of sadness, usually after a frustrating event, from a true, persistent depressive mood. The younger the children, the more imprecise their time estimates are likely to be.

Mood disorders tend to be chronic if they begin early. Childhood onset may be the most severe form of mood disorder and tends to appear in families with a high incidence of mood disorders and alcohol abuse. The children are likely to have such secondary complications as conduct disorder, alcohol and other substance abuse, and antisocial behavior. Functional impairment associated with a depressive disorder in childhood extends to practically all areas of a child's psychosocial world; school performance and behavior, peer relationships, and family relationships all suffer. Only highly intelligent and academically oriented children with no more than a moderate depression can compensate for their difficulties in learning by substantially increasing their time and effort. Otherwise, school performance is invariably affected by a combination of difficulty in concentrating, slowed thinking, lack of interest and motivation, fatigue, sleepiness, depressive ruminations, and preoccupations. Depression in a child may be misdiagnosed as a learning disorder. Learning problems secondary to depression, even when long-standing, are corrected rapidly after a child's recovery from the depressive episode.

Children and adolescents with major depressive disorder may have hallucinations and delusions. In most cases, these psychotic symptoms are thematically consistent with the depressed mood, occur with the depressive episode (usually at its worst), and do not include certain types of hallucinations, such as conversing voices and a commenting voice, which are specific to schizophrenia. Depressive hallucinations usually consist of a single voice speaking to the person from outside his or her head, with derogatory or suicidal content. Depressive delusions center on themes of guilt, physical disease, death, nihilism, deserved punishment, personal inadequacy, and sometimes persecution. These delusions are rare in prepuberty, probably because of cognitive immaturity, but are present in about one half of all psychotically depressed adolescents.

Adolescent onset of a mood disorder may be difficult to diagnose when first seen if the adolescent has attempted self-medication with alcohol or other illicit substances. In a recent study, 17 percent of young people with a mood disorder first received medical attention because of substance abuse. Only after detoxification could the psychiatric symptoms be assessed properly and the mood disorder diagnosed correctly.

Dysthymic Disorder. Dysthymic disorder in children and adolescents consists of a depressed or irritable mood for most of the day, for more days than not, over a period of at least 1 year. DSM-IV notes that, in children and adolescents, irritable mood can replace the depressed mood criterion for adults and that the duration criterion is not 2 years but 1 year for children and adolescents. According to the DSM-IV diagnostic criteria, at least three of the following symptoms must accompany the depressed or irritable mood: poor self-esteem, pessimism or hopelessness, loss of interest, social withdrawal, chronic fatigue, feelings of guilt or brooding about the past, irritability or excessive anger, decreased activity or productivity, and poor concentration or memory. During the year of the disturbance, these symptoms do not resolve for more than 2 months at a time. In addition, no major depressive episode is present during the first year of the disturbance. To meet the DSM-IV diagnostic criteria for dysthymic disorder, a child must not have a history of a manic or hypomanic episode. Dysthymic disorder is also not diagnosed if the symptoms occur exclusively during a chronic psychotic disorder or if they are the direct effects of a substance or a general medical condition. DSM-IV provides for the specification of early onset (before 21 years of age) or late onset (after 21 years of age) (see Table 15.3–1).

A child or adolescent with dysthymic disorder may have had a previous major depressive episode before the onset of dysthymic disorder, but it is much more common for a child with dysthymic disorder for more than 1 year to have major depressive disorder. In this case, both depressive diagnoses are given (*double depression*). Dysthymic disorder in children is known to have an average age of onset that is several years earlier than the age of onset of major depressive disorder. Clinicians disagree about whether dysthymic disorder is a chronic and insidious version of major depressive disorder or a separate disorder. Occasionally, young people fulfill the criteria for dysthymic disorder, except that their episodes last only 2 weeks to several months, with symptom-free intervals lasting for 2 to 3 months. These minor mood presentations in children are likely to indicate severe mood disorder episodes in the future. Current knowledge suggests that the longer, the more recurrent, the more frequent, and perhaps the less related to social stress these episodes are, the greater the likelihood of a severe mood disorder in the future. When minor depressive episodes follow a significant stressful life event by less than 3 months, however, they do not indicate future mood disorder episodes and therefore should be diagnosed as *adjustment disorder with depressed mood or bereavement.*

Bipolar I Disorder. Bipolar I disorder is rarely diagnosed in prepubertal children; manic episodes are uncommon in this age group, even when depressive symptoms have already appeared. In general, a major depressive episode precedes a manic episode in an adolescent who experiences bipolar I disorder. But when a classic manic episode occurs in an adolescent, it is recognized as a definite change from a preexisting state and often appears with grandiose and paranoid delusions and hallucinatory phenomena. According to DSM-IV, the diagnostic criteria for a manic episode are the same for children and adolescents as for adults (see Table 15.2–4). The diagnostic criteria for a manic episode include a distinct period of an abnormally elevated, expansive, or irritable mood that lasts at least 1 week or for any duration if hospitalization is necessary. In addition, during periods of mood disturbance, at least three of the following significant and persistent symptoms must be present: inflated self-esteem or grandiosity, decreased need for sleep, pressure to talk, flight of ideas or racing thoughts, distractibility, an increase in goal-directed activity, and excessive involvement in pleasurable activities that may result in painful consequences. The mood disturbance is sufficient to cause marked impairment, and it is not due to the direct effect of a substance or a general medical condition. Therefore, manic states precipitated by somatic medications (for example, antidepressants) cannot be interpreted as indicating a diagnosis of bipolar I disorder.

In contrast to a classic manic episode, childhood manic episodes may be variants that are related to bipolar I disorder. The atypical manic episodes are sometimes observed in children with family histories of classic bipolar I disorder; the atypical manic episodes consist of extreme mood variability, cyclic aggressive behavior, high levels of distractibility, and poor attention span. These episodes are not likely to be clearly episodic, and they may be less treatment-responsive than classic manic episodes. Children with atypical hypomanic episodes must be differentiated from children with severe attention-deficit/hyperactivity disorder, who share some features of mania but exhibit their behaviors on a long-term basis rather than on an episodic basis. In attention-deficit/hyperactivity disorder, family histories of bipolar I disorder are uncommon.

In general, when manic episodes appear in an adolescent, they are often accompanied by psychotic features, and hospitalization is often necessary. Delusions and hallucinations of adolescents may involve grandiose notions about their power, worth, knowledge, family, or relationships. Persecutory delusions and flight of ideas are common. Overall, gross impairment of reality testing is common in adolescent manic episodes. In adolescents with major depressive disorder destined for bipolar I disorder, those at highest risk have family histories of bipolar I disorder and exhibit acute severe depressive episodes with psychosis, hypersomnia, and psychomotor retardation.

Cyclothymic Disorder. The only difference in the DSM-IV diagnostic criteria for child or adolescent cyclothymic disorder is that a period of 1 year of numerous mood swings is necessary, instead of the adult criterion of 2 years. Some adolescents with cyclothymic disorder probably experience bipolar I disorder.

Schizoaffective Disorder. The criteria for schizoaffective disorder in children and adolescents are identical to those in adults. Although some adolescents and probably some children do fit the criteria for schizoaffective disorder, little is known about the natural course of their illness, family history, psychobiology, and treatment. In DSM-IV, schizoaffective disorder in children is classified as a psychotic disorder.

Bereavement. Bereavement is a state of grief related to the death of a loved one that may occur with symptoms characteristic of a major depressive episode. Typical depressive symptoms associated with bereavement include feelings of sadness, insomnia, diminished appetite, and in some cases, weight loss. Grieving children may become withdrawn and appear sad, and they are not easily drawn into even favorite activities.

In DSM-IV, bereavement is not a mental disorder but is in the category of additional conditions that may be a focus of clinical attention. Children in the midst of a typical bereavement period may also meet the criteria for major depressive disorder when the symptoms persist longer than 2 months after the loss. In some instances, severe depressive symptoms within 2 months of the loss are considered to be beyond the scope of normal grieving, and a diagnosis of major depressive disorder is warranted. Symptoms indicative of major depressive disorder exceeding usual bereavement include guilt related to issues beyond those surrounding the death of the loved one, preoccupation with death other than thoughts about being dead to be with the deceased person, morbid preoccupation with worthlessness, marked psychomotor retardation, prolonged serious functional impairment, and hallucinations other than transient perceptions of the voice of the deceased person.

The duration of a normal period of bereavement varies; in children, the duration may depend partly on the support system in place. For example, a child who must be removed from home because of the death of the only parent in the home may feel devastated and abandoned for a long time. Children who lose loved ones may feel that the death occurred because they were bad or did not perform as expected. The reaction to the loss of a loved one may be influenced partly by a child's being prepared for the death in cases of chronic illness. (Bereavement is also discussed in Chapter 32 and Chapter 2, Section 2.7.)

Pathology and Laboratory Examination. No single laboratory test is useful in making a diagnosis of a mood disorder. A screening test for thyroid function can rule out the possibility of an endocrinological contribution to a mood disorder. Dexamethasone-suppression tests may be performed serially in cases of major depressive disorder to document whether an initial nonsuppressor becomes a suppressor with treatment or with resolution of the symptoms.

Differential Diagnosis

Psychotic forms of depressive and manic episodes must be differentiated from schizophrenia. Substance-induced mood disorder can sometimes be differentiated from other mood disorders only after detoxification. Anxiety symptoms and conduct-disordered behavior can coexist with depressive disorders and frequently can pose problems in differentiating those disorders from nondepressed emotional and conduct disorders.

Of particular importance is the distinction between agitated depressive or manic episodes and attention-deficit/hyperactivity disorder, in which the persistent excessive activity and restlessness can cause confusion. Prepubertal children do not show classic forms of agitated depression, such as hand wringing and pacing. Instead, an inability to sit still and frequent temper tantrums are the most common symptoms. Sometimes, the correct diagnosis becomes evident only after remission of the depressive episode. If a child has no difficulty concentrating, is not hyperactive when recovered from a depressive episode, and is in a drug-free state, attention-deficit/hyperactivity disorder probably is not present.

Course and Prognosis

The course and prognosis of mood disorders in children and adolescents depend on the age of onset, the severity of the episode, and the presence of comorbid disorders; a young age of onset and multiple disorders predict a poorer prognosis. The mean length of an episode of major depression in children and adolescents is about 9 months; the cumulative probability of recurrence is 40 percent by 2 years and 70 percent by 5 years. It has been reported that depressed children who live in families with high levels of chronic conflict are more likely to have relapses. Follow-up studies have found that in 20 to 40 percent of adolescents who have a major depression, bipolar I disorder will develop in a period of 5 years after the index depression. Clinical characteristics of the depressive episode that are suggestive of the highest risk of developing bipolar I disorder include delusionality and psychomotor retardation in addition to a family history of bipolar illness. Depressive disorders are associated with short-term and long-term peer relationship difficulties and complications, poor academic achievement, and persistent poor self-esteem. Dysthymic disorder has an even more protracted recovery than major depression; the mean episode length is about 4 years. Early-onset dysthymic disorder is associated with significant risks of comorbidity with major depression (70 percent), bipolar disorder (13 percent), and eventual substance abuse (15 percent). The risk of suicide, which represents 12 percent of mortalities in the adolescent age range, is significant among adolescents with depressive disorders.

Treatment

Hospitalization. The important immediate consideration is often whether hospitalization is indicated to keep the child or adolescent safe or whether it is the only setting in which it is possible to initiate treatment. When a patient is suicidal, hospitalization is indicated to provide maximum protection against the patient's own self-destructive impulses and behavior. Hospitalization also may be needed when a child or adolescent has coexisting substance abuse or dependence.

Psychotherapy. Several open studies supporting certain types of psychosocial interventions in the treatment of childhood depression have been performed. Preliminary findings from one large controlled study comparing cognitive-behavioral interventions with nondirective supportive psychotherapy and systemic behavioral family therapy showed that 70 percent of adolescents had some improvement with each of the interventions; cognitive-behavioral intervention had the most rapid effect. Another controlled study comparing a brief course of cognitive-behavioral therapy with relaxation therapy favored the cognitive-behavioral intervention. At a 3- to 6-month follow-up, however, there were no significant differences between the two treatment groups. This effect was due to relapse in the cognitive-behavioral group, along with some continued recovery in some patients in the relaxation group. Factors that seem to interfere with treatment responsiveness include the presence of comorbid anxiety disorder that probably was present before the depressive episode.

Family intervention is almost always a component of treatment for childhood depression, for educating families about mood disorders as well as encouraging more effective conflict resolution; family intervention is especially important to deal with conflict because persistent conflict may hasten or increase relapse in depression. As depressed children's psychosocial function may remain impaired for long periods, even after the depressive episode has remitted, long-term social skills interventions are needed. In some treatment programs, modeling and role playing can help establish good problem-solving skills.

Pharmacotherapy. The serotonin-specific reuptake inhibitors (SSRIs) are increasingly compelling as a first-line pharmacological intervention for depressive disorders in children and adolescents. SSRIs are reported to be effective in treating depression in adults; they have a benign side effect profile and a relatively low lethality potential in overdose.

Open studies have reported a 70 to 90 percent response with fluoxetine (Prozac) among children and adolescents. Currently, at least one double-blind, placebo-controlled study of an adolescent sample shows statistically significant improvement with fluoxetine compared with placebo. The degree of improvement was variable, and there were no differences between males and females. Although additional investigation is needed, the SSRIs remain promising as safe and beneficial medications for children and adolescents.

No other controlled studies show the efficacy of other antidepressants for depressive disorders in children and adolescents. Tricyclic antidepressants have been used less frequently since the SSRIs came on the market. The use of tricyclic antidepressants requires baseline studies, gradual titration of the drug, and monitoring of electrocardiogram (ECG) changes, blood pressure, side effects, and, whenever possible, serum levels. Because toxicity produces serious cardiac arrhythmias, seizures, coma, and death, monitoring is essential. The clinical response may be correlated with plasma level. In one uncontrolled study using imipramine (Tofranil) to treat prepubertal major depressive disorder, good responses were seen when blood levels were 140 to 150 ng/mL. Because some children and adolescents who have depressive episodes eventually experience bipolar II disorder, clinicians must note hypomanic symptoms that may occur during the use of fluoxetine and other antidepressants. In these cases, the medication should be discontinued to determine whether the hypomanic episode then resolves. Hypomanic responses to antidepressants, however, do not necessarily predict that bipolar II disorder has developed.

Bipolar I disorder and bipolar II disorder in childhood and adolescence are treated with lithium (Eskalith) with good results. Children with early-onset bipolar disorder and preexisting disruptive behavior disorders (for example, conduct disorder and attention-deficit/hyperactivity disorder) who experience bipolar disorders early in adolescence are less likely to respond well to lithium than those without the behavior disorders.

Electroconvulsive Therapy. Electroconvulsive therapy (ECT) has been used for a variety of psychiatric illnesses in adults, primarily severe depressive and manic mood disorders and catatonia. ECT rarely is used for adolescents, although there have been published case reports of its efficacy in adolescents with depression and mania. Currently, case reports suggest that ECT may be a relatively safe and useful treatment for adolescents with severe, treatment-resistant affective disorders with psychosis, catatonic symptoms, and persistent suicidality.

SUICIDE

The suicide rate among adolescents has quadrupled since 1950, from 2.5 to 11.2 per 100,000 adolescents. Suicide currently accounts for 12 percent of deaths in the adolescent age group. Adolescent suicide attempt rates have also increased in recent years; 1-year prevalence rates range from 1.7 to 5.9 percent and lifetime prevalence rates range from 3.0 to 7.1 percent. Suicidal ideation, gestures, and attempts frequently are associated with depressive disorders, and these suicidal phenomena, particularly in adolescence, are a growing public mental health problem.

Suicidal ideation occurs in all age groups and with greatest frequency when the depressive disorder is severe. More than 12,000 children and adolescents are hospitalized in the United States each year because of suicidal threats or behavior, but completed suicide is rare in children younger than 12 years of age. A young child is hardly capable of designing and carrying out a realistic suicide plan. Cognitive immaturity seems to play a protective role in preventing even children who wish they were dead from committing suicide. Completed suicide occurs about 5 times more often in adolescent boys than in girls, although the rate of suicide attempts is at least 3 times higher among adolescent girls than among boys. Suicidal ideation is not a static phenomenon; it may wax and wane with time. The decision to engage in suicidal behavior may be made impulsively, without much forethought, or the decision may be the culmination of prolonged rumination.

The method of the suicide attempt influences the morbidity and completion rates independent of the severity of the intent to die at the time of the suicidal behavior. Therefore, the most common method of completed suicide in children and adolescents is the use of firearms, which accounts for about two thirds of all suicides in boys and almost one half of suicides in girls. The second most common method of suicide in boys, occurring in about one fourth of all cases, is hanging; in girls, about one fourth commit suicide through ingestion of toxic substances. Carbon monoxide poisoning is the next most common method of suicide in boys, but it occurs in less than 10 percent; suicide by hanging and carbon monoxide poisoning are equally frequent among girls and account for about 10 percent each. Additional risk factors in suicide include a family history of suicidal behavior, exposure to family violence, impulsivity, substance abuse, and availability of lethal methods.

Epidemiology

Recently, the suicide rate among adolescents in the United States has risen dramatically, although this is not the case in some other countries. There has been a steady increase in the suicide rate for persons 15 to 19 years of age in the United States. The rate is currently 13.6 per 100,000 for boys and 3.6 per 100,000 for girls. More than 5,000 adolescents commit suicide each year in the United States—1 every 90 minutes. These increased suicide rates are believed to reflect changes in the social environment, changing attitudes toward suicide, and the increasing availability of the means to commit suicide; for example, in the United States, 66 percent of adolescent suicides by boys are committed with firearms, compared with 6 percent in the United Kingdom. Suicide is the third leading cause of death in the United States for persons 15 to 24 years of age and is second among white males in this age group. The rates for suicide depend on age, and they increase significantly after puberty. Whereas fewer than 1 completed suicide per 100,000 occurs in persons younger than 14 years of age, about 10 per 100,000 completed suicides occur in adolescents between 15 and 19 years of age. In adolescents younger than 14 years of age, suicide attempts are at least 50 times more common than suicide completions. Between 15 and 19 years of age, however, the rate of suicide attempts is about 15 times greater than the rate of suicide completions. The number of adolescent suicides over the past several decades has increased threefold or fourfold.

Etiology

Universal features in suicidal adolescents are the inability to synthesize solutions to problems and the lack of coping strategies to deal with immediate stressors. Therefore, a narrow view of the options available to deal with recurrent family discord, rejection, or failure contributes to a decision to commit suicide.

Genetic Factors. Evidence of a genetic contribution to suicidal behavior is based on family suicide risk studies and the higher concordance for suicide among monozygotic twins compared with dizygotic twins. Although the risk for suicide is high in people with mental disorders—including schizophrenia, major depressive disorder, and bipolar I disorder—the risk for suicide is much higher in the relatives of those with mood disorders than in the relatives of people with schizophrenia.

Other Biological Factors. Neurochemical findings show some overlap between people with aggressive, impulsive behaviors and those who complete suicide. Low levels of serotonin (5-HT) and its major metabolite, 5-hydroxyindoleacetic acid (5-HIAA), have been found postmortem in the brains of persons who complete suicide. Low levels of 5-HIAA have been found in the cerebrospinal fluid of depressed people who attempted suicide by violent methods. Alcohol and other psychoactive substances may lower 5-HIAA, perhaps by increasing the vulnerability for suicidal behavior in an already predisposed person. The mechanism linking decreased serotonergic function and aggressive or suicidal behavior is unknown, and low serotonin may turn out to be a marker, rather than a cause, of aggression and suicidal propensity. The dexamethasone-suppression test has produced less reliable findings in depressed children and adolescents than in adults, but some studies of children and adolescents indicate an association of nonsuppression on the dexamethasone-suppression test and potentially lethal suicide attempts. In children and adolescents, the association between suicidality and nonsuppression is not necessarily in the context of a major mood disorder.

Social Factors. Children and adolescents are vulnerable to overwhelmingly chaotic, abusive, and neglectful environments. A wide range of psychopathological symptoms may occur secondary to exposure to violent and abusive homes. Aggressive, self-destructive, and suicidal behaviors seem to occur with greatest frequency in those who have endured chronically stressful family lives.

Diagnosis and Clinical Features

Direct questioning of children and adolescents about suicidal thoughts is necessary, because studies have consistently shown that parents are frequently unaware of such ideas in their children. Suicidal thoughts (that is, children's talking about wanting to harm themselves) and suicidal threats (that is, children's statements that they want to jump in front of a car) are more common than suicide completion.

The characteristics of adolescents who attempt suicide and those who complete suicide are similar, and about one third of those who completed suicide had made previous attempts. Mental disorders in some persons who attempt or complete suicide include major depressive disorder, manic episodes, and psychotic disorders. Those with mood disorders in combination with substance abuse and a history of aggressive behavior are particularly high-risk adolescents. Those without mood disorders who are violent, aggressive, and impulsive may be prone to suicide during family or peer conflicts. High levels of hopelessness, poor problem-solving skills, and a history of aggressive behavior are risk factors for suicide. Depression alone is a more serious risk factor for suicide in girls than in boys, but boys often have more severe psychopathology than girls who commit suicide. The profile of an adolescent who commits suicide is occasionally one of high achievement and perfectionistic character traits; such an adolescent may have been humiliated recently by a perceived failure, such as diminished academic performance.

In psychiatrically disturbed and vulnerable adolescents, suicide attempts are often related to recent stressors. The precipitants of suicidal behavior include conflicts and arguments with family members and boyfriends or girlfriends. Alcohol and other substance use may further predispose an already vulnerable adolescent to suicidal behavior. In other cases, an adolescent attempts suicide in anticipation of punishment after being caught by the police or other authority figures for a forbidden behavior.

About 40 percent of youthful persons who complete suicide had previous psychiatric treatment, and about 40 percent had made a previous suicide attempt. A child who has lost a parent by any means before age 13 has a high risk for mood disorders and suicide. The precipitating factors include loss of face with peers, a broken romance, school difficulties, unemployment, bereavement, separation, and rejection. Clusters of suicides among adolescents who know one another and go to the same school have been reported. Suicidal behavior may precipitate other such attempts within a peer group through identification—so-called copycat suicides. Some studies have found an increase in adolescent suicide after television programs in which the main theme was the suicide of a teenager. In general, however, many other factors are involved, including a necessary substrate of psychopathology.

One recent study investigated two clusters of teenage suicide in Texas. The researchers found that indirect exposure to suicide through the media was not significantly associated with suicide. Factors that were associated included previous suicidal threats or attempts, self-injury, exposure to someone who had died violently, recent romantic breakups, and a high frequency of moves, schools attended, and parental figures lived with.

The tendency of disturbed young people to imitate highly publicized suicides has been called the Werther syndrome, after the protagonist in Johann Wolfgang von Goethe's novel, *The Sorrows of Young Werther.* The novel, in which the hero kills himself, was banned in some European countries after its publication more than 200 years ago because of a rash of suicides by young men who read it; some dressed like Werther before killing themselves or left the book open at the passage describing his death. In general, although imitation may play a role in the timing of suicide attempts by vulnerable adolescents, the overall suicide rate does not seem to increase when media exposure increases.

Treatment

Adolescents who attempt suicide must be evaluated before the decision is made regarding hospitalization or return to home. Those who fall into high-risk groups should be hospitalized until the suicidality is no longer present. High-risk persons include those who have made previous suicide attempts; boys older than 12 years of age with histories of aggressive behavior or substance abuse; those who have made an attempt with a lethal method, such as a gun or a toxic ingested substance; those with major depressive disorder characterized by social withdrawal, hopelessness, and a lack of energy; girls who have run away from home, are pregnant, or have made an attempt with a method other than ingesting a toxic substance; and any person who exhibits persistent suicidal ideation. A child or an adolescent with suicidal ideation must be hospitalized if a clinician has any doubt about the family's ability to supervise the child or to cooperate with treatment in an outpatient setting. In such a situation, child protective services must be involved before the child can be discharged. When adolescents with suicidal ideation report that they are no longer suicidal, discharge can be considered only after a complete discharge plan is in place. The plan must include psychotherapy, pharmacotherapy, and family therapy as indicated. A written contract with the adolescent, outlining the adolescent's agreement not to engage in suicidal behavior and providing an alternative if suicidal ideation reoccurs, should be in place. In addition, a follow-up outpatient appointment should be made before the discharge, and a telephone hot-line number should be provided to the adolescent and the family in case suicidal ideation reappears before treatment begins.

References

Birmaher B, Ryan ND, Williamson DE, Brent DA, Kaufman J: Childhood and adolescent depression: A review of the past 10 years. Part II. J Am Acad Child Adolesc Psychiatry *35:* 1575, 1996.

Birmaher B, Ryan ND, Williamson DE, Brent DA, Kaufman J, Dahl RE, Nelson B: Childhood and adolescent depression: A review of the past 10 years. Part I. J Am Acad Child Adolesc Psychiatry *35:* 1427, 1996.

Blumenthal SJ: Youth suicide: Risk factors, assessment, and treatment of adolescent and young adult suicidal patients. Psychiatr Clin North Am *13:* 511, 1990.

Casat CD, Arana GW, Powell K: The DST in children and adolescents with major depressive disorder. Am J Psychiatry *146:* 505, 1989.

Dorn LD, Burgess ES, Dichek HL, Putnam FW, Chrousos GP, Gold PW: Thyroid hormone concentrations in depressed and nondepressed adolescents: Group differences and behavioral relations. J Am Acad Child Adolesc Psychiatry *35:* 299, 1996.

Emslie GJ, Rush AJ, Weinberg WA, Rintelmann JW, Roffwarg HP: Children with major depression show reduced rapid eye movement latencies. Arch Gen Psychiatry *47:* 199, 1990.

Garland AF, Zigler E: Adolescent suicide prevention: Current research and social policy implications. Am Psychol *48:* 169, 1993.

Harrington RC: Depressive disorder in children and adolescents. Br J Hosp Med *43:* 108, 1990.

Hendin H: Psychodynamics of suicide, with particular reference to the young. Am J Psychiatry *48:* 1150, 1991.

Kazdin AE: Childhood depression. J Child Psychol Psychiatry *31:* 121, 1990.

Kovacs M, Goldston D, Gatsonis C: Suicidal behaviors and childhood-onset depressive disorders: A longitudinal investigation. J Am Acad Child Adolesc Psychiatry *32:* 8, 1993.

Lewinsohn PM, Rohde P, Seeley JR: Psychosocial characteristics of adolescents with a history of suicide attempt. J Am Acad Child Adolesc Psychiatry *32:* 60, 1993.

Marttunen MJ, Aro HM, Henrisksson MM, Lonnqvist JK: Mental disorders in adolescent suicide. Arch Gen Psychiatry *48:* 834, 1991.

Mitchell J, McCauley E, Burke P, Calderon R, Schloredt K: Psychopathy in parents of depressed children adolescents. J Am Acad Child Adolesc Psychiatry *28:* 352, 1989.

Moise FN, Petrides G: Case study: Electroconvulsive therapy in adolescents. J Am Acad Child Adolesc Psychiatry *35:* 312, 1996.

Pataki CS, Carlson GA: Affective disorders in children and adolescents. In *Handbook on Studies on Child Psychiatry,* B Tonge, GD Burrows, JS Werry, editors, p 137. Elsevier, Amsterdam, 1990.

Pataki CS, Carlson GA: Bipolar disorder in children and adolescents. In *Clinical Guide to Depression in Children and Adolescents,* M Shafii, S Shafii, editors, p 269. American Psychiatric Press, Washington, 1992.

Pfeffer CR, Klerman GL, Hurt SW, Kakuma T, et al: Suicidal children grow up: Rates and psychosocial risk factors for suicide attempts during follow-up. J Am Acad Child Adolesc Psychiatry *32:* 106, 1993.

Rotheram-Borus MJ: Suicidal behavior and risk factors among runaway youths. Am J Psychiatry *150:* 103, 1993.

Ryland DH, Kruesi MJ: Suicide among adolescents. Int Rev Psychiatry *4:* 185, 1992.

Shaffer D, Garland A, Gould M, Fisher P, Trautman P: Preventing teenage suicide: A critical review. J Am Acad Child Adolesc Psychiatry *27:* 675, 1988.

Steingard RJ, Renshaw PF, Yurgelun-Todd D, Applemans KE, Lyoo IK, Shorrock KL, Bucci JP, Cesena M, Abebe D, Zurakowski D, Pussaint TY, Barnes P: Structural abnormalities in brain magnetic resonance images in depressed children. J Am Acad Child Adolesc Psychiatry *35:* 307, 1996.

Varanka TM, Weller RA, Weller EB, Fristad MA: Lithium treatment of manic episodes with psychotic features in prepubertal children. Am J Psychiatry *145:* 1557, 1988.

Walker M, Moreau D, Weissman MM: Parents' awareness of children's suicide attempts. Am J Psychiatry *147:* 1364, 1990.

49

Schizophrenia with Childhood Onset

According to the fourth edition of *Diagnostic and Statistical Manual of Mental Disorders* (DSM-IV), the onset of schizophrenia is typically between the late teens and mid-30s, but the disorder can occur as early as 5 or 6 years of age. Although the characteristics are the same in children and adults, diagnosis may be more difficult. In children, delusions and hallucinations usually are less elaborate, and visual hallucinations are more common.

Schizophrenia with childhood onset is conceptually the same as schizophrenia in adolescence and adulthood. Although rare, schizophrenia in prepubertal children includes the presence of at least two of the following: hallucinations, delusions, grossly disorganized speech or behavior, and severe withdrawal for at least 1 month. Social or academic dysfunction must be present, and continuous signs of the disturbance must persist for at least 6 months. The diagnostic criteria for schizophrenia in children are identical to the criteria for the adult form, except that instead of showing deteriorating functioning, children may fail to achieve their expected levels of social and academic functioning.

Before the 1960s, the term *childhood psychosis* was applied to a heterogeneous group of pervasive developmental disorders without hallucinations and delusions. In the 1960s and 1970s, children with evidence of a profound psychotic disturbance early in life often were observed to be mentally retarded, socially dysfunctional with severe communication and language impairments, and without a family history of schizophrenia. In children with psychoses that emerged after the age of 5, however, auditory hallucinations, delusions, inappropriate affects, thought disorder, and normal intelligence were manifest, and these children often had a family history of schizophrenia; they were viewed as exhibiting schizophrenia, whereas the younger children were identified as having an entirely different disorder, either autistic disorder or a pervasive developmental disorder.

In the 1980s, schizophrenia with childhood onset was formally separated from autistic disorder. This change reflected evidence accrued during the 1960s and 1970s that the clinical picture, family history, age of onset, and course of the two disorders were different. After the separation of the disorders, two controversies ensued. First, a minority of researchers remained of the opinion that a subgroup of autistic children will eventually have schizophrenia, as evidence shows for a small group. In general, schizophrenia is easily differentiated from autistic disorder (Table 41–3). Most children with autistic disorder are impaired in all areas of adaptive functioning from early life onward. The onset is almost always before 3 years of age, whereas the onset of schizophrenia usually is in adolescence or young adulthood. Schizophrenia in prepubertal children is much more rare than in adolescence and young adulthood, and there are practically no reports of an onset of schizophrenia before 5 years of age. According to DSM-IV, schizophrenia can be diagnosed in the presence of autistic disorder.

The second controversy concerned applying adult diagnostic criteria for schizophrenia to children. Several reports indicate that some children do have hallucinations, delusions, and thought disorders typical of schizophrenia, but normal developmental immaturities in language development and in separating reality from fantasy sometimes make it difficult to diagnose schizophrenia in children ages 5 to 7 years.

EPIDEMIOLOGY

Schizophrenia in prepubertal children is exceedingly rare; it is estimated to occur less frequently than autistic disorder. In adolescents, the prevalence of schizophrenia is estimated to be 50 times greater than in younger children, with probable rates of 1 to 2 per 1,000. Boys seem to have a slight preponderance among children with schizophrenia, with an estimated ratio of about 1.67 boys to 1 girl. Boys often become symptomatic at a younger age than girls. Schizophrenia rarely is diagnosed in children younger than 5 years of age; it is commonly diagnosed in adolescents older than 15 years of age. The symptoms usually emerge insidiously, and the diagnostic criteria are met gradually over time. Occasionally, the onset of schizophrenia is sudden and occurs in a previously well-functioning child. Schizophrenia also may be diagnosed in a child who has had chronic difficulties and then experiences a significant exacerbation. The prevalence of schizophrenia among the parents of children with schizophrenia is about 8 percent, which is close to double the prevalence in the parents of patients with adult-onset schizophrenia.

Schizotypal personality disorder is similar to schizophrenia in its inappropriate affects, excessive magical thinking, odd beliefs, social isolation, ideas of reference, and unusual perceptual experiences, such as illusions. Schizotypal personality disorder, however, does not have psychotic features; still, the disorder seems to aggregate in families with adult-onset schizophrenia. Therefore, there is an unclear relation between the two disorders.

ETIOLOGY

Although family and genetic studies provide substantial evidence of a biological contribution to the development of schizophrenia, no specific biological markers have been identified, and the precise mechanisms of transmission of schizophrenia are not understood. Schizophrenia is significantly more prevalent among first-degree relatives of those with schizophrenia than in the general population. Adoption studies of patients with adult-onset schizophrenia have shown that schizophrenia occurs in the biological relatives, not the adoptive relatives. Additional genetic evidence is supported by the higher concordance rates for schizophrenia in monozygotic twins than in dizygotic twins. The genetic transmission pattern of schizophrenia remains unknown; but more genetic loading is seen in the relatives of those with childhood-onset schizophrenia than in the relatives of those with adult-onset schizophrenia.

Currently, no reliable method can identify people at the highest risk for schizophrenia in a given family. Nevertheless, higher-than-expected rates of neurological soft signs and impairments in sustaining attention and in strategies for information processing appear among high-risk groups of children. Increased rates of disturbed communication styles are found in families with a patient with schizophrenia. High expressed emotion, characterized by overly critical responses in families, negatively affects the prognosis of patients with schizophrenia.

Various abnormal, nonspecific results on computed tomography (CT) scans and electroencephalograms (EEGs) have been noted in patients with schizophrenia. Children and adolescents with schizophrenia are more apt to have a premorbid history of social rejection, poor peer relationships, clingy withdrawn behavior, and academic trouble than those with adult-onset schizophrenia. Some children with schizophrenia that is first seen in middle childhood have early histories of motor milestones and delayed language acquisition that are similar to some symptoms of autistic disorder. The mechanisms of biological vulnerability and environmental influences producing manifestations of schizophrenia remain under investigation.

DIAGNOSIS AND CLINICAL FEATURES

All of the symptoms included in adult-onset schizophrenia may be manifest in children with the disorder. The onset is frequently insidious; after first exhibiting inappropriate affects of unusual behavior, a child may take months or years to meet all of the diagnostic criteria for schizophrenia. Children who eventually meet the criteria often are socially rejected and clingy and have limited social skills. They may have histories of delayed motor and verbal milestones and do poorly in school despite normal intelligence. Although children with schizophrenia and autistic disorder may be similar in their early histories, children with schizophrenia have normal intelligence and do not meet the criteria for a pervasive developmental disorder.

According to DSM-IV, a child with schizophrenia may experience a deterioration of function, along with the emergence of psychotic symptoms, or the child may never achieve the expected level of functioning (see Table 13–6). Auditory hallucinations commonly are manifest in children with schizophrenia. They may hear several voices making an ongoing critical commentary, or command hallucinations may tell children to kill themselves or others. The voices may be of a bizarre nature, identified as "a computer in my head," Martians, or the voice of someone familiar, such as a relative. Visual hallucinations are experienced by a significant number of children with schizophrenia and often are frightening; the children may see the devil, skeletons, scary faces, or space creatures. Transient phobic visual hallucinations also occur in traumatized children who do not eventually have a major psychotic disorder.

Delusions are present in more than one half of all children with schizophrenia; the delusions take various forms, including persecutory, grandiose, and religious. Delusions increase in frequency with increased age. Blunted or inappropriate affects are almost universally present in children with schizophrenia. Children with schizophrenia may giggle inappropriately or cry without being able to explain why. Formal thought disorders, including loosening of associations and thought blocking, are common features among children with schizophrenia. Illogical thinking and poverty of thought are also often present. Unlike adults with schizophrenia, children with schizophrenia do not have poverty of content of speech, but they speak less than other children of the same intelligence and are ambiguous in the way they refer to people, objects, and events. The communication deficits observable in children with schizophrenia include unpredictably changing the topic of conversation without introducing the new topic to the listener (loose associations). Children with schizophrenia also exhibit illogical thinking and speaking and tend to underuse self-initiated repair strategies to aid in their communication. Therefore, when an utterance is unclear or vague, normal children attempt to clarify their communication with repetitions, revision, and more detail. Children with schizophrenia, on the other hand, fail to aid in communication with revision, fillers, or starting over. These deficits may be conceptualized as negative symptoms in childhood schizophrenia.

The core phenomena for schizophrenia seem to be the same among various age groups, but a child's developmental level influences the presentation of the symptoms. Therefore, delusions of young children are less complex than those of older children. Age-appropriate content, such as animal imagery and monsters, is likely to be a source of delusional fear in children. Other features that seem to be present with a high frequency in children with schizophrenia are poor motor functioning, visuospatial impairments, and attention deficits.

DSM-IV delineates five types of schizophrenia: paranoid, disorganized, catatonic, undifferentiated, and residual.

Joe was a 12-year-old boy who was referred for evaluation after he was found doing bizarre things such as urinating in jars in his room and becoming increasingly disorganized in school. Joe had always been a distant and quiet child who his parents believed was highly intelligent, thoughtful, and talented in writing poetry. As a young child, he had been socially isolated but was able to relate to his teachers and other adults. When he entered the sixth grade, however, he began to be avoided actively by his classmates, who saw him as strange. Joe could still attend school, but his grades started to deteriorate because he was not as attentive as he used to be. At home, he became more isolated, resisted family meals because of a newly adopted vegetarianism, and spent more time alone in his room. He was still writing poetry, and he seemed to be deep in thought most of the time.

Joe began to warn his parents to be careful because he and they were being followed. He increasingly resisted leaving his room, and his parents finally confronted him about his concerns. He explained that he had been communicating with God and that he was here for a larger purpose. He admitted to hearing several voices that would argue and warn him when there was danger. He began to be mistrustful of everyone, including his parents; he feared that they might poison him and believed that he would be safer if he did not eat meat. He began to eat less and lost 5 pounds.

Joe was finally admitted to the adolescent psychiatric inpatient unit because of his inability to eat appropriately or to function in school. He was started on a trial of risperidone (Risperdal), 1 mg twice daily, which was increased to 2 mg twice daily. Joe seemed to be responding: the voices were less predominant, and he seemed to be less paranoid. He developed troubling akathisia and required benztropine (Cogentin) in addition to the risperidone. Joe was responsive to the medication, but he clearly would not be able to return to his original school. He was referred to a private school for adolescents with severe emotional disturbances.

Pathology and Laboratory Examinations

No specific laboratory tests are helpful in the diagnosis of schizophrenia with childhood onset. High incidences of pregnancy and birth complications have been reported in the histories of children with schizophrenia, but presently, no specificity has been found in these risks for childhood schizophrenia. EEG studies also have not been helpful in distinguishing children with schizophrenia from other children. A recent report of endocrine and neuroimaging tests in adolescents with first-time psychosis did not reveal specific utility of these tests either in making a diagnosis of schizophrenia or in detecting occult medical causes for the psychosis.

DIFFERENTIAL DIAGNOSIS

Children with schizotypal personality disorder and with schizophrenia have many similarities. Blunted affect, social isolation, eccentric thoughts, ideas of reference, and bizarre behavior may be seen in both disorders; however, in schizophrenia, overt psychotic symptoms such as hallucinations, delusions, and incoherence must be present at some point. When they are present, they exclude a diagnosis of schizotypal personality disorder. Hallucinations alone, however, are not evidence of schizophrenia; patients must show either a deterioration of function or an inability to meet an expected developmental level to warrant the diagnosis of schizophrenia. Auditory and visual hallucinations can appear as self-limited events in nonpsychotic young children who are faced with extreme psychosocial stressors, such as the breakup of their parents, and in children experiencing a major loss or significant change in lifestyle.

Psychotic phenomena are common among children with major depressive disorder, in which both hallucinations and, less commonly, delusions may occur. The congruence of mood with psychotic features is most pronounced in depressed children, although children with schizophrenia may also seem sad. The hallucinations and delusions of schizophrenia are more likely to have a bizarre quality than those of children with depressive disorders. In children and adolescents with bipolar I disorder, it often is difficult to distinguish a first episode of mania with psychotic features from schizophrenia if the child has no history of previous depressions. Grandiose delusions and hallucinations are typical of manic episodes, but clinicians often must follow the natural history of the disorder to confirm the presence of a mood disorder. Pervasive developmental disorders, including autistic disorder with normal intelligence, may share some features with schizophrenia. Most notably, difficulty with social relationships, an early history of delayed language acquisition, and ongoing communication deviance are manifest in both disorders; however, hallucinations, delusions, and formal thought disorder are core features of schizophrenia and are not expected features of pervasive developmental disorders. Pervasive developmental disorders usually are diagnosed by 3 years of age, but schizophrenia with childhood onset is rarely diagnosable before 5 years of age.

The abuse of alcohol and other substances sometimes can result in a deterioration of function, psychotic symptoms, and paranoid delusions. Amphetamines, lysergic acid diethylamide (LSD), and phencyclidine (PCP) may lead to a psychotic state. A sudden, flagrant onset of paranoid psychosis is more suspicious of substance-induced psychotic disorder than an insidious onset.

Medical conditions that may induce psychotic features include thyroid disease, systemic lupus erythematosus, and temporal lobe disease.

COURSE AND PROGNOSIS

Important predictors of the course and outcome of childhood-onset schizophrenia include the child's level of functioning before the onset of schizophrenia, the age of onset, the child's degree of functioning regained after the first episode, and the degree of support available from the family. Children with developmental delays, learning disorders, and premorbid behavioral disorders, such as attention-deficit/hyperactivity disorder and conduct disorder, seem to be poor responders to medication treatment of schizophrenia and are likely to have the most guarded prognoses. In a long-term outcome study of patients with schizophrenia with onset before 14 years of age, the worst prognoses occurred in children with schizophrenia that was diagnosed before they were 10 years of age and who had preexisting personality disorders.

An additional issue in outcome studies is the stability of the diagnosis of schizophrenia. As many as one third of all children who receive a diagnosis of schizophrenia may end up with a diagnosis of a mood disorder (instead of schizophrenia) in adolescence. Children and adolescents with bipolar I disorder may have a better long-term prognosis than children and adolescents with schizophrenia. In adult-onset schizophrenia, family interactions, such as high expressed emotion, may be associated with increased relapse rates. No clear-cut data are available regarding childhood schizophrenia, but the degree of supportiveness, as opposed to critical and overinvolved family responses, probably influences the prognosis.

In general, schizophrenia with childhood onset seems to be less medication-responsive than adult-onset and adolescent-onset schizophrenia, and the prognosis may be poorer. Positive symptoms—that is, hallucinations and delusions—are likely to be more responsive to medication than are negative symptoms such as withdrawal. In a recent report of 38 children with schizophrenia who had been hospitalized, two thirds required placement in residential facilities, and only one third were improved enough to return home.

TREATMENT

The treatment of schizophrenia with childhood onset includes a multimodality approach. Antipsychotic medications are indicated and may be effective, although many patients show little or no response. In addition, family education and ongoing supportive family meetings are needed to maximize the level of support that the family can give the patient. The proper educational setting for the child is also important, because social skills deficits, attention deficits, and academic difficulties often accompany childhood schizophrenia.

Pharmacotherapy

Several open trials and at least one double-blind, placebo-controlled study have shown haloperidol (Haldol) to be effective in the treatment of childhood schizophrenia. Several recent studies have suggested that risperidone, a benzisoxazole derivative, is as effective and has less troublesome side effects than haloperidol in the treatment of schizophrenia in older adolescents and adults. Published case reports have shown the efficacy of risperidone in the treatment of psychosis in children and adolescents.

High-potency medications, such as haloperidol, risperidone, and trifluoperazine (Stelazine), are favored because of their decreased sedative side effects. The dosage for haloperidol ranges from about 1 to 10 mg a day in divided doses. Acute dystonic reactions do occur in children, and 1 to 2 mg a day of benztropine usually is enough to treat the extrapyramidal side effects. Children and adolescents who are treated with antipsychotic medications are at risk for withdrawal dyskinesis when the medication is withdrawn. The long-term side effects, including tardive dyskinesia, are perpetual risks for any patients who are treated with an antipsychotic medication.

Another relatively new antipsychotic medication, clozapine (Clozaril), has been used with some success in adults with schizophrenia who are resistant to treatment with multiple conventional antipsychotics. Clozapine has the advantage of generally not inducing extrapyramidal side effects, and it is unlikely to cause tardive dyskinesia. However, because of its serious, potentially fatal side effect, agranulocytosis, patients' white blood cell count must be monitored before treatment and frequently while the medication is being used. Agranulocytosis occurs in 1 to 2 percent of all patients. Other side effects associated with clozapine include somnolence, tachycardia, postural hypotension, hypersalivation, hyperthermia, and seizures. No available data evaluate its efficacy for treatment-resistant children and adolescents with schizophrenia. One published case study has reported on three successfully treated adolescents with schizophrenia who were resistant to traditional antipsychotic treatment. The adolescents who were treated with clozapine reported sedation and increased salivation but were able to tolerate the medication. Because of the serious nature of agranulocytosis, however, patients and families should be counseled extensively, and clinicians should report that the families understand the risks and the need for close monitoring.

Psychotherapy

Psychotherapists who work with children with schizophrenia must take into account a child's developmental level. They must continually support the child's good reality testing and must have sensitivity to the child's sense of self.

References

Adams M, Kutcher S, Antonis E, Bird D: Diagnostic utility of endocrine and neuroimaging screening tests in first-onset adolescent psychosis. J Am Acad Child Adolesc Psychiatry *35:* 67, 1996.

Birmaher B, Baker R, Kapur S, Quintana H, Ganguli R: Clozapine for the treatment of adolescents with schizophrenia. J Am Acad Child Adolesc Psychiatry *31:* 160, 1992.

Burd L, Kerbeshian J: A North Dakota prevalence study of schizophrenia presenting in childhood. J Am Acad Child Adolesc Psychiatry *26:* 347, 1987.

Burke P, DelBeccaro M, McCauley E, Clark C: Hallucinations in children. J Am Acad Child Adolesc Psychiatry *24:* 71, 1985.

Campbell M, Grega DM, Green WH, Bennett WG: Neuroleptic-induced dyskinesias in children. Clin Neuropharmacol *6:* 207, 1983.

Cantor S, Kestenbaum C: Psychotherapy with schizophrenic children. J Am Acad Child Adolesc Psychiatry *25:* 623, 1986.

Caplan R, Guthrie D, Foy JG: Communication deficits and formal thought disorder in schizophrenic children. J Am Acad Child Adolesc Psychiatry *31:* 151, 1992.

Caplan R, Guthrie D, Komo S: Conversational repair in schizophrenic and normal children. J Am Acad Child Adolesc Psychiatry *35:* 950, 1996.

Eggers C: Course and prognosis of childhood schizophrenia. J Autism Child Schizophr *8:* 21, 1978.

Fish B: Antecedents of a schizophrenic break. J Am Acad Child Adolesc Psychiatry *25:* 595, 1986.

Green WH, Padron-Gayol M, Hardesty AS, Bassiri M: Schizophrenia with childhood onset: A phenomenological study of 38 cases. J Am Acad Child Adolesc Psychiatry *31:* 968, 1992.

Hellgren L, Gillberg C, Enerskog I: Antecedents of adolescent psychoses: A population-based study of school health problems in children who develop psychosis in adolescence. J Am Acad Child Adolesc Psychiatry *26:* 351, 1987.

Kemph J: Hallucinations in psychotic children. J Am Acad Child Adolesc Psychiatry *26:* 556, 1987.

Kydd RR, Werry JS: Schizophrenia in children under 16 years. J Autism Dev Disord *12:* 343, 1982.

Lykes WC, Cuerva JE: Risperidone in children with schizophrenia. J Am Acad Child Adolesc Psychiatry *35:* 405, 1996.

Moise FN, Petrides G: Case study: Electroconvulsive therapy in adolescents. J Am Acad Child Adolesc Psychiatry *35:* 312, 1996.

Petty LP, Ornitz EM, Michelman JD, Zimmerman EG: Autistic children who became schizophrenic. Arch Gen Psychiatry *41:* 129, 1984.

Quintana H, Keshavan M: Case study: Risperidone in children and adolescents with schizophrenia. J Am Acad Adolesc Psychiatry *34:* 292, 1995.

Schreier HA, Libow JA: Acute phobic hallucinations in very young children. J Am Acad Child Adolesc Psychiatry *25:* 574, 1986.

Towbin KE, Dykens EM, Pearson GS, Cohen DJ: Conceptualizing "borderline syndrome of childhood" and "childhood schizophrenia" as a developmental disorder. J Am Acad Child Adolesc Psychiatry *32:* 775, 1993.

Volkmar FR: Childhood and adolescent psychosis: A review of the past 10 years. J Am Acad Child Adolesc Psychiatry *35:* 843, 1996.

Watkins J, Asarnow JR, Tanguay P: Symptoms development in childhood onset schizophrenia. J Child Psychol Psychiatry *29:* 865, 1988.

Welner A, Welner Z, Fishman R: Psychiatric adolescent inpatients: Eight to ten year follow-up. Arch Gen Psychiatry *36:* 698, 1979.

Werry JS, McClellan JM: Predicting outcome in child and adolescent (early onset) schizophrenia and bipolar disorder. J Am Acad Child Adolesc Psychiatry *31:* 147, 1992.

50

Adolescent Substance Abuse

Studies of alcohol use among adolescents in the United States have shown that by 13 years of age, one third of boys and almost one fourth of girls have tried alcohol. By 18 years of age, 92 percent of males and 73 percent of females reported using alcohol, and 4 percent reported using alcohol daily. Of high school seniors, 41 percent reported using marijuana; 2 percent reported using the drug daily.

Drinking among adolescents follows adult demographic drinking patterns: The highest proportion of alcohol use occurs among adolescents in the Northeast; whites are more likely to drink than are other groups; among whites, Roman Catholics are the least likely nondrinkers. The four most common causes of death in people between the ages of 10 and 24 years are motor vehicle accidents (37 percent), homicide (14 percent), suicide (12 percent), and other injuries or accidents (12 percent). Of adolescents treated in pediatric trauma centers, more than one third are treated for alcohol or drug use.

Studies considering alcohol and illicit drug use by adolescents as psychiatric disorders, supported by family studies of genetic contributions, by adoption studies, and by observing children of substance users reared outside the biological home, have demonstrated a greater prevalence of substance use, particularly alcoholism, among biological children of alcoholics than among adopted youngsters.

During the past decade, several risk factors have been identified for adolescent substance abuse. These include high levels of family conflict, academic difficulties, comorbid psychiatric disorders such as conduct disorder and depression, parental and peer substance use, impulsivity, and early onset of cigarette smoking. The greater the number of risk factors, the more likely it is that an adolescent will be a substance user.

In the 1990s, some degree of downward trend in the prevalence of drug use is still apparent; this trend began in the 1980s. Despite the report implying that adolescents use less alcohol, marijuana, and cocaine than they once used, a significant number of adolescents still continue to use illicit drugs and experience serious sequelae.

EPIDEMIOLOGY

Alcohol

In a recent survey, drinking was shown to be a significant problem for 10 to 20 percent of adolescents. In the age range of 13 to 17 years, in the United States, there are 3 million problem drinkers and 300,000 adolescents with alcohol dependence.

The gap between male and female alcohol consumers is narrowing. Drinking was reported by 70 percent of 8th-grade students: 54 percent reported drinking within the past year, 27 percent reported having gotten drunk at least once, and 13 percent reported binge drinking in the 2 weeks before the survey. By the 12th grade, 88 percent of high school students reported drinking and 77 percent drank within the past year; 5 percent of 8th-grade students, 1.3 percent of 10th-grade students, and 3.6 percent of 12th-grade students reported daily alcohol use.

Marijuana

Marijuana is the most widely used illicit drug among high school students. It has been termed a ''gateway drug,'' because the strongest predictor of future cocaine use is frequent marijuana use during adolescence. Of 8th-grade, 10th-grade, and 12th-grade students, 10 percent, 23 percent, and 36 percent, respectively, report using marijuana, a slight decrease from the year preceding the survey. Of 8th-grade, 10th-grade, and 12th-grade students, 0.2 percent, 0.8 percent, and 2 percent, respectively, report daily marijuana use. Prevalence rates for marijuana are highest among Native American males and females; these rates are nearly as high in white males and females and Mexican-American males. The lowest annual rates are reported by Latin-American females, African-American females, and Asian-American males and females.

Cocaine

The annual cocaine use reported by high school seniors decreased more than 30 percent between 1990 and 1991. In 1991, 2.3 percent of 8th-grade students, 4.1 percent of 10th-grade students, and 7.8 percent of 12th-grade students reported using cocaine. One tenth of a percent of high school students reported daily use of cocaine. The prevalence rates for crack cocaine use are about one half those for cocaine.

Lysergic Acid Diethylamide (LSD)

Lysergic acid diethylamide (LSD) is reportedly used by 2.7 percent of 8th-grade students, 5.6 percent of 10th-grade students, and 8.8 percent of 12th-grade students. Of 12th-grade students, 0.1 percent report daily use. The current LSD rates are lower than rates of LSD use during the past 2 decades.

Inhalants

The use of inhalants in the form of glue, aerosols, and gasoline is relatively more common among younger than older adolescents. Among 8th-grade, 10th-grade, and 12th-grade students, 17.6 percent, 15.7 percent, and 17.6 percent, respectively, report using inhalants; 0.2 percent of 8th-grade students, 0.1 percent of 10th-grade students, and 0.2 percent of 12th-grade students report daily use of inhalants.

Among adolescents enrolled in substance abuse treatment programs, 96 percent are polydrug users; 97 percent of adolescents who abuse drugs also use alcohol.

ETIOLOGY

Genetic Factors

The concordance for alcoholism has been reported to be higher among monozygotic than dizygotic twins. Considerably fewer studies have been conducted of families of drug abusers. One twin study of drug users showed that the drug-abuse concordance for male monozygotic twins was twice that for dizygotic twins. Studies of children of alcoholics reared away from their biological homes have shown that these children have about a 25 percent chance of becoming alcoholics.

Psychosocial Factors

A recent study concluded that children in families with the lowest measures of parental supervision and monitoring initiated alcohol, tobacco, and other drug use earlier than children from families with more supervision. The risk was greatest for children younger than 11 years of age. With more rigorous parental monitoring, young adolescents might be delayed in or prevented from initiating drug and alcohol use. Furthermore, increased supervision during middle childhood years may diminish drug and alcohol sampling and ultimately diminish the risk of using marijuana, cocaine, or inhalants in the future.

Comorbidity

Rates of alcohol and drug use are reportedly higher in relatives of children with depression and bipolar disorders. On the other hand, mood disorders are common among those with alcoholism. There is evidence of a strong link between early antisocial behavior, conduct disorder, and substance abuse. Substance abuse may be viewed as one form of behavioral deviance that, unsurprisingly, is associated with other forms of social and behavioral deviance. Early intervention with children who show early signs of social deviance and antisocial behavior may conceivably impede the processes that contribute to later substance abuse.

The prevalence of comorbidity, that is, the occurrence of more than one substance use disorder or the combination of a substance use disorder and another psychiatric disorder, is common. It is important to know about all comorbid disorders, which may show differential responses to treatment.

Surveys of adolescents with alcoholism show rates of 50 percent or greater for additional psychiatric disorders, especially mood disorders. In a recent survey of adolescents who used alcohol, more than 80 percent met criteria for another disorder. The disorders most frequently present were depressive disorders, disruptive behavior disorders, and drug use disorders. These rates of comorbidity are even higher than those for adults. The diagnosis of alcohol abuse or dependence was likely to follow rather than precede other disorders; the fact that a large proportion of adolescents with alcoholism have a previous childhood disorder may have etiological as well as treatment implications. In this survey, the onset of alcohol disorders did not systematically precede drug abuse or dependence. In 50 percent of cases, alcohol use followed drug use. Alcohol use may be a gateway to drug use, but not in most cases. The presence of other psychiatric disorders was associated with an earlier onset or alcohol disorder, but it did not seem to indicate a more protracted course of alcoholism.

DIAGNOSIS AND CLINICAL FEATURES

According to the fourth edition of *Diagnostic and Statistical Manual of Mental Disorders* (DSM-IV), substance-related disorders include the disorders of substance dependence, substance abuse, substance intoxication, and substance withdrawal. *Substance dependence* refers to a cluster of cognitive, behavioral, and physiological symptoms indicating that a person continues the use of a substance despite significant substance-related problems. A pattern of repeated self-administration may result in tolerance, withdrawal, and compulsive drug-taking behavior. Dependence can be applied to every substance, with the exception of caffeine. It requires the presence of at least three symptoms of the maladaptive pattern, which can occur at any time during the same 12-month period. Symptoms of dependence can include tolerance, withdrawal, greater use of the substance than was intended, an unsuccessful desire to cut down or control use and reduction of social or occupational activities because of substance use. In addition, the user knows that the substance causes significant impairment but does not give it up. Physiological dependence (evidence of tolerance or withdrawal) may or may not be present.

Substance abuse refers to a maladaptive pattern of substance use leading to clinically significant impairment or distress, as manifest by one or more of the following symptoms within a 12-month period: recurrent substance use in situations that cause physical danger to the user, recurrent substance use in the face of obvious impairment in school or work situations, recurrent substance use despite resulting legal problems, or recurrent substance use despite social or interpersonal problems. To meet the criteria for substance abuse, the symptoms must not, now or in the past, have met the criteria for substance dependence for this class of substance.

Substance intoxication refers to the development of a reversible, substance-specific syndrome caused by use of a substance. Clinically significant maladaptive behavioral or psychological changes must be present.

Substance withdrawal refers to a substance-specific syndrome caused by the cessation of, or reduction in, prolonged substance use. The substance-specific syndrome causes clinically significant distress or impairment in social or occupational functioning.

The diagnosis of alcohol or drug use in adolescents is made through careful interview, observations, laboratory findings, and history provided by reliable sources. Many nonspecific signs may point to alcohol or drug use, and clinicians must be careful to corroborate hunches before jumping to conclusions. Substance use may be viewed on a continuum with experimentation, the mildest use, regular use without obvious impairment, abuse, and finally, dependence. Changes in academic performance, nonspecific physical ailments, changes in relationships with family members, changes in peer group, unexplained phone calls, or changes in personal hygiene may indicate substance use in an adolescent. Many of these indicators, however, also can be consistent with the onset of depression, adjustment to school, or the prodrome of a psychotic illness. Therefore, it is important to keep the channels of communication with an adolescent open when substance use is suspected.

There is a relation between substance use and a variety of high-risk behaviors, including the use of a weapon, suicidal behavior, early sexual experimentation, risky driving, "heavy metal" or alternative music, and occasionally, preoccupation with cults or Satanism. Although none of these behaviors necessarily predicts substance use, suspicion may be raised.

Adolescents with inadequate social skills may use a substance as a way to try to fit in with a peer group. In some cases, adolescents begin their substance use at home with their parents, who also use substances to enhance their social interactions.

Although there is no evidence of a typical adolescent user of alcohol or drugs, most substance users seem to have underlying social skills deficits and less-than-optimal peer relationships.

TREATMENT

Treatment settings that serve adolescents with alcohol or drug use disorders include inpatient units, residential treatment facilities, halfway houses, group homes, partial hospital programs, and outpatient settings. Basic components of adolescent alcohol or drug use treatment include individual psychotherapy, drug-specific counseling, self-help groups (Alcoholics Anonymous [AA], Narcotics Anonymous [NA], Alateen, Al-Anon), substance abuse education and relapse prevention programs, and random urine drug testing. Family therapy and psychopharmacological intervention may be added.

Before deciding on the most appropriate treatment setting for a particular adolescent, a screening process must take place in which structured and unstructured interviews help to determine the types of substances being used and the quantities and frequencies. Determining coexisting psychiatric disorders is also critical. Rating scales are typically used to document pretreatment and posttreatment severity of abuse. The Teen Addiction Severity Index (T-ASI), the Adolescent Drug and Alcohol Diagnostic Assessment (ADAD), and the Adolescent Problem Severity Index (APSI) are several severity-oriented rating scales. The T-ASI is broken down into dimensions that include a family function, school or employment status, psychiatric status, peer-social relationships, and legal status.

After most of the information about substance use and the patient's overall psychiatric status has been obtained, a treatment strategy must be chosen and an appropriate setting must be decided on. Two very different approaches to the treatment of substance abuse are embodied in the Minnesota model and the multidisciplinary professional model. The Minnesota model is based on the premise of AA; it is an intensive 12-step program with a counselor who functions as the primary therapist. The program uses self-help participation and group processes. Inherent in this treatment strategy is the need for adolescents to admit that substance use is problematic and that help is necessary. Furthermore, they must be willing to work toward altering their lifestyle to eradicate substance use. The multidisciplinary professional model consists of a team of mental health professionals that usually is led by a physician. Following a case-management model, each member of the team has specific areas of treatment for which he or she is responsible. Interventions may include cognitive-behavioral therapy, family therapy, and pharmacological intervention. This approach usually is suited for adolescents with comorbid psychiatric diagnoses.

Cognitive-behavioral approaches to psychotherapy for adolescents with substance use generally require that adolescents be motivated to participate in treatment and refrain from further substance use. The therapy focuses on relapse prevention and maintaining abstinence.

Psychopharmacological interventions for adolescent alcohol and drug users are still in their early stages. When mood disorders are present, there are clear indications for antidepressants, and generally, the serotonin reuptake inhibitors are the first line of treatment. In the past, some pharmacological interventions have been aimed at aiding the abstinence process. For example, disulfiram has been used in alcoholism to cause an aversive reaction if alcohol is ingested. In certain instances, administration of a medication has been used to block the reinforcing effect of the illicit drug, for instance, giving naltrexone (ReVia) for opioid abuse. Some medications mitigate the craving or withdrawal symptoms for a drug that is no longer being used. Clonidine (Catapres) has been used transiently during heroin withdrawal. Occasionally, an intervention is made to substitute the illicit drug with another drug that is more amenable to the treatment situation, for example, using methadone instead of heroin. Adolescents are required to have two documented attempts at detoxification and consent from an adult before they can enter such a treatment program.

Because comorbidity influences treatment outcome, it is important to pay attention to other disorders such as mood disorders, anxiety disorders, conduct disorder, or attention-deficit/hyperactivity disorder during the treatment of substance use disorders.

References

Brook JS, Whiteman M, Finch SJ, Cohen P: Young adult drug use and delinquency: Childhood antecedents and adolescent mediators. J Am Acad Child Adolesc Psychiatry *35:* 1584, 1996.

Chilcoat HD, Anthony J: Impact of parent monitoring on initiation of drug use through late childhood. J Am Acad Child Adolesc Psychiatry *35:* 91, 1996.

Copans SA, Kinney J: Adolescents. In *Clinical Manual of Substance Abuse,* J Kinney, editor, p 288. Mosby-Year Book, St. Louis, 1996.

Duffy A, Milin R: Case study: Withdrawal syndrome in adolescent chronic cannabis users. J Am Acad Child Adolesc Psychiatry *35:* 1618, 1996.

Kaminer Y: *Adolescent Substance Abuse: A Comprehensive Guide to Theory and Practice.* Plenum, New York, 1994.

Kaminer Y, Bukstein OG, Tarter TE: The teen addiction severity index (T-ASI): Rationale and reliability. Int J Addict *26:* 219, 1991.

King CA, Ghaziuddin N, McGovern L, Brand E, Hill E, Naylor M: Predictors of comorbid alcohol and substance abuse in depressed adolescents. J Am Acad Child Adolesc Psychiatry *35:* 743, 1996.

Novins DK, Beals J, Shore JH, Manson SM: Substance abuse treatment of American Indian adolescents: Comorbid symptomatology, gender differences, and treatment patterns. J Am Acad Child Adolesc Psychiatry *35:* 1593, 1996.

Piacentini J, Pataki C: Substance abuse in depressed adolescents. In *Depression in Children and Adolescents,* HS Koplewicz, E Klass, editors, p 133. Harwood, Philadelphia, 1993.

Rohde P, Lewinsohn PM, Seeley JR: Psychiatric comorbidity with problematic alcohol use in high school students. J Am Acad Child Adolesc Psychiatry *35:* 101, 1996.

Todd RD, Geller B, Neuman R, Fox LW, Hickok J: Increased prevalence of alcoholism in relatives of depressed and bipolar children. J Am Acad Child Adolesc Psychiatry *35:* 716, 1996.

Webb JA, Baer PE, Getz JG, McKelvey RS: Do fifth graders' attitudes and intentions toward alcohol use predict seventh-grade use? J Am Acad Child Adolesc Psychiatry *35:* 1611, 1996.

51

Child Psychiatry: Additional Conditions That May Be a Focus of Clinical Attention

BORDERLINE INTELLECTUAL FUNCTIONING

According to the fourth edition of *Diagnostic and Statistical Manual of Mental Disorders* (DSM-IV), a child with borderline intellectual functioning has an intelligence quotient (IQ) in the range of 71 to 84. Impaired adaptive functioning accompanies the disorder, which is diagnosed when difficulties in academic, social, or vocational areas pertaining to borderline intellectual functioning become the focus of clinical attention.

Clinicians must assess a patient's intellectual level and current and past levels of adaptive functioning to diagnose borderline intellectual functioning. In cases of major mental disorders in which the current level of adaptive functioning has deteriorated, the diagnosis of borderline intellectual functioning may not be clearly evident. In such situations, clinicians must evaluate a patient's history to determine whether a compromised level of adaptive functioning was present even before the onset of the mental disorder.

Only about 6 to 7 percent of the population are found to have a borderline IQ, as determined by the Stanford-Binet test or the Wechsler scales. The premise behind the inclusion of borderline intellectual functioning in DSM-IV is that people may experience difficulties in their adaptive capacities as a result of the intellectual deficits and thus may require attention. In the absence of specific intrapsychic conflicts, developmental traumas, biochemical abnormalities, and other factors linked to any other mental disorder, such people may experience severe emotional distress. Frustration and embarrassment over their difficulties may shape their life choices and lead to circumstances warranting psychiatric intervention.

Etiology

Genetic factors are increasingly found to play a role in intellectual deficits. Environmental deprivation and infectious and toxic exposures can also contribute to cognitive impairments. Twin and adoption studies support hypotheses that many genes contribute to the development of a particular IQ. Specific infectious processes (such as congenital rubella), prenatal exposures (such as fetal alcohol syndrome), and specific chromosomal abnormalities (such as fragile X syndrome) result in mental retardation.

Diagnosis

In DSM-IV, the following statement about borderline intellectual functioning appears:

> This category can be used when the focus of clinical attention is associated with borderline intellectual functioning, that is, an IQ in the 71 to 84 range. Differential diagnosis between Borderline Intellectual Functioning and Mental Retardation (an IQ of 70 or below) is especially difficult when the coexistence of certain mental disorders (e.g., Schizophrenia) is involved. ***Coding note:*** *This is coded on Axis II.*

Treatment

The main focus of treatment is to improve practical adaptive skills, social skills, and self-esteem. The goal is to improve the match between the person's capabilities and lifestyle. After the underlying problem becomes known to the therapist, psychiatric treatment can be useful. Many people with borderline intellectual functioning are able to function at a superior level in some areas while being markedly deficient in other areas. By directing such persons to appropriate areas of endeavor, by pointing out socially acceptable behavior, and by teaching them living skills, the therapist can help improve their self-esteem.

ACADEMIC PROBLEM

The editors of DSM-IV refer to *academic problem* as a problem that is not caused by a mental disorder or, if caused by a mental disorder, is severe enough to warrant clinical attention.

This diagnostic category is used when a child or adolescent is having significant academic difficulties that are not deemed to be due to a specific learning disorder or communication disorder or directly related to a psychiatric disorder. Nevertheless, intervention is necessary because the child's achievement is significantly impaired in school. Therefore, a child or an adolescent who is of normal intelligence and is free of a learning disorder or a communication disorder but is failing in school or doing poorly falls into this category.

Etiology

Many emotional factors contribute to a child's confidence, competence, and academic success. A child who is troubled by family conflict, social isolation, or shyness may not fulfill his or her potential. Academic problems have many contributing factors and may arise at any time during a child's school years. School is the major occupation of children and adolescents and is their main social and educational instrument. Adjustment and success in the school setting depend on children's physical, cognitive, social, and emotional adjustment. Children's general coping mechanisms in many developmental tasks usually are reflected in their academic and social success in school. Boys and girls must cope with the process of separation from parents, adjustments to new environments, adaptation to social contacts, competition, assertion, and intimacy, and exposure to unfamiliar attitudes. A corresponding relation often exists between school performance and how well these tasks are mastered.

Anxiety may play a major role in interfering with children's academic performances. Anxiety may hamper their abilities to perform well on tests, to speak in public, and to ask questions when they do not understand something. Some children are so concerned about the way others view them that they are unable to attend to their academic tasks. For some children, conflicts about success and fears of the consequences imagined to accompany the attainment of success may hamper academic success. Sigmund Freud described people with such conflicts as "those wrecked by success." For example, an adolescent girl may be unable to succeed in school because she fears social rejection or the loss of femininity, or both, and she perceives success as being involved with aggression and competition with boys.

Depressed children also may withdraw from academic pursuits; they require specific interventions to improve their academic performances and to treat their depression. Children who do not have major depressive disorder but who are consumed by family problems such as financial troubles, marital discord in their parents, and mental illness in family members may be distracted and unable to attend to academic tasks. Children who receive mixed messages from their parents about accepting criticism and redirection from their teachers may become confused and unable to perform well in school. The loss of the parents as the primary and predominant teachers in a child's life may result in identity conflicts for some children. Some students lack a stable sense of self and are unable to identify goals for themselves, a situation that leads to a sense of boredom or futility. Cultural and economic background can play a role in how well accepted a child feels in school and can affect the child's academic achievement. Familial socioeconomic level, parental education, race, religion, and family functioning can influence a child's sense of fitting in and can affect preparation to meet school demands.

Schools, teachers, and clinicians can share insights about how to foster productive and cooperative environments for all students in a classroom. Teacher's expectations about their students' performance influence these performances. Teachers serve as agents whose varying expectations can shape the differential development of students' skills and abilities. Such conditioning early in school, especially when negative, can disturb academic performance. Therefore, a teacher's affective response to a child can prompt the appearance of an academic problem. Most important is the teachers' humane approach to students at all levels of education, including medical school.

Diagnosis

In DSM-IV, the following statement about academic problem appears:

> This category can be used when the focus of clinical attention is an academic problem that is not due to a mental disorder or, if due to a mental disorder, is sufficiently severe to warrant independent clinical attention. An example is a pattern of failing grades or of significant underachievement in a person with adequate intellectual capacity in the absence of a Learning or Communication Disorder or any other mental disorder that would account for the problem.

Treatment

The initial step in determining a useful intervention for an academic problem is a comprehensive diagnostic evaluation. After it has been determined that another disorder is not directly influencing academic performance, an appropriate intervention can be developed. Although not considered a mental disorder, an academic problem often can be alleviated by psychological means. Psychotherapeutic techniques can be used successfully for scholastic difficulties related to poor motivation, poor self-concept, and underachievement. Early efforts to relieve the problem are critical: Sustained problems in learning and school performance frequently are compounded and precipitate severe difficulties. Feelings of anger, frustration, shame, loss of self-respect, and helplessness—emotions that most often accompany school failures—emotionally and cognitively damage self-esteem, disabling future performance and clouding expectations for success. Generally, children with academic problems require either school-based intervention or individual attention.

In dealing with academic problems, tutoring is an effective technique and should be considered in most cases. Tutoring is of proven value in preparing for objective multiple choice examinations, such as the Scholastic Aptitude Test (SAT) and Medical College Aptitude Test. Taking such examinations repetitively and using relaxation skills are two behavioral techniques of great value in diminishing anxiety.

CHILDHOOD OR ADOLESCENT ANTISOCIAL BEHAVIOR

According to DSM-IV, *child or adolescent antisocial behavior* refers to behavior that is not caused by a mental disorder and includes isolated antisocial acts, not a pattern of behavior. This category covers many acts by children and adolescents that violate the rights of others, such as overt acts of aggression and violence and covert acts of lying, stealing, truancy, and running away from home. Certain antisocial acts, such as fire setting, possession of a weapon, or a severe act of aggression toward another child, require intervention, even if only a single occurrence. Sometimes, children without a pattern of recurrent aggression or antisocial behavior become involved in occasional less severe behaviors that nevertheless require some intervention. The DSM-IV definition of conduct disorder requires a repetitive pattern of at least three antisocial behaviors for at least 6 months, but childhood or adolescent antisocial behavior may consist of isolated events that do not constitute a mental disorder but do become the focus of clinical attention. The emergence of occasional antisocial symptoms is common among children who have a variety of mental disorders, including psychotic disorders, depressive disorders, impulse-control disorders, and disruptive behavior and attention-deficit disorders, such as attention-deficit/hyperactivity disorder and oppositional defiant disorder.

A child's age and developmental level affect the manifestations of disturbed conduct and influence the child's likelihood to meet the diagnostic criteria for a conduct disorder, as opposed to childhood antisocial behavior. Therefore, a child of 5 or 6 years of age is not likely to meet the criteria for three antisocial symptoms—for example, physical confrontations, the use of weapons, and forcing someone into sexual activity—but a single symptom, such as initiating fights, is common in the 5- to 6-year-old age group. The term *juvenile delinquent* is defined by the legal system as a youth who has violated the law in some way, but the term does not imply that the youth meets the criteria for a mental disorder.

Epidemiology

Estimates of antisocial behavior range from 5 to 15 percent of the general population and somewhat less among children and adolescents. Reports have documented the increased frequency of antisocial behaviors in urban settings, compared with rural areas. In one report, the risk of coming into contact with the police for an antisocial behavior was estimated to be 20 percent for teenage boys and 4 percent for teenage girls.

Etiology

Antisocial behaviors may occur in the context of a mental disorder or in its absence. Antisocial behavior is multidetermined and occurs most frequently in children or adolescents with many risk factors. Among the most common risk factors are harsh and physically abusive parenting, parental criminality, and a child's tendency toward impulsive and hyperactive behavior. Additional associated features of children and adolescents with antisocial behavior are low IQ, academic failure, and low levels of adult supervision. (See Chapter 32 for a discussion of genetic and social factors as causes of adult antisocial behavior.)

Psychological Factors. If their parenting experience is poor, children experience emotional deprivation, which leads to low self-esteem and unconscious anger. When children are not given any limits, their consciences are deficient because they have not internalized parental prohibitions that account for superego formation. Therefore, they have so-called superego lacunae, which allow them to commit antisocial acts without guilt. At times, such children's antisocial behavior is a vicarious source of pleasure and gratification for parents who act out their own forbidden wishes and impulses through their children. A consistent finding in people who perform repeated acts of violent behavior is a history of physical abuse.

Diagnosis and Clinical Features

In DSM-IV, the following statement about childhood or adolescent antisocial behavior appears:

> This category can be used when the focus of clinical attention is antisocial behavior in a child or adolescent that is not due to a mental disorder (e.g., Conduct Disorder or an Impulse-Control Disorder). Examples include isolated antisocial acts of children or adolescents (not a pattern of antisocial behavior).

The childhood behaviors most associated with antisocial behavior are theft, incorrigibility, arrests, school problems, impulsiveness, promiscuity, oppositional behavior, lying, suicide attempts, substance abuse, truancy, running away, associated with undesirable people, and staying out late at night. The greater the number of symptoms present in childhood, the greater is the probability of adult antisocial behavior; however, the presence of many symptoms also indicates the development of other mental disorders in adult life.

Differential Diagnosis

Substance-related disorders (including alcohol, cannabis, and cocaine use disorders), bipolar I disorder, and schizophrenia in childhood often manifest themselves as antisocial behavior.

Treatment

Disturbances of conduct frequently accompany the onset of various other psychiatric disorders. The first step in determining the appropriate treatment for a child or an adolescent who is manifesting antisocial behavior is to evaluate the need to treat any coexisting mental disorder, such as bipolar I disorder, a psychotic disorder, or a depressive disorder that may be contributing to the antisocial behavior. The treatment of antisocial behavior usually involves behavioral management, which is most effective when the patient is in a controlled environment or when the child's family members cooperate in maintaining the behavioral program. Schools can help modify antisocial behavior in classrooms. Rewards for prosocial behaviors and positive reinforcement for the control of unwanted behaviors have merit.

In cases of rare or occasional antisocial behaviors, medications generally are not used. When repetitive episodes of explosive behavior, aggression, or violent outbursts ensue, medications have been used with some success. Lithium (Eskalith) and haloperidol (Haldol) may reduce explosive behavior and rage outbursts. When hyperactivity and impulsivity are a contributing factor, methylphenidate (Ritalin) may be helpful to reduce impulsivity and decrease aggression in some cases.

It is more difficult to treat children and adolescents with long-term patterns of antisocial behavior, particularly covert behaviors such as stealing and lying. Group therapy has been used to treat these behaviors, and cognitive problem-solving approaches are potentially helpful.

IDENTITY PROBLEM

According to DSM-IV, *identity problem* refers to uncertainty about issues relating to identity, such as goals, career choice, friendships, sexual behavior, moral values, and group loyalties. An identity problem can cause severe distress for a young person and can lead a person to seek psychotherapy or guidance. Identity problem is, however, not recognized as a mental disorder in DSM-IV. It is sometimes manifest in the context of such mental disorders as mood disorders, psychotic disorders, and borderline personality disorder.

Epidemiology

No reliable information is available regarding predisposing factors, familial pattern, sex ratio, or prevalence, but problems with identity formation seem to be a result of life in modern society. Today, children and adolescents often experience great instability in family life, problems with identity formation, conflicts between adolescent peer values and the values of parents and society, and exposure through the media and education to various moral, behavioral, and lifestyle possibilities.

Etiology

The causes of identity problems often are multifactorial and include the pressures of a highly dysfunctional family and the influences of coexisting mental disorders. In general, adolescents who suffer from major depressive disorder, psychotic disorders, and other mental disorders report feeling alienated from family members and experience a degree of turmoil. Children who have had difficulties in mastering expected developmental tasks all along are likely to have difficulties with the pressure to establish a well-defined identity during adolescence. Erik Erikson used the term *identity versus role diffusion* to describe the developmental and psychosocial tasks challenging adolescents to incorporate past experiences and present goals into a coherent sense of self.

Diagnosis and Clinical Features

In DSM-IV, the following statement about identity problem appears:

> This category can be used when the focus of clinical attention is uncertainty about multiple issues relating to identity such as long-term goals, career choice, friendship patterns, sexual orientation and behavior, moral values, and group loyalties.

The essential features of identity problem seem to revolve around the question "Who am I?" Conflicts are experienced as irreconcilable aspects of the self that the adolescent is unable to integrate into a coherent identity. If the symptoms are not recognized and resolved, a full-blown identity crisis may develop. As Erikson described, youth manifests severe doubting and an inability to make decisions (abulia), a sense of isolation and inner emptiness, a growing inability to relate to others, disturbed sexual functioning, a distorted time perspective, a sense of urgency, and the assumption of a negative identity. The associated features frequently include marked discrepancy between the adolescent's self-perception and the views that others have of the adolescent; moderate anxiety and depression that are usually related to inner preoccupation, rather than external realities; and self-doubt and uncertainty about the future, with either difficulty in making choices or impulsive experiments in an attempt to establish an independent identity. Some persons with identity problem join cultlike groups.

Differential Diagnosis

Identity problem must be differentiated from a mental disorder (such as borderline personality disorder, schizophreniform disorder, schizophrenia, or a mood disorder). At times, what initially seems to be an identity problem may be the prodromal manifestations of one of these disorders. Intense but normal conflicts associated with maturing, such as adolescent turmoil and midlife crisis, may be confusing, but they usually are not associated with marked deterioration in school, vocational, or social functioning or with severe subjective distress. Considerable evidence indicates that adolescent turmoil often is not a phase that is outgrown but an indication of true psychopathology.

Course and Prognosis

The onset of identity problem is most frequently in late adolescence, as teenagers separate from the nuclear family and attempt to establish an independent identity and value system. The onset usually is manifest by a gradual increase in anxiety, depression, regressive phenomena (such as loss of interest in friends, school, and activities), irritability, sleep difficulties, and changes in eating habits. The course usually is relatively brief, as developmental lags are responsive to support, acceptance, and the provision of a psychosocial moratorium.

An extensive prolongation of adolescence with continued identity problem may lead to the chronic state of role diffusion that may indicate a disturbance of early developmental stages and the presence of borderline personality disorder, a mood disorder, or schizophrenia. An identity problem usually resolves by the mid-20s. If it persists, the person with the identity problem may be unable to make career commitments or lasting attachments.

Treatment

Individual psychotherapy directed toward encouraging growth and development usually is considered the therapy of choice. Adolescents with identity problems often feel developmentally unprepared to deal with the increasing demands for social, emotional, and sexual independence. Issues of separation and individuation from their families can be challenging and overwhelming. Treatment is aimed at helping these adolescents develop a sense of competence and mastery about necessary social and vocational choices. A therapist's empathic acknowledgment of an adolescent's struggle can be helpful in the process.

References

Anderson JC: The conduct disorder. In *Handbook of Studies on Child Psychiatry*, BJ Tonge, GD Burrows, JS Werry, editors, p 283. Elsevier Science, New York, 1990.

Benasich AA, Curtiss S, Tallal P: Language, learning and behavioral disturbances in childhood. J Am Acad Child Adolesc Psychiatry *32:* 585, 1993.

Blos P: *On Adolescence.* Free Press, Glen Cove, NY, 1962.

Bow JN: A comparison of intellectually superior male reading achievers and underachievers from a neuropsychological perspective. J Learn Disabil *21:* 118, 1988.

Brent DA, Johnson B, Bartles S, Bridge J, Rather C, Matta J, Connolly J, Constantine D: Personality disorder, tendency to impulsive violence and suicidal behavior in adolescents. J Am Acad Child Adolesc Psychiatry *32:* 69, 1993.

DuPaul G, Rapport M: Does methylphenidate normalize the classroom performance of children with attention deficit disorder. J Am Acad Child Adolesc Psychiatry *32:* 190, 1993.

Egan J: Etiology and treatment of borderline personality disorder in adolescents. Hosp Community Psychiatry *37:* 6, 1986.

Eiserman WD: Three types of peer tutoring: Effects on the attitudes of students with learning disabilities and their regular class peers. J Learn Disabil *21:* 249, 1988.

Erikson EH: The problems of ego identity. J Am Psychoanal Assoc *4:* 428, 1956.

Galanter M: Cults and zealous self-help movements: A psychiatric perspective. Am J Psychiatry *147:* 543, 1990.

Hoge RD, Andrews DA, Leschied AW: Tests of three hypotheses regarding the predictors of delinquency. J Abnorm Child Psychol *22:* 547, 1994.

Keogh BK: Improving services for problem learners: Rethinking and restructuring. J Learn Disabil *21:* 19, 1988.

Lewis DO: *Vulnerabilities to Delinquency.* Spectrum, New York, 1981.

Lewis DO, Yeager CA, Lovely R, Stein A, Coham-Portorreal CS: A clinical follow-up of delinquent males: Ignored vulnerabilities, unmet needs, and the perpetuation of violence. J Am Acad Child Adolesc Psychiatry *33:* 518, 1994.

Lundy MS, Pfohl B, Kuperman S: Adult criminality among formerly hospitalized child psychiatric patients. J Am Acad Child Adolesc Psychiatry *32:* 568, 1993.

Masterson JF: *The Psychiatric Dilemma of Adolescence.* Little, Brown, Boston, 1967.

Newcorn JH, Halpern JM: Comorbidity among disruptive behavior. Child Adolesc Clin North Am *3:* 227, 1994.

Petti TA, Vela RM: Borderline disorders of childhood: An overview. J Am Acad Child Adolesc Psychiatry *29:* 327, 1990.

Rende RD: Longitudinal relations between temperamental traits and behavioral syndromes in middle childhood. J Am Acad Child Adolesc Psychiatry *32:* 287, 1993.

Robson KS: *The Borderline Child: Approaches to Etiology, Diagnosis, and Treatment.* McGraw-Hill, New York, 1983.

Sadock VA: Other additional conditions that may be a focus of clinical attention. In *Comprehensive Textbook of Psychiatry,* ed 6, HI Kaplan, BJ Sadock, editors, p 1633. Williams & Wilkins, Baltimore, 1995.

Soloff PH, George A, Nathan RS, Schulz PM: Progress in pharmacotherapy of borderline disorders. Arch Gen Psychiatry *43:* 7, 1986.

Stone MH: *The Borderline Syndromes.* McGraw-Hill, New York, 1980.

Tremblay RE, Masse B, Perron D, Leblanc M, et al: Early disruptive behavior, poor school achievement, delinquent behavior, and delinquent personality: Longitudinal analyses. J Consult Clin Psychol *60:* 64, 1992.

Verhulst IC, Eussen MLJM, Berden GFMG, Sanders-Woodstra J, van der Ende J: Pathways of problem behaviors from childhood to adolescence. J Am Acad Child Adolesc Psychiatry *32:* 388, 1993.

52 Psychiatric Treatment of Children and Adolescents

▲ 52.1 Individual Psychotherapy

Individual psychotherapy with children is focused on improving children's adaptive skills in and outside the family setting. Treatment reflects an understanding of children's developmental levels and shows sensitivity toward families and environments in which children live. Most children do not seek psychiatric treatment; they are taken to a psychotherapist because of a disturbance noted by a family member, a schoolteacher, or a pediatrician. Children often believe that they are being taken for treatment because of their misbehavior or as a punishment for wrongdoing.

Children are able to disclose their own thoughts, feelings, moods, and perceptual experiences better than others; however, even when external behavior problems have been identified by others, children's internal experiences may be largely unknown. Children often are able to describe their feelings in a particular situation but are unable to make changes without an advocate's help. Therefore, child psychotherapists function as advocates for their child patients in interactions with schools, legal agencies, and community organizations. Child psychotherapists may be called on to make recommendations that affect various aspects of children's lives.

THEORIES AND TECHNIQUES

Because a combination of therapeutic interventions often is used to treat children, clinicians must have a working knowledge of several psychotherapeutic techniques and their applications in childhood. Psychodynamic approaches are sometimes mixed with supportive components and behavioral management techniques to build a comprehensive treatment plan for children. Individual psychotherapy with children frequently takes place in conjunction with family therapy, group therapy, and, when indicated, psychopharmacology. Several theoretical systems underlie psychotherapeutic approaches with children, including psychoanalytic theories, behavioral theories, family systems theories, and developmental theories.

Psychoanalytic Theories

In classic psychoanalytic theory, exploratory psychotherapy applies to patients of all ages by reversing the evolution of psychopathologic processes. A principal difference noted with advancing age is a sharpening distinction between psychogenetic and psychodynamic factors. The younger the child, the more the genetic and dynamic forces are intertwined. The development of these pathological processes generally is believed to begin with experiences that have proved to be particularly significant to children and have affected them adversely. Although in one sense the experiences were real, in another sense, they may have been misinterpreted or imagined. In any event, to children, these were traumatic experiences that caused unconscious complexes. Being inaccessible to conscious awareness, the unconscious elements readily escape rational adaptive maneuvers and are subject to pathological misuse of adaptive and defensive mechanisms. The result is the development of conflicts leading to distressing symptoms, character attitudes, or patterns of behavior that constitute the emotional disturbance.

The psychoanalytic view of emotional disturbances in children has increasingly assumed a developmental orientation. Therefore, the maladaptive defensive functioning is directed against conflicts between impulses that are characteristic of a specific developmental phase and environmental influences or a child's internalized representations of environment. In this framework, disorders result from environmental interferences with maturational timetables or conflicts with the environment engendered by developmental progress. The result is difficulty in achieving or resolving developmental tasks and fulfilling capacities that are specific to later phases of development. These developmental stages can be expressed in various ways, from Anna Freud's lines of development to Erik Erikson's concept of sequential psychosocial capacities.

The goal of therapy is to help develop good conflict-resolution skills in children so they can function at their appropriate developmental levels. Therapy may again be necessary as children face the challenges of subsequent developmental periods.

Psychoanalytic psychotherapy is a modified form of psychotherapy that is expressive and exploratory and that endeavors to reverse the evolution of emotional disturbance through reenacting and desensitizing traumatic events by freely expressing thoughts and feelings in an interview-play situation. Ultimately, therapists help patients understand the warded-off feelings, fears, and wishes that have beset them.

Whereas the psychoanalytic psychotherapeutic approach seeks improvement by exposure and resolution of buried conflicts, suppressive-supportive-educative psychotherapy works in an opposite fashion by aiming to facilitate repression. Therapists, capitalizing on patients' desire to please, encourage patients to substitute new adaptive and defensive mechanisms. In this therapy, clinicians use interpretations minimally; instead, they emphasize suggestion, persuasion, exhortation, operant reinforcement, counseling, education, direction, advice, abreaction, environmental manipulation, intellectual review, gratification of patient's current dependent needs, and similar techniques.

Behavioral Theories

All behavior, whether adaptive or maladaptive, is a consequence of the same basic principles of behavior acquisition and maintenance. Behavior is either learned or unlearned: What renders behavior abnormal or disturbed is its social significance. Although theories and their derivative therapeutic intervention techniques have become increasingly complex over the years, all learning can be subsumed in two global basic mechanisms. One is classic respondent conditioning, akin to Ivan Pavlov's famous experiments, and the second is operant instrumental learning, which is associated with B. F. Skinner, although it is basic to both Edward Thorndike's law of effect, which is about the influence of reinforcing consequences of behavior, and to Sigmund Freud's pain–pleasure principle. Both of these basic mechanisms assign the highest priority to the immediate precipitants of behavior and deemphasize remote underlying causal determinants that are important in the psychoanalytic tradition.

The respondent conditioning theory asserts that there are only two types of abnormal behavior: behavioral deficits that result from a failure to learn and deviant maladaptive behaviors that are a consequence of learning inappropriate things. Such concepts have always been an implicit part of the rationale underlying all child psychotherapy. Intervention strategies derive much of their success, particularly with children, from rewarding previously unnoticed good behavior, thereby highlighting it, and making it occur more frequently than in the past.

Family Systems Theories

Although families have long been an interest of child psychotherapists, the understanding of transactional family processes has been greatly enhanced by conceptual contributions from cybernetics, systems theory, communications theory, object relations theory, social role theory, ethology, and ecology. The bedrock premise entails the idea of a family's functioning as a self-regulating open system that possesses its own unique history and structure. This structure is constantly evolving as a consequence of dynamic interaction between the family's mutually interdependent systems and people who share a complementarity of needs. From this conceptual foundation, a wealth of ideas has emerged under rubrics such as family development, life cycle, homeostasis, functions, identity, values, goals, congruence, symmetry, myths, rules, roles (spokesperson, symptoms bearer, scapegoat, affect barometer, pet, persecutor, victim, arbitrator, distractor, saboteur, rescuer, breadwinner, disciplinarian, nurturer), structure (boundaries, splits, pairings, alliances, coalitions, enmeshed, disengaged), double bind, scapegoating, pseudomutuality, and mystification. Increasingly, appreciation of the family system sometimes explains why a minute therapeutic input at a critical junction may result in far-reaching changes, whereas in other situations, huge amounts of therapeutic effort seem to be absorbed with minimal evidence of change.

Developmental Theories

Underlying child psychotherapy is the assumption that, in the absence of unusual interferences, children mature in basically orderly, predictable ways that are codifiable in a variety of interrelated psychosociobiological sequential systematizations. The central, overriding role of a developmental frame of reference in child psychotherapy distinguishes it from adult psychotherapy. A therapist's orientation should entail more than a knowledge of age-appropriate behavior derived from such studies as Arnold Gesell's description of the morphology of behavior. It should encompass more than psychosexual development with ego psychological and sociocultural amendments, exemplified by Erikson's epigenetic schema. It extends beyond familiarity with Jean Piaget's sequence of intellectual evolution as a basis for knowing the level of abstraction at which children of various ages may be expected to function or for assessing their capacities for moral orientation.

TYPES OF PSYCHOTHERAPY

Developing a psychotherapeutic intervention for a particular child includes evaluation of the child's age, developmental level, type of problem, and the communication style. Whichever style or combination of techniques a therapist chooses to use in psychotherapy, the relationship between child and therapist is a critical element. The relationship itself often is the primary if not the sole ingredient in psychotherapy. The therapist provides a safe space in which to listen, empathize, and solve problems with the child.

Cognitive-behavioral therapy is an amalgam of behavior therapy and cognitive psychology. It emphasizes how children may use thinking processes and cognitive modalities to reframe, restructure, and solve problems. A child's distortions are addressed by generating alternative ways of dealing with problematic situations. Cognitive-behavioral strategies have been useful in the treatment of mood disorders and anxiety disorders.

Remedial, educational, and patterning psychotherapy is focused on teaching new attitudes and patterns of behavior to children who persist in using immature and inefficient patterns that are often presumed to be due to a maturational lag. Supportive psychotherapy is particularly helpful in enabling a well-adjusted youngster to cope with emotional turmoil engendered by a crisis. It also is used with disturbed youngsters whose less-than-adequate ego functioning may be seriously disrupted by an expressive-exploratory mode or by other forms of therapeutic intervention.

At the beginning of most psychotherapy, regardless of a patient's age and the nature of the therapeutic interventions, the principal therapeutic elements perceived by patients tend to be supportive as a consequence of therapists' universal efforts to be reliably and sensitively responsive. In fact, some therapy may never proceed beyond the supportive level, whereas other therapy develops an expressive-exploratory or behavioral modification flavor on top of the supportive foundation.

Release therapy, described initially by David Levy, facilitates the abreaction of pent-up emotions. Although abreaction is an aspect of many therapeutic undertakings, in release therapy, the treatment situation is structured to encourage only this factor. It is indicated primarily for preschool-age children who have a distorted emotional reaction to an isolated trauma.

Preschool-age children are sometimes treated through the parents, a process called *filial therapy.* Therapists using the strategy should be alert to the possibility that apparently successful filial treatment can obscure a significant diagnosis because patients are not treated directly. The first case of filial therapy was that of Little Hans, reported by Freud in 1905. Hans was a 5-year-old phobic child who was treated by his father under Freud's supervision.

Psychotherapy with children often is psychoanalytically oriented: It is focused on, through the vehicle of self-understanding, enabling children to develop their potential. This development is accomplished by liberating, for constructive use, psychic energy presumed to be expended in defenses against fantasied dangers. Children generally are unaware of these unreal dangers, their fear of them, and the psychological defenses they use to avoid both the danger and the fear. With the awareness that is facilitated, patients can evaluate the usefulness of their defensive maneuvers and can relinquish unnecessary maneuvers that constitute the symptoms of their emotional disturbance.

Child psychoanalysis, an intensive, uncommon form of psychoanalytic psychotherapy, works on unconscious resistance and defenses during three to four sessions a week. Under these circumstances, therapists anticipate unconscious resistance and allow transference manifestations to mature to a full transference neurosis, through which neurotic conflicts are resolved. Interpretations of dynamically relevant conflicts are emphasized in psychoanalytic descriptions, elements that are predominant in other types of psychotherapies are not overlooked. Indeed, in all psychotherapy, children should derive support from the consistently understanding and accepting relationship with their therapists. Remedial educational guidance is provided when necessary.

Probably the most vivid examples of the integration of psychodynamic and behavioral approaches, although they are not always explicitly conceptualized as such, appear in the milieu of child and adolescent psychiatric therapy in inpatient, residential, and day treatment facilities. Behavioral change is initiated in these settings, and its repercussions are explored concurrently in individual psychotherapeutic sessions, so that the action in one arena and the information stemming from it augment and illuminate what transpires in the other arena.

Cognitive therapy has been used with children, adolescents, and adults. The approach attempts to correct cognitive distortions, particularly negative conceptions of self, and is used mainly in depressive disorders.

DIFFERENCES BETWEEN CHILDREN AND ADULTS

Logic suggests that psychotherapy with children, who generally are more flexible than adults and who have simpler defenses and other mental mechanisms, should consume less time than comparable treatment of adults. Experience usually does not confirm this expectation, because children usually lack some elements that contribute to successful treatment. A child, for example, typically does not seek help. As a consequence, one of a therapist's first tasks is to stimulate a child's motivation for treatment. Children commonly begin therapy involuntarily, often without the benefit of true parental support. Although parents may want their children to be helped or changed, the desire often is generated by frustrated anger toward the children. Typically, the anger is accompanied by relative insensitivity to what therapists perceive as the children's need and the basis for a therapeutic alliance. Therefore, whereas adult patients frequently perceive advantages in getting well, children may envision therapeutic change as nothing more than conforming to a disagreeable reality, an attitude that heightens the likelihood of their perceiving a therapist as the parent's punitive agent. This is hardly the most fertile soil in which to nurture a therapeutic alliance.

Children tend to externalize internal conflicts in search of alloplastic adaptations, and they find it difficult to conceive of problem resolution except by altering an obstructing environment. A passive, masochistic boy who is the constant butt of his schoolmates' teasing finds it inconceivable that the situation can be rectified by altering his mode of handling his aggressive impulses rather than by someone's controlling his tormentors, a view that may be reinforced by significant adults in his environment. The tendency of children to reenact their feelings in new situations facilitates the early appearance of spontaneous and global transference reactions that may be troublesome. Concurrently, children's eagerness for new experiences, coupled with their natural developmental fluidity, tends to limit the intensity and therapeutic usefulness of subsequent transference developments.

Children have a limited capacity for self-observation, with the notable exception of some obsessive children who resemble adults in this ability. Such obsessive children, however, usually isolate the vital emotional components. In exploratory-interpretative psychotherapies, the development of a capacity for ego splitting—that is, simultaneous emotional involvement and self-observation—is most helpful. Only by means of identification with a trusted adult and in alliance with this adult can children approach such an ideal. A therapist's gender and the relatively superficial aspects of the therapist's demeanor may be important elements in the development of a trusting relationship with a child.

Regressive behavioral and communicative modes can be wearing on child therapists. Typically motor-minded, even when they do not require external controls, children may demand a degree of physical stamina that is not a significant factor in therapy with adults. The age appropriateness of such primitive mechanisms as denial, projection, and isolation hinders the process of working through, which relies on a patient's synthesizing and integrating capacities, both of which are immature in children. Environmental pressures on therapists are also generally greater in psychotherapeutic work with children than in work with adults.

Although children compare unfavorably with adults in many qualities that are generally considered desirable in therapy, children have the advantage of their active maturational and developmental forces. The history of psychotherapy for children is punctuated by efforts to harness these assets and to overcome the liabilities. Recognition of the importance of play constituted a major forward stride in these efforts.

PLAYROOM

The structure, design, and furnishing of the playroom are important. Some therapists maintain that the toys should be few, simple, and carefully selected to facilitate the communication of fantasy. Other therapists suggest that a wide variety of playthings should be available to increase the range of feelings that children can express. These contrasting recommendations have been attributed to differences in therapeutic methods. Some therapists tend to avoid interpretation, even of conscious ideas, whereas others recommend the interpretation of unconscious content directly and quickly.

Therapists tend to change their preferences in equipment as they accumulate experience and develop confidence in their abilities. Although special equipment—such as genital dolls, amputation dolls, and see-through anatomically complete (except for genitalia) models—have been used in therapy, many therapists have observed that the unusual nature of such items risks making children wary and suspicious of a therapist's motives. Until dolls available to children in their own homes include genitalia, the psychological content that special dolls are designed to elicit may be more available at the appropriate time with conventional dolls.

Although the choices of play materials vary among therapists, the following equipment can constitute a well-balanced playroom or play area: multigenerational families of flexible but sturdy dolls of various races; additional dolls representing special roles and feelings, such as police officer, doctor, and soldier; dollhouse furnishings with or without a dollhouse; toy animals; puppets; paper, crayons, paint, and blunt-ended scissors; a spongelike ball; clay or something comparable; tools like rubber hammers, rubber knives, and guns; building blocks, cars, trucks, and airplanes; and eating utensils. The toys should enable children to communicate through play. Therapists should avoid toys and materials that are fragile or break easily, that can result in physical injury to a child, or that can increase a child's guilt.

Each child should have a special drawer or box, if space is available, in which to store items the child brings to the therapy session or to store projects, such as drawings and stories, for future retrieval. Limits must be set so that the private storage area is not used to hoard communal play equipment and thus deprive the other patients. Some therapists assert that absence of such arrangements evokes material about sibling rivalry; others believe that this assertion is a rationalization for not respecting children's privacy, inasmuch as sibling feelings can be expressed in other ways.

INITIAL APPROACH

Various approaches are associated with each therapist's individual style and perception of children's needs, from approaches in which a therapist endeavors to direct children's thought content and activity (release therapy, some behavior therapy, and certain educational patterning techniques) to exploratory methods in which a therapist endeavors to follow children's leads. Even though children determine the focus, therapists structure the situation. Encouraging children to say whatever they wish and to play freely, as in exploratory psychotherapy, establishes a definite structure. Therapists create an atmosphere in which they get to know all about a child—the good side as well as the bad side, as children would put it. A therapist may communicate to a child that the child's response elicits neither anger or pleasure but only understanding from the therapist. Such an assertion does not imply that therapists have no emotions, but it assures the young patient that the therapist's personal feelings and standards are subordinate to understanding the youngster.

THERAPEUTIC INTERVENTIONS

Psychotherapy with children and adolescents generally is more directed and active than it often is with adults. Children usually are unable to synthesize histories of their own lives, but they are excellent reporters of their current internal states. Even with adolescents, a therapist often takes an active role, is somewhat less open-ended than with adults, and offers more direction and advocacy than with adults. A child or adolescent therapist often makes exclamations and expresses confrontations in which the therapist directs attention to data of which patients are cognizant. A therapist may use interpretations, designed to expand patients' conscious awareness of themselves, by making explicit the elements that have previously been expressed implicitly in the patients' thoughts, feelings, and behavior. Beyond interpretation, therapists may educatively offer new information to which patients have not been exposed previously. At the most active end of the continuum are advising, counseling, and directing, which are designed to help patients adopt a course of action or a conscious attitude.

Nurturing and maintaining a therapeutic alliance may require educating children about the process of therapy. Another educational intervention may entail assigning labels to affects that have not been part of a youngster's past experience. Rarely does therapy have to compensate for a real absence of education about acceptable decorum and playing games. Children usually are not in therapy because they have never been exposed to educational efforts but because repeated educational efforts have failed. Therefore, therapy generally need not include additional teaching efforts, despite the frequent temptation to offer them.

Adults' natural educational fervor with children often is accompanied by a paradoxical tendency to protect children from learning about some of life's realities. In the past, this tendency contributed to the stork's role in childbirth, the story that people who have died are taking a long trip, and similar fairy-tale explanations about natural phenomena that adults are uncomfortable communicating to children. Although adults are more honest with children today, therapists can find themselves in situations in which their overwhelming urge to protect a hurt child may be as disadvantageous to the child as the stork myth. Alternatively, information given to the child must account for individual problems and developmental levels.

The temptation for a therapist to offer himself or herself as a model for identification may also stem from helpful educational attitudes toward children. Although this may sometimes be an appropriate therapeutic strategy, therapists should not lose sight of the pitfalls of this apparently innocuous maneuver.

PARENTS

Psychotherapy with children requires parental involvement, which does not necessarily reflect parental culpability for a youngster's emotional difficulties but is a reality of a child's dependent state. This fact cannot be stressed too much because of an occupational hazard shared by many who work with children—the urge to rescue children from their parents' negative influences, a desire that sometimes is related to an unconscious competitive desire to be a better parent than the child's or the therapist's own parents.

Parents are involved in child psychotherapy in varying degrees. For preschool-age children, the entire therapeutic effort may be directed toward the parents, without any direct treatment of the child. At the other extreme, children can be treated in psychotherapy without any parental involvement beyond the payment of fees and perhaps transporting the child to the therapy sessions. Most practitioners, however, prefer to maintain an informative alliance with parents for the purpose of obtaining additional information about the child.

Probably the most frequent parental arrangements are those developed in child guidance clinics—that is, parent guidance focused on the child or on the parent–child interaction and therapy for the parents' own individual needs concurrent with the child's therapy. Parents may be seen by their child's therapist or by someone else. Recently, there have been increasing efforts to shift the focus from the child as the primary patient to the child as the family's emissary to the clinic. In such family therapy, all or selected members of the family are treated simultaneously as a family group. Although the preferences of specific clinics and practitioners for either an individual or a family therapeutic approach may be unavoidable, the final decision regarding which therapeutic strategy or combination to use should be derived from the clinical assessment.

CONFIDENTIALITY

The issue of confidentiality takes on greater meaning as children grow older. Very young children are unlikely to be as concerned about this issue, as are adolescents. Confidentiality usually is preserved until the point at which a child is believed to be in danger or to be a danger to someone else. In other situations, a child's permission usually is sought before a specific issue is raised with parents. There are advantages to creating an atmosphere in which children can feel that all words and actions are viewed by therapists as simultaneously both serious and tentative. In other words, children's communications do not bind therapists to a commitment; nevertheless, they are too important to be communicated to a third party without a patient's permission. Although such an attitude may be conveyed implicitly, sometimes therapists should explicitly discuss confidentiality with children. The bulk of what children do and say in psychotherapy is common knowledge to the parents.

The therapist should try to enlist parents' cooperation in respecting the privacy of children's therapeutic sessions. The respect is not always readily honored, because parents are naturally curious about what transpires and they may be threatened by a therapist's apparently privileged position.

Routinely reporting to a child the essence of communications with third parties about the child underscores the therapist's reliability and respect for the child's autonomy. In certain treatments, the report may be combined with soliciting the child's guesses about these transactions. A therapist also may find it fruitful to invite children, particularly older children, to participate in discussions about them with third parties.

INDICATIONS

Psychotherapy usually is indicated for children with emotional disorders that seem to be permanent enough to impede maturational and developmental forces. Psychotherapy also may be indicated when a child's development is not impeded but is inducing reactions in the environment that are considered pathogenic. Such disharmonies ordinarily are dealt with by the child with parental assistance; however, when these efforts are persistently inadequate, psychotherapeutic interventions may be indicated.

Psychotherapy should be limited to instances in which positive indicators point to its potential usefulness. For a child to benefit from psychotherapy, the home situation must provide a certain amount of nurturance, stability, and motivation for therapy. A child must have adequate cognitive resources to participate in the process and profit from it. Psychotherapy must be judged with common sense. If a psychotherapy situation is not effective, it must be determined whether the therapist and patient are poorly matched, whether the type of psychotherapy is inappropriate to the nature of the problems, and whether the child is cognitively inappropriate for the treatment.

REFERENCES

Adams PL: *A Primer of Child Psychotherapy.* Little, Brown, Boston, 1982.

Beardslee WR, Salt P, Porterfield K, Rothberg PC, van de Velde P, Swatling S, Hoke L, Moilanen DL, Wheelock I: Comparison of preventive interventions for families with parental affective disorder. J Am Acad Child Adolesc Psychiatry *32:* 254, 1993.

Berlin LN: Some transference and countertransference issues in the playroom. J Am Acad Child Adolesc Psychiatry *26:* 101, 1987.

Cohen JA, Mannarino AP: A treatment model for sexually abused preschoolers. J Interpers Violence *8:* 115, 1993.

Eyberg SM: Assessing therapy outcome with preschool children: Progress and problems. J Clin Child Psychol *21:* 306, 1992.

Fonagy P, Target M: The efficacy of psychoanalysis for children with disruptive behavior disorders. J Am Acad Child Adolesc Psychiatry *33:* 45, 1994.

Forehand R, Wierson M: The role of developmental factors in planning behavioral interventions for children: Disruptive behavior as an example. Behav Ther *24:* 117, 1993.

Gabel S, Bemporad JR: Variations in countertransference reactions in psychotherapy with children. Am J Psychother *48:* 11, 1994.

Kazdin AE: Effectiveness of psychotherapy with children and adolescents. J Consult Clin Psychol *59:* 785, 1991.

Kazdin AE: Psychotherapy for children and adolescents: Current progress and future research directions. Am Psychol *48:* 644, 1993.
Kendall PC, Morris RJ: Child therapy: Issues and recommendations. J Consult Clin Psychol *59:* 777, 1991.
Kernberg PF: A reevaluation of estimates of child therapy effectiveness: Discussion. J Am Acad Child Adolesc Psychiatry *31:* 710, 1992.
Kernberg PF, Chazan SE, Frankel A, Hariton JR, Kruger RS, Scholl H: *Children with Conduct Disorders: A Psychotherapy Manual.* Basic Books, New York, 1991.
Leichtman M: Psychotherapeutic interventions with brain-injured children and their families: II. Psychotherapy. Bull Menninger Clin *56:* 338, 1992.
Mullins LL, Olson RA, Chaney JM: A social learning/family systems approach to the treatment of somatoform disorders in children and adolescents. Fam Syst Med *10:* 201, 1992.
Ronen T: Cognitive therapy with young children. Child Psychiatry Hum Dev *23:* 19, 1992.
Shapiro T, Esman A: Psychoanalysis and child and adolescent psychiatry. J Am Acad Child Adolesc Psychiatry *31:* 6, 1992.
Shirk SR, Phillips JS: Child therapy training: Closing the gaps with research and practice. J Consult Clin Psychol *59:* 766, 1991.
Shirk SR, Russell RL: A reevaluation of estimates of child therapy effectiveness. J Am Acad Child Adolesc Psychiatry *31:* 703, 1992.
Shirk SR, Saiz CC: Clinical, empirical, and developmental perspectives on the therapeutic relationship in child psychotherapy. Dev Psychopathol *4:* 713, 1992.
Sholevar GP, Burland JA, Frank JL, Etezady MH, Goldstein J: Psychoanalytic treatment of children and adolescents. J Am Acad Child Adolesc Psychiatry *28:* 685, 1989.
Target M, Fonagy P: The efficacy of psychoanalysis for children with emotional disorders. J Am Child Adolesc Psychiatry *33:* 361, 1994.
Weiss JR, Weiss B, Donenberg GR: The lab versus the clinic: Effects of child and adolescent psychotherapy. Am Psychol *47:* 1578, 1992.

▲ 52.2 Group Psychotherapy

Group therapy is an effective modality in which to address issues of interpersonal style, peer relationships, and social skills. Group psychotherapy can be modified to suit groups of children in various age groups and can focus on behavioral, educational, and social skills and on psychodynamic issues. The mode in which the group functions depends on children's developmental levels, intelligence, and problems to be addressed. In behaviorally oriented groups, the group leader is a directive, active participant who facilitates prosocial interactions and desired behaviors. In groups using psychodynamic approaches, the leader may monitor interpersonal interactions less actively than in behavior therapy groups.

Groups are highly effective in providing peer feedback and support to children who are either socially isolated or unaware of their effects on their peers. Groups with very young children generally are highly structured by the leader and use imagination and play to foster socially acceptable peer relationships and positive behavior. Therapists must be keenly aware of the level of children's attention span and the need for consistency and limit setting. Leaders of preschool-age groups can model supportive adult behavior in meaningful ways for children who have been deprived or neglected. School-age children's groups may be single sex or may include both boys and girls. School-age children are more sophisticated in verbalizing their feelings than preschoolers, but they also benefit from structured therapeutic games. Children of school age need frequent reminders about rules, and they are quick to point out infractions of the rules to each other. Interpersonal skills can be addressed nicely in group settings with school-age children.

Among early adolescents, same-sex groups are often used. In early adolescence, physiological changes and the new demands of high school lead to stress that may be ameliorated when groups of same-age peers compare and share. In older adolescence, groups more often include both boys and girls. Even with older adolescents, the leader often uses structure and direct intervention to maximize the therapeutic value of the group. Adolescents who are feeling dejected or alienated may find a special sense of belonging in a therapy group.

PRESCHOOL-AGE AND EARLY SCHOOL-AGE GROUPS

Work with a preschool-age group usually is structured by a therapist through the use of a particular technique, such as puppets or artwork, or is couched in terms of a permissive play atmosphere. In therapy with puppets, children project their fantasies onto the puppets in a way not unlike ordinary play. The main value lies in the cathexis afforded children, especially if they show difficulty in expressing their feelings. Here, the group aids the child less by interaction with other members than by action with the puppets.

In play group therapy, the emphasis rests on children's interactional qualities with each other and with the therapist in the permissive playroom setting. A therapist should be a person who can allow children to produce fantasies verbally and in play but who can also use active restraint when children undergo excessive tension. The toys are the traditional ones used in individual play therapy. The children use the toys to act out aggressive impulses and to relive their home difficulties with group members and with the therapist. The children selected for group treatment have a common social hunger and need to be like their peers and to be accepted by them. The children selected for group psychotherapy usually include those with phobias, effeminate boys, shy and withdrawn children, and children with disruptive behavior disorders.

Modifications of these criteria have been used in group psychotherapy for autistic children, parent group therapy, and art therapy. A modification of group psychotherapy has been used for toddlers with physical disabilities who show speech and language delays. The experience of twice-a-week group activities involves mothers and children in a mutual teaching-learning setting. This experience has proved effective for mothers who received supportive psychotherapy in the group experience; their formerly hidden fantasies about their children emerged and were dealt with therapeutically.

LATENCY-AGE GROUPS

Activity group psychotherapy is based on the idea that poor and divergent experiences have led to deficits in children's appropriate personality development; therefore, corrective experiences in a therapeutically conditioned environment modify them. Because some latency-age children have deep disturbances involving fears, high anxiety levels, and guilt, a modification of activity-interview group psychotherapy has evolved. The format uses interview techniques, verbal explanations of fantasies, group play, work, and other communications. In this type of group psychotherapy, children verbalize in a problem-oriented manner, with the awareness that problems brought them together and that the group aims to change them. They report dreams, fantasies, daydreams, and traumatic and unpleasant experiences. Open discussion includes both the experiences and the group behavior.

Therapists vary in their use of time, cotherapists, food, and materials. Most groups meet after school for at least 1 hour, although other group leaders prefer a 90-minute session. Some therapists serve food during the last 10 minutes; others prefer serving times when the children are together for talking. Food, however, does not become a major feature and is never central to the group's activities.

PUBERTAL AND ADOLESCENT GROUPS

Group therapy methods similar to those used in latency-age groups can be used with pubertal children, who are often grouped monosexually. Their problems resemble those of late latency-age children, but they are also beginning, especially the girls, to feel the effects and pressures of early adolescence. Groups offer help during a transitional period; they seem to satisfy the social appetite of preadolescents, who compensate for feelings of inferiority and self-doubt by forming groups. This therapy takes advantage of the influence of the socialization process during these years. Because pubertal children experience difficulties in conceptualizing, pubertal therapy groups tend to use play, drawing, psychodrama, and other nonverbal modes of expression. The therapist's role is active and directive.

Activity group psychotherapy has been the recommended group therapy for pubertal children who do not have significantly disturbed personality patterns. The children, usually of the same sex and in groups of not more than eight, freely engage in activities in a setting especially designed and planned for its physical and environmental characteristics. Samuel Slavson, a pioneer in group psychotherapy, pictured the group as a substitute family in which the passive, neutral therapist becomes the surrogate for parents. The therapist assumes various roles, mostly in a nonverbal manner, as each child interacts with the therapist and other group members. Currently, however, therapists tend to see the group as a form of peer group, with its attendant socializing processes, rather than as a reenactment of the family.

Late adolescents, 16 years of age and older, often may be included in groups of adults. Group therapy has been useful in the treatment of substance-related disorders. Combined therapy (the use of group and individual therapy) also has been used successfully with adolescents.

OTHER GROUP SITUATIONS

Groups are also helpful in more focused treatments, such as specific social skills training for children with attention-deficit/hyperactivity disorder, and for children with bereavement problems or eating disorders. In these more specialized groups, the issues are more specific, and actual tasks (as in social skills groups) may be practiced within the group. Some residential and day treatment units use group psychotherapy techniques. Group psychotherapy in schools for underachievers and for children from low socioeconomic levels has relied on reinforcement and on modeling theory, in addition to traditional techniques, and has been supplemented by parent groups.

In controlled conditions, residential treatment units have been used for specific studies in group psychotherapy, such as behavioral contracting. Behavioral contracting with reward–punishment reinforcement provides positive reinforcements among preadolescent boys with severe concerns in basic trust, low self-esteem, and dependence conflicts. Somewhat akin to formal residential treatment units are social group work homes. For children who undergo many psychological assaults before placement, supportive group psychotherapy offers ventilation and catharsis, but more often it succeeds in letting children become aware of the enjoyment of sharing activities and developing skills.

Public schools—also a structured environment, although not usually considered the best site for group psychotherapy—have been used by several workers. Group psychotherapy as group counseling readily lends itself to school settings. One such group used gender- and problem-homogeneous selection for groups of six to eight students, who met once a week during school hours over 2 to 3 years.

INDICATIONS

Many indications exist for the use of group psychotherapy as a treatment modality. Some indications are situational; a therapist may work in a reformatory setting, in which group psychotherapy seems to reach adolescents better than does individual treatment. Another indication is time economics; more patients can be reached in a given time by the use of groups than by individual therapy. Group therapy best helps a child at a given age and developmental stage and with a given type of problem. In young age groups, children's social hunger and their potential need for peer acceptance help determine their suitability for group therapy. Criteria for unsuitability are controversial and have been loosened progressively.

PARENT GROUPS

In group psychotherapy, as in most treatment procedures for children, parental difficulties present obstacles. Sometimes, uncooperative parents refuse to bring a child or to participate in their own therapy. The extreme of this situation reveals itself when severely disturbed parents use a child as their channel of communication to work out their own needs. In such circumstances, a child is in the intolerable position of receiving positive group experiences that seem to create havoc at home.

Parent groups, therefore, can be a valuable aid to group psychotherapy for their children. Parents of children in therapy often have difficulty in understanding the nature of children's ailments, in discerning the line of demarcation between normal and pathological behavior, in relating to the medical establishment, and in coping with feelings of guilt. Parent groups assist in these areas and help members formulate guidelines for action.

REFERENCES

Abramowitz CV: The effectiveness of group psychotherapy with children. Arch Gen Psychiatry *33:* 320, 1976.

Blotcky M, Sheinbein M, Wiggins K, Forgotson J: A verbal group technique for ego-disturbed children: Action to words. Int J Psychoanal Psychother *8:* 203, 1980.
Bromfield R, Pfeifer G: Combining group and individual psychotherapy: Impact on the individual treatment experience. J Am Acad Child Adolesc Psychiatry *27:* 220, 1988.
Cerda RA, Nemiroff HW, Richmond AH: Therapeutic group approaches in an inpatient facility for children and adolescents: A 15-year perspective. Group *15:* 71, 1991.
Chase JL: Inpatient adolescent and latency-age children's perspectives on the curative factors in group psychotherapy. Group *15:* 95, 1991.
Clifford MW: A model for group therapy with latency-age boys. Group *15:* 116, 1991.
Garland JA: The establishment of individual and collective competency in children's groups as a prelude to entry into intimacy, disclosure, and bonding. Int J Group Psychother *42:* 395, 1992.
Kraft IA: Group therapy. In *Basic Handbook of Child Psychiatry,* JD Noshpitz, editor, vol 3, p 159. Basic Books, New York, 1979.
Kraft IA: Some special considerations in adolescent group psychotherapy. Int J Group Psychother *11:* 196, 1961.
Kymissis P, Licamele WL, Boots S, Kessler E: Training in child and adolescent group therapy: Two surveys and a model. Group *15:* 163, 1991.
Schamess G: Reflections on a developing body of group-as-a-whole theory for children's therapy groups: An introduction. Int J Group Psychother *42:* 351, 1992.
Scheidlinger S: An overview of nine decades of group psychotherapy. Hosp Community Psychiatry *45:* 217, 1994.
Scheidlinger S: Group treatment of adolescents. Am J Orthopsychiatry *55:* 102, 1985.
Scheidlinger S: Short-term group psychotherapy for children: An overview. Int J Group Psychother *34:* 573, 1984.
Slavson SR, Schiffer M: *Group Psychotherapies for Children.* International Universities Press, New York, 1985.
Suger M: Research in child and adolescent group psychotherapy. J Child Adolesc Group Ther *3:* 207, 1993.
Trad PV: Diagnostic peer group assessments in preschoolers with anxiety disorders. J Child Adolesc Group Ther *3:* 207, 1992.
Yalom ID: *Inpatient Group Psychotherapy.* Basic Books, New York, 1983.
Zimpfer DG: Group work with juvenile delinquents. J Spec Group Work *17:* 116, 1992.

▲ 52.3 Residential, Day, and Hospital Treatment

Residential treatment centers and facilities are appropriate settings for children and adolescents with mental disorders, who require a highly structured and supervised setting for a substantial time. Such settings have the advantage of providing a stable, consistent environment with a high level of psychiatric monitoring but less intensive than in a hospital. Children and adolescents with serious psychiatric disturbances often end up in residential facilities because of difficulties in managing their own psychiatric problems and because of family situations in which appropriate supervision and parenting are impossible. Residential settings offer many treatments, including behavioral management, psychotherapy, medication, special education, and the therapeutic milieu itself. Children and adolescents who benefit from residential settings have a wide variety of psychiatric problems and commonly have difficulties with impulse control and structuring their own time. Many residents of such programs also have families with serious psychiatric, financial, and parenting difficulties.

Day treatment programs are excellent alternatives for children and adolescents, who require more intensive support, monitoring, and supervision than is available in the community but are able to live successfully at home if they receive the proper level of intervention. In most cases, children and adolescents who attend day hospital programs have serious mental disorders and might warrant psychiatric hospitalization without the programs support. Family therapy, group and individual psychotherapy, psychopharmacology, behavioral management programs, and special education are integral parts of these programs.

Psychiatric hospitalization is needed when a child or an adolescent exhibits dangerous behavior, is contemplating suicide, or is experiencing an exacerbation of a psychotic disorder or another serious mental disorder. Safety, stabilization, and effective treatment are the goals of hospitalization. Recently, the length of stay for child and adolescent psychiatric patients has decreased because of financial pressures and increased availability of day treatment programs. Psychiatric hospitalization may be some children's first opportunity to experience a stable, safe environment. Hospitals often are the most appropriate places to start new medications, and they provide an around-the-clock setting in which to observe a child's behavior. Children may show a remission of some symptoms by virtue of their removal from a stressful or abusive environment. After a child has been observed for several weeks, the best treatment and disposition may become clear.

RESIDENTIAL TREATMENT

More than 20,000 emotionally disturbed children are in residential treatment centers in the United States, and this number is increasing. Deteriorating social conditions, particularly in cities, often make it impossible for a child with a serious mental disorder to live at home. In these cases, residential treatment centers serve a real need. They provide a structured living environment in which children may form strong attachments to and receive commitments from staff members. The purpose of the center is to provide treatment and special education for children and their families.

Staff and Setting

Staffing patterns include various combinations of child care workers, teachers, social workers, psychiatrists, pediatricians, nurses, and psychologists; therefore, residential treatment can be very expensive. The Joint Commission on the Mental Health of Children made the following structural and setting recommendations: In addition to space for therapy programs, there should be facilities for a first-rate school and a rich evening activity program, and there should be ample space for play, both indoors and out. Facilities should be small, seldom exceeding 60 patients in capacity with a limit of 100 patients, and they should make provisions for children to live in small groups. The centers should be located near the families they serve and should be readily accessible by public transportation. They should be located for ready access to special medical and educational services and to various community resources, including consultants. The centers should be open institutions whenever possible; locked buildings, wards, or rooms should be required only rarely. In designing residential programs, the guiding principle should be that children should be removed from their normal life settings the least possible distance in space, in time, and in the psychological texture of the experience.

Indications

Most children who are referred for residential treatment have had multiple evaluations by professionals such as school psychologists, outpatient psychotherapists, juvenile court officials, or state welfare agency staff. Attempts at outpatient treatment and foster home placement usually precede residential treatment. Sometimes, the severity of a child's problems or the inability of a family to provide for the child's needs prohibits sending a child home. Many children sent to residential treatment centers have disruptive behavior problems in addition to other problems, including mood disorders and psychotic disorders. In some cases, serious psychosocial problems such as physical or sexual abuse, neglect, indigence, or homelessness necessitate out-of-home placement. The age range of the children varies among institutions, but most children are between 5 and 15 years of age. Boys are referred more frequently than are girls.

An initial review of data enables the intake staff to determine whether a particular child is likely to benefit from the treatment program; often, for every child accepted for admission, three are rejected. The next step usually is interviews with the child and the parents by various staff members, such as a therapist, a group-living worker, and a teacher. Psychological testing and neurological examinations are given, when indicated, if they have not already been performed. The child and parents should be prepared for these interviews.

Group Living

Most of a child's time in a residential treatment setting is spent in group living. The group-living staff consists of child care workers who offer a structured environment that forms a therapeutic milieu; the environment places boundaries and limitations on the children. Tasks are defined within the limits of children's abilities; incentives, such as additional privileges, encourage them to progress rather than regress. In milieu therapy, the environment is structured, limits are set, and a therapeutic atmosphere is maintained.

The children often select one or more staff members with whom to form a relationship; through this relationship, they express, consciously and unconsciously, many of their feelings about their parents. The child care staff should be trained to recognize such transference reactions and to respond to them in a way that is different from the children's expectations, which are based on their previous or even current relationships with their parents.

To maintain consistency and balance, the group-living staff members must communicate freely and regularly with each other and with the other professional and administrative staff members of the residential setting, particularly the children's teachers and therapists. The child care staff members must recognize any tendencies toward becoming the good (or bad) parent in response to a child's splitting behavior. This tendency may be manifest as a pattern of blaming other staff members for a child's disruptive behavior. Similarly, the child care staff must recognize and avoid such individual and group countertransference reactions as sadomasochistic and punitive behavior toward a child.

The structured setting should offer a corrective emotional experience and opportunities for facilitating and improving children's adaptive behavior, particularly when such problems as speech and language deficits, intellectual retardation, inadequate peer relationships, bed-wetting, poor feeding habits, and attention deficits are present. Some attention deficits are the basis of a child's poor academic performance and unsocialized behavior, including temper tantrums, fighting, and withdrawal.

Behavior modification principles also have been used, particularly in group work with children. Behavior therapy is part of a residential center's total therapeutic effort.

Education

Children in residential treatment frequently have severe learning disorders, disruptive behavior, and attention-deficit disorders. Usually, the children cannot function in a regular community school and consequently need a special on-grounds school. A major goal of the on-grounds school is to motivate children to learn. The educational process in residential treatment is complex; Table 52.3–1 shows some of its components.

Therapy

Most residential facilities use a basic behavior modification program to set guidelines and to give the residents a concrete sense of how to earn privileges. These behavioral programs range in detail and intensity. Some programs operate with level systems that are associated with privileges and responsibilities. Some programs use a token economy system in which residents earn points for appropriate behavior and for meeting specific goals. In most programs, the program includes basic tasks of living as well as specific therapeutic goals for the residents.

Psychotherapy offered in the program generally is supportive and oriented toward reunion with the family when possible. Insight-oriented psychotherapy is included when it can be used by a resident.

Parents

Concomitant work with parents is essential. Children usually have a strong tie to at least one parent, no matter how disturbed the parent may be. Sometimes, a child idealizes the parent, who repeatedly fails the child. Other times, the parent has an ambivalent or unrealistic expectation that the child will return home. In some instances, the parent must be helped to enable the child to live in another setting when it is in the child's best interest. Most residential treatment centers offer individual or group therapy for parents, couples or marital therapy, and in some cases, conjoint family therapy.

DAY TREATMENT

The concept of daily comprehensive therapeutic experiences that do not require removing children from their homes or families is derived partly from experiences with a therapeutic nursery school. Day hospital programs for children were then developed, and the number of programs continues to grow.

Table 52.3–1
Education Process in Residential Treatment

Preentry Assessment →	Intervention Program Planning ↔		Evaluation Reevaluation →	Educational Placement →	Follow-up
Nature of emotional conflict	Educational skill development	—Anxiety reduction program	Weekly staff meetings	Regular school	
Nature of learning difficulties	—Remedial reading —Basic skill development —Perceptual motor and impulse–control teaching —Arts and crafts skills —Music skills —Total group project —Academic skills built on six instructional cycles of 25 days in which assessment diagnosis, individual objectives and prescription, and new objectives or alternatives are planned	—Supportive adult relationships —Stable, trusted models —Life-space interviewing —Individual psychotherapy —Removal from classroom area —Guidance room standardized —Quiet room safety in unit	Interdisciplinary meetings and conferences Daily teacher reports Psychological testing Continuous criterion testing Semiannual educational testing Semiannual total staff evaluation	Special class Private school State institution	

Courtesy of Melvin Lewis, M.B., B.S. (London), F.R.C.Psych., D.C.H.

The main advantages of day treatment are that children remain with their families and the families can be more involved in day treatment than they are in residential or hospital treatment. Day treatment also is much less expensive than residential treatment. At the same time, the risks of day treatment are a child's social isolation and confinement to a narrow band of social contacts in the program's disturbed peer population.

Indications

The primary indication for day treatment is the need for a more structured, intensive, and specialized treatment program than can be provided on an outpatient basis. At the same time, the home in which the child is living should be able to provide an environment that is at least not destructive to the child's development. Children who are likely to benefit from day treatment may have a wide range of diagnoses, including autistic disorder, conduct disorder, attention-deficit/hyperactivity disorder, and mental retardation. Exclusion symptoms include behavior that is likely to be destructive to the children themselves or to others under the treatment conditions. Therefore, some children who threaten to run away, set fires, attempt suicide, hurt others, or disrupt to a significant degree the lives of their families while they are at home may not be suitable for day treatment.

Programs

The same ingredients that lead to a successful residential treatment program apply to day treatment. These ingredients include clear administrative leadership, team collaboration, open communication, and an understanding of children's behavior. Indeed, having a single agency offer both residential and day treatment has advantages.

A major function of child care staff in day treatment for psychiatrically disturbed children is to provide positive experiences and a structure that enables the children and their families to internalize controls and to function better than in the past regarding themselves and the outside world. Again, the methods used are essentially similar to those in full residential treatment programs.

Because the ages, needs, and range of diagnoses of children who may benefit from some form of day treatment vary, many day treatment programs have been developed. Some programs specialize in special educational and structured environmental needs of mentally retarded children. Others offer special therapeutic efforts required to treat children with autism and schizophrenia. Still other programs provide the total spectrum of treatment usually found in full residential treatment, of which they may be a part. Children may move from one part of the program to another and may be in residential treatment or day treatment according to their needs. The school program always is a major component of day treatment, and psychiatric treatment varies according to a child's needs and diagnosis.

Results

Recently, attempts have been made to analyze the treatment outcome of day treatment and partial hospitalization. There are many different dimensions to analyzing overall benefits of such programs. Assessment of level of improvement in clinical status, academic progress, peer relationships, community interactions (legal difficulties), and family relationships are some pertinent areas to measure. In a recent follow-up 1 year after discharge from a partial hospital program, patients compared at admission and at 1 year postdischarge showed improvement in clinical symptoms to a statistically significant degree on each subscale of the Child Behavior Checklist except for sex problems. These improvements included mood symptoms, somatic complaints, attention problems, thought problems, delinquent behavior, and aggressive behavior. The assessment of long-term effectiveness of day treatment is fraught with difficulties, from the point of view of a child's maintenance of gains, a therapist's view of psychological gains, or cost–benefit ratios.

At the same time, the advantage of day treatment has encouraged further development of programs. Moreover, the lessons learned from day treatment programs have moved mental health disciplines toward having services follow children, rather than perpetuating discontinuities of care. The experiences of day treatment for psychiatric conditions of children and adolescents have also encouraged pediatric hospitals and departments to adopt a model that promotes continuity of care for the medical treatment of children with chronic physical illnesses.

HOSPITAL TREATMENT

Beginning in the 1920s, inpatient psychiatric treatment of children includes two types of units: acute-care hospital units and long-term hospital units. Acute-care units generally accept children who exhibit dangerous (suicidal, assaultive, or psychotically disorganized) behavior. Diagnosis, stabilization, and formulation and initiation of a treatment plan are the goals of acute-care units. Disposition usually is to home, to residential treatment centers, or to long-term (usually state) hospitals for continued care. Acute-care hospitalization generally lasts from 6 to 12 weeks and often is extended because of the wait for beds in residential treatment centers and state hospitals.

Long-term hospitalization generally lasts many months to years. The staffs of inpatient units are interdisciplinary and include psychiatrists, psychologists, social workers, nurses, activity therapists, and teachers.

REFERENCES

Ascherman LI: The impact of unstructured games of fantasy and role playing on an inpatient unit for adolescents. Int J Group Psychother *43:* 335, 1993.

Bishop EG, McNally G: An in-home crisis intervention program for children and their families. Hosp Community Psychiatry *44:* 182, 1993.

Costello AJ, Dulcan MK, Kalas R: A checklist of hospitalization criteria for use with children. Hosp Community Psychiatry *42:* 823, 1991.

Evangelakis MG: A *Manual for Residential and Day Treatment of Children.* Thomas, Springfield, IL, 1974.

Gold J, Shera D, Clarkson B: Private psychiatric hospitalization of children: Predictors of length of stay. J Am Acad Child Adolesc Psychiatry *32:* 135, 1993.

Grizenko N, Papineau D, Sayegh L: Effectiveness of a multimodal day treatment program for children with disruptive behavior problems. J Am Acad Child Adolesc Psychiatry *32:* 127, 1993.

Hunger DS, Webster CD, Konstantareas MM, Sloman L: Ten years later: What becomes of the psychiatrically disturbed child in day treatment. J Child Care *1:* 45, 1982.

Kayser JA, Teitelman M: Design and implementation of a continuum of care for children and youth in private mental health settings. Continuum *1:* 15, 1994.

Kiser LJ, Heston JD, Millsap PA, Pruitt DB: Testing the limits: Special treatment procedures for child and adolescent partial hospitalization. Int J Partial Hosp *7:* 37, 1991.

Kiser LJ, Millsap PA, Hickerson S, Heston JD, Nunn W, Pruitt DB, Rohr M: Results of treatment one year later: Child and adolescent partial hospitalization. J Am Acad Child Adolesc Psychiatry *35:* 81, 1996.

Lewis M, Lewis DO, Shanok SS, Klatskin E, Osborn JR: The undoing of residential treatment. J Am Acad Child Adolesc Psychiatry *19:* 160, 1980.

Lundy M, Pumariega AJ: Psychiatric hospitalization of children and adolescents: Treatment in search of a rationale. J Child Family Stud *2:* 1, 1993.

Lyman RD, Prentice-Dunn S, Gabel S, editors: *Residential and Inpatient Treatment of Children and Adolescents.* Plenum, New York, 1989.

Mikkelsen EJ, Bereika GM, McKenzie JC: Short-term family-based residential treatment: An alternative to psychiatric hospitalization for children. Am J Orthopsychiatry *63:* 28, 1993.

Nurcombe B: Goal-directed treatment planning and the principles of brief hospitalization. J Am Acad Child Adolesc Psychiatry *28:* 26, 1989.

Perrin EC: Children in hospitals. J Dev Behav Pediatr *14:* 50, 1993.

Pfeiffer SI, Strzelecki SC: Inpatient psychiatric treatment of children and adolescents: A review of outcome studies. J Am Acad Child Adolesc Psychiatry *29:* 847, 1990.

Prentice-Dunn S, Wilson DR, Lyman RD: Client factors related to outcome in a residential and day treatment program for children. J Clin Child Psychol *10:* 188, 1981.

Zang LD: The antisocial aggressive school-age child: Day hospitals. In *Handbook of Treatment of Mental Disorders and Adolescence,* B Wolman, J Egan, A Ross, editors, p 317. Prentice-Hall, Englewood Cliffs, NJ, 1978.

Zimet SG, Farley GK: Academic achievement of children with emotional disorders treated in a day hospital program: An outcome study. Child Psychiatry Hum Dev *23:* 183, 1993.

▲ 52.4 Biological Therapies

PHARMACOTHERAPY

In the 1990s, there are many important interests and concerns about child and adolescent psychopharmacotherapy, including the use of serotonin-specific reuptake inhibitors (SSRIs) in the treatment of depressive disorders, obsessive-compulsive disorders, and other syndromes. At least one double-blind, placebo-controlled study showed the efficacy of fluoxetine (Prozac) in treating child and adolescent depression. The tricyclic antidepressants have significantly decreased in frequency of use since SSRIs appeared on the market, mainly because of the potentially less serious risks of SSRIs compared with tricyclic antidepressants. Fluoxetine (Prozac), sertraline (Zoloft), paroxetine (Paxil), fluvoxamine (Luvox), and nefazodone (Serzone) are being relatively frequently used with children and adolescents. Concern has increased about the safety of medications, particularly tricyclic drugs, the cardiotoxicity of which may have contributed to the sudden deaths of four children who were taking desipramine (Norpramin, Pertofrane) as part of the treatment of attention-deficit/hyperactivity disorder. Another medication commonly used to treat attention-deficit/hyperactivity disorder as well as depressive disorders is bupropion (Wellbutrin).

The management of severe aggression, disruptive behavior, and attention-deficit/hyperactivity disorders remains a challenge. Multiple drugs are sometimes used in these cases, although few studies attest to the efficacy or safety of drug combinations. Newer antipsychotic medications such as clozapine (Clozaril) and risperidone (Risperdal) have enabled a wider range of treatment-resistant patients to benefit from neuroleptic treatment. Risperidone is also considered to be a drug with less extrapyramidal side effects and less potential for the eventual development of tardive dyskinesia. The goals of pediatric psychopharmacotherapy have not changed: One aim is to decrease maladaptive behaviors and promote adaptive behaviors in such areas as school performance. To this end, clinicians must try to avoid cognitive dulling. The medications used in pediatric psychopharmacotherapy often are associated with a specific disorder or with target symptoms that appear in several disorders. For example, haloperidol (Haldol) is used to treat Tourette's disorder and severe aggression, which may occur in many disorders.

Therapeutic Considerations

An evaluation for psychopharmacotherapy must first include an assessment of a child's psychopathology and physical condition to rule out any predisposition for side effects (Table 52.4–1). An assessment of the child's caregivers focuses on their ability to provide a safe and consistent environment in which a clinician can conduct a drug trial. The physician must consider the benefit–risk ratio and must explain it to the patient, if he or she is old enough, and to the child's caregivers and others (for example, child welfare workers) who may be involved in the decision to medicate.

The clinician must obtain baseline ratings before medicating. Behavioral rating scales help objectify the child's response to medication. The physician generally starts at a low dose and titrates upward on the basis of the child's response and the appearance of adverse effects. Optimal drug trials cannot be rushed (for example, by insurance-imposed inadequately short hospital stays or by infrequent outpatient visits), nor can drug trials be prolonged by the physician's insufficient contact with the patient and the caregivers. The success of drug trials often hinges on the physician's daily accessibility.

Table 52.4–1
Diagnostic Processes of Biological Therapy

1. Diagnostic evaluation
2. Symptom measurement
3. Risk–benefit ratio analysis
4. Establishment of a contract for therapy
5. Periodic reevaluation
6. Termination and tapered drug withdrawal

Childhood Pharmacokinetics

Children, compared with adults, have greater hepatic capacity, more glomerular filtration, and less fatty tissue. Therefore, stimulants, antipsychotics, and tricyclic drugs are eliminated more rapidly by children than by adults; lithium (Eskalith) may be eliminated more rapidly, and children may have less ability to store drugs in their fat. Because of children's quick elimination, the half-lives of many medications may be shorter in children than in adults.

Little evidence indicates that clinicians can predict a child's blood level from the dosage or a treatment response from the plasma level. Relatively low serum levels of haloperidol seem to be adequate to treat Tourette's disorder in children. No correlation is seen between the methylphenidate (Ritalin) serum level and a child's response. The data are incomplete and conflicting about major depressive disorder and serum levels of tricyclic drugs. A serum-level-to-response relation has been found for tricyclic drugs in the treatment of enuresis.

With lithium therapy, a saliva-to-serum-lithium ratio can be established for a child by averaging three to four individual ratios. The average ratio can then be used to convert subsequent saliva levels to serum levels and thus avoid some venipunctures in children who are stressed by blood tests. As with serum levels, regular clinical monitoring for adverse effects is necessary. Table 52.4–2 lists representative drugs and their indications, dosages, adverse reactions, and monitoring requirements.

Indications

Mental Retardation. The psychopharmacotherapy for mental retardation most often addresses behavioral problems, especially aggression, and the coexistence of other mental disorders. Medications are overused to control the behavior of institutionalized children who are retarded because other therapies and services are not available. For severe aggression, antipsychotics are most commonly used, and cognitive dulling can best be avoided with high-potency drugs. β-Adrenergic receptor antagonists have reduced aggression in uncontrolled studies of adults and children with mental retardation. Lithium and anticonvulsants such as carbamazepine (Tegretol) may also be tried.

Antipsychotics have the advantage of a fast onset of action and little need for laboratory monitoring of their adverse effects, but the use of other drugs eliminates the risk for tardive dyskinesia.

The endogenous opioid antagonists, such as naltrexone (ReVia), and the SSRIs, such as fluoxetine, reduce self-injurious behavior in some patients with mental retardation. When attention-deficit/hyperactivity disorder coexists with mental retardation, methylphenidate often is effective, and a small study showed behavioral improvements with fenfluramine (Pondimin).

Recent attempts have been made to treat the behavioral problems associated with fragile X syndrome with folic acid supplements. Some prepubescent children experienced less active or less aggressive behavior and concentrated better when they took folic acid than they did before treatment.

Learning Disorders. No pharmacological agent significantly improves any learning disorder, but many children with other mental disorders also have learning disorders, and many who have learning disorders also have behavioral problems. These associations and the importance of school and learning in children's lives raise questions about the cognitive effects of psychotropics. Table 52.4–3 summarizes the effects of drugs on cognitive tests of learning functions. In children with learning disorders but no other mental disorder, methylphenidate facilitates performance on several standard cognitive, psycholinguistic, memory, and vigilance tests but does not improve children's academic achievement ratings or teacher ratings. Cognitive impairment from psychotropic drugs, especially antipsychotics, may be an even greater problem for people who are mentally retarded than for those with learning disorders.

Autistic Disorder. The behavioral problems of children with autistic disorder can be extreme. In short-term and long-term studies, haloperidol, often in nonsedating dosages, has proved to be efficacious in reducing temper tantrums, ag-

Table 52.4–2
Common Psychoactive Drugs in Childhood and Adolescence

Drugs	Indications	Dosage	Adverse Reactions and Monitoring
Antipsychotics—also known as major tranquilizers, neuroleptics; divided into (1) high-potency, low-dosage, eg, haloperidol (Haldol), trifluoperazine (Stelazine), thiothixene (Navane); (2) low-potency, high-dosage (more sedating), eg, chlorpromazine (Thorazine), thioridazine (Mellaril); (3) clozapine (Clozaril); and (4) risperidone (Risperdal)	Psychoses; agitated, aggressive, self-injurious behaviors in mental retardation (MR), pervasive developmental disorders (PDD), and conduct disorder (CD) Studies support following indications: Haloperidol—schizophrenia, PDD, CD with severe aggression, Tourette's disorder Clozapine—refractory schizophrenia in adolescence Risperidone—anecdotal reports of success in PDD	All can be given in 2 to 4 divided doses or combined into one dose after gradual buildup Haloperidol—child 0.5–6 mg a day, adolescent 0.5–6 mg a day Thiothixene—5–42 mg a day Chlorpromazine and thioridazine—child, 10–200 mg a day; adolescent 50–600 mg a day, over 16 years of age, 100–700 mg a day Clozapine—dosage not determined in children; 600 mg a day in adolescents Risperidone—1–3 mg a day in several children with PDD	Sedation, weight gain, hypotension, lowered seizure threshold, constipation, extrapyramidal symptoms, jaundice, agranulocytosis, dystonic reaction, tardive dyskinesia; with clozapine, no extrapyramidal adverse effects Monitor: blood pressure, complete blood count (CBC), liver function tests (LFTs), electroencephalogram (EEG), if indicated; with thioridazine pigmentary retinopathy is rare but dictates ceiling of 800 mg in adults and proportionately lower in children; with clozapine weekly white blood counts (WBCs) for development of agranulocytosis and EEG monitoring due to lowering of seizure threshold
Stimulants Dextroamphetamine (Dexedrine) FDA approved for children 3 years and older Methylphenidate (Ritalin) and pemoline (Cylert) FDA approved for children 6 years and older	In attention-deficit/hyperactivity disorder (ADHD) for hyperactivity, impulsivity, and inattentiveness	Dextroamphetamine and methylphenidate generally are given at 8 AM and noon (the usefulness of sustained-release preparations is not proved) Dextroamphetamine—2.5–40 mg a day up to 0.5 mg/kg a day Methylphenidate—10–60 mg a day or up to 1.0 mg/kg a day Pemoline—37.5–112.5 mg given at 8 AM;	Insomnia, anorexia, weight loss (and possibly growth delay), headache, tachycardia, precipitation or exacerbation of tic disorders With pemoline, monitor LFTs, because hepatoxicity is possible
Lithium—considered an antipsychotic drug, also has antiaggression properties	Studies support use in MR and CD for aggressive and self-injurious behaviors; can be used for same in PDD; also indicated for early-onset bipolar I disorder	600–2,100 mg in 2 or 3 divided doses; keep serum concentrations to 0.4–1.2 mEq/L	Nausea, vomiting, enuresis, headache, tremor, weight gain, hypothyroidism Experience with adults suggests renal function monitoring
Tricyclic drugs Imipramine (Tofranil) has been used in most child studies Nortriptyline (Pamelor) has been studied in children Clomipramine (Anafranil) is effective in child obsessive-compulsive disorder (OCD)	Major depressive disorder, separation anxiety disorder, bulimia nervosa, enuresis; sometimes used in ADHD, sleepwalking disorder, and sleep terror disorder Clomipramine is effective in child OCD and sometimes in PDD	Imipramine—start with divided dosages totaling about 1.5 mg/kg a day; can build up to not more than 5 mg/kg a day and eventually combine in one dose; not FDA approved for children except for enuresis; dosage is usually 50–100 mg before sleep Clomipramine—start at 50 mg a day; can raise to not more than 3 mg/kg a day or 200 mg a day	Dry mouth, constipation, tachycardia, drowsiness, postural hypotension, hypertension, mania Electrocardiogram (ECG) monitoring is needed because of risk for cardiac conduction slowing; consider lowering dosage if PR interval 0.20 s or QRS interval 0.12 s; baseline EEG is advised, as it can lower seizure threshold (especially with clomipramine); blood levels of drug are sometimes useful

(continued)

Table 52.4–2 *(continued)*

Drugs	Indications	Dosage	Adverse Reactions and Monitoring
Serotonin-specific reuptake inhibitors—fluoxetine (Prozac), sertraline (Zoloft), and fluvoxamine (Luvox)	OCD; may be useful in major depressive disorder, anorexia, bulimia nervosa, repetitive behaviors in MR or PDD	Appears less than adult dosages	Nausea, headache, nervousness, insomnia, dry mouth, diarrhea, drowsiness
Carbamazepine (Tegretol)—an anticonvulsant	Aggression or dyscontrol in MR or CD, bipolar disorder	Start with 10 mg/kg a day; can build to 20–30 mg/kg a day; therapeutic serum concentration range seems to be 4–12 mg/L	Drowsiness, nausea, rash, vertigo, irritability Monitor: CBC and LFTs for possible blood dyscrasias and hepatotoxicity; blood levels are necessary
Benzodiazepines—have been studied insufficiently in childhood and adolescence	Sometimes effective in parasomnias: sleepwalking disorder or sleep terror disorder; can be tried in generalized anxiety disorder Clonazepam (Klonopin) can be tried in all anxiety disorders, especially panic disorder Alprazolam (Xanax) can be tried in separation anxiety disorder	Parasomnias: diazepam (Valium) 2–10 mg before bedtime	Can cause drowsiness, ataxia, tremor, dyscontrol; can be abused
Fenfluramine (Pondimin)—an amphetamine congener	Withdrawn from market because of severe heart valve damage as adverse effect (see Chapter 35)		
Propranolol (Inderal)—a β-adrenergic receptor antagonist	Aggression in MR, PDD, and cognitive disorder; awaits controlled studies	Effective dosage in children and adolescents is not yet established; range is probably 40–320 mg a day	Bradycardia, hypotension, nausea, hypoglycemia, depression; avoid in asthma
Clonidine (Catapres)—a presynaptic α-adrenergic blocking agent	Some success in ADHD; clonidine in Tourette's disorder	Clonidine—0.1–0.3 mg/kg a day; 3–5.5 μg/kg a day Guanfacine—up to 3 mg/kg a day	Orthostatic hypotension, sedation, dry mouth
Cyproheptadine (Periactin)	Anorexia nervosa	Dosages up to 8 mg 4 times a day	Antihistaminic side effects, including sedation and dryness of the mouth
Naltrexone (ReVia)	Self-injurious behaviors in MR and PDD; currently being studied in PDD	0.5–2.0 mg/kg a day	Sleepiness, aggressivity Monitor LFTs, as hepatotoxicity has been reported in adults at high dosages
Desmopressin (DDAVP)	Nocturnal enuresis	20–40 μg intranasally	Headache; hyponatremic seizures (rare)

Courtesy of Richard Perry, M.D.

Table 52.4–3
Effects of Psychotropic Drugs on Cognitive Tests of Learning Functions[a]

		Test Function				
Drug Class	Continuous Performance Test (Attention)	Matching Familiar Figures (Impulsivity)	Paired Associates (Verbal Learning)	Porteus Maze (Planning Capacity)	Short Term Memory[a]	WISC (Intelligence)
Stimulant	↑	↑	↑	↑	↑	↑
Antidepressant	↑	0		0	0	0
Antipsychotic	↑↓		↓	↓	↓	0

Adapted from Amar MG: Drugs, learning and the psychotherapies. In *Pediatric Psychopharmacology: The Use of Behavior Modifying Drugs in Children*, JS Werry, editor, p 355. Brunner/Mazel, New York, 1978.
↑ Improved; ↑↓ inconsistent; ↓ worse; 0, no effect.
[a] Various tests; digit span, word recall, etc.

gression, stereotypies, self-injurious behavior, hyperactivity, and withdrawal, but dyskinesia is a risk. Recently, the SSRIs have been studied in autistic disorder, as researchers posited an association between the compulsive behaviors in obsessive-compulsive disorder and stereotypic behaviors common in children with autism. To date, clomipramine (Anafranil) and fluoxetine have shown promise in ending stereotypies and other behaviors in autistic children and adults.

The opioid antagonists naloxone (Narcan) and naltrexone are effective in reducing self-injurious behavior in some autistic children, but to what degree other behaviors are benefited is not yet clear. Improvements seem to be modest. The behavioral difficulties of children with autism can be difficult to manage. Much effort, firmness, and consistency are required from caregivers, and psychiatrists may need to try many medications. β-Blockers, lithium, or anticonvulsants may be helpful. Polypharmacy is not unusual but has not been studied formally. Stimulants can be tried to reduce hyperactivity and inattentiveness in relatively manageable children with autism.

Attention-Deficit/Hyperactivity Disorder. Studies continue to support the use of stimulants in treating attention-deficit/hyperactivity disorder. The most frequently researched and used stimulant is methylphenidate. Dextroamphetamine (Dexedrine) is of comparable efficacy and, unlike methylphenidate, is approved by the Food and Drug Administration (FDA) for children 3 years of age and older; the starting age for methylphenidate is 6 years. Pemoline (Cylert) is a less effective but longer-acting stimulant that carries a small risk for hepatotoxicity. Stimulants reduce hyperactivity, inattentiveness, and impulsivity in about 75 percent of children with attention-deficit/hyperactivity disorder. The effects are not paradoxical, as normal children respond similarly. The dose-related side effects of stimulants are listed in Table 52.4–4.

Attention-deficit/hyperactivity disorder often coexists with oppositional defiant disorder or conduct disorder. With these added disorders comes aggression. In some cases, stimulants seem to reduce aggression, but a common mistake is to prolong stimulant trials when the aggression is not subsiding and when a switch to or the addition of a more specifically antiaggression drug is indicated.

For children with attention-deficit/hyperactivity disorder, who are resistant to stimulants, and for children with preexisting tic disorders, antidepressants can be tried. Bupropion is not uncommonly tried when stimulants are ineffective in treating attention-deficit/hyperactivity disorder. Desipramine has been shown to be somewhat effective in the treatment of attention-deficit/hyperactivity disorder, but its use is limited because of the associated risks. Since the sudden death of four children being treated with desipramine for attention-deficit/hyperactivity disorder, extra caution must be recommended. Other tricyclic drugs, including nortriptyline (Pamelor) and clomipramine (Anafranil), have been tried with some success. The response of children with attention-deficit/hyperactivity disorder to antidepressants can occur within days of the beginning of treatment.

A few studies have shown that clonidine (Catapres) has been used with some success in attention-deficit/hyperactivity disorder. Antipsychotics can be used to treat attention-deficit/hyperactivity disorder, but only after other treatments have failed because of the risks of sedation and tardive dyskinesia.

Attention-deficit/hyperactivity disorder often precedes and then coexists with tic disorders. (Chapter 45 discusses the pharmacotherapy for children with both conditions.)

The dietary management of hyperactivity has received much of public attention, but controlled studies have not substantiated its benefit. Similarly, in most controlled studies, caffeine was not determined to be superior to placebo for alleviating attention-deficit/hyperactivity disorder.

Table 52.4–4
Common Dose-Related Side Effects of Stimulants

Insomnia
Decreased appetite
Irritability or nervousness
Weight loss

Conduct Disorder. The assaultiveness frequently associated with conduct disorder is targeted by pharmacotherapy. Antipsychotics such as haloperidol can quell aggression, but sedation and the risk of tardive dyskinesia are major drawbacks. With newer antipsychotics such as risperidone on the market, the hope of less long-term adverse effects supports its use. Lithium has reduced aggression in conduct disorder, and propranolol (Inderal) and carbamazepine have been effective in open studies.

When conduct disorder is associated with attention-deficit/hyperactivity disorder and when the aggression is mild, a trial of a stimulant may be indicated; stimulants are faster acting and easier to monitor than the previously noted drugs. Clonidine may be effective and deserves further study.

The aggression associated with conduct disorder often is difficult to control. Therefore, polypharmacy is common although no studies have demonstrated the benefits of this approach.

Tourette's Disorder. The strongly antidopaminergic antipsychotics haloperidol and pimozide (Orap) are the most effective medications for Tourette's disorder. Pimozide prolongs the QT interval and thus requires electrocardiographic (ECG) monitoring. Clonidine, a presynaptic α-adrenergic blocking agent, is less effective than the two antipsychotics but avoids the risk for tardive dyskinesia; sedation is a frequent side effect of clonidine.

Tic disorders often coexist with attention-deficit/hyperactivity disorder in children and adolescents. Stimulants, which can precipitate tics, should be avoided in these cases, although recent studies indicate that the prohibition may not be totally warranted. Clonidine reduces tics in both attention-deficit/hyperactivity disorder and the comorbid cases. A small study supports the use of nortriptyline.

Enuresis. Before initiating psychopharmacotherapy in treating enuresis, clinicians must consider the merits of waiting for a possible spontaneous remission and of using behavioral techniques; bell-and-pad conditioning (a bell awakens the child when the mattress becomes wet) is perhaps the most elaborate behavioral treatment and seems to be more successful than medication.

Tricyclic drugs are effective in reducing enuresis in about 60 percent of patients, and desmopressin (DDAVP) is effective in about 50 percent of patients. Improvement ranges from complete cessation of wetting to continued wetting but with less urine volume. Tricyclic drugs are given about 1 hour before bedtime. The starting dosage usually is 25 mg a day, a lower dosage than that used in trials for depression. The dosage can be increased to 75 mg a day for an adolescent but should not exceed 2 mg/kg a day. Children usually respond within days. Desmopressin is taken intranasally in dosages of 10 to 40 mg a day. When used over months, nasal discomfort can occur, and water retention is potentially a problem. Patients who respond with full dryness should continue to take the medication for several months to prevent relapses.

Separation Anxiety Disorder. Few studies support the use of anxiolytics in pediatric psychopharmacology. A recent double-blind, placebo-controlled study did not replicate a similar study performed by the same workers 20 years before, when imipramine (Tofranil) was shown to be effective for school refusal. Alprazolam (Xanax) may be helpful in separation anxiety disorder, but the data are conflicting.

Schizophrenia. Antipsychotics are used commonly for schizophrenia in childhood and adolescence, but only two double-blind studies showed a modest effectiveness of antipsychotics in adolescent schizophrenia, and only one of these studies was placebo-controlled. In the only double-blind placebo-controlled study of childhood schizophrenia, haloperidol was significantly superior to the placebo. Schizophrenia with onset in late adolescence is treated like adult-onset schizophrenia.

Mood Disorders. The SSRIs currently are the drugs of choice in the pharmacological treatment of depressive disorders in children and adolescents. One controlled study supports the efficacy of fluoxetine in this population. Tricyclic drugs have not been shown to be superior to a placebo in double-blind, placebo-controlled studies of children and adolescents with major depressive disorder. In children, developmental differences in neurotransmitters and neuroendocrine systems may be associated with responses to antidepressants. In any case, the 1990s undoubtedly will present several studies of SSRIs in the treatment of early-onset major depressive disorder.

Most clinicians advocate a trial of antidepressant medication in severe, prolonged major depressive disorder. The SSRIs are favored because of their apparent efficacy, mild side effect profile, and less risk in overdose. When treating a child or an adolescent at risk for suicide, care must always be taken to use medication with the greatest degree of safety.

Manic episodes in childhood and adolescence are treated as they are in adulthood. No double-blind, placebo-controlled studies have demonstrated the effectiveness of lithium in treating adolescent mania, but many open trials support its use. Divalproex (Depakote) is another medication currently used frequently to treat bipolar disorder in children and adolescents.

Obsessive-Compulsive Disorder. In a growing number of studies, clomipramine has been proved effective in diminishing obsessions and compulsions in children and adolescents. Fluoxetine has been studied less than clomipramine but also seems to be effective. Clomipramine generally is well tolerated. The side effects of fluoxetine seem to be more frequent, bothersome, and dramatic than side effects of clomipramine. Other SSRIs probably will be studied for their use in treating early-onset obsessive-compulsive disorder.

Eating Disorders. The treatment of anorexia nervosa does not primarily focus on pharmacologic interventions, but drugs can be important adjuncts in many cases. The SSRIs are not used uncommonly in this population; the target symptoms are obsessions and compulsions and high levels of anxiety and depressive symptoms. Cyproheptadine (Periactin) was used historically and reported to be of benefit to some patients with anorexia, and antidepressants may benefit those with comorbid depressive disorders. However, the compromised metabolism of many patients with anorexia can put them at high risk for cardiac arrhythmias if tricyclic drugs are administered.

Many antidepressants—imipramine, desipramine, trazodone (Desyrel), fluoxetine, and monoamine oxidase inhibitors (MAOIs)—reduce binge eating and purging in bulimia nervosa. In one large study of patients with bulimia nervosa, bupropion was associated with a dramatic incidence of seizures.

Sleep Terror Disorder and Sleepwalking Disorder. Sleep terror disorder and sleepwalking disorder occur in the transition from deep delta-wave sleep (stages 3 and 4) to light sleep. Benzodiazepines and tricyclic drugs are effective in these disorders. They work by reducing both delta-wave sleep and arousals between sleep stages. The medications should be used temporarily and in only severe cases, because tolerance to the medications develops, cessation of the medications can lead to severe rebound worsening of the disorders, and reducing delta sleep in children may have deleterious effects. Therefore, behavioral approaches are preferred for these disorders.

Other Disorders. Buspirone (BuSpar) has been effective in an open trial of adolescents with generalized anxiety disorder. Patients with early-onset panic disorder and panic attacks have benefited from clonazepam (Klonopin) in several open trials.

Adverse Effects and Complications

Antidepressants. The adverse effects of antidepressants for children usually are similar to those for adults and result from the antidepressants' anticholinergic properties. The adverse effects include dry mouth, constipation, palpitations, tachycardia, loss of accommodation, and sweating. The most serious adverse effects are cardiovascular, although in children, diastolic hypertension is more common and postural hypotension occurs more rarely than in adults. ECG changes are most apt to be seen in children receiving high dosages. Slowed cardiac conduction (PR interval 0.20 seconds or QRS interval 0.12) may necessitate lowering the dosage. FDA guidelines limit dosages to a maximum of 5 mg/kg a day. The drugs can be toxic in an overdose, and in small children, ingestion of 200 to 400 mg can be fatal. When the dosage is lowered too rapidly, withdrawal effects are manifest mainly by gastrointestinal symptoms: cramping, nausea, vomiting, and sometimes apathy and weakness. Treatment is a slower tapering of the dosage.

Antipsychotics. The best studied antipsychotics given to pediatric age groups are chlorpromazine (Thorazine), thioridazine (Mellaril), and haloperidol. High-potency and low-potency antipsychotics are believed to differ in their adverse-effect profiles. The phenothiazine derivatives (chlorpromazine and thioridazine) have the most pronounced sedative and atropinic actions, whereas the high-potency antipsychotics are commonly believed to be associated with extrapyramidal reactions, such as parkinsonian symptoms, akathisia, and acute dystonias. Caution is warranted in assuming that these reactions are also true for children. In particular, when comparisons are made at low-dosage levels of equivalent potency, differences may not be detected.

Even if the frequency of the adverse effects differs among medications, the effects are always caused by the antipsychotics. Evidence in children of impaired cognitive function and, most importantly, of tardive dyskinesia calls for great caution in the use of drugs. Tardive dyskinesia—which is characterized by persistent abnormal involuntary movements of the tongue, face, mouth, or jaw and sometimes the extremities—is a known hazard when giving antipsychotics to patients of all age groups. No known treatment is effective. Tardive dyskinesia has not been reported in patients taking less than 375 to 400 grams of chlorpromazine equivalents. Because nonpersistent choreiform movements of the extremities and trunk are common after an abrupt discontinuation of antipsychotics, clinicians must distinguish these symptoms from persistent dyskinesias.

Whenever clinically feasible, children receiving antipsychotics should be periodically withdrawn from the medication, so that clinicians can assess the patient's current clinical needs and the possible development of tardive dyskinesia.

Stimulants. Problems with retarded growth associated with taking stimulants have been reported, although little evidence for the problems is available. The current belief is that any growth suppression is temporary and that children taking stimulants eventually reach their normal height.

OTHER BIOLOGICAL THERAPIES

Electroconvulsive therapy (ECT) is not indicated in childhood or adolescence. Psychosurgery for severe and intransigent obsessive-compulsive disorder should probably be delayed until adulthood, after all attempts at less drastic treatment have failed and when the patient can participate fully in the process of informed consent.

Little evidence indicates that food allergies or sensitivities play a role in childhood mental disorders. Diets that eliminate food additives, colorings, and sugar are difficult to maintain and usually have no effect. Megavitamin therapy usually is ineffective (unless child has a frank vitamin deficiency) and can cause bad adverse effects.

REFERENCES

Aman MG, Kern RA, McGhee OE, Arnold LEA: Fenfluramine and methylphenidate in children with mental retardation and ADHD: Clinical and side effects. J Am Acad Child Adolesc Psychiatry *32:* 851, 1993.

American Psychiatric Association: Practice guidelines for eating disorders. Am J Psychiatry *150:* 212, 1993.

Biederman J, Baldessarini RJ, Goldblatt A, Lapey KA, Doyle A, Hesslein PS: A naturalistic study of 24-hour electrocardiographic recordings and echocardiographic findings in children and adolescents treated with desipramine. J Am Acad Child Adolesc Psychiatry *32:* 805, 1993.

Campbell M, Small AM, Green WH, Jennings SJ, Perry R, Bennett WG, Anderson L: Behavioral efficacy of haloperidol and lithium carbonate: A comparison in hospitalized aggressive children with conduct disorder. Arch Gen Psychiatry *41:* 650, 1984.

Clein PD, Riddle MA: Pharmacokinetics in children and adolescents. Child Adolesc Psychiatr Clin North Am *4:* 59, 1995.

Colle LM, Belair JF, DiFeo M, Weiss J, LaRoache C: Extended open-label fluoxetine treatment of adolescents with major depression. J Child Adolesc Psychopharmacol *4:* 225, 1994.

Geller B: Psychopharmacology of children and adolescents: Pharmacokinetics and relationships of plasma/serum levels to response. Psychopharmacol Bull *27:* 401, 1991.

Geller B, Cooper TB, Graham DL, Fetner H, Marsteller FA, Wells JM: Pharmacokinetically designed double-blind placebo controlled study of nortriptyline in 6- to 12-year olds with major depressive disorder. J Am Acad Child Adolesc Psychiatry *31:* 34, 1992.

Gordon CT, State RC, Nelson JE, Hamburger SD, Rapoport JL: A double-blind comparison of clomipramine, desipramine, and placebo in the treatment of autistic disorder. Arch Gen Psychiatry *50:* 441, 1993.

Green WH: *Child and Adolescent Clinical Psychopharmacology.* Williams & Wilkins, Baltimore, 1991.

Green WH: Nonstimulant drugs in the treatment of attention-deficit/hyperactivity disorder. Child Adolesc Psychiatr Clin North Am *1:* 449, 1992.

Greenhill L: Pharmacotherapy: Stimulants. Child Adolesc Psychiatr Clin North Am *1:* 411, 1992.

Hardan A, Johnson K, Johnson C, Krecznyj B: Case study: Risperidone treatment of children and adolescents with developmental disorders. J Am Acad Child Adolesc Psychiatry *35:* 1551, 1996.

Jensen PS, Ryan WD, Prien R: Psychopharmacology of child and adolescent major depression: Present and future directions. J Child Adolesc Psychopharmacol *2:* 31, 1992.

Ratey JJ, Gordon A: The psychopharmacology of aggression: Toward a new day. Psychopharmacol Bull *29:* 65, 1993.

Riddle MA, Geller B, Rayn N: Another sudden death in a child treated with desipramine. J Am Acad Child Adolesc Psychiatry *32:* 792, 1993.

Spencer T, Biederman J, Wilens T, Steingard R, Geist D: Nortriptyline treatment of children with attention-deficit/hyperactivity disorder and tic disorder or Tourette's syndrome. J Am Acad Child Adolesc Psychiatry *32:* 205, 1993.

Steingard R, Biederman J, Spencer T, Wilens T, Gonzalez A: Comparison of clonidine response in the treatment of attention-deficit/hyperactivity disorder with and without comorbid tic disorders. J Am Acad Child Adolesc Psychiatry *32:* 350, 1993.

▲ 52.5 Psychiatric Treatment of Adolescents

Environmental demands increase during adolescence, and many serious mental disorders have their onset during this time. Schizophrenia, bipolar I disorder, and the risk for completed suicide all drastically increase in adolescence. Although some degree of stress is virtually universal in adolescence, most teenagers without mental disorders are able to cope well with the environmental demands. Teenagers with preexisting mental disorders may experience exacerbations during adolescence and may become frustrated, alienated, and demoralized.

People must be sensitive to adolescents' perceptions of themselves: In a group of teenagers of the same age, there is a range of emotional maturity. Issues that are specific to adolescents are related to their new evolving identities, the development of sexual activities, and their plans to meet future life goals.

DIAGNOSIS

Adolescents can be assessed in both their specific stage-appropriate functions and their general progress in accomplishing the tasks of adolescence. For almost all adolescents in today's culture, at least until their late teens, school performance is the prime barometer of healthy functioning. Intellectually normal adolescents who are not functioning satisfactorily in some form of schooling have significant psychological problems, the nature and causes of which should be identified.

Questions to be asked regarding adolescents' stage-specific tasks are the following: What degree of separation from their parents have adolescents achieved? What sort of identifies are evolving? How do they perceive their past? Do they perceive themselves as being responsible for their own development or as being only the passive recipients of their parents' influences? How do they perceive themselves with regard to the future, and how do they anticipate their future responsibilities for themselves and others? Can they think about the varying consequences of different ways of living? How do they express their sexual and affectionate interests? These tasks occupy all adolescents and normally are performed at varying times.

Adolescents' object relations must be evaluated. Do they perceive and accept both good and bad qualities in their parents? Do they see their peers and boyfriends or girlfriends as separate people with needs and identities of their own, or do others exist only for the adolescents' own needs?

A respect for and, if possible, some actual understanding of an adolescent's subcultural and ethnic background are essential. For example, in some groups, depression is acceptable; in other groups, overt depression is a sign of weakness and is masked by antisocial acts, substance misuse, and self-destructive risks. A psychiatrist need not be of the same race or group identity as an adolescent to treat him or her effectively. Respect and knowledgeable concern are human qualities and are not group restricted.

INTERVIEWS

Whenever circumstances permit, both an adolescent patient and his or her parents should be interviewed. Other family members also may be included, depending on their degree of involvement in the teenager's life and difficulties. Clinicians should see the adolescent first, however; preferential treatment helps avoid the appearance of being the parents' agent. In psychotherapy with an older adolescent, the therapist and the parents usually have little contact after the initial part of the therapy, because ongoing contact inhibits the adolescent's desire to open up.

Interview Techniques

All patients test and mistrust therapists, but adolescents often manifest these reactions crudely, intensely, provocatively, and for prolonged periods. Clinicians must establish themselves as trustworthy and helpful adults to promote a therapeutic alliance. They should encourage adolescents to tell their own stories, without interrupting to check discrepancies; such a tactic seems like correcting and expressing disbelief. Clinicians should ask patients for explanations and theories about what happened. Why did these behaviors or feelings occur? When did things change? What caused the identified problems to begin when they did?

Sessions with adolescents generally follow the adult model: The therapist sits across from the patient. In early adolescence, however, board games (such as checkers) may help to stimulate conversation in an otherwise quiet, anxious patient.

Language is crucial. Even when a teenager and a clinician come from the same socioeconomic group, their languages are seldom the same. Psychiatrists should use their own language, explain any specialized terms or concepts, and ask for an explanation of unfamiliar in-group jargon or slang. Many adolescents do not talk spontaneously about illicit substances and suicidal tendencies but do respond honestly to a therapist's questions. A therapist may need to ask specifically about each substance and the amount and frequency of its use.

The sexual histories and current sexual activities of adolescents are increasingly important pieces of information for adequate evaluation. The nature of adolescents' sexual behaviors often is a vignette of their whole personality structures and ego development, but a long time may elapse in therapy before adolescents begin to talk about their sexual behavior.

TREATMENT

Usually, no single therapy modality is specific to a particular disorder. The best choice often is what best fits the characteristics of the individual adolescent and the family or social milieu. Real dependence needs of adolescents may press clinicians to strive to maintain even the sickest youngster in a satisfactory home. But for the same reason, clinicians may be forced to remove adolescents from pathogenic homes, even when the severity of the illness alone does not dictate it, because the youngsters are not developmentally capable of handling the double burden of working to overcome their illness and being traumatized at home. Also, adolescents' striving for autonomy may so complicate problems of compliance with therapy that they force involuntary inpatient treatment of difficulties for which such treatment may not be necessary at a different stage of life. Therefore, the following discussion is less a set of guidelines than a brief summary of what each treatment modality can or should offer.

Individual Psychotherapy

Few, if any, adolescent patients are trusting or open without considerable time and testing, and it is helpful to anticipate the testing period by letting patients know that it is to be expected and is natural and healthy. Pointing out the likelihood of therapeutic problems—for instance, impatience and disappointment with the psychiatrist, with the therapy, with the time required, and with the often-intangible results—may help keep problems under control. Therapeutic goals should be stated in terms that adolescents understand and value. Although they may not see the point in exercising self-control, enduring dysphoric emotions, or forgoing impulsive gratification, they may value feeling more confident than in the past and gaining more control over their lives and the events that affect them.

Typical adolescent patients need a real relationship with a therapist they can perceive as a real person. The therapist becomes another parent, because adolescents still need appropriate parenting or reparenting. Therefore, a professional who is impersonal and anonymous is a less useful model than one who can accept and respond rationally to an angry challenge or confrontation without fear or false conciliation, can impose limits and controls when adolescents cannot, can admit mistakes and ignorance, and can openly express the gamut of human emotions. Adolescents perceive the failure to take a stand about self-damaging and self-destructive behavior or to respond actively to manipulative and dishonest behavior as indifference or collusion.

Countertransference reactions can be intense in psychotherapeutic work with adolescents, and therapists must be aware of them. An adolescent often expresses hostile feelings toward adults, such as parents and teachers. A therapist may react with an overidentification with the adolescent or with the parents. Such reactions are determined, at least in part, by a therapist's own experiences during adolescence or, when applicable, by the therapist's own experiences as a parent.

Individual outpatient therapy is appropriate for adolescents whose problems are manifest in conflicted emotions and nondangerous behavior, who are not too disorganized to be maintained outside a structured setting, and whose families or other living environments are not disturbed enough to negate the influence of therapy. Such therapy characteristically focuses on intrapsychic conflicts and inhibitions; on the meanings of emotions, attitudes, and behavior; and on the influence of the past and the present. Antianxiety agents can be considered in adolescents whose anxiety may be high at certain times during psychotherapy, but adolescents' potential for abusing these drugs must be weighed carefully.

Group Psychotherapy

In many ways group psychotherapy is a natural setting for adolescents. Most teenagers are more comfortable with peers than with adults. A group diminishes the sense of unequal power between the adult therapist and the adolescent patient. Participation varies, depending on an adolescent's readiness. Not all interpretations and confrontations should come from the parent-figure therapist; group members often are adept at noticing symptomatic behavior in each other, and adolescents may find it easier to hear and consider critical or challenging comments from their peers.

Group psychotherapy usually addresses interpersonal and current life issues. However, some adolescents are too fragile for group psychotherapy or have symptoms or social traits that are too likely to elicit peer group ridicule; they need individual therapy to attain enough ego strength to struggle with peer relationships. Conversely, other adolescents must resolve interpersonal issues in a group before they can tackle intrapsychic issues in the intensity of one-to-one therapy.

Family Therapy

Family therapy is the primary modality when adolescents' difficulties are mainly a reflection of a dysfunctional family (for example, teenagers with simple school phobia, runaways). The same may be true when developmental issues, such as adolescent sexuality and striving for autonomy, trigger family conflicts or when family pathology is severe, as in cases of incest and child abuse. In these instances, adolescents usually need individual therapy as well, but family therapy is mandatory if an adolescent is to remain in the home or return to it. Serious character pathology, such as that underlying antisocial and borderline personality disorders, often develops from highly pathogenic early parenting. Family therapy is strongly indicated whenever possible for such disorders, but most authorities consider it adjunctive to intensive individual psychotherapy when individual psychopathology has become so internalized that it persists regardless of the current family status.

Inpatient Treatment

Residential treatment schools often are preferable for long-term therapy, but hospitals are more suitable for emergencies, although some adolescent inpatient hospital units also provide educational, recreational, and occupational facilities for long-term patients. Adolescents whose families are too disturbed or incompetent, who are dangerous to themselves or others, who are out of control in ways that preclude further healthy development, or who are seriously disorganized require, at least temporarily, the external controls of structured environment.

Long-term inpatient therapy is the treatment of choice for severe disorders that are considered wholly or largely psychogenic in origin, such as major ego deficits that are caused by early massive deprivation and that respond poorly or not at all to medication. Severe borderline personality disorder, for example, regardless of the behavioral symptoms, requires a full-time corrective environment in which regression is possible and safe and in which ego development can take place. Psychotic disorders in adolescence often require hospitalization, but psychotic adolescents often respond to appropriate medication so that therapy usually is feasible in an outpatient setting, except during exacerbation. Schizophrenic adolescents who show a long-term deteriorating course may require hospitalization periodically.

Day Hospitals

In day hospitals, which have become increasingly popular, adolescents spend the day in class, individual and group psychotherapy, and other programs, but they go home in the evenings. Compared with full hospitalization, day hospitals are less expensive and usually are preferred by patients.

CLINICAL PROBLEMS

Atypical Puberty

Pubertal changes that occur 2½ years earlier or later than the average age are within the normal range. However, body image is so important to adolescents that extremes of the norm may be distressing to some, either because markedly early maturation subjects them to social and sexual pressures for which they are unready or because late maturation makes them feel inferior and excludes them from some peer activities. Medical reassurance, even if based on examination and testing to rule out pathophysiology, may be insufficient. An adolescent's distress may show as sexual or delinquent acting out, withdrawal, or problems at school of such a degree as to warrant therapeutic intervention. Therapy also may be prompted by similar disturbances in some adolescents who fail to achieve peer-valued stereotypes of physical development despite normal pubertal physiology.

Substance-Related Disorders

Some experimentation with psychoactive substances is almost ubiquitous among adolescents, especially if this category of behavior includes alcohol use. However, most adolescents do not become abusers, particularly of prescription drugs and illegal substances. Regular substance abuse of any degree represents disturbance. Substance abuse sometimes is self-medication against depression or schizophrenic deterioration and sometimes is a sign of characterological disorder in teenagers whose ego deficits render them unequal to the stresses of puberty and the tasks of adolescence. But many substances, especially cocaine, have a physiologically reinforcing action that acts independently of preexisting psychopathology. Regardless of why the abuse developed, it becomes a problem in itself. Ego development depends on confronting and learning to cope adaptively with reality. The substances become both a substitute for reality and an avoidance of it and thus impair ego development and perpetuate the abuse to conceal poor coping skills.

When substance abuse covers an underlying illness or is a maladaptive response to current stresses or disturbed family dynamics, treatment of the underlying cause may take care of the substance abuse. Outpatient psychotherapy, however, generally is useless with long-term abusers, who require a structured setting in which the substances are not available.

Suicide

Suicide currently is the second leading cause of death among adolescents. Many hospital admissions of adolescents result from suicidal ideation or behavior. Suicide is the final common pathway for a number of disorders, and its high incidence reflects grave psychopathology. Some authorities believe that in adolescence, in contrast to adulthood, schizophrenia more often underlies suicide than major mood disorders. Among adolescents who are not psychotic, the highest suicidal risks occur in those adolescents who have a history of parental suicide, who are unable to form stable attachments, who display impulsive behavior or episodic dyscontrol, and who abuse alcohol or other substances. Many adolescent suicides show a common pattern of long-standing family and social problems throughout childhood and the escalation of subjective distress under the pressure and stresses of puberty and adolescence, followed by a suicide attempt precipitated by the sudden real or perceived loss of a person or social support believed to be the one source of meaning or closeness.

Normal developmental losses—of childhood dependence, of parents, of childhood—also can cause psychogenic depression in adolescents. The rapid and extreme mood swings in adolescence, coupled with adolescents' difficulties in seeing beyond the intensity of the moment, contribute to catastrophic despair and impulsive suicide attempts over losses that adults could withstand. Moreover, alcohol and other substances can decrease the resistance to suicidal impulses. Normally persistent magical thinking may impair the sense of permanence of death and may allow adolescents to contemplate suicide more lightly than do adults.

During both evaluation and treatment, suicidal thoughts, plans, and past attempts must be discussed directly when the concern arises and information is not volunteered. Long-term or recurring thoughts should be taken seriously, and an agreement or contract should be negotiated with adolescents not to attempt suicide without first calling and talking about it with the psychiatrist. Adolescents usually are honest about making and keeping, or refusing, such agreements; if they refuse, closed hospitalization is indicated. Hospitalization is a sign of serious, protective concern and may be as therapeutic as the opportunity to conduct or plan further treatment in a safe environment.

References

Bird HR: Psychiatric treatment of adolescents. In *Comprehensive Textbook of Psychiatry,* ed 6, HI Kaplan, BJ Sadock, editors, p 2439. Williams & Wilkins, Baltimore, 1995.

Blos P: *On Adolescence.* Free Press, New York, 1962.

Davis M, Raffe IH: The holding environment in the inpatient treatment of adolescents. Adolesc Psychiatry *12:* 434, 1985.

Erikson EH: The problem of ego identity. J Am Psychoanal Assoc *4:* 56, 1966.

Feldman LB: Integrating individual and family therapy in the treatment of symptomatic children and adolescents. Am J Psychother *42:* 272, 1988.

Freud A: Adolescence. Psychoanal Study Child *16:* 225, 1958.

Gartner AF: Countertransference issues in the psychotherapy of adolescents. J Child Adolesc Psychother *2:* 187, 1985.

Group for the Advancement of Psychiatry: *Normal Adolescence,* vol 6, report 68. Group for the Advancement of Psychiatry, New York, 1968.

Kazdin AE: Psychotherapy for children and adolescents. Annu Rev Psychol *41:* 21, 1990.

Lyman RD, Prentice-Dunn S, Gabel S: *Residential and Inpatient Treatment of Children and Adolescents.* Plenum, New York, 1989.

March JS, Mulle K, Herbel B: Behavioral psychotherapy for children and adolescents with obsessive-compulsive disorder: An open trial of a new protocol-driven package. J Am Acad Child Adolesc Psychiatry *33:* 333, 1994.

Moreau D, Mufson L, Weissman MM, Klerman GL: Interpersonal psychotherapy for adolescent depression: Description of modification and preliminary application. J Am Acad Child Adolesc Psychiatry *30:* 642, 1991.

Mufson L, Moreau D, Weissman MM, Wickramaratne P, Martin J, Samoilov A: Modification of interpersonal psychotherapy with depressed adolescents (IPT-A): Phase I and II studies. J Am Acad Child Adolesc Psychiatry *33:* 695, 1994.

O'Brien JD: Current prevention concepts in child and adolescent psychiatry. Am J Psychother *45:* 261, 1991.

Peterson AC, Taylor B: The biological approach to adolescence. In *Handbook of Adolescent Development,* J Adelson, editor, p 68. Wiley, New York, 1980.

Schowalter JE, Anyan WR: *The Family Handbook of Adolescence.* Knopf, New York, 1979.

Shaffer D, Garland A, Vieland V, Underwood M, Busner C: The impact of curriculum-based suicide prevention programs for teenagers. J Am Acad Child Adolesc Psychiatry *30:* 588, 1991.

Sholevar GP, Burland A, Frank JL, Etezady MH, Goldstein J: Psychoanalytic treatment of children and adolescents. J Am Acad Child Adolesc Psychiatry *28:* 685, 1989.

53 Forensic Issues in Child Psychiatry

In medicine, ethics historically has alluded to moral obligations as well as to the accepted behavior that physicians follow; on the broadest scale, the Hippocratic oath summarizes ethical values in medicine. During the past few decades, however, new ethical and moral dilemmas have arisen with the growth of medical knowledge and technology. The traditional ethical tenet that physicians must consider each patient above all else has often been challenged. For example, a patient may be kept alive for long periods while in a coma, or a pregnant woman's life may be saved by aborting her fetus.

Society's view of children and their rights has evolved dramatically in the 20th century. The institution of a juvenile court system about 100 years ago was an acknowledgment that children must be protected and provided for in ways different from adults. In 1980, the American Academy of Child and Adolescent Psychiatry published a code of ethics that was developed to publicly endorse the ethical standards of this discipline. The code is based on the assumption that children are vulnerable and unable to take adequate care of themselves, but as they mature, their capacities to make judgments of and choices about their well-being develop as well. There are several caveats in the code: From the standpoint of child and adolescent psychiatrists, issues of consent, confidentiality, and professional responsibility must be seen in the context of overlapping and potentially conflicting rights of children, parents, and society.

Confidentiality, or intensive trust, refers to the relationship between two people with respect to the ''entrustment of secrets.'' Until the 1970s, little attention was paid to issues of confidentiality pertaining to minors. In 1980, among the items in the American Academy of Child and Adolescent Psychiatry's Code of Ethics, six principles were related to confidentiality. Breaches and limits of confidentiality can take place when any of the following situations occur: child abuse, maltreatment, or for purposes of appropriate education. Although unnecessary with a child or adolescent, consent for disclosure should be obtained when possible. In 1979, the American Psychiatric Association (APA) stated that a child 12 years of age could give consent for disclosure of confidential information and that, with the exception of safety issues, a minor's consent is required for disclosure of information to others, including the child's parents. According to the Academy of Child Psychiatry's Code of Ethics, the consent of a minor is not required for disclosure for confidential information. Specific ages for consent are not addressed in the code. Child and adolescent psychiatrists often face the dilemma of weighing the potential benefits and possible harm in sharing with the child's parents information obtained confidentially from a child. Although the smoothest transition occurs when the child and the physician agree that certain information can be shared, in many situations that border on ''dangerousness to the child or others,'' the child or adolescent does not agree to share the information with a parent or another responsible adult. Among adolescents, these secrets that are sometimes shared with a psychiatrist may involve drug or alcohol use, unsafe sex practices, or a thrill-seeking act that places the adolescent in danger. A psychiatrist may choose to work with the child or adolescent toward agreeing to share confidential information when it is determined by the treating psychiatrist that the probable outcome would be beneficial. The initial treatment contract, however, limits confidentiality to situations of ''danger'' to the child or others.

Other arenas that can pose confidentiality dilemmas include educational and scientific settings, research activities, and third-party agencies. Professional settings such as annual psychiatric conventions often include individual case presentations. In the context of a clinical symposium, doctors should realize that confidentiality means more than changing or dropping a patient's name; other information in a case study may pose a threat to a patient's privacy. Research projects sometimes are impeded by laws designed to protect the privacy of children and their families. In some cases, long-term follow-up studies may no longer be ''legal'' because of a time limitation on a written consent for study.

Third-party payers are requiring more and more confidential information before they consider reimbursement of psychiatric services. Information disclosed to insurance companies often is shared with many reviewers in the company; it also is in danger of being merged into a database in a computer system that is not highly restricted or confidential.

In general, there is no way to simplify the many difficult and complex confidentiality issues that may emerge in treating children and adolescents. Child and adolescent psychiatrists function as advocates for their patients and must always remain aware of minors' vulnerabilities and of the importance of maintaining trust in the treatment relationship.

CHILD CUSTODY

The evolution of child custody decision making has been influenced by increasing awareness and recognition of the rights of children and women, as well as by a broadening perspective on the developmental and psychological needs of the children involved. Historically, children were considered to be their fathers' property. At the beginning of this century, the ''tender years'' doctrine became the standard for determining child custody. According to this doctrine, the relationship between mother and infant, later generalized to mother and child, is responsible for the optimal emotional development of the child; the doctrine thus supported custody decisions in the mother's favor in most cases.

With this doctrine as its guide, psychological issues in developing children became an acceptable dimension to consider in the determination of custody. In controversial and unclear cases, psychological expert testimony began to be accepted as a valuable part of child custody decision making.

The "best interest of the child" standard replaced the "tender years" doctrine and expanded considerations of the optimal parent to include assessing issues of emotional climate, safety, and educational and social opportunities for the children. The "best interest of the child" grew from the movement to support legislation about the rights of children in the areas of compulsory education, child labor laws, and child abuse and neglect protection laws. Therefore, although "best interest" standards have broadened the dimensions considered in evaluating which parent is most capable to serve the best interest of the child, there is vagueness about how to measure these qualities in a parent. In view of the lack of clarity regarding what specific parameters in a parent best correspond to the interest of the child, child and adolescent psychiatrists to have increasingly been asked to help make decisions by defining relevant psychological conditions in parents and in the relationships between parents and children.

Psychiatric evaluators may be asked to give an opinion about child custody at various points during the separation and divorce process. Sometimes, a psychiatric evaluation is requested by the parents before any legal action occurs. When the parents and an evaluator can agree on custody decisions before the legal process, a court is likely to go along with these decisions rather than launch an additional investigation. A psychiatric evaluation may be ordered by the court or by the attorneys representing feuding parents. In such cases, an evaluator is faced with two disgruntled parents who often are consumed by their mutual conflict to the point that neither is willing to compromise, even in the child's interest. The advantage in such cases, however, is that evaluators represent the court and can act as advocate for the child without the same pressures as when an evaluator is hired by only one parent. A psychiatric evaluation also may be initiated by a guardian ad litem, an attorney who is appointed by the court to represent the child. Psychiatric evaluators also may be requested to give an opinion about custody during a mediation process. Mediation is a legal process that usually involves one attorney and one evaluator. Because mediation can occur outside the judicial system, some families may prefer it to going through a trial. In addition to custody, psychiatric evaluators often are asked to give opinions about visitation.

In undertaking a custody evaluation, an evaluator is expected to determine the best interests of the child while keeping in mind the standard elements that the court considers. These considerations include the wishes of the parents and the child; relationships with significant others in the child's life; the child's adjustment to the current home, school, and community; the psychiatric and physical health of all parties; the level of conflict and potential danger to the child under the care of either parent. A psychiatric evaluator must maintain his or her role as an advocate for the best interest of the child and does not consider the fairest outcome for parents. The psychiatric evaluator conducts a series of interviews, often including at least one separate interview with each parent and the child alone and one interview with the child and both parents. The evaluator may obtain a written waiver of confidentiality from all parties because he or she may have made disclosures to opposing attorneys and in court before the judge. The evaluator uses direct questioning as well as observations of the relationships between the child and each parent. The age and developmental needs of the child are considered in making a judgment regarding which parent may better serve the child's interests. As part of the psychiatric assessment of the child custody evaluation, the evaluator determines the need for psychiatric treatment for any of the parties involved.

The child custody evaluation generally is provided in a written report. This document is not confidential and may be used in court. The report contains a description of the relationship between the child and parents, the capabilities of the parents, and finally, the custody recommendations. In view of data supporting the importance of continuing a relationship with both parents in most cases, it is recommended that joint custody be considered before other options. When there is enough cooperation to negotiate for joint custody, the best interests of the child often are served. Joint custody may not be the best option for a child when the relationship of the child with either parent is jeopardized and undermined by the other. The next most frequent choice when joint custody is not advisable is full custody by one parent with visitation rights for the other parent. The parent awarded full custody should be capable of supporting the visitations and relationship with the noncustodial parent. In custody disputes involving a biological parent and a nonbiological parent, the biological parent generally has the right to custody unless he or she is shown to be unable to provide for the child. After the custody evaluation has been submitted in writing, the results must be communicated to the parents, the child, and possibly their respective attorneys. The evaluator may be called on to testify in court, and the parties may use the custody evaluation to mediate other areas of their dispute.

Many complications can occur in an ongoing bitter dispute between divorcing or divorced parents. Both true and false allegations of psychiatric illness, drug or alcohol abuse, or sexual or physical abuse are not uncommon during custody battles. The evaluator must be prepared to verify any allegations and to carefully discuss their effects on custody and visitation. Evidence suggests that markedly elevated numbers of unfounded allegations of child sexual abuse occur during the course of custody disputes.

JUVENILE OFFENDERS

The creation of a separate juvenile court system in the United States occurred by statute in the state of Illinois in the late 1800s. Its mandate was to rehabilitate rather than to punish. The omission of various constitutional safeguards, such as the rights to counsel, confrontation, and cross-examination of a accuser, eventually led to criticism and disillusionment with this system. Juvenile offenders of small and significant crimes often were sent to state-run residential programs that were criticized for being overcrowded, neglectful, and frankly abusive.

Despite the strong sentiment to increase due process protection for juveniles rather than pretrial, trial, and sentencing, the juvenile court system includes intake, adjudication, and disposition. The intake is a determination of whether there probably is cause that a youth committed a crime. If they confess, juveniles can be diverted from the court system altogether at this time, and appropriate plans for rehabilitation can be made in a community setting. For more serious crimes or when juveniles deny perpetrating a crime, the process continues. Juveniles must be represented by counsel, and an attorney is provided if the family cannot afford to provide their own. Unlike adult court, the determination of guilt or innocence is determined by a judge, not a jury. The case is argued by a prosecuting attorney and a defense attorney, and the judge is bound by the same standards as in adult court; that is, a judgment of delinquency requires proof beyond a reasonable doubt. When the charge is substantiated and the judgment is for delinquency, the juvenile is an ''adjudicated delinquent.'' Disposition must next be determined. Dispositions include a wide range of options, from placement in youth correctional facilities, to residential treatment settings, to psychiatric hospitalizations for further evaluation. *Delinquent acts* refer to ordinary crimes committed by juveniles; *status offenses* refer to behaviors that would not be criminal if perpetrated by adults, such as truancy, running away, or drinking alcohol. Sometimes, youths who are believed to have committed a serious crime are turned over (receive a waiver) to adult criminal court.

Psychiatrists are not infrequently consulted to provide recommendations at any phase of the juvenile justice process. A psychiatrist may be asked to evaluate a juvenile to make recommendations about appropriate diversion plans. Psychiatric evaluation may be sought for adjudicated delinquents to determine whether treatment for a psychiatric illness would work in favor of preventing future delinquent acts and, if so, in what setting. Psychiatric evaluations also may be requested when the court is considering a waiver to adult court. In some states, such decisions are based, in part, on the juvenile's psychiatric history and current mental status.

References

American Academy of Child and Adolescent Psychiatry: *Code of Ethics.* American Academy of Child and Adolescent Psychiatry, Washington, 1980.

Barnum R: Clinical evaluation of juvenile delinquents facing transfer to adult court. J Am Acad Child Adolesc Psychiatry *26:* 922, 1987.

Berlin FS, Malin MH, Dean S: Effects of statutes requiring psychiatrists to report suspected sexual abuse of children. Am J Psychiatry *148:* 449, 1991.

Billick SB, Perry CD: Role of the psychiatric evaluator in child custody disputes. In *Principles and Practice of Forensic Psychiatry,* R Rosner, editor, p 271. Chapman & Hall, New York, 1994.

Cohen R, Parmaleed I, et al: Characteristics of children and adolescents in a psychiatric hospital and a corrections facility. J Am Acad Child Adolesc Psychiatry *29:* 909, 1990.

Grisso T, Miller MO, Sabos B: Competency to stand trial in juvenile court. Int J Law Psychiatry *10:* 1, 1987.

Guyer MJ: Child psychiatry and legal liability: Implications of recent case law. J Am Child Adolesc Psychiatry *29:* 958, 1990.

Herman SP: Special issues in child custody evaluations. J Am Acad Child Adolesc Psychiatry *29:* 969, 1990.

Kalogerakis M: Juvenile delinquency. In *Clinical Handbook of Child Psychiatry and the Law,* DH Schetky, EP Benedek, editors, p 97. Brunner/Mazel, New York, 1992.

Lewis DO, Lovely R, Yeager G: Toward a theory of the genesis of violence: A follow-up study of delinquents. J Am Acad Child Adolesc Psychiatry *28:* 744, 1989.

Ratner RA: Juvenile delinquency. In *Principles and Practice of Forensic Psychiatry,* R Rosner, editor, p 36. Chapman & Hall, New York, 1994.

Schetky DH, Guyer MJ: Civil litigation and the child psychiatrist. J Am Acad Child Adolesc Psychiatry *29:* 963, 1990.

Shields JM, Johnson A: Collision between law and ethics: Consent for treatment with adolescents. Bull Am Acad Psychiatry Law *20:* 309, 1992.

Taylor L, Adelman HS: Reframing the confidentiality dilemma for work in children's best interests. Prof Psychol Res Pract *20:* 79, 1987.

Weintrob A: Confidentiality and its dilemmas in child and adolescent psychiatry. In *Principles and Practice of Forensic Psychiatry,* R Rosner, editor, p 197. Chapman & Hall, New York, 1994.

54

Geriatric Psychiatry

The term *geriatric* stems from the Greek *geras* (''old age'') and *iatros* (''physician'') and thus refers to treating or healing older people. In 1978, the Institute of Medicine of the National Academy of Sciences recommended including more information about geriatrics in medical school curricula, and in 1989, the American Board of Psychiatry and Neurology (ABPN) declared geriatric psychiatry a subspecialty. The first certification examination, given in 1991, produced the earliest group of certified geropsychiatrists, and today, geriatric psychiatry is the fastest growing field in psychiatry.

As the branch of medicine concerned with promoting longevity and preventing, diagnosing, and treating physical and psychological disorders in older adults, geriatric psychiatry requires a special knowledge; mental disorders of these patients often differ in clinical manifestations, pathogenesis, and pathophysiology from disorders of younger adults. Many disorders of older people do not match the categories in the fourth edition of *Diagnostic and Statistical Manual of Mental Disorders* (DSM-IV), and diagnosing and treating older adults can present more difficulties than treating younger people. Older people may have coexisting chronic medical diseases and disabilities, may take many medications, and may show cognitive impairments.

The life expectancy in the United States has increased from 47 years in 1900 to 75.8 years in 1996. Since 1960, the population age 65 and older has grown 89 percent, whereas the total population has increased only 39 percent. According to the 1990 U.S. census, the oldest old people—at least 85 years of age—are the fastest growing group of the population age 65 and older; although the oldest old people comprise only 1.2 percent of the population, their number has increased 232 percent since 1960. People at least 85 years of age currently constitute 10 percent of those age 65 and older; there are 39 men for every 100 women age 85 or older.

PSYCHIATRIC ASSESSMENT

Psychiatric history-taking and the mental status examination of older adults follow the same format as those of younger adults, but because of the high prevalence of cognitive disorders in older people, psychiatrists must determine whether a patient understands the nature and purpose of the examination. When a patient is cognitively impaired, an independent history should be obtained from a family member or caretaker. The patient still should be seen alone—even if there is clear evidence of impairment—to preserve the privacy of the doctor–patient relationship and to elicit any suicidal thoughts or paranoid ideation, which may not be voiced in the presence of a relative or a nurse.

Laboratory Studies

Laboratory and imaging studies can help clinicians establish a diagnosis and detect treatable conditions, especially disorders that might otherwise be regarded as part of normal aging. Computed tomography, magnetic resonance imaging, or single photon emission computed tomography scans probably are indicated whenever a person's mental status has changed noticeably.

Psychiatric History

A complete psychiatric history includes preliminary identification (name, age, sex, marital status), chief complaint, history of the present illness, history of previous illnesses, personal history, and family history. A review of medications (including over-the-counter medications) that the patient is currently using or has used in the recent past is also important.

Patients older than age 65 often have subjective complaints of minor memory impairments, such as forgetting people's names and misplacing objects. Minor cognitive problems also may occur because of anxiety in the interview situation. These age-associated memory impairments are of no significance; the term *benign senescent forgetfulness* has been used to describe them.

A patient's medical history should note all major illnesses, especially seizure disorders, loss of consciousness, headaches, visual problems, and hearing loss. The clinician should determine whether the patient has a history of alcohol use. Although substance abuse is less of a problem in older than younger adults, a history of prolonged substance abuse may account for current deficits.

A patient's childhood and adolescent history can provide information about personality organization and give important clues about coping strategies and defense mechanisms used under stress. A history of learning disability or minimal cerebral dysfunction is significant. The psychiatrist should inquire about friends, sports, hobbies, social activity, and work. The occupational history should include the patient's feeling about work, relationships with peers, problems with authority, and attitudes toward retirement. The patient also should be questioned about plans for the future. What are the patient's hopes and fears?

The family history should include a patient's description of parents' attitudes and adaptation to their old age and, if applicable, information about the causes of their deaths. Alzheimer's disease is transmitted as an autosomal dominant trait in 10 to 30 percent of the offspring of parents with Alzheimer's disease; depression and alcohol dependence also run in families. The patient's current social situation should be evaluated: Who cares for the patient? Does the patient have children? What are the characteristics of patient–child relationships? A financial history helps the psychiatrist evaluate the role of economic hardship in the patient's illness and to make realistic treatment recommendations.

The marital history includes a description of the spouse and the characteristics of the relationship. If the patient is a widow or a widower, the psychiatrist should explore how grieving was handled. If the loss of the spouse occurred within the past year, the patient is at high risk for an adverse physical or psychological event.

The patient's sexual history includes sexual activity, orientation, libido, masturbation, extramarital affairs, and sexual symptoms (such as impotence and anorgasmia). Young clinicians may have to overcome their own biases about taking a sexual history: Sexuality is an area of concern for many geriatric patients, who welcome the chance to talk about their sexual feelings and attitudes.

Mental Status Examination

The mental status examination offers a cross-sectional view of how a patient thinks, feels, and behaves during the examination. With older adults, a psychiatrist may not be able to rely on a single examination to answer all of the diagnostic questions. Repeat mental status examinations may have to be performed because of fluctuating changes in the patient's mental status. The longitudinal history from the patient or the patient's family is important.

General Description. A general description of the patient includes appearance, psychomotor activity, attitude toward the examiner, and speech activity.

Motor disturbances—such as shuffling gait, stooped posture, pill-rolling movements of the fingers, tremors, and body asymmetry—should be noted. Involuntary movements of the mouth or tongue may be side effects of phenothiazine medication. Many depressed patients seem to be slow in speech and movement. A masklike facies occurs in Parkinson's disease.

The patient's speech may be pressured in agitated, manic, and anxious states. Tearfulness and overt crying occur in depressive and cognitive disorders, especially if the patient feels frustrated about being unable to answer one of the examiner's questions. The presence of a hearing aid or another indication that the patient has a hearing problem, such as requesting the repetition of questions, should be noted.

The patient's attitude toward the examiner—cooperative, suspicious, guarded, ingratiating—can give clues about possible transference reactions. Because of transference, older adults can react to younger physicians as if the physicians were parent figures, despite the age difference.

Functional Assessment. Patients older than 65 years of age should be evaluated for their capacity to maintain independence and to perform the activities of daily life, which include toileting, preparing meals, dressing, grooming, and eating. The degree of functional competence in their everyday behaviors is an important consideration in formulating a plan of treatment for these patients.

Mood, Feelings, and Affect. Suicide is a leading cause of death of older people, and an evaluation of a patient's suicidal ideation is essential. Loneliness is the most common reason cited by older adults who consider suicide. Feelings of loneliness, worthlessness, helplessness, and hopelessness are symptoms of depression, which carries a high risk for suicide. Nearly 75 percent of all suicide victims suffer from depression, alcohol abuse, or both. The examiner should specifically ask the patient about any thoughts of suicide, whether the patient feels life is no longer worth living, and whether a person is better off dead or, when dead, is no longer a burden to others. Such thoughts—especially when associated with alcohol abuse, living alone, the recent death of a spouse, physical illness, and somatic pain—are indicative of a high suicidal risk.

Disturbances in mood states, most notably depression and anxiety, may interfere with memory functioning. An expansive or euphoric mood may indicate a manic episode or may be a sign of a dementing disorder. Frontal lobe dysfunction often produces *witzelsucht,* which is the tendency to make puns and jokes and then laugh aloud at them.

The patient's affect may be flat, blunted, constricted, shallow, or inappropriate, all of which can indicate a depressive disorder, schizophrenia, or brain dysfunction. Such affects are important abnormal findings, even though they are not pathognomonic of a specific disorder. Dominant lobe dysfunction causes dysprosody, an inability to express emotional feelings through speech intonation.

Perceptual Disturbances. Hallucinations and illusions by older adults may be transitory phenomena resulting from decreased sensory acuity. The examiner should note whether the patient is confused about time or place during the hallucinatory episode; confusion points to an organic condition. It is particularly important to ask the patient about distorted body perceptions. Because hallucinations may be caused by brain tumors and other focal pathology, a diagnostic workup may be indicated. Brain diseases cause perceptive impairments; agnosia, the inability to recognize and interpret the significance of sensory impressions, is associated with organic brain diseases. The examiner should note the type of agnosia—the denial of illness (anosognosia), the denial of a body part (atopognosia), or the inability to recognize objects (visual agnosia) or faces (prosopagnosia).

Language Output. This category of the geriatric mental status examination covers the aphasias, which are disorders of language output related to organic lesions of the brain. The best described are nonfluent or Broca's aphasia, fluent or Wernicke's aphasia, and global aphasia, a combination of fluent and nonfluent aphasias. In nonfluent or Broca's aphasia, the patient's understanding remains intact, but the ability to speak is impaired. The patient is unable to pronounce "Methodist Episcopalian." Speech generally is mispronounced and may be telegraphic in nature. A simple test for Wernicke's aphasia is to point to some common objects—such as a pen or a pencil, a doorknob, and a light switch—and ask the patient to name them. The patient also may be unable to demonstrate the use of simple objects, such as a key and a match (ideomotor apraxia).

Visuospatial Functioning. Some decline in visuospatial capability is normal with aging. Asking a patient to copy figures or a drawing may be helpful in assessing the function. A neuropsychological assessment should be performed when visuospatial functioning is obviously impaired.

Thought. Disturbances in thinking include neologisms, word salad, circumstantiality, tangentiality, loosening of associations, flight of ideas, clang associations, and blocking. The loss of the ability to appreciate nuances of meaning (abstract thinking) may be an early sign of dementia. Thinking is then described as concrete or literal.

Thought content should be examined for phobias, obsessions, somatic preoccupations, and compulsions. Ideas about suicide or homicide should be discussed. The examiner should determine whether delusions are present and how such delusions affect the patient's life. Delusions may be present in nursing home patients and may have been a reason for admission. Ideas of reference or of influence should be described. Patients who are hard of hearing may be classified mistakenly as paranoid or suspicious.

Sensorium and Cognition. Sensorium concerns the functioning of the special senses; cognition concerns information processing and intellect. The survey of both areas is known as the neuropsychiatric examination and consists of the clinician's assessment and a comprehensive battery of psychological tests.

CONSCIOUSNESS. A sensitive indicator of brain dysfunction is an altered state of consciousness in which the patient does not seem to be alert, shows fluctuations in levels of awareness, or seems to be lethargic. In severe cases, the patient is somnolescent or stuporous.

ORIENTATION. Impairment in orientation to time, place, and person is associated with cognitive disorders. Cognitive impairment often is observed in mood disorders, anxiety disorders, factitious disorders, conversion disorder, and personality disorders, especially during periods of severe physical or environmental stress. The examiner should test for orientation to place by asking the patient to describe his or her present location. Orientation to person may be approached in two ways: Does the patient know his or her own name, and are nurses and doctors identified as such? Time is tested by asking the patient the date, the year, the month, and the day of the week. The patient also should be asked about the length of time spent in a hospital, during what season of the year, and how the patient knows these facts. Greater significance is given to difficulties concerning person than to difficulties of time and place, and more significance is given to orientation to place than to orientation to time.

MEMORY. Memory usually is evaluated in terms of immediate, recent, and remote memory. Immediate retention and recall are tested by giving the patient six digits to repeat forward and backward. The examiner should record the result of the patient's capacity to remember. People with unimpaired memory usually can recall six digits forward and five or six digits backward. The clinician should be aware that the ability to do well on digit-span tests is impaired in extremely anxious patients. Remote memory can be tested by asking for the patient's place and date of birth, the patient's mother's name before she was married, and names and birthdays of the patient's children.

In cognitive disorders, recent memory deteriorates first. Recent memory assessment can be approached in several ways. Some examiners give the patient the names of three items early in the interview and ask for recall later. Others prefer to tell a brief story and ask the patient to repeat it verbatim. Memory of the recent past also can be tested by asking for the patient's place of residence, including the street number; the method of transportation to the hospital; and some current events. If the patient has a deficit in memory such as amnesia, careful testing should be performed to determine whether it is retrograde amnesia (loss of memory before an event) or anterograde amnesia (loss of memory after the event). Retention and recall also can be tested by having the patient retell a simple story. Patients who confabulate make up new material in the retelling of the story.

INTELLECTUAL TASKS, INFORMATION, AND INTELLIGENCE. Various intellectual tasks may be presented to estimate the patient's fund of general knowledge and intellectual functioning. Counting and calculation can be tested by asking the patient to subtract 7 from 100 and to continue subtracting 7 from the result until the number 2 is reached. The examiner records the responses as a baseline for future testing. The examiner can also ask the patient to count backward from 20 to 1, and can record the time necessary to complete the exercise. The patient also can be asked to do simple arithmetic—for example, to state the number of nickels in $1.35.

The patient's fund of general knowledge is related to intelligence. The patient can be asked to name the president of the United States, to name the three largest cities in the United States, to give the population of the United States, and to give the distance from New York to Paris. The examiner must take into account the patient's educational level, socioeconomic status, and general life experience in assessing the results of some of these tests.

READING AND WRITING. It may be important for the clinician to examine the patient's reading and writing and to determine whether the patient has a specific speech deficit. The examiner may have the patient read a simple story aloud or write a short sentence to test for a reading or writing disorder. Whether the patient is right-handed or left-handed should be noted.

Judgment. Judgment is the capacity to act appropriately in various situations: Does the patient show impaired judgment? What would the patient do if a stamped, sealed, addressed envelope was found in the street? What would the patient do if smoke was smelled in a theater? Can the patient discriminate? What is the difference between a dwarf and a boy? Why are couples required to get a marriage license?

Neuropsychological Assessment

A thorough neuropsychological examination includes a comprehensive battery of tests that can be replicated by various examiners and can be repeated over time to assess the course of a specific illness. The most widely used test of current cognitive functioning is the Mini-Mental State Examination (MMSE), which assesses orientation, attention, calculation, immediate and short-term recall, language, and the ability to follow simple commands (see Table 10.12). The MMSE is used to detect impairments, follow the course of an illness, and monitor the patient's treatment responses. It is not used to make a formal diagnosis. The maximum MMSE score is 30. Age and educational level influence cognitive performance as measured by the MMSE. It is useful to compare an individual patient's score with a population reference group (Figs. 54–1 and 54–2).

The assessment of intellectual abilities is performed with the Wechsler adult intelligence scale–revised (WAIS-R), which gives verbal, performance, and full-scale intelligence quotient (IQ) scores. Some test results, such as those of vocabulary

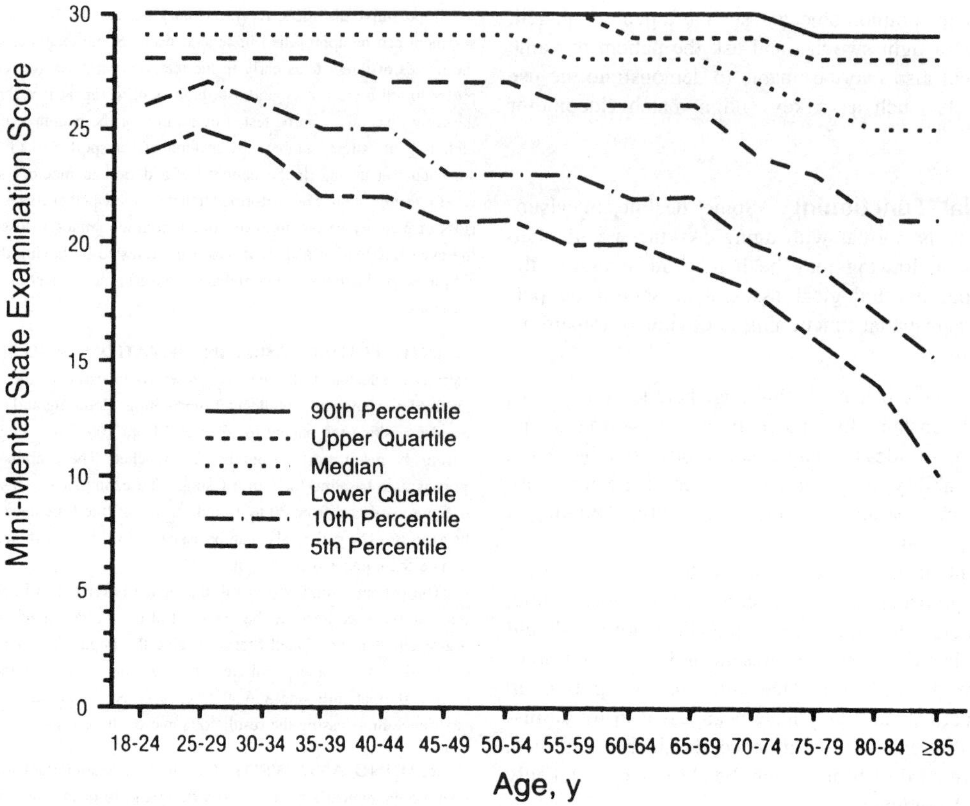
Mini-Mental State Examination Score
30
25
20
15
10
5
0
90th Percentile
Upper Quartile
Median
Lower Quartile
10th Percentile
5th Percentile
18-24 25-29 30-34 35-39 40-44 45-49 50-54 55-59 60-64 65-69 70-74 75-79 80-84 ≥85
Age, y

FIGURE 54–1
Mini-Mental State Examination score by age and selected percentiles. Data from the Epidemiologic Catchment Area surveys, 1980 to 1984, with weights based on the 1980 U.S. population distributions for age, sex, and race. (Reprinted with permission from Crum RM, Anthony JC, Bassett SS, Folstein MF: Population-based norms for the Mini-Mental State Examination by age and educational level. JAMA *269:* 2388, 1993.)

tests, hold up as aging progresses; results of other tests, such as tests of similarities and digit-symbol substitution, do not. The performance part of the WAIS-R is a more sensitive indicator of brain damage than the verbal part.

Visuospatial functions are sensitive to the normal aging process. The Bender Gestalt test is one of a large number of instruments used to test visuospatial functions; another is the Halstead-Reitan battery, which is the most complex battery of tests covering the entire spectrum of information processing and cognition. Depression, even in the absence of dementia, often impairs psychomotor performance, especially visuospatial functioning and timed motor performance. The Geriatric Depression Scale is a useful screening instrument that excludes somatic complaints from its list of items. The presence of somatic complaints on a rating scale tends to confound the diagnosis of a depressive disorder.

Current Medications Used

Older adults are susceptible to the adverse behavioral and cognitive effects of drugs. The most commonly used class of psychoactive drugs among older people, the benzodiazepines, can cause sedation, behavioral disinhibition, depression, and memory impairment as side effects. Benzodiazepine discontinuation can cause insomnia and anxiety. Many antidepressant drugs cause nervousness and insomnia, and medications used to treat cardiovascular, pulmonary, and endocrine disorders are also known to cause psychiatric side effects. The clinician must obtain a complete list of all current medications used by the patient.

MENTAL DISORDERS OF OLD AGE

The National Institute of Mental Health's Epidemiologic Catchment Area (ECA) program has found that the most common mental disorders of old age are depressive disorders, cognitive disorders, phobias, and alcohol use disorders. Older adults also have a high risk for suicide and drug-induced psychiatric symptoms. Many metal disorders of old age can be prevented, ameliorated, or even reversed. Of special importance are the reversible causes of delirium and dementia; but if not diagnosed accurately and treated in a timely fashion, these conditions can progress to an irreversible state requiring a patient's institutionalization.

Several psychosocial risk factors also predispose older people to mental disorders. These risk factors include loss of social roles, loss of autonomy, the deaths of friends and relatives, declining health, increased isolation, financial constraints, and decreased cognitive functioning.

Many drugs can cause psychiatric symptoms in older

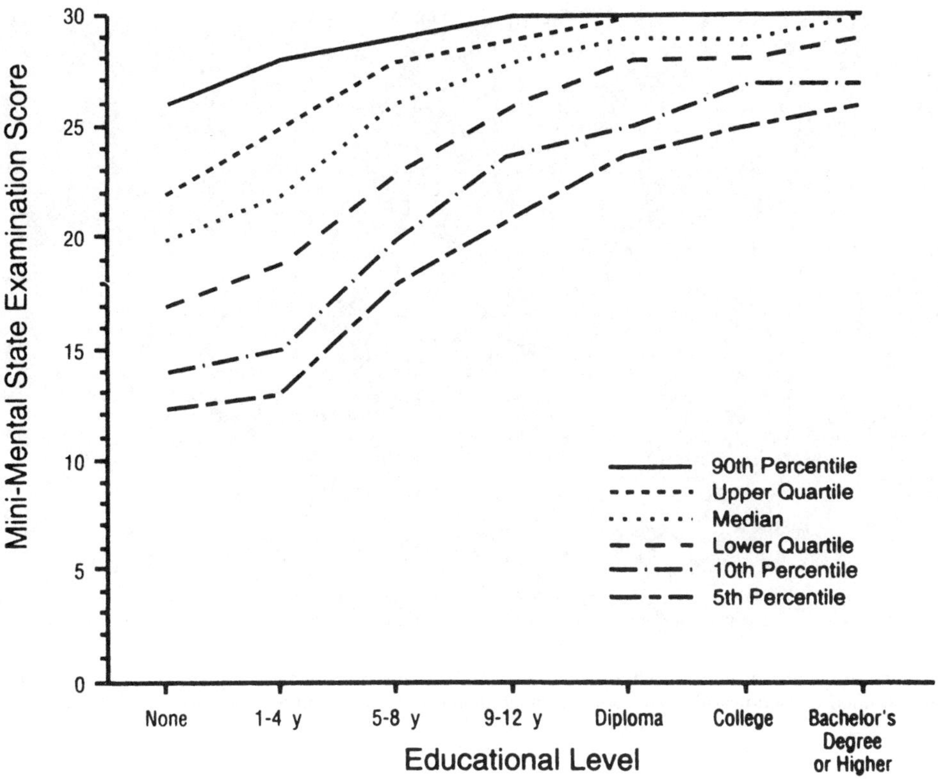
Mini-Mental State Examination Score
30
25
20
15
10
5
0
90th Percentile
Upper Quartile
Median
Lower Quartile
10th Percentile
5th Percentile
None
1-4 y
5-8 y
9-12 y
Diploma
College
Bachelor's Degree or Higher
Educational Level

FIGURE 54–2

Mini-Mental State Examination score by educational level and selected percentiles. Data from the Epidemiologic Catchment Area surveys, 1980 to 1984, with weights based on the 1980 U.S. population distributions for age, sex, and race. (Reprinted with permission from Crum RM, Anthony JC, Bassett SS, Folstein MF: Population-based norms for the Mini-Mental State Examination by age and educational level. JAMA *269:* 2388, 1993.)

adults. These symptoms occur as a result of a patient's age-related alterations in drug absorption, a prescribed dosage that is too large, the patient's not following instructions and taking too large a dose, the patient's sensitivity to the medication, and conflicting regimens presented by several physicians. Almost the entire spectrum of mental disorders can be caused by drugs.

Dementing Disorders

Only arthritis is a more common cause of disability among adults age 65 and older than dementia, which is a generally progressive and irreversible impairment of the intellect, the prevalence of which increases with age. Of people in the United States older than age 65, about 5 percent have severe dementia and 15 percent have mild dementia. Of people older than age 80, about 20 percent have severe dementia. Known risk factors for dementia are age, family history, and female sex.

In contrast to mental retardation, the intellectual impairment of dementia develops over time—that is, previously achieved mental functions are lost gradually. The characteristic changes of dementia involve cognition, memory, language, and visuospatial functions, but behavioral disturbances are common as well and include agitation, restlessness, wandering, rage, violence, shouting, social and sexual disinhibition, impulsiveness, sleep disturbances, and delusions. Delusions and hallucinations occur during the course of the dementias in nearly 75 percent of all patients.

Cognition is impaired by many conditions, including brain injuries, cerebral tumors, acquired immune deficiency syndrome (AIDS), alcohol, medications, infections, chronic pulmonary diseases, and inflammatory diseases. Although dementias associated with advanced age typically are caused by primary degenerative central nervous system (CNS) disease and vascular disease, many factors contribute to cognitive impairment; in older people, mixed causes of dementia are common.

About 10 to 15 percent of all patients who exhibit symptoms of dementia have potentially treatable conditions. The treatable conditions include systemic disorders, such as heart disease, renal disease, and congestive heart failure; endocrine disorders, such as hypothyroidism; vitamin deficiency; medication misuse; and primary mental disorders, most notably depressive disorders.

Depending on the site of the cerebral lesion, dementias are classified as cortical and subcortical. A subcortical dementia occurs in Huntington's disease, Parkinson's disease, normal pressure hydrocephalus, multi-infarct dementia, and Wilson's disease. The subcortical dementias are associated with movement disorders, gait apraxia, psychomotor retardation, apathy, and akinetic mutism, which can be confused with catatonia.

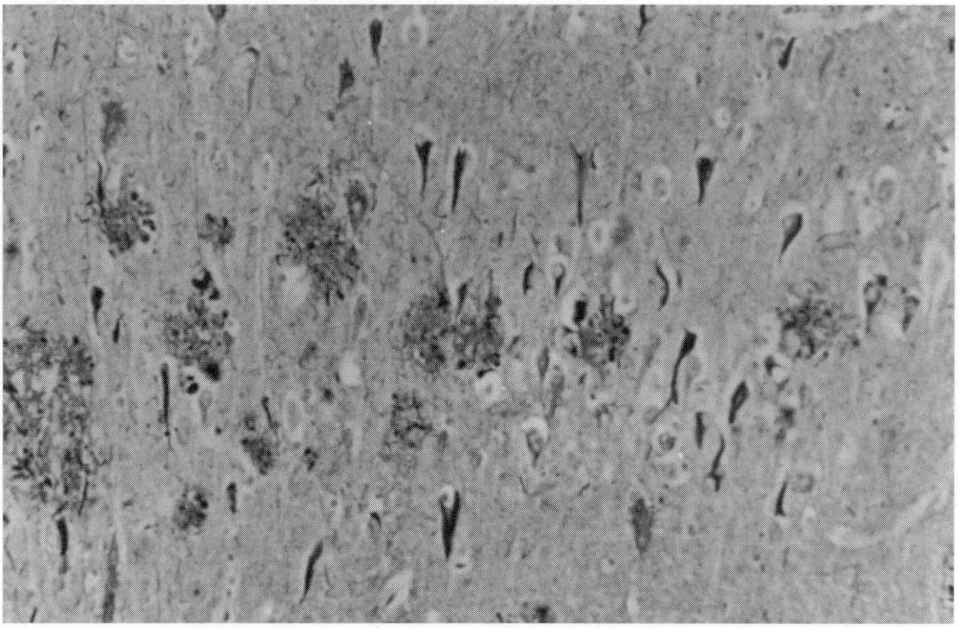

FIGURE 54–3
Microscopic appearance of the hippocampus from a patient with Alzheimer's disease, showing large numbers of neurofibrillary tangles and senile plaques (modified Bielschowsky's stain, original magnification ×190). (Courtesy of Daniel Perl, M.D.)

The cortical dementias occur in dementias of the Alzheimer's type, Creutzfeldt-Jakob disease (CJD), and Pick's disease, which frequently manifest aphasia, agnosia, and apraxia. In clinical practice, the two types of dementia overlap, and in most cases, an accurate diagnosis can be made only by autopsy. Human prion diseases result from coding mutations in the prion protein gene (PRNP) and may be inherited, acquired, or sporadic. They include familial CJD, Gerstmann-Sträussler-Scheinker syndrome, and fatal familial insomnia. These are inherited as autosomal dominant mutations. The acquired diseases include kuru and iatrogenic CJD. Kuru was an epidemic prion disease of the Fore people of Papua, New Guinea, caused by cannibalistic funereal rituals, which peaked in incidence in the 1950s. Iatrogenic disease is rare and is caused by, for example, the use of contaminated dura mater and corneal grafts and treatment with human cadaveric pituitary-derived growth hormone and gonadotrophin. Sporadic CJD accounts for 85% of the human prion diseases and occurs worldwide with a uniform distribution and incidence of around 1 in 1 million per annum, with a mean age at onset of 65 years. It is exceedingly rare in individuals under 30 years of age. (Additional information on dementia is contained in Chapter 10, Section 10.3.)

Dementia of the Alzheimer's Type. Of all patients with dementia, 50 to 60 percent have dementia of the Alzheimer's type, which is the most common type of dementia. About 5 percent of all people who reach age 65 have dementia of the Alzheimer's type, compared with 15 to 25 percent of all those age 85 or older. The prevalence of dementia of the Alzheimer's type is higher in women than in men. Patients with dementia of the Alzheimer's type occupy more than 50 percent of all nursing home beds.

This dementia has an insidious onset and is progressive. The mean survival for people with dementia of the Alzheimer's type is approximately 8 years (range, 1 to 20 years). The diagnosis is made on the basis of the patient's history and a mental status examination. Brain-imaging techniques also may be useful.

Dementia of the Alzheimer's type is characterized by the gradual onset and progressive decline of cognitive functions. Memory is impaired, and at least one of the following is seen: aphasia, apraxia, agnosia, and disturbances in executive functioning. The general sequence of deficits is memory, language, and visuospatial functions. Initially, a patient may have an inability to learn and recall new information; then, he or she develops impaired naming, followed by an inability to copy figures. Early dementia of the Alzheimer's type may be difficult to diagnose because a patient's IQ may be normal.

Personality changes—such as depression, obsessiveness, and suspiciousness—occur. Outbursts of anger are common, and there is a risk of violent acts. Disorientation leads to wandering; a patient may be discovered far from home in a dazed condition. Loss of initiative is common. Neurological defects—such as gait disturbances, aphasia, apraxia, and agnosia—eventually appear.

ETIOLOGY. The cause of Alzheimer's disease is unknown, although postmortem neuropathological and biochemical studies have shown a selective loss of cholinergic neurons. Structural and functional changes occur. Gross anatomical findings include reduced gyral volume in the frontal and temporal lobes, with relative sparing of the primary motor and sensory cortex. Typical microscopic alterations include senile plaques and neurofibrillary tangles, which are derived from tau proteins (Figs. 54–3 and 10.3–1). Blocking the aberrant phosphorylation of tau proteins is being explored as a possible therapeutic intervention in dementia of the Alzheimer's type.

TREATMENT. Dementia of the Alzheimer's type has no known prevention or cure. Treatment is palliative and consists of proper nutrition, exercise, and supervision of daily activity. Medication may be helpful in managing agitation and behavioral disturbances. Propranolol (Inderal), pindolol (Visken), buspirone (BuSpar), and valproate (Depakene) all have been reported to help reduce agitation and aggression. Haloperidol (Haldol) and other high-potency dopamine-blocking agents may be used to control acute behavior disturbances. Some patients with dementia of the Alzheimer's type show improvement in cognitive and functional measures when treated with tacrine (Cognex) or donepezil (Aricept). Recent reports of vitamin E supplementation (400 to 600 mg a day) retarding the progress of dementia are encouraging.

Vascular Dementia. The second most common type of dementia is vascular dementia. It is characterized by the same cognitive deficits as dementia of the Alzheimer's type, but vascular dementia has focal neurological signs and symptoms, such as an exaggeration of deep tendon reflexes, extensor plantar response, pseudobulbar palsy, gait abnormalities, and weakness of an extremity. Compared with dementia of the Alzheimer's type, vascular dementia has an abrupt onset and a stepwise deteriorating course. Vascular dementia may be prevented through the reduction of known risk factors, such as hypertension, diabetes, cigarette smoking, and arrhythmias. Diagnosis can be confirmed with magnetic resonance imaging (MRI) and cerebral blood flow studies.

Dementia Due to Pick's Disease. Pick's disease causes a slowly progressing dementia and is associated with focal cortical lesions, primarily on the frontal lobe, that produce aphasia, apraxia, and agnosia. The disease lasts from 2 to 10 years; the average duration is 5 years. Clinically, Pick's disease is difficult to distinguish from Alzheimer's disease. On autopsy, however, the brain reveals intraneuronal inclusions called *Pick bodies,* which are different from the neurofibrillary tangles of Alzheimer's dementia. Pick's disease is much rarer than Alzheimer's dementia, and no treatment is available.

Dementia Due to Creutzfeldt-Jakob Disease. CJD is caused by a slow-growing infectious virus and is a diffuse degenerative disease that affects the pyramidal and extrapyramidal systems. Some cases have been traced to the transplantation of the cornea of an infected person to a previously noninfected person. The disease usually affects people in their 50s, and the usual course is approximately 1 year. Dementia due to Creutzfeldt-Jakob disease is not associated with aging, and its incidence actually decreases after age 60. The terminal stage is characterized by severe dementia, generalized hypertonicity, and profound speech disturbances.

G. R. Mallucci and J. Collinge reported on a new variant of CJD that appeared in 1995 in the United Kingdom. The patients affected all died; they were young (under 40), and none had risk factors of CJD. At autopsy, prion disease was found. The disease was attributed to the transmission in the 1980s in the United Kingdom of bovine spongiform encephalopathy (BSE) between cattle and from cattle to other species by contaminated feed and exposure to bovine prions resulted in transmission of BSE to humans.

They suggested that clinicians be alert for behavioral and psychiatric abnormalities in young people (or even in older individuals) in association with cerebellar or cognitive abnormalities. The psychiatric presentation of CJD is not specific, and diagnosis relies on the development of progressive neurodegenerative features. Suspected patients should be reviewed regularly over the months after presentation. A rapid progression will confirm the new variant.

Dementia Due to Huntington's Disease. Huntington's disease is a hereditary disease associated with progressive degeneration of the basal ganglia and the cerebral cortex. The onset of Huntington's disease occurs between 35 and 50 years of age, but the disease may begin later in rare cases. It is characterized by progressive dementia, muscular hypertonicity, and bizarre choreiform movements; death usually occurs 15 to 20 years after the onset of the disease. No treatment is available. Huntington's disease is transmitted as an autosomal dominant gene (traced to the G8 fragment of chromosome 4). Each offspring of an affected parent has a 50 percent chance of getting the disease, and everyone with the gene eventually has the disease. A genetic screening test for the disorder is now available. Currently, 25,000 Americans have Huntington's disease, and approximately 125,000 children are at risk.

Dementia Due to Normal Pressure Hydrocephalus. In older people, normal pressure hydrocephalus causes gait disturbances (unstable or shuffling gait), urinary incontinence, and dementia. Enlargement of the ventricles with increased cerebrospinal fluid (CSF) pressure is found.

Dementia Due to Parkinson's Disease. Parkinson's disease is characterized primarily by motor dysfunction, but cognitive disturbances, including dementia, may be part of the disorder. Frontal lobe symptoms and memory deficits are common. Nearly one half of all affected patients are depressed, and depression is the most common mental disturbance in Parkinson's disease. Patients are also at increased risk for anxiety. Medications used to treat Parkinson's disease—particularly drugs that facilitate dopaminergic neurotransmission, such as levodopa, amantadine (Symmetrel), and bromocriptine (Parlodel)—may cause psychosis and delirium.

Depressive Disorders

Depressive symptoms are present in about 15 percent of all older adult community residents and nursing home patients. Age itself is not a risk factor for the development of depression, but being widowed and having a chronic medical illness are associated with vulnerability to depressive disorders. Late-onset depression is characterized by high rates of recurrence.

The common signs and symptoms of depressive disorders include reduced energy and concentration, sleep problems (especially early morning awakening and multiple awakenings), decreased appetite, weight loss, and somatic complaints. The presenting symptoms may be different in older depressed patients from those seen in younger adults because of an increased emphasis on somatic complaints in older people. They are particularly vulnerable to major depressive episodes with melancholic features, characterized by depression, hypochondriasis, low self-esteem, feelings of worthlessness, and self-accusatory trends (especially about sex and sinfulness) with paranoid and suicidal ideation.

Cognitive impairment in depressed geriatric patients is referred to as the dementia syndrome of depression (pseudodementia), which can be confused easily with true dementia. In true dementia, intellectual performance usually is global in nature, and impairment is consistently poor; in pseudodementia, deficits in attention and concentration are variable. Compared with patients who have true dementia, patients with pseudodementia are less likely to have language impairment and to confabulate; when uncertain, they are more likely to say "I don't know;" memory difficulties are more limited to free recall, as compared with recognition on cued recall tests. Pseudodementia occurs in about 15 percent of depressed older patients, and 25 to 50 percent of patients with dementia are depressed. Table 10.3–14 compares dementia and pseudodementia.

Depression may be associated with physical illness and with the medications used for treating illness. Clinicians must be aware of the many pharmacological agents that are common causes of depression (see Table 15.1–10).

Bipolar I Disorder

Bipolar I disorder usually begins in middle adulthood, although the lifetime prevalence of 1 percent remains steady throughout life. A vulnerability to recurrences remains, so patients with a history of bipolar I disorder may display a manic episode late in life. In most instances, a first episode of manic behavior after age 65 should alert clinicians to search for an associated physiological or organic cause, such as the side effects of medication or an early dementia. The signs and symptoms of mania in older people are similar to those in younger adults and include an elevated, expansive, or irritable mood; a decreased need to sleep; distractibility; impulsivity; and, often, excessive alcohol intake. Hostile or paranoid behavior usually is present. Cognitive impairment, disorientation, or fluctuating levels of awareness should make clinicians suspicious of an organic cause.

Lithium (Eskalith) remains a treatment of choice for mania, but its use by older patients must be monitored carefully, because their reduced renal clearance makes lithium toxicity a significant risk. Neurotoxic effects are also more common in older people than in younger adults.

Schizophrenia

Schizophrenia usually begins in late adolescence or young adulthood and persists throughout life. Although first episodes diagnosed after age 65 are rare, a late-onset type beginning after age 45 has been described. Women are more likely to have a late onset of schizophrenia than men. Another difference between early-onset and late-onset schizophrenia is the greater prevalence of paranoid schizophrenia in the late-onset type. About 20 percent of people with schizophrenia show no active symptoms by age 65; 80 percent show varying degrees of impairment. Psychopathology becomes less marked as patients age.

The residual type of schizophrenia occurs in about 30 percent of all people with schizophrenia. Its signs and symptoms include emotional blunting, social withdrawal, eccentric behavior, and illogical thinking. Delusions and hallucinations are uncommon. Because most residual people with schizophrenia are unable to care for themselves, long-term hospitalization is required.

Older people with schizophrenic symptoms respond well to antipsychotic drugs. Medication must be administered judiciously, and lower-than-usual dosages often are effective for older adults.

Delusional Disorder

The age of onset of delusional disorder usually is between ages 40 and 55, but it can occur at any time during the geriatric period. Delusions can take many forms; the most common is persecutory in nature—patients believe that they are being spied on, followed, poisoned, or harassed in some way. People with delusional disorder may become violent toward their supposed persecutors. Some people lock themselves in their rooms and live reclusive lives. Somatic delusions, in which people believe they have a fatal illness, also may occur in older people. In one study of people older than 65 years of age, pervasive persecutory ideation was present in 4 percent of people sampled.

Among those who are vulnerable, delusional disorder can occur under physical or psychological stress and may be precipitated by the death of a spouse, loss of a job, retirement, social isolation, adverse financial circumstances, debilitating medical illness or surgery, visual impairment, and deafness. Delusions also may accompany other disorders—such as dementia of the Alzheimer's type, alcohol use disorders, schizophrenia, depressive disorders, and bipolar I disorder—which need to be ruled out. Delusional syndromes also may result from prescribed medications or from early signs of a brain tumor.

The prognosis is fair to good in most cases; best results are achieved through a combination of psychotherapy and pharmacotherapy.

A late-onset delusional disorder called *paraphrenia* is characterized by persecutory delusions. It develops over several years and is not associated with dementia. Some workers believe the disorder to be a variant of schizophrenia that first becomes manifest after age 60. Patients with a family history of schizophrenia show an increased rate of paraphrenia.

Anxiety Disorders

The anxiety disorders include panic disorder, phobias, obsessive-compulsive disorder, generalized anxiety disorder, acute stress disorder, and posttraumatic stress disorder. Anxiety disorders begin in early or middle adulthood, but some appear for the first time after age 60. An initial onset of panic disorder in older people is rare but can occur. The ECA study determined that the 1-month prevalence of anxiety disorders in people age 65 and older is 5.5 percent. By far the most common disorders are phobias (4 to 8 percent). The rate for panic disorder is 1 percent.

The signs and symptoms of phobias in older adults are less severe than those that occur in younger people, but the effects are equally, if not more, debilitating for older patients. Existential theories help explain anxiety when there is no specifically identifiable stimulus for a chronically anxious feeling.

Older people must come to grips with death. The person may deal with the thought of death and with a sense of despair and anxiety, rather than with equanimity and Erik Erikson's sense of integrity. The fragility of the autonomic nervous system in older people may account for the development of anxiety after a major stressor. Because of concurrent physically disability, older people react more severely to posttraumatic stress disorder than younger people.

Obsessions and compulsions may appear for the first time in older adults, although older adults with obsessive-compulsive disorder usually had demonstrated evidence of obsessive-compulsive disorder, such as being orderly, perfectionistic, punctual, and parsimonious, when they were younger. When symptomatic, patients become excessive in their desire for orderliness, rituals, and sameness. They may become generally inflexible and rigid and have compulsions to check things again and again. Obsessive-compulsive disorder, in contrast to obsessive-compulsive personality disorder, is characterized by ego-dystonic rituals and obsessions and may begin late in life.

Treatment of anxiety disorders must be individually tailored to patients and must take into account the biopsychosocial interplay producing the disorder. Both pharmacotherapy and psychotherapy are required.

Somatoform Disorders

Somatoform disorders, characterized by physical symptoms resembling medical diseases, are relevant to geriatric psychiatry because somatic complaints are common among older adults. More than 80 percent of people older than 65 years of age have at least one chronic disease—usually arthritis or cardiovascular problems. After the age of 75 years, 20 percent have diabetes and an average of four diagnosable chronic illnesses that require medical attention.

Hypochondriasis is common in people older than 60 years of age, although the peak incidence is in the 40- to 50-year-old age group. The disorder usually is chronic, and the prognosis is guarded. Repeated physical examinations are useful in reassuring patients that they do not have a fatal illness, but invasive and high-risk diagnostic procedures should be avoided unless medically indicated.

Telling patients that their symptoms are imaginary and counterproductive usually meets with resentment. Clinicians should acknowledge that the complaint is real, that the pain is really there and perceived as such by the patient, and that a psychological or pharmacological approach to the problem is indicated.

Alcohol and Other Substance Use Disorders

Older adults with alcohol dependence usually give a history of excessive drinking that began in young or middle adulthood. They usually are medically ill, primarily with liver disease, and are either divorced, widowers, or men who never married. Many have arrest records and are numbered among homeless people. A large number have chronic dementing illness such as Wernicke's encephalopathy and Korsakoff's syndrome. Twenty percent of nursing home patients have alcohol dependence.

Over all, alcohol and other substance use disorders account for 10 percent of all emotional problems in older people, and dependence on such substances as hypnotics, anxiolytics, and narcotics is more common in old age than is generally recognized. Substance-seeking behavior characterized by crime, manipulativeness, and antisocial behavior is relatively rare in older adults compared with younger adults. Older patients may abuse anxiolytics to allay chronic anxiety or to ensure sleep. The maintenance of chronically ill cancer patients with narcotics prescribed by a physician produces dependence, but the need to provide pain relief takes precedence over the possibility of narcotic dependence and is entirely justified.

The clinical presentation of older patients with alcohol and other substance use disorders is varied and includes confusion, poor personal hygiene, depression, malnutrition, and the effects of exposure and falls. The sudden onset of delirium in older people hospitalized for medical illness is most often caused by alcohol withdrawal. Alcohol abuse also should be considered in older adults with chronic gastrointestinal problems.

Older people may misuse over-the-counter substances, including nicotine and caffeine. Thirty-five percent use over-the-counter analgesics, and thirty percent use laxatives. Unexplained gastrointestinal, psychological, and metabolic problems should alert clinicians to over-the-counter substance abuse.

Sleep Disorders

Advanced age is the single most important factor associated with the increased prevalence of sleep disorders. Sleep-related phenomena that are reported more frequently by older than by younger adults are sleeping problems, daytime sleepiness, daytime napping, and the use of hypnotic drugs. Clinically, older people experience higher rates of breathing-related sleep disorder and medication-induced movement disorders than younger adults.

In addition to altered regulatory and physiological systems, the causes of sleep disturbances in older people include primary sleep disorders, other mental disorders, general medical disorders, and social and environmental factors. Among the primary sleep disorders, dyssomnias are the most frequent, especially primary insomnia, nocturnal myoclonus, restless legs syndrome, and sleep apnea. Of the parasomnias, rapid eye movement (REM) sleep behavior disorder occurs almost exclusively among elderly men. The conditions that commonly interfere with sleep in older adults also include pain, nocturia, dyspnea, and heartburn. The lack of a daily structure and of social or vocational responsibilities contributes to poor sleep.

As a result of the decreased length of their daily sleep–wake cycle, older people without daily routines, especially patients in nursing homes, may experience an advanced sleep phase, in which they go to sleep early and awaken during the night.

Even modest amounts of alcohol can interfere with the quality of sleep and can cause sleep fragmentation and early morning awakening. Alcohol may also precipitate or aggravate obstructive sleep apnea. Many older people use alcohol, hypnotics, and other central nervous system depressants to help them fall asleep, but data show that these people experience more early morning awakening than trouble falling sleep. When prescribing sedative-hypnotic drugs for older people, clinicians must monitor the patients for unwanted cognitive, behavioral, and psychomotor effects, including memory impairment (anterograde amnesia), residual sedation, rebound insomnia, daytime withdrawal, and unsteady gait.

Dementia may be associated with sundowning, an increase in confusion and agitation after nightfall. Dementia is associated with an increased frequency of arousals, increased stage 1 sleep, and decreased stages 3 and 4 sleep. Many demented patients, however, have no sleep disturbance.

Changes in sleep structure among people older than 65 years of age involve both REM sleep and non–rapid eye movement (NREM) sleep. The REM changes include the redistribution of REM sleep throughout the night, an increased number of REM episodes, a decreased length of REM episodes, and reduced total REM sleep. The NREM changes include the decreased amplitude of delta waves, a decreased percentage of stages 3 and 4 sleep, and an increased percentage of stages 1 and 2 sleep. In addition, older people experience increased awakening after sleep onset.

Much of the observed deterioration in the quality of sleep in older people is due to the altered timing and consolidation of sleep. For example, with advanced age, people have a lower amplitude of circadian rhythms, a 12-hour sleep-propensity rhythm, and a decreased length of circadian cycles.

OTHER DISORDERS OF OLD AGE

Vertigo

Feelings of vertigo or dizziness, a common complaint of older adults, cause many older adults to become inactive because they fear falling. The causes of vertigo are varied and include anemia, hypotension, cardiac arrhythmia, cerebrovascular disease, basilar artery insufficiency, middle ear disease, acoustic neuroma, and Ménière's disease. Most cases of vertigo have a strong psychological component, and clinicians should ascertain any secondary gain from the symptom. The overuse of anxiolytics can cause dizziness and daytime somnolence. Treatment with meclizine (Antivert), 25 to 100 mg daily, has been successful in many cases of vertigo.

Syncope

The sudden loss of consciousness associated with syncope results from a reduction of cerebral blood flow and brain hypoxia. A thorough medical workup is required to rule out the various causes listed in Table 54–1.

Table 54–1
Common Causes of Syncope

Epilepsy
Cerebral ischemia
Coronary artery insufficiency; valvular disease
Anemia
Carotid sinus syndrome
Cardiac arrhythmia
Stokes-Adams conduction defect
Hyperventillation
Hypoglycemia
Anxiety attack
Cerebrovascular disease; vertebral-basilar insufficiency

ELDER ABUSE

An estimated 10 percent of people older than 65 years of age are abused. *Elder abuse* is defined by the American Medical Association as "an act or omission which results in harm or threatened harm to the health or welfare of an elderly person." Mistreatment includes abuse and neglect—physically, psychologically, financially, and materially. Sexual abuse does occur. Acts of omission include the withholding of food, medicine, clothing, and other necessities. The types of elder abuse are listed in Table 54–2.

Family conflicts and other problems often underlie elder abuse. The victims tend to be very old and frail. They often live with their assailants, who may be financially dependent on the victims. Both the victim and the perpetrator tend to deny or minimize the presence of abuse. Interventions include providing legal services, housing, and medical, psychiatric, and social services.

PSYCHOPHARMACOLOGICAL TREATMENT OF GERIATRIC DISORDERS

In older adults, certain guidelines should be followed regarding the use of all drugs. A pretreatment medical evaluation is essential, including an electrocardiogram (ECG). It is especially useful to have an older patient or the family bring in all currently used medications, because multiple drug use may be contributing to the symptoms.

Most psychotropic drugs should be given in equally divided doses 3 or 4 times over a 24-hour period. Older patients may not be able to tolerate a sudden rise in drug blood level resulting from one large daily dose. Any changes in blood pressure and pulse rate and other side effects should be watched. For patients with insomnia, however, giving the major portion of an antipsychotic or antidepressant at bedtime takes advantage of its sedating and soporific effects. Liquid preparations are useful for older patients who cannot or who refuse to swallow tablets. Clinicians should frequently reassess all patients to determine the need for maintenance medication, changes in dosage, and development of side effects. If a patient is taking psychotropic drugs at the time of the evaluation, the clinician should, if possible, discontinue these medications and, after a washout period, reevaluate the patient during a drug-free baseline state.

Adults older than 65 years of age use the greatest number of medications of any age group; 25 percent of all prescriptions are written for them. Adverse drug reactions caused by medications result in the hospitalization of nearly 250,000 persons in the United States each year. Psychotropic drugs are among the most commonly prescribed, along with cardiovascular and diuretic medications; 40 percent of all hypnotics dispensed in the United States each year are to those older than 65 years of age, and 70 percent of older people use over-the-counter med-

Table 54–2
Types of Elder Abuse

Physical or Sexual Abuse
- Bruises (bilateral and at various stages of healing)
- Welts
- Lacerations
- Punctures
- Fractures
- Evidence of excessive drugging
- Burns
- Physical restraints (tying to beds, etc.)
- Malnutrition and dehydration
- Lack of personal care
- Inadequate heating
- Lack of food and water
- Unclean clothes or bedding
- Lack of needed medication
- Lack of eyeglasses, hearing aids, false teeth
- Difficulty in walking or sitting
- Venereal disease
- Pain or itching, bruises, or bleeding of external genitalia, vaginal area, or anal area

Psychological Abuse (vulnerable adults react by exhibiting resignation, fear, depression, mental confusion, anger, ambivalence, insomnia)
- Threats
- Insults
- Harassment
- Withholding of security and affection
- Harsh orders
- Refusal on the part of the family or those caring for the adult to allow travel, visits by friends or other family members, attendance at church

Exploitation
- Misuse of vulnerable adult's income or other financial resources (victim is best source of information but in most cases has turned management of financial affairs over to another person; as a result, there may be some confusion about finances)

Medical Abuse
- Withholding or improper administration of medications or necessary medical treatments for a condition or the withholding of aids the person would medically require, such as false teeth, glasses, hearing aids
- May be a cause of:
  - Confusion
  - Disorientation
  - Memory impairment
  - Agitation
  - Lethargy
  - Self-neglect

Neglect
- Conduct of vulnerable adult or others that results in deprivation of care necessary to maintain physical and mental health
- May be manifest by:
  - Malnutrition
  - Poor personal hygiene
  - Any of the indicators for medical abuse

Reprinted with permission from Washington State Medical Association: *Elder Abuse: Guidelines for Intervention by Physicians and Other Service Providers.* Washington State Medical Association, Seattle, 1985.

ications, compared with only 10 percent of young adults. (Chapter 35 presents a comprehensive survey of the psychopharmacological agents.)

Principles

The major goals of the pharmacological treatment of older people are to improve the quality of life, maintain people in the community, and delay or avoid their placement in nursing homes. Individualization of dosage is the basic tenet of geriatric psychopharmacology.

Alterations of drug dosages are required because of the physiological changes that occur as the people age. Renal disease is associated with decreased renal clearance of drugs; liver disease results in a decreased ability to metabolize drugs; cardiovascular disease and reduced cardiac output can effect both renal and hepatic drug clearance; and gastrointestinal disease and decreased gastric acid secretion influence drug absorption. As a person ages, the ratio of lean to fat body mass also changes. With normal aging, lean body mass decreases and body fat increases. Changes in the ratio of lean to fat body mass that accompany aging affect the distribution of drugs. Many lipid-soluble psychotropic drugs are distributed more widely in fat than in lean tissue, so a drug's action can be unexpectedly prolonged in older people. Similarly, changes in end-organ or receptor-site sensitivity must be taken into account. In older people, the increased risk of orthostatic hypotension from psychotropic drugs is related to reduced functioning of blood-pressure–regulating mechanisms.

As a general rule, the lowest possible dose should be used to achieve the desired therapeutic response. Clinicians must know the pharmacodynamics, pharmacokinetics, and biotransformation of each drug prescribed and the effects of the interaction of the drug with other drugs that a patient is taking.

Antidepressants

All antidepressant drugs are equally effective in treating depression; therefore, side effects are a dominant consideration in selecting a drug. Older patients often are more susceptible to some antidepressant side effects than younger adults. The consequences of adverse drug reactions in older people also are potentially more severe than in younger adults. Among the factors that contribute to adverse effect prevalence and severity in older people are altered drug metabolism, compromised physiological functions, altered body composition, and drug interactions. The geriatric dosages of commonly used antidepressants are listed in Table 54–3.

Tricyclic drugs are among the oldest psychopharmacological agents. When used by older people, the secondary amine agents desipramine (Norpramin) and nortriptyline (Aventyl, Pamelor) are preferred because of their low propensity to cause anticholinergic, orthostatic, and sedative side effects. Nortriptyline is less likely than other tricyclic agents to cause orthostatic hypotension in patients with congestive heart failure. Because of the quinidine-like effect of all tricyclics, a pretreatment electroencephalogram (EEG) is essential to determine whether a patient has a preexisting cardiac conduction defect.

Table 54–3
Geriatric Dosages of Commonly Used Antidepressants

Generic Name	Trade Name	Geriatric Dosage Range (mg a day)
Tricyclics[c]		
Imipramine	Tofranil	25–300
Desipramine	Norpramin, Pertofrane	10–300
Trimipramine	Surmontil	25–300
Amitriptyline	Elavil	25–300
Nortriptyline	Pamelor, Aventyl	10–150
Protriptyline	Vivactil	10–40
Doxepin	Adapin, Sinequan	10–300
Tetracyclic		
Maprotiline	Ludiomil	25–150
Serotonin-specific reuptake inhibitors		
Fluoxetine	Prozac	5–80
Fluvoxamine	Luvox	25–150
Paroxetine	Paxil	5–20
Sertraline	Zoloft	50–200
Trazodone	Desyrel	100–500
Bupropion	Wellbutrin	75–450
Nefazodone	Serzone	100–400
Monoamine oxidase inhibitors (MAOIs)[a]		
Phenelzine	Nardil	15–45
Tranylcypromine[b]	Parnate	10–20

[a] Persons taking MAOIs should be on a tyramine-free diet.
[b] Not recommended in persons older than age 60 because of pressor effects.
[c] Exact range may vary among laboratories.

Monoamine oxidase inhibitors (MAOIs) are also useful in treating depression because monoamine oxidase (MAO) decreases in the aging brain and may account for diminished catecholamines and a resultant depression. MAOIs may be used with caution in older patients. Orthostatic hypotension is common and severe with MAOIs; patients must adhere to a tyramine-free diet to avoid hypertensive crises. The potential for serious drug interactions involving certain analgesics, such as meperidine (Demerol) and sympathomimetics, also requires that patients understand what food and drugs they may use. Tranylcypromine (Parnate) and phenelzine (Nardil) are representative drugs that should be used cautiously for patients who are prone to hypertension. Any kind of cognitive impairment precludes MAOI therapy. Table 54–3 lists the geriatric dosages of the MAOIs.

Major side effect considerations with some other antidepressants are as follows: for trazodone (Desyrel), sedation and orthostatic hypotension; for amoxapine (Asendin), extrapyramidal effects; and for maprotiline (Ludiomil), seizures. With the exception of the risk of seizures at high dosages, bupropion (Wellbutrin) generally is well tolerated. It is nonsedating and does not produce orthostasis, but it should be given in three divided doses.

In general, the serotonin-specific reuptake inhibitors (SSRIs) are safe and well tolerated by older patients. As a group, these drugs may cause nausea and other gastrointestinal symptoms, nervousness, agitation, headache, and insomnia, most often to mild degrees. Fluoxetine (Prozac) is the drug most likely to cause nervousness, insomnia, and loss of appetite, particularly early in treatment. Sertraline (Zoloft) is the drug most likely to produce nausea and diarrhea. Paroxetine (Paxil) causes some anticholinergic effects. SSRIs do not cause the characteristic side effects of tricyclic agents. The absence of orthostatic hypotension is a clinically significant factor in older people's use of SSRIs.

Psychostimulants

The psychostimulants, also called sympathomimetics and analeptics, include amphetamines (for example, dextroamphetamine [Dexedrine]), methylphenidate (Ritalin), and pemoline (Cylert). In selected cases, they can improve the mood, apathy, and anhedonia of depressed older patients, especially when these symptoms are caused by an associated chronic medical illness such as rheumatoid arthritis or multiple sclerosis. Amphetamines also may augment analgesia for patients who require pain medication. The use of psychostimulants is controversial because of the risk of abuse, but when prescribed judiciously in small dosages, they are of value. The geriatric dosages of the psychostimulants are listed in Table 54–4.

Antimanics

The use of lithium in elderly patients is more hazardous than its use in young patients because of the common occurrence of age-related morbidity and physiological changes of the heart, the thyroid, and the kidneys. Lithium is excreted by the kidneys, and decreased renal clearance and renal disease can increase the risk of toxicity. Thiazide diuretics decrease the renal clearance of lithium; consequently, the concomitant use of these medications can necessitate adjustments in lithium dosage. Other medications also may interfere with lithium clearance. Lithium may cause CNS effects, to which older people often are especially sensitive. Because of these factors, frequent serum monitoring of lithium levels is recommended. In addition, cardiac, kidney, and thyroid workups are essential before initiating therapy. The geriatric dosages of drugs used in bipolar I disorder are listed in Table 54–5.

Antipsychotics

In addition to treating overt signs of psychosis such as hallucinations and delusions, antipsychotics have been used to

Table 54–4
Geriatric Dosages of Psychostimulants

Generic Name	Trade Name	Geriatric Dosage Range (mg a day)
Dextroamphetamine	Dexedrine	2.5–10
Pemoline	Cylert	18.75–37
Methylphenidate	Ritalin	2.5–20

Table 54–5
Drugs Used to Treat Bipolar Disorder

Generic Name	Trade Name	Geriatric Dosage Range (mg a day)
Lithium carbonate	Eskalith, Lithane, Lithotabs	75–900
Carbamazepine	Tegretol	200–1,200
Valproate, divalproex	Depakene, Depakote	250–1,000
Clonazepam	Klonopin	0.5–1.5

deal effectively with violent, agitated, and abusive geriatric patients.

In general, psychosis in older people frequently responds to much lower dosages of medication than those used for younger patients. Older adults also are much more sensitive to many of the side effects of antipsychotic medications than young patients, specifically to the extrapyramidal (parkinsonian) side effects. Older patients have been known to stop speaking, ambulating, and swallowing as a result of these side effects. The same dosages of medication are not likely to produce significant problems for young patients.

Neurological Adverse Effects. The most common side effects of antipsychotic drugs are extrapyramidal signs, such as akathisia and acute dystonia. Akathisia may be misinterpreted as psychotic agitation, and the acute dyskinesias (especially of the face, tongue, and neck) may simulate the bizarre movements of schizophrenia. Parkinsonian symptoms are a late complication of drug therapy. The dyskinesias, manifest mainly by buccolingual movements, are noted late in the course of high-dosage antipsychotic therapy, especially in older people. Autonomic adverse effects are particularly troublesome because they may upset the homeostasis of organs innervated by the autonomic nervous system, such as the bladder, the gastrointestinal tract, and the cardiovascular system. Alterations in sleep—such as insomnia, bizarre dreams, and sleepwalking—can occur. All drugs with anticholinergic properties may produce a toxic confusional state, which may also cause mydriasis and blurring of vision. Other drugs have adrenergic properties causing miosis.

Hip fracture resulting from falls, partly associated with medication use, is a major cause of morbidity in older people and can be a proximal or distal factor associated with demise. Consequently, to minimize the potentially deleterious and even life-threatening adverse effects, clinicians should monitor drug use. Hip fractures are least often associated with short half-life anxiolytics and most often associated with antipsychotics.

Clinical experience indicates that the therapeutic effects of antipsychotic medications in older people may not become evident on a given dosage of medication for 4 weeks or longer. Because of the therapeutic factors and risks, the dictum in treating psychosis in people older than 65 years of age is to start low and go slow. As in younger patients, adverse effect profiles should help determine the choice of medication, but no consensus exists about the choice or the dose level of antipsychotics for older adults. There is no need to administer prophylactic antiparkinsonian agents on a regular basis when prescribing antipsychotics. The anticholinergic aspects of these drugs can create unwanted side effects, especially memory impairment. The geriatric dosages for commonly used antipsychotic agents are listed in Table 54–6.

Anxiolytics

The population older than 65 years of age constitutes less than 12 percent of the total population but includes 15 percent of long-term anxiolytic drug users. Their rate of regular use is 5 times that the general population. Furthermore, among men with equivalent degrees of high emotional distress, those older than 60 years of age are 4 times more likely to use an antianxiety drug than men between the ages of 18 and 29.

Geriatric patients with mild or moderate anxiety can benefit from anxiolytics, among which the benzodiazepines are the most widely used. Most patients are treated for brief periods, although some may have to be maintained on small dosages for long periods. The long-term use of benzodiazepines is controversial, because they are controlled substances with a potential for abuse; therefore, benzodiazepines with short or intermediate half-lives are preferable for use as hypnotics. Benzodiazepines may cause short periods of memory impairment, such as anterograde amnesia, which may aggravate an existing cognitive disorder in an older patient. Elderly patients accumulate the long-acting benzodiazepines (such as diazepam [Valium]) in adipose tissues, and this process increases such

Table 54–6
Geriatric Dosages of Commonly Used Antipsychotics

Generic Name	Trade Name	Geriatric Dosage Range (mg a day)
Phenothiazines		
Aliphatic		
Chlorpromazine	Thorazine	30–300
Triflupromazine	Vesprin	1–15
Piperazine		
Perphenazine	Trilafon	8–32
Trifluoperazine	Stelazine	1–15
Fluphenazine	Prolixin, Permitil	1–10
Piperidine		
Thioridazine	Mellaril	25–300
Mesoridazine	Serentil	50–400
Thioxanthenes		
Chlorprothixene	Taractan	30–300
Thiothixene	Navane	2–20
Dibenzoxazepine		
Loxapine	Loxitane	50–250
Dihydroindole		
Molindone	Moban	50–225
Butyrophenone		
Haloperidol	Haldol	2–20
Benzisoxazole		
Risperidone	Risperdal	2–4

unwanted effects as ataxia, insomnia, and confusion (sundowner syndrome). These effects can be avoided if the lowest possible dosage is prescribed and if intake is monitored until a therapeutic response is achieved.

Barbiturates may be substituted for the benzodiazepines in the few patients who do not respond to benzodiazepines. Geriatric patients are particularly prone to paradoxical dysphoria and cognitive disorganization, which can result from barbiturates. Compared with the benzodiazepines, the barbiturates have a higher abuse potential. Barbiturates are controlled substances (schedule II), and the Drug Enforcement Agency (DEA) imposes constraints on their use.

Buspirone (BuSpar) is an anxiolytic drug without sedative properties. It has a longer onset of action—up to 3 weeks—than either the benzodiazepines or the barbiturates and does not cause cognitive impairment. Moreover, it does not have any potential for abuse. A summary of the geriatric dosages of drugs used to treat anxiety and insomnia is presented in Table 54–7.

Pharmacological Management of Agitation and Aggression in Dementia

A common issue in the treatment of older patients with dementia is the management of agitation and aggression. The use of antipsychotics is generally unsatisfactory because of their limited efficacy and their parkinsonian side effects. Benzodiazepines, although frequently used to treat behavior disturbances, may produce cognitive impairment, sedation, and paradoxical worsening of the patient's behavior. Buspirone, trazodone, and some β-adrenergic antagonists, such as propranolol and pindolol, have been reported to reduce agitation, aggression, and impulsivity in patients with dementia and other cognitive disorders.

Table 54–7
Geriatric Dosages of Drugs Used to Treat Anxiety and Insomnia

Generic Name	Trade Name	Geriatric Dosage Range (mg a day)
Benzodiazepines		
Alprazolam	Xanax	0.5–6
Chlordiazepoxide	Librium	15–100
Clorazepate	Tranxene	7.5–60
Diazepam	Valium	2–60
Flurazepam	Dalmane	15–30
Halazepam	Paxipam	60–160
Lorazepam	Ativan	2–6
Oxazepam	Serax	30–120
Prazepam	Centrax	20–60
Temazepam	Restoril	15–30
Triazolam	Halcion	0.125–0.25
Nonbenzodiazepines		
Buspirone	BuSpar	5–60
Secobarbital	Seconal	50–300
Meprobamate	Miltown	400–800
Chloral hydrate	Noctec	500–1,000
Zolpidem	Ambien	2.5–5
β-Adrenergic blockers		
Propranolol	Inderal	40–160
Atenolol	Tenormin	25–100

PSYCHOTHERAPY FOR GERIATRIC PATIENTS

The standard psychotherapeutic interventions—such as insight-oriented psychotherapy, supportive psychotherapy, cognitive therapy, group therapy, and family therapy—should be available to geriatric patients. According to Sigmund Freud, people older than 50 years of age are not suited for psychoanalysis because their mental processes lack elasticity. In the view of many who followed Freud, however, psychoanalysis is possible after 50. Advanced age certainly limits plasticity of the personality, but as Otto Fenichel stated, "It does so in varying degrees and at very different ages so that no general rule can be given." Insight-oriented psychotherapy may help remove a specific symptom, even for older people. It is of most benefit when patients have possibilities for libidinal and narcissistic gratification, but it is contraindicated if it would bring only the insight that life has been a failure and that the patient has no opportunity to make up for it.

Common age-related issues in therapy involve the need to adapt to recurrent and diverse losses (such as the deaths of friends and loved ones), the need to assume new roles (such as the adjustment to retirement and the disengagement from previously defined roles), and the need to accept mortality. Psychotherapy helps older people deal with these issues and the emotional problems surrounding them and to understand their behavior and the effects of their behavior on others. In addition to improving interpersonal relationships, psychotherapy increases self-esteem and self-confidence, decreases feelings of helplessness and anger, and improves the quality of life. As described by Alvin Goldfarb, geriatric psychotherapy has the general aim of assisting older adults to have minimal complaints, to help them make and keep friends of both sexes, and to have sexual relations when they have interest and capacity.

Psychotherapy helps relieve tensions of biological and cultural origins and helps older people work and play within the limits of their functional status and as determined by their past training, activities, and self-concept in society. In patients with impaired cognition, psychotherapy can produce remarkable gains in both physical and mental symptoms. In one study conducted in an old-age home, 43 percent of the patients receiving psychotherapy showed decreased urinary incontinence, improved gait, greater mental alertness, improved memory, and better hearing than before psychotherapy.

Therapists must be more active, supportive, and flexible in conducting therapy with older than with younger adults, and they must be prepared to act decisively at the first sign of an incapacity that requires the active involvement of another physician, such as an internist, or that requires consulting or with enlisting the aid of a family member.

Older people usually seek therapy for a therapist's unqualified and unlimited support, reassurance, and approval. Patients often expect a therapist to be all powerful, all knowing, and able to affect a magical cure. Most patients eventually learn to recognize that the therapist is human and that they are engaged in a collaborative effort. In some cases, however, the therapist may have to assume the idealized role, especially when the patient is unable or unwilling to test reality effectively. With the help of the therapist, the patient deals with problems that had been avoided previously. As the therapist offers direct encouragement, reassurance, and advice, the patient's self-confidence increases as conflicts are resolved.

Transference

In most cases, older patients parentify a younger psychiatrist and transfer the infantile responses from the past relationship with the parent to the present relationship with the physician. A childlike dependence can then develop or, conversely, a childlike defiance and disobedience may appear. The patient can be shown how the infantile behavior is at work in relation to the psychiatrist and to others in the patient's life. Other transferential reactions include the patient's reacting to the therapist as a brother, sister, uncle, or even grandparent.

Group Therapy

Group therapy with older people provides an opportunity for mutual support and helps patients deal with the stresses of adapting to declining resources. Group members provide new friendships at a time when old friends have died. Patients have the opportunity to help each other and to increase their self-esteem. Even patients with mild to moderate dementia can be helped to remain stimulated, active, and oriented through group interaction.

Family Therapy

Engaging a patient's family in treatment is frequently desirable and often necessary. Issues in family therapy are myriad. They include the distribution of family resources in providing care for the patient, the attitudes of the children toward their parent and their parent's need for therapy, the grandparenting role, and the examination of family conflicts.

Brief Therapy

Short-term therapy approaches, such as cognitive therapy, help older adults by correcting distortions in thinking, especially self-induced prejudices about the aging process. People who believe that they are too old for sports, sex, learning new things, acquiring new skills, helping others, and working at new jobs can have these cognitive distortions modified by direct therapeutic interventions. Patients can learn to use adaptive defense mechanisms and can be persuaded to make an effort to fight phobic avoidances and other inhibitions.

INSTITUTIONAL CARE OF GERIATRIC PATIENTS

Institutionalizing an older person often is viewed as a failure in management, but it often is a carefully planned and executed treatment option that improves the person's quality of life. There are several types of institutions.

Old-age homes and board-and-care homes are voluntary nonprofit institutions in which older people are expected to live together for the rest of their lives, with no attempt to rehabilitate them for discharge. Instead, they are helped to adjust to the protective setting and to have a better social life than they could have in their own homes.

Nursing homes and extended-care facilities are institutions for the long-term care of people who are chronically ill or permanently impaired. These institutions emphasize the admission of short-term convalescent patients and persons with the potential for rehabilitation to community life. Nevertheless, only 50 percent stay less than 3 months, and 50 percent stay on as permanent residents. The government divides nursing homes into skilled nursing facilities and intermediate-care facilities. Seventy percent are proprietary, and thirty percent are nonproprietary or governmental. In 1988, the average cost for a year's stay in a nursing home was $22,000; now, that cost is over $40,000 a year. A total of $38 billion is spent annually on nursing home care, half of which is paid by the government (through Medicaid). An increasing number of private insurance companies now offer long-term care insurance to help cover nursing home and in-home care costs.

Day-care centers and community centers are places where older people congregate, enjoy socializing experiences, and deal with feelings of depression, anxiety, boredom, and loneliness.

State psychiatric hospitals once had a large geriatric population with various cognitive disorders. Today, these hospitals exclude older people with dementia unless the dementia is mild or reversible and the patient is not likely to become a permanent resident. As a result, both old-age homes and nursing homes have received patients who are similar to the disorganized, bizarre, and violent patients formerly in mental hospitals. The likelihood that these brain-damaged patients will ever be discharged from long-term care facilities is slim, because even willing and effective families cannot cope with the many around-the-clock needs of such patients.

A new trend to help avoid institutionalization is the so-called retirement community composed of relatively healthy older people. The communities usually are run on a nonprofit basis and may have an associated medical facility for the treatment of medical problems. Increasingly, profit-making companies are also establishing such retirement communities.

Restraints

Restraints are belts and vests that keep patients from falling out of bed and wheelchairs or from wandering away. For some patients (such as patients who would pull out feeding or oxygen tubes), such restraints are necessary, but for most patients, they are not used excessively. Some federal surveys have revealed that about 40 percent of all nursing home residents are put in restraints each year. The alternatives include tilted recliners, safe wandering paths, and floor alarms. Patients without restraints have better muscle tone from the exercise of walking and, psychologically, have less rage and a greater sense of mastery than patients in restraints.

Psychosocial Therapy

Institutions can provide a total-push approach to patients, which involves a variety of professional staff members, including psychologists; social workers; psychiatric aides; occupational, vocational, and activity therapists; nutritionists; and exercise therapists. Each has skills that, when brought to bear on institutionalized residents either individually or in a group, can markedly improve a patient's quality of life.

Psychiatrists who work with older people must be especially aware of their own attitudes toward the aging process and toward older people, particularly their own parents and grandparents. If psychiatrists have unresolved resentments or unconscious anger toward older adults in their own lives, they are likely to have countertransference problems that interfere with their ability to do good psychotherapy. Similarly, if they have unresolved fears of death, dying, or chronic illness, they may have blind spots that interfere with therapy. Psychiatrists must have an optimistic view of the last stage of life and a genuine belief that older people have a rightful place in society and a reservoir of wisdom from their accumulated years of experience, which enables them to change.

References

Addonizio G, Alexopoulos GS: Affective disorders in the elderly. Int J Geriatr Psychiatry *8:* 41, 1993.

American Association for Geriatric Psychiatry Board of Directors, American Geriatrics Society Clinical Practice Committee: Psychotherapeutic medications in the nursing home. J Am Geriatr Soc *40:* 946, 1992.

Chapman J, Arlazoroff A, Goldfarb LG, Cervenakova L, Neufeld MT, Weber E, Herbert M, Brown P, Gajdusek DC, Korczyn AD: Fatal insomnia in a case of familial Creutzfeldt-Jakob disease with the codon 200^{Lys} mutation. Neurology *46:* 758, 1996.

Collinge J, Palmer MS: Human prion diseases. In *Prion Diseases,* J Collinge, MS Palmer, editors, p 18. Oxford University Press, Oxford, 1996.

Coyne AC, Reichman WE, Berbig LJ: The relationship between dementia and elder abuse. Am J Psychiatry *150:* 643, 1993.

Francis J, Kapoor WN: Delirium in hospitalized elderly. J Gen Intern Med *5:* 65, 1990.

Francis J, Kapoor WN: Prognosis after hospital discharge of older medical patients with delirium. J Am Geriatr Soc *40:* 601, 1992

Goldberg R: Geriatric consultation/liaison psychiatry. Adv Psychosom Med *19:* 138, 1989.

Hsich G, Kenney K, Gibbs CJ Jr, Lee KH, Harrington MG: The 14-3-3 brain protein in cerebrospinal fluid as a marker for transmissible spongiform encephalopathies. N Engl J Med *335:* 921, 1996.

Koenig HG, Breitner JC: Use of antidepressants in medically ill older patients. Psychosomatics *31:* 22, 1990.

Mallucci GR, Collinge J: Neuropsychiatric presentations of prion disease. Curr Opin Psychiatry *10:* 59, 1997.

Ramsdell JW, Rothrock JF, Ward HW, Volk DM: Evaluation of cognitive impairment in the elderly. J Gen Intern Med *5:* 55, 1990.

Rosenberg DR, Wright B, Gershon S: Depression in the elderly. Dementia *3:* 157, 1992.

Rovner BW, Katz IR: Psychiatric disorders in the nursing home: A selective review of studies related to clinical care. Int J Geriatr Psychiatry *8:* 75, 1993.

Salzman C: Practical considerations in the pharmacologic treatment of depression and anxiety in the elderly. J Clin Psychiatry *51:* 40, 1990.

Solomon K, Manepalli J, Ireland GA, Mahon GM: Alcoholism and prescription drug abuse in the elderly: St. Louis University grand rounds. J Am Geriatr Soc *41:* 57, 1993.

Thomas C, Kelman HR, Kennedy GJ, Ahn C: Depressive symptoms and mortality in elderly persons. J Gerontol *47:* S80, 1992.

Weiss LJ, Lazarus LW: Psychosocial treatment of the geropsychiatric patient. Int J Geriatr Psychiatry *8:* 95, 1993.

Will RG, Ironside JW, Zeidler M, Cousens SN, Estibeiro K, Alperovitch A, Poser S, Pocchiari M, Hofman A, Smith PG: A new variant of Creutzfeldt-Jakob disease in the UK. Lancet *347:* 921, 1996.

55

Forensic Psychiatry

Forensic psychiatry conventionally refers to the services of professionals who evaluate cases and testify in court about legal matters such as competency determinations, criminal responsibility, and malpractice litigation. Forensic psychiatrists are certified by the American Board of Forensic Psychiatry and, in contrast to the psychiatrist–patient therapeutic alliance at the heart of most psychiatric work, aim only to evaluate a person to gather information for the party that retained the psychiatrist. In this situation, there is no doctor–patient relationship with the aims of elucidating causes and thus improving mental and emotional functioning and there is no rule of confidentiality.

The word *forensic* (from the Latin *forum*) means "belonging to, or suitable for, the courts or public discussion"; forensic psychiatry thus deals with mental disorders as related to legal principles. Both psychiatrists and lawyers have a stake in dealing with those who, by violating the rules of society because of a mental disorder, adversely affect the functioning of the community. For psychiatrists, however, this legal alliance has had a serious side effect—psychiatrists increasingly practice defensive medicine and convert patients into adversaries against whom clinicians must defend themselves. When patients sense a shift in a physician's motives from helping the patient to self-protection, their feelings alone may trigger litigation and thereby destroy the very elements that allow psychiatrists to avoid lawsuits: the therapeutic alliance.

PSYCHIATRISTS AND THE COURTS

Most psychiatric work with patients is based on the therapeutic alliance between clinicians and the patient, but forensic psychiatry adopts an adversarial position. The complexity of medicolegal matters is inevitably divided (or, more often, polarized) into two sides, which pull against each other in the effort to place the truth in the hands of the fact finder (the judge or the jury). For clinicians exposed to merciless cross-examination scenes in all media, this element of the U.S. legal system can evoke fear, revulsion, and dismay, but insights into the process may somewhat temper these feelings. Psychiatrists can act as two kinds of witnesses: witnesses of fact and expert witnesses.

Witness of Fact

As a witness of fact or an ordinary witness, a psychiatrist's role is the same as that of any witness who, for example, saw an accident on the street and is called to court to testify about the facts. A psychiatrist also may act as a witness of fact by reading portions of a medical record aloud in court to enter them into the legal record. In theory, any psychiatrist at any level of training can fulfill this role.

Expert Witness

On the other hand, a psychiatrist may qualify as an expert witness under certain circumstances. The qualifying process refers not to popular recognition in his or her clinical field but to acceptance by the court and by advocates for both sides of the case as suitable to perform expert functions. Therefore, the term *expert* has particular legal meaning independent of a clinician's actual or presumed expertise in a given area. The expertise of an expert witness is elucidated during direct and cross-examination; psychiatrists are questioned about education, publications, and certifications. In the courtroom context, an expert witness (unlike witnesses of fact, who cannot express opinions or report others' statements) may draw conclusions from data and thereby render an opinion—for example, that a patient meets the required criteria for a commitment or for an insanity defense under the standards of a jurisdiction. Expert psychiatric witnesses play a role in determining the standard of care and the reasonable practice of psychiatry.

Psychiatrists most commonly act as experts in court proceedings, not as witnesses of fact. One side in the case usually asks a psychiatrist to serve as an expert; clinicians rarely act as independent examiners reporting directly to the court. Often, each side hires a psychiatric expert, and in the ensuing battle of the experts, each gives an opposing opinion. A battle of the experts can leave a jury in a quandary and can cause it to discount both experts' testimony and to decide the case on other evidence and testimony. Testimony elicited by the hiring attorney is known as direct examination; the opposing attorney draws out additional material through cross-examination.

Direct Examination. Direct examination is the first questioning of a witness by the attorney for the party on whose behalf the witness is called. Direct examination is a friendly interrogation that is rehearsed routinely with the attorney before the trial and generally consists of open-ended questions that require narrative answers.

Cross-Examination. Cross-examination is the questioning of a witness by the attorney for the opposing party. Cross-examination usually involves long, possibly leading questions that demand a "yes" or "no" answer. Few experiences can be as demoralizing for clinicians as cross-examination by an eager, aggressive, and sarcastic attorney for the opposing side. This segment of the total experience, more than any other, makes many clinicians leery of appearing in the courtroom in any role. For a clinician in this situation, some helpful principles may be kept in mind.

First, a clinician should listen closely to the question being asked and always pause a moment before answering, not only to replay the question mentally for clarity but to allow the other side to object. Then, he or she should answer only the question asked. The expert witness should stop talking the moment the judge begins to speak.

Second, the clinician should remember the limits of his or her field and should be particularly careful about words such as ''always'' and ''never,'' which identify predictions the clinician is asked to make. If pressed to give a ''yes'' or ''no'' answer to a complex question, the clinician should recall that he or she is permitted to answer, ''That question cannot be answered with a yes or a no.''

Third, the clinician should not be afraid or reluctant to say, ''I don't know'' when the response is true: Not all questions asked by attorneys have answers.

Fourth, the clinician should insist on pretrial preparation by the hiring attorney. Few situations are as needlessly traumatic as being sent into court unprepared. When testifying, the clinician should speak simply, avoid jargon, and be tactful. He or she should be careful about accepting professional literature as authoritative and should ask to see or hear relevant sections before conceding that an entire work is an authority.

Expert witnesses have several rights in court. If they are uncertain about how to answer a question or whether they must answer the question posed, they may ask the judge for guidance. They may ask the judge whether material the attorney has asked for is privileged. They may refuse to answer questions that they do not understand. They may ask the examining counsel to clarify or repeat the question. They may state that they do not know the answer to the question. They may ask the judge whether they can qualify the answer when a ''yes'' or ''no'' answer is requested. They have a right to complete their answers and should protest if they are interrupted. They may refer to written records to refresh their recollections or memories.

The attorneys in a case generally guide a psychiatrist in proper courtroom procedure and the admissibility of testimony. Attorneys are free to object at any point in the examination when they think that certain lines of inquiry, evidence, or content are inappropriate for the court's consideration.

Court-Mandated Evaluations. In several legal situations, a judge asks clinicians to act as consultants to the court, a position that raises the issue of whom a clinician works for. Because clinical information may have to be revealed to the court, clinicians may not enjoy the same confidential relationship with their patients in these situations that they have in private practice. Clinicians who make such court-ordered evaluations are under an ethical obligation and, in some states, a legal obligation to so inform the patients at the outset of the examinations and to make sure that the patients understand this condition. Such court-mandated evaluations were supported by the Supreme Court of the United States in *Ake v. Oklahoma.* The Court held that, when a state allows a defense of sanity, it must provide funds for a psychiatric expert for an indigent defendant. Such an expert may be part of the defense if appropriate.

Evaluation of Witnesses' Credibility. It is up to the trial judge to grant a psychiatric examination requested by one of the parties to the action. Before ordering such an examination, the trial judge asks for evidence that such an examination is necessary to determine the merits of the case and that the imposition on or inconvenience to the witness does not outweigh the examination's value. Many courts limit psychiatric examinations to complaining witnesses in rape and other sex-offense cases, in which corroborative proof is nearly always circumstantial. In cases of incest, for example, the father and the daughter may jointly deny the incest that the mother persistently alleges; or the father may steadfastly deny the act, and the mother may support his denial; or, after accusing her father, the daughter may retract her accusation. Only a thorough psychiatric examination of the family can eliminate the confusion. Recognizing that false charges may stem from the psychodynamics of a victim who seems normal to a layperson, the courts permit psychiatrists to expose mental processes and defenses in complaining witnesses. The liberal attitude in this area probably results from the gravity of the charge or the general lack of corroborating evidence. Psychiatrists cannot testify regarding whether someone is telling the truth, but they can discuss personality or psychological factors affecting the way information is reported. For example, patients with dissociative disorders may report factually incorrect situations with deep conviction.

PRIVILEGE AND CONFIDENTIALITY

Privilege

Privilege is the right to maintain secrecy or confidentiality in the face of a subpoena. Privileged communications are statements made by certain people within a relationship—such as husband–wife, priest–penitent, or doctor–patient—that the law protects from forced disclosure on the witness stand. The right of privilege belongs to the patient, not to the physician, and so the patient can waive the right.

Psychiatrists, who are licensed to practice medicine, may claim medical privilege, but the privilege is so riddled with qualifications that it is practically meaningless. Purely federal cases have no psychotherapist–patient privilege. Moreover, the privilege does not exist at all in military courts, regardless of whether the physician is military or civilian and whether the privilege is recognized in the state in which the court-martial takes place. The privilege has numerous exceptions, which often are viewed as implied waivers. In the most common exception, patients are said to waive the privilege by injecting their mental condition into the litigation, thereby making their condition an element of their claim or defense. Another exception involves proceedings for hospitalization, in which the interests of both the patient and the public are said to call for a departure from confidentiality. In several contexts, clinicians may be ordered to give the court information that is ordinarily considered privileged. Yet another exception is made in child-custody and child-protection proceedings in regard to the best interest of the child. Furthermore, the privilege does not apply to *actions* between a therapist and a patient. Therefore, in a fee dispute or a malpractice claim, the complainant's lawyer can obtain the necessary therapy records to resolve the dispute.

Under medical privilege, psychiatrists and other physicians do not legally enjoy the same privilege that exists between client and attorney, priest and churchgoer, and husband and wife. Most physicians are not aware of this fact.

Confidentiality

A long-held premise of medical ethics binds physicians to hold secret all information given by patients. This professional obligation is called confidentiality. Confidentiality applies to certain populations and not to others; a group that is within the circle of confidentiality shares information without receiving specific permission from a patient. Such groups include, in addition to the physician, other staff members treating the patient, clinical supervisors, and consultants. Parties outside the circle include the patient's family, attorney, and previous therapist; sharing information with such people requires the patient's permission. Nevertheless, in numerous instances, a psychiatrist may be asked to divulge information imparted by a patient. Although a court demand for information is most worrisome to psychiatrists, demands most frequently come from sources such as insurers, who cannot compel disclosure but can withhold a benefit without it. A patient generally makes a disclosure or authorizes the psychiatrist to make disclosures to receive a benefit, such as employment, welfare benefits, or insurance.

A subpoena can force a psychiatrist to breach confidentiality, and courts must be able to compel witnesses to testify for the law to function adequately. A subpoena (''under penalty'') is an order to appear as a witness in court or at a deposition. Physicians usually are served with a *subpoena duces tecum,* which requires that they also produce their relevant records and documents. Although the power to issue subpoenas belongs to a judge, they are routinely issued at the request of an attorney representing a party to an action.

In bona fide emergencies, information may be released in as limited a way as feasible to carry out necessary interventions. Sound clinical practice holds that psychiatrists should make the effort, time allowing, to obtain the patient's permission anyway and should debrief the patient after the emergency.

As a rule, clinical information may be shared with the patient's permission—preferably written permission, although oral permission suffices with proper documentation. Each release is good for only one bolus of information, and permission should be reobtained for each subsequent release, even to the same party. Permission overcomes only the legal barrier, not the clinical one; the release is permission, not obligation. If a clinician believes that the information may be destructive, the matter should be discussed, and the release may be refused with some exceptions.

Third-Party Payers and Supervision. Increased insurance coverage for health care is precipitating a concern about confidentiality and the conceptual model of psychiatric practice. Today, insurance covers about 70 percent of all health care bills; to provide coverage, an insurance carrier must be able to obtain information with which it can assess the administration and costs of various programs.

Quality control of care necessitates that confidentiality not be absolute; it also requires a review of individual patients and therapists. The therapist in training must breach a patient's confidence by discussing the case with a supervisor. Institutionalized patients who have been ordered by a court to get treatment must have their individualized treatment programs submitted to a mental health board.

Discussions About Patients. In general, psychiatrists have multiple loyalties: to patients, to society, and to the profession. Through their writings, teaching, and seminars, they can share their acquired knowledge and experience and provide information that may be valuable to other professionals and to the public. However, it is not easy to write or talk about a psychiatric patient without breaching the confidentiality of the relationship. Unlike physical ailments, which can be discussed without anyone's recognizing the patient, a psychiatric history usually entails a discussion of distinguishing characteristics. Psychiatrists have an obligation not to disclose identifiable patient information (and, perhaps, any descriptive patient information) without appropriate informed consent. Failure to obtain informed consent may result in claims based on breach of privacy, defamation, or both.

Child Abuse. In the state of New York, all physicians are legally required to take a course on child abuse for medical licensure. All states now legally require that psychiatrists, among others, who have reason to believe that a child has been the victim of physical or sexual abuse, make an immediate report to an appropriate agency. In this situation, confidentiality is decisively limited by legal statute on the ground that potential or actual harm to vulnerable children outweighs the value of confidentiality in a psychiatric setting. Although many complex psychodynamic nuances accompany the required reporting of suspected child abuse, such reports generally are considered ethically justified.

Disclosure to Safeguard. In some situations, a physician must report to the authorities, as specifically required by law. The classic example of mandatory reporting involves a patient with epilepsy who operates a motor vehicle. Another example of mandatory reporting—one in which penalties are imposed for failing to report—involves child abuse. Expanded definitions of what constitutes child abuse under the law have been amended in some jurisdictions to include both emotional and physical child abuse. Under the legislation, practitioners who learn that a patient is engaged in sexual activity with a child are obliged to report it. In the absence of a specific statute that mandates reporting, a report is optional. As a general principle, a person has no duty to come to the aid of another unless a special relationship mandates this duty. After a person has come to the aid of another, however, a relationship is established, and a duty may be imposed.

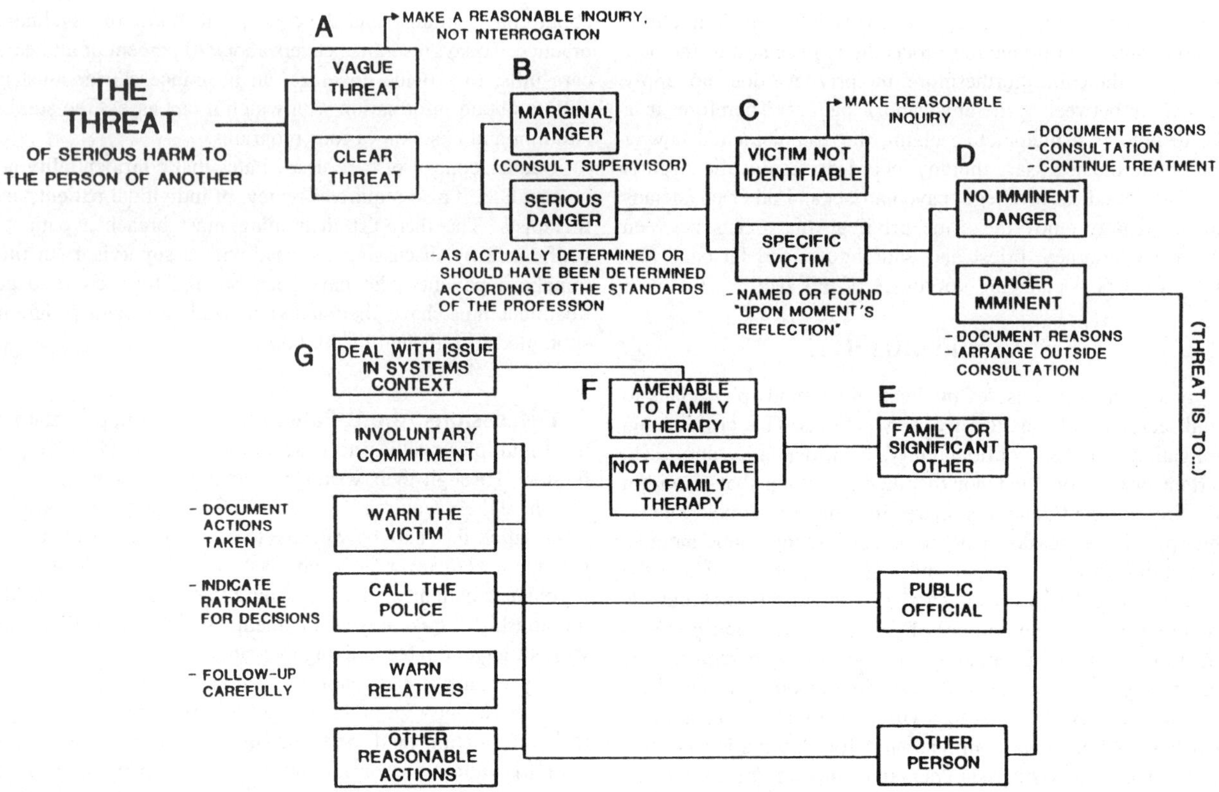
THE THREAT
OF SERIOUS HARM TO THE PERSON OF ANOTHER
A
VAGUE THREAT
MAKE A REASONABLE INQUIRY, NOT INTERROGATION
CLEAR THREAT
B
MARGINAL DANGER
(CONSULT SUPERVISOR)
SERIOUS DANGER
- AS ACTUALLY DETERMINED OR SHOULD HAVE BEEN DETERMINED ACCORDING TO THE STANDARDS OF THE PROFESSION
C
MAKE REASONABLE INQUIRY
VICTIM NOT IDENTIFIABLE
SPECIFIC VICTIM
- NAMED OR FOUND "UPON MOMENT'S REFLECTION"
D
- DOCUMENT REASONS
- CONSULTATION
- CONTINUE TREATMENT
NO IMMINENT DANGER
DANGER IMMINENT
- DOCUMENT REASONS
- ARRANGE OUTSIDE CONSULTATION
(THREAT IS TO...)
E
FAMILY OR SIGNIFICANT OTHER
PUBLIC OFFICIAL
OTHER PERSON
F
AMENABLE TO FAMILY THERAPY
NOT AMENABLE TO FAMILY THERAPY
G
DEAL WITH ISSUE IN SYSTEMS CONTEXT
INVOLUNTARY COMMITMENT
WARN THE VICTIM
CALL THE POLICE
WARN RELATIVES
OTHER REASONABLE ACTIONS
- DOCUMENT ACTIONS TAKEN
- INDICATE RATIONALE FOR DECISIONS
- FOLLOW-UP CAREFULLY

FIGURE 55–1

Tarasoff II decision chart. (Reprinted with permission from Gross BH, Weiberjer LE, editors: *The Mental Health Professional and the Legal System,* p 98. Jossey-Bass, San Francisco, 1982.)

TARASOFF I. Does the establishment of a therapist–patient relationship obligate the therapist to care for the safety of not only the patient but also others? This issue was raised in 1976 in the case of *Tarasoff v. Regents of University of California* (now known as *Tarasoff I*). In this case, Prosenjit Poddar, a student and a voluntary outpatient at the mental health clinic of the University of California, told his therapist that he intended to kill a student readily identified as Tatiana Tarasoff. Realizing the seriousness of the intention, the therapist, with the concurrence of a colleague, concluded that Poddar should be committed for observation under a 72-hour emergency psychiatric detention provision of the California commitment law. The therapist notified the campus police both orally and in writing that Poddar was dangerous and should be committed.

Concerned about the breach of confidentiality, the therapist's supervisor vetoed the recommendation and ordered all records relating to Poddar's treatment destroyed. At the same time, the campus police temporarily detained Poddar but released him on his assurance that he would "stay away from that girl." Poddar stopped going to the clinic when he learned from the police about his therapist's recommendation to commit him. Two months later, he carried out his previously announced threat to kill Tatiana. The young woman's parents thereupon sued the university for negligence.

As a consequence, the California Supreme Court, which deliberated the case for the unprecedented time of about 14 months, ruled that a physician or a psychotherapist who has reason to believe that a patient may injure or kill someone must notify the potential victim, the victim's relatives or friends, or the authorities.

The discharge of the duty imposed on the therapist to warn intended victims against danger may take one or more various steps, depending on the case. Therefore, stated the court, it may call for the therapist to notify the intended victim or others likely to notify the victim of the danger, to notify the police, or to take whatever other steps are reasonably necessary under the circumstances.

The *Tarasoff I* decision has not drastically affected psychiatrists; it has long been their practice to warn the appropriate people or law enforcement authorities when a patient presents a distinct and immediate threat to someone. According to the American Psychiatric Association, confidentiality may, with careful judgment, be broken in the following ways. A patient probably will commit murder, and the act can be stopped only by the psychiatrist's notification of the police. A patient probably will commit suicide, and the act can be stopped only by the psychiatrist's notification of the police. A patient, such as a bus driver or an airline pilot, who has potentially life-threatening responsibilities, shows marked impairment of judgment.

The *Tarasoff I* ruling does not require a therapist to report a patient's fantasies; instead, it requires him or her to report an intended homicide and it is the therapist's duty to exercise good judgment.

TARASOFF II. In 1982, the California Supreme Court issued a second ruling in the case of *Tarasoff v. Regents of University of California* (now known as *Tarasoff II*), which broadened its earlier ruling, the duty to *warn,* to include the duty to *protect* (Fig. 55–1).

The *Tarasoff II* ruling has stimulated intense debates in the medicolegal field. Lawyers, judges, and expert witnesses argue the definition of protection, the nature of the relationship between the therapist and the patient, and the balance between public safety and individual privacy.

Clinicians argue that the duty to protect hinders treatment because a patient may not trust a doctor if confidentiality is not maintained. Furthermore, because it is not easy to determine whether a patient is dangerous enough to justify long-term incarceration, unnecessary involuntary hospitalization because of a therapist's defensive practices may occur.

As a result of such debates in the medicolegal field, since 1976, the state courts have not made a uniform interpretation of the *Tarasoff II* ruling (the duty to protect). Generally, clinicians should note whether a specific identifiable victim seems to be in imminent and probable danger from the threat of an action contemplated by a mentally ill patient; the harm, in addition to being imminent, should be potentially serious or severe. Usually, the patient must be a danger to another person and not to property; and the therapist should take clinically reasonable actions.

In a few cases (none successful so far), claims have already been advanced that a *Tarasoff*-like duty applies to the infection of partners with human immunodeficiency virus (HIV) by patients under mental health treatment. The breach of confidentiality in *Tarasoff* cases is justified only by the threat of violence. Laws vary confusingly by jurisdiction. The ideal solution is to persuade the patient to make the disclosure and report the matter to the public health authorities.

HOSPITALIZATION

As part of their police power, all states provide for some form of involuntary hospitalization. Such action usually is taken when psychiatric patients present a danger to themselves or others in their environment to the degree that their urgent need for treatment in a closed institution is evident. Certain states allow for involuntary hospitalization when patients are unable to care for themselves adequately.

The doctrine of *parens patriae* allows the state to intervene and to act as a surrogate parent for those who are unable to care for themselves or who may harm themselves. In English common law, *parens patriae* (''father of his country'') dates to the time of King Edward I and originally referred to a monarch's duty to protect the people. In U.S. common law, the doctrine has been transformed into a paternalism in which the state acts for people who are mentally ill and for minors.

The statutes governing hospitalization of people who are mentally ill generally have been designated commitment laws, but psychiatrists have long considered the term to be undesirable: Commitment legally means a warrant for imprisonment. The American Bar Association and the American Psychiatric Association have recommended that the term *commitment* be replaced by the less offensive and more accurate term *hospitalization,* which most states have adopted. Although this change in terminology does not correct the punitive attitudes of the past, the emphasis on hospitalization is in keeping with psychiatrists' views of treatment rather than punishment.

False imprisonment is the legal action arising from the claim that a patient has been hospitalized negligently. It is an uncommon basis for malpractice litigation and is rarely successful when invoked; presently, society tends to emphasize social protection more than individual rights. For instances in which hospitalization is necessary, a clinician's guidelines are to obtain an emergency or involuntary hospitalization in good faith, for reasonable cause, with data obtained from personal examination or a reliable report of danger; seclude the patient for proper indications according to local regulations; and obtain consultation on ambiguous cases.

Procedures of Admission

Four procedures of admission to psychiatric facilities have been endorsed by the American Bar Association to safeguard civil liberties and to make sure that no person is railroaded into a mental hospital. Although each of the 50 states has the power to enact its own laws on psychiatric hospitalization, the procedures outlined here are gaining much acceptance.

Informal Admission. Informal admission operates on the general hospital model, in which a patient is admitted to a psychiatric unit of a general hospital in the same way that a medical or surgical patient is admitted. Under such circumstances, the ordinary doctor–patient relationship applies, with the patient free to enter and to leave, even against medical advice.

Voluntary Admission. In cases of voluntary admission, patients apply in writing for admission to a psychiatric hospital. They may come to the hospital on the advice of a personal physician, or they may seek help on their own. In either case, patients are examined by a psychiatrist on the hospital staff and are admitted if the examination reveals the need for hospital treatment.

Temporary Admission. Temporary admission is used for patients who are so senile or so confused that they require hospitalization and are not able to make decisions of their own and for patients who are so acutely disturbed that they must be immediately admitted to a psychiatric hospital on an emergency basis. Under the procedure, a person is admitted to the hospital on the written recommendation of one physician. Once the patient has been admitted, the need for hospitalization must be confirmed by a psychiatrist on the hospital staff. The procedure is temporary because patients cannot be hospitalized against their will for more than 15 days.

Involuntary Admission. Involuntary admission involves the question of whether patients are suicidal and thus a danger to themselves or homicidal and thus a danger to others. Because these people do not recognize their need for hospital care, the application for admission to a hospital may be made by a relative or a friend. Once the application is made, the patients must be examined by two physicians, and, if both physicians confirm the need for hospitalization, the patients can then be admitted.

Involuntary hospitalization involves an established procedure for written notification of the next of kin. Furthermore, the patients have access at any time to legal counsel, who can bring the case before a judge. If the judge does not think that hospitalization is indicated, the patient's release can be ordered.

Involuntary admission allows a patient to be hospitalized for 60 days. After this time, if the patient is to remain hospitalized, the case must be reviewed periodically by a board consisting of psychiatrists, nonpsychiatric physicians, lawyers, and other citizens not connected with the institution. In New York State, the board is called the Mental Health Information Service.

People who have been hospitalized involuntarily and who believe that they should be released have the right to file a petition for a writ of habeas corpus. Under law, a writ of habeas corpus may be proclaimed by those who believe that they have been illegally deprived of liberty. The legal procedure asks a court to decide whether a patient has been hospitalized without due process of law. The case must be heard by a court at once, regardless of the manner or the form in which the motion is filed. Hospitals are obligated to submit the petitions to the court immediately.

Involuntary Discharge

Under a variety of circumstances, patients may have to be discharged from a hospital against their will—if they have intentionally broken a major hospital rule (for example, smuggled drugs or assaulted another patient), refused treatment, or been restored to health but still wish to remain hospitalized. People may wonder why many patients wish to remain in a psychiatric hospital. For some patients, such a protective environment is preferable to the streets, jail, or the family's home. Although the focus here is on discharge from an inpatient unit, similar issues are involved in unilateral termination with an outpatient.

Abandonment as Cause of Action. For clinicians, the potential pitfall of involuntary discharge or involuntary termination is the charge of abandonment. This claim can be a particularly fertile ground for malpractice litigation when the inevitable bad feelings are combined with a bad outcome. A clinician's vulnerability in this context is augmented by the jury's tendency to project a prejudicial distaste for the mentally ill person onto the physician and to view the physician as someone who probably wants to get rid of the patient to be free to play golf. This popular perception places an additional onus on clinicians to exercise special care in such charged situations.

Ending the Relationship. An involuntary discharge entails all the pain of the usual therapy termination process with far less opportunity for healing and growth and for gaining perspective. Most important, in this situation, the clinician directly opposes the patient's proclaimed wishes and thereby severely strains the therapeutic alliance. Consultation and documentation of the rationale for the action are the two safeguards against liability.

''Going the extra mile'' means smoothing the way for the patient to obtain care in the future. Termination does not mean abandonment when a good-faith transfer of services is made through an appropriate referral to another hospital or therapist. Furthermore, when possible, the patient should be told that the door is open for a negotiated return at some future time after restitution has been made or the problem has otherwise been redressed.

The clinician is not obliged to accept any patient back into full treatment. Patients are owed only an evaluation to determine their needs. Referral to an appropriate source of care may then follow. Blanket refusal to see a patient is a dangerous course and, short of serious risk of bodily harm to the clinician, should be avoided.

Emergencies. The one circumstance in which clinicians cannot terminate patients is a state of emergency. A typical example is the instance of a patient who attacks a therapist. The therapist cannot terminate the patient's care, no matter how severe the assault, until the emergency situation has been resolved (for example, by hospitalizing the patient or by arranging for seclusion or restraint). Only then can the therapist terminate the relationship and transfer the patient.

RIGHT TO TREATMENT

Among the rights of patients, the right to the standard quality of care is fundamental. This right has been litigated in much-publicized cases in recent years under the slogan of ''right to treatment.''

In 1966, Judge David Bazelon, speaking for the District of Columbia Court of Appeals in *Rouse v. Cameron,* noted that the purpose of involuntary hospitalization is treatment and concluded that the absence of treatment draws into question the constitutionality of the confinement. Treatment in exchange for liberty is the logic of the ruling. In this case, the patient was discharged on a writ of habeas corpus, the basic legal remedy to ensure liberty. Judge Bazelon further held that, if alternative treatments that infringe less on personal liberty are available, involuntary hospitalization cannot take place.

Alabama Federal District Court Judge Frank Johnson was more venturesome in the decree he rendered in 1971 in *Wyatt v. Stickney.* The *Wyatt* case was a class-action proceeding brought under newly developed rules that sought not release but treatment. Judge Johnson ruled that people civilly committed to a mental institution have a constitutional right to receive such individual treatment as will give them a reasonable opportunity to be cured or to have their mental condition improved. Judge Johnson set out minimum requirements for staffing, specified physical facilities and nutritional standards, and required individualized treatment plans.

The new codes, more detailed than the old ones, include the right to be free from excessive or unnecessary medication; the right to privacy and dignity; the right to the least restrictive environment; the unrestricted right to be visited by attorneys, clergy, and private physicians; and the right not to be subjected to lobotomies, electroconvulsive treatments, and other procedures without fully informed consent. Patients can be required to perform therapeutic tasks but not hospital chores, unless they volunteer for them and are paid the federal minimum wage. This requirement is an attempt to eliminate the practice of peonage, in which psychiatric patients were forced to work at menial tasks, without payment, for the benefit of the state.

In a number of states today, medication or electroconvulsive therapy cannot be forcibly administered to a patient without first obtaining court approval, which may take as long as 10 days. The right to refuse treatment is a legal doctrine that holds that, except in emergencies, people cannot be forced to accept treatment against their will. An emergency is defined as a condition in clinical practice that requires immediate intervention to prevent death or serious harm to the patient or others or to prevent deterioration of the patient's clinical state.

In the 1976 case of *O'Connor v. Donaldson,* the Supreme Court of the United States ruled that harmless mentally ill patients cannot be confined against their will without treatment if they can survive outside. According to the Court, a finding of mental illness alone cannot justify a state's confining people in a hospital against their will. Instead, involuntarily confined patients must be considered dangerous to themselves or others or possibly so unable to care for themselves that they cannot survive outside. As a result of the 1979 case of *Rennie v. Klein,* patients have the right to refuse treatment and to use an appeal process. As a result of the 1981 case of *Roger v. Oken,* patients have an absolute right to refuse treatment, but a guardian may authorize treatment. Questions have been raised about psychiatrists' ability to accurately predict dangerousness and about the risk to psychiatrists, who may be sued for monetary damages if people are thereby deprived of their civil rights.

The ethical controversy concerning applications of the law to psychiatric patients came to the fore through Thomas Szasz, a professor of psychiatry at the State University of New York. In his book *The Myth of Mental Illness,* Szasz argued that the various psychiatric diagnoses are totally devoid of significance and contended that psychiatrists have no place in the courts of law and that all forced confinements because of mental illness are unjust. Szasz's opposition to suicide prevention and the imposition of treatment, with or without confinement, is interesting but is viewed by the psychiatric community with strong misgivings.

CIVIL RIGHTS OF PATIENTS

Thanks to several clinical, public, and legal movements, criteria for the civil rights of people who are mentally ill, apart from their rights as patients, have been both established and affirmed.

Least Restrictive Alternative

Clinicians often are puzzled by the right of least strict alternative, which is perhaps the most legalistic civil right; nothing in clinical work or training prepares psychiatrists to think in terms of restrictiveness. Instead, clinical interventions are undertaken according to their effectiveness, positive benefit–risk ratio, and other operational certainties. A series of legal decisions on state intervention in organizations maneuvered the concept of the least restrictive alternative into mental health law, where it has taken solid root.

The principle holds that patients have the right to receive the least restrictive means of treatment for the requisite clinical effect. Therefore, if a patient can be treated as an outpatient, commitment should not be used; if a patient can be treated on an open ward, seclusion should not be used.

Although apparently fairly straightforward on first reading, difficulty arises when clinicians attempt to apply the concept to choose among involuntary medication, seclusion, and restraint as the intervention of choice. Distinguishing among these interventions on the basis of restrictiveness proves to be a purely subjective exercise fraught with personal bias. Moreover, each of these three interventions is both more and less restrictive than each of the other two. Nevertheless, the effort should be made to think in terms of restrictiveness when deciding how to treat patients.

Visitation Rights

Patients have the right to receive visitors and to do so at reasonable hours (customary hospital visiting hours). Allowance must be made for the possibility that, at certain times, a patient's clinical condition may not permit visits. This fact should be clearly documented, however, because such rights must not be suspended without good reason.

Certain categories of visitors are not limited to the regular visiting hours; these include a patient's attorney, private physician, and members of the clergy—all of whom have, broadly speaking, unrestricted access to the patient, including the right to privacy in their discussions. Even here, a bona fide emergency may delay such visits. Again, the patient's needs come first. Under similar reasoning, certain noxious visits may be curtailed (for example, a patient's relative bringing drugs into the ward).

Communication Rights

Patients should, in general, have free and open communication with the outside world by telephone or mail, but this right varies regionally to some degree. Some jurisdictions charge the hospital administration with a responsibility for monitoring the communications of patients. In some areas, hospitals are expected to make available reasonable supplies of paper, envelopes, and stamps for patients' use.

Specific circumstances affect communication rights. A patient who is hospitalized in relation to a criminal charge of making harassing or threatening phone calls should not be given unrestricted access to the telephone, and similar considerations apply to mail. As a rule, however, patients should be allowed private telephone calls, and their incoming and outgoing mail should not be opened by hospital staff members.

Private Rights

Patients have several rights to privacy. In addition to confidentiality, they are allowed private bathroom and shower space, secure storage space for clothing and other belongings, and adequate floor space per person. They also have the right to wear their own clothes and to carry their own money.

Economic Rights

Apart from special considerations related to incompetence, psychiatric patients generally are permitted to manage their own financial affairs. One feature of this fiscal right is the requirement that patients be paid if they work in the institution (for example, gardening or preparing food). This right often creates tension between the valid therapeutic need for activity, including jobs, and exploitative labor. A consequence of this tension is that valuable occupational, vocational, and rehabilitative therapeutic programs may have to be eliminated because of the failure of legislatures to supply the funding to pay wages to patients who participate in these programs.

SECLUSION AND RESTRAINT

Seclusion refers to placing and keeping an inpatient in a bare room for the purpose of containing a clinical situation that may result in a state of emergency. Restraint involves measures designed to confine a patient's bodily movements, such as the use of leather cuffs and anklets or straitjackets. Seclusion and restraint are issues that raise questions of safety. The American Psychiatric Association's *Task Force Report on Seclusion and Restraint* provides standards for the use of these interventions. Clinicians practicing in institutions that use such measures should be familiar with this report and with local statutes. In most areas, the doctrine of the least restrictive alternatives is invoked. According to this concept, commitment should be used only when no less restrictive alternative is available, but clinicians facing a genuine emergency should act conservatively. A patient can always be released from restraints or seclusion, whereas the harm caused by uncontained violence may be irreversible.

INFORMED CONSENT

Lawyers representing an injured claimant now invariably add to a claim of negligent performance of procedures (malpractice) an informed consent claim as another possible area of liability. Ironically, this is one claim under which the requirement of expert testimony may be avoided. The usual claim of medical malpractice requires the litigant to produce an expert to establish that the defendant physician departed from accepted medical practice. But in a case in which the physician did not obtain informed consent, the fact that the treatment was technically well performed, in accord with the generally accepted standard of care, and affected a complete cure is immaterial. As a practical matter, however, unless the treatment had adverse consequences, a complainant will not get far with a jury in an action based solely on an allegation that the treatment was performed without consent.

In classic tort theory (a *tort* is a civil wrongful act other than a breach of contract), an intentional touching to which a person has not given consent is *battery.* Therefore, the administration of electroconvulsive therapy or chemotherapy, although therapeutic, is a battery when performed without consent. Indeed, any unauthorized touching outside conventional social intercourse constitutes a battery and is an offense to the dignity of the person, an invasion of the person's right of self-determination, for which punitive and actual damages may be imposed. Justice Benjamin Cardozo wrote: ''Every human being of adult years and sound mind has a right to determine what shall be done with his own body; and a surgeon who performs an operation without his patient's consent commits [a battery] for which he is liable in damages.'' Because informed consent has become a broadly recognized part of the standard of care, a procedure performed without informed consent may be malpractice as well as battery.

According to Justice Cardozo, the patient's consent to the treatment, not the effectiveness or the timeliness of the treatment, allows a physician to take care of a patient. Therefore, a mentally competent adult may refuse treatment, even though it is effective and involves little risk. But, for example, when gangrene sets in and the patient is psychotic, treatment—even of such momentous proportions as amputation—may be ordered to save the patient's life. The state also is said to have a compelling interest in preventing its citizens from committing suicide, and such interest allows for treatment without consent in this situation as well.

In the case of minors, the parent or guardian is legally empowered to give consent to medical treatment. By statute, most states, however, list specific diseases and conditions that a minor can consent to have treated—including venereal disease, pregnancy, substance dependence, alcohol abuse, and contagious diseases. In an emergency, a physician can treat a minor without parental consent. The trend is to adopt the so-called mature minor rule, which allows minors to consent to treatment under ordinary circumstances. As a result of the Supreme Court's 1967 *Gault* decision, all juveniles must now be represented by counsel, must be able to confront witnesses, and must be given proper notice of any charges. Emancipated minors have the rights of an adult when it can be shown that they are living as adults with control over their own lives.

In the past, to obviate a claim of battery, physicians needed only to relate what they proposed to do and then to obtain the patient's consent thereto. Simultaneously with the growth of product liability and consumer law, however, the courts began to require that physicians also relate sufficient information to allow patients to decide whether such a procedure is acceptable in the light of the risks, the benefits, and the available alternatives, including no treatment at all. In general, informed consent requires that there be an understanding of the nature and the foreseeable risks and benefits of a procedure; a knowledge of alternative procedures; awareness of the consequences of withholding consent; and the recognition that the consent is voluntary. Physicians must convey to patients a readiness to listen and to discuss anything a patient may fear as a risk, a side effect, or a concern about the proposed treatment.

Consent Form

The introduction of consent forms followed revelations of harm done to patients during clinical experimentation. Consent forms are written documents outlining a patient's informed consent to a proposed procedure. These forms usually are designed by attorneys, whose aim is to protect an institution from liability; therefore, the forms often are exhaustive and require a level of reading comprehension that is beyond many patients. Paradoxically, if such a form truly covered all possible eventualities, it probably would be too long to be comprehensible, and if it were short enough to be comprehensible, it might be incomplete; some theorists have therefore recommended that the form be replaced by a standardized discussion and a progress note.

The basic elements of a consent form should include a fair explanation of the procedures to be followed and their purposes, including identification of any procedures that are experimental; a description of any attendant discomforts and risks reasonably to be expected; a description of any benefits reasonably to be expected; a disclosure of any appropriate alternative procedures that may be advantageous to the patient; an offer to answer any inquiries concerning the procedures; and an instruction that the patient is free to withdraw patient consent and to discontinue participation in the project or activity at any time without prejudice. The patient has the right to refuse treatment.

CHILD CUSTODY

The action of a court in a child-custody dispute is now predicated on the child's best interests. The maxim reflects the idea that a natural parent does not have an inherent right to be named as a custodial parent, but the presumption, although a bit eroded, remains in favor of the mother in the case of young children. As a rule, the courts presume that the welfare of a child of tender years generally is best served by maternal custody when the mother is a good and fit parent. The best interest of the mother may be served by naming her as the custodial parent, because a mother may never resolve the effects of the loss of a child, but her best interest is not to be equated ipso facto with the best interest of the child. Care and protection proceedings are the court's interventions in the welfare of a child when the parents are unable to care for the child.

More fathers are asserting custodial claims. In about 5 percent of all cases, fathers are named custodians. The movement supporting women's rights also is enhancing the chances of paternal custody. With more women going to work outside the home, the traditional rationale for maternal custody has less force today than it did in the past.

Currently, every state has a statute allowing a court, usually a juvenile court, to assume jurisdiction over a neglected or abused child and to remove the child from parental custody. Most states provide several grounds for assuming jurisdiction, such as parental abuse and an injurious living environment. When a court removes a child from parental custody, it usually orders that the care and custody of the child be supervised by the welfare or probation department.

TESTAMENTARY AND CONTRACTUAL CAPACITY AND COMPETENCE

Psychiatrists may be asked to evaluate patients' testamentary capacities and their competence to make a will. Three psychological abilities are necessary to prove this competence. Patients must know the nature and the extent of their bounty (property), the fact that they are making a bequest, and the identities of their natural beneficiaries (spouse, children, and other relatives).

When a will is being probated, one of the heirs or another person often challenges its validity. A judgment in such cases must be based on a reconstruction, using data from documents and from expert psychiatric testimony, of the testator's mental state at the time the will was written. When a person is unable to or does not exercise the right to make a will, the law in all states provides for the distribution of property to the heirs; if there are no heirs, the estate goes to the public treasury.

Witnesses at the signing of a will, who might include a psychiatrist, may attest that the testator was rational at the time the will was executed. In unusual cases, a lawyer may videotape the signing to safeguard the will from attack. Ideally, people who are thinking of making a will and believe that questions may be raised about their testamentary competence hire a forensic psychiatrist to perform a dispassionate examination antemortem to validate and record their capacity.

An incompetence proceeding and the appointment of a guardian may be considered necessary when a family member is spending the family's assets and property is in danger of dissipation, as in the case of aged, retarded, alcohol-dependent, and psychotic people. At issue is whether such people are capable of managing their own affairs. A guardian appointed to take control of the property of one deemed incompetent, however, cannot make a will for the ward (the incompetent person).

Competence is determined on the basis of a person's ability to make a sound judgment—to weigh, to reason, and to make reasonable decisions. Competence is task specific, not general: The capacity to weigh decision-making factors (competence) often is best demonstrated by a person's ability to ask pertinent and knowledgeable questions after the risks and the benefits have been explained. Although physicians (especially psychiatrists) often give opinions on competence, only a judge's ruling converts the opinion into a finding; a patient is not competent or incompetent until the court so rules. The diagnosis of a mental disorder is not, in itself, sufficient to warrant a finding of incompetence. Instead, the mental disorder must cause an impairment in judgment for the specific issues involved. After they have been declared incompetent, people are deprived of certain rights: They cannot make contracts, marry, start a divorce action, drive a vehicle, handle their own property, or practice their professions. Incompetence is decided at a formal courtroom proceeding, and the court usually appoints a guardian who will best serve a patient's interests. Another hearing is necessary to declare a patient competent. Admission to a mental hospital does not automatically mean that a person is incompetent.

Competence also is essential in contracts, because a contract is an agreement between parties to do a specific act. A contract is declared invalid if, when it was signed, one of the parties was unable to comprehend the nature and effect of his or her act. The marriage contract is subject to the same standard and, thus, can be voided if either party did not understand the nature, duties, obligations, and other characteristics entailed at the time of the marriage. In general, however, the courts are unwilling to declare a marriage void on the basis of incompetence.

Whether competence is related to wills, contracts, or the making or breaking of marriages, the fundamental concern is a person's state of awareness and capacity to comprehend the significance of the particular commitment made.

Durable Power of Attorney

A modern development that permits people to make provisions for their own anticipated loss of decision-making capacity is called a *durable power of attorney.* The document permits the advance selection of a substitute decision maker who can act without the necessity of court proceedings when the signatory becomes incompetent through illness, progressive dementia, or perhaps a relapse of bipolar I disorder.

Competence to Inform

Competence to inform is a relatively new concept involving a patient's interaction with a clinician; it is useful in ambiguous situations that may have a poor outcome. A clinician first explains to a patient the value of being honest with the clinician and then attempts to determine whether the patient is competent to weigh the risks and benefits of withholding information about suicidal or homicidal intent. The process must be documented.

CRIMINAL LAW

Competence to Stand Trial

The Supreme Court of the United States stated that the prohibition against trying someone who is mentally incompetent is fundamental to the U.S. system of justice. Accordingly, the Court, in *Dusky v. United States,* approved a test of competence that seeks to ascertain whether a criminal defendant "has sufficient present ability to consult with his lawyer with a reasonable degree of rational understanding—and whether he has a rational as well as factual understanding of the proceedings against him."

One of the most useful clinical guides for determining a patient's competence to stand trial is the McGarry instrument, which identifies 13 areas of functioning:

1. Ability to appraise the legal defenses available
2. Level of unmanageable behavior
3. Quality of relating to the attorney
4. Ability to plan legal strategy
5. Ability to appraise the roles of various participants in the courtroom proceedings
6. Understanding of court procedure
7. Appreciation of the charges
8. Appreciation of the range and the nature of the possible penalties
9. Ability to appraise the likely outcome
10. Capacity to disclose to the attorney available pertinent facts surrounding the offense
11. Capacity to challenge prosecution witnesses realistically
12. Capacity to testify relevantly
13. Manifestation of self-serving versus self-defeating motivation

One strength of such a guide is that it helps clinicians, even without courtroom experience, picture the effects of the familiar forms of psychopathology on these parameters.

Clinicians merely offer opinions about competence. The judge is free to honor, modify, or disregard these opinions, and a patient is not competent or incompetent until the judge so rules. Psychiatrists would do well to refrain from protesting a competence judgment that contradicts clinical opinion. Disagreeing with a judgment is a matter for appeals courts, not for clinical objections.

Competence to Be Executed

One of the new areas of competence to emerge in the interface between psychiatry and the law is the question of people's competence to be executed. The requirement for competence in this area is believed to rest on three general principles. First, a person's awareness of what is happening is supposed to heighten the retributive element of the punishment. Punishment is meaningless unless the person is aware of it and knows the punishment's purpose. Second, a competent person who is about to be executed is believed to be in the best position to make whatever peace is appropriate with religious beliefs, including confession and absolution. Third, a competent person who is about to be executed preserves, until the end, the possibility (admittedly slight) of recalling a forgotten detail of the events or the crime that may prove exonerating.

The need to preserve competence was supported recently in the Supreme Court case of *Ford v. Wainwright.* But no matter the outcome of legal struggles with this question, most medical bodies have gravitated toward the position that it is unethical for any clinician to participate, no matter how remotely, in state-mandated executions; a physician's duty to preserve life transcends all other competing requirements. Therefore, there is ethical guidance for psychiatrists on this point. The ethical dilemmas of a psychiatrist's involvement in such situations are readily predictable. A psychiatrist who examines a patient slated for execution may find the person incompetent on the basis of a mental disorder but may incur a medical obligation to recommend a treatment plan, which, if implemented, would ensure the person's fitness to be executed. There is room for a difference of opinion regarding whether treatment under these circumstances is humane or inhumane.

Criminal Responsibility

According to criminal law, committing an act that is socially harmful is not the sole criterion of whether a crime has been committed. Instead, the objectionable act must have two components: voluntary conduct *(actus reus)* and evil intent *(mens rea).* There cannot be an evil intent when an offender's mental status is so deficient, so abnormal, or so diseased as to have deprived the offender of the capacity for rational intent. The law can be invoked only when an illegal intent is implemented. Neither behavior, however harmful, nor the intent to do harm is, in itself, a ground for criminal action.

Until recently, in most U.S. jurisdictions, people could be found not guilty by reason of insanity if they had a mental illness, did not know the difference between right and wrong, and did not know the nature and consequences of their acts. The persistence of the insanity defense seems to derive from two profound medicolegal forces. One is the moral imperative: The insanity defense is perhaps more nearly a moral than either a clinical or a legal issue. The moral dimension speaks to the reluctance to hold blameworthy or culpable those in society who do not seem to merit such labels because of their psychological or neurological conditions—a state the law calls mental disease or defect. Children and people who are severely retarded have traditionally occupied this moral niche; people who are mentally ill have always been in an ambiguous position. The second force sustaining the insanity defense is the perception of fairness. Society's sense of the fairness of its courts is undermined when, as one judge stated, "drooling idiots are treated as if they were responsible defendants." Ultimately, the legal system requires a class of nonculpable people and a system and standards for defining this class—in short, the theory and practice of an insanity defense.

From a societal viewpoint, the insanity defense generates two common misconceptions that make it unpopular. First, many hardened criminals are believed to use the legal loophole to escape conviction. In reality, the insanity defense is used in only a tiny fraction of cases, and it prevails in a tiny fraction of this fraction—precisely because of its unpopularity. Second, the insanity defense is believed to allow psychiatrists to get criminals off by acting as apologists for their evil actions. This view fails because the adversarial system requires two psychiatric opinions and because no psychiatrist ever decides a case.

M'Naghten Rule. The precedent for determining legal responsibility was established in 1843 in the British courts.

The so-called M'Naghten rule, which has, until recently, determined criminal responsibility in most of the United States, holds that people are not guilty by reason of insanity if they labored under a mental disease such that they were unaware of the nature, the quality, and the consequences of their acts or if they were incapable of realizing that their acts were wrong. Moreover, to absolve people from punishment, a delusion used as evidence must be one that, if true, would be an adequate defense. If the delusional idea does not justify the crime, such people are presumably held responsible, guilty, and punishable. The M'Naghten rule is known commonly as the right-wrong test.

The M'Naghten rule derives from the famous M'Naghten case of 1843 (Fig. 55–2). When Daniel M'Naghten murdered Edward Drummond, the private secretary of Robert Peel, M'Naghten had been suffering from delusions of persecution for several years, had complained to many people about his "persecutors," and finally had decided to correct the situation by murdering Robert Peel. When Drummond came out of Peel's home, M'Naghten shot Drummond, whom he mistook for Peel. The jury, as instructed under the prevailing law, found M'Naghten not guilty by reason of insanity. M'Naghten was later committed to a hospital for the insane. The case aroused great interest and caused the House of Lords to debate the problems of criminality and insanity. In response to questions about what guidelines could be used to determine whether a person could plead insanity as a defense against criminal responsibility, the English chief judge wrote:

1. To establish a defense on the ground of insanity, it must be clearly proved that, at the time of committing the act, the party accused was laboring under such a defect of reason, from disease of the mind, as not to know the nature and quality of the act he was doing, or if he did know it, he did not know he was doing what was wrong.
2. Where a person labors under partial delusions only and is not in other respects insane and as a result commits an offense, he must be considered in the same situation regarding responsibility as if the facts with respect to which the delusion exists were real.

According to the M'Naghten rule, the question is not whether the accused knows the difference between right and wrong in general, it is whether the defendant understood the nature and the quality of the act and whether the defendant knew the difference between right and wrong with respect to the act—that is, specifically whether the defendant knew the act was wrong or perhaps thought the act was correct, a delusion causing the defendant to act in legitimate self-defense.

Irresistible Impulse. In 1922, a committee of jurists in England reexamined the M'Naghten rule. The committee suggested broadening the concept of insanity in criminal cases to include the irresistible impulse tests, which rules that a person charged with a criminal offense is not responsible for an act if the act was committed under an impulse that the person was unable to resist because of mental disease. The courts have chosen to interpret this concept in such a way that it has been called the policeman-at-the-elbow law. In other words, the court grants an impulse to be irresistible only when it can be determined that the accused would have committed the act even if a policeman had been at the accused's elbow. To most psychiatrists, this interpretation is unsatisfactory because it covers only a small, special group of those who are mentally ill.

FIGURE 55–2
Daniel M'Naghten. His 1843 murder trial led to the establishment of rules still generally observed in legal insanity pleas. (Courtesy of Culver Pictures.)

Durham Rule. In the case of *Durham v. United States,* Judge David Bazelon handed down a decision in 1954 in the District of Columbia Court of Appeals. The decision resulted in the product rule of criminal responsibility: An accused is not criminally responsible if his or her unlawful act was the product of mental disease or mental defect.

In the *Durham* case, Judge Bazelon expressly stated that the purpose of the rule was to get good and complete psychiatric testimony. He sought to release the criminal law from the theoretical straitjacket of the M'Naghten rule, but judges and juries in cases using the *Durham* rule became mired in confusion over the terms "product," "disease," and "defect." In 1972, some 18 years after the rule's adoption, the Court of Appeals for the District of Columbia, in *United States v. Brawner,* discarded the rule. The court—all nine members, including Judge Bazelon—decided in a 143-page opinion to throw out its *Durham* rule and to adopt in its place the test recommended in 1962 by the American Law Institute in its model penal code, which is the law in the federal courts today.

Model Penal Code. In its model penal code, the American Law Institute recommended the following test of criminal responsibility: People are not responsible for criminal conduct if, at the time of such conduct, as a result of mental disease or defect, they lacked substantial capacity either to appreciate the criminality (wrongfulness) of their conduct or to conform their conduct to the requirement of the law. The term *mental disease or defect* does not include an abnormality manifest only by repeated criminal or otherwise antisocial conduct.

Subsection 1 of the American Law Institute rule contains five operative concepts: mental disease or defect, lack of substantial capacity, appreciation, wrongfulness, and conformity of conduct to the requirements of law. The rule's second subsection, stating that repeated criminal or antisocial conduct is not, of itself, to be taken as mental disease or defect, aims to keep the sociopath or psychopath within the scope of criminal responsibility.

Other Tests. The test of criminal responsibility and other tests of criminal liability refer to the time of the offense's commission, whereas the test of competence to stand trial refers to the time of the trial.

The 1982 verdict of a District of Columbia jury, which found John W. Hinckley, Jr., the would-be assassin of President Ronald Reagan, not guilty by reason of insanity, ignited moves to limit or abolish the special plea (Fig. 55–3). Hinckley's trial by jury also turned out to be a trial of law and psychiatry. The psychiatrists and the law that allows their testimony were made the culprits for the unpopular verdict. "The psychiatrists spun sticky webs of pseudoscientific jargon," wrote a prominent columnist, "and in these webs the concept of justice, like a moth, fluttered feebly and was trapped." The American Bar Association and the American Psychiatric Association quickly issued statements calling for a change in the law. More than 40 bills were introduced in Congress to amend the law; none was passed, but the bills helped defuse the public criticism. At present, Hinckley is hospitalized indefinitely at the federal St. Elizabeth's Hospital in Washington, DC.

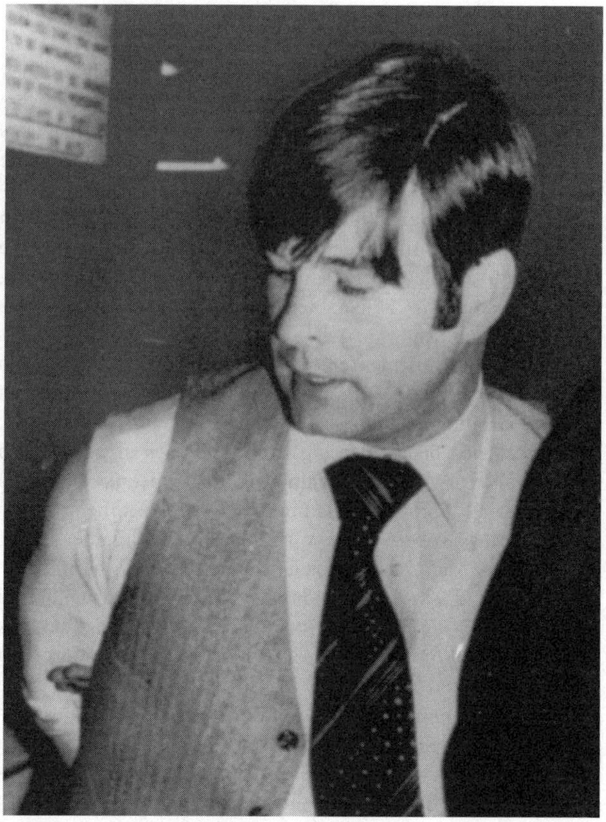

FIGURE 55–4
Dan White. The former San Francisco supervisor killed San Francisco mayor George Moscone and supervisor Harvey Milk at City Hall in 1978. White's "Twinkie defense" helped reduce his crime for murder to manslaughter, for which he served 5 years. White committed suicide a few days after he was released from prison. (Courtesy of Wide World Photos.)

FIGURE 55–3
John Hinckley, Jr. In 1980, he shot President Ronald Reagan and Secretary James Brady. Hinckley was found not guilty by reason of insanity in 1982. The Brady Bill, a gun control bill, became law in 1993. (Courtesy of Wide World Photos.)

Attempts at legal reform have included the plea of guilty but mentally ill, which is already used in some jurisdictions. This standard has the advantage of identifying guilt while allowing some adaptation to psychiatric conditions; for example, it allows for treatment in restricted settings while permitting the courts to maintain an active role. "Guilty but insane" is a contradiction in terms: Insanity has no legal meaning except as exculpation. The defense of diminished capacity is based on the claim that the defendant suffered an impairment (usually but not always because of mental illness) sufficient to interfere with the ability to formulate a specific element (such as forethought) of the particular crime charged. Therefore, the defense finds its most common use with so-called specific-intent crimes, such as first-degree murder.

Under this concept, the crime of Dan White, who had killed

two city officials of San Francisco, was reduced from murder to manslaughter (Fig. 55–4). White's "Twinkie defense" involved psychiatrists who testified that he was depressed and that his compulsive eating of junk foods was a symptom of depression. His depression led to a manslaughter conviction, rather than a first-degree murder conviction. After he was released from prison, White committed suicide.

The American Medical Association has proposed yet another reform: limiting the insanity exculpation to cases in which the person is so ill as to lack the necessary criminal intent (*mens rea*). This approach would all but eliminate the insanity defense and place a burden on the prisons to accept large numbers of people who are mentally ill.

The American Bar Association and the American Psychiatric Association, in their 1982 statements, recommended a defense of nonresponsibility, which focuses solely on whether defendants, as a result of mental disease or defect, are unable to appreciate the wrongfulness of their conduct. These proposals would limit the evidence of mental illness to cognition and would exclude control, but apparently a defense would still be available under a not-guilty plea—such as extreme emotional disturbance, automatism, provocation, or self-defense—that would be established without psychiatric testimony about mental illness. The American Psychiatric Association also urged that "mental illness" be limited to severely abnormal mental conditions. These proposals still are controversial, and the issue probably will arise again with each sensational case in which the insanity defense is used.

Figures 55–5 through 55–8 represent a variety of cases in which mental illness was a factor.

FIGURE 55–6

Colin Ferguson. He was determined competent and elected to represent himself during his murder trial for the 1993 Long Island Railroad massacre. Ferguson was convicted and is presently serving a 200-year sentence. (Courtesy of Wide World Photos.)

FIGURE 55–5

Richard Speck. He was convicted in 1966 of slaying eight nurses in Chicago by stabbing and strangulation. He was sentenced to death in the electric chair. His legal defense was based on his genetic makeup which was "XYY." Individuals with these genes have been reported to be tall, be mentally retarded, have acne, and show aggressive behavior. (Courtesy of Wide World Photos.)

MALPRACTICE

Malpractice is the term commonly used to refer to professional negligence. Legally, negligence is defined by what a reasonably prudent person would or would not do in the same or similar circumstances. An action based on negligence, whatever the specific situation, involves basic problems of the relationship among the parties, the risk, and the reason. A negligence action often is precipitated by a bad outcome and resultant bad feelings.

The usual claim of malpractice requires a litigant to produce an expert to establish the four *D*s of malpractice: that there was the *d*ereliction (negligent performance or omission) of a *d*uty that *d*irectly led to *d*amages. In negligence, a standard of care requisite under the particular circumstances must exist; a duty must have been owed by the defendant or by someone for whose conduct the defendant is answerable; the duty must have been owed to the plaintiff; and a breach of the duty must be the legal cause of the plaintiff's asserted damage or injury.

The requisite standard of care under the circumstances may be established in the federal or state constitution, statutes, administrative regulations, court decisions, or the custom of the community. The law, however, with few exceptions, does not specifically define the particular duties, and it is impossible to define the way in which a person should act under various circumstances and conditions. As a rule, professionals have the duty to exercise the degree of skill ordinarily used under similar circumstances by similar professionals.

Complainants in a malpractice action must prove their allegations by a preponderance of evidence. To sustain the burden of proof, the plaintiff must show an act or omission on the part of the defendant or of someone for whose conduct the defendant is answerable; a causal relation between the conduct and the damage or injury allegedly suffered by the plaintiff; and the negligent quality of the conduct. Because most professional conduct is not within the common knowledge of laypeople, expert testimony must usually provide such information.

In relative frequency of malpractice suits, psychiatry ranks eighth among the medical specialties; in almost every suit for psychiatric malpractice in which liability was imposed, tangible physical injury was proved. The number of suits against psychiatrists is said to be small because of patients' reluctance to expose a psychiatric history, the skill of psychiatrists in dealing with patients' negative feelings, and the difficulty in linking injury with treatment. Psychiatrists have been sued for malpractice for faulty diagnosis and screening, improper certification in hospitalization, suicide, harmful effects of electroconvulsive treatments and psychotropic drugs, improper divulgence of information, and sexual intimacy with patients.

FIGURE 55–8
Jeffrey Dahmer. His murder trial for the deaths of 17 young men and boys gained widespread notoriety after accusations of cannibalistic practices were made. Dahmer was killed in prison by a psychotic inmate in 1994. (Courtesy of Wide World Photos.)

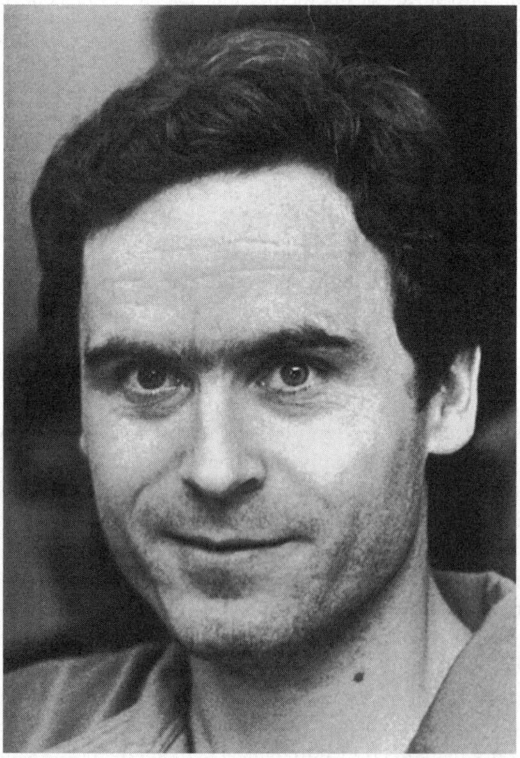

FIGURE 55–7
Theodore Bundy. Bundy was a serial killer responsible for the deaths of at least 22 young women. He represented himself at trials in Utah, Colorado, and Florida. Found guilty of murder, he was executed by the state of Florida in 1989. (Courtesy of Wide World Photos.)

In a recent line of cases, third parties have been able to sue psychotherapists for allegedly implanting false memories of childhood sexual abuse in their patients. In one case, a father won a $425,000 jury verdict against his daughter's therapists for negligently reinforcing or implanting false memories of his sexually abusing her. Several other cases have allowed third parties to sue as direct victims of therapists' negligence. The implications of these cases to psychotherapeutic practice are far-reaching, controversial, and, as yet, unresolved.

Respondeat Superior

The Latin phrase *respondeat superior* expresses the axiom, "Let the master answer for the deeds of the servant." This doctrine holds that a person occupying a high position in a chain or hierarchy of responsibility is liable for the actions of a person in a lower position. A typical example is the psychiatric attending physician who supervises a resident. By the same reasoning, when a state hospital, for instance, is named in a lawsuit, the list of cited defendants may extend upward to include the commissioner of mental health and the governor of the state. After the traditional first response, the attorneys usually weed out the irrelevant defendants.

A few critical issues should be noted here: First, consultation from outside the line of clinical responsibility often does not fit the model for this doctrine. The consultant is an adviser, not a superior. Second, the question of the particular defendant's authority (whether the person can hire and fire, censure, or control subordinates in the system) is relevant to the assignment of blame. Third, as a rule, psychiatrists should remove themselves from situations in which they bear responsibility (liability) for the practice of other professionals but cannot control the activities of these persons or perform their own assessments of the patients. In such situations, a psychiatrist may consider carrying vicarious liability insurance, which protects psychiatrists against liability for actions against clinicians they supervise directly or indirectly. In addition, psychiatrists should clarify ambiguities of responsibility at the point of entry into a system.

Suicide and Suicidal Attempts by Patients

Suicide and suicidal attempts are the most frequent causes of lawsuits against psychiatrists. An estimated one of every two suicides leads to a malpractice action. Psychiatrists may be charged with negligence because they did not properly control a patient under treatment; such negligence causes injury, and the suicidal behavior must have been predictable. A psychiatrist may be accused of malpractice even though suicide occurs during the patient's hospitalization.

Misdiagnosis

For clinicians who are still grappling with the often counterintuitive complexities of the various editions of the *Diagnostic and Statistical Manual of Mental Disorders,* the idea that misdiagnosis can result in litigation may precipitate needless anxiety. Cases on this point are not concerned with whether a patient unambiguously suffered from schizophrenia or bipolar I disorder. Instead, the imputation is that a clinician negligently missed some diagnostic point. Typical examples include failures to discover a patient's suicidal or homicidal intent, a concomitant or underlying medical condition, or a side effect of consequence. The diagnoses, by inference, would be obvious to an average practitioner.

Negligent Treatment

After diagnosis comes treatment, which may be claimed to be negligent in various ways, perhaps most succinctly summarized as "too much, too little, or wrong." Typical claims allege inadequate or insufficient treatment (undertreatment), excessive or overly aggressive treatment (overtreatment), and variations on the theme of improper treatment, such as using the wrong medication, failing to anticipate or respond to side effects appropriately, and creating iatrogenic harms or addictions.

Clinicians often worry about being sued for drug-produced harm detected years after the drug was introduced, such as unsuspected, late-appearing side effects; however, here the law is logical. The relevant standard is information available to an average practitioner at the time of the event. In court, for example, the latest edition of an appropriate textbook that was available at the time of the alleged negligence may be used to illuminate the issue.

Among the treatment modalities that are a source of professional liability are various antipsychotic medications associated with the development of tardive dyskinesia. Accordingly, psychiatrists should monitor their patients receiving such medications after warning the patients and their guardians of the risk. Documented evidence of informed consent should be in the patients' medical records. Other risks—such as retinopathy, teratogenicity, and kidney failure—should be noted when appropriate. Informed consent should be obtained before initiating electroconvulsive therapy. Recently, a hospital was judged liable for withholding antipsychiatric medication in a case of depression when psychotherapy was the sole treatment used.

Preventing Liability

Although eliminating malpractice is impossible, some preventive approaches have proven valuable in clinical practice: Clinicians should provide only those kinds of care that they are qualified to offer. They should not overload their practices or overstretch their abilities; they should take reasonable care of themselves; and they should treat their patients with respect. The documentation of good care is a strong deterrent to liability. Such documentation should include the decision-making process, the clinician's rationale for treatment, and an evaluation of the costs and the benefits. A consultation affords protection against liability, because it allows a clinician to obtain information about the peer group's standard of practice. It also provides a second opinion and enables the clinician to submit any judgment to the scrutiny of a peer. A clinician who takes the trouble to obtain a consultation in a difficult and complex case is unlikely to be viewed by a jury as careless or negligent. The informed-consent process involves a discussion of the inherent uncertainty of psychiatric practice. Such a dialogue helps prevent a liability suit.

OTHER AREAS OF FORENSIC PSYCHIATRY

Emotional Damage and Distress

There has been a rapidly rising trend to sue for psychological and emotional damage in recent years, both secondary to physical injury or as a consequence of witnessing a stressful act and from the suffering endured under the stress of such circumstances as concentration camp experiences. The West German government heard many of these claims from people detained in Nazi camps during World War II. In the United States, the courts have moved from a conservative to a liberal position in awarding damages for such claims. Psychiatric examinations and testimony are sought in these cases, often by both the plaintiffs and the defendants.

Workmen's Compensation

The stresses of employment may cause or accentuate mental illness. Patients are entitled to be compensated for their job-related disabilities or to receive disability retirement benefits. A psychiatrist is often called upon to evaluate such situations.

References

Colella U: HIV-related information and the tension between confidentiality and liberal discovery: The need for a uniform approach. J Leg Med *16:* 33, 1995.

Conte HR, Plutchik R, Picard S, Karasu TB: Ethics in the practice of psychotherapy: A survey. Am J Psychother *43:* 32, 1989.

Daniolos PT, Holmes VF: HIV public policy and psychiatry: An examination of ethical issues and professional guidelines. Psychosomatics *36:* 12, 1995.

Fink PJ: On being ethical in an unethical world. Am J Psychiatry *146:* 1097, 1989.

Goldstein RL: Paranoids in the legal system: The litigious paranoid and the paranoid criminal. Psychiatr Clin North Am *18:* 303, 1995.

Gutheil TG: Approaches to forensic assessment of false claims of sexual misconduct by therapists. Bull Am Acad Psychiatry Law *20:* 289, 1992.

Gutheil TG: Legal issues in psychiatry. In *Comprehensive Textbook of Psychiatry,* ed 6, HI Kaplan, BJ Sadock, editors, p 2747. Williams & Wilkins, Baltimore, 1995.

Husted JR, Nehemkis A: Civil commitment viewed from three perspectives: professional, family, and police. Bull Am Acad Psychiatry Law *23:* 533, 1995.

Jaworoski S, Zabow A: Involuntary psychiatric hospitalization of minors. Med Law *14:* 635, 1995.

Jobes DA, Berman AL: Suicide and malpractice liability: Assessing and revising policies, procedures, and practice in outpatient settings. Prof Psychol Res Pract *24:* 91, 1993.

Kantor JE: *Medical Ethics for Physicians-in-Training.* Plenum, New York, 1989.

Kluft RP: Treating the patient who has been sexually exploited by a previous therapist. Psychiatr Clin North Am *12:* 1483, 1989.

Kunjukrishnan R, Varan LR: Major effective disorders and forensic psychiatry. Psychiatr Clin North Am *15:* 569, 1992.

Miller RD: Need-for-treatment criteria for involuntary civil commitment: Impact in practice. Am J Psychiatry *149:* 1380, 1992.

Oppenheimer K, Swanson G: Duty to warn: When should confidentiality be breached? J Fam Pract *30:* 179, 1990.

Palermo GB, Perracuti S, Palermo MT: Malingering a challenge for the forensic examiner. Med Law *15:* 143, 1996.

Perlin ML: Tarasoff and the dilemma of the dangerous patient: New directions for the 1990's. Law Psychol Rev *16:* 29, 1992.

Reid WH, Wise M, Sutton B: The use and reliability of psychiatric diagnosis in forensic settings. Psychiatr Clin North Am *15:* 529, 1992.

Roback HB, Moore RF, Bloch FS, Shelton M: Confidentiality in group psychotherapy: empirical findings and the law. Int J Group Psychother *46:* 117, 1996.

Saks E: The criminal responsibility of people with multiple personality disorder. Psychiatr Q *66:* 119, 1995.

Stone A: *Law Psychiatry and Morality.* American Psychiatric Press, Washington, 1984.

Weiner IB: On competence and ethicality in psychodiagnostic assessment. J Pers Assess *53:* 827, 1989.

Werner PD, Meloy JR: Decision making about dangerousness in releasing patients from long-term psychiatric hospitalization. J Psychiatry Law *20:* 35, 1992.

56

Ethics in Psychiatry

The Hippocratic oath, which originated in ancient Greece perhaps as early as the fourth century B.C., set forth an ethical code for physicians and, among other requirements, prohibited doctors from participating in surgery or abortions. For centuries, most physicians in Christian Europe probably followed versions of the Hippocratic principles. Thomas Percival, an 18th century English Physician, wrote a code of ethics that the founders of the American Medical Association (AMA) drew on for their version of Hippocratic traditions; the AMA's ethical code was first enunciated in 1847 and has been revised through the years. The American Psychiatric Association's (APA) ethical code is formulated in the 1995 edition of the *Principles of Medical Ethics with Annotations Especially Applicable to Psychiatry.*

Although medicine has been practiced to some degree in almost every known culture and although surgeons and doctors practiced in ancient civilizations such as Egypt and Mesopotamia (and Egyptian medicine was famous in antiquity), the idea that the practice of medicine was based on moral principles seems to have been confined to the Western world. Underlying the practice of Western medicine, ethical principles provide a foundation and direction for complex, often painful decisions about human beings, but perhaps no area of medicine is so concerned with ethics as the field of psychiatry. Treating psychiatric patients routinely requires psychiatrists to confront basic ethical dilemmas, such as restricting individual freedom through involuntary commitment and administering medicine to patients deemed not competent to refuse intervention. Such issues illustrate the most pervasive ethical conflict in psychiatry, that between autonomy and beneficence, the right of patients to self-determination and the duty of physicians to act in the best interests of their patients. Hospitalizing patients and treating them against their will are common practices in psychiatry, practices that fuel the debate about the limits and extent of rights for those who are mentally ill.

Because ethics implies a set of principles that people rely on to determine right and wrong and good and bad, physicians often are tempted to seek answers in legal or professional codes of ethics. Currently, these codes do not necessarily help to solve the medical problems. Laws may change, as they have in regard to involuntary hospitalization and treatment, or they may be ambiguous, as they are in regard to the limits of patient confidentiality. Codes of ethics also are subject to change and often are ambiguous. Does the rule "Do no harm" help a physician to decide whether to force hospitalization on a patient to protect society? Is a physician to "do no harm" to a patient or to society?

The law does not always establish positive duties (what people should do) to the extent that professional (especially medical) ethical standards do. Physicians' positive duties are based on specific ethical principles, including *beneficence* or nonmalfeasance (the duty to do no harm) and *autonomy* (the duty to protect a patient's freedom to choose). Other ethical principles are derived from specific underlying principles, including those shaping the parameters of truth telling, disclosure, informed consent, involuntary hospitalization, the right to receive and refuse treatment, and duties to third parties.

Because of the unique nature of the disorders of people who are mentally ill, the principles of beneficence and autonomy in psychiatry may be interpreted in opposing ways and can lead to potential or actual conflicts in values and beliefs about appropriate care. To understand the ethical dilemmas inherent in the practice of psychiatry, it is necessary to understand the theories that are the sources of most ethical issues.

UTILITARIAN THEORY

According to utilitarian theory, a fundamental obligation in making decisions is to try to produce the greatest possible happiness for the greatest number of people. When considering which decisions to make, laws to enact, or policies to follow, utilitarian theory requires that people consider all of the available evidence relevant to decisions about the consequences of alternative courses of action and on the basis of this evidence, make the decision, law, or policy most likely to produce the greatest happiness in society. When the alternative course of action is dismal, people must choose the way that produces the least amount of pain.

The predictions about consequences are sometimes controversial and difficult to make. For example, the debates about mandatory human immunodeficiency virus (HIV) testing and reporting and about mandatory substance testing center partly on the question of whether mandatory policies discourage people from seeking medical treatment and, thus, have counterproductive consequences. Utilitarian theory recognizes no fundamental rights to truth, to informed consent, and to confidentiality. Truth-telling, confidentiality, and informed consent are recognized only when and if they result in the most happiness or the least pain. Utilitarianism also has been used to justify medical paternalism, which is discussed next.

Utilitarian approaches to physician–patient relationships are being replaced by approaches based on a second major ethical theory—the autonomy theory. However, the utilitarian theory is still the basis for macro decisions about the allocation of society's resources for treatment and medical research.

Paternalism

Paternalism may be defined as a person's performing actions for another's benefit without the person's consent. Paternalism in medicine takes two forms: state and individual. Requirements that patients go to licensed practitioners for treatment and that certain drugs be given only through prescriptions are examples of state paternalism. Individual paternalism has been the traditional model for the physician–patient relationship. In this model, physicians are supposed to treat patients as a caring parent would treat a young child. A physician has a duty of beneficence to a patient, just as a parent has a duty of beneficence toward a child. The physician or parent is presumed to know what is best for the patient or child and has no obligation to explain each decision or to ask permission to perform beneficial actions. Like a parent, a physician is presumed to have knowledge that the patient may be incapable of understanding or, in the physician's judgment, is better off not knowing.

AUTONOMY THEORY

Based on the writings of Immanuel Kant, autonomy theory conceives of the relationship between a physician and a normal adult patient as a relationship between two responsible people, not as one between a parent and a child. The relationship is deontological, implying a moral obligation between the two parties.

Normal adult patients are presumed to have the ability and the right to make rational, responsible life decisions. They are autonomous (self-governing), and their right to self-determination must be respected, even when a physician believes that a decision will work against a patient's best interests. The legal assumption of adults' competence, the right to informed consent in treatment and research, the right to refuse treatment, and the limitations on the ability of psychiatrists to involuntarily hospitalize and involuntarily treat people are all examples of the growing recognition of adults' fundamental rights to self-determination in medical decision making.

Autonomy theory accepts the idea that people have obligations to produce happiness and diminish pain, but unlike utilitarian theory, autonomy theory prohibits forcing people to achieve these goals against their will. To lie to normal adults, even for their benefit, is to show a lack of respect for their ability to be responsible beings. According to autonomy theory, subjecting people to research without their consent is to treat them as things, not as human beings, and is thereby absolutely wrong. In utilitarian theory, such research can be pursued when it produces happiness in society.

Autonomy theory also holds that treating people paternalistically is justified only when these people lack the capacity to be autonomous (for example, young children, those who are profoundly retarded, and some people who are psychotic).

FURTHER ETHICAL PRINCIPLES

Ethical principles can both support and further the goals of psychiatric practice and research. In particular situations, awareness of the relevance and conscious application of those principles can help clarify treatment options and justify particular decisions.

Justice

An ethical principle that is especially relevant to the ethics of mental health policy is *justice,* in this context, a fair distribution and application of psychiatric services. Justice in the sense of fair procedures enters into the involuntary hospitalization and treatment of people who, as a result of mental illness, are dangerous to themselves or others. The rules of procedural justice are central in this situation because involuntary treatment restricts both the liberty and the choices of such people.

Respect

Another additional ethical principle is respect for people, displayed through efforts to restore or maximize patients' competence or other capacities. The more that psychiatric treatment moves toward the restoration of a patient's capacity to function, the more the treatment approximates the ethical ideal of respect. The task is difficult, however, when patients suffer from enduring or permanent disabilities, such as adults who are autistic, whose capacity for insight, motivation, and judgment is permanently impaired. Doctors may be tempted to suggest that such people be institutionalized to control their behavior by forcing them to function within a highly structured and sheltered environment; for some patients, this treatment option may be preferable. For others, however, despite their autistic tendencies and habits, it may be preferable to recommend a living situation that combines therapy and behavioral management with the preferences of the patient that, although eccentric, are socially permissible. Treatments that maximize patients' capacities and choices are ethically preferable to treatments designed primarily for the convenience of caretakers.

PROFESSIONAL CODES

Most professional organizations and many business groups have codes of ethics. Such codes reflect a consensus about the general standards of appropriate professional conduct. The *AMA's Principles of Medical Ethics,* the *APA's Principles of Medical Ethics with Annotations Especially Applicable to Psychiatry,* and the *American College of Physicians Ethics Manual* articulate ideal standards of practice and professional virtues of practitioners. These codes include exhortations to use skillful and scientific techniques, to self-regulate misconduct within the profession, and to respect the rights and needs of patients, families, colleagues, and society. Such exhortations are reinforced by ethical principles, such as beneficence, utility, autonomy, respect, and justice.

In recent years, there has been increased interest in the use of professional codes of ethics as a standard of criticism and as a means to regulate professional misconduct. For ethical violations, the APA may expel members from its organization or, for less severe violations, suspend membership for a time. During this period, a member may be required to undergo supervision or extra training. For still less severe violations, a member may be reprimanded or admonished, with no effect on membership status. Expulsion from the APA is reported publicly, but whether less severe violations are reported is left to the discretion of the local APA branch. Some hospitals withdraw privileges from a psychiatrist who has been expelled for ethical reasons, and malpractice coverage may be denied.

The 1995 edition of *Principles of Medical Ethics with Annotations Especially Applicable to Psychiatry* provides a useful and comprehensive example of a professional code geared to the psychiatric profession. The manual covers a broad array of psychiatric ethical issues, from fee splitting and sex with former patients to psychiatrists' participation in executions, all of which are unethical. Another useful manual is the 1995 edition of the *Opinions of the Ethics Committee on the Principles of Medical Ethics with Annotations Especially Applicable to Psychiatry.* This manual, developed by APA Ethics Committee members and consultants, provides answers to commonly asked ethical questions. A summary of ethical questions and answers is provided in Table 56–1.

PATIENT–THERAPIST SEXUAL RELATIONS

For a psychiatrist to engage a patient in a sexual relationship is clearly unethical. Furthermore, legal sanctions against such behavior make the ethical question moot. Various criminal law statutes have been used against psychiatrists who violate this ethical principle. Rape charges may be and have been brought against such psychiatrists; sexual assault and battery charges also have been used to convict psychiatrists.

In addition, patients who have been victimized sexually by psychiatrists and other physicians have won damages in malpractice suits. Insurance carriers for the APA and the AMA no longer insure against patient–therapist sexual relations, and the carriers exclude liability for any such sexual activity.

Finally, professional boards and associations have formulated procedures to review charges made by patients, and these groups can censure or suspend physicians. Ultimately, licenses to practice medicine may be revoked. In one case involving patient–therapist sexual relations, a court stated: ''There is a public policy to protect the patient from the deliberate and malicious abuse of power and breach of trust by a psychiatrist when the patient entrusts to him her body and mind in the hope that he will use his best efforts to find a cure.''

The issue of whether sexual relations between an ex-patient and a therapist violate an ethical principle remains an area of controversy. Proponents of the view ''Once a patient always a patient'' insist that any involvement with an ex-patient—even one that leads to marriage—should be prohibited. They maintain that a transferential reaction that always exists between the patient and the therapist prevents a rational decision about their emotional or sexual union. Others insist that, if a transferential reaction still exists, the therapy is incomplete and that, as autonomous human beings, ex-patients should not be subjected to paternalistic moralizing by physicians. Accordingly, they believe that no sanctions should prohibit emotional or sexual involvements by ex-patients and their psychiatrists. Some psychiatrists maintain that a reasonable time should elapse before such a liaison. The length of the ''reasonable'' period remains controversial: Some have suggested 2 years. Other psychiatrists maintain that any period of prohibited involvement with an ex-patient is an unnecessary restriction. The *Principles of Medical Ethics with Annotations Especially Applicable to Psychiatry,* however, states: ''Sexual activity with a current or *former* [italics added] patient is unethical.''

INFORMED CONSENT

Informed consent is the cornerstone of autonomy theory. Adult patients are assumed to have the right to consent or refuse to consent to treatment. U.S. law reflects strong popular beliefs about the commitment to self-determination. To permit competent adults to make important personal choices about lifestyles, careers, relationships, and other values is one way to demonstrate respect for people. True informed consent offers when a patient's choice is intentional, free of undue outside influence, and made with rational understanding. The disabling effects of illness, especially mental illness, however, confuse the issue. How is it possible for psychiatrists to show respect for people whose capacity to choose is compromised by the very condition for which the treatment is offered?

A document of informed consent serves only as a record of the completion of a process. This process should include obtaining enough uncoerced information during a sufficiently long time to make an informed choice about treatment. Information about the diagnosis, the prognosis, and the risks and benefits of accepting or rejecting alternative courses of treatment enables patients to make informed choices.

As physicians, psychiatrists are educated to respond to people in need of help, often in emergency or crisis situations. People who require medical care frequently do not want to make choices; they want physicians to take care of them and to tell them what to do to get well. Therefore, patients often regress in response to mental and physical illness and may become especially vulnerable to influence and exploitation. The psychological authority of psychiatrists, in particular, is well documented. Psychiatrists must guard against the tendency to dominate their patients' decision making.

The legal doctrine of informed consent is a reminder that psychiatrists must respect the rights of patients, including their right to be informed and to make treatment choices. However, the law does not provide guidance about the complex and subtle ethical responsibility to show respect for patients, especially when their competence is, to some degree, compromised by their illness. A psychiatrist's first ethical task is to treat patients properly. To show respect is to listen, to try to understand, and to avoid stereotyping and making a premature diagnosis. Psychiatrists also convey respect by the way they talk, try to explain, and seek to provide patients, even questionably competent ones, realistic options.

Physicians must take precautions against presuming that patients are incompetent to decide for themselves until proven otherwise or protected by courts. Respect for patients is achieved by reciprocity, communication, and concern, not by domination. Even toward patients with minimal mental disorders who are undergoing psychotherapy, psychiatrists primarily display respect not through informed consent but through their attentive and sensitive responses to the nuances of their patients' verbal and nonverbal behavior.

Table 56–1
Ethical Questions and Answers

Topic	Question	Answer
Abandonment	How can psychiatrists avoid being charged with patient abandonment upon retirement?	Retiring psychiatrists are not abandoning patients if they provide their patients with sufficient notice and make every reasonable effort to find follow-up care for the patients.
	Is it ethical to provide only outpatient care to a seriously ill patient, who may require hospitalization?	This could constitute abandonment unless the outpatient practitioner or agency arranges for their patients to receive inpatient care from another provider.
Bequests	A dying patient bequeaths his or her estate to his or her treating psychiatrist. Is this ethical?	No. Accepting the bequest seems improper and exploitational of the therapeutic relationship. However, it may be ethical to accept a token bequest from a deceased patient who named his or her psychiatrist in the will without that psychiatrist's knowledge.
Competency	Is it ethical for psychiatrists to perform vaginal exams? Hospital physicals?	Psychiatrists may provide nonpsychiatric medical procedures if they are competent to do so and if the procedures do not preclude effective psychiatric treatment by distorting the transference. Pelvic exams carry a high risk of distorting the transference and would be better performed by another clinician.
	Can ethics committees review issues of physician competency?	Yes. Incompetency is an ethical issue.
Confidentiality	Must confidentiality be maintained after the death of a patient?	Yes. Ethically, confidences survive a patient's death. Exceptions include protecting others from imminent harm or proper legal compulsions.
	Is it ethical to release information about a patient to an insurance company?	Yes, if the information provided is limited to that which is needed to process the insurance claim.
	Can a videotaped segment of a therapy session be used at a workshop for professionals?	Yes, if informed, uncoerced consent has been obtained, anonymity is maintained, the audience is advised that editing makes this an incomplete session, and the patient knows the purpose of the videotape.
	Should a physician report mere suspicion of child abuse in a state requiring reporting of child abuse?	No. A physician must make several assessments before deciding whether to report suspected abuse. One must consider whether abuse is ongoing, whether abuse is responsive to treatment, and whether reporting will cause potential harm. Check specific statutes. Make safety for potential victims the top priority.
Conflict of Interest	Is there a potential ethical conflict if a psychiatrist has both psychotherapeutic and administrative duties in dealing with students or trainees?	Yes. You must define your role in advance to the trainees or students. Administrative opinions should be obtained from a psychiatrist who is not involved in a treatment relationship with the trainee or student.
Diagnosis without Examination	Is it ethical to offer a diagnosis based only upon review of records to determine, for insurance purposes, if suicide was the result of illness?	Yes.
	Is it ethical for a supervising psychiatrist to sign a diagnosis on an insurance form for services provided by a supervisee when the psychiatrist has not examined the patient?	Yes, if the psychiatrist ensures that proper care is given and the insurance form clearly indicates the role of supervisor and supervisee.

Exploitation (also see Bequests)	What constitutes exploitation of the therapeutic relationship?	Exploitation occurs when the psychiatrist uses the therapeutic relationship for personal gain. This includes adopting or hiring a patient as well as sexual or financial relationships.
Fee splitting	What is fee splitting?	Fee splitting occurs when one physician pays another for a patient referral. This would also apply to lawyers giving a forensic psychiatrist referrals in exchange for a percentage of the fee. Fee splitting may occur in an office setting if the psychiatrist takes a percentage of his or her office-mates' fees for supervision or expenses. Costs for such items or services must be arranged separately. Otherwise, it would appear that the office owner could benefit from referring patients to a colleague in the office. Fee splitting is illegal.
Informed consent	Is it ethical to refuse to divulge information about a patient who has agreed to give this information to those requesting it?	No. It is the patient's decision, not the therapist's.
	Is informed consent needed when presenting or writing about case material?	Not if the patient is aware of the supervisory/teaching process and confidentiality is preserved.
Moonlighting	Can psychiatric residents ethically "moonlight?"	They can if their duties are not beyond their ability, if they are properly supervised, and if the moonlighting does not interfere with their residency training.
Reporting	Should psychiatrists expose or report unethical behavior of a colleague or colleagues? Can a spouse bring an ethical complaint?	Psychiatrists are obligated to report colleagues' unethical behavior. A spouse with knowledge of unethical behavior can bring an ethical complaint as well.
Research	How can ethical research be performed with subjects who cannot give informed consent?	Consent can be given by a legal guardian or via a living will. Incompetent persons have the right to withdraw from the research project at any time.
Retirement	See Abandonment.	
Supervision	What are the ethical requirements when a psychiatrist supervises other mental health professionals?	The psychiatrist must spend sufficient time to ensure that proper care is given and that the supervisee is not providing services that are outside the scope of their training. It is ethical to charge a fee for supervision.
Taping and Recording	Can videotapes of patient interviews be used for training purposes on a national level (eg, workshops, board exam preparation)?	Appropriate and explicit informed consent must be obtained. The purpose and scope of exposure of the tape must be emphasized in addition to the resulting loss of confidentiality.

Courtesy of Eugene Rubin, M.D. (Data derived from American Psychiatric Association *Opinions of the Ethics Committee on the Principles of Medical Ethics with Annotations Especially Applicable to Psychiatry.* American Psychiatric Association, Washington, 1995.)

RIGHT TO DIE

A patient's right to refuse treatment is part of the rationale used to support seriously ill patients' right to forgo life-sustaining treatment. That is, patients who believe that their quality of life would be compromised by continued treatment have the right to demand that such treatment be withheld or withdrawn. Patients who are expected to lose their capacity to make decisions may express their wishes prospectively, usually through the use of an advanced directive or living will. These directives have full legal standing in some states and may be used as evidence about a patient's wishes in the states that do not recognize the directives. Living wills, however, present problems: They often are too general to cover all of the eventualities in the course of a serious illness.

On June 25, 1990, the Supreme Court of the United States made a determination on the right-to-die issue raised by *Cruzan v. Missouri Board of Health.* The Court upheld the right of a competent person to have "a constitutionally protected liberty interest in refusing unwanted medical treatment." The Supreme Court applied this principle to all patients who have made their wishes clearly known, whether or not they ever regain consciousness.

In the case of *Cruzan v. Missouri Board of Health,* the issue under dispute was determining who has the right to decide on the care of an unconscious person who has not previously made his or her wishes known. The Supreme Court found that, when a permanently unconscious person has left no clear instructions, a state may carry out its interest in "the protection and preservation of human life" by denying a request by others, including family members, to withhold treatment. It was later determined, however, that Cruzan had indicated to family and friends that she did not want life support, and she died in December 1990 after the withdrawal of treatment.

This Supreme Court ruling enables each state to decide the rigor of the evidentiary standards it wishes to apply when asked to withhold or withdraw treatment from a person in a persistent vegetative state who has not previously stated his or her wishes on the subject. Physicians are encouraged to consider the laws pertaining to the preservation of life in the states in which they practice before advising patients about writing a living will. The lack of clear documentation of a patient's wishes may cause these wishes to be set aside by surrogate decision makers or by the state.

A further extension of this issue involves physician-assisted suicide. The media and the courts have focused much attention on Dr. Jack Kevorkian, a retired Michigan pathologist who has assisted in more than 45 suicides to date and has been acquitted of criminal charges on several occasions. Physician-assisted suicide raises several ethical questions, including the assessment of decisional capacity in weighing autonomy versus beneficence, as well as the conflicting roles of physicians in preserving life versus ending suffering. Psychiatry has been involved in cases in which issues such as depression and spousal abuse were believed to influence patients' decisions to seek physician-assisted suicide. For a more complete discussion of this issue, see Chapter 2, Section 27.

SURROGATE DECISION MAKING

A surrogate is sometimes designated to make treatment decisions for patients who have lost decisional capabilities. The surrogate may be designated by the patient before losing capacity or may be chosen by a court. States sometimes allow surrogates to be designated by a hospital. The designated surrogate usually is a next of kin, although next of kin may not always be the appropriate decision makers. Relatives may have psychological and other agendas that interfere with their ability to make just decisions. In the past, surrogates made decisions for patients on a best-interests principle. The surrogate was supposed to decide which treatments could be reasonably expected to be in the patient's best interests. Present autonomy-based legal approaches require surrogates to decide on the basis of what the patient would have wished, a decision known as *substituted judgment.* Therefore, a surrogate should be familiar with the patient's values and attitudes. Substituted judgments present problems because it may be difficult to determine whether a surrogate is really able to decide what the patient would have wished. If a substituted judgment cannot be made, the surrogate uses the best-interests approach.

INVOLUNTARY TREATMENT

The principle of beneficence is invoked to justify the treatment of some people against their will. If a person has a mental disorder that is dangerous to self or others, the law permits involuntary treatment. The legal ground for the treatment of people who are dangerous to others is to protect public safety; the legal basis for the treatment of suicidal and gravely disabled people is to protect their lives and safety. In both cases, the decisions rest on the ethical basis of benefiting patients by treating their mental disorders.

There are, however, legal and ethical limits to involuntary hospitalization. Involuntarily hospitalized patients have a right to a judicial review of the grounds for their confinement and treatment. Because involuntary treatment restricts a person's liberty and personal choice, the law requires that it be done for good reasons. Moreover, the hospitalization may not be indefinite, as was the case before the late 1960s. From an ethical perspective, involuntary treatment is permitted on a time-limited trial basis to determine whether the treatment is beneficial. The law usually permits a longer duration of involuntary treatment for people who are dangerous to others than it does for patients who are dangerous only to themselves. In both cases, the benefits of treatment must accrue within a finite time, but a voluntary and consenting patient can be treated as long as it is deemed medically necessary.

Some mentally disordered, disruptive, and dangerous patients cannot benefit from treatment unless their behavior and the underlying psychoses can be brought under control; their sedation or restraint may be unavoidable. At the same time, behavior control alone is not a sufficient goal of ethical psychiatric care. It may, in some instances, be all that can be achieved; mental illness sometimes defies psychiatry's best efforts to control it. Treating the mental illness, restoring competence and ability to function, and helping a mentally ill person cope with or even conquer mental illness are the ultimate goals of psychiatric intervention. (Issues involved in psychiatric hospitalization are discussed in greater detail in Chapter 55.)

CONFIDENTIALITY

Issues of confidentiality often generate ethical dilemmas for the psychiatric profession. Therapist–patient confidentiality governs all situations except those in which another ethical or legal principle overrides the principle of autonomy. Breeches of confidentiality are justified when a psychiatrist maximizes the overall benefit to society or a subsegment of society by resorting to other core ethical principles instead of patient autonomy.

When patients threaten to harm themselves, individual freedom is curtailed by a psychiatrist's beneficent action. When patients threaten others, the principle of beneficence shifts in focus from a patient's welfare to the subsegment of society at risk. The principle of distributive justice means that all members of society are allocated an equal share of public safety. The Tarasoff decision and the APA's policy allowing psychiatrists to notify an identifiable third party at risk of exposure to an HIV-infected patient who is unable or unwilling to take autonomy-preserving precautions are examples of these principles in action.

LIAISON PSYCHIATRY

Liaison psychiatrists often are called upon to evaluate a patient's ability to make decisions about medical care. A physician may request a psychiatric consultation because a patient refuses to consent to a procedure. Such evaluations often present ethical and conceptual problems. Under law, adults are considered competent until proved otherwise. This presumption of competence is reflected in the law's recognition that patients have the right to consent or refuse to consent to medical treatment. Incompetence is a legal concept and can be established only by the courts, but psychiatrists often are given leeway to establish whether a patient has decisional capacity. If a psychiatrist evaluates a patient as incapable of decision making, the burden of disproof effectively rests with the patient. The patient must then ask a patient advocate or a lawyer to request a competence hearing before a court.

In such cases, the autonomy ethic, backed by both the law and contemporary psychiatric diagnosis, is clear: No matter how beneficial a physician believes a treatment will be and no matter how dangerous the probable consequences of rejecting this treatment, a patient has a presumptive right to reject it. Refusal of treatment is not sufficient justification for claiming that a patient is decisionally incapacitated. What is at question in this evaluation is the patient's ability to give informed consent. That is, can the patient understand and appreciate the diagnosis, the prognosis, and the risks and benefits of accepting or rejecting the offered treatment? Patients who can do so have the right to refuse treatment.

IMPAIRED PHYSICIANS

Impairment in a physician may occur as the result of psychiatric or of medical disorders or the use of mind-altering and habit-forming substances (such as alcohol and drugs). Many organic illnesses may interfere with the cognitive and motor skills required to provide competent medical care. Although the legal responsibility to report an impaired physician varies depending on the state, the ethical responsibility remains universal. An incapacitated physician should be reported to an appropriate authority, and the reporting physician is required to follow specific hospital, state, and legal procedures. A physician who treats an impaired physician should not be required to monitor the impaired physician's progress or fitness to return to work. This monitoring should be performed by an independent physician or group of physicians who have no conflicts of interest.

The Office of Professional Medical Conduct (OPMC) in New York State regulated the practice of medicine by investigating illegal or unethical practice by physicians and other health professionals, such as physician assistants. Similar regulatory agencies exist in other states. Professional misconduct in New York State is defined as one of the following:

1. Practicing fraudulently and with gross negligence or incompetence.
2. Practicing while the ability to practice is impaired.
3. Being habitually drunk, or being dependent on or a habitual user of narcotics or other drugs having similar effects.
4. Immoral conduct in the practice of the profession.
5. Permitting, aiding, or abetting an unlicensed person to perform activities requiring a license.
6. Refusing a client or patient service because of creed, color, or national origin.
7. Practicing beyond the scope of practice permitted by law.
8. Being convicted of a crime or being the subject of disciplinary action in another jurisdiction.

The source of professional misconduct complaints derive mainly from the public in addition to others (Fig. 56–1 and Table 56–2).

PHYSICIANS IN TRAINING

It is unethical to delegate authority for patient care to anyone who is not appropriately qualified and experienced, such as a medical student or a resident, without adequate supervision from an attending physician. Residents are physicians in training and, as such, must provide a good deal of patient care. Within a healthy, ethical teaching environment, residents and medical students may be involved with and responsible for the

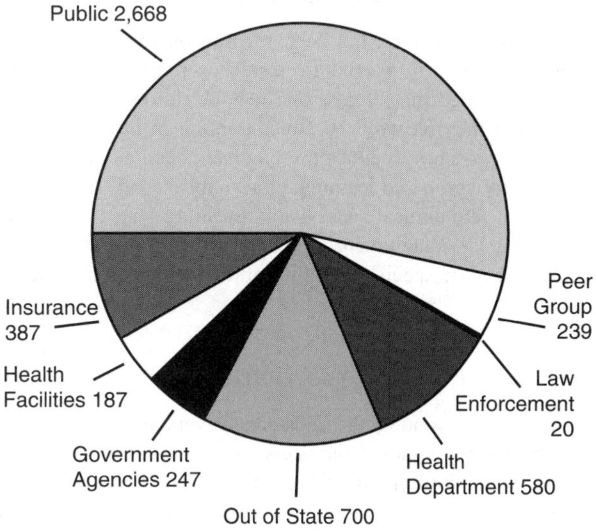
Public 2,668
Peer Group 239
Insurance 387
Health Facilities 187
Law Enforcement 20
Government Agencies 247
Health Department 580
Out of State 700

FIGURE 56–1

Office of Professional Medical Conduct—Source of Complaints 1995. (Reprinted from Office of Professional Medical Conduct, New York State Department of Health, Albany, NY.)

Table 56–2
Summary Statistics from New York State Department of Health Office of Professional Medical Conduct

	1992	1993	1994	1995
Complaints received	4,606	5,117	4,675	5,028
Investigations completed	4,167	4,694	4,852	6,014
Licensees referred for charges	204	297	328	334
Administrative warnings/consultations	81	96	79	88
Summary suspensions	3	12	8	10
Disciplinary actions				
Surrender	34	42	66	75
Revocation	25	56	73	94
Suspension	47	61	79	94
Censure and reprimand/probation	7	14	25	30
Censure and reprimand/other	5	30	21	25
Dismissal	6	6	7	6
Subtotal	124	209	271	324
Temporary/permanent surrenders	27	23	28	36
Monitoring agreements	10	11	8	3
Total actions	161	243	307	363

day-to-day care of many ill patients, but they are supervised, supported, and directed by highly trained and experienced physicians. Patients have the right to know the level of training of their care providers and should be made aware of the resident's or medical student's level of training. Residents and medical students should know and acknowledge their limitations and should ask for supervision from experienced colleagues as necessary.

Ethics in Psychiatry Training

Increasing attention has been focused on the relative lack of ethics training in psychiatric residency programs. A recent survey indicated that almost one half of residents polled reported that they received no ethics training in their curricula. Several approaches to ethics training have been advocated, including problem-based learning, case analysis, and ethics training woven into clinical supervision. Special issues include the ethics of cost containment in mental health care as well as ethical questions specifically applicable to child and adolescent psychiatry.

Abortion

Abortion is among the most controversial ethical issues confronting physicians, lawmakers, and the general public. In *Roe v. Wade,* the Supreme Court of the United States, basing its decision on common-law precedents that gave no legal standing to early-stage fetuses, ruled that there are no legal obligations toward fetuses in the early stages of development. Early abortions, therefore, can be regulated only for the purpose of ensuring the safety of pregnant women. The Court ruled that common-law precedents give limited obligations to the fetus after it becomes viable. Therefore, states are permitted to regulate late-stage abortions.

Since *Roe v. Wade,* antiabortion advocates have tried to limit abortions in various ways. Congress passed laws in 1993 that impose harsh penalties on people blockading or physically obstructing access to facilities performing abortions. The following case vignette illustrates several potential ethical dilemmas a psychiatrist may face when a mentally ill patient seeks an abortion.

A psychiatric consultant was called to evaluate a 35-year-old woman with catatonic paranoid schizophrenia who was 16 weeks pregnant. She was requesting her fifth abortion and had a history of multiple abortions secondary to the delusional belief that the fetus had become a devil. Her present request was based on the same delusional belief.

DISCUSSION

Autonomy and beneficence clearly come into conflict here. A woman's right to choose is opposed by evidence of delusional incapacity interfering with her ability to give informed consent. Confidentiality becomes an issue when deciding whether to involve her sexual partner or her family. The psychiatrist's recommendations here would require a close assessment of this patient's support system, the need for a legal guardian, and the use of antipsychotic medication until decisional capacity is regained. The psychiatrist would have to weigh the risks and benefits of medication to both mother and fetus. If a decision were to be postponed while awaiting a medication response, the gestation could progress beyond the stage at which it could be terminated. Consultation with a hospital ethics committee, colleagues, and professional societies is recommended in such a difficult situation.

In 1993, President Bill Clinton overturned the gag rule that prohibited the use of public funds by clinics that included abortion as a family-planning option. He also lifted the ban on federal funding of research involving tissue from aborted fetuses. Many researchers consider fetal tissue transplants to be a promising treatment for Parkinson's disease and dementia of the Alzheimer's type.

References

Adler G, Beckett A: Psychotherapy of the patient with an HIV infection: Some ethical and therapeutic dilemmas. Psychosomatics *30:* 202, 1989.

American College of Physicians: American College of Physicians Ethics Manual, third edition. Ann Intern Med *117:* 947, 1992.

Balint J, Shalton W: Regaining the initiative. Forging a new model of the patient-physician relationship. JAMA *275:* 887, 1996.

Brabbins C, Butler J, Bentall R: Consent to neuroleptic medication for schizophrenia: clinical, ethical and legal issues. Br J Psychiatry *168:* 540, 1996.

Conte HR, Plutchik R, Picard S, Karasu TB: Ethics in the practice of psychotherapy: A survey. Am J Psychother *43:* 32, 1989.

Fink PJ: On being ethical in an unethical world. Am J Psychiatry *146:* 1097, 1989.

Fitten LJ: The ethics of conducting research with older psychiatric patients. Int J Geriatr Psychiatry *8* (1, Suppl): 33, 1993.

Gutheil TG, Gabbard GO: Obstacles to the dynamic understanding of therapist–patient sexual relations. Am J Psychother *46:* 515, 1992.

James DS, Leadbeatter S: Confidentiality, death and the doctor. J Clin Pathol *49:* 1, 1996.

Jonsen AR, Siegler M, Winslade WJ: *Clinical Ethics,* ed 2. Macmillan, New York, 1986.

Hartmann L: Presidential address: Reflections on humane values and biopsychosocial integration. Am J Psychiatry *149:* 1135, 1992.

Hendin H, Klerman G: Physician-assisted suicide: The dangers of legalization. Am J Psychiatry *150:* 143, 1993.

Hoge SK, Feucht-Haviar TC: Long-term, assenting psychiatric patients: decisional capacity and the quality of care. Bull Am Assoc Psychiatry Law *23:* 343, 1995.

Kant I: *Foundations of the Metaphysics of Morals.* Bobbs-Merrill, Indianapolis. 1959.

Kantor JE: *Medical Ethics for Physicians-in-Training.* Plenum, New York, 1989.

Kluft RP: Treating the patient who has been sexually exploited by a previous therapist. Psychiatr Clin North Am *12:* 1483, 1989.

Lazarus JA: Ethical issues in doctor-patient sexual relationships. Psychiatr Clin North Am *18:* 55, 1995.

Mill JS: *Essential Works of John Stuart Mill,* M Lerner, editor. Bantam, New York, 1961.

Oppenheimer K, Swanson G: Duty to warn: When should confidentiality be breached? J Fam Pract *30:* 179, 1990.

Redden K, Frankel C: Liability of psychiatrists for sexual relations with patients. Psychiatry Digest *3:* 89, 1977.

Rosenberg JE, Eth S: Ethics in psychiatry. In *Comprehensive Textbook of Psychiatry,* ed 6, HI Kaplan, BJ Sadock, editors, p 2767. Williams & Wilkins, Baltimore, 1995.

Schwartz IM: Hospitalization of adolescents for psychiatric and substance abuse treatment: Legal and ethical issues. J Adolesc Health Care *10:* 473, 1989.

Stone A: *Law, Psychiatry and Morality.* American Psychiatric Press, Washington, 1984.

Thoreson RW, Shaughnessy P, Heppner PP, Cook SW: Sexual contact during and after the professional relationship: Attitudes and practices of male counselors. J Counsel Dev *71:* 429, 1993.

Weiner IB: On competence and ethicality in psychodiagnostic assessment. J Pers Assess *53:* 827, 1989.

Index

Page numbers followed by *t* and *f* indicate tables and figures, respectively. Page numbers in **boldface** indicate main discussions.

D

H

M

U

V